Where Once We Walked

**A Guide
to the
Jewish Communities
Destroyed
in The
Holocaust**

by Gary Mokotoff and Sallyann Amdur Sack

Avotaynu, Inc.
P.O. Box 900
Teaneck, NJ 07666

Printed in the United States of America

Second Printing

Picture Credits: Photos of Frankfurt am Main, Glogow, Mikulov, Prague and Sarajevo are courtesy of Leo Baeck Institute. Photos of Brailov, Kazimierz Dolny, Vilnius and Yelgava are courtesy of Boris Feldblyum. Photo of Vienna courtesy of Bildarchiv der Österreichischen Nationalbibliothek. All other photos courtesy of YIVO Institute for Jewish Research.

Library of Congress Cataloging-in-Publication Data
Mokotoff, Gary
     Where once we walked: a guide to the Jewish communities destroyed in the holocaust / Gary Mokotoff, Sallyann Amdur Sack.
ISBN 0-9626373-1-9 (acid free paper)
     1. Jews—Europe, Eastern—Directories. 2. Europe, Eastern—Gazetteers. 3. Jews—Germany—Directories. 4. Germany—Gazetteers. 5. Jews—Austria—Directories. 6. Austria—Directories. I. Sack, Sallyann Amdur. II. Title.
DS135.E83M65 1991   914.7'0003—dc20   91-70405

To our families:

Amdur of Braslov
Cemnic of Jalowka
Dubner of Plock
Mokotow of Warka
Shulkin of Polotsk
Slomovitz of Solotvina
Taratotsky of Bialystok
Wlodower of Praga

Table of Contents

Essential to optimum use of this gazetteer is an understanding of all elements in the listings for the towns. Detailed, easy-to-read descriptions are given here.

If the locality name does not appear in the Listing of Towns, these strategies may be helpful.

An explanation of the geographic term that is misunderstood by many.

Sources referred to in the Listing of Towns are described in detail.

Understanding the process of how this gazetteer was compiled will enhance the researcher's success in locating towns and comprehending the entries. Computer technology made this gazetteer possible; many of the considerations necessary to organize and analyze its more than 150,000 pieces of information are also presented here.

A phonetic index of the 37,000 town names in this book.

Acknowledgments

We are grateful for the enthusiastic support and active, expert help of many people. Randy Daitch spent many valuable hours transliterating into English the more than 2,000 town names listed by the Chamber of the Holocaust as well as the landsmanshaftn records of Yad Vashem. Randy, along with Gary Mokotoff, is the coauthor of the Daitch-Mokotoff Soundex System used in this book as a phonetic index to town names. His extensive knowledge of the collection in the U.S. Library of Congress Geography and Map Division enabled us to discover many otherwise unknown resources.

Harold Rhode of the Jewish Genealogy Society of Greater Washington remained an active collaborator throughout the project. He spent hours and hours verifying the accuracy of Estonian, Latvian and Lithuanian entries. He also translated from the Hebrew, portions of various *Pinkasim Hakehillot* entries and searched *Ohalei Shem* to track down numerous citations from *Latter Day Leaders, Sages and Scholars*. We are grateful for his contribution.

Several other members of the Jewish Genealogy Society of Greater Washington assisted substantially. Suzan Wynne provided us with her list of 6,000 town names in Galicia that was especially useful in resolving questions where more than one town in that area had the same name. Boris Feldblyum shared his knowledge of geography of the Soviet Union, which helped us find many elusive towns. Paul Klein supplied the mathematical formulas used to determine the direction and distance between a town and its closest major city. Hans Hirsch devoted hours to locating obscure German communities cited in the *Gedenkbuch*.

Dr. Ronald Grim, director of the Reading Room of the Library of Congress Geography and Map Division, and his staff devoted many hours and much energy to seeking out maps and offering indispensable advice. Those who helped so much were Michael Buscher, Barbara Christie, Patrick Dempsey, Kathryn Engston, Gary Fitzpatrick, James Flatness, Robert Morris and W. Ronald Roberts. We especially want to thank Thomas DeClaire, whose extraordinary knowledge and unfailingly good-natured willingness to share it, transformed otherwise tedious research into challenging detective work. His efforts exalt the term "public servant." Research librarians at the Library of Congress Hebraic Section, Peggy Pearlstein and Sharon Horowitz, were unstinting in their efforts on this project. George Kovtun, David Krause, Harold Leich and Kenneth Nyardi, of the Library of Congress European Reading Room, also supplied valuable advice. Thank you also to Linda Chanowitz of the U.S. Defense Mapping Agency for her assistance in obtaining copies of the U.S. Board on Geographic Names computer tapes.

Many other librarians advised us. Our thanks go to the staff of Leo Baeck Institute, YIVO Institute for Jewish Research, New York Public Library Jewish Division and American Jewish Historical Society. Daniel Schlyter of the LDS (Mormon) Family History Library offered much valuable guidance.

Chester Cohen graciously allowed us to include the names from his book *Shtetl Finder*. Neil Rosenstein helped us locate many obscure communities listed in his book *Latter Day Leaders, Sages and Scholars*. Eileen Polakoff provided ongoing encouragement and advice on the production side of the book. Miriam Weiner permitted us to use her library to research a number of communities.

Our Israeli experts were extremely encouraging and forthcoming. Rabbi Naftali Gal, director of the Chamber of the Holocaust, demonstrated great trust and generosity in permitting us to use his notebooks. Hadassah Assouline allowed us to copy her unpublished list of holdings at the Central Archives for the History of the Jewish People. She made many helpful suggestions and willingly supplied information about the location of communities we could not find. Rabbi Meir Wunder told us about the second (unpublished) *Hebrew Subscription Lists*; its author Shlomo Katzov kindly allowed us to use the list. Yad Vashem librarian Orah Alcalay assisted us with yizkor book research, and Esther Ramon, president of the Israel Genealogical Society, contributed expertise about Baden-Württemberg.

Editors of the Yad Vashem *Pinkas Hakehillot* project were unfailingly splendid; several made special trips on short notice to meet with Americans who had only a few days in Jerusalem. Thanks to Jan Ancel, Gabriel Bar-Sheked, Henry Wasserman and Avram Wein. Dov Levin, editor of the *Pinkas Hakehillot* for Latvia-Estonia and *Yahadut Lita*, was especially generous with his time and efforts on our behalf. Above all, we are grateful to Shmuel Spector, director of the *Pinkas Hakehillot* project, who gave not only information and direction, but substantial encouragement and moral support.

Rose Marie Ciecierski furnished highly accurate data entry, without which producing this work would have been a nightmare. She often identified questionable material, which helped minimize errors. If these many explanations are comprehensible, the credit must go to our excellent editor, Irene Saunders Goldstein. Responsibility for obscurities, however, must remain ours.

Most importantly, we offer gratitude and love to our long-suffering spouses, Ruth Mokotoff and Lawrence Sack, M.D., who have tolerated and even encouraged our seemingly endless obsession with the map of Jewish Europe.

Introduction

Two major upheavals have characterized Jewish life of the past two centuries: massive emigration and the Holocaust. Most Jews today live in countries to which their ancestors moved less than 150 years ago, but exactly where relatives lived in the "old country" is a question whose answer is frequently difficult to determine. Sometimes a town name was transmitted orally, but no such place can be found on a map. In other cases, a name was written on a document, such as a naturalization application or a ship's passenger manifest, but again, the place cannot be located on any current map.

In the two centuries before the murder of six million Jews during the Holocaust, most Jews lived in Central and Eastern Europe—the area of numerous wars and resulting boundary changes that altered maps dramatically over the years. It was not until late in the 19th century, for example, that Germany existed as a unified country. For more than a century (1795-1918), Poland did not exist at all. Czechoslovakia was created after World War I from Bohemia, Moravia, Slovakia, and parts of Silesia and Transcarpathian Ruthenia.

With virtually every boundary change, place names changed, too, and maps were redrawn. Sovereigns often renamed towns and cities in their conquered territories in an effort to legitimize their new regimes. Even when place names were not substantively changed, they often were spelled differently to reflect the language of the new rulers. To complicate matters, most languages of the region use diacritical marks—dots, slashes, hooks and accent marks—that change the pronunciation of a given letter. Into this complexity, add the Russians' Cyrillic alphabet, a system whose letters are almost totally different from the Roman alphabet used throughout the rest of this region.

It is difficult enough to identify a single town that may have been Hungarian before World War I, Czechoslovakian in the interwar period and part of the Ukrainian Soviet Socialist Republic today. But one must also consider that Jews often gave their own names to many towns. Indura, for example, a town on today's Polish-Russian border, is called Amdur in Yiddish. The Polish town of Gora Kalwaria, which means Mount Calvary, lost its Christian overtones when the Jews called it Ger.

Not only did boundaries and official town names change; not only did our ancestors assign Yiddish names to places, some places disappeared entirely. As the Industrial Revolution progressed throughout the world, people moved from the farm to the city, from rural areas to urban communities. Consequently, many small villages ceased to exist altogether. In more populous countries such as Germany, cities grew out to swallow up, and eliminate from the map, various villages and hamlets. In the USSR, some villages destroyed by the Germans were never rebuilt, and others were depopulated as part of the collective farm movement.

To add to this confusion, many town names are not unique. For example, we have identified 31 different towns named Adamow in Poland and 111 towns named Aleksandrow in the USSR. Did your Romanian family come from the Calinesti in Transylvania or the Calinesti in Bukovina?

It is no wonder that immigrant ancestors identified a single place name in countless different ways. We have found the Polish city of Czestochowa spelled 100 different ways by Holocaust survivors listed in the National Registry of the American Gathering/Federation of Jewish Holocaust Survivors.

These geographical identity problems were severely compounded by the human and archival devastation of the Holocaust. Had it not been for the Holocaust, most Jews today would be able to contact relatives in Europe to learn about their family histories. Records still would be available for research. It is the annihilation of the Jewish people and destruction of many records about them that makes a definitive gazetteer of Jewish Central and Eastern Europe necessary. These considerations led us to include in this book all the European countries where Jewish communities were destroyed.

The title of our book, *Where Once We Walked*, has a double meaning. To some, it may merely refer to the towns of our ancestors. To the authors, it signifies that, if not for the Holocaust, this gazetteer would not have been necessary.

Gary Mokotoff
Sallyann Amdur Sack
March 1991
Adar 5751

xi

How to Use This Gazetteer

Directions for using this gazetteer and a description of its unique features and conventions are given below. The first section of text is an alphabetical Listing of Towns. The second section is comprised of a phonetic index (soundex) of town names that uses the Daitch-Mokotoff Soundex System. The soundex is helpful when town names cannot be located in the main listing.

Researchers should first look up the name of the town in the "Listing of Towns." There may be more than one listing for a particular town name, so a quick perusal of nearby entries may be fruitful, especially if the first listing does not match information known about the town in question. A description of the information and abbreviations included in the list is provided below. If a town name cannot be found in the "Listing of Towns," turn to "What To Do When You Cannot Find Your Town" for additional strategies.

Information in Listing of Towns

This section is comprised of more than 22,000 individual communities listed alphabetically. Contemporary town names are listed using the spelling as defined by the U.S. Board on Geographic Names. Also included are former names of communities and names of communities no longer in existence. Many variant spellings or synonyms of town names are also listed, together with references to the current name, if known. Many Yiddish names are also listed.

Where there is more than one town with the same name, the name may be uniquely identified by a qualifier in parentheses following the name. This qualifier is usually the name of a nearby town, province or region in which the town is located. See "How this Book was Compiled" for additional discussion of town names, including qualifiers.

A sample entry appears in the box. Many entries include some or all of the data described below.

Belgorod Dnestrovskiy, Ukr. (Akerman, Akkerman, Belgorod Dnestrovski, Belgorod, Dnestrovskii, Cetatea Alba, Ir Lavan); pop. 4,239; 45 km SSW of Odessa; 46°12'/30°21'; AMG, EDRD, EJ, GUM4, HSL, JGFF, LDL, PHR2, SF, YB.

Town Name

Towns are listed alphabetically in bold face type, using the contemporary town name as defined by the United States Board on Geographic Names (BGN).

Country

With the exception of Greece, names of countries are abbreviated. Communities within the USSR are defined by the republic (indicated by *) in which they are located.

Abbreviation	Country
Aus.	Austria
Bulg.	Bulgaria
Byel.	Byelorussia* (White Russia)
Cz.	Czechoslovakia
Est.	Estonia*
Germ.	Germany
Hung.	Hungary
Lat.	Latvia*
Lith.	Lithuania*
Mold.	Moldavia*
Pol.	Poland
Rom.	Romania
Ukr.	Ukraine*
USSR	Soviet Union (general area)
Yug.	Yugoslavia

Alternate Names (Synonyms)

Alternate names are enclosed within parentheses and separated by commas. If there is doubt as to whether a name is truly a synonym, a question mark is included. Alternate names include Yiddish names and all distinct variants cited in the references used.

Distance/Direction

Towns are identified by proximity to major towns within their country. Major towns are shown on the map "Central and Eastern Europe Today." Town names are of contemporary vintage, although earlier versions of the names are listed on the pre-World War I and interwar maps where appropriate. The major towns were chosen for geographical diversity within each country, not necessarily because they were the largest Jewish population centers.

Distance is noted in kilometers. To convert kilometers to miles, multiply by 0.6 (six-tenths). Almost all localities listed in the gazetteer are within 100 km (60 miles) of a major town.

Latitude/Longitude

This information was extracted from U.S. government gazetteers. When the town could not be located in a gazetteer but was found on a map, the coordinates were taken from the map. In all cases, latitude is north of the equator and longitude is east of Greenwich.

Jewish Population

In most cases, the source is *The Black Book of Localities Whose Jewish Population Was Destroyed by the Nazis (Black Book)*, or its successor, *Jewish Communities Destroyed in the Holocaust*, known colloquially as the *Grey Book*. These two sources are described in detail under Population Statistics in "References"; others are noted as well. In some cases, especially for highly populated towns not listed in the *Black Book*, various additional sources were used. See "References" for more information on these sources.

Source Codes

Alphabetical codes (e.g., EJ, CAHJP) refer to sources that provide information about Jewish communities. A complete description of these codes and the sources they refer to are listed in "References." Not all entries include source codes.

***See* References**

Alternate names and spellings for towns are included in the alphabetical listing. *See* references direct the reader to the official, contemporary name. If the reference includes the word *possibly*, it means that while the authors were unable to locate the town on a map exactly as spelled, there was a town nearby with a similar spelling.

Akkerman, *see* Belgorod Dnestrovskiy.

Listing of Town Names by the Daitch-Mokotoff Soundex System

A listing of all town names, contemporary as well as alternate forms, is grouped phonetically according to the Daitch-Mokotoff Soundex System in the last section of this gazetteer. The soundex system makes it possible to search for a town according to the sound, rather than the spelling, of the name. Use of this soundex may help the researcher solve problems associated with misspelled town names.

What To Do If You Cannot Find Your Town Listed

Phonetic Index

For many months prior to the publication of this gazetteer, the authors tested its use by processing inquiries from persons unable to find the towns of their ancestors. By far, the most common reason the towns could not be located was that the names were misspelled. By using the phonetic (soundex) index in the last section of this book, however, the authors invariably were able to locate the towns.

If the town name cannot be located in the main listing of the book, use the soundex system. The rules for encoding the town name are very simple. Begin with the name as it is believed to be spelled, then delete all the vowels in the name (unless the first letter of the name is a vowel) and then convert the remaining consonants to numbers that represent like-sounding consonants. Using this constructed code, consult the numerical soundex index for the listing of town names that sound like the one under investigation. See the final section of this book for the soundex.

Check Spelling

One should consider the source of the name's spelling. If the source is a handwritten document, has the handwriting been read correctly? Was the source a document, such as a passport, completed by a government official who almost certainly knew the correct spelling of the town name? Or was the source a document, such as an application for citizenship, where the name was spoken in an interview and the recorder spelled the name as he heard it? Was the source a name passed down by word of mouth?

In a case where the spelling is based on what a person said, one should take into account the possible accent of the individual. One tough problem was solved, for example, when it was learned that the source was an aged aunt who lived in the Boston area. Many New Englanders drop the sound of the letter 'r' when it follows an 'a'. "Park the car" becomes "pahk the cah." The town of Kahlovka was nowhere to be found, but by adding an 'r' at the appropriate point, the town of Karlovka was identified and located on the map.

Consult Maps

When the researcher is convinced that the spelling is accurate, a number of options still remain. The first is to consult a library with an extensive map collection. Look on a detailed map of the region *in the time period in question*. In general, three time periods are delineated in the past 150 years: (1) the era before World War I, (2) the period between the two world wars (interwar) and (3) the years after World War II.

Town May Not Be Listed

More than 22,000 towns are identified in this book, but U.S. government gazetteers include in excess of 350,000 town names for the countries dealt with in this book. The complete list is available on microfiche from Avotaynu, P.O. Box 1134, Teaneck, NJ 07666. It includes all names in alphabetical as well as soundex sequence. The price is $24.00, subject to change.

Library of Congress

As a final resort, the U.S. Library of Congress Geography and Map Division accepts research inquiries. If the library staff succeeds in locating the town, they generally send to the patron a photocopy of a map showing the town's location. There is no charge for this service. Mail requests to Library of Congress Geography and Map Division, Washington, DC 20540. The telephone number is 201-707-MAPS.

No, Your Family Did Not Come from "Guberniya"

Frequently, novice genealogists or family historians declare that their family came from Guberniya or from the town of Grodnoguberniya. This is a common misconception. There is no place named "Guberniya!" Guberniya is the Russian word for "province." When immigrant ancestors said they came from Grodnoguberniya, it meant they came from the region near the Byelorussian city of Grodno.

An equally common error is to think one's ancestral town was Minsk, Vilna or Grodno, based on information supplied by ancestors. Often these were understood to be town names, when in fact what was meant was the guberniya or region of that name. On a similar note, ancestors may have said they were from Riga or Vienna or Iasi, when they may have actually come from a small village of another name near the major population center.

References

More than three dozen significant sources were used to compile this gazetteer. Where available, each town's Jewish population statistics and latitude/longitude are provided. In addition, where a listed town name was obtained from a particular source, the code of that source is indicated in the entry. The codes and the sources represented are described in this section.

Population Statistics

Jewish population statistics were taken primarily from the *Black Book of Localities Whose Jewish Population Was Exterminated by the Nazis [Black Book]*, published by Yad Vashem in Jerusalem. These population figures originally were derived from various government censuses taken during the 1920s and 1930s.

Some of these census figures are controversial, especially the statistics based on the 1921 census of Poland. The head count was undertaken shortly after the conclusion of World War I; significant war-related population displacements are believed to have distorted the population counts. Experts at Yad Vashem Martyrs' and Heroes' Remembrance Authority in Jerusalem assert that many Jews had not yet returned to their former homes by the time of the 1921 census, resulting in Jewish population statistics lower than they might have been had the census been taken just a few years later.

Population figures have been adjusted in this work, usually upward, for the 4,000 communities listed in *Jewish Communities Destroyed in the Holocaust*.

Black Book of Localities Whose Jewish Population Was Exterminated by the Nazis. Jerusalem: Yad Vashem, 1965.

Avraham Klevan, ed., *Jewish Communities Destroyed in the Holocaust*, prelim. ed. Jerusalem: Yad Vashem, 1982.

Town Name, Latitude/Longitude

Contemporary town names were extracted from gazetteers published by U.S. government agencies; official town names are standards as defined by the U.S. Board on Geographic Names. Gazetteers are published for every country in the world, indicating latitude and longitude of every population center as well as other natural and man-made landmarks.

AMG — *American Gathering/Federation of Jewish Holocaust Survivors*

This organization maintains a National Registry of more than 70,000 Holocaust survivors and their families living in the United States and Canada. The National Registry's database includes individuals' names before World War II (including maiden names of women), places of birth, towns before the war and places during the Holocaust. Extracted from the database for this book were birthplaces and town names before the war.

The organization is located at 122 West 30 Street, New York, NY 10001.

BGN — *U.S. Board on Geographic Names*

This source is a series of gazetteers published by the U.S. government using the official names as defined by the U.S. Board on Geographic Names. A list of these gazetteers appears in "Atlases, Gazetteers, Maps and Other Sources." They may be purchased from the U.S. Government Printing Office.

CAHJP — *Central Archives for the History of the Jewish People*

This facility contains original source material and microfilms, categorized and filed by locality, of material relating to Jews held in non-Jewish archives throughout the world. The material is often handwritten, generally in the language of the particular country. The Central Archives can supply information as to the existence of material about locations relevant to correspondents' queries, but cannot engage in actual research.

CAHJP is located in the Sprinzak Building, Hebrew University Givat Ram campus, Jerusalem, Israel. The mailing address is P.O. Box 1149, Jerusalem, Israel. Polish holdings are summarized in A. Teller, H. Volovici, and H. Assouline, *Guide to the Sources for the History of the Jews in Poland in the Central Archives*. Jerusalem: Central Archives for the History of the Jewish People, 1988.

COH — *Chamber of the Holocaust*

More than 2,000 memorial plaques at this museum/memorial in Jerusalem commemorate destroyed Jewish communities, primarily in Central and Eastern Europe. Community survivors gather to hold memorial services here on the anniversary of the destruction of the individual communities. Attendance at memorial services is a good way to meet survivors from individual communities.

For information, contact Rabbi Naphtali Gal, Chamber of the Holocaust, Mount Zion, Jerusalem, Israel.

EDRD — *Every Day Remembrance Day: A Chronicle of Jewish Martyrdom*

This book is a calendar of anti-Semitic events that have taken place every day of the year throughout history. Primary emphasis is placed on the Holocaust; many yahrzeit (anniversary) dates of the deportation and destruction of the Jewish community are indicated. Place names have been extracted from this work.

Simon Wiesenthal, *Every Day Remembrance Day: A Chronicle of Jewish Martyrdom*. New York: Henry Holt and Company, 1986.

EGRS — *Encyclopedia of Galician Rabbis and Scholars*

Rabbi Meir Wunder, *Encyclopedia of Galician Rabbis and Scholars*, 3 vols. Jerusalem: Institute for Commemoration of Galician Jewry, 1978-1986.

EJ — *Encyclopaedia Judaica*

This work is considered by some as the definitive encyclopedia of Jewish history. Extracted from the index were the names of towns in Central and Eastern Europe.

Encyclopaedia Judaica, 16 vols. Jerusalem: Keter Publishing House, 1971-1972.

FRG — *From A Ruined Garden: The Memorial Books of Polish Jewry*

This is an anthology of stories excerpted from yizkor (memorial) books.

Jack Kugelmass and Jonathan Boyarin, *From A Ruined Garden: The Memorial Books of Polish Jewry*. New York: Schocken Books, 1983.

GA — *Ghetto Anthology*

This book provides statistical information and describes sites of ghettos, labor camps, concentration camps and annihilation centers of the Holocaust.

Roman Mogilanski, *Ghetto Anthology*. Los Angeles: American Congress of Jews from Poland and Survivors of Concentration Camps, Inc., 1985.

GED — *Gedenkbuch: Opfer der Verfolgung der Juden, 1933-1945*

This book is a compilation of information on more than 128,000 German Jews who died in the Holocaust. Birthplaces of these Jews have been extracted for this gazetteer.

Gedenkbuch: Opfer der Verfolgung der Juden, 1933-1945, 2 vols. Koblenz, Germany: Bundesarchiv, 1986.

GUM — *Guide to Unpublished Materials of the Holocaust Period*

Volumes III-VI of the *Guide to Unpublished Materials of the Holocaust Period* provide an index to archival material at Yad Vashem about Jewish communities affected by the Holocaust. The series is edited by Yehuda Bauer and published in Jerusalem by The Hebrew University of Jerusalem and Yad Vashem.

GUM3   *Yad Vashem Archival Material, Part 1*, Vol. III, 1975.
GUM4   *Yad Vashem Archival Material, Part 2*, Vol. IV, 1977.
GUM5   *Yad Vashem Archival Material, Part 3*, Vol. V, 1979.
GUM6   *Moreshet Archives in Giv'at Haviva*, Vol. VI, 1981.

GYLA — *A Guide to YIVO's Landsmanshaftn Archive*

The guide describes the archival collection at YIVO Institute for Jewish Research of material concerning landsmanshaftn societies located primarily in New York City. Landsmanshaftn societies are Jewish immigrant organizations composed of individuals from the same locality.

Rosaline Schwartz and Susan Milamed, *A Guide to YIVO's Landsmanshaftn Archive*. New York: YIVO Institute for Jewish Research, 1986.

HSL — *Hebrew Subscription Lists*

Noted in this book are the Yiddish names of more than 8,700 towns whose residents subscribed to Yiddish and Hebrew-language books published during the 19th century. An appendix lists the Roman-alphabet names of about 5,500 towns which have been incorporated in *Where Once We Walked*.

Berl Kagan, *Hebrew Subscription Lists*. New York: Ktav Publishing House, 1975.

HSL2 — *Hebrew Subscription Lists: Book 2*

This book is comparable in structure to its predecessor, *Hebrew Subscription Lists*. Copies may be consulted at Hebrew University Library in Jerusalem and Jewish Theological Seminary Library in New York.

Shlomo Katzov, *Hebrew Subscription Lists: Book 2*, unpublished.

ISH1, ISH2, ISH3 — *Illustrated Sourcebook of the Holocaust*

Three volumes of pictures illustrate events of the Holocaust during the period 1933-1945.

Zosa Szajkowski, *Illustrated Sourcebook of the Holocaust*. New York: Ktav Publishing House, 1977.

JGFF — *Jewish Genealogical Family Finder*

This reference is an up-to-date, computerized database of towns and surnames being researched by more than 1,500 Jewish genealogists throughout the world. Extracted from the database are the names of Central and Eastern European towns.

The Jewish Genealogical Family Finder is maintained and published by the Jewish Genealogical Society, Inc., P.O. Box 6398, New York, NY 10128.

LDL — *Latter Day Leaders, Sages and Scholars*

This book lists the names of rabbis and scholars alphabetically by town name and surname.

Emanuel Rosenstein and Neil Rosenstein, *Latter Day Leaders, Sages and Scholars*. Elizabeth, N.J.: Computer Center for Jewish Genealogy, 1983.

LDS — *Latter-day Saints Family History Library Locality Catalog*

The Family History Library of the Church of Jesus Christ of Latter-day Saints (Mormons) has a vast microfilm collection of birth, marriage and death registers for towns throughout the world. These records are copies of documents kept at official archives in the countries of origin and are also available through these repositories. The LDS holdings are especially rich in Jewish vital statistics records from Germany, Hungary and Poland. The films may be consulted at the Family History Library in Salt Lake City, Utah, and at LDS Family History Centers all over the world. By policy of the church, these facilities are open to the public in a secular environment.

LJEE — *Last Jews of Eastern Europe*

This book presents a photographic essay of the remnants of the European Jewish community following the Holocaust.

Brian Blue and Yale Strom, *Last Jews of Eastern Europe*. New York: Philosophical Library, 1986.

LYV — *Landsmanshaftn Societies on File at Yad Vashem*

Yad Vashem Martyrs' and Heroes' Remembrance Authority in Jerusalem maintains a list of landsmanshaftn societies located in Israel. Landsmanshaftn societies are Jewish immigrant organizations composed of individuals from the same locality. Yad Vashem, P.O. Box 84, Jerusalem, Israel.

PH — *Pinkas Hakehillot (Encyclopedia of Communities)*

This remarkable collection of books, published by Yad Vashem Martyrs' and Heroes' Remembrance Authority in Jerusalem, eventually will document all the towns in Eastern Europe where at least 100 Jews lived before the Holocaust. As of June 1990, 11 volumes were completed with at least 7 more planned. The volumes cited in this book are:

PHGB	*Pinkas Hakehillot: Germany—Bavaria* Baruch Zvi Ophir, ed., 1972.
PHGBW	*Pinkas Hakehillot: Germany—Württemberg, Hohenzollern, Baden* Joseph Walk, ed., 1986.
PHH	*Pinkas Hakehillot: Hungary* Theodore Lavi, ed., 1976.
PHLE	*Pinkas Hakehillot: Latvia and Estonia* Dov Levin, ed., 1988.
PHP1	*Pinkas Hakehillot: Poland—Vol. I, The Communities of Lodz and its Region* Danuta Dabrowska and Abraham Wein, eds., 1976.
PHP2	*Pinkas Hakehillot: Poland—Vol. II, Eastern Galicia* Danuta Dabrowska, Abraham Wein and Aharon Weiss, eds., 1980.
PHP3	*Pinkas Hakehillot: Poland—Vol. III, Western Galicia & Silesia* Abraham Wein and Aharon Weiss, eds., 1984.
PHP4	*Pinkas Hakehillot: Poland—Vol. IV, Warszawa and its Region* Abraham Wein, ed., 1989.
PHR1	*Pinkas Hakehillot: Rumania—Vol. I* Theodore Lavi and Aviva Broshni, ed., 1969.
PHR2	*Pinkas Hakehillot: Rumania—Vol. II* Jan Ancel and Theodore Lavi, ed., 1980.
PHY	*Pinkas Hakehillot: Yugoslavia* Zvi Loker, ed., 1988.

POCEM — *Informacja Dotyczaca Cmentarzy Wyznania Mojzeszowego w Polsce [Jewish Cemeteries in Poland]*

This publication is a compilation of reports on the condition of various Jewish cemetery sites in Poland.

Informacja Dotyczaca Cmentarzy Wyznania Mojzeszowego w Polsce. Warsaw, 1981.

SF — *Shtetl Finder*

For many years *Shtetl Finder* was the only gazetteer of Eastern European Jewry. Town names are listed alphabetically by Roman alphabet version of the Yiddish name.

Chester G. Cohen, *Shtetl Finder.* Los Angeles: Periday Company, 1980; Bowie, Md.: Heritage Books, 1989.

SM — *Sefer Marmarosh*

This book presents the histories of towns in the Marmarosh region of Romania/Ukraine.

S. Y. Gross and Y. Yosef Cohen, *Sefer Marmarosh.* Tel Aviv: Beit Marmarosh, 1983.

WS — *Wooden Synagogues*

This book offers photographs and drawings of the exteriors and interiors of wooden synagogues in Eastern Europe.

Maria Piechotka and Kazimierz Piechotka, *Wooden Synagogues.* Warsaw: Arkady, 1959.

YB — *Yizkor Books*

More than 700 yizkor (memorial) books have been published for towns in Central and Eastern Europe where Jews lived before the Holocaust. Almost all of the books are written in Yiddish or Hebrew. While there is no standard format for these works, each typically includes a history of the Jewish population of the town from its inception, the events of the Holocaust itself and, occasionally, chronicles of Jewish life after the Holocaust. Individual stories by survivors that memorialize their deceased relatives are included. Those families with no survivors are remembered by name, where possible, together with brief biographies of the families. Many yizkor books close with a necrology—an alphabetical list of victims from the town.

The largest collection of yizkor books is at Yad Vashem in Jerusalem, Israel. A list of the towns represented in this collection is published in *A Guide to Jewish Genealogical Research in Israel*. The largest collections in the United States are at YIVO Institute for Jewish Research in New York and the Library of Congress in Washington. *Genealogical Resources in the New York Metropolitan Area* is considered to have the most complete annotated list of yizkor books, including bibliographical citations.

Sallyann Amdur Sack, *A Guide to Jewish Genealogical Research in Israel*. Baltimore: Genealogical Publishing Co., 1987.

Estelle M. Guzik, ed., *Genealogical Resources in the New York Metropolitan Area*. New York: Jewish Genealogical Society, Inc., 1989.

YL — *Yahadut Lita [Lithuanian Jewry]*

This is a four-volume work on the history of Lithuanian Jewry. Volume 3 provides detailed descriptions of more than 200 Lithuanian Jewish communities.

R. Hasman, D. Lipec, et al., *Yahadut Lita*, vol. 3. Tel Aviv: Association for Mutual Help of Former Residents of Lithuania in Israel, 1967.

How This Book Was Compiled

Jewish genealogists have talked about producing a comprehensive gazetteer of Jewish Europe for more than ten years, but until recently the obstacles seemed insurmountable. The successful compilation of this book ultimately was made possible by the use of a computer.

The technology permitted the collection, collation and analysis of the book's more than 150,000 pieces of information, including pre-World War I town names, interwar names, and current names, as well as Yiddish names and old historical synonyms (alternate, or variant, names). Included in this volume are the names and locations of more than 22,000 towns culled from the sources described in detail in "References."

Identifying Towns and their Locations

The town names, compiled by the authors from dozens of sources, were matched electronically against a computer file of the more than 350,000 names listed in gazetteers produced by the United States government. These gazetteers provide the official spellings as defined by the U.S. Board on Geographic Names (BGN); they show the latitude and longitude of *every* town in Central and Eastern Europe circa 1960, as well as selected alternate town names, interwar and pre-World War I names.

Latitude and longitude. Certain assumptions were made to determine the latitude and longitude of towns. If only one entry appeared on the BGN list with the same spelling as an entry on the compiled list, it was assumed that the computer had successfully located the town in question.

This might seem an obvious conclusion, but it was not necessarily foolproof. For a brief 48 hours during this project, the great Ukrainian city of Lvov was placed in Czechoslovakia! It seems that there is, indeed, a town of Lvov in Czechoslovakia—but since BGN spelled its Ukrainian town as *L'vov*, a mismatch resulted. The computer also erroneously matched the town of Jerusalem, Czechoslovakia, with Israel's capital city! In addition, an erroneous match could have occurred if a misspelled town name or other incorrect data coincided with a valid town name. (The efforts of many knowledgeable experts were enlisted to double-check the accuracy of the entries. The authors, nevertheless, invite readers to inform them about the omissions and errors inevitable in a project of this magnitude.)

If more than one entry appeared on the BGN list for the town name, all available information about the town in question was evaluated to determine which of the BGN entries was the one sought. Clues included country, province and often information about the town's proximity to another town. In those cases where information was inadequate, *The New York Times Atlas of the World* was used to assist in resolving the ambiguity. If only one entry appeared in this atlas, it was assumed to be the town in question (i.e., it was assumed for the purposes of this gazetteer that Jews lived in the largest towns, those listed in atlases). Where the *Black Book of Localities Whose Jewish Population was Exterminated by the Nazis [Black Book]* listed more than one town and the atlas listed only one town, it was assumed that the location with the largest Jewish population was the one listed in the atlas.

Where the town name did not appear in *The New York Times Atlas of the World*, a variety of detailed atlases was consulted. These supplementary resources included contemporary road maps, as well as interwar and prewar maps of Europe.

Multiple listings of town names. In countries with duplicate town names, these ambiguities often are resolved by adding a word or phrase that uniquely identifies its location. This qualifier may be another town name (Baden bei Wien), a region (Aleksandrow Lodzki), a county (Marmaros Sziget) or a river (Frankfurt am Main). Where the qualifier is a town name, it was found in the BGN gazetteer, and the duplicate town closest in distance to the qualifier town was selected. A similar rule was applied to rivers and regions. Errors may have occurred in the case of region qualifiers, however, since regions usually have discrete boundaries and the chosen town may be outside those boundaries, even though located closest to the qualifier town.

Synonyms or Variant Names

Because this gazetteer is intended to be a research tool and not a scholarly work, synonyms or variant town names have been included, although they may not necessarily be official names. Some variant spellings may merely reflect the way different authors referred to a town name in the sources used to compile this gazetteer. Not all variant town names were included, however, especially Yiddish names.

The spelling of many Yiddish names is a product of the phonetic transliteration of the original town name into the Hebrew alphabet and then the retransliteration back to the Roman alphabet using non-Slavic pronunciations. For example, the Yiddish name Devenishki refers to the Polish town of Dziewieniszki, which is pronounced "Devenishki." Other Yiddish names are based on the way residents of the towns pronounced the names. These were included in the gazetteer to aid the reader who might know the town name only as it was communicated orally. This is the equivalent of considering "Noo Yawk" to be a synonym for New York since that is the way many New Yorkers pronounce the name of their city. Yes, the authors would include Noo Yawk as a synonym in a gazetteer of the United States!

It was sometimes difficult to distinguish between variant spellings and typographical errors. The town of Kramaszowka, Poland, as listed in the *Black Book*, is almost certainly Kramarzowka. Are they synonyms or is Kramaszowka a typographical error? In making such subjective decisions, the authors favored including the listings as synonyms to help the reader who might look for the town under an alternate spelling. Of course, the negative side of this decision is that it perpetuates typographical errors.

Diacritical Marks

The spellings used for all town names are those designated by the U.S. Board on Geographic Names. The languages of most countries covered in this book use a variety of diacritical marks that affect pronunciation. For example, Dąbrowa is properly pronounced "Dambrowa" because of the ogonek under the initial 'a'; Białystok is pronounced "Biawystok" because of the stroke through the 'l' and Württemberg is pronounced Wuerttemberg because of the umlaut over the 'u'. No diacritical marks have been used in the town listings. Localities are spelled and alphabetized as if there were no such marks.

Atlases, Gazetteers, Maps and Other Sources:
A Select Bibliography

Atlases

Andree, Richard. *Andrees Allgemeiner Handatlas*. Leipzig: Velhagen & Klasing, 1924.

Atlas Polski (Road Atlas of Poland). Warsaw: Panstwowe Przedsiebiorstwo Wydawnictw Kartograficznych.

Auto Atlas CSSR. Bratislava: Geodeticky a Kartograficky Podnik v. Praze, 1971.

Bartholomew, John C., ed. dir. *The New York Times Atlas of the World*. New York: Times Books, 1985.

Der Grosse ADAC General Atlas, Bundesrepublik Deutschland. Munich: Mairs Geographischer Verlag, 1985. Scale: 1:200,000.

National Geographic Atlas of the World. 2d ed., enl. Washington, D.C.: National Geographic Society, 1966.

Kendler, Josef von and Carl von Kendler. *Orts- und Verkehrs-Lexikon von Eosterreich-Ungarn*. 3d. ed. Vienna: 1905.

Polska: Mapa Topograficzna, Komunikacyjna i Administracyjna. E Romera. Lvov; Warsaw: Ksiaznica Atlas, 1929.

Stieler, Adolf. *Hand-Atlas uber alle Theile der Erde*. Gotha: Justes Perthe, 1913.

Treharne, R.F. and H. Fullard, eds. *Muir's Historical Atlas*. 11th ed. London: George Philip and Son, Ltd., 1967.

Gazetteers

Andree, Richard. *Andrees Allgemeiner Handatlas*. Leipzig: Velhagen & Klasing, 1924.

Chlebowskiego, Bronislawa. *Slownik Geograficzny*. 14 vols. Warsaw: Druk, 1892.

Cohen, Chester G. *Shtetl Finder*. Los Angeles: Periday Company, 1980; Bowie, Md.: Heritage Books, 1989.

Czechoslovakia. Washington, D.C.: U.S. Army Topographic Command, June 1970.

Flynn, R.E. and G. Quinting. *Gazetteer of Yugoslavia*. 2 vols. 2d ed. Washington, D.C.: U.S. Defense Mapping Agency, March 1983.

Gazetteer of Austria, No. 66. Washington, D.C.: U.S. Department of the Interior, May 1962.

Gazetteer of Bulgaria. 2d ed. Washington, D.C.: U.S. Defense Mapping Agency, April 1987.

Gazetteer of Poland. 2 vols. 2d ed. Washington, D.C.: U.S. Defense Mapping Agency, August 1988.

Gazetteer of Western Czechoslovakia. Washington, D.C.: U.S. Army Map Service, July 1954. Typescript. Based on 1:25,000 map series AMS M872, M641, M671 and M508.

Germany--Federal Republic and West Berlin. 2 vols. Washington, D.C.: U.S. Department of the Interior, May 1960.

Hungary, Gazetteer No. 52. Washington, D.C.: U.S. Department of the Interior, May 1961.

Index to Maps of Eastern Europe 1:250,000 (Series N501). Washington, D.C.: U.S. Defense Mapping Agency, 1973.

Index to Maps of Western Europe 1:250,000 (Series M501). Washington, D.C.: U.S. Defense Mapping Agency, 1973.

Index to Names on AMS 1:250,000 Maps of Eastern Europe (Series N501). 2 vols. Washington, D.C.: U.S. Army Map Service, October 1966.

Klotz, R.G. and G. Quinting. *Gazetteer of the German Democratic Republic and Berlin*. 2 vols. 2d ed. Washington, D.C.: U.S. Defense Mapping Agency, October 1983.

Lakoma, M. and D. Piekarz. *Skorowidz do Mapy Polski w Pidzialce*. Warsaw: Panstwowe Przedsiebiorstwo Wydawnictw Kartograficznych, 1956. Scale: 1:500,000.

Magyarorszag Helysegnevtara 1944. Budapest: Hornyanszky Viktor RT Nyomdai Muintezet.

Retrospektivny Lexikon Obci: 1850-1970. Vol. II, Part 1. [Bohemia.] Prague: 1978.

Retrospektivny Lexikon Obci: 1850-1970. Vol. II, Part 2. [Slovakia and Moravia.] Prague: 1978.

Ritters Geographisch-Statistisches Lexikon. Leipzig: Verlag von Otto Wigand, 1910.

Royal Geographic Society. "Permanent Commission on Geographic Names: Lists of Names (New Series): 12, Moldavian SSR." London: 1966. Typescript.

Rudolph, H. *Orts-Lexikon von Deutschland*. Leipzig: Louis Zander, 1870.

Russisches Geographisches Namenbuch. Wiesbaden: Otto Harrassowitz, 1964.

U.S. Army Topographic Command. *USSR*. 7 vols. Washington, D.C.: June 1970.

U.S. Department of the Interior. *NIS Gazetteer of Greece*. Washington, D.C.: Central Intelligence Agency, December 1960.

U.S. Department of the Interior. *NIS Gazetteer of Rumania*. Washington: Central Intelligence Agency, July 1960.

Maps

Most of the following maps are part of the collection of the Geography and Map Division, U.S. Library of Congress, Washington, DC. The majority of the Library's holdings of several million maps is uncatalogued; if a map listed below is catalogued, the call number is provided (LC#).

Austria

Austria. Hallwag. Scale: 1:450,000. Index.

Bulgaria

Generalstab des Heeres. *Bulgaria*. Nuremberg: Gesellschaft fur Konsum-Markt-und Absatzforschung Kreiskate, 1986. Scale: 1:500,000.

Romania and Bulgaria. Hallwag. Scale: 1:1,000,000. Index.

Czechoslovakia

Czechoslovakia. G. Freytag & Berndt, [1934]. Scale: 1:600,000. Index. Czechoslovakian names.

Czechoslovakia. G. Freytag & Berndt, [1934]. Scale: 1:600,000. Index. German names.

Czechoslovakia: Bohemia [prov.]. Perco, 1905. German names.

Czechoslovakia: Moravia. R. Tampler, 1902. Scale: 1:900,000.

Czechoslovakia: Slovakia [prov.] & Podkarpat. Rus. 1924. Scale: 1:400,000. Postal.

Pretrov, A.L. *Karpatoruske Pomistni Nazvy*. Prague: Nakladem Ceske Akademie Ved a Umeni, 1929.

Germany

German Democratic Republic. Hallwag. Scale: 1:500,000. Index.

Southern Germany. Hallwag. Scale: 1:500,000. Index.

Bartholomew World Travel Map: Germany West and East. Edinburgh: John Bartholomew and Son, 1989. Scale: 1:1,000,000. Index.

Germany: Silesia [prov.]. R & A OSS #G119, 1945. Scale: 1:1,900,000.

Hungary

Hungary. Budapest: Magyar Kir. Allami Nyomdd, 1914. Scale: 1:400,000.

Hungary. Hallwag. Scale: 1:500,000. Index.

JRO Organisationskarte Deutschland. Munich: JRO-Kartografische Verlagsgesellschaft, 1984. Scale: 1:750,000. LC# G6 081.F7 .J7.

Magyar Foldrajzi Intezet R.T. Kogutowicz: Megyei Terkepek, 1914. Scale: 1:340,000.

Poland

Lakoma, M. and D. Piekarz. *Poland*. Warsaw: Panstwowe Przed Siebiorstwo Wydawnictw Kartograficznych, [1972]. LC# G6520, 1972, .p3.

Romania

Dostal, Jarosla. *Podkarpatski Rus*. Prague: 1936. Scale: 1:300,000. LC# 7103.z3 1936 .D6.

Harta Fizica, Politica si Etnografica a Banatul [prov.]. Pau, Virgil, 1936. Scale: 1:300,000. Administrative.

La Bucovine. Bucharest: Academie Roumaine, 1937.

Northern Romania and Bucovina. Int. Geo. al Armalei, 1900. Scale: 1:600,000.

Romania and Bulgaria. Hallwag. Scale: 1:1,000,000. Index.

Rumania, Northern and Bucovina. Freytag and Berndt, [Pre-World War I]. Scale: 1:400,000. German language.

Tufescu, Victor. *Republica Socialista Romania*. Bucharest: Editura Didactica si Pedagogica, 1985. Scale: 1:80,000.

Russia (*see also under* USSR)

Imperial Army Map Series. [Pre-World War I.] Scale: 1:126,000. LC# G7010 S126 .R8.

USSR (*see also under* Russia)

Kubiiovych, V. and A. Zhukov'kyi. *Ukraina. Karta Ukrainy*. Munich; Paris: 1978.

Martin, L. "Moldavian SSR." *Foreign Affairs*, 3 (April 1925): 511. Scale: ca 1:1,300,000. Boundaries with the Ukraine and Bessarabia.

Moldavian SSR. Directorul Statisticei Din Basarabia, 1922. Scale: 1:300,000. Economic.

Moldavian SSR. Carl Fleming, [1917]. Scale: 1:600,000.

Poland: Poznan [prov.]. Romer, 1939. Scale: 1:600,000.

Ukranian SSR [Western]: Volyn and Podilla, 1856. Stulp Nagel, 1863. Scale: 1:1,250,000.

Ukrainian SSR: Crimea. Gugsk: NKVD, 1937. Scale: 1:500,000.

Western Soviet Union. Bad Soden: Ravenstein Verlag. Scale: 1:2,000,000. Index.

Yugoslavia

Yugoslavia. Hallwag. Scale: 1:1,000,000. Index.

Other Sources

Indicator Alfabetic Al Localitatilor Din Republica Populara Romina. Bucharest: Editura Stiintifica, 1956.

Deak, Istvan. *The Lawful Revolution: Louis Kossuth and the Hungarians 1848-1849*. New York: Coumbia University Press, 1979.

Gardiner, Duncan B. *German Towns in Slovakia and Upper Hungary*. Lakewood, Ohio, 12961 Lake Avenue, 1988.

Gotlieb, Shmuel Noah. *Ohalei Shem*. Pinsk: Glouberman, 1912; Israel: T'futsa, 1983.

Kredel, Otto and Franz Thierfelder. *Deutsch-fremdsprachiges Ortsnamenverzeichnis*. Berlin: Deutche Verlagsgesellschaft, 1931.

Martinovici, C. and N. Istrati. *Dictionarul: Transilvaniei, Banatului: Si Celorlalte Tinuturi Alipite*. Cluj: Institut de arte grafice, 1921.

Mosse, S.A., ed. *Anuarul Romaniei 1931-32: Pentru Comert, Industrie, Meserii si Agricultura*. Bucharest: Editura Stiintifica.

Orth, Donald J., comp. *Geographic Names and the Federal Government: A Bibliography*. Washington, D.C.: Library of Congress, September 1990.

Rospom, Stanislaw. *Skorowidz Ustalonych Nazw Miejscowosci na Ziemiach Odzyskanych*. Wroclaw: Instytut Kartografic.

CENTRAL & EASTERN EUROPE

BEFORE WORLD WAR I

St. Petersburg

Reval

Dorpat

o Pskov

RUSSIAN

Tver

Moskva

Riga

Velikiye Luki

Shavli

Dvinsk

Kovno

Vitebsk

Smolensk

EMPIRE

Vilna

Rostock

Danzig

Königsberg

Minsk

Bryansk

Hamburg

Stettin

Belostok

Gomel

Kursk

Voronezh

Hannover

GERMANY

Posen

Warszawa

Pinsk

Konotop

Berlin

Lodz

Köln

Leipzig

Breslau

Lublin

Kiev

Frankfurt-am-Main

Chenstokhov

Rovno

Kharkov

Nürnberg

Prague

Cracow

Przemysl

Lemberg

Stuttgart

Brünn

Kaschau

Munkacs

Czernowitz

Vinnitsa

Yekaterinoslav

München

Wien

o Pressburg

o Miskolcz

o Uman

Salzburg

Budapest

Jassy

Odessa

Innsbruck

Graz

Koloszvar

Kishinev

Nagykanizsa

Szeged

AUSTRIA-HUNGARY

Simferopol

Agram

RUMANIA

Belgrade

Bucharest

SERBIA

BULGARIA

Varna

MONTE-
NEGRO

Skoplje

Sofia

ALBANIA

Salonika

GREECE

Janina

Athens

CENTRAL & EASTERN EUROPE

BETWEEN THE WARS

Leningrad

Tallinn
ESTONIA
Tartu

Pskov

Kalinin

Moskva

U. S. S. R.

LATVIA

Riga

Velikiye Luki

Siauliai

Daugavpils

LITHUANIA

Vitebsk

Smolensk

Kovno

Wilno

Minsk

Bryansk

Rostock

Königsberg

(GERMANY)

BYELORUSSIA
S.S.R.

Gomel

Kursk

Voronezh

Danzig

Hamburg

Stettin

Bialystok

Hannover

Poznan

Warszawa

Pinsk

Konotop

Berlin

GERMANY

Lodz

POLAND

Rowne

Kiyev

Köln

Leipzig

Breslau

Lublin

Kharkov

Czestochowa

UKRAINE
S.S.R.

Frankfurt-am-Main

Dnepropetrovsk

Nürnberg

Praha

Krakow

Przemysl

Lwow

Stuttgart

CZECHOSLOVAKIA

Vinnitsa

Uman

München

Brno

Kosice

Mukachevo

Salzburg

Wien

Bratislava

Miskolc

Cernauti

Innsbruck

AUSTRIA

Graz

HUNGARY

Cluj

Iasi

Chisinau

Odessa

Nagykanizsa

Szeged

Zagreb

Budapest

RUMANIA

Simferopol

Beograd

Bucharest

YUGOSLAVIA

BULGARIA

Varna

Skoplje

Sofija

ALBANIA

Thessaloniki

GREECE

Ioannina

Athens

xxvii

CENTRAL &
EASTERN EUROPE

1991

Listing of Towns

Aachen, Germ. (Aix la Chapelle); pop. 1,352; 62 km SW of Koln; 50°46'/06°06'; AMG, EJ, GED, GUM3, HSL, HSL2, JGFF.

Aalaiy Torna, *see* Turna nad Bodvou.

Aalen, Germ.; pop. 7; 62 km ENE of Stuttgart; 48°50'/10°06'; AMG, PHGBW.

Aba, Hung.; pop. 59; 69 km SSW of Budapest; 47°02'/18°31'; LDS, PHH.

Abadaja, *see* Apalina.

Abadszalok, Hung.; pop. 103; HSL, PHH. This town was not found in BGN gazetteers under the given spelling.

Abafalva, *see* Abovce.

Abaujdevecser, Hung.; pop. 4; 45 km NNE of Miskolc; 48°21'/21°06'.

Abaujker, Hung.; pop. 30; 45 km NE of Miskolc; 48°18'/21°12'.

Abaujlak, Hung.; pop. 5; 38 km N of Miskolc; 48°24'/20°58'.

Abaujsap, *see* Rasonysapberencs.

Abaujszanto, Hung. (Szanto); pop. 771; 38 km NE of Miskolc; 48°17'/21°12'; AMG, COH, GUM5, HSL, HSL2, JGFF, LDL, LDS, PHH.

Abaujszolnok, Hung.; pop. 6; 38 km NNE of Miskolc; 48°22'/20°59'.

Abaujvar, Hung.; pop. 44; 62 km NNE of Miskolc; 48°32'/21°19'; AMG, JGFF.

Abbazia, *see* Opatija.

Abda, Hung.; pop. 5; 114 km W of Budapest; 47°42'/17°33'.

Abeil, *see* Obeliai.

Abel, *see* Obeliai.

Abeli, *see* Obeliai.

Abeliai, *see* Obeliai.

Abenheim, Germ.; 50 km SSW of Frankfurt am Main; 49°40'/08°17'; JGFF.

Abensberg, Germ.; 82 km N of Munchen; 48°49'/11°51'; PHGB.

Abertamy, Cz.; pop. 5; 120 km W of Praha; 50°22'/12°49'.

Abod, Hung.; pop. 6; 38 km N of Miskolc; 48°24'/20°48'; HSL.

Abony, Hung.; pop. 431; 75 km ESE of Budapest; 47°11'/20°00'; AMG, GUM3, HSL, LDL, LDS, PHH.

Abosfalva, *see* Abus.

Abovce, Cz. (Abafalva); 82 km SW of Kosice; 48°19'/20°20'; HSL.

Abram, Rom.; pop. 12; 114 km WNW of Cluj; 47°19'/22°23'.

Abramovce, (Abrany); HSL. This pre-World War I community was not found in BGN gazetteers.

Abramowka, Pol.; pop. 16; 45 km ENE of Lublin; 51°19'/23°09'.

Abramowo, Pol.; pop. 97; Described in the *Black Book* as being in the Polesie region of Poland, this town was not found in BGN gazetteers.

Abramut, Rom.; pop. 19; 120 km WNW of Cluj; 47°19'/22°15'.

Abrany, *see* Abramovce.

Abrany Borsod, LDL. This pre-World War I community was not found in BGN gazetteers.

Abrehnen, *see* Abrini.

Abrene, *see* Abrini.

Abrini, Lat. (Abrehnen, Abrene, Jaunlatgale, Neu Lettgallen, Pitalovo); 139 km NNE of Daugavpils; 56°58'/27°37'; PHLE.

Abrud, Rom. (Abrudbanya); BGN lists two possible localities with this name located at 44°09'/27°59' and 46°16'/23°04'. HSL.

Abrudbanya, *see* Abrud.

Abrud Sat, Rom. (Gross Schlatten); 69 km SSW of Cluj; 46°17'/23°04'; HSL.

Abterode, Germ.; pop. 93; 139 km S of Hannover; 51°12'/09°56'; JGFF, LDS.

Abud, Rom.; pop. 5; 101 km E of Cluj; 46°31'/24°55'.

Abus, Rom. (Abosfalva); 75 km ESE of Cluj; 46°21'/24°23'; HSL.

Acas, *see* Acis.

Acatari, Rom. (Akosfalva); pop. 17; 88 km ESE of Cluj; 46°29'/24°38'; HSL.

Achern, Germ.; pop. 15; 82 km WSW of Stuttgart; 48°38'/08°04'; LDS, PHGBW.

Achim, Germ.; pop. 44; 88 km SW of Hamburg; 53°02'/09°01'.

Achneish, *see* Akniste.

Acholshausen, Germ.; pop. 11; 82 km W of Nurnberg; 49°39'/10°00'; JGFF, PHGB.

Achremowce, *see* Akhremovtsy.

Achtyrka, *see* Akhtyrka.

Acis, Rom. (Acas, Akos); pop. 84; 107 km NW of Cluj; 47°32'/22°47'; HSL, PHR2.

Aciua, Rom.; pop. 2; 107 km NNW of Cluj; 47°41'/23°22'.

Acs, Hung.; pop. 127; 82 km W of Budapest; 47°42'/18°01'; AMG, HSL, LDS, PHH.

Acsa, Hung.; pop. 12; 45 km NNE of Budapest; 47°48'/19°23'.

Acsad, Hung.; pop. 107 km NNW of Nagykanizsa; 47°19'/16°44'; HSL, HSL2.

Acsteszer, Hung.; pop. 6; 82 km WSW of Budapest; 47°24'/18°01'.

Ada, Yug.; pop. 342; 114 km NNW of Beograd; 45°48'/20°08'; COH, EJ, GUM5, HSL, HSL2, LDL, PHY.

Adacs, Hung.; pop. 16; 69 km NE of Budapest; 47°42'/19°59'.

Adamos, *see* Adamus.

Adamov, *see* Adamow.

Adamow, Pol. (Adamov, Yadimov); pop. 664; 62 km NNW of Lublin; 51°44'/22°16'; AMG, EDRD, GUM3, GUM5, HSL, JGFF, LYV, PHP4, POCEM, SF. A number of towns in Poland and the USSR are named Adamov or Adamow. References most often indicate the town described here.

Adams, *see* Adamus.

Adamus, Rom. (Adamos, Adams); 69 km SE of Cluj; 46°18'/24°14'; HSL.

Adancata, *see* Glybokaya.

Adancata Storojinet, *see* Glybokaya.

Adancata Strojinet, *see* Glybokaya.

Adand, Hung.; pop. 21; 94 km SSW of Budapest; 46°52'/18°10'; LDS.

Adaseni, Rom.; pop. 24; 114 km NW of Iasi; 48°04'/26°56'.

Adasztevel, Hung.; pop. 9; 107 km N of Nagykanizsa; 47°18'/17°33'.

Ade, Yug.; pop. 342; 82 km NW of Skopje; 42°40'/21°02'.

Adelebsen, Germ.; pop. 40; 94 km S of Hannover; 51°35'/09°45'; GUM5.

Adelnau, *see* Odolanow.

Adelsberg, Germ.; pop. 35; 75 km E of Frankfurt am Main; 50°02'/09°45'; GUM5, JGFF, LDS, PHGB.

Adelsdorf, Germ.; pop. 64; 32 km NW of Nurnberg; 49°43'/10°54'; GUM5, HSL, HSL2, JGFF, PHGB.

Adelsheim, Germ.; pop. 27; 75 km N of Stuttgart; 49°24'/09°23'; AMG, JGFF, LDS, PHGBW.

Adjud, *see* Adjudu Vechi.

Adjudu Vechi, Rom. (Adjud, Adzud); 120 km S of Iasi; 46°08'/27°11'; GUM3, GUM4, GUM5, LDL, PHR1.

Admont, Aus.; 94 km WNW of Graz; 47°34'/14°27'; GUM4, GUM5.

Adolfow, Pol.; pop. 5; 75 km SW of Bialystok; 52°39'/22°18'.

Adoni, Rom. (Eraadony); pop. 24; 133 km WNW of Cluj; 47°26'/22°11'.

Adony, Hung. (Racadony); pop. 37; 50 km S of Budapest; 47°07'/18°52'; HSL, LDS, PHH.

Adorjas, Hung.; pop. 101 km ESE of Nagykanizsa; 45°51'/18°04'; HSL.

Adrianopol, Ukr.; 251 km ESE of Kharkov; 48°22'/38°43'; HSL, LDL.

Adrianu Mare, Rom. (Nagyabajom, Nagyadorjan); pop. 112; 94 km ESE of Cluj; 46°29'/24°48'.

Adutiskis, Lith. (Goduzischki, Haydutsishok, Heidotzishok, Hidotzishok, Hoduciszki); 94 km NE of Vilnius; 55°09'/26°36'; AMG, GUM3, HSL, JGFF, LDL, SF, YB.

Adzud, *see* Adjudu Vechi.

Aegidienberg, *see* Agidienberg.

Aegina, *see* Aiyina.

Aerzen, *see* Arzen.

Affaltrach, Germ.; pop. 27; 45 km N of Stuttgart; 49°08'/09°23';

PHGBW.

Agard, Hung.; 56 km SSW of Budapest; 47°11'/18°37'; HSL.

Agasfalva, *see* Aldea.

Agenhof, *see* Igene.

Agfalva, Hung.; pop. 11; 146 km NNW of Nagykanizsa; 47°41'/16°31'.

Aggtelek, Hung. (Agtelek); pop. 8; 50 km NW of Miskolc; 48°28'/20°31'; HSL.

Aghiresu, Rom. (Aghiresu Cluj, Egeres); pop. 127; 32 km WNW of Cluj; 46°53'/23°15'; PHR2.

Aghiresu Cluj, *see* Aghiresu.

Agidienberg, Germ. (Aegidienberg); 45 km SE of Koln; 50°40'/07°18'; GED.

Aglona, *see* Somerseta.

Agram, *see* Zagreb.

Agries, Rom. (Egreshely); pop. 20; 82 km NNE of Cluj; 47°24'/24°09'.

Agrij, Rom.; pop. 30; 50 km WNW of Cluj; 47°04'/23°08'.

Agrinion, Greece; 126 km SSE of Ioannina; 38°38'/21°25'; GUM5.

Agris, Rom. (Belegregy, Felsoegregy); pop. 20; 133 km NNW of Cluj; 47°53'/23°01'; HSL.

Agtelek, *see* Aggtelek.

Agustov, *see* Augustow.

Agyagfalva, *see* Lutita.

Ahaus, Germ.; pop. 91; 126 km N of Koln; 52°04'/07°00'; GED, GUM3.

Ahausen, Germ.; 120 km S of Stuttgart; 47°44'/09°19'; PHGBW.

Ahlden, Germ.; pop. 4; 50 km NNW of Hannover; 52°46'/09°33'.

Ahlem, Germ. (Ahlon); pop. 117; 6 km WNW of Hannover; 52°23'/09°40'; EJ, GED, GUM3, GUM5, GUM6.

Ahlen, Germ.; pop. 117; 114 km NNE of Koln; 51°45'/07°55'; AMG, GUM5, JGFF.

Ahlon, *see* Ahlem.

Ahmecetca, GUM4. This town was not found in BGN gazetteers under the given spelling.

Ahrensburg, Germ.; pop. 23; 26 km NE of Hamburg; 53°41'/10°15'.

Ahrensdorf, Germ.; 75 km N of Berlin; 53°07'/13°32'; GUM3.

Ahrweiler, Germ.; pop. 42; 50 km SSE of Koln; 50°33'/07°05'; EJ.

Ai, *see* Ay.

Aichach, Germ.; 50 km NW of Munchen; 48°28'/11°08'; GUM3, PHGB.

Aidhausen, Germ.; pop. 31; 88 km NW of Nurnberg; 50°09'/10°26'; GUM5, HSL, LDS, PHGB.

Aigen, Aus.; 6 km ESE of Salzburg; 47°47'/13°05'; EJ.

Ailringen, Germ.; 75 km NNE of Stuttgart; 49°22'/09°45'; PHGBW.

Ainazi, Lat.; pop. 7; 107 km N of Riga; 57°52'/24°21'.

Airiogala, *see* Ariogala.

Aisheshuk, *see* Eisiskes.

Aishishak, *see* Eisiskes.

Aishishuk, *see* Eisiskes.

Aislingen, Germ.; 88 km WNW of Munchen; 48°30'/10°27'; PHGB.

Aispute, *see* Aizpute.

Aiud, Rom. (Strassburg); 56 km SSE of Cluj; 46°18'/23°43'; GUM4, PHR1.

Aix La Chapelle, *see* Aachen.

Aiyina, Greece (Aegina); 38 km SSW of Athens; 37°45'/23°26'; EJ.

Aizkalni, Lat. (Jasmuiza); pop. 9; 45 km NNE of Daugavpils; 56°12'/26°47'.

Aizkraukle, Lat.; pop. 1; 75 km ESE of Riga; 56°36'/25°11'.

Aizpute, Lat. (Aispute, Gazenpot, Hasenpoth, Hasenpoth, Hazenpot, Hoznpot); pop. 580; 150 km WSW of Riga; 56°43'/21°36'; COH, HSL, LDL, PHLE, SF.

Ajak, Hung.; pop. 63; 94 km ENE of Miskolc; 48°11'/22°04'; LDS, PHH.

Ajka, Hung.; pop. 41; 88 km NNE of Nagykanizsa; 47°06'/17°34'.

Ajkarendek, Hung.; pop. 3; 88 km NNE of Nagykanizsa; 47°08'/17°34'.

Ajszyn, *see* Gaysin.

Aka, Hung.; pop. 9; 75 km WSW of Budapest; 47°24'/18°04'.

Akali, *see* Balatonakali.

Akarattya, Hung.; 88 km SW of Budapest; 47°01'/18°10'; HSL.

Akaszto, Hung.; 88 km WNW of Szeged; 46°42'/19°12'; HSL, LDS.

Akemene, *see* Akmene.

Aken, Germ.; pop. 9; 69 km NNW of Leipzig; 51°51'/12°03'.

Akerman, *see* Belgorod Dnestrovskiy.

Akhremovtsy, Byel. (Achremowce); pop. 14; 195 km NNW of Minsk; 55°35'/27°07'.

Akhtyrka, Ukr. (Achtyrka); pop. 369; 101 km WNW of Kharkov; 50°18'/34°54'; GUM4.

Akimovici, *see* Yakimovtsy.

Akimovka, Ukr.; 195 km S of Dnepropetrovsk; 46°42'/35°10'; HSL.

Akkerman, *see* Belgorod Dnestrovskiy.

Aklin, HSL. This pre-World War I community was not found in BGN gazetteers.

Akmene, Lith. (Akemene, Akmian, Okmian, Okmiyan, Okmjan); pop. 360; 50 km WNW of Siauliai; 56°15'/22°45'; GUM3, HSL, JGFF, LDL, SF, YL.

Akmian, *see* Akmene.

Akna Raho, *see* Rakhov.

Aknasugatag, *see* Ocna Sugatag.

Akna Szlatina, *see* Solotvina.

Aknist, *see* Akniste.

Akniste, Lat. (Achneish, Aknist, Aknistes); pop. 176; 56 km WNW of Daugavpils; 56°10'/25°45'; JGFF, PHLE, SF.

Aknistes, *see* Akniste.

Akos, *see* Acis.

Akosfalva, *see* Acatari.

Akovo, Yug. (Dakovo, Djakovo); pop. 254; 170 km WNW of Beograd; 45°19'/18°25'; CAHJP, GUM4, GUM5, GUM6, PHY.

Aktenstadt, Germ.; pop. 74; Described in the *Black Book* as being in the Hessen region of Germany, this town was not found in BGN gazetteers.

Alacska, Hung.; pop. 4; 19 km NW of Miskolc; 48°13'/20°39'; HSL.

Alag, Hung.; pop. 27; 19 km N of Budapest; 47°38'/19°09'.

Alanta, Lith. (Alunta, Avanta, Ovanta, Owanta); pop. 222; 82 km N of Vilnius; 55°21'/25°18'; LDL, SF, YL.

Alap, Hung.; pop. 40; 82 km S of Budapest; 46°48'/18°42'.

Alattyan, Hung.; pop. 8; 69 km E of Budapest; 47°26'/20°03'.

Alave, *see* Alove.

Alba, Rom.; pop. 30; 139 km NW of Iasi; 48°10'/26°28'.

Alba Iulia, Rom. (Alba Julia, Albaiulia, Carlosburg, Gyulafehervar, Karlsburg); pop. 1,558; 82 km S of Cluj; 46°04'/23°35'; AMG, EJ, GUM3, GUM4, GUM6, JGFF, LDL, PHR1.

Albaiulia, *see* Alba Iulia.

Alba Julia, *see* Alba Iulia.

Albersweiler, Germ.; pop. 36; 101 km WNW of Stuttgart; 49°13'/08°02'.

Albertfalva, Hung.; pop. 99; 13 km SSW of Budapest; 47°27'/19°02'; PHH.

Alberti, *see* Albertirsa.

Albertirsa, Hung. (Alberti); pop. 45; 50 km ESE of Budapest; 47°15'/19°37'; HSL, JGFF, LDL, LDS, PHH.

Albesti, Rom.; 82 km ENE of Bucuresti; 44°32'/27°08'; HSL.

Albestii Bistritei, Rom. (Feherlak); pop. 10; 69 km NE of Cluj; 46°59'/24°28'.

Albigowa, Pol.; pop. 94; 50 km WNW of Przemysl; 50°01'/22°14'; HSL.

Albishe, Germ.; pop. 34; Described in the *Black Book* as being in the Rheinland-Pfalz region of Germany, this town was not found in BGN gazetteers.

Albisheim, Germ.; 69 km SSW of Frankfurt am Main; 49°39'/08°06'; GED.

Albota, *see* Verkhnyaya Albota.

Alcedar, *see* Alchedary.

Alchedary, Mold. (Alcedar); pop. 174; 101 km N of Kishinev; 47°52'/28°53'.

Alcsut, Hung.; pop. 7; 38 km WSW of Budapest; 47°26'/18°36'.

Aldea, Rom. (Agasfalva); pop. 2; 150 km ESE of Cluj; 46°15'/25°26'.

Aldebro, Hung.; 50 km SW of Miskolc; 47°48'/20°14'; HSL.

Aldekerk, Germ.; pop. 10; 62 km NW of Koln; 51°26'/06°26'.

Aldingen, Germ.; 19 km N of Stuttgart; 48°52'/09°15'; HSL, JGFF, PHGBW.

Aldoboly, *see* Dobolii de Sus.

Aleksander, *see* Aleksandrow Lodzki.

Aleksandreni, USSR. JGFF. A number of towns share this name. It was not possible to determine from available information which one is being referenced.

Aleksandreny, Mold. (Alexandreni Targ); pop. 1,018; 107 km NW of Kishinev; 47°49'/28°06'.

Aleksandreshty, Mold. (Alexandresti); pop. 2; 114 km S of Kishinev; 46°03'/28°25'.

Aleksandria, *see* Aleksandriya.

Aleksandriia, *see* Aleksandriya.

Aleksandrija, *see* Aleksandriya.

Aleksandriya, Ukr. (Aleksandria, Aleksandriia, Aleksandrija, Aleksandrya); pop. 2,000; 133 km NW of Rovno; 51°30'/24°60'; COH, EDRD, EJ, GUM3, GUM5, HSL, JGFF, LDL, SF, YB.

Aleksandrov, *see* Aleksandrow.

Aleksandrovka, (Aleksandrowki); SF. A number of towns share this name. It was not possible to determine from available information which one is being referenced. *See also* Bolschaja Aleksandrovka.

Aleksandrovki, *see* Aleksandrowka.

Aleksandrovo, *see* Aleksandrow Kujawski.

Aleksandrovsk, *see* Zaporozhye.

Aleksandrovski, HSL, LDL. This pre-World War I community was not found in BGN gazetteers.

Aleksandrow, (Aleksandrov); pop. 57; AMG, LDL. A number of towns share this name. It was not possible to determine from available information which one is being referenced. The name Aleksandrow usually refers to the town of Aleksandrow Lodzki. *See* Aleksandrow Lodzki.

Aleksandrowice, Pol.; pop. 81; 69 km SW of Krakow; 49°49'/19°01'.

Aleksandrowka, (Aleksandrovki); LDL. A number of towns share this name. It was not possible to determine from available information which one is being referenced. The *Black Book* notes two towns in contemporary Poland with this name. Neither appears in modern gazetteers. One (pop. 71) is listed in Lublin province, the other (pop. 63) in Warszawa province near Nieszawa.

Aleksandrowki, *see* Aleksandrowka.

Aleksandrow Kujawski, Pol. (Aleksandrovo); pop. 977; 126 km NE of Poznan; 52°52'/18°42'; COH, GUM5, JGFF, PHP1, PHP4, SF.

Aleksandrow Lodzki, Pol. (Aleksander); pop. 2,635; 13 km WNW of Lodz; 51°49'/19°18'; CAHJP, COH, EDRD, EJ, GA, GUM3, GUM4, GUM6, ISH2, JGFF, LDL, LDS, LYV, PHP1, POCEM, SF, YB.

Aleksandrowo, HSL. A number of towns share this name. It was not possible to determine from available information which one is being referenced.

Aleksandrowsk, *see* Zaporozhye.

Aleksandrya, *see* Aleksandriya.

Aleksat, *see* Aleksotas.

Alekseyevka, Ukr. (Mansburg); pop. 19; 62 km SW of Odessa; 46°07'/30°04'.

Aleksin, USSR; pop. 68; 146 km S of Moskva; 54°31'/37°07'.

Aleksinac, Yug.; pop. 6; 170 km SE of Beograd; 43°32'/21°43'.

Aleksince, Cz. (Elecske, Valaksincz); 69 km NE of Bratislava; 48°22'/17°57'; HSL.

Aleksnitz, *see* Novyy Oleksinets.

Aleksotas, Lith. (Aleksat); 6 km SSW of Kaunas; 54°53'/23°54'; GUM3, HSL, JGFF, SF.

Alerheim, Germ.; 82 km SSW of Nurnberg; 48°51'/10°37'; PHGB.

Alesd, Rom. (Elesd); pop. 372; 94 km WNW of Cluj; 47°04'/22°25'; HSL, HSL2, PHR2.

Alesheim, Germ.; 50 km S of Nurnberg; 49°03'/10°52'; GUM3, PHGB.

Aleshki, *see* Tsyurupinsk.

Aleus, Rom. (Elyus); pop. 8; 82 km WNW of Cluj; 47°09'/22°38'.

Alexandreni, Ukr. BGN lists two possible localities with this name located at 45°54'/28°57' and 46°27'/29°28'. PHR2.

Alexandreni Targ, *see* Aleksandreny.

Alexandresti, *see* Aleksandreshty.

Alexandria, Rom.; 82 km SW of Bucuresti; 43°59'/25°20'; GUM4, HSL, LDL.

Alexandroupolis, Greece; pop. 176; 246 km E of Thessaloniki; 40°15'/25°53'; EDRD, EJ.

Alexandrovka, Ukr.; pop. 1,157; 101 km NW of Odessa; 47°09'/29°51'; AMG, GUM4, HSL, LDL, PHR1.

Alexandrovsk, *see* Zaporozhye.

Alflen, Germ.; pop. 4; 88 km S of Koln; 50°11'/07°02'.

Alfter, Germ.; 32 km SSE of Koln; 50°44'/07°01'; GED.

Algyo, Hung.; pop. 11; 13 km N of Szeged; 46°20'/20°13'.

Algyogyafalu, *see* Geoagiu.

Algyogyalfalu, *see* Geoagiu.

Alibanfa, Hung.; pop. 1; 56 km N of Nagykanizsa; 46°53'/16°56'.

Alibunar, Yug.; pop. 31; 45 km NE of Beograd; 45°04'/20°58'.

Alikendorf, Germ.; 107 km WNW of Leipzig; 51°59'/11°17'; LDS.

Alistal, *see* Hrobonovo.

Alita, *see* Alytus.

Alite, *see* Alytus.

Alitus, *see* Alytus.

Aljmas, Yug.; pop. 2; 146 km WNW of Beograd; 45°32'/18°57'.

Alker, *see* Cheriu.

Alland, Aus.; pop. 5; 32 km SW of Wien; 48°03'/16°05'.

Allendorf, *see* Allendorf an der Lumda.

Allendorf an der Lumda, Germ. (Allendorf); pop. 57; 69 km N of Frankfurt am Main; 50°41'/08°50'; GUM3, GUM4, GUM5, GUM6, HSL, LDS.

Allendorf an der Werra, Germ.; pop. 24; 126 km SSE of Hannover; 51°17'/09°59'; LDS.

Allenstein, *see* Olsztyn.

Allersheim, Germ.; 88 km W of Nurnberg; 49°38'/09°54'; GUM5, LDS, PHGB, PHGBW.

Allesk, *see* Olesko.

Allmannshofen, Germ.; 75 km WNW of Munchen; 48°37'/10°48'; PHGB.

Allmendshofen, Germ.; pop. 2; 107 km SSW of Stuttgart; 47°56'/08°30'.

Almas, Hung. AMG, HSL, HSL2, JGFF. A number of towns share this name. It was not possible to determine from available information which one is being referenced.

Almasel, Rom. (Kisalmas); 120 km SW of Cluj; 46°05'/22°26'; HSL.

Almas Galgo, *see* Galgau.

Almasmalom, *see* Malin.

Almasmezo, *see* Poiana.

Almasrakos, *see* Racas.

Almasszent Tamasi, *see* Tamasa.

Almasu, Rom.; pop. 30; 45 km WNW of Cluj; 46°57'/23°08'.

Almasu Mare, Rom.; pop. 29; 101 km WNW of Cluj; 47°19'/22°32'.

Almaszeg, *see* Voivozi.

Almaujvaros, HSL. This pre-World War I community was not found in BGN gazetteers.

Almosd, Hung.; pop. 83; 120 km ESE of Miskolc; 47°25'/21°59'; HSL, LDS, PHH.

Aloja, Lat.; pop. 2; 101 km NNE of Riga; 57°46'/24°53'.

Alor, *see* Urisor.

Alove, Lith. (Alave, Ohlau, Olawa); pop. 78; 69 km SSE of Kaunas; 54°21'/24°12'; HSL.

Alpar, Hung.; pop. 49; 69 km NNW of Szeged; 46°49'/20°00'; LDS.

Alparet, *see* Olpret.

Alpen, Germ.; pop. 31; 75 km NNW of Koln; 51°35'/06°31'; GUM5.

Alpenrod, Germ.; pop. 4; 75 km ESE of Koln; 50°38'/07°52'.

Alsbach, Germ.; pop. 20; 45 km S of Frankfurt am Main; 49°44'/08°38'; LDS.

Alsdorf, Germ.; pop. 39; 56 km WSW of Koln; 50°53'/06°10'.

Alsedziai, Lith. (Alshad, Alsiad); pop. 199; 82 km W of Siauliai; 56°02'/22°03'; GUM4, LDL, SF, YL.

Alsenai, *see* Olshany.

Alsenz, Germ.; pop. 23; 75 km SW of Frankfurt am Main; 49°43'/07°49'; JGFF.

Alsfeld, Germ.; pop. 224; 88 km NNE of Frankfurt am Main; 50°45'/09°16'; CAHJP, LDS.

Alshad, *see* Alsedziai.

Alsheim, Germ.; pop. 25; 50 km SSW of Frankfurt am Main; 49°46'/08°20'.

Alsiad, *see* Alsedziai.

Alsoabrany, Hung.; pop. 16; 32 km S of Miskolc; 47°53'/20°41'; HSL.

Alsoapsa, *see* Nizhna Apsha.

Alsobajom, *see* Boian.

Alsoberecki, Hung.; pop. 19; 75 km NE of Miskolc; 48°21'/21°42'; AMG.

Alsobisztra, *see* Nizhnyaya Bystraya.

Alsobolkeny, *see* Beica de Jos.

Alsobudak, *see* Bistrita.

Alsocece, Hung.; pop. 5; 45 km NE of Miskolc; 48°21'/21°12'.

Alsocsora, *see* Ciubanca.

Alsodabas, *see* Dabas.

Alsoderna, *see* Dernisoara.

Alsodobsza, Hung.; pop. 9; 19 km NE of Miskolc; 48°11'/21°00'.

Alsofernezely, *see* Firiza.

Alsogagy, Hung.; pop. 8; 38 km NNE of Miskolc; 48°24'/21°02'; HSL.

Alsogalla, Hung.; pop. 27; 50 km W of Budapest; 47°34'/18°24'.

Alsogod, Hung.; pop. 38; 26 km N of Budapest; 47°41'/19°08'.

Alsogorzsony, *see* Nemesgorzsony.

Alsogyertany, *see* Nizny Hrabovec.

Alsohagymas, *see* Hasmas.

Alsohahot, *see* Hahot.

Alsohangony, *see* Hangony.

Alsohidegpatak, *see* Nizhne Studenyy.

Alsohomorod, *see* Homorodu de Jos.

Alsoidecs, *see* Ideciu de Jos.

Alsok, Hung.; pop. 4; 26 km SSE of Nagykanizsa; 46°14'/17°07'.

Alsokalinfalva, *see* Kaliny.

Alsokalocsa, *see* Kolochava.

Alsokortvelyes, *see* Sarbogard.

Alsokosaly, *see* Caseiu.

Also Kubin, *see* Dolny Kubin.

Alsokubin, *see* Dolny Kubin.

Alsolapos, *see* Lapos.

Also Lendva, *see* Lendava.

Alsolieszko, *see* Dolny Lieskov.

Alsomera, Hung.; pop. 12; 45 km NNE of Miskolc; 48°21'/21°09'.

Alsomislye, *see* Nizna Mysla.

Also Mochnya, *see* Chminany.

Alsonemedi, Hung.; pop. 58; 26 km SSE of Budapest; 47°19'/19°10'; PHH.

Alsonemesapati, Hung.; pop. 5; 50 km N of Nagykanizsa; 46°51'/16°56'.

Alsoneresznice, *see* Neresnica.

Alsonovaj, *see* Novajidrany.

Alsonyarlo, *see* Chichisa.

Alsonyek, Hung.; pop. 6; 114 km WSW of Szeged; 46°12'/18°44'.

Alsoolcsva, *see* Olcsva.

Alsoorbo, *see* Garbova de Jos.

Alsoors, Hung.; pop. 7; 101 km SW of Budapest; 46°59'/17°59'.

Alsopahok, Hung.; pop. 12; 45 km N of Nagykanizsa; 46°46'/17°11'.

Alsopaty, Hung.; pop. 2; 101 km N of Nagykanizsa; 47°18'/16°56'; AMG.

Alsopeteny, Hung.; pop. 8; 45 km N of Budapest; 47°53'/19°15'.

Alsopojeni, *see* Poeni.

Alsorajk, Hung.; pop. 5; 32 km N of Nagykanizsa; 46°39'/17°00'.

Alsorakos, *see* Racosul de Jos.

Alsoregmec, Hung. (Regmec, Regmitz); pop. 14; 75 km NE of Miskolc; 48°28'/21°37'; JGFF.

Alsoremete, *see* Remete.

Alsorepa, *see* Ripa de Jos.

Alsoribnyicze, *see* Rybnica.

Alsorona, *see* Rona de Jos.

Alsoronok, Hung.; pop. 4; 82 km NW of Nagykanizsa; 46°59'/16°22'.

Alsosack, Hung.; pop. 36; 88 km N of Nagykanizsa; 47°11'/17°11'.

Alsosag, Hung.; pop. 109; 94 km N of Nagykanizsa; 47°14'/17°09'; PHH.

Alsosajo, *see* Nizna Slana.

Alsosarad, HSL. This pre-World War I community was not found in BGN gazetteers.

Alsosegesd, Hung.; pop. 11; 32 km ESE of Nagykanizsa; 46°20'/17°21'.

Alsosofalva, *see* Ocna de Jos.

Alsoszalok, *see* Nizny Slavkov.

Alsoszeleste, Hung.; pop. 10; 101 km N of Nagykanizsa; 47°18'/16°50'.

Alsoszelistye, *see* Nizhneye Selishche.

Alsoszenterzsebet, Hung.; pop. 3; 56 km WNW of Nagykanizsa; 46°45'/16°29'.

Alsoszinever, *see* Sinevir Polyana.

Alsoszopor, *see* Supuru de Jos.

Alsoszouor, *see* Supuru de Jos.

Alsoszuha, Hung.; pop. 7; 38 km NW of Miskolc; 48°22'/20°31'.

Alsotelekes, Hung.; pop. 8; 45 km NNW of Miskolc; 48°25'/20°40'.

Alsoujfalu, *see* Satu Nou de Jos.

Alsoujlak, Hung.; pop. 16; 82 km NNW of Nagykanizsa; 47°05'/16°51'.

Alsovadasz, Hung.; pop. 17; 26 km NNE of Miskolc; 48°15'/20°55'.

Alsovalko, *see* Valcau de Jos.

Alsovamos, Hung. (Vamos); 114 km W of Budapest; 47°45'/17°39'; HSL.

Alsovaradja, *see* Oarta de Jos.

Alsovarany, *see* Vrani.

Alsovereczke, *see* Nizhniye Veretski.

Alsoviso, *see* Viseu de Jos.

Alsowartberg, HSL, LDL. This pre-World War I community was not found in BGN gazetteers.

Alsozopor, *see* Soporul de Jos.

Alsozsolca, Hung. (Alsozsolcza); pop. 75; 6 km ESE of Miskolc; 48°04'/20°53'; HSL, PHH.

Alsozsolcza, *see* Alsozsolca.

Alsozsuk, *see* Jucu de Jos.

Alsvika, *see* Alsviki.

Alsviki, Lat. (Alsvika, Kemeri); pop. 1; 176 km N of Daugavpils; 57°24'/26°53'.

Altaussee, GUM5. This town was not found in BGN gazetteers under the given spelling.

Altberun, HSL. This pre-World War I community was not

Amtchislav (Mstislavl), Byelorussia: Wintertime view of wooden synagogue built in the first half of the seventeenth century.

found in BGN gazetteers.

Alt Breisach, *see* Breisach.

Altdamm, *see* Dabie.

Altdorf, Germ.; pop. 68; 114 km SW of Stuttgart; 48°16'/07°49'; AMG, GED, HSL, LDS, PHGBW.

Altdorf (Bavaria), Germ.; pop. 2; 19 km ESE of Nurnberg; 49°23'/11°21'; PHGB.

Altdorf (Romania), Rom.; pop. 37; 82 km NE of Cluj; 47°10'/24°31'.

Altena, Germ.; pop. 23; 62 km NE of Koln; 51°18'/07°40'.

Altenahr, Germ.; pop. 5; 56 km S of Koln; 50°31'/07°00'; GED.

Altenbamberg, Germ.; pop. 6; 69 km SW of Frankfurt am Main; 49°47'/07°50'; GED.

Altenbogge, Germ.; pop. 8; 88 km NNE of Koln; 51°36'/07°45'.

Altenburg, Germ.; pop. 100; 38 km SSE of Leipzig; 50°59'/12°27'; AMG, EJ, GUM3, GUM5, GUM6, HSL, LDS.

Alten Buseck, Germ.; pop. 19; 62 km N of Frankfurt am Main; 50°37'/08°45'; LDS.

Altendorf, HSL2. There are 28 towns in five Central and Eastern European countries called Altendorf.

Altengronau, Germ.; pop. 46; 69 km ENE of Frankfurt am Main; 50°15'/09°37'.

Altenhasslau, Germ.; pop. 7; 45 km ENE of Frankfurt am Main; 50°11'/09°12'.

Altenkirchen, Germ.; pop. 92; 56 km ESE of Koln; 50°42'/07°39'; GED.

Altenkunstadt, *see* Burgkunstadt.

Altenlotheim, Germ.; pop. 22; 120 km N of Frankfurt am Main; 51°07'/08°55'.

Altenmuhr, Germ.; pop. 49; 45 km SSW of Nurnberg; 49°10'/10°42'; GUM5, HSL, PHGB.

Altenschonbach, Germ.; pop. 18; 62 km WNW of Nurnberg; 49°49'/10°24'; GUM5, HSL, PHGB.

Altenstadt, Germ.; 101 km ESE of Stuttgart; 48°10'/10°07'; CAHJP, EJ, GED, GUM5, HSL, JGFF, LDS.

Altenstadt (Hessen), Germ.; 26 km NE of Frankfurt am Main; 50°17'/08°57'; LDS.

Altenstein, Germ.; 82 km NNW of Nurnberg; 50°10'/10°44'; HSL, JGFF, PHGB.

Altenundem, Germ. GED. This town was not found in BGN gazetteers under the given spelling.

Althaif, *see* Vecamuiza.

Althof, *see* Vecamuiza.

Altkettenhof, Aus.; pop. 4; 13 km SE of Wien; 48°07'/16°28'.

Alt Kolziglow, Pol.; pop. 10; 94 km WSW of Gdansk; 54°15'/17°14'.

Altkrautheim, Germ.; 75 km NNE of Stuttgart; 49°23'/09°38'; PHGBW.

Alt Landsberg, Germ. LDS. This town was not found in BGN gazetteers under the given spelling.

Altleiningen, Germ.; pop. 2; 75 km SSW of Frankfurt am Main; 49°31'/08°05'; JGFF.

Altlengbach, Aus.; pop. 6; 32 km WSW of Wien; 48°09'/15°55'.

Alt Lesle, *see* Wloclawek.

Altlichtenwarth, Aus.; pop. 7; 62 km NNE of Wien; 48°38'/16°48'.

Altmamayeshti, Ukr. (Mamaestii Vechi, Staromamayevtsy); pop. 39; 13 km WNW of Chernovtsy; 48°21'/25°48'.

Altmark, *see* Stary Targ.

Altmemelhof, *see* Vecmemele.

Altmuhldorf, Germ.; pop. 1; 69 km ENE of Munchen; 48°15'/12°30'.

Alt Ofen, *see* Budapest.

Altona, Germ.; pop. 5,000; 133 km N of Hannover; 53°33'/10°00'; AMG, CAHJP, EJ, GED, GUM3, GUM5, HSL, HSL2, JGFF, LDL, PHGBW, PHP1, PHP2.

Alt Oytch, *see* Auce.

Alt Oytz, *see* Auce.

Altpaka, *see* Stara Paka.

Alt Sandez, *see* Stary Sacz.

Alt Sanz, *see* Stary Sacz.

Altshtat, *see* Staryy Sambor.

Altshtot, *see* Sambor.

Altspeyer, *see* Speyer.

Altstadt, *see* Sambor.

Altwied, Germ.; 62 km SE of Koln; 50°29'/07°28'; AMG.

Altwiedermus, Germ.; pop. 27; 32 km NE of Frankfurt am Main; 50°14'/09°03'.

Aluksna, *see* Aluksne.

Aluksne, Lat. (Aluksna); pop. 183; 176 km N of Daugavpils; 57°25'/27°03'; PHLE, SF.

Alukst, *see* Ilukste.

Alunis, *see* Alunish.

Alunish, Mold. (Alunis, Magyaro); pop. 29; 133 km NW of Kishinev; 47°51'/27°39'; HSL.

Alunisu, Rom. (Alunisu Mures); pop. 44; 50 km W of Cluj; 46°50'/22°57'.

Alunisu Mures, *see* Alunisu.

Alunta, *see* Alanta.

Alushta, Ukr.; pop. 242; 45 km SE of Simferopol; 44°40'/34°25'; AMG, GUM4.

Alvinc, *see* Vintu de Jos.

Alvitas, Lith.; pop. 31; 75 km SW of Kaunas; 54°38'/22°55'.

Alwernia, Pol.; pop. 70; 26 km WSW of Krakow; 50°04'/19°32'.

Alytus, Lith. (Alita, Alite, Alitus, Olita); pop. 1,715; 62 km SSE of Kaunas; 54°24'/24°03'; COH, GUM3, GUM4, GUM5, HSL, JGFF, LDL, SF, YL.

Alzenau, *see* Alzenau in Unterfranken.

Alzenau in Unterfranken, Germ. (Alzenau); pop. 97; 26 km E of Frankfurt am Main; 50°05'/09°04'; AMG, GUM5, LDS, PHGB.

Alzey, Germ.; pop. 192; 56 km SW of Frankfurt am Main; 49°45'/08°07'; GUM4, GUM5, HSL.

Amacz, *see* Amati.

Amati, Rom. (Amacz); pop. 23; 120 km NW of Cluj; 47°45'/22°55'.

Amberg, Germ.; pop. 94; 56 km E of Nurnberg; 49°27'/11°52'; CAHJP, EJ, GUM3, GUM5, PHGB.

Ambrozfalva, Hung.; pop. 3; 45 km ENE of Szeged; 46°21'/20°44'.

Ambud, Rom.; pop. 64; 120 km NNW of Cluj; 47°46'/22°57'.

Ambukow, *see* Ambukuv.

Ambukuv, Ukr. (Ambukow); pop. 7; 107 km N of Lvov; 50°46'/24°00'.

Amdor, *see* Indura.

Amdur, *see* Indura.

Amendingen, Germ.; 107 km WSW of Munchen; 48°00'/10°11'; PHGB.

Ammendorf, Germ.; pop. 2; 32 km WNW of Leipzig; 51°26'/11°59'; GUM3.

Ammersee, GUM5. This town was not found in BGN gazetteers under the given spelling.

Amoneburg, Germ. BGN lists two possible localities with this name located at 50°02'/08°16' and 50°48'/08°54'. HSL.

Amorbach, Germ.; 62 km SE of Frankfurt am Main; 49°39'/09°14'; PHGB.

Ampfelwang, Aus.; pop. 1; 50 km NE of Salzburg; 48°05'/13°34'.

Ampfing, Germ.; 62 km ENE of Munchen; 48°16'/12°25'; GUM3.

Amsana, *see* Mszana.

Amschelberg, *see* Kosova Hora.

Amshana, *see* Mszana.

Amshinov, *see* Mszczonow.

Amstetten, Aus.; pop. 28; 114 km WSW of Wien; 48°07'/14°52'; GUM4.

Amtchislav, *see* Mstislavl.

Amtzislov, *see* Mstislavl.

Amur, Byel. (Amur Nishni Dnjeprowsk); 88 km WSW of Gomel; 52°13'/29°46'; HSL, LDL, SF.

Amur Nishni Dnjeprowsk, *see* Amur.

Ananiev, *see* Ananyev.

Ananyev, Ukr. (Ananiev); pop. 3,516; 120 km S of Uman; 47°43'/29°58'; EDRD, EJ, GUM4, GUM5, HSL, LDL, SF.

Anapol, *see* Annopol.

Anarcs, Hung.; pop. 91; 101 km ENE of Miskolc; 48°11'/22°07'; HSL, HSL2, JGFF, LDS, PHH.

Ance, Lat. (Ances); pop. 26; 139 km WNW of Riga; 57°31'/22°01'.

Ances, *see* Ance.

Anciokrak, *see* Tarutino.

Andau, Aus.; pop. 10; 69 km ESE of Wien; 47°46'/17°02'.

Andernach, Germ.; pop. 115; 69 km SE of Koln; 50°26'/07°24'; EJ.

Andocs, Hung.; pop. 2; 75 km NE of Nagykanizsa; 46°39'/17°56'.

Andornak, HSL. This pre-World War I community was not found in BGN gazetteers.

Andranishok, *see* Andrioniskis.

Andrashida, Hung.; pop. 7; 56 km NNW of Nagykanizsa; 46°52'/16°48'.

Andrasocz, HSL. This pre-World War I community was not found in BGN gazetteers.

Andreapol, USSR; pop. 327; 107 km ENE of Velikiye Luki; 56°39'/32°15'.

Andreev, *see* Jedrezejow.

Andrespol, Pol.; pop. 17; 13 km E of Lodz; 51°44'/19°39'.

Andreyev, *see* Jedrezejow.

Andrichov, *see* Andrychow.

Andrid, Rom. (Erendred); pop. 74; 126 km WNW of Cluj; 47°31'/22°21'.

Andriejava, Lith.; pop. 66; This town was not found in BGN gazetteers under the given spelling.

Andrijasevci, Yug.; pop. 7; 146 km WNW of Beograd; 45°13'/18°44'.

Andrikhov, *see* Andrychow.

Andrionishkis, *see* Andrioniskis.

Andrioniskis, Lith. (Andranishok, Andrionishkis, Andronischki); pop. 35; 107 km NE of Kaunas; 55°36'/25°03'; SF.

Andronischki, *see* Andrioniskis.

Andruha, *see* Zeleno.

Andrukha, *see* Zeleno.

Andrupene, Lat.; pop. 8; 62 km NE of Daugavpils; 56°11'/27°23'.

Andrushovka, Ukr. (Andruszowka); pop. 7; 50 km S of Rovno; 50°14'/26°10'.

Andruszkowice, Pol.; pop. 10; 88 km SSW of Lublin; 50°40'/21°42'.

Andruszowka, *see* Andrushovka.

Andrychow, Pol. (Andrichov, Andrikhov, Yendrikhov); pop. 409; 50 km SW of Krakow; 49°51'/19°21'; COH, EGRS, EJ, GA, GUM4, HSL, LDL, LYV, PHP3, POCEM, SF, YB.

Andryjanki, Pol.; pop. 4; 62 km S of Bialystok; 52°37'/23°00'.

Andrzejewo, Pol.; pop. 277; 69 km SW of Bialystok; 52°51'/22°12'; GUM4, JGFF, LDS, PHP4.

Andrzejow (Lodz area), Pol.; pop. 99; 13 km E of Lodz; 51°44'/19°38'; GUM3, GUM5, PHP1, SF.

Andrzejow (Lublin area), Pol.; pop. 26; 56 km S of Lublin; 50°46'/22°26'.

Anenska Studanka, Cz. (Konigsfeld); 82 km N of Brno; 49°51'/16°33'; COH, HSL, HSL2, LYV.

Angelberg, *see* Tussenhausen.

Angelsdorf, Germ.; pop. 6; 26 km WSW of Koln; 50°56'/06°33'.

Angelturn, Germ.; 82 km N of Stuttgart; 49°29'/09°36'; JGFF, LDS.

Angenrod, Germ.; pop. 70; 88 km NNE of Frankfurt am Main; 50°46'/09°12'.

Angerburg, *see* Wegorzewo.

Angereii Noui, *see* Lazovsk.

Angermunde, Germ.; pop. 60; 69 km NNE of Berlin; 53°02'/14°00'; HSL.

Angern, Aus.; pop. 63; 45 km NE of Wien; 48°22'/16°50'.

Anghelus, Rom. (Angyalos); pop. 1; 170 km N of Bucuresti; 45°53'/25°53'.

Angyalos, *see* Anghelus.

Anhalt, *see* Anholt.

Anholt, Germ. (Anhalt); 107 km NNW of Koln; 51°51'/06°26'; COH, GED, GUM3.

Anikshchyai, *see* Anyksciai.

Aniksht, *see* Anyksciai.

Anikst, *see* Anyksciai.

Anin, Pol.; pop. 8; 13 km E of Warszawa; 52°14'/21°10'.

Anklam, Germ.; pop. 43; 107 km E of Rostock; 53°52'/13°42'; JGFF.

Annaberg, Germ. (Annaberg Buchholz); pop. 57; 94 km SE of Leipzig; 50°34'/13°00'; GUM3, GUM4, GUM5, LDS, PHP3.

Annaberg Buchholz, *see* Annaberg.

Annapol, Pol.; 62 km SE of Poznan; 51°59'/17°32'; JGFF.

Annapoli, LDL, SF. This town was not found in BGN gazetteers under the given spelling.

Annopol, Ukr. (Anapol); See listings below.

Annopol (Bialystok), Pol.; pop. 50; 50 km NE of Warszawa; 52°26'/21°42'.

Annopol (Lublin), Pol.; pop. 1,251; 62 km SW of Lublin; 50°53'/21°51'; AMG, GA, GUM3, GUM5, JGFF, LDL, LDS, POCEM, SF, YB.

Annopol (Ukraine), Ukr.; pop. 1,250; 50 km ESE of Rovno; 50°27'/26°54'; EDRD.

Annweiler, Germ.; pop. 15; 101 km WNW of Stuttgart; 49°12'/07°58'.

Anrochte, Germ.; pop. 53; 120 km NE of Koln; 51°34'/08°20'; AMG.

Ansbach, Germ.; pop. 197; 45 km SW of Nurnberg; 49°18'/10°35'; AMG, CAHJP, EJ, GUM3, GUM5, HSL, HSL2, JGFF, LDS, PHGB, PHGBW, PHGB, PHP2.

Antakalnis, Lith. (Antokol); 6 km NW of Vilnius; 54°42'/25°19'; JGFF.

Antalept, *see* Antaliepte.

Antaliepte, Lith. (Antalept); pop. 367; 114 km N of Vilnius; 55°40'/25°51'; HSL, SF, YL.

Antanava, *see* Paupis.

Antapoli, *see* Antopol.

Antas, Rom.; pop. 7; 45 km N of Cluj; 47°07'/23°35'; HSL.

Antau, Aus.; pop. 4; 56 km SSE of Wien; 47°46'/16°29'.

Antchikrok, *see* Tarutino.

Antepolye, *see* Antopol.

Antin, Yug.; pop. 2; 150 km WNW of Beograd; 45°23'/18°45'.

Antipolye, *see* Antopol.

Antokol, *see* Antakalnis.

Antolka, Pol.; pop. 23; 38 km N of Krakow; 50°24'/20°06'.

Antonin, *see* Antoniny.

Antoninek, GA, GUM4. This town was not found in BGN gazetteers under the given spelling.

Antonin Nowy, Pol.; pop. 7; 45 km NNW of Lublin; 51°34'/22°25'.

Antonin Stary, Pol.; pop. 9; 45 km NNW of Lublin; 51°35'/22°27'.

Antoniny, Ukr. (Antonin); 101 km SE of Rovno; 49°48'/26°52'; SF.

Antoniow, Pol.; pop. 77; 69 km SSW of Lublin; 50°45'/21°54'.

Antonivka, *see* Antonuvka.

Antonopol, Byel.; 45 km NE of Minsk; 54°11'/28°04'; COH, EDRD, HSL, SF.

Antonov, *see* Antonuv.

Antonovka, *see* Antonuvka.

Antonovo, Byel. (Antonowo); pop. 5; 82 km SW of Minsk; 53°37'/26°22'.

Antonovtsy, Ukr. (Antonowce); pop. 7; 50 km SSW of Rovno; 50°13'/25°56'.

Antonow, *see* Antonuv.

Antonowce, *see* Antonovtsy.

Antonowiecka, *see* Antonuvka.

Antonowka; Also *see* Antonuvka, Antonowka (Polesie).

Antonowka (Polesie), Ukr.; pop. 63; 82 km N of Rovno; 51°19'/26°20'.

Antonowo, *see* Antonovo.

Antonuv, Ukr. (Antonov, Antonow); pop. 24; 69 km NNW of Chernovtsy; 48°53'/25°41'.

Antonuvka, Ukr. (Antonivka, Antonovka, Antonowiecka, Biisk, Bisk, Biysk); pop. 482; 26 km NNE of Rovno; 50°48'/26°30';

CAHJP, HSL, JGFF, SF.

Antopol, Byel. (Antapoli, Antepolye, Antipolye, Antopole); pop. 1,792; 94 km W of Pinsk; 52°12'/24°47'; COH, EDRD, FRG, GA, GUM3, GUM4, GUM5, GYLA, HSL, HSL2, LDL, LYV, SF, YB.

Antopol (Wolyn), Ukr.; pop. 68; 13 km E of Rovno; 50°36'/26°26'.

Antopole, *see* Antopol.

Antosin, *see* Antosino.

Antosino, Byel. (Antosin); pop. 6; 26 km SSW of Minsk; 53°43'/27°18'.

Antunovac, Yug. (Autunowatz); pop. 7; 82 km ESE of Zagreb; 45°29'/17°00'.

Anturke, Lith. (Intorok, Inturik, Inturk, Inturke); 62 km N of Vilnius; 55°10'/25°33'; SF, YL.

Anufrehifka, *see* Onufriewka.

Anyksciai, Lith. (Anikshchyai, Aniksht, Anikst, Anykst, Onikshty); pop. 1,748; 101 km NE of Kaunas; 55°32'/25°06'; AMG, COH, GUM4, GUM5, GYLA, HSL, HSL2, JGFF, LDL, SF, YL.

Anykst, *see* Anyksciai.

Apa, Rom.; pop. 110; 114 km NNW of Cluj; 47°46'/23°12'; HSL, HSL2, PHR2.

Apacatorna, Hung.; pop. 9; 82 km N of Nagykanizsa; 47°07'/17°18'.

Apagy, Hung.; pop. 109; 88 km E of Miskolc; 47°58'/21°56'; HSL, LDS, PHH.

Apahegy, *see* Viile Apei.

Apahida, Rom.; 13 km NE of Cluj; 46°49'/23°45'; HSL, HSL2, PHR2.

Apalina, Rom. (Abadaja); pop. 26; 88 km E of Cluj; 46°45'/24°42'.

Apanagyfalu, *see* Nusfalau.

Apanagyfalva, *see* Nusfalau.

Apateu, (Apati, Olahapati); LDL. A number of towns share this name. It was not possible to determine from available information which one is being referenced.

Apatfalu, *see* Apatfalva.

Apatfalva, Hung. (Apatfalu); pop. 40; 32 km ESE of Szeged; 46°10'/20°35'; HSL.

Apati, Hung.; 82 km NE of Szeged; 46°34'/21°07'; HSL. *See also* Apateu.

Apatin, Yug.; pop. 94; 150 km WNW of Beograd; 45°40'/18°59'; PHY.

Apatistvanfalva, Hung.; pop. 1; 75 km WNW of Nagykanizsa; 46°54'/16°15'.

Apatiu, Rom.; pop. 10; 50 km NE of Cluj; 47°00'/24°11'.

Apatkeresztur, *see* Cristur.

Apc, Hung.; pop. 116; 56 km NE of Budapest; 47°48'/19°42'; COH, HSL, PHH.

Ape, Lat. (Apes, Appenhof); pop. 90; 163 km NE of Riga; 57°32'/26°40'; PHLE.

Apes, *see* Ape.

Apetlon, Aus.; pop. 4; 62 km SE of Wien; 47°45'/16°50'.

Apfelberg, Aus.; 50 km WNW of Graz; 47°12'/14°50'; PHP4.

Apheim, HSL. This pre-World War I community was not found in BGN gazetteers.

Apolda, Germ.; pop. 59; 69 km SW of Leipzig; 51°01'/11°30'; GUM5, LDS.

Aporka, Hung.; pop. 3; 38 km S of Budapest; 47°14'/19°01'.

Apostag, Hung.; pop. 94; 75 km S of Budapest; 46°53'/18°57'; HSL, LDS, PHH.

Apostolovo, Ukr.; 126 km SW of Dnepropetrovsk; 47°40'/33°44'; AMG.

Appenhof, *see* Ape.

Appenweier, Germ.; pop. 5; 88 km SW of Stuttgart; 48°32'/07°59'; PHGBW.

Apsicsa, *see* Apsilsa.

Apsilsa, Ukr. (Apsicsa, Kisapsa); 150 km WSW of Chernovtsy; 48°01'/23°58'; COH, GUM5.

Apt, *see* Opatow.

Apta, *see* Opatow.

Arad, Rom.; pop. 6,430; 182 km SW of Cluj; 46°11'/21°19'; AMG, CAHJP, EJ, GUM4, GUM5, GUM6, HSL, HSL2, JGFF, LDL, PHR1.

Aradac, Yug.; pop. 4; 69 km NNW of Beograd; 45°23'/20°19'.

Arahida, Rom.; pop. 56; Described in the *Black Book* as being in the Transylvania region of Romania, this town was not found in BGN gazetteers.

Arak, Hung.; pop. 1; 133 km WNW of Budapest; 47°52'/17°23'.

Arandelovac, Yug.; pop. 3; 62 km S of Beograd; 44°18'/20°35'.

Arannnyosmeggyes, *see* Medisa.

Aranyidka, *see* Zlata Idka.

Aranylona, *see* Lunca.

Aranymegges, *see* Medisa.

Aranyod, Hung.; pop. 2; 62 km N of Nagykanizsa; 46°57'/17°04'.

Aranyomeggyes, *see* Mediesu Aurit.

Aranyos, Ukr.; 101 km SSW of Uman; 47°59'/29°42'; HSL, HSL2. This town was located on a pre-World War I map, but does not appear in contemporary gazetteers.

Aranyosgyeres, *see* Ghiris.

Aranyosmarot, *see* Zlate Moravce.

Aranyosmegyes, *see* Mediesu Aurit.

Aranyos Torda, *see* Turda.

Aranzenii Vechi, *see* Bratislava.

Arbesbach, Aus.; pop. 3; 107 km WNW of Wien; 48°29'/14°57'.

Arbore, Rom.; pop. 107; 139 km WNW of Iasi; 47°44'/25°56'.

Arborea, Rom.; pop. 12; 126 km NW of Iasi; 48°03'/26°31'.

Arcalia, Rom. (Arokaja); pop. 3; 69 km NE of Cluj; 47°05'/24°21'.

Archid, Rom.; pop. 6; 82 km NW of Cluj; 47°21'/23°01'.

Archshofen, Germ.; pop. 24; 75 km WSW of Nurnberg; 49°27'/10°04'; GED, PHGBW.

Arciz, *see* Artsiz.

Arcus, Rom. (Arkos); pop. 12; 170 km NNW of Bucuresti; 45°54'/25°46'.

Ardan, Rom. (Ardany); 88 km NE of Cluj; 47°02'/24°41'; HSL.

Ardanhaza, *see* Ardanovo.

Ardanovce, Cz.; 75 km NE of Bratislava; 48°32'/17°54'; HSL, HSL2.

Ardanovo, Ukr. (Ardanhaza); 189 km SSW of Lvov; 48°20'/22°56'; HSL. This town was located on a pre-World War I map, but does not appear in contemporary gazetteers.

Ardany, *see* Ardan.

Arded, *see* Ardud.

Ardo, *see* Ardovo.

Ardovo, Cz. (Ardo); 62 km SW of Kosice; 48°32'/20°25'; HSL, HSL2.

Ardud, Rom. (Arded, Erdod); pop. 124; 114 km NW of Cluj; 47°38'/22°53'; HSL, HSL2, LDL, PHR2.

Ardusat, Rom. (Erdoszada); pop. 51; 101 km NNW of Cluj; 47°39'/23°22'; HSL.

Arduzel, Rom.; pop. 10; 82 km NNW of Cluj; 47°27'/23°16'.

Arenberg, Germ.; 82 km WNW of Frankfurt am Main; 50°22'/07°39'; GED.

Argel, Rom.; pop. 11; 170 km WNW of Iasi; 47°46'/25°28'.

Argelsried, Germ.; pop. 1; 19 km WSW of Munchen; 48°06'/11°18'.

Argenau, *see* Gniewkowo.

Argenschwang, Germ.; pop. 29; 75 km SW of Frankfurt am Main; 49°53'/07°42'.

Argos, Greece; 94 km SW of Athens; 37°38'/22°43'; EJ.

Arheilgen, Germ.; pop. 30; 26 km S of Frankfurt am Main; 49°55'/08°39'.

Arinis, Rom. (Egerhart?, Egerhat); pop. 99; 88 km NNW of Cluj; 47°30'/23°14'; HSL, PHR2.

Ariogala, Lith. (Airiogala, Iragola, Ragola, Ragole?); pop. 462; 50 km NW of Kaunas; 55°16'/23°28'; GUM5, HSL, HSL2, JGFF, LDL, SF, YL.

Arioneshty, Mold. (Arionesti); pop. 24; 170 km NW of Kishinev; 48°23'/27°51'.

Arionesti, *see* Arioneshty.

Ariseni, *possibly* Oraseni.

Arka, Hung.; pop. 13; 50 km NE of Miskolc; 48°21'/21°15'.

Arkos, *see* Arcus.

Arlamowska Wola, *see* Volya Arlamovskaya.

Arlava, Lat.; pop. 4; 107 km WNW of Riga; 57°24'/22°36'.

Arlo, Hung.; pop. 30; 45 km W of Miskolc; 48°11'/20°16'; HSL.

Arloff, Germ.; 45 km S of Koln; 50°36'/06°47'; GED.

Armenis, Rom. BGN lists two possible localities with this name located at 45°12'/22°19' and 46°26'/24°50'. HSL.

Armensk, HSL. This pre-World War I community was not found in BGN gazetteers.

Armiansk Bazar, *see* Armyansk.

Armsheim, Germ.; pop. 4; 56 km SW of Frankfurt am Main; 49°48'/08°04'.

Armyansk, Ukr. (Armiansk Bazar); pop. 156; 133 km NNW of Simferopol; 46°06'/33°42'; GUM4, LDL, SF.

Arnau, *see* Ornowo.

Arneburg, Germ.; 94 km W of Berlin; 52°40'/12°00'; LDS.

Arnoldowo, Pol.; 88 km NE of Poznan; 52°58'/17°55'; POCEM.

Arnoldstein, Aus.; 146 km SW of Graz; 46°33'/13°43'; GUM4.

Arnoldsweiler, Germ.; 32 km SW of Koln; 50°50'/06°30'; GED.

Arnostovice, Cz.; pop. 9; 56 km SSE of Praha; 49°37'/14°36'.

Arnot, Hung.; pop. 4; 13 km NE of Miskolc; 48°08'/20°52'.

Arnsberg, Germ.; pop. 39; 94 km NE of Koln; 51°23'/08°05'; CAHJP, GUM5, LDS.

Arnsfelde, *see* Gostomia.

Arnstadt, Germ.; pop. 78; 114 km SW of Leipzig; 50°50'/10°57'; AMG, EDRD, EJ.

Arnstein, Germ.; pop. 32; 94 km E of Frankfurt am Main; 49°59'/09°59'; LDS, PHGB.

Arnswalde, *see* Choszczno.

Arokaja, *see* Arcalia.

Arokhaza, HSL. This pre-World War I community was not found in BGN gazetteers.

Arokszallas, HSL. This pre-World War I community was not found in BGN gazetteers.

Arokto, Hung.; pop. 28; 45 km SSE of Miskolc; 47°44'/20°57'; HSL.

Arolsen, Germ.; pop. 26; 126 km SSW of Hannover; 51°22'/09°01'; GUM5, HSL, JGFF.

Arosheviz, HSL. This pre-World War I community was not found in BGN gazetteers.

Arpasteu, (Arpasti, Arpasto); HSL. This pre-World War I community was not found in BGN gazetteers.

Arpasti, *see* Arpasteu.

Arpasto, *see* Arpasteu.

Arta, Greece; pop. 389; 62 km SSE of Ioannina; 39°10'/20°59'; EJ, GUM4.

Artand, Hung.; pop. 8; 133 km SE of Miskolc; 47°07'/21°46'.

Artasow, *see* Artasuv.

Artasuv, Ukr. (Artasow); pop. 24; 26 km NNE of Lvov; 50°01'/24°08'.

Artemovsk, Ukr. (Artemowsk, Bachmut, Bakhmut); pop. 6,631; 195 km SE of Kharkov; 48°35'/38°00'; EJ, GUM4, HSL, HSL2, LDL, SF.

Artemowsk, *see* Artemovsk.

Artsiz, Ukr. (Arciz, Artziz); pop. 842; 114 km SW of Odessa; 45°59'/29°25'; PHR2, YB.

Artyshchuv, Ukr. (Artyszczow); 26 km SW of Lvov; 49°46'/23°41'; PHP2.

Artyszczow, *see* Artyshchuv.

Artziz, *see* Artsiz.

Arva, Rom. BGN lists two possible localities with this name located at 44°59'/26°09' and 45°46'/26°58'. PHR1.

Arvanagyfalu, HSL. This pre-World War I community was not found in BGN gazetteers.

Arys, *see* Orzysz.

Arzen, Germ. (Aerzen); pop. 7; 50 km SSW of Hannover; 52°02'/09°16'; JGFF.

Arzheim, Germ. BGN lists two possible localities with this name located at 49°12'/08°05' and 50°21'/07°38'. GED.

As, Cz.; pop. 51; 163 km W of Praha; 50°13'/12°11'.

Asakert, *see* Nove Sady.

Asare, Lat. (Aseri, Assern); pop. 18; 50 km WNW of Daugavpils; 56°07'/25°54'; GUM4, PHLE.

Asch, Germ.; pop. 38; A number of towns share this name. It was not possible to determine from available information which one is being referenced.

Aschach, GUM5. A number of towns share this name. It was not possible to determine from available information which one is being referenced.

Aschaffenburg, Germ.; pop. 591; 38 km ESE of Frankfurt am Main; 49°59'/09°09'; AMG, CAHJP, EJ, GUM4, GUM5, HSL, HSL2, JGFF, PHGB, PHGBW.

Aschbach, Germ.; pop. 60; 50 km WNW of Nurnberg; 49°46'/10°34'; CAHJP, GUM5, PHGB.

Aschendorf, Germ.; 176 km WNW of Hannover; 53°04'/07°22'; LDS.

Aschenhausen, Germ.; pop. 12; 120 km NE of Frankfurt am Main; 50°36'/10°12'; CAHJP, EJ, LDS.

Aschersleben, Germ.; pop. 106; 82 km WNW of Leipzig; 51°45'/11°28'; EJ, GUM3, GUM4, GUM5, LDS.

Aschileu Mare, Rom. (Magyarujfalu); 32 km NNW of Cluj; 46°59'/23°30'; HSL.

Asen, Bulg. (Assen); 82 km NE of Sofija; 43°00'/24°12'; HSL.

Asenovgrad, Bulg. (Stanimaka); 150 km ESE of Sofija; 42°01'/24°52'; EJ.

Asenz, Germ. GED. This town was not found in BGN gazetteers under the given spelling.

Aseri, *see* Asare.

Ashendorf, Germ. LDS. This town was not found in BGN gazetteers under the given spelling.

Asite, Lat.; pop. 3; 157 km SW of Riga; 56°28'/21°40'.

Askovitz, *see* Noskovtsy.

Asmena, *see* Oshmyany.

Asminta, Lith.; pop. 14; 32 km SSE of Kaunas; 54°41'/24°00'.

Aspang Markt, Aus.; pop. 4; 75 km NNE of Graz; 47°33'/16°05'.

Asperg, Germ.; 19 km NNW of Stuttgart; 48°54'/09°07'; GUM3.

Asperhofen, Aus.; pop. 1; 32 km W of Wien; 48°14'/15°55'.

Aspern, *see* Aspern an der Donau.

Aspern an der Donau, Aus. (Aspern); 13 km ENE of Wien; 48°13'/16°30'; HSL.

Assakurt, *see* Nove Sady.

Assen, *see* Asen.

Assenheim, Germ.; pop. 20; 32 km NNE of Frankfurt am Main; 50°18'/08°49'; JGFF, LDS.

Assern, *see* Asare.

Assinghausen, Germ.; pop. 7; 114 km NE of Koln; 51°18'/08°30'.

Asslar, Germ.; pop. 20; 62 km NNW of Frankfurt am Main; 50°36'/08°28'.

Asszonyfa, Hung.; 107 km N of Nagykanizsa; 47°20'/17°24'; LDS.

Astileu, Rom. (Eskullo); pop. 20; 101 km WNW of Cluj; 47°02'/22°23'; HSL.

Astrik, *see* Ustrzyki Dolne.

Astrin, *see* Ostryna.

Asune, Lat. (Asunes); pop. 24; 69 km ENE of Daugavpils; 56°02'/27°37'; PHLE.

Asunes, *see* Asune.

Asvany, HSL. A number of towns share this name. It was not possible to determine from available information which one is being referenced.

Asvar, HSL. This pre-World War I community was not found in BGN gazetteers.

Aszalo, Hung.; pop. 28; 19 km NE of Miskolc; 48°13'/20°58'; HSL.

Aszanfo, HSL. This pre-World War I community was not found in BGN gazetteers.

Aszar, Hung.; pop. 19; 82 km W of Budapest; 47°31'/18°00'; HSL.

Aszod, Hung.; pop. 365; 38 km NE of Budapest; 47°39'/19°30'; COH, EJ, GUM5, HSL, LDL, LDS, PHH.

Aszubeszterce, *see* Dorolea.

Atachi, *see* Ataki.

Ataki, Mold. (Atachi, Otach Tyrg, Otaci Sat, Otaci Targ); pop. 2,785; 176 km NW of Kishinev; 48°27'/27°47'; EJ, GUM3, GUM4, GUM5, JGFF, SF.

Atany, Hung.; pop. 6; 62 km SSW of Miskolc; 47°37'/20°22'; HSL.

Atasiene, Lat.; pop. 17; 75 km NNW of Daugavpils; 56°32'/26°24'.

Atea, Rom.; pop. 26; 139 km NW of Cluj; 47°52'/22°47'.

Athens, Greece; pop. 1,578; 302 km SSE of Thessaloniki; 38°00'/23°44'; AMG, EDRD, GUM3, GUM4, GUM6, JGFF.

Atia, Rom. (Atya); pop. 8; 120 km E of Cluj; 46°29'/25°08'; HSL.

Atid, Rom. (Eted); 120 km ESE of Cluj; 46°27'/25°03'; HSL.

Atkar, Hung.; pop. 14; 69 km NE of Budapest; 47°43'/19°54'.

Atratzheim, HSL. This pre-World War I community was not found in BGN gazetteers.

Attala, Hung.; pop. 6; 82 km E of Nagykanizsa; 46°23'/18°04'.

Attendorn, Germ.; 69 km NE of Koln; 51°07'/07°54'; GED.

Attnang, Aus.; 56 km NE of Salzburg; 48°01'/13°43'; GUM5.

Atya, *see* Atia.

Atzenbrugg, Aus.; pop. 10; 38 km W of Wien; 48°17'/15°54'.

Atzgersdorf, Aus.; pop. 137; 13 km SSW of Wien; 48°09'/16°18'.

Aub, Germ.; pop. 78; 75 km W of Nurnberg; 49°33'/10°04'; CAHJP, GUM5, HSL, HSL2, PHGB.

Aubach, USSR. JGFF. A number of towns share this name. It was not possible to determine from available information which one is being referenced.

Aubstadt, Germ.; pop. 1; 107 km NW of Nurnberg; 50°20'/10°26'.

Auce, Lat. (Alt Oytch, Alt Oytz, Autz, Oitz, Oytz); pop. 151; 94 km SW of Riga; 56°28'/22°53'; LDL, PHLE, SF.

Aue, Germ.; 50 km SSE of Nurnberg; 49°05'/11°16'; PHGB.

Auerbach, Germ.; pop. 45; JGFF. A number of towns share this name. It was not possible to determine from available information which one is being referenced.

Auerbach (Schwaben), Germ.; 32 km N of Munchen; 48°24'/11°40'; PHGB.

Auerbach an der Bergstrasse, Germ.; 75 km N of Stuttgart; 49°24'/09°13'; CAHJP.

Auf dem Bock, Germ. (Bock); 107 km SSW of Koln; 50°10'/06°11'; COH.

Aufeld, Germ. (Auffeld); 69 km N of Hamburg; 54°05'/10°01'; HSL.

Auffeld, *see* Aufeld.

Aufhausen, Germ.; 88 km SSW of Nurnberg; 48°45'/10°29'; HSL, HSL2, JGFF, PHGB, PHGBW.

Aufkirchen, Germ.; 62 km SW of Nurnberg; 49°03'/10°28'; PHGB.

Aufsess, Germ.; pop. 20; 56 km N of Nurnberg; 49°54'/11°13'; GUM5, PHGB.

Augsburg, Germ.; pop. 910; 56 km WNW of Munchen; 48°22'/10°53'; AMG, EDRD, EJ, GED, GUM3, GUM4, GUM5, HSL, HSL2, JGFF, LDS, PHGB, PHGBW.

Augspil, (Augspils); pop. 59; This town was not found in BGN gazetteers under the given spelling.

Augspils, *see* Augspil.

Augustov, *see* Augustow.

Augustow, Pol. (Agustov, Augustov, Oygstova, Yagestov, Yagistov, Yagustova); pop. 2,261; 88 km NNW of Bialystok; 53°51'/23°00'; AMG, CAHJP, COH, EDRD, EJ, GA, GUM3, GUM5, GUM6, HSL, HSL2, ISH1, ISH3, JGFF, LDL, LYV, PHP4, POCEM, SF, YB.

Augustowa Ad Ratam, *see* Velikiye Mosty.

Aukshtadvaris, *see* Aukstadvaris.

Aukstadvaris, Lith. (Aukshtadvaris, Visoki Dvor, Visokidvar,

9

Visokidvor, Wysokidwor); pop. 297; 50 km WSW of Vilnius; 54°35'/24°32'; GUM3, LDL, LYV, SF, YL.

Aukstoji Panemune, Lith. (Ponemon); 13 km SE of Kaunas; 54°51'/23°58'; JGFF.

Auleja, Lat.; pop. 4; 50 km NE of Daugavpils; 56°03'/27°17'.

Aumeisteri, Lat. (Cirgali); pop. 7; 139 km NE of Riga; 57°31'/26°12'.

Aumund, *see* Vegesack.

Aurach, Germ.; 56 km SW of Nurnberg; 49°15'/10°25'; PHGB.

Aurelin, Pol.; pop. 6; 82 km ESE of Lublin; 50°56'/23°41'.

Aurelow, Pol.; pop. 39; 26 km NE of Czestochowa; 50°55'/19°21'; GUM5, PHP1.

Aurich, Germ.; pop. 400; 163 km WSW of Hamburg; 53°28'/07°29'; AMG, CAHJP, EJ, GED, GUM5, HSL, JGFF, LDS.

Ausbach, Germ.; 120 km NE of Frankfurt am Main; 50°50'/09°55'; AMG, HSL.

Auscha, *see* Ustek.

Auschwitz, *see* Oswiecim.

Auseu, Rom.; pop. 14; 88 km WNW of Cluj; 47°02'/22°30'.

Aushvits, *see* Oswiecim.

Auspitz, *see* Hustopece.

Aussee, *see* Usov.

Aussig, *see* Usti nad Labem.

Austerlitz, *see* Slavkov u Brna.

Austile, *see* Ustilug.

Autunowatz, *see* Antunovac.

Autz, *see* Auce.

Avafelsofalu, *see* Negresti.

Avanta, *see* Alanta.

Avas, HSL. A number of towns share this name. It was not possible to determine from available information which one is being referenced.

Avasujfalu, *see* Certeze.

Avasujvaros, *see* Orasu Nou.

Avdarma, Mold.; pop. 15; 88 km S of Kishinev; 46°15'/28°50'.

Ay, Germ. (Ai); BGN lists two possible localities with this name located at 47°41'/08°11' and 48°19'/10°02'. HSL.

Ayibator, LDL. This pre-World War I community was not found in BGN gazetteers.

Aynzingen, Ukr. (Einsingen, Eynzingen); pop. 11; 56 km NW of Lvov; 50°13'/23°29'.

Aysyn, *see* Gaysin.

Azarce, *see* Azartsy.

Azartsy, Byel. (Azarce); pop. 3; 120 km N of Minsk; 54°53'/27°41'.

Azipolia, *see* Zhovten.

Baba, Rom.; pop. 30; 69 km N of Cluj; 47°21'/23°45'; HSL.

Babadag, Rom.; 208 km ENE of Bucuresti; 44°54'/28°43'; GUM4, HSL.

Babahalma, *see* Bobohalma.

Babanka, Ukr. (Babynka, Bobinka); 19 km ESE of Uman; 48°42'/30°27'; SF.

Babarc, Hung.; pop. 5; 126 km WSW of Szeged; 46°00'/18°33'.

Babasesti, Rom.; pop. 13; 114 km NNW of Cluj; 47°46'/23°06'.

Babche, Ukr. (Babcze); pop. 54; 114 km WNW of Chernovtsy; 48°40'/24°28'.

Babcza, *see* Babta.

Babcze, *see* Babche.

Babdiu, Rom.; pop. 9; 45 km N of Cluj; 47°07'/23°42'.

Babelsberg, Germ. (Nowawes); pop. 142; 26 km SW of Berlin; 52°24'/13°06'.

Babenhausen, Germ.; pop. 52; 26 km ESE of Frankfurt am Main; 49°58'/08°57'; GUM3.

Babeni, Rom.; pop. 87; 62 km NNW of Cluj; 47°18'/23°24'; HSL.

Babesti, Rom. (Kisbanya); pop. 14; 139 km NNW of Cluj; 47°58'/23°05'; HSL.

Babiak, Pol. (Frauendorf); pop. 237; 82 km NW of Lodz; 52°21'/18°40'; GUM4, HSL, JGFF, LDS, PHP1, SF.

Babice, Pol.; pop. 20; 50 km WSW of Krakow; 50°03'/19°12';

GUM3, GUM5, GUM6, HSL. *See also* Babiche.

Babiche, Ukr. (Babice); pop. 39; 56 km NNE of Lvov; 50°13'/24°32'.

Babicheva, Ukr. (Babichova, Babuchow); pop. 21; 45 km SW of Chernovtsy; 48°10'/25°23'.

Babichova, *see* Babicheva.

Babichy, Pol.; 19 km S of Lodz; 51°39'/19°29'; GA.

Babimost, Pol. (Bomst); 88 km SW of Poznan; 52°10'/15°49'; HSL, LDS.

Babin (Bessarabia), Ukr. (Babony); pop. 112; 75 km NE of Chernovtsy; 48°32'/26°52'; HSL, HSL2.

Babin (Bucovina), Ukr.; pop. 64; 32 km W of Chernovtsy; 48°20'/25°29'.

Babina Greda, Yug.; pop. 5; 157 km W of Beograd; 45°07'/18°32'.

Babince, *see* Babintsy.

Babinovichi, Byel. (Babinowicze); pop. 332; 45 km SE of Vitebsk; 54°50'/30°35'; SF.

Babinowicze, *see* Babinovichi.

Babintse, *see* Babintsy.

Babintsy, Ukr. (Babince, Babintse); pop. 37; 45 km N of Chernovtsy; 48°41'/26°03'; PHP2.

Babi Yar, Ukr.; 6 km E of Kiyev; 50°26'/30°33'; EDRD, EJ, GUM4, GUM5, GUM6. Not a town, but a ravine on the outskirts of Kiyev notorious for the murder of tens of thousands of Jews during the Holocaust.

Babocsa, Hung.; pop. 53; 56 km SE of Nagykanizsa; 46°02'/17°22'; PHH.

Babolna, Hung. (Bobalna); 82 km W of Budapest; 47°38'/17°59'; HSL.

Babony, *see* Babin (Bessarabia).

Babonymegyer, Hung. (Nagybabony); pop. 38; 94 km NE of Nagykanizsa; 46°45'/18°07'; LDS.

Babot, Hung.; pop. 8; 133 km N of Nagykanizsa; 47°34'/17°05'.

Babstadt, Germ.; 56 km NNW of Stuttgart; 49°15'/09°04'; LDS.

Babta, Rom. (Babcza); pop. 17; 94 km NW of Cluj; 47°28'/22°56'.

Babtai, Lith. (Bobt, Bobty); pop. 153; 26 km NNW of Kaunas; 55°06'/23°48'; GUM3, HSL, JGFF, LDL, SF, YL.

Babuchow, *see* Babicheva.

Babule, Pol.; pop. 3; 107 km WNW of Przemysl; 50°24'/21°32'.

Babynka, *see* Babanka.

Bac, Yug. (Bacs); 120 km WNW of Beograd; 45°23'/19°14'; HSL, JGFF, PHY.

Bacau, Rom.; pop. 9,593; 82 km SSW of Iasi; 46°34'/26°54'; CAHJP, EJ, GUM3, GUM4, GUM5, GYLA, HSL, JGFF, LDL.

Bacesti, Rom.; pop. 426; 50 km SSW of Iasi; 46°51'/27°14'; PHR1.

Bacharach, Germ.; pop. 35; 62 km WSW of Frankfurt am Main; 50°04'/07°46'; EDRD, EJ.

Bachchysaray, *see* Bakhchisaray.

Bachlowa, Pol.; pop. 5; 50 km SSW of Przemysl; 49°26'/22°21'.

Bachmac, *see* Bakhmach.

Bachmatch, *see* Bakhmach.

Bachmut, *see* Artemovsk.

Bachnowate, *see* Bagnovate.

Bachory, Pol.; pop. 11; 38 km N of Przemysl; 50°07'/22°55'.

Bachorz, Pol.; pop. 12; 38 km W of Przemysl; 49°50'/22°17'.

Bachow, Pol.; pop. 82; 19 km W of Przemysl; 49°48'/22°30'; AMG, HSL.

Bachoy, Mold. (Bachoyu, Bacioiu); pop. 24; 13 km SE of Kishinev; 46°55'/28°54'.

Bachoyu, *see* Bachoy.

Bachtchisarai, *see* Bakhchisaray.

Bachtshisarai, *see* Bakhchisaray.

Bachuv, Ukr. (Baczow); pop. 27; 62 km ESE of Lvov; 49°32'/24°39'.

Bacia, Rom. (Bacsi, Deva); pop. 120 km S of Cluj; 45°48'/23°01'; GUM4, HSL, HSL2, PHR1.

Bacieczki, Pol.; 6 km WNW of Bialystok; 53°09'/23°06'; GUM3.

Bacioiu, *see* Bachoy.

Backa Palanka, Yug. (Backa Polana?); pop. 191; 101 km WNW of Beograd; 45°15'/19°22'; COH, GUM4, PHY.

Backa Polana, *possibly* Backa Palanka.

Backa Topola, Yug.; pop. 411; 126 km NW of Beograd; 45°49'/19°39'; PHY.

Backau, *see* Backov.

Backi Monostor, Yug. (Monostorszeg); pop. 22; 163 km WNW of Beograd; 45°48'/18°56'; HSL.

Backi Petrovac, Yug.; pop. 100; 94 km WNW of Beograd; 45°22'/19°36'; PHY.

Backnang, Germ.; pop. 2; 26 km NNE of Stuttgart; 48°57'/09°26'; GUM3.

Backo Gradiste, Yug. (Bacs Folovar); pop. 49; 88 km NNW of Beograd; 45°32'/20°02'.

Backo Petrovo Selo, Yug. (Bacs Peczello); pop. 282; 101 km NNW of Beograd; 45°42'/20°05'; CAHJP, PHY.

Backov, Cz. (Backau); 82 km ESE of Praha; 49°44'/15°28'; HSL.

Backowice, Pol.; pop. 5; 107 km SW of Lublin; 50°48'/21°14'.

Bacs, *see* Bac.

Bacsa, Hung.; pop. 12; 107 km W of Budapest; 47°43'/17°40'; HSL.

Bacsalmas, Hung.; pop. 169; 62 km WSW of Szeged; 46°08'/19°20'; COH, HSL, HSL2, PHH.

Bacsbokod, Hung. (Bikity); pop. 29; 75 km WSW of Szeged; 46°07'/19°10'; LDS.

Bacseni, *see* Baksheny.

Bacs Folovar, *see* Backo Gradiste.

Bacsi, *see* Bacia.

Bacskamadaras, *see* Pasareni.

Bacs Peczello, *see* Backo Petrovo Selo.

Bacstopolya, GUM6, HSL. This pre-World War I community was not found in BGN gazetteers.

Bacza, Pol.; 82 km ESE of Krakow; 49°33'/20°45'; HSL.

Baczal Gorny, Pol.; pop. 16; 101 km WSW of Przemysl; 49°47'/21°22'.

Baczkamadaras, *see* Pasareni.

Baczki, Pol.; pop. 133; 94 km SSW of Bialystok; 52°22'/22°27'.

Baczow, *see* Bachuv.

Badacin, Rom.; pop. 4; 75 km WNW of Cluj; 47°15'/22°51'.

Badacsonytomaj, Hung.; pop. 31; 62 km NE of Nagykanizsa; 46°48'/17°31'.

Badacsonytordemic, Hung. (Nemestordemic); pop. 12; 56 km NNE of Nagykanizsa; 46°49'/17°29'.

Bad Aibling, Germ.; pop. 10; 45 km SE of Munchen; 47°52'/12°00'; GUM3.

Badalo, HSL. This pre-World War I community was not found in BGN gazetteers.

Badan, Cz.; 133 km ENE of Bratislava; 48°20'/18°51'; HSL.

Badbergen, Germ.; 120 km W of Hannover; 52°38'/07°59'; JGFF, LDS.

Bad Berneck, *see* Bad Berneck im Fichtelgebirge.

Bad Berneck im Fichtelgebirge, Germ. (Bad Berneck); 75 km NNE of Nurnberg; 50°03'/11°40'; PHGB.

Bad Buchau, *see* Buchau.

Bad Deutsch Altenburg, Aus.; 45 km E of Wien; 48°08'/16°54'; GUM5.

Bad Durkheim, Germ. (Durkheim); pop. 184; 82 km SSW of Frankfurt am Main; 49°28'/08°12'; GED, GUM5, HSL, HSL2, LDL, LDS.

Bad Durrheim, Germ.; 94 km SSW of Stuttgart; 48°01'/08°32'; PHGBW.

Bad Ems, Germ. (Ems); pop. 116; 69 km WNW of Frankfurt am Main; 50°20'/07°43'; GUM5, HSL, LDS.

Baden, Aus.; pop. 1,108; 26 km SSW of Wien; 48°01'/16°14'; AMG, CAHJP, GUM3, GUM4, GUM4, HSL2, JGFF.

Baden-Wurttemburg; Not a town, but a region of southwestern Germany.

Baden Baden, Germ.; pop. 435; 69 km WSW of Stuttgart; 48°45'/08°15'; AMG, EJ, GUM3, GUM5, HSL, ISH1, LDS, PHGBW.

Badenweiler, Germ.; pop. 11; 157 km SW of Stuttgart; 47°48'/07°41'; PHGBW.

Badfalva, *see* Berbesti.

Bad Freienwalde, Germ. (Freienwalde); pop. 67; 56 km NE of Berlin; 52°47'/14°02'; LDS.

Bad Friedrichshall, Germ.; 56 km N of Stuttgart; 49°14'/09°13'; JGFF.

Bad Gandersheim, Germ. (Gandersheim); 62 km SSE of Hannover; 51°52'/10°02'; LDS.

Badgastein, Aus.; pop. 7; 82 km S of Salzburg; 47°07'/13°08'.

Bad Godesberg, Germ. (Godesberg); pop. 109; 38 km SE of Koln; 50°41'/07°09'; GED, GUM3.

Bad Harzburg, Germ.; 82 km ESE of Hannover; 51°53'/10°34'; GUM5.

Bad Hersfeld, Germ. (Hersfeld); pop. 360; 114 km NNE of Frankfurt am Main; 50°52'/09°42'; COH, GUM3.

Bad Homburg, *see* Bad Homburg vor der Hohe.

Bad Homburg vor der Hohe, Germ. (Bad Homburg, Homburg, Homburg vor der Hohe); pop. 400; 19 km NNW of Frankfurt am Main; 50°13'/08°37'; EJ, GED, GUM3, HSL, JGFF, LDS.

Bad Honnef, Germ.; 45 km SE of Koln; 50°38'/07°14'; GED.

Bad Hornburg, *see* Hornburg.

Badiceni, *see* Badichany.

Badichany, Mold. (Badiceni); pop. 47; 146 km NNW of Kishinev; 48°13'/28°04'.

Badicu, *see* Badyku Moldavskoye.

Badin, Cz.; 150 km WSW of Kosice; 48°40'/19°08'; HSL.

Bad Ischl, Aus.; pop. 36; 45 km E of Salzburg; 47°43'/13°37'; GUM5.

Bad Kissingen, Germ. (Kissingen); pop. 504; 101 km ENE of Frankfurt am Main; 50°12'/10°05'; CAHJP, EDRD, EJ, GUM3, GUM4, GUM5, HSL, JGFF, LDL, PHGB.

Bad Koenigswart, *see* Lazne Kynzvart.

Bad Konig, Germ. (Konig); pop. 85; 45 km SE of Frankfurt am Main; 49°45'/09°01'; LDS.

Bad Kreuznach, Germ. (Kreutznach, Kreuznach); pop. 680; 62 km SW of Frankfurt am Main; 49°50'/07°52'; AMG, CAHJP, EDRD, EJ, HSL, HSL2, JGFF.

Bad Lauchstadt, Germ. (Langensalza); pop. 34; 38 km W of Leipzig; 51°23'/11°51'; GUM3.

Bad Lippspringe, Germ. (Lippspringe); pop. 14; 88 km SW of Hannover; 51°47'/08°49'.

Badljevina, Yug.; pop. 6; 94 km ESE of Zagreb; 45°31'/17°12'.

Bad Mergentheim, Germ. (Mergentheim); pop. 205; 88 km NNE of Stuttgart; 49°29'/09°46'; AMG, EDRD, EJ, GED, GUM3, GUM4, GUM5, HSL, HSL2, JGFF, LDL, PHGBW.

Bad Mingolsheim, *see* Mingolsheim.

Bad Nauheim, Germ. (Nauheim); pop. 300; 38 km N of Frankfurt am Main; 50°22'/08°45'; AMG, EJ, GUM3, GUM4.

Bad Neuenahr, Germ.; pop. 70; 50 km SSE of Koln; 50°33'/07°08'.

Bad Neustadt an der Saale, Germ. (Neustadt an der Saale); pop. 162; 114 km ENE of Frankfurt am Main; 50°20'/10°13'; GED, GUM3, GUM5, PHGB.

Bad Oeynhausen, Germ.; pop. 71; 62 km WSW of Hannover; 52°12'/08°48'.

Bad Orb, Germ. (Orb); pop. 79; 50 km ENE of Frankfurt am Main; 50°13'/09°21'.

Bad Polzin, *see* Polczyn Zdroj.

Bad Pyrmont, Germ.; pop. 42; 56 km SSW of Hannover; 51°59'/09°15'; GUM5.

Badragaii Vechi, *see* Braga.

Badragii Noui, *see* Braga.

Badragii Vechi, *see* Staryy Badrazh.

Bad Rappenau, Germ. (Rappenau); pop. 56; 56 km N of Stuttgart; 49°14'/09°06'; GUM3, LDS, PHGBW.

Bad Reichenhall, Germ.; pop. 49; 107 km ESE of Munchen; 47°44'/12°53'; AMG, GUM3, GUM5, GUM6, PHGB.

Badrzychowice, Pol.; pop. 6; 69 km NE of Krakow; 50°21'/20°47'.

Bad Salzschlirf, Germ. (Salzschlirf); 82 km NE of Frankfurt am Main; 50°37'/09°30'; GUM3.

Bad Salzuflen, Germ. (Salzuflen); pop. 114; 69 km SW of Hannover; 52°05'/08°46'; GUM4, LDS.

Bad Salzungen, Germ.; pop. 22; 139 km NE of Frankfurt am Main; 50°49'/10°14'.

Bad Schwalbach, Germ.; pop. 96; 45 km W of Frankfurt am Main; 50°08'/08°04'; AMG.

Bad Segeberg, Germ. (Segeberg); pop. 23; 50 km NNE of Hamburg; 53°56'/10°19'; HSL, JGFF.

Bad Soden, see Bad Soden am Taunus.

Bad Soden am Taunus, Germ. (Bad Soden); pop. 50; 19 km W of Frankfurt am Main; 50°08'/08°30'; GUM5.

Bad Sulzburg, Germ. (Sulzburg Baden); 150 km SW of Stuttgart; 47°49'/07°45'; JGFF.

Bad Tennstedt, Germ.; pop. 47; 107 km WSW of Leipzig; 51°09'/10°50'.

Bad Tolz, Germ.; pop. 21; 50 km S of Munchen; 47°46'/11°34'; ISH1, PHGB.

Bad Vilbel, Germ. (Vilbel); pop. 23; 19 km NNE of Frankfurt am Main; 50°11'/08°45'; GUM5.

Bad Voslau, Aus.; pop. 99; 32 km SSW of Wien; 47°58'/16°12'.

Bad Wildungen, Germ.; pop. 150; 120 km N of Frankfurt am Main; 51°07'/09°07'.

Bad Wimpfen, Germ. (Wimpfen); 56 km N of Stuttgart; 49°14'/09°08'; AMG, LDS, PHGBW.

Bad Worishofen, Germ.; pop. 7; 75 km WSW of Munchen; 48°01'/10°36'; GED, JGFF, PHGB.

Badyku Moldavskoye, Mold. (Badicu); pop. 11; 114 km S of Kishinev; 46°06'/28°17'.

Bagailaviskis, see Bagaslaviskis.

Bagamer, Hung.; pop. 91; 114 km ESE of Miskolc; 47°27'/22°00'; HSL, PHH.

Bagaslavishkis, see Bagaslaviskis.

Bagaslaviskis, Lith. (Bagailaviskis, Bagaslavishkis, Bogoslavishok); 56 km NW of Vilnius; 55°05'/24°46'; YL.

Bagatele, Pol.; pop. 32; Described in the Black Book as being in the Bialystok region of Poland, this town was not found in BGN gazetteers.

Bagdad, Rom.; 126 km NE of Bucuresti; 45°08'/27°22'; HSL, LDL.

Bagdoniske, Lith. (Bogdananrz); 26 km SSW of Siauliai; 55°46'/23°11'; JGFF.

Bagienica, Pol.; pop. 118; 75 km ENE of Krakow; 50°06'/21°00'; PHP3. This town was located on an interwar map of Poland but does not appear in contemporary gazetteers. Map coordinates are approximate.

Baglyasalja, Hung.; pop. 17; 75 km WSW of Miskolc; 48°06'/19°47'.

Bagna, Pol.; pop. 57; 32 km WNW of Czestochowa; 50°53'/18°43'.

Bagnovate, Ukr. (Bachnowate, Bakhnovate, Bochnovata); pop. 26; 107 km SSW of Lvov; 49°04'/23°09'; HSL, SF.

Bagolasanc, Hung.; pop. 3; 6 km ESE of Nagykanizsa; 46°26'/17°02'.

Bagolyfalu, see Hurez.

Bagolyuk, GUM4. This town was not found in BGN gazetteers under the given spelling.

Bagota, see Bohata.

Bagrationovsk, USSR (Preussisch Eylau); pop. 12; 45 km SSE of Kaliningrad; 54°23'/20°39'.

Bagrineshti, see Bagrineshty.

Bagrineshty, Mold. (Bagrineshti, Bagrinesti); pop. 34; 107 km NW of Kishinev; 47°52'/28°15'.

Bagrinesti, see Bagrineshty.

Bagrinovka, Ukr. (Bahrinesti); pop. 21; 45 km S of Chernovtsy; 47°59'/25°57'.

Bahmutea, see Mikhaylovka (Bessarabia).

Bahn, Pol. (Banie); 45 km SSE of Szczecin; 53°06'/14°39'; LDS.

Bahnbrucken, Germ.; 50 km NW of Stuttgart; 49°07'/08°47'; LDS.

Bahnea, Rom.; 82 km ESE of Cluj; 46°22'/24°29'; HSL, HSL2.

Bahrinesti, see Bagrinovka.

Baia Mare, Rom. (Nagy Banya, Nagybanya); pop. 2,030; 107 km N of Cluj; 47°40'/23°35'; AMG, COH, EJ, GUM4, GUM5, GUM6, HSL, LDL, PHR2, YB.

Baiasesti, see Baisesti.

Baia Sprie, see Sajoszentpeter.

Baiersdorf, Germ.; 32 km NNW of Nurnberg; 49°40'/11°02'; EJ, HSL, HSL2, JGFF, PHGB.

Baiertal, see Baierthal.

Baierthal, Germ. (Baiertal, Bayertal); pop. 31; 88 km ESE of Frankfurt am Main; 49°41'/09°45'; GED, HSL, JGFF, LDS, PHGBW.

Baimaclia, see Baymakliya.

Bain, see Banovce nad Bebravou.

Bainet, Rom. (Baineti); pop. 23; 150 km WNW of Iasi; 47°58'/25°57'; PHR2.

Baineti, see Bainet.

Bairamcea, see Nikolayevka Novorossiyskaya.

Baisa Gala, see Baisogala.

Baisagole, see Baisogala.

Baisesti, Rom. (Baiasesti); pop. 43; 114 km WNW of Iasi; 47°29'/26°07'.

Baisingen, Germ.; pop. 100; 45 km SW of Stuttgart; 48°30'/08°47'; GUM5, PHGBW.

Baisk, see Bauska.

Baisogala, Lith. (Baisa Gala, Baisagole, Baisogola, Beisogala); pop. 106; 45 km SE of Siauliai; 55°38'/23°43'; HSL, JGFF, LDL, SF, YL.

Baisogola, see Baisogala.

Baita (Satu Mare), Rom.; pop. 25; 88 km NNW of Cluj; 47°32'/23°09'.

Baita Salaj, Rom.; pop. 36; 38 km NNE of Cluj; 47°02'/23°52'.

Baius, see Bayush.

Baiut, Rom. (Erzsebetbanya); pop. 20; 101 km N of Cluj; 47°37'/24°00'.

Baj, Hung.; 56 km WNW of Budapest; 47°39'/18°22'; HSL.

Baja, Hung.; pop. 1,648; 88 km WSW of Szeged; 46°11'/18°58'; AMG, COH, EDRD, EJ, GUM4, GUM5, HSL, JGFF, LDS, PHH.

Bajdy, Pol.; pop. 9; 82 km WSW of Przemysl; 49°46'/21°40'.

Bajkowce, Pol. PHP2. This town was not found in BGN gazetteers under the given spelling.

Bajkowitz, see Bojkovice.

Bajmok, Yug.; pop. 131; 150 km NW of Beograd; 45°58'/19°26'; PHY.

Bajna, Hung.; pop. 3; 38 km WNW of Budapest; 47°39'/18°36'; HSL.

Bajot, Hung.; pop. 6; 50 km WNW of Budapest; 47°44'/18°34'; HSL.

Bajramtscha, see Nikolayevka Novorossiyskaya.

Bak, Hung.; 38 km NNW of Nagykanizsa; 46°43'/16°51'; HSL.

Baka, Hung.; 101 km ENE of Miskolc; 48°09'/22°09'; HSL, HSL2, LDS.

Bakalarzewo, Pol. (Baklerava, Baklerove, Baklrovo); pop. 141; 114 km NNW of Bialystok; 54°06'/22°39'; CAHJP, HSL, JGFF, LDL, LDS, PHP4, POCEM, SF, YB.

Bakar, Yug.; pop. 1; 126 km SW of Zagreb; 45°18'/14°32'.

Bakavsk, see Bukowsko.

Bakhchisaray, see Bakhchisaray.

Bakhchisaray, Ukr. (Bachchysaray, Bachtchisarai, Bachtshisarai, Bakhchisarai); pop. 275; 32 km SSW of Simferopol; 44°45'/33°52'; EDRD, EJ, GUM4, GUM5, HSL, SF.

Bakhmach, Ukr. (Bachmac, Bachmatch); pop. 612; 32 km WSW of Konotop; 51°11'/32°47'; HSL, LDL, SF.

Bakhmut, see Artemovsk.

Bakhnovate, see Bagnovate.

Baki, see Buki.

Baklerava, see Bakalarzewo.

Baklerove, *see* Bakalarzewo.

Baklrovo, *see* Bakalarzewo.

Bakoca, Hung.; pop. 6; 82 km ESE of Nagykanizsa; 46°13'/18°00'.

Bakonszeg, Hung.; 114 km SE of Miskolc; 47°11'/21°27'; LDS.

Bakonybank, Hung.; pop. 3; 88 km WSW of Budapest; 47°28'/17°54'.

Bakonybel, Hung.; pop. 12; 107 km WSW of Budapest; 47°15'/17°44'.

Bakonycsernye, Hung.; pop. 37; 75 km WSW of Budapest; 47°19'/18°05'.

Bakonygyirot, Hung.; pop. 7; 94 km WSW of Budapest; 47°25'/17°48'.

Bakonyjako, Hung.; pop. 3; 101 km NNE of Nagykanizsa; 47°13'/17°36'.

Bakonykoppany, Hung.; pop. 6; 107 km WSW of Budapest; 47°20'/17°41'.

Bakonykuti, Hung.; pop. 2; 75 km SW of Budapest; 47°15'/18°12'.

Bakonynana, Hung.; pop. 6; 88 km SW of Budapest; 47°17'/17°58'.

Bakonyoszlop, Hung.; pop. 4; 88 km WSW of Budapest; 47°21'/17°56'.

Bakonyszentivan, Hung.; pop. 7; 107 km WSW of Budapest; 47°24'/17°40'.

Bakonyszentkiraly, Hung.; pop. 25; 88 km WSW of Budapest; 47°22'/17°53'; LDS.

Bakonyszentlaszlo, Hung.; pop. 19; 94 km WSW of Budapest; 47°23'/17°48'.

Bakonyszombathely, Hung.; pop. 20; 82 km WSW of Budapest; 47°28'/17°58'.

Bakonytamasi, Hung.; pop. 20; 101 km WSW of Budapest; 47°25'/17°44'.

Bakow, Pol. (Bankau); pop. 2; 38 km SE of Wroclaw; 50°46'/17°17'.

Bakowa Gora, *see* Bakowa Gorna.

Bakowa Gorna, Pol. (Bakowa Gora); pop. 9; 69 km NE of Czestochowa; 51°09'/19°52'.

Bakowce, Pol.; pop. 21; Described in the *Black Book* as being in the Lwow region of Poland, this town was not found in BGN gazetteers.

Bakowice, *see* Bankwitz.

Bakowski Mlyn, Pol.; pop. 3; 88 km S of Gdansk; 53°35'/18°35'.

Baksa, Hung.; 101 km ESE of Nagykanizsa; 45°57'/18°05'; HSL, HSL2, LDS.

Baksheny, Mold. (Bacseni); pop. 2; 62 km W of Kishinev; 47°05'/28°01'.

Baksht, *see* Bakshty.

Baksht Borishoka, *see* Bakshty.

Bakshty, Byel. (Baksht, Baksht Borishoka, Bakszty); 94 km W of Minsk; 53°56'/26°11'; GUM4, LDL, SF.

Bakszty, *see* Bakshty.

Bakta, Hung.; pop. 28; 38 km NNE of Miskolc; 48°22'/21°02'; HSL.

Baktaloranthaza, Hung.; pop. 211; 94 km E of Miskolc; 48°00'/22°05'; AMG, PHH.

Bala, HSL. This pre-World War I community was not found in BGN gazetteers.

Balabanca, *see* Balabanka.

Balabaneshty, Mold. (Balabanesti); pop. 7; 26 km NE of Kishinev; 47°04'/29°08'.

Balabanesti, *see* Balabaneshty.

Balabanka, Ukr. (Balabanca); pop. 4; 101 km SSW of Odessa; 45°46'/29°51'.

Bala Banovka, *see* Balabanovka.

Balabanovka, Ukr. (Bala Banovka, Balabanowka); 56 km WNW of Uman; 49°07'/29°37'; LDL, SF.

Balabanowka, *see* Balabanovka.

Balaceana, Rom.; pop. 134; 126 km WNW of Iasi; 47°38'/26°03'; PHR2.

Balajt, Hung.; pop. 7; 32 km N of Miskolc; 48°19'/20°48'.

Balaklava, USSR; pop. 70; This town was not found in BGN gazetteers under the given spelling.

Balakleya, *see* Balakliya.

Balakliya, Ukr. (Balakleya); 163 km NW of Dnepropetrovsk; 49°37'/33°45'; JGFF.

Balanca Grosi, Rom. (Grosi Satu Mare); pop. 20; 75 km W of Cluj; 46°56'/22°36'.

Balaneshty, Mold. (Balanesti); pop. 48; 62 km WNW of Kishinev; 47°13'/28°05'.

Balanesti, *see* Balaneshty.

Balanovca, GUM4. This town was not found in BGN gazetteers under the given spelling.

Balashadzharmat, *see* Balassagyarmat.

Balasineshty, Ukr. (Balasinesti); pop. 28; 82 km E of Chernovtsy; 48°15'/26°58'.

Balasinesti, *see* Balasineshty.

Balassagyarmat, Hung. (Balashadzharmat, Boloshodyormot, Dyormot, Dzhormot); pop. 2,013; 69 km N of Budapest; 48°05'/19°18'; AMG, COH, EJ, HSL, HSL2, LDL, LDS, LYV, PHH.

Balatina, *see* Bolotino.

Balaton, Hung.; 38 km WSW of Miskolc; 48°06'/20°19'; HSL.

Balatonakali, Hung. (Akali); pop. 4; 75 km NE of Nagykanizsa; 46°53'/17°45'.

Balatonalmadi, Hung.; pop. 6; 94 km SW of Budapest; 47°02'/18°01'; GUM3.

Balatonaracs, Hung.; pop. 6; 88 km NE of Nagykanizsa; 46°58'/17°54'.

Balatonbereny, Hung.; pop. 14; 45 km NNE of Nagykanizsa; 46°43'/17°19'.

Balatonboglar, Hung. (Boglar); pop. 213; 62 km NE of Nagykanizsa; 46°47'/17°40'; GUM4, HSL, LDS, PHH.

Balatonbozsok, Hung.; pop. 10; 88 km SW of Budapest; 46°57'/18°14'.

Balatoncsicso, Hung.; pop. 2; 75 km NNE of Nagykanizsa; 46°56'/17°40'.

Balatonendred, Hung.; pop. 10; 88 km NE of Nagykanizsa; 46°50'/17°59'.

Balatonfokajar, Hung.; pop. 43; 88 km SW of Budapest; 47°01'/18°13'; LDS.

Balatonfured, Hung.; pop. 143; 88 km NE of Nagykanizsa; 46°57'/17°53'; HSL, LDS, PHH.

Balatonkenese, Hung.; pop. 17; 88 km SW of Budapest; 47°02'/18°07'.

Balatonkeresztur, Hung.; pop. 7; 45 km NE of Nagykanizsa; 46°42'/17°23'.

Balatonkiliti, Hung.; pop. 53; 101 km SW of Budapest; 46°53'/18°05'; PHH.

Balatonlelle, Hung.; pop. 13; 69 km NE of Nagykanizsa; 46°47'/17°42'.

Balatonmagyarod, Hung.; pop. 4; 26 km NNE of Nagykanizsa; 46°36'/17°11'.

Balatonszabadi, Hung.; pop. 8; 101 km SW of Budapest; 46°53'/18°08'.

Balatonszarszo, Hung.; pop. 27; 75 km NE of Nagykanizsa; 46°50'/17°50'.

Balatonszemes, Hung.; pop. 57; 75 km NE of Nagykanizsa; 46°49'/17°47'; PHH.

Balatonszentgyorgy, Hung.; pop. 17; 45 km NNE of Nagykanizsa; 46°41'/17°18'.

Balatonudvari, Hung.; pop. 4; 82 km NE of Nagykanizsa; 46°54'/17°49'.

Balatonujhely, Hung.; 94 km NE of Nagykanizsa; 46°54'/18°02'; GUM5.

Balatonujlak, Hung.; pop. 4; 38 km NE of Nagykanizsa; 46°40'/17°23'.

Balatonzamardi, *see* Zamardi.

Balaureshty, Mold. (Balauresti); pop. 14; 56 km WSW of Kishinev; 46°56'/28°08'.

Balauresti, *see* Balaureshty.

Balauseri, Rom. (Balavasar); 88 km ESE of Cluj; 46°24'/24°41';

HSL.

Balavasar, *see* Balauseri.

Balazsfalva, *see* Blaj.

Balazstelke, *see* Blajel.

Balbieriskis, Lith. (Balberiskis, Balbirishok, Balbirishuk, Balbirshuk, Balkerishki, Barbircheff); pop. 507; 45 km S of Kaunas; 54°32'/23°53'; GUM3, HSL, JGFF, LDL, SF, YL.

Balbirishok, *see* Balbieriskis.

Balbirishuk, *see* Balbieriskis.

Balbirshuk, *see* Balbieriskis.

Balc, Rom.; pop. 23; 101 km WNW of Cluj; 47°17'/22°32'.

Balcauti, *see* Balkautsy.

Balcautii de Jos, *see* Balkauts de Zhos.

Balceana, *see* Bolchany.

Balchi, *see* Balki.

Baldenburg, Pol.; pop. 48; 126 km SW of Gdansk; 53°53'/16°50'; LDS.

Baldingen, Germ.; 75 km SSW of Nurnberg; 48°52'/10°29'; PHGB.

Baldone, Lat.; pop. 9; 32 km ESE of Riga; 56°45'/24°24'.

Baleliai Antrieji, Lith. (Varnenai); 82 km NE of Kaunas; 55°26'/24°43'; GUM3.

Balf, Hung.; 139 km NNW of Nagykanizsa; 47°39'/16°40'; GUM4, HSL.

Balice, *see* Balichi.

Baliche Podruzhne, Ukr. (Balicze Podrozne); pop. 25; 82 km S of Lvov; 49°10'/24°03'.

Baliche Zazhechne, Ukr. (Balicze Podgorne); pop. 24; 82 km S of Lvov; 49°10'/24°06'.

Balichi, Ukr. (Balice); pop. 90; 75 km WSW of Lvov; 49°46'/23°01'; HSL2.

Balicze Podgorne, *see* Baliche Zazhechne.

Balicze Podrozne, *see* Baliche Podruzhne.

Baligrod, Pol. (Beligrod); pop. 515; 62 km SSW of Przemysl; 49°20'/22°17'; COH, EGRS, GUM5, HSL, HSL2, JGFF, LYV, PHP2, PHP3, POCEM, SF, YB.

Balin, Ukr.; pop. 1,258; 88 km NNE of Chernovtsy; 48°52'/26°41'; COH, HSL, LDL, SF, YB.

Balinesti, Rom.; pop. 7; 139 km WNW of Iasi; 47°54'/26°10'.

Balingen, Germ.; 62 km SSW of Stuttgart; 48°17'/08°51'; PHGBW.

Balintfalva, *see* Valentova.

Balkany, Hung.; pop. 531; 88 km ESE of Miskolc; 47°46'/21°52'; HSL, HSL2, LDL, LDS, PHH.

Balkauts de Zhos, Mold. (Balcautii de Jos); pop. 30; 182 km NW of Kishinev; 48°17'/27°12'.

Balkautsy, Mold. (Balcauti); pop. 33; 189 km NW of Kishinev; 48°19'/27°12'.

Balkerishki, *see* Balbieriskis.

Balki, Ukr. (Balchi); 56 km SW of Vinnitsa; 49°04'/27°41'; GUM4, PHR1.

Balki (Lublin); Described in HSL as near Lublin, it is not listed in interwar or contemporary gazetteers.

Balki (near Lublin), Pol. HSL.

Balkunai, Lith. (Balkuny); pop. 1; 62 km S of Kaunas; 54°23'/23°53'.

Balkuny, *see* Balkunai.

Ballenberg, Germ.; 75 km N of Stuttgart; 49°24'/09°33'; JGFF, PHGBW.

Ballenstedt, Germ.; pop. 11; 88 km WNW of Leipzig; 51°43'/11°14'; HSL, LDS.

Balmazujvaros, Hung.; pop. 395; 69 km SE of Miskolc; 47°37'/21°21'; AMG, GUM5, HSL, LDS, PHH, YB.

Balnaca, Rom.; pop. 13; 75 km W of Cluj; 46°57'/22°35'.

Balninkai, Lith. (Bolnik); pop. 237; 75 km NNW of Vilnius; 55°18'/25°08'; YL.

Balog, *see* Blh nad Iplom.

Balon, Cz.; 50 km ESE of Bratislava; 47°50'/17°40'; HSL, HSL2.

Balozsameggyes, Hung.; pop. 3; 88 km N of Nagykanizsa; 47°09'/16°52'.

Balsa, Hung.; pop. 44; 56 km ENE of Miskolc; 48°11'/21°33';

HSL.

Balta, Ukr.; pop. 9,116; 107 km SSW of Uman; 47°56'/29°37'; EDRD, EJ, GUM4, GUM5, HSL, JGFF, LDL, PHP2, PHR1, SF.

Balti, *see* Beltsy.

Baltiiskii Port, *see* Paldiski.

Baltinava, Lat. (Baltinavas, Baltinova, Baltinove); pop. 207; 139 km NNE of Daugavpils; 56°57'/27°39'; COH, PHLE.

Baltinavas, *see* Baltinava.

Baltinova, *see* Baltinava.

Baltinove, *see* Baltinava.

Baltisch Port, *see* Paldiski.

Baltiysk, USSR (Pillau); pop. 13; 38 km WSW of Kaliningrad; 54°39'/19°55'.

Baltoja Voke, Lith. (Belaya Vaka, Biala Waka); 13 km SSW of Vilnius; 54°36'/25°12'; GUM3, GUM5.

Baltoji Voke, Lith.; 13 km SSW of Vilnius; 54°36'/25°12'; GUM5.

Baltow, Pol.; pop. 30; 75 km SW of Lublin; 51°01'/21°33'; GUM5.

Baltowka, GUM5. This town was not found in BGN gazetteers under the given spelling.

Baltrimontz, *see* Butrimoniai.

Baluchin, Ukr. (Baluczyn); pop. 29; 38 km ENE of Lvov; 49°51'/24°34'.

Baluczyn, *see* Baluchin.

Balut, *see* Baluty.

Baluti, *see* Baluty.

Baluty, Pol. (Balut, Baluti); 13 km NNW of Lodz; 51°48'/19°28'; EJ.

Balvanyosvaralja, *see* Unguras.

Balvi, Lat. (Balvu, Balwa, Bolovsk, Bolowsk, Bolve, Bolvi); pop. 387; 146 km N of Daugavpils; 57°08'/27°15'; LDL, PHLE.

Balvu, *see* Balvi.

Balwa, *see* Balvi.

Bamberg, Germ.; pop. 812; 50 km NNW of Nurnberg; 49°52'/10°52'; AMG, CAHJP, EDRD, EJ, GED, GUM3, GUM4, GUM5, HSL, HSL2, JGFF, LDS, PHGB, PHP3.

Ban, Rom. (Felsoban); pop. 3; 69 km WNW of Cluj; 47°06'/22°49'; LDS.

Bana, Hung.; pop. 39; 88 km W of Budapest; 47°39'/17°55'.

Banachi, HSL. This pre-World War I community was not found in BGN gazetteers.

Banat; Not a town, but a region between the Transylvanian Alps and the Danube, Tisza and Mures Rivers. Formerly part of Hungary, it is now divided among Romania, Yugoslavia and Hungary.

Banatski Karlovac, Yug.; pop. 10; 50 km NE of Beograd; 45°04'/21°02'.

Banatsko Arandelovo, Yug.; pop. 39; 146 km NNW of Beograd; 46°04'/20°15'.

Band, Rom.; pop. 81; 62 km ESE of Cluj; 46°35'/24°23'; HSL.

Bandrow Narodowy, Pol.; pop. 38; 50 km S of Przemysl; 49°24'/22°42'.

Baneshty, Mold. (Banesti); pop. 32; 75 km NW of Kishinev; 47°34'/28°23'.

Banesti, *see* Baneshty.

Banfalu, HSL. This pre-World War I community was not found in BGN gazetteers.

Banfalva, Hung.; pop. 21; 26 km WNW of Miskolc; 48°13'/20°31'; HSL.

Banfe, Germ.; pop. 6; 94 km N of Frankfurt am Main; 50°54'/08°51'.

Banffyhunyad, *see* Huedin.

Banhegyes, *see* Magyarbanhegyes.

Banhida, Hung.; pop. 85; 56 km W of Budapest; 47°34'/18°23'; PHH.

Banhorvat, Hung.; pop. 16; 32 km WNW of Miskolc; 48°14'/20°31'; HSL.

Bania Berezow, *see* Banya Berezov.

Bania Kotowska, Ukr. (Kotov); pop. 247; 114 km S of Lvov;

48°55'/23°25'; LDL, SF. This town was located on an interwar map of Poland but does not appear in contemporary gazetteers. Map coordinates are approximate.

Banie, *see* Bahn.

Banila, *see* Banilov.

Banila pe Ceremus, *see* Banilov (Ceremus).

Banila pe Siret, *see* Banilov (Siret).

Banilov, Ukr. (Banila); AMG, COH, GUM4, HSL, LYV. Two towns in Bukovina are named Banilov (Banila). The sources of information do not distinguish between the two. See listings below.

Banilov (Ceremus), Ukr. (Banila pe Ceremus); pop. 517; 45 km W of Chernovtsy; 48°22'/25°21'; PHR2.

Banilov (Siret), Ukr. (Banila pe Siret); pop. 688; 45 km SW of Chernovtsy; 48°05'/25°29'; PHR2.

Banin, Cz.; pop. 2; 62 km NNW of Brno; 49°40'/16°28'.

Banja, Yug.; 157 km SSW of Beograd; 43°33'/19°36'; GUM4, GUM5.

Banja Koviljaca, Yug. (Koviljaca); pop. 3; 107 km SW of Beograd; 44°30'/19°11'.

Banja Luka, Yug. (Banya Luka, Bonya Luka); pop. 368; 146 km SE of Zagreb; 44°46'/17°10'; EJ, GUM4, HSL, PHY.

Bank, Germ. BGN lists two possible localities with this name located at 47°56'/19°11' and 50°50'/06°03'. HSL.

Banka, Cz.; 75 km NE of Bratislava; 48°35'/17°51'; HSL.

Bankau, *see* Bakow.

Bankwitz, (Bakowice); pop. 20; A number of towns share this name. It was not possible to determine from available information which one is being referenced. Near Khirov (Chyrow), according to a list of Galician towns. Bankwitz does not appear in interwar or contemporary gazetteers.

Banlaktolmecs, *see* Lazaret.

Banokszentgyorgy, Hung.; pop. 9; 19 km WNW of Nagykanizsa; 46°33'/16°47'.

Banova Jaruga, Yug.; pop. 18; 82 km ESE of Zagreb; 45°26'/16°54'.

Banovce, *see* Banovce nad Bebravou.

Banovce nad Bebravou, Cz. (Bain, Banovce); pop. 686; 107 km NE of Bratislava; 48°43'/18°16'; GUM5, HSL, HSL2.

Banovce nad Ondavou, Cz.; pop. 52; 45 km E of Kosice; 48°41'/21°49'.

Banovichi, USSR; pop. 340; This town was not found in BGN gazetteers under the given spelling.

Banreve, Hung.; pop. 11; 45 km WNW of Miskolc; 48°18'/20°22'; HSL, HSL2.

Banska Bystrica, Cz. (Besztercebanya, Neusohl); pop. 1,264; 150 km W of Kosice; 48°44'/19°09'; AMG, EDRD, EJ, GUM4, GUM5, GUM6.

Banska Stiavnica, Cz. (Schemnitz, Selmecbanya); pop. 434; 139 km ENE of Bratislava; 48°27'/18°54'; GUM4.

Bantapolcsany, Hung.; pop. 7; 26 km WNW of Miskolc; 48°11'/20°29'.

Banunin, Ukr.; pop. 9; 32 km NE of Lvov; 49°57'/24°24'.

Banya, COH, HSL. A number of towns share this name. It was not possible to determine from available information which one is being referenced.

Banya Berezov, Ukr. (Bania Berezow, Banya Berezuv); pop. 20; 88 km W of Chernovtsy; 48°25'/24°45'.

Banya Berezuv, *see* Banya Berezov.

Banya Luka, *see* Banja Luka.

Bar, Ukr. (Ber); pop. 5,270; 62 km SW of Vinnitsa; 49°04'/27°40'; EDRD, EJ, GUM4, GUM5, HSL, HSL2, JGFF, LDL, PHP3, PHR1, SF.

Bara, Rom. (Barafalva, Berekeresztur); 163 km SW of Cluj; 45°54'/21°53'; PHR1.

Barabas, Hung.; pop. 88; 120 km ENE of Miskolc; 48°14'/22°26'; HSL, PHH.

Baraboi, *see* Baraboy.

Baraboy, Mold. (Baraboi); pop. 44; 150 km NW of Kishinev; 48°05'/27°37'.

Baracska, Hung.; pop. 33; 38 km SSW of Budapest;

47°17'/18°46'; HSL, LDS.

Barafalva, *see* Bara.

Baraki, Pol.; pop. 36; 62 km SSW of Lublin; 50°48'/22°03'.

Baran, Byel.; 82 km S of Vitebsk; 54°29'/30°18'; GUM4.

Baranca, Rom. (Barancea); pop. 60; 146 km NW of Iasi; 48°08'/26°19'.

Barancea, *see* Baranca.

Barancha, Mold. (Baroncea); pop. 57; 133 km NW of Kishinev; 48°02'/27°55'.

Baranczyce, Pol.; pop. 31; Described in the *Black Book* as being in the Lwow region of Poland, this town was not found in BGN gazetteers.

Barand, Hung.; pop. 3; 94 km SSE of Miskolc; 47°18'/21°14'; HSL, LDS, PHH.

Baranivka, *possibly* Baranovka.

Baranov, *see* Baranow.

Baranovich, *see* Baranovichi.

Baranovichi, Byel. (Baranovich, Baranovitch, Baranovitsh, Baranowicze); pop. 7,796; 120 km N of Pinsk; 53°08'/26°02'; AMG, COH, EDRD, EJ, FRG, GA, GUM3, GUM4, GUM5, GUM6, HSL, HSL2, ISH3, JGFF, LDL, SF, YB.

Baranovitch, *see* Baranovichi.

Baranovitsh, *see* Baranovichi.

Baranovka, Ukr. (Baranivka?, Baranowka, Baronovka); pop. 602; 107 km ESE of Rovno; 50°18'/27°40'; GUM4, HSL, LDL, SF, YB.

Baranow, Pol. (Baranov, Baranow nad Wieprzem); pop. 1,028; 50 km NW of Lublin; 51°34'/22°09'; AMG, CAHJP, COH, EDRD, GUM4, GUM5, HSL2, LDS, POCEM, SF.

Baranow (Monasterzyska area), Ukr.; pop. 21; 101 km NW of Chernovtsy; 49°05'/25°05'. This town was located on an interwar map of Poland but does not appear in contemporary gazetteers. Map coordinates are approximate.

Baranowice, Pol. (Baranowitz); 82 km WSW of Krakow; 50°01'/18°43'; LDS, PHP4.

Baranowicze, *see* Baranovichi.

Baranowitz, *see* Baranowice.

Baranowka, *see* Baranovka.

Baranow nad Wieprzem, *see* Baranow.

Baranowo, Pol.; pop. 92; 107 km N of Warszawa; 53°11'/21°18'; CAHJP, HSL, JGFF, LDL, YB.

Baranow Sandomierski, Pol. (Barniv, Bornov); pop. 745; 114 km SSW of Lublin; 50°29'/21°32'; GA, GUM3, GUM6, PHP3, POCEM, SF.

Baranyamagocs, HSL. This pre-World War I community was not found in BGN gazetteers.

Baranyaszentgyorgy, Hung.; pop. 1; 82 km ESE of Nagykanizsa; 46°14'/18°01'.

Baraolt, Rom. (Barot); pop. 34; 170 km ESE of Cluj; 46°05'/25°36'; HSL.

Barashi, Ukr. (Barasj); 126 km ENE of Rovno; 50°43'/28°01'; LDL, SF.

Barasj, *see* Barashi.

Baratos, *see* Brates.

Barbele, Lat.; pop. 1; 69 km SE of Riga; 56°27'/24°36'.

Barbesti, Rom.; pop. 78; 56 km S of Cluj; 46°17'/23°19'.

Barbircheff, *see* Balbieriskis.

Barby, Germ.; pop. 15; 82 km NW of Leipzig; 51°58'/11°53'.

Barca, Cz.; pop. 55; 13 km SE of Kosice; 48°41'/21°16'; AMG, HSL.

Barcanfalva, *see* Barczanfalva.

Barchaczow, Pol.; pop. 82 km SE of Lublin; 50°41'/23°22'; PHP2.

Barchfeld, Germ.; pop. 65; 139 km NE of Frankfurt am Main; 50°48'/10°18'; HSL, JGFF, LDS.

Barchholz, HSL. This pre-World War I community was not found in BGN gazetteers.

Barchovice, Cz.; pop. 3; 38 km ESE of Praha; 49°57'/14°58'.

Barchow, Pol.; pop. 4; 50 km NE of Warszawa; 52°31'/21°39'.

Barciai, Lith. (Bartele, Barteliai, Bortele); pop. 4; 75 km SSW of Vilnius; 54°11'/24°41'; GUM3.

Barciany, Pol. (Barten); pop. 4; 170 km WNW of Bialystok;

Berdichev, Ukraine: View from the Gnilopyat River.

54°13'/21°21'.

Barcice, Pol.; pop. 22; 82 km SE of Krakow; 49°32'/20°39'; AMG.

Barcika, Hung.; pop. 24; 26 km NW of Miskolc; 48°16'/20°38'; HSL.

Barcin, Pol. (Bartschin); pop. 20; 82 km NE of Poznan; 52°52'/17°58'; JGFF, POCEM.

Barcs, Hung.; pop. 493; 62 km SE of Nagykanizsa; 45°58'/17°28'; GUM4, JGFF, PHH.

Barczaca, Pol.; pop. 9; 50 km E of Warszawa; 52°10'/21°38'.

Barczanfalva, Rom. (Barcanfalva, Barsana, Birsana); pop. 423; 120 km N of Cluj; 47°49'/24°04'; AMG, PHR2.

Barczewo, Pol.; 146 km ESE of Gdansk; 53°50'/20°42'; POCEM.

Barczkow, Pol.; pop. 15; 50 km ENE of Krakow; 50°08'/20°33'.

Bardar, Mold.; pop. 20; 19 km SW of Kishinev; 46°54'/28°40'.

Bardejov, Cz. (Bartfa, Bartfeld, Bartfeldt); pop. 2,264; 69 km N of Kosice; 49°17'/21°17'; AMG, COH, EJ, GUM4, HSL, HSL2, JGFF.

Bardenberg, Germ.; pop. 4; 62 km WSW of Koln; 50°51'/06°07'.

Bardesti, Rom.; pop. 5; 69 km ESE of Cluj; 46°35'/24°31'.

Bardfalva, *see* Berbesti.

Bardichev, *see* Berdichev.

Bardiow, Pol. PHP3. This town was not found in BGN gazetteers under the given spelling.

Bardo Dolne, *see* Kolonia Bardo Dolne.

Bardos, Hung.; 94 km NNW of Nagykanizsa; 47°12'/16°45'; HSL.

Bardudvarnok, Hung.; pop. 2; 56 km E of Nagykanizsa; 46°20'/17°41'.

Baremel, Ukr. (Beremel?, Beremelia, Boremel, Boromel, Mochalivka); pop. 6; 75 km WSW of Rovno; 50°28'/25°12'; AMG, JGFF, LDL, SF, YB.

Bargau, Rom.; pop. 11; HSL, HSL2. A number of towns share this name. It was not possible to determine from available information which one is being referenced.

Barglow Dworny, Pol.; 75 km NNW of Bialystok; 53°47'/22°52'; LDS.

Barishevka, Byel. (Baryschewka, Borishovka, Borisovka, Borshivka); pop. 436; 157 km SE of Vitebsk; 53°52'/31°05'; LDL, SF.

Barkasovo, GUM3. This town was not found in BGN gazetteers under the given spelling.

Barkaszo, HSL. This pre-World War I community was not found in BGN gazetteers.

Barkava, Lat. (Barkavas); pop. 76; 101 km N of Daugavpils; 56°43'/26°36'.

Barkavas, *see* Barkava.

Barki, Pol.; pop. 36; A number of towns share this name. It was not possible to determine from available information which one is being referenced.

Barlad, *see* Birlad.

Barladeni, *see* Barlyadyany.

Barlafalu, *see* Borlesti.

Barlibas, Rom.; 50 km E of Cluj; 46°43'/24°16'; HSL.

Barlinek, Pol. (Berlinchen); pop. 26; 75 km SE of Szczecin; 52°59'/15°12'; LDS.

Barlyadyany, Mold. (Barladeni); pop. 60; 176 km NW of Kishinev; 48°16'/27°25'.

Barmen, Germ.; 45 km W of Koln; 50°57'/06°18'; EJ.

Barna, Hung. (Barnafalva); pop. 5; 62 km WSW of Miskolc; 48°06'/19°56'.

Barnabas, GUM5. This town was not found in BGN gazetteers under the given spelling.

Barnafalva, *see* Barna.

Barnag, Hung. (Nemetbarnag); pop. 12; 88 km NNE of Nagykanizsa; 46°59'/17°45'.

Barniv, *see* Baranow Sandomierski.

Barnova Soroca, *see* Byrnovo.

Barntrup, Germ.; pop. 17; 62 km SW of Hannover; 51°59'/09°07'; GUM4, LDS.

Barodbeznye, *see* Beznea.

Barodeinka, *see* Borodyanka.

Barodsomos, *see* Cornitel.

Baromlak, *see* Borumlaca.

Baroncea, *see* Barancha.

Baronovka, *see* Baranovka.

Barot, *see* Baraolt.

Barsad, *see* Bershad.

Barsana, *see* Barczanfalva.

16

Barsaul de Sus, *see* Birsau de Sus.

Barsbaracska, GUM4. This town was not found in BGN gazetteers under the given spelling.

Barshchovitse, *see* Borshchovichi.

Barsinghausen, Germ.; pop. 58; 19 km SW of Hannover; 52°18'/09°27'; GED.

Barstaszar, *see* Tesare nad Zitavou.

Barstyciai, Lith. (Breshtitz); pop. 87; 94 km W of Siauliai; 56°10'/21°52'; YL.

Barszczowice, *see* Borshchovichi.

Bartele, *see* Barciai.

Barteliai, *see* Barciai.

Barten, *see* Barciany.

Bartenstein, Germ.; 82 km NNE of Stuttgart; 49°21'/09°53'; GUM4. *See also* Bartoszyce.

Bartfa, *see* Bardejov.

Bartfeld, *see* Bardejov.

Bartfeldt, *see* Bardejov.

Barth, Germ.; pop. 12; 50 km NE of Rostock; 54°22'/12°44'; GUM3, GUM4, GUM5.

Bartininkai, Lith.; pop. 93; 75 km SW of Kaunas; 54°30'/23°02'.

Bartishaw, *see* Botosani.

Bartkowa Posadowa, Pol.; pop. 20; 69 km ESE of Krakow; 49°46'/20°45'.

Bartkowice, Pol.; pop. 10; 26 km NE of Czestochowa; 50°55'/19°23'.

Bartne, Pol.; pop. 12; 107 km WSW of Przemysl; 49°34'/21°20'.

Bartnitz, HSL. This pre-World War I community was not found in BGN gazetteers.

Bartodzieje, *see* Bartodzieje Podlesne.

Bartodzieje Podlesne, Pol. (Bartodzieje); pop. 104; 45 km NNE of Czestochowa; 51°05'/19°28'; GUM3.

Bartoldy, Pol.; pop. 5; 82 km NNW of Warszawa; 52°58'/20°51'.

Bartolovec, Yug.; pop. 9; 69 km NNE of Zagreb; 46°18'/16°26'.

Bartosovce, Cz.; 56 km N of Kosice; 49°12'/21°17'; HSL.

Bartoszewo, GUM4. This town was not found in BGN gazetteers under the given spelling.

Bartoszyce, Pol. (Bartenstein); pop. 64; 139 km E of Gdansk; 54°15'/20°48'; LDS.

Bartschin, *see* Barcin.

Baruth, Germ.; 56 km SSE of Berlin; 52°03'/13°30'; GUM4.

Barwald Dolny, Pol.; pop. 10; 38 km SW of Krakow; 49°52'/19°34'.

Barwalde, *see* Barwice.

Barwica, *see* Barwice.

Barwice, Pol. (Barwalde, Barwica); 126 km ENE of Szczecin; 53°44'/16°21'; LDS.

Barwinek, Pol.; 88 km SW of Przemysl; 49°26'/21°42'; PHP3.

Barycz, Pol.; pop. 22; 50 km NE of Czestochowa; 50°56'/19°47'; AMG, GUM3, PHP3.

Barylow, *see* Baryluv.

Baryluv, Ukr. (Barylow); pop. 90; 88 km NE of Lvov; 50°21'/24°53'; YB.

Baryschewka, *see* Barishevka.

Barysh, Ukr. (Barysz); pop. 229; 94 km NW of Chernovtsy; 49°02'/25°16'; GUM3, GYLA, PHP2.

Barysz, *see* Barysh.

Barzan, *see* Berezhany.

Barzila, HSL. This pre-World War I community was not found in BGN gazetteers.

Barzna, USSR. EDRD. This town was not found in BGN gazetteers under the given spelling.

Basaid, Yug.; pop. 25; 101 km N of Beograd; 45°39'/20°25'.

Bascalia, *see* Bashkaliya.

Basesti, Rom. (Bazosd); pop. 55; 82 km NNW of Cluj; 47°29'/23°09'.

Baseu, Rom.; pop. 23; 139 km NW of Iasi; 48°08'/26°29'.

Bashkaliya, Mold. (Bascalia); pop. 13; 82 km S of Kishinev; 46°18'/28°47'.

Bashkany, Mold. (Boscana); pop. 20; 19 km NNE of Kishinev; 47°08'/29°00'.

Bashova, Ukr. (Baszowa); pop. 19; 82 km WNW of Rovno; 50°53'/25°11'.

Bashuki, Ukr. (Baszuki); pop. 26; 101 km SSW of Rovno; 49°49'/25°32'.

Basnia, Pol.; pop. 115; 56 km NNE of Przemysl; 50°11'/23°14'.

Basnia Gorna, Pol.; pop. 58; 50 km NNE of Przemysl; 50°10'/23°15'.

Basnice, Cz.; 82 km NE of Praha; 50°20'/15°36'; HSL.

Bason Chadash, *see* Novaya Basan.

Bassenheim, Germ.; 75 km SE of Koln; 50°22'/07°28'; GED, JGFF.

Bassum, Germ.; pop. 18; 88 km WNW of Hannover; 52°51'/08°44'.

Bastheim, Germ.; pop. 22; 114 km ENE of Frankfurt am Main; 50°24'/10°12'; GUM5, JGFF, LDS, PHGB.

Bastunai, Lith. (Bastuny); pop. 34; 62 km NNW of Vilnius; 55°11'/25°12'.

Bastuny, *see* Bastunai.

Baszowa, *see* Bashova.

Baszuki, *see* Bashuki.

Bataapati, Hung.; pop. 3; 120 km WSW of Szeged; 46°13'/18°36'.

Batak, *see* Batakiai.

Batakai, *see* Batakiai.

Batakiai, Lith. (Batak, Batakai, Batok, Betok, Botak, Botik, Botoka, Botoken, Botoki); pop. 88; 82 km SSW of Siauliai; 55°21'/22°31'; HSL, JGFF, LDL, SF, YL.

Batanii Mari, Rom.; pop. 8; 176 km ESE of Cluj; 46°05'/25°41'.

Batar, *see* Batyr.

Batarci, Rom. (Batarciu, Batarcs); pop. 201; 146 km NNW of Cluj; 48°02'/23°10'; HSL, HSL2, PHR2.

Batarciu, *see* Batarci.

Batarcs, *see* Batarci.

Bataszek, Hung.; pop. 122; 114 km WSW of Szeged; 46°11'/18°44'; LDS, PHH.

Batelov, Cz. (Battelau); 88 km W of Brno; 49°19'/15°24'; HSL.

Batiatycze, *see* Batyatychi.

Batin, Rom. (Batony); pop. 37; 50 km NE of Cluj; 47°04'/24°04'.

Batiz, Rom. (Botiz); 120 km S of Cluj; 45°46'/23°00'; HSL, PHR2.

Batiza, *see* Botiza.

Batka, Cz. (Felso Batka); 88 km SW of Kosice; 48°23'/20°11'; HSL.

Batmonostor, Hung.; pop. 18; 94 km WSW of Szeged; 46°06'/18°56'; LDS.

Batok, *see* Batakiai.

Batony, *see* Batin.

Bator, Hung.; pop. 8; 45 km SW of Miskolc; 47°59'/20°16'; HSL2.

Batorkeszi, *see* Vojnice.

Batorove Kesy, *see* Vojnice.

Batorz, Pol.; pop. 48; 50 km S of Lublin; 50°51'/22°29'.

Batovo, Cz. AMG, GUM3. A number of towns share this name. It was not possible to determine from available information which one is being referenced.

Batowice, Pol.; pop. 9; 13 km NE of Krakow; 50°07'/20°02'.

Battelau, *see* Batelov.

Battenberg, Germ.; pop. 32; 107 km N of Frankfurt am Main; 51°01'/08°39'; HSL, JGFF, LDS.

Battenfeld, Germ.; pop. 19; 107 km N of Frankfurt am Main; 51°02'/08°40'; HSL, JGFF.

Battonya, Hung.; pop. 152; 62 km ENE of Szeged; 46°17'/21°01'; LDL, LDS, PHH.

Baturin, Ukr.; 26 km WNW of Konotop; 51°21'/32°53'; LDL, SF.

Baturnin, GUM4. This town was not found in BGN gazetteers under the given spelling.

Baturyn, Byel.; pop. 21; 50 km NNW of Minsk; 54°15'/27°25'. This town was located on an interwar map of Poland but does not appear in contemporary gazetteers. Map coordinates are approximate.

Batya, Hung.; pop. 17; 101 km WNW of Szeged; 46°29'/18°57'; HSL, HSL2.

Batyatychi, Ukr. (Batiatycze); pop. 195; 32 km NNE of Lvov; 50°06'/24°16'; PHP2.

Batyjow, *see* Batyyuv.

Batyn, COH. This town was not found in BGN gazetteers under the given spelling.

Batyr, Mold. (Batar); pop. 24; 50 km SSE of Kishinev; 46°35'/29°00'.

Batyu, *see* Uzlovoye.

Batyyuv, Ukr. (Batyjow); pop. 14; 75 km NE of Lvov; 50°17'/24°52'.

Bauerbach, Germ.; 45 km NW of Stuttgart; 49°04'/08°45'; HSL, LDS, PHGBW.

Bauerwitz, Pol.; pop. 4; 107 km SW of Czestochowa; 50°10'/18°00'.

Baumbach, Germ.; pop. 65; 126 km NNE of Frankfurt am Main; 51°02'/09°40'.

Baunach, Germ.; pop. 62 km NNW of Nurnberg; 49°59'/10°51'; PHGB.

Bauni, Lat.; pop. 1; 114 km NNE of Riga; 57°45'/25°11'.

Baurcei, *see* Baurchi.

Baurchi, Mold. (Baurcei); pop. 20; 107 km S of Kishinev; 46°06'/28°41'.

Bausendorf, Germ.; pop. 33; 107 km S of Koln; 50°01'/07°00'.

Bausk, *see* Bauska.

Bauska, Lat. (Baisk, Bausk, Bauske, Boisk, Boysk); pop. 770; 69 km S of Riga; 56°24'/24°11'; COH, EJ, HSL, JGFF, LDL, PHLE, SF.

Bauske, *see* Bauska.

Bautzen, Germ.; pop. 73; 146 km E of Leipzig; 51°11'/14°26'; AMG, GUM6.

Bavaria; Not a town, but a state in southern Germany.

Bavorov, Cz.; pop. 8; 114 km S of Praha; 49°07'/14°05'.

Bavorovice, Cz.; pop. 8; 120 km S of Praha; 49°02'/14°26'.

Baworow, Ukr.; pop. 99; 88 km NNW of Chernovtsy; 49°05'/25°45'. This town was located on an interwar map of Poland but does not appear in contemporary gazetteers. Map coordinates are approximate.

Baych, *see* Biecz.

Bayern; *See* Bavaria.

Bayertal, *see* Baierthal.

Baymakliya, Mold. (Baimaclia); pop. 509; 94 km S of Kishinev; 46°11'/28°24'.

Baymakliya (near Taraclia Tighina), Rom.; pop. 21; Described in the *Black Book* as being in the Bessarabia region of Romania, this town was not found in BGN gazetteers.

Bayreuth, Germ.; pop. 261; 69 km NNE of Nurnberg; 49°57'/11°35'; AMG, CAHJP, EJ, GUM3, GUM4, GUM5, HSL, JGFF, PHGB.

Bayrischzell, Germ.; pop. 1; 62 km SE of Munchen; 47°40'/12°01'.

Baytsh, *see* Biecz.

Bayush, Mold. (Baius); pop. 3; 62 km S of Kishinev; 46°28'/28°29'.

Baza, *see* Bazakerettye.

Bazakerettye, Hung. (Baza); 26 km WNW of Nagykanizsa; 46°32'/16°44'; HSL.

Bazalia, *see* Bazaliya.

Bazaliia, *see* Bazaliya.

Bazalija, *see* Bazaliya.

Bazaliya, Ukr. (Bazalia, Bazaliia, Bazalija, Bazilia, Bazylia); 107 km SSE of Rovno; 49°43'/26°28'; HSL, JGFF, SF.

Bazanowice, Pol.; pop. 6; 94 km SW of Krakow; 49°44'/18°43'.

Bazantov, Cz.; pop. 1; 146 km WSW of Praha; 49°45'/12°34'.

Bazar, Ukr.; pop. 22; 75 km NNW of Chernovtsy; 48°57'/25°34'; HSL, SF.

Bazavluchok, Ukr. (Buzuluk); 88 km SW of Dnepropetrovsk; 47°56'/34°02'; GUM5.

Bazesti, Rom.; 62 km SSW of Cluj; 46°21'/23°02'; HSL, HSL2.

Bazilia, *see* Bazaliya.

Bazilian, *see* Padubysys.

Bazilionai, *see* Padubysys.

Bazin, *see* Pezinok.

Bazna, Rom.; 82 km SE of Cluj; 46°12'/24°17'; EJ.

Bazos, Rom.; 195 km SW of Cluj; 45°44'/21°29'; HSL.

Bazosd, *see* Basesti.

Bazow, Pol.; pop. 16; 107 km SW of Lublin; 50°36'/21°27'.

Bazsi, Hung.; pop. 5; 62 km N of Nagykanizsa; 46°56'/17°15'.

Bazylia, *see* Bazaliya.

Bdeneves, Cz.; pop. 4; 94 km SW of Praha; 49°46'/13°14'.

Bebra, Germ.; pop. 120; 126 km NNE of Frankfurt am Main; 50°58'/09°48'; COH, GUM3, JGFF.

Bebrene, Lat.; pop. 8; 32 km WNW of Daugavpils; 56°04'/26°07'.

Becej, Yug.; pop. 500; 94 km NNW of Beograd; 45°37'/20°03'; CAHJP, EDRD, PHY.

Becherov, Cz.; pop. 82 km N of Kosice; 49°25'/21°19'; HSL.

Bechhofen, Germ. (Beckhofen); pop. 28; 50 km SW of Nurnberg; 49°09'/10°33'; EJ, GUM5, HSL, HSL2, PHGB, WS.

Bechovice, Cz.; pop. 3; 13 km E of Praha; 50°05'/14°37'.

Bechtheim, Germ. BGN lists two possible localities with this name located at 49°44'/08°18' and 50°17'/08°11'. JGFF.

Bechtolsheim, Germ.; pop. 16; 50 km SW of Frankfurt am Main; 49°48'/08°12'.

Bechyne, Cz.; pop. 39; 94 km S of Praha; 49°18'/14°29'; JGFF.

Beckhofen, *see* Bechhofen.

Beckov, Cz.; pop. 68; 88 km NNE of Bratislava; 48°47'/17°54'; COH, JGFF.

Beckum, Germ.; pop. 90; 114 km NNE of Koln; 51°45'/08°02'; AMG, GUM5, LDS.

Beclean, Rom. (Bethlen, Betlen); pop. 671; 62 km NNE of Cluj; 47°11'/24°11'; AMG, COH, GUM5, HSL, HSL2, LDL, PHR2, YB.

Becov, *see* Becov nad Teplou.

Becov nad Teplou, Cz. (Becov, Petschau); pop. 26; 114 km WSW of Praha; 50°05'/12°49'; EJ, HSL, HSL2.

Becske, Hung.; pop. 7; 50 km NNE of Budapest; 47°55'/19°23'; HSL, HSL2, LDS.

Becvary, Cz.; pop. 21; 45 km ESE of Praha; 49°57'/15°05'.

Beczkow, Pol.; pop. 17; 107 km NNE of Krakow; 50°52'/20°48'.

Bedahaza, *see* Bedevlya.

Bedburdyck, Germ.; pop. 9; 32 km WNW of Koln; 51°07'/06°34'; GED.

Bedburg, Germ.; 26 km W of Koln; 51°00'/06°35'; GED.

Beddelhausen, Germ.; pop. 8; 107 km NNW of Frankfurt am Main; 51°00'/08°30'.

Bedeval, *see* Bedevlya.

Bedevla, *see* Bedevlya.

Bedevle, *see* Bedevlya.

Bedevlia, *see* Bedevlya.

Bedevlya, Ukr. (Bedahaza, Bedeval, Bedevla, Bedevle, Bedevlia, Bidevle); 170 km WSW of Chernovtsy; 48°01'/23°40'; AMG, COH, HSL, LYV, SM. This town was located on a pre-World War I map, but does not appear in contemporary gazetteers.

Bedkow, Pol. (Bendkow); pop. 228; 26 km ESE of Lodz; 51°35'/19°45'; CAHJP, GA, LDS, PHP1, SF.

Bedkowice, Pol.; pop. 9; 13 km WNW of Krakow; 50°10'/19°45'; PHP3.

Bedlenko, Pol.; pop. 5; 88 km ESE of Lodz; 51°12'/20°19'.

Bedlne, *see* Bedlno.

Bedlno, Pol. (Bedlne); pop. 31; 69 km N of Lublin; 51°49'/22°33'.

Bednarka, Pol.; pop. 13; 107 km WSW of Przemysl; 49°38'/21°20'.

Bednarov, Ukr. (Bednarow, Bednaruv); pop. 31; 101 km SE of Lvov; 49°02'/24°33'.

Bednarow, *see* Bednarov.

Bednaruv, *see* Bednarov.

Bedo, Hung. (Bedohaza); 126 km SE of Miskolc; 47°10'/21°45'; GUM5, LDS.

Bedohaza, *see* Bedo.

Bedrc, Cz.; pop. 3; 38 km SE of Praha; 49°49'/14°43'.

Bedrykowce, *see* Berdykovtse.

Bedziechow, Pol.; pop. 5; 69 km W of Lodz; 51°53'/18°27'.

Bedziemysl, Pol.; pop. 22; 75 km WNW of Przemysl; 50°03'/21°47'.

Bedzin, Pol. (Bendin, Bendzin); pop. 17,298; 56 km S of Czestochowa; 50°20'/19°09'; AMG, CAHJP, COH, EDRD, EJ, FRG, GA, GUM3, GUM4, GUM5, GUM6, HSL, HSL2, ISH1, JGFF, LDL, LDS, LYV, PHP1, PHP3, PHP4, POCEM, SF, YB.

Beelen, Germ.; pop. 4; 120 km SW of Hannover; 51°56'/08°08'.

Beelitz, Germ.; pop. 79; 45 km SW of Berlin; 52°14'/12°58'; EJ.

Beerfelden, Germ.; pop. 91; 62 km SSE of Frankfurt am Main; 49°34'/08°59'; JGFF, LDS.

Beeskow, Germ.; 69 km ESE of Berlin; 52°10'/14°15'; JGFF.

Befegsurany, Hung.; pop. 65; This town was not found in BGN gazetteers under the given spelling.

Begno, Pol.; pop. 5; 56 km NNW of Warszawa; 52°45'/20°50'.

Begoml, Byel.; 101 km N of Minsk; 54°44'/28°04'; GUM4.

Behanky, Cz.; pop. 4; 82 km NW of Praha; 50°41'/13°49'.

Beharov, Cz.; pop. 4; 126 km SW of Praha; 49°21'/13°10'.

Behringersdorf, Germ.; pop. 7; 13 km NE of Nurnberg; 49°29'/11°12'; PHGB.

Behynce, Cz. (Beje); 75 km SW of Kosice; 48°25'/20°18'; HSL.

Beica de Jos, Rom. (Alsobolkeny); pop. 12; 88 km E of Cluj; 46°44'/24°48'.

Beica de Sus, Rom.; pop. 6; 94 km E of Cluj; 46°44'/24°49'.

Beienheim, Germ.; pop. 7; 38 km N of Frankfurt am Main; 50°22'/08°49'; LDS.

Beilngries, Germ.; 56 km SE of Nurnberg; 49°02'/11°29'; PHGB.

Beiramich, *see* Nikolayevka Novorossiyskaya.

Beiramtch, *see* Nikolayevka Novorossiyskaya.

Beiseforth, Germ.; pop. 21; 126 km NNE of Frankfurt am Main; 51°05'/09°33'; AMG, LDS.

Beisogala, *see* Baisogala.

Beitch, *see* Biecz.

Beius, Rom. (Belenyes); 94 km WSW of Cluj; 46°40'/22°21'; HSL, LDL.

Bejcgyertyanos, Hung.; pop. 10; 88 km N of Nagykanizsa; 47°09'/16°55'.

Bejdy, Pol.; pop. 32; 107 km N of Lublin; 52°10'/22°36'.

Beje, *see* Behynce.

Bejsce, Pol.; pop. 9; 56 km NE of Krakow; 50°15'/20°37'.

Bekasmegyer, Hung. (Bekesmegyer); pop. 136; 19 km NNW of Budapest; 47°36'/19°03'; GUM5, PHH.

Bekecs, Hung.; pop. 101; 32 km ENE of Miskolc; 48°09'/21°11'; GUM5, HSL, HSL2, PHH.

Bekeny, *see* Bekenypuszta.

Bekenypuszta, Hung. (Bekeny); 13 km SW of Miskolc; 48°01'/20°39'; HSL.

Bekes, Hung.; pop. 228; 94 km NE of Szeged; 46°46'/21°08'; LDS, PHH.

Bekescsaba, Hung.; pop. 2,458; 88 km NE of Szeged; 46°41'/21°06'; AMG, COH, EJ, GUM3, GUM4, GUM5, GUM6, HSL, JGFF, LDS, PHH.

Bekesmegyer, *see* Bekasmegyer.

Bekessamson, Hung.; pop. 5; 45 km NE of Szeged; 46°25'/20°38'.

Bekesszentandras, Hung.; pop. 50; 75 km N of Szeged; 46°52'/20°29'; LDS, PHH.

Bekheve, *see* Bychawa.

Bekiesza, Pol.; pop. 37; 45 km ENE of Lublin; 51°18'/23°13'.

Bekolce, Hung.; pop. 4; 38 km WSW of Miskolc; 48°05'/20°17'.

Bektez, Yug. (Bekteze); pop. 25; 157 km ESE of Zagreb; 45°24'/17°56'.

Bekteze, *see* Bektez.

Bel, *see* Beliu.

Bela, *see* Bela pod Bezdezem.

Bela Cerkva, *see* Byala Cherkova.

Bela Crkva, *possibly* Byala Cherkova.

Belaia Tserkov, *see* Belaya Tserkov.

Belapatfalva, Hung.; pop. 43; 32 km WSW of Miskolc; 48°03'/20°22'.

Bela pod Bezdezem, Cz. (Bela); pop. 25; 50 km NNE of Praha; 50°30'/14°48'; GUM5.

Belasovice, HSL. This pre-World War I community was not found in BGN gazetteers.

Belauti, *see* Belauts.

Belauts, Ukr. (Belauti); pop. 20; 45 km ENE of Chernovtsy; 48°21'/26°29'.

Belavar, Hung.; pop. 2; 38 km SE of Nagykanizsa; 46°07'/17°13'.

Belaya, Ukr.; pop. 78; 38 km NW of Lvov; 50°06'/23°40'. See *also* Bielsko Biala.

Belaya Krinitsa, Ukr. (Belokrinitsa, Bialokrynica, Fantana Alba); pop. 27; 45 km S of Chernovtsy; 47°58'/25°53'; GUM4.

Belaya Tserkov, Ukr. (Belaia Tserkov, Biala Cerkiew, Biala Tserkov, Sde Lavan, Shwartz Stimme, White Field); pop. 15,624; 75 km S of Kiyev; 49°47'/30°07'; EDRD, EJ, GUM4, GUM5, HSL, HSL2, JGFF, LDL, PHP1, SF.

Belaya Vaka, *see* Baltoja Voke.

Belber, *see* Bilbor.

Belchatov, *see* Belchatow.

Belchatow, Pol. (Belchatov, Belkhatov); pop. 3,688; 50 km S of Lodz; 51°22'/19°23'; AMG, CAHJP, COH, EDRD, EJ, FRG, GA, GUM3, GUM4, GUM5, HSL, HSL2, JGFF, LDS, LYV, PHP1, SF, YB.

Belchatowek, Pol.; 45 km S of Lodz; 51°23'/19°22'; PHP1.

Belchowka, Pol.; pop. 3; 62 km SW of Przemysl; 49°29'/22°06'.

Belcus, *see* Belusa.

Belda, Pol.; pop. 10; 75 km NW of Bialystok; 53°41'/22°37'.

Beldno, Pol.; pop. 9; 50 km ESE of Krakow; 49°49'/20°24'.

Beldow, Pol.; 19 km WNW of Lodz; 51°50'/19°12'; PHP1.

Belecke, Germ.; 114 km NE of Koln; 51°29'/08°20'; LDS.

Belecko, Cz.; pop. 7; 107 km ENE of Praha; 50°09'/15°57'.

Belecska, Hung. (Gorbo Belecska); 107 km SSW of Budapest; 46°39'/18°25'; LDS.

Beled, Hung.; pop. 336; 120 km N of Nagykanizsa; 47°28'/17°06'; AMG, EJ, GUM5, HSL, HSL2, LDL, LDS, PHH.

Belegregy, *see* Agris.

Belejow, *see* Beleyev.

Beleni, HSL. This pre-World War I community was not found in BGN gazetteers.

Belenyes, *see* Beius.

Belev, USSR; pop. 238; 133 km NE of Bryansk; 53°50'/36°08'.

Beleyev, Ukr. (Belejow); pop. 40; 88 km S of Lvov; 49°06'/24°02'.

Belezna, Hung.; pop. 1; 19 km S of Nagykanizsa; 46°20'/16°57'; AMG.

Belfort, Germ.; 88 km ENE of Hannover; 52°31'/11°01'; LDL.

Belgard, *see* Bialogard.

Belgorod, USSR; pop. 631; 126 km SSE of Kursk; 50°36'/36°34'; HSL.

Belgorod Dnestrovski, *see* Belgorod Dnestrovskiy.

Belgorod Dnestrovskii, *see* Belgorod Dnestrovskiy.

Belgorod Dnestrovskiy, Ukr. (Akerman, Akkerman, Belgorod Dnestrovski, Belgorod Dnestrovskii, Cetatea Alba, Ir Lavan); pop. 4,239; 45 km SSW of Odessa; 46°12'/30°21'; AMG, EDRD, EJ, GUM4, HSL, JGFF, LDL, PHR2, SF, YB.

Belgorodka, *see* Belogorodka.

Belgrad, *see* Bialogard.

Belgrade, *see* Beograd.

Belice, Cz.; pop. 9; 45 km S of Praha; 49°46'/14°28'.

Beligrod, *see* Baligrod.

Belilovka, Ukr.; pop. 1,894; 62 km NNE of Vinnitsa;

49°41'/29°02'; HSL, LDL, SF.

Beli Manastir, Yug.; pop. 38; 182 km WNW of Beograd; 45°46'/18°37'.

Belin, Ukr. (Bilin, Byelin); 126 km WSW of Chernovtsy; 48°07'/24°15'; SM.

Belina, Cz. (Bena); 114 km SW of Kosice; 48°15'/19°51'; AMG, GUM5, HSL.

Belinek, Byel. (Bielinek); pop. 3; 69 km W of Pinsk; 52°15'/25°06'.

Belinitch, *see* Belynichi.

Belinkovitch, *see* Belynkovichi.

Belisce, Yug.; pop. 96; 189 km WNW of Beograd; 45°41'/18°25'.

Belitsa, Byel. (Belitza, Bielica, Bilitza); pop. 483; 150 km WSW of Minsk; 53°39'/25°19'; AMG, COH, EDRD, EJ, GUM3, HSL, HSL2, LDL, LYV, SF, YB.

Belitza, *see* Belitsa.

Beliu, Rom. (Bel); 126 km WSW of Cluj; 46°29'/21°59'; AMG.

Belkhatov, *see* Belchatow.

Belkiralymezo, *see* Craiova.

Bellersheim, Germ.; pop. 7; 45 km N of Frankfurt am Main; 50°27'/08°50'.

Belobozhnitsa, Ukr. (Bialoboznica); pop. 19; 88 km NNW of Chernovtsy; 49°03'/25°40'.

Belochitz, Ukr. EDRD. This town was not found in BGN gazetteers under the given spelling.

Belogorodka, Ukr. (Belgorodka, Bielogorodka, Bilhorodki, Byelogorodka); pop. 2,000; 26 km WSW of Kiyev; 50°23'/30°13'; JGFF, LDL, SF.

Belogorsk, Ukr. (Karassu Basar, Karasu Bazar, Karasubazar, Kraso Bazar); pop. 350; 38 km NE of Simferopol; 45°03'/34°36'; EJ, GUM4, HSL, HSL2, LDL, SF.

Belogorye, Ukr. (Lachovitch, Lachowcy, Lakhovtsy, Liachovitz, Ljachowzy, Lyakhovtsy); pop. 844; 75 km SSE of Rovno; 50°00'/26°25'; SF.

Belogusha, Byel. (Bialohusza); pop. 162; 56 km ESE of Pinsk; 51°56'/26°55'.

Belokorets, Byel. (Bialokorzec); pop. 6; 75 km W of Minsk; 54°01'/26°31'.

Belokorovichi, Ukr. (Bilokorovitch); 139 km NE of Rovno; 51°07'/28°02'; GUM4, SF.

Belokrinitsa, *see* Belaya Krinitsa.

Beloky, Cz.; pop. 2; 19 km WNW of Praha; 50°08'/14°14'.

Belopolye, Ukr. (Bialopole, Byelopolye); pop. 1,260; 75 km N of Vinnitsa; 49°51'/28°52'; GA, GUM5.

Belostok, Ukr.; pop. 12; 94 km W of Rovno; 50°42'/24°59'. See *also* Bialystok.

Belovarec, Ukr. (Bilovarets, Bilvaritz, Kiskirva, Mala Kriva); 163 km WSW of Chernovtsy; 48°03'/23°44'; LYV, SM.

Belovizh, Ukr. (Bialowiz); pop. 19; 126 km NE of Rovno; 51°23'/27°28'.

Belovtse, *see* Belovtsy.

Belovtsy, Ukr. (Belovtse, Bielowce, Bilavati); pop. 11; 38 km NE of Chernovtsy; 48°30'/26°22'.

Belowschtschina, USSR. EDRD. This town was not found in BGN gazetteers under the given spelling.

Belozera, *see* Belozerye.

Belozerka, Ukr. (Bialozorka, Bieloserka, Bielozierka, Bielozorka); pop. 869; 101 km S of Rovno; 49°46'/26°11'; COH, SF.

Belozerye, Ukr. (Belozera, Bilazor); 139 km NE of Uman; 49°19'/31°55'; LDL, SF.

Belsbocs, *see* Bocs.

Belsk, *see* Bielsk.

Belskaya Volya, Ukr. (Bielska Wola); pop. 44; 101 km NNW of Rovno; 51°27'/25°49'.

Belsobocs, *see* Bocs.

Beltekhodos, *see* Hodisa.

Beltinci, Yug.; pop. 3; 94 km N of Zagreb; 46°36'/16°15'.

Beltiug, Rom.; pop. 20; 107 km NW of Cluj; 47°33'/22°51'.

Beltsy, Mold. (Balti, Beltz, Belzy, Bielce); pop. 14,259; 107 km NW of Kishinev; 47°46'/27°56'; AMG, EDRD, EJ, GUM4,

HSL, JGFF, PHR2, SF.

Beltz, *see* Beltsy; Belz.

Beluj, Cz.; 139 km ENE of Bratislava; 48°21'/18°54'; HSL.

Belus, *see* Belut.

Belusa, Cz. (Belcus); pop. 56; 126 km E of Brno; 49°04'/18°20'; JGFF.

Belut, Yug. (Belus); 101 km NE of Skopje; 42°29'/22°31'; HSL.

Belvardgyula, Hung.; pop. 5; 126 km ESE of Nagykanizsa; 45°58'/18°26'.

Bely, *see* Biel.

Belynichi, Byel. (Belinitch); pop. 816; 139 km ENE of Minsk; 54°00'/29°42'; LDL, SF.

Belynkovichi, Byel. (Belinkovitch); 120 km NNE of Gomel; 53°15'/32°08'; SF.

Belyye Oslavy, Ukr. (Oslav Byaly, Oslaw Bialy); pop. 187; 94 km W of Chernovtsy; 48°29'/24°42'; PHP2.

Belyy Kamen, Ukr. (Bialikomin, Bialy Kamien, Bialykamien, Bilkamin); pop. 292; 62 km ENE of Lvov; 49°54'/24°50'; EDRD, EGRS, GUM3, GUM6, HSL, HSL2, LDL, PHP2, SF.

Belz, Ukr. (Beltz); pop. 2,104; 62 km N of Lvov; 50°23'/24°01'; CAHJP, COH, EDRD, EGRS, GUM3, GUM5, GYLA, HSL, HSL2, LDL, LYV, PHP2, SF, YB.

Belza, Cz.; 19 km SSE of Kosice; 48°35'/21°17'; AMG.

Belzec, Pol. (Belzhets, Belzhetz); pop. 109; 82 km NNE of Przemysl; 50°23'/23°26'; AMG, COH, EJ, FRG, GA, GUM4, GUM5, GUM6, HSL, HSL2, JGFF, PHP1, PHP2, PHP3, PHP4, SF.

Belzhets, *see* Belzec.

Belzhetz, *see* Belzec.

Belzhits, *see* Belzyce.

Belzhitse, *see* Belzyce.

Belzhitza, *see* Belzyce.

Belzig, Germ.; pop. 5; 62 km SW of Berlin; 52°08'/12°36'.

Belzy, *see* Beltsy.

Belzyce, Pol. (Belzhits, Belzhitse, Belzhitza); pop. 1,882; 19 km SW of Lublin; 51°11'/22°17'; AMG, CAHJP, EDRD, EJ, GA, GUM3, GUM4, GUM5, GUM6, HSL, LDS, LYV, SF.

Bena, *see* Belina.

Benadikovce, Cz. (Benedikovce); 62 km N of Kosice; 49°14'/21°33'; AMG, HSL.

Benakani, *see* Benyakoni.

Benatky nad Jizerou, Cz. (Nove Benatky); pop. 21; 32 km NE of Praha; 50°17'/14°50'.

Bender, *see* Bendery.

Benderi, *see* Bendery.

Bendery, Mold. (Bender, Benderi, Tehinia, Tighina, Tiginia); pop. 8,294; 56 km ESE of Kishinev; 46°49'/29°29'; EJ, GUM4, GUM5, HSL, HSL2, JGFF, LDL, PHR2, SF, YB.

Bendin, *see* Bedzin.

Bendkov, *see* Bedkow.

Bendorf, Germ.; pop. 250; 75 km SE of Koln; 50°26'/07°34'; GED, GUM3.

Bendorf Sayn, Germ.; 75 km SE of Koln; 50°26'/07°35'; GED, PHGBW.

Bendzin, *see* Bedzin.

Bene, *see* Beregbene.

Benediki, Ukr. JGFF, LDL. This pre-World War I community was not found in BGN gazetteers.

Benedikovce, *see* Benadikovce.

Benesat, Rom.; pop. 7; 75 km NNW of Cluj; 47°25'/23°18'.

Benesov, Cz.; pop. 300; 38 km SE of Praha; 49°47'/14°41'; EJ, GUM4, HSL, HSL2.

Benesov nad Ploucnici, Cz. (Frantiskov); pop. 54; 75 km NNW of Praha; 50°44'/14°19'.

Benfeld, *possibly* Bonfeld.

Bengel, Germ.; pop. 18; 107 km S of Koln; 50°01'/07°04'.

Benhausen, *see* Bobenhausen Zwei.

Beniakon, *see* Benyakoni.

Beniowa, Pol.; pop. 73; 88 km S of Przemysl; 49°03'/22°53'.

Benkovce, Cz.; 45 km NE of Kosice; 48°57'/21°43'; HSL.

Benkovtse, Byel. (Bienkowce); pop. 5; 94 km N of Pinsk; 52°55'/26°05'.

Bennigsen, Germ.; pop. 6; 26 km S of Hannover; 52°14'/09°40'.

Benrath Hilden, *see* Benroth.

Benroth, Germ. (Benrath Hilden); pop. 91; 45 km E of Koln; 50°51'/07°31'.

Bensberg, Germ.; pop. 2; 13 km ENE of Koln; 50°58'/07°10'.

Bensheim, Germ.; pop. 180; 50 km S of Frankfurt am Main; 49°41'/08°37'; AMG, GED, JGFF, LDS.

Bentheim, Germ.; pop. 20; 157 km N of Koln; 52°19'/07°10'; CAHJP, GED, LDS.

Bentschen, *see* Zbaszyn.

Beny, *see* Bina.

Benyakoni, Byel. (Benakani, Beniakon, Bieniakonie); pop. 49; 150 km W of Minsk; 54°15'/25°22'; AMG, COH, GUM3, HSL, SF.

Benye, Hung.; pop. 3; 45 km ESE of Budapest; 47°21'/19°33'; HSL, HSL2, JGFF.

Beocin, Yug.; pop. 37; 75 km WNW of Beograd; 45°12'/19°44'.

Beodra, *see* Novo Milosevo.

Beograd, Yug. (Belgrade, Nandorfehervar); pop. 7,906; 322 km NNW of Skopje; 44°50'/20°30'; AMG, CAHJP, COH, EDRD, EJ, GUM4, GUM5, GUM6, HSL, HSL2, ISH2, JGFF, LDL, LJEE, PHY.

Ber, *see* Bar.

Beravci, Yug.; pop. 1; 170 km W of Beograd; 45°09'/18°26'.

Berbesht, *see* Berbesti.

Berbesti, Rom. (Badfalva, Bardfalva, Berbesht); pop. 539; 126 km N of Cluj; 47°51'/23°56'; COH, GUM3, GUM4, HSL, LYV, PHR2, SM.

Bercel, Hung. (Nogradberczel, Nogradbertsel); pop. 179; 45 km NNE of Budapest; 47°52'/19°25'; COH, GUM5, HSL, HSL2, LDL, LDS, LYV, PHH.

Berchan, *see* Brichany.

Berchez, Rom.; pop. 36; 88 km N of Cluj; 47°31'/23°30'.

Berchezoaia, Rom. (Berkeszpataka); pop. 12; 88 km N of Cluj; 47°30'/23°32'.

Berching, Germ.; 50 km SE of Nurnberg; 49°07'/11°27'; EDRD, PHGB.

Berchisesti, Rom.; pop. 18; 126 km WNW of Iasi; 47°32'/26°02'.

Berchtesgaden, Germ.; pop. 2; 120 km ESE of Munchen; 47°38'/13°00'; GUM3.

Bercu, Rom.; pop. 76; 139 km NNW of Cluj; 47°55'/22°53'.

Berd Ansk, *see* Berdyansk.

Berdechow, Pol.; 82 km SSW of Lublin; 50°40'/21°56'; GUM4.

Berdiansk, *see* Berdyansk.

Berdichev, Ukr. (Bardichev, Berditchev, Berditchov, Berdyczow); pop. 30,812; 82 km N of Vinnitsa; 49°54'/28°35'; AMG, COH, EDRD, EJ, GUM3, GUM4, GUM5, GUM6, HSL, HSL2, JGFF, LDL, LYV, PHP2, SF.

Berditchev, *see* Berdichev.

Berditchov, *see* Berdichev.

Berdjansk, *see* Berdyansk.

Berdowszczyzna, *possibly* Burdykovshchina.

Berdyansk, Ukr. (Berd Ansk, Berdiansk, Berdjansk, Bierdjansk, Osipenko, Osipienko); pop. 2,138; 227 km SE of Dnepropetrovsk; 46°45'/36°47'; GUM4, JGFF, SF.

Berdyczow, *see* Berdichev.

Berdykovtse, Ukr. (Bedrykowce); pop. 8; 50 km NNW of Chernovtsy; 48°42'/25°47'.

Bere, *see* Berea.

Berea, Rom. (Bere); pop. 13; 139 km NW of Cluj; 47°41'/22°21'; HSL.

Berecyk, *see* Bretcu.

Bereg, Hung. (Bereh); AMG, HSL, HSL2. A number of towns share this name. It was not possible to determine from available information which one is being referenced.

Bereg (Wolyn), Ukr.; pop. 5; 62 km SSW of Rovno; 50°12'/25°40'.

Beregbene, Hung. (Bene); 146 km ENE of Miskolc; 48°10'/22°47'; HSL.

Beregboszormeny, *see* Berekboszormeny.

Beregdaroc, Hung.; pop. 38; 133 km ENE of Miskolc; 48°12'/22°32'.

Bereg Hasva, LDL. This pre-World War I community was not found in BGN gazetteers.

Beregi, Ukr. (Nagy Bereg, Nagybereg); 202 km SSW of Lvov; 48°14'/22°45'; AMG, HSL.

Beregomet, Ukr. (Bergomet, Berhomet, Berhomet pe Prut, Berhomete pe Siret, Berkhomet); pop. 979; 50 km SW of Chernovtsy; 48°10'/25°19'; COH, GUM4, LDL, PHR2, SF.

Beregovo, Ukr. (Beregszasz, Berehovo, Berehowo, Sachsisch-Bereg); pop. 9,427; 208 km SSW of Lvov; 48°13'/22°39'; AMG, COH, EJ, GUM3, GUM4, GUM5, GUM6, HSL, HSL2, JGFF, LDL.

Beregrakos, HSL. This pre-World War I community was not found in BGN gazetteers.

Beregsurany, Hung.; 133 km ENE of Miskolc; 48°10'/22°33'; PHH.

Beregszasz, *see* Beregovo.

Beregszentmiklos, HSL. This pre-World War I community was not found in BGN gazetteers.

Beregszollos, *see* Vinogradov.

Beregujfalu, Hung.; 150 km ENE of Miskolc; 48°17'/22°48'; AMG, COH, HSL.

Bereh, *see* Bereg.

Berehovo, *see* Beregovo.

Berehowo, *see* Beregovo.

Berehy Dolne, Pol.; pop. 22; 45 km S of Przemysl; 49°26'/22°38'; PHP2.

Berehy Gorne, Pol.; pop. 28; 75 km S of Przemysl; 49°09'/22°34'.

Berejow, Pol.; pop. 6; 38 km NNE of Lublin; 51°31'/22°45'.

Berekboszormeny, Hung. (Beregboszormeny); 133 km SE of Miskolc; 47°04'/21°41'; LDS, PHH.

Berekeresztur, *see* Bara.

Beremel, *possibly* Baremel.

Beremelia, *see* Baremel.

Beremend, Hung.; pop. 18; 133 km ESE of Nagykanizsa; 45°47'/18°26'.

Beremiany, *see* Beremyany.

Beremyany, Ukr. (Beremiany); pop. 58; 75 km NW of Chernovtsy; 48°53'/25°26'; AMG, GUM3.

Berenbostel, Germ.; 13 km NW of Hannover; 52°27'/09°37'; GED.

Berencs, *see* Branc.

Berend, *see* Berindan.

Bereni, Rom.; pop. 2; 101 km E of Cluj; 46°33'/24°52'.

Berent, *see* Koscierzyna.

Berente, Hung.; pop. 10; 26 km NW of Miskolc; 48°14'/20°40'; HSL.

Berescie, *see* Berestye.

Beresdowo, *see* Berezdov.

Beresino, *see* Berezino.

Beresk, Ukr. (Beresko); pop. 9; 101 km WNW of Rovno; 50°53'/24°54'.

Bereska, Pol.; pop. 26; 56 km SSW of Przemysl; 49°24'/22°23'.

Beresko, *see* Beresk.

Beresnegowatoje, *see* Bereznegovatoye.

Beresovka, *see* Berezovka.

Berest, Pol.; pop. 17; 101 km ESE of Krakow; 49°31'/20°59'.

Berestechko, Ukr. (Beresteczko, Berestetchka, Brestitski); pop. 1,975; 82 km SW of Rovno; 50°21'/25°07'; AMG, COH, EDRD, EJ, GA, GUM3, GUM5, HSL, LDL, LYV, SF, YB.

Beresteczko, *see* Berestechko.

Berestetchka, *see* Berestechko.

Berestovets, Ukr. (Berestovitz, Berestowiec); pop. 27; 38 km N of Rovno; 50°52'/26°18'; SF.

Berestovitsa, *see* Bolshaya Berestovitsa.

Berestovitz, *see* Berestovets.

Berestovitza, *see* Bolshaya Berestovitsa.

Berestowiec, *see* Berestovets.

Berestye, Ukr. (Berescie); pop. 44; 107 km N of Rovno; 51°32'/26°33'.

Beresztelke, *see* Breaza.

Beret, Hung.; pop. 16; 38 km NNE of Miskolc; 48°21'/21°02'.

Beretke, *see* Bretka.

Berettykohany, *see* Cohani.

Berettyodeda, *see* Ghida.

Berettyoszentmarton, Hung. LDS. This town was not found in BGN gazetteers under the given spelling.

Berettyoszeplak, *see* Suplacu de Barcau.

Berettyoujfalu, Hung.; pop. 1,083; 114 km SE of Miskolc; 47°13'/21°33'; AMG, COH, EJ, GUM3, HSL, LDL, LDS, PHH.

Berettyovaralja, HSL. This pre-World War I community was not found in BGN gazetteers.

Bereza, Byel. (Bereza Kartuska, Bereza Kartuskaya, Brezah, Kartoz Brezah, Kartusskaya Bereza, Kartuz Bereze); pop. 2,163; 94 km WNW of Pinsk; 52°32'/24°59'; AMG, COH, EDRD, EJ, GA, GUM3, GUM4, GUM5, HSL, JGFF, LDL, PHP1, PHP2, SF, YB.

Bereza Kartuska, *see* Bereza.

Bereza Kartuskaya, *see* Bereza.

Berezan, Ukr.; 69 km E of Kiyev; 50°19'/31°28'; EJ.

Berezany, *see* Berezhany.

Berezce, *see* Velikiye Berezhtsy.

Berezcy, *see* Velikiye Berezhtsy.

Berezdiv, *see* Berezdov.

Berezdov, Ukr. (Beresdowo, Berezdiv); 62 km E of Rovno; 50°28'/27°07'; JGFF, LDL, SF.

Berezene, *see* Berezno.

Berezhany, Ukr. (Barzan, Berezany, Berson, Berzhan, Brezan, Brzesciany?, Brzezany, Brzezhany, Bzezan, Bzhezhani); pop. 3,582; 82 km ESE of Lvov; 49°27'/24°56'; CAHJP, COH, EDRD, EGRS, EJ, GUM3, GUM4, GUM5, GYLA, HSL, HSL2, JGFF, LDL, PHP2, PHP3, SF, YB.

Berezhki, Ukr. (Berezki); pop. 27; 107 km N of Rovno; 51°31'/26°37'.

Berezhnits, *see* Berezhnitsa.

Berezhnitsa, Byel. (Berezhnits, Bereznica, Bereznitsa, Berznits); pop. 1,372; 114 km WNW of Pinsk; 52°50'/24°55'; AMG, COH, EDRD, FRG, GUM3, SF.

Berezhtse, *see* Velikiye Berezhtsy.

Berezin, *see* Berezino.

Berezina, Ukr.; pop. 125; 120 km WSW of Odessa; 46°14'/29°12'.

Berezino, Byel. (Beresino, Berezin); pop. 1,565; 126 km N of Minsk; 54°54'/28°12'; AMG, EDRD, EJ, GUM4, JGFF, LDL, SF.

Bereziv, *see* Berezovo.

Berezki, *see* Berezhki.

Berezlogi, *see* Berezlozhi.

Berezlozhi, Mold. (Berezlogi); pop. 2; 56 km N of Kishinev; 47°26'/28°56'.

Berezna, Ukr.; pop. 697; 107 km WNW of Konotop; 51°34'/31°47'; EDRD, GUM4, GUM5, LDL, SF.

Berezne, *see* Berezno.

Bereznegovatoye, Ukr. (Beresnegowatoje, Brezhnovata); 182 km NE of Odessa; 47°18'/32°51'; SF.

Bereznek, Cz. AMG, COH. This town was not found in BGN gazetteers under the given spelling.

Berezniak, Pol.; pop. 33; Described in the *Black Book* as being in the Polesie region of Poland, this town was not found in BGN gazetteers.

Berezniaki, *see* Bereznyaki.

Bereznica, *see* Berezhnitsa.

Bereznica Nizna, Pol.; pop. 20; 56 km SSW of Przemysl; 49°25'/22°25'.

Bereznica Rustykalna, Pol.; pop. 25; Described in the *Black Book* as being in the Lwow region of Poland, this town was not found in BGN gazetteers.

Bereznica Wyzna, Pol.; pop. 7; 62 km SSW of Przemysl; 49°21'/22°22'.

Bereznitsa, *see* Berezhnitsa.

Berezno, Ukr. (Berezene, Berezne, Brezhna, Brezne); pop. 2,360; 56 km NNE of Rovno; 51°00'/26°45'; AMG, COH, FRG, GUM3, GUM4, GUM5, HSL, HSL2, JGFF, LYV, SF, YB.

Bereznyaki, Byel. (Berezniaki); pop. 12; 107 km NE of Pinsk; 52°30'/27°30'.

Berezny Velky, Cz.; pop. 2,404; 88 km ENE of Kosice; 48°48'/22°25'; AMG, COH.

Berezo, *see* Brezova pod Bradlom.

Berezov, *see* Brzozow.

Berezovca, *see* Berezovka.

Berezovitsa, *see* Berezovitsa Mala.

Berezovitsa Mala, Ukr. (Berezovitsa); 107 km SSW of Rovno; 49°46'/25°34'; JGFF.

Berezovitsa Velka, *see* Velikaya Berezovitsa.

Berezovka, Ukr. (Beresovka, Berezovca, Berozovka); pop. 3,223; 88 km N of Odessa; 47°12'/30°55'; EJ, GUM3, GUM4, GUM4, GUM6, HSL, LDL, PHR1, SF.

Berezovka (near Lida), Byel.; 107 km N of Minsk; 54°47'/27°40'; SF.

Berezovo, Ukr. (Beriziv, Berezuv); pop. 58; 133 km NNE of Rovno; 51°35'/27°21'; CAHJP, GUM3, JGFF, SM.

Berezow, Pol.; pop. 102; 120 km NNE of Krakow; 51°02'/20°51'. *See also* Berezuv.

Berezowica Wielka, *see* Velikaya Berezovitsa.

Berezow Nizny, *see* Berezuv Nizhny.

Berezow Sredni, Ukr.; pop. 75; 75 km W of Chernovtsy; 48°25'/24°55'.

Berezow Wyzny, *see* Verkhniy Berezov.

Berezuv, *see* Berezovo.

Berezuv Nizhny, Ukr. (Berezow Nizny); pop. 82; 75 km W of Chernovtsy; 48°24'/24°51'.

Berezuv Vyzhny, *see* Verkhniy Berezov.

Berfa, Germ.; 88 km NNE of Frankfurt am Main; 50°46'/09°21'; JGFF.

Berge, Germ.; 139 km W of Hannover; 52°37'/07°43'; GUM5.

Bergen, Germ.; pop. 145; 56 km N of Hannover; 52°49'/09°58'; LDS.

Bergen Enkheim, Germ.; 13 km NE of Frankfurt am Main; 50°09'/08°45'; GED, GUM5.

Berghausen, Germ.; 56 km WNW of Stuttgart; 49°00'/08°32'; EJ.

Bergheim, Germ.; 26 km W of Koln; 50°58'/06°39'; AMG, GED, HSL, JGFF, YB.

Bergheim (near Bonn), Germ.; 26 km SE of Koln; 50°46'/07°06'; GED.

Berghia, Rom.; pop. 2; 69 km ESE of Cluj; 46°32'/24°26'.

Berg im Gau, Germ.; pop. 1; 62 km NW of Munchen; 48°38'/11°15'.

Bergisch Gladbach, Germ.; pop. 4; 19 km NE of Koln; 50°59'/07°08'.

Bergkamen, Germ.; pop. 4; 88 km NNE of Koln; 51°38'/07°38'.

Bergkirchen, Germ. GED. A number of towns share this name. It was not possible to determine from available information which one is being referenced.

Berglern, Germ. (Lern); 38 km NE of Munchen; 48°23'/11°56'; PHGB.

Bergomet, *see* Beregomet.

Bergrothenfels, Germ.; 69 km ESE of Frankfurt am Main; 49°54'/09°35'; PHGB.

Berg vor Nideggen, Germ. GED. This town was not found in BGN gazetteers under the given spelling.

Bergzabern, Germ.; pop. 43; 94 km WNW of Stuttgart; 49°06'/08°00'; CAHJP, GED.

Berhida, Hung.; pop. 32; 82 km SW of Budapest; 47°07'/18°08'.

Berhomet, *see* Beregomet.

Berhomete pe Siret, *see* Beregomet.

Berhomet pe Prut, *see* Beregomet.

22

Berindan, Rom. (Berend); pop. 22; 126 km NNW of Cluj; 47°47'/23°01'.

Berindu, Rom.; pop. 2; 26 km NW of Cluj; 46°57'/23°26'.

Berinta, Rom.; pop. 20; 94 km N of Cluj; 47°33'/23°41'.

Berislav, Ukr. (Beryslaw); pop. 395; 208 km ENE of Odessa; 46°50'/33°26'; LDL, SF.

Berkach, Germ.; pop. 20; 120 km NW of Nurnberg; 50°26'/10°24'; LDS.

Berkesd, Hung.; pop. 14; 120 km ESE of Nagykanizsa; 46°04'/18°25'.

Berkesz, Hung.; pop. 8; 88 km E of Miskolc; 48°06'/21°59'; HSL.

Berkeszpataka, see Berchezoaia.

Berkheim, Germ.; 107 km SE of Stuttgart; 48°03'/10°05'; HSL.

Berkhomet, see Beregomet.

Berkovitsa, Bulg.; pop. 79; 62 km NNW of Sofija; 43°14'/23°07'; EJ, JGFF.

Berlad, see Birlad.

Berlebas, see Rakhov.

Berleburg, Germ.; pop. 44; 101 km ENE of Koln; 51°03'/08°24'; GUM5, HSL.

Berlichingen, Germ.; pop. 67; 69 km N of Stuttgart; 49°20'/09°29'; HSL, JGFF, PHGBW.

Berlin, Germ.; pop. 172,672; 150 km NNE of Leipzig; 52°31'/13°24'; AMG, CAHJP, EDRD, EJ, GED, GUM3, GUM4, GUM5, GUM6, HSL, HSL2, ISH1, ISH2, ISH3, JGFF, LDL, LDS, LYV, PHGBW, PHP1, PHP2, PHP3, PHP4, YB.

Berlinchen, see Barlinek.

Berlinti, possibly Berlintsy.

Berlintsy, Mold. (Berlinti?); pop. 88; 202 km NW of Kishinev; 48°19'/26°56'.

Berlochy, see Berlogy.

Berlogy, Ukr. (Berlochy, Berlohy); pop. 25; 107 km SSE of Lvov; 48°58'/24°15'.

Berlohy, see Berlogy.

Bermuthshain, Germ.; pop. 6; 62 km NE of Frankfurt am Main; 50°28'/09°19'.

Bernadzki Most, Pol.; pop. 4; 50 km ESE of Bialystok; 52°51'/23°41'.

Bernartice, Cz.; pop. 40; 88 km S of Praha; 49°22'/14°24'; EJ.

Bernatfalva, see Bernatovice.

Bernatovice, (Bernatfalva); HSL. This pre-World War I community was not found in BGN gazetteers.

Bernau, Germ.; pop. 57; 26 km NNE of Berlin; 52°40'/13°35'; GUM3.

Bernburg, Germ.; pop. 206; 69 km NW of Leipzig; 51°48'/11°44'; AMG, EJ, GUM3, HSL, HSL2, JGFF, LDS.

Berndorf, Aus.; pop. 38; 32 km SSW of Wien; 47°57'/16°06'; GUM5.

Bernecebarati, Hung.; pop. 24; 62 km NNW of Budapest; 48°02'/18°55'.

Bernhausen, Germ.; 19 km SSE of Stuttgart; 48°41'/09°13'; GUM3, PHGBW.

Bernkastel Cues, see Bernkastel Kues.

Bernkastel Kues, Germ. (Bernkastel Cues); pop. 61; 120 km WSW of Frankfurt am Main; 49°55'/07°04'; GUM5.

Bernow, Pol.; pop. 4; 82 km ESE of Lodz; 51°19'/20°26'.

Bernstadt, see Bernstadt in Schlesien.

Bernstadt in Schlesien, Pol. (Bernstadt, Bierutow); pop. 80; 38 km ENE of Wroclaw; 51°07'/17°32'; AMG, HSL, HSL2, LDS.

Bernstein, see Pelczyce.

Beroea, see Veroia.

Berolzheim, see Markt Berolzheim.

Beroun, Cz.; pop. 133; 32 km SW of Praha; 49°57'/14°05'.

Berovo, Yug.; pop. 1; 114 km ESE of Skopje; 41°43'/22°51'.

Berozovka, see Berezovka.

Berrendorf, Germ.; pop. 11; 26 km WSW of Koln; 50°55'/06°35'; GED.

Bersad, see Bershad.

Bershad, Ukr. (Barsad, Bersad, Berszad, Berszada); pop. 7,016; 69 km SW of Uman; 48°22'/29°31'; EDRD, EJ, GUM3, GUM4, GUM5, GYLA, HSL, JGFF, LDL, PHR1, SF, YB.

Bershty, Byel. (Berszty); pop. 30; 208 km WSW of Minsk; 53°52'/24°24'.

Berson, see Berezhany.

Berstadt, Germ.; 45 km N of Frankfurt am Main; 50°26'/08°52'; LDS.

Berszad, see Bershad.

Berszada, see Bershad.

Berszty, see Bershty.

Berta, see Burty.

Bertotovce, Cz.; 38 km NW of Kosice; 49°01'/21°02'; JGFF.

Berveni, Rom. (Borvely); pop. 79; 139 km NW of Cluj; 47°45'/22°28'.

Berwangen, Germ.; pop. 35; BGN lists two possible localities with this name located at 47°38'/08°30' and 49°11'/08°59'. GUM5, LDS, PHGBW.

Beryansk, HSL. This pre-World War I community was not found in BGN gazetteers.

Beryslaw, see Berislav.

Berzai, see Birzai.

Berzasca, Rom. (Berzaska); 264 km SSW of Cluj; 44°39'/21°57'; HSL.

Berzaska, see Berzasca.

Berzaune, Lat.; pop. 9; 107 km NNW of Daugavpils; 56°48'/26°02'.

Berzek, Hung.; pop. 4; 13 km ESE of Miskolc; 48°01'/20°57'.

Berzence, Hung.; pop. 36; 32 km SSE of Nagykanizsa; 46°12'/17°09'.

Berzete, see Brzotin.

Berzevicze, HSL, LDL. This pre-World War I community was not found in BGN gazetteers.

Berzgale, Lat.; pop. 16; 101 km NNE of Daugavpils; 56°38'/27°30'.

Berzhan, see Berezhany.

Berzhnitse, see Brzeznica.

Berzin, see Brzeziny.

Berzniki, Pol.; 114 km N of Bialystok; 54°05'/23°28'; JGFF, POCEM.

Berznits, see Berezhnitsa.

Berzpils, Lat. (Dompole); pop. 95; 114 km N of Daugavpils; 56°51'/27°05'; PHLE.

Bes, see Gabcikovo.

Besalma, see Beshalma.

Besenov, Cz. (Besenyo); 88 km E of Bratislava; 48°03'/18°16'; HSL.

Besenyo, see Besenov.

Besenyod, Hung.; pop. 23; 94 km E of Miskolc; 47°58'/22°01'; LDS.

Besenyotelek, Hung.; pop. 6; 56 km SSW of Miskolc; 47°42'/20°26'.

Besenyszog, Hung.; pop. 31; 94 km E of Budapest; 47°18'/20°16'.

Bes Ghioz, see Besh Gioz.

Beshalma, Mold. (Besalma); pop. 6; 94 km S of Kishinev; 46°10'/28°39'.

Beshenkovichi, Byel. (Beshenkowitschi, Bishenkovitz, Bjeschenkowitschi); pop. 1,487; 50 km SW of Vitebsk; 55°03'/29°27'; GYLA, HSL, JGFF, LDL, SF.

Beshenkowitschi, see Beshenkovichi.

Besh Gioz, Mold. (Bes Ghioz); pop. 12; 101 km S of Kishinev; 46°07'/28°52'.

Beshtemak, Mold. (Bestemac); pop. 16; 56 km S of Kishinev; 46°32'/28°32'.

Besiekiery, Pol.; pop. 12; 56 km NW of Lodz; 52°09'/18°58'.

Besiny, Cz.; pop. 12; 126 km SSW of Praha; 49°18'/13°19'.

Beska, Yug.; pop. 1; 50 km WNW of Beograd; 45°07'/20°04'.

Besno, Cz.; pop. 14; 69 km W of Praha; 50°11'/13°31'.

Bessarabia; Not a town but a region now part of the Moldavian SSR. Bordered by the Black Sea and the Dniester, Danube and Prut Rivers, it has alternately been part of Romania (1856-1878, 1918-1940) and Russia (1812-1856, 1878-1918, 1940-present).

Bessarabka, Mold. (Romanesti); pop. 1,995; 82 km SSE of Kishinev; 46°20'/28°58'; GUM4.

Bessingen, Germ.; 38 km SSW of Hannover; 52°06'/09°30'; LDS.

Bestemac, *see* Beshtemak.

Bestovice, Cz.; pop. 59; 101 km NNW of Brno; 50°01'/16°13'.

Bestvina, Cz.; pop. 10; 82 km ESE of Praha; 49°50'/15°36'.

Bestwina, Pol.; pop. 25; 62 km SW of Krakow; 49°54'/19°04'.

Beszowa, Pol.; pop. 7; 94 km NE of Krakow; 50°25'/21°07'.

Besztece, *see* Bistrita.

Besztercebanya, *see* Banska Bystrica.

Beszterce Naszod, LDL. This pre-World War I community was not found in BGN gazetteers.

Beszterec, Hung.; pop. 31; 82 km ENE of Miskolc; 48°09'/21°51'.

Beszyce, Pol.; pop. 10; 101 km SW of Lublin; 50°36'/21°31'.

Betfia, Rom.; pop. 3; 120 km W of Cluj; 46°58'/22°02'.

Bethlen, *see* Beclean.

Betigola, *see* Betygala.

Betlen, *see* Beclean.

Betok, *see* Batakiai.

Betsche, *see* Pszczew.

Bettenhausen, Germ.; 120 km NE of Frankfurt am Main; 50°33'/10°17'; LDS.

Bettingen, Germ.; pop. 25; 146 km SW of Frankfurt am Main; 49°26'/06°51'.

Betygala, Lith. (Betigola, Betygola); pop. 83; 62 km NW of Kaunas; 55°22'/23°22'; YL.

Betygola, *see* Betygala.

Betzdorf, Germ.; pop. 43; 69 km E of Koln; 50°47'/07°53'; GED.

Betziesdorf, Germ.; 88 km N of Frankfurt am Main; 50°51'/08°50'; LDS.

Beudiu, Rom.; pop. 69; 50 km NE of Cluj; 47°04'/24°10'.

Beuel, Germ.; pop. 130; 32 km SE of Koln; 50°44'/07°08'; GED.

Beuern, Germ.; 62 km N of Frankfurt am Main; 50°38'/08°49'; LDS.

Beurig, Germ.; pop. 29; 157 km SW of Frankfurt am Main; 49°36'/06°34'.

Beuthen, *see* Bytom.

Beutzenburg, GUM4. This town was not found in BGN gazetteers under the given spelling.

Beverungen, Germ.; pop. 61; 82 km S of Hannover; 51°40'/09°22'; CAHJP, EJ, HSL, JGFF.

Beytch, *see* Biecz.

Bezbrudy, Ukr.; pop. 7; 38 km ENE of Lvov; 49°55'/24°33'.

Bezdan, Yug.; pop. 75; 170 km WNW of Beograd; 45°51'/18°56'; COH, GUM4, PHY.

Bezded, *see* Tiszabezded.

Bezdedtelek, *see* Tiszabezded.

Bezdonys, Lith.; 19 km NE of Vilnius; 54°48'/25°32'; GUM3.

Bezdruzice, Cz.; pop. 24; 107 km WSW of Praha; 49°54'/12°58'.

Bezejow, *possibly* Bozhuv.

Bezeny, Mold. (Bezin); pop. 7; 38 km NNW of Kishinev; 47°18'/28°40'.

Bezenye, Hung.; pop. 3; 146 km WNW of Budapest; 47°58'/17°13'.

Bezered, Hung.; pop. 10; 56 km N of Nagykanizsa; 46°52'/17°01'.

Bezhezhin, *see* Brzeziny.

Bezhitsa, USSR; pop. 768; 13 km NW of Bryansk; 53°19'/34°18'.

Bezi, Hung.; pop. 30; 126 km W of Budapest; 47°40'/17°24'; LDS.

Bezid, Rom. (Bezidul Nou, Bozodujfalu); pop. 10; 107 km ESE of Cluj; 46°24'/24°55'.

Bezidul Nou, *see* Bezid.

Bezidu Nou, *see* Bezidu Nov.

Bezidu Nov, Rom. (Bezidu Nou); pop. 96; 107 km ESE of Cluj;

46°25'/24°54'; EJ, PHR2.

Bezin, *see* Bezeny.

Bezivce, *see* Bezovce.

Bezmichowa Dolna, Pol.; pop. 8; 45 km SW of Przemysl; 49°31'/22°23'.

Bezmichowa Gorna, Pol.; pop. 15; 45 km SSW of Przemysl; 49°31'/22°24'.

Bezmir, Cz.; pop. 4; 56 km S of Praha; 49°39'/14°32'.

Beznea, Rom. (Barodbeznye); pop. 36; 75 km W of Cluj; 46°57'/22°38'; AMG.

Bezovce, Cz. (Bezivce); pop. 83; 62 km E of Kosice; 48°38'/22°09'; AMG, HSL.

Bezoyn, *see* Biezun.

Bezwola, Pol.; pop. 4; 62 km N of Lublin; 51°46'/22°48'.

Bia, Hung.; pop. 32; 19 km WSW of Budapest; 47°28'/18°49'; HSL.

Biadoliny Radlowskie, *see* Lopon.

Biala, Pol. AMG. A number of towns share this name. It was not possible to determine from available information which one is being referenced. *See also* Bielsko Biala. Biala, which means "white" in Slavic tongues, is not only the name of a number of towns in Eastern Europe, but is also used as a nickname for a number of towns that include Biala as part of their names, e.g., Biala Rawska.

Biala (near Krakow), Pol.; pop. 1,363; 69 km SW of Krakow; 49°49'/19°02'.

Biala (near Lodz), Pol.; pop. 27; 26 km N of Lodz; 51°56'/19°27'.

Biala (near Myslenice), Pol.; pop. 69; 234 km ESE of Przemysl; 49°02'/25°46'.

Biala (Prudnik), Pol.; 88 km SE of Wroclaw; 50°23'/17°39'; CAHJP, EJ, HSL, HSL2, JGFF.

Biala Bielsko, *see* Bielsko Biala.

Biala Bilits, *see* Bielsko Biala.

Bialabzheg, *see* Bialobrzegi.

Biala Cerkiew, *see* Belaya Tserkov.

Bialaczow, Pol. (Bialatchov, Bialoczev); pop. 166; 75 km ESE of Lodz; 51°18'/20°18'; EDRD, GA, GUM5, PHP1, PHP4, SF.

Biala D'Lita, *see* Biala Podlaska.

Biala Gadol, *see* Biala Podlaska.

Biala Gora, Pol.; pop. 38; 38 km WNW of Lodz; 51°59'/19°04'.

Biala Katan, *see* Biala Rawska.

Biala Krakowska, *see* Bielsko Biala.

Biala Opolskie, Pol.; 32 km SW of Czestochowa; 50°40'/18°42'; JGFF.

Biala Podlaska, Pol. (Biala D'Lita, Biala Gadol, Podlyashe); pop. 6,874; 101 km NNE of Lublin; 52°02'/23°08'; AMG, CAHJP, COH, EDRD, EJ, GA, GUM3, GUM4, GUM5, HSL, HSL2, JGFF, LDL, LDS, LYV, PHP3, PHP4, POCEM, SF, YB.

Biala Poshet, *see* Biala Rawska.

Biala Ravska, *see* Biala Rawska.

Biala Rawska, Pol. (Biala Katan, Biala Poshet, Biala Ravska); pop. 1,429; 62 km SSW of Warszawa; 51°48'/20°29'; AMG, CAHJP, COH, EDRD, GA, GUM3, GUM4, GUM5, HSL, LDS, LYV, PHP1, PHP2, POCEM, SF, YB.

Bialatchov, *see* Bialaczow.

Biala Tserkov, *see* Belaya Tserkov.

Biala Waka, *see* Baltoja Voke.

Biala Wielka, Pol.; pop. 6; 38 km E of Czestochowa; 50°42'/19°40'.

Biala Wyzna, Pol.; pop. 19; 94 km ESE of Krakow; 49°37'/20°58'.

Biale Blota, Pol.; pop. 20; 133 km N of Bialystok; 54°18'/23°03'.

Bialikomin, *see* Belyy Kamen.

Bialistok, *see* Bialystok.

Bialka, Pol.; pop. 20; 50 km W of Przemysl; 49°53'/22°03'; GUM5.

Bialki Dolne, Pol.; pop. 5; 50 km NW of Lublin; 51°36'/22°04'.

Bialki Gorne, Pol.; pop. 8; 50 km NW of Lublin; 51°36'/22°05'.

Bialoboznica, *see* Belobozhnitsa.

Bialobrodzie, Pol.; pop. 36; Described in the *Black Book* as being in the Wilen region of Poland, this town was not found in BGN gazetteers.

Bialobrzeg, Pol.; 62 km ESE of Poznan; 52°11'/17°47'; JGFF.

Bialobrzegi, Pol. (Bialabzheg); pop. 2,200; 75 km S of Warszawa; 51°39'/20°57'; AMG, COH, EDRD, GA, GUM3, GUM4, GUM5, HSL, HSL2, LDS, PHP4, SF.

Bialobrzegi (Lancut area), Pol.; pop. 69; 45 km NW of Przemysl; 50°06'/22°21'.

Bialoczev, *see* Bialaczow.

Bialogard, Pol. (Belgard, Belgrad); pop. 112; 114 km NE of Szczecin; 54°00'/16°00'; GUM3, HSL, LDS.

Bialogon, Pol.; pop. 252; 94 km NNE of Krakow; 50°51'/20°34'; GUM5.

Bialogorne, Pol.; pop. 6; 50 km SSW of Warszawa; 51°54'/20°34'.

Bialohusza, *see* Belogusha.

Bialokorzec, *see* Belokorets.

Bialokrynica, *see* Belaya Krinitsa.

Bialoleka, Pol.; pop. 10; 13 km N of Warszawa; 52°19'/21°02'.

Bialopole, *see* Belopolye.

Bialostok, *see* Vinogradov.

Bialowieza, Pol.; 69 km SE of Białystok; 52°41'/23°49'; COH, EJ, GUM3, HSL.

Bialowiz, *see* Belovizh.

Bialoworce, GUM3. This town was not found in BGN gazetteers under the given spelling.

Bialozorka, *see* Belozerka.

Bialy Bor, Pol.; 126 km SW of Gdansk; 53°53'/16°50'; LDS.

Bialy Dunajec, Pol.; pop. 7; 88 km S of Krakow; 49°22'/20°01'.

Bialy Kamien, *see* Belyy Kamen.

Bialykamien, *see* Belyy Kamen.

Bialystok, Pol. (Belostok, Bialistok); pop. 39,602; 170 km NE of Warszawa; 53°08'/23°09'; AMG, CAHJP, COH, EDRD, EJ, GA, GUM3, GUM4, GUM5, GUM6, HSL, HSL2, JGFF, LDL, LDS, LYV, PHP1, PHP2, PHP4, POCEM, YB.

Bialyszewo, Pol.; pop. 7; 101 km WNW of Warszawa; 52°47'/19°45'.

Biberach, *see* Biberach an der Riss.

Biberach an der Riss, Germ. (Biberach); 88 km SE of Stuttgart; 48°06'/09°48'; PHGBW.

Bibergau, Germ.; pop. 6; 82 km WNW of Nurnberg; 49°48'/10°06'; PHGB.

Bibice, Pol.; pop. 2; 13 km N of Krakow; 50°08'/19°57'.

Biblis, Germ.; pop. 100; 50 km S of Frankfurt am Main; 49°41'/08°27'; CAHJP, HSL, JGFF.

Bibra, Germ.; pop. 57; 126 km NNW of Nurnberg; 50°28'/10°26'; JGFF, LDS.

Bicai, Rom. (Bicaz Salaj); pop. 23; 88 km NW of Cluj; 47°28'/23°02'.

Bicaz Salaj, *see* Bicai.

Bichava, *see* Bychawa.

Bicheva, *see* Bichevaya.

Bichevaya, Ukr. (Bicheva); 120 km NW of Dnepropetrovsk; 49°22'/34°05'; EDRD.

Bichlbach, Aus.; pop. 1; 50 km WNW of Innsbruck; 47°25'/10°47'.

Bichov, *see* Bykhov.

Bickenbach, Germ.; 45 km S of Frankfurt am Main; 49°45'/08°37'; LDS.

Bicsad, Rom.; pop. 119; 182 km SW of Iasi; 46°06'/25°52'; HSL, HSL2.

Bicske, Hung.; pop. 241; 32 km WSW of Budapest; 47°29'/18°38'; HSL, HSL2, LDS, PHH.

Bicskof, *see* Velikiy Bychkov.

Biczyce, Pol.; pop. 44; 62 km SE of Krakow; 49°38'/20°29'.

Bidevle, *see* Bedevlya.

Bidgoshch, *see* Bydgoszcz.

Biebesheim, Germ.; pop. 21; 38 km S of Frankfurt am Main; 49°47'/08°28'; LDS.

Biebrich, Germ. (Biebrich am Rhein); pop. 100; 56 km WNW of Frankfurt am Main; 50°19'/07°57'; AMG, EJ, HSL, HSL2, JGFF.

Biebrich am Rhein, *see* Biebrich.

Biechow, Pol.; 82 km NE of Krakow; 50°23'/20°59'; GA.

Biecz, Pol. (Baych, Baytsh, Beitch, Beytch); pop. 632; 101 km ESE of Krakow; 49°44'/21°15'; AMG, CAHJP, COH, EDRD, EGRS, EJ, GA, GUM4, GUM5, GYLA, HSL, HSL2, JGFF, LDL, LDS, LYV, PHP3, POCEM, SF, YB.

Biedaszki, Pol.; pop. 11; 88 km SW of Lodz; 51°24'/18°16'.

Biedermannsdorf, Aus.; pop. 14; 19 km S of Wien; 48°05'/16°20'.

Biedrusko, Pol.; pop. 1; 19 km N of Poznan; 52°33'/16°57'.

Biedrzykowice, Pol.; pop. 7; 45 km NNE of Krakow; 50°24'/20°19'.

Biegonice, Pol.; pop. 23; 82 km ESE of Krakow; 49°35'/20°41'.

Biejkow, Pol.; pop. 25; 69 km S of Warszawa; 51°42'/21°01'.

Biel, Cz. (Bely); pop. 95; 62 km ESE of Kosice; 48°25'/22°03'; GUM5, HSL.

Bielany Budy, *see* Budy Bielanskie.

Bielatycze, Ukr.; pop. 40; 56 km NNE of Rovno; 51°05'/26°35'. This town was located on an interwar map of Poland but does not appear in contemporary gazetteers. Map coordinates are approximate.

Bielavi, *see* Bielawy.

Bielawa, Pol.; pop. 4; 26 km SE of Warszawa; 52°07'/21°08'.

Bielawa Dolna, Pol. (Langenbielau); pop. 8; 139 km W of Wroclaw; 51°18'/15°02'; GUM3, GUM4, GUM6.

Bielawki, Pol.; pop. 2; 56 km N of Lodz; 52°14'/19°25'; PHP1.

Bielawy, Pol. (Bielavi); 38 km N of Lodz; 52°04'/19°39'; JGFF, LDS, PHP4, SF.

Bielce, *see* Beltsy.

Bielcza, Pol.; pop. 15; 62 km E of Krakow; 50°02'/20°44'.

Bielefeld, Germ. (Bielfeld); pop. 860; 88 km SW of Hannover; 52°02'/08°32'; AMG, CAHJP, EJ, GED, GUM3, GUM4, HSL, HSL2, LDS, YB.

Bielfeld, *see* Bielefeld.

Bielica, *see* Belitsa.

Bielice, Pol. AMG. A number of towns share this name. It was not possible to determine from available information which one is being referenced.

Bieliczna, Pol.; pop. 5; 107 km ESE of Krakow; 49°27'/21°06'.

Bielin, Pol.; pop. 24; 82 km E of Lublin; 51°03'/23°46'.

Bielinek, *see* Belinek.

Bieliniec, Pol.; pop. 15; 88 km S of Lublin; 50°28'/22°16'.

Bieliny, Pol.; pop. 82; 82 km NW of Przemysl; 50°27'/22°18'; PHP3, PHP4.

Bieliny Kapitulne, Pol.; pop. 68; 107 km NNE of Krakow; 50°51'/20°55'.

Bielitz, *see* Bielsko Biala.

Bielitz Biala, *see* Bielsko Biala.

Bielniki, Pol. PHP3. This town was not found in BGN gazetteers under the given spelling.

Bielogorodka, *see* Belogorodka.

Bieloserka, *see* Belozerka.

Bieloserka Bolshoi, (Bielozerka Hagdolah); SF. This town was not found in BGN gazetteers under the given spelling.

Bielowce, *see* Belovtsy.

Bielowice, Pol.; pop. 10; 75 km ESE of Lodz; 51°24'/20°23'.

Bielowizna, Pol.; pop. 52; 50 km SSE of Czestochowa; 50°23'/19°15'.

Bielowy, Pol.; pop. 6; 107 km ESE of Krakow; 49°46'/21°20'.

Bielozerka Hagdolah, *see* Bieloserka Bolshoi.

Bielozierka, *see* Belozerka.

Bielozorka, *see* Belozerka.

Bielsk, Pol. (Belsk); pop. 249; 94 km WNW of Warszawa; 52°40'/19°48'; COH, EJ, GA, GUM3, HSL, JGFF, LDL, LDS, PHP4.

Bielska Wola, *see* Belskaya Volya.

Bielsko, *see* Bielsko Biala.

Bielsko Biala, Pol. (Belaya, Biala, Biala Bielsko, Biala Bilits, Biala Krakowska, Bielitz, Bielitz Biala, Bielsko, Bilitz, Byala, Byelits Biala, Byelsko, Byelsko Biala, Zuelz); pop. 3,982; 69 km SW of Krakow; 49°49'/19°02'; CAHJP, COH, EGRS, EJ, GUM3, GUM4, GUM5, GUM6, HSL, HSL2, JGFF, LDL, LDS, LYV, PHP1, PHP2, PHP3, POCEM, SF, YB.

Bielsko Podlaskie, *see* Bielsk Podlaski.

Bielsk Podlaski, Pol. (Bielsko Podlaskie, Bilsk, Byelsk, Byelsk Podlaski); pop. 2,392; 45 km S of Bialystok; 52°46'/23°12'; AMG, CAHJP, COH, EDRD, EJ, GA, GUM3, GUM4, GUM5, GUM6, GYLA, HSL, HSL2, JGFF, LDL, LDS, LYV, POCEM, SF, YB.

Bielszowice, Pol.; 62 km S of Czestochowa; 50°16'/18°50'; AMG, GUM3.

Bieluniszki, Pol.; pop. 28; Described in the *Black Book* as being in the Wilen region of Poland, this town was not found in BGN gazetteers.

Bieniakonie, *see* Benyakoni.

Bieniasze, Pol.; pop. 3; 50 km NNE of Bialystok; 53°33'/23°31'.

Bieniaszowice, Pol.; pop. 21; 62 km ENE of Krakow; 50°13'/20°46'.

Bieniec, Pol.; pop. 6; 50 km NW of Czestochowa; 51°07'/18°39'.

Bienkowce, *see* Benkovtse.

Bierdjansk, *see* Berdyansk.

Bieringen, Germ.; 45 km SSW of Stuttgart; 48°27'/08°51'; PHGBW.

Biernaty Stare, Pol.; pop. 4; 107 km S of Bialystok; 52°14'/22°41'.

Bierstadt, Germ.; pop. 48; 26 km WSW of Frankfurt am Main; 50°05'/08°17'; JGFF.

Bierun Nowy, Pol.; 50 km WSW of Krakow; 50°05'/19°11'; LDS.

Bierutow, *see* Bernstadt in Schlesien.

Bierwce, Pol.; pop. 6; 82 km SSE of Warszawa; 51°34'/21°10'.

Biery, Pol.; pop. 8; 82 km SW of Krakow; 49°48'/18°55'.

Bierzanow, *see* Biezanow.

Bierznik, LDL. This pre-World War I community was not found in BGN gazetteers.

Biesiadka, Pol.; 101 km WNW of Przemysl; 50°16'/21°34'; GA, GUM3, PHP3.

Biesti, *see* Biyeshty.

Biestrzykow Wielki, Pol.; pop. 7; 50 km NE of Czestochowa; 51°05'/19°41'.

Bietigheim, Germ.; 26 km NNW of Stuttgart; 48°57'/09°07'; GUM3, JGFF, PHGBW.

Biezanow, Pol. (Bierzanow); pop. 13; 13 km ESE of Krakow; 50°01'/20°03'; GUM3, GUM4, GUM5, PHP3.

Biezdziedza, Pol.; pop. 15; 94 km W of Przemysl; 49°49'/21°30'.

Biezun, Pol. (Bezoyn, Bizun, Byezhun); pop. 779; 107 km WNW of Warszawa; 52°58'/19°55'; COH, FRG, HSL, LDS, LYV, PHP1, PHP4, SF, YB.

Bigge, Germ.; pop. 35; 114 km NE of Koln; 51°21'/08°28'; HSL.

Bihac, Yug.; pop. 149; 114 km S of Zagreb; 44°49'/15°52'; HSL, PHY.

Bihale, Pol.; pop. 39; 38 km NNE of Przemysl; 50°05'/23°02'.

Bihar, *see* Biharea.

Bihardancshaza, Hung. (Dancshaza); pop. 2; 107 km SSE of Miskolc; 47°14'/21°19'.

Bihardioszeg, *see* Diosig.

Biharea, Rom. (Bihar); 133 km WNW of Cluj; 47°09'/21°55'; HSL, PHR2.

Biharkeresztes, Hung. (Keresztes); pop. 164; 133 km SE of Miskolc; 47°08'/21°43'; HSL, HSL2, LDS, PHH.

Biharnagybajom, Hung.; pop. 144; 101 km SSE of Miskolc; 47°13'/21°14'; HSL, LDS, PHH.

Biharpuspoki, *see* Episcopia Bihorului.

Bihartorda, Hung.; pop. 35; 107 km SSE of Miskolc; 47°13'/21°22'; LDS.

Biharudvary, (Biharudvori); HSL, LDL. This pre-World War I community was not found in BGN gazetteers.

Biharudvori, *see* Biharudvary.

Biharugra, Hung. (Ugra); pop. 8; 133 km NE of Szeged;

46°58'/21°36'; LDS.

Biisk, *see* Antonuvka.

Bijeljina, Yug.; pop. 321; 101 km WSW of Beograd; 44°45'/19°13'; CAHJP, EJ, PHY.

Bikhava, *see* Bychawa.

Bikity, *see* Bacsbokod.

Bikivics, *see* Velikiy Bychkov.

Bikovsk, *see* Bukowsko.

Bikowek, Pol.; pop. 10; 45 km S of Warszawa; 51°54'/20°50'.

Biksad, *see* Bixad.

Biksti, Lat.; pop. 1; 75 km SW of Riga; 56°42'/22°58'.

Bikszad, *see* Bixad.

Bila, HSL. A number of towns share this name. It was not possible to determine from available information which one is being referenced.

Bila Cirkev, Ukr. (Biserica Alba, Sdeh Lavan, Shwartz Tomah, Tiszafeyeenyhaz); 157 km WSW of Chernovtsy; 47°57'/23°55'; SM.

Bilaevka, GUM4. This town was not found in BGN gazetteers under the given spelling.

Bilak, *see* Bileag.

Bilan, *see* Bylany.

Bilavati, *see* Belovtsy.

Bilazor, *see* Belozerye.

Bilbor, Rom. (Belber); pop. 52; 150 km ENE of Cluj; 47°03'/25°31'.

Bilca, Rom.; pop. 33; 163 km WNW of Iasi; 47°55'/25°45'.

Bilche, Ukr. (Bilcze); pop. 39; 56 km S of Lvov; 49°24'/23°50'.

Bilche Zolotoye, Ukr. (Bilcze Zlote); pop. 133; 56 km N of Chernovtsy; 48°47'/25°53'; GUM3, PHP2.

Bilcze, *see* Bilche.

Bilcze Zlote, *see* Bilche Zolotoye.

Bilczow, Pol.; pop. 7; 69 km NE of Krakow; 50°24'/20°46'.

Bilczyn, CAHJP. This town does not appear in contemporary or interwar gazetteers of Poland. It was located in the Wolyn province of interwar Poland.

Bildugi, *see* Bildyugi.

Bildyugi, Byel. (Bildugi, Bildzhugi, Bildzhugis, Bildzhuis, Bildziugi, Bildziuki); pop. 154; 176 km W of Vitebsk; 55°29'/27°23'.

Bildzhugi, *see* Bildyugi.

Bildzhugis, *see* Bildyugi.

Bildzhuis, *see* Bildyugi.

Bildziugi, *see* Bildyugi.

Bildziuki, *see* Bildyugi.

Bileag, Rom. (Bilak); HSL. This pre-World War I community was not found in BGN gazetteers.

Bileca, Yug.; pop. 19; 264 km WNW of Skopje; 42°53'/18°26'.

Bilence, Cz.; pop. 16; 75 km WNW of Praha; 50°26'/13°30'.

Bilenec, Cz.; pop. 3; 69 km W of Praha; 50°08'/13°28'.

Bilghez, Rom. (Burgezd); pop. 14; 82 km WNW of Cluj; 47°14'/22°43'.

Bilgoraj, Pol. (Bilgoray); pop. 3,715; 82 km S of Lublin; 50°33'/22°42'; AMG, COH, EDRD, EJ, FRG, GA, GUM3, GUM4, GUM5, HSL, HSL2, JGFF, LDS, LYV, POCEM, SF, YB.

Bilgoray, *see* Bilgoraj.

Bilhorodki, *see* Belogorodka.

Biliceni, *see* Staryye Bilicheny.

Bilichi, Ukr. (Bilicz, Bylice, Bylitse); pop. 53; 94 km SW of Lvov; 49°26'/22°53'; PHP4.

Bilichov, Cz.; pop. 3; 45 km WNW of Praha; 50°16'/13°55'.

Bilicz, *see* Bilichi.

Bilin, *see* Belin.

Bilina, Cz.; pop. 78; 69 km NW of Praha; 50°32'/13°48'.

Bilina Velikaya, *see* Bolshaya Belina.

Bilina Velka, *see* Bolshaya Belina.

Bilina Wielka, *see* Bolshaya Belina.

Biliniec, *see* Ilintsy (near Chernovtsy).

Bilinka Mala, Ukr.; pop. 27; 82 km SSW of Lvov; 49°15'/23°25'. This town was located on an interwar map of Poland but does not appear in contemporary gazetteers. Map coordinates are approximate.

Bilitz, *see* Bielsko Biala.

Bilitza, *see* Belitsa.

Bilka, Ukr.; pop. 23; 114 km N of Chernovtsy; 49°16'/26°15'; HSL.

Bilka Krolewska, *see* Nizhnyaya Belka.

Bilka Krulevska, *see* Nizhnyaya Belka.

Bilkamin, *see* Belyy Kamen.

Bilka Shlyakhetska, Ukr. (Bilka Szlachecka); pop. 61; 26 km E of Lvov; 49°49'/24°18'.

Bilka Szlachecka, *see* Bilka Shlyakhetska.

Bilke, *see* Bilki.

Bilki, Ukr. (Bilke, Bilky); 182 km S of Lvov; 48°19'/23°08'; AMG, COH, GUM4, HSL, HSL2, JGFF.

Bilky, *see* Bilki.

Billerbeck, Germ.; pop. 30; 120 km N of Koln; 51°58'/07°18'.

Billigheim (Baden), Germ.; pop. 27; 69 km N of Stuttgart; 49°21'/09°15'; GED, LDS, PHGBW.

Billigheim (Rhineland Pfalz), Germ.; pop. 35; 88 km WNW of Stuttgart; 49°08'/08°06'; GUM5.

Billstedt, Germ.; pop. 8; 13 km E of Hamburg; 53°33'/10°08'.

Bilogorshche, Ukr. (Bilohorszcze); pop. 76; 6 km WNW of Lvov; 49°51'/23°56'.

Bilohorszcze, *see* Bilogorshche.

Bilokorovitch, *see* Belokorovichi.

Bilovarets, *see* Belovarec.

Bilovec, Cz. (Wagstadt); pop. 85; 120 km NE of Brno; 49°46'/18°02'.

Bilsk, *see* Bielsk Podlaski.

Bilsko, Pol.; pop. 26; 62 km SE of Krakow; 49°40'/20°32'. This town was located on an interwar map of Poland but does not appear in contemporary gazetteers. Map coordinates are approximate.

Bilvaritz, *see* Belovarec.

Bina, Cz. (Beny); 114 km E of Bratislava; 47°55'/18°39'; HSL.

Binarea, Rom.; pop. 108; Described in the *Black Book* as being in the Transylvania region of Romania, this town was not found in BGN gazetteers.

Binarowa, Pol.; pop. 18; 101 km ESE of Krakow; 49°45'/21°14'; JGFF.

Binau, Germ.; pop. 27; 69 km NNW of Stuttgart; 49°22'/09°03'; JGFF, LDS, PHGBW.

Binczarowa, Pol.; pop. 6; 69 km SE of Krakow; 49°34'/20°28'.

Bindermichl, GUM5. This town was not found in BGN gazetteers under the given spelling.

Bingen, Germ.; pop. 471; 56 km SW of Frankfurt am Main; 49°58'/07°54'; CAHJP, EJ, GUM4, GUM5, HSL, HSL2, JGFF, PHGBW.

Binsforth, Germ.; pop. 11; 126 km NNE of Frankfurt am Main; 51°04'/09°35'.

Binswangen, Germ.; pop. 49; 82 km WNW of Munchen; 48°34'/10°39'; GED, HSL, HSL2, JGFF, PHGB.

Bira, Rom.; 45 km SW of Iasi; 47°02'/27°03'; HSL.

Birca, Rom.; 202 km WSW of Bucuresti; 43°58'/23°37'; COH, HSL, HSL2.

Bircza, Pol. (Birtch); pop. 1,038; 26 km SW of Przemysl; 49°41'/22°28'; AMG, EGRS, GUM3, GYLA, JGFF, LDL, PHP2, PHP3, POCEM, SF.

Bircza Stara, Pol.; pop. 78; 26 km SW of Przemysl; 49°42'/22°27'.

Biri, Hung.; pop. 18; 88 km ESE of Miskolc; 47°49'/21°51'.

Birini, Lat.; pop. 2; 45 km NE of Riga; 57°14'/24°39'.

Birkenau, Germ.; pop. 37; 62 km S of Frankfurt am Main; 49°34'/08°43'; EJ. *See also* Brzezinka. The better known Birkenau is the concentration camp near Oswiecim (Auschwitz), Poland.

Birkenfeld, Germ.; pop. 42; 120 km SW of Frankfurt am Main; 49°39'/07°11'; HSL, JGFF.

Birkenwerder, Germ.; pop. 50; 26 km NW of Berlin; 52°41'/13°17'.

Birkesdorf, Germ.; 38 km SW of Koln; 50°49'/06°28'; GED.

Birklar, Germ.; 50 km N of Frankfurt am Main; 50°30'/08°49'; LDS.

Birlad, Rom. (Barlad, Berlad); pop. 3,727; 107 km S of Iasi; 46°14'/27°40'; AMG, EJ, GYLA, HSL, HSL2, JGFF, LDL, PHR1.

Birlovka, *see* Bysen.

Birnbaum, *see* Miedzychod.

Birsana, *see* Barczanfalva.

Birsau de Sus, Rom. (Barsaul de Sus, Felsoberekszo); pop. 40; 101 km NNW of Cluj; 47°36'/23°13'.

Birschton, *see* Birstonas.

Birshtan, *see* Birstonas.

Birshton, *see* Birstonas.

Birstein, Germ.; pop. 115; 56 km NE of Frankfurt am Main; 50°21'/09°18'; LDS.

Birstonas, Lith. (Birschton, Birshtan, Birshton); 38 km SSE of Kaunas; 54°37'/24°02'; SF, YL.

Birsula, *see* Kotovsk (Ukraine).

Birtch, *see* Bircza.

Biruintsa, Mold. (Borceag); pop. 6; 114 km S of Kishinev; 46°03'/28°32'.

Birzai, Lith. (Berzai, Birze, Birzh, Birzhi); pop. 1,807; 94 km ENE of Siauliai; 56°12'/24°45'; AMG, COH, EJ, GUM3, GUM4, GUM6, HSL, HSL2, JGFF, LDL, SF, YL.

Birze, *see* Birzai.

Birzgale, Lat.; pop. 5; 56 km ESE of Riga; 56°38'/24°46'.

Birzh, *see* Birzai.

Birzhi, *see* Birzai.

Birzi, Lat. (Birzu Muiza); pop. 14; 75 km NW of Daugavpils; 56°24'/25°47'.

Birzula, *see* Kotovsk (Ukraine).

Birzu Muiza, *see* Birzi.

Bisamberg, Aus.; pop. 2; 19 km N of Wien; 48°20'/16°21'.

Bischberg, Germ.; pop. 56 km NNW of Nurnberg; 49°55'/10°50'; HSL, PHGB.

Bischbrunn, Germ.; 62 km ESE of Frankfurt am Main; 49°52'/09°29'; PHGB.

Bischhausen, Germ.; 146 km NNE of Frankfurt am Main; 51°08'/09°56'; HSL, LDS.

Bischitz, *see* Bysice.

Bischofsberg, Aus.; 101 km WSW of Graz; 46°52'/14°05'; HSL.

Bischofsburg, *see* Biskupiec.

Bischofsheim, Germ.; pop. 32; 13 km NE of Frankfurt am Main; 50°09'/08°48'; EDRD, HSL, JGFF, LDS, PHGB.

Bischofstetten, Aus.; pop. 6; 69 km WSW of Wien; 48°07'/15°28'.

Bischofswerder, *see* Biskupiec.

Bischwind, Germ.; 69 km NW of Nurnberg; 49°55'/10°24'; LDS, PHGB.

Bisenz, *see* Bzenec.

Biserica Alba, *see* Bila Cirkev.

Bishenkovitz, *see* Beshenkovichi.

Bishkiv, Ukr. (Bishkuv, Biszkow); 45 km NNW of Lvov; 50°11'/23°52'; HSL.

Bishkuv, *see* Bishkiv.

Bisk, *see* Antonuvka.

Biska Wolka, *see* Wolka Biska.

Biskopitza, *see* Biskupice.

Biskovichi, Ukr. (Biskovitse, Biskowice); pop. 38; 69 km SW of Lvov; 49°32'/23°12'; HSL, HSL2.

Biskovitse, *see* Biskovichi.

Biskowice, *see* Biskovichi.

Biskupice, Pol. (Biskopitza); pop. 26; 19 km ESE of Krakow; 49°58'/20°07'; AMG, GUM5, JGFF.

Biskupice Lubelskie, Pol.; pop. 129; 32 km ESE of Lublin; 51°08'/22°57'; AMG, LDS, POCEM, SF.

Biskupice Melsztynskie, Pol.; pop. 15; 62 km ESE of Krakow; 49°52'/20°43'.

Biskupice Radlowskie, Pol.; pop. 6; 69 km ENE of Krakow; 50°08'/20°52'.

Biskupiec, Pol. (Bischofsburg, Bischofswerder, Biskupitz); pop. 30; 157 km ESE of Gdansk; 53°52'/20°58'; LDS, POCEM.

Biskupitz, see Biskupiec.

Bismarch Hutte, Pol. PHP3. This town was not found in BGN gazetteers under the given spelling.

Bisses, Germ.; pop. 12; 38 km NNE of Frankfurt am Main; 50°24'/08°54'.

Bissingen, Germ.; 94 km WNW of Munchen; 48°43'/10°37'; PHGB.

Bistina, see Bushtyna.

Bistra, Rom. (Bisztra); pop. 303; 133 km N of Cluj; 47°52'/24°12'; PHR2, SM.

Bistrita, Rom. (Alsobudak, Besztece); pop. 2,198; 75 km NE of Cluj; 47°08'/24°29'; AMG, COH, EJ, GUM3, GUM4, GUM6, HSL, HSL2, LDL, PHR2.

Bistrita Bargaului, see Bistrita Birgaului.

Bistrita Birgaului, Rom. (Bistrita Bargaului); pop. 33; 101 km NE of Cluj; 47°13'/24°46'.

Bistritch, see Bystryca.

Bistuszowa, Pol.; pop. 5; 88 km E of Krakow; 49°53'/21°05'.

Biszca, HSL. This pre-World War I community was not found in BGN gazetteers.

Biszcza, Pol.; pop. 170; 75 km NNW of Przemysl; 50°25'/22°39'.

Biszkow, see Bishkiv.

Bisztra, see Bistra.

Bisztraterebes, see Chiribis.

Bitburg, Germ.; pop. 65; 114 km S of Koln; 49°58'/06°32'; GED.

Biten, see Byten.

Bitetice, Cz.; 88 km SE of Praha; 49°28'/15°09'; HSL.

Bitkov, Ukr. (Bitkow, Bytkow); pop. 44; 114 km WNW of Chernovtsy; 48°38'/24°28'; HSL.

Bitkow, see Bitkov.

Bitla, see Botla.

Bitola, Yug. (Bitolj, Bitolja, Monastir); pop. 3,778; 114 km S of Skopje; 41°02'/21°20'; EJ, GUM4, GUM5, ISH2, PHY.

Bitolj, see Bitola.

Bitolja, see Bitola.

Bitshutsh, see Buchach.

Bitterfeld, Germ.; pop. 60; 45 km N of Leipzig; 51°37'/12°19'; GUM3.

Biusa, Rom. (Boshaza); pop. 5; 75 km NNW of Cluj; 47°25'/23°15'.

Bivolari, Rom.; pop. 826; 45 km NNW of Iasi; 47°32'/27°26'; GUM4, LDL, PHR1, YB.

Bivolu Mare, Rom.; pop. 8; 126 km NW of Iasi; 48°10'/26°44'.

Bivolu Mic, Rom.; pop. 12; 126 km NW of Iasi; 48°09'/26°48'.

Bixad, Rom. (Biksad, Bikszad); 133 km N of Cluj; 47°56'/23°24'; AMG, LDL, PHR2.

Biyesht, see Biyeshty.

Biyeshty, Mold. (Biesti, Biyesht); pop. 86; 62 km N of Kishinev; 47°31'/28°52'.

Biysk, see Antonuvka.

Bizeljsko, Yug.; pop. 1; 38 km NW of Zagreb; 46°01'/15°42'.

Bizerewicze, see Bizherevichi.

Bizherevichi, Byel. (Bizerewicze); pop. 6; 26 km ESE of Pinsk; 52°03'/26°27'.

Bizinev, see Budanov.

Bizinov, see Budanov.

Biznov, see Budanov.

Bizovac, Yug.; pop. 4; 176 km WNW of Beograd; 45°35'/18°28'.

Bizun, see Biezun.

Bjelina, Yug.; 195 km S of Zagreb; 44°03'/15°51'; HSL.

Bjelovar, Yug.; pop. 360; 62 km ENE of Zagreb; 45°54'/16°51'; PHY.

Bjeschenkowitschi, see Beshenkovichi.

Blachownia Slaska, Pol.; 75 km SW of Czestochowa; 50°22'/18°17'; PHP3.

Bladiau, see Pyatidorozhnoye.

Blagoevgrad, Bulg. (Gorna Dzhumaya); 82 km S of Sofija; 42°01'/23°06'; EJ.

Blagovshchina, GUM4. This town was not found in BGN gazetteers under the given spelling.

Blaj, Rom. (Balazsfalva, Blasendorf); 69 km SSE of Cluj; 46°11'/23°55'; HSL, HSL2, LDL, PHR1.

Blajel, Rom. (Balazstelke); 82 km SE of Cluj; 46°13'/24°19'; HSL.

Blajenii de Jos, Rom.; pop. 11; 75 km NE of Cluj; 47°10'/24°21'.

Blajenii de Sus, Rom.; pop. 4; 75 km NE of Cluj; 47°10'/24°23'.

Blanowice, Pol.; pop. 10; 45 km SE of Czestochowa; 50°31'/19°28'.

Blansko, Cz.; pop. 54; 26 km N of Brno; 49°22'/16°40'.

Blasendorf, see Blaj.

Blashka, see Blaszki.

Blaszki, Pol. (Blashka); pop. 2,186; 69 km WSW of Lodz; 51°40'/18°27'; CAHJP, COH, GUM4, HSL2, JGFF, PHP1, SF.

Blaszkowa, Pol. (Blazkowa); pop. 41; 101 km W of Przemysl; 49°51'/21°23'.

Blatna, Cz.; pop. 48; 82 km SSW of Praha; 49°26'/13°53'.

Blatne Revistia, Cz. (Sarosreviscse); 62 km ENE of Kosice; 48°44'/22°05'; HSL.

Blatzheim, Germ. (Blotzheim?); pop. 2; 26 km SW of Koln; 50°51'/06°38'; GED, HSL, PHGBW.

Blazek, Pol.; pop. 14; 50 km S of Lublin; 50°51'/22°26'.

Blazev, see Blazowa.

Blazhova, see Blazowa.

Blazice, Cz. (Bologd); 13 km ESE of Kosice; 48°40'/21°25'; HSL.

Blazki, GUM3. This town was not found in BGN gazetteers under the given spelling.

Blazkowa, see Blaszkowa.

Blazov, HSL. A number of towns share this name. It was not possible to determine from available information which one is being referenced.

Blazow, possibly Blazowa.

Blazowa, Pol. (Blazev, Blazhova, Blazow?); pop. 930; 50 km W of Przemysl; 49°53'/22°06'; EGRS, GA, GUM3, GUM5, HSL, HSL2, JGFF, LDL, PHP3, POCEM, SF.

Bled, Yug.; pop. 5; 157 km WNW of Zagreb; 46°22'/14°08'.

Bledostowo, Pol.; pop. 12; 45 km NNW of Warszawa; 52°35'/20°56'.

Bledov, see Bledow.

Bledow, Pol. (Bledov, Blendov); pop. 815; 101 km W of Lublin; 51°17'/21°05'; COH, GA, HSL, JGFF, LYV, PHP1, PHP4, SF, YB.

Bledowa, Pol. PHP3. This town was not found in BGN gazetteers under the given spelling.

Bledzew, Pol. (Blesen); pop. 6; 107 km W of Poznan; 52°31'/15°24'; LDS.

Bleich, Germ.; 88 km ESE of Nurnberg; 49°13'/12°16'; PHGBW.

Bleicherode, Germ.; pop. 107; 120 km W of Leipzig; 51°26'/10°35'.

Blendov, see Bledow.

Blenkemezo, see Poiana Blenchii.

Blesen, see Bledzew.

Bleshchanovka, Ukr.; 82 km NE of Chernovtsy; 48°46'/26°48'; JGFF.

Bleshtenautsy, Mold. (Blesteni); pop. 16; 176 km NW of Kishinev; 48°07'/27°13'.

Blesteni, see Bleshtenautsy.

Blexen, Germ.; pop. 5; 94 km WSW of Hamburg; 53°32'/08°32'.

Blezhovo, Ukr. (Blezowo); pop. 101; 120 km NNE of Rovno; 51°26'/27°21'.

Blezowo, see Blezhovo.

Blh nad Iplom, Cz. (Balog); 150 km E of Bratislava; 48°05'/19°08'; HSL.

Bliedersdorf, Germ.; 32 km WSW of Hamburg; 53°29'/09°34'; HSL.

Blieskastel, Germ.; pop. 8; 146 km SW of Frankfurt am Main;

49°14'/07°15'; HSL.

Blihusz, Pol. EDRD. This town was not found in BGN gazetteers under the given spelling.

Blinow, Pol.; pop. 12; 45 km S of Lublin; 50°52'/22°24'.

Bliskowice, Pol.; pop. 8; 62 km SW of Lublin; 50°57'/21°50'.

Blizejov, Cz.; pop. 7; 120 km SW of Praha; 49°30'/12°59'.

Blizhin, *see* Blizyn.

Blizianka, Pol.; pop. 47; 62 km W of Przemysl; 49°53'/21°57'.

Blizin, *see* Blizyn.

Blizna, *see* Blizne.

Blizne, Pol. (Blizna); pop. 56; 56 km WSW of Przemysl; 49°45'/21°59'; HSL, HSL2, SF.

Blizocin, Pol.; pop. 4; 50 km NW of Lublin; 51°36'/22°13'.

Blizow, Pol.; pop. 3; 82 km SE of Lublin; 50°36'/23°07'.

Blizyn, Pol. (Blizhin, Blizin); pop. 47; 114 km ESE of Lodz; 51°07'/20°45'; GA, GUM3, GUM4, GUM5, GUM6, PHP1, SF.

Blochy, Pol.; pop. 6; 69 km NNE of Warszawa; 52°44'/21°36'.

Blodno, *see* Bluden.

Blomberg, Germ.; pop. 28; 69 km SSW of Hannover; 51°56'/09°05'; LDS.

Blonie, Pol. (Bloyna); pop. 1,262; 26 km WSW of Warszawa; 52°12'/20°37'; AMG, COH, EDRD, GA, GUM3, GUM4, GUM5, HSL, HSL2, JGFF, PHP4, POCEM, SF.

Bloshniki, Byel. (Bloszniki); pop. 40; 126 km W of Vitebsk; 55°21'/28°13'.

Bloszniki, *see* Bloshniki.

Blotnia, *see* Bolotnya.

Blotnya, *see* Bolotnya.

Blotzheim, *possibly* Blatzheim.

Blovice, Cz.; pop. 48; 88 km SW of Praha; 49°35'/13°33'; HSL.

Bloyna, *see* Blonie.

Blozew Gorna, Ukr.; pop. 29; 107 km SW of Lvov; 49°15'/22°55'. This town was located on an interwar map of Poland but does not appear in contemporary gazetteers. Map coordinates are approximate.

Blsany, Cz.; pop. 50; 75 km W of Praha; 50°13'/13°28'.

Bluden, Byel. (Blodno, Pogodino); pop. 122; 101 km WNW of Pinsk; 52°32'/24°54'; SF.

Bludenz, Aus.; pop. 1; 120 km WSW of Innsbruck; 47°09'/09°49'.

Bludna, Cz.; 120 km WNW of Praha; 50°24'/12°49'; LDL.

Bludniki, Ukr.; pop. 46; 94 km SE of Lvov; 49°07'/24°38'.

Bludov, Ukr. (Bludow); pop. 46; 94 km WSW of Rovno; 50°37'/24°55'; COH, EDRD, SF.

Bludow, *see* Bludov.

Blumenthal, Germ.; pop. 36; 101 km SW of Hamburg; 53°11'/08°35'; GED.

Blumenthal Bei Hellenthall, GUM5. This town was not found in BGN gazetteers under the given spelling.

Blutenam, *see* Kwieciszewo.

Blyshchyvody, Ukr. (Blyszczywody); pop. 37; 26 km N of Lvov; 50°03'/24°04'.

Blyszczywody, *see* Blyshchyvody.

Bobalna, *see* Babolna.

Bobbin, Germ.; 107 km NE of Rostock; 54°34'/13°32'; JGFF.

Bobenhausen, *see* Bobenhausen Zwei.

Bobenhausen Zwei, Germ. (Benhausen, Bobenhausen); pop. 32; 69 km NNE of Frankfurt am Main; 50°35'/09°08'.

Bobenheim, *see* Bobenheim am Berg.

Bobenheim am Berg, Germ. (Bobenheim); pop. 7; 75 km SSW of Frankfurt am Main; 49°31'/08°09'; HSL.

Bober, *see* Bobr.

Boberka, *see* Bobrka.

Bobeshti, *see* Bobovtsy.

Bobesti, *see* Bobovtsy.

Bobiatyn, *see* Bobyatyn.

Bobinka, *see* Babanka.

Bobino Wielkie, Pol.; pop. 48; 94 km N of Warszawa; 53°03'/21°04'.

Bobletichi, Mold. (Bobletici); pop. 5; 75 km WNW of Kishinev;

47°28'/28°03'.

Bobletici, *see* Bobletichi.

Bobly, Ukr.; pop. 28; 133 km N of Lvov; 51°00'/24°29'.

Bobohalma, Rom. (Babahalma); 69 km ESE of Cluj; 46°21'/24°14'; HSL.

Bobota, Rom.; pop. 65; 94 km NW of Cluj; 47°23'/22°46'.

Bobov, *see* Bobowa.

Bobova, *see* Bobowa.

Bobovna, *see* Bobovnya.

Bobovnya, Byel. (Bobovna); 82 km SSW of Minsk; 53°15'/26°57'; SF.

Bobovtsy, Ukr. (Bobeshti, Bobesti); pop. 38; 19 km WSW of Chernovtsy; 48°16'/25°42'.

Bobowa, Pol. (Bobov, Bobova); pop. 565; 82 km ESE of Krakow; 49°42'/20°56'; COH, EGRS, GA, GUM3, GUM4, GUM5, HSL, HSL2, LDL, PHP3, SF.

Bobowo, Pol.; 56 km S of Gdansk; 53°53'/18°34'; POCEM.

Bobr, Byel. (Bober); pop. 1,018; 114 km SSW of Vitebsk; 54°20'/29°16'; GUM5, HSL, JGFF, LDL, SF.

Bobrek, Pol. (Bobrek Karf); pop. 28; 94 km SW of Krakow; 49°46'/18°40'; GA, JGFF.

Bobrek Karf, *see* Bobrek.

Bobri, Lat. (Bobry); 26 km ESE of Daugavpils; 55°44'/26°49'; JGFF, PHP1.

Bobrik, *see* Bobrik Pervyy.

Bobrik Pervyy, Ukr. (Bobrik); 82 km NW of Konotop; 51°55'/32°44'; EDRD.

Bobrinets, Ukr. (Bobrinitz, Bobrynetz, Bobrzyniec); pop. 2,265; 170 km ESE of Uman; 48°03'/32°12'; EDRD, HSL, JGFF, SF.

Bobrinitz, *see* Bobrinets.

Bobrinskaia, Ukr. EDRD. This town was not found in BGN gazetteers under the given spelling.

Bobrka, Ukr. (Boberka, Boiberik, Boyberik, Prachnik); pop. 1,480; 38 km ESE of Lvov; 49°38'/24°18'; AMG, COH, EDRD, EGRS, GUM3, GUM4, GUM5, HSL, JGFF, LDL, PHP2, PHP3, SF, YB.

Bobrka (Krosno area), Pol.; pop. 8; 82 km WSW of Przemysl; 49°38'/21°42'.

Bobrka (Lesko area), Pol.; pop. 27; 50 km SSW of Przemysl; 49°25'/22°27'.

Bobroidy, *see* Bobroydy.

Bobroisk, *see* Bobruysk.

Bobrokut, USSR; pop. 2,288; This town was not found in BGN gazetteers under the given spelling.

Bobrovica, *see* Bobrovitsa.

Bobrovichi, Byel. (Bobrowicze);

Bobrovichi (Nowogrodek), Byel.; pop. 5; 69 km W of Minsk; 54°03'/26°34'.

Bobrovichi (Polesie), Byel.; pop. 37; 62 km NNW of Pinsk; 52°37'/25°47'.

Bobrovitsa, Ukr. (Bobrovica, Bobrovitsy, Bobrovitza); 126 km W of Konotop; 51°31'/31°22'; EDRD, SF.

Bobrovitsy, *see* Bobrovitsa.

Bobrovitza, *see* Bobrovitsa.

Bobrovnik, *see* Bobrowniki.

Bobrovy Jut, *see* Bobrovyy Kut.

Bobrovy Kut, *see* Bobrovyy Kut.

Bobrovyy Kut, Ukr. (Bobrovy Jut, Bobrovy Kut); pop. 2,288; 182 km NE of Odessa; 47°06'/32°57'; EJ.

Bobrowe, Pol.; pop. 34; 38 km ESE of Lublin; 50°59'/22°59'.

Bobrowicze, *see* Bobrovichi.

Bobrowka, Pol.; pop. 24; 32 km N of Przemysl; 50°02'/22°52'; GA.

Bobrowniki, Pol. (Bobrovnik); pop. 164; 62 km WNW of Lublin; 51°34'/21°56'; HSL, LDS, SF. A number of towns in Poland with this name had small Jewish populations (fewer than 20). One Bobrowniki, located near Konskie (pop. 30), does not appear in contemporary gazetteers.

Bobrowniki Wielkie, Pol.; pop. 12; 69 km E of Krakow; 50°04'/20°55'.

Bobroydy, Ukr. (Bobroidy); pop. 30; 38 km NNW of Lvov; 50°09'/23°51'.

Bobruisk, *see* Bobruysk.

Bobrujsk, *see* Bobruysk.

Bobruysk, Byel. (Bobroisk, Bobruisk, Bobrujsk); pop. 21,558; 139 km WNW of Gomel; 53°09'/29°14'; COH, EDRD, EJ, GUM3, GUM4, GUM5, GYLA, HSL, JGFF, LDL, PHP4, SF, YB.

Bobry, *see* Bobri.

Bobrynetz, *see* Bobrinets.

Bobryszce, Pol.; pop. 23; Described in the *Black Book* as being in the Lodz region of Poland, this town was not found in BGN gazetteers.

Bobrzyniec, *see* Bobrinets.

Bobt, *see* Babtai.

Bobty, *see* Babtai.

Bobuleshty, Mold. (Bobulesti); pop. 12; 101 km NNW of Kishinev; 47°53'/28°21'.

Bobulesti, *see* Bobuleshty.

Bobulince, Ukr.; pop. 32; 82 km NW of Chernovtsy; 48°55'/25°25'. This town was located on an interwar map of Poland but does not appear in contemporary gazetteers. Map coordinates are approximate.

Bobyatyn, Ukr. (Bobiatyn); pop. 76; 75 km N of Lvov; 50°30'/24°26'.

Boc, Cz. BGN lists two possible localities with this name located at 46°34'/23°21' and 50°22'/13°05'. AMG.

Bocecea, Rom. PHR1. This town was not found in BGN gazetteers under the given spelling.

Bocfolde, Hung.; pop. 3; 45 km NNW of Nagykanizsa; 46°47'/16°50'.

Bochanow, Pol. POCEM. This town was not found in BGN gazetteers under the given spelling.

Bochavitz, *see* Bykovtsy.

Bocheykovo, Byel. (Botcheikev, Botcheikovo); 69 km WSW of Vitebsk; 55°01'/29°09'; LDL, SF.

Bochingen, Germ.; pop. 47; 94 km WNW of Stuttgart; 49°14'/08°06'.

Bochkuv, *see* Velikiy Bychkov.

Bochnia, Pol. (Bokhnia, Kolanow, Salzberg); pop. 2,459; 45 km ESE of Krakow; 49°58'/20°26'; AMG, CAHJP, EDRD, EGRS, EJ, GA, GUM3, GUM4, GUM5, GUM6, HSL, HSL2, JGFF, LDL, LYV, PHP1, PHP3, POCEM, SF.

Bochnovata, *see* Bagnovate.

Bocholt, Germ.; pop. 300; 101 km NNW of Koln; 51°50'/06°36'; AMG, EJ, GED, GUM5, LDS.

Bochotnica, Pol. (Bochotnica Koscielna); pop. 90; 45 km W of Lublin; 51°20'/21°59'.

Bochotnica Koscielna, *see* Bochotnica.

Bochov, Cz.; pop. 37; 101 km W of Praha; 50°09'/13°03'.

Bochum, Germ.; pop. 1,152; 62 km N of Koln; 51°29'/07°13'; AMG, EJ, GED, GUM3, GUM4, GUM5, GUM6, LDS.

Bocian, Pol. PHP4. This town was not found in BGN gazetteers under the given spelling.

Bocicau, Rom.; pop. 7; 150 km NNW of Cluj; 48°06'/23°09'.

Bocicoiel, Rom.; pop. 54; 114 km NNE of Cluj; 47°42'/24°19'.

Bocicoiul Mare, *see* Bocicoiu Mare.

Bocicoiu Mare, Rom. (Bocicoiul Mare, Nagybocsko); pop. 286; 139 km N of Cluj; 47°58'/24°00'; PHR2.

Bock, *see* Auf Dem Bock.

Bockenheim, Germ. (Gross Bockenheim, Kleinbockenheim); pop. 30; 69 km SSW of Frankfurt am Main; 49°36'/08°11'; GED, HSL, HSL2, JGFF.

Bocki, Pol. (Bodki); pop. 725; 56 km S of Bialystok; 52°39'/23°03'; CAHJP, COH, GA, HSL, LDL, POCEM, SF.

Bockow, Pol.; pop. 14; 45 km S of Lublin; 50°53'/22°38'; AMG.

Bockum, Germ. AMG. A number of towns share this name. It was not possible to determine from available information which one is being referenced.

Boconad, Hung.; pop. 6; 69 km SSW of Miskolc; 47°38'/20°12'.

Bocs, Hung. (Belsbocs, Belsobocs); pop. 58; 19 km ESE of Miskolc; 48°03'/20°58'; HSL, LDS, PHH.

Bocsarlapujto, *see* Karancslapujto.

Bocska, Hung.; pop. 3; 19 km NNW of Nagykanizsa; 46°33'/16°55'.

Bocsko Raho, *see* Rakhov.

Bocsum, HSL. This pre-World War I community was not found in BGN gazetteers.

Boczki Swidrowo, Pol.; 75 km WNW of Bialystok; 53°36'/22°23'; GUM3, HSL.

Boczow, *see* Bottschow.

Bod, Rom. (Borfalu, Brenndorf); 157 km NNW of Bucuresti; 45°46'/25°39'; HSL.

Bodajk, Hung.; pop. 27; 62 km SW of Budapest; 47°19'/18°14'.

Bodak, *see* Bodiky.

Boden, HSL. A number of towns share this name. It was not possible to determine from available information which one is being referenced.

Bodendorf, Germ. JGFF. A number of towns share this name. It was not possible to determine from available information which one is being referenced.

Bodenfelde, Germ.; pop. 29; 88 km S of Hannover; 51°38'/09°34'.

Bodenheim, Germ.; pop. 39; 32 km SW of Frankfurt am Main; 49°56'/08°18'; JGFF.

Bodenmais, Germ.; 150 km NE of Munchen; 49°04'/13°06'; JGFF.

Bodersweier, Germ.; pop. 46; 94 km WSW of Stuttgart; 48°36'/07°52'; PHGBW.

Bodesti, HSL. A number of towns share this name. It was not possible to determine from available information which one is being referenced.

Bodhaza, Rom. (Bothaza); 176 km WNW of Bucuresti; 45°01'/24°02'; HSL. This town was located on a pre-World War I map, but does not appear in contemporary gazetteers.

Bodia, Rom.; pop. 9; 50 km WNW of Cluj; 47°03'/23°04'.

Bodigheim, Germ.; pop. 32; 82 km N of Stuttgart; 49°29'/09°19'; LDS, PHGBW.

Bodiky, Cz. (Bodak); 38 km ESE of Bratislava; 47°55'/17°28'; HSL.

Bodjentin, *see* Bodzentyn.

Bodki, *see* Bocki.

Bodmer, Hung.; pop. 2; 45 km WSW of Budapest; 47°27'/18°33'.

Bodolz, Germ.; pop. 1; 139 km SSE of Stuttgart; 47°34'/09°40'.

Bodonci, Yug.; pop. 3; 107 km N of Zagreb; 46°44'/16°07'.

Bodony, Hung.; pop. 9; 56 km SW of Miskolc; 47°57'/20°02'.

Bodos, Rom.; 176 km ESE of Cluj; 46°05'/25°40'; HSL.

Bodroghalom, Hung.; pop. 42; 75 km NE of Miskolc; 48°18'/21°43'.

Bodrogkeresztur, Hung.; pop. 535; 45 km ENE of Miskolc; 48°10'/21°22'; AMG, EJ, GUM5, HSL, LDS, PHH.

Bodrogkisfalud, Hung.; pop. 32; 45 km ENE of Miskolc; 48°11'/21°22'.

Bodrogolaszi, Hung.; pop. 31; 56 km NE of Miskolc; 48°17'/21°31'.

Bodrogszerdahely, *see* Streda nad Bodrogom.

Bodrog Vecs, HSL. This pre-World War I community was not found in BGN gazetteers.

Bodrogzsadany, *see* Sarazsadany.

Boduszow, Pol.; pop. 13; 101 km SW of Lublin; 50°43'/21°21'.

Bodvalenke, Hung.; pop. 3; 56 km N of Miskolc; 48°33'/20°49'.

Bodvarako, Hung.; pop. 2; 56 km N of Miskolc; 48°31'/20°45'.

Bodvaszilas, Hung.; pop. 24; 56 km N of Miskolc; 48°32'/20°44'.

Bodzanov, *see* Bodzanow.

Bodzanow, Pol. (Bodzanov); pop. 807; 75 km WNW of Warszawa; 52°30'/20°01'; AMG, COH, GUM3, HSL, LDL, LDS, PHP4, SF.

Bodzasujlak, *see* Novosad.

Bodzechow, *see* Kraskow.

Bodzentin, *see* Bodzentyn.

Bodzentyn, Pol. (Bodjentin, Bodzentin); pop. 934; 114 km WSW of Lublin; 50°57'/20°58'; AMG, CAHJP, EDRD, GA, GUM3, GUM5, JGFF, LDS, PHP4, POCEM, SF.

Bodziaczow, *see* Bodzyachuv.

Bodziejowice, Pol.; pop. 3; 38 km ESE of Czestochowa; 50°37'/19°37'.

Bodzyachuv, Ukr. (Bodziaczow); pop. 24; 82 km NNE of Lvov; 50°28'/24°34'.

Boehl, GUM5. This town was not found in BGN gazetteers under the given spelling.

Boehmisch Leipa, *see* Ceska Lipa.

Boesing, *see* Pezinok.

Boffzen, Germ.; pop. 11; 75 km S of Hannover; 51°45'/09°23'.

Bogacs, Hung.; pop. 21; 32 km SSW of Miskolc; 47°54'/20°32'; HSL.

Bogad, Hung.; 107 km ESE of Nagykanizsa; 46°05'/18°20'; HSL.

Bogarja, Pol.; pop. 450; COH. Described in the *Black Book* as being in the Kielce region of Poland, this town was not found in BGN gazetteers.

Bogata, Rom. (Bogata Muras, Marosbogat, Marosbogata); 56 km SE of Cluj; 46°27'/24°04'; HSL.

Bogata de Jos, Rom.; pop. 12; 50 km N of Cluj; 47°11'/23°40'.

Bogata de Sus, Rom.; pop. 32; 56 km N of Cluj; 47°12'/23°43'.

Bogata Muras, *see* Bogata.

Bogate, Pol.; pop. 24; 82 km N of Warszawa; 52°57'/20°59'.

Bogat Koze, *see* Bogatkozetanya.

Bogatkozetanya, Hung. (Bogat Koze); 38 km SE of Miskolc; 47°51'/21°07'; LDS.

Bogdaj, Pol.; pop. 5; 62 km NNE of Wroclaw; 51°32'/17°34'.

Bogdan, Ukr. (Bohdan, Tiszabogdany); pop. 357; 120 km WSW of Chernovtsy; 48°02'/24°22'; AMG, GUM4, GUM5, HSL, HSL2, SM.

Bogdanantz, *see* Bagdoniske.

Bogdand, Rom.; pop. 18; 88 km NW of Cluj; 47°25'/22°56'.

Bogdaneasca Veche, *see* Staraya Bogdanovka.

Bogdanhaza, *see* Stirciu.

Bogdanovca, Rom. PHR1. This town was not found in BGN gazetteers under the given spelling.

Bogdanovka, Byel. (Bohdanowka);

Bogdanovka (Polesie), Byel.; pop. 20; 38 km NNE of Pinsk; 52°22'/26°27'.

Bogdanovka (Tarnopol), Ukr. (Sinkov, Sinkow); pop. 37; 38 km N of Chernovtsy; 48°37'/25°57'; GUM5.

Bogdanovka (Wolyn), Ukr.; pop. 12; 107 km SSE of Rovno; 49°40'/26°29'; EDRD.

Bogdanowka, *see* Bogdanuvka.

Bogdanuvka, (Bogdanowka);

Bogdanuvka (Skalat area), Ukr.; pop. 62; 94 km E of Lvov; 49°41'/25°18'.

Bogdanuvka (Zboruv area), Ukr.; pop. 24; 94 km E of Lvov; 49°41'/25°18'; GUM4, GUM4, GUM6, PHP2.

Bogdany, HSL. A number of towns share this name. It was not possible to determine from available information which one is being referenced.

Bogdasa, Hung.; pop. 6; 88 km SE of Nagykanizsa; 45°53'/17°48'.

Bogeiu, Rom. (Bozsaly); pop. 27; 107 km WNW of Cluj; 47°16'/22°21'.

Bogel, Germ.; pop. 13; 62 km W of Frankfurt am Main; 50°11'/07°48'.

Bogen, Germ.; 120 km NNE of Munchen; 48°55'/12°41'; PHGB.

Boghiceni, *see* Bogicheny.

Bogicheny, Mold. (Boghiceni); pop. 27; 38 km WSW of Kishinev; 46°57'/28°20'.

Boglar, *see* Balatonboglar.

Boglewice, Pol. (Boglewicki Tartak); pop. 27; 56 km S of Warszawa; 51°49'/20°59'.

Boglewicki Tartak, *see* Boglewice.

Bogoduchow, *see* Bogodukhov.

Bogodukhov, Ukr. (Bogoduchow); pop. 259; 56 km WNW of Kharkov; 50°10'/35°32'.

Bogojevo, Yug.; pop. 10; 133 km WNW of Beograd; 45°32'/19°08'.

Bogojina, Yug.; pop. 3; 107 km N of Zagreb; 46°41'/16°17'.

Bogoniowice, Pol.; pop. 25; 82 km ESE of Krakow; 49°49'/20°59'.

Bogopol, *see* Pervomaysk.

Bogoria, Pol. (Bogorja, Bogoryja); 114 km NE of Krakow; 50°40'/21°16'; AMG, GA, GUM5, LDS, SF, WS.

Bogorja, *see* Bogoria.

Bogorodchany, Ukr. (Bohorodczany, Bohorodczany Stare, Brodshin, Brotchin); pop. 730; 114 km WNW of Chernovtsy; 48°48'/24°32'; EDRD, EGRS, GUM3, GUM4, HSL, HSL2, LDL, PHP2, SF.

Bogoroditsk, USSR; pop. 54; 227 km SSE of Moskva; 53°46'/38°08'.

Bogoroditsyn, *see* Bogorodychyn.

Bogorodychyn, Ukr. (Bogoroditsyn, Bohorodyczyn); pop. 33; 82 km WNW of Chernovtsy; 48°43'/25°01'; AMG.

Bogoryja, *see* Bogoria.

Bogoslavishok, *see* Bagaslaviskis.

Bogosza, Pol. PHP4. This town was not found in BGN gazetteers under the given spelling.

Bogoszyn, Pol. PHP4. This town was not found in BGN gazetteers under the given spelling.

Bogoz, *see* Mugeni.

Bogrovice, HSL. This pre-World War I community was not found in BGN gazetteers.

Bogrowka, HSL. This pre-World War I community was not found in BGN gazetteers.

Boguchwala, Pol.; pop. 33; 62 km WNW of Przemysl; 49°59'/21°57'.

Bogucice, Pol. (Bogutschuetz); 62 km NE of Krakow; 50°29'/20°36'; EJ, PHP3.

Boguschewitschi, *see* Bogushevichi.

Bogushe, *see* Bogushi.

Bogushevichi, Byel. (Boguschewitschi, Bohoshevitch, Boshevitch); 82 km E of Minsk; 53°42'/28°49'; LDL, SF.

Bogushevsk, Byel. (Bogushevskoye); pop. 390; 45 km S of Vitebsk; 54°51'/30°13'.

Bogushevskoye, *see* Bogushevsk.

Bogushi, Ukr. (Bogushe, Boguszowka, Bohusze); pop. 4; 69 km NNE of Rovno; 51°06'/26°45'.

Boguslav, Ukr. (Boguslaw, Bohslov, Bohuslaw, Boslev); pop. 6,432; 101 km SSE of Kiyev; 49°33'/30°53'; EJ, HSL, JGFF, LDL, SF.

Boguslaw, *see* Boguslav.

Boguslawowka, Pol.; pop. 31; Described in the *Black Book* as being in the Wolyn region of Poland, this town was not found in BGN gazetteers.

Boguszowka, *see* Bogushi.

Bogutschuetz, *see* Bogucice.

Bogutyn, Ukr. (Bohutyn); pop. 4; 69 km E of Lvov; 49°40'/24°57'.

Bogwidzowy, Pol.; pop. 8; 45 km NNE of Czestochowa; 51°06'/19°26'.

Bogyan, HSL. This pre-World War I community was not found in BGN gazetteers.

Bogyiszlo, Hung.; pop. 7; 101 km W of Szeged; 46°23'/18°50'.

Bogyoszlo, Hung.; pop. 3; 133 km N of Nagykanizsa; 47°34'/17°11'.

Bogzeshty, Mold. (Bogzesti); pop. 13; 56 km NW of Kishinev; 47°25'/28°26'.

Bogzesti, *see* Bogzeshty.

Bohata, Cz. (Bagota); 88 km ESE of Bratislava; 47°53'/18°12'; HSL.

Bohatery Lesne, Pol.; pop. 5; 82 km N of Bialystok; 53°48'/23°33'.

Bohatice, Cz.; pop. 1; 69 km N of Praha; 50°40'/14°40'.

Bohatkowce, Ukr.; pop. 25; 94 km NNW of Chernovtsy; 49°05'/25°25'. This town was located on an interwar map of Poland but does not appear in contemporary gazetteers.

Map coordinates are approximate.

Bohdan, *see* Bogdan.

Bohdanowka, *see* Bogdanovka.

Bohemia; Not a town, but a region of the Austro-Hungarian Empire that existed until World War I. It is now a constituent republic of Czechoslovakia.

Bohl, Germ.; 82 km S of Frankfurt am Main; 49°23'/08°18'; CAHJP.

Bohmisch Brod, *see* Cesky Brod.

Bohmisch Leipa, *see* Ceska Lipa.

Bohopolia, *see* Pervomaysk.

Bohorodczany, *see* Bogorodchany.

Bohorodczany Stare, *see* Bogorodchany.

Bohorodyczyn, *see* Bogorodychyn.

Bohoshevitch, *see* Bogushevichi.

Bohslov, *see* Boguslav.

Bohumin, Cz. (Neu Oderberg, Novy Bohumin, Oderberg); pop. 984; 146 km NE of Brno; 49°55'/18°20'; EJ, GUM4.

Bohunovo, Cz. (Lekenye); 69 km SW of Kosice; 48°31'/20°23'; HSL.

Bohuslaw, *see* Boguslav.

Bohusov, Cz.; 146 km NNE of Brno; 50°15'/17°43'; HSL.

Bohusze, *see* Bogushi.

Bohutycze, Pol.; pop. 3; 94 km ESE of Lublin; 50°48'/23°44'.

Bohutyn, *see* Bogutyn.

Boian, *see* Boyany.

Boianceni, *see* Boyany.

Boiberik, *see* Bobrka.

Boid, *see* Budslav.

Boimie, *see* Bojmie.

Boinesti, Rom. (Bujanhaza); pop. 36; 133 km NNW of Cluj; 47°55'/23°21'.

Boisk, *see* Bauska.

Boiska Stare, Pol.; pop. 17; 50 km SW of Lublin; 50°59'/21°58'.

Boiu Mare, Rom. (Bun, Nagybuny); pop. 17; 75 km N of Cluj; 47°24'/23°35'; HSL, HSL, HSL2.

Boizenburg, Germ.; pop. 6; 50 km ESE of Hamburg; 53°23'/10°43'; GUM3, GUM4, LDS.

Bojan, *see* Boyany.

Bojaniec, *see* Boyanets.

Bojanow, Pol.; pop. 122; 94 km NW of Przemysl; 50°26'/21°57'; HSL2.

Bojanowka, Pol.; pop. 9; 69 km N of Lublin; 51°47'/22°45'.

Bojanowo, LDL. A number of towns share this name. It was not possible to determine from available information which one is being referenced.

Bojkovice, Cz. (Bajkowitz); pop. 36; 88 km E of Brno; 49°02'/17°49'.

Bojmie, Pol. (Boimie); pop. 52; 62 km E of Warszawa; 52°12'/21°58'.

Bojonye, Hung.; pop. 41; This town was not found in BGN gazetteers under the given spelling.

Bojowice, *see* Boyovichi.

Bojt, Hung.; pop. 14; 120 km SE of Miskolc; 47°12'/21°44'; LDS.

Boka, Yug.; pop. 3; 62 km N of Beograd; 45°21'/20°50'.

Bokhnia, *see* Bochnia.

Bokinichi, Byel. (Bokinicze); pop. 16; 26 km NE of Pinsk; 52°17'/26°24'.

Bokinicze, *see* Bokinichi.

Bokinka Krolewska, Pol.; 94 km NNE of Lublin; 51°54'/23°22'; HSL, HSL2, JGFF.

Bokiny, Pol.; pop. 12; 19 km SW of Bialystok; 53°03'/22°55'.

Bokony, Hung.; pop. 137; 82 km ESE of Miskolc; 47°44'/21°45'; AMG, HSL, HSL2, PHH.

Bokor, Hung.; 56 km NNE of Budapest; 47°56'/19°33'; HSL.

Bokov, Ukr. (Bokow, Bokuv); pop. 22; 94 km ESE of Lvov; 49°15'/24°54'.

Bokow, *see* Bokov.

Bokuv, *see* Bokov.

Bol, Cz.; pop. 61; 56 km ESE of Kosice; 48°28'/21°57'.

Bolanowice, *see* Bolyanovichi.

Bolboaca, *see* Kotlovina.

Bolbochi, Mold. (Bolbocii Vechi); pop. 47; 133 km NW of Kishinev; 48°04'/28°05'.

Bolbocii Vechi, *see* Bolbochi.

Bolchany, Mold. (Balceana); pop. 3; 38 km SW of Kishinev; 46°50'/28°25'.

Bolcske, Hung. (Havas); pop. 44; 94 km S of Budapest; 46°44'/18°58'; HSL, LDS.

Bolda, Rom.; pop. 13; 94 km NW of Cluj; 47°32'/22°55'; AMG, HSL.

Boldog, Hung.; 50 km ENE of Budapest; 47°36'/19°42'; HSL.

Boldogasszony, *see* Frauenkirchen.

Boldogkoujfalu, Hung.; pop. 9; 45 km NE of Miskolc; 48°19'/21°15'.

Boldogkovaralja, Hung.; pop. 28; 45 km NE of Miskolc; 48°20'/21°14'.

Boldureshti, *see* Boldureshty.

Boldureshty, Mold. (Boldureshti, Bolduresti); pop. 51; 62 km W of Kishinev; 47°08'/28°04'.

Bolduresti, *see* Boldureshty.

Boldva, Hung.; pop. 62; 19 km N of Miskolc; 48°13'/20°48'; HSL, HSL2, PHH.

Bolechov, *see* Bolekhov.

Bolechow, *see* Bolekhov.

Bolechow Ruski, *see* Bolekhov.

Bolekhov, Ukr. (Bolechov, Bolechow, Bolechow Ruski); pop. 2,394; 94 km S of Lvov; 49°04'/23°52'; CAHJP, COH, EDRD, EGRS, GUM3, GUM4, GUM5, HSL, HSL2, JGFF, LDL, LYV, PHP2, SF, YB. There was also a town named Bolechow Ruski (pop. 585) shown in the 1921 Polish census as being in the area.

Bolesiny, Cz.; pop. 2; 114 km SW of Praha; 49°24'/13°22'.

Boleslav, Cz.; pop. 312; 107 km N of Praha; 51°00'/15°02'.

Boleslaw, Pol. (Boleslev);

Boleslaw (Katowice area), Pol.; pop. 74; 38 km WNW of Krakow; 50°18'/19°29'.

Boleslaw (Tarnow area), Pol.; pop. 73; 75 km NE of Krakow; 50°17'/20°55'; HSL, SF.

Boleslawiec, Pol.; pop. 546; 75 km WNW of Czestochowa; 51°12'/18°12'; AMG, GUM3, GUM4, GUM5, HSL, HSL2, JGFF, LDS, PHP1, SF.

Boleslev, *see* Boleslaw.

Bolestraszyce, Pol.; pop. 17; 6 km NE of Przemysl; 49°49'/22°52'; HSL.

Boletice, Cz.; pop. 12; 146 km S of Praha; 48°49'/14°13'.

Bolevec, Cz.; pop. 1; 88 km SW of Praha; 49°46'/13°22'.

Bolewice, Pol.; 56 km WSW of Poznan; 52°24'/16°08'; GA.

Bolganymajor, Hung. (Furstenfelde); 120 km W of Budapest; 47°46'/17°31'; GUM5.

Bolgrad, Ukr.; pop. 1,222; 182 km SW of Odessa; 45°41'/28°37'; COH, GUM4, GUM5, LDL, SF.

Bolho, Hung.; pop. 1; 50 km SE of Nagykanizsa; 46°02'/17°18'.

Bolimov, *see* Bolimow.

Bolimow, Pol. (Bolimov); pop. 259; 62 km NE of Lodz; 52°05'/20°10'; CAHJP, COH, EDRD, GA, LDS, PHP1, POCEM, SF, YB.

Bolizuby, Ukr.; pop. 37; 126 km N of Chernovtsy; 49°25'/25°45'. This town was located on an interwar map of Poland but does not appear in contemporary gazetteers. Map coordinates are approximate.

Boljevci, Yug.; pop. 2; 26 km SW of Beograd; 44°43'/20°14'.

Bolkenhain, Pol.; 62 km WSW of Wroclaw; 50°55'/16°06'; GUM3, GUM4, GUM5, HSL.

Bolkhov, USSR; pop. 39; 114 km ENE of Bryansk; 53°27'/36°01'.

Bolkovce, Cz. (Bolyk); 114 km SW of Kosice; 48°20'/19°47'; HSL.

Bolkow, Pol.; pop. 21; 69 km NW of Czestochowa; 51°19'/18°38'; GA, JGFF, PHP1.

Bollendorf, Germ.; pop. 65; 133 km S of Koln; 49°51'/06°22'.

Bollstadt, Germ.; 88 km SSW of Nurnberg; 48°45'/10°30'; PHGB.

Bollweiler, HSL, PHGBW. This town was not found in BGN gazetteers under the given spelling.

Bolnik, *see* Balninkai.

Bolochow, *see* Bolokhuv.

Bologd, *see* Blazice.

Bolokhuv, Ukr. (Bolochow); pop. 25; 88 km SSE of Lvov; 49°06'/24°11'; AMG.

Boloshodyormot, *see* Balassagyarmat.

Bolotino, Mold. (Balatina); pop. 131; 139 km WNW of Kishinev; 47°42'/27°20'.

Bolotnya, Ukr. (Blotnia, Blotnya); pop. 35; 56 km ESE of Lvov; 49°33'/24°41'.

Bolovsk, *see* Balvi.

Bolowsk, *see* Balvi.

Bolozhinov, Ukr. (Bolozynow); pop. 39; 56 km NE of Lvov; 50°01'/24°44'.

Bolozynow, *see* Bolozhinov.

Bolschaja Aleksandrovka, Ukr. (Aleksandrovka, Bolshoya Aleksandrovka); pop. 1,157; 176 km SSW of Dnepropetrovsk; 47°19'/33°18'; HSL, LDL, SF.

Bolsewits, *see* Bolshovtsy.

Bolsewitz, *see* Bolshovtsy.

Bolshakovo, USSR (Kreuzingen); 75 km ENE of Kaliningrad; 54°53'/21°40'; PHGBW.

Bolshaly Seidemenukha, *see* Kalininskoye.

Bolshaya Belina, Ukr. (Bilina Velikaya, Bilina Velka, Bilina Wielka); pop. 85; 56 km SW of Lvov; 49°32'/23°28'.

Bolshaya Berestovit, *see* Brzostowica.

Bolshaya Berestovitsa, Byel. (Berestovitsa, Berestovitza, Brestovits, Brzostowica Wielka, Bzhostovitsa Vyelka, Velikaya Berestovitsa); pop. 720; 182 km WNW of Pinsk; 53°11'/24°01'; EJ, JGFF, LDL, SF.

Bolshaya Lenina, Ukr. (Lenina Velka, Lenina Wielka); pop. 57; 94 km SW of Lvov; 49°24'/22°56'.

Bolshaya Romanowka, SF. This town was not found in BGN gazetteers under the given spelling.

Bolshaya Seidemenukha, *see* Kalininskoye.

Bolshaya Turya, Ukr. (Turza Wielka, Tuzha Velka); pop. 201; 88 km S of Lvov; 49°08'/24°04'.

Bolshaya Verbcha, Ukr. (Verbche Velke, Werbcze, Werbcze Wielkie); pop. 27; 69 km N of Rovno; 51°12'/26°16'; GUM3.

Bolshevetz, *see* Bolshovtsy.

Bolshiye Asnashany, Mold. (Hasnasenii Mari); pop. 52; 120 km NW of Kishinev; 47°55'/27°59'.

Bolshiye Luki, Byel. (Luki Wielkie, Velikiye Luki); pop. 1,627; 107 km N of Pinsk; 53°00'/26°03'; GUM4, PHLE.

Bolshiye Orly, Byel. (Orly Wielkie); pop. 66; 62 km E of Pinsk; 52°03'/27°04'.

Bolshiye Sittsy, Byel. (Sitce); pop. 6; 126 km N of Minsk; 54°56'/27°32'.

Bolshiye Zhukhovichi, Byel. (Zhuchovitch, Zhukovitchi, Zuchowicze); 94 km SW of Minsk; 53°25'/26°19'; SF.

Bolshoi Lepeticha, (Lepeticha Hagdola, Lipetitcha); SF. This town was not found in BGN gazetteers under the given spelling.

Bolshoi Tokmak, *see* Tokmak.

Bolshovtse, *see* Bolshovtsy.

Bolshovtsy, Ukr. (Bolsewits, Bolsewitz, Bolshevetz, Bolshovtse, Bolshovtzi, Bolszowce); pop. 825; 94 km SE of Lvov; 49°11'/24°45'; AMG, EGRS, GUM3, GYLA, HSL, HSL2, JGFF, LDL, PHP2, SF.

Bolshovtzi, *see* Bolshovtsy.

Bolshoya Aleksandrovka, *see* Bolschaja Aleksandrovka.

Bolshoya Znamenka, *see* Znamenka.

Bolshoye Osovo, Byel. (Ossovo); 157 km W of Minsk; 54°05'/25°13'; EDRD, SF.

Bolshoy Stydin, Ukr. (Stydyn Velki, Stydyn Wielki); pop. 31; 56 km N of Rovno; 51°03'/26°10'.

Bolshoy Zhelutsk, Ukr. (Zholudek, Zoludzik?); pop. 418; 82 km N of Rovno; 51°19'/26°07'.

Bolszow, Pol. PHP2. This town was not found in BGN gazetteers under the given spelling.

Bolszowce, *see* Bolshovtsy.

Bolve, *see* Balvi.

Bolvi, *see* Balvi.

Boly, Hung. (Nemetboly); pop. 22; 126 km ESE of Nagykanizsa; 45°58'/18°31'; AMG.

Bolya, *see* Buia.

Bolyanovichi, Ukr. (Bolanowice, Bolyanovitse); pop. 44; 69 km WSW of Lvov; 49°41'/23°04'.

Bolyanovitse, *see* Bolyanovichi.

Bolyk, *see* Bolkovce.

Bolyok, Hung.; pop. 281; 45 km WNW of Miskolc; 48°14'/20°16'; HSL, HSL2, LDS.

Bomberg, Germ.; 26 km NE of Koln; 51°04'/07°11'; AMG.

Bomst, *see* Babimost.

Bonarowka, Pol.; pop. 9; 69 km W of Przemysl; 49°49'/21°48'.

Bonbaden, Germ.; 50 km NW of Frankfurt am Main; 50°30'/08°25'; AMG.

Boncodfolde, Hung.; pop. 3; 56 km NNW of Nagykanizsa; 46°52'/16°44'.

Boncza, Pol.; pop. 21; 62 km S of Warszawa; 51°44'/21°04'.

Bonczida, *see* Bontida.

Bondarovca, Rom. PHR1. This town was not found in BGN gazetteers under the given spelling.

Bondorf, Germ.; 38 km SSW of Stuttgart; 48°31'/08°50'; PHGBW.

Bondyrz, Pol.; pop. 19; 88 km SE of Lublin; 50°34'/23°06'.

Bonenburg, Germ.; 107 km SSW of Hannover; 51°33'/09°03'; GED.

Bonevichi, Ukr. (Boniowice); pop. 40; 88 km SW of Lvov; 49°35'/22°50'.

Bonfeld, Germ. (Benfeld?); pop. 37; 56 km N of Stuttgart; 49°13'/09°06'; AMG, HSL, JGFF, LDS, PHGBW.

Bonin, Pol.; pop. 2; 101 km S of Bialystok; 52°15'/23°02'.

Boniowice, *see* Bonevichi.

Bonkowo Podlesne, Pol.; pop. 3; 94 km NW of Warszawa; 52°58'/20°11'.

Bonn, Germ.; pop. 1,167; 32 km SE of Koln; 50°44'/07°06'; AMG, EDRD, EJ, GED, GUM3, GUM5, HSL, HSL2, LDS, PHGBW.

Bonnland, Germ.; pop. 10; 82 km E of Frankfurt am Main; 50°03'/09°52'; LDS, PHGB.

Bonnya, Hung.; pop. 8; 69 km ENE of Nagykanizsa; 46°35'/17°54'.

Bonow, *see* Bunov.

Bonstadt, Germ.; pop. 4; 26 km NNE of Frankfurt am Main; 50°17'/08°51'.

Bontaieni, Rom.; pop. 2; 101 km N of Cluj; 47°37'/23°44'.

Bontida, Rom. (Bonczida); pop. 40; 26 km NNE of Cluj; 46°55'/23°48'; HSL, HSL2, PHR2.

Bonuv, *see* Bunov.

Bonya Luka, *see* Banja Luka.

Bonyhad, Hung.; pop. 1,022; 120 km E of Nagykanizsa; 46°18'/18°32'; AMG, COH, EDRD, EJ, GUM3, GUM5, HSL, HSL2, JGFF, LDL, LDS, PHH.

Bonyretalap, Hung.; pop. 32; 94 km W of Budapest; 47°39'/17°52'.

Boohom, LDL. This pre-World War I community was not found in BGN gazetteers.

Bopfingen, Germ.; 88 km SSW of Nurnberg; 48°51'/10°21'; PHGBW.

Boppard, Germ.; pop. 92; 75 km W of Frankfurt am Main; 50°14'/07°36'; EDRD, EJ, GUM5, JGFF.

Bor, Cz.; pop. 35; A number of towns share this name. It was not possible to determine from available information which one is being referenced.

Bor (Yugoslavia), Yug.; 159 km ESE of Beograd; 44°06'/22°06'; EDRD, GUM3, GUM4, GUM5, GUM6.

Boradianka, see Borodyanka.

Borak, Yug.; 182 km SE of Zagreb; 44°29'/17°24'; EJ.

Boratyn (Jaroslaw area), Pol.; pop. 31; 19 km NW of Przemysl; 49°56'/22°40'.

Boratyn (Sokal area), Ukr.; pop. 35; 69 km N of Lvov; 50°25'/24°12'; HSL.

Boratyniec Lacki, Pol.; pop. 14; 82 km S of Bialystok; 52°25'/22°57'.

Borauti, see Borovtse.

Borbest, LDL. This pre-World War I community was not found in BGN gazetteers.

Borceag, see Biruintsa.

Borchow, *possibly* Borshchuv.

Borchtchagovka, Ukr. EDRD. This town was not found in BGN gazetteers under the given spelling.

Borcut, Rom.; pop. 6; 82 km N of Cluj; 47°29'/23°51'.

Bordosiu, Rom.; pop. 12; 94 km ESE of Cluj; 46°24'/24°47'.

Bordulaki, see Bordulyaki.

Bordulyaki, Ukr. (Bordulaki); pop. 4; 75 km NE of Lvov; 50°11'/24°57'.

Borek, Pol. (Borek Wielkopolski, Waldwinkel); pop. 34; 62 km SSE of Poznan; 51°55'/17°15'; CAHJP, HSL, HSL2, JGFF, LDS.

Borek Falecki, Pol.; pop. 58; 13 km SSE of Krakow; 50°02'/19°56'; GUM5, PHP3.

Borek Kuty, Ukr.; pop. 2; 45 km NE of Rovno; 50°52'/26°41'.

Borek Nowy, Pol.; pop. 6; 50 km WNW of Przemysl; 49°55'/22°06'.

Borek Stary, Pol.; pop. 13; 50 km WNW of Przemysl; 49°57'/22°07'.

Borek Szlachecki, Pol.; pop. 22; 19 km SSW of Krakow; 49°58'/19°47'.

Borek Wielkopolski, see Borek.

Boremel, see Baremel.

Borfalu, see Bod.

Borgentreich, Germ.; pop. 14; 94 km S of Hannover; 51°34'/09°15'; GED, HSL, JGFF.

Borgholz, Germ.; pop. 25; 88 km S of Hannover; 51°37'/09°16'.

Borgholzhausen, Germ.; pop. 7; 101 km WSW of Hannover; 52°06'/08°18'.

Borghorst, Germ.; pop. 42; 139 km N of Koln; 52°08'/07°25'; LDS.

Borgo Mijloceni, (Kozepborgo); HSL. This pre-World War I community was not found in BGN gazetteers.

Borgo Muraseni, see Muresenii Birgaului.

Borgoprund, see Prundu Birgaului.

Borgotiha, see Tiha Birgaului.

Borhid, Rom.; 114 km NNW of Cluj; 47°44'/23°12'; HSL. This town was located on a pre-World War I map, but does not appear in contemporary gazetteers.

Boria, Pol. (Borja); pop. 57; 75 km SW of Lublin; 50°59'/21°33'.

Borinya, Ukr. (Borynia); pop. 318; 114 km SSW of Lvov; 49°04'/23°00'; AMG, HSL, PHP2, SF.

Borishovka, see Barishevka.

Borislav, Ukr. (Boryslaw); pop. 7,170; 75 km SSW of Lvov; 49°17'/23°25'; AMG, COH, EDRD, EGRS, EJ, GA, GUM3, GUM4, GUM5, GUM6, GYLA, HSL, HSL2, JGFF, LDL, LYV, PHP2, PHP3, SF, YB.

Borisov, Byel.; pop. 8,355; 75 km NE of Minsk; 54°15'/28°30'; AMG, COH, EDRD, EJ, GUM4, HSL, HSL2, JGFF, LDL, SF.

Borisovka, see Barishevka.

Borispol, Ukr.; 32 km ESE of Kiyev; 50°21'/30°57'; HSL, JGFF, LDL, SF.

Borivka, see Borovaja.

Borja, see Boria.

Bork, Germ.; 94 km NNE of Koln; 51°40'/07°30'; HSL.

Borka, Cz.; 38 km WSW of Kosice; 48°38'/20°46'; HSL, HSL2.

Borken, Germ.; pop. 130; 120 km N of Frankfurt am Main; 51°03'/09°17'; GED, JGFF.

Borken (near Essen), Germ.; pop. 102; 107 km N of Koln; 51°51'/06°52'; GUM5.

Borkenhagen, Germ.; pop. 3; 69 km WSW of Rostock; 53°57'/11°04'.

Borki (Lublin area), Pol.; pop. 30; 56 km N of Lublin; 51°43'/22°31'; GUM4.

Borki (Lvov area), Ukr.; pop. 20; 32 km NW of Lvov; 50°07'/23°45'; GUM3.

Borki Nizinskie, Pol.; pop. 21; 114 km NE of Krakow; 50°23'/21°26'.

Borki Wielkie, see Velikiye Borki.

Borki Wyrki, Pol.; pop. 4; 94 km E of Warszawa; 52°07'/22°21'.

Borkowizna, Pol.; pop. 23; 32 km S of Lublin; 51°01'/22°25'.

Borla, Rom.; pop. 23; 75 km NW of Cluj; 47°17'/22°57'.

Borlesti, Rom. (Barlafalu); pop. 58; 94 km SW of Iasi; 46°46'/26°29'.

Bornheim, Germ.; pop. 60; 26 km SSE of Koln; 50°46'/07°00'; LDS.

Bornich, Germ.; pop. 2; 62 km W of Frankfurt am Main; 50°08'/07°46'.

Bornitz, HSL. A number of towns share this name. It was not possible to determine from available information which one is being referenced.

Bornov, see Baranow Sandomierski.

Borochiche, Ukr. (Boroczyce); pop. 6; 88 km NNE of Lvov; 50°27'/24°50'.

Boroczyce, see Borochiche.

Borod, Rom. (Borodul Mare?, Nagybarod); pop. 204; 75 km WNW of Cluj; 46°59'/22°38'; AMG, HSL, PHR2.

Borodina, GUM4. This town was not found in BGN gazetteers under the given spelling.

Borodino, Ukr.; pop. 50; 114 km WSW of Odessa; 46°18'/29°15'.

Borodul Mare, *possibly* Borod.

Borodyanka, Ukr. (Barodeinka, Boradianka); 50 km WNW of Kiyev; 50°39'/29°56'; JGFF, LDL, SF.

Borofka, see Borovaja.

Borogani, see Borogany.

Borogany, Mold. (Borogani); pop. 6; 75 km S of Kishinev; 46°22'/28°31'.

Borohradek, Cz.; pop. 6; 114 km NNW of Brno; 50°06'/16°06'.

Borolea, Rom.; pop. 6; 101 km NW of Iasi; 47°57'/27°02'.

Boromel, see Baremel.

Boronka, Hung.; 45 km NE of Nagykanizsa; 46°35'/17°27'; HSL.

Boronow, Pol.; 19 km SSW of Czestochowa; 50°40'/18°56'; JGFF.

Borosneu Mare, Rom.; pop. 50; 157 km N of Bucuresti; 45°49'/26°00'; HSL.

Borossebes, see Sebis.

Borosznok, see Brusturesti.

Borota, Hung.; pop. 11; 75 km W of Szeged; 46°16'/19°14'.

Borov, Cz.; 82 km NNE of Kosice; 49°18'/21°54'; JGFF.

Borovaja, Lat. (Borivka, Borofka); 101 km NE of Daugavpils; 56°15'/28°02'; JGFF, PHLE.

Borovaya, Ukr.; pop. 150; 120 km ESE of Kharkov; 49°24'/37°40'.

Borove, Ukr. (Borowe); pop. 25; 50 km N of Lvov; 50°16'/24°12'; PHP2.

Borovichi, USSR; pop. 317; 202 km NW of Kalinin; 58°22'/34°00'.

Borovka, Ukr.; 69 km W of Kiyev; 50°27'/29°33'; COH, EDRD.

Borovoye, Ukr. (Borowe); pop. 38; 88 km NE of Rovno; 51°06'/27°13'.

Borovsk, USSR; pop. 43; 94 km SW of Moskva; 55°12'/36°30'.

Borovtse, Ukr. (Borauti); pop. 114; 38 km NW of Chernovtsy; 48°35'/25°38'.

Borow, Pol.; pop. 34; 45 km SE of Lublin; 50°56'/22°57'; HSL.

Borowa (Brzesko area), Pol.; pop. 25; 69 km ESE of Krakow; 49°48'/20°47'.

Borowa (Mielec area), Pol.; pop. 186; 107 km NE of Krakow; 50°23'/21°22'; PHP2, PHP3.

Borowa (Pilzno area), Pol.; pop. 25; 101 km E of Krakow;

50°05'/21°18'.

Borowa Gora, Pol.; pop. 43; 50 km NNE of Przemysl; 50°09'/23°13'.

Borowe, Pol.; pop. 20; 88 km NNE of Warszawa; 52°59'/21°36'; HSL, HSL2. *See also* Borove; Borovoye.

Borowe (Lwow); *Black Book* notes a town by this name (pop. 25) in the interwar Polish province of Lwow. BGN shows two possible locations: 50°07'/23°58' and 50°16'/24°12'.

Borowica, Pol.; pop. 16; 45 km ESE of Lublin; 51°04'/23°07'.

Borowiec, Pol.; pop. 27; 69 km N of Przemysl; 50°21'/23°03'; COH.

Borowirowszczyzna, Pol.; pop. 25; Described in the *Black Book* as being in the Nowogrodek region of Poland, this town was not found in BGN gazetteers.

Borownica, Pol.; pop. 39; 62 km S of Lublin; 50°43'/22°23'.

Borrstadt, Germ.; 75 km SSW of Frankfurt am Main; 49°35'/07°57'; JGFF.

Bors, Rom.; pop. 3; 139 km WNW of Cluj; 47°07'/21°49'.

Borsa, *see* Borsa Maramures.

Borsa Cluj, Rom.; pop. 57; 26 km N of Cluj; 46°56'/23°40'; PHR2.

Borsa Maramures, Rom. (Borsa, Borsha, Borsha Maramuresh, Borsha Marmorosh, Kolozsborsa); pop. 2,486; 126 km NNE of Cluj; 47°39'/24°40'; AMG, COH, GUM3, GUM4, HSL, HSL2, JGFF, LYV, PHR2.

Borschtschagowka, *see* Borshchagovka.

Borsec, Rom. (Borszek); pop. 151; 150 km ENE of Cluj; 46°57'/25°34'; HSL, PHR2.

Borsha, *see* Borsa Maramures.

Borshagovka, *see* Borshchagovka.

Borsha Maramuresh, *see* Borsa Maramures.

Borsha Marmorosh, *see* Borsa Maramures.

Borshchagovka, Ukr. (Borschtschagowka, Borshagovka); 82 km NE of Vinnitsa; 49°29'/29°32'; JGFF, LDL, SF.

Borshchev, Ukr. (Borshchov, Borshtchev, Borszczow); pop. 1,656; 56 km N of Chernovtsy; 48°48'/26°03'; AMG, CAHJP, EDRD, EGRS, GUM3, GUM4, GUM5, GUM6, HSL, HSL2, JGFF, LDL, PHP2, SF, YB.

Borshchev (near Rogatin), Ukr.; pop. 56; 50 km ESE of Lvov; 49°40'/24°36'.

Borshchevka, Ukr. (Borszczowka); 88 km WNW of Rovno; 51°03'/25°11'; GUM4.

Borshchov, *see* Borshchev.

Borshchovichi, Ukr. (Barshchovitse, Barszczowice); pop. 57; 19 km ENE of Lvov; 49°52'/24°16'.

Borshchuv, Ukr. (Borchow?, Borshov, Borszow); pop. 58; 56 km N of Chernovtsy; 48°48'/26°03'; HSL.

Borshivka, *see* Barishevka.

Borshov, *see* Borshchuv.

Borshtchev, *see* Borshchev.

Borsod, Hung.; pop. 8; 32 km N of Miskolc; 48°19'/20°45'; HSL.

Borsodbota, Hung. (Bota); 32 km WNW of Miskolc; 48°13'/20°24'; HSL.

Borsodcsaba, HSL. This pre-World War I community was not found in BGN gazetteers.

Borsodgeszt, Hung.; pop. 14; 19 km S of Miskolc; 47°57'/20°42'.

Borsodharsany, HSL. This pre-World War I community was not found in BGN gazetteers.

Borsodivanka, Hung.; pop. 9; 50 km S of Miskolc; 47°42'/20°40'.

Borsodnadasd, Hung.; pop. 51; 45 km W of Miskolc; 48°07'/20°15'; HSL, HSL2.

Borsodszemere, *see* Mezoszemere.

Borsodszentmarton, *see* Bukkszentmarton.

Borsodszirak, Hung.; pop. 5; 26 km N of Miskolc; 48°16'/20°46'.

Borsosbereny, Hung.; pop. 7; 56 km N of Budapest; 47°58'/19°07'.

Borsosgyor, Hung.; pop. 5; 107 km N of Nagykanizsa; 47°19'/17°26'.

Borsuchizna, Byel. (Borsuczyzna); pop. 2; 176 km N of Minsk; 55°26'/27°27'.

Borsuczyzna, *see* Borsuchizna.

Borszczow, *see* Borshchev.

Borszczowka, *see* Borshchevka.

Borszeg, *see* Burzuc.

Borszek, *see* Borsec.

Borszorcsok, Hung.; pop. 3; 82 km N of Nagykanizsa; 47°08'/17°24'.

Borszow, *see* Borshchuv.

Borszyn, Pol.; pop. 7; 32 km NW of Lodz; 51°59'/19°11'.

Bortaycze, GA. This town was not found in BGN gazetteers under the given spelling.

Bortele, *see* Barciai.

Bortkov, Ukr. (Bortkow, Bortkuv); pop. 81; 50 km ENE of Lvov; 49°51'/24°38'.

Bortkow, *see* Bortkov.

Bortkuv, *see* Bortkov.

Bortniki (near Chodoruv), Ukr.; pop. 73; 62 km SSE of Lvov; 49°21'/24°18'.

Bortniki (near Tlumach), Ukr.; pop. 27; 82 km WNW of Chernovtsy; 48°46'/25°02'.

Bortnow, *see* Bortnuv.

Bortnuv, Ukr. (Bortnow); pop. 15; 107 km N of Lvov; 50°47'/24°06'.

Bortyatin, Ukr. (Bortiatyn); pop. 51; 45 km WSW of Lvov; 49°49'/23°24'.

Bor u Chroustovic, Cz.; pop. 76; 94 km NW of Brno; 49°56'/15°59'.

Boruja Koscielna, Pol.; pop. 2; 62 km WSW of Poznan; 52°16'/16°08'.

Borumlaca, Rom. (Baromlak); pop. 1; 101 km WNW of Cluj; 47°13'/22°29'.

Borusowa, Pol.; pop. 35; 69 km NE of Krakow; 50°17'/20°48'; AMG.

Borvalaszut, *see* Crucisor.

Borvely, *see* Berveni.

Boryczewicze, Byel.; pop. 20; 32 km ESE of Pinsk; 51°55'/26°25'. This town was located on an interwar map of Poland but does not appear in contemporary gazetteers. Map coordinates are approximate.

Borynia, *see* Borinya.

Boryniche, Ukr. (Borynicze); pop. 12; 45 km SSE of Lvov; 49°30'/24°13'.

Borynicze, *see* Boryniche.

Boryslaw, *see* Borislav.

Boryslawice, Pol.; pop. 75; 75 km WSW of Lodz; 51°40'/18°26'.

Boryslawka, Pol.; pop. 10; 26 km SSW of Przemysl; 49°39'/22°38'.

Borysowka, *see* Borysuvka.

Borysowo, Pol.; pop. 69; 126 km NW of Bialystok; 54°09'/22°25'.

Borysowszczyzna, Pol.; pop. 15; 82 km S of Bialystok; 52°26'/23°06'; HSL.

Borysuvka, Byel. (Borysowka); 120 km WSW of Pinsk; 51°55'/24°27'; GUM5.

Bor Zapilski, Pol.; pop. 31; 19 km W of Czestochowa; 50°50'/18°51'.

Borzava, HSL. This pre-World War I community was not found in BGN gazetteers.

Borzavar, Hung.; pop. 4; 94 km WSW of Budapest; 47°18'/17°50'.

Borzechow, Pol.; pop. 21; 26 km SW of Lublin; 51°06'/22°17'.

Borzecin, Pol.; pop. 84; 56 km E of Krakow; 50°05'/20°42'; JGFF.

Borzecinek, Pol.; pop. 1; 32 km SSE of Lublin; 50°59'/22°43'.

Borzna, Ukr.; pop. 697; 56 km W of Konotop; 51°15'/32°26'; JGFF, SF.

Borzychy, Pol.; pop. 11; 62 km NE of Warszawa; 52°28'/21°55'.

Bosaca, Cz.; pop. 55; 94 km NNE of Bratislava; 48°50'/17°50'.

Bosanska Gradiska, Yug.; pop. 28; 120 km ESE of Zagreb; 45°09'/17°15'.

Bosanska Krupa, Yug.; pop. 5; 107 km S of Zagreb; 44°53'/16°10'.

Bosanski Brod, Yug.; pop. 79; 176 km ESE of Zagreb; 45°08'/18°01'.

Bosanski Novi, Yug.; pop. 12; 88 km SSE of Zagreb; 45°03'/16°22'.

Bosanski Petrovac, Yug.; pop. 9; 139 km SSE of Zagreb; 44°34'/16°21'.

Bosanski Samac, Yug.; pop. 29; 163 km W of Beograd; 45°04'/18°28'.

Bosarkany, Hung.; pop. 22; 139 km W of Budapest; 47°41'/17°15'.

Boscana, *see* Bashkany.

Bosen, Germ.; pop. 40; 133 km SW of Frankfurt am Main; 49°34'/07°03'; GUM5, JGFF.

Boshaza, *see* Biusa.

Boshevitch, *see* Bogushevichi.

Bosiacz, *see* Bosyach.

Bosilec, Cz.; pop. 3; 107 km S of Praha; 49°09'/14°39'.

Bosing, *see* Pezinok.

Bosingfeld, Germ.; pop. 28; 56 km SW of Hannover; 52°04'/09°07'.

Boska Wola, Pol.; pop. 11; 69 km SSE of Warszawa; 51°43'/21°10'.

Boskovice, Cz. (Boskowitz); pop. 452; 38 km N of Brno; 49°29'/16°40'; AMG, CAHJP, EJ, HSL, HSL2, LDL.

Boskowitz, *see* Boskovice.

Boslar, Germ.; 45 km W of Koln; 50°58'/06°20'; GED.

Boslev, *see* Boguslav.

Bosna Serai, *see* Sarajevo.

Bosnia; Part of the Austro-Hungarian Empire prior to the end of World War I, Bosnia now is a constituent republic of Yugoslavia.

Bosta, Hung.; pop. 5; 107 km ESE of Nagykanizsa; 45°57'/18°13'.

Bostyn, Byel.; pop. 42; 56 km NE of Pinsk; 52°23'/26°45'.

Bosyach, Byel. (Bosiacz); pop. 22; 120 km W of Pinsk; 52°16'/24°24'.

Bosyne, Cz.; pop. 4; 45 km N of Praha; 50°25'/14°33'.

Bosyry, Ukr.; pop. 10; 75 km N of Chernovtsy; 48°56'/26°09'.

Boszormeny, *see* Hajduboszormeny.

Bota, *see* Borsodbota.

Botak, *see* Batakiai.

Botany, Cz.; pop. 67; 69 km ESE of Kosice; 48°27'/22°06'; AMG.

Botcheikev, *see* Bocheykovo.

Botcheikovo, *see* Bocheykovo.

Botfa, Hung. (Zalabesenyo); pop. 1; 50 km NNW of Nagykanizsa; 46°48'/16°52'.

Bothaza, *see* Bodhaza.

Botik, *see* Batakiai.

Botiz, *see* Batiz.

Botiza, Rom. (Batiza, Botiza Maramures, Butiza); pop. 121; 114 km N of Cluj; 47°40'/24°09'; COH, HSL, HSL2, PHR2, SM.

Botiza Maramures, *see* Botiza.

Botiz Satu Mare, Rom.; pop. 145; 133 km NNW of Cluj; 47°50'/22°57'.

Botla, (Bitla); SF. This town was not found in BGN gazetteers under the given spelling.

Botoka, *see* Batakiai.

Botoken, *see* Batakiai.

Botoki, *see* Batakiai.

Botosana, Rom.; pop. 4; 133 km WNW of Iasi; 47°41'/25°57'.

Botosani, Rom. (Bartishaw, Botoshani); pop. 11,840; 94 km WNW of Iasi; 47°45'/26°40'; AMG, CAHJP, EJ, GUM3, GUM4, GUM5, GUM6, GYLA, HSL, HSL2, JGFF, PHR1.

Botoshani, *see* Botosani.

Botpalad, Hung.; pop. 26; 150 km E of Miskolc; 48°02'/22°48'.

Botragy, Cz. AMG, HSL. This pre-World War I community was not found in BGN gazetteers.

Bottingheim, Cz.; 163 km WNW of Kosice; 49°45'/19°40'; PHGB.

Bottrop, Germ.; pop. 350; 69 km N of Koln; 51°31'/06°55'; GED.

Bottschow, Pol. (Boczow); 133 km SSE of Szczecin; 52°19'/14°56'; GA.

Bous, Germ. (Buss); pop. 5; 157 km SW of Frankfurt am Main; 49°17'/06°48'.

Bovenden, Germ.; 94 km SSE of Hannover; 51°35'/09°56'; GED.

Boxberg, Germ.; 82 km N of Stuttgart; 49°29'/09°38'; GED, LDS.

Boyan, *see* Boyany.

Boyanets, Ukr. (Bojaniec, Boyanitz); pop. 43; 38 km N of Lvov; 50°10'/24°06'; HSL, LDL, SF.

Boyanitz, *see* Boyanets.

Boyany, Ukr. (Boian, Boianceni, Bojan, Boyan); pop. 127; 19 km E of Chernovtsy; 48°17'/26°08'; EJ, GUM4, HSL, HSL2, LDL, PHR2.

Boyarka, Ukr. (Boyarka Budayevka); pop. 53; 19 km SW of Kiyev; 50°19'/30°19'; HSL, SF.

Boyarka Budayevka, *see* Boyarka.

Boyberik, *see* Bobrka.

Boyevitse, *see* Boyovichi.

Boyovichi, Ukr. (Bojowice, Boyevitse); pop. 22; 75 km WSW of Lvov; 49°44'/22°59'.

Boysk, *see* Bauska.

Boze, Pol.; pop. 29; 69 km SSE of Warszawa; 51°42'/21°08'.

Bozejovice, Cz.; pop. 1; 75 km S of Praha; 49°28'/14°29'.

Bozhev, *see* Bozhuv.

Bozhuv, Ukr. (Bezejow?, Bozhev); pop. 26; 94 km NNE of Lvov; 50°31'/24°51'.

Bozicany, Cz.; pop. 6; 120 km W of Praha; 50°16'/12°47'.

Bozieni, Rom. AMG. A number of towns share this name. It was not possible to determine from available information which one is being referenced.

Bozieni Bals, *see* Bozienii de Sus.

Bozienii de Sus, Rom. (Bozieni Bals); pop. 122; 69 km SW of Iasi; 46°58'/26°41'; PHR1.

Bozinta Mare, Rom.; pop. 6; 101 km N of Cluj; 47°38'/23°27'.

Bozkovice, Cz.; pop. 2; 50 km SSE of Praha; 49°42'/14°37'.

Bozodujfalu, *see* Bezid.

Bozovice, *see* Bozovici.

Bozovici, Rom. (Bozovice, Bozoviciu, Bozovics); 240 km SSW of Cluj; 44°56'/22°00'; HSL.

Bozoviciu, *see* Bozovici.

Bozovics, *see* Bozovici.

Bozsaly, *see* Bogeiu.

Bozsor, *see* Bujor.

Bozykow, Pol.; pop. 22; Described in the *Black Book* as being in the Tarnopol region of Poland, this town was not found in BGN gazetteers.

Brackel, Germ.; 32 km S of Hamburg; 53°18'/10°02'; JGFF.

Brackwede, Germ.; pop. 18; 94 km SW of Hannover; 51°59'/08°31'; LDS.

Braclav, *see* Bratslav.

Braclaw, *see* Bratslav.

Brad, Rom. (Fenyofalva); pop. 102; 94 km SSW of Cluj; 46°08'/22°47'; GUM4, JGFF, PHR1.

Braesti, Rom. (Braesti Dorohoi); pop. 25; 120 km WNW of Iasi; 47°30'/26°05'.

Braesti Dorohoi, *see* Braesti.

Braga, Ukr. (Badragii Vechi, Badragii Noui); pop. 30; 50 km NE of Chernovtsy; 48°31'/26°30'.

Bragin, Byel. (Brohin); pop. 2,165; 88 km SSW of Gomel; 51°47'/30°16'; EJ, HSL, JGFF, SF.

Brahin, LDL. This pre-World War I community was not found in BGN gazetteers.

Braila, Rom. (Breila, Ibraila); pop. 7,134; 176 km NE of Bucuresti; 45°16'/27°59'; AMG, EJ, GUM4, HSL, JGFF, LDL, PHR1.

Brailov, Ukr. (Brailow, Bralov); pop. 2,393; 26 km SW of Vinnitsa; 49°06'/28°10'; EDRD, EJ, HSL, HSL2, JGFF, LDL, PHR1, SF.

Brailov, Ukraine: Jewish family outside their home.

Brailow, *see* Brailov.

Brak, LDL. This pre-World War I community was not found in BGN gazetteers.

Brake, Germ.; 101 km WSW of Hamburg; 53°20'/08°29'; LDS.

Brakel, Germ.; pop. 93; 88 km SSW of Hannover; 51°43'/09°11'; AMG, HSL.

Bralin, Pol.; pop. 4; 69 km NE of Wroclaw; 51°17'/17°54'.

Bralov, *see* Brailov.

Branc, Cz. (Berencs); 82 km ENE of Bratislava; 48°13'/18°09'; LDL.

Brancovenesti, *see* Brincovenesti.

Brandeis, HSL, HSL2. A number of towns share this name. It was not possible to determine from available information which one is being referenced.

Brandenburg, Germ.; pop. 350; 56 km WSW of Berlin; 52°25'/12°33'; EJ, GUM3, GUM5, GUM6, HSL, HSL2, LDS, PHGBW.

Brandwica, Pol.; 82 km SSW of Lublin; 50°37'/22°04'; PHP3.

Brandysek, Cz.; pop. 9; 26 km WNW of Praha; 50°11'/14°11'.

Brandys nad Labem, Cz.; pop. 69; 19 km NE of Praha; 50°11'/14°40'; GUM4, GUM5, GUM6.

Brandys nad Orlici, Cz.; pop. 264; 94 km NNW of Brno; 50°00'/16°18'.

Braneshty, Mold. (Branistea); pop. 101; 150 km WNW of Kishinev; 47°48'/27°15'.

Branewka, Pol.; pop. 6; 62 km S of Lublin; 50°43'/22°33'.

Braniewa, *see* Braniewo.

Braniewo, Pol. (Braniewa, Braunsberg); pop. 75; 75 km ENE of Gdansk; 54°23'/19°50'; HSL.

Branistea, Rom.; pop. 20; 56 km NNE of Cluj; 47°10'/24°04'. *See also* Braneshty.

Branjin Vrh, Yug.; pop. 10; 182 km WNW of Beograd; 45°48'/18°37'.

Brankow, Pol.; pop. 7; 69 km S of Warszawa; 51°43'/21°02'.

Bransk, Pol. (Braynsk, Breinsk); pop. 2,165; 50 km SSW of Bialystok; 52°44'/22°51'; AMG, COH, EJ, GA, GUM3, GUM4, GUM5, GYLA, HSL2, JGFF, LDL, LYV, POCEM, SF, YB.

Branska, HSL. This pre-World War I community was not found in BGN gazetteers.

Branszczyk, Pol.; pop. 140; 56 km NE of Warszawa; 52°38'/21°36'; HSL, PHP4.

Branzeni, *see* Brynzeny.

Branzenii Vechi, *see* Staryye Brynzeny.

Braskov, Cz.; pop. 2; 26 km W of Praha; 50°06'/14°06'.

Braslav, Byel. (Braslaw, Breslav, Breslev); pop. 1,130; 202 km NNW of Minsk; 55°38'/27°02'; AMG, COH, EDRD, EJ, GA, GUM3, GUM5, GUM6, HSL, JGFF, LDL, SF, YB.

Braslaw, *see* Braslav.

Brasov, Rom. (Brasso, Kronstadt, Orasul Stalin); pop. 2,594; 139 km NW of Bucuresti; 45°38'/25°35'; EJ, GUM4, HSL, HSL2, LDL, PHR1.

Brasso, *see* Brasov.

Braszewice, Pol.; pop. 8; 75 km SW of Lodz; 51°30'/18°27'.

Bratca, Rom.; pop. 34; 75 km W of Cluj; 46°56'/22°37'; AMG.

Brates, Rom. (Baratos); 163 km N of Bucuresti; 45°50'/26°04'; HSL.

Bratian, Pol. (Bratjan); pop. 2; 114 km SE of Gdansk; 53°28'/19°37'.

Bratislava, Cz. (Aranzenii Vechi, Bratyslawa, Pozsony, Pressburg); pop. 14,882; 120 km SSE of Brno; 48°09'/17°07'; AMG, EJ, GUM3, GUM4, GUM5, GUM6, GYLA, HSL, HSL2, ISH1, ISH3, JGFF, LDL, LJEE, PHP2, PHP3, YB.

Bratjan, *see* Bratian.

Bratka, HSL. This pre-World War I community was not found in BGN gazetteers.

Bratkovtse, Ukr. (Bratkowce); pop. 126; 107 km WNW of Chernovtsy; 48°48'/24°43'.

Bratkowce, *see* Bratkovtse.

Bratkow Gorny, Pol.; pop. 16; 38 km W of Lodz; 51°49'/18°54'.

Bratkowice, Pol.; pop. 37; 69 km WNW of Przemysl; 50°07'/21°52'.

Bratkowka, Pol.; pop. 10; 75 km WSW of Przemysl; 49°46'/21°43'.

Bratnik, Pol.; pop. 25; Described in the *Black Book* as being in the Lublin region of Poland, this town was not found in

37

BGN gazetteers.

Bratolyubovka, Ukr.; 150 km WSW of Dnepropetrovsk; 48°13'/32°58'; LDL, SF.

Bratronice, Cz.; 32 km WSW of Praha; 50°04'/14°01'; JGFF.

Bratslav, Ukr. (Braclav, Braclaw, Bratslow, Bratzlav); pop. 1,840; 56 km SE of Vinnitsa; 48°50'/28°57'; EDRD, EJ, GYLA, JGFF, LDL, PHR1, SF.

Bratslow, *see* Bratslav.

Bratuleni, *see* Bratuleny.

Bratuleny, Mold. (Bratuleni); pop. 6; 69 km W of Kishinev; 47°08'/27°58'.

Bratuseni, *see* Bratushany.

Bratushany, Mold. (Bratuseni); pop. 21; 157 km NW of Kishinev; 48°05'/27°25'.

Bratyslawa, *see* Bratislava.

Bratz, *see* Brojce.

Bratzlav, *see* Bratslav.

Braubach, Germ.; pop. 4; 75 km W of Frankfurt am Main; 50°17'/07°40'; EDRD.

Braunau, *see* Broumov.

Brauneberg, Germ.; pop. 20; 120 km WSW of Frankfurt am Main; 49°55'/06°59'; GUM4.

Braunfels, Germ.; pop. 29; 50 km NW of Frankfurt am Main; 50°31'/08°24'.

Braunlage, Germ.; 94 km SE of Hannover; 51°44'/10°37'; GUM3.

Braunsbach, Germ.; pop. 53; 62 km NNE of Stuttgart; 49°12'/09°48'; GUM5, HSL, HSL2, JGFF, LDL, PHGBW.

Braunsberg, *see* Braniewo.

Braunschweig, Germ. (Brunswick); pop. 1,000; 56 km E of Hannover; 52°16'/10°32'; AMG, EJ, GED, GUM3, GUM4, GUM5, HSL, HSL2, LDS, PHGBW.

Bravica, *see* Bravicha.

Bravicea, *see* Bravicha.

Braviceni, *see* Bravicheny.

Bravicha, Mold. (Bravica, Bravicea, Bravitcha, Brawicza?); pop. 413; 50 km NW of Kishinev; 47°22'/28°27'; LDL, SF.

Bravicheny, Mold. (Braviceni); pop. 19; 56 km NNW of Kishinev; 47°26'/28°39'.

Bravitcha, *see* Bravicha.

Brawicza, *possibly* Bravicha.

Braynsk, *see* Bransk.

Brcko, Yug.; pop. 112; 133 km W of Beograd; 44°52'/18°49'; EDRD, GUM4, GUM5, PHY.

Brdov, *see* Brdow.

Brdovec, Yug.; pop. 13; 19 km WNW of Zagreb; 45°52'/15°46'.

Brdow, Pol. (Brdov); pop. 24; 82 km NW of Lodz; 52°21'/18°43'; CAHJP, EDRD.

Breanova, *see* Bryanovo.

Breaza, Rom. (Beresztelke); pop. 94; 163 km NE of Cluj; 47°37'/25°20'; PHR2.

Breaza Somes, Rom.; pop. 49; 75 km NNE of Cluj; 47°21'/24°04'.

Breb, Rom. (Breb Maramures); pop. 154; 114 km N of Cluj; 47°45'/23°54'.

Breb Maramures, *see* Breb.

Breckenheim, Germ.; pop. 6; 26 km WSW of Frankfurt am Main; 50°05'/08°22'.

Breclav, Cz. (Lundenburg); pop. 838; 50 km SSE of Brno; 48°46'/16°53'; CAHJP, EJ, GUM4, HSL, HSL2.

Bredelar, Germ.; pop. 9; 126 km SSW of Hannover; 51°25'/08°46'.

Bredtheim, Pol.; pop. 46; Described in the *Black Book* as being in the Stanislawow region of Poland, this town was not found in BGN gazetteers.

Bregenz, Aus.; pop. 10; 126 km W of Innsbruck; 47°30'/09°46'; EJ.

Brehy, Cz.; pop. 50; 114 km ENE of Bratislava; 48°24'/18°39'.

Breidenbach, Germ.; pop. 94 km NNW of Frankfurt am Main; 50°53'/08°28'; JGFF.

Breila, *see* Braila.

Breinsk, *see* Bransk.

Breisach, Germ. (Alt Breisach); pop. 287; 146 km SW of Stuttgart; 48°02'/07°35'; CAHJP, EJ, HSL, JGFF, PHGBW.

Breitenau, Germ.; 62 km SW of Nurnberg; 49°13'/10°16'; GUM3, LDS, PHGB.

Breitenbach, *see* Breitenbach am Herzberg.

Breitenbach am Herzberg, Germ. (Breitenbach); pop. 72; 94 km NNE of Frankfurt am Main; 50°46'/09°31'; LDS.

Breitenberg, Germ.; 176 km NE of Munchen; 48°42'/13°48'; GUM3.

Breitenlee, Aus.; pop. 1; 13 km NE of Wien; 48°15'/16°30'.

Breitenwaida, Aus.; pop. 2; 38 km NW of Wien; 48°30'/16°04'.

Breitenwang, Aus.; pop. 3; 56 km WNW of Innsbruck; 47°29'/10°44'.

Brejeni, *see* Brezheny.

Brelikow, Pol.; 38 km SSW of Przemysl; 49°31'/22°31'; HSL.

Bremen, Germ.; pop. 1,328; 94 km SW of Hamburg; 53°05'/08°48'; AMG, EJ, GED, GUM3, GUM4, GUM5, HSL, JGFF, PHP1, PHP2.

Bremerhaven, Germ. (Wesermunde); pop. 432; 94 km WSW of Hamburg; 53°33'/08°35'; AMG, GUM5, JGFF.

Bremervorde, Germ.; pop. 23; 56 km WSW of Hamburg; 53°29'/09°08'; HSL, JGFF.

Bremke, Germ.; pop. 36; 45 km S of Hannover; 52°02'/09°33'.

Brenken, Germ.; pop. 11; 120 km SSW of Hannover; 51°35'/08°36'.

Brennberg, Germ.; 101 km ESE of Nurnberg; 49°04'/12°24'; PHGB.

Brenndorf, *see* Bod.

Brenn Poritschen, HSL. This pre-World War I community was not found in BGN gazetteers.

Bren Osuchowski, Pol.; pop. 31; 101 km ENE of Krakow; 50°19'/21°16'.

Breshtitz, *see* Barstyciai.

Breslau, *see* Wroclaw.

Breslav, *see* Braslav.

Breslev, *see* Braslav.

Bresslau, *see* Wroclaw.

Brest, Byel. (Brest Litovsk, Brest Litowsk, Brisk, Brisk D Lita, Brisk Dlita, Brist nad Bugie, Brzesc Litewski, Brzesc nad Bugiem, Bzheshch nad Bugyem); pop. 15,630; 163 km WSW of Pinsk; 52°06'/23°42'; AMG, CAHJP, COH, EDRD, EJ, FRG, GA, GUM3, GUM4, GUM5, GUM6, GYLA, HSL, HSL2, JGFF, LDL, LYV, PHP3, PHP4, YB.

Brestanica, Yug. (Rajhenburg, Reichenburg); pop. 2; 45 km WNW of Zagreb; 45°59'/15°29'; HSL.

Brestitski, *see* Berestechko.

Brest Kujavsk, *see* Brzesc Kujawski.

Brest Litovsk, *see* Brest.

Brest Litowsk, *see* Brest.

Brestovac Pozeski, Yug. (Pozeski Brestovac); pop. 3; 133 km ESE of Zagreb; 45°20'/17°36'.

Brestovits, *see* Bolshaya Berestovitsa.

Bretcu, Rom. (Berecyk); pop. 13; 163 km SSW of Iasi; 46°03'/26°18'.

Bretka, Cz. (Beretke); pop. 13; 69 km SW of Kosice; 48°29'/20°21'; HSL, HSL2.

Bretten, Germ.; pop. 155; 50 km WNW of Stuttgart; 49°03'/08°42'; HSL, HSL2, JGFF, PHGBW.

Bretzenheim, Germ.; pop. 27; 62 km SW of Frankfurt am Main; 49°52'/07°54'.

Breza, Yug.; 195 km SW of Beograd; 44°01'/18°16'; HSL, HSL2.

Brezah, *see* Bereza.

Brezan, *see* Berezhany.

Brezezowicz, LDL. This pre-World War I community was not found in BGN gazetteers.

Brezhen, *see* Brezheny.

Brezheny, Mold. (Brejeni, Brezhen); pop. 30; 82 km NW of Kishinev; 47°35'/28°09'.

Brezhin, *see* Brzeziny.

Brezhna, *see* Berezno.

Brezhnovata, *see* Bereznegovatoye.

Brezice, Yug.; pop. 1; 38 km WNW of Zagreb; 45°54'/15°35'.

Brezin, Cz.; pop. 4; 94 km WSW of Praha; 49°58'/13°08'; AMG.

Brezina, Cz. (Kolbas); 32 km ESE of Kosice; 48°33'/21°34'; HSL, JGFF.

Brezinka, HSL. A number of towns share this name. It was not possible to determine from available information which one is being referenced.

Breziny, *see* Brzeziny.

Brezitz, *see* Velikiye Berezhtsy.

Brezne, *see* Berezno.

Breznice, Cz. (Breznitz); pop. 57; 69 km SSW of Praha; 49°33'/13°58'; EJ, HSL, HSL2.

Breznicki Hum, *see* Hum Breznicki.

Breznitz, *see* Breznice.

Brezno, Cz.; pop. 24; 50 km NE of Praha; 50°24'/15°00'.

Brezno nad Hronom, Cz.; pop. 281; 114 km W of Kosice; 48°49'/19°39'; GUM4, GUM5, HSL.

Brezoaia, *see* Brezoya.

Brezov, Cz.; 56 km N of Kosice; 49°09'/21°30'; HSL.

Brezova, *see* Brezova pod Bradlom.

Brezova pod Bradlom, Cz. (Berezo, Brezova, Bruesau); pop. 100; 69 km NNE of Bratislava; 48°40'/17°32'; COH, GUM4, HSL, HSL2, JGFF, YB.

Brezovica nad Torysou, Cz.; pop. 90; 56 km NW of Kosice; 49°09'/20°51'.

Brezowice, COH, PHP2. This town was not found in BGN gazetteers under the given spelling.

Brezoya, Mold. (Brezoaia); pop. 6; 69 km SE of Kishinev; 46°31'/29°27'.

Briancovenesti, *see* Brincovenesti.

Brianska Gora, *see* Brunska Gora.

Briaza, HSL. This pre-World War I community was not found in BGN gazetteers.

Briceni, *see* Brichany.

Briceni Sat, *see* Brichany.

Briceni Targ, *see* Brichany.

Briceva, *see* Bricheva.

Brichany, Mold. (Berchan, Briceni, Briceni Sat, Briceni Targ, Bricheni, Bricheni Sat, Bricheni Targ, Britshan, Britshani, Britsiteni); pop. 5,354; 202 km NW of Kishinev; 48°22'/27°06'; EDRD, EJ, GUM3, GUM4, GYLA, HSL, JGFF, LYV, PHR2, SF, YB.

Bricheni, *see* Brichany.

Bricheni Sat, *see* Brichany.

Bricheni Targ, *see* Brichany.

Bricheva, Mold. (Briceva, Brichevo, Britcheva); pop. 2,431; 157 km NW of Kishinev; 48°07'/27°39'; AMG, COH, EJ, PHR2, SF, YB.

Brichevo, *see* Bricheva.

Brieg, *see* Brzeg.

Briegel, *see* Brzesko.

Brieni, *see* Chervono Glinskoye.

Briesen, *see* Brzezin.

Brigel, *see* Brzesko.

Brigi, *see* Ratniceni.

Brigu, *see* Ratniceni.

Bril, Byel. (Brylki); pop. 7; 69 km WNW of Minsk; 54°07'/26°34'.

Brilice, Cz.; pop. 2; 126 km SSE of Praha; 49°01'/14°44'.

Brilon, Germ.; pop. 73; 126 km NE of Koln; 51°24'/08°35'; GUM5, JGFF, LDS.

Brin, Ukr. (Bryn); pop. 5; 101 km SE of Lvov; 49°03'/24°34'.

Brincovenesti, Rom. (Brancovenesti, Briancovenesti, Marosvecs); pop. 20; 88 km ENE of Cluj; 46°52'/24°46'; HSL.

Brisk, *see* Brest.

Brisk D Koya, *see* Brzesc Kujawski.

Brisk D Lita, *see* Brest.

Brisk Dlita, *see* Brest.

Brisk Kuyavsk, *see* Brzesc Kujawski.

Brister, *see* Brustury.

Bristev, Cz.; pop. 3; 56 km NE of Praha; 50°17'/15°14'.

Brist nad Bugie, *see* Brest.

Britavca, *see* Britovka.

Britavka, *see* Britovka.

Britcheva, *see* Bricheva.

Britovka, Ukr. (Britavca, Britavka); 107 km SW of Uman; 48°10'/29°11'; PHR1.

Britshan, *see* Brichany.

Britshani, *see* Brichany.

Britsiteni, *see* Brichany.

Briukhovo, GUM4. This town was not found in BGN gazetteers under the given spelling.

Brizdowitz, *see* Brzozowiec.

Brnenec, Cz. (Brunnlitz); pop. 17; 56 km NNW of Brno; 49°38'/16°31'; GUM3, GUM4, GUM5.

Brnik, Pol.; pop. 37; 75 km ENE of Krakow; 50°08'/21°00'.

Brno, Cz. (Bruenn, Brunn); pop. 11,003; 120 km NNW of Bratislava; 49°12'/16°38'; AMG, EJ, GUM3, GUM4, GUM5, GUM6, HSL, HSL2, JGFF, PHGB.

Brno Venkov, Cz.; pop. 863; Described in the *Black Book* as being in the Moravia-Silesia region of Czechoslovakia, this town was not found in BGN gazetteers.

Broceni, Lat.; pop. 4; 101 km WSW of Riga; 56°42'/22°32'.

Brod, *see* Brody.

Broda, *see* Uhersky Brod.

Brodanci, Yug.; pop. 1; 176 km WNW of Beograd; 45°32'/18°27'.

Brodenbach, Germ.; pop. 18; 88 km W of Frankfurt am Main; 50°14'/07°27'.

Brodina, Rom.; pop. 231; 182 km NE of Cluj; 47°53'/25°25'; PHR2.

Brodla, Pol.; pop. 19; 26 km WSW of Krakow; 50°03'/19°36'.

Brodnica, Pol.; pop. 56; 38 km WSW of Gdansk; 54°16'/18°05'; GUM4, LDS. *See also* Brodnitsa.

Brodnica (near Poznan), Pol.; 38 km S of Poznan; 52°09'/16°53'; CAHJP.

Brodnitsa, Byel. (Brodnica); pop. 26; 32 km W of Pinsk; 52°09'/25°42'.

Brodok, Ukr. (Vadul Nistrului); pop. 14; 38 km N of Chernovtsy; 48°37'/25°58'; HSL.

Brodshin, *see* Bogorodchany.

Brodski Varos, Yug.; pop. 1; 170 km ESE of Zagreb; 45°10'/18°00'.

Brod Slavonski, *see* Slavonski Brod.

Brod Uhersky, *see* Uhersky Brod.

Brody, Ukr. (Brod, Prode); pop. 7,202; 88 km NE of Lvov; 50°05'/25°09'; AMG, CAHJP, COH, EDRD, EGRS, EJ, GA, GUM3, GUM4, GUM5, HSL, HSL2, JGFF, LDL, LYV, PHP1, PHP2, PHP3, SF, YB.

Brody (near Bielsko Biala), Pol.; pop. 26; 32 km SSW of Krakow; 49°52'/19°42'.

Brody (near Radom), Pol.; pop. 91; 94 km WSW of Lublin; 51°02'/21°14'.

Brohin, *see* Bragin.

Brojce, Pol. (Bratz); 13 km ESE of Lodz; 51°40'/19°38'; HSL, LDS.

Brok, Pol.; pop. 873; 45 km SW of Bialystok; 52°56'/22°35'; COH, GUM3, HSL, HSL2, JGFF, SF.

Brok (Warszawa area), Pol.; 75 km NE of Warszawa; 52°42'/21°51'; GUM3, LDS, PHP4.

Brokeln, Germ.; 50 km S of Hannover; 51°58'/09°28'; LDS.

Brolniki, Byel.; pop. 41; 120 km SW of Minsk; 53°25'/25°55'. This town was located on an interwar map of Poland but does not appear in contemporary gazetteers. Map coordinates are approximate.

Bromberg, *see* Bydgoszcz.

Bromskirchen, Germ.; 114 km N of Frankfurt am Main; 51°05'/08°37'; JGFF, LDS.

Bronczyce, Pol.; pop. 9; 19 km NNE of Krakow; 50°14'/20°07'.

Bronica, *see* Bronitsa.

Broniewo, Pol.; 107 km ENE of Poznan; 52°40'/18°31'; GA.

Broniow, Pol.; pop. 4; 107 km ESE of Lodz; 51°17'/20°48'.

Bronislawowka, GUM5. This town was not found in BGN gazetteers under the given spelling.

Bronitsa, Ukr. (Bronica); pop. 50; 62 km SW of Lvov; 49°27'/23°20'; GA.

Bronka, Ukr. (Sico Branko, Sucha Bronka, Szuhabaranka); 170 km S of Lvov; 48°25'/23°16'; SM.

Bronnbach, Germ.; 75 km ESE of Frankfurt am Main; 49°43'/09°33'; PHGBW.

Bronnweiler, Germ.; 45 km S of Stuttgart; 48°27'/09°08'; PHGBW.

Bronocice, Pol.; pop. 24; 38 km NE of Krakow; 50°20'/20°21'.

Bronowice, Pol. AMG. A number of towns share this name. It was not possible to determine from available information which one is being referenced.

Bronowo Plewnik, Pol. (Pelvac Pelyva, Plewnik); 107 km N of Warszawa; 53°10'/20°53'; HSL.

Broos, *see* Orastie.

Broscauti, Rom. (Broscauti Dorohoi); pop. 24; 126 km NW of Iasi; 47°57'/26°27'.

Broscauti Dorohoi, *see* Broscauti.

Broscautii Noui, Rom.; pop. 68; This town was not found in BGN gazetteers under the given spelling.

Broscautii Vechi, *see* Bruskovtsy.

Broshnev Osada, Ukr. (Broshnyuv, Broszniow); pop. 223; 101 km SSE of Lvov; 48°59'/24°12'; GUM5, HSL, PHP2, YB.

Broshnyuv, *see* Broshnev Osada.

Broszecin, Pol.; pop. 15; 56 km SSW of Lodz; 51°17'/19°05'.

Broszniow, *see* Broshnev Osada.

Brotchin, *see* Bogorodchany.

Brotdorf, Germ.; pop. 26; 163 km SW of Frankfurt am Main; 49°28'/06°40'; GED.

Broumov, Cz. (Braunau); pop. 68; 146 km NE of Praha; 50°35'/16°20'; AMG, GUM6.

Brovari, *see* Brovary.

Brovary, Ukr. (Brovari, Browary); pop. 526; 19 km NE of Kiyev; 50°30'/30°46'; SF.

Browary, *see* Brovary.

Brtec, Cz.; pop. 63; BGN lists two possible localities with this name located at 49°29'/14°29' and 49°55'/16°07'.

Bruchhausen, Germ.; 69 km WNW of Hannover; 52°50'/09°01'; HSL.

Bruchsal, Germ.; pop. 603; 56 km WNW of Stuttgart; 49°08'/08°36'; AMG, HSL, HSL2, JGFF, PHGBW.

Bruck, Germ.; 75 km WNW of Nurnberg; 49°49'/10°09'; CAHJP, HSL, HSL2, PHGB. *See also* Bruck an der Grossglocknerstrasse.

Bruck an der Grossglocknerstrasse, Aus. (Bruck); pop. 42; 62 km S of Salzburg; 47°17'/12°49'.

Brucken, Germ. GED, JGFF. A number of towns share this name. It was not possible to determine from available information which one is being referenced.

Bruckenau, Germ.; pop. 128; 82 km ENE of Frankfurt am Main; 50°18'/09°48'; GUM5, PHGB.

Bruckneudorf, Aus.; pop. 33; 38 km ESE of Wien; 48°01'/16°47'.

Brudnica, *see* Brudnice.

Brudnice, Pol. (Brudnica); 120 km NW of Warszawa; 53°05'/19°53'; HSL.

Brudzen Duzy, Pol.; pop. 11; 107 km N of Lodz; 52°40'/19°31'.

Brudzew, Pol.; pop. 132; 75 km WNW of Lodz; 52°07'/18°36'; PHP1.

Brudzice, Pol.; pop. 7; 50 km N of Czestochowa; 51°10'/19°20'.

Bruel, Germ.; 50 km SSW of Rostock; 53°44'/11°43'; LDS.

Bruenn, *see* Brno.

Bruesau, *see* Brezova pod Bradlom.

Bruex, *see* Most.

Bruhl, Germ.; pop. 108; 19 km S of Koln; 50°50'/06°54'; GUM5, HSL, PHGBW.

Brunau, HSL. A number of towns share this name. It was not possible to determine from available information which one

is being referenced.

Brunava, Lat. (Brunaviski, Brunavitzik, Brunovishok, Brunovitshok, Brunovitzik); 69 km SSE of Riga; 56°22'/24°24'; JGFF, PHLE.

Brunaviski, *see* Brunava.

Brunavitzik, *see* Brunava.

Brunen, Germ.; pop. 14; 88 km NNW of Koln; 51°43'/06°41'.

Brunn, *see* Brno.

Brunn am Gebirge, Aus.; pop. 25; 19 km SSW of Wien; 48°06'/16°17'.

Brunnau, Germ.; pop. 69 km WNW of Nurnberg; 49°52'/10°21'; LDS, PHGB.

Brunnlitz, *see* Brnenec.

Brunovishok, *see* Brunava.

Brunovitshok, *see* Brunava.

Brunovitzik, *see* Brunava.

Brunsdorf, Pol. PHP1. This town was not found in BGN gazetteers under the given spelling.

Brunska Gora, Byel. (Brianska Gora); EDRD. A number of towns share this name. It was not possible to determine from available information which one is being referenced.

Brunswick, *see* Braunschweig.

Bruntal, Cz. (Freudenthal); pop. 81; 107 km NNE of Brno; 49°59'/17°28'; HSL, HSL2, JGFF.

Brus, Pol. (Bruss); pop. 29; 56 km NE of Lublin; 51°29'/23°18'; SF.

Brusilov, Ukr.; pop. 379; 75 km WSW of Kiyev; 50°17'/29°32'; EDRD, HSL, JGFF, LDL, SF.

Brusko Nowe, *see* Brusno Nowe.

Brusko Stare, *see* Brusno Stare.

Bruskovtsy, Ukr. (Broscautii Vechi); pop. 115; 19 km WSW of Chernovtsy; 48°15'/25°40'.

Brusnica, Cz.; 62 km NNE of Kosice; 49°09'/21°42'; AMG.

Brusnik, Pol.; 82 km ESE of Krakow; 49°45'/20°55'; GUM4.

Brusno Nowe, Pol. (Brusko Nowe); pop. 42; 62 km NNE of Przemysl; 50°14'/23°20'.

Brusno Stare, Pol. (Brusko Stare); pop. 54; 69 km NNE of Przemysl; 50°15'/23°22'.

Bruss, *see* Brus.

Brustura, *see* Lopukhov.

Brusturesti, Rom. (Borosznok); HSL. This pre-World War I community was not found in BGN gazetteers.

Brusturoasa, Rom.; 126 km SW of Iasi; 46°31'/26°12'; JGFF.

Brustury, Ukr. (Brister, Brusztura); pop. 52; 75 km WSW of Chernovtsy; 48°18'/24°53'; AMG, COH, LYV, SM.

Brusy, Pol.; pop. 24; 82 km SW of Gdansk; 53°53'/17°43'.

Bruszczewo, Pol.; 50 km SSW of Poznan; 52°01'/16°35'; GA.

Brusztura, *see* Brustury.

Bruttig, Germ.; pop. 7; 94 km SSE of Koln; 50°08'/07°14'.

Bruzdovitz, *see* Brzozowiec.

Bruzyca, Pol.; 13 km WNW of Lodz; 51°49'/19°19'; CAHJP. Bruzyca is now part of the town of Aleksandrow Lodzki. *See* Aleksandrow Lodzki.

Brvany, Cz.; pop. 1; 62 km WNW of Praha; 50°24'/13°44'.

Brwinow, Pol.; pop. 54; 26 km SW of Warszawa; 52°09'/20°43'; GUM4.

Bryanovo, Mold. (Breanova); pop. 6; 50 km NNW of Kishinev; 47°25'/28°39'.

Bryansk, USSR; pop. 2,500; 6 km SSW of Bryansk; 53°14'/34°21'.

Brykon, Ukr.; pop. 20; 50 km ENE of Lvov; 49°55'/24°41'.

Brykov, Ukr. (Brykow); pop. 23; 62 km S of Rovno; 50°06'/26°08'.

Brykow, *see* Brykov.

Brykuta Stara, Pol.; pop. 37; Described in the *Black Book* as being in the Tarnopol region of Poland, this town was not found in BGN gazetteers.

Brylince, Pol.; pop. 7; 19 km SW of Przemysl; 49°43'/22°40'.

Brylki, *see* Bril.

Bryn, *see* Brin.

Brynzeny, Mold. (Branzeni); pop. 29; 176 km WNW of

Kishinev; 48°05'/27°08'.

Bryshce, Ukr. (Bryszcze Samojlowka); pop. 23; Described in the *Black Book* as being in the Wolyn region of Poland, this town was not found in BGN gazetteers.

Bryszcze, Ukr.; pop. 24; 69 km WSW of Rovno; 50°35'/25°15'. This town was located on an interwar map of Poland but does not appear in contemporary gazetteers. Map coordinates are approximate.

Bryszcze Samojlowka, *see* Bryshce.

Bryukhovichi, Ukr. (Brzuchowice); pop. 60; 13 km NNW of Lvov; 49°54'/23°58'.

Brzaczowice, Pol.; pop. 15; 32 km SE of Krakow; 49°52'/20°04'.

Brzana, Pol.; pop. 49; 82 km ESE of Krakow; 49°43'/20°56'. The 1921 census of Poland shows two towns, Brzana Dolna and Brzana Gorna. The population figure shown here is the combined population.

Brzechow, Pol.; pop. 2; 107 km NNE of Krakow; 50°50'/20°47'.

Brzeg, Pol. (Brieg, Bzheg); pop. 255; 38 km ESE of Wroclaw; 50°52'/17°27'; EJ, GUM3, HSL, HSL2, LDS, POCEM.

Brzeg Dolny, Pol. (Brzegi, Dyhernfurth); 26 km WNW of Wroclaw; 51°11'/16°41'; EJ, GUM3, GUM4, GUM5, HSL.

Brzegi, *see* Brzeg Dolny.

Brzerzusnia, Pol.; pop. 36; Described in the *Black Book* as being in the Kielce region of Poland, this town was not found in BGN gazetteers.

Brzesc, Pol.; 101 km ENE of Poznan; 52°34'/18°25'; LDL.

Brzesciany, *possibly* Berezhany.

Brzescie (near Miechow), Pol.; pop. 26; 50 km N of Krakow; 50°31'/20°08'.

Brzescie (near Zwolen), Pol.; pop. 30; 88 km W of Lublin; 51°18'/21°18'.

Brzesc Kujawski, Pol. (Brest Kujavsk, Brisk D Koya, Brisk Kuyavsk); pop. 794; 101 km NNW of Lodz; 52°36'/18°54'; CAHJP, EDRD, EJ, GA, HSL, LDL, PHP4, SF, YB.

Brzesc Litewski, *see* Brest.

Brzesc nad Bugiem, *see* Brest.

Brzesko, Pol. (Briegel, Brigel); pop. 1,935; 50 km E of Krakow; 49°58'/20°37'; AMG, CAHJP, COH, EDRD, EGRS, GA, GUM3, GUM4, GUM5, HSL, HSL2, JGFF, LDL, LDS, PHP3, POCEM, SF, YB.

Brzesko Nowe, Pol.; pop. 457; 38 km ENE of Krakow; 50°08'/20°23'; GUM5.

Brzeszcze, Pol.; pop. 42; 56 km WSW of Krakow; 49°59'/19°09'.

Brzezany, *see* Berezhany.

Brzezawa, Pol.; pop. 36; 32 km SW of Przemysl; 49°41'/22°22'.

Brzezce, Pol.; 75 km WSW of Krakow; 49°59'/18°51'; EDRD.

Brzezhany, *see* Berezhany.

Brzezie, Pol.; pop. 28; 26 km ESE of Krakow; 49°59'/20°14'.

Brzezie Laskowa, Pol.; pop. 27; Described in the *Black Book* as being in the Kielce region of Poland, this town was not found in BGN gazetteers.

Brzezin, Pol. (Briesen); 120 km SSE of Szczecin; 52°25'/15°05'; CAHJP, HSL.

Brzezina, *see* Bzhezina.

Brzezinka, Pol. (Birkenau); pop. 233; 26 km SW of Krakow; 49°58'/19°39'; PHP3.

Brzezinki, Pol.; 56 km SSE of Warszawa; 51°48'/21°06'; GUM3.

Brzeziny, Pol. (Berzin, Bezhezhin, Brezhin, Breziny, Bzhezini, Bzheziny, Loewenstadt); pop. 4,979; 19 km ENE of Lodz; 51°48'/19°45'; AMG, CAHJP, EJ, GA, GUM3, GUM4, GUM5, GUM6, GYLA, HSL, HSL2, JGFF, LDS, LYV, PHP1, SF, YB.

Brzeziny (Krakow), Pol.; pop. 65; 56 km ESE of Czestochowa; 50°32'/19°49'.

Brzeziny (near Garwolin), Pol.; pop. 20; 69 km WNW of Lublin; 51°38'/21°50'.

Brzeziny (near Lublin), Pol.; pop. 23; 62 km ESE of Lublin; 50°56'/23°20'.

Brzezna, Pol.; pop. 8; 75 km SE of Krakow; 49°36'/20°37'.

Brzeznica, Pol. (Berzhnitse, Bzhezhnitsa); pop. 406; 69 km SW of Lodz; 51°26'/18°43'; CAHJP, COH, GUM3, GUM4, LDS, LYV, PHP1, YB.

Brzeznica (near Bielsko Biala), Pol.; pop. 24; 26 km SW of Krakow; 49°58'/19°38'; PHP3.

Brzeznica Bychawska, Pol.; pop. 25; 38 km N of Lublin; 51°32'/22°45'.

Brzeznica Ksiazeca, Pol.; pop. 5; 38 km N of Lublin; 51°33'/22°45'.

Brzeznica Stara, Pol. PHP1. This town was not found in BGN gazetteers under the given spelling.

Brzezowiec, Pol.; pop. 24; 50 km E of Krakow; 49°58'/20°38'.

Brzezowka, Pol.; pop. 21; 88 km ENE of Krakow; 50°16'/21°06'.

Brzhostik, *see* Brzostek.

Brzoski Tatary, Pol.; pop. 29; Described in the *Black Book* as being in the Bialystok region of Poland, this town was not found in BGN gazetteers.

Brzostek, Pol. (Brzhostik); pop. 479; 94 km W of Przemysl; 49°53'/21°25'; AMG, EGRS, HSL, LDL, PHP3, SF.

Brzostowa, Pol.; pop. 24; 82 km SW of Lublin; 50°54'/21°29'.

Brzostowa Gora, Pol.; pop. 3; 94 km WNW of Przemysl; 50°23'/21°47'.

Brzostowica, Byel. (Bolshaya Berestovit, Brzostowica Mala, Bzhostovitsa, Bzhostovitsa Mala, Bzhostovitsa Vielka, Mala Berestovitsa, Velikaya Berestovit); pop. 32; 182 km WNW of Pinsk; 53°11'/24°01'; COH, HSL, LYV.

Brzostowica Mala, *see* Brzostowica.

Brzostowica Wielka, *see* Bolshaya Berestovitsa.

Brzotice, Cz.; pop. 3; 62 km ESE of Praha; 49°40'/15°08'.

Brzotin, Cz. (Berzete); 56 km WSW of Kosice; 48°38'/20°30'; HSL.

Brzoza Krolewska, Pol.; pop. 69; 62 km NW of Przemysl; 50°15'/22°20'.

Brzoza Stadnicka, Pol.; pop. 25; 56 km NW of Przemysl; 50°12'/22°17'.

Brzozdowce, *possibly* Brzozowiec.

Brzozdowce Miasto, EGRS. This town was not found in BGN gazetteers under the given spelling.

Brzozki Brzezinskie, Pol.; pop. 22; Described in the *Black Book* as being in the Bialystok region of Poland, this town was not found in BGN gazetteers.

Brzozow, Pol. (Berezov); pop. 1,127; 56 km WSW of Przemysl; 49°42'/22°01'; AMG, CAHJP, COH, EDRD, EGRS, GA, GUM4, GUM5, HSL, HSL2, JGFF, LDL, PHP3, SF, YB.

Brzozowica Duza, Pol. (Brzozowica Wielka); pop. 8; 88 km N of Lublin; 51°58'/22°37'.

Brzozowica Mala, Pol.; pop. 12; 82 km N of Lublin; 51°57'/22°39'.

Brzozowica Wielka, *see* Brzozowica Duza.

Brzozowiec, Pol. (Brizdowitz, Bruzdovitz, Brzozdowce?); pop. 440; 56 km SW of Przemysl; 49°26'/22°12'; EDRD, LDL, PHP2, SF, WS.

Brzozow Stary, Pol.; pop. 8; 62 km W of Warszawa; 52°18'/20°03'.

Brzuchowice, *see* Bryukhovichi.

Brzuska, Pol.; pop. 61; 26 km WSW of Przemysl; 49°46'/22°29'.

Brzydzyn Nowy, Pol.; pop. 29; Described in the *Black Book* as being in the Kielce region of Poland, this town was not found in BGN gazetteers.

Brzyna, Pol.; pop. 15; 75 km SE of Krakow; 49°32'/20°30'.

Brzyska, Pol. (Brzyski); pop. 13; 101 km W of Przemysl; 49°50'/21°23'.

Brzyska Wola, Pol.; pop. 42; 62 km NNW of Przemysl; 50°20'/22°35'.

Brzyski, *see* Brzyska.

Brzyzna, Pol.; pop. 1; 88 km WNW of Przemysl; 50°03'/21°38'.

Bubel Lukowisko, Pol.; pop. 3; 107 km S of Bialystok; 52°14'/23°12'.

Bubel Stary, Pol.; pop. 3; 101 km S of Bialystok; 52°16'/23°12'.

Bublelai, *see* Bubleliai.

Bubleliai, Lith. (Bublelai); pop. 29; 62 km WSW of Kaunas; 54°50'/22°56'.

Buc, Yug.; 107 km WNW of Zagreb; 46°13'/14°44'; HSL, HSL2.

Bucea, Rom.; pop. 16; 69 km WNW of Cluj; 46°57'/22°44'.

Bucecea, Rom.; 107 km WNW of Iasi; 47°46'/26°26'; GUM4.

Bucha, HSL. A number of towns share this name. It was not possible to determine from available information which one is being referenced.

Buchach, Ukr. (Bitshutsh, Buczacz, Butchatch); pop. 3,858; 94 km NW of Chernovtsy; 49°04'/25°24'; AMG, CAHJP, COH, EDRD, EGRS, EJ, GA, GUM3, GUM4, GUM5, GUM6, GYLA, HSL, HSL2, JGFF, LDL, LYV, PHP2, SF, YB.

Bucharest, *see* Bucuresti.

Buchau, Germ. (Bad Buchau); pop. 247; 82 km SSE of Stuttgart; 48°04'/09°37'; GED, GUM4, HSL, JGFF, PHGBW.

Buchberg, (Bukkhegy); GUM3, GUM5. A number of towns share this name. It was not possible to determine from available information which one is being referenced.

Buchel, GUM4. A number of towns share this name. It was not possible to determine from available information which one is being referenced.

Buchen, Germ.; pop. 40; 82 km SE of Frankfurt am Main; 49°31'/09°20'; GED, HSL, LDS, PHGBW.

Buchenau, Germ.; 94 km N of Frankfurt am Main; 50°53'/08°36'; LDS.

Buchenbach, Germ.; 19 km NW of Nurnberg; 49°35'/10°58'; JGFF, PHGB.

Buchenbeuren, Germ.; pop. 5; 101 km WSW of Frankfurt am Main; 49°55'/07°16'.

Buchholz, Germ.; 26 km S of Hamburg; 53°20'/09°52'; LDS.

Buchlicze, Ukr.; pop. 24; 94 km N of Rovno; 51°25'/26°45'. This town was located on an interwar map of Poland but does not appear in contemporary gazetteers. Map coordinates are approximate.

Buchloe, Germ.; pop. 1; 62 km WSW of Munchen; 48°02'/10°44'; GUM3.

Buchowice, Ukr.; pop. 37; 82 km SW of Lvov; 49°25'/23°05'. This town was located on an interwar map of Poland but does not appear in contemporary gazetteers. Map coordinates are approximate.

Buchowo, *see* Bukhovo.

Buchowszczyzna Nowa, Byel.; pop. 41; 50 km WNW of Minsk; 54°05'/26°55'. This town was located on an interwar map of Poland but does not appear in contemporary gazetteers. Map coordinates are approximate.

Bucici, Yug.; pop. 9; 195 km SE of Zagreb; 44°20'/17°23'.

Bucium, Rom. (Bucsum); 157 km SE of Cluj; 45°44'/25°05'; HSL, HSL2.

Buciumi, Rom. (Varmezo); BGN lists two possible localities with this name located at 46°12'/26°47' and 47°28'/23°29'. HSL, HSL2, LDL, PHR2.

Buciumi Salaj, Rom.; pop. 41; 50 km WNW of Cluj; 47°02'/23°04'.

Buciumi Satu Mare, Rom.; pop. 35; 82 km N of Cluj; 47°28'/23°29'.

Buck, *possibly* Buk.

Buckeburg, Germ.; pop. 63; 50 km WSW of Hannover; 52°16'/09°03'; AMG, GED, GUM4, HSL, JGFF.

Bucki, Pol.; 133 km NNW of Bialystok; 54°17'/22°45'; GUM3.

Bucniow, *see* Butsnev.

Bucovat, *see* Bykovets.

Bucovice, Cz. (Butschowitz); pop. 87; 26 km E of Brno; 49°09'/17°00'; EJ, GUM5, HSL, HSL2.

Bucovina (Bukovina); Not a town but a region now in northeastern Romania and the southwestern Ukraine. It was part of the Austro-Hungarian Empire prior to the end of World War I and then part of Romania until the end of World War II.

Bucow, *possibly* Bukova.

Bucsitura, Rom. (Bucsoaia); 146 km WNW of Iasi; 47°33'/25°49'; PHR2.

Bucsko, COH. This town was not found in BGN gazetteers under the given spelling.

Bucsoaia, *see* Bucsitura.

Bucsum, *see* Bucium.

Bucsuszentlaszlo, Hung.; pop. 19; 45 km N of Nagykanizsa; 46°47'/16°57'.

Bucuresti, Rom. (Bucharest); pop. 74,480; 133 km S of Iasi; 46°03'/27°35'; AMG, CAHJP, EDRD, EJ, GUM3, GUM4, GUM5, GUM6, GYLA, HSL, HSL2, ISH1, ISH3, JGFF, LDL, LJEE, PHP1, PHP2, PHR1.

Bucyki, *see* Butsyki.

Bucyn, *see* Butsyn.

Buczacz, *see* Buchach.

Buczkow, Pol.; pop. 19; 50 km E of Krakow; 50°03'/20°34'.

Buczkowice, Pol.; pop. 15; 69 km SW of Krakow; 49°44'/19°04'.

Buczkowska Wola, Pol.; pop. 9; 38 km SSW of Lodz; 51°32'/19°09'.

Buda, *see* Budapest.

Budaabrany, Hung.; 114 km ESE of Miskolc; 47°32'/22°00'; LDS.

Budachi, *see* Primorskoye (Bessarabia I).

Budafok, Hung.; pop. 366; 13 km S of Budapest; 47°26'/19°03'; GUM5, PHH.

Budahaz, *see* Budince.

Budakalasz, Hung.; pop. 52; 19 km NNW of Budapest; 47°37'/19°03'; GUM5, PHH.

Budakeszi, Hung.; pop. 25; 13 km W of Budapest; 47°31'/18°56'.

Buda Koshelevo, Byel.; 45 km NW of Gomel; 52°43'/30°34'; GUM4.

Budanov, Ukr. (Bizinev, Bizinov, Biznov, Budzanov, Budzanow, Budzanuv); pop. 1,156; 101 km NNW of Chernovtsy; 49°10'/25°43'; EDRD, EGRS, EJ, GUM3, GUM4, GUM5, GYLA, HSL, JGFF, LDL, LYV, PHP1, PHP2, SF, YB.

Budaors, Hung.; pop. 1; 13 km SW of Budapest; 47°27'/18°58'.

Budapest, Hung. (Alt Ofen, Buda, Budon, Kobanya, Obuda, Ofen, Pest); pop. 184,453; 139 km SW of Miskolc; 47°30'/19°05'; AMG, EDRD, EJ, GUM3, GUM4, GUM5, GUM6, HSL, HSL2, ISH1, ISH2, ISH3, JGFF, LDL, LDS, LJEE, PHH, PHP2, PHP3, YB, YL.

Budatelec, Rom. (Budatelke); 50 km ENE of Cluj; 46°52'/24°15'; HSL. This town was located on a pre-World War I map, but does not appear in contemporary gazetteers.

Budatelke, *see* Budatelec.

Budateteny, Hung.; pop. 11; 19 km SSW of Budapest; 47°25'/19°01'.

Budcha, Byel. (Budcza); pop. 6; 88 km NNE of Pinsk; 52°45'/26°50'.

Budcza, *see* Budcha.

Bude, *see* Budey.

Budejovice, *see* Ceske Budejovice.

Buderaz, *see* Buderazh.

Buderazh, Ukr. (Buderaz); pop. 13; 38 km S of Rovno; 50°20'/26°08'.

Buderich, Germ.; 82 km NNW of Koln; 51°38'/06°35'; GED.

Budes, *see* Budesti Maramures.

Budesheim, Germ.; pop. 51; 88 km S of Koln; 50°13'/06°33'.

Budesti, *see* Budesti Maramures.

Budesti Maramures, Rom. (Budes, Budesti, Budfalva); pop. 405; 114 km N of Cluj; 47°44'/23°57'; AMG, GUM4, HSL, PHR2, SM.

Budevitz, *see* Budvieciai.

Budey, Mold. (Bude); 26 km SE of Kishinev; 46°49'/28°59'; HSL.

Budfalva, *see* Budesti Maramures.

Budi, *see* Budy.

Budimci, Yug.; pop. 2; 182 km WNW of Beograd; 45°28'/18°20'.

Budin, *see* Budyne nad Ohri.

Budina, *see* Budyne nad Ohri.

Budince, Cz. (Budahaz); 69 km ESE of Kosice; 48°32'/22°07'; HSL.

Buding, HSL. This pre-World War I community was not found

42

in BGN gazetteers.

Budingen, Germ.; pop. 150; 38 km NE of Frankfurt am Main; 50°18'/09°07'; HSL.

Budinscina, Yug.; pop. 3; 45 km N of Zagreb; 46°07'/16°12'.

Budis, Cz.; 146 km NE of Bratislava; 48°52'/18°46'; HSL.

Budisava, Yug.; pop. 7; 62 km NW of Beograd; 45°17'/20°00'.

Budislav, *see* Budslav.

Budiul de Campie, Rom. (Mezobodon); 50 km ESE of Cluj; 46°33'/24°12'; HSL. This town was located on a pre-World War I map, but does not appear in contemporary gazetteers.

Budki Neznanovske, Ukr. (Budki Nieznanowskie); pop. 9; 50 km NNE of Lvov; 50°10'/24°29'.

Budki Nieznanowskie, *see* Budki Neznanovske.

Budkov, Ukr. (Budkow, Budkuv); pop. 27; 26 km SE of Lvov; 49°41'/24°11'.

Budkovce, Cz. (Butka); pop. 99; 50 km E of Kosice; 48°38'/21°56'; HSL.

Budkow, *see* Budkov.

Budkuv, *see* Budkov.

Budniki, Byel.; 45 km SW of Vitebsk; 55°00'/29°35'; HSL.

Budomierz, Pol.; pop. 66; 50 km NE of Przemysl; 50°07'/23°17'.

Budon, *see* Budapest.

Budslav, Byel. (Boid, Budislav, Budslaw, Butslav, Butzlav); pop. 140; 107 km N of Minsk; 54°47'/27°27'; COH, HSL, LDL, LYV, SF.

Budslaw, *see* Budslav.

Budszentmihaly, Hung.; pop. 673; 45 km ESE of Miskolc; 47°58'/21°22'; COH, HSL, LDL, LDS, PHH.

Buduri, *see* Kochkovatoye.

Budus, Rom.; pop. 41; 82 km NE of Cluj; 47°05'/24°32'.

Buduslau, Rom.; pop. 25; 126 km WNW of Cluj; 47°24'/22°16'.

Budva, Yug.; pop. 1; 214 km W of Skopje; 42°17'/18°51'.

Budvieciai, Lith. (Budevitz, Budvitch); JGFF. A number of towns share this name. It was not possible to determine from available information which one is being referenced.

Budvietis, Lith.; pop. 20; 82 km SSW of Kaunas; 54°18'/23°20'.

Budvitch, *see* Budvieciai.

Budweis, *see* Ceske Budejovice.

Budwiecie, Pol.; 139 km NNW of Bialystok; 54°19'/22°31'; SF.

Budy, Ukr. (Budi); pop. 21; 19 km SW of Kharkov; 49°53'/36°02'; GUM3, JGFF, PHR1.

Budy Augustowskie, Pol.; pop. 1; 69 km SSE of Warszawa; 51°41'/21°12'.

Budy Barczackie, Pol.; pop. 5; 50 km E of Warszawa; 52°10'/21°38'.

Budy Bielanskie, Pol. (Bielany Budy, Siniec); 50 km N of Warszawa; 52°41'/20°55'; PHP3.

Budy Krepskie, Pol.; pop. 5; 69 km SE of Warszawa; 51°46'/21°34'.

Budy Lancuckie, Pol.; pop. 74; 45 km NW of Przemysl; 50°07'/22°26'.

Budylov, Ukr. (Budylow); pop. 24; 94 km ESE of Lvov; 49°31'/25°15'.

Budylow, *see* Budylov.

Budymle, *see* Budymlya.

Budymlya, Ukr. (Budymle); pop. 23; 133 km NNE of Rovno; 51°40'/26°59'.

Budyne nad Ohri, Cz. (Budin, Budina); pop. 46; 38 km NW of Praha; 50°24'/14°09'; EJ, HSL, HSL2.

Budynin, *see* Budzynin.

Budy Usniackie, Pol.; pop. 9; 50 km SE of Warszawa; 51°55'/21°28'.

Budy Wielgoleskie, Pol. (Wielgolaskie Budki); pop. 8; 56 km ESE of Warszawa; 52°02'/21°42'.

Budy Zaklasztorne, Pol.; pop. 3; 56 km SW of Warszawa; 52°00'/20°19'.

Budzanov, *see* Budanov.

Budzanow, *see* Budanov.

Budzanuv, *see* Budanov.

Budzhin, *see* Budzyn.

Budzin, *see* Budzyn.

Budziska, Pol.; pop. 119; 56 km NE of Warszawa; 52°32'/21°40'.

Budziszyn, Pol.; pop. 6; 50 km S of Warszawa; 51°53'/21°04'.

Budziszynek, Pol.; pop. 5; 50 km S of Warszawa; 51°52'/21°04'.

Budzyn, Pol. (Budzhin, Budzin); See listings below.

Budzyn (Lublin area), Pol.; pop. 27; 45 km SSW of Lublin; 50°57'/22°12'; FRG, GUM3, GUM4, GUM5, GUM6, HSL.

Budzyn (Poznan area), Pol.; pop. 21; 56 km N of Poznan; 52°53'/16°59'.

Budzynin, Pol. (Budynin); pop. 55; 107 km NE of Przemysl; 50°26'/23°57'.

Buer, Germ.; pop. 150; 88 km WSW of Hannover; 52°15'/08°24'; AMG, LDS.

Buetow, *see* Butow.

Bugai, *see* Skaudvile.

Bugaj, Pol.; pop. 48; 45 km NE of Czestochowa; 50°55'/19°38'; EDRD, GUM5, PHP1, POCEM.

Bugakov, Ukr. (Bugakow); 50 km SE of Vinnitsa; 48°54'/28°56'; PHR1.

Bugakow, *see* Bugakov.

Buglov, Ukr. (Bugluv, Buhlow); pop. 23; 101 km S of Rovno; 49°46'/26°03'.

Bugluv, *see* Buglov.

Bugojno, Yug.; pop. 46; 221 km SE of Zagreb; 44°03'/17°27'; EJ, PHY.

Bugryn, Ukr. (Buhryn); pop. 4; 19 km ESE of Rovno; 50°33'/26°32'.

Bugyi, Hung.; pop. 601; 38 km SSE of Budapest; 47°13'/19°09'; PHH.

Buhl, Germ.; pop. 111; 75 km WSW of Stuttgart; 48°42'/08°09'; AMG, GUM5, HSL, HSL2, LDS, PHGBW.

Buhlow, *see* Buglov.

Buhryn, *see* Bugryn.

Buhusi, Rom.; 82 km SW of Iasi; 46°43'/26°42'; EJ, GUM4, HSL, JGFF, LDL, PHR1.

Buia, Rom. (Bolya); 101 km SE of Cluj; 45°58'/24°17'; HSL.

Buj, Hung.; pop. 104; 69 km E of Miskolc; 48°06'/21°39'; PHH.

Bujakow, Pol.; pop. 69 km S of Czestochowa; 50°11'/18°49'; GUM3.

Bujaly Gniewosze, Pol.; pop. 5; 94 km SSW of Bialystok; 52°28'/22°21'.

Bujaly Mikosze, Pol.; pop. 8; 94 km SSW of Bialystok; 52°28'/22°22'.

Bujanhaza, *see* Boinesti.

Bujawa, Pol.; pop. 33; Described in the *Black Book* as being in the Lwow region of Poland, this town was not found in BGN gazetteers.

Bujniczki, Pol.; pop. 9; 62 km NNE of Czestochowa; 51°13'/19°38'.

Bujor, Rom. (Bozsor); 150 km SSE of Iasi; 45°52'/27°54'; PHR1.

Bujoru, *see* Buzhory.

Buk, (Buck?); HSL. A number of towns share this name. It was not possible to determine from available information which one is being referenced.

Bukachevtsy, Ukr. (Bukaczowce, Bukotchovitz, Bukshevitz); pop. 733; 82 km SE of Lvov; 49°15'/24°30'; COH, EGRS, GUM3, JGFF, LDL, PHP2, SF, YB.

Bukaczowce, *see* Bukachevtsy.

Bukavitz, *see* Bykovka.

Bukharino, USSR; pop. 81; This town was not found in BGN gazetteers under the given spelling.

Bukhovo, Bulg. (Buchowo); 26 km NE of Sofija; 42°46'/23°34'; HSL, HSL2.

Buki, Ukr. (Baki); 38 km N of Uman; 49°05'/30°25'; SF.

Bukin, *see* Mladenovo.

Bukkaranyos, Hung.; pop. 19; 19 km S of Miskolc; 47°59'/20°47'.

Bukkfalva, *see* Bykovets.

Bukkhegy, *see* Buchberg.

Bukkormenyes, *see* Urmenis.

Bukkosd, Hung.; pop. 10; 88 km ESE of Nagykanizsa;

46°06'/17°59'.

Bukkospatak, *see* Velikiy Bychkov.

Bukkszenterzsebet, Hung.; pop. 14; 45 km WSW of Miskolc; 48°03'/20°10'.

Bukkszentmarton, Hung. (Borsodszentmarton); pop. 4; 32 km WSW of Miskolc; 48°04'/20°21'.

Bukkzserc, Hung.; pop. 2; 26 km SW of Miskolc; 47°58'/20°30'.

Bukmuiza, Lat.; pop. 7; 75 km NE of Daugavpils; 56°11'/27°39'.

Bukotchovitz, *see* Bukachevtsy.

Bukov, Cz.; pop. 24; 45 km WNW of Brno; 49°27'/16°13'.

Bukova, Ukr. (Bucow?); pop. 55; 82 km SW of Lvov; 49°35'/23°00'.

Bukovec, *see* Velikiy Bychkov.

Bukovecz, *see* Bykovets.

Bukovina, Cz. (Gugel); pop. 8; 62 km NNW of Praha; 50°37'/14°18'. This name usually refers to the region of interwar Romania rather than this particular town. *See* Bucovina.

Bukovinka, Ukr. (Bukowinka); 114 km SSW of Lvov; 49°00'/23°06'; GUM4, HSL.

Bukovnica, Yug.; pop. 1; 107 km N of Zagreb; 46°42'/16°20'.

Bukovska, *see* Bukowsko.

Bukowa (near Piotrkow Trybunalski), Pol.; pop. 30; 56 km S of Lodz; 51°19'/19°28'.

Bukowa (near Zamosc), Pol.; pop. 29; 75 km S of Lublin; 50°35'/22°34'; GA.

Bukowa Mala, Pol.; pop. 10; 69 km ENE of Lublin; 51°18'/23°31'.

Bukowice, Pol.; pop. 13; 107 km N of Lublin; 52°09'/23°00'; JGFF.

Bukowiec, Pol.; pop. 31; 62 km SSW of Przemysl; 49°19'/22°25'; GA, PHP1.

Bukowina, Pol.; pop. 42; 82 km NW of Przemysl; 50°26'/22°19'. This name usually refers to the region of interwar Romania rather than this particular town. *see* Bucovina.

Bukowinka, *see* Bukovinka.

Bukowski Las, Pol.; pop. 54; 62 km ENE of Lublin; 51°22'/23°27'.

Bukowsko, Pol. (Bakavsk, Bikovsk, Bukovska); pop. 623; 62 km SW of Przemysl; 49°29'/22°04'; COH, EGRS, GA, GUM5, HSL, HSL2, JGFF, LDL, PHP3, POCEM, SF, YB.

Bukshevitz, *see* Bukachevtsy.

Buksztel, Pol.; pop. 15; 26 km NNE of Bialystok; 53°19'/23°19'.

Bul'boka, Mold. (Bulboaca); pop. 3; 38 km ESE of Kishinev; 46°53'/29°18'.

Bulaesti, *see* Bulayeshty.

Bulayeshty, Mold. (Bulaesti); pop. 30; 56 km N of Kishinev; 47°28'/28°59'.

Bulboaca, *see* Bul'boka.

Bulkovo, Byel. (Bulkowo); pop. 45; 150 km WSW of Pinsk; 52°07'/23°56'.

Bulkowo, *see* Bulkovo.

Bullenheim, Germ.; pop. 54; 62 km WNW of Nurnberg; 49°38'/10°14'; HSL, PHGB.

Bultrimantz, *see* Butrimoniai.

Bulz, Rom. (Csarnohaza); pop. 7; 69 km W of Cluj; 46°55'/22°41'.

Bumsla, *see* Mlada Boleslav.

Bun, *see* Boiu Mare.

Bunde, Germ.; pop. 72; 75 km WSW of Hannover; 52°12'/08°35'; GUM5, LDS.

Bunde (near Emden), Germ.; pop. 52; 182 km WSW of Hamburg; 53°11'/07°16'.

Bundorf, Germ.; 94 km NW of Nurnberg; 50°13'/10°31'; PHGB.

Bunkas, Lat.; pop. 1; 163 km WSW of Riga; 56°35'/21°28'.

Bunov, Ukr. (Bonow, Bonuv); pop. 37; 50 km W of Lvov; 49°54'/23°16'.

Burakowka, *see* Buryakovka.

Burczyce Stare, Ukr.; pop. 25; 88 km SSW of Lvov; 49°15'/23°15'. This town was located on an interwar map of Poland but does not appear in contemporary gazetteers.

Map coordinates are approximate.

Burdiakowce, *see* Burdyakovtsy.

Burdujeni, Rom.; pop. 1,244; 114 km WNW of Iasi; 47°41'/26°17'; AMG, EDRD, GUM4, GUM6, GYLA, HSL, LDL.

Burdyakovtse, *see* Burdyakovtsy.

Burdyakovtsy, Ukr. (Burdiakowce, Burdyakovtse); pop. 29; 69 km N of Chernovtsy; 48°54'/26°10'; PHP2.

Burdykovshchina, Byel. (Berdowszczyzna?); pop. 30; 126 km SW of Minsk; 53°21'/25°52'.

Buren, Germ.; pop. 54; 126 km SSW of Hannover; 51°33'/08°34'; GED, GUM5, JGFF, LDS.

Burenice, Cz.; pop. 5; 75 km SE of Praha; 49°33'/15°04'.

Burg, Germ.; pop. 84; 107 km WSW of Berlin; 52°16'/11°51'; GUM3, GUM5.

Burgambach, Germ.; 56 km WNW of Nurnberg; 49°41'/10°25'; JGFF, PHGB.

Burgas, Bulg.; pop. 1,520; 88 km S of Varna; 42°30'/27°28'; EJ, GUM4.

Burgau, Germ.; 94 km WNW of Munchen; 48°26'/10°24'; GUM3, GUM4, GUM5, GUM6, PHGB.

Burgbernheim, Germ.; pop. 1; 56 km WSW of Nurnberg; 49°27'/10°19'; CAHJP, PHGB.

Burgbrohl, Germ.; pop. 16; 62 km SE of Koln; 50°27'/07°17'.

Burgdorf, Germ.; pop. 40; 26 km NE of Hannover; 52°27'/10°01'.

Burgebrach, Germ.; pop. 5; 50 km NW of Nurnberg; 49°50'/10°45'; PHGB.

Burgel, Germ.; pop. 83; 6 km E of Frankfurt am Main; 50°07'/08°47'; CAHJP, JGFF.

Burgellern, Germ.; 62 km N of Nurnberg; 49°59'/11°03'; PHGB.

Burgeln, Germ.; 88 km N of Frankfurt am Main; 50°51'/08°49'; AMG.

Burgenland; Not a town, but an area in Austria that was part of Hungary until 1920.

Burgezd, *see* Bilghez.

Burg Grafenrode, Germ. (Burggrafenrode); pop. 150; 26 km NNE of Frankfurt am Main; 50°16'/08°48'; LDS.

Burggrafenrode, *see* Burg Grafenrode.

Burghaslach, Germ. (Furstenforst); pop. 73; 50 km WNW of Nurnberg; 49°44'/10°36'; CAHJP, GUM5, JGFF, PHGB.

Burghaun, Germ.; pop. 112; 101 km NE of Frankfurt am Main; 50°42'/09°43'.

Burghausen, Germ.; 94 km ENE of Munchen; 48°10'/12°50'; PHGB.

Burgheim, Germ.; 75 km NW of Munchen; 48°42'/11°01'; PHGB.

Burgholzhausen, Germ.; 26 km N of Frankfurt am Main; 50°15'/08°40'; LDS.

Burgkundstadt, *see* Burgkunstadt.

Burgkunstadt, Germ. (Altenkunstadt, Burgkundstadt); pop. 59; 82 km N of Nurnberg; 50°08'/11°15'; CAHJP, GED, GUM4, GUM5, HSL, HSL2, JGFF, LDL, PHGB.

Burglesau, Germ.; 62 km N of Nurnberg; 50°00'/11°05'; PHGB.

Burgpreppach, Germ.; pop. 89; 82 km NNW of Nurnberg; 50°08'/10°39'; CAHJP, GUM4, GUM5, HSL, HSL2, PHGB.

Burgsinn, Germ.; pop. 42; 69 km ENE of Frankfurt am Main; 50°09'/09°39'; GUM5, PHGB.

Burgsteinfurt, Germ.; pop. 122; 139 km N of Koln; 52°09'/07°20'; AMG, CAHJP, GED, GUM5, HSL.

Burgugi, *see* Vinogradovka.

Burhave, Germ.; pop. 4; 107 km W of Hamburg; 53°35'/08°22'.

Burin, *see* Buryn.

Burkanow, *see* Burkanuv.

Burkanuv, Ukr. (Burkanow); pop. 110; 114 km NNW of Chernovtsy; 49°17'/25°23'; PHP2.

Burkhardsfelden, Germ.; 62 km N of Frankfurt am Main; 50°35'/08°49'; LDS.

Burlaneshty, Rom. (Burlanesti); pop. 22; 114 km NNW of Iasi; 48°08'/27°07'.

Burlanesti, *see* Burlaneshty.

Burniszki, Pol.; pop. 8; 146 km NNW of Bialystok; 54°23'/22°51'.

Burnosy, Byel.; pop. 7; 133 km WSW of Minsk; 53°49'/25°35'.

Burshtin, see Burshtyn.

Burshtyn, Ukr. (Burshtin, Bursztyn); pop. 379; 82 km SE of Lvov; 49°16'/24°38'; AMG, COH, EDRD, EGRS, GUM4, GUM5, HSL, HSL2, LDL, PHP2, SF, YB.

Burstadt, Germ.; pop. 38; 56 km S of Frankfurt am Main; 49°38'/08°27'; JGFF, LDS.

Bursz, Pol.; pop. 5; 114 km NW of Warszawa; 53°11'/20°12'.

Bursztyn, see Burshtyn.

Burty, Ukr. (Berta); 101 km NE of Uman; 49°07'/31°27'; LDL, SF.

Burwin, Pol.; pop. 3; 82 km NNE of Lublin; 51°56'/23°04'.

Buryakovka, Ukr. (Burakowka); pop. 60; 75 km NNW of Chernovtsy; 48°55'/25°35'.

Buryn, Ukr. (Burin); pop. 33; 45 km E of Konotop; 51°12'/33°49'.

Burzec, Pol.; pop. 10; 69 km NNW of Lublin; 51°48'/22°16'.

Burzenin, Pol.; pop. 228; 56 km SW of Lodz; 51°28'/18°50'; AMG, LDL, LDS, PHP1, SF.

Burzuc, Rom. (Borszeg); pop. 20; 114 km WNW of Cluj; 47°09'/22°11'.

Burzysk, Pol. PHP4. This town was not found in BGN gazetteers under the given spelling.

Busag, Rom.; pop. 22; 101 km NNW of Cluj; 47°39'/23°25'.

Busenberg, Germ.; pop. 28; 107 km WNW of Stuttgart; 49°08'/07°50'.

Busendorf, HSL. A number of towns share this name. It was not possible to determine from available information which one is being referenced.

Busenhausen, Germ.; pop. 4; 56 km ESE of Koln; 50°43'/07°38'.

Bushche, Ukr. (Buszcze); pop. 41; 69 km ESE of Lvov; 49°33'/24°54'; PHP2.

Bushila, Mold. (Busila); pop. 4; 94 km WNW of Kishinev; 47°24'/27°48'.

Bushovka, Mold. (Busovca); pop. 22; 69 km N of Kishinev; 47°35'/28°48'.

Bushtina, see Bushtyna.

Bushtyna, Ukr. (Bistina, Bushtina, Bustina, Bustino, Bustyahaza); pop. 500; 189 km WSW of Chernovtsy; 48°03'/23°28'; AMG, COH, HSL, HSL2, SM.

Bushyki, Byel. (Buszyki); pop. 9; 157 km N of Minsk; 55°16'/27°41'.

Busila, see Bushila.

Busk, Ukr.; pop. 1,533; 50 km NE of Lvov; 49°58'/24°38'; AMG, COH, EDRD, EGRS, EJ, GA, GUM3, GUM4, GUM5, HSL, HSL2, JGFF, LDL, LYV, PHP2, SF. See also Busko Zdroj.

Busko, see Busko Zdroj.

Buskovice, Cz.; pop. 82 km W of Praha; 50°13'/13°22'; GUM4.

Busko Zdroj, Pol. (Busk, Busk Zadroi, Busko); pop. 1,464; 69 km NE of Krakow; 50°28'/20°43'; AMG, CAHJP, EDRD, GA, GUM3, GUM4, GUM5, GYLA, JGFF, LYV, PHP4, POCEM, SF, YB.

Busk Zadroi, see Busko Zdroj.

Busno, Pol.; 88 km ESE of Lublin; 50°58'/23°45'; GA.

Busovca, see Bushovka.

Busovisko, Ukr. (Busowisko); pop. 28; 88 km SW of Lvov; 49°23'/22°59'.

Busowisko, see Busovisko.

Busowno, Pol. (Bussowno); pop. 28; 50 km ENE of Lublin; 51°16'/23°18'.

Buss, see Bous.

Bussowno, see Busowno.

Bussu, Hung.; pop. 5; 75 km ENE of Nagykanizsa; 46°28'/17°58'.

Bustehrad, Cz.; pop. 10; 19 km WNW of Praha; 50°09'/14°11'.

Bustina, see Bushtyna.

Bustino, see Bushtyna.

Bustyahaza, see Bushtyna.

Buszcze, see Bushche.

Buszkow, Pol.; pop. 5; 45 km NNE of Krakow; 50°23'/20°18'.

Buszkowice, Pol.; pop. 35; 6 km N of Przemysl; 49°49'/22°48'.

Buszkowiczki, Pol.; pop. 24; 6 km NNE of Przemysl; 49°49'/22°49'.

Buszyki, see Bushyki.

Butani, Rom.; pop. 2; 94 km WNW of Cluj; 47°01'/22°26'.

Butchatch, see Buchach.

Butelka Nizna, Ukr.; pop. 81; 146 km SSW of Lvov; 48°45'/22°55'. This town was located on an interwar map of Poland but does not appear in contemporary gazetteers. Map coordinates are approximate.

Butelka Wyzna, Ukr.; pop. 66; 146 km SSW of Lvov; 48°45'/22°55'. This town was located on an interwar map of Poland but does not appear in contemporary gazetteers. Map coordinates are approximate.

Buten, see Byten.

Buteni, Rom.; pop. 120 km SW of Cluj; 46°19'/22°07'; HSL2, PHR1.

Butenkovo, see Kobelyaki.

Butiza, see Botiza.

Butka, see Budkovce.

Butla, Ukr.; pop. 182; 157 km SSW of Lvov; 48°35'/23°05'; HSL, PHP2. This town was located on an interwar map of Poland but does not appear in contemporary gazetteers. Map coordinates are approximate.

Butmer, see Pripyat.

Butow, Pol. (Buetow, Bytow); pop. 114; 82 km WSW of Gdansk; 54°10'/17°30'; LDS.

Butrimants, see Butrimoniai.

Butrimoniai, Lith. (Baltrimontz, Bultrimantz, Butrimants, Butrimonicai, Butrimontz, Butrimonys, Butyrmantsy); pop. 948; 69 km N of Kaunas; 55°29'/24°08'; GUM3, HSL, JGFF, SF, YL.

Butrimonicai, see Butrimoniai.

Butrimontz, see Butrimoniai.

Butrimonys, see Butrimoniai.

Butschowitz, see Bucovice.

Butsin, see Butsyn.

Butslav, see Budslav.

Butsnev, Ukr. (Bucniow); pop. 22; 120 km ESE of Lvov; 49°28'/25°33'.

Butsyki, Ukr. (Bucyki); pop. 36; 114 km N of Chernovtsy; 49°19'/26°02'.

Butsyn, Ukr. (Bucyn, Butsin); pop. 46; 146 km WNW of Rovno; 51°25'/24°36'.

Buttelborn, Germ.; pop. 27; 26 km SSW of Frankfurt am Main; 49°54'/08°31'; JGFF.

Buttenhausen, Germ.; pop. 92; 50 km SE of Stuttgart; 48°22'/09°29'; JGFF, PHGBW.

Buttenheim, Germ.; pop. 17; 45 km N of Nurnberg; 49°48'/11°02'; HSL, HSL2, JGFF, PHGB.

Buttenwiesen, Germ.; pop. 98; 82 km WNW of Munchen; 48°36'/10°43'; AMG, GED, HSL, PHGB, PHGBW.

Butthard, see Butthart.

Butthart, Germ. (Butthard); pop. 8; 88 km W of Nurnberg; 49°36'/09°53'; GUM5, LDS, PHGB.

Buttos, Hung.; pop. 19; 50 km N of Miskolc; 48°29'/21°01'.

Butyny, Ukr.; pop. 80; 45 km N of Lvov; 50°14'/23°59'.

Butyrmantsy, see Butrimoniai.

Butzbach, Germ.; pop. 139; 45 km N of Frankfurt am Main; 50°26'/08°41'; GED, JGFF, LDS.

Butzlav, see Budslav.

Butzow, Germ.; 32 km S of Rostock; 53°51'/11°59'; HSL, LDS.

Butzweiler, Germ.; pop. 50; 133 km S of Koln; 49°49'/06°37'.

Buxtehude, Germ.; pop. 26 km SW of Hamburg; 53°27'/09°42'; GUM4.

Buza, Rom. (Buzahaza); pop. 34; 45 km NE of Cluj; 46°54'/24°09'.

Buzafalva, see Buzice.

Buzahaza, see Buza.

Buzaki, Ukr.; pop. 4; 150 km NW of Rovno; 51°38'/24°49'.

Buzany, *see* Buzhany.

Buzau, Rom.; 101 km NNE of Bucuresti; 45°09'/26°50'; EJ, GUM4, PHR1.

Buzhany, Ukr. (Buzany); pop. 32; 82 km NE of Lvov; 50°22'/24°50'.

Buzhory, Mold. (Bujoru); pop. 24; 45 km WSW of Kishinev; 46°56'/28°16'.

Buzias, Rom. (Buziasfurdo); 195 km SW of Cluj; 45°39'/21°36'; PHR1.

Buziasfurdo, *see* Buzias.

Buzica, Cz. (Buzita); 26 km SSW of Kosice; 48°32'/21°04'; HSL.

Buzice, Cz. (Buzafalva); 13 km SE of Kosice; 48°39'/21°18'; HSL.

Buzita, *see* Buzica.

Buzovita, *see* Buzovitsa.

Buzovitsa, Ukr. (Buzovita); pop. 32; 75 km NE of Chernovtsy; 48°30'/26°56'.

Buzsak, Hung.; pop. 19; 50 km NE of Nagykanizsa; 46°39'/17°35'.

Buzuluk, *see* Bazavluchok.

Byala, *see* Bielsko Biala.

Byala (near Chortkov), Ukr.; pop. 32; 88 km NNW of Chernovtsy; 49°02'/25°46'; GUM3.

Byala (near Sarny), Ukr.; pop. 29; 126 km N of Rovno; 51°40'/26°44'.

Byala Cherkova, Yug. (Bela Cerkva, Bela Crkva?); pop. 67; 75 km ENE of Beograd; 44°54'/21°26'; PHY.

Byblo, Ukr.; pop. 26; 94 km SE of Lvov; 49°15'/24°51'; HSL.

Bychawa, Pol. (Bekheve, Bichava, Bikhava, Byckov); pop. 1,876; 32 km S of Lublin; 51°01'/22°32'; AMG, COH, GA, GUM3, GUM4, GUM5, HSL, HSL2, LDS, LYV, PHP1, SF, YB.

Bychory, Cz.; pop. 1; 56 km E of Praha; 50°04'/15°16'.

Bychow, *see* Bykhov.

Byckov, *see* Bychawa.

Byckov Malyj, HSL. This pre-World War I community was not found in BGN gazetteers.

Byczow, Pol.; pop. 20; 56 km NE of Krakow; 50°25'/20°30'; HSL. *See also* Bykuv.

Byczyna, Pol.; pop. 4; 45 km W of Krakow; 50°10'/19°19'; PHP1, POCEM.

Bydgoszcz, Pol. (Bidgoshch, Bromberg); pop. 745; 107 km NNE of Poznan; 53°09'/18°00'; AMG, CAHJP, COH, EDRD, EJ, FRG, GA, GUM3, GUM4, GUM5, GUM6, HSL, ISH1, JGFF, LDS, LYV, PHP1.

Byelin, *see* Belin.

Byelits Biala, *see* Bielsko Biala.

Byelogorodka, *see* Belogorodka.

Byelopolye, *see* Belopolye.

Byelorussia; Not a town, but a republic of the Soviet Union. The western half was part of Poland prior to the end of World War II. Also known as White Russia.

Byelov, USSR; pop. 2,338; 315 km SW of Smolensk; 52°42'/28°47'. This town was located on a pre-World War I map, but does not appear in contemporary gazetteers.

Byelsk, *see* Bielsk Podlaski.

Byelsko, *see* Bielsko Biala.

Byelsko Biala, *see* Bielsko Biala.

Byelsk Podlaski, *see* Bielsk Podlaski.

Byezhun, *see* Biezun.

Byk, Ukr.; pop. 3; 170 km N of Lvov; 51°20'/24°10'.

Bykev, Cz.; pop. 4; 38 km N of Praha; 50°21'/14°25'.

Bykhov, Byel. (Bichov, Bychow, Bykjov, Staryi Bykhov); pop. 2,575; 133 km NW of Gomel; 53°31'/30°15'; COH, EJ, GUM4, HSL, JGFF, SF.

Bykhov (Polesie), Ukr.; pop. 44; 146 km NW of Rovno; 51°45'/25°16'.

Byki, Byel.; 45 km ESE of Gomel; 52°15'/31°36'; GUM5.

Bykjov, *see* Bykhov.

Bykos, Cz.; pop. 9; 38 km SW of Praha; 49°53'/14°04'.

Bykov, Ukr. (Bykow);

Bykov (near Przemysl), Ukr.; pop. 37; 75 km WSW of Lvov; 49°46'/22°56'.

Bykov (near Sambor), Ukr.; pop. 44; 62 km SSW of Lvov; 49°28'/23°28'.

Bykovets, Mold. (Bucovat, Bukkfalva, Bukovecz); pop. 57; 38 km WNW of Kishinev; 47°11'/28°27'.

Bykovice, HSL. A number of towns share this name. It was not possible to determine from available information which one is being referenced.

Bykovka, Ukr. (Bukavitz); 120 km NNW of Vinnitsa; 50°17'/27°59'; SF.

Bykovtse, *see* Bykovtsy.

Bykovtsy, Ukr. (Bochavitz, Bykovtse, Bykowcy); 62 km S of Rovno; 50°04'/26°07'; SF.

Bykow, *see* Bykov.

Bykowcy, *see* Bykovtsy.

Bykuv, Ukr. (Byczow); pop. 27; 62 km SSW of Lvov; 49°28'/23°28'. *See also* Byczow.

Bylany, Cz. (Bilan); 94 km E of Praha; 49°58'/15°44'; HSL.

Bylice, *see* Bilichi.

Byliny Stare, Pol.; pop. 9; 45 km E of Lodz; 51°44'/20°09'.

Bylitse, *see* Bilichi.

Byrnovo, Mold. (Barnova Soroca); pop. 51; 189 km NW of Kishinev; 48°25'/27°32'.

Bysen, Cz. (Birlovka); 32 km WNW of Praha; 50°14'/14°02'; GUM4.

Bysice, Cz. (Bischitz); pop. 4; 32 km N of Praha; 50°19'/14°37'; HSL, HSL2.

Byst, Cz.; pop. 8; 107 km ENE of Praha; 50°08'/15°55'.

Bystra, Pol.; pop. 36; 94 km ESE of Krakow; 49°40'/21°06'; GUM4, HSL, HSL2, PHP3.

Bystra (near Bielsko Biala), Pol.; pop. 20; 69 km SW of Krakow; 49°46'/19°05'.

Bystra (Slaskie), Pol.; pop. 22; 88 km SSW of Krakow; 49°31'/19°05'.

Bystraki, Ukr.; pop. 18; 139 km N of Lvov; 51°03'/23°55'.

Bystre, Cz.; pop. 54; 45 km NNE of Kosice; 49°01'/21°33'.

Bystrica, *see* Povazska Bystrica.

Bystrice, Cz.; pop. 27; A number of towns share this name. It was not possible to determine from available information which one is being referenced.

Bystrice Mala, HSL. This pre-World War I community was not found in BGN gazetteers.

Bystrice Nove, *see* Nova Bystrice.

Bystrice pod Hostynem, Cz.; pop. 34; 82 km ENE of Brno; 49°24'/17°41'.

Bystrichi, Ukr. (Bystritschi, Bystrzece); pop. 47; 56 km NE of Rovno; 50°53'/26°55'; SF.

Bystritschi, *see* Bystrichi.

Bystrowice, Pol.; pop. 49; 19 km NW of Przemysl; 49°56'/22°35'.

Bystry, Ukr.; 133 km SW of Lvov; 49°01'/22°46'; HSL, HSL2.

Bystrzece, *see* Bystrichi.

Bystrzejowice, Pol.; pop. 17; 19 km ESE of Lublin; 51°09'/22°46'.

Bystrzyca, Pol. (Bistritch); pop. 22; 75 km W of Przemysl; 49°59'/21°44'; AMG, GUM3, LDL, SF.

Byszyce, Pol.; pop. 4; 26 km SSE of Krakow; 49°56'/20°01'.

Byten, Byel. (Biten, Buten); pop. 739; 101 km NW of Pinsk; 52°53'/25°30'; AMG, COH, GUM3, GUM4, HSL, LYV, SF, YB.

Byten (Kovel area), Ukr.; pop. 60; 107 km WNW of Rovno; 51°08'/24°58'; EDRD, GUM3.

Bytkov, *see* Bitkov.

Bytom, Pol. (Beuthen); pop. 3,500; 50 km S of Czestochowa; 50°21'/18°58'; AMG, CAHJP, EJ, GUM3, GUM4, HSL, JGFF, LDS, PHP2, PHP3, POCEM.

Bytom Odrzanski, Pol.; 107 km SW of Poznan; 51°44'/15°50'; LDS.

Bytomsko, Pol.; pop. 10; 50 km ESE of Krakow; 49°49'/20°28'; HSL.

Byton, Pol.; 107 km NW of Lodz; 52°34'/18°36'; JGFF.

Bytow, *see* Butow.

Bzau, see Zau de Cimpie.

Bzenec, Cz. (Bisenz); pop. 138; 50 km ESE of Brno; 48°59'/17°16'; EJ, HSL, HSL2.

Bzesko Nowe, GUM3. This town was not found in BGN gazetteers under the given spelling.

Bzezan, see Berezhany.

Bzheg, see Brzeg.

B Zhesha Nova, see Nowe Brzesko.

Bzheshch nad Bugyem, see Brest.

Bzhezhani, see Berezhany.

Bzhezhnitsa, see Brzeznica.

Bzhezina, Ukr. (Brzezina); pop. 30; 50 km S of Lvov; 49°26'/24°04'.

Bzhezini, see Brzeziny.

Bzheziny, see Brzeziny.

Bzhostovitsa, see Brzostowica.

Bzhostovitsa Mala, see Brzostowica.

Bzhostovitsa Vielka, see Brzostowica.

Bzhostovitsa Vyelka, see Bolshaya Berestovitsa.

Bzin, Pol.; pop. 6; 120 km ESE of Lodz; 51°07'/20°51'; HSL, HSL2, JGFF, SF.

Bzinek, Pol.; pop. 14; 120 km ESE of Lodz; 51°06'/20°51'.

Bzite, Pol.; pop. 5; 45 km ESE of Lublin; 51°03'/23°11'.

Bzowiec, Pol. (Bzowiec Gorny); pop. 28; 50 km SE of Lublin; 50°50'/22°56'; JGFF.

Bzowiec Gorny, see Bzowiec.

Cabesti, see Kabeshti.

Cabin, HSL. This pre-World War I community was not found in BGN gazetteers.

Cabov, Cz.; 32 km NE of Kosice; 48°48'/21°39'; HSL.

Cabuna, Yug.; pop. 36; 120 km E of Zagreb; 45°45'/17°35'.

Cacak, Yug.; pop. 7; 107 km S of Beograd; 43°54'/20°21'.

Cachrov, Cz.; pop. 3; 126 km SSW of Praha; 49°16'/13°18'.

Cacica, Rom.; pop. 40; 139 km WNW of Iasi; 47°38'/25°54'.

Cacinci, Yug.; pop. 8; 146 km E of Zagreb; 45°36'/17°53'.

Cacova, Rom. (Kakova); 240 km SSW of Cluj; 45°07'/21°35'; HSL.

Cacuciu, Rom. (Gorgenykakucs); pop. 2; 94 km E of Cluj; 46°44'/24°51'.

Cadca, Cz.; pop. 570; 157 km ENE of Brno; 49°26'/18°47'; GUM4.

Cadea, Rom.; pop. 29; 133 km WNW of Cluj; 47°20'/22°05'.

Cadobesti, see Kadobovtsy.

Cadolzburg, Germ.; pop. 1; 13 km WSW of Nurnberg; 49°27'/10°52'; LDS, PHGB.

Cadow, Pol.; pop. 19; 38 km NE of Czestochowa; 51°01'/19°33'.

Caffa, see Feodosiya.

Caglic, see Donji Caglic.

Cahul, see Kagul.

Caian, HSL. This pre-World War I community was not found in BGN gazetteers.

Caianul Mic, see Caianu Mic.

Caianu Mic, Rom. (Caianul Mic, Kiskajan); pop. 61; 69 km NNE of Cluj; 47°14'/24°09'; HSL.

Cainari, see Kaynary.

Cainarii Vechi, see Kaynariy Vek.

Caiuti, see Caiuti Tirg.

Caiuti Tirg, Rom. (Caiuti); pop. 111; 120 km SSW of Iasi; 46°11'/26°56'; HSL, PHR1.

Cajba, see Kazhba.

Cajvana, Rom.; pop. 21; 133 km WNW of Iasi; 47°42'/25°58'.

Cako, Hung.; 114 km NNE of Szeged; 47°01'/21°11'; HSL.

Cakova, Cz.; 120 km NNE of Brno; 50°04'/17°33'; HSL.

Cakovci, Yug.; pop. 2; 126 km WNW of Beograd; 45°15'/19°04'.

Cakovec, Yug. (Csakathurn, Csaktornya); pop. 533; 75 km NNE of Zagreb; 46°23'/16°26'; COH, GUM3, HSL, PHY, YB.

Calabasi, Rom. HSL2. This pre-World War I community was not found in BGN gazetteers.

Calafat, Rom.; 258 km WSW of Bucuresti; 43°59'/22°56'; PHR1.

Calafindesti, Rom.; pop. 12; 133 km WNW of Iasi;

47°51'/26°07'.

Calarasi, see Kalarash.

Calarasi Sat, possibly Kalarash.

Calarasi Targ, see Kalarash.

Calata, Rom. (Calatele); 45 km W of Cluj; 46°48'/23°01'; PHR1.

Calatele, see Calata.

Calbe, Germ. (Calbe an der Saale); pop. 22; 82 km NW of Leipzig; 51°54'/11°46'; GUM4.

Calbe an der Saale, see Calbe.

Calceva, see Kalchevaya.

Caldern, Germ. (Kaldern); 88 km N of Frankfurt am Main; 50°51'/08°40'; LDS.

Calimanesti, Rom. (Kelementelke); 94 km ESE of Cluj; 46°25'/24°44'; HSL.

Calinesti, Rom. (Kalinest); 182 km S of Cluj; 45°09'/23°53'; AMG, COH, HSL, SM. See also Kalineshty.

Calinesti (Budesti area), Rom.; pop. 24; This town was not found in BGN gazetteers under the given spelling.

Calinesti Cuparencu, Rom.; pop. 22; 133 km WNW of Iasi; 47°48'/26°09'.

Calinesti Enache, Rom.; pop. 39; 133 km WNW of Iasi; 47°47'/26°08'.

Calinesti I, Rom. (Kanyahaza); pop. 187; HSL, HSL2, PHR2. Described in the *Black Book* as being in the Transylvania region of Romania, this town was not found in BGN gazetteers.

Calinesti II, Rom. (Felsokalinfalva); pop. 148; PHR2. Described in the *Black Book* as being in the Transylvania region of Romania, this town was not found in BGN gazetteers.

Calkar, see Kalkar.

Calle, Germ.; 101 km NE of Koln; 51°20'/08°13'; GUM5.

Calma, Yug.; pop. 12; 88 km WNW of Beograd; 45°05'/19°30'.

Calmatui, see Kalmatsuy.

Calna, Rom.; pop. 3; 50 km N of Cluj; 47°11'/23°39'.

Calomija, HSL. This pre-World War I community was not found in BGN gazetteers.

Calovo, Cz. (Nagy Megyer, Nagymegyer, Velky Mader, Velky Meder); pop. 510; 56 km ESE of Bratislava; 47°52'/17°46'; HSL, JGFF.

Calvaria, see Kalvarija.

Calvorde, Germ.; 107 km ENE of Hannover; 52°24'/11°18'; LDS.

Calw, Germ.; 32 km WSW of Stuttgart; 48°43'/08°44'; GUM3, GUM4, PHGBW.

Camar, Rom. (Kemer); pop. 71; 94 km WNW of Cluj; 47°18'/22°37'; HSL.

Camarasu, Rom.; 45 km ENE of Cluj; 46°47'/24°08'; HSL.

Camarzana, Rom. (Komorzan); pop. 134; 146 km NNW of Cluj; 48°00'/23°19'; HSL, PHR2.

Camberg, Germ. (Kamberg); pop. 57; 38 km WNW of Frankfurt am Main; 50°18'/08°16'; GED.

Camcic, see Zarya.

Camena, see Kamennaya.

Camenca, see Kamenka.

Camgorodok, (Shandrovka); JGFF. This town was not found in BGN gazetteers under the given spelling.

Camitz, Germ. (Kamitz); 62 km NE of Leipzig; 51°31'/13°06'; HSL.

Cammer, Germ.; 56 km SW of Berlin; 52°15'/12°40'; GED.

Cammin, see Kamien Pomorski.

Campalung Moldovenesc, see Cimpulung Moldovenesc.

Campalyngul, see Cimpulung Moldovenesc.

Campani, (Felsomezos); HSL. This pre-World War I community was not found in BGN gazetteers.

Campia Turzii, see Cimpia Truzii.

Campina, see Cimpinita.

Camplungul, see Cimpulung Moldovenesc.

Campulung La Tisa, see Cimpulung La Tisa.

Canciu, Rom. (Gancs); pop. 36; 62 km NNE of Cluj;

47°17'/23°59'; HSL.

Canea, Greece (Chania, Khania); pop. 267; 277 km S of Athens; 35°31'/24°01'; EDRD.

Cania, *see* Kaniya.

Cankova, Yug.; pop. 3; 107 km N of Zagreb; 46°43'/16°01'.

Cannstatt, *see* Stuttgart.

Cantavir, Yug. (Csantaver); pop. 78; 133 km NW of Beograd; 45°55'/19°46'; PHY.

Capasul de Campi, *see* Capusu de Cimpie.

Caplani, *see* Kaplany.

Capnic, *see* Cavnic.

Capowce, *see* Tsapovka.

Capresti, *see* Kapreshty.

Capresti Colonie, *see* Kapreshty.

Capu Campului, *see* Capu Cimpului.

Capu Cimpului, Rom. (Capu Campului); pop. 23; 126 km WNW of Iasi; 47°30'/26°00'.

Capu Codrului, Rom.; pop. 17; 126 km WNW of Iasi; 47°32'/25°59'.

Capustani, *see* Kapustyany.

Capustiani, *see* Kapustyany.

Capusu de Cimpie, Rom. (Capasul de Campi, Mezokapus); 62 km ESE of Cluj; 46°33'/24°19'; HSL.

Caputh, Germ. (Kaputh); pop. 4; 32 km SW of Berlin; 52°21'/13°00'; GUM4.

Carabeteni, *see* Karabetovka.

Caracal, Rom.; 146 km WSW of Bucuresti; 44°07'/24°21'; GUM4, PHR1.

Caracui, *see* Karakuy.

Caracuseni, *see* Karakushany.

Caragacii Vechi (Bessarabia), *see* Nagornoye.

Cara Hasan, *see* Karagasany.

Caramahmet, *see* Shevchenkovo (Bessarabia).

Caram Sebes, Rom. PHR1. This town was not found in BGN gazetteers under the given spelling.

Caransebes, Rom.; 189 km SSW of Cluj; 45°25'/22°13'; GUM4.

Carapciu pe Ceremus, *see* Kharapchou pe Ceremus.

Carapciu pe Siret, *see* Karapchiv.

Caraseu, Rom. (Szamoskrasso); pop. 91; 114 km NNW of Cluj; 47°44'/23°06'; PHR2.

Carastelec, Rom.; pop. 7; 88 km WNW of Cluj; 47°18'/22°42'.

Carbuna, *see* Karbuna.

Carcedea, *see* Kerecsend.

Carei, Rom. (Carei Mare, Karalnnstadt, Nagykaroly); pop. 2,394; 133 km NW of Cluj; 47°41'/22°28'; AMG, COH, EJ, HSL, HSL2, JGFF, LDL, PHR2.

Carei Mare, *see* Carei.

Carevo Selo, *see* Delcevo.

Carierde Piatra, Rom. PHR1. This town was not found in BGN gazetteers under the given spelling.

Carlibaba, *see* Cirlibaba.

Carlibaba Noua, *see* Cirlibaba Noua.

Carlosburg, *see* Alba Iulia.

Carlovca, *see* Karlovka.

Carlsbad, *see* Karlovy Vary.

Carlsberg, Germ.; 150 km E of Leipzig; 51°06'/14°28'; JGFF.

Carlsruhe, *see* Pokoj.

Carmeiu, Rom. PHR1. This town was not found in BGN gazetteers under the given spelling.

Carna, *see* Sarisske Cierne.

Carnateni, *see* Kirnatseny.

Carnesti, *see* Kyrneshty.

Carno, *see* Sarisske Cierne.

Carolath, *see* Siedlisko.

Carpesti, *see* Karpeshty.

Carpineni, *see* Karpineny.

Carsicov, *see* Karyshkov.

Cartofleanca, *see* Novyye Sochi.

Carynskie, Pol.; pop. 21; 75 km S of Przemysl; 49°10'/22°38'.

Cascalia, *see* Kashkaliya.

Caseiu, Rom. (Alsokosaly); pop. 69; 50 km N of Cluj;

47°11'/23°52'.

Casel, Germ.; pop. 80; 101 km SE of Berlin; 51°41'/14°08'.

Caslav, Cz.; pop. 194; 69 km E of Praha; 49°55'/15°24'.

Caslavsko, Cz.; pop. 4; 69 km SE of Praha; 49°36'/15°00'.

Caslita Dunare, *see* Kislitsa.

Caslovce, HSL. This pre-World War I community was not found in BGN gazetteers.

Cassel, *see* Kassel.

Casta, Cz. (Schattmannsdorf); 32 km NNE of Bratislava; 48°24'/17°22'; HSL.

Castellaum, *see* Kastellaun.

Castoria, *see* Kastoria.

Castrop Rauxel, Germ.; pop. 160; 69 km N of Koln; 51°33'/07°19'; GED, LDS.

Castrov, Cz.; pop. 1; 101 km SE of Praha; 49°18'/15°11'.

Casunca, *see* Kashunka.

Casva, Rom.; pop. 2; 101 km ENE of Cluj; 46°47'/24°52'.

Cataleni, *see* Katsaleny.

Catalu, Rom. (Catalul, Cataly); pop. 28; 62 km WNW of Cluj; 47°08'/22°59'.

Catalul, *see* Catalu.

Catalusa, Rom.; pop. 26; 62 km WNW of Cluj; 47°09'/22°59'.

Cataly, *see* Catalu.

Catcau, *see* Citcau.

Catina, Rom. (Katona); 45 km ENE of Cluj; 46°51'/24°11'; HSL.

Catzbach, *see* Luzhanka.

Cauas, Rom. (Ergkavas); pop. 6; 120 km NW of Cluj; 47°34'/22°33'.

Causani, *see* Kaushany.

Causanii Noui, *see* Kaushany.

Causani Noui, *see* Kaushany.

Causani Novi, *see* Kaushany.

Cavala, Greece; 208 km WSW of Athens; 37°51'/21°23'; AMG, LDL.

Cavalla, *see* Kavalla.

Cavnic, Rom. (Capnic, Kapnikbanya); pop. 85; 107 km N of Cluj; 47°40'/23°52'; HSL.

Cazaci, *see* Starokazachye.

Cazaciovca, Rom. PHR1. This town was not found in BGN gazetteers under the given spelling.

Cazaclia, *see* Kazakliya.

Cazanesti, *see* Kazaneshty.

Cazangic, *see* Kazanzhik.

Cazin, Yug.; pop. 1; 94 km S of Zagreb; 44°58'/15°57'.

Cazma, Yug.; pop. 16; 50 km E of Zagreb; 45°45'/16°37'.

Ceaba, Rom.; pop. 5; 50 km NE of Cluj; 47°03'/24°06'.

Ceaca, Rom.; pop. 14; 50 km N of Cluj; 47°11'/23°34'.

Ceadar, *see* Chadyr.

Ceadar Lunga, *see* Chadyr Lunga.

Ceaga, *see* Petrovka.

Cean, Rom.; pop. 11; 114 km WNW of Cluj; 47°27'/22°31'.

Ceanu Mare, Rom. (Mezocsan); 32 km ESE of Cluj; 46°40'/23°57'; HSL.

Ceblow, *see* Tsebluv.

Cece, Hung.; pop. 60; 88 km S of Budapest; 46°46'/18°39'; HSL, HSL2, LDS, PHH.

Cecehov, Cz.; 50 km ENE of Kosice; 48°44'/21°59'; AMG.

Cecejovce, Cz. (Csecs); 19 km SW of Kosice; 48°36'/21°04'; HSL.

Cecelice, Cz.; pop. 6; 32 km NNE of Praha; 50°18'/14°37'.

Cechesti, Rom.; pop. 10; 120 km ESE of Cluj; 46°19'/25°01'.

Cechowka, Pol.; pop. 143; 26 km E of Warszawa; 52°15'/21°19'; GUM5, PHP4.

Cechtice, Cz.; pop. 16; 69 km SE of Praha; 49°38'/15°03'.

Cecur Menjir, *see* Chekur Menzhir.

Cecylowka, Pol.; pop. 22; 82 km SSE of Warszawa; 51°34'/21°22'; GUM4.

Cedzyna, Pol.; pop. 3; 107 km NNE of Krakow; 50°52'/20°44'.

Cefa, Rom. (Cseffa); pop. 12; 146 km W of Cluj; 46°55'/21°44'.

Cegenydanyad, Hung.; pop. 45; 133 km E of Miskolc;

47°56'/22°33'.

Cegielnia, Pol.; pop. 57; 69 km SW of Lublin; 50°58'/21°43'.

Cegled, Hung.; pop. 856; 69 km ESE of Budapest; 47°10'/19°48'; GUM4, HSL, JGFF, LDS, PHH.

Cegledbercel, Hung.; pop. 3; 56 km ESE of Budapest; 47°13'/19°41'.

Ceglow, Pol.; pop. 89; 50 km E of Warszawa; 52°09'/21°44'; GA, GUM4, LDS, PHP4.

Cegoreni, see Chegoreny.

Cehal, Rom.; pop. 13; 101 km WNW of Cluj; 47°23'/22°36'.

Cehalut, Rom.; pop. 11; 107 km WNW of Cluj; 47°25'/22°34'.

Ceheiu, Rom.; pop. 19; 82 km WNW of Cluj; 47°15'/22°47'.

Cehetel, Rom. (Csehetfalva); pop. 6; 120 km ESE of Cluj; 46°24'/25°08'.

Cehul Silvaniei, see Cehu Silvaniei.

Cehul Sivaniei, see Cehu Silvaniei.

Cehu Silvaniei, Rom. (Cehu Sivaniei, Cehu Sivaniei, Cehul Silvaniei, Cehul Sivaniei, Szilagycseh); pop. 553; 75 km NNW of Cluj; 47°25'/23°11'; AMG, HSL, JGFF, PHR2.

Cehu Silvaniei, see Cehu Silvaniei.

Cehu Sivaniei, see Cehu Silvaniei.

Ceica, Rom.; pop. 130; 107 km W of Cluj; 46°51'/22°11'; PHR1.

Cejkov, Cz.; pop. 83; 50 km ESE of Kosice; 48°28'/21°46'.

Cejov, Cz.; pop. 11; 88 km ESE of Praha; 49°34'/15°23'.

Cekanice, Cz.; pop. 5; 75 km SSE of Praha; 49°26'/14°41'; HSL.

Cekiske, Lith. (Tsiekishok, Tzeikishok); pop. 324; 45 km NW of Kaunas; 55°10'/23°31'; HSL, SF, YL.

Cekoniskes, Lith. (Tschanovik); 19 km WNW of Vilnius; 54°44'/25°05'; JGFF.

Cekow, Pol.; pop. 46; 82 km W of Lodz; 51°54'/18°18'; HSL, PHP1.

Cel, Hung.; 107 km E of Nagykanizsa; 46°23'/18°23'; HSL.

Celakovice, Cz.; pop. 10; 26 km NE of Praha; 50°10'/14°46'.

Celestynow, Pol.; pop. 24; 56 km ESE of Lodz; 51°26'/20°05'.

Celiny, Pol.; pop. 32; 88 km N of Lublin; 51°59'/22°28'; EDRD.

Celiv, Cz.; pop. 2; 114 km WSW of Praha; 49°53'/12°57'.

Celivo, Cz.; pop. 3; 50 km SE of Praha; 49°42'/14°48'.

Celje, Yug.; pop. 25; 75 km WNW of Zagreb; 46°14'/15°16'; PHY.

Celkovice, Cz.; pop. 3; 82 km SSE of Praha; 49°24'/14°39'.

Celldomolk, Hung. (Czelldomolk, Kiscell, Kisczell, Nemesdomolk, Zellin); pop. 451; 94 km N of Nagykanizsa; 47°15'/17°09'; EDRD, GUM3, HSL, LDS, PHH.

Celle, Germ.; pop. 80; 38 km NNE of Hannover; 52°37'/10°05'; AMG, EJ, GED, GUM4, JGFF.

Cemerne, Cz.; pop. 53; 38 km NE of Kosice; 48°53'/21°40'; HSL.

Cenac, see Chenak.

Cenalos, Rom.; pop. 11; 120 km WNW of Cluj; 47°15'/22°09'.

Ceniawa, see Tsenyava.

Ceniow, see Tsenyuv.

Centa, Yug.; pop. 19; 38 km NNW of Beograd; 45°07'/20°23'.

Center, Hung.; pop. 5; 38 km WNW of Miskolc; 48°15'/20°22'; HSL.

Cepari, Rom. (Tschippendorf); pop. 34; 82 km NE of Cluj; 47°14'/24°26'.

Ceparia, see Chepariya.

Cepcewicze Male, see Tseptsevichi.

Cepcewicze Wielkie Obolonie, Ukr.; pop. 53; 56 km N of Rovno; 51°05'/26°03'. This town was located on an interwar map of Poland but does not appear in contemporary gazetteers. Map coordinates are approximate.

Cepcewicze Wielkie Smolki, Ukr.; pop. 29; 56 km N of Rovno; 51°05'/26°25'. This town was located on an interwar map of Poland but does not appear in contemporary gazetteers. Map coordinates are approximate.

Cepeleuti, see Chepeleutsy.

Cepice, Cz.; pop. 4; 114 km SSW of Praha; 49°16'/13°36'.

Cepin, Yug. (Tschepin); pop. 9; 170 km WNW of Beograd; 45°32'/18°34'.

Ceradice, Cz.; 69 km WNW of Praha; 50°19'/13°30'; AMG.

Ceranow, Pol.; 82 km SW of Bialystok; 52°38'/22°14'; GUM5.

Cercany, Cz.; pop. 8; 32 km SE of Praha; 49°51'/14°43'.

Cere, Lat.; pop. 2; 75 km W of Riga; 57°07'/22°52'.

Cered, Hung. (Czered); pop. 25; 62 km W of Miskolc; 48°09'/19°58'; HSL.

Cerepcauti, see Cherepkovtsy.

Cerevic, Yug.; pop. 7; 82 km WNW of Beograd; 45°13'/19°40'.

Cergowa, possibly Tsekhuv.

Cerhenice, Cz.; pop. 25; 45 km E of Praha; 50°05'/15°05'.

Cerkiewnik, Pol. (Munsterberg); pop. 59; 120 km ESE of Gdansk; 53°55'/20°24'; HSL.

Cerlina, see Cherlina.

Cernauca, see Chernavka.

Cernauti, see Chernovtsy.

Cernawicy, see Chernavchitsy.

Cernesti, Rom.; pop. 28; 88 km N of Cluj; 47°31'/23°45'.

Cernevcy, see Chernevtsy.

Cernevti, see Chernevtsy.

Cernici, Cz.; pop. 5; 69 km SE of Praha; 49°37'/15°04'.

Cerniny, Cz.; pop. 5; 62 km ESE of Praha; 49°51'/15°13'.

Cerni Potok, see Czarny Potok.

Cernoleuca, see Chernolevka.

Cernosin, Cz.; pop. 16; 120 km WSW of Praha; 49°49'/12°53'.

Cernov, Cz.; 94 km W of Brno; 49°21'/15°19'; HSL.

Cernovice, Cz.; pop. 42; 88 km SE of Praha; 49°22'/14°58'.

Cernowitze Bukovina, see Chernovtsy.

Cernuchi, see Chernukhi.

Certege, Rom. (Csertesz); 56 km SW of Cluj; 46°25'/23°02'; HSL.

Certeze, Rom. (Avasujfalu); pop. 254; 133 km N of Cluj; 47°54'/23°28'; PHR2.

Certizne, Cz.; pop. 88; 82 km NNE of Kosice; 49°21'/21°50'; HSL, JGFF.

Certlov, see Rybnik.

Cerveny Kostelec, Cz.; pop. 21; 126 km NE of Praha; 50°29'/16°06'; EJ.

Cesarka, Pol.; pop. 24; Described in the *Black Book* as being in the Lodz region of Poland, this town was not found in BGN gazetteers.

Cesis, Lat. (Venden, Wenden); pop. 171; 82 km NE of Riga; 57°18'/25°15'; JGFF, LDL, PHLE, SF.

Ceska Lipa, Cz. (Boehmisch Leipa, Bohmisch Leipa); pop. 305; 69 km N of Praha; 50°41'/14°33'; AMG, EJ, HSL, HSL2.

Ceska Skalice, Cz.; 114 km NE of Praha; 50°24'/16°03'; EJ.

Ceska Trebova, Cz.; pop. 27; 88 km NNW of Brno; 49°54'/16°27'.

Ceske Budejovice, Cz. (Budejovice, Budweis); pop. 1,423; 126 km S of Praha; 48°59'/14°28'; EDRD, EJ, GUM3, JGFF.

Ceske Velenice, Cz.; pop. 49; 133 km SW of Brno; 48°46'/14°58'.

Cesky Brod, Cz. (Bohmisch Brod); pop. 82; 26 km E of Praha; 50°04'/14°51'; HSL.

Cesky Heralec, Cz.; 75 km NW of Brno; 49°41'/15°59'; AMG.

Cesky Krumlov, Cz. (Krumlov); pop. 120; 146 km S of Praha; 48°49'/14°19'.

Cesky Sternberk, Cz.; pop. 21; 50 km ESE of Praha; 49°49'/14°56'.

Cesky Tesin, Cz. (Tesin, Tesin Cesky); pop. 1,148; 157 km NE of Brno; 49°45'/18°37'; HSL. On the border with Poland, its twin city is Cieszyn.

Cesvaine, Lat.; pop. 15; 126 km NNW of Daugavpils; 56°58'/26°19'.

Cetariu, Rom. (Hegykozcsatar); pop. 7; 126 km WNW of Cluj; 47°08'/22°01'.

Cetatea Alba, see Belgorod Dnestrovskiy.

Cetatele, Rom. (Gyorkefalva); pop. 4; 101 km N of Cluj; 47°36'/23°45'.

Cetinje, Yug.; pop. 13; 214 km W of Skopje; 42°24'/18°55'.

Cetireni, see Chetyreny.

Cetvertinovca, see Chetvertinovka.

Cewkow, Pol.; pop. 159; 56 km N of Przemysl; 50°15'/22°52';

PHP2.

Chabarovice, Cz.; pop. 43; 75 km NW of Praha; 50°41'/13°56'.

Chabielice, Pol.; pop. 52; 56 km SSW of Lodz; 51°16'/19°07'; PHP1.

Chabna, see Polesskoye.

Chabnoje, see Polesskoye.

Chabowka, Pol.; pop. 50; 62 km S of Krakow; 49°36'/19°56'; GUM4, GUM5.

Chabowo Swiniary, Pol.; pop. 1; 94 km WNW of Warszawa; 52°47'/19°55'.

Chadorowka, Pol.; pop. 22; Described in the *Black Book* as being in the Lwow region of Poland, this town was not found in BGN gazetteers.

Chadyr, Mold. (Ceadar); pop. 4; 50 km SSW of Kishinev; 46°40'/28°24'.

Chadyr Lunga, Mold. (Ceadar Lunga); pop. 524; 114 km S of Kishinev; 46°03'/28°50'.

Chagrov, Ukr. (Chagruv, Czahrow); pop. 38; 75 km SE of Lvov; 49°18'/24°32'.

Chagruv, see Chagrov.

Chajety, Pol.; pop. 9; 26 km NNE of Warszawa; 52°28'/21°16'.

Chalcis, see Khalkis.

Chalkis, see Khalkis.

Chaltch, see Cholotschje.

Chaltz, see Cholotschje.

Cham, Germ.; pop. 82; 120 km E of Nurnberg; 49°13'/12°40'; AMG, GUM3, PHGB.

Chan, see Teofipol.

Chanava, Cz. (Hanva); 82 km SW of Kosice; 48°20'/20°18'; HSL.

Chancza, Pol.; pop. 7; 107 km NE of Krakow; 50°39'/21°05'.

Chania, see Canea.

Chaniszka, see Haniska.

Chanov, Cz.; pop. 2; 69 km WNW of Praha; 50°30'/13°41'.

Chanyzh, Ukr. (Czanyz); pop. 23; 56 km NE of Lvov; 50°05'/24°41'.

Chapayevsk, USSR (Trotsk); pop. 184; 781 km ENE of Voronezh; 52°58'/49°41'.

Chapli, Ukr. (Czaple); pop. 65; 75 km SW of Lvov; 49°31'/23°02'; HSL.

Chaplino, Ukr.; pop. 59; 101 km ESE of Dnepropetrovsk; 48°09'/36°15'.

Charbinowice, Pol.; pop. 5; 56 km NE of Krakow; 50°17'/20°37'.

Charciabalda, Pol.; pop. 5; 126 km W of Bialystok; 53°21'/21°17'.

Chari, see Chereya.

Charishkifka, see Goryshkovka.

Charkow, see Kharkov.

Charlejow, Pol.; pop. 20; 56 km NW of Lublin; 51°40'/22°17'.

Charlottenburg, Germ.; 6 km WSW of Berlin; 52°31'/13°18'; HSL.

Charlupia Wielka, Pol.; pop. 13; 62 km SW of Lodz; 51°34'/18°38'.

Charna, see Czarna.

Charni Dunayets, see Czarny Dunajec.

Charnokontse, see Velikiye Chornokontsy.

Charnokontse Velk, see Velikiye Chornokontsy.

Charnushovitse, Ukr. (Czarnuszowice); pop. 26; 26 km E of Lvov; 49°49'/24°20'.

Charpaczka, see Kharpachka.

Charsnitza, see Charsznica.

Charsznica, Pol. (Charsnitza, Kharshnitse); pop. 446; 45 km N of Krakow; 50°25'/19°56'; AMG, COH, GUM4, GUM5, HSL, LYV, SF, YB.

Chartariya Chadasha, see Tschertorija Novaya.

Chartorisk, see Sta yy Chartoriysk.

Chartoriysk, see Staryy Chartoriysk.

Charukuv, Ukr. (Czarukow); pop. 28; 82 km WSW of Rovno; 50°37'/25°06'.

Charz, Pol.; pop. 3; 26 km W of Lublin; 51°17'/22°14'.

Charzewice (near Brzesko), Pol.; pop. 32; 62 km ESE of Krakow; 49°53'/20°45'.

Charzewice (near Tarnobrzeg), Pol.; pop. 21; 82 km SSW of Lublin; 50°36'/22°03'.

Charzyno, Pol. (Garrin); 101 km NE of Szczecin; 54°05'/15°34'; LDS.

Chashnik, see Chashniki.

Chashniki, Byel. (Chashnik, Tschaschniki); pop. 1,646; 75 km SW of Vitebsk; 54°52'/29°10'; GYLA, LDL, SF.

Chaszczow, see Khashchuv.

Chaussy, see Chausy.

Chausy, Byel. (Chaussy, Choss, Czausy); pop. 1,757; 157 km N of Gomel; 53°48'/30°58'; GYLA, JGFF, SF.

Chaykovichi, Ukr. (Chaykovitse, Czajkowice); pop. 49; 50 km SW of Lvov; 49°36'/23°31'.

Chaykovitse, see Chaykovichi.

Chcebuz, Cz.; pop. 14; 50 km N of Praha; 50°29'/14°26'.

Cheb, Cz. (Eger); pop. 505; 150 km WSW of Praha; 50°04'/12°22'; EJ.

Chebabcea, see Shirokoye.

Chebin, see Trzebinia.

Chebinya, see Trzebinia.

Chechanovitz, see Ciechanowiec.

Chechelevka, Ukr. (Kokalofka); JGFF. A number of towns share this name. It was not possible to determine from available information which one is being referenced.

Chechelnik, Ukr. (Chetschelnik, Chichelnik, Chitchilnik, Cicelnic?, Czeczelnik, Tschetschelnik); pop. 2,301; 88 km SW of Uman; 48°13'/29°22'; GUM3, GUM4, GUM6, GYLA, SF.

Chechersk, Byel. (Czeczersk); pop. 1,313; 56 km N of Gomel; 52°55'/30°55'; LDL, SF.

Chechersk (Lwow), Ukr. CAHJP. CAHJP has 18th century documents for this town, which does not appear in interwar or contemporary gazetteers.

Chechiav, see Czchow.

Chechinov, see Ciechanow.

Chechis, Rom. (Chechis Salaj); pop. 42; 94 km N of Cluj; 47°35'/23°36'.

Chechis Salaj, see Chechis.

Chechlowo, Pol.; pop. 4; 82 km SSW of Bialystok; 52°31'/22°35'.

Chechly, Pol.; pop. 27; 88 km WNW of Przemysl; 50°03'/21°35'.

Chechochinek, see Ciechocinek.

Chechov, see Czechowka Dolna.

Checiny, Pol. (Chenciny, Chentchin); pop. 2,825; 88 km NNE of Krakow; 50°48'/20°27'; AMG, CAHJP, COH, EDRD, EJ, GA, GUM3, GUM4, GUM5, GYLA, HSL, HSL2, JGFF, LDL, LDS, PHP1, POCEM, SF.

Chege, see Tiszacsege.

Chegea, Rom.; pop. 2; 101 km NW of Cluj; 47°28'/22°41'.

Chegoreny, Mold. (Cegoreni); pop. 37; 62 km N of Kishinev; 47°30'/28°52'.

Chekhanov, see Ciechanow.

Chekhanove, see Ciechanow.

Chekhanovits, see Ciechanowiec.

Chekhanovtse, see Ciechanowiec.

Chekhovo, USSR (Uderwangen); pop. 4; 26 km SE of Kaliningrad; 54°33'/20°43'.

Chekolteny, Mold. (Ciocalteni); pop. 60; 56 km NNW of Kishinev; 47°29'/28°37'.

Chekur Menzhir, Mold. (Cecur Menjir); pop. 5; 69 km S of Kishinev; 46°26'/28°45'.

Chelb, Pol.; pop. 3; 94 km ESE of Lodz; 51°13'/20°30'.

Chelem, see Chelm.

Chelinta, Rom. (Kelencze); pop. 20; 82 km NNW of Cluj; 47°27'/23°19'; HSL.

Chelitch, see Galich.

Chelm, Pol. (Chelem, Khelem, Khelm, Kholm); pop. 12,064; 69 km E of Lublin; 51°08'/23°30'; AMG, CAHJP, COH, EDRD, EJ, FRG, GA, GUM3, GUM4, GUM5, GUM6, HSL, HSL2, JGFF, LDL, LDS, LYV, PHGBW, PHP2, POCEM, SF, YB.

Chelmce, Pol.; 101 km ENE of Czestochowa; 50°56'/20°30'; PHP3.

Chelmek, Pol.; pop. 48; 50 km W of Krakow; 50°06'/19°14'; GUM4, GUM5.

Chelmeniti, see Kelmentsy.

Chelmenti, see Kelmentsy.

Chelmiec, Pol. (Chelmiec Polski); pop. 79; 75 km ESE of Krakow; 49°38'/20°41'; PHP3. A second town of Chelmiec Niemiecki (pop. 21) appears in the 1921 census of Poland.

Chelmiec Polski, see Chelmiec.

Chelmno, Pol.; pop. 74; 114 km S of Gdansk; 53°21'/18°26'; GA, GUM3, GUM4, GUM5, GUM6, HSL, PHP1, PHP4, SF.

Chelmo, Pol.; pop. 33; 56 km NE of Czestochowa; 51°04'/19°45'.

Chelmza, Pol.; pop. 72; 133 km S of Gdansk; 53°11'/18°37'; GUM4.

Chelodz, see Czeladz.

Chemenik, see Czemierniki.

Chemerintsy, Ukr. (Ciemierzynce, Ciemierzyniec, Tsemezhintse); pop. 100; 56 km ESE of Lvov; 49°40'/24°47'.

Chemernik, see Czemierniki.

Chemerovitz, see Chemerovtsy.

Chemerovtsy, Ukr. (Chemerovitz, Czemerowce); pop. 1,258; 82 km N of Chernovtsy; 49°00'/26°22'; EDRD, SF.

Chemilov, see Cmielow.

Chemnitz, see Karl-Marx-Stadt.

Chemyerniki, see Czemierniki.

Chenak, Mold. (Cenac); pop. 7; 62 km S of Kishinev; 46°28'/28°38'.

Chenciny, see Checiny.

Chendul Mare, see Chendu Mare.

Chendul Mic, see Chendu Mic.

Chendu Mare, Rom. (Chendul Mare, Nagykend); 94 km ESE of Cluj; 46°23'/24°44'; HSL.

Chendu Mic, Rom. (Chendul Mic, Kiskend); 94 km ESE of Cluj; 46°24'/24°43'; HSL.

Chenga, see Csenger.

Chenger, see Csenger.

Chenstchov, see Czestochowa.

Chenstochov, see Czestochowa.

Chenstokhov, see Czestochowa.

Chentatzitza, see Czestocice.

Chentchin, see Checiny.

Chepariya, Mold. (Ceparia); pop. 3; 133 km NW of Kishinev; 47°56'/27°43'.

Chepeleuts, see Chepeleutsy.

Chepeleutsy, Mold. (Cepeleuti, Chepeleuts); 182 km NW of Kishinev; 48°18'/27°18'; PHR2.

Chepelov, see Ciepielow.

Cherche, Ukr. (Chernche, Czercze, Czerncze); pop. 35; 163 km NW of Rovno; 51°44'/24°52'; PHP2.

Cherechiu, Rom. (Erdokerek); pop. 3; 133 km WNW of Cluj; 47°23'/22°08'.

Cheremoshno, Ukr. (Czeremoszno); pop. 102; 114 km WNW of Rovno; 51°19'/25°01'.

Cherepkovo, Mold. (Chiripkeu, Ciripcau); pop. 22; 114 km NNW of Kishinev; 47°59'/28°23'.

Cherepkovtsy, Ukr. (Cerepcauti); pop. 34; 38 km S of Chernovtsy; 48°00'/25°58'.

Chereposhetz, see Kharpachka.

Cheres, Byel. (Czeress); pop. 5; 163 km W of Vitebsk; 55°38'/27°43'.

Cheresh, Ukr. (Cires, Ciresi); pop. 106; 38 km SW of Chernovtsy; 48°06'/25°36'; PHR2.

Cheretezh, Ukr. (Czertez); pop. 9; 82 km SSE of Lvov; 49°10'/24°15'.

Chereusa, Rom.; pop. 10; 120 km WNW of Cluj; 47°30'/22°27'.

Chereya, Byel. (Chari, Tschereja); pop. 1,098; 88 km SW of Vitebsk; 54°37'/29°17'; SF.

Cherikov, Byel. (Czerykow); pop. 1,594; 133 km N of Gomel; 53°34'/31°23'; JGFF, SF.

Cherin, see Chigirin.

Cherinka, see Chernevka.

Cheriu, Rom. (Alker); pop. 8; 120 km W of Cluj; 47°01'/22°02'.

Cherkassy, Ukr. (Cherkoss, Czerkasy); pop. 10,886; 157 km ESE of Kiyev; 49°26'/32°04'; AMG, EDRD, EJ, GUM5, GYLA, HSL, JGFF, LDL, SF.

Cherkhava, Ukr. (Czerchawa); pop. 53; 75 km SW of Lvov; 49°25'/23°14'.

Cherkoss, see Cherkassy.

Cherlina, Mold. (Cerlina); pop. 27; 126 km NNW of Kishinev; 48°05'/28°37'.

Cherna, see Cierna.

Chernavchitse, see Chernavchitsy.

Chernavchitsy, Byel. (Cernawicy, Chernavchitse, Czernawczyce, Tsarnovitz); pop. 428; 163 km W of Pinsk; 52°13'/23°44'; JGFF, SF.

Chernavka, Ukr. (Cernauca); pop. 74; 19 km NNE of Chernovtsy; 48°25'/26°02'.

Chernche, see Cherche.

Chernelitsa, Ukr. (Czernelica); pop. 528; 69 km NW of Chernovtsy; 48°49'/25°26'; AMG, EGRS, GUM4, HSL, HSL2, PHP2, SF.

Chernev, Ukr. (Czerniow); pop. 52; 69 km SE of Lvov; 49°16'/24°27'.

Chernevka, Byel. (Cherinka, Czernewka); 126 km SSE of Vitebsk; 54°05'/30°46'; JGFF, LDL, SF.

Chernevtsi, see Chernevtsy.

Chernevtsy, Ukr. (Cernevcy, Cernevti, Chernevtsi, Chernivitz, Tschernewzi); pop. 1,917; 82 km S of Vinnitsa; 48°32'/28°07'; LDL, PHR1, SF.

Cherneyev, Ukr. (Cherneyuv, Czerniejow); pop. 336; 107 km WNW of Chernovtsy; 48°51'/24°43'.

Cherneyuv, see Cherneyev.

Chernich, see Chernukhi.

Chernichov, see Chernikhov.

Chernigov, Ukr. (Czernihow, Tschernigov); pop. 10,607; 133 km NNE of Kiyev; 51°30'/31°18'; COH, EDRD, GUM4, GUM5, HSL, JGFF, LDL, SF.

Chernigovka, HSL. A number of towns share this name. It was not possible to determine from available information which one is being referenced.

Chernikhov, Ukr. (Chernichov, Czernichow); pop. 32; 56 km SW of Lvov; 49°37'/23°21'; AMG, HSL, SF.

Chernikhovtsy, Ukr. (Czernichowce); pop. 10; 114 km S of Rovno; 49°38'/25°44'.

Chernilyava, Ukr. (Czernilawa); pop. 47; 50 km WNW of Lvov; 49°59'/23°20'.

Chernitsa, Ukr. (Czernica); pop. 39; 88 km ENE of Lvov; 49°58'/25°15'.

Chernivitz, see Chernevtsy.

Cherniyuv, Ukr. (Czernijow); pop. 19; 120 km WNW of Rovno; 50°58'/24°41'.

Chernobil, see Chernobyl.

Chernobyl, Ukr. (Chernobil); pop. 1,765; 101 km NNW of Kiyev; 51°16'/30°14'; HSL, JGFF, LDL, SF.

Chernokinits, see Dzialoszyn.

Chernolevka, Mold. (Cernoleuca); pop. 89; 176 km NW of Kishinev; 48°19'/27°34'.

Chernovitsy, see Chernovtsy.

Chernovitz, see Chernovtsy.

Chernovtsky, see Chernovtsy.

Chernovtsy, Ukr. (Cernauti, Cernovcy, Cernowitze Bukovina, Chernovitsy, Chernovitz, Chernovtsky, Czerniowce, Czernovitz, Czernowitz); pop. 42,932; 214 km SW of Vinnitsa; 48°18'/25°56'; AMG, EDRD, EJ, GUM3, GUM4, GUM5, GUM6, GYLA, HSL, HSL2, JGFF, LDL, PHP2, PHP3, PHR2, SF, YB.

Chernukhi, Ukr. (Cernuchi, Chernich); 114 km S of Konotop; 50°16'/32°57'; LDL, SF.

Chernyakhov, Ukr.; pop. 437; 133 km W of Kiyev;

51

50°27'/28°40'; GUM4, JGFF.

Chernyakhovsk, USSR (Insterburg); pop. 310; 82 km E of Kaliningrad; 54°38'/21°49'; CAHJP, HSL, JGFF, LDS.

Chernyany, Byel. (Czerniany); pop. 105; 133 km WSW of Pinsk; 51°59'/24°12'.

Chernyatin, Ukr. (Czerniatyn); pop. 105; 50 km NW of Chernovtsy; 48°39'/25°27'; PHP2.

Cherny Ostrov, see Chernyy Ostrov.

Chernyshevskoye, USSR (Eydtkuhen, Eydtkuhnen); pop. 112; 139 km E of Kaliningrad; 54°39'/22°44'; HSL, JGFF.

Chernyye Oslavy, Ukr. (Oslavy Charne, Oslaw Gzarny); pop. 29; 88 km W of Chernovtsy; 48°28'/24°44'.

Chernyy Ostrov, Ukr. (Cherny Ostrov, Chorny Ostrov, Cornyj Ostrov, Czarna Ostrov); 126 km SSE of Rovno; 49°30'/26°45'; JGFF, LDL, SF.

Chersk, see Czersk.

Cherson, see Kherson.

Chertezh, Ukr.; 82 km SSE of Lvov; 49°10'/24°15'; AMG.

Cherven, Byel. (Czerwien, Eihumen, Igumen, Ihumen); pop. 2,027; 62 km ESE of Minsk; 53°42'/28°26'; EDRD, GUM4, GYLA, HSL, HSL2, JGFF, LDL, SF.

Chervin, see Czerwin.

Chervona, Ukr. (Grabiuti, Grabovtsy); 56 km SW of Vinnitsa; 48°52'/27°54'; PHR1.

Chervonoarmeisk, Ukr. (Radevil, Radivil, Radvil, Radzhivilov, Radzivilov, Radziwillow, Rodvil); pop. 2,036; 88 km SW of Rovno; 50°08'/25°15'; AMG, COH, EJ, GA, GUM3, GUM4, GUM5, GUM6, GYLA, HSL, HSL2, JGFF, LDL, PHP2, SF, YB.

Chervonoarmeysk, Ukr. (Pulin); pop. 1,056; 146 km E of Rovno; 50°28'/28°16'; EDRD.

Chervonoarmeyskoye, Ukr. (Cubei); pop. 11; 170 km SW of Odessa; 45°47'/28°44'.

Chervono Glinskoye, Ukr. (Brieni); pop. 7; 114 km SW of Odessa; 45°58'/29°26'.

Chervonograd, Ukr. (Czerwonohrad, Krisnipolye, Kristinopol, Krystynopol); pop. 2,086; 62 km N of Lvov; 50°23'/24°14'; COH, EGRS, GUM3, GYLA, HSL, HSL2, LDL, PHP2, SF.

Chervony Prapor, see Chervonyy Prapor.

Chervonyy Prapor, Ukr. (Chervony Prapor); pop. 25; 189 km N of Simferopol; 46°37'/34°41'.

Chesa, Rom. (Kishaza); 120 km WSW of Cluj; 46°45'/22°02'; HSL.

Chesereu, Rom. (Erkeseru); pop. 13; 133 km WNW of Cluj; 47°26'/22°07'.

Cheshanov, see Cieszanow.

Cheshin, see Cieszyn.

Chesniki, Ukr. (Czesniki); pop. 90; 75 km ESE of Lvov; 49°23'/24°43'.

Chestokhova, see Czestochowa.

Chesybesy, see Zhovten.

Chet, Rom.; pop. 19; 120 km WNW of Cluj; 47°25'/22°21'.

Chetrosu, see Ketrosy.

Chetschelnik, see Chechelnik.

Chetvertinovka, Ukr. (Cetvertinovca); 69 km WSW of Uman; 48°36'/29°17'; GUM4, PHR1.

Chetvertnya, Ukr. (Czetwiertnia); pop. 23; 75 km WNW of Rovno; 51°03'/25°28'.

Chetyreny, Mold. (Cetireni); pop. 31; 69 km WNW of Kishinev; 47°13'/27°55'.

Cheuchis, see Chiochis.

Cheud, Rom.; pop. 32; 75 km NNW of Cluj; 47°23'/23°20'.

Cheznovice, Cz.; pop. 6; 56 km SW of Praha; 49°47'/13°47'.

Chianovca, Rom. PHR1. This town was not found in BGN gazetteers under the given spelling.

Chibed, Rom.; pop. 1; 107 km E of Cluj; 46°32'/24°58'.

Chibene, Ukr. EDRD. This town was not found in BGN gazetteers under the given spelling.

Chiced, see Chiesd.

Chichelnik, see Chechelnik.

Chichisa, Rom. (Alsonyarlo); pop. 29; 50 km NW of Cluj; 47°08'/23°12'.

Chidea, Rom. (Kide); pop. 5; 32 km N of Cluj; 46°59'/23°36'; HSL.

Chidry, see Khidry.

Chiend, (Kovend); HSL. This pre-World War I community was not found in BGN gazetteers.

Chiesd, Rom. (Chiced, Keccsed, Kecsed); pop. 26; 88 km NW of Cluj; 47°23'/22°53'; HSL.

Chigirin, Ukr. (Cherin, Czehryn); pop. 408; 182 km WNW of Dnepropetrovsk; 49°04'/32°40'; JGFF, LDL, SF.

Chigirleni, see Chigirleny.

Chigirleny, Mold. (Chigirleni); pop. 14; 32 km S of Kishinev; 46°45'/28°50'.

Chilia Noua, see Kiliya.

Chilia Nova, see Kiliya.

Chilioara, Rom.; pop. 43; 75 km NW of Cluj; 47°20'/23°02'.

Chimiashla, see Chimishliya.

Chimisheny, Mold. (Cimiseni); pop. 8; 26 km ENE of Kishinev; 47°01'/29°08'.

Chimishli, see Chimishliya.

Chimishliya, Mold. (Chimiashla, Chimishli, Cimislia, Cimislija); pop. 925; 56 km S of Kishinev; 46°32'/28°47'; PHR2, SF.

Chinari, Rom.; pop. 5; 82 km E of Cluj; 46°36'/24°35'.

Chincis, Rom. (Kincses); pop. 101 km E of Cluj; 46°44'/24°54'; HSL. This town was located on a pre-World War I map, but does not appear in contemporary gazetteers.

Chinisheutsy, Mold. (Ciniseuti); pop. 486; 82 km N of Kishinev; 47°41'/28°52'.

Chinkeu, Ukr. (Chinkov, Cincau, Concau); pop. 57; 38 km NNW of Chernovtsy; 48°36'/25°49'; PHR2.

Chinkov, see Chinkeu.

Chinocz, see Khinoch.

Chintelnic, Rom.; pop. 3; 69 km NE of Cluj; 47°06'/24°20'.

Chiny, see Tsna.

Chinyadevo, (Cinadovo); COH, GUM3, HSL, HSL2. This pre-World War I community was not found in BGN gazetteers.

Chiochis, Rom. (Cheuchis, Kekes); pop. 27; 50 km NE of Cluj; 46°59'/24°11'; HSL.

Chios, see Khios.

Chioselia, see Kisseliya.

Chiperceni, see Kipercheny.

Chirales, Rom. (Kyrieleis); pop. 17; 69 km NE of Cluj; 47°05'/24°18'.

Chiraleu, Rom.; pop. 5; 114 km WNW of Cluj; 47°18'/22°18'.

Chircaesti, see Kirkayeshty.

Chirianca, see Kiriyanka.

Chiribis, Rom. (Bisztraterebes); pop. 12; 114 km WNW of Cluj; 47°19'/22°21'.

Chiriet Lunga, see Kiriyet Lunga.

Chirileu, Rom. (Kerelo); 69 km ESE of Cluj; 46°28'/24°23'; HSL.

Chiripkeu, see Cherepkovo.

Chirov, see Khyrov.

Chirpan, Bulg.; pop. 210; 176 km ESE of Sofija; 42°12'/25°20'; EJ.

Chirsova, see Kirsova.

Chirutnea, see Kiryutnya.

Chisalau, see Kiselev.

Chiscareni, see Lazo.

Chishki, Ukr. (Czyszki); pop. 39; 82 km SW of Lvov; 49°38'/22°58'. See also Chizhki.

Chisinau, see Kishinev.

Chisindia, Rom. (Kiszindia); pop. 126 km SW of Cluj; 46°17'/22°06'; HSL.

Chisineu Cris, Rom.; pop. 171; 163 km WSW of Cluj; 46°32'/21°31'; PHR1.

Chisla Salieva, see Podvornoye.

Chislavici, see Khislavichi.

Chislaz, Rom. (Vamoslaz); pop. 1; 120 km WNW of Cluj;

47°17'/22°14'; HSL.

Chistag, Rom. (Keszteg); pop. 29; 101 km WNW of Cluj; 47°03'/22°22'; HSL.

Chistelnita, see Kishtelnitsa.

Chistovodnoye, Ukr. (Suiunduc); pop. 2; 75 km WSW of Odessa; 46°26'/29°46'.

Chitcani, see Kitskany.

Chitcani Vechi, see Staryye Kitskany.

Chitch, see Czudec.

Chitchilnik, see Chechelnik.

Chiuesti, Rom.; pop. 91; 62 km N of Cluj; 47°18'/23°53'; PHR2.

Chiuza, Rom.; pop. 37; 69 km NNE of Cluj; 47°14'/24°15'.

Chizeve, see Czyzew.

Chizheva, see Czyzew.

Chizhevo, see Czyzew.

Chizhki, Ukr. (Chishki); pop. 26; 13 km ESE of Lvov; 49°48'/24°10'.

Chlaniow, Pol.; pop. 50 km SE of Lublin; 50°50'/22°53'; JGFF.

Chlebiczyn Lesny, see Lesnoy Khlebichin.

Chlebiczyn Polny, see Lesnoy Khlebichin.

Chlebna, Pol.; pop. 13; 88 km WSW of Przemysl; 49°43'/21°38'.

Chlebowice Swirskie, see Khlebovitse Svizhske.

Chlebowice Wielkie, see Velikiye Glibovichi.

Chlebowka, see Glebuvka.

Chlevieska, see Chlewska Wola.

Chlewczany, see Khlevchany.

Chlewice, Pol.; pop. 88; 62 km E of Czestochowa; 50°40'/20°01'.

Chlewiska, Pol.; pop. 55; 107 km ESE of Lodz; 51°15'/20°46'.

Chlewska Wola, Pol. (Chlevieska); pop. 20; 62 km E of Czestochowa; 50°41'/19°58'; SF.

Chlina, Pol.; pop. 13; 45 km NNW of Krakow; 50°27'/19°50'.

Chliple, see Khliple.

Chlopczyce, Ukr.; pop. 79; 82 km SSW of Lvov; 49°15'/23°25'. This town was located on an interwar map of Poland but does not appear in contemporary gazetteers. Map coordinates are approximate.

Chlopeniczi, see Kholopenichi.

Chlopiatyn, Pol.; pop. 11; 107 km NE of Przemysl; 50°27'/23°59'.

Chlopice, Pol.; pop. 5; 26 km NNW of Przemysl; 49°58'/22°41'.

Chlopkow, Pol.; pop. 21; 101 km S of Bialystok; 52°16'/22°52'; HSL.

Chlopowka, Ukr.; pop. 26; 75 km N of Chernovtsy; 48°55'/25°55'. This town was located on an interwar map of Poland but does not appear in contemporary gazetteers. Map coordinates are approximate.

Chlopy, see Peremozhnoye.

Chlumec, see Chlumec nad Cidlinou.

Chlumec nad Cidlinou, Cz. (Chlumec, Kulm); pop. 71; 69 km ENE of Praha; 50°09'/15°27'; EJ, HSL.

Chmelnik, see Khmelnik.

Chmelnitski, see Khmelnitskiy.

Chmelov, Cz.; 45 km N of Kosice; 49°04'/21°27'; AMG.

Chmelovec, Cz. (Komlos, Komloskeresztes); 45 km N of Kosice; 49°05'/21°22'; HSL.

Chmielek, Pol.; pop. 51; 69 km N of Przemysl; 50°23'/22°53'.

Chmielen Wielki, Pol.; pop. 3; 107 km NNW of Warszawa; 53°11'/20°45'.

Chmieliska, Ukr.; pop. 41; 126 km S of Rovno; 49°30'/26°01'; GUM3. This town was located on an interwar map of Poland but does not appear in contemporary gazetteers. Map coordinates are approximate.

Chmielnicki, see Khmelnitskiy.

Chmielnik, Pol.; pop. 5,908; 82 km NE of Krakow; 50°38'/20°45'; AMG, CAHJP, COH, EDRD, EGRS, EJ, FRG, GA, GUM3, GUM4, GUM5, GUM6, GYLA, HSL, HSL2, JGFF, LDL, LDS, PHP1, PHP2, PHP3, PHP4, POCEM, SF, YB.

Chmielnik (Lodz area), Pol.; pop. 21; 94 km W of Lodz; 51°47'/18°06'.

Chmielnik (Rzeszow area), Pol.; pop. 20; 50 km WNW of Przemysl; 49°59'/22°09'.

Chmielnik Potoki, GUM4. This town was not found in BGN gazetteers under the given spelling.

Chmielno, see Khmelno.

Chmielno (near Stawiski), Pol. PHP4. This town was not found in BGN gazetteers under the given spelling.

Chmielow, see Khmelyuv.

Chmielowice, Pol.; pop. 5; 88 km NNE of Krakow; 50°42'/20°33'.

Chmielowka, see Khmelevka.

Chmiliv, see Khmelyuv.

Chmilov, see Cmielow.

Chminany, Cz. (Also Mochnya, Mohnya, Monyhad); 38 km NNW of Kosice; 49°00'/21°04'; HSL.

Chne, Germ. HSL2. This pre-World War I community was not found in BGN gazetteers.

Chobedza, Pol.; 32 km N of Krakow; 50°20'/19°54'; GUM3.

Chobowicze, see Khabovichi.

Chobruchi, Mold. (Cioburciu); pop. 42; 82 km ESE of Kishinev; 46°36'/29°42'.

Chobultow, see Khobultova.

Chocen, Cz. (Chotzen); pop. 24; 94 km NNW of Brno; 50°00'/16°14'; HSL.

Chocerady, Cz.; pop. 7; 38 km ESE of Praha; 49°53'/14°48'.

Chocholow, Pol.; pop. 25; 88 km S of Krakow; 49°22'/19°49'; HSL.

Chocianow, see Chocianowice.

Chocianowice, Pol. (Chocianow); pop. 6; 13 km SW of Lodz; 51°43'/19°25'; GUM3.

Chociencyze, see Khotenchitsy.

Chocieszow, see Khoteshov.

Chocim, Ukr. CAHJP. CAHJP has eighteenth-century documents that describe Chocim as being in Stanislawow province. It does not appear in interwar or contemporary gazetteers.

Chocim (Lodz area), Pol.; 62 km W of Lodz; 51°49'/18°33'; GUM5.

Chocimierz, see Khotimir.

Chocimow, Pol.; pop. 3; 94 km SW of Lublin; 50°56'/21°15'.

Chocimsk, Pol. PHP2. This town was not found in BGN gazetteers under the given spelling.

Chocz, Pol. (Chotch); pop. 99; 82 km ESE of Poznan; 51°58'/17°52'; GA, GUM3, HSL, HSL2, SF.

Chocznia, Pol.; pop. 4; 45 km SW of Krakow; 49°53'/19°28'.

Chodaczkow Maly, see Velikaya Khodachka.

Chodaczkow Wielki, see Velikaya Khodachka.

Chodaczow, Pol.; pop. 12; 45 km NW of Przemysl; 50°09'/22°31'.

Chodecz, Pol. (Chodetch); pop. 459; 75 km NNW of Lodz; 52°24'/19°02'; CAHJP, HSL, JGFF, LDL, PHP4, SF, YB.

Chodel, Pol. (Chodla); pop. 646; 32 km SW of Lublin; 51°07'/22°08'; COH, EDRD, GA, GUM4, GUM5, HSL, HSL2, JGFF, SF.

Chodenice, Pol.; pop. 6; 38 km ESE of Krakow; 49°59'/20°23'.

Choderev, see Khodorov.

Choderkowce, see Khoderkovtse.

Chodetch, see Chodecz.

Chodkow, see Chodkow Nowy.

Chodkow Nowy, Pol. (Chodkow); 101 km SSW of Lublin; 50°32'/21°36'; GUM5, HSL.

Chodkow, Pol.; 69 km WNW of Warszawa; 52°30'/20°02'; POCEM.

Chodla, see Chodel.

Chodorkov, see Khodorkov.

Chodorkow, see Khodorkov.

Chodorov, see Khodorov.

Chodorow, see Khodorov.

Chodoun, Cz.; pop. 7; 38 km SW of Praha; 49°54'/13°59'.

Chodov, Cz.; pop. 54; 120 km W of Praha; 50°15'/12°45'.

Chodova Plana, Cz. (Kuttenplan); 126 km WSW of Praha; 49°53'/12°44'; EJ, HSL, JGFF.

Chodywance, Pol.; pop. 55; 94 km NNE of Przemysl; 50°25'/23°38'.

Chodziez, Pol. (Kolmar); pop. 92; 62 km N of Poznan; 52°59'/16°55'; CAHJP, GA, JGFF.

Choinik, see Khoyniki.

Choiniki, see Khoyniki.

Chojewo, Pol.; pop. 4; 50 km S of Bialystok; 52°43'/22°58'.

Chojna, Pol.; 62 km S of Szczecin; 52°58'/14°26'; POCEM.

Chojnata, Pol.; pop. 16; 56 km SW of Warszawa; 51°54'/20°27'.

Chojnica, see Chojnik.

Chojnice, Pol. (Konitz); pop. 110; 101 km SW of Gdansk; 53°42'/17°34'; AMG, EDRD, EJ, HSL, HSL2, POCEM.

Chojnik, Pol. (Chojnica); pop. 21; 82 km E of Krakow; 49°53'/20°59'.

Chojniki, see Khoyniki.

Chojno Nowe, Pol.; pop. 7; 38 km E of Lublin; 51°11'/23°04'.

Chojno Stare, Pol.; pop. 9; 38 km E of Lublin; 51°11'/23°06'.

Chojnow, Pol. (Haynau); pop. 66; 75 km W of Wroclaw; 51°16'/15°56'; HSL, LDS.

Chojnowo, Pol.; 114 km NW of Warszawa; 53°07'/20°04'; GA.

Chojny, Pol.; pop. 104; 13 km SSE of Lodz; 51°43'/19°29'.

Chojny Stare, Pol.; pop. 34; 13 km SSE of Lodz; 51°43'/19°29'.

Chok Maydan, Mold. (Cioc Maidan); pop. 21; 75 km S of Kishinev; 46°22'/28°49'.

Cholewiana Gora, Pol.; pop. 71; 82 km NW of Przemysl; 50°21'/22°04'; HSL.

Choliv, see Uzlovoye.

Cholmetch, see Kholmech.

Cholojow, see Uzlovoye.

Choloniow, see Kholonev.

Cholopenitch, see Kholopenichi.

Cholopenitschi, see Kholopenichi.

Cholotschje, (Chaltch, Chaltz); LDL, SF. This town was not found in BGN gazetteers under the given spelling.

Cholowice, Pol.; pop. 16; 19 km WSW of Przemysl; 49°46'/22°35'.

Cholui, (Cholvi); LDL, SF. This town was not found in BGN gazetteers under the given spelling.

Cholvi, see Cholui.

Chomczyn, see Khimchin.

Chomeciska Duze, Pol. (Chomeciska Wielkie); pop. 10; 69 km SE of Lublin; 50°48'/23°10'.

Chomeciska Wielkie, see Chomeciska Duze.

Chomentowek, Pol.; pop. 5; 75 km NE of Krakow; 50°33'/20°40'.

Chomiakow, see Khomyakuv.

Chomiakowka, see Khomyakovka.

Chomle, Cz.; pop. 5; 62 km SW of Praha; 49°52'/13°38'.

Chomsk, see Khomsk.

Chomutice, Cz.; pop. 4; 82 km NE of Praha; 50°22'/15°30'.

Chomutov, Cz. (Komotau); pop. 483; 82 km WNW of Praha; 50°27'/13°26'; AMG, CAHJP, EJ, ISH1.

Chop, Ukr. (Cop, Csap, Csop); pop. 433; 208 km SSW of Lvov; 48°26'/22°12'; AMG, HSL, HSL2, JGFF, LDL.

Chopniow, Ukr.; pop. 51; 45 km WSW of Rovno; 50°35'/25°35'. This town was located on an interwar map of Poland but does not appear in contemporary gazetteers. Map coordinates are approximate.

Chopovichi, Ukr. (Chopovitch); pop. 1,302; 120 km WNW of Kiyev; 50°50'/28°57'; HSL, JGFF, SF.

Chopovitch, see Chopovichi.

Choragwica, Pol.; pop. 1; 19 km SE of Krakow; 49°57'/20°05'.

Choral, see Khorol.

Choreshty, Mold. (Ciorasti); pop. 43; 50 km WNW of Kishinev; 47°10'/28°14'.

Chorewo, see Khorevo.

Chorherrn, Aus.; pop. 1; 19 km WNW of Wien; 48°17'/16°05'.

Chorki, Pol.; pop. 6; 50 km NW of Lodz; 52°06'/19°04'.

Chorkowka, Pol.; pop. 9; 82 km WSW of Przemysl; 49°39'/21°41'.

Chorna, Mold. (Ciorna); pop. 10; 88 km N of Kishinev; 47°46'/28°58'.

Chorny Ostrov, see Chernyy Ostrov.

Chorobrow, see Pravda.

Chorochoryn, see Khorokhorin.

Chorodetz, see Gorodets.

Chorodishtch, see Gorodishche.

Chorol, see Khorol.

Choromsk, see Khoromsk.

Choronow, Ukr.; pop. 38; 13 km NW of Lvov; 49°55'/23°55'. This town was located on an interwar map of Poland but does not appear in contemporary gazetteers. Map coordinates are approximate.

Chorosciec, see Khorostsets.

Choroshtch, see Choroszcz.

Chorosnica, see Khorosnitsa.

Chorostkov, see Khorostkov.

Chorostkow, see Khorostkov.

Chorostow, see Khorostov.

Choroszcz, Pol. (Choroshtch); pop. 450; 13 km W of Bialystok; 53°09'/22°59'; CAHJP, COH, EJ, GUM3, HSL, LDL, LDS, SF.

Choroszewicze, Byel.; pop. 32; 101 km NW of Pinsk; 52°55'/25°25'. This town was located on an interwar map of Poland but does not appear in contemporary gazetteers. Map coordinates are approximate.

Choroszewszczyce, see Khoroshovchitsy.

Chorow, see Goruv.

Chortitz, see Khortitsa.

Chortkev, see Chortkov.

Chortkov, Ukr. (Chortkev, Czortkow, Czortkow Stary); pop. 3,314; 82 km N of Chernovtsy; 49°01'/25°48'; AMG, COH, EDRD, EGRS, EJ, GA, GUM3, GUM4, GUM5, GUM6, HSL, HSL2, JGFF, LDL, LYV, PHP2, SF, YB.

Chortotza, see Khortitsa.

Chortovets, Ukr. (Czortowiec); pop. 317; 69 km WNW of Chernovtsy; 48°42'/25°17'; COH, PHP2.

Chortzel, see Chorzele.

Chorzele, Pol. (Chortzel, Khorzel, Khorzele, Khorzhel, Khozhel); pop. 928; 114 km N of Warszawa; 53°16'/20°54'; COH, GUM4, HSL, JGFF, LDS, LYV, PHP4, SF, YB.

Chorzelow, Pol.; pop. 3; 114 km ENE of Krakow; 50°21'/21°27'.

Chorzen, Pol.; pop. 37; 94 km E of Poznan; 52°14'/18°14'.

Chorzewa, Pol.; pop. 44; 69 km N of Krakow; 50°41'/20°14'.

Chorzow, Pol. (Huta Krolewska, Konigshutte, Krolewska Huta); pop. 2,811; 56 km S of Czestochowa; 50°18'/18°58'; AMG, EJ, GUM3, GUM4, GUM5, HSL, JGFF, LDS, PHP3.

Chorzow (Lwow), Pol.; pop. 23; 19 km WNW of Przemysl; 49°55'/22°35'.

Chorzyna, Pol.; pop. 3; 62 km NNW of Czestochowa; 51°18'/18°51'.

Choslovitz, see Khislavichi.

Choss, see Chausy.

Choszczno, Pol. (Arnswalde); pop. 118; 69 km ESE of Szczecin; 53°10'/15°25'; CAHJP, GUM3, GUM4, HSL, LDS.

Choszczow, Pol.; pop. 6; 38 km WNW of Lublin; 51°28'/22°12'; HSL.

Chotch, see Chocz.

Chotcza Dolna, Pol. (Chotcza Nowa); pop. 29; 56 km WSW of Lublin; 51°14'/21°48'.

Chotcza Gorna, Pol.; pop. 16; 56 km WSW of Lublin; 51°15'/21°47'.

Chotcza Nowa, see Chotcza Dolna.

Chotebor, Cz.; pop. 65; 88 km WNW of Brno; 49°43'/15°40'.

Chotel Czerwony, Pol.; pop. 4; 62 km NE of Krakow; 50°23'/20°43'.

Chotesice, Cz.; pop. 1; 56 km NE of Praha; 50°17'/15°16'.

Chotimierz, see Khotimir.

Chotimsk, see Khotimsk.

Chotin, see Khotin.

Chotomow, Pol.; pop. 3; 26 km NW of Warszawa; 52°25'/20°53'.

Chotoviny, Cz.; pop. 15; 75 km SSE of Praha; 49°29'/14°41'.

Chotowitz, LDL. This pre-World War I community was not found in BGN gazetteers.

Chotutice, Cz.; pop. 6; 38 km E of Praha; 50°04'/14°59'.

Chotycze, Pol.; pop. 7; 107 km S of Bialystok; 52°12'/22°47'.

Chotylow, Pol.; pop. 85; 101 km NNE of Lublin; 52°00'/23°22'.

Chotylub, Pol.; pop. 45; 62 km NNE of Przemysl; 50°15'/23°15'.

Chotymyr, *see* Khotimir.

Chotyn, *see* Khotin.

Chotynicze, *see* Khotynichi.

Chotyniec, Pol.; pop. 67; 26 km NNE of Przemysl; 49°57'/23°01'.

Chotynin, Pol.; pop. 4; 82 km WNW of Czestochowa; 51°13'/18°12'.

Chotys, Cz.; pop. 4; 32 km E of Praha; 50°01'/14°54'.

Chotysany, Cz.; pop. 12; 50 km SE of Praha; 49°45'/14°49'.

Chotzen, *see* Chocen.

Choustnik, Cz.; pop. 11; 88 km SSE of Praha; 49°20'/14°50'.

Choziez, HSL. This pre-World War I community was not found in BGN gazetteers.

Chraboly, Pol. BGN lists two possible localities with this name located at 52°52'/23°12' and 53°16'/22°58'. JGFF.

Chramec, Cz. (Harmacz); 94 km SW of Kosice; 48°17'/20°11'; HSL.

Chrancovice, Cz.; pop. 14; 94 km WSW of Praha; 49°51'/13°10'.

Chrapon, Pol.; pop. 3; 120 km WNW of Warszawa; 53°00'/19°43'.

Chrapun, *see* Khrapun.

Chrapy, Pol.; pop. 26; 45 km WNW of Lodz; 51°56'/18°57'.

Chrast, Cz.; pop. 85; 75 km SW of Praha; 49°48'/13°30'.

Chrastany, Cz.; pop. 23; A number of towns share this name. It was not possible to determine from available information which one is being referenced.

Chrastava, Cz. (Kratzau); pop. 22; 94 km NNE of Praha; 50°49'/14°59'.

Chrbonin, Cz.; pop. 3; 88 km SSE of Praha; 49°22'/14°52'.

Chreniow, Pol.; pop. 20; Described in the *Black Book* as being in the Tarnopol region of Poland, this town was not found in BGN gazetteers.

Chrewt, Pol.; pop. 56; 56 km S of Przemysl; 49°20'/22°32'.

Chribska, Cz.; pop. 12; 94 km N of Praha; 50°52'/14°29'.

Christburg, *see* Dzierzgon.

Christianstadt, *see* Krzystkowice.

Chroberz, Pol.; pop. 21; 62 km NE of Krakow; 50°26'/20°34'.

Chrolowice, Pol.; pop. 13; 88 km SSW of Bialystok; 52°26'/22°34'.

Chromowka, Pol.; pop. 24; 82 km ESE of Lublin; 50°55'/23°35'. This town was located on an interwar map of Poland but does not appear in contemporary gazetteers. Map coordinates are approximate.

Chroscice, Pol.; pop. 6; 50 km E of Warszawa; 52°15'/21°48'.

Chrosla, Pol.; pop. 8; 32 km E of Warszawa; 52°11'/21°28'.

Chrostkowo, Pol.; pop. 7; 139 km N of Lodz; 52°57'/19°15'.

Chroustovice, Cz.; pop. 8; 101 km NW of Brno; 49°58'/16°00'.

Chrudim, Cz.; pop. 150; 94 km E of Praha; 49°57'/15°48'.

Chruslanki Jozefowskie, Pol.; pop. 30; 45 km SW of Lublin; 51°00'/22°01'.

Chruslanki Mazanowskie, Pol.; pop. 8; 50 km SW of Lublin; 51°02'/21°58'.

Chruslice, Pol.; 101 km S of Warszawa; 51°25'/20°59'; GA.

Chruslina, Pol.; pop. 29; 45 km SW of Lublin; 51°03'/22°00'.

Chrustne, Pol.; pop. 6; 62 km WNW of Lublin; 51°37'/21°59'.

Chrusty Nowe, Pol.; pop. 9; 26 km E of Lodz; 51°42'/19°48'.

Chruszczobrod, Pol.; pop. 17; 45 km SSE of Czestochowa; 50°25'/19°19'.

Chruszczow, Pol.; pop. 3; 26 km W of Lublin; 51°17'/22°13'.

Chrypalicze, *see* Khrypaliche.

Chryplin, *see* Khryplin.

Chrzanow, Pol. (Hrycowola, K Shonev, Keshanov, Khshanov, Khshanuv, Krashanov, Kreshanov, Kshanev, Kshanov); pop. 6,328; 38 km W of Krakow; 50°08'/19°24'; AMG, CAHJP, COH, EDRD, EGRS, EJ, FRG, GA, GUM3, GUM4, GUM5, GUM6, HSL, HSL2, LDL, LYV, PHP2, PHP3, POCEM, SF, YB.

Chrzanow (near Janow Lubelski), Pol.; pop. 120; 56 km S of Lublin; 50°47'/22°37'.

Chrzczanka, Pol.; pop. 4; 69 km NNE of Warszawa; 52°47'/21°30'.

Chrzczony, Pol.; pop. 5; 94 km WSW of Bialystok; 53°02'/21°46'.

Chszczonow, Pol. AMG, JGFF. This town was not found in BGN gazetteers under the given spelling.

Chubin, *see* Trzebinia.

Chuchel, Cz.; pop. 3; 88 km ESE of Praha; 49°48'/15°38'.

Chuchuleny, Mold. (Ciuciuleni); pop. 291; 32 km W of Kishinev; 47°02'/28°25'.

Chuchulya, Mold. (Ciuciulea); pop. 120; 126 km WNW of Kishinev; 47°40'/27°29'.

Chudel, Ukr. (Czudel); pop. 65; 82 km NNE of Rovno; 51°15'/26°44'.

Chudenice, Cz.; pop. 5; 114 km SW of Praha; 49°28'/13°11'.

Chudin, *see* Mezhirechye.

Chudlovo, Cz. AMG, HSL. This pre-World War I community was not found in BGN gazetteers.

Chudnov, Ukr. (Chudnow, Cudnov, Cudnow); pop. 4,067; 94 km NNW of Vinnitsa; 50°03'/28°07'; COH, EJ, HSL, JGFF, LDL, SF.

Chudnow, *see* Chudnov.

Chudovo, USSR; pop. 120; 120 km ESE of Leningrad; 59°10'/31°41'.

Chufleshty, Mold. (Ciuflesti); pop. 17; 50 km SSE of Kishinev; 46°37'/29°00'.

Chuguyev, Ukr. (Czugujew); pop. 322; 32 km ESE of Kharkov; 49°50'/36°39'; GUM4.

Chukalovka, *see* Chukaluvka.

Chukaluvka, Ukr. (Chukalovka, Czukalowka); pop. 29; 114 km WNW of Chernovtsy; 48°52'/24°41'.

Chukhovo, Byel. (Czuchowo); pop. 17; 32 km N of Pinsk; 52°20'/26°15'.

Chulovichi, Ukr. (Chulovitse, Czulowice); pop. 20; 26 km SW of Lvov; 49°40'/23°44'.

Chulovitse, *see* Chulovichi.

Churovichi, USSR; pop. 227; 202 km SW of Bryansk; 52°10'/32°00'.

Chust, *see* Khust.

Chutuleshty, Mold. (Ciutulesti); pop. 40; 88 km NNW of Kishinev; 47°46'/28°24'.

Chvalec, Cz.; pop. 1; 126 km NE of Praha; 50°35'/16°02'.

Chvalenice, Cz.; pop. 4; 88 km SW of Praha; 49°39'/13°29'.

Chvateruby, Cz.; pop. 4; 19 km NW of Praha; 50°14'/14°21'.

Chvojenec, Cz.; pop. 3; 107 km ENE of Praha; 50°07'/15°56'.

Chwalowice, Pol.; pop. 81; 69 km SSW of Lublin; 50°46'/21°54'.

Chwalowo, *see* Khvalovo Pervoye.

Chwedkowicze, *see* Khvedkovichi.

Chworostow, *see* Khvorostov.

Chybice, Pol.; pop. 14; 107 km SW of Lublin; 50°56'/21°07'.

Chybie, Pol.; pop. 53; 82 km WSW of Krakow; 49°54'/18°49'; AMG.

Chyliczki, Pol.; pop. 39; 26 km SSE of Warszawa; 52°05'/21°03'.

Chylin, Pol.; pop. 26; 56 km ENE of Lublin; 51°17'/23°20'.

Chylin Stary, Pol.; pop. 5; 69 km WNW of Warszawa; 52°27'/20°02'.

Chylonia, Pol. (Chylonja); pop. 5; 32 km NW of Gdansk; 54°32'/18°29'.

Chylonja, *see* Chylonia.

Chynava, Cz.; pop. 4; 26 km WSW of Praha; 50°01'/14°05'.

Chynov, Cz.; pop. 21; 82 km SSE of Praha; 49°24'/14°49'; JGFF.

Chynow, Pol.; 32 km S of Lodz; 51°31'/19°20'; PHP4.

Chyrow, *see* Khirov.

Chyrzyna, Pol. (Chyrzyna Korytniki); pop. 17; 19 km W of Przemysl; 49°48'/22°33'.

Chyrzyna Korytniki, *see* Chyrzyna.

Chyse, Cz.; pop. 20; 88 km W of Praha; 50°06'/13°15'.

Chyste, Byel. (Czyste); 133 km WSW of Vitebsk; 55°05'/28°05'; HSL.

Chystovice, Cz.; pop. 2; 75 km SE of Praha; 49°35'/15°05'.

Chyzyny, Pol.; 56 km ESE of Warszawa; 52°01'/21°44'; GA, GUM4, GUM5.

Ciacova, Rom.; 240 km SW of Cluj; 45°31'/21°08'; PHR1.

Ciazen, Pol.; pop. 11; 62 km ESE of Poznan; 52°13'/17°49'.

Cibakhaza, Hung.; pop. 15; 82 km N of Szeged; 46°58'/20°12'.

Cibla, see Eversmuiza.

Cibu, Rom. (Cseb, Csob); pop. 6; 101 km ESE of Cluj; 46°23'/24°48'.

Cicarlau, see Circirlau.

Cicarovce, Cz.; pop. 66; 62 km ESE of Kosice; 48°33'/22°02'.

Cicelnic, possibly Chechelnik.

Cicenice, Cz.; pop. 12; 107 km S of Praha; 49°09'/14°14'.

Ciceu, Rom.; pop. 1; 157 km SW of Iasi; 46°25'/25°47'.

Ciceu Corabia, Rom.; pop. 4; 56 km NNE of Cluj; 47°15'/23°57'.

Ciceu Giurgesti, Rom. (Csicsogyongyfalva); pop. 110; 62 km NNE of Cluj; 47°15'/24°01'.

Ciceuvic, Rom. PHR1. This town was not found in BGN gazetteers under the given spelling.

Cichawa, Pol.; pop. 5; 32 km ESE of Krakow; 49°57'/20°16'.

Cichoborz, see Cichoburz.

Cichoburz, Pol. (Cichoborz); pop. 46; 114 km ESE of Lublin; 50°43'/23°59'.

Cichostow, Pol.; pop. 14; 56 km N of Lublin; 51°41'/22°49'.

Cicirlau, see Circirlau.

Cidreag, Rom. (Cseoreg); pop. 22; 146 km NNW of Cluj; 47°59'/22°58'; JGFF.

Ciechanki Krzesimowskie, Pol.; pop. 1; 26 km ENE of Lublin; 51°17'/22°52'.

Ciechanow, Pol. (Chechinov, Chekhanov, Chekhanove, Tshekhanov, Ziechenau); pop. 4,403; 75 km NNW of Warszawa; 52°53'/20°37'; AMG, COH, EDRD, EJ, GA, GUM3, GUM4, GUM5, GUM6, HSL, HSL2, JGFF, LDL, LDS, LYV, PHP1, PHP4, POCEM, SF, YB.

Ciechanowiec, Pol. (Chechanovitz, Chekhanovits, Chekhanovtse, Rudelstadt, Tshekhanovets, Tshekhanovits); pop. 1,649; 69 km SSW of Bialystok; 52°40'/22°31'; CAHJP, COH, EDRD, FRG, GA, GUM3, GUM5, HSL, JGFF, LDL, LDS, LYV, PHP4, POCEM, SF, YB.

Ciechlin, Pol.; pop. 9; 50 km SSW of Warszawa; 51°52'/20°41'.

Ciechocinek, Pol. (Chechochinek); pop. 769; 133 km NNW of Lodz; 52°52'/18°48'; AMG, EDRD, GUM4, HSL, HSL2, PHP4, POCEM, SF, YB.

Ciechomice, Pol.; pop. 5; 88 km N of Lodz; 52°29'/19°42'.

Ciechomin, Pol.; pop. 27; 62 km SE of Lodz; 51°16'/20°02'.

Ciechostowice, Pol.; pop. 5; 107 km ESE of Lodz; 51°10'/20°47'.

Ciecina, Pol.; pop. 24; 75 km SW of Krakow; 49°37'/19°09'.

Cieciorki, Pol. BGN lists two possible localities with this name located at 52°40'/20°23' and 53°02'/22°16'. PHP4.

Cieciszew, Pol.; pop. 21; 32 km SE of Warszawa; 52°03'/21°11'.

Cieciulow, Pol.; pop. 3; 45 km WNW of Czestochowa; 51°01'/18°37'.

Cieklin, Pol.; pop. 16; 101 km WSW of Przemysl; 49°39'/21°23'.

Cielaz, see Tselenzh.

Cielcza, Pol.; pop. 4; 56 km SE of Poznan; 52°01'/17°29'.

Cieletniki, Pol.; pop. 10; 38 km NE of Czestochowa; 50°54'/19°35'; PHP1.

Cieloszka, Pol.; pop. 8; 101 km W of Bialystok; 53°23'/21°42'.

Ciemierzowice, Pol.; pop. 8; 19 km NNW of Przemysl; 49°54'/22°44'.

Ciemierzynce, see Chemerintsy.

Ciemierzyniec, see Chemerintsy.

Ciemietniki, Pol.; pop. 8; 56 km NE of Czestochowa; 50°57'/19°52'.

Ciemiezowice, Pol. PHP3. This town was not found in BGN gazetteers under the given spelling.

Cieniawa, Pol.; pop. 22; 88 km ESE of Krakow; 49°37'/20°51';

PHP3.

Ciepelow, see Ciepielow.

Ciepielewo, Pol. (Cieplewo Dworskie); pop. 23; 69 km N of Warszawa; 52°50'/21°08'.

Ciepielow, Pol. (Chepelov, Ciepelow, Czepielow); pop. 339; 69 km WSW of Lublin; 51°15'/21°34'; EDRD, EJ, GA, GUM4, GUM5, HSL, LDS, SF.

Cieplewo Dworskie, see Ciepielewo.

Cieplice, Pol.; pop. 107; 56 km NNW of Przemysl; 50°15'/22°38'; PHP3.

Ciepliny, Pol.; pop. 8; 82 km NW of Lodz; 52°22'/18°51'.

Cierna, Cz. (Cherna); 69 km ESE of Kosice; 48°26'/22°06'; AMG.

Ciesle, Pol.; 26 km WSW of Poznan; 52°22'/16°37'; GA.

Cieszanow, Pol. (Cheshanov, Tseshanov, Tsheshanov, Tzieshinov); pop. 939; 50 km NNE of Przemysl; 50°14'/23°08'; COH, EGRS, GA, GUM3, GUM5, HSL, HSL2, LDL, LYV, PHP1, PHP2, PHP3, POCEM, SF, YB.

Cieszkowy, Pol.; pop. 6; 50 km NE of Krakow; 50°20'/20°32'.

Cieszowa, Pol. (Czieschowa, Tzishova); 26 km SW of Czestochowa; 50°40'/18°50'; SF, WS.

Cieszybiesy, Pol. PHP2. This town was not found in BGN gazetteers under the given spelling.

Cieszyn, Pol. (Cheshin, Teschen, Teshin); pop. 1,591; 101 km SW of Krakow; 49°46'/18°36'; AMG, CAHJP, EGRS, EJ, GUM3, GUM4, GUM5, LYV, PHP3, POCEM. On the Czechoslovakian border, its twin city is Cesky Tesin.

Cieszyna, Pol.; pop. 40; 82 km W of Przemysl; 49°52'/21°37'; GA, PHP3.

Cieszyny, Pol.; pop. 4; 126 km SSE of Gdansk; 53°13'/19°13'; GUM3.

Ciezkowice, Pol. (Tzezhkovitz); pop. 218; 45 km WNW of Krakow; 50°13'/19°22'; COH, EDRD, GUM3, GUM5, HSL, PHP3, SF. This location and the location below are both in the vicinity of Krakow. It is not possible to distinguish which town is indicated in the source references.

Ciezkowice (near Tarnow), Pol.; pop. 95; 82 km ESE of Krakow; 49°47'/20°58'.

Cifer, Cz.; 32 km NE of Bratislava; 48°19'/17°30'; HSL.

Cig, Rom. (Csog); pop. 19; 107 km NW of Cluj; 47°32'/22°38'.

Cigand, Hung.; pop. 229; 88 km ENE of Miskolc; 48°15'/21°54'; HSL, JGFF, PHH.

Cigla, Cz.; 75 km N of Kosice; 49°22'/21°24'; JGFF.

Ciheiu, Rom.; pop. 3; 126 km W of Cluj; 46°59'/21°58'.

Cihost, Cz.; pop. 8; 75 km ESE of Praha; 49°44'/15°20'.

Cihrin, Ukr. EDRD. This town was not found in BGN gazetteers under the given spelling.

Ciisia, see Ogorodnoye.

Cikolasziget, Hung.; pop. 4; 133 km WNW of Budapest; 47°56'/17°23'.

Cimelice, Cz.; pop. 7; 75 km S of Praha; 49°28'/14°04'.

Cimiseni, see Chimisheny.

Cimislia, see Chimishliya.

Cimislija, see Chimishliya.

Cimochy, Pol. BGN lists two possible localities with this name located at 52°55'/23°35' and 53°58'/22°41'. JGFF.

Cimpia Truzii, Rom. (Campia Turzii); 32 km SE of Cluj; 46°33'/23°53'; PHR1.

Cimpinita, Rom. (Campina); 88 km NNW of Bucuresti; 45°09'/25°43'; GUM4, PHR1.

Cimpulung La Tisa, Rom. (Campulung La Tisa, Depoyla, Hosszumezo); pop. 317; 139 km N of Cluj; 47°59'/23°46'; HSL, PHR2, SM.

Cimpulung Moldovenesc, Rom. (Campalung Moldovenesc, Campalyngul, Camplungul, Kimpulung); pop. 1,488; 157 km W of Iasi; 47°32'/25°34'; AMG, EDRD, EJ, GUM4, GUM5, HSL, JGFF, SF.

Cinadovo, see Chinyadevo.

Cincau, see Chinkeu.

Cineves, Cz.; pop. 15; 56 km NE of Praha; 50°14'/15°13'.

Ciniseuti, see Chinisheutsy.

Cinkota, Hung.; pop. 432; 13 km ENE of Budapest; 47°31'/19°14'; LDS, PHH.

Cioara Murza, *see* Nadrechnoye.

Cioara Murzei, *see* Nadrechnoye.

Cioburciu, *see* Chobruchi.

Ciocaia, Rom. (Csokaly); pop. 36; 133 km WNW of Cluj; 47°20'/22°03'.

Ciocalteni, *see* Chekolteny.

Cioc Maidan, *see* Chok Maydan.

Ciocmani, Rom. (Csokmany); pop. 12; 62 km NNW of Cluj; 47°17'/23°21'; HSL.

Ciocotis, Rom. (Csokas); pop. 46; 94 km N of Cluj; 47°33'/23°48'.

Ciolacu Nou, *see* Novaya Chelakovka.

Ciolacu Vechi, *see* Staraya Chelakovka.

Ciolacu Vechiu, *see* Staraya Chelakovka.

Ciolkowicze Wielkie, *see* Tselkoviche Velikoye.

Ciolt, Rom. (Csolt); pop. 29; 82 km N of Cluj; 47°29'/23°31'.

Ciomirna, Rom. (Ciumara, Ciumarna, Csomorlo); pop. 27; 56 km NW of Cluj; 47°07'/23°08'.

Ciorasti, *see* Choreshty.

Ciorna, *see* Chorna.

Ciornita, Mold.; pop. 52; 114 km NNW of Kishinev; 47°58'/28°28'.

Ciornohuzi, *possibly* Khoroshovtsy.

Cioropcanii Noui, *see* Novyye Choropkany.

Cioropcanii Vechi, *see* Staryye Choropkany.

Ciotusza, Pol.; pop. 17; 82 km N of Przemysl; 50°28'/23°12'.

Cirak, Hung.; pop. 4; 120 km N of Nagykanizsa; 47°28'/17°02'.

Cirava, Lat.; pop. 5; 163 km WSW of Riga; 56°44'/21°23'.

Circ, Cz.; pop. 55; 69 km NNW of Kosice; 49°17'/20°55'.

Circirlau, Rom. (Cicarlau, Cicirlau); pop. 42; 107 km NNW of Cluj; 47°42'/23°24'.

Cires, *see* Cheresh.

Ciresi, *see* Cheresh.

Ciresoaia, Rom. (Ciresoaia Somes); pop. 20; 56 km NNE of Cluj; 47°09'/24°03'.

Ciresoaia Somes, *see* Ciresoaia.

Cirgali, *see* Aumeisteri.

Ciripcau, *see* Cherepkovo.

Cirlibaba, Rom. (Carlibaba, Kirlibaba); pop. 154; 146 km NE of Cluj; 47°35'/25°08'; PHR2.

Cirlibaba Noua, Rom. (Carlibaba Noua); pop. 111; 146 km NE of Cluj; 47°34'/25°08'.

Cisiec, Pol.; pop. 24; 82 km SW of Krakow; 49°35'/19°07'.

Cismele, *see* Strumok.

Cisna, Pol.; pop. 118; 69 km SSW of Przemysl; 49°13'/22°20'; PHP2, PHP3.

Cisovice, Cz.; pop. 4; 32 km SSW of Praha; 49°52'/14°19'.

Cisow, *see* Tysov.

Cisow Las, *see* Tysov.

Cista, Cz.; pop. 22; 62 km WSW of Praha; 50°02'/13°35'; HSL.

Citavjan, *see* Tytuvenai.

Citcau, Rom. (Catcau, Kaczko); pop. 91; 56 km N of Cluj; 47°12'/23°47'; HSL, HSL2, JGFF.

Citoliby, Cz.; pop. 1; 56 km WNW of Praha; 50°20'/13°48'.

Ciubanca, Rom. (Alsocsora); pop. 12; 50 km N of Cluj; 47°09'/23°34'.

Ciucea, Rom. (Csucsa); pop. 134; 62 km WNW of Cluj; 46°57'/22°49'.

Ciuciulea, *see* Chuchulya.

Ciuciuleni, *see* Chuchuleny.

Ciudeiu, *see* Mezhirechye.

Ciudin, GUM4. This town was not found in BGN gazetteers under the given spelling.

Ciuflesti, *see* Chufleshty.

Ciula, Rom.; pop. 12; 69 km NNW of Cluj; 47°21'/23°25'.

Ciuleni, Rom.; 45 km WSW of Cluj; 46°46'/22°59'; PHR1.

Ciulesti, Rom.; pop. 39; A number of towns share this name. It was not possible to determine from available information which one is being referenced.

Ciumara, *see* Ciomirna.

Ciumarna, *see* Ciomirna.

Ciumeni, Rom. (Csomafalva, Csomeny); pop. 7; 69 km N of Cluj; 47°19'/23°36'.

Ciumesti, Rom. (Csomakoz); pop. 26; 139 km NW of Cluj; 47°39'/22°20'.

Ciuslice, Pol.; pop. 5; 50 km NE of Krakow; 50°20'/20°29'.

Ciutelec, Rom.; pop. 11; 107 km WNW of Cluj; 47°16'/22°23'.

Ciutulesti, *see* Chutuleshty.

Ciz, Cz. (Csiz); 82 km SW of Kosice; 48°19'/20°17'; HSL.

Cizer, Rom. (Csizer); pop. 37; 62 km WNW of Cluj; 47°04'/22°53'.

Cizkovice, Cz.; pop. 10; 56 km NW of Praha; 50°29'/14°02'.

Ckyne, Cz.; pop. 15; 120 km S of Praha; 49°07'/13°50'.

Clausthal Zellerfeld, Germ.; pop. 5; 82 km SE of Hannover; 51°49'/10°21'.

Cleastitz, *see* Veselaya Dolina.

Cleve, Germ.; pop. 200; 101 km SW of Hannover; 52°05'/08°18'.

Cleves, *see* Kleve.

Climauti, *see* Klimautsy.

Cliscauti, *see* Klishkovtsy.

Clivesti, *see* Khliveshte.

Clivodin, *see* Klivodin.

Cloppenburg, Germ.; pop. 30; 126 km WNW of Hannover; 52°51'/08°02'; GED.

Cluj, Rom. (Cluj Napoca, Klausenberg, Klausenburg, Kluyzenburg, Kluzh, Kolozhvar, Kolozsvar, Kolozvar); pop. 13,504; 302 km WSW of Iasi; 46°46'/23°36'; AMG, COH, EDRD, EJ, GUM3, GUM4, GUM5, GUM6, HSL, HSL2, ISH1, JGFF, LDL, LJEE, LYV, PHP3, PHR2, YB.

Cluj Napoca, *see* Cluj.

Clus, Germ. BGN lists two possible localities with this name located at 51°53'/10°01' and 52°16'/08°59'. AMG.

Cmielow, Pol. (Chemilov, Chmilov, Tshmelev); pop. 664; 82 km SW of Lublin; 50°53'/21°31'; AMG, COH, GA, GUM5, HSL, JGFF, SF, YB.

Cmien, *possibly* Tsmen Pervsha.

Cmolas, Pol.; pop. 32; 94 km WNW of Przemysl; 50°18'/21°45'.

Cna, *see* Tsna.

Coadjuthen, *see* Katyciai.

Coas, Rom.; pop. 43; 88 km N of Cluj; 47°32'/23°35'.

Cobalca, *see* Kobylka.

Cobalceni, *see* Kobalchin.

Cobalea Noua, *see* Kobylnya.

Cobalea Veche, *see* Kobylnya.

Cobatesti, Rom.; pop. 10; 126 km ESE of Cluj; 46°21'/25°09'.

Coblenz, *see* Koblenz.

Coburg, Germ.; pop. 233; 94 km N of Nurnberg; 50°15'/10°58'; AMG, EJ, GUM3, GUM4, GUM5, PHGB.

Cobusca Noua, *see* Novaya Kobuska.

Cobusca Veche, *see* Staraya Kobuska.

Cochem, Germ.; pop. 49; 94 km SSE of Koln; 50°08'/07°09'; EJ, GUM3.

Cociulia, *see* Kochuliya.

Cocuetii Vechi, Rom.; pop. 21; Described in the *Black Book* as being in the Bessarabia region of Romania, this town was not found in BGN gazetteers.

Codaesti, Rom. (Codaiesti); pop. 325; 38 km SSE of Iasi; 46°52'/27°45'; GUM4, HSL, PHR1.

Codaiesti, *see* Codaesti.

Codor, Rom.; pop. 22; 45 km N of Cluj; 47°07'/23°49'.

Coesfeld, Germ.; pop. 60; 114 km N of Koln; 51°56'/07°09'; EJ, GED.

Cohani, Rom. (Berettykohany); pop. 14; 107 km WNW of Cluj; 47°19'/22°24'.

Cojocna, Rom. (Kolozs, Santa Maria); pop. 32; 32 km NNE of Cluj; 46°56'/23°50'; HSL.

Coka, Yug.; pop. 49; 126 km NNW of Beograd; 45°56'/20°09'; HSL.

Colcauti, *see* Kolikoutsy.

Coldau, Rom.; pop. 4; 62 km NNE of Cluj; 47°11'/24°08'.

Colencauti, *see* Kolinkovtsy.

Colmberg, Germ.; pop. 11; 50 km WSW of Nurnberg; 49°22'/10°25'; PHGB.

Coln, *see* Koln.

Cologne, *see* Koln.

Colonita, *see* Kolonitsa (Bessarabia).

Coltau, Rom.; pop. 24; 101 km N of Cluj; 47°36'/23°31'.

Coltirea, Rom. (Kolczer); pop. 29; 101 km NNW of Cluj; 47°37'/23°24'; HSL.

Coltovo, Cz. (Csolto); 69 km SW of Kosice; 48°30'/20°23'; HSL.

Comalovo, Ukr. (Comanfalva, Csmolif); 176 km WSW of Chernovtsy; 48°12'/23°33'; SM. This town was located on a pre-World War I map, but does not appear in contemporary gazetteers.

Comandau, Rom.; pop. 73; 157 km N of Bucuresti; 45°46'/26°16'.

Comanesti, Rom. (Homorodkemenyfalva); 120 km SW of Iasi; 46°25'/26°26'; PHR2.

Comanesti Suceava, Rom.; pop. 121; 133 km WNW of Iasi; 47°40'/25°59'.

Comanfalva, *see* Comalovo.

Comaresti, *see* Komarovtsi.

Comarova, *see* Komarow.

Combahn, Germ. GED. This town was not found in BGN gazetteers under the given spelling.

Comlausa, Rom. (Vgocsakomlos); pop. 117; 146 km NNW of Cluj; 48°03'/23°10'; PHR2.

Comori, Rom.; pop. 4; 101 km E of Cluj; 46°44'/24°54'.

Comotini, Greece; 208 km ENE of Thessaloniki; 41°06'/25°25'; CAHJP, EDRD.

Comrat, *see* Komrat.

Conatcauti, Ukr.; 82 km SSW of Vinnitsa; 48°35'/28°00'; PHR1. This town was located on a pre-World War I map, but does not appear in contemporary gazetteers.

Concau, *see* Chinkeu.

Condratesti, *see* Kondrateshty.

Conoplja, Yug. (Csonopyca); pop. 49; 146 km NW of Beograd; 45°49'/19°15'; PHY.

Constance, *see* Konstanz.

Constanta, Rom. (Kuestendje); 202 km E of Bucuresti; 44°11'/28°39'; EJ, GUM4, GUM5, HSL, JGFF, PHR1.

Constanza, GUM6. This town was not found in BGN gazetteers under the given spelling.

Convatin, GUM4. This town was not found in BGN gazetteers under the given spelling.

Cop, *see* Chop.

Copaceni, *see* Kopacheny.

Copaigorod, *see* Kopaygorod.

Copalnic, Rom.; pop. 18; 88 km N of Cluj; 47°31'/23°39'.

Copalnic Manastur, Rom. (Kapolnokhonostor, Kapolnokmonostor); pop. 319; 88 km N of Cluj; 47°30'/23°41'; HSL, HSL2, PHR2.

Copanca, *see* Kopanka.

Copcui, *see* Kupkuy.

Copeleuti, Rom.; pop. 175; Described in the *Black Book* as being in the Bessarabia region of Romania, this town was not found in BGN gazetteers.

Coplean, Rom.; pop. 9; 56 km N of Cluj; 47°12'/23°50'.

Copou, Rom. (Copou Targ, Copu Targ); pop. 182; 6 km WNW of Iasi; 47°11'/27°34'; PHR1.

Copou Targ, *see* Copou.

Coppenbrugge, Germ. (Koppenbrugge); 38 km S of Hannover; 52°07'/09°33'; HSL.

Copru, Rom.; pop. 4; 50 km ENE of Cluj; 46°52'/24°12'.

Copu Targ, *see* Copou.

Corabia, Rom.; 146 km SW of Bucuresti; 43°47'/24°30'; GUM3.

Corbach, Germ.; pop. 135; LDS. Described in the *Black Book* as being in the Hessen region of Germany, this town was not found in BGN gazetteers.

Corbesti, Rom. (Csokva); 88 km ESE of Cluj; 46°26'/24°35'; HSL.

Corbu, Rom. (Gyergyohollo); pop. 40; 146 km WSW of Iasi; 46°59'/25°42'.

Corcesti, *see* Corocaesti.

Corcmaz, *see* Krokmazy.

Cordau, Rom.; pop. 6; 126 km W of Cluj; 46°57'/21°59'.

Corestauti, *see* Korestautsy.

Corfu, *see* Kerkira.

Corinth, GUM6. This town was not found in BGN gazetteers under the given spelling.

Corjauti, Rom.; pop. 3; 139 km WNW of Iasi; 48°02'/26°16'.

Corjeuti, *see* Korzhevtsy.

Corjeva, *see* Korzhevo.

Corlateni, Rom.; pop. 6; 114 km NW of Iasi; 47°56'/26°33'.

Cormani, *see* Korman.

Corneni, Rom.; pop. 2; 38 km N of Cluj; 47°04'/23°44'.

Cornest, *see* Cornesti.

Cornesti, Rom. (Cornest, Sinfalva); 32 km SSE of Cluj; 46°31'/23°42'; HSL.

Cornesti Gara, *see* Kyrneshty.

Cornesti Targ, *see* Korneshty.

Corni, Rom. JGFF. A number of towns share this name. It was not possible to determine from available information which one is being referenced.

Cornitel, Rom. (Barodsomos); pop. 5; 75 km WNW of Cluj; 46°59'/22°38'.

Cornova, *see* Kornovo.

Cornyj Ostrov, *see* Chernyy Ostrov.

Corocaesti, Rom. (Corcesti); pop. 65; 101 km WNW of Iasi; 47°38'/26°29'.

Corod, Rom. (Szamoskorod); pop. 41; 120 km NNW of Cluj; 47°46'/23°01'; HSL.

Coropceni, *see* Korobcheny.

Corpaci, *see* Karpach.

Coruia, Rom.; pop. 24; 94 km N of Cluj; 47°34'/23°36'.

Corvinesti, Rom.; pop. 21; 56 km NE of Cluj; 47°01'/24°16'.

Cosarnita, *see* Koshernitsa.

Cosauti, *see* Kosoutsy.

Cosbuc, Rom.; pop. 4; 88 km NNE of Cluj; 47°22'/24°24'.

Coseiu, Rom.; pop. 10; 82 km NW of Cluj; 47°19'/22°59'.

Cosel, *see* Kozle.

Coseni, *see* Kosheny.

Costesti, *see* Kostintsy.

Costesti Balti, *see* Kosteshty.

Costesti Lapusna, *see* Kosteshty Lapusna.

Costiceni, *see* Kotyudzhen.

Costini, HSL. This pre-World War I community was not found in BGN gazetteers.

Costiui, Rom. (Rona Sek, Ronaszek); pop. 17; 126 km N of Cluj; 47°53'/24°02'; SM.

Costrijeni, *see* Kostrizhevka.

Cosuleni, *see* Kostuleny.

Coswig, Germ.; 69 km N of Leipzig; 51°53'/12°27'; LDS.

Cothen, *see* Kothen.

Cotiugeni, *see* Kotyugany.

Cotiugenii Mari, *see* Kotyuzhany.

Cotiugeni Mari, *see* Kotyuzhany.

Cotman, *see* Kitsman.

Cotova, *see* Kotova.

Cottbus, Germ. (Kottbus); pop. 450; 107 km SE of Berlin; 51°46'/14°20'; AMG, EJ, GUM3, HSL.

Cotu Lung, *see* Cotu Lung.

Cotu Lung, Rom. (Cotul Lung); 170 km NE of Bucuresti; 45°23'/27°49'; GUM4.

Cotu Miculinti, Rom.; pop. 1; 126 km NNW of Iasi; 48°11'/26°57'.

Cotusca, Rom.; pop. 4; 126 km NW of Iasi; 48°08'/26°51'.

Couasna, *see* Covasna.

Courland; Courland is not a town, but a region of Latvia.

Covasna, Rom. (Couasna); pop. 66; 163 km N of Bucuresti; 45°51'/26°11'; HSL.

Covurlui, *see* Kovyrluy.

Crimea: View of the temporary Agudes Akhim (Union of Brothers) Settlement of the Novy Bit (New Life) Association.

Cozmeni, *see* Kitsman.

Cracalia, Rom.; pop. 8; 126 km NW of Iasi; 48°01'/26°31'.

Cracesti, Rom. (Kracest, Kracsfalva); pop. 95; 114 km N of Cluj; 47°45'/23°50'; SM.

Craciunel, Rom. (Karacsonfalva); pop. 3; 150 km ESE of Cluj; 46°11'/25°26'; HSL.

Craciunesti, Rom. (Karacson Falva, Kretsnif, Tiszakaracsonfalva); pop. 889; 139 km N of Cluj; 47°58'/23°59'; AMG, SM.

Cracow, *see* Krakow.

Craidorlt, *see* Craidorol.

Craidorol, Rom. (Craidorlt, Craidorolt, Craidorott, Kiralydarocz, Kyralydarocz); pop. 133; 120 km NW of Cluj; 47°37'/22°42'; HSL, PHR2.

Craidorolt, *see* Craidorol.

Craidorott, *see* Craidorol.

Crailsheim, Germ.; pop. 175; 82 km SW of Nurnberg; 49°09'/10°05'; AMG, JGFF, PHGBW.

Crainfeld, Germ.; pop. 57; 62 km NE of Frankfurt am Main; 50°29'/09°21'; LDS.

Crainimat, Rom.; pop. 8; 69 km NE of Cluj; 47°04'/24°24'.

Craiova, Rom. (Belkiralymezo); 126 km WSW of Cluj; 46°35'/21°58'; EJ, GUM3, GUM4, HSL, JGFF, PHR1.

Crasna, Rom. (Kraszna); pop. 418; 69 km WNW of Cluj; 47°10'/22°54'; COH, GUM3, PHR2.

Crasna Iliesti, *possibly* Krasnoilsk.

Crasna Ilschi, *see* Krasnoilsk.

Crasnaleuca, Rom.; pop. 14; 120 km NNW of Iasi; 48°09'/26°58'.

Crasna Putnei, *see* Krasnoputna.

Crasnaseni, *see* Krasnosheny.

Creaca, Rom.; pop. 12; 56 km NW of Cluj; 47°12'/23°15'.

Creglingen, Germ.; pop. 74; 75 km W of Nurnberg; 49°28'/10°02'; EJ, GUM5, JGFF, PHGBW.

Crehange, HSL. This pre-World War I community was not found in BGN gazetteers.

Cremenciuc, *see* Kremenchug.

Cremenia, HSL. This pre-World War I community was not found in BGN gazetteers.

Crensovci, Yug.; pop. 9; 94 km N of Zagreb; 46°35'/16°18'.

Crepaja, Yug.; pop. 23; 26 km NNE of Beograd; 45°01'/20°39'.

Crestur, Rom.; pop. 4; 120 km WNW of Cluj; 47°21'/22°14'.

Creussen, Germ.; 62 km NNE of Nurnberg; 49°51'/11°37'; GUM3, PHGB.

Crijopol, *see* Kryzhopol.

Crikvenica, Yug.; pop. 30; 120 km SW of Zagreb; 45°11'/14°42'.

Crimea; Not a town, but a peninsula in the southern Ukraine that juts into the Black Sea.

Crimmitschau, Germ.; pop. 9; 56 km S of Leipzig; 50°49'/12°23'.

Cris, Rom. (Keresd); 75 km SSW of Cluj; 46°17'/22°54'; HSL.

Criscauti, *see* Krishkautsy.

Crisceatec, *see* Kreshchatik.

Cristelec, Rom.; pop. 11; 88 km WNW of Cluj; 47°16'/22°43'.

Cristesti, GUM4, JGFF. A number of towns share this name. It was not possible to determine from available information which one is being referenced.

Cristinesti, Rom.; pop. 47; 139 km NW of Iasi; 48°06'/26°23'.

Cristolt, Rom.; 56 km NNW of Cluj; 47°12'/23°26'; HSL.

Cristoltel, Rom. (Cristottul Mare); pop. 26; 56 km NNW of Cluj; 47°15'/23°24'.

Cristorel, Rom.; pop. 6; 26 km NNW of Cluj; 46°58'/23°28'.

Cristottul Mare, *see* Cristoltel.

Cristur, Rom. (Apatkeresztur, Szekelykeresztur); pop. 155; 120 km SSW of Cluj; 45°49'/22°57'; HSL, HSL2, LDL, PHR2.

Criuleni, *see* Kriulyany.

Criva, Mold.; pop. 32; 214 km WNW of Kishinev; 48°15'/26°40'.

Crivitz, Germ.; 69 km SSW of Rostock; 53°35'/11°39'; LDS.

Crivoje Ozero, *see* Krivoye Ozero.

Crna Gora, Yug.; 214 km SSW of Beograd; 43°13'/19°01'; GUM4.

Crnomelj, Yug.; pop. 1; 62 km SW of Zagreb; 45°34'/15°12'.

Croatia; Not a town, but a region of the Austro-Hungarian Empire that existed until World War I. It is now a constituent republic of Yugoslavia.

Cronheim, Germ.; pop. 48; 50 km SSW of Nurnberg; 49°06'/10°40'; AMG, CAHJP, GUM5, PHGB.

Crossen, *see* Krosno Odrzanskie.

Crucisor, Rom. (Borvalaszut); pop. 23; 107 km NNW of Cluj; 47°41'/23°15'.

Cruglic Hotin, *see* Kruglik.

Cruglic Orhei, *see* Kruglyak.

Crumstadt, Germ.; pop. 44; 38 km S of Frankfurt am Main; 49°49'/08°31'; JGFF.

Crvenka, Yug. (Cservenka); pop. 34; 126 km NW of Beograd; 45°39'/19°28'; EDRD.

Csaba, Hung.; 88 km ENE of Nagykanizsa; 46°39'/18°05'; HSL, HSL2, LDS.

Csabacsud, Hung.; pop. 13; 75 km NNE of Szeged; 46°50'/20°39'.

Csabdi, Hung.; pop. 9; 38 km W of Budapest; 47°31'/18°37'.

Csabrendek, Hung.; pop. 107; 69 km N of Nagykanizsa; 47°01'/17°18'; JGFF, LDS, PHH.

Csaholc, Hung.; pop. 29; 146 km E of Miskolc; 47°59'/22°44'; HSL.

Csajag, Hung.; pop. 9; 82 km SW of Budapest; 47°03'/18°11'.

Csakany, Hung.; pop. 8; 26 km NE of Nagykanizsa; 46°32'/17°17'; HSL.

Csakathurn, *see* Cakovec.

Csakbereny, Hung.; pop. 5; 62 km SW of Budapest; 47°21'/18°20'.

Csaktornya, *see* Cakovec.

Csakvar, Hung.; pop. 56; 50 km WSW of Budapest; 47°24'/18°27'; PHH.

Csallokozposfa, *see* Posfa.

Csanadapaca, Hung.; pop. 27; 62 km NE of Szeged; 46°33'/20°53'.

Csanadpalota, Hung.; pop. 31; 45 km E of Szeged; 46°15'/20°44'.

Csanalos, *see* Urziceni.

Csantaver, *see* Cantavir.

Csany, Hung.; pop. 63; 56 km NE of Budapest; 47°39'/19°50'; HSL, HSL2, PHH.

Csanytelek, Hung.; pop. 7; 45 km N of Szeged; 46°36'/20°07'.

Csap, *see* Chop.

Csapi, Hung.; 19 km NNE of Nagykanizsa; 46°32'/17°06'; HSL.

Csapod, Hung.; pop. 7; 126 km N of Nagykanizsa; 47°31'/16°55'.

Csarda, *possibly* Csaroda.

Csarnohaza, *see* Bulz.

Csaroda, Hung. (Csarda?); pop. 82; 126 km ENE of Miskolc; 48°10'/22°28'; HSL.

Csaszar, Hung.; pop. 15; 69 km WSW of Budapest; 47°30'/18°09'; HSL.

Csaszartoltes, Hung.; pop. 29; 82 km W of Szeged; 46°25'/19°11'; HSL.

Csaszlo, Hung.; pop. 16; 146 km E of Miskolc; 47°55'/22°44'; HSL.

Csatalja, Hung.; pop. 8; 101 km WSW of Szeged; 46°02'/18°57'; LDS.

Csatar, Hung.; 45 km NNW of Nagykanizsa; 46°47'/16°53'; HSL.

Csatka, Hung.; pop. 8; 88 km WSW of Budapest; 47°22'/17°59'.

Csavoly, Hung.; pop. 8; 75 km WSW of Szeged; 46°11'/19°09'.

Cseb, *see* Cibu.

Csebeny, Hung.; 75 km ESE of Nagykanizsa; 46°11'/17°56'; HSL.

Csecs, *see* Cecejovce.

Csecse, Hung.; pop. 23; 56 km NE of Budapest; 47°52'/19°38'; HSL, LDL, LDS.

Cseffa, *see* Cefa.

Csege, *see* Tiszacsege.

Csegold, Hung.; pop. 21; 146 km E of Miskolc; 47°54'/22°41'.

Csehbanya, Hung.; pop. 6; 101 km NNE of Nagykanizsa; 47°11'/17°41'.

Csehetfalva, *see* Cehetel.

Cseke, Hung. BGN lists two possible localities with this name located at 47°48'/19°14' and 48°22'/21°59'. HSL.

Csekut, Hung.; pop. 4; 82 km NNE of Nagykanizsa; 47°04'/17°33'.

Csenger, Hung. (Chenga, Chenger); pop. 611; 146 km E of Miskolc; 47°50'/22°41'; AMG, COH, GUM5, HSL, HSL2, LDS, LYV, PHH, YB.

Csengersima, Hung.; pop. 22; 150 km E of Miskolc; 47°52'/22°44'.

Csengerujfalu, Hung.; pop. 34; 139 km E of Miskolc; 47°48'/22°38'.

Csengod, Hung.; pop. 11; 88 km WNW of Szeged; 46°43'/19°16'.

Csenyete, Hung.; pop. 7; 45 km NNE of Miskolc; 48°26'/21°03'.

Cseoreg, *see* Cidreag.

Csep, Hung.; pop. 12; 75 km W of Budapest; 47°35'/18°04'.

Csepa, Hung.; pop. 16; 69 km N of Szeged; 46°48'/20°08'; HSL, HSL2.

Csepel, Hung.; pop. 638; 19 km S of Budapest; 47°25'/19°05'; GUM5, PHH.

Csepreg, Hung.; pop. 61; 114 km NNW of Nagykanizsa; 47°24'/16°43'; LDS, PHH.

Cserep, *see* Cserepfalu.

Cserepfalu, Hung. (Cserep); pop. 9; 32 km SW of Miskolc; 47°56'/20°32'; HSL.

Cserhathalap, Hung.; pop. 26; 56 km N of Budapest; 47°59'/19°22'.

Cserhatszentivan, Hung.; pop. 14; 56 km NNE of Budapest; 47°56'/19°35'.

Cserjes, *see* Lozansky.

Csernely, Hung.; pop. 12; 32 km W of Miskolc; 48°09'/20°21'.

Csertesz, *see* Certege.

Cservenka, *see* Crvenka.

Csesznek, Hung.; pop. 15; 88 km WSW of Budapest; 47°21'/17°53'.

Csesztreg, Hung.; pop. 14; 50 km WNW of Nagykanizsa; 46°43'/16°31'.

Csesztve, Hung.; pop. 7; 62 km N of Budapest; 48°01'/19°17'.

Cseteny, Hung.; pop. 23; 82 km WSW of Budapest; 47°19'/18°00'.

Csetnik, *see* Stitnik.

Csibrak, Hung.; pop. 9; 101 km ENE of Nagykanizsa; 46°28'/18°21'.

Csicsogombas, *see* Gostila.

Csicsogyongyfalva, *see* Ciceu Giurgesti.

Csiger Szollos, *see* Seleus.

Csikarlo, *see* Sikarlo.

Csikfalva, *see* Vargata.

Csiksomlyo, HSL. This pre-World War I community was not found in BGN gazetteers.

Csikszentdomokos, *see* Sindominic.

Csikszentmihaly, *see* Mihaileni.

Csikszereda, *see* Miercurea Ciuc.

Csiktaplocza, *see* Toplita Ciuc.

Csikvand, Hung.; pop. 4; 120 km WSW of Budapest; 47°28'/17°27'.

Csillaghegy, Hung. BGN lists two possible localities with this name located at 46°52'/16°55' and 47°03'/16°54'. AMG, GUM5.

Csimpo, HSL. This pre-World War I community was not found in BGN gazetteers.

Csipkerek, Hung.; pop. 3; 75 km N of Nagykanizsa; 47°04'/16°57'.

Csitar, Hung.; pop. 4; 62 km N of Budapest; 48°03'/19°26'; HSL.

Csiz, *see* Ciz.

Csizer, *see* Cizer.

Csmolif, *see* Comalovo.

Csob, *see* Cibu.

Csobad, Hung.; pop. 22; 32 km NNE of Miskolc; 48°17'/21°02'; HSL.

Csobaj, Hung.; pop. 23; 45 km E of Miskolc; 48°03'/21°21'; HSL.

Csobanka, Hung. BGN lists two possible localities with this name located at 47°15'/20°30' and 47°38'/18°58'. HSL.

Csog, *see* Cig.

Csogle, Hung.; pop. 23; 94 km N of Nagykanizsa; 47°13'/17°16'.

Csokako, Hung.; pop. 5; 62 km WSW of Budapest; 47°21'/18°16'.

Csokaly, *see* Ciocaia.

Csokas, *see* Ciocotis.

Csokmany, *see* Ciocmani.

Csokmo, Hung.; pop. 65; 120 km SSE of Miskolc; 47°02'/21°18'; LDS, PHH.

Csokoly, Hung.; pop. 10; 45 km ESE of Nagykanizsa; 46°18'/17°33'.

Csokonyavisonta, Hung. (Erdocsokonya); pop. 6; 56 km SE of Nagykanizsa; 46°05'/17°27'.

Csokva, *see* Corbesti.

Csolnok, Hung.; pop. 5; 38 km WNW of Budapest; 47°42'/18°43'.

Csolt, *see* Ciolt.

Csolto, *see* Coltovo.

Csoma, Hung. BGN lists two possible localities with this name located at 46°22'/18°03' and 47°01'/21°30'. HSL.

Csomafalva, *see* Ciumeni.

Csomakoz, *see* Ciumesti.

Csomend, Hung.; pop. 4; 45 km NE of Nagykanizsa; 46°34'/17°30'.

Csomeny, *see* Ciumeni.

Csomoder, Hung.; pop. 12; 32 km WNW of Nagykanizsa; 46°37'/16°39'.

Csomonya, Cz.; 101 km ESE of Kosice; 48°24'/22°28'; HSL. This town was located on a pre-World War I map, but does not appear in contemporary gazetteers.

Csomor, Hung.; pop. 77; 13 km NE of Budapest; 47°33'/19°14'; PHH.

Csomorlo, *see* Ciomirna.

Csonge, Hung.; pop. 2; 107 km N of Nagykanizsa; 47°21'/17°04'; HSL.

Csongrad, Hung.; pop. 345; 56 km N of Szeged; 46°42'/20°09'; HSL, LDS, PHH.

Csonkahegyhat, Hung.; pop. 6; 50 km NW of Nagykanizsa; 46°48'/16°43'.

Csonopyca, *see* Conoplja.

Csop, *see* Chop.

Csor, Hung.; pop. 2; 69 km SW of Budapest; 47°12'/18°16'.

Csorba, *see* Strba.

Csorna, Hung.; pop. 795; 133 km W of Budapest; 47°37'/17°15'; AMG, EDRD, HSL, LDS, PHH.

Csornyefold, Hung.; pop. 5; 32 km W of Nagykanizsa; 46°30'/16°38'.

Csorvas, Hung.; pop. 38; 69 km NE of Szeged; 46°38'/20°50'.

Csosz, Hung.; pop. 9; 69 km SSW of Budapest; 47°02'/18°25'.

Csot, Hung.; pop. 2; 114 km WSW of Budapest; 47°22'/17°37'; HSL.

Csota, Hung.; 82 km NNE of Nagykanizsa; 47°04'/17°30'; HSL.

Csovar, Hung.; pop. 2; 38 km NNE of Budapest; 47°49'/19°20'.

Csucsa, *see* Ciucea.

Csurgo, Hung.; pop. 229; 26 km SSE of Nagykanizsa; 46°16'/17°06'; GUM5, JGFF, LDS, PHH.

Csurgonagymarton, Hung.; pop. 3; 19 km SSE of Nagykanizsa; 46°18'/17°05'.

Csurog, *see* Curug.

Csuszka, *see* Tuska.

Csuz, *see* Dubnik.

Cubani, *see* Kuban.

Cubei, *see* Chervonoarmeyskoye.

Cubles Somesani, Rom. (Cublesul Ungureasca, Magyarkoblos); 38 km N of Cluj; 47°03'/23°38'; HSL.

Cublesul Ungureasca, *see* Cubles Somesani.

Cubolta, *see* Kubolta.

Cubulcut, Rom. (Erkobolkut); pop. 38; 126 km WNW of Cluj; 47°19'/22°12'.

Cucavca, *see* Kukavka.

Cucerdea, Rom. (Olahkocsard, Szekelykocsard); 62 km ESE of Cluj; 46°24'/24°16'; HSL.

Cuceu, Rom.; pop. 7; 62 km NW of Cluj; 47°16'/23°12'.

Cuci, Rom. (Kutyfalva); 50 km ESE of Cluj; 46°28'/24°09'; HSL.

Cucioaia, *see* Kuchoya.

Cuciulat, Rom.; pop. 4; 69 km NNW of Cluj; 47°19'/23°25'.

Cuciurul Mare, *see* Velikiy Kochurov.

Cuciurul Mic, *see* Malyy Kochurov.

Cucniow, *see* Tsutsnyuv.

Cuconestii Vechi, *see* Staryye Kukoneshty (Bessarabia).

Cucu, Rom.; pop. 9; 126 km NNW of Cluj; 47°47'/22°58'.

Cucuruzeni, *see* Kokorozeny.

Cucylow, *see* Tsutsyluv.

Cudnov, *see* Chudnov.

Cudnow, *see* Chudnov.

Cudzynowice, Pol.; pop. 4; 50 km NE of Krakow; 50°18'/20°29'.

Cufoaia, Rom.; pop. 3; 82 km N of Cluj; 47°29'/23°48'.

Cuhca, *see* Cuhea.

Cuhea, Rom. (Cuhca, Izakonyha, Izakonyka, Kechnie); pop. 321; 114 km NNE of Cluj; 47°42'/24°16'; GUM4, LDL, PHR2, SM.

Cuhnesti, *see* Kukhneshty.

Cuhurestii de Jos, *see* Nizhniye Kugureshty.

Cuizovca, *see* Kuyzovka.

Cukmantl, *see* Zlate Hory (Moravia).

Culcea, Rom.; pop. 8; 94 km N of Cluj; 47°34'/23°33'.

Culciul Mare, *see* Culciu Mare.

Culciu Mare, Rom. (Culciul Mare); pop. 20; 120 km NNW of Cluj; 47°45'/23°03'.

Culevcea, *see* Kolesnoye.

Culmea, *see* Podgornoye.

Culpiu, Rom.; pop. 5; 62 km E of Cluj; 46°38'/24°26'.

Cuman, *see* Tsuman.

Cunicea, *see* Kunicha.

Cupca, *see* Kupka.

Cupcina, *see* Kupchino.

Cuple, Pol.; pop. 15; 26 km SW of Lublin; 51°10'/22°12'.

Cuporani, *see* Rovnoye.

Cupseni, Rom.; pop. 4; 94 km N of Cluj; 47°33'/23°56'.

Curatura, *see* Kuratura.

Curtici, Rom.; 182 km WSW of Cluj; 46°21'/21°18'; PHR1.

Curtuiuseni, Rom. (Curtuiusieni, Curtusieni, Erkortvelyes); pop. 32; 139 km WNW of Cluj; 47°33'/22°12'.

Curtuiusieni, *see* Curtuiuseni.

Curtusieni, *see* Curtuiuseni.

Curug, Yug. (Csurog); pop. 72; 82 km NW of Beograd; 45°28'/20°04'; PHY.

Cusdrioara, Rom. (Cuzdrioada, Cuzdrioara, Cuzorioara, Kozarvar); pop. 84; 50 km NNE of Cluj; 47°10'/23°55'; HSL.

Cusma, Rom. (Kusma); pop. 16; 94 km NE of Cluj; 47°08'/24°42'; HSL.

Cusmed, Rom.; pop. 4; 114 km ESE of Cluj; 46°28'/25°03'.

Cusmirca, *see* Kushmirka.

Cut, Rom.; 101 km S of Cluj; 45°56'/23°40'; HSL.

Cuta, Rom.; pop. 6; 94 km NW of Cluj; 47°32'/23°00'.

Cuxhaven, Germ.; pop. 39; 94 km WNW of Hamburg; 53°53'/08°42'.

Cuzap, Rom.; pop. 18; 101 km WNW of Cluj; 47°12'/22°25'.

Cuzaplac, Rom. (Cuzaplacu, Kozeplak); pop. 22; 38 km WNW of Cluj; 46°58'/23°12'; HSL.

Cuzaplacu, *see* Cuzaplac.

Cuzdrioada, *see* Cusdrioara.

Cuzdrioara, *see* Cusdrioara.

Cuzminti, *see* Kuzmintsy.

Cuzorioara, *see* Cusdrioara.

Cvikov, Cz.; pop. 17; 82 km N of Praha; 50°47'/14°38'.

Cvrstec, Yug. (Sveti Petar Cvrstec); pop. 5; 56 km NE of Zagreb; 46°00'/16°40'.

Cybulice, Pol.; pop. 1; 32 km WNW of Warszawa; 52°23'/20°38'.

Cychry, Pol.; pop. 6; 45 km SSW of Warszawa; 51°54'/20°40'.

Cycow, Pol. (Tzitzov, Wiszniewice); pop. 181; 45 km ENE of

Lublin; 51°18'/23°09'; COH, GA, GUM5, GUM5, HSL, HSL2, JGFF, POCEM, SF.

Cygany, *see* Rudka (Tarnopol).

Cyprki, Pol.; pop. 12; 75 km NW of Bialystok; 53°40'/22°22'.

Cyr, *see* Tsyr.

Cyranka, Pol.; 114 km ENE of Krakow; 50°18'/21°26'; GA.

Cyryn, *see* Tsirin.

Czachulec, Pol. PHP1. This town was not found in BGN gazetteers under the given spelling.

Czahrow, *see* Chagrov.

Czaje Wolka, Pol.; pop. 14; 62 km SSW of Bialystok; 52°41'/22°42'.

Czajkin, GUM3. This town was not found in BGN gazetteers under the given spelling.

Czajki, Pol.; pop. 26; 82 km SW of Lodz; 51°29'/18°20'.

Czajkowa, Pol.; pop. 15; 114 km ENE of Krakow; 50°23'/21°31'.

Czajkowice, *see* Chaykovichi.

Czaniec, Pol.; pop. 11; 56 km SW of Krakow; 49°51'/19°15'.

Czanyz, *see* Chanyzh.

Czaplaki, Pol.; pop. 17; 32 km NE of Przemysl; 49°59'/23°09'.

Czaple, *see* Chapli.

Czaple Male, Pol.; pop. 7; 32 km N of Krakow; 50°18'/19°57'.

Czaple Ruskie, Pol.; pop. 39; Described in the *Black Book* as being in the Lublin region of Poland, this town was not found in BGN gazetteers.

Czaple Wielkie, Pol.; pop. 7; 32 km N of Krakow; 50°18'/19°59'.

Czaplice, Pol.; pop. 23; 75 km WSW of Bialystok; 53°07'/21°59'.

Czaplinek, Pol. (Tempelburg); pop. 63; 114 km ENE of Szczecin; 53°33'/16°14'; HSL, LDS.

Czarkow, Pol.; 94 km E of Poznan; 52°14'/18°15'; GA, GUM3, LDL.

Czarna, Pol. (Charna);

Czarna (near Konskie), Pol.; pop. 39; 101 km ESE of Lodz; 51°08'/20°32'.

Czarna (near Lesko), Pol.; pop. 122; 56 km S of Przemysl; 49°20'/22°40'; COH, HSL, HSL2, PHP2.

Czarna (near Lublin), Pol.; pop. 22; 56 km NNW of Lublin; 51°43'/22°16'.

Czarna (near Pilzno), Pol.; pop. 65; 94 km E of Krakow; 50°04'/21°16'; GUM3, SF.

Czarna (near Radom), Pol.; pop. 22; 82 km W of Lublin; 51°26'/21°27'.

Czarna (near Ropczyce), Pol.; pop. 33; 88 km WNW of Przemysl; 50°08'/21°45'.

Czarna Ostrov, *see* Chernyy Ostrov.

Czarna Srednia, Pol.; pop. 21; 62 km S of Bialystok; 52°36'/22°49'.

Czarna Struga, Pol.; pop. 2; 19 km NNE of Warszawa; 52°22'/21°06'.

Czarna Wielka, *see* Czarna Wielkie.

Czarna Wielkie, Pol. (Czarna Wielka); pop. 26; 69 km S of Bialystok; 52°34'/22°50'.

Czarnca, Pol.; pop. 32; 56 km ENE of Czestochowa; 50°49'/19°56'.

Czarne, Pol. (Hammerstein); pop. 55; 133 km SW of Gdansk; 53°41'/16°56'; GUM3, GUM4.

Czarnia, Pol.; pop. 37; 126 km N of Warszawa; 53°22'/21°12'; JGFF.

Czarniecka Gora, Pol.; 101 km ESE of Lodz; 51°08'/20°32'; PHP1.

Czarniewice, *see* Czarnowiec.

Czarnikau, *see* Czarnkow.

Czarnkow, Pol. (Czarnikau); pop. 321; 56 km NW of Poznan; 52°54'/16°34'; CAHJP, HSL, JGFF.

Czarnoglow, Pol.; pop. 18; 50 km ENE of Warszawa; 52°18'/21°46'.

Czarnokonce Wielkie, *see* Velikiye Chornokontsy.

Czarnokoniecka Wola, Pol.; pop. 28; Described in the *Black Book* as being in the Tarnopol region of Poland, this town was not found in BGN gazetteers.

Czarnolas, Pol.; pop. 7; 62 km WNW of Lublin; 51°26'/21°43'.

Czarnolozy, Pol.; pop. 23; 75 km ESE of Lublin; 50°56'/23°30'; EJ.

Czarnowaz, Pol.; pop. 6; 75 km E of Warszawa; 52°13'/22°04'.

Czarnowiec, Pol. (Czarniewice); pop. 66; 50 km SE of Warszawa; 51°56'/21°26'.

Czarnuszowice, *see* Charnushovitse.

Czarny, COH. This town was not found in BGN gazetteers under the given spelling.

Czarny Dunajec, Pol. (Charni Dunayets, Dunayets, Tzarna Dunayetz); pop. 341; 75 km S of Krakow; 49°26'/19°52'; EGRS, GA, GUM3, GUM4, HSL, LYV, PHP3, SF, YB.

Czarny Potok, Pol. (Cerni Potok); pop. 5; 69 km SE of Krakow; 49°35'/20°29'; AMG.

Czartorysk, *see* Staryy Chartoriysk.

Czartowczyk, Pol.; pop. 6; 101 km ESE of Lublin; 50°35'/23°36'.

Czarukow, *see* Charukuv.

Czaryz, Pol.; pop. 21; 56 km E of Czestochowa; 50°43'/19°54'.

Czaslaw, Pol.; pop. 7; 32 km SE of Krakow; 49°52'/20°09'.

Czastary, Pol. (Tshastar); pop. 16; 82 km WNW of Czestochowa; 51°16'/18°19'; FRG.

Czastkowice, Pol.; pop. 14; 26 km NW of Przemysl; 49°57'/22°34'.

Czausy, *see* Chausy.

Czchow, Pol. (Chechiav); pop. 136; 62 km ESE of Krakow; 49°50'/20°41'; EGRS, GUM3, GUM4, GUM5, HSL, PHP3, SF.

Czechow, Pol.; pop. 26; 75 km NNE of Krakow; 50°35'/20°36'; HSL2.

Czechowice, Pol.; pop. 172; 69 km SW of Krakow; 49°53'/19°01'; PHP3, POCEM.

Czechowka Dolna, Pol. (Chechov, Vinovi); 13 km NNE of Lublin; 51°16'/22°35'; SF.

Czeczelnik, *see* Chechelnik.

Czeczersk, *see* Chechersk.

Czeczke, *see* Tetche.

Czege, *see* Taga.

Czehryn, *see* Chigirin.

Czekaje, Pol.; 82 km SW of Lodz; 51°27'/18°23'; PHP1.

Czekarzewice, Pol.; pop. 10; 69 km SW of Lublin; 51°02'/21°41'.

Czeladz, Pol. (Chelodz); pop. 753; 56 km S of Czestochowa; 50°19'/19°06'; AMG, COH, GA, GUM3, GUM4, HSL, HSL2, JGFF, POCEM, SF.

Czelatyce, Pol.; pop. 11; 19 km NW of Przemysl; 49°55'/22°37'.

Czelldomolk, *see* Celldomolk.

Czemerowce, *see* Chemerovtsy.

Czemery, HSL. This pre-World War I community was not found in BGN gazetteers.

Czemierniki, Pol. (Chemenik, Chemernik, Chemyerniki); pop. 1,004; 56 km N of Lublin; 51°41'/22°37'; AMG, COH, EDRD, GUM3, GUM4, GUM5, LDS, LYV, PHP4, POCEM, SF.

Czemierniki (Krasnystaw area), Pol.; pop. 26; 32 km ESE of Lublin; 51°09'/23°00'.

Czempin, Pol. (Schempin); 38 km SSW of Poznan; 52°09'/16°46'; CAHJP, JGFF.

Czempisz, Pol.; pop. 10; 82 km WSW of Lodz; 51°35'/18°17'.

Czente, *see* Tentea.

Czepel, *see* Shepel.

Czepiele, Pol.; pop. 2; 56 km NE of Bialystok; 53°27'/23°40'.

Czepielow, *see* Ciepielow.

Czepow Dolny, Pol.; pop. 3; 56 km WNW of Lodz; 52°03'/18°47'.

Czepowiczi, LDL. This pre-World War I community was not found in BGN gazetteers.

Czerbin, *see* Czerwin.

Czerchawa, *see* Cherkhava.

Czercze, *see* Cherche.

Czered, *see* Cered.

Czeremcha, Pol.; pop. 25; 75 km SSE of Bialystok; 52°31'/23°21'; GUM4.

Czeremoszno, *see* Cheremoshno.

Czeress, *see* Cheres.

Czerkasy, *see* Cherkassy.

Czermin, Pol.; pop. 44; 107 km ENE of Krakow; 50°21'/21°21'; PHP3.

Czermna, Pol.; pop. 56; 107 km ESE of Krakow; 49°49'/21°18'.

Czermno, Pol.; pop. 27; 101 km ESE of Lublin; 50°40'/23°42'.

Czerna, Pol.; pop. 10; 32 km SW of Krakow; 49°54'/19°37'.

Czernawczyce, *see* Chernavchitsy.

Czerncze, *see* Cherche.

Czernelica, *see* Chernelitsa.

Czernewka, *see* Chernevka.

Czernia, Pol. PHP4. This town was not found in BGN gazetteers under the given spelling.

Czerniachow, Pol. PHP3. This town was not found in BGN gazetteers under the given spelling.

Czerniany, *see* Chernyany.

Czerniatyn, *see* Chernyatin.

Czernica, *see* Chernitsa.

Czernice, GA. A number of towns share this name. It was not possible to determine from available information which one is being referenced.

Czernichow, *see* Chernikhov.

Czernichowce, *see* Chernikhovtsy.

Czernichowek, Pol.; pop. 2; 26 km SW of Krakow; 50°00'/19°41'.

Czerniczyn, Pol.; pop. 37; 107 km ESE of Lublin; 50°46'/23°55'.

Czerniec, Pol.; pop. 3; 69 km SE of Krakow; 49°34'/20°26'.

Czerniecin, Pol.; pop. 10; 56 km SSE of Lublin; 50°48'/22°49'.

Czerniejewo, Pol. (Schwarzenau); 38 km ENE of Poznan; 52°26'/17°30'; CAHJP, GUM5, HSL.

Czerniejow, Pol.; pop. 28; 75 km E of Lublin; 51°05'/23°38'; GA, GUM3, PHP2. *See also* Cherneyev.

Czerniewicze, GUM3. This town was not found in BGN gazetteers under the given spelling.

Czerniewo, Pol. BGN lists two possible localities with this name located at 52°36'/19°57' and 54°10'/18°30'. AMG.

Czernihow, *see* Chernigov.

Czernijow, *see* Cherniyuv.

Czernik, Pol.; pop. 3; 50 km NE of Warszawa; 52°25'/21°38'.

Czernikowo, Pol.; pop. 14; 139 km NNW of Lodz; 52°57'/18°56'.

Czernilawa, *see* Chernilyava.

Czerniow, *see* Chernev.

Czerniowce, *see* Chernovtsy.

Czernovitz, *see* Chernovtsy.

Czernowitz, *see* Chernovtsy.

Czersk, Pol. (Chersk); 45 km SE of Warszawa; 51°57'/21°14'; LDS, PHP4, SF.

Czersk Pomorski, Pol.; 75 km SSW of Gdansk; 53°48'/17°59'; POCEM.

Czersl, Pol.; pop. 2; 82 km NNW of Lublin; 51°54'/22°18'.

Czertez, *see* Cheretezh.

Czertyzne, Pol.; pop. 4; 107 km ESE of Krakow; 49°29'/21°05'.

Czerwien, *see* Cherven.

Czerwin, Pol. (Chervin, Czerbin); pop. 218; 94 km WSW of Bialystok; 52°57'/21°45'; GUM4, LDL, SF, YB.

Czerwinsk, *see* Czerwinsk nad Wisla.

Czerwinsk nad Wisla, Pol. (Czerwinsk, Tshervinsk); pop. 388; 50 km WNW of Warszawa; 52°24'/20°18'; AMG, COH, EDRD, EJ, FRG, LDS, PHP4.

Czerwona, Pol.; pop. 50; 75 km WSW of Lublin; 51°12'/21°26'.

Czerwona Gora, Pol.; pop. 11; 94 km SW of Lublin; 50°51'/21°20'.

Czerwona Wola, Pol.; pop. 20; 45 km N of Przemysl; 50°09'/22°43'.

Czerwonka, Pol.; 75 km N of Warszawa; 52°54'/21°14'; PHP4.

Czerwonohrad, *see* Chervonograd.

Czerwony Bor, GUM4, PHP4. This town was not found in BGN gazetteers under the given spelling.

Czerykow, *see* Cherikov.

Czesniki, *see* Chesniki.

Czestoborowice, Pol.; pop. 54; 38 km SE of Lublin; 51°01'/22°52'.

Czestochowa, Pol. (Chenstchov, Chenstochov, Chenstokhov, Chestokhova, Tshenstokhov); pop. 22,663; 94 km NW of Krakow; 50°48'/19°07'; AMG, CAHJP, COH, EDRD, EJ, FRG, GA, GUM3, GUM4, GUM5, GUM6, GYLA, HSL, HSL2, ISH1, ISH2, ISH3, JGFF, LDL, LDS, LYV, PHP1, PHP4, POCEM, SF, YB.

Czestocice, Pol. (Chentatzitza); 88 km SW of Lublin; 50°56'/21°22'; SF.

Czestoniew, Pol.; pop. 41; 50 km S of Warszawa; 51°52'/20°58'; GA, GUM5. The 1921 Polish census also shows a town of Czestoniew Nowy (pop. 73).

Czesybiesy, *see* Zhovten.

Czetwiertnia, *see* Chetvertnya.

Czezwin, Pol. PHP4. This town was not found in BGN gazetteers under the given spelling.

Czieschowa, *see* Cieszowa.

Czilka, EGRS. This town was not found in BGN gazetteers under the given spelling.

Czimisli, LDL. This pre-World War I community was not found in BGN gazetteers.

Czlopa, Pol. (Schloppe); pop. 100; 88 km NW of Poznan; 53°05'/16°07'; HSL, LDS.

Czmielov, *see* Khmelyuv.

Czmon, Pol. (Schlochau); pop. 125; 32 km SSE of Poznan; 52°11'/17°04'; HSL.

Czolczyn, Pol.; pop. 11; 26 km W of Lodz; 51°46'/19°10'.

Czolhany, Ukr.; pop. 124; 126 km S of Lvov; 48°45'/23°55'; PHP2. This town was located on an interwar map of Poland but does not appear in contemporary gazetteers. Map coordinates are approximate.

Czolowiec, Byel.; pop. 49; 88 km NE of Pinsk; 52°25'/27°15'. This town was located on an interwar map of Poland but does not appear in contemporary gazetteers. Map coordinates are approximate.

Czoptelke, *see* Top.

Czorsztyn, Pol.; pop. 11; 75 km SSE of Krakow; 49°26'/20°19'; PHP3.

Czortkow, *see* Chortkov.

Czortkow Stary, *see* Chortkov.

Czortowiec, *see* Chortovets.

Czosnow, Pol.; pop. 6; 26 km WNW of Warszawa; 52°23'/20°44'.

Czubin, Pol.; 26 km SW of Warszawa; 52°10'/20°40'; HSL.

Czubrowice, Pol.; pop. 10; 26 km WNW of Krakow; 50°13'/19°41'.

Czuchowo, *see* Chukhovo.

Czuchow Pienki, Pol.; pop. 13; 101 km S of Bialystok; 52°17'/22°47'.

Czuczewicze Male, Byel.; pop. 21; 88 km NE of Pinsk; 52°25'/27°15'. This town was located on an interwar map of Poland but does not appear in contemporary gazetteers. Map coordinates are approximate.

Czuczewicze Wielkie, Byel.; pop. 64; 88 km NE of Pinsk; 52°25'/27°15'. This town was located on an interwar map of Poland but does not appear in contemporary gazetteers. Map coordinates are approximate.

Czudec, Pol. (Chitch, Czudez); pop. 332; 69 km W of Przemysl; 49°57'/21°50'; AMG, EGRS, GUM5, LDL, PHP3, POCEM, SF.

Czudel, *see* Chudel.

Czudez, *see* Czudec.

Czudyn, *see* Mezhirechye.

Czudzin, *see* Mezhirechye.

Czugujew, *see* Chuguyev.

Czukalowka, *see* Chukaluvka.

Czukow, Ukr.; 50 km SE of Vinnitsa; 48°55'/28°57'; PHR1. This town was located on a pre-World War I map, but does not appear in contemporary gazetteers.

Czulczyce, Pol.; pop. 33; 62 km E of Lublin; 51°13'/23°27'.

Czulowice, *see* Chulovichi.

Czumsk Duzy, Pol.; pop. 11; 126 km WNW of Warszawa; 52°58'/19°30'.

Czyrczyk, HSL. This pre-World War I community was not found in BGN gazetteers.

Czyrna, Pol.; pop. 11; 107 km ESE of Krakow; 49°29'/21°02'; HSL.

Czystadebina, Pol.; pop. 33; 45 km SE of Lublin; 50°57'/22°57'.

Czyste, *see* Chyste.

Czystohorb, Pol.; pop. 22; 75 km SW of Przemysl; 49°22'/22°02'.

Czystylow, GUM3, GUM4. This town was not found in BGN gazetteers under the given spelling.

Czyszki, *see* Chishki.

Czyze, Pol.; pop. 22; 45 km SE of Bialystok; 52°47'/23°25'.

Czyzew, Pol. (Chizeve, Chizheva, Chizhevo, Czyzewo, Tshizheva, Tzizhav); pop. 1,595; 69 km SW of Bialystok; 52°48'/22°19'; AMG, EDRD, GA, GUM3, GUM4, HSL, JGFF, LDL, LDS, LYV, PHP4, SF, YB.

Czyzewo, *see* Czyzew.

Czyzewo Koscielne Wies, Pol.; pop. 59; Described in the *Black Book* as being in the Bialystok region of Poland, this town was not found in BGN gazetteers.

Czyzow, Pol.; pop. 29; 69 km ENE of Krakow; 50°10'/20°51'; PHP1.

Czyzowice, Pol. BGN lists two possible localities with this name located at 49°59'/18°26' and 50°16'/20°37'. HSL.

Czyzowka, Pol.; pop. 3; 32 km WNW of Krakow; 50°13'/19°28'.

Czyzyki, Pol.; pop. 10; 50 km SE of Bialystok; 52°47'/23°32'.

Czyzykow, GUM6. This town was not found in BGN gazetteers under the given spelling.

Czyzyny, Pol.; pop. 22; 6 km E of Krakow; 50°04'/20°01'; GUM3, GUM5.

Dabaca, HSL. This pre-World War I community was not found in BGN gazetteers.

Dabas, Hung. (Alsodabas); pop. 44; 45 km SE of Budapest; 47°11'/19°19'; HSL, HSL2, LDS, PHH.

Daber, *see* Dobra (near Szczecin).

Dabie, Pol. (Altdamm, Dabie Miasto, Dambia, Dambye, Dombe, Dombie, Dombye); pop. 1,163; 62 km WNW of Lodz; 52°05'/18°50'; AMG, CAHJP, COH, GA, GUM3, GUM5, GUM5, GYLA, HSL, HSL2, JGFF, LDS, LYV, PHP1, SF.

Dabie Miasto, *see* Dabie.

Dabjon, *see* Domnin.

Dabki, *see* Dubka.

Dabronc, Hung.; pop. 7; 75 km N of Nagykanizsa; 47°02'/17°10'.

Dabrova Gornicha, *see* Dabrowa Gornicza.

Dabrovica, *see* Dabrowica.

Dabrowa, Pol. (Dombrove); pop. 1,218; 62 km N of Bialystok; 53°40'/23°21'; AMG, COH, GUM4, HSL, HSL2, JGFF, LDL, PHP4, SF. At least 135 towns in Poland are named Dabrowa, which means "oak grove." See listings below.

Dabrowa (near Jaroslaw), Pol.; pop. 34; 26 km NNE of Przemysl; 49°59'/22°59'.

Dabrowa (near Kielce), Pol.; pop. 63; 107 km NNE of Krakow; 50°55'/20°41'; GUM3, GUM5.

Dabrowa (near Niepolomice), Pol.; pop. 52; 26 km ESE of Krakow; 50°00'/20°15'.

Dabrowa (near Opoczno), Pol.; pop. 27; 62 km ESE of Lodz; 51°20'/20°08'.

Dabrowa Bialostocka, Pol. POCEM. This town was not found in BGN gazetteers under the given spelling.

Dabrowa Dzieciel, Pol.; pop. 7; 56 km SW of Bialystok; 52°54'/22°27'.

Dabrowa Gornicza, Pol. (Dabrova Gornicha, Dambrova Gurnicha, Dombrava Gornitsha, Dombrova, Dombrove Gur, Dombrowa Gornicza); pop. 4,304; 56 km S of Czestochowa; 50°20'/19°12'; AMG, CAHJP, EDRD, EJ, GA, GUM3, GUM4, GUM5, GUM6, HSL, HSL2, JGFF, LDL, LYV, POCEM, SF, YB.

Dabrowa Kozlowska, Pol.; 94 km W of Lublin; 51°28'/21°17'; GA.

Dabrowa K Pabianic, Pol. PHP1. This town was not found in BGN gazetteers under the given spelling.

Dabrowa Lazy, Pol.; pop. 24; 56 km SW of Bialystok; 52°51'/22°27'.

Dabrowa Rusiecka, Pol.; pop. 8; 56 km SSW of Lodz; 51°20'/18°57'; PHP1.

Dabrowa Szlachecka, Pol.; pop. 2; 19 km SW of Krakow; 50°00'/19°46'.

Dabrowa Tarnowska, Pol.; pop. 2,099; 75 km ENE of Krakow; 50°10'/20°59'; AMG, COH, EGRS, GA, GUM3, GUM5, HSL, JGFF, LDL, PHP3, POCEM, SF.

Dabrowa Tworki, Pol.; pop. 5; 56 km SW of Bialystok; 52°49'/22°29'.

Dabrowa Wielka, Pol.; pop. 64; 62 km SW of Bialystok; 52°51'/22°24'.

Dabrowica, Pol. (Dabrovica, Dambrovitsa, Dubrovits); pop. 40; 107 km SSW of Lublin; 50°29'/21°37'; CAHJP, EDRD, LYV. *See also* Dubrovitsa.

Dabrowice, Pol. (Dombrovits); pop. 184; 50 km NE of Lodz; 51°56'/20°06'; GA, GUM4, GUM5, PHP4.

Dabrowiece, Pol. PHP1. This town was not found in BGN gazetteers under the given spelling.

Dabrowka Dolna, GA. This town was not found in BGN gazetteers under the given spelling.

Dabrowka Koscielna, Pol.; pop. 55; 50 km SW of Bialystok; 52°51'/22°34'; GA.

Dabrowka Lug, Pol.; pop. 10; 82 km E of Warszawa; 52°07'/22°09'.

Dabrowka Morska, Pol.; pop. 17; 50 km ENE of Krakow; 50°08'/20°34'.

Dabrowka Niemiecka, Pol.; pop. 85; 75 km ESE of Krakow; 49°37'/20°40'.

Dabrowka Ruska, Pol.; pop. 19; 50 km SW of Przemysl; 49°34'/22°10'.

Dabrowka Stany, Pol.; pop. 31; 82 km E of Warszawa; 52°07'/22°06'.

Dabrowka Starzenska, Pol.; pop. 12; 38 km WSW of Przemysl; 49°47'/22°15'.

Dabrowka Szczepanowska, Pol.; pop. 1; 69 km E of Krakow; 49°55'/20°52'.

Dabrowka Szlachecka, Pol.; pop. 11; 13 km NNW of Warszawa; 52°21'/20°57'.

Dabrowka Tuchowska, Pol.; pop. 21; 82 km E of Krakow; 49°54'/21°03'.

Dabrowka Wylazy, Pol.; pop. 2; 82 km E of Warszawa; 52°09'/22°10'.

Dabrowki Brenskie, Pol.; pop. 13; 75 km ENE of Krakow; 50°15'/20°57'.

Dabrowno, Pol. (Gilgenburg); pop. 47; 139 km ESE of Gdansk; 53°26'/20°03'; LDS.

Dab Wielki, Pol.; pop. 7; 101 km N of Lodz; 52°37'/19°21'.

Dachau, Germ.; pop. 15; 19 km NW of Munchen; 48°16'/11°26'; EJ, GED, GUM3, GUM4, GUM5, HSL, PHGB, PHGBW, PHP1, PHP4. Most sources refer to the concentration camp at Dachau.

Dachev, USSR; EDRD. This town was not found in BGN gazetteers under the given spelling.

Dachnow, Pol.; pop. 39; 50 km NNE of Przemysl; 50°12'/23°07'.

Dachsbach, Germ.; 32 km WNW of Nurnberg; 49°39'/10°42'; PHGB.

Dacice, Cz. (Datschitz); pop. 51; 88 km WSW of Brno; 49°05'/15°26'.

Dad, Hung.; pop. 12; 62 km W of Budapest; 47°31'/18°14'.

Dagda, Lat. (Dagdas, Dagde, Dedga); pop. 668; 69 km NE of Daugavpils; 56°06'/27°32'; COH, JGFF, LDL, PHLE, SF.

Dagdas, *see* Dagda.

Dagde, *see* Dagda.

Dahn, Germ.; pop. 70; 114 km WNW of Stuttgart; 49°09'/07°47'.

Dahnovici, *see* Dakhnovichi.

Daia, Rom.; 50 km S of Bucuresti; 44°00'/25°59'; HSL.

Dailydai, Lith. (Dojlidy, Doylidy); pop. 5; 50 km SE of Vilnius; 54°17'/25°36'.

Dainiai, (Dainjenai, Dauyen); YL. A number of towns share this name. It was not possible to determine from available information which one is being referenced.

Dainjenai, *see* Dainiai.

Daka, Hung.; pop. 6; 101 km N of Nagykanizsa; 47°17'/17°26'.

Dakhnovichi, Mold. (Dahnovici); pop. 6; 32 km WSW of Kishinev; 46°58'/28°29'.

Dakovo, *see* Akovo.

Dalachow, Pol.; pop. 12; 50 km WNW of Czestochowa; 51°05'/18°36'.

Dalanowka, Pol. PHP4. This town was not found in BGN gazetteers under the given spelling.

Dale, Pol.; pop. 9; 38 km NNE of Krakow; 50°21'/20°13'.

Dalechowice, Pol.; pop. 5; 45 km NE of Krakow; 50°12'/20°27'.

Dalechowy, Pol.; pop. 6; 69 km NNE of Krakow; 50°36'/20°23'.

Dalekowice, Pol.; pop. 35; Described in the *Black Book* as being in the Lublin region of Poland, this town was not found in BGN gazetteers.

Daleshova, Ukr. (Daleszowa); pop. 23; 62 km NW of Chernovtsy; 48°47'/25°29'.

Daleszewice, Pol.; pop. 24; 69 km ESE of Lodz; 51°18'/20°09'; HSL, PHP1.

Daleszowa, *see* Daleshova.

Daleszyce, Pol. (Dalishitza); pop. 306; 107 km NNE of Krakow; 50°49'/20°48'; GUM4, GUM5, LDS, PHP4, POCEM, SF.

Dalimerice, Cz.; pop. 3; 75 km NNE of Praha; 50°36'/15°09'.

Daliowa, Pol. (Daljowa); pop. 24; 82 km SW of Przemysl; 49°27'/21°48'; PHP3, SF.

Dalishitza, *see* Daleszyce.

Dalj, Yug.; pop. 16; 139 km WNW of Beograd; 45°29'/18°59'.

Daljowa, *see* Daliowa.

Dalmatia; Not a town, but a section of Croatia (now in Yugoslavia) between Bosnia-Herzegovina and the Adriatic Sea.

Dalnich, Ukr. (Dalnicz); pop. 53; 32 km NNE of Lvov; 50°04'/24°16'.

Dalnicz, *see* Dalnich.

Dalnik, Ukr.; 13 km WSW of Odessa; 46°28'/30°34'; EJ.

Dalnow, *see* Dolginovo.

Damacuseni, Rom. (Domokos); pop. 94; 82 km N of Cluj; 47°27'/23°55'; HSL.

Damak, Hung.; pop. 13; 32 km N of Miskolc; 48°19'/20°50'; HSL.

Dambach, HSL. A number of towns share this name. It was not possible to determine from available information which one is being referenced.

Dambia, *see* Dabie.

Damborice, Cz. (Damboritz); 26 km ESE of Brno; 49°02'/16°55'; GUM4.

Damboritz, *see* Damborice.

Dambraveni, *see* Dumbraveny.

Dambrova Gurnicha, *see* Dabrowa Gornicza.

Dambrovitsa, *see* Dabrowica.

Dambye, *see* Dabie.

Damenice, Cz.; pop. 8; 69 km SE of Praha; 49°35'/14°53'.

Damgarten, *see* Ribnitzdamgarten.

Damianow, Pol.; pop. 6; 75 km WNW of Lublin; 51°43'/21°46'.

Damice, Cz. BGN lists two possible localities with this name located at 50°12'/19°57' and 50°20'/13°01'. HSL.

Damienesti, Rom.; pop. 136; 69 km SSW of Iasi; 46°44'/26°59'; PHR1.

Damieni, Rom. (Demenyhaza); pop. 1; 101 km E of Cluj; 46°38'/24°52'.

Damienice, Pol.; pop. 3; 38 km ESE of Krakow; 49°59'/20°24'.

Damis, Rom.; 82 km W of Cluj; 46°52'/22°34'; HSL.

Damnov, Cz.; pop. 11; 126 km WSW of Praha; 49°47'/12°48'.

Damoc, Hung.; pop. 45; 94 km NE of Miskolc; 48°22'/22°02'; AMG, HSL.

Dancauti, *see* Dankovtsy.

Danceni, *see* Dancheny.

Dancheny, Mold. (Danceni); pop. 8; 13 km SW of Kishinev; 46°58'/28°43'.

Dancshaza, *see* Bihardancshaza.

Dancu, *see* Danku.

Danczypol, Pol.; pop. 10; 82 km ESE of Lublin; 50°49'/23°35'.

Dandowka, Pol.; pop. 145; 56 km WNW of Krakow; 50°16'/19°11'; GUM3.

Danestii Chioarului, Rom.; pop. 12; 94 km NNW of Cluj; 47°33'/23°21'.

Danichuv, Ukr. (Daniczow); pop. 42; 56 km ENE of Rovno; 50°40'/27°00'.

Daniczow, *see* Danichuv.

Danielow, Pol. (Danilov); pop. 4; 56 km NNE of Czestochowa; 51°15'/19°29'.

Danila, Rom.; pop. 9; 133 km WNW of Iasi; 47°45'/26°06'.

Danilcze, Pol.; pop. 20; Described in the *Black Book* as being in the Stanislawow region of Poland, this town was not found in BGN gazetteers.

Danilevitch, *see* Dunilovichi.

Danilov, *see* Danielow.

Danilovo, Ukr.; 182 km WSW of Chernovtsy; 48°09'/23°27'; SM.

Danilovtse, Ukr. (Danilowce); pop. 15; 94 km E of Lvov; 49°40'/25°18'.

Danilowce, *see* Danilovtse.

Danilowicze, GUM4, GUM6. This town was not found in BGN gazetteers under the given spelling.

Danilowka, Pol.; 88 km SW of Bialystok; 52°44'/22°02'; PHP4.

Daniszewice, Pol.; pop. 2; 62 km NNE of Czestochowa; 51°14'/19°40'.

Dankera, *see* Gostini.

Dankere, *see* Gostini.

Dankovtsy, Ukr. (Dancauti); pop. 30; 45 km NE of Chernovtsy; 48°27'/26°31'.

Dankow, Pol.; pop. 21; 62 km SSW of Warszawa; 51°50'/20°31'.

Danku, Mold. (Dancu); 50 km SW of Kishinev; 46°46'/28°13'; JGFF.

Dannstadt, Germ.; pop. 5; 75 km S of Frankfurt am Main; 49°26'/08°19'.

Danowice, Pol.; pop. 5; 82 km WNW of Lodz; 51°59'/18°16'.

Danpataka, *see* Valeni.

Danszentmiklos, Hung.; pop. 4; 50 km ESE of Budapest; 47°13'/19°33'.

Dantova, *see* Dotnuva.

Danul, Mold. (Danul Vechi, Danul Vechiu); pop. 104; 139 km WNW of Kishinev; 47°50'/27°30'.

Danul Vechi, *see* Danul.

Danul Vechiu, *see* Danul.

Dany, Hung.; pop. 24; 38 km ENE of Budapest; 47°31'/19°33'.

Danzig, *see* Gdansk.

Dapalovce, Cz.; 50 km NNE of Kosice; 49°04'/21°45'; JGFF.

Dara, Rom.; pop. 40; 133 km NW of Cluj; 47°49'/22°45'.

Darabani, Rom.; pop. 1,917; 139 km NW of Iasi; 48°11'/26°35'; COH, EDRD, EJ, GUM4.

Darachow, *see* Darakhov.

Darag, *see* Hajdudorog.

Darakhov, Ukr. (Darachow); pop. 109; 114 km NNW of Chernovtsy; 49°18'/25°33'; PHP2.

Darany, Hung.; pop. 10; 69 km SE of Nagykanizsa; 45°59'/17°35'.

Darbenai, Lith. (Darbian, Darbyenay, Dorbenai, Dorbian, Dorbyan, Dorbyany, Drobian, Drobyan); pop. 601; 133 km W of Siauliai; 56°01'/21°15'; HSL, JGFF, LYV, SF, YL.

Darbian, *see* Darbenai.

Darbyenay, *see* Darbenai.

Darcauti, *see* Derkautsy.

Darda, Yug.; pop. 23; 163 km WNW of Beograd; 45°38'/18°42'; GUM4, HSL, HSL2, LDS.

Darevnaya, Byel. (Derevna, Derewna); pop. 21; 114 km NNW of Pinsk; 53°05'/25°50'; GUM3.

Darevo, Byel. (Darewo); pop. 8; 133 km N of Minsk; 55°02'/27°23'.

Darewo, *see* Darevo.

Dargun, Germ.; 56 km ESE of Rostock; 53°54'/12°51'; HSL, LDS.

Darkauts, *see* Derkautsy.

Darkehmen, *see* Ozersk.

Darlowo, Germ. (Rugenwalde); pop. 36; 277 km ENE of Rostock; 54°26'/16°23'; LDS.

Darmanesti, Rom.; pop. 92; 126 km WNW of Iasi; 47°44'/26°09'; PHR1, PHR2.

Darmstadt, Germ.; pop. 1,646; 32 km S of Frankfurt am Main; 49°52'/08°39'; AMG, CAHJP, EJ, GED, GUM3, GUM4, GUM5, HSL, HSL2, JGFF, LDS, PHGBW, PHP1, YB.

Darmysl, Cz.; pop. 2; 126 km SW of Praha; 49°39'/12°53'.

Darnica, *see* Darnitsa.

Darnitsa, Ukr. (Darnica); 13 km E of Kiyev; 50°26'/30°38'; EDRD, GUM4.

Darot, Rom.; 50 km NNE of Cluj; 47°07'/24°03'; HSL.

Darow, Pol.; pop. 11; 69 km SW of Przemysl; 49°28'/21°57'.

Darshonishok, *see* Darsuniskis.

Darshunishok, *see* Darsuniskis.

Darsuniskis, Lith. (Darshonishok, Darshunishok); 26 km SE of Kaunas; 54°44'/24°07'; LDL, SF, YL.

Daruvar, Yug.; pop. 136; 101 km E of Zagreb; 45°35'/17°14'; GUM4, HSL, PHY.

Darva, *see* Kolodne.

Darvas, Hung.; 120 km SSE of Miskolc; 47°06'/21°21'; LDS.

Daschkowka, *see* Dashkovka.

Dascova, *see* Dyshkovo.

Daseburg, Germ.; pop. 4; 101 km S of Hannover; 51°31'/09°14'.

Dasev, *see* Dashev.

Dashava, Ukr. (Daszawa); pop. 14; 69 km S of Lvov; 49°16'/24°00'.

Dashev, Ukr. (Dasev, Dashiev, Dosha, Staraya Dashevka); pop. 2,168; 62 km WNW of Uman; 49°00'/29°27'; JGFF, LDL, SF.

Dashiev, *see* Dashev.

Dashkavka, *see* Dashkovka.

Dashkeviche, *see* Dashkevichi.

Dashkevichi, Byel. (Dashkeviche, Daszkiewicze); 146 km WNW of Pinsk; 52°57'/24°32'; GUM4.

Dashkovka, Byel. (Daschkowka, Dashkavka); 157 km NNW of Gomel; 53°44'/30°16'; LDL, SF.

Dasice, Cz.; pop. 11; 107 km NW of Brno; 50°02'/15°55'.

Dassel, Germ.; pop. 17; 69 km S of Hannover; 51°48'/09°41'.

Daszawa, *see* Dashava.

Daszkiewicze, *see* Dashkevichi.

Daszowka, Pol.; pop. 63; 50 km S of Przemysl; 49°23'/22°35'; HSL.

Datnuva, *see* Dotnuva.

Datschitz, *see* Dacice.

Datteln, Germ.; pop. 45; 88 km N of Koln; 51°40'/07°23'; GED.

Dattenfeld, Germ.; 45 km ESE of Koln; 50°48'/07°34'; GED.

Datterode, Germ.; pop. 10; 146 km SSE of Hannover; 51°07'/10°01'.

Datyn, Ukr.; pop. 45; 146 km WNW of Rovno; 51°31'/24°46'; GUM3.

Dauborn, Germ.; pop. 14; 45 km WNW of Frankfurt am Main; 50°20'/08°11'.

Daubringen, Germ.; 69 km N of Frankfurt am Main; 50°39'/08°44'; LDS.

Daudzese, Lat.; pop. 4; 88 km ESE of Riga; 56°28'/25°14'.

Daug, *see* Daugai.

Daugai, Lith. (Daug, Daugi, Doig, Doyg); pop. 363; 62 km SE of Kaunas; 54°22'/24°20'; COH, HSL, JGFF, LDL, SF, YL.

Daugailiai, Lith.; pop. 73; 107 km N of Vilnius; 55°36'/25°50'; GUM3.

Daugapils, *see* Daugavpils.

Daugava, *see* Daugavpils.

Daugavpils, Lat. (Daugapils, Daugava, Dinaburg, Duenaburg, Dunaberg, Dunaburg, Dvinsk, Dwinsk, Dzvinsk); pop. 11,585; 189 km ESE of Riga; 55°53'/26°32'; AMG, COH, EDRD, EJ, GUM3, GUM4, GUM5, GUM6, HSL, HSL2, JGFF, LDL, PHLE, SF, YB.

Daugeliszki, *see* Naujasis Daugeliskis.

Daugi, *see* Daugai.

Daujenai, Lith.; pop. 25; 75 km ENE of Siauliai; 55°58'/24°31'.

Daujoji Vilnia, SF. This town was not found in BGN gazetteers under the given spelling.

Dausenau, Germ.; 69 km WNW of Frankfurt am Main; 50°20'/07°46'; JGFF.

Dautmergen, Germ. (Schomberg Dautmergen); 69 km SSW of Stuttgart; 48°14'/08°45'; GUM3, GUM4, GUM6.

Dautova, *see* Davod.

Dauyen, *see* Dainiai.

Davideni, *see* Davidovka.

Davideshte, Ukr. (Davidesti); pop. 48; 26 km NW of Chernovtsy; 48°29'/25°42'; GUM4, HSL, PHR2, SF.

Davidesti, *see* Davideshte.

David Gorodok, Byel. (David Horodok, Davidgrodek, Davidgrudek, Dawidgrodek); pop. 3,500; 75 km E of Pinsk; 52°03'/27°13'; EDRD, EJ, GUM3, GUM4, GUM5, HSL, JGFF, LDL, SF, WS, YB.

Davidgrodek, *see* David Gorodok.

Davidgrudek, *see* David Gorodok.

Davidhaza, Hung.; 62 km WNW of Nagykanizsa; 46°49'/16°22'; HSL.

David Horodok, *see* David Gorodok.

Davidka, USSR; EDRD, GUM4. This town was not found in BGN gazetteers under the given spelling.

Davidkovo, Bulg.; 176 km ESE of Sofija; 41°40'/24°58'; AMG.

Davidkovtse, Ukr. (Dawidkowce); pop. 21; 75 km N of Chernovtsy; 48°56'/25°59'.

Davidov, Ukr. (Dawidow); pop. 27; 19 km ESE of Lvov; 49°45'/24°08'; HSL, PHP2.

Davidovka, Ukr. (Davideni, Davydovka); pop. 99; 32 km SW of Chernovtsy; 48°07'/25°35'; COH, GUM4, SF.

Davitkov, HSL. This pre-World War I community was not found in BGN gazetteers.

Davle, Cz.; pop. 9; 32 km S of Praha; 49°53'/14°24'.

Davod, Hung. (Dautova); pop. 16; 101 km SW of Szeged; 46°00'/18°55'; LDS.

Davor, Yug.; pop. 7; 139 km ESE of Zagreb; 45°07'/17°31'.

Davydovka, *see* Davidovka.

Dawidgrodek, *see* David Gorodok.

Dawidkowce, *see* Davidkovtse.

Dawidow, *see* Davidov.

Dealu Mare, Rom. (Dulofalva); 69 km N of Cluj; 47°22'/23°49'; HSL.

Dealumare, (Gyalumare).

Deba, Pol.; 101 km WNW of Przemysl; 50°26'/21°46'; PHP3.

Debeikiai, Lith. (Dobeik, Dvyk); pop. 175; 45 km S of Siauliai; 55°37'/23°21'; LDL, SF, YL.

Debeljaca, Yug.; pop. 185; 32 km N of Beograd; 45°04'/20°36'; PHY.

Debercseny, Hung.; pop. 4; 56 km N of Budapest; 47°58'/19°19'; HSL.

Debeslavtse, Ukr. (Debeslawce); pop. 42; 62 km WNW of Chernovtsy; 48°28'/25°10'.

Debeslawce, *see* Debeslavtse.

Debe Wielkie, Pol.; pop. 76; 32 km E of Warszawa; 52°12'/21°27'; PHP4.

Debica, Pol. (Debitsa, Dembica, Dembits, Dembitsa, Dembitz, Dembiza); pop. 1,561; 101 km WNW of Przemysl; 50°03'/21°25'; AMG, COH, EDRD, EGRS, EJ, GA, GUM3, GUM4, GUM5, GYLA, HSL, HSL2, JGFF, LDL, LYV, PHP1, PHP3, PHP4, POCEM, SF, YB.

Debicze, Pol.; pop. 42; 94 km SW of Lodz; 51°28'/18°11'.

Debie, Pol.; pop. 5; 38 km NW of Czestochowa; 51°03'/18°56'; POCEM.

Debienica, Pol.; pop. 46; 69 km NNE of Warszawa; 52°44'/21°38'.

Debina, Pol. (Dembina, Dembinka); HSL, HSL2, LYV. A number of towns share this name. It was not possible to determine from available information which one is being referenced.

Debina (near Janow Lubelski), Pol.; pop. 54; 38 km S of Lublin; 50°56'/22°28'.

Debina (near Lancut), Pol.; pop. 21; 50 km WNW of Przemysl; 50°06'/22°18'; PHP2.

Debitsa, *see* Debica.

Deblin, Pol. (Demblin, Modrzyc, Modzhits, Modzhitz, Modzits); pop. 34; 62 km ENE of Krakow; 50°13'/20°44'; AMG, COH, EDRD, FRG, GA, GUM3, GUM4, GUM5, GUM6, HSL, HSL2, JGFF, LYV, SF, YB.

Debna, Pol.; pop. 11; 45 km SW of Przemysl; 49°37'/22°14'.

Debnik, Pol.; 26 km NNW of Czestochowa; 50°58'/19°01'; GUM3.

Debniki, Pol.; pop. 93; 13 km S of Krakow; 50°03'/19°55'.

Debno, Pol. (Dembno).

Debno (Kielce), Pol.; 114 km SW of Lublin; 50°54'/21°00'; CAHJP.

Debno (near Gorzow Wielkopolskie), Pol. (Neudamm); 88 km SSE of Szczecin; 52°44'/14°41'; HSL, POCEM.

Debno (near Przemysl), Pol.; pop. 73; 50 km NNW of Przemysl; 50°12'/22°31'.

Deborzyn, Pol.; pop. 8; 101 km E of Krakow; 49°55'/21°20'.

Debow, Pol.; pop. 43; 38 km NW of Przemysl; 50°02'/22°26'.

Debowa, Pol.; pop. 10; 101 km E of Krakow; 49°51'/21°20'; POCEM.

Debowce, Pol.; pop. 25; 69 km ESE of Warszawa; 52°04'/21°56'; HSL.

Debowica, Pol.; pop. 4; 82 km N of Lublin; 51°57'/22°28'.

Debowiec, Pol.; pop. 39; 88 km SW of Krakow; 49°49'/18°43'.

Debrad, Cz. (Debrod); 19 km WSW of Kosice; 48°39'/20°59'; HSL.

Debrecen, Hung. (Debretsin); pop. 9,142; 88 km ESE of Miskolc; 47°32'/21°38'; AMG, COH, EDRD, GUM3, GUM4, GUM5, GUM6, HSL, HSL2, JGFF, LDL, LDS, LJEE, LYV, PHH, YB.

Debren, Bulg.; 133 km SSE of Sofija; 41°36'/23°51'; HSL.

Debretsin, *see* Debrecen.

Debrisch, HSL. This pre-World War I community was not found in BGN gazetteers.

Debrod, *see* Debrad.

Debrzno, Pol. (Preussisch Friedland); pop. 118; 126 km N of Poznan; 53°32'/17°14'.

Debska Wola, Pol.; pop. 12; 88 km NNE of Krakow; 50°44'/20°36'.

Debur, Bulg. (Derbent); 170 km ESE of Sofija; 42°05'/25°12'; LDL.

Deby Wolskie, Pol.; pop. 3; 62 km NNW of Czestochowa; 51°19'/18°56'.

Decin, Cz.; pop. 161; 82 km NNW of Praha; 50°47'/14°13'; EJ.

Decs, Hung.; pop. 56; 107 km W of Szeged; 46°17'/18°46'; AMG, PHH.

Deda, Rom.; pop. 170; 101 km ENE of Cluj; 46°56'/24°54'; HSL, HSL2, PHR2.

Deda Bisztra, HSL. This pre-World War I community was not found in BGN gazetteers.

Dederkaly Male, Ukr.; pop. 8; 69 km S of Rovno; 50°03'/26°06'.

Dedes, Hung.; pop. 27; 26 km WNW of Miskolc; 48°11'/20°30'; HSL.

Dedesdorf, Germ.; pop. 5; 94 km WSW of Hamburg; 53°27'/08°31'.

Dedga, *see* Dagda.

Dedilov, Ukr. (Dzedziluv, Dziedzilow); pop. 83; 26 km NE of Lvov; 49°56'/24°22'.

Dedkovitchu, *see* Priluki (near Ovruch).

Dedova, Cz.; pop. 1; 82 km NW of Brno; 49°46'/15°59'.

Dedukhi, *see* Priluki (near Ovruch).

Deg, Hung.; pop. 25; 88 km SSW of Budapest; 46°52'/18°27'.

Deggendorf, Germ.; pop. 15; 126 km NE of Munchen; 48°50'/12°58'; EDRD, EJ, GED, GUM3, PHGB, PHGBW.

Deggingen, Germ.; 45 km ESE of Stuttgart; 48°36'/09°43'; HSL, HSL2, JGFF.

Dehrn, Germ.; pop. 2; 56 km WNW of Frankfurt am Main; 50°25'/08°07'.

Deidesheim, Germ.; pop. 10; 88 km SSW of Frankfurt am Main; 49°25'/08°12'; GED, HSL.

Deinzendorf, Aus.; 69 km NW of Wien; 48°42'/15°55'; HSL.

Deisel, Germ.; pop. 10; 94 km S of Hannover; 51°36'/09°25'; GED, HSL, LDS.

Deisenhausen, Germ.; 94 km W of Munchen; 48°15'/10°20'; PHGB.

Dej, Rom. (Des); pop. 3,360; 50 km NNE of Cluj; 47°09'/23°52'; AMG, COH, EJ, GUM4, HSL, HSL2, JGFF, LDL, PHR2, YB.

Deja, Rom. (Deshaza); pop. 7; 75 km NW of Cluj; 47°21'/23°11'.

Dejtar, Hung.; pop. 25; 62 km N of Budapest; 48°02'/19°10'.

Deksznie, GUM3. This town was not found in BGN gazetteers under the given spelling.

Delacheu, *see* Delakeu.

Delakeu, Mold. (Delacheu); pop. 12; 38 km NE of Kishinev; 47°06'/29°18'.

Delatycze, *see* Delyatichi.

Delatyn, *see* Delyatin.

Delcevo, Yug. (Carevo Selo); pop. 1; 107 km E of Skopje; 41°58'/22°47'.

Delejow, *see* Deleyuv.

Deleyuv, Ukr. (Delejow); pop. 30; 107 km SE of Lvov; 49°06'/24°52'.

Deliatin, *see* Delyatin.

Delitzsch, Germ.; pop. 24; 32 km N of Leipzig; 51°32'/12°21'.

Deljiler, *see* Dmitriyevka.

Delkenheim, Germ.; pop. 5; 26 km SW of Frankfurt am Main; 50°03'/08°22'; JGFF.

Dellmensingen, Germ.; 75 km ESE of Stuttgart; 48°18'/09°54'; PHGBW.

Delmenhorst, Germ.; pop. 197; 107 km SW of Hamburg; 53°03'/08°37'; GUM5, YB.

Delovoye, Ukr. (Terebesfejer Patak, Trebusa, Trebusan, Trebusany); pop. 311; 139 km SW of Chernovtsy; 47°56'/24°11'; AMG, COH, HSL, HSL2, JGFF, SM.

Delyatichi, Byel. (Delatycze, Delyatyche); pop. 104; 107 km WSW of Minsk; 53°47'/25°59'; CAHJP, GUM5, GYLA, HSL, JGFF, LDL, SF, YB.

Delyatin, Ukr. (Delatyn, Deliatin); pop. 1,576; 101 km W of Chernovtsy; 48°32'/24°38'; AMG, COH, EGRS, EJ, GUM3, GUM4, GUM5, HSL, HSL2, JGFF, LDL, PHP2, SF.

Delyatyche, *see* Delyatichi.

Demantsfurth, Germ.; 38 km WNW of Nurnberg; 49°40'/10°43'; PHGB.

Dembica, *see* Debica.

Dembina, *see* Debina.

Dembinka, *see* Debina.

Dembits, *see* Debica.

Dembitsa, *see* Debica.

Dembitz, *see* Debica.

Dembiza, *see* Debica.

Demblin, *see* Deblin.

Dembno, *see* Debno.

Demecser, Hung.; pop. 368; 82 km ENE of Miskolc; 48°07'/21°55'; HSL, PHH.

Demene, Lat.; pop. 8; 26 km S of Daugavpils; 55°44'/26°32'.

Demenka, Byel.; 114 km ESE of Minsk; 53°11'/28°51'; SF.

Demenyhaza, *see* Damieni.

Demete, *see* Demjata.

Demeterfalva, *see* Dumitrita.

Demidov, USSR; pop. 416; 62 km NW of Smolensk; 55°16'/31°31'; GUM4.

Demidovka, Ukr. (Demidowka, Demiduvka); pop. 592; 62 km SW of Rovno; 50°25'/25°20'; COH, EDRD, JGFF, LYV, SF.

Demidovshchina, Byel. (Demidovshchyzna, Demidowszyzna); pop. 25; 101 km W of Pinsk; 52°16'/24°41'.

Demidovshchyzna, *see* Demidovshchina.

Demidow, *see* Demiduv.

Demidowka, *see* Demidovka.

Demidowszyzna, *see* Demidovshchina.

Demiduv, Ukr. (Demidow); pop. 23; 62 km SSE of Lvov; 49°22'/24°15'.

Demiduvka, *see* Demidovka.

Demievka, EJ. EJ describes Demievka as a suburb of Kiyev. There is no reference in BGN.

Demjata, Cz. (Demete); 50 km N of Kosice; 49°06'/21°19'; HSL.

Demmelsdorf, Germ.; pop. 29; 62 km N of Nurnberg; 49°58'/11°03'; AMG, GUM5, JGFF, PHGB.

Demmin, Germ.; pop. 8; 62 km ESE of Rostock; 53°54'/13°02'; HSL, LDS.

Demnia, *see* Demnya.

Demnya, Ukr. (Demnia); pop. 36; 114 km S of Lvov; 48°54'/24°09'; HSL.

Demotika, GUM4. This town was not found in BGN gazetteers under the given spelling.

Demyansk, USSR; pop. 20; 189 km NNE of Velikiye Luki; 57°38'/32°28'; GUM4.

Demycze, Pol.; pop. 443; PHP2. Described in the *Black Book* as being in the Stanislawow region of Poland, this town was not found in BGN gazetteers.

Dencshaza, Hung.; pop. 4; 75 km ESE of Nagykanizsa; 46°00'/17°50'.

Deneslak, Hung.; pop. 4; 62 km NNW of Nagykanizsa; 46°56'/16°51'.

Denevitz, *see* Pryamobalka.

Deniskovichi, Byel. (Deniskowicze); pop. 34; 82 km NNE of Pinsk; 52°44'/26°41'.

Deniskowicze, *see* Deniskovichi.

Denkow, Pol.; pop. 260; 82 km SW of Lublin; 50°56'/21°26'; GUM4, GUM5, PHP1.

Denkowek, Pol.; pop. 13; 88 km SW of Lublin; 50°55'/21°24'.

Dennenlohe, Germ.; pop. 3; 50 km SSW of Nurnberg; 49°06'/10°37'; GUM5, PHGB.

Dentlein, *see* Dentlein am Forst.

Dentlein am Forst, Germ. (Dentlein); 56 km SW of Nurnberg; 49°09'/10°26'; PHGB.

Denysow, Ukr.; pop. 34; 94 km NNW of Chernovtsy; 49°05'/25°25'. This town was located on an interwar map of Poland but does not appear in contemporary gazetteers. Map coordinates are approximate.

Depoyla, *see* Cimpulung La Tisa.

Depultycze Krolewskie, Pol.; pop. 3; 62 km E of Lublin; 51°05'/23°27'.

Derazhna, *see* Derazhno.

Derazhnia, *see* Derazhnya.

Derazhno, Ukr. (Derazhna, Derazne); pop. 624; 38 km NW of Rovno; 50°52'/26°03'; COH, GUM4, SF.

Derazhnya, Ukr. (Derazhnia, Dereshnja); pop. 3,250; 75 km W of Vinnitsa; 49°16'/27°26'; EJ, JGFF, SF.

Derazne, *see* Derazhno.

Derbent, *see* Debur.

Derc, *see* Dert.

Dercen, HSL. This pre-World War I community was not found in BGN gazetteers.

Derebchin, Ukr. (Derebcin); 56 km S of Vinnitsa; 48°46'/28°21'; PHR1.

Derebcin, *see* Derebchin.

Derechin, Byel. (Dereczyn, Deretchin, Derhichin, Dretchin); pop. 1,346; 150 km NW of Pinsk; 53°15'/24°55'; AMG, COH, EDRD, GUM3, GUM4, GUM5, HSL, JGFF, LYV, SF, YB.

Derechin (Wolyn), Ukr.; pop. 7; 94 km NNE of Lvov; 50°36'/24°38'.

Derecske, Hung.; pop. 562; 101 km SE of Miskolc; 47°21'/21°34'; AMG, GUM3, HSL, HSL2, LDL, LDS, PHH, YB.

Dereczanka, Pol.; pop. 9; 114 km NNE of Lublin; 52°05'/23°25'.

Dereczyn, *see* Derechin.

Derekegyhaz, Hung.; pop. 4; 45 km N of Szeged; 46°35'/20°22'.

Derenburg, Germ.; pop. 1; 101 km ESE of Hannover; 51°52'/10°54'.

Dereneu, *see* Derenev.

Derenev, Mold. (Dereneu); pop. 110; 62 km WNW of Kishinev; 47°23'/28°15'.

Derenie, Pol.; pop. 23; Described in the *Black Book* as being in the Bialystok region of Poland, this town was not found in BGN gazetteers.

Dereniowka, Ukr.; pop. 28; 75 km NNW of Chernovtsy; 48°55'/25°45'. This town was located on an interwar map of Poland but does not appear in contemporary gazetteers. Map coordinates are approximate.

Dereshnja, *see* Derazhnya.

Deresk, *see* Drzkovce.

Deretchin, *see* Derechin.

Derevlyany, *see* Volitsa Derevlyanska.

Derevna, Pol. (Derevnaya, Derewina, Derewno, Glubokoye); See listings below. *See also* Darevnaya.

Derevna (near Slonim), Byel.; pop. 44; 133 km NNW of Pinsk; 53°12'/25°29'.

Derevna (near Volozhin), Byel.; pop. 288; 69 km SW of Minsk; 53°42'/26°34'.

Derevnaya, *see* Derevna.

Derevno, Byel.; 75 km N of Minsk; 54°31'/27°35'; LDL, LYV, SF, YB.

Derevok, Ukr. (Derewek); pop. 68; 146 km NW of Rovno; 51°45'/25°21'; GUM4.

Derewek, *see* Derevok.

Derewina, *see* Derevna.

Derewlany, *see* Volitsa Derevlyanska.

Derewna, *see* Darevnaya.

Derewno, *see* Derevna.

Dereznianska Wola, *see* Wola Dereznianska.

Dereznia Solska, Pol.; pop. 3; 82 km N of Przemysl; 50°30'/22°42'.

Derezyce, Pol.; pop. 45; Described in the *Black Book* as being in the Lwow region of Poland, this town was not found in BGN gazetteers.

Derhichin, *see* Derechin.

Derkautsy, Mold. (Darcauti, Darkauts); pop. 42; 150 km NW of Kishinev; 48°14'/27°59'.

Derlo, Pol.; pop. 8; 114 km SSE of Bialystok; 52°10'/23°23'.

Derman, *see* Ustenskoye Pervoye.

Dermanka, Ukr.; 62 km ENE of Rovno; 50°47'/27°09'; GUM4.

Derna, Rom. (Felsoderna); pop. 24; 107 km WNW of Cluj; 47°12'/22°18'; HSL.

Dernau, Germ.; pop. 14; 50 km SSE of Koln; 50°32'/07°03'; GUM3, GUM4, GUM6.

Dernisoara, Rom. (Alsoderna); pop. 11; 114 km WNW of Cluj; 47°13'/22°15'.

Dernow, *see* Dernuvka.

Dernuvka, Ukr. (Dernow); pop. 30; 26 km N of Lvov; 50°02'/24°06'.

Derpt, *see* Tartu.

Dersida, Rom.; pop. 3; 94 km NW of Cluj; 47°23'/22°48'.

Dert, Ukr. (Derc); pop. 33; 101 km NE of Rovno; 51°12'/27°20'.

Dertingen, Germ.; pop. 4; 75 km ESE of Frankfurt am Main; 49°46'/09°37'; JGFF, LDS, PHGBW.

Derventa, Yug.; pop. 143; 176 km ESE of Zagreb; 44°59'/17°55'; PHY.

Derylaki, Pol.; pop. 8; 82 km NNW of Przemysl; 50°29'/22°28'.

Derzow, *see* Dezhov.

Derzs, *see* Nyirderzs.

Des, *see* Dej.

Desakna, *see* Ocna Dejului.

Desantnoye, Ukr. (Galilesti); pop. 1; 139 km SSW of Odessa; 45°34'/29°32'.

Desenice, Cz.; pop. 47; 126 km SW of Praha; 49°16'/13°10'.

Desest, *see* Desesti.

Desesti, Rom. (Desest, Desze); pop. 91; 114 km N of Cluj;

47°46'/23°51'; SM.

Deshaza, see Deja.

Desna, Ukr.; 56 km N of Kiyev; 50°55'/30°45'; JGFF.

Dessau, Germ.; pop. 400; 62 km N of Leipzig; 51°50'/12°15'; CAHJP, COH, EJ, HSL, HSL2, ISH1, JGFF, PHP1, PHP2.

Destna, Cz.; 94 km SSE of Praha; 49°16'/14°56'; AMG.

Destnice, Cz.; pop. 3; 62 km W of Praha; 50°14'/13°37'.

Desze, see Desesti.

Deszk, Hung.; pop. 3; 13 km ESE of Szeged; 46°13'/20°15'.

Deszkowice, Pol.; pop. 19; 62 km SE of Lublin; 50°46'/23°01'.

Desznica, Pol.; pop. 8; 94 km WSW of Przemysl; 49°34'/21°29'.

Deszno (Kielce), Pol.; pop. 28; 62 km N of Krakow; 50°37'/20°09'.

Deszno (Lwow), Pol.; pop. 21; 75 km SW of Przemysl; 49°33'/21°51'.

Deta, Rom. (Detta); 240 km SW of Cluj; 45°24'/21°14'; PHR1.

Detek, Hung.; pop. 6; 32 km NNE of Miskolc; 48°20'/21°02'; HSL.

Deter, see Gemerske Dechtare.

Detk, Hung.; pop. 1; 62 km SW of Miskolc; 47°45'/20°06'.

Detmold, Germ.; pop. 207; 75 km SW of Hannover; 51°56'/08°53'; HSL, JGFF, LDS.

Detskoye Selo, see Pushkin.

Detta, see Deta.

Dettelbach, Germ.; pop. 60; 75 km WNW of Nurnberg; 49°48'/10°11'; GUM5, HSL, HSL2, PHGB.

Dettenhausen, Germ.; 26 km S of Stuttgart; 48°36'/09°06'; PHGBW.

Dettensee, Germ.; pop. 2; CAHJP, EJ, LDS, PHGBW. Described in the *Black Book* as being in the Baden-Wurttemberg region of Germany, this town was not found in BGN gazetteers. A village in the district of Hechingen in the principality of Hohenzollern, it does not appear in BGN.

Detter, Germ.; 75 km ENE of Frankfurt am Main; 50°14'/09°46'; PHGB.

Dettingen, Germ.; 56 km SW of Stuttgart; 48°25'/08°38'; JGFF.

Detva, Cz.; pop. 59; 133 km WSW of Kosice; 48°34'/19°25'.

Deutenheim, Germ.; 50 km WNW of Nurnberg; 49°35'/10°25'; PHGB.

Deutsch Eylau, see Ilawa.

Deutsch Jahrndorf, Aus.; pop. 2; 56 km ESE of Wien; 48°01'/17°06'.

Deutsch Kaltenbrunn, Aus.; pop. 2; 50 km ENE of Graz; 47°05'/16°06'.

Deutschkreitz, see Deutschkreutz.

Deutschkreutz, Aus. (Deutschkreitz, Sopronkeresztur); 69 km SSE of Wien; 47°36'/16°38'; EJ, GUM5, HSL, HSL2, LDL, LDS.

Deutsch Tschantschendorf, Aus.; pop. 4; 62 km ENE of Graz; 47°06'/16°17'.

Deutsch Wagram, Aus.; pop. 23; 19 km NE of Wien; 48°18'/16°34'.

Deutsch Wartenberg, see Otyn.

Deutz, HSL. This pre-World War I community was not found in BGN gazetteers.

Deva, see Bacia.

Devavanya, Hung.; pop. 213; 107 km NNE of Szeged; 47°02'/20°58'; GUM5, HSL, LDS, PHH.

Devecser, Hung. (Deveczer); pop. 230; 82 km NNE of Nagykanizsa; 47°06'/17°26'; GUM5, HSL, HSL2, LDL, PHH.

Deveczer, see Devecser.

Devenishki, see Dieveniskes.

Devyatniki, Ukr. (Dzeventniki, Dziewietniki); pop. 30; 45 km SE of Lvov; 49°31'/24°17'.

Dewenishki, see Dieveniskes.

Dewin, see Divin.

Dezanovac, Yug.; pop. 14; 88 km ESE of Zagreb; 45°35'/17°06'.

Dezghinge, see Dezginzhe.

Dezginzhe, Mold. (Dezghinge); pop. 9; 69 km S of Kishinev;

46°26'/28°37'.

Dezhov, Ukr. (Derzow); pop. 29; 56 km S of Lvov; 49°24'/24°00'.

Dezmer, see Dezmir.

Dezmir, Rom. (Dezmer); 13 km E of Cluj; 46°46'/23°43'; HSL.

Dhidhimotikon, Greece; pop. 651; 302 km NE of Thessaloniki; 41°22'/26°26'; COH.

Diakovce, Cz.; pop. 90; 56 km E of Bratislava; 48°08'/17°51'; HSL.

Diatkowice, see Dyatkovtsy.

Dibenka, see Dubienka.

Dibetsk, see Dubetsko.

Dicio, Rom. (Dicso); HSL. This pre-World War I community was not found in BGN gazetteers.

Dicio St Martin, Rom. (Dicsoszentmarton); HSL, HSL2. This pre-World War I community was not found in BGN gazetteers.

Dicso, see Dicio.

Dicsoszentmarton, see Dicio St Martin.

Didkovitch, see Priluki (near Ovruch).

Didkovitz, see Priluki (near Ovruch).

Didymoteikhou, see Didymotihou.

Didymotihou, Greece (Didymoteikhou); pop. 651; 302 km NE of Thessaloniki; 41°21'/26°30'; AMG, GUM3.

Dieburg, Germ.; pop. 271; 26 km SE of Frankfurt am Main; 49°54'/08°51'; GUM3.

Diedelsheim, Germ.; pop. 10; 50 km WNW of Stuttgart; 49°02'/08°41'; LDS, PHGBW.

Diedenbergen, Germ.; pop. 13; 19 km WSW of Frankfurt am Main; 50°04'/08°25'.

Diefflen, Germ.; pop. 29; 157 km SW of Frankfurt am Main; 49°22'/06°45'.

Dielkirchen, Germ.; pop. 36; 75 km SW of Frankfurt am Main; 49°40'/07°49'; GED.

Dielmissen, Germ.; 50 km S of Hannover; 51°58'/09°37'; LDS.

Diemantstein, Germ.; pop. 2; 94 km SSW of Nurnberg; 48°43'/10°33'; PHGB.

Diemerode, Germ.; pop. 19; 139 km NNE of Frankfurt am Main; 51°04'/09°51'.

Dienheim, Germ.; pop. 2; 38 km SSW of Frankfurt am Main; 49°50'/08°21'.

Diepenau, Germ.; 69 km W of Hannover; 52°25'/08°43'; JGFF.

Diepholz, Germ.; pop. 33; 94 km W of Hannover; 52°36'/08°22'; GUM5.

Dierdorf, Germ.; pop. 84; 69 km ESE of Koln; 50°33'/07°40'; GUM5.

Diersburg, Germ.; pop. 43; 101 km SW of Stuttgart; 48°24'/07°56'; ISH1, JGFF, LDS, PHGBW.

Diespeck, Germ.; pop. 5; 32 km WNW of Nurnberg; 49°36'/10°38'; GUM5, PHGB.

Diessen, Germ.; 45 km SW of Munchen; 47°57'/11°06'; PHGB.

Dietenheim, Germ.; 94 km ESE of Stuttgart; 48°13'/10°04'; GUM4.

Dietenhofen, Germ.; 32 km WSW of Nurnberg; 49°24'/10°41'; PHGB.

Dietzenbach, Germ.; pop. 19; 13 km SE of Frankfurt am Main; 50°01'/08°47'; GED.

Dieveniskes, Lith. (Devenishki, Dewenishki, Divenishok, Dziewieniszki); 56 km SSE of Vilnius; 54°12'/25°37'; AMG, COH, GUM3, JGFF, YB.

Diez, Germ.; pop. 50; 56 km WNW of Frankfurt am Main; 50°22'/08°01'; JGFF, LDS.

Differten, Germ.; pop. 8; 170 km SW of Frankfurt am Main; 49°14'/06°47'; GED.

Dignaja, Lat.; pop. 12; 50 km NW of Daugavpils; 56°18'/26°10'.

Diguri Putna, GUM4. This town was not found in BGN gazetteers under the given spelling.

Dihtinet, see Dikhtenets.

Dihtineti, see Dikhtenets.

Dijir, Rom. (Dizser); pop. 19; 107 km WNW of Cluj; 47°21'/22°28'.

Dikhtenets, Ukr. (Dihtinet, Dihtineti); pop. 56; 75 km SW of Chernovtsy; 48°03'/25°02'; PHR2.

Dikla, *see* Dukla.

Dikow, *see* Tarnobrzeg.

Dilif, *see* Dulovo.

Dillich, Germ.; pop. 25; 114 km NNE of Frankfurt am Main; 51°00'/09°17'; AMG.

Dillingen, Germ. (Dillingen an der Donau); pop. 135; 163 km SW of Frankfurt am Main; 49°21'/06°44'; GED, GUM5, PHGB.

Dillingen an der Donau, *see* Dillingen.

Dilsberg, Germ.; 75 km NNW of Stuttgart; 49°24'/08°50'; PHGBW.

Dimacheni, Rom.; pop. 10; 114 km NW of Iasi; 47°54'/26°33'.

Dimer, *see* Dymer.

Dimidovca, Ukr.; 82 km SW of Uman; 48°28'/29°13'; GUM4, PHR1. This town was located on a pre-World War I map, but does not appear in contemporary gazetteers.

Dimitravas, *see* Tarvydai.

Dinaburg, *see* Daugavpils.

Dinauti, *see* Dinovtsy.

Dindesti, Rom. (Eradengeleg); pop. 42; 126 km WNW of Cluj; 47°32'/22°23'.

Dinewitz, *see* Dunayevtsy.

Dinglingen, Germ.; 107 km SW of Stuttgart; 48°21'/07°50'; PHGBW.

Dingolfing, Germ.; 88 km NE of Munchen; 48°38'/12°30'; PHGB.

Dinkelsbuhl, Germ.; pop. 54; 69 km SW of Nurnberg; 49°04'/10°19'; AMG, GED, GUM4, GUM5, LDS, PHGB, PHGBW.

Dinnyeberki, Hung.; pop. 4; 82 km ESE of Nagykanizsa; 46°05'/17°57'.

Dinov, *see* Dynow.

Dinovits, *see* Dunayevtsy.

Dinovitz, *see* Dunayevtsy.

Dinovtsy, Ukr. (Dinauti); pop. 22; 26 km ENE of Chernovtsy; 48°20'/26°18'.

Dinskivola, *see* Zdunska Wola.

Dinslaken, Germ.; pop. 234; 75 km NNW of Koln; 51°34'/06°44'; GED.

Diosgyor, Hung.; pop. 274; 6 km WSW of Miskolc; 48°06'/20°41'; GUM5, GUM6, HSL, LDL, LDS, PHH.

Diosig, Hung. (Bihardioszeg, Dioszeg); pop. 196; 126 km ESE of Miskolc; 47°18'/22°00'; HSL, PHR2.

Diosjeno, Hung.; pop. 43; 56 km N of Budapest; 47°57'/19°03'.

Dioskal, Hung.; pop. 17; 32 km N of Nagykanizsa; 46°40'/17°03'.

Diosod, Rom.; pop. 6; 75 km NW of Cluj; 47°18'/23°01'; HSL.

Diospatak, *see* Valea Rea.

Diosviszlo, Hung.; pop. 2; 114 km ESE of Nagykanizsa; 45°52'/18°10'.

Dioszeg, *see* Diosig.

Dipsa, Rom. (Dipse); pop. 6; 69 km NE of Cluj; 46°58'/24°26'.

Dipse, *see* Dipsa.

Dirchau, *see* Tczew.

Dirmstein, Germ.; pop. 14; 69 km SSW of Frankfurt am Main; 49°34'/08°15'; GED, GUM5, JGFF.

Dirna, Cz.; pop. 3; 101 km SSE of Praha; 49°15'/14°51'.

Dirschau, *see* Tczew.

Dirschaw, *see* Tczew.

Disna, Byel. (Disne, Disneg, Dzisna); pop. 2,742; 133 km W of Vitebsk; 55°34'/28°13'; AMG, COH, EDRD, EJ, FRG, GA, GUM3, GUM4, GUM5, GYLA, HSL, JGFF, LDL, LYV, SF, YB.

Disne, *see* Disna.

Disneg, *see* Disna.

Diszel, Hung.; pop. 31; 69 km NNE of Nagykanizsa; 46°53'/17°30'; HSL.

Disznajo, *see* Porcesti.

Disznopataka, *see* Valea Porcului.

Disznosd, HSL, HSL2. This pre-World War I community was

not found in BGN gazetteers.

Disznoshorvat, Hung.; pop. 41; 32 km NNW of Miskolc; 48°18'/20°40'.

Ditrau, Rom. (Ditro); pop. 157; 146 km ENE of Cluj; 46°49'/25°31'; HSL, PHR2.

Ditro, *see* Ditrau.

Ditrohodas, HSL. This pre-World War I community was not found in BGN gazetteers.

Dittenheim, Germ.; 50 km SSW of Nurnberg; 49°03'/10°48'; HSL, HSL2, JGFF, PHGB.

Ditterswind, Germ.; 82 km NNW of Nurnberg; 50°10'/10°38'; PHGB.

Dittlofsroda, Germ.; pop. 18; 75 km ENE of Frankfurt am Main; 50°09'/09°46'; GUM3, GUM5, PHGB.

Diuksyn, *see* Dyuksin.

Diulmeni, *see* Yarovoye.

Divenishok, *see* Dieveniskes.

Diviciorii Mari, Rom.; pop. 13; 45 km NE of Cluj; 46°59'/24°05'.

Diviciorii Mici, Rom.; pop. 16; 45 km NE of Cluj; 46°58'/24°06'.

Divin, Byel. (Dewin, Diwin, Dyvin, Dywin); pop. 786; 107 km WSW of Pinsk; 51°58'/24°35'; EJ, GUM4, HSL, JGFF, LDL, SF.

Divisov, Cz.; pop. 42; 45 km SE of Praha; 49°47'/14°53'.

Divisovice, Cz.; pop. 62 km S of Praha; 49°36'/14°32'; HSL.

Divizia, *see* Diviziya.

Diviziya, Ukr. (Divizia); pop. 23; 82 km SSW of Odessa; 45°57'/29°58'.

Diwin, *see* Divin.

Diz Gramzda, Lat. (Gramzdas); pop. 4; 163 km SW of Riga; 56°22'/21°37'.

Dizser, *see* Dijir.

Djakovo, *see* Akovo.

Djoltai, *see* Dzholtay.

Djulaves, *see* Miokovicevo.

Djurdjevac, *see* Urdevac.

Djurin, *see* Dzhurin.

Dlazkovice, Cz.; pop. 4; 56 km NW of Praha; 50°28'/13°58'.

Dlazov, Cz.; pop. 9; 126 km SW of Praha; 49°22'/13°10'.

Dlha, Cz. (Hossufalu, Hosszufalu); 45 km NNE of Bratislava; 48°25'/17°26'; HSL.

Dlhe, Cz.; 120 km NE of Bratislava; 48°51'/18°23'; AMG.

Dlouha, Cz.; 114 km W of Praha; 50°19'/12°54'; HSL.

Dlouha Lhota, JGFF. A number of towns share this name. It was not possible to determine from available information which one is being referenced.

Dlouha Ves, JGFF. A number of towns share this name. It was not possible to determine from available information which one is being referenced.

Dlouhonovice, Cz.; pop. 2; 107 km NNW of Brno; 50°04'/16°27'.

Dluga Szlachecka, Pol.; pop. 5; 26 km E of Warszawa; 52°15'/21°19'.

Dluga Wies, Pol.; pop. 32; 94 km ESE of Poznan; 51°56'/18°05'.

Dlugie, HSL. A number of towns share this name. It was not possible to determine from available information which one is being referenced.

Dlugie Kamienskie, Pol.; pop. 13; 82 km SW of Bialystok; 52°40'/22°16'.

Dlugoborz, Pol.; pop. 18; 62 km SW of Bialystok; 52°57'/22°15'.

Dlugosiodlo, Pol.; pop. 801; 69 km NNE of Warszawa; 52°46'/21°36'; COH, GUM3, HSL, PHP4.

Dlugovolya, *see* Dolgovolya.

Dlugowola, Pol.; pop. 23; 62 km S of Warszawa; 51°46'/20°53'. *See also* Dolgovolya.

Dlutow, Pol.; pop. 44; 26 km S of Lodz; 51°34'/19°24'; JGFF.

Dluzniewice, Pol.; pop. 15; 75 km SE of Lodz; 51°15'/20°07'.

Dmenin, Pol.; 45 km NE of Czestochowa; 51°04'/19°34'; JGFF.

Dminin, Pol.; pop. 21; 75 km N of Lublin; 51°52'/22°27'; GA.

Dmitriev, USSR; pop. 180; This town was not found in BGN

gazetteers under the given spelling.

Dmitriyevka, Ukr. (Deljiler, Dmitrovka, Dmitrowka); pop. 17; 120 km SW of Odessa; 45°50'/29°29'; HSL, JGFF, LDL, SF.

Dmitrov, Ukr. (Dmytrow); pop. 92; 56 km NE of Lvov; 50°12'/24°37'; AMG, YB.

Dmitrovka, see Dmitriyevka.

Dmitrovsk, see Dmitrovsk Orlovskiy.

Dmitrovsk Orlovskiy, USSR (Dmitrovsk); pop. 21; 101 km SE of Bryansk; 52°30'/35°09'.

Dmitrowka, see Dmitriyevka.

Dmochy Glinki, Pol.; pop. 3; 62 km SW of Bialystok; 52°50'/22°21'.

Dmytrow, see Dmitrov.

Dmytrowice, Pol.; pop. 38; 19 km NNW of Przemysl; 49°54'/22°45'.

Dneprodzerzhinsk, Ukr. (Dnieprodzierzynsk, Dnyeprodzerzinsk, Kamenskoe, Kamenskoye, Kamianskoc, Kamienskie); pop. 1,348; 32 km W of Dnepropetrovsk; 48°30'/34°37'; EDRD.

Dnepropetrovsk, Ukr. (Dniepropetrovsk, Ekaterinoslav, Jekaterynoslaw, Keterinoslav, Secheslav, Siczeslaw, Yekaterinoslav); pop. 62,073; 195 km SSW of Kharkov; 48°27'/34°59'; AMG, COH, EDRD, EJ, GUM3, GUM4, GUM5, HSL, HSL2, JGFF, LDL, LYV, PHP2, SF, YB.

Dnesice, Cz.; pop. 8; 101 km SW of Praha; 49°36'/13°17'; HSL.

Dnieprodzierzynsk, see Dneprodzerzhinsk.

Dniepropetrovsk, see Dnepropetrovsk.

Dniestrzyk Holowiecki, Pol.; pop. 43; Described in the *Black Book* as being in the Stanislawow region of Poland, this town was not found in BGN gazetteers.

Dno, USSR; pop. 96; 94 km E of Pskov; 57°50'/29°59'.

Dnyeprodzerzinsk, see Dneprodzerzhinsk.

Doaga, Rom.; 157 km S of Iasi; 45°49'/27°17'; GUM4.

Dob, Yug.; 114 km WNW of Zagreb; 46°09'/14°38'; HSL.

Doba, Rom. (Szamosdob); 126 km NW of Cluj; 47°44'/22°43'; HSL.

Doba Mare, Rom.; pop. 5; 69 km NW of Cluj; 47°17'/23°05'.

Doba Mica, Rom.; pop. 11; 69 km NW of Cluj; 47°18'/23°05'.

Dobanovci, Yug.; pop. 5; 19 km WSW of Beograd; 44°50'/20°13'.

Dobcza, Pol.; pop. 49; 50 km N of Przemysl; 50°14'/22°45'.

Dobczyce, Pol. (Dobshitz, Dopshitz); 32 km SE of Krakow; 49°52'/20°05'; AMG, GUM5, HSL, PHP3, SF.

Dobeik, see Debeikiai.

Dobele, Lat. (Dobeln, Doblen); pop. 80; 62 km SW of Riga; 56°37'/23°16'; GUM4, LDL, PHLE, SF.

Dobeln, see Dobele.

Dobeni, Rom.; pop. 7; 133 km ESE of Cluj; 46°17'/25°11'.

Doberschutz, see Dobrzyca.

Dobiecin, Pol.; pop. 8; 50 km S of Lodz; 51°22'/19°26'; EDRD.

Dobiegniew, Pol. (Woldenberg, Woldenburg); pop. 51; 101 km WNW of Poznan; 52°58'/15°45'; GUM4, LDS.

Dobieslawice, Pol.; pop. 7; 50 km NE of Krakow; 50°13'/20°35'.

Dobieszowice, Pol.; pop. 26; 50 km S of Czestochowa; 50°24'/19°00'.

Dobieszyn, Pol.; pop. 20; 82 km WSW of Przemysl; 49°43'/21°41'.

Dobkov, Cz.; pop. 2; 88 km WNW of Brno; 49°42'/15°41'.

Dobkowice, Ukr.; pop. 22; 94 km SW of Lvov; 49°35'/22°45'. This town was located on an interwar map of Poland but does not appear in contemporary gazetteers. Map coordinates are approximate.

Doblen, see Dobele.

Dobocza, see Dubovec.

Doboj, Yug.; pop. 54; 189 km WSW of Beograd; 44°44'/18°05'; PHY.

Dobolii de Sus, Rom. (Aldoboly, Feldoboly); pop. 1; 157 km N of Bucuresti; 45°47'/26°02'.

Dobolt, Rom.; pop. 10; 139 km NNW of Cluj; 47°59'/23°02'.

Doborcseny, see Dobrocina.

Doborhegy, Hung.; pop. 3; 69 km NNW of Nagykanizsa; 46°59'/16°42'.

Doboseni, Rom.; pop. 1; 163 km ESE of Cluj; 46°07'/25°35'.

Doboz, Hung.; pop. 17; 94 km NE of Szeged; 46°44'/21°15'.

Dobra, Pol.; pop. 1,207; 62 km WNW of Lodz; 51°55'/18°37'; AMG, COH, EDRD, GUM3, HSL2, JGFF, PHP3, POCEM, SF.

Dobra (near Limanowa), Pol.; pop. 184; 50 km SE of Krakow; 49°43'/20°16'; EGRS, GUM3, PHP1, SF.

Dobra (near Sanok), Pol.; pop. 25; 38 km SW of Przemysl; 49°40'/22°18'.

Dobra (near Szczecin), Pol. (Daber); 50 km ENE of Szczecin; 53°35'/15°18'; LDS.

Dobraczyn, see Dobrochin.

Dobra Mala, HSL. This pre-World War I community was not found in BGN gazetteers.

Dobra Misla, LDL. This pre-World War I community was not found in BGN gazetteers.

Dobra nad Ondavou, Cz.; pop. 90; 45 km NNE of Kosice; 49°01'/21°42'.

Dobranka, see Dobryanka.

Dobranowka, GUM3. This town was not found in BGN gazetteers under the given spelling.

Dobrany, Cz.; pop. 30; 101 km SW of Praha; 49°39'/13°18'; HSL.

Dobra Rustykalna, Pol.; pop. 34; Described in the *Black Book* as being in the Lwow region of Poland, this town was not found in BGN gazetteers.

Dobrassen, see Dobrosov.

Dobra Szlachecka, Pol.; pop. 30; 38 km SW of Przemysl; 49°39'/22°18'.

Dobrava, USSR; pop. 2,442; A number of towns share this name. It was not possible to determine from available information which one is being referenced.

Dobra Velka, HSL. This pre-World War I community was not found in BGN gazetteers.

Dobrcz, Pol. (Dobrz); pop. 5; 120 km NNE of Poznan; 53°16'/18°09'; EDRD.

Dobre, Pol.; pop. 373; 45 km ENE of Warszawa; 52°20'/21°41'; GA, HSL, PHP4, SF.

Dobre Miasto, Pol. (Guttstadt); pop. 70; 120 km ESE of Gdansk; 53°59'/20°24'; AMG, LDS.

Dobreni, GUM4. A number of towns share this name. It was not possible to determine from available information which one is being referenced.

Dobricany, Cz.; pop. 9; 62 km WNW of Praha; 50°18'/13°37'.

Dobricel, Rom.; pop. 12; 69 km NNE of Cluj; 47°18'/24°07'.

Dobrich, see Tolbukhin.

Dobrichovice, Cz.; pop. 12; 26 km SSW of Praha; 49°56'/14°17'.

Dobricionesti, Rom.; pop. 11; 88 km WNW of Cluj; 46°59'/22°28'.

Dobrin, see Dobrzyn nad Wisla.

Dobrin Bay Dervents, see Golub Dobrzyn.

Dobrinka, see Dobryanka.

Dobris, Cz.; pop. 115; 45 km SSW of Praha; 49°46'/14°11'.

Dobriv, Cz.; pop. 6; 69 km SW of Praha; 49°43'/13°41'.

Dobriya, see Dobryanka.

Dobrjanka, see Dobryanka.

Dobrkow, Pol.; pop. 3; 107 km E of Krakow; 49°59'/21°21'.

Dobrochin, Ukr. (Dobraczyn); pop. 17; 69 km N of Lvov; 50°25'/24°14'.

Dobrociesz, Pol.; pop. 19; 56 km ESE of Krakow; 49°48'/20°34'.

Dobrocina, Rom. (Doborcseny); pop. 2; 62 km N of Cluj; 47°16'/23°43'.

Dobrocovice, Cz.; pop. 5; 19 km E of Praha; 50°03'/14°42'.

Dobrodzien, Pol. (Guttentag); pop. 40; 50 km WSW of Czestochowa; 50°44'/18°27'; HSL, LDS, POCEM.

Dobrohostow, Ukr.; pop. 48; 107 km S of Lvov; 48°55'/23°35'; HSL. This town was located on an interwar map of Poland but does not appear in contemporary gazetteers. Map coordinates are approximate.

Dobrokoz, Hung.; pop. 36; 101 km E of Nagykanizsa; 46°59'/16°42'.

46°25'/18°15'.

Dobromil, Ukr. (Dobromyl); pop. 2,119; 94 km SW of Lvov; 49°34'/22°47'; AMG, CAHJP, COH, EDRD, EGRS, GUM3, GUM4, GUM5, GUM6, HSL, HSL2, JGFF, LDL, PHP2, PHP3, SF, YB.

Dobromirka, Ukr.; pop. 28; 114 km S of Rovno; 49°38'/25°55'. This town was located on an interwar map of Poland but does not appear in contemporary gazetteers. Map coordinates are approximate.

Dobromyl, *see* Dobromil.

Dobromysl, Byel.; 45 km ESE of Vitebsk; 54°56'/30°40'; GUM4.

Dobron, Pol.; 19 km SW of Lodz; 51°38'/19°15'; HSL.

Dobronauti, *see* Dobronovtsy.

Dobronouts, *see* Dobronovtsy.

Dobronovtsy, Ukr. (Dobronauti, Dobronouts); pop. 89; 26 km N of Chernovtsy; 48°29'/26°01'.

Dobron Velika, HSL. This pre-World War I community was not found in BGN gazetteers.

Dobropole Mateuszowka, Ukr.; pop. 26; 101 km NNW of Chernovtsy; 49°12'/25°26'.

Dobrose, *see* Dobrosov.

Dobrosin, Ukr.; pop. 26; 38 km NNW of Lvov; 50°08'/23°51'; HSL.

Dobrosov, Cz. (Dobrassen, Dobrose); 157 km W of Praha; 50°07'/12°15'; HSL.

Dobrostany, Ukr.; pop. 20; 26 km W of Lvov; 49°52'/23°38'.

Dobroszyce, Pol.; 38 km NE of Wroclaw; 51°16'/17°20'; PHP2.

Dobrotow, *see* Dobrotuv.

Dobrotuv, Ukr. (Dobrotow); pop. 54; 94 km WNW of Chernovtsy; 48°33'/24°42'; HSL.

Dobrotvor, Ukr. (Dobrotwor); pop. 216; 50 km NNE of Lvov; 50°14'/24°22'; HSL, JGFF, LDL, PHP2, SF.

Dobrotwor, *see* Dobrotvor.

Dobrovelichkovka, Ukr.; pop. 2,060; 82 km ESE of Uman; 48°23'/31°11'.

Dobrovice, Cz.; pop. 10; 50 km NE of Praha; 50°22'/14°57'.

Dobrovitov, Cz.; pop. 16; 69 km ESE of Praha; 49°47'/15°20'.

Dobrovlyany, *see* Drogobych.

Dobrovlyany (near Bobrka), Ukr.; pop. 20; 62 km SSE of Lvov; 49°22'/24°18'.

Dobrovlyany (near Drogobych), Ukr.; pop. 54; 69 km SSW of Lvov; 49°21'/23°30'.

Dobrovlyany (near Stryy), Ukr.; pop. 21; 56 km SSW of Lvov; 49°26'/23°34'.

Dobrovnik, Yug.; pop. 7; 101 km N of Zagreb; 46°39'/16°21'.

Dobrovody, Ukr. (Dobrowody); pop. 25; 107 km NW of Chernovtsy; 49°09'/25°13'.

Dobrovolsk, USSR (Pillkallen); pop. 26; 133 km ENE of Kaliningrad; 54°46'/22°31'.

Dobrowlany, *see* Drogobych.

Dobrowoda, Pol.; pop. 20; 69 km NE of Krakow; 50°24'/20°46'.

Dobrowody, *see* Dobrovody.

Dobrowola, Pol.; pop. 6; 26 km SSW of Lublin; 51°03'/22°18'.

Dobruchow, Pol.; pop. 2; 26 km WSW of Lodz; 51°44'/19°06'.

Dobrush, Byel.; pop. 372; 26 km E of Gomel; 52°25'/31°19'.

Dobrusha, Mold. (Slobozia Dobrusa); pop. 12; 94 km NNW of Kishinev; 47°47'/28°35'.

Dobruska, Cz.; pop. 48; 120 km ENE of Praha; 50°18'/16°10'; HSL, HSL2.

Dobry, Pol.; 88 km E of Gdansk; 54°08'/19°56'; LDL.

Dobryanka, Ukr. (Dobranka, Dobrinka, Dobriya, Dobrjanka); pop. 367; 114 km S of Vinnitsa; 48°17'/28°23'; JGFF, LDL, SF.

Dobrylow, Pol.; pop. 6; 75 km E of Lublin; 51°13'/23°41'.

Dobrynin, Pol.; pop. 22; 101 km WNW of Przemysl; 50°12'/21°32'.

Dobrynka, Pol.; pop. 20; 101 km NNE of Lublin; 52°00'/23°29'.

Dobrz, *see* Dobrcz.

Dobrzanka, Pol.; pop. 23; 32 km SW of Przemysl; 49°40'/22°24'.

Dobrzankowo, Pol.; pop. 21; 82 km N of Warszawa; 52°59'/20°58'.

Dobrzany, Pol.; pop. 6; 62 km E of Szczecin; 53°22'/15°25'. *See also* Dobzhany.

Dobrzechow, Pol.; pop. 6; 75 km W of Przemysl; 49°53'/21°45'; GUM5, PHP3.

Dobrzelow, Pol.; 45 km S of Lodz; 51°23'/19°24'; PHP1.

Dobrzeszow, Pol.; pop. 3; 88 km ENE of Czestochowa; 50°59'/20°20'.

Dobrzyca, Pol. (Doberschutz); pop. 6; 82 km SE of Poznan; 51°52'/17°36'; CAHJP, LDL, LDS.

Dobrzyce, Pol.; pop. 346; EGRS. Described in the *Black Book* as being in the Krakow region of Poland, this town was not found in BGN gazetteers.

Dobrzykow, Pol.; pop. 26; 82 km N of Lodz; 52°28'/19°45'.

Dobrzyn, *See* Dobrzyn nad Wisla; Golub Dobrzyn.

Dobrzyn Golub, *see* Golub Dobrzyn.

Dobrzyn nad Drewca, *see* Golub Dobrzyn.

Dobrzyn nad Drweca, *see* Golub Dobrzyn.

Dobrzyn nad Wisla, Pol. (Dobrin); pop. 775; 107 km N of Lodz; 52°39'/19°20'; COH, EJ, GUM3, GUM4, HSL, PHP4, POCEM, SF, YB. *See also* Golub-Dobrzyn.

Dobschau, *see* Dobsina.

Dobshitz, *see* Dobczyce.

Dobsina, Cz. (Dobschau); 69 km W of Kosice; 48°49'/20°22'; GUM4, HSL.

Dobspuda, Pol. PHP4. This town was not found in BGN gazetteers under the given spelling.

Dobsza, HSL. This pre-World War I community was not found in BGN gazetteers.

Dobuzek, Pol.; pop. 16; 107 km NNE of Przemysl; 50°34'/23°45'.

Dobyasser, *see* Dubossary.

Dobzhany, Ukr. (Dobrzany); pop. 32; 38 km WSW of Lvov; 49°45'/23°31'.

Dobzhin, *see* Golub Dobrzyn.

Dobzhin Golub, *see* Golub Dobrzyn.

Dobzhin nad Drvents, *see* Golub Dobrzyn.

Dockingen, Germ.; 62 km S of Nurnberg; 48°56'/10°45'; HSL, HSL2, PHGB.

Doda, HSL. This pre-World War I community was not found in BGN gazetteers.

Doerzbach, *see* Dorzbach.

Doge, Hung.; pop. 17; 94 km ENE of Miskolc; 48°16'/22°05'; LDS.

Doging, Germ.; 146 km E of Munchen; 47°58'/13°30'; HSL.

Dogwizdow, Pol. PHP3. This town was not found in BGN gazetteers under the given spelling.

Doh, Rom.; pop. 11; 94 km WNW of Cluj; 47°19'/22°43'.

Dohlen, Germ. JGFF. A number of towns share this name. It was not possible to determine from available information which one is being referenced.

Doig, *see* Daugai.

Dojazdow, Pol.; pop. 20; 13 km ENE of Krakow; 50°07'/20°07'.

Dojlidy, *see* Dailydai.

Doksany, Cz.; pop. 6; 45 km NW of Praha; 50°27'/14°10'.

Dokshits, *see* Dokshitsy.

Dokshitse, *see* Dokshitsy.

Dokshitsy, Byel. (Dokshits, Dokshitse, Dokshitsya, Dokshitz, Dokszyce, Dugscitz); pop. 2,055; 120 km N of Minsk; 54°54'/27°46'; AMG, COH, GUM3, GUM4, HSL, JGFF, LDL, LYV, SF, YB.

Dokshitz, *see* Dokshitsy.

Dokszyce, *see* Dokshitsy.

Dokudow, Pol.; pop. 7; 88 km NNE of Lublin; 51°57'/23°13'; GA.

Doles, *see* Vecdoles.

Dolesheim, GUM3. This town was not found in BGN gazetteers under the given spelling.

Dolge, Ukr. (Dolgoye, Dolhe); HSL. *See also* Dolgov; Dolgoye; Dovge.

Dolge (Tarnopol), Ukr.; pop. 23; 107 km NNW of Chernovtsy; 49°13'/25°43'.

Dolgesheim, Germ.; pop. 15; 62 km W of Stuttgart;

48°48'/08°16'.

Dolginov, *see* Dolginovo.

Dolginovo, Byel. (Dalnow, Dolginov, Dolhinov, Dolhinow, Dolhinuv, Dolne); pop. 1,747; 94 km N of Minsk; 54°39'/27°29'; AMG, COH, EDRD, EJ, GUM3, GUM4, GUM5, GUM6, HSL, JGFF, LYV, SF, YB.

Dolgorukovo, USSR (Stablack); 38 km S of Kaliningrad; 54°26'/20°31'; GUM3.

Dolgov, Ukr. (Dolge); pop. 21; 114 km NW of Chernovtsy; 49°02'/24°55'.

Dolgovolya, Ukr. (Dlugovolya, Dlugowola); pop. 45; 94 km NNW of Rovno; 51°25'/26°04'.

Dolgoye, Ukr. (Dolge, Dolhe Podbuskie, Dovhe); pop. 144; 88 km SSW of Lvov; 49°10'/23°21'; HSL, JGFF, LYV, PHP2, SM. *See also* Dolge.

Dolgoye (II), Ukr. (Dolha); 176 km S of Lvov; 48°22'/23°17'; AMG, HSL, HSL2.

Dolha, *see* Dolgoye (II).

Dolhe, *see* Dolge; Dovge.

Dolhe Podbuskie, *see* Dolgoye.

Dolhinov, *see* Dolginovo.

Dolhinow, *see* Dolginovo.

Dolhinuv, *see* Dolginovo.

Dolhobrody, Pol. (Dolhobrot); pop. 44; 82 km NE of Lublin; 51°41'/23°31'; HSL, SF.

Dolhobrot, *see* Dolhobrody.

Dolhobyczow, Pol.; pop. 99; 126 km ESE of Lublin; 50°35'/24°02'; GA, GUM5.

Dolin, Cz.; pop. 2; 32 km WNW of Praha; 50°15'/14°07'.

Dolina, Ukr.; pop. 2,014; 107 km S of Lvov; 48°58'/24°01'; AMG, COH, EDRD, EGRS, EJ, GUM3, GUM4, GUM5, HSL, HSL2, JGFF, LDL, PHP2, SF.

Dolina (near Ivano Frankovsk), Ukr.; pop. 20; 75 km NW of Chernovtsy; 48°51'/25°12'.

Dolina (Tarnopol), Ukr.; pop. 26; 75 km NNW of Chernovtsy; 48°57'/25°43'.

Dolinen, Ukr. (Dolineni); pop. 33; 38 km NE of Chernovtsy; 48°25'/26°26'.

Dolineni, *see* Dolinen.

Doliniany, *see* Dolinyany.

Dolinskoye, Ukr. (Hotzila, Valegotsulovo, Valehotzulovo, Volegotsulovo, Walegozulowo); pop. 2,545; 133 km NW of Odessa; 47°32'/29°55'; EDRD, LDL, SF.

Dolinyany, Ukr. (Doliniany); pop. 71; 62 km SE of Lvov; 49°25'/24°25'.

Dolishnev, Ukr. (Laszki Gorne, Lyashki Gurne); pop. 70; 50 km SSE of Lvov; 49°29'/24°11'.

Dolmatovshchina, Byel. (Dolmatowszczyzna); pop. 22; 101 km SW of Minsk; 53°26'/26°14'.

Dolmatowszczyzna, *see* Dolmatovshchina.

Dolna, Pol.; pop. 86; 69 km SW of Czestochowa; 50°28'/18°14'; GA, JGFF.

Dolna Ludova, GUM6. This town was not found in BGN gazetteers under the given spelling.

Dolna Tuzla, HSL. This pre-World War I community was not found in BGN gazetteers.

Dolne, *see* Dolginovo.

Dolne Zahorany, Cz. (Hegymeg); 107 km SW of Kosice; 48°21'/19°55'; HSL.

Dolni Bousov, Cz.; 62 km NE of Praha; 50°26'/15°08'; JGFF.

Dolni Kounice, Cz. (Kanitz, Kuniz); pop. 53; 19 km SSW of Brno; 49°04'/16°28'; EJ, HSL.

Dolni Kralovice, Cz.; pop. 52; 62 km ESE of Praha; 49°40'/15°09'.

Dolni Kubin, *see* Dolny Kubin.

Dolni Lukavice, Cz.; pop. 9; 101 km SW of Praha; 49°36'/13°21'.

Dolni Zandov, Cz.; pop. 20; 139 km WSW of Praha; 50°01'/12°33'.

Dolnja Lendava, *see* Lendava.

Dolny Kubin, Cz. (Also Kubin, Alsokubin, Dolni Kubin); pop.

418; 150 km WNW of Kosice; 49°12'/19°18'; AMG, EJ, GUM4, HSL.

Dolny Lieskov, Cz. (Alsoliszko); 133 km E of Brno; 49°03'/18°25'; HSL.

Dolovo, Cz. AMG. A number of towns share this name. It was not possible to determine from available information which one is being referenced.

Dolsk, Ukr. (Dolzig); pop. 56; 146 km N of Lvov; 51°07'/24°23'.

Dolu, Rom.; pop. 4; 32 km NW of Cluj; 46°59'/23°20'.

Doly, Cz. (Karvinna, Karwina); pop. 172; 150 km NE of Brno; 49°50'/18°29'; HSL, PHP3.

Doly (Poland), Pol.; pop. 20; 56 km ESE of Krakow; 49°56'/20°42'.

Doly Biskupie, Pol.; pop. 15; 94 km SW of Lublin; 50°59'/21°13'.

Doly Slatinski, *see* Solotvina.

Dolzhka, Ukr. (Dolzka, Dolzki); pop. 141; 88 km SE of Lvov; 49°10'/24°29'; PHP2.

Dolzhki, Ukr. (Dolzhok); 50 km E of Rovno; 50°30'/26°54'; GUM4.

Dolzhok, *see* Dolzhki.

Dolzig, *see* Dolsk.

Dolzka, *see* Dolzhka.

Dolzki, *see* Dolzhka.

Dolzyca, Pol.; pop. 22; 75 km SW of Przemysl; 49°20'/22°02'; HSL.

Domacheva, *see* Domachevo.

Domacheve, *see* Domachevo.

Domachevo, Byel. (Domacheva, Domacheve, Domachuv, Domaczewo, Domaczow, Domatcheva, Domatchov); pop. 1,337; 176 km WSW of Pinsk; 51°45'/23°36'; COH, EDRD, GUM3, GUM4, HSL, JGFF, LDL, LYV, SF.

Domachuv, *see* Domachevo.

Domacyny, Pol.; pop. 18; 114 km SSW of Lublin; 50°28'/21°29'.

Domaczewo, *see* Domachevo.

Domaczow, *see* Domachevo.

Domahida, *see* Domanesti.

Domamysl, Cz.; pop. 4; 75 km SE of Praha; 49°28'/14°53'.

Domanesti, Rom. (Domahida); pop. 11; 133 km NW of Cluj; 47°43'/22°36'.

Domanevka, Ukr. (Domanovca, Domonovca, Dumanovka); pop. 1,191; 133 km N of Odessa; 47°38'/30°59'; EDRD, EJ, GUM4, GUM5, PHR1.

Domanjsevci, Yug. (Domanjsovci); pop. 2; 114 km N of Zagreb; 46°47'/16°18'.

Domanjsovci, *see* Domanjsevci.

Domanovca, *see* Domanevka.

Domanowo, *see* Domanowo Stare.

Domanowo Stare, Pol. (Domanowo); pop. 6; 50 km SSW of Bialystok; 52°47'/22°45'.

Domaradz, Pol.; pop. 123; 62 km WSW of Przemysl; 49°47'/21°57'; PHP3.

Domashe, Byel. (Domasze); pop. 7; 75 km WNW of Minsk; 54°19'/26°45'.

Domashov, Ukr. (Domashuv, Domaszow); pop. 40; 56 km NNW of Lvov; 50°20'/23°51'.

Domashuv, *see* Domashov.

Domasze, *see* Domashe.

Domaszewnica, Pol.; pop. 25; 75 km NNW of Lublin; 51°51'/22°23'.

Domaszewska Wolka, Pol.; pop. 20; Described in the *Black Book* as being in the Lublin region of Poland, this town was not found in BGN gazetteers.

Domaszno, Pol.; pop. 2; 75 km ESE of Lodz; 51°30'/20°31'.

Domaszow, *see* Domashov.

Domaszowce Nowe, GUM6. This town was not found in BGN gazetteers under the given spelling.

Domatcheva, *see* Domachevo.

Domatchov, *see* Domachevo.

Domatkow, Pol.; pop. 25; 82 km WNW of Przemysl; 50°12'/21°46'.

Domazhir, Ukr. (Domazyr); pop. 25; 13 km WNW of Lvov; 49°53'/23°51'.

Domazlice, Cz.; pop. 94; 133 km SW of Praha; 49°26'/12°56'.

Domazyr, *see* Domazhir.

Dombe, *see* Dabie.

Dombegyhaz, Hung.; pop. 36; 75 km ENE of Szeged; 46°20'/21°08'.

Dombie, *see* Dabie.

Dombiratos, Hung.; pop. 3; 75 km ENE of Szeged; 46°25'/21°07'.

Dombo, *possibly* Valendorf.

Dombovar, Hung.; pop. 722; 88 km E of Nagykanizsa; 46°23'/18°07'; AMG, COH, GUM5, GUM6, LDS, PHH.

Dombrad, Hung.; pop. 234; 88 km ENE of Miskolc; 48°14'/21°56'; AMG, HSL, HSL2, JGFF, LDL, LDS, PHH.

Dombrava Gornitsha, *see* Dabrowa Gornicza.

Dombrova, *see* Dabrowa Gornicza.

Dombrove, *see* Dabrowa.

Dombrove Gur, *see* Dabrowa Gornicza.

Dombroven, *see* Dumbraveny.

Dombroveni, *see* Dumbraveny.

Dombrovits, *see* Dabrowice.

Dombrovitsa, *see* Dubrovitsa.

Dombrovitza, *see* Dubrovitsa.

Dombrowa Gornicza, *see* Dabrowa Gornicza.

Dombye, *see* Dabie.

Domefolde, Hung.; pop. 5; 32 km WNW of Nagykanizsa; 46°35'/16°40'.

Dominteni, *see* Dominteny.

Dominteny, Mold. (Dominteni); pop. 71; 126 km NW of Kishinev; 47°57'/27°57'.

Domitz, Germ.; 94 km ESE of Hamburg; 53°08'/11°15'; LDS.

Domnau, *see* Domnovo.

Domnin, Rom. (Dabjon); pop. 19; 75 km NW of Cluj; 47°20'/23°11'.

Domnovo, USSR (Domnau); pop. 7; 45 km SE of Kaliningrad; 54°25'/20°50'.

Domokos, *see* Damacuseni.

Domonovca, *see* Domanevka.

Domony, Hung.; pop. 20; 32 km NE of Budapest; 47°39'/19°26'; HSL, LDS.

Domos, Hung.; pop. 20; 32 km NNW of Budapest; 47°46'/18°55'.

Domostawa, Pol.; pop. 4; 75 km S of Lublin; 50°37'/22°17'.

Domosu, Rom.; pop. 1; 45 km W of Cluj; 46°50'/23°01'.

Domoszlo, Hung.; pop. 29; 56 km SW of Miskolc; 47°50'/20°07'; HSL.

Domotori, Hung.; pop. 4; 82 km NNW of Nagykanizsa; 47°08'/16°43'.

Domousice, Cz.; pop. 18; 50 km WNW of Praha; 50°14'/13°44'.

Dompole, *see* Berzpils.

Domsod, Hung.; pop. 94; 50 km S of Budapest; 47°05'/19°00'; GUM5, HSL, LDS, PHH.

Domulugeni, *see* Domuluzhany.

Domuluzhany, Mold. (Domulugeni); pop. 10; 94 km NNW of Kishinev; 47°48'/28°26'.

Donaueschingen, Germ.; pop. 16; 101 km SSW of Stuttgart; 47°57'/08°30'; PHGBW.

Donauworth, Germ.; pop. 94; 88 km NW of Munchen; 48°42'/10°48'; GUM3, PHGB.

Donbki, *see* Dubka.

Dondosani Gara, *see* Dondyushany.

Dondusani, *see* Dondyushany.

Dondyushany, Mold. (Dondosani Gara, Dondusani); pop. 277; 170 km NW of Kishinev; 48°14'/27°36'.

Donetsk, Ukr. (Donieck, Iuzovka, Juzowka, Stalin Donezk, Stalino, Yuzovka); pop. 12,100; 214 km E of Dnepropetrovsk; 48°00'/37°48'; EDRD, EJ, GUM4, GUM5.

Donieck, *see* Donetsk.

Donja Dubrava, Yug.; pop. 21; 88 km NE of Zagreb; 46°19'/16°49'.

Donja Stubica, Yug.; pop. 18; 26 km N of Zagreb; 45°59'/15°58'.

Donji Caglic, Yug. (Caglic); pop. 5; 101 km ESE of Zagreb; 45°23'/17°09'.

Donji Grad, Yug. (Osijekdonji Grad); pop. 160; 163 km WNW of Beograd; 45°34'/18°43'.

Donji Miholjac, Yug.; pop. 119; 163 km E of Zagreb; 45°45'/18°10'; PHY.

Donji Milanovac, Yug.; pop. 1; 133 km ESE of Beograd; 44°28'/22°07'.

Donji Skugric, Yug.; pop. 2; 170 km W of Beograd; 44°54'/18°22'.

Donji Vakuf, Yug.; pop. 3; 214 km SE of Zagreb; 44°08'/17°24'.

Donji Vidovec, Yug.; pop. 9; 82 km NNE of Zagreb; 46°20'/16°47'.

Donji Zemunik, Yug. (Zemunik); pop. 1; 189 km S of Zagreb; 44°07'/15°23'.

Dopshitz, *see* Dobczyce.

Dor, Hung.; pop. 2; 133 km W of Budapest; 47°36'/17°18'.

Dora, Ukr.; pop. 87; 101 km W of Chernovtsy; 48°28'/24°35'; GUM3, GUM4, GUM5, GUM6, SF. Dora is also the name of a concentration camp.

Doraganova, *see* Nowyja Dorogi.

Dorbenai, *see* Darbenai.

Dorbian, *see* Darbenai.

Dorbozy, Pol.; pop. 3; 69 km N of Przemysl; 50°21'/22°57'.

Dorbyan, *see* Darbenai.

Dorbyany, *see* Darbenai.

Dorfe Haaren, GUM5. This town was not found in BGN gazetteers under the given spelling.

Dorfel, HSL. A number of towns share this name. It was not possible to determine from available information which one is being referenced.

Dorfen, Germ.; 45 km NE of Munchen; 48°16'/12°09'; PHGB.

Dorgo, *see* Tallya.

Dormagen, Germ.; pop. 42; 26 km NW of Koln; 51°06'/06°50'; GED.

Dormand, Hung.; 50 km SSW of Miskolc; 47°43'/20°25'; HSL.

Dormitz, Germ.; 19 km N of Nurnberg; 49°36'/11°07'; PHGB.

Dorna, HSL. A number of towns share this name. It was not possible to determine from available information which one is being referenced.

Dorna Candrenilor, *see* Dorna Cindrenilor.

Dornach, Germ.; 32 km S of Stuttgart; 48°34'/09°12'; HSL, PHGBW.

Dorna Cindrenilor, Rom. (Dorna Candrenilor); pop. 112; 139 km NE of Cluj; 47°21'/25°15'.

Dorna Vatra, *see* Vatra Dornei.

Dorna Watra, *see* Vatra Dornei.

Dornbach, Pol.; 56 km NNW of Przemysl; 50°16'/22°28'; HSL, JGFF. A number of towns in Germany and Austria also have this name. It is not possible to determine which one was referenced.

Dornberg, Germ.; 75 km ESE of Frankfurt am Main; 49°38'/09°26'; LDS.

Dornbirn, Aus.; pop. 7; 126 km W of Innsbruck; 47°25'/09°44'.

Dorndorf, Germ.; 62 km SE of Nurnberg; 48°57'/11°29'; PHGB.

Dornesti, Rom. (Hadikfalva); pop. 84; 139 km WNW of Iasi; 47°52'/26°01'; PHR2, SF.

Dornfeld, *see* Ternopolye.

Dornheim, Germ.; pop. 31; 32 km SSW of Frankfurt am Main; 49°53'/08°29'; CAHJP, GUM5, GUM5, PHGB.

Dornigheim, Germ.; 13 km ENE of Frankfurt am Main; 50°08'/08°50'; LDS.

Dornum, Germ.; pop. 36; 170 km W of Hamburg; 53°39'/07°25'; LDS.

Dorobertovo, *see* Dorogobratovo.

Dorobratovo, *see* Dorogobratovo.

Dorog, Hung.; pop. 31; 38 km WNW of Budapest; 47°43'/18°44'.

Doroghaza, Hung.; pop. 4; 69 km WSW of Miskolc; 47°59'/19°54'; HSL.

Dorogma, Hung.; 101 km S of Miskolc; 47°14'/20°52'; HSL. This town was located on a pre-World War I map, but does not appear in contemporary gazetteers.

Dorogobratovo, Ukr. (Dorobertovo, Dorobratovo); 182 km SSW of Lvov; 48°21'/22°54'; AMG, LYV.

Dorogobuzh, USSR; pop. 231; 82 km ENE of Smolensk; 54°54'/33°18'; JGFF.

Dorogov, Ukr. (Doroguv, Dorohow); pop. 37; 88 km SE of Lvov; 49°09'/24°32'.

Doroguv, see Dorogov.

Dorohoi, Rom.; pop. 5,820; 126 km WNW of Iasi; 47°57'/26°24'; EDRD, EJ, GUM4, GUM5, HSL, JGFF, LDL, LJEE, PHR1.

Dorohow, see Dorogov.

Dorohucza, Pol.; pop. 24; 32 km E of Lublin; 51°10'/23°01'; GA, GUM4.

Dorohusk, Pol.; pop. 54; 88 km E of Lublin; 51°10'/23°49'; GA.

Dorok, see Kmetovo.

Dorolea, Rom. (Aszubeszterce); pop. 16; 94 km NE of Cluj; 47°11'/24°38'.

Dorolt, Rom.; pop. 23; 133 km NW of Cluj; 47°51'/22°49'.

Dorosauti, Ukr.; pop. 58; 38 km N of Chernovtsy; 48°35'/25°53'; PHR2.

Doroshitse, GUM4, GUM5, GUM6. This town was not found in BGN gazetteers under the given spelling.

Dorosinie, see Novyye Dorosini.

Doroslovo, Yug.; pop. 9; 133 km WNW of Beograd; 45°37'/19°12'.

Dorozhev, Ukr. (Dorozow); pop. 92; 56 km SSW of Lvov; 49°28'/23°32'.

Dorozow, see Dorozhev.

Dorpa, see Tartu.

Dorpat, see Tartu.

Dorpen, Germ.; pop. 6; 170 km WNW of Hannover; 52°57'/07°19'.

Dorrmoschel, Germ.; pop. 5; 88 km SW of Frankfurt am Main; 49°37'/07°45'; JGFF.

Dorsten, Germ.; pop. 47; 88 km N of Koln; 51°40'/06°58'; GED, GUM4.

Dorstfeld, Germ.; pop. 59; 75 km NNE of Koln; 51°31'/07°25'.

Dorszyn, Pol.; pop. 13; 62 km SE of Lodz; 51°14'/19°50'.

Dortmund, Germ.; pop. 3,820; 75 km NNE of Koln; 51°31'/07°27'; AMG, EDRD, EJ, GED, GUM3, GUM4, GUM5, GUM6, ISH1.

Dorzbach, Germ. (Doerzbach); 82 km NNE of Stuttgart; 49°23'/09°42'; JGFF, PHGBW.

Dosha, see Dashev.

Dossenheim, Germ.; pop. 5; 75 km S of Frankfurt am Main; 49°27'/08°41'; LDS, PHGBW.

Dotnava, see Dotnuva.

Dotneva, see Dotnuva.

Dotnuva, Lith. (Dantova, Datnuva, Dotnava, Dotneva); pop. 204; 56 km N of Kaunas; 55°21'/23°54'; COH, HSL, JGFF, LDL, SF, YL.

Dottenheim, Germ.; 45 km W of Nurnberg; 49°33'/10°31'; PHGB.

Doubrava, Cz.; pop. 69; 150 km NE of Brno; 49°52'/18°29'.

Doubravcany, Cz.; pop. 1; 45 km ESE of Praha; 49°58'/15°00'.

Doubravcice, Cz.; pop. 2; 26 km ESE of Praha; 50°01'/14°48'.

Doudleby, Cz.; pop. 9; 139 km S of Praha; 48°54'/14°30'.

Doudleby nad Orlici, Cz.; pop. 2; 107 km NNW of Brno; 50°07'/16°16'; HSL.

Doupov, Cz.; pop. 6; 94 km W of Praha; 50°15'/13°09'.

Doveny, Hung.; pop. 3; 38 km NW of Miskolc; 48°21'/20°33'.

Dovgaliszek, possibly Naujasis Daugiliskis.

Dovge, Ukr. (Dolge, Dolhe, Dovhe); pop. 20; 56 km SSW of Lvov; 49°24'/23°41'.

Dovhe, see Dolgoye; Dovge.

Dovsk, Byel. (Dowsk); 88 km NW of Gomel; 53°09'/30°28'; SF.

Dowgieliszki, see Naujasis Daugiliskis.

Dowsk, see Dovsk.

Doyg, see Daugai.

Doylidy, see Dailydai.

Dozice, Cz.; pop. 2; 88 km SSW of Praha; 49°32'/13°42'.

Drabesi, Lat.; pop. 2; 75 km NE of Riga; 57°14'/25°17'.

Drabinianka, Pol.; pop. 44; 62 km WNW of Przemysl; 50°01'/22°01'.

Drabov, Ukr.; 126 km ESE of Kiyev; 49°58'/32°08'; HSL.

Drabovshchyzna, Byel. (Drabowszczyzna); pop. 11; 101 km NNE of Pinsk; 52°54'/26°42'.

Drabowszczyzna, see Drabovshchyzna.

Draceni, Rom. (Drancenii de Sus?); pop. 26; 120 km W of Iasi; 47°27'/26°01'.

Drachinets, Ukr. (Dracinet, Dracineti); pop. 232; 19 km W of Chernovtsy; 48°19'/25°42'; PHR2.

Dracic, Yug.; pop. 2; 88 km SSW of Beograd; 44°13'/19°55'.

Dracinet, see Drachinets.

Dracineti, see Drachinets.

Draculea, see Trudovoye.

Draga, Yug.; pop. 1; 107 km WSW of Zagreb; 45°38'/14°40'; HSL.

Dragalic, Yug.; pop. 1; 114 km ESE of Zagreb; 45°15'/17°18'.

Draganeshti, see Dragoneshty.

Draganesti, see Dragoneshty.

Dragany, Pol.; pop. 10; 45 km SSE of Lublin; 50°54'/22°40'.

Dragasymuv, Ukr. (Drahasymow); pop. 38; 45 km W of Chernovtsy; 48°24'/25°24'.

Dragavilma, see Vima Mica.

Dragimiresht, see Dragomiresti.

Dragoesti, Rom. (Dragonyfalva); pop. 24; 120 km WNW of Iasi; 47°33'/26°05'.

Dragomerfalva, see Dragomiresti.

Dragomirest, see Dragomiresti.

Dragomiresti, Rom. (Dragimiresht, Dragomerfalva, Dragomirest); pop. 739; 114 km NNE of Cluj; 47°41'/24°18'; COH, GUM3, GUM4, GUM5, HSL, HSL2, LDL, LYV, PHR2, SM.

Dragoneshty, Mold. (Draganeshti, Draganesti); pop. 89; 94 km NW of Kishinev; 47°43'/28°15'.

Dragonyfalva, see Dragoesti.

Dragosen, see Dragusheny.

Dragoseni, Rom. PHR1. This town was not found in BGN gazetteers under the given spelling.

Dragovo, Ukr. (Drahiv, Drahova, Drahovo, Kovesliget); 176 km WSW of Chernovtsy; 48°14'/23°33'; AMG, JGFF, LYV, SM.

Dragu, Rom.; pop. 10; 32 km NW of Cluj; 47°01'/23°24'.

Dragunia, Pol. PHP4. This town was not found in BGN gazetteers under the given spelling.

Dragusenii Noui, see Novyye Dragusheny.

Dragusenii Vechi, see Dragusheny.

Dragusheni Nouy, see Novyye Dragusheny.

Dragusheny, Mold. (Dragosen, Dragusenii Vechi); pop. 8; 32 km WSW of Kishinev; 46°59'/28°27'.

Dragutinovo, see Novo Milosevo.

Drahasymow, see Dragasymuv.

Drahisevo, GUM3. This town was not found in BGN gazetteers under the given spelling.

Drahiv, see Dragovo.

Drahlin, Cz.; pop. 2; 50 km SSW of Praha; 49°44'/13°58'.

Drahnov, Cz.; pop. 59; 56 km E of Kosice; 48°35'/21°58'.

Drahnovice, Cz.; pop. 9; 45 km ESE of Praha; 49°49'/14°54'.

Drahobudice, Cz.; pop. 5; 50 km ESE of Praha; 49°56'/15°04'.

Drahobuz, Cz.; pop. 5; 56 km NNW of Praha; 50°32'/14°19'.

Drahomysl, Cz.; pop. 2; 62 km WNW of Praha; 50°19'/13°39'.

Drahov, Cz. BGN lists two possible localities with this name located at 48°44'/21°35' and 49°11'/14°45'. HSL.

Drahova, see Dragovo.

Drahovce, Cz.; pop. 65; 69 km NE of Bratislava; 48°31'/17°48'.

Drahovec, GUM4. This town was not found in BGN gazetteers under the given spelling.

Drahovo, see Dragovo.

Drama (Bulgaria), Bulg.; pop. 500; 163 km SW of Varna; 42°14'/26°26'.

Drama (Greece), Greece; pop. 672; 120 km NE of Thessaloniki; 41°10'/24°11'; EDRD, GUM3.

Dramburg, *see* Drawsko Pomorskie.

Dramin, Pol. (Dramino); pop. 7; 75 km NW of Warszawa; 52°46'/20°14'.

Dramino, *see* Dramin.

Dranceni, *see* Drinceni.

Drancenii de Sus, *possibly* Draceni.

Dransfeld, Germ.; pop. 48; 101 km S of Hannover; 51°30'/09°46'; JGFF.

Dransheva, *see* Drazdzewo.

Drasenhofen, Aus.; pop. 2; 69 km N of Wien; 48°45'/16°34'.

Drasliceni, *see* Draslicheny.

Draslicheny, Mold. (Drasliceni); pop. 4; 26 km NNW of Kishinev; 47°09'/28°46'.

Drassburg, Aus.; pop. 7; 56 km SSE of Wien; 47°44'/16°29'.

Drassmarkt, Aus.; pop. 5; 82 km S of Wien; 47°31'/16°24'.

Dratow, Pol.; pop. 64; 32 km NE of Lublin; 51°21'/22°57'.

Dravacsehi, Hung.; pop. 4; 114 km ESE of Nagykanizsa; 45°49'/18°10'.

Dravafok, Hung.; pop. 4; 82 km SE of Nagykanizsa; 45°53'/17°46'.

Dravakeresztur, Hung.; pop. 1; 88 km SE of Nagykanizsa; 45°50'/17°46'.

Dravapiski, Hung.; pop. 1; 107 km ESE of Nagykanizsa; 45°50'/18°06'.

Dravaszabolcs, Hung.; pop. 6; 120 km ESE of Nagykanizsa; 45°48'/18°13'.

Dravasztara, Hung.; pop. 7; 94 km SE of Nagykanizsa; 45°49'/17°49'.

Dravograd, Yug.; pop. 2; 120 km NW of Zagreb; 46°35'/15°01'.

Drawno, Pol. (Neuwedell); pop. 38; 88 km E of Szczecin; 53°13'/15°45'.

Drawsko, Pol.; 75 km WNW of Poznan; 52°51'/16°02'; GUM3.

Drawsko Pomorskie, Pol. (Dramburg); pop. 24; 88 km ENE of Szczecin; 53°32'/15°48'; HSL, LDS.

Drazdzewo, Pol. (Dransheva); pop. 15; 94 km N of Warszawa; 53°05'/21°07'; SF.

Drazgow, Pol.; pop. 32; 50 km NW of Lublin; 51°35'/22°08'.

Drazniew, Pol.; pop. 35; 88 km S of Bialystok; 52°22'/22°42'; HSL.

Drebsk, Byel.; pop. 12; 62 km ENE of Pinsk; 52°14'/27°01'.

Dregelypalank, Hung.; pop. 36; 62 km N of Budapest; 48°03'/19°03'.

Dreisen, Germ.; pop. 6; 75 km SSW of Frankfurt am Main; 49°36'/08°01'; GED.

Dreissigacker, Germ.; 133 km NE of Frankfurt am Main; 50°34'/10°23'; LDS.

Drelow, Pol.; pop. 24; 82 km N of Lublin; 51°55'/22°53'.

Dremcice, Cz.; pop. 10; 62 km NW of Praha; 50°28'/13°55'.

Drengfurth, *see* Srokowo.

Drensteinfurt, Germ.; 114 km NNE of Koln; 51°48'/07°45'; GUM5.

Drepcauti, *see* Drepkovtsy.

Drepkovtsy, Ukr. (Drepcauti); pop. 24; 56 km E of Chernovtsy; 48°16'/26°43'.

Dresden, Germ. (Drezden); pop. 5,120; 101 km E of Leipzig; 51°03'/13°45'; AMG, CAHJP, COH, EDRD, EJ, GUM3, GUM4, GUM5, GUM6, HSL, HSL2, JGFF, LDL, LDS, LYV, PHP1, PHP4.

Dresnitz, *see* Partizanska Dreznica.

Dreszew, Pol.; pop. 13; 38 km NNE of Warszawa; 52°31'/21°18'.

Dretchin, *see* Derechin.

Drewnica, Pol.; 13 km NE of Warszawa; 52°19'/21°07'; GA.

Drewnik, Pol.; pop. 5; 45 km NW of Lublin; 51°36'/22°17'.

Drezden, *see* Dresden.

Drezdenko, Pol. (Driesen); pop. 85; 88 km WNW of Poznan; 52°50'/15°49'; HSL.

Dreznica, *see* Partizanska Dreznica.

Drhovy, Cz.; pop. 8; 45 km S of Praha; 49°44'/14°14'.

Dribin, Byel. (Dribino, Drybin); pop. 664; 126 km SE of Vitebsk; 54°08'/31°06'; CAHJP, HSL. CAHJP refers to a Drybin in Lwow province that does not appear in interwar or contemporary gazetteers.

Dribino, *see* Dribin.

Driceni, Lat.; pop. 4; 94 km NNE of Daugavpils; 56°39'/27°11'.

Dridu, *see* Dridu Movila.

Dridu Movila, Rom. (Dridu); 45 km NNE of Bucuresti; 44°42'/26°27'; HSL.

Drienove, Cz. (Somfalu); 133 km E of Brno; 49°10'/18°30'; HSL.

Driesen, *see* Drezdenko.

Drighiu, Rom.; pop. 8; 82 km WNW of Cluj; 47°10'/22°39'.

Drilch, *see* Ilza.

Drildzh, *see* Ilza.

Driltch, *see* Ilza.

Drinceni, Rom. (Dranceni); 56 km SE of Iasi; 46°49'/28°06'; PHR1.

Drinja, *possibly* Drinjaca.

Drinjaca, Yug. (Drinja?); 120 km SW of Beograd; 44°17'/19°09'; EJ.

Drissa, *see* Verkhnedvinsk.

Drisviat, *see* Drisvyaty.

Drisvyaty, Byel. (Drisviat, Dryswiaty); pop. 5; 202 km NNW of Minsk; 55°35'/26°40'; HSL, LDL, SF.

Drisy, Cz.; pop. 11; 26 km NNE of Praha; 50°15'/14°39'.

Driten, Cz.; pop. 17; 107 km S of Praha; 49°09'/14°21'.

Drmoul, Cz. (Duerrmaul); pop. 48; 133 km WSW of Praha; 49°56'/12°40'; EJ.

Drnis, Yug.; pop. 1; 221 km S of Zagreb; 43°52'/16°09'; GUM4.

Drnje, Yug.; pop. 8; 82 km NE of Zagreb; 46°13'/16°55'.

Drobian, *see* Darbenai.

Drobich, *see* Drogobych.

Drobin, Pol. (Drobnin); pop. 1,095; 88 km WNW of Warszawa; 52°45'/19°59'; AMG, COH, GA, GUM4, GUM5, HSL, LDL, LDS, LYV, PHP1, PHP4, POCEM, SF.

Drobnin, *see* Drobin.

Drobovice, Cz.; pop. 2; 75 km ESE of Praha; 49°53'/15°25'.

Drobyan, *see* Darbenai.

Drochia, *see* Drokiya II.

Drochia Gara, *see* Drokiya I.

Drochlin, Pol.; pop. 28; 38 km E of Czestochowa; 50°44'/19°38'.

Drochow Dolny, Pol.; pop. 1; 88 km NNE of Krakow; 50°42'/20°35'.

Drodzyn, *see* Drozdin.

Droesing, *see* Drosing.

Drogichevka, *see* Drogichuvka.

Drogichin, Byel. (Drohichin, Drohiczyn, Drohitchin); pop. 1,521; 69 km W of Pinsk; 52°11'/25°09'; AMG, COH, GA, GUM3, GUM4, GUM5, GUM6, HSL, HSL2, JGFF, LDL, LYV, SF, YB.

Drogichuvka, Ukr. (Drogichevka, Drohiczowka); pop. 31; 69 km NW of Chernovtsy; 48°51'/25°31'.

Droginia, Pol.; pop. 23; 32 km SSE of Krakow; 49°52'/20°02'; HSL, PHP3.

Drogobich, *see* Drogobych.

Drogobych, Ukr. (Dobrovlyany, Dobrowlany, Drobich, Drogobich, Drogobycz, Drohobich, Drohobitch, Drohobycz); pop. 11,833; 69 km SSW of Lvov; 49°21'/23°30'; AMG, CAHJP, COH, EDRD, EGRS, EJ, GA, GUM3, GUM4, GUM5, GUM6, GYLA, HSL, HSL2, JGFF, LDL, PHP2, PHP3, SF, YB.

Drogobycz, *see* Drogobych.

Drogomirchany, Ukr. (Drohomirczany); pop. 39; 114 km WNW of Chernovtsy; 48°53'/24°38'.

Drogomyshl, Ukr. (Drohomysl); pop. 98; 56 km WNW of Lvov; 50°03'/23°18'; HSL.

Drogoszewo, Pol.; pop. 15; 94 km W of Bialystok; 53°09'/21°46'.

Drogowle, Pol.; pop. 8; 101 km NE of Krakow; 50°41'/20°59'.

Drohichin, *see* Drogichin.

Drohiczowka, *see* Drogichuvka.

Drohiczyn, Pol. (Drohiczyn nad Bugiem); pop. 814; 88 km SSW of Białystok; 52°24'/22°39'; GUM5, POCEM, SF, YB. *See also* Drogichin.

Drohiczyn nad Bugiem, *see* Drohiczyn.

Drohitchin, *see* Drogichin.

Drohobich, *see* Drogobych.

Drohobitch, *see* Drogobych.

Drohobycz, *see* Drogobych.

Drohobyczka, Pol.; pop. 17; 32 km WNW of Przemysl; 49°52'/22°21'.

Drohojow, Pol.; pop. 16; 19 km N of Przemysl; 49°54'/22°48'.

Drohomirczany, *see* Drogomirchany.

Drohomysl, *see* Drogomyshl.

Drohowyze, Pol. PHP2. This town was not found in BGN gazetteers under the given spelling.

Drokiya I, Mold. (Drochia Gara); pop. 113; 150 km NW of Kishinev; 48°07'/27°49'.

Drokiya II, Mold. (Drochia); pop. 56; 139 km NW of Kishinev; 48°02'/27°48'.

Dromersheim, Germ.; pop. 13; 56 km SW of Frankfurt am Main; 49°55'/07°58'; GUM5, JGFF.

Droshkopol, *see* Druzhkopol.

Drosing, Aus. (Droesing); pop. 12; 56 km NE of Wien; 48°32'/16°54'.

Drossen, *see* Osno.

Drove, Germ.; 38 km SW of Koln; 50°44'/06°31'; GED, LDS.

Drozdin, Ukr. (Drodzyn, Drozdyn); pop. 33; 133 km NNE of Rovno; 51°39'/27°14'; SF, YB.

Drozdni, Ukr. (Drozdnie); pop. 70; 114 km WNW of Rovno; 51°06'/24°52'.

Drozdnie, *see* Drozdni.

Drozdov, Cz.; pop. 50; 56 km SW of Praha; 49°52'/13°50'.

Drozdy, GUM3. A number of towns share this name. It was not possible to determine from available information which one is being referenced.

Drozdyn, *see* Drozdin.

Drozen, Pol. (Drozyn); pop. 3; 88 km WNW of Lodz; 52°11'/18°27'.

Drozgenik, *see* Druskininkai.

Drozyn, *see* Drozen.

Druchowa, *see* Drukhov.

Druckenik, *see* Druskininkai.

Drugnia, Pol.; pop. 6; 94 km NE of Krakow; 50°40'/20°51'.

Druitory, Mold. (Duritoarya Veke, Duruitoarea Veche); pop. 69; 150 km WNW of Kishinev; 47°52'/27°16'.

Druja, *see* Druya.

Drujsk, *see* Druysk.

Drukhov, Ukr. (Druchowa, Drukhova); pop. 22; 50 km NE of Rovno; 50°54'/26°48'.

Drukhova, *see* Drukhov.

Drupia, Pol.; pop. 16; 82 km E of Warszawa; 52°04'/22°10'.

Drushkopla, *see* Druzhkopol.

Drushkopol, *see* Druzhkopol.

Druskieniki, *see* Druskininkai.

Druskininkai, Lith. (Drozgenik, Druckenik, Druskieniki); pop. 294; 101 km S of Kaunas; 54°01'/23°58'; AMG, COH, GUM3, HSL, JGFF, LDL, PHLE, SF.

Drusti, Lat.; pop. 7; 114 km ENE of Riga; 57°14'/25°52'.

Druszkopol, *see* Druzhkopol.

Druta, *see* Drutsa.

Drutarnia, Pol.; pop. 3; 26 km SSW of Czestochowa; 50°35'/18°51'.

Drutsa, Mold. (Druta); pop. 22; 157 km WNW of Kishinev; 47°58'/27°18'.

Druya, Byel. (Druja); pop. 1,011; 182 km WNW of Vitebsk; 55°47'/27°27'; COH, EDRD, EJ, GUM3, GUM4, GUM6, HSL, LDL, LYV, SF, YB.

Druysk, Byel. (Drujsk); pop. 412; 189 km W of Vitebsk; 55°44'/27°17'; GUM3, GUM5, LYV, YB.

Druzbin, Pol.; pop. 4; 45 km W of Lodz; 51°50'/18°49'.

Druzec, Cz.; pop. 3; 32 km W of Praha; 50°06'/14°03'.

Druzhilovichi, Byel. (Druzylowicze); pop. 18; 38 km WNW of Pinsk; 52°14'/25°33'.

Druzhkopol, Ukr. (Droshkopol, Drushkopla, Drushkopol, Druszkopol, Druzkopol); pop. 779; 82 km NNE of Lvov; 50°26'/24°41'; COH, EDRD, LDL, LYV, SF, YB.

Druzhnaya Gorka, USSR; pop. 5; 75 km S of Leningrad; 59°17'/30°08'.

Druzkopol, *see* Druzhkopol.

Druzkow Pusty, Pol.; pop. 13; 62 km ESE of Krakow; 49°48'/20°37'.

Druzykowa, Pol.; pop. 10; 50 km E of Czestochowa; 50°41'/19°51'.

Druzylowicze, *see* Druzhilovichi.

Drwinia, Pol.; pop. 25; 38 km ENE of Krakow; 50°06'/20°27'.

Drybin, *see* Dribin.

Dryshchuv, *see* Podlesnoye.

Dryssa, *see* Verkhnedvinsk.

Dryswiaty, *see* Drisvyaty.

Dryszczow, *see* Podlesnoye.

Drzazna, Pol.; pop. 5; 62 km SW of Lodz; 51°34'/18°39'.

Drzewica, Pol. (Dzhevitza, Zhevitza); pop. 1,013; 75 km ESE of Lodz; 51°27'/20°29'; COH, GA, GUM4, GUM5, HSL, PHP1, PHP4, SF.

Drzkovce, Cz. (Deresk); 75 km WSW of Kosice; 48°33'/20°14'; HSL.

Dshankoi, *see* Dzhankoy.

Duba, Cz.; pop. 23; 50 km N of Praha; 50°31'/14°33'; HSL.

Dubanevitse, Ukr. (Dubaniowice); pop. 20; 38 km SW of Lvov; 49°42'/23°31'.

Dubaniowice, *see* Dubanevitse.

Dubanti, Rom.; pop. 28; This town was not found in BGN gazetteers under the given spelling.

Dubarsi, Rom.; 45 km SE of Iasi; 46°53'/28°00'; PHR1. This town was located on a pre-World War I map, but does not appear in contemporary gazetteers.

Dubas, Pol.; pop. 19; 94 km WNW of Przemysl; 50°16'/21°45'.

Dubasari, *see* Dubossary.

Dubbelin, HSL. This pre-World War I community was not found in BGN gazetteers.

Dubeczno, Pol. (Dubetchna); pop. 440; 62 km NE of Lublin; 51°26'/23°26'; GUM3, GUM5, SF.

Dubejovice, Cz.; pop. 9; 62 km ESE of Praha; 49°42'/15°03'.

Dubene, *see* Dubinovo.

Dubenka, *see* Dubienka.

Dubetchna, *see* Dubeczno.

Dubetsk, *see* Dubetsko.

Dubetsko, Pol. (Dibetsk, Dubetsk, Dubiecko, Dubietzko, Dubyetsko); pop. 977; 26 km W of Przemysl; 49°49'/22°23'; COH, EGRS, GUM3, GUM4, HSL, JGFF, LDL, LYV, PHP3, POCEM, SF, YB.

Dubi, Cz.; pop. 54; 82 km NW of Praha; 50°41'/13°47'.

Dubiciai, Lith. (Dubicze); pop. 10; 82 km SSW of Vilnius; 54°01'/24°44'.

Dubicsany, Hung.; pop. 6; 32 km WNW of Miskolc; 48°17'/20°30'; HSL.

Dubicze, *see* Dubiciai.

Dubiecko, *see* Dubetsko.

Dubienka, Pol. (Dibenka, Dubenka, Dubyenka); pop. 1,204; 94 km E of Lublin; 51°03'/23°53'; AMG, CAHJP, COH, EDRD, GA, GUM3, GUM4, GUM5, HSL, HSL2, JGFF, LDL, LDS, LYV, PHP3, SF.

Dubietzko, *see* Dubetsko.

Dubin, Pol. (Dupin); 69 km N of Wroclaw; 51°37'/17°08'; GA.

Dubina, *see* Dubinovo.

Dubines, *see* Dubinovo.

Dubingai, *see* Dubingiai.

Dubingiai, Lith. (Dubingai, Dubinik); 50 km N of Vilnius; 55°04'/25°27'; YL.

Dubinik, *see* Dubingiai.

Dubinovo, Byel. (Dubene, Dubina, Dubines, Dubinowo); pop. 362; 214 km NNW of Minsk; 55°46'/26°57'; GUM3, LYV.

Dubinowo, *see* Dubinovo.

Dubiny, Pol.; pop. 20; 50 km SE of Bialystok; 52°46'/23°36'.

Dubka, Ukr. (Dabki, Donbki); pop. 55; 62 km NW of Chernovtsy; 48°47'/25°27'.

Dublany, see Dublyany.

Dublovice, Cz.; 50 km S of Praha; 49°40'/14°22'; JGFF.

Dublyany, Ukr. (Dublany); pop. 79; 56 km SW of Lvov; 49°30'/23°24'; AMG.

Dubna, see Dubno.

Dubnica nad Vahom, Cz.; pop. 69; 120 km NNE of Bratislava; 48°58'/18°11'.

Dubnik, Cz. (Csuz); 101 km E of Bratislava; 47°57'/18°25'; AMG, HSL, LDL.

Dubno, Ukr. (Dubna); pop. 5,315; 38 km SW of Rovno; 50°25'/25°45'; AMG, CAHJP, COH, EDRD, EJ, GA, GUM3, GUM4, GUM5, GUM6, HSL, HSL2, JGFF, LDL, PHP4, SF, YB.

Duboj, see Duboy.

Dubosar, see Dubossary.

Dubosevica, Yug.; pop. 17; 182 km WNW of Beograd; 45°53'/18°42'.

Dubossary, Mold. (Dobyasser, Dubasari, Dubosar); pop. 3,630; 26 km NE of Kishinev; 47°07'/29°10'; COH, EJ, GUM4, HSL, SF, YB.

Dubova, see Dubovo.

Dubova Balka, USSR; pop. 35; This town was not found in BGN gazetteers under the given spelling.

Dubove, see Dubovoye.

Dubovec, Cz. (Dobocza); 94 km SW of Kosice; 48°17'/20°10'; HSL.

Dubovo, Ukr. (Dubova, Dubowo); 26 km ESE of Uman; 48°38'/30°27'; EDRD, SF.

Dubovoje, see Dubovoye.

Dubovoye, Ukr. (Dubove, Dubovoje, Dubowa, Dubowe); pop. 2,500; 150 km WSW of Chernovtsy; 48°10'/23°53'; AMG, COH, GUM3, SM.

Dubovtsy, Ukr. (Dubowce); pop. 49; 107 km SE of Lvov; 49°05'/24°46'; COH.

Dubowa, see Dubovoye.

Dubowce, see Dubovtsy.

Dubowe, see Dubovoye.

Dubowo, see Dubovo.

Duboy, Byel. (Duboj); pop. 25; 56 km E of Pinsk; 52°02'/26°52'; GYLA.

Dubranec, Yug.; pop. 7; 26 km S of Zagreb; 45°37'/15°58'.

Dubrava, see Dubrave.

Dubrave, Yug. (Dubrava); pop. 20; 146 km WSW of Beograd; 44°49'/18°37'; AMG, HSL.

Dubravka, Cz. (Dubroka); 50 km E of Kosice; 48°38'/21°53'; HSL.

Dubrojsk, see Dubrovsk.

Dubroka, see Dubravka.

Dubrova, see Dubrovo.

Dubrovits, see Dabrowica.

Dubrovitsa, Ukr. (Dabrowica, Dombrovitsa, Dombrovitza, Dubrowica); pop. 2,536; 114 km N of Rovno; 51°34'/26°34'; AMG, COH, FRG, GUM3, GUM4, GUM6, HSL, HSL2, JGFF, LDL, SF, YB.

Dubrovka, USSR; pop. 542; COH, GUM4, HSL, JGFF, SF. A number of towns share this name. It was not possible to determine from available information which one is being referenced.

Dubrovka (Lwow), Ukr. (Uhrynow); pop. 6; 82 km N of Lvov; 50°34'/24°06'.

Dubrovnik, Yug. (Ragusa); pop. 120; 283 km WNW of Skopje; 42°39'/18°07'; CAHJP, EJ, GUM4, JGFF, PHY.

Dubrovno, Byel.; pop. 3,105; 75 km SE of Vitebsk; 54°35'/30°41'; EJ, HSL, JGFF, LDL, SF.

Dubrovo, Byel. (Dubrova, Dubrowa); pop. 94; 45 km WNW of Minsk; 54°06'/27°06'.

Dubrovsk, Ukr. (Dubrojsk); pop. 47; 126 km N of Rovno; 51°41'/26°09'.

Dubrowa, see Dubrovo.

Dubrowica, see Dubrovitsa.

Dubrowo, LDL. This pre-World War I community was not found in BGN gazetteers.

Dubryniow, Ukr.; pop. 71; 107 km SE of Lvov; 49°05'/24°45'. This town was located on an interwar map of Poland but does not appear in contemporary gazetteers. Map coordinates are approximate.

Dubyenka, see Dubienka.

Dubyetsko, see Dubetsko.

Duchcov, Cz.; pop. 134; 75 km NW of Praha; 50°36'/13°45'.

Ducherow, Germ.; pop. 7; 114 km ESE of Rostock; 53°46'/13°47'.

Duchnice, Pol.; pop. 3; 19 km SW of Warszawa; 52°12'/20°48'.

Duchnow, Pol.; pop. 14; 26 km E of Warszawa; 52°11'/21°21'.

Ducka Wola, Pol.; pop. 23; 69 km SSE of Warszawa; 51°42'/21°07'.

Dudar, Hung.; 88 km WSW of Budapest; 47°18'/17°57'; AMG.

Dudelsheim, Germ.; pop. 70; 38 km NE of Frankfurt am Main; 50°18'/09°02'; GUM5.

Dudenhofen, Germ.; 82 km NW of Stuttgart; 49°19'/08°24'; EJ, GED.

Duderstadt, Germ.; pop. 30; 101 km SSE of Hannover; 51°31'/10°16'; GUM5, GUM6.

Duenaburg, see Daugavpils.

Duerrmaul, see Drmoul.

Duga Resa, Yug.; pop. 5; 56 km SSW of Zagreb; 45°27'/15°30'.

Dugo Selo, Yug.; pop. 23; 19 km E of Zagreb; 45°48'/16°15'.

Dugscitz, see Dokshitsy.

Duhren, Germ.; 56 km NW of Stuttgart; 49°15'/08°50'; LDS.

Duisburg, Germ.; pop. 3,176; 56 km NNW of Koln; 51°26'/06°45'; AMG, EDRD, EJ, GED, GUM3, GUM4, ISH1, LDS, YB.

Duisburg Ruhrort, Germ.; pop. 150; 56 km NNW of Koln; 51°26'/06°45'.

Duka, Hung.; pop. 6; 82 km N of Nagykanizsa; 47°07'/17°07'.

Dukhovshchina, USSR; pop. 195; 202 km E of Leningrad; 59°40'/33°55'.

Dukla, Pol. (Dikla); pop. 1,509; 82 km SW of Przemysl; 49°34'/21°41'; AMG, COH, EGRS, EJ, GA, GUM3, GUM5, GUM6, GYLA, HSL, HSL2, JGFF, LDL, PHP2, PHP3, POCEM, SF.

Dukor, see Dukora.

Dukora, Byel. (Dukor); 38 km ESE of Minsk; 53°40'/27°57'; LDL, SF.

Dukrowo, Pol.; pop. 37; Described in the *Black Book* as being in the Nowogrodek region of Poland, this town was not found in BGN gazetteers.

Duksht, see Dukstas.

Dukstas, Lith. (Duksht, Dukszty); pop. 416; 114 km NNE of Vilnius; 55°32'/26°20'; AMG, COH, GUM3, HSL, JGFF, SF, YB.

Dukstos, Lith.; 32 km WNW of Vilnius; 54°50'/24°58'; GUM4.

Dukszty, see Dukstas.

Dulabka, Pol.; pop. 16; 101 km WSW of Przemysl; 49°40'/21°24'.

Dulaves, see Miokovicevo.

Dulcza Mala, Pol.; pop. 37; 94 km ENE of Krakow; 50°13'/21°13'.

Dulcza Wielka, Pol.; pop. 44; 94 km ENE of Krakow; 50°11'/21°14'.

Dulfalva, see Dulovo.

Duliby (near Bobrka), Ukr.; pop. 27; 50 km SE of Lvov; 49°27'/24°23'.

Duliby (near Pomortsy), Ukr.; pop. 25; 82 km NW of Chernovtsy; 48°56'/25°26'.

Duliby (near Stryy), Ukr.; pop. 22; 75 km S of Lvov; 49°14'/23°51'.

Dulken, Germ.; pop. 70; 56 km WNW of Koln; 51°15'/06°21'.

Dulmen, Germ.; pop. 60; 101 km N of Koln; 51°50'/07°18'; GED, GUM5.

Dulofalva, *see* Dealu Mare.

Dulovo, Ukr. (Dilif, Dulfalva); 176 km WSW of Chernovtsy; 48°09'/23°35'; SM.

Dulowa, Pol.; pop. 6; 26 km W of Krakow; 50°09'/19°31'.

Dumanovka, *see* Domanevka.

Dumbraveni, *see* Dumbraveny.

Dumbraveny, Mold. (Dambraveni, Dombroven, Dombroveni, Dumbraveni, Elisabethstadt); pop. 1,198; 126 km NNW of Kishinev; 48°03'/28°14'; COH, EJ, GUM4, JGFF, LDL, PHR1, PHR2, SF, YB.

Dumbravioara, Rom.; pop. 1; 82 km E of Cluj; 46°38'/24°38'.

Dumitreni, Rom. (Szentdemeter); pop. 15; 94 km ESE of Cluj; 46°24'/24°45'; HSL.

Dumitrita, Rom. (Demeterfalva); pop. 16; 82 km NE of Cluj; 47°04'/24°37'.

Dunaalmas, Hung.; pop. 6; 62 km WNW of Budapest; 47°44'/18°20'.

Dunaberg, *see* Daugavpils.

Dunaburg, *see* Daugavpils.

Dunaegyhaza, Hung.; pop. 7; 82 km S of Budapest; 46°50'/18°57'.

Dunafoldvar, Hung.; pop. 363; 82 km S of Budapest; 46°48'/18°56'; HSL, LDS, PHH.

Dunaharaszti, Hung.; pop. 151; 26 km S of Budapest; 47°21'/19°05'; GUM3, PHH.

Dunaiv, *see* Dunayev.

Dunajevcy, *see* Dunayevtsy.

Dunajow, *see* Dunayev.

Dunajska Streda, Cz. (Duna Szerdahely, Dunaszerdahely, Schutt Szerdahly); pop. 3,222; 45 km ESE of Bratislava; 47°59'/17°37'; AMG, COH, EJ, GUM4, HSL, JGFF, LDL, YB.

Dunakeszi, Hung.; pop. 100; 19 km N of Budapest; 47°38'/19°08'; PHH.

Dunakiliti, Hung.; pop. 3; 146 km WNW of Budapest; 47°58'/17°17'.

Dunalka, Lat.; pop. 8; 170 km WSW of Riga; 56°41'/21°20'.

Dunalovitch, *see* Dunilovichi.

Dunamocs, *see* Moca.

Dunapataj, Hung.; pop. 126; 101 km S of Budapest; 46°38'/19°00'; LDS, PHH.

Dunapentele, *see* Sztalinvaros.

Dunarea, Rom.; 157 km E of Bucuresti; 44°26'/28°07'; GUM4.

Dunareanca, *see* Zadunayevka.

Dunaszeg, Hung.; pop. 5; 114 km W of Budapest; 47°46'/17°33'.

Dunaszekcso, Hung.; pop. 56; 107 km WSW of Szeged; 46°05'/18°46'; PHH.

Dunaszentbenedek, Hung.; pop. 4; 107 km S of Budapest; 46°36'/18°54'.

Dunaszentgyorgy, Hung.; pop. 12; 107 km WNW of Szeged; 46°32'/18°50'.

Duna Szerdahely, *see* Dunajska Streda.

Dunaszerdahely, *see* Dunajska Streda.

Dunaujvaros, *see* Sztalinvaros.

Dunavecse, Hung.; pop. 94; 69 km S of Budapest; 46°55'/18°59'; PHH.

Dunayets, *see* Czarny Dunajec.

Dunayev, Ukr. (Dunaiv, Dunajow, Duneiav); pop. 95; 62 km ESE of Lvov; 49°37'/24°50'; COH, EGRS, GUM3, GUM4, JGFF, LDL, PHP2, SF.

Dunayevitz, *see* Dunayevtsy.

Dunayevtsy, Ukr. (Dinewitz, Dinovits, Dinovitz, Dunajevcy, Dunayevitz); pop. 5,186; 94 km NE of Chernovtsy; 48°54'/26°50'; COH, EDRD, EJ, GUM4, GYLA, JGFF, PHP1, SF.

Dundaga, Lat. (Dundagas); pop. 64; 126 km WNW of Riga; 57°31'/22°21'; GUM3, PHLE.

Dundagas, *see* Dundaga.

Duneiav, *see* Dunayev.

Dungenheim, Germ.; pop. 5; 82 km SSE of Koln; 50°16'/07°10'.

Dunika, Lat.; pop. 6; 182 km SW of Riga; 56°17'/21°20'.

Dunilovichi, Byel. (Danilevitch, Dunalovitch, Dunilovicze, Dunilowicze, Dunovits); pop. 685; 139 km NNW of Minsk; 55°04'/27°14'; AMG, COH, EDRD, GUM3, GUM4, HSL, JGFF, SF, YB.

Dunilovicze, *see* Dunilovichi.

Dunilowicze, *see* Dunilovichi.

Duninow, *see* Duninow Duzy.

Duninow Duzy, Pol. (Duninow); pop. 27; 94 km N of Lodz; 52°32'/19°26'.

Duninow Nowy, Pol.; pop. 21; 101 km N of Lodz; 52°35'/19°29'.

Dunkov, USSR; EDRD. This town was not found in BGN gazetteers under the given spelling.

Dunkowice, Pol.; 26 km N of Przemysl; 49°58'/22°54'; HSL.

Dunkowiczki, Pol.; pop. 11; 13 km NNW of Przemysl; 49°52'/22°47'.

Dunovits, *see* Dunilovichi.

Dunsbach, Germ.; 75 km NE of Stuttgart; 49°13'/09°53'; JGFF, PHGBW.

Duoly, Pol. EDRD. This town was not found in BGN gazetteers under the given spelling.

Dupin, *see* Dubin.

Dupliska, Ukr.; pop. 7; 50 km NNW of Chernovtsy; 48°43'/25°46'; HSL.

Dupljaja, Yug.; pop. 6; 62 km ENE of Beograd; 44°56'/21°17'.

Dupnitsa, *see* Stanke Dimitrov.

Duraczow, Pol.; 101 km ESE of Lodz; 51°06'/20°31'; PHP1.

Durand, *see* Tvarozna.

Durbach, HSL, JGFF, PHGBW. This town was not found in BGN gazetteers under the given spelling.

Durbe, Lat. (Durben); pop. 8; 170 km WSW of Riga; 56°35'/21°21'; JGFF, PHLE.

Durben, *see* Durbe.

Durboslar, Germ.; pop. 50 km WSW of Koln; 50°54'/06°15'; GED.

Durdenovac, *see* Urdenovac.

Durdevac, *see* Urdevac.

Durdy, Pol.; pop. 8; 107 km WNW of Przemysl; 50°25'/21°36'.

Durelsdorf, *see* Tvarozna.

Duren, Germ.; pop. 330; 38 km SW of Koln; 50°48'/06°29'; GED, LDS.

Duritoarya Veke, *see* Druitory.

Durkheim, *see* Bad Durkheim.

Durkov, Cz. BGN lists two possible localities with this name located at 48°42'/21°27' and 49°14'/20°52'. JGFF.

Durlach, Germ.; pop. 57; 56 km WNW of Stuttgart; 49°00'/08°29'; PHGBW.

Durmaul, *see* Trmova.

Durnau, HSL. A number of towns share this name. It was not possible to determine from available information which one is being referenced.

Durnkrut, Aus.; pop. 27; 50 km NE of Wien; 48°29'/16°51'.

Durova, LDL. This pre-World War I community was not found in BGN gazetteers.

Durrwangen, Germ.; 62 km SW of Nurnberg; 49°07'/10°23'; PHGB.

Dursztyn, Pol.; pop. 9; 82 km SSE of Krakow; 49°25'/20°12'.

Duruitoarea Veche, *see* Druitory.

Durusa, Rom.; pop. 2; 75 km NNW of Cluj; 47°25'/23°28'.

Dusanow, Ukr. (Dusanow); pop. 50; 56 km ESE of Lvov; 49°32'/24°36'; JGFF.

Dusanow, *see* Dusanov.

Duschnik, *see* Dusniky.

Dusetai, *see* Dusetos.

Dusetoi, *see* Dusetos.

Dusetos, Lith. (Dusetai, Dusetoi, Dusiat, Dusjaty, Dusyat); pop. 704; 126 km N of Vilnius; 55°45'/25°51'; HSL, SF, YL.

Dusiat, *see* Dusetos.

Dusjaty, *see* Dusetos.

Dusmani, *see* Voroshilovo.

Dusniky, Cz. (Duschnik); 19 km SW of Praha; 50°02'/14°14';

Dvinsk (Daugavpils), Latvia: The courtyard of an ORT vocational school. On the right, a man sits with a stack of lumber, and on the left, a group of women at a table in the garden.

HSL.

Dusnok, Hung.; pop. 34; 88 km W of Szeged; 46°23'/18°58'.

Dusowce, Pol.; pop. 11; 13 km NNE of Przemysl; 49°53'/22°53'.

Dusseldorf, Germ.; pop. 5,500; 38 km NNW of Koln; 51°13'/06°46'; AMG, EDRD, EJ, GED, GUM3, GUM4, GUM5, GUM6, HSL, HSL2, ISH1, JGFF, PHGBW, PHP1.

Dusyat, *see* Dusetos.

Duzy Dol, Pol.; pop. 7; 45 km S of Warszawa; 51°55'/20°53'; JGFF.

Dvart, *see* Warta.

Dvilne, *see* Nadezhnaya.

Dvinsk, *see* Daugavpils.

Dvorce, Cz. (Hof); pop. 20; 101 km NNE of Brno; 49°50'/17°34'.

Dvorets, Byel. (Dvoretz, Dworzec); pop. 388; 139 km SW of Minsk; 53°24'/25°34'; COH, EDRD, GUM3, GUM4, GUM5, GUM6, HSL, HSL2, SF. The *Black Book* notes two towns named Dworzec in Wolyn province with Jewish populations of 73 and 92. Neither could be found in interwar or contemporary gazetteers.

Dvoretz, *see* Dvorets.

Dvorniky, Cz. (Udvarnok); 38 km SW of Kosice; 48°36'/20°50'; HSL.

Dvory nad Zitavou, Cz. (Udvard); pop. 119; 88 km E of Bratislava; 47°59'/18°16'; COH, HSL.

Dvozhyshche, Byel. (Dworzyszcze); pop. 9; 69 km WNW of Minsk; 54°10'/26°39'.

Dvur Kralove, Cz. (Dvur Kralove nad Lab, Dvur Kralove nad Labem, Koniginhof, Koniginhof an der Elbe); pop. 182; 101 km NE of Praha; 50°26'/15°49'; HSL.

Dvur Kralove nad Lab, *see* Dvur Kralove.

Dvur Kralove nad Labem, *see* Dvur Kralove.

Dvurt, *see* Warta.

Dvyk, *see* Debeikiai.

Dwernik, Pol.; pop. 27; 75 km S of Przemysl; 49°12'/22°38'.

Dwikozy, Pol.; pop. 25; 82 km SW of Lublin; 50°44'/21°47'.

Dwinsk, *see* Daugavpils.

Dworaki, Pol. (Dworaki Staski); pop. 30; 32 km SW of Bialystok; 52°57'/22°45'.

Dworaki Staski, *see* Dworaki.

Dworszowice Koscielne, Pol.; pop. 23; 38 km N of Czestochowa; 51°05'/19°08'.

Dworszowice Pakoszowe, Pol.; pop. 51; 50 km N of Czestochowa; 51°10'/19°06'.

Dworzec, *see* Dvorets.

Dworzysk, Pol.; 26 km NE of Bialystok; 53°18'/23°25'; GUM3.

Dworzyska, Pol.; pop. 21; 56 km ESE of Lublin; 50°56'/23°09'.

Dworzyszcze, *see* Dvozhyshche.

Dyadkovichi, Ukr. (Dziatkowicze); pop. 21; 13 km WSW of Rovno; 50°36'/26°04'.

Dyatkovo, USSR; pop. 72; 45 km N of Bryansk; 53°36'/34°20'.

Dyatkovtse, *see* Dyatkovtsy.

Dyatkovtsy, Ukr. (Diatkowice, Dyatkovtse); pop. 61; 75 km WNW of Chernovtsy; 48°33'/25°00'.

Dyatlovichi, Byel. (Dziatlowicze); pop. 26; 56 km NE of Pinsk; 52°20'/26°50'.

Dyatlovo, Byel. (Zdzhentsiol, Zetl, Zhetl, Zietil, Zitl, Zozhetsiol, Zsetl); pop. 2,376; 146 km SW of Minsk; 53°28'/25°24'; AMG, COH, EDRD, EJ, GUM3, GUM4, GUM5, GUM6, GYLA, HSL, HSL2, JGFF, SF, YB.

Dybki, Pol.; pop. 5; 69 km NNE of Warszawa; 52°44'/21°43'.

Dybkow, Pol.; pop. 42; 45 km NNW of Przemysl; 50°10'/22°37'; PHP3.

Dyczkow, Ukr.; pop. 62; 107 km N of Chernovtsy; 49°15'/25°45'; PHP2. This town was located on an interwar map of Poland but does not appear in contemporary gazetteers. Map coordinates are approximate.

Dydiowa, Ukr.; pop. 76; 139 km SSW of Lvov; 48°55'/22°45'; HSL. This town was located on an interwar map of Poland but does not appear in contemporary gazetteers. Map coordinates are approximate.

Dyhernfurth, *see* Brzeg Dolny.

Dylagowka, Pol.; pop. 45; 45 km WNW of Przemysl; 49°55'/22°13'.

Dylazki, Pol.; pop. 4; 32 km SW of Lublin; 51°09'/22°13'.

Dyle, Pol.; pop. 13; 75 km SSE of Lublin; 50°36'/22°48'.

Dymer, Ukr. (Dimer); 45 km NNW of Kiyev; 50°47'/30°18'; EDRD, GYLA, JGFF, LDL, SF.

Dymitrow Duzy, Pol.; pop. 7; 114 km SSW of Lublin; 50°28'/21°31'.

Dymitrow Maly, Pol.; pop. 9; 114 km SSW of Lublin; 50°29'/21°30'.

Dymokury, Cz.; pop. 5; 56 km NE of Praha; 50°15'/15°12'.

Dyniska, Pol.; pop. 73; 101 km NNE of Przemysl; 50°25'/23°43'.

Dynow, Pol. (Dinov); pop. 1,273; 38 km W of Przemysl; 49°49'/22°14'; CAHJP, COH, EDRD, EGRS, GUM3, GUM4, HSL, HSL2, JGFF, LDL, PHP2, PHP3, POCEM, SF, YB.

Dyormot, *see* Balassagyarmat.

Dyshkovo, Mold. (Dascova); pop. 53; 45 km NNW of Kishinev; 47°22'/28°36'.

Dysina, Cz.; 82 km SW of Praha; 49°47'/13°29'; HSL.

Dyszobaba, Pol.; pop. 8; 75 km N of Warszawa; 52°55'/21°24'.

Dytiatyn, Ukr.; pop. 38; 101 km WNW of Chernovtsy; 48°55'/24°55'. This town was located on an interwar map of Poland but does not appear in contemporary gazetteers. Map coordinates are approximate.

Dyuksin, Ukr. (Diuksyn); pop. 4; 32 km NW of Rovno; 50°50'/26°06'.

Dyvin, *see* Divin.

Dywin, *see* Divin.

Dzaudhikau, *see* Ordzhonikidze.

Dzbow, Pol.; pop. 6; 6 km SSW of Czestochowa; 50°46'/19°05'.

Dzedushitse Male, Ukr. (Dzieduszyce Male, Dzieduszyce Wielkie?); pop. 27; 82 km S of Lvov; 49°09'/24°01'.

Dzedziluv, *see* Dedilov.

Dzelzava, Lat.; pop. 5; 133 km N of Daugavpils; 57°00'/26°26'.

Dzerbene, Lat.; pop. 8; 101 km ENE of Riga; 57°12'/25°40'.

Dzerves, Lat.; pop. 1; 120 km WSW of Riga; 56°42'/22°11'.

Dzerzhinsk, Byel. (Kaidanovo, Kaydanovo, Keidanov, Koidanovo, Koydanovo, Romanov); pop. 1,778; 38 km SW of Minsk; 53°41'/27°08'; EDRD, EJ, GUM4, HSL, HSL2, JGFF, LDL, SF, YB.

Dzeventniki, *see* Devyatniki.

Dzevice, Pol. EDRD. This town was not found in BGN gazetteers under the given spelling.

Dzhamany, Mold. (Geamana); pop. 49; 32 km ESE of Kishinev; 46°49'/29°08'.

Dzhankoi, *see* Dzhankoy.

Dzhankoy, Ukr. (Dshankoi, Dzhankoi); pop. 3,000; 94 km N of Simferopol; 45°43'/34°24'; EDRD, GUM4.

Dzhevitza, *see* Drzewica.

Dzhikev, *see* Tarnobrzeg.

Dzholtay, Mold. (Djoltai); pop. 4; 94 km S of Kishinev; 46°11'/28°52'.

Dzhormot, *see* Balassagyarmat.

Dzhurin, Ukr. (Djurin); pop. 1,470; 69 km S of Vinnitsa; 48°41'/28°18'; EJ, GUM3, GUM4, GUM5, GUM6, GYLA, JGFF, PHR1.

Dzhuruv, Ukr. (Dzurow, Zhurov, Zurow); pop. 71; 45 km W of Chernovtsy; 48°24'/25°19'; GYLA, HSL, PHP2.

Dzialdowo, Pol.; pop. 35; 120 km NW of Warszawa; 53°14'/20°11'; GUM3, GUM4, GUM6, PHP4, POCEM.

Dzialki Morozowalskie, GUM4. This town was not found in BGN gazetteers under the given spelling.

Dzialoshitz, *see* Dzialoszyce.

Dzialoszyce, Pol. (Dzialoshitz, Dzyaloshitse, Zalazhtsy, Zaleshits,

Zaloshits, Zaloshitz, Zalshits); pop. 5,618; 45 km NE of Krakow; 50°22'/20°21'; AMG, CAHJP, COH, EDRD, EJ, FRG, GA, GUM3, GUM4, GUM5, GUM6, HSL, JGFF, LDL, LDS, LYV, POCEM, SF, YB.

Dzialoszyn, Pol. (Chernokinits, Dzyaloshin); pop. 1,909; 45 km NW of Czestochowa; 51°07'/18°52'; CAHJP, COH, EDRD, HSL, LDS, LYV, PHP1, POCEM, SF.

Dzialyn, Pol.; pop. 42; 45 km N of Lublin; 51°36'/22°42'.

Dzianisz, Pol.; pop. 7; 88 km S of Krakow; 49°20'/19°51'.

Dziasloszyce, Pol. PHP1. This town was not found in BGN gazetteers under the given spelling.

Dziatkowicze, *see* Dyadkovichi.

Dziatlowicze, *see* Dyatlovichi.

Dzibice, Pol.; pop. 4; 38 km ESE of Czestochowa; 50°36'/19°35'.

Dzibulki, Ukr.; pop. 33; 26 km NNE of Lvov; 50°01'/24°10'.

Dziczki, GUM3. This town was not found in BGN gazetteers under the given spelling.

Dziecinin, Pol.; pop. 4; 38 km ESE of Lublin; 51°04'/23°00'.

Dzieciol, Byel. EDRD. This town was not found in BGN gazetteers under the given spelling.

Dzieczyna, Pol. (Furstenfeld); 82 km S of Poznan; 51°46'/16°51'; GA, GUM3, GUM5.

Dzieduszyce Male, *see* Dzedushitse Male.

Dzieduszyce Wielkie, *possibly* Dzedushitse Male.

Dziedzice, Pol.; pop. 234; 69 km WSW of Krakow; 49°55'/19°01'; AMG, PHP3.

Dziedzilow, *see* Dedilov.

Dziekanka, Pol.; pop. 46; This town was not found in BGN gazetteers under the given spelling.

Dziekanow, Pol.; pop. 65; 107 km ESE of Lublin; 50°50'/23°55'.

Dziekanow Niemiecki, Pol.; pop. 3; 13 km NW of Warszawa; 52°21'/20°52'.

Dziekanow Polski, Pol.; pop. 6; 19 km NW of Warszawa; 52°22'/20°50'.

Dziembowo, Pol.; pop. 4; 75 km NNW of Poznan; 53°05'/16°50'.

Dziembrow, Byel.; pop. 31; 182 km NW of Pinsk; 53°25'/24°25'. This town was located on an interwar map of Poland but does not appear in contemporary gazetteers. Map coordinates are approximate.

Dziemiany, Pol.; 126 km S of Gdansk; 53°13'/18°40'; GA.

Dziemionna, Pol.; pop. 4; 94 km NE of Poznan; 52°58'/18°05'.

Dziepulc, Pol.; pop. 6; 45 km NE of Czestochowa; 51°04'/19°32'.

Dziergova, *see* Dzierzgowo.

Dzierzaniny, Pol.; pop. 18; 69 km ESE of Krakow; 49°48'/20°46'.

Dzierzbin, Pol.; pop. 16; 88 km WNW of Lodz; 52°00'/18°15'.

Dzierzbotki, Pol.; 69 km W of Lodz; 51°55'/18°31'; GUM3, PHP1.

Dzierzby, Pol. (Dzierzby Szlacheckie); pop. 21; 82 km SSW of Bialystok; 52°32'/22°26'.

Dzierzby Szlacheckie, *see* Dzierzby.

Dzierzgon, Pol. (Christburg); pop. 50; 62 km ESE of Gdansk; 53°56'/19°21'; JGFF, LDS, POCEM.

Dzierzgow, Pol.; pop. 61; 56 km E of Czestochowa; 50°43'/19°58'.

Dzierzgowo, Pol. (Dziergova); pop. 45; 107 km NNW of Warszawa; 53°10'/20°40'; SF.

Dzierzkowice, Pol.; pop. 78; 50 km SW of Lublin; 50°58'/22°05'.

Dzierzoniow, Cz. (Reichenbach); pop. 70; 170 km NE of Praha; 50°43'/16°39'; EJ, GUM3, GUM4, GUM5, GUM6, HSL, LDS, LJEE, PHP3, POCEM.

Dzietrzkowice, Pol.; pop. 15; 69 km WNW of Czestochowa; 51°10'/18°19'.

Dzietrzniki, Pol.; pop. 38; 50 km WNW of Czestochowa; 51°07'/18°37'.

Dziewiecierz, Pol.; pop. 54; 69 km NE of Przemysl; 50°13'/23°29'.

Dziewiecioly, Pol.; pop. 15; 32 km NNE of Krakow; 50°18'/20°11'.

Dziewieczyce, Pol.; pop. 57; 50 km NNE of Krakow; 50°25'/20°22'; PHP2.

Dziewieniszki, *see* Dieveniskes.

Dziewietniki, *see* Devyatniki.

Dziewin, Pol.; pop. 19; 38 km E of Krakow; 50°05'/20°28'.

Dziewule, Pol.; pop. 22; 94 km NNW of Lublin; 52°03'/22°24'.

Dziewuliny, Pol.; pop. 5; 38 km S of Lodz; 51°29'/19°28'.

Dzigorzew, Pol.; pop. 7; 56 km WSW of Lodz; 51°37'/18°43'.

Dzikov, *see* Dzikow Stary.

Dzikow, *see* Dzikow Stary.

Dzikowiec, Pol.; pop. 4; 88 km WNW of Przemysl; 50°17'/21°51'.

Dzikow Nowy, Pol. (Nowy Dzikow); pop. 38; 50 km N of Przemysl; 50°14'/22°58'; GA.

Dzikow Stary, Pol. (Dzikov, Dzikow, Stary Dzikow); pop. 347; 56 km N of Przemysl; 50°15'/22°56'; EGRS, GA, GUM3, HSL, LDL, PHP1, PHP2, SF, YB.

Dzilbowiec, LDL. This pre-World War I community was not found in BGN gazetteers.

Dzisna, *see* Disna.

Dziunkow, LDL. This pre-World War I community was not found in BGN gazetteers.

Dziwnow, *see* Dziwnowek.

Dziwnowek, Pol. (Dziwnow); 69 km N of Szczecin; 54°02'/14°48'; GUM6.

Dzukste, Lat.; pop. 9; 56 km SW of Riga; 56°47'/23°15'; JGFF.

Dzurkiv, Ukr. (Dzurkow, Dzurkuv); pop. 100; 62 km WNW of Chernovtsy; 48°38'/25°12'; HSL, PHP2.

Dzurkow, *see* Dzurkiv.

Dzurkuv, *see* Dzurkiv.

Dzurow, *see* Dzhuruv.

Dzuryn, Ukr.; pop. 52; 56 km NW of Chernovtsy; 48°45'/25°35'. This town was located on an interwar map of Poland but does not appear in contemporary gazetteers. Map coordinates are approximate.

Dzvinogorod, Ukr. (Dzvinogrud); pop. 17; 94 km NW of Chernovtsy; 49°05'/25°24'.

Dzvinogrud, Ukr. (Dzvinogrod); pop. 116; 26 km ESE of Lvov; 49°44'/24°15'; CAHJP, GUM3, PHP2. *See also* Dzvinogorod.

Dzvinsk, *see* Daugavpils.

Dzvinyach, Ukr. (Dzwiniacz, Zviniatch); pop. 63; 120 km WNW of Chernovtsy; 48°45'/24°26'; HSL, SF.

Dzvinyach (Tarnopol), Ukr.; pop. 11; 50 km NNW of Chernovtsy; 48°42'/25°44'.

Dzwiniacz, *see* Dzvinyach.

Dzwiniacz Dolny, Pol.; pop. 45; 45 km SSW of Przemysl; 49°28'/22°34'.

Dzwiniacz Gorny, *see* Gorishnyy Dzvinyach.

Dzwiniaczka, *see* Zvinyachka.

Dzwinogrod, *see* Dzvinogrud.

Dzwonek, Pol.; pop. 26; 94 km NNE of Warszawa; 52°58'/21°43'.

Dzwonowa, Pol.; pop. 3; 101 km E of Krakow; 49°55'/21°18'.

Dzyaloshin, *see* Dzialoszyn.

Dzyaloshitse, *see* Dzialoszyce.

Dzygovka, Ukr.; pop. 1,561; 101 km S of Vinnitsa; 48°22'/28°20'.

Ebeczk, HSL. This pre-World War I community was not found in BGN gazetteers.

Ebelsbach, Germ.; pop. 23; 62 km NW of Nurnberg; 49°59'/10°41'; GUM5, PHGB.

Ebenfurth, Aus.; pop. 9; 45 km S of Wien; 47°52'/16°22'; EJ.

Ebensee, Aus. AMG, EDRD, GUM3, GUM4, GUM5, GUM6. This town was not found in BGN gazetteers under the given spelling.

Ebensfeld, Germ.; pop. 5; 75 km NNW of Nurnberg; 50°04'/10°57'; PHGB.

Eberau, Aus.; pop. 3; 75 km ENE of Graz; 47°06'/16°28'; GUM4.

Eberbach, Germ.; pop. 72; 75 km SSE of Frankfurt am Main; 49°28'/08°59'; GED, GUM5, LDS, PHGBW.

Ebereichsdorf, Aus.; pop. 20; This town was not found in BGN gazetteers under the given spelling.

Ebergassing, Aus.; pop. 4; 26 km SE of Wien; 48°02'/16°31'.

Ebermannstadt, Germ.; 45 km N of Nurnberg; 49°47'/11°12'; PHGB.

Ebern, Germ.; 75 km NNW of Nurnberg; 50°05'/10°48'; PHGB.

Ebernburg, Germ.; pop. 14; 69 km SW of Frankfurt am Main; 49°49'/07°50'; GED.

Ebersbach, Germ.; 88 km SW of Munchen; 47°51'/10°28'; PHGB.

Eberschutz, Germ.; 101 km S of Hannover; 51°33'/09°22'; GED.

Ebersheim, Germ.; pop. 29; 38 km SW of Frankfurt am Main; 49°55'/08°15'; GUM5, JGFF.

Eberstadt, Germ.; pop. 99; 38 km S of Frankfurt am Main; 49°49'/08°39'; GED, HSL, JGFF, LDS, PHGBW.

Eberswalde, Germ.; pop. 192; 50 km NNE of Berlin; 52°50'/13°50'; GUM3, GUM4, HSL.

Ebingen, Germ.; pop. 12; 69 km S of Stuttgart; 48°13'/09°02'.

Ebneth, Germ.; 82 km N of Nurnberg; 50°10'/11°15'; PHGB.

Ebrach, Germ.; 62 km WNW of Nurnberg; 49°50'/10°30'; PHGB.

Ebsdorf, Germ.; 75 km N of Frankfurt am Main; 50°44'/08°49'; LDS.

Ecaterineanca, *see* Yekaterinovka.

Echimauti, *see* Yekimoutsy.

Echterdingen, Germ.; 19 km S of Stuttgart; 48°41'/09°10'; PHGBW.

Echzell, Germ.; pop. 59; 38 km NNE of Frankfurt am Main; 50°24'/08°54'; GUM5.

Ecka, Yug.; pop. 33; 62 km N of Beograd; 45°19'/20°28'.

Eckardroth, *see* Romsthal.

Eckarts Rupboden, Germ.; 75 km ENE of Frankfurt am Main; 50°16'/09°43'; PHGB.

Eckau, *see* Iecava.

Eckengraf, *see* Viesite.

Ecsed, Hung.; pop. 26; 62 km NE of Budapest; 47°44'/19°47'; HSL, HSL2.

Ecseg, Hung.; pop. 24; 62 km NNE of Budapest; 47°54'/19°36'; HSL.

Ecseny, Hung.; pop. 4; 69 km ENE of Nagykanizsa; 46°33'/17°51'; HSL.

Ecser, Hung.; 19 km ESE of Budapest; 47°27'/19°20'; LDS.

Eddelak, Germ.; 69 km WNW of Hamburg; 53°57'/09°09'; JGFF.

Eddersheim, Germ.; pop. 11; 19 km SW of Frankfurt am Main; 50°02'/08°28'.

Edeleny, Hung.; pop. 298; 32 km NNW of Miskolc; 48°18'/20°44'; AMG, COH, GUM4, GUM5, HSL, HSL2, PHH.

Edelfingen, Germ.; pop. 85; 94 km W of Nurnberg; 49°31'/09°45'; GED, PHGBW.

Edelstal, Aus.; pop. 3; 45 km E of Wien; 48°06'/16°59'.

Edenkoben, Germ.; pop. 69; 94 km WNW of Stuttgart; 49°17'/08°09'; EJ, GED, HSL.

Ederding, Aus.; pop. 5; 56 km W of Wien; 48°17'/15°40'.

Ederheim, Germ.; 82 km SSW of Nurnberg; 48°49'/10°28'; CAHJP, JGFF, PHGB.

Edesheim, Germ.; 94 km WNW of Stuttgart; 49°16'/08°08'; GED, HSL.

Ediger, Germ.; 101 km SSE of Koln; 50°06'/07°10'; AMG.

Edineti, *see* Yedintsy.

Edineti Sat, *possibly* Yedintsy.

Edineti Targ, *see* Yedintsy.

Edingen, Germ.; 75 km S of Frankfurt am Main; 49°27'/08°37'; HSL, PHGBW.

Edinita, *see* Yedintsy.

Edinita Targ, *see* Yedintsy.

Edole, Lat. (Edwahlen); pop. 5; 146 km W of Riga; 57°01'/21°42'.

Edwahlen, *see* Edole.

Efringen, Germ.; pop. 10; 170 km SSW of Stuttgart; 47°40'/07°34'; GED, PHGBW.

Egbeli, *see* Gbely.

Egeln, Germ.; pop. 17; 94 km NW of Leipzig; 51°57'/11°26';

HSL, LDS.

Egelsbach, Germ.; pop. 52; 19 km S of Frankfurt am Main; 49°58'/08°40'; GED, LDS.

Egen, Germ.; 38 km NE of Koln; 51°10'/07°24'; EJ, HSL, YB.

Egenhausen, Germ.; 45 km WSW of Nurnberg; 49°26'/10°28'; GUM3, JGFF, PHGB.

Eger, Hung. (Erlau); pop. 2,128; 32 km SW of Miskolc; 47°54'/20°23'; AMG, EJ, GUM4, GUM5, HSL, HSL2, ISH1, JGFF, LDL, LDS, PHH, YB. *See also* Cheb.

Egerag, Hung.; pop. 5; 114 km ESE of Nagykanizsa; 45°59'/18°18'.

Egerbegy, *see* Iobageni.

Egerbocs, Hung.; pop. 2; 45 km WSW of Miskolc; 48°02'/20°16'.

Egercsehi, Hung.; pop. 18; 38 km WSW of Miskolc; 48°03'/20°17'.

Egeres, *see* Aghiresu.

Egerhart, *possibly* Arinis.

Egerhat, *see* Arinis.

Egerlovo, Hung.; pop. 3; 45 km S of Miskolc; 47°43'/20°38'.

Egersee, HSL, HSL2. This pre-World War I community was not found in BGN gazetteers.

Egerszeg, Hung.; 26 km NE of Budapest; 47°38'/19°25'; HSL.

Egerszog, Hung.; pop. 4; 45 km NNW of Miskolc; 48°27'/20°35'.

Egervar, Hung.; pop. 4; 62 km NNW of Nagykanizsa; 46°56'/16°52'.

Egervolgy, Hung.; pop. 6; 82 km N of Nagykanizsa; 47°07'/16°55'.

Eges, HSL. This pre-World War I community was not found in BGN gazetteers.

Eggenburg, Aus.; pop. 33; 62 km NW of Wien; 48°38'/15°49'.

Eggenfelden, Germ.; pop. 16; 88 km NE of Munchen; 48°24'/12°46'; GUM3, PHGB.

Eggern, Aus.; pop. 1; 120 km WNW of Wien; 48°54'/15°08'.

Eggesin, Germ.; pop. 3; 139 km ESE of Rostock; 53°41'/14°05'.

Eggolsheim, Germ.; 38 km N of Nurnberg; 49°46'/11°03'; PHGB.

Eglaine, Lat. (Jalovka); 26 km W of Daugavpils; 55°57'/26°08'; JGFF.

Egloffstein, Germ.; 32 km N of Nurnberg; 49°42'/11°15'; PHGB.

Egregy, *see* Magyaregregy.

Egreshely, *see* Agries.

Egyed, Hung.; pop. 10; 126 km N of Nagykanizsa; 47°31'/17°21'.

Egyeduta, Hung.; pop. 5; 19 km WSW of Nagykanizsa; 46°25'/16°45'.

Egyek, Hung.; pop. 123; 56 km SSE of Miskolc; 47°38'/20°54'; HSL, PHH.

Egyhazasdengeleg, Hung.; pop. 11; 50 km NE of Budapest; 47°48'/19°34'.

Egyhazashetye, Hung.; pop. 2; 88 km N of Nagykanizsa; 47°10'/17°07'.

Ehingen, Germ.; 69 km SE of Stuttgart; 48°17'/09°44'; PHGB.

Ehrenbreitstein, Germ. CAHJP, HSL. This pre-World War I community was not found in BGN gazetteers.

Ehrenfeld, Ukr.; pop. 11; 26 km N of Lvov; 50°03'/24°04'. This town was located on an interwar map of Poland but does not appear in contemporary gazetteers. Map coordinates are approximate.

Ehrstadt, Germ.; 56 km NNW of Stuttgart; 49°15'/08°59'; LDS, PHGBW.

Ehrsten, *see* Meimbressen.

Eibelstadt, Germ.; 82 km WNW of Nurnberg; 49°44'/10°00'; CAHJP, PHGB.

Eibenschitz, *see* Ivancice.

Eich, Germ.; pop. 35; 45 km SSW of Frankfurt am Main; 49°45'/08°24'.

Eichenbuhl, Germ.; 62 km ESE of Frankfurt am Main; 49°42'/09°20'; PHGB.

Eichenhausen, Germ.; pop. 11; 114 km NW of Nurnberg; 50°19'/10°18'; GUM3, GUM5, PHGB.

Eichstatt, Germ.; pop. 30; 69 km S of Nurnberg; 48°53'/11°11'; EJ, GUM3, PHGB.

Eichstetten, Germ.; pop. 129; 133 km SW of Stuttgart; 48°05'/07°44'; HSL, JGFF, LDS, PHGBW.

Eichtersheim, Germ.; pop. 21; 62 km NW of Stuttgart; 49°14'/08°46'; PHGBW.

Eichweiler, Germ.; pop. 110; Described in the *Black Book* as being in the Neidersachsen-Westfallen region of Germany, this town was not found in BGN gazetteers.

Eidlitz, *see* Udlice.

Eigenheim, *see* Starokazachye.

Eigentovka, *see* Ignatovka.

Eihumen, *see* Cherven.

Eilendorf, Germ.; pop. 23; 56 km SW of Koln; 50°47'/06°10'.

Eimeldingen, Germ.; 170 km SSW of Stuttgart; 47°38'/07°36'; LDS.

Eimelrod, Germ.; pop. 16; 126 km NE of Koln; 51°18'/08°42'; AMG.

Einartshausen, Germ.; pop. 400; 50 km NNE of Frankfurt am Main; 50°30'/09°04'.

Einbeck, Germ.; pop. 58; 69 km SSE of Hannover; 51°49'/09°52'.

Einsiedel, *see* Mnisek nad Hnilcom.

Einsingen, *see* Aynzingen.

Eisbergen, Germ.; pop. 1; 50 km SW of Hannover; 52°12'/09°01'.

Eisenach, Germ.; pop. 360; 146 km WSW of Leipzig; 50°59'/10°19'; JGFF, LDS.

Eisenarzt, Germ.; pop. 1; 88 km ESE of Munchen; 47°48'/12°38'.

Eisenbach, Germ.; pop. 360; 75 km NNE of Frankfurt am Main; 50°36'/09°23'; EJ, GUM5, GUM6.

Eisenberg, Germ.; 75 km SSW of Frankfurt am Main; 49°33'/08°06'; GUM5.

Eisenburg, Germ.; 101 km WSW of Munchen; 48°01'/10°13'; PHGB.

Eisenerz, Aus.; 69 km NW of Graz; 47°32'/14°53'; GUM4.

Eisenhuttenstadt, Germ. (Fuerstenberg); 94 km ESE of Berlin; 52°09'/14°39'; JGFF.

Eisenkappel, Aus.; pop. 3; 94 km SSW of Graz; 46°29'/14°35'.

Eisenstadt, Aus. (Weniger Maertersdorf); pop. 204; 45 km SSE of Wien; 47°51'/16°31'; CAHJP, EJ, HSL, HSL2, JGFF.

Eiserfeld, Germ.; 75 km E of Koln; 50°50'/07°59'; GED.

Eisfeld, Germ.; pop. 10; 114 km N of Nurnberg; 50°25'/10°55'.

Eishishki, *see* Eisiskes.

Eishishuk, *see* Eisiskes.

Eishyshok, *see* Eisiskes.

Eisiskes, Lith. (Aisheshuk, Aishishak, Aishishuk, Eishishki, Eishishuk, Eishyshok, Ejszyszki, Eshishuk, Eyshishkes, Eyshishok); pop. 1,591; 62 km S of Vilnius; 54°10'/25°00'; AMG, COH, EDRD, EJ, GUM3, GUM4, GUM5, GUM6, HSL, HSL2, JGFF, LDL, LYV, SF, YB.

Eisleben, Germ.; pop. 101; 62 km WNW of Leipzig; 51°32'/11°33'.

Eiterfeld, Germ.; pop. 56; 114 km NE of Frankfurt am Main; 50°46'/09°48'; LDS.

Eitorf, Germ.; 38 km ESE of Koln; 50°46'/07°27'; GED.

Eiwanowitz, *see* Ivanovice na Hane.

Ejszyszki, *see* Eisiskes.

Ejwidowicze, *see* Eyvidovichi.

Ekaterinoslav, *see* Dnepropetrovsk.

Ekel, *see* Okolicna na Ostrove.

Elasson, Greece; 107 km SSW of Thessaloniki; 39°53'/22°10'; GUM4.

Elben, Germ.; 133 km N of Frankfurt am Main; 51°14'/09°12'; LDS.

Elberfeld, *see* Wuppertal.

Elbing, *see* Elblag.

Elblag, Pol. (Elbing); pop. 460; 50 km ESE of Gdansk; 54°10'/19°23'; AMG, CAHJP, EJ, GUM3, GUM4, GUM5, LDS, PHGBW, PHP2, PHP4, POCEM.

Eldagsen, Germ.; pop. 56; 32 km S of Hannover; 52°10'/09°39'; GED.

Elecske, *see* Aleksince.

Eleja, Lat.; pop. 6; 69 km SSW of Riga; 56°24'/23°41'.

Elek, Hung.; pop. 40; 88 km NE of Szeged; 46°32'/21°15'.

Eleonorowka, Ukr.; pop. 22; 26 km WSW of Rovno; 50°35'/25°55'. This town was located on an interwar map of Poland but does not appear in contemporary gazetteers. Map coordinates are approximate.

Elesd, *see* Alesd.

Elesdlok, *see* Luncsoara.

Elesdszurdok, *see* Surduc.

Elgersburg, Germ.; pop. 7; 120 km SW of Leipzig; 50°42'/10°51'.

Elgershausen, Germ.; 126 km S of Hannover; 51°17'/09°22'; LDS.

Elisabethstadt, *see* Dumbraveny.

Elizabetgrod, *see* Kirovograd.

Elizarow, *see* Yelizarov.

Elk, Pol. (Lyck); pop. 150; 94 km NW of Bialystok; 53°50'/22°21'; EJ, HSL, JGFF.

Elksni, Lat. (Elksnu); pop. 2; 69 km WNW of Daugavpils; 56°13'/25°36'.

Elksnu, *see* Elksni.

Elkush, *see* Olkusz.

Ellar, Germ.; pop. 16; 62 km NW of Frankfurt am Main; 50°31'/08°06'; AMG, GUM5.

Ellend, Hung.; pop. 1; 120 km ESE of Nagykanizsa; 46°03'/18°23'.

Ellerbach, Germ.; 82 km WNW of Munchen; 48°30'/10°34'; PHGB.

Ellersheim, Germ. PHGBW. This town was not found in BGN gazetteers under the given spelling.

Ellerstadt, Germ.; pop. 2; 75 km S of Frankfurt am Main; 49°28'/08°16'; GED.

Ellingen, Germ.; pop. 38; 50 km S of Nurnberg; 49°04'/10°58'; GUM3, GUM5, ISH1, PHGB.

Ellrich, Germ.; pop. 14; 114 km SE of Hannover; 51°35'/10°39'; AMG, GUM5, LDS.

Ellwangen, Germ.; 69 km NE of Stuttgart; 48°57'/10°08'; PHGBW.

Elmendshofen, Germ.; 126 km S of Stuttgart; 47°40'/08°47'; PHGBW.

Elmshagen, Germ.; 126 km S of Hannover; 51°16'/09°19'; LDS.

Elmshorn, Germ.; pop. 80; 38 km WNW of Hamburg; 53°45'/09°39'; GED, GUM5, HSL.

Elnhausen, Germ.; 82 km N of Frankfurt am Main; 50°48'/08°41'; LDS.

Elsdorf, Germ.; pop. 43; 56 km SW of Hamburg; 53°14'/09°21'; GED.

Eltendorf, Aus.; pop. 3; 56 km E of Graz; 47°00'/16°12'.

Eltmann, Germ.; 69 km NW of Nurnberg; 49°58'/10°40'; GUM3, PHGB.

Eltville, Germ.; pop. 60; 38 km WSW of Frankfurt am Main; 50°02'/08°07'; GUM5.

Elva, Est.; 26 km SW of Tartu; 58°13'/26°25'; PHLE.

Elyus, *see* Aleus.

Elzach, Germ.; 107 km SW of Stuttgart; 48°11'/08°04'; PHGBW.

Embken, Germ.; 45 km SW of Koln; 50°41'/06°34'; GED.

Emden, Germ.; pop. 700; 182 km WSW of Hamburg; 53°22'/07°13'; AMG, EJ, GED, GUM4, GUM5, GUM6, HSL, HSL2, JGFF, LDS, PHP1.

Emersacker, Germ.; 75 km WNW of Munchen; 48°30'/10°40'; PHGB.

Emes, *see* Emmes.

Emilia, Pol. (Emilja); pop. 9; 26 km NNW of Lodz; 51°55'/19°22'.

Emilin, Pol.; pop. 12; 94 km N of Lodz; 52°32'/19°33'.

Emilja, *see* Emilia.

Emiltchina, *see* Yemilchino.

Emiltchine, Ukr. EDRD. This town was not found in BGN gazetteers under the given spelling.

Emlichheim, Germ.; 189 km N of Koln; 52°37'/06°51'; GED.

Emmendingen, Germ.; pop. 364; 120 km SW of Stuttgart; 48°08'/07°51'; HSL, JGFF, LDS, PHGBW.

Emmerdingen, Germ.; 133 km SW of Stuttgart; 48°00'/07°51'; HSL. This town was located on a pre-World War I map, but does not appear in contemporary gazetteers.

Emmerich, Germ.; pop. 90; 107 km NW of Koln; 51°50'/06°15'; AMG, GED.

Emmerstedt, Germ.; pop. 6; 82 km E of Hannover; 52°15'/10°58'.

Emmes, Ukr. (Emes); pop. 1,268; 114 km SW of Dnepropetrovsk; 47°52'/33°41'.

Emmetzheim, GUM3. This town was not found in BGN gazetteers under the given spelling.

Emod, Hung.; pop. 72; 26 km SSE of Miskolc; 47°56'/20°49'; HSL, PHH.

Ems, *see* Bad Ems.

Enciu, Rom.; pop. 3; 62 km NE of Cluj; 47°03'/24°15'.

Encovany, Cz.; pop. 2; 56 km NNW of Praha; 50°32'/14°15'.

Encs, Hung.; pop. 272; 38 km NE of Miskolc; 48°20'/21°08'; HSL, HSL2, PHH.

Encsencs, Hung.; pop. 62; 107 km ESE of Miskolc; 47°44'/22°07'; AMG, HSL, LDS, PHH.

Endingen, Germ.; 126 km SW of Stuttgart; 48°08'/07°42'; EJ, HSL, HSL2, PHGBW.

Endred, *see* Ondrejovce.

Endrefalva, Hung.; pop. 12; 82 km NNE of Budapest; 48°08'/19°35'.

Endrod, Hung.; pop. 80; 88 km NNE of Szeged; 46°56'/20°47'; PHH.

Endsee, Germ.; 62 km WSW of Nurnberg; 49°26'/10°14'; PHGB.

Enese, Hung.; pop. 2; 126 km W of Budapest; 47°39'/17°25'.

Engelhartstetten, Aus.; pop. 1; 45 km E of Wien; 48°10'/16°53'.

Engels, *see* Gor'kiy.

Engetried, Germ.; 88 km WSW of Munchen; 47°56'/10°24'; PHGB.

Engure, Lat.; pop. 5; 56 km WNW of Riga; 57°10'/23°13'.

Enichioi, *see* Novoselovka.

Enmianki, Pol.; pop. 89; Described in the *Black Book* as being in the Warszawa region of Poland, this town was not found in BGN gazetteers.

Enniger, Germ.; 120 km NNE of Koln; 51°50'/07°57'; JGFF.

Enns, Aus.; pop. 3; 120 km NE of Salzburg; 48°12'/14°28'; EJ.

Enskirchen, GUM3. This town was not found in BGN gazetteers under the given spelling.

Entradam, *see* Rebreanu.

Enyed, *see* Enyedszentkiraz.

Enyedszentkiraz, Rom. (Enyed); HSL, HSL2. This pre-World War I community was not found in BGN gazetteers.

Enying, Hung.; pop. 178; 88 km SSW of Budapest; 46°56'/18°15'; LDS, PHH.

Enzenreith, Aus.; pop. 2; 69 km SSW of Wien; 47°40'/15°57'.

Epe, Germ.; 146 km N of Koln; 52°11'/07°02'; GED.

Eperies, *see* Presov.

Eperjes, *see* Presov.

Eperjeske, Hung.; pop. 8; 114 km ENE of Miskolc; 48°21'/22°13'.

Eperyos, *see* Presov.

Epfenbach, Germ.; 69 km NNW of Stuttgart; 49°20'/08°55'; LDS.

Epfishe, HSL. This pre-World War I community was not found in BGN gazetteers.

Episcopia Bihoruliu, *see* Episcopia Bihorului.

Episcopia Bihorului, Rom. (Biharpuspoki, Episcopia Bihoruliu, Piscopia); pop. 40; 133 km WNW of Cluj; 47°06'/21°54'; HSL, PHR2.

Eppelsheim, Germ.; pop. 21; 62 km SSW of Frankfurt am Main; 49°42'/08°10'; JGFF.

Eppertshausen, Germ.; pop. 30; 19 km SE of Frankfurt am Main; 49°57'/08°51'.

Eppingen, Germ.; pop. 60; 45 km NW of Stuttgart; 49°08'/08°54'; GUM5, HSL, HSL2, LDS, PHGBW.

Eppstein, Germ.; 19 km W of Frankfurt am Main; 50°08'/08°24'; JGFF.

Equarhofen, Germ.; 69 km W of Nurnberg; 49°30'/10°07'; PHGB.

Eraadony, see Adoni.

Eradengeleg, see Dindesti.

Erbach, Germ. CAHJP. A number of towns share this name. It was not possible to determine from available information which one is being referenced.

Erbendorf, Germ.; pop. 25; 82 km NE of Nurnberg; 49°50'/12°03'; PHGB.

Erbenheim, Germ.; pop. 35; 26 km WSW of Frankfurt am Main; 50°03'/08°18'.

Erbes Budesheim, Germ.; pop. 13; 62 km SW of Frankfurt am Main; 49°45'/08°02'.

Erbstadt, Germ.; 26 km NNE of Frankfurt am Main; 50°16'/08°52'; LDS.

Ercsi, Hung.; pop. 133; 38 km SSW of Budapest; 47°15'/18°54'; GUM5, LDS, PHH.

Erd, Hung.; pop. 110; 26 km SSW of Budapest; 47°22'/18°56'; PHH.

Erdberg, Aus.; 50 km N of Wien; 48°37'/16°38'; EJ.

Erdevik, Yug.; pop. 27; 88 km WNW of Beograd; 45°07'/19°25'.

Erding, Germ.; pop. 3; 32 km NE of Munchen; 48°18'/11°56'; PHGB.

Erdmannrode, Germ.; 114 km NE of Frankfurt am Main; 50°48'/09°47'; JGFF.

Erdmannsdorf, Germ.; 69 km ESE of Leipzig; 50°49'/13°04'; GUM3, GUM5, GUM5.

Erdobenye, Hung.; pop. 153; 50 km NE of Miskolc; 48°16'/21°22'; AMG, HSL, HSL2, LDL, LDS, PHH.

Erdocsokonya, see Csokonyavisonta.

Erdod, see Ardud.

Erdohorvati, Hung.; pop. 14; 56 km NE of Miskolc; 48°19'/21°26'.

Erdokerek, see Cherechiu.

Erdokovesd, Hung.; pop. 11; 50 km WSW of Miskolc; 48°02'/20°06'.

Erdokurt, Hung.; pop. 7; 38 km NNE of Budapest; 47°46'/19°28'.

Erdoszada, see Ardusat.

Erdoszallas, see Salnita.

Erdoszentgyorgy, see Singeorgiu de Padure.

Erdotarcsa, Hung.; pop. 11; 45 km NE of Budapest; 47°46'/19°33'.

Erdotelek, Hung.; pop. 40; 56 km SSW of Miskolc; 47°41'/20°19'; HSL, LDS.

Erdudka, see Oravska Lesna.

Eremieni, Rom.; pop. 6; 101 km E of Cluj; 46°32'/24°52'.

Erendred, see Andrid.

Ererjes, see Presov.

Erfelden, Germ.; pop. 31; 32 km SSW of Frankfurt am Main; 49°50'/08°28'.

Erfurt, Germ.; pop. 819; 94 km SW of Leipzig; 50°59'/11°02'; AMG, CAHJP, EDRD, EJ, GUM3, HSL, JGFF, LDS, PHP1.

Ergkavas, Rom. (Erkavas); HSL. This pre-World War I community was not found in BGN gazetteers. See also Cauas.

Ergli, Lat.; pop. 6; 94 km E of Riga; 56°54'/25°38'.

Ergoldsbach, Germ.; pop. 3; 75 km NNE of Munchen; 48°41'/12°12'.

Erk, Hung.; pop. 3; 75 km ENE of Budapest; 47°37'/20°05'; LDS.

Erkavas, see Ergkavas.

Erkelenz, Germ.; pop. 60; 50 km WNW of Koln; 51°05'/06°19'; GUM5.

Erkeln, Germ.; pop. 12; 82 km SSW of Hannover; 51°41'/09°14'.

Erkeseru, see Chesereu.

Erkner, Germ.; 26 km ESE of Berlin; 52°25'/13°45'; GUM5.

Erkobolkut, see Cubulcut.

Erkortvelyes, see Curtuiuseni.

Erkrath, Germ.; 38 km N of Koln; 51°13'/06°54'; GUM5.

Erksdorf, Germ.; 88 km N of Frankfurt am Main; 50°51'/09°01'; JGFF, LDS.

Erlaa, see Erlaa Bei Wien.

Erlaa Bei Wien, Aus. (Erlaa); pop. 81; 13 km SSW of Wien; 48°08'/16°19'.

Erlabrunn, Germ.; 88 km ESE of Frankfurt am Main; 49°51'/09°51'; PHGB.

Erlangen, Germ.; pop. 130; 19 km NNW of Nurnberg; 49°36'/11°01'; AMG, CAHJP, EJ, GED, GUM3, HSL, HSL2, LDS, PHGB.

Erlau, see Eger.

Erlauf, Aus.; pop. 12; 88 km WSW of Wien; 48°11'/15°11'.

Erlbach, Germ.; 88 km ENE of Munchen; 48°18'/12°47'; LDS.

Erlenbach, Germ. (Erlenbach Bei Dahn); pop. 25; 101 km WNW of Stuttgart; 49°07'/07°52'; GED, HSL, PHGB.

Erlenbach Bei Dahn, see Erlenbach.

Erlui, LDL. This pre-World War I community was not found in BGN gazetteers.

Ermershausen, Germ.; pop. 67; 88 km NNW of Nurnberg; 50°13'/10°37'; GUM5, HSL, JGFF, PHGB.

Ermetzhofen, Germ.; pop. 35; 62 km W of Nurnberg; 49°30'/10°16'; GUM5, JGFF, LDS, PHGB.

Ermihalydalva, see Valea Lui Mihai.

Ermihalyfalva, see Mihaifalau.

Ermoclia, see Yermokliya.

Ermreuth, Germ.; pop. 25; 26 km N of Nurnberg; 49°39'/11°12'; GED, HSL, PHGB.

Erndtebruck, Germ.; pop. 9; 88 km ENE of Koln; 50°59'/08°16'.

Ernei, Rom.; pop. 15; 82 km E of Cluj; 46°36'/24°39'.

Ernestinehof, see Ernestinovo.

Ernestinovo, Yug. (Ernestinehof); pop. 3; 157 km WNW of Beograd; 45°27'/18°40'.

Ernsbach, Germ.; 62 km N of Stuttgart; 49°18'/09°31'; JGFF, PHGBW.

Ernsthausen, Germ.; 107 km N of Frankfurt am Main; 50°59'/08°44'; LDS.

Erolaszi, see Olosig.

Erp, Germ.; 26 km SSW of Koln; 50°46'/06°44'; GED.

Erpatak, Hung. (Hugyaj); pop. 31; 82 km ESE of Miskolc; 47°48'/21°46'; HSL, LDS.

Erpuzice, Cz.; pop. 16; 107 km SW of Praha; 49°48'/13°03'.

Ersekcsanad, Hung.; pop. 9; 88 km WSW of Szeged; 46°15'/18°59'; GUM4.

Ersekujvar, see Nove Zamky.

Ersekvadkert, Hung.; pop. 57; 62 km N of Budapest; 48°00'/19°12'; HSL, PHH.

Erselend, see Silindru.

Ersszodoro, see Sudurau.

Erstarcsa, see Tarcea.

Ersvasad, see Vasad.

Erteny, Hung.; pop. 5; 94 km ENE of Nagykanizsa; 46°37'/18°08'.

Ervenice, Cz.; pop. 24; 82 km WNW of Praha; 50°31'/13°32'.

Erwitte, Germ.; pop. 20; 126 km SW of Hannover; 51°37'/08°21'.

Erzhausen, Germ.; 19 km S of Frankfurt am Main; 49°57'/08°38'; LDS.

Erzhvilek, see Erzvilkas.

Erzhvilkas, see Erzvilkas.

Erzsebetbanya, see Baiut.

Erzvilkas, Lith. (Erzhvilek, Erzhvilkas, Erzvilki); pop. 222; 82 km WNW of Kaunas; 55°16'/22°43'; GUM3, GUM4, GUM5, HSL, LDL, SF, YL.

Erzvilki, see Erzvilkas.

Esbach, Germ. JGFF. A number of towns share this name. It was not possible to determine from available information which one is being referenced.

Eyshishok (Eisiskes), Lithuania: An outdoor class at a "folkshul."

Eschau, Germ.; pop. 21; 56 km ESE of Frankfurt am Main; 49°49'/09°16'; GUM5, PHGB.

Eschelbach, *see* Eschelbach an der Ilm.

Eschelbach an der Ilm, Germ. (Eschelbach); 56 km N of Munchen; 48°35'/11°35'; LDS.

Eschelbronn, Germ.; 62 km NNW of Stuttgart; 49°19'/08°52'; PHGBW.

Eschenau, Germ.; 19 km NNE of Nurnberg; 49°34'/11°12'; PHGB, PHGBW.

Eschenhausen, Germ.; 82 km WNW of Hannover; 52°50'/08°46'; HSL.

Eschershausen, Germ.; 56 km S of Hannover; 51°55'/09°39'; GUM3, LDS.

Eschollbrucken, Germ.; 38 km S of Frankfurt am Main; 49°49'/08°34'; LDS.

Eschwege, Germ.; pop. 390; 139 km SSE of Hannover; 51°11'/10°04'; AMG, GED, GUM3, GUM4, GUM6, HSL, JGFF, LDS.

Eschweiler, Germ.; 50 km WSW of Koln; 50°49'/06°17'; JGFF.

Escu, Rom. (Veczke); pop. 6; 45 km N of Cluj; 47°08'/23°32'; HSL.

Esen, Bulg.; 101 km SW of Varna; 42°50'/26°47'; HSL.

Esens, Germ.; pop. 80; 157 km W of Hamburg; 53°39'/07°36'; LDS.

Eshishuk, *see* Eisiskes.

Eskullo, *see* Astileu.

Eslarn, Germ.; pop. 1; 107 km ENE of Nurnberg; 49°35'/12°32'.

Esseg, *see* Osijek.

Essen, Germ.; pop. 5,045; 62 km N of Koln; 51°27'/07°01'; AMG, CAHJP, EJ, GED, GUM3, GUM4, GUM5, ISH1, JGFF.

Essenheim, Germ.; pop. 21; 45 km SW of Frankfurt am Main; 49°56'/08°09'.

Essen Heisingen, Germ.; pop. 4; 56 km N of Koln; 51°25'/07°04'.

Essen Kray, *see* Kray.

Essen Steele, Germ.; pop. 140; 56 km N of Koln; 51°26'/07°05'.

Essingen, Germ.; 62 km ENE of Stuttgart; 48°48'/10°02'; GED, HSL, JGFF.

Esslingen, Germ. (Esslingen am Neckar); pop. 128; 13 km E of Stuttgart; 48°45'/09°18'; CAHJP, EDRD, EJ, GUM3, GUM5, HSL, HSL2, JGFF, PHGBW.

Esslingen am Neckar, *see* Esslingen.

Essweiler, Germ.; 101 km SW of Frankfurt am Main; 49°33'/07°34'; JGFF.

Estenfeld, Germ.; pop. 16; 88 km WNW of Nurnberg; 49°50'/10°01'; GUM5, PHGB.

Esterdin, *see* Sterdyn.

Esterwegen, Germ.; pop. 4; 150 km WNW of Hannover; 52°59'/07°37'; GUM3, GUM5, GUM6.

Estrik, *see* Ustrzyki Dolne.

Eszek, *see* Osijek.

Esztar, Hung.; pop. 26; 120 km SE of Miskolc; 47°17'/21°47'; LDS.

Eszteny, *see* Stoiana.

Eszteregnye, Hung.; pop. 8; 13 km W of Nagykanizsa; 46°28'/16°53'.

Esztergom, Hung.; pop. 523; 45 km NW of Budapest; 47°48'/18°45'; EJ, HSL, HSL2, LDS, PHH.

Ete, Hung.; pop. 12; 75 km W of Budapest; 47°32'/18°04'.

Eted, *see* Atid.

Eterdam, LDL. This pre-World War I community was not found in BGN gazetteers.

Etes, Hung.; pop. 14; 82 km W of Miskolc; 48°07'/19°43'.

Etingen, Germ.; 101 km ENE of Hannover; 52°23'/11°10'; GUM3, PHP2.

Ettenheim, Germ.; pop. 44; 114 km SW of Stuttgart; 48°15'/07°49'; LDS, PHGBW.

Ettlingen, Germ.; pop. 62; 62 km WNW of Stuttgart; 48°57'/08°24'; EJ, GUM5, PHGBW.

Etyek, Hung.; pop. 21; 26 km WSW of Budapest; 47°27'/18°45'.

Etzenricht, Germ.; pop. 1; 75 km ENE of Nurnberg; 49°38'/12°06'.

Eubigheim, Germ.; pop. 34; 88 km SE of Frankfurt am Main;

49°31'/09°32'; LDS, PHGBW.

Euerbach, Germ.; pop. 2; 101 km WNW of Nurnberg; 50°04'/10°08'; CAHJP, PHGB.

Eupatoria, *see* Yevpatoriya.

Euskirchen, Germ.; pop. 250; 38 km S of Koln; 50°40'/06°47'; AMG, GED.

Eustachow, Pol.; pop. 6; 82 km ENE of Czestochowa; 50°56'/20°16'.

Eutin, Germ.; 82 km NNE of Hamburg; 54°08'/10°37'; GED.

Eversmuiza, Lat. (Cibla); pop. 6; 114 km NE of Daugavpils; 56°33'/27°53'.

Evghenita, *see* Yevgenyevka.

Evpatoriia, *see* Yevpatoriya.

Ewelin, Pol.; pop. 6; 56 km ESE of Warszawa; 51°54'/21°32'.

Exin, *see* Kcynia.

Eydtkuhen, *see* Chernyshevskoye.

Eydtkuhnen, *see* Chernyshevskoye.

Eynzingen, *see* Aynzingen.

Eyshishkes, *see* Eisiskes.

Eyshishok, *see* Eisiskes.

Eysolden, Germ.; 45 km SSE of Nurnberg; 49°08'/11°13'; PHGB.

Eyvidovichi, Byel. (Ejwidowicze); pop. 8; 182 km NNW of Minsk; 55°29'/26°56'.

Ezerenai, *see* Zarasai.

Ezherena, *see* Zarasai.

Ezherene, *see* Zarasai.

Ezreni, *see* Zarasai.

Ezupol, *see* Zhovten.

Fabianhaza, Hung.; pop. 86; 120 km E of Miskolc; 47°50'/22°22'; HSL, LDL, PHH.

Fabianki, Pol. (Fabjanki); pop. 34; 114 km NNW of Lodz; 52°44'/19°07'.

Fabiansebestyen, Hung.; pop. 3; 56 km NNE of Szeged; 46°41'/20°28'.

Fabjanki, *see* Fabianki.

Fachbach, Germ.; pop. 9; 75 km WNW of Frankfurt am Main; 50°20'/07°41'.

Facimiech, Pol.; pop. 7; 19 km SW of Krakow; 49°58'/19°43'.

Facsad, *see* Faget.

Fadd, Hung.; pop. 58; 107 km W of Szeged; 46°28'/18°50'; LDS, PHH.

Fagaras, Rom. (Fagarasi, Fogaras); 146 km SE of Cluj; 45°51'/24°58'; CAHJP, EJ, HSL, PHR1.

Fagarasi, *see* Fagaras.

Faget, Rom. (Facsad); pop. 95; 150 km SW of Cluj; 45°51'/22°11'; PHR1.

Fahrenwalde, Germ.; 114 km NNE of Berlin; 53°26'/14°04'; AMG.

Fajnica, Pol. PHP4. This town was not found in BGN gazetteers under the given spelling.

Fajslawice, Pol.; pop. 2; 32 km ESE of Lublin; 51°06'/22°58'; GA, GUM5.

Fajsz, Hung.; pop. 37; 94 km W of Szeged; 46°25'/18°55'.

Falatycze, Pol.; pop. 3; 107 km S of Bialystok; 52°13'/22°50'.

Falcio, *possibly* Falciu.

Falciu, Rom. (Falcio?); pop. 154; 107 km SSE of Iasi; 46°18'/28°08'; JGFF, PHR1.

Falecice, Pol.; pop. 7; 69 km S of Warszawa; 51°41'/20°57'.

Falejowka, Pol.; pop. 9; 50 km SW of Przemysl; 49°38'/22°10'.

Falencia Miedzeszyn, Pol. PHP4. This town was not found in BGN gazetteers under the given spelling.

Falenica, Pol. (Falenits, Falenitsa, Falenitz); pop. 1,108; 26 km ESE of Warszawa; 52°10'/21°14'; AMG, COH, EDRD, FRG, GUM4, GUM5, HSL, ISH2, ISH3, LDL, LYV, PHP4, SF, YB.

Falenits, *see* Falenica.

Falenitsa, *see* Falenica.

Falenitz, *see* Falenica.

Falenty, GUM5. This town was not found in BGN gazetteers under the given spelling.

Faleshti, *see* Faleshty.

Faleshty, Mold. (Faleshti, Falesti); pop. 3,258; 107 km WNW of Kishinev; 47°34'/27°42'; EDRD, EJ, GUM4, GUM5, JGFF, LDL, PHR2, SF.

Falesti, *see* Faleshty.

Faliszew, Pol. (Faliszow); pop. 3; 69 km NE of Czestochowa; 51°10'/19°55'.

Faliszow, *see* Faliszew.

Faliszowka, Pol.; pop. 7; 88 km WSW of Przemysl; 49°39'/21°37'.

Falkenau, *see* Sokolov (Czechoslovakia).

Falkenberg, Germ.; pop. 34; 120 km NNE of Frankfurt am Main; 51°04'/09°23'; AMG, GUM3, GUM4, GUM5.

Falkenburg, *see* Zlocieniec.

Falkensee, Germ.; pop. 21; 26 km W of Berlin; 52°34'/13°05'; GUM3.

Falkenstein, Germ.; pop. 102; 94 km S of Leipzig; 50°29'/12°22'; GUM3, GUM5.

Falknov nad Ohri, *see* Sokolov (Czechoslovakia).

Falkusovce, Cz.; 45 km E of Kosice; 48°37'/21°51'; HSL.

Falticeni, Rom. (Palticeni); 101 km WNW of Iasi; 47°27'/26°18'; EJ, GUM4, GUM5, HSL, HSL2, JGFF, LDL, PHR1.

Falusugatag, *see* Satu Sugatag.

Falu Szlatina, *see* Solotvina.

Faluzsolcza, *see* Felsozsolca.

Fancsika, Hung.; 94 km ESE of Miskolc; 47°31'/21°45'; AMG, HSL.

Fandul Moldovei, *see* Fundu Moldovei.

Fantana Alba, *see* Belaya Krinitsa.

Fantanele Nasaud, Rom.; pop. 20; Described in the *Black Book* as being in the Transylvania region of Romania, this town was not found in BGN gazetteers.

Farad, Hung.; pop. 34; 139 km W of Budapest; 47°36'/17°12'; HSL, PHH.

Faragau, Rom. (Farago); pop. 6; 69 km E of Cluj; 46°46'/24°31'.

Farago, *see* Faragau.

Farcasa, Rom.; pop. 35; 94 km NNW of Cluj; 47°35'/23°20'; HSL.

Farkasd, *see* Vlcany.

Farkasgyepu, Hung.; pop. 3; 101 km NNE of Nagykanizsa; 47°12'/17°38'.

Farkaslaka, *see* Lupeni.

Farkasrev, *see* Vad Maramures.

Farkazd, *see* Vlcany.

Farladani Tighina, *see* Farladyany.

Farladeny, *see* Farladyany.

Farladyany, Mold. (Farladani Tighina, Farladeny); pop. 44; 50 km ESE of Kishinev; 46°47'/29°22'.

Farmos, Hung.; pop. 18; 62 km E of Budapest; 47°22'/19°51'; LDS.

Farna, Cz. (Papfalva); 107 km E of Bratislava; 48°00'/18°31'; HSL.

Farynki, Ukr.; pop. 47; 139 km NW of Rovno; 51°40'/25°16'.

Fasciszowa, Pol.; pop. 18; 75 km ESE of Krakow; 49°51'/20°51'.

Fashchevka, Ukr. (Faszczowka); pop. 20; 126 km N of Chernovtsy; 49°23'/26°14'.

Fassoldshof, Germ.; 75 km N of Nurnberg; 50°07'/11°21'; PHGB.

Fastov, Ukr.; pop. 3,545; 56 km SW of Kiyev; 50°05'/29°55'; EJ, GYLA, JGFF, LDL, SF.

Faszczowka, *see* Fashchevka.

Fatezh, USSR; pop. 39; 50 km NW of Kursk; 52°05'/35°52'; GUM4.

Fauerbach, *see* Fauerbach Bei Nidda.

Fauerbach Bei Nidda, Germ. (Fauerbach); 45 km NNE of Frankfurt am Main; 50°24'/09°04'; JGFF.

Fauresti, Rom.; pop. 45; 94 km N of Cluj; 47°34'/23°45'.

Fechenbach, Germ.; pop. 9; 62 km ESE of Frankfurt am Main; 49°46'/09°20'; GUM5, PHGB.

Fechenheim, Germ.; 13 km NE of Frankfurt am Main;

50°08'/08°45'; LDS.

Fechheim, Germ.; 94 km N of Nurnberg; 50°16'/11°07'; JGFF.

Fedemes, Hung.; pop. 2; 45 km WSW of Miskolc; 48°02'/20°12'.

Fedvernik, HSL. This pre-World War I community was not found in BGN gazetteers.

Fegernic, Rom.; pop. 5; 120 km WNW of Cluj; 47°12'/22°08'.

Fegyvernek, Hung.; pop. 85; 94 km S of Miskolc; 47°16'/20°32'; PHH.

Fehergyarmat, Hung. (Feheryarmat); pop. 679; 133 km E of Miskolc; 47°59'/22°31'; AMG, COH, GUM4, HSL, HSL2, LDL, LDS, PHH, YB.

Feherlak, see Albestii Bistritei.

Fehervarcsurgo, Hung.; pop. 2; 69 km SW of Budapest; 47°18'/18°16'.

Feheryarmat, see Fehergyarmat.

Fehrbellin, Germ.; pop. 4; 56 km WNW of Berlin; 52°48'/12°46'; GUM4.

Fehring, Aus.; 45 km ESE of Graz; 46°56'/16°01'; GUM5.

Feiurd, possibly Feiurdeni.

Feiurdeni, Rom. (Feiurd?, Fejerd); pop. 6; 19 km N of Cluj; 46°53'/23°38'; HSL.

Fejercse, Hung.; pop. 14; 126 km ENE of Miskolc; 48°08'/22°28'.

Fejerd, see Feiurdeni.

Fejerfalva, see Feresti.

Fekete Ardo, Hung.; 170 km E of Miskolc; 48°05'/23°03'; AMG, GUM3.

Feketeerdo, AMG, HSL, JGFF. A number of towns share this name. It was not possible to determine from available information which one is being referenced.

Feketegyarmat, see Iermata Neagra.

Feketepatak, HSL. This pre-World War I community was not found in BGN gazetteers.

Feketeszek, Hung.; 82 km ESE of Miskolc; 47°53'/21°48'; HSL.

Feketeto, possibly Taut.

Feketic, Yug.; pop. 48; 114 km NW of Beograd; 45°40'/19°42'.

Felcsut, Hung.; pop. 51; 38 km WSW of Budapest; 47°27'/18°35'.

Felczyn, GUM5. This town was not found in BGN gazetteers under the given spelling.

Feldafing, Germ.; pop. 9; 32 km SSW of Munchen; 47°57'/11°18'; AMG, GUM3, GUM4, GUM5, GUM6.

Feldbach, Aus.; 38 km ESE of Graz; 46°57'/15°53'; GUM5.

Feldebro, Hung.; pop. 10; 50 km SW of Miskolc; 47°49'/20°15'; HSL.

Feldesz, GUM3. This town was not found in BGN gazetteers under the given spelling.

Feldkirch, Aus.; 139 km WSW of Innsbruck; 47°14'/09°36'; EDRD.

Feldmoching, Germ.; pop. 2; 13 km NW of Munchen; 48°13'/11°32'; GUM3.

Feldoboly, see Dobolii de Sus.

Feldru, Rom. (Foldra); pop. 50; 94 km NE of Cluj; 47°17'/24°36'; HSL.

Feleac, Rom. (Szaszfellak); pop. 13; 62 km NE of Cluj; 47°05'/24°15'; HSL.

Feled, see Jesenske.

Feledince, see Jesenske.

Felfalu, Cz.; 114 km NE of Bratislava; 48°36'/18°29'; HSL. This town was located on a pre-World War I map, but does not appear in contemporary gazetteers.

Felgyogy, see Geoagiu.

Felicjanow, Pol.; 26 km ENE of Lodz; 51°46'/19°50'; PHP1.

Felicjanow Nowy, Pol.; pop. 8; 26 km E of Lodz; 51°45'/19°50'.

Felixdorf, Aus.; pop. 2; 45 km S of Wien; 47°53'/16°14'.

Felizienthal, Ukr.; pop. 20; 94 km WNW of Chernovtsy; 48°35'/24°45'. This town was located on an interwar map of Poland but does not appear in contemporary gazetteers. Map coordinates are approximate.

Felk, see Velka Pri Poprade.

Felka, see Velka Pri Poprade.

Fellbach, Germ.; 6 km NE of Stuttgart; 48°48'/09°17'; PHGBW.

Fellheim, Germ.; pop. 20; 107 km WSW of Munchen; 48°05'/10°09'; EJ, GUM3, GUM5, HSL, HSL2, JGFF, PHGB.

Fellin, see Viljandi.

Felling, Aus.; 88 km NW of Wien; 48°52'/15°48'; HSL.

Felnemet, Hung.; pop. 23; 38 km SW of Miskolc; 47°56'/20°22'.

Felpec, Hung.; pop. 12; 107 km W of Budapest; 47°31'/17°36'.

Fels, see Fels am Wagram.

Fels am Wagram, Aus. (Fels); pop. 3; 50 km WNW of Wien; 48°26'/15°49'.

Felsberg, Germ.; pop. 98; 126 km NNE of Frankfurt am Main; 51°08'/09°25'; GUM5, ISH1, LDS.

Felshevisho, see Viseu de Sus.

Felshtin, see Gvardeyskoye.

Felshtyn, see Skelivka.

Felsoabrany, Hung.; pop. 48; 26 km S of Miskolc; 47°54'/20°41'; HSL.

Felso Apsa, see Verkhneye Vodyanoye.

Felsoapsa, see Verkhneye Vodyanoye.

Felsoban, see Ban.

Felsobanya, see Sajoszentpeter.

Felso Batka, see Batka.

Felsoberecki, Hung.; pop. 10; 75 km NE of Miskolc; 48°22'/21°42'.

Felsoberekszo, see Birsau de Sus.

Felsobisztra, see Verkhnyaya Bystra.

Felsobisztre, see Nizhne Bystraya.

Felsocece, Hung.; pop. 3; 45 km NE of Miskolc; 48°22'/21°12'.

Felsodabas, see Felsodobos.

Felsoderna, see Derna.

Felsodobos, Hung. (Felsodabas); pop. 36; 69 km WSW of Budapest; 47°26'/18°07'; LDS.

Felsodobsza, Hung.; pop. 14; 32 km NE of Miskolc; 48°16'/21°04'.

Felsodorgicse, Hung.; pop. 2; 82 km NE of Nagykanizsa; 46°55'/17°43'.

Felsoegregy, see Agris.

Felsogagy, Hung.; pop. 23; 45 km NNE of Miskolc; 48°26'/21°01'; HSL.

Felsogalla, Hung.; pop. 192; 50 km W of Budapest; 47°33'/18°27'; AMG, PHH.

Felsogod, Hung.; pop. 149; 26 km N of Budapest; 47°42'/19°09'; GUM5, PHH.

Felsohahot, see Hahot.

Felsohidegpatak, see Verkhne Studenyy.

Felsohrabonicza, HSL. This pre-World War I community was not found in BGN gazetteers.

Felsoilosva, see Tirlisua.

Felsoireg, Hung.; pop. 62; PHH. This town was not found in BGN gazetteers under the given spelling.

Felsoiszkaz, see Iszkaz.

Felsojanosfa, Hung.; pop. 4; 56 km NW of Nagykanizsa; 46°51'/16°34'.

Felsojozsa, see Jozsa.

Felsokalinfalva, see Calinesti II.

Felsokalocsa, see Negrovets.

Felsokelecseny, Hung.; pop. 3; 38 km NW of Miskolc; 48°22'/20°36'.

Felsolapos, HSL. This pre-World War I community was not found in BGN gazetteers.

Felsomarosujvar, see Uioara de Sus.

Felsomera, Hung.; pop. 34; 45 km NNE of Miskolc; 48°22'/21°09'.

Felsomezos, see Campani.

Felsomindszent, Hung.; pop. 7; 88 km ESE of Nagykanizsa; 46°13'/18°04'; LDS.

Felsomislye, see Vysna Mysla.

Felsomocsolad, Hung.; pop. 11; 69 km ENE of Nagykanizsa; 46°35'/17°50'.

Felsomonoster, see Manasturel.

Felsonana, Hung.; pop. 5; 120 km ENE of Nagykanizsa; 46°28'/18°32'.

Felsonyarad, Hung.; pop. 18; 32 km NW of Miskolc; 48°20'/20°36'; HSL, JGFF.

Felsonyarto, see Stina.

Felsonyek, Hung.; pop. 14; 101 km SSW of Budapest; 46°47'/18°18'.

Felsoors, Hung.; pop. 5; 94 km NE of Nagykanizsa; 47°01'/17°57'.

Felsopahok, Hung.; pop. 4; 45 km N of Nagykanizsa; 46°47'/17°10'.

Felsopaty, Hung.; pop. 6; 107 km N of Nagykanizsa; 47°19'/16°56'.

Felsopenc, see Penc.

Felsopeteny, Hung.; pop. 6; 45 km N of Budapest; 47°53'/19°12'.

Felsorajk, Hung.; pop. 7; 38 km N of Nagykanizsa; 46°41'/17°00'.

Felsoregec, Hung.; pop. 21; JGFF. This town was not found in BGN gazetteers under the given spelling.

Felsoremete, see Vysne Remety.

Felsorepa, see Ripa de Sus.

Felsorevisce, HSL. This pre-World War I community was not found in BGN gazetteers.

Felsoreviscse, see Vysne Revistia.

Felsoribnycze, see Vysna Rybnica.

Felsorona, see Rona de Sus.

Felsoronok, Hung.; pop. 3; 82 km NW of Nagykanizsa; 46°59'/16°21'.

Felsosajo, see Vysna Slana.

Felsosegesd, Hung.; pop. 27; 32 km ESE of Nagykanizsa; 46°21'/17°21'.

Felsosofalu, see Ocna de Sus.

Felsoszek, see Sag.

Felso Szeli, see Horne Saliby.

Felsoszeli, see Horne Saliby.

Felso Szelistye, see Salistea de Sus.

Felsoszelistye, see Salistea de Sus.

Felsoszelt, see Horne Saliby.

Felsoszemenye, Hung.; pop. 30; 32 km W of Nagykanizsa; 46°28'/16°38'.

Felsoszentmarton, Hung.; pop. 4; 88 km SE of Nagykanizsa; 45°51'/17°42'.

Felsoszinever, see Sinevir.

Felsoszocs, see Suciu de Sus.

Felsoszopor, see Supuru de Sus.

Felsoszovat, Rom.; 32 km E of Cluj; 46°46'/23°58'; HSL. This town was located on a pre-World War I map, but does not appear in contemporary gazetteers.

Felsoszucs, see Suciu de Sus.

Felso Szuha, see Szuhafo.

Felsoszuha, see Szuhafo.

Felsotarkany, Hung.; pop. 7; 32 km SW of Miskolc; 47°58'/20°25'.

Felsotatarlaka, see Tartaria.

Felsotokes, see Vysny Klatov.

Felsotold, Hung.; pop. 4; 69 km NNE of Budapest; 47°58'/19°37'.

Felsovadasz, Hung.; pop. 24; 38 km N of Miskolc; 48°22'/20°56'.

Felsovaradja, see Oarta de Sus.

Felsovizniecze, see Nizhnyaya Viznitse.

Felsoviznieczee, HSL. This pre-World War I community was not found in BGN gazetteers.

Felsozsolca, Hung. (Faluzsolcza); pop. 65; 6 km E of Miskolc; 48°06'/20°52'; HSL, PHH.

Felszopor, Hung.; pop. 3; 120 km N of Nagykanizsa; 47°27'/16°49'.

Felsztein, see Skelivka.

Felsztin, see Skelivka.

Felsztyn, see Skelivka.

Felvincz, see Vintul de Sus.

Fenesel, see Finisel.

Fensel, see Finisel.

Fenyeslitke, Hung.; pop. 58; 94 km ENE of Miskolc; 48°16'/22°06'; HSL, LDS, PHH.

Fenyofalva, see Brad.

Fenyofo, Hung.; pop. 3; 101 km WSW of Budapest; 47°21'/17°46'.

Feodosia, see Feodosiya.

Feodosiia, see Feodosiya.

Feodosiya, Ukr. (Caffa, Feodosia, Feodosiia, Feodosya, Kaffa, Oaffa, Theodosia); pop. 3,248; 101 km ENE of Simferopol; 45°02'/35°23'; EJ, GUM3, GUM4, HSL, HSL2, JGFF, SF.

Feodosja, see Feodosiya.

Feodosya, see Feodosiya.

Ferdinand, see Mikhaylovgrad.

Ferdinandovac, Yug.; pop. 10; 94 km NE of Zagreb; 46°03'/17°12'.

Ferencztelep, see Pocskai.

Ferest, see Feresti.

Feresti, Rom. (Fejerfalva, Ferest); pop. 31; 126 km N of Cluj; 47°50'/23°57'; SM.

Fericanci, Yug.; pop. 14; 157 km E of Zagreb; 45°32'/17°59'.

Fericea, Rom.; pop. 4; 75 km NNW of Cluj; 47°24'/23°24'.

Ferndorf, Germ.; 75 km ENE of Koln; 50°58'/08°00'; GED.

Ferneziu, Rom.; pop. 31; 107 km N of Cluj; 47°41'/23°38'.

Fersig, Rom.; pop. 15; 88 km NNW of Cluj; 47°32'/23°23'.

Fertoendred, Hung.; pop. 6; 139 km N of Nagykanizsa; 47°36'/16°55'.

Fertoszentmiklos, Hung.; pop. 62; 133 km N of Nagykanizsa; 47°35'/16°53'; PHH.

Fertoszeplak, Hung.; pop. 1; 139 km N of Nagykanizsa; 47°37'/16°50'.

Feshtelitsa, Mold. (Festelita); pop. 16; 75 km ESE of Kishinev; 46°32'/29°34'.

Festelita, see Feshtelitsa.

Festenberg, see Twardogora.

Feteshty, Ukr. (Fetesti); pop. 39; 88 km E of Chernovtsy; 48°10'/27°05'.

Fetesti, see Feteshty.

Feuchtwangen, Germ.; pop. 46; 62 km SW of Nurnberg; 49°10'/10°20'; CAHJP, GUM5, HSL, HSL2, JGFF, LDS, PHGB.

Feudenheim, Germ.; pop. 49; 75 km S of Frankfurt am Main; 49°29'/08°27'; LDS, PHGBW.

Feuerbach, Germ. PHGBW. A number of towns share this name. It was not possible to determine from available information which one is being referenced.

Fiatfalva, see Filia.

Fiddichow, see Widuchowa.

Filakovo, Cz. (Fulek); pop. 248; 114 km SW of Kosice; 48°16'/19°50'; HSL, HSL2, LDL, LDS.

Filea, Rom. (Fulehaz); pop. 106; 101 km ENE of Cluj; 46°56'/24°54'.

Filehne, see Wielen.

Filesti, Rom.; 182 km NE of Bucuresti; 45°27'/27°59'; GUM3.

Filia, Rom. (Fiatfalva); pop. 2; 170 km ESE of Cluj; 46°09'/25°37'.

Filibe, see Plovdiv.

Filipec, see Pilipets.

Filipetz, see Pilipets.

Filipkowce, see Pilipche.

Filipova, see Filipow.

Filipow, Pol. (Filipova); pop. 280; 120 km NNW of Bialystok; 54°11'/22°37'; HSL, JGFF, LDL, LDS, PHP4, POCEM, SF, YB.

Filipowice, Pol.; pop. 28; 62 km ESE of Krakow; 49°51'/20°44'.

Filipowka, Pol.; pop. 8; 62 km ESE of Warszawa; 51°56'/21°48'.

Finisel, Rom. (Fenesel, Fensel, Kisfenes); 19 km SW of Cluj; 46°41'/23°25'; HSL.

Finke, Hung.; pop. 23; 26 km N of Miskolc; 48°17'/20°45'.

Finthen, Germ.; 45 km SW of Frankfurt am Main;

49°59'/08°10'; GUM5.

Firiza, Rom. (Alsofernezely); pop. 10; 114 km N of Cluj; 47°45'/23°36'.

Firleev, *see* Lipovka.

Firlej, Pol.; pop. 180; 38 km NNW of Lublin; 51°33'/22°29'; AMG, GA, GUM5, LDS, PHP4.

Firlej (near Radom), Pol.; pop. 53; 101 km W of Lublin; 51°26'/21°11'.

Firlejow, *see* Lipovka.

Firlejowka, *see* Firleyuvka.

Firleyuvka, Ukr. (Firlejowka); pop. 63; 50 km ENE of Lvov; 49°53'/24°38'.

Firminis, Rom. (Furmenyes); pop. 2; 62 km NW of Cluj; 47°15'/23°08'; HSL.

Firnitz, Aus.; 101 km SW of Graz; 46°34'/14°17'; HSL. This town was located on a pre-World War I map, but does not appear in contemporary gazetteers.

Firtusu, Rom.; pop. 5; 126 km ESE of Cluj; 46°25'/25°09'.

Fischach, Germ.; pop. 127; 69 km W of Munchen; 48°17'/10°40'; AMG, GED, HSL, HSL2, JGFF, PHGB.

Fischamend Markt, Aus.; pop. 19; 19 km ESE of Wien; 48°07'/16°36'.

Fischbach, Germ.; pop. 153; 69 km ESE of Nurnberg; 49°10'/11°57'.

Fischbachau, Germ.; pop. 1; 56 km SE of Munchen; 47°43'/11°57'.

Fischborn, Germ.; pop. 24; 56 km NE of Frankfurt am Main; 50°23'/09°18'.

Fischingen, Germ. BGN lists two possible localities with this name located at 47°39'/07°36' and 48°23'/08°41'. PHGBW.

Fitkow, *see* Fitkuv.

Fitkuv, Ukr. (Fitkow); pop. 21; 107 km WNW of Chernovtsy; 48°42'/24°36'.

Fiuk, Pol.; pop. 5; 75 km ENE of Krakow; 50°08'/20°57'.

Fiume, *see* Rijeka.

Fizesu Gherlii, Rom. (Fizesul Gherlei); pop. 38; 38 km NE of Cluj; 47°01'/23°59'.

Fizesul Gherlei, *see* Fizesu Gherlii.

Flacht, Germ.; pop. 40; 56 km WNW of Frankfurt am Main; 50°21'/08°03'.

Fladungen, Germ.; 114 km NE of Frankfurt am Main; 50°31'/10°10'; PHGB.

Flamanzeni, *see* Flamynzeny.

Flamersheim, Germ.; pop. 87; 45 km S of Koln; 50°37'/06°51'; GED.

Flammersfeld, Germ.; pop. 3; 56 km ESE of Koln; 50°38'/07°33'.

Flamynzeny, Mold. (Flamanzeni); pop. 1; 82 km WNW of Kishinev; 47°30'/28°04'.

Flatau, *see* Zlotow.

Flatow, *see* Zlotow.

Flehingen, Germ.; pop. 83; 50 km NW of Stuttgart; 49°06'/08°48'; LDS, PHGBW.

Flensburg, Germ.; pop. 61; 146 km NNW of Hamburg; 54°47'/09°26'; GUM5.

Flieden, Germ.; pop. 50; 75 km NE of Frankfurt am Main; 50°25'/09°34'; AMG, JGFF.

Fliesteden, Germ.; 19 km WNW of Koln; 50°59'/06°44'; GED.

Floisdorf, Germ. (Florisdorf); 45 km SSW of Koln; 50°38'/06°37'; PHP2.

Flondora, Rom.; pop. 10; 107 km NW of Iasi; 48°00'/27°02'.

Flonheim, Germ.; pop. 51; 56 km SW of Frankfurt am Main; 49°47'/08°02'; JGFF.

Florentynowo, Pol. (Narty); 50 km NW of Warszawa; 52°38'/20°36'; GA.

Floreshty, Mold. (Floresti, Floresti Noui); pop. 380; 107 km NNW of Kishinev; 47°53'/28°17'; GUM4.

Floresti, *see* Floreshty.

Floresti Cluj, Rom.; pop. 28; 13 km SW of Cluj; 46°44'/23°29'.

Floresti Noui, *see* Floreshty.

Floresti Sat, Mold.; pop. 149; 114 km NNW of Kishinev; 47°54'/28°18'.

Floridsdorf, Aus.; 13 km N of Wien; 48°15'/16°24'; GUM3, GUM4, GUM5.

Florina, Greece; pop. 293; 126 km W of Thessaloniki; 40°48'/21°26'; EDRD.

Florisdorf, *see* Floisdorf.

Florsheim, Germ.; pop. 45; 19 km SW of Frankfurt am Main; 50°01'/08°26'; AMG, GUM5.

Floryjanowa, *see* Narol.

Florynka, Pol.; pop. 24; 94 km ESE of Krakow; 49°34'/20°59'.

Floss, Germ.; pop. 23; 88 km NE of Nurnberg; 49°44'/12°17'; CAHJP, EJ, HSL, HSL2, LDS, PHGB.

Flossenburg, Germ.; pop. 101 km NE of Nurnberg; 49°44'/12°21'; GUM3, GUM4, GUM5, PHP3.

Flotzheim, Germ.; pop. 75 km S of Nurnberg; 48°51'/10°49'; PHGB.

Focsani, Rom.; pop. 163 km NNE of Bucuresti; 45°42'/27°11'; EJ, GUM3, GUM4, HSL, JGFF, LDL, PHR1.

Fodorhaz, Rom. (Fodorhaza); 246 km SW of Cluj; 45°27'/20°59'; HSL.

Fodorhaza, *see* Fodorhaz.

Fogaras, *see* Fagaras.

Fohnsdorf, Aus.; pop. 6; 62 km W of Graz; 47°12'/14°41'.

Foi, Rom. (Folyfalva); pop. 4; 82 km ESE of Cluj; 46°29'/24°36'; HSL.

Fokinsk, USSR; pop. 258; This town was not found in BGN gazetteers under the given spelling.

Fokovci, Yug.; pop. 6; 107 km N of Zagreb; 46°44'/16°16'.

Fokto, Hung.; pop. 37; 101 km WNW of Szeged; 46°31'/18°55'.

Foldeak, Hung.; pop. 15; 26 km NE of Szeged; 46°19'/20°30'.

Foldes, Hung.; pop. 269; 101 km SE of Miskolc; 47°18'/21°22'; AMG, HSL, LDL, LDS, PHH.

Foldra, *see* Feldru.

Foldvar, HSL. A number of towns share this name. It was not possible to determine from available information which one is being referenced.

Folmava, Cz.; pop. 9; 146 km SW of Praha; 49°21'/12°51'.

Foltesti, Rom.; pop. 100; 163 km SSE of Iasi; 45°45'/28°03'; GUM4, PHR1.

Folusz, GA. A number of towns share this name. It was not possible to determine from available information which one is being referenced.

Folvark, *see* Strutin.

Folvarki, *see* Strutin.

Folvark Karasin, Ukr. (Forwarki Wielkie?); pop. 41; 101 km N of Rovno; 51°26'/26°47'.

Folwarki, *see* Monastyriska.

Folwarki Male, *see* Strutin.

Folwark Raducki, Pol.; pop. 27; 56 km NW of Czestochowa; 51°13'/18°46'.

Folyas, Hung.; 45 km SE of Miskolc; 47°48'/21°08'; HSL.

Folyfalva, *see* Foi.

Fonovice, Cz.; pop. 126 km NE of Brno; 49°46'/18°09'; HSL.

Fony, Hung.; pop. 27; 50 km NE of Miskolc; 48°24'/21°18'.

Fonyed, Hung.; pop. 3; 32 km NE of Nagykanizsa; 46°38'/17°16'.

Fonyod, Hung.; pop. 16; 50 km NE of Nagykanizsa; 46°44'/17°33'.

Forbach, Germ.; 62 km WSW of Stuttgart; 48°41'/08°21'; GUM3, HSL.

Forchheim, Germ.; pop. 79; 32 km N of Nurnberg; 49°43'/11°04'; AMG, CAHJP, GUM3, GUM5, JGFF, PHGB.

Fordon, Pol.; pop. 100; 114 km NE of Poznan; 53°09'/18°11'; CAHJP, JGFF, PHP4.

Forgacskut, *see* Ticu.

Forgolany, Hung.; 163 km E of Miskolc; 47°58'/23°01'; HSL. This town was located on a pre-World War I map, but does not appear in contemporary gazetteers.

Fornad, Hung.; 101 km ENE of Nagykanizsa; 46°41'/18°17'; HSL.

Foroeucs, LDL. This pre-World War I community was not found in BGN gazetteers.

Frankfurt am Main, Germany: Marketplace with Börneplatz Synagogue and cemetery in background.

Forostna, Ukr.; pop. 19; 38 km ENE of Chernovtsy; 48°19'/26°27'.

Forro, Hung.; pop. 57; 38 km NNE of Miskolc; 48°19'/21°05'; AMG, HSL, PHH.

Forroencs, HSL. This pre-World War I community was not found in BGN gazetteers.

Forst, Germ.; pop. 205; 120 km ESE of Berlin; 51°44'/14°38'.

Forteni, Rom.; pop. 5; 133 km ESE of Cluj; 46°18'/25°14'.

Forth, Germ.; pop. 44; 19 km NNE of Nurnberg; 49°36'/11°14'; AMG, JGFF, LDS, PHGB.

Forwarki Wielkie, *possibly* Folvark Karasin.

Fot, Hung.; pop. 40; 19 km NNE of Budapest; 47°37'/19°12'.

Fragel, HSL. This pre-World War I community was not found in BGN gazetteers.

Frain, *see* Vranov nad Toplou.

Framersheim, Germ.; pop. 28; 50 km SSW of Frankfurt am Main; 49°46'/08°11'; GUM5.

Frampol, Pol. (Franpol); pop. 1,465; 69 km S of Lublin; 50°41'/22°40'; AMG, COH, EDRD, GUM4, GUM5, HSL, LDL, LDS, LYV, POCEM, SF, YB.

Franconia; Not a town, but a section of the German state of Bavaria.

Franken; *See* Franconia.

Frankenau, Germ.; pop. 55; 120 km N of Frankfurt am Main; 51°06'/08°56'; LDS.

Frankenberg, Germ.; pop. 120; 114 km N of Frankfurt am Main; 51°04'/08°48'; GUM5, LDS.

Frankenthal, Germ.; pop. 300; 69 km S of Frankfurt am Main; 49°32'/08°21'; GED, GUM5, HSL.

Frankenwinheim, Germ.; pop. 51; 69 km WNW of Nurnberg; 49°53'/10°19'; GUM5, HSL, PHGB.

Frankershausen, Germ.; pop. 27; 133 km S of Hannover; 51°14'/09°55'; LDS.

Frankfort on the Main, *see* Frankfurt am Main.

Frankfurt am Hochst, Germ.; pop. 200; 13 km WSW of Frankfurt am Main; 50°06'/08°32'.

Frankfurt am Main, Germ. (Frankfort on the Main); pop. 29,385; 150 km NNW of Stuttgart; 50°07'/08°41'; AMG, CAHJP, EDRD, GED, GUM3, GUM4, GUM5, GUM6, HSL, HSL2, ISH2, ISH3, JGFF, LDL, LDS, PHGBW, PHP1, PHP2, YB.

Frankfurt am Rodelheim, Germ.; pop. 100; 6 km WSW of Frankfurt am Main; 50°07'/08°35'.

Frankfurt an der Oder, Germ.; pop. 800; 82 km E of Berlin; 52°21'/14°33'; CAHJP, GUM5, HSL, HSL2, LDS, PHP1.

Frankisch Crumbach, Germ.; pop. 55; 45 km SSE of Frankfurt am Main; 49°45'/08°52'.

Frankova, *see* Sec.

Frankstadt, *see* Frenstat Pod Radhostem.

Franpol, *see* Frampol.

Frantiskov, *see* Benesov nad Ploucnici.

Frantiskovy Lazne, Cz.; pop. 95; 150 km W of Praha; 50°07'/12°22'.

Franusin, Pol.; pop. 4; 114 km NNE of Przemysl; 50°33'/23°52'.

Franzburg, Germ.; pop. 5; 50 km ENE of Rostock; 54°11'/12°53'.

Frasan, *see* Frasin.

Frasin, Rom. (Frasan); pop. 156; 139 km WNW of Iasi; 47°32'/25°48'; JGFF, PHR2.

Frastak, *see* Hlohovec.

Frata, Rom. (Magyarfrata); pop. 36; 32 km E of Cluj; 46°42'/24°03'; HSL.

Fratautii Noi, Rom. (Fratautii Noui, Fratuatii Noui); pop. 104; 157 km WNW of Iasi; 47°57'/25°51'.

Fratautii Noui, *see* Fratautii Noi.

Fratautii pe Suceava, Rom.; pop. 40; 150 km WNW of Iasi;

47°54'/25°53'.

Fratautii Vechi, Rom.; pop. 28; 150 km WNW of Iasi; 47°54'/25°53'; AMG.

Fratuatii Noui, *see* Fratautii Noi.

Frauenberg, Aus.; 101 km WNW of Graz; 47°35'/14°23'; COH, JGFF.

Frauenburg, *see* Saldus.

Frauendorf, *see* Babiak.

Frauenkirchen, Aus. (Boldogasszony); pop. 386; 56 km ESE of Wien; 47°50'/16°55'; AMG, EJ, HSL, LDL, LDS.

Fraulautern, Germ.; pop. 37; 157 km SW of Frankfurt am Main; 49°20'/06°46'.

Fraustadt, *see* Wschowa.

Fraydorf, *see* Novoselovskoye.

Frechen, Germ.; pop. 105; 13 km WSW of Koln; 50°55'/06°49'; AMG.

Freckenhorst, Germ.; pop. 12; 133 km SW of Hannover; 51°55'/07°58'.

Fredropol, Pol.; pop. 10; 19 km S of Przemysl; 49°42'/22°45'.

Freiberg, *see* Pribor.

Freiburg, *see* Freiburg im Breisgau.

Freiburg im Breisgau, Germ. (Freiburg); pop. 1,399; 133 km SW of Stuttgart; 48°00'/07°51'; AMG, EDRD, EJ, GED, GUM3, GUM5, HSL, JGFF, LDL, LDS, PHGBW.

Freienohl, Germ.; pop. 2; 94 km NE of Koln; 51°22'/08°10'.

Freienwalde, Germ.; pop. 34; 56 km NE of Berlin; 52°47'/14°02'. *See also* Bad Freienwalde.

Freilassing, Germ.; 107 km ESE of Munchen; 47°51'/12°59'; GUM3.

Frei Laubersheim, Germ.; pop. 11; 62 km SW of Frankfurt am Main; 49°48'/07°54'.

Freising, Germ.; 32 km N of Munchen; 48°24'/11°44'; PHGB.

Freistadt, Aus.; 133 km NE of Salzburg; 48°30'/14°30'; HSL2. *See also* Karvina.

Freistett, Germ. (Neu Freistett); pop. 30; 88 km WSW of Stuttgart; 48°40'/07°57'; PHGBW.

Freital, Germ.; pop. 18; 94 km ESE of Leipzig; 51°01'/13°39'.

Freiwaldau, *see* Jesenik.

Frelichow, Pol.; pop. 15; 82 km WSW of Krakow; 49°55'/18°48'.

Fremdingen, Germ.; 75 km SSW of Nurnberg; 48°58'/10°28'; PHGB.

Frensdorf, Germ.; 45 km NNW of Nurnberg; 49°49'/10°52'; JGFF, PHGB.

Frenstat, *see* Frenstat Pod Radhostem.

Frenstat Pod Radhostem, Cz. (Frankstadt, Frenstat); pop. 21; 120 km NE of Brno; 49°33'/18°13'.

Freren, Germ.; pop. 17; 146 km W of Hannover; 52°29'/07°33'; GED, LDS.

Freudenberg, Germ.; 62 km ESE of Frankfurt am Main; 49°45'/09°19'; PHGBW.

Freudenburg, Germ.; pop. 60; 157 km S of Koln; 49°33'/06°32'; GUM5.

Freudenstadt, Germ.; pop. 6; 69 km SW of Stuttgart; 48°26'/08°25'; PHGBW.

Freudental, Germ.; pop. 90; GUM3, PHGBW. A number of towns share this name. It was not possible to determine from available information which one is being referenced.

Freudenthal, Germ.; 32 km NNW of Stuttgart; 49°01'/09°03'; CAHJP, GUM3, GUM4, YB. *See also* Bruntal.

Freuenburg, *see* Saldus.

Freystadt, Germ.; pop. 45 km ESE of Nurnberg; 49°12'/11°30'; CAHJP, PHGB.

Freyung, Germ.; pop. 4; 163 km NE of Munchen; 48°48'/13°33'.

Frickhofen, Germ.; pop. 24; 62 km WNW of Frankfurt am Main; 50°30'/08°01'.

Fricovce, Cz. (Frics); 38 km NW of Kosice; 49°01'/20°58'; HSL.

Frics, *see* Fricovce.

Fridman, *see* Frydman.

Fridolfing, Germ.; pop. 2; 94 km E of Munchen; 48°00'/12°49'.

Fridrikhshtadt, *see* Jaunjelgava.

Friedberg, Germ.; 38 km N of Frankfurt am Main; 50°21'/08°46'; CAHJP, EJ, GED, GUM3, GUM4, HSL, JGFF, LDS.

Friedberg (Baden), Germ.; 88 km SSE of Stuttgart; 48°00'/09°25'; PHGBW.

Friedberg an der Ach, Germ.; 50 km WNW of Munchen; 48°21'/10°59'; PHGB.

Friedburg, Aus.; 32 km NNE of Salzburg; 48°01'/13°15'; HSL.

Friedeberg, Germ.; pop. 400; A number of towns share this name. It was not possible to determine from available information which one is being referenced. *See also* Strzelce Krajenskie.

Friedek, *see* Frydek.

Friedensfeld, *see* Mirnopolye.

Friedland, *see* Korfantow.

Friedland (East Prussia), *see* Pravdinsk.

Friedrichsburg, Germ.; 45 km SW of Hannover; 52°08'/09°11'; PHGBW.

Friedrichsgmund, Germ.; 38 km S of Nurnberg; 49°11'/11°01'; PHGB.

Friedrichshafen, Germ.; 133 km SSE of Stuttgart; 47°39'/09°29'; EDRD.

Friedrichshof, JGFF. A number of towns share this name. It was not possible to determine from available information which one is being referenced.

Friedrichstadt, Germ.; pop. 35; 114 km NW of Hamburg; 54°22'/09°05'; CAHJP, GED, LDS. *See also* Jaunjelgava. This town name is more frequently associated with Jaunjelgava, Latvia.

Friedrusk, *see* Piedruja.

Frielendorf, Germ.; pop. 85; 114 km NNE of Frankfurt am Main; 50°59'/09°20'; LDS.

Friesen, Germ.; 50 km N of Nurnberg; 49°50'/11°02'; JGFF, PHGB.

Friesenhausen, Germ.; 88 km NW of Nurnberg; 50°10'/10°29'; PHGB.

Friesenheim, Germ.; pop. 48; 107 km SW of Stuttgart; 48°22'/07°53'; JGFF, LDS, PHGBW.

Friesheim, Germ.; 26 km SSW of Koln; 50°45'/06°46'; GED.

Friesoythe, Germ.; pop. 4; 146 km WNW of Hannover; 53°01'/07°51'; GED.

Frille, Germ.; pop. 11; 50 km WSW of Hannover; 52°20'/09°00'; GED.

Frimmersdorf, Germ.; pop. 7; 32 km WNW of Koln; 51°03'/06°35'; GED.

Fristik, *see* Frysztak.

Fritzlar, Germ.; pop. 140; 126 km N of Frankfurt am Main; 51°08'/09°17'; LDS.

Frohnhausen, Germ.; 82 km N of Frankfurt am Main; 50°47'/08°37'; LDS.

Frohnleiten, Aus.; pop. 6; 32 km NNW of Graz; 47°16'/15°19'.

Froienburg, *see* Saldus.

Frombork, Pol.; 62 km ENE of Gdansk; 54°22'/19°41'; LDS.

Frondenberg, Germ.; pop. 23; 82 km NE of Koln; 51°28'/07°46'; GUM3.

Fruhbuss, *see* Prebuz.

Frumosica, *see* Frumushika.

Frumosu, Rom. (Frumosul); pop. 88; 157 km WNW of Iasi; 47°37'/25°39'; AMG.

Frumosul, *see* Frumosu.

Frumushika, Mold. (Frumosica, Frumusica); pop. 57; 120 km NW of Kishinev; 47°57'/28°07'; GUM4, HSL, PHR1.

Frumusica, *see* Frumushika.

Frumusica Noua, *see* Krasnyanka.

Frumusica Veche, *see* Staroselye.

Frunza, Rom.; 94 km SSW of Cluj; 46°08'/22°47'; PHR1.

Frydek, Cz. (Friedek); pop. 307; 133 km NE of Brno; 49°41'/18°21'; HSL.

Frydek Mistek, HSL. This pre-World War I community was not found in BGN gazetteers.

Frydlant, Cz.; pop. 26; 101 km NNE of Praha; 50°55'/15°05'.

Frydman, Pol. (Fridman); pop. 20; 75 km SSE of Krakow;

49°27'/20°14'; HSL.

Frydrychowice, Pol.; pop. 21; 38 km SW of Krakow; 49°55'/19°26'.

Fryedek, Germ. HSL2. This pre-World War I community was not found in BGN gazetteers.

Frystat, see Karvina.

Fryszerka, Pol.; pop. 20; 50 km NNE of Czestochowa; 51°08'/19°29'.

Frysztak, Pol. (Fristik); pop. 1,500; 82 km W of Przemysl; 49°50'/21°37'; AMG, COH, EGRS, GA, GUM3, GUM4, GUM5, HSL, JGFF, PHP3, SF.

Fryvaldov, see Jesenik.

Fuchsstadt, Germ.; 88 km E of Frankfurt am Main; 50°06'/09°56'; HSL, HSL2.

Fuerstenberg, see Eisenhuttenstadt.

Fuerth, see Furth.

Fuge, HSL. This pre-World War I community was not found in BGN gazetteers.

Fughiu, Rom. (Fugyi); pop. 3; 126 km W of Cluj; 47°03'/22°03'.

Fugod, Hung.; 38 km NE of Miskolc; 48°19'/21°07'; HSL.

Fugyi, see Fughiu.

Fugyivasarhely, see Osorheiu.

Fujna, see Fuyna.

Fulda, Germ.; pop. 1,100; 88 km NE of Frankfurt am Main; 50°33'/09°40'; AMG, CAHJP, EDRD, EJ, GED, GUM4, HSL, HSL2, JGFF, LDL, PHGBW, YB.

Fule, Hung.; pop. 4; 82 km SW of Budapest; 47°03'/18°15'.

Fulehaz, see Filea.

Fulek, see Filakovo.

Fulesd, Hung. (Velezd?); pop. 50; 146 km E of Miskolc; 48°01'/22°41'; HSL, PHH.

Fulnek, Cz.; pop. 35; 107 km NE of Brno; 49°43'/17°55'.

Fulokercs, Hung.; pop. 6; 45 km NNE of Miskolc; 48°26'/21°07'.

Fulopfalu, HSL. This pre-World War I community was not found in BGN gazetteers.

Fulopfalva, see Pilipets.

Fulopszallas, Hung.; pop. 83; 82 km SSE of Budapest; 46°49'/19°15'; HSL, HSL2, PHH.

Fulpos, see Szatmarokorito.

Fulposdaroc, Hung.; pop. 8; 126 km E of Miskolc; 47°56'/22°30'; HSL.

Fundu Galbena, Mold.; pop. 11; 19 km SW of Kishinev; 46°53'/28°37'.

Fundukleewka, (Fundukleyevka); SF. This town was not found in BGN gazetteers under the given spelling.

Fundukleyevka, see Fundukleewka.

Fundul Moldovei, see Fundu Moldovei.

Fundu Moldovei, Rom. (Fandul Moldovei, Fundul Moldovei); pop. 107; 157 km NE of Cluj; 47°32'/25°24'.

Funduri, see Staryye Fundury.

Funfkirchen, see Pecs.

Furceni, see Furcheny.

Furcheny, Mold. (Furceni); pop. 30; 45 km N of Kishinev; 47°20'/28°56'.

Furfeld, Germ.; pop. 75; 62 km SW of Frankfurt am Main; 49°47'/07°54'.

Furged, Hung.; pop. 1; 101 km NE of Nagykanizsa; 46°43'/18°18'.

Furmanow, Pol.; pop. 7; 101 km ESE of Lodz; 51°12'/20°37'.

Furmany, Pol.; pop. 7; 88 km SSW of Lublin; 50°37'/21°48'.

Furmenyes, see Firminis.

Furstenau, Germ.; pop. 48; 133 km W of Hannover; 52°31'/07°43'.

Furstenberg, Germ.; pop. 82 km NNW of Berlin; 53°11'/13°09'; GUM5, LDS.

Furstenfeld, see Dzieczyna.

Furstenfeldbruck, Germ.; pop. 8; 26 km W of Munchen; 48°11'/11°15'; GUM3.

Furstenfelde, see Bolganymajor.

Furstenforst, see Burghaslach.

Furstenwalde, Germ.; pop. 150; 45 km ESE of Berlin;

52°22'/14°04'.

Furstenzell, Germ.; 139 km NE of Munchen; 48°32'/13°19'; GUM3.

Furta, Hung.; pop. 8; 120 km SE of Miskolc; 47°08'/21°28'; HSL, LDS.

Furth, Germ. (Fuerth); pop. 1,990; 6 km WNW of Nurnberg; 49°28'/11°00'; AMG, CAHJP, EDRD, EJ, GUM3, GUM4, GUM5, HSL, HSL2, JGFF, LDL, LDS, PHGB, PHGBW, PHP1.

Furth im Wald, Germ.; 126 km E of Nurnberg; 49°18'/12°51'; PHGB.

Furtwangen, Germ.; pop. 1; 114 km SSW of Stuttgart; 48°03'/08°12'; PHGBW.

Fussgonheim, Germ.; pop. 11; 75 km S of Frankfurt am Main; 49°28'/08°18'; GED.

Futoma, Pol.; pop. 58; 50 km W of Przemysl; 49°51'/22°08'; AMG, HSL.

Fuves, see Varzari.

Fuyna, Ukr. (Fujna); pop. 42; 26 km NW of Lvov; 50°02'/23°49'.

Fuzerkomlos, Hung.; pop. 4; 69 km NE of Miskolc; 48°31'/21°28'.

Fuzerradvany, Hung.; pop. 11; 75 km NE of Miskolc; 48°29'/21°32'.

Fuzes, Hung. BGN lists two possible localities with this name located at 46°52'/20°29' and 48°12'/21°40'. HSL.

Fuzesabony, Hung.; pop. 203; 50 km SSW of Miskolc; 47°45'/20°25'; HSL, LDS, PHH.

Fuzeser, see Vrbnica.

Fuzesgyarmat, Hung.; pop. 217; 114 km SSE of Miskolc; 47°06'/21°13'; HSL, LDS, PHH.

Fuzovka, Mold.; pop. 31; BGN lists two possible localities with this name located at 47°37'/28°49' and 47°45'/28°45'.

Fuzvolgy, Hung.; pop. 5; 19 km NNW of Nagykanizsa; 46°31'/16°57'.

Gabcikovo, Cz. (Bes); pop. 79; 45 km ESE of Bratislava; 47°54'/17°35'; HSL.

Gabin, Pol. (Gambin, Gombin); pop. 2,564; 75 km N of Lodz; 52°24'/19°44'; AMG, CAHJP, EDRD, EJ, GA, GUM3, GUM4, GUM5, GYLA, HSL, HSL2, JGFF, LYV, PHP1, PHP4, POCEM, SF, WS.

Gablitz, Aus.; pop. 9; 19 km W of Wien; 48°13'/16°09'.

Gabon, Pol.; pop. 3; 82 km SE of Krakow; 49°32'/20°35'.

Gaborjan, Hung.; pop. 12; 120 km SE of Miskolc; 47°14'/21°40'; LDS.

Gabrovo, Bulg.; 163 km ENE of Sofija; 42°52'/25°19'; GUM4.

Gabultow, Pol.; pop. 13; 50 km NE of Krakow; 50°17'/20°33'; HSL.

Gac, Pol.; pop. 29; HSL. A number of towns share this name. It was not possible to determine from available information which one is being referenced.

Gacs, Hung. PHH. This town was not found in BGN gazetteers under the given spelling.

Gacsaly, Hung.; pop. 68; 146 km E of Miskolc; 47°56'/22°46'.

Gac Sokola, Pol.; pop. 226; 62 km WSW of Bialystok; 53°05'/22°15'; PHP4.

Gad, see Geoagiu.

Gadac, (Hodiatch); LDL, SF. This town was not found in BGN gazetteers under the given spelling.

Gadalin, Rom.; pop. 10; 19 km NE of Cluj; 46°51'/23°51'.

Gadany, Hung.; pop. 10; 38 km ENE of Nagykanizsa; 46°31'/17°24'.

Gadebusch, Germ.; 75 km ENE of Hamburg; 53°42'/11°07'; LDS.

Gadiach, see Gadyach.

Gadna, Hung.; pop. 7; 38 km N of Miskolc; 48°24'/20°56'; HSL.

Gadoros, Hung.; pop. 13; 56 km NNE of Szeged; 46°40'/20°36'.

Gadyach, Ukr. (Gadiach, Hadziacz); pop. 1,764; 114 km SE of Konotop; 50°22'/34°00'; EJ, GUM4, JGFF.

Gaesti, Rom. (Gocs); 69 km WNW of Bucuresti; 44°43'/25°19'; GUM4, PHR1.

Gaflenz, Aus.; pop. 1; 107 km NW of Graz; 47°53'/14°43'.

Gagarin, USSR (Gzhatsk); pop. 276; 157 km SSW of Kalinin; 55°33'/35°00'.

Gaggenau, Germ.; pop. 8; 62 km W of Stuttgart; 48°48'/08°20'; PHGBW.

Gagybator, Hung.; pop. 14; 45 km N of Miskolc; 48°26'/20°57'.

Gagyvendegi, Hung.; pop. 7; 45 km N of Miskolc; 48°26'/20°59'.

Gaibach, Germ.; 75 km WNW of Nurnberg; 49°53'/10°14'; PHGB.

Gaiganz, Germ.; 32 km N of Nurnberg; 49°40'/11°08'; PHGB.

Gaiki, Lat.; pop. 1; 94 km WSW of Riga; 56°47'/22°35'.

Gailingen, Germ.; pop. 375; 126 km S of Stuttgart; 47°42'/08°45'; GED, GUM3, GUM4, HSL, JGFF, LDL, LDS, PHGBW, YB.

Gainfarn, Aus.; pop. 21; 32 km S of Wien; 47°57'/16°12'.

Gairing, *see* Gajary.

Gaischin, *see* Gayshin.

Gaisin, *see* Gaysin.

Gaissin, *see* Gaysin.

Gajar, *see* Gajary.

Gajary, Cz. (Gairing, Gajar); 45 km NNW of Bratislava; 48°28'/16°56'; AMG, HSL.

Gaje, Pol.; pop. 34; 26 km NNE of Przemysl; 49°57'/22°59'.

Gajec, GA. This town was not found in BGN gazetteers under the given spelling.

Gajecice, Pol.; pop. 8; 38 km NNW of Czestochowa; 51°05'/19°03'.

Gaje Nizne, *see* Gay Nizhniye.

Gaje Smolenskie, Pol.; pop. 23; Described in the *Black Book* as being in the Tarnopol region of Poland, this town was not found in BGN gazetteers.

Gaje Wielkie, Pol. PHP2. This town was not found in BGN gazetteers under the given spelling.

Gaje Wyzne, *see* Gay Nizhniye.

Gajkowice, Pol.; pop. 79; 32 km SE of Lodz; 51°30'/19°41'.

Gajsin, *see* Gaysin.

Galacs, *see* Golet.

Galambok, Hung.; pop. 2; 19 km NE of Nagykanizsa; 46°31'/17°08'.

Galanesti, Rom.; pop. 6; 157 km WNW of Iasi; 47°55'/25°48'.

Galanta, Cz.; pop. 3,473; 45 km ENE of Bratislava; 48°12'/17°43'; COH, EJ, GUM3, GUM4, GUM5, HSL, HSL2, LDL.

Galaseni, *see* Galashany.

Galashany, Mold. (Galaseni); pop. 25; 150 km WNW of Kishinev; 47°52'/27°20'.

Galati, Rom. (Galatz); 195 km NE of Bucuresti; 45°27'/28°03'; AMG, EJ, GUM3, GUM4, HSL, JGFF, PHR1.

Galatii Bistritei, Rom.; pop. 41; 62 km NE of Cluj; 46°59'/24°24'.

Galatz, *see* Galati.

Galautas, Rom.; pop. 183; 139 km ENE of Cluj; 46°55'/25°26'.

Galben, GUM4. This town was not found in BGN gazetteers under the given spelling.

Galczyn, Pol. PHP4. This town was not found in BGN gazetteers under the given spelling.

Galeny, Byel. (Haleny); pop. 9; 146 km WNW of Pinsk; 52°42'/24°11'.

Galeshty, *see* Galesti.

Galesti, Rom. (Galeshty, Nyaradgalfalva); 94 km ESE of Cluj; 46°31'/24°45'; HSL.

Galewice, Pol.; pop. 13; 88 km WNW of Czestochowa; 51°21'/18°15'; PHP1.

Galgaguta, Hung.; pop. 12; 45 km NNE of Budapest; 47°51'/19°24'.

Galgagyork, Hung. (Totgyork); pop. 6; 38 km NNE of Budapest; 47°44'/19°23'; LDS.

Galgaheviz, Hung.; pop. 8; 38 km NE of Budapest; 47°37'/19°34'.

Galgamacsa, Hung.; pop. 18; 32 km NE of Budapest; 47°42'/19°23'.

Galgau, Rom. (Almas Galgo, Galgo); pop. 121; 62 km N of Cluj; 47°17'/23°43'; PHR2.

Galgauska, Lat.; pop. 5; 150 km N of Daugavpils; 57°11'/26°34'.

Galgo, *see* Galgau.

Galgoc, *see* Hlohovec.

Galgocz, *see* Hlohovec.

Galibicy, USSR; EDRD. This town was not found in BGN gazetteers under the given spelling.

Galich, Ukr. (Chelitch, Halicz, Helitch); pop. 582; 101 km SE of Lvov; 49°07'/24°44'; AMG, CAHJP, COH, EGRS, EJ, HSL, JGFF, LDL, PHP2, PHP3, SF.

Galicia; Not a town, but a region that since World War II has been part of southern Poland and the Ukraine. Prior to 1772, it constituted the southern part of the Kingdom of Poland, then became part of the Austro-Hungarian Empire until the end of World War I. It was then returned to Poland until the end of World War II.

Galilesti, *see* Desantnoye.

Galina, *see* Galiniai.

Galiniai, Lith. (Galina); 26 km S of Vilnius; 54°30'/25°18'; AMG.

Galinovolya, Ukr. (Halinowola); pop. 29; 163 km WNW of Rovno; 51°25'/24°20'.

Galkovshchina, Byel. (Hatowszczyzna?); pop. 21; 157 km WNW of Vitebsk; 55°59'/28°08'.

Galkowek, Pol.; 19 km E of Lodz; 51°45'/19°44'; PHP1.

Galoc, *see* Hlohovec.

Galosfa, Hung.; pop. 6; 69 km ESE of Nagykanizsa; 46°15'/17°54'.

Galos Petrei, *see* Galospetreu.

Galos Petreu, *see* Galospetreu.

Galospetreu, Rom. (Galos Petrei, Galos Petreu, Galospetri); pop. 35; 133 km WNW of Cluj; 47°29'/22°13'; AMG, HSL.

Galospetri, *see* Galospetreu.

Galszecs, Hung.; 62 km ENE of Miskolc; 48°12'/21°37'; HSL, JGFF, LDL. This town was located on a pre-World War I map, but does not appear in contemporary gazetteers.

Galvacs, Hung.; pop. 5; 45 km N of Miskolc; 48°25'/20°47'; HSL.

Gamas, Hung.; pop. 37; 62 km NE of Nagykanizsa; 46°37'/17°46'.

Gambach, Germ.; pop. 68; 50 km N of Frankfurt am Main; 50°28'/08°44'; GUM5, JGFF.

Gambin, *see* Gabin.

Ganachevka, Ukr. (Ganachuv, Hanaczow); pop. 68; 38 km ESE of Lvov; 49°43'/24°25'; G'JM3, GUM4, GUM6.

Ganachuv, *see* Ganachevka.

Ganachuvka, Ukr. (Hanaczowka); pop. 37; 38 km ESE of Lvov; 49°42'/24°25'.

Ganack⎯, Germ.; 107 km NE of Munchen; 48°43'/12°41'; EDRD, GUM3, GUM5.

Ganaseny de Pedure, Mold. (Hanasenii de Padure); pop. 6; 82 km SSW of Kishinev; 46°21'/28°20'.

Gancheshty, *see* Kotovsk (Bessarabia).

Gancs, *see* Canciu.

Gandersheim, *see* Bad Gandersheim.

Gandesti, *see* Gindeshty.

Gangelt, Germ.; pop. 22; 69 km W of Koln; 50°59'/06°00'.

Gangura, Mold.; pop. 22; 38 km SE of Kishinev; 46°44'/29°01'.

Ganice, *see* Ganichi.

Ganicha, *see* Ganicsa.

Ganichi, Ukr. (Ganice, Ganics, Ganya); pop. 4,400; 157 km WSW of Chernovtsy; 48°08'/23°49'; GUM3, GUM5, LDL, SM.

Ganics, *see* Ganichi.

Ganicsa, (Ganicha, Ganits); COH, HSL, LYV. This town was not found in BGN gazetteers under the given spelling.

Ganits, *see* Ganicsa.

Gankovitsa, Ukr. (Hankowice); pop. 26; 150 km SSW of Lvov; 48°38'/23°03'.

Gankovtse, *see* Gankovtsy.

Gankovtsy, Ukr. (Gankovtse, Hankowce); pop. 82; 50 km WNW of Chernovtsy; 48°32'/25°25'.

Ganserndorf, Aus.; pop. 52; 32 km NE of Wien; 48°21'/16°44'.

Gantsevichi, Byel. (Hancewicze); pop. 485; 75 km N of Pinsk; 52°45'/26°26'; COH, EDRD, GUM5, HSL, LYV, SF.

Ganunin, Ukr. (Hanunin); pop. 12; 62 km NNE of Lvov; 50°16'/24°36'.

Ganushovtse, Ukr. (Hanuszowce); pop. 22; 114 km WNW of Chernovtsy; 49°01'/24°49'.

Ganya, see Ganichi.

Gappenach, Germ.; pop. 1; 82 km SSE of Koln; 50°16'/07°21'.

Gapsal, see Haapsalu.

Gara, Hung.; pop. 4; 88 km SW of Szeged; 46°02'/19°03'; LDS.

Garabonc, Hung.; pop. 8; 26 km NNE of Nagykanizsa; 46°35'/17°08'.

Garadna, Hung.; pop. 27; 50 km NNE of Miskolc; 48°25'/21°11'; HSL.

Garany, Cz.; 45 km ESE of Kosice; 48°33'/21°47'; GUM3, GUM4, GUM5, GUM6, HSL.

Garasymuv, Ukr. (Harasymow, Harszymow); pop. 55; 75 km WNW of Chernovtsy; 48°46'/25°14'; PHP2.

Garba, see Gurba.

Garbatka, Pol.; pop. 111; 69 km WNW of Lublin; 51°29'/21°38'; AMG, EDRD, GUM3, GUM5, HSL.

Garbatowka, Pol.; pop. 10; 38 km NE of Lublin; 51°22'/23°07'.

Garbenteich, Germ.; 56 km N of Frankfurt am Main; 50°32'/08°45'; LDS.

Garbocz, HSL. This pre-World War I community was not found in BGN gazetteers.

Garbolc, Hung.; pop. 33; 157 km E of Miskolc; 47°57'/22°52'.

Garbou, see Girbou.

Garbov, see Garbow.

Garbova, possibly Garbovat.

Garbova de Jos, (Alsoorbo);

Garbovat, Mold. (Garbova?); pop. 11; 45 km ESE of Kishinev; 46°51'/29°22'. A number of towns share this name. It was not possible to determine from available information which one is being referenced.

Garbow, Pol. (Garbov); pop. 27; 19 km WNW of Lublin; 51°21'/22°21'; FRG.

Garcin, Yug.; pop. 3; 182 km ESE of Zagreb; 45°12'/18°12'.

Gardanfalva, see Girdani.

Gardani, see Girdani.

Gardeja, Pol. (Garnsee); 82 km SSE of Gdansk; 53°37'/18°57'; LDS.

Gardelegen, Germ.; pop. 39; 114 km ENE of Hannover; 52°32'/11°22'; GUM4, GUM5, LDS.

Gardony, Hung.; pop. 32; 45 km SSW of Budapest; 47°12'/18°39'.

Gardzienice, Pol.; pop. 20; 26 km ESE of Lublin; 51°06'/22°51'.

Gardzienice Stare, Pol.; pop. 7; 69 km W of Lublin; 51°16'/21°33'.

Garesnica, Yug.; pop. 34; 75 km ESE of Zagreb; 45°35'/16°56'.

Gargzdai, Lith. (Gargzhday, Garsden, Garzdai, Gorzad, Gorzd, Gorzed, Gorzh D, Gorzhdy); pop. 1,049; 120 km WSW of Siauliai; 55°43'/21°24'; AMG, COH, EDRD, GUM5, HSL, LYV, SF, YB, YL.

Gargzhday, see Gargzdai.

Garki, Pol.; pop. 2; 69 km NNE of Wroclaw; 51°32'/17°39'.

Garlele Garariei; pop. 179; PHR1. This town was not found in BGN gazetteers under the given spelling.

Garliava, Lith. (Godilieva, Godlawo, Godlewo, Gorliava); pop. 311; 19 km S of Kaunas; 54°49'/23°52'; GUM4, HSL, LDL, SF, YL.

Garmisch Partenkirchen, Germ.; 82 km SSW of Munchen; 47°30'/11°06'; GUM3, GUM4.

Garnek, Pol.; 32 km NE of Czestochowa; 50°53'/19°28'; PHP1.

Garnsee, see Gardeja.

Garrin, see Charzyno.

Garsa Mare, see Ghirisa.

Garsden, see Gargzdai.

Garsene, Lat.; pop. 6; 50 km WNW of Daugavpils; 56°06'/25°50'.

Gartz, Germ.; pop. 26; 101 km NNE of Berlin; 53°12'/14°23'; HSL.

Garvilin, see Garwolin.

Garvolin, see Garwolin.

Garwolin, Pol. (Garvilin, Garvolin); pop. 4,000; 62 km ESE of Warszawa; 51°54'/21°38'; COH, EDRD, FRG, GUM3, GUM4, GUM5, HSL, HSL2, JGFF, LYV, PHP4, SF, YB.

Garz, HSL. A number of towns share this name. It was not possible to determine from available information which one is being referenced.

Garzdai, see Gargzdai.

Garzweiler, Germ.; pop. 22; 32 km WNW of Koln; 51°04'/06°30'.

Gasawa, Pol. (Gonsawa); pop. 2; 62 km NE of Poznan; 52°46'/17°46'; AMG.

Gasewo, Pol. BGN lists two possible localities with this name located at 52°29'/20°00' and 52°59'/21°13'. PHP4.

Gasiorowo, Pol.; pop. 46; 38 km N of Warszawa; 52°33'/21°06'.

Gaski, Pol.; pop. 23; 50 km SSE of Warszawa; 51°51'/21°11'.

Gasocin, Pol.; pop. 68; 56 km NNW of Warszawa; 52°44'/20°43'; GUM4.

Gasowka Oleksin, Pol.; pop. 1; 26 km SSW of Bialystok; 52°57'/22°53'.

Gasowka Skwarki, Pol.; pop. 9; 32 km SW of Bialystok; 52°59'/22°48'.

Gassendorf, Ukr.; pop. 6; 75 km S of Lvov; 49°14'/23°39'.

Gata, see Gattendorf.

Gatarta, Lat.; pop. 5; 114 km ENE of Riga; 57°13'/25°54'.

Gatchina, USSR; 45 km S of Leningrad; 59°34'/30°08'; GUM4.

Gatkow, Pol. PHP4. This town was not found in BGN gazetteers under the given spelling.

Gattendorf, Aus. (Gata, Lajtakata); 50 km ESE of Wien; 48°01'/16°59'; EJ, HSL, LDS.

Gau Algesheim, Germ.; pop. 25; 50 km SW of Frankfurt am Main; 49°57'/08°01'; HSL.

Gaubitsch, Aus.; pop. 3; 56 km N of Wien; 48°39'/16°23'.

Gauersheim, Germ.; pop. 17; 62 km SSW of Frankfurt am Main; 49°40'/08°04'; GED, GUM4, JGFF.

Gaugrehweiler, Germ.; 75 km SW of Frankfurt am Main; 49°42'/07°52'; GED, JGFF.

Gaujiena, Lat.; pop. 2; 150 km NE of Riga; 57°31'/26°24'.

Gaukonigshofen, Germ.; pop. 67; 82 km W of Nurnberg; 49°38'/10°00'; GUM5, PHGB.

Gau Odernheim, Germ.; pop. 43; 50 km SSW of Frankfurt am Main; 49°46'/08°12'.

Gaure, Lith.; pop. 17; 94 km SSW of Siauliai; 55°15'/22°28'; YL.

Gaureni de Sus, see Gaureny.

Gaureny, Mold. (Gaureni de Sus); pop. 5; 62 km WNW of Kishinev; 47°12'/28°05'.

Gauri, see Gaurini.

Gaurini, Lat. (Gauri); pop. 19; 69 km SSW of Riga; 56°29'/23°28'.

Gauting, Germ.; pop. 4; 19 km SW of Munchen; 48°04'/11°22'; GUM3.

Gauzeni, see Gauzeny.

Gauzeny, Mold. (Gauzeni); pop. 42; 88 km NNW of Kishinev; 47°45'/28°34'.

Gava, Hung.; pop. 186; 62 km ENE of Miskolc; 48°10'/21°36'; GUM5, HSL, HSL2, LDL, LDS, PHH.

Gavanoasa, see Gavanosy.

Gavanosy, Mold. (Gavanoasa); pop. 10; 139 km S of Kishinev; 45°46'/28°23'.

Gavieze, Lat. (Gaviezes); pop. 1; 182 km WSW of Riga; 56°30'/21°15'.

Gaviezes, see Gavieze.

Gavrilchitsy, Byel. (Hawrylczyce); pop. 7; 88 km NE of Pinsk; 52°38'/27°06'.

Gavrileshte, Ukr. (Gavrilesti); pop. 47; 26 km WNW of Chernovtsy; 48°28'/25°39'.

Gavrilesti, *see* Gavrileshte.

Gavrilovka, Ukr. (Gavryluvka, Hawrylowka); pop. 38; 101 km WNW of Chernovtsy; 48°41'/24°43'.

Gavryluvka, *see* Gavrilovka.

Gawlow, Pol.; pop. 39; 38 km E of Krakow; 50°02'/20°28'.

Gawluszowice, Pol.; 114 km NE of Krakow; 50°25'/21°23'; JGFF.

Gaworzyna, Pol.; pop. 12; 94 km WSW of Lublin; 51°13'/21°13'.

Gawrony, Pol.; 62 km ESE of Lodz; 51°24'/20°12'; PHP1.

Gawrzylowa, Pol.; pop. 28; 101 km WNW of Przemysl; 50°03'/21°25'.

Gaya, *see* Kyjov.

Gaye Nizhne, *see* Gay Nizhniye.

Gayna, Byel. (Hajna, Hayna); 45 km N of Minsk; 54°14'/27°43'; SF.

Gaynin, Byel. (Hajnin); pop. 7; 94 km N of Pinsk; 52°55'/26°23'.

Gay Nizhniye, Ukr. (Gaje Nizne, Gaje Wyzne, Gaye Nizhne); pop. 33; 62 km S of Lvov; 49°20'/23°41'.

Gayshin, Byel. (Gaischin, Heishin); 107 km N of Gomel; 53°21'/30°59'; SF.

Gaysin, Ukr. (Ajszyn, Aysyn, Gaisin, Gaissin, Gajsin, Haissin, Haisyn, Hajsyn, Heisin); pop. 5,190; 62 km W of Uman; 48°48'/29°23'; EDRD, EJ, GUM4, GUM5, JGFF, LDL, SF.

Gazenpot, *see* Aizpute.

Gbely, Cz. (Egbeli); 62 km SE of Brno; 48°43'/17°08'; HSL.

Gdansk, Pol. (Danzig); pop. 4,000; 240 km NNE of Poznan; 54°21'/18°40'; AMG, CAHJP, EDRD, EJ, FRG, GUM3, GUM4, GUM5, GUM6, HSL, HSL2, JGFF, LDS, PHP1, PHP2, PHP3, PHP4.

Gdeshichi, Ukr. (Gdeshitse, Gdeszyce); pop. 27; 82 km WSW of Lvov; 49°39'/22°56'.

Gdeshitse, *see* Gdeshichi.

Gdeszyce, *see* Gdeshichi.

Gdeszyn, Pol.; pop. 18; 88 km ESE of Lublin; 50°47'/23°39'.

G Dov, *see* Gdow.

Gdov, USSR; pop. 86; 107 km NNW of Pskov; 58°46'/27°48'.

Gdow, Pol. (G Dov); pop. 245; 26 km ESE of Krakow; 49°55'/20°12'; EGRS, GUM4, GUM5, HSL, PHP3, SF.

Gdynia, Pol.; 26 km NW of Gdansk; 54°30'/18°33'; AMG, GUM3, GUM5, JGFF.

Geamana, *see* Dzhamany.

Gebe, *see* Nyirkata.

Gebeltov, *see* Giebultow.

Geberjen, Hung.; pop. 16; 126 km E of Miskolc; 47°56'/22°28'.

Gebice, Pol. (Gembic, Gembitz); pop. 22; 75 km ENE of Poznan; 52°35'/18°02'; HSL, LDS.

Gebiczyna, Pol.; pop. 8; 101 km W of Przemysl; 49°58'/21°24'.

Gecse, Hung.; 120 km WSW of Budapest; 47°27'/17°32'; HSL.

Gederlak, Hung.; pop. 8; 101 km WNW of Szeged; 46°37'/18°55'.

Gedern, Germ.; pop. 130; 56 km NE of Frankfurt am Main; 50°26'/09°12'; CAHJP, JGFF, LDS.

Gedrevitz, *see* Giedraiciai.

Gedrovitz, *see* Giedraiciai.

Gegeny, Hung.; pop. 103; 88 km ENE of Miskolc; 48°09'/21°57'; AMG, HSL, PHH.

Gehaus, Germ.; pop. 23; 126 km NE of Frankfurt am Main; 50°45'/10°05'; JGFF, LDS.

Gehrden, Germ.; 13 km SW of Hannover; 52°19'/09°36'; GED, LDS.

Geidekrug, *see* Silute.

Geilenkirchen, Germ.; pop. 125; 56 km W of Koln; 50°58'/06°09'; GED, GUM5.

Geilshausen, Germ.; pop. 11; 69 km N of Frankfurt am Main; 50°39'/08°54'.

Geinsheim, Germ.; pop. 30; 32 km SSW of Frankfurt am Main; 49°53'/08°24'; GED.

Geisa, Germ.; pop. 90; 114 km NE of Frankfurt am Main; 50°43'/09°58'; AMG, JGFF, LDS.

Geiselhoring, Germ.; 94 km NNE of Munchen; 48°50'/12°23'; GUM3.

Geiselwind, Germ.; 56 km WNW of Nurnberg; 49°46'/10°28'; PHGB.

Geisenfeld, Germ.; 62 km N of Munchen; 48°41'/11°37'; PHGB.

Geisenheim, Germ.; pop. 20; 50 km WSW of Frankfurt am Main; 49°59'/07°58'; GUM3, GUM5.

Geisig, Germ.; pop. 18; 69 km W of Frankfurt am Main; 50°15'/07°48'.

Geisingen, Germ.; 107 km S of Stuttgart; 47°55'/08°38'; PHGBW.

Geislar, Germ.; 26 km SE of Koln; 50°46'/07°07'; GED.

Geislingen a Steige, GUM3, GUM5. This town was not found in BGN gazetteers under the given spelling.

Geismar, Germ.; 114 km N of Frankfurt am Main; 51°04'/08°51'; GED, LDS.

Geiss Nidda, Germ.; pop. 19; 38 km NNE of Frankfurt am Main; 50°24'/08°58'.

Geistingen, Germ.; pop. 30; Described in the *Black Book* as being in the Neidersachsen-Westfallen region of Germany, this town was not found in BGN gazetteers.

Geisweid, Germ.; 75 km E of Koln; 50°55'/08°02'; GED.

Gejovce, HSL. This pre-World War I community was not found in BGN gazetteers.

Geldern, Germ.; pop. 48; 75 km NW of Koln; 51°31'/06°20'; EDRD, EJ, GUM3, YB.

Geldersheim, Germ.; pop. 4; 94 km WNW of Nurnberg; 50°03'/10°09'; GUM5, PHGB.

Gelej, Hung.; pop. 23; 32 km S of Miskolc; 47°50'/20°47'; HSL.

Gelencze, *see* Ghelinta.

Gelenes, Hung.; pop. 37; 126 km ENE of Miskolc; 48°12'/22°27'; HSL.

Gelenuvka Stara, *see* Staraya Yelenovka.

Geleven, *see* Gelvonai.

Geleziai, Lith.; 88 km E of Siauliai; 55°50'/24°42'; JGFF.

Gellenhaza, Hung.; pop. 12; 45 km NNW of Nagykanizsa; 46°46'/16°47'.

Gelmyazov, Ukr. (Glemjasow?, Glemyazovo, Helmiazov, Holishev); 94 km SE of Kiyev; 49°49'/31°21'; LDL, SF.

Gelnhausen, Germ.; pop. 200; 38 km ENE of Frankfurt am Main; 50°12'/09°11'; CAHJP, EJ, HSL, HSL2, JGFF, LDS.

Gelnica, Cz. (Gollnitz); pop. 887; 26 km WNW of Kosice; 48°51'/20°56'; HSL.

Gelsdorf, Germ.; 45 km SSE of Koln; 50°35'/07°02'; JGFF.

Gelse, Hung.; pop. 31; 26 km N of Nagykanizsa; 46°36'/17°00'; HSL, HSL2, LDS.

Gelsenkirchen, Germ.; pop. 1,440; 69 km N of Koln; 51°31'/07°06'; AMG, EDRD, EJ, GED, GUM4, GUM5, ISH1.

Gelsungen, Germ.; 126 km NNE of Frankfurt am Main; 51°09'/09°26'; LDS.

Gelvan, *see* Gelvonai.

Gelvonai, Lith. (Geleven, Gelvan, Gelvoniai, Gelvonis, Gelvonys, Gevonai, Gevonis, Gielwany, Gilvan); pop. 473; 56 km NE of Kaunas; 55°04'/24°42'; HSL, JGFF, LDL, SF, YL.

Gelvoniai, *see* Gelvonai.

Gelvonis, *see* Gelvonai.

Gelvonys, *see* Gelvonai.

Gembic, *see* Gebice.

Gembitz, *see* Gebice.

Gemeinlebarn, Aus.; pop. 2; 45 km WNW of Wien; 48°20'/15°48'.

Gemen, Germ.; pop. 39; 107 km N of Koln; 51°51'/06°52'; AMG, EJ, GUM5.

Gemer, Cz. (Sajogomor); 75 km SW of Kosice; 48°27'/20°19'; HSL.

Gemerske Dechtare, Cz. (Deter); 101 km SW of Kosice; 48°15'/20°03'; HSL.

Gemmerich, Germ.; pop. 12; 69 km W of Frankfurt am Main; 50°14'/07°45'.

Gemmingen, Germ.; pop. 57; 50 km NNW of Stuttgart; 49°09'/08°59'; GUM5, JGFF, LDS, PHGBW.

Gemund, Germ.; pop. 28; 56 km SSW of Koln; 50°34'/06°30';

GED, GUM5, HSL.

Gemunden, Germ. AMG, JGFF.

Gemunden (Bavaria), Germ.; pop. 74; 69 km E of Frankfurt am Main; 50°03'/09°42'; GUM5, PHGB.

Gemunden (Rhineland Pfalz), Germ.; pop. 55; 88 km WSW of Frankfurt am Main; 49°54'/07°28'.

Gemunden an der Wohra, Germ.; pop. 49; 101 km N of Frankfurt am Main; 50°58'/08°58'.

Gemzse, Hung.; pop. 79; 107 km ENE of Miskolc; 48°08'/22°12'; HSL, LDS, PHH.

Genderkingen, Germ.; pop. 1; 82 km NW of Munchen; 48°42'/10°53'.

General Poetas, see Kureshnitsa.

Gengenbach, Germ.; pop. 35; 94 km SW of Stuttgart; 48°24'/08°01'; PHGBW.

Genichesk, Ukr. (Genitchesk, Genitzshek); pop. 1,779; 150 km N of Simferopol; 46°11'/34°46'; HSL, HSL2, LDL, SF.

Genin, Germ.; 56 km NE of Hamburg; 53°51'/10°39'; LDS.

Genitchesk, see Genichesk.

Genitzshek, see Genichesk.

Gensingen, Germ.; pop. 21; 56 km SW of Frankfurt am Main; 49°54'/07°56'.

Gensungen, Germ.; 126 km NNE of Frankfurt am Main; 51°08'/09°26'; LDS.

Genterovci, Yug.; pop. 4; 94 km N of Zagreb; 46°37'/16°25'.

Genthin, Germ.; pop. 29; 82 km WSW of Berlin; 52°24'/12°10'; GUM3, GUM5.

Geoagiu, Rom. (Algyogyafalu, Algyogyalfalu, Felgyogy, Gad); 101 km S of Cluj; 45°55'/23°12'; PHR1.

Georgenberg, see Spisska Sobota.

Georgenhausen, Germ.; 32 km SSE of Frankfurt am Main; 49°51'/08°48'; LDS.

Georgensgmund, Germ.; pop. 44; 38 km S of Nurnberg; 49°12'/11°01'; CAHJP, GUM3, PHGB.

Georgswalde, see Jirikov.

Gepiu, Rom.; pop. 3; 139 km W of Cluj; 46°55'/21°48'.

Ger, see Gora Kalwaria.

Gera, Germ.; pop. 510; 50 km S of Leipzig; 50°52'/12°05'; AMG, GUM4.

Gerabronn, Germ.; 75 km NE of Stuttgart; 49°15'/09°55'; EJ, PHGBW.

Geranony, Byel. (Gieranony); pop. 24; 133 km W of Minsk; 54°07'/25°35'.

Geras, Aus.; pop. 3; 82 km NW of Wien; 48°47'/15°40'.

Gerausa, Rom.; pop. 17; 107 km NW of Cluj; 47°36'/22°56'.

Gerbach, Germ.; 75 km SW of Frankfurt am Main; 49°40'/07°52'; JGFF.

Gerbovets, Mold. (Harbovat); pop. 9; 56 km WNW of Kishinev; 47°20'/28°19'; COH.

Gerbstedt, Germ.; pop. 16; 62 km WNW of Leipzig; 51°38'/11°37'.

Gerce, Hung.; pop. 18; 94 km N of Nagykanizsa; 47°13'/17°01'; HSL.

Gerdauen, see Zheleznodorozhnyy.

Gerde, Hung.; pop. 3; 94 km ESE of Nagykanizsa; 45°59'/18°02'.

Gerend, see Grind.

Gerendkeresztur, see Grindeni.

Gerenyes, Hung.; pop. 1; 88 km E of Nagykanizsa; 46°18'/18°11'.

Geres, see Ghirisa.

Geresdorf, Germ.; 101 km ESE of Nurnberg; 49°09'/12°27'; HSL.

Gergely, see Gergelyiugornya.

Gergelyi, see Gergelyiugornya.

Gergelyiugornya, Hung. (Gergely, Gergelyi, Ugornya); pop. 114; 120 km ENE of Miskolc; 48°08'/22°21'; HSL, PHH.

Gergo, see Hrhov.

Gerjen, Hung.; pop. 8; 101 km WNW of Szeged; 46°30'/18°54'.

Gerla, see Gherla.

Gerlenhofen, Germ.; pop. 1; 82 km ESE of Stuttgart; 48°20'/10°02'.

Gerleve, Germ.; 114 km N of Koln; 51°56'/07°14'; HSL.

Germakovka, Ukr. (Germakowka, Germanowka); pop. 76; 50 km N of Chernovtsy; 48°42'/26°11'; AMG, PHP2.

Germakowka, see Germakovka.

Germanovichi, Byel. (Hermanowicze); pop. 209; 150 km W of Vitebsk; 55°24'/27°48'; GUM4, HSL, JGFF.

Germanovka, Ukr. (Guermanovka); EDRD. A number of towns share this name. It was not possible to determine from available information which one is being referenced.

Germanowka, see Germakovka.

Germanuv, Ukr. (Hermanow); pop. 30; 26 km E of Lvov; 49°48'/24°20'; GUM4, PHP2, PHP4.

Germersheim, Germ.; pop. 58; 82 km WNW of Stuttgart; 49°13'/08°22'; EDRD, GED, HSL, JGFF.

Gernrode, Germ.; 94 km WNW of Leipzig; 51°44'/11°08'; GUM3, LDS.

Gernsbach, Germ.; pop. 65; 62 km WSW of Stuttgart; 48°46'/08°20'; GUM4, LDS, PHGBW.

Gernsheim, Germ.; pop. 30; 45 km S of Frankfurt am Main; 49°45'/08°29'; JGFF.

Geroda, Germ.; pop. 49; 88 km ENE of Frankfurt am Main; 50°17'/09°54'; GUM5, JGFF, PHGB.

Geroldshausen, Germ.; pop. 12; 88 km WNW of Nurnberg; 49°41'/09°54'; GUM5, PHGB.

Gerolfingen, Germ.; 62 km SSW of Nurnberg; 49°03'/10°31'; PHGB.

Gerolstein, Germ.; pop. 41; 88 km S of Koln; 50°13'/06°40'; GED.

Gerolzhofen, Germ.; pop. 115; 75 km WNW of Nurnberg; 49°54'/10°21'; GUM5, HSL, HSL2, PHGB.

Gerse, Hung.; pop. 6; 69 km NNW of Nagykanizsa; 46°59'/16°44'; GUM3.

Gersfeld, Germ.; pop. 97; 101 km NE of Frankfurt am Main; 50°27'/09°57'; GUM3, HSL, JGFF.

Gerstetten, Germ.; pop. 62 km E of Stuttgart; 48°38'/10°02'; PHGBW.

Gerthe, Germ.; pop. 60; Described in the *Black Book* as being in the Neidersachsen-Westfallen region of Germany, this town was not found in BGN gazetteers.

Gertop, Mold. (Hartop, Hartop Soroca); pop. 22; 101 km NNW of Kishinev; 47°53'/28°28'.

Gertop Mare, Mold. (Hartop Mare?, Hartopul Mare); pop. 125; 32 km N of Kishinev; 47°14'/28°56'.

Gertsa, Ukr. (Herta); 32 km ESE of Chernovtsy; 48°09'/26°15'; EJ, GUM3, GUM4, HSL, LDL.

Gescher, Germ.; 114 km N of Koln; 51°57'/07°01'; GED.

Geseke, Germ.; pop. 50; 114 km SW of Hannover; 51°39'/08°31'; JGFF, LDS.

Gesia Wolka, Pol.; 75 km NW of Lublin; 51°47'/22°00'; GUM3.

Gesstemunde und Lehe, Germ.; pop. 247; Described in the *Black Book* as being in the Bremen region of Germany, this town was not found in BGN gazetteers.

Gestorf, Germ.; 26 km S of Hannover; 52°14'/09°42'; GED.

Geszt, Hung.; 126 km NE of Szeged; 46°53'/21°35'; HSL, LDS.

Gesztely, Hung.; pop. 69; 19 km E of Miskolc; 48°06'/20°58'; HSL, HSL2, PHH.

Gesztered, Hung.; pop. 42; 82 km ESE of Miskolc; 47°46'/21°47'; HSL, LDS.

Gesztes, see Hostisovce.

Getlovo, Mold. (Ghetlova); pop. 33; 45 km NW of Kishinev; 47°22'/28°32'.

Getye, Hung.; pop. 4; 45 km N of Nagykanizsa; 46°46'/17°04'.

Gevelsberg, Germ.; pop. 26; 50 km NNE of Koln; 51°19'/07°20'.

Gevonai, see Gelvonai.

Gevonis, see Gelvonai.

Gewitsch, see Jevicko.

Gey, Germ.; 45 km SW of Koln; 50°45'/06°25'; GED.

Geyche, Ukr. (Guyche, Hujcze); pop. 25; 50 km NNW of Lvov; 50°15'/23°46'.

Gezlev, see Yevpatoriya.

Gheghie, Rom.; pop. 11; 82 km WNW of Cluj; 47°01'/22°31'.

Ghelinta, Rom. (Gelencze); pop. 8; 170 km SSW of Iasi; 45°57'/26°14'.

Ghenci, Rom.; pop. 13; 126 km NW of Cluj; 47°38'/22°32'.

Gheorgheni, Rom. (Gyergyoszentmiklos); pop. 619; 150 km E of Cluj; 46°43'/25°37'; AMG, HSL, PHR2.

Gheria Mare, Rom.; pop. 51; 139 km NNW of Cluj; 47°58'/23°13'.

Gherla, Rom. (Gerla, Somoshuyvar, Szamosujvar); pop. 1,037; 45 km NNE of Cluj; 47°02'/23°55'; AMG, COH, EJ, HSL, LYV, PHR2, YB.

Gherta Mica, Rom. (Kisgercze); pop. 64; 133 km NNW of Cluj; 47°56'/23°14'; HSL.

Ghetlova, see Getlovo.

Ghida, Rom. (Berettyodeda); pop. 4; 107 km WNW of Cluj; 47°18'/22°27'.

Ghidighici, see Gidigich.

Ghiduleni, see Giduleny.

Ghilvaci, Rom.; pop. 6; 126 km NW of Cluj; 47°41'/22°40'.

Ghimes, Rom. (Ghimes Faget, Gyimes, Gyimesbukk); pop. 224; 133 km SW of Iasi; 46°35'/26°02'; GUM3, HSL, PHR2.

Ghimes Faget, see Ghimes.

Ghincauti, see Ginkautsi.

Ghinda, Rom.; pop. 4; 82 km NE of Cluj; 47°08'/24°34'.

Ghioli, Rom.; pop. 23; 45 km NE of Cluj; 46°57'/24°04'.

Ghipes, Rom.; pop. 3; 150 km ESE of Cluj; 46°16'/25°24'.

Ghirasa Ghira, GUM4. This town was not found in BGN gazetteers under the given spelling.

Ghireni, Rom.; pop. 10; 120 km NW of Iasi; 48°09'/26°53'.

Ghiris, Rom. (Aranyosgyeres, Gyeres, Gyeresszentkiraly); 38 km SE of Cluj; 46°33'/23°54'; HSL.

Ghirisa, Rom. (Garsa Mare, Geres); pop. 40; 114 km NW of Cluj; 47°36'/22°48'; HSL.

Ghiriseni, see Girisheny.

Ghirova, see Girovo.

Ghitcauti, Rom. (Hancauti); pop. 31; 120 km NW of Iasi; 48°06'/26°41'.

Gialacuta, Rom. (Gyalakuta); 107 km SSW of Cluj; 46°00'/22°47'; HSL.

Gibart, Hung.; pop. 25; 38 km NE of Miskolc; 48°19'/21°10'; HSL.

Gibaszew, see Gibaszewo.

Gibaszewo, Pol. (Gibaszew); pop. 3; 50 km WNW of Lodz; 51°54'/18°49'.

Giby, Pol.; pop. 3; 107 km N of Bialystok; 54°02'/23°22'; JGFF.

Gichitse, see Gichitsy.

Gichitsy, Byel. (Gichitse, Hiezyce?); pop. 21; 82 km NW of Pinsk; 52°40'/25°26'.

Gicze, Cz.; 69 km WSW of Kosice; 48°34'/20°18'; HSL. This town was located on a pre-World War I map, but does not appear in contemporary gazetteers.

Gidigich, Mold. (Ghidighici); 19 km NNW of Kishinev; 47°06'/28°46'; GUM4.

Gidla, see Gidle.

Gidle, Pol. (Gidla, Gidzel); pop. 192; 32 km NE of Czestochowa; 50°58'/19°29'; GA, GUM5, JGFF, PHP1, SF.

Giduleny, Mold. (Ghiduleni); pop. 23; 75 km N of Kishinev; 47°37'/28°45'.

Gidzel, see Gidle.

Giebelstadt, Germ.; pop. 37; 88 km W of Nurnberg; 49°40'/09°56'; CAHJP, GUM5, PHGB.

Gieben, see Giessen.

Giebultow, Pol. (Gebeltov); 13 km NNW of Krakow; 50°09'/19°53'; FRG.

Giedlarowa, Pol.; pop. 39; 50 km NW of Przemysl; 50°13'/22°24'.

Giedraicai, see Giedraiciai.

Giedraiciai, Lith. (Gedrevitz, Gedrovitz, Giedraicai); pop. 421; 50 km N of Vilnius; 55°05'/25°15'; GUM3, HSL, LDL, SF, YL.

Gielczyn, Pol.; pop. 34; 45 km W of Bialystok; 53°14'/22°29'.

Gielniov, see Gielniow.

Gielniow, Pol. (Gielniov); pop. 3,500; 82 km ESE of Lodz; 51°24'/20°29'; GA, GUM5, HSL, PHP1, PHP4, SF.

Gielwany, see Gelvonai.

Gielzow, Pol. BGN lists two possible localities with this name located at 51°19'/20°24' and 51°28'/20°23'. PHP1.

Giemzow, Pol.; pop. 4; 13 km ESE of Lodz; 51°42'/19°36'.

Gier, see Gora Kalwaria.

Gieraltowiczki, Pol.; pop. 3; 45 km SW of Krakow; 49°57'/19°24'.

Gieranony, see Geranony.

Gieraszowice, Pol.; pop. 2; 107 km SW of Lublin; 50°36'/21°27'.

Gierlachow Blizszy, Pol.; pop. 28; Described in the *Black Book* as being in the Kielce region of Poland, this town was not found in BGN gazetteers.

Giershagen, Germ.; pop. 12; 126 km SSW of Hannover; 51°24'/08°49'.

Giershofen, Germ.; pop. 2; 69 km ESE of Koln; 50°32'/07°40'.

Giesebitz, see Izbica.

Giesenkirchen, Germ.; pop. 10; 38 km WNW of Koln; 51°09'/06°30'.

Gieski, Pol.; pop. 68; Described in the *Black Book* as being in the Lodz region of Poland, this town was not found in BGN gazetteers.

Giessen, Germ. (Gieben); pop. 1,017; 62 km N of Frankfurt am Main; 50°35'/08°39'; AMG, EJ, GED, GUM3, GUM4, GUM5, HSL, JGFF, LDS, PHGBW, YB.

Gige, Hung.; pop. 4; 50 km ESE of Nagykanizsa; 46°18'/17°37'; LDS.

Gigen, Bulg.; 146 km NNE of Sofija; 43°42'/24°29'; EJ.

Gilau, Rom. (Gyalu); pop. 161; 19 km WSW of Cluj; 46°45'/23°23'; HSL, PHR2.

Gildehaus, Germ.; 157 km N of Koln; 52°18'/07°07'; GED.

Gilgau, Rom.; 56 km NNW of Cluj; 47°12'/23°20'; HSL.

Gilgenburg, see Dabrowno.

Gilowka Dolna, Pol.; pop. 5; 69 km W of Warszawa; 52°22'/20°01'.

Gilsa, Germ.; pop. 7; 107 km N of Frankfurt am Main; 51°01'/09°11'.

Gilserberg, Germ.; pop. 37; 101 km N of Frankfurt am Main; 50°57'/09°04'.

Gilvan, see Gelvonai.

Gimbsheim, Germ.; pop. 30; 38 km SSW of Frankfurt am Main; 49°47'/08°23'.

Gindeshty, Mold. (Gandesti); pop. 10; 101 km NNW of Kishinev; 47°50'/28°22'.

Gindorf, Germ.; pop. 30; 32 km WNW of Koln; 51°03'/06°33'.

Ginivishov, see Gniewoszow.

Ginkautsi, Mold. (Ghincauti); pop. 42; 182 km NW of Kishinev; 48°17'/27°20'.

Ginki, Byel.; pop. 9; 150 km N of Minsk; 55°13'/27°42'.

Ginkovtse, Ukr. (Hinkowce); pop. 55; 56 km NNW of Chernovtsy; 48°47'/25°45'; PHP2.

Giorocuta, Rom. (Girokuta); pop. 14; 94 km NW of Cluj; 47°26'/22°48'.

Giraltovce, Cz.; pop. 1,009; 50 km N of Kosice; 49°07'/21°31'; GUM4, HSL.

Girbou, Rom. (Garbou, Hegykoz); pop. 108; 50 km NNW of Cluj; 47°09'/23°26'.

Girdani, Rom. (Gardanfalva, Gardani); pop. 28; 94 km NNW of Cluj; 47°33'/23°19'; AMG.

Gireshkov, see Gorzkow.

Girincs, Hung.; pop. 13; 19 km ESE of Miskolc; 47°58'/20°59'; HSL.

Girisheni, see Girisheny.

Girisheny, Mold. (Ghiriseni, Girisheni); pop. 52; 69 km NW of Kishinev; 47°26'/28°17'.

Girkalnis, Lith. (Girtagola, Girtakol); pop. 270; 62 km WNW of Kaunas; 55°19'/23°13'; HSL, JGFF, SF, YL.

Girokuta, see Giorocuta.

Girovo, Mold. (Ghirova); pop. 68; 62 km NW of Kishinev; 47°25'/28°16'.

Girtagola, *see* Girkalnis.

Girtakol, *see* Girkalnis.

Giruliai, Lith.; 139 km WSW of Siauliai; 55°46'/21°05'; GUM3, GUM4.

Gissigheim, Germ.; 88 km ESE of Frankfurt am Main; 49°36'/09°35'; JGFF, PHGBW.

Giulesti, Rom. (Maragyulafalva, Zsulest); pop. 176; 120 km N of Cluj; 47°49'/23°56'; GUM4, PHR2, SM.

Giulvaz, Rom.; 240 km SW of Cluj; 45°33'/20°59'; HSL.

Giumiurdzhina, Bulg.; pop. 775; This town was not found in BGN gazetteers under the given spelling.

Giungi, Rom. (Gyongy); pop. 14; 107 km NW of Cluj; 47°34'/22°47'.

Giurgiu, Rom.; pop. 113; BGN lists two possible localities with this name located at 43°53'/25°58' and 46°30'/22°57'.

Givozits, *see* Gwozdziec.

Gizhdiyany, Mold. (Hajdieni); pop. 137; 133 km WNW of Kishinev; 47°46'/27°27'.

Gizycko, Pol. (Loetzen, Lotzen, Luczany); 139 km WNW of Bialystok; 54°02'/21°46'; AMG.

Gladbeck, Germ.; pop. 264; 75 km N of Koln; 51°34'/06°59'; AMG, GED.

Gladenbach, Germ.; pop. 108; 82 km N of Frankfurt am Main; 50°46'/08°34'; GUM5, JGFF.

Gladyszow, Pol.; pop. 5; 114 km ESE of Krakow; 49°32'/21°16'.

Glan Munchweiler, Germ.; pop. 33; 114 km SW of Frankfurt am Main; 49°28'/07°26'; GED.

Glasmanka, *see* Gostini.

Glatz, *see* Klodzko.

Glauberg, Germ.; pop. 22; 38 km NE of Frankfurt am Main; 50°19'/09°00'; LDS.

Glauchau, Germ.; pop. 30; 56 km SSE of Leipzig; 50°49'/12°32'; JGFF.

Glavan, Mold. (Tarigrad); pop. 94; 139 km NW of Kishinev; 48°03'/27°46'.

Glavtchev, *see* Glowaczow.

Glayvits, *see* Gleiwitz.

Glazmanka, *see* Gostini.

Glazmanke, *see* Gostini.

Glazminka, *see* Gostini.

Glaznow, HSL, HSL2. This pre-World War I community was not found in BGN gazetteers.

Gleboczek, *see* Glubochek.

Gleboka, Pol.; pop. 32; 19 km NE of Krakow; 50°08'/20°09'. *See also* Glemboka.

Glebokie, Byel. (Glebokoye, Glembokie, Glubokie); pop. 2,844; 146 km N of Minsk; 55°08'/27°41'; AMG, COH, EDRD, EJ, GA, GUM3, GUM4, GUM5, GUM6, HSL, JGFF, LDL, LYV, SF, YB. *See also* Glemboke.

Glebokie (Lwow), Pol.; pop. 5; 69 km SW of Przemysl; 49°33'/21°55'.

Glebokie (near Chelm), Pol.; pop. 11; 38 km ENE of Lublin; 51°18'/23°06'.

Glebokie (near Wlodawa), Pol.; pop. 16; 38 km NE of Lublin; 51°29'/22°56'.

Glebokoye, *see* Glebokie.

Glebowice, Pol. (Glebowicze, Glubowce); pop. 9; 45 km SW of Krakow; 49°57'/19°20'; GUM3.

Glebowicze, *see* Glebowice.

Glebuvka, Ukr. (Chlebowka, Khlebwka); pop. 47; 120 km WNW of Chernovtsy; 48°48'/24°27'.

Gledeny, *see* Gledin.

Gledin, Rom. (Gledeny); pop. 3; 88 km ENE of Cluj; 46°58'/24°43'; HSL.

Glehn, Germ. BGN lists two possible localities with this name located at 50°36'/06°36' and 51°10'/06°35'. AMG.

Gleichenberg, *see* Gleichenberg Dorf.

Gleichenberg Dorf, Aus. (Gleichenberg); 38 km ESE of Graz; 46°53'/15°54'; EJ.

Gleicherwiesen, Germ.; pop. 26; 107 km NNW of Nurnberg; 50°22'/10°38'; JGFF, LDS.

Gleidingen, Germ.; pop. 18; 19 km SE of Hannover; 52°17'/09°50'.

Gleina, Germ.; 32 km S of Leipzig; 51°03'/12°11'; GUM3.

Gleiwitz, *see* Gliwice.

Glemboka, Ukr. (Gleboka); pop. 29; 82 km SW of Lvov; 49°32'/22°59'.

Glemboke, Ukr. (Glebokie); pop. 22; 120 km SSE of Lvov; 48°49'/24°25'.

Glembokie, *see* Glebokie.

Glemjasow, *possibly* Gelmyazov.

Glemyazovo, *see* Gelmyazov.

Glenbochek, *see* Glubochek.

Glesch, Germ.; 26 km W of Koln; 50°58'/06°35'; GED.

Gleusdorf, Germ.; 75 km NNW of Nurnberg; 50°05'/10°51'; PHGB.

Glina, *see* Glinyany.

Glinah, *see* Glinyany.

Glina Mare, *see* Glinoya.

Glina Stara, Pol.; pop. 21; Described in the *Black Book* as being in the Kielce region of Poland, this town was not found in BGN gazetteers.

Gline, *see* Glinyany.

Glingeni Balti, *see* Glinzheny (Balti).

Glingeni Orhei, *see* Glinzheny (Orhei).

Glini, *see* Glinne.

Glinianka, Pol.; pop. 45; 32 km ESE of Warszawa; 52°08'/21°26'; PHP4.

Glinianki, Pol.; 62 km NE of Lublin; 51°26'/23°25'; PHP4.

Gliniany, *see* Glinyany.

Glinice, Pol.; 88 km S of Warszawa; 51°30'/20°52'; GUM3.

Glinik, Pol.; pop. 23; 88 km W of Przemysl; 49°58'/21°35'.

Glinik Charzewski, Pol.; pop. 4; 69 km W of Przemysl; 49°55'/21°50'.

Glinik Gorny, Pol.; pop. 17; 82 km W of Przemysl; 49°51'/21°35'.

Glinik Sredni, Pol.; pop. 18; 82 km W of Przemysl; 49°51'/21°36'.

Glinitsa, Ukr. (Hlinita); pop. 140; 19 km W of Chernovtsy; 48°20'/25°42'; PHR2.

Glinka, Byel. (Linkah); pop. 88; 45 km ESE of Pinsk; 51°56'/26°40'; SF.

Glinki, Ukr.; pop. 317; 13 km ESE of Rovno; 50°35'/26°25'.

Glinki (Stanislawow), Ukr.; pop. 30; 94 km WNW of Chernovtsy; 48°39'/24°46'.

Glinna, Ukr.; pop. 24; 88 km ESE of Lvov; 49°35'/25°11'; PHP2.

Glinne, Ukr. (Glini, Glinnoye); pop. 34; 62 km SSW of Lvov; 49°27'/23°29'; SF.

Glinne (Polesie), Ukr.; pop. 66; 133 km NNE of Rovno; 51°31'/27°25'; WS.

Glinno Wielkie, Pol.; 114 km NE of Poznan; 52°58'/18°21'; GA.

Glinnoye, *see* Glinne.

Glinojeck, Pol. (Glinovietzk); pop. 68; 82 km NW of Warszawa; 52°49'/20°18'; GUM3, GUM4, SF.

Glinovietzk, *see* Glinojeck.

Glinoya, Mold. (Glina Mare); pop. 22; 182 km NW of Kishinev; 48°14'/27°16'.

Glinsko, *see* Glinskoye.

Glinskoye, Ukr. (Glinsko); pop. 124; 32 km NNW of Lvov; 50°04'/23°54'; PHP2.

Glinyanka, Ukr. (Zaglinki); pop. 19; 146 km N of Lvov; 51°08'/24°12'.

Glinyany, Ukr. (Glina, Glinah, Gline, Gliniany); pop. 1,679; 38 km E of Lvov; 49°49'/24°31'; COH, EDRD, EGRS, EJ, GA, GUM3, GUM4, HSL, HSL2, JGFF, LDL, PHP1, PHP2, SF, YB.

Gliny Male, Pol.; pop. 8; 107 km NE of Krakow; 50°25'/21°19'.

Gliny Wielkie, Pol.; pop. 27; 107 km NE of Krakow; 50°24'/21°19'.

Glinzheny (Balti), Mold. (Glingeni Balti); pop. 57; 101 km WNW of Kishinev; 47°36'/27°53'.

Glinzheny (Orhei), Mold. (Glingeni Orhei); pop. 62; 94 km N of Kishinev; 47°49'/28°53'.

Glisk, *see* Glusk.

Gliwice, Pol. (Glayvits, Gleiwitz); pop. 1,899; 69 km SSW of Czestochowa; 50°17'/18°40'; AMG, EJ, FRG, GA, GUM3, GUM4, GUM5, GUM6, HSL, HSL2, JGFF, LDL, LDS, PHP3, POCEM.

Globikowa, Pol.; pop. 10; 101 km W of Przemysl; 49°58'/21°27'.

Globino, Ukr.; 163 km WNW of Dnepropetrovsk; 49°23'/33°17'; GUM4.

Glodeni, Rom.; pop. 22; A number of towns share this name. It was not possible to determine from available information which one is being referenced. *See also* Glodyany.

Glod Maramures, Rom.; pop. 218; 114 km N of Cluj; 47°43'/24°05'; COH, GUM3.

Glodowo, Pol.; 120 km WNW of Bialystok; 53°44'/21°40'; GUM4.

Glod Somes, Rom.; pop. 38; 62 km N of Cluj; 47°17'/23°39'.

Glodyany, Mold. (Glodeni); pop. 214; 133 km WNW of Kishinev; 47°47'/27°31'.

Glogau, *see* Glogow.

Gloggnitz, Aus.; pop. 35; 69 km SSW of Wien; 47°40'/15°56'.

Glogo, *see* Glogow.

Glogov, *see* Glogow.

Glogow, Pol. (Glogau, Glogo, Glogov, Glogow Malopolski); pop. 648; 69 km WNW of Przemysl; 50°09'/21°58'; AMG, EGRS, EJ, FRG, GA, GUM4, GUM5, HSL, HSL2, JGFF, LDL, LDS, PHP1, PHP2, PHP3, SF.

Glogow (Kielce area), Pol.; 101 km S of Warszawa; 51°25'/20°52'; GUM5.

Glogow (Lower Silesia), Germ.; pop. 600; CAHJP, GUM3. This town was not found in BGN gazetteers under the given spelling.

Glogowek, Pol. (Oberglogau); pop. 50; 101 km SW of Czestochowa; 50°22'/17°52'; POCEM.

Glogowice, Pol.; pop. 5; 19 km NE of Lodz; 51°50'/19°39'.

Glogow Malopolski, *see* Glogow.

Glomcha, *see* Hlomcza.

Glott, Germ.; pop. 3; 88 km WNW of Munchen; 48°30'/10°29'.

Glovna, *see* Glowno.

Glovno, *see* Glowno.

Glowaczow, Pol. (Glavtchev); pop. 1,411; 75 km SSE of Warszawa; 51°38'/21°19'; AMG, COH, HSL, JGFF, SF.

Glowaczowa, Pol.; pop. 11; 101 km E of Krakow; 50°03'/21°19'.

Glowienka, Pol.; pop. 3; 75 km WSW of Przemysl; 49°40'/21°46'.

Glowno, Pol. (Glovna, Glovno); pop. 1,430; 32 km NNE of Lodz; 51°58'/19°44'; AMG, CAHJP, COH, EDRD, EJ, GA, GUM3, GUM5, HSL, HSL2, JGFF, LDS, PHP1, SF.

Glubczyce, Pol. (Leobschuetz, Leobschutz); pop. 111; 114 km SW of Czestochowa; 50°12'/17°49'; AMG, HSL, JGFF, LDS.

Glubochek, Ukr. (Gleboczek, Glenbochek); pop. 83; 62 km N of Chernovtsy; 48°49'/25°56'; GUM3, GUM4, GUM6.

Glubokie, *see* Glebokie.

Glubokoye, *see* Derevna.

Glubowce, *see* Glebowice.

Gluchov, *see* Glukhov.

Gluchow, *see* Glukhov.

Gluchowice, *see* Glukhovitse.

Gluchow Stawki, Pol.; pop. 27; Described in the *Black Book* as being in the Kielce region of Poland, this town was not found in BGN gazetteers.

Gluckstadt, Germ. (Glueckstadt); 50 km WNW of Hamburg; 53°47'/09°25'; EJ.

Glueckstadt, *see* Gluckstadt.

Glukhov, Ukr. (Gluchov, Gluchow, Hluchov); pop. 2,551; 69 km NE of Konotop; 51°41'/33°55'; EJ, HSL, JGFF, LDL, SF.

Glukhovitse, Ukr. (Gluchowice); pop. 22; 26 km ESE of Lvov; 49°46'/24°15'.

Glusha, Byel.; pop. 53; 126 km ESE of Minsk; 53°05'/28°52'.

Glushitsa, Ukr. (Gluszyca); pop. 66; 94 km N of Rovno; 51°24'/26°39'.

Glushkov, *see* Glushkovskoye.

Glushkovo, Ukr. (Hluzkowo); pop. 41; 69 km NE of Rovno; 50°52'/27°09'.

Glushkovskoye, Ukr. (Glushkov, Gluszkow); pop. 35; 50 km NW of Chernovtsy; 48°39'/25°28'.

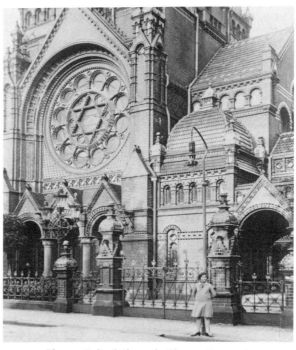

Glogow, Poland (formerly Glogau, Germany): Exterior of synagogue.

Glusk, Pol. (Glisk); pop. 390; 13 km SSE of Lublin; 51°11'/22°36'; AMG, EDRD, GUM5, HSL, LDL, LDS, POCEM, SF. *See also* Glussk.

Glusko Duze, Pol.; pop. 7; 38 km WSW of Lublin; 51°13'/22°00'.

Glussk, Byel. (Glusk, Halusk, Hlusk); pop. 2,581; 133 km SE of Minsk; 52°54'/28°41'; EJ, HSL, HSL2, JGFF, PHP4, SF, YB.

Gluszkow, *see* Glushkovskoye.

Gluszyca, *see* Glushitsa.

Gluszyn, Pol.; 107 km NW of Lodz; 52°32'/18°38'; GA.

Gluzy, Pol. BGN lists two possible localities with this name located at 50°22'/20°15' and 50°24'/20°43'. HSL.

Glybokaya, Ukr. (Adancata, Adancata Storojinet, Adancata Strojinet); pop. 263; 32 km S of Chernovtsy; 48°05'/25°56'.

Gmund (Baden), Germ.; pop. 78; BGN lists two possible localities with this name located at 47°37'/09°32' and 48°48'/09°47'.

Gmund (Bavaria), *see* Gnadenberg.

Gmunden, Aus.; pop. 53; 56 km ENE of Salzburg; 47°55'/13°48'; AMG.

Gnadenberg, Germ. (Gmund [Bavaria]); 114 km SW of Munchen; 47°36'/10°14'; GUM5.

Gnadendorf, Aus.; pop. 2; 50 km N of Wien; 48°37'/16°24'.

Gnaszyn Dolny, Pol.; pop. 7; 6 km WSW of Czestochowa; 50°48'/19°03'.

Gncsen, *see* Gniezno.

Gnesen, *see* Gniezno.

Gnevetchov, *see* Gniewoszow.

Gnevkovy, *see* Gniewkowo.

Gniazdkow, Pol.; pop. 16; 56 km W of Lublin; 51°16'/21°48'.

Gniew, Pol.; pop. 20; 62 km SSE of Gdansk; 53°50'/18°50'.

Gniewczyna Lancucka, Pol.; pop. 35; 38 km NW of Przemysl; 50°07'/22°29'.

Gniewczyna Tryniecka, Pol.; pop. 36; 38 km NW of Przemysl; 50°06'/22°30'.

Gniewiecin, Pol.; pop. 27; 56 km N of Krakow; 50°32'/20°04'.

Gniewkowo, Pol. (Argenau, Gnevkovy, Nefcover); pop. 41; 114 km NE of Poznan; 52°53'/18°26'; AMG, GUM4, GUM5, HSL, JGFF, LDS.

Gniewoszow, Pol. (Ginivishov, Gnevetchov); pop. 3,500; 62 km WNW of Lublin; 51°28'/21°48'; AMG, COH, EDRD, GA, GUM4, HSL, HSL2, JGFF, LDS, SF, WS, YB.

Gniezdziska, Pol.; pop. 2; 82 km ENE of Czestochowa; 50°52'/20°16'.

Gniezno, Pol. (Gncsen, Gnesen); pop. 395; 45 km NE of Poznan; 52°33'/17°36'; CAHJP, EDRD, EJ, GUM5, HSL, JGFF, LDS, PHP1, PHP4.

Gnigl, Aus.; pop. 2; 6 km E of Salzburg; 47°48'/13°05'.

Gnilche, Ukr. (Hnilcze); pop. 39; 101 km SE of Lvov; 49°12'/24°56'.

Gnilichki, Ukr. (Hnilice Male); pop. 21; 107 km S of Rovno; 49°40'/26°06'.

Gnilitse Velke, see Gnilitsy.

Gnilitsy, Ukr. (Gnilitse Velke, Hnilice Wielkie); pop. 47; 107 km S of Rovno; 49°42'/26°06'.

Gnivan, Ukr.; pop. 142; 19 km SSW of Vinnitsa; 49°06'/28°20'.

Gnizdichev, Ukr. (Gnizdychuv, Hnizdyczow); pop. 100; 62 km SSE of Lvov; 49°21'/24°07'; PHP2.

Gnizdychuv, see Gnizdichev.

Gnodstadt, Germ.; pop. 12; 69 km W of Nurnberg; 49°38'/10°07'; PHGB.

Gnoien, Germ.; 45 km ESE of Rostock; 53°58'/12°43'; LDS.

Gnojnice, see Gnoynitse.

Gnojnik, Pol.; pop. 34; 56 km ESE of Krakow; 49°54'/20°37'.

Gnojno, Pol.; pop. 10; 88 km NE of Krakow; 50°37'/20°51'; JGFF. *See also* Gnoyno.

Gnotzheim, Germ.; 56 km SSW of Nurnberg; 49°04'/10°43'; PHGB.

Gnoynitse, Ukr. (Gnojnice); pop. 35; 62 km W of Lvov; 49°57'/23°07'.

Gnoyno, Ukr. (Gnojno); pop. 21; 120 km N of Lvov; 50°54'/24°29'.

Goagiu, Rom.; pop. 5; 114 km ESE of Cluj; 46°22'/25°01'.

Gobelsburg, Aus.; 56 km WNW of Wien; 48°27'/15°41'; EJ.

Goch, Germ.; pop. 65; 101 km NW of Koln; 51°40'/06°10'; GUM3, GUM5.

Gochevo, Ukr. EDRD. This town was not found in BGN gazetteers under the given spelling.

Gochsheim, Germ.; pop. 20; 88 km NW of Nurnberg; 50°01'/10°17'; GUM5, HSL, PHGB, PHGBW.

Goclawek, Pol.; pop. 4; 13 km E of Warszawa; 52°14'/21°08'.

Gocs, Cz.; 62 km W of Kosice; 48°46'/20°25'; HSL. This town was located on a pre-World War I map, but does not appear in contemporary gazetteers. *See also* Gaesti.

Gocz, HSL, JGFF. This town was not found in BGN gazetteers under the given spelling.

Goddelau, Germ.; pop. 17; 32 km S of Frankfurt am Main; 49°50'/08°30'; JGFF.

Godeliai, Lith.; pop. 177; 62 km SW of Siauliai; 55°42'/22°22'; HSL.

Godeliai (II), Lith.; pop. 22; 94 km W of Siauliai; 55°59'/21°47'.

Godemesterhaza, see Stinceni.

Godesberg, see Bad Godesberg.

Godilieva, see Garliava.

Goding, Aus.; 50 km SW of Graz; 46°47'/14°55'; HSL.

Godlawo, see Garliava.

Godlewo, see Garliava.

Godlewo Backi, Pol.; pop. 11; 62 km SW of Bialystok; 52°48'/22°25'.

Godlewo Mierniki, Pol.; pop. 7; 69 km SW of Bialystok; 52°43'/22°18'.

Godlewo Wielkie, Pol.; pop. 20; 69 km SW of Bialystok; 52°44'/22°19'.

Godollo, Hung.; pop. 276; 26 km NE of Budapest; 47°36'/19°22'; GUM4, GUM6, LDS, PHH.

Godowa, Pol.; 69 km W of Przemysl; 49°51'/21°49'; PHP3.

Godre, Hung.; pop. 6; 75 km E of Nagykanizsa; 46°17'/17°59'.

Goduv, Ukr. (Hodow); pop. 57; 75 km ESE of Lvov; 49°37'/25°01'.

Goduzischki, see Adutiskis.

Godzhineshty, Mold. (Hodjinesti); pop. 77; 56 km NW of Kishinev; 47°22'/28°19'.

Godziesze Wielkie, Pol.; pop. 33; 88 km WSW of Lodz; 51°39'/18°11'.

Godzisz, Pol.; pop. 2; 82 km WNW of Lublin; 51°43'/21°40'.

Goeding, see Hodonin.

Goerlitz, see Gorlitz.

Goettingen, see Gottingen.

Goggingen, Germ.; pop. 21; 56 km WNW of Munchen; 48°20'/10°52'; PHGB.

Gogikev, LDL. This pre-World War I community was not found in BGN gazetteers.

Gogolevo, Ukr. (Hohalov); 157 km SSE of Konotop; 49°55'/33°50'; EDRD, SF.

Gogolin, Pol.; 82 km SW of Czestochowa; 50°29'/18°02'; GA, GUM3, GUM4, GUM5, PHP3, POCEM.

Gogolow, Pol.; pop. 42; 94 km W of Przemysl; 49°51'/21°31'.

Golab, Pol.; 38 km NW of Lublin; 51°30'/22°23'; GA, GUM3, GUM5.

Golaia Pristan, see Golaya Pristan.

Golancz, Pol. (Gollantsch); pop. 50; 62 km N of Poznan; 52°57'/17°18'; JGFF.

Gola Pristan, see Golaya Pristan.

Gola Przystan, see Golaya Pristan.

Golaya Pristan, Ukr. (Gola Pristan, Gola Przystan, Golaia Pristan, Holia Pristan); pop. 291; 139 km ENE of Odessa; 46°31'/32°31'; SF.

Golbice, Pol.; pop. 7; 50 km NW of Lodz; 52°06'/19°06'.

Golcowa, Pol.; pop. 59; 50 km WSW of Przemysl; 49°46'/22°03'.

Golcuv Jenikov, Cz. (Golcuvjenikov, Goltsch Jenikau); pop. 133; 82 km ESE of Praha; 49°49'/15°29'; EJ.

Golcuvjenikov, see Golcuv Jenikov.

Golcza, Pol.; pop. 22; 32 km N of Krakow; 50°20'/19°56'.

Goldap, Pol.; pop. 48; 146 km NW of Bialystok; 54°19'/22°18'; POCEM.

Goldbach, Germ.; pop. 39; 38 km ESE of Frankfurt am Main; 50°00'/09°11'; GUM5, JGFF, PHGB, PHGBW.

Goldberg, see Zlotoryja.

Goldenhof, Pol. PHP1. This town was not found in BGN gazetteers under the given spelling.

Goldenstadt, Germ.; pop. 82 km SSW of Rostock; 53°28'/11°31'; GED.

Gol Dingen, see Kuldiga.

Goldingen, see Kuldiga.

Goldkops, GUM3. This town was not found in BGN gazetteers under the given spelling.

Goldstein, HSL. This pre-World War I community was not found in BGN gazetteers.

Golecin, Pol.; pop. 6 km W of Poznan; 52°26'/16°52'; GA.

Goleczyna, Pol.; pop. 14; 107 km E of Krakow; 49°58'/21°21'.

Golejow, Pol.; 107 km NE of Krakow; 50°34'/21°12'; GUM4.

Goleniow, Pol. (Gollnow); pop. 73; 26 km NE of Szczecin; 53°34'/14°49'; LDS.

Golerkany, Mold. (Holercani); pop. 14; 45 km NNE of Kishinev; 47°19'/29°05'.

Goleshuv, Ukr. (Holeszow); pop. 27; 69 km SSE of Lvov; 49°19'/24°16'.

Goleszow, Pol.; pop. 44; 94 km SW of Krakow; 49°44'/18°45'; GUM3, GUM4, GUM5, PHP3.

Goleszow (near Tarnow), Pol.; pop. 30; 107 km ENE of Krakow; 50°14'/21°27'.

Golet, Rom. (Galacs); 195 km SSW of Ciuj; 45°17'/22°15'; HSL.

Golgau, (Golgory); EGRS, LDL. This pre-World War I

101

community was not found in BGN gazetteers.

Golgora, *see* Gologory.

Golgory, *see* Golgau.

Goligor, *see* Gologory.

Golin, *see* Golina.

Golina, Pol. (Golin, Gollin); pop. 695; 75 km E of Poznan; 52°15'/18°06'; COH, EDRD, GUM3, HSL, HSL2, LDL, LDS, PHP1, SF.

Golina Wielka, Pol.; pop. 8; 75 km NNW of Wroclaw; 51°42'/16°47'; GA.

Golinka, Pol.; 75 km NNW of Wroclaw; 51°42'/16°49'; EDRD.

Golizna, Pol.; pop. 67; Described in the *Black Book* as being in the Lublin region of Poland, this town was not found in BGN gazetteers.

Golkovice, *see* Golkowice.

Golkow, Pol.; 32 km S of Warszawa; 52°03'/20°59'; GA.

Golkowice, (Golkovice); HSL. A number of towns share this name. It was not possible to determine from available information which one is being referenced.

Gollantsch, *see* Golancz.

Golle, Hung.; pop. 22; 82 km E of Nagykanizsa; 46°26'/18°01'; HSL.

Gollheim, Germ.; pop. 19; 75 km SSW of Frankfurt am Main; 49°35'/08°03'.

Gollin, *see* Golina.

Gollnitz, *see* Gelnica.

Gollnow, *see* Goleniow.

Gollub, *see* Golub Dobrzyn.

Golne, Byel. (Golnie); pop. 34; 195 km WNW of Pinsk; 53°18'/24°01'.

Golnie, *see* Golne.

Golobi, *see* Goloby.

Golobudy, Byel. (Holobudy); pop. 109; 163 km WNW of Pinsk; 53°00'/24°13'.

Goloby, Ukr. (Golobi, Holobi, Holoby); pop. 209; 101 km WNW of Rovno; 51°05'/25°01'; AMG, SF.

Gologorica, Yug. (Moncalvo); 163 km SW of Zagreb; 45°15'/14°02'; HSL.

Gologorki, *see* Gologurki.

Gologory, Ukr. (Golgora, Goligor); pop. 505; 50 km E of Lvov; 49°45'/24°43'; GUM3, HSL, JGFF, PHP2, SF.

Gologurki, Ukr. (Gologorki); pop. 27; 50 km E of Lvov; 49°46'/24°43'.

Golonki, Pol.; pop. 7; 56 km S of Bialystok; 52°40'/22°52'.

Golonog, Pol.; pop. 95; 50 km SSE of Czestochowa; 50°21'/19°14'.

Golop, Hung.; pop. 11; 38 km NE of Miskolc; 48°14'/21°12'; COH.

Goloshnitsa, Mold. (Holosnita); pop. 33; 150 km NNW of Kishinev; 48°15'/28°10'.

Goloskov, Ukr.; pop. 1,572; 82 km W of Vinnitsa; 49°23'/27°21'.

Goloskovo, Ukr. (Goloskowo, Holoskov); 75 km SSE of Uman; 48°10'/30°27'; LDL, SF.

Goloskowo, *see* Goloskovo.

Goloskuv, Ukr. (Holoskow); pop. 34; 88 km WNW of Chernovtsy; 48°42'/24°52'.

Golotczyzna, Pol.; pop. 6; 62 km NNW of Warszawa; 52°47'/20°42'.

Golotki, Ukr. (Holotki); pop. 23; 114 km S of Rovno; 49°39'/26°10'.

Golovanevsk, Ukr. (Holavenevsk); pop. 3,474; 50 km SE of Uman; 48°23'/30°28'; COH, EDRD, EJ, JGFF, SF.

Golovatchino, Byel. (Golowtschin, Holovtchin, Jablonitsa); 62 km WNW of Vitebsk; 55°23'/29°14'; LDL, SF.

Golovchyntse, Ukr. (Holowczynce); 62 km NNW of Chernovtsy; 48°49'/25°44'; GUM3, GUM4, PHP2.

Golovetsko, *see* Golovetskoye.

Golovetskoye, Ukr. (Golovetsko, Holowiecko); pop. 73; 101 km SW of Lvov; 49°18'/22°53'.

Golovkino, USSR (Nemonien); pop. 2; 56 km NE of Kaliningrad; 54°59'/21°16'.

Golovno, Ukr. (Holowno); pop. 23; 170 km N of Lvov; 51°20'/24°05'.

Golowierzchy, Pol.; pop. 16; 94 km N of Lublin; 52°01'/22°30'.

Golowtschin, *see* Golovatchino.

Gols, Aus.; pop. 16; 56 km ESE of Wien; 47°53'/16°54'.

Golshany, Byel. (Holshan, Holshani, Holszany, Olshan, Olshani); 114 km WNW of Minsk; 54°15'/26°01'; AMG, GUM3, GUM4, HSL, HSL2, LDL, SF, YB.

Golta, Ukr. (Halta); 94 km SE of Uman; 48°03'/30°53'; EDRD, GUM4, HSL, LDL, PHR1, SF. Golta is now part of Pervomaysk.

Goltsch Jenikau, *see* Golcuv Jenikov.

Golub, *see* Golub Dobrzyn.

Golub Dobrzyn, Pol. (Dobrin Bay Dervents, Dobrzyn Golub, Dobrzyn nad Drewca, Dobrzyn nad Drweca, Dobzhin, Dobzhin Golub, Dobzhin Nad Drvents, Gollub, Golub, Golub Dobzhin); pop. 1,976; 139 km SSE of Gdansk; 53°07'/19°03'; AMG, CAHJP, HSL, HSL2, JGFF, LDL, LDS, LYV, PHP1, PHP4, SF, YB. This entry represents the twin cities of Golub and Dobrzyn. Population figures are given for Dobrzyn. Golub's pre-War Jewish population was 104. *See also* Dobrzyn nad Wisla.

Golub Dobzhin, *see* Golub Dobrzyn.

Golubichi, Byel. (Holubicze); 139 km WSW of Vitebsk; 55°07'/27°58'; COH, HSL. The *Black Book* shows a town called Holubicze in Wilen province near Dunilowicze. No such town appears in interwar gazetteers of Poland nor in BGN.

Golubie, Pol.; 45 km SW of Gdansk; 54°13'/18°02'; GUM3.

Golubinci, Yug.; pop. 7; 38 km WNW of Beograd; 44°59'/20°04'.

Golubitsa, Ukr. (Holubica); pop. 35; 82 km ENE of Lvov; 49°55'/25°10'.

Golymin Polnoc, Pol. (Golymin Stary); pop. 44; 62 km NNW of Warszawa; 52°48'/20°53'.

Golymin Stary, *see* Golymin Polnoc.

Golyn, *see* Kotyatiche Golyn.

Golynka, Byel. (Holinka, Holynka); pop. 224; 176 km WSW of Minsk; 53°30'/24°56'; COH, HSL, JGFF, SF, YB.

Golystok, Pol.; pop. 14; 56 km NNE of Warszawa; 52°44'/21°21'.

Gomaringen, Germ.; 45 km S of Stuttgart; 48°27'/09°07'; PHGBW.

Gombas, *see* Hubova.

Gombin, *see* Gabin.

Gomel, Byel. (Homel, Homiyah); pop. 37,745; 277 km ESE of Minsk; 52°25'/31°00'; AMG, CAHJP, EJ, GUM4, GUM5, HSL, HSL2, JGFF, LDL, SF, YB.

Gomirje, Yug.; pop. 3; 88 km SW of Zagreb; 45°20'/15°08'.

Gomla, LDL. This pre-World War I community was not found in BGN gazetteers.

Gommersheim, Germ.; pop. 24; 88 km WNW of Stuttgart; 49°17'/08°16'; GED.

Gomorszollos, Hung.; pop. 4; 45 km NW of Miskolc; 48°23'/20°26'.

Gomunica, *possibly* Gomunice.

Gomunice, Pol. (Gomunica?); pop. 278; 50 km NNE of Czestochowa; 51°10'/19°29'; GUM5, PHP1.

Gonbach, Germ.; 82 km SSW of Frankfurt am Main; 49°33'/07°54'; JGFF.

Gonc, Hung.; pop. 229; 56 km NNE of Miskolc; 48°28'/21°17'; AMG, COH, HSL, LDS, PHH.

Gonchi Brud, *see* Gonchiy Brod.

Gonchiy Brod, Ukr. (Gonchi Brud, Gonczy Brod); pop. 28; 107 km WNW of Rovno; 51°04'/24°53'.

Goncruszka, Hung.; pop. 53; 56 km NNE of Miskolc; 48°27'/21°15'; HSL, PHH.

Gonczy Brod, *see* Gonchiy Brod.

Gonczyce, Pol.; pop. 16; 69 km ESE of Warszawa; 51°47'/21°44'.

Gondelsheim, Germ.; 50 km WNW of Stuttgart; 49°04'/08°40'; LDS, PHGBW.

Gondovo, Cz. (Salmos); 120 km ENE of Bratislava;

48°17'/18°40'; HSL.

Goniadz, Pol. (Goniondzh, Gonyadz, Gonyandz, Gonyondzh); pop. 1,135; 45 km NW of Bialystok; 53°29'/22°45'; AMG, EDRD, GA, GUM3, GUM4, HSL, HSL2, JGFF, LYV, POCEM, SF, YB.

Goniondzh, *see* Goniadz.

Gonsawa, *see* Gasawa.

Gonyadz, *see* Goniadz.

Gonyandz, *see* Goniadz.

Gonyondzh, *see* Goniadz.

Goorlitz, *see* Gorlitz.

Goppingen, Germ.; pop. 382; 38 km E of Stuttgart; 48°42'/09°40'; GED, GUM3, JGFF, PHGBW.

Gor, Hung.; pop. 3; 107 km NNW of Nagykanizsa; 47°22'/16°48'.

Gor'kiy, (Engels);

Gora, Pol. (Guhrau); pop. 57; 82 km NW of Wroclaw; 51°40'/16°32'; HSL, HSL2, JGFF.

Gorai, *see* Goraj Lubelski.

Goraj, *see* Goraj Lubelski.

Gorajec Stara, Pol.; pop. 52; Described in the *Black Book* as being in the Lublin region of Poland, this town was not found in BGN gazetteers.

Gorajec Zagroble, Pol.; pop. 73; Described in the *Black Book* as being in the Lublin region of Poland, this town was not found in BGN gazetteers.

Goraj Lubelski, Pol. (Gorai, Goraj, Goray); pop. 394; 62 km S of Lublin; 50°43'/22°40'; CAHJP, COH, EDRD, FRG, GUM5, HSL, HSL2, PHR1, POCEM, SF.

Gora Kalwaria, Pol. (Ger, Gier, Gora Kalwarja, Gur, Gura Kalvaria); pop. 2,961; 38 km SE of Warszawa; 51°59'/21°14'; AMG, COH, EDRD, EJ, FRG, GA, GUM5, HSL, LDS, LYV, PHP1, PHP4, POCEM, SF, YB.

Gora Kalwarja, *see* Gora Kalwaria.

Gora Motyczna, Pol.; pop. 9; 107 km ENE of Krakow; 50°06'/21°23'.

Gorane, Byel. (Horanie); pop. 8; 120 km NW of Minsk; 54°45'/26°32'.

Goranin, Pol.; pop. 10; 88 km E of Poznan; 52°22'/18°15'.

Gora Pulawska, Pol.; pop. 41; 45 km WNW of Lublin; 51°25'/21°57'.

Gora Ropczycka, Pol.; pop. 16; 82 km WNW of Przemysl; 50°03'/21°41'.

Gora Siewierska, Pol.; pop. 5; 50 km S of Czestochowa; 50°24'/19°05'.

Gora Strykowa, Pol. (Strekowa Gora); pop. 27; 45 km W of Bialystok; 53°13'/22°33'.

Gora Wisniowa, *see* Wisniowa Gora.

Goray, *see* Goraj Lubelski.

Gorbakha, Byel. (Horbacka); pop. 27; 50 km WSW of Pinsk; 52°06'/25°22'.

Gorbakov, Ukr. (Horbakow); pop. 5; 26 km E of Rovno; 50°36'/26°39'.

Gorbenpinczehely, *see* Pincehely.

Gorbkuv, Ukr. (Horbkow); pop. 42; 75 km N of Lvov; 50°29'/24°22'.

Gorbo Belecska, *see* Belecska.

Gorbopincehely, *see* Pincehely.

Gorbovo, Byel. (Horbow?); pop. 7; 69 km WNW of Pinsk; 52°26'/25°16'; GA.

Gorchtchik, Ukr. EDRD. This town was not found in BGN gazetteers under the given spelling.

Gorcsony, Hung.; pop. 4; 101 km ESE of Nagykanizsa; 45°58'/18°08'; HSL.

Gorczenica, Pol.; pop. 2; 133 km SSE of Gdansk; 53°13'/19°23'.

Gorczyn, Pol. BGN lists two possible localities with this name located at 51°35'/19°09' and 52°23'/16°53'. POCEM.

Gordineshty, Mold. (Gordinesti Hotin); pop. 30; BGN lists two possible localities with this name located at 47°42'/28°48' and 48°10'/27°10'.

Gordinesti Hotin, *see* Gordineshty.

Gordinya, *see* Gordynya.

Gordynya, Ukr. (Gordinia, Hordynia Rustykalna, Hordynia Szlachecka); pop. 32; 56 km SW of Lvov; 49°32'/23°23'.

Gorecko, GUM3. This town was not found in BGN gazetteers under the given spelling.

Gorecko Stare, Pol.; pop. 5; 82 km SSE of Lublin; 50°32'/23°00'.

Gorgenyhodak, *see* Hodac.

Gorgenykakucs, *see* Cacuciu.

Gorgenyoroszdalu, *see* Solovastru.

Gorgenyorsova, *see* Orsova.

Gorgenyszentimre, *see* Gurghiu.

Gorgeteg, Hung.; pop. 7; 45 km ESE of Nagykanizsa; 46°09'/17°26'.

Gorican, Yug.; pop. 4; 82 km NNE of Zagreb; 46°23'/16°41'.

Gorica Svetojanska, Yug. (Sveta Jana); pop. 5; 32 km SW of Zagreb; 45°43'/15°36'.

Gorinchovo, Ukr. (Horincovo); 182 km WSW of Chernovtsy; 48°16'/23°26'; AMG, LYV, SM.

Goringrod, *see* Goryngrad.

Gorischkowka, *see* Goryshkovka.

Gorishnyy Dzvinyach, Pol. (Dzwiniacz Gorny); pop. 171; 75 km S of Przemysl; 49°09'/22°47'; PHP2.

Gorizia, *see* Gorizy.

Gorizy, (Gorizia); HSL. This pre-World War I community was not found in BGN gazetteers.

Gorka Koscielowska, Pol.; pop. 12; 38 km NE of Krakow; 50°19'/20°16'.

Gorka Lubartowska, Pol.; pop. 7; 38 km N of Lublin; 51°31'/22°39'.

Gorki, Byel.; pop. 2,343; 114 km SE of Vitebsk; 54°17'/30°59'; AMG, EDRD, EJ, HSL, HSL2, JGFF, LDL, PHP1, SF.

Gorki (Lwow), Pol.; pop. 56; 56 km WSW of Przemysl; 49°39'/22°02'.

Gorki (near Garwolin), Pol.; pop. 16; 62 km ESE of Warszawa; 51°52'/21°35'.

Gorki (near Grubaki), Pol.; pop. 14; 32 km E of Warszawa; 52°11'/21°25'.

Gorki (near Kielce), Pol.; pop. 5; 88 km NNE of Krakow; 50°43'/20°43'.

Gorki (near Konskie), Pol.; pop. 11; 114 km ESE of Lodz; 51°08'/20°43'.

Gorki (near Mogielnica), Pol.; pop. 1; 75 km S of Warszawa; 51°38'/20°47'.

Gorki (near Sandomierz), Pol.; pop. 19; 101 km SW of Lublin; 50°40'/21°26'.

Gorki (near Sochaczew), Pol.; pop. 5; 32 km W of Warszawa; 52°20'/20°32'.

Gorki (near Stopnica), Pol.; pop. 8; 69 km NE of Krakow; 50°22'/20°45'.

Gorki (near Wlodawa), Pol.; pop. 4; 69 km NE of Lublin; 51°27'/23°28'.

Gorki (Wolyn), Ukr.; pop. 25; 88 km E of Rovno; 50°31'/27°28'.

Gorki Borze, Pol.; pop. 21; 62 km NE of Warszawa; 52°27'/21°51'.

Gorki Grabienskie, Pol.; pop. 7; 50 km SW of Lodz; 51°28'/18°57'.

Gorki Srednie, Pol.; pop. 7; 62 km NE of Warszawa; 52°27'/21°52'.

Gorki Szczukowskie, Pol. (Szczukowskie Gorki); pop. 3; 101 km ENE of Czestochowa; 50°53'/20°32'.

Gorki Wielkie, Pol.; pop. 6; 82 km SW of Krakow; 49°47'/18°52'.

Gorkiy, Ukr.; 170 km ESE of Dnepropetrovsk; 47°30'/36°46'; JGFF.

Gorliava, *see* Garliava.

Gorlice, Pol. (Gorlits, Gorlitse, Gorlitza); pop. 2,300; 101 km ESE of Krakow; 49°40'/21°10'; COH, EDRD, EGRS, EJ, GA, GUM3, GUM4, GUM5, HSL, HSL2, LDL, LYV, PHP2, PHP3, POCEM, SF, YB.

Gorliczyna, Pol.; pop. 14; 38 km NW of Przemysl; 50°04'/22°29'.

Gorlits, *see* Gorlice.

Gorlitse, *see* Gorlice.

Gorlitz, Germ. (Goerlitz, Goorlitz, Zgorzelec); pop. 450; 182 km SE of Berlin; 51°10'/15°00'; AMG, EJ, GUM3, GUM4, GUM5, GUM6, HSL, JGFF, LDS, PHP3. Gorlitz is on the Polish border. Across the Neisse River in Poland is the twin city of Zgorzelec.

Gorlitza, *see* Gorlice.

Gorlovka, Ukr.; 227 km E of Dnepropetrovsk; 48°18'/38°03'.

Gorna Dzhumaya, *see* Blagoevgrad.

Gorna Wies, Pol.; pop. 28; 13 km N of Krakow; 50°10'/19°56'.

Gornesti, Rom.; pop. 6; 82 km E of Cluj; 46°40'/24°39'.

Gorniki, Ukr.; pop. 52; 170 km WNW of Rovno; 51°43'/24°29'.

Gornja Stubica, Yug.; pop. 1; 26 km N of Zagreb; 45°58'/16°02'.

Gornji Miholjac, Yug.; pop. 7; 133 km E of Zagreb; 45°46'/17°40'.

Gornji Milanovac, Yug.; pop. 3; 94 km S of Beograd; 44°02'/20°27'.

Gornji Petrovci, Yug.; pop. 2; 120 km N of Zagreb; 46°49'/16°12'.

Gorno, Pol.; pop. 71; 75 km NW of Przemysl; 50°18'/22°09'; PHP3.

Gornostayevka, Ukr.; 182 km N of Simferopol; 46°31'/34°18'; GUM4.

Gornostaypol, Ukr. (Hornistopol); 75 km NNW of Kiyev; 51°04'/30°15'; EDRD, JGFF, LDL, SF.

Gorod, Ukr. (Gorodye, Horodz, Horodzhyey); 62 km WSW of Chernovtsy; 48°18'/25°03'; LYV.

Gorodeia, *see* Gorodeya.

Gorodenka, Ukr. (Horodenka); pop. 3,048; 50 km NW of Chernovtsy; 48°40'/25°30'; AMG, COH, EDRD, EGRS, EJ, GA, GUM3, GUM4, GUM5, GUM6, GYLA, HSL, HSL2, JGFF, LDL, PHP2, SF, YB.

Gorodets, Ukr. (Chorodetz, Horodziec); pop. 607; 82 km N of Rovno; 51°17'/26°19'; COH, SF.

Gorodets (Polesie), *see* Merkulovichi.

Gorodeya, Byel. (Gorodeia, Horodia, Horodzei, Horodziej); pop. 796; 94 km SW of Minsk; 53°19'/26°32'; COH, HSL, LDL, SF.

Gorodilovo, Byel. (Horodzilow); pop. 1; 75 km WNW of Minsk; 54°14'/26°37'.

Gorodisce, Byel. JGFF, SF. This town was not found in BGN gazetteers under the given spelling.

Gorodischtsche, *see* Gorodishche.

Gorodishche, Ukr. (Chorodishtch, Gorodischtsche, Horodyszcze); pop. 1,194; 107 km NE of Uman; 49°17'/31°27'; AMG, JGFF, LDL. There are no less than 35 towns in the USSR with this name. See listings below.

Gorodishche (Bessarabia), Mold. (Horodistea Lapusna); pop. 43; 50 km WNW of Kishinev; 47°13'/28°14'.

Gorodishche (Dnepropetrovsk area), Ukr.; 94 km S of Dnepropetrovsk; 47°39'/34°35'; GUM4.

Gorodishche (Lwow), Ukr.; pop. 71; 62 km SW of Lvov; 49°28'/23°20'; HSL.

Gorodishche (Moldavia), Mold. (Horodistea); pop. 43; 50 km WNW of Kishinev; 47°13'/28°14'.

Gorodishche (near Berezno), Ukr.; pop. 3; 56 km NNE of Rovno; 51°01'/26°45'.

Gorodishche (near Bobruysk), Byel.; 146 km E of Minsk; 53°44'/29°48'; SF.

Gorodishche (near Charukuv), Ukr.; pop. 6; 69 km W of Rovno; 50°42'/25°16'.

Gorodishche (near Kustyn), Ukr.; pop. 30; 13 km ENE of Rovno; 50°38'/26°22'.

Gorodishche (near Lubny), Ukr.; pop. 120 km S of Konotop; 50°11'/33°04'; SF.

Gorodishche (Nowogrodek), Byel.; pop. 760; 120 km SW of Minsk; 53°19'/26°00'; COH, GUM3, GUM5, GYLA, HSL, HSL2, SF.

Gorodishche (Polesie), Byel.; pop. 44; 13 km NE of Pinsk; 52°10'/26°16'.

Gorodishche (Wilen), Byel.; pop. 12; 101 km NNW of Minsk; 54°44'/27°08'.

Gorodka, Mold. (Horodca); pop. 6; 32 km W of Kishinev; 47°03'/28°29'.

Gorodkovka, Ukr. (Mestkovka, Miastkovka, Myastkovka); pop. 1,602; 101 km SSE of Vinnitsa; 48°23'/28°42'; EDRD.

Gorodlo, *see* Horodlo.

Gorodlovitse, Ukr. (Horodlowice); pop. 46; 82 km N of Lvov; 50°34'/24°16'.

Gorodna, *see* Gorodnya.

Gorodnista, *see* Gorodnitsa.

Gorodnitsa, Ukr. (Gorodnista, Horodnica, Horodnitza); pop. 1,126; 75 km ENE of Rovno; 50°48'/27°19'; GUM4, HSL, JGFF, LDL, SF, YB. The *Black Book* also notes a town named Horodnica (pop. 30) in the interwar Polish province of Nowogrodek. The town does not appear in interwar or contemporary gazetteers.

Gorodnitsa (Stanislawow), Ukr.; pop. 81; 45 km NW of Chernovtsy; 48°41'/25°38'; PHP2.

Gorodno, Byel. (Horodno); pop. 583; 38 km ESE of Pinsk; 51°52'/26°30'; EJ, LDL, SF, YB.

Gorodno (Lyubomyl area), Ukr.; pop. 24; 163 km N of Lvov; 51°16'/24°08'.

Gorodnya, Ukr. (Gorodna, Horodna); pop. 1,359; 133 km WNW of Konotop; 51°53'/31°36'; EDRD, GUM4, HSL, SF.

Gorodok; pop. 2,494; AMG, COH, GUM4, HSL2, JGFF, LDL, PHP3, PHP4, SF. *See also* Grodek; Grudek.

Gorodok (near Bobruysk), Byel.; pop. 120 km SE of Minsk; 53°03'/28°46'; HSL, HSL, SF.

Gorodok (near Kamenets Podolskiy), Ukr. (Graydung, Graydunk); 107 km NNE of Chernovtsy; 49°10'/26°34'; SF.

Gorodok (near Lvov), Ukr. (Graydik, Grayding, Greiding, Grodek Jagiellonski, Grodig, Grudek Yagyelonski, Horodok, Hrudek); pop. 2,545; 26 km WSW of Lvov; 49°47'/23°39'; CAHJP, COH, EDRD, EGRS, EJ, HSL, PHP2, YB.

Gorodok (near Molodechno), Byel.; pop. 990; 56 km WNW of Minsk; 54°09'/26°55'; GUM3, GUM5, GUM6, SF.

Gorodok (near Rovno), Ukr.; pop. 62; 13 km NW of Rovno; 50°41'/26°11'; SF.

Gorodok (near Vitebsk), Byel.; pop. 2,660; 38 km NW of Vitebsk; 55°28'/29°59'; EJ, GUM4, HSL, JGFF.

Gorodye, *see* Gorod.

Gorodyshche Krulevske, Ukr. (Gorodyshche Krulevski, Horodyszcze Krolewskie); pop. 20; 50 km SSE of Lvov; 49°26'/24°16'.

Gorodyshche Krulevski, *see* Gorodyshche Krulevske.

Gorodyslavichi, Ukr. (Gorodyslavitse, Horodystawice); pop. 68; 26 km ESE of Lvov; 49°45'/24°18'.

Gorodyslavitse, *see* Gorodyslavichi.

Gorodzuv, Ukr. (Horodzow); pop. 14; 38 km NW of Lvov; 50°08'/23°47'.

Gorokholina, Ukr. (Horocholina); pop. 58; 114 km WNW of Chernovtsy; 48°45'/24°35'.

Gorokhov, Ukr. (Horchov, Horkhov, Horkhuv, Horochow, Orikhov); pop. 2,377; 88 km NNE of Lvov; 50°30'/24°46'; AMG, COH, EDRD, EJ, GUM3, HSL, HSL2, LDL, SF, YB.

Goromboly, Hung.; pop. 27; 13 km S of Miskolc; 48°03'/20°47'; HSL.

Gorond, *see* Goronda.

Goronda, Ukr. (Gorond); 195 km SSW of Lvov; 48°22'/22°34'; AMG, HSL.

Gorosheve, Ukr. (Horoszowa); pop. 39; 32 km NNE of Chernovtsy; 48°32'/26°06'.

Goroshki, *see* Volodarsk Volynskiy.

Gorowo Ilaweckie, Pol. (Landsberg Ost Preussen); pop. 21; 120 km E of Gdansk; 54°17'/20°30'.

Gorozhanka, Ukr. (Horozanka); pop. 94; 101 km SE of Lvov; 49°09'/24°55'.

Gorozhanna Volka, *see* Velikaya Gorozhanka.

Gorpin, Ukr. (Horpin); pop. 26; 32 km NE of Lvov;

50°00'/24°22'.

Gorsdorf, Germ. JGFF. A number of towns share this name. It was not possible to determine from available information which one is being referenced.

Gorshkov, *see* Gorzkow.

Gorsk, Byel. (Horsk); pop. 9; 101 km WNW of Pinsk; 52°24'/24°44'.

Gorskoye, Ukr. (Gorutsko, Horucko); pop. 41; 50 km S of Lvov; 49°28'/23°48'.

Gorszkowice, *possibly* Gorzkowice.

Goruna, Rom. (Gorund); pop. 21; 82 km NNW of Bucuresti; 45°05'/25°56'.

Gorund, *see* Goruna.

Gorutsko, *see* Gorskoye.

Goruv, Ukr. (Chorow); pop. 22; 107 km NNE of Lvov; 50°42'/24°39'.

Gorval, Byel. (Gorwal, Horval); 56 km W of Gomel; 52°34'/30°11'; LDL, SF.

Gorwal, *see* Gorval.

Gory, USSR; pop. 355; A number of towns share this name. It was not possible to determine from available information which one is being referenced.

Gory (near Kielce), Pol.; pop. 23; 56 km NNE of Krakow; 50°29'/20°25'.

Gory Luszowskie, Pol.; pop. 10; 38 km WNW of Krakow; 50°11'/19°25'.

Gory Morskie, Pol.; pop. 29; Described in the *Black Book* as being in the Kielce region of Poland, this town was not found in BGN gazetteers.

Goryngrad, Ukr. (Goringrod, Horyngrad Krupa, Horyngrod, Kripa); pop. 307; 19 km ENE of Rovno; 50°39'/26°31'; GUM3, SF, YB.

Gorynska Wola, Pol.; pop. 5; 88 km SSE of Warszawa; 51°33'/21°15'.

Goryshkovka, Ukr. (Charishkifka, Gorischkowka, Horyschkowka); 69 km SSE of Vinnitsa; 48°38'/28°37'; LDL, SF.

Goryslawice, Pol.; pop. 3; 62 km NE of Krakow; 50°21'/20°42'.

Gorzad, *see* Gargzdai.

Gorzakiew, Pol.; pop. 23; 88 km NE of Krakow; 50°36'/20°53'.

Gorzanka, Pol.; pop. 15; 56 km SSW of Przemysl; 49°20'/22°23'.

Gorzd, *see* Gargzdai.

Gorzed, *see* Gargzdai.

Gorzedow, Pol.; pop. 6; 62 km NNE of Czestochowa; 51°13'/19°33'.

Gorzejowa, Pol.; pop. 20; 101 km W of Przemysl; 49°56'/21°22'.

Gorzelnia, Pol.; pop. 20; Described in the *Black Book* as being in the Lublin region of Poland, this town was not found in BGN gazetteers.

Gorzen Dolny, Pol.; pop. 17; 45 km SW of Krakow; 49°52'/19°30'; PHP3.

Gorzen Gorny, Pol.; pop. 1; 45 km SW of Krakow; 49°51'/19°30'.

Gorzh D, *see* Gargzdai.

Gorzhdy, *see* Gargzdai.

Gorzkow, Pol. (Gireshkov, Gorshkov); pop. 434; 45 km ESE of Lublin; 50°57'/23°01'; AMG, EDRD, GUM5, HSL, JGFF, LDS, SF.

Gorzkow (Kielce area), Pol.; pop. 23; 114 km NE of Krakow; 50°41'/21°15'; GUM4, GUM5, PHP3.

Gorzkowice, Pol. (Gorszkowice?); pop. 648; 62 km NNE of Czestochowa; 51°13'/19°36'; GUM5, HSL, HSL2, PHP1, SF.

Gorzno, Pol.; pop. 25; 69 km ESE of Warszawa; 51°51'/21°43'.

Gorzow, Pol.; 50 km WSW of Krakow; 50°04'/19°14'; JGFF.

Gorzow Slaski, Pol. (Landsberg [Schleisen], Landsberg an der Prosna); pop. 20; 50 km WNW of Czestochowa; 51°02'/18°26'; HSL, LDS.

Gorzow Wielkopolski, Pol. (Landsberg an der Warthe); pop. 600; 94 km SE of Szczecin; 52°44'/15°14'; CAHJP, EJ, HSL, POCEM.

Gorzyce (near Przeworsk), Pol.; pop. 25; 45 km NNW of Przemysl; 50°08'/22°35'.

Gorzyce (near Tarnobrzeg), Pol.; pop. 31; 82 km SSW of Lublin; 50°40'/21°51'.

Gorzyczany, Pol.; pop. 12; 94 km SW of Lublin; 50°38'/21°36'.

Gosan, Pol.; pop. 8; 107 km NE of Czestochowa; 51°06'/20°35'.

Gosca, *see* Goshcha.

Goscienczyce, Pol.; pop. 15; 45 km S of Warszawa; 51°55'/20°57'.

Goscieradow, Pol.; 56 km SSW of Lublin; 50°52'/22°01'; GUM3.

Goscino, Pol. (Gross Jestin); pop. 5; 101 km NE of Szczecin; 54°03'/15°40'.

Gosciszka, Pol.; pop. 10; 120 km NW of Warszawa; 53°07'/20°01'.

Goshcha, Ukr. (Gosca, Hoshch, Hoshcha, Hosht, Hoshtch, Hoszcza, Osht); pop. 811; 32 km E of Rovno; 50°36'/26°40'; GUM3, GUM4, GUM5, HSL, LYV, SF, YB.

Goshchevo, Byel. (Hoszczewo); pop. 9; 94 km WNW of Pinsk; 52°42'/25°13'; GUM3.

Goshevo, Byel. (Hoszewo); pop. 6; 69 km WNW of Pinsk; 52°18'/25°14'.

Goshov, Ukr. (Hoszow); pop. 83; 94 km S of Lvov; 49°02'/23°53'; HSL.

Goslar, Germ.; pop. 46; 69 km ESE of Hannover; 51°54'/10°26'; AMG, EJ, GUM4, GUM5.

Goslin, HSL. This pre-World War I community was not found in BGN gazetteers.

Goslow, *see* Yevpatoriya.

Gospic, Yug.; 150 km S of Zagreb; 44°33'/15°23'; EDRD, GUM4, GUM5.

Gospodinci, Yug.; pop. 17; 75 km NW of Beograd; 45°24'/20°00'.

Gosprzydowa, Pol.; pop. 33; 56 km ESE of Krakow; 49°53'/20°35'.

Gossfelden, Germ.; pop. 14; 94 km N of Frankfurt am Main; 50°52'/08°44'; LDS.

Gossmannsdorf, *see* Gossmannsdorf am Main.

Gossmannsdorf am Main, Germ. (Gossmannsdorf); 82 km WNW of Nurnberg; 49°41'/10°02'; CAHJP, GUM5, JGFF, PHGB.

Gostila, Rom. (Csicsogombas); pop. 2; 69 km N of Cluj; 47°20'/23°49'.

Gostini, Lat. (Dankera, Dankere, Glasmanka, Glazmanka, Glazmanke, Glazminka); 94 km NW of Daugavpils; 56°37'/25°47'; AMG, JGFF, LDL, PHLE, SF.

Gostinin, *see* Gostynin.

Gostkow, Pol.; 114 km ESE of Lodz; 51°08'/20°46'; GA.

Gostomel, Ukr. (Hostomlia); 26 km WNW of Kiyev; 50°35'/30°16'; LDL, SF.

Gostomia, Pol. (Arnsfelde); pop. 3; 94 km NW of Poznan; 53°11'/16°26'.

Gostov, Ukr. (Hostow); pop. 40; 88 km WNW of Chernovtsy; 48°46'/24°56'.

Gostwica, Pol.; pop. 12; 69 km SE of Krakow; 49°37'/20°36'.

Gostyn, Pol.; 69 km S of Poznan; 51°53'/17°02'; JGFF.

Gostynie, Pol.; pop. 4; 82 km W of Lodz; 51°55'/18°17'.

Gostynin, Pol. (Gostinin); pop. 1,831; 82 km N of Lodz; 52°26'/19°29'; AMG, COH, EDRD, EJ, FRG, GA, GUM4, HSL, HSL2, JGFF, LDL, LYV, PHP1, PHP4, POCEM, SF, YB.

Goszczyn, Pol.; pop. 185; 62 km S of Warszawa; 51°44'/20°51'; JGFF, PHP4.

Goteshty, Mold. (Gotesti); pop. 35; 107 km SSW of Kishinev; 46°09'/28°10'.

Gotesti, *see* Goteshty.

Gotha, Germ.; pop. 350; 120 km SW of Leipzig; 50°57'/10°43'; AMG, EJ, GUM3, LDS.

Gotse Delchev, Bulg. (Nevrokop); pop. 514; 133 km SSE of Sofija; 41°34'/23°44'; EJ, GUM6.

Gotsk, Byel. (Hock); pop. 12; 88 km NE of Pinsk; 52°31'/27°09'.

Gottingen, Germ. (Goettingen); pop. 411; 101 km SSE of Hannover; 51°32'/09°56'; EJ, GUM3, GUM4, GUM5, HSL,

HSL2, LDL.

Gottwaldov, Cz. (Zlin); pop. 109; 75 km ENE of Brno; 49°13'/17°40'; GUM5.

Govartchov, see Gowarczow.

Govorova, see Goworowo.

Govorove, see Goworowo.

Gowarczow, Pol. (Govartchov); pop. 508; 82 km ESE of Lodz; 51°17'/20°26'; GUM3, GUM5, HSL, HSL2, LDS, PHP1, SF.

Goworowo, Pol. (Govorove); pop. 1,085; 82 km NNE of Warszawa; 52°54'/21°34'; AMG, COH, FRG, GUM3, GUM4, HSL, HSL2, JGFF, LYV, PHP4, SF, YB.

Goworowo Probostwo, Pol.; pop. 93; 82 km NNE of Warszawa; 52°54'/21°34'.

Gozd Lipinski, Pol.; pop. 31; 75 km NNW of Przemysl; 50°27'/22°34'.

Gozdowska Wola, GA. This town was not found in BGN gazetteers under the given spelling.

Gozd Stary, Pol.; pop. 5; 82 km S of Warszawa; 51°34'/21°03'.

Gozdzielin, Pol.; pop. 9; 88 km SW of Lublin; 50°54'/21°26'.

Gozdzik, Pol.; pop. 22; 62 km ESE of Warszawa; 51°55'/21°44'.

Gozha, Byel. (Hoza); pop. 2; 240 km WSW of Minsk; 53°49'/23°52'.

Grabce Wreckie, GUM4. This town was not found in BGN gazetteers under the given spelling.

Graben, Germ.; 69 km WNW of Stuttgart; 49°10'/08°29'; GUM3, GUM4, GUM5, GUM6, LDS, PHGBW.

Grabianka, Pol.; pop. 2; 50 km ESE of Warszawa; 51°59'/21°29'.

Grabianow, Pol.; pop. 7; 88 km E of Warszawa; 52°08'/22°17'.

Grabie, Pol.; 38 km ESE of Krakow; 49°51'/20°16'; HSL.

Grabiec, Pol.; 50 km ESE of Czestochowa; 50°37'/19°45'; JGFF.

Grabie Stare, Pol.; pop. 6; 26 km NE of Warszawa; 52°22'/21°20'.

Grabiny, Pol.; pop. 25; 62 km NE of Warszawa; 52°38'/21°47'.

Grabiuti, see Chervona.

Grabki, see Grabkow.

Grabki Duze, Pol.; pop. 5; 94 km NE of Krakow; 50°35'/20°57'.

Grabkow, Pol. (Grabki); 56 km NNW of Lodz; 52°12'/19°19'; GUM3.

Grabniki, Ukr.; pop. 31;

Grabocin, Pol.; 56 km SSE of Czestochowa; 50°18'/19°15'; AMG.

Graboszyce, Pol.; pop. 18; 38 km SW of Krakow; 49°57'/19°27'.

Grabov, (Grabow);

Grabov (near Dolina), Ukr.; 114 km S of Lvov; 48°54'/24°00'; CAHJP.

Grabov (Polesie), Byel.; pop. 45; 114 km NE of Pinsk; 52°31'/27°37'.

Grabova, Ukr. (Grabowa); pop. 43; 50 km NE of Lvov; 50°04'/24°36'.

Grabovets, Ukr. (Grabovits, Grabovitz, Grabovyets, Grabowiec); pop. 105; 107 km WNW of Chernovtsy; 48°45'/24°37'. The *Black Book* also notes a town southeast of Ternopol at approximately 49°46'/26°11'. It appears on an interwar map of Poland, but not in contemporary gazetteers. *See also* Grabowiec.

Grabovits, see Grabovets.

Grabovitz, see Grabovets.

Grabovka, Ukr. (Grabowka); pop. 64; 114 km SSE of Lvov; 48°54'/24°23'.

Grabovtsy, see Chervona.

Grabovyets, see Grabovets.

Grabow, Pol.; pop. 915; 94 km WSW of Lodz; 51°31'/18°07'; AMG, COH, FRG, GA, GUM3, HSL, HSL2, LYV, PHP1, SF. *See also* Grabov.

Grabow (Bialystok area), GUM3. This town was not found in BGN gazetteers under the given spelling.

Grabow (near Dabie), Pol.; pop. 35; 56 km N of Lodz; 52°13'/19°37'.

Grabow (Poznan), Pol.; pop. 59; 94 km WSW of Lodz; 51°31'/18°07'.

Grabow (Schwerin), Germ.; 94 km SSW of Rostock; 53°17'/11°34'; JGFF, LDS.

Grabowa, Pol.; pop. 5; 101 km NE of Krakow; 50°25'/21°11'; GUM5. *See also* Grabova.

Grabowce, Pol. (Grabowce Dolne); pop. 20; 56 km NW of Lublin; 51°38'/22°07'; PHP2.

Grabowce Dolne, see Grabowce.

Grabowie, Pol.; pop. 7; 56 km SSW of Lodz; 51°22'/18°56'.

Grabowiec, Pol.; pop. 1,721; 82 km ESE of Lublin; 50°50'/23°34'; AMG, COH, EDRD, GA, GUM3, GUM5, HSL, HSL2, JGFF, LDL, LDS, LYV, PHP2, SF. *See also* Grabovets.

Grabowiec (near Radom), Pol.; pop. 43; 82 km WSW of Lublin; 51°06'/21°24'.

Grabowka, Pol.; pop. 30; 56 km SW of Lublin; 50°56'/21°58'. *See also* Grabovka.

Grabowka (near Bialystok), Pol.; 13 km ENE of Bialystok; 53°09'/23°16'; GUM3.

Grabownica Starzenska, Pol.; pop. 47; 56 km WSW of Przemysl; 49°39'/22°05'.

Grabow Rycki, Pol.; pop. 8; 62 km NW of Lublin; 51°41'/22°06'.

Gracanica, Yug.; pop. 22; 214 km SW of Beograd; 43°44'/18°17'.

Gractz, see Grodzisk.

Gracze, GA. This town was not found in BGN gazetteers under the given spelling.

Gradacac, Yug.; pop. 45; 163 km W of Beograd; 44°53'/18°26'.

Gradin, Yug. (Gradina); pop. 22; 170 km WSW of Zagreb; 45°27'/13°51'.

Gradina, see Gradin.

Gradistea, Rom.; 146 km W of Bucuresti; 44°27'/24°14'; GUM4.

Gradki, Ukr. (Hradki); pop. 26; 107 km N of Rovno; 51°30'/26°46'.

Grady, Pol.; pop. 29; 75 km ENE of Krakow; 50°15'/20°56'.

Grady Nowe, Pol.; pop. 7; 94 km W of Lodz; 52°00'/18°07'.

Grady Polewne, Pol.; pop. 16; 62 km NNE of Warszawa; 52°44'/21°26'.

Gradysk, Ukr.; pop. 8; 107 km NW of Rovno; 51°23'/25°20'.

Grady Stare, Pol.; pop. 5; 94 km ESE of Poznan; 52°01'/18°07'.

Graetz, see Grodzisk Wielkopolski.

Grafelfing, Germ.; pop. 4; 13 km SW of Munchen; 48°06'/11°27'; GUM3, GUM5.

Grafenberg, Germ.; 26 km NNE of Nurnberg; 49°39'/11°15'; PHGB.

Grafenhausen, Germ.; pop. 44; 26 km S of Frankfurt am Main; 49°56'/08°36'; LDS.

Grafenwoerth, see Grafenworth.

Grafenwohr, Germ.; 62 km NE of Nurnberg; 49°43'/11°54'; PHGB.

Grafenworth, Aus. (Grafenwoerth); 50 km WNW of Wien; 48°24'/15°47'; EJ.

Grain, Germ. (Krain); 69 km E of Nurnberg; 49°20'/12°03'; EJ.

Graisbach, Germ.; 82 km S of Nurnberg; 48°45'/10°54'; PHGB.

Grajewo, Pol. (Grayavah); pop. 2,834; 75 km NW of Bialystok; 53°39'/22°27'; AMG, COH, EDRD, EJ, GA, GUM3, GUM4, GUM5, HSL, JGFF, LDL, LDS, PHP4, SF.

Grala Dabrowizna, Pol.; pop. 5; 82 km E of Warszawa; 52°05'/22°06'.

Gralewo, Pol.; 82 km WNW of Warszawa; 52°43'/20°07'; GA, GUM5.

Gramatneusiedl, Aus.; pop. 9; 26 km SSE of Wien; 48°01'/16°29'.

Gramzdas, see Diz Gramzda.

Gran, Ukr. (Hranie); pop. 28; 107 km N of Rovno; 51°32'/26°21'.

Granaut, see Grinautsy.

Granauti, see Grinautsy.

Granica, (Gronitza); pop. 764; HSL, LDS, SF. A number of towns share this name. It was not possible to determine from available information which one is being referenced.

Granice, Pol.; 56 km NE of Czestochowa; 51°06'/19°44'; PHP1.

Granicesti, Rom.; pop. 9; 133 km WNW of Iasi; 47°49'/26°04'.

Granne, Pol.; pop. 14; 82 km SSW of Białystok; 52°32'/22°31'.

Granov, Ukr. (Granow, Granuv); 50 km W of Uman; 48°52'/29°34'; LDL, SF.

Granow, see Granov.

Granowiec, Pol.; pop. 6; 69 km NE of Wroclaw; 51°31'/17°40'.

Granuv, see Granov.

Grasmannsdorf, Germ.; 50 km NW of Nurnberg; 49°50'/10°46'; PHGB.

Gratkorn, Aus.; pop. 1; 13 km WNW of Graz; 47°08'/15°21'.

Gratz, see Grodzisk Wielkopolski.

Graudenz, see Grudziadz.

Gravenwiesbach, Germ.; pop. 17; 38 km NW of Frankfurt am Main; 50°24'/08°27'.

Grayavah, see Grajewo.

Graydik, see Gorodok (near Lvov).

Grayding, see Gorodok (near Lvov).

Graydung, see Gorodok (near Kamenets Podolskiy).

Graydunk, see Gorodok (near Kamenets Podolskiy).

Graz, Aus.; pop. 1,720; 146 km SSW of Wien; 47°04'/15°27'; AMG, EDRD, EJ, GUM3, GUM4, GUM5, HSL.

Graziowa, Pol.; pop. 75; 32 km SSW of Przemysl; 49°36'/22°33'. See also Gronzeva.

Grebenau, Germ.; pop. 92; 94 km NNE of Frankfurt am Main; 50°45'/09°28'.

Grebenhain, Germ.; pop. 14; 62 km NE of Frankfurt am Main; 50°29'/09°21'.

Grebenka, Ukr.; pop. 27; 139 km E of Kiyev; 50°07'/32°26'.

Grebenki, Ukr.; 56 km S of Kiyev; 49°57'/30°12'; GUM4.

Grebenov, Ukr. (Hrebenow); pop. 43; 114 km S of Lvov; 48°58'/23°29'; HSL.

Grebenstein, Germ.; pop. 48; 107 km S of Hannover; 51°27'/09°25'; GED, GUM3, HSL, JGFF, LDS.

Grebien, Pol.; pop. 10; 56 km WNW of Czestochowa; 51°09'/18°35'.

Grebkow, Pol.; pop. 48; 62 km ENE of Warszawa; 52°16'/21°55'; GA, HSL.

Greboszow, Pol.; pop. 22; 69 km NE of Krakow; 50°15'/20°47'; GUM5.

Grebow, Pol.; pop. 172; 94 km SSW of Lublin; 50°34'/21°52'; GUM5, JGFF, PHP3.

Greding, Germ.; 50 km SSE of Nurnberg; 49°03'/11°21'; LDS, PHGB.

Greene, Germ.; 62 km SSE of Hannover; 51°51'/09°56'; LDS.

Greetsiel, Germ.; 189 km WSW of Hamburg; 53°30'/07°06'; LDS.

Gregorov, Ukr. (Gregoruv, Hrehorow); pop. 25; 69 km SE of Lvov; 49°20'/24°25'; GUM5.

Gregoruv, see Gregorov.

Greiding, see Gorodok (near Lvov).

Greiditz, HSL. This pre-World War I community was not found in BGN gazetteers.

Greifenberg, see Gryfice.

Greifenhagen, see Gryfino.

Greifswald, Germ.; pop. 46; 82 km ENE of Rostock; 54°06'/13°23'; GUM4, HSL.

Greiz, Germ.; pop. 44; 75 km S of Leipzig; 50°39'/12°12'; GUM4.

Gremheim, Germ.; pop. 2; 88 km WNW of Munchen; 48°38'/10°40'.

Gremyach, Ukr.; 126 km N of Konotop; 52°20'/33°17'; GUM4.

Grenci, Lat.; pop. 8; 75 km WSW of Riga; 56°54'/22°53'.

Grenkeshek, see Grinkiskis.

Grenzach, Germ.; pop. 7; 176 km SSW of Stuttgart; 47°33'/07°40'; PHGBW.

Grenzhausen, see Hohr Grenzhausen.

Gresk, Byel. (Gressk); pop. 386; 82 km S of Minsk; 53°10'/27°29'.

Gressenich, Germ.; pop. 8; 50 km SW of Koln; 50°46'/06°18'.

Gressk, see Gresk.

Greussenheim, Germ.; pop. 12; 82 km ESE of Frankfurt am Main; 49°49'/09°46'; GUM5.

Grevenbroich, Germ.; pop. 88; 32 km WNW of Koln; 51°05'/06°35'; GED, JGFF.

Grezegerzova, see Grzegorzew.

Grezow, Pol.; pop. 9; 75 km E of Warszawa; 52°11'/22°08'.

Grezowka, Pol.; pop. 29; 88 km NNW of Lublin; 51°59'/22°18'.

Grgurevci, Yug.; pop. 3; 75 km WNW of Beograd; 45°06'/19°39'.

Gribev, see Grybow.

Gribiv, see Grybow.

Gribo, see Grybow.

Gribov, see Grybow.

Gribuv, see Grybow.

Griby, see Grybai.

Gricev, see Gritsev.

Grichinovichi, Byel. (Hryczynowicze); pop. 35; 88 km NE of Pinsk; 52°23'/27°21'.

Griedel, Germ.; pop. 29; 45 km N of Frankfurt am Main; 50°26'/08°42'.

Griesheim, Germ.; pop. 67; 32 km S of Frankfurt am Main; 49°52'/08°33'; LDS.

Grigore Gika Vode, see Nepolokovtsy.

Grigori Ghica Voda, see Nepolokovtsy.

Grigoriopol, Mold.; 45 km NE of Kishinev; 47°09'/29°18'; EJ, LDL, SF.

Grimancauti, see Grimankautsy.

Grimankautsy, Mold. (Grimancauti); pop. 47; 202 km NW of Kishinev; 48°23'/27°06'.

Grimaylov, Ukr. (Grzymalow, Gzhimalov, Rimalov); pop. 1,494; 120 km N of Chernovtsy; 49°20'/26°00'; AMG, COH, EGRS, FRG, GUM3, GUM4, GUM5, HSL, HSL2, JGFF, LDL, PHP2, SF.

Grimma, Germ.; pop. 23; 26 km E of Leipzig; 51°14'/12°43'.

Grimmen, Germ.; pop. 8; 56 km ENE of Rostock; 54°06'/13°03'.

Grimnoye, Ukr. (Rumno); pop. 24; 38 km SSW of Lvov; 49°36'/23°46'.

Grinauti Raia, see Grinautsi.

Grinauts, see Grinautsy.

Grinautsi, Mold. (Grinauti Raia); pop. 30; 176 km NW of Kishinev; 48°17'/27°23'.

Grinautsy, Mold. (Granaut, Granauti, Grinauts); pop. 78; 126 km NW of Kishinev; 47°53'/27°47'.

Grind, Rom. (Gerend); 133 km SSW of Cluj; 45°52'/22°29'; HSL.

Grind Cristur, see Grindeni.

Grindeni, Rom. (Gerendkeresztur, Grind Cristur); 45 km ESE of Cluj; 46°30'/24°00'; HSL.

Grinki, Ukr. (Hrynkowce); pop. 22; 88 km S of Rovno; 49°51'/26°08'.

Grinkishok, see Grinkiskis.

Grinkiskis, Lith. (Grenkeshek, Grinkishok); pop. 235; 45 km SE of Siauliai; 55°34'/23°38'; GUM5, HSL, JGFF, LDL, SF, YL.

Grischino, see Grishino.

Grishino, Ukr. (Grischino); pop. 1,620; 150 km E of Dnepropetrovsk; 48°20'/37°05'; HSL, LDL, SF.

Grishkabod, see Griskabudis.

Grishkabud, see Griskabudis.

Griskabodis, see Griskabudis.

Griskabudis, Lith. (Grishkabod, Grishkabud, Griskabodis); pop. 92; 45 km WSW of Kaunas; 54°51'/23°10'; JGFF, YL.

Gritsa, see Grojec.

Gritsev, Ukr. (Gricev, Grizew, Haritzev, Ritzov); pop. 1,578; 101 km SE of Rovno; 49°58'/27°13'; HSL, JGFF, LDL, SF.

Gritza, see Grojec.

Gritze, see Grojec.

Griva, Lat. (Grivo, Griwa, Grzywka); pop. 227; 6 km SSW of Daugavpils; 55°51'/26°30'; COH, HSL, JGFF, PHLE, SF.

Griva (Polesie), Ukr. (Hrywa); pop. 9; 120 km NW of Rovno; 51°31'/25°25'.

Grivita Noua, Rom.; pop. 10; 120 km NW of Iasi; 48°01'/26°35'.

Grivo, *see* Griva.

Griwa, *see* Griva.

Grizew, *see* Gritsev.

Grobin, *see* Grobina.

Grobina, Lat. (Grobin, Grobinas, Grovin); pop. 116; 182 km WSW of Riga; 56°33'/21°10'; COH, HSL, JGFF, LDL, PHLE, SF.

Grobinas, *see* Grobina.

Grobla, Pol.; pop. 39; 38 km ENE of Krakow; 50°08'/20°25'.

Grobzig, Germ.; pop. 10; 56 km NW of Leipzig; 51°41'/11°52'; HSL, HSL2.

Grocholice, Pol. (Grocholitza); pop. 51; 50 km S of Lodz; 51°20'/19°22'; LDS, PHP1, SF.

Grocholitza, *see* Grocholice.

Grochov, *see* Grochow.

Grochow, Pol. (Grochov, Grochow Wloscianski); pop. 21; 75 km ENE of Warszawa; 52°25'/22°08'; EJ, GUM3, GUM5, HSL, PHP4, SF.

Grochowka, Pol.; pop. 76; 94 km N of Lublin; 52°03'/22°39'.

Grochow Wloscianski, *see* Grochow.

Grochy Stare, Pol.; pop. 9; 62 km N of Warszawa; 52°47'/20°56'.

Grodek, Pol.; pop. 1,508; 170 km NE of Warszawa; 53°08'/23°09'; FRG, GA, GUM3, HSL, LYV, SF, YB. Also *see* Gorodok, Grudek.

Grodek (Kielce), Pol.; pop. 21; 45 km E of Czestochowa; 50°43'/19°42'.

Grodek (Warszawa), Pol.; pop. 4; 56 km NNE of Warszawa; 52°43'/21°19'.

Grodek Jagiellonski, *see* Gorodok (near Lvov).

Grodek Nadbuzny, Pol.; pop. 30; Described in the *Black Book* as being in the Lublin region of Poland, this town was not found in BGN gazetteers.

Grodig, *see* Gorodok (near Lvov).

Grodkow, Pol. (Grottkau); pop. 40; 50 km SE of Wroclaw; 50°42'/17°23'; AMG, JGFF.

Grodkowice, Pol.; pop. 3; 26 km ESE of Krakow; 50°01'/20°15'; GUM4.

Grodne, *see* Grodno.

Grodno, Byel. (Grodne, Horodne, Hurodno); pop. 18,697; 234 km NW of Pinsk; 53°41'/23°50'; AMG, CAHJP, COH, EDRD, EJ, GA, GUM3, GUM4, GUM5, GUM6, GYLA, HSL, HSL2, ISH3, JGFF, LDL, LYV, PHP1, PHP2, PHP4, WS, YB.

Grodowice, Pol.; pop. 30; 56 km NE of Krakow; 50°16'/20°37'.

Grodyslawice, Pol.; pop. 35; 101 km NNE of Przemysl; 50°32'/23°37'.

Grodzhisk, *see* Grodzisk Mazowiecki.

Grodzhisk Mazovyets, *see* Grodzisk Mazowiecki.

Grodziec, Pol. AMG, JGFF, PHP1. A number of towns share this name. It was not possible to determine from available information which one is being referenced.

Grodziec (Kielce), Pol.; pop. 162; 50 km S of Czestochowa; 50°21'/19°06'.

Grodziec (near Konin), Pol.; pop. 107; 88 km ESE of Poznan; 52°02'/18°04'; GA, GUM3.

Grodzisk, Pol. (Gractz); pop. 3,600; 13 km NNE of Warszawa; 52°20'/21°04'; AMG, COH, EDRD, GYLA, HSL2, JGFF, LDL, PHP4. Grodzisk may also refer to Grodzisk Wielkopolski and a small town in the Bialystok region called Grodzisk. The Grodzisk referred to in SF is Grodzisko Dolne. *See also* Grodzisko Dolne.

Grodzisk (near Bialystok), Pol.; pop. 16; 62 km SSW of Bialystok; 52°35'/22°44'; GA.

Grodzisk Mazowiecki, Pol. (Grodzhisk, Grodzhisk Mazovyets, Grozitsk); pop. 2,756; 32 km SW of Warszawa; 52°07'/20°38'; AMG, EDRD, EJ, GA, GUM3, GUM4, GUM5, HSL, LDS, LYV, POCEM, SF.

Grodzisko, Pol.; pop. 600; 75 km W of Przemysl; 49°55'/21°43'; CAHJP.

Grodzisko Dolne, Pol. (Grodzisko Miasto); pop. 101; 45 km NW of Przemysl; 50°10'/22°28'; GUM4, GUM5, PHP3, SF.

Grodzisko Gorne, Pol. PHP3. This town was not found in BGN gazetteers under the given spelling.

Grodzisko Miasteczko, Pol.; pop. 367; EGRS, PHP3. Described in the *Black Book* as being in the Lwow region of Poland, this town was not found in BGN gazetteers.

Grodzisko Miasto, *see* Grodzisko Dolne.

Grodzisk Wielkopolski, Pol. (Graetz, Gratz); pop. 61; 50 km SW of Poznan; 52°14'/16°22'; CAHJP, EJ, LDS.

Grodzkie Nowe, Pol.; pop. 4; 45 km WSW of Bialystok; 53°03'/22°32'.

Grodztwo Kowal, Pol.; pop. 31; Described in the *Black Book* as being in the Warszawa region of Poland, this town was not found in BGN gazetteers.

Grojec, Pol. (Gritsa, Gritza, Gritze, Grutse, Gruyets); pop. 4,922; 50 km S of Warszawa; 51°52'/20°52'; AMG, CAHJP, COH, EDRD, EJ, GA, GUM3, GUM4, GUM5, HSL, ISH3, JGFF, LDL, LDS, LYV, PHP1, PHP4, SF, WS, YB.

Grombach, Germ.; pop. 28; BGN lists two possible localities with this name located at 48°35'/08°33' and 49°14'/09°00'. PHGBW.

Gromiec, Pol.; pop. 9; 45 km WSW of Krakow; 50°03'/19°18'.

Gromnik, Pol.; pop. 140; 82 km ESE of Krakow; 49°51'/20°58'; GUM5, HSL, PHP3.

Gromovo, USSR (Lauknen); pop. 13; 62 km NE of Kaliningrad; 54°58'/21°25'.

Gronau, Germ.; pop. 44; 38 km SSE of Hannover; 52°05'/09°47'; GED, GUM5.

Gronenbach, Germ.; 107 km SW of Munchen; 47°53'/10°13'; PHGB.

Groningen, Germ.; 107 km WNW of Leipzig; 51°56'/11°13'; HSL, HSL2, JGFF, LDL, LDS.

Gronitza, *see* Granica.

Gronov, Byel.; 133 km N of Gomel; 53°34'/31°28'; JGFF.

Gronow, Pol.; 62 km SW of Lodz; 51°25'/18°44'; GA.

Gronzeva, Ukr. (Graziowa); pop. 29; 107 km SW of Lvov; 49°19'/22°49'.

Grosi Satu Mare, *see* Balanca Grosi.

Grosi Somes, Rom.; pop. 40; 88 km WNW of Cluj; 47°02'/22°29'.

Grosolovo, GUM4, PHR1. This town was not found in BGN gazetteers under the given spelling.

Grosow, Germ.; 88 km NE of Rostock; 54°29'/13°16'; JGFF.

Gross, AMG. A number of towns share this name. It was not possible to determine from available information which one is being referenced.

Grossalsleben, Germ.; 107 km WNW of Leipzig; 51°59'/11°14'; LDS.

Grossau, Aus. GUM6. A number of towns share this name. It was not possible to determine from available information which one is being referenced.

Gross Becskerek, *see* Zrenjanin.

Grossbeti, LDL. This pre-World War I community was not found in BGN gazetteers.

Gross Bieberau, Germ.; pop. 48; 38 km SSE of Frankfurt am Main; 49°48'/08°50'; LDS.

Gross Bockenheim, *see* Bockenheim.

Gross Breesen, Germ.; 107 km ESE of Berlin; 51°59'/14°42'; GUM5.

Grosseicholzheim, Germ.; pop. 56; 82 km SE of Frankfurt am Main; 49°27'/09°17'; AMG, LDS, PHGBW.

Grosselfingen, Germ.; 82 km SSW of Nurnberg; 48°51'/10°33'; PHGB.

Grossen Buseck, Germ.; pop. 53; 62 km N of Frankfurt am Main; 50°36'/08°47'; GUM3, GUM5, LDS.

Grosseneder, Germ.; 101 km SSE of Hannover; 51°33'/10°10'; LDS.

Grossenenglis, Germ.; 120 km N of Frankfurt am Main; 51°04'/09°16'; LDS.

Grossenkneten, Germ.; pop. 1; 120 km WNW of Hannover; 52°57'/08°16'.

Grossen Linden, *see* Grossenlinden.

Grossenlinden, Germ. (Grossen Linden); pop. 22; 56 km N of Frankfurt am Main; 50°32'/08°39'; GUM5, LDS.

Grossenzersdorf, Aus.; pop. 221; 19 km E of Wien; 48°12'/16°33'.

Grossgartach, Germ.; 50 km N of Stuttgart; 49°09'/09°08'; PHGBW.

Gross Gerau, *see* Grossgerau.

Grossgerau, Germ. (Gross Gerau); pop. 200; 26 km SSW of Frankfurt am Main; 49°55'/08°29'; LDS.

Grossheubach, Germ.; 56 km SE of Frankfurt am Main; 49°44'/09°13'; AMG.

Gross Jestin, *see* Goscino.

Gross Kackschen, Germ.; pop. 30; Described in the *Black Book* as being in the Ostpreussen region of Germany, this town was not found in BGN gazetteers.

Grosskadolz, Aus.; pop. 2; 62 km NNW of Wien; 48°42'/16°11'.

Gross Karben, *see* Grosskarben.

Grosskarben, Germ. (Gross Karben); pop. 60; 19 km NNE of Frankfurt am Main; 50°14'/08°48'; GED, GUM5, JGFF.

Grosskarlbach, Germ.; pop. 8; 69 km SSW of Frankfurt am Main; 49°33'/08°15'; GUM5.

Gross Krotzenburg, *see* Grosskrotzenburg.

Grosskrotzenburg, Germ. (Gross Krotzenburg); pop. 110; 26 km E of Frankfurt am Main; 50°05'/08°59'; JGFF, YB.

Grosskrut, Aus.; pop. 12; 56 km NNE of Wien; 48°38'/16°43'.

Grosslangheim, Germ.; pop. 17; 69 km WNW of Nurnberg; 49°45'/10°14'; HSL, PHGB.

Gross Leine, Germ.; pop. 2; 75 km SE of Berlin; 52°00'/14°04'.

Grosslomnitz, *see* Velka Lomnica.

Gross Magendorf, *see* Rastice.

Gross Mesereitsch, *see* Velke Mezirici.

Gross Mosty, *see* Velikiye Mosty.

Grossmuhlingen, Germ.; 82 km NW of Leipzig; 51°57'/11°42'; LDS.

Grossostheim, Germ.; pop. 28; 32 km ESE of Frankfurt am Main; 49°55'/09°05'; GUM5, JGFF, PHGB.

Gross Ottersleben, *see* Ottersleben.

Grosspetersdorf, Aus.; pop. 47; 69 km NE of Graz; 47°14'/16°19'.

Grosspoppen, Aus.; pop. 2; 94 km WNW of Wien; 48°40'/15°20'.

Gross Radomysl, *see* Radomysl Wielki.

Gross Rhuden, Germ.; pop. 4; 56 km SE of Hannover; 51°57'/10°07'.

Gross Rohrheim, Germ.; 50 km S of Frankfurt am Main; 49°43'/08°29'; GUM3.

Grossropperhausen, Germ.; 107 km NNE of Frankfurt am Main; 50°56'/09°22'; LDS.

Gross Rosen, *see* Rogoznica.

Grossrussbach, Aus.; pop. 10; 38 km N of Wien; 48°28'/16°25'.

Grosssachsen, Germ.; 69 km S of Frankfurt am Main; 49°31'/08°40'; JGFF.

Gross Sallo, *see* Tekovske Luzany.

Gross Schlatten, *see* Abrud Sat.

Gross Schogen, *see* Sieu.

Grossschutzen, *see* Velke Levare.

Grosssiegharts, Aus.; 94 km WNW of Wien; 48°47'/15°24'; AMG.

Gross Strehlitz, *see* Strzelce Opolskie.

Gross Surany, *see* Surany.

Grosstaxen, Aus.; pop. 3; 120 km NW of Wien; 48°57'/15°16'.

Gross Umstadt, Germ.; pop. 60; 32 km SE of Frankfurt am Main; 49°52'/08°56'.

Grosswarasdorf, Aus.; pop. 4; 82 km SSE of Wien; 47°32'/16°33'.

Grosswardein, *see* Oradea.

Gross Wartenberg, *see* Sycow.

Grossweikersdorf, Aus.; pop. 7; 45 km NW of Wien; 48°28'/15°59'.

Gross Wierau, *see* Wiry.

Gross Zimmern, Germ.; pop. 71; 32 km SSE of Frankfurt am Main; 49°52'/08°50'; JGFF.

Groszowice, Pol.; pop. 23; 94 km W of Lublin; 51°26'/21°18'.

Grosz Wartenberg, *see* Sycow.

Grotniki Duze, Pol.; pop. 21; 69 km NE of Krakow; 50°19'/20°50'; PHP1.

Grotowice, Pol.; pop. 8; 62 km E of Lodz; 51°36'/20°22'.

Grottkau, *see* Grodkow.

Grotzingen, Germ.; pop. 31; 56 km WNW of Stuttgart; 49°00'/08°30'; LDS, PHGBW.

Grovin, *see* Grobina.

Grozeshti, *see* Grozeshty.

Grozeshty, Mold. (Grozeshti, Grozesti); pop. 24; 56 km WSW of Kishinev; 47°00'/28°05'.

Grozesti, *see* Grozeshty.

Grozinti, *see* Grozintsi.

Grozintsi, Ukr. (Grozinti); pop. 22; 26 km NE of Chernovtsy; 48°25'/26°10'.

Grozitsk, *see* Grodzisk Mazowiecki.

Grozny, *see* Groznyy.

Groznyy, Ukr. (Grozny); 202 km E of Dnepropetrovsk; 48°15'/37°42'; EJ.

Grozov, *see* Grozovo.

Grozovo, Byel. (Grozov, Hrozow); pop. 704; 82 km S of Minsk; 53°10'/27°20'; AMG, JGFF, SF, YB.

Grubisno Polje, Yug.; pop. 31; 94 km E of Zagreb; 45°42'/17°10'.

Grubna, Ukr.; pop. 4; 82 km ENE of Chernovtsy; 48°28'/27°04'.

Grubov, *see* Grybow.

Gruczno, Pol.; pop. 4; 114 km S of Gdansk; 53°21'/18°19'.

Grudek, Ukr.; pop. 77; 38 km NNW of Chernovtsy; 48°37'/25°52'. *Also see* Gorodok; Grodek.

Grudek Yagyelonski, *see* Gorodok (near Lvov).

Grudna Gorna, Pol.; pop. 18; 94 km W of Przemysl; 49°57'/21°29'.

Grudna Kepska, Pol.; pop. 8; 107 km ESE of Krakow; 49°45'/21°19'.

Grudziadz, Pol. (Graudenz); pop. 297; 101 km S of Gdansk; 53°29'/18°46'; AMG, GUM3, GUM5, HSL, JGFF.

Gruenberg, *see* Zielona Gora.

Gruensfeld, *see* Grunsfeld.

Gruenstadt, *see* Grunstadt.

Gruesen, *see* Grusen.

Gruisor, Rom.; pop. 3; 88 km ESE of Cluj; 46°27'/24°37'.

Grun, Ukr.; 94 km ESE of Konotop; 50°42'/34°16'; GUM4.

Grunberg, *see* Zielona Gora.

Grundsheim, Germ.; 82 km SE of Stuttgart; 48°10'/09°40'; PHGBW.

Grundzales, Lat.; pop. 2; 139 km NE of Riga; 57°28'/26°13'.

Gruningen, Germ.; 69 km SW of Berlin; 52°18'/12°27'; LDS.

Grunow Spiegelberg, GUM3. This town was not found in BGN gazetteers under the given spelling.

Grunsfeld, Germ. (Gruensfeld); pop. 30; 94 km ESE of Frankfurt am Main; 49°36'/09°45'; EJ, GED, JGFF, PHGBW.

Grunstadt, Germ. (Gruenstadt); pop. 135; 69 km SSW of Frankfurt am Main; 49°34'/08°10'; CAHJP, GED, HSL, HSL2, JGFF.

Grunwald, *see* Jesiona.

Grusen, Germ. (Gruesen); pop. 22; 107 km N of Frankfurt am Main; 51°00'/08°57'; LDS.

Gruseva, *see* Grushevo.

Grushatichi, Ukr. (Grushatytse, Hruszatyce); pop. 22; 82 km WSW of Lvov; 49°38'/22°54'.

Grushatytse, *see* Grushatichi.

Grushev, Ukr. (Hrushov, Hruszow); pop. 164; 56 km WNW of Lvov; 50°05'/23°19'; AMG, HSL, PHP2, SF.

Grushevka, Ukr. (Grushuvka, Hruszowka); pop. 24; 45 km NE of Rovno; 50°49'/26°49'.

Grushevo, Mold. (Gruseva); pop. 10; 26 km N of Kishinev; 47°09'/28°56'.

Grushevtsy, Ukr.; 69 km NE of Chernovtsy; 48°33'/26°49'; JGFF.

Grushka, Ukr.; pop. 37; 50 km S of Uman; 48°21'/30°17'.

Grushuvka, *see* Grushevka.

Grushvitsy Pervyye, Ukr. (Hruszwica); pop. 42; 19 km SW of Rovno; 50°33'/26°02'.

Grusyatychi, Ukr. (Hrusiatycze); pop. 52; 50 km SE of Lvov; 49°29'/24°23'.

Gruszczyn, Pol.; pop. 29; 69 km WSW of Lublin; 51°08'/21°38'; GA.

Gruszow, Pol.; 38 km SE of Krakow; 49°52'/20°13'; HSL.

Gruszow Wielki, Pol.; pop. 17; 82 km ENE of Krakow; 50°12'/21°03'.

Gruta, Pol.; pop. 2; 101 km SSE of Gdansk; 53°28'/18°58'.

Grutse, *see* Grojec.

Gruyets, *see* Grojec.

Gruz, *see* Gruzdziai.

Gruzd, *see* Gruzdziai.

Gruzdziai, Lith. (Gruz, Gruzd); pop. 150; 26 km NNW of Siauliai; 56°06'/23°16'; HSL, LDL, SF, YL.

Grybai, Lith. (Griby); 62 km NE of Vilnius; 55°05'/25°59'; JGFF.

Grybovitsa, Ukr. (Grzybowice); pop. 30; 94 km N of Lvov; 50°41'/24°15'.

Grybow, Pol. (Gribev, Gribiv, Gribo, Gribov, Gribuv, Grubov); pop. 847; 94 km ESE of Krakow; 49°38'/20°57'; COH, EDRD, EGRS, GUM5, HSL, HSL2, LDL, LYV, PHP3, POCEM, SF.

Gryfice, Pol. (Greifenberg); pop. 68; 75 km NE of Szczecin; 53°55'/15°21'; JGFF, LDS.

Gryfin, *possibly* Gryfino.

Gryfino, Pol. (Greifenhagen, Gryfin?); pop. 35; 32 km S of Szczecin; 53°15'/14°29'; HSL, PHP4.

Grygorowicze, GUM4. This town was not found in BGN gazetteers under the given spelling.

Grynyava, Ukr. (Hryniawa); pop. 29; 88 km SW of Chernovtsy; 47°59'/24°53'; PHP2.

Gryvyatki, Ukr. (Hrywiatki); pop. 10; 114 km WNW of Rovno; 51°15'/25°01'.

Grywald, Pol.; pop. 4; 75 km SE of Krakow; 49°27'/20°22'.

Grzebienie, Pol.; pop. 4; 62 km N of Bialystok; 53°37'/23°27'.

Grzeda, *see* Gzhenda.

Grzegorzew, Pol. (Grezegerzova); pop. 10; 69 km WNW of Lodz; 52°12'/18°44'; SF.

Grzegorzewice (Kielce), Pol.; pop. 21; 107 km SW of Lublin; 50°53'/21°10'.

Grzegorzewice (Warszawa), Pol.; pop. 28; 62 km SSE of Warszawa; 51°46'/21°08'.

Grzeska, Pol.; pop. 8; 38 km NW of Przemysl; 50°04'/22°28'.

Grzmiaca, Pol.; pop. 22; 75 km S of Warszawa; 51°37'/20°47'.

Grzybow, Pol.; 56 km N of Lodz; 52°13'/19°45'; GA, JGFF.

Grzybowice, *see* Grybovitsa.

Grzybowo, Pol. AMG, JGFF. A number of towns share this name. It was not possible to determine from available information which one is being referenced.

Grzymala, Pol.; pop. 11; 88 km NE of Krakow; 50°32'/20°59'.

Grzymalkow, Pol. (Grzymalowka); pop. 10; 94 km ENE of Czestochowa; 51°01'/20°24'.

Grzymalow, *see* Grimaylov.

Grzymalowka, *see* Grzymalkow.

Grzywka, *see* Griva.

Grzywkowicze, *see* Gzhivkoviche.

Gualdo Tadino, GUM4, GUM5. This town was not found in BGN gazetteers under the given spelling.

Guben, *see* Wilhelmpieckstadt Guben.

Guberniya; Not a town, but the Russian word for "province." It is commonly but mistakenly believed to be a town name. Similarly, Grodnogubernia is not a town name, but refers to the province of Grodno. A more complete discussion is presented in the first section of this book.

Gubiche, Ukr. (Hubice, Hubicze); pop. 226; 75 km SSW of Lvov; 49°19'/23°27'.

Gubin, Ukr. (Hubin, Hubin Czeski); pop. 22; 114 km W of Rovno; 50°49'/24°39'.

Guchok, Ukr. (Huczko?); pop. 202; 94 km SW of Lvov; 49°34'/22°47'; PHP2.

Gudenieki, Lat.; pop. 3; 150 km WSW of Riga; 56°54'/21°38'.

Gudensberg, Germ.; pop. 122; 133 km N of Frankfurt am Main; 51°11'/09°22'; LDS.

Gudigai, GUM6. This town was not found in BGN gazetteers under the given spelling.

Gudovac, Yug.; pop. 8; 62 km ENE of Zagreb; 45°53'/16°47'.

Gudzion, *see* Gudziunai.

Gudziunai, Lith. (Gudzion); pop. 103; 56 km SE of Siauliai; 55°31'/23°48'; YL.

Guermanovka, *see* Germanovka.

Gugel, Germ.; 56 km NNW of Nurnberg; 49°56'/10°56'; PHGB. *See also* Bukovina.

Guhrau, *see* Gora.

Guklivyy, Ukr. (Hukliva); 139 km SSW of Lvov; 48°42'/23°14'; AMG.

Gulacs, Hung.; pop. 59; 126 km E of Miskolc; 48°05'/22°28'; HSL, JGFF, PHH.

Gulay Pole, *see* Gulyay Pole.

Gulbene, Lat. (Schwaneburg, Schwanenburg, Shvaneburg, Vecgulbene); pop. 65; 150 km N of Daugavpils; 57°11'/26°45'; GUM4, PHLE.

Gulbiny, Pol.; pop. 14; 139 km SSE of Gdansk; 53°07'/19°19'.

Gulboka, Mold. (Hulboca); pop. 34; 19 km NNW of Kishinev; 47°07'/28°48'.

Gulcha Pervaya, Ukr. (Hulcza Wloscianska); pop. 62; 26 km S of Rovno; 50°26'/26°17'.

Gulevichi, Ukr. (Hulewicze, Hulievca); pop. 8; 101 km WNW of Rovno; 51°15'/25°13'; AMG, EDRD.

Guljai Polje, *see* Gulyay Pole.

Guls, Germ.; pop. 4; 82 km WNW of Frankfurt am Main; 50°20'/07°33'.

Gulyay Pole, Ukr. (Gulay Pole, Guljai Polje, Holiapol); pop. 1,182; 69 km SW of Dnepropetrovsk; 48°07'/34°08'; HSL, HSL2, SF.

Gulzow, Germ.; pop. 25; 69 km E of Rostock; 54°02'/13°07'.

Gumbinnen, *see* Gusev.

Gummersbach, Germ.; pop. 6; 45 km ENE of Koln; 51°02'/07°33'.

Gumna, Pol.; pop. 7; 94 km SW of Krakow; 49°47'/18°42'.

Gumniska, Pol. (Humniska); 82 km E of Krakow; 50°01'/21°02'; GUM5.

Gumowo Szlacheckie, Pol.; pop. 9; 75 km NW of Warszawa; 52°50'/20°29'.

Gumpoldskirchen, Aus.; pop. 9; 26 km S of Wien; 48°03'/16°17'.

Gundelfingen, Germ.; 88 km E of Stuttgart; 48°33'/10°22'; PHGB.

Gundelsheim, Germ.; 62 km N of Stuttgart; 49°17'/09°10'; PHGBW.

Gundelsheim (Bavaria), Germ.; 45 km SSW of Nurnberg; 49°07'/10°50'; PHGB.

Gunja, Yug.; pop. 2; 126 km W of Beograd; 44°53'/18°52'.

Guns, *see* Koszeg.

Guntersblum, Germ.; pop. 40; 38 km SSW of Frankfurt am Main; 49°48'/08°21'; GUM5, JGFF.

Guntramsdorf, Aus.; pop. 18; 26 km S of Wien; 48°02'/16°18'.

Gunzburg, Germ.; pop. 8; 88 km ESE of Stuttgart; 48°27'/10°16'; PHGB, PHGBW.

Gunzendorf, Germ.; 56 km WSW of Nurnberg; 49°22'/10°17'; HSL, PHGB, PHGB.

Gunzenhausen, Germ.; pop. 219; 45 km SSW of Nurnberg; 49°06'/10°45'; AMG, CAHJP, GUM3, GUM5, HSL, HSL2, ISH1, JGFF, LDS, PHGB.

Gur, *see* Gora Kalwaria.

Gura Bacului, *see* Gura Bykuluy.

Gura Bykuluy, Mold. (Gura Bacului); pop. 19; 50 km E of

Kishinev; 46°56'/29°28'.

Gura Cainari, *see* Gura Kaynary.

Gura Camenca, *see* Gura Kamenka.

Gura Galbena, Mold.; pop. 111; 38 km S of Kishinev; 46°42'/28°42'.

Gurahont, Rom.; 114 km SW of Cluj; 46°16'/22°21'; HSL.

Gura Humora, *see* Gura Humorului.

Gurahumora, *see* Gura Humorului.

Gura Humorului, Rom. (Gura Humora, Gurahumora); pop. 1,951; 133 km WNW of Iasi; 47°33'/25°54'; AMG, EDRD, EJ, GUM4, GUM5, HSL, JGFF, LDL, PHR2, SF.

Gura Kalvaria, *see* Gora Kalwaria.

Gura Kalwariska, LDL. This pre-World War I community was not found in BGN gazetteers.

Gura Kamenka, Mold. (Gura Camenca); pop. 9; 101 km NNW of Kishinev; 47°53'/28°21'.

Gura Kaynary, Mold. (Gura Cainari); pop. 68; 107 km NW of Kishinev; 47°52'/28°11'.

Gura Putein, *see* Gura Putnei.

Gura Putilei, *see* Gura Putnei.

Gura Putnei, Rom. (Gura Putein, Gura Putilei); pop. 21; 170 km WNW of Iasi; 47°54'/25°35'; PHR2.

Gura Rosie, *see* Kazatskoye.

Gura Vailor, *see* Yelizavetovka.

Gurba, Rom. (Garba); 139 km WSW of Cluj; 46°28'/21°47'; HSL.

Gurghiu, Rom. (Gorgenyszentimre); pop. 72; 94 km E of Cluj; 46°46'/24°51'.

Guruslau, Rom.; pop. 5; 75 km NW of Cluj; 47°17'/22°59'.

Gurzenich, Germ.; 38 km SW of Koln; 50°47'/06°27'; GED.

Gurzuf, Ukr.; pop. 30; 50 km SSE of Simferopol; 44°33'/34°17'.

Gusak, Byel. (Husaki); pop. 19; 139 km WSW of Pinsk; 51°56'/24°04'.

Gusakov, Ukr. (Husakov, Hussakow); pop. 249; 75 km WSW of Lvov; 49°43'/23°00'; EGRS, HSL, HSL2, JGFF, LDL, PHP2, PHP3, SF.

Gusev, USSR (Gumbinnen); pop. 208; 107 km E of Kaliningrad; 54°36'/22°12'; AMG, HSL, HSL2.

Gushcha, Ukr. (Huszcza); pop. 43; 163 km N of Lvov; 51°16'/23°44'; EDRD.

Gusiatyn, *see* Gusyatin.

Gusino, USSR; pop. 427; 50 km WSW of Smolensk; 54°44'/31°22'.

Gussing, Aus. (Nemetujvar); pop. 74; 69 km E of Graz; 47°04'/16°20'; EJ, HSL, LDL, LDS.

Gustanj, *see* Ravne na Koroskem.

Gusten, Germ.; 75 km WNW of Leipzig; 51°47'/11°36'; HSL.

Gustorf, Germ.; pop. 4; 32 km WNW of Koln; 51°04'/06°34'.

Gustrow, Germ.; pop. 120; 38 km S of Rostock; 53°48'/12°10'; CAHJP, EJ, HSL, JGFF, LDS.

Gusyatin, Ukr. (Gusiatyn, Husiatin, Husiatyn); pop. 368; 88 km N of Chernovtsy; 49°04'/26°13'; AMG, CAHJP, COH, EGRS, GUM3, GUM4, GUM5, GUM6, GYLA, HSL, HSL2, JGFF, LDL, PHP2, SF, YB.

Gusztyn, Pol. PHP2. This town was not found in BGN gazetteers under the given spelling.

Gut, *see* Gut am Steg.

Guta (Czechoslovakia), *see* Kolarovo.

Gutahaza, Hung.; pop. 2; 82 km NNW of Nagykanizsa; 47°07'/16°48'.

Guta Mikhalin, Byel. (Huta Michalinska); pop. 22; 107 km WNW of Pinsk; 52°42'/24°56'.

Gut am Steg, Aus. (Gut); 75 km W of Wien; 48°22'/15°23'; HSL.

Guta Polonetska, Ukr. (Huta Polonicka, Huta Poloniecka); pop. 20; 56 km NE of Lvov; 50°07'/24°39'.

Guta Sukhodolska, *see* Khuta Sukhodolska.

Guta Zelena, Ukr. (Huta Zielona); pop. 8; 50 km NW of Lvov; 50°14'/23°34'.

Gutenbrunn, *see* Kobyle Pole.

Gutersloh, Germ.; pop. 80; 107 km SW of Hannover;

51°54'/08°23'; GED, GUM5, HSL, LDS.

Gutorfolde, Hung.; pop. 14; 32 km NW of Nagykanizsa; 46°39'/16°44'.

Gutsisko, Ukr. (Hucisko); pop. 35; 82 km ESE of Lvov; 49°24'/24°50'; PHP3.

Gutsisko Brodzke, Ukr. (Hucisko Brodzkie); pop. 27; 88 km ENE of Lvov; 49°57'/25°11'.

Gutsisko Penyatske, Ukr. (Hucisko Pikulskie?); pop. 39; 82 km ENE of Lvov; 49°54'/25°09'.

Guttentag, *see* Dobrodzien.

Guttstadt, *see* Dobre Miasto.

Guty Bujno, Pol.; pop. 5; 82 km SW of Bialystok; 52°51'/22°02'.

Guxhagen, Germ.; pop. 190; 133 km NNE of Frankfurt am Main; 51°12'/09°29'; LDS.

Guyche, *see* Geyche.

Guzar, GUM4. This town was not found in BGN gazetteers under the given spelling.

Gvardeiskoye, *see* Gvardeyskoye.

Gvardeysk, USSR (Tapiau); pop. 28; 38 km E of Kaliningrad; 54°39'/21°05'; HSL.

Gvardeyskoye, Ukr. (Felshtin, Gvardeiskoye); 126 km NNE of Chernovtsy; 49°19'/26°43'; EDRD, EJ, HSL, HSL2, JGFF, YB.

Gvodzhits, *see* Gwozdziec.

Gvodzhzhyets Miasta, *see* Gvozdets.

Gvozd, Ukr. (Hwozd); pop. 49; 107 km WNW of Chernovtsy; 48°41'/24°32'.

Gvozdets, Ukr. (Gvodzhzhyets Miasta, Gvozdetz, Gwozdziec Miasta); pop. 1,234; 56 km WNW of Chernovtsy; 48°35'/25°17'; COH, EGRS, HSL, JGFF, LDL, SF.

Gvozdetz, *see* Gvozdets.

Gvozdits, *see* Gwozdziec.

Gvozdova, *see* Gvozdovo.

Gvozdovka, *see* Gvozdovka Vtoraya.

Gvozdovka Vtoraya, Ukr. (Gvozdovka, Gvozdovke, Gwozdowka); 107 km S of Uman; 47°53'/30°05'; SF.

Gvozdovke, *see* Gvozdovka Vtoraya.

Gvozdovo, Mold. (Gvozdova); pop. 7; 107 km NNW of Kishinev; 47°54'/28°21'.

Gvozduts, *see* Gwozdziec.

Gvozhdzhyets, *see* Gwozdziec.

Gvozhdzhyets Miasto, *see* Gwozdziec.

Gvozhdziyets Malyy, *see* Malyy Gvozdets.

Gwizdalki, Pol.; pop. 9; 75 km NW of Czestochowa; 51°20'/18°36'.

Gwizdaly, Pol.; pop. 22; 56 km NE of Warszawa; 52°33'/21°38'.

Gwizdzilny, Pol. EDRD. This town was not found in BGN gazetteers under the given spelling.

Gwozdowka, *see* Gvozdovka Vtoraya.

Gwozdziec, Pol. (Givozits, Gvodzhits, Gvozdits, Gvozduts, Gvozhdzhyets, Gvozhdzhyets Miasto); pop. 55; 88 km NW of Przemysl; 50°23'/21°59'; AMG, GUM5, HSL2, LYV, PHP2, WS.

Gwozdziec Maly, *see* Malyy Gvozdets.

Gwozdziec Miasto, *see* Gvozdets.

Gwoznica Dolna, Pol.; pop. 2; 56 km W of Przemysl; 49°51'/21°59'.

Gwoznica Gorna, Pol.; pop. 23; 56 km W of Przemysl; 49°50'/22°01'.

Gyala, *see* Gyalaret.

Gyalakuta, *see* Gialacuta.

Gyalaret, Hung. (Gyala); 13 km SSW of Szeged; 46°12'/20°07'; HSL.

Gyalu, *see* Gilau.

Gyalumare, *see* Dealumare.

Gyar, Hung.; 26 km NNE of Budapest; 47°41'/19°16'; JGFF.

Gyarmat, Hung.; 120 km WSW of Budapest; 47°28'/17°30'; HSL.

Gyekes, *see* Steinbach.

Gyenesdias, Hung.; pop. 6; 45 km NNE of Nagykanizsa; 46°46'/17°17'.

Gyeres, *see* Ghiris.

Gyeresszentkiraly, *see* Ghiris.

Gyergyoalfalu, *see* Josenii Birgaului.

Gyergyohollo, *see* Corbu.

Gyergyoszentmiklos, *see* Gheorgheni.

Gyergyotol, *see* Tulghes.

Gyerkes, *see* Steinbach.

Gyerofalva, *see* Panic.

Gyertyanliget, *see* Kobyletskaya Polyana.

Gyimes, *see* Ghimes.

Gyimesbukk, *see* Ghimes.

Gyimeskozeplak, *see* Lunca de Jos.

Gyimeskozeplock, *see* Lunca de Jos.

Gyirmot, Hung.; pop. 10; 114 km W of Budapest; 47°38'/17°35'.

Gymnich, Germ.; 19 km SW of Koln; 50°50'/06°44'; AMG, GED.

Gyod, Hung.; pop. 1; 101 km ESE of Nagykanizsa; 46°00'/18°11'.

Gyoma, Hung.; pop. 189; 94 km NNE of Szeged; 46°56'/20°50'; GUM4, HSL, LDS, PHH.

Gyomore, Hung.; pop. 126; 114 km WSW of Budapest; 47°30'/17°34'; HSL, LDL, LDS, PHH.

Gyomro, Hung.; pop. 175; 26 km ESE of Budapest; 47°25'/19°24'; HSL, LDS, PHH.

Gyon, Hung.; pop. 53; 45 km SE of Budapest; 47°10'/19°20'; LDS, PHH.

Gyongy, *see* Giungi.

Gyongyos, Hung.; pop. 2,136; 69 km NE of Budapest; 47°47'/19°56'; AMG, EJ, HSL, HSL2, JGFF, LDL, LDS, PHH.

Gyongyoshalasz, Hung.; pop. 10; 69 km NE of Budapest; 47°44'/19°56'.

Gyongyoshalmaj, Hung.; pop. 2; 69 km SW of Miskolc; 47°46'/20°03'.

Gyongyosherman, Hung.; pop. 6; 94 km NNW of Nagykanizsa; 47°12'/16°39'.

Gyongyosmellek, Hung.; 75 km ESE of Nagykanizsa; 45°59'/17°42'; LDS.

Gyongyosoroszi, Hung.; pop. 4; 69 km SW of Miskolc; 47°50'/19°54'.

Gyongyospata, Hung.; pop. 11; 62 km NE of Budapest; 47°49'/19°48'; HSL.

Gyongyostarjan, Hung.; pop. 3; 69 km NE of Budapest; 47°48'/19°52'.

Gyonk, Hung.; pop. 77; 114 km ENE of Nagykanizsa; 46°33'/18°29'; AMG, HSL, LDL, LDS, PHH.

Gyor, Hung. (Gyorsziget, Raab); pop. 4,688; 114 km W of Budapest; 47°41'/17°38'; AMG, COH, EJ, GUM3, GUM4, GUM5, HSL, HSL2, JGFF, LDL, LDS, PHH.

Gyorasszonyfa, Hung.; pop. 14; 94 km WSW of Budapest; 47°30'/17°48'; LDS, PHH.

Gyore, Hung.; pop. 1; 107 km E of Nagykanizsa; 46°18'/18°24'; HSL.

Gyorkefalva, *see* Cetatele.

Gyorkony, Hung.; pop. 13; 101 km S of Budapest; 46°38'/18°42'.

Gyoro, Hung.; pop. 1; 126 km N of Nagykanizsa; 47°30'/17°01'.

Gyorocske, Hung.; pop. 3; 107 km NE of Miskolc; 48°23'/22°09'.

Gyorsag, Hung.; pop. 7; 101 km W of Budapest; 47°34'/17°45'.

Gyorsovenyhaz, Hung.; pop. 13; 126 km W of Budapest; 47°42'/17°22'.

Gyorszabadi, Hung.; pop. 3; 114 km W of Budapest; 47°46'/17°39'.

Gyorszemere, Hung.; pop. 37; 114 km W of Budapest; 47°33'/17°34'.

Gyorszentivan, Hung.; pop. 4; 101 km W of Budapest; 47°42'/17°44'.

Gyorszentmarton, Hung.; pop. 94; 101 km W of Budapest; 47°33'/17°45'; HSL, LDL, LDS, PHH.

Gyorsziget, *see* Gyor.

Gyortelek, Hung.; pop. 28; 120 km E of Miskolc; 47°56'/22°26'; HSL.

Gyorujfalu, Hung.; pop. 2; 114 km W of Budapest; 47°43'/17°37'.

Gyorvar, Hung.; pop. 9; 69 km NNW of Nagykanizsa; 46°59'/16°51'.

Gyorzamoly, Hung.; pop. 8; 114 km W of Budapest; 47°44'/17°35'.

Gyrbovets, Mold.; pop. 41; 45 km ESE of Kishinev; 46°51'/29°22'.

Gyugy, Hung.; pop. 14; 62 km NE of Nagykanizsa; 46°41'/17°41'.

Gyugye, Hung.; pop. 2; 133 km E of Miskolc; 47°56'/22°34'; HSL.

Gyula, Hung.; pop. 670; 94 km NE of Szeged; 46°39'/21°17'; HSL, LDS, PHH.

Gyulafehervar, *see* Alba Iulia.

Gyulafiratot, Hung.; pop. 10; 94 km SW of Budapest; 47°09'/17°57'.

Gyulahaza, Hung.; pop. 74; 101 km ENE of Miskolc; 48°08'/22°07'; HSL, LDS, PHH.

Gyulaj, Hung.; pop. 14; 101 km ENE of Nagykanizsa; 46°30'/18°18'.

Gyulakeszi, Hung.; pop. 3; 62 km NNE of Nagykanizsa; 46°52'/17°29'.

Gyulavari, Hung.; pop. 7; 101 km NE of Szeged; 46°39'/21°20'.

Gyulevesz, Hung.; pop. 6; 50 km N of Nagykanizsa; 46°51'/17°07'.

Gyure, Hung.; pop. 122; 114 km ENE of Miskolc; 48°11'/22°17'; HSL, JGFF, PHH.

Gyurkapataka, *see* Jurca.

Gyuro, Hung.; pop. 6; 32 km SW of Budapest; 47°23'/18°44'; HSL.

Gzhatsk, *see* Gagarin.

Gzhenda, Ukr. (Grzeda); pop. 24; 50 km NNW of Lvov; 50°16'/23°48'.

Gzhimalov, *see* Grimaylov.

Gzhivkoviche, Byel. (Grzywkowicze); pop. 30; 26 km ESE of Pinsk; 52°01'/26°28'.

Haag, Germ.; 56 km NNE of Nurnberg; 49°52'/11°34'; LDS.

Haan, Germ.; pop. 5; 32 km N of Koln; 51°12'/07°00'.

Haapsalu, Est. (Gapsal, Hapsal, Hapsil); 88 km SW of Tallinn; 58°56'/23°33'; PHLE.

Haar, Germ.; pop. 36; 13 km ESE of Munchen; 48°06'/11°44'.

Haaren, Germ.; pop. 40; 114 km SSW of Hannover; 51°34'/08°44'.

Habartov, Cz. (Habersbirk); pop. 11; 139 km W of Praha; 50°12'/12°33'.

Haber, *see* Habrina.

Habern, *see* Habry.

Habersbirk, *see* Habartov.

Habic, Rom. (Hetbukk); pop. 3; 88 km E of Cluj; 46°42'/24°47'; HSL.

Habitzheim, Germ.; pop. 22; 32 km SE of Frankfurt am Main; 49°51'/08°53'; LDS.

Habrina, Cz. (Haber); 62 km NNW of Praha; 50°36'/14°19'; HSL.

Habry, Cz. (Habern); pop. 39; 82 km ESE of Praha; 49°45'/15°29'; EJ, HSL, HSL2.

Hacava, Cz.; pop. 56; 94 km WSW of Kosice; 48°38'/19°57'.

Hachenburg, Germ.; pop. 111; 69 km ESE of Koln; 50°39'/07°50'.

Hachtchevaty, Ukr. EDRD. This town was not found in BGN gazetteers under the given spelling.

Hacki, Pol.; pop. 6; 38 km S of Bialystok; 52°50'/23°11'.

Hac Wielka, Byel.; pop. 24; 56 km WNW of Pinsk; 52°25'/25°35'. This town was located on an interwar map of Poland but does not appear in contemporary gazetteers. Map coordinates are approximate.

Haczow, Pol.; pop. 72; 62 km WSW of Przemysl; 49°40'/21°54'.

Hadad, *see* Hodod.

Hadamar, Germ.; pop. 25; 62 km WNW of Frankfurt am Main; 50°27'/08°03'; AMG, JGFF, PHGBW.

Hadersdorf, Aus.; pop. 54; 13 km W of Wien; 48°13'/16°14'.

Hadersfeld, Aus.; pop. 1; 19 km NW of Wien; 48°20'/16°16'.

Hadich, Germ. EJ. This town was not found in BGN gazetteers under the given spelling.

Hadikfalva, *see* Dornesti.

Hadle Kanczuckie, *see* Hadle Szklarskie.

Hadle Szklarskie, Pol. (Hadle Kanczuckie); pop. 35; 38 km WNW of Przemysl; 49°55'/22°18'; PHP3.

Hadmersleben, Germ.; 107 km WNW of Leipzig; 51°59'/11°18'; GUM3, LDS.

Hadynkowce, Ukr.; pop. 38; 56 km N of Chernovtsy; 48°45'/25°55'; HSL. This town was located on an interwar map of Poland but does not appear in contemporary gazetteers. Map coordinates are approximate.

Hadynow, Pol.; pop. 5; 107 km N of Lublin; 52°10'/22°41'.

Hadziacz, *see* Gadyach.

Hage, Germ.; pop. 6; 176 km W of Hamburg; 53°37'/07°16'.

Hagen, Germ.; pop. 650; 56 km NNE of Koln; 51°21'/07°28'; AMG, CAHJP, EJ, GED, GUM3, GUM4.

Hagenau, Germ.; 56 km WSW of Nurnberg; 49°19'/10°19'; HSL, HSL2.

Hagenbach, Germ.; pop. 43; 75 km WNW of Stuttgart; 49°01'/08°15'; CAHJP, EJ, GUM5, HSL, JGFF, PHGB.

Hagenburg, Germ.; 26 km W of Hannover; 52°26'/09°20'; GED, LDS.

Hagenow, Germ.; 82 km E of Hamburg; 53°26'/11°11'; JGFF, LDS.

Hagi Curda, *see* Kamyshevka.

Hagnaufurt, Germ.; 101 km SE of Stuttgart; 47°59'/09°43'; JGFF.

Hagyaros, *see* Hagyarosborond.

Hagyarosborond, Hung. (Hagyaros); pop. 2; 56 km NNW of Nagykanizsa; 46°54'/16°43'.

Hagymadfalva, *see* Spinus.

Hagymas, *see* Hasmas.

Hagymaslapos, *see* Lapusel.

Hahn, Germ.; 38 km S of Frankfurt am Main; 49°48'/08°33'; LDS.

Hahnheim, Germ.; pop. 20; 45 km SW of Frankfurt am Main; 49°52'/08°14'.

Hahnlein, Germ.; 45 km S of Frankfurt am Main; 49°44'/08°34'; JGFF, LDS.

Hahot, Hung. (Alsohahot, Felsohahot); pop. 45; 32 km NNW of Nagykanizsa; 46°38'/16°56'; LDS, PHH.

Haidershofen, Aus.; pop. 3; 107 km ENE of Salzburg; 48°04'/14°27'.

Haieu, Rom. (Hajo); pop. 10; 120 km W of Cluj; 46°59'/22°00'.

Haiger, Germ.; pop. 28; 88 km NW of Frankfurt am Main; 50°45'/08°13'.

Haigerloch, Germ.; pop. 300; 56 km SSW of Stuttgart; 48°22'/08°48'; AMG, EJ, GUM5, PHGBW.

Hainburg, *see* Hainburg an der Donau.

Hainburg an der Donau, Aus. (Hainburg); pop. 3; 45 km E of Wien; 48°09'/16°56'.

Hainchen, Germ.; 32 km NE of Frankfurt am Main; 50°16'/09°00'; LDS.

Hain Grundau, Germ.; pop. 12; 38 km NE of Frankfurt am Main; 50°15'/09°09'.

Hainhausen, Germ.; pop. 6; 19 km ESE of Frankfurt am Main; 50°03'/08°53'.

Hainsfarth, Germ. (Heinsfarth); pop. 42; 69 km SSW of Nurnberg; 48°58'/10°37'; GED, GUM5, HSL, HSL2, PHGB.

Hainstadt, Germ.; pop. 39; 82 km SE of Frankfurt am Main; 49°32'/09°20'; HSL, JGFF, LDS, PHGBW.

Haissin, *see* Gaysin.

Haisyn, *see* Gaysin.

Hajdabesernin, GUM3. This town was not found in BGN gazetteers under the given spelling.

Hajdananasz, *see* Hajdunanas.

Hajdeu de Sus, *see* Khazhdeu de Sus.

Hajdieni, *see* Gizhdiyany.

Hajdubagos, Hung. (Hajdubogosz); pop. 50; 101 km SE of Miskolc; 47°24'/21°40'; GUM3, HSL, LDS, PHH.

Hajdubogosz, *see* Hajdubagos.

Hajduboszormeny, Hung. (Boszormeny); pop. 906; 69 km ESE of Miskolc; 47°40'/21°31'; AMG, COH, GUM3, GUM5, HSL, LDS, PHH.

Hajdubozormeny, LDL. This pre-World War I community was not found in BGN gazetteers.

Hajduczok, Byel. EDRD. This town was not found in BGN gazetteers under the given spelling.

Hajdudorog, Hung. (Darag); pop. 414; 62 km ESE of Miskolc; 47°49'/21°30'; GUM3, GUM5, HSL, LDL, LDS, PHH.

Hajduhadhaz, Hung. (Hajduhodkaz); pop. 523; 82 km ESE of Miskolc; 47°41'/21°40'; AMG, GUM3, GUM5, HSL, HSL2, LDS, PHH.

Hajduhaz, *see* Szeremle.

Hajduhodkaz, *see* Hajduhadhaz.

Hajdunanas, Hung. (Hajdananasz); pop. 1,131; 56 km ESE of Miskolc; 47°51'/21°26'; AMG, GUM3, HSL, HSL2, JGFF, LDS, PHH, YB.

Hajdusamson, Hung. (Samson); pop. 268; 88 km ESE of Miskolc; 47°36'/21°46'; AMG, HSL, LDL, LDS, PHH, YB.

Hajduszoboszlo, Hung.; pop. 480; 82 km SE of Miskolc; 47°27'/21°24'; COH, HSL, LDL, LDS, PHH.

Hajduszovat, Hung. (Szovat); pop. 144; 94 km SE of Miskolc; 47°23'/21°29'; HSL, HSL2, LDS, PHH.

Hajduteglas, HSL. This pre-World War I community was not found in BGN gazetteers.

Hajmas, Hung.; pop. 2; 75 km E of Nagykanizsa; 46°17'/17°55'.

Hajmasker, Hung.; pop. 5; 88 km SW of Budapest; 47°09'/18°01'.

Hajna, *see* Gayna.

Hajnin, *see* Gaynin.

Hajnowka, Pol.; pop. 41; 56 km SE of Bialystok; 52°44'/23°35'; AMG, GUM3, HSL.

Hajo, *see* Haieu.

Hajos, Hung.; pop. 30; 82 km W of Szeged; 46°24'/19°07'.

Hajowniki, Pol.; pop. 11; 75 km ESE of Lublin; 50°50'/23°26'.

Hajsyn, *see* Gaysin.

Halamky, Cz.; pop. 1; 126 km SW of Brno; 48°51'/14°55'.

Halaszi, Hung.; pop. 4; 139 km WNW of Budapest; 47°53'/17°20'.

Halberstadt, Germ.; pop. 720; 107 km ESE of Hannover; 51°54'/11°03'; AMG, CAHJP, EJ, GUM3, GUM4, HSL, HSL2, ISH1, JGFF, LDS, PHP4.

Halbow, Pol. PHP3. This town was not found in BGN gazetteers under the given spelling.

Halcnow, Pol.; pop. 9; 62 km SW of Krakow; 49°51'/19°06'.

Haldensleben, Germ. (Neuhaldensleben); pop. 11; 114 km E of Hannover; 52°18'/11°25'.

Haldern, Germ.; pop. 10; 94 km NNW of Koln; 51°46'/06°28'.

Haleny, *see* Galeny.

Halesz, *see* Tapioszollos.

Halic, Cz.; 133 km SW of Kosice; 48°21'/19°35'; GUM4.

Halicz, *see* Galich.

Haligovce, Cz.; 88 km NW of Kosice; 49°22'/20°27'; HSL.

Halimba, Hung.; pop. 4; 82 km NNE of Nagykanizsa; 47°02'/17°32'.

Halinowola, *see* Galinovolya.

Hall, *see* Schwabisch Hall.

Halle, Germ. (Halle an der Saale); pop. 1,300; 38 km WNW of Leipzig; 51°30'/12°00'; AMG, CAHJP, EJ, HSL, HSL2, JGFF, LDL, LDS, PHGBW.

Halle an der Saale, *see* Halle.

Hallein, Aus.; pop. 7; 19 km SSE of Salzburg; 47°41'/13°06'; EDRD, EJ.

Hallenberg, Germ.; pop. 39; 120 km N of Frankfurt am Main; 51°07'/08°38'; GUM5.

Hallerndorf, Germ.; 38 km NNW of Nurnberg; 49°46'/10°59'; PHGB.

Hallstadt, Germ.; 56 km NNW of Nurnberg; 49°56'/10°53'; PHGB.

Hallstatt, Aus.; pop. 1; 50 km ESE of Salzburg; 47°33'/13°39'.

Halmaj, Hung.; pop. 58; 26 km NNE of Miskolc; 48°15'/21°00'; HSL, PHH.

Halmasd, Rom. (Halmosd); 88 km WNW of Cluj; 47°09'/22°37'; HSL.

Halmeu, Rom. (Halmi); pop. 1,373; 146 km NNW of Cluj; 47°58'/23°01'; AMG, HSL, HSL2, JGFF, LDL, PHR2, YB.

Halmi, *see* Halmeu.

Halmosd, *see* Halmasd.

Halom, Hung.; 94 km WNW of Szeged; 46°31'/19°03'; HSL.

Hals, Germ.; 146 km NE of Munchen; 48°36'/13°28'; PHGB.

Halsdorf, Germ.; pop. 38; 94 km N of Frankfurt am Main; 50°55'/08°57'; HSL.

Halta, *see* Golta.

Haltern, Germ.; pop. 27; 94 km N of Koln; 51°44'/07°11'; AMG, GED.

Haluboki, *see* Rastice.

Halusk, *see* Glussk.

Haluszczynce, Pol.; pop. 23; Described in the *Black Book* as being in the Tarnopol region of Poland, this town was not found in BGN gazetteers.

Haly, Ukr.; pop. 20; 38 km NNW of Rovno; 50°55'/26°05'. This town was located on an interwar map of Poland but does not appear in contemporary gazetteers. Map coordinates are approximate.

Halze, Cz.; pop. 10; 133 km WSW of Praha; 49°50'/12°35'.

Hamborn, Germ.; pop. 800; 101 km SSW of Hannover; 51°40'/08°46'; GUM3.

Hambro, HSL. This pre-World War I community was not found in BGN gazetteers.

Hambuch, Germ.; pop. 9; 88 km SSE of Koln; 50°14'/07°11'.

Hamburg, Germ.; pop. 17,904; 133 km N of Hannover; 53°33'/10°00'; AMG, CAHJP, EJ, GED, GUM3, GUM4, GUM5, GUM6, HSL, HSL2, ISH1, JGFF, LDL, LDS, PHGBW, PHP1, PHP2, PHP4.

Hamelerwald, Germ.; pop. 2; 26 km E of Hannover; 52°21'/10°07'.

Hamelin, *see* Hameln.

Hameln, Germ. (Hamelin); pop. 170; 45 km SSW of Hannover; 52°06'/09°21'; CAHJP, EJ, GED, LDS.

Hamm, Germ.; pop. 61; 56 km ESE of Koln; 50°46'/07°40'; AMG, CAHJP, GED, GUM5, HSL, JGFF.

Hammelburg, Germ.; pop. 98; 88 km E of Frankfurt am Main; 50°07'/09°54'; AMG, CAHJP, GUM5, HSL, HSL2, PHGB.

Hammerstein, *see* Czarne.

Hamminkeln, Germ.; pop. 9; 94 km NNW of Koln; 51°44'/06°35'.

Hamor, Hung.; pop. 36; 13 km WSW of Miskolc; 48°06'/20°39'; HSL.

Hanaczow, *see* Ganachevka.

Hanaczowka, *see* Ganachuvka.

Hanasenii de Padure, *see* Ganaseny de Pedure.

Hanashishok, *see* Onuskis.

Hanau, *see* Hanau am Main.

Hanau am Main, Germ. (Hanau); pop. 630; 19 km ENE of Frankfurt am Main; 50°08'/08°55'; AMG, CAHJP, EJ, GUM4, HSL, HSL2, JGFF, LDS.

Han Casla, *see* Udobnoye.

Hancauti, *see* Ghitcauti.

Hancesti, *see* Kotovsk (Bessarabia).

Hancewicze, *see* Gantsevichi.

Hanczeschty, *see* Kotovsk (Bessarabia).

Hanczowa, Pol.; pop. 15; 114 km ESE of Krakow; 49°29'/21°10'.

Handlova, Cz. (Krickerhau, Kriegerhay, Nyitrabanya); pop. 92; 139 km NE of Bratislava; 48°44'/18°46'; AMG, GUM6.

Handzlowka, Pol.; pop. 33; 45 km WNW of Przemysl; 49°59'/22°14'.

Hanesti, *see* Hantesti.

Hangacs, Hung.; pop. 25; 32 km N of Miskolc; 48°18'/20°50'; HSL.

Hangony, Hung. (Alsohangony); pop. 28; 50 km WNW of Miskolc; 48°14'/20°12'; HSL.

Haniska, Cz. (Chaniszka); 19 km S of Kosice; 48°37'/21°15'; HSL.

Hankowce, *see* Gankovtsy.

Hankowice, *see* Gankovitsa.

Hanna, Pol.; pop. 48; 82 km NE of Lublin; 51°43'/23°30'.

Hannover, Germ. (Hanover); pop. 5,521; 133 km S of Hamburg; 52°22'/09°43'; AMG, CAHJP, COH, EJ, GED, GUM3, GUM4, GUM5, GUM6, HSL, HSL2, JGFF, LYV, PHGBW, PHP1, PHP2.

Hannoversch Munden, *see* Munden.

Hanover, *see* Hannover.

Han Pijesak, Yug.; 150 km SW of Beograd; 44°05'/18°57'; GUM4.

Hansdorf, *see* Hanusovice.

Hansk, Pol. (Heinsk); pop. 10; 62 km ENE of Lublin; 51°24'/23°25'; GUM5, SF.

Hanspach, *see* Lipova.

Hantesti, Rom. (Hanesti); pop. 74; 114 km WNW of Iasi; 47°45'/26°22'; EJ, GUM4, PHR1.

Hanunin, *see* Ganunin.

Hanusovce, *see* Hanusovce nad Toplou.

Hanusovce nad Toplou, Cz. (Hanusovce, Hanustalu); pop. 271; 45 km NNE of Kosice; 49°02'/21°30'; COH, GUM4, HSL, LDL.

Hanusovice, Cz. (Hansdorf); 107 km N of Brno; 50°05'/16°57'; GUM3, GUM4.

Hanustalu, *see* Hanusovce nad Toplou.

Hanuszeschty, *possibly* Kotovsk (Bessarabia).

Hanuszowce, *see* Ganushovtse.

Hanuszyszki, *see* Onuskis.

Hanva, *see* Chanava.

Hapai, Rom.; pop. 6; 126 km WNW of Iasi; 47°53'/26°16'.

Hapsal, *see* Haapsalu.

Hapsil, *see* Haapsalu.

Hara Kbira, HSL. This pre-World War I community was not found in BGN gazetteers.

Harangod, Hung. BGN lists two possible localities with this name located at 47°54'/21°50' and 48°08'/21°05'. EDRD.

Hara Sghira, HSL. This pre-World War I community was not found in BGN gazetteers.

Harastas, (Harasztos); HSL. This pre-World War I community was not found in BGN gazetteers.

Harasymow, *see* Garasymuv.

Harasztkerek, *see* Roteni.

Harasztos, *see* Harastas.

Harbovat, *see* Gerbovets.

Harburg, Germ.; 82 km S of Nurnberg; 48°46'/10°40'; CAHJP, GUM5, HSL, HSL2, PHGB.

Harburg Wilhelmsburg, Germ.; pop. 400; 13 km S of Hamburg; 53°28'/09°59'.

Harbutowice, Pol.; 88 km SW of Krakow; 49°48'/18°49'; HSL.

Harc, Hung.; pop. 7; 120 km W of Szeged; 46°24'/18°38'.

Harczo, *see* Hartau.

Hardenberg, Germ.; pop. 17; BGN lists two possible localities with this name located at 51°06'/07°44' and 51°19'/07°05'.

Harderode, Germ.; 45 km S of Hannover; 52°03'/09°33'; LDS.

Hardheim, Germ.; pop. 65; 75 km ESE of Frankfurt am Main; 49°37'/09°29'; LDS, PHGBW.

Haren, Germ.; pop. 30; 176 km W of Hannover; 52°47'/07°14'; GUM5, LDS.

Harhaj, Cz.; 56 km N of Kosice; 49°11'/21°25'; HSL.

Harheim, Germ.; pop. 7; 19 km NNW of Frankfurt am Main; 50°11'/08°41'.

Harina, *see* Herina.

Harisof, *see* Htusovo.

Haritzev, *see* Gritsev.

Harka, *see* Magyarfalva.

Harkabuz, Pol.; pop. 7; 62 km S of Krakow; 49°33'/19°51'.

Harkacs, *see* Hrkac.

Harkany, Hung.; pop. 39; 114 km ESE of Nagykanizsa;

45°51'/18°14'.

Harlau, *see* Hirlau.

Harmacz, *see* Chramec.

Harmas, HSL. A number of towns share this name. It was not possible to determine from available information which one is being referenced.

Harmaspatak, *see* Valea Ternei.

Harmuthsachsen, Germ.; pop. 34; 146 km NNE of Frankfurt am Main; 51°09'/09°51'; JGFF, LDS.

Harnicesti, Rom. (Hernecs, Hornicest); pop. 63; 120 km N of Cluj; 47°47'/23°53'; SM.

Haromfa, Hung.; pop. 2; 50 km SE of Nagykanizsa; 46°06'/17°20'.

Haromhuta, Hung.; pop. 3; 56 km NE of Miskolc; 48°23'/21°26'.

Harpstedt, Germ.; pop. 11; 94 km WNW of Hannover; 52°54'/08°35'.

Harsany, Hung.; pop. 56; 19 km S of Miskolc; 47°58'/20°45'; HSL, PHH.

Harsewinkel, Germ.; pop. 10; 107 km SW of Hannover; 51°58'/08°14'.

Harsfalva, HSL. This pre-World War I community was not found in BGN gazetteers.

Har Shafer, *see* Ingulets.

Harszymow, *see* Garasymuv.

Hartau, (Harczo); HSL. A number of towns share this name. It was not possible to determine from available information which one is being referenced.

Hartfeld, *see* Tverdopillya.

Harthausen, Germ.; 82 km WNW of Stuttgart; 49°18'/08°21'; EJ.

Hartmanice, Cz.; pop. 59; 126 km SSW of Praha; 49°10'/13°28'.

Hartmanov, Cz.; pop. 3; 107 km W of Praha; 50°14'/13°01'.

Hartop, *see* Gertop.

Hartop Mare, *possibly* Gertop Mare.

Hartop Soroca, *see* Gertop.

Hartopul Mare, *see* Gertop Mare.

Harz, Germ.; pop. 49; 101 km WNW of Leipzig; 51°34'/10°57'.

Harzgerode, Germ.; pop. 10; 88 km WNW of Leipzig; 51°38'/11°09'.

Hasan Batar, *see* Vinogradnoye.

Haselbach, Germ.; 94 km NE of Frankfurt am Main; 50°23'/10°00'; PHGB.

Hasenhecke Siedlung, GUM3. This town was not found in BGN gazetteers under the given spelling.

Hasenpot, *see* Aizpute.

Hasenpoth, *see* Aizpute.

Haskovo, *see* Khaskovo.

Haslach, Germ.; 101 km SW of Stuttgart; 48°17'/08°05'; GUM3, GUM5, PHGBW.

Hasmas, Rom. (Alsohagymas, Hagymas); pop. 34; 120 km WSW of Cluj; 46°30'/22°05'; AMG, HSL.

Hasnasenii Mari, *see* Bolshiye Asnashany.

Hassfurt, Germ.; pop. 93; 75 km NW of Nurnberg; 50°02'/10°30'; GUM5, HSL, JGFF, PHGB.

Hassloch, Germ.; pop. 62; 88 km S of Frankfurt am Main; 49°22'/08°16'; GED, GUM5, JGFF.

Hasznos, Hung.; pop. 6; 69 km NE of Budapest; 47°56'/19°44'.

Hat, Cz.; 146 km NE of Brno; 49°57'/18°15'; AMG.

Hatowszczyzna, *possibly* Galkovshchina.

Hatten, Germ.; 120 km SW of Hamburg; 53°03'/08°23'; HSL.

Hattingen, Germ.; pop. 73; 56 km N of Koln; 51°24'/07°10'; LDS.

Hatuica, Rom.; pop. 3; 170 km N of Bucuresti; 45°56'/26°08'.

Hatvan, Hung.; pop. 647; 50 km NE of Budapest; 47°40'/19°41'; AMG, GUM4, GUM5, HSL, HSL2, LDS, PHH.

Hatzbach, Germ.; pop. 2; 94 km N of Frankfurt am Main; 50°53'/09°01'; HSL, LDS.

Hatzenport, Germ.; pop. 2; 88 km SSE of Koln; 50°14'/07°25'.

Hausberge, *see* Hausberge an der Porta.

Hausberge an der Porta, Germ. (Hausberge); pop. 28; 56 km

WSW of Hannover; 52°14'/08°55'; AMG, GUM3, HSL.

Hausen, Germ.; 157 km SSW of Stuttgart; 47°41'/07°51'; HSL, PHGB, PHGB.

Hausmannstatten, Aus.; pop. 1; 13 km SSE of Graz; 46°59'/15°30'.

Hausmenning, Aus.; pop. 3; 120 km WSW of Wien; 48°04'/14°48'.

Haustenbeck, Germ.; pop. 5; 94 km SW of Hannover; 51°50'/08°46'.

Hautzendorf, Aus.; pop. 3; 32 km N of Wien; 48°26'/16°29'.

Hauzenberg, Germ.; 157 km NE of Munchen; 48°39'/13°38'; GUM3.

Havad, *see* Neaua.

Havadto, HSL. This pre-World War I community was not found in BGN gazetteers. *See also* Viforoasa.

Havarna, *see* Havirna.

Havas, *see* Bolcske.

Havasmezo, *see* Poienile de Sub Munte.

Havasnagydalu, *see* Mariselu.

Havelberg, Germ.; 94 km WNW of Berlin; 52°49'/12°05'; HSL.

Havirna, Rom. (Havarna); pop. 57; 126 km NW of Iasi; 48°04'/26°39'.

Havlickuv Brod, Cz. (Nemecky Brod); pop. 160; 94 km WNW of Brno; 49°37'/15°35'.

Hawlowice, Pol.; pop. 6; 26 km WNW of Przemysl; 49°56'/22°32'.

Hawrylczyce, *see* Gavrilchitsy.

Hawrylowka, *see* Gavrilovka.

Haydutsishok, *see* Adutiskis.

Hayna, *see* Gayna.

Haynau, *see* Chojnow.

Hazenau, *see* Aizpute.

Hazin, Cz.; 56 km ENE of Kosice; 48°45'/22°01'; HSL.

Hazlach, Pol.; pop. 6; 94 km SW of Krakow; 49°48'/18°40'.

Hazlov, Cz.; pop. 7; 157 km W of Praha; 50°09'/12°16'.

Hazslin, HSL. This pre-World War I community was not found in BGN gazetteers.

Hebdow, Pol.; pop. 11; 38 km ENE of Krakow; 50°09'/20°25'.

Hebenshausen, Germ.; pop. 6; 114 km SSE of Hannover; 51°23'/09°55'.

Hechingen, Germ.; pop. 106; 50 km S of Stuttgart; 48°21'/08°59'; CAHJP, GUM5, HSL, HSL2, JGFF, PHGBW.

Hechlingen, Germ.; 62 km SSW of Nurnberg; 48°58'/10°44'; PHGB.

Hechtsheim, Germ.; pop. 58; 32 km SW of Frankfurt am Main; 49°58'/08°17'.

Heci, Rom. (Heci Lespezi); pop. 1,011; 75 km WNW of Iasi; 47°21'/26°40'; GUM5, PHR1.

Heci Lespezi, *see* Heci.

Heciu Nou, *see* Novyye Gechi.

Hecznarowice, Pol.; pop. 1; 56 km SW of Krakow; 49°54'/19°10'.

Heddernheim, *see* Hedernheim.

Hedernheim, (Heddernheim); pop. 132; HSL, HSL2, JGFF. Described in the *Black Book* as being in the Hessen region of Germany, this town was not found in BGN gazetteers.

Hedervar, Hung.; 126 km WNW of Budapest; 47°50'/17°28'; LDS.

Hedrehely, Hung.; pop. 15; 56 km ESE of Nagykanizsa; 46°11'/17°40'.

Heegheim, Germ.; 32 km NE of Frankfurt am Main; 50°18'/08°58'; LDS.

Heepen, Germ.; 88 km SW of Hannover; 52°02'/08°37'; LDS.

Heessen, Germ. BGN lists two possible localities with this name located at 51°43'/07°51' and 52°14'/09°06'. JGFF.

Hefziba, Pol. PHP2. This town was not found in BGN gazetteers under the given spelling.

Hegy, HSL. A number of towns share this name. It was not possible to determine from available information which one is being referenced.

Hegyalja, Hung. AMG. A number of towns share this name. It was not possible to determine from available information which one is being referenced.

Hegyeshalom, Hung. (Strass Somerein); 150 km WNW of Budapest; 47°55'/17°10'; EJ, GUM3, GUM4, GUM6.

Hegyfalu, Hung.; pop. 12; 107 km N of Nagykanizsa; 47°21'/16°53'.

Hegyhatszentjakab, Hung.; pop. 1; 62 km NW of Nagykanizsa; 46°52'/16°33'.

Hegyhatszentpeter, Hung.; pop. 6; 69 km NNW of Nagykanizsa; 46°59'/16°49'.

Hegykoz, see Girbou.

Hegykozcsatar, see Cetariu.

Hegykozpalyi, see Paleu.

Hegykozszentimre, see Sintimreu.

Hegykoztottelek, see Tautelec.

Hegymeg, see Dolne Zahorany.

Hehalom, Hung.; pop. 17; 45 km NE of Budapest; 47°46'/19°35'.

Hehlen, Germ.; pop. 33; 50 km S of Hannover; 51°59'/09°29'; LDS.

Heideck, Germ.; 45 km S of Nurnberg; 49°07'/11°07'; PHGB.

Heidekrug, see Silute.

Heidelberg, Germ.; pop. 1,354; 82 km S of Frankfurt am Main; 49°25'/08°42'; AMG, GED, GUM4, GUM5, HSL, HSL2, JGFF, LDS, PHGBW, YB.

Heidelsheim, Germ.; pop. 9; 56 km WNW of Stuttgart; 49°06'/08°39'; LDS, PHGBW.

Heidemuhle, see Kowale Panskie.

Heidenheim, Germ.; pop. 25; 56 km SSW of Nurnberg; 49°01'/10°45'; AMG, GUM4, GUM5, HSL, HSL2, LDS, PHGB, PHGBW.

Heidenreichstein, Aus.; pop. 28; 120 km WNW of Wien; 48°52'/15°07'.

Heidesheim, Germ. BGN lists two possible localities with this name located at 49°35'/08°12' and 50°00'/08°07'. JGFF.

Heidingsfeld, Germ.; pop. 83; 88 km WNW of Nurnberg; 49°46'/09°58'; CAHJP, EJ, HSL, PHGB, PHGBW.

Heidotzishok, see Adutiskis.

Heilbronn, Germ.; pop. 980; 45 km N of Stuttgart; 49°08'/09°13'; AMG, EDRD, EJ, GED, GUM5, JGFF, PHGBW.

Heiligenstadt, Germ.; pop. 34; 114 km SSE of Hannover; 51°23'/10°08'; LDS.

Heiligenstadt (Bavaria), Germ.; 50 km N of Nurnberg; 49°52'/11°10'; GUM5, PHGB.

Heilsberg, see Lidzbark Warminski.

Heilsbronn, Germ.; 26 km SW of Nurnberg; 49°20'/10°48'; LDS, PHGB.

Heimertingen, Germ.; 107 km WSW of Munchen; 48°02'/10°09'; PHGB.

Heimerzheim, Germ.; 32 km S of Koln; 50°43'/06°55'; GED.

Heinebach, Germ.; pop. 37; 133 km NNE of Frankfurt am Main; 51°03'/09°40'; LDS.

Heinichen, GUM3. This town was not found in BGN gazetteers under the given spelling.

Heinrichs, Germ.; 133 km NNW of Nurnberg; 50°36'/10°39'; HSL, HSL2.

Heinrichs B Weitra, Aus. HSL. This pre-World War I community was not found in BGN gazetteers.

Heinsberg, Germ.; pop. 54; 62 km W of Koln; 51°04'/06°05'; GUM5, HSL.

Heinsdorf, Germ.; 69 km S of Berlin; 51°56'/13°20'; HSL.

Heinsfarth, see Hainsfarth.

Heinsheim, Germ.; pop. 21; 62 km N of Stuttgart; 49°16'/09°09'; JGFF, LDS, PHGBW.

Heinsk, see Hansk.

Heishin, see Gayshin.

Heisin, see Gaysin.

Hejce, Hung.; pop. 5; 56 km NE of Miskolc; 48°26'/21°17'.

Hejobaba, Hung.; pop. 31; 26 km SE of Miskolc; 47°54'/20°57'; AMG, GUM5, HSL.

Hejocsaba, Hung.; pop. 272; 6 km SSE of Miskolc; 48°04'/20°48'; GUM4, HSL, JGFF, LDS, PHH.

Hejokeresztur, Hung.; pop. 5; 19 km SE of Miskolc; 47°58'/20°53'.

Hejopapi, Hung.; pop. 22; 26 km SSE of Miskolc; 47°54'/20°55'; HSL.

Hejoszalonta, Hung.; pop. 5; 26 km SSE of Miskolc; 47°56'/20°53'.

Hel, Pol.; 38 km N of Gdansk; 54°37'/18°47'; GUM3.

Heldenbergen, Germ.; pop. 75; 19 km NE of Frankfurt am Main; 50°14'/08°52'; GUM5, JGFF, LDS.

Helenow, Pol.; 69 km N of Lodz; 52°19'/19°38'; GUM4, PHP1.

Helenowka Stara, see Staraya Yelenovka.

Helesfa, Hung.; pop. 3; 88 km ESE of Nagykanizsa; 46°05'/17°59'.

Helitch, see Galich.

Hellenthal, Germ.; 62 km SSW of Koln; 50°29'/06°26'; AMG.

Hellstein, Germ.; pop. 20; 50 km NE of Frankfurt am Main; 50°19'/09°18'.

Helmarshausen, see Karlshafen.

Helmern, Germ.; pop. 6; BGN lists two possible localities with this name located at 51°34'/08°46' and 51°37'/09°05'.

Helmiazov, see Gelmyazov.

Helmstadt, Germ.; 62 km NNW of Stuttgart; 49°19'/08°59'; AMG.

Helmstedt, Germ.; pop. 18; 88 km E of Hannover; 52°14'/11°00'; EJ, GUM3, GUM4, LDS.

Hemau, Germ.; pop. 3; 69 km ESE of Nurnberg; 49°03'/11°47'.

Hemer, Germ.; pop. 8; 75 km NE of Koln; 51°23'/07°46'; GUM3, GUM4.

Hemmerden, Germ.; pop. 11; 32 km WNW of Koln; 51°07'/06°36'; GED.

Hemsbach, Germ.; pop. 86; 62 km S of Frankfurt am Main; 49°36'/08°39'; GED, JGFF, PHGBW.

Hencida, Hung.; pop. 81; 120 km SE of Miskolc; 47°15'/21°42'; AMG, LDS, PHH.

Henesz, Hung.; pop. 16; 38 km ESE of Nagykanizsa; 46°14'/17°23'.

Hengersberg, Germ.; pop. 4; 126 km NE of Munchen; 48°47'/13°03'.

Hengstfeld, Germ.; 75 km SW of Nurnberg; 49°13'/10°06'; JGFF, PHGBW.

Hennef, Germ.; 32 km ESE of Koln; 50°47'/07°17'; GED.

Hennweiler, Germ.; pop. 36; 94 km SW of Frankfurt am Main; 49°49'/07°26'.

Henrykow, Pol.; pop. 234; 13 km NNW of Warszawa; 52°20'/20°58'; COH, PHP4. Located very close to Warszawa, the town does not appear in contemporary gazetteers.

Heppenheim, see Heppenheim an der Bergstrasse.

Heppenheim an der Bergstrasse, Germ. (Heppenheim); pop. 103; 56 km S of Frankfurt am Main; 49°38'/08°39'; GED, GUM3, GUM5, HSL, PHGBW, YB.

Heppenheim an der Wiese, Germ.; pop. 28; 69 km SSW of Frankfurt am Main; 49°36'/08°16'.

Herbede, Germ.; pop. 37; 56 km N of Koln; 51°25'/07°16'.

Herbern, Germ.; pop. 16; 101 km NNE of Koln; 51°45'/07°41'.

Herborn, Germ.; pop. 93; 69 km NNW of Frankfurt am Main; 50°41'/08°19'; HSL.

Herbstein, Germ.; 69 km NE of Frankfurt am Main; 50°33'/09°21'; LDS.

Hercegcut, see Hercegkut.

Hercegfalva, see Mezofalva.

Hercegkut, Hung. (Hercegcut); pop. 8; 62 km NE of Miskolc; 48°20'/21°32'; HSL.

Hercegovac, Yug.; pop. 17; 82 km E of Zagreb; 45°39'/17°01'.

Hercegszanto, Hung.; pop. 44; 101 km SW of Szeged; 45°57'/18°56'.

Herdecke, Germ.; pop. 20; 62 km NNE of Koln; 51°24'/07°26'.

Hered, Hung.; pop. 11; 45 km NE of Budapest; 47°42'/19°38'; HSL.

Hereg, Hung.; pop. 1; 45 km WNW of Budapest; 47°39'/18°31'.

Herend, Hung.; pop. 12; 94 km NNE of Nagykanizsa; 47°08'/17°45'.

Heresznye, Hung.; pop. 3; 50 km SE of Nagykanizsa; 46°03'/17°17'.

Herford, Germ.; pop. 204; 75 km SW of Hannover; 52°08'/08°41'; AMG.

Hergershausen, Germ.; pop. 33; BGN lists two possible localities with this name located at 49°57'/08°55' and 51°01'/09°41'.

Herina, Rom. (Harina); pop. 87; 69 km NE of Cluj; 47°01'/24°25'; HSL.

Herink, Cz.; pop. 3; 19 km SE of Praha; 49°58'/14°35'.

Herkheim, Germ. (Kleinerdlingen); pop. 5; 82 km SSW of Nurnberg; 48°50'/10°29'; HSL, JGFF, PHGB.

Herleshausen, Germ.; pop. 60; 146 km NE of Frankfurt am Main; 51°01'/10°10'; LDS.

Herlinghausen, Germ.; 107 km S of Hannover; 51°28'/09°12'; GED.

Hermagor, Aus.; pop. 3; 139 km SSE of Salzburg; 46°37'/13°22'; AMG.

Hermann Mestetz, *see* Hermanuv Mestec.

Hermannstadt, *see* Sibiu.

Hermanovce, Cz.; 45 km NNW of Kosice; 49°03'/21°01'; AMG, HSL, JGFF.

Hermanovice, Pol. (Hermanowice); pop. 14; 13 km SSE of Przemysl; 49°44'/22°49'; EDRD.

Hermanovka, *see* Krasnoye (near Belaya Tserkov).

Hermanow, *see* Germanuv.

Hermanowa, Pol.; pop. 30; 56 km WNW of Przemysl; 49°57'/22°01'.

Hermanowice, *see* Hermanovice.

Hermanowicze, *see* Germanovichi.

Hermanstadt, *see* Sibiu.

Hermanszeg, Hung.; pop. 16; 139 km E of Miskolc; 47°54'/22°38'.

Hermanuv Mestec, Cz. (Hermann Mestetz); pop. 87; 82 km E of Praha; 49°57'/15°40'; EJ.

Hermeskeil, Germ.; pop. 40; 133 km SW of Frankfurt am Main; 49°39'/06°57'.

Hernadcsany, Cz.; 19 km SE of Kosice; 48°36'/21°20'; GUM5, HSL.

Hernadkak, Hung.; pop. 12; 19 km E of Miskolc; 48°05'/20°58'.

Hernadkercs, Hung.; pop. 5; 32 km NE of Miskolc; 48°15'/21°03'.

Hernadnemeti, Hung.; pop. 58; 19 km E of Miskolc; 48°04'/20°59'; HSL, HSL2, PHH.

Hernadpetri, Hung.; pop. 6; 56 km NNE of Miskolc; 48°29'/21°10'.

Hernadszentandras, Hung.; pop. 12; 32 km NE of Miskolc; 48°17'/21°06'.

Hernadvecse, Hung.; pop. 83; 50 km NNE of Miskolc; 48°27'/21°10'; PHH.

Hernadzsadany, *see* Zdana.

Herne, Germ.; pop. 450; 69 km N of Koln; 51°33'/07°13'; AMG, GED, GUM3.

Hernecs, *see* Harnicesti.

Herrenalb, Germ.; 56 km W of Stuttgart; 48°48'/08°26'; PHGBW.

Herrieden, Germ.; pop. 1; 50 km SW of Nurnberg; 49°14'/10°31'; LDS, PHGB.

Herrlingen, Germ.; 62 km ESE of Stuttgart; 48°25'/09°54'; GUM4, PHGBW.

Herrlisheim, HSL. This pre-World War I community was not found in BGN gazetteers.

Herrnbaumgarten, Aus.; pop. 4; 56 km N of Wien; 48°41'/16°41'.

Hersbruck, Germ.; pop. 20; 32 km ENE of Nurnberg; 49°31'/11°26'; GUM3, GUM4, GUM5, GUM6, PHGB.

Herschberg, Germ.; 120 km SSW of Frankfurt am Main; 49°18'/07°33'; GED.

Herschfeld, Germ.; 114 km ENE of Frankfurt am Main; 50°20'/10°14'; HSL.

Hersel, Germ.; pop. 7; 26 km SSE of Koln; 50°46'/07°02'; GED.

Hersfeld, *see* Bad Hersfeld.

Herstelle, Germ.; pop. 4; 88 km S of Hannover; 51°39'/09°25'; JGFF.

Herta, *see* Gertsa.

Herten, Germ.; pop. 30; 75 km N of Koln; 51°36'/07°08'; GED.

Hertnik, Cz.; 62 km N of Kosice; 49°13'/21°15'; HSL.

Hervest, Germ.; pop. 3; 88 km N of Koln; 51°40'/07°01'.

Herxheim, Germ. BGN lists two possible localities with this name located at 49°09'/08°13' and 49°31'/08°11'. GUM5, JGFF.

Herzegovina; Not a town, but part of the Austro-Hungarian Empire prior to the end of World War I. Now a constituent republic of Yugoslavia.

Herzfeld, Germ.; 88 km S of Rostock; 53°20'/11°46'; GUM4.

Herzogenaurach, Germ.; 19 km WNW of Nurnberg; 49°33'/10°53'; PHGB.

Herzogenburg, Aus.; pop. 11; 50 km W of Wien; 48°16'/15°41'.

Herzogenrath, Germ.; pop. 6; 56 km WSW of Koln; 50°52'/06°06'.

Hessdorf, Germ.; pop. 56; 26 km NW of Nurnberg; 49°38'/10°55'; GUM5, HSL, HSL2, JGFF, PHGB.

Hesse; Not a town, but a region of central Germany.

Hesse Darmstadt, Germ. CAHJP, JGFF. This town was not found in BGN gazetteers under the given spelling.

Hessen, Germ.; 82 km ESE of Hannover; 52°01'/10°47'; JGFF, PHGBW.

Hessental, Germ.; 56 km NE of Stuttgart; 49°06'/09°46'; GUM5, PHGBW.

Hessheim, Germ.; pop. 4; 62 km SSW of Frankfurt am Main; 49°33'/08°18'.

Hessisch Lichtenau, Germ.; 139 km S of Hannover; 51°12'/09°43'; GUM3, GUM5.

Hessisch Oldendorf, Germ.; pop. 21; 45 km SW of Hannover; 52°10'/09°15'.

Hessloch, Germ.; pop. 33; 50 km SSW of Frankfurt am Main; 49°44'/08°15'; JGFF.

Het, Hung.; pop. 4; 32 km WNW of Miskolc; 48°17'/20°23'; HSL.

Hetbukk, *see* Habic.

Hete, Hung.; pop. 13; 126 km ENE of Miskolc; 48°07'/22°29'.

Hetenyegyhaza, Hung.; 75 km SE of Budapest; 46°55'/19°35'; HSL, HSL2.

Hetes, Hung.; pop. 4; 56 km E of Nagykanizsa; 46°25'/17°42'.

Hethars, Cz.; 56 km NNW of Kosice; 49°09'/20°58'; HSL, HSL2.

Hettmannsdorf, Aus.; pop. 1; 56 km SSW of Wien; 47°46'/16°03'.

Hettstadt, Germ.; 88 km ESE of Frankfurt am Main; 49°48'/09°49'; PHGB, PHGBW.

Heubach, Germ.; pop. 25; 82 km NE of Frankfurt am Main; 50°22'/09°43'; LDS.

Heuberg, Germ. BGN lists two possible localities with this name located at 49°10'/09°30' and 48°29'/09°35'. GUM3, PHGBW.

Heuchelheim, *see* Hochelheim.

Heusenstamm, Germ.; pop. 32; 13 km ESE of Frankfurt am Main; 50°04'/08°48'; GED.

Heves, Hung.; pop. 426; 62 km SSW of Miskolc; 47°36'/20°17'; EDRD, HSL, HSL2, PHH.

Hevesugra, Hung.; pop. 2; 69 km SW of Miskolc; 47°46'/20°04'.

Heviz, Hung. (Heviz Szent Andras, Hevizszentandras); pop. 23; 45 km N of Nagykanizsa; 46°47'/17°11'; HSL.

Hevizgyork, Hung.; pop. 36; 38 km NE of Budapest; 47°38'/19°31'.

Heviz Szent Andras, *see* Heviz.

Hevizszentandras, *see* Heviz.

Hida, Rom. (Hidalmas); pop. 338; 45 km NW of Cluj; 47°04'/23°17'; HSL, HSL2, JGFF, LDL, PHR2.

Hidalmas, *see* Hida.

Hidas, Hung.; 120 km E of Nagykanizsa; 46°16'/18°30'; HSL, LDS.

Hidashollos, Hung.; pop. 2; 75 km NNW of Nagykanizsa; 47°03'/16°42'.

Hidasnemeti, Hung.; pop. 45; 56 km NNE of Miskolc; 48°30'/21°14'; HSL.

Hideaga, Rom.; pop. 59; 94 km NNW of Cluj; 47°35'/23°25'.

Hidotzishok, *see* Adutiskis.

Hidveg, *see* Ipelske Predmostie.

Hidvegardo, Hung.; pop. 14; 56 km N of Miskolc; 48°34'/20°51'; HSL.

Hiezyce, *possibly* Gichitsy.

Hilbringen, Germ.; pop. 28; 163 km SW of Frankfurt am Main; 49°26'/06°37'; GED.

Hilchenbach, Germ.; pop. 25; 82 km ENE of Koln; 50°59'/08°06'; AMG, GED.

Hildburghausen, Germ.; pop. 60; 114 km NNW of Nurnberg; 50°25'/10°45'; HSL, HSL2, LDS.

Hilden, Germ.; pop. 44; 32 km N of Koln; 51°10'/06°56'; GED.

Hildesheim, Germ.; pop. 600; 32 km SE of Hannover; 52°09'/09°58'; AMG, CAHJP, GUM3, GUM4, GUM5, GUM6, HSL, HSL2, ISH1, JGFF, LDL, PHP1.

Hildmannsfeld, Germ.; 82 km WSW of Stuttgart; 48°44'/08°03'; LDS.

Hiliuti, *see* Khiliutsy.

Hillesheim, Germ.; pop. 22; 75 km S of Koln; 50°18'/06°40'.

Hilpoltstein, Germ.; 38 km SSE of Nurnberg; 49°12'/11°12'; JGFF, PHGB.

Hilsbach, Germ.; 56 km NW of Stuttgart; 49°12'/08°50'; LDS.

Hiltenfingen, Germ.; 69 km W of Munchen; 48°10'/10°43'; PHGB.

Hilzingen, Germ.; 120 km S of Stuttgart; 47°46'/08°47'; PHGBW.

Himbach, Germ.; pop. 28; 32 km NE of Frankfurt am Main; 50°16'/09°00'; GUM5.

Himberg, Aus.; pop. 20; 19 km SSE of Wien; 48°05'/16°26'.

Himeshaza, Hung.; pop. 6; 120 km WSW of Szeged; 46°05'/18°34'.

Himmelkron, Germ.; pop. 2; 82 km NNE of Nurnberg; 50°04'/11°36'.

Himmelstadt, Germ.; 82 km E of Frankfurt am Main; 49°56'/09°48'; PHGB.

Himod, Hung.; pop. 2; 126 km N of Nagykanizsa; 47°31'/17°01'.

Hindenburg, *see* Zabrze.

Hindesdorf, GUM6. This town was not found in BGN gazetteers under the given spelling.

Hinkovice, HSL. This pre-World War I community was not found in BGN gazetteers.

Hinkowce, *see* Ginkovtse.

Hinterbruhl, Aus.; pop. 24; 19 km SSW of Wien; 48°05'/16°14'.

Hintersdorf, Aus.; pop. 1; 19 km WNW of Wien; 48°18'/16°13'.

Hintersteinau, Germ.; pop. 16; 69 km NE of Frankfurt am Main; 50°25'/09°28'; LDS.

Hinzert, Germ.; 139 km SW of Frankfurt am Main; 49°42'/06°54'; GUM3.

Hird, Hung.; pop. 1; 107 km ESE of Nagykanizsa; 46°06'/18°21'.

Hirics, Hung.; pop. 4; 107 km ESE of Nagykanizsa; 45°49'/18°00'.

Hirlau, Rom. (Harlau); 62 km WNW of Iasi; 47°26'/26°54'; EJ, GUM4, HSL, JGFF, PHR1.

Hirschaid, Germ.; pop. 65; 45 km NNW of Nurnberg; 49°49'/11°00'; GUM5, HSL, HSL2, PHGB.

Hirschberg, *see* Jelenia Gora.

Hirschhorn, Germ.; pop. 22; 75 km SSE of Frankfurt am Main; 49°27'/08°54'; JGFF, LDS, PHGBW.

Hirtenberg, Aus.; pop. 2; 38 km S of Wien; 47°55'/16°11'.

Hitdorf, Germ.; 19 km N of Koln; 51°04'/06°56'; JGFF.

Hivnev, *see* Ugnev.

Hivniv, *see* Ugnev.

Hlasivo, Cz.; pop. 5; 69 km SSE of Praha; 49°30'/14°45'.

Hlavatce, Cz.; pop. 10; 94 km SSE of Praha; 49°18'/14°38'.

Hlavenec, Cz.; pop. 1; 26 km NE of Praha; 50°14'/14°42'.

Hlemyzdi, Cz.; pop. 2; 75 km N of Praha; 50°43'/14°43'.

Hleszczawa, Pol.; pop. 66; Described in the *Black Book* as being in the Tarnopol region of Poland, this town was not found in BGN gazetteers.

Hlibow, Ukr.; pop. 27; 88 km N of Chernovtsy; 49°05'/25°55'. This town was located on an interwar map of Poland but does not appear in contemporary gazetteers. Map coordinates are approximate.

Hlina, Cz.; 38 km WNW of Praha; 50°13'/13°58'; HSL.

Hlinita, *see* Glinitsa.

Hlinsko, Cz.; pop. 56; 82 km NW of Brno; 49°46'/15°54'.

Hlizov, Cz.; pop. 4; 62 km E of Praha; 49°59'/15°18'.

Hlohovec, Cz. (Frastak, Galgoc, Galgocz, Galoc); pop. 1,199; 56 km NE of Bratislava; 48°26'/17°48'; AMG, EJ, GUM4, GUM5, HSL, LDL.

Hlohovicky, Cz.; pop. 9; 56 km SW of Praha; 49°54'/13°40'.

Hlomcza, Pol. (Glomcha); pop. 18; 38 km SW of Przemysl; 49°38'/22°17'.

Hlubieniec, Pol.; pop. 37; Described in the *Black Book* as being in the Bialystok region of Poland, this town was not found in BGN gazetteers.

Hluboczek Wielki, Ukr.; 114 km E of Lvov; 49°38'/25°32'; GUM3, GUM4, GUM5, PHP2.

Hluboka, *see* Hluboka nad Vltavou.

Hluboka nad Vltavou, Cz. (Hluboka); pop. 29; 120 km S of Praha; 49°03'/14°26'; AMG, COH, HSL, HSL2.

Hluboki, *see* Rastice.

Hluchov, *see* Glukhov.

Hlucin, Cz.; pop. 38; 139 km NE of Brno; 49°54'/18°11'; HSL.

Hludno, Pol.; pop. 41; 50 km WSW of Przemysl; 49°47'/22°09'.

Hluk, Cz.; pop. 69 km ESE of Brno; 48°59'/17°32'; HSL.

Hlusk, *see* Glussk.

Hluzkowo, *see* Glushkovo.

Hnatnice, Cz.; pop. 2; 101 km NNW of Brno; 50°01'/16°26'.

Hnevanov, Cz.; pop. 5; 163 km S of Praha; 48°41'/14°25'.

Hnidawa, GUM3. This town was not found in BGN gazetteers under the given spelling.

Hnidousy, Cz.; pop. 12; 26 km WNW of Praha; 50°10'/14°08'.

Hnilcze, *see* Gnilche.

Hnilice Male, *see* Gnilichki.

Hnilice Wielkie, *see* Gnilitsy.

Hnizdyczow, *see* Gnizdichev.

Hnyla, Ukr.; pop. 60; 157 km SSW of Lvov; 48°35'/22°55'; HSL. This town was located on an interwar map of Poland but does not appear in contemporary gazetteers. Map coordinates are approximate.

Hobbach, Germ.; 50 km ESE of Frankfurt am Main; 49°51'/09°17'; PHGB.

Hobodovka, *see* Obodovka.

Hobol, Hung.; pop. 3; 75 km ESE of Nagykanizsa; 46°01'/17°46'.

Hochberg, Germ.; pop. 85; 88 km ESE of Frankfurt am Main; 49°47'/09°53'; CAHJP, GUM5, HSL, JGFF, PHGB, PHGBW.

Hochelheim, Germ. (Heuchelheim); pop. 16; 50 km N of Frankfurt am Main; 50°31'/08°37'; LDS.

Hocherberg, *see* Mittelbexbach.

Hochhausen, Germ.; 62 km N of Stuttgart; 49°19'/09°06'; HSL, JGFF, LDS, PHGBW.

Hochheim, Germ.; pop. 25; 114 km NW of Nurnberg; 50°22'/10°27'; GUM5, PHGB.

Hochheim am Main, Germ.; pop. 21; 26 km SW of Frankfurt am Main; 50°01'/08°21'; GUM5.

Hochkirchen, Germ. BGN lists two possible localities with this name located at 50°48'/06°38' and 50°53'/06°56'. GED.

Hochneukirch, Germ.; pop. 20; 38 km WNW of Koln; 51°06'/06°27'; GED.

Hochspeyer, Germ.; pop. 32; 88 km SSW of Frankfurt am Main; 49°27'/07°54'; AMG, GED.

Hochst, *see* Hochst im Odenwald.

Hochstadt, *see* Hochstadt an der Donau.

Hochstadt am Main, Germ.; 82 km N of Nurnberg; 50°09'/11°10'; PHGB.

Hochstadt an der Aisch, Germ.; 32 km NW of Nurnberg; 49°42'/10°48'; PHGB.

Hochstadt an der Donau, Germ. (Hochstadt); 94 km WNW of Munchen; 48°36'/10°33'; LDS.

Hochstatten, Germ.; 69 km SW of Frankfurt am Main; 49°46'/07°50'; JGFF.

Hochst im Odenwald, Germ. (Hochst); pop. 110; 38 km SE of Frankfurt am Main; 49°48'/08°59'; GED, GUM5, HSL, LDS, YB.

Hochwolkersdorf, Aus.; pop. 8; 69 km S of Wien; 47°39'/16°17'.

Hock, see Gotsk.

Hockenheim, Germ.; pop. 50; 75 km NW of Stuttgart; 49°19'/08°33'; GUM5, LDS, PHGBW.

Hoczew, Pol.; pop. 59; 50 km SSW of Przemysl; 49°26'/22°19'.

Hodac, Rom. (Gorgenyhodak); pop. 16; 101 km E of Cluj; 46°46'/24°55'.

Hodarauti, see Khodoroutsy.

Hodasz, Hung.; pop. 191; 107 km E of Miskolc; 47°55'/22°13'; HSL, LDS, PHH.

Hodgya, see Hoghia.

Hodi, see Hody.

Hodiatch, see Gadac.

Hodisa, Rom. (Beltekhodos); pop. 19; 101 km NW of Cluj; 47°35'/22°59'.

Hodisu, Rom.; pop. 5; 50 km WNW of Cluj; 46°54'/22°55'.

Hodjinesti, see Godzhineshty.

Hodmezovasarhely, Hung.; pop. 1,501; 26 km NNE of Szeged; 46°25'/20°20'; EDRD, EJ, GUM3, GUM4, GUM5, HSL, LDS, PHH.

Hodod, Rom. (Hadad, Kreigsdorf); pop. 102; 82 km NW of Cluj; 47°24'/23°02'; HSL, PHR2.

Hodonin, Cz. (Goeding, Hudonin); pop. 736; 50 km ESE of Brno; 48°52'/17°08'; EJ, GUM4, HSL.

Hodorkov, see Khodorkov.

Hodosa, Rom. (Hodosa de Ciuc); pop. 216; 94 km E of Cluj; 46°38'/24°49'.

Hodosa de Ciuc, see Hodosa.

Hodousice, Cz.; pop. 3; 126 km SW of Praha; 49°18'/13°11'.

Hodow, see Goduv.

Hodowica, Pol.; pop. 21; Described in the *Black Book* as being in the Lwow region of Poland, this town was not found in BGN gazetteers.

Hoduciszki, see Adutiskis.

Hody, Cz. (Hodi, Homburg Hohe); 45 km ENE of Bratislava; 48°12'/17°43'; HSL.

Hodyszewo, Pol.; pop. 11; 45 km SSW of Bialystok; 52°50'/22°47'.

Hof, Germ.; 114 km S of Leipzig; 50°19'/11°55'; EJ, GED, GUM3, PHGB. *See also* Dvorce.

Hofamt Priel, Aus. EDRD. This town was not found in BGN gazetteers under the given spelling.

Hoff, Germ.; pop. 96; 50 km E of Koln; 50°52'/07°35'.

Hoffenheim, Germ.; pop. 51; 62 km NNW of Stuttgart; 49°16'/08°51'; AMG, GUM5, PHGBW.

Hofgeismar, Germ.; pop. 34; 107 km S of Hannover; 51°29'/09°24'; GED, GUM3, HSL, LDS.

Hofheim, see Hofheim am Taunus.

Hofheim (Bavaria), Germ.; pop. 54; 88 km NW of Nurnberg; 50°08'/10°32'; PHGB.

Hofheim am Taunus, Germ. (Hofheim); pop. 32; 19 km WSW of Frankfurt am Main; 50°05'/08°27'; GUM5.

Hofnungstal, see Nadezhdovka.

Hofstetten, Germ.; 50 km ESE of Frankfurt am Main; 49°52'/09°12'; PHGB.

Hoghia, Rom. (Hodgya); pop. 3; 133 km ESE of Cluj; 46°17'/25°14'.

Hogyesz, Hung.; pop. 309; 114 km ENE of Nagykanizsa; 46°29'/18°25'; HSL, HSL2, JGFF, LDL, LDS, PHH.

Hogyoliomad, COH. This town was not found in BGN gazetteers under the given spelling.

Hohalov, see Gogolevo.

Hohe, Germ.; 56 km S of Hannover; 51°57'/09°28'; LDS.

Hohebach, Germ.; pop. 32; 75 km NNE of Stuttgart; 49°22'/09°44'; HSL, JGFF, PHGBW.

Hoheinod, Germ.; pop. 21; 120 km SSW of Frankfurt am Main; 49°17'/07°36'; GED.

Hohenau, Aus.; pop. 70; 62 km NNE of Wien; 48°37'/16°55'; EJ, HSL.

Hohenberg, Germ. PHGBW. A number of towns share this name. It was not possible to determine from available information which one is being referenced.

Hoheneich, Aus.; pop. 4; 120 km WNW of Wien; 48°46'/15°01'.

Hohenems, Aus.; pop. 18; 126 km W of Innsbruck; 47°22'/09°41'; CAHJP, EJ, HSL, PHGBW.

Hohenfeld, Germ.; 69 km WNW of Nurnberg; 49°43'/10°10'; PHGB.

Hohenhameln, Germ.; pop. 1; 32 km ESE of Hannover; 52°16'/10°04'.

Hohenhausen, Germ.; 62 km SW of Hannover; 52°07'/08°57'; LDS.

Hohenlimburg, Germ.; pop. 70; 62 km NE of Koln; 51°21'/07°36'; GED, GUM5.

Hohenraunau, Germ.; 94 km W of Munchen; 48°13'/10°22'; PHGB.

Hohenruppersdorf, Aus.; pop. 5; 32 km NNE of Wien; 48°27'/16°39'.

Hohensalza, see Inowroclaw.

Hohensolms, Germ.; pop. 8; 69 km NNW of Frankfurt am Main; 50°39'/08°31'; HSL.

Hohenstadt, see Zabreh.

Hohenstein, see Olsztynek.

Hohen Sulzen, Germ.; pop. 7; 62 km SSW of Frankfurt am Main; 49°37'/08°13'.

Hohentrudingen, Germ.; 56 km SSW of Nurnberg; 49°00'/10°42'; PHGB.

Hohr Grenzhausen, Germ. (Grenzhausen); pop. 21; 75 km SE of Koln; 50°26'/07°40'.

Hojesin, Cz.; pop. 3; 88 km ESE of Praha; 49°49'/15°39'.

Hokov, Cz.; pop. 8; 62 km W of Praha; 50°09'/13°34'.

Hola, Pol.; pop. 70; 50 km NE of Lublin; 51°33'/23°11'.

Holashitz, see Oleszyce.

Holatin, Ukr. (Huliatin, Tarfalu); 139 km S of Lvov; 48°39'/23°26'; SM.

Holavenevsk, see Golovanevsk.

Holberg, GUM6. This town was not found in BGN gazetteers under the given spelling.

Holendry, Pol.; pop. 21; 94 km E of Lublin; 51°02'/23°50'.

Hole Rawskie, Ukr.; pop. 50; 45 km NW of Lvov; 50°14'/23°42'.

Holercani, see Golerkany.

Holesov, Cz. (Holleschau); pop. 282; 69 km ENE of Brno; 49°20'/17°35'; AMG, EDRD, EJ, HSL, HSL2, JGFF.

Holeszow, Pol.; pop. 118; 75 km NE of Lublin; 51°41'/23°24'; PHP3, SF. *See also* Goleshuv.

Holiapol, see Gulyay Pole.

Holia Pristan, see Golaya Pristan.

Holic, Cz.; pop. 386; 62 km SE of Brno; 48°48'/17°10'; EJ, HSL, HSL2.

Holice, Cz.; pop. 73; 107 km E of Praha; 50°05'/16°00'.

Holinka, see Golynka.

Holishev, see Gelmyazov.

Hollabrunn, Aus. (Oberhollabrunn); pop. 78; 45 km NW of Wien; 48°33'/16°05'; HSL.

Hollad, Hung.; pop. 8; 38 km NE of Nagykanizsa; 46°38'/17°19'.

Hollenbach, Germ. PHGBW. A number of towns share this name. It was not possible to determine from available information which one is being referenced.

Hollenberg, Germ.; 45 km NNE of Nurnberg; 49°46'/11°29'; GUM5.

Holleschau, see Holesov.

Hollfeld, Germ.; 56 km N of Nurnberg; 49°56'/11°18'; PHGB.

Hollohaza, Hung.; pop. 12; 69 km NNE of Miskolc; 48°33'/21°25'.

Hollrich, Germ.; 82 km E of Frankfurt am Main; 50°04'/09°48'; PHGB.

Hollstadt, Germ.; 120 km ENE of Frankfurt am Main; 50°21'/10°18'; PHGB.

Holmi, Rom. AMG, JGFF. This town was not found in BGN gazetteers under the given spelling.

Holobi, *see* Goloby.

Holobudy, *see* Golobudy.

Holobutow, GUM3. This town was not found in BGN gazetteers under the given spelling.

Holoby, *see* Goloby.

Holojow, *see* Uzlovoye.

Holonie, Byel. EDRD. This town was not found in BGN gazetteers under the given spelling.

Holoskov, *see* Goloskovo.

Holoskow, *see* Goloskuv.

Holosnita, *see* Goloshnitsa.

Holoszynce, Ukr.; pop. 25; 107 km N of Chernovtsy; 49°15'/26°05'. This town was located on an interwar map of Poland but does not appear in contemporary gazetteers. Map coordinates are approximate.

Holotin, Cz.; 82 km E of Praha; 49°57'/15°35'; HSL.

Holotki, *see* Golotki.

Holoubkov, Cz.; pop. 6; 62 km SW of Praha; 49°47'/13°42'.

Holovke, *see* Holowienki.

Holovtchin, *see* Golovatchino.

Holowczynce, *see* Golovchyntse.

Holowiecko, *see* Golovetskoye.

Holowienki, Pol. (Holovke); 88 km NE of Warszawa; 52°30'/22°17'; LDL.

Holowno, *see* Golovno.

Holshan, *see* Golshany.

Holshani, *see* Golshany.

Holsice, Cz.; 56 km ESE of Praha; 49°45'/15°03'; HSL.

Holszany, *see* Golshany.

Holten, Germ.; pop. 16; 69 km NNW of Koln; 51°32'/06°48'; JGFF.

Holubica, *see* Golubitsa.

Holubicze, *see* Golubichi.

Holubie, Pol.; pop. 20; 126 km ESE of Lublin; 50°38'/24°05'.

Holubin, Cz. (Holubina, Holubine); 120 km WSW of Praha; 49°55'/12°45'; AMG, HSL.

Holubina, *see* Holubin.

Holubine, *see* Holubin.

Holubla, Pol.; pop. 12; 101 km ENE of Warszawa; 52°17'/22°26'.

Holuczkow, Pol.; pop. 12; 45 km SW of Przemysl; 49°35'/22°20'.

Holudza, Pol.; pop. 8; 62 km NE of Krakow; 50°24'/20°43'.

Holyn, *see* Kotyatiche Golyn.

Holynka, *see* Golynka.

Holynka (near Augustow), Byel.; pop. 75; 234 km NW of Pinsk; 53°47'/23°55'.

Holynka (near Grodno), Byel.; pop. 49; 189 km WNW of Pinsk; 53°11'/23°55'; SF.

Holzappel, Germ.; pop. 24; 62 km WNW of Frankfurt am Main; 50°21'/07°54'.

Holzhausen, Germ.; pop. 24; 114 km WSW of Hannover; 52°13'/08°00'; GED, LDS.

Holzhausen (near Koblenz), Germ.; pop. 24; 56 km W of Frankfurt am Main; 50°13'/07°55'.

Holzheim, Germ.; pop. 20; BGN lists two possible localities with this name located at 50°29'/08°43' and 50°47'/09°40'. LDS.

Holzing, *see* Otterskirchen.

Holzminden, Germ.; pop. 100; 69 km S of Hannover; 51°49'/09°27'; HSL, LDS.

Homberg, Germ.; pop. 30; 75 km N of Frankfurt am Main; 50°44'/09°00'; GED, GUM3, GUM5.

Homberg Kassel, Germ.; pop. 34; 75 km N of Frankfurt am Main; 50°44'/09°00'.

Homburg, *see* Bad Homburg vor der Hohe.

Homburg am Main, Germ.; pop. 25; 75 km ESE of Frankfurt am Main; 49°47'/09°37'; GUM5, LDS, PHGB.

Homburg an der Saar, Germ.; pop. 128; 133 km SW of Frankfurt am Main; 49°19'/07°20'; GED.

Homburg Hohe, *see* Hody.

Homburg Pfalz, HSL. This pre-World War I community was not found in BGN gazetteers.

Homburg vor der Hohe, *see* Bad Homburg vor der Hohe.

Homel, *see* Gomel.

Homiyah, *see* Gomel.

Hommonarokito, HSL. This pre-World War I community was not found in BGN gazetteers.

Homne, *see* Humenne.

Homok, HSL. A number of towns share this name. It was not possible to determine from available information which one is being referenced.

Homokbodoge, Hung.; pop. 15; 107 km NNE of Nagykanizsa; 47°18'/17°36'.

Homokkomarom, Hung.; pop. 4; 13 km NW of Nagykanizsa; 46°30'/16°55'.

Homokmegy, Hung.; pop. 9; 88 km WNW of Szeged; 46°29'/19°05'.

Homokszentgyorgy, Hung.; pop. 4; 56 km ESE of Nagykanizsa; 46°07'/17°35'.

Homokterenye, Hung.; pop. 33; 62 km WSW of Miskolc; 48°02'/19°57'; GUM5, HSL.

Homonna, *see* Humenne.

Homorod, Rom. (Homorodokland?); 150 km ESE of Cluj; 46°03'/25°16'; HSL.

Homorodalmas, *see* Meresti.

Homorodkemenyfalva, *see* Comanesti.

Homorodokland, *possibly* Homorod.

Homorodszentmarton, *see* Martinis.

Homorodu de Jos, Rom. (Alsohomorod, Homorodul de Jos); pop. 61; 114 km NNW of Cluj; 47°40'/23°05'.

Homorodul de Jos, *see* Homorodu de Jos.

Homorud, Hung.; 107 km SW of Szeged; 45°59'/18°48'; HSL.

Homoty, Pol.; pop. 2; 88 km S of Bialystok; 52°24'/22°58'.

Hompesch, Germ.; pop. 45; 45 km W of Koln; 50°59'/06°21'; GED.

Homrod, *see* Miske.

Homrogd, Hung.; pop. 21; 26 km NNE of Miskolc; 48°17'/20°55'; HSL.

Honigsberg, Aus.; 69 km N of Graz; 47°36'/15°38'; HSL.

Honnef, Germ.; pop. 46; 45 km SE of Koln; 50°38'/07°14'.

Honningen, GUM5. A number of towns share this name. It was not possible to determine from available information which one is being referenced.

Hont, Hung.; pop. 8; 62 km N of Budapest; 48°03'/19°00'.

Hontchest, *see* Kotovsk (Bessarabia).

Hoof, Germ.; pop. 120; 126 km S of Hannover; 51°17'/09°21'; LDS.

Hoor, *see* Horovce.

Hopkie, Pol.; pop. 6; 101 km NNE of Przemysl; 50°31'/23°40'.

Hoppstadten, Germ.; pop. 82; 114 km SW of Frankfurt am Main; 49°37'/07°12'; GED, JGFF.

Hora Kutna, Cz.; pop. 188; 56 km E of Praha; 49°57'/15°16'; HSL.

Horanie, *see* Gorane.

Horazdovice, Cz.; pop. 154; 107 km SSW of Praha; 49°19'/13°43'.

Horb, Germ.; pop. 100; 50 km SW of Stuttgart; 48°26'/08°41'; CAHJP, EDRD, GUM5, PHGB, PHGBW.

Horbacka, *see* Gorbakha.

Horbakow, *see* Gorbakov.

Horbkow, *see* Gorbkuv.

Horbow, *possibly* Gorbovo.

Horburg, Germ.; 13 km WNW of Leipzig; 51°22'/12°10'; HSL.

Horchov, *see* Gorokhov.

Horde, Germ.; pop. 237; 69 km NNE of Koln; 51°29'/07°30';

GUM3.

Horden, Germ.; 62 km W of Stuttgart; 48°47'/08°21'; LDS, PHGBW.

Hordynia Rustykalna, *see* Gordynya.

Hordynia Szlachecka, *see* Gordynya.

Horelice, Cz.; pop. 17; 19 km SW of Praha; 50°02'/14°13'.

Horepniky, Cz.; pop. 36; Described in the *Black Book* as being in the Bohemia region of Czechoslovakia, this town was not found in BGN gazetteers.

Horesedly, Cz. (Horosedl); pop. 1; 62 km W of Praha; 50°10'/13°37'; HSL.

Horesovicky, Cz.; pop. 2; 38 km WNW of Praha; 50°17'/13°58'.

Horgos, Yug.; pop. 42; 150 km NNW of Beograd; 46°09'/19°58'; PHY.

Horhat, *see* Hrochot.

Horia, HSL. A number of towns share this name. It was not possible to determine from available information which one is being referenced.

Horice, Cz.; pop. 107; 88 km NE of Praha; 50°22'/15°38'; JGFF.

Horincevo, GUM3. This town was not found in BGN gazetteers under the given spelling.

Horincovo, *see* Gorinchovo.

Horinghausen, Germ.; pop. 28; 133 km S of Hannover; 51°16'/08°59'; CAHJP, JGFF.

Horitschon, Aus.; pop. 1; 75 km SSE of Wien; 47°35'/16°33'.

Horkheim, Germ.; 45 km N of Stuttgart; 49°07'/09°10'; EJ, PHGBW.

Horkhov, *see* Gorokhov.

Horkhuv, *see* Gorokhov.

Horlacea, Rom.; pop. 3; 45 km W of Cluj; 46°49'/23°02'.

Horn (Austria), Aus.; pop. 55; 75 km WNW of Wien; 48°39'/15°39'.

Horn (Germany), Germ.; 126 km S of Stuttgart; 47°42'/09°00'; JGFF, LDS.

Horna, Cz. (Hornya); 69 km ENE of Kosice; 48°46'/22°12'; HSL.

Hornburg, Germ. (Bad Hornburg); 69 km ESE of Hannover; 52°01'/10°37'; LDS, PHGBW.

Horne Saliby, Cz. (Felso Szeli, Felsoszeli, Felsoszelt, Hornie Saliby); pop. 153; 50 km E of Bratislava; 48°07'/17°45'; HSL.

Hornheim, *see* Raczki.

Horni Benesov, Cz.; pop. 23; 114 km NNE of Brno; 49°58'/17°36'.

Horni Cepen, *see* Horny Cepen.

Horni Cerekev, Cz.; pop. 29; 94 km W of Brno; 49°19'/15°20'; JGFF.

Hornicest, *see* Harnicesti.

Hornie Saliby, *see* Horne Saliby.

Hornigi, Pol.; pop. 4; 50 km SSE of Warszawa; 51°51'/21°10'.

Horni Hincina, *see* Horni Hyncina.

Horni Hyncina, Cz. (Horni Hincina); 62 km N of Brno; 49°40'/16°33'; GUM4.

Horni Litvinov, Cz.; pop. 127; 82 km WNW of Praha; 50°36'/13°37'.

Hornistopol, *see* Gornostaypol.

Hornostaje, Pol.; pop. 9; 45 km NW of Bialystok; 53°27'/22°48'.

Hornowo, Pol.; pop. 17; 69 km S of Bialystok; 52°33'/22°59'.

Hornya, *see* Horna.

Horny Cepen, Cz. (Horni Cepen); 50 km NE of Bratislava; 48°19'/17°43'; HSL.

Horobatowice, Pol. PHP2. This town was not found in BGN gazetteers under the given spelling.

Horocholina, *see* Gorokholina.

Horochow, *see* Gorokhov.

Horodca, *see* Gorodka.

Horodec, *see* Merkulovichi.

Horodek, Pol.; pop. 37; 56 km SSW of Przemysl; 49°21'/22°29'.

Horodenka, *see* Gorodenka.

Horodets, *see* Merkulovichi.

Horodia, *see* Gorodeya.

Horodistea, *see* Gorodishche (Moldavia).

Horodistea Lapusna, *see* Gorodishche (Bessarabia).

Horodle, *see* Horodlo.

Horodlo, Pol. (Gorodlo, Horodle); pop. 747; 107 km ESE of Lublin; 50°53'/24°02'; CAHJP, COH, HSL, HSL2, LDS, LYV, POCEM, SF, YB.

Horodlowice, *see* Gorodlovitse.

Horodna, *see* Gorodnya.

Horodne, *see* Grodno.

Horodnica, *see* Gorodnitsa.

Horodnitza, *see* Gorodnitsa.

Horodno, *see* Gorodno.

Horodoc; *See* Gorodok; Grodek; Grudek.

Horodok, *see* Gorodok (near Lvov).

Horodystawice, *see* Gorodyslavichi.

Horodyszcze, Pol.; pop. 19; 62 km E of Lublin; 51°11'/23°27'; GUM3. *See also* Gorodishche. This town most often refers to the town of Gorodishche in the former Polish province of Nowogrodek. *See also* Gorodishche.

Horodyszcze Krolewskie, *see* Gorodyshche Krulevske.

Horodz, *see* Gorod.

Horodzei, *see* Gorodeya.

Horodzhyey, *see* Gorod.

Horodziec, *see* Gorodets.

Horodziej, *see* Gorodeya.

Horodzilow, *see* Gorodilovo.

Horodzow, *see* Gorodzuv.

Horosauti, *see* Khoroshovtsy.

Horoscauti, *see* Khoroshovtsy.

Horoschki, *see* Volodarsk Volynskiy.

Horosedl, *see* Horesedly.

Horoshki, *see* Volodarsk Volynskiy.

Horostyta, Pol.; pop. 14; 62 km NE of Lublin; 51°36'/23°15'.

Horoszczyce, Pol.; pop. 14; 120 km NE of Przemysl; 50°34'/24°00'.

Horoszki Male, Pol.; pop. 14; 107 km S of Bialystok; 52°14'/23°02'.

Horoszowa, *see* Gorosheve.

Horovce, Cz. (Hoor); 38 km ENE of Kosice; 48°43'/21°47'; HSL.

Horovice, Cz.; pop. 56; 50 km SW of Praha; 49°50'/13°55'; JGFF, PHP3.

Horozanka, *see* Gorozhanka.

Horozanna Wielka, *see* Velikaya Gorozhanka.

Horpacs, Hung.; pop. 7; 62 km N of Budapest; 48°00'/19°08'.

Horpin, *see* Gorpin.

Horrem, Germ.; 19 km WSW of Koln; 50°55'/06°42'; GED.

Horrenbach, Germ.; 82 km NNE of Stuttgart; 49°25'/09°39'; LDS.

Horschitz, HSL, HSL2. This pre-World War I community was not found in BGN gazetteers.

Horsice, Cz.; pop. 14; 101 km SW of Praha; 49°32'/13°23'.

Horsk, *see* Gorsk.

Horsovsky Tyn, Cz.; pop. 66; 126 km SW of Praha; 49°32'/12°57'; JGFF.

Horstein, Germ.; pop. 118; 26 km E of Frankfurt am Main; 50°03'/09°05'; GUM5, JGFF, PHGB.

Horst Emscher, Germ.; pop. 90; 101 km NNE of Koln; 51°42'/07°42'; AMG.

Horstmar, Germ.; pop. 30; 133 km N of Koln; 52°05'/07°19'; GUM5.

Hort, Hung.; pop. 46; 56 km NE of Budapest; 47°42'/19°47'.

Horucko, *see* Gorskoye.

Horval, *see* Gorval.

Horvatkimle, Hung.; pop. 2; 133 km W of Budapest; 47°49'/17°22'.

Horvatkut, Hung.; pop. 5; 38 km NE of Nagykanizsa; 46°35'/17°21'.

Horvatlovo, Hung.; pop. 2; 94 km NW of Nagykanizsa; 47°11'/16°27'.

Horvatzsidany, Hung.; pop. 4; 114 km NNW of Nagykanizsa;

47°25'/16°37'.

Hory Matky Bozi, Cz.; pop. 5; 120 km SSW of Praha; 49°16'/13°26'.

Horyngrad Krupa, see Goryngrad.

Horyngrod, see Goryngrad.

Horyniec, Pol.; pop. 120; 62 km NNE of Przemysl; 50°11'/23°22'; COH, PHP2.

Horyschkowka, see Goryshkovka.

Horyszow Polski, Pol.; pop. 47; 75 km ESE of Lublin; 50°45'/23°25'.

Horyszow Ruski, Pol.; pop. 38; 88 km ESE of Lublin; 50°45'/23°37'.

Hosbach, Germ.; pop. 12; 45 km ESE of Frankfurt am Main; 50°00'/09°12'; PHGB.

Hoshch, see Goshcha.

Hoshcha, see Goshcha.

Hosht, see Goshcha.

Hoshtch, see Goshcha.

Hoslovitz, LDL. This pre-World War I community was not found in BGN gazetteers.

Hossufalu, see Dlha.

Hosszuaszo, see Husasau.

Hosszufalu, see Dlha.

Hosszuheteny, Hung.; pop. 25; 107 km ESE of Nagykanizsa; 46°09'/18°21'; HSL.

Hosszumezo, see Cimpulung La Tisa.

Hosszupalyi, Hung.; pop. 98; 107 km SE of Miskolc; 47°24'/21°45'; LDS, PHH.

Hosszupereszteg, Hung.; pop. 9; 82 km N of Nagykanizsa; 47°06'/17°01'.

Hostau, see Hostoun.

Hostinne, Cz.; pop. 72; 107 km NE of Praha; 50°33'/15°44'.

Hostisovce, Cz. (Gesztes); 88 km WSW of Kosice; 48°30'/20°07'; HSL.

Hostivice, Cz.; pop. 6; 13 km WSW of Praha; 50°05'/14°16'.

Hostka, Cz.; pop. 31; BGN lists two possible localities with this name located at 49°42'/12°36' and 50°30'/14°20'.

Hostomice, Cz. (Hostomitz); pop. 68; 45 km SW of Praha; 49°50'/14°03'; HSL.

Hostomitz, see Hostomice.

Hostomlia, see Gostomel.

Hostoun, Cz. (Hostau); pop. 24; 133 km SW of Praha; 49°34'/12°45'; HSL.

Hostovce nad Bodvou, Cz. (Vendegi); 32 km SW of Kosice; 48°34'/20°52'; HSL.

Hostow, see Gostov.

Hostynne, Pol.; pop. 4; 94 km ESE of Lublin; 50°45'/23°42'.

Hoszcza, see Goshcha.

Hoszczewo, see Goshchevo.

Hoszewo, see Goshevo.

Hoszow, see Goshov.

Hoszow (near Staryy Sambor), Pol.; pop. 23; 50 km S of Przemysl; 49°24'/22°39'.

Hoszowczyk, Pol.; pop. 19; 50 km S of Przemysl; 49°24'/22°37'.

Hoteni, Rom. (Hotinka, Huten); 114 km N of Cluj; 47°46'/23°54'; HSL, SM.

Hotin, see Khotin.

Hotinka, see Hoteni.

Hottenbach, Germ.; pop. 16; 101 km SW of Frankfurt am Main; 49°50'/07°18'.

Hotzenplotz, see Osoblaha.

Hotzila, see Dolinskoye.

Hovestadt, Germ.; pop. 5; 120 km NE of Koln; 51°40'/08°09'.

Hovniv, see Ugnev.

Hoxter, Germ.; pop. 65; 75 km S of Hannover; 51°46'/09°23'; GUM5, JGFF.

Hoya, Germ.; pop. 40; 56 km NW of Hannover; 52°48'/09°09'; AMG.

Hoyerswerda, Germ.; pop. 1; 133 km SE of Berlin; 51°26'/14°15'.

Hoym, Germ.; 94 km WNW of Leipzig; 51°47'/11°18'; LDS.

Hoyren, Germ.; 139 km SSE of Stuttgart; 47°34'/09°41'; AMG.

Hoza, see Gozha.

Hoznpot, see Aizpute.

Hrabesin, Cz.; pop. 6; 69 km ESE of Praha; 49°51'/15°20'.

Hrabkov, Cz.; 32 km NW of Kosice; 48°58'/21°01'; JGFF.

Hrabovec, Cz. BGN lists two possible localities with this name located at 49°06'/21°57' and 49°16'/21°23'. AMG.

Hradec Kralove, Cz. (Koniggratz); pop. 314; 94 km ENE of Praha; 50°13'/15°50'; EJ, HSL, HSL2.

Hradek, Cz.; 56 km SSW of Brno; 48°46'/16°16'; HSL.

Hradenin, Cz.; pop. 3; 38 km E of Praha; 50°02'/15°02'.

Hradesin, Cz.; pop. 3; 19 km E of Praha; 50°02'/14°45'.

Hradiste Mnichovo, HSL, HSL2. This pre-World War I community was not found in BGN gazetteers.

Hradki, see Gradki.

Hranice, Cz. (Maehrisch Weisskirchen); pop. 211; 94 km NE of Brno; 49°33'/17°44'; EJ.

Hranie, see Gran.

Hrastin, Yug.; pop. 9; 163 km WNW of Beograd; 45°26'/18°36'.

Hrebenow, see Grebenov.

Hrebla, HSL. This pre-World War I community was not found in BGN gazetteers.

Hrehorow, see Gregorov.

Hrejkovice, Cz.; pop. 6; 75 km S of Praha; 49°28'/14°17'.

Hrhov, Cz. (Gergo); 38 km SW of Kosice; 48°36'/20°45'; HSL.

Hrimezdice, Cz.; pop. 11; 50 km S of Praha; 49°42'/14°17'.

Hrinovca, see Khrenovka.

Hrip, Rom.; pop. 23; 120 km NNW of Cluj; 47°43'/23°00'.

Hriskov, Cz.; pop. 18; 50 km WNW of Praha; 50°18'/13°52'; AMG.

Hristici, see Khristichi.

Hriteni, Rom.; pop. 4; 107 km NNW of Iasi; 48°00'/27°05'.

Hrivcice, Cz.; pop. 5; 50 km WNW of Praha; 50°20'/13°55'.

Hrivno, Cz.; pop. 2; 38 km NNE of Praha; 50°19'/14°46'.

Hrkac, Cz. (Harkacs); 75 km SW of Kosice; 48°29'/20°17'; HSL.

Hrob, Cz.; pop. 23; 82 km NW of Praha; 50°40'/13°43'.

Hrobce, Cz. (Hrobec); 50 km NNW of Praha; 50°28'/14°14'; HSL.

Hrobec, see Hrobce.

Hrobonovo, Cz. (Alistal); 50 km ESE of Bratislava; 47°56'/17°43'; EJ, HSL, HSL2, LDL.

Hrochot, Cz. (Horhat); 139 km WSW of Kosice; 48°40'/19°19'; HSL.

Hronov, Cz.; pop. 70; 126 km NE of Praha; 50°29'/16°11'; EJ.

Hroszowka, Pol.; pop. 15; 45 km WSW of Przemysl; 49°42'/22°16'.

Hrotovice, Cz. (Hrottowitz); pop. 10; 45 km WSW of Brno; 49°08'/16°03'.

Hrottowitz, see Hrotovice.

Hroubovice, Cz.; pop. 51; 88 km NW of Brno; 49°53'/16°00'; HSL.

Hroznetin, Cz. (Lash, Lichtenstadt); 114 km W of Praha; 50°18'/12°52'; EJ, HSL, JGFF.

Hrozovo, LDL. This pre-World War I community was not found in BGN gazetteers.

Hrozow, see Grozovo.

Hrtkovci, Yug.; pop. 3; 56 km W of Beograd; 44°53'/19°46'.

Hrubieszow, Pol. (Hrubishov, Hrubyeshuv, Rubashov, Rubeshov, Rubischoff, Rubishov, Rubishoyv); pop. 5,679; 107 km ESE of Lublin; 50°48'/23°55'; AMG, COH, EDRD, EJ, GA, GUM3, GUM4, GUM5, GUM6, HSL, HSL2, JGFF, LDL, LDS, LYV, PHP1, PHP2, PHP3, PHP4, POCEM, SF, YB.

Hrubishov, see Hrubieszow.

Hrubyeshuv, see Hrubieszow.

Hrud, Pol.; pop. 6; 101 km N of Lublin; 52°06'/23°07'.

Hrudek, see Gorodok (near Lvov).

Hrushov, see Grushev.

Hrusiatycze, see Grusyatychi.

Hrusov, Cz.; pop. 219; 146 km NE of Brno; 49°52'/18°18'; HSL.

Hruszatyce, see Grushatichi.

Hruszew, Pol.; pop. 25; 94 km S of Bialystok; 52°19'/22°43'.

Husiatin (Gusyatin), Ukraine: A sixteenth-century fortress synagogue.

Hruszow, *see* Grushev.

Hruszowice, Pol.; pop. 38; 26 km NNE of Przemysl; 49°57'/23°00'.

Hruszowka, *see* Grushevka.

Hruszwica, *see* Grushvitsy Pervyye.

Hrycowola, *see* Chrzanow.

Hryczynowicze, *see* Grichinovichi.

Hryniawa, *see* Grynyava.

Hryniow, Pol.; pop. 39; Described in the *Black Book* as being in the Lwow region of Poland, this town was not found in BGN gazetteers.

Hrynkowce, *see* Grinki.

Hrywa, *see* Griva (Polesie).

Hrywiatki, *see* Gryvyatki.

Htusovo, Ukr. (Harisof, Rortieyes Szentmihaly); 182 km WSW of Chernovtsy; 48°08'/23°27'; SM.

Hubice, *see* Gubiche.

Hubicze, *see* Gubiche.

Hubienice, Pol.; pop. 11; 69 km NE of Krakow; 50°16'/20°50'.

Hubin, *see* Gubin.

Hubin Czeski, *see* Gubin.

Hubo, *see* Hubovo.

Hubova, Cz. (Gombas); 157 km WNW of Kosice; 49°07'/19°11'; HSL.

Hubovo, Cz. (Hubo); 75 km SW of Kosice; 48°24'/20°22'; HSL.

Huciska, Pol.; 19 km NNE of Poznan; 52°33'/17°05'; GUM4.

Hucisko, *see* Gutsisko.

Hucisko Brodzkie, *see* Gutsisko Brodzke.

Hucisko Jawornickie, Pol.; pop. 9; 32 km WNW of Przemysl; 49°54'/22°21'.

Hucisko Pikulskie, *possibly* Gutsisko Penyatske.

Huckelhoven, Germ.; 50 km W of Koln; 51°03'/06°13'; GED, GUM3.

Huczko, *possibly* Guchok.

Huczwice, Pol.; pop. 24; 69 km SSW of Przemysl; 49°19'/22°14'.

Hudcov, Cz.; pop. 12; 75 km NW of Praha; 50°38'/13°47'.

Hudonin, *see* Hodonin.

Huedin, Rom. (Banffyhunyad); pop. 1,026; 45 km W of Cluj; 46°52'/23°03'; HSL, JGFF, PHR2.

Huffenhardt, Germ.; pop. 21; 62 km N of Stuttgart; 49°18'/09°05'; GUM5, LDS, PHGBW.

Hugyag, Hung.; pop. 14; 69 km N of Budapest; 48°05'/19°26'; HSL.

Hugyaj, *see* Erpatak.

Hujcze, *see* Geyche.

Hujsko, Pol.; pop. 14; 26 km S of Przemysl; 49°38'/22°45'.

Hukliva, *see* Guklivyy.

Hulboca, *see* Gulboka.

Hulchrath, Germ.; pop. 16; 38 km NW of Koln; 51°15'/06°40'.

Hulcza Wloscianska, *see* Gulcha Pervaya.

Hulcze, Pol.; pop. 44; 120 km NE of Przemysl; 50°30'/24°01'.

Hulewicze, *see* Gulevichi.

Huliatin, *see* Holatin.

Hulice, Cz.; pop. 5; 62 km ESE of Praha; 49°43'/15°05'.

Hulievca, *see* Gulevichi.

Huls, Germ.; 56 km NW of Koln; 51°22'/06°31'; GUM5.

Hulsede, Germ.; 32 km SW of Hannover; 52°15'/09°22'; GED.

Hulskie, Pol.; pop. 30; 69 km S of Przemysl; 49°15'/22°33'.

Human, *see* Uman.

Hum Breznicki, Yug. (Breznicki Hum); pop. 6; 45 km NNE of Zagreb; 46°07'/16°17'.

Humenne, Cz. (Homne, Homonna); pop. 2,197; 56 km NE of Kosice; 48°56'/21°55'; AMG, COH, EJ, GUM4, GUM6, HSL, HSL2, JGFF, LDL.

Humme, Germ.; 101 km S of Hannover; 51°32'/09°24'; HSL.

Humniska, Pol.; pop. 70; 50 km WSW of Przemysl; 49°40'/22°04'; AMG. *See also* Gumniska. The *Black Book* also shows a second town named Humniska (pop. 30) in the interwar Polish province of Tarnopol. The town was near Kamenka Bugskaya and does not appear in contemporary gazetteers.

Humpolec, Cz. (Humpoletz); pop. 148; 88 km ESE of Praha; 49°33'/15°22'; JGFF.

Humpoletz, *see* Humpolec.

Huncovce, Cz. (Hunfalu, Hunsdorf); pop. 194; 82 km WNW of Kosice; 49°07'/20°23'; EJ, GUM4, HSL, HSL2, JGFF, LDL.

Hundsbach, Germ. JGFF. A number of towns share this name. It was not possible to determine from available information which one is being referenced.

Hundsfeld, Germ.; 82 km E of Frankfurt am Main; 50°04'/09°52'; GUM4, GUM6, LDS.

Hunedeara, *see* Hunedoara.

Hunedoara, Rom. (Hunedeara); 126 km SSW of Cluj; 45°45'/22°54'; PHR1.

Hunfalu, *see* Huncovce.

Hunfeld, Germ.; pop. 60; 101 km NE of Frankfurt am Main; 50°40'/09°46'; GUM3, HSL.

Hungen, Germ.; pop. 52; 50 km N of Frankfurt am Main; 50°28'/08°54'; GED, GUM5.

Hungheim, Germ.; 75 km N of Stuttgart; 49°25'/09°31'; LDS,

PHGBW.

Hunsdorf, *see* Huncovce.

Hurbanovo, Cz. (Stara Dala); pop. 1,012; 88 km ESE of Bratislava; 47°52'/18°12'; CAHJP.

Hurben, Germ.; 75 km E of Stuttgart; 48°35'/10°12'; HSL, HSL2, JGFF.

Hurby, GUM4. This town was not found in BGN gazetteers under the given spelling.

Hureczko, Pol.; pop. 26; 6 km NE of Przemysl; 49°48'/22°52'.

Hurez, Rom. (Bagolyfalu); pop. 27; 150 km SE of Cluj; 45°48'/24°57'.

Hurka, Cz.; 150 km S of Praha; 48°45'/14°05'; JGFF.

Hurko, Pol.; pop. 21; 6 km NE of Przemysl; 49°49'/22°53'.

Hurnheim, Germ.; 88 km SSW of Nurnberg; 48°48'/10°29'; PHGB.

Hurnie, Ukr.; pop. 20; 107 km S of Lvov; 48°55'/23°45'. This town was located on an interwar map of Poland but does not appear in contemporary gazetteers. Map coordinates are approximate.

Hurodno, *see* Grodno.

Hurth, Germ.; pop. 44; 13 km SSW of Koln; 50°52'/06°52'.

Husaki, *see* Gusak.

Husakov, *see* Gusakov.

Husasau, Rom. (Hosszuaszo); HSL. This pre-World War I community was not found in BGN gazetteers.

Husen, Germ.; pop. 4; A number of towns share this name. It was not possible to determine from available information which one is being referenced.

Husi, Rom.; 62 km SE of Iasi; 46°41'/28°04'; EJ, HSL, HSL2, JGFF, PHP2, PHR1.

Husia, Rom.; pop. 2; 62 km NNW of Cluj; 47°17'/23°18'.

Husiatin, *see* Gusyatin.

Husiatyn, *see* Gusyatin.

Husinka, Pol.; pop. 4; 101 km NNE of Lublin; 52°04'/23°18'.

Husne Wyzne, Ukr.; pop. 60; 157 km SSW of Lvov; 48°35'/23°05'. This town was located on an interwar map of Poland but does not appear in contemporary gazetteers. Map coordinates are approximate.

Husovice, Cz.; pop. 81; 13 km NNE of Brno; 49°13'/16°39'.

Husow, Pol. (Hussow); pop. 42; 38 km WNW of Przemysl; 49°59'/22°17'.

Hussakow, *see* Gusakov.

Hussingen, Germ.; 62 km SSW of Nurnberg; 48°58'/10°41'; PHGB.

Hussow, *see* Husow.

Hust, *see* Khust.

Huste, *see* Khust.

Husten, Germ.; pop. 6; 56 km ENE of Koln; 50°59'/07°45'.

Hustopece, Cz. (Auspitz); pop. 149; 32 km SSE of Brno; 48°56'/16°44'.

Husynne (near Chelm), Pol.; pop. 56; 88 km E of Lublin; 51°08'/23°51'.

Husynne (near Hrubieszow), Pol.; pop. 40; 107 km ESE of Lublin; 50°50'/23°59'.

Huszcza, *see* Gushcha.

Huszlew, Pol.; pop. 6; 107 km N of Lublin; 52°08'/22°50'; CAHJP.

Huszt, *see* Khust.

Husztkoz, *see* Nankovo.

Huta; Huta means "foundry" in Polish. There are no less than 127 towns in interwar Poland with this word in their names. GUM3 refers to a town in Volhynia (Wolyn); GUM4 references two towns, one in the Kielce area and the other a camp in the Lvov area. Population figures are for a town in the Rovno district of Volhynia. Map coordinates are for the town closest to the town of Rovno, which is today the Ukrainian town of Guta.

Huta (Lwow), Pol.; pop. 13; 26 km SW of Przemysl; 49°42'/22°33'; GUM4.

Huta (near Kielce), Pol.; pop. 107 km ESE of Lodz; 51°13'/20°44'; GUM4.

Huta (Wolyn), GUM3. This town was not found in BGN gazetteers under the given spelling. A number of towns share this name. It was not possible to determine from available information which one is being referenced.

Huta Bankowa, Pol. CAHJP. Located in the vicinity of Lodz, this town does not appear in contemporary gazetteers.

Huta Brzuska, Pol.; pop. 13; 19 km WSW of Przemysl; 49°44'/22°31'.

Huta Dabrowa, Pol.; pop. 41; 75 km NW of Lublin; 51°49'/22°03'.

Huta Deregowska, Pol.; pop. 17; 82 km S of Lublin; 50°33'/22°15'.

Huta Gogolowska, Pol.; pop. 13; 88 km W of Przemysl; 49°53'/21°32'.

Huta Golcieynow, Pol.; pop. 47; Described in the *Black Book* as being in the Lublin region of Poland, this town was not found in BGN gazetteers.

Huta Jozefow, Pol.; pop. 24; 50 km S of Lublin; 50°49'/22°18'.

Huta Komarowska, Pol.; pop. 94 km SE of Lublin; 50°36'/23°24'; PHP3.

Huta Komorowska, Pol.; 101 km WNW of Przemysl; 50°24'/21°43'; GA, GUM3, GUM5, GUM6.

Huta Krolewska, *see* Chorzow.

Huta Michalinska, *see* Guta Mikhalin.

Huta Obedynska, Ukr.; pop. 34; 45 km WNW of Lvov; 50°05'/23°35'. This town was located on an interwar map of Poland but does not appear in contemporary gazetteers. Map coordinates are approximate.

Huta Plebanska, Pol.; pop. 20; 82 km NNW of Przemysl; 50°31'/22°27'.

Huta Polonicka, *see* Guta Polonetska.

Huta Poloniecka, *see* Guta Polonetska.

Hutar, Ukr.; pop. 40; 150 km S of Lvov; 48°35'/23°15'. This town was located on an interwar map of Poland but does not appear in contemporary gazetteers. Map coordinates are approximate.

Huta Suchodolska, *see* Khuta Sukhodolska.

Huta Szklana, Pol.; pop. 33; A number of towns share this name. It was not possible to determine from available information which one is being referenced.

Huta Voivozi, *see* Sinteu.

Huta Zakowska, Pol. (Zakowska Huta); pop. 2; 56 km ESE of Warszawa; 52°04'/21°42'.

Huta Zielona, *see* Guta Zelena.

Huten, *see* Hoteni.

Hutkow, Pol.; pop. 76; 88 km N of Przemysl; 50°34'/23°16'.

Huttenbach, Germ.; pop. 41; 26 km NNE of Nurnberg; 49°37'/11°18'; CAHJP, HSL, PHGB.

Huttenberg, Germ. LDS. A number of towns share this name. It was not possible to determine from available information which one is being referenced.

Huttendorf, Germ.; 13 km NW of Nurnberg; 49°32'/10°58'; GUM3.

Huttengesass, Germ.; pop. 46; 32 km NE of Frankfurt am Main; 50°13'/09°03'; LDS.

Huttenheim, Germ. (Huttenheim in Bayern); pop. 24; 62 km WNW of Nurnberg; 49°39'/10°15'; GUM5, PHGB.

Huttenheim in Bayern, *see* Huttenheim.

Hutting, Germ.; 82 km NW of Munchen; 48°48'/11°07'; PHGB.

Huwniki, Pol.; 26 km S of Przemysl; 49°39'/22°42'; GA.

Huzele, Pol.; pop. 70; 50 km SW of Przemysl; 49°29'/22°19'.

Huziejow Stary, Ukr.; pop. 33; 126 km S of Lvov; 48°45'/23°55'. This town was located on an interwar map of Poland but does not appear in contemporary gazetteers. Map coordinates are approximate.

Hvar, Yug.; pop. 6; 296 km S of Zagreb; 43°11'/16°27'.

Hwozd, *see* Gvozd.

Hybralec, Cz.; pop. 5; 82 km WNW of Brno; 49°26'/15°34'.

Hylvaty, Cz.; pop. 18; 94 km NNW of Brno; 49°57'/16°23'.

Hyskov, Cz.; pop. 8; 32 km SW of Praha; 49°59'/14°03'.

Hyza, Pol.; pop. 6; 75 km SE of Lublin; 50°44'/23°14'.

Hyzne, Pol.; pop. 39; 45 km WNW of Przemysl; 49°56'/22°11'.

Iablona Noua, *see* Novaya Yablona.

Iablona Veche, *see* Staraya Yablona.

Iablonita, Rom.; pop. 72; Described in the *Black Book* as being in the Bessarabia region of Romania, this town was not found in BGN gazetteers.

Iachmir, *see* Jacmierz.

Iacobeni, Rom. (Jacobeni); pop. 228; 150 km NE of Cluj; 47°26'/25°19'; AMG, GUM4, HSL.

Iacobesti, Rom.; 133 km WNW of Iasi; 47°46'/26°05'; HSL.

Iad, Rom.; 82 km NE of Cluj; 47°11'/24°34'; HSL.

Iadara, Rom.; pop. 11; 82 km NNW of Cluj; 47°29'/23°24'.

Iakobshtadt, *see* Jekabpils.

Ialoveni, *see* Yaloveny.

Ialpugeni, *see* Yalpuzheny.

Ialta, *see* Yalta.

Iambol, *see* Yambol.

Iampol, *see* Yampol.

Ianauti, *see* Ivanovtsy.

Iara de Mures, Rom. (Marosjara); pop. 4; 88 km E of Cluj; 46°39'/24°44'; HSL.

Iargara, *see* Yargora.

Iarisav, *see* Yaryshev.

Iarisev, Rom. PHR1. This town was not found in BGN gazetteers under the given spelling.

Iaroslava, *see* Yaroslavka.

Iasi, Rom. (Jasi, Jassy); pop. 32,369; 302 km ENE of Cluj; 47°10'/27°36'; AMG, CAHJP, EJ, GUM3, GUM4, GUM5, GUM6, HSL, HSL2, JGFF, LDL, LJEE, PHP2, PHP3, PHR1.

Iasin, *see* Yasinya.

Iasinia, *see* Yasinya.

Iasliska, *see* Jasliska.

Iaslovat, Rom.; pop. 16; 139 km WNW of Iasi; 47°46'/25°58'.

Iaz, HSL. A number of towns share this name. It was not possible to determine from available information which one is being referenced.

Iba, Germ.; 126 km NNE of Frankfurt am Main; 50°58'/09°52'; HSL, LDS.

Ibanesti (Bucovina), Rom.; pop. 61; 88 km S of Iasi; 46°24'/27°36'.

Ibanesti (Transylvania), Rom. (Libanfalva); pop. 49; 101 km E of Cluj; 46°46'/24°56'; HSL.

Ibbenburen, Germ.; pop. 39; 133 km WSW of Hannover; 52°16'/07°44'.

Ibraila, *see* Braila.

Ibrany, Hung.; pop. 215; 69 km ENE of Miskolc; 48°08'/21°43'; GUM5, HSL, PHH.

Ibrony, *see* Nyiribrony.

Iburg, Germ.; 120 km WSW of Hannover; 52°09'/08°03'; LDS.

Ichenhausen, Germ.; pop. 356; 94 km ESE of Stuttgart; 48°22'/10°19'; GED, GUM3, GUM5, HSL, HSL2, JGFF, PHGB.

Ichnya, Ukr.; pop. 250; 69 km SW of Konotop; 50°52'/32°24'.

Ickelheim, Germ.; 50 km W of Nurnberg; 49°29'/10°26'; PHGB.

Ickowice, Pol. PHP4. This town was not found in BGN gazetteers under the given spelling.

Iclod, Rom. (Iclodul Mare, Nagyiklod, Nagyikold); pop. 176; 32 km NNE of Cluj; 46°59'/23°48'; HSL, PHR2.

Iclodul Mare, *see* Iclod.

Iclozel, Rom.; pop. 4; 26 km NNE of Cluj; 46°58'/23°49'.

Icna, (Itchnia); EDRD, LDL, SF. This town was not found in BGN gazetteers under the given spelling.

Ida, *see* Velka Pri Poprade.

Idalin, Pol.; pop. 17; 45 km SW of Lublin; 51°01'/22°00'.

Idar Oberstein, Germ.; pop. 154; 107 km SW of Frankfurt am Main; 49°42'/07°18'; GED, GUM5.

Ideciu de Jos, Rom. (Alsoidecs, Ideciul de Jos); 88 km ENE of Cluj; 46°48'/24°45'; HSL.

Ideciul de Jos, *see* Ideciu de Jos.

Idos, Yug.; pop. 2; 120 km N of Beograd; 45°50'/20°19'.

Idrany, Hung.; pop. 28; This town was not found in BGN gazetteers under the given spelling.

Idstein, Germ.; pop. 75; 32 km WNW of Frankfurt am Main; 50°14'/08°16'.

Idunum, *see* Judenburg.

Idzesti, *see* Izhevtsy.

Idzikowice, Pol.; pop. 26; 56 km NW of Warszawa; 52°39'/20°32'.

Iecava, Lat. (Eckau); 45 km SSE of Riga; 56°36'/24°12'; PHLE.

Iegheriste, Rom.; pop. 10; 101 km NNW of Cluj; 47°39'/23°16'.

Iermata Neagra, Rom. (Feketegyarmat); 157 km WSW of Cluj; 46°38'/21°30'; HSL.

Iermut, Rom. PHR1. This town was not found in BGN gazetteers under the given spelling.

Iernuteni, Rom. (Radnotfaja); pop. 143; 88 km E of Cluj; 46°46'/24°43'; PHR2.

Ieud, Rom. (Yoed, Yoid); pop. 286; 114 km NNE of Cluj; 47°41'/24°14'; PHR2, SM.

Ievve, *see* Johvi.

Igal, Hung.; pop. 4; 75 km ENE of Nagykanizsa; 46°32'/17°57'.

Igelsbach, Germ. PHGBW. A number of towns share this name. It was not possible to determine from available information which one is being referenced.

Igene, Lat. (Agenhof); 88 km WNW of Riga; 57°18'/22°50'; PHLE.

Igersheim, Germ.; 94 km W of Nurnberg; 49°30'/09°49'; GED, JGFF, PHGBW.

Igesti, *see* Izhevtsy.

Iggelheim, Germ.; pop. 16; 88 km S of Frankfurt am Main; 49°22'/08°18'; CAHJP, GED, JGFF.

Ighiu, Rom. (Magyarigen); 75 km S of Cluj; 46°09'/23°31'; HSL.

Igla, *see* Uglya.

Iglau, *see* Jihlava.

Igle, *see* Uglya.

Igling, Germ.; 56 km WSW of Munchen; 48°04'/10°48'; GUM5.

Iglita, Rom.; 182 km NE of Bucuresti; 45°08'/28°11'; GUM4.

Iglo, *see* Spisska Nova Ves.

Ignacow, Pol.; pop. 27; A number of towns share this name. It was not possible to determine from available information which one is being referenced.

Ignacow Szlachecki, Pol.; pop. 3; 62 km NE of Czestochowa; 51°11'/19°48'.

Ignalina, Lith. (Ignalinko); 94 km NNE of Vilnius; 55°21'/26°10'; COH, GUM3, HSL.

Ignalinko, *see* Ignalina.

Ignatei, *see* Ignatsey.

Ignatki, Pol. PHP4. A number of towns share this name. It was not possible to determine from available information which one is being referenced.

Ignatovka, Ukr. (Eigentovka, Ignatowka, Jgnatowka, Kolonie Ignitowka, Lozisht); pop. 900; AMG, COH, EDRD, GUM3, GUM5, SF. Described in SF as an agricultural community 30 km northeast of Lutsk, this town does not appear in current gazetteers.

Ignatow, Pol.; pop. 16; 69 km E of Lublin; 51°08'/23°35'.

Ignatowka, *see* Ignatovka.

Ignatsey, Mold. (Ignatei); pop. 42; 82 km NNW of Kishinev; 47°41'/28°40'.

Ignecz, HSL. This pre-World War I community was not found in BGN gazetteers.

Igolomia, Pol.; pop. 27; 26 km E of Krakow; 50°05'/20°15'; HSL.

Igren, Ukr.; pop. 81; 19 km ENE of Dnepropetrovsk; 48°28'/35°12'.

Igrici, Hung.; pop. 7; 32 km SSE of Miskolc; 47°52'/20°53'.

Igricze, *see* Ihriste.

Igrovitsa, Ukr. (Ihrowica); pop. 46; 114 km E of Lvov; 49°43'/25°31'.

Igstadt, Germ.; pop. 5; 26 km WSW of Frankfurt am Main; 50°05'/08°19'.

Igumen, *see* Cherven.

Iharosbereny, Hung.; pop. 2; 13 km ESE of Nagykanizsa; 46°22'/17°07'.

Ihrhove, Germ.; pop. 3; 170 km WSW of Hamburg; 53°10'/07°27'.

Ihringen, Germ.; pop. 102; 139 km SW of Stuttgart; 48°03'/07°39'; HSL, JGFF, LDS, PHGBW.

Ihriste, Cz. (Igricze); 120 km E of Brno; 49°09'/18°18'; HSL.

Ihrowica, *see* Igrovitsa.

Ihumen, *see* Cherven.

Iik, *see* Ukk.

Ikazan, *see* Ikazn.

Ikazn, Byel. (Ikazan); pop. 37; 189 km W of Vitebsk; 55°37'/27°16'.

Ikervar, Hung.; pop. 6; 94 km N of Nagykanizsa; 47°12'/16°54'.

Iklad, Hung.; pop. 8; 38 km NE of Budapest; 47°40'/19°27'; COH, GUM4, HSL, YB.

Iklodbordoce, Hung. (Kerkaiklod); pop. 2; 38 km WNW of Nagykanizsa; 46°36'/16°37'.

Ikskile, Lat.; pop. 5; 32 km ESE of Riga; 56°49'/24°30'; PHLE.

Ilanets, GUM4. This town was not found in BGN gazetteers under the given spelling.

Ilava, Cz.; pop. 359; 114 km E of Brno; 49°00'/18°14'; GUM4, HSL, HSL2.

Ilawa, Pol. (Deutsch Eylau); pop. 100; 101 km SE of Gdansk; 53°36'/19°34'; AMG, GUM4, PHP4.

Ilawcze, Ukr.; pop. 51; 88 km N of Chernovtsy; 49°05'/25°55'. This town was located on an interwar map of Poland but does not appear in contemporary gazetteers. Map coordinates are approximate.

Ilba, Rom. (Illoba); pop. 10; 114 km NNW of Cluj; 47°43'/23°21'; HSL.

Ileanda, Rom. (Ileanda Mare, Nagyilonda); pop. 308; 69 km N of Cluj; 47°20'/23°38'; GUM4, HSL, PHR2, YB.

Ileanda Mare, *see* Ileanda.

Ilia, *see* Ilya.

Ilina, *see* Ilino.

Ilince, *see* Ilintsy.

Ilinets, *see* Ilintsy.

Ilineuca, *see* Yelenovka.

Ilineuka, *see* Yelenovka.

Iliniec, Pol. PHP2. This town was not found in BGN gazetteers under the given spelling.

Ilino, USSR (Ilina, Iljino); pop. 378; 82 km ESE of Velikiye Luki; 55°57'/31°40'; LDL, PHP1, SF.

Ilintse, *see* Ilintsy (near Chernovtsy).

Ilintsy, Ukr. (Ilince, Ilinets, Iljincy, Linitz); pop. 5,407; 56 km E of Vinnitsa; 49°07'/29°12'; EDRD, EJ, GUM4, GYLA, JGFF, LDL, SF.

Ilintsy (near Chernovtsy), Ukr. (Biliniec, Ilintse); pop. 77; 50 km WNW of Chernovtsy; 48°26'/25°17'.

Ilioara, Rom.; pop. 1; 88 km E of Cluj; 46°38'/24°45'.

Ilisesti, Rom.; pop. 131; 126 km WNW of Iasi; 47°36'/26°03'; PHR2.

Ilja, *see* Ilya.

Iljincy, *see* Ilintsy.

Iljino, *see* Ilino.

Ilk, Hung.; pop. 65; 107 km ENE of Miskolc; 48°07'/22°14'; HSL, JGFF.

Illereichen, Germ.; pop. 49; 101 km ESE of Stuttgart; 48°10'/10°07'; GED, HSL, HSL2, JGFF, PHGB, PHGBW.

Illerich, Germ.; pop. 6; 88 km SSE of Koln; 50°12'/07°11'.

Illingen, Germ.; pop. 107; 146 km SW of Frankfurt am Main; 49°22'/07°03'; AMG, GED, JGFF.

Illmitz, Aus.; pop. 6; 62 km SE of Wien; 47°45'/16°48'.

Illoba, *see* Ilba.

Illocska, Hung.; pop. 4; 139 km SW of Szeged; 45°48'/18°32'.

Illok, *see* Ylakiai.

Illoki, *see* Ylakiai.

Illukst, *see* Ilukste.

Illuxt, *see* Ilukste.

Ilmenau, Germ.; pop. 80; 126 km SW of Leipzig; 50°41'/10°54'.

Ilnica, Cz. AMG, COH, HSL. This pre-World War I community was not found in BGN gazetteers.

Ilnik, Ukr.; pop. 206; 107 km SSW of Lvov; 49°06'/23°06'; HSL, PHP2.

Ilniki, Ukr.; pop. 2; 56 km NNE of Rovno; 51°01'/26°40'.

Ilok, Yug.; pop. 292; 101 km WNW of Beograd; 45°13'/19°23'; EJ, HSL, JGFF, PHY.

Ilokst, *see* Ilukste.

Ilosva, *see* Irshava.

Ilow, Pol.; pop. 450; 62 km W of Warszawa; 52°20'/20°02'; PHP4.

Ilowa, Pol.; 69 km ENE of Lublin; 51°16'/23°33'; GA, PHP2.

Ilukst, *see* Ilukste.

Ilukste, Lat. (Alukst, Illukst, Illuxt, Ilokst, Ilukst, Ilukstes); pop. 58; 26 km WNW of Daugavpils; 55°58'/26°18'; LDL, PHLE, SF.

Ilukstes, *see* Ilukste.

Ilva Mare, Rom. (Nagyilva); pop. 109; 120 km NE of Cluj; 47°22'/24°54'; HSL, PHR2.

Ilva Mica, Rom. (Kisilva); pop. 126; 101 km NE of Cluj; 47°19'/24°40'; HSL, PHR2.

Ilvesheim, Germ.; pop. 23; 75 km S of Frankfurt am Main; 49°28'/08°34'; GUM5, JGFF, LDS, PHGBW.

Ilvov, GUM3. This town was not found in BGN gazetteers under the given spelling.

Ilya, Byel. (Ilia, Ilja); pop. 586; 62 km NNW of Minsk; 54°25'/27°18'; AMG, COH, EDRD, EJ, GUM4, HSL, LDL, LYV, SF, YB.

Ilza, Pol. (Drilch, Drildzh, Driltch, Ilzha); pop. 1,545; 88 km WSW of Lublin; 51°10'/21°15'; AMG, COH, EDRD, GA, GUM3, GUM5, HSL, JGFF, LDS, LYV, SF.

Ilzha, *see* Ilza.

Imbradas, Lith.; pop. 50; 133 km NNE of Vilnius; 55°47'/26°06'.

Imbshausen, Germ.; pop. 1; 75 km SSE of Hannover; 51°45'/10°03'.

Imeni, Rom.; pop. 1; 176 km N of Bucuresti; 45°57'/26°10'.

Imerinka, Ukr. EDRD. This town was not found in BGN gazetteers under the given spelling.

Imielnica, Pol.; 88 km N of Lodz; 52°31'/19°46'; EDRD, PHP4.

Imling, *see* Immling.

Immendorf, Germ.; 56 km W of Koln; 50°57'/06°10'; GED.

Immenhausen, Germ.; 114 km S of Hannover; 51°25'/09°30'; GED, LDS.

Immenroda, *see* Immenrode.

Immenrode, Germ. (Immenroda); 114 km SE of Hannover; 51°30'/10°38'; LDS.

Immling, Germ. (Imling); 56 km ESE of M..ıchen; 47°56'/12°16'; HSL.

Imola, Hung.; pop. 3; 45 km NW of Miskolc; 48°25'/20°33'; HSL.

Impfingen, Germ.; pop. 3; 88 km ESE of Frankfurt am Main; 49°39'/09°39'; PHGBW.

Imputita, *see* Vladychen.

Imsady, HSL. This pre-World War I community was not found in BGN gazetteers.

Imsbach, Germ.; 82 km SW of Frankfurt am Main; 49°35'/07°53'; JGFF.

Inacovce, Cz.; 56 km E of Kosice; 48°42'/22°02'; HSL.

Inancs, Hung.; pop. 31; 32 km NE of Miskolc; 48°17'/21°04'; HSL.

Indarapnici, *see* Indarepnish.

Indarepnish, Mold. (Indarapnici); pop. 13; 75 km NNW of Kishinev; 47°36'/28°35'.

India, *see* Indija.

Indija, Yug. (India); pop. 39; 45 km WNW of Beograd; 45°03'/20°05'.

Indra, Lat.; 62 km E of Daugavpils; 55°52'/27°32'; PHLE.

Indura, Pol. (Amdor, Amdur); pop. 1,709; 62 km NE of Bialystok; 53°27'/23°53'; CAHJP, COH, GUM3, GUM5, HSL, HSL2, JGFF, LDL, SF.

Ineshty, Mold. (Inesti); pop. 29; 69 km NW of Kishinev;

47°30'/28°24'.

Inesti, *see* Ineshty.

Ineu, Rom.; 139 km WSW of Cluj; 46°26'/21°51'; PHR1.

Ingelheim, Germ. (Ober Ingelheim); pop. 118; 50 km SW of Frankfurt am Main; 49°58'/08°03'; GUM5, JGFF.

Ingenheim, Germ.; pop. 83; 88 km WNW of Stuttgart; 49°08'/08°05'; GED, HSL.

Ingersheim, Germ.; 75 km NE of Stuttgart; 49°07'/10°04'; JGFF, PHGBW.

Ingolstadt, Germ.; pop. 100; 75 km NNW of Munchen; 48°46'/11°26'; EJ, HSL, PHGB.

Ingulec, *see* Ingulets.

Ingulets, Ukr. (Har Shafer, Ingulec); pop. 2,157; 150 km SW of Dnepropetrovsk; 47°44'/33°15'; LDL, SF.

Inheiden, Germ.; pop. 6; 45 km N of Frankfurt am Main; 50°27'/08°54'; GUM5.

Inke, Hung.; pop. 18; 19 km ESE of Nagykanizsa; 46°24'/17°12'.

Innsbruck, Aus.; pop. 317; 133 km SW of Salzburg; 47°16'/11°24'; AMG, EJ, GUM3, GUM5, JGFF.

Inota, Hung.; pop. 3; 75 km SW of Budapest; 47°12'/18°11'.

Inowlodz, Pol.; pop. 408; 56 km ESE of Lodz; 51°32'/20°13'; CAHJP, GA, GUM5, HSL, JGFF, PHP1, POCEM, SF.

Inowroclaw, Pol. (Hohensalza); pop. 252; 94 km NE of Poznan; 52°48'/18°16'; AMG, CAHJP, EJ, GA, GUM3, GUM4, HSL, JGFF, PHP1, PHP4.

Insko, Pol. (Norenberg); pop. 33; 69 km E of Szczecin; 53°25'/15°32'.

Insterburg, *see* Chernyakhovsk.

Intorok, *see* Anturke.

Inturik, *see* Anturke.

Inturk, *see* Anturke.

Inturke, *see* Anturke.

Inucu, Rom.; pop. 8; 32 km WNW of Cluj; 46°51'/23°15'.

Invancice, GUM5. This town was not found in BGN gazetteers under the given spelling.

Inwald, Pol.; pop. 28; 50 km SW of Krakow; 49°52'/19°24'.

Inzersdorf, *see* Inzersdorf Bei Wien.

Inzersdorf Bei Wien, Aus. (Inzersdorf); pop. 81; 13 km S of Wien; 48°08'/16°21'.

Ioannina, Greece (Janina, Joanina, Yanina); pop. 1,970; 208 km SW of Thessaloniki; 39°40'/20°51'; AMG, CAHJP, COH, EDRD, GUM5, HSL.

Iobageni, Rom. (Egerbegy); pop. 3; 94 km E of Cluj; 46°34'/24°48'; HSL.

Ioda, *see* Iody.

Iody, Byel. (Ioda, Jod, Jody, Yod, Yodi); pop. 238; 182 km NNW of Minsk; 55°27'/27°14'; AMG, COH, EDRD, GUM3, GUM4, LYV.

Iojib, Rom.; pop. 20; 120 km NNW of Cluj; 47°49'/23°10'.

Ioneasca, *see* Ionyaska.

Ionyaska, Mold. (Ioneasca); pop. 4; 32 km S of Kishinev; 46°45'/28°42'.

Iorcani, Rom.; 82 km W of Iasi; 47°20'/26°31'; HSL.

Iordaneni, *see* Iordanovka.

Iordaneshte, Ukr. (Iordanesti); pop. 99; 32 km S of Chernovtsy; 48°06'/25°48'; COH, PHR2.

Iordanesti, *see* Iordaneshte.

Iordanovka, Mold. (Iordaneni); pop. 3; 75 km S of Kishinev; 46°23'/28°55'.

Iosipovka, Ukr. (Juzefpol, Lidvinka, Yuzefpol); pop. 1,041; 69 km SE of Uman; 48°15'/30°47'; HSL, LDL, SF.

Ip, Rom. (Ipp); pop. 58; 88 km WNW of Cluj; 47°14'/22°39'; HSL.

Ipel, Cz. (Ipoly); 114 km WSW of Kosice; 48°34'/19°43'; HSL.

Ipelske Predmostie, Cz. (Hidveg); 146 km E of Bratislava; 48°04'/19°04'; HSL.

Ipelske Ulany, Cz. (Ipoly Fodemes); 146 km E of Bratislava; 48°08'/19°03'; HSL.

Iphofen, Germ.; 62 km WNW of Nurnberg; 49°41'/10°17'; EDRD, PHGB.

Ipolnyak, COH. This town was not found in BGN gazetteers under the given spelling.

Ipoly, *see* Ipel.

Ipolydamasd, Hung.; pop. 7; 45 km NW of Budapest; 47°51'/18°50'.

Ipoly Fodemes, *see* Ipelske Ulany.

Ipolysag, *see* Sahy.

Ipolyszog, Hung.; pop. 7; 62 km N of Budapest; 48°03'/19°14'.

Ipolytarnoc, Hung.; pop. 7; 88 km W of Miskolc; 48°14'/19°38'.

Ipp, *see* Ip.

Ipsheim, Germ.; 45 km W of Nurnberg; 49°32'/10°29'; PHGB.

Ipthausen, Germ.; 107 km NW of Nurnberg; 50°18'/10°29'; PHGB.

Iragola, *see* Ariogala.

Ir Chadash, *see* Nowe Miasto.

Ir Chadash Sugind, *see* Zemaiciu Naumiestis.

Iregszemcse, Hung.; 94 km NE of Nagykanizsa; 46°42'/18°11'; PHH.

Irena, Pol. (Virena); pop. 2,702; BGN lists two possible localities with this name located at 50°45'/22°03' and 51°34'/21°52'. LYV.

Irhocz, *see* Vilkovtsy.

Irholch, *see* Vilkovtsy.

Irholcz, *see* Vilkovtsy.

Irholo, *see* Vilkovtsy.

Irig, Yug.; pop. 1; 62 km WNW of Beograd; 45°06'/19°52'.

Irina, Rom.; pop. 22; 126 km WNW of Cluj; 47°33'/22°24'.

Ir Khadash, *see* Nowy Korczyn.

Ir Lavan, *see* Belgorod Dnestrovskiy.

Irota, Hung.; pop. 1; 38 km N of Miskolc; 48°24'/20°53'.

Irpen, Ukr.; pop. 45; 19 km WNW of Kiyev; 50°31'/30°15'.

Irrel, Germ.; pop. 18; 126 km S of Koln; 49°51'/06°28'.

Irsa, Hung.; pop. 195; 50 km ESE of Budapest; 47°14'/19°37'; HSL, HSL2, LDS.

Irsava, *see* Irshava.

Irshava, Ukr. (Ilosva, Irsava); pop. 7,078; 182 km S of Lvov; 48°19'/23°03'; AMG, COH, GUM3, GUM4, HSL, HSL2, LDL, LYV.

Irshe, *see* Orsha.

Irsi, Lat.; pop. 6; 94 km E of Riga; 56°47'/25°36'.

Irsya, *see* Orsha.

Ir Yashan, *see* Sambor.

Irza, (Tarzik).

Irzadze, Pol.; pop. 21; 45 km ESE of Czestochowa; 50°38'/19°41'.

Isaccea, Rom.; 208 km NE of Bucuresti; 45°16'/28°28'; GUM4.

Isaje, *see* Isayev.

Isakov, Ukr. (Isakow, Isakuv); pop. 36; 75 km NW of Chernovtsy; 48°49'/25°13'.

Isakovo, Mold.; pop. 102; 45 km NNW of Kishinev; 47°22'/28°43'.

Isakow, *see* Isakov.

Isakuv, *see* Isakov.

Isaszeg, Hung.; pop. 74; 26 km ENE of Budapest; 47°32'/19°24'; PHH.

Isayev, Ukr. (Isaje); pop. 68; 94 km SSW of Lvov; 49°13'/23°07'.

Isep, *see* Ispina. Not found in contemporary gazetteers, it is most likely the modern town of Ispina.

Iserlia, *see* Volnoye.

Iserlia Noua, *see* Novaya Iserliya.

Iserlohn, Germ.; pop. 188; 69 km NE of Koln; 51°22'/07°42'; AMG, CAHJP, GED, LDS.

Ishcholnyany, Byel. (Iszczolna); pop. 14; 176 km WSW of Minsk; 53°40'/24°54'.

Ishkold, Byel. (Iszkoldz); pop. 12; 101 km SW of Minsk; 53°20'/26°21'.

Ishnovets, Mold. (Isnovat); pop. 15; 32 km N of Kishinev; 47°14'/28°52'.

Ishtcha Solna, *see* Uscie Solne.

Ishtcha Zilona, *see* Ustse Zelene.

Isjum, *see* Izyum.

Iska, *see* Izky.

Iskan, Pol.; pop. 43; 26 km WSW of Przemysl; 49°47'/22°27'; HSL, SF.

Iski, *see* Izky.

Iskorost, *see* Korosten.

Iskrzyczyn, Pol.; pop. 5; 88 km SW of Krakow; 49°49'/18°45'.

Iskrzynia, Pol.; pop. 10; 62 km WSW of Przemysl; 49°42'/21°52'.

Isky, *see* Izky.

Ismail, *see* Izmail.

Ismaning, Germ.; 19 km NNE of Munchen; 48°14'/11°41'; PHGB.

Isnovat, *see* Ishnovets.

Isnuchpol, Ukr. EDRD. This town was not found in BGN gazetteers under the given spelling.

Isola, *see* Izola.

Ispanmezo, *see* Spermezeu.

Ispas, Ukr.; pop. 143; 50 km WSW of Chernovtsy; 48°17'/25°17'; COH, HSL, PHR2.

Isper, Aus.; pop. 4; 94 km W of Wien; 48°17'/15°03'.

Ispina, Pol. (Isep); pop. 90; 38 km ENE of Krakow; 50°07'/20°24'; PHP3.

Israelovca, *see* Izrailovka.

Israilovka, *see* Izrailovka.

Issel, Germ.; pop. 6; 133 km S of Koln; 49°49'/06°44'.

Isselbach, Germ.; pop. 26; 62 km WNW of Frankfurt am Main; 50°24'/07°54'.

Isselburg, Germ.; pop. 11; 101 km NNW of Koln; 51°50'/06°28'; GED.

Issum, Germ.; pop. 11; 75 km NW of Koln; 51°32'/06°26'.

Istabnik, *see* Izdebnik.

Istebna, Pol.; pop. 18; 94 km SW of Krakow; 49°34'/18°54'.

Istenmezeje, Hung.; pop. 5; 56 km WSW of Miskolc; 48°05'/20°03'; HSL.

Istra, Lat. (Istras); pop. 50; 101 km NE of Daugavpils; 56°15'/27°58'.

Istras, *see* Istra.

Istrik, *see* Ustrzyki Dolne.

Istrin, *see* Ostryna.

Istryk, *see* Ustrzyki Dolne.

Istvandi, Hung.; pop. 4; 69 km ESE of Nagykanizsa; 46°01'/17°38'.

Iszczolna, *see* Ishcholnyany.

Iszka, *see* Izky.

Iszkaz, Hung. (Felsoiszkaz); pop. 5; 88 km N of Nagykanizsa; 47°10'/17°18'.

Iszkoldz, *see* Ishkold.

Isztimer, Hung.; pop. 3; 69 km SW of Budapest; 47°17'/18°12'.

Itcani, Rom. (Itcani Gara, Itcani Noui); pop. 414; 114 km WNW of Iasi; 47°41'/26°15'; GUM4, HSL.

Itcani Gara, *see* Itcani.

Itcani Noui, *see* Itcani.

Itchnia, *see* Icna.

Itel, LDL. This pre-World War I community was not found in BGN gazetteers.

Ittlingen, Germ.; pop. 46; 50 km NNW of Stuttgart; 49°11'/08°56'; LDS, PHGBW.

Iuda, Rom.; pop. 12; 69 km ENE of Cluj; 46°56'/24°29'; HSL.

Iujineti, *see* Yuzhenitse.

Iurcauti, *see* Yurkovtsy.

Iurceni, *see* Yurcheny.

Iuzovka, *see* Donetsk.

Ivan, Hung.; pop. 24; 120 km N of Nagykanizsa; 47°27'/16°55'.

Ivana Franka, Ukr. (Naguyevichi, Nahujowice); pop. 66; 75 km SSW of Lvov; 49°22'/23°19'.

Ivanbattyan, Hung.; pop. 3; 126 km ESE of Nagykanizsa; 45°54'/18°25'.

Ivanc, Hung.; pop. 2; 69 km NW of Nagykanizsa; 46°56'/16°30'.

Ivancauti, Rom.; pop. 66; 139 km NW of Iasi; 48°14'/26°39'.

Ivancea, *see* Ivancha.

Ivancha, Mold. (Ivancea); pop. 7; 38 km N of Kishinev; 47°17'/28°51'.

Ivancice, Cz. (Eibenschitz); pop. 141; 19 km SW of Brno; 49°06'/16°23'; EJ, HSL, HSL2.

Ivancsa, Hung.; pop. 24; 45 km SSW of Budapest; 47°09'/18°49'.

Ivandarda, Hung.; 126 km SW of Szeged; 45°50'/18°36'; LDS.

Ivanec, Yug.; pop. 35; 50 km N of Zagreb; 46°13'/16°07'.

Ivane Puste, Ukr. (Iwanie Puste); pop. 28; 45 km N of Chernovtsy; 48°39'/26°10'; PHP2.

Ivaneshti, Mold. (Ivanesti); pop. 11; 114 km NW of Kishinev; 47°54'/28°09'.

Ivanesti, *see* Ivaneshti.

Ivanestii Noui, *see* Novaya Ivanovka.

Ivanestii Vechi, *see* Russko Ivanovka.

Ivangorod, Ukr. (Iwanogorod); PHR1. A number of towns share this name. It was not possible to determine from available information which one is being referenced.

Ivanhkovitz, *see* Ivashkovtsy.

Ivanice, Cz. (Ivanyi); 88 km SW of Kosice; 48°20'/20°15'; HSL.

Ivanichi, Ukr. (Iwanicze); pop. 40; 94 km N of Lvov; 50°39'/24°21'; GUM4.

Ivanici, *see* Ivano Zolot.

Ivaniki, Byel. (Iwaniki); pop. 235; 19 km NNW of Pinsk; 52°11'/26°05'; EDRD.

Ivaniska, *see* Iwaniska.

Ivanitz, *see* Ivenets.

Ivanka, *see* Ivanka Pri Dunaji.

Ivanka Pri Dunaji, Cz. (Ivanka); 13 km NE of Bratislava; 48°11'/17°16'; AMG, COH, GUM4, GUM6, HSL.

Ivankov, Ukr. (Iwankow); pop. 6; 62 km N of Chernovtsy; 48°49'/26°10'; EDRD, HSL, JGFF, LDL, SF.

Ivankoviche, *see* Ivankovichi.

Ivankovichi, Byel. (Ivankoviche, Iwankowicze); pop. 25; 133 km NNW of Pinsk; 53°13'/25°41'.

Ivankovtsy, Ukr. (Jankowce); pop. 31; 94 km S of Rovno; 49°48'/26°08'.

Ivano Frankovo, Ukr. (Janow [Lwow]); pop. 490; 19 km WNW of Lvov; 49°55'/23°44'; COH, EGRS, GUM3, GUM4, GUM5, HSL, LYV, PHP2, SF.

Ivano Frankovsk, Ukr. (Iwano Frankowsk, Stanislau, Stanislav, Stanislavov, Stanislawow, Stanisle, Stanislo, Stanislowow); pop. 23,248; 114 km WNW of Chernovtsy; 48°56'/24°43'; AMG, COH, EGRS, EJ, GA, GUM3, GUM4, GUM5, GUM6, GYLA, HSL, HSL2, JGFF, LDL, LDS, PHP2, PHP3, PHP4, SF, YB.

Ivanopol, Ukr.; pop. 1,400; 75 km NNW of Vinnitsa; 49°51'/28°13'; SF.

Ivanovice, Ukr.; pop. 85; 56 km SSE of Lvov; 49°23'/24°06'.

Ivanovice na Hane, Cz. (Eiwanowitz); pop. 64; 38 km NE of Brno; 49°19'/17°06'; HSL.

Ivanovka, Ukr. (Iwanowka, Janczyn, Janowka, Yanofka, Yanovka); pop. 55; 88 km WNW of Rovno; 51°05'/25°16'; SF.

Ivanovka (near Skalat), Ukr.; pop. 26; 133 km N of Chernovtsy; 49°26'/26°08'.

Ivanovka (near Terebovlya), Ukr. (Janow Trembowelski); pop. 525; 107 km NNW of Chernovtsy; 49°13'/25°43'; AMG, EDRD, HSL, LYV, SF, WS, YB.

Ivanovka (near Zhitomir), Ukr. (Yanushevichi); GUM4. This town was not found in BGN gazetteers under the given spelling.

Ivanovka (Tarnopol), Ukr. (Yanchin); pop. 95; 56 km ESE of Lvov; 49°34'/24°37'.

Ivanovo, Byel. (Janow, Janow [Polesie], Janow Polski); pop. 1,988; 45 km W of Pinsk; 52°09'/25°32'; COH, EDRD, EJ, GUM4, GUM5, GUM6, HSL, JGFF, SF, YB.

Ivanovo Selo, Yug.; pop. 8; 94 km E of Zagreb; 45°40'/17°15'.

Ivanovtse, (Iwanowice); pop. 85; A number of towns share this name. It was not possible to determine from available information which one is being referenced.

Ivanovtsy, Ukr. (Ianauti); pop. 267; 82 km ENE of Chernovtsy; 48°30'/27°03'.

Ivano Zolot, Ukr. (Ivanici, Iwanie); pop. 26; 50 km NW of Chernovtsy; 48°43'/25°38'; EJ.

Ivansk, *see* Iwaniska.

Bdinska, Yug.; pop. 3; 62 km E of Zagreb; 45°47'/16°49'.

Ivantchik, Ukr. EDRD. This town was not found in BGN gazetteers under the given spelling.

Ivantseviche, Byel. (Iwancewicze); pop. 7; 50 km WNW of Minsk; 54°13'/27°04'.

Ivanusca, *see* Ivanushka.

Ivanushka, Mold. (Ivanusca); pop. 50; 139 km NW of Kishinev; 47°56'/27°33'.

Ivanyi, *see* Ivanice.

Ivashkovtsy, Byel. (Ivanhkovitz, Ivaskovice, Iwaszkowce); 114 km WNW of Minsk; 54°30'/26°10'; HSL, SF.

Ivaskovice, *see* Ivashkovtsy.

Ivatsevichi, Byel. (Ivatzvitch, Iwacewicze); 88 km NW of Pinsk; 52°43'/25°21'; GUM3, GUM4, HSL, SF, YB.

Ivatzvitch, *see* Ivatsevichi.

Ivenets, Byel. (Ivanitz, Ivienic, Iwieniec); pop. 945; 56 km WSW of Minsk; 53°53'/26°45'; AMG, COH, EDRD, GUM3, GUM4, GUM6, HSL, HSL2, JGFF, LDL, SF, YB.

Ivesti, Rom.; pop. 325; 170 km S of Iasi; 45°41'/27°31'; HSL, PHR1.

Ivia, *see* Ivye.

Ivienic, *see* Ivenets.

Ivnica, Yug. (Ivnitza); 202 km SW of Beograd; 44°11'/18°09'; LDL, SF.

Ivnitza, *see* Ivnica.

Ivot, USSR; pop. 5; 50 km NNW of Bryansk; 53°40'/34°13'.

Ivye, Byel. (Ivia, Iwia, Iwie, Iwje); pop. 2,076; 120 km W of Minsk; 53°56'/25°46'; AMG, COH, EDRD, EJ, GUM3, GUM4, GUM5, GUM6, HSL, JGFF, LDL, PHP4, SF, YB.

Iwacewicze, *see* Ivatsevichi.

Iwancewicze, *see* Ivantseviche.

Iwanicze, *see* Ivanichi.

Iwanie, *see* Ivano Zolot.

Iwanie Puste, *see* Ivane Puste.

Iwaniki, *see* Ivaniki.

Iwaniska, Pol. (Ivaniska, Ivansk, Iwanisko); pop. 1,518; 107 km SW of Lublin; 50°44'/21°17'; AMG, COH, EDRD, GA, GUM4, GUM5, JGFF, LDL, POCEM, SF.

Iwanisko, *see* Iwaniska.

Iwankow, *see* Ivankov.

Iwankowicze, *see* Ivankovichi.

Iwano Frankowsk, *see* Ivano Frankovsk.

Iwanogorod, *see* Ivangorod.

Iwanowice, *see* Ivanovtse.

Iwanowice (near Kalisz), Pol.; pop. 65; 75 km WSW of Lodz; 51°39'/18°20'; PHP1.

Iwanowice (near Krakow), Pol.; pop. 34; 19 km N of Krakow; 50°13'/19°59'.

Iwanowka, *see* Ivanovka.

Iwaszkowce, *see* Ivashkovtsy.

Iwia, *see* Ivye.

Iwie, *see* Ivye.

Iwieniec, *see* Ivenets.

Iwierzyce, Pol.; pop. 18; 75 km WNW of Przemysl; 50°02'/21°46'.

Iwje, *see* Ivye.

Iwkowa, Pol.; pop. 36; 56 km ESE of Krakow; 49°49'/20°31'.

Iwla, Pol.; pop. 3; 88 km WSW of Przemysl; 49°34'/21°38'.

Iwonicz, Pol.; pop. 61; 69 km WSW of Przemysl; 49°37'/21°49'; EGRS, PHP3.

Iwonicz Zdroj, GUM5. This town was not found in BGN gazetteers under the given spelling.

Iwowe, Pol.; pop. 7; 69 km ESE of Warszawa; 51°59'/21°53'.

Iza, Ukr.; 189 km S of Lvov; 48°12'/23°19'; AMG, COH, GUM6.

Izabelin, Byel. (Zabelin); pop. 272; 157 km WNW of Pinsk; 53°06'/24°33'; GUM4, HSL, JGFF, PHP4, SF.

Izakonyha, *see* Cuhea.

Izakonyka, *see* Cuhea.

Izaslaw, *see* Zaslavl.

Izasopatak, *see* Slatioara.

Izabelin, Byelorussia: Interior of synagogue showing bima.

Izaszacsal, *see* Sacel.

Izbeshty, Mold. (Izbestea, Izbishtya); pop. 117; 32 km NNE of Kishinev; 47°13'/29°00'.

Izbestea, *see* Izbeshty.

Izbica, Pol. (Giesebitz, Izbitsa, Izbitz, Izbitza); pop. 4,000; 56 km ESE of Lublin; 50°53'/23°10'; AMG, COH, EDRD, GUM3, HSL, JGFF, LYV, PHGBW, PHP4, POCEM, SF.

Izbica (Lubelska), Pol. (Izbica Lubelska, Izbica Lubelski); pop. 2,862; 56 km ESE of Lublin; 50°53'/23°10'; AMG, EDRD, GUM3, GUM4, GUM5, HSL2, LDS, PHP1.

Izbica Kujawska, Pol.; pop. 1,378; 88 km NW of Lodz; 52°25'/18°47'; CAHJP, EDRD, GA, GUM4, GUM5, HSL2, PHP1.

Izbica Lubelska, *see* Izbica (Lubelska).

Izbica Lubelski, *see* Izbica (Lubelska).

Izbica Nowa, Pol.; pop. 53; Described in the *Black Book* as being in the Lublin region of Poland, this town was not found in BGN gazetteers.

Izbishtya, *see* Izbeshty.

Izbitsa, *see* Izbica.

Izbitz, *see* Izbica.

Izbitza, *see* Izbica.

Izbugya, *see* Zbudza.

Izby, *see* Izdby.

Izdby, Pol. (Izby); pop. 11; 107 km ESE of Krakow; 49°27'/21°04'.

Izdebki, Pol.; pop. 71; 50 km WSW of Przemysl; 49°45'/22°08'; HSL.

Izdebki Blazeje, Pol.; pop. 24; 101 km N of Lublin; 52°07'/22°35'.

Izdebki Kosmy, Pol.; pop. 4; 101 km N of Lublin; 52°07'/22°36'.

Izdebki Wasy, Pol.; pop. 10; 101 km N of Lublin; 52°06'/22°34'.

Izdebnik, Pol. (Istabnik); 32 km SSW of Krakow; 49°52'/19°46'; GUM4, GUM5, PHP3.

Izdeshkovo, USSR; pop. 102; 107 km NE of Smolensk; 55°09'/33°37'.

Izhevtsy, Ukr. (Idzesti, Igesti, Jgesti); pop. 100; 38 km SSW of Chernovtsy; 48°02'/25°39'; COH.

Iziaslav, *see* Zaslavl.

Izky, Ukr. (Iska, Iski, Isky, Iszka); pop. 300; 139 km S of Lvov; 48°39'/23°23'; AMG, HSL, SM.

Izluchistoye, Ukr. (Stalindorf); pop. 1,694; 107 km SW of Dnepropetrovsk; 47°55'/33°46'; GUM4.

Izmail, Ukr. (Ismail); pop. 1,680; 195 km SW of Odessa; 45°21'/28°50'; EJ, HSL, LDL, SF.

Izola, Yug. (Isola); 182 km WSW of Zagreb; 45°32'/13°40'; PHY.

Izow, see Izuv.

Izrailovka, Ukr. (Israelovca, Israilovka); pop. 1,227; 94 km SSW of Vinnitsa; 48°32'/27°44'; PHR1.

Izsak, Hung.; pop. 27; 82 km SSE of Budapest; 46°48'/19°22'; HSL, LDS, PHH.

Izsakfa, Hung.; pop. 3; 94 km N of Nagykanizsa; 47°13'/17°10'.

Izsep, see Zipov.

Izuv, Ukr. (Izow); pop. 21; 114 km N of Lvov; 50°50'/24°06'; HSL.

Izvalta, Lat.; pop. 7; 32 km ENE of Daugavpils; 55°57'/27°02'.

Izvoare, see Izvory.

Izvoarele, see Izvory.

Izvory, Mold. (Izvoare, Izvoarele); pop. 57; 69 km N of Kishinev; 47°33'/28°58'.

Izyaslav, Ukr. (Izyaslavl, Zaslav, Zaslaw, Zaslov); pop. 3,820; 69 km SE of Rovno; 50°07'/26°48'; EJ, GUM4, JGFF, LDL, SF.

Izyaslavl, see Izyaslav.

Izyum, Ukr. (Isjum); pop. 268; 120 km SE of Kharkov; 49°12'/37°19'.

Jaba, Hung.; 94 km NE of Nagykanizsa; 46°49'/18°01'; HSL.

Jabar, Rom. (Zsabar); 176 km SW of Cluj; 45°43'/21°48'; HSL.

Jabenita, Rom.; pop. 4; 88 km ENE of Cluj; 46°47'/24°48'.

Jablanow, see Yablonov.

Jablon, Pol.; pop. 43; 69 km NNE of Lublin; 51°44'/23°06'; GUM5, PHP1.

Jabloncza, see Silicka Jablonica.

Jablon Dabrowa, Pol.; pop. 6; 38 km SW of Bialystok; 52°55'/22°42'.

Jablonec, see Jablonec nad Nisou.

Jablonec nad Nisou, Cz. (Jablonec); pop. 801; 88 km NNE of Praha; 50°43'/15°11'; AMG, HSL, HSL2.

Jablonewo, see Yablonovo.

Jablonica, Pol.; pop. 23; 107 km ESE of Krakow; 49°48'/21°20'. See also Yablonitsa.

Jablonica Polska, Pol.; pop. 39; 62 km WSW of Przemysl; 49°42'/21°55'.

Jablonica Ruska, Pol.; pop. 15; 45 km WSW of Przemysl; 49°43'/22°14'.

Jablonice, see Yablonitsa.

Jablonitsa, see Golovatchino.

Jablonitza, see Yablonitsa.

Jablonka, Pol. (Jablonka Koscielna, Yoblonka); pop. 157; 56 km SW of Bialystok; 52°57'/22°22'; AMG, CAHJP, HSL, JGFF, LDS, PHP4, POCEM, SF, YB. See also Yablonka.

Jablonka (Krakow), Pol.; pop. 42; 75 km S of Krakow; 49°29'/19°42'.

Jablonka Koscielna, see Jablonka.

Jablonka Nizna, see Nizna Jablonka.

Jablonka Swierszczewo, Pol. LDS. This town was not found in BGN gazetteers under the given spelling.

Jablonka Wyzna, see Wyzna Jablonka.

Jablon Koscielna, Pol.; pop. 52; 45 km SW of Bialystok; 52°55'/22°39'.

Jablonna, Pol. (Yablanna); pop. 572; 19 km NNW of Warszawa; 52°22'/20°56'; COH, GA, GUM4, GUM5, HSL, LYV, PHP4, SF.

Jablonna Lacka, Pol.; pop. 131; 94 km E of Warszawa; 52°15'/22°25'. This town was located on an interwar map of Poland but does not appear in contemporary gazetteers. Map coordinates are approximate.

Jablonna Legionowo, Pol.; 19 km NNW of Warszawa; 52°24'/20°56'; GUM3.

Jablonna Ruska, Pol.; pop. 22; 94 km E of Warszawa; 52°15'/22°25'. This town was located on an interwar map of Poland but does not appear in contemporary gazetteers. Map coordinates are approximate.

Jablonne V Podjestedi, Cz. (Nemecke Jablonne); pop. 30; 82 km N of Praha; 50°46'/14°47'.

Jablonow, Pol.; pop. 56; 62 km WNW of Lublin; 51°25'/21°43'; AMG, JGFF. See also Yablonov.

Jablonowka, see Yablonovka.

Jablunkov, Cz.; pop. 134; 163 km ENE of Brno; 49°35'/18°46'; GUM4, PHP3.

Jabocritch, Ukr. EDRD. This town was not found in BGN gazetteers under the given spelling.

Jabuka, Yug.; pop. 20; A number of towns share this name. It was not possible to determine from available information which one is being referenced.

Jac, Rom.; pop. 13; 56 km NW of Cluj; 47°10'/23°14'; HSL.

Jachimowka, Pol.; pop. 23; Described in the Black Book as being in the Wolyn region of Poland, this town was not found in BGN gazetteers.

Jachymov, Cz.; pop. 25; 114 km W of Praha; 50°22'/12°55'.

Jaciazek, Pol.; pop. 82 km N of Warszawa; 52°58'/21°05'; GA.

Jackowo Gorne, Pol.; pop. 1; 38 km NNE of Warszawa; 52°33'/21°15'.

Jacmierz, Pol. (Iachmir, Posada Jacmierska); pop. 45; 56 km SW of Przemysl; 49°37'/22°01'.

Jacnia, Pol.; pop. 5; 82 km SE of Lublin; 50°35'/23°10'.

Jacobeni, see Iacobeni.

Jacobshagen, see Khoroshovtsy.

Jacovce, Cz.; pop. 53; 94 km NE of Bratislava; 48°35'/18°09'; AMG.

Jaczew, Pol.; pop. 7; 62 km NE of Warszawa; 52°28'/21°50'.

Jadlowa, Pol.; pop. 450; EGRS, LDL. Described in the Black Book as being in the Krakow region of Poland, this town was not found in BGN gazetteers.

Jadlowice, Pol. PHP3. This town was not found in BGN gazetteers under the given spelling.

Jadova, see Zhadova.

Jadova Noua, see Zhadova.

Jadovo, see Jadow.

Jadow, Pol. (Jadovo, Yadov, Yadove); pop. 1,492; 50 km NE of Warszawa; 52°28'/21°38'; AMG, COH, EDRD, GA, GUM3, GUM4, GUM5, HSL, HSL2, JGFF, LYV, PHP4, SF, YB.

Jadowniki, Pol.; pop. 86; 56 km E of Krakow; 49°58'/20°40'; PHP3.

Jadowniki Mokre, Pol.; pop. 29; 62 km ENE of Krakow; 50°09'/20°44'.

Jadwinow, Pol.; pop. 2; 62 km W of Lublin; 51°25'/21°41'.

Jadwinowka, see Yadvinuvka.

Jadziwia, Pol. PHP4. This town was not found in BGN gazetteers under the given spelling.

Jaegerndorf, see Krnov.

Jagerndorf, Germ.; 101 km NE of Munchen; 48°32'/12°47'; AMG, COH, HSL, HSL2.

Jagiela, Pol. (Jagiella); pop. 63; 38 km NW of Przemysl; 50°06'/22°34'.

Jagiella, see Jagiela.

Jagielnica, see Yagelnitsa.

Jagielnica Stara, see Yagelnitsa Stara.

Jaglewicze, see Yaglevichi.

Jagodina, see Svetozarevo.

Jagodne, Pol.; 88 km NNW of Lublin; 51°59'/22°11'; HSL.

Jagodzin, see Yagodin.

Jagodziniec, Pol.; pop. 13; 88 km WSW of Lodz; 51°36'/18°14'.

Jagonak, Hung.; pop. 5; 88 km E of Nagykanizsa; 46°19'/18°05'.

Jagotin, see Yagotin.

Jahlow, HSL. This pre-World War I community was not found in BGN gazetteers.

Jajce, Yug.; pop. 31; 189 km SE of Zagreb; 44°21'/17°17'.

Jajczaki, Pol.; pop. 26; 56 km NW of Czestochowa; 51°10'/18°39'.

Jajeczkowicze, *see* Yayechkovichi.

Jajinci, Yug.; 13 km S of Beograd; 44°44'/20°29'; EJ, GUM4, GUM5.

Jajkowce, *see* Yaykovtse.

Jak, Hung.; pop. 3; 82 km NNW of Nagykanizsa; 47°08'/16°35'.

Jakac Stara, Pol.; pop. 16; 82 km WSW of Bialystok; 53°01'/21°57'.

Jakfa, Hung.; pop. 9; 107 km N of Nagykanizsa; 47°20'/16°58'.

Jakfalva, Hung.; pop. 4; 32 km NW of Miskolc; 48°20'/20°35'.

Jakimczyce, *see* Yakimchitsy.

Jaklovce, Cz.; pop. 52; 32 km WNW of Kosice; 48°52'/21°00'.

Jakobowka, *see* Yakubovka.

Jakobstadt, *see* Jekabpils.

Jakowicze, *see* Yakoviche.

Jakowki, Pol.; pop. 8; 107 km S of Bialystok; 52°12'/23°08'.

Jakowlewo, (Yakovlevo); pop. 155; COH, LYV. Described in the *Black Book* as being in the Polesie region of Poland, this town was not found in BGN gazetteers.

Jaksice, Pol.; 94 km NE of Poznan; 52°52'/18°12'; GA, GUM4.

Jaksmanice, Pol.; pop. 53; 13 km ESE of Przemysl; 49°45'/22°53'.

Jaktorow, *see* Yaktoruv.

Jakubben, *see* Jakuby.

Jakubin, *possibly* Jakuby.

Jakubow, Pol.; pop. 30; 69 km NNE of Krakow; 50°36'/20°25'; PHP4.

Jakubowka, *see* Yakubovka.

Jakuby, Pol. (Jakubben, Jakubin?); pop. 13; 88 km WNW of Bialystok; 53°32'/22°02'.

Jalocz, *see* Yaloch.

Jalovka, *see* Eglaine.

Jalow, Pol. PHP2. This town was not found in BGN gazetteers under the given spelling.

Jalowe, Pol.; pop. 38; 50 km S of Przemysl; 49°25'/22°40'; HSL.

Jalowka, Pol. (Yaluvka); pop. 588; 56 km E of Bialystok; 53°01'/23°54'; COH, GUM3, HSL, JGFF, LDL, POCEM, SF.

Jalta, *see* Yalta.

Jaltichkov, *see* Yaltuchkov.

Jaltuskow, *see* Yaltushkov.

Jalzabet, Yug.; pop. 2; 62 km NNE of Zagreb; 46°15'/16°29'.

Jamielnica, *see* Yamelnitsa.

Jammince, HSL. This pre-World War I community was not found in BGN gazetteers.

Jamna Dolna, Pol.; pop. 11; 26 km SSW of Przemysl; 49°38'/22°34'.

Jamna Gorna, Pol.; pop. 29; 32 km SSW of Przemysl; 49°36'/22°37'.

Jamne, *see* Yamne.

Jamniki, Pol.; pop. 7; 45 km NE of Lublin; 51°28'/23°06'.

Jamnitz, *see* Jemnice.

Jampol, *see* Yampol.

Jancewicze, *see* Yantsevichi.

Janczowa, Pol.; pop. 5; 75 km ESE of Krakow; 49°43'/20°47'.

Janczyn, *see* Ivanovka.

Jand, Hung.; pop. 48; 120 km ENE of Miskolc; 48°07'/22°23'; HSL.

Janiewicze, *see* Yanevichi.

Janikowice, Pol.; pop. 26 km NNE of Krakow; 50°17'/20°10'; HSL.

Janikowo, Pol.; 88 km NE of Poznan; 52°45'/18°07'; GA, PHP4.

Janina, *see* Ioannina.

Janinow (near Blonie), Pol.; pop. 23; 38 km N of Lodz; 52°04'/19°37'.

Janinow (near Rava Russkaya), Pol.; pop. 24; 38 km E of Lodz; 51°41'/20°01'.

Janischki, *see* Joniskis.

Janisze, Pol.; pop. 6; 56 km NW of Lublin; 51°38'/22°00'.

Jank, Hung.; pop. 70; 139 km E of Miskolc; 47°56'/22°40'; HSL, PHH.

Jankai, Lith.; pop. 8; 38 km WSW of Kaunas; 54°51'/23°20'.

Janki Mlode, Pol.; pop. 19; 88 km NNE of Warszawa; 52°59'/21°40'.

Jankowa, Pol.; pop. 13; 82 km ESE of Krakow; 49°42'/20°56'.

Jankowce, *see* Ivankovtsy.

Jankowice, Pol.; 38 km N of Czestochowa; 51°03'/19°16'; PHP1.

Jankowka, Pol.; pop. 5; 26 km SE of Krakow; 49°56'/20°05'.

Janochy, Pol.; pop. 4; 101 km WSW of Bialystok; 53°04'/21°43'.

Janoshalma, Hung.; pop. 382; 62 km W of Szeged; 46°18'/19°20'; AMG, HSL, PHH.

Janoshaza, Hung.; pop. 466; 82 km N of Nagykanizsa; 47°07'/17°10'; GUM3, GUM4, HSL, LDS, PHH.

Janoshida, Hung.; pop. 30; 75 km E of Budapest; 47°23'/20°04'; HSL.

Janosi, *see* Rimavske Janovce.

Janov, *see* Janow Lubelski.

Janova, *see* Jonava.

Janovice, *see* Janovice nad Uhlavou.

Janovice nad Uhlavou, Cz. (Janovice); pop. 21; 120 km SW of Praha; 49°21'/13°13'; EJ.

Janovichi, *see* Yanovichi.

Janovo, *see* Jonava.

Janow, GYLA, HSL2, LDL, POCEM. A number of towns share this name. It was not possible to determine from available information which one is being referenced. *See also* Ivanovo. No less than 20 towns in interwar Poland were named Janow. The towns with the larger Jewish populations are shown below.

Janow (Bialostockie), *see* Janow Sokolski.

Janow (Koninske), Pol.; 69 km WNW of Lodz; 52°07'/18°40'; PHP1.

Janow (Lwow), *see* Ivano Frankovo.

Janow (near Czestochowa), Pol.; pop. 264; 26 km ESE of Czestochowa; 50°44'/19°27'; CAHJP, HSL, PHP3, POCEM, SF.

Janow (Polesie), *see* Ivanovo.

Janow (Sieradzkie), Pol.; pop. 21; 75 km NW of Czestochowa; 51°22'/18°36'.

Janowa, *see* Jonava.

Janowice, Pol.; pop. 38; 69 km E of Krakow; 49°54'/20°53'; GUM3, GUM4, HSL.

Janowicze, *see* Yanoviche.

Janowiczi, *see* Yanovichi.

Janowiec, Pol. (Janowiec nad Wisla, Yanovitch); pop. 261; 50 km W of Lublin; 51°20'/21°53'; CAHJP, COH, HSL, LDS, SF. *See also* Janowiec Wielkopolski.

Janowiec nad Wisla, *see* Janowiec.

Janowiec Wielkopolski, Pol. (Janowiec, Janowitz); pop. 90; 50 km NE of Poznan; 52°45'/17°30'; AMG.

Janowitz, *see* Janowiec Wielkopolski.

Janowka, *see* Ivanovka.

Janow Lubelski, Pol. (Janov, Yanev, Yaniv, Yanov Polski, Yanuv, Yonev); pop. 2,881; 62 km S of Lublin; 50°43'/22°25'; AMG, CAHJP, COH, GUM3, GUM4, GUM5, HSL, JGFF, LYV, SF.

Janow Nowy, Pol.; pop. 8; 56 km S of Lodz; 51°17'/19°19'.

Janowo, Pol.; pop. 24; 120 km NNW of Warszawa; 53°19'/20°40'; GUM3, LDL, POCEM, SF.

Janow Podlaski, Pol. (Yanev Podlaski, Yanev Shedletzki, Yanov, Yanov Podlaski, Yanuv Podolsk); pop. 1,707; 107 km S of Bialystok; 52°12'/23°13'; AMG, COH, EDRD, HSL, JGFF, LDS, LYV, PHP4, POCEM, SF.

Janow Polski, *see* Ivanovo.

Janow Sokolski, Pol. (Janow [Bialostockie], Yanov Sokolski); pop. 1,027; 45 km N of Bialystok; 53°28'/23°14'; COH, GUM3, HSL, JGFF, LYV, POCEM, SF, WS.

Janow Trembowelski, *see* Ivanovka (near Terebovlya).

Janukow, Pol. PHP4. This town was not found in BGN gazetteers under the given spelling.

Januszew, Pol. (Yanishov?); pop. 48; 56 km W of Warszawa; 52°22'/20°09'; LDL, PHP4.

Januszkowice, Pol.; pop. 54; 94 km W of Przemysl; 49°52'/21°28'.

Januszno, Pol.; pop. 6; 82 km WNW of Lublin; 51°30'/21°31'.

Japca, *see* Zhabka.

Japoloc, *see* Yapolots.

Jaraczew, Pol. (Jaraczewo, Jaratschewo); pop. 21; 56 km SE of Poznan; 51°58'/17°18'; JGFF.

Jaraczewo, *see* Jaraczew.

Jaratschewo, *see* Jaraczew.

Jarczew, Pol. (Novi Yarichev, Yarchev, Yarichuv, Yarichuv Novi, Yarichuv Novy); 75 km NW of Lublin; 51°49'/21°58'; GUM5, JGFF, LYV.

Jarczow, Pol. (Yartchovka); pop. 208; 94 km NNE of Przemysl; 50°25'/23°36'; AMG, EDRD, LDS, SF.

Jardanhaza, Hung.; pop. 16; 45 km W of Miskolc; 48°09'/20°15'; HSL.

Jaremcze, *see* Yaremcha.

Jareniowka, Pol.; pop. 5; 94 km WSW of Przemysl; 49°46'/21°27'.

Jarentowskie Pole, *see* Jaretowskie Pole.

Jaretowskie Pole, Pol. (Jarentowskie Pole); pop. 16; 56 km WSW of Lublin; 51°13'/21°47'.

Jarewiszcze, Ukr.; pop. 29; 157 km N of Lvov; 51°15'/24°15'. This town was located on an interwar map of Poland but does not appear in contemporary gazetteers. Map coordinates are approximate.

Jarkendorf, Germ.; 69 km WNW of Nurnberg; 49°51'/10°20'; PHGB.

Jarkovac, Yug.; pop. 5; 56 km N of Beograd; 45°16'/20°46'.

Jarmi, Hung.; pop. 58; 107 km E of Miskolc; 47°58'/22°15'; AMG, HSL, LDS, PHH.

Jarmolince, *see* Yarmolintsy.

Jarnice, Pol.; pop. 27; 69 km ENE of Warszawa; 52°22'/21°59'.

Jarnuty, Pol. BGN lists two possible localities with this name located at 52°59'/21°39' and 53°09'/22°01'. HSL.

Jarocin, Pol. (Jarotschin); pop. 113; 62 km SE of Poznan; 51°58'/17°31'; AMG, CAHJP, HSL, LDS, POCEM.

Jarocin (near Tarnobrzeg), Pol.; pop. 70; 82 km S of Lublin; 50°34'/22°20'; GUM3, GUM4, HSL.

Jaromer, Cz.; pop. 34; 107 km NE of Praha; 50°22'/15°55'.

Jaronowice, Pol.; pop. 23; 62 km E of Czestochowa; 50°39'/20°02'.

Jaroslav, *see* Jaroslaw.

Jaroslavice, Cz. (Joslowitz); pop. 50; 56 km SSW of Brno; 48°45'/16°14'.

Jaroslaw, Pol. (Jaroslav, Yaroslav, Yereslev); pop. 6,577; 32 km NNW of Przemysl; 50°01'/22°41'; AMG, CAHJP, COH, EDRD, EGRS, EJ, GUM3, GUM4, GUM5, HSL, HSL2, JGFF, LDL, LYV, PHP1, PHP2, PHP3, PHP4, POCEM, SF, YB.

Jaroslawiec, Pol.; pop. 30; 88 km ESE of Lublin; 50°55'/23°42'.

Jaroszyn, Pol.; 45 km WNW of Lublin; 51°26'/21°57'; GUM3.

Jarotschin, *see* Jarocin.

Jarovnice, Cz.; 45 km NNW of Kosice; 49°03'/21°04'; JGFF.

Jarowica, Pol.; pop. 56; Described in the *Black Book* as being in the Wolyn region of Poland, this town was not found in BGN gazetteers.

Jarpice, Cz.; pop. 2; 38 km WNW of Praha; 50°19'/14°05'.

Jartypory, Pol.; pop. 5; 75 km ENE of Warszawa; 52°25'/22°06'.

Jaruga, *see* Yaruga.

Jaryczow, *see* Novyy Yarychev.

Jaryczow Nowy, *see* Novyy Yarychev.

Jaryczow Stary, *see* Novyy Yarychev.

Jaryschew, *see* Yaryshev.

Jarzt, Germ.; 32 km N of Munchen; 48°22'/11°34'; GUM3.

Jarzyly, Pol.; pop. 9; 88 km N of Warszawa; 53°02'/21°19'.

Jasa Tomic, Yug.; pop. 56; 75 km N of Beograd; 45°27'/20°52'.

Jasd, Hung.; pop. 5; 82 km SW of Budapest; 47°17'/18°02'.

Jasenovac, Yug.; 88 km ESE of Zagreb; 45°16'/16°54'; EDRD, EJ, GUM4, GUM5, GUM6.

Jashkov, Ukr. EDRD. This town was not found in BGN gazetteers under the given spelling.

Jasi, *see* Iasi.

Jasiel, Pol.; pop. 3; 82 km SW of Przemysl; 49°22'/21°55'.

Jasien (near Dolina), Ukr.; pop. 98; 126 km S of Lvov; 48°45'/24°10'.

Jasien (near Staryy Sambor), Pol.; pop. 64; 45 km S of Przemysl; 49°26'/22°38'.

Jasien (near Wielun), Pol.; pop. 60; 62 km NW of Czestochowa; 51°17'/18°45'; HSL, HSL2.

Jasienica, *see* Jasienica Rosielna.

Jasienica (Bialystok area), Pol.; pop. 22; 82 km SW of Bialystok; 52°48'/22°03'; GUM3.

Jasienica (Kielce area), Pol.; 107 km SSW of Lublin; 50°33'/21°34'; GUM3.

Jasienica (near Warszawa), Pol.; pop. 45; 32 km NE of Warszawa; 52°25'/21°24'.

Jasienica Rosielna, Pol. (Jasienica, Yashnitza, Yasinitza); pop. 479; 62 km WSW of Przemysl; 49°45'/21°57'; EGRS, GA, HSL, JGFF, LDL, PHP3, SF.

Jasienica Solna, *see* Yasenitsa Solna.

Jasienica Sufczynska, Pol.; pop. 7; 26 km WSW of Przemysl; 49°46'/22°27'.

Jasienica Zamkowa, *possibly* Yasenitsa Solna.

Jasienice, *see* Yasenitsa.

Jasieniec Nowy, Pol.; pop. 12; 94 km WSW of Lublin; 51°08'/21°13'.

Jasieniow Gorny, *see* Verkhniy Yasenov.

Jasieniow Polny, *see* Yasenev Polnyy.

Jasiennik Stary, Pol.; pop. 16; 75 km NNW of Przemysl; 50°25'/22°26'.

Jasienow, *see* Verkhniy Yasenov; Yasenov.

Jasienowka, *see* Jasionowka.

Jasienow Polny, Pol. PHP2. This town was not found in BGN gazetteers under the given spelling.

Jasiewicze, *see* Yasevichi.

Jasina, *see* Yasinya.

Jasine, HSL. This pre-World War I community was not found in BGN gazetteers.

Jasinowka, *see* Yasinuvka.

Jasionka, Pol.; pop. 51; 62 km WNW of Przemysl; 50°07'/22°04'; GA.

Jasionka Masiowa, *see* Yasenitsa.

Jasionowk, COH. This town was not found in BGN gazetteers under the given spelling.

Jasionowka, Pol. (Jasienowka, Yashinovka, Yashinovke, Yashinowka); pop. 1,306; 32 km NNW of Bialystok; 53°23'/23°02'; AMG, COH, EDRD, GA, GUM4, HSL, JGFF, LDL, LYV, SF.

Jasiorowka, Pol.; pop. 92; 56 km NE of Warszawa; 52°33'/21°43'.

Jasiow, Pol.; pop. 42; Described in the *Black Book* as being in the Kielce region of Poland, this town was not found in BGN gazetteers.

Jasiunai, Lith. (Jaszuny); 32 km S of Vilnius; 54°27'/25°20'; GUM3, GUM5, HSL.

Jaskowice, Pol.; 75 km S of Czestochowa; 50°09'/18°45'; GA.

Jaskowicze, *see* Yaskovichi.

Jaslany, Pol. (Yaslany); pop. 74; 114 km NE of Krakow; 50°24'/21°29'; AMG, HSL, JGFF, SF.

Jaslikow, Pol.; pop. 17; 45 km ESE of Lublin; 51°00'/23°04'.

Jasliska, Pol. (Iasliska, Posada Jasliska, Yoshlisk); pop. 224; 82 km SW of Przemysl; 49°27'/21°48'; EGRS, GUM4, HSL, HSL2.

Jaslo, Pol. (Yasla, Yaslo); pop. 2,445; 94 km WSW of Przemysl; 49°45'/21°28'; AMG, COH, EDRD, EGRS, EJ, GA, GUM3, GUM4, GUM5, HSL, HSL2, JGFF, LDL, PHP3, POCEM, SF, YB.

Jaslowiec, *see* Pomortsy.

Jasmuiza, *see* Aizkalni.

Jasna Podlopien, Pol.; pop. 17; 50 km SE of Krakow; 49°44'/20°18'.

Jasnogorka, *see* Yasnogorka.

Jasov, Cz. (Jaszo); pop. 67; 19 km WSW of Kosice;

Jassy (Iasi), Romania: Distinguished men posing in front of the oldest synagogue in Jassy, built nearly 200 years ago.

48°41'/20°59'; HSL, HSL2.

Jasova, Cz. (Jaszfalu); 101 km E of Bratislava; 47°59'/18°24'; HSL.

Jassy, *see* Iasi.

Jastary, Lith. EDRD. This town was not found in BGN gazetteers under the given spelling.

Jastkow, Pol.; pop. 42; 13 km WNW of Lublin; 51°19'/22°28'; GUM4.

Jastkowice, Pol. (Yostkovitz); pop. 37; 82 km SSW of Lublin; 50°37'/22°06'; JGFF, SF.

Jastrebarsko, Yug.; pop. 18; 32 km SW of Zagreb; 45°40'/15°39'.

Jastrow, *see* Jastrowo.

Jastrowie, *see* Jastrowo.

Jastrowo, Pol. (Jastrow, Jastrowie); pop. 200; 38 km WNW of Poznan; 52°36'/16°31'; HSL, HSL2, JGFF, LDS.

Jastrzab, Pol.; pop. 97; 114 km ESE of Lodz; 51°15'/20°57'.

Jastrzabka Nowa, Pol.; pop. 14; 88 km E of Krakow; 50°05'/21°09'.

Jastrzabka Stara, Pol.; pop. 97; 94 km ENE of Krakow; 50°08'/21°15'.

Jastrzebia, Pol.; pop. 21; 82 km ESE of Krakow; 49°47'/20°54'.

Jastrzebica, *see* Yastshembitsa.

Jastrzebice, Pol.; pop. 13; 62 km NNW of Czestochowa; 51°18'/19°00'.

Jastrzebie, Pol. (Jastrzebie Smiary); pop. 46; 88 km E of Warszawa; 52°03'/22°15'.

Jastrzebiec, Pol.; pop. 20; 69 km NNW of Przemysl; 50°21'/22°40'.

Jastrzebie Smiary, *see* Jastrzebie.

Jastrzebik, Pol.; pop. 6; 107 km SE of Krakow; 49°24'/20°55'.

Jastrzebska Wola, Pol.; pop. 9; 114 km NE of Krakow; 50°44'/21°11'.

Jastrzebsko Stare, Pol.; pop. 1; 62 km WSW of Poznan;

52°18'/16°04'.

Jasvainiai, *see* Josvainiai.

Jaswily, Pol.; 45 km NNW of Bialystok; 53°28'/22°56'; HSL.

Jaswojki, LDL. This pre-World War I community was not found in BGN gazetteers.

Jaszalsoszentgyorgy, Hung.; pop. 84; 75 km E of Budapest; 47°22'/20°06'; HSL, PHH.

Jaszapati, Hung.; pop. 209; 82 km ENE of Budapest; 47°31'/20°09'; LDS, PHH.

Jaszarokszallas, Hung.; pop. 189; 69 km ENE of Budapest; 47°38'/19°59'; PHH.

Jaszbereny, Hung.; pop. 676; 62 km E of Budapest; 47°30'/19°55'; GUM3, GUM6, LDS, PHH.

Jaszczew, Pol.; pop. 3; 82 km WSW of Przemysl; 49°44'/21°39'.

Jaszczulty, Pol.; pop. 10; 62 km NNE of Warszawa; 52°43'/21°31'.

Jaszdozsa, Hung.; pop. 27; 69 km ENE of Budapest; 47°34'/20°01'.

Jaszfalu, *see* Jasova.

Jaszfelsoszentgyorgy, Hung.; pop. 15; 56 km E of Budapest; 47°30'/19°48'.

Jaszfenyszaru, Hung.; pop. 89; 50 km ENE of Budapest; 47°34'/19°43'; PHH.

Jaszjakohalma, Hung.; pop. 16; 69 km ENE of Budapest; 47°31'/20°00'.

Jaszkarajeno, Hung.; pop. 142; 94 km ESE of Budapest; 47°03'/20°04'; HSL, HSL2, PHH.

Jaszkerekegyhaza, *see* Kerekegyhaza.

Jaszkiser, Hung.; pop. 60; 82 km E of Budapest; 47°27'/20°13'; HSL, PHH.

Jaszladany, Hung.; pop. 122; 82 km E of Budapest; 47°22'/20°10'; PHH.

Jaszo, *see* Jasov.

Jaszsag, LDS. Not a town, but a district of Hungary. A major town in the district is Jaszbereny.

Jaszszentandras, Hung.; pop. 9; 75 km SSW of Miskolc; 47°35'/20°11'; LDS.

Jaszszentlaszlo, Hung.; pop. 2; 50 km NW of Szeged; 46°34'/19°46'.

Jasztelek, Hung.; pop. 12; 69 km E of Budapest; 47°29'/20°00'.

Jaszuny, *see* Jasiunai.

Jata, Pol.; pop. 40; 82 km NW of Przemysl; 50°23'/22°04'; HSL.

Jatra, *see* Yatra.

Jauer, *see* Jawor.

Jaunauce, Lat.; pop. 1; 101 km SW of Riga; 56°27'/22°42'.

Jaungulbene, Lat. (Jaungulbenes); pop. 8; 139 km N of Daugavpils; 57°04'/26°36'.

Jaungulbenes, *see* Jaungulbene.

Jaunijelgaua, *see* Jaunjelgava.

Jaunijelgava, *see* Jaunjelgava.

Jaunjelgava, Lat. (Fridrikhshtadt, Friedrichstadt, Jaunijelgaua, Jaunijelgava, Jaunjelgavas, Naira); pop. 619; 75 km ESE of Riga; 56°37'/25°05'; EJ, HSL, HSL2, JGFF, LDL, PHLE, SF.

Jaunjelgavas, *see* Jaunjelgava.

Jaunlaicene, Lat.; pop. 2; 176 km NE of Riga; 57°32'/26°52'.

Jaunlatgale, *see* Abrini.

Jaunpiebalga, Lat. (Jaunpiebalgas); pop. 25; 120 km ENE of Riga; 57°11'/26°03'.

Jaunpiebalgas, *see* Jaunpiebalga.

Jaunsvirlauka, Lat.; pop. 1; 56 km S of Riga; 56°30'/23°56'.

Javaravas, Lith.; pop. 29; This town was not found in BGN gazetteers under the given spelling.

Javgur, *see* Zhavgur.

Javor, Cz.; pop. 76; BGN lists two possible localities with this name located at 49°20'/13°15' and 50°34'/16°11'.

Javorov, *see* Yavorov.

Jawcze, *see* Yavche.

Jawiszowice, Pol.; pop. 22; 56 km WSW of Krakow; 49°57'/19°09'; GUM3, GUM4, GUM5, GUM6.

Jawor, Pol. (Jauer); pop. 68; 56 km WSW of Wroclaw; 51°03'/16°11'; HSL, LDS, POCEM.

Jawora, *see* Yavora.

Jaworki, Pol.; pop. 5; 88 km SE of Krakow; 49°25'/20°34'.

Jawornik, *see* Jawornik Polski.

Jawornik Polski, Pol. (Jawornik, Jawornik Przedmiescie?, Yavornik); pop. 155; 38 km WNW of Przemysl; 49°53'/22°17'; AMG, EGRS, GUM4, GUM5, JGFF, LDL, PHP3, SF.

Jawornik Przedmiescie, *possibly* Jawornik Polski.

Jawornik Ruski, Pol.; pop. 125; 38 km WSW of Przemysl; 49°44'/22°19'; PHP2.

Jaworow, *see* Yavorov.

Jaworowka, *see* Yavoruvka.

Jaworsko, Pol.; pop. 4; 62 km ESE of Krakow; 49°55'/20°46'.

Jawor Solecki, Pol.; pop. 5; 75 km WSW of Lublin; 51°09'/21°29'.

Jaworze, Pol. BGN lists two possible localities with this name located at 49°48'/18°58' and 53°18'/19°02'. HSL.

Jaworzec, Pol.; pop. 4; 69 km S of Przemysl; 49°13'/22°27'.

Jaworze Dolne, Pol.; pop. 75; 101 km W of Przemysl; 49°58'/21°22'.

Jaworze Gorne, Pol.; pop. 16; 101 km W of Przemysl; 49°57'/21°22'.

Jaworznik, Pol.; pop. 4; 32 km ESE of Czestochowa; 50°37'/19°25'.

Jaworzno, Pol. (Yavarzna, Yavorzhne, Yavorzno, Yavozhne); pop. 1,346; 50 km WNW of Krakow; 50°13'/19°17'; AMG, COH, EGRS, GUM3, GUM4, GUM5, GUM6, HSL, HSL2, JGFF, LDL, LYV, PHP3, PHP4, POCEM, SF.

Jaworzno (near Czestochowa), Pol.; pop. 30; 45 km WNW of Czestochowa; 51°02'/18°39'.

Jaworzyna Slaska, Pol. (Konigszelt); pop. 1; 45 km SW of Wroclaw; 50°55'/16°28'; GUM3.

Jazienica Ruska, Pol.; pop. 28; Described in the *Black Book* as

being in the Tarnopol region of Poland, this town was not found in BGN gazetteers.

Jazlovice, Cz.; pop. 2; 19 km SE of Praha; 49°58'/14°38'.

Jazlowiec, *see* Pomortsy.

Jazovo, Yug.; pop. 15; 126 km NNW of Beograd; 45°53'/20°14'.

Jazow Nowy, *possibly* Stariy Yarov.

Jazowsko, Pol.; pop. 47; 75 km SE of Krakow; 49°32'/20°31'.

Jazow Stary, *see* Stariy Yarov.

Jazwie, Pol.; pop. 4; 38 km NE of Warszawa; 52°24'/21°29'.

Jazwinki, *see* Yazvinki.

Jazwiny, Pol.; pop. 30; 94 km E of Krakow; 50°05'/21°15'.

Jebenhausen, Germ.; 38 km E of Stuttgart; 48°41'/09°38'; GED, JGFF, PHGBW.

Jedelina, *see* Jedlina.

Jedenspeigen, Aus.; pop. 1; 50 km NE of Wien; 48°30'/16°52'.

Jedincy, *see* Yedintsy.

Jedlany, Cz.; pop. 2; 69 km SSE of Praha; 49°30'/14°43'.

Jedle, Pol.; pop. 4; 82 km ENE of Czestochowa; 50°56'/20°14'.

Jedlice, GA. This town was not found in BGN gazetteers under the given spelling.

Jedlicze, Pol. (Yedlitch); pop. 148; 82 km WSW of Przemysl; 49°43'/21°39'; AMG, EGRS, GUM3, GUM5, HSL, LDL, PHP3, SF.

Jedlina, Pol. (Jedelina); 56 km WSW of Krakow; 50°03'/19°09'; EDRD.

Jedlinki, Pol.; pop. 5; 75 km NNW of Przemysl; 50°25'/22°33'.

Jedlinsk, Pol. (Yedlinsk); pop. 762; 88 km S of Warszawa; 51°31'/21°07'; AMG, COH, EDRD, GA, HSL, HSL2, LDL, SF.

Jedlnia, Pol.; pop. 88 km W of Lublin; 51°28'/21°22'; AMG, GUM4, GUM6.

Jedlnia Letnisko, Pol.; 88 km W of Lublin; 51°26'/21°20'; GA.

Jedlno, Pol.; 38 km N of Czestochowa; 51°05'/19°15'; HSL.

Jedrezejow, Ukr. (Andreev, Andreyev); 126 km W of Kiyev; 50°30'/28°41'; EJ, LDL.

Jedrzejewo, Pol. (Putzig); pop. 6; 50 km NW of Poznan; 52°51'/16°37'.

Jedrzejow, Pol. (Jendrzejov, Yedzheyov, Yendzheva, Yendzheyev, Yendzhiov, Yendziv); pop. 4,585; 62 km NNE of Krakow; 50°38'/20°18'; AMG, COH, EDRD, EJ, GA, GUM3, GUM4, GUM5, HSL, HSL2, LYV, PHP4, SF, YB.

Jedwabne, Pol. (Yedvabna, Yedwabne); pop. 757; 56 km W of Bialystok; 53°17'/22°18'; GA, GUM3, GUM4, HSL, HSL2, JGFF, LDL, PHP4, POCEM, SF, WS, YB.

Jedziszcze, Pol. PHP4. This town was not found in BGN gazetteers under the given spelling.

Jejse, Byel. (Yeysi); pop. 119; 176 km NNW of Minsk; 55°25'/27°05'; LYV. This town was located on an interwar map of Poland but does not appear in contemporary gazetteers. Map coordinates are approximate.

Jekabpils, Lat. (Iakobshtadt, Jakobstadt, Jekobpils, Yakovshtat, Yekabpils); pop. 794; 82 km NW of Daugavpils; 56°29'/25°51'; COH, EJ, GYLA, HSL, HSL2, JGFF, LDL, PHLE, SF.

Jekaterynoslaw, *see* Dnepropetrovsk.

Jeke, Hung.; pop. 7; 107 km ENE of Miskolc; 48°14'/22°10'; LDS.

Jekobpils, *see* Jekabpils.

Jelcza, Pol.; pop. 11; 45 km N of Krakow; 50°27'/19°53'.

Jelec, Yug.; 208 km SSW of Beograd; 43°30'/18°37'; HSL, HSL2.

Jelechowice, *see* Yelekhovichi.

Jelen, Pol. (Yelin); pop. 43; 50 km W of Krakow; 50°10'/19°15'; HSL, SF.

Jelenia Gora, Pol. (Hirschberg); pop. 360; 94 km WSW of Wroclaw; 50°54'/15°44'; GA, GUM3, GUM5, HSL, LDS, POCEM.

Jeleniec, Pol.; pop. 15; 75 km NNW of Lublin; 51°52'/22°16'.

Jeleniewo, Pol.; pop. 250; 126 km NNW of Bialystok; 54°12'/22°55'; JGFF, PHP4, POCEM.

Jelenje, Yug.; pop. 1; 126 km SW of Zagreb; 45°23'/14°28'.

Jelenkowate, Ukr.; pop. 21; 163 km S of Lvov; 48°25'/23°25'. This town was located on an interwar map of Poland but does not appear in contemporary gazetteers. Map coordinates are approximate.

Jelesnia, Pol.; pop. 90; 69 km SSW of Krakow; 49°39'/19°20'; PHP3.

Jelewo, Pol. PHP4. This town was not found in BGN gazetteers under the given spelling.

Jelgava, Lat. (Jelgavas, Mitau, Mitava, Mitawa, Mitoi, Yelgava); pop. 1,979; 45 km SSW of Riga; 56°39'/23°42'; AMG, COH, EJ, GUM3, GUM4, GUM5, HSL, HSL2, JGFF, LDL, PHLE, SF.

Jelgavas, *see* Jelgava.

Jelissawetgrad, *see* Kirovograd.

Jelka, Cz.; pop. 210; 32 km E of Bratislava; 48°09'/17°31'; HSL.

Jelna, Pol.; pop. 44; 69 km NW of Przemysl; 50°18'/22°22'; HSL.

Jelnia, Pol.; 82 km ESE of Lodz; 51°26'/20°27'; AMG, GUM3.

Jelno, *see* Yelno.

Jelochowice, Pol. PHP2. This town was not found in BGN gazetteers under the given spelling.

Jelonka Mala, Pol.; pop. 30; Described in the *Black Book* as being in the Polesie region of Poland, this town was not found in BGN gazetteers.

Jelonki, Pol.; pop. 46; 88 km NNE of Warszawa; 52°53'/21°48'.

Jelsava, Cz. (Jolsva); pop. 219; 75 km WSW of Kosice; 48°38'/20°14'; AMG, GUM3, GUM4, HSL, HSL2.

Jemgum, Germ.; 176 km WSW of Hamburg; 53°16'/07°23'; LDS.

Jemilcino, *see* Yemilchino.

Jemnice, Cz. (Jamnitz); pop. 63; 75 km WSW of Brno; 49°02'/15°34'; EJ.

Jena, Germ.; pop. 150; 69 km SW of Leipzig; 50°56'/11°35'; EJ, HSL.

Jendrzejov, *see* Jedrzejow.

Jenikau, HSL, HSL2. This pre-World War I community was not found in BGN gazetteers.

Jenke, *see* Jenkovce.

Jenki, Pol.; pop. 9; 26 km SW of Bialystok; 53°03'/22°49'.

Jenkovce, Cz. (Jenke); 69 km E of Kosice; 48°39'/22°13'; HSL.

Jennersdorf, Aus.; pop. 9; 50 km ESE of Graz; 46°56'/16°08'; GUM4, GUM5.

Jeno, Hung.; 75 km SW of Budapest; 47°06'/18°15'; HSL.

Jenstejn, Cz.; pop. 3; 13 km NE of Praha; 50°09'/14°36'.

Jerchy, *see* Yerkhi.

Jeremicze, *see* Yeremichi.

Jeremjejewka, *see* Veremiyevka.

Jerice, Cz.; pop. 2; 94 km NE of Praha; 50°21'/15°41'.

Jeruzal, Pol.; pop. 25; 62 km ESE of Warszawa; 52°04'/21°51'.

Jeruzalema, Lat. PHLE. This town was not found in BGN gazetteers under the given spelling.

Jeryze, *see* Jerzyce.

Jerzyce, Pol. (Jeryze); pop. 5; 101 km ENE of Poznan; 52°34'/18°27'.

Jesberg, Germ.; pop. 74; 107 km N of Frankfurt am Main; 51°00'/09°09'; GUM5.

Jesenice, Cz.; pop. 42; 69 km W of Praha; 50°06'/13°29'.

Jesenik, Cz. (Freiwaldau, Fryvaldov); pop. 138; 120 km N of Brno; 50°14'/17°12'; GUM4.

Jesenske, Cz. (Feled, Feledince); pop. 564; 94 km SW of Kosice; 48°18'/20°05'; HSL.

Jesentuki, USSR; EDRD. This town was not found in BGN gazetteers under the given spelling.

Jesin, Cz.; pop. 8; 26 km NW of Praha; 50°16'/14°12'.

Jesiona, Pol. (Grunwald); 69 km NE of Wroclaw; 51°28'/17°48'; PHP3, PHP4.

Jessnitz, Germ.; pop. 28; 50 km N of Leipzig; 51°41'/12°18'; HSL, HSL2, JGFF.

Jetzelsdorf, Aus.; pop. 5; 62 km NNW of Wien; 48°42'/16°03'.

Jeutendorf, Aus.; pop. 1; 50 km W of Wien; 48°15'/15°44'.

Jever, Germ.; pop. 126; 139 km W of Hamburg; 53°35'/07°54';

GED, GUM5, JGFF.

Jevicko, Cz. (Gewitsch); pop. 107; 56 km N of Brno; 49°38'/16°44'; HSL, HSL2.

Jevineves, Cz.; pop. 5; 38 km NNW of Praha; 50°21'/14°20'.

Jevpatorija, *see* Yevpatoriya.

Jevreni, *see* Zhevreny.

Jewe, *see* Johvi.

Jezena, Byel.; pop. 21; This town, in the Nowogrodek province of interwar Poland, does not appear in interwar or contemporary gazetteers.

Jezerance, (Jezerne); HSL. This pre-World War I community was not found in BGN gazetteers.

Jezerne, *see* Jezerance.

Jezierna, *see* Ozernyany.

Jeziernica, *see* Ozernitsa.

Jezierzanka, *see* Yezezhanka.

Jezierzany, *see* Ozeryany; Ozeryany (Wolyn).

Jeziorany, Pol.; 139 km E of Gdansk; 53°59'/20°45'; GYLA, POCEM.

Jeziorko, Pol.; pop. 33; 94 km SSW of Lublin; 50°34'/21°49'. The *Black Book* notes a second town named Jeziorko (pop. 42) in the interwar Polish province of Polesie. It does not appear in contemporary gazetteers.

Jeziorna, *see* Jeziorna Krolewska.

Jeziorna Krolewska, Pol. (Jeziorna, Yeziorna); pop. 137; 26 km SSE of Warszawa; 52°05'/21°06'; AMG, COH, EDRD, GUM5, HSL, HSL2, PHP1, PHP4, SF.

Jeziorna Oborska, Pol.; pop. 4; 26 km SE of Warszawa; 52°05'/21°07'.

Jezioro, *see* Ozero.

Jeziorosy, *see* Zarasai.

Jeziory, *see* Ozery.

Jeznas, *see* Jieznas.

Jezor, Pol.; 50 km WNW of Krakow; 50°14'/19°12'; AMG.

Jezow, Pol. (Yezhov); pop. 1,048; 38 km ENE of Lodz; 51°49'/19°58'; CAHJP, GA, HSL, HSL2, LDS, PHP1, PHP4, POCEM, SF.

Jezowe, Pol.; pop. 161; 82 km NW of Przemysl; 50°22'/22°09'; PHP3, PHP4.

Jezupol, *see* Zhovten.

Jgesti, *see* Izhevtsy.

Jgnatowka, *see* Ignatovka.

Jiblea, GUM4. This town was not found in BGN gazetteers under the given spelling.

Jibou, Rom. (Zsibo); pop. 640; 62 km NW of Cluj; 47°16'/23°15'; AMG, COH, GUM6, HSL, HSL2, PHR2.

Jicin, Cz.; pop. 136; 75 km NE of Praha; 50°26'/15°22'.

Jidovita, *see* Rebreanu.

Jieznas, Lith. (Jeznas, Yezna, Yeznas); pop. 286; 38 km SE of Kaunas; 54°36'/24°10'; COH, GUM3, HSL, JGFF, LDL, SF, YB, YL.

Jihlava, Cz. (Iglau); pop. 1,102; 82 km W of Brno; 49°24'/15°35'; AMG, EJ, JGFF.

Jilava, Rom.; 13 km S of Bucuresti; 44°20'/26°05'; GUM3, GUM4.

Jilemnice, Cz.; pop. 1; 94 km NE of Praha; 50°36'/15°31'.

Jimlin, Cz.; pop. 5; 56 km WNW of Praha; 50°19'/13°45'.

Jince, Cz.; pop. 6; 50 km SW of Praha; 49°47'/13°59'.

Jindrichuv Hradec, Cz.; pop. 247; 114 km SSE of Praha; 49°09'/15°00'; JGFF.

Jirikov, Cz. (Georgswalde); pop. 2; 107 km N of Praha; 50°59'/14°35'.

Jirkov, Cz.; pop. 44; 82 km WNW of Praha; 50°30'/13°27'.

Jistebnice, Cz.; pop. 28; 75 km S of Praha; 49°29'/14°32'.

Jisterpy, Cz.; pop. 3; 56 km NNW of Praha; 50°32'/14°17'.

Jitomir, *see* Zhitomir.

Jivatov, *see* Zhivacher.

Jklad, Hung. HSL2. This pre-World War I community was not found in BGN gazetteers.

Jleanda, Rom. HSL2. This pre-World War I community was not found in BGN gazetteers.

Jlok, Hung. HSL2, LDL. This pre-World War I community was not found in BGN gazetteers.

Joanin, Pol.; pop. 7; 50 km SE of Lublin; 50°54'/22°57'.

Joanina, *see* Ioannina.

Jobahaza, Hung.; pop. 1; 133 km N of Nagykanizsa; 47°35'/17°12'.

Jobbagyi, Hung.; pop. 21; 62 km NE of Budapest; 47°50'/19°41'; HSL.

Jochsberg, Germ.; pop. 2; 50 km SW of Nurnberg; 49°19'/10°24'; PHGB.

Jod, *see* Iody.

Jodlowa, Pol. (Yodlava); pop. 301; 101 km E of Krakow; 49°52'/21°18'; EDRD, GUM3, GUM4, GUM5, HSL, JGFF, PHP3, SF.

Jodlowka (near Bochnia), Pol.; pop. 8; 50 km E of Krakow; 49°59'/20°33'.

Jodlowka (near Pruchnik), Pol.; pop. 35; 26 km WNW of Przemysl; 49°53'/22°28'; HSL.

Jodlowka (near Tarnow), Pol.; pop. 22; 82 km E of Krakow; 50°04'/21°07'.

Jodlowka Tuchowska, Pol.; pop. 15; 88 km ESE of Krakow; 49°50'/21°04'.

Jodlownik, Pol.; pop. 14; 38 km SE of Krakow; 49°47'/20°14'; GUM3.

Jody, *see* Iody.

Jogeva, Est. (Laisgol M, Laisholm); pop. 5; 45 km NW of Tartu; 58°45'/26°24'.

Johannisburg, *see* Pisz.

Johlingen, Germ.; pop. 18; 56 km WNW of Stuttgart; 49°02'/08°35'; JGFF, LDS, PHGBW.

Johvi, Est. (Ievve, Jewe); pop. 8; 120 km NNE of Tartu; 59°22'/27°27'.

Jolo, Hung. HSL2. This pre-World War I community was not found in BGN gazetteers.

Jolsva, *see* Jelsava.

Jonava, Lith. (Janova, Janovo, Janowa, Yanova, Yanove, Yonava); pop. 2,701; 32 km NE of Kaunas; 55°05'/24°17'; AMG, COH, EJ, GUM3, GUM5, GUM6, HSL, HSL2, JGFF, LDL, LYV, PHP4, SF, YB, YL.

Joniec, Pol.; pop. 9; 50 km NW of Warszawa; 52°36'/20°35'.

Jonik, Pol. (Jonnik); pop. 6; 75 km NNW of Lublin; 51°51'/22°15'.

Joniny, Pol.; pop. 5; 94 km E of Krakow; 49°54'/21°11'.

Joniskelis, Lith. (Yaneskel, Yohonishkel, Yonishkel, Yonushkel); pop. 162; 56 km ENE of Siauliai; 56°02'/24°10'; HSL, JGFF, LDL, SF, YL.

Joniskis, Lith. (Janischki, Yanishke, Yanishki, Yanishok, Yenishok, Yonishkis, Yonishok); pop. 978; 38 km NNE of Siauliai; 56°14'/23°37'; COH, FRG, GUM3, GUM5, HSL, JGFF, LDL, LYV, SF, YL.

Jonnik, *see* Jonik.

Jora de Jos, *see* Nizhniye Zhory.

Jora de Mijloc, *see* Sredniye Zhory.

Jora de Sus, *see* Verkhniye Zhory.

Jordanow, Pol. (Yordanev, Yordanov); pop. 238; 56 km S of Krakow; 49°39'/19°50'; COH, EGRS, GUM4, GUM5, HSL, LDL, LYV, PHP3, POCEM, SF, YB.

Jordanowo, GA. This town was not found in BGN gazetteers under the given spelling.

Jormannsdorf, Aus.; pop. 1; 69 km NE of Graz; 47°21'/16°13'.

Josbach, Germ.; pop. 25; 94 km N of Frankfurt am Main; 50°54'/09°00'; AMG, LDS.

Josefov, Cz.; pop. 31; 107 km ENE of Praha; 50°20'/15°55'.

Josefow, Pol. EDRD, HSL2. This pre-World War I community was not found in BGN gazetteers.

Josenii Bargaului, *see* Josenii Birgaului.

Josenii Birgaului, Rom. (Gyergyoalfalu, Josenii Bargaului); pop. 21; 94 km NE of Cluj; 47°13'/24°41'.

Joslowitz, *see* Jaroslavice.

Josvafo, Hung.; pop. 10; 50 km NNW of Miskolc; 48°29'/20°34'.

Josvainiai, Lith. (Jasvainiai, Yasvainiai, Yasven, Yosvain, Yosven); pop. 341; 45 km N of Kaunas; 55°15'/23°50'; HSL, JGFF, SF, YL.

Jovsa, Cz.; pop. 59; 62 km ENE of Kosice; 48°50'/22°06'.

Jozefin, *see* Yuzefin.

Jozefka, GUM4. This town was not found in BGN gazetteers under the given spelling.

Jozefow, Pol. (Yozefov, Yuzefov, Yuzefov Ardinatzki, Yuzefuv); pop. 1,050; 82 km N of Przemysl; 50°28'/23°02'; AMG, COH, HSL, LDS, PHP1, PHP4, POCEM, SF, YB.

Jozefow (Nad Wisla), Pol. (Yozifif Veisil); pop. 736; 62 km W of Lublin; 51°25'/21°39'; COH, GA, GUM3, GUM5, JGFF, LDS, POCEM, SF.

Jozefow (near Bedzin), Pol.; pop. 6; 56 km S of Czestochowa; 50°19'/19°10'.

Jozefow (near Brzeziny), Pol.; pop. 15; 32 km ENE of Lodz; 51°49'/19°53'.

Jozefow (near Konskie), Pol.; pop. 17; 94 km ESE of Lodz; 51°15'/20°30'.

Jozefow (near Krasnystaw), Pol.; pop. 8; 45 km ESE of Lublin; 51°04'/23°11'.

Jozefow (near Lublin), Pol.; pop. 2; 13 km WNW of Lublin; 51°19'/22°24'.

Jozefow (near Otwock), Pol.; 26 km ESE of Warszawa; 52°09'/21°20'; HSL, SF.

Jozefow (near Swidry Male), Pol.; pop. 14; 26 km WSW of Warszawa; 52°12'/20°42'.

Jozefow (near Wielun), Pol.; pop. 5; 56 km WNW of Czestochowa; 51°09'/18°34'.

Jozefowka, *see* Yuzefuvka.

Jozefow Stary (Kielce), Pol.; pop. 12; 75 km NE of Czestochowa; 51°11'/19°58'; GUM3.

Jozefow Stary (Warszawa), Pol.; pop. 3; 38 km E of Lodz; 51°41'/19°58'.

Jozsa, Hung. (Felsojozsa); pop. 31; 75 km ESE of Miskolc; 47°36'/21°34'; HSL, LDS.

Juchen, Germ.; pop. 50; 38 km WNW of Koln; 51°06'/06°30'; GED.

Juchnowicze, *see* Yukhnovichi.

Juchowitschi, *see* Yukhovichi.

Jucica Veche, Rom.; pop. 325; This town was not found in BGN gazetteers under the given spelling.

Jucu de Jos, Rom. (Alsozsuk, Jucul de Jos); 19 km NE of Cluj; 46°52'/23°48'; HSL.

Jucul de Jos, *see* Jucu de Jos.

Judenau, Aus.; pop. 1; 32 km WNW of Wien; 48°17'/16°00'.

Judenbach, Germ.; 107 km N of Nurnberg; 50°24'/11°13'; EJ.

Judenburg, Aus. (Idunum); pop. 50; 62 km W of Graz; 47°10'/14°40'; EJ, GUM5, GUM6.

Judendorf, Aus.; 13 km WNW of Graz; 47°07'/15°21'; EJ.

Judovka, Lat.; 6 km SE of Daugavpils; 55°51'/26°34'; PHLE.

Juelich, *see* Julich.

Jueterbog, *see* Juterbog.

Jugenheim, Germ.; 45 km S of Frankfurt am Main; 49°45'/08°38'; GUM5.

Jugesheim, Germ.; pop. 1; 19 km ESE of Frankfurt am Main; 50°02'/08°53'.

Jugoszow, Pol.; pop. 5; 101 km SW of Lublin; 50°41'/21°32'.

Jugovici, Yug. (Jugowice); 234 km SSW of Beograd; 43°16'/18°28'; PHP3.

Jugowice, *see* Jugovici.

Julich, Germ. (Juelich); pop. 135; 45 km WSW of Koln; 50°56'/06°22'; EDRD, EJ, GED, HSL, LDS.

Juliszew, Pol.; pop. 66; 62 km NNE of Lodz; 52°15'/19°55'. This town was located on an interwar map of Poland but does not appear in contemporary gazetteers. Map coordinates are approximate.

Juljopol, *see* Liliopol.

Jumprava, Lat. (Jumpravas, Jungfernhof); pop. 5; 62 km NNE of Riga; 57°29'/24°36'.

Jumpravas, *see* Jumprava.

Jumpravmuiza, Lat.; 69 km S of Riga; 56°25'/24°07'; GUM3,

GUM4, PHLE.

Jumurda, Lat.; pop. 1; 240 km NNE of Riga; 58°56'/25°44'.

Jungbunzlau, *see* Mlada Boleslav.

Jungfernhof, *see* Jumprava.

Junikowo, Pol. PHP1. This town was not found in BGN gazetteers under the given spelling.

Juodupis, Lith.; pop. 194; 114 km WSW of Siauliai; 55°37'/21°33'.

Juraciszki, *see* Yuratishki.

Jurbarkas, Lith. (Jurborg, Jurburg, Yorburg, Yorvorig, Yurbarkas, Yurburg); pop. 1,887; 75 km W of Kaunas; 55°04'/22°46'; COH, EJ, GUM3, GUM5, HSL, JGFF, LDL, SF, WS, YL.

Jurborg, *see* Jurbarkas.

Jurburg, *see* Jurbarkas.

Jurca, Rom. (Gyurkapataka); pop. 3; 45 km N of Cluj; 47°08'/23°33'.

Jurcauti, GUM4. This town was not found in BGN gazetteers under the given spelling.

Jure, Lith.; 32 km SW of Kaunas; 54°46'/23°29'; JGFF.

Jureczkowa, Pol.; pop. 43; 69 km S of Przemysl; 49°15'/22°35'. This town was located on an interwar map of Poland but does not appear in contemporary gazetteers. Map coordinates are approximate.

Juriew, *see* Tartu.

Jurjew, *see* Tartu.

Jurkalne, Lat. (Jurkalnes); pop. 11; 163 km W of Riga; 57°00'/21°23'.

Jurkalnes, *see* Jurkalne.

Jurki, Pol.; pop. 21; 45 km N of Lublin; 51°35'/22°45'. This town was located on an interwar map of Poland but does not appear in contemporary gazetteers. Map coordinates are approximate.

Jurkow, Pol. AMG, HSL. This pre-World War I community was not found in BGN gazetteers.

Jurmala, Lat.; pop. 279; 32 km W of Riga; 56°58'/23°34'.

Jurovice, *see* Yurevichi.

Jurydyka, Ukr.; pop. 41; 107 km SSW of Rovno; 49°45'/25°35'; HSL. This town was located on an interwar map of Poland but does not appear in contemporary gazetteers. Map coordinates are approximate.

Justingrad, *see* Sokolovka.

Juszkiewicze, *see* Yushkevichi.

Jut, *see* Siojut.

Jutas, Hung.; 101 km SW of Budapest; 47°07'/17°54'; GUM5.

Juterbog, Germ. (Jueterbog); pop. 12; 62 km S of Berlin; 51°59'/13°05'; GUM4.

Jutroschin, *see* Jutrosin.

Jutrosin, Pol. (Jutroschin); pop. 29; 69 km N of Wroclaw; 51°39'/17°10'; HSL.

Juzefpol, *see* Iosipovka.

Juzintai, Lith. (Yozint); pop. 55; 126 km N of Vilnius; 55°47'/25°41'; YL.

Juzmin, *see* Kozmin.

Juzowka, *see* Donetsk.

Kaal, HSL. This pre-World War I community was not found in BGN gazetteers.

Kaba, Hung.; pop. 314; 94 km SSE of Miskolc; 47°21'/21°17'; HSL, LDL, LDS, PHH.

Kabeliai, Lith. (Kobiele); pop. 14; 107 km SSW of Vilnius; 53°57'/24°18'.

Kaberneeme, Est.; 32 km NE of Tallinn; 59°31'/25°16'; PHLE.

Kabeshti, Ukr. (Cabesti); pop. 120; 19 km WSW of Chernovtsy; 48°16'/25°39'; PHR2.

Kabold, *see* Kobersdorf.

Kac, Yug.; pop. 25; 69 km NW of Beograd; 45°18'/19°58'.

Kachanovka, Ukr. (Kaczanowka); pop. 22; 133 km N of Chernovtsy; 49°28'/26°07'.

Kachin, Ukr. (Kaczyn); pop. 6; 139 km WNW of Rovno; 51°29'/24°48'.

Kachovka, *see* Kakhovka.

Kacice, Pol.; pop. 31; 50 km N of Warszawa; 52°40'/21°05'.

Kaclowa, Pol.; pop. 17; 94 km ESE of Krakow; 49°36'/20°58'.

Kacorlak, Hung.; pop. 3; 26 km N of Nagykanizsa; 46°34'/16°58'.

Kacs, Hung.; pop. 6; 19 km SSW of Miskolc; 47°57'/20°37'.

Kacwin, Pol.; pop. 10; 88 km SSE of Krakow; 49°22'/20°18'.

Kaczanowka, *see* Kachanovka.

Kaczka, Pol.; pop. 42; 75 km NNE of Warszawa; 52°51'/21°35'.

Kaczko, *see* Citcau.

Kaczonowy, Pol. (Kaczorowy); pop. 36; 94 km WSW of Przemysl; 49°45'/21°26'.

Kaczorowy, *see* Kaczonowy.

Kaczy Dol, Pol.; pop. 47; Described in the *Black Book* as being in the Warszawa region of Poland, this town was not found in BGN gazetteers.

Kaczyn, *see* Kachin.

Kadan, Cz.; pop. 113; 88 km WNW of Praha; 50°23'/13°16'; COH, EJ, HSL.

Kadar, *see* Kitanchevo.

Kadarkut, Hung.; pop. 69; 56 km ESE of Nagykanizsa; 46°14'/17°38'; GUM4, LDS, PHH.

Kadarta, Hung.; pop. 1; 94 km SW of Budapest; 47°07'/17°57'.

Kadcza, Pol.; pop. 21; 88 km SE of Krakow; 49°25'/20°35'. This town was located on an interwar map of Poland but does not appear in contemporary gazetteers. Map coordinates are approximate.

Kadino, Yug.; 13 km ESE of Skopje; 41°58'/21°37'; LDL.

Kadlburg, HSL. This pre-World War I community was not found in BGN gazetteers.

Kadlubek, Pol.; pop. 41; 82 km S of Warszawa; 51°36'/21°05'.

Kadlubiska (Lublin), Pol.; pop. 23; 94 km ESE of Lublin; 50°40'/23°31'.

Kadlubiska (Lwow), Pol.; pop. 23; 75 km NNE of Przemysl; 50°22'/23°21'.

Kadobeste, *see* Kadobovtsy.

Kadobna, Ukr.; pop. 14; 94 km SSE of Lvov; 49°02'/24°13'.

Kadobovtsy, Ukr. (Cadobesti, Kadobeste); pop. 92; 38 km NNW of Chernovtsy; 48°35'/25°46'; GUM4.

Kadysz, Pol. PHP4. This town was not found in BGN gazetteers under the given spelling.

Kadzhidla, *see* Kadzidlo.

Kadzice, Pol.; pop. 5; 38 km NE of Krakow; 50°15'/20°22'.

Kadzidlo, Pol. (Kadzhidla); pop. 133; 114 km W of Bialystok; 53°14'/21°28'; AMG, PHP4, SF, YB.

Kadzielnia, GUM4. This town was not found in BGN gazetteers under the given spelling.

Kadziolki, Pol.; pop. 1; 107 km ENE of Krakow; 50°13'/21°23'.

Kaerpen B Bergheim, GUM5. This town was not found in BGN gazetteers under the given spelling.

Kaffa, *see* Feodosiya.

Kaganovich, *see* Polesskoye.

Kagarlyk, Ukr. (Karlik); 69 km SSE of Kiyev; 49°51'/30°50'; LDL, SF.

Kagerava, *see* Libavske Udoli.

Kagul, Mold. (Cahul, Kahul); pop. 803; 133 km S of Kishinev; 45°54'/28°11'.

Kahme, *see* Kamionna.

Kahul, *see* Kagul.

Kaidan, *see* Kedainiai.

Kaidanovo, *see* Dzerzhinsk.

Kainbach, Aus.; pop. 7; 13 km NE of Graz; 47°05'/15°31'.

Kainreith, Aus.; pop. 3; 75 km NW of Wien; 48°43'/15°43'.

Kairlindach, Germ.; 26 km NW of Nurnberg; 49°38'/10°51'; JGFF, PHGB.

Kaiserau, *see* Kolonie Kaiserau.

Kaiserlautern, *see* Kaiserslautern.

Kaisersdorf, Aus.; pop. 45; 82 km S of Wien; 47°32'/16°24'.

Kaisersesch, Germ.; pop. 50; 88 km SSE of Koln; 50°14'/07°09'.

Kaiserslautern, Germ. (Kaiserlautern); pop. 756; 101 km SSW of Frankfurt am Main; 49°27'/07°45'; AMG, EJ, GED, GUM3, GUM5, HSL, JGFF, LDS.

Kazimierz Dolny, Poland: Street crowd follows a klezmer band that has just arrived in town.

Kaiserwald, *see* Mezaparks.

Kaishiadorys, *see* Kaisiadorys.

Kaisiadoris, *see* Kaisiadorys.

Kaisiadorys, Lith. (Kaishiadorys, Kaisiadoris, Kashedar, Koisedary, Koschedary, Koshedar, Koshedary, Koshidar, Koszedary); pop. 596; 38 km E of Kaunas; 54°52'/24°27'; GUM3, GUM4, GUM5, GUM6, HSL, HSL2, JGFF, SF, YL.

Kajar, Hung.; pop. 15; 107 km WSW of Budapest; 47°29'/17°38'.

Kajaszo, Hung. (Kajaszoszentpeter); pop. 27; 38 km SW of Budapest; 47°19'/18°44'; LDS.

Kajaszoszentpeter, *see* Kajaszo.

Kajdacs, Hung. (Sanc); pop. 17; 107 km S of Budapest; 46°34'/18°38'; HSL.

Kajetanka, Pol.; pop. 2; 114 km S of Bialystok; 52°10'/23°17'.

Kajna, *see* Slovensky Kajna.

Kak, *see* Mesztegnyo.

Kakad, *see* Kokad.

Kakasd, Hung.; pop. 10; 120 km W of Szeged; 46°21'/18°36'.

Kakawa, Pol.; pop. 20; 94 km WSW of Lodz; 51°37'/18°08'.

Kakhovka, Ukr. (Kachovka); pop. 2,441; 208 km ENE of Odessa; 46°49'/33°29'; GUM4, HSL, HSL2, JGFF, LDL, SF.

Kakics, Hung.; pop. 4; 88 km ESE of Nagykanizsa; 45°54'/17°52'.

Kakolewnica, Pol. (Kakolownica); pop. 11; 82 km N of Lublin; 51°54'/22°42'.

Kakolowka, Pol.; pop. 29; 50 km W of Przemysl; 49°51'/22°05'.

Kakolownica, *see* Kakolewnica.

Kakova, *see* Cacova.

Kakucs, Hung. (Kakush); pop. 23; 38 km SE of Budapest; 47°15'/19°22'; AMG.

Kakush, *see* Kakucs.

Kal, Hung.; pop. 130; 56 km SSW of Miskolc; 47°44'/20°16'; PHH.

Kalacsin, *see* Kelechin.

Kaladei, *see* Kolodeje nad Luznici.

Kalagarovka, Ukr. (Kalaharowka); pop. 19; 107 km N of Chernovtsy; 49°15'/26°14'.

Kalaharowka, *see* Kalagarovka.

Kalamata, *see* Kalami.

Kalami, Greece (Kalamata); 176 km SW of Athens; 37°02'/22°07'; GUM4.

Kalaniec Litewski, Pol.; pop. 1,902; Described in the *Black Book* as being in the Polesie region of Poland, this town was not found in BGN gazetteers.

Kalaras, *see* Kalarash.

Kalarash, Mold. (Calarasi, Calarasi Sat?, Calarasi Targ, Kalaras, Tuzora); pop. 3,662; 50 km WNW of Kishinev; 47°16'/28°19'; EDRD, EJ, GUM3, GUM4, HSL, JGFF, LYV, PHR1, PHR2, SF, YB.

Kalaszyce, EGRS. This town was not found in BGN gazetteers under the given spelling.

Kalawaria, Pol. PHP4. This town was not found in BGN gazetteers under the given spelling.

Kalchevaya, Ukr. (Calceva); pop. 7; 170 km SW of Odessa; 45°44'/28°49'.

Kald, Hung.; pop. 19; 88 km N of Nagykanizsa; 47°10'/17°03'.

Kaldenkirchen, Germ.; 62 km WNW of Koln; 51°19'/06°13'; GUM5.

Kaldern, *see* Caldern.

Kaletnik, Pol.; 26 km E of Lodz; 51°43'/19°47'; PHP1.

Kaletten Bei Libau, HSL. This pre-World War I community was not found in BGN gazetteers.

Kalevi, Est. (Kalevi Liiva); 163 km SW of Tallinn; 58°21'/22°48'; PHLE.

Kalevi Liiva, *see* Kalevi.

Kalicsava, *see* Kolochava.

Kalikal, LDL. This pre-World War I community was not found in BGN gazetteers.

Kalin, *see* Kaliny.

Kalina, Cz. AMG. A number of towns share this name. It was not possible to determine from available information which one is being referenced.

Kalina Wielka, Pol.; pop. 4; 38 km NNE of Krakow; 50°23'/20°09'.

Kalinciakovo, *see* Varsany.

Kalineshty, Mold. (Calinesti); pop. 37; 120 km WNW of Kishinev; 47°34'/27°29'.

Kalinest, *see* Calinesti.

Kalinin, USSR (Tver); pop. 1,443; 157 km NW of Moskva; 56°52'/35°55'.

Kalinindorf, *see* Kalininskoye.

Kaliningrad, USSR (Koenigsberg, Konigsberg); pop. 4,049; 586 km SW of Pskov; 54°43'/20°30'; AMG, CAHJP, EJ, GUM3, HSL, HSL2, JGFF, LDL, LDS, PHP1, PHP2, PHP4, YB.

Kalininskoye, Ukr. (Bolshaly Seidemenukha, Bolshaya Seidemenukha, Kalinindorf, Sde Menucha, Sdeh Menocha); pop. 3,891; 182 km NE of Odessa; 47°07'/32°59'; EJ, SF.

Kalinka, HSL. A number of towns share this name. It was not possible to determine from available information which one is being referenced.

Kalinkovichi, Byel. (Kalinkovitch); pop. 3,102; 120 km WSW of Gomel; 52°08'/29°19'; AMG, EJ, LDL, SF.

Kalinkovitch, *see* Kalinkovichi.

Kalinovka, Ukr. (Kolenivka); pop. 1,097; 32 km N of Vinnitsa; 49°28'/28°32'; EDRD, HSL, SF.

Kalinovo, Cz.; 120 km SW of Kosice; 48°24'/19°43'; JGFF.

Kalinovshchizna, Ukr. (Kalinowszczyzna); pop. 9; 88 km NNW of Chernovtsy; 49°03'/25°41'.

Kalinow, Pol.; pop. 28; 69 km S of Przemysl; 49°13'/22°33'.

Kalinowice, *see* Kalinowiec.

Kalinowiec, Pol. (Kalinowice); pop. 51; 62 km NE of Warszawa; 52°29'/21°50'.

Kalinowka, *see* Kalinuvka.

Kalinowszczyzna, *see* Kalinovshchizna.

Kalinuvka, Ukr. (Kalinowka); pop. 37; 19 km N of Lvov; 49°57'/24°01'.

Kaliny, Ukr. (Alsokalinfalva, Kalin); pop. 250; 150 km WSW of Chernovtsy; 48°09'/23°53'; AMG, LYV, SM. This town was located on a pre-World War I map, but does not appear in contemporary gazetteers.

Kalios, *see* Kalyus.

Kalis, *see* Kalyus.

Kalisch, *see* Kalisz.

Kalish, *see* Kalush.

Kalisk, *see* Kolyshki.

Kalisko, Pol.; pop. 8; 56 km S of Lodz; 51°16'/19°25'.

Kaliste, Cz. (Kallos); 150 km W of Kosice; 48°50'/19°13'; HSL.

Kalisz, Pol. (Kalisch, Kolish); pop. 15,566; 94 km WSW of Lodz; 51°45'/18°05'; AMG, CAHJP, COH, EDRD, EJ, GA, GUM3, GUM4, GUM5, GUM6, GYLA, HSL, HSL2, ISH1, ISH2, JGFF, LDL, LDS, LYV, PHP1, PHP2, PHP3, PHP4, POCEM, SF, YB. *See also* the Ukrainian town of Kalush.

Kalisz Pomorski, Pol. (Kallies); pop. 26; 69 km SW of Gdansk; 54°03'/17°48'; LDS.

Kalius, USSR; pop. 1,192; This town was not found in BGN gazetteers under the given spelling.

Kalkar, Germ. (Calkar); pop. 65; 101 km NW of Koln; 51°44'/06°18'; GED, GUM5.

Kalksburg, Aus.; pop. 1; 13 km SW of Wien; 48°08'/16°15'.

Kall, Germ.; pop. 34; 50 km SSW of Koln; 50°33'/06°33'.

Kalladorf, Aus.; pop. 4; 56 km NNW of Wien; 48°39'/16°05'.

Kallies, *see* Kalisz Pomorski.

Kallo, Hung.; pop. 56; 45 km NE of Budapest; 47°45'/19°30'; GUM3, HSL, PHH.

Kallos, *see* Kaliste.

Kallosemjen, Hung.; pop. 112; 88 km ESE of Miskolc; 47°52'/21°56'; AMG, GUM5, HSL, LDS, PHH.

Kallwang, *see* Kalwang.

Kalmatsuy, Mold. (Calmatui); 56 km SW of Kishinev; 46°48'/28°12'; JGFF.

Kalme, Germ.; 69 km ESE of Hannover; 52°05'/10°39'; LDS.

Kalna, Pol.; pop. 23; COH. A number of towns share this name. It was not possible to determine from available information which one is being referenced.

Kalnalis, Lith. (Kalnel); 107 km W of Siauliai; 56°02'/21°33'; JGFF.

Kalne, Ukr.; pop. 30; 75 km ESE of Lvov; 49°38'/24°58'.

Kalnel, *see* Kalnalis.

Kalni, Lith. JGFF. A number of towns share this name. It was not possible to determine from available information which one is being referenced.

Kalniboloto, *see* Katerinopol.

Kalnica, Pol.; pop. 23; 69 km S of Przemysl; 49°13'/22°25'.

Kalnicki, *see* Kalnik.

Kalnik, Ukr. (Kalnicki); 176 km SSW of Lvov; 48°31'/22°36'; AMG, COH, GUM3, HSL.

Kalnikow, Pol.; pop. 30; 26 km NE of Przemysl; 49°55'/23°02'.

Kalocfa, Hung.; pop. 3; 50 km NW of Nagykanizsa; 46°45'/16°34'.

Kalocsa, Hung.; pop. 484; 94 km WNW of Szeged; 46°32'/19°00'; EDRD, GUM5, HSL, LDS, PHH.

Kalocsalaz, HSL. This pre-World War I community was not found in BGN gazetteers.

Kalov, *see* Nagykallo.

Kaloz, Hung.; pop. 40; 82 km SSW of Budapest; 46°57'/18°29'.

Kalsnava, Lat. (Kalsnavas); pop. 17; 107 km NW of Daugavpils; 56°45'/25°54'.

Kalsnavas, *see* Kalsnava.

Kaltanenai, Lith. (Koltiniani, Koltininai?); pop. 130; 75 km NNE of Vilnius; 55°16'/26°00'; SF.

Kaltenleutgeben, Aus.; pop. 14; 19 km SW of Wien; 48°07'/16°11'.

Kaltennordheim, Germ.; pop. 35; 120 km NE of Frankfurt am Main; 50°38'/10°10'.

Kaltensundheim, Germ.; pop. 5; 120 km NE of Frankfurt am Main; 50°37'/10°10'.

Kaltinenai, Lith. (Keltinan, Koltinenai, Koltyniany); pop. 130; 69 km SW of Siauliai; 55°34'/22°27'; COH, EDRD, GUM3, GUM4, GUM5, JGFF, YB, YL.

Kaltwasser, *see* Zimna Voda.

Kaluga, USSR; pop. 833; 163 km SSW of Moskva; 54°31'/36°16'; JGFF, LDL.

Kalusa, *see* Kaluza.

Kalusa Vulchovce, COH. This town was not found in BGN gazetteers under the given spelling.

Kalush, Ukr. (Kalish, Kalusz, Kalusz Nowy); pop. 3,277; 101 km SSE of Lvov; 49°01'/24°22'; AMG, CAHJP, COH, EDRD, EGRS, EJ, GUM3, GUM4, GUM5, GYLA, HSL, JGFF, LDL, LYV, PHP2, SF. *See also* the Polish town of Kalisz.

Kalushin, *see* Kaluszyn.

Kalushki, *see* Koluszki.

Kaluska Wola, *see* Wola Kaluska.

Kalusz, *see* Kalush.

Kalusz Nowy, *see* Kalush.

Kaluszyn, Pol. (Kalushin); pop. 5,033; 56 km E of Warszawa; 52°13'/21°49'; AMG, COH, EDRD, EJ, FRG, GA, GUM3, GUM4, GUM5, HSL, HSL2, JGFF, LDS, LYV, PHP1, PHP4, POCEM, SF, YB.

Kaluszyn (near Nowy Dwor Mazowiecki), Pol.; pop. 217; 26 km NNW of Warszawa; 52°27'/20°52'.

Kaluv, *see* Nagykallo.

Kaluza, Cz. (Kalusa); 56 km ENE of Kosice; 48°49'/22°00'; HSL.

Kaluze, Pol.; pop. 5; 50 km WNW of Czestochowa; 51°05'/18°39'.

Kalvaria, *see* Kalvarija.

Kalvarija, Lith. (Calvaria, Kalvaria, Kalvariya, Kalwaria, Kalwariya); pop. 1,233; 75 km SSW of Kaunas; 54°24'/23°14'; AMG, COH, EJ, GUM3, GUM4, GUM6, HSL, HSL2, ISH2, JGFF, LDL, LYV, SF, YB, YL.

Kalvariya, *see* Kalvarija.

Kalvene, Lat. (Kalvini); pop. 10; 150 km WSW of Riga; 56°37'/21°42'; PHLE.

Kalvini, *see* Kalvene.

Kalwang, Aus. (Kallwang); pop. 1; 69 km WNW of Graz; 47°25'/14°45'.

Kalwaria, *see* Kalvarija.

Kalwaria Paclawska, Pol. (Kalwarja Paclawska); pop. 3; 26 km S of Przemysl; 49°38'/22°43'.

Kalwaria Zebrzydowska, Pol. (Kalwarja Zebrzydowska); pop. 486; 32 km SSW of Krakow; 49°52'/19°41'; EGRS, GUM4, GUM5, PHP3, SF.

Kalwariya, *see* Kalvarija.

Kalwarja, Lith.; 75 km SSW of Kaunas; 54°24'/23°14'; COH, EDRD, LDL. EDRD refers to a town in the Minsk district. No such town appears in BGN near Minsk.

Kalwarja Paclawska, *see* Kalwaria Paclawska.

Kalwarja Zebrzydowska, *see* Kalwaria Zebrzydowska.

Kalwarya, *see* Zemaiciu Kalvarija.

Kaly, Pol.; pop. 28; 13 km WNW of Lodz; 51°49'/19°22'.

Kalynivka, Ukr. (Porudno); pop. 41; 50 km W of Lvov; 49°54'/23°19'.

Kalyszyce, LDL. This pre-World War I community was not found in BGN gazetteers.

Kalyus, Ukr. (Kalios, Kalis, Kolis, Kulus); 107 km NE of Chernovtsy; 48°38'/27°19'; HSL, SF.

Kamai, *see* Kamajai.

Kamajai, Lith. (Kamai, Kamje, Kemai, Komajai, Komaje); pop. 336; 133 km N of Vilnius; 55°49'/25°30'; JGFF, LDL, SF, YL.

Kamberg, *see* Camberg.

Kamberk, *see* Zlate Hory (Bohemia).

Kamczatka, Byel.; pop. 25; 214 km NW of Pinsk; 53°35'/24°05'. This town was located on an interwar map of Poland but does not appear in contemporary gazetteers. Map coordinates are approximate.

Kame, LDL. This pre-World War I community was not found in BGN gazetteers.

Kamecze, GUM3. This town was not found in BGN gazetteers under the given spelling.

Kamelishki, Byel.; 150 km WNW of Minsk; 54°51'/25°53'; COH.

Kamelowka, *see* Kamelyuvka.

Kamelyuvka, Ukr. (Kamelowka); pop. 3; 120 km N of Lvov; 50°53'/24°27'.

Kamen, Byel.; pop. 426; 82 km WSW of Vitebsk; 55°01'/28°53'; GUM4, GUM6, JGFF, PHP3, SF, YB. *See also* Kamien.

Kamen (near Rudnik), Pol.; pop. 201; 75 km NW of Przemysl; 50°20'/22°08'; CAHJP, HSL.

Kamen (Nowogrodek), Byel.; pop. 59; 56 km WSW of Minsk; 53°52'/26°39'.

Kamen (Westfalen), Germ.; pop. 78; 88 km NNE of Koln; 51°36'/07°40'; LDS.

Kamenec, HSL. A number of towns share this name. It was not possible to determine from available information which one is being referenced.

Kamenets, Byel. (Kamenets Litovsk, Kamenetz, Kamieniec Litewski, Kamyenyets Litevski, Komenitz, Komenitz D Lita); 157 km W of Pinsk; 52°24'/23°49'; COH, EDRD, GUM3, GYLA, HSL, JGFF, LDL, LYV, SF, WS, YB.

Kamenets Litovsk, *see* Kamenets.

Kamenets Podolsk, *see* Kamenets Podolskiy.

Kamenets Podolski, *see* Kamenets Podolskiy.

Kamenets Podolskiy, Ukr. (Kamenets Podolsk, Kamenets Podolski, Kamieniec Podolski, Komenitz Podolsk); pop. 12,774; 62 km NE of Chernovtsy; 48°40'/26°34'; COH, EDRD, EJ, GUM3, GUM4, GUM5, GUM6, GYLA, HSL, JGFF, LDL, LYV, PHP2, SF, YB.

Kamenetz, *see* Kamenets.

Kamenice, *see* Kamenice nad Lipou.

Kamenice nad Lipou, Cz. (Kamenice); pop. 35; 101 km SE of Praha; 49°18'/15°05'.

Kamenka, Mold. (Camenca); pop. 36; 146 km WNW of Kishinev; 47°50'/27°22'; SF.

Kamenka (near Cherkassy), Ukr.; 139 km ENE of Uman; 49°02'/32°06'; SF.

Kamenka Bugskaia, *see* Kamenka Bugskaya.

Kamenka Bugskaya, Ukr. (Kamenka Bugskaia, Kaminka, Kamionka, Kamionka Buska, Kamionka Strumilowa, Kamionka Strumiowa, Kamyonka, Kamyonka Strumilova); pop. 2,685; 38 km NNE of Lvov; 50°06'/24°21'; EDRD, EGRS, EJ, GA, GUM3, GUM4, GUM5, GUM6, HSL, JGFF, LDL, PHP2, SF, WS.

Kamenka Cherkaskyi, Ukr.; pop. 1,106; 139 km ENE of Uman; 49°02'/32°06'.

Kamenka Dneprovskaja, Ukr.; 107 km S of Dnepropetrovsk; 47°34'/34°24'; GUM5, HSL, JGFF, LDL, SF.

Kamen Kashirskiy, Ukr. (Kamien Koszyrski, Kamin Kashirski, Kamin Koshirski, Kamyen Koshirsk); pop. 617; 146 km NW of Rovno; 51°38'/24°58'; AMG, COH, EDRD, FRG, GUM3, GUM4, GUM6, HSL, JGFF, LDL, SF, YB.

Kamenki, Ukr. (Kamionka, Kamionki); pop. 103; 120 km S of Rovno; 49°33'/26°01'; AMG, COH, EDRD, GA, GUM3, GUM4, GUM5, HSL, LDS, PHP2, PHP3, SF.

Kamennaya, Ukr. (Camena); pop. 56; 13 km SSW of Chernovtsy; 48°14'/25°51'.

Kamennoye, Ukr. (Millerovo); 290 km ESE of Kharkov; 48°10'/39°10'; GUM4, GUM5.

Kamenny Brod, *see* Kamennyy Brod.

Kamennyy Brod, Ukr. (Kamenny Brod, Kameny Brod, Kammeny Brod); pop. 1,021; 114 km W of Kiyev; 50°28'/28°57'; SF, YB.

Kamennyye Budy, Ukr. (Kamienna Gora); pop. 25; 45 km NNW of Lvov; 50°12'/23°48'.

Kamenobrod, Ukr. (Kamienobrod); pop. 6; 26 km W of Lvov; 49°51'/23°38'.

Kamensk, USSR; pop. 1,413; 69 km E of Kaliningrad; 54°39'/21°33'.

Kamenskoe, *see* Dneprodzerzhinsk.

Kamenskoya, *see* Kamensk Saporoshi.

Kamenskoye, *see* Dneprodzerzhinsk.

Kamenskoye (Bessarabia), Ukr. (Taslac); pop. 51; 139 km SW of Odessa; 45°49'/29°15'; AMG.

Kamensk Saporoshi, (Kamenskoya); LDL, SF. This town was not found in BGN gazetteers under the given spelling.

Kameny Brod, *see* Kamennyy Brod.

Kamesznica, Pol.; pop. 19; 82 km SW of Krakow; 49°35'/19°04'; HSL.

Kamianna, Pol.; pop. 9; 101 km ESE of Krakow; 49°32'/20°57'.

Kamianskoc, *see* Dneprodzerzhinsk.

Kamien, AMG. A number of towns share this name. It was not possible to determine from available information which one is being referenced. *See also* Kamen. The towns with larger Jewish populations are shown below.

Kamien (near Chelm), Pol.; pop. 8; 75 km E of Lublin; 51°06'/23°36'; GA.

Kamien (near Kalisz), Pol.; pop. 33; 88 km W of Lodz; 51°50'/18°14'.

Kamien (near Wlodawa), Pol.; pop. 14; 56 km NE of Lublin; 51°32'/23°16'.

Kamienczyk, Pol.; pop. 124; 56 km NE of Warszawa; 52°36'/21°33'; PHP4.

Kamienica, Pol.; pop. 118; 69 km SW of Krakow; 49°48'/19°02'; HSL, HSL2, PHP3.

Kamienica (near Nowy Sacz), Pol.; pop. 35; 69 km SE of Krakow; 49°35'/20°21'.

Kamienica Dolna, Pol.; pop. 9; 101 km W of Przemysl; 49°55'/21°22'.

Kamienica Polska, Pol.; pop. 29; 19 km SSE of Czestochowa; 50°41'/19°09'.

Kamieniec, Pol. AMG, JGFF. A number of towns share this name. It was not possible to determine from available information which one is being referenced.

Kamieniec Litewski, *see* Kamenets.

Kamieniec Podolski, *see* Kamenets Podolskiy.

Kamien Koszyrski, *see* Kamen Kashirskiy.

Kamienna, Ukr. (Skarzhisk, Skarzisko Kamyena, Skarzysko); pop. 47; 107 km WNW of Chernovtsy; 48°45'/24°42'; JGFF.

Kamienna Gora, Pol. (Landeshut); pop. 74; 75 km SW of Wroclaw; 50°47'/16°02'; LDS. *See also* Kamennyye Budy.

Kamiennowola, Pol.; pop. 7; 45 km N of Lublin; 51°35'/22°38'.

Kamienobrod, *see* Kamenobrod.

Kamien Pomorski, Pol. (Cammin); pop. 33; 62 km N of Szczecin; 53°58'/14°47'; LDS.

Kamiensk, Pol.; pop. 856; 56 km NNE of Czestochowa; 51°13'/19°30'; CAHJP, EDRD, EJ, GUM5, GUM5, PHP1, SF, YB.

Kamienskie, *see* Dneprodzerzhinsk.

Kamiensko, Pol.; pop. 5; 26 km WSW of Czestochowa; 50°48'/18°44'.

Kamien Szlachecki, Byel.; pop. 41; 101 km WSW of Pinsk; 52°05'/24°35'. This town was located on an interwar map of Poland but does not appear in contemporary gazetteers. Map coordinates are approximate.

Kamien Wielki, Pol.; pop. 24; 82 km NE of Czestochowa; 51°05'/20°15'. This town was located on an interwar map of Poland but does not appear in contemporary gazetteers. Map coordinates are approximate.

Kamilonisi, GUM4. This town was not found in BGN gazetteers under the given spelling.

Kaminka, *see* Kamenka Bugskaya; Kamionka (Bialystok).

Kamin Kashirski, *see* Kamen Kashirskiy.

Kamin Koshirski, *see* Kamen Kashirskiy.

Kaminsk, Pol.; 94 km S of Warszawa; 51°29'/21°05'; AMG, HSL.

Kamionek, Pol.; 75 km ENE of Poznan; 52°34'/18°00'; GA.

Kamionka, *see* Kamenka Bugskaya; Kamenki.

Kamionka (Bialystok), Pol. (Kaminka); pop. 236; 19 km ESE of Bialystok; 53°05'/23°20'; EJ, GUM3, HSL, HSL2, JGFF, SF.

Kamionka (Chelm), Pol.; pop. 20; 32 km E of Lublin; 51°14'/23°03'.

Kamionka Buska, *see* Kamenka Bugskaya.

Kamionka Mala, *see* Malaya Kamenka.

Kamionka Strumilowa, *see* Kamenka Bugskaya.

Kamionka Strumiowa, *see* Kamenka Bugskaya.

Kamionka Wielka, Ukr.; pop. 58; 75 km WNW of Chernovtsy; 48°38'/25°06'.

Kamionka Wielka (near Nowy Sacz), Pol.; pop. 31; 88 km ESE of Krakow; 49°35'/20°49'; GUM4.

Kamionka Wolowska, Pol. PHP2. This town was not found in BGN gazetteers under the given spelling.

Kamionki, *see* Kamenki.

Kamionna, Pol. (Kahme); pop. 27; 50 km ESE of Krakow; 49°49'/20°23'.

Kamishacha, *see* Kamyshevka.

Kamitz, *see* Camitz.

Kamje, *see* Kamajai.

Kammeny Brod, *see* Kamennyy Brod.

Kammerich, Germ. BGN lists two possible localities with this name located at 50°50'/07°27' and 53°53'/12°46'. JGFF.

Kamocin, Pol.; pop. 4; 38 km SSE of Lodz; 51°28'/19°35'.

Kamocsa, HSL. This pre-World War I community was not found in BGN gazetteers.

Kamon, Hung.; pop. 20; 94 km NNW of Nagykanizsa; 47°15'/16°37'.

Kamoroc, HSL. This pre-World War I community was not found in BGN gazetteers.

Kampinos, Pol.; pop. 56; 38 km W of Warszawa; 52°16'/20°28'; GUM4, GUM5.

Kamskoye, HSL. This pre-World War I community was not found in BGN gazetteers.

Kamyen Koshirsk, *see* Kamen Kashirskiy.

Kamyenyets Litevski, *see* Kamenets.

Kamyk, Pol.; pop. 345; 19 km NW of Czestochowa; 50°55'/19°02'; CAHJP, JGFF.

Kamyonka, *see* Kamenka Bugskaya.

Kamyonka Strumilova, *see* Kamenka Bugskaya.

Kamysevacha, *see* Kamyshevka.

Kamyshevka, Ukr. (Hagi Curda, Kamishacha, Kamysevacha); pop. 4; 163 km SW of Odessa; 45°31'/29°08'; SF.

Kanczuga, Pol. (Kantchika, Kontchuga); pop. 967; 32 km WNW of Przemysl; 49°59'/22°25'; AMG, COH, EGRS, GUM3, GUM5, HSL, HSL2, JGFF, LDL, PHP2, PHP3, SF.

Kanda, Hung.; 114 km WSW of Szeged; 46°02'/18°44'; HSL.

Kandau, *see* Kandava.

Kandava, Lat. (Kandau, Kandavas, Kandoi); pop. 67; 82 km W of Riga; 57°02'/22°46'; HSL, PHLE, SF.

Kandavas, *see* Kandava.

Kandoi, *see* Kandava.

Kanev, Ukr. (Kaniow); pop. 1,395; 101 km SE of Kiyev; 49°45'/31°28'; EJ, HSL, HSL2, LDL, SF.

Kanice Stare, Pol.; pop. 15; 82 km E of Czestochowa; 50°45'/20°13'.

Kanie, Pol.; 38 km E of Lublin; 51°09'/23°07'; GUM4.

Kaniow, *see* Kanev.

Kaniowka, GUM3. This town was not found in BGN gazetteers under the given spelling.

Kanitz, *see* Dolni Kounice.

Kaniya, Mold. (Cania); pop. 22; 88 km SSW of Kishinev; 46°17'/28°14'.

Kanjiza, Yug. (Stara Kanjiza); pop. 223; 146 km NNW of Beograd; 46°04'/20°03'; HSL, PHY.

Kano, Hung.; pop. 5; 45 km NNW of Miskolc; 48°26'/20°36'; HSL.

Kanonichi, Ukr. (Kanonicze); pop. 32; 94 km N of Rovno; 51°26'/26°13'.

Kanonicze, *see* Kanonichi.

Kansk, *see* Konskie.

Kantankusenka, (Kontikoziva); SF. This town was not found in BGN gazetteers under the given spelling.

Kantchika, *see* Kanczuga.

Kanth, *see* Katy Wroclawskie.

Kantorjanosi, Hung.; pop. 213; 101 km E of Miskolc; 47°56'/22°09'; LDS, PHH.

Kany, Hung.; pop. 2; 56 km N of Miskolc; 48°31'/21°01'; HSL.

Kanya, Hung.; pop. 4; 88 km NE of Nagykanizsa; 46°42'/18°04'; HSL.

Kanyahaza, *see* Calinesti I.

Kanyar, Hung.; 75 km S of Miskolc; 47°29'/20°29'; JGFF, LDS.

Kanyavar, Hung.; pop. 2; 32 km WNW of Nagykanizsa; 46°34'/16°41'.

Kapani, COH, HSL. This pre-World War I community was not found in BGN gazetteers.

Kapashne, *see* Kopasnovo.

Kapciamiestis, Lith. (Koptchevo, Koptsiva); pop. 187; 107 km S of Kaunas; 54°00'/23°39'; HSL, JGFF, LDL, SF, YL.

Kapellen, Germ.; pop. 2; 82 km NW of Koln; 51°34'/06°22'; GED.

Kapelln, Aus.; pop. 1; 45 km W of Wien; 48°15'/15°45'.

Kaperowce, Pol.; pop. 98; Described in the *Black Book* as being in the Tarnopol region of Poland, this town was not found in BGN gazetteers.

Kapfenberg, Aus.; pop. 7; 50 km NNW of Graz; 47°26'/15°18'.

Kapi, Est.; 126 km SW of Tallinn; 58°38'/23°14'; HSL.

Kapiel, Pol.; 38 km ENE of Poznan; 52°26'/17°31'; CAHJP.

Kapini, Lat. (Kapinu); pop. 95; 45 km NE of Daugavpils; 56°08'/27°06'.

Kapinu, *see* Kapini.

Kapisova, Cz.; pop. 57; 75 km N of Kosice; 49°20'/21°36'; HSL.

Kaplanoviche, Byel. (Kaplanowicze); pop. 4; 107 km N of Pinsk; 53°00'/26°40'.

Kaplanowicze, *see* Kaplanoviche.

Kaplany, Mold. (Caplani); pop. 43; 107 km ESE of Kishinev; 46°23'/29°52'.

Kaplava, Lat. (Kaplavas); pop. 28; 32 km E of Daugavpils; 55°52'/27°00'; PHLE.

Kaplavas, *see* Kaplava.

Kaplica, Pol.; pop. 2; 38 km SW of Gdansk; 54°14'/18°11'.

Kaplice, Cz.; pop. 25; 157 km S of Praha; 48°44'/14°29'.

Kaplonosy, Pol. (Koplancy, Koplanus); pop. 25; 69 km NE of Lublin; 51°36'/23°21'; SF.

Kapnikbanya, *see* Cavnic.

Kapolcs, Hung.; pop. 21; 75 km NNE of Nagykanizsa; 46°57'/17°37'; LDS.

Kapoli, *see* Kopyl.

Kapolia, *see* Kopyl.

Kapolna, Hung.; 56 km SW of Miskolc; 47°46'/20°15'; HSL.

Kapolnasnyek, Hung.; pop. 100; 45 km SW of Budapest; 47°14'/18°41'; LDS, PHH.

Kapolnokhonostor, *see* Copalnic Manastur.

Kapolnokmonostor, *see* Copalnic Manastur.

Kapoly, Hung.; pop. 1; 82 km NE of Nagykanizsa; 46°44'/17°58'.

Kaposfo, Hung. (Szomajom); pop. 7; 50 km E of Nagykanizsa; 46°22'/17°40'.

Kaposfured, Hung.; pop. 5; 56 km E of Nagykanizsa; 46°25'/17°47'.

Kaposkeresztur, Hung.; pop. 5; 75 km E of Nagykanizsa; 46°20'/17°58'.

Kaposmero, Hung.; pop. 26; 56 km E of Nagykanizsa; 46°22'/17°43'; AMG, LDS.

Kapospula, Hung.; pop. 4; 88 km E of Nagykanizsa; 46°23'/18°06'.

Kaposszekcso, Hung.; pop. 3; 88 km E of Nagykanizsa; 46°20'/18°08'.

Kaposszentbenedek, Hung.; pop. 3; 56 km E of Nagykanizsa; 46°20'/17°42'.

Kaposszerdahely, Hung.; pop. 3; 62 km E of Nagykanizsa; 46°19'/17°45'.

Kaposujlak, Hung.; pop. 4; 62 km E of Nagykanizsa; 46°22'/17°44'.

Kaposvar, Hung.; pop. 3,055; 62 km E of Nagykanizsa; 46°22'/17°48'; AMG, EDRD, EJ, GUM4, GUM5, GUM6, HSL, LDS, PHH.

Kappel, Germ.; 94 km WSW of Frankfurt am Main; 50°00'/07°22'; PHGBW.

Kapreschty, *see* Kapreshty.

Kapresht, *see* Kapreshty.

Kapreshti, *see* Kapreshty.

Kapreshty, Mold. (Capresti, Capresti Colonie, Kapreschty, Kapresht, Kapreshti); pop. 1,815; 88 km NNW of Kishinev; 47°45'/28°28'; COH, LDL, PHR2, SF, YB.

Kaproncza, *see* Koprivnica.

Kapsukas, *see* Marijampole.

Kaptalanfa, Hung.; pop. 11; 75 km N of Nagykanizsa; 47°04'/17°21'.

Kaptalantoti, Hung.; pop. 12; 62 km NNE of Nagykanizsa; 46°51'/17°31'.

Kapulovka, Ukr. (Kopylovka); 114 km SSW of Dnepropetrovsk; 47°33'/34°14'; JGFF.

Kapulye, *see* Kopyl.

Kapusany, *see* Velke Kapusany.

Kapust, *see* Kopys.

Kapustyany, Ukr. (Capustani, Capustiani); 88 km WSW of Uman; 48°32'/29°02'; GUM4, PHR1.

Kaputh, *see* Caputh.

Kapuvar, Hung.; pop. 428; 139 km N of Nagykanizsa; 47°36'/17°02'; AMG, HSL, JGFF, LDS, PHH.

Karabetovka, Mold. (Carabeteni); pop. 3; 69 km S of Kishinev; 46°24'/28°55'.

Karachev, USSR; pop. 522; 45 km ESE of Bryansk; 53°07'/34°59'.

Karachinuv, Ukr. (Karaczynow); pop. 44; 13 km WNW of Lvov; 49°52'/23°50'.

Karack Maly, Byel.; pop. 21; 82 km NNE of Pinsk; 52°45'/26°35'. This town was located on an interwar map of Poland but does not appear in contemporary gazetteers. Map coordinates are approximate.

Karacsond, Hung.; 69 km SW of Miskolc; 47°44'/20°02'; HSL.

Karacson Falva, *see* Craciunesti.

Karacsonfalva, *see* Craciunel.

Karaczynow, *see* Karachinuv.

Karad, Hung.; pop. 83; 75 km NE of Nagykanizsa; 46°41'/17°51'; HSL, LDS, PHH.

Karagasany, Mold. (Cara Hasan); pop. 11; 94 km ESE of Kishinev; 46°28'/29°49'.

Karait, GUM4. This town was not found in BGN gazetteers under the given spelling.

Karajewicze, Ukr.; pop. 20; 26 km SSW of Rovno; 50°25'/26°05'. This town was located on an interwar map of Poland but does not appear in contemporary gazetteers. Map coordinates are approximate.

Karakushany, Mold. (Caracuseni, Karakushen); pop. 70; 189 km NW of Kishinev; 48°16'/27°05'.

Karakushen, *see* Karakushany.

Karakuy, Mold. (Caracui); pop. 12; 38 km SSW of Kishinev; 46°42'/28°33'.

Karalnnstadt, *see* Carei.

Karanac, Yug.; 176 km WNW of Beograd; 45°45'/18°41'; GUM4.

Karancsalja, Hung.; pop. 7; 82 km W of Miskolc; 48°08'/19°45'.

Karancsbereny, Hung.; pop. 4; 82 km W of Miskolc; 48°11'/19°45'.

Karancskeszi, Hung.; 82 km NNE of Budapest; 48°10'/19°42'; HSL.

Karancslapujto, Hung. (Bocsarlapujto); pop. 14; 82 km W of Miskolc; 48°09'/19°44'.

Karancssag, Hung.; pop. 15; 82 km NNE of Budapest; 48°07'/19°40'.

Karapchiv, Ukr. (Carapciu pe Siret, Kharapchiu pe Siret); pop. 61; 32 km SSE of Chernovtsy; 48°06'/26°01'.

Karapchu, Ukr.; 32 km S of Chernovtsy; 48°05'/25°49'; JGFF.

Karasin, Ukr.; pop. 37; 107 km NNE of Rovno; 51°29'/26°51'.

Karassu Basar, *see* Belogorsk.

Karasu Bazar, *see* Belogorsk.

Karasubazar, *see* Belogorsk.

Karasz, Hung.; 107 km E of Nagykanizsa; 46°16'/18°19'; HSL, HSL2, LDS.

Karasznokvajda, Hung.; pop. 21; This town was not found in BGN gazetteers under the given spelling.

Karatfold, Hung.; pop. 5; 62 km NNW of Nagykanizsa; 46°58'/16°45'.

Karavukovo, Yug.; pop. 16; 126 km WNW of Beograd; 45°30'/19°12'.

Karb, Pol.; 50 km S of Czestochowa; 50°21'/18°52'; HSL.

Karbach, Germ.; pop. 36; 75 km ESE of Frankfurt am Main; 49°52'/09°38'; GUM5, JGFF, PHGB.

Karbuna, Mold. (Carbuna); pop. 20; 38 km SSE of Kishinev; 46°43'/28°57'.

Karcag, Hung.; pop. 910; 88 km S of Miskolc; 47°19'/20°56'; AMG, COH, GUM5, HSL, LDL, LDS, PHH, YB.

Karcsa, Hung.; pop. 48; 82 km NE of Miskolc; 48°19'/21°48'; HSL.

Karcsava, *see* Krcava.

Karczemka, Pol.; 120 km S of Gdansk; 53°17'/18°06'; PHP1.

Karczew, Pol. (Kartchev, Kartshev); pop. 836; 26 km ESE of Warszawa; 52°05'/21°15'; COH, EDRD, FRG, GA, GUM3, GUM5, GUM6, HSL, LDL, LDS, PHP4, POCEM, SF, YB.

Karczmiska, Pol.; pop. 24; 45 km WSW of Lublin; 51°15'/21°59'; GA.

Karczowice, Pol.; pop. 30; 50 km N of Krakow; 50°30'/19°58'.

Kardasova Recice, Cz.; pop. 22; 107 km SSE of Praha; 49°12'/14°53'.

Karditsa, Greece; pop. 49; 94 km ESE of Ioannina; 39°22'/21°55'.

Karelic, *see* Korelichi.

Karelits, *see* Korelichi.

Karez, Cz.; pop. 6; 56 km SW of Praha; 49°49'/13°47'.

Karge, *see* Kargowa.

Kargowa, Pol. (Karge, Kargowa Zielona, Unruhstadt, Unrukstadt); pop. 22; 88 km SW of Poznan; 52°04'/15°51'; HSL, HSL2, JGFF, LDS.

Kargowa Zielona, *see* Kargowa.

Karitchin, *see* Korycin.

Kariv, *see* Kurow.

Karkaziskes, Lith.; 45 km NNE of Vilnius; 54°58'/25°44'; JGFF.

Karla Marksa, USSR; pop. 28; 1600 km S of Kursk; 37°12'/36°58'.

Karlburg, *see* Rusovce.

Karlich, Germ.; 75 km SE of Koln; 50°23'/07°29'; GED.

Karlik, *see* Kagarlyk.

Karlikow, Pol.; pop. 11; 62 km SW of Przemysl; 49°27'/22°04'; HSL.

Karlin, Byel. (Karlin Pinsk); 6 km E of Pinsk; 52°07'/26°08'; CAHJP, COH, EJ, HSL, LDL.

Karlino, Pol. (Korlin); pop. 18; 107 km NE of Szczecin; 54°02'/15°52'; HSL, JGFF.

Karlin Pinsk, *see* Karlin.

Karl-Marx-Stadt, Germ. (Chemnitz); pop. 2,796; 69 km SE of Leipzig; 50°50'/12°55'; AMG, EJ, GUM3, GUM4, GUM5, HSL, JGFF.

Karlovac, Yug. (Karlstadt); pop. 347; 45 km SSW of Zagreb; 45°29'/15°33'; HSL, PHY.

Karlovka, Ukr. (Carlovca); 101 km SW of Kharkov; 49°27'/35°08'; GUM4, PHR1.

Karlovy Vary, Cz. (Carlsbad, Karlsbad, Karlzbad); pop. 2,115; 114 km W of Praha; 50°13'/12°54'; AMG, EJ, GUM3, GUM5, GUM6, HSL, HSL2, JGFF.

Karlow, *see* Karluv.

Karlowice, Pol. PHP2. This town was not found in BGN gazetteers under the given spelling.

Karlsbad, *see* Karlovy Vary.

Karlsburg, Germ.; 94 km E of Rostock; 53°58'/13°37'; HSL, HSL2. *See also* Alba Iulia.

Karlsdorf, HSL. A number of towns share this name. It was not possible to determine from available information which one is being referenced.

Karlshafen, Germ. (Helmarshausen); pop. 10; 88 km S of Hannover; 51°38'/09°27'; GED, LDS.

Karlsrode, *see* Naberezhnoye.

Karlsruhe, Germ.; pop. 3,386; 62 km WNW of Stuttgart; 49°01'/08°24'; AMG, CAHJP, EJ, GED, GUM3, GUM4, HSL, HSL2, JGFF, LDL, LDS, PHGBW.

Karlstadt, Germ.; 75 km E of Frankfurt am Main; 49°57'/09°46'; GUM5, PHGB. *See also* Karlovac.

Karlstein, Aus.; 101 km NW of Wien; 48°52'/15°24'; HSL.

Karluv, Ukr. (Karlow); pop. 52; 38 km WNW of Chernovtsy; 48°27'/25°28'.

Karlzbad, *see* Karlovy Vary.

Karmacs, Hung.; pop. 14; 50 km N of Nagykanizsa; 46°50'/17°11'; GUM3, HSL.

Karmanowice, Pol.; pop. 1; 32 km WNW of Lublin; 51°21'/22°07'.

Karnich, GUM4. This town was not found in BGN gazetteers under the given spelling.

Karniewo, Pol.; pop. 29; 69 km N of Warszawa; 52°50'/20°59'; GUM4, HSL, JGFF, PHP4.

Karniow, Pol.; 19 km NE of Krakow; 50°08'/20°10'; PHP3.

Karniszewice, Pol.; pop. 28; 13 km SW of Lodz; 51°40'/19°20'.

Karnobat, *see* Polyanovgrad.

Karnozia, Pol. PHP4. This town was not found in BGN gazetteers under the given spelling.

Karolin, Pol.; pop. 26 km NE of Lublin; 51°20'/22°50'; GA, HSL.

Karolinka, Byel.; 120 km WNW of Minsk; 54°25'/25°55'; GUM3. This town was located on an interwar map of Poland but does not appear in contemporary gazetteers. Map coordinates are approximate.

Karolinow Stary, Pol.; pop. 29; 56 km SW of Warszawa; 51°58'/20°19'.

Karolowka, *see* Karolyuvka.

Karolyuvka, Ukr. (Karolowka); 62 km NNW of Chernovtsy; 48°49'/25°43'; GUM3.

Karos, Hung.; pop. 7; 75 km NE of Miskolc; 48°20'/21°45'; HSL.

Karow, *see* Karuv.

Karpach, Mold. (Corpaci); pop. 66; 163 km WNW of Kishinev; 47°59'/27°08'.

Karpathy, *possibly* Karpety.

Karpeshty, (Carpesti); pop. 24; Described in the *Black Book* as being in the Bessarabia region of Romania, this town was not found in BGN gazetteers.

Karpety, Ukr. (Karpathy?); 150 km WSW of Kharkov; 49°57'/34°06'; HSL.

Karpfen, *see* Krupina.

Karpilovka, (Karpilowka); *See also* Oktyabrskiy.

Karpilovka (near Kisorichi), Ukr.; pop. 92; 88 km NE of Rovno; 51°09'/27°12'.

Karpilovka (near Sarny), Ukr.; pop. 68; 94 km N of Rovno; 51°25'/26°42'.

Karpilowka, *see* Karpilovka.

Karpineny, Mold. (Carpineni); pop. 271; 45 km SW of Kishinev; 46°46'/28°22'.

Karpovichi, Byel. (Karpowicze); 50 km NNW of Minsk; 54°17'/27°20'; HSL.

Karpowicze, *see* Karpovichi.

Karsakiskis, Lith.; 82 km E of Siauliai; 55°48'/24°36'; JGFF.

Karsava, Lat. (Karsavas, Karsavka, Korshovka, Korsove, Korsovka, Korsovke, Korsowka); pop. 52; 126 km NNE of Daugavpils; 56°47'/27°40'; LDL, PHLE, SF.

Karsavas, *see* Karsava.

Karsavka, *see* Karsava.

Karsfeld Allach, GUM4. This town was not found in BGN gazetteers under the given spelling.

Karsin, Pol.; pop. 3; 62 km SW of Gdansk; 53°55'/17°56'.

Karsy, Pol.; pop. 54; 88 km NE of Krakow; 50°23'/21°04'; GUM5.

Kartchev, *see* Karczew.

Kartchin, *see* Korycin.

Kartena, Lith.; pop. 35; 114 km WSW of Siauliai; 55°55'/21°28'.

Kartoflyanka, *see* Novyye Sochi.

Kartoz Brezah, *see* Bereza.

Kartshev, *see* Karczew.

Kartusskaya Bereza, *see* Bereza.

Kartuz Bereze, *see* Bereza.

Kartuzy, Pol.; pop. 35; 32 km WSW of Gdansk; 54°20'/18°12'; AMG, GUM3, LDS.

Karuv, Ukr. (Karow); 62 km NNW of Lvov; 50°21'/23°48'; EGRS.

Karvina, Cz. (Freistadt, Frystat); pop. 1,155; 157 km NE of Brno; 49°52'/18°33'; EJ, HSL, PHP3.

Karvinna, *see* Doly.

Karwina, *see* Doly.

Karwodrza, Pol.; pop. 11; 88 km E of Krakow; 49°56'/21°05'.

Karwowo Krzywanice, Pol.; pop. 14; 69 km WNW of Warszawa; 52°38'/20°09'.

Karyshkov, Ukr. (Carsicov); 62 km SSW of Vinnitsa; 48°49'/27°55'; PHR1.

Karzdaba, Lat. (Karzdabas); pop. 3; 126 km NNW of Daugavpils; 56°59'/26°13'.

Karzdabas, *see* Karzdaba.

Kaschau, *see* Kosice.

Kaschowka, *see* Kozachuvka.

Kasdanov, Ukr. EDRD. This town was not found in BGN gazetteers under the given spelling.

Kasejovice, Cz. (Kasselowitz, Kossowitz); pop. 48; 88 km SSW of Praha; 49°28'/13°44'; EJ, HSL2, JGFF.

Kasely, *see* Koshelevo.

Kasendorf, Germ.; 69 km N of Nurnberg; 50°02'/11°21'; PHGB.

Kasentin, *see* Konstantynow.

Kasha, *see* Kosice.

Kashau, *see* Kosice.

Kashedar, *see* Kaisiadorys.

Kasheli, *see* Koshelevo.

Kashivka, Ukr. (Kaszowka); pop. 15; 88 km WNW of Rovno; 51°10'/25°21'.

Kashkaliya, Mold. (Cascalia); pop. 4; 45 km SE of Kishinev; 46°41'/29°10'.

Kashofka, *see* Kozachuvka.

Kashov, *see* Kosice.

Kashoy, *see* Kosice.

Kashperovka, Ukr. JGFF. A number of towns share this name. It was not possible to determine from available information which one is being referenced.

Kashunka, Mold. (Casunca); pop. 13; 94 km NNW of Kishinev; 47°47'/28°23'.

Kasilan, Pol.; pop. 48; 62 km ESE of Lublin; 51°03'/23°29'.

Kasimirov, *see* Kazimirovo.

Kasin, *possibly* Kasina.

Kasina, Yug. (Kasin?); 19 km N of Zagreb; 45°55'/16°00'; HSL.

Kasina Wielka, *see* Kosina Wielka.

Kasinka, Pol.; pop. 4; 50 km SSE of Krakow; 49°43'/20°03'.

Kaslomkzo, *see* Kosovskaya Polyana.

Kasmark, *see* Kezmarok.

Kasna Dolna, Pol.; pop. 4; 82 km ESE of Krakow; 49°48'/20°56'.

Kasna Gorna, Pol.; pop. 9; 82 km ESE of Krakow; 49°47'/20°55'.

Kasperske Hory, Cz.; pop. 33; 120 km SSW of Praha; 49°09'/13°34'.

Kassa, *see* Kosice.

Kassel, Germ. (Cassel); pop. 3,000; 126 km S of Hannover; 51°19'/09°30'; AMG, EJ, GUM3, GUM4, GUM5, HSL, HSL2, JGFF, LDS.

Kasselowitz, *see* Kasejovice.

Kastav, Yug.; pop. 1; 133 km SW of Zagreb; 45°22'/14°21'.

Kastellaun, Germ. (Castellaum); pop. 85; 88 km WSW of Frankfurt am Main; 50°04'/07°27'; AMG, GUM5.

Kastelyosdombo, Hung.; pop. 4; 75 km SE of Nagykanizsa; 45°57'/17°37'.

Kastoria, Greece (Castoria); pop. 655; 101 km N of Ioannina; 40°33'/21°15'; COH, GUM4, JGFF.

Kasubassa, GUM4. This town was not found in BGN gazetteers under the given spelling.

Kaszahaza, Hung.; pop. 6; 50 km NNW of Nagykanizsa; 46°51'/16°50'.

Kaszew, Pol.; pop. 7; 62 km W of Lodz; 51°49'/18°33'.

Kaszony, *see* Kosyno.

Kaszowka, *see* Kashivka.

Kaszyce, Pol.; 19 km NNW of Przemysl; 49°55'/22°45'; HSL.

Katadfa, Hung.; pop. 3; 82 km ESE of Nagykanizsa; 46°00'/17°52'.

Katarzynow, Pol. (Katarzynow Nowy); pop. 46; 26 km E of Lodz; 51°44'/19°50'; PHP1.

Katarzynow Nowy, *see* Katarzynow.

Katerburg, *see* Katerinovka.

Katerina, *see* Katerini.

Katerini, Greece (Katerina, Katherine); pop. 41; 62 km SSW of Thessaloniki; 40°15'/22°30'; AMG, EJ.

Katerinopol, Ukr. (Kalniboloto, Piaterota, Yekaterinopol); pop. 1,759; 62 km NE of Uman; 48°56'/30°58'; JGFF.

Katerinovka, Ukr. (Katerburg, Katrynburg); pop. 384; 75 km S of Rovno; 50°00'/25°53'; HSL, JGFF, LDL, SF.

Katherine, *see* Katerini.

Katlakalna, *see* Katlakalns.

Katlakalns, Lat. (Katlakalna); pop. 10; 19 km SE of Riga; 56°52'/24°11'.

Katoly, Hung.; pop. 1; 120 km ESE of Nagykanizsa; 46°04'/18°27'.

Katona, *see* Catina.

Katovice, Cz.; pop. 1; 101 km SSW of Praha; 49°16'/13°50'.

Katowice, Pol. (Kattowitz, Stalinogrod); pop. 5,716; 62 km S of Czestochowa; 50°16'/19°01'; AMG, CAHJP, EJ, GA, GUM3, GUM4, GUM5, GUM6, HSL, HSL2, JGFF, LDL, LDS, PHP1, PHP3, PHP4, POCEM.

Katrynburg, *see* Katerinovka.

Katsaleny, Mold. (Cataleni); pop. 4; 50 km WSW of Kishinev; 46°55'/28°11'.

Katscher, *see* Kietrz.

Kattowitz, *see* Katowice.

Katy, Pol.; pop. 23; 69 km SSE of Lublin; 50°39'/22°43'.

Katyciai, Lith. (Coadjuthen); 120 km SW of Siauliai; 55°17'/21°49'; JGFF.

Katy Kupce, *see* Kupce.

Katy Nowe, Pol.; pop. 4; 82 km NE of Krakow; 50°27'/20°58'.

Katy Wroclawskie, Pol. (Kanth); pop. 33; 19 km SW of Wroclaw; 51°02'/16°46'; LDS.

Katzelsdorf, Aus. AMG. A number of towns share this name. It was not possible to determine from available information which one is being referenced.

Kaubenheim, Germ.; 45 km W of Nurnberg; 49°32'/10°28'; PHGB.

Kauen, *see* Kaunas.

Kaufbeuren, Germ.; pop. 8; 75 km SW of Munchen; 47°53'/10°37'; GUM3, GUM5.

Kaufering, Germ.; 56 km WSW of Munchen; 48°05'/10°53'; GUM3, GUM4, GUM5, ISH3.

Kaukehmen, *see* Yasnoye.

Kauleliskiai, Lith.; 45 km ESE of Siauliai; 55°42'/23°47'; COH.

Kaumberg, Aus.; pop. 4; 45 km SW of Wien; 48°01'/15°53'.

Kaunas, Lith. (Kauen, Kovno, Kowno); pop. 25,044; 94 km W of Vilnius; 54°54'/23°54'; AMG, CAHJP, EDRD, EJ, FRG, GUM3, GUM3, GUM4, GUM5, GUM6, HSL, HSL2, ISH1, ISH2, ISH3, JGFF, LDL, PHP1, PHP4, SF, YL.

Kaunata, Lat. (Kaunatas, Kobnat, Kovnat); pop. 101; 82 km NE of Daugavpils; 56°20'/27°32'; PHLE.

Kaunatas, *see* Kaunata.

Kaunitz, Germ. BGN lists two possible localities with this name located at 50°06'/14°51' and 51°51'/08°34'. JGFF.

Kausany, *see* Kaushany.

Kaushany, Mold. (Causani, Causani Noui, Causani Novi, Causanii Noui, Kausany, Koshany); pop. 1,870; 62 km ESE of Kishinev; 46°38'/29°25'; EDRD, EJ, GUM4, PHR2, SF.

Kautzen, Aus.; pop. 3; 120 km WNW of Wien; 48°55'/15°14'.

Kavala, Bulg.; pop. 1,700; This town was not found in BGN gazetteers under the given spelling.

Kavalla, Greece (Cavalla); pop. 2,135; 126 km NE of Thessaloniki; 40°56'/24°25'; AMG, COH, EDRD, GUM4.

Kavarsk, *see* Kavarskas.

Kavarskas, Lith. (Kavarsk, Kovarsk, Kovarskas, Koverskas); pop. 436; 88 km NE of Kaunas; 55°26'/24°55'; HSL, JGFF, LDL, SF, YL.

Kavas, Hung.; pop. 4; 56 km NNW of Nagykanizsa; 46°52'/16°43'.

Kavsko, Ukr. (Kawsko); 62 km S of Lvov; 49°21'/23°48'; HSL.

Kawczyce, Pol.; pop. 5; 69 km NE of Krakow; 50°26'/20°45'.

Kawec, Pol.; pop. 12; 38 km SE of Krakow; 49°51'/20°14'.

Kaweczyn, Pol. (Kaweczyn Debicki, Kaweczyn Sedziszowski); pop. 190; 82 km WNW of Przemysl; 50°05'/21°44'; PHP3.

Kaweczyn Debicki, *see* Kaweczyn.

Kaweczyn Sedziszowski, *see* Kaweczyn.

Kawsko, *see* Kavsko.

Kaydanovo, *see* Dzerzhinsk.

Kaynariy Vek, Mold. (Cainarii Vechi); pop. 96; 126 km NW of Kishinev; 48°01'/28°07'.

Kaynary, Mold. (Cainari); pop. 32; 38 km SE of Kishinev; 46°41'/29°03'.

Kazakliya, Mold. (Cazaclia); pop. 12; 114 km S of Kishinev; 46°00'/28°40'.

Kazan, USSR; 712 km E of Moskva; 55°45'/49°08'; EJ, GUM4, HSL, HSL2.

Kazaneshty, Mold. (Cazanesti); pop. 44; 75 km NNW of Kishinev; 47°37'/28°28'.

Kazanka, Ukr.; 170 km SW of Dnepropetrovsk; 47°50'/32°50'; SF.

Kazanki, Pol.; pop. 8; 82 km NW of Lodz; 52°24'/18°49'.

Kazanlik, see Kazanluk.

Kazanluk, Bulg. (Kazanlik); pop. 520; 170 km E of Sofija; 42°37'/25°24'; EJ.

Kazanov, see Kazanow.

Kazanow, Pol. (Kazanov); pop. 336; 75 km W of Lublin; 51°17'/21°28'; AMG, EDRD, GUM5, HSL, LDS, SF.

Kazanzhik, Mold. (Cazangic); pop. 9; 56 km SSW of Kishinev; 46°31'/28°26'.

Kazatin, Ukr.; pop. 3,012; 56 km NNE of Vinnitsa; 49°43'/28°50'; EJ, HSL, HSL2, SF.

Kazatskoye, Ukr. (Gura Rosie); pop. 29; 50 km WSW of Odessa; 46°21'/30°03'.

Kazhaneradok, see Kozhan Gorodok.

Kazhba, Mold. (Cajba); pop. 28; 133 km WNW of Kishinev; 47°43'/27°27'.

Kazimierowka, Pol. (Kazimierzowka); 101 km ESE of Lublin; 50°41'/23°39'; GUM3, GUM4, GUM5, PHP3.

Kazimierz, see Kazimierz Dolny.

Kazimierza, LDL. This pre-World War I community was not found in BGN gazetteers.

Kazimierza Mala, Pol.; pop. 31; 50 km NE of Krakow; 50°16'/20°32'.

Kazimierza Wielka, Pol.; pop. 293; 45 km NE of Krakow; 50°16'/20°29'; AMG, GUM3, GUM5, SF.

Kazimierz Biskupi, Pol.; 82 km E of Poznan; 52°19'/18°10'; PHP1.

Kazimierz Dolny, Pol. (Kazimierz, Kazimierz nad Wisla, Kazimyerz, Kazimyerz Dolni, Kazmir, Kuzmir); pop. 1,382; 45 km W of Lublin; 51°19'/21°57'; AMG, CAHJP, COH, EDRD, GA, GUM3, GUM4, GUM5, HSL, HSL2, JGFF, LDS, LYV, PHP4, POCEM, SF, YB.

Kazimierz nad Wisla, see Kazimierz Dolny.

Kazimierzowka, see Kazimierowka.

Kazimirka, Ukr.; 62 km N of Rovno; 51°07'/26°28'; GUM3.

Kazimirov, see Kazimirovo.

Kazimirovo, Byel. (Kasimirov, Kazimirov); 94 km WNW of Gomel; 52°54'/29°50'; LDL, SF.

Kazimyerz, see Kazimierz Dolny.

Kazimyerz Dolni, see Kazimierz Dolny.

Kazincbarcika, Hung. (Sajokazinc); pop. 62; 26 km NW of Miskolc; 48°15'/20°38'; HSL, JGFF, LDS, PHH.

Kazlu Ruda, Lith. (Kozlova Ruda, Kozlowa Ruda); 26 km SW of Kaunas; 54°46'/23°30'; GUM3, GUM4, HSL, SF.

Kazmierz, Pol.; pop. 16; 26 km WNW of Poznan; 52°31'/16°35'.

Kazmir, see Kazimierz Dolny.

Kaznejov, Cz.; pop. 8; 82 km WSW of Praha; 49°53'/13°24'.

Kaznow, Pol.; 38 km NNE of Lublin; 51°30'/22°46'; GA.

Kazsok, Hung.; pop. 4; 75 km ENE of Nagykanizsa; 46°29'/17°58'.

Kcynia, Pol. (Exin); pop. 77; 69 km NNE of Poznan; 52°59'/17°30'; HSL, HSL2, POCEM.

Kdyne, Cz.; pop. 45; 133 km SW of Praha; 49°24'/13°02'.

Kebharec, see Skalka.

Keblov, Cz.; pop. 5; 62 km ESE of Praha; 49°41'/15°04'.

Keccsed, see Chiesd.

Kecel, Hung.; pop. 100; 75 km WNW of Szeged; 46°32'/19°16'; PHH.

Kechnie, see Cuhea.

Keci, Lat.; pop. 5; 75 km ENE of Riga; 57°06'/25°19'.

Kecovo, Cz. (Kecso); 62 km SW of Kosice; 48°30'/20°29'; HSL.

Kecsed, see Chiesd.

Kecsege, Hung. (Majsamiklosvar); pop. 39; 101 km ENE of Nagykanizsa; 46°41'/18°18'.

Kecskemet, Hung.; pop. 1,346; 82 km SE of Budapest; 46°54'/19°42'; AMG, COH, GUM4, GUM5, HSL, HSL2, JGFF, LDS, PHH.

Kecso, see Kecovo.

Kedainai, see Kedainiai.

Kedainiai, Lith. (Kaidan, Kedainai, Keidan, Keidany, Keydan, Kiejdany, Kuidany, Kuidany); pop. 4,028; 50 km N of Kaunas; 55°17'/23°58'; COH, EJ, GUM3, GUM4, GUM5, GUM6, GYLA, HSL, HSL2, JGFF, LDL, SF, YB.

Kedzierz, Pol.; pop. 4; 101 km WNW of Przemysl; 50°05'/21°26'.

Kedzierzyn Kozle, GA. This town was not found in BGN gazetteers under the given spelling.

Kehida, Hung.; pop. 5; 50 km N of Nagykanizsa; 46°51'/17°06'.

Kehl, Germ.; pop. 113; 101 km WSW of Stuttgart; 48°35'/07°49'; GUM3, PHGBW.

Keidan, see Kedainiai.

Keidanov, see Dzerzhinsk.

Keidany, see Kedainiai.

Keiltchiglov, see Kielczyglow.

Keipene, Lat.; pop. 14; 62 km E of Riga; 56°53'/25°11'.

Kejzlice, Cz.; pop. 7; 88 km ESE of Praha; 49°35'/15°24'.

Kek, Hung.; pop. 68; 82 km ENE of Miskolc; 48°07'/21°53'; HSL.

Kekcse, Hung.; pop. 19; 94 km ENE of Miskolc; 48°15'/22°00'; HSL, LDS.

Kekenyes, see Trnava.

Kekes, see Chiochis.

Kelbassen, see Kielbasy.

Kelc, Cz.; 88 km NE of Brno; 49°29'/17°49'; HSL.

Kelebia, Hung.; pop. 19; 45 km WSW of Szeged; 46°12'/19°37'.

Kelechin, Ukr. (Kalacsin, Kelecin); 139 km S of Lvov; 48°38'/23°23'; HSL, SM.

Kelecin, see Kelechin.

Kelecseny, see Klacany.

Keled, Hung.; pop. 1; 82 km N of Nagykanizsa; 47°05'/17°07'; HSL.

Kelementelke, see Calimanesti.

Kelemer, Hung.; pop. 1; 45 km NW of Miskolc; 48°21'/20°26'; HSL.

Kelemes, see Lubotice.

Kelencze, see Chelinta.

Keleviz, Hung.; pop. 3; 38 km ENE of Nagykanizsa; 46°31'/17°25'.

Kelheim, Germ.; 82 km SE of Nurnberg; 48°55'/11°52'; PHGB.

Kelin, see Koln.

Kelm, see Kelme.

Kelme, Lith. (Kelm, Kelmy); pop. 2,000; 45 km SSW of Siauliai; 55°38'/22°56'; COH, EJ, GUM3, GUM5, HSL, HSL2, JGFF, SF, YL.

Kelmentsy, Ukr. (Chelmeniti, Chelmenti); pop. 318; 69 km ENE of Chernovtsy; 48°28'/26°50'.

Kelmy, see Kelme.

Keln, see Koln.

Kelsterbach, Germ.; pop. 49; 13 km SW of Frankfurt am Main; 50°04'/08°32'.

Keltinan, see Kaltinenai.

Kelts, see Kielce.

Keltz, see Kielce.

Kemai, see Kamajai.

Kemecse, Hung.; pop. 367; 75 km E of Miskolc; 48°04'/21°48'; AMG, GUM3, HSL, HSL2, LDS, PHH.

Kemence, Hung.; pop. 17; 62 km NNW of Budapest; 48°01'/18°54'.

Kemendollar, Hung.; pop. 2; 56 km N of Nagykanizsa; 46°54'/16°58'.

Kemeneshogyesz, Hung.; pop. 23; 107 km N of Nagykanizsa; 47°21'/17°18'.

Kemenesmagasi, Hung.; pop. 15; 107 km N of Nagykanizsa; 47°20'/17°13'.

Kemenesmihalyfa, Hung. (Mihalyfa); pop. 6; 101 km N of Nagykanizsa; 47°17'/17°07'; HSL, LDS.

Kemenespalfa, Hung.; pop. 2; 82 km N of Nagykanizsa; 47°08'/17°11'.

Kemenesszentpeter, Hung.; pop. 5; 120 km N of Nagykanizsa;

47°26'/17°14'.

Kemer, *see* Camar.

Kemeri, *see* Alsviki.

Kemes, Hung.; 107 km ESE of Nagykanizsa; 45°50'/18°06'; HSL.

Kemnade, Germ.; 50 km S of Hannover; 51°59'/09°31'; LDS.

Kempen, *see* Kepno.

Kempfenhausen, Germ.; pop. 1; 26 km SSW of Munchen; 47°59'/11°22'.

Kempten, Germ.; pop. 56; 107 km SW of Munchen; 47°43'/10°19'; AMG, EDRD, GED, GUM3, PHGB.

Kenderes, Hung.; pop. 49; 101 km S of Miskolc; 47°15'/20°41'; HSL.

Kenese, Hung.; 88 km SSW of Budapest; 46°56'/18°15'; HSL. This town was located on a pre-World War I map, but does not appear in contemporary gazetteers.

Kenez, Hung.; 94 km NNW of Nagykanizsa; 47°12'/16°47'; HSL.

Kenezlo, Hung.; pop. 31; 56 km ENE of Miskolc; 48°12'/21°32'.

Kenigsfeld, *see* Ustchorna.

Kenten, Germ.; 19 km W of Koln; 50°57'/06°40'; GED.

Kenti, *see* Kety.

Kenty, *see* Kety.

Kenyeri, Hung.; pop. 5; 114 km N of Nagykanizsa; 47°23'/17°05'.

Kenzingen, Germ.; pop. 19; 120 km SW of Stuttgart; 48°12'/07°46'; PHGBW.

Kepa, Pol.; pop. 22; 32 km SW of Lublin; 51°04'/22°16'.

Kepa Celejowska, Pol.; pop. 33; 50 km SE of Warszawa; 51°52'/21°20'.

Kepa Chotecka, Pol.; 50 km WSW of Lublin; 51°15'/21°50'; GA.

Kepa Falenicka, Pol.; 19 km SE of Warszawa; 52°08'/21°09'; GA.

Kepa Lubawska, Pol.; pop. 12; 82 km NE of Krakow; 50°20'/21°03'.

Kepa Rzeczycka, Pol.; pop. 8; 75 km SSW of Lublin; 50°39'/22°02'.

Kepa Tarchominska, GUM4. This town was not found in BGN gazetteers under the given spelling.

Kepki, Pol.; pop. 23; 75 km N of Lublin; 51°52'/22°29'.

Kepno, Pol. (Kempen); pop. 262; 75 km NE of Wroclaw; 51°17'/17°59'; AMG, CAHJP, EJ, GED, GUM3, GUM5, HSL, HSL2, JGFF, LDS, PHP1.

Ker, *see* Kersemjen.

Kerch, Ukr. (Kercz, Kertsh); pop. 3,067; 189 km ENE of Simferopol; 45°21'/36°28'; EDRD, EJ, GUM4, GUM5, HSL, LDL, SF.

Kercsed, *see* Kerecsend.

Kercseliget, Hung.; pop. 4; 82 km E of Nagyka zsa; 46°20'/18°04'.

Kercz, *see* Kerch.

Kerdzhali, *see* Kurdzhali.

Kerecke, *see* Keretski.

Kerecki, *see* Keretski.

Kerecky, *see* Keretski.

Kerecsend, Hung. (Carcedea, Kercsed); pop. 8; 45 km SSW of Miskolc; 47°48'/20°21'; HSL.

. . eseny, Hung.; pop. 4; 26 km N of Nagykanizsa; .6°37'/17°03'.

k egky, *see* Keretski.

Kerekegyhaza, Hung. (Jaszkerekegyhaza); pop. 14; 69 km SE of Budapest; 46°56'/19°29'; LDS.

Kerekheg, *see* Okrouhla.

Kerekhegy, *see* Okrouhla.

Kereknye, Cz.; 82 km E of Kosice; 48°33'/22°18'; AMG, HSL. This town was located on a pre-World War I map, but does not appear in contemporary gazetteers.

Kerekteleki, Hung.; pop. 8; 88 km W of Budapest; 47°31'/17°56'.

Kerelo, *see* Chirileu.

Keremjen, Hung.; pop. 20; This town was not found in BGN gazetteers under the given spelling.

Kerepec, *see* Kerepes.

Kerepes, Hung. (Kerepec); pop. 46; 19 km NE of Budapest; 47°34'/19°17'; HSL.

Kereplye, *see* Kravany.

Keresd, *see* Cris.

Kerestur, Cz. (Szecskeresztur); 26 km E of Kosice; 48°39'/21°34'; HSL.

Kereszteny, Hung.; pop. 8; 120 km NNW of Nagykanizsa; 47°27'/16°47'.

Kereszter, Hung.; 133 km SSE of Miskolc; 47°01'/21°30'; HSL.

Keresztes, *see* Biharkeresztes.

Keresztespuspoki, Hung.; pop. 4; 38 km S of Miskolc; 47°49'/20°41'.

Keresztete, Hung.; 50 km N of Miskolc; 48°30'/20°57'; HSL.

Keresztur, Hung.; 94 km WSW of Budapest; 47°23'/17°52'; AMG, EJ, HSL, HSL2, LDL.

Keresztut, *see* Kotaj.

Keretski, Ukr. (Kerecke, Kerecki, Kerecky, Keregky, Keretzky); 163 km S of Lvov; 48°29'/23°13'; AMG, COH, HSL, SM.

Keretzky, *see* Keretski.

Kerkaiklod, *see* Iklodbordoce.

Kerkakutas, Hung.; pop. 1; 56 km WNW of Nagykanizsa; 46°46'/16°30'.

Kerkatotfalu, Hung. (Totfalu); 38 km WNW of Nagykanizsa; 46°35'/16°35'; HSL.

Kerkira, Greece (Corfu); pop. 1,819; 88 km WSW of Ioannina; 39°40'/19°50'; EDRD, GUM4, GUM6, LDL.

Kernasovca, Rom. PHR1. This town was not found in BGN gazetteers under the given spelling.

Kernitsa, Ukr. (Kiernica); pop. 40; 26 km SW of Lvov; 49°46'/23°43'.

Kerpen, Germ.; pop. 103; 19 km SW of Koln; 50°52'/06°41'; AMG, EDRD, EJ.

Kersemjen, Hung. (Ker); 120 km E of Miskolc; 48°01'/22°25'; HSL.

Kert, *see* Strekov.

Kerta, Hung.; pop. 9; 88 km N of Nagykanizsa; 47°10'/17°17'.

Kertsh, *see* Kerch.

Kertvaros, Hung. (Sopronbanfalva); pop. 12; 146 km NNW of Nagykanizsa; 47°41'/16°33'.

Kerzenheim, Germ.; pop. 5; 75 km SSW of Frankfurt am Main; 49°35'/08°04'.

Kesellymeszo, COH. This town was not found in BGN gazetteers under the given spelling.

Keshanov, *see* Chrzanow.

Keshenev, *see* Kishinev.

Keshepitz, *see* Krzepice.

Kesheshovitz, *see* Krzeszowiec.

Keshinov, *see* Kishinev.

Keshionzh, *see* Ksiaz Wielki.

Kesmark, *see* Kezmarok.

Kesov, *see* Polny Kesov.

Kesselbach, Germ.; pop. 28; 69 km N of Frankfurt am Main; 50°40'/08°52'; JGFF.

Kestrich, Germ.; pop. 24; 75 km NNE of Frankfurt am Main; 50°39'/09°11'.

Keszeg, Hung.; pop. 5; 45 km N of Budapest; 47°50'/19°15'.

Kesznyeten, Hung.; pop. 27; 26 km ESE of Miskolc; 47°58'/21°03'; HSL.

Keszohidegkut, Hung.; pop. 7; 114 km SSW of Budapest; 46°37'/18°26'.

Keszteg, *see* Chistag.

Keszter, Rom.; 94 km WNW of Cluj; 47°04'/22°25'; HSL. This town was located on a pre-World War I map, but does not appear in contemporary gazetteers.

Keszthely, Hung.; pop. 872; 45 km NNE of Nagykanizsa; 46°46'/17°15'; AMG, EDRD, GUM4, HSL, HSL2, LDS, PHH.

Kesztolc, Hung.; pop. 7; 32 km NW of Budapest; 47°43'/18°48'.

Ketbodony, Hung.; pop. 18; 50 km N of Budapest;

Kherson, Ukraine: Worker sawing logs at an Agro-Joint sawmill.

47°56'/19°17'.

Ketegyhaza, Hung.; pop. 41; 82 km NE of Szeged; 46°32'/21°11'; HSL.

Keterinoslav, *see* Dnepropetrovsk.

Kethely, Hung.; pop. 50; 45 km NE of Nagykanizsa; 46°39'/17°24'; PHH.

Ketrosy, Mold. (Chetrosu); pop. 140; 139 km NW of Kishinev; 48°05'/27°54'.

Ketrzyn, Pol. (Rastenburg); pop. 106; 157 km WNW of Bialystok; 54°05'/21°23'; GUM3, LDS.

Ketsch, Germ.; pop. 16; 82 km NW of Stuttgart; 49°22'/08°32'; PHGBW.

Kettenbach, Germ.; pop. 24; 50 km WNW of Frankfurt am Main; 50°15'/08°04'.

Kettlasbrunn, Aus.; pop. 6; 45 km NNE of Wien; 48°33'/16°39'.

Kettwig, Germ. (Kettwig a/d Ruhr); pop. 45; 50 km N of Koln; 51°22'/06°57'; GED, YB.

Kettwig a/d Ruhr, *see* Kettwig.

Keturiasdesimt Totoriu, Lith. (Sorok Tatary); 19 km SSW of Vilnius; 54°34'/25°10'; GUM4.

Keturvalakiai, Lith.; pop. 6; 62 km SW of Kaunas; 54°33'/23°09'.

Kety, Pol. (Kenti, Kenty); pop. 329; 56 km SW of Krakow; 49°53'/19°14'; AMG, EGRS, HSL, LDL, PHP3, POCEM, SF.

Kevermes, Hung.; pop. 32; 82 km ENE of Szeged; 46°25'/21°11'; AMG.

Keydan, *see* Kedainiai.

Kezmarok, Cz. (Kasmark, Kesmark); pop. 1,796; 75 km WNW of Kosice; 49°08'/20°26'; AMG, COH, EJ, GUM4, GUM5, HSL, JGFF, LDL.

Khabne, *see* Polesskoye.

Khabnoye, *see* Polesskoye.

Khabovichi, Byel. (Chobowicze); pop. 23; 114 km WSW of Pinsk; 52°04'/24°29'.

Khalkis, Greece (Chalcis, Chalkis); pop. 325; 56 km NNW of Athens; 38°28'/23°36'; EDRD, GUM6.

Khamovka, USSR; EDRD. This town was not found in BGN gazetteers under the given spelling.

Khania, *see* Canea.

Kharapchiu pe Siret, *see* Karapchiv.

Kharapchou pe Ceremus, Ukr. (Carapciu pe Ceremus); pop. 290; COH. This town was not found in BGN gazetteers under the given spelling.

Kharkov, Ukr. (Charkow); pop. 81,130; 195 km NNE of Dnepropetrovsk; 50°00'/36°15'; AMG, COH, EDRD, GUM3, GUM4, GUM5, HSL, JGFF, PHP4.

Kharpachka, Ukr. (Charpaczka, Chereposhetz); 75 km WSW of Uman; 48°45'/29°13'; SF.

Kharshnitse, *see* Charsznica.

Khashchevatoye, *possibly* Khashchevoye.

Khashchevoye, Ukr. (Khashchevatoye?); pop. 3,170; 45 km NNE of Dnepropetrovsk; 48°42'/35°20'.

Khashchuv, Ukr. (Chaszczow); pop. 19; 107 km SW of Lvov; 49°16'/22°47'.

Khaskovo, Bulg. (Haskovo); pop. 1,030; 195 km ESE of Sofija; 41°56'/25°33'; EJ.

Khazhdeu de Sus, Ukr. (Hajdeu de Sus); pop. 45; 45 km ENE of Chernovtsy; 48°22'/26°32'.

Khelem, *see* Chelm.

Khelm, *see* Chelm.

Kherson, Ukr. (Cherson); pop. 14,837; 146 km ENE of Odessa; 46°38'/32°36'; EDRD, GUM4, GUM5, HSL, JGFF, LDL, PHP1, SF.

Khidry, Byel. (Chidry); pop. 8; 150 km WNW of Pinsk; 52°32'/24°03'.

Khiliutsy, Mold. (Hiliuti); pop. 66; 150 km WNW of Kishinev; 47°56'/27°23'.

Khimchin, Ukr. (Chomczyn, Khomchin); pop. 44; 56 km W of Chernovtsy; 48°23'/25°09'.

Khinoch, Ukr. (Chinocz); pop. 36; 114 km N of Rovno; 51°35'/26°08'.

Khios, Greece (Chios); pop. 39; 208 km ENE of Athens; 38°23'/26°07'.

Khirov, Ukr. (Chyrow); AMG, COH, EGRS, JGFF. This town was not found in BGN gazetteers under the given spelling.

Khisinau, *see* Kishinev.

Khislavichi, USSR (Chislavici, Choslovitz); pop. 2,102; 75 km S of Smolensk; 54°11'/32°10'; GUM5, JGFF, LDL, SF.

Khlebovitse Svizhske, Ukr. (Chlebowice Swirskie); pop. 49; 45 km ESE of Lvov; 49°37'/24°26'.

Khlebovitse Velki, *see* Velikiye Glibovichi.

Khlebwka, *see* Glebuvka.

Khlevchany, Ukr. (Chlewczany); pop. 125; 56 km N of Lvov; 50°19'/23°58'; PHP2.

Khliple, Ukr. (Chliple); pop. 37; 56 km SW of Lvov; 49°40'/23°12'.

Khliveshte, Ukr. (Clivesti); pop. 24; 32 km WNW of Chernovtsy; 48°29'/25°38'.

Khlopy, *see* Peremozhnoye.

Khmelevka, Ukr. (Chmielowka, Khmelyuvka); pop. 23; 126 km WNW of Chernovtsy; 48°48'/24°23'.

Khmelnik, Ukr. (Chmelnik, Khmyelnik); pop. 6,011; 56 km WNW of Vinnitsa; 49°33'/27°58'; AMG, EJ, HSL, JGFF, SF.

Khmelnitski, *see* Khmelnitskiy.

Khmelnitskii, *see* Khmelnitskiy.

Khmelnitskiy, Ukr. (Chmelnitski, Chmielnicki, Khmelnitski, Khmelnitskii, Kiemieliszki, Kimlishuk, Ploskirow, Proskurov); pop. 13,408; 107 km W of Vinnitsa; 49°25'/27°00'; AMG, COH, EDRD, EJ, GUM3, GUM4, GUM5, GYLA, HSL, HSL2, JGFF, PHP4, SF, YB.

Khmelno, Ukr. (Chmielno); 75 km NE of Lvov; 50°15'/24°50'; GUM3, JGFF.

Khmelyuv, Ukr. (Chmielow, Chmiliv, Czmielov); pop. 21; 107 km N of Lvov; 50°48'/24°28'; EDRD, HSL, JGFF, SF.

Khmelyuvka, *see* Khmelevka.

Khmyelnik, *see* Khmelnik.

Khobultova, Ukr. (Chobultow); pop. 9; 114 km N of Lvov; 50°49'/24°27'.

Khodachkuv Velki, *see* Velikaya Khodachka.

Khoderkovtse, Ukr. (Choderkowce); pop. 30; 38 km SE of Lvov; 49°35'/24°17'.

Khodoreuts, *see* Khodoroutsy.

Khodorkov, Ukr. (Chodorkov, Chodorkow, Hodorkov); pop. 2,000; 94 km SW of Kiyev; 50°06'/29°18'; EDRD, JGFF, PHP4, SF.

Khodoroutsy, Mold. (Hodarauti, Khodoreuts); pop. 27; 189 km NW of Kishinev; 48°22'/27°20'.

Khodorov, Ukr. (Choderev, Chodorov, Chodorow, Khodorow); pop. 1,230; 56 km SE of Lvov; 49°24'/24°19'; AMG, CAHJP, COH, EDRD, EGRS, GUM3, GUM5, HSL, HSL2, JGFF, PHP2, SF, WS.

Khodorow, *see* Khodorov.

Khodorozha, Mold. (Slobozia Hodjinesti, Slobozia Horodistea); pop. 31; 62 km N of Kishinev; 47°30'/28°53'.

Khoiniki, *see* Khoyniki.

Kholm, USSR; pop. 103; 234 km E of Leningrad; 59°46'/34°25'. *See also* Chelm.

Kholmech, Byel. (Cholmetch); 45 km SSW of Gomel; 52°09'/30°37'; SF.

Kholmy, Ukr.; 69 km W of Konotop; 51°22'/32°14'; GUM4.

Kholonev, Ukr. (Choloniow); pop. 10; 94 km NNE of Lvov; 50°30'/24°52'.

Kholopenichi, Byel. (Chlopeniczi, Cholopenitch, Cholopenitschi); pop. 860; 114 km NE of Minsk; 54°31'/28°58'; LDL, SF.

Khomchin, *see* Khimchin.

Khomsk, Byel. (Chomsk); pop. 1,048; 69 km WNW of Pinsk; 52°20'/25°14'; COH, GUM3, GUM4, GUM5, HSL, HSL2, JGFF, PHP4, SF.

Khomyakov, *see* Khomyakuv.

Khomyakovka, Ukr. (Chomiakowka); pop. 74; 56 km WNW of Chernovtsy; 48°34'/25°18'.

Khomyakuv, Ukr. (Chomiakow, Khomyakov); pop. 83; 107 km WNW of Chernovtsy; 48°49'/24°42'.

Khorevo, Byel. (Chorewo); pop. 15; 120 km WNW of Pinsk; 52°38'/24°35'.

Khorli, *see* Khorly.

Khorly, Ukr. (Khorli); pop. 118; 139 km NW of Simferopol; 46°05'/33°18'.

Khorokhorin, Ukr. (Chorochoryn); pop. 61; 94 km W of Rovno; 50°50'/24°58'; GUM3.

Khorol, Ukr. (Choral, Chorol); pop. 2,081; 163 km S of Konotop; 49°47'/33°17'; GUM4, HSL, JGFF, LDL, SF.

Khoromsk, Byel. (Choromsk); pop. 15; 69 km E of Pinsk; 52°02'/27°07'.

Khoroshoutsi, *see* Khoroshovtsy.

Khoroshovchitsy, Byel. (Choroszewszczyce, Kurovischtscha); pop. 21; 139 km SW of Minsk; 53°20'/25°38'; EDRD.

Khoroshovtsy, Ukr. (Ciornohuzi?, Horosauti, Horoscauti, Jacobshagen, Khoroshoutsi); pop. 58; 26 km N of Chernovtsy; 48°28'/25°59'; GUM4, PHR2.

Khoroskiv, *see* Khorostkov.

Khorosnitsa, Ukr. (Chorosnica); pop. 20; 50 km WSW of Lvov; 49°49'/23°16'.

Khorostkov, Ukr. (Chorostkov, Chorostkow, Khoroskiv, Khroskev); pop. 1,979; 107 km N of Chernovtsy; 49°14'/25°55'; AMG, COH, EDRD, EGRS, FRG, GUM3, GUM4, GUM5, GUM6, HSL, HSL2, JGFF, LDL, LYV, PHP2, SF, YB.

Khorostov, Byel. (Chorostow); pop. 70; 94 km NE of Pinsk; 52°30'/27°17'.

Khorostsets, Ukr. (Chorosciec); pop. 24; 88 km ESE of Lvov; 49°36'/25°08'.

Khorov (near Ostrog), Ukr.; pop. 15; 32 km SE of Rovno; 50°24'/26°30'.

Khorshyluvka, USSR (Korszylow?); pop. 21; Described in the *Black Book* as being in the Tarnopol region of Poland, this town was not found in BGN gazetteers.

Khortitsa, Ukr. (Chortitz, Chortotza); 69 km S of Dnepropetrovsk; 47°50'/34°56'; SF.

Khorzel, *see* Chorzele.

Khorzele, *see* Chorzele.

Khorzhel, *see* Chorzele.

Khoslavichi, GUM4. This town was not found in BGN gazetteers under the given spelling.

Khotenchitsy, Byel. (Chocienczyce); pop. 35; 56 km NNW of Minsk; 54°19'/27°23'.

Khoteshov, Ukr. (Chocieszow); pop. 56; 157 km NW of Rovno; 51°43'/24°48'; HSL.

Khotimir, Ukr. (Chocimierz, Chotimierz, Chotymyr, Khotsimezh); pop. 160; 82 km WNW of Chernovtsy; 48°45'/25°06'; EGRS, HSL, HSL2, PHP2.

Khotimsk, Byel. (Chotimsk); pop. 1,792; 150 km NE of Gomel; 53°24'/32°35'; GUM4, HSL, LDL, SF.

Khotin, Ukr. (Chotin, Chotyn, Hotin); pop. 5,786; 45 km NE of Chernovtsy; 48°29'/26°30'; COH, EJ, GUM3, GUM4, GUM5, GUM6, GYLA, HSL, HSL2, JGFF, LDL, LYV, PHR2, SF, YB.

Khotsimezh, *see* Khotimir.

Khotynichi, Byel. (Chotynicze); pop. 11; 62 km N of Pinsk; 52°38'/26°18'.

Khoyniki, Byel. (Choinik, Choiniki, Chojniki, Khoiniki); pop. 2,053; 94 km SW of Gomel; 51°54'/29°58'; GUM5, JGFF, LDL, SF.

Khozhel, *see* Chorzele.

Khrapun, Byel. (Chrapun); pop. 29; 101 km ESE of Pinsk; 51°42'/27°29'.

Khrenovka, Ukr. (Hrinovca); 69 km SSW of Vinnitsa; 48°47'/27°49'; PHR1.

Khristichi, Mold. (Hristici); pop. 9; 139 km NNW of Kishinev;

48°08'/28°11'.

Khristinovka, Ukr.; pop. 211; 19 km WNW of Uman; 48°50'/29°58'.

Khroskev, *see* Khorostkov.

Khrypaliche, Ukr. (Chrypalicze); pop. 15; 120 km N of Lvov; 50°52'/24°14'.

Khryplin, Ukr. (Chryplin); pop. 70; 107 km WNW of Chernovtsy; 48°53'/24°44'.

Khshanov, *see* Chrzanow.

Khshanuv, *see* Chrzanow.

Khust, Ukr. (Chust, Hust, Huste, Huszt); pop. 11,276; 195 km WSW of Chernovtsy; 48°10'/23°18'; AMG, COH, EJ, GUM3, GUM4, GUM5, HSL, JGFF, LDL, SM.

Khuta Sukhodolska, Ukr. (Guta Sukhodolska, Huta Suchodolska); pop. 26; 38 km SSE of Lvov; 49°35'/24°10'.

Khutor Novinki, Byel. (Novinki); 13 km NNW of Minsk; 53°56'/27°33'; EDRD.

Khutor Shevchenko, Ukr. (Volynskiy); 133 km NNE of Kiyev; 51°33'/31°19'; COH, JGFF.

Khutor Tarasivka, Ukr. (Tarasivka, Terasiwka); 62 km NW of Uman; 49°13'/29°44'; GUM3.

Khvalovo Pervoye, Byel. (Chwalowo); pop. 24; 150 km WNW of Pinsk; 52°39'/24°08'.

Khvaydan, *see* Kvedarna.

Khvedkovichi, Byel. (Chwedkowicze); pop. 8; 146 km W of Pinsk; 52°09'/24°03'.

Khvorostov, Ukr. (Chworostow); pop. 29; 150 km N of Lvov; 51°12'/24°14'.

Khyrov, Ukr. (Chirov); pop. 919; 94 km SW of Lvov; 49°32'/22°51'; CAHJP, HSL, LDL, PHP2, SF, WS.

Kibart, *see* Kybartai.

Kibarti, *see* Kybartai.

Kibarty, *see* Kybartai.

Kichary, Pol.; pop. 30; 82 km SW of Lublin; 50°44'/21°45'.

Kicin, Pol.; 6 km NNE of Poznan; 52°28'/17°01'; GA.

Kiczki, Pol.; pop. 39; 50 km ESE of Warszawa; 52°05'/21°44'.

Kide, *see* Chidea.

Kidry, Ukr.; pop. 12; 101 km N of Rovno; 51°27'/26°20'.

Kiduliai, Lith.; pop. 307; 75 km W of Kaunas; 55°04'/22°47'.

Kieferstadtel, *see* Sosnicowice.

Kiejdany, *see* Kedainiai.

Kiel, Germ.; pop. 605; 94 km N of Hamburg; 54°20'/10°08'; AMG, CAHJP, EJ, GUM3, GUM4, GUM5, HSL, LDS.

Kielbasa, Pol.; pop. 97; Described in the *Black Book* as being in the Lodz region of Poland, this town was not found in BGN gazetteers.

Kielbasin, *possibly* Kielbasy.

Kielbasy, Pol. (Kelbassen, Kielbasin?); 139 km W of Bialystok; 53°29'/21°12'; GUM3, GUM4, GUM5, GUM6.

Kielbaszyn, *possibly* Vielbassen.

Kielbow, Pol.; pop. 42; 82 km S of Warszawa; 51°34'/21°01'.

Kielce, Pol. (Kelts, Keltz, Kilts, Kiltz); pop. 15,530; 101 km NNE of Krakow; 50°50'/20°40'; AMG, COH, EDRD, EJ, FRG, GA, GUM3, GUM4, GUM5, GUM6, GYLA, HSL, HSL2, ISH3, JGFF, LDL, LDS, LYV, PHP1, PHP4, POCEM, SF, YB.

Kielczawa, Pol.; pop. 2; 62 km SSW of Przemysl; 49°22'/22°15'.

Kielczew, *possibly* Kielczewice.

Kielczewek, Pol.; pop. 5; 69 km WNW of Lodz; 52°14'/18°44'.

Kielczewice, Pol. (Kielczew?); pop. 24; 32 km S of Lublin; 51°01'/22°26'.

Kielczyglow, Pol. (Keiltchiglov, Kielsztyglov); pop. 241; 56 km NNW of Czestochowa; 51°14'/18°59'; AMG, COH, EDRD, PHP1, SF.

Kielczyglowek, Pol.; pop. 23; 62 km NNW of Czestochowa; 51°17'/18°55'.

Kielkow, Pol.; pop. 11; 101 km WNW of Przemysl; 50°14'/21°28'.

Kielnarowa, Pol.; pop. 14; 56 km WNW of Przemysl; 49°58'/22°04'.

Kielno, Pol.; pop. 1; 26 km WNW of Gdansk; 54°27'/18°21'.

Kielpiniec, Pol.; pop. 6; 75 km SW of Bialystok; 52°37'/22°21'.

Kielsztyglov, *see* Kielczyglow.

Kiemieliszki, *see* Khmelnitskiy.

Kiena, *see* Kine.

Kierling, Aus.; pop. 2; 19 km NW of Wien; 48°18'/16°16'.

Kiernica, *see* Kernitsa.

Kiernozia, Pol.; pop. 284; 62 km NNE of Lodz; 52°16'/19°52'; AMG, GA, PHP4, POCEM, SF, YB.

Kietrz, Pol. (Katscher); pop. 42; 114 km SW of Czestochowa; 50°05'/18°00'; LDS.

Kiev, *see* Kiyev.

Kigyos, Hung.; 107 km NNE of Szeged; 47°02'/20°58'; HSL.

Kijany Blizsze, Pol.; pop. 10; 26 km NE of Lublin; 51°21'/22°48'.

Kije, Pol.; pop. 40; 75 km NNE of Krakow; 50°37'/20°35'.

Kijew, *see* Kiyev.

Kijow, *see* Kiyev.

Kikinda, Yug. (Nagy Kikinda, Velika Kikinda); pop. 418; 120 km N of Beograd; 45°50'/20°29'; PHY.

Kikol, Pol.; pop. 267; 133 km NNW of Lodz; 52°54'/19°07'; HSL, JGFF, PHP4, POCEM.

Kilb, Aus.; pop. 2; 69 km WSW of Wien; 48°06'/15°24'.

Kilija, *see* Kiliya.

Kiliman, Hung.; pop. 1; 32 km N of Nagykanizsa; 46°38'/17°00'.

Kilingi Nomme, Est.; pop. 1; 107 km WSW of Tartu; 58°09'/24°58'.

Kiliya, Ukr. (Chilia Noua, Chilia Nova, Kilija); pop. 1,969; 163 km SSW of Odessa; 45°27'/29°16'; EJ, HSL, JGFF, LDL, SF.

Kilts, *see* Kielce.

Kiltz, *see* Kielce.

Kimeliszek, Lith. EDRD. This town was not found in BGN gazetteers under the given spelling.

Kimirz, *see* Kimizh.

Kimizh, Ukr. (Kimirz); pop. 51; 45 km ESE of Lvov; 49°39'/24°30'.

Kimle, *see* Kumling.

Kimlishuk, *see* Khmelnitskiy.

Kimpulung, *See* Cimpulung Moldovenesc.

Kincses, *see* Chincis.

Kindenheim, Germ. (Kinderheim); pop. 6; 62 km SSW of Frankfurt am Main; 49°37'/08°10'; HSL.

Kinderheim, *see* Kindenheim.

Kine, Lith. (Kiena); 19 km E of Vilnius; 54°39'/25°38'; GUM3, GUM4.

Kinev, *see* Kunow.

Kingisepp, USSR; pop. 65; 107 km SW of Leningrad; 59°22'/28°36'.

Kiniki, Pol.; pop. 5; 82 km WNW of Warszawa; 52°46'/20°10'.

Kinsk, *see* Konskie.

Kintsk, *see* Konskie.

Kipercheny, Mold. (Chiperceni); pop. 208; 62 km N of Kishinev; 47°31'/28°50'.

Kippenheim, Germ.; pop. 153; 114 km SW of Stuttgart; 48°18'/07°50'; AMG, JGFF, PHGBW.

Kirald, Hung.; pop. 15; 32 km WNW of Miskolc; 48°15'/20°24'; HSL.

Kiraly, HSL. This pre-World War I community was not found in BGN gazetteers.

Kiralydarocz, *see* Craidorol.

Kiralyfala, Rom.; pop. 69 km SE of Cluj; 46°18'/24°13'; HSL. This town was located on a pre-World War I map, but does not appear in contemporary gazetteers.

Kiralyhaza, *see* Korolevo.

Kiraly Helmec, *see* Kralovsky Chlmec.

Kiralyhelmec, Cz.; 62 km ESE of Kosice; 48°25'/21°57'; COH, HSL2.

Kiraly Mezo, *see* Ustchorna.

Kiralyret, Hung. BGN lists two possible localities with this name located at 47°07'/18°59' and 47°54'/18°59'. HSL.

Kirchardt, Germ.; 50 km NNW of Stuttgart; 49°12'/09°00';

LDS.

Kirchberg, Germ.; pop. 72; 94 km WSW of Frankfurt am Main; 49°57'/07°24'; GED, GUM5, HSL, JGFF.

Kirchdorf, Germ. HSL2. A number of towns share this name. It was not possible to determine from available information which one is being referenced.

Kirchdrauf, *see* Spisske Podhradie.

Kircheimbolanden, *see* Kirchheimbolanden.

Kirchen, Germ.; pop. 66; 176 km SSW of Stuttgart; 47°39'/07°34'; GED, HSL, JGFF, LDS, PHGBW.

Kirchenbirk, *see* Kostelni Briza.

Kirchendorf, LDL. This pre-World War I community was not found in BGN gazetteers.

Kirch Gons, *see* Pohl Gons.

Kirchhain, Germ.; pop. 250; 88 km N of Frankfurt am Main; 50°49'/08°58'; GUM5, HSL, JGFF, LDS.

Kirchheim, *see* Kirchheim an der Weinstrasse.

Kirchheim (Unterfranken), Germ.; 88 km W of Nurnberg; 49°39'/09°52'; GUM5, PHGB.

Kirchheim an der Weinstrasse, Germ. (Kirchheim); pop. 34; 75 km SSW of Frankfurt am Main; 49°32'/08°11'; AMG, GED, HSL, PHGBW, WS.

Kirchheimbolanden, Germ. (Kircheimbolanden); pop. 58; 62 km SSW of Frankfurt am Main; 49°40'/08°01'; GED, HSL, JGFF.

Kirchheim im Schwaben, Germ.; 82 km W of Munchen; 48°11'/10°29'; PHG1.

Kirchherten, Germ.; 38 km W of Koln; 51°00'/06°29'; GED.

Kirchohsen, Germ.; pop. 6; 45 km SSW of Hannover; 52°03'/09°23'.

Kircholm, *see* Salaspils.

Kirchschlag, *see* Kirchschlag Bei Linz.

Kirchschlag Bei Linz, Aus. (Kirchschlag); 114 km NE of Salzburg; 48°24'/14°16'; HSL.

Kirchschonbach, Germ.; 62 km WNW of Nurnberg; 49°49'/10°23'; PHGB.

Kirchtrudering, Germ. (Trudering); pop. 5; 6 km ESE of Munchen; 48°08'/11°40'.

Kirdzhali, *see* Kurdzhali.

Kirf, Germ.; pop. 84; 157 km S of Koln; 49°33'/06°29'.

Kirilovka, Germ. EDRD. A number of towns share this name. It was not possible to determine from available information which one is being referenced.

Kiriyanka, Mold. (Chirianca); pop. 2; 38 km NW of Kishinev; 47°15'/28°32'.

Kiriyet Lunga, Mold. (Chiriet Lunga); pop. 16; 94 km S of Kishinev; 46°13'/28°57'.

Kirkayeshty, Mold. (Chircaesti); pop. 15; 62 km ESE of Kishinev; 46°43'/29°32'.

Kirkilai, Lith. (Kirklyay, Kurkil, Kurkla); 94 km NE of Siauliai; 56°14'/24°42'; LDL, SF.

Kirklyay, *see* Kirkilai.

Kirlibaba, *see* Cirlibaba.

Kirn, Germ.; pop. 147; 94 km SW of Frankfurt am Main; 49°47'/07°27'; EDRD, GUM5, LDS.

Kirnatseny, Mold. (Carnateni); pop. 5; 62 km ESE of Kishinev; 46°40'/29°30'.

Kirnberg, Germ.; 62 km WSW of Nurnberg; 49°21'/10°14'; PHGB.

Kirov, Germ. PHLE. This town was not found in BGN gazetteers under the given spelling.

Kirovograd, Ukr. (Elizabetgrod, Jelissawetgrad, Kirowo, Kirowograd, Yelisavetgrod, Yelizavelgrad, Zinovyevsk, Zinowjewsk); pop. 18,358; 157 km E of Uman; 48°30'/32°18'; EDRD, EJ, GUM4, GUM5, GYLA, HSL, HSL2, JGFF, LDL, SF.

Kirowo, *see* Kirovograd.

Kirowograd, *see* Kirovograd.

Kirschberg, GUM5. This town was not found in BGN gazetteers under the given spelling.

Kirsova, Mold. (Chirsova); pop. 10; 88 km S of Kishinev;

46°14'/28°39'.

Kirtorf, Germ.; pop. 37; 82 km N of Frankfurt am Main; 50°46'/09°07'; JGFF, LDS.

Kiryutnya, Mold. (Chirutnea); pop. 2; 114 km S of Kishinev; 46°01'/28°44'.

Kis, *see* Kuktiskes.

Kisac, Yug. (Kisag); pop. 42; 82 km NW of Beograd; 45°21'/19°44'.

Kisag, *see* Kisac.

Kisalmas, *see* Almasel.

Kisapati, Hung.; pop. 5; 56 km NNE of Nagykanizsa; 46°51'/17°28'.

Kisapsa, *see* Apsilsa.

Kisar, Hung.; pop. 37; 133 km E of Miskolc; 48°03'/22°31'; AMG, HSL.

Kisasszond, Hung.; pop. 4; 50 km E of Nagykanizsa; 46°20'/17°38'.

Kisbagyon, Hung.; pop. 5; 50 km NE of Budapest; 47°49'/19°35'.

Kisbajom, Hung.; pop. 2; 45 km ESE of Nagykanizsa; 46°18'/17°30'.

Kisbanya, *see* Babesti.

Kisbarapati, Hung.; pop. 7; 69 km ENE of Nagykanizsa; 46°36'/17°52'.

Kisbarathegy, Hung.; pop. 7; 107 km W of Budapest; 47°36'/17°37'.

Kisber, Hung.; pop. 198; 82 km WSW of Budapest; 47°30'/18°02'; HSL, LDS, PHH.

Kisberenzna, *see* Velikiy Bereznyy.

Kisberezna, *see* Velikiy Bereznyy.

Kisberki, Hung.; pop. 3; 82 km E of Nagykanizsa; 46°21'/18°01'.

Kisberzseny, Hung.; pop. 3; 82 km N of Nagykanizsa; 47°06'/17°16'.

Kisbodak, Hung.; pop. 14; 133 km WNW of Budapest; 47°54'/17°25'.

Kisbudmer, Hung.; pop. 2; 126 km ESE of Nagykanizsa; 45°55'/18°27'.

Kiscell, *see* Celldomolk.

Kisczell, *see* Celldomolk.

Kisecsed, *possibly* Kisecset.

Kisecset, Hung. (Kisecsed?); pop. 4; 50 km N of Budapest; 47°56'/19°19'; HSL.

Kiselev, Ukr. (Chisalau); pop. 113; 38 km NW of Chernovtsy; 48°35'/25°40'.

Kiselin, Ukr. (Kisielin); pop. 94; 107 km W of Rovno; 50°52'/24°49'; GUM3, HSL, LDL, SF.

Kisenzhopol, *see* Ksiezpol.

Kisfalu, HSL. This pre-World War I community was not found in BGN gazetteers.

Kisfenes, *see* Finisel.

Kisgalambfalva, *see* Porumbenii Mici.

Kisgercze, *see* Gherta Mica.

Kisgorbo, Hung.; pop. 7; 62 km N of Nagykanizsa; 46°56'/17°10'.

Kisgyalan, Hung.; pop. 3; 75 km E of Nagykanizsa; 46°25'/17°59'.

Kisgyor, Hung.; pop. 18; 13 km SSW of Miskolc; 48°01'/20°42'; HSL.

Kishartyan, Hung.; pop. 17; 82 km NNE of Budapest; 48°05'/19°43'.

Kishaza, *see* Chesa.

Kishegyes, *see* Mali Idos.

Kishind, *see* Male Chyndice.

Kishinev, Mold. (Chisinau, Keshenev, Keshinov, Khisinau, Kiszyniow); pop. 41,405; 47°00'/28°50'; AMG, EDRD, EJ, GUM3, GUM4, GUM5, GUM6, HSL, HSL2, JGFF, LDL, LJEE, LYV, PHP2, PHP3, PHR2, SF, YB.

Kishla Saliyeva, *see* Podvornoye.

Kishtelnitsa, Mold. (Chistelnita); pop. 105; 69 km NNW of Kishinev; 47°34'/28°40'.

Kishuta, Hung.; pop. 3; 62 km NE of Miskolc; 48°27'/21°29'.

Kishvarda, *see* Kisvarda.

Kisida, *see* Mala Ida.

Kisielew, Pol.; pop. 2; 94 km S of Bialystok; 52°19'/22°48'.

Kisielice, Pol.; 94 km SE of Gdansk; 53°36'/19°16'; LDS.

Kisielin, *see* Kiselin.

Kisielow, Pol.; pop. 6; 88 km SW of Krakow; 49°47'/18°46'.

Kisielowka, Pol.; pop. 20; A number of towns share this name. It was not possible to determine from available information which one is being referenced.

Kisigmand, Hung.; pop. 7; 75 km W of Budapest; 47°39'/18°06'.

Kisilva, *see* Ilva Mica.

Kiskajan, *see* Caianu Mic.

Kiskallo, Hung.; pop. 6; 82 km ESE of Miskolc; 47°53'/21°52'.

Kiskend, *see* Chendu Mic.

Kiskinizs, Hung.; pop. 12; 32 km NE of Miskolc; 48°15'/21°03'.

Kiskirva, *see* Belovarec.

Kiskomarom, Hung.; pop. 41; 19 km NE of Nagykanizsa; 46°33'/17°11'.

Kiskore, Hung.; pop. 24; 69 km S of Miskolc; 47°30'/20°30'; HSL.

Kiskoros, Hung.; pop. 588; 75 km WNW of Szeged; 46°37'/19°18'; GUM4, HSL, HSL2, LDL, LDS, PHH.

Kiskorpad, Hung.; pop. 10; 50 km E of Nagykanizsa; 46°21'/17°37'.

Kiskundorozsma, Hung.; pop. 41; 13 km WNW of Szeged; 46°17'/20°04'; AMG.

Kiskunfelegyhaza, Hung.; pop. 996; 56 km NW of Szeged; 46°43'/19°51'; COH, HSL, LDS, PHH.

Kiskunhalas, Hung.; pop. 668; 56 km WNW of Szeged; 46°26'/19°30'; AMG, GUM6, HSL, LDS, PHH.

Kiskunlachaza, Hung. (Szentivan); pop. 100; 38 km S of Budapest; 47°12'/19°01'; HSL, PHH.

Kiskunmajsa, Hung.; pop. 168; 45 km WNW of Szeged; 46°29'/19°45'; AMG, HSL, LDS, PHH.

Kisladany, HSL. This pre-World War I community was not found in BGN gazetteers.

Kislang, Hung.; pop. 14; 82 km SSW of Budapest; 46°58'/18°23'.

Kislau, Germ.; 62 km NW of Stuttgart; 49°13'/08°39'; PHGBW.

Kisleta, Hung.; pop. 68; 94 km ESE of Miskolc; 47°50'/22°01'; HSL, LDS, PHH.

Kislitsa, Ukr. (Caslita Dunare); pop. 13; 176 km SW of Odessa; 45°25'/29°02'.

Kislod, Hung.; pop. 12; 101 km NNE of Nagykanizsa; 47°09'/17°37'.

Kislonya, *see* Lonya.

Kislovchina, *see* Kozlovshchina.

Kislovodsk, USSR; pop. 2,000; 914 km SSE of Voronezh; 43°56'/42°44'; GUM4, GUM5, GUM6.

Kislovshchizna, *see* Kozlovshchina.

Kislowszczyzna, *see* Kozlovshchina.

Kismarja, Hung.; pop. 53; 126 km SE of Miskolc; 47°15'/21°50'; HSL, LDS, PHH.

Kismarton, Aus.; 45 km SSE of Wien; 47°51'/16°32'; EJ, LDL, LDS.

Kisnameny, Hung.; pop. 43; 146 km E of Miskolc; 47°57'/22°42'.

Kisnana, Hung.; pop. 41; 56 km SW of Miskolc; 47°51'/20°09'.

Kisnarda, Hung.; pop. 1; 101 km NW of Nagykanizsa; 47°14'/16°27'.

Kisnemedi, Hung.; pop. 10; 32 km NNE of Budapest; 47°44'/19°18'.

Kisorichi, Ukr. (Kisorycze); pop. 39; 94 km NE of Rovno; 51°11'/27°16'.

Kisorycze, *see* Kisorichi.

Kisovce, HSL. This pre-World War I community was not found in BGN gazetteers.

Kispalad, Hung.; pop. 22; 150 km E of Miskolc; 48°01'/22°50'; HSL.

Kispast, *see* Valea Mica.

Kis Patak, *see* Valea Mica.

Kispatak, *see* Ricky.

Kispec, Hung.; pop. 6; 107 km WSW of Budapest; 47°29'/17°38'.

Kispest, Hung.; pop. 3,456; 13 km SE of Budapest; 47°27'/19°08'; AMG, COH, GUM5, JGFF, PHH.

Kispirit, Hung.; pop. 4; 94 km N of Nagykanizsa; 47°12'/17°15'.

Kisraska, *see* Male Raskovce.

Kisrebra, *see* Rebrisoara.

Kisrecse, Hung.; pop. 4; 13 km NE of Nagykanizsa; 46°30'/17°04'.

Kisrozvagy, Hung.; pop. 36; 94 km NE of Miskolc; 48°21'/21°57'.

Kissarmas, *see* Sarmasel.

Kisseben, *see* Sabinov.

Kissebes, *see* Poieni.

Kisseliya, Mold. (Chioselia); pop. 4; 101 km S of Kishinev; 46°09'/28°24'.

Kissenheim, HSL. This pre-World War I community was not found in BGN gazetteers.

Kissikator, Hung.; pop. 5; 50 km W of Miskolc; 48°12'/20°08'.

Kissingen, *see* Bad Kissingen.

Kisskowo, *see* Kiszkowo.

Kisszallas, Hung.; pop. 11; 50 km W of Szeged; 46°17'/19°30'.

Kisszekeres, Hung. (Szekeres); pop. 25; 139 km E of Miskolc; 47°58'/22°38'; HSL.

Kisszentgrot, Hung. (Szentgrot); pop. 9; 62 km N of Nagykanizsa; 46°56'/17°05'; HSL, LDS.

Kistapolca, Hung.; pop. 1; 126 km ESE of Nagykanizsa; 45°49'/18°23'.

Kistapolcsany, *see* Topolcianky.

Kistarcsa, Hung.; pop. 88; 19 km ENE of Budapest; 47°32'/19°16'; EDRD, GUM4, GUM5, GUM6, PHH.

Kistelek, Hung.; pop. 218; 32 km NW of Szeged; 46°28'/19°59'; HSL, LDS, PHH.

Kisterenye, Hung. (Kistoronya); pop. 87; 69 km WSW of Miskolc; 48°01'/19°50'; GUM5, PHH.

Kistokaj, Hung.; pop. 11; 13 km SE of Miskolc; 48°03'/20°51'; HSL.

Kistormas, Hung.; pop. 3; 120 km ENE of Nagykanizsa; 46°30'/18°34'.

Kistoronya, *see* Kisterenye.

Kistotfalu, Hung.; pop. 1; 120 km ESE of Nagykanizsa; 45°54'/18°19'.

Kisujszallas, Hung.; pop. 310; 101 km S of Miskolc; 47°13'/20°46'; HSL, LDS, PHH.

Kisungvar, HSL. This pre-World War I community was not found in BGN gazetteers.

Kisunyom, Hung.; pop. 8; 88 km NNW of Nagykanizsa; 47°09'/16°39'.

Kisvarda, Hung. (Kishvarda, Klaynvardayn, Kleinwardein, Virdayn Katan); pop. 3,658; 94 km ENE of Miskolc; 48°13'/22°05'; AMG, COH, EJ, GUM3, GUM4, GUM5, GUM6, HSL, JGFF, LDL, LDS, LYV, PHH, YB.

Kisvarsany, Hung.; pop. 54; 114 km ENE of Miskolc; 48°09'/22°18'; HSL, JGFF, LDS, PHH.

Kisvasarhely, Hung.; pop. 5; 69 km N of Nagykanizsa; 47°00'/17°12'.

Kisvaszar, Hung.; pop. 4; 94 km E of Nagykanizsa; 46°17'/18°13'.

Kisvejke, Hung.; pop. 3; 114 km E of Nagykanizsa; 46°23'/18°25'.

Kiszindia, *see* Chisindia.

Kiszkowo, Pol. (Kisskowo); pop. 3; 26 km NE of Poznan; 52°35'/17°15'; JGFF.

Kiszolow, Pol. PHP3. This town was not found in BGN gazetteers under the given spelling.

Kiszombor, Hung.; pop. 20; 19 km ESE of Szeged; 46°11'/20°26'.

Kiszsidany, Hung. (Nemetzsidany); pop. 3; 114 km NNW of Nagykanizsa; 47°25'/16°39'.

Kiszte, *see* Kysta.

Kiszyniow, *see* Kishinev.

Kitai Gorod, *see* Kitay Gorod.

Kitaigorod, *see* Kitay Gorod.

Kitanchevo, Bulg. (Kadar); 101 km WNW of Varna; 43°44'/26°53'; HSL.

Kitay Gorod, Ukr. (Kitai Gorod, Kitaigorod); pop. 1,595; 94 km SW of Uman; 48°29'/29°01'; COH, EDRD, JGFF, LDL, SF, YB.

Kitev, *see* Kuty.

Kitki, Pol.; pop. 3; 101 km NNW of Warszawa; 53°08'/20°36'.

Kitov, *see* Kuty.

Kitow, Pol.; pop. 9; 56 km SE of Lublin; 50°48'/22°56'.

Kitsee, *see* Kittsee.

Kitskan, *see* Kitskany.

Kitskani Vek, *see* Staryye Kitskany.

Kitskany, Mold. (Chitcani, Kitskan); pop. 35; 62 km ESE of Kishinev; 46°47'/29°36'.

Kitsman, Ukr. (Cotman, Cozmeni, Kosman, Kotzman, Kozmeny, Kucmeh); pop. 640; 19 km NW of Chernovtsy; 48°26'/25°46'; JGFF, LYV, PHR2, SF.

Kittsee, Aus. (Kitsee); pop. 62; 56 km E of Wien; 48°05'/17°04'; CAHJP, EJ, LDS.

Kitzingen, Germ.; pop. 360; 69 km WNW of Nurnberg; 49°44'/10°10'; EDRD, EJ, GUM5, HSL, PHGB.

Kivercy, *see* Kivertsy.

Kivertsy, Ukr. (Kivercy, Kivertzi, Kiwerce); pop. 175; 62 km WNW of Rovno; 50°50'/25°28'; GUM4, HSL, SF.

Kivertzi, *see* Kivertsy.

Kiwaczow, Pol. PHP2. This town was not found in BGN gazetteers under the given spelling.

Kiwerce, *see* Kivertsy.

Kiydantsy, Ukr. (Kujdance, Kuydantse); pop. 40; 75 km WNW of Chernovtsy; 48°32'/24°58'; JGFF.

Kiyev, Ukr. (Kiev, Kijew, Kijow, Kjew); pop. 140,256; 189 km N of Uman; 50°26'/30°31'; AMG, EDRD, EJ, GUM3, GUM4, GUM5, GUM6, HSL, HSL2, ISH1, JGFF, LDL, LYV, PHP1, PHP2, PHP4, SF.

Kizil Orda, Pol. PHP3. This town was not found in BGN gazetteers under the given spelling.

Kjew, *see* Kiyev.

Klacany, Cz. (Kelecseny); 69 km ESE of Kosice; 48°32'/22°07'; HSL.

Kladam, Germ. LDS. This town was not found in BGN gazetteers under the given spelling.

Kladanj, Yug.; pop. 12; 157 km SW of Beograd; 44°14'/18°42'.

Kladnev, Ukr. (Kladniow); pop. 57; 133 km N of Lvov; 51°01'/23°56'.

Kladniow, *see* Kladnev.

Kladno, Cz.; pop. 257; 26 km W of Praha; 50°09'/14°06'; COH, GUM3, GUM6, HSL.

Kladovo, Yug.; pop. 1; 163 km E of Beograd; 44°37'/22°37'.

Kladowa, Pol. PHP4. This town was not found in BGN gazetteers under the given spelling.

Kladruby, Cz.; pop. 21; 120 km SW of Praha; 49°43'/12°58'.

Klagenfurt, Aus.; pop. 180; 101 km SW of Graz; 46°38'/14°18'; EJ, GUM4, GUM5, HSL.

Klaipeda, Lith. (Klajpeda, Memel); pop. 2,402; 139 km WSW of Siauliai; 55°43'/21°07'; AMG, COH, EJ, GUM3, GUM4, GUM5, GUM6, HSL, JGFF, LDL, PHP2, YL.

Klaj, Pol.; pop. 37; 32 km ESE of Krakow; 49°59'/20°19'; PHP3.

Klajpeda, *see* Klaipeda.

Klakar, Yug.; pop. 1; 182 km ESE of Zagreb; 45°06'/18°08'.

Klamos, Cz.; pop. 7; 75 km ENE of Praha; 50°07'/15°30'.

Klanjec, Yug.; pop. 4; 38 km NW of Zagreb; 46°04'/15°45'.

Klanovice, Cz.; pop. 9; 13 km ENE of Praha; 50°06'/14°40'.

Klapowka, Pol.; pop. 9; 75 km WNW of Przemysl; 50°13'/21°52'; JGFF.

Klapy, Pol.; pop. 3; 50 km NW of Praha; 50°26'/14°01'.

Klarysew, Pol.; pop. 2; 26 km SE of Warszawa; 52°06'/21°07'.

Klasna, *see* Klasno.

Klasni, *see* Klasno.

Klasno, (Klasna, Klasni); pop. 396; EGRS, HSL, PHP3, SF. Described in the *Black Book* as being in the Krakow region of Poland, this town was not found in BGN gazetteers.

Klaster, Cz.; 88 km SW of Praha; 49°30'/13°35'; HSL, HSL2.

Klaszkovce, Ukr. EDRD. This town was not found in BGN gazetteers under the given spelling.

Klatovy, Cz. (Klattau); pop. 416; 114 km SW of Praha; 49°24'/13°18'; EJ, GUM5, HSL, HSL2, JGFF.

Klattau, *see* Klatovy.

Klausenberg, *see* Cluj.

Klausenburg, *see* Cluj.

Klavdiyevo Tarasovo, Ukr. (Klavdyevo Tarasovka); pop. 26; 38 km WNW of Kiyev; 50°35'/30°01'.

Klavdyevo Tarasovka, *see* Klavdiyevo Tarasovo.

Klaynvardayn, *see* Kisvarda.

Klebanovka, Ukr. (Klebanowka, Klebanuvka); pop. 46; 120 km S of Rovno; 49°35'/26°01'.

Klebanowka, *see* Klebanovka.

Klebanuvka, *see* Klebanovka.

Klecany, Cz.; pop. 16; 19 km NNW of Praha; 50°11'/14°25'.

Klecenov, *see* Kosicky Klecenov.

Kleck, *see* Kletsk.

Klecko, Pol. (Kletzko); pop. 26; 38 km NE of Poznan; 52°38'/17°26'.

Klecz, Pol.; pop. 4; 56 km SSW of Lodz; 51°22'/19°01'.

Klecza Dolna, Pol.; pop. 8; 38 km SW of Krakow; 49°53'/19°34'.

Kleczany, Pol.; 69 km ESE of Krakow; 49°40'/20°38'; PHP3.

Kleczew, Pol. (Kleczow, Kletchei, Kletcheva); pop. 894; 82 km E of Poznan; 52°22'/18°10'; AMG, COH, GUM3, HSL2, JGFF, PHP1, SF.

Kleczewo, Pol.; 75 km SE of Gdansk; 53°44'/19°11'; PHP4.

Kleczkowo, Pol. (Kletchkovo); pop. 25; 88 km WSW of Bialystok; 53°04'/21°51'; HSL, SF.

Kleczow, *see* Kleczew.

Kleinalsleben, Germ.; 107 km WNW of Leipzig; 51°59'/11°16'; LDS.

Kleinbardorf, Germ.; 101 km NW of Nurnberg; 50°16'/10°24'; CAHJP, GUM5, PHGB.

Kleinbockenheim, *see* Bockenheim.

Kleindexen, GUM4. This town was not found in BGN gazetteers under the given spelling.

Kleineibstadt, Germ.; pop. 26; 107 km NW of Nurnberg; 50°18'/10°22'; GUM5, HSL, JGFF, PHGB.

Kleineicholzheim, Germ.; pop. 38; 82 km SE of Frankfurt am Main; 49°26'/09°17'; LDS, PHGBW.

Kleinerdlingen, *see* Herkheim.

Kleinheubach, Germ.; pop. 45; 62 km SE of Frankfurt am Main; 49°43'/09°13'; GUM5, HSL, PHGB.

Kleinkarlbach, Germ.; pop. 2; 75 km SSW of Frankfurt am Main; 49°32'/08°09'.

Klein Krotzenburg, *see* Kleinkrotzenburg.

Kleinkrotzenburg, Germ. (Klein Krotzenburg); pop. 26; 19 km E of Frankfurt am Main; 50°05'/08°58'; GED.

Kleinlangheim, Germ.; pop. 50; 62 km WNW of Nurnberg; 49°46'/10°17'; GUM5, PHGB.

Kleinneusiedl, Aus.; pop. 7; 26 km ESE of Wien; 48°05'/16°36'.

Klein Nordlingen, HSL. This pre-World War I community was not found in BGN gazetteers.

Kleinostheim, Germ.; 32 km ESE of Frankfurt am Main; 50°00'/09°04'; PHGB.

Klein Reken, Germ.; 101 km N of Koln; 51°47'/07°02'; GED.

Kleinrust, Aus.; pop. 1; 56 km W of Wien; 48°16'/15°37'.

Kleinschlag, Aus.; pop. 3; 56 km NE of Graz; 47°23'/15°57'.

Kleinsteinach, Germ.; pop. 45; 88 km NW of Nurnberg; 50°07'/10°27'; GUM5, HSL, HSL2, JGFF, PHGB.

Klein Umstadt, Germ.; pop. 6; 32 km SE of Frankfurt am Main; 49°53'/08°57'.

Kleinwallstadt, Germ.; pop. 50; 45 km ESE of Frankfurt am Main; 49°53'/09°10'; AMG, GUM5, PHGB.

Kleinwarasdorf, Aus.; pop. 3; 82 km SSE of Wien; 47°32'/16°35'.

Kleinwardein, *see* Kisvarda.

Kleinweikersdorf, Aus.; pop. 2; 56 km NNW of Wien; 48°38'/16°12'.

Klejniki, *see* Kleyniki.

Klejpeda, Pol.; pop. 6; 133 km NNW of Bialystok; 54°18'/22°49'.

Klekacz, *see* Klekacze.

Klekacze, Pol. (Klekacz); pop. 6; 94 km NNE of Przemysl; 50°28'/23°33'.

Klembovka, *see* Klubovka.

Klembow, *see* Klembow Koscielny.

Klembow Koscielny, Pol. (Klembow); pop. 7; 32 km NE of Warszawa; 52°25'/21°20'.

Klemensow, Pol.; 69 km SE of Lublin; 50°44'/23°02'; GUM4, GUM5, GUM6.

Klementov, *see* Klimontow.

Klementowice, Pol.; 32 km WNW of Lublin; 51°21'/22°09'; GA.

Klenec, Cz.; pop. 9; 38 km NW of Praha; 50°24'/14°15'.

Klenocz, *see* Klenovec.

Klenova, Cz.; 82 km NE of Kosice; 48°57'/22°20'; HSL.

Klenovec, Cz. (Klenocz); 101 km WSW of Kosice; 48°36'/19°54'; HSL.

Klenowitz, HSL, HSL2. This pre-World War I community was not found in BGN gazetteers.

Kleparov, Ukr. (Kleparow); pop. 1,120; 6 km NW of Lvov; 49°51'/23°59'; EGRS.

Kleparow, *see* Kleparov.

Klepie Gorne, Pol.; pop. 2; 88 km NE of Krakow; 50°26'/21°01'.

Kleshchel, *see* Kleszczele.

Kleshchele, *see* Kleszczele.

Kleshchi, Byel. (Kleszcze); pop. 21; 50 km W of Pinsk; 52°11'/25°24'.

Kleshchuvna, *see* Klishchevna.

Kleshkovtsy, LDL. This pre-World War I community was not found in BGN gazetteers.

Kleshtchel, *see* Kleszczele.

Kleshtchov, *see* Kleszczow.

Klesov, Ukr. (Klesow, Klisov, Klosova); pop. 90; 94 km NNE of Rovno; 51°20'/26°56'; AMG, COH, GUM3, SF. The *Black Book* notes a second town in Polesie province named Klesow (pop. 52) that does not appear in interwar or contemporary gazetteers.

Klesow, *see* Klesov.

Kleszcze, *see* Kleshchi.

Kleszczele, Pol. (Kleshchel, Kleshchele, Kleshtchel); pop. 621; 62 km SSE of Bialystok; 52°35'/23°19'; GA, GUM3, GUM4, GUM5, HSL, LDL, LYV, SF.

Kleszczow, Pol. (Kleshtchov); pop. 232; 56 km N of Czestochowa; 51°14'/19°18'; AMG, CAHJP, HSL, HSL2, PHP1, SF.

Kleszczowna, *see* Klishchevna.

Kleszewo, Pol. (Kleszewo Stare); pop. 28; 56 km N of Warszawa; 52°45'/21°06'.

Kleszewo Stare, *see* Kleszewo.

Kletchei, *see* Kleczew.

Kletcheva, *see* Kleczew.

Kletchkovo, *see* Kleczkowo.

Kletna, *see* Kletnaya.

Kletnaya, Byel. (Kletna); pop. 12; 50 km NW of Pinsk; 52°25'/25°44'.

Kletnya, GUM4. This town was not found in BGN gazetteers under the given spelling.

Kletsk, Byel. (Kleck, Kletzk, Klezk); pop. 4,190; 107 km SSW of Minsk; 53°04'/26°38'; AMG, COH, EJ, GA, GUM3, GUM4, GUM5, GUM6, HSL, HSL2, JGFF, LDL, LYV, SF, YB.

Kletzk, *see* Kletsk.

Kletzko, *see* Klecko.

Klevan, Ukr. (Klewan); pop. 1,520; 26 km WNW of Rovno; 50°45'/25°59'; COH, GUM3, GUM4, GYLA, HSL, JGFF, LDL, SF.

Kleve, Germ. (Cleves); pop. 200; 114 km NW of Koln;

51°47'/06°09'; CAHJP, GED, GUM5, HSL.

Klevov, Pol. EDRD. This town was not found in BGN gazetteers under the given spelling.

Klew, Pol.; pop. 10; 69 km SE of Lodz; 51°13'/20°03'.

Klewan, *see* Klevan.

Klewinowo, Pol.; pop. 2; 26 km SSE of Bialystok; 52°59'/23°11'.

Kleyniki, Byel. (Klejniki); pop. 4; 170 km W of Pinsk; 52°09'/23°36'.

Klezk, *see* Kletsk.

Klicany, Cz.; pop. 12; 19 km NNW of Praha; 50°12'/14°26'.

Klichev, Byel.; pop. 126 km ESE of Minsk; 53°29'/29°21'; SF.

Klichy, Pol.; pop. 4; 56 km S of Bialystok; 52°40'/22°55'.

Klicin, Cz.; 75 km WNW of Praha; 50°17'/13°28'; HSL.

Kliczkow Wielki, Pol.; pop. 3; 69 km SW of Lodz; 51°32'/18°34'.

Klikol, *see* Klykoliai.

Klikole, *see* Klykoliai.

Klikov, Cz.; pop. 9; 126 km WSW of Brno; 48°55'/14°55'.

Klimautsy, Mold. (Climauti); pop. 33; 170 km NW of Kishinev; 48°19'/27°37'.

Klimentov, *see* Klimontow.

Klimentow, *see* Klimontow.

Klimetow, *see* Klimontow.

Klimiec, Ukr.; 94 km S of Lvov; 49°04'/23°31'; HSL. This town was located on a pre-World War I map, but does not appear in contemporary gazetteers.

Klimkovice, Cz.; pop. 139; 133 km NE of Brno; 49°48'/18°08'.

Klimkovka, *see* Klimkowka.

Klimkovtse, Ukr. (Klimkowce); pop. 41; 120 km S of Rovno; 49°36'/26°06'.

Klimkowce, *see* Klimkovtse.

Klimkowka, Pol. (Klimkovka); pop. 22; 75 km SW of Przemysl; 49°35'/21°50'; HSL.

Klimontow, Pol. (Klementov, Klimentov, Klimentow, Klimetow); pop. 2,652; 101 km SW of Lublin; 50°40'/21°27'; AMG, COH, EDRD, GA, GUM3, GUM5, GYLA, HSL, JGFF, LDL, LDS, LYV, PHP4, SF.

Klimontow (near Bedzin), Pol.; pop. 67; 56 km WNW of Krakow; 50°17'/19°12'.

Klimontow (near Jedrzejow), Pol.; pop. 13; 32 km NE of Krakow; 50°14'/20°20'.

Klimontow (near Miechow), Pol.; pop. 29; 50 km N of Krakow; 50°31'/20°03'.

Klimonty, Pol.; 101 km E of Warszawa; 52°11'/22°31'; GA, GUM3, GUM4.

Klimov, *see* Klimovka.

Klimovichi, Byel. (Klimovitch, Klimovitz, Klimowice?, Klimowicze); pop. 2,587; 150 km NNE of Gomel; 53°37'/31°58'; HSL, LDL, SF.

Klimovitch, *see* Klimovichi.

Klimovitz, *see* Klimovichi.

Klimovka, USSR (Klimov, Klimow); pop. 431; 875 km NE of Moskva; 58°52'/51°09'; LDL, SF.

Klimovo, USSR; pop. 431; 170 km SW of Bryansk; 52°24'/32°13'; GUM4, HSL.

Klimow, *see* Klimovka.

Klimowice, *possibly* Klimovichi.

Klimowicze, *see* Klimovichi.

Klin, USSR; pop. 94; 75 km ESE of Kalinin; 56°20'/36°45'; GUM3.

Klinec, Cz.; pop. 3; 26 km SSW of Praha; 49°54'/14°20'.

Klingenberg am Main, Germ.; 50 km ESE of Frankfurt am Main; 49°47'/09°12'; GUM5, PHGB.

Klingenmunster, Germ.; pop. 3; 94 km WNW of Stuttgart; 49°08'/08°01'; GED.

Klingenthal, Germ.; pop. 6; 107 km S of Leipzig; 50°22'/12°28'.

Klintsy, USSR (Klintzi, Klinzy); pop. 5,248; 150 km SW of Bryansk; 52°45'/32°15'; EDRD, EJ, GUM5, HSL, JGFF, SF.

Klintzi, *see* Klintsy.

Kliny, Pol. PHP1. A number of towns share this name. It was not possible to determine from available information which one is being referenced.

Klinzy, *see* Klintsy.

Klischkowcy, *see* Klishkovtsy.

Klishchevna, Ukr. (Kleshchuvna, Kleszczowna); pop. 24; 62 km ESE of Lvov; 49°29'/24°36'.

Klishkovtsy, Ukr. (Cliscauti, Klischkowcy, Klishkutz, Klushkevitz); pop. 452; 26 km NE of Chernovtsy; 48°26'/26°16'; SF.

Klishkutz, *see* Klishkovtsy.

Klisov, *see* Klesov.

Kliszow, Pol.; 114 km NE of Krakow; 50°25'/21°24'; JGFF.

Klivodin, Ukr. (Clivodin); pop. 46; 26 km NW of Chernovtsy; 48°29'/25°45'.

Klobouk, *see* Klobouky.

Klobouky, Cz. (Klobouk); pop. 89; 32 km SE of Brno; 48°59'/16°52'.

Klobuck, Pol. (Klobucko, Klobutsk, Klobutzk); pop. 1,647; 19 km WNW of Czestochowa; 50°54'/18°56'; AMG, CAHJP, COH, GA, GUM3, GUM4, GUM5, JGFF, LDS, LYV, PHP1, SF, YB.

Klobucko, *see* Klobuck.

Klobukowice, Pol.; pop. 9; 19 km ENE of Czestochowa; 50°50'/19°20'.

Klobuky, Cz.; pop. 15; 45 km WNW of Praha; 50°18'/13°59'.

Klobutsk, *see* Klobuck.

Klobutzk, *see* Klobuck.

Kloczew, Pol.; 69 km NW of Lublin; 51°44'/21°58'; GUM5.

Kloda, (Klode); FRG. A number of towns share this name. It was not possible to determine from available information which one is being referenced.

Klodau, *see* Klodawa.

Klodava, *see* Klodawa.

Klodawa, Pol. (Klodau, Klodava, Klodeve, Klodove, Klodowa); pop. 1,800; 69 km NW of Lodz; 52°15'/18°55'; AMG, COH, EDRD, EJ, HSL, HSL2, JGFF, LDL, LDS, LYV, PHP1, PHP4, SF.

Klode, *see* Kloda.

Klodeve, *see* Klodawa.

Klodne, Pol.; pop. 20; Described in the *Black Book* as being in the Krakow region of Poland, this town was not found in BGN gazetteers.

Klodnica, Pol.; pop. 51; PHP3. A number of towns share this name. It was not possible to determine from available information which one is being referenced.

Klodno, *see* Klodno Velikoye.

Klodno Velikoye, Ukr. (Klodno, Klodno Velke, Klodno Wielkie); pop. 37; 26 km NE of Lvov; 50°00'/24°17'; PHP2.

Klodno Velke, *see* Klodno Velikoye.

Klodno Wielkie, *see* Klodno Velikoye.

Klodove, *see* Klodawa.

Klodowa, *see* Klodawa.

Klodzice, Pol.; pop. 8; 50 km SE of Lodz; 51°21'/19°47'.

Klodzienko, *see* Kolodentse.

Klodzko, Pol. (Glatz); pop. 176; 75 km S of Wroclaw; 50°26'/16°39'; AMG, EJ, HSL, LDS, POCEM.

Klokocevci, Yug.; pop. 6; 163 km E of Zagreb; 45°34'/18°07'.

Klokotnia, *see* Klokotyna.

Klokotyna, (Klokotnia); GUM4, PHR1. This town was not found in BGN gazetteers under the given spelling.

Klomnice, Pol.; pop. 137; 26 km NE of Czestochowa; 50°56'/19°22'; PHP1.

Klonice, *see* Kolonitsa.

Klonitse, *see* Kolonitsa.

Klonowa, Pol.; 82 km NW of Czestochowa; 51°25'/18°26'; PHP1.

Klooga, Est.; 32 km SW of Tallinn; 59°19'/24°16'; EDRD, GUM3, GUM4, GUM5, GUM6, ISH2, PHLE.

Kloppenheim, Germ.; 19 km N of Frankfurt am Main; 50°14'/08°45'; JGFF.

Kloski Mlynowieta, Pol.; pop. 10; 38 km WSW of Bialystok; 53°03'/22°37'.

Klosno, Pol.; pop. 2; 139 km WNW of Warszawa; 53°08'/19°29'.

Klosova, *see* Klesov.

Klostar Ivanic, Yug.; pop. 5; 32 km E of Zagreb; 45°44'/16°25'.

Klosterlechfeld, *see* Lager Lechfeld.

Klosterneuburg, Aus.; pop. 227; 19 km NNW of Wien; 48°18'/16°19'; JGFF.

Klovainiai, Lith. (Klovian); pop. 21; 38 km E of Siauliai; 55°56'/23°56'; YL.

Klovian, *see* Klovainiai.

Klubovka, Ukr. (Klembovka); 69 km SE of Rovno; 50°05'/26°46'; AMG.

Klucek, Cz.; pop. 3; 69 km WNW of Praha; 50°17'/13°36'.

Klucko, Pol.; pop. 4; 88 km ENE of Czestochowa; 51°02'/20°22'.

Kluczbork, Pol.; 69 km WNW of Czestochowa; 50°59'/18°13'; LDS.

Kluczkowice, Pol.; pop. 2; 50 km SW of Lublin; 51°05'/21°56'.

Klucznikowice, Pol.; pop. 121; 50 km WSW of Krakow; 50°03'/19°14'; PHP3.

Kluczow Maly, Pol.; pop. 26; Described in the *Black Book* as being in the Stanislawow region of Poland, this town was not found in BGN gazetteers.

Kluczow Wielki, *see* Klyuchev.

Kluczyce, Pol.; pop. 5; 50 km E of Czestochowa; 50°44'/19°48'.

Kludzice, Pol.; pop. 7; 50 km SE of Lodz; 51°21'/19°47'.

Klukowo, Pol.; 56 km SW of Bialystok; 52°47'/22°30'; LDS.

Klunya, *see* Koln.

Klushkevitz, *see* Klishkovtsy.

Klusk, *see* Klyusk.

Klusow, Ukr.; pop. 27; 120 km WNW of Chernovtsy; 48°51'/24°28'. This town was located on an interwar map of Poland but does not appear in contemporary gazetteers. Map coordinates are approximate.

Klusserath, Germ.; 126 km S of Koln; 49°50'/06°51'; JGFF.

Kluszkowce, Pol.; pop. 20; 75 km SSE of Krakow; 49°27'/20°19'.

Kluwince, Ukr.; pop. 49; 75 km N of Chernovtsy; 48°55'/25°55'. This town was located on an interwar map of Poland but does not appear in contemporary gazetteers. Map coordinates are approximate.

Kluyzenburg, *see* Cluj.

Kluzh, *see* Cluj.

Klwatecka Wolka, Pol.; pop. 79; Described in the *Black Book* as being in the Kielce region of Poland, this town was not found in BGN gazetteers.

Klwatka, Pol.; pop. 20; 88 km W of Lublin; 51°24'/21°19'.

Klwow, Pol. (Kviv); pop. 297; 88 km E of Lodz; 51°32'/20°38'; GA, JGFF, LDS, PHP1, SF.

Klykoliai, Lith. (Klikol, Klikole); 62 km NW of Siauliai; 56°22'/22°50'; JGFF, YL.

Klyuchev, Ukr. (Kluczow Wielki, Klyuchuv Velki); pop. 21; 75 km W of Chernovtsy; 48°28'/24°57'.

Klyuchuv Velki, *see* Klyuchev.

Klyusk, Ukr. (Klusk); pop. 15; 126 km WNW of Rovno; 51°04'/24°36'.

Klyz, Pol.; pop. 21; 62 km ENE of Krakow; 50°12'/20°50'.

Klyzow, Pol.; pop. 43; 82 km S of Lublin; 50°33'/22°10'.

Kmetovo, Cz. (Dorok); 88 km ENE of Bratislava; 48°10'/18°17'; HSL.

Kmiczyn, Pol.; pop. 32; 107 km NNE of Przemysl; 50°33'/23°47'.

Knaj, Pol.; pop. 3; 88 km WSW of Krakow; 49°53'/18°44'.

Knazice, Cz.; 101 km NE of Bratislava; 48°24'/18°25'; AMG.

Knenitsh, *see* Knyazhnychi.

Kneselo, Ukr. (Kniesiolo?); pop. 55; 50 km SE of Lvov; 49°31'/24°22'.

Knetzgau, Germ.; 69 km NW of Nurnberg; 49°59'/10°33'; PHGB.

Knezevi Vinogradi, Yug.; pop. 25; 170 km WNW of Beograd; 45°45'/18°45'.

Kniaza Krinica, *see* Knyazha.

Kniazdwor, *see* Knyazhdvur.

Kniaze, *see* Knyazhe.

Kniazha, *see* Knyazha.

Kniaziowo, COH. This town was not found in BGN gazetteers under the given spelling.

Kniazitch, *see* Knyazhitsy.

Kniazpol, *see* Knyazhpol.

Kniazyce, Pol.; pop. 7; 19 km S of Przemysl; 49°43'/22°45'.

Kniehenitch, *see* Knyazhnychi.

Kniephof, *see* Konarzewo.

Kniesiolo, *possibly* Kneselo.

Knihinin, Pol.; pop. 6,478; GYLA, PHP2. Described in the *Black Book* as being in the Stanislawow region of Poland, this town was not found in BGN gazetteers.

Knihinin Kolonia, Pol.; pop. 910; Described in the *Black Book* as being in the Stanislawow region of Poland, this town was not found in BGN gazetteers.

Knihynicze, *see* Knyazhnychi.

Knishin, *see* Knyszyn.

Knisin, *see* Knyszyn.

Kniszyn, *see* Knyszyn.

Knittelfeld, Aus.; pop. 26; 56 km WNW of Graz; 47°13'/14°49'.

Knjashizy, *see* Knyazhitsy.

Knoblauch, Germ.; 38 km WSW of Berlin; 52°30'/12°52'; EJ.

Knoviz, Cz.; pop. 11; 26 km WNW of Praha; 50°13'/14°08'.

Knurow, Pol.; 69 km SSW of Czestochowa; 50°13'/18°40'; AMG.

Knyaschewo, SF. This town was not found in BGN gazetteers under the given spelling.

Knyazha, Ukr. (Kniaza Krinica, Kniazha); 75 km NE of Vinnitsa; 49°28'/29°30'; LDL, SF.

Knyazhdvur, Ukr. (Kniazdwor); pop. 106; 75 km WNW of Chernovtsy; 48°33'/24°56'; PHP2.

Knyazhe, Ukr. (Kniaze); pop. 126; 38 km WNW of Chernovtsy; 48°24'/25°27'; PHP2.

Knyazhitsy, Byel. (Kniazitch, Knjashizy); 139 km S of Vitebsk; 53°58'/30°09'; LDL, SF.

Knyazhnychi, Ukr. (Knenitsh, Kniehenitch, Knihynicze); pop. 414; 62 km SE of Lvov; 49°23'/24°28'; EGRS, HSL, LDL, PHP2, SF, YB.

Knyazhpol, Ukr. (Kniazpol); pop. 33; 94 km SW of Lvov; 49°34'/22°45'.

Knyszewicze, Pol.; pop. 2; 45 km NE of Bialystok; 53°20'/23°40'.

Knyszyn, Pol. (Knishin, Knisin, Kniszyn); pop. 1,235; 26 km NW of Bialystok; 53°19'/22°55'; AMG, COH, EDRD, GA, GUM3, GUM4, GUM5, HSL, HSL2, LYV, SF.

Kobaj, GUM4. This town was not found in BGN gazetteers under the given spelling.

Kobaki, Ukr.; pop. 60; 50 km W of Chernovtsy; 48°20'/25°13'; GUM4.

Kobalchin, Ukr. (Cobalceni); pop. 24; 107 km SSW of Vinnitsa; 48°31'/27°28'.

Kobanya, *see* Budapest.

Kobelaki, *see* Kobelyaki.

Kobeliaki, *see* Kobelyaki.

Kobelyaki, Ukr. (Butenkovo, Kobelaki, Kobeliaki, Kobielaki, Kobiliak, Kobylaki); pop. 1,400; 101 km NW of Dnepropetrovsk; 49°09'/34°12'; GUM4, HSL, LDL, SF.

Kobern, Germ.; pop. 68; 82 km SE of Koln; 50°19'/07°28'; EDRD, GED, GUM5.

Kobersdorf, Aus. (Kabold); pop. 172; 69 km S of Wien; 47°36'/16°24'; EJ, HSL, HSL2, LDL, LDS.

Kobialki Nowe, Pol.; pop. 15; 82 km ESE of Warszawa; 51°57'/22°02'.

Kobiel, HSL. This pre-World War I community was not found in BGN gazetteers.

Kobielaki, *see* Kobelyaki.

Kobiele, *see* Kabeliai.

Kobiele Male, Pol.; pop. 4; 45 km NE of Czestochowa; 51°01'/19°38'.

Kobiele Wielkie, Pol.; pop. 33; 45 km NE of Czestochowa; 51°02'/19°38'; JGFF.

Kobierzyn, Pol.; pop. 155; 13 km S of Krakow; 50°01'/19°54'; PHP3.

Kobiletsa Polyana, *see* Kobyletskaya Polyana.

Kobiliack, *see* Kobiljak.

Kobiliak, *see* Kobelyaki.

Kobiljak, (Kobiliack); GUM4. A number of towns share this name. It was not possible to determine from available information which one is being referenced.

Kobilnik, *see* Kobylnik.

Kobilniki, *see* Kobylnik.

Kobilnye, *see* Sladkovodnaya.

Kobiztcha, *see* Kobyzhcha.

Kobleny, Hung.; pop. 4; 101 km E of Nagykanizsa; 46°18'/18°18'.

Koblenz, Germ. (Coblenz); pop. 547; 82 km WNW of Frankfurt am Main; 50°21'/07°36'; AMG, CAHJP, EDRD, EJ, GED, GUM4, GUM5, HSL, HSL2, ISH1, JGFF, LDS, PHGBW.

Koblo, Pol.; pop. 6; 107 km ESE of Lublin; 50°53'/23°58'.

Koblo Stare, Ukr.; pop. 56; 82 km SW of Lvov; 49°25'/23°05'. This town was located on an interwar map of Poland but does not appear in contemporary gazetteers. Map coordinates are approximate.

Kobnat, *see* Kaunata.

Kobrin, Byel. (Kobryn); pop. 5,431; 120 km W of Pinsk; 52°13'/24°21'; AMG, COH, EDRD, EJ, FRG, GA, GUM3, GUM4, GUM5, GUM6, HSL, HSL2, JGFF, LDL, LYV, SF, YB.

Kobryn, *see* Kobrin.

Kobrzyniec Nowy, Pol.; pop. 2; 139 km N of Lodz; 52°58'/19°19'.

Kobrzyniec Stary, Pol.; pop. 24; 139 km N of Lodz; 52°59'/19°20'.

Kobuzie, Pol.; pop. 3; 19 km WNW of Bialystok; 53°15'/22°56'.

Kobyla, Pol.; pop. 24; A number of towns share this name. It was not possible to determine from available information which one is being referenced.

Kobylaki, *see* Kobelyaki.

Kobylany, Pol.; 107 km N of Lublin; 52°10'/22°54'; GA, GUM4. GUM4 refers to a second town located in the Crimea. It does not appear in contemporary gazetteers.

Kobylany Gorne, Pol.; pop. 3; 94 km ENE of Warszawa; 52°20'/22°22'.

Kobyla Wola, Pol.; pop. 2; 62 km ESE of Warszawa; 51°51'/21°40'.

Kobylczyna, Pol.; pop. 5; 62 km ESE of Krakow; 49°45'/20°34'; GUM4.

Kobyle, Pol.; pop. 20; 69 km ESE of Krakow; 49°44'/20°44'.

Kobylea, *see* Kobylnya.

Kobylecka Polana, *see* Kobyletskaya Polyana.

Kobyle Pole, Pol. (Gutenbrunn, Kobylepole); 13 km ESE of Poznan; 52°23'/17°01'; GA, GUM3, GUM4, PHP1, PHP4.

Kobylepole, *see* Kobyle Pole.

Kobyletskaya Polyana, Ukr. (Gyertyanliget, Kobiletsa Polyana, Kobylecka Polana, Polana Kobilecka, Polien Kabileczky); 139 km WSW of Chernovtsy; 48°03'/24°04'; AMG, HSL, SM.

Kobylice, Cz.; 82 km ENE of Praha; 50°15'/15°35'; GA.

Kobylin, Pol.; 32 km WSW of Bialystok; 53°07'/22°41'; GUM4.

Kobylino, Pol.; pop. 82; 32 km WSW of Bialystok; 53°07'/22°41'.

Kobylka, Mold. (Cobalca); pop. 151; 38 km NW of Kishinev; 47°17'/28°35'; GA.

Kobylnica, Pol.; 13 km NE of Poznan; 52°27'/17°06'; GA, PHP2.

Kobylnica Ruska, Pol.; pop. 44; 38 km NNE of Przemysl; 50°01'/23°05'.

Kobylnica Woloska, Pol.; pop. 36; 32 km NE of Przemysl; 50°00'/23°07'.

Kobylnik, Byel. (Kobilnik, Kobilniki); 133 km NW of Minsk; 54°56'/26°41'; AMG, EDRD, GUM3, GUM4, JGFF, LDL, LYV, SF, YB.

Kobylniki, Pol.; 56 km WNW of Warszawa; 52°28'/20°14'; AMG, JGFF, SF.

Kobylniki (Minsk area), Byel.; 133 km NW of Minsk; 54°56'/26°41'; EDRD.

Kobylnya, Mold. (Cobalea Noua, Cobalea Veche, Kobylea); pop. 103; 101 km N of Kishinev; 47°52'/28°40'.

Kobylowloki, Ukr.; pop. 25; 75 km NNW of Chernovtsy; 48°55'/25°45'. This town was located on an interwar map of Poland but does not appear in contemporary gazetteers. Map coordinates are approximate.

Kobyzhcha, Ukr. (Kobiztcha, Kobyzszcza); 82 km NE of Kiyev; 50°50'/31°30'; LDL, SF.

Kobyzszcza, see Kobyzhcha.

Kocborowo, Pol.; pop. 126; 45 km S of Gdansk; 53°59'/18°31'.

Koce Schaby, Pol.; pop. 5; 56 km SSW of Bialystok; 52°42'/22°39'.

Kochanov, see Kokhanovo.

Kochanova, see Kokhanovo.

Kochanovce, Cz.; pop. 83; 56 km NE of Kosice; 48°57'/21°56'; HSL.

Kochanovichi, Byel. (Koczanowicze); pop. 41; 26 km E of Pinsk; 52°07'/26°26'.

Kochanovitch, see Kokhanovichi.

Kochanowka, Pol.; pop. 51; 13 km WNW of Lodz; 51°48'/19°21'; HSL, PHP1. See also Kokhanovka.

Kochel, Germ.; pop. 9; 56 km S of Munchen; 47°40'/11°22'; HSL.

Kochendorf, Germ.; pop. 114 km NNW of Hamburg; 54°29'/09°46'; GUM3, GUM5, GUM6, PHGBW.

Kochkovatoye, Ukr. (Buduri); pop. 6; 101 km SSW of Odessa; 45°48'/29°53'.

Kochlew, Pol.; pop. 9; 50 km NW of Czestochowa; 51°12'/18°46'.

Kochlowice, Pol.; 62 km S of Czestochowa; 50°15'/18°55'; PHP3.

Kochon, Pol.; pop. 11; 114 km N of Lodz; 52°42'/19°20'.

Kochstadt, HSL. This pre-World War I community was not found in BGN gazetteers.

Kochuliya, Mold. (Cociulia); pop. 16; 82 km S of Kishinev; 46°22'/28°25'.

Kocin, see Kocin Stary.

Kocin Nowy, Pol.; pop. 3; 26 km N of Czestochowa; 50°56'/19°06'.

Kocin Stary, Pol. (Kocin); pop. 44; 26 km N of Czestochowa; 50°57'/19°07'; HSL.

Kociubince, see Kotsyubinchiki.

Kociubinczyki, see Kotsyubinchiki.

Kock, Pol. (Kotsk, Kotzk); pop. 2,092; 50 km NNW of Lublin; 51°38'/22°27'; AMG, CAHJP, COH, EDRD, EJ, GA, GUM3, GUM4, GUM5, HSL, HSL2, JGFF, LDL, LDS, LYV, PHP1, PHP4, POCEM, SF, YB.

Kockelburg, HSL. This pre-World War I community was not found in BGN gazetteers.

Koclerov, Cz.; pop. 1; 101 km NE of Praha; 50°29'/15°47'.

Kocmyrzow, Pol.; pop. 14; 19 km NE of Krakow; 50°08'/20°08'; GUM3.

Koconia, Pol.; pop. 7; 56 km NE of Czestochowa; 51°04'/19°47'.

Kocs, Hung.; pop. 21; 69 km W of Budapest; 47°36'/18°13'; HSL.

Kocser, Hung.; pop. 6; 88 km ESE of Budapest; 47°00'/19°55'.

Kocsola, Hung.; pop. 13; 88 km ENE of Nagykanizsa; 46°32'/18°11'.

Kocsord, Hung.; pop. 56; 120 km E of Miskolc; 47°57'/22°23'; HSL, PHH.

Kocudza, see Kocudza Dolna.

Kocudza Dolna, Pol. (Kocudza); pop. 7; 69 km S of Lublin; 50°41'/22°37'.

Kocurow, Pol.; pop. 27; 62 km SW of Krakow; 49°42'/19°15'.

Koczanow, Pol.; pop. 6; 45 km ENE of Krakow; 50°11'/20°29'; GUM4.

Koczanowicze, see Kochanovichi.

Koczargi Nowe, Pol.; pop. 8; 13 km WSW of Warszawa; 52°15'/20°48'.

Koczow, Pol.; pop. 4; 75 km ESE of Lublin; 51°02'/23°35'.

Koden, Pol. (Kodni, Kodnia); pop. 541; 107 km NE of Lublin; 51°54'/23°36'; COH, GA, GUM5, HSL, JGFF, LDS, LYV, POCEM, SF.

Kodeniec, Pol.; pop. 105; 56 km NE of Lublin; 51°36'/23°08'.

Kodima, see Kodyma.

Kodni, see Koden.

Kodnia, see Koden.

Kodnja, see Kodnya.

Kodnya, Ukr. (Kodnja); 101 km N of Vinnitsa; 50°05'/28°43'; SF.

Kodrab, Pol.; pop. 9; 56 km NE of Czestochowa; 51°06'/19°38'; PHP1.

Kodyma, Ukr. (Kodima); pop. 1,986; 114 km SW of Uman; 48°06'/29°07'; GUM5, LDL, SF.

Kodzborg, see Kuczbork.

Koeln, see Koln.

Koenigsberg, see Kaliningrad. The 1921 census of Poland notes a town (pop. 29) named Koenigsberg in Lwow province. Nineteenth-century documents note a town near Rudnick in Lwow province. No town by this name appears on a detailed 1929 map of Poland or in contemporary gazetteers.

Koenigswart, *possibly* Kralovske Porici.

Koeslin, see Koszanowo.

Koflach, Aus.; 32 km WSW of Graz; 47°04'/15°05'; GUM4.

Kogilno, Ukr. (Kohilno); pop. 8; 120 km N of Lvov; 50°52'/24°25'.

Koglhof, Aus.; pop. 1; 38 km NNE of Graz; 47°19'/15°41'.

Kohfidisch, Aus.; pop. 1; 69 km ENE of Graz; 47°10'/16°21'.

Kohilno, see Kogilno.

Kohiszyn, USSR; HSL2. This pre-World War I community was not found in BGN gazetteers.

Kohlo, see Kolo.

Kohlscheid, Germ.; pop. 6; 62 km WSW of Koln; 50°50'/06°06'.

Koidanovo, see Dzerzhinsk.

Koil, see Kolo.

Koisedary, see Kaisiadorys.

Kojetein, see Kojetin.

Kojetin, Cz. (Kojetein); pop. 143; 50 km NE of Brno; 49°21'/17°19'; EJ, HSL.

Kojly, Pol.; pop. 6; 45 km SE of Bialystok; 52°47'/23°29'.

Koka, Hung.; pop. 69; 38 km E of Budapest; 47°29'/19°35'; LDS, PHH.

Kokad, Hung. (Kakad); pop. 13; 120 km ESE of Miskolc; 47°24'/21°57'; LDS.

Kokalofka, see Chechelevka.

Kokasice, Cz.; pop. 1; 114 km WSW of Praha; 49°53'/12°57'.

Kokava nad Rimavicou, Cz. (Kokava na Rimavica); pop. 63; 107 km WSW of Kosice; 48°34'/19°50'.

Kokava na Rimavica, see Kokava nad Rimavicou.

Kokengauzen, see Koknese.

Kokenhausen, see Koknese.

Kokenhusen, see Koknese.

Kokenyes, see Ternovo.

Kokenyesd, see Porumbesti.

Kokhanavka, see Kokhanovka.

Kokhanovichi, Byel. (Kochanovitch); 150 km WNW of Vitebsk; 55°52'/28°08'; LDL, SF.

Kokhanovka, Ukr. (Kochanowka, Kokhanavka); pop. 31; 56 km WNW of Lvov; 49°59'/23°15'.

Kokhanovo, Byel. (Kochanov, Kochanova); pop. 480; 88 km S of Vitebsk; 54°28'/29°59'; LDL, SF.

Koknese, Lat. (Kokengauzen, Kokenhausen, Kokenhusen, Kokneses); pop. 26; 88 km ESE of Riga; 56°39'/25°26'; PHLE.

Kokneses, see Koknese.

Kokorin, Cz.; pop. 2; 45 km N of Praha; 50°26'/14°34'.

Kokorozeny, Mold. (Cucuruzeni); pop. 43; 56 km NNW of Kishinev; 47°29'/28°44'.

Kokoszki, *see* Kokuszka.

Kokot, Pol.; pop. 14; 75 km NNE of Krakow; 50°36'/20°33'.

Koktishka, *see* Kuktiskes.

Kokuszka, Pol. (Kokoszki); pop. 6; 94 km SE of Krakow; 49°28'/20°44'; PHP3.

Kol, *see* Kuliai.

Kolacsko, HSL. This pre-World War I community was not found in BGN gazetteers.

Kolacze, Pol.; 62 km NE of Lublin; 51°28'/23°19'; GUM4.

Kolaczkowice, Pol.; pop. 47; 82 km NE of Krakow; 50°30'/20°52'.

Kolaczyce, Pol. (Kolashitz, Kolatchitz); pop. 104; 94 km W of Przemysl; 49°49'/21°26'; GA, HSL, HSL2, JGFF, PHP3, SF.

Kolaje, Cz.; pop. 6; 56 km ENE of Praha; 50°09'/15°14'.

Kolaki, Pol. (Kolaki Zagnatowo); pop. 25; 88 km N of Warszawa; 53°00'/21°28'.

Kolaki Koscielne, Pol.; pop. 88; 56 km SW of Bialystok; 52°55'/22°25'. This town was located on an interwar map of Poland but does not appear in contemporary gazetteers. Map coordinates are approximate.

Kolaki Zagnatowo, *see* Kolaki.

Kolanki, *see* Kolyanki.

Kolano, Pol.; pop. 15; 62 km NNE of Lublin; 51°41'/23°04'.

Kolano Swierczyno, Pol.; pop. 15; 94 km WSW of Lodz; 51°37'/18°08'.

Kolanow, *see* Bochnia.

Kolarovgrad, Bulg. (Shumen, Shumla); pop. 540; 82 km W of Varna; 43°16'/26°55'; EJ, LDL.

Kolarovo, Cz. (Guta [Czechoslovakia]); pop. 320; 69 km ESE of Bratislava; 47°55'/18°00'; COH, HSL.

Kolashitz, *see* Kolaczyce.

Kolatchitz, *see* Kolaczyce.

Kolbas, *see* Brezina.

Kolbasov, Cz.; 88 km NE of Kosice; 49°01'/22°23'; HSL, HSL2, JGFF.

Kolbasuv, *see* Kolbuszowa.

Kolberg, *see* Kolobrzeg.

Kolbiel, Pol. (Kolobeel); pop. 1,130; 45 km ESE of Warszawa; 52°04'/21°29'; COH, EDRD, GA, GUM5, GUM6, HSL, LDL, LDS, PHP1, PHP4, SF.

Kolbishov, *see* Kolbuszowa.

Kolbovichi, Byel. (Kolbowicze); pop. 6; 101 km NNW of Pinsk; 52°57'/25°36'.

Kolbowicze, *see* Kolbovichi.

Kolbushov, *see* Kolbuszowa.

Kolbushova, *see* Kolbuszowa.

Kolbuszowa, Pol. (Kolbasuv, Kolbishov, Kolbushov, Kolbushova, Kolbuszowa Dolna); pop. 1,415; 88 km WNW of Przemysl; 50°15'/21°46'; AMG, CAHJP, COH, EDRD, EGRS, FRG, GA, GUM4, GUM5, GYLA, HSL, HSL2, JGFF, LDL, LYV, PHP3, POCEM, SF, YB.

Kolbuszowa Dolna, *see* Kolbuszowa.

Kolbuszowa Gorna, Pol.; pop. 66; 82 km WNW of Przemysl; 50°14'/21°48'.

Kolby, Byel.; pop. 19; 19 km ESE of Pinsk; 52°02'/26°22'.

Kolchino, Ukr. (Kolcino); 176 km SSW of Lvov; 48°28'/22°46'; HSL.

Kolcino, *see* Kolchino.

Kolcse, Hung.; pop. 47; 146 km E of Miskolc; 48°03'/22°43'; HSL.

Kolczer, *see* Coltirea.

Koldin, Cz.; pop. 3; 101 km NNW of Brno; 50°02'/16°15'.

Koldychevo, Byel. (Koldyczewo); 120 km SW of Minsk; 53°17'/26°03'; EDRD, GA, GUM3, GUM4.

Koldyczewo, *see* Koldychevo.

Kolechowice, Pol. (Kolechowice Folwark); pop. 5; 32 km NNE of Lublin; 51°28'/22°51'.

Kolechowice Folwark, *see* Kolechowice.

Koledziany, *see* Kolendzyany.

Kolek, *see* Kolets.

Kolendzyany, Ukr. (Koledziany); pop. 71; 75 km N of Chernovtsy; 48°58'/25°57'; GUM3.

Kolenivka, *see* Kalinovka.

Kolesd, Hung.; pop. 32; 114 km S of Budapest; 46°31'/18°35'.

Kolesniki, Byel.; pop. 28; 146 km WSW of Minsk; 53°53'/25°18'. This town was located on a pre-World War I map, but does not appear in contemporary gazetteers.

Kolesnoye, Ukr. (Culevcea); pop. 57; 82 km SW of Odessa; 46°02'/29°56'.

Kolesovice, Cz.; pop. 63; 62 km W of Praha; 50°08'/13°37'.

Kolets, Ukr. (Kolek); pop. 33; 82 km N of Rovno; 51°19'/26°31'.

Kolibabovce, Cz.; 75 km ENE of Kosice; 48°43'/22°16'; JGFF.

Kolikoutsy, Mold. (Colcauti); pop. 35; 195 km NW of Kishinev; 48°19'/27°09'.

Kolimeya, *see* Kolomyya.

Kolimia, *see* Kolomyya.

Kolin, Cz. (Neukollin); pop. 482; 50 km E of Praha; 50°02'/15°12'; AMG, CAHJP, COH, EJ, HSL.

Kolinec, Cz.; pop. 20; 120 km SSW of Praha; 49°18'/13°26'.

Kolinkovtsy, Ukr. (Colencauti); pop. 103; 19 km NE of Chernovtsy; 48°25'/26°08'.

Kolis, *see* Kalyus.

Kolish, *see* Kalisz.

Kolishki, *see* Kolyshki.

Koliszowy, Pol.; pop. 9; 82 km SE of Lodz; 51°11'/20°14'.

Kolk, *see* Kolki.

Kolke, *see* Kolki.

Kolked, Hung.; pop. 2; 120 km SW of Szeged; 45°57'/18°43'.

Kolki, Ukr. (Kolk, Kolke); pop. 723; 69 km NW of Rovno; 51°06'/25°40'; AMG, CAHJP, COH, FRG, GUM4, JGFF, LDL, LYV, SF.

Kolki (Polesie), Ukr.; pop. 38; 114 km N of Rovno; 51°35'/26°37'.

Kolleda, Germ.; 82 km WSW of Leipzig; 51°11'/11°14'; GUM3.

Kolmar, *see* Chodziez.

Koln, Germ. (Coln, Cologne, Kelin, Keln, Klunya, Koeln); pop. 19,500; 157 km WNW of Frankfurt am Main; 50°56'/06°57'; AMG, CAHJP, COH, EJ, GED, GUM3, GUM5, HSL, HSL2, ISH1, ISH3, JGFF, LDL, LDS, LYV, PHGBW, PHP1.

Kolna, *see* Kolno.

Koln Deutz, Germ.; pop. 400; 157 km WNW of Frankfurt am Main; 50°56'/06°57'.

Kolne, *see* Kolno.

Kolnica, Pol. BGN lists two possible localities with this name located at 52°05'/18°35' and 53°47'/23°03'. JGFF.

Koln Mulheim, Germ.; pop. 200; 157 km WNW of Frankfurt am Main; 50°56'/06°57'.

Kolno, Pol. (Kolna, Kolne); pop. 2,216; 88 km WNW of Bialystok; 53°25'/21°56'; COH, GUM3, GUM4, GUM5, HSL, JGFF, LDL, LYV, PHP4, POCEM, SF, YB.

Kolo, Pol. (Kohlo, Koil, Koyl, Kuyl); pop. 5,159; 75 km WNW of Lodz; 52°11'/18°37'; AMG, CAHJP, COH, EDRD, EJ, GA, GUM3, GUM4, GUM5, GYLA, HSL, HSL2, JGFF, LDL, LDS, LYV, PHP1, PHP4, SF, YB.

Kolobeel, *see* Kolbiel.

Kolobrzeg, Pol. (Kolberg); pop. 200; 107 km NNE of Szczecin; 54°11'/15°35'; EJ, GUM3, HSL.

Kolocava, *see* Kolochava.

Kolochava, Ukr. (Alsokalocsa, Kalicsava, Kolocava); 163 km W of Chernovtsy; 48°26'/23°41'; SM.

Kolodeje, Cz.; pop. 23; 13 km E of Praha; 50°04'/14°39'.

Kolodeje nad Luznici, Cz. (Kaladei); 101 km S of Praha; 49°15'/14°25'; EJ.

Kolodentse, Ukr. (Klodzienko); pop. 8; 26 km NE of Lvov; 50°00'/24°16'.

Kolodeyevka, Ukr. (Kolodziejowka);

Kolodeyevka (near Ivano Frankovsk), Ukr.; pop. 11; 114 km WNW of Chernovtsy; 48°58'/24°46'.

Kolodeyevka (near Skalat), Ukr.; pop. 21; 133 km N of Chernovtsy; 49°28'/25°55'.

Kolodishchi, Byel.; 19 km ENE of Minsk; 53°56'/27°46'; GUM4.

Kolodja, *see* Kolodya.

Kolodna, *see* Kolodne.

Kolodne, Ukr. (Darva, Kolodna); 176 km WSW of Chernovtsy; 48°10'/23°35'; HSL, SM. This town was located on a pre-World War I map, but does not appear in contemporary gazetteers.

Kolodnica, *see* Kolodnitsa.

Kolodnitsa, Byel. (Kolodnica); BGN lists two possible localities with this name located at 51°14'/24°45' and 54°33'/29°12'. HSL.

Kolodrobka, Ukr.; pop. 29; 45 km N of Chernovtsy; 48°38'/26°01'.

Kolodruby, Ukr.; pop. 18; 45 km S of Lvov; 49°30'/23°48'; HSL.

Kolodya, Ukr. (Kolodja); pop. 24; 88 km NNW of Rovno; 51°22'/25°48'.

Kolodzeyuv, Ukr. (Kolodziejow); pop. 23; 88 km SE of Lvov; 49°10'/24°33'.

Kolodziejow, *see* Kolodzeyuv.

Kolodziejowka, *see* Kolodeyevka.

Kologury, Ukr. (Kolohury); pop. 25; 38 km SE of Lvov; 49°34'/24°17'.

Kolohury, *see* Kologury.

Kolokolin, Ukr.; pop. 28; 75 km SE of Lvov; 49°18'/24°30'.

Kolomai, *see* Kolomyya.

Koloman, Pol.; pop. 3; 107 km ENE of Czestochowa; 51°01'/20°36'.

Kolomea, *see* Kolomyya.

Kolomey, *see* Kolomyya.

Kolomyia, *see* Kolomyya.

Kolomyja, *see* Kolomyya.

Kolomyya, Ukr. (Kolimeya, Kolimia, Kolomai, Kolomea, Kolomey, Kolomyia, Kolomyja); pop. 18,246; 69 km WNW of Chernovtsy; 48°32'/25°02'; AMG, CAHJP, COH, EDRD, EGRS, EJ, GA, GUM3, GUM4, GUM5, GUM6, GYLA, HSL, HSL2, JGFF, LDL, PHP2, PHP3, SF, YB.

Kolonia, Pol. AMG, HSL. A number of towns share this name. It was not possible to determine from available information which one is being referenced.

Kolonia Bardo Dolne, Pol. (Bardo Dolne); pop. 3; 107 km NE of Krakow; 50°44'/21°02'.

Kolonia Synajska, *see* Kolonja Synajska.

Kolonia Synyska, *see* Kolonja Synajska.

Kolonia Szczerbacka, Pol.; pop. 7; 94 km ESE of Lodz; 51°15'/20°35'.

Kolonice, Pol.; pop. 4; 69 km SSW of Przemysl; 49°16'/22°16'.

Koloniec, Pol.; pop. 11; 82 km SE of Lodz; 51°11'/20°09'.

Kolonie Ignitowka, *see* Ignatovka.

Kolonie Kaiserau, Germ. (Kaiserau); pop. 4; 82 km NNE of Koln; 51°34'/07°36'.

Kolonie Lvovo, *see* Lvovo.

Kolonie Synaska, *see* Kolonja Synajska.

Kolonie Wertizany, *see* Vertyuzhany.

Kolonie Zgurica, *see* Zguritsa.

Kolonie Zoludzk, (Zholudsk, Zoludzk); GUM4, SF, YB. This town was not found in BGN gazetteers under the given spelling.

Kolonitsa, Ukr. (Klonice, Klonitse); pop. 20; 56 km WNW of Lvov; 50°04'/23°19'.

Kolonitsa (Bessarabia), Mold. (Colonita); pop. 2; 13 km NE of Kishinev; 47°02'/28°58'.

Kolonja Izaaka, Pol.; pop. 142; Described in the *Black Book* as being in the Bialystok region of Poland, this town was not found in BGN gazetteers.

Kolonja Izraelska, Pol.; pop. 55; Described in the *Black Book* as being in the Bialystok region of Poland, this town was not found in BGN gazetteers.

Kolonja Synajska, Byel. (Kolonia Synajska, Kolonia Synyska, Kolonie Synaska); pop. 78; SF, YB. This town could not be found in contemporary gazetteers although it is listed in the yizkor book for Derechin.

Kolonsk, Byel.; pop. 4; 45 km NW of Pinsk; 52°28'/25°47'.

Koloverta, *see* Koloverti.

Koloverti, Ukr. (Koloverta, Kolowerta); pop. 33; 50 km ENE of Rovno; 50°41'/26°57'.

Kolowerta, *see* Koloverti.

Kolozhvar, *see* Cluj.

Kolozs, *see* Cojocna.

Kolozsborsa, *see* Borsa Maramures.

Kolozsvar, *see* Cluj.

Kolozs Zsombor, *see* Zimbor.

Kolozuby, Byel.; pop. 14; 114 km WNW of Pinsk; 52°49'/25°00'; SF.

Kolozvar, *see* Cluj.

Kolpino, USSR; 26 km ESE of Leningrad; 59°45'/30°36'; GUM4.

Kolpytov, Ukr. (Kopytow?); pop. 23; 101 km NNE of Lvov; 50°36'/24°46'; AMG, JGFF.

Kolta, Cz.; pop. 130; 94 km E of Bratislava; 48°01'/18°25'; HSL, HSL2, LDL.

Koltchin, *see* Kulchiny.

Koltinenai, *see* Kaltinenai.

Koltiniani, *see* Kaltanenai.

Koltininai, *possibly* Kaltanenai.

Koltov, Ukr. (Koltow); 75 km ENE of Lvov; 49°51'/25°03'; HSL.

Koltow, *see* Koltov.

Koltyniany, *see* Kaltinenai.

Kolumna, Pol.; 26 km SW of Lodz; 51°37'/19°11'; PHP1.

Kolushki, *see* Koluszki.

Koluszki, Pol. (Kalushki, Kolushki); pop. 387; 26 km ENE of Lodz; 51°46'/19°48'; GA, GUM5, PHP1, PHP4, SF.

Kolut, Yug.; 170 km NW of Beograd; 45°53'/18°57'; JGFF.

Kolyanki, Ukr. (Kolanki); pop. 24; 62 km NW of Chernovtsy; 48°47'/25°30'.

Kolyshki, Byel. (Kalisk, Kolishki); pop. 1,006; 50 km E of Vitebsk; 55°10'/30°58'; SF.

Komadi, Hung.; pop. 257; 133 km SSE of Miskolc; 47°00'/21°30'; HSL, LDS, PHH.

Komajai, *see* Kamajai.

Komaje, *see* Kamajai.

Komajsk, *see* Komaysk.

Komancza, Pol.; pop. 74; 75 km SW of Przemysl; 49°20'/22°04'.

Komara Osada, Pol. POCEM. This town was not found in BGN gazetteers under the given spelling.

Komareshti, *see* Komarovtsi.

Komar Gorod, *see* Komargorod.

Komargorod, Ukr. (Komar Gorod, Komeirid); 82 km S of Vinnitsa; 48°32'/28°37'; LDL, SF.

Komarichi, USSR; pop. 172; 101 km SSE of Bryansk; 52°24'/34°50'.

Komarin, Byel.; 251 km N of Vitebsk; 57°26'/30°34'; LDL.

Komarne, *see* Komarno.

Komarnik, *see* Komarniki.

Komarniki, Ukr. (Komarnik); pop. 76; 120 km SSW of Lvov; 48°59'/23°03'; AMG, GUM3, HSL, SF.

Komarno, Cz. (Komarne, Komorn); pop. 3,204; 88 km ESE of Bratislava; 47°46'/18°08'; COH, EJ, GUM4, GUM5, GUM6, HSL2. Komarno is the twin city of Komarom, Hungary. *See also* Komarom.

Komarno (near Chelm), Pol.; pop. 6; 107 km N of Lublin; 52°09'/23°07'; AMG.

Komarno (near Lvov), Ukr.; pop. 2,047; 38 km SW of Lvov; 49°38'/23°42'; AMG, COH, EDRD, EGRS, EJ, GA, GUM4, GUM5, HSL, JGFF, LDL, LYV, PHP2, SF, YB.

Komarom, Hung. (Ujvaros); pop. 192; 75 km WNW of Budapest; 47°44'/18°07'; AMG, GUM3, GUM4, HSL, HSL2, JGFF, PHH. Komarom is the twin city of Komarno, Czechoslovakia. *See also* Komarno.

Komarom Csicso, LDL. This pre-World War I community was not found in BGN gazetteers.

Komaromszemere, *see* Semerovo.

Komarov, Ukr.; pop. 22; 75 km NW of Rovno; 51°10'/25°45'.

See also Komarow.

Komarove, *see* Komarow.

Komarovec, COH, HSL. This pre-World War I community was not found in BGN gazetteers.

Komarovka, Ukr.; 75 km WSW of Konotop; 51°14'/32°09'; HSL, SF.

Komarovo, Byel. (Komarowo, Komrov); 107 km NNW of Minsk; 54°46'/27°23'; LDL, SF.

Komarovtsi, Ukr. (Comaresti, Komareshti); pop. 65; 32 km SW of Chernovtsy; 48°12'/25°34'; COH.

Komarow, Pol. (Comarova, Komarov, Komarove); pop. 1,752; 94 km SE of Lublin; 50°37'/23°28'; AMG, CAHJP, COH, EDRD, FRG, GUM3, GUM4, GUM5, HSL, HSL2, JGFF, LDS, LYV, SF.

Komarowka, Pol. (Komarowka Podlaska); pop. 412; 45 km NE of Lublin; 51°29'/23°03'; GA, GUM3.

Komarowka Podlaska, *see* Komarowka.

Komarowo, *see* Komarovo.

Komarow Osada, GA. This town was not found in BGN gazetteers under the given spelling.

Komarvaros, Hung.; pop. 9; 19 km NE of Nagykanizsa; 46°32'/17°11'.

Komaysk, Byel. (Komajsk); pop. 4; 120 km N of Minsk; 54°53'/27°54'.

Kombornia, Pol.; pop. 18; 62 km WSW of Przemysl; 49°44'/21°53'; HSL.

Komeirid, *see* Komargorod.

Komenitz, *see* Kamenets.

Komenitz D Lita, *see* Kamenets.

Komenitz Podolsk, *see* Kamenets Podolskiy.

Komiatice, *see* Komjatice.

Kominterna Kopalnya, USSR; pop. 40; This town was not found in BGN gazetteers under the given spelling.

Komjat, *see* Komjati.

Komjath, *see* Komjatice.

Komjati, Hung. (Komjat); pop. 8; 56 km N of Miskolc; 48°33'/20°46'; AMG, COH, HSL.

Komjatice, Cz. (Komiatice, Komjath); pop. 69; 82 km E of Bratislava; 48°09'/18°11'; JGFF.

Komletinci, Yug.; pop. 1; 133 km WNW of Beograd; 45°09'/18°57'.

Komlevshchyzna, Byel. (Komlewszczyzna); pop. 30; 107 km NNE of Pinsk; 52°56'/26°49'.

Komlewszczyzna, *see* Komlevshchyzna.

Komlo, Hung.; pop. 26; 101 km ESE of Nagykanizsa; 46°12'/18°16'; HSL.

Komlod, Hung.; pop. 12; 62 km W of Budapest; 47°33'/18°16'.

Komlos, *see* Chmelovec.

Komloska, Hung.; pop. 4; 56 km NE of Miskolc; 48°20'/21°28'.

Komloskeresztes, *see* Chmelovec.

Kommern, Germ.; 45 km SSW of Koln; 50°37'/06°39'; GED.

Kommunarsk, Ukr. (Voroshilovsk); 246 km ESE of Kharkov; 48°30'/38°47'; GUM4, GUM4.

Komo, Hung.; pop. 20; This town was not found in BGN gazetteers under the given spelling.

Komora; The *Black Book* notes two towns in Poland with this name, one in Lublin province (pop. 123) and another in Kielce province (pop. 24). The name Komora does not appear in contemporary or interwar gazetteers.

Komorn, *see* Komarno.

Komorniki, *see* Rogow Komorniki.

Komoro, Hung.; pop. 20; 101 km ENE of Miskolc; 48°18'/22°07'; HSL, LDS.

Komorowo, Pol.; pop. 70; 88 km NNE of Warszawa; 52°50'/21°51'; JGFF, PHP4.

Komory, Pol.; pop. 8; 62 km NE of Warszawa; 52°26'/21°50'.

Komorzan, *see* Camarzana.

Komotau, *see* Chomutov.

Komotini, Greece; pop. 1,148; 208 km ENE of Thessaloniki; 41°06'/25°25'.

Kompolt, Hung.; 56 km SSW of Miskolc; 47°44'/20°15'; HSL.

Komrat, Mold. (Comrat); pop. 392; 82 km S of Kishinev; 46°18'/28°39'.

Komrov, *see* Komarovo.

Konar, Pol. PHP3. This town was not found in BGN gazetteers under the given spelling.

Konary, Pol.; pop. 24; 50 km SSE of Warszawa; 51°53'/21°14'; GUM5, HSL, PHP1.

Konarzewo, Pol. (Kniephof); 26 km SW of Poznan; 52°20'/16°43'; CAHJP.

Konatice, Yug.; pop. 1; 38 km SSW of Beograd; 44°33'/20°15'.

Konczyce Male, Pol.; pop. 5; 94 km WSW of Krakow; 49°51'/18°38'.

Konczyska, Pol.; pop. 7; 69 km ESE of Krakow; 49°51'/20°50'.

Kondo, Hung.; pop. 4; 19 km NW of Miskolc; 48°12'/20°39'.

Kondorfa, Hung.; pop. 4; 69 km NW of Nagykanizsa; 46°54'/16°24'.

Kondoros, Hung.; pop. 31; 75 km NNE of Szeged; 46°46'/20°48'.

Kondraciszki, GUM3. This town was not found in BGN gazetteers under the given spelling.

Kondrajec Szlachecki, Pol.; pop. 2; 75 km NW of Warszawa; 52°48'/20°16'.

Kondrateshty, Mold. (Condratesti); pop. 11; 69 km WNW of Kishinev; 47°25'/28°06'.

Konela, Ukr.; 38 km NNW of Uman; 49°04'/30°06'; JGFF.

Konen, Germ.; pop. 72; 146 km S of Koln; 49°41'/06°33'.

Konetspol, Ukr. (Konezpol, Parnivka, Pavlova); 94 km SE of Uman; 48°00'/30°48'; LDL, SF.

Konev, *see* Konyuv.

Konezpol, *see* Konetspol.

Kongernheim, Germ.; pop. 5; 45 km SW of Frankfurt am Main; 49°51'/08°15'.

Koniaczow, Pol.; pop. 6; 32 km NNW of Przemysl; 50°02'/22°44'; PHP3.

Konice, Cz.; pop. 23; 50 km N of Brno; 49°35'/16°53'; CAHJP, EJ.

Koniecbor, Pol.; pop. 9; 107 km NNW of Bialystok; 54°01'/22°50'.

Koniecmosty, Pol.; pop. 8; 62 km NE of Krakow; 50°20'/20°40'.

Koniecpol, Pol. (Konietzpol, Konyetzpol); pop. 1,077; 38 km E of Czestochowa; 50°47'/19°41'; AMG, CAHJP, EDRD, GA, GUM3, GUM4, GUM5, GUM6, HSL, JGFF, LDS, LYV, PHP1, PHP1, SF.

Konieczkowa, Pol.; pop. 28; 69 km SW of Przemysl; 49°35'/21°55'. This town was located on an interwar map of Poland but does not appear in contemporary gazetteers. Map coordinates are approximate.

Konieczna, Pol.; pop. 3; 114 km SW of Przemysl; 49°28'/21°19'.

Konieczno, Pol.; pop. 12; 69 km E of Czestochowa; 50°48'/20°03'.

Konietzpol, *see* Koniecpol.

Konig, *see* Bad Konig.

Koniggratz, *see* Hradec Kralove.

Konigheim, Germ.; pop. 44; 88 km ESE of Frankfurt am Main; 49°36'/09°37'; LDS, PHGBW.

Koniginhof, *see* Dvur Kralove.

Koniginhof an der Elbe, *see* Dvur Kralove.

Konigsbach, Germ.; pop. 162; 45 km WNW of Stuttgart; 48°58'/08°37'; HSL, LDS, PHGBW.

Konigsberg, *see* Kaliningrad; Nova Bana.

Konigsberg (Bavaria), Germ.; 82 km NW of Nurnberg; 50°05'/10°35'; GUM4, GUM5, PHGB.

Konigsfeld, Germ.; 62 km N of Nurnberg; 49°57'/11°10'; GUM3. *See also* Anenska Studanka.

Konigshofen, Germ.; pop. 108; 107 km NW of Nurnberg; 50°18'/10°29'; GUM5, HSL, LDS, PHGB, PHGBW.

Konigshutte, *see* Chorzow.

Konigslutter, Germ.; 75 km E of Hannover; 52°15'/10°49'; LDS.

Konigstein im Taunus, Germ.; pop. 75; 19 km WNW of Frankfurt am Main; 50°11'/08°28'; GED.

Konigswart, *possibly* Kralovske Porici.

Konigswerth, *see* Kralovske Porici.

Konigswinter, Germ.; 38 km SE of Koln; 50°41'/07°11'; GED.

Konigszelt, *see* Jaworzyna Slaska.

Konin, Pol.; pop. 2,902; 94 km WNW of Lodz; 52°13'/18°16'; AMG, CAHJP, COH, EDRD, EJ, GUM3, GUM4, HSL2, JGFF, LDS, LYV, PHP1, PHP4, SF.

Konina, Pol.; pop. 7; 56 km SSE of Krakow; 49°37'/20°08'.

Koniow, *see* Konyuv.

Konitz, *see* Chojnice.

Koniuchy, Pol.; pop. 25; 94 km ESE of Lublin; 50°44'/23°37'. *See also* Konyushki.

Koniuszki, Pol. (Koniuszki Tuliglowskie); pop. 36; A number of towns share this name. It was not possible to determine from available information which one is being referenced. *See also* Koniuchy; Konyushki.

Koniuszki (Bialystok), *see* Konyukhi.

Koniuszki Krolewskie, *see* Konyushki.

Koniuszki Tuliglowskie, *see* Koniuszki.

Koniuszowa, Pol.; pop. 16; 75 km ESE of Krakow; 49°40'/20°48'.

Koniv, *see* Kunev.

Konjic, Yug.; pop. 6; 240 km SW of Beograd; 43°39'/17°58'.

Konken, Germ.; pop. 7; 114 km SW of Frankfurt am Main; 49°31'/07°21'; GED, JGFF.

Konkolniki, Ukr.; pop. 43; 114 km WNW of Chernovtsy; 48°55'/24°45'. This town was located on an interwar map of Poland but does not appear in contemporary gazetteers. Map coordinates are approximate.

Konopiska, Pol.; pop. 17; 13 km SW of Czestochowa; 50°44'/19°01'.

Konopki, GUM4. A number of towns share this name. It was not possible to determine from available information which one is being referenced.

Konopne, Pol.; pop. 6; 94 km ESE of Lublin; 50°45'/23°42'.

Konopnica, Pol.; pop. 22; 6 km WSW of Lublin; 51°14'/22°28'.

Konotop, Ukr.; pop. 5,763; 208 km NE of Kiyev; 51°14'/33°12'; EJ, HSL, JGFF, LDL, SF.

Konotopie, Pol.; pop. 6; 133 km NNW of Lodz; 52°53'/19°07'.

Konrac, Cz.; pop. 4; 107 km WSW of Brno; 49°01'/15°10'.

Konradow, Pol.; pop. 23; 50 km NNE of Czestochowa; 51°06'/19°32'.

Konsk, *see* Konskie.

Konskevole, *see* Konskowola.

Konski, *see* Konskie.

Konskie, Pol. (Kansk, Kinsk, Kintsk, Konsk, Konski, Kuntsk); pop. 5,037; 94 km ESE of Lodz; 51°12'/20°25'; AMG, CAHJP, COH, EDRD, EJ, FRG, GA, GUM3, GUM4, GUM5, GUM6, GYLA, HSL, HSL2, JGFF, LDL, LDS, LYV, PHP1, PHP4, SF, WS.

Konskovola, *see* Konskowola.

Konskowola, Pol. (Konskevole, Konskovola); pop. 876; 38 km WNW of Lublin; 51°25'/22°04'; COH, EDRD, EJ, GA, GUM3, GUM4, GUM5, GUM6, HSL, HSL2, LDL, LDS, LYV, SF.

Konstadt, *see* Wolczyn.

Konstancin, Pol.; pop. 399; 26 km SE of Warszawa; 52°05'/21°07'; GA, PHP4.

Konstancja, *see* Konstantsya.

Konstantin, *see* Konstantynow.

Konstantin Chadash, *see* Novyy Konstantinov.

Konstantinivka, *see* Konstantinovka.

Konstantin Khadash, *see* Novyy Konstantinov.

Konstantinograd, *see* Krasnograd.

Konstantinogrod, *see* Krasnograd.

Konstantinov, *see* Konstantynow.

Konstantinovka, Ukr. (Konstantinivka, Konstantinowka); pop. 1,920; 126 km SE of Uman; 47°50'/31°09'; EDRD, GUM4, HSL, JGFF, LDL, SF.

Konstantinovo, Ukr. (Konstantynowo); pop. 217; SF. A number of towns share this name. It was not possible to determine from available information which one is being referenced.

Konstantinowka, *see* Konstantinovka.

Konstantinuvka (near Sarny), Ukr.; pop. 24; 45 km NNE of Lvov; 50°12'/24°18'.

Konstantin Yashan, *see* Konstantynow.

Konstantsya, Ukr. (Konstancja); pop. 6; 62 km N of Chernovtsy; 48°51'/25°56'.

Konstantyna, Pol.; 13 km SE of Lodz; 51°42'/19°31'; HSL.

Konstantynogrod, *see* Krasnograd.

Konstantynovka, GUM3. This town was not found in BGN gazetteers under the given spelling.

Konstantynow, Pol. (Kasentin, Konstantin, Konstantin Yashan, Konstantinov, Konstantynow nad Bugiem, Konstantynow Podlaska, Kosintin, Kosnitin, Kostantin Yashan, Kostentin); pop. 783; 107 km S of Bialystok; 52°13'/23°05'; AMG, COH, GUM3, GUM4, GUM5, HSL, HSL2, JGFF, LDL, LDS, LYV, PHP2, PHP4, POCEM, SF.

Konstantynow Lodzki, Pol.; pop. 942; 13 km WSW of Lodz; 51°45'/19°20'; CAHJP, GUM5, HSL, JGFF, LDS, PHP1, SF.

Konstantynow nad Bugiem, *see* Konstantynow.

Konstantynowo, *see* Konstantinovo.

Konstantynow Podlaska, *see* Konstantynow.

Konstantynuvka (near Sarny), LDL. This pre-World War I community was not found in BGN gazetteers.

Konstanz, Germ. (Constance); pop. 537; 126 km S of Stuttgart; 47°40'/09°11'; AMG, EJ, GED, GUM4, JGFF, LDS, PHGBW.

Kontchuga, *see* Kanczuga.

Kontikoziva, *see* Kantankusenka.

Kontopa, Pol. PHP4. This town was not found in BGN gazetteers under the given spelling.

Konus, Cz.; pop. 109; 75 km ENE of Kosice; 48°47'/22°16'; AMG.

Konvelishok, LDL. This pre-World War I community was not found in BGN gazetteers.

Kony, Hung.; pop. 4; 126 km W of Budapest; 47°38'/17°22'.

Konyar, Hung.; pop. 80; 107 km SE of Miskolc; 47°19'/21°40'; AMG, LDS, PHH, YB.

Konyetspol, *see* Koniecpol.

Konyukhi, Byel. (Koniuszki [Bialystok]); pop. 34; 146 km WNW of Pinsk; 53°00'/24°39'.

Konyushki, Ukr. (Koniuszki, Koniuszki Krolewskie, Konyushki Nanovske); See listings below. *See also* Koniuchy.

Konyushki (Stanislawow), Ukr.; pop. 38; 69 km WSW of Lvov; 49°45'/23°04'.

Konyushki (Tarnopol), Ukr.; pop. 44; 75 km SE of Lvov; 49°19'/24°36'; GUM3.

Konyushki Nanovske, *see* Konyushki.

Konyuv, Ukr. (Konev, Koniow); pop. 34; 82 km SW of Lvov; 49°34'/22°58'; EDRD.

Konz, Germ.; 146 km S of Koln; 49°42'/06°35'; GUM5.

Koovi, Hung. (Kovi); AMG, HSL.

Kopache, *see* Kopachi.

Kopacheny, Mold. (Copaceni); pop. 45; 82 km NW of Kishinev; 47°37'/28°14'.

Kopachi, Byel. (Kopache, Kopacze); pop. 10; 170 km NW of Pinsk; 53°19'/24°37'.

Kopachintsy, Ukr. (Kopachynitse, Kopaczynce); pop. 22; 69 km NW of Chernovtsy; 48°50'/25°23'.

Kopachovka, Ukr. (Kopaczowka); pop. 274; 82 km WNW of Rovno; 50°53'/25°13'; GUM5.

Kopachynitse, *see* Kopachintsy.

Kopacze, *see* Kopachi.

Kopaczowka, *see* Kopachovka.

Kopaczynce, *see* Kopachintsy.

Kopai Gorod, *see* Kopaygorod.

Kopaigorod, *see* Kopaygorod.

Kopaliny, Pol.; 50 km E of Krakow; 49°59'/20°36'; GUM5, PHP3.

Kopalow, Pol. PHP4. This town was not found in BGN gazetteers under the given spelling.

Kopanka, Mold. (Copanca); pop. 149; 69 km ESE of Kishinev; 46°43'/29°38'.

Kopasnovo, Ukr. (Kapashne, Yernyes); 182 km WSW of Chernovtsy; 48°13'/23°28'; SM.

Kopatkevichi, Byel. (Kopatkevitch); pop. 820; 150 km WSW of Gomel; 52°19'/28°49'; HSL, LDL, SF.

Kopatkevitch, *see* Kopatkevichi.

Kopaygorod, Ukr. (Copaigorod, Kopai Gorod, Kopaigorod, Koprod); pop. 1,595; 62 km SW of Vinnitsa; 48°52'/27°47'; EDRD, GUM4, GUM5, GUM6, HSL, JGFF, LDL, PHR1, SF.

Kopchak, Mold. (Tatar Copceac); pop. 7; 133 km S of Kishinev; 45°51'/28°42'.

Kopcseny Kittse, LDL. This pre-World War I community was not found in BGN gazetteers.

Kopczany, Pol.; pop. 3; 75 km N of Bialystok; 53°47'/23°32'.

Kopczynce, Pol. PHP4. This town was not found in BGN gazetteers under the given spelling.

Kopeisk, GUM4. This town was not found in BGN gazetteers under the given spelling.

Koper, Yug.; 176 km WSW of Zagreb; 45°33'/13°44'; PHY.

Kopetkowa, GUM3. This town was not found in BGN gazetteers under the given spelling.

Kopidlno, Cz.; pop. 15; 62 km NE of Praha; 50°20'/15°16'.

Kopiec, Pol.; pop. 21; A number of towns share this name. It was not possible to determine from available information which one is being referenced.

Kopil, *see* Kopyl.

Kopin, Ukr.; pop. 1,094; YB. Described in the yizkor book for Kamenets Podolskiy, it does not appear in the BGN gazetteer.

Kopis, *see* Kopys.

Kopishche, Byel.; 82 km NW of Minsk; 54°26'/26°49'; GUM4.

Kopisty, Cz.; 75 km WNW of Praha; 50°33'/13°38'; GYLA.

Kopitshinets, *see* Kopychintsy.

Kopkas, *see* Poienile de Sub Munte.

Kopki, Pol.; pop. 17; 82 km NW of Przemysl; 50°25'/22°19'.

Koplancy, *see* Kaplonosy.

Koplanus, *see* Kaplonosy.

Kopocsapati, Hung.; pop. 72; 107 km ENE of Miskolc; 48°13'/22°16'; PHH.

Kopojno, Pol.; pop. 13; 75 km ESE of Poznan; 52°10'/17°59'.

Koppanyszanto, Hung.; pop. 24; 88 km ENE of Nagykanizsa; 46°36'/18°07'.

Koppenbrugge, *see* Coppenbrugge.

Koprivnica, Yug. (Kaproncza); pop. 339; 75 km NE of Zagreb; 46°10'/16°50'; AMG, PHY.

Koprod, *see* Kopaygorod.

Koprusa, Pol.; pop. 29; 107 km NE of Czestochowa; 51°08'/20°34'.

Koprzywnica, Pol. (Kopshevnitza, Kopshivnitsa, Pokshivnits, Pokshivnitsa, Pokshivnitza); pop. 812; 101 km SSW of Lublin; 50°35'/21°35'; AMG, EDRD, GA, GUM3, GUM5, GYLA, JGFF, LDS, LYV, PHP3, POCEM, SF, YB.

Kopshevnitza, *see* Koprzywnica.

Kopshivnitsa, *see* Koprzywnica.

Koptchevo, *see* Kapciamiestis.

Koptchintz, *see* Kopychintsy.

Koptsevichi, USSR; pop. 279; A number of towns share this name. It was not possible to determine from available information which one is being referenced.

Koptsiva, *see* Kapciamiestis.

Kopust, *see* Kopys.

Kopychintsy, Ukr. (Kopitshinets, Koptchintz, Kopyczynce); pop. 2,471; 94 km N of Chernovtsy; 49°06'/25°56'; AMG, COH, EDRD, EGRS, FRG, GUM3, GUM4, GUM5, GUM6, GYLA, HSL, HSL2, JGFF, LDL, PHP2, SF.

Kopyczynce, *see* Kopychintsy.

Kopyl, Byel. (Kapoli, Kapolia, Kapulye, Kopil); pop. 1,680; 88 km S of Minsk; 53°09'/27°05'; COH, EJ, GUM3, GUM5, GUM6, GYLA, HSL, JGFF, LDL, SF, YB.

Kopylovka, *see* Kapulovka.

Kopylow, Pol.; 107 km ESE of Lublin; 50°54'/23°58'; CAHJP.

Kopyly, Byel.; pop. 5; 182 km W of Pinsk; 52°28'/23°27'.

Kopys, Byel. (Kapust, Kopis, Kopust); pop. 813; 101 km S of Vitebsk; 54°19'/30°18'; GUM4, HSL, LDL, SF.

Kopytow, *possibly* Kolpytov.

Kopytowa, Pol.; pop. 17; 88 km WSW of Przemysl; 49°40'/21°37'.

Korabina, Pol.; pop. 5; 88 km NW of Przemysl; 50°24'/21°58'.

Korablew, *see* Korablew Zagrodniki.

Korablew Zagrodniki, Pol. (Korablew); pop. 7; 56 km SSW of Lodz; 51°21'/19°02'.

Korb, Germ.; 94 km WSW of Munchen; 48°08'/10°21'; LDS, PHGBW.

Korbach, Germ.; pop. 135; 133 km SSW of Hannover; 51°17'/08°52'; HSL.

Korbecke, Germ.; pop. 3; 107 km NE of Koln; 51°30'/08°07'.

Korchyn, Ukr. (Korczyn Rustykalny); pop. 20; 88 km S of Lvov; 49°06'/23°32'.

Korchynie, Pol.; pop. 3; 88 km NNE of Przemysl; 50°25'/23°32'.

Korcula, Yug.; pop. 3; 322 km SSE of Zagreb; 42°58'/17°08'; GUM4, GUM6.

Korczew, Pol.; pop. 39; 101 km SSW of Bialystok; 52°21'/22°37'.

Korczow, Pol.; pop. 45; BGN lists two possible localities with this name located at 50°23'/23°50' and 50°30'/22°44'.

Korczyce Wielkie, *see* Velikiye Korchitsy.

Korczyn, Pol.; pop. 20; 88 km ENE of Czestochowa; 50°56'/20°21'; AMG, CAHJP, EDRD, GUM3, PHP3. CAHJP describes a town named Korczyn in the Bialystok area which does not appear in interwar or contemporary gazetteers.

Korczyn (near Skole), Ukr.; pop. 34; 88 km S of Lvov; 49°06'/23°32'.

Korczyna, Pol.; pop. 796; 69 km WSW of Przemysl; 49°43'/21°49'; AMG, EGRS, GA, GUM5, HSL, HSL2, JGFF, LDL, PHP3, POCEM, SF, YB.

Korczyn Rustykalny, *see* Korchyn.

Korczyska, Pol.; pop. 9; 45 km SSW of Lodz; 51°27'/19°04'.

Kordorf, Germ.; pop. 18; 56 km WNW of Frankfurt am Main; 50°17'/07°55'.

Kordowka, Pol.; pop. 31; Described in the *Black Book* as being in the Stanislawow region of Poland, this town was not found in BGN gazetteers.

Korec, *see* Korets.

Koreliche, *see* Korelichi.

Korelichi, Byel. (Karelic, Karelits, Koreliche, Korelicze, Korelitz, Korzelice, Kozhelitse); pop. 535; 101 km SW of Minsk; 53°34'/26°08'; AMG, CAHJP, COH, EDRD, GUM3, GUM4, HSL, HSL2, JGFF, LDL, SF, YB.

Korelicze, *see* Korelichi.

Korelitz, *see* Korelichi.

Koren, Cz.; 120 km WSW of Praha; 49°51'/12°51'; HSL.

Korenetz, *see* Kurenets.

Korenice, Cz.; pop. 16; 50 km E of Praha; 49°58'/15°08'.

Korestautsy, Mold. (Corestauti); pop. 24; 195 km NW of Kishinev; 48°21'/27°16'.

Korets, Ukr. (Korec, Koretz, Koric, Koritz, Korzec, Korzets, Korzhets, Korzysc?); pop. 3,888; 62 km E of Rovno; 50°37'/27°10'; AMG, COH, EJ, GUM3, GUM4, GUM5, GUM6, HSL, HSL2, JGFF, LYV, SF, YB.

Koretz, *see* Korets.

Korezule, GUM3. This town was not found in BGN gazetteers under the given spelling.

Korfantow, Pol. (Friedland); 75 km SE of Wroclaw; 50°29'/17°36'; AMG, EJ, GUM3, GUM4, GUM6, HSL, HSL2.

Koric, *see* Korets.

Koricin, LDL. This pre-World War I community was not found in BGN gazetteers.

Korilifka, *see* Oleyevo Korolevka.

Koristchan, *see* Korycany.

Koritschan, *see* Korycany.

Koritz, *see* Korets.

Koriv, *see* Kurow.

Korlat, Hung.; pop. 27; 50 km NE of Miskolc; 48°23'/21°15'.

Korlin, *see* Karlino.

Korma, Byel.; pop. 1,248; 82 km NNW of Gomel; 53°08'/30°48'; HSL, LDL, SF.

Korman, Ukr. (Cormani); pop. 1; 94 km NE of Chernovtsy; 48°35'/27°10'.

Kormanice, Pol.; pop. 5; 19 km SSW of Przemysl; 49°43'/22°44'.

Kormend, Hung.; pop. 389; 69 km NW of Nagykanizsa; 47°01'/16°36'; GUM5, HSL, LDS, PHH.

Kormocbanya, *see* Kremnica.

Kornalowice, Ukr.; pop. 44; 82 km SSW of Lvov; 49°15'/23°25'. This town was located on an interwar map of Poland but does not appear in contemporary gazetteers. Map coordinates are approximate.

Kornburg, Germ.; 19 km S of Nurnberg; 49°21'/11°06'; PHGB.

Kornelimunster, Germ.; pop. 22; 62 km SW of Koln; 50°44'/06°11'.

Kornelowka, *see* Korolyuvka.

Kornesht, *see* Korneshty.

Kornesht Targ, *see* Korneshty.

Kornesht Tyrg, *see* Korneshty.

Korneshty, Mold. (Cornesti Targ, Kornesht, Kornesht Targ, Kornesht Tyrg, Kornesty); pop. 338; 75 km WNW of Kishinev; 47°22'/28°00'; SF.

Korneshty Sabany, *see* Kyrneshty.

Kornesty, *see* Korneshty.

Korneuburg, Aus.; pop. 42; 26 km NNW of Wien; 48°21'/16°20'.

Kornevo, USSR (Zinten); pop. 32; 38 km SSW of Kaliningrad; 54°27'/20°18'; HSL.

Korniaktow, Pol.; pop. 26; 45 km NW of Przemysl; 50°05'/22°22'.

Kornica, Pol.; pop. 28; 107 km S of Bialystok; 52°11'/22°56'.

Kornice, *see* Kornichi.

Kornichi, Ukr. (Kornice); pop. 9; 62 km SW of Lvov; 49°38'/23°14'.

Kornie, Pol.; pop. 41; 82 km NE of Przemysl; 50°19'/23°36'.

Kornik, Pol. (Kurnik); pop. 57; 26 km SE of Poznan; 52°15'/17°06'; EJ, HSL, HSL2, JGFF, LDS, PHP1, WS.

Kornin, Ukr.; 82 km SW of Kiyev; 50°05'/29°32'; EDRD.

Korniow, *see* Kornyuv.

Kornitsa, Bulg. (Kornitza, Korniza); 120 km SSE of Sofija; 41°39'/23°41'; SF.

Kornitz, *see* Kurenets.

Kornitza, *see* Kornitsa.

Korniza, *see* Kornitsa.

Kornova, *see* Kornovo.

Kornovo, Mold. (Cornova, Kornova); pop. 20; 69 km WNW of Kishinev; 47°24'/28°11'.

Kornwestheim, Germ.; pop. 7; 19 km N of Stuttgart; 48°52'/09°11'; GUM3, PHGBW.

Kornye, Hung.; pop. 22; 56 km W of Budapest; 47°33'/18°20'.

Kornyuv, Ukr. (Korniow); pop. 81; 69 km NW of Chernovtsy; 48°48'/25°20'.

Korobcheny, Mold. (Coropceni); pop. 46; 56 km NNW of Kishinev; 47°29'/28°31'; GUM4.

Korolevo, Ukr. (Kiralyhaza, Kralovo nad Tisou); 202 km S of Lvov; 48°09'/23°08'; AMG, GUM3, HSL, HSL2, JGFF.

Korolovka, *see* Oleyevo Korolevka.

Korolowka, *see* Oleyevo Korolevka.

Korolyuvka, Ukr. (Kornelowka); pop. 15; 88 km WNW of Chernovtsy; 48°48'/25°00'.

Korom, Hung.; pop. 17; 19 km SE of Miskolc; 47°59'/20°57'; HSL.

Korompa, *see* Krompachy.

Koronco, Hung.; pop. 8; 120 km W of Budapest; 47°36'/17°32'.

Korond, GUM3. This town was not found in BGN gazetteers under the given spelling.

Koronowo, Pol. (Krone an der Brahe); pop. 56; 120 km NNE of Poznan; 53°19'/17°57'; GUM5, HSL, LDS, POCEM.

Korop, Ukr.; pop. 787; 45 km NW of Konotop; 51°34'/32°58'; LDL, SF.

Koropets, Ukr. (Koropiec, Koropitz, Kropitz); pop. 176; 88 km NW of Chernovtsy; 48°56'/25°10'; COH, EDRD, EGRS, GUM3, GYLA, HSL, JGFF, LDL, PHP2, SF.

Koropiec, *see* Koropets.

Koropitz, *see* Koropets.

Koropki, HSL. This pre-World War I community was not found in BGN gazetteers.

Koropuz, *see* Koropuzh.

Koropuzh, Ukr. (Koropuz); pop. 30; 38 km SW of Lvov; 49°41'/23°34'.

Koros, *see* Krizevci.

Koroshegy, Hung.; pop. 33; 82 km NE of Nagykanizsa; 46°50'/17°54'; HSL.

Korosladany, Hung.; pop. 119; 101 km NNE of Szeged; 46°58'/21°05'; HSL, LDS, PHH.

Korosmezo, *see* Yasinya.

Korosnagyharsany, Hung.; pop. 8; 139 km SE of Miskolc; 47°00'/21°39'; LDS.

Korosszakal, Hung. (Szakal); pop. 15; 139 km SE of Miskolc; 47°01'/21°36'; LDS.

Korosszegapati, Hung.; pop. 24; 133 km SE of Miskolc; 47°02'/21°38'; LDS.

Korost, Ukr.; pop. 60; 69 km N of Rovno; 51°12'/26°20'; AMG, GUM3.

Korostarcsa, Hung.; pop. 21; 101 km NNE of Szeged; 46°53'/21°02'.

Korosten, Ukr. (Iskorost); pop. 6,089; 146 km WNW of Kiyev; 50°57'/28°39'; EJ, GUM4, JGFF, SF.

Korostishov, *see* Korostyshev.

Korostov, Ukr. (Korostowice?, Korostuv); pop. 32; 107 km SSW of Lvov; 49°01'/23°25'.

Korostowice, *possibly* Korostov.

Korostuv, *see* Korostov.

Korostyshev, Ukr. (Korostishov, Korostyszow, Korshev, Krostchov); pop. 3,017; 107 km WSW of Kiyev; 50°19'/29°04'; GUM4, GYLA, HSL, JGFF, LDL, SF.

Korostyszow, *see* Korostyshev.

Korotichi, Byel. (Korotycze); pop. 25; 101 km E of Pinsk; 52°01'/27°33'.

Korotycze, *see* Korotichi.

Korouhev, Cz.; pop. 3; 62 km NW of Brno; 49°40'/16°15'.

Korozluky, Cz.; pop. 3; 69 km WNW of Praha; 50°29'/13°43'.

Korpoi, COH. This town was not found in BGN gazetteers under the given spelling.

Korpona, *see* Krupina.

Korrenzig, Germ.; 45 km W of Koln; 51°00'/06°16'; GED.

Korschenbroich, Germ.; pop. 20; 38 km WNW of Koln; 51°11'/06°31'.

Korshev, Ukr. (Korshuv, Korszow); pop. 30; 75 km WNW of Chernovtsy; 48°39'/25°01'. *See also* Korostyshev.

Korshev (Wolyn), Ukr.; pop. 9; 82 km W of Rovno; 50°40'/25°07'.

Korshovka, *see* Karsava.

Korshuv, *see* Korshev.

Korshyluvka, Ukr. (Koszylowce); pop. 45; 120 km S of Rovno; 49°34'/26°04'.

Korsov, Ukr. (Korsow); pop. 24; 88 km NE of Lvov; 50°14'/25°08'.

Korsove, *see* Karsava.

Korsovka, *see* Karsava.

Korsovke, *see* Karsava.

Korsow, *see* Korsov.

Korsowka, *see* Karsava.

Korsun, *see* Korsun Shevchenkovskiy.

Korsun Shevchenkovskiy, Ukr. (Korsun); pop. 2,449; 107 km NE of Uman; 49°26'/31°15'; EJ, GYLA, HSL, SF.

Korszow, *see* Korshev.

Korszylow, *possibly* Khorshyluvka.

Kortelisy, *see* Kortilisy.

Kortilisy, Ukr. (Kortelisy); pop. 195; 189 km NW of Rovno; 51°52'/24°26'; JGFF.

Kortovian, *see* Kurtuvenai.

Kortvelyes, HSL. A number of towns share this name. It was not possible to determine from available information which one is being referenced.

Koruv, *see* Kurow.

Korva, *see* Kurow.

Korycany, Cz. (Koristchan, Koritschan); 38 km E of Brno; 49°07'/17°11'; HSL.

Korycin, Pol. (Karitchin, Kartchin); pop. 265; 45 km N of Bialystok; 53°27'/23°06'; COH, GUM3, GUM5, JGFF, POCEM, SF.

Koryciny, Pol.; pop. 5; 62 km SSW of Bialystok; 52°39'/22°44'.

Koryczany, Pol.; pop. 66; 75 km NW of Lublin; 51°48'/22°02'.

Korynkovka, GUM4. This town was not found in BGN gazetteers under the given spelling.

Koryst, Ukr.; 56 km E of Rovno; 50°36'/27°00'; JGFF.

Korytki, *see* Korytki Lesne.

Korytki Lesne, Pol. (Korytki); pop. 23; 88 km W of Bialystok; 53°11'/21°51'.

Korytnica, *see* Korytnitsa.

Korytnica (Kielce area), Pol.; pop. 24; 101 km NE of Krakow; 50°37'/21°04'.

Korytnica (Lublin area), Pol.; pop. 53; 82 km WNW of Lublin; 51°44'/21°47'.

Korytniki, Pol.; pop. 33; 13 km WSW of Przemysl; 49°47'/22°39'.

Korytnitsa, Ukr. (Korytnica); pop. 279; 101 km NNE of Lvov; 50°38'/24°48'.

Koryukovka, Ukr.; pop. 712; 88 km WNW of Konotop; 51°46'/32°16'.

Korzec, *see* Korets.

Korzelice, *see* Korelichi.

Korzenica, Pol.; pop. 31; 32 km N of Przemysl; 50°02'/22°56'.

Korzeniec, Pol.; pop. 30; 26 km SW of Przemysl; 49°43'/22°31'; EDRD, GUM5.

Korzeniew, Pol.; pop. 9; 88 km W of Lodz; 51°57'/18°13'.

Korzeniow, Pol.; pop. 23; 101 km WNW of Przemysl; 50°09'/21°27'.

Korzeniste, Pol.; pop. 3; 82 km WNW of Bialystok; 53°22'/22°01'.

Korzenna, Pol.; pop. 7; 82 km ESE of Krakow; 49°41'/20°51'; GUM5.

Korzenno, Pol.; pop. 2; 101 km NE of Krakow; 50°44'/20°56'.

Korzets, *see* Korets.

Korzhets, *see* Korets.

Korzhevo, Mold. (Corjeva); pop. 31; 32 km NE of Kishinev; 47°06'/29°11'.

Korzhevtsy, Mold. (Corjeuti); pop. 209; 195 km NW of Kishinev; 48°14'/27°03'.

Korzkiew, Pol.; pop. 9; 13 km NNW of Krakow; 50°10'/19°53'.

Korzysc, *possibly* Korets.

Kos, Greece; 334 km ESE of Athens; 36°53'/27°19'; GUM4.

Kosani, Yug.; 88 km SE of Skopje; 41°21'/22°01'; LDL.

Kosarovce, Cz.; 56 km NE of Kosice; 49°03'/21°47'; HSL.

Kosauts, *see* Kosoutsy.

Koschedary, *see* Kaisiadorys.

Koschmin, *see* Kozmin.

Koscian, Pol. (Kosten); pop. 35; 45 km SSW of Poznan; 52°06'/16°38'; CAHJP, HSL.

Kosciejow, Pol.; pop. 27; 38 km NNE of Krakow; 50°20'/20°16'.

Koscieliska, Pol.; pop. 33; 50 km SE of Warszawa; 51°55'/21°28'.

Koscielisko, *see* Zakopane.

Koscielniki, Pol.; pop. 29; 19 km ENE of Krakow; 50°06'/20°11'.

Koscieniewicze, *see* Kostenevichi.

Koscierzyna, Pol. (Berent); pop. 18; 50 km SW of Gdansk; 54°07'/17°59'; HSL, JGFF, LDS.

Kosciewicze, *see* Kostevichi.

Koscifiniki, *see* Kostselniki.

Kosciolkow, Pol.; 69 km ESE of Poznan; 52°10'/17°52'; POCEM.

Kosciow, Pol. PHP2. This town was not found in BGN gazetteers under the given spelling.

Kosciukowicze, Pol.; pop. 4; 69 km S of Bialystok; 52°34'/23°05'.

Kosd, Hung.; pop. 20; 38 km N of Budapest; 47°48'/19°11'.

Kosel, *see* Kozle.

Koselovo, *see* Koshelevo.

Kosemin, Pol.; pop. 14; 101 km WNW of Warszawa; 52°52'/19°54'.

Koserz, Pol.; pop. 6; 62 km NW of Lodz; 52°16'/19°04'.

Kosev, *see* Kosov.

Koseva, *see* Kozova.

Kosevo, Yug.; 82 km ESE of Skopje; 41°42'/22°21'; EJ.

Kosewo, Pol. (Kosewo Wloscianskie [Warsaw area], Kossewo); pop. 143; 88 km WSW of Bialystok; 52°55'/21°54'.

Kosewo (Warszawa area), Pol.; pop. 4; 45 km NNW of Warszawa; 52°36'/20°46'; PHP4.

Kosewo Wloscianskie (Warsaw area), *see* Kosewo.

Koshany, *see* Kaushany.

Koshedar, *see* Kaisiadorys.

Koshedary, *see* Kaisiadorys.

Koshelevo, Ukr. (Kasely, Kasheli, Koselovo, Koshelovo); 182 km S of Lvov; 48°14'/23°20'; AMG, GUM3, LYV, SM.

Koshelovo, *see* Koshelevo.

Kosheny, Mold. (Coseni); pop. 9; 82 km WNW of Kishinev; 47°26'/27°56'.

Koshernitsa, Mold. (Cosarnita); pop. 68; 107 km NNW of Kishinev; 47°56'/28°28'.

Koshidar, *see* Kaisiadorys.

Koshitse, *see* Koszyce.

Koshitz, *see* Koszyce.

Koshlyaki, Ukr. (Kozlaki); pop. 56; 107 km S of Rovno; 49°41'/26°09'.

Koshnik, *see* Krasnik.

Kosice, Cz. (Kaschau, Kasha, Kashau, Kashov, Kashoy, Kassa); pop. 11,195; 309 km ENE of Bratislava; 48°42'/21°15'; AMG, COH, EDRD, EJ, GUM3, GUM4, GUM5, GUM6, GYLA, HSL, HSL2, JGFF, LDL, LJEE, LYV.

Kosiche Velke, Byel. (Kosicze Wielkie); pop. 8; 157 km W of Pinsk; 52°08'/23°49'.

Kosicky Klecenov, Cz. (Klecenov); 19 km ENE of Kosice; 48°45'/21°31'; HSL.

Kosicze Wielkie, *see* Kosiche Velke.

Kosienice, Pol.; pop. 18; 13 km NW of Przemysl; 49°53'/22°42'.

Kosin, Pol.; 62 km SW of Lublin; 50°50'/21°55'; GA.

Kosina, Pol.; pop. 94; 45 km WNW of Przemysl; 50°04'/22°20'.

Kosina Wielka, Pol. (Kasina Wielka); pop. 16; 45 km SSE of Krakow; 49°44'/20°09'.

Kosino, *see* Kosiny.

Kosintin, *see* Konstantynow.

Kosiny, Ukr. (Kosino, Mezokaszony); 208 km SSW of Lvov; 48°15'/22°28'; AMG, GUM5, LDL.

Koslar, Germ.; 50 km WSW of Koln; 50°55'/06°19'; GED.

Koslin, *see* Koszanowo.

Koslov, *see* Yevpatoriya.

Koslow, *see* Yevpatoriya.

Koslowszczyzna, *see* Kozlovshchina.

Kosmach, Ukr. (Kosmacz); pop. 223; 82 km W of Chernovtsy; 48°20'/24°50'.

Kosmach (near Bogorodchany), Ukr.; pop. 23; 126 km WNW of Chernovtsy; 48°45'/24°22'.

Kosmacz, *see* Kosmach.

Kosman, *see* Kitsman.

Kosmonosy, Cz.; pop. 18; 50 km NNE of Praha; 50°26'/14°56'.

Kosna, Pol. BGN lists two possible localities with this name located at 45°06'/16°16' and 52°34'/23°16'. HSL.

Kosnitin, *see* Konstantynow.

Kosobudy, Pol.; pop. 3; 82 km SE of Lublin; 50°38'/23°05'.

Kosogorka, Ukr.; pop. 1,160; 107 km NNE of Chernovtsy; 49°06'/26°45'.

Kosorice, Cz.; pop. 2; 45 km NE of Praha; 50°20'/14°58'.

Kosoutsy, Mold. (Cosauti, Kosauts); pop. 22; 139 km NNW of Kishinev; 48°13'/28°18'.

Kosov, Ukr. (Kosev, Kosow Huculski, Kosow Stary, Kossow Stary, Kossuv, Kosuv Hutsulski); pop. 2,166; 62 km W of Chernovtsy; 48°19'/25°06'; AMG, COH, EDRD, EGRS, EJ, GUM3, GUM4, GUM5, GUM6, HSL, JGFF, LDL, LYV, PHP2, SF, YB. *See also* Kosow; Kossovo; Kossow.

Kosova Hora, Cz. (Amschelberg); 56 km S of Praha; 49°39'/14°29'; EJ.

Kosovka, Ukr. JGFF. A number of towns share this name. It was not possible to determine from available information which one is being referenced.

Kosov Lacki, *see* Kosow Lacki.

Kosov Latski, *see* Kosow Lacki.

Kosov Polski, *see* Kossovo.

Kosovska Mitrovica, Yug.; pop. 106; 107 km NW of Skopje; 42°53'/20°52'.

Kosovska Polana, *see* Kosovskaya Polyana.

Kosovska Polyana, *see* Kosovskaya Polyana.

Kosovskaya Polyana, Ukr. (Kaslomkzo, Kosovska Polana, Kosovska Polyana, Polana Kosovska, Polien Kosoviczki); 139 km WSW of Chernovtsy; 48°00'/24°06'; SM.

Kosow, Ukr. (Kossov, Kossow); pop. 81; 94 km NNW of Chernovtsy; 49°06'/25°40'; AMG, HSL2, JGFF, LDS, PHP4, SF. The name Kosow is also associated with a number of other locations with much larger Jewish populations than the town shown here. *See also* Kosov; Kosow Lacki; Kossovo; Kossow.

Kosow Huculski, *see* Kosov.

Kosow Lacki, Pol. (Kosov Lacki, Kosov Latski, Kossow Lacki); pop. 10; 88 km SW of Bialystok; 52°36'/22°09'; EDRD, GA, GUM3, HSL.

Kosow Stary, *see* Kosov.

Kosowy, Pol.; pop. 46; 94 km WNW of Przemysl; 50°17'/21°39'; HSL2.

Kospallag, Hung.; pop. 7; 45 km NNW of Budapest; 47°53'/18°56'.

Kossaki, Pol.; 50 km WSW of Bialystok; 53°07'/22°21'; PHP4.

Kossewo, *see* Kosewo.

Kossov, *see* Kosow.

Kossovo, Byel. (Kosov Polski); pop. 1,473; 94 km WNW of Pinsk; 52°45'/25°09'; AMG, COH, EDRD, GUM3, GUM4, GUM5, GUM6, HSL, JGFF, LDL, SF, YB. The Polish name for this town is Kossow. *See also* Kosov; Kosow; Kossow.

Kossow, *see* Kosow. The *Black Book* also shows the towns of Kossow Ruski (pop. 41) and Kossow Hulidow (pop. 56) within the interwar Polish province of Lubelskie. *See also* Kosov; Kosow; Kossovo.

Kossow (near Kielce), Pol.; 62 km E of Czestochowa; 50°43'/20°02'; AMG. A contemporary Polish road map also shows another town named Kossow in the interwar province of Kielce near Radom at 51°22'/21°04'.

Kossowitz, *see* Kasejovice.

Kossow Lacki, *see* Kosow Lacki.

Kossow Ruski, Pol.; pop. 41; Described in the *Black Book* as being in the Lublin region of Poland, this town was not found in BGN gazetteers.

Kossow Stary, *see* Kosov.

Kossuthfalva, *see* Stara Moravica.

Kossuv, *see* Kosov.

Kossyn, Pol.; pop. 71; 75 km E of Lublin; 51°05'/23°35'. This town was located on an interwar map of Poland but does not appear in contemporary gazetteers. Map coordinates are approximate.

Kostajnica, Yug.; pop. 30; 75 km SE of Zagreb; 45°13'/16°33'.

Kostantin Yashan, *see* Konstantynow.

Kostany, Cz.; pop. 26; A number of towns share this name. It

was not possible to determine from available information which one is being referenced.

Kostarowce, Pol.; pop. 19; 56 km SW of Przemysl; 49°36'/22°07'.

Kostatin, *see* Novyy Konstantinov.

Kostedt, Germ.; pop. 5; 62 km WSW of Hannover; 52°14'/08°52'.

Kostel, *see* Podivin.

Kostelan, HSL. This pre-World War I community was not found in BGN gazetteers.

Kostelec, (Kosteletz); HSL, HSL2. A number of towns share this name. It was not possible to determine from available information which one is being referenced.

Kostelec nad Cernymi Lesy, Cz.; pop. 30; 32 km ESE of Praha; 49°59'/14°52'.

Kostelec nad Labem, Cz.; pop. 33; 19 km NNE of Praha; 50°14'/14°36'.

Kostelec nad Orlici, Cz.; pop. 44; 114 km NNW of Brno; 50°08'/16°14'.

Kosteletz, *see* Kostelec.

Kostelni Briza, Cz. (Kirchenbirk); pop. 2; 133 km W of Praha; 50°07'/12°37'.

Kostelniki, Ukr. (Kostselniki); pop. 39; 75 km NW of Chernovtsy; 48°53'/25°21'.

Kostely, HSL. This pre-World War I community was not found in BGN gazetteers.

Kosten, *see* Koscian.

Kostenevichi, Byel. (Koscieniewicze); pop. 30; 82 km NNW of Minsk; 54°35'/27°12'.

Kostenice, Cz.; pop. 2; 107 km NW of Brno; 50°01'/15°54'.

Kostintin, *see* Konstantynow.

Kostera, Pol.; pop. 13; 82 km NE of Krakow; 50°33'/20°48'.

Kostesht, *see* Kosteshty.

Kosteshti, *see* Kostintsy.

Kosteshty, Mold. (Costesti Balti, Kostesht); pop. 20; 157 km WNW of Kishinev; 47°51'/27°13'.

Kosteshty Lapusna, Mold. (Costesti Lapusna); pop. 68; 19 km S of Kishinev; 46°52'/28°46'.

Kostevichi, Byel. (Kosciewicze); pop. 6; 146 km NW of Minsk; 54°53'/26°16'.

Kostiantinograd, *see* Krasnograd.

Kostintsy, Ukr. (Costesti, Kosteshti); pop. 274; 26 km WSW of Chernovtsy; 48°17'/25°36'; PHR2.

Kostiukovitch, *see* Kostyukovichi.

Kostolany, *see* Kostolna Pri Dunaji.

Kostolna, Cz.; 101 km ESE of Brno; 48°52'/17°59'; GUM4, GUM6.

Kostolna Pri Dunaji, Cz. (Kostolany, Kosztelany?); 26 km ENE of Bratislava; 48°11'/17°26'; HSL.

Kostomloty, Pol.; pop. 2; 114 km NE of Lublin; 51°58'/23°40'.

Kostopol, Ukr.; pop. 1,185; 38 km NNE of Rovno; 50°53'/26°27'; AMG, COH, EDRD, GUM3, GUM4, GUM5, GUM6, LDL, LYV, PHP2, SF, YB.

Kostrina, Ukr.; 146 km SW of Lvov; 48°57'/22°36'; AMG, HSL.

Kostrizhevka, Ukr. (Costrijeni); pop. 72; 45 km NNW of Chernovtsy; 48°39'/25°43'.

Kostroma, HSL. This pre-World War I community was not found in BGN gazetteers.

Kostry, Pol.; pop. 7; 56 km NNE of Lublin; 51°42'/22°55'.

Kostrza Ryje, Pol.; pop. 4; 45 km SE of Krakow; 49°47'/20°17'.

Kostrzeszyn, Pol.; pop. 5; 56 km NE of Krakow; 50°22'/20°32'.

Kostrzyna, Pol.; pop. 6; 32 km W of Czestochowa; 50°51'/18°42'.

Kostselniki, *see* Kostelniki.

Kostuleny, Mold. (Cosuleni); pop. 15; 69 km W of Kishinev; 47°05'/27°55'.

Kostyukovichi, Byel. (Kostiukovitch); pop. 1,608; 126 km NNE of Gomel; 53°20'/32°03'; JGFF, LDL, SF.

Kosuv Hutsulski, *see* Kosov.

Kosyno, (Kaszony); COH, HSL, HSL2. This pre-World War I community was not found in BGN gazetteers.

164

Koszalin, *see* Koszanowo.

Koszanowo, Pol. (Koeslin, Koslin, Koszalin); pop. 140; 56 km SSW of Poznan; 52°02'/16°33'; HSL, HSL2, LDS.

Koszarawa, *see* Koszarowa.

Koszarowa, Pol. (Koszarawa); pop. 6; 62 km SSW of Krakow; 49°39'/19°25'.

Koszary, Pol.; pop. 30; 88 km WSW of Lublin; 51°07'/21°16'.

Koszedary, *see* Kaisiadorys.

Koszeg, Hung. (Guns); pop. 131; 114 km NNW of Nagykanizsa; 47°23'/16°33'; EJ, GUM3, GUM4, GUM5, GUM6, HSL, HSL2, JGFF, LDS, PHH.

Koszegdoroszlo, Hung.; pop. 1; 107 km NNW of Nagykanizsa; 47°21'/16°33'.

Koszegszerdahely, Hung.; pop. 11; 107 km NNW of Nagykanizsa; 47°20'/16°31'.

Koszelewy, Pol.; pop. 5; 139 km SE of Gdansk; 53°20'/19°58'.

Koszoly, Pol.; pop. 6; 94 km NNE of Lublin; 51°54'/23°17'.

Koszow, GUM3. This town was not found in BGN gazetteers under the given spelling.

Kosztelany, *possibly* Kostolna Pri Dunaji.

Kosztowa, Pol.; pop. 49; 50 km SW of Przemysl; 49°35'/22°15'; HSL. This town was located on an interwar map of Poland but does not appear in contemporary gazetteers. Map coordinates are approximate.

Koszyce, Pol. (Koshitse, Koshitz); pop. 678; 50 km ENE of Krakow; 50°10'/20°34'; AMG, COH, EDRD, GUM3, GUM4, GUM5, GUM5, PHP3, SF.

Koszylowce, *see* Korshyluvka.

Kotaj, Hung. (Keresztut); pop. 166; 69 km E of Miskolc; 48°03'/21°43'; GUM5, HSL, PHH.

Kotcse, Hung.; pop. 8; 75 km NE of Nagykanizsa; 46°45'/17°52'.

Kotegyan, Hung.; pop. 14; 114 km NE of Szeged; 46°44'/21°29'; LDS.

Kotel, Bulg. (Kozyan); 126 km SW of Varna; 42°53'/26°27'; JGFF.

Kotelek, Hung.; pop. 22; 88 km S of Miskolc; 47°20'/20°27'.

Kotelnia, *see* Staraya Kotelnya.

Kotelnice, HSL. This pre-World War I community was not found in BGN gazetteers.

Kotelnja, *see* Staraya Kotelnya.

Kotelnua, *see* Staraya Kotelnya.

Kotelnya, *see* Staraya Kotelnya.

Koteschau, HSL. This pre-World War I community was not found in BGN gazetteers.

Kothen, Germ. (Cothen); pop. 180; 56 km NW of Leipzig; 51°45'/11°58'; COH, HSL, LDS.

Kotkowska Wola, *see* Wola Kotkowska.

Kotlice, Pol.; pop. 21; 88 km ESE of Lublin; 50°43'/23°35'.

Kotlovina, Ukr. (Bolboaca); pop. 33; 195 km SW of Odessa; 45°30'/28°34'.

Kotolina Hayashana, *see* Staraya Kotelnya.

Kotoriba, Yug.; pop. 7; 88 km NNE of Zagreb; 46°22'/16°49'.

Kotormany, Hung.; pop. 4; 69 km WNW of Nagykanizsa; 46°49'/16°21'.

Kotov, *see* Bania Kotowska.

Kotova, Mold. (Cotova); pop. 31; 146 km NW of Kishinev; 48°10'/27°57'.

Kotovsk (Bessarabia), Mold. (Gancheshty, Hancesti, Hanczeschty, Hontchest, Hanuszeschty?, Kotowsk); pop. 1,523; 32 km SSW of Kishinev; 46°50'/28°36'; LDL, PHR1.

Kotovsk (Ukraine), Ukr. (Birsula, Birzula); pop. 2,507; 126 km SSW of Uman; 47°45'/29°32'; EJ, LDL, SF.

Kotovskoye, Ukr.; 82 km N of Odessa; 47°10'/30°36'; EJ.

Kotowa Wola, Pol.; pop. 12; 82 km SSW of Lublin; 50°37'/21°56'.

Kotowka, *see* Kotuv.

Kotowsk, *see* Kotovsk (Bessarabia).

Kotowy, Pol.; pop. 11; 139 km WNW of Warszawa; 53°06'/19°34'.

Kotozovo, *see* Volodarsk Volynskiy.

Kotra, Byel.; pop. 4; 139 km WNW of Pinsk; 52°42'/24°19'.

Kotsk, *see* Kock.

Kotsyubinchiki, Ukr. (Kociubince, Kociubinczyki, Kotsyubinchyki); pop. 44; 75 km N of Chernovtsy; 48°57'/26°10'.

Kotsyubinchyki, *see* Kotsyubinchiki.

Kottbus, *see* Cottbus.

Kottendorf, Aus.; 62 km ENE of Salzburg; 47°57'/13°53'; EJ.

Kottingbrunn, Aus.; pop. 2; 32 km S of Wien; 47°57'/16°13'.

Kotun, Pol.; pop. 138; 75 km E of Warszawa; 52°11'/22°04'.

Kotuv, Ukr. (Kotowka); pop. 7; 88 km ESE of Lvov; 49°21'/24°58'.

Kotyatiche Golyn, Ukr. (Golyn, Holyn); pop. 122; 101 km SSE of Lvov; 49°01'/24°15'; PHP2.

Kotyudzhen, Mold. (Costiceni); pop. 25; 208 km NW of Kishinev; 48°21'/26°57'.

Kotyugany, Mold. (Cotiugeni); pop. 80; 133 km S of Kishinev; 45°56'/28°15'.

Kotyuzhany, Mold. (Cotiugeni Mari, Cotiugenii Mari); pop. 367; 101 km NNW of Kishinev; 47°51'/28°33'.

Kotzk, *see* Kock.

Kotzman, *see* Kitsman.

Kotzschenbroda, Germ.; pop. 8; 94 km E of Leipzig; 51°06'/13°37'.

Kotzting, Germ.; pop. 12; 133 km E of Nurnberg; 49°10'/12°51'; GUM3, PHGB.

Koumice, Cz.; pop. 20; 19 km E of Praha; 50°05'/14°42'.

Kourim, Cz.; pop. 17; 45 km E of Praha; 50°00'/14°59'.

Kovac, Yug.; 50 km SSW of Skopje; 41°41'/21°09'; HSL, HSL2.

Kovacica, Yug.; pop. 37; 38 km N of Beograd; 45°06'/20°38'.

Kovacshaza, HSL, HSL2. This pre-World War I community was not found in BGN gazetteers.

Kovacsret, *see* Kushnitsa.

Kovacsvagas, Hung.; pop. 14; 69 km NE of Miskolc; 48°27'/21°32'.

Kovagoors, Hung.; pop. 72; 62 km NE of Nagykanizsa; 46°51'/17°36'; HSL, JGFF, LDS, PHH.

Koval, *see* Kowal.

Kovalishki, Byel. (Kowaliszki); pop. 5; 202 km W of Vitebsk; 55°46'/27°10'.

Kovarberence, GUM5. This town was not found in BGN gazetteers under the given spelling.

Kovarremete, HSL. This pre-World War I community was not found in BGN gazetteers.

Kovarsk, *see* Kavarskas.

Kovarskas, *see* Kavarskas.

Kovaszo, HSL. This pre-World War I community was not found in BGN gazetteers.

Kovchitsy, *see* Kovchitsy Vtoryye.

Kovchitsy Vtoryye, Byel. (Kovchitsy); 133 km WNW of Gomel; 52°50'/29°11'.

Kovecses, Hung.; pop. 9; 139 km W of Budapest; 47°37'/17°12'; HSL.

Kovel, Ukr. (Kovla, Kovle, Kowel); pop. 12,758; 126 km WNW of Rovno; 51°13'/24°43'; AMG, COH, EDRD, EJ, FRG, GA, GUM3, GUM4, GUM5, GUM6, GYLA, HSL, HSL2, JGFF, LDL, LYV, SF.

Kovend, *see* Chiend.

Koverskas, *see* Kavarskas.

Kovesd, Hung.; 114 km WSW of Szeged; 46°12'/18°42'; HSL.

Koveskal, Hung.; pop. 15; 69 km NNE of Nagykanizsa; 46°53'/17°36'.

Kovesliget, *see* Dragovo.

Kovi, *see* Koovi. AMG states it is in Hungary. It is not in contemporary gazetteers.

Koviljaca, *see* Banja Koviljaca.

Kovin, Yug.; pop. 75; 38 km E of Beograd; 44°45'/20°59'; EDRD, HSL, HSL2.

Kovla, *see* Kovel.

Kovle, *see* Kovel.

Kovnat, *see* Kaunata.

Kovno, *see* Kaunas.

Kovnyatin, Byel. (Kowniatyn); pop. 5; 32 km NNW of Pinsk;

52°20'/26°03'.

Kovyrluy, Mold. (Covurlui); pop. 10; 56 km SSW of Kishinev; 46°36'/28°23'.

Kowal, Pol. (Koval, Kval); pop. 1,227; 94 km NNW of Lodz; 52°32'/19°10'; AMG, CAHJP, COH, HSL, HSL2, JGFF, LYV, PHP1, PHP4, POCEM, SF, YB.

Kowald, Aus.; pop. 1; 26 km WSW of Graz; 47°02'/15°07'.

Kowale Panskie, Pol. (Heidemuhle); 62 km WNW of Lodz; 51°56'/18°33'; EDRD, GA, GUM3, PHP1.

Kowaliszki, see Kovalishki.

Kowalkow, Pol.; pop. 7; 82 km WSW of Lublin; 51°15'/21°24'.

Kowalowy, Pol.; pop. 59; 94 km E of Krakow; 49°53'/21°12'.

Kowel, see Kovel.

Kownaciska, Pol.; pop. 18; 94 km E of Warszawa; 52°15'/22°20'.

Kownaty, HSL. A number of towns share this name. It was not possible to determine from available information which one is being referenced.

Kowniatyn, see Kovnyatin.

Kowno, see Kaunas.

Koydanovo, see Dzerzhinsk.

Koyl, see Kolo.

Kozachizna, Ukr. (Kozaczyzna); pop. 60; 62 km N of Chernovtsy; 48°51'/26°00'; SF.

Kozachovka, see Kozachuvka.

Kozachuvka, Ukr. (Kaschowka, Kashofka, Kozachovka, Kozaczowka); pop. 6; 45 km NE of Chernovtsy; 48°32'/26°25'; SF.

Kozaczowka, see Kozachuvka.

Kozaczyzna, see Kozachizna.

Kozaki, Ukr. GUM3, GUM5, PHP2. Kozaki is a concentration camp described in PHP1 as being near Yavorov.

Kozangrodek, see Kozhan Gorodok.

Kozara, see Kozari.

Kozari, Ukr. (Kozara); pop. 13; 75 km SE of Lvov; 49°15'/24°26'.

Kozarmisleny, Hung.; pop. 4; 107 km ESE of Nagykanizsa; 46°02'/18°18'.

Kozarvar, see Cusdrioara.

Kozelec, see Kozelets.

Kozelets, Ukr. (Kozelec, Kozeletz, Kozielec, Mushkev, Myszkow Nowy); pop. 748; 69 km NNE of Kiyev; 50°55'/31°07'; HSL, LDL, SF.

Kozeletz, see Kozelets.

Kozelsk, USSR; pop. 115; 133 km NE of Bryansk; 54°02'/35°48'.

Kozepapsa, see Stredni Apsa.

Kozepborgo, see Borgo Mijloceni.

Kozeplak, see Cuzaplac.

Kozepviso, see Viseu de Mijloc. Described in EJ as being near Viseu de Sus, Kozepviso does not apppear in contemporary gazetteers.

Kozeve, see Kozova.

Kozhan Gorodok, Byel. (Kazhaneradok, Kozangrodek, Kozhangrudek, Kozhanhorodok, Kurzanhradek); pop. 783; 62 km ENE of Pinsk; 52°13'/27°01'; COH, EDRD, FRG, HSL, JGFF, SF, WS, YB.

Kozhangrudek, see Kozhan Gorodok.

Kozhanhorodok, see Kozhan Gorodok.

Kozhanka, Ukr.; 56 km ENE of Vinnitsa; 49°18'/29°17'; JGFF.

Kozhelitse, see Korelichi.

Kozhenits, see Kozienice.

Kozhenitz, see Kozienice.

Kozhnitz, see Kozienice.

Kozia Gora, GUM4, PHP2. A number of towns share this name. It was not possible to determine from available information which one is being referenced.

Kozian, see Kozyany.

Koziany, see Kozyany.

Koziarnia, Pol.; pop. 4; 69 km NW of Przemysl; 50°23'/22°20'.

Kozia Wies, Pol.; pop. 8; 62 km ENE of Czestochowa; 50°56'/20°02'.

Kozice Dolne, Pol.; pop. 17; 26 km ESE of Lublin; 51°07'/22°48'.

Kozice Gorne, Pol.; pop. 15; 19 km ESE of Lublin; 51°07'/22°46'.

Kozieglowy, Pol.; pop. 343; 26 km SSE of Czestochowa; 50°36'/19°10'; AMG, COH, LDL.

Kozielec, see Kozelets.

Kozielniki, Pol.; pop. 37; Described in the Black Book as being in the Lwow region of Poland, this town was not found in BGN gazetteers.

Kozienice, Pol. (Kozhenits, Kozhenitz, Kozhnitz, Koznitz); pop. 3,811; 82 km WNW of Lublin; 51°35'/21°34'; AMG, CAHJP, COH, EDRD, EJ, FRG, GA, GUM3, GUM4, GUM5, GUM6, HSL, HSL2, LDL, LDS, LYV, PHP1, POCEM, SF, YB.

Kozieniec, Pol. BGN lists two possible localities with this name located at 51°00'/23°21' and 51°32'/20°42'. PHP4.

Koziki Majdan, Pol.; pop. 40; 75 km NNE of Warszawa; 52°48'/21°45'.

Kozin, Ukr.; pop. 525; 69 km SW of Rovno; 50°16'/25°28'; AMG, COH, GUM3, GUM4, HSL, LDL, LYV, SF.

Kozin (near Kiev), Ukr.; pop. 525; 69 km SW of Rovno; 50°16'/25°28'; SF.

Kozinowo Nowe, Pol.; pop. 34; Described in the Black Book as being in the Nowogrodek region of Poland, this town was not found in BGN gazetteers.

Koziny, GUM3. This town was not found in BGN gazetteers under the given spelling.

Koziol, Pol.; pop. 12; 94 km WNW of Bialystok; 53°26'/21°51'.

Koziowa, see Kozova.

Kozirynek, see Radzyn Podlaski.

Kozlaki, see Koshlyaki.

Kozle, Pol. (Cosel, Kosel); pop. 80; 82 km SW of Czestochowa; 50°20'/18°10'; EJ, HSL, HSL2, LDS.

Kozlin, Ukr.; pop. 36; 19 km NE of Rovno; 50°43'/26°26'.

Kozliniche, see Kozlinichi.

Kozlinichi, Ukr. (Kozliniche, Kozlinicze); pop. 51; 82 km NNW of Rovno; 51°16'/25°56'.

Kozlinicze, see Kozlinichi.

Kozlov, (Kozlow); See also Yevpatoriya.

Kozlov (Tarnopol), Ukr.; pop. 25; 45 km NE of Lvov; 49°58'/24°32'.

Kozlova Ruda, see Kazlu Ruda.

Kozlovshchina, Byel. (Kislovchina, Kislovshchizna, Kislowszczyzna, Koslowszczyzna, Kozlowstchine, Kozlowszczyzna); 146 km NW of Pinsk; 53°19'/25°18'; COH, EDRD, GUM3, GUM4, GUM6, HSL, JGFF, SF.

Kozlovshchyzna, Byel.; pop. 71; 150 km N of Minsk; 55°11'/27°22'; LYV.

Kozlow, Ukr.; pop. 715; 101 km ESE of Lvov; 49°33'/25°21'; AMG, EGRS, GUM3, GUM4, HSL, LDL, LYV, PHP2. See also Kozlov; Kozluv.

Kozlow (near Miechow), Pol.; pop. 86; 50 km N of Krakow; 50°29'/20°02'; GUM3.

Kozlowa, Pol. PHP4. This town was not found in BGN gazetteers under the given spelling.

Kozlowa Ruda, see Kazlu Ruda.

Kozlowek, Pol.; 82 km W of Przemysl; 49°51'/21°41'; PHP3.

Kozlowstchine, see Kozlovshchina.

Kozlowszczyzna, see Kozlovshchina.

Kozlow Szlachecki, Pol.; pop. 10; 56 km WSW of Warszawa; 52°10'/20°09'.

Kozluv, Ukr. (Kozlow); pop. 66; 107 km NNE of Lvov; 50°43'/24°41'.

Kozma, see Kuzmice.

Kozmadombja, Hung.; pop. 3; 50 km NW of Nagykanizsa; 46°46'/16°33'.

Kozmeny, see Kitsman.

Kozmice, see Kozmice Male.

Kozmice Male, Pol. (Kozmice); 26 km SE of Krakow; 49°56'/20°04'; EDRD.

Kozmin, Pol. (Juzmin, Koschmin); pop. 135; 82 km SE of Poznan; 51°49'/17°27'; CAHJP, HSL, LDS, POCEM.

Kozminek, Pol. (Kozminka); pop. 729; 75 km W of Lodz; 51°48'/18°20'; AMG, EJ, GA, GUM3, GUM4, GUM5, HSL, HSL2, JGFF, PHP1, SF.

Kozminka, *see* Kozminek.

Koznitz, *see* Kozienice.

Kozodrza, Pol.; pop. 7; 88 km WNW of Przemysl; 50°06'/21°37'.

Kozolupy, Cz.; pop. 43; 94 km SW of Praha; 49°46'/13°15'; HSL.

Kozomin, Cz.; pop. 3; 19 km NNW of Praha; 50°14'/14°23'.

Kozova, Ukr. (Koseva, Kozeve, Koziowa, Kozovo, Kozowa); pop. 1,391; 94 km ESE of Lvov; 49°26'/25°09'; AMG, COH, EDRD, EGRS, GUM3, GUM4, HSL, HSL2, JGFF, LDL, LYV, PHP2, SF.

Kozovka, Pol.; pop. 40; Described in the *Black Book* as being in the Tarnopol region of Poland, this town was not found in BGN gazetteers.

Kozovo, *see* Kozova.

Kozowa, *see* Kozova.

Kozowowice, Pol. PHP3. This town was not found in BGN gazetteers under the given spelling.

Kozubata, Pol.; pop. 13; 45 km NE of Lublin; 51°23'/23°11'.

Kozuchow, Pol. (Kozuchow Wielki); pop. 8; 94 km ENE of Warszawa; 52°21'/22°20'.

Kozuchow (near Nowa Sol), Pol.; 120 km SW of Poznan; 51°45'/15°36'; LDS.

Kozuchowek, Pol.; pop. 2; 94 km ENE of Warszawa; 52°21'/22°21'.

Kozuchow Wielki, *see* Kozuchow.

Kozyan, *see* Kotel.

Kozyany, Byel. (Kozian, Koziany); pop. 165; 163 km NNW of Minsk; 55°18'/26°52'; COH, EDRD, GUM3, GUM6, SF, YB.

Kracest, *see* Cracesti.

Kracie, *see* Kratie.

Kracinovce, COH, HSL. This pre-World War I community was not found in BGN gazetteers.

Kracsfalva, *see* Cracesti.

Kraczew, Pol. (Kraczow); pop. 3; 101 km ESE of Lublin; 50°36'/23°34'.

Kraczewice, Pol.; pop. 9; 32 km WSW of Lublin; 51°13'/22°07'.

Kraczkowa, Pol.; pop. 52; 50 km WNW of Przemysl; 50°02'/22°10'.

Kraczow, *see* Kraczew.

Kragujevac, Yug.; pop. 95; 94 km SSE of Beograd; 44°01'/20°55'; EDRD.

Kraiburg, *see* Kraiburg am Inn.

Kraiburg am Inn, Germ. (Kraiburg); 62 km ENE of Munchen; 48°11'/12°26'; PHGB.

Krailling, Germ.; pop. 9; 19 km SW of Munchen; 48°06'/11°24'.

Krain, *see* Grain.

Kraisdorf, Germ.; 82 km NNW of Nurnberg; 50°08'/10°44'; PHGB.

Kraitzburg, *see* Krustpils.

Krajenka, Pol. (Krajenka Chelmno, Krojanke); pop. 260; 101 km N of Poznan; 53°18'/16°59'; AMG, HSL, JGFF, LDS.

Krajenka Chelmno, *see* Krajenka.

Krajnikov, Ukr. (Mihalka, Mikif); 182 km WSW of Chernovtsy; 48°07'/23°26'; SM.

Krajno, Pol.; pop. 108; 114 km NNE of Krakow; 50°53'/20°51'; COH.

Krajowice, Pol.; 56 km NE of Przemysl; 49°57'/23°30'; GUM5, PHP3.

Krajow Nowy, GUM4. This town was not found in BGN gazetteers under the given spelling.

Krakanova, *see* Krekenava.

Krakau, *see* Krakow.

Krakenovo, *see* Krekenava.

Krakes, Lith. (Krok); 62 km NNW of Kaunas; 55°24'/23°44'; GYLA, HSL, JGFF, SF, YL.

Krakiai, Lith.; pop. 659; 69 km WNW of Siauliai; 56°17'/22°24'; COH.

Krakinava, *see* Krekenava.

Krakinova, *see* Krekenava.

Krakinovo, *see* Krekenava.

Krako, *see* Krakow.

Krakovets, Ukr. (Krakovitz, Krakowiec); pop. 529; 62 km W of Lvov; 49°58'/23°10'; AMG, COH, EDRD, EGRS, HSL, JGFF, LDL, SF, YB.

Krakovitz, *see* Krakovets.

Krakow, Pol. (Cracow, Krakau, Krako, Krakoy, Krakuv, Kroke); pop. 45,229; 94 km SE of Czestochowa; 50°05'/19°55'; AMG, CAHJP, COH, EDRD, EGRS, EJ, FRG, GA, GUM3, GUM4, GUM5, GUM6, HSL, HSL2, ISH1, ISH2, ISH3, JGFF, LDL, LDS, LJEE, LYV, PHP1, PHP2, PHP3, PHP4, POCEM, SF, YB.

Krakowice, Pol. PHP2. This town was not found in BGN gazetteers under the given spelling.

Krakowiec, *see* Krakovets.

Krakoy, *see* Krakow.

Krakuv, *see* Krakow.

Krali, LDL. This pre-World War I community was not found in BGN gazetteers.

Kraliky, Cz.; pop. 28; 107 km N of Brno; 50°05'/16°46'.

Kraljevcani, Yug.; pop. 2; 56 km SSE of Zagreb; 45°20'/16°18'.

Kraljevica, Yug.; pop. 2; 126 km SW of Zagreb; 45°16'/14°34'; EJ, GUM4, GUM5.

Kralovo nad Tisou, *see* Korolevo.

Kralovske Porici, Cz. (Koenigswart?, Konigswart?, Konigswerth); 126 km W of Praha; 50°11'/12°41'; EJ, HSL, HSL2.

Kralovsky Chlmec, Cz. (Kiraly Helmec, Kralovsky Chlumec, Krulovsky); 62 km ESE of Kosice; 48°25'/21°59'; AMG, GUM5, HSL, JGFF, LDL.

Kralovsky Chlumec, *see* Kralovsky Chlmec.

Kralupy, *see* Kralupy nad Vltavou.

Kralupy nad Vltavou, Cz. (Kralupy); pop. 119; 19 km NW of Praha; 50°14'/14°19'.

Kramaszowka, Pol.; pop. 27; Described in the *Black Book* as being in the Lwow region of Poland, this town was not found in BGN gazetteers.

Kramatorsk, Ukr.; 170 km SE of Kharkov; 48°43'/37°32'.

Kramkowka Duza, Pol. (Kramkowka Wielka); pop. 6; 45 km WNW of Bialystok; 53°26'/22°42'.

Kramkowka Wielka, *see* Kramkowka Duza.

Kramsk, Pol.; pop. 61; 94 km WNW of Lodz; 52°16'/18°26'; GUM3.

Kranj, Yug.; pop. 16; 139 km WNW of Zagreb; 46°14'/14°22'.

Kranjska Gora, Yug.; 182 km WNW of Zagreb; 46°29'/13°47'; GUM6.

Kransberg, *see* Krantsberg.

Krantsberg, Ukr. (Kransberg, Kranzberg); pop. 27; 62 km SW of Lvov; 49°29'/23°23'.

Kranzberg, *see* Krantsberg.

Krape, Lat.; pop. 1; 69 km ESE of Riga; 56°44'/25°07'.

Krapina, Yug.; pop. 33; 50 km NNW of Zagreb; 46°10'/15°53'.

Krapkowice, Pol. (Krappitz, Kreitzburg, Kreuzburg); pop. 160; 88 km SW of Czestochowa; 50°29'/17°58'; COH, EJ, GUM4, GUM6, HSL, JGFF, LDS, PHLE, POCEM, SF.

Krappitz, *see* Krapkowice.

Krasew, Pol.; pop. 24; 62 km N of Lublin; 51°46'/22°28'.

Krashanov, *see* Chrzanow.

Krashnik, *see* Krasnik.

Krasic, Yug.; pop. 5; 38 km SW of Zagreb; 45°39'/15°31'.

Krasichin, *see* Krasiczyn.

Krasiczyn, Pol. (Krasichin); pop. 32; 13 km WSW of Przemysl; 49°46'/22°40'; CAHJP, EDRD.

Krasienin, Pol.; pop. 30; 19 km NW of Lublin; 51°22'/22°28'.

Krasilov, Ukr. (Krasilova, Krasilow, Kresilov); pop. 1,550; 120 km SE of Rovno; 49°39'/26°58'; COH, HSL, JGFF, SF.

Krasilova, *see* Krasilov.

Krasilow, *see* Krasilov.

Krasinstav, *see* Krasnystav.

Kraskow, Pol. (Bodzechow); pop. 44; 88 km SW of Lublin; 50°55'/21°28'; GA, GUM3, GUM4, POCEM.

Kraslau, *see* Kraslava.

Kraslava, Lat. (Kraslau, Kraslave, Kraslavka, Kraslavke, Kreslavaka, Kreslavka, Kreslawa); pop. 1,549; 45 km ENE of Daugavpils; 55°54'/27°10'; EJ, JGFF, LDL, PHLE, SF.

Kraslave, *see* Kraslava.

Kraslavka, *see* Kraslava.

Kraslavke, *see* Kraslava.

Kraslice, Cz.; pop. 66; 146 km W of Praha; 50°20'/12°31'.

Krasna, Ukr. (Krasnisora, Taracz Krazna); 146 km WSW of Chernovtsy; 48°13'/23°56'; HSL, HSL2, JGFF, SM. The entries in HSL refer to towns in the Lublin district of Poland and in Czechoslovakia. Neither of these is mentioned in the *Black Book*.

Krasna (near Kalush), Ukr.; pop. 59; 120 km SSE of Lvov; 48°51'/24°17'.

Krasna (near Nadvorna), Ukr.; pop. 51; 94 km WNW of Chernovtsy; 48°35'/24°42'.

Krasna (near Turka), Ukr.; pop. 69; 94 km WNW of Chernovtsy; 48°35'/24°42'.

Krasna (Tarnopol), Ukr.; pop. 30; 88 km ESE of Lvov; 49°36'/25°11'.

Krasna Hora nad Vltavoa, HSL. A number of towns share this name. It was not possible to determine from available information which one is being referenced.

Krasna Hora nad Vltavou, Cz. (Schonberg); 62 km S of Praha; 49°36'/14°18'; COH.

Krasna Ilski, *see* Krasnoilsk.

Krasna Kamienka, LDL. This pre-World War I community was not found in BGN gazetteers.

Krasna Lipa, Cz.; pop. 28; 94 km N of Praha; 50°54'/14°31'.

Krasnaluk, *see* Krasnoluki.

Krasnapole, (Krasnapoli); JGFF, SF. This town was not found in BGN gazetteers under the given spelling.

Krasnapoli, *see* Krasnapole.

Krasna Putna, *see* Krasnoputna.

Krasna Wies, Pol.; pop. 12; 56 km S of Bialystok; 52°39'/23°10'.

Krasna Wola, *see* Krasnaya Volya.

Krasnaya Sloboda, Byel.; pop. 615; 107 km NNE of Pinsk; 52°51'/27°10'.

Krasnaya Volya, Byel. (Krasna Wola); pop. 31; 69 km NE of Pinsk; 52°23'/27°04'.

Krasnaye, Pol. PHP2. This town was not found in BGN gazetteers under the given spelling.

Krasne, Pol. AMG. A number of towns share this name. It was not possible to determine from available information which one is being referenced.

Krasne (near Krakow), Pol.; pop. 24; 38 km SE of Krakow; 49°49'/20°14'.

Krasne (near Molodechno), Byel. (Krasnei); pop. 319; 50 km NW of Minsk; 54°14'/27°05'; COH, GUM4, GUM6, SF.

Krasne (near Rzeszow), Pol.; pop. 30; 56 km WNW of Przemysl; 50°03'/22°06'.

Krasne (near Skalat), Ukr.; pop. 71; 114 km N of Chernovtsy; 49°18'/26°10'.

Krasne (near Vilnius), Lith.; 26 km WSW of Vilnius; 54°41'/24°57'; GUM5.

Krasne (near Wlodawa), Pol.; pop. 50; 45 km E of Lublin; 51°08'/23°11'.

Krasne (near Zolochev), Ukr.; pop. 67; 45 km ENE of Lvov; 49°55'/24°37'.

Krasne (Wolyn), Ukr.; pop. 312; 62 km WSW of Rovno; 50°32'/25°21'; COH, EDRD, GUM3, GUM4, LYV.

Krasnei, *see* Krasne (near Molodechno).

Krasne Potockie, Pol.; pop. 16; 62 km ESE of Krakow; 49°40'/20°35'.

Krasnica, Pol.; pop. 25; 62 km ESE of Lodz; 51°27'/20°15'; PHP1.

Krasniczyn, Pol.; pop. 540; 62 km ESE of Lublin; 50°56'/23°22';

COH, GA, GUM5, LDS, POCEM.

Krasnik, Pol. (Koshnik, Krashnik, Kroshnik, Krushnik); pop. 4,200; 45 km SSW of Lublin; 50°55'/22°14'; AMG, CAHJP, COH, EDRD, EJ, FRG, GA, GUM3, GUM4, GUM5, GUM6, GYLA, HSL, HSL2, ISH1, ISH3, JGFF, LDS, LYV, PHP2, PHP3, POCEM, SF, YB.

Krasnishore, *see* Taracs Kraszna.

Krasnisora, *see* Krasna.

Krasnistav, *see* Krasnystaw.

Krasnistov, *see* Krasnystaw.

Krasnitsa, Byel. JGFF. A number of towns share this name. It was not possible to determine from available information which one is being referenced.

Krasno, Cz.; pop. 66; 101 km NE of Brno; 49°29'/17°59'; EJ.

Krasnoarmeyskoye, Mold. (Principele Carol); pop. 3; 45 km SW of Kishinev; 46°50'/28°17'.

Krasnobrod, Pol.; pop. 1,148; 88 km SE of Lublin; 50°33'/23°12'; AMG, COH, EDRD, GUM3, GUM5, GYLA, HSL, HSL2, JGFF, LDS, SF, YB.

Krasnocz, HSL. This pre-World War I community was not found in BGN gazetteers.

Krasnodar, USSR (Yekaterinodar); pop. 1,746; 738 km S of Voronezh; 45°02'/39°00'; EDRD, EJ, GUM4, GUM5.

Krasnoe Selo, USSR; pop. 58; This town was not found in BGN gazetteers under the given spelling.

Krasnograd, Ukr. (Konstantinograd, Konstantinogrod, Konstantynogrod, Kostiantinograd, Krasnogrod); pop. 1,576; 88 km SSW of Kharkov; 49°22'/35°27'; GUM4, LDL, SF.

Krasnogrod, *see* Krasnograd.

Krasnoilsk, Ukr. (Crasna Iliesti?, Crasna Ilschi, Krasna Ilski); pop. 97; 45 km SSW of Chernovtsy; 48°00'/25°34'; PHR2.

Krasnokuck, *see* Krasnokutsk.

Krasnokutsk, Ukr. (Krasnokuck); pop. 9; 82 km W of Kharkov; 50°04'/35°09'.

Krasnoluka, Ukr.; pop. 25; 82 km S of Rovno; 49°54'/26°04'.

Krasnoluki, Byel. (Krasnaluk); 107 km SW of Vitebsk; 54°37'/28°50'; LDL, SF.

Krasnopol, Pol.; pop. 79; 114 km N of Bialystok; 54°07'/23°12'; HSL, HSL2, JGFF, LDL, LDS, POCEM, SF.

Krasnopole, *see* Krasnopolye.

Krasnopole Malastowki, Byel.; 150 km NNE of Gomel; 53°42'/31°54'; CAHJP.

Krasnopolye, Ukr. (Krasnopole, Krassnapolje, Krosnopolia); pop. 1,715; 264 km NW of Konotop; 53°20'/31°24'; GUM4, HSL, LDL, SF.

Krasnoputna, Ukr. (Crasna Putnei, Krasna Putna); pop. 160; 45 km SSW of Chernovtsy; 48°01'/25°34'.

Krasnoselka, Ukr.; 146 km ESE of Dnepropetrovsk; 47°37'/36°34'; JGFF.

Krasnoselye, Ukr.; pop. 35; 69 km N of Lvov; 50°26'/24°08'.

Krasnoshelets, *see* Krasnosielc.

Krasnoshelts, *see* Krasnosielc.

Krasnosheny, Mold. (Crasnaseni); pop. 38; 62 km NW of Kishinev; 47°26'/28°24'.

Krasnosielc, Pol. (Krasnoshelets, Krasnoshelts, Krosnoshiltz); pop. 926; 88 km N of Warszawa; 53°02'/21°10'; AMG, COH, EDRD, GUM3, GUM4, GUM5, GUM6, HSL, LYV, PHP4, SF.

Krasnostav, Ukr.; pop. 1,204; 69 km ESE of Rovno; 50°24'/27°11'; EDRD, JGFF. *See also* Krasnystaw.

Krasnostavtse, *see* Krasnostavtsy.

Krasnostavtsy, Ukr. (Krasnostavtse, Krasnostawce); pop. 33; 45 km WNW of Chernovtsy; 48°32'/25°29'.

Krasnostawce, *see* Krasnostavtsy.

Krasnovce, Cz. (Krasznoc); 50 km ENE of Kosice; 48°43'/21°53'; HSL.

Krasnoya, *see* Krasnoye.

Krasnoye, Ukr. (Krasnoya); pop. 2,002; 45 km S of Vinnitsa; 48°54'/28°25'; EJ, LDL, SF.

Krasnoye (near Belaya Tserkov), Ukr. (Hermanovka); 62 km S of Kiyev; 49°55'/30°25'; LDL, SF.

Krasny, USSR; pop. 298; 50 km SW of Smolensk; 54°35'/31°28'; COH, JGFF.

Krasnyanka, Ukr. (Frumusica Noua); pop. 14; 101 km WSW of Odessa; 46°16'/29°25'.

Krasny Brod, Cz.; pop. 72; 75 km NNE of Kosice; 49°14'/21°54'; JGFF.

Krasny Gorodok, see Raygorodok.

Krasny Oktyabr, see Krasnyy Oktyabr.

Krasny Ostrov, see Kukizov.

Krasnystav, (Krasinstav);

Krasnystaw, Pol. (Krasnistav, Krasnistov, Krasnostav); pop. 1,754; 50 km ESE of Lublin; 50°59'/23°11'; AMG, CAHJP, COH, EJ, GA, GUM4, GUM5, GYLA, HSL, HSL2, JGFF, LDL, LDS, LYV, PHP1, POCEM, SF, YB. The Black Book notes a town named Krasnystaw in the former Polish province of Nowogrodek, now Byelorussia. It does not appear in interwar or contemporary gazetteers.

Krasnyye Okny, Ukr. (Okne, Okny); pop. 1,972; 150 km NW of Odessa; 47°32'/29°27'; JGFF.

Krasnyy Oktyabr, Byel. (Krasny Oktyabr, Oktyabr); pop. 90; 163 km WSW of Gomel; 52°14'/28°36'.

Kraso Bazar, see Belogorsk.

Krasocin, Pol.; pop. 49; 69 km ENE of Czestochowa; 50°54'/20°07'.

Krasowo Czestki, Pol.; pop. 15; 45 km SW of Bialystok; 52°51'/22°41'.

Krasowo Wielkie, Pol.; pop. 31; 45 km SW of Bialystok; 52°51'/22°42'.

Krassnapolje, see Krasnopolye.

Krastine, see Krastini.

Krastini, Lith. (Krastine); 88 km NE of Siauliai; 56°19'/24°30'; JGFF.

Kraszewice, Pol.; pop. 135; 88 km WSW of Lodz; 51°31'/18°14'.

Kraszewo Czubaki, Pol.; pop. 1; 88 km WNW of Warszawa; 52°49'/20°03'.

Kraszkowice, Pol.; pop. 36; 50 km NW of Czestochowa; 51°12'/18°43'.

Kraszna, see Crasna.

Krasznafalu, HSL. This pre-World War I community was not found in BGN gazetteers.

Krasznamihalyfalva, HSL. This pre-World War I community was not found in BGN gazetteers.

Krasznisora, see Taracs Kraszna.

Krasznoc, see Krasnovce.

Krata, see Krutnoye.

Kratecko, Yug.; pop. 4; 69 km ESE of Zagreb; 45°24'/16°38'.

Kratie, Pol. (Kracie); pop. 18; 62 km NE of Lublin; 51°25'/23°24'.

Kratka Kesy, see Kratke Kesy.

Kratke Kesy, Cz. (Kratka Kesy, Kurta Keszi); pop. 56; 94 km ESE of Bratislava; 47°47'/18°17'.

Kratonohy, Cz.; pop. 5; 82 km ENE of Praha; 50°10'/15°36'.

Kratzau, see Chrastava.

Krauszow, Pol. (Krauzow); pop. 20; 75 km S of Krakow; 49°29'/19°58'.

Krautheim, Germ.; 75 km NNE of Stuttgart; 49°23'/09°38'; EDRD, LDS, PHGB, PHGBW.

Krautostheim, Germ.; 56 km W of Nurnberg; 49°35'/10°23'; PHGB.

Krauzow, see Krauszow.

Kravany, Cz. (Kereplye); 32 km ENE of Kosice; 48°46'/21°39'; HSL.

Kravarsko, Yug.; pop. 2; 32 km SSE of Zagreb; 45°35'/16°03'.

Krawara, Pol.; pop. 4; 107 km ESE of Lodz; 51°17'/20°50'.

Kray, Germ. (Essen Kray); pop. 40; 69 km N of Koln; 51°32'/07°17'.

Kraziai, Lith. (Kroz, Kroze, Krozhe, Kruce, Kruz); pop. 660; 56 km SW of Siauliai; 55°36'/22°42'; COH, GUM5, GUM6, HSL, JGFF, LDL, SF, YL.

Krc, Cz.; pop. 7; 107 km S of Praha; 49°12'/14°15'.

Krcava, Cz. (Karcsava); 75 km E of Kosice; 48°40'/22°15'; HSL.

Krcin, Cz.; 120 km ENE of Praha; 50°21'/16°07'; HSL, HSL2.

Krec, Cz.; pop. 5; 82 km SSE of Praha; 49°23'/14°55'.

Krechow, see Krekhov.

Krechowce, see Krekhovtse.

Krechowice, see Krekhovichi.

Krecow, Pol.; pop. 25; 38 km SW of Przemysl; 49°37'/22°22'.

Krefeld, Germ.; pop. 1,720; 50 km NW of Koln; 51°20'/06°34'; AMG, GED, GUM3, GUM5, HSL, HSL2.

Kregi, Pol.; pop. 9; 45 km NNE of Warszawa; 52°34'/21°21'.

Kreigsdorf, see Hodod.

Kreinik, LDL. This pre-World War I community was not found in BGN gazetteers.

Kreisbach, Aus.; pop. 3; 56 km WSW of Wien; 48°05'/15°37'.

Kreitsburg, see Krustpils.

Kreitzburg, see Krapkowice.

Krekenava, Lith. (Krakanova, Krakenovo, Krakinava, Krakinova, Krakinovo, Krekenova); pop. 527; 69 km ESE of Siauliai; 55°33'/24°06'; COH, GUM4, GUM5, HSL, HSL2, JGFF, LDL, SF, YB, YL.

Krekenova, see Krekenava.

Krekhov, Ukr. (Krechow); pop. 99; 32 km NW of Lvov; 50°04'/23°50'.

Krekhovichi, Ukr. (Krechowice, Krekhovitse); pop. 175; 101 km S of Lvov; 49°00'/24°09'; GUM4, HSL, PHP2.

Krekhovitse, see Krekhovichi.

Krekhovtse, Ukr. (Krechowce); pop. 58; 114 km WNW of Chernovtsy; 48°54'/24°40'.

Kremenchug, Ukr. (Cremenciuc, Kremenchuk, Krementchug, Kremienczuk, Krzemienczuk); pop. 28,969; 133 km WNW of Dnepropetrovsk; 49°04'/33°25'; AMG, EDRD, EJ, GUM4, GYLA, HSL, HSL2, JGFF, LDL, SF.

Kremenchuk, see Kremenchug.

Kremenets, Ukr. (Kremenits, Kremenitz, Krzemieniec, Kshemyenyets); pop. 6,616; 69 km SSW of Rovno; 50°06'/25°43'; AMG, CAHJP, COH, EJ, GA, GUM3, GUM4, GUM5, GUM6, GYLA, HSL, JGFF, LDL, LYV, PHP2, SF, YB.

Kremenits, see Kremenets.

Kremenitz, see Kremenets.

Krementchug, see Kremenchug.

Kremienczuk, see Kremenchug.

Kremintsy, Ukr. (Tartarov, Tatarow?); pop. 129; 101 km W of Chernovtsy; 48°20'/24°34'; GUM4, GUM5, PHP2.

Kremmen, Germ.; 45 km NW of Berlin; 52°46'/13°02'; LDS.

Kremna, Cz. (Lublo Krempach); 82 km NW of Kosice; 49°21'/20°42'; HSL.

Kremnica, Cz. (Kormocbanya, Kremnitz); pop. 374; 146 km NE of Bratislava; 48°42'/18°55'; EDRD, GUM4, GUM5.

Kremnitz, see Kremnica.

Kremno, Ukr. BGN lists two possible localities with this name located at 52°16'/25°19' and 51°03'/28°14'. COH.

Krempachy, Pol.; pop. 6; 75 km SSE of Krakow; 49°27'/20°10'.

Krempna, Pol.; pop. 4; 101 km SW of Przemysl; 49°31'/21°31'; JGFF.

Krems, see Krems an der Donau.

Krems an der Donau, Aus. (Krems); pop. 197; 62 km WNW of Wien; 48°25'/15°36'; EDRD, EJ.

Kremsier, see Kromeriz.

Kremyanitsa, Byel. (Krimianitza, Krzemienica); 163 km NW of Pinsk; 53°13'/24°41'; SF, YB.

Kremyz, Cz.; pop. 2; 75 km NW of Praha; 50°36'/13°49'.

Krenglbach, Aus.; pop. 1; 82 km NE of Salzburg; 48°12'/13°57'.

Krenice, Cz. BGN lists two possible localities with this name located at 49°30'/13°12' and 50°02'/14°40'. HSL.

Krenitz, see Krynica Wies.

Krepa Dolna, Pol.; pop. 23; Described in the Black Book as being in the Kielce region of Poland, this town was not found in BGN gazetteers.

Krepa Koscielna, Pol.; pop. 17; 69 km WSW of Lublin; 51°09'/21°34'.

Krepice, Pol.; 50 km NE of Krakow; 50°20'/20°27'; AMG.

Kreshanov, *see* Chrzanow.

Kreshchatik, Ukr. (Crisceatec); pop. 72; 38 km NNW of Chernovtsy; 48°37'/25°44'.

Kreshiv, *see* Krzeszow.

Kreshov, *see* Krzeszow.

Kresilov, *see* Krasilov.

Kreslavaka, *see* Kraslava.

Kreslaval, LDL. This pre-World War I community was not found in BGN gazetteers.

Kreslavka, *see* Kraslava.

Kreslawa, *see* Kraslava.

Krestyanovka, Ukr. (Larindorf); pop. 125; 94 km N of Simferopol; 45°43'/33°57'.

Kreta Sloboda, Ukr.; pop. 24; 69 km NE of Rovno; 50°55'/27°05'. This town was located on an interwar map of Poland but does not appear in contemporary gazetteers. Map coordinates are approximate.

Kretinga, Lith. (Kretingale, Kretinge, Kretingen, Krettingen, Krottingen); pop. 904; 133 km WSW of Siauliai; 55°53'/21°15'; COH, EDRD, EJ, GUM5, HSL2, JGFF, LYV, SF, YL.

Kretingale, *see* Kretinga.

Kretinge, *see* Kretinga.

Kretingen, *see* Kretinga.

Kretki Duze, Pol. (Kretki Wielkie); pop. 5; 139 km SSE of Gdansk; 53°11'/19°26'.

Kretki Wielkie, *see* Kretki Duze.

Kretowce, (Kretowka); EJ, GUM3, PHP2. This town was not found in BGN gazetteers under the given spelling.

Kretowka, *see* Kretowce.

Kretsnif, *see* Craciunesti.

Krettingen, *see* Kretinga.

Kreutzburg, HSL, HSL2. This pre-World War I community was not found in BGN gazetteers.

Kreutznach, *see* Bad Kreuznach.

Kreuzau, Germ.; 38 km SW of Koln; 50°45'/06°29'; GED.

Kreuzberg, *see* Krustpils.

Kreuzburg, *see* Krapkowice.

Kreuzenort, *see* Krzyzanowice.

Kreuzingen, *see* Bolshakovo.

Kreuznach, *see* Bad Kreuznach.

Kreva, *see* Krevo.

Krevo, Byel. (Kreva, Krewo); 101 km WNW of Minsk; 54°19'/26°17'; AMG, COH, GUM3, HSL, HSL2, JGFF, LDL, SF.

Krevz, *see* Krizevci.

Krewo, *see* Krevo.

Kreznica Jara, Pol.; pop. 19; 19 km SSW of Lublin; 51°09'/22°29'.

Krhanice, Cz.; pop. 2; 32 km SSE of Praha; 49°51'/14°33'.

Kriaunai, *see* Kriaunos.

Kriaunos, Lith. (Kriaunai); pop. 13; 139 km N of Vilnius; 55°51'/25°48'.

Krichev, Byel. (Kritchev); pop. 1,546; 150 km N of Gomel; 53°42'/31°43'; EJ, HSL, LDL, SF.

Krichevo, Ukr. (Krichovo, Kricovo, Kricsfalva, Kricsif, Kriesfalva); 176 km WSW of Chernovtsy; 48°11'/23°34'; GUM5, SM.

Krichilsk, Ukr. (Kryczylsk); pop. 100; 75 km N of Rovno; 51°14'/26°22'.

Krichka, Ukr. (Krychka, Kryczka); pop. 57; 126 km WNW of Chernovtsy; 48°40'/24°19'.

Krichovo, *see* Krichevo.

Krickerhau, *see* Handlova.

Kricov, Cz.; 75 km ENE of Praha; 50°16'/15°28'; HSL.

Kricovo, *see* Krichevo.

Kricsfalva, *see* Krichevo.

Kricsif, *see* Krichevo.

Kriegerhay, *see* Handlova.

Kriegshaber, Germ.; 56 km WNW of Munchen; 48°22'/10°56'; HSL, PHGB.

Krienek, *see* Krynki.

Kriesfalva, *see* Krichevo.

Krievei, *see* Repedea.

Kriewen, *see* Krzywin.

Krifch, *see* Krzywcza.

Kriftch, *see* Krzywcza.

Kriftel, Germ.; pop. 3; 13 km WSW of Frankfurt am Main; 50°05'/08°29'.

Krilev, *see* Krylow.

Krilov, *see* Krylow.

Kriltsin, *see* Krincinas.

Krimianitza, *see* Kremyanitsa.

Krimice, Cz.; pop. 5; 94 km SW of Praha; 49°45'/13°18'.

Krimilev, *see* Kromolow.

Krimilov, *see* Kromolow.

Krimulda, Lat.; pop. 4; 50 km NE of Riga; 57°10'/24°50'.

Krincinas, Lith. (Kriltsin); pop. 37; 82 km ENE of Siauliai; 56°05'/24°32'; YL.

Krinec, Cz.; pop. 8; 50 km NE of Praha; 50°16'/15°09'.

Krinek, *see* Krynki.

Krinichki, Ukr.; 45 km WSW of Dnepropetrovsk; 48°22'/34°27'; JGFF.

Krinitza, *see* Krynica Wies.

Krinki, *see* Krynki.

Krinok, *see* Krynki.

Kripa, *see* Goryngrad.

Kripuli, Byel. (Krypule); pop. 8; 107 km N of Minsk; 54°47'/27°38'; GUM4.

Krise, Cz.; pop. 17; 69 km SW of Praha; 49°50'/13°33'.

Krishkautsy, Mold. (Criscauti); pop. 65; 157 km NW of Kishinev; 48°16'/27°51'.

Krisnipolye, *see* Chervonograd.

Kristiania, HSL. This pre-World War I community was not found in BGN gazetteers.

Kristinopol, *see* Chervonograd.

Kritchev, *see* Krichev.

Kritzendorf, Aus.; pop. 24; 19 km NNW of Wien; 48°20'/16°18'.

Kriukai, Lith. (Kruk, Kruki); pop. 184; 50 km NNE of Siauliai; 56°18'/23°50'; GUM4, HSL, LDL, SF, YL.

Kriukav, *see* Kryukov.

Kriulyany, Mold. (Criuleni); pop. 240; 38 km NE of Kishinev; 47°13'/29°10'.

Kriva, Mold.; pop. 32; 214 km WNW of Kishinev; 48°15'/26°40'.

Kriva (Czechoslovakia), COH, HSL. This pre-World War I community was not found in BGN gazetteers.

Kriva (Yugoslavia), Yug.; 146 km SW of Zagreb; 45°23'/14°16'; HSL2.

Kriva Palanka, Yug.; pop. 4; 75 km NE of Skopje; 42°12'/22°21'.

Krivay Rog, *see* Krivoy Rog.

Krivazer, *see* Krivoye Ozero.

Krivch, *see* Krzywcza.

Krive, Cz. (Nagykirva); 69 km N of Kosice; 49°17'/21°09'; AMG, LYV.

Krivich, *see* Krzywcza.

Krivichi, Byel. (Krivitch, Krivitsh, Krszywcze Gorne, Krzywcze, Krzywicze, Kshivche, Kshivche Gurne); pop. 278; 101 km NNW of Minsk; 54°43'/27°17'; AMG, COH, GUM3, GUM4, GUM5, GUM6, GYLA, JGFF, LYV, SF, YB.

Krivichi (Nowogrodek), Byel.; pop. 18; 120 km WSW of Minsk; 53°51'/25°42'.

Krivitch, *see* Krivichi.

Krivitsa, Byel. (Krzywica); pop. 28; 50 km WNW of Pinsk; 52°15'/25°28'; GUM4.

Krivitsh, *see* Krivichi.

Krivka, *see* Krywka.

Krivoe Ozero, *see* Krivoye Ozero.

Krivoi, *see* Krivoy Rog.

Krivoie Oziero, *see* Krivoye Ozero.

Krivoi Rog, *see* Krivoy Rog.

Krivoje Ozero, *see* Krivoye Ozero.

Krivoj Rog, *see* Krivoy Rog.

Krivoklat, Cz.; 45 km WSW of Praha; 50°02'/13°53'; GUM3, GUM6.

Krivorovnya, Ukr. (Krzyworownia); pop. 38; 82 km WSW of Chernovtsy; 48°11'/24°54'.

Krivoshin, Byel. (Krzywoszyn); pop. 18; 88 km N of Pinsk; 52°52'/26°08'.

Krivoye Ozero, Ukr. (Crivoje Ozero, Krivazer, Krivoe Ozero, Krivoie Oziero, Krivoje Ozero); pop. 3,917; 101 km S of Uman; 47°56'/30°21'; EJ, GUM3, GUM4, GYLA, JGFF, LDL, PHR1, SF.

Krivoy Rog, Ukr. (Krivay Rog, Krivoi, Krivoi Rog, Krivoj Rog, Krzywy Rog); pop. 6,430; 133 km SW of Dnepropetrovsk; 47°55'/33°21'; EDRD, EJ, GUM4, GUM5, JGFF, SF.

Krivsoudov, Cz.; pop. 10; 69 km SE of Praha; 49°38'/15°06'.

Krizevci, Yug. (Koros, Krevz); pop. 126; 50 km NE of Zagreb; 46°02'/16°32'; CAHJP, HSL, PHY.

Krizhopol, *see* Kryzhopol.

Krjukow, *see* Kryukov.

Krjupow, USSR; EDRD. This town was not found in BGN gazetteers under the given spelling.

Krnany, Cz.; pop. 3; 32 km S of Praha; 49°51'/14°29'.

Krnjak, Yug.; pop. 4; 62 km SSW of Zagreb; 45°20'/15°36'.

Krnov, Cz. (Jaegerndorf); pop. 323; 126 km NNE of Brno; 50°06'/17°43'; AMG, GUM4.

Krnsko, Cz.; pop. 9; 45 km NNE of Praha; 50°23'/14°51'.

Kroatisch Minihof, Aus.; pop. 5; 82 km SSE of Wien; 47°32'/16°38'.

Krobanow, Pol.; 38 km SW of Lodz; 51°36'/19°00'; PHP1.

Kroben, *see* Krobia.

Krobia, Pol. (Kroben, Krocben, Kroeben); pop. 21; 82 km S of Poznan; 51°46'/17°00'; CAHJP.

Krobia (near Wloclawek), Pol.; pop. 36; 139 km NE of Poznan; 53°03'/18°48'.

Krobonosz, Pol. (Krobonosza); pop. 24; 56 km E of Lublin; 51°13'/23°23'.

Krobonosza, *see* Krobonosz.

Krocben, *see* Krobia.

Krocehlavy, Cz.; pop. 23; 26 km W of Praha; 50°06'/14°06'.

Krocienko, LDL. This pre-World War I community was not found in BGN gazetteers.

Kroczyce Stare, Pol.; 45 km ESE of Czestochowa; 50°34'/19°35'; CAHJP.

Kroczyn, Pol.; pop. 23; 82 km E of Lublin; 51°07'/23°40'.

Kroeben, *see* Krobia.

Krojanke, *see* Krajenka.

Krok, *see* Krakes.

Kroke, *see* Krakow.

Krokmazy, Mold. (Corcmaz); pop. 59; 107 km ESE of Kishinev; 46°27'/29°59'.

Krokocka Wola, Pol.; 32 km WSW of Lodz; 51°44'/18°59'; HSL.

Krole Duze, Pol.; pop. 8; 75 km SW of Bialystok; 52°50'/22°04'; GUM4.

Krole Stare, Pol.; pop. 22; 75 km N of Przemysl; 50°26'/22°46'.

Krolevets, Ukr. (Krolewiec); pop. 1,304; 38 km N of Konotop; 51°33'/33°23'; HSL.

Krolewice, Pol.; pop. 7; 107 km SW of Lublin; 50°36'/21°26'.

Krolewiec, *see* Krolevets.

Krolewska Huta, *see* Chorzow.

Krolewskie Bagno, Pol.; pop. 14; 26 km E of Warszawa; 52°13'/21°18'.

Krolewszczyzna, *see* Krulevshchina.

Krolikow, Pol.; pop. 14; 88 km ESE of Poznan; 52°03'/18°01'; GUM3.

Krolik Polski, Pol.; pop. 18; 75 km SW of Przemysl; 49°31'/21°49'; HSL.

Krolik Woloski, Pol.; pop. 5; 75 km SW of Przemysl; 49°30'/21°49'.

Krolowa Ruska, Pol.; pop. 33; 88 km ESE of Krakow; 49°35'/20°51'.

Kromau, *see* Moravsky Krumlov.

Kromau Mahrisch, *see* Moravsky Krumlov.

Krombach, Germ.; 69 km ENE of Koln; 51°00'/07°57'; GED.

Kromeriz, Cz. (Kremsier); pop. 403; 56 km ENE of Brno; 49°18'/17°24'; CAHJP, EJ, HSL, HSL2, PHP2.

Kromolow, Pol. (Krimilev, Krimilov); pop. 275; 45 km SE of Czestochowa; 50°29'/19°31'; AMG, CAHJP, EDRD, EJ, HSL, HSL2, JGFF, LDL, LDS, SF.

Krompach, Cz.; pop. 88 km N of Praha; 50°50'/14°42'; HSL.

Krompachy, Cz. (Korompa); pop. 365; 38 km WNW of Kosice; 48°55'/20°52'; JGFF.

Kromszewice, Pol.; pop. 5; 75 km NNW of Lodz; 52°23'/19°03'.

Kromy, USSR; pop. 56; 114 km ESE of Bryansk; 52°40'/35°46'.

Kron, *see* Kruonis.

Kronach, Germ.; pop. 32; 88 km N of Nurnberg; 50°14'/11°19'; CAHJP, JGFF, PHGB.

Kronberg, Germ.; pop. 20; 19 km WNW of Frankfurt am Main; 50°11'/08°30'.

Krone an der Brahe, *see* Koronowo.

Kronstadt, *see* Brasov.

Kronstetten, Germ.; pop. 1; 82 km E of Nurnberg; 49°19'/12°09'.

Kropelin, Germ.; 26 km WSW of Rostock; 54°04'/11°48'; LDS.

Kropevnik, Ukr. (Kropivnik, Kropiwnik, Kropiwnik Nowy, Kropiwnik Stary); pop. 80; 101 km SW of Lvov; 49°35'/22°44'; GUM3, GUM4, HSL.

Kropine, *see* Kruopine.

Kropitz, *see* Koropets.

Kropivna, Ukr. (Kropiwna); pop. 10; 56 km E of Lvov; 49°41'/24°48'.

Kropivnik, *see* Kropevnik.

Kropiwna, *see* Kropivna.

Kropiwnik, *see* Kropevnik.

Kropiwnik Nowy, *see* Kropevnik.

Kropiwnik Stary, *see* Kropevnik.

Kroppenstedt, Germ.; pop. 4; 101 km WNW of Leipzig; 51°56'/11°18'; LDS.

Kropstadt, Germ.; pop. 75 km SSW of Berlin; 51°58'/12°44'; HSL.

Kroschenke, *see* Kroscienko.

Kroscienko, Pol. (Kroschenke, Kroshchenke, Kroshinka, Kroshtzinka); pop. 241; 45 km S of Przemysl; 49°28'/22°40'; AMG, COH, EGRS, HSL, HSL2, PHP2.

Kroscienko (near Nowy Targ), Pol.; pop. 233; 82 km SE of Krakow; 49°26'/20°25'; GUM4, GUM5, LYV, PHP3, SF, YB.

Kroscienko Nizne, Pol.; pop. 31; 75 km WSW of Przemysl; 49°41'/21°48'.

Kroscienko Wyzne, Pol.; pop. 8; 69 km WSW of Przemysl; 49°41'/21°50'.

Krosenko, Ukr. (Krosienko); pop. 42; 38 km ESE of Lvov; 49°42'/24°30'; GUM3, GUM6.

Kroshchenke, *see* Kroscienko.

Kroshinka, *see* Kroscienko.

Kroshnik, *see* Krasnik.

Kroshnivitz, *see* Krosniewice.

Kroshtzinka, *see* Kroscienko.

Krosienko, *see* Krosenko.

Krosin, Pol.; pop. 4; 45 km NW of Poznan; 52°48'/16°40'.

Krosinek, Pol.; pop. 2; 50 km NW of Poznan; 52°49'/16°41'.

Krosna, Lith.; pop. 72; 62 km SSW of Kaunas; 54°23'/23°33'.

Krosnica, Pol.; pop. 4; 75 km SE of Krakow; 49°27'/20°21'.

Krosnice, Pol. BGN lists two possible localities with this name located at 51°29'/17°21' and 52°58'/20°29'. PHP4.

Krosniewice, Pol. (Kroshnivitz); pop. 1,259; 62 km NNW of Lodz; 52°15'/19°11'; AMG, COH, EDRD, GA, GUM3, GUM4, GUM5, HSL, HSL2, JGFF, LDL, PHP1, POCEM, SF, YB.

Krosno, Pol.; pop. 1,725; 75 km WSW of Przemysl; 49°41'/21°47'; AMG, COH, EDRD, EGRS, EJ, GA, GUM3, GUM4, GUM5, GUM6, HSL, JGFF, LDL, PHP3, POCEM, SF.

Krosno Odrzanskie, Pol. (Crossen); pop. 67; 133 km SW of

Poznan; 52°03'/15°05'; HSL, LDS, POCEM.

Krosnopolia, *see* Krasnopolye.

Krosnoshiltz, *see* Krasnosielc.

Krosnowa, Pol.; pop. 6; 38 km NE of Lodz; 51°52'/19°56'.

Krostchov, *see* Korostyshev.

Krotoschin, *see* Krotoszyn.

Krotoszyn, Pol. (Krotoschin); pop. 110; 75 km NNE of Wroclaw; 51°42'/17°27'; CAHJP, EJ, HSL, HSL2, JGFF, LDL, LDS, PHP1, PHP3, POCEM.

Krotovo, Byel. (Krotowo); pop. 10; 32 km WNW of Pinsk; 52°14'/25°46'.

Krotowo, *see* Krotovo.

Krottingen, *see* Kretinga.

Krotzenburg, GUM5. This town was not found in BGN gazetteers under the given spelling.

Krouna, Cz.; pop. 8; 75 km NW of Brno; 49°46'/16°02'.

Krovatka, Ukr. (Krowatka); pop. 21; 88 km WNW of Rovno; 50°55'/25°05'.

Krowatka, *see* Krovatka.

Krowica Holodowska Wies, Ukr.; pop. 87; 56 km WSW of Lvov; 49°45'/23°15'. This town was located on an interwar map of Poland but does not appear in contemporary gazetteers. Map coordinates are approximate.

Krowica Lasowa, Ukr.; pop. 53; 56 km WSW of Lvov; 49°45'/23°15'. This town was located on an interwar map of Poland but does not appear in contemporary gazetteers. Map coordinates are approximate.

Krowica Sama, Ukr.; pop. 62; 56 km WSW of Lvov; 49°45'/23°15'. This town was located on an interwar map of Poland but does not appear in contemporary gazetteers. Map coordinates are approximate.

Krowice, Pol. PHP2. This town was not found in BGN gazetteers under the given spelling.

Krowinka, Ukr.; pop. 25; 75 km NNW of Chernovtsy; 48°55'/25°45'. This town was located on an interwar map of Poland but does not appear in contemporary gazetteers. Map coordinates are approximate.

Krowniki, Pol.; pop. 21; 6 km E of Przemysl; 49°47'/22°50'.

Kroz, *see* Kraziai.

Kroze, *see* Kraziai.

Krozhe, *see* Kraziai.

Krpy, Cz.; pop. 1; 32 km NNE of Praha; 50°20'/14°41'.

Krstur, Yug.; pop. 11; 150 km NNW of Beograd; 46°08'/20°06'.

Krsy, Cz.; pop. 6; 101 km WSW of Praha; 49°56'/13°04'.

Krszywcze Gorne, *see* Krivichi.

Kruce, *see* Kraziai.

Krucha, Byel.; pop. 297; 114 km SSW of Vitebsk; 54°15'/29°32'; COH, HSL.

Kruchenicze, *see* Krukhinichi.

Kruczy Borek, Pol.; pop. 9; 45 km N of Warszawa; 52°37'/21°08'.

Krufch, *see* Krzywcza.

Krugel, Ukr. (Kruhel); pop. 12; 139 km WNW of Rovno; 51°15'/24°31'.

Krugla, *see* Krugloye.

Krugle, Pol. PHP2. This town was not found in BGN gazetteers under the given spelling.

Kruglik, Mold. (Cruglic Hotin); pop. 20; 32 km NNE of Kishinev; 47°13'/29°02'.

Krugloe, *see* Krugloye.

Krugloye, Byel. (Krugla, Krugloe, Krula); pop. 428; 107 km S of Vitebsk; 54°15'/29°48'; GUM4, LDL, SF.

Kruglyak, Mold. (Cruglic Orhei); pop. 38; 88 km N of Kishinev; 47°45'/29°15'.

Krugov, Ukr. (Kruguv, Kruhow); 82 km E of Lvov; 49°50'/25°08'; CAHJP.

Kruguv, *see* Krugov.

Kruhel, *see* Krugel.

Kruhel Wielki, Pol.; pop. 10; 13 km SW of Przemysl; 49°46'/22°44'.

Kruhlany, Pol.; pop. 5; 56 km NNE of Bialystok; 53°30'/23°38'.

Kruhle, Pol.; pop. 31; 62 km N of Bialystok; 53°37'/23°22'; HSL.

Kruhow, *see* Krugov.

Kruk, *see* Kriukai.

Krukenitsa, Ukr. (Krukienice); pop. 264; 62 km WSW of Lvov; 49°41'/23°10'; EDRD, EGRS, PHP2.

Krukhinichi, Ukr. (Kruchenicze); pop. 4; 114 km NNE of Lvov; 50°45'/24°40'.

Kruki, *see* Kriukai.

Krukienice, *see* Krukenitsa.

Krukow, Pol.; pop. 24; 69 km SW of Lublin; 50°54'/21°45'.

Krukowka, HSL. A number of towns share this name. It was not possible to determine from available information which one is being referenced.

Krukowszczyzna, Pol.; pop. 8; 38 km N of Bialystok; 53°26'/23°06'.

Krula, *see* Krugloye.

Krulevshchina, Byel. (Krolewszczyzna); pop. 32; 133 km N of Minsk; 55°02'/27°45'.

Krulovsky, *see* Kralovsky Chlmec.

Krumbach, Germ.; pop. 79; 94 km W of Munchen; 48°15'/10°22'; GUM3, JGFF, PHGB. *See also* Krumbach Markt.

Krumbach Markt, Aus. (Krumbach); pop. 20; 75 km NE of Graz; 47°31'/16°11'; HSL, JGFF.

Krumlov, *see* Cesky Krumlov.

Krumlov Moravsky, *see* Moravsky Krumlov.

Krumpach, HSL. This pre-World War I community was not found in BGN gazetteers.

Kruonis, Lith. (Kron); pop. 241; 26 km ESE of Kaunas; 54°46'/24°14'; YL.

Kruopine, Lith. (Kropine); 26 km WSW of Siauliai; 55°55'/22°53'; JGFF.

Krupa, Byel. (Krupka); 75 km ENE of Minsk; 53°57'/28°42'; JGFF, LDL, SF.

Krupe, Pol.; pop. 27; 50 km ESE of Lublin; 51°02'/23°15'.

Krupina, Cz. (Karpfen, Korpona); pop. 1,331; 146 km ENE of Bratislava; 48°21'/19°04'; COH.

Krupka, *see* Krupa.

Krupki, Byel.; pop. 885; 114 km NE of Minsk; 54°19'/29°08'; EDRD, GUM4.

Krupove, Ukr. (Krupowie); pop. 32; 114 km N of Rovno; 51°34'/26°29'.

Krupowie, *see* Krupove.

Krupsko, Ukr.; pop. 7; 50 km S of Lvov; 49°28'/24°02'.

Kruschwitz, *see* Kruszwica.

Krushelnitsa, Ukr. (Kruszelnica, Kruszelnica Rustykalna, Kruszelnica Szlachecka); pop. 34; 94 km SSW of Lvov; 49°06'/23°29'; HSL.

Krushnik, *see* Krasnik.

Krusicany, Cz.; pop. 12; 38 km SSE of Praha; 49°48'/14°36'.

Krusk, USSR; EDRD. This town was not found in BGN gazetteers under the given spelling.

Krustpils, Lat. (Kraitzburg, Kreitsburg, Kreuzberg); pop. 1,149; 82 km NW of Daugavpils; 56°30'/25°51'; EJ, GYLA, JGFF, LDL, PHLE.

Kruswica, *see* Kruszwica.

Kruszelnica, *see* Krushelnitsa.

Kruszelnica Rustykalna, *see* Krushelnitsa.

Kruszelnica Szlachecka, *see* Krushelnitsa.

Krusznik, Pol.; 107 km N of Bialystok; 54°01'/23°07'; GUM3.

Kruszwica, Pol. (Kruschwitz, Kruswica); pop. 23; 94 km NE of Poznan; 52°41'/18°18'; GA, PHP4.

Kruszyna, Pol.; pop. 47; 50 km NE of Czestochowa; 51°02'/19°48'; EDRD, GUM3, GUM4, GUM6, PHP1, PHP4.

Kruszyniany, Pol.; pop. 21; 45 km ENE of Bialystok; 53°11'/23°49'.

Krutiye, *see* Krutnoye.

Krutnoye, Ukr. (Krata, Krutiye, Krutuje, Krutyje, Krutyye); pop. 1,958; 114 km SSW of Uman; 47°58'/29°12'; LDL, SF.

Krutuje, *see* Krutnoye.

Krutyje, *see* Krutnoye.

Krutyye, *see* Krutnoye.

Kruz, *see* Kraziai.

Kruzlowa, Pol.; pop. 27; 88 km ESE of Krakow; 49°39'/20°54'.

Krychka, *see* Krichka.

Krychow, Pol. EDRD, GA, GUM4, GUM5, GUM6. This town was not found in BGN gazetteers under the given spelling.

Kryczka, *see* Krichka.

Kryczylsk, *see* Krichilsk.

Kryg, Pol.; pop. 9; 107 km ESE of Krakow; 49°40'/21°16'.

Krylovo, USSR (Nordenburg); pop. 41; 82 km ESE of Kaliningrad; 54°20'/21°34'; LDS.

Krylow, Pol. (Krilev, Krilov); pop. 622; 126 km ESE of Lublin; 50°41'/24°04'; COH, GUM3, GUM4, HSL, HSL2, LDL, LDS, SF.

Krymno, Ukr.; pop. 37; BGN lists two possible localities with this name located at 51°31'/24°18' and 51°40'/25°10'.

Krynica, *see* Krynica Wies.

Krynica Wies, Pol. (Krenitz, Krinitza, Krynica); pop. 95; 107 km ESE of Krakow; 49°24'/20°58'; AMG, COH, GUM3, GUM4, GUM5, POCEM, SF.

Krynica Zdroj, Pol.; pop. 1,023; 101 km ESE of Krakow; 49°26'/20°58'; EGRS, HSL, PHP3.

Krynka, Pol.; pop. 7; 94 km NNW of Lublin; 52°01'/22°24'.

Krynki, Pol. (Krienek, Krinek, Krinki, Krinok); pop. 3,495; 45 km NE of Bialystok; 53°16'/23°47'; AMG, EDRD, EJ, FRG, GA, GUM3, GUM4, GUM5, HSL, HSL2, JGFF, LDL, LYV, POCEM, SF, YB.

Krynki Sobole, Pol.; pop. 2; 69 km S of Bialystok; 52°32'/22°47'.

Krypule, *see* Kripuli.

Kryry, Cz.; pop. 24; 75 km W of Praha; 50°11'/13°26'.

Kryry (Poland), Pol.; 82 km WSW of Krakow; 50°01'/18°49'; EDRD.

Krysk, Pol.; 50 km WNW of Warszawa; 52°32'/20°25'; LDS.

Krysovitse, Ukr. (Krysowice, Krzywczyce); pop. 20; 62 km WSW of Lvov; 49°46'/23°09'.

Krysowice, *see* Krysovitse.

Kryspinow, Pol.; pop. 9; 13 km SW of Krakow; 50°03'/19°48'.

Krystkowice, GA. This town was not found in BGN gazetteers under the given spelling.

Krystynopol, *see* Chervonograd.

Kryukov, Ukr. (Kriukav, Krjukow); pop. 1,166; 69 km SSE of Dnepropetrovsk; 47°50'/35°19'; SF.

Krywa, Pol.; pop. 9; 107 km WSW of Przemysl; 49°31'/21°19'.

Krywe Ad Tworylne, Pol.; pop. 20; Described in the *Black Book* as being in the Lwow region of Poland, this town was not found in BGN gazetteers.

Krywka, Pol. (Krivka); pop. 24; 62 km S of Przemysl; 49°16'/22°45'; HSL, SF. The *Black Book* notes a town named Krywka (pop. 39) in the interwar Polish province of Stanislawow. It does not appear in interwar or contemporary gazetteers.

Kryzhopol, Ukr. (Crijopol, Krizhopol, Kryzopol); pop. 1,539; 101 km SSE of Vinnitsa; 48°23'/28°53'; GUM3, GUM4, LDL, PHR1, SF.

Kryzopol, *see* Kryzhopol.

Krzak, Pol.; pop. 22; 62 km SE of Lublin; 50°48'/23°06'.

Krzatka, Pol.; pop. 6; 94 km WNW of Przemysl; 50°24'/21°51'.

Krzciecice, Pol.; pop. 4; 62 km N of Krakow; 50°35'/20°11'.

Krzcin, Pol.; pop. 22; 101 km SSW of Lublin; 50°34'/21°36'.

Krzczonow, Pol.; pop. 96; 32 km SSE of Lublin; 51°00'/22°43'; GA.

Krzecin, Pol.; pop. 14; 19 km SSW of Krakow; 49°57'/19°45'.

Krzeczanowo, Pol.; pop. 3; 88 km WNW of Warszawa; 52°51'/20°06'.

Krzeczkowo Mianowskie, Pol.; pop. 5; 62 km SW of Bialystok; 52°51'/22°20'.

Krzeczow (near Nowy Targ), Pol.; pop. 34; 50 km S of Krakow; 49°41'/19°56'.

Krzeczow (near Sieradz), Pol.; pop. 40; 50 km NW of

Czestochowa; 51°11'/18°46'.

Krzemienczuk, *see* Kremenchug.

Krzemienica (near Mielec), Pol.; 114 km NE of Krakow; 50°26'/21°25'; GUM3.

Krzemieniec, *see* Kremenets.

Krzemienna, Pol.; pop. 27; 45 km WSW of Przemysl; 49°42'/22°12'.

Krzepice, Pol. (Keshepitz, Kshepits, Kshepitse); pop. 1,772; 32 km WNW of Czestochowa; 50°58'/18°44'; AMG, CAHJP, COH, FRG, GUM3, GUM4, HSL, HSL2, JGFF, LDS, LYV, PHP1, POCEM, SF, YB.

Krzepin, Pol.; pop. 5; 56 km E of Czestochowa; 50°45'/19°57'.

Krzesinki, Pol.; 19 km SSE of Poznan; 52°20'/17°00'; GA.

Krzesiny, Pol.; 19 km SSE of Poznan; 52°21'/16°59'; GA.

Krzesk, *see* Krzesk Krolowa Niwa.

Krzesk Krolowa Niwa, Pol. (Krzesk); pop. 5; 94 km N of Lublin; 52°04'/22°37'; GA.

Krzeslin, Pol.; pop. 18; 94 km E of Warszawa; 52°15'/22°21'.

Krzeszow, Pol. (Kreshiv, Kreshov); pop. 281; 69 km NW of Przemysl; 50°24'/22°21'; AMG, COH, EDRD, GA, GUM3, GUM5, GUM6, HSL, HSL2, LDS, PHP3, POCEM, SF.

Krzeszow Gorny, Pol.; 75 km NNW of Przemysl; 50°25'/22°23'; LDS.

Krzeszowice, *see* Krzeszowiec.

Krzeszowiec, Pol. (Kesheshovitz, Krzeszowice); pop. 506; 19 km W of Krakow; 50°08'/19°38'; AMG, EGRS, GUM4, HSL, JGFF, PHP3, SF.

Krzeszowka, Pol. (Kshesivka); 45 km NNE of Krakow; 50°27'/20°12'; FRG, GUM5.

Krzetow, Pol.; pop. 23; 56 km NE of Czestochowa; 51°00'/19°51'.

Krzewianki, Pol. PHP1. This town was not found in BGN gazetteers under the given spelling.

Krzewica, Pol.; pop. 26; 101 km NE of Przemysl; 50°26'/23°52'.

Krzykawka, Pol.; pop. 35; 45 km WNW of Krakow; 50°19'/19°25'.

Krzymosze, Pol.; pop. 15; 101 km E of Warszawa; 52°10'/22°28'.

Krzymow, Pol.; pop. 3; 88 km WNW of Lodz; 52°12'/18°26'.

Krzymowskie, Pol.; pop. 5; 94 km N of Lublin; 52°03'/22°53'.

Krzyncze Gorne, Pol. PHP2. This town was not found in BGN gazetteers under the given spelling.

Krzynowloga Mala, Pol.; pop. 38; 107 km NNW of Warszawa; 53°10'/20°48'; HSL.

Krzynowloga Wielka, Pol.; pop. 6; 114 km N of Warszawa; 53°13'/20°51'.

Krzystkowice, Pol. (Christianstadt); pop. 5; 133 km SW of Poznan; 51°47'/15°15'; GUM3, GUM4, GUM6.

Krzywcza, Pol. (Krifch, Kriftch, Krivch, Krivich, Krufch, Kshivcha); pop. 203; 19 km W of Przemysl; 49°48'/22°33'; COH, HSL, LYV, PHP2, PHP3, POCEM, SF.

Krzywcze, *see* Krivichi.

Krzywcze Dolne, *see* Nizhneye Krivche.

Krzywcze Gorne, *see* Verkhneye Krivche.

Krzywczyce, *see* Krysovitse.

Krzywda, Pol.; pop. 72; 62 km SE of Warszawa; 51°49'/21°32'; HSL, HSL2.

Krzywe (near Brzozow), Pol.; pop. 25; 45 km SW of Przemysl; 49°40'/22°12'.

Krzywe (near Rava Russkaya), Pol.; pop. 38; 62 km NNE of Przemysl; 50°13'/23°19'.

Krzywe (Tarnopol), Ukr.; pop. 49; 62 km NE of Lvov; 50°14'/24°39'.

Krzywica, *see* Krivitsa.

Krzywice, Pol.; pop. 29; AMG. A number of towns share this name. It was not possible to determine from available information which one is being referenced.

Krzywicze, *see* Krivichi.

Krzywiczki, Pol.; 62 km ESE of Lublin; 51°04'/23°29'; GUM5.

Krzywiecka Wola, *see* Wola Krzywiecka.

Krzywin, Pol. (Kriewen); 62 km S of Poznan; 51°57'/16°49';

LDS.

Krzywoluka, *see* Kshyvoluka.

Krzyworownia, *see* Krivorovnya.

Krzywoszyn, *see* Krivoshin.

Krzywowolka, Pol.; pop. 9; 94 km NE of Lublin; 51°49'/23°31'.

Krzywulanka, Pol.; pop. 75; Described in the *Black Book* as being in the Tarnopol region of Poland, this town was not found in BGN gazetteers.

Krzywy Rog, *see* Krivoy Rog.

Krzyz, Pol.; pop. 32; 75 km E of Krakow; 50°03'/20°59'.

Krzyzanowice, Pol. (Kreuzenort); pop. 2; 107 km SSW of Czestochowa; 49°59'/18°16'.

Krzyzewo Nadrzeczne, Pol.; pop. 5; 82 km N of Warszawa; 52°56'/21°05'.

Krzyzowa, Pol.; pop. 14; 69 km SSW of Krakow; 49°37'/19°20'.

Krzyzowka, Pol.; 101 km ESE of Krakow; 49°29'/20°57'; PHP1.

Krzyzowniki, GA. A number of towns share this name. It was not possible to determine from available information which one is being referenced.

Ksanti, Bulg.; pop. 500; This town was not found in BGN gazetteers under the given spelling.

Ksawerow Stary, Pol.; pop. 11; 69 km SSE of Warszawa; 51°40'/21°09'.

Ksebki, Pol.; pop. 2; 107 km WNW of Bialystok; 53°27'/21°38'.

Kshanev, *see* Chrzanow.

Kshanov, *see* Chrzanow.

Kshanzh, *see* Ksiaz Wielki.

Kshanzh Vyelki, *see* Ksiaz Wielki.

Kshaz, *see* Ksiaz Wielki.

Kshaz Vyelki, *see* Ksiaz Wielki.

Kshemyenyets, *see* Kremenets.

Kshepits, *see* Krzepice.

Kshepitse, *see* Krzepice.

Kshesivka, *see* Krzeszowka.

Kshivcha, *see* Krzywcza.

Kshivche, *see* Krivichi.

Kshivche Gurne, *see* Krivichi.

K Shonev, *see* Chrzanow.

Kshoynzh, *see* Ksiaz Wielki.

Kshyvche Dolne, *see* Nizhneye Krivche.

Kshyvoluka, Ukr. (Krzywoluka); pop. 24; 75 km NNW of Chernovtsy; 48°58'/25°32'; HSL.

Ksiaz, *see* Ksiaz Wielki.

Ksiaznice Male, Pol.; pop. 6; 45 km ENE of Krakow; 50°11'/20°32'.

Ksiaz Wielki, Pol. (Keshionzh, Kshanzh, Kshanzh Vyelki, Kshaz, Kshaz Vyelki, Kshoynzh, Ksiaz, Xiaz, Xions); pop. 852; 45 km N of Krakow; 50°26'/20°08'; AMG, FRG, GA, GUM4, GUM5, HSL, HSL2, JGFF, LYV, SF, YB.

Ksice, Cz.; pop. 2; 107 km SW of Praha; 49°48'/13°00'.

Ksiezomierz, Pol.; pop. 8; 56 km SW of Lublin; 50°55'/21°59'.

Ksiezopole Smolaki, Pol.; pop. 3; 75 km ENE of Warszawa; 52°19'/22°05'; HSL.

Ksiezostany, Pol.; pop. 4; 94 km SE of Lublin; 50°37'/23°25'.

Ksiezpol, Pol. (Kisenzhopol); pop. 5; 75 km N of Przemysl; 50°25'/22°45'; SF.

Kubajowka, *see* Kubayuvka.

Kuban, Mold. (Cubani); pop. 61; 139 km WNW of Kishinev; 47°46'/27°19'; GUM4, GUM5.

Kubanovo, Cz. (Szete); 126 km E of Bratislava; 48°04'/18°49'; HSL.

Kubarty, GUM5. This town was not found in BGN gazetteers under the given spelling.

Kubayuvka, Ukr. (Kubajowka); 88 km WNW of Chernovtsy; 48°37'/24°48'; GUM3.

Kubeczki, Pol.; 62 km N of Wroclaw; 51°34'/16°59'; GA.

Kubekhaza, Hung.; pop. 1; 19 km SE of Szeged; 46°09'/20°17'.

Kublich, Ukr.; 50 km WSW of Uman; 48°43'/29°34'; JGFF.

Kublichi, Byel. (Kublitch, Kublitschi); pop. 2,000; 120 km WSW of Vitebsk; 55°10'/28°20'; COH, GUM4, JGFF, LDL, SF.

Kublitch, *see* Kublichi.

Kublitschi, *see* Kublichi.

Kubolta, Mold. (Cubolta); pop. 53; 114 km NW of Kishinev; 47°53'/28°02'.

Kubyn, Pol. EDRD. This town was not found in BGN gazetteers under the given spelling.

Kucewicze, *see* Kutsevichi.

Kuchany, Ukr. (Kuczany); pop. 26; 170 km N of Lvov; 51°20'/24°04'.

Kuchary, Pol.; pop. 37; A number of towns share this name. It was not possible to determine from available information which one is being referenced.

Kuchary (near Plonsk), Pol. (Kuchary Zydowskie); 56 km NW of Warszawa; 52°40'/20°30'; GA, PHP4.

Kuchary Zydowskie, *see* Kuchary (near Plonsk).

Kuchecka Wola, *see* Kukhotskaya Volya.

Kuchenheim, Germ.; pop. 4; 38 km S of Koln; 50°39'/06°50'; GED.

Kuchoya, Mold. (Cucioaia, Kuchoyya); pop. 3; 69 km NW of Kishinev; 47°27'/28°11'.

Kuchoyya, *see* Kuchoya.

Kuciunai, Lith.; pop. 20; 88 km S of Kaunas; 54°08'/23°31'.

Kucmeh, *see* Kitsman.

Kucow, Pol.; pop. 53; 56 km N of Czestochowa; 51°14'/19°18'.

Kuczany, *see* Kuchany.

Kuczbork, Pol. (Kodzborg); pop. 32; 114 km NW of Warszawa; 53°05'/20°03'; LDS, SF.

Kuczewola, Pol.; pop. 7; 82 km WSW of Lodz; 51°40'/18°16'.

Kudirkos Naumiestis, Lith. (Naumestis, Naumiestis Kudirkos, Nayshtot Ponivez, Nayshtot Shaki, Neishtat Kudirko, Neishtat Shervint, Neyshtadt Shaki, Novoe Mesto, Vladislavov, Vlodislovov); pop. 991; 62 km WSW of Kaunas; 54°46'/22°53'; AMG, GUM3, GYLA, HSL, JGFF, SF, YL.

Kudrintsy, Ukr. (Kudrintz, Kudrynce); pop. 52; 45 km NNE of Chernovtsy; 48°37'/26°18'; EGRS, GYLA, HSL, SF.

Kudrintz, *see* Kudrintsy.

Kudrynce, *see* Kudrintsy.

Kuestendje, *see* Constanta.

Kuflew, Pol.; pop. 24; 62 km E of Warszawa; 52°06'/21°49'; AMG.

Kuhl, *see* Kuliai.

Kuidany, *see* Kedainiai.

Kujawien, *see* Piotrkow Kujawski.

Kujdance, *see* Kiydantsy.

Kujdanow, *see* Kuydanuv.

Kukaly, Pol.; pop. 12; 50 km S of Warszawa; 51°53'/21°01'.

Kukavka, Ukr. (Cucavca); 88 km SSW of Vinnitsa; 48°37'/27°43'; PHR1.

Kukec, Yug.; pop. 1; 114 km N of Zagreb; 46°46'/16°12'.

Kuketse, *see* Kukuci.

Kuketze, *see* Kukuci.

Kukhneshty, Mold. (Cuhnesti); pop. 76; 133 km WNW of Kishinev; 47°40'/27°23'.

Kukhotskaya Volya, Ukr. (Kuchecka Wola); pop. 32; 126 km NNW of Rovno; 51°40'/25°42'.

Kukizov, Ukr. (Krasny Ostrov, Kukizow); pop. 46; 19 km NE of Lvov; 49°56'/24°16'; EJ, PHP2, SF.

Kukizow, *see* Kukizov.

Kuklichi, Byel. (Kuklicze); pop. 12; 133 km WNW of Pinsk; 52°50'/24°32'.

Kuklicze, *see* Kuklichi.

Kuktiskes, Lith. (Kis, Koktishka, Kuktiskiai); pop. 172; 88 km N of Vilnius; 55°24'/25°40'; YL.

Kuktiskiai, *see* Kuktiskes.

Kukuci, Lith. (Kuketse, Kuketze); 82 km NE of Siauliai; 56°20'/24°26'; JGFF.

Kukucze, GUM3. This town was not found in BGN gazetteers under the given spelling.

Kukulloszeplak, HSL. This pre-World War I community was not found in BGN gazetteers.

Kukunjevac, Yug.; pop. 9; 94 km ESE of Zagreb; 45°27'/17°06'.

174

Kukyenyes, *see* Trnava.

Kul, *see* Kuliai.

Kula, Yug.; pop. 88; 114 km NW of Beograd; 45°37'/19°32'; PHY.

Kulachkovtsy, Ukr. (Kulaczkowce); pop. 124; 56 km WNW of Chernovtsy; 48°33'/25°18'; GYLA, PHP2.

Kulaczkowce, *see* Kulachkovtsy.

Kulakovtse, Ukr. (Kulakowce); pop. 47; 45 km NNW of Chernovtsy; 48°38'/25°52'.

Kulakowce, *see* Kulakovtse.

Kulaschi, LDL. This pre-World War I community was not found in BGN gazetteers.

Kulaszne, Pol.; pop. 29; 62 km SW of Przemysl; 49°25'/22°10'.

Kulawa, *see* Kulyava.

Kulchin, *see* Kulchiny.

Kulchiny, Ukr. (Koltchin, Kulchin, Kultschiny); pop. 1,266; 107 km SE of Rovno; 49°45'/26°54'; HSL, LDL, SF.

Kulchitse Shlyakhetske, *see* Kulchitsy.

Kulchitsy, Ukr. (Kulchitse Shlyakhetske, Kulczyce Szlacheckie); pop. 67; 62 km SW of Lvov; 49°30'/23°17'.

Kulczyce Rustykalne, Pol.; pop. 50; Described in the *Black Book* as being in the Lwow region of Poland, this town was not found in BGN gazetteers.

Kulczyce Szlacheckie, *see* Kulchitsy.

Kulczyn, Pol.; pop. 8; 56 km ENE of Lublin; 51°23'/23°19'.

Kuldiga, Lat. (Gol Dingen, Goldingen); pop. 1; 126 km W of Riga; 56°58'/21°59'; COH, HSL, JGFF, LDL, PHLE, SF.

Kuleje, Pol.; pop. 2; 26 km W of Czestochowa; 50°51'/18°48'.

Kulesz, Pol. PHP4. This town was not found in BGN gazetteers under the given spelling.

Kulesze Koscielne, Pol.; pop. 185; 45 km WSW of Bialystok; 53°02'/22°31'; GUM3, PHP4.

Kulesze Litewka, Pol.; pop. 36; Described in the *Black Book* as being in the Bialystok region of Poland, this town was not found in BGN gazetteers.

Kulgai, Byel. (Kulhaje Wielkie); pop. 3; 120 km W of Vitebsk; 55°19'/28°17'.

Kulhaje Wielkie, *see* Kulgai.

Kuliai, Lith. (Kol, Kuhl, Kul); pop. 142; 107 km WSW of Siauliai; 55°48'/21°39'; HSL, JGFF, SF, YL.

Kulichkov, Ukr. (Kuliczkow); pop. 35; 56 km N of Lvov; 50°18'/24°05'.

Kulichow, Pol. PHP2. This town was not found in BGN gazetteers under the given spelling.

Kuliczkow, *see* Kulichkov.

Kuligow, Pol.; pop. 15; 32 km NNE of Warszawa; 52°31'/21°11'.

Kulikov, Ukr. (Kulikow); pop. 509; 19 km N of Lvov; 49°59'/24°05'; EGRS, GA, GUM3, GUM4, HSL, HSL2, LDL, PHP2, PHP3, SF.

Kulikovka, Ukr.; 107 km W of Konotop; 51°22'/31°39'; JGFF.

Kulikovo Pole, Ukr.; pop. 1,266; 416 km NNE of Kharkov; 53°25'/38°43'.

Kulikow, *see* Kulikov.

Kulimaz, Pol. PHP4. This town was not found in BGN gazetteers under the given spelling.

Kulm, *see* Chlumec nad Cidlinou.

Kulmain, Germ.; 82 km NE of Nurnberg; 49°54'/11°54'; PHGB.

Kulmbach, Germ.; 75 km N of Nurnberg; 50°06'/11°27'; EJ, PHGB.

Kulno, Pol.; 62 km NNW of Przemysl; 50°20'/22°29'; HSL.

Kulparkow, *see* Kulparkuv.

Kulparkuv, Ukr. (Kulparkow); pop. 343; 13 km SSW of Lvov; 49°49'/23°59'.

Kulro, Pol.; pop. 90; Described in the *Black Book* as being in the Lublin region of Poland, this town was not found in BGN gazetteers.

Kulsheim, Germ.; pop. 44; 75 km ESE of Frankfurt am Main; 49°40'/09°31'; HSL, HSL2, JGFF, PHGB, PHGBW.

Kulsobocs, Hung.; pop. 13; 19 km ESE of Miskolc; 48°02'/20°58'; LDS.

Kulsovat, Hung.; pop. 6; 101 km N of Nagykanizsa;

47°18'/17°14'.

Kultschiny, *see* Kulchiny.

Kulus, *see* Kalyus.

Kulyava, Ukr. (Kulawa); pop. 17; 38 km N of Lvov; 50°10'/24°00'.

Kumelsk, Pol.; pop. 5; 82 km WNW of Bialystok; 53°29'/22°05'.

Kumling, Hung. (Kimle); 133 km WNW of Budapest; 47°50'/17°25'; HSL.

Kumow, *see* Kumow Majoracki.

Kumow Majoracki, Pol. (Kumow); pop. 38; 75 km ESE of Lublin; 51°02'/23°33'; GUM5.

Kunagota, Hung.; pop. 92; 69 km NE of Szeged; 46°26'/21°03'; HSL, PHH.

Kunbaja, Hung.; pop. 9; 62 km SW of Szeged; 46°05'/19°25'.

Kuncsorba, Hung.; pop. 9; 101 km N of Szeged; 47°08'/20°34'.

Kunev, Ukr. (Koniv, Kuniew, Kunyev); pop. 1,314; 45 km SSE of Rovno; 50°15'/26°22'; SF.

Kunfelegyhaza, HSL, LDL. This pre-World War I community was not found in BGN gazetteers.

Kungos, Hung.; pop. 9; 82 km SW of Budapest; 47°04'/18°11'.

Kunhegyes, Hung.; pop. 273; 88 km S of Miskolc; 47°22'/20°38'; HSL, LDS, PHH.

Kunicha, Mold. (Cunicea, Kunichya); pop. 21; 107 km NNW of Kishinev; 47°54'/28°39'.

Kunichya, *see* Kunicha.

Kuniczki, Pol.; 62 km ESE of Lodz; 51°25'/20°11'; PHP1.

Kuniew, *see* Kunev.

Kunin, Ukr.; pop. 51; 32 km NW of Lvov; 50°06'/23°48'.

Kuniz, *see* Dolni Kounice.

Kunkowce, Pol.; pop. 12; 6 km WNW of Przemysl; 49°48'/22°43'.

Kunmadaras, Hung.; pop. 302; 75 km S of Miskolc; 47°26'/20°48'; EJ, GUM5, HSL, LDS, PHH.

Kunmajsa, HSL. This pre-World War I community was not found in BGN gazetteers.

Kunov, *see* Kunow.

Kunow, Pol. (Kinev, Kunov); pop. 510; 94 km SW of Lublin; 50°57'/21°17'; AMG, GA, GUM5, PHP1, SF, YB.

Kunowa, Pol.; pop. 6; 107 km ESE of Krakow; 49°44'/21°20'.

Kunreuth, Germ.; 32 km N of Nurnberg; 49°41'/11°09'; JGFF, PHGB.

Kunszentmarton, Hung.; pop. 202; 69 km N of Szeged; 46°50'/20°17'; HSL, LDS, PHH.

Kunszentmiklos, Hung.; pop. 155; 56 km S of Budapest; 47°02'/19°08'; HSL, LDS, PHH.

Kunsziget, Hung.; pop. 3; 120 km W of Budapest; 47°44'/17°31'.

Kuntsk, *see* Konskie.

Kunyev, *see* Kunev.

Kunzak, Cz.; pop. 1; 107 km WSW of Brno; 49°07'/15°12'.

Kunzelsau, Germ.; pop. 70; 69 km NNE of Stuttgart; 49°17'/09°41'; AMG, JGFF, PHGBW.

Kupa, Hung.; 32 km N of Miskolc; 48°20'/20°55'; HSL.

Kupce, Pol. (Katy Kupce); pop. 3; 56 km NE of Warszawa; 52°27'/21°45'.

Kupchina, *see* Kupchino.

Kupchino, Mold. (Cupcina, Kupchina); pop. 23; 163 km NW of Kishinev; 48°06'/27°23'.

Kupchintsy, Ukr. (Kupczynce); pop. 25; 107 km ESE of Lvov; 49°27'/25°21'.

Kupczynce, *see* Kupchintsy.

Kupel, Ukr. (Kupil); pop. 1,828; 120 km SSE of Rovno; 49°36'/26°31'; GUM4, JGFF, LDL, SF.

Kupen, Bulg. BGN lists two possible localities with this name located at 42°51'/25°07' and 41°36'/24°59'. JGFF.

Kupiansk, *see* Kupyansk.

Kupichov, Ukr. (Kupiczow); pop. 236; 114 km WNW of Rovno; 51°00'/24°43'.

Kupichvolya, Ukr. (Kupiczwola); pop. 25; 38 km N of Lvov; 50°10'/24°11'.

Kupiczow, *see* Kupichov.

Kupiczwola, *see* Kupichvolya.

Kupil, *see* Kupel.

Kupin, Ukr.; pop. 1,830; 101 km NNE of Chernovtsy; 49°06'/26°35'; COH, GYLA, HSL, JGFF, SF.

Kupishki, *see* Kupiskis.

Kupishok, *see* Kupiskis.

Kupiskis, Lith. (Kupishki, Kupishok); pop. 1,444; 101 km E of Siauliai; 55°50'/24°58'; COH, HSL, JGFF, LDL, SF, YL.

Kupjansk, *see* Kupyansk.

Kupka, Ukr. (Cupca); pop. 71; 38 km S of Chernovtsy; 48°02'/25°47'; COH.

Kupkuy, Mold. (Copcui); pop. 9; 62 km SSW of Kishinev; 46°31'/28°21'.

Kupna, Pol.; pop. 23; 13 km WSW of Przemysl; 49°47'/22°34'; HSL.

Kupnovichi Staryye, Ukr. (Kupnovitse Stare, Kupnowice Stare); pop. 21; 56 km SW of Lvov; 49°39'/23°20'.

Kupnovitse Stare, *see* Kupnovichi Staryye.

Kupnowice Stare, *see* Kupnovichi Staryye.

Kuppenheim, Germ.; pop. 70; 69 km W of Stuttgart; 48°50'/08°15'; GUM5, PHGBW.

Kups, Germ.; 88 km N of Nurnberg; 50°12'/11°17'; JGFF, PHGB.

Kupusina, Yug.; pop. 7; 150 km WNW of Beograd; 45°44'/19°01'.

Kupyansk, Ukr. (Kupiansk, Kupjansk); pop. 152; 107 km ESE of Kharkov; 49°42'/37°38'.

Kurantice, Cz.; pop. 23; Described in the *Black Book* as being in the Bohemia region of Czechoslovakia, this town was not found in BGN gazetteers.

Kurash, Ukr. (Kurasz); pop. 30; 101 km N of Rovno; 51°27'/26°32'.

Kurasz, *see* Kurash.

Kuraszkow, Pol.; pop. 7; 82 km ESE of Lodz; 51°20'/20°25'.

Kuratura, Mold. (Curatura); pop. 28; 101 km N of Kishinev; 47°53'/28°55'.

Kurchino, Byel. (Kurczyno); pop. 7; 107 km N of Minsk; 54°46'/27°26'.

Kurczyno, *see* Kurchino.

Kurd, Hung.; pop. 12; 101 km E of Nagykanizsa; 46°27'/18°19'.

Kurdwanow, Pol.; pop. 46; 19 km SSE of Krakow; 50°00'/19°57'.

Kurdwanowka, GUM3. This town was not found in BGN gazetteers under the given spelling.

Kurdyban, GUM4. This town was not found in BGN gazetteers under the given spelling.

Kurdzhali, Bulg. (Kerdzhali, Kirdzhali); pop. 152; 202 km ESE of Sofija; 41°39'/25°22'; EJ.

Kurenets, Byel. (Korenetz, Kornitz, Kurzeniec); pop. 1,131; 88 km NW of Minsk; 54°33'/26°57'; AMG, COH, EDRD, GUM3, GUM4, GUM5, GUM6, HSL, JGFF, LDL, SF, YB.

Kuresare, *see* Kuressaare.

Kureshnitsa, Mold. (General Poetas); pop. 12; 150 km NNW of Kishinev; 48°14'/28°10'.

Kuressaare, Est. (Kuresare); pop. 100; 189 km SW of Tallinn; 58°15'/22°28'; PHLE.

Kurima, Cz.; pop. 180; 62 km N of Kosice; 49°14'/21°27'; AMG, COH, HSL, LDL.

Kurityan, Hung.; pop. 10; 32 km NW of Miskolc; 48°19'/20°38'; HSL.

Kurivody, Cz.; pop. 1; 62 km NNE of Praha; 50°35'/14°49'.

Kurki, Pol.; pop. 29; 82 km WNW of Bialystok; 53°33'/22°10'.

Kurkil, *see* Kirkilai.

Kurkla, *see* Kirkilai.

Kurkli, *see* Kurkliai.

Kurkliai, Lith. (Kurkli); pop. 181; 88 km NNW of Vilnius; 55°25'/25°03'; HSL2, YL.

Kurland; Not a town, but a region of modern day Latvia.

Kurlandia, PHLE.

Kurmeni, Lat. (Kurzeme); 101 km E of Riga; 56°40'/25°42'; PHLE.

Kurnik, *see* Kornik.

Kurniki Iwanczanskie, Ukr.; pop. 22; 126 km NNW of Chernovtsy; 49°25'/25°35'. This town was located on an interwar map of Poland but does not appear in contemporary gazetteers. Map coordinates are approximate.

Kuropatniki, Ukr.; pop. 17; 82 km ESE of Lvov; 49°30'/25°01'.

Kuropole, *see* Kuropolye.

Kuropolye, Byel. (Kuropole); pop. 5; 157 km NNW of Minsk; 55°13'/26°52'.

Kurov, *see* Kurovtsy.

Kurovichi, Ukr. (Kurovitse, Kurowice); pop. 53; 32 km E of Lvov; 49°46'/24°26'; GUM3, GUM4, GUM5, GUM6, PHP2.

Kurovischtscha, *see* Khoroshovchitsy.

Kurovitse, *see* Kurovichi.

Kurovtsy, Ukr. (Kurov, Kurowce); pop. 14; 107 km E of Lvov; 49°38'/25°29'; LDL.

Kurow, Pol. (Kariv, Koriv, Koruv, Korva, Kuruv); pop. 2,230; 32 km WNW of Lublin; 51°23'/22°12'; AMG, CAHJP, COH, EDRD, FRG, GA, GUM3, GUM4, GUM4, GUM5, HSL, JGFF, LDS, LYV, PHP4, SF, YB.

Kurowce, *see* Kurovtsy.

Kurowice, *see* Kurovichi.

Kurozvany, Ukr. (Kurozwany); pop. 26; 38 km E of Rovno; 50°34'/26°44'.

Kurozwany, *see* Kurozvany.

Kurozweki, Pol.; pop. 224; 101 km NE of Krakow; 50°35'/21°06'; JGFF, LDS.

Kursenai, Lith. (Kurseniai, Kurshan, Kurshany, Kurshjan); pop. 841; 26 km W of Siauliai; 56°00'/22°56'; COH, GUM3, GUM5, HSL, JGFF, SF, YL.

Kurseniai, *see* Kursenai.

Kurshan, *see* Kursenai.

Kurshany, *see* Kursenai.

Kurshjan, *see* Kursenai.

Kursk, USSR; pop. 4,154; 88 km SW of Leningrad; 59°19'/29°08'; GUM4, GUM6, JGFF, LDL.

Kurta Keszi, *see* Kratke Kesy.

Kurtavenai, *see* Kurtuvenai.

Kurtuvenai, Lith. (Kortovian, Kurtavenai, Kurtuvian); pop. 103; 19 km SW of Siauliai; 55°50'/23°03'; GUM5, HSL.

Kurtuvian, *see* Kurtuvenai.

Kurtvvenai, Lith. YL. This town was not found in BGN gazetteers under the given spelling.

Kuruv, *see* Kurow.

Kuryany, Ukr. (Kurzany?); pop. 45; 69 km ESE of Lvov; 49°26'/24°48'.

Kurylowka, Pol.; pop. 101; 62 km NNW of Przemysl; 50°18'/22°28'; PHP3.

Kurzanhradek, *see* Kozhan Gorodok.

Kurzany, *possibly* Kuryany.

Kurzatki Rawy, *see* Rawy.

Kurzelaty, Pol.; pop. 4; 69 km NW of Lublin; 51°43'/21°54'.

Kurzelow, Pol.; pop. 191; 56 km ENE of Czestochowa; 50°53'/19°53'.

Kurzeme, *see* Kurmeni.

Kurzeniec, *see* Kurenets.

Kurzyna, Pol. (Kurzyna Mala?); pop. 31; 82 km NNW of Przemysl; 50°30'/22°22'; GUM3.

Kurzyna Mala, *possibly* Kurzyna.

Kusel, Germ.; pop. 66; 107 km SW of Frankfurt am Main; 49°33'/07°24'; GED.

Kusgyarmat, COH. This town was not found in BGN gazetteers under the given spelling.

Kushmirka, Mold. (Cusmirca); pop. 63; 107 km N of Kishinev; 47°54'/28°43'.

Kushnitsa, Ukr. (Kovacsret, Kusnice, Kusnive); 170 km S of Lvov; 48°27'/23°15'; AMG, COH, JGFF, SM.

Kusin, Cz.; 62 km ENE of Kosice; 48°49'/22°04'; HSL.

Kusma, *see* Cusma.

Kusnice, *see* Kushnitsa.

Kusnive, *see* Kushnitsa.

Kustanszeg, Hung.; pop. 1; 45 km NW of Nagykanizsa;

46°47'/16°41'.

Kustany, Hung.; pop. 4; 50 km N of Nagykanizsa; 46°50'/17°07'.

Kustendil, *see* Kyustendil.

Kusti, Cz.; 88 km SW of Praha; 49°48'/13°17'; AMG.

Kustrawa, Pol.; pop. 3; 69 km NNW of Przemysl; 50°24'/22°23'.

Kustrin, Pol.; pop. 150; 101 km S of Szczecin; 52°35'/14°39'; HSL, JGFF, LDS, POCEM.

Kusze, Pol.; pop. 9; 82 km NNW of Przemysl; 50°28'/22°26'.

Kuta, Ukr. JGFF. A number of towns share this name. It was not possible to determine from available information which one is being referenced.

Kutaski Grady, Pol.; pop. 7; 82 km NE of Warszawa; 52°39'/22°01'.

Kutaski Stare, Pol.; pop. 11; 88 km SW of Bialystok; 52°39'/22°02'.

Kutaso, Hung.; pop. 3; 62 km NNE of Budapest; 47°57'/19°33'.

Kutev, *see* Kuty.

Kutina, Yug.; pop. 50; 69 km ESE of Zagreb; 45°29'/16°47'; PHY.

Kutjevo, Yug.; pop. 8; 150 km ESE of Zagreb; 45°25'/17°53'.

Kutna Hora, Cz.; pop. 140; 56 km E of Praha; 49°57'/15°16'.

Kutno, Pol.; pop. 6,784; 56 km NNW of Lodz; 52°14'/19°22'; AMG, COH, EDRD, EJ, GA, GUM3, GUM4, GUM5, GYLA, HSL, HSL2, ISH1, ISH3, JGFF, LDL, LDS, LYV, PHP1, PHP4, POCEM, SF, YB.

Kutow, *see* Kuty.

Kutsevichi, Byel. (Kucewicze); pop. 4; 114 km WNW of Minsk; 54°23'/26°07'.

Kuttenplan, *see* Chodova Plana.

Kutuzovo, USSR (Scherwind, Schirwindt); pop. 13; 150 km ENE of Kaliningrad; 54°47'/22°51'; HSL.

Kutuzov Volodarsk, *see* Volodarsk Volynskiy.

Kutuzowe Volodarskoe, *see* Volodarsk Volynskiy.

Kuty, Ukr. (Kitev, Kitov, Kutev, Kutow); pop. 2,605; 56 km WSW of Chernovtsy; 48°16'/25°11'; AMG, COH, EDRD, EGRS, EJ, GA, GUM3, GUM4, GUM5, GUM6, GYLA, HSL, JGFF, LDL, LYV, PHP2, PHP3, SF, YB.

Kutyfalva, *see* Cuci.

Kutylowo Perysie, Pol.; pop. 13; 62 km SW of Bialystok; 52°46'/22°26'.

Kutyn, Ukr.; pop. 9; 139 km NNW of Rovno; 51°49'/25°46'.

Kutyska, Ukr.; pop. 4; 88 km NW of Chernovtsy; 48°54'/25°07'.

Kutyski, Pol.; pop. 5; 82 km NE of Warszawa; 52°32'/22°08'.

Kuty Stare, *see* Kuty Stary.

Kuty Stary, Ukr. (Kuty Stare); pop. 84; 56 km WSW of Chernovtsy; 48°17'/25°09'.

Kutzberg, Germ.; 101 km WNW of Nurnberg; 50°05'/10°07'; PHGB.

Kuydantse, *see* Kiydantsy.

Kuydanuv, Ukr. (Kujdanow); pop. 9; 107 km NNW of Chernovtsy; 49°11'/25°22'.

Kuyl, *see* Kolo.

Kuyzovka, Mold. (Cuizovca); pop. 127; 75 km N of Kishinev; 47°37'/28°49'.

Kuzary, Pol. PHP4. This town was not found in BGN gazetteers under the given spelling.

Kuzhnitsa, *see* Kuznica.

Kuziai, Lith.; 13 km WNW of Siauliai; 55°59'/23°08'; GUM5.

Kuzie, Pol.; pop. 73; 101 km W of Bialystok; 53°18'/21°40'.

Kuzmice, Cz. (Kozma); 26 km ESE of Kosice; 48°35'/21°34'; HSL.

Kuzmichi, Byel. (Kuzmicze); pop. 3; 94 km NW of Minsk; 54°37'/26°57'.

Kuzmicze, *see* Kuzmichi.

Kuzmin, Ukr.; 114 km WNW of Vinnitsa; 49°42'/27°05'; JGFF, LDL, SF.

Kuzmina, Pol.; pop. 15; 32 km SW of Przemysl; 49°37'/22°26'.

Kuzmino, Cz. AMG, JGFF. A number of towns share this name. It was not possible to determine from available information which one is being referenced.

Kuzmintsy, Ukr. (Cuzminti); 62 km SW of Vinnitsa;

48°57'/27°41'; GUM4, PHR1.

Kuzmir, *see* Kazimierz Dolny.

Kuznia, Pol.; pop. 5; 88 km ESE of Poznan; 51°57'/17°55'; PHP3.

Kuzniaki, Pol.; pop. 43; 88 km ENE of Czestochowa; 50°59'/20°21'.

Kuznica, Pol. (Kuzhnitsa, Kuznitse, Kuznitza); pop. 450; 56 km NNE of Bialystok; 53°31'/23°39'; COH, GUM3, GUM5, HSL, HSL2, JGFF, LDL, LYV, POCEM, SF.

Kuznica Blonska, Pol.; pop. 8; 82 km SW of Lodz; 51°28'/18°25'.

Kuznica Grabowska, Pol.; pop. 20; 88 km SW of Lodz; 51°30'/18°17'.

Kuznica Stara, Pol.; pop. 36; A number of towns share this name. It was not possible to determine from available information which one is being referenced.

Kuznitse, *see* Kuznica.

Kuznitza, *see* Kuznica.

Kuzova, Cz.; pop. 6; 69 km WSW of Praha; 50°02'/13°32'.

Kvacany, Cz.; 133 km WNW of Kosice; 49°10'/19°33'; JGFF.

Kvacice, Cz.; 62 km ESE of Brno; 48°59'/17°25'; AMG.

Kvakovce, Cz.; 45 km NE of Kosice; 48°59'/21°41'; HSL.

Kval, *see* Kowal.

Kvasi, *see* Kvasy.

Kvasiny, Cz.; pop. 11; 120 km NNW of Brno; 50°13'/16°16'.

Kvasnovice, Cz.; pop. 3; 101 km SSW of Praha; 49°25'/13°38'.

Kvasuv, Ukr. (Kwasow); pop. 25; 82 km NNE of Lvov; 50°27'/24°39'.

Kvasy, Ukr. (Kvasi, Tiszaborkut); 120 km WSW of Chernovtsy; 48°08'/24°17'; SM.

Kvatchali, *see* Kwaczala.

Kvatki, *see* Kvetkai.

Kvedarna, Lith. (Khvaydan); pop. 394; 94 km SW of Siauliai; 55°33'/22°00'; HSL, YL.

Kvetinov, Cz.; pop. 5; 94 km WNW of Brno; 49°34'/15°31'.

Kvetkai, Lith. (Kvatki, Kvietiski); pop. 97; 114 km ENE of Siauliai; 56°10'/25°09'; LDL, SF.

Kvietiski, *see* Kvetkai.

Kvilda, Cz.; pop. 11; 139 km SSW of Praha; 49°01'/13°35'.

Kviv, *see* Klwow.

Kvrievka, Rom. PHR1. This town was not found in BGN gazetteers under the given spelling.

Kwaczala, Pol. (Kvatchali); pop. 79; 32 km WSW of Krakow; 50°04'/19°30'; HSL, SF.

Kwasow, *see* Kvasuv.

Kwaszenina, Pol.; pop. 46; 32 km S of Przemysl; 49°33'/22°40'.

Kwidzyn, Pol. (Marienwerder); pop. 210; 69 km SSE of Gdansk; 53°44'/18°55'; EJ, JGFF, LDS.

Kwieciszewo, Pol. (Blutenam); pop. 13; 75 km ENE of Poznan; 52°37'/18°03'; LDS.

Kwikow, Pol.; pop. 9; 56 km ENE of Krakow; 50°09'/20°40'.

Kwilina, Pol.; pop. 6; 62 km E of Czestochowa; 50°41'/20°01'.

Kybartai, Lith. (Kibart, Kibarti, Kibarty); pop. 1,253; 82 km SW of Kaunas; 54°39'/22°45'; EJ, GUM3, GUM5, HSL, JGFF, LDL, SF.

Kyburg, Aus. EDRD. This town was not found in BGN gazetteers under the given spelling.

Kyjov, Cz. (Gaya); pop. 357; 45 km ESE of Brno; 49°01'/17°07'; CAHJP, EJ, HSL, HSL2.

Kyllburg, Germ.; pop. 54; 107 km S of Koln; 50°02'/06°35'.

Kynsperk, *see* Kynsperk nad Ohri.

Kynsperk nad Ohri, Cz. (Kynsperk); pop. 38; 139 km W of Praha; 50°07'/12°32'.

Kyralydarocz, *see* Craidorol.

Kyrieleis, *see* Chirales.

Kyritz, Germ.; 88 km WNW of Berlin; 52°57'/12°24'; LDS.

Kyrneshty, Mold. (Carnesti, Cornesti Gara, Korneshty Sabany); pop. 87; 62 km WNW of Kishinev; 47°10'/28°00'.

Kysak, Cz.; 19 km NNW of Kosice; 48°51'/21°13'; EDRD.

Kysibl, *see* Struzna.

Kysperk, *see* Letohrad.

Kysta, Cz. (Kiszte); 45 km ESE of Kosice; 48°31'/21°43'; HSL.

Kysucke Nove Mesto, Cz.; pop. 144; 157 km ENE of Brno; 49°18'/18°47'.

Kytinbf, Cz.; 32 km SSW of Praha; 49°51'/14°13'; HSL.

Kyustendil, Bulg. (Kustendil); pop. 2,869; 69 km SW of Sofija; 42°17'/22°41'; EJ.

Laa, *see* Laa an der Thaya.

Laa an der Thaya, Aus. (Laa); pop. 62; 62 km N of Wien; 48°43'/16°23'.

Laage, Germ.; 26 km SE of Rostock; 53°56'/12°21'; LDS.

Laasan, Germ.; pop. 3; 62 km SW of Leipzig; 50°57'/11°39'.

Laasphe, Germ.; pop. 125; 101 km NNW of Frankfurt am Main; 50°56'/08°24'; GUM5.

Labach, Ukr. (Labacz); pop. 14; 69 km NE of Lvov; 50°02'/24°52'.

Labacz, *see* Labach.

Labatlan, Hung.; pop. 23; 50 km WNW of Budapest; 47°45'/18°30'; HSL.

Labedz, Pol.; pop. 51; BGN lists two possible localities with this name located at 50°23'/20°21' and 50°50'/19°39'.

Labes, *see* Labetz.

Labetz, Germ. (Labes); pop. 38; 69 km N of Leipzig; 51°52'/12°42'.

Labiau, *see* Polessk.

Labischin, *see* Labiszyn.

Labiszyn, Pol. (Labischin); pop. 85; 88 km NE of Poznan; 52°57'/17°56'; HSL, JGFF, POCEM.

Labod, Hung.; pop. 24; 45 km ESE of Nagykanizsa; 46°12'/17°27'.

Labowa, *see* Maciejowa.

Labun, *see* Yurovshchina.

Labunie, Pol.; pop. 37; 82 km SE of Lublin; 50°39'/23°22'; GA.

Labunki, Pol.; pop. 9; 82 km SE of Lublin; 50°41'/23°21'; GUM3.

Lac, *see* Vysochanskoye.

Laca, Hung.; pop. 58; 94 km NE of Miskolc; 48°22'/22°00'; HSL, PHH.

Lacarak, Yug.; pop. 7; 75 km W of Beograd; 45°00'/19°34'.

Lachawa, Pol.; pop. 17; 38 km SW of Przemysl; 49°39'/22°22'.

Lachen, Germ.; 94 km S of Frankfurt am Main; 49°19'/08°12'; GED, PHGB.

Lachovici, *see* Lyakhovichi.

Lachovitch, *see* Belogorye.

Lachowce, Pol.; pop. 19; 107 km NE of Przemysl; 50°30'/23°52'.

Lachowcy, *see* Belogorye.

Lachowice, *see* Lyakhovitse.

Lachowice Podrozne, *see* Podorozhnoye.

Lachowice Zarzeczne, *see* Lyakhovitse Zazhechke.

Lachowicze, *see* Lyakhovichi.

Lachva, *see* Lakhva.

Lachwa, *see* Lakhva.

Lackenbach, Aus. (Lakompak); pop. 346; 75 km S of Wien; 47°35'/16°28'; AMG, CAHJP, HSL, HSL2, JGFF, LDL, LDS.

Lackie Szlacheckie, *see* Leki Szlacheckie.

Lackie Wielkie, GUM3, GUM4, GUM5, GUM6, PHP2. This town was not found in BGN gazetteers under the given spelling.

Lacko, Pol.; pop. 232; 69 km SE of Krakow; 49°33'/20°27'; AMG, EGRS, GUM5, PHP3. The *Black Book* notes a town named Lacko (pop. 26) in the interwar Polish province of Lwow. The town appears in a list of Galician towns as located near Dobromil, but does not appear in interwar or contemporary gazetteers.

Laczhaz, *see* Lascaia.

Laczka, Pol.; pop. 26; BGN lists two possible localities with this name located at 52°09'/21°57' and 52°45'/21°37'.

Laczki Brzeskie, Pol.; pop. 57; 107 km ENE of Krakow; 50°11'/21°23'.

Laczna, Pol.; pop. 90; 120 km ENE of Czestochowa; 50°59'/20°47'.

Lad, Pol. (Lad nad Warta); pop. 21; 69 km ESE of Poznan; 52°13'/17°54'; GUM4.

Lada, Cz. (Laden); 82 km N of Praha; 50°47'/14°45'; HSL.

Ladance, *see* Ladantsy.

Ladantse, *see* Ladantsy.

Ladantsy, Ukr. (Ladance, Ladantse); pop. 48; 56 km ESE of Lvov; 49°38'/24°38'.

Ladany, Hung.; 26 km ESE of Szeged; 46°10'/20°28'; HSL, HSL2.

Ladanybene, Hung.; pop. 7; 56 km SE of Budapest; 47°02'/19°27'.

Ladbesenyo, Hung.; pop. 6; 38 km N of Miskolc; 48°21'/20°47'.

Ladce, Cz.; 120 km E of Brno; 49°02'/18°17'; GUM5.

Ladejn, *see* Ladyzhin.

Ladek, Pol.; pop. 37; 88 km ESE of Poznan; 52°02'/18°01'; JGFF.

Ladek Zdroj, Pol. (Landek im Schlesien); pop. 25; 82 km S of Wroclaw; 50°21'/16°53'; LDS.

Laden, *see* Lada.

Ladenburg, Germ.; pop. 91; 75 km S of Frankfurt am Main; 49°28'/08°37'; AMG, GED, GUM5, LDS, PHGBW.

Ladendorf, Aus.; pop. 10; 45 km N of Wien; 48°32'/16°29'.

Ladhaza, *see* Malom.

Ladimirevci, Yug. (Ladimirewzi); pop. 8; 182 km WNW of Beograd; 45°37'/18°27'.

Ladimirewzi, *see* Ladimirevci.

Ladizhnenka, Ukr. (Ladyzinka, Lodishenka); pop. 2,798; 38 km SSW of Uman; 48°30'/30°00'; SF.

Ladmir, *see* Vladimir Volynskiy.

Ladmoc, *see* Ladmovce.

Ladmovce, Cz. (Ladmoc); pop. 185; 50 km ESE of Kosice; 48°25'/21°47'; AMG, HSL.

Lad nad Warta, *see* Lad.

Ladomer, Cz.; 139 km NE of Bratislava; 48°35'/18°53'; COH, HSL.

Ladomirova, Cz.; 75 km N of Kosice; 49°20'/21°38'; AMG.

Ladosno, GUM4. This town was not found in BGN gazetteers under the given spelling.

Ladowicze, *see* Lyadovichi.

Ladyczyn, *possibly* Lanchin.

Ladyshin, *see* Lanchin.

Ladyzhin, Ukr. (Ladejn); 69 km WSW of Uman; 48°40'/29°15'; GUM4, PHR1.

Ladyzhinka, Ukr.; 32 km S of Uman; 48°33'/30°15'; JGFF.

Ladyzinka, *see* Ladizhnenka.

Ladzkie Szlacheckie, *see* Lipovka (near Ivano Frankovsk).

Laehn, *see* Lahn.

Laferte, HSL. This pre-World War I community was not found in BGN gazetteers.

Lage, Germ.; pop. 13; 75 km WSW of Hannover; 52°17'/08°39'; LDS.

Lagedi, Est.; 13 km E of Tallinn; 59°24'/24°56'; GUM3, GUM4, PHLE.

Lager Lechfeld, Germ. (Klosterlechfeld, Lechfeld); 56 km W of Munchen; 48°10'/10°51'; GUM3, GUM3, GUM5.

Lagiewniki, HSL, PHP1. A number of towns share this name. It was not possible to determine from available information which one is being referenced.

Lagisza, Pol. (Lagisza Cmentarna); pop. 31; 50 km S of Czestochowa; 50°21'/19°08'; GUM3.

Lagisza Cmentarna, *see* Lagisza.

Lagow, Pol. (Logiv); pop. 1,269; 114 km NE of Krakow; 50°47'/21°05'; COH, EDRD, FRG, GUM4, GUM5, HSL, JGFF.

Lagowica Nowa, Pol.; pop. 25; 114 km NE of Krakow; 50°42'/21°10'.

Laguszow, Pol.; pop. 35; 56 km W of Lublin; 51°22'/21°47'.

Lahiszyn, *see* Telekhany.

Lahlapos, *see* Lapus.

Lahn, Germ. (Laehn); 150 km WNW of Hannover; 52°49'/07°37'; EJ.

Lahodow, Pol.; pop. 54; Described in the *Black Book* as being in the Tarnopol region of Poland, this town was not found in BGN gazetteers.

Lahoisk, *see* Logoysk.

178

Lahovec, Ukr. (Lahoviz, Lengyelszallas); 139 km S of Lvov; 48°42'/23°25'; SM. This town was located on a pre-World War I map, but does not appear in contemporary gazetteers.

Lahoviz, see Lahovec.

Lahr, Germ.; pop. 118; 107 km SW of Stuttgart; 48°20'/07°52'; GED, LDS, PHGBW.

Laibach, see Ljubljana.

Laidzes, see Laidzesciems.

Laidzesciems, Lat. (Laidzes); pop. 2; 133 km W of Riga; 57°10'/21°52'.

Laimbach, Germ.; 94 km SSE of Stuttgart; 47°59'/09°41'; PHGBW.

Laisa, Germ.; pop. 5; 107 km N of Frankfurt am Main; 50°59'/08°37'.

Laisgol M, see Jogeva.

Laisholm, see Jogeva.

Laizuva, Lith. (Latzkeva, Latzkova, Latzuva, Layzheve, Leizeva); pop. 127; 69 km WNW of Siauliai; 56°23'/22°34'; HSL, JGFF, LDL, SF.

Lajoskomarom, Hung.; pop. 9; 94 km SSW of Budapest; 46°51'/18°21'.

Lajosmizse, Hung.; pop. 60; 69 km SE of Budapest; 47°01'/19°33'; PHH.

Lajsce, Pol.; pop. 17; 88 km WSW of Przemysl; 49°40'/21°33'.

Lajtakata, see Gattendorf.

Lak, Hung.; pop. 25; 38 km N of Miskolc; 48°21'/20°52'; HSL.

Laka, Pol. (Laka Rustykalna?, Lanka); pop. 150; 56 km WNW of Przemysl; 50°05'/22°06'; PHP2, SF.

Laka Rustykalna, possibly Laka.

Laka Szlachecka, Pol.; pop. 44; Described in the Black Book as being in the Lwow region of Poland, this town was not found in BGN gazetteers.

Lakhoviche, see Lyakhovitse.

Lakhovtsy, see Belogorye.

Lakhva, Byel. (Lachva, Lachwa, Lakhwa); pop. 1,126; 69 km ENE of Pinsk; 52°13'/27°06'; AMG, COH, EDRD, EJ, GA, GUM3, GUM4, GUM5, GUM6, HSL, JGFF, LDL, LYV, SF, YB.

Lakhwa, see Lakhva.

Lakocsa, Hung.; pop. 2; 82 km SE of Nagykanizsa; 45°54'/17°42'.

Lakompak, see Lackenbach.

Lakta, Pol.; 56 km N of Wroclaw; 51°33'/16°59'; GA.

Lakta Dolna, Pol.; pop. 16; 45 km ESE of Krakow; 49°50'/20°25'.

Lakta Gorna, Pol. (Lankti); pop. 18; 50 km ESE of Krakow; 49°50'/20°26'; HSL, SF.

Lalin, Pol.; pop. 20; HSL. Described in the Black Book as being in the Lwow region of Poland, this town was not found in BGN gazetteers.

Lalova, see Lalovo.

Lalovo, Mold. (Lalova, Madchendorf, Preraslia, Psherosla, Rozvaduv, Rozvidev, Shedlishtza); pop. 19; 69 km N of Kishinev; 47°34'/29°01'.

Lambsheim, Germ.; 69 km S of Frankfurt am Main; 49°31'/08°17'; GED, HSL.

Lampertheim, Germ.; pop. 90; 62 km S of Frankfurt am Main; 49°36'/08°28'; GUM3, GUM5, LDS.

Lampertice, Cz.; pop. 1; 120 km NE of Praha; 50°40'/15°57'.

Lamprechtshausen, Aus.; pop. 4; 26 km NNW of Salzburg; 47°59'/12°57'.

Lamsheim, Germ.; pop. 28; Described in the Black Book as being in the Rheinland-Pfalz region of Germany, this town was not found in BGN gazetteers.

Lamspringe, Germ.; pop. 12; 50 km SE of Hannover; 51°58'/10°01'.

Lan, Byel.; pop. 11; 101 km SSW of Minsk; 53°09'/26°41'.

Lanchin, Ukr. (Ladyczyn?, Ladyshin, Lanczyn, Lanshin, Lantchin); pop. 383; 88 km WNW of Chernovtsy; 48°33'/24°45'; GUM3, GUM4, HSL, JGFF, LDL, PHP2, SF.

Lanchkorun, see Zarechanka.

Lanckorona, Pol.; pop. 9; 32 km SSW of Krakow; 49°51'/19°43'; PHP2, WS.

Lancut, Pol. (Lantsut, Lantzut); pop. 1,925; 50 km WNW of Przemysl; 50°04'/22°14'; AMG, CAHJP, COH, EDRD, EGRS, EJ, GA, GUM3, GUM4, GUM5, HSL, HSL2, JGFF, LDL, LYV, PHP3, POCEM, SF, YB.

Lanczyn, see Lanchin.

Landau, AMG, CAHJP, EJ, GED, HSL, PHGBW. A number of towns named Landau are located in Germany, Austria and the area of Poland that was formerly eastern Germany. Many of the sources above do not indicate which town is refered to.

Landau an der Isar, Germ.; 101 km NE of Munchen; 48°41'/12°41'; GUM3, GUM5, LDS, PHGB.

Landau in der Pfalz, Germ.; pop. 638; 88 km WNW of Stuttgart; 49°12'/08°07'; JGFF.

Landeck (Austria), Aus.; 62 km WSW of Innsbruck; 47°08'/10°34'; GUM3.

Landek im Schlesien, see Ladek Zdroj.

Landek im Westpreussen, see Ledyczek.

Landeshut, see Kamienna Gora.

Landestreu, Ukr. (Landstrew); pop. 31; 107 km SSE of Lvov; 48°56'/24°19'.

Landsberg, Germ.; pop. 600; 32 km NW of Leipzig; 51°31'/12°10'; AMG, HSL.

Landsberg (Schleisen), see Gorzow Slaski.

Landsberg am Lech, Germ.; pop. 21; 56 km WSW of Munchen; 48°03'/10°52'; GUM3, GUM5, GUM6, PHGB.

Landsberg an der Prosna, see Gorzow Slaski.

Landsberg an der Warthe, see Gorzow Wielkopolski.

Landsberg Ost Preussen, see Gorowo Ilaweckie.

Landshut, Germ.; 62 km NNE of Munchen; 48°32'/12°09'; EJ, GED, GUM3, GUM4, PHGB, PHP3.

Landstrew, see Landestreu.

Landstuhl, Germ.; pop. 55; 114 km SW of Frankfurt am Main; 49°25'/07°34'; GED, GUM5.

Landvarov, see Liutavariskes.

Landvorova, see Liutavariskes.

Landwarow, see Liutavariskes.

Lanek, Pol. PHP4. This town was not found in BGN gazetteers under the given spelling.

Langadas, Greece; 19 km NNE of Thessaloniki; 40°45'/23°04'.

Langen, Germ.; pop. 80; 19 km S of Frankfurt am Main; 49°59'/08°40'; GED, GUM5.

Langenaltheim, Germ.; 69 km S of Nurnberg; 48°54'/10°56'; GUM3.

Langenberg, Germ.; pop. 16; 50 km N of Koln; 51°21'/07°08'.

Langen Bergheim, Germ.; 26 km NE of Frankfurt am Main; 50°14'/09°00'; LDS.

Langenbielau, see Bielawa Dolna.

Langenbrucken, Germ.; pop. 11; 62 km NW of Stuttgart; 49°12'/08°39'; PHGBW.

Langendiebach, Germ.; pop. 36; 26 km ENE of Frankfurt am Main; 50°10'/08°59'; GUM5, LDS.

Langendorf, Pol.; pop. 30; 50 km SW of Czestochowa; 50°31'/18°38'; LDS.

Langenfeld, Germ.; pop. 71; 69 km NE of Koln; 51°22'/07°42'.

Langenfeld (Rhineland), Germ.; 69 km SSE of Koln; 50°23'/07°06'; GUM5.

Langenlois, Aus.; pop. 9; 62 km WNW of Wien; 48°28'/15°40'.

Langenlonsheim, Germ.; pop. 40; 56 km SW of Frankfurt am Main; 49°54'/07°54'; JGFF.

Langenrohr, Aus.; pop. 4; 32 km WNW of Wien; 48°18'/16°00'.

Langensalza, see Bad Lauchstadt.

Langenscheid, Germ.; pop. 5; 62 km WNW of Frankfurt am Main; 50°21'/07°57'.

Langenschwalbach, Germ.; pop. 90; Described in the Black Book as being in the Hessen region of Germany, this town was not found in BGN gazetteers.

Langenschwarz, Germ.; 94 km NE of Frankfurt am Main; 50°43'/09°38'; JGFF.

Langenselbold, Germ.; pop. 200; 32 km ENE of Frankfurt am Main; 50°11'/09°02'; GUM5, LDS.

Langenzenn, Germ.; pop. 2; 19 km W of Nurnberg; 49°30'/10°48'; HSL, HSL2, JGFF, PHGB.

Langenzersdorf, Aus.; pop. 25; 19 km N of Wien; 48°18'/16°21'.

Langerwehe, Germ.; 45 km SW of Koln; 50°49'/06°21'; GED.

Lang Gons, Germ.; pop. 10; 50 km N of Frankfurt am Main; 50°30'/08°40'; LDS.

Langsdorf, Germ.; pop. 25; 50 km N of Frankfurt am Main; 50°30'/08°51'; LDS.

Langside, HSL. This pre-World War I community was not found in BGN gazetteers.

Langweiler, Germ.; pop. 113; 50 km WSW of Koln; 50°52'/06°14'; GED.

Lania, Pol.; pop. 8; 88 km NW of Lodz; 52°25'/18°56'.

Lanieta, Pol.; 75 km NNW of Lodz; 52°22'/19°17'; EDRD.

Lanka, *see* Laka.

Lanki Male, Ukr.; pop. 27; 75 km SSE of Lvov; 49°15'/24°15'. This town was located on an interwar map of Poland but does not appear in contemporary gazetteers. Map coordinates are approximate.

Lankti, *see* Lakta Gorna.

Lanovits, *see* Lanovtsy.

Lanovitz, *see* Lanovtsy.

Lanovtse, *see* Lanovtsy.

Lanovtse (Tarnopol), Ukr.; pop. 54; 62 km N of Chernovtsy; 48°51'/26°00'.

Lanovtsy, Ukr. (Lanovits, Lanovitz, Lanovtse, Lanowce); pop. 629; 88 km S of Rovno; 49°52'/26°05'; COH, EDRD, GUM4, HSL, JGFF, SF, YB.

Lanowce, *see* Lanovtsy.

Lanowice, GUM5. This town was not found in BGN gazetteers under the given spelling.

Lanowicze, Pol.; 126 km NNW of Bialystok; 54°13'/22°44'; HSL.

Lanowiec, Pol. PHP2. This town was not found in BGN gazetteers under the given spelling.

Lanshin, *see* Lanchin.

Lansk, *see* Rybaki.

Lanskroun, Cz.; pop. 50; 88 km N of Brno; 49°55'/16°37'; EDRD.

Lantchin, *see* Lanchin.

Lantskorun, *see* Zarechanka.

Lantsut, *see* Lancut.

Lantzekronia, *see* Zarechanka.

Lantzut, *see* Lancut.

Lany (near Bobrka), Ukr.; pop. 22; 38 km SE of Lvov; 49°36'/24°18'.

Lany (near Lvov), Ukr.; pop. 50; 32 km S of Lvov; 49°38'/23°52'.

Lany Polske, Ukr. (Lany Polskie); pop. 6; 45 km NNE of Lvov; 50°08'/24°22'.

Lany Polskie, *see* Lany Polske.

Lany Wielkie, Pol.; pop. 8; 50 km N of Krakow; 50°31'/19°51'.

Lanzenkirchen, Aus.; pop. 2; 56 km S of Wien; 47°44'/16°14'.

Lapanow, Pol. (Lapnov); pop. 114; 38 km ESE of Krakow; 49°52'/20°18'; GUM3, HSL, PHP3, SF.

Lapczyca, Pol.; pop. 9; 32 km ESE of Krakow; 49°58'/20°22'.

Lapi, *see* Lapy.

Lapiai, Lith.; pop. 39; 120 km WSW of Siauliai; 55°46'/21°28'.

Lapichi, Byel. (Lapitch); pop. 709; 82 km ESE of Minsk; 53°26'/28°33'; JGFF, LDL, SF, YB.

Lapiguz, Pol.; pop. 7; 82 km NNW of Lublin; 51°56'/22°21'.

Lapinoz, Pol.; pop. 1; 139 km SSE of Gdansk; 53°11'/19°22'.

Lapiszow, Pol.; pop. 24; Described in the *Black Book* as being in the Lwow region of Poland, this town was not found in BGN gazetteers.

Lapitch, *see* Lapichi.

Lapnov, *see* Lapanow.

Lapos, Hung. (Alsolapos); 56 km ESE of Budapest; 47°19'/19°46'; HSL, HSL2.

Lapovo, Yug.; pop. 4; 88 km SE of Beograd; 44°11'/21°06'.

Lapshin, Ukr. (Lapszyn); pop. 20; 75 km ESE of Lvov; 49°29'/24°55'.

Lapsze Nizne, Pol.; pop. 6; 82 km SSE of Krakow; 49°24'/20°15'.

Lapsze Wyzne, Pol.; pop. 8; 82 km SSE of Krakow; 49°24'/20°12'.

Lapszow, Pol.; pop. 8; 50 km ENE of Krakow; 50°11'/20°33'.

Lapszyn, *see* Lapshin.

Lapus, Rom. (Lahlapos); pop. 95; 88 km N of Cluj; 47°30'/24°01'; HSL.

Lapusel, Rom. (Hagymaslapos); pop. 83; 101 km N of Cluj; 47°37'/23°29'; HSL.

Lapushna, Mold. (Lapusna); pop. 165; 38 km SW of Kishinev; 46°53'/28°25'.

Lapusna, *see* Lapushna.

Lapy, Pol. (Lapi); pop. 623; 26 km SW of Bialystok; 52°59'/22°52'; CAHJP, GA, GUM4, HSL, HSL2, JGFF, LDL, LYV, PHP4, SF.

Lapy Debowizna, Pol.; pop. 4; 26 km SW of Bialystok; 52°58'/22°54'.

Larga, Mold.; pop. 81; 214 km NW of Kishinev; 48°23'/26°52'.

Larindorf, *see* Krestyanovka.

Larissa, Greece; pop. 767; 120 km S of Thessaloniki; 39°38'/22°25'; GUM4.

Lascaia, Rom. (Laczhaz); HSL. This pre-World War I community was not found in BGN gazetteers.

Laschia, Rom.; pop. 6; 88 km N of Cluj; 47°32'/23°44'.

Laschinca, *see* Lesechniki.

Las Debowy, Pol.; pop. 21; 56 km WSW of Lublin; 51°13'/21°49'.

Lash, *see* Hroznetin.

Lasha, *see* Losha.

Lashchov, *see* Laszczow.

Lashkuv, Ukr. (Laszkow); pop. 53; 75 km NE of Lvov; 50°15'/24°55'.

Lasi, Lat. (Lasu); pop. 25; 26 km W of Daugavpils; 55°57'/26°08'; PHLE.

Lasick, *see* Lasitsk.

Lasin, Pol.; pop. 23; 94 km SSE of Gdansk; 53°32'/19°06'; LDS.

Lasitsk, Byel. (Lasick); pop. 29; 26 km SE of Pinsk; 51°56'/26°17'.

Lask, Pol. (Laski, Lusk); pop. 59; 32 km SW of Lodz; 51°35'/19°08'; AMG, CAHJP, COH, EDRD, EJ, GA, GUM3, GUM4, GUM5, HSL, HSL2, JGFF, LDL, LDS, LYV, PHP1, PHP4, SF, YB.

Laskaczev, *see* Laskarzew.

Laskarov, *see* Laskarzew.

Laskarzev, *see* Laskarzew.

Laskarzew, Pol. (Laskaczev, Laskarov, Laskarzev, Laskazhev, Laskerov, Laskirov); pop. 1,352; 69 km SE of Warszawa; 51°48'/21°36'; AMG, COH, EDRD, GA, GUM3, GUM4, GUM5, HSL, LDL, LYV, SF, YB.

Laska Wola, *see* Wola Laska.

Laskazhev, *see* Laskarzew.

Laskerov, *see* Laskarzew.

Laski, *see* Lask.

Laskirov, *see* Laskarzew.

Lasko, Yug.; pop. 3; 69 km WNW of Zagreb; 46°09'/15°14'.

Lasko (Poland), Pol.; 88 km SW of Poznan; 51°58'/15°56'; AMG.

Laskod, Hung.; pop. 58; 94 km E of Miskolc; 48°03'/22°03'; AMG, HSL, LDS, PHH.

Laskorun, *see* Zarechanka.

Laskovtsy, Ukr. (Laskowce); pop. 3; 101 km NNW of Chernovtsy; 49°09'/25°34'; PHP2.

Laskow, *see* Laskuv.

Laskowce, *see* Laskovtsy.

Laskowice, Pol.; 94 km S of Gdansk; 53°30'/18°27'; GA.

Laskowice Olawskie, Pol. (Markstadt); 26 km E of Wroclaw; 51°02'/17°21'; GA, GUM3, GUM4, GUM5, PHP3.

Laskowicze, *see* Lyaskovichi.

Laskowicze Wielkie, *see* Leskovichi.

Laskowiec, Pol.; 45 km W of Bialystok; 53°14'/22°34'; AMG.

Laskowka, Pol.; pop. 12; 38 km W of Przemysl; 49°52'/22°18'.

Laskuv, Ukr. (Laskow); pop. 24; 107 km N of Lvov; 50°48'/24°11'.

Laslovo, Yug.; pop. 1; 157 km WNW of Beograd; 45°25'/18°42'.

Lasochow, Pol.; pop. 7; 75 km E of Czestochowa; 50°48'/20°11'.
Lasocin, Pol. (Lasoczyn); pop. 123; 69 km SW of Lublin; 50°54'/21°45'; EDRD, GUM5.
Lasoczyn, see Lasocin.
Lasotki, Pol.; pop. 17; 101 km N of Lodz; 52°37'/19°33'.
Lasowice, Pol.; 45 km S of Czestochowa; 50°27'/18°53'; PHP3.
Lasse, see Lassee.
Lassee, Aus. (Lasse); pop. 44; This town was not found in BGN gazetteers under the given spelling.
Lastivka, Ukr. (Lastowki, Lastuvki); pop. 44; 88 km SSW of Lvov; 49°14'/23°12'.
Las Toczylowo, Pol.; pop. 15; 38 km W of Bialystok; 53°13'/22°37'.
Lastomir, Cz.; pop. 56; 50 km E of Kosice; 48°42'/21°56'; AMG, HSL.
Lastovce, Cz.; 32 km ESE of Kosice; 48°33'/21°38'; AMG.
Lastovo, Yug.; 347 km SSE of Zagreb; 42°46'/16°55'; GUM4.
Lastowki, see Lastivka.
Lastuvki, see Lastivka.
Lasu, see Lasi.
Laszcza, Pol.; pop. 3; 26 km S of Warszawa; 52°07'/20°55'.
Laszczow, Pol. (Lashchov, Loshtchov); pop. 1,041; 107 km NNE of Przemysl; 50°32'/23°43'; AMG, COH, EDRD, GUM3, GUM4, HSL, JGFF, LDS, LYV, SF.
Laszczowka, Pol.; pop. 10; 88 km NNE of Przemysl; 50°27'/23°26'.
Laszczyn, Pol.; pop. 5; 69 km NNW of Wroclaw; 51°38'/16°52'; GA.
Laszki, Pol.; pop. 60; 32 km N of Przemysl; 50°01'/22°54'.
Laszki Dolne, see Lyashki Dolne.
Laszki Gorne, see Dolishnev.
Laszki Goscincowe, Pol.; pop. 28; Described in the Black Book as being in the Lwow region of Poland, this town was not found in BGN gazetteers.
Laszki Krolewskie, Pol.; pop. 35; Described in the Black Book as being in the Tarnopol region of Poland, this town was not found in BGN gazetteers.
Laszkow, see Lashkuv.
Laszow, Pol.; pop. 27; 50 km NW of Czestochowa; 51°09'/18°39'.
Laszowka, Pol.; pop. 5; 75 km SSE of Warszawa; 51°39'/21°24'.
Latach, Ukr. (Latacz); pop. 25; 69 km NW of Chernovtsy; 48°50'/25°29'.
Latacz, see Latach.
Latanka, Pol.; pop. 21; Described in the Black Book as being in the Warszawa region of Poland, this town was not found in BGN gazetteers.
Latchorzew, Pol.; pop. 7; 13 km WSW of Warszawa; 52°14'/20°51'.
Latczyn, Pol.; pop. 26; 88 km WSW of Bialystok; 53°06'/21°48'.
Latgale; Latgale is not a town, but a province of Latvia.
Latgalia; Not a town, but the the southeastern portion of Latvia.
Lathen, Germ.; pop. 40; 170 km WNW of Hannover; 52°52'/07°19'; GUM5, LDS.
Latoszek, Pol.; pop. 39; Described in the Black Book as being in the Warszawa region of Poland, this town was not found in BGN gazetteers.
Latowicz, Pol. (Lotovitch); pop. 416; 56 km ESE of Warszawa; 52°02'/21°48'; GA, GUM5, HSL, LDS, PHP4, SF.
Latowicze, Pol. CAHJP. This town was not found in BGN gazetteers under the given spelling.
Latrany, Hung.; pop. 8; 69 km NE of Nagykanizsa; 46°45'/17°45'.
Latvija; Not a town, but a county within Latvia.
Latyczow, see Letichev.
Latyczyn, Pol.; pop. 5; 62 km SSE of Lublin; 50°44'/22°50'.
Latzkawa, see Liskiava.
Latzkeva, see Laizuva.
Latzkova, see Laizuva.
Latzuva, see Laizuva.
Laubach, Germ.; pop. 42; 56 km NNE of Frankfurt am Main; 50°33'/08°59'; GUM5, JGFF.
Lauban, see Luban.

Laubere, Lat.; pop. 6; 62 km E of Riga; 56°48'/25°03'.
Lauberg, Germ.; 56 km ESE of Munchen; 47°47'/12°12'; LDS.
Lauchheim, Germ.; 82 km ENE of Stuttgart; 48°52'/10°15'; PHGBW.
Lauda, Germ.; 94 km ESE of Frankfurt am Main; 49°34'/09°42'; EDRD, EJ, PHGBW.
Laudenbach, Germ.; pop. 71; 82 km WSW of Nurnberg; 49°27'/09°56'; GED, GUM5, JGFF, PHGB, PHGBW, PHGB.
Laudona, Lat. (Laudonas); pop. 49; 94 km NNW of Daugavpils; 56°42'/26°11'; PHLE.
Laudonas, see Laudona.
Lauenau, Germ.; pop. 20; 32 km SW of Hannover; 52°16'/09°22'; GED.
Lauenberg, see Lebork.
Lauenburg, see Lebork.
Lauf, Germ.; 19 km NE of Nurnberg; 49°31'/11°17'; LDS, PHGB.
Laufenselden, Germ.; pop. 56; 50 km W of Frankfurt am Main; 50°13'/08°00'; GUM5.
Laufersweiler, Germ.; pop. 80; 101 km WSW of Frankfurt am Main; 49°54'/07°18'; JGFF.
Lauingen, Germ.; 94 km E of Stuttgart; 48°34'/10°26'; EJ, PHGB.
Lauknen, see Gromovo.
Laukuba, see Laukuva.
Laukuva, Lith. (Laukuba, Lavkovo, Loykeva, Loykova); pop. 305; 75 km SW of Siauliai; 55°37'/22°14'; GUM3, GUM4, GUM5, LDL, SF, YL.
Laun, see Louny.
Laupheim, Germ.; pop. 280; 75 km SE of Stuttgart; 48°14'/09°53'; CAHJP, HSL, HSL2, JGFF, PHGBW.
Laurahutte, see Siemianowice Slaskie.
Lautenburg, see Lidzbark.
Lauterbach, Germ.; pop. 132; 75 km NNE of Frankfurt am Main; 50°38'/09°24'; AMG, JGFF.
Lauterbach (Bavaria), Germ.; 82 km WNW of Munchen; 48°38'/10°45'; PHGB.
Lauterbrunn, Germ.; 75 km WNW of Munchen; 48°28'/10°43'; PHGB.
Lauterecken, Germ.; pop. 8; 94 km SW of Frankfurt am Main; 49°39'/07°36'.
Lavini, see Livani.
Lavkov, see Luoke.
Lavkovo, see Laukuva.
Lavochne, Ukr. (Lawoczne); pop. 140; 126 km S of Lvov; 48°49'/23°22'; AMG, EDRD, GUM4, GUM6, HSL, PHP2.
Lavrov, Ukr. (Lawrow, Lawrykow?); pop. 5; 69 km WSW of Rovno; 50°37'/25°15'; GUM4.
Lavruv, Ukr.; pop. 79; 94 km SW of Lvov; 49°24'/22°53'.
Lawoczne, see Lavochne.
Lawrow, see Lavrov.
Lawrykow, possibly Lavrov.
Laxenburg, Aus.; pop. 11; 19 km S of Wien; 48°04'/16°21'.
Layptsig, see Leipzig.
Layptsik, see Leipzig.
Layzheve, see Laizuva.
Lazany, Pol.; pop. 26; 26 km ESE of Krakow; 49°57'/20°09'; HSL.
Lazarea, Rom.; pop. 71; 146 km E of Cluj; 46°45'/25°32'.
Lazaret, Rom. (Banlaktolmecs, Talmaciu); 133 km SSE of Cluj; 45°39'/24°16'; EJ.
Lazdei, see Lazdijai.
Lazdey, see Lazdijai.
Lazdijai, Lith. (Lazdei, Lazdey, Lazhdai, Lezdi, Lozdzee, Lozdzieje); pop. 1,141; 82 km S of Kaunas; 54°14'/23°31'; COH, HSL, HSL2, JGFF, LDL, LDS, SF, YL.
Lazdona, Lat.; pop. 7; 114 km NNW of Daugavpils; 56°50'/26°15'.
Lazduny, Byel.; pop. 10; 101 km W of Minsk; 53°55'/25°59'.
Lazhdai, see Lazdijai.
Lazi, Hung.; 94 km WSW of Budapest; 47°28'/17°50'; HSL.
Laziska, Pol.; 45 km NNE of Poznan; 52°47'/17°15'; HSL.
Lazne Kynzvart, Cz. (Bad Koenigswart); pop. 23; 126 km WSW

of Praha; 50°01'/12°38'; EJ.

Laznowska Wola, Pol.; pop. 18; 26 km ESE of Lodz; 51°39'/19°45'.

Lazo, Mold. (Chiscareni); pop. 75; 88 km NW of Kishinev; 47°33'/28°02'.

Lazovsk, Mold. (Angereii Noui, Sangerei); pop. 144; 88 km NW of Kishinev; 47°38'/28°09'; HSL.

Lazow, Pol.; pop. 98; 82 km SSW of Bialystok; 52°34'/22°23'; HSL.

Lazow (near Bilgoraj), Pol.; pop. 32; 69 km NNW of Przemysl; 50°21'/22°25'.

Lazuri, Rom.; pop. 48; 133 km NW of Cluj; 47°51'/22°52'.

Lazy, Pol.; pop. 234; 50 km SSE of Czestochowa; 50°21'/19°25'; AMG.

Lazy (near Bochnia), Pol.; pop. 5; 45 km ESE of Krakow; 49°58'/20°31'.

Lazy (near Jaroslaw), Pol.; pop. 12; 26 km N of Przemysl; 49°59'/22°52'.

Lazy (near Oswiecim), Pol.; pop. 9; 50 km WSW of Krakow; 49°59'/19°16'; GA, PHP3.

Lazy (near Warszawa), Pol.; pop. 22; 45 km W of Warszawa; 52°16'/20°24'.

Lazy pod Makytou, Cz.; 114 km ENE of Brno; 49°14'/18°14'; HSL.

Le, *see* Leh.

Leba, Pol.; pop. 3; 88 km WNW of Gdansk; 54°45'/17°33'.

Lebedevo, Byel. (Lebedov, Lebedowa, Lebiedziew); pop. 740; 75 km WNW of Minsk; 54°19'/26°42'; COH, GUM4, GUM5, HSL.

Lebedin, Ukr. (Lebiedyn); pop. 310; 114 km ESE of Konotop; 50°35'/34°29'; GUM4.

Lebedov, *see* Lebedevo.

Lebedowa, *see* Lebedevo.

Lebenhan, Germ.; 114 km ENE of Frankfurt am Main; 50°22'/10°11'; PHGB.

Lebeny, Hung.; pop. 33; 126 km W of Budapest; 47°44'/17°23'.

Lebiedyn, *see* Lebedin.

Lebiedziew, *see* Lebedevo.

Lebork, Pol. (Lauenberg, Lauenburg); pop. 239; 62 km WNW of Gdansk; 54°33'/17°46'; EJ, GUM3, GUM4, JGFF, LDS.

Lecava, *see* Leckava.

Lecavas, *see* Leckava.

Lechenich, Germ.; pop. 70; 26 km SSW of Koln; 50°48'/06°47'; GED.

Lechfeld, *see* Lager Lechfeld.

Lechicha, *see* Leczyca.

Lechinta, Rom. (Lecninta, Szaszlekence); pop. 162; 62 km NE of Cluj; 47°01'/24°21'; HSL, PHR2.

Lechna, *see* Leczna.

Lechovice, Cz.; 69 km N of Brno; 49°44'/16°33'; HSL.

Lechovich, *see* Lyakhovichi.

Lechovicz, *see* Lyakhovichi.

Lechow, Pol.; 114 km NE of Krakow; 50°49'/21°01'; GUM4, GUM5.

Lechowek, Pol.; pop. 4; 114 km NE of Krakow; 50°48'/21°01'; GUM4.

Lechowitz, *see* Lyakhovichi.

Lecka, Pol.; pop. 2; 56 km W of Przemysl; 49°52'/22°01'.

Leckava, Lith. (Lecava, Lecavas, Leckawa, Letzkova); pop. 38; 82 km WNW of Siauliai; 56°23'/22°15'; HSL, YL.

Leckawa, *see* Leckava.

Lecninta, *see* Lechinta.

Lecsmer, GUM5. This town was not found in BGN gazetteers under the given spelling.

Lecycza, *see* Leczyca.

Leczna, Pol. (Lechna, Lenchna, Lenczna, Lentchna); pop. 2,019; 26 km ENE of Lublin; 51°18'/22°53'; CAHJP, COH, EDRD, EJ, GA, GUM4, GUM5, HSL, HSL2, JGFF, LDL, LDS, LYV, PHP3, SF.

Lecznowola, Pol.; pop. 35; 94 km N of Lublin; 52°03'/22°28'.

Leczyca, Pol. (Lechicha, Lecycza, Lenchicha, Lenchitsa, Lentshits, Linchits, Lintchitz, Lunchich, Luntzitz); pop. 4,051; 38 km NW of Lodz; 52°04'/19°13'; AMG, CAHJP, EDRD, EJ, GA, GUM3, GUM5, HSL, HSL2, JGFF, LDL, LDS, LYV, PHP1, PHP4, SF, YB.

Leczyn, *see* Lencin.

Ledec, *see* Ledec nad Sazavou.

Ledec nad Sazavou, Cz. (Ledec); pop. 68; 75 km ESE of Praha; 49°42'/15°17'.

Lednica, Pol.; 19 km ESE of Krakow; 49°59'/20°05'; PHP3.

Ledurga, Lat.; pop. 1; 56 km NE of Riga; 57°19'/24°45'.

Ledvice, Cz.; pop. 7; 75 km NW of Praha; 50°35'/13°47'.

Ledyczek, Pol. (Landek im Westpreussen); pop. 45; 126 km N of Poznan; 53°32'/16°57'; POCEM.

Leeheim, Germ.; pop. 21; 32 km SSW of Frankfurt am Main; 49°52'/08°27'.

Leer, Germ.; pop. 280; 170 km WSW of Hamburg; 53°14'/07°26'; AMG, GED, LDS.

Legden, Germ.; 126 km N of Koln; 52°02'/07°06'; GED, GUM5.

Legend, Hung.; pop. 11; 45 km N of Budapest; 47°53'/19°19'.

Legenyealsomihal, LDL. This pre-World War I community was not found in BGN gazetteers.

Legenyemihly, *see* Luhyna.

Leghea, Rom.; pop. 5; 32 km WNW of Cluj; 46°51'/23°12'.

Legina, *see* Luhyna.

Legionowo, Pol.; 88 km NNE of Warszawa; 52°50'/21°52'; EDRD, GA, GUM3, GUM4, GUM5, PHP4.

Legnica, Pol. (Legniszewo, Liegnitz); pop. 850; 62 km W of Wroclaw; 51°10'/16°11'; AMG, EJ, GUM4, GUM6, HSL, HSL2, LDS, POCEM.

Legniszewo, *see* Legnica.

Legonice, Pol.; pop. 8; 75 km E of Lodz; 51°37'/20°32'.

Legrad, Yug.; pop. 18; 88 km NE of Zagreb; 46°18'/16°52'; HSL.

Legyesbenye, Hung.; pop. 60; 32 km ENE of Miskolc; 48°10'/21°09'; HSL, PHH.

Leh, Hung. (Le, Sirokyluh, Szeleslonka); 26 km NNE of Miskolc; 48°17'/20°59'; GUM5, HSL, LYV, SM.

Leh Lunka, *see* Luh.

Lehocz, HSL. This pre-World War I community was not found in BGN gazetteers.

Lehrberg, Germ.; pop. 11; 45 km SW of Nurnberg; 49°20'/10°31'; JGFF, PHGB.

Lehrensteinsfeld, Germ.; pop. 23; 45 km N of Stuttgart; 49°08'/09°19'; LDS, PHGBW.

Lehrte, Germ.; pop. 31; 19 km ENE of Hannover; 52°23'/09°58'; AMG.

Leibitz, *see* Lubica.

Leibnitz, Aus.; pop. 1; 38 km SSE of Graz; 46°46'/15°32'.

Leidenhofen, Germ.; 75 km N of Frankfurt am Main; 50°44'/08°49'; LDS.

Leiha, Germ.; 32 km WSW of Leipzig; 51°16'/11°52'; GUM3, GUM6.

Leihgestern, Germ.; pop. 21; 50 km N of Frankfurt am Main; 50°31'/08°40'; GUM5, LDS.

Leimen, Germ.; pop. 114 km SSW of Frankfurt am Main; 49°17'/07°46'; GED, LDS, PHGBW.

Leimersheim, Germ.; pop. 26; 69 km WNW of Stuttgart; 49°08'/08°21'; GED, GUM5, JGFF.

Leipalingis, Lith. (Leipolingis, Lipon); pop. 153; 94 km S of Kaunas; 54°05'/23°51'; JGFF, YL.

Leipheim, Germ.; 82 km ESE of Stuttgart; 48°26'/10°12'; GUM3, GUM4, PHGB.

Leipnik, *see* Lipnik nad Becou.

Leipolingis, *see* Leipalingis.

Leiptig, *see* Serpnevoye.

Leipzig, Germ. (Layptsig, Layptsik); pop. 13,030; 150 km SSW of Berlin; 51°18'/12°20'; AMG, CAHJP, EJ, GUM3, GUM4, GUM5, GUM6, HSL, HSL2, JGFF, LYV, PHP1, PHP2, PHP3, PHP4.

Leitershofen, Germ.; 62 km WNW of Munchen; 48°21'/10°50'; PHGB.

Leitmeritz, *see* Litomerice.

Leiwen, Germ.; pop. 42; 133 km WSW of Frankfurt am Main; 49°49'/06°53'; GUM5.

Leizeva, *see* Laizuva.

Lejasciems, Lat. (Neuhof); 157 km ENE of Riga; 57°17'/26°35'; PHLE.

Lekarovce, Cz. (Lekart); 69 km E of Kosice; 48°37'/22°10'; HSL.

Lekart, *see* Lekarovce.

Leka Szczucinska, Pol.; pop. 13; 94 km NE of Krakow; 50°20'/21°08'.

Lekawa, Pol.; pop. 3; 56 km S of Lodz; 51°17'/19°24'.

Lekawica, Pol.; pop. 22; 38 km SSW of Krakow; 49°50'/19°35'.

Lekeciai, Lith.; pop. 24; 26 km W of Kaunas; 54°58'/23°30'.

Lekenik, Yug.; pop. 11; 26 km SE of Zagreb; 45°36'/16°12'.

Lekenye, *see* Bohunovo.

Lekhevich, *see* Lyakhovitse.

Lekhovich, *see* Lyakhovitse.

Leki (Krakow area), Pol.; 50 km WSW of Krakow; 49°57'/19°13'; GUM5.

Leki (Lwow), Pol.; pop. 30; BGN lists two possible localities with this name located at 49°37'/21°40' and 49°49'/21°41'. GUM5, HSL.

Leki (near Siedlce), Pol.; 69 km E of Warszawa; 52°07'/21°57'; GA.

Leki Dolne, Pol.; pop. 38; 94 km E of Krakow; 49°59'/21°14'.

Leki Gorne, Pol.; pop. 18; 94 km E of Krakow; 49°59'/21°11'.

Leki Krolewskie, Pol.; pop. 7; 69 km NE of Czestochowa; 51°11'/19°51'.

Lekinsko, Pol.; pop. 8; 56 km N of Czestochowa; 51°13'/19°21'.

Leki Szlacheckie, Pol. (Lackie Szlacheckie); pop. 8; 62 km NE of Czestochowa; 51°11'/19°48'; PHP2.

Leki Wielkie, Pol.; pop. 1; 45 km SW of Poznan; 52°08'/16°31'.

Leksandrowa, Pol.; pop. 17; 45 km ESE of Krakow; 49°54'/20°28'.

Lelchitsy, Byel. (Leltchitz, Leltzitz); pop. 1,500; 150 km E of Pinsk; 51°47'/28°20'; SF.

Lelechowka, *see* Lelekhovka.

Leleiu, Rom.; pop. 21; 82 km NW of Cluj; 47°23'/23°04'.

Lelekhovka, Ukr. (Lelechowka); pop. 14; 26 km WNW of Lvov; 49°57'/23°41'.

Leles, Cz. (Lelesz); pop. 195; 62 km ESE of Kosice; 48°28'/22°02'; HSL, JGFF, LDL.

Lelesz, *see* Leles.

Lelev, *see* Lelow.

Lelewo, Pol.; pop. 17; 38 km NW of Warszawa; 52°34'/20°42'; HSL.

Lelikov, Byel. (Lelikow, Lelikuv); pop. 35; 101 km WSW of Pinsk; 51°55'/24°42'.

Lelikow, *see* Lelikov.

Lelikuv, *see* Lelikov.

Leliunai, Lith.; pop. 63; 94 km N of Vilnius; 55°28'/25°24'.

Leliwa, Pol.; pop. 6; 88 km NW of Czestochowa; 51°25'/18°22'.

Lelow, Pol. (Lelev); pop. 638; 38 km ESE of Czestochowa; 50°41'/19°37'; AMG, CAHJP, EDRD, EJ, GUM5, HSL, HSL2, LDS, PHP1, SF.

Lelowice, Pol.; pop. 6; 32 km NE of Krakow; 50°17'/20°15'.

Leltchitz, *see* Lelchitsy.

Leltzitz, *see* Lelchitsy.

Lembeck, Germ.; pop. 2; 94 km N of Koln; 51°46'/07°00'.

Lemberg, *see* Lvov.

Lemes, *see* Lemesany.

Lemesany, Cz. (Lemes); pop. 57; 19 km N of Kosice; 48°51'/21°16'; COH, HSL, LDL.

Lemeshevichi, Byel. (Lemieszewicze); pop. 67; 13 km E of Pinsk; 52°05'/26°19'.

Lemforde, Germ.; pop. 20; 94 km W of Hannover; 52°28'/08°23'; GUM5.

Lemgo, Germ.; pop. 52; 69 km SW of Hannover; 52°02'/08°54'; GUM4, LDS.

Lemieszewicze, *see* Lemeshevichi.

Lemniu, Rom. (Lemniu Somes); pop. 61; 69 km NNW of Cluj; 47°21'/23°29'.

Lemniu Somes, *see* Lemniu.

Lempino, Pol.; pop. 6; 82 km WNW of Warszawa; 52°46'/20°06'.

Lemsal, *see* Limbazi.

Lemzal, *see* Limbazi.

Lenarczyce, Pol.; pop. 21; 88 km SW of Lublin; 50°42'/21°40'.

Lenarddaroc, Hung.; pop. 11; 32 km W of Miskolc; 48°09'/20°23'.

Lenardfalu, HSL. This pre-World War I community was not found in BGN gazetteers.

Lencauti, *see* Lenkovtsy.

Lencauti Hotin, *see* Lenkovtsy.

Lenchicha, *see* Leczyca.

Lenchitsa, *see* Leczyca.

Lenchna, *see* Leczna.

Lenci, Lat.; pop. 1; 82 km NE of Riga; 57°23'/25°12'.

Lencin, Ukr. (Leczyn); pop. 27; 62 km ESE of Rovno; 50°16'/26°57'; CAHJP. CAHJP refers to a town named Leczyn in Stanislawow province that does not appear in interwar or contemporary gazetteers.

Lencze, Pol. (Lencze Gorne); pop. 10; 26 km SSW of Krakow; 49°54'/19°43'.

Lencze Gorne, *see* Lencze.

Lenczna, *see* Leczna.

Lendava, Yug. (Also Lendva, Dolnja Lendava); pop. 171; 94 km N of Zagreb; 46°34'/16°27'; PHY.

Lendersdorf, Germ.; 38 km SW of Koln; 50°46'/06°29'; GED.

Lendershausen, Germ.; pop. 10; 88 km NW of Nurnberg; 50°08'/10°31'; GUM5, PHGB.

Lenesice, Cz.; pop. 14; 62 km WNW of Praha; 50°22'/13°46'.

Lengerich, Germ.; pop. 47; 126 km WSW of Hannover; 52°11'/07°52'; GUM3.

Lengfeld, Germ.; pop. 30; 32 km SE of Frankfurt am Main; 49°50'/08°54'.

Lengsfeld, *see* Stadtlengsfeld.

Lengyelszallas, *see* Lahovec.

Lengyeltoti, Hung.; pop. 48; 56 km NE of Nagykanizsa; 46°40'/17°39'; LDS.

Lenin, Byel.; pop. 928; 94 km ENE of Pinsk; 52°20'/27°29'; AMG, COH, GUM3, GUM4, GUM5, HSL, LYV, SF, YB.

Lenina Mala, *see* Lenina Malaya.

Lenina Malaya, Ukr. (Lenina Mala); pop. 9; 101 km SW of Lvov; 49°22'/22°52'.

Lenina Velka, *see* Bolshaya Lenina.

Lenina Wielka, *see* Bolshaya Lenina.

Lenindorf, *see* Leninskoye.

Leningrad, USSR (Peterburg, St.Petersburg); pop. 84,505; 251 km NNE of Pskov; 59°55'/30°15'; AMG, EJ, GUM4, GUM5, HSL2, JGFF, PHP2, PHP4.

Lenino, Ukr.; 139 km NE of Simferopol; 45°18'/35°47'; EDRD.

Leninskaya Kopalnya, USSR; pop. 41; This town was not found in BGN gazetteers under the given spelling.

Leninskoye, Ukr. (Lenindorf); pop. 110; 45 km N of Simferopol; 45°17'/34°03'.

Lenke, EGRS, HSL, LDL. This pre-World War I community was not found in BGN gazetteers.

Lenkersheim, Germ.; 45 km W of Nurnberg; 49°30'/10°29'; PHGB.

Lenkovtsy, Ukr. (Lencauti, Lencauti Hotin); pop. 134; 62 km NE of Chernovtsy; 48°30'/26°45'.

Lentchna, *see* Leczna.

Lentestii de Jos, Rom.; pop. 171; This town was not found in BGN gazetteers under the given spelling.

Lenti, Hung.; pop. 40; 38 km WNW of Nagykanizsa; 46°37'/16°33'.

Lentikapolna, Hung.; pop. 2; 45 km WNW of Nagykanizsa; 46°40'/16°33'.

Lentshits, *see* Leczyca.

Lentupis, *see* Lyntupy.

Lenzingen, Pol. PHP1. This town was not found in BGN gazetteers under the given spelling.

Leoben, Aus.; pop. 130; 107 km SSE of Salzburg; 46°56'/13°36'; AMG, EJ.

Leobersdorf, Aus.; pop. 12; 38 km S of Wien; 47°55'/16°13'.

Leobschuetz, *see* Glubczyce.

Leobschutz, *see* Glubczyce.

Leoncin, Pol.; pop. 149; 32 km WNW of Warszawa;

52°24'/20°33'; PHP4.

Leonhoff, COH. This town was not found in BGN gazetteers under the given spelling.

Leonin, Pol.; pop. 1; 38 km SW of Lublin; 51°07'/22°00'.

Leonpol, Byel. (Levinpol); pop. 138; 163 km WNW of Vitebsk; 55°48'/27°47'; AMG, COH, LDL, SF, YB.

Leontina, see Leontyevo.

Leontyevo, Mold. (Leontina); pop. 9; 69 km ESE of Kishinev; 46°40'/29°36'.

Leopol, see Lvov.

Leopoldow, HSL. A number of towns share this name. It was not possible to determine from available information which one is being referenced.

Leopoldowo, Pol.; pop. 10; 82 km W of Bialystok; 53°09'/21°54'.

Leopoldsdorf, see Leopoldsdorf im Marchfelde.

Leopoldsdorf im Marchfelde, Aus. (Leopoldsdorf); pop. 22; 26 km ENE of Wien; 48°13'/16°41'.

Leopoldshall, Germ.; pop. 2; 82 km NW of Leipzig; 51°51'/11°35'.

Leordina, Rom. (Lerdene, Lerdine); pop. 324; 126 km N of Cluj; 47°47'/24°15'; AMG, COH, GUM4, HSL, JGFF, PHR2, SM.

Leova, see Leovo.

Leovo, Mold. (Leova, Levo); pop. 2,326; 75 km SSW of Kishinev; 46°28'/28°15'; EDRD, EJ, JGFF, PHR2, SF, YB.

Lepel, Byel.; pop. 1,923; 101 km SW of Vitebsk; 54°53'/28°42'; EDRD, EJ, GUM4, LDL, SF.

Lepeticha Hagdola, see Bolshoi Lepeticha.

Leplevka, Byel. (Leplowka); pop. 14; 170 km WSW of Pinsk; 51°46'/23°40'.

Leplowka, see Leplevka.

Lepna, see Lipno.

Lepseny, Hung.; pop. 48; 88 km SW of Budapest; 47°00'/18°15'; LDS.

Lerche, Germ.; 94 km NNE of Koln; 51°37'/07°43'; GUM5.

Lerdene, see Leordina.

Lerdine, see Leordina.

Lern, see Berglern.

Leros, GUM4. This town was not found in BGN gazetteers under the given spelling.

Les, Rom.; pop. 11; 133 km W of Cluj; 46°57'/21°51'.

Leschnitz, see Lesnica.

Lesechniki, Ukr. (Laschinca); pop. 33; 45 km NNW of Chernovtsy; 48°41'/25°51'.

Lesenceistvand, Hung.; pop. 9; 62 km NNE of Nagykanizsa; 46°52'/17°21'.

Lesencetomaj, Hung.; pop. 10; 56 km NNE of Nagykanizsa; 46°51'/17°22'.

Lesenice, Cz.; 157 km E of Bratislava; 48°06'/19°15'; HSL.

Leshchantse, Ukr. (Leszczance); pop. 27; 88 km NW of Chernovtsy; 48°59'/25°23'.

Leshchatuv, Ukr. (Leszczatka?, Leszczatow); pop. 32; 82 km NNE of Lvov; 50°29'/24°30'.

Leshchin, Ukr. (Leszczyn); pop. 13; 50 km SE of Lvov; 49°29'/24°21'.

Leshchkuv, Ukr. (Leszczkow); pop. 22; 75 km N of Lvov; 50°28'/24°06'.

Leshnev, Ukr. (Leshnov, Lesniow, Leszniow); pop. 179; 88 km NE of Lvov; 50°14'/25°05'; EDRD, EGRS, EJ, GYLA, HSL, HSL2, JGFF, LDL, PHP2, SF.

Leshnov, see Leshnev.

Leshnya, Byel. (Leszna); pop. 13; 101 km S of Minsk; 53°00'/27°00'.

Lesienice, Ukr.; pop. 51; 38 km SSE of Lvov; 49°35'/24°05'; GUM4. This town was located on an interwar map of Poland but does not appear in contemporary gazetteers. Map coordinates are approximate.

Lesko, Pol. (Linsk, Lisk, Lisko); pop. 2,338; 50 km SSW of Przemysl; 49°27'/22°19'; AMG, CAHJP, COH, EDRD, EGRS, EJ, GA, GUM3, GUM4, GUM5, HSL, JGFF, LYV, PHP2, PHP3, POCEM, SF, YB.

Leskovac, Yug.; pop. 93; 114 km N of Skopje; 42°59'/21°57'; PHY.

Leskovichi, Byel. (Laskowicze Wielkie, Lyaskoviche Velke); pop. 20; 82 km W of Pinsk; 52°20'/24°55'.

Leslau, see Wloclawek.

Leslo, see Wloclawek.

Lesluya, see Wloclawek.

Lesmir, Rom.; pop. 11; 94 km WNW of Cluj; 47°15'/22°34'.

Lesna, Pol. PHP4. A number of towns share this name. It was not possible to determine from available information which one is being referenced.

Lesna Podlaska, Pol.; pop. 107 km N of Lublin; 52°08'/23°02'; GA.

Lesnaya Slobodka, Ukr. (Slobodka Lesna, Slobudka Lesna); pop. 37; 82 km WNW of Chernovtsy; 48°37'/24°57'; PHP2.

Lesnevichi, Ukr. (Lesniovitse, Lesniowice); pop. 64; 32 km W of Lvov; 49°52'/23°34'; HSL.

Lesnica, Pol. (Leschnitz, Lesnica Opolska); 75 km SW of Czestochowa; 50°26'/18°11'; LDS, POCEM.

Lesnica Opolska, see Lesnica.

Lesniovitse, see Lesnevichi.

Lesniow, see Leshnev.

Lesniowice, Pol.; pop. 24; 69 km ESE of Lublin; 50°59'/23°30'. *See also* Lesnevichi.

Lesno Brdo, GUM6. This town was not found in BGN gazetteers under the given spelling.

Lesnowo, Pol. (Reimerswalde); 32 km ESE of Gdansk; 54°15'/19°05'; GUM3.

Lesnoye, Ukr. (Manzar); pop. 193; 107 km WSW of Odessa; 46°28'/29°21'.

Lesnoy Khlebichin, Ukr. (Chlebiczyn Lesny, Chlebiczyn Polny); pop. 47; 82 km WNW of Chernovtsy; 48°41'/24°55'; GUM4.

Lesnyaki, see Lisnyaki.

Lespezi, Rom.; pop. 114 km S of Iasi; 46°10'/27°14'; GUM4.

Lessen, Germ.; 45 km SSW of Leipzig; 50°58'/12°04'; HSL, LDS.

Lestina, Cz.; pop. 23; 75 km ESE of Praha; 49°46'/15°24'.

Lesu, Rom.; pop. 16; 107 km NE of Cluj; 47°19'/24°45'.

Leszczance, see Leshchantse.

Leszczanka, Pol.; pop. 30; 82 km NNE of Lublin; 51°56'/23°02'.

Leszczatka, *possibly* Leshchatuv.

Leszczatow, see Leshchatuv.

Leszczawa Dolna, Pol.; pop. 31; 26 km SW of Przemysl; 49°40'/22°27'.

Leszczawa Gorna, Pol.; pop. 51; 32 km SW of Przemysl; 49°39'/22°27'.

Leszczawka, Pol.; pop. 8; 32 km SW of Przemysl; 49°38'/22°25'.

Leszczkow, see Leshchkuv.

Leszczowate, Pol.; pop. 39; 38 km SSW of Przemysl; 49°30'/22°34'.

Leszczyn, see Leshchin.

Leszinow, see Lezhanovka.

Leszkowice, Pol.; pop. 30; 38 km N of Lublin; 51°33'/22°37'.

Leszna, see Leshnya.

Leszniow, see Leshnev.

Leszno, Pol. (Lissa); pop. 299; 69 km SSW of Poznan; 51°51'/16°35'; AMG, CAHJP, EDRD, EJ, GA, HSL2, JGFF, LDL, PHP1.

Leszno (near Blonie), Pol.; pop. 258; 26 km W of Warszawa; 52°16'/20°36'; HSL, HSL2, PHP4.

Let, Rom.; pop. 3; 163 km N of Bucuresti; 45°51'/26°01'.

Letca, Rom.; pop. 13; 69 km NNW of Cluj; 47°20'/23°27'; AMG, HSL.

Letenye, Hung.; pop. 52; 19 km WSW of Nagykanizsa; 46°26'/16°44'; PHH.

Letichev, Ukr. (Latyczow, Letichuv, Letitchev); pop. 2,434; 69 km W of Vinnitsa; 49°23'/27°37'; COH, EJ, GUM4, GYLA, HSL, JGFF, LYV, SF.

Letichuv, see Letichev.

Letiny, Cz.; pop. 7; 94 km SW of Praha; 49°32'/13°27'; JGFF.

Letitchev, see Letichev.

Letky, Cz.; 19 km NW of Praha; 50°11'/14°23'; HSL.

Letmathe, Germ.; pop. 3; 62 km NE of Koln; 51°22'/07°37'.

Letnia, see Letnya.

Letnya, Ukr. (Letnia); pop. 53; 56 km S of Lvov; 49°24'/23°44'.

Letohrad, Cz. (Kysperk); pop. 33; 101 km N of Brno;

50°02'/16°30'.

Letov, Cz.; pop. 5; 75 km W of Praha; 50°14'/13°27'.

Letowice, Pol.; pop. 37; 69 km E of Krakow; 49°59'/20°51'.

Letownia, Pol.; pop. 78; 69 km NW of Przemysl; 50°20'/22°15'; PHP3.

Letschin, Germ.; pop. 12; 62 km ENE of Berlin; 52°38'/14°22'.

Lettau, *see* Lietuva.

Letzkova, *see* Leckava.

Leubsdorf, Germ.; 50 km SE of Koln; 50°33'/07°18'; GUM5.

Leuseni, *see* Leusheny.

Leuseni Orhei, *see* Leusheny.

Leusheni, *see* Leusheny.

Leusheny, Mold. (Leuseni, Leuseni Orhei, Leusheni); pop. 37; 56 km NW of Kishinev; 47°29'/28°26'; JGFF.

Leutershausen, Germ.; pop. 54; 50 km SW of Nurnberg; 49°18'/10°25'; GUM5, JGFF, LDS, PHGB.

Leutershausen (Baden), Germ.; pop. 40; 69 km S of Frankfurt am Main; 49°30'/08°40'; PHGBW.

Leutkirch, Germ.; 120 km SW of Munchen; 47°50'/10°02'; PHGBW.

Leutschau, *see* Levoca.

Leva, *see* Levice.

Level, Hung.; pop. 6; 146 km WNW of Budapest; 47°54'/17°12'.

Levelek, Hung.; pop. 103; 94 km E of Miskolc; 47°58'/22°00'; AMG, HSL, LDL, PHH.

Leverkusen, Germ.; pop. 62; 13 km N of Koln; 51°01'/06°59'; GUM4, GUM5, LDS.

Levertev, *see* Lubartow.

Levertov, *see* Lubartow.

Levice, Cz. (Leva); pop. 1,651; 107 km ENE of Bratislava; 48°13'/18°36'; COH, GUM4, GUM6, HSL, LDL.

Levinpol, *see* Leonpol.

Levkiev, *see* Lewkow.

Levkov, Ukr. BGN lists two possible localities with this name located at 48°26'/29°04' and 50°15'/28°50'. JGFF.

Levo, *see* Leovo.

Levoca, Cz. (Leutschau); pop. 1,100; 62 km WNW of Kosice; 49°02'/20°36'; AMG, EJ, GUM5, HSL.

Lewin Brzeski, Pol. (Lowen); pop. 39; 56 km ESE of Wroclaw; 50°45'/17°37'; GA, LDS.

Lewkow, Pol. (Levkiev); 94 km NNE of Wroclaw; 51°42'/17°52'; LDL, SF.

Lewniowa, Pol.; pop. 41; 56 km ESE of Krakow; 49°53'/20°39'.

Lezachow, Pol.; pop. 12; 45 km NNW of Przemysl; 50°09'/22°37'.

Lezajsk, Pol. (Lezansk, Lezhaysk, Lizhensk, Lzhansk); pop. 1,575; 56 km NW of Przemysl; 50°16'/22°25'; AMG, CAHJP, COH, EDRD, EGRS, EJ, FRG, GUM3, GUM4, GUM5, HSL, HSL2, JGFF, LDL, LDS, LYV, PHP2, PHP3, POCEM, SF, YB.

Lezanowka, *see* Lezhanovka.

Lezany, Pol.; pop. 34; 75 km WSW of Przemysl; 49°39'/21°48'.

Lezce, Pol.; pop. 21; 45 km NNW of Czestochowa; 51°08'/19°02'.

Lezdi, *see* Lazdijai.

Lezhanovka, Ukr. (Leszinow, Lezanowka, Lezhanuvka); pop. 20; 114 km N of Chernovtsy; 49°19'/26°04'; GUM3.

Lezhanuvka, *see* Lezhanovka.

Lezhaysk, *see* Lezajsk.

Lezyny, Pol.; pop. 7; 88 km WSW of Przemysl; 49°40'/21°32'.

Lgov, USSR; pop. 183; 62 km WSW of Kursk; 51°41'/35°16'.

Lhota, Cz.; 82 km NE of Brno; 49°30'/17°37'; HSL.

Lhuta, Cz.; 88 km NW of Brno; 49°55'/16°08'; HSL.

Liachovitch, *see* Lyakhovichi.

Liachovitz, *see* Belogorye.

Liady, *see* Lyady.

Liban, *see* Liepaja.

Libanfalva, *see* Ibanesti (Transylvania).

Libatchov, *see* Lubaczow.

Libau, *see* Liepaja.

Libava, *see* Liepaja.

Libavske Udoli, Cz. (Kagerava); pop. 22; 139 km W of Praha;

50°07'/12°34'.

Libawa, *see* Liepaja.

Libceves, Cz.; pop. 13; 62 km WNW of Praha; 50°27'/13°50'.

Libechov, Cz.; pop. 26; 45 km N of Praha; 50°25'/14°27'.

Libechuyv, *see* Lubaczow.

Libedice, Cz.; pop. 4; 82 km WNW of Praha; 50°19'/13°23'.

Libejovice, Cz.; pop. 4; 114 km S of Praha; 49°06'/14°12'.

Liben, Cz. (Lieben); 26 km S of Praha; 49°56'/14°28'; EJ, HSL.

Liberec, Cz.; pop. 1,312; 88 km NNE of Praha; 50°47'/15°03'; EJ, GUM4, GUM5.

Libertow, Pol.; pop. 5; 19 km S of Krakow; 49°58'/19°53'.

Libesice, Cz.; pop. 21; 56 km NNW of Praha; 50°34'/14°18'.

Libesovice, Cz.; pop. 16; 69 km W of Praha; 50°15'/13°30'.

Libevne, *see* Lyuboml.

Libez, Cz.; pop. 4; 50 km SE of Praha; 49°46'/14°55'.

Libiaz, Pol. (Libiaz Wielki); pop. 39; 45 km W of Krakow; 50°06'/19°18'; HSL. The 1921 census of Poland also shows a town of Libiaz Maly (Little Libiaz) with a Jewish population of 36.

Libiaz Wielki, *see* Libiaz.

Libickozma, Hung.; pop. 1; 45 km ENE of Nagykanizsa; 46°31'/17°32'.

Libidza, Pol.; pop. 15; 19 km WNW of Czestochowa; 50°53'/18°59'.

Libien, Pol. PHP4. This town was not found in BGN gazetteers under the given spelling.

Libinky, Cz.; pop. 1; 56 km NNW of Praha; 50°32'/14°17'.

Libiszow, Pol.; pop. 19; 75 km ESE of Lodz; 51°26'/20°20'.

Liblar, Germ.; 19 km SSW of Koln; 50°49'/06°48'; GED, JGFF.

Libna, Cz. (Liebenau); BGN lists two possible localities with this name located at 45°57'/15°32' and 50°39'/16°08'. GUM5, JGFF.

Libocany, Cz.; pop. 2; 69 km WNW of Praha; 50°20'/13°31'.

Libochora, Ukr. (Libohora); pop. 35; 94 km S of Lvov; 49°03'/23°31'. This town was located on an interwar map of Poland but does not appear in contemporary gazetteers. Map coordinates are approximate. *See also* Libukhora.

Libochovany, Cz.; pop. 1; 62 km NW of Praha; 50°34'/14°02'.

Libochovice, Cz.; pop. 57; 45 km NW of Praha; 50°24'/14°02'.

Libodrice, Cz.; pop. 5; 45 km E of Praha; 50°00'/15°05'.

Libohora, *see* Libochora.

Liboi, *see* Liepaja.

Libokhora, *see* Libukhora.

Libomysl, Cz.; pop. 3; 45 km SW of Praha; 49°52'/14°00'.

Liborice, Cz.; pop. 7; 69 km W of Praha; 50°15'/13°31'.

Libouchec, Cz.; pop. 1; 82 km NNW of Praha; 50°46'/14°02'.

Liboun, Cz.; pop. 8; 56 km SE of Praha; 49°38'/14°49'.

Libov, Cz.; 75 km NNW of Praha; 50°42'/14°04'; HSL.

Libova, *see* Liepaja.

Libovne, *see* Lyuboml.

Liboya, *see* Liepaja.

Librantowa, Pol.; pop. 37; 75 km ESE of Krakow; 49°40'/20°46'; GUM5, PHP3.

Librava Mesto, *see* Mesto Libava.

Libuchora, *see* Libukhora.

Libukhora, Ukr. (Libokhora, Libuchora, Liebochora); pop. 210; 126 km SSW of Lvov; 48°55'/22°58'; AMG, HSL, PHP2, SF. *See also* Libochora.

Libusin, Cz.; pop. 6; 32 km WNW of Praha; 50°10'/14°03'.

Libusza, Pol.; pop. 13; 107 km ESE of Krakow; 49°41'/21°15'.

Libyne, *see* Lubenec.

Lich, Germ.; pop. 74; 50 km N of Frankfurt am Main; 50°31'/08°50'; GUM5, LDS.

Lichenroth, Germ.; pop. 42; 62 km NE of Frankfurt am Main; 50°26'/09°20'; JGFF.

Lichkovtse, *see* Luchkovtsy.

Lichtenau, Germ.; pop. 109; 88 km WSW of Stuttgart; 48°44'/08°01'; JGFF, PHGBW.

Lichtenau (Bavaria), Germ.; 32 km SW of Nurnberg; 49°17'/10°41'; LDS, PHGB.

Lichtenau (Westphalia), Germ.; pop. 20; 101 km SSW of Hannover; 51°37'/08°54'; GUM5.

Lichtenberg, Germ.; 45 km SSE of Frankfurt am Main;

49°46'/08°48'; LDS.

Lichtenberg (Brandenburg area), Germ.; 75 km E of Berlin; 52°19'/14°27'; GUM3.

Lichtenfels, Germ.; pop. 74; 82 km N of Nurnberg; 50°09'/11°04'; GED, GUM4, GUM5, JGFF, PHGB.

Lichtenstadt, *see* Hroznetin.

Lichtental, *see* Svetlodolinskoye.

Lichterfelde, Germ.; 75 km S of Berlin; 51°53'/13°13'; GUM5.

Lichty, Pol.; pop. 9; 56 km N of Lublin; 51°43'/22°38'.

Lichwin, Pol.; pop. 23; 82 km ESE of Krakow; 49°53'/20°57'.

Lickov, Cz.; pop. 26; 62 km WNW of Praha; 50°17'/13°38'.

Liczkowce, *see* Luchkovtsy.

Lida, Byel.; pop. 5,419; 146 km WSW of Minsk; 53°53'/25°18'; AMG, COH, EDRD, GA, GUM3, GUM4, GUM5, GUM6, HSL, HSL2, JGFF, LDL, LYV, PHP4, SF, YB.

Lidice, Cz.; 19 km W of Praha; 50°08'/14°12'; GUM3, GUM5.

Liduvian, *see* Lyduvenai.

Lidvinka, *see* Iosipovka.

Lidvinov, *see* Lyduvenai.

Lidzbark, Pol. (Lautenburg); pop. 60; 133 km NW of Warszawa; 53°16'/19°49'; HSL, POCEM.

Lidzbark Warminski, Pol. (Heilsberg); pop. 39; 126 km E of Gdansk; 54°08'/20°35'; HSL.

Liebarska Lucka, GUM4. This town was not found in BGN gazetteers under the given spelling.

Liebau, *see* Liepaja.

Lieben, *see* Liben.

Liebenau, Germ.; 107 km S of Hannover; 51°29'/09°17'; HSL, JGFF, LDS. *See also* Libna.

Liebenau (Austria), Aus.; 120 km WNW of Wien; 48°31'/14°48'; GUM3, GUM5.

Liebenwalde, Germ.; 45 km N of Berlin; 52°52'/13°24'; LDS.

Lieberose, Germ.; pop. 5; 82 km ESE of Berlin; 51°59'/14°18'; GUM3, GUM5.

Lieber Tov, *see* Lyubar.

Liebesice, HSL. This pre-World War I community was not found in BGN gazetteers.

Liebing, Aus.; 88 km NE of Graz; 47°25'/16°30'; JGFF.

Lieblos, Germ.; pop. 7; 32 km ENE of Frankfurt am Main; 50°12'/09°08'.

Liebochora, *see* Libukhora.

Liebochowitz, HSL. This pre-World War I community was not found in BGN gazetteers.

Liebstadt, Germ.; pop. 32; 114 km ESE of Leipzig; 50°52'/13°52'; CAHJP.

Liedolsheim, Germ.; 75 km WNW of Stuttgart; 49°10'/08°25'; LDS, PHGBW.

Liege, *see* Liegi.

Liegi, Lat. (Liege); 176 km WSW of Riga; 56°35'/21°20'; JGFF.

Liegnitz, *see* Legnica.

Lielauce, Lat.; pop. 1; 88 km SW of Riga; 56°31'/22°54'.

Lielkokini, Ukr. EJ. A number of towns share this name. It was not possible to determine from available information which one is being referenced.

Lielstraupe, Lat. (Roop, Straupe); pop. 1; 69 km NE of Riga; 57°21'/24°57'.

Lielvarde, Lat. (Rembate); pop. 9; 50 km ESE of Riga; 56°43'/24°48'.

Lienz, Aus.; pop. 3; 114 km S of Salzburg; 46°50'/12°47'.

Liepaja, Lat. (Liban, Libau, Libava, Libawa, Liboi, Libova, Liboya, Liebau); pop. 7,825; 195 km WSW of Riga; 56°31'/21°01'; AMG, COH, EJ, GUM3, GUM4, GUM5, HSL, HSL2, JGFF, LDL, PHLE, PHP1, PHP3, SF.

Liepas, Lat.; pop. 1; 94 km NE of Riga; 57°23'/25°26'.

Liepkalne, *see* Liepkalns.

Liepkalns, Lat. (Liepkalne); pop. 5; 94 km E of Riga; 56°49'/25°37'.

Liepna, Lat. (Liepnas); pop. 21; 176 km N of Daugavpils; 57°21'/27°28'.

Liepnas, *see* Liepna.

Lieser, Germ.; pop. 6; 120 km WSW of Frankfurt am Main;

49°55'/07°01'.

Liesing, Aus.; pop. 87; 13 km SSW of Wien; 48°09'/16°18'; AMG.

Lieskova, Cz. (Mogyoros); 56 km E of Kosice; 48°35'/22°02'; HSL, JGFF.

Lietuva, (Lettau, Litva, Litwa); AMG. Not a town, but a region of Lithuania.

Lievenhof, *see* Livani.

Liezen, Aus.; pop. 2; 94 km ESE of Salzburg; 47°34'/14°14'; GUM4, GUM5.

Liezere, Lat. (Liezeres); pop. 4; 120 km ENE of Riga; 57°01'/26°04'; PHLE.

Liezeres, *see* Liezere.

Liflandia, (Livonia); PHLE. Not a town, but a province of Latvia.

Liga, Pol. EDRD. A number of towns share this name. It was not possible to determine from available information which one is being referenced.

Ligatne, Lat.; pop. 11; 62 km NE of Riga; 57°11'/25°02'; PHLE.

Ligem, *see* Lygumai.

Ligmian, *see* Linkmenys.

Ligmiany, *see* Linkmenys.

Ligum, *see* Lygumai.

Ligumai, *see* Lygumai.

Lika, GUM4. This town was not found in BGN gazetteers under the given spelling.

Likavitos, GUM4. This town was not found in BGN gazetteers under the given spelling.

Likeva, *see* Lukow.

Likeve, *see* Lukow.

Likova, *see* Lukow.

Liksna, Lat.; pop. 15; 19 km WNW of Daugavpils; 55°59'/26°23'.

Lilienfeld, Aus.; pop. 2; 56 km SW of Wien; 48°01'/15°38'.

Liliopol, Pol. (Juljopol, Liljopol); pop. 54; 69 km NW of Lodz; 52°18'/19°03'.

Liljopol, *see* Liliopol.

Liman, Ukr. (Zolocari); pop. 38; 120 km SSW of Odessa; 45°41'/29°45'.

Limanowa, Pol. (Limonov); pop. 905; 62 km SE of Krakow; 49°42'/20°26'; EGRS, GA, GUM3, GUM4, GUM5, HSL, JGFF, LDL, PHP3, SF.

Limbach, Germ.; 69 km NW of Nurnberg; 49°59'/10°38'; PHGB.

Limbazhi, *see* Limbazi.

Limbazi, Lat. (Lemsal, Lemzal, Limbazhi); pop. 105; 75 km NNE of Riga; 57°31'/24°42'; COH, PHLE, SF.

Limbenii Vechi, *see* Staryye Limbeny.

Limberk, *see* Pomezi.

Limburg, *see* Limburg an der Lahn.

Limburg an der Lahn, Germ. (Limburg); pop. 300; 56 km WNW of Frankfurt am Main; 50°23'/08°03'; AMG, EJ, GUM5, HSL, HSL2, JGFF.

Limmer, Germ.; 50 km SSE of Hannover; 52°00'/09°48'; HSL.

Limonov, *see* Limanowa.

Linchits, *see* Leczyca.

Lindach, Germ.; 75 km NNW of Stuttgart; 49°25'/09°01'; LDS.

Lindau, Germ.; 139 km SSE of Stuttgart; 47°33'/09°41'; EDRD, EJ, GED, GUM3, PHGB, PHGBW.

Linden, Germ.; 38 km W of Nurnberg; 49°30'/10°35'; HSL, JGFF.

Linden bei Hannover, Germ.; 6 km WSW of Hannover; 52°22'/09°41'; HSL.

Lindenschied, Germ.; 94 km WSW of Frankfurt am Main; 49°54'/07°24'; JGFF.

Lindheim, Germ.; pop. 35; 38 km NE of Frankfurt am Main; 50°18'/08°59'; GUM5, JGFF, LDS.

Lindhorst, Germ.; 32 km WSW of Hannover; 52°22'/09°17'; GED.

Line, Cz.; pop. 18; 94 km SW of Praha; 49°42'/13°16'; HSL, HSL2.

Linevo, Byel. (Linowo); pop. 96; 120 km WNW of Pinsk; 52°29'/24°30'.

Lingen, Germ.; pop. 39; 163 km W of Hannover; 52°31'/07°19'; GUM4, GUM5.

Lingenfeld, Germ.; 82 km WNW of Stuttgart; 49°15'/08°21'; GED.

Linitz, *see* Ilintsy.

Linkah, *see* Glinka.

Linkani, *see* Lipkany.

Linkeve, *see* Linkuva.

Linkiskiai, Lith. (Linkitz); JGFF. This town was not found in BGN gazetteers under the given spelling.

Linkitz, *see* Linkiskiai.

Linkmenai, *see* Linkmenys.

Linkmenys, Lith. (Ligmian, Ligmiany, Linkmenai, Lyngmiany); pop. 80; 82 km NNE of Vilnius; 55°18'/25°57'; COH, GUM3, SF, YB.

Linkova, *see* Linkuva.

Linkovo, *see* Linkuva.

Linkowo, *see* Linkuva.

Linkuva, Lith. (Linkeve, Linkova, Linkovo, Linkowo); pop. 625; 45 km NE of Siauliai; 56°05'/23°59'; GUM5, HSL, JGFF, SF, YL.

Linnich, Germ.; pop. 100; 45 km W of Koln; 50°59'/06°16'; AMG, GED, JGFF.

Linow, Pol.; pop. 30; 69 km SW of Lublin; 50°52'/21°49'.

Linowo, *see* Linevo.

Linsk, *see* Lesko.

Lintchitz, *see* Leczyca.

Linz, Aus.; pop. 671; 114 km NE of Salzburg; 48°18'/14°18'; AMG, GUM3, GUM4, GUM5, GUM6, ISH2. *See also* Linz am Rhein.

Linz am Rhein, Germ. (Linz); pop. 65; 50 km SE of Koln; 50°34'/07°17'; EJ.

Liozna, *see* Liozno.

Liozno, Byel. (Liozna, Lozniany); pop. 1,204; 45 km ESE of Vitebsk; 55°02'/30°48'; EJ, GUM4, SF.

Lipa, Pol.; pop. 33; 32 km WSW of Przemysl; 49°43'/22°23'; HSL.

Lipa (Stanislawow), Ukr.; pop. 27; 101 km NW of Chernovtsy; 48°59'/25°04'.

Lipa Krepa, Pol.; pop. 11; 69 km WSW of Lublin; 51°10'/21°37'.

Lipa Miklas, Pol.; pop. 16; 69 km WSW of Lublin; 51°10'/21°37'.

Lipau, Rom.; pop. 23; 114 km NNW of Cluj; 47°43'/23°08'.

Lipca, *see* Lipsha.

Lipcani, *see* Lipkany.

Lipcani Sat, *possibly* Lipcheny.

Lipcani Targ, *see* Lipkany.

Lipcany, *see* Lipkany.

Lipceni, *see* Lipcheny.

Lipcheny, Mold. (Lipcani Sat?, Lipceni); pop. 28; 94 km N of Kishinev; 47°48'/28°53'.

Lipcse, *see* Lipsha.

Lipcsemezo, *see* Lipsha.

Lipec, HSL. A number of towns share this name. It was not possible to determine from available information which one is being referenced.

Lipecka Palana, *see* Lipsha.

Lipen, Byel.; pop. 441; 94 km ESE of Minsk; 53°25'/28°49'.

Lipence, Cz.; pop. 9; 19 km S of Praha; 49°57'/14°23'.

Lipetitcha, *see* Bolshoi Lepeticha.

Lipica, Pol. (Lippehne); pop. 46; 157 km E of Gdansk; 54°20'/21°06'.

Lipica Dolna, *see* Lipitsa Dolna.

Lipica Gorna, *see* Lipitsa Gurna.

Lipiczany, GUM3, GUM4. This town was not found in BGN gazetteers under the given spelling.

Lipie, Pol.; pop. 9; 69 km ESE of Krakow; 49°44'/20°44'; GA, PHP3.

Lipik, Yug.; pop. 47; 101 km ESE of Zagreb; 45°25'/17°10'.

Lipina Nowa, Pol.; pop. 7; 75 km ESE of Lublin; 50°51'/23°24'.

Lipinki, Pol.; pop. 56; 107 km ESE of Krakow; 49°41'/21°18'.

Lipiny, Pol.; 56 km S of Czestochowa; 50°19'/18°55'; COH, HSL, PHP3.

Lipiny Dolne, Pol.; pop. 9; 75 km NNW of Przemysl; 50°25'/22°29'.

Lipiny Gorne, Pol.; pop. 55; 75 km NNW of Przemysl; 50°26'/22°29'.

Lipiny Nowe, Pol.; pop. 5; 45 km WSW of Lodz; 51°43'/18°50'.

Lipitsa Dolna, Ukr. (Lipica Dolna); pop. 66; 82 km ESE of Lvov; 49°20'/24°48'.

Lipitsa Gurna, Ukr. (Lipica Gorna); pop. 84; 82 km ESE of Lvov; 49°21'/24°47'.

Lipkan, *see* Lipkany.

Lipkany, Mold. (Linkani, Lipcani, Lipcani Targ, Lipcany, Lipkan); pop. 4,698; 208 km WNW of Kishinev; 48°16'/26°48'; AMG, COH, EDRD, EJ, GUM6, GYLA, HSL, HSL2, JGFF, LYV, PHR2, SF, YB.

Lipki, Pol.; pop. 59; 69 km NE of Warszawa; 52°34'/21°57'.

Lipkow, Pol.; pop. 2; 13 km W of Warszawa; 52°16'/20°49'.

Liplas, Pol.; pop. 8; 26 km ESE of Krakow; 49°57'/20°13'.

Lipljan, Yug.; pop. 3; 69 km NNW of Skopje; 42°32'/21°08'.

Lipna, *see* Lipno.

Lipne, *see* Lipno.

Lipniaki, Pol.; pop. 11; 82 km N of Lublin; 51°54'/22°36'.

Lipnic, *see* Lipnik (Bessarabia).

Lipnica, *see* Lipnica Murowana.

Lipnica (near Kielce), Pol.; pop. 17; 82 km E of Czestochowa; 50°45'/20°17'.

Lipnica Dolna, Pol.; pop. 31; 101 km WSW of Przemysl; 49°47'/21°23'.

Lipnica Mala, Pol.; pop. 3; 69 km S of Krakow; 49°32'/19°38'.

Lipnica Murowana, Pol. (Lipnica, Lipnitza); pop. 68; 50 km ESE of Krakow; 49°52'/20°32'; AMG, HSL, HSL2, SF.

Lipnica Wielka, Pol.; pop. 23; 69 km S of Krakow; 49°30'/19°37'.

Lipnicka, Cz.; pop. 1; 75 km ESE of Praha; 49°40'/15°23'.

Lipniczka, Pol.; pop. 7; 82 km ESE of Krakow; 49°43'/20°54'.

Lipnik, Pol.; pop. 502; 38 km SSE of Krakow; 49°48'/20°06'; HSL, JGFF, PHP3, PHP4.

Lipnik (Bessarabia), Mold. (Lipnic); pop. 15; 182 km NW of Kishinev; 48°24'/27°31'.

Lipnik (Lodz), Pol.; pop. 31; 56 km NNW of Czestochowa; 51°14'/18°53'.

Lipnik (near Brzozow), Pol.; pop. 9; 45 km WSW of Przemysl; 49°42'/22°15'.

Lipnik (near Rava Russkaya), Ukr.; pop. 72; 32 km NNE of Lvov; 50°07'/24°14'.

Lipniki, Pol.; pop. 24; HSL, HSL2. A number of towns share this name. It was not possible to determine from available information which one is being referenced.

Lipnik Maly, *see* Maly Lipnik.

Lipnik nad Becou, Cz. (Leipnik); pop. 154; 82 km NE of Brno; 49°32'/17°36'; EJ, HSL, HSL2, JGFF, PHP4.

Lipniscek, *see* Lipnishki.

Lipnishki, Byel. (Lipniscek, Lipnishky, Lipnishok, Lipnishuk, Lipniszki, Lipniszok); pop. 412; 133 km W of Minsk; 54°00'/25°37'; COH, GUM3, GUM4, HSL, LDL, LYV, PHP4, SF, YB.

Lipnishky, *see* Lipnishki.

Lipnishok, *see* Lipnishki.

Lipnishuk, *see* Lipnishki.

Lipniszki, *see* Lipnishki.

Lipniszok, *see* Lipnishki.

Lipnitza, *see* Lipnica Murowana.

Lipno, Pol. (Lepna, Lipna, Lipne); pop. 2,443; 126 km NNW of Lodz; 52°50'/19°12'; AMG, COH, EJ, GA, GUM4, GUM5, GUM5, GUM6, HSL, HSL2, JGFF, LDL, LYV, PHP1, PHP4, SF.

Lipno (Wolyn), Ukr.; pop. 24; 50 km NNW of Rovno;

51°01'/26°02'.

Lipon, *see* Leipalingis.

Lipot, Hung.; pop. 3; 126 km WNW of Budapest; 47°52'/17°28'.

Lipova, Cz. (Hanspach); pop. 4; 107 km N of Praha; 51°01'/14°21'; GUM4.

Lipovat, Rom.; 69 km S of Iasi; 46°34'/27°42'; JGFF.

Lipovec, *see* Lipovets.

Lipovets, Ukr. (Lipovec, Lipovetz, Lipowiec); pop. 3,605; 38 km E of Vinnitsa; 49°14'/29°03'; EDRD, EJ, HSL, HSL2, JGFF, SF.

Lipovetz, *see* Lipovets.

Lipovka, Ukr. (Firleev, Firlejow, Lipowka, Mateev); pop. 45; 56 km ESE of Lvov; 49°31'/24°34'; HSL, JGFF, SF.

Lipovka (near Ivano Frankovsk), Ukr. (Ladzkie Szlacheckie, Lyadske Shlyakhetske); pop. 133; 101 km WNW of Chernovtsy; 48°47'/24°46'.

Lipovtse, *see* Lipovtsy.

Lipovtsy, Ukr. (Lipovtse, Lipowce); pop. 58; 50 km ESE of Lvov; 49°42'/24°40'.

Lipowa, COH, GUM3. A number of towns share this name. It was not possible to determine from available information which one is being referenced.

Lipowce, *see* Lipovtsy.

Lipowczyce, Pol.; pop. 10; 56 km NE of Czestochowa; 51°09'/19°39'.

Lipowice, Pol. PHP2. This town was not found in BGN gazetteers under the given spelling.

Lipowiec, *see* Lipovets.

Lipowka, *see* Lipovka.

Lippehne, *see* Lipica.

Lipperode, Germ.; 120 km SW of Hannover; 51°42'/08°23'; LDS.

Lippo, Hung.; pop. 8; 126 km SW of Szeged; 45°52'/18°34'.

Lippspringe, *see* Bad Lippspringe.

Lippstadt, Germ.; pop. 126; 120 km SW of Hannover; 51°40'/08°21'; GED, GUM3, GUM4, GUM5, HSL, JGFF.

Lipsa, *see* Lipsha.

Lipsha, Ukr. (Lipca, Lipcse, Lipcsemezo, Lipecka Palana, Lipsa, Polien Lipsa); 182 km S of Lvov; 48°16'/23°23'; SM.

Lipsk, Pol. (Lipsk nad Biebrza); pop. 87; 75 km N of Bialystok; 53°44'/23°24'; HSL, HSL2, PHP4, POCEM, SF.

Lipskie Budy, Pol.; pop. 12; 75 km SSE of Warszawa; 51°39'/21°14'.

Lipsk nad Biebrza, *see* Lipsk.

Lipsko, Pol.; pop. 1,376; 62 km WSW of Lublin; 51°10'/21°39'; AMG, COH, EDRD, EGRS, GA, GUM3, GUM4, HSL, JGFF, LDS, LYV, SF, WS.

Lipsko (near Zamosc), Pol.; pop. 248; 75 km NNE of Przemysl; 50°21'/23°20'; COH, GA, GUM5, HSL, PHP2, SF.

Lipsko nad Wisla, Pol. AMG, GUM5. This town was not found in BGN gazetteers under the given spelling.

Liptod, Hung.; pop. 2; 126 km WSW of Szeged; 46°03'/18°31'.

Liptorosenberg, *see* Ruzomberok.

Liptoszentmiklos, *see* Liptovsky Svaty Mikulas.

Liptotepla, *see* Liptovska Tepla.

Liptoteplicska, *see* Liptovska Teplicka.

Liptovska Anna, (Szentanna); HSL. This pre-World War I community was not found in BGN gazetteers.

Liptovska Tepla, Cz. (Liptotepla); 139 km WNW of Kosice; 49°06'/19°25'; HSL.

Liptovska Teplicka, Cz. (Liptoteplicska); 88 km WNW of Kosice; 48°58'/20°06'; HSL.

Liptovsky Hradok, Cz.; pop. 56; 120 km WNW of Kosice; 49°02'/19°44'; GUM4.

Liptovsky Mikulas, *see* Liptovsky Svaty Mikulas.

Liptovsky Svaty Mikulas, Cz. (Liptoszentmiklos, Liptovsky Mikulas); pop. 1,259; 126 km WNW of Kosice; 49°05'/19°37'; EJ, GUM4, GUM5, HSL, PHP3.

Lisaveta, *see* Livezi.

Lisberg, Germ.; pop. 1; 62 km WNW of Nurnberg; 49°53'/10°24'; PHGB.

Lisdorf, Germ.; pop. 9; 163 km SW of Frankfurt am Main; 49°18'/06°46'.

Lisek, HSL. A number of towns share this name. It was not possible to determine from available information which one is being referenced.

Lisen, Cz. (Losch); 6 km E of Brno; 49°12'/16°42'; HSL.

Lisets, Ukr. (Lisitz, Lysets, Lysiec, Lysiec Stary); pop. 275; 120 km WNW of Chernovtsy; 48°52'/24°36'; EGRS, HSL, HSL2, LDL, PHP2, SF.

Lishki, *see* Liszki.

Lishnevka, Ukr. (Lishniovka, Lishnivka, Lisnovka, Liszniowka); pop. 3; 114 km NW of Rovno; 51°29'/25°24'; LDL, SF.

Lishniovka, *see* Lishnevka.

Lishnivka, *see* Lishnevka.

Lishnya, Ukr. (Lisznia); pop. 30; 94 km N of Lvov; 50°41'/24°11'; AMG, JGFF.

Lishnya (Wolyn), Ukr.; pop. 8; 62 km SW of Rovno; 50°26'/25°21'.

Lisia Gora, Pol.; 82 km E of Krakow; 50°05'/21°03'; PHP3.

Lisianka, *see* Lysyanka.

Lisiatycze, *see* Lisyatychi.

Lisichansk, Ukr.; 195 km ESE of Kharkov; 48°55'/38°26'; HSL.

Lisicovo, Ukr. (Lisitse, Rokamezo); 163 km S of Lvov; 48°29'/23°16'; AMG, SM.

Lisienica, Pol. PHP2. This town was not found in BGN gazetteers under the given spelling.

Lisinka, *see* Lysyanka.

Lisitse, *see* Lisicovo.

Lisitz, *see* Lisets.

Lisk, *see* Lesko.

Liska, LDL. A number of towns share this name. It was not possible to determine from available information which one is being referenced.

Liskava, *see* Liskiava.

Liskeva, *see* Liskovo.

Liski (near Rava Russkaya), Pol.; pop. 23; 114 km NE of Przemysl; 50°31'/23°58'.

Liski (Stanislawow), Ukr.; pop. 38; 75 km WNW of Chernovtsy; 48°39'/25°02'.

Liskiava, Lith. (Latzkawa, Liskava); pop. 146; 94 km S of Kaunas; 54°06'/24°03'; JGFF, SF.

Lisko, *see* Lesko.

Liskova, *see* Lyskovo.

Liskovitz, *see* Lyszkowice.

Liskovo, Byel. (Liskeva); pop. 146; 107 km N of Pinsk; 53°01'/26°33'; COH.

Liskowate, Pol.; pop. 67; 38 km S of Przemysl; 49°31'/22°37'.

Lisna, Rom.; pop. 30; 133 km NW of Iasi; 48°06'/26°28'.

Lisnice, Cz. (Sepekov); pop. 20; 82 km S of Praha; 49°25'/14°25'; HSL.

Lisnik Duzy, Pol.; pop. 22; 50 km SSW of Lublin; 50°53'/22°05'.

Lisnovka, *see* Lishnevka.

Lisnowo, Pol.; pop. 7; 101 km SSE of Gdansk; 53°28'/19°10'.

Lisnyaki, Ukr. (Lesnyaki); 94 km E of Kiyev; 50°16'/31°48'; GUM4.

Lisobiki, *see* Lysobyki.

Lisoviki, Pol. EDRD. This town was not found in BGN gazetteers under the given spelling.

Lisovitse, Ukr. (Lisowice); pop. 24; 88 km S of Lvov; 49°07'/23°53'; HSL.

Lisow, Pol.; 82 km NNE of Krakow; 50°41'/20°40'; LDS.

Lisowa, HSL. This pre-World War I community was not found in BGN gazetteers.

Lisowce, GUM3, GUM4, PHP2. This town was not found in BGN gazetteers under the given spelling.

Lisowice, *see* Lisovitse.

Lisowo, Pol.; pop. 6; 88 km SSW of Bialystok; 52°28'/22°38'.

Lispeszentadorjan, Hung. (Szentadorjan); pop. 4; 26 km WNW of Nagykanizsa; 46°32'/16°42'.

Lissa, Pol. PHP2. A number of towns share this name. It was

not possible to determine from available information which one is being referenced. *See also* Leszno.

Listany, Cz.; pop. 22; 94 km SW of Praha; 49°50'/13°11'.

Listvin, Ukr. (Listwin); pop. 8; 32 km SSW of Rovno; 50°24'/26°00'.

Listwin, *see* Listvin.

Lisyatychi, Ukr. (Lisiatycze); pop. 138; 62 km S of Lvov; 49°20'/23°57'; PHP2.

Liszki, Pol. (Lishki, Litzki); pop. 33; 13 km SW of Krakow; 50°02'/19°46'; PHP3, SF.

Liszki (near Siedlce), Pol.; pop. 28; 94 km SSW of Bialystok; 52°23'/22°30'.

Liszko, *see* Liszkopuszta.

Liszkopuszta, Hung. (Liszko); 56 km NNE of Budapest; 47°57'/19°29'; HSL.

Liszna, Pol.; pop. 24; 94 km NE of Lublin; 51°47'/23°34'.

Lisznia, *see* Lishnya.

Liszniowka, *see* Lishnevka.

Liszno, Pol.; pop. 51; 38 km ESE of Lublin; 51°07'/23°07'; GUM4.

Lita; Not a town, but the Yiddish word for Lithuania.

Lite, Cz.; 88 km WSW of Praha; 49°55'/13°16'; HSL. Not a town, but the Yiddish word for Lithuania.

Liten, Cz.; pop. 11; 32 km SW of Praha; 49°54'/14°09'; HSL.

Litene, Lat.; pop. 16; 150 km N of Daugavpils; 57°11'/27°02'; PHLE.

Liteni, Rom.; 88 km WNW of Iasi; 47°32'/26°32'; PHR1.

Litetiny, Cz.; pop. 1; 107 km NW of Brno; 50°01'/16°02'.

Litevisk, *see* Lutowiska.

Litiatyn, *see* Lityatin.

Litija, Yug.; pop. 1; 94 km WNW of Zagreb; 46°03'/14°50'.

Litin, Ukr. (Lityn); pop. 2,487; 32 km WNW of Vinnitsa; 49°20'/28°04'; EDRD, EJ, HSL, HSL2, JGFF, LDL, SF.

Lititov, *see* Lututow.

Litka, Hung.; pop. 4; 45 km NNE of Miskolc; 48°27'/21°04'; HSL.

Litke, Hung.; 88 km NNE of Budapest; 48°13'/19°36'; HSL.

Litohlavy, Cz.; pop. 1; 75 km SW of Praha; 49°46'/13°34'.

Litol, Cz.; pop. 13; 32 km NE of Praha; 50°11'/14°51'.

Litomerice, Cz. (Leitmeritz); pop. 462; 56 km NW of Praha; 50°32'/14°08'; EJ, GUM3, GUM4, GUM5, GUM6.

Litomysl, Cz.; pop. 182; 82 km NNW of Brno; 49°52'/16°19'; HSL.

Litovel, Cz. (Littau); pop. 36; 69 km NNE of Brno; 49°43'/17°05'.

Litovice, Cz.; pop. 3; 19 km WSW of Praha; 50°05'/14°14'.

Litovisk, *see* Lutowiska.

Litovizh, Ukr. (Litowiz); pop. 32; 88 km N of Lvov; 50°38'/24°11'.

Litowiz, *see* Litovizh.

Litschau, Aus.; pop. 23; 126 km WNW of Wien; 48°56'/15°03'; HSL, HSL2.

Litshenitz, *see* Luchinets.

Littau, *see* Litovel.

Littfeld, Germ.; 75 km ENE of Koln; 51°00'/07°59'; GED.

Litva, *see* Lietuva.

Litvinki, Byel. (Litwinki); pop. 2; 133 km W of Pinsk; 52°14'/24°11'.

Litvonovo, LDL. This pre-World War I community was not found in BGN gazetteers.

Litwa, *see* Lietuva.

Litwinki, *see* Litvinki.

Lityatin, Ukr. (Litiatyn); pop. 9; 94 km ESE of Lvov; 49°23'/25°03'.

Lityn, *see* Litin.

Litynia, *see* Litynya.

Litynya, Ukr. (Litynia); pop. 29; 50 km SSW of Lvov; 49°27'/23°40'.

Litzki, *see* Liszki.

Litzmannstadt, *see* Lodz.

Litzmanstadt, *see* Lodz.

Liubachev, *see* Lubaczow.

Liuban, *see* Lyuban.

Liubar, *see* Lyubar.

Liubavas, Lith. (Liubova, Lubova); pop. 90; 82 km SW of Kaunas; 54°22'/23°03'; JGFF, SF.

Liubitch, *see* Lyubech.

Liublin Colonie, Mold.; pop. 274; 133 km NNW of Kishinev; 48°07'/28°30'.

Liuboml, *see* Lyuboml.

Liubonitch, *see* Lyubonichi.

Liubova, *see* Liubavas.

Liudvinavas, Lith.; pop. 85; 56 km SSW of Kaunas; 54°29'/23°21'; HSL, LDL, SF, YL.

Liuta, *see* Vladimirovo.

Liutavariskes, Lith. (Landvarov, Landvorova, Landwarow); 19 km WSW of Vilnius; 54°39'/25°03'; HSL, JGFF, LDL, SF.

Liutchin, *see* Ludza.

Liutsyn, *see* Ludza.

Liuzii Homoru Lui, Rom.; pop. 31; This town was not found in BGN gazetteers under the given spelling.

Livada, Rom. (Livada Satu Mare, Sarkoz); pop. 192; 126 km NNW of Cluj; 47°52'/23°08'; PHR2.

Livada Noua, (Sarkozujlac); HSL. This pre-World War I community was not found in BGN gazetteers.

Livada Satu Mare, *see* Livada.

Livani, Lat. (Lavini, Lievenhof, Livenhof, Liwenhof); pop. 1,015; 62 km NW of Daugavpils; 56°22'/26°11'; AMG, JGFF, LDL, PHLE, SF.

Livberze, Lat.; pop. 1; 45 km SW of Riga; 56°43'/23°30'.

Livenhof, *see* Livani.

Livenii Vechi, Rom.; pop. 4; 107 km NNW of Iasi; 48°03'/27°05'.

Livezi, Mold. (Lisaveta); pop. 20; 150 km NNW of Kishinev; 48°15'/28°05'.

Livno, Yug.; pop. 7; 234 km SSE of Zagreb; 43°50'/17°01'.

Livny, USSR; pop. 302; 94 km NW of Voronezh; 52°25'/37°37'.

Livonia, *see* Liflandia. Not a town, but an area of Latvia.

Liw, Pol.; pop. 125; 62 km ENE of Warszawa; 52°23'/21°58'; HSL.

Liwcze, Pol.; pop. 46; 120 km NE of Przemysl; 50°30'/24°02'.

Liwenhof, *see* Livani.

Liwki Szlacheckie, Pol.; pop. 5; 107 km N of Lublin; 52°08'/22°48'.

Lizansk, *see* Lozansky.

Liza Stara, Pol.; pop. 2; 45 km SSW of Bialystok; 52°52'/22°48'.

Lizhensk, *see* Lezajsk.

Ljachowzy, *see* Belogorye.

Ljuban, *see* Lyuban.

Ljubescica, Yug.; pop. 5; 56 km NNE of Zagreb; 46°10'/16°23'.

Ljubischin; Ljubischin is a few kilometers northeast of Chervin (formerly Igumjen). It is not found in contemporary gazetteers.

Ljubljana, Yug. (Laibach, Lubiana); pop. 93; 120 km W of Zagreb; 46°02'/14°30'; AMG, CAHJP, EJ, GUM3, GUM4, PHGBW, PHY.

Ljubonitschi, *see* Lyubonichi.

Ljudwipol, *see* Sosnovoye.

Ljutomer, Yug.; pop. 12; 88 km N of Zagreb; 46°31'/16°12'.

Ljuzyn, *see* Ludza.

Lnare, Cz.; pop. 6; 88 km SSW of Praha; 49°28'/13°47'; JGFF.

Lniano, Pol.; pop. 11; 94 km S of Gdansk; 53°32'/18°13'.

Lobachevka, Ukr. (Lobaczowka); pop. 45; 94 km NE of Lvov; 50°25'/24°59'.

Lobaczowka, *see* Lobachevka.

Lobau, Germ.; 163 km E of Leipzig; 51°06'/14°40'; JGFF.

Lobodno, Pol.; pop. 9; 26 km NW of Czestochowa; 50°56'/19°00'.

Lobositz, *see* Lovosice.

Lobozew, Pol.; pop. 45; 50 km SSW of Przemysl; 49°25'/22°31'; HSL.

Lobsens, *see* Lobzenica.

Lobsenz, *see* Lobzenica.

Lobzenica, Pol. (Lobsens, Lobsenz); pop. 77; 94 km N of Poznan; 53°16'/17°16'; AMG, HSL, JGFF.

Lochocin, Pol.; pop. 23; 114 km NNW of Lodz; 52°45'/19°06'.

Lochotin, Cz.; pop. 3; 94 km W of Praha; 50°11'/13°10'.

Lochov, *see* Lochow.

Lochovice, Cz.; pop. 18; 45 km SW of Praha; 49°51'/13°59'.

Lochow, Pol. (Lochov); pop. 33; 56 km NE of Warszawa; 52°31'/21°43'; GA, GUM3, GUM5, HSL, HSL2, PHP1, PHP3, SF.

Lochtynowo, Pol.; pop. 1; 75 km W of Bialystok; 53°09'/22°01'.

Lochvitza, *see* Lokhvitza.

Lochwica, *see* Lokhvitsa.

Lochynsko, Pol.; pop. 14; 56 km SSE of Lodz; 51°18'/19°41'.

Lockenhaus, Aus.; pop. 27; 82 km NE of Graz; 47°24'/16°25'.

Locknitz, Germ.; 120 km NNE of Berlin; 53°27'/14°13'; JGFF.

Locs, Hung.; pop. 3; 114 km N of Nagykanizsa; 47°24'/16°49'.

Lode, Lat. (Lodes); pop. 1; 50 km NE of Riga; 57°16'/24°45'.

Lodenice, Cz.; 26 km SW of Praha; 49°59'/14°10'; HSL.

Lodes, *see* Lode.

Lodherov, Cz.; pop. 2; 101 km SSE of Praha; 49°13'/14°58'.

Lodishenka, *see* Ladizhnenka.

Lodmer, *see* Vladimir Volynskiy.

Lodomeria, *see* Vladimir Volynskiy.

Lodus, *see* Mladonov.

Lodygowice, Pol.; pop. 15; 69 km SW of Krakow; 49°43'/19°09'; JGFF.

Lodyna, Pol.; pop. 36; 45 km S of Przemysl; 49°29'/22°36'.

Lodyna Nova, Ukr. (Lodyna Nowa); pop. 22; 32 km NE of Lvov; 50°02'/24°23'.

Lodyna Nowa, *see* Lodyna Nova.

Lodz, Pol. (Litzmannstadt, Litzmanstadt, Lodzh); pop. 156,155; 114 km N of Czestochowa; 51°45'/19°28'; AMG, CAHJP, COH, EDRD, EJ, GA, GUM3, GUM4, GUM5, GUM6, GYLA, HSL, HSL2, ISH2, ISH3, JGFF, LDL, LDS, LYV, PHP1, PHP2, PHP3, PHP4, POCEM, SF, YB.

Lodzh, *see* Lodz.

Lodzinka Gorna, Pol.; pop. 15; 26 km SW of Przemysl; 49°41'/22°32'.

Loetzen, *see* Gizycko.

Loewenstadt, *see* Brzeziny.

Lof, Germ.; pop. 5; 88 km W of Frankfurt am Main; 50°14'/07°26'.

Loganeshty, Mold. (Loganesti); pop. 16; 19 km SW of Kishinev; 46°55'/28°33'.

Loganesti, *see* Loganeshty.

Logig, Rom.; pop. 5; 75 km ENE of Cluj; 46°53'/24°34'.

Logishin, *see* Telekhany.

Logiv, *see* Lagow.

Logoisk, *see* Logoysk.

Logosk, GUM5. This town was not found in BGN gazetteers under the given spelling.

Logoysk, Byel. (Lahoisk, Logoisk); pop. 1,022; 45 km NNE of Minsk; 54°12'/27°51'; GUM4, JGFF, SF.

Logvinoviche, Byel. (Lohwinowicze); pop. 4; 101 km NNE of Pinsk; 52°55'/26°46'.

Lohishin, *see* Telekhany.

Lohiszyn, *see* Telekhany.

Lohnberg, Germ.; pop. 10; 56 km NW of Frankfurt am Main; 50°31'/08°16'.

Lohne, Germ.; 75 km WSW of Hannover; 52°11'/08°40'; LDS.

Lohnsfeld, Germ.; pop. 5; 82 km SSW of Frankfurt am Main; 49°33'/07°51'; JGFF.

Lohr, Germ. (Lohr am Main); pop. 66; 62 km E of Frankfurt am Main; 49°59'/09°35'; GED, GUM5, PHGB.

Lohra, Germ.; 75 km N of Frankfurt am Main; 50°44'/08°38'; LDS.

Lohr am Main, *see* Lohr.

Lohrhaupten, Germ.; pop. 20; 56 km ENE of Frankfurt am Main; 50°08'/09°29'; JGFF.

Lohwinowicze, *see* Logvinoviche.

Loimersdorf, Aus.; pop. 1; 38 km E of Wien; 48°10'/16°50'.

Lojowa, HSL. This pre-World War I community was not found in BGN gazetteers.

Loka, Yug.; 94 km NW of Zagreb; 46°31'/15°31'; HSL.

Lokach, *see* Lokachi.

Lokachi, Ukr. (Lokach, Lokacze, Lokatchi, Lukach); pop. 1,265; 107 km NNE of Lvov; 50°44'/24°39'; CAHJP, COH, HSL, JGFF, LDL, SF.

Lokacze, *see* Lokachi.

Lokatchi, *see* Lokachi.

Loket, Cz.; pop. 55; 120 km W of Praha; 50°11'/12°45'.

Lokhvitsa, Ukr. (Lochwica); pop. 2,095; 101 km S of Konotop; 50°22'/33°16'; GUM4, JGFF.

Lokhvitza, (Lochvitza); SF. This town was not found in BGN gazetteers under the given spelling.

Lokietka, Pol.; pop. 7; 56 km ESE of Lodz; 51°27'/20°09'.

Loknica, *see* Loknitsa.

Loknik, *see* Luoke.

Loknitsa, Ukr. (Loknica); pop. 39; 139 km NNW of Rovno; 51°49'/25°50'.

Lokstedt, Germ.; pop. 34; 13 km NNW of Hamburg; 53°36'/09°59'.

Loktyshi, Byel. (Loktysze); pop. 5; 94 km NNE of Pinsk; 52°50'/26°43'.

Loktysze, *see* Loktyshi.

Lollar, Germ.; pop. 21; 69 km N of Frankfurt am Main; 50°39'/08°42'; LDS.

Lom, Bulg.; pop. 416; 133 km N of Sofija; 43°49'/23°14'; EJ, GUM4.

Lomaz, *see* Lomazy.

Lomazy, Pol. (Lomaz); pop. 829; 88 km NNE of Lublin; 51°54'/23°10'; AMG, COH, EDRD, GA, GUM3, GUM5, GYLA, HSL, HSL2, JGFF, LDL, LDS, POCEM, SF.

Lomianek, *see* Lomianki.

Lomianki, Pol. (Lomianek, Lomianki Gorne); pop. 130; 13 km NW of Warszawa; 52°21'/20°54'; GUM4, PHP4, SF. The *Black Book* also lists a town of Lomianki Gorne (pop. 130).

Lomianki Gorne, *see* Lomianki.

Lommersum, Germ.; 32 km SSW of Koln; 50°43'/06°48'; GED.

Lomna, Pol.; pop. 235; 26 km SW of Przemysl; 49°38'/22°31'; EGRS, HSL, PHP2. The *Black Book* notes a town named Lomna (pop. 235) in the interwar Polish province of Stanislawow that does not appear in contemporary gazetteers.

Lomna (Lwow), Pol.; pop. 42; 26 km SW of Przemysl; 49°41'/22°28'.

Lomnica, *see* Lomnica Zdroj.

Lomnica Zdroj, Pol. (Lomnica); 94 km SE of Krakow; 49°27'/20°45'; PHP3.

Lomnice, Cz. (Lomnitz); 32 km NW of Brno; 49°25'/16°25'; HSL, HSL2.

Lomnitz, *see* Lomnice.

Lompirt, Rom.; pop. 4; 88 km NW of Cluj; 47°19'/22°51'.

Lom u Mostu, Cz.; pop. 30; 82 km WNW of Praha; 50°36'/13°40'.

Lomza, Pol. (Lomzha); pop. 9,131; 69 km W of Bialystok; 53°11'/22°05'; AMG, CAHJP, EDRD, EJ, GA, GUM3, GUM4, GUM5, GUM6, GYLA, HSL, HSL2, ISH1, JGFF, LDL, LDS, LYV, PHP1, PHP4, POCEM, SF, YB.

Lomzha, *see* Lomza.

Lomzyca, Pol.; pop. 93; 75 km W of Bialystok; 53°11'/22°03'; HSL.

Lomzycza Wyzna, Pol. PHP4. This town was not found in BGN gazetteers under the given spelling.

Londorf, Germ.; pop. 67; 69 km N of Frankfurt am Main; 50°40'/08°52'.

Lone, Ukr. (Lonie); pop. 70; 50 km E of Lvov; 49°44'/24°40'.

Lonie, *see* Lone.

Loningen, Germ.; pop. 2; 139 km W of Hannover; 52°44'/07°46'; GED.

Lonnerstadt, Germ.; 38 km NW of Nurnberg; 49°42'/10°46'; PHGB.

Lonya, Hung. (Kislonya, Nagylonya); pop. 61; 114 km ENE of Miskolc; 48°19'/22°17'; HSL.

Loosdorf, Aus.; 69 km WSW of Wien; 48°12'/15°24'; JGFF.

Lopatchna, *see* Lopuszno.

Lopatin, Ukr. (Lopatyn); pop. 462; 69 km NE of Lvov; 50°13'/24°51'; AMG, EDRD, EGRS, EJ, GUM3, GUM4, HSL, JGFF, PHP2, SF, YB.

Lopatki, Pol.; 32 km SW of Lodz; 51°34'/19°07'; POCEM.

Lopatna, Mold.; pop. 8; 62 km N of Kishinev; 47°30'/29°02'.

Lopatnic, *see* Lopatnik.

Lopatnik, Mold. (Lopatnic); pop. 21; 182 km WNW of Kishinev; 48°09'/27°04'.

Lopatno, Pol.; pop. 4; 107 km SW of Lublin; 50°42'/21°16'.

Lopaty, HSL. A number of towns share this name. It was not possible to determine from available information which one is being referenced.

Lopatyche, Byel. (Lopatycze); pop. 1; 94 km N of Pinsk; 52°54'/26°25'.

Lopatycze, *see* Lopatyche.

Lopatyn, *see* Lopatin.

Lopayton, LDL. This pre-World War I community was not found in BGN gazetteers.

Lopenitsa Mala, *see* Malaya Lopenitsa.

Lopianka, Pol.; pop. 224; 56 km NE of Warszawa; 52°33'/21°44'; COH. The *Black Book* notes a town of Lopianka (pop. 23) in the interwar Polish province of Stanislawow that does not appear in interwar or contemporary gazetteers.

Lopienica Mala, *see* Malaya Lopenitsa.

Lopienka, Pol.; pop. 8; 69 km SSW of Przemysl; 49°16'/22°22'.

Lopiennik, Pol.; 32 km SW of Lublin; 51°04'/22°14'; JGFF.

Lopiennik Gorny, Pol. (Lopiennik Lacki); pop. 65; 38 km ESE of Lublin; 51°03'/23°02'.

Lopiennik Lacki, *see* Lopiennik Gorny.

Lopon, Pol. (Biadoliny Radlowskie); pop. 27; 62 km E of Krakow; 49°59'/20°47'; HSL.

Loposhna, *see* Lopuszno.

Lopsingen, Germ.; 75 km SSW of Nurnberg; 48°53'/10°32'; PHGB.

Lopuchowa, Pol.; pop. 12; 94 km WNW of Przemysl; 50°02'/21°33'.

Lopukhov, Ukr. (Brustura); 146 km W of Chernovtsy; 48°22'/23°58'; AMG.

Lopushnitsa, Ukr. (Lopusznica); pop. 22; 101 km SW of Lvov; 49°30'/22°44'.

Lopuszanka Lechniowa, Pol.; pop. 10; 62 km S of Przemysl; 49°17'/22°47'.

Lopuszka Mala, Pol.; pop. 36; 32 km WNW of Przemysl; 49°58'/22°26'.

Lopuszka Wielka, Pol.; pop. 43; 32 km WNW of Przemysl; 49°56'/22°24'.

Lopuszna, Pol.; pop. 47; 75 km SSE of Krakow; 49°29'/20°08'; GYLA.

Lopusznica, *see* Lopushnitsa.

Lopuszno, Pol. (Lopatchna, Loposhna); pop. 397; 82 km ENE of Czestochowa; 50°57'/20°15'; AMG, COH, GUM5, HSL, JGFF, PHP1, SF.

Lorau, Rom.; pop. 11; 75 km W of Cluj; 46°55'/22°39'.

Loretto, Aus.; 38 km SSE of Wien; 47°54'/16°31'; GUM4.

Lorev, Hung.; pop. 5; 50 km S of Budapest; 47°07'/18°54'.

Lorinci, Hung.; pop. 254; 50 km NE of Budapest; 47°44'/19°41'; HSL, LDS, PHH.

Lorrach, Germ.; pop. 151; 170 km SSW of Stuttgart; 47°37'/07°40'; LDS, PHGBW.

Lorsch, Germ.; pop. 70; 56 km S of Frankfurt am Main; 49°39'/08°34'; JGFF.

Losch, *see* Lisen.

Loschitz, *see* Lostice.

Losha, Byel. (Lasha); 56 km S of Minsk; 53°25'/27°24'; LDL, SF.

Loshits, *see* Losice.

Loshitz, *see* Losice.

Loshnev, Ukr. (Loszniow); pop. 55; 120 km N of Chernovtsy; 49°22'/25°44'.

Loshtchov, *see* Laszczow.

Losiacz, *see* Losyach.

Losice, Pol. (Loshits, Loshitz, Lositse); pop. 2,708; 107 km S of Bialystok; 52°13'/22°43'; AMG, CAHJP, COH, EDRD, EJ, FRG, GA, GUM3, GUM4, GUM5, HSL, JGFF, LDS, LYV, PHP1, SF, YB.

Losie, Pol.; pop. 65; 101 km ESE of Krakow; 49°35'/21°06'.

Losiniec, Pol.; pop. 65; A number of towns share this name. It was not possible to determine from available information which one is being referenced.

Lositse, *see* Losice.

Losk, Byel.; pop. 9; 88 km WNW of Minsk; 54°16'/26°26'.

Loslau, HSL. This pre-World War I community was not found in BGN gazetteers.

Losno, *see* Lozno.

Losonc, *see* Lucenec.

Losoncz, *see* Lucenec.

Lososina Dolna, Pol.; pop. 6; 62 km ESE of Krakow; 49°45'/20°37'.

Lososina Gorna, Pol.; pop. 8; 50 km SE of Krakow; 49°44'/20°24'.

Lososna, *see* Lososno.

Lososno, Byel. (Lososna); pop. 2; 234 km WNW of Pinsk; 53°40'/23°47'; GUM4, HSL.

Lostice, Cz. (Loschitz); pop. 55; 69 km N of Brno; 49°45'/16°56'; EJ, HSL, HSL2.

Lostowka, Pol.; pop. 5; 50 km SSE of Krakow; 49°41'/20°09'.

Losyach, Ukr. (Losiacz); pop. 104; 75 km N of Chernovtsy; 48°55'/26°05'; PHP2.

Loszniow, *see* Loshnev.

Lotatniki, HSL. This pre-World War I community was not found in BGN gazetteers.

Lothard, Hung.; pop. 7; 114 km ESE of Nagykanizsa; 46°00'/18°21'.

Lotovitch, *see* Latowicz.

Lotow, Pol.; pop. 19; 94 km ESE of Lublin; 50°44'/23°40'.

Lotwa Mala, Byel.; pop. 100; 94 km N of Pinsk; 52°55'/26°15'. This town was located on an interwar map of Poland but does not appear in contemporary gazetteers. Map coordinates are approximate.

Lotzen, *see* Gizycko.

Loucen, Cz.; pop. 2; 45 km NE of Praha; 50°17'/15°02'.

Loucim, Cz.; pop. 4; 126 km SW of Praha; 49°22'/13°07'.

Loucna nad Desnou, Cz. (Vizmberk); pop. 4; 107 km N of Brno; 50°04'/17°06'.

Lounin, Cz.; pop. 38 km SW of Praha; 49°54'/14°01'; HSL.

Lounovice, Cz.; pop. 11; 26 km ESE of Praha; 49°59'/14°46'.

Louny, Cz. (Laun); pop. 253; 56 km WNW of Praha; 50°21'/13°48'; EJ.

Lovasbereny, Hung.; pop. 53; 50 km SW of Budapest; 47°18'/18°33'; EJ, HSL, LDS, PHH.

Lovaszpatona, Hung.; pop. 10; 107 km WSW of Budapest; 47°26'/17°38'.

Lovich, *see* Lowicz.

Lovo, Hung.; pop. 10; 126 km N of Nagykanizsa; 47°30'/16°47'; AMG, COH, HSL.

Lovopetri, Hung.; pop. 9; 107 km ENE of Miskolc; 48°11'/22°12'; HSL.

Lovosice, Cz. (Lobositz); pop. 225; 50 km NW of Praha; 50°31'/14°04'; AMG, EJ, GUM3, HSL, HSL2.

Lovyn, *see* Lubny.

Lowce, Pol.; pop. 20; 19 km NNW of Przemysl; 49°56'/22°44'.

Lowcza, Pol.; pop. 83; 69 km NNE of Przemysl; 50°18'/23°19'; GUM4.

Lowcza (near Chelm), Pol.; pop. 25; 62 km ENE of Lublin; 51°20'/23°28'.

Lowczow, Pol.; pop. 31; 75 km E of Krakow; 49°55'/21°00'.

Lowczowek, Pol.; pop. 26; 75 km E of Krakow; 49°55'/20°59'.

Lowczyce, see Lowczyk.

Lowczyk, (Lowczyce); pop. 26; Described in the *Black Book* as being in the Stanislawow region of Poland, this town was not found in BGN gazetteers.

Lowen, see Lewin Brzeski.

Lowenberg, see Lwowek Slaski.

Lowicz, Pol. (Lovich, Loyvitch, Luyvich); pop. 4,517; 50 km NNE of Lodz; 52°07'/19°56'; AMG, CAHJP, COH, EDRD, EJ, GA, GUM3, GUM4, GUM5, GUM6, HSL, HSL2, ISH2, JGFF, LDS, LYV, PHP1, POCEM, SF, YB.

Lowinia, Pol.; pop. 18; 62 km N of Krakow; 50°36'/20°07'.

Lowisko, Pol.; pop. 25; 75 km NW of Przemysl; 50°18'/22°11'; AMG, HSL.

Loyev, Byel.; pop. 1,064; 62 km S of Gomel; 51°56'/30°48'; GUM4, HSL, JGFF, LDL, SF.

Loykeva, see Laukuva.

Loykova, see Laukuva.

Loyvitch, see Lowicz.

Loza, Cz.; 88 km WSW of Praha; 49°54'/13°17'; HSL.

Lozansky, Ukr. (Cserjes, Lizansk); 150 km S of Lvov; 48°34'/23°27'; SM. This town was located on a pre-World War I map, but does not appear in contemporary gazetteers.

Lozdzee, see Lazdijai.

Lozdzieje, see Lazdijai.

Lozin, Cz.; 45 km E of Kosice; 48°40'/21°50'; AMG, HSL.

Lozina, Ukr.; pop. 25; 19 km WNW of Lvov; 49°57'/23°49'.

Lozisht, see Ignatovka.

Lozna, Rom. (Lozna Mare, Nagylozna); pop. 60; 69 km NNW of Cluj; 47°19'/23°28'; HSL.

Lozna Mare, see Lozna.

Lozniany, see Liozno.

Lozno, Bulg. (Losno); 69 km SW of Sofija; 42°18'/22°39'; LDL.

Lozno Aleksandrovka, Ukr.; 176 km E of Kharkov; 49°50'/38°44'; GUM4.

Lozorno, Cz.; 26 km NNW of Bratislava; 48°20'/17°03'; HSL.

Lozova, see Lozovo.

Lozovaja, see Lozovaya.

Lozovaya, Ukr. (Lozovaja, Lozovia); pop. 1,453; 114 km NE of Dnepropetrovsk; 48°53'/36°23'; LDL, SF.

Lozovia, see Lozovaya.

Lozovo, Mold. (Lozova, Luhova?); pop. 34; 38 km WNW of Kishinev; 47°08'/28°23'; PHR1.

Lscin, Pol.; pop. 25; 69 km NNE of Krakow; 50°38'/20°24'.

Lubachov, see Lubaczow.

Lubachowy, Pol.; pop. 6; 62 km E of Czestochowa; 50°39'/19°58'.

Lubaczow, Pol. (Libatchov, Libechuyv, Liubachev, Lubachov, Lubatchov, Lubichuv); pop. 1,715; 50 km NNE of Przemysl; 50°10'/23°08'; COH, EDRD, EGRS, EJ, GA, GUM3, GUM4, GUM5, HSL, HSL2, LDL, LYV, PHP2, PHP3, PHP4, POCEM, SF.

Lubaczyn, see Lyubachin.

Luban, (Lauban);

Luban (near Jelenia Gora), Germ.; pop. 30; GYLA. This town was not found in BGN gazetteers under the given spelling.

Lubana, Lat. (Lubanas); pop. 41; 120 km N of Daugavpils; 56°54'/26°43'; PHLE.

Lubanas, see Lubana.

Lubanow, Pol.; pop. 31; 32 km SSE of Lodz; 51°30'/19°33'.

Lubartov, see Lubartow.

Lubartow, Pol. (Levertev, Levertov, Lubartov, Lyubartov); pop. 3,269; 32 km N of Lublin; 51°28'/22°38'; AMG, CAHJP, COH, EDRD, EJ, GA, GUM3, GUM4, GUM5, HSL, HSL2, JGFF, LDL, LDS, LYV, POCEM, SF, YB.

Lubasch, see Lubasz.

Lubashov, see Lyubeshov.

Lubashovka, see Lyubashevka.

Lubasz, Pol. (Lubasch); pop. 41; 56 km NW of Poznan; 52°52'/16°31'; JGFF, POCEM.

Lubaszewo, see Lyubashevo.

Lubaszowa, Pol.; pop. 6; 82 km ESE of Krakow; 49°52'/21°03'.

Lubatchov, see Lubaczow.

Lubatowa, Pol.; pop. 3; 75 km SW of Przemysl; 49°33'/21°46'; AMG.

Lubau, Germ.; pop. 27; 101 km ESE of Leipzig; 50°57'/13°37'.

Lubavich, see Lubavichi.

Lubavichi, USSR (Lubavich, Lubavitch, Lyubavichi, Lyubavitch); pop. 1,069; 75 km S of Smolensk; 54°11'/31°43'; COH, EDRD, EJ, GUM4, GUM6, HSL, LDL, SF.

Lubavitch, see Lubavichi.

Lubawa, Pol.; pop. 26; 114 km SE of Gdansk; 53°30'/19°45'; HSL, JGFF.

Lubbecke, Germ.; pop. 48; 75 km WSW of Hannover; 52°18'/08°37'.

Lubben, Germ.; pop. 26; 75 km SE of Berlin; 51°57'/13°54'.

Lubca, HSL, JGFF. This town was not found in BGN gazetteers under the given spelling.

Lubce, see Lyubcha.

Lubch, see Lyubcha.

Lubcz, see Lyubcha.

Lubcza, Pol.; pop. 57; 56 km NNE of Krakow; 50°28'/20°21'; AMG, YB. *See also* Lyubcha.

Lubec, see Lyubech.

Lubeck, Germ. (Luebeck); pop. 650; 62 km NE of Hamburg; 53°52'/10°42'; AMG, CAHJP, EJ, GUM3, GUM4, GUM5, HSL, JGFF, LDL.

Lubeczov, see Lyubashevo.

Lubela, Cz.; 133 km WNW of Kosice; 49°03'/19°29'; AMG.

Lubella, see Lyubelya.

Lubelski, Pol. AMG, COH. This town was not found in BGN gazetteers under the given spelling.

Luben, see Lubny.

Lubenec, Cz. (Libyne); pop. 40; 82 km W of Praha; 50°09'/13°19'.

Lubenets, Ukr. (Lubience); pop. 27; 120 km WNW of Chernovtsy; 48°41'/24°23'.

Lubenia, Pol.; pop. 55; 62 km W of Przemysl; 49°56'/21°57'.

Lubenichi, see Lyubonichi.

Lubenitchi, see Lyubonichi.

Luber, see Lyubar.

Lubezere, Lat.; pop. 2; 101 km WNW of Riga; 57°25'/22°38'.

Lubiana, see Ljubljana.

Lubiane, Pol.; pop. 6; 69 km WNW of Bialystok; 53°29'/22°14'.

Lubianki Nizsze, Pol.; pop. 29; Described in the *Black Book* as being in the Tarnopol region of Poland, this town was not found in BGN gazetteers.

Lubiaz, see Lyubyaz.

Lubica, Cz. (Leibitz); pop. 52; 75 km WNW of Kosice; 49°07'/20°27'.

Lubichuv, see Lubaczow.

Lubicz, see Osada Lubicz.

Lubiczko, Pol.; pop. 13; 62 km ENE of Krakow; 50°14'/20°47'.

Lubiczyn, Pol.; pop. 25; 56 km NNE of Lublin; 51°37'/23°05'.

Lubien, see Lubien Kujawski.

Lubien (Lwow), see Velikiy Lyuben.

Lubien (near Chelm), Pol.; pop. 49; 62 km NE of Lublin; 51°33'/23°19'.

Lubien (near Nowy Targ), Pol.; pop. 9; 50 km S of Krakow; 49°43'/19°59'.

Lubience, see Lubenets.

Lubienia, Pol.; pop. 10; 101 km WSW of Lublin; 51°04'/21°11'.

Lubienka, Pol.; pop. 4; 88 km NNE of Lublin; 51°54'/23°14'.

Lubienko, Pol.; pop. 4; 88 km WSW of Przemysl; 49°40'/21°35'.

Lubien Kujawski, Pol. (Lubien, Lubin); pop. 797; 75 km NNW of Lodz; 52°24'/19°11'; COH, HSL, HSL2, SF.

Lubien Wielki, see Velikiy Lyuben.

Lubieszow, see Lyubeshov.

Lubikowicze, see Lyubikovichi.

Lubin, *see* Lubien Kujawski.

Lubinka, Pol.; pop. 16; 75 km E of Krakow; 49°54'/20°54'.

Lubishov, *see* Lyubeshov.

Lubitow, *see* Lyubitov.

Lubitowska Wolka, *possibly* Lyubitov.

Lubla, Pol.; pop. 2; 82 km W of Przemysl; 49°49'/21°36'.

Lublica, Pol.; pop. 8; 88 km W of Przemysl; 49°48'/21°32'.

Lublin, Pol.; pop. 37,337; 157 km ESE of Warszawa; 51°15'/22°34'; AMG, CAHJP, COH, EDRD, EJ, GA, GUM3, GUM4, GUM5, GUM6, HSL, HSL2, ISH1, ISH2, ISH3, JGFF, LDL, LDS, LYV, PHP1, PHP2, PHP3, POCEM, SF, YB.

Lubliniec, Pol. (Lublinitz); pop. 240; 32 km SW of Czestochowa; 50°40'/18°41'; HSL, HSL2, LDL, LDS, PHP3, POCEM, SF.

Lubliniec Nowy, Pol.; pop. 66; 56 km N of Przemysl; 50°17'/23°06'.

Lubliniec Stary, Pol.; pop. 57; 56 km N of Przemysl; 50°17'/23°05'.

Lublinitz, *see* Lubliniec.

Lublo Krempach, *see* Kremna.

Lubnie, *see* Lubny.

Lubno, Pol.; pop. 61; 45 km W of Przemysl; 49°49'/22°10'; JGFF.

Lubno (Warszawa), Pol.; pop. 23; 50 km NE of Lodz; 52°03'/20°02'.

Lubno Opace, Pol.; pop. 4; 88 km WSW of Przemysl; 49°40'/21°35'.

Lubny, Ukr. (Lovyn, Luben, Lubnie); pop. 5,341; 139 km S of Konotop; 50°01'/33°00'; EJ, GUM4, HSL, JGFF, LDL, SF.

Lubochiny, *see* Lyubokhiny.

Lubocz, Pol.; pop. 10; 62 km E of Lodz; 51°37'/20°23'.

Lubola, Pol.; pop. 2; 56 km W of Lodz; 51°46'/18°43'.

Lubomierz, Pol.; 56 km SSE of Krakow; 49°37'/20°12'; PHP3.

Lubomirka, Pol.; pop. 22; 50 km WSW of Lublin; 51°14'/21°51'.

Luboml, *see* Lyuboml.

Luboml Wies, *see* Lyuboml Wies.

Lubonik, HSL. This pre-World War I community was not found in BGN gazetteers.

Luborzitza, *see* Luborzyca.

Luborzyca, Pol. (Luborzitza); 19 km NE of Krakow; 50°09'/20°07'; SF.

Lubostron, Pol.; 82 km NE of Poznan; 52°54'/17°53'; CAHJP.

Lubotice, Cz. (Kelemes); 38 km N of Kosice; 49°01'/21°17'; HSL, JGFF.

Lubotin, *see* Lyubotin.

Lubotyn, Pol. (Lubotyn Stary); pop. 60; 82 km WSW of Bialystok; 52°56'/21°56'.

Lubotyn Stary, *see* Lubotyn.

Lubova, *see* Liubavas.

Lubow, Ukr.; pop. 28; Described in the *Black Book* as being in Lwow province, it does not appear in interwar or contemporary gazetteers. A list of Galician towns indicates it was near Sokal.

Lubowicz Wielki, Pol.; pop. 6; 62 km SW of Bialystok; 52°45'/22°33'.

Lubraniec, Pol. (Lubranitz, Lyubranets); pop. 834; 101 km NW of Lodz; 52°33'/18°51'; AMG, CAHJP, COH, EJ, HSL, HSL2, JGFF, PHP4, SF, YB.

Lubranitz, *see* Lubraniec.

Lubrza, Pol.; 101 km WSW of Poznan; 52°18'/15°26'; GA.

Lubsza, *see* Lyubsha.

Lubtch, *see* Lyubcha.

Lubtheen, Germ.; 75 km ESE of Hamburg; 53°18'/11°05'; LDS.

Lubtse, *see* Lyubcha.

Lubycza Kam, Pol.; pop. 35; 75 km NNE of Przemysl; 50°20'/23°31'. This town was located on an interwar map of Poland but does not appear in contemporary gazetteers. Map coordinates are approximate.

Lubycza Kniazie, Pol.; pop. 11; 75 km NNE of Przemysl; 50°20'/23°31'.

Lubycza Krolewska, Pol.; pop. 649; 82 km NNE of Przemysl; 50°20'/23°32'; EDRD, EGRS, HSL, PHP2.

Luby Kurki, Pol.; pop. 5; 88 km W of Bialystok; 53°09'/21°52'.

Lubz, Germ.; pop. 3; 75 km S of Rostock; 53°27'/12°02'; JGFF, LDS.

Lubzina, Pol.; pop. 6; 94 km WNW of Przemysl; 50°04'/21°32'.

Luc, Yug.; 189 km WNW of Beograd; 45°47'/18°32'; HSL.

Luca, *see* Lucha.

Lucaceni, *see* Lukacheny.

Lucavatul de Jos, *see* Lukavets.

Lucavatul de Sus, *see* Lukavets.

Lucavita, *see* Lukovitsa.

Lucenec, Cz. (Losonc, Losoncz); pop. 2,742; 126 km SW of Kosice; 48°20'/19°40'; AMG, COH, EJ, GUM4, GUM5, HSL, HSL2, LDS.

Lucfalva, Hung.; pop. 2; 75 km NNE of Budapest; 48°02'/19°42'.

Lucha, Ukr. (Luca); pop. 27; 75 km W of Chernovtsy; 48°24'/24°54'.

Luchcze, *see* Lyukhcha.

Luchin, *see* Ludza.

Luchinchik, Ukr. (Lucincic); 75 km SSW of Vinnitsa; 48°43'/27°48'; PHR1.

Luchine, Ukr. (Luchini); pop. 3,097; 126 km N of Lvov; 50°58'/24°26'.

Luchinets, Ukr. (Litshenitz, Lucinet, Lutschinez); 75 km SSW of Vinnitsa; 48°43'/27°50'; GUM4, LDL, PHR1, SF.

Luchini, *see* Luchine.

Luchkovtsy, Ukr. (Lichkovtse, Liczkowce); pop. 44; 94 km N of Chernovtsy; 49°08'/26°10'; GUM4.

Luchow Dolny, Pol.; pop. 5; 62 km NNW of Przemysl; 50°19'/22°38'.

Luchow Gorny, Pol.; pop. 6; 62 km N of Przemysl; 50°20'/22°42'.

Lucincic, *see* Luchinchik.

Lucinet, *see* Luchinets.

Luck, *see* Lutsk.

Lucka, Germ.; 26 km S of Leipzig; 51°06'/12°21'; HSL.

Luckenwalde, Germ.; pop. 140; 50 km S of Berlin; 52°05'/13°10'; GUM3, GUM4, LDS.

Lucmierz, Pol.; 19 km NW of Lodz; 51°52'/19°22'; GUM3.

Luczanowice, Pol.; pop. 3; 13 km ENE of Krakow; 50°06'/20°07'.

Luczany, *see* Gizycko.

Luczyce, Pol.; pop. 26; 13 km ESE of Przemysl; 49°45'/22°50'; GUM3.

Ludad, Hung.; pop. 1; 101 km NE of Szeged; 46°49'/21°10'.

Ludany, Hung.; pop. 6; 75 km NNE of Budapest; 48°08'/19°32'.

Ludberg, *see* Ludbreg.

Ludbreg, Yug. (Ludberg); pop. 74; 69 km NNE of Zagreb; 46°15'/16°37'; PHY.

Ludcrinetz, GUM3. This town was not found in BGN gazetteers under the given spelling.

Ludendorf, Germ.; 38 km S of Koln; 50°40'/06°54'; ISH2.

Ludeniewicze, *see* Lyudenevichi.

Ludenscheid, Germ.; pop. 112; 56 km NE of Koln; 51°13'/07°37'; GUM3.

Ludin, Ukr. (Ludzin); pop. 29; 107 km N of Lvov; 50°48'/24°03'.

Ludinghausen, Germ.; pop. 25; 101 km N of Koln; 51°46'/07°28'; GUM5.

Ludinka, USSR; pop. 386; 208 km NE of Moskva; 56°45'/40°28'.

Ludinovo, USSR; pop. 189; This town was not found in BGN gazetteers under the given spelling.

Ludmilowka, Pol.; pop. 27; 50 km SW of Lublin; 50°56'/22°01'.

Ludomir, *see* Vladimir Volynskiy.

Ludosul de Muras, Rom. (Marosludas); HSL, LDL. This pre-World War I community was not found in BGN gazetteers.

Ludus, Rom.; pop. 523; 50 km ESE of Cluj; 46°29'/24°06'; EJ,

GUM4, HSL, PHR1.

Ludvipol, *see* Sosnovoye.

Ludvisin, *see* Ludwisin.

Ludwigsburg, Germ.; pop. 175; 19 km N of Stuttgart; 48°54'/09°11'; EJ, GED, GUM3, GUM6, HSL, HSL2, PHGBW.

Ludwigshafen, Germ.; pop. 1,400; 75 km S of Frankfurt am Main; 49°29'/08°27'; AMG, GED, GUM5, HSL, JGFF, PHGBW.

Ludwigshorst, Germ.; pop. 6; 75 km NNW of Berlin; 53°06'/13°01'.

Ludwigslust, Germ.; pop. 29; 101 km SSW of Rostock; 53°19'/11°30'; GUM3, GUM4, GUM5, HSL, LDS.

Ludwikow, Pol.; 50 km ESE of Lodz; 51°32'/20°04'; PHP1.

Ludwikowo, Pol.; 101 km N of Lodz; 52°35'/19°37'; GUM6.

Ludwin, Pol.; pop. 4; 32 km NE of Lublin; 51°21'/22°55'.

Ludwinow, HSL. A number of towns share this name. It was not possible to determine from available information which one is being referenced.

Ludwipol, *see* Sosnovoye.

Ludwisin, (Ludvisin, Ludwiszyn); EDRD, GUM3, GUM5, PHP4. This town was not found in BGN gazetteers under the given spelling.

Ludwiszyn, *see* Ludwisin.

Ludynia, Pol.; pop. 15; 69 km ENE of Czestochowa; 50°51'/20°07'.

Ludynie, *see* Lyudyn.

Ludza, Lat. (Liutchin, Liutsyn, Ljuzyn, Luchin, Ludzen, Lutsen, Lyutsin); pop. 1,630; 107 km NE of Daugavpils; 56°33'/27°43'; COH, EJ, HSL, JGFF, LDL, PHLE, SF.

Ludzen, *see* Ludza.

Ludzimierz, Pol.; pop. 6; 75 km S of Krakow; 49°28'/19°59'.

Ludzin, *see* Ludin.

Luebeck, *see* Lubeck.

Lueneburg, *see* Luneburg.

Lueta, Rom.; pop. 6; 150 km ESE of Cluj; 46°16'/25°29'.

Luga, USSR; pop. 379; 133 km S of Leningrad; 58°44'/29°52'; HSL, LDL.

Lugansk, *see* Voroshilovgrad.

Luga Wola, Pol. EDRD. This town was not found in BGN gazetteers under the given spelling.

Lugazi, Lat.; pop. 2; 146 km NE of Riga; 57°46'/25°57'.

Lugde, Germ.; pop. 16; 62 km SSW of Hannover; 51°57'/09°15'; HSL.

Lugi, Ukr. (Luhy?); 114 km WSW of Chernovtsy; 48°04'/24°26'; COH.

Lugi Golasze, Pol.; pop. 57; Described in the *Black Book* as being in the Lublin region of Poland, this town was not found in BGN gazetteers.

Luginy, Ukr. (Luhin); 157 km NE of Rovno; 51°05'/28°24'; GUM5, HSL, SF.

Lugi Wielkie, Pol.; pop. 4; 101 km NNW of Lublin; 52°07'/22°23'.

Lugoj, *see* Voroshilovgrad.

Lugos, *see* Voroshilovgrad.

Lugosch, *see* Voroshilovgrad.

Luh, Rom. (Leh Lunka, Lunca, Tisralunka); pop. 39; 88 km SW of Cluj; 46°31'/22°28'; AMG, SM.

Luhansk, *see* Voroshilovgrad.

Luhe, Germ.; 75 km ENE of Nurnberg; 49°35'/12°09'; PHGB.

Luhin, *see* Luginy.

Luhova, *possibly* Lozovo.

Luhy, *possibly* Lugi.

Luhyna, Cz. (Legenyemihly, Legina); 38 km ESE of Kosice; 48°29'/21°38'; HSL.

Lujeni, *see* Luzhany.

Lujerdiu, Rom.; pop. 12; 32 km N of Cluj; 46°59'/23°43'.

Luka, Cz.; pop. 50; 94 km W of Praha; 50°10'/13°10'; CAHJP, EJ.

Luka (Stanislawow), Ukr.; pop. 20; 101 km NW of Chernovtsy; 49°01'/24°59'; GUM3, PHP2.

Lukach, *see* Lokachi.

Lukacheny, Mold. (Lucaceni); pop. 4; 107 km WNW of Kishinev; 47°27'/27°36'.

Lukachevka, Ukr. EDRD. This town was not found in BGN gazetteers under the given spelling.

Lukaczin, Ukr. EDRD. This town was not found in BGN gazetteers under the given spelling.

Luka Mala, *see* Malaya Luka.

Lukanowice, Pol.; pop. 34; 69 km E of Krakow; 49°58'/20°53'.

Lukashevka, Ukr. (Lukaszewka); 75 km WSW of Uman; 48°39'/29°12'; HSL, JGFF, SF.

Lukaszewka, *see* Lukashevka.

Lukatz Kreuz, Pol.; pop. 20; 88 km WNW of Poznan; 52°53'/15°59'.

Lukavec, Cz.; pop. 33; 69 km SE of Praha; 49°34'/15°00'.

Lukavets, Ukr. (Lucavatul de Jos, Lucavatul de Sus); pop. 215; 45 km WSW of Chernovtsy; 48°13'/25°25'.

Lukavets Maydan, *see* Maydan.

Lukavitsa, *see* Lukovitsa.

Lukavytsa, Ukr. (Lukawica); pop. 24; 75 km SW of Lvov; 49°24'/23°14'.

Lukawica, *see* Lukavytsa.

Lukawiec (near Cieszanow), Pol.; pop. 61; 38 km NNE of Przemysl; 50°05'/23°07'; HSL.

Lukawiec (near Rzeszow), Pol.; pop. 20; 69 km NW of Przemysl; 50°16'/22°07'.

Luka Wielka, Ukr.; pop. 25; 88 km NNW of Chernovtsy; 49°05'/25°35'. This town was located on an interwar map of Poland but does not appear in contemporary gazetteers. Map coordinates are approximate.

Lukiszki, HSL, HSL2. This pre-World War I community was not found in BGN gazetteers.

Luki Wielkie, *see* Bolshiye Luki.

Lukjanowicze, *see* Lukyanovichi.

Luknif, *see* Luoke.

Luknik, *see* Luoke.

Lukoszyn, Pol.; pop. 4; 107 km N of Lodz; 52°41'/19°35'.

Lukov, Cz. (Lukov nad Toplou); pop. 51; 69 km NNW of Kosice; 49°18'/21°05'. Lukov is the more commonly used Yiddish spelling for Lukow, Poland.

Lukova, *see* Lukow.

Lukovitsa, Ukr. (Lucavita, Lukavitsa); pop. 26; 19 km ESE of Chernovtsy; 48°12'/26°05'; GUM4.

Lukov nad Toplou, *see* Lukov.

Lukovo, Byel. (Lukowo); pop. 35; 126 km WSW of Pinsk; 51°54'/24°14'.

Lukow, Pol. (Likeva, Likeve, Likova, Lukova); pop. 6,145; 82 km NNW of Lublin; 51°55'/22°23'; AMG, CAHJP, COH, EDRD, EJ, GA, GUM3, GUM4, GUM5, HSL, HSL2, JGFF, LDS, LYV, PHP1, PHP4, POCEM, SF, YB.

Lukowa, Pol.; pop. 174; 69 km N of Przemysl; 50°22'/22°57'; HSL, SF.

Lukowe, Pol.; pop. 26; 62 km SW of Przemysl; 49°25'/22°14'.

Lukowek, Pol.; pop. 67; 69 km ENE of Lublin; 51°18'/23°33'.

Lukowica, Pol.; pop. 79; 62 km SE of Krakow; 49°37'/20°29'.

Lukowo, Pol.; 26 km NNW of Poznan; 52°38'/16°53'; GUM3. *See also* Lukovo.

Lukoy, USSR; HSL2. This pre-World War I community was not found in BGN gazetteers.

Lukshi, *see* Luksiai.

Luksiai, Lith. (Lukshi, Luszki); pop. 42; 6 km W of Siauliai; 55°57'/23°13'; EDRD, YL.

Lukvitsa, Ukr. (Prislup, Przyslup); pop. 36; 133 km WNW of Chernovtsy; 48°44'/24°15'; COH, HSL.

Luky, Ukr.; pop. 29; 50 km SW of Lvov; 49°37'/23°23'; HSL, SF.

Lukyanovichi, Byel. (Lukjanowicze); pop. 7; 114 km NNW of Minsk; 54°51'/27°01'.

Lulsfeld, Germ.; pop. 16; 69 km WNW of Nurnberg;

Lvov, Ukraine (formerly Lwow, Poland, previously Lemberg, Austro-Hungary): Bagel peddlers in front of a fountain.

49°52'/10°20'; GUM5, PHGB.

Luna, Rom. (Negresti Satu Mare); pop. 538; 126 km N of Cluj; 47°52'/23°26'; AMG, HSL.

Luna de Jos, Rom. (Lunga Cernei de Jos); pop. 14; 26 km NNE of Cluj; 46°57'/23°45'.

Luna de Sus, Rom. (Szaszlona); pop. 12; 13 km SW of Cluj; 46°44'/23°26'; HSL.

Lunavolia, *see* Lunna.

Lunca, *see* Luh.

Lunca Bradului, Rom. (Palotailva); pop. 175; 120 km ENE of Cluj; 46°57'/25°06'; PHR2.

Lunca de Jos, Rom. (Gyimeskozeplak, Gyimeskozeplock); pop. 286; 69 km SW of Cluj; 46°22'/22°55'; HSL, PHR2.

Lunchich, *see* Leczyca.

Luncsoara, Rom. (Elesdlok); pop. 33; 94 km SW of Cluj; 46°19'/22°37'.

Lundenburg, *see* Breclav.

Luneburg, Germ. (Lueneburg); pop. 147; 45 km SE of Hamburg; 53°15'/10°24'; EJ, GED, GUM4, ISH2.

Luneburger Heide, GUM4. This town was not found in BGN gazetteers under the given spelling.

Lunen, Germ.; pop. 140; 88 km NNE of Koln; 51°37'/07°31'; GED, GUM5.

Lunga Cernei de Jos, *see* Luna de Jos.

Luniewo Wielkie, Pol.; pop. 7; 62 km SW of Bialystok; 52°45'/22°28'.

Lunin, Byel.; pop. 51; 45 km NE of Pinsk; 52°18'/26°38'.

Luninets, Byel. (Luniniec, Luninits, Luninitz, Luninyets); pop. 2,045; 50 km NE of Pinsk; 52°15'/26°48'; AMG, COH, EDRD, FRG, GUM3, GUM4, GUM5, GUM6, HSL, JGFF, LDL, SF, YB.

Luniniec, *see* Luninets.

Luninits, *see* Luninets.

Luninitz, *see* Luninets.

Luninyets, *see* Luninets.

Lunna, Byel. (Lunavolia, Lunna Wola, Lunno, Volia); pop. 1,373; 195 km NW of Pinsk; 53°27'/24°16'; JGFF, SF, WS.

Lunna Wola, *see* Lunna.

Lunno, *see* Lunna.

Luntzitz, *see* Leczyca.

Luoka, *see* Luoke.

Luoke, Lith. (Lavkov, Loknik, Luknif, Luknik, Luoka, Luykeve); pop. 513; 50 km WSW of Siauliai; 55°53'/22°31'; GUM3, GUM4, GUM5, HSL, HSL2, JGFF, SF, YL.

Lupeni, Rom. (Farkaslaka); pop. 20; 163 km S of Cluj; 45°21'/23°14'; HSL, HSL2, PHR1.

Lupianka Stara, Pol.; pop. 14; 19 km SW of Bialystok; 53°03'/22°52'.

Lupisuki, Ukr.; pop. 29; 94 km NNW of Rovno; 51°24'/26°02'.

Lupkow, Pol.; pop. 43; 82 km SSW of Przemysl; 49°15'/22°04'; JGFF.

Lupolovo, Byel.; 150 km S of Vitebsk; 53°53'/30°20'; HSL.

Lusca, Rom.; pop. 6; 88 km NE of Cluj; 47°17'/24°25'; EJ.

Luschan, *see* Luzhany.

Lusci Palanka, Yug.; pop. 6; 120 km SSE of Zagreb; 44°45'/16°25'.

Lushki, *see* Luzhki.

Lusino, *see* Lyusino.

Lusk, *see* Lask.

Luslawice, Pol.; pop. 38; 75 km ESE of Krakow; 49°53'/20°51'.

Lustadt, *see* Oberlustadt.

Lustenau, Aus.; pop. 1; 133 km W of Innsbruck; 47°26'/09°39'.

Lustenice, Cz.; pop. 6; 45 km NE of Praha; 50°20'/14°56'.

Luszawa, Pol. (Luszawa Karczma); pop. 12; 45 km N of Lublin; 51°35'/22°34'.

Luszawa Karczma, *see* Luszawa.

Luszki, *see* Luksiai.

Luszniewo, *see* Lyushnevo.

Luszowice, *see* Luszowice Gorne.

Luszowice Gorne, Pol. (Luszowice); pop. 68; 82 km ENE of Krakow; 50°08'/21°06'.

Luta, Pol.; 69 km NE of Lublin; 51°28'/23°29'; GA, GUM5, GUM6.

Lutamiersk, *see* Lutomiersk.

Lutcza, Pol.; pop. 92; 62 km W of Przemysl; 49°49'/21°54'; PHP3.

Lutherstadt Wittenberg, Germ. (Wittenberg); pop. 70; 69 km N of Leipzig; 51°52'/12°39'; GUM3, GUM4, GUM5, GUM6, ISH1, PHP4.

Luthorst, Germ.; pop. 7; 62 km S of Hannover; 51°51'/09°43'.

Lutita, Rom. (Agyagfalva); pop. 6; 133 km ESE of Cluj; 46°15'/25°11'.

Lutki, Byel.; pop. 12; 101 km E of Pinsk; 52°02'/27°36'.

Lutkowka, Pol.; pop. 5; 50 km SSW of Warszawa; 51°55'/20°37'.

Lutomiersk, Pol. (Lutamiersk); pop. 775; 19 km WSW of Lodz; 51°45'/19°13'; CAHJP, COH, GA, GUM4, GUM5, HSL, HSL2, LDL, LDS, PHP1, SF.

Lutoryz, Pol.; pop. 14; 69 km WNW of Przemysl; 49°58'/21°55'.

Lutoviska, *see* Lutowiska.

Lutowiska, Pol. (Litevisk, Litovisk, Lutoviska); pop. 1,220; 69 km S of Przemysl; 49°15'/22°42'; COH, EGRS, GYLA, HSL, HSL2, JGFF, LDL, LYV, PHP2, POCEM, SF, YB.

Lutowo, Pol.; pop. 3; 120 km N of Poznan; 53°27'/17°26'.

Lutrini, Lat.; pop. 11; 107 km WSW of Riga; 56°44'/22°24'.

Lutschinez, *see* Luchinets.

Lutsen, *see* Ludza.

Lutsk, Ukr. (Luck, Lutzk, Luytsk, Luytsk Vilka, Luzk); pop. 14,860; 62 km W of Rovno; 50°45'/25°20'; AMG, COH, EJ, GA, GUM3, GUM4, GUM5, GUM6, GYLA, HSL, JGFF, LYV, PHP2, PHP3, PHP4, SF, YB.

Luttange, HSL. This pre-World War I community was not found in BGN gazetteers.

Luttich, HSL. This pre-World War I community was not found in BGN gazetteers.

Lututov, *see* Lututow.

Lututow, Pol. (Lititov, Lututov); pop. 1,466; 82 km NW of Czestochowa; 51°22'/18°26'; AMG, CAHJP, COH, EDRD, GA, GUM3, GUM4, GUM5, HSL, HSL2, JGFF, LDL, LYV, PHP1, POCEM, SF.

Lutynsk, *see* Lyutynsk.

Lutzelsachsen, Germ.; pop. 21; 69 km S of Frankfurt am Main; 49°32'/08°40'; PHGBW.

Lutzk, *see* Lutsk.

Luxheim, Germ.; 32 km SW of Koln; 50°46'/06°38'; GED.

Luykeve, *see* Luoke.

Luytsk, *see* Lutsk.

Luytsk Vilka, *see* Lutsk.

Luyvich, *see* Lowicz.

Luzan, *see* Luzhany.

Luzany, Cz.; 82 km NE of Bratislava; 48°31'/18°01'; HSL.

Luze, Cz.; pop. 59; 94 km NW of Brno; 49°54'/16°02'; HSL, HSL2.

Luzek Dolny, *see* Luzhek Dolny.

Luzhanka, Ukr. (Catzbach); pop. 7; 126 km SW of Odessa; 46°03'/29°12'.

Luzhany, Ukr. (Lujeni, Luschan, Luzan); pop. 381; 13 km WNW of Chernovtsy; 48°22'/25°47'; GUM4, PHR2.

Luzhek Dolny, Ukr. (Luzek Dolny); pop. 40; 62 km SW of Lvov; 49°27'/23°23'.

Luzhki, Byel. (Lushki, Luzki, Luzkye); pop. 442; 146 km W of Vitebsk; 55°21'/27°52'; AMG, COH, HSL, LYV, SF.

Luzk, *see* Lutsk.

Luzki, *see* Luzhki.

Luzkye, *see* Luzhki.

Luzna, Pol.; pop. 38; 94 km ESE of Krakow; 49°43'/21°03'.

Lviv, *see* Lvov.

Lvov, Ukr. (Lemberg, Leopol, Lviv, Lwow); pop. 76,854; 182 km SW of Rovno; 49°50'/24°00'; AMG, CAHJP, COH, EDRD, EGRS, EJ, FRG, GA, GUM3, GUM4, GUM5, GUM6, HSL, HSL2, ISH1, ISH2, ISH3, JGFF, LDL, LDS, LYV, PHP1, PHP2, PHP3, PHP4, SF, YB.

Lvovo, Ukr. (Kolonie Lvovo, Lwowo); pop. 2,134; 189 km ENE of Odessa; 46°47'/33°10'; JGFF, LDL, SF.

Lwow, *see* Lvov.

Lwowek, Pol. (Ncustadt bei Pinne, Neustadt bei Pinne); pop. 72; 50 km W of Poznan; 52°27'/16°11'; CAHJP, HSL, JGFF.

Lwowek Slaski, Pol. (Lowenberg); pop. 20; 101 km W of Wroclaw; 51°07'/15°35'; LDS.

Lwowo, *see* Lvovo.

Lyadi, *see* Lyady.

Lyadovichi, Byel. (Ladowicze); pop. 75; 56 km WNW of Pinsk; 52°19'/25°24'.

Lyadske Shlyakhetske, *see* Lipovka (near Ivano Frankovsk).

Lyady, Byel. (Liady, Lyadi); pop. 2,020; 38 km ESE of Minsk; 53°47'/28°05'; HSL, JGFF, SF.

Lyakhoviche, *see* Lyakhovichi.

Lyakhoviche (Polesie), Byel.; pop. 28; 38 km W of Pinsk; 52°11'/25°36'.

Lyakhovichi, Byel. (Lachovici, Lachowicze, Lechovich, Lechovicz, Lechovith, Liachovitch, Lyakhoviche); pop. 1,656; 107 km N of Pinsk; 53°02'/26°16'; AMG, COH, EDRD, EJ, GUM3, GUM4, GYLA, HSL, JGFF, LDL, SF, YB.

Lyakhovitse, Ukr. (Lachowice, Lakhoviche, Lekhevich, Lekhovich); pop. 38; 114 km WNW of Chernovtsy; 48°48'/24°31'; EDRD, HSL, LYV, PHP3.

Lyakhovitse Podruzhne, *see* Podorozhnoye.

Lyakhovitse Zazhechke, Ukr. (Lachowice Zarzeczne); pop. 25; 75 km SSE of Lvov; 49°13'/24°12'.

Lyakhovtsy, *see* Belogorye.

Lyashki Dolne, Ukr. (Laszki Dolne); pop. 36; 50 km SSE of Lvov; 49°29'/24°12'.

Lyashki Gurne, *see* Dolishnev.

Lyaskoviche Velke, *see* Leskovichi.

Lyaskovichi, Byel. (Laskowicze); pop. 10; 38 km W of Pinsk; 52°10'/25°34'.

Lyck, *see* Elk.

Lyduvenai, Lith. (Liduvian, Lidvinov); 56 km S of Siauliai; 55°30'/23°06'; JGFF, YL.

Lyebed, Ukr. EJ. Described in EJ as a suburb of Kiyev, this town does not appear in contemporary gazetteers.

Lygumai, Lith. (Ligem, Ligum, Ligumai, Lymgumai); pop. 240; 19 km NE of Siauliai; 56°00'/23°39'; GUM5, HSL, JGFF, LDL, SF, YL.

Lykoszyn, Pol.; pop. 4; 114 km NNE of Przemysl; 50°34'/23°50'.

Lymgumai, *see* Lygumai.

Lyngmiany, *see* Linkmenys.

Lyniew, Pol. (Lyniow); pop. 4; 75 km NNE of Lublin; 51°44'/23°15'.

Lyniow, *see* Lyniew.

Lynki, Byel. YB. This town could not be found in contemporary gazetteers. It is listed in the yizkor book for Stolin.

Lyntupy, Byel. (Lentupis); 157 km NW of Minsk; 55°03'/26°19'; COH, GUM3, HSL, LDL, SF, YB.

Lyptosztmiklo, LDL. This pre-World War I community was not found in BGN gazetteers.

Lysa, Cz.; pop. 33; 56 km SSE of Praha; 49°38'/14°40'.

Lysa Gora, Pol.; 88 km WSW of Przemysl; 49°35'/21°35'; HSL.

Lysaja Gora, Ukr. EDRD. This town was not found in BGN gazetteers under the given spelling.

Lysakow, Pol.; 56 km SSW of Lublin; 50°46'/22°11'; GA, HSL.

Lysakowek, Pol.; pop. 12; 107 km NE of Krakow; 50°23'/21°19'.

Lysanka, *see* Lysyanka.

Lyse, Pol.; pop. 46; 107 km W of Bialystok; 53°22'/21°34'.

Lysets, *see* Lisets.

Lysica, Cz.; 163 km ENE of Brno; 49°15'/18°55'; COH, HSL.

Lysiec, *see* Lisets.

Lysiec Stary, *see* Lisets.

Lyskornia, Pol.; pop. 6; 75 km WNW of Czestochowa; 51°16'/18°24'.

Lyskovo, Byel. (Liskova, Lyskow); pop. 450; 133 km WNW of Pinsk; 52°51'/24°37'; GUM4, HSL, JGFF, SF, YB.

Lyskow, *see* Lyskovo.

Lyskuv (near Zurawno), Ukr.; pop. 37; 82 km SSE of Lvov; 49°11'/24°12'.

Lysobyki, Pol. (Lisobiki); pop. 438; 50 km NW of Lublin; 51°37'/22°17'; AMG, GUM5, HSL, SF.

Lysow, Pol.; pop. 34; 94 km S of Bialystok; 52°18'/22°42'.

Lysowiec, Pol.; pop. 21; Described in the *Black Book* as being in the Kielce region of Poland, this town was not found in BGN gazetteers.

Lysyanka, Ukr. (Lisianka, Lisinka, Lysanka); 69 km NNE of Uman; 49°15'/30°50'; EJ, JGFF, LDL, SF.

Lyszkowice, Pol. (Liskovitz, Lyszkowicze?); pop. 545; 38 km NE of Lodz; 51°59'/19°55'; GA, HSL, HSL2, PHP1, SF, YB.

Lyszkowicze, *possibly* Lyszkowice.

Lyubachin, Byel. (Lubaczyn); pop. 12; 69 km ENE of Pinsk; 52°16'/27°04'; JGFF.

Lyuban, Byel. (Liuban, Ljuban); pop. 1,032; 126 km SSE of Minsk; 52°48'/28°00'; JGFF, LDL, SF, YB.

Lyuban (near Volozhin), Byel.; 88 km NW of Minsk; 54°35'/26°52'; GUM4.

Lyubar, Ukr. (Lieber Tov, Liubar, Luber); pop. 4,146; 94 km NW of Vinnitsa; 49°55'/27°45'; GYLA, SF.

Lyubartov, *see* Lubartow.

Lyubashevka, Ukr. (Lubashovka); 107 km S of Uman; 47°51'/30°15'; LDL, SF.

Lyubashevo, Byel. (Lubaszewo, Lubeczov); 82 km N of Pinsk; 52°47'/26°26'; EDRD, GUM4.

Lyubavichi, *see* Lubavichi.

Lyubavitch, *see* Lubavichi.

Lyubch, *see* Lyubcha.

Lyubcha, Byel. (Lubce, Lubch, Lubcz, Lubcza, Lubtch, Lubtse, Lyubch); pop. 496; 101 km WSW of Minsk; 53°45'/26°04'; EDRD, GUM3, GUM4, GUM5, JGFF, LDL, SF.

Lyubech, Ukr. (Liubitch, Lubec); 146 km N of Kiyev; 51°42'/30°39'; SF.

Lyubelya, Ukr. (Lubella); pop. 112; 45 km N of Lvov; 50°12'/23°57'; PHP2.

Lyubeshov, Ukr. (Lubashov, Lubieszow, Lubishov); pop. 17; 139 km NNW of Rovno; 51°46'/25°31'; GUM3, GUM4, GUM5, GUM6, LDL, SF.

Lyubichev, GUM4. This town was not found in BGN gazetteers under the given spelling.

Lyubikovichi, Ukr. (Lubikowicze); pop. 33; 101 km N of Rovno; 51°29'/26°37'.

Lyubitov, Ukr. (Lubitow, Lubitowska Wolka?, Lyubitovka); pop. 26; 114 km WNW of Rovno; 51°09'/24°50'.

Lyubitovka, *see* Lyubitov.

Lyubokhiny, Ukr. (Lubochiny); pop. 17; 170 km WNW of Rovno; 51°28'/24°13'.

Lyuboml, Ukr. (Libevne, Libovne, Liubomil, Luboml); pop. 3,141; 157 km N of Lvov; 51°14'/24°02'; AMG, COH, EDRD, EJ, GUM3, GUM4, GUM5, HSL, JGFF, LDL, SF, YB.

Lyuboml Wies, (Luboml Wies); pop. 255; Described in the *Black Book* as being in the Wolyn region of Poland, this town was not found in BGN gazetteers.

Lyubonichi, Byel. (Liubonitch, Ljubonitschi, Lubenichi, Lubenitchi); 126 km ESE of Minsk; 53°17'/29°14'; SF, YB.

Lyubotin, Ukr. (Lubotin); pop. 42; 19 km WSW of Kharkov; 49°57'/35°58'; HSL.

Lyubranets, *see* Lubraniec.

Lyubsha, Ukr. (Lubsza); pop. 57; 50 km SE of Lvov; 49°30'/24°27'.

Lyubyaz, Ukr. (Lubiaz); 146 km NNW of Rovno; 51°50'/25°28'; GUM4.

Lyudenevichi, Byel. (Ludeniewicze); 107 km ENE of Pinsk; 52°13'/27°42'; JGFF.

Lyudvipol, *see* Sosnovoye.

Lyudyn, Ukr. (Ludynie, Lyudyne); pop. 27; 126 km N of Rovno; 51°41'/26°34'.

Lyudyne, *see* Lyudyn.

Lyukhcha, Ukr. (Luchcze, Lyukhche); pop. 40; 94 km N of Rovno; 51°23'/26°38'.

Lyukhche, *see* Lyukhcha.

Lyushnevo, Byel. (Luszniewo); pop. 21; 133 km NNW of Pinsk; 53°14'/25°42'.

Lyusino, Byel. (Lusino); pop. 5; 62 km NNE of Pinsk; 52°38'/26°31'.

Lyutsin, *see* Ludza.

Lyutynsk, Ukr. (Lutynsk); pop. 36; 120 km N of Rovno; 51°39'/26°37'.

Lzhansk, *see* Lezajsk.

Lzin, Cz.; pop. 4; 101 km SSE of Praha; 49°14'/14°48'.

Macau, Rom.; pop. 5; 26 km WNW of Cluj; 46°50'/23°18'.

Macedonia; Not a town, but a region at the southern end of the Balkan Peninsula divided among Bulgaria, Greece and Yugoslavia.

Machev, *see* Maciejow.

Macheyuv, *see* Maciejow.

Machnin, Cz.; pop. 4; 88 km NNE of Praha; 50°48'/14°59'.

Machnow, Pol.; pop. 72; 88 km NNE of Przemysl; 50°21'/23°37'.

Machnowek, Pol.; pop. 18; 107 km NE of Przemysl; 50°26'/23°55'.

Machnowka, *see* Makhnovka.

Machory, Pol.; pop. 9; 26 km NE of Krakow; 50°11'/20°12'.

Machowa, Pol.; pop. 55; 94 km E of Krakow; 50°01'/21°13'.

Machyov, *see* Maciejow.

Maciejow, Pol. (Machev, Macheyuv, Machyov, Maczev, Matiejow, Matseyev, Motchiov); pop. 2,206; 62 km WNW of Czestochowa; 51°02'/18°17'; HSL2. *See also* Matsiov.

Maciejowa, Pol. (Labowa, Matsyeyuv); pop. 221; 94 km ESE of Krakow; 49°32'/20°52'; EGRS, FRG, GUM5, HSL, PHP3.

Maciejowice, Pol. (Motchevitz); pop. 799; 75 km SE of Warszawa; 51°42'/21°33'; AMG, GUM3, HSL, PHP4, SF.

Maciejow Stary, Pol.; pop. 16; 45 km SSE of Lublin; 50°54'/22°44'.

Macin, Rom.; pop. 182 km NE of Bucuresti; 45°15'/28°09'; GUM4.

Mackenzell, Germ.; 101 km NE of Frankfurt am Main; 50°40'/09°48'; JGFF.

Mackowice, Pol.; pop. 37; 13 km NW of Przemysl; 49°51'/22°42'.

Maconka, Hung.; pop. 7; 69 km WSW of Miskolc; 47°59'/19°50'.

Macs, Hung.; 82 km SE of Miskolc; 47°35'/21°30'; HSL.

Macsola, HSL. This pre-World War I community was not found in BGN gazetteers.

Maczev, *see* Maciejow.

Maczevice, Pol. EDRD. This town was not found in BGN gazetteers under the given spelling.

Mad, Hung. (Nagynad); pop. 370; 38 km NE of Miskolc; 48°12'/21°17'; AMG, COH, GUM3, GUM4, HSL, HSL2, LDL, LDS, LYV, PHH, YB.

Mada, Rom.; pop. 101 km S of Cluj; 45°59'/23°08'; HSL, HSL2.

Madalin, Pol.; pop. 9; 75 km W of Lodz; 51°53'/18°25'.

Madaras, Hung.; pop. 48; 75 km SW of Szeged; 46°03'/19°16'; HSL, LDS.

Madaras Satu Mare, Rom.; pop. 36; 120 km NW of Cluj; 47°41'/22°51'.

Madarsky Seldin, (Magyarszogyen); HSL. This pre-World War I community was not found in BGN gazetteers.

Madchendorf, *see* Lalovo.

Madei, Rom.; pop. 139 km W of Iasi; 47°13'/25°45'; HSL.

Madfeld, Germ.; pop. 21; 126 km SSW of Hannover; 51°26'/08°44'.

Madliena, Lat.; pop. 5; 69 km E of Riga; 56°51'/25°10'.

Madocsa, Hung.; pop. 12; 94 km S of Budapest; 46°41'/18°58'.

Madohn, *see* Madona.

Madon, *see* Madona.

Madona, Lat. (Madohn, Madon, Modohn); pop. 97; 114 km NNW of Daugavpils; 56°51'/26°13'; COH, PHLE.

Maehrisch Budwitz, *see* Moravske Budejovice.

Maehrisch Kromau, *see* Moravsky Krumlov.

Maehrisch Neustadt, *see* Unicov.

Maehrisch Ostrau, *see* Ostrava.

Maehrisch Truebau, *see* Moravska Trebova.

Maehrisch Weisskirchen, *see* Hranice.

Maeriste, Rom.; pop. 7; 88 km NW of Cluj; 47°19'/22°48'.

Maerkisch Friedland, *see* Miroslawiec.

Maga, Hung.; 75 km E of Miskolc; 48°04'/21°46'; LDS.

Magare, *see* Magarei.

Magarei, Rom. (Magare); HSL. This pre-World War I community was not found in BGN gazetteers.

Magdalowka, Ukr.; pop. 37; 88 km NNW of Chernovtsy; 49°05'/25°45'. This town was located on an interwar map of Poland but does not appear in contemporary gazetteers. Map coordinates are approximate.

Magdeburg, Germ.; pop. 2,361; 107 km NW of Leipzig; 52°10'/11°40'; AMG, EDRD, EJ, GUM3, GUM4, GUM5, GUM6, HSL, ISH1, JGFF, LDS.

Magendorf, HSL, HSL2, JGFF. This town was not found in BGN gazetteers under the given spelling.

Magerov, Ukr. (Magierow, Magriv); pop. 600; 32 km NW of Lvov; 50°07'/23°43'; COH, EDRD, EGRS, HSL, HSL2, LDL, PHP2, SF.

Maghera, Rom.; pop. 10; 126 km WNW of Iasi; 47°52'/26°18'.

Magierow, *see* Magerov.

Maglod, Hung.; pop. 86; 19 km E of Budapest; 47°27'/19°22';

PHH.

Magnashev, *see* Magnuszew.

Magne, HSL. This pre-World War I community was not found in BGN gazetteers.

Magnesia, LDL. This pre-World War I community was not found in BGN gazetteers.

Magnuszew, Pol. (Magnashev); pop. 731; 62 km SE of Warszawa; 51°46'/21°24'; AMG, GA, GUM4, HSL, HSL2, LDL, LDS, SF.

Magocs, Hung.; pop. 116; 94 km E of Nagykanizsa; 46°21'/18°14'; HSL, JGFF, LDS, PHH.

Magosliget, Hung.; pop. 5; 157 km E of Miskolc; 48°03'/22°52'.

Magriv, *see* Magerov.

Magura, COH, HSL. A number of towns share this name. It was not possible to determine from available information which one is being referenced.

Magura Ilvei, Rom.; pop. 39; 114 km NE of Cluj; 47°23'/24°48'.

Magy, Hung.; pop. 22; 88 km E of Miskolc; 47°56'/21°59'; HSL, LDS.

Magyaralmas, Hung.; pop. 8; 62 km SW of Budapest; 47°18'/18°20'.

Magyaratad, Hung.; pop. 21; 69 km ENE of Nagykanizsa; 46°28'/17°54'.

Magyarbanhegyes, Hung. (Banhegyes); pop. 74; 62 km NE of Szeged; 46°27'/20°58'; HSL, HSL2, PHH.

Magyarbolkeny, HSL. This pre-World War I community was not found in BGN gazetteers.

Magyarboly, Hung.; pop. 6; 133 km ESE of Nagykanizsa; 45°50'/18°30'.

Magyarcsanad, Hung.; pop. 7; 32 km E of Szeged; 46°10'/20°37'.

Magyarcseke, LDL. This pre-World War I community was not found in BGN gazetteers.

Magyardombegyhaz, Hung.; pop. 5; 69 km ENE of Szeged; 46°23'/21°04'.

Magyaregregy, Hung. (Egregy); pop. 8; 107 km E of Nagykanizsa; 46°15'/18°19'; HSL.

Magyarfalva, Hung. (Harka); 139 km NNW of Nagykanizsa; 47°38'/16°36'; GUM3, GUM4, GUM5, HSL.

Magyarfenes, *see* Vlaha.

Magyarfold, Hung.; pop. 10; 56 km WNW of Nagykanizsa; 46°47'/16°25'.

Magyarfrata, *see* Frata.

Magyargencs, Hung.; pop. 14; 107 km N of Nagykanizsa; 47°22'/17°18'; LDS.

Magyarhomorog, Hung.; pop. 15; 133 km SE of Miskolc; 47°01'/21°33'; LDS.

Magyarigen, *see* Ighiu.

Magyarkeresztur, Hung.; pop. 6; 126 km N of Nagykanizsa; 47°31'/17°10'.

Magyarkeszi, Hung.; pop. 28; 101 km NE of Nagykanizsa; 46°45'/18°14'.

Magyarkimle, Hung.; pop. 23; 133 km WNW of Budapest; 47°50'/17°22'.

Magyarkoblos, *see* Cubles Somesani.

Magyarlapos, *see* Tirgu Lapus.

Magyarmecske, Hung.; pop. 22; 94 km ESE of Nagykanizsa; 45°57'/17°58'.

Magyarnagyszombor, *see* Zimbor.

Magyarnandor, Hung.; pop. 8; 56 km N of Budapest; 47°58'/19°21'.

Magyarnemegye, *see* Nimigea de Jos.

Magyaro, *see* Alunish.

Magyarovar, *see* Mosonmagyarovar.

Magyarpatak, *see* Valea Ungurului.

Magyarpolany, Hung.; pop. 8; 94 km NNE of Nagykanizsa; 47°10'/17°33'.

Magyarsard, *see* Sard.

Magyarszek, Hung.; pop. 14; 101 km ESE of Nagykanizsa; 46°12'/18°12'; GUM5.

Magyarszerdahely, Hung.; pop. 7; 19 km NNW of Nagykanizsa; 46°33'/16°56'.

Magyarszogyen, *see* Madarsky Seldin.

Magyarszombatfa, Hung.; pop. 3; 62 km WNW of Nagykanizsa; 46°46'/16°20'.

Magyartes, Hung.; pop. 1; 56 km N of Szeged; 46°44'/20°13'.

Magyarujfalu, *see* Aschileu Mare.

Magyarvalko, *see* Valcaul Ungureasca.

Mahal, Rom.; pop. 8; 45 km NE of Cluj; 46°59'/24°02'.

Mahlberg, Germ.; 114 km SW of Stuttgart; 48°17'/07°49'; ISH1.

Mahnaym, Pol. PHP2. This town was not found in BGN gazetteers under the given spelling.

Mahrendorf, HSL. This pre-World War I community was not found in BGN gazetteers.

Mahrisch Ostrau, *see* Ostrava.

Mahrisch Schonberg, *see* Sumperk.

Mahrish Ostrau, *see* Ostrava.

Maia, Rom.; pop. 94 km E of Cluj; 46°35'/24°51'; HSL.

Maiad, Rom.; pop. 4; 88 km ESE of Cluj; 46°31'/24°43'.

Maidan, *see* Majdan Krolewski.

Maieru, Rom.; pop. 57; 114 km NE of Cluj; 47°24'/24°45'; HSL.

Maihingen, Germ.; 75 km SSW of Nurnberg; 48°56'/10°30'; PHGB.

Maikammer, Germ.; 94 km WNW of Stuttgart; 49°18'/08°08'; GED, JGFF.

Maikop, GUM4, HSL. This pre-World War I community was not found in BGN gazetteers.

Mailberg, Aus.; pop. 3; 56 km NNW of Wien; 48°40'/16°11'.

Mainbernheim, Germ.; pop. 32; 62 km WNW of Nurnberg; 49°42'/10°15'; GUM5, HSL, JGFF, PHGB.

Maineck, Germ.; 75 km N of Nurnberg; 50°07'/11°18'; PHGB.

Mainroth, Germ.; 75 km N of Nurnberg; 50°07'/11°19'; PHGB.

Mainstockheim, Germ.; pop. 72; 75 km WNW of Nurnberg; 49°47'/10°09'; GUM5, HSL, HSL2, PHGB.

Mainz, Germ. (Mayence); pop. 2,738; 32 km SW of Frankfurt am Main; 50°00'/08°15'; AMG, CAHJP, EDRD, EJ, GED, GUM3, GUM4, GUM5, HSL, HSL2, JGFF, LDS, PHGBW.

Mainzlar, Germ.; 69 km N of Frankfurt am Main; 50°40'/08°44'; LDS.

Mainz Weisenau, Germ.; pop. 22; 32 km SW of Frankfurt am Main; 49°59'/08°18'; GUM5.

Maioresti, Rom.; pop. 10; 94 km ENE of Cluj; 46°54'/24°49'.

Maishad, *see* Mosedis.

Maishagola, *see* Maisiagala.

Maisiagala, Lith. (Maishagola, Maisiogala, Mejszagola); 26 km NW of Vilnius; 54°52'/25°04'; GUM3, GUM4, HSL, JGFF, LDL, SF.

Maisiogala, *see* Maisiagala.

Majaczewice, Pol.; pop. 62 km SW of Lodz; 51°26'/18°49'; PHP1.

Majdan, Ukr.; 146 km S of Lvov; 48°36'/23°29'; JGFF. *See also* Majdan Krolewski. The name Majdan, which means "square" in Polish, is the name of 37 towns on an interwar map of Poland. The *Black Book* shows census figures for about ten towns. The name Majdan tends to be associated with Majdan Krolewski. *See also* Majdan Krolewski.

Majdanek, Pol. (Majdan Tatarski, Maydan Tatarski); pop. 7; 6 km ESE of Lublin; 51°14'/22°36'; AMG, EDRD, GA, GUM3, GUM4, GUM5, GUM6, PHP3, PHP4. Most sources refer to the concentration camp at Majdanek.

Majdan Gorny, *see* Verkhniy Maydan.

Majdan Kozic Dolnych, Pol.; pop. 6; 19 km SE of Lublin; 51°07'/22°42'.

Majdan Krasieninski, Pol.; pop. 11; 19 km NNW of Lublin; 51°21'/22°30'.

Majdan Krolewski, Pol. (Maidan, Majdan); pop. 565; 101 km WNW of Przemysl; 50°23'/21°45'; AMG, EGRS, FRG, GUM3, HSL, HSL2, LDL, PHP3, SF, SM. *See also* Majdan.

Majdan Krzywski, Pol.; pop. 16; 38 km ESE of Lublin;

51°00'/23°00'.

Majdan Kukawiecki, Pol. (Majdan Kukawski); pop. 7; 75 km ESE of Lublin; 50°54'/23°29'.

Majdan Kukawski, *see* Majdan Kukawiecki.

Majdan Lesniowski, Pol.; pop. 2; 69 km ESE of Lublin; 51°00'/23°32'.

Majdan Lipiwiecki, *possibly* Maydan Stary.

Majdan Maly, Pol.; pop. 2; 94 km SE of Lublin; 50°32'/23°18'.

Majdan Ostrowski, Pol.; pop. 10; 69 km ESE of Lublin; 50°57'/23°29'.

Majdan Radlinski, Pol.; pop. 4; 32 km SW of Lublin; 51°03'/22°14'.

Majdan Sieniawski, Pol.; pop. 114; 56 km N of Przemysl; 50°17'/22°45'.

Majdan Skierbieszowski, Pol.; pop. 5; 69 km ESE of Lublin; 50°53'/23°23'.

Majdan Skordiow, Pol. (Majdan Skordjow); pop. 20; 82 km E of Lublin; 51°07'/23°45'.

Majdan Skordjow, *see* Majdan Skordiow.

Majdan Sopocki, Pol.; pop. 18; 82 km N of Przemysl; 50°28'/23°10'.

Majdan Sredni, *see* Maydan Sredni.

Majdan Starowiejski, Pol.; pop. 8; 38 km S of Lublin; 50°57'/22°29'.

Majdan Stary, *see* Maydan Stary.

Majdan Tatarski, *see* Majdanek.

Majdan Wierzchowinski, Pol. (Majdan Wierzchowski); pop. 10; 45 km SE of Lublin; 50°52'/22°51'.

Majdan Wierzchowski, *see* Majdan Wierzchowinski.

Majkow, *see* Maykov.

Majnicz, *see* Maynich.

Majoshaza, Hung.; pop. 3; 32 km S of Budapest; 47°16'/19°00'.

Majowka, GUM3, GUM5. This town was not found in BGN gazetteers under the given spelling.

Majs, Hung.; pop. 6; 126 km SW of Szeged; 45°54'/18°36'; HSL.

Majsamiklosvar, *see* Kecsege.

Majtis, Hung.; pop. 18; 139 km E of Miskolc; 47°57'/22°39'.

Makad, Hung.; pop. 7; 50 km S of Budapest; 47°05'/18°56'.

Makarki, Pol.; pop. 17; 69 km SSW of Bialystok; 52°34'/22°46'.

Makarov, Ukr.; 50 km W of Kiyev; 50°28'/29°49'; EJ, HSL, JGFF, LDL, SF.

Makarowka, Pol.; pop. 13; 101 km N of Lublin; 52°07'/22°53'.

Makarska, Yug.; pop. 25; 290 km SSE of Zagreb; 43°18'/17°02'.

Makasan, *see* Makaseni.

Makaseni, Lat. (Makasan); pop. 3; 88 km NNE of Daugavpils; 56°35'/27°19'; PHLE.

Makeyevka, Ukr. (Makiyevka); 114 km S of Konotop; 50°15'/32°46'; JGFF.

Makhnovka, Ukr. (Machnowka, Mochnovka); pop. 2,025; HSL, LDL, SF. A number of towns share this name. It was not possible to determine from available information which one is being referenced.

Makiyevka, *see* Makeyevka.

Makkoshotyka, Hung.; pop. 4; 62 km NE of Miskolc; 48°21'/21°31'.

Maklar, Hung.; pop. 2; 45 km SSW of Miskolc; 47°48'/20°25'.

Mako, Hung.; pop. 2,503; 26 km E of Szeged; 46°13'/20°29'; COH, EJ, GUM5, GUM6, HSL, HSL2, JGFF, LDL, LDS, PHH.

Makocice, Pol.; pop. 113; 32 km NE of Krakow; 50°13'/20°16'.

Makod, *see* Mocod.

Makolusky, Cz.; pop. 7; 50 km ESE of Praha; 49°50'/15°01'.

Makoszka, Pol.; pop. 5; 50 km NNE of Lublin; 51°35'/22°56'.

Makoszyn, Pol.; pop. 26; 114 km NNE of Krakow; 50°49'/20°58'; GUM4.

Makov, *see* Makow Mazowiecki. There are also towns in Czechoslovakia called Makov.

Makova, *see* Makow Mazowiecki.

Makovi, *see* Makow Mazowiecki.

Makov Mazovyetsk, *see* Makow Mazowiecki.

Makow, *see* Makow Podhalanski.

Makowa Rustykalna, Pol.; pop. 20; 26 km S of Przemysl; 49°38'/22°41'.

Makowiec Duzy, Pol.; pop. 2; 50 km ENE of Warszawa; 52°21'/21°44'.

Makow Mazowiecki, Pol. (Makov, Makov Mazovyetsk, Makova, Makovi); pop. 3,369; 69 km N of Warszawa; 52°52'/21°06'; AMG, CAHJP, COH, EDRD, EJ, GA, GUM3, GUM4, GYLA, HSL, JGFF, LYV, PHP4, SF, YB.

Makow Podhalanski, Pol. (Makow); pop. 189; 45 km S of Krakow; 49°44'/19°41'; AMG, GUM3, GUM5, HSL, JGFF, PHP3, YB.

Makrancz, *see* Mokrance.

Maksimets, Ukr. (Maksymowka, Maksymuvka?); pop. 19; 126 km W of Chernovtsy; 48°31'/24°16'; GUM3, GUM4, JGFF.

Maksimovichi, Ukr. (Maksymovitse, Maksymowice); pop. 41; 69 km SW of Lvov; 49°34'/23°11'.

Maksymovitse, *see* Maksimovichi.

Maksymowice, *see* Maksimovichi.

Maksymowka, *see* Maksimets.

Maksymuvka, *possibly* Maksimets.

Mala, Pol.; 94 km W of Przemysl; 49°58'/21°31'; GUM5.

Mala Berestovitsa, *see* Brzostowica.

Mala Cerkwica, Pol.; pop. 6; 114 km SSW of Gdansk; 53°31'/17°35'.

Malachowice, Pol.; 32 km NNW of Lodz; 52°00'/19°22'; JGFF.

Malachy, (Malatzka);

Malacka, *possibly* Malacky.

Malacky, Cz. (Malacka?); pop. 791; 38 km NNW of Bratislava; 48°26'/17°01'; GUM4, GUM5, HSL, HSL2.

Malaesti Balti, *see* Malayeshty.

Mala Glusza, *see* Malaya Glusha.

Mala Hlusza, *see* Malaya Glusha.

Mala Ida, Cz. (Kisida); 13 km SW of Kosice; 48°40'/21°10'; HSL.

Mala Khlusha, *see* Malaya Glusha.

Malakhovka, Ukr.; 157 km NE of Rovno; 51°12'/28°22'; EJ.

Mala Kriva, *see* Belovarec.

Malanowo Stare, Pol.; pop. 5; 114 km WNW of Warszawa; 52°47'/19°31'.

Malastow, Pol.; pop. 4; 114 km ESE of Krakow; 49°34'/21°15'.

Malaszewicze, Pol. (Malaszewicze Duze); pop. 53; 114 km NNE of Lublin; 52°02'/23°31'; GA.

Malaszewicze Duze, *see* Malaszewicze.

Malat, *see* Moletai.

Mala Torona, *see* Mala Trna.

Mala Trna, Cz. (Mala Torona); 45 km ESE of Kosice; 48°27'/21°41'; JGFF.

Malatzka, *see* Malachy.

Malawa, Pol.; pop. 22; BGN lists two possible localities with this name located at 49°41'/22°25' and 50°02'/22°06'.

Mala Wies (near Plock), Pol.; pop. 20; 62 km WNW of Warszawa; 52°28'/20°06'.

Mala Wies (near Radom), Pol.; pop. 30; 56 km S of Warszawa; 51°50'/20°48'. Contemporary maps show another Mala Wies near Czestochowa at 50°57'/19°37'. Also in the interwar province of Kielce.

Malaya Glusha, Ukr. (Mala Glusza, Mala Hlusza, Mala Khlusha); pop. 135; 163 km NW of Rovno; 51°48'/24°59'; GUM4.

Malaya Kamenka, Ukr. (Kamionka Mala); pop. 49; 75 km WNW of Chernovtsy; 48°36'/25°01'.

Malaya Lopenitsa, Byel. (Lopenitsa Mala, Lopienica Mala); pop. 47; 150 km WNW of Pinsk; 53°02'/24°30'.

Malaya Luka, Ukr. (Luka Mala); pop. 38; 120 km N of Chernovtsy; 49°22'/26°14'.

Malaya Plavucha, Ukr. (Plaucha Male, Plaucza Mala); pop. 29; 88 km ESE of Lvov; 49°35'/25°12'.

Malaya Vishera, USSR; pop. 156; 157 km ESE of Leningrad; 58°53'/32°08'.

Malayeshty, Mold. (Malaesti Balti); pop. 24; 146 km WNW of Kishinev; 47°53'/27°21'.

Malborg, Pol. PHP4. This town was not found in BGN gazetteers under the given spelling.

Malbork, Pol. (Marienberg, Marienburg); pop. 170; 45 km SE of Gdansk; 54°02'/19°03'; LDS, PHLE.

Malchin, Germ.; pop. 8; 56 km ESE of Rostock; 53°44'/12°47'; EJ, HSL, JGFF, LDS.

Malchitse, Ukr. (Malczyce); pop. 2; 38 km W of Lvov; 49°51'/23°26'.

Malchow, Germ.; 75 km SSE of Rostock; 53°29'/12°26'; GUM3, GUM4, GUM5, LDS.

Malcin, Cz.; pop. 3; 82 km ESE of Praha; 49°41'/15°28'.

Malczew, Pol.; pop. 6; 19 km ENE of Lodz; 51°47'/19°43'.

Malczow, Pol.; pop. 7; 101 km W of Lublin; 51°22'/21°11'.

Malczyce, see Malchitse.

Malczyn, Pol.; pop. 7; 45 km NW of Warszawa; 52°35'/20°43'.

Male, Cz.; 69 km W of Brno; 49°20'/15°42'; HSL.

Male Blahovo, Cz. (Sikabony); 38 km ESE of Bratislava; 48°00'/17°37'; HSL.

Male Brezno, see Povrly.

Malec, Pol.; pop. 31; 50 km SW of Krakow; 49°56'/19°15'.

Malech, Byel. (Malecz, Moletch); pop. 479; 107 km WNW of Pinsk; 52°29'/24°42'; COH, HSL, JGFF, LDL, SF, YB.

Malechow, see Malekhuv.

Malechy, Pol.; pop. 12; 69 km N of Warszawa; 52°51'/20°59'.

Male Chyndice, Cz. (Kishind); 88 km ENE of Bratislava; 48°18'/18°17'; HSL.

Malecz, see Malech.

Malejowa, Pol.; pop. 13; 50 km S of Krakow; 49°40'/19°53'.

Malekhuv, Ukr. (Malechow); pop. 20; 50 km SSE of Lvov; 49°29'/24°07'.

Male Lunawy, Pol.; pop. 8; 114 km S of Gdansk; 53°23'/18°36'.

Maleniec, Pol. (Malenitz); pop. 185; 82 km SE of Lodz; 51°11'/20°11'; AMG, HSL, SF.

Malenitz, see Maleniec.

Male Raskovce, Cz. (Kisraska); 50 km ESE of Kosice; 48°34'/21°55'; HSL.

Male Sedlishche, Ukr. (Siedliszcze Male); pop. 641; 38 km NE of Rovno; 50°49'/26°38'; GUM4.

Malesice, Cz.; 94 km SW of Praha; 49°46'/13°18'; HSL.

Malesov, Cz.; 56 km ESE of Praha; 49°55'/15°14'; HSL.

Malesze, Pol.; pop. 14; 45 km S of Bialystok; 52°48'/22°58'.

Maleszewo Male, see Malyy Malyshev.

Maleszowa, Pol.; pop. 13; 88 km NNE of Krakow; 50°41'/20°44'.

Maletai, see Moletai.

Male Tarpno, Pol.; pop. 14; 94 km S of Gdansk; 53°31'/18°48'.

Maletos, see Moletai.

Mali Bukovec, Yug.; pop. 12; 82 km NNE of Zagreb; 46°18'/16°44'.

Malic, Cz.; pop. 3; 56 km NW of Praha; 50°33'/14°05'.

Malice Koscielne, Pol.; pop. 11; 88 km SW of Lublin; 50°46'/21°31'.

Maligoshtcht, see Malogoszcz.

Mali Idjos, see Mali Idos.

Mali Idos, Yug. (Kishegyes, Mali Idjos); pop. 67; 120 km NW of Beograd; 45°43'/19°40'; PHY.

Malin, Ukr. (Almasmalom); pop. 4,582; 101 km WNW of Kiyev; 50°46'/29°14'; GUM5, HSL, JGFF, LDL, SF.

Malin (Romania), Rom.; pop. 23; 56 km NE of Cluj; 47°07'/24°09'.

Malina, USSR; EDRD. A number of towns share this name. It was not possible to determine from available information which one is being referenced.

Malinec, Cz.; 120 km WSW of Kosice; 48°30'/19°41'; JGFF.

Malinka, see Malyinka.

Malinovka, Ukr. (Malinuv, Malnow, Malpa); pop. 52; 45 km SW of Lvov; 49°35'/23°37'.

Malinowka, Pol.; pop. 87; 62 km ENE of Lublin; 51°19'/23°27'. See also Malinuvka.

Malinsk, see Malynsk.

Malinti, see Malintsy.

Malintsy, Ukr. (Malinti); pop. 169; 26 km NE of Chernovtsy; 48°26'/26°15'.

Malinuv, see Malinovka.

Malinuvka, Ukr. (Malinowka); pop. 25; 26 km SSW of Lvov; 49°42'/23°50'.

Maliszow, Pol.; pop. 7; 101 km W of Lublin; 51°18'/21°08'.

Maljaty, see Moletai.

Maljuny, Byel. EDRD. This town was not found in BGN gazetteers under the given spelling.

Malken, see Malki.

Malkevichi, Byel. (Malkiewicze); pop. 8; 170 km NW of Pinsk; 53°24'/24°48'.

Malki, Pol. (Malken); 126 km SSE of Gdansk; 53°14'/19°15'; EDRD, GUM3.

Malkiewicze, see Malkevichi.

Malkinia, see Malkinia Gorna.

Malkinia Dolna, Pol.; pop. 25; 88 km SW of Bialystok; 52°43'/22°00'.

Malkinia Gorna, Pol. (Malkinia); pop. 275; 82 km NE of Warszawa; 52°41'/22°01'; AMG, GUM3, GUM4, GUM5, HSL, PHP1, PHP4, SF.

Malkow (near Chelm), Pol.; pop. 37; 45 km ENE of Lublin; 51°19'/23°14'.

Malkow (near Hrubieszow), Pol.; pop. 21; 120 km ESE of Lublin; 50°39'/24°01'.

Malkowice, Pol.; pop. 33; 13 km N of Przemysl; 49°52'/22°50'.

Mallwischken, see Mayskoye.

Malmo, AMG, HSL, LDL. This pre-World War I community was not found in BGN gazetteers.

Malnas, Rom.; pop. 6; 182 km N of Bucuresti; 46°01'/25°50'.

Malnow, see Malinovka.

Maloarkhangelsk, USSR; pop. 28; 82 km N of Kursk; 52°24'/36°30'.

Malocice, Pol.; pop. 7; 26 km WNW of Warszawa; 52°22'/20°42'; HSL.

Malociechowo, Pol.; pop. 2; 114 km S of Gdansk; 53°21'/18°16'.

Malodruzy, Pol. PHP4. This town was not found in BGN gazetteers under the given spelling.

Malogoszcz, Pol. (Maligoshtch); pop. 415; 82 km ENE of Czestochowa; 50°49'/20°17'; EDRD, GUM3, GUM5, LDL, LDS, SF.

Malom, Hung. (Ladhaza); pop. 17; 13 km SSE of Miskolc; 48°00'/20°51'; HSL.

Malomierzyce, Pol.; pop. 7; 88 km WSW of Lublin; 51°12'/21°21'.

Malonty, Cz.; pop. 4; 157 km SW of Brno; 48°41'/14°35'.

Malopole, Pol.; pop. 13; 38 km NNE of Warszawa; 52°29'/21°18'.

Malorita, Byel. (Maloryta); pop. 753; 146 km WSW of Pinsk; 51°47'/24°05'; COH, HSL, LYV, SF.

Maloryta, see Malorita.

Malova, LDL. This pre-World War I community was not found in BGN gazetteers.

Malovata, Mold. (Molovata); pop. 103; 45 km NNE of Kishinev; 47°21'/29°07'.

Malowa Gora, Pol.; pop. 3; 114 km NNE of Lublin; 52°06'/23°29'.

Maloyaroslavets, USSR; pop. 120; 107 km SW of Moskva; 55°01'/36°28'; GUM4.

Maloyaroslavets Pervyy, Ukr. (Malu Mare); pop. 19; 139 km SW of Odessa; 46°05'/29°00'.

Maloyaroslavets Vtordy, Ukr. (Malu Mic); pop. 18; 133 km SW of Odessa; 46°09'/29°05'.

Malpa, see Malinovka.

Malsch, Germ.; pop. 101; 62 km W of Stuttgart; 48°53'/08°20'; GED, GUM5, JGFF, PHGWH.

Malsch bei Heidelberg, Germ. PHGWH. This town was not found in BGN gazetteers under the given spelling.

Malsch bei Wiesloch, Germ.; pop. 52; 62 km NW of Stuttgart; 49°15'/08°41'; PHGBW.

Malsfeld, Germ.; pop. 9; 126 km NNE of Frankfurt am Main; 51°05'/09°32'.

Malsice, Cz.; pop. 6; 88 km S of Praha; 49°22'/14°35'.

Malta, *see* Silmala.

Malu Mare, *see* Maloyaroslavets Pervyy.

Malu Mic, *see* Maloyaroslavets Vtordy.

Malusy Wielkie, Pol.; pop. 11; 13 km E of Czestochowa; 50°48'/19°20'.

Maluszyn, Pol.; pop. 62; 50 km ENE of Czestochowa; 50°55'/19°48'.

Malut, Rom.; pop. 3; 56 km NNE of Cluj; 47°10'/24°06'.

Maluzyn, Pol.; pop. 16; 69 km NW of Warszawa; 52°45'/20°25'.

Malyat, *see* Moletai.

Maly Gyres, *see* Maly Hores.

Maly Hores, Cz. (Maly Gyres); pop. 74; 62 km ESE of Kosice; 48°24'/21°57'; JGFF.

Malyi, Hung.; pop. 31; 13 km SSE of Miskolc; 48°01'/20°50'; HSL.

Malyinka, Hung. (Malinka); pop. 7; 19 km W of Miskolc; 48°09'/20°30'; HSL.

Maly Lipnik, Cz. (Lipnik Maly); 75 km NW of Kosice; 49°20'/20°48'; HSL.

Malyn, Pol.; pop. 10; 32 km W of Lodz; 51°47'/19°02'.

Malynsk, Ukr. (Malinsk, Malynska); pop. 39; 62 km N of Rovno; 51°06'/26°33'; GUM3, GUM4, SF.

Malynska, *see* Malynsk.

Maly Plock, Pol.; 75 km W of Bialystok; 53°19'/22°02'; PHP4.

Maly Saris, Cz.; 38 km NNW of Kosice; 49°01'/21°11'; HSL.

Maly Trostenets, *see* Malyy Trostenets.

Maly Trostinec, *see* Malyy Trostenets.

Maly Trostyanets, *see* Malyy Trostenets.

Malyye Mileshty, Mold. (Milestii Mici); pop. 7; 19 km S of Kishinev; 46°54'/28°49'.

Malyye Orly, Byel. (Orly Male); pop. 30; 62 km E of Pinsk; 52°02'/27°02'.

Malyy Gvozdets, Ukr. (Gvozhdziyets Malyy, Gwozdziec Maly); pop. 21; 56 km WNW of Chernovtsy; 48°34'/25°16'.

Malyy Kochurov, Ukr. (Cuciurul Mic); pop. 40; 26 km NNW of Chernovtsy; 48°28'/25°54'.

Malyy Malyshev, Byel. (Maleszewo Male); pop. 32; 94 km E of Pinsk; 52°05'/27°32'.

Malyy Trostenets, Byel. (Maly Trostenets, Maly Trostinec, Maly Trostyanets); 13 km ESE of Minsk; 53°50'/27°43'; EDRD, GUM4, PHGBW.

Mamaestii Vechi, *see* Altmamayeshti.

Mamaliga, *see* Mamalyga.

Mamalyga, Ukr. (Mamaliga); pop. 53; 50 km E of Chernovtsy; 48°15'/26°36'.

Mamino, Pol.; pop. 17; 94 km N of Warszawa; 53°03'/21°19'.

Manasi, *see* Monashi.

Manasterczany, Pol.; pop. 42; Described in the *Black Book* as being in the Stanislawow region of Poland, this town was not found in BGN gazetteers.

Manasterek, *see* Monasterek.

Manasterz, Pol.; pop. 64; 38 km NNW of Przemysl; 50°07'/22°40'; AMG, JGFF.

Manasterzec, *see* Monastyrets.

Manasterzh (near Lisko), Pol.; pop. 51; 38 km WNW of Przemysl; 49°57'/22°22'.

Manastezhets, *see* Monastyrets. According to the *Black Book*, a second town of Manastezhets (pop. 26) was located near Zhidechuv.

Manasturel, Rom. (Felsomonoster); pop. 8; 56 km NNE of Cluj; 47°10'/23°57'.

Manau, *see* Minau.

Mand, Hung.; pop. 10; 133 km E of Miskolc; 48°00'/22°37'.

Mandac, *see* Myndyk.

Mandok, Hung.; pop. 401; 107 km ENE of Miskolc; 48°19'/22°12'; AMG, HSL, HSL2, LDL, LDS, PHH.

Mandresti, *see* Myndreshty.

Manetin, Cz.; pop. 7; 88 km WSW of Praha; 49°59'/13°14'.

Maneuti, Rom.; pop. 64; 150 km WNW of Iasi; 47°54'/25°56'.

Manevichi, Ukr. (Maniewicze, Manivits, Manyevich, Manyevichi, Monavitz, Monevitch); pop. 62; 101 km NW of Rovno; 51°22'/25°32'; AMG, GUM3, GUM4, GUM6, SF.

Manevichi (Polesie), Ukr.; pop. 6; 94 km NW of Rovno; 51°17'/25°32'.

Mangali, Lat. (Mangalu); pop. 1; 13 km N of Riga; 57°03'/24°09'.

Mangalu, *see* Mangali.

Manicovca, *see* Mankovka.

Maniewicze, *see* Manevichi.

Maniowy, Pol.; pop. 32; 75 km SSE of Krakow; 49°27'/20°16'.

Manivits, *see* Manevichi.

Mank, Aus.; pop. 5; 82 km WSW of Wien; 48°06'/15°20'.

Mankoviche, Byel. (Mankowicze); pop. 52; 133 km NNW of Minsk; 55°02'/26°54'.

Mankovka, Ukr. (Manicovca); 56 km SW of Uman; 48°29'/29°38'; GUM4, PHR1.

Mankowicze, *see* Mankoviche.

Mannelsdorf, *see* Zvonickov.

Mannersdorf am Leithagebirge, Aus.; pop. 2; 32 km SE of Wien; 47°58'/16°36'.

Mannersdorf an der March, Aus.; pop. 3; 45 km NE of Wien; 48°23'/16°50'.

Mannheim, Germ.; pop. 6,972; 75 km S of Frankfurt am Main; 49°29'/08°28'; AMG, CAHJP, EJ, GED, GUM3, GUM5, GUM6, HSL, HSL2, ISH1, JGFF, LDL, LDS, PHGBW.

Mansbach, Germ.; pop. 40; 114 km NE of Frankfurt am Main; 50°47'/09°55'; JGFF, LDS.

Mansburg, *see* Alekseyevka.

Mantov, Cz. (Mantova?); pop. 7; 107 km SW of Praha; 49°39'/13°12'; HSL, LDL.

Mantova, *possibly* Mantov.

Mantua, LDL. This pre-World War I community was not found in BGN gazetteers.

Manyevich, *see* Manevichi.

Manyevichi, *see* Manevichi.

Manzar, *see* Lesnoye.

Maradik, Yug.; pop. 3; 50 km WNW of Beograd; 45°06'/20°00'.

Maragyulafalva, *see* Giulesti.

Maramaros Sighet, *see* Sighet.

Maramarossziget, *see* Sighet.

Marandeni, *see* Marandeny.

Marandeny, Mold. (Marandeni); pop. 11; 107 km WNW of Kishinev; 47°40'/27°50'.

Marasesti, Rom.; pop. 146 km S of Iasi; 45°53'/27°14'; PHR1.

Maravianka, *see* Marwianka.

Maravna Krilovitz, *see* Murovanyye Kurilovtsy.

Maraza, Hung.; pop. 4; 120 km ESE of Nagykanizsa; 46°04'/18°31'.

Marazlaveni, *see* Marazleyevka.

Marazleyevka, Ukr. (Marazlaveni, Marazli); pop. 5; 69 km SW of Odessa; 46°06'/30°03'.

Marazli, *see* Marazleyevka.

Marbach, Germ. PHGBW. A number of towns share this name. It was not possible to determine from available information which one is being referenced.

Marbach am Walde, Aus.; pop. 1; 101 km WNW of Wien; 48°32'/15°05'.

Marbach an der Donau, Aus.; pop. 6; 88 km W of Wien; 48°13'/15°09'.

Marburg, *see* Maribor.

Marburg an der Lahn, Germ.; pop. 325; 88 km N of Frankfurt am Main; 50°49'/08°46'; AMG, GUM3, GUM4, GUM5, GUM6, HSL, HSL2, LDL, LDS, PHP4.

Marca, Rom.; pop. 18; 94 km WNW of Cluj; 47°13'/22°34'.

Marcalgergelyi, Hung.; pop. 5; 107 km N of Nagykanizsa; 47°19'/17°16'.

Marcali, Hung.; pop. 279; 38 km NE of Nagykanizsa; 46°35'/17°25'; GUM5, LDS, PHH.

Marcalto, Hung.; pop. 17; 120 km N of Nagykanizsa; 47°26'/17°22'.

Marcauti, *see* Markeutsy.

Marcauti Hotin, *see* Markeutsy.

Marcelina, *see* Martynovka.

Marchegg, Aus.; pop. 35; 45 km ENE of Wien; 48°16'/16°54'; EJ.

Marciena, Lat.; pop. 19; 107 km NNW of Daugavpils; 56°46'/26°06'.

Marcinkance, *see* Marcinkonys.

Marcinkonys, Lith. (Marcinkance); 94 km SW of Vilnius; 54°04'/24°23'; AMG, GUM3.

Marcinkowice, Pol.; pop. 28; 69 km ESE of Krakow; 49°40'/20°40'; EDRD, PHP3.

Marcinowice, Pol.; pop. 15; 50 km N of Krakow; 50°30'/20°00'.

Marciszow, Pol.; pop. 13; 38 km SE of Czestochowa; 50°30'/19°24'.

Marculesti, Rom.; 114 km ENE of Bucuresti; 44°34'/27°31'; EDRD.

Marculesti Colonie, *see* Markuleshty.

Mardorf, Germ.; pop. 25; 82 km N of Frankfurt am Main; 50°46'/08°55'; HSL, LDS.

Marek, *see* Stanke Dimitrov.

Marenberg, *see* Radlje Ob Dravi.

Mareniceni, *see* Merinitseni.

Marenicheni, *see* Merinitseni.

Margareten, *see* Marghita.

Margaretten, *see* Marghita.

Margecany, Cz. (Margitfalva, Margitfaul); 32 km NW of Kosice; 48°53'/21°00'; AMG, HSL.

Marghita, Rom. (Margareten, Margaretten, Marghuta, Margita); pop. 1,623; 120 km WNW of Cluj; 47°21'/22°20'; AMG, EJ, HSL, HSL2, JGFF, LDL, PHR2, YB.

Marghuta, *see* Marghita.

Margine, Rom.; pop. 27; 107 km WNW of Cluj; 47°18'/22°25'.

Marginea, Rom.; pop. 23; 150 km WNW of Iasi; 47°49'/25°49'.

Margita, *see* Marghita.

Margitfalu, HSL. This pre-World War I community was not found in BGN gazetteers.

Margitfalva, *see* Margecany.

Margitfaul, *see* Margecany.

Margonin, Pol.; pop. 12; 62 km N of Poznan; 52°58'/17°06'.

Margonya, *see* Marhan.

Marhan, Cz. (Margonya); 56 km N of Kosice; 49°10'/21°28'; HSL.

Maria Anzbach, Aus.; pop. 2; 32 km WSW of Wien; 48°11'/15°55'.

Mariakalnok, Hung.; pop. 2; 139 km WNW of Budapest; 47°52'/17°19'.

Mariakemend, Hung.; pop. 7; 120 km ESE of Nagykanizsa; 46°02'/18°28'.

Mariampol, *see* Marijampole.

Mariampole, *see* Marijampole.

Marianca de Sus, *see* Verkhnyaya Maryanovka.

Marianosztra, Hung.; pop. 17; 45 km NNW of Budapest; 47°52'/18°53'.

Marianowo, Pol. (Marjanowo); pop. 38; 62 km NNE of Warszawa; 52°45'/21°28'.

Marianow Rogowski, Pol. (Marjanow Rogowski); pop. 46; 32 km ENE of Lodz; 51°49'/19°54'.

Marianske Lazne, Cz. (Marienbad); pop. 495; 126 km WSW of Praha; 49°58'/12°42'; EJ, GUM4, HSL.

Mariapocs, Hung. (Pocs Megyer); pop. 84; 94 km E of Miskolc; 47°53'/22°02'; AMG, HSL, PHH.

Maria Theresiopol, *see* Subotica.

Maribor, Yug. (Marburg); pop. 81; 88 km NNW of Zagreb; 46°33'/15°39'; EJ, JGFF, PHY.

Marienbad, *see* Marianske Lazne.

Marienberg, *see* Malbork.

Marienburg, *see* Malbork.

Mariengauzen, *see* Vilaka.

Marienhafe, Germ.; pop. 25; 176 km WSW of Hamburg; 53°32'/07°16'.

Marienhausen, *see* Vilaka.

Marienthal, Germ. JGFF. A number of towns share this name. It was not possible to determine from available information which one is being referenced.

Marienwerder, *see* Kwidzyn.

Marijampol, Lith. PHP4. This town was not found in BGN gazetteers under the given spelling.

Marijampole, Lith. (Kapsukas, Mariampol, Mariampole); pop. 2,545; 50 km SW of Kaunas; 54°34'/23°21'; AMG, COH, EJ, GA, GUM3, GUM4, GUM5, GUM6, HSL, HSL2, JGFF, LDL, PHP2, SF, YL.

Marina Gorka, Byel.; 56 km ESE of Minsk; 53°31'/28°09'; GUM4.

Marinhoiz, *see* Vilaka.

Marinopol, Ukr. (Marjampol Miasto, Maryampol); pop. 241; 107 km SE of Lvov; 49°02'/24°51'; CAHJP, EGRS, HSL, LDL. *See also* the major Lithuanian town of Marijampole.

Marinovca, *see* Maryanovka.

Marinovka, *see* Maryanovka.

Mariolana, *see* Plandiste.

Mariselu, Rom. (Havasnagydalu); pop. 2; 69 km NE of Cluj; 47°01'/24°31'.

Marisfeld, Germ.; 126 km NNW of Nurnberg; 50°33'/10°34'; LDS.

Maritei, Rom.; pop. 64; 126 km WNW of Iasi; 47°45'/26°08'; PHR2.

Mariupol, *see* Zhdanov.

Marius, Rom.; pop. 14; 107 km NNW of Cluj; 47°40'/23°11'.

Mariyanovo, *see* Vilaka.

Marjampol Miasto, *see* Marinopol.

Marjanci, Yug.; pop. 2; 176 km E of Zagreb; 45°40'/18°18'.

Marjanka Nowa, Pol.; pop. 93; Described in the *Black Book* as being in the Lublin region of Poland, this town was not found in BGN gazetteers.

Marjanowka, *see* Maryanuvka.

Marjanowo, *see* Marianowo.

Marjanow Rogowski, *see* Marianow Rogowski.

Markauciskes, Lith. (Markovshchizna, Markowszczyzna); 45 km SW of Vilnius; 54°31'/24°48'; GUM3.

Markelsheim, Germ.; pop. 30; 88 km W of Nurnberg; 49°28'/09°50'; CAHJP, GED, PHGBW.

Markendorf, *see* Markowa.

Markeutsy, Mold. (Marcauti, Marcauti Hotin); pop. 41; 189 km NW of Kishinev; 48°20'/27°14'.

Markgrafneusiedl, Aus.; pop. 17; 19 km NE of Wien; 48°16'/16°38'.

Marki, Pol.; pop. 156; 13 km NE of Warszawa; 52°19'/21°08'; GA, GUM4.

Marki Grojeckie, Pol.; pop. 23; Described in the *Black Book* as being in the Warszawa region of Poland, this town was not found in BGN gazetteers.

Marki Pustelnik, Pol. PHP4. This town was not found in BGN gazetteers under the given spelling.

Markisch Friedland, *see* Miroslawiec.

Markivka, *see* Novo Markovka.

Markkleeberg, Germ.; pop. 49; 6 km ESE of Leipzig; 51°17'/12°24'; GUM4, GUM5.

Markneukirchen, Germ.; pop. 5; 114 km S of Leipzig;

50°19'/12°19'.

Markobel, Germ.; pop. 62; 26 km NE of Frankfurt am Main; 50°13'/08°59'; LDS.

Markoldendorf, Germ.; pop. 20; 69 km S of Hannover; 51°49'/09°47'.

Markopol, Ukr.; pop. 6; 94 km ENE of Lvov; 49°51'/25°17'; JGFF.

Markostav, Ukr. (Markostaw); pop. 2; 101 km N of Lvov; 50°43'/24°23'.

Markostaw, see Markostav.

Markoviche, Ukr. (Markowicze); pop. 7; 94 km NNE of Lvov; 50°32'/24°45'. The *Black Book* notes another town of Markoviche (pop. 22) in the interwar Polish province of Polesie that does not appear in interwar or contemporary gazetteers.

Markovka, see Novo Markovka.

Markovshchizna, see Markauciskes.

Markowa, Pol. (Markendorf); pop. 126; 45 km WNW of Przemysl; 50°01'/22°19'; GUM3, GUM4, HSL, PHP3.

Markowice, Pol.; pop. 31; 75 km N of Przemysl; 50°26'/22°44'; HSL.

Markowicze, see Markoviche.

Markowka, see Novo Markovka.

Markowo Wolka, Pol.; pop. 6; 45 km SSW of Bialystok; 52°49'/22°43'.

Markowszczyzna, see Markauciskes.

Marksdorf, see Markusovce.

Markstadt, see Laskowice Olawskie.

Markt, Germ.; 170 km SSW of Stuttgart; 47°38'/07°35'; LDS.

Markt Berolzheim, Germ. (Berolzheim); pop. 72; 56 km S of Nurnberg; 49°01'/10°51'; GUM3, HSL, HSL2, JGFF, PHGB.

Marktbreit, see Obernbreit.

Markt Erlbach, Germ.; 32 km W of Nurnberg; 49°29'/10°39'; GUM5, HSL, PHGB.

Marktheidenfeld, Germ.; pop. 14; 75 km ESE of Frankfurt am Main; 49°50'/09°37'; GUM5, PHGB.

Markt Piesting, Aus. (Unterpiesting); pop. 8; 45 km SSW of Wien; 47°52'/16°07'.

Marktredwitz, Germ.; pop. 13; 94 km NE of Nurnberg; 50°00'/12°05'; GUM3, PHGB.

Markt Rettenbach, Germ.; pop. 1; 88 km WSW of Munchen; 47°57'/10°24'.

Marktsteft, Germ.; pop. 2; 69 km WNW of Nurnberg; 49°40'/10°10'; GUM5, JGFF, PHGB.

Markuleshti, see Markuleshty.

Markuleshty, Mold. (Marculesti Colonie, Markuleshti, Markulesty, Markulisti); pop. 2,337; 107 km NNW of Kishinev; 47°53'/28°15'; GUM6, PHR2, SF, YB.

Markulesty, see Markuleshty.

Markulisti, see Markuleshty.

Markuniow, Pol.; pop. 40; Described in the *Black Book* as being in the Lwow region of Poland, this town was not found in BGN gazetteers.

Markusfalu, see Markusovce.

Markushev, see Markuszow.

Markushov, see Markuszow.

Markusica, Yug.; pop. 4; 157 km WNW of Beograd; 45°22'/18°42'.

Markusovce, Cz. (Marksdorf, Markusfalu); 50 km WNW of Kosice; 48°55'/20°38'; HSL.

Markuszow, Pol. (Markushev, Markushov); pop. 1,001; 26 km WNW of Lublin; 51°22'/22°16'; COH, EDRD, FRG, GA, GUM3, GUM4, GUM5, HSL, HSL2, JGFF, LDS, LYV, POCEM, SF, YB.

Markuszowa, Pol.; 75 km W of Przemysl; 49°52'/21°43'; PHP3.

Marl, Germ.; pop. 32; 82 km N of Koln; 51°39'/07°05'; GED.

Marloffstein, Germ.; 26 km N of Nurnberg; 49°37'/11°04'; PHGB.

Marlow, Germ.; 32 km ENE of Rostock; 54°09'/12°35'; JGFF, LDS.

Marna Noua, Rom.; pop. 2; 133 km NW of Cluj; 47°39'/22°24'.

Marnheim, Germ.; pop. 1; 69 km SSW of Frankfurt am Main; 49°38'/08°02'.

Marok, Hung.; pop. 6; 133 km SW of Szeged; 45°52'/18°31'.

Marokpapi, Hung.; pop. 12; 133 km ENE of Miskolc; 48°09'/22°31'.

Maroldsweisach, Germ.; pop. 25; 88 km NNW of Nurnberg; 50°12'/10°40'; GUM5, JGFF, PHGB.

Marosbogat, see Bogata.

Marosbogata, see Bogata.

Marosborgo, see Muresenii Birgaului.

Maroshevitz, see Toplita.

Marosheviz, see Toplita.

Marosjara, see Iara de Mures.

Marosludas, see Ludosul de Muras.

Marosszentbenedeko, *possibly* Szentbenedek.

Marosugra, see Ogra.

Marosujvar, see Uioara de Sus.

Marosvasarhely, see Tirgu Mures.

Marosvecs, see Brincovenesti.

Marshintsy, Ukr. (Marsinita); pop. 86; 32 km ESE of Chernovtsy; 48°13'/26°17'.

Marsinita, see Marshintsy.

Marsneni, Lat.; pop. 1; 107 km NE of Riga; 57°26'/25°37'.

Martijanec, Yug.; pop. 13; 69 km NNE of Zagreb; 46°17'/16°33'.

Martineni, Rom.; pop. 2; 170 km N of Bucuresti; 45°55'/26°06'.

Martinesti, Rom.; pop. 28; 126 km NNW of Cluj; 47°47'/22°56'.

Martinis, Rom. (Homorodszentmarton, Martinus); pop. 9; 150 km ESE of Cluj; 46°14'/25°23'; HSL.

Martinova, Cz. (Martonfalva); 88 km ENE of Bratislava; 48°12'/18°17'; HSL.

Martinovca, Ukr.; 56 km SW of Vinnitsa; 49°00'/27°45'; PHR1. This town was located on a pre-World War I map, but does not appear in contemporary gazetteers.

Martinus, see Martinis.

Martonfalva, see Martinova.

Martonos, Yug.; pop. 17; 150 km NNW of Beograd; 46°07'/20°03'.

Martonvasar, Hung.; pop. 79; 32 km SW of Budapest; 47°19'/18°47'; PHH.

Martonyi, Hung.; pop. 21; 50 km N of Miskolc; 48°28'/20°46'; HSL.

Martselin, see Martynovka.

Martynovka, Ukr. (Marcelina, Martselin); pop. 23; 56 km SSW of Rovno; 50°13'/25°49'; GUM4.

Martynow, see Martynuv Stary.

Martynow Nowy, see Martynuv Novy.

Martynow Stary, see Martynuv Stary.

Martynuv Novy, Ukr. (Martynow Nowy); pop. 62; 82 km SE of Lvov; 49°13'/24°33'.

Martynuv Stary, Ukr. (Martynow, Martynow Stary); pop. 35; 88 km SE of Lvov; 49°12'/24°34'.

Maruszyna, Pol.; pop. 9; 82 km S of Krakow; 49°25'/19°57'.

Marvile, Lith. (Marwile); JGFF. This town was not found in BGN gazetteers under the given spelling.

Marvits, see Murawica.

Marvitz, see Murawica.

Marwianka, Lith. (Maravianka); 6 km WSW of Kaunas; 54°54'/23°52'; LDL, SF.

Marwile, see Marvile.

Marwino, Pol.; pop. 41; Described in the *Black Book* as being in the Bialystok region of Poland, this town was not found in BGN gazetteers.

Marxheim, Germ. AMG. A number of towns share this name. It was not possible to determine from available information which one is being referenced.

Maryampol, *see* Marinopol.

Maryanovka, Ukr. (Marinovca, Marinovka); 182 km SW of Odessa; 45°35'/28°47'; PHR1.

Maryanuvka, Ukr. (Marjanowka); pop. 82; 114 km WNW of Rovno; 51°12'/24°58'.

Maryanuvka (near Kolki), Ukr.; pop. 26; 50 km N of Rovno; 51°02'/26°25'.

Marzecin, Pol.; pop. 5; 69 km NE of Krakow; 50°28'/20°37'.

Marzysz, Pol.; pop. 4; 94 km NNE of Krakow; 50°46'/20°43'.

Mascauti, *see* Mashkautsy.

Maschau, *see* Mastov.

Maseviche, *see* Masevichi.

Masevichi, Byel. (Maseviche, Masiewicze); pop. 38; 26 km NW of Pinsk; 52°15'/25°58'.

Mashev, Ukr. (Mashuv, Maszow); pop. 48; 150 km N of Lvov; 51°11'/24°07'.

Mashkautsy, Mold. (Mascauti); pop. 239; 38 km N of Kishinev; 47°17'/29°00'.

Mashuv, *see* Mashev.

Masiewicze, *see* Masevichi.

Masiewo, Pol.; pop. 26; 62 km ESE of Bialystok; 52°49'/23°55'; COH.

Maslomiaca, Pol.; pop. 10; 13 km NNE of Krakow; 50°10'/20°00'.

Maslovice, Cz.; pop. 4; 19 km NW of Praha; 50°12'/14°23'.

Maslow, Pol.; pop. 31; 107 km NNE of Krakow; 50°54'/20°43'.

Maslowice, Pol.; 62 km NE of Czestochowa; 51°06'/19°48'; PHP1.

Masluchy, Pol.; pop. 4; 38 km NE of Lublin; 51°28'/22°57'.

Massbach, Germ.; pop. 33; 101 km NW of Nurnberg; 50°11'/10°17'; GUM3, GUM5, PHGB.

Massenbach, Germ.; 50 km NNW of Stuttgart; 49°10'/09°04'; JGFF, PHGBW.

Massenbachhausen, Germ.; 50 km NNW of Stuttgart; 49°11'/09°03'; JGFF, PHGBW.

Massing, Germ. BGN lists two possible localities with this name located at 48°00'/12°31' and 48°24'/12°36'. PHGB.

Massow, *see* Maszewo.

Mast, Cz.; 19 km NW of Bratislava; 48°16'/17°02'; HSL.

Mastov, Cz. (Maschau); pop. 68; 88 km W of Praha; 50°16'/13°17'; JGFF.

Maszaniec, Pol.; pop. 46; Described in the *Black Book* as being in the Tarnopol region of Poland, this town was not found in BGN gazetteers.

Maszew, Pol.; pop. 1; 56 km W of Lodz; 51°49'/18°38'.

Maszewo, Pol. (Massow); pop. 22; 38 km ENE of Szczecin; 53°29'/15°03'.

Maszewo Duze, Pol.; pop. 8; 94 km N of Lodz; 52°34'/19°38'.

Maszewo Male, Pol.; pop. 22; 94 km N of Lodz; 52°34'/19°39'.

Maszki, Pol.; pop. 10; 26 km WSW of Lublin; 51°15'/22°16'.

Maszkienice, Pol.; pop. 3; 56 km E of Krakow; 49°59'/20°42'.

Maszow, *see* Mashev.

Matcze, Pol.; pop. 22; 101 km ESE of Lublin; 50°57'/23°59'.

Mateev, *see* Lipovka.

Matei, Rom.; pop. 39; 56 km NE of Cluj; 46°59'/24°16'.

Mateszalka, Hung.; pop. 1,621; 120 km E of Miskolc; 47°57'/22°20'; AMG, COH, GUM3, GUM4, GUM5, GUM6, HSL, HSL2, JGFF, LDL, LDS, PHH.

Matetelke, Hung.; pop. 4; 69 km WSW of Szeged; 46°10'/19°17'.

Mateuti, *see* Mateutsy.

Mateutsy, Mold. (Mateuti); pop. 79; 94 km N of Kishinev; 47°48'/28°56'.

Matiejow, *see* Maciejow.

Matkiv, *see* Matkow.

Matkow, Ukr. (Matkiv); pop. 83; 157 km SSW of Lvov; 48°35'/23°05'; HSL, SF. This town was located on an interwar map of Poland but does not appear in contemporary gazetteers. Map coordinates are approximate.

Matkule, Lat. (Matkules); pop. 2; 94 km W of Riga; 56°58'/22°36'.

Matkules, *see* Matkule.

Matolcs, Hung.; pop. 14; 126 km E of Miskolc; 47°58'/22°28'; LDS.

Matraballa, Hung.; pop. 5; 56 km WSW of Miskolc; 47°59'/20°02'.

Mataderecske, Hung.; pop. 11; 56 km SW of Miskolc; 47°57'/20°05'.

Matramindszent, Hung.; pop. 10; 62 km WSW of Miskolc; 47°58'/19°56'.

Matranovak, Hung.; pop. 35; 56 km WSW of Miskolc; 48°02'/19°59'; HSL.

Matraszollos, Hung.; pop. 6; 69 km NNE of Budapest; 47°58'/19°41'.

Matraverebely, Hung.; pop. 9; 75 km NNE of Budapest; 47°59'/19°47'.

Matseyev, *see* Maciejow.

Matsiov, Ukr. (Maciejow); pop. 2,206; 150 km WNW of Rovno; 51°13'/24°20'; COH, EDRD, GUM3, GUM4, GUM5, GUM6.

Matsyeyuv, *see* Maciejowa.

Mattersburg, Aus. (Mattersdorf, Nagymarton); pop. 511; 56 km S of Wien; 47°44'/16°24'; EJ, HSL, HSL2, JGFF, LDL, LDS, PHP3.

Mattersdorf, *see* Mattersburg.

Matuizai, Lith. (Matujzy); pop. 8; 62 km SW of Vilnius; 54°17'/24°41'.

Matujzy, *see* Matuizai.

Matuk, *see* Matukai.

Matukai, Lith. (Matuk); 50 km NW of Vilnius; 55°06'/24°59'; JGFF.

Matwica, Pol.; 82 km W of Bialystok; 53°13'/21°55'; PHP4.

Matwijowce, Ukr.; pop. 22; 120 km S of Rovno; 49°35'/25°55'. This town was located on an interwar map of Poland but does not appear in contemporary gazetteers. Map coordinates are approximate.

Matyjowce, Ukr.; pop. 28; 50 km WSW of Chernovtsy; 48°15'/25°15'. This town was located on an interwar map of Poland but does not appear in contemporary gazetteers. Map coordinates are approximate.

Matysowka, Pol.; pop. 17; 56 km WNW of Przemysl; 50°01'/22°04'.

Matyus, Hung.; pop. 5; 114 km ENE of Miskolc; 48°17'/22°17'; HSL.

Matzenheim, HSL. This pre-World War I community was not found in BGN gazetteers.

Mauerbach, Aus.; pop. 3; 19 km W of Wien; 48°14'/16°09'.

Mauer bei Amstetten, Aus.; pop. 26; 120 km WSW of Wien; 48°05'/14°48'.

Mauer bei Wein, Aus.; pop. 169; 13 km SW of Wien; 48°09'/16°16'.

Mauruciai, Lith. (Mevrotsh); 19 km SSW of Kaunas; 54°47'/23°45'; YL.

Maustrenk, Aus.; pop. 4; 45 km NNE of Wien; 48°34'/16°42'.

Mauthausen, Aus.; 120 km NE of Salzburg; 48°14'/14°31'; AMG, GUM3, GUM4, GUM5, GUM6, PHP3.

Mavruciai, HSL. This pre-World War I community was not found in BGN gazetteers.

Maxdorf, Germ.; 75 km S of Frankfurt am Main; 49°29'/08°18'; GUM5.

Maxglan, Aus.; pop. 9; 133 km NE of Innsbruck; 47°48'/13°02'.

Maxsain, Germ.; pop. 10; 75 km ESE of Koln; 50°33'/07°47'.

Maydan, (Lukavets Maydan);

Maydan Gurny, *see* Verkhniy Maydan.

Maydan Sredni, Ukr. (Majdan Sredni); pop. 68; 94 km WNW of Chernovtsy; 48°38'/24°45'.

Maydan Stary, Ukr. (Majdan Lipiwiecki?, Majdan Stary); pop. 20; 62 km NE of Lvov; 50°10'/24°46'.

Maydan Tatarski, *see* Majdanek.

Mayen, Germ.; pop. 250; 75 km SSE of Koln; 50°20'/07°13';

GED, JGFF.

Mayence, *see* Mainz.

Mayfeld, *see* Mayskoye (Crimea).

Maykov, Ukr. (Majkow, Maykuv); pop. 46; 45 km E of Rovno; 50°31'/26°47'.

Maykuv, *see* Maykov.

Maynich, Ukr. (Majnicz); pop. 21; 50 km SSW of Lvov; 49°31'/23°33'; JGFF.

Mayskoye, USSR (Mallwischken); pop. 3; 114 km ENE of Kaliningrad; 54°44'/22°14'.

Mayskoye (Crimea), Ukr. (Mayfeld); 88 km NNE of Simferopol; 45°36'/34°34'.

Maytshet, *see* Molchad.

Maza, Hung.; 107 km E of Nagykanizsa; 46°16'/18°24'; HSL.

Mazanow, Pol.; pop. 9; 50 km SW of Lublin; 51°01'/21°55'.

Mazeikai, *see* Mazeikiai.

Mazeiki, *see* Mazeikiai.

Mazeikiai, Lith. (Mazeikai, Mazeiki, Mazheik, Mazheiki, Mazheyk, Mazheyki, Mazik, Mezyk, Mozejki, Murav Evo, Muravievo); pop. 682; 26 km NW of Siauliai; 56°06'/23°06'; AMG, GUM3, HSL, LYV, SF, YL.

Mazheik, *see* Mazeikiai.

Mazheiki, *see* Mazeikiai.

Mazheyk, *see* Mazeikiai.

Mazheyki, *see* Mazeikiai.

Maziarnia Wawrzkowa, *see* Mazyarnya Vavrshkova.

Mazik, *see* Mazeikiai.

Mazoviechi, *see* Nowy Dwor Mazowiecki.

Mazowiecki, COH, JGFF. This town was not found in BGN gazetteers under the given spelling.

Mazurowka, *see* Mazuruvka.

Mazuruvka, Ukr. (Mazurowka); pop. 6; 101 km N of Chernovtsy; 49°09'/25°59'.

Mazury, Pol.; pop. 52; 75 km NW of Przemysl; 50°16'/22°05'; GUM5, PHP3.

Mazyarnya Vavrshkova, Ukr. (Maziarnia Wawrzkowa); pop. 3; 50 km NE of Lvov; 50°06'/24°36'.

Mazzesinsel, YB. This town was not found in BGN gazetteers under the given spelling.

Mcely, Cz.; pop. 8; 50 km NE of Praha; 50°18'/15°05'.

Mchawa, Pol.; pop. 31; 62 km SSW of Przemysl; 49°22'/22°16'.

Mdzewo, Pol.; pop. 6; 94 km NW of Warszawa; 52°57'/20°18'.

Mechenried, Germ.; 82 km NW of Nurnberg; 50°05'/10°29'; HSL, PHGB.

Mechernich, Germ.; 45 km SSW of Koln; 50°36'/06°39'; GUM5.

Mechetinskaya, GUM4. This town was not found in BGN gazetteers under the given spelling.

Mechishchev, Ukr. (Mechishchuv, Mieczyszczow); pop. 53; 88 km ESE of Lvov; 49°22'/24°53'.

Mechishchuv, *see* Mechishchev.

Mechnov, Cz.; pop. 4; 45 km ESE of Praha; 49°48'/14°54'.

Mecholupy, Cz. (Michelob); 69 km WNW of Praha; 50°16'/13°33'; HSL, JGFF.

Mecin, Cz.; pop. 7; 101 km SW of Praha; 49°29'/13°24'.

Mecina, Pol.; pop. 32; 62 km ESE of Krakow; 49°41'/20°34'.

Mecina Wielka, Pol.; pop. 7; 107 km ESE of Krakow; 49°38'/21°16'.

Meciszow, Pol.; pop. 24; 101 km WNW of Przemysl; 50°10'/21°29'.

Meckenhausen, Germ.; 38 km SE of Nurnberg; 49°10'/11°17'; PHGB.

Meckenheim, Germ.; pop. 86; 45 km SSE of Koln; 50°38'/07°01'; GED, JGFF.

Meckesheim, Germ.; pop. 24; 69 km NNW of Stuttgart; 49°20'/08°49'; GED, LDS.

Mecklenburg, Germ.; 50 km SW of Rostock; 53°51'/11°28'; EDRD, EJ, GUM3, GUM5, GUM6, LDS.

Meclov, Cz. (Metzling); pop. 6; 133 km SW of Praha; 49°30'/12°53'; HSL, HSL2.

Mecsekalja, Hung.; pop. 3; 101 km ESE of Nagykanizsa; 46°04'/18°10'.

Mecseknadasd, Hung. (Puspoknadasd); pop. 3; 114 km E of Nagykanizsa; 46°13'/18°28'.

Mecsekszabolcs, Hung.; pop. 12; 101 km ESE of Nagykanizsa; 46°07'/18°16'.

Medebach, Germ.; 126 km N of Frankfurt am Main; 51°12'/08°43'; GUM5.

Medenica, *see* Medenitsa.

Medenice, Ukr.; pop. 216; 50 km S of Lvov; 49°26'/23°45'; AMG, EGRS, HSL, HSL2, PHP2, YB.

Medenitsa, Ukr. (Medenica, Mednitz); 50 km S of Lvov; 49°26'/23°45'; HSL, SF.

Medgyes, Rom. (Megyes); HSL, HSL2, LDL. This pre-World War I community was not found in BGN gazetteers.

Medgyesegyhaza, Hung. (Medgyeshaza); pop. 60; 75 km NE of Szeged; 46°30'/21°02'; PHH.

Medgyeshaza, *see* Medgyesegyhaza.

Medias, Rom. (Mediasch); 88 km SE of Cluj; 46°10'/24°21'; GUM4, PHR1.

Mediasch, *see* Medias.

Mediasul Aurit, *see* Mediesu Aurit.

Mediedischki, LDL. This pre-World War I community was not found in BGN gazetteers.

Mediesu Aurit, Rom. (Aranyomeggyes, Aranyosmegyes, Mediasul Aurit, Mediesul Aurit); pop. 260; 120 km NNW of Cluj; 47°47'/23°09'; HSL, LDL, PHR2.

Mediesul Aurit, *see* Mediesu Aurit.

Medin, Ukr.; pop. 32; 120 km S of Rovno; 49°36'/26°09'; GUM4.

Medina, Ukr. (Medynia, Medynya); pop. 29; 101 km SE of Lvov; 49°05'/24°35'; HSL.

Medingenai, Lith.; 75 km WSW of Siauliai; 55°49'/22°05'; YL.

Medininkai, *see* Varniai.

Medisa, Rom. (Arannnyosmeggyes, Aranymegges); pop. 9; 107 km NW of Cluj; 47°36'/23°00'.

Medlesice, Cz.; pop. 3; 94 km E of Praha; 49°59'/15°46'.

Medna, Byel. (Miedna); 163 km WSW of Pinsk; 51°52'/23°45'; SF.

Medni, Lat. (Ungurmuiza); 88 km NNW of Daugavpils; 56°37'/26°05'; PHLE.

Mednitz, *see* Medenitsa.

Medrzechow, Pol.; pop. 36; 82 km NE of Krakow; 50°18'/20°57'; CAHJP, HSL.

Meducha, *see* Medukha.

Medukha, Ukr. (Meducha); pop. 37; 101 km SE of Lvov; 49°09'/24°49'.

Medvedevka, *see* Medvedka.

Medvedichi, Byel. (Medveditch, Medwiedischki, Niedzwiedzica); pop. 116; 101 km N of Pinsk; 52°56'/26°18'; SF.

Medveditch, *see* Medvedichi.

Medvedka, Ukr. (Medvedevka); 26 km N of Vinnitsa; 49°23'/28°28'; EJ.

Medvedovce, *see* Medvedzie.

Medvedovka, Ukr. (Medwjedowka); 163 km NE of Uman; 49°10'/32°23'; HSL, SF.

Medvedzie, Cz. (Medvedovce); 139 km WNW of Kosice; 49°20'/19°33'; HSL.

Medvezhaya Gora, USSR; pop. 31; This town was not found in BGN gazetteers under the given spelling.

Medvinovtsy, Byel. (Miedwinowicze); pop. 8; 150 km NNW of Pinsk; 53°23'/25°18'.

Medwiedischki, *see* Medvedichi.

Medwjedowka, *see* Medvedovka.

Medyka, Pol.; pop. 132; 13 km ENE of Przemysl; 49°48'/22°56'; PHP2.

Medynia, *see* Medina.

Medynia Glogowska, Pol.; pop. 47; 62 km WNW of Przemysl; 50°10'/22°08'.

Medynia Lancucka, Pol.; pop. 5; 62 km WNW of Przemysl; 50°08'/22°08'.

Medynya, *see* Medina.

Medze, Lat.; pop. 1; 182 km WSW of Riga; 56°39'/21°08'.

Medzhibozh, Ukr. (Medzibezh, Medzibozh, Mezhibezh, Miedzyboz, Smiedzyborz); pop. 4,614; 82 km W of Vinnitsa; 49°26'/27°25'; COH, EJ, HSL, JGFF, LDL.

Medzibezh, *see* Medzhibozh.

Medziboz, *see* Miedzyborz.

Medzibozh, *see* Medzhibozh.

Medzilaborce, Cz. (Mezolaborc, Mezolabore); pop. 1,661; 82 km NNE of Kosice; 49°16'/21°55'; AMG, COH, GUM4, GUM5, GUM5, GUM6, HSL, HSL2, JGFF.

Medzula, Lat.; pop. 3; 114 km ENE of Riga; 57°01'/25°57'.

Meerane, Germ.; pop. 27; 56 km SSE of Leipzig; 50°51'/12°28'.

Meerbeck, Germ.; 38 km WSW of Hannover; 52°20'/09°09'; GED.

Meerholz, Germ.; pop. 56; 32 km ENE of Frankfurt am Main; 50°11'/09°08'; JGFF.

Meersburg, Germ.; 126 km S of Stuttgart; 47°42'/09°16'; PHGBW.

Megesheim, Germ.; 69 km SSW of Nurnberg; 48°56'/10°39'; PHGB.

Meggyesfalva, Rom. (Megyesfalva); HSL. This pre-World War I community was not found in BGN gazetteers.

Megyaszo, Hung.; pop. 99; 26 km NE of Miskolc; 48°11'/21°03'; AMG, HSL, PHH.

Megyer, Hung.; 75 km N of Nagykanizsa; 47°04'/17°12'; HSL.

Megyes, *see* Medgyes.

Megyesfalva, *see* Meggyesfalva.

Mehlauken, *see* Zalesye.

Mehlsack, *see* Pieniezno.

Mehr, Germ.; 94 km NNW of Koln; 51°44'/06°29'; EDRD, EJ.

Mehringen, Germ.; pop. 30; 126 km NNE of Koln; 51°55'/07°54'.

Mehtelek, Hung.; pop. 26; 157 km E of Miskolc; 47°56'/22°51'.

Meidling, Aus. BGN lists two possible localities with this name located at 48°10'/16°20' and 48°20'/15°37'. PHP2.

Meienci, Yug.; pop. 32; This town was not found in BGN gazetteers under the given spelling.

Meiliski, *see* Meiliskiai.

Meiliskiai, Lith. (Meiliski); 56 km SSE of Siauliai; 55°29'/23°32'; JGFF.

Meilnik, HSL. This pre-World War I community was not found in BGN gazetteers.

Meimbressen, Germ. (Ehrsten); pop. 62; 114 km S of Hannover; 51°24'/09°21'; GED, JGFF, LDS.

Meinerzhagen, Germ.; pop. 46; 56 km NE of Koln; 51°07'/07°39'; GED.

Meiningen, Germ.; pop. 293; 133 km NE of Frankfurt am Main; 50°33'/10°25'; GUM3, LDS.

Meinsen, Germ.; 32 km SW of Hannover; 52°15'/09°21'; GED.

Meinz, Pol. PHP2. This town was not found in BGN gazetteers under the given spelling.

Meirani, Lat. (Meiranu); pop. 22; 114 km N of Daugavpils; 56°50'/26°37'.

Meiranu, *see* Meirani.

Meisad, *see* Mosedis.

Meisenheim, Germ.; pop. 38; 82 km SW of Frankfurt am Main; 49°43'/07°40'; HSL.

Meissen, Germ.; pop. 40; 82 km E of Leipzig; 51°09'/13°29'; EJ.

Mejszagola, *see* Maisiagala.

Mekhev, *see* Miechow.

Melbach, Germ.; 38 km N of Frankfurt am Main; 50°23'/08°49'; LDS.

Melbeck, Germ.; 45 km SE of Hamburg; 53°11'/10°24'; JGFF.

Meleghegy, Hung. BGN lists two possible localities with this name located at 46°48'/17°07' and 46°58'/17°52'. HSL.

Meleseni, *see* Melesheny.

Meleshen, *see* Melesheny.

Melesheny, Mold. (Meleseni, Meleshen); pop. 48; 50 km NW of Kishinev; 47°22'/28°23'.

Melgiew, Pol.; pop. 58; 13 km E of Lublin; 51°14'/22°47'.

Meliat, *see* Moletai.

Meliata, Cz. (Mellete); 69 km SW of Kosice; 48°31'/20°20';

HSL.

Melitopol, Ukr.; pop. 8,583; 182 km SSE of Dnepropetrovsk; 46°50'/35°22'; AMG, EJ, GUM4, HSL, HSL2, JGFF, SF.

Melits, *see* Mielec.

Melitz, *see* Mielec.

Melle, Germ.; pop. 8; 94 km WSW of Hannover; 52°12'/08°21'.

Mellete, *see* Meliata.

Mellrichstadt, Germ.; pop. 151; 120 km NE of Frankfurt am Main; 50°26'/10°19'; CAHJP, EDRD, GUM3, GUM5, PHGB.

Melnich, Ukr. (Mielniczne?); pop. 110; 75 km SSE of Lvov; 49°14'/24°17'; PHP2.

Melnik, *see* Mielnik.

Melnitsa, Ukr.; pop. 871; 101 km WNW of Rovno; 51°09'/25°06'; COH, HSL, LDL, SF. *See also* Melnitsa Podolskaya.

Melnitsa Podolskaya, Ukr. (Melnitsa, Melnitse, Melnitza, Mielnica, Mielnice, Myelnitsa); pop. 1,411; 38 km NNE of Chernovtsy; 48°37'/26°10'; AMG, COH, EDRD, EGRS, GUM3, GUM4, GUM5, HSL2, JGFF, LDL, LYV, PHP2, YB.

Melnitse, *see* Melnitsa Podolskaya.

Melnitza, *see* Melnitsa Podolskaya.

Melonek, Pol.; pop. 5; 114 km NE of Krakow; 50°44'/21°09'.

Melperts, Germ.; pop. 3; 107 km NE of Frankfurt am Main; 50°31'/10°01'.

Melsungen, Germ.; pop. 76; 133 km NNE of Frankfurt am Main; 51°08'/09°33'; CAHJP, LDS.

Meltsy, Ukr. (Mielce); pop. 23; 146 km WNW of Rovno; 51°27'/24°45'.

Melykut, Hung.; pop. 71; 62 km WSW of Szeged; 46°13'/19°23'; PHH.

Mema, LDL. This pre-World War I community was not found in BGN gazetteers.

Memel, *see* Klaipeda.

Memmelsdorf, Germ.; pop. 33; 56 km NNW of Nurnberg; 49°56'/10°57'; CAHJP, GUM5, HSL, JGFF, PHGB, PHGB.

Memmingen, Germ.; pop. 161; 107 km WSW of Munchen; 47°59'/10°10'; EJ, GED, GUM3, GUM5, PHGB, PHGBW.

Mena, Ukr. (Myena); pop. 1,321; 75 km WNW of Konotop; 51°31'/32°13'; SF.

Mende, Hung.; pop. 13; 32 km ESE of Budapest; 47°25'/19°27'.

Menden, Germ.; pop. 32; 75 km NE of Koln; 51°26'/07°48'; GUM5.

Mendicauti, *see* Mendikauts.

Mendikauts, Ukr. (Mendicauti); pop. 21; 101 km ENE of Chernovtsy; 48°24'/27°16'.

Menes, HSL. This pre-World War I community was not found in BGN gazetteers.

Mengele, Lat.; pop. 15; 82 km E of Riga; 56°49'/25°24'.

Mengen, Germ.; 88 km SSE of Stuttgart; 48°03'/09°20'; EDRD.

Mengeringhausen, Germ.; pop. 23; 126 km SSW of Hannover; 51°21'/08°59'.

Menschede, GUM5. This town was not found in BGN gazetteers under the given spelling.

Mensengesass, Germ.; pop. 4; 38 km E of Frankfurt am Main; 50°04'/09°10'.

Menslage, Germ.; 133 km W of Hannover; 52°41'/07°49'; JGFF.

Men Yryczy, LDL. This pre-World War I community was not found in BGN gazetteers.

Menzhirichi, *see* Mezherichi.

Menzingen, Germ.; pop. 6; 56 km NW of Stuttgart; 49°09'/08°46'; LDS, PHGBW.

Menzyryczy, *see* Mezherichi.

Meppen, Germ.; pop. 53; 163 km W of Hannover; 52°41'/07°19'; GUM5, LDS.

Merch, *see* Merkine.

Merchingen, Germ.; pop. 62; 75 km N of Stuttgart; 49°24'/09°30'; HSL, HSL2, LDS, PHGBW.

Merchweiler, Germ.; pop. 26; 146 km SW of Frankfurt am Main; 49°21'/07°03'; GED.

Mercin, Cz.; 88 km SSW of Praha; 49°31'/13°41'; HSL.

Mercurea Ciuc, *see* Miercurea Ciuc.

Mercurea Nirajului, *see* Miercurea Nirajului.

Merdzene, Lat.; pop. 9; 120 km NE of Daugavpils; 56°41'/27°45'.

Merech, *see* Merkine.

Merefa, Ukr.; pop. 42; 26 km SSW of Kharkov; 49°48'/36°03'.

Merenberg, Germ.; pop. 8; 56 km NW of Frankfurt am Main; 50°31'/08°11'.

Meresti, Rom. (Homorodalmas); 150 km ESE of Cluj; 46°14'/25°27'; HSL.

Meretch, *see* Merkine.

Meretske, Byel. (Miereckie); pop. 3; 150 km N of Minsk; 55°12'/27°38'.

Mergentheim, *see* Bad Mergentheim.

Merinitseni, Ukr. (Mareniceni, Marenicheni); pop. 25; 69 km WSW of Chernovtsy; 48°08'/25°03'; PHR2.

Meritz, *see* Merkine.

Merk, Hung.; pop. 85; 120 km ESE of Miskolc; 47°47'/22°22'; HSL, PHH.

Merken, Germ.; 45 km WSW of Koln; 50°51'/06°25'; GED.

Merkengersch, Aus.; pop. 1; 107 km WNW of Wien; 48°53'/15°19'.

Merkine, Lith. (Merch, Merech, Meretch, Meritz, Merts, Mertsh); pop. 1,430; 88 km SSE of Kaunas; 54°10'/24°10'; COH, GUM5, HSL, HSL2, JGFF, LDL, LYV, SF, YL.

Merkulovichi, Byel. (Gorodets [Polesie], Horodec, Horodets); pop. 264; 101 km W of Pinsk; 52°12'/24°40'; EDRD, FRG, HSL, JGFF, LDL, SF, YB.

Merlau, Germ.; pop. 6; 62 km NNE of Frankfurt am Main; 50°37'/09°02'; AMG.

Mernye, Hung.; pop. 5; 62 km ENE of Nagykanizsa; 46°30'/17°50'.

Merovce, Cz.; 133 km ENE of Bratislava; 48°10'/18°54'; HSL.

Merseburg, Germ.; pop. 64; 26 km WNW of Leipzig; 51°22'/12°00'; EJ.

Mersevat, Hung.; pop. 4; 101 km N of Nagykanizsa; 47°17'/17°13'.

Mertloch, Germ.; pop. 10; 82 km SSE of Koln; 50°16'/07°19'.

Merts, *see* Merkine.

Mertsh, *see* Merkine.

Merunice, Cz.; pop. 3; 62 km WNW of Praha; 50°29'/13°49'.

Merxheim, Germ.; pop. 31; 88 km SW of Frankfurt am Main; 49°47'/07°34'; JGFF.

Merzbach, Germ. BGN lists two possible localities with this name located at 49°28'/10°35' and 50°36'/06°56'. HSL.

Merzhausen, Germ.; pop. 53; 32 km NW of Frankfurt am Main; 50°19'/08°28'; LDS.

Merzig, Germ.; pop. 204; 163 km SW of Frankfurt am Main; 49°27'/06°38'; AMG, GED, GUM5, JGFF, YB.

Meschede, Germ.; pop. 52; 107 km NE of Koln; 51°21'/08°17'; AMG.

Meschigorie, *see* Mezhgorye.

Meseni, *see* Misheny.

Meseritz, *see* Mezhirichi.

Mesetice, Cz.; pop. 4; 62 km S of Praha; 49°35'/14°31'.

Meshana Dolna, *see* Mszana Dolna.

Meshchovsk, USSR; pop. 48; 133 km NNE of Bryansk; 54°19'/35°17'.

Mesherov, *see* Mezhirov.

Meshkots, *see* Meskuiciai.

Meshkov, Ukr. (Myszkow); pop. 25; 56 km NNW of Chernovtsy; 48°46'/25°50'.

Meskai, Lith.; pop. 15; 101 km SSW of Siauliai; 55°12'/22°21'.

Meskoviche, Byel. (Mieskowicze); pop. 13; 13 km S of Pinsk; 52°02'/26°05'.

Meskuiciai, Lith. (Meshkots); 50 km SW of Siauliai; 55°42'/22°40'; YL.

Mesno, Cz.; pop. 4; 82 km SW of Praha; 49°39'/13°37'.

Messel, Germ.; pop. 21; 26 km SSE of Frankfurt am Main; 49°56'/08°45'; LDS.

Messelhausen, Germ.; pop. 13; 94 km W of Nurnberg; 49°35'/09°47'; PHGBW.

Messenkamp, Germ.; 26 km SW of Hannover; 52°15'/09°23'; GED.

Messern, Aus.; pop. 4; 82 km WNW of Wien; 48°43'/15°31'.

Messinghausen, Germ.; pop. 4; 126 km NE of Koln; 51°23'/08°40'.

Messingwerk, HSL. This pre-World War I community was not found in BGN gazetteers.

Messkirch, Germ.; pop. 4; 94 km S of Stuttgart; 47°59'/09°07'; EDRD.

Mestec, *see* Mestec Kralove.

Mesteceni, Rom.; pop. 82; 94 km WNW of Iasi; 47°24'/26°25'.

Mestec Kralove, Cz. (Mestec); pop. 47; 62 km ENE of Praha; 50°12'/15°18'; HSL.

Mesterhaza, Hung.; pop. 7; 107 km N of Nagykanizsa; 47°22'/16°52'.

Mestkovka, *see* Gorodkovka.

Mesto Libava, Cz. (Librava Mesto); pop. 74; 88 km NE of Brno; 49°43'/17°31'.

Mesto Stare, Cz.; pop. 22; Described in the *Black Book* as being in the Bohemia region of Czechoslovakia, this town was not found in BGN gazetteers.

Mesto Touskov, Cz.; pop. 45; 94 km SW of Praha; 49°47'/13°15'.

Mesto Zdar, Cz. (Zdar); pop. 29; 69 km WNW of Brno; 49°34'/15°57'; JGFF.

Mestys Stankov, *see* Stankov.

Meszes, Hung.; pop. 21; 45 km N of Miskolc; 48°26'/20°48'; HSL.

Meszna Opacka, Pol.; pop. 13; 75 km E of Krakow; 49°54'/20°59'.

Meszna Szlachecka, Pol.; pop. 11; 75 km E of Krakow; 49°55'/20°58'.

Mesztegnyo, Hung. (Kak); pop. 7; 32 km ENE of Nagykanizsa; 46°30'/17°26'; HSL.

Meteliai, Lith.; pop. 62; 75 km S of Kaunas; 54°18'/23°45'.

Metkow, Pol.; pop. 4; 38 km WSW of Krakow; 50°03'/19°22'.

Metriena, Lat.; pop. 17; 94 km NNW of Daugavpils; 56°40'/26°19'.

Mettmann, Germ.; pop. 8; 38 km N of Koln; 51°15'/06°58'.

Metzerwisse, HSL. This pre-World War I community was not found in BGN gazetteers.

Metzingen, Germ.; 32 km SSE of Stuttgart; 48°32'/09°16'; PHGBW.

Metzling, *see* Meclov.

Meudt, Germ.; pop. 43; 69 km WNW of Frankfurt am Main; 50°30'/07°54'; GUM5, JGFF.

Meuselwitz, Germ.; pop. 30; 32 km S of Leipzig; 51°03'/12°18'; GUM4.

Mevrotsh, *see* Mauruciai.

Meytshet, *see* Molchad.

Mezapark, *see* Mezaparks.

Mezaparks, Lat. (Kaiserwald, Mezapark); 13 km NNE of Riga; 57°00'/24°10'; GUM3, PHLE.

Mezciems, Lat. (Pogulianka, Pogulyanka); 13 km WNW of Daugavpils; 55°55'/26°27'; PHLE.

Mezerich, *see* Miedzyrzec.

Mezerich Gadol, *see* Mezhirichi.

Mezerich Korets, *see* Mezhirichi.

Mezeritch Katan, *see* Mezherichi.

Mezeritz D'lita, *see* Miedzyrzec Podlaski.

Mezeritz Gadol, *see* Miedzyrzecz Volhyn.

Mezgorje, *see* Mezhgorye.

Mezherichi, Ukr. (Menzhirichi, Menzyryczy, Mezeritch Katan, Mezyryczy); pop. 208; 38 km SE of Rovno; 50°18'/26°29'; SF.

Mezheyki, Byel. (Mierzejki); pop. 39; 62 km WNW of Minsk; 54°06'/26°39'.

Mezhgorye, Ukr. (Meschigorie, Mezgorje, Okormezo, Volove, Volovo, Wolowa, Wolowe); pop. 4,966; 150 km S of Lvov; 48°32'/23°30'; AMG, COH, EDRD, GUM3, GUM4, GUM6, HSL, LDL, PHP2, SM.

Mezhibezh, *see* Medzhibozh.

Mezhibozh, *see* Miedzyborz.

Mezhirech, *see* Miedzyrzec.

Mezhirechye, Ukr. (Chudin, Ciudeiu, Czudyn, Czudzin); pop. 570; 45 km SSW of Chernovtsy; 48°03'/25°37'; COH, EDRD, EJ, LDL, PHR2, SF.

Mezhirichi, Ukr. (Meseritz, Mezerich Gadol, Mezerich Korets, Mezyrycz Korecki, Miedzyrzec Korzecki, Miedzyrzec Wolyn, Miedzyrzecz); pop. 1,743; 45 km ENE of Rovno; 50°39'/26°52'; CAHJP, GUM4, HSL, JGFF, SF, YB.

Mezhirov, Ukr. (Mesherov, Mezirov); pop. 1,015; 45 km SW of Vinnitsa; 49°05'/28°01'; LDL, SF.

Mezhrechye, Byel. (Miedzyrzecz [Bialystok]); pop. 13; 139 km NW of Pinsk; 53°04'/24°46'.

Mezhvitsa, Ukr. (Mierzwica); pop. 20; 19 km N of Lvov; 50°00'/24°02'.

Mezica, Yug.; pop. 1; 120 km WNW of Zagreb; 46°31'/14°52'.

Meziklasi, Cz.; pop. 3; 82 km ESE of Praha; 49°38'/15°21'.

Mezimesti, Cz.; pop. 2; 139 km NE of Praha; 50°37'/16°15'.

Mezimosti, *see* Mezimosti nad Nezarkou.

Mezimosti nad Nezarkou, Cz. (Mezimosti); pop. 23; 107 km SSE of Praha; 49°11'/14°42'.

Mezirici Valesske, *see* Valasske Mezirici.

Mezirov, *see* Mezhirov.

Mezobereny, Hung.; pop. 166; 94 km NE of Szeged; 46°49'/21°02'; HSL, LDS, PHH.

Mezobodon, *see* Budiul de Campie.

Mezocsan, *see* Ceanu Mare.

Mezocsat, Hung.; pop. 536; 38 km SSE of Miskolc; 47°49'/20°55'; COH, GUM4, HSL, LDL, LDS, PHH.

Mezocsokonya, Hung.; pop. 16; 50 km E of Nagykanizsa; 46°26'/17°39'.

Mezoermenyas, HSL. This pre-World War I community was not found in BGN gazetteers.

Mezofalva, Hung. (Hercegfalva); pop. 14; 69 km S of Budapest; 46°56'/18°46'.

Mezogyan, Hung.; 126 km NE of Szeged; 46°52'/21°32'; LDS.

Mezohegyes, Hung.; pop. 17; 50 km ENE of Szeged; 46°19'/20°49'.

Mezokapus, *see* Capusu de Cimpie.

Mezokaszony, *see* Kosiny.

Mezokemenytelke, HSL. This pre-World War I community was not found in BGN gazetteers.

Mezokeresztes, Hung.; pop. 257; 32 km S of Miskolc; 47°50'/20°42'; GUM3, GUM5, HSL, LDL, LDS, PHH.

Mezokomarom, Hung.; pop. 23; 94 km SSW of Budapest; 46°50'/18°17'.

Mezokovacs, HSL. This pre-World War I community was not found in BGN gazetteers.

Mezokovacshaza, Hung.; pop. 382; 62 km NE of Szeged; 46°24'/20°55'; HSL, PHH.

Mezokovesd, Hung.; pop. 874; 38 km SSW of Miskolc; 47°49'/20°35'; AMG, COH, GUM4, HSL, HSL2, LDL, LDS, PHH.

Mezolaborc, *see* Medzilaborce.

Mezolabore, *see* Medzilaborce.

Mezoladany, Hung. (Orladany); pop. 133; 107 km ENE of Miskolc; 48°17'/22°13'; GUM5, HSL, LDS, PHH.

Mezolak, Hung.; pop. 29; 107 km N of Nagykanizsa; 47°20'/17°22'; HSL.

Mezomegyer, Hung.; pop. 3; 88 km NE of Szeged; 46°43'/21°04'.

Mezomehes, *see* Miheseul de Campi.

Mezonagymihaly, Hung.; pop. 17; 38 km S of Miskolc; 47°49'/20°44'; HSL.

Mezonyarad, Hung.; pop. 34; 32 km S of Miskolc; 47°52'/20°41'; HSL.

Mezonyek, Hung.; pop. 70; HSL. This pre-World War I community was not found in BGN gazetteers.

Mezoors, Hung.; pop. 23; 88 km W of Budapest; 47°34'/17°53'.

Mezopeterd, Hung.; 120 km SE of Miskolc; 47°10'/21°37'; LDS.

Mezosaly, *see* Saulia.

Mezosas, Hung.; pop. 33; 126 km SE of Miskolc; 47°07'/21°34'.

Mezoseg, HSL. This pre-World War I community was not found in BGN gazetteers.

Mezoszabad, *see* Voiniceni.

Mezoszakal, *see* Sacalul de Campi.

Mezoszemere, Hung. (Borsodszemere); pop. 13; 45 km SSW of Miskolc; 47°45'/20°32'.

Mezoszentgyorgy, Hung.; pop. 14; 82 km SW of Budapest; 47°00'/18°17'; AMG.

Mezoszentmarton, *see* Sinmartin.

Mezoszilas, Hung. (Szilas Balhas, Szilasbalhas); pop. 54; 88 km SSW of Budapest; 46°49'/18°29'; HSL, LDL, LDS, PHH.

Mezoszopor, *see* Soporu de Cimpie.

Mezotarkany, Hung.; pop. 33; 45 km SSW of Miskolc; 47°43'/20°29'; HSL.

Mezo Telegd, *see* Tileagd.

Mezotelegd, *see* Tileagd.

Mezotohat, *see* Taureni.

Mezotur, Hung.; pop. 584; 94 km N of Szeged; 47°00'/20°38'; AMG, GUM5, HSL, HSL2, LDS, PHH.

Mezovari, HSL. This pre-World War I community was not found in BGN gazetteers.

Mezovelker, *see* Velcherul de Campi.

Mezozah, *see* Zau de Cimpie.

Mezozombor, Hung.; pop. 7; 38 km ENE of Miskolc; 48°09'/21°16'; HSL.

Mezrich, *see* Miedzyrzec.

Mezritsh, *see* Miedzyrzec.

Mezyk, *see* Mazeikiai.

Mezyrycz Korecki, *see* Mezhirichi.

Mezyryczy, *see* Mezherichi.

Mglin, USSR; pop. 1,244; 101 km WSW of Bryansk; 53°04'/32°51'.

Miaczyn, Pol.; pop. 76; 82 km ESE of Lublin; 50°45'/23°30'.

Miadziol, GUM3, GUM4, GUM5, HSL. This pre-World War I community was not found in BGN gazetteers.

Miadziol Nowy, Byel.; pop. 133; 107 km NW of Minsk; 54°45'/26°55'; COH, GUM3. This town was located on an interwar map of Poland but does not appear in contemporary gazetteers. Map coordinates are approximate.

Miadziol Stary, Byel.; pop. 35; 107 km NW of Minsk; 54°45'/26°55'; GUM3. This town was located on an interwar map of Poland but does not appear in contemporary gazetteers. Map coordinates are approximate.

Mianowek, Pol. PHP4. This town was not found in BGN gazetteers under the given spelling.

Mianowice, Pol.; pop. 13; 94 km W of Gdansk; 54°27'/17°13'.

Miase, Pol.; pop. 2; 32 km NE of Warszawa; 52°24'/21°27'.

Miaskivka, *see* Mjaskowka.

Miaskowo, Pol. BGN lists two possible localities with this name located at 51°56'/16°48' and 52°10'/17°23'. GUM3.

Miasowa, Pol.; pop. 26; 75 km NNE of Krakow; 50°43'/20°22'.

Miastko, Pol. (Rummelsberg, Rummelsburg); pop. 60; 114 km SW of Gdansk; 54°00'/16°59'.

Miastkovka, *see* Gorodkovka.

Miastkow Stary, Pol.; pop. 4; 62 km ESE of Warszawa; 51°55'/21°48'.

Miava, *see* Myjava.

Mica, Rom.; 45 km NNE of Cluj; 47°08'/23°56'; HSL.

Micasasa, Rom. (Mikeszasza); 88 km SE of Cluj; 46°05'/24°07'; HSL.

Micauti, *see* Mikautsy.

Micestii de Campie, *see* Micestii de Cimpie.

Micestii de Cimpie, Rom. (Micestii de Campie); pop. 72; 56 km ENE of Cluj; 46°52'/24°19'.

Micfalau, Rom.; pop. 6; 182 km N of Bucuresti; 46°03'/25°50'.

Michaelsdorf, JGFF. A number of towns share this name. It was not possible to determine from available information which one is being referenced.

Michailowka, LDL. This pre-World War I community was not found in BGN gazetteers.

Michajlowka, *see* Mikhalovka.

Michalany, Cz.; pop. 96; 32 km ESE of Kosice; 48°31'/21°38'; AMG.

Michalcze, *see* Mikhalche.

Michalczowa, Pol.; pop. 4; 62 km ESE of Krakow; 49°46'/20°37'.

Michalin, *see* Mikhalin. The *Black Book* indicates a town named Michalin (pop. 55) in the interwar Polish province of Lublin that does not appear in interwar or contemporary gazetteers.

Michaliszki, *see* Mikhalishki.

Michalkovice, Cz.; pop. 61; 146 km NE of Brno; 49°50'/18°21'.

Michalkowice, Pol.; 94 km SSW of Czestochowa; 50°02'/18°34'; PHP3.

Michalok, Cz. (Mihalko); 45 km NNE of Kosice; 48°59'/21°38'; HSL.

Michalova, *see* Michalowo.

Michalovce, Cz. (Michalowitz, Mihalevich, Mikhalovich, Mikhalowitz, Nadimihali, Nadzhmihali, Nagymihaly); pop. 4,761; 50 km ENE of Kosice; 48°45'/21°56'; AMG, COH, EJ, GUM4, GUM5, GUM6, HSL, HSL2, JGFF, LDL, LYV, YB.

Michalowek, Pol. PHP4. A number of towns share this name. It was not possible to determine from available information which one is being referenced.

Michalowice, Pol.; 13 km NNE of Krakow; 50°10'/19°59'; CAHJP. *See also* Mikhaylovichi.

Michalowitz, *see* Michalovce.

Michalowka, *see* Mikhaylovka (Wolyn).

Michalowo, Pol. (Michalova, Mihalytelke, Nezbodka); pop. 887; 32 km ESE of Bialystok; 53°02'/23°36'; GA, GUM3, HSL, LDL, POCEM, SF.

Michalpol, *see* Mikhaylovka.

Michaylovka, *see* Mikhaylovka.

Michelbach, *see* Michelbach an der Lucke.

Michelbach (Bavaria), GUM3. This town was not found in BGN gazetteers under the given spelling.

Michelbach an der Lucke, Germ. (Michelbach); pop. 42; 75 km SW of Nurnberg; 49°14'/10°07'; LDS, PHGBW.

Michelbach Markt, Aus.; 45 km WSW of Wien; 48°06'/15°45'; JGFF.

Michelfeld, Germ.; 56 km NW of Stuttgart; 49°14'/08°47'; LDS, PHGBW.

Michelhausen, Aus.; pop. 6; 32 km WNW of Wien; 48°17'/15°56'.

Michelob, *see* Mecholupy.

Michelpolia, *see* Mikhaylovka.

Michelstadt, Germ.; pop. 90; 50 km SE of Frankfurt am Main; 49°41'/09°01'; CAHJP, GED, GUM5, HSL, YB.

Michendorf, Germ.; pop. 9; 32 km SW of Berlin; 52°18'/13°01'.

Michle, HSL. This pre-World War I community was not found in BGN gazetteers.

Michniowice, Pol.; pop. 35; Described in the *Black Book* as being in the Stanislawow region of Poland, this town was not found in BGN gazetteers.

Michov, *see* Michow Lubartowski.

Michow, *see* Michow Lubartowski.

Michowice, Pol.; pop. 6; 45 km ENE of Lodz; 51°50'/20°06'.

Michow Lubartowski, Pol. (Michov, Michow, Mikhov); pop. 1,711; 38 km NW of Lublin; 51°32'/22°18'; AMG, COH, GUM5, HSL, LDS, POCEM, SF.

Miclesti, *see* Mikleshty.

Micola, Rom. (Mikola); HSL. This pre-World War I community was not found in BGN gazetteers.

Micske, *see* Ujfeherto.

Micula, Rom.; pop. 138; 139 km NNW of Cluj; 47°54'/22°57'; PHR2.

Micus, Rom. (Mikes); HSL. This pre-World War I community was not found in BGN gazetteers.

Miechocin, Pol.; pop. 5; 101 km SSW of Lublin; 50°34'/21°40'.

Miechov, *see* Miechow.

Miechow, Pol. (Mekhev, Miechov, Myekhov); pop. 2,383; 38 km N of Krakow; 50°22'/20°02'; AMG, COH, FRG, GA, GUM3, GUM4, GUM5, GUM6, HSL, LYV, PHP3, PHP4, SF, YB.

Miechow Charsznica, Pol.; 38 km N of Krakow; 50°24'/19°57'; AMG.

Miechowice, Pol. (Miechowiec, Miechowitz); pop. 29; 50 km S of Czestochowa; 50°22'/18°52'; LDS.

Miechowice Male, Pol.; pop. 22; 62 km ENE of Krakow; 50°10'/20°46'.

Miechowice Wielkie, Pol.; pop. 15; 62 km ENE of Krakow; 50°11'/20°45'.

Miechowiec, *see* Miechowice.

Miechowitz, *see* Miechowice.

Mieczyn, Pol.; pop. 9; 75 km ENE of Czestochowa; 50°55'/20°12'.

Mieczyszczow, *see* Mechishchev.

Miedna, *see* Medna.

Miedniki, *see* Varniai.

Miedwinowicze, *see* Medvinovtsy.

Miedzechow, Pol.; pop. 7; 56 km S of Warszawa; 51°50'/21°02'.

Miedzeszyn, Pol.; 19 km ESE of Warszawa; 52°10'/21°09'; GUM4, GUM5.

Miedzeszynek, Pol.; pop. 100; PHP4. Described in the *Black Book* as being in the Warszawa region of Poland, this town was not found in BGN gazetteers.

Miedzianka, Pol.; 88 km ENE of Czestochowa; 50°50'/20°22'; GUM4.

Miedzierza, Pol.; pop. 28; 94 km NE of Czestochowa; 51°05'/20°24'; PHP1.

Miedzna, Pol.; pop. 27; 75 km NE of Warszawa; 52°28'/22°06'; HSL.

Miedzna Murowana, Pol.; pop. 6; 75 km ESE of Lodz; 51°18'/20°14'.

Miedzno, Pol.; pop. 124; 32 km NW of Czestochowa; 50°59'/18°59'; AMG, GUM4.

Miedzyborz, (Medziboz, Mezhibozh); HSL2, SF. A number of towns share this name. It was not possible to determine from available information which one is being referenced. This town name normally refers to Medzhibozh in the Ukraine, but there is at least one town in Poland with the same name. *See* Miedzyborz (Kalisz area).

Miedzyborz (Kalisz area), Pol. (Neumittelwalde); 62 km NE of Wroclaw; 51°24'/17°40'; CAHJP, LDS.

Miedzyboz, *see* Medzhibozh.

Miedzychod, Pol. (Birnbaum); pop. 42; 75 km W of Poznan; 52°36'/15°54'; GUM3, HSL, LDS.

Miedzygorz, Pol.; pop. 40; 88 km SW of Lublin; 50°44'/21°34'.

Miedzyles, HSL. A number of towns share this name. It was not possible to determine from available information which one is being referenced.

Miedzyrzec, Ukr. (Mezerich, Mezhirech, Mezrich, Mezritsh, Myedzirzets, Myendzirzets); The names Meseritz, Mezerich, Mezhirech, Mezrich, Miedzyrzec, Myedzirzets and Myendzirzets may be associated with one of five towns: Miedzyrzec Podlaski, Miedzyrzec Wolyn, Miedzyrzecz (now called Mezherichi), Menzyryczy (now called Mezhirichi) and Miedzyrzecz (Poznan). Properly, those town names ending with "ts" or "c" are associated with the first two towns and those synonyms with a "ch" or "cz" suffix with the remaining towns. Miedzyrzec means "between the rivers."

Miedzyrzec (Wolyn), Pol. (Miedzyrzec Wolynski); pop. 1,743; EJ, LDL. Described in the *Black Book* as being in the Wolyn region of Poland, this town was not found in BGN gazetteers.

Miedzyrzec Korzecki, *see* Mezhirichi.

Miedzyrzec Podlaski, Pol. (Mezeritz D'lita, Myedzirzets Podlask, Myendzirzets Podlas, Stolpno); pop. 9,415; 88 km N of Lublin; 51°59'/22°47'; AMG, CAHJP, COH, EDRD, EJ, FRG, GA, GUM3, GUM4, GUM5, GUM6, GYLA, HSL, HSL2, ISH2, ISH3, JGFF, LDL, LDS, LYV, PHP1, PHP3, PHP4, SF, YB.

Miedzyrzec Wolyn, *see* Mezhirichi.

Miedzyrzec Wolynski, *see* Miedzyrzec (Wolyn).

Miedzyrzecz, *see* Mezhirichi.

Miedzyrzecz (Bialystok), *see* Mezhrechye.

Miedzyrzecz (Poznan), Pol. (Miedzyrzecz Wielkopolski); pop. 105; 94 km W of Poznan; 52°26'/15°35'; LDS. The German name of this town is Meseritz.

Miedzyrzecze Gorne, Pol.; pop. 14; 75 km SW of Krakow; 49°51'/18°57'.

Miedzyrzecz Volhyn, (Mezeritz Gadol);

Miedzyrzecz Wielkopolski, *see* Miedzyrzecz (Poznan).

Miedzyswiec, Pol.; pop. 5; 88 km SW of Krakow; 49°48'/18°48'.

Miedzyzdroje, Pol. (Misdroy); pop. 1; 56 km N of Szczecin; 53°56'/14°27'.

Miehlen, Germ.; pop. 47; 62 km W of Frankfurt am Main; 50°13'/07°50'.

Miejsce, Pol. (Staedtel); 26 km WSW of Krakow; 50°01'/19°31'; LDS, POCEM.

Miekina, *see* Miekinia.

Miekinia, Pol. (Miekina); pop. 1; 26 km WNW of Krakow; 50°10'/19°36'.

Miekisz Nowy, Pol.; pop. 36; 32 km NNE of Przemysl; 50°02'/22°59'.

Miekisz Stary, Pol.; pop. 21; 32 km NNE of Przemysl; 50°02'/22°58'.

Mielce, *see* Meltsy.

Mielciesko, *see* Miescisko.

Mielcuchy, Pol.; pop. 15; 88 km SW of Lodz; 51°28'/18°19'.

Mielec, Pol. (Melits, Melitz, Myelets); pop. 2,807; 107 km ENE of Krakow; 50°17'/21°25'; AMG, COH, EDRD, EGRS, EJ, GA, GUM3, GUM4, GUM5, HSL, HSL2, ISH3, JGFF, LDL, LYV, PHP2, PHP3, SF, YB.

Mieleszki, Pol.; pop. 16; 38 km E of Bialystok; 53°04'/23°42'.

Mielnica, *see* Melnitsa Podolskaya.

Mielnice, *see* Melnitsa Podolskaya.

Mielniczne, *possibly* Melnich.

Mielnik, Pol. (Melnik); pop. 233; 94 km S of Bialystok; 52°20'/23°03'; POCEM, SF.

Mielnow, Pol.; 13 km WSW of Przemysl; 49°46'/22°37'; HSL.

Mien, Pol.; pop. 8; 50 km SSW of Bialystok; 52°47'/22°42'.

Mienia, Pol.; pop. 4; 50 km E of Warszawa; 52°09'/21°42'; GUM4.

Mieniany, Pol.; pop. 2; 114 km ESE of Lublin; 50°44'/23°57'.

Miercurea Ciuc, Rom. (Csikszereda, Mercurea Ciuc); pop. 268; 163 km SW of Iasi; 46°21'/25°48'; GUM4, HSL, PHR2.

Miercurea Nirajului, Rom. (Mercurea Nirajului, Nyaradszereda); pop. 225; 94 km ESE of Cluj; 46°32'/24°48'; HSL, PHR2.

Miereckie, *see* Meretske.

Mierlau, Rom. (Nyarlo); 120 km W of Cluj; 46°55'/22°01'; HSL.

Miernow, Pol.; pop. 7; 56 km NE of Krakow; 50°20'/20°38'.

Mieroszow, Cz.; 139 km NE of Praha; 50°40'/16°11'; POCEM.

Mierzejki, *see* Mezheyki.

Mierzen, Pol.; pop. 6; 32 km SE of Krakow; 49°52'/20°12'.

Mierzwica, *see* Mezhvitsa.

Mierzyce, Pol.; pop. 39; 56 km NW of Czestochowa; 51°10'/18°42'.

Mieschkow, *see* Mieszkow.

Miescisko, Pol. (Mielciesko); 45 km NNE of Poznan; 52°44'/17°20'; POCEM.

Miesenheim, Germ.; 75 km SE of Koln; 50°24'/07°25'; JGFF.

Mieskowicze, *see* Meskoviche.

Mieszkow, Pol. (Mieschkow); pop. 4; 56 km SE of Poznan; 52°02'/17°28'.

Mietustwo, Pol.; pop. 7; 82 km S of Krakow; 49°24'/19°53'.

Migovoye, Ukr. (Mihova, Mikhova, Mikova); pop. 243; 45 km SW of Chernovtsy; 48°09'/25°22'; EDRD, GUM4, PHR2.

Mihaifalau, Rom. (Ermihalyfalva); AMG, GUM3, HSL, HSL2, LDL. This pre-World War I community was not found in BGN gazetteers.

Mihaileanca, *see* Mikhaylyanka.

Mihaileni, Rom. (Csikszentmihaly); pop. 1,490; 139 km WNW of Iasi; 47°58'/26°09'; GUM4, JGFF, LDL. *See also* Mikhayleny.

Mihalaseni, *see* Mikhayleny.

Mihalcea, *see* Mikhalche.

Mihald, Hung.; pop. 18; 13 km E of Nagykanizsa; 46°27'/17°08'.

Mihalevich, *see* Michalovce.

Mihalka, *see* Krajnikov.

Mihalko, *see* Michalok.

Mihalyfa, *see* Kemenesmihalyfa.

Mihalytelke, *see* Michalowo.

Miheseul de Campi, Rom. (Mezomehes); HSL. This pre-World War I community was not found in BGN gazetteers.

Mihoesti, Rom.; 62 km SSW of Cluj; 46°22'/23°03'; HSL.

Mihova, *see* Migovoye.

Mihoveni, Rom.; pop. 4; 126 km WNW of Iasi; 47°41'/26°10'.

Mijaczow, Pol.; pop. 27; 26 km SE of Czestochowa; 50°35'/19°19'.

Mijlocenii Bargaului, *see* Mijlocenii Birgaului.

Mijlocenii Birgaului, Rom. (Mijlocenii Bargaului); pop. 43; 94 km NE of Cluj; 47°13'/24°40'.

Mikaliskis, Lith. (Mykaliskiai); pop. 27; 56 km E of Siauliai; 55°54'/24°14'; JGFF.

Mikashevichi, Byel. (Mikaszewicze); pop. 178; 94 km ENE of Pinsk; 52°13'/27°28'; COH, GUM4, HSL.

Mikaszewicze, *see* Mikashevichi.

Mikautsy, Mold. (Micauti); pop. 22; 26 km NNW of Kishinev; 47°10'/28°45'.

Mikepercs, Hung.; pop. 29; 94 km SE of Miskolc; 47°27'/21°38'; GUM3, JGFF, LDS, YB.

Mikes, *see* Micus.

Mikeszasza, *see* Micasasa.

Mikhailovgrad, *see* Mikhaylovgrad.

Mikhailovka, *see* Mikhaylovka.

Mikhalche, Ukr. (Michalcze, Mihalcea); pop. 30; 56 km NW of Chernovtsy; 48°47'/25°36'; HSL, PHP2.

Mikhalevichi, *see* Mikhaylovichi.

Mikhalin, Ukr. (Michalin); pop. 24; 62 km NE of Rovno; 51°02'/26°56'.

Mikhalishki, Byel. (Michaliszki); 139 km WNW of Minsk; 54°49'/26°10'; AMG, COH, GUM3, GUM4, HSL.

Mikhalovich, *see* Michalovce.

Mikhalovka, Ukr. (Michajlowka); 82 km NE of Chernovtsy; 48°48'/26°47'; PHR1.

Mikhalowitz, *see* Michalovce.

Mikhalpol, *see* Mikhaylovka.

Mikhayleny, Mold. (Mihaileni, Mihalaseni); pop. 143; 146 km NW of Kishinev; 48°03'/27°37'.

Mikhaylovgrad, Bulg. (Ferdinand, Mikhailovgrad); pop. 101; 88 km N of Sofija; 43°25'/23°13'; EJ.

Mikhaylovichi, Ukr. (Michalowice, Mikhalevichi); pop. 23; 62 km SSW of Lvov; 49°22'/23°36'.

Mikhaylovka, Ukr. (Michalpol, Michaylovka, Michelpolia, Mikhailovka, Mikhalpol); pop. 1,153; 133 km SSE of Dnepropetrovsk; 47°16'/35°14'; EDRD, GUM4, GUM4, GYLA, HSL, HSL2, JGFF, LDL, SF, WS. There are 111 towns named Mikhaylovka in the republics of the USSR encompassed by this book. Each of the sources cited above seem to refer to a different town. GYLA refers to the Mikhaylovka near Kamenets Poloskiy; GUM4, the Mikhaylovka near Zaporozhe; SF, the town south of Dnepropetrovsk. The map coordinates shown refer to SF.

Mikhaylovka (Bessarabia), Mold. (Bahmutea); pop. 52; 56 km SSE of Kishinev; 46°33'/28°56'.

Mikhaylovka (Wolyn), Ukr. (Michalowka); pop. 857; 82 km SW of Rovno; 50°09'/25°22'; HSL.

Mikhaylyanka, Ukr. (Mihaileanca); pop. 48; 50 km ENE of Chernovtsy; 48°23'/26°36'.

Mikhov, *see* Michow Lubartowski.

Mikhova, *see* Migovoye.

Mikif, *see* Krajnikov.

Mikulov (formerly Nikolsburg), Czechoslovakia: Tempelgasse.

Mikleshty, Mold. (Miclesti); pop. 22; 32 km N of Kishinev; 47°14'/28°49'.

Mikleus, Yug. (Miklos); 139 km E of Zagreb; 45°37'/17°48'; HSL, HSL2.

Miklos, *see* Mikleus.

Miklusy, Pol.; pop. 19; 94 km N of Lublin; 52°03'/22°30'.

Mikluszowice, Pol.; pop. 41; 38 km E of Krakow; 50°04'/20°29'.

Mikofalva, Hung.; pop. 8; 38 km WSW of Miskolc; 48°03'/20°19'; HSL.

Mikohaza, Hung.; pop. 26; 75 km NE of Miskolc; 48°27'/21°36'.

Mikola, *see* Micola.

Mikolajki, Pol. (Nikolaiken); pop. 43; 133 km WNW of Bialystok; 53°48'/21°35'; POCEM.

Mikolajow, *see* Nikolayev.

Mikolajowice, Pol.; pop. 6; 69 km E of Krakow; 49°59'/20°53'.

Mikolajow Wielkie, EGRS. This town was not found in BGN gazetteers under the given spelling.

Mikolapatak, *see* Valeni.

Mikolasov, Ukr. EDRD. This town was not found in BGN gazetteers under the given spelling.

Mikolayev, *see* Nikolayev.

Mikolintza, *see* Mikulintsy.

Mikolow, Pol.; 69 km W of Krakow; 50°10'/18°54'; AMG, GUM5, PHP3, POCEM.

Mikoly, Cz.; 163 km SW of Brno; 48°40'/14°32'; HSL.

Mikova, *see* Migovoye.

Mikow, Pol.; pop. 14; 75 km SSW of Przemysl; 49°18'/22°08'.

Mikstat, Pol. (Mixstadt); pop. 61; 88 km NE of Wroclaw; 51°32'/17°59'; LDS.

Mikula, Cz.; 120 km E of Bratislava; 48°04'/18°40'; HSL.

Mikulasovice, Cz.; pop. 4; 101 km N of Praha; 50°57'/14°22'.

Mikulczyce, Pol. (Mikultschutz); pop. 67; 56 km SSW of Czestochowa; 50°20'/18°47'.

Mikulec, Cz.; pop. 2; 75 km NNW of Brno; 49°48'/16°25'.

Mikulichin, Ukr. (Mikuliczyn); pop. 552; 101 km W of Chernovtsy; 48°24'/24°36'; EGRS, GUM4, GUM5, HSL, PHP2.

Mikuliczyn, *see* Mikulichin.

Mikulince, *see* Mikulintsy.

Mikulino, USSR; pop. 403; 69 km WNW of Smolensk; 55°02'/31°05'.

Mikulintsy, Ukr. (Mikolintza, Mikulince, Mikulincie); pop. 1,891; 126 km NNW of Chernovtsy; 49°24'/25°36'; AMG, EDRD, EGRS, GUM3, GUM4, GUM5, GUM6, GYLA, HSL, HSL2, JGFF, LDL, PHP2, SF, YB. The *Black Book* refers to a town named Mikulince (pop. 73) in the interwar Polish province of Stanislawow. The town does not appear in interwar or contemporary gazetteers, but does appear in a list of Galician towns as being near Sniatyn.

Mikulov, Cz. (Nikolsburg, Svati Mikulow); pop. 535; 50 km S of Brno; 48°48'/16°38'; CAHJP, COH, EJ, GUM4, HSL, HSL2, JGFF, YB.

Mikultschutz, *see* Mikulczyce.

Mikuszowice, Pol.; pop. 28; 69 km SW of Krakow; 49°47'/19°05'.

Milacze, Pol.; pop. 53; Described in the *Black Book* as being in the Polesie region of Poland, this town was not found in BGN gazetteers.

Milaczew, Pol. (Milaczewskie Mlyny); pop. 23; 75 km W of Lodz; 51°56'/18°25'.

Milaczewskie Mlyny, *see* Milaczew.

Milakowo, Pol.; 94 km ESE of Gdansk; 54°01'/20°04'; POCEM.

Milanow, Pol.; pop. 31; 56 km NNE of Lublin; 51°42'/22°53'; EDRD, GUM5.

Milanowek, Pol.; pop. 37; 26 km SW of Warszawa; 52°08'/20°41'; GUM4, PHP4.

Milanowicze, *see* Milyanovichi.

Milas, Rom.; pop. 10; 62 km ENE of Cluj; 46°49'/24°26'.

Milasel, Rom.; pop. 11; 62 km E of Cluj; 46°44'/24°27'.

Milatycze, *see* Milyatyche.

Milatyn, *see* Milyatyn.

Milawa, Pol.; 62 km ENE of Poznan; 52°32'/17°55'; HSL.

Milawczyce, Pol.; pop. 2; 50 km NE of Krakow; 50°21'/20°28'.

Milaytchitz, *see* Milejczyce.

Milcha, Byel. (Milcza); 94 km N of Minsk; 54°41'/27°37'; GUM4.

Milcza, *see* Milcha.

Mileanca, Rom.; pop. 27; 120 km NW of Iasi; 48°05'/26°42'.

Milej, Hung.; pop. 1; 50 km NNW of Nagykanizsa; 46°48'/16°45'.

Milejczyce, Pol. (Milaytchitz); pop. 648; 75 km S of Bialystok; 52°31'/23°08'; COH, GA, HSL, JGFF, POCEM, SF.

Milejow, Pol.; 50 km SSE of Lodz; 51°21'/19°43'; GA, GUM3, GUM4, PHP1.

Milesauti, *see* Milisauti.

Mileshty, Mold. (Milestii Mari); pop. 54; 62 km WNW of Kishinev; 47°13'/28°03'.

Milestii Mari, *see* Mileshty.

Milestii Mici, *see* Malyye Mileshty.

Mileszki, Pol.; 13 km ENE of Lodz; 51°46'/19°35'; PHP1.

Milevichi, Byel. (Milewicze); pop. 58; 107 km NE of Pinsk; 52°28'/27°36'.

Milevsko, Cz.; pop. 103; 75 km S of Praha; 49°27'/14°22'; JGFF.

Milewicze, *see* Milevichi.

Milewo, GA. A number of towns share this name. It was not possible to determine from available information which one is being referenced.

Milewo Brzegedy, Pol.; pop. 13; 69 km N of Warszawa; 52°52'/20°53'.

Miliana, HSL. This pre-World War I community was not found in BGN gazetteers.

Milica, Pol.; pop. 13; 120 km ESE of Lodz; 51°08'/20°51'.

Milicin, Cz.; pop. 10; 62 km SSE of Praha; 49°34'/14°40'.

Milicz, Pol. (Militsch); pop. 73; 56 km N of Wroclaw; 51°32'/17°16'; CAHJP.

Milie, *see* Miliye.

Milik, Pol.; pop. 20; 107 km SE of Krakow; 49°21'/20°51'.

Milin, Cz.; pop. 21; 62 km SSW of Praha; 49°38'/14°03'; HSL, HSL2.

Milisauti, Rom. (Milesauti); pop. 46; 139 km WNW of Iasi; 47°47'/26°00'.

Militsch, *see* Milicz.

Miliye, Ukr. (Milie); pop. 197; 50 km W of Chernovtsy; 48°20'/25°17'; COH, PHR2.

Milkow, Pol.; pop. 29; 50 km N of Przemysl; 50°12'/22°53'.

Millerovo, *see* Kamennoye.

Milno, Ukr.; pop. 54; 107 km E of Lvov; 49°48'/25°29'.

Milnowo, Pol.; pop. 22; Described in the *Black Book* as being in the Wilen region of Poland, this town was not found in BGN gazetteers.

Milochniewice, Pol.; pop. 5; 45 km ENE of Lodz; 51°47'/20°06'.

Milodroz, Pol.; pop. 3; 101 km WNW of Warszawa; 52°39'/19°39'.

Miloslavichi, Byel. (Miloslavitch, Miloslawicze); 163 km NNE of Gomel; 53°41'/32°15'; LDL, SF.

Miloslavitch, *see* Miloslavichi.

Miloslaw, Pol.; 45 km ESE of Poznan; 52°12'/17°29'; HSL2.

Miloslawicze, *see* Miloslavichi.

Milosna, Pol.; pop. 122; 56 km NNW of Lodz; 52°13'/19°11'; AMG, GUM3, GUM4, GUM5, GUM6, LYV, PHP4, SF, YB.

Milostin, Cz.; pop. 5; 56 km W of Praha; 50°12'/13°40'.

Milota, Hung.; pop. 8; 146 km E of Miskolc; 48°06'/22°47'.

Milovka, *see* Milowka.

Milowka, Pol. (Milovka); pop. 163; 82 km SW of Krakow; 49°34'/19°05'; EGRS, HSL, PHP3, SF.

Miltenberg, Germ.; pop. 100; 62 km SE of Frankfurt am Main; 49°42'/09°15'; GUM5, PHGB.

Milyanovichi, Ukr. (Milanowicze); pop. 91; 139 km WNW of Rovno; 51°11'/24°27'.

Milyatin, Ukr. (Milyatyn Buryny); pop. 30; 32 km ESE of Rovno; 50°27'/26°37'.

Milyatyche, Ukr. (Milatycze); pop. 21; 26 km SE of Lvov; 49°42'/24°06'.

Milyatyn, Ukr. (Milatyn); pop. 82; 88 km NNE of Lvov; 50°34'/24°34'.

Milyatyn (Lwow), Ukr.; pop. 9; 45 km WSW of Lvov; 49°46'/23°24'.

Milyatyn Buryny, *see* Milyatin.

Milyatyn Pochapki, *see* Pochapka.

Milzkalne, Lat.; pop. 1; 56 km W of Riga; 56°59'/23°14'.

Mimon, Cz.; pop. 17; 69 km N of Praha; 50°39'/14°44'.

Minaj, *possibly* Monaj.

Minau, Rom. (Manau); pop. 25; 82 km NNW of Cluj; 47°29'/23°16'; COH.

Mindelheim, Germ.; pop. 6; 82 km WSW of Munchen; 48°03'/10°29'; GED, GUM3, PHGB.

Minden, Germ.; pop. 229; 56 km WSW of Hannover; 52°17'/08°55'; EDRD, EJ, GUM3, GUM6, HSL, JGFF.

Mindszent, Hung.; pop. 103; 38 km N of Szeged; 46°32'/20°12'; HSL, LDS, PHH.

Mineu, Rom.; pop. 12; 75 km NW of Cluj; 47°21'/23°06'.

Mingir, *see* Minzhir.

Mingolsheim, Germ. (Bad Mingolsheim); pop. 24; 62 km NW of Stuttgart; 49°14'/08°40'; JGFF, LDS, PHGBW.

Minkovitz, *see* Minkovtsy.

Minkovtsy, Ukr. (Minkovitz, Minkowce); pop. 1,796; 101 km NE of Chernovtsy; 48°51'/27°06'; COH, GUM4, JGFF, SF, YB.

Minkowce, *see* Minkovtsy.

Minoga, Pol.; pop. 5; 26 km N of Krakow; 50°15'/19°55'.

Minsk, Byel.; pop. 53,686; 221 km NNE of Pinsk; 53°54'/27°34'; AMG, CAHJP, COH, EDRD, EJ, GUM3, GUM4, GUM5, GUM6, GYLA, HSL, HSL2, ISH1, ISH2, ISH3, JGFF, LDL, LYV, PHGBW, PHP1, PHP4, SF, YB.

Minsk Khadash, *see* Minsk Mazowiecki.

Minsk Mazovyets, *see* Minsk Mazowiecki.

Minsk Mazovyetsk, *see* Minsk Mazowiecki.

Minsk Mazowiecki, Pol. (Minsk Khadash, Minsk Mazovyets, Minsk Mazovyetsk, Novo Minsk, Novominsk); pop. 4,130; 38 km E of Warszawa; 52°11'/21°34'; AMG, COH, EDRD, EJ, GA, GUM3, GUM4, GUM5, GUM6, HSL, JGFF, LDL, LDS, LYV, PHP4, POCEM, SF, YB.

Minster, Germ.; pop. 600; Described in the *Black Book* as being in the Neidersachsen-Westfalen region of Germany, this town was not found in BGN gazetteers.

Mintia, Rom.; 114 km SSW of Cluj; 45°56'/22°51'; HSL.

Mintiu, Rom.; pop. 1; 75 km NE of Cluj; 47°14'/24°22'.

Minzhir, Mold. (Mingir); pop. 97; 56 km SW of Kishinev; 46°40'/28°20'.

Miody, Lith. EDRD. This town was not found in BGN gazetteers under the given spelling.

Miokovicevo, Yug. (Djulaves, Dulaves); pop. 26; 114 km E of Zagreb; 45°40'/17°26'.

Mior, *see* Miory.

Miorcani, Rom.; pop. 5; 133 km NW of Iasi; 48°12'/26°51'.

Miory, Byel. (Mior); pop. 371; 163 km W of Vitebsk; 55°37'/27°38'; AMG, COH, EDRD, GUM4, HSL, LDL, LYV, SF, YB.

Mir, Byel.; pop. 2,074; 88 km SW of Minsk; 53°27'/26°28'; AMG, CAHJP, COH, EDRD, EJ, GA, GUM3, GUM4, GUM5, GUM6, HSL, HSL2, JGFF, LDL, LYV, SF, YB.

Mirarid, *see* Mirgorod.

Mirashasa, GUM4. This town was not found in BGN gazetteers under the given spelling.

Mircze, Pol.; pop. 77; 114 km ESE of Lublin; 50°39'/23°55'; GA, GUM5.

Miresul Mare, *see* Miresu Mare.

Miresu Mare, Rom. (Miresul Mare, Nagyniyres); pop. 71; 88 km NNW of Cluj; 47°30'/23°20'; HSL.

Mirgorod, Ukr. (Mirarid, Mirhorod Yashan); pop. 1,994; 146 km SSE of Konotop; 49°58'/33°36'; GUM4, JGFF, LDL, SF.

Mirhorod Yashan, *see* Mirgorod.

Mirkow, Pol.; 75 km NW of Czestochowa; 51°16'/18°26'; PHP1.

Mirnopolye, Ukr. (Friedensfeld); pop. 6; 88 km SW of Odessa; 46°10'/29°39'.

Mirocice, Pol.; 114 km SW of Lublin; 50°53'/21°02'; GUM4.

Mirocin, Pol.; pop. 18; 32 km NW of Przemysl; 50°02'/22°34'.

Miron, Rom.; pop. 7; 120 km WNW of Iasi; 47°29'/26°01'.

Mironim, Byel.; pop. 4; 107 km NW of Pinsk; 52°57'/25°26'.

Miropol, Ukr.; pop. 1,143; 69 km SSW of Dnepropetrovsk; 47°57'/34°20'; HSL, JGFF, SF.

Miroslav, Cz. (Misslitz); pop. 291; 38 km SSW of Brno; 48°57'/16°19'; EJ, GUM3, HSL, HSL2, ISH1.

Miroslavas, Lith.; pop. 124; 69 km S of Kaunas; 54°20'/23°54'; GUM4.

Miroslawiec, Pol. (Maerkisch Friedland, Markisch Friedland); pop. 72; 107 km E of Szczecin; 53°20'/16°06'; CAHJP, EJ, HSL, JGFF, LDS, POCEM.

Mirotyn, Ukr.; pop. 4; 26 km SSE of Rovno; 50°26'/26°19'.

Mirow Stary, Pol.; pop. 7; 107 km WSW of Lublin; 51°11'/21°04'.

Mirsid, Rom.; pop. 9; 62 km NW of Cluj; 47°14'/23°08'.

Miryn, Ukr.; pop. 7; 101 km WNW of Rovno; 51°12'/25°08'.

Mirzec, Pol.; pop. 2; 107 km WSW of Lublin; 51°08'/21°04'.

Misburg, Germ.; pop. 2; 13 km ENE of Hannover; 52°23'/09°51'.

Misca, Rom.; pop. 23; A number of towns share this name. It was not possible to determine from available information which one is being referenced.

Misdroy, *see* Miedzyzdroje.

Mishenits, *see* Myszyniec.

Mishenitz, *see* Myszyniec.

Misheny, Mold. (Meseni); pop. 15; 69 km S of Kishinev; 46°25'/28°28'.

Mishev, *see* Mniszow.

Mishinyets, *see* Myszyniec.

Mishkovitz, *see* Myshkovtse.

Mishkovtsy, *see* Myshkovtse.

Mishlenitse, *see* Myslenice.

Mishlenitz, *see* Myslenice.

Mishlinits, *see* Myslenice.

Mishnits, *see* Myszyniec.

Mishov, *see* Mniszow.

Misiad, *see* Mosedis.

Misiankov, *see* Mizyakov.

Misiewicze, Pol.; pop. 22; Described in the *Black Book* as being in the Nowogrodek region of Poland, this town was not found in BGN gazetteers.

Misjakow, *see* Mizyakov.

Miske, Hung. (Homrod); pop. 20; 88 km W of Szeged; 46°27'/19°02'; GUM4, HSL, HSL2.

Miskiniai, Lith. (Miszkinie); 45 km S of Siauliai; 55°34'/23°21'; JGFF.

Miskolc, Hung. (Miskolcz); pop. 10,428; 139 km NE of Budapest; 48°06'/20°47'; AMG, COH, GUM3, GUM4, GUM5, GUM6, HSL, HSL2, JGFF, LDL, LDS, LJEE, PHH, YB.

Miskolcz, *see* Miskolc.

Misslitz, *see* Miroslav.

Mistelbach, *see* Mistelbach an der Zaya.

Mistelbach an der Zaya, Aus. (Mistelbach); pop. 94; 45 km N of Wien; 48°34'/16°34'; CAHJP.

Mistelfeld, Germ.; 82 km N of Nurnberg; 50°08'/11°06'; JGFF, PHGB.

Mistow, Pol.; pop. 14; 45 km E of Warszawa; 52°14'/21°37'.

Miszewo, Pol.; 50 km NW of Warszawa; 52°39'/20°37'; GUM3.

Miszkinie, *see* Miskiniai.

Miszla, Hung.; pop. 14; 107 km SSW of Budapest; 46°38'/18°29'.

Miszory, Pol. (Myszory); pop. 7; 45 km W of Warszawa; 52°20'/20°20'.

Mitau, *see* Jelgava.

Mitava, *see* Jelgava.

Mitawa, *see* Jelgava.

Mitburger, YB. This town was not found in BGN gazetteers under the given spelling.

Mitcau, *see* Mittsau.

Mitel Apsa, *see* Stredni Apsa.

Mitel Wisho, *see* Viseu de Mijloc.

Mititei, Rom.; pop. 7; 82 km NNE of Cluj; 47°17'/24°19'.

Mitkovka, USSR; pop. 22; 170 km SW of Bryansk; 52°25'/32°09'.

Mitoc, Rom.; pop. 57; 120 km WNW of Iasi; 47°50'/26°26'.

Mitocu Balan, Rom.; 114 km WSW of Iasi; 47°07'/26°10'; GUM4.

Mitoi, *see* Jelgava.

Mitropolit, *see* Porumbrey.

Mitrovica, GUM4. A number of towns share this name. It was not possible to determine from available information which one is being referenced.

Mitshat, *see* Molchad.

Mittelbexbach, Germ. (Hocherberg); 133 km SW of Frankfurt am Main; 49°21'/07°16'; GED.

Mittel Biberach, Germ.; 114 km SW of Stuttgart; 48°06'/08°01'; PHGBW.

Mittelehrenbach, Germ.; 32 km N of Nurnberg; 49°41'/11°10'; PHGB.

Mittelsinn, Germ.; pop. 107; 69 km ENE of Frankfurt am Main; 50°12'/09°37'; GUM5, LDS, PHGB.

Mittelstreu, Germ.; pop. 19; 114 km ENE of Frankfurt am Main; 50°23'/10°16'; PHGB.

Mittenwald, Germ.; 82 km S of Munchen; 47°26'/11°15'; GUM3, GUM5, PHGB.

Mitterndorf an der Fischa, Aus.; pop. 8; 32 km SSE of Wien; 47°59'/16°28'.

Mitterscholtz, HSL. This pre-World War I community was not found in BGN gazetteers.

Mitterteich, Germ.; pop. 3; 101 km NE of Nurnberg; 49°57'/12°15'; PHGB.

Mittsau, Ukr. (Mitcau); pop. 25; 38 km N of Chernovtsy; 48°36'/26°01'.

Mittweida, Germ.; pop. 24; 56 km ESE of Leipzig; 50°59'/12°59'.

Mitulin, Ukr.; pop. 41; 50 km E of Lvov; 49°46'/24°38'; GUM4.

Mitwitz, Germ.; 94 km N of Nurnberg; 50°15'/11°13'; JGFF, PHGB.

Mixstadt, *see* Mikstat.

Mizach, *see* Mizoch.

Mizhinets, Ukr. (Mizyniec); pop. 25; 75 km WSW of Lvov; 49°41'/22°55'.

Mizikov, *see* Mizyakov.

Mizoch, Ukr. (Mizach, Mizocz, Mizotch); pop. 845; 32 km S of Rovno; 50°24'/26°09'; AMG, COH, EDRD, GUM3, GUM4, GUM5, HSL, LYV, SF, YB.

Mizocz, *see* Mizoch.

Mizotch, *see* Mizoch.

Mizun, Pol. PHP2. This town was not found in BGN gazetteers under the given spelling.

Mizun Stary, Ukr.; pop. 182; 146 km S of Lvov; 48°35'/23°45'; HSL, PHP2. This town was located on an interwar map of Poland but does not appear in contemporary gazetteers. Map coordinates are approximate.

Mizyakov, Ukr. (Misiankov, Misjakow, Mizikov); 26 km NW of Vinnitsa; 49°24'/28°22'; LDL, SF.

Mizyniec, *see* Mizhinets.

Mjaskowka, (Miaskivka); LDL, SF. This town was not found in BGN gazetteers under the given spelling.

Mlada Boleslav, Cz. (Bumsla, Jungbunzlau); pop. 264; 50 km NNE of Praha; 50°25'/14°54'; EJ, HSL, HSL2.

Mlada Vozice, Cz.; pop. 79; 69 km SSE of Praha; 49°32'/14°49'.

Mladenovo, Yug. (Bukin); 107 km WNW of Beograd; 45°18'/19°16'; HSL.

Mladonov, Cz. (Lodus); 163 km SW of Brno; 48°41'/14°30'; HSL.

Mlava, *see* Mlawa.

Mlawa, Pol. (Mlava); pop. 5,923; 107 km NW of Warszawa; 53°07'/20°23'; AMG, COH, EDRD, EJ, GA, GUM3, GUM4, GUM5, HSL, HSL2, ISH1, JGFF, LDL, LDS, LYV, PHP1, PHP4, SF, YB.

Mlcechvosty, Cz.; pop. 4; 32 km NNW of Praha; 50°19'/14°20'.

Mlekosrby, Cz.; pop. 2; 75 km ENE of Praha; 50°12'/15°30'.

Mlenauti, Rom.; pop. 7; 139 km NW of Iasi; 48°08'/26°29'.

Mlinov, Ukr. (Mlinuv, Mlynow); pop. 615; 50 km WSW of Rovno; 50°30'/25°36'; AMG, CAHJP, GUM3, GUM4, GUM5, HSL, JGFF, LYV, SF, YB.

Mlinuv, *see* Mlinov.

Mlodiatyn, *see* Mlodyatyn.

Mlodnice, Pol.; pop. 6; 101 km S of Warszawa; 51°26'/20°52'.

Mlodochow, Pol.; pop. 2; 114 km NE of Krakow; 50°25'/21°26'.

Mlodow, Pol.; pop. 63; Described in the *Black Book* as being in the Lwow region of Poland, this town was not found in BGN gazetteers.

Mlodyatyn, Ukr. (Mlodiatyn); pop. 36; 88 km WNW of Chernovtsy; 48°31'/24°49'.

Mlodzawy Duze, Pol. (Mlodzowy Duze); pop. 7; 56 km NE of Krakow; 50°26'/20°31'.

Mlodzianowo, Pol.; pop. 15; 75 km N of Warszawa; 52°55'/21°04'.

Mlodziszyn, Pol. PHP4. This town was not found in BGN gazetteers under the given spelling.

Mlodzowy, Pol.; pop. 4; 45 km NNE of Czestochowa; 51°06'/19°26'.

Mlodzowy Duze, *see* Mlodzawy Duze.

Mlynary, Pol. (Muhlhausen); pop. 31; 69 km E of Gdansk; 54°12'/19°43'; LDS.

Mlynarze, Pol.; pop. 42; 82 km N of Warszawa; 52°58'/21°26'.

Mlyniec, Pol.; pop. 3; 146 km S of Gdansk; 53°05'/18°49'.

Mlynne, Pol.; pop. 24; 50 km ESE of Krakow; 49°45'/20°25'.

Mlynovtse, Ukr. (Mlynowce, Muehlbach); pop. 48; 50 km ESE of Lvov; 49°43'/24°36'.

Mlynow, *see* Mlinov.

Mlynowce, *see* Mlynovtse.

Mlyn Spindleruv, Cz.; pop. 63; 88 km SSE of Praha; 49°20'/14°53'.

Mlyn Wojtostwo, Pol.; pop. 48; Described in the *Black Book* as being in the Kielce region of Poland, this town was not found in BGN gazetteers.

Mlyny, Pol.; pop. 33; 75 km NE of Krakow; 50°34'/20°44'; GUM3.

Mnetes, Cz.; pop. 2; 38 km NNW of Praha; 50°22'/14°17'.

Mnichovo Hradiste, Cz.; pop. 42; 62 km NNE of Praha; 50°32'/14°59'.

Mnichow, Pol.; pop. 22; 75 km NNE of Krakow; 50°42'/20°22'.

Mnin, Pol.; pop. 97; 82 km ENE of Czestochowa; 50°59'/20°12'.

Mniow, Pol.; pop. 52; 101 km ENE of Czestochowa; 51°01'/20°29'.

Mnisek nad Hnilcom, Cz. (Einsiedel, Remet); 32 km WNW of Kosice; 48°48'/20°48'; HSL.

Mniszek, Pol.; pop. 51; 62 km SSW of Lublin; 50°50'/21°57'.

Mniszew, *see* Mniszow.

Mniszki, Pol.; pop. 3; 94 km ENE of Poznan; 52°30'/18°21'.

Mniszkow, Pol.; pop. 6; 56 km SE of Lodz; 51°22'/20°02'.

Mniszow, Pol. (Mishev, Mishov, Mniszew); pop. 275; 50 km SE of Warszawa; 51°51'/21°17'; HSL, SF.

Moara de Piatra, *see* Moara de Pyatre.

Moara de Pyatre, Mold. (Moara de Piatra); pop. 40; 120 km NW of Kishinev; 47°54'/28°00'.

Moca, Cz. (Dunamocs); pop. 79; 107 km ESE of Bratislava; 47°46'/18°25'; HSL.

Mochalivka, *see* Baremel.

Mochnaczka Wyzna, Pol.; pop. 22; 101 km ESE of Krakow; 49°27'/20°59'.

Mochnata, Ukr. (Mochnate); pop. 42; 114 km SSW of Lvov; 48°55'/23°20'; HSL.

Mochnate, *see* Mochnata.

Mochnovka, *see* Makhnovka.

Mochowo, Pol.; pop. 5; 114 km WNW of Warszawa; 52°46'/19°34'.

Mochula, Byel. (Moczula); pop. 9; 82 km E of Pinsk; 52°01'/27°21'.

Mochulki, Ukr. (Moczulki); pop. 116; 114 km W of Rovno; 50°54'/24°41'.

Mochy, Pol.; 75 km SW of Poznan; 52°00'/16°11'; EDRD.

Mocidlec, Cz.; pop. 4; 88 km WSW of Praha; 50°03'/13°14'.

Mocira, Rom.; pop. 9; 101 km N of Cluj; 47°37'/23°32'.

Mociu, Rom. (Mocs); 32 km ENE of Cluj; 46°48'/24°02'; HSL, PHR1.

Mocod, Rom. (Makod); pop. 8; 82 km NNE of Cluj; 47°16'/24°18'; HSL.

Mocovice, Cz.; pop. 5; 69 km ESE of Praha; 49°54'/15°21'.

Mocs, *see* Mociu.

Mocsa, Hung.; pop. 19; 69 km W of Budapest; 47°40'/18°11'.

Mocsar, *possibly* Moczary.

Mocsonok, *see* Sladkovicovo.

Moczalec, Pol.; pop. 10; 88 km WSW of Lodz; 51°35'/18°13'.

Moczary, Pol. (Mocsar?); pop. 38; 50 km S of Przemysl; 49°23'/22°40'; HSL.

Moczula, *see* Mochula.

Moczuliszcze, Ukr.; pop. 48; 75 km N of Rovno; 51°15'/26°25'. This town was located on an interwar map of Poland but does not appear in contemporary gazetteers. Map coordinates are approximate.

Moczulki, *see* Mochulki.

Moczulniki, Byel.; pop. 29; 101 km WSW of Pinsk; 52°05'/24°36'. This town was located on an interwar map of Poland but does not appear in contemporary gazetteers. Map coordinates are approximate.

Moczydla Nowe, Pol.; pop. 5; 50 km S of Lublin; 50°51'/22°25'.

Moczydly, Pol.; 101 km NNW of Bialystok; 53°58'/22°45'; POCEM.

Model, HSL. This pre-World War I community was not found in BGN gazetteers.

Modena, COH, HSL, ISH2. This town was not found in BGN gazetteers under the given spelling.

Moderowka, Pol.; pop. 8; 82 km WSW of Przemysl; 49°46'/21°38'.

Modlany, Cz.; pop. 1; 75 km NW of Praha; 50°39'/13°54'.

Modliborzitse, *see* Modliborzyce.

Modliborzyce, Pol. (Modliborzitse, Modliboshitz, Modlibozhits); pop. 957; 56 km S of Lublin; 50°45'/22°20'; CAHJP, COH, GA, GUM3, GUM5, HSL, JGFF, LYV, POCEM, SF.

Modliboshitz, *see* Modliborzyce.

Modlibozhits, *see* Modliborzyce.

Modlin, Pol.; pop. 9; 32 km WNW of Warszawa; 52°26'/20°41'; GUM4, PHP4.

Modling, Aus.; pop. 302; 19 km SSW of Wien; 48°05'/16°17'; HSL.

Modlin Nowy, *see* Nowy Modlin.

Modliszewice, Pol.; pop. 8; 82 km ESE of Lodz; 51°13'/20°22'.

Modlnica, Pol.; pop. 12; 13 km NW of Krakow; 50°08'/19°52'.

Modlniczka, Pol.; pop. 6; 6 km WNW of Krakow; 50°07'/19°52'.

Modohn, *see* Madona.

Modor, *see* Modra.

Modra, Cz. (Modor); pop. 577; 26 km NNE of Bratislava;

48°20'/17°19'; HSL, LDS.

Modrice, Cz.; 13 km S of Brno; 49°08'/16°37'; GUM4.

Modrych, *see* Modrychi.

Modrychi, Ukr. (Modrych, Modrycz); pop. 80; 75 km SSW of Lvov; 49°19'/23°29'.

Modrycz, *see* Modrychi.

Modry Kamen, Cz.; pop. 382; 150 km SW of Kosice; 48°15'/19°20'.

Modryn, Pol.; pop. 37; 114 km ESE of Lublin; 50°41'/23°54'.

Modrzejow, Pol.; 56 km WNW of Krakow; 50°15'/19°09'; AMG, CAHJP, GUM3, PHP3.

Modrzyc, *see* Deblin.

Modzele Wygoda, Pol.; pop. 173; PHP4. Described in the *Black Book* as being in the Bialystok region of Poland, this town was not found in BGN gazetteers.

Modzhits, *see* Deblin.

Modzhitz, *see* Deblin.

Modzits, *see* Deblin.

Moers, Germ. (Mors); pop. 191; 62 km NNW of Koln; 51°27'/06°39'; EDRD, GED.

Moftinul Mic, *see* Moftinu Mic.

Moftinu Mic, Rom. (Moftinul Mic); pop. 35; 126 km NW of Cluj; 47°41'/22°36'.

Mogelnitsa, *see* Mogielnica.

Mogelnitse, *see* Mogielnica.

Mogelnitza, *see* Mogielnica.

Mogendorf, Germ.; pop. 24; 75 km WNW of Frankfurt am Main; 50°30'/07°46'.

Mogielnica, Pol. (Mogelnitsa, Mogelnitse, Mogelnitza); pop. 2,722; 69 km S of Warszawa; 51°42'/20°44'; AMG, CAHJP, COH, GA, GUM3, GUM4, GUM5, GYLA, HSL, JGFF, LDL, LDS, LYV, PHP1, PHP4, SF, WS, YB.

Mogielnica (near Trembovlya), Ukr.; pop. 77; 107 km NNW of Chernovtsy; 49°13'/25°35'.

Mogila, Pol.; pop. 23; 13 km E of Krakow; 50°04'/20°05'; GUM3.

Mogilev, Byel. (Mohilev, Mohylew, Mohylow, Molev); pop. 17,105; 150 km S of Vitebsk; 53°54'/30°21'; EDRD, EJ, GUM3, GUM4, GUM5, GUM6, GYLA, HSL, JGFF, LDL, PHP1, SF, WS.

Mogilev Podolski, *see* Mogilev Podolskiy.

Mogilev Podolskiy, Ukr. (Mogilev Podolski, Mohilev Podolsk); pop. 9,622; 101 km SSW of Vinnitsa; 48°27'/27°48'; EJ, GUM3, GUM4, GUM5, GUM6, HSL, JGFF, LDL, PHR1, SF.

Mogilna, *see* Mogilno.

Mogilno, Ukr. (Mogilna, Mohilno); pop. 29; 120 km N of Lvov; 50°55'/24°26'; JGFF, PHP1, PHP4.

Mogilno (near Poznan), Pol.; 75 km NE of Poznan; 52°40'/17°58'; GUM3, GUM4.

Mogilno (near Stolbtsy), Byel.; 62 km SSW of Minsk; 53°25'/26°59'; SF.

Mogilyany, Ukr. (Mohylany); pop. 15; 32 km ESE of Rovno; 50°26'/26°34'.

Mogneszty, GUM3. This town was not found in BGN gazetteers under the given spelling.

Mogos, Rom.; 170 km SSE of Iasi; 45°41'/28°00'; HSL.

Mogosesti, Rom.; pop. 29; 94 km NNW of Cluj; 47°35'/23°24'; HSL.

Mogyorod, Hung.; pop. 5; 19 km NE of Budapest; 47°36'/19°15'.

Mogyoros, *see* Lieskova.

Mohacs, Hung.; pop. 741; 120 km WSW of Szeged; 45°59'/18°42'; AMG, EDRD, GUM4, GUM5, JGFF, LDS, PHH.

Mohast Rabati, *see* Velikiye Mosty.

Mohelnice, Cz. (Mueglitz, Muglitz?); pop. 142; 75 km N of Brno; 49°47'/16°55'; EJ, HSL.

Mohilev, *see* Mogilev.

Mohilev Podolsk, *see* Mogilev Podolskiy.

Mohilno, *see* Mogilno.

Mohnya, *see* Chminany.

Mohol, *see* Mol.

Mohora, Hung.; pop. 28; 56 km N of Budapest; 47°59'/19°20'.

Mohrin, *see* Moryn.

Mohringen, Germ.; 13 km SSW of Stuttgart; 48°44'/09°09'; PHGBW.

Mohrungen, *see* Morag.

Mohylany, *see* Mogilyany.

Mohylew, *see* Mogilev.

Mohylow, *see* Mogilev.

Moigrad, Rom.; pop. 13; 62 km NW of Cluj; 47°12'/23°09'.

Moinesti, Rom.; pop. 114 km SW of Iasi; 46°28'/26°29'; EJ, GUM4, HSL, HSL2, JGFF, LDL, PHR1.

Moisei, *see* Moiseiu.

Moiseiu, Rom. (Moisei, Moiseu); pop. 1,216; 120 km NNE of Cluj; 47°39'/24°33'; GUM4, PHR2, SM.

Moiseni, Rom.; pop. 26; 133 km N of Cluj; 47°56'/23°28'.

Moiseu, *see* Moiseiu.

Moisling, Germ.; 56 km NE of Hamburg; 53°51'/10°39'; EJ.

Mojmirovce, Cz. (Urmeny); 69 km ENE of Bratislava; 48°13'/18°04'; HSL, HSL2, LDL.

Mojslawice, Pol.; pop. 39; 94 km ESE of Lublin; 50°53'/23°47'.

Mojzeszow, Pol.; pop. 29; 69 km NE of Czestochowa; 51°01'/20°00'.

Mokca, HSL. This pre-World War I community was not found in BGN gazetteers.

Mokobody, Pol. (Monkavid); pop. 290; 75 km ENE of Warszawa; 52°17'/22°07'; GUM3, GUM5, LDS, SF.

Mokotow, Pol.; 13 km SSE of Warszawa; 52°12'/21°01'; AMG.

Mokra, COH, HSL, LYV. A number of towns share this name. It was not possible to determine from available information which one is being referenced.

Mokra Germ, *see* Nemetskaya Mokra.

Mokrance, Cz. (Makrancz); 19 km SW of Kosice; 48°36'/21°02'; HSL.

Mokrany, Byel.; pop. 93; 133 km WSW of Pinsk; 51°51'/24°16'; HSL.

Mokrany Nove, Byel.; pop. 10; 107 km NNE of Pinsk; 52°56'/26°52'.

Mokra Russ, *see* Russkaya Mokraya.

Mokra Strona, Pol.; pop. 20; 32 km NW of Przemysl; 50°03'/22°30'.

Mokra Wies, Pol.; pop. 10; 38 km NE of Warszawa; 52°28'/21°30'.

Mokre, Pol. (Mokre Niwki); pop. 21; 56 km SW of Przemysl; 49°27'/22°10'; GA, HSL.

Mokrelipie, Pol.; pop. 17; 56 km SSE of Lublin; 50°45'/22°52'.

Mokre Niwki, *see* Mokre.

Mokrets, Ukr. (Mokrzec, Mokshets); pop. 24; 133 km N of Lvov; 51°01'/24°24'.

Mokrin, Yug.; pop. 38; 126 km N of Beograd; 45°56'/20°25'.

Mokroc, *see* Mokrotyn.

Mokrosek, Pol.; pop. 36; 88 km S of Warszawa; 51°32'/21°03'.

Mokrotyn, Ukr. (Mokroc); pop. 20; 26 km NNW of Lvov; 50°01'/23°57'.

Mokrovo, Byel. (Mokrowo); 75 km ENE of Pinsk; 52°13'/27°14'; GUM5.

Mokrowo, *see* Mokrovo.

Mokrsko, Pol. (Mokrsko Rzadowe); pop. 37; 62 km WNW of Czestochowa; 51°11'/18°29'.

Mokrsko Rzadowe, *see* Mokrsko.

Mokryany, Ukr. (Mokrzany, Mokzhany); pop. 23; 75 km SW of Lvov; 49°25'/23°17'.

Mokrzany, *see* Mokryany.

Mokrzec, *see* Mokrets.

Mokrzesz, Pol.; pop. 4; 19 km ENE of Czestochowa; 50°49'/19°24'.

Mokrzyska, Pol.; pop. 23; 50 km E of Krakow; 50°02'/20°38'.

Mokrzyszow, Pol.; pop. 20; 94 km SSW of Lublin; 50°34'/21°43'.

Mokshets, *see* Mokrets.

Mokwin, *see* Pershotravnevoye.

Mokzhany, *see* Mokryany.

Mol, Yug. (Mohol); pop. 117; 114 km NNW of Beograd; 45°46'/20°08'; HSL, HSL2, PHY.

Molchad, Byel. (Maytshet, Meytshet, Mitshat, Molchadz, Molczadz, Molczadz Stacja Kolejowa, Moltchad, Motsit); pop. 1,020; 139 km SW of Minsk; 53°19'/25°42'; AMG, COH, EDRD, GUM3, GUM4, GUM6, HSL, JGFF, LDL, LYV, SF, YB.

Molchadz, *see* Molchad.

Molchanovka, Ukr. (Molczanowka); pop. 31; 126 km S of Rovno; 49°31'/26°02'.

Molczadz, *see* Molchad.

Molczadz Stacja Kolejowa, *see* Molchad.

Molczanowka, *see* Molchanovka.

Moldauischbanid, LDL. This pre-World War I community was not found in BGN gazetteers.

Moldautein, *see* Tyn nad Vltavou.

Moldava, *see* Moldava nad Bodvou.

Moldava nad Bodvou, Cz. (Moldava); pop. 842; 94 km NW of Praha; 50°43'/13°39'; AMG, HSL.

Moldavia; Not a town, but a republic of the USSR.

Moldawsko, Pol.; pop. 20; Described in the *Black Book* as being in the Stanislawow region of Poland, this town was not found in BGN gazetteers.

Moldova, *see* Moldova Sulita.

Moldova Sulita, Rom. (Moldova); pop. 55; 157 km NE of Cluj; 47°41'/25°15'.

Moldovita, Rom. (Rusl Moldovita); pop. 452; 163 km WNW of Iasi; 47°41'/25°32'; PHR2.

Moleshty, Mold. (Molesti); pop. 22; 32 km S of Kishinev; 46°47'/28°47'.

Molesti, *see* Moleshty.

Moletai, Lith. (Malat, Maletai, Maletos, Maljaty, Malyat, Meliat, Moliat); pop. 1,343; 69 km N of Vilnius; 55°14'/25°25'; COH, HSL, JGFF, LDL, LYV, SF, YL.

Moletch, *see* Malech.

Molev, *see* Mogilev.

Moliat, *see* Moletai.

Moliatitch, *see* Molyatichi.

Molnari, Hung.; pop. 11; 13 km SW of Nagykanizsa; 46°23'/16°50'.

Molnaszecsod, Hung.; pop. 8; 75 km NNW of Nagykanizsa; 47°03'/16°41'.

Molocneea, Rom. PHR1. This town was not found in BGN gazetteers under the given spelling.

Molodechno, Byel. (Molodeczno, Molodetchno); pop. 357; 69 km WNW of Minsk; 54°19'/26°51'; COH, GUM3, GUM4, GUM5, GUM6, HSL, LDL, SF.

Molodeczno, *see* Molodechno.

Molodetchno, *see* Molodechno.

Molodiya, Ukr. (Plaiul Cosmin, Plaiul Cosminului); pop. 88; 19 km SE of Chernovtsy; 48°13'/26°02'.

Molodkov, Ukr. (Molotkow, Molotkuv); pop. 30; 114 km WNW of Chernovtsy; 48°39'/24°29'.

Molodova, *see* Molodovo (Bessarabia).

Molodovo (Bessarabia), Ukr. (Molodova); pop. 21; 88 km NE of Chernovtsy; 48°33'/27°05'.

Molodovo (Polesie), Byel. (Molodow); pop. 13; 38 km WNW of Pinsk; 52°17'/25°41'.

Molodow, *see* Molodovo (Polesie).

Molodycz, Pol.; pop. 16; 45 km N of Przemysl; 50°10'/22°50'.

Molodylow, *see* Molodyluv.

Molodyluv, Ukr. (Molodylow); pop. 36; 88 km WNW of Chernovtsy; 48°41'/24°51'.

Molodziatycze, Pol.; pop. 73; 88 km ESE of Lublin; 50°49'/23°42'; GUM5.

Mologhia, GUM5. This town was not found in BGN gazetteers under the given spelling.

Molotkow, *see* Molodkov.

Molotkuv, *see* Molodkov.

Molotow, Ukr.; pop. 24; 62 km SSE of Lvov; 49°21'/24°17'.

Molotychki, *see* Molyatichi.

Molovata, *see* Malovata.

Molozew, Pol.; pop. 11; 88 km SSW of Bialystok; 52°27'/22°31'.

Molozow, Pol.; pop. 17; 114 km ESE of Lublin; 50°37'/23°49'.

Molsheim, Germ.; pop. 7; 62 km SSW of Frankfurt am Main; 49°39'/08°10'.

Moltchad, *see* Molchad.

Molyatichi, Byel. (Moliatitch, Molotychki, Molyatichki, Molytichki); 163 km N of Gomel; 53°51'/31°32'; LDL, SF.

Molyatichki, *see* Molyatichi.

Molytichki, *see* Molyatichi.

Momberg, Germ.; 94 km N of Frankfurt am Main; 50°52'/09°06'; LDS.

Momlingen, Germ.; 38 km ESE of Frankfurt am Main; 49°51'/09°05'; PHGB.

Mommenheim, Germ.; pop. 4; 45 km SW of Frankfurt am Main; 49°53'/08°16'.

Monaco, *see* Munchen.

Monaj, Hung. (Minaj?); pop. 7; 32 km NNE of Miskolc; 48°18'/20°57'; HSL.

Monariu, Rom.; pop. 4; 75 km NE of Cluj; 47°04'/24°28'.

Monashi, Ukr. (Manasi); pop. 3; 62 km SW of Odessa; 46°10'/30°04'.

Monast, USSR; pop. 2,005; This town was not found in BGN gazetteers under the given spelling.

Monasterek, Ukr. (Manasterek); pop. 15; 45 km NW of Lvov; 50°10'/23°37'.

Monasterishtche, *see* Monastyriska.

Monasteriska, *see* Monastyriska.

Monasteryska, *see* Monastyriska.

Monasterzec, Pol.; pop. 25; 45 km SW of Przemysl; 49°31'/22°22'.

Monasterzyska, *see* Monastyriska.

Monastir, *see* Bitola.

Monastiristch, *see* Monastyrishche.

Monastirshtchina, *see* Monastyrshchina.

Monastrishch, *see* Monastyriska.

Monastrishtch, *see* Monastyriska.

Monastyrets, Ukr. (Manasterzec, Manastezhets); pop. 55; 45 km SSW of Lvov; 49°32'/23°42'.

Monastyrisce, *see* Monastyriska.

Monastyrishche, Ukr. (Monastiristch); 88 km SW of Konotop; 50°50'/32°10'; COH, EDRD.

Monastyriska, Ukr. (Folwarki, Monasterishtche, Monasteriska, Monasteryska, Monasterzyska, Monastrishch, Monastrishtch, Monastyrisce); pop. 1,168; 101 km NW of Chernovtsy; 49°05'/25°10'; AMG, COH, EGRS, EJ, GUM3, GUM4, GUM5, GUM6, HSL, HSL2, JGFF, LDL, LYV, PHP2, SF, YB.

Monastyrshchina, USSR (Monastirshtchina); pop. 1,715; 50 km S of Smolensk; 54°22'/31°51'; HSL, JGFF, LDL, SF.

Monavitz, *see* Manevichi.

Moncalvo, *see* Gologorica.

Monchberg, Germ.; 56 km ESE of Frankfurt am Main; 49°48'/09°16'; PHGB.

Monchen Gladbach, Germ. (Monchengladbach, Munchen Gladbach); pop. 954; 45 km WNW of Koln; 51°12'/06°26'; AMG, GUM3, GUM5, PHGBW.

Monchengladbach, *see* Monchen Gladbach.

Monchsdeggingen, Germ.; 88 km SSW of Nurnberg; 48°47'/10°35'; PHGB.

Monchsroth, Germ.; pop. 42; 75 km SW of Nurnberg; 49°01'/10°22'; GUM5, PHGB.

Mondorf, Germ.; pop. 20; 26 km SE of Koln; 50°47'/07°04'; GED.

Monevitch, *see* Manevichi.

Monheim, Germ.; 75 km S of Nurnberg; 48°50'/10°50'; PHGB.

Moniaki, Pol.; pop. 28; 45 km SW of Lublin; 51°02'/22°06'.

Moniatycze, Pol.; pop. 4; 101 km ESE of Lublin; 50°52'/23°52'.

Monkavid, *see* Mokobody.

Monkobody, HSL. This pre-World War I community was not found in BGN gazetteers.

Monok, Hung.; pop. 87; 32 km NE of Miskolc; 48°13'/21°09'; COH, HSL, HSL2, PHH.

Monor, Hung.; pop. 445; 38 km ESE of Budapest; 47°21'/19°27'; GUM3, GUM5, HSL, LDS, PHH.

Monosbel, Hung.; pop. 10; 32 km WSW of Miskolc; 48°02'/20°21'.

Monostor, Hung.; 82 km ESE of Miskolc; 47°41'/21°40'; COH, HSL, LDL.

Monostorapati, Hung.; pop. 7; 75 km NNE of Nagykanizsa; 46°55'/17°34'.

Monostorpalyi, Hung.; pop. 27; 107 km SE of Miskolc; 47°24'/21°47'; HSL, LDS.

Monostorszeg, *see* Backi Monostor.

Monowice, Pol.; pop. 3; 45 km WSW of Krakow; 50°02'/19°18'.

Montabaur, Germ. (Montebaur); pop. 85; 69 km WNW of Frankfurt am Main; 50°26'/07°50'; GED.

Montebaur, *see* Montabaur.

Montenegro; Not a town, but the smallest Yugoslavian constituent republic.

Monyhad, *see* Chminany.

Monzel, Germ.; pop. 9; 120 km S of Koln; 49°55'/06°57'; HSL.

Monzernheim, Germ.; pop. 5; 56 km SSW of Frankfurt am Main; 49°43'/08°14'.

Moosburg, Germ.; 50 km NNE of Munchen; 48°28'/11°56'; GUM3, GUM4, PHGB.

Mor, Hung.; pop. 182; 69 km WSW of Budapest; 47°23'/18°12'; HSL, HSL2, LDL, LDS, PHH.

Morag, Pol. (Mohrungen); pop. 50; 94 km ESE of Gdansk; 53°55'/19°56'.

Moragy, Hung.; pop. 8; 114 km WSW of Szeged; 46°13'/18°39'; JGFF.

Moranwica, LDL. This pre-World War I community was not found in BGN gazetteers.

Moravany, Cz.; 101 km NW of Brno; 50°00'/15°57'; HSL.

Moravec, Cz.; 50 km WNW of Brno; 49°27'/16°09'; HSL.

Moraveves, Cz.; pop. 7; 69 km WNW of Praha; 50°25'/13°37'.

Moravia; Not a town, but a region in Czechoslovakia.

Moravica, Ukr. EDRD. This town was not found in BGN gazetteers under the given spelling.

Moravitza, *see* Morawica.

Moravska Ostrava, *see* Ostrava.

Moravska Trebova, Cz. (Maehrisch Truebau); pop. 64; 69 km N of Brno; 49°45'/16°40'; GUM4.

Moravske Budejovice, Cz. (Maehrisch Budwitz); pop. 99; 62 km WSW of Brno; 49°03'/15°48'; EJ.

Moravske Lieskove, Cz.; 94 km NNE of Bratislava; 48°49'/17°48'; JGFF.

Moravsky Krumlov, Cz. (Kromau, Kromau Mahrisch, Krumlov Moravsky, Maehrisch Kromau); pop. 359; 26 km SW of Brno; 49°03'/16°19'; EJ, HSL.

Morawczyna, Pol.; pop. 2; 69 km S of Krakow; 49°30'/19°57'.

Morawianki, Pol.; pop. 8; 50 km ENE of Krakow; 50°13'/20°38'.

Morawiany, Pol.; pop. 5; 50 km ENE of Krakow; 50°13'/20°37'.

Morawica, Pol. (Moravitza); pop. 73; 94 km NNE of Krakow; 50°45'/20°38'; SF.

Morawiec, Pol. PHP4. This town was not found in BGN gazetteers under the given spelling.

Morawska Ostrawa, *see* Ostrava.

Morchenstern, *see* Smrzovka.

Mord, *see* Mordy.

Mordarka, Pol.; pop. 37; 62 km ESE of Krakow; 49°43'/20°28'; EDRD.

Mordy, Pol. (Mord); pop. 1,746; 101 km E of Warszawa; 52°13'/22°31'; COH, EDRD, FRG, GA, GUM4, GUM5, HSL, HSL2, JGFF, LDS, LYV, PHP4, POCEM, SF.

Mordzejow, COH, HSL. This pre-World War I community was not found in BGN gazetteers.

Moreni, Rom.; 75 km NW of Bucuresti; 44°59'/25°39'; GUM4, PHR1.

Morfelden, Germ.; pop. 38; 19 km SSW of Frankfurt am Main; 49°59'/08°34'.

Morgownik, Pol. PHP4. This town was not found in BGN gazetteers under the given spelling.

Morichida, Hung.; pop. 6; 126 km W of Budapest; 47°31'/17°25'.

Moringen, Germ.; pop. 22; 82 km SSE of Hannover; 51°42'/09°52'; GUM3, GUM5.

Morlaca, Rom.; pop. 14; 50 km W of Cluj; 46°52'/22°57'.

Mornsheim, Germ.; 69 km S of Nurnberg; 48°53'/11°00'; PHGB.

Morochna Velka, *see* Morochno.

Morochno, Ukr. (Morochna Velka, Moroczna Wielka); pop. 49; 139 km NNW of Rovno; 51°50'/25°54'.

Morochow, Pol.; pop. 25; 56 km SW of Przemysl; 49°28'/22°12'.

Moroczna Wielka, *see* Morochno.

Moroczyn, Pol.; pop. 6; 107 km ESE of Lublin; 50°50'/23°56'; HSL.

Moroshevis, *see* Toplita.

Moroshhevis, *see* Toplita.

Moroski, Byel.; pop. 4; 75 km WNW of Minsk; 54°20'/26°42'.

Morovic, Yug.; 101 km W of Beograd; 45°00'/19°13'; AMG.

Morozeni, *see* Morozeny.

Morozeny, Mold. (Morozeni); pop. 31; 50 km NNW of Kishinev; 47°23'/28°39'.

Morozovsk, USSR; pop. 248; 448 km SE of Voronezh; 48°21'/41°50'.

Mors, *see* Moers.

Morshin, Ukr. (Morszyn, Morszyn Zdroj); 82 km S of Lvov; 49°09'/23°52'; GUM4, GUM5.

Morszkow, Pol.; pop. 4; 94 km SSW of Bialystok; 52°28'/22°25'.

Morszyn, *see* Morshin.

Morszyn Zdroj, *see* Morshin.

Mortini, Lat.; 82 km NE of Daugavpils; 56°14'/27°39'; PHLE.

Moryn, Pol. (Mohrin); pop. 9; 75 km S of Szczecin; 52°51'/14°23'; POCEM.

Morzyczyn, Pol.; pop. 26; 75 km NE of Warszawa; 52°41'/21°54'.

Morzywol, Pol.; pop. 4; 88 km ESE of Lodz; 51°15'/20°27'.

Mosalsk, HSL. This pre-World War I community was not found in BGN gazetteers.

Mosaneti, *see* Moshanets.

Mosbach, Germ.; pop. 159; 69 km N of Stuttgart; 49°21'/09°09'; AMG, EDRD, HSL, PHGBW.

Mosberg, Ukr.; pop. 11; Described in a list of Galician towns as being near Yavorov, this town does not appear in interwar or contemporary gazetteers.

Moscanci, Yug.; pop. 3; 114 km N of Zagreb; 46°45'/16°10'.

Moscenica, Yug.; pop. 5; 50 km SE of Zagreb; 45°27'/16°21'.

Moschin, *see* Mosina.

Mosciany, *see* Mostsyany.

Moscice, Pol.; 69 km E of Krakow; 50°01'/20°56'; GUM5.

Mosciska, *see* Mostiska.

Mosciska (near Radzyn), Pol.; pop. 24; 82 km N of Lublin; 51°57'/22°37'.

Mosciska (near Wlodawa), Pol.; pop. 14; 50 km NNE of Lublin; 51°34'/23°00'.

Moscow, *see* Moskva.

Mosedis, Lith. (Maishad, Meisad, Misiad); pop. 175; 114 km W of Siauliai; 56°10'/21°35'; HSL, LDL, SF, YL.

Moshanets, Ukr. (Mosaneti); pop. 30; 62 km NE of Chernovtsy; 48°28'/26°42'.

Moshchisk, *see* Mostiska.

Moshkuv, Ukr. (Moszkow); pop. 26; 75 km N of Lvov; 50°29'/24°09'. The *Black Book* notes a town (pop. 11) named Moszkow in the interwar Polish province of Wolyn that does not appear in interwar or contemporary gazetteers.

Moshtchisk, *see* Mostishche.

Moshtsiska, *see* Mostiska.

Mosina, Pol. (Moschin); pop. 22; 26 km SSW of Poznan; 52°15'/16°51'; AMG, LDS.

Moskalowka, *see* Moskalyuvka.

Moskaluvka, *see* Moskalyuvka.

Moskalyuvka, Ukr. (Moskalowka, Moskaluvka); pop. 158; 62 km WSW of Chernovtsy; 48°18'/25°06'; PHP2.

Moskarzew, *see* Moskorzew.

Moskorzew, Pol. (Moskarzew); pop. 5; 62 km E of Czestochowa; 50°39'/19°56'.

Moskva, USSR (Moscow); 157 km SE of Kalinin; 55°45'/37°35'; AMG, EDRD, EJ, HSL, ISH1, LDL, PHP1.

Moslavina Podravska, Yug. (Podravska Moslavina); pop. 16; 150 km E of Zagreb; 45°47'/17°59'.

Moson, *see* Mosonmagyarovar.

Mosonmagyarovar, Hung. (Magyarovar, Moson); pop. 549; 139 km WNW of Budapest; 47°52'/17°17'; AMG, GUM5, HSL, JGFF, LDS, PHH.

Mosonszentjanos, Hung. (Sankt Johann); pop. 24; 150 km W of Budapest; 47°47'/17°08'.

Mosonszentmiklos, Hung.; pop. 16; 126 km W of Budapest; 47°44'/17°26'.

Mosonszentpeter, Hung. (Sankt Peter); pop. 5; 146 km W of Budapest; 47°47'/17°09'.

Mosonszolnok, Hung.; pop. 2; 146 km W of Budapest; 47°51'/17°11'.

Mosoreni, Ukr.; pop. 17; 38 km N of Chernovtsy; 48°37'/26°02'.

Mosorin, Yug.; pop. 10; 56 km NW of Beograd; 45°18'/20°11'.

Mossbach, Germ.; 82 km SSW of Leipzig; 50°41'/11°49'; HSL, LDL.

Most, Cz. (Bruex); pop. 737; 75 km WNW of Praha; 50°32'/13°39'; EJ.

Mostar, Yug.; pop. 136; 270 km SW of Beograd; 43°21'/17°49'; EJ, GUM4, PHY.

Mostek, Cz. (Schwanenbruckl); pop. 10; 139 km SW of Praha; 49°33'/12°40'.

Most Gadol, *see* Velikiye Mosty.

Mostishche, Ukr. (Moshatzik, Moshtchisk); 94 km SSE of Lvov; 49°04'/24°20'; SF.

Mostiska, Ukr. (Mosciska, Moshchisk, Moshtsiska); pop. 2,328; 62 km WSW of Lvov; 49°48'/23°09'; AMG, COH, EDRD, EGRS, EJ, GUM3, GUM4, GUM5, HSL, HSL2, JGFF, LDL, PHP2.

Mosti Vielkie, *see* Velikiye Mosty.

Mostki, Pol.; pop. 41; 107 km NE of Krakow; 50°37'/21°14'.

Mostki (Lwow); There were two towns in the Polish interwar province of Lwow; one was near Nawarya at 49°43'/23°51', and a second was near Ulanow at 50°35'/22°22'.

Mostovoi, *see* Mostovoye.

Mostovoye, Ukr. (Mostovoi); 107 km N of Odessa; 47°25'/31°00'; GUM3, GUM4, PHR1.

Mostow, Pol.; pop. 16; 101 km N of Lublin; 52°06'/22°45'.

Mostowlany, Pol.; pop. 4; 50 km E of Bialystok; 53°05'/23°53'.

Most Rabati, *see* Velikiye Mosty.

Mostsyany, Byel. (Mosciany); 150 km NW of Minsk; 54°57'/26°13'; PHP3.

Mosty, Byel.; pop. 171; 182 km NW of Pinsk; 53°25'/24°32'. *See also* Velikiye Mosty. This name often referred to the Ukrainian town of Velikiye Mosty.

Mosty Male, Pol.; pop. 147; 82 km NNE of Przemysl; 50°19'/23°33'; HSL, PHP2.

Mosty Wielkie, *see* Velikiye Mosty.

Mosuni, Rom.; pop. 5; 88 km E of Cluj; 46°34'/24°44'.

Moszczanica, Pol.; pop. 55; 62 km N of Przemysl; 50°18'/22°54'.

Moszczaniec, Pol.; pop. 7; 75 km SW of Przemysl; 49°26'/21°55'.

Moszczenica, Pol.; pop. 61; 94 km ESE of Krakow; 49°44'/21°07'.

Moszczenica (Lodz area), Pol.; 32 km SE of Lodz; 51°30'/19°43'; GUM5.

Moszczenica Nizna, Pol.; pop. 4; 75 km SE of Krakow; 49°33'/20°38'.

Moszczona Panska, Pol.; pop. 6; 82 km S of Bialystok; 52°27'/23°01'.

Moszenki, Pol.; pop. 32; Described in the *Black Book* as being in the Lublin region of Poland, this town was not found in BGN gazetteers.

Moszkow, *see* Moshkuv.

Motchevitz, *see* Maciejowice.

Motchiov, *see* Maciejow.

Motel, *see* Motol.

Motele, *see* Motol.

Motila, *see* Motyli.

Motis, Rom.; pop. 15; 88 km NW of Cluj; 47°26'/23°08'; HSL.

Motol, Byel. (Motel, Motele); pop. 1,140; 45 km WNW of Pinsk; 52°19'/25°36'; COH, EDRD, HSL, HSL2, JGFF, LDL, LYV, SF, YB.

Motsit, *see* Molchad.

Motvarjavci, *see* Motvarjevci.

Motvarjevci, Yug. (Motvarjavci); pop. 3; 107 km N of Zagreb; 46°43'/16°21'.

Motwica, Pol.; pop. 30; 75 km NE of Lublin; 51°43'/23°20'.

Motycz, Pol.; pop. 22; 13 km WSW of Lublin; 51°15'/22°24'.

Motycze Poduchowne, Pol.; pop. 10; 82 km SSW of Lublin; 50°40'/21°51'.

Motyle, *see* Motyli.

Motyli, Byel. (Motila, Motyle); pop. 14; 195 km W of Minsk; 53°56'/24°38'; SF.

Movorzhev, USSR; pop. 204; This town was not found in BGN gazetteers under the given spelling.

Mozdzierz, Pol.; pop. 6; 94 km N of Lodz; 52°33'/19°35'.

Mozejki, *see* Mazeikiai.

Mozgawa, Pol.; pop. 8; 56 km NE of Krakow; 50°26'/20°31'.

Mozir, *see* Mozyr.

Mozyr, Byel. (Mozir, Mozyrz); pop. 5,901; 126 km SW of Gomel; 52°03'/29°16'; AMG, EJ, HSL, JGFF, LDL, SF.

Mozyrz, *see* Mozyr.

Mradice, Cz.; pop. 2; 62 km WNW of Praha; 50°20'/13°41'.

Mragowo, Pol. (Sensburg); pop. 66; 150 km WNW of Bialystok; 53°52'/21°18'; HSL.

Mratin, Cz.; pop. 5; 19 km NNE of Praha; 50°12'/14°33'.

Mrazhnitsa, Ukr. (Mraznica); pop. 176; 82 km SSW of Lvov; 49°15'/23°23'; HSL.

Mraznica, *see* Mrazhnitsa.

Mricna, Cz.; pop. 2; 94 km NE of Praha; 50°36'/15°29'.

Mrigolod, *see* Mrzyglod.

Mrocza, Pol. (Mrotschen); pop. 49; 101 km NNE of Poznan; 53°15'/17°37'; POCEM.

Mroczkow, Pol.; pop. 10; 114 km ESE of Lodz; 51°09'/20°43'.

Mroczkowice, Pol.; 62 km E of Lodz; 51°40'/20°21'; GA.

Mrotschen, *see* Mrocza.

Mrowla, Pol.; pop. 16; 69 km WNW of Przemysl; 50°06'/21°56'.

Mrozowa Wola, Pol.; pop. 7; 69 km NE of Warszawa; 52°35'/21°52'.

Mrozy, Pol.; pop. 306; 56 km E of Warszawa; 52°10'/21°48'; GA, GUM4, GUM5, HSL, PHP4, SF.

Mrzyglod, Pol. (Mrigolod); pop. 75; 32 km SE of Czestochowa; 50°33'/19°22'.

Mrzyglody, Pol.; pop. 60; 69 km NNE of Przemysl; 50°17'/23°28'.

Mscibow, *see* Mstibovo.

Msciow, Pol.; pop. 2; 82 km SSW of Lublin; 50°43'/21°49'.

Mscislaw, *see* Mstislavl.

Msciwoje, Pol. PHP4. This town was not found in BGN gazetteers under the given spelling.

Mseno, Cz.; pop. 11; 45 km N of Praha; 50°27'/14°38'.

Mshanets, Ukr. (Mszaniec); pop. 22; 107 km SW of Lvov; 49°20'/22°46'.

Mshchonov, *see* Mszczonow.

Mstibovo, Byel. (Mscibow, Mszibowo, Omstibova); pop. 255; 170 km WNW of Pinsk; 53°07'/24°15'; HSL, JGFF, SF.

Mstishaw, *possibly* Mstyczow.

Mstislavl, Byel. (Amtchislav, Amtzislov, Mscislaw, Omtchislav); pop. 3,371; 163 km SE of Vitebsk; 54°02'/31°44'; EJ, JGFF, LDL, SF.

Mstisov, Cz.; pop. 1; 82 km NW of Praha; 50°40'/13°46'.

Mstow, Pol. (Omstov); pop. 740; 19 km ENE of Czestochowa;

50°50'/19°18'; CAHJP, GUM3, GUM5, JGFF, LDS, PHP1, SF.

Mstyczow, Pol. (Mstishaw?); pop. 8; 56 km N of Krakow; 50°32'/19°59'; HSL.

Mszadla Nowa, Pol.; pop. 14; 56 km W of Lublin; 51°20'/21°47'.

Mszadla Stara, Pol.; pop. 24; 56 km W of Lublin; 51°21'/21°47'.

Mszana, Pol. (Amsana, Amshana); pop. 39; 88 km SW of Przemysl; 49°29'/21°39'; SF.

Mszana Dolna, Pol. (Meshana Dolna); pop. 410; 50 km SSE of Krakow; 49°41'/20°05'; AMG, EGRS, GUM3, GUM4, GUM5, HSL, HSL2, LDL, PHP3, POCEM, SF.

Mszana Gorna, Pol.; pop. 34; 50 km SSE of Krakow; 49°40'/20°06'.

Mszaniec, see Mshanets.

Mszanna, Pol.; pop. 33; BGN lists two possible localities with this name located at 52°09'/22°45' and 51°20'/23°32'.

Mszczonow, Pol. (Amshinov, Mshchonov); pop. 2,188; 50 km SW of Warszawa; 51°59'/20°31'; COH, EDRD, FRG, GUM4, GUM5, HSL, HSL2, LDL, LDS, LYV, PHP1, PHP4, POCEM, SF, YB.

Mszibowo, see Mstibovo.

Mtsensk, USSR; pop. 151; 146 km ENE of Bryansk; 53°17'/36°35'.

Much, Germ.; 32 km E of Koln; 50°55'/07°24'; GED, GUM3.

Muchawka, see Mukhavka.

Muchea, Rom.; 170 km NE of Bucuresti; 45°20'/27°48'; GUM4.

Mucsony, Hung.; pop. 19; 26 km NNW of Miskolc; 48°16'/20°41'; HSL.

Muddersheim, Germ.; 26 km SW of Koln; 50°45'/06°40'; GED.

Mueglitz, see Mohelnice.

Muehlbach, see Mlynovtse.

Muenster, see Munster.

Mugeni, Rom. (Bogoz); pop. 14; 139 km ESE of Cluj; 46°15'/25°13'.

Muggensturm, Germ.; pop. 3; 69 km W of Stuttgart; 48°52'/08°17'; JGFF, PHGBW.

Muglinov, Cz.; pop. 62; 146 km NE of Brno; 49°51'/18°18'.

Muglitz, *possibly* Mohelnice.

Muhi, Hung.; pop. 8; 19 km SE of Miskolc; 47°59'/20°56'.

Muhlbach, Germ.; 114 km NNE of Frankfurt am Main; 50°56'/09°33'; LDS, PHGBW.

Muhldorf, Germ.; 69 km ENE of Munchen; 48°15'/12°32'; GUM3, GUM4, GUM5, GUM6, PHGB.

Muhlen, Germ. PHGBW. A number of towns share this name. It was not possible to determine from available information which one is being referenced.

Muhlfeld, Germ.; 120 km NW of Nurnberg; 50°27'/10°21'; JGFF, PHGB.

Muhlhausen, Germ.; pop. 168; 133 km WSW of Leipzig; 51°13'/10°27'; EDRD, EJ, GUM3, GUM5, HSL, HSL2, LDS. *See also* Mlynary.

Muhlhausen (Bavaria), Germ.; pop. 52; 45 km SE of Nurnberg; 49°10'/11°27'; GUM5, PHGB.

Muhlheim am Main, Germ.; pop. 74; 13 km E of Frankfurt am Main; 50°07'/08°50'; LDS.

Muhlheim an der Ruhr, see Mulheim an der Ruhr.

Muhlstetten, Germ.; 38 km S of Nurnberg; 49°09'/11°02'; PHGB.

Muhringen, Germ.; pop. 48; 50 km SSW of Stuttgart; 48°25'/08°46'; GUM5, HSL, HSL2, JGFF, PHGBW.

Mukacevo, see Mukachevo.

Mukachevo, Ukr. (Mukacevo, Mukaczewo, Munkacs, Munkacz, Munkatsch); pop. 11,313; 182 km SSW of Lvov; 48°27'/22°43'; AMG, COH, EJ, GUM3, GUM4, GUM5, GUM6, HSL, HSL2, JGFF, LDL, PHP2, PHP3, YB.

Mukaczewo, see Mukachevo.

Mukane, Ukr. (Mukanie); pop. 31; 69 km NE of Lvov; 50°14'/24°45'.

Mukanie, see Mukane.

Mukhavka, Ukr. (Muchawka); pop. 26; 69 km NNW of Chernovtsy; 48°54'/25°43'.

Mulawicze, Pol.; pop. 4; 38 km S of Bialystok; 52°52'/23°05'.

Mulchitsy, Ukr. (Mulczyce); pop. 8; 107 km NNW of Rovno; 51°32'/25°53'.

Mulczyce, see Mulchitsy.

Mulfingen, Germ.; 75 km NNE of Stuttgart; 49°20'/09°48'; EJ, PHGBW.

Mulheim, Germ. EJ, GED.

Mulheim (near Koblenz), Germ.; pop. 100; 75 km SE of Koln; 50°23'/07°30'; GUM5.

Mulheim am Mosel, Germ.; pop. 23; 120 km WSW of Frankfurt am Main; 49°55'/07°01'.

Mulheim an der Ruhr, Germ. (Muhlheim an der Ruhr); pop. 626; 56 km N of Koln; 51°26'/06°53'; GUM3, GUM5, LDS.

Mullheim, Germ.; pop. 110; 157 km SW of Stuttgart; 47°48'/07°38'; HSL, HSL2, JGFF, LDS, PHGBW.

Mullrose, Germ.; 75 km ESE of Berlin; 52°15'/14°25'; LDS.

Mumling Grumbach, Germ.; pop. 22; 45 km SE of Frankfurt am Main; 49°46'/09°00'; LDS.

Mumor, Hung.; pop. 2; 45 km WNW of Nagykanizsa; 46°38'/16°34'.

Munchberg, Germ.; 101 km NNE of Nurnberg; 50°12'/11°47'; GUM3, PHGB.

Muncheberg, Germ.; pop. 34; 50 km E of Berlin; 52°30'/14°08'.

Munchen, Germ. (Monaco, Munich); pop. 9,005; 150 km SSE of Nurnberg; 48°09'/11°35'; AMG, EDRD, EJ, GED, GUM3, GUM4, GUM5, GUM6, HSL, HSL2, ISH1, ISH3, JGFF, LDL, LDS, PHGB, PHGBW.

Munchen Gladbach, see Monchen Gladbach.

Munchreith an der Thaya, Aus.; pop. 4; 107 km NW of Wien; 48°53'/15°23'.

Munchweiler, Germ.; 120 km SSW of Frankfurt am Main; 49°13'/07°42'; HSL, JGFF.

Munchweiler an der Alsenz, Germ.; 82 km SSW of Frankfurt am Main; 49°33'/07°53'; GED.

Munden, Germ. (Hannoversch Munden); pop. 95; 114 km S of Hannover; 51°25'/09°41'; GED, HSL, HSL2.

Munich, see Munchen.

Munina, Pol.; pop. 3; 26 km N of Przemysl; 49°59'/22°45'.

Munkacs, see Mukachevo.

Munkacz, see Mukachevo.

Munkatsch, see Mukachevo.

Munnerstadt, Germ.; 107 km ENE of Frankfurt am Main; 50°15'/10°11'; PHGB.

Munsingen, Germ.; 45 km SE of Stuttgart; 48°25'/09°30'; PHGBW.

Munster, Germ. (Muenster); pop. 600; 126 km N of Koln; 51°58'/07°38'; AMG, CAHJP, EJ, GED, GUM4, GUM5, JGFF, LDS.

Munsterberg, see Cerkiewnik.

Munstereifel, Germ.; pop. 48; 50 km S of Koln; 50°33'/06°46'; GED.

Munsterhausen, Germ.; pop. 6; 88 km W of Munchen; 48°19'/10°27'; PHGB.

Munstermaifeld, Germ.; pop. 50; 82 km SSE of Koln; 50°15'/07°22'; EDRD.

Muntenia, GUM4. This town was not found in BGN gazetteers under the given spelling.

Muntz, Germ.; 45 km W of Koln; 50°59'/06°22'; GED.

Munus, Ukr.; 88 km NW of Simferopol; 45°37'/33°31'.

Munzenberg, Germ.; pop. 33; 45 km N of Frankfurt am Main; 50°27'/08°47'.

Munzesheim, Germ.; pop. 23; 50 km NW of Stuttgart; 49°07'/08°43'; LDS, PHGBW.

Murafa, Ukr.; pop. 1,421; 62 km W of Kharkov; 50°03'/35°20'; EDRD, GUM4, GUM6, LDL, PHR1, SF.

Murakeresztur, Hung.; pop. 10; 13 km SSW of Nagykanizsa; 46°22'/16°52'.

Mura Mare, Rom.; pop. 3; 88 km E of Cluj; 46°39'/24°47'.

Muran, Cz. (Murany); 88 km W of Kosice; 48°44'/20°03'; HSL.

Murany, see Muran.

Muraratka, Hung.; pop. 4; 26 km WSW of Nagykanizsa;

46°27'/16°41'.

Muraszombat, *see* Murska Sobota.

Murau, Aus.; 101 km W of Graz; 47°06'/14°10'; GUM5.

Murava, Ukr. (Murawa); pop. 167; 139 km N of Lvov; 51°04'/23°59'; GUM3, GUM4, LYV, YB.

Murava (Bialystok), Byel.; pop. 9; 146 km WNW of Pinsk; 52°38'/24°13'.

Murav Evo, *see* Mazeikiai.

Muravica, *see* Murawica.

Muravievo, *see* Mazeikiai.

Muravitsa, *see* Murawica.

Murawa, *see* Murava.

Murawica, Pol. (Marvits, Marvitz, Muravica, Muravitsa); SF. Described in SF as adjacent to the town of Mlinow, Murawica does not appear in contemporary gazetteers.

Murawjewo, LDL. This pre-World War I community was not found in BGN gazetteers.

Murawskie Nadbuzne, Pol.; pop. 7; 75 km SW of Bialystok; 52°38'/22°23'.

Murczyn, Pol.; 75 km NE of Poznan; 52°52'/17°47'; GA.

Mureseni, Rom.; pop. 22; 75 km ESE of Cluj; 46°31'/24°31'.

Muresenii Bargaului, *see* Muresenii Birgaului.

Muresenii Birgaului, Rom. (Borgo Muraseni, Marosborgo, Muresenii Bargaului); pop. 82; 107 km NE of Cluj; 47°14'/24°50'; HSL.

Mur Kirilovtsy, *see* Murovanyye Kurilovtsy.

Murnau, Germ.; pop. 1; 56 km SSW of Munchen; 47°41'/11°12'; GUM5.

Murovano Kurilovtsy, *see* Murovanyye Kurilovtsy.

Murovanyye Kurilovtsy, Ukr. (Maravna Krilovitz, Mur Kirilovtsy, Murovano Kurilovtsy); pop. 1,239; 88 km SW of Vinnitsa; 48°44'/27°31'; HSL, JGFF, LDL, SF.

Murowana Goslin, *see* Murowana Goslina.

Murowana Goslina, Pol. (Murowana Goslin); pop. 44; 19 km N of Poznan; 52°34'/17°01'; CAHJP, POCEM.

Murowin, Ukr.; pop. 23; 94 km NNW of Rovno; 51°25'/26°05'. This town was located on an interwar map of Poland but does not appear in contemporary gazetteers. Map coordinates are approximate.

Murska Sobota, Yug. (Muraszombat); pop. 159; 101 km N of Zagreb; 46°40'/16°10'; HSL, LDS, PHY.

Murski Crnci, Yug.; pop. 3; 101 km N of Zagreb; 46°38'/16°07'.

Murstetten, Aus.; pop. 3; 45 km W of Wien; 48°14'/15°49'.

Muryjovo, GUM3. This town was not found in BGN gazetteers under the given spelling.

Murzzuschlag, Aus.; pop. 15; 69 km N of Graz; 47°36'/15°41'.

Musbach, Germ.; 94 km SSE of Stuttgart; 47°59'/09°35'; HSL.

Muschenheim, Germ.; 50 km N of Frankfurt am Main; 50°29'/08°48'; LDS.

Musfalau, Rom.; pop. 214; Described in the *Black Book* as being in the Transylvania region of Romania, this town was not found in BGN gazetteers.

Mush, *see* Novaya Mysh.

Mushina, *see* Muszyna.

Mushkatovtse, *see* Slobodka Mushkatovka.

Mushkev, *see* Kozelets.

Musnik, *see* Musninkai.

Musninkai, Lith. (Musnik, Musninuai); pop. 351; 45 km WNW of Vilnius; 54°57'/24°51'; GUM5, YL.

Musninuai, *see* Musninkai.

Mussbach, Germ.; 94 km SSW of Frankfurt am Main; 49°22'/08°10'; JGFF.

Musteata, *see* Mustyatsa.

Mustvee, Est.; pop. 6; 56 km N of Tartu; 58°51'/26°56'; PHLE.

Mustyatsa, Mold. (Musteata); pop. 12; 107 km WNW of Kishinev; 47°31'/27°39'.

Muszaly, Hung. (Nagymuzsaly); 88 km SSE of Miskolc; 47°19'/21°07'; GUM3, GUM5.

Muszkatowce, *see* Slobodka Mushkatovka.

Muszkatowka, Pol. PHP2. This town was not found in BGN gazetteers under the given spelling.

Muszne, Pol.; pop. 26; Described in the *Black Book* as being in the Polesie region of Poland, this town was not found in BGN gazetteers.

Muszyna, Pol. (Mushina); pop. 423; 114 km SE of Krakow; 49°21'/20°55'; CAHJP, COH, EGRS, GUM5, HSL, JGFF, LDL, PHP3, POCEM, SF.

Muszynka, Pol.; pop. 10; 114 km ESE of Krakow; 49°23'/21°05'.

Mutejovice, Cz.; pop. 7; 56 km W of Praha; 50°12'/13°42'.

Mutenin, Cz.; pop. 19; 133 km SW of Praha; 49°33'/12°45'.

Mutterstadt, Germ.; pop. 90; 75 km S of Frankfurt am Main; 49°27'/08°21'; GED, GUM5.

Mutvitsa, Ukr. (Mutwica); pop. 6; 146 km NNW of Rovno; 51°51'/26°00'.

Mutwica, *see* Mutvitsa.

Muzijovo, Cz. AMG, COH. This town was not found in BGN gazetteers under the given spelling.

Muzylow, Ukr.; pop. 23; 94 km NW of Chernovtsy; 48°55'/25°05'. This town was located on an interwar map of Poland but does not appear in contemporary gazetteers. Map coordinates are approximate.

Myadel, Byel. (Myadl); 120 km NNW of Minsk; 54°53'/26°57'; JGFF, SF.

Myadl, *see* Myadel.

Myastkovka, *see* Gorodkovka.

Mychow, Pol.; pop. 7; 101 km SW of Lublin; 50°55'/21°17'.

Mycow, Pol.; pop. 23; 114 km NE of Przemysl; 50°27'/24°00'.

Myczkow, Pol.; pop. 6; 56 km SSW of Przemysl; 49°23'/22°25'.

Myczkowce, Pol.; pop. 49; 50 km SSW of Przemysl; 49°27'/22°25'.

Myczow, Ukr.; pop. 42; 38 km ESE of Rovno; 50°25'/26°45'. This town was located on an interwar map of Poland but does not appear in contemporary gazetteers. Map coordinates are approximate.

Mydlniki, Pol.; pop. 16; 6 km WSW of Krakow; 50°05'/19°51'.

Mydlow, Pol.; pop. 4; 101 km SW of Lublin; 50°43'/21°23'.

Mydlowiec, Pol.; pop. 2; 101 km SW of Lublin; 50°44'/21°23'.

Mydzk Maly, Ukr.; pop. 24; 56 km N of Rovno; 51°05'/26°11'.

Myedzirzets, *see* Miedzyrzec.

Myedzirzets Podlask, *see* Miedzyrzec Podlaski.

Myekhov, *see* Miechow.

Myelets, *see* Mielec.

Myelnitsa, *see* Melnitsa Podolskaya.

Myena, *see* Mena.

Myendzirzets, *see* Miedzyrzec.

Myendzirzets Podlas, *see* Miedzyrzec Podlaski.

Myjava, Cz. (Miava); pop. 307; 75 km NNE of Bratislava; 48°45'/17°34'; GUM4, HSL, HSL2, JGFF, LDL, YB.

Mykaliskiai, *see* Mikaliskis.

Myketyntse, Ukr. (Mykietynce); pop. 64; 107 km WNW of Chernovtsy; 48°54'/24°45'.

Mykietynce, *see* Myketyntse.

Myndreshty, Mold. (Mandresti); pop. 14; 69 km NW of Kishinev; 47°30'/28°17'.

Myndyk, Mold. (Mandac); pop. 41; 150 km NW of Kishinev; 48°09'/27°47'.

Myodla, *see* Zelenopol Ye.

Mysenec, Cz.; pop. 2; 101 km S of Praha; 49°13'/14°12'.

Myshakuvka, Ukr. (Myszakowka); pop. 25; 75 km NE of Rovno; 50°52'/27°12'.

Myshev, Ukr. (Myszow); pop. 33; 94 km N of Lvov; 50°41'/24°20'; HSL.

Myshin, Ukr. (Myszyn); pop. 21; 69 km W of Chernovtsy; 48°27'/25°00'.

Myshkovtse, Ukr. (Mishkovitz, Mishkovtsy, Myszkowce, Myszkowice); pop. 20; 101 km N of Chernovtsy; 49°09'/26°02'; GUM3, HSL, JGFF, PHP2, SF.

Myshlyatichi, Ukr. (Myslatycze, Myslyatyche); pop. 36; 69 km WSW of Lvov; 49°44'/23°04'.

Myslachowice, Pol.; pop. 18; 32 km WNW of Krakow; 50°11'/19°29'.

Myslakow, Pol.; 56 km NE of Lodz; 52°06'/20°02'; GA.

Myslakowice, Pol.; 69 km E of Lodz; 51°37'/20°29'; GA.

Myslatycze, *see* Myshlyatichi.

Myslenice, Pol. (Mishlenitse, Mishlenitz, Mishlinits); pop. 675; 32 km S of Krakow; 49°50'/19°56'; COH, EGRS, GUM5, HSL, HSL2, LYV, PHP3, POCEM, SF, YB.

Mysliborz, Pol. (Soldin); pop. 36; 69 km SSE of Szczecin; 52°55'/14°52'; HSL, LDS.

Myslina, *see* Mysliny.

Mysliny, Ukr. (Myslina); pop. 5; 94 km WSW of Rovno; 50°29'/24°58'.

Myslkovice, Cz.; pop. 6; 94 km SSE of Praha; 49°18'/14°45'.

Mysloboje, *see* Mysloboye.

Mysloboye, Byel. (Mysloboje); pop. 7; 101 km N of Pinsk; 52°59'/26°15'.

Myslow, Pol.; 82 km NW of Lublin; 51°51'/21°59'; GUM5.

Myslowa, HSL. This pre-World War I community was not found in BGN gazetteers.

Myslowice, Pol. (Myslowitz, Slupna); pop. 463; 56 km WNW of Krakow; 50°14'/19°09'; AMG, CAHJP, GUM3, HSL, HSL2, JGFF, LDS, PHP3, POCEM.

Myslowitz, *see* Myslowice.

Myslyatyche, *see* Myshlyatichi.

Mystkow, Pol.; pop. 7; 82 km ESE of Krakow; 49°37'/20°48'.

Mystkowiec Stary, Pol.; pop. 11; 45 km NNE of Warszawa; 52°38'/21°16'.

Mystkowska Wola, *see* Wola Mystkowska.

Myszakowka, *see* Myshakuvka.

Myszkow, Pol.; pop. 563; 26 km SE of Czestochowa; 50°35'/19°21'; AMG, COH, GUM3, HSL, HSL2, LYV, PHP3, SF. *See also* Meshkov.

Myszkowce, *see* Myshkovtse.

Myszkowice, *see* Myshkovtse.

Myszkow Nowy, *see* Kozelets.

Myszory, *see* Miszory.

Myszow, *see* Myshev.

Myszyn, *see* Myshin.

Myszyniec, Pol. (Mishenits, Mishenitz, Mishinyets, Mishnits); pop. 600; 120 km W of Bialystok; 53°23'/21°21'; COH, GYLA, HSL, JGFF, LDL, LYV, PHP4, SF, YB.

Myta, Ukr.; pop. 49; 107 km S of Lvov; 48°58'/23°55'; HSL. This town was located on an interwar map of Poland but does not appear in contemporary gazetteers. Map coordinates are approximate.

Mytarz, Pol.; pop. 13; 94 km WSW of Przemysl; 49°37'/21°31'.

Mzurow, Pol.; pop. 12; 32 km ESE of Czestochowa; 50°40'/19°30'.

Nabburg, Germ.; pop. 5; 82 km E of Nurnberg; 49°27'/12°11'; PHGB.

Naberezhnoye, USSR (Karlsrode); pop. 4; 56 km NE of Kaliningrad; 54°57'/21°21'.

Nabla, *see* Nebel.

Nabrad, Hung.; pop. 33; 126 km E of Miskolc; 48°00'/22°27'; HSL.

Nabroz, Pol.; pop. 22; 114 km ESE of Lublin; 50°35'/23°47'.

Naceradec, Cz.; pop. 30; 62 km SE of Praha; 49°37'/14°55'.

Nacha, Byel. (Nacza); pop. 41; 176 km W of Minsk; 54°04'/24°50'; GUM4.

Nachod, Cz.; pop. 362; 126 km NE of Praha; 50°25'/16°10'; AMG, EJ, HSL, HSL2, JGFF.

Nacina Ves, Cz. (Nacyna Ves, Natafalva, Nazina Ves); pop. 84; 45 km NE of Kosice; 48°49'/21°51'; GUM4, HSL.

Nackenheim, Germ.; pop. 6; 32 km SW of Frankfurt am Main; 49°55'/08°21'.

Nackowo, HSL. This pre-World War I community was not found in BGN gazetteers.

Nacpolsk, Pol.; 56 km WNW of Warszawa; 52°30'/20°15'; PHP4.

Nacyna Ves, *see* Nacina Ves.

Nacza, *see* Nacha.

Nadalj, Yug.; pop. 2; 88 km NW of Beograd; 45°31'/19°56'.

Nadarzyn, Pol. (Nadazhin, Nadzin); pop. 431; 26 km SSW of Warszawa; 52°06'/20°48'; CAHJP, HSL, JGFF, LDS, PHP4, SF, YB.

Nadas, Hung.; pop. 2; 94 km NE of Nagykanizsa; 46°59'/17°56'; HSL,
HSL2.

Nadasd, *see* Trstena na Ostrove.

Nadasu, Rom.; pop. 4; 32 km W of Cluj; 46°51'/23°09'.

Nadasu Sasesc, (Szasznadas); HSL. This pre-World War I community was not found in BGN gazetteers.

Nadazhin, *see* Nadarzyn.

Nadbrzezie, Pol.; pop. 28; 82 km SSW of Lublin; 50°40'/21°46'.

Nadejkov, Cz.; pop. 12; 69 km S of Praha; 49°30'/14°29'.

Nadezhdovka, Ukr. (Hofnungstal); pop. 5; 107 km WSW of Odessa; 46°19'/29°21'.

Nadezhnaya, Ukr. (Dvilne); 170 km ESE of Dnepropetrovsk; 47°35'/36°50'; JGFF.

Nadimihali, *see* Michalovce.

Nadis, Rom.; pop. 2; 75 km NW of Cluj; 47°23'/23°10'.

Nadlac, Rom. (Nagylak); 227 km SW of Cluj; 46°10'/20°45'; HSL, PHR1.

Nadma, Pol.; pop. 15; 19 km NE of Warszawa; 52°22'/21°11'.

Nadolany, Pol.; pop. 14; 62 km SW of Przemysl; 49°32'/22°03'.

Nadrechnoye, Ukr. (Cioara Murza, Cioara Murzei); pop. 21; 126 km WSW of Odessa; 46°22'/29°06'.

Nadrybie, Pol. (Nadrybie Dwor); pop. 47; 38 km NE of Lublin; 51°21'/23°02'; AMG.

Nadrybie Dwor, *see* Nadrybie.

Nadstawem, Pol.; pop. 69 km N of Wroclaw; 51°38'/17°11'; GA.

Nadudvar, Hung.; pop. 291; 82 km SSE of Miskolc; 47°25'/21°10'; AMG, HSL, HSL2, LDL, LDS, PHH.

Nadujfalu, Hung.; pop. 1; 56 km WSW of Miskolc; 48°01'/19°59'.

Nadushita, Mold. (Nadusita); pop. 126; 133 km NW of Kishinev; 48°02'/27°56'.

Nadusita, *see* Nadushita.

Nadvorna, *see* Nadvornaya.

Nadvornaya, Ukr. (Nadvorna, Nadworna, Nodvorna); pop. 2,042; 107 km WNW of Chernovtsy; 48°38'/24°34'; AMG, COH, EDRD, EGRS, EJ, GUM3, GUM4, GUM5, HSL, HSL2, JGFF, LDL, PHP2, SF, YB.

Nadworna, *see* Nadvornaya.

Nadzhmihali, *see* Michalovce.

Nadzin, *see* Nadarzyn.

Nadzow, Pol.; pop. 9; 32 km NE of Krakow; 50°15'/20°19'.

Nagachev, Ukr. (Nahaczow); pop. 131; 56 km WNW of Lvov; 50°01'/23°18'; PHP2.

Nagawczyna, Pol.; pop. 3; 101 km WNW of Przemysl; 50°03'/21°27'.

Nagelsberg, Germ.; 69 km NNE of Stuttgart; 49°18'/09°41'; PHGBW.

Nagelsberg Bei Runzelsau, HSL. This pre-World War I community was not found in BGN gazetteers.

Naglowice, Pol. (Noglovitz); pop. 79; 69 km E of Czestochowa; 50°41'/20°07'; SF.

Nagnajow, Pol.; pop. 14; 107 km SSW of Lublin; 50°31'/21°37'.

Nagold, Germ.; 45 km SW of Stuttgart; 48°33'/08°43'; PHGBW.

Nagor, USSR; pop. 1,769; This town was not found in BGN gazetteers under the given spelling.

Nagorki, Pol.; pop. 29; 69 km W of Bialystok; 53°16'/22°04'.

Nagorna, *see* Nagornoye.

Nagornoye, Byel. (Caragacii Vechi [Bessarabia], Nagorna); pop. 27; 107 km NNE of Pinsk; 52°58'/26°47'.

Nagornoye (Bessarabia), Ukr.; pop. 1; 208 km SW of Odessa; 45°26'/28°27'.

Nagortse Male, Ukr. (Nahorce Male); pop. 43; 32 km NE of Lvov; 50°00'/24°23'.

Nagorzanka, *see* Naguzhanka.

Nagorzany, Pol.; pop. 23; 62 km SW of Przemysl; 49°31'/22°03'.

Nagoszyn, Pol.; pop. 59; 101 km WNW of Przemysl; 50°08'/21°26'.

Nagov, Cz.; 75 km NNE of Kosice; 49°15'/21°57'; JGFF.

Nagovo, *see* Olnkhovtsy.

Naguyevichi, *see* Ivana Franka.

Naguzhanka, Ukr. (Nagorzanka); pop. 237; 88 km NNW of Chernovtsy; 49°03'/25°47'; PHP2.

Naguzhanka (near Czortkow), Ukr.; pop. 51; 75 km NNW of Chernovtsy; 48°56'/25°44'.

Nagyabajom, *see* Adrianu Mare.

Nagyacsad, Hung.; pop. 10; 107 km N of Nagykanizsa; 47°22'/17°22'.

Nagyadorjan, *see* Adrianu Mare.

Nagyalasony, Hung.; pop. 3; 94 km N of Nagykanizsa; 47°14'/17°21'.

Nagyar, Hung.; pop. 16; 133 km E of Miskolc; 48°03'/22°34'; HSL.

Nagyatad, Hung.; pop. 256; 38 km ESE of Nagykanizsa; 46°13'/17°22'; LDS, PHH.

Nagybabony, *see* Babonymegyer.

Nagybajcs, Hung.; pop. 2; 107 km WNW of Budapest; 47°46'/17°42'.

Nagybajom, Hung.; pop. 112; 45 km E of Nagykanizsa; 46°23'/17°31'; HSL, JGFF, LDS, PHH.

Nagybakonak, Hung.; pop. 12; 19 km N of Nagykanizsa; 46°33'/17°03'.

Nagybanhegyes, Hung.; pop. 15; 62 km NE of Szeged; 46°28'/20°54'; HSL.

Nagy Banya, *see* Baia Mare.

Nagybanya, *see* Baia Mare.

Nagybaracska, Hung.; pop. 77; 101 km WSW of Szeged; 46°03'/18°54'; PHH.

Nagybarca, Hung.; pop. 91; 32 km WNW of Miskolc; 48°15'/20°32'.

Nagybarod, *see* Borod.

Nagybatony, Hung.; pop. 13; 69 km WSW of Miskolc; 47°58'/19°50'.

Nagybecskerek, *see* Zrenjanin.

Nagy Bereg, *see* Beregi.

Nagybereg, *see* Beregi.

Nagybereny, Hung.; pop. 33; 101 km SSW of Budapest; 46°48'/18°10'.

Nagyberki, Hung.; pop. 13; 82 km E of Nagykanizsa; 46°22'/18°01'.

Nagybicserd, Hung.; pop. 4; 94 km ESE of Nagykanizsa; 46°01'/18°05'.

Nagy Bocska, *see* Velikiy Bychkov.

Nagybocsko, *see* Bocicoiu Mare.

Nagyborzsony, Hung.; pop. 9; 50 km NNW of Budapest; 47°56'/18°50'.

Nagyborzsova, GUM5. This town was not found in BGN gazetteers under the given spelling.

Nagybudmer, Hung.; pop. 2; 126 km ESE of Nagykanizsa; 45°56'/18°27'.

Nagybuny, *see* Boiu Mare.

Nagycenk, Hung.; pop. 3; 139 km NNW of Nagykanizsa; 47°36'/16°42'.

Nagycsecs, Hung.; pop. 23; 19 km SE of Miskolc; 47°58'/20°57'; HSL, JGFF.

Nagycsepely, Hung.; pop. 6; 75 km NE of Nagykanizsa; 46°45'/17°50'.

Nagycsomote, Hung.; pop. 7; 107 km NNW of Nagykanizsa; 47°20'/16°35'.

Nagyczigand, HSL. This pre-World War I community was not found in BGN gazetteers.

Nagydem, Hung.; pop. 17; 107 km WSW of Budapest; 47°26'/17°41'.

Nagydobos, Hung.; pop. 108; 114 km E of Miskolc; 48°03'/22°19'; HSL, JGFF, LDS, PHH.

Nagydorog, Hung.; pop. 87; 101 km S of Budapest; 46°38'/18°40'; HSL, PHH.

Nagyecsed, Hung.; pop. 533; 126 km E of Miskolc; 47°52'/22°24'; COH, GUM4, GUM5, HSL, LDS, PHH.

Nagyenyed, HSL. This pre-World War I community was not found in BGN gazetteers.

Nagyesztergar, Hung.; pop. 4; 94 km WSW of Budapest; 47°17'/17°54'.

Nagyfalu, *see* Velka Ves nad Iplom.

Nagy Fodemes, *see* Velke Ulany.

Nagyfuged, Hung.; pop. 8; 69 km SW of Miskolc; 47°41'/20°07'.

Nagygec, Hung.; pop. 45; 150 km E of Miskolc; 47°51'/22°45'.

Nagy Geres, *see* Velky Hores.

Nagygeresd, Hung.; pop. 6; 114 km N of Nagykanizsa; 47°23'/16°55'.

Nagyhalasz, Hung.; pop. 312; 75 km ENE of Miskolc; 48°08'/21°46'; AMG, HSL, LDL, PHH.

Nagyharsany, Hung.; pop. 27; 126 km ESE of Nagykanizsa; 45°50'/18°24'; LDS.

Nagyhodos, Hung.; pop. 23; 157 km E of Miskolc; 47°58'/22°51'.

Nagyida, *see* Velka Ida.

Nagyigmand, Hung.; pop. 49; 75 km W of Budapest; 47°38'/18°05'.

Nagyiklod, *see* Iclod.

Nagyikold, *see* Iclod.

Nagyilonda, *see* Ileanda.

Nagyilva, *see* Ilva Mare.

Nagyivan, Hung.; pop. 7; 75 km SSE of Miskolc; 47°29'/20°56'; HSL.

Nagykallo, Hung. (Kalov, Kaluv); pop. 977; 82 km ESE of Miskolc; 47°53'/21°51'; AMG, COH, EJ, GUM3, GUM5, HSL, HSL2, JGFF, LDL, LDS, LJEE, PHH, YB.

Nagykamond, Hung.; pop. 1; 82 km N of Nagykanizsa; 47°08'/17°12'.

Nagykanizsa, Hung.; pop. 2,838; 202 km SW of Budapest; 46°27'/16°59'; AMG, EDRD, EJ, GUM3, GUM4, GUM5, GUM6, HSL, LDS, PHH.

Nagykapornak, Hung.; pop. 21; 50 km N of Nagykanizsa; 46°49'/17°00'.

Nagy Kapos, *see* Velke Kapusany.

Nagykapos, *see* Velke Kapusany.

Nagykaroly, *see* Carei.

Nagykata, Hung.; pop. 253; 50 km E of Budapest; 47°25'/19°45'; GUM3, LDL, LDS, PHH.

Nagykend, *see* Chendu Mare.

Nagykereki, Hung.; pop. 26; 126 km SE of Miskolc; 47°11'/21°48'.

Nagy Kikinda, *see* Kikinda.

Nagykinizs, Hung.; pop. 19; 32 km NE of Miskolc; 48°14'/21°02'.

Nagykirva, *see* Krive.

Nagykokenyes, Hung.; pop. 11; 50 km NE of Budapest; 47°44'/19°36'.

Nagykolked, Hung.; pop. 3; 75 km NW of Nagykanizsa; 47°04'/16°33'.

Nagykonyi, Hung.; pop. 29; 94 km ENE of Nagykanizsa; 46°35'/18°12'.

Nagykoros, Hung.; pop. 540; 75 km ESE of Budapest; 47°02'/19°47'; HSL, LDS, PHH.

Nagykorpad, Hung.; pop. 5; 45 km ESE of Nagykanizsa; 46°16'/17°28'.

Nagykoru, Hung.; pop. 24; 94 km S of Miskolc; 47°16'/20°27'.

Nagykosztolany, *see* Velke Kostolany.

Nagykovacsi, Hung.; pop. 11; 19 km WNW of Budapest; 47°35'/18°53'.

Nagykovesd, HSL, LDL. This pre-World War I community was not found in BGN gazetteers.

Nagylak, *see* Nadlac.

Nagylang, Hung.; pop. 4; 75 km SSW of Budapest; 47°00'/18°27'.

Nagylaz, HSL. This pre-World War I community was not found in BGN gazetteers.

Nagylengyel, Hung.; pop. 10; 45 km NNW of Nagykanizsa; 46°47'/16°46'.

Nagyleta, Hung. (Nagyletavertes); pop. 276; 114 km ESE of Miskolc; 47°23'/21°54'; HSL, JGFF, LDS, PHH.

Nagyletavertes, *see* Nagyleta.

Nagylevard, *see* Velke Levare.

Nagyloc, Hung.; pop. 4; 69 km NNE of Budapest; 48°02'/19°35'.

Nagylok, Hung.; pop. 2; 75 km SSW of Budapest; 46°58'/18°40'.

Nagylonya, *see* Lonya.

Nagylozna, *see* Lozna.

Nagy Lucs, *see* Velka Luc.

Nagylucs, *see* Velka Luc.

Nagymagocs, Hung.; pop. 1; 45 km NNE of Szeged; 46°35'/20°30'.

Nagymagyar, *see* Rastice.

Nagymanyok, Hung.; pop. 1; 114 km E of Nagykanizsa; 46°17'/18°28'.

Nagymaros, Hung.; pop. 34; 38 km NNW of Budapest; 47°47'/18°58'; HSL.

Nagymarton, *see* Mattersburg.

Nagy Megyer, *see* Calovo.

Nagymegyer, *see* Calovo.

Nagymihaly, *see* Michalovce.

Nagymuzsaly, *see* Muszaly.

Nagynad, *see* Mad.

Nagyniyres, *see* Miresu Mare.

Nagy Olved, *see* Velke Ludince.

Nagyoroszi, Hung.; pop. 68; 62 km N of Budapest; 48°00'/19°06'; AMG, GUM5, HSL, LDL, LDS, PHH.

Nagypali, Hung.; pop. 4; 62 km NNW of Nagykanizsa; 46°55'/16°51'.

Nagypall, Hung.; pop. 5; 114 km ESE of Nagykanizsa; 46°09'/18°27'.

Nagypirit, Hung.; pop. 8; 94 km N of Nagykanizsa; 47°12'/17°14'.

Nagyrabe, Hung.; pop. 59; 107 km SSE of Miskolc; 47°12'/21°20'; LDS, PHH.

Nagyrada, Hung.; pop. 9; 26 km NNE of Nagykanizsa; 46°37'/17°07'.

Nagyrakocz, *see* Rakovo.

Nagyrakos, Hung.; pop. 3; 62 km NW of Nagykanizsa; 46°50'/16°28'.

Nagyrede, Hung.; pop. 9; 62 km NE of Budapest; 47°46'/19°51'.

Nagyret, HSL. A number of towns share this name. It was not possible to determine from available information which one is being referenced.

Nagyrocze, Cz.; pop. 547; 82 km WSW of Kosice; 48°41'/20°07'; HSL.

Nagyrozvagy, Hung.; pop. 67; 88 km NE of Miskolc; 48°20'/21°55'.

Nagysajo, *see* Sieul Mare.

Nagysap, Hung.; pop. 16; 45 km WNW of Budapest; 47°41'/18°36'.

Nagysarmas, *see* Sarmasel.

Nagysimonyi, Hung.; pop. 101; 101 km N of Nagykanizsa; 47°16'/17°04'; HSL, LDS, PHH.

Nagysomkut, *see* Somcuta Mare.

Nagy Surany, *see* Surany.

Nagysurany, *see* Surany.

Nagyszakacsi, Hung.; pop. 19; 26 km ENE of Nagykanizsa; 46°29'/17°19'.

Nagyszalonta, *see* Ujszalonta.

Nagyszeben, *see* Sibiu.

Nagyszekeres, Hung.; pop. 15; 133 km E of Miskolc; 47°58'/22°37'; HSL.

Nagyszenas, Hung.; pop. 15; 62 km NNE of Szeged; 46°41'/20°40'.

Nagyszentmiklos, *see* Sinnicolaw Mare.

Nagyszokoly, Hung.; pop. 15; 101 km NE of Nagykanizsa; 46°43'/18°13'.

Nagyszollos, *see* Vinogradov.

Nagyszombat, *see* Trnava.

Nagytapolcsany, *see* Topolcany.

Nagytarna, *see* Tarna Mare.

Nagyteremi, *see* Tirimia Mare.

Nagyteteny, Hung.; pop. 159; 19 km SSW of Budapest; 47°24'/18°59'; LDS, PHH.

Nagy Varad, *see* Oradea.

Nagyvarad, *see* Oradea.

Nagyvarsany, Hung.; pop. 33; 114 km ENE of Miskolc; 48°10'/22°17'; GUM6, HSL, LDS.

Nagyvazsony, Hung.; pop. 46; 82 km NNE of Nagykanizsa; 46°59'/17°42'; LDS, PHH.

Nagyveleg, Hung.; pop. 10; 75 km WSW of Budapest; 47°22'/18°07'.

Nagyvisnyo, Hung.; pop. 27; 32 km W of Miskolc; 48°08'/20°26'.

Nagyzerind, *see* Zerind.

Nahaczow, *see* Nagachev.

Nahorce Male, *see* Nagortse Male.

Nahoruby, Cz.; pop. 6; 45 km S of Praha; 49°44'/14°27'.

Naila, Germ.; 107 km NNE of Nurnberg; 50°19'/11°42'; PHGB.

Naira, *see* Jaunjelgava.

Nak, Hung.; pop. 3; 82 km ENE of Nagykanizsa; 46°29'/18°04'.

Nakel, *see* Naklo.

Nakel Netze, *see* Naklo.

Nakiel, Pol.; pop. 8; 101 km N of Warszawa; 53°09'/21°09'.

Nakielnica, Pol.; pop. 8; 19 km WNW of Lodz; 51°52'/19°16'.

Naklik, Pol.; pop. 6; 69 km NNW of Przemysl; 50°23'/22°28'.

Naklo, Pol. (Nakel, Nakel Netze, Naklo nad Notecia); pop. 58; 88 km NNE of Poznan; 53°09'/17°36'; HSL, LDS, PHP1, POCEM.

Naklo nad Notecia, *see* Naklo.

Nakory, Pol.; pop. 27; 94 km ENE of Warszawa; 52°17'/22°20'.

Nakri, Cz.; pop. 7; 114 km S of Praha; 49°07'/14°19'; AMG.

Nakvasha, Ukr. (Nakwasza); pop. 21; 94 km ENE of Lvov; 49°58'/25°19'.

Nakwasza, *see* Nakvasha.

Nalbach, Germ.; pop. 29; 157 km SW of Frankfurt am Main; 49°23'/06°47'; GED.

Nalchik, USSR; pop. 2,000; 989 km SE of Voronezh; 43°31'/43°38'.

Nalechov, *see* Naleczow.

Nalechuv, *see* Naleczow.

Naleczow, Pol. (Nalechov, Nalechuv, Nalenchov, Nalenchuv, Nalenczow, Nalentchov, Naleynchiv); pop. 268; 26 km W of Lublin; 51°17'/22°13'; AMG, GA, GUM4, HSL, LDL, LYV, SF.

Nalenchov, *see* Naleczow.

Nalenchuv, *see* Naleczow.

Nalenczow, *see* Naleczow.

Nalentchov, *see* Naleczow.

Naleynchiv, *see* Naleczow.

Nalibok, *see* Naliboki.

Naliboki, Byel. (Nalibok); pop. 185; 126 km WSW of Minsk; 53°42'/25°42'; COH, GUM4, GUM6, HSL, LDL, LYV, SF, YB.

Nalzovice, Cz.; pop. 16; 50 km S of Praha; 49°42'/14°22'.

Namest, *see* Namest nad Oslavou.

Namest nad Oslavou, Cz. (Namest); pop. 21; 38 km W of Brno; 49°13'/16°09'.

Namestovo, Cz.; pop. 319; 150 km WNW of Kosice; 49°24'/19°30'.

Namslau, *see* Namyslow.

Namyslow, Pol. (Namslau); pop. 68; 50 km E of Wroclaw; 51°05'/17°43'; HSL, LDS.

Nana, Cz.; pop. 1,047; 126 km ESE of Bratislava; 47°48'/18°44'; HSL.

Nanas, LDL. This pre-World War I community was not found in BGN gazetteers.

Nanchulka, Ukr. (Nanczulka Mala); pop. 44; 101 km SW of Lvov; 49°24'/22°49'.

Nancy, Cz.; 139 km W of Praha; 50°23'/12°33'; AMG, HSL, LDL.

Nanczulka Mala, *see* Nanchulka.

Nandorfehervar, *see* Beograd.

Nandras, *see* Nandraz.

Nandraz, Cz. (Nandras); 82 km WSW of Kosice; 48°36'/20°11'; HSL.

Nanest, *see* Nanesti.

Nanesti, Rom. (Nanest, Nanfalva); pop. 74; 126 km N of Cluj; 47°50'/24°01'; SM.

Nanfalva, *see* Nanesti.

Nankif, *see* Nankovo.

Nankovo, Ukr. (Husztkoz, Nankif); 189 km WSW of Chernovtsy; 48°12'/23°24'; COH, HSL, SM.

Nanova, Ukr. (Nanowa); pop. 13; 101 km SW of Lvov; 49°26'/22°44'.

Nanowa, *see* Nanova.

Napadeni, *see* Napadeny.

Napadeny, Mold. (Napadeni); pop. 28; 69 km WNW of Kishinev; 47°24′/28°09′.

Napadova, *see* Napadovo.

Napadovo, Mold. (Napadova); pop. 7; 120 km NNW of Kishinev; 48°01′/28°35′.

Napajedla, Cz.; pop. 54; 62 km E of Brno; 49°10′/17°32′.

Napekow, Pol.; pop. 22; 107 km NNE of Krakow; 50°49′/20°54′.

Napkor, Hung.; pop. 206; 88 km E of Miskolc; 47°56′/21°53′; HSL, PHH.

Naprad, *see* Neporadza.

Napradea, Rom.; pop. 44; 69 km NNW of Cluj; 47°22′/23°19′; AMG.

Naprawa, Pol.; pop. 17; 50 km S of Krakow; 49°40′/19°52′; PHP3.

Narai, Hung.; pop. 3; 94 km NNW of Nagykanizsa; 47°12′/16°34′.

Narajewka, *see* Narayevka.

Narajow, *see* Narayev.

Narajow Miasto, *see* Narayev.

Naramice, Pol.; pop. 4; 75 km NW of Czestochowa; 51°18′/18°26′.

Narayev, Ukr. (Narajow, Narajow Miasto, Narayuv, Nariav); pop. 21; 69 km ESE of Lvov; 49°32′/24°46′; COH, EDRD, EGRS, GUM3, HSL, HSL2, JGFF, LDL, PHP2, SF, YB.

Narayevka, Ukr. (Narajewka); 45 km WNW of Uman; 48°54′/29°40′; GUM4, PHR1.

Narayuv, *see* Narayev.

Narev, *see* Narew.

Narevka, *see* Narewka Mala.

Narevka Mala, *see* Narewka Mala.

Narevke, *see* Narewka Mala.

Narew, Pol. (Narev); pop. 419; 38 km ESE of Bialystok; 52°55′/23°31′; COH, GA, GUM3, GYLA, LDL, SF.

Narewka, *see* Narewka Mala.

Narewka Mala, Pol. (Narevka, Narevka Mala, Narevke, Narewka); pop. 758; 50 km ESE of Bialystok; 52°50′/23°45′; CAHJP, COH, HSL, JGFF, LYV, POCEM, SF.

Nariav, *see* Narayev.

Narinsk, *see* Norinsk.

Narocz, Byel.; 126 km NW of Minsk; 54°54′/26°43′; GUM4.

Narodichi, Ukr. (Narodici, Naroditch); pop. 2,508; 133 km WNW of Kiyev; 51°12′/29°05′; HSL, JGFF, LDL, SF.

Narodici, *see* Narodichi.

Naroditch, *see* Narodichi.

Narol, Pol. (Floryjanowa, Narol Miasto, Narol Myasto); pop. 734; 75 km NNE of Przemysl; 50°21′/23°19′; AMG, COH, EDRD, EGRS, EJ, GA, GUM3, GUM4, HSL, JGFF, LDL, LYV, PHP1, PHP2, SF.

Narol Miasto, *see* Narol.

Narol Myasto, *see* Narol.

Narol Wies, Pol.; pop. 16; 75 km NNE of Przemysl; 50°23′/23°19′.

Narovl, *see* Narovlya.

Narovla, *see* Narovlya.

Narovlya, Byel. (Narovl, Narovla, Narowla); pop. 1,357; 126 km SW of Gomel; 51°48′/29°30′; SF, WS.

Narowla, *see* Narovlya.

Nart Nowy, Pol.; pop. 18; 82 km NW of Przemysl; 50°20′/22°01′.

Nart Stary, Pol.; pop. 13; 88 km NW of Przemysl; 50°21′/22°00′.

Narty, *see* Florentynowo.

Narva, Est. (Narve, Narwa); pop. 188; 139 km NNE of Tartu; 59°23′/28°12′; EDRD, GUM4, GUM5, PHLE.

Narva Joesu, *see* Narva Joesuu.

Narva Joesuu, Est. (Narva Joesu); 139 km NNE of Tartu; 59°27′/28°03′; PHLE.

Narve, *see* Narva.

Narwa, *see* Narva.

Nasal, Rom.; pop. 5; 45 km NE of Cluj; 46°57′/24°07′.

Nasaud, Rom.; pop. 425; 82 km NE of Cluj; 47°17′/24°24′; EJ, PHR2.

Naselsk, *see* Nasielsk.

Nashelsk, *see* Nasielsk.

Nashlavcha, Mold. (Naslavcea); pop. 57; 189 km NW of Kishinev; 48°28′/27°35′.

Nasice, Yug.; pop. 161; 163 km E of Zagreb; 45°30′/18°06′; PHY.

Nasiczne, Pol.; pop. 8; 75 km S of Przemysl; 49°11′/22°37′.

Nasielsk, Pol. (Naselsk, Nashelsk, Nasielska Wola, Nasyelsk); pop. 2,691; 45 km NNW of Warszawa; 52°35′/20°48′; AMG, COH, EDRD, EJ, GUM3, GUM5, GYLA, HSL, HSL2, JGFF, LDL, LYV, PHP1, PHP4, SF, WS.

Nasielska Wola, *see* Nasielsk.

Naslavcea, *see* Nashlavcha.

Naslawice, Pol.; pop. 33; 101 km SW of Lublin; 50°41′/21°32′.

Nassau, Germ.; pop. 71; 69 km WNW of Frankfurt am Main; 50°19′/07°48′; GUM5, JGFF.

Nastashchin, *see* Nastashino.

Nastashino, Ukr. (Nastashchin, Nastaszczyn); pop. 38; 75 km SE of Lvov; 49°18′/24°36′; HSL.

Nastaszczyn, *see* Nastashino.

Nastatten, Germ.; pop. 55; 62 km W of Frankfurt am Main; 50°12′/07°52′.

Nasyelsk, *see* Nasielsk.

Naszaly, Hung.; pop. 12; 62 km WNW of Budapest; 47°42′/18°16′.

Natafalva, *see* Nacina Ves.

Nauen, Germ.; pop. 35; 38 km W of Berlin; 52°36′/12°53′; HSL, JGFF.

Naugard, *see* Nowogard.

Nauheim, *see* Bad Nauheim.

Naujamiestis, Lith.; pop. 157; 56 km ESE of Siauliai; 55°41′/24°09′; HSL.

Naujasis Daugeliskis, Lith. (Daugeliszki); 101 km NNE of Vilnius; 55°22′/26°18′; GUM3, SF, YB.

Naujasis Dauguliskis, (Dovgaliszek?, Dowgieliszki); pop. 48; EDRD. Described in the *Black Book* as being in the Nowogrodek region of Poland, this town was not found in BGN gazetteers.

Naujoji Vilnia, Lith. (Nei Vileika, Nova Vilejka, Nowa Wilejka, Vileika); 6 km ENE of Vilnius; 54°42′/25°25′; EDRD, GUM4, HSL, HSL2.

Naukseni, Lat.; pop. 3; 133 km NNE of Riga; 57°53′/25°27′.

Naumburg, Germ.; pop. 36; 133 km N of Frankfurt am Main; 51°15′/09°10′; GUM3, JGFF, LDS.

Naumestis, *see* Kudirkos Naumiestis.

Naumiestis Kudirkos, *see* Kudirkos Naumiestis.

Nautreni, (Nautrenu); pop. 26; PHLE. This town was not found in BGN gazetteers under the given spelling.

Nautrenu, *see* Nautreni.

Navahredek, *see* Novogrudok.

Navaredok, *see* Novogrudok.

Navaria, *see* Navariya.

Navariya, Ukr. (Navaria, Navarja, Navria, Nawaria, Nawarja, Nawarya); pop. 340; 19 km SSW of Lvov; 49°45′/23°56′; EGRS, HSL, LDL, PHP2, SF.

Navarja, *see* Navariya.

Navarnet, *see* Navyrnets.

Navaselicza, *see* Neresnitsa.

Navria, *see* Navariya.

Navyrnets, Mold. (Navarnet); pop. 20; 120 km WNW of Kishinev; 47°36′/27°33′.

Nawaria, *see* Navariya.

Nawarja, *see* Navariya.

Nawarya, *see* Navariya.

Nawarzyce, Pol.; pop. 6; 50 km NNE of Krakow; 50°31′/20°17′.

Nawodzice, Pol.; pop. 9; 107 km SW of Lublin; 50°37′/21°27′.

Nawojowa, Pol.; pop. 16; 82 km ESE of Krakow; 49°34′/20°45′; JGFF.

Nawsie Brzosteckie, Pol.; pop. 23; 94 km W of Przemysl; 49°53′/21°28′.

Nawsie Kolaczyckie, Pol.; pop. 73; 94 km W of Przemysl; 49°48′/21°28′.

Naya Radomsk, *see* Radomsko.
Naya Sandets, *see* Nowy Sacz.
Naydorf, *see* Novaya Derevnya.
Naymark, *see* Neumark.
Naymarkt, *see* Tirgu Mures.
Nay Sants, *see* Nowy Sacz.
Nayshtot Ponivez, *see* Kudirkos Naumiestis.
Nayshtot Shaki, *see* Kudirkos Naumiestis.
Nayshtut, *see* Nowy Korczyn.
Nazavizuv, *see* Nezavizov.
Nazawizow, *see* Nezavizov.
Nazina Ves, *see* Nacina Ves.
Ncustadt Bei Pinne, *see* Lwowek.
Neagra Sarului, Rom.; pop. 3; 139 km NE of Cluj; 47°14'/25°20'.
Neamtz, LDL. This pre-World War I community was not found in BGN gazetteers.
Nea Orestias, *see* Orestias.
Neaua, Rom. (Havad); pop. 3; 101 km ESE of Cluj; 46°29'/24°50'.
Nebel, Ukr. (Nabla); 146 km NNW of Rovno; 51°52'/25°46'; LDL, SF.
Nebersdorf, Aus.; pop. 5; 82 km SSE of Wien; 47°31'/16°34'.
Nebiliec, *see* Niebylec.
Nebilitz, *see* Niebylec.
Nebilovy, Cz.; 94 km SW of Praha; 49°38'/13°26'; HSL.
Nebylov, Ukr. (Nebyluv, Niebylow); pop. 26; 120 km SSE of Lvov; 48°49'/24°13'; GUM5, HSL, PHP2.
Nebyluv, *see* Nebylov.
Necemice, Cz.; pop. 17; 62 km W of Praha; 50°14'/13°38'.
Necin, Cz.; pop. 4; 50 km S of Praha; 49°42'/14°14'.
Neckarau, Germ.; 69 km S of Frankfurt am Main; 49°30'/08°28'; PHGBW.
Neckarbischofsheim, Germ.; pop. 40; 62 km NNW of Stuttgart; 49°18'/08°58'; GUM3, LDS, PHGBW.
Neckargemund, Germ.; 75 km NNW of Stuttgart; 49°23'/08°48'; PHGBW.
Neckar Steinach, *see* Neckarsteinach.
Neckarsteinach, Germ. (Neckar Steinach); pop. 30; 75 km NNW of Stuttgart; 49°24'/08°51'; JGFF, LDS.
Neckarsulm, Germ.; 50 km N of Stuttgart; 49°11'/09°14'; EDRD, PHGBW.
Neckarzimmern, Germ.; pop. 29; 62 km N of Stuttgart; 49°19'/09°08'; LDS, PHGBW.
Necrasovca Noua, *see* Novaya Nekrasovka.
Nectiny, Cz.; pop. 25; 94 km WSW of Praha; 49°58'/13°10'.
Nedabauti, *see* Nedoboyevtsy.
Nedanovce, Cz.; 101 km NE of Bratislava; 48°36'/18°18'; HSL.
Nedecz, *see* Nededza.
Neded, Cz. (Negyed); pop. 114; 69 km E of Bratislava; 48°01'/17°59'; HSL.
Nededza, Cz. (Nedecz); 157 km ENE of Brno; 49°13'/18°50'; HSL.
Nedezow, Pol.; pop. 52; 94 km NNE of Przemysl; 50°28'/23°35'.
Nedinge, Lith. (Nedzinge); pop. 49; 75 km SSE of Kaunas; 54°15'/24°20'.
Nedoboyevtsy, Ukr. (Nedabauti); pop. 48; 38 km NE of Chernovtsy; 48°26'/26°21'.
Nedomice, Cz.; pop. 5; 26 km NNE of Praha; 50°16'/14°37'.
Nedrahovice, Cz.; pop. 5; 56 km S of Praha; 49°37'/14°27'.
Nedrazice, Cz.; pop. 9; 114 km SW of Praha; 49°39'/13°02'.
Nedzinge, *see* Nedinge.
Nefcover, *see* Gniewkowo.
Nefta, HSL. This pre-World War I community was not found in BGN gazetteers.
Negerfalva, *see* Negrilesti.
Negnevichi, Byel. (Negniavitch, Niehniewicze); pop. 112; 101 km WSW of Minsk; 53°39'/26°05'; LDL, SF.
Negniavitch, *see* Negnevichi.
Negoslavci, Yug.; pop. 1; 133 km WNW of Beograd; 45°17'/19°00'.
Negostina, Rom.; pop. 16; 139 km WNW of Iasi; 47°56'/26°05'.

Negreia, Rom.; pop. 7; 101 km N of Cluj; 47°38'/23°45'.
Negreni, Rom.; 120 km W of Bucuresti; 44°34'/24°36'; HSL.
Negressi, *see* Negresti.
Negresti, Rom. (Avafelsofalu, Negressi); 45 km S of Iasi; 46°50'/27°26'; COH, GUM4, HSL, PHR1, PHR2.
Negresti Satu Mare, *see* Luna.
Negreviz, *see* Negrovets.
Negrileasa, Rom.; pop. 13; 139 km W of Iasi; 47°25'/25°49'.
Negril Esti, *see* Negrilesti.
Negrilesti, Rom. (Negerfalva, Negril Esti); pop. 42; 69 km NNE of Cluj; 47°16'/24°03'; HSL.
Negrivits, *see* Negrovets.
Negriviz, *see* Negrovets.
Negrovec, *see* Negrovets.
Negrovets, Ukr. (Felsokalocsa, Negreviz, Negrivits, Negriviz, Negrovec); 163 km W of Chernovtsy; 48°27'/23°40'; HSL, LYV, SM.
Negrovo, Ukr.; 88 km SW of Odessa; 46°12'/29°39'; AMG, COH, HSL.
Negurenii Vechi Orhei, *see* Staryye Negu?eny.
Negureni Vek, *see* Staryye Negureny.
Negyed, *see* Neded.
Negyes, Hung.; pop. 13; 50 km S of Miskolc; 47°42'/20°43'; HSL.
Neheim, *see* Neheim Husten.
Neheim Husten, Germ. (Neheim); pop. 62; 94 km NE of Koln; 51°27'/07°59'; JGFF.
Nehoiu, Rom.; 114 km N of Bucuresti; 45°25'/26°18'; GUM4, PHR1.
Nehrybka, Pol.; pop. 27; 13 km SE of Przemysl; 49°46'/22°48'.
Nehvizdy, Cz.; pop. 12; 19 km ENE of Praha; 50°08'/14°44'.
Neidenburg, *see* Nidzica.
Neidenstein, Germ.; pop. 75; 62 km NNW of Stuttgart; 49°19'/08°53'; GUM5, JGFF, LDS, PHGBW.
Neidlingen, Germ.; 32 km ESE of Stuttgart; 48°35'/09°34'; PHGBW.
Neisantz, *see* Nowy Sacz.
Neishtat, *see* Neustadt.
Neishtat Kudirko, *see* Kudirkos Naumiestis.
Neishtat Oif der Piltza, *see* Nowe Miasto nad Pilica.
Neishtat Shervint, *see* Kudirkos Naumiestis.
Neishtat Sugind, *see* Zemaiciu Naumiestis.
Neishtetel, *see* Nikolayev.
Neisse, *see* Nysa.
Neitersen, Germ.; pop. 5; 56 km ESE of Koln; 50°41'/07°34'.
Nei Ushitz, *see* Novaya Ushitsa.
Nei Vileika, *see* Naujoji Vilnia.
Nei Zhagar, *see* Zagare.
Nejdek, Cz.; pop. 37; 120 km W of Praha; 50°20'/12°45'.
Nejepin, Cz.; pop. 1; 88 km ESE of Praha; 49°45'/15°36'.
Nekezseny, Hung.; pop. 4; 32 km W of Miskolc; 48°10'/20°26'.
Nekhachevo, Byel. (Niechaczewo); pop. 42; 88 km WNW of Pinsk; 52°39'/25°13'.
Nekhvoroshcha, Ukr.; 88 km NNW of Dnepropetrovsk; 49°09'/34°44'; GUM4.
Nekvasovy, Cz.; pop. 4; 94 km SSW of Praha; 49°26'/13°37'.
Nelahozeves, Cz.; pop. 4; 26 km NW of Praha; 50°16'/14°18'.
Nelepino, *see* Nelipeno.
Nelidovo, USSR; pop. 194; This town was not found in BGN gazetteers under the given spelling.
Nelipeno, (Nelepino); pop. 250; AMG. This town was not found in BGN gazetteers under the given spelling.
Nellingen, Germ. BGN lists two possible localities with this name located at 48°32'/09°47' and 48°43'/09°18'. GUM4.
Nemajunai, Lith. (Niemonany, Niemoniany, Nimayin); 45 km SSE of Kaunas; 54°34'/24°05'; JGFF, LDL, SF.
Nemakscai, *see* Nemaksciai.
Nemaksciai, Lith. (Nemakscai, Nemaksht, Nemoksht, Nemokshty, Nemuksht); pop. 704; 69 km SSW of Siauliai; 55°26'/22°46'; GUM3, HSL, HSL2, LDL, SF, YL.
Nemaksht, *see* Nemaksciai.
Nemecka Mokra, *see* Nemetskaya Mokra.

Nemecka Poruba, see Poruba Pod Vihorlatom.

Nemecke Jablonne, see Jablonne V Podjestedi.

Nemecky Brod, see Havlickuv Brod.

Nemecky Rohozec, see Podboransky Rohozec.

Nemencine, Lith. (Nementchin, Nemenzin, Niemenczyn); 26 km NNE of Vilnius; 54°51'/25°29'; AMG, COH, GUM3, GUM4, GUM5, GYLA, HSL, LDL, SF.

Nemenitz, see Nemunaitis.

Nementchin, see Nemencine.

Nemenzin, see Nemencine.

Nemerchi, see Nemerichi.

Nemerci, see Nemerichi.

Nemerichi, Ukr. (Nemerchi, Nemerci); 88 km SSW of Vinnitsa; 48°41'/27°43'; PHR1.

Nemes, Rom.; 69 km SW of Cluj; 46°22'/22°53'; HSL.

Nemesapati, Hung.; pop. 3; 56 km N of Nagykanizsa; 46°52'/16°57'; HSL.

Nemesbikk, Hung.; pop. 15; 32 km SE of Miskolc; 47°53'/20°58'; HSL.

Nemesborzova, Hung.; pop. 5; 139 km E of Miskolc; 47°59'/22°38'.

Nemesbuk, Hung.; pop. 11; 50 km N of Nagykanizsa; 46°49'/17°09'.

Nemesded, Hung.; pop. 40; 19 km E of Nagykanizsa; 46°26'/17°15'; PHH.

Nemesdomolk, see Celldomolk.

Nemesgorzsony, Hung. (Alsogorzsony); pop. 3; 114 km N of Nagykanizsa; 47°24'/17°22'.

Nemesgulacs, Hung.; pop. 12; 56 km NNE of Nagykanizsa; 46°50'/17°29'.

Nemeshany, Hung.; pop. 9; 75 km N of Nagykanizsa; 47°04'/17°22'.

Nemeske, Hung.; pop. 6; 69 km ESE of Nagykanizsa; 46°01'/17°43'.

Nemesker, Hung.; pop. 9; 120 km N of Nagykanizsa; 47°29'/16°48'.

Nemeskocs, Hung.; pop. 4; 94 km N of Nagykanizsa; 47°12'/17°11'.

Nemeskolta, Hung.; pop. 8; 88 km NNW of Nagykanizsa; 47°09'/16°46'.

Nemesladony, Hung.; pop. 7; 114 km N of Nagykanizsa; 47°24'/16°53'.

Nemesleanyfalu, Hung.; pop. 5; 82 km NNE of Nagykanizsa; 46°59'/17°41'.

Nemesnadudvar, Hung.; pop. 11; 88 km W of Szeged; 46°20'/19°03'.

Nemesocsa, see Zemianska Olca.

Nemespatro, see Patro.

Nemespecsely, see Pecsely.

Nemessandorhaza, Hung.; pop. 5; 45 km N of Nagykanizsa; 46°47'/16°57'.

Nemesszalok, Hung.; pop. 73; 101 km N of Nagykanizsa; 47°17'/17°18'; HSL, LDL, LDS, PHH.

Nemesszentandras, Hung.; pop. 4; 45 km N of Nagykanizsa; 46°46'/16°57'.

Nemestordemic, see Badacsonytordemic.

Nemesvamos, Hung.; pop. 9; 101 km SW of Budapest; 47°03'/17°53'.

Nemesvid, Hung.; pop. 29; 19 km ENE of Nagykanizsa; 46°30'/17°16'; GUM5.

Nemetbarnag, see Barnag.

Nemetboly, see Boly.

Nemetfalu, Hung.; pop. 1; 50 km NW of Nagykanizsa; 46°49'/16°41'.

Nemeti, Hung.; 114 km ESE of Nagykanizsa; 45°57'/18°15'; HSL.

Nemetlad, Hung.; pop. 9; 62 km ESE of Nagykanizsa; 46°08'/17°39'.

Nemetmokra, see Nemetskaya Mokra.

Nemetskaya Mokra, Ukr. (Mokra Germ, Nemecka Mokra, Nemetmokra); 150 km W of Chernovtsy; 48°23'/23°50'; SM.

Nemetujvar, see Gussing.

Nemetzsidany, see Kiszsidany.

Nemiluv, Ukr. (Niemilow); pop. 10; 69 km NE of Lvov; 50°16'/24°46'.

Nemir, Ukr. (Niemir); pop. 7; 101 km WNW of Rovno; 50°59'/24°59'.

Nemirov, Ukr.; pop. 4,176; 45 km SE of Vinnitsa; 48°58'/28°51'; EDRD, EJ, GUM4, GYLA, HSL, HSL2, JGFF, SF, YB.

Nemirov (near Lvov), Ukr. (Nemirova, Niemirow, Nyemiruv); pop. 1,298; 50 km WNW of Lvov; 50°07'/23°27'; AMG, COH, EGRS, EJ, GUM3, HSL, JGFF, LYV, PHP1, PHP2, PHR1, SF.

Nemirova, see Nemirov (near Lvov).

Nemiz, Cz.; 50 km SE of Praha; 49°45'/14°56'; HSL.

Nemnovo, Byel. (Niemnowo); pop. 8; 246 km WSW of Minsk; 53°52'/23°46'.

Nemoksht, see Nemaksciai.

Nemokshty, see Nemaksciai.

Nemonien, see Golovkino.

Nemosice, Cz.; pop. 1; 94 km E of Praha; 50°01'/15°48'.

Nemovichi, Ukr. (Niemowicze); pop. 94; 82 km N of Rovno; 51°16'/26°38'.

Nemsova, Cz.; 107 km E of Brno; 48°58'/18°07'; HSL.

Nemteni, see Nemtseny.

Nemti, Hung.; pop. 5; 69 km WSW of Miskolc; 48°01'/19°54'.

Nemtseny, Mold. (Nemteni); pop. 90; 56 km WSW of Kishinev; 46°55'/28°07'.

Nemuksht, see Nemaksciai.

Nemunaitis, Lith. (Nemenitz, Nemunayts, Niemenietz); pop. 142; 75 km SSE of Kaunas; 54°18'/24°02'; JGFF, LDL, SF, YL.

Nemunayts, see Nemunaitis.

Nemunelio Radviliskis, Lith. (Nemunelis Radviliskis, Radvilishok Nemunelis); pop. 205; 107 km NE of Siauliai; 56°24'/24°46'; YL.

Nemunelis Radviliskis, see Nemunelio Radviliskis.

Nentershausen, Germ.; pop. 37; 133 km NNE of Frankfurt am Main; 51°01'/09°56'; HSL, JGFF.

Nenzenheim, Germ. (Neunzenheim); pop. 29; 56 km WNW of Nurnberg; 49°38'/10°17'; GUM5, HSL, PHGB.

Nepolcauti, see Nepolokovtsy.

Nepolkouts, see Nepolokovtsy.

Nepolokouts, see Nepolokovtsy.

Nepolokovtsy, Ukr. (Grigore Gika Vode, Grigori Ghica Voda, Nepolcauti, Nepolkouts, Nepolokouts); pop. 316; 26 km WNW of Chernovtsy; 48°23'/25°38'; COH, GUM4, LDL.

Nepolomits, see Niepolomice.

Nepomuk, Cz.; pop. 32; 94 km SSW of Praha; 49°29'/13°36'.

Nepomysl, Cz.; pop. 15; 82 km W of Praha; 50°13'/13°19'.

Neporadza, Cz. (Naprad); 75 km SW of Kosice; 48°22'/20°24'; AMG, HSL.

Neporotova, see Neporotovo.

Neporotovo, Ukr. (Neporotova); pop. 135; 107 km NE of Chernovtsy; 48°36'/27°18'.

Nepos, Rom.; pop. 5; 94 km NE of Cluj; 47°17'/24°32'.

Nera, HSL. This pre-World War I community was not found in BGN gazetteers.

Neratovice, Cz.; pop. 12; 26 km N of Praha; 50°16'/14°31'.

Neresnica, Cz. (Alsoneresznice); BGN lists two possible localities with this name located at 44°27'/21°44' and 48°26'/19°12'. HSL.

Neresnice, see Neresnitsa.

Neresnitsa, Ukr. (Navaselicza, Neresnice, Neresniza, Novoselice, Novoseliza, Nyereshaza, Taracujfalu, Taruj Falu); pop. 356; 157 km WSW of Chernovtsy; 48°07'/23°46'; AMG, COH, HSL, LYV, SM.

Neresniza, see Neresnitsa.

Nereta, Lat. (Neretas); pop. 70; 82 km WNW of Daugavpils; 56°10'/25°18'; PHLE.

Neretas, see Nereta.

Nerezice, GUM3. This town was not found in BGN gazetteers under the given spelling.

Nerusai, *see* Nerushay.

Nerushay, Ukr. (Nerusai); pop. 14; 133 km SW of Odessa; 45°40'/29°31'.

Nesfoaia, *see* Nesfoyya.

Nesfoyya, Ukr. (Nesfoaia); pop. 47; 50 km ENE of Chernovtsy; 48°20'/26°34'.

Neshviz, *see* Nesvizh.

Nesselroden, Germ.; pop. 14; 146 km NE of Frankfurt am Main; 51°01'/10°06'; LDS.

Nestanishki, Byel. (Niestaniszki); 126 km NW of Minsk; 54°45'/26°19'; HSL.

Nestanitse, Ukr. (Niestanice); pop. 87; 50 km NNE of Lvov; 50°14'/24°29'.

Nestedice, Cz.; pop. 2; 69 km NNW of Praha; 50°40'/14°09'.

Nestemice, Cz.; pop. 19; 69 km NNW of Praha; 50°40'/14°06'.

Nesterov, Ukr. (Nesterow, Zalkove, Zalkva, Zholkev, Zholkeva, Zholkva, Zholkve, Zhulkev, Zhulkyev, Zolkiew); pop. 3,718; 32 km N of Lvov; 50°04'/23°58'; CAHJP, COH, EDRD, EGRS, EJ, GUM3, GUM4, GUM5, GUM6, HSL, JGFF, LDL, PHP1, PHP2, PHP3, PHP4, SF, YB.

Nesterov (RFSR), USSR (Stalluponen); pop. 48; 133 km E of Kaliningrad; 54°38'/22°34'; AMG.

Nesterovtsy, Ukr. (Nesterowce); pop. 17; 101 km E of Lvov; 49°42'/25°23'.

Nesterow, *see* Nesterov.

Nesterowce, *see* Nesterovtsy.

Nestervarca, *see* Nestervarka.

Nestervarka, Ukr. (Nestervarca); 69 km SE of Vinnitsa; 48°41'/28°52'; PHR1.

Nestrasovice, Cz.; pop. 2; 69 km SSW of Praha; 49°34'/14°02'.

Nesuchonzhi, *see* Nesukhoyezhe.

Nesukhoyezhe, Ukr. (Nesuchonzhi, Nezkizh, Niesuchojeze); pop. 435; 139 km WNW of Rovno; 51°23'/24°49'; COH, HSL, PHP4, SF.

Nesvizh, Byel. (Neshviz, Niesviez, Nieswiez, Nishviz, Nyeshvyezh); pop. 3,346; 94 km SSW of Minsk; 53°13'/26°40'; EDRD, EJ, GA, GUM3, GUM4, GUM5, GUM6, HSL, HSL2, JGFF, LDL, LYV, PHP4, SF, YB.

Neszmely, Hung.; pop. 4; 62 km WNW of Budapest; 47°44'/18°22'; HSL.

Neteni, Rom.; pop. 5; 69 km NE of Cluj; 47°01'/24°27'.

Netphen, Germ.; 82 km E of Koln; 50°55'/08°06'; GED.

Netra, Germ.; pop. 32; 146 km SSE of Hannover; 51°06'/10°06'; LDS.

Netreba, Ukr.; pop. 33; 94 km NE of Rovno; 51°06'/27°20'.

Netvorice, Cz.; pop. 1; 38 km SSE of Praha; 49°49'/14°32'.

Netzwalde, *see* Rynarzewo.

Neubeuern, Germ.; pop. 2; 62 km SE of Munchen; 47°46'/12°09'.

Neu Bidschow, HSL, HSL2. This pre-World War I community was not found in BGN gazetteers.

Neubitschow, *see* Novy Bydzov.

Neubrandenburg, Germ.; pop. 182; 94 km ESE of Rostock; 53°34'/13°16'; GUM4, JGFF.

Neubruck, *see* Wartoslaw.

Neubrunn, Germ.; 82 km ESE of Frankfurt am Main; 49°44'/09°40'; PHGB.

Neubukow, Germ.; pop. 21; 32 km WSW of Rostock; 54°02'/11°40'; JGFF, LDS.

Neu Bukowitz, *see* Spisicbukovica.

Neuburg an der Donau, Germ.; 69 km NW of Munchen; 48°44'/11°11'; PHGB.

Neuburg an der Kammel, Germ.; 94 km W of Munchen; 48°18'/10°22'; PHGB.

Neudamm, *see* Debno (near Gorzow Wielkopolskie).

Neudenau, Germ.; pop. 12; 62 km N of Stuttgart; 49°18'/09°17'; PHGBW.

Neu Dorf, Cz. HSL2. This pre-World War I community was not found in BGN gazetteers.

Neudorf, *see* Spisska Nova Ves.

Neudorf Bei Parndorf, Aus.; pop. 7; 45 km ESE of Wien; 48°01'/16°56'.

Neudorfl, Aus.; pop. 33; 50 km S of Wien; 47°47'/16°17'; HSL.

Neuenbrunslar, Germ.; 133 km NNE of Frankfurt am Main; 51°10'/09°26'; LDS.

Neuendettelsau, Germ.; pop. 2; 32 km SW of Nurnberg; 49°17'/10°47'.

Neuendorf Uber Furstenwald, GUM6. This town was not found in BGN gazetteers under the given spelling.

Neuengamme, Germ. EDRD, GUM3, GUM5. This town was not found in BGN gazetteers under the given spelling.

Neuenhaus, Germ.; pop. 27; 176 km N of Koln; 52°30'/06°58'; GED, LDS.

Neuenkirchen, Germ.; 150 km N of Koln; 52°15'/07°22'; CAHJP, HSL, JGFF.

Neuenmarkt, Germ.; 82 km NNE of Nurnberg; 50°06'/11°36'; PHGB.

Neuenried, Germ.; 88 km SW of Munchen; 47°50'/10°30'; PHGB.

Neufeld, *see* Neufeld an der Leitha.

Neufeld an der Leitha, Aus. (Neufeld); pop. 18; 45 km S of Wien; 47°51'/16°22'; EJ.

Neu Freistett, *see* Freistett.

Neuhaldensleben, *see* Haldensleben.

Neuhammer, Germ.; 157 km SE of Berlin; 51°24'/14°48'; GUM3, GUM4.

Neuhaus, GUM5, HSL, HSL2, PHGB, PHGBW. A number of towns share this name. It was not possible to determine from available information which one is being referenced.

Neuhausen, Germ.; 82 km ESE of Stuttgart; 48°23'/10°06'; PHGB.

Neuhemsbach, Germ.; pop. 12; 88 km SSW of Frankfurt am Main; 49°31'/07°55'; GED.

Neuhof, Germ.; pop. 34; 75 km NE of Frankfurt am Main; 50°26'/09°37'; GUM3, PHGBW. *See also* Lejasciems; Nowy Dwor.

Neuhofen, Germ.; 82 km S of Frankfurt am Main; 49°25'/08°26'; GED.

Neuhofen an der Krems, Aus.; pop. 1; 94 km NE of Salzburg; 48°08'/14°13'.

Neu Isenburg, Germ.; pop. 133; 13 km SSE of Frankfurt am Main; 50°03'/08°42'; GED, GUM3.

Neukalen, Germ.; 56 km ESE of Rostock; 53°49'/12°47'; LDS.

Neukirchen, Germ.; pop. 108; 101 km NNE of Frankfurt am Main; 50°52'/09°20'; GED, HSL, LDS.

Neukollin, *see* Kolin.

Neu Leiningen, HSL. This pre-World War I community was not found in BGN gazetteers.

Neuleiningen, Germ.; pop. 3; 69 km SSW of Frankfurt am Main; 49°33'/08°08'; CAHJP, GED.

Neulengbach, Aus.; pop. 20; 38 km WSW of Wien; 48°12'/15°54'; CAHJP.

Neu Lettgallen, *see* Abrini.

Neulingen, Germ.; 126 km WNW of Berlin; 52°52'/11°34'; HSL.

Neumagen, Germ.; pop. 45; 126 km S of Koln; 49°51'/06°54'; GUM5.

Neumark, (Naymark, Noymarkt); EJ, GUM3, GUM3, HSL, HSL2, PHP1. A number of towns share this name. It was not possible to determine from available information which one is being referenced.

Neumark am Mures, *see* Tirgu Mures.

Neumarkt, *see* Nowy Targ; Sroda Slaska; Tirgu Mures.

Neumarkt an der Raab, Aus.; pop. 4; 56 km ESE of Graz; 46°55'/16°10'.

Neumarkt an der Ybbs, Aus.; pop. 9; 94 km WSW of Wien; 48°08'/15°03'.

Neumarkt im Schlesien, *see* Nowe Marcinkowo.

Neumarkt in der Oberpfalz, Germ.; pop. 114; 32 km ESE of Nurnberg; 49°17'/11°28'; CAHJP, GUM5.

Neumarkt Sankt Veit, Germ.; 69 km NE of Munchen; 48°22'/12°30'; PHGB.

Neumerice, Cz.; pop. 6; 26 km WNW of Praha; 50°14'/14°13'.

Neumetely, Cz.; pop. 2; 45 km SW of Praha; 49°51'/14°03'.

Neumittelwalde, *see* Miedzyborz (Kalisz area).

Neumorschen, Germ.; pop. 14; 126 km NNE of Frankfurt am Main; 51°04'/09°36'; JGFF.

Neumuenster, *see* Neumunster.

Neumunster, Germ. (Neumuenster); pop. 43; 62 km N of Hamburg; 54°04'/09°59'.

Neunburg Vorm Wald, Germ.; 94 km E of Nurnberg; 49°21'/12°23'; PHGB.

Neunkirchen (Austria), Aus.; pop. 204; 56 km S of Wien; 47°43'/16°05'; AMG.

Neunkirchen (Germany), Germ.; pop. 213; 139 km SW of Frankfurt am Main; 49°21'/07°11'; EDRD, GUM4, GUM5.

Neunstetten, Germ.; 75 km N of Stuttgart; 49°25'/09°37'; LDS.

Neunzenheim, *see* Nenzenheim.

Neu Oderberg, *see* Bohumin.

Neuotting, Germ.; 82 km ENE of Munchen; 48°14'/12°42'; PHGB.

Neuraussnitz, HSL. This pre-World War I community was not found in BGN gazetteers.

Neuruppin, Germ.; 69 km NW of Berlin; 52°56'/12°48'; AMG, JGFF.

Neusalz, *see* Nowa Sol.

Neu Sandez, *see* Nowy Sacz.

Neusatz, *see* Novi Sad.

Neu Sedlitz, *see* Slavkov u Brna.

Neusiedl, Aus.; pop. 37; 50 km SSW of Wien; 47°53'/15°57'.

Neusohl, *see* Banska Bystrica.

Neuss, Germ.; pop. 250; 32 km NW of Koln; 51°12'/06°42'; EDRD, EJ, GED, YB.

Neustadt, Germ. (Neishtat); 120 km SSW of Stuttgart; 47°54'/08°13'; AMG, EDRD, GUM3, JGFF, PHGBW. *See also* Nowy Korczyn. There are scores of towns with this name, which means "new city" in German. See listings below.

Neustadt am Kulm, Germ.; 69 km NE of Nurnberg; 49°49'/11°50'; PHGB.

Neustadt am Rubenberge, Germ.; pop. 37; 26 km WNW of Hannover; 52°30'/09°28'; GED.

Neustadt an der Aisch, Germ.; pop. 111; 38 km WNW of Nurnberg; 49°35'/10°36'; EJ, GUM3, GUM5, PHGB.

Neustadt an der Dibau, Germ. PHGB. This town was not found in BGN gazetteers under the given spelling.

Neustadt an der Haardt, *see* Neustadt an der Weinstrasse.

Neustadt an der Saale, *see* Bad Neustadt an der Saale.

Neustadt an der Waldnaab, Germ.; 82 km NE of Nurnberg; 49°44'/12°10'; PHGB.

Neustadt an der Weinstrasse, Germ. (Neustadt an der Haardt); pop. 375; 94 km SSW of Frankfurt am Main; 49°21'/08°09'; GED, GUM5, HSL.

Neustadt a Warthe, *see* Nowe Miasto nad Warta.

Neustadt Bei Coburg, Germ.; 101 km N of Nurnberg; 50°19'/11°07'; GUM3, GUM4, GUM5.

Neustadt Bei Pinne, *see* Lwowek.

Neustadtel, Germ. BGN lists two possible localities with this name located at 50°35'/12°37' and 51°13'/14°12'. HSL, HSL2.

Neustadtgodens, Germ.; pop. 14; 133 km WSW of Hamburg; 53°29'/07°59'; HSL, LDS.

Neustadt in der Pfalz, HSL. This pre-World War I community was not found in BGN gazetteers.

Neustadt in Hessen, Germ.; pop. 119; 88 km N of Frankfurt am Main; 50°51'/09°07'.

Neustadt in Oberschlesien, *see* Prudnik.

Neustadt in Oldenwald, Germ.; pop. 20; 45 km SE of Frankfurt am Main; 49°48'/09°04'.

Neustadtles, Germ.; 120 km NE of Frankfurt am Main; 50°30'/10°13'; PHGB.

Neustadt Sugind, *see* Zemaiciu Naumiestis.

Neustettin, *see* Szczecinek.

Neustift an der Rosalia, Aus.; pop. 6; 56 km S of Wien; 47°43'/16°20'.

Neustrelitz, Germ.; pop. 62; 101 km NNW of Berlin; 53°22'/13°05'; HSL.

Neustupov, Cz.; pop. 12; 56 km SSE of Praha; 49°37'/14°42'.

Neutal, Aus.; pop. 11; 82 km S of Wien; 47°32'/16°26'.

Neuteich, *see* Nowy Staw.

Neuteich Freistaat, *see* Nowy Staw.

Neuterhausen, HSL. This pre-World War I community was not found in BGN gazetteers.

Neutitschein, *see* Novy Jicin.

Neutitschin, *see* Novy Jicin.

Neutomischel, *see* Nowy Tomysl.

Neutra, *see* Nitra.

Neu Ulm, Germ.; 75 km ESE of Stuttgart; 48°24'/10°01'; GED, GUM3, PHGB.

Neuwarp, *see* Nowe Warpno.

Neuwedell, *see* Drawno.

Neuwied, Germ.; pop. 300; 69 km SE of Koln; 50°26'/07°28'; AMG, CAHJP, EJ, GUM3, GUM5, HSL, JGFF.

Neuzedlisch, *see* Nove Sedliste.

Nevaran, *see* Nevarenai.

Nevarenai, Lith. (Nevaran); pop. 95; 69 km W of Siauliai; 56°06'/22°17'; YL.

Neveklov, Cz. (Nevekolov); pop. 40; 45 km SSE of Praha; 49°45'/14°32'.

Nevekolov, *see* Neveklov.

Nevel, USSR; pop. 6,169; 50 km SW of Velikiye Luki; 56°00'/29°59'; AMG, EDRD, GUM4, HSL, JGFF, LDL, SF.

Nevesinje, Yug.; pop. 1; 251 km SW of Beograd; 43°16'/18°07'.

Nevetlefalu, Ukr. (Nevetlen); 214 km S of Lvov; 48°01'/23°00'; HSL.

Nevetlen, *see* Nevetlefalu.

Neviges, Germ.; pop. 14; 45 km N of Koln; 51°19'/07°05'.

Nevir, Ukr.; 163 km NW of Rovno; 51°52'/24°59'; JGFF.

Nevrokop, *see* Gotse Delchev.

New Tredegar, LDL. This pre-World War I community was not found in BGN gazetteers.

Neyshtadt Shaki, *see* Kudirkos Naumiestis.

Nezavizov, Ukr. (Nazavizuv, Nazawizow); pop. 58; 107 km WNW of Chernovtsy; 48°40'/24°36'.

Nezbavetice, Cz.; pop. 1; 88 km SW of Praha; 49°39'/13°28'.

Nezbodka, *see* Michalowo.

Nezhin, Ukr. (Nezin, Niezyn, Nizyn); pop. 6,131; 94 km WSW of Konotop; 51°03'/31°53'; EDRD, EJ, GUM4, HSL, JGFF, LDL, SF.

Nezin, *see* Nezhin.

Nezkizh, *see* Nesukhoyezhe.

Neznanuv, Ukr. (Nieznanow); pop. 46; 50 km NE of Lvov; 50°10'/24°33'.

Neznasov, Cz. (Neznazov); 101 km S of Praha; 49°14'/14°23'; EJ.

Neznazov, *see* Neznasov.

Nezsa, Hung.; pop. 4; 45 km N of Budapest; 47°51'/19°18'.

Nezvestice, Cz.; pop. 4; 88 km SW of Praha; 49°39'/13°31'.

Nezvir, Ukr. (Niezwir); pop. 30; 75 km WNW of Rovno; 51°03'/25°25'.

Nezviska, Ukr. (Niezwiska); pop. 74; 69 km NW of Chernovtsy; 48°46'/25°15'; GUM3, PHP2.

Ngytad, HSL. This pre-World War I community was not found in BGN gazetteers.

Niagova, *see* Olnkhovtsy.

Nica, Lat.; pop. 6; 195 km SW of Riga; 56°21'/21°04'.

Nichelsburg, Pol. PHP4. This town was not found in BGN gazetteers under the given spelling.

Nichiteni, Rom.; pop. 4; 114 km NW of Iasi; 48°06'/26°52'.

Nickelsburg, Pol. PHP3. This town was not found in BGN gazetteers under the given spelling.

Nicolaenca, *see* Nikolayevka.

Nicolaevca, Mold.; pop. 24; 88 km NW of Kishinev; 47°40'/28°14'; PHR1.

Nicoreni, *see* Nikoreny.

Nicoresti, Rom.; 146 km S of Iasi; 45°56'/27°17'; JGFF.

Nidda, Germ.; pop. 60; 45 km NNE of Frankfurt am Main; 50°25'/09°00'.

Nideggen, Germ.; 45 km SW of Koln; 50°42'/06°29'; GED.

Nidek, Pol.; pop. 9; 50 km SW of Krakow; 49°55'/19°20'.

Nidzica, Pol. (Neidenburg); pop. 125; 126 km NNW of Warszawa; 53°22'/20°26'; GUM5, POCEM.

Niebieszczany, Pol.; pop. 8; 56 km SW of Przemysl; 49°31'/22°10'.

Niebocko, Pol.; pop. 6; 50 km WSW of Przemysl; 49°41'/22°07'; HSL.

Niebrow, Pol.; pop. 30; 45 km ESE of Lodz; 51°33'/19°58'; PHP1.

Niebylec, Pol. (Nebiliec, Nebilitz); pop. 283; 62 km W of Przemysl; 49°52'/21°54'; AMG, EGRS, GA, GUM5, HSL, LDL, PHP3, SF.

Niebylow, *see* Nebylov.

Niechaczewo, *see* Nekhachevo.

Niechcice, Pol.; pop. 60; 56 km SSE of Lodz; 51°17'/19°35'; PHP1.

Niechcicka Wola Nowa, *see* Wola Niechcicka Nowa.

Niechmirow, Pol.; pop. 28; 62 km SW of Lodz; 51°23'/18°46'.

Niechobrz, Pol.; pop. 82; 69 km WNW of Przemysl; 49°59'/21°53'.

Niechodzin, Pol.; pop. 12; 69 km NW of Warszawa; 52°51'/20°35'.

Nieciecz, Pol.; pop. 32; 88 km ENE of Warszawa; 52°28'/22°19'.

Nieciecza, Pol.; pop. 11; 69 km ENE of Krakow; 50°09'/20°51'.

Niecieslawice, Pol.; pop. 6; 94 km NE of Krakow; 50°30'/21°02'.

Nieczajna, Pol.; 82 km ENE of Krakow; 50°10'/21°04'; PHP3.

Niedabyl, Pol.; pop. 23; 69 km S of Warszawa; 51°40'/21°05'.

Niedarczow Gorny, Pol.; pop. 4; 88 km W of Lublin; 51°17'/21°21'.

Niedary, Pol.; pop. 11; 45 km ENE of Krakow; 50°07'/20°30'.

Niedenstein, Germ. (Niederstein); pop. 70; 133 km S of Hannover; 51°14'/09°19'; JGFF.

Niederabsdorf, Aus.; pop. 7; 56 km NNE of Wien; 48°34'/16°51'.

Niederaula, Germ.; pop. 88; 101 km NNE of Frankfurt am Main; 50°48'/09°36'.

Niederbieber, Germ.; 62 km SE of Koln; 50°29'/07°29'; GUM5.

Niederbronn, HSL. This pre-World War I community was not found in BGN gazetteers.

Niederbuhl, Germ.; 69 km W of Stuttgart; 48°50'/08°13'; GUM3, PHGBW.

Niederelsungen, Germ.; pop. 10; 114 km S of Hannover; 51°24'/09°12'.

Niederemmel, Germ.; pop. 55; 126 km WSW of Frankfurt am Main; 49°53'/06°55'.

Nieder Eschbach, Germ.; 19 km NNW of Frankfurt am Main; 50°12'/08°40'; LDS.

Niederflorstadt, Germ.; pop. 33; 32 km NNE of Frankfurt am Main; 50°19'/08°52'.

Niederhagenthal, HSL. This pre-World War I community was not found in BGN gazetteers.

Niederhochstadt, Germ.; pop. 45; 88 km WNW of Stuttgart; 49°14'/08°13'; CAHJP, GED, HSL.

Niederholm, Germ.; pop. 24; Described in the *Black Book* as being in the Rheinland-Pfalz region of Germany, this town was not found in BGN gazetteers.

Niederkirchen, *see* Niederkruchten.

Niederklein, Germ.; pop. 15; 82 km N of Frankfurt am Main; 50°47'/08°59'; JGFF, LDS.

Niederkreuzstetten, Aus.; pop. 2; 38 km N of Wien; 48°28'/16°28'.

Niederkruchten, Germ. (Niederkirchen); 56 km WNW of Koln; 51°12'/06°13'; AMG, HSL.

Niederlahnstein, Germ.; pop. 19; 82 km W of Frankfurt am Main; 50°18'/07°36'; GUM5.

Niederleis, Aus.; pop. 7; 45 km N of Wien; 48°33'/16°24'.

Niederlustadt, Germ.; pop. 3; 82 km WNW of Stuttgart; 49°15'/08°17'; JGFF.

Niedermarsberg, Germ.; pop. 90; 120 km SSW of Hannover; 51°27'/08°51'; GUM5.

Niedermeiser, Germ.; 107 km S of Hannover; 51°28'/09°18'; HSL, LDS.

Niedermemmel, GUM5. This town was not found in BGN gazetteers under the given spelling.

Niedermendig, Germ.; pop. 40; 69 km SSE of Koln; 50°22'/07°17'; JGFF.

Niedermittlau, Germ.; pop. 13; 32 km ENE of Frankfurt am Main; 50°10'/09°08'.

Nieder Mockstadt, Germ.; pop. 35; 32 km NNE of Frankfurt am Main; 50°20'/08°57'; GUM5, LDS.

Nieder Moos, Germ.; pop. 1; 69 km NE of Frankfurt am Main; 50°29'/09°23'.

Niedermoschel, Germ.; 75 km SW of Frankfurt am Main; 49°44'/07°48'; GED.

Niedernberg, Germ.; 38 km ESE of Frankfurt am Main; 49°55'/09°09'; PHGB.

Niederntudorf, Germ.; 114 km SSW of Hannover; 51°38'/08°41'; LDS.

Nieder Ohmen, Germ.; pop. 69; 69 km N of Frankfurt am Main; 50°39'/09°02'; JGFF.

Nieder Olm, Germ.; 38 km SW of Frankfurt am Main; 49°54'/08°13'; GUM5.

Nieder Ramstadt, Germ.; 38 km S of Frankfurt am Main; 49°49'/08°42'; LDS.

Niederrodenbach, Germ.; 26 km ENE of Frankfurt am Main; 50°09'/09°02'; LDS.

Niederrodern, HSL, HSL2. This pre-World War I community was not found in BGN gazetteers.

Nieder Saulheim, Germ.; pop. 26; 50 km SW of Frankfurt am Main; 49°53'/08°09'.

Niederschleinz, Aus.; pop. 5; 56 km NW of Wien; 48°36'/15°53'.

Nieder Selters, GUM5. This town was not found in BGN gazetteers under the given spelling.

Niederstein, *see* Niedenstein.

Niederstetten, Germ.; pop. 90; 88 km WSW of Nurnberg; 49°24'/09°55'; EJ, GED, HSL, JGFF, PHGBW.

Niedersulz, Aus.; pop. 4; 38 km NNE of Wien; 48°29'/16°40'.

Niedertaufkirchen, Germ.; pop. 1; 75 km ENE of Munchen; 48°20'/12°33'.

Niederweidbach, Germ.; pop. 28; 75 km NNW of Frankfurt am Main; 50°42'/08°29'; JGFF.

Nieder Weisel, Germ.; pop. 37; 45 km N of Frankfurt am Main; 50°25'/08°41'.

Niederwerrn, Germ.; pop. 51; 94 km NW of Nurnberg; 50°04'/10°11'; CAHJP, GUM5, HSL, JGFF, PHGB.

Nieder Wiesen, Germ.; pop. 50; 62 km SW of Frankfurt am Main; 49°44'/07°59'; GED.

Niederwollstadt, Germ.; pop. 30; 26 km N of Frankfurt am Main; 50°17'/08°46'; HSL.

Niederzissen, Germ.; pop. 50; 56 km SSE of Koln; 50°28'/07°14'; JGFF.

Niedrzwica Duza, Pol. (Niedrzwica Wielka); pop. 65; 19 km SSW of Lublin; 51°07'/22°24'.

Niedrzwica Koscielna, Pol.; pop. 22; 26 km SSW of Lublin; 51°05'/22°22'.

Niedrzwica Wielka, *see* Niedrzwica Duza.

Niedrzwice, Pol.; pop. 12; 101 km SW of Lublin; 50°37'/21°31'.

Niedzica, Pol.; pop. 43; 82 km SSE of Krakow; 49°25'/20°18'.

Niedziela, Germ. PHP1. This town was not found in BGN gazetteers under the given spelling.

Niedzwiada, Pol.; pop. 61; 94 km W of Przemysl; 49°59'/21°31'.

Niedzwiadka, Pol.; pop. 5; 82 km NW of Lublin; 51°55'/22°07'.

Niedzwiedz, Pol.; pop. 33; 19 km NNE of Krakow; 50°14'/20°06'.

Niedzwiedz (near Kielce), Pol.; pop. 24; 94 km ENE of Czestochowa; 50°58'/20°26'.

Niedzwiedzica, *see* Medvedichi.

Nieglowice, Pol.; pop. 44; 94 km WSW of Przemysl;

49°44'/21°28'; HSL, PHP3.

Niegowic, Pol.; pop. 16; 32 km ESE of Krakow; 49°56'/20°15'.

Niegowoniczki, Pol.; pop. 28; 50 km SE of Czestochowa; 50°23'/19°26'.

Nieheim, Germ.; pop. 77; 75 km SSW of Hannover; 51°48'/09°07'; HSL.

Niehniewicze, *see* Negnevichi.

Nieklan Wielki, Pol.; pop. 21; 101 km ESE of Lodz; 51°11'/20°37'.

Niekrasow, Pol.; pop. 3; 114 km NE of Krakow; 50°29'/21°24'.

Niekurza, Pol.; pop. 3; 114 km NE of Krakow; 50°27'/21°25'.

Nieledwia, Pol.; pop. 13; 82 km SW of Krakow; 49°33'/19°05'.

Nielepkowice, Pol.; pop. 9; 38 km NNW of Przemysl; 50°06'/22°42'.

Nielisz, Pol.; pop. 27; 62 km SE of Lublin; 50°48'/23°03'.

Niemce, Pol.; pop. 105; 50 km WNW of Krakow; 50°17'/19°15'; AMG.

Niemcza, Pol. (Nimptsch); pop. 2; 50 km S of Wroclaw; 50°41'/16°51'.

Niemen, GUM3. This town was not found in BGN gazetteers under the given spelling.

Niemenczyn, *see* Nemencine.

Niemenietz, *see* Nemunaitis.

Niemianowice, Pol.; pop. 7; 88 km W of Lublin; 51°23'/21°20'.

Niemienice, Pol. (Niemnietz); pop. 27; 45 km ESE of Lublin; 50°59'/23°06'.

Niemilow, *see* Nemiluv.

Niemir, *see* Nemir.

Niemirki, Pol.; pop. 6; 88 km SSW of Bialystok; 52°28'/22°28'; GUM4.

Niemirow, *see* Nemirov (near Lvov).

Niemirow (near Bialystok), Pol.; pop. 149; 94 km S of Bialystok; 52°18'/23°09'; SF.

Niemiryczow, Pol.; pop. 6; 56 km W of Lublin; 51°16'/21°43'.

Niemnietz, *see* Niemienice.

Niemnowo, *see* Nemnovo.

Niemojki, Pol.; pop. 36; 101 km S of Bialystok; 52°16'/22°42'; GUM5.

Niemonany, *see* Nemajunai.

Niemoniany, *see* Nemajunai.

Niemowicze, *see* Nemovichi.

Niemstow, Pol.; pop. 58; 56 km N of Przemysl; 50°16'/23°04'; HSL.

Nienadowa, Pol.; pop. 75; 26 km W of Przemysl; 49°50'/22°26'.

Nienadowka, Pol.; pop. 71; 62 km WNW of Przemysl; 50°12'/22°06'.

Nienborg, Germ.; 139 km N of Koln; 52°08'/07°06'; GED.

Nienburg, Germ.; pop. 107; 45 km WNW of Hannover; 52°38'/09°13'; GUM3, HSL.

Nienowice, Pol.; pop. 29; 19 km NNE of Przemysl; 49°56'/22°56'.

Nieplomitza, *see* Niepolomice.

Niepolomice, Pol. (Nepolomits, Nieplomitza, Nyepolomitse); pop. 484; 26 km E of Krakow; 50°02'/20°14'; AMG, CAHJP, COH, EGRS, GUM3, GUM4, GUM5, HSL, LDL, LYV, PHP3, POCEM, SF.

Nieporaz, Pol.; pop. 2; 26 km W of Krakow; 50°06'/19°32'.

Nieporet, Pol.; pop. 65; 26 km N of Warszawa; 52°26'/21°03'.

Nieprzesnia, GUM5. This town was not found in BGN gazetteers under the given spelling.

Nierendorf, GUM5. This town was not found in BGN gazetteers under the given spelling.

Nierodzim, Pol.; 88 km SW of Krakow; 49°46'/18°49'; AMG.

Nieskurzow Stary, Pol.; pop. 5; 107 km SW of Lublin; 50°49'/21°12'.

Niestanice, *see* Nestanitse.

Niestaniszki, *see* Nestanishki.

Niesten, Germ.; 75 km N of Nurnberg; 50°04'/11°16'; PHGB.

Niesuchash, LDL. This pre-World War I community was not found in BGN gazetteers.

Niesuchojeze, *see* Nesukhoyezhe.

Niesulkow, Pol.; pop. 6; 19 km NE of Lodz; 51°53'/19°40'.

Niesulowo, Pol.; pop. 15; 94 km N of Warszawa; 53°04'/21°16'.

Niesviez, *see* Nesvizh.

Nieswicz, Ukr.; pop. 26; 45 km S of Rovno; 50°15'/26°15'. This town was located on an interwar map of Poland but does not appear in contemporary gazetteers. Map coordinates are approximate.

Nieswiez, *see* Nesvizh.

Nieswin, Pol.; pop. 7; 88 km ESE of Lodz; 51°14'/20°28'; COH.

Nieszawa, Pol. (Nishava); pop. 262; 126 km NNW of Lodz; 52°50'/18°54'; HSL, HSL2, LDL, PHP1, PHP4, SF.

Nieszkodna, Pol.; pop. 4; 94 km SW of Lodz; 51°30'/18°11'.

Nieszkow, Pol.; pop. 13; 45 km NNE of Krakow; 50°23'/20°17'.

Nieszkowice Male, Pol.; pop. 7; 32 km ESE of Krakow; 49°57'/20°20'.

Nietiahy, Pol.; pop. 12; 50 km NE of Lublin; 51°35'/23°04'.

Nietkow, GUM6. This town was not found in BGN gazetteers under the given spelling.

Nievern, Germ.; pop. 8; 75 km WNW of Frankfurt am Main; 50°20'/07°41'.

Nieweglosz, Pol.; pop. 6; 62 km N of Lublin; 51°44'/22°39'.

Niewiatrowice, Pol.; pop. 22; 45 km NNE of Krakow; 50°23'/20°20'.

Niewierz, GUM3, GUM4. A number of towns share this name. It was not possible to determine from available information which one is being referenced.

Niewiescin, Pol.; pop. 2; 120 km S of Gdansk; 53°18'/18°14'.

Niewirkow, Pol.; pop. 44; 88 km ESE of Lublin; 50°42'/23°31'; GUM4.

Niewistka, Pol.; pop. 19; 38 km WSW of Przemysl; 49°44'/22°14'.

Niewodna, Pol.; pop. 82 km W of Przemysl; 49°54'/21°40'; PHP3.

Niezabitow, Pol.; pop. 6; 32 km WSW of Lublin; 51°15'/22°08'.

Niezdara, Pol.; pop. 24; 45 km S of Czestochowa; 50°27'/18°59'; AMG.

Nieznanow, *see* Neznanuv.

Nieznanowice, Pol.; pop. 24; 32 km ESE of Krakow; 49°56'/20°16'.

Niezwir, *see* Nezvir.

Niezwiska, *see* Nezviska.

Niezyn, *see* Nezhin.

Nifribony, *see* Nyiribrony.

Nigovichi, *see* Nikhovichi.

Nihowice, *see* Nikhovichi.

Nihzni Vierecki, *see* Nizhniye Veretski.

Nijemci, Yug.; pop. 8; 120 km WNW of Beograd; 45°09'/19°02'.

Nikhovichi, Ukr. (Nigovichi, Nihowice); pop. 38; 56 km SW of Lvov; 49°40'/23°15'.

Nikinci, Yug.; pop. 4; 50 km W of Beograd; 44°51'/19°50'.

Nikisialka Duza, Pol.; pop. 9; 88 km SW of Lublin; 50°47'/21°30'.

Nikisialka Mala, Pol.; pop. 10; 88 km SW of Lublin; 50°47'/21°30'.

Nikitsch, Aus.; pop. 6; 82 km SSE of Wien; 47°32'/16°40'; JGFF.

Nikityche, Ukr. (Nikitycze); pop. 10; 126 km N of Lvov; 50°57'/24°04'.

Nikitycze, *see* Nikityche.

Nikla, Hung.; pop. 12; 45 km NE of Nagykanizsa; 46°35'/17°31'.

Niklovichi, Ukr. (Niklovitse, Niklowice); pop. 50; 45 km WSW of Lvov; 49°44'/23°25'.

Niklovitse, *see* Niklovichi.

Niklowice, *see* Niklovichi.

Nikolaev, *see* Nikolayev.

Nikolai, Germ. HSL2. This pre-World War I community was not found in BGN gazetteers.

Nikolaiken, *see* Mikolajki.

Nikolajev, *see* Nikolayev.

Nikolajew, *see* Nikolayev.

Nikolayev, Ukr. (Mikolajow, Mikolayev, Neishtetel, Nikolaev, Nikolajev, Nikolajew); pop. 21,786; 114 km NE of Odessa;

46°58'/32°00'; AMG, EDRD, EJ, GUM3, GUM4, GUM5, GUM6, GYLA, HSL, HSL2, JGFF, PHP2, SF.

Nikolayev (Lwow), Ukr.; pop. 315; 94 km NE of Lvov; 50°21'/24°59'; CAHJP, COH, EGRS, HSL, LDL, YB.

Nikolayev (Nowogrodek), Byel.; pop. 63; 114 km WSW of Minsk; 53°50'/25°50'.

Nikolayev (Podolia), Ukr.; pop. 1,262; 126 km SSE of Rovno; 49°35'/26°51'; HSL, SF.

Nikolayev (Stanislawow), Ukr.; pop. 498; 45 km S of Lvov; 49°31'/23°59'; HSL.

Nikolayev (Tarnopol), Ukr.; pop. 59; 26 km ESE of Lvov; 49°46'/24°20'.

Nikolayevka, Ukr. (Nicolaenca); 120 km SE of Uman; 47°48'/30°57'; HSL.

Nikolayevka Novorossiyskaya, Ukr. (Bairamcea, Bajramtscha, Beiramich, Beiramtch); pop. 806; 75 km SW of Odessa; 46°08'/29°54'; EDRD, LDL, SF, YB.

Nikolsburg, see Mikulov.

Nikolskaya, Ukr. (Nikolskaya Sloboda, Nikolskaya Slobodka, Nikolski Slobodka, Slobodka Nikolskaya); 6 km NE of Kiyev; 50°27'/30°35'; SF.

Nikolskaya Sloboda, see Nikolskaya.

Nikolskaya Slobodka, see Nikolskaya.

Nikolski Slobodka, see Nikolskaya.

Nikopol, Ukr.; pop. 2,699; 107 km S of Dnepropetrovsk; 47°34'/34°24'; GUM4, HSL, ISH1, SF.

Nikopol (Bulgaria), Bulg. (Nikopolis); 170 km NE of Sofija; 43°42'/24°54'; EJ.

Nikopolis, see Nikopol (Bulgaria).

Nikoreny, Mold. (Nicoreni); pop. 75; 139 km NW of Kishinev; 47°58'/27°42'.

Nikrace, Lat.; pop. 7; 139 km SW of Riga; 56°32'/21°56'.

Niksdorf, GUM6. This town was not found in BGN gazetteers under the given spelling.

Niksic, Yug.; pop. 3; 221 km WNW of Skopje; 42°46'/18°58'.

Niksowizna, Pol.; pop. 6; 88 km W of Bialystok; 53°21'/21°53'.

Nima, Rom.; pop. 4; 38 km NNE of Cluj; 47°04'/23°52'.

Nimayin, see Nemajunai.

Nimerice, Cz.; pop. 8; 45 km NNE of Praha; 50°24'/14°49'.

Nimigea de Jos, Rom. (Magyarnemegye, Nimizshe); pop. 234; 75 km NNE of Cluj; 47°15'/24°18'; PHR2.

Nimigea de Sus, Rom.; pop. 28; 82 km NNE of Cluj; 47°17'/24°19'.

Nimizshe, see Nimigea de Jos.

Nimoreni, see Nimoreny.

Nimoreny, Mold. (Nimoreni); pop. 18; 13 km W of Kishinev; 47°01'/28°41'.

Nimptsch, see Niemcza.

Nires, Rom. (Szasznyires); pop. 27; 50 km NNE of Cluj; 47°06'/23°59'; HSL.

Nirza, Lat. (Nirzas); pop. 33; 107 km NE of Daugavpils; 56°24'/27°56'; PHLE.

Nirzas, see Nirza.

Nis, Yug.; pop. 373; 150 km N of Skopje; 43°19'/21°54'; EDRD, GUM4, PHY.

Niscani, see Nishkany.

Nishava, see Nieszawa.

Nishkany, Mold. (Niscani); pop. 16; 50 km WNW of Kishinev; 47°16'/28°19'.

Nishtot Tavrig, see Zemaiciu Naumiestis.

Nishviz, see Nesvizh.

Nisk, see Nisko.

Niska, see Nisko.

Niskenichi, Ukr. (Niskienicze, Niskiewicze); pop. 25; 107 km N of Lvov; 50°45'/24°12'.

Niskienicze, see Niskenichi.

Niskiewicze, see Niskenichi.

Nisko, Pol. (Nisk, Niska); pop. 528; 82 km S of Lublin; 50°32'/22°09'; COH, EDRD, EGRS, FRG, GUM4, GUM5, HSL, HSL2, JGFF, LDL, PHP3, SF.

Nisporeni, see Nisporeny.

Nisporeny, Mold. (Nisporeni); pop. 380; 50 km W of Kishinev; 47°05'/28°11'.

Niszczyce, Pol.; pop. 1; 94 km WNW of Warszawa; 52°39'/19°46'.

Nitaure, Lat.; pop. 4; 69 km ENE of Riga; 57°04'/25°12'.

Nitra, Cz. (Neutra, Nyitra); pop. 4,661; 75 km ENE of Bratislava; 48°19'/18°05'; AMG, COH, EJ, GUM3, GUM4, GUM5, GUM6, HSL, HSL2, JGFF, LDL.

Niuved, Rom.; pop. 3; 139 km WNW of Cluj; 47°14'/21°53'.

Nivetsk, Ukr. (Niweck); pop. 17; 107 km N of Rovno; 51°31'/26°26'.

Nivitse, Ukr. (Niwice); pop. 32; 62 km NE of Lvov; 50°10'/24°46'; COH.

Nivki, Byel. (Niwki); pop. 76; 94 km NNW of Minsk; 54°39'/27°07'.

Nivki (Polesie), Byel.; pop. 40; 75 km WNW of Pinsk; 52°28'/25°10'.

Nivra, Ukr. (Niwra); pop. 44; 50 km NNE of Chernovtsy; 48°43'/26°13'.

Nivy, Byel. (Niwy); pop. 24; 75 km WNW of Pinsk; 52°28'/25°10'.

Niweck, see Nivetsk.

Niwice, see Nivitse.

Niwiska, Pol.; pop. 25; 94 km WNW of Przemysl; 50°14'/21°37'.

Niwka, Pol.; pop. 329; 50 km ESE of Lodz; 51°32'/20°03'; AMG, CAHJP, COH, GUM3.

Niwki, see Nivki.

Niwra, see Nivra.

Niwy, see Nivy.

Nizankowice, see Nizhankovichi.

Nizatycze, Pol.; pop. 20; Described in the *Black Book* as being in the Lwow region of Poland, this town was not found in BGN gazetteers.

Nizborg Nowy, see Nizhborg Novyy.

Nizborg Stary, see Staryy Nizhborok.

Nizborg Szlachecki, see Nizhborg Novyy.

Nizhankovichi, Ukr. (Nizankowice, Nizhankovitz, Nozankovitz); pop. 408; 88 km WSW of Lvov; 49°41'/22°49'; EGRS, HSL, HSL2, PHP2, SF.

Nizhankovitz, see Nizhankovichi.

Nizhborg, see Nizhborg Novyy.

Nizhborg Novy, see Nizhborg Novyy.

Nizhborg Novyy, Ukr. (Nizborg Nowy, Nizborg Szlachecki, Nizhborg, Nizhborg Novy); pop. 28; 94 km N of Chernovtsy; 49°07'/26°01'; HSL.

Nizhborg Stary, see Staryy Nizhborok.

Nizhna Apsha, Ukr. (Alsoapsa, Nizni Apsa, Unter Apsa); 157 km WSW of Chernovtsy; 48°00'/23°50'; COH, HSL, SM.

Nizhne Bystraya, Ukr. (Felsobisztre, Nizhniye Bistri); 170 km S of Lvov; 48°22'/23°32'; HSL.

Nizhne Studenyy, Ukr. (Alsohidegpatak, Nizni Studeny, Studena); 139 km S of Lvov; 48°42'/23°22'; HSL, SM.

Nizhnev, Ukr. (Nizhnov, Nizniow); pop. 451; 94 km NW of Chernovtsy; 48°57'/25°06'; EGRS, GUM3, GUM4, HSL, HSL2, LDL, PHP2, SF.

Nizhneye, Ukr.; 214 km ESE of Kharkov; 48°46'/38°37'; HSL.

Nizhneye Krivche, Ukr. (Krzywcze Dolne, Kshyvche Dolne); pop. 23; 50 km N of Chernovtsy; 48°42'/26°06'; PHP2.

Nizhneye Selishche, Ukr. (Alsoszelistye, Nizni Seliste); 182 km WSW of Chernovtsy; 48°11'/23°27'; GUM5, SM.

Nizhni Verecki, see Nizhni Vereki.

Nizhni Vereki, (Nizhni Verecki); GUM5. This town was not found in BGN gazetteers under the given spelling.

Nizhni Veretski, see Nizhniye Veretski.

Nizhniy Bistri, see Nizhnyaya Bystraya.

Nizhniye Bistri, see Nizhne Bystraya.

Nizhniye Kugureshty, Mold. (Cuhurestii de Jos); pop. 20; 107 km NNW of Kishinev; 47°56'/28°36'.

Nizhniye Veretski, Ukr. (Alsovereczke, Nihzni Vierecki, Nizhni Veretski, Nizni Verecki, Nizni Verecky, Verecky Nizni, Vereeze?); 139 km SSW of Lvov; 48°46'/23°06'; AMG,

COH, GUM3, HSL.

Nizhniye Zhory, Mold. (Jora de Jos, Zhora de Zhos); pop. 40; 56 km N of Kishinev; 47°28'/29°06'.

Nizhnov, *see* Nizhnev.

Nizhnyaya Belka, Ukr. (Bilka Krolewska, Bilka Krulevska); pop. 21; 19 km ENE of Lvov; 49°51'/24°17'.

Nizhnyaya Bystraya, Ukr. (Alsobisztra, Nizhniy Bistri, Nizni Bystry, Unter Bistra); 170 km S of Lvov; 48°21'/23°32'; COH, SM.

Nizhnyaya Viznitse, Ukr. (Felsovizniecze); 170 km SSW of Lvov; 48°31'/22°46'. This town was not found in BGN gazetteers under the given spelling.

Nizkov, Cz.; pop. 2; 69 km WNW of Brno; 49°32'/15°48'.

Nizna Jablonka, Cz. (Jablonka Nizna); pop. 253; 75 km NE of Kosice; 49°08'/22°06'; EGRS, HSL.

Nizna Mysla, Cz. (Alsomislye); 19 km SE of Kosice; 48°37'/21°22'; HSL.

Nizna Sebastova, Cz. (Nizni Sebes); pop. 59; 38 km N of Kosice; 49°01'/21°17'.

Nizna Slana, Cz. (Alsosajo); 62 km W of Kosice; 48°44'/20°25'; HSL.

Nizne Cabiny, Cz.; pop. 51; 69 km NNE of Kosice; 49°10'/21°55'.

Nizni Apsa, *see* Nizhna Apsha.

Nizni Bystry, *see* Nizhnyaya Bystraya.

Nizni Orlik, *see* Nizny Orlik.

Nizniow, *see* Nizhnev.

Nizni Sebes, *see* Nizna Sebastova.

Nizni Seliste, *see* Nizhneye Selishche.

Nizni Slavkov, *see* Nizny Slavkov.

Nizni Studeny, *see* Nizhne Studenyy.

Nizni Verecki, *see* Nizhniye Veretski.

Nizni Verecky, *see* Nizhniye Veretski.

Nizny Hrabovec, Cz. (Alsogyertany); pop. 70; 45 km NE of Kosice; 48°51'/21°46'; HSL.

Nizny Orlik, Cz. (Nizni Orlik); 75 km N of Kosice; 49°20'/21°32'; JGFF.

Nizny Slavkov, Cz. (Alsoszalok, Nizni Slavkov); 56 km NW of Kosice; 49°06'/20°51'; HSL.

Nizyn, *see* Nezhin.

Noara Noua, Rom.; pop. 111; Described in the *Black Book* as being in the Bessarabia region of Romania, this town was not found in BGN gazetteers.

Nochern, Germ.; pop. 8; 69 km W of Frankfurt am Main; 50°10'/07°43'.

Nockowa, Pol.; pop. 21; 75 km WNW of Przemysl; 50°01'/21°47'.

Nocoleav, Rom. PHR1. This town was not found in BGN gazetteers under the given spelling.

Nodvorna, *see* Nadvornaya.

Nogaysk, *see* Primorskoye.

Noglovitz, *see* Naglowice.

Nograd, Hung.; pop. 34; 50 km N of Budapest; 47°55'/19°03'.

Nogradadsap, *see* Nogradsap.

Nogradberczel, *see* Bercel.

Nogradbertsel, *see* Bercel.

Nogradkovesd, Hung.; pop. 9; 45 km NNE of Budapest; 47°52'/19°23'.

Nogradmarcal, Hung.; pop. 3; 62 km N of Budapest; 48°02'/19°24'.

Nogradmegyer, Hung.; pop. 14; 75 km NNE of Budapest; 48°04'/19°38'; AMG.

Nogradpatak, HSL. This pre-World War I community was not found in BGN gazetteers.

Nogradsap, Hung. (Nogradadsap); pop. 20; 45 km NNE of Budapest; 47°50'/19°21'.

Nogradszakal, Hung.; pop. 9; 82 km N of Budapest; 48°11'/19°32'.

Nogradveroce, Hung.; pop. 61; 45 km N of Budapest; 47°50'/19°02'.

Nohfelden, Germ.; pop. 6; 126 km SW of Frankfurt am Main;

49°35'/07°09'.

Noiszew, *see* Nojszew.

Nojszew, Pol. (Noiszew); pop. 4; 56 km ENE of Warszawa; 52°22'/21°49'.

Nomme, Est.; pop. 34; 13 km SW of Tallinn; 59°23'/24°40'; PHLE.

Noniucha, Pol. PHP2. This town was not found in BGN gazetteers under the given spelling.

Nonnenweier, Germ.; pop. 88; 114 km SW of Stuttgart; 48°21'/07°46'; GED, JGFF, PHGBW, YB.

Norap, Hung.; pop. 6; 101 km N of Nagykanizsa; 47°16'/17°28'.

Nord, Pol.; pop. 23; Described in the *Black Book* as being in the Lwow region of Poland, this town was not found in BGN gazetteers.

Nordeck, Germ.; pop. 17; 69 km N of Frankfurt am Main; 50°41'/08°50'; LDS.

Norden, Germ.; pop. 231; 182 km W of Hamburg; 53°36'/07°12'; CAHJP, GUM5, HSL, LDS.

Nordenburg, *see* Krylovo.

Nordenham, Germ.; pop. 21; 101 km WSW of Hamburg; 53°30'/08°29'.

Nordenstadt, Germ.; pop. 37; 26 km WSW of Frankfurt am Main; 50°04'/08°21'.

Nordhausen, Germ.; pop. 438; 107 km W of Leipzig; 51°31'/10°48'; AMG, GUM3, GUM4, GUM5, GUM6, HSL, JGFF, LDS.

Nordheim, *see* Nordheim vor der Rhon.

Nordheim vor der Rhon, Germ. (Nordheim); pop. 32; 120 km NE of Frankfurt am Main; 50°29'/10°11'; GUM3, GUM5, PHGB.

Nordhorn, Germ.; pop. 50; 170 km N of Koln; 52°26'/07°05'; GED, GUM5, LDS.

Nordlingen, Germ.; pop. 233; 82 km SSW of Nurnberg; 48°51'/10°30'; GED, GUM5, HSL, JGFF, PHGB, PHGBW.

Nordrach, Germ.; 94 km SW of Stuttgart; 48°22'/08°00'; PHGBW.

Nordstemmen, Germ.; pop. 6; 32 km SSE of Hannover; 52°10'/09°47'.

Nordstetten, Germ.; 50 km SSW of Stuttgart; 48°26'/08°42'; JGFF, PHGBW.

Norenberg, *see* Insko.

Norinsk, Ukr. (Narinsk); 163 km WNW of Kiyev; 51°16'/28°36'; LDL, SF.

Norta, Pol.; pop. 6; 50 km N of Krakow; 50°30'/20°05'.

Norten Hardenberg, Germ.; pop. 1; 88 km SSE of Hannover; 51°38'/09°56'.

Northeim, Germ.; pop. 128; 82 km SSE of Hannover; 51°42'/10°00'.

Norvenich, Germ.; 32 km SW of Koln; 50°48'/06°39'; GED.

Nosaczewicze, Pol.; pop. 38; Described in the *Black Book* as being in the Wolyn region of Poland, this town was not found in BGN gazetteers.

Nosalewice, Pol.; pop. 11; 69 km NE of Czestochowa; 51°07'/19°57'.

Nosarzewo, GUM4, PHP4. This town was not found in BGN gazetteers under the given spelling.

Noski, *see* Noski Snietne.

Noski Snietne, Pol. (Noski); pop. 2; 38 km SW of Bialystok; 52°58'/22°42'.

Noskov, Cz.; pop. 1; 62 km SSE of Praha; 49°33'/14°48'.

Noskovtsy, Ukr. (Askovitz, Noskowcy); 50 km SW of Vinnitsa; 48°58'/27°59'; SF.

Noskowcy, *see* Noskovtsy.

Nosov, Ukr. (Nosow); pop. 43; 101 km ESE of Lvov; 49°14'/25°00'.

Nosovka, Ukr.; 94 km NE of Kiyev; 50°56'/31°35'; LDL, SF.

Nosow, *see* Nosov.

Noszlop, Hung.; 94 km N of Nagykanizsa; 47°11'/17°28'; HSL.

Noszvaj, Hung.; pop. 15; 32 km SW of Miskolc; 47°56'/20°29'; HSL.

Noszyce, Pol. PHP4. This town was not found in BGN

gazetteers under the given spelling.

Notig, Rom.; pop. 16; 69 km NNW of Cluj; 47°22'/23°13'.

Nottuln, Germ.; pop. 5; 114 km N of Koln; 51°56'/07°21'; GED.

Noua Sulita, see Novoseltsy.

Noul Caragaci, see Vishnevoye.

Noul Sasesc, Rom. (Szaszujfalu); 107 km ESE of Cluj; 46°07'/24°36'; HSL.

Nova, Hung.; pop. 21; 45 km NW of Nagykanizsa; 46°41'/16°41'; HSL, JGFF.

Nova Bana, Cz. (Konigsberg); pop. 250; 114 km ENE of Bratislava; 48°26'/18°39'.

Nova Bason, see Novaya Basan.

Nova Bukovica, see Spisicbukovica.

Nova Bystrice, Cz. (Bystrice Nove); pop. 76; 114 km WSW of Brno; 49°01'/15°06'.

Nova Cerekev, Cz.; pop. 34; 88 km SE of Praha; 49°25'/15°07'.

Nova Crnja, Yug.; pop. 15; 101 km N of Beograd; 45°40'/20°37'.

Nova Gorica, Yug.; 182 km W of Zagreb; 45°57'/13°39'; PHY.

Nova Gradiska, Yug.; pop. 207; 126 km ESE of Zagreb; 45°16'/17°23'; GUM4, PHY.

Novaharod Siversk, see Novgorod Severskiy.

Novaia Greblia, see Nowa Grobla.

Novaj, Hung.; pop. 24; 38 km SSW of Miskolc; 47°51'/20°29'; HSL.

Novaja Usica, see Novaya Ushitsa.

Novajidrany, Hung. (Alsonovaj); pop. 3; 45 km NNE of Miskolc; 48°24'/21°11'.

Novak, Hung. BGN lists two possible localities with this name located at 41°26'/20°37' and 47°12'/18°09'. HSL.

Nova Kanjiza, see Novi Knezevac.

Nova Kapela, Yug.; pop. 4; 146 km ESE of Zagreb; 45°12'/17°39'.

Novaky, Cz. (Nyitra Novak); 126 km NE of Bratislava; 48°43'/18°33'; EDRD, GUM4, GUM5, GUM6, LDL.

Nova Muzh, see Novaya Mysh.

Nova Oshitza, see Novaya Ushitsa.

Nova Pazova, Yug.; pop. 8; 26 km WNW of Beograd; 44°56'/20°14'.

Nova Praga, see Novaya Praga.

Nova Raca, Yug.; pop. 9; 75 km E of Zagreb; 45°48'/16°57'.

Novaredok, see Novogrudok.

Nova Ukrainka, see Novoukrainka.

Nova Ukreinka, see Novoukrainka.

Nova Ves, Cz.; pop. 37; BGN lists 99 population centers in Czechoslovakia named Nova Ves, which means "new town."

Nova Vilejka, see Naujoji Vilnia.

Novaya Aleksandriya, see Pulawy.

Novaya Basan, Ukr. (Bason Chadash, Nova Bason, Novo Basan); 69 km ENE of Kiyev; 50°34'/31°31'; EDRD, JGFF, LDL, SF.

Novaya Chelakovka, Mold. (Ciolacu Nou); pop. 14; 94 km WNW of Kishinev; 47°29'/27°50'.

Novaya Derevnya, Ukr. (Naydorf); pop. 125; 101 km NNW of Simferopol; 45°46'/33°55'.

Novaya Iserliya, Mold. (Iserlia Noua); pop. 4; 62 km SSE of Kishinev; 46°29'/28°57'.

Novaya Ivanovka, Ukr. (Ivanestii Noui); pop. 6; 139 km SW of Odessa; 45°55'/29°05'.

Novaya Kobuska, Mold. (Cobusca Noua); pop. 10; 32 km E of Kishinev; 46°56'/29°13'.

Novaya Mysh, Byel. (Mush, Nova Muzh, Nowa Mysz); pop. 632; 120 km NNW of Pinsk; 53°08'/25°54'; HSL, SF.

Novaya Nekrasovka, Ukr. (Necrasovca Noua); pop. 8; 202 km SW of Odessa; 45°21'/28°42'.

Novaya Odessa, Ukr. (Novi Odessa); 126 km NNE of Odessa; 47°19'/31°47'; JGFF, LDL, SF.

Novaya Praga, Ukr. (Nova Praga, Novi Praga); pop. 591; 150 km W of Dnepropetrovsk; 48°34'/32°55'; SF.

Novaya Sarata, Mold. (Sarata Noua, Tomai); pop. 28; 101 km WNW of Kishinev; 47°30'/27°48'.

Novaya Strelishcha, see Novyye Strelishcha.

Novaya Ushitsa, Ukr. (Nei Ushitz, Nova Oshitza, Novaja Usica, Oyshitz); pop. 1,844; 94 km SW of Vinnitsa; 48°50'/27°17'; EJ, JGFF, SF.

Novaya Vyzhva, Ukr. (Wyzwa Nowa, Wyzwa Stara?); pop. 358; 150 km WNW of Rovno; 51°24'/24°25'.

Novaya Yablona, Mold. (Iablona Noua); pop. 41; 126 km NW of Kishinev; 47°49'/27°37'.

Nova Zagora, Bulg.; pop. 412; 176 km SW of Varna; 42°29'/26°01'; EJ.

Nove Benatky, see Benatky nad Jizerou.

Nove Hrady, Cz.; pop. 24; A number of towns share this name. It was not possible to determine from available information which one is being referenced.

Nove Mesto, Cz. AMG, GUM3, HSL, JGFF. A number of towns share this name. It was not possible to determine from available information which one is being referenced.

Nove Mesto nad Metuji, Cz.; pop. 35; 120 km ENE of Praha; 50°20'/16°10'.

Nove Mesto nad Vahom, Cz. (Vag Ujhely); pop. 1,581; 88 km NNE of Bratislava; 48°45'/17°50'; CAHJP, EJ, GUM4, GUM5, HSL, LDL.

Nove Mesto na Morave, Cz.; pop. 39; 62 km WNW of Brno; 49°34'/16°05'.

Nove Miasto, AMG, EDRD. This town was not found in BGN gazetteers under the given spelling.

Nove Miesto, Cz. HSL2. This pre-World War I community was not found in BGN gazetteers.

Nove Sady, Cz. (Asakert, Assakurt); 75 km NE of Bratislava; 48°29'/17°59'; HSL.

Nove Sedlice, see Slavkov u Brna.

Nove Sedliste, Cz. (Neuzedlisch); 133 km SW of Praha; 49°44'/12°40'; EJ, HSL, HSL2.

Nove Sedlo, Cz.; pop. 31; 126 km W of Praha; 50°13'/12°44'.

Nove Strakonice, Cz.; pop. 122; 101 km SSW of Praha; 49°16'/13°54'.

Nove Straseci, Cz.; pop. 24; 38 km W of Praha; 50°09'/13°55'.

Nove Zamky, Cz. (Ersekujvar); pop. 2,535; 82 km E of Bratislava; 47°59'/18°10'; COH, EJ, GUM4, GUM6, HSL, HSL2, JGFF, LDL.

Novgorod, Ukr.; pop. 926; 176 km ESE of Dnepropetrovsk; 47°33'/36°56'; GUM4, HSL, LDL.

Novgorod Seversk, see Novgorod Severskiy.

Novgorod Severski, see Novgorod Severskiy.

Novgorod Severskiy, Ukr. (Novaharod Siversk, Novgorod Seversk, Novgorod Severski); pop. 2,089; 88 km N of Konotop; 52°00'/33°16'; EJ, HSL, LDL, SF.

Novi Becej, Yug. (Torok Becse, Torokbecse, Vranjevo); pop. 167; 94 km NNW of Beograd; 45°36'/20°08'; GUM4, HSL, PHY.

Novi Bezdan, Yug.; pop. 38; 189 km WNW of Beograd; 45°44'/18°28'.

Novi Bug, see Novyy Bug.

Novi Dvor, see Sarmasel.

Novi Dvur, see Sarmasel.

Novi Knezevac, Yug. (Nova Kanjiza, Novi Knezvac, Torok Kanyizsa); pop. 167; 139 km NNW of Beograd; 46°03'/20°06'; PHY.

Novi Knezvac, see Novi Knezevac.

Novi Korchin, see Nowy Korczyn.

Novi Kortchin, see Nowy Korczyn.

Novi Marof, Yug.; pop. 5; 45 km NNE of Zagreb; 46°09'/16°20'.

Novi Miasto, see Nowe Miasto.

Novinki, see Khutor Novinki.

Novi Odessa, see Novaya Odessa.

Novi Pazar, Yug.; pop. 249; 150 km NW of Skopje; 43°08'/20°31'; PHY.

Novi Pikov, see Novyy Pikov.

Novi Pohost, see Pogost.

Novi Praga, see Novaya Praga.

Novi Sach, see Nowy Sacz.

233

Novoaleksandrovsk (Zarasai), Lithuania: The corner of a broad street across from A. Feldsher's drugstore (sign above entrance).

Beograd; 45°15'/19°50'; AMG, CAHJP, COH, EDRD, EJ, GUM4, GUM5, GUM6, HSL, LDS, LJEE, PHY.

Novi Sadi, *see* Novosady.

Novi Sansh, *see* Nowy Sacz.

Novi Senzhari, *see* Novyye Sanzhary.

Novitanitz, *see* Nowotaniec.

Novi Targ, *see* Nowy Targ.

Novitsa, Ukr. (Nowica); pop. 51; 107 km SSE of Lvov; 48°57'/24°20'.

Novi Vitebsk, *see* Novo Vitebsk.

Novi Vrbas, Yug.; pop. 189; 107 km NW of Beograd; 45°35'/19°40'.

Novi Yarichev, *see* Jarczew.

Novo, *see* Zaronovo.

Novo Aleksandrovsk, *see* Zarasai.

Novoaleksandrovsk, *see* Zarasai.

Novo Basan, *see* Novaya Basan.

Novobrzesk, *see* Nowe Brzesko.

Novo Cice, Yug.; pop. 5; 19 km SE of Zagreb; 45°42'/16°07'.

Novoe Mesto, *see* Kudirkos Naumiestis.

Novo Fastov, Ukr. EDRD. This town was not found in BGN gazetteers under the given spelling.

Novogeorgievsk, *see* Svetlovodsk.

Novo Georgijevsk, *see* Svetlovodsk.

Novogeorgiyevsk, *see* Svetlovodsk.

Novogorod, USSR (Nowgorod); pop. 926; 163 km SE of Leningrad; 58°31'/31°17'.

Novograd Volynsk, *see* Novograd Volynskiy.

Novograd Volynskiy, Ukr. (Novograd Volynsk, Novograd Volynskij, Zviagel, Zvihil, Zvil, Zwiahl); pop. 6,553; 94 km E of Rovno; 50°36'/27°37'; COH, EDRD, GUM4, GUM5, HSL, JGFF, LDL, SF, YB.

Novogrod, *see* Nowogrod.

Novogrudek, *see* Novogrudok.

Novogrudok, Byel. (Navahredek, Navaredok, Novaredok, Novogrudek, Novohorodek, Novohorodok, Novradok, Nowogrodek, Nowogrudok); pop. 3,405; 120 km WSW of Minsk; 53°36'/25°50'; AMG, CAHJP, COH, EDRD, EJ, FRG, GA, GUM3, GUM4, GUM5, GUM6, HSL, HSL2, JGFF, LDL, SF, YB.

Novohorodek, *see* Novogrudok.

Novohorodok, *see* Novogrudok.

Novo Konstantinov, *see* Novyy Konstantinov.

Novokonstantinov, *see* Novyy Konstantinov.

Novo Labun, Ukr.; 101 km ESE of Rovno; 50°01'/27°21'; JGFF.

Novo Malin, Ukr. (Nowomalin); pop. 12; 38 km SSE of Rovno; 50°18'/26°22'.

Novo Markovka, Ukr. (Markivka, Markovka, Markowka); pop. 20; 82 km W of Chernovtsy; 48°30'/24°52'; LDL, SF.

Novo Mesto, Yug.; pop. 1; 62 km WSW of Zagreb; 45°48'/15°10'.

Novomigrod, Ukr. EDRD. This town was not found in BGN gazetteers under the given spelling.

Novo Milosevo, Yug. (Beodra, Dragutinovo); pop. 13; 107 km NNW of Beograd; 45°43'/20°18'.

Novo Minsk, *see* Minsk Mazowiecki.

Novominsk, *see* Minsk Mazowiecki.

Novo Mirgorod, *see* Novomirgorod.

Novomirgorod, Ukr. (Novo Mirgorod, Novomirogorod, Nowomirgorod); pop. 858; 107 km ENE of Uman; 48°47'/31°39'; HSL, HSL2, JGFF, LDL, SF.

Novomirogorod, *see* Novomirgorod.

Novomoskovsk, Ukr. (Nowomoskowsk); pop. 1,421; 26 km NNE of Dnepropetrovsk; 48°37'/35°12'; EDRD, GUM4, SF.

Novo Pashkovo, Byel.; 146 km S of Vitebsk; 53°57'/30°15'; GUM4.

Novo Poltavka, *see* Novopoltavka.

Novopoltavka, Ukr. (Novo Poltavka); pop. 1,906; 176 km NE of Odessa; 47°33'/32°30'; SF.

Novo Priluki, USSR; pop. 1,563; EDRD. This town was not found in BGN gazetteers under the given spelling.

Novo Radomsk, *see* Radomsko.

Novorodchitsy, Ukr. (Noworodczyce); pop. 21; 50 km S of Rovno; 50°14'/26°16'.

Novorossiysk, Ukr.; pop. 1,915; 150 km E of Odessa; 46°07'/32°38'; LDL.

Novosad, Cz. (Bodzasujlak); 45 km ESE of Kosice; 48°32'/21°44'; HSL.

Novo Sadi, *see* Novosady.

Novosady, Byel. (Novi Sadi, Novo Sadi); 26 km SW of Minsk; 53°48'/27°10'; SF.

Novosedlice, Cz.; pop. 32; 82 km NW of Praha; 50°39'/13°49'.

Novoselica, *see* Novoseltsy.

Novoselice, *see* Neresnitsa.

Novo Selitsa, *see* Novoseltsy.

Novoselitsa (near Khodorov), Ukr.; pop. 24; 107 km S of Lvov; 48°57'/23°55'.

Novoseliza, *see* Neresnitsa.

Novoselka Kostyukova, Ukr. (Nowociolka Kosciukowa); pop. 98; 50 km N of Chernovtsy; 48°43'/25°55'.

Novoselki, Ukr. (Novoselki Gostsinne, Nowosiolki, Nowosiolki Goscinne); pop. 40; 50 km SW of Lvov; 49°38'/23°28'.

Novoselki Gostsinne, *see* Novoselki.

Novoselovka, Ukr. (Enichioi); pop. 2; 146 km SW of Odessa; 45°41'/29°16'.

Novoselovskoye, Ukr. (Fraydorf); pop. 400; 69 km NW of Simferopol; 45°26'/33°36'; GUM4.

Novoseltsy, Ukr. (Noua Sulita, Novo Selitsa, Novoselica); pop. 39; 32 km ESE of Chernovtsy; 48°13'/26°17'; AMG, COH, EJ, GUM3, GUM4, GUM5, GYLA, HSL, JGFF, LYV, PHR2, SF, YB.

Novoshitse, Ukr. (Nowoszyce); pop. 21; 62 km SW of Lvov; 49°28'/23°25'.

Novosokolniki, USSR; pop. 339; 26 km WSW of Velikiye Luki; 56°19'/30°09'.

Novosyulka, Ukr. (Nowosiolka); pop. 10; 75 km N of Chernovtsy; 48°58'/25°57'; HSL, HSL2. These references could apply to any of the towns with this name listed here and below.

Novosyulka (near Podgaytsy), Ukr.; pop. 44; 101 km E of Lvov; 49°47'/25°24'.

Novosyulka (near Przemyslany), Ukr.; pop. 43; 45 km ESE of Lvov; 49°40'/24°33'.

Novosyulka Yazlovets, *see* Novsyulka Yazlovetska.

Novosyulki, Ukr.; 50 km E of Lvov; 49°47'/24°39'; GUM3.

Novosyulki Ruske, Ukr. (Nowosiolki); pop. 32; 94 km WSW of Rovno; 50°28'/24°59'.

Novosyulki Yazlovets, *see* Novsyulka Yazlovetska.

Novo Ukrainka, Ukr.; pop. 2,800; 107 km ESE of Uman; 48°19'/31°32'; GUM4, GUM5, SF.

Novoukrainka, Ukr. (Nova Ukrainka, Nova Ukreinka, Varenzh, Warez); pop. 520; 75 km N of Lvov; 50°31'/24°06'; GUM3, GUM5, LDL, PHP2, YB.

Novo Ukrainka (Lwow), Pol. (Varenz, Varenz Miasto, Varez, Varez Miasto, Warez Miasto); pop. 520; 120 km NE of Przemysl; 50°31'/24°06'; EGRS, LYV.

Novo Vileisk, LDL. This pre-World War I community was not found in BGN gazetteers.

Novo Vitebsk, Ukr. (Novi Vitebsk, Novyy Vitebsk); pop. 1,334; 94 km SW of Dnepropetrovsk; 47°58'/33°54'.

Novo Vorontsovka, HSL. This pre-World War I community was not found in BGN gazetteers.

Novoyelnya, Byel. (Nowojelnia); pop. 135; 139 km SW of Minsk; 53°28'/25°35'; FRG, GUM3, GUM6, JGFF.

Novo Zhagory, *see* Zagare.

Novozibkov, *see* Novozybkov.

Novo Zlatopol, Ukr. (Novyy Zlatopol, Perve Numer); 146 km ESE of Dnepropetrovsk; 47°40'/36°34'; JGFF.

Novo Zlatopolskaya, HSL. This pre-World War I community was not found in BGN gazetteers.

Novozybkov, USSR (Novozibkov, Novozybkow, Nowosybkow); pop. 4,825; 182 km SW of Bryansk; 52°32'/31°56'; EDRD, EJ, HSL, JGFF, LDL, SF.

Novozybkow, *see* Novozybkov.

Novradeker, *see* Sarmasel.

Novradok, *see* Novogrudok.

Novska, Yug.; pop. 26; 94 km ESE of Zagreb; 45°20'/16°59'.

Novsyulka Yazlovetska, (Novosyulka Yazlovets, Novosyulki Yazlovets, Nowosiclka Jazlowiecka, Nowosiolka Jazlowiecka); pop. 56; Described in the *Black Book* as being in the Tarnopol region of Poland, this town was not found in BGN gazetteers.

Novy Bohumin, *see* Bohumin.

Novy Bug, *see* Novyy Bug.

Novy Bydzov, Cz. (Neubitschow); pop. 148; 75 km ENE of Praha; 50°15'/15°30'; EJ.

Novy Dvor, *see* Sarmasel. There are no less than 80 towns in Poland, the USSR and Czechoslovakia called Novy Dvor, Novy Dvur or Nowy Dwor, all of which mean "new court."

Novy Dvur; *See* Novy Dvor.

Novye Strelishche, *see* Novyye Strelishcha.

Novy Hrozenkov, Cz.; 114 km ENE of Brno; 49°21'/18°13'; GUM3.

Novy Jicin, Cz. (Neutitschein, Neutitschin); pop. 206; 114 km NE of Brno; 49°36'/18°01'; EJ, HSL.

Novy Oleksiniec, *see* Novyy Oleksinets.

Novy Oskol, USSR; pop. 27; This town was not found in BGN gazetteers under the given spelling.

Novy Sacz, *see* Nowy Sacz.

Novy Targ, *see* Nowy Targ.

Novyy Aleksinets, *see* Novyy Oleksinets.

Novyy Bug, Ukr. (Novi Bug, Novy Bug, Nowyi Bug); 189 km NNE of Odessa; 47°41'/32°30'; HSL, SF.

Novyy Dvor, Byel. (Nowy Dwor); pop. 370; 195 km WSW of Minsk; 53°48'/24°34'; AMG, EJ, HSL, JGFF, LYV, SF, YB.

Novyy Choropkany, Mold. (Cioropcanii Noui); pop. 13; 94 km WNW of Kishinev; 47°24'/27°42'.

Novyye Dorosini, Ukr. (Dorosinie); pop. 39; 94 km WNW of Rovno; 50°57'/25°01'.

Novyye Dragusheny, Mold. (Dragusenii Noui, Dragusheni Nouy); pop. 16; 32 km W of Kishinev; 47°03'/28°25'; JGFF.

Novyye Gechi, Mold. (Heciu Nou); pop. 30; 107 km NW of Kishinev; 47°47'/28°04'.

Novyye Popeshty, Mold. (Popeshti Nouy, Popesti de Jos, Popestii Noui); pop. 4; 126 km NW of Kishinev; 47°59'/27°59'.

Novyye Ruseshty, Mold. (Rusestii Noui); pop. 16; 19 km SW of Kishinev; 46°56'/28°39'.

Novyye Sanzhary, Ukr. (Novi Senzhari); pop. 24; 114 km NW of Dnepropetrovsk; 49°20'/34°20'.

Novyye Selishty, Mold. (Sulita, Sulita Targ, Sulita Tirg); pop. 4,154; 50 km WNW of Kishinev; 47°15'/28°18'; GUM4, HSL, JGFF, LDL, PHR1.

Novyye Sochi, Mold. (Cartofleanca, Kartoflyanka); pop. 22; 107 km WNW of Kishinev; 47°32'/27°40'.

Novyye Strelishcha, Ukr. (Novaya Strelishcha, Novye Strelishche, Strelisk, Strzeliska, Strzeliska Nowe, Strzylcze?); pop. 828; 50 km SE of Lvov; 49°31'/24°24'; AMG, COH, EGRS, GYLA, HSL, HSL2, JGFF, PHP2, SF.

Novyye Veledniki, Ukr. (Vladnik, Veledniki); 170 km WNW of Kiyev; 51°19'/28°28'; SF.

Novyy Konstantinov, Ukr. (Konstantin Chadash, Konstantin Khadash, Kostatin, Novo Konstantinov, Novokonstantinov, Nowo Konstantinow); pop. 1,612; 62 km WNW of Vinnitsa; 49°29'/27°44'; EDRD, HSL, JGFF, LDL, LYV, SF.

Novyy Oleksinets, Ukr. (Aleksnitz, Novy Oleksiniec, Novyy Aleksinets, Nowy Aleksiniec, Oleksinets Novy); pop. 6; 101 km SSW of Rovno; 49°50'/25°30'; EJ, SF.

Novyy Pikov, Ukr. (Novi Pikov, Novyy Pykiv); pop. 1,614; 45

km NNW of Vinnitsa; 49°34'/28°16'.

Novyy Pochayev, Ukr. (Poczajow Nowy); pop. 1,083; 88 km SSW of Rovno; 50°00'/25°31'; COH.

Novyy Pogost, Byel. (Pogost Novy, Pohost Nowy); pop. 159; 176 km W of Vitebsk; 55°30'/27°29'.

Novyy Pykiv, *see* Novyy Pikov.

Novyy Rozhan, Byel. (Rozan Nowy); pop. 13; 101 km NE of Pinsk; 52°47'/27°07'.

Novyy Sverzhen, Byel. (Nowy Swershen, Sverzhna, Swiercna, Swierzan Nowy, Swierzen Nowy, Swierzen Stary?); pop. 425; 69 km SW of Minsk; 53°27'/26°44'; EDRD, GUM3, GUM4, GUM5, GUM6, SF.

Novyy Vitebsk, *see* Novo Vitebsk.

Novyy Vitkov, Ukr. (Vitkov, Vitkuv Novy, Witkow Nowy, Witkow Stary); pop. 987; 62 km NNE of Lvov; 50°19'/24°29'; EGRS, GUM4, PHP2, SF, YB.

Novyy Yarychev, Ukr. (Jaryczow, Jaryczow Nowy, Jaryczow Stary, Yartchev); pop. 926; 26 km NE of Lvov; 49°55'/24°18'; CAHJP, COH, EDRD, EGRS, GUM3, GUM4, HSL, LDL, PHP2, SF, WS.

Novyy Zlatopol, *see* Novo Zlatopol.

Nowa Biala, Pol.; pop. 6; 75 km SSE of Krakow; 49°27'/20°09'.

Nowa Brzeznica, Pol. POCEM, SF. This town was not found in BGN gazetteers under the given spelling.

Nowa Gora, Pol.; 26 km WNW of Krakow; 50°11'/19°36'; CAHJP, PHP3.

Nowa Grobla, Pol. (Novaia Greblia); pop. 10; 38 km NNE of Przemysl; 50°05'/23°01'.

Nowa Maliszewa, GA. This town was not found in BGN gazetteers under the given spelling.

Nowa Mysz, *see* Novaya Mysh.

Nowa Schita, LDL. This pre-World War I community was not found in BGN gazetteers.

Nowa Slupia, *see* Slupia Nowa.

Nowa Sol, Pol. (Neusalz); pop. 46; 107 km SW of Poznan; 51°48'/15°43'; EDRD, GUM3, GUM4, GUM6.

Nowawes, *see* Babelsberg.

Nowa Wies, Pol.; 50 km SE of Lodz; 51°24'/19°50'; EJ, PHP3, PHP4. According to BGN, there are 118 towns in Poland today named Nowa Wies, which means "new village."

Nowa Wies (near Bedzin), Pol.; pop. 20; 50 km S of Czestochowa; 50°21'/19°06'.

Nowa Wies (near Czestochowa), Pol.; pop. 7; 13 km SE of Czestochowa; 50°44'/19°10'.

Nowa Wies (near Dobromil), Ukr.; pop. 29; 38 km SSW of Lvov; 49°35'/23°40'.

Nowa Wies (near Grojec), Pol.; pop. 5; 56 km S of Warszawa; 51°49'/21°05'.

Nowa Wies (near Ilza), Pol.; pop. 6; 69 km WSW of Lublin; 51°06'/21°33'.

Nowa Wies (near Jedrzejow), Pol.; pop. 5; 50 km NNE of Krakow; 50°30'/20°18'.

Nowa Wies (near Katowice), Pol. (Wirek); pop. 30; 62 km S of Czestochowa; 50°16'/18°52'. This town is now called Wirek.

Nowa Wies (near Kolbuszowa), Pol.; pop. 8; 88 km WNW of Przemysl; 50°14'/21°44'.

Nowa Wies (near Krasnystaw), Pol.; pop. 12; 62 km SE of Lublin; 50°49'/23°09'.

Nowa Wies (near Ostroleka), Pol.; pop. 30; 101 km N of Warszawa; 53°06'/21°25'; GA.

Nowa Wies (near Pultusk), Pol.; pop. 29; 94 km WNW of Warszawa; 52°46'/19°58'.

Nowa Wies (near Sandomierz), Pol.; pop. 9; 88 km SSW of Lublin; 50°41'/21°45'.

Nowa Wies (near Sedziszow), Pol.; pop. 21; 69 km E of Czestochowa; 50°39'/20°08'.

Nowa Wies (near Sochaczew), Pol.; pop. 7; 50 km WSW of Warszawa; 52°15'/20°16'.

Nowa Wies (near Turobin), Pol.; pop. 21; 101 km N of Warszawa; 53°06'/21°25'.

Nowa Wies Czudecka, Pol.; pop. 4; 69 km W of Przemysl;

49°56'/21°49'.

Nowa Wilejka, *see* Naujoji Vilnia.

Nowd Bychow, LDL. This pre-World War I community was not found in BGN gazetteers.

Nowe, Pol.; pop. 31; 82 km S of Gdansk; 53°39'/18°45'; GYLA, POCEM.

Nowe Brzesko, (B Zhesha Nova, Novobrzesk); GA, LDL, SF. This town was not found in BGN gazetteers under the given spelling.

Nowe Marcinkowo, Pol. (Neumarkt im Schlesien); pop. 62; 157 km ESE of Gdansk; 53°50'/20°54'.

Nowe Miasto, Pol. (Ir Chadash, Novi Miasto); pop. 780; 50 km NW of Warszawa; 52°39'/20°38'; AMG, CAHJP, COH, EJ, GUM3, GUM4, GUM5, GUM6, HSL, HSL, JGFF, PHP4, SF, WS, YB. Nowe Miasto means "new town" in Polish, which explains the large number of locations with that name. See listings below.

Nowe Miasto (Lwow), Ukr.; pop. 259; 82 km SW of Lvov; 49°37'/22°52'; EGRS, HSL, PHP2, PHP3, SF.

Nowe Miasto Lubawskie, Pol.; pop. 61; 120 km SE of Gdansk; 53°25'/19°36'.

Nowe Miasto nad Pilica, Pol. (Neishtat Oif der Piltza); pop. 1,667; 75 km E of Lodz; 51°38'/20°35'; GA, LDS, PHP1, SF.

Nowe Miasto nad Warta, Pol. (Neustadt a Warthe); pop. 16; 50 km SE of Poznan; 52°06'/17°25'; EJ, HSL, LDS.

Nowe Mlyny, Pol.; pop. 27; Described in the *Black Book* as being in the Kielce region of Poland, this town was not found in BGN gazetteers.

Nowe Polaszki, Pol.; pop. 3; 50 km SW of Gdansk; 54°02'/18°08'.

Nowe Pole, Pol. (Nowopole); pop. 4; 62 km WSW of Lublin; 51°10'/21°41'; HSL.

Nowe Siolo (Lwow), Pol.; pop. 125; 50 km NNE of Przemysl; 50°14'/23°10'; PHP2.

Nowe Siolo (Stanislawow), Ukr.; pop. 46; 38 km SSW of Lvov; 49°35'/23°40'.

Nowe Siolo (Tarnopol), Ukr.; pop. 109; 114 km S of Rovno; 49°39'/26°04'.

Nowe Swieciany, *see* Svencioneliai.

Nowe Warpno, Pol. (Neuwarp); pop. 3; 38 km NW of Szczecin; 53°44'/14°18'.

Nowgorod, *see* Novogorod.

Nowica, *see* Novitsa.

Nowiny, Pol.; 75 km N of Przemysl; 50°27'/23°08'; HSL.

Nowiny Brdowskie, Pol.; 82 km NW of Lodz; 52°20'/18°45'; GA, PHP1.

Nowiny Horynieckie, Pol.; pop. 44; 62 km NNE of Przemysl; 50°14'/23°23'.

Nowiny Pokarczmiska, Pol.; pop. 113; 75 km NW of Lublin; 51°49'/22°03'.

Nowociolka Kosciukowa, *see* Novoselka Kostyukova.

Nowogard, Pol. (Naugard); pop. 26; 45 km NE of Szczecin; 53°39'/15°07'.

Nowogrod, Pol. (Novogrod); pop. 514; 88 km W of Bialystok; 53°14'/21°52'; CAHJP, COH, HSL, LDL, LDS, PHP4, POCEM, SF, WS, YB.

Nowogrodek, *see* Novogrudok.

Nowogrudok, *see* Novogrudok.

Nowojelnia, *see* Novoyelnya.

Nowojowa Gora, Pol.; pop. 20; 19 km W of Krakow; 50°07'/19°40'.

Nowo Konstantinow, *see* Novyy Konstantinov.

Nowomalin, *see* Novo Malin.

Nowomirgorod, *see* Novomirgorod.

Nowomodna, Pol.; pop. 4; 88 km SSW of Bialystok; 52°26'/22°29'.

Nowomoskowsk, *see* Novomoskovsk.

Nowopole, *see* Nowe Pole.

Nowo Radomsko, *see* Radomsko.

Noworodczyce, *see* Novorodchitsy.

Nowosiadlo, Pol.; pop. 36; 75 km W of Warszawa; 52°26'/19°55'.

Nowosiclka Jazlowiecka, see Novsyulka Yazlovetska.

Nowosielce, Pol.; pop. 36; 45 km NW of Przemysl; 50°04'/22°25'; EGRS.

Nowosielce Gniewosz, Pol.; pop. 56; 56 km SW of Przemysl; 49°34'/22°04'.

Nowosielce Kozickie, Pol.; pop. 12; 32 km SSW of Przemysl; 49°34'/22°32'.

Nowosielec, Pol.; pop. 24; 82 km NW of Przemysl; 50°27'/22°10'; HSL, LDL, SF.

Nowosielica, Ukr.; pop. 43; 62 km SW of Lvov; 49°35'/23°15'. This town was located on an interwar map of Poland but does not appear in contemporary gazetteers. Map coordinates are approximate.

Nowo Sinjawa, (Siniava); SF. This town was not found in BGN gazetteers under the given spelling.

Nowosiolka, see Novosyulka.

Nowosiolka Jazlowiecka, see Novsyulka Yazlovetska.

Nowosiolki, AMG, GA, GUM3. See also Novoselki; Novosyulki Ruske. An interwar map of Poland notes 68 towns named Nowosiolki, which means "new little hamlet." The AMG reference is unknown. GA refers to a town near Chelm. GUM3 refers to a town in the Bialystok area. in addition to the towns lised below, the Black Book notes a town in the interwar Polish province of Polesie (pop. 98).

Nowosiolki (near Konstantynow), Pol.; pop. 21; 69 km S of Bialystok; 52°33'/23°11'.

Nowosiolki (near Lisko), Pol.; pop. 35; 50 km SSW of Przemysl; 49°25'/22°28'.

Nowosiolki (near Przemysl), Pol.; pop. 31; 26 km S of Przemysl; 49°38'/22°44'.

Nowosiolki (near Slonim), Byel.; pop. 25; 114 km NW of Pinsk; 52°57'/25°09'.

Nowosiolki (near Tomaszow Lubelski), Pol.; pop. 33; 114 km NE of Przemysl; 50°32'/23°55'.

Nowosiolki Dydynskie, Pol.; pop. 9; 26 km S of Przemysl; 49°38'/22°44'.

Nowosiolki Goscinne, see Novoselki.

Nowosiolki Kadynalskie, Pol.; pop. 45; Described in the Black Book as being in the Lwow region of Poland, this town was not found in BGN gazetteers.

Nowosiolki Liskie, Pol.; pop. 45; Described in the Black Book as being in the Tarnopol region of Poland, this town was not found in BGN gazetteers.

Nowosiolki Nowoczeskie, Pol.; pop. 31; Described in the Black Book as being in the Wolyn region of Poland, this town was not found in BGN gazetteers.

Nowosiolki Przednie, Pol.; pop. 29; 88 km NNE of Przemysl; 50°23'/23°40'.

Nowosybkow, see Novozybkov.

Nowoszyce, see Novoshitse.

Nowotaniec, Pol. (Novitanitz); pop. 42; 62 km SW of Przemysl; 49°31'/22°02'; EGRS, HSL, LDL, SF.

Nowy Aleksiniec, see Novyy Oleksinets.

Nowy Bartkow, GA. This town was not found in BGN gazetteers under the given spelling.

Nowy Bytom, Pol.; pop. 62 km S of Czestochowa; 50°17'/18°53'; PHP3.

Nowy Dwor, Pol. (Neuhof); pop. 402; 62 km NNE of Bialystok; 53°38'/23°33'; GA, GUM4, LDL, PHP1, SF, YB. See also Novyy Dvor; Nowy Dwor Maziowecki. There are no less than 80 towns in Poland, the USSR and Czechoslovakia called Novy Dvor, Novy Dvur or Nowy Dwor, all of which mean "new court." Shown here is the town near Bialystok. This name also commonly refers to Nowy Dwor Mazowiecki near Warszawa. The GUM4 entry refers to a town in the interwar Polish province of Polesie. The LDL entry does not specify which Nowy Dwor.

Nowy Dwor Maziowecki, (Nowy Dwor);

Nowy Dwor Mazowiecki, Pol. (Mazoviechi); pop. 3,916; 26 km WNW of Warszawa; 52°26'/20°43'; AMG, CAHJP, COH, EJ, FRG, GA, GUM3, GUM4, GUM5, GUM6, HSL, HSL2, JGFF, LYV, PHP4, POCEM, SF.

Nowy Dzikow, see Dzikow Nowy.

Nowyi Bug, see Novyy Bug.

Nowyja Dorogi, (Doraganova); LDL, SF. This town was not found in BGN gazetteers under the given spelling.

Nowy Korczyn, Pol. (Ir Khadash, Nayshtut, Neustadt, Novi Korchin, Novi Kortchin); pop. 2,478; 69 km NE of Krakow; 50°18'/20°49'; AMG, CAHJP, EDRD, GA, GUM3, GUM5, GYLA, JGFF, LDS, LYV, SF.

Nowy Korzec, Pol.; pop. 232; Described in the Black Book as being in the Wolyn region of Poland, this town was not found in BGN gazetteers.

Nowy Lupkow, Pol.; pop. 82 km SSW of Przemysl; 49°15'/22°05'; AMG.

Nowy Modlin, Pol. (Modlin Nowy); pop. 10; 32 km NW of Warszawa; 52°28'/20°42'.

Nowy Pohost, see Pogost.

Nowy Sacz, Pol. (Nay Sants, Naya Sandets, Neisantz, Neu Sandez, Novi Sach, Novi Sansh, Novy Sacz, Sandets, Sandz, Sants, Sanz, Tsants, Tzanz); pop. 9,009; 75 km ESE of Krakow; 49°38'/20°43'; AMG, CAHJP, COH, EDRD, EGRS, EJ, FRG, GA, GUM3, GUM4, GUM5, GYLA, HSL, HSL2, JGFF, LDL, LYV, PHP2, PHP3, POCEM, SF, YB.

Nowy Staw, Pol. (Neuteich, Neuteich Freistaat); pop. 40; 32 km ESE of Gdansk; 54°08'/19°01'.

Nowy Swershen, see Novyy Sverzhen.

Nowy Swiat, Pol.; 75 km NNE of Poznan; 52°59'/17°44'; GA.

Nowy Swierzen, GUM4, GUM5, GUM6. This town was not found in BGN gazetteers under the given spelling.

Nowy Targ, Pol. (Neumarkt, Novi Targ, Novy Targ, Noymark); pop. 1,342; 75 km S of Krakow; 49°29'/20°02'; AMG, CAHJP, COH, EGRS, GA, GUM3, GUM4, GUM5, HSL, JGFF, LDS, LYV, PHGB, PHP3, POCEM, SF, YB.

Nowy Tomysl, Pol. (Neutomischel); pop. 28; 56 km WSW of Poznan; 52°19'/16°09'; GUM4, HSL.

Nowy Wisnicz, see Wisnicz Nowy.

Nowy Zagorz, Pol.; 50 km SW of Przemysl; 49°32'/22°16'; YB.

Nowy Zmigrod, see Zmigrod Nowy.

Noyaya Mysh, LDL. This pre-World War I community was not found in BGN gazetteers.

Noymark, see Nowy Targ.

Noymarkt, see Neumark.

Nozankovitz, see Nizhankovichi.

Nozdrzec, Pol.; pop. 10; 38 km WSW of Przemysl; 49°47'/22°13'.

Nsagyszeben, LDL. This pre-World War I community was not found in BGN gazetteers.

Nudysze, see Nudyzhi Peski.

Nudyzhe, see Nudyzhi Peski.

Nudyzhi Peski, Ukr. (Nudysze, Nudyzhe); pop. 21; 176 km N of Lvov; 51°23'/24°07'.

Nujno, see Nuyno.

Numbrecht, Germ.; pop. 15; 45 km E of Koln; 50°54'/07°33'.

Nupaky, Cz.; pop. 5; 19 km ESE of Praha; 50°00'/14°36'.

Nur, Pol.; pop. 400; 75 km SW of Bialystok; 52°40'/22°19'; GUM5, JGFF, LDL, LDS, PHP4, POCEM, SF.

Nuremberg, see Nurnberg.

Nurmuiza, Lat.; pop. 1; 88 km WNW of Riga; 57°14'/22°46'.

Nurnberg, Germ. (Nuremberg, Wohrd); pop. 7,502; 150 km NNW of Munchen; 49°27'/11°05'; AMG, CAHJP, EJ, GED, GUM3, GUM4, GUM5, GUM6, HSL, HSL2, ISH1, JGFF, LDS, PHGB, PHGBW, PHP1, PHP2, PHP4.

Nurtingen, Germ.; 19 km SE of Stuttgart; 48°38'/09°21'; PHGBW.

Nurzec, Pol.; pop. 38; 75 km S of Bialystok; 52°29'/23°10'; GA.

Nurzyna, Pol.; pop. 9; 88 km N of Lublin; 51°58'/22°28'.

Nuseni, Rom.; pop. 48; 62 km NE of Cluj; 47°06'/24°12'.

Nusfalau, Rom. (Apanagyfalu, Apanagyfalva, Szilagynagyfalu); 82 km WNW of Cluj; 47°12'/22°44'; AMG, HSL, JGFF, PHR2.

Nusmice, Pol.; pop. 31; Described in the *Black Book* as being in the Lwow region of Poland, this town was not found in BGN gazetteers.

Nussdorf an der Traisen, Aus.; pop. 5; 50 km WNW of Wien; 48°21'/15°42'.

Nussloch, Germ.; pop. 21; 75 km NW of Stuttgart; 49°20'/08°42'; GED, LDS, PHGBW.

Nustar, Yug.; pop. 6; 139 km WNW of Beograd; 45°20'/18°51'.

Nuttlar, Germ.; pop. 7; 114 km NE of Koln; 51°22'/08°26'.

Nuyno, Ukr. (Nujno); pop. 19; 139 km NW of Rovno; 51°33'/24°54'.

Nyagova, *see* Olnkhovtsy.

Nyarad, Hung.; pop. 4; 101 km N of Nagykanizsa; 47°17'/17°22'; HSL.

Nyaradgalfalva, *see* Galesti.

Nyaradszentlaszlo, *see* Sanvasii.

Nyaradszereda, *see* Miercurea Nirajului.

Nyaradto, Rom.; 75 km ESE of Cluj; 46°29'/24°28'; HSL, HSL2. This town was located on a pre-World War I map, but does not appear in contemporary gazetteers.

Nyaregyhaza, Hung.; pop. 8; 45 km ESE of Budapest; 47°15'/19°30'.

Nyarlo, *see* Mierlau.

Nyek, *see* Vinica.

Nyekladhaza, Hung.; 19 km SSE of Miskolc; 47°59'/20°50'; HSL, PHH.

Nyemiruv, *see* Nemirov (near Lvov).

Nyepolomitse, *see* Niepolomice.

Nyereshaza, *see* Neresnitsa.

Nyergesujfalu, Hung.; pop. 39; 50 km WNW of Budapest; 47°46'/18°33'; HSL.

Nyeshvyezh, *see* Nesvizh.

Nyim, Hung.; pop. 2; 94 km NE of Nagykanizsa; 46°48'/18°07'.

Nyirabrany, Hung. (Szentgyorgyabrany); pop. 167; 107 km ESE of Miskolc; 47°33'/22°02'; LDS, PHH.

Nyiracsad, Hung.; pop. 210; 101 km ESE of Miskolc; 47°36'/21°59'; AMG, HSL, LDS, PHH.

Nyirad, Hung.; pop. 2; 75 km NNE of Nagykanizsa; 47°00'/17°27'.

Nyiradony, Hung.; pop. 229; 94 km ESE of Miskolc; 47°41'/21°55'; AMG, HSL, LDS, PHH.

Nyirbator, Hung.; pop. 1,873; 101 km ESE of Miskolc; 47°50'/22°08'; AMG, COH, GUM3, HSL, HSL2, JGFF, LDL, LDS, PHH.

Nyirbeltek, Hung.; pop. 128; 107 km ESE of Miskolc; 47°42'/22°08'; HSL, PHH.

Nyirbogat, Hung.; pop. 322; 101 km ESE of Miskolc; 47°48'/22°04'; HSL, LDL, LDS, PHH.

Nyirbogdany, Hung.; pop. 150; 82 km E of Miskolc; 48°03'/21°53'; AMG, HSL, PHH.

Nyircsaholy, Hung.; pop. 133; 120 km E of Miskolc; 47°54'/22°20'; PHH.

Nyircsaszari, Hung.; pop. 45; 107 km E of Miskolc; 47°52'/22°11'; HSL.

Nyirderzs, Hung. (Derzs); pop. 57; 107 km E of Miskolc; 47°54'/22°10'; LDS, PHH.

Nyiregyhaza, Hung.; pop. 5,134; 69 km E of Miskolc; 47°57'/21°43'; AMG, COH, EDRD, EJ, GUM3, GUM4, GUM6, HSL, HSL2, JGFF, LDL, LDS, LJEE, PHH.

Nyires, *possibly* Nyirjes.

Nyirgelse, Hung.; pop. 52; 94 km ESE of Miskolc; 47°45'/21°59'; HSL, LDS, PHH.

Nyirgyulaj, Hung.; pop. 89; 101 km E of Miskolc; 47°53'/22°06'; HSL, PHH.

Nyiri, Hung.; pop. 5; 69 km NE of Miskolc; 48°30'/21°27'.

Nyiribrony, Hung. (Ibrony, Nifribony); pop. 34; 88 km E of Miskolc; 48°01'/21°58'; LDS.

Nyirjako, Hung.; pop. 74; 94 km E of Miskolc; 48°02'/22°05'; PHH.

Nyirjes, Hung. (Nyires?); BGN lists two possible localities with this name located at 47°54'/19°58' and 47°55'/21°46'. EDRD,

HSL.

Nyirkarasz, Hung.; pop. 164; 94 km E of Miskolc; 48°06'/22°06'; HSL, LDS, PHH.

Nyirkata, Hung. (Gebe); pop. 137; 114 km E of Miskolc; 47°52'/22°16'; HSL, HSL2, PHH.

Nyirkercs, Hung.; pop. 35; 94 km E of Miskolc; 48°01'/22°03'.

Nyirlovo, Hung.; pop. 46; 107 km ENE of Miskolc; 48°12'/22°11'.

Nyirlugos, Hung.; pop. 145; 107 km ESE of Miskolc; 47°42'/22°03'; HSL, LDL, LDS, PHH.

Nyirmada, Hung.; pop. 531; 107 km E of Miskolc; 48°04'/22°12'; AMG, GUM3, GUM4, HSL, HSL2, JGFF, LDL, LDS, PHH.

Nyirmartonfalva, Hung.; pop. 54; 101 km ESE of Miskolc; 47°35'/21°54'; PHH.

Nyirmeggyes, Hung.; pop. 139; 107 km E of Miskolc; 47°55'/22°16'; AMG, HSL, LDL, LDS, PHH.

Nyirmihalydi, Hung.; pop. 74; 94 km ESE of Miskolc; 47°44'/21°59'; LDS, PHH.

Nyirparasznya, Hung.; pop. 34; 114 km E of Miskolc; 48°02'/22°17'.

Nyirpazony, Hung.; pop. 33; 75 km E of Miskolc; 47°59'/21°48'.

Nyirpilis, Hung.; pop. 33; 107 km ESE of Miskolc; 47°47'/22°11'; HSL.

Nyirszollos, Hung.; pop. 9; 69 km E of Miskolc; 48°01'/21°42'.

Nyirtass, Hung.; pop. 248; 94 km ENE of Miskolc; 48°07'/22°02'; AMG, HSL, LDS, PHH.

Nyirtet, Hung.; pop. 28; 88 km E of Miskolc; 48°01'/21°56'.

Nyirtura, Hung.; pop. 40; 82 km E of Miskolc; 48°01'/21°50'.

Nyirvaja, LDL. This pre-World War I community was not found in BGN gazetteers.

Nyirvasvari, Hung.; pop. 44; 107 km ESE of Miskolc; 47°49'/22°11'.

Nyitra, *see* Nitra.

Nyitrabanya, *see* Handlova.

Nyitra Novak, *see* Novaky.

Nymburk, Cz.; pop. 106; 45 km ENE of Praha; 50°11'/15°03'.

Nyoger, Hung.; pop. 4; 88 km N of Nagykanizsa; 47°11'/16°56'.

Nyomar, Hung.; pop. 3; 26 km N of Miskolc; 48°17'/20°49'; HSL.

Nyomja, Hung.; pop. 1; 120 km ESE of Nagykanizsa; 46°00'/18°27'.

Nyrany, Cz.; pop. 39; 101 km SW of Praha; 49°43'/13°12'.

Nyrkov, Ukr. (Nyrkow); pop. 53; 62 km NNW of Chernovtsy; 48°49'/25°36'.

Nyrkow, *see* Nyrkov.

Nyrsko, Cz.; pop. 139; 126 km SW of Praha; 49°18'/13°09'.

Nysa, Pol. (Neisse); pop. 220; 69 km SSE of Wroclaw; 50°30'/17°20'; GUM3, GUM4, HSL, HSL2, JGFF, LDS.

Oaffa, *see* Feodosiya.

Oaia, Rom.; pop. 17; 88 km ESE of Cluj; 46°27'/24°39'.

Oar, Rom.; pop. 32; 133 km NW of Cluj; 47°49'/22°43'.

Oarta de Jos, Rom. (Alsovaradja); pop. 25; 88 km NW of Cluj; 47°27'/23°08'.

Oarta de Sus, Rom. (Felsovaradja); pop. 13; 88 km NW of Cluj; 47°28'/23°04'.

Obanya, Hung.; 114 km E of Nagykanizsa; 46°13'/18°25'; HSL, HSL2.

Obarzym, Pol.; pop. 6; 45 km WSW of Przemysl; 49°43'/22°11'.

Obava, Ukr.; 170 km SSW of Lvov; 48°31'/22°48'; AMG.

Obbach, Germ.; pop. 113; 101 km E of Frankfurt am Main; 50°04'/10°06'; GUM5, PHGB.

Obbornhofen, Germ.; pop. 6; 45 km N of Frankfurt am Main; 50°27'/08°50'.

Obdach, Aus.; pop. 4; 56 km WSW of Graz; 47°04'/14°41'.

Obdenice, Cz.; pop. 5; 62 km S of Praha; 49°33'/14°22'.

Obecnice, Cz.; pop. 8; 62 km SSW of Praha; 49°43'/13°57'.

Obecse, *see* Obesce.

Obel, *see* Obeliai.

Obeliai, Lith. (Abeil, Abel, Abeli, Abeliai, Obel); pop. 680; 146 km N of Vilnius; 55°56'/25°48'; AMG, GUM5, HSL, JGFF,

SF, YL.

Obelniki, Pol.; pop. 3; 88 km N of Lublin; 51°59'/22°35'.

Obenhausen, Germ.; 94 km ESE of Stuttgart; 48°14'/10°11'; PHGB.

Oberaltertheim, Germ.; pop. 27; 88 km ESE of Frankfurt am Main; 49°44'/09°46'; GUM5, HSL, PHGB.

Oberammergau, Germ.; pop. 5; 69 km SSW of Munchen; 47°36'/11°04'; EJ.

Ober Apsa, *see* Verkhneye Vodyanoye.

Ober Asphe, *see* Oberasphe.

Oberasphe, Germ. (Ober Asphe); pop. 22; 101 km N of Frankfurt am Main; 50°57'/08°39'; LDS.

Oberaula, Germ.; pop. 91; 101 km NNE of Frankfurt am Main; 50°51'/09°28'; HSL, LDS.

Oberberg, Aus.; pop. 33; 45 km SSE of Wien; 47°51'/16°30'.

Oberbieber, Germ.; 62 km SE of Koln; 50°29'/07°30'; GED.

Oberbildein, Aus.; pop. 2; 75 km ENE of Graz; 47°08'/16°28'.

Ober Bistra, *see* Verkhnyaya Bystra.

Oberbrechen, Germ.; 50 km WNW of Frankfurt am Main; 50°21'/08°12'; GED.

Oberdollendorf, Germ.; 32 km SE of Koln; 50°42'/07°11'; GED.

Oberdorf, Germ.; pop. 148; 133 km SSE of Stuttgart; 47°37'/09°34'; AMG, HSL2, JGFF, PHGBW.

Oberdorf in Wurtemberg, HSL. This pre-World War I community was not found in BGN gazetteers.

Oberehrenbach, Germ.; 32 km N of Nurnberg; 49°41'/11°12'; PHGB.

Oberelsbach, Germ.; pop. 41; 114 km NE of Frankfurt am Main; 50°26'/10°08'; GUM5, PHGB.

Obererlenbach, Germ.; 19 km N of Frankfurt am Main; 50°14'/08°41'; LDS.

Oberessfeld, Germ.; pop. 4; 101 km NNW of Nurnberg; 50°16'/10°33'.

Obereuerheim, Germ.; 75 km NW of Nurnberg; 50°00'/10°22'; PHGB.

Obergimpern, Germ.; pop. 23; 56 km NNW of Stuttgart; 49°15'/09°02'; PHGBW.

Ober Gleen, *see* Obergleen.

Obergleen, Germ. (Ober Gleen); pop. 32; 82 km NNE of Frankfurt am Main; 50°45'/09°08'.

Oberglogau, *see* Glogowek.

Obergrombach, Germ.; pop. 3; 56 km WNW of Stuttgart; 49°05'/08°35'; LDS, PHGBW.

Obergunzburg, Germ.; 94 km SW of Munchen; 47°51'/10°25'; PHGB.

Oberhaching, Germ.; pop. 3; 19 km S of Munchen; 48°02'/11°36'.

Oberhausen, Germ.; pop. 625; 62 km N of Koln; 51°28'/06°51'; GED, JGFF, PHGBW.

Oberhausen (near Augsburg), Germ.; 50 km SW of Munchen; 47°57'/10°59'; PHGB.

Oberhausen (Wallhalben), Germ.; pop. 33; 126 km SSW of Frankfurt am Main; 49°19'/07°31'.

Oberhollabrunn, *see* Hollabrunn.

Oberingelbach, Germ.; pop. 5; 62 km ESE of Koln; 50°41'/07°43'.

Ober Ingelheim, *see* Ingelheim.

Oberkaufungen, Germ.; pop. 1; 126 km S of Hannover; 51°16'/09°38'.

Ober Klingen, Germ.; pop. 28; 38 km SSE of Frankfurt am Main; 49°49'/08°53'; LDS.

Oberkotzau, Germ.; pop. 4; 107 km NNE of Nurnberg; 50°16'/11°56'; PHGB.

Oberlahnstein, Germ.; pop. 44; 82 km W of Frankfurt am Main; 50°18'/07°37'; GUM5.

Oberlangenstadt, Germ.; pop. 18; 88 km N of Nurnberg; 50°11'/11°15'; JGFF, PHGB.

Oberlanzendorf, Aus.; pop. 1; 19 km SE of Wien; 48°06'/16°27'.

Oberlauringen, Germ.; pop. 65; 101 km NW of Nurnberg; 50°13'/10°23'; AMG, GUM5, JGFF, PHGB.

Oberlenningen, Germ.; 32 km SE of Stuttgart; 48°33'/09°27';

PHGBW.

Oberlistingen, Germ.; pop. 3; 107 km S of Hannover; 51°27'/09°14'.

Oberloisdorf, Aus.; pop. 6; 88 km S of Wien; 47°27'/16°30'.

Oberlustadt, Germ. (Lustadt); pop. 26; 82 km WNW of Stuttgart; 49°15'/08°16'; GUM5, JGFF.

Obermassing, Germ.; 45 km SE of Nurnberg; 49°07'/11°19'; PHGB.

Ober Mockstadt, Germ.; pop. 22; 38 km NNE of Frankfurt am Main; 50°21'/08°58'.

Obermoschel, Germ.; pop. 35; 75 km SW of Frankfurt am Main; 49°44'/07°46'; GED, HSL.

Obernalb, Aus.; pop. 1; 75 km NW of Wien; 48°45'/15°56'.

Obernau, Germ.; 38 km ESE of Frankfurt am Main; 49°56'/09°08'; PHGB.

Obernbreit, Germ. (Marktbreit); pop. 164; 69 km WNW of Nurnberg; 49°39'/10°10'; GUM4, GUM5, HSL, HSL2, JGFF, PHGB.

Oberndorf, Germ.; pop. 75 km SSW of Stuttgart; 48°17'/08°34'; CAHJP, HSL, JGFF, PHGBW.

Oberndorf an der Melk, Aus.; pop. 2; 88 km WSW of Wien; 48°03'/15°13'.

Obernkirchen, Germ.; pop. 60; 45 km WSW of Hannover; 52°16'/09°08'.

Obernzell, Germ.; 157 km NE of Munchen; 48°34'/13°39'; GUM3.

Obernzenn, Germ.; 45 km WSW of Nurnberg; 49°27'/10°28'; HSL, PHGB.

Ober Olm, Germ.; pop. 39; 38 km SW of Frankfurt am Main; 49°57'/08°11'.

Oberowisheim, Germ.; 56 km NW of Stuttgart; 49°09'/08°41'; PHGBW.

Oberpetersdorf, Aus.; pop. 6; 69 km S of Wien; 47°37'/16°23'.

Oberpfaffenhofen, Germ.; pop. 1; 26 km SW of Munchen; 48°04'/11°16'.

Oberpleichfeld, Germ.; 88 km WNW of Nurnberg; 49°53'/10°05'; PHGB.

Oberpullendorf, Aus.; pop. 16; 82 km SSE of Wien; 47°30'/16°31'.

Oberrabnitz, Aus.; pop. 4; 82 km NE of Graz; 47°29'/16°21'.

Ober Ramstadt, Germ.; pop. 65; 32 km SSE of Frankfurt am Main; 49°50'/08°45'; LDS.

Oberramstadt, Germ.; 50 km SW of Nurnberg; 49°19'/10°26'; AMG.

Oberreidenbach, Germ.; 101 km SW of Frankfurt am Main; 49°42'/07°28'; GED.

Oberriedenberg, Germ.; pop. 8; 88 km ENE of Frankfurt am Main; 50°20'/09°52'; GUM5.

Ober Rina, *see* Rona de Sus.

Oberrine, *see* Rona de Sus.

Oberschwarzach, Germ.; 62 km WNW of Nurnberg; 49°52'/10°25'; PHGB.

Ober Seemen, *see* Oberseemen.

Oberseemen, Germ. (Ober Seemen); pop. 76; 56 km NE of Frankfurt am Main; 50°25'/09°14'; CAHJP, LDS.

Obersiebenbrunn, Aus.; pop. 20; 26 km NE of Wien; 48°16'/16°42'.

Obersitzko, *see* Obrzycko.

Oberstdorf, Germ.; pop. 2; 126 km SW of Munchen; 47°24'/10°17'; ISH1.

Oberstein, HSL. A number of towns share this name. It was not possible to determine from available information which one is being referenced.

Obersteinabrunn, Aus.; pop. 3; 56 km NW of Wien; 48°38'/16°01'.

Oberstockstall, Aus.; pop. 3; 45 km WNW of Wien; 48°27'/15°55'.

Oberstotzingen, Germ.; 82 km ESE of Stuttgart; 48°32'/10°13'; PHGBW.

Oberstreu, Germ.; 120 km ENE of Frankfurt am Main; 50°24'/10°19'; PHGB.

Oberthulba, Germ.; pop. 41; 94 km ENE of Frankfurt am Main; 50°12'/09°58'; GUM5, PHGB.

Obertin, Ukr. (Obertyn); pop. 1,131; 75 km WNW of Chernovtsy; 48°42'/25°10'; AMG, COH, EGRS, GUM5, GUM6, HSL, HSL2, JGFF, PHP2, SF.

Obertraun, Aus.; pop. 7; 56 km ESE of Salzburg; 47°33'/13°41'.

Obertshausen, Germ.; pop. 2; 13 km ESE of Frankfurt am Main; 50°04'/08°51'.

Obertyn, see Obertin.

Oberursel, Germ.; pop. 40; 19 km NW of Frankfurt am Main; 50°12'/08°35'.

Ober Visho, see Viseu de Sus.

Obervorschutz, Germ.; 126 km N of Frankfurt am Main; 51°09'/09°21'; LDS.

Oberwaldbehrungen, Germ.; pop. 11; 114 km NE of Frankfurt am Main; 50°26'/10°11'; PHGB.

Oberwaltersdorf, Aus.; pop. 30; 32 km S of Wien; 47°58'/16°19'.

Oberwart, Aus.; pop. 138; 62 km NE of Graz; 47°17'/16°12'.

Oberwarth, see Warth.

Oberweiler, Germ. JGFF. A number of towns share this name. It was not possible to determine from available information which one is being referenced.

Oberweilersbach, Germ.; 38 km N of Nurnberg; 49°45'/11°08'; PHGB.

Oberwesel, Germ.; pop. 44; 69 km WSW of Frankfurt am Main; 50°06'/07°44'; AMG, EDRD, EJ, JGFF.

Oberwia, Pol. (Obierwia); pop. 6; 107 km N of Warszawa; 53°10'/21°26'.

Oberwikon, LDL. This pre-World War I community was not found in BGN gazetteers.

Ober Wisho, see Viseu de Sus.

Oberwollstadt, Germ.; 32 km N of Frankfurt am Main; 50°18'/08°45'; LDS.

Oberzell, Germ.; 120 km SSE of Stuttgart; 47°45'/09°34'; LDS.

Oberzissen, Germ.; pop. 6; 62 km SSE of Koln; 50°27'/07°12'.

Obesce, Yug. (Obecse); 94 km NNW of Beograd; 45°37'/20°03'; EDRD, HSL2. This town was located on a pre-World War I map, but does not appear in contemporary gazetteers.

Obice, Pol.; pop. 16; 82 km NNE of Krakow; 50°40'/20°35'.

Obiechow, Pol.; pop. 9; 56 km N of Krakow; 50°34'/19°52'.

Obierwia, see Oberwia.

Obilic, Yug. (Obilicevo); pop. 35; 82 km NNW of Skopje; 42°41'/21°05'.

Obilicevo, see Obilic.

Oblajovice, Cz.; pop. 4; 75 km SSE of Praha; 49°27'/14°53'.

Oblarn, Aus. (Oeblarn); pop. 2; 82 km ESE of Salzburg; 47°27'/13°59'.

Oblekon, Pol.; pop. 18; 82 km NE of Krakow; 50°19'/21°01'.

Obnize, Pol.; pop. 13; 82 km SSW of Bialystok; 52°30'/22°36'.

Obodovka, Ukr. (Hobodovka); 126 km E of Lvov; 49°32'/25°40'; COH, EJ, GUM4, LDL, PHR1, SF. This town was located on an interwar map of Poland but does not appear in contemporary gazetteers. Map coordinates are approximate.

Obodovka (Tarnopol), Ukr. (Obodowka); pop. 24; 114 km S of Rovno; 49°38'/25°55'. This town was located on an interwar map of Poland but does not appear in contemporary gazetteers. Map coordinates are approximate.

Obodowka, see Obodovka (Tarnopol).

Obodr, Cz.; pop. 1; 32 km NE of Praha; 50°17'/14°49'.

Oboltsy, Byel. (Oboltzi, Obolzy); 69 km S of Vitebsk; 54°36'/29°50'; SF.

Oboltzi, see Oboltsy.

Obolzy, see Oboltsy.

Obora, Cz.; 82 km WSW of Praha; 49°53'/13°25'; HSL.

Obornik, see Oborniki.

Oborniki, Pol. (Obornik); pop. 137; 32 km NNW of Poznan; 52°39'/16°49'; CAHJP, HSL, LDS.

Oboyan, USSR; pop. 118; 62 km S of Kursk; 51°12'/36°16'.

Obra, Pol.; pop. 5; 69 km SW of Poznan; 52°05'/16°03'.

Obradovci, Yug.; pop. 6; 150 km E of Zagreb; 45°37'/17°57'.

Obran, HSL. This pre-World War I community was not found

in BGN gazetteers.

Obratan, Cz.; pop. 6; 82 km SE of Praha; 49°27'/14°58'.

Obrazow, Pol.; pop. 10; 88 km SW of Lublin; 50°42'/21°39'.

Obreja Veche, see Staraya Obrezha.

Obrigheim, Germ.; 69 km SSW of Frankfurt am Main; 49°36'/08°12'; HSL, JGFF.

Obristvi, Cz.; pop. 6; 32 km N of Praha; 50°18'/14°29'.

Obritz, Aus.; pop. 3; 62 km NNW of Wien; 48°42'/16°09'.

Obritzberg, Aus.; pop. 2; 56 km W of Wien; 48°17'/15°35'.

Obrocz, Pol.; pop. 11; 82 km SE of Lublin; 50°37'/23°02'.

Obrow, Pol.; pop. 11; 62 km NNW of Czestochowa; 51°17'/19°00'.

Obrowiec, Pol.; pop. 9; 101 km ESE of Lublin; 50°48'/23°50'; GA.

Obryn, Byel.; pop. 13; 88 km SW of Minsk; 53°33'/26°20'.

Obryte, Pol.; pop. 65; 56 km N of Warszawa; 52°43'/21°16'.

Obrzycko, Pol. (Obersitzko); pop. 75; 45 km WNW of Poznan; 52°42'/16°32'; CAHJP, HSL, JGFF.

Obsza, Pol.; pop. 84; 62 km N of Przemysl; 50°19'/22°58'; JGFF.

Obszanska Wola, see Wola Obszanska.

Obuda, see Budapest.

Obukhov, Ukr. BGN lists two possible localities with this name located at 48°47'/27°45' and 50°06'/30°38'. JGFF.

Obych, Ukr. (Obycz); pop. 3; 56 km S of Rovno; 50°09'/26°01'.

Obycz, see Obych.

Obytce, Cz.; pop. 6; 114 km SW of Praha; 49°24'/13°22'.

Ochakov, Ukr. (Oczakowbia, Otchakov, Otschakow); pop. 667; 62 km ENE of Odessa; 46°37'/31°33'; GUM3, HSL, LDL, SF.

Ochedzyn, Pol.; pop. 7; 82 km WNW of Czestochowa; 51°18'/18°16'.

Ochiul Alb, see Okyu Alb.

Ochlopow, see Okhlopov.

Ochmanow, Pol.; pop. 3; 26 km ESE of Krakow; 50°00'/20°09'.

Ochota, Pol.; 13 km S of Warszawa; 52°13'/20°59'; HSL.

Ochotnica, see Ochotnica Dolna.

Ochotnica Dolna, Pol. (Ochotnica); pop. 103; 69 km SE of Krakow; 49°32'/20°19'; GUM5, PHP3.

Ochoza, Pol.; pop. 5; 56 km E of Lublin; 51°13'/23°21'.

Ochsenfeld, Germ.; pop. 1; 75 km S of Nurnberg; 48°51'/11°10'.

Ochsenfurt, Germ.; pop. 5; 75 km WNW of Nurnberg; 49°39'/10°05'; EDRD, GUM5, PHGB.

Ochsenhausen, Germ.; 94 km SE of Stuttgart; 48°04'/09°57'; PHGBW.

Ochtendung, Germ.; pop. 50; 69 km SE of Koln; 50°21'/07°23'.

Ochtrup, Germ.; pop. 41; 146 km N of Koln; 52°13'/07°11'.

Ocieka, Pol.; pop. 26; 94 km WNW of Przemysl; 50°08'/21°35'.

Ociesc, Pol.; pop. 39; 88 km S of Warszawa; 51°32'/20°48'.

Ocieseki, Pol.; pop. 20; 107 km NE of Krakow; 50°45'/20°59'.

Ociete, Pol.; pop. 15; 62 km NE of Warszawa; 52°38'/21°48'.

Ockenheim, Germ.; pop. 31; 56 km SW of Frankfurt am Main; 49°56'/07°58'.

Ockershausen, Germ.; 82 km N of Frankfurt am Main; 50°48'/08°45'; LDS.

Ocna, see Okno.

Ocna de Jos, Rom. (Alsosofalva); pop. 9; 120 km E of Cluj; 46°32'/25°08'.

Ocna Dejului, Rom. (Desakna); 45 km NNE of Cluj; 47°07'/23°51'; HSL.

Ocna de Sus, Rom. (Felsosofalu); pop. 3; 120 km E of Cluj; 46°32'/25°09'.

Ocna Sibiului, Rom. (Vizakna); 101 km SSE of Cluj; 45°53'/24°03'; HSL.

Ocna Sugatag, Rom. (Aknasugatag, Okna Sugatag); pop. 169; 120 km N of Cluj; 47°47'/23°56'; COH, HSL, PHR2, SM.

Ocnita, see Oknitsa.

Ocnita Gara, possibly Oknitsa.

Ocs, Hung.; pop. 4; 82 km NNE of Nagykanizsa; 47°00'/17°37'.

Ocsa, Hung.; pop. 94; 32 km SE of Budapest; 47°18'/19°14'; HSL, HSL2, PHH.

Ocseny, Hung.; pop. 27; 107 km W of Szeged; 46°19'/18°46'.

Ocsod, Hung.; pop. 114; 75 km N of Szeged; 46°54'/20°24'; LDS, PHH.

Oczakowbia, see Ochakov.

Oczkow, Pol.; pop. 3; 62 km SW of Krakow; 49°44'/19°15'.

Odechowiec, Pol.; pop. 4; 88 km W of Lublin; 51°19'/21°20'.

Odelsk, Byel.; pop. 163; 214 km WNW of Pinsk; 53°24'/23°46'; HSL, LDL, SF, WS.

Odenbach, Germ.; pop. 27; 88 km SW of Frankfurt am Main; 49°41'/07°39'; GED, JGFF.

Odenberg, Germ.; 13 km NNE of Nurnberg; 49°32'/11°12'; JGFF.

Odenburg, see Sopron.

Odenheim, Germ.; pop. 36; 56 km NW of Stuttgart; 49°11'/08°45'; LDS, PHGBW.

Odenkirchen, Germ.; pop. 90; 38 km WNW of Koln; 51°08'/06°27'.

Odenwald, see Rapla.

Odenwaldstettin, GUM5, PHGBW. This town was not found in BGN gazetteers under the given spelling.

Oderady, Ukr.; pop. 5; 82 km W of Rovno; 50°41'/25°06'.

Oderberg, see Bohumin.

Odernheim, Germ.; 82 km SW of Frankfurt am Main; 49°46'/07°42'; GED, JGFF.

Odess, see Odessa.

Odessa, Ukr. (Odess); pop. 153,243; 258 km SSE of Uman; 46°28'/30°44'; AMG, CAHJP, COH, EDRD, EJ, GUM3, GUM4, GUM5, GUM6, GYLA, HSL, HSL2, ISH1, JGFF, LDL, LJEE, PHP2, PHP4, PHR1, SF, YB.

Odesti, Rom.; pop. 18; 94 km NNW of Cluj; 47°31'/23°06'.

Odheim, Germ. (Oedheim); pop. 17; 56 km N of Stuttgart; 49°14'/09°15'; HSL, PHGBW.

Odjivol, see Odrzywol.

Odobesti, Rom.; 157 km S of Iasi; 45°46'/27°03'; GUM4, HSL, PHR1.

Odolanow, Pol. (Adelnau); pop. 27; 75 km NNE of Wroclaw; 51°34'/17°42'; AMG, CAHJP, HSL, JGFF.

Odombovar, see Ujdombovar.

Odonow, Pol.; pop. 9; 45 km NE of Krakow; 50°15'/20°28'.

Odorau, see Odoreu.

Odoreu, Rom. (Odorau, Szatmar Udvari, Szatmarudvari); pop. 115; 126 km NNW of Cluj; 47°48'/23°00'; HSL, HSL2, LDL, PHR2.

Odorhei, Rom. (Szekelyudvarhely); pop. 313; 139 km ESE of Cluj; 46°18'/25°18'; GUM3, HSL, LDL, PHR2.

Odrekhova, see Odrzechowa.

Odrizhin, Byel. (Odryzyn, Odyzyn?); pop. 38; 50 km SW of Pinsk; 51°58'/25°28'.

Odrowaz, Pol.; pop. 20; 107 km ESE of Lodz; 51°08'/20°39'; PHP1.

Odrowazek, Pol.; pop. 7; 107 km ESE of Lodz; 51°06'/20°39'.

Odryzyn, see Odrizhin.

Odrzechowa, Pol. (Odrekhova); pop. 32; 62 km SW of Przemysl; 49°33'/21°59'.

Odrzykon, Pol.; pop. 3; 75 km WSW of Przemysl; 49°45'/21°45'.

Odrzywol, Pol. (Odjivol); pop. 389; 75 km ESE of Lodz; 51°32'/20°33'; AMG, GA, PHP1, SF.

Odyzyn, possibly Odrizhin.

Oeblarn, see Oblarn.

Oedheim, see Odheim.

Oelde, Germ.; pop. 41; 126 km SW of Hannover; 51°49'/08°09'; AMG, GUM5.

Oels, see Olesnica.

Oepfershausen, Germ.; pop. 2; 126 km NE of Frankfurt am Main; 50°39'/10°15'.

Oerlinghausen, Germ.; pop. 19; 88 km SW of Hannover; 51°58'/08°40'.

Oestinghausen, Germ.; pop. 3; 114 km NE of Koln; 51°38'/08°06'.

Oestrich, see Ostrich.

Oettershausen, Germ.; 82 km WNW of Nurnberg; 49°54'/10°13'; PHGB.

Oettingen, see Ottingen.

Oeventrop, Germ. (Oventrop); pop. 5; 94 km NE of Koln; 51°24'/08°08'.

Ofeherto, Hung.; pop. 120; 101 km E of Miskolc; 47°56'/22°03'; HSL, PHH.

Ofen, see Budapest.

Offenau, Germ.; 56 km N of Stuttgart; 49°15'/09°10'; PHGBW.

Offenbach, Germ. (Offenbach am Main); pop. 1,434; 6 km ESE of Frankfurt am Main; 50°06'/08°46'; AMG, CAHJP, EJ, GED, GUM3, GUM4, HSL, HSL2, JGFF.

Offenbach am Glan, Germ. (Offenbach in der Pfalz); pop. 25; 94 km SW of Frankfurt am Main; 49°37'/07°33'; HSL, JGFF, PHGBW.

Offenbach am Main, see Offenbach.

Offenbach in der Pfalz, see Offenbach am Glan.

Offenburg, Germ.; pop. 291; 94 km SW of Stuttgart; 48°29'/07°56'; AMG, EJ, GED, GUM3, GUM5, JGFF, PHGBW.

Offingen, Germ.; 94 km ESE of Stuttgart; 48°29'/10°22'; PHGB.

Oficjalow, Pol.; pop. 7; 94 km SW of Lublin; 50°47'/21°26'.

Ofienburg, LDL. This pre-World War I community was not found in BGN gazetteers.

Ogarka, Pol.; pop. 14; 69 km E of Czestochowa; 50°47'/20°04'.

Oger, see Ogre.

Ogershof, see Ogre.

Oggau, Aus.; pop. 3; 45 km SE of Wien; 47°50'/16°40'.

Oglyadov, Ukr. (Ohladow); pop. 82; 62 km NE of Lvov; 50°12'/24°42'.

Ogonowice, Pol.; pop. 9; 75 km ESE of Lodz; 51°21'/20°19'; PHP1.

Ogony, Pol.; pop. 5; 82 km N of Warszawa; 52°57'/21°26'.

Ogorodnoye, Ukr. (Ciisia); pop. 5; 157 km SW of Odessa; 45°53'/28°51'.

Ogorodnya Gomelskaya, Byel.; pop. 65; 38 km E of Gomel; 52°20'/31°33'.

Ogorzeliny, Pol.; pop. 3; 114 km SSW of Gdansk; 53°36'/17°34'.

Ogra, Rom. (Marosugra); 69 km ESE of Cluj; 46°26'/24°19'; HSL.

Ogre, Lat. (Oger, Ogershof, Ogres); pop. 38; 38 km ESE of Riga; 56°49'/24°36'; GUM4, PHLE.

Ogres, see Ogre.

Ogrodniczki, Pol.; pop. 4; 13 km NE of Bialystok; 53°12'/23°16'.

Ogrody, Pol.; pop. 80; 82 km SSW of Poznan; 51°50'/16°29'.

Ogrodzieniec, Pol.; pop. 45; 50 km SE of Czestochowa; 50°27'/19°31'; HSL, JGFF.

Ogulin, Yug.; pop. 21; 82 km SSW of Zagreb; 45°16'/15°14'; PHY.

Ohare, Cz.; pop. 1; 56 km ENE of Praha; 50°06'/15°18'.

Oharice, Cz.; pop. 2; 69 km NE of Praha; 50°27'/15°15'.

Ohatkocs, HSL. This pre-World War I community was not found in BGN gazetteers.

Ohladow, see Oglyadov.

Ohlau, see Alove.

Ohrdruf, Germ.; pop. 120 km SW of Leipzig; 50°49'/10°44'; EDRD, GUM3, GUM4, GUM5.

Ohrid, Yug.; pop. 3; 114 km SSW of Skopje; 41°07'/20°48'.

Ohringen, Germ.; pop. 177; 50 km NNE of Stuttgart; 49°12'/09°30'; PHGBW.

Oitz, see Auce.

Ojcow, Pol.; 19 km NNW of Krakow; 50°13'/19°50'; PHP3.

Ojdula, Rom.; pop. 2; 170 km SSW of Iasi; 45°59'/26°15'.

Okalewo, Pol.; pop. 24; 133 km WNW of Warszawa; 53°04'/19°37'.

Okany, Hung.; pop. 64; 114 km NE of Szeged; 46°54'/21°21'; LDS, PHH.

Okecske, Hung.; pop. 82 km N of Szeged; 46°56'/20°07'; LDS.

Okhlopov, Ukr. (Ochlopow); pop. 8; 88 km NNE of Lvov; 50°28'/24°39'.

Okhrimovka, Ukr. BGN lists two possible localities with this name located at 47°38'/33°21' and 50°15'/35°31'. COH.

Okip, see Okopy.

Oklesna, Pol.; pop. 11; 26 km WSW of Krakow; 50°02'/19°31'.

Okmian, see Akmene.

Okmianica, see Okmyanitsa.

Okmiyan, see Akmene.

Okmjan, see Akmene.

Okmyanitsa, Byel. (Okmianica); pop. 11; 208 km NNW of Minsk; 55°42'/27°00'.

Okna, see Okno.

Okna Sugatag, see Ocna Sugatag.

Okne, see Krasnyye Okny.

Oknitsa, Mold. (Ocnita, Ocnita Gara?); pop. 263; 182 km NW of Kishinev; 48°23'/27°26'.

Okno, Ukr. (Ocna, Okna); pop. 115; 32 km N of Chernovtsy; 48°34'/25°58'; GUM3, HSL, HSL2, LDL, PHP2, SF.

Okno (Stanislawow), Ukr.; pop. 28; 56 km WNW of Chernovtsy; 48°40'/25°22'.

Okny, see Krasnyye Okny.

Okocim, Pol.; pop. 35; 50 km E of Krakow; 49°57'/20°37'; PHP3.

Okolica, see Okolitsa.

Okolicna na Ostrove, Cz. (Ekel); 75 km ESE of Bratislava; 47°48'/17°56'; HSL.

Okolitsa, (Okolica); GUM5. This town was not found in BGN gazetteers under the given spelling.

Okonek, (Ratzebuhr); pop. 22; This town was not found in BGN gazetteers under the given spelling.

Okopy, Ukr. (Okip, Okup, Okupy); pop. 69; 45 km NE of Chernovtsy; 48°32'/26°24'; SF.

Okopy (near Chelm), Pol.; pop. 28; 75 km E of Lublin; 51°11'/23°40'.

Okopy (near Magierow); pop. 59; This town does not appear in interwar or contemporary gazetteers, but does appear in a list of Galician towns.

Okorag, Hung.; pop. 4; 88 km ESE of Nagykanizsa; 45°55'/17°53'.

Okorito, HSL. This pre-World War I community was not found in BGN gazetteers.

Okormezo, see Mezhgorye.

Okorsk, Ukr. (Okorsk Wielki); pop. 11; 94 km W of Rovno; 50°45'/24°56'.

Okorsk Wielki, see Okorsk.

Okrajnik, Pol.; pop. 4; 56 km SW of Krakow; 49°44'/19°18'.

Okrouhla, Ukr. (Kerekheg, Kerekhegy, Okruhla); 170 km WSW of Chernovtsy; 48°05'/23°40'; AMG, LYV, SM.

Okrouhlicka, Cz. (Sejdorf); pop. 9; 88 km WNW of Brno; 49°32'/15°33'.

Okruhla, see Okrouhla.

Okrzeja, Pol.; pop. 133; 69 km NW of Lublin; 51°45'/22°06'; GUM3, GUM4, GUM5.

Oksa, Pol.; pop. 61; 69 km E of Czestochowa; 50°44'/20°07'.

Oksentiya, Mold. (Oxintea); pop. 23; 50 km NNE of Kishinev; 47°23'/29°07'.

Oksiutycze, Pol.; pop. 6; 82 km S of Bialystok; 52°25'/22°59'.

Oktyabr, see Krasnyy Oktyabr.

Oktyabrdorf, see Pshenichnoye.

Oktyabrskiy, Byel. (Karpilovka); 146 km W of Gomel; 52°38'/28°53'; GUM4, SF.

Oktyabrskoi Revolyutsii, USSR; pop. 35; This town was not found in BGN gazetteers under the given spelling.

Okuniev, see Okuniew.

Okuniew, Pol. (Okuniev, Okunyev); pop. 498; 26 km ENE of Warszawa; 52°16'/21°18'; AMG, COH, GA, GUM4, GUM5, HSL, HSL2, LDS, LYV, PHP4, SF, YB.

Okuninka, Pol.; pop. 7; 75 km NE of Lublin; 51°30'/23°31'.

Okuniuwek, Pol. PHP4. This town was not found in BGN gazetteers under the given spelling.

Okunyev, see Okuniew.

Okup, see Okopy.

Okupy, see Okopy.

Okyu Alb, Mold. (Ochiul Alb); pop. 41; 146 km NW of Kishinev; 48°02'/27°40'.

Olad, Hung.; pop. 5; 94 km NNW of Nagykanizsa; 47°14'/16°35'.

Olahapati, see Apateu.

Olahkocsard, see Cucerdea.

Olahlapos, Rom.; 82 km N of Cluj; 47°29'/24°01'; HSL. This town was located on a pre-World War I map, but does not appear in contemporary gazetteers.

Olahpatak, see Vlachovo.

Olahszentgyorg, see Singeorz Bai.

Olahujfalu, see Voul Romin.

Olaine, Lat.; pop. 1; 26 km SSW of Riga; 56°48'/23°59'; PHLE.

Olanesti, see Oloneshty.

Olapolia, see Olgopol.

Olaszfa, Hung. (Olaszka); pop. 14; 69 km N of Nagykanizsa; 47°01'/16°53'.

Olaszka, see Olaszfa.

Olaszliszka, Hung.; pop. 277; 50 km NE of Miskolc; 48°15'/21°26'; AMG, HSL, LDL, LDS, PHH.

Olawa, Pol.; 26 km ESE of Wroclaw; 50°58'/17°18'; LDS, POCEM. See also Alove.

Olbernhau, Germ.; pop. 7; 101 km ESE of Leipzig; 50°40'/13°20'.

Olbersdorf, Germ.; 176 km E of Leipzig; 50°53'/14°46'; HSL.

Olbiecin, Pol.; pop. 24; 50 km SSW of Lublin; 50°53'/22°07'.

Olbo, Hung.; pop. 14; 101 km N of Nagykanizsa; 47°18'/16°52'.

Olbramovice, Cz.; pop. 2; 32 km SSW of Brno; 48°59'/16°24'.

Olching, Germ.; pop. 4; 19 km WNW of Munchen; 48°12'/11°20'; GUM3.

Olchowce, Pol.; pop. 42; 50 km SW of Przemysl; 49°34'/22°14'. See also Olkoviche.

Olchowczyk, GUM4. This town was not found in BGN gazetteers under the given spelling.

Olchowiec, Pol.; pop. 32; 50 km E of Lublin; 51°14'/23°17'; PHP2. See also Olkhovets.

Olchowka, see Olkhovtsy.

Olcsva, Hung. (Alsoolcsva); pop. 39; 120 km E of Miskolc; 48°05'/22°20'; HSL.

Olcsvaapati, Hung.; pop. 5; 120 km E of Miskolc; 48°05'/22°21'.

Oldenburg, Germ.; pop. 391; 126 km SW of Hamburg; 53°10'/08°12'; CAHJP, EJ, GUM3, GUM4, GUM5, GUM6.

Oldersum, Germ.; pop. 9; 176 km WSW of Hamburg; 53°20'/07°20'.

Oldrichov, see Oldrisov.

Oldrisov, Cz. (Oldrichov); pop. 20; 133 km NE of Brno; 49°59'/17°58'.

Oleanita, see Olyanitsa.

Olecko, Pol. (Treuburg); pop. 94; 114 km NW of Bialystok; 54°02'/22°31'; GUM5, HSL.

Oledzkie, Pol.; pop. 8; 45 km SSW of Bialystok; 52°48'/22°53'.

Olejow, see Oleyev.

Olejowa Korniow, see Oleyeva Kornyuv.

Olejowa Korolowka, see Oleyeva Korolevka.

Olekshin, see Oleksianka.

Olekshitsa, Byel. (Olekszyce); pop. 12; 202 km WNW of Pinsk; 53°20'/23°57'.

Oleksianka, Pol. (Olekshin); pop. 7; 62 km ESE of Warszawa; 52°00'/21°51'; FRG.

Oleksince, see Oleksintse.

Oleksinets Novy, see Novyy Oleksinets.

Oleksintse, Ukr. (Oleksince); pop. 36; 56 km NNW of Chernovtsy; 48°48'/25°50'.

Olekszyce, see Olekshitsa.

Olenowka, Pol.; pop. 13; 75 km E of Lublin; 51°08'/23°37'.

Olesha, Ukr. (Olesza); pop. 35; 82 km WNW of Chernovtsy; 48°50'/25°08'.

Oleshiche, see Oleszyce.

Oleshki, see Oleshkuv.

Oleshkuv, Ukr. (Oleshki); pop. 586; 50 km WNW of Chernovtsy; 48°28'/25°21'.

Oleshonki, Byel. (Olszynka); pop. 1; 101 km WNW of Minsk;

54°25'/26°20'.

Olesk, Ukr.; pop. 68; 146 km N of Lvov; 51°07'/24°11'; JGFF.

Oleski, see Olesko.

Olesko, Ukr. (Allesk, Oleski); pop. 636; 62 km ENE of Lvov; 49°58'/24°53'; COH, EDRD, EGRS, EJ, HSL, HSL2, JGFF, LDL, LYV, PHP2, SF.

Olesnica, Pol. (Oels, Ols); pop. 120; 32 km NE of Wroclaw; 51°12'/17°23'; EJ, GUM3, GUM4, HSL, JGFF, LDS, PHP4.

Olesnica (near Garwolin), Pol.; pop. 79; 75 km ESE of Warszawa; 52°03'/22°00'.

Olesnica (near Staszow), Pol.; pop. 67; 94 km NE of Krakow; 50°27'/21°04'.

Olesniki, Pol.; pop. 17; 38 km ESE of Lublin; 51°07'/23°02'; HSL.

Olesno, Pol.; pop. 52; 75 km ENE of Krakow; 50°12'/20°56'; LDS, POCEM.

Olesza, see Olesha.

Oleszki, see Tsyurupinsk.

Oleszkowo, Pol.; pop. 5; 32 km N of Bialystok; 53°20'/23°11'.

Olesznica, GUM5, GUM5. This town was not found in BGN gazetteers under the given spelling.

Oleszno, Pol.; pop. 114; 69 km ENE of Czestochowa; 50°57'/20°03'.

Oleszyce, Pol. (Holashitz, Oleshiche); pop. 1,590; 45 km N of Przemysl; 50°10'/23°02'; AMG, COH, EGRS, GUM3, HSL, JGFF, LDL, PHP2, POCEM, SF.

Oleszyce Stare, Pol.; pop. 105; 45 km N of Przemysl; 50°10'/23°00'.

Olevsk, Ukr. (Olewsk, Olivsk); pop. 2,916; 120 km NE of Rovno; 51°13'/27°39'; LDL, SF.

Olewsk, see Olevsk.

Oleyev, Ukr. (Olejow); pop. 51; 88 km E of Lvov; 49°45'/25°15'.

Oleyeva Kornyuv, Ukr. (Olejowa Korniow); pop. 48; 62 km NW of Chernovtsy; 48°44'/25°22'.

Oleyeva Korolevka, Ukr. (Olejowa Korolowka, Oleyeva Korolyuvka); pop. 29; 62 km NW of Chernovtsy; 48°45'/25°22'.

Oleyeva Korolyuvka, see Oleyeva Korolevka.

Oleyevo Korolevka, Ukr. (Korilifka, Korolovka, Korolowka); pop. 1,161; 50 km N of Chernovtsy; 48°44'/25°59'; AMG, COH, EGRS, GUM4, GUM5, HSL, HSL2, JGFF, LDL, PHP2, SF.

Olganow, Pol.; pop. 3; 69 km NE of Krakow; 50°25'/20°46'.

Olgapol, see Olgopol.

Olgomel, Byel. (Ozdamicze); pop. 50; 94 km E of Pinsk; 52°03'/27°29'.

Ol Gopol, see Olgopol.

Olgopol, Ukr. (Ol Gopol, Olapolia, Olgapol, Olhopol); pop. 1,660; 82 km SSW of Uman; 48°12'/29°30'; AMG, EDRD, GUM4, HSL, LDL, PHR1, SF.

Olhopol, see Olgopol.

Olik, see Olyka.

Olika, see Olyka.

Oliki, USSR; EDRD. A number of towns share this name. It was not possible to determine from available information which one is being referenced.

Oliscani, see Olishkany.

Olishkany, Mold. (Oliscani); pop. 266; 94 km N of Kishinev; 47°48'/28°43'.

Olita, see Alytus.

Olivsk, see Olevsk.

Olizarka, Ukr. (Ulizerka); pop. 321; 56 km NW of Rovno; 51°05'/25°55'; GUM4, LYV, SF. This town was located on an interwar map of Poland but does not appear in contemporary gazetteers. Map coordinates are approximate.

Olkenik, see Valkininkas.

Olkeniki, see Valkininkas.

Olkhovets, Ukr. (Olchowiec); pop. 52; 32 km NNE of Chernovtsy; 48°33'/26°10'.

Olkhovets (near Bobrka), Ukr.; pop. 25; 32 km SE of Lvov; 49°38'/24°11'.

Olkhovets (Stanislawow), Ukr.; pop. 21; 62 km NW of Chernovtsy; 48°48'/25°23'.

Olkhovtsy, Byel. (Olchowka); 101 km N of Pinsk; 52°59'/26°09'; GUM3.

Olkieniki, see Valkininkas.

Olkienniki, see Valkininkas.

Olkinik, see Valkininkas.

Olknik, see Valkininkas.

Olkoviche, see Olkovichi.

Olkovichi, Byel. (Olkoviche); pop. 27; 75 km NNW of Minsk; 54°30'/27°26'.

Olkush, see Olkusz.

Olkusz, Pol. (Elkush, Olkush); pop. 2,707; 32 km WNW of Krakow; 50°17'/19°34'; AMG, CAHJP, COH, EDRD, EJ, GA, GUM3, GUM4, GUM5, HSL, HSL2, JGFF, LDS, LYV, PHP1, PHP3, PHP4, POCEM, SF, YB.

Olmany, Byel.; pop. 64; 75 km ESE of Pinsk; 51°48'/27°04'.

Olmuetz, see Olomouc.

Olmutz, see Olomouc.

Olnhausen, Germ.; pop. 17; 62 km N of Stuttgart; 49°19'/09°27'; PHGBW.

Olnkhovtsy, Ukr. (Nagovo, Niagova, Nyagova); 163 km WSW of Chernovtsy; 48°04'/23°43'; AMG, HSL, SM.

Olomouc, Cz. (Olmuetz, Olmutz); pop. 2,216; 62 km NE of Brno; 49°35'/17°15'; AMG, EDRD, EJ, GUM3, GUM4, HSL, PHP2.

Oloneshty, Mold. (Olanesti); pop. 110; 101 km ESE of Kishinev; 46°30'/29°55'.

Olosig, Rom. (Erolaszi); pop. 6; 126 km WNW of Cluj; 47°21'/22°11'.

Olovi, Cz.; pop. 22; 139 km W of Praha; 50°15'/12°33'; HSL.

Olovo, Yug.; pop. 30; 170 km SW of Beograd; 44°07'/18°35'.

Olpe, Germ.; 62 km ENE of Koln; 51°02'/07°51'; GED.

Olpin, see Olpiny.

Olpini, see Olpiny.

Olpiny, Pol. (Olpin, Olpini); pop. 185; 101 km ESE of Krakow; 49°49'/21°12'; EGRS, GUM4, HSL, LDL, PHP3, SF.

Olpret, Rom. (Alparet); pop. 38; 45 km N of Cluj; 47°08'/23°39'; HSL.

Ols, see Olesnica.

Olsana, see Olshana.

Olsberg, Germ.; pop. 16; 120 km NE of Koln; 51°21'/08°30'.

Olshan, see Golshany.

Olshana, Ukr. (Olsana, Vilshana); 88 km NE of Uman; 49°13'/31°13'; LDL, SF.

Olshani, see Golshany.

Olshanik, Ukr. (Olszanik); pop. 36; 69 km SW of Lvov; 49°26'/23°13'.

Olshanitsa, (Olszanica);

Olshanitsa (near Lisko), Ukr.; pop. 73; 50 km E of Lvov; 49°48'/24°40'.

Olshanitsa (near Yavorov), Ukr.; pop. 45; 45 km WNW of Lvov; 49°57'/23°27'.

Olshany, Ukr. (Alsenai, Olszany); pop. 1,069; 26 km W of Kharkov; 50°03'/35°53'; COH, LYV, PHP4.

Olshany (near Vilnius), Byel.; pop. 114; 114 km WNW of Minsk; 54°15'/26°01'; GUM3, GUM4.

Olshany (Polesie), Byel.; pop. 60; 114 km WNW of Pinsk; 52°30'/24°34'; AMG, JGFF.

Olshevo, Byel. (Olszewo); pop. 31; 69 km WNW of Pinsk; 52°28'/25°12'.

Olsov, Cz.; 56 km NW of Kosice; 49°11'/20°53'; HSL.

Olszana, Pol.; pop. 10; 75 km SE of Krakow; 49°34'/20°31'.

Olszanica, see Olshanitsa.

Olszanik, see Olshanik.

Olszanka Mala, Ukr.; pop. 22; 56 km ESE of Lvov; 49°35'/24°35'. This town was located on an interwar map of Poland but does not appear in contemporary gazetteers. Map coordinates are approximate.

Olszany, Pol.; pop. 4; 13 km SW of Przemysl; 49°45'/22°39'. See also Olshany.

Olszewnica, Pol. (Olszewnica Wielka); pop. 42; 82 km N of Lublin; 51°55'/22°35'.

Olszewnica Mala, Pol.; pop. 5; 82 km N of Lublin; 51°56'/22°38'.

Olszewnica Wielka, *see* Olszewnica.

Olszewo, *see* Olshevo.

Olszow Dolny, Pol.; pop. 131; 69 km SW of Krakow; 49°48'/19°03'.

Olszowiec, HSL. A number of towns share this name. It was not possible to determine from available information which one is being referenced.

Olszowka, Pol.; pop. 27; 94 km SW of Lublin; 50°54'/21°21'.

Olszowno, Pol.; pop. 9; 101 km SW of Lublin; 50°49'/21°15'.

Olsztyn, Pol. (Allenstein); pop. 612; 133 km ESE of Gdansk; 53°47'/20°29'; CAHJP, GUM3, GUM4, LDS, PHP1.

Olsztyn (Kielce area), Pol.; pop. 100; 13 km ESE of Czestochowa; 50°45'/19°16'; GUM5.

Olsztynek, Pol. (Hohenstein); pop. 33; 133 km ESE of Gdansk; 53°35'/20°18'; GUM3, GUM4.

Olszyc, Pol. (Olszyc Szlachecki, Olszyce); pop. 38; 82 km ESE of Warszawa; 52°02'/22°07'; AMG, JGFF.

Olszyce, *see* Olszyc.

Olszyc Szlachecki, *see* Olszyc.

Olszyn, Pol.; pop. 8; 114 km SSE of Bialystok; 52°08'/23°23'.

Olszynka, *see* Oleshonki.

Olszyny, Pol.; pop. 20; 94 km ESE of Krakow; 49°49'/21°09'; PHP3.

Oltarzew, Pol.; pop. 47; 19 km WSW of Warszawa; 52°13'/20°47'.

Oltenita, Rom.; 56 km ESE of Bucuresti; 44°05'/26°38'; PHR1.

Olviopol, *see* Pervomaysk.

Olwiopol, *see* Pervomaysk.

Olyanitsa, Ukr. (Oleanita); 75 km WSW of Uman; 48°37'/29°14'; PHR1.

Olyka, Ukr. (Olik, Olika); pop. 2,086; 32 km WNW of Rovno; 50°43'/25°49'; AMG, CAHJP, COH, EDRD, EJ, GUM3, GUM4, GUM5, GUM6, HSL, HSL2, LDL, LYV, SF, WS, YB.

Ombod, Rom.; 195 km S of Cluj; 45°02'/22°56'; HSL. This town was located on a pre-World War I map, but does not appear in contemporary gazetteers.

Omniszonka, Pol. PHP3. This town was not found in BGN gazetteers under the given spelling.

Omoravicza, *see* Stara Moravica.

Omstibova, *see* Mstibovo.

Omstov, *see* Mstow.

Omtchislav, *see* Mstislavl.

Omuli, Lat.; pop. 1; 146 km NE of Riga; 57°55'/25°45'.

Oncesti, Rom. (Uncsest, Vancsfalva); pop. 123; 126 km N of Cluj; 47°51'/23°59'; SM.

Ond, Hung.; pop. 49; 38 km NE of Miskolc; 48°11'/21°13'.

Ondava, GUM5. This town was not found in BGN gazetteers under the given spelling.

Ondod, Hung.; pop. 3; 94 km NNW of Nagykanizsa; 47°14'/16°33'.

Ondrejovce, Cz. (Endred); 107 km E of Bratislava; 48°08'/18°31'; HSL.

Oneshty, Mold. (Onesti); pop. 39; 38 km NW of Kishinev; 47°17'/28°33'; HSL.

Onesti, *see* Oneshty.

Onga, Hung.; pop. 62; 13 km ENE of Miskolc; 48°07'/20°55'; HSL, HSL2, PHH.

Oni, LDL. This pre-World War I community was not found in BGN gazetteers.

Onikshty, *see* Anyksciai.

Oniscani, *see* Onishkany.

Onishkany, Mold. (Oniscani); pop. 153; 56 km NW of Kishinev; 47°22'/28°19'.

Oniskis, *see* Onuskis.

Onitcani, *see* Onitskany.

Onitskany, Mold. (Onitcani); pop. 28; 32 km NE of Kishinev; 47°09'/29°05'.

Onod, Hung.; pop. 184; 13 km SE of Miskolc; 48°00'/20°55'; HSL, LDL, LDS, PHH.

Onuca, Rom.; pop. 5; 75 km E of Cluj; 46°44'/24°35'.

Onufriewka, (Anufrehifka); SF. This town was not found in BGN gazetteers under the given spelling.

Onuskis, Lith. (Hanashishok, Hanuszyszki, Oniskis, Onusky); pop. 342; 50 km SW of Vilnius; 54°29'/24°36'; AMG, JGFF, LDL, SF, YL.

Onusky, *see* Onuskis.

Onut, Ukr.; 32 km N of Chernovtsy; 48°34'/26°03'; AMG, GUM4.

Onyszki, Pol.; pop. 9; 38 km N of Przemysl; 50°05'/22°57'.

Oos, Germ.; pop. 10; 75 km W of Stuttgart; 48°47'/08°12'.

Opachi, Mold. (Opaci); pop. 43; 62 km SE of Kishinev; 46°35'/29°21'.

Opaci, *see* Opachi.

Opacie, Pol.; pop. 10; 101 km WSW of Przemysl; 49°46'/21°24'.

Opacionka, Pol.; pop. 30; Described in the *Black Book* as being in the Krakow region of Poland, this town was not found in BGN gazetteers.

Opaka, Ukr.; pop. 80; 82 km SSW of Lvov; 49°17'/23°18'.

Opaki, Ukr.; pop. 7; 75 km ENE of Lvov; 49°52'/25°03'.

Opalenica, Pol. (Opalenitza); pop. 2; 38 km SW of Poznan; 52°18'/16°26'.

Opaleniska, Pol. (Opalenisko); pop. 4; 50 km NW of Przemysl; 50°08'/22°25'.

Opalenisko, *see* Opaleniska.

Opalenitza, *see* Opalenica.

Opalin, Ukr.; pop. 516; 163 km NNW of Lvov; 51°17'/23°42'; CAHJP, GUM5, JGFF.

Opalya, *possibly* Opalyi.

Opalyi, Hung. (Opalya?); pop. 160; 114 km E of Miskolc; 48°00'/22°19'; HSL, LDS, PHH.

Oparany, Cz.; pop. 18; 82 km S of Praha; 49°24'/14°29'.

Oparszczyzna, Pol.; pop. 20; Described in the *Black Book* as being in the Tarnopol region of Poland, this town was not found in BGN gazetteers.

Opary, *see* Opory.

Opatija, Yug. (Abbazia); 139 km SW of Zagreb; 45°20'/14°19'; HSL, PHY.

Opatkowice, *see* Zakliczyn.

Opatkowice Drewniane, Pol.; pop. 21; 62 km NNE of Krakow; 50°33'/20°22'.

Opatkowice Pojalowskie, Pol.; pop. 11; 62 km NNE of Krakow; 50°33'/20°22'.

Opatov, *see* Opatow.

Opatow, Pol. (Apt, Apta, Opatov); pop. 5,462; 94 km SW of Lublin; 50°48'/21°26'; AMG, CAHJP, COH, EDRD, EJ, FRG, GA, GUM3, GUM4, GUM5, GUM6, HSL, HSL2, JGFF, LDL, LDS, LYV, PHP1, PHP2, PHP3, PHP4, SF, YB.

Opatowek, Pol.; pop. 186; 82 km WSW of Lodz; 51°44'/18°14'; CAHJP, GUM3, GUM4.

Opatowice, Pol.; pop. 170; 45 km SSW of Czestochowa; 50°27'/18°49'.

Opatowiec, Pol.; pop. 166; 62 km NE of Krakow; 50°15'/20°44'; CAHJP, COH, GUM3.

Opava, Cz. (Troppau); pop. 1,035; 126 km NE of Brno; 49°57'/17°55'; EJ, GUM5, HSL, PHP1.

Opechowo, Pol.; pop. 12; 88 km WSW of Bialystok; 53°04'/21°48'.

Opladen, Germ.; pop. 39; 19 km N of Koln; 51°04'/07°01'; GED, GUM3, GUM5.

Oplany, Cz.; pop. 5; 32 km ESE of Praha; 49°56'/14°52'.

Oploty, Cz.; pop. 9; 75 km WNW of Praha; 50°17'/13°27'.

Oplucko, *see* Oplutsko.

Oplutsko, Ukr. (Oplucko); pop. 36; 69 km NE of Lvov; 50°12'/24°45'.

Opochka, USSR; pop. 577; 120 km W of Velikiye Luki; 56°39'/28°38'.

Opochno, *see* Opoczno.

Opocnice, Cz.; pop. 2; 56 km ENE of Praha; 50°11'/15°15'.

Opoczka, *see* Opoczka Mala.

Opoczka Mala, Pol. (Opoczka); 62 km SW of Lublin; 50°53'/21°51'; LDL.

Opoczno, Pol. (Opochno, Opotchna); pop. 3,376; 75 km ESE of Lodz; 51°22'/20°17'; AMG, COH, EDRD, GA, GUM4, GUM5, HSL, HSL2, JGFF, LDS, LYV, PHP1, PHP3, SF.

Opola, *see* Opole Lubelskie.

Opole, Pol. (Oppein, Oppeln); pop. 607; 82 km WSW of Czestochowa; 50°40'/17°57'; AMG, COH, EDRD, GUM3, GYLA, HSL, HSL2, ISH1, JGFF, LDS, LYV, PHP3, POCEM.

Opole Lubelski, *see* Opole Lubelskie.

Opole Lubelskie, Pol. (Opola, Opole Lubelski); pop. 3,766; 45 km WSW of Lublin; 51°09'/21°58'; AMG, CAHJP, EDRD, GA, GUM4, GUM5, GUM6, JGFF, LDL, LDS, POCEM, SF.

Oporets, Ukr. (Oporzec); pop. 56; 133 km S of Lvov; 48°47'/23°20'.

Opory, Ukr. (Opary); pop. 9; 56 km SSW of Lvov; 49°25'/23°42'; GUM4.

Oporzec, *see* Oporets.

Oposhno, *see* Oposhnya.

Oposhnya, Ukr. (Oposhno, Oposna); 114 km WSW of Kharkov; 49°58'/34°37'; SF.

Oposna, *see* Oposhnya.

Opotchna, *see* Opoczno.

Opozdzew, Pol.; pop. 5; 56 km SSE of Warszawa; 51°47'/21°06'.

Oppein, *see* Opole.

Oppeln, *see* Opole.

Oppenheim, Germ.; pop. 68; 38 km SSW of Frankfurt am Main; 49°51'/08°21'; EJ, GUM5, JGFF.

Oppertshofen, Germ.; 88 km S of Nurnberg; 48°42'/10°40'; PHGB.

Opsa, Byel. (Opshe); pop. 334; 189 km NNW of Minsk; 55°32'/26°50'; GUM3, HSL, LDL, LYV, SF.

Opshe, *see* Opsa.

Or, Hung.; pop. 70; 107 km E of Miskolc; 47°59'/22°12'; PHH.

Oracov, Cz.; pop. 9; 62 km W of Praha; 50°07'/13°33'.

Oracu, *see* Orak.

Oradea, Rom. (Grosswardein, Nagy Varad, Nagyvarad); pop. 19,838; 133 km W of Cluj; 47°04'/21°56'; AMG, CAHJP, COH, EDRD, EJ, GUM3, GUM4, GUM5, GUM6, HSL, HSL2, JGFF, LDL, PHR2, YB.

Oradna, *see* Rodna.

Oradovka, Ukr. (Orodowka); 13 km W of Uman; 48°47'/30°00'; PHR1.

Orahovica, Yug.; pop. 53; 195 km WSW of Beograd; 44°25'/18°03'.

Orak, Mold. (Oracu); pop. 4; 50 km SSW of Kishinev; 46°40'/28°28'.

Oran, *see* Varena.

Oranchitsy, Byel. (Oranczyce); pop. 25; 114 km WNW of Pinsk; 52°28'/24°33'; HSL.

Oranczyce, *see* Oranchitsy.

Oranienburg, Germ.; pop. 105; 32 km NW of Berlin; 52°45'/13°14'; EDRD, HSL, HSL2, JGFF, LDL, LDS, PHP1.

Orany, *see* Varena.

Oras, *see* Orasa.

Orasa, Rom. (Oras); pop. 113; 107 km SSW of Iasi; 46°25'/26°45'.

Oraseni, Rom. (Ariseni?); pop. 127; 146 km ESE of Cluj; 46°10'/25°21'; GUM3, HSL.

Orastie, Rom. (Broos); 107 km S of Cluj; 45°50'/23°12'; GUM4, PHR1.

Orasul Nou, *see* Orasu Nou.

Orasul Nou Satu Mare, *see* Orasu Nou.

Orasul Stalin, *see* Brasov.

Orasu Nou, Rom. (Avasujvaros, Orasul Nou, Orasul Nou Satu Mare); pop. 254; 126 km NNW of Cluj; 47°50'/23°17'; HSL, JGFF, PHR2.

Oravita, Rom. (Orawitza); 240 km SSW of Cluj; 45°02'/21°42'; HSL, PHR1.

Oravska Lesna, Cz. (Erdudka); 170 km WNW of Kosice; 49°23'/19°11'; HSL.

Orawa, *see* Oryava.

Orawczyk, Pol.; pop. 54; Described in the *Black Book* as being in the Stanislawow region of Poland, this town was not found in BGN gazetteers.

Orawitza, *see* Oravita.

Orawka, Pol.; pop. 4; 69 km S of Krakow; 49°31'/19°43'.

Orb, *see* Bad Orb.

Orchowek, Pol.; pop. 27; 75 km NE of Lublin; 51°31'/23°34'; CAHJP.

Orci, Hung.; pop. 5; 69 km E of Nagykanizsa; 46°24'/17°52'.

Orda, Byel.; 107 km SSW of Minsk; 53°07'/26°29'; HSL.

Ordasei, *see* Ordashey.

Ordashey, Mold. (Ordasei); pop. 5; 82 km NNW of Kishinev; 47°41'/28°30'.

Ordejov, Cz.; 88 km ESE of Brno; 48°58'/17°45'; HSL.

Ordogfala, HSL. This pre-World War I community was not found in BGN gazetteers.

Ordogkut, HSL. This pre-World War I community was not found in BGN gazetteers.

Ordow, *see* Orduv.

Ordshonikidze, *see* Ordzhonikidze.

Orduv, Ukr. (Ordow); pop. 22; 69 km NNE of Lvov; 50°22'/24°31'.

Ordzhonikidze, Ukr. (Dzaudhikau, Ordshonikidze, Vladikavkaz); 107 km SSW of Dnepropetrovsk; 47°40'/34°03'; EJ, GUM4, HSL.

Oregcserto, Hung.; pop. 2; 88 km WNW of Szeged; 46°31'/19°07'.

Oreglak, Hung.; pop. 13; 56 km NE of Nagykanizsa; 46°36'/17°37'.

Orekhovets, Ukr. (Orzechowiec); pop. 30; 133 km N of Chernovtsy; 49°28'/26°11'.

Orekhovno, Byel. (Orzechowno); pop. 101; 114 km W of Vitebsk; 55°22'/28°23'.

Orel, USSR (Oryol); pop. 3,597; 120 km E of Bryansk; 52°58'/36°04'.

Orelec, Pol.; pop. 30; 45 km SSW of Przemysl; 49°27'/22°27'.

Oreske, Cz. BGN lists two possible localities with this name located at 48°45'/17°18' and 48°52'/21°54'. HSL.

Orestias, Greece (Nea Orestias); pop. 197; 309 km NE of Thessaloniki; 41°30'/26°31'.

Orfalu, Hung.; pop. 9; 75 km WNW of Nagykanizsa; 46°53'/16°17'.

Orgeyev, Mold. (Orhaiv, Orhei); pop. 6,408; 45 km N of Kishinev; 47°22'/28°49'; EDRD, EJ, GUM4, GUM5, HSL, JGFF, LDL, PHR2, SF, YB.

Orhaiv, *see* Orgeyev.

Orhalom, Hung.; pop. 23; 69 km N of Budapest; 48°05'/19°25'; HSL.

Orhei, *see* Orgeyev.

Oriachov, *see* Orjechow.

Oriechowno, Byel. (Oriekhov, Oriekhovno); pop. 712; 114 km W of Vitebsk; 55°22'/28°23'.

Oriekhov, *see* Oriechowno.

Oriekhovno, *see* Oriechowno.

Orikhov, *see* Gorokhov.

Orinin, Ukr.; pop. 1,797; 62 km NNE of Chernovtsy; 48°46'/26°24'; COH, EDRD, EJ, JGFF, SF.

Orishche, Ukr. (Oryszcze); pop. 4; 94 km N of Lvov; 50°41'/24°27'.

Orishkovtsy, Ukr. (Orishovtsy?, Oryshkovtse, Oryszkowce); pop. 23; 88 km S of Rovno; 49°50'/26°08'.

Orishovtsy, *possibly* Orishkovtsy.

Orjechow, (Oriachov); LDL, SF. This town was not found in BGN gazetteers under the given spelling.

Orkeny, Hung.; pop. 108; 56 km SE of Budapest; 47°08'/19°26'; HSL, PHH.

Orla, Pol.; pop. 1,167; 50 km SSE of Bialystok; 52°42'/23°20'; CAHJP, COH, GA, GUM3, GYLA, HSL, JGFF, LDS, LYV, POCEM, SF.

Orladany, see Mezoladany.

Orle, see Orlya.

Orlicky, Cz.; pop. 1; 101 km N of Brno; 50°02'/16°41'.

Orliczko, Pol.; pop. 6; 50 km WNW of Poznan; 52°37'/16°20'.

Orlingerhausen, see Ortlingerhausen.

Orlova, Cz. (Orlowa); pop. 394; 150 km NE of Brno; 49°51'/18°26'; AMG, COH, HSL, HSL2, LDL, SF, YB.

Orlove, Cz.; 133 km E of Brno; 49°08'/18°26'; HSL.

Orlovichi, Byel. (Orlowicze); pop. 2; 120 km NW of Pinsk; 53°01'/25°11'.

Orlovo, Byel.; 82 km WNW of Vitebsk; 55°31'/29°00'; EDRD, JGFF.

Orlovskaya, HSL. This pre-World War I community was not found in BGN gazetteers.

Orlowa, see Orlova.

Orlow Drewniany, Pol.; pop. 11; 62 km ESE of Lublin; 50°54'/23°13'.

Orlowicze, see Orlovichi.

Orlowka, see Orluvka.

Orlowko, see Orluvka.

Orluvka, Ukr. (Orlowka, Orlowko); pop. 8; 62 km NNE of Rovno; 51°03'/26°43'.

Orlya, Byel. (Orle); pop. 195; 176 km WSW of Minsk; 53°30'/24°59'; GUM3, GUM6, JGFF.

Orly Male, see Malyye Orly.

Orly Wielkie, see Bolshiye Orly.

Ormenyes, Hung.; 101 km S of Miskolc; 47°12'/20°35'; HSL.

Ormezo, see Strazske.

Ornbau, Germ.; 45 km SW of Nurnberg; 49°10'/10°39'; PHGB.

Orneta, Pol. (Wormditt); pop. 45; 101 km E of Gdansk; 54°07'/20°08'.

Ornontowice, Pol.; 69 km S of Czestochowa; 50°11'/18°46'; GA, GUM4.

Ornowo, Pol. (Arnau); 114 km ESE of Gdansk; 53°40'/19°57'; HSL.

Orodowka, see Oradovka.

Oroftiana de Sus, Rom.; pop. 4; 150 km NW of Iasi; 48°11'/26°20'.

Oros, Hung.; pop. 113; 75 km E of Miskolc; 47°57'/21°48'; HSL, PHH.

Orosfaia, Rom.; pop. 8; 62 km ENE of Cluj; 46°51'/24°25'.

Orosfala, Rom. (Oroszfala); 120 km NW of Cluj; 47°43'/22°57'; HSL. This town was located on a pre-World War I map, but does not appear in contemporary gazetteers.

Oroshaza, Hung.; pop. 727; 56 km NE of Szeged; 46°34'/20°40'; HSL, LDL, LDS, PHH.

Oroslavje, Yug.; pop. 40; 32 km NNW of Zagreb; 46°00'/15°56'.

Oroszfala, see Orosfala.

Oroszko, see Repedea.

Oroszlany, Hung.; pop. 7; 56 km WSW of Budapest; 47°29'/18°19'.

Oroszlo, Hung.; pop. 2; 94 km ESE of Nagykanizsa; 46°13'/18°08'.

Oroszmezo, Rom.; 88 km WNW of Cluj; 47°17'/22°43'; HSL. This town was located on a pre-World War I map, but does not appear in contemporary gazetteers.

Oroszmokra, see Russkaya Mokraya.

Orosztony, Hung.; pop. 8; 32 km N of Nagykanizsa; 46°38'/17°04'.

Oroszvar, see Rusovce.

Oroszveg, Ukr.; 182 km SSW of Lvov; 48°27'/22°43'; HSL. This town was located on a pre-World War I map, but does not appear in contemporary gazetteers.

Orow, Ukr.; pop. 101; 107 km S of Lvov; 48°55'/23°35'; PHP2. This town was located on an interwar map of Poland but does not appear in contemporary gazetteers. Map

coordinates are approximate.

Orsava, GUM3. This town was not found in BGN gazetteers under the given spelling.

Orschweier, Germ.; 120 km SW of Stuttgart; 48°17'/07°48'; LDS, PHGBW.

Orsha, Byel. (Irshe, Irsya, Orsza, Urshe); pop. 6,780; 82 km SSE of Vitebsk; 54°31'/30°26'; EDRD, EJ, GUM4, GUM5, HSL, HSL2, JGFF, LYV, SF.

Orsova, Rom. (Gorgenyorsova); 246 km S of Cluj; 44°42'/22°25'; HSL, HSL2, PHR1.

Orsoy, Germ.; 69 km NNW of Koln; 51°32'/06°42'; GED, JGFF.

Orsza, see Orsha.

Orszentmiklos, Hung.; pop. 9; 26 km NNE of Budapest; 47°41'/19°16'.

Orszulewo, Pol.; pop. 14; 107 km NNW of Lodz; 52°40'/19°09'.

Ortelec, Rom.; pop. 7; 62 km NW of Cluj; 47°12'/23°06'.

Ortel Krolewski, Pol.; pop. 10; 94 km NNE of Lublin; 51°57'/23°16'.

Ortel Ksiazecy, Pol.; pop. 16; 94 km NNE of Lublin; 51°59'/23°15'; GA, GUM5.

Ortelsburg, see Szczytno.

Ortenberg, Germ.; pop. 42; 45 km NE of Frankfurt am Main; 50°21'/09°03'.

Ortenburg, Germ.; pop. 1; 126 km NE of Munchen; 48°33'/13°14'; LDS.

Ortilos, Hung.; pop. 1; 19 km S of Nagykanizsa; 46°17'/16°56'.

Ortiteag, Rom.; pop. 5; 94 km WNW of Cluj; 47°02'/22°27'.

Ortlingerhausen, Germ. (Orlingerhausen); 75 km W of Hannover; 52°27'/08°37'; LDS.

Orvanitsa, Ukr. (Orwianica); pop. 34; 107 km N of Rovno; 51°30'/26°33'.

Orwianica, see Orvanitsa.

Oryava, Ukr. (Orawa); pop. 60; 114 km SSW of Lvov; 48°55'/23°18'; HSL.

Oryol, see Orel.

Oryshkovtse, see Orishkovtsy.

Oryszcze, see Orishche.

Oryszew, see Oryszew Nowy.

Oryszew Nowy, Pol. (Oryszew); pop. 8; 45 km SW of Warszawa; 52°07'/20°23'.

Oryszkowce, see Orishkovtsy.

Orzechow, Pol.; pop. 15; 69 km SSW of Lublin; 50°45'/21°53'; HSL, PHP4.

Orzechowce, Pol.; pop. 15; 13 km NNW of Przemysl; 49°52'/22°47'.

Orzechowiec, see Orekhovets.

Orzechowno, see Orekhovno.

Orzechow Nowy, Pol.; pop. 14; 38 km NE of Lublin; 51°28'/23°01'.

Orzel, see Pervomaysk.

Orzendov, see Urzedow.

Orzeszkowka, Pol. (Orzeszowka); pop. 3; 75 km NE of Warszawa; 52°28'/22°08'; GUM5.

Orzeszowka, see Orzeszkowka.

Orzistchov, see Rzhishchev.

Orzysz, Pol. (Arys); pop. 30; 107 km WNW of Bialystok; 53°49'/21°57'; GUM4.

Osada Lubicz, Pol. (Lubicz); pop. 362; 139 km NE of Poznan; 53°02'/18°45'; COH, GUM3, GUM4, GUM5, GUM6, HSL, HSL2, LDL, PHP4, SF.

Osagard, Hung.; pop. 5; 45 km N of Budapest; 47°52'/19°12'.

Osandarfalva, see Sandrovo.

Osann, Germ.; 120 km S of Koln; 49°55'/06°57'; GUM5, JGFF.

Oschatz, Germ.; pop. 15; 56 km E of Leipzig; 51°18'/13°07'; GUM5.

Oschersleben, Germ.; pop. 41; 114 km NW of Leipzig; 52°02'/11°15'; GUM3.

Oscislowo, Pol. BGN lists two possible localities with this name located at 52°27'/18°16' and 52°50'/20°27'. PHP4.

Osecna, Cz.; pop. 5; 75 km NNE of Praha; 50°42'/14°55'.

Osehlib, *see* Oshekhliby.

Osek, Cz.; pop. 41; 62 km NE of Praha; 50°28'/15°09'.

Osekruv, Ukr. (Osiekrow); pop. 9; 114 km WNW of Rovno; 50°55'/24°41'.

Oselce, Cz.; pop. 8; 88 km SSW of Praha; 49°26'/13°41'.

Oselin, Cz.; pop. 9; 120 km SW of Praha; 49°46'/12°52'.

Osencin, Germ. EDRD. This town was not found in BGN gazetteers under the given spelling.

Oserdow, Pol.; pop. 22; 107 km NE of Przemysl; 50°26'/23°59'.

Oseredek, Pol.; pop. 12; 75 km N of Przemysl; 50°26'/23°10'.

Oshekhlib, *see* Oshekhliby.

Oshekhliby, Ukr. (Osehlib, Oshekhlib); pop. 81; 26 km WNW of Chernovtsy; 48°25'/25°42'.

Oshetsk, *see* Osieck.

Oshetzk, *see* Osieck.

Oshik, *see* Osieck.

Oshiokov, *see* Osjakow.

Oshmana, *see* Oshmyany.

Oshmene, *see* Oshmyany.

Oshmiana, *see* Oshmyany.

Oshmina, *see* Oshmyany.

Oshmyany, Byel. (Asmena, Oshmana, Oshmene, Oshmiana, Oshmina, Osmiana, Osmiany, Oszmiana, Ozmiana); pop. 4,000; 120 km WNW of Minsk; 54°25'/25°56'; AMG, EJ, GUM3, GUM4, GUM5, GUM6, HSL, HSL2, JGFF, LDL, SF, YB.

Oshpetzin, *see* Oswiecim.

Oshpitsin, *see* Oswiecim.

Oshpol, *see* Uzpaliai.

Osht, *see* Goshcha.

Oshvitsin, *see* Oswiecim.

Oshvitzin, *see* Oswiecim.

Oshvotsk, *see* Otwock.

Oshvyentsim, *see* Oswiecim.

Osiakow, Pol.; pop. 759; 32 km WNW of Czestochowa; 50°55'/18°45'; GUM3, PHP1. This town was located on an interwar map of Poland but does not appear in contemporary gazetteers. Map coordinates are approximate.

Osie, Pol.; pop. 26; 88 km S of Gdansk; 53°36'/18°21'.

Osieciny, Pol.; pop. 436; 107 km NW of Lodz; 52°38'/18°43'; GUM3, LDS, PHP1, SF.

Osieck, Pol. (Oshetsk, Oshetzk, Oshik); pop. 324; 45 km SE of Warszawa; 51°58'/21°25'; HSL, HSL2, LYV, SF.

Osiecza, Pol.; pop. 7; 82 km ESE of Poznan; 52°11'/18°07'.

Osieczna, Pol. (Storchnest); 62 km S of Poznan; 51°54'/16°41'; HSL.

Osiek, Pol. (Osyetsk); pop. 539; 114 km SSW of Lublin; 50°29'/21°32'; COH, GA, GUM3, GUM5, YB.

Osiek (Kalisz area), Pol.; 88 km WNW of Czestochowa; 51°22'/18°12'; PHP1.

Osiek (near Krakow), Pol.; pop. 213; 50 km SW of Krakow; 49°57'/19°17'; EGRS, LYV, PHP3.

Osiek Grodowski, Pol.; 94 km WSW of Przemysl; 49°38'/21°29'; GA.

Osiekrow, *see* Osekruv.

Osielec, Pol.; pop. 9; 50 km S of Krakow; 49°41'/19°46'; PHP3.

Osijek, Yug. (Esseg, Eszek); pop. 2,445; 163 km WNW of Beograd; 45°33'/18°42'; AMG, CAHJP, EJ, GUM4, PHY.

Osijekdonji Grad, *see* Donji Grad.

Osinki, Pol.; pop. 20; 56 km SSW of Lublin; 50°48'/22°11'.

Osipenko, *see* Berdyansk.

Osipienko, *see* Berdyansk.

Osipovichi, Byel.; pop. 1,126; 94 km ESE of Minsk; 53°18'/28°38'; HSL, SF, YB.

Osjakov, *see* Osjakow.

Osjakow, Pol. (Oshiokov, Osjakov, Osyakow, Shakev, Ushiokov); 62 km NNW of Czestochowa; 51°17'/18°48'; AMG, LDL, SF.

Oskrzesince, *see* Oskzhesintse.

Oskzhesintse, Ukr. (Oskrzesince); pop. 20; 69 km SE of Lvov; 49°21'/24°26'.

Oslany, Cz.; pop. 90; 114 km NE of Bratislava; 48°38'/18°28'.

Oslav Byaly, *see* Belyye Oslavy.

Oslavy Charne, *see* Chernyye Oslavy.

Oslaw Bialy, *see* Belyye Oslavy.

Oslaw Gzarny, *see* Chernyye Oslavy.

Oslawica, Pol.; pop. 13; 75 km SSW of Przemysl; 49°18'/22°05'.

Osli, Hung.; 139 km N of Nagykanizsa; 47°38'/17°05'; HSL.

Oslip, Aus.; pop. 6; 45 km SE of Wien; 47°50'/16°37'.

Osmiana, *see* Oshmyany.

Osmiany, *see* Oshmyany.

Osmola, Pol.; pop. 8; 69 km S of Bialystok; 52°34'/22°58'.

Osmolice, Pol.; 19 km S of Lublin; 51°07'/22°30'; GUM6.

Osmolin, Pol.; pop. 63; 69 km N of Lodz; 52°18'/19°50'.

Osnabruck, Germ.; pop. 450; 114 km WSW of Hannover; 52°16'/08°03'; CAHJP, GUM4, GUM5, LDS, YB.

Osnica Wielka, *see* Velikaya Osnitsa.

Osnick, *see* Osnitsk.

Osnitsk, Ukr. (Osnick); pop. 37; 101 km NNE of Rovno; 51°17'/27°09'.

Osno, Pol. (Drossen); pop. 28; 120 km SSE of Szczecin; 52°27'/14°52'; HSL, LDS.

Osoblaha, Cz. (Hotzenplotz); pop. 13; 146 km NNE of Brno; 50°17'/17°43'; EJ, HSL, HSL2.

Osobnica, Pol.; pop. 18; 94 km WSW of Przemysl; 49°42'/21°25'.

Osochniki, Byel. (Osoczniki); pop. 24; 133 km WNW of Pinsk; 52°52'/24°39'.

Osoczniki, *see* Osochniki.

Osoj, Yug. BGN lists two possible localities with this name located at 41°32'/20°39' and 41°32'/20°56'. COH, HSL.

Osorheiu, Rom. (Fugyivasarhely); pop. 73; 126 km W of Cluj; 47°02'/22°03'; PHR2.

Osova, Ukr.; 56 km NNW of Rovno; 51°05'/25°58'; CAHJP, SF.

Osovtse, Ukr. (Osowce); pop. 58; 107 km NNW of Chernovtsy; 49°09'/25°22'.

Osovtsy, (Osowce); *See also* Osovtsy Pervyye.

Osovtsy Pervyye, Byel. (Osovtsy); pop. 29; 62 km WSW of Pinsk; 52°05'/25°15'.

Osowa, Pol.; 69 km ENE of Lublin; 51°25'/23°31'; GA, HSL, SF.

Osowa (near Sarny), Ukr.; pop. 23; 101 km N of Rovno; 51°28'/26°22'.

Osowa Wysksa, GUM3. This town was not found in BGN gazetteers under the given spelling.

Osowa Wyszka, Pol.; pop. 700; COH. Described in the *Black Book* as being in the Wolyn region of Poland, this town was not found in BGN gazetteers.

Osowce, *see* Osovtse; Osovtsy.

Osowek, Pol.; 114 km NE of Krakow; 50°29'/21°22'; POL.

Osowka, Pol. (Ossowka Nowa); pop. 22; 94 km NE of Krakow; 50°36'/21°00'.

Ospinzi, *see* Oswiecim.

Ossa, Cz. AMG. A number of towns share this name. It was not possible to determine from available information which one is being referenced.

Ossala, Pol.; pop. 27; 114 km NE of Krakow; 50°29'/21°22'.

Ossan, Germ.; pop. 22; Described in the *Black Book* as being in the Rheinland-Pfalz region of Germany, this town was not found in BGN gazetteers.

Ossendorf, Germ.; 107 km SSW of Hannover; 51°31'/09°05'; GED.

Ossovo, *see* Bolshoye Osovo.

Ossowa, Pol.; pop. 32; 69 km N of Lublin; 51°49'/22°51'; GA, GUM5, GUM6.

Ossowka Nowa, *see* Osowka.

Ostalovitse, Ukr. (Ostalowice); pop. 43; 50 km ESE of Lvov; 49°36'/24°32'.

Ostalowice, *see* Ostalovitse.

Ostape, *see* Ostapovo.

Ostapie, *see* Ostapovo.

Ostapkowce, Pol.; pop. 28; Described in the *Black Book* as being in the Stanislawow region of Poland, this town was not found in BGN gazetteers.

Ostapovo, Ukr. (Ostape, Ostapie); pop. 31; 126 km N of Chernovtsy; 49°23'/26°02'; GUM4.

Ostashin, Byel. (Ostaszyn); pop. 21; BGN lists two possible localities with this name located at 53°28'/26°10' and 53°41'/26°01'.

Ostaszyn, *see* Ostashin.

Ostende, Byel. AMG. A number of towns share this name. It was not possible to determine from available information which one is being referenced.

Oster, Ukr. (Ostor, Ostrz); pop. 1,267; 62 km NNE of Kiyev; 50°57'/30°53'; SF.

Osterberg, Germ.; 101 km ESE of Stuttgart; 48°09'/10°10'; JGFF, LDS, PHGB.

Osterburken, Germ.; pop. 7; 82 km N of Stuttgart; 49°26'/09°25'; PHGBW.

Ostercappeln, Germ. (Osterkappeln); 101 km WSW of Hannover; 52°21'/08°14'; LDS.

Osterdorf, Germ. BGN lists two possible localities with this name located at 47°33'/10°06' and 48°57'/10°58'. PHGBW.

Ostereiden, Germ.; 126 km SW of Hannover; 51°34'/08°26'; JGFF.

Osterfeld, Germ.; pop. 48; 114 km N of Frankfurt am Main; 51°03'/08°39'; GED.

Osterholz Scharmbeck, Germ.; pop. 38; 82 km SW of Hamburg; 53°14'/08°48'.

Osterkappeln, *see* Ostercappeln.

Oster Novoselitz, LDL. This pre-World War I community was not found in BGN gazetteers.

Osterode, *see* Ostroda.

Osterode am Harz, Germ.; pop. 48; 82 km SE of Hannover; 51°44'/10°11'; GUM4, GUM5, GUM6, LDS.

Ostffyasszonyfa, Hung.; pop. 18; 107 km N of Nagykanizsa; 47°19'/17°03'.

Osthafen, *possibly* Osthofen.

Ostheim, *see* Ostheim vor der Rhon.

Ostheim vor der Rhon, Germ. (Ostheim); 120 km NE of Frankfurt am Main; 50°28'/10°13'; GUM5, HSL, PHGB, PHGBW.

Osthofen, Germ. (Osthafen?); pop. 95; 50 km SSW of Frankfurt am Main; 49°42'/08°20'; GUM3, GUM5, HSL.

Ostila, *see* Ustilug.

Ostin, Germ.; pop. 1; 50 km SSE of Munchen; 47°45'/11°46'.

Ostinghausen, Germ.; 114 km NE of Koln; 51°38'/08°12'; JGFF.

Ostobuz, *see* Ostobuzh.

Ostobuzh, Ukr. (Ostobuz); pop. 11; 62 km NNW of Lvov; 50°22'/23°53'.

Ostoje, Pol.; pop. 13; 62 km N of Wroclaw; 51°34'/17°09'.

Ostojicevo, Yug. (Potiski Sveti Nikola); pop. 27; 126 km NNW of Beograd; 45°53'/20°10'.

Ostojow, Pol.; pop. 22; 120 km ENE of Czestochowa; 51°01'/20°49'.

Ostor, *see* Oster.

Ostoros, Hung.; pop. 9; 38 km SW of Miskolc; 47°52'/20°26'; AMG.

Ostorw Polnochy, LDL. This pre-World War I community was not found in BGN gazetteers.

Ostra, *see* Ostrog.

Ostraha, *see* Ostrog.

Ostra Mogila, Ukr.; 94 km WNW of Chernovtsy; 48°46'/24°54'; GUM4.

Ostrava, Cz. (Maehrisch Ostrau, Mahrisch Ostrau, Mahrish Ostrau, Moravska Ostrava, Morawska Ostrawa); pop. 6,865; 139 km NE of Brno; 49°50'/18°17'; AMG, EJ, GUM3, GUM4, GUM5, GUM6, HSL, ISH2, JGFF, PHP3, PHP4.

Ostrava Slezska, Cz.; pop. 668; Described in the *Black Book* as being in the Moravia-Silesia region of Czechoslovakia, this town was not found in BGN gazetteers.

Ostre, *see* Ostrog.

Ostredek, Cz.; pop. 6; 38 km SE of Praha; 49°50'/14°50'.

Ostretin, Cz.; pop. 2; 107 km NW of Brno; 50°03'/16°02'.

Ostreznica, Pol.; pop. 4; 32 km WNW of Krakow; 50°11'/19°34'.

Ostrich, Germ. (Oestrich); 50 km WSW of Frankfurt am Main; 50°01'/08°02'; CAHJP.

Ostrin, *see* Ostryna.

Ostringen, Germ.; pop. 20; 62 km NW of Stuttgart; 49°13'/08°43'; LDS, PHGBW.

Ostroda, Pol. (Osterode); pop. 156; 107 km ESE of Gdansk; 53°42'/19°59'; HSL.

Ostrog, Ukr. (Ostra, Ostraha, Ostre); pop. 7,991; 38 km SE of Rovno; 50°20'/26°31'; AMG, CAHJP, EDRD, EJ, GA, GUM3, GUM4, GUM5, GYLA, HSL, HSL2, JGFF, LDL, PHP2, SF, YB.

Ostrogorsk, USSR (Ostrogozhsk, Ostrogozsk); pop. 221; 114 km SE of Voronezh; 50°49'/39°00'.

Ostrogozhsk, *see* Ostrogorsk.

Ostrogozsk, *see* Ostrogorsk.

Ostroleka, Pol. (Ostrolenka); pop. 3,352; 101 km NNE of Warszawa; 53°05'/21°34'; AMG, COH, EJ, GUM3, GUM4, GUM5, GYLA, HSL, HSL2, JGFF, LDL, LYV, PHP4, SF, YB.

Ostrolenka, *see* Ostroleka.

Ostromech Krulevski, *see* Ostromichi.

Ostromecz Krolewski, *see* Ostromichi.

Ostromeczyn, Pol.; pop. 5; 101 km S of Bialystok; 52°16'/22°50'; HSL.

Ostromer, Cz.; pop. 2; 82 km NE of Praha; 50°22'/15°32'.

Ostromichi, Byel. (Ostromech Krulevski, Ostromecz Krolewski); pop. 29; 114 km W of Pinsk; 52°17'/24°28'.

Ostronek, Pol. EDRD. This town was not found in BGN gazetteers under the given spelling.

Ostropol, Ukr. (Ostropolia); pop. 1,325; 88 km WNW of Vinnitsa; 49°48'/27°34'; GUM5, HSL, JGFF, LDL, SF, WS.

Ostropolia, *see* Ostropol.

Ostrorog, Pol. (Scharfenort); pop. 15; 38 km WNW of Poznan; 52°38'/16°28'.

Ostroshitskiy Gorodok, Byel.; pop. 665; 26 km NNE of Minsk; 54°04'/27°42'.

Ostrov; *See also* Ostrow and listings under Ostruv.

Ostrov (near Minsk), Byel.; pop. 4; 45 km SE of Minsk; 53°36'/27°55'.

Ostrov (near Rudki), Ukr.; pop. 26; 56 km SW of Lvov; 49°37'/23°21'.

Ostrova, *see* Ostrow Lubelski.

Ostrovchik Polny, Ukr. (Ostrowczyk Polny); pop. 20; 50 km ENE of Lvov; 49°54'/24°43'.

Ostrovets, Byel. (Ostrowiec [Vilnius Area]); 133 km WNW of Minsk; 54°37'/25°57'; GUM5.

Ostrovitz, *see* Ostrowiec Swietokrzyski.

Ostrovitza, *see* Ostrowiec Swietokrzyski.

Ostrov Lubelski, *see* Ostrow Lubelski.

Ostrov Mazovyetska, *see* Ostrow Mazowiecka.

Ostrovna, *see* Ostrovno.

Ostrovno, Byel. (Ostrovna); 26 km SW of Vitebsk; 55°08'/29°53'; SF.

Ostrovtse, *see* Ostrowiec Swietokrzyski.

Ostrovy, *see* Ostrowy.

Ostrow, Pol. AMG, COH, JGFF, LDL. A number of towns share this name. It was not possible to determine from available information which one is being referenced. There are at least 50 towns with Ostrow (also Ostrov, Ostruv) as the name or part of the name. *See also* Ostrow Lubelski, Ostrow Mazowiecka and Ostrow Wielkopolski, which were the most populous. It was not possible to determine which Ostrow is indicated in the AMG, COH, JGFF and LDL entries. *See also* Ostrov and the listings under Ostruv.

Ostrow (near Chelm), Pol.; pop. 16; 88 km E of Lublin; 51°07'/23°47'.

Ostrow (near Dubno), Ukr.; pop. 6; 82 km SW of Rovno; 50°20'/25°13'.

Ostrow (near Janow Lubelski), Pol.; pop. 18; 38 km SSW of Lublin; 51°00'/22°15'.

Ostrow (near Jaroslaw), Pol.; pop. 74; 38 km WNW of Przemysl; 50°01'/22°25'.

Ostrow (near Konstantynow), Pol.; pop. 2; 107 km S of Bialystok; 52°11'/23°20'.

Ostrow (near Lubartow), Pol.; pop. 24; 45 km NNW of Lublin; 51°36'/22°20'.

Ostrow (near Luninets), Byel.; pop. 3; 26 km SSE of Pinsk; 51°55'/26°13'.

Ostrow (near Miechow), Pol.; pop. 5; 32 km NE of Krakow; 50°14'/20°22'.

Ostrow (near Przemysl), Pol.; pop. 65; 6 km WNW of Przemysl; 49°48'/22°44'.

Ostrow (near Ropczyce), Pol.; pop. 27; 88 km WNW of Przemysl; 50°05'/21°35'.

Ostrow (near Sokal), Ukr.; pop. 41; 75 km N of Lvov; 50°29'/24°17'.

Ostrow (near Tarnopol), Ukr.; pop. 3; 82 km SW of Rovno; 50°20'/25°13'.

Ostrow (Nowogrodek), Byel.; pop. 8; 94 km N of Pinsk; 52°53'/25°59'.

Ostrowczyk Polny, *see* Ostrovchik Polny.

Ostrowek, Pol.; pop. 90; 94 km ENE of Warszawa; 52°19'/22°25'; COH, HSL.

Ostrowek (near Kalisz), Pol.; 88 km W of Lodz; 51°54'/18°09'; PHP1.

Ostrowek (near Sokolow), Pol.; pop. 44; 62 km NE of Warszawa; 52°33'/21°47'.

Ostrowek (near Wegrow), Pol.; pop. 56; 75 km NW of Lublin; 51°46'/21°52'; GUM3.

Ostrowek (near Wielun), Pol.; 75 km NW of Czestochowa; 51°21'/18°37'; PHP1.

Ostrowiec, *see* Ostrowiec Swietokrzyski. Ostrowiec usually refers to the town of Ostrowiec Swietokrzyski.

Ostrowiec (Lvov area), Pol.; pop. 53; 50 km NNE of Przemysl; 50°09'/23°09'.

Ostrowiec (Vilnius area), *see* Ostrovets.

Ostrowiec Kielecki, Pol. AMG, PHP1. This town was not found in BGN gazetteers under the given spelling.

Ostrowiec Swietokrzyski, Pol. (Ostrovitz, Ostrovitza, Ostrovtse, Ostrowiec); pop. 10,095; 88 km SW of Lublin; 50°56'/21°24'; AMG, COH, EDRD, EJ, FRG, GA, GUM3, GUM4, GUM5, GUM6, HSL, HSL2, LDL, PHP4, POCEM, SF, YB.

Ostrowik, Pol.; 56 km WNW of Bialystok; 53°25'/22°29'; HSL.

Ostrow Kaliski, Pol.; pop. 22; 88 km WSW of Lodz; 51°33'/18°13'.

Ostrow Krolewski, Pol.; pop. 2; 38 km E of Krakow; 50°01'/20°29'.

Ostrow Lubelski, Pol. (Ostrov Lubelski, Ostrova); pop. 1,267; 32 km NNE of Lublin; 51°29'/22°51'; GA, GUM3, GUM5, GUM6, HSL, HSL2, JGFF, LDL, LYV, POCEM, SF.

Ostrow Mazowiecka, Pol. (Ostrov Mazovyetska, Ostrow Mazowiecki); pop. 6,812; 82 km NE of Warszawa; 52°48'/21°54'; AMG, EDRD, EJ, GUM3, GUM4, GUM5, HSL, HSL2, JGFF, LDL, LDS, LYV, PHP1, PHP4, SF, YB.

Ostrow Mazowiecki, *see* Ostrow Mazowiecka.

Ostrowo, *see* Ostrow Wielkopolski.

Ostrow Polnocny, Pol.; 38 km NE of Bialystok; 53°16'/23°41'; SF.

Ostrow Poludniowy, Pol.; pop. 6; 38 km NE of Bialystok; 53°15'/23°42'.

Ostrowsko, Pol.; pop. 11; 75 km SSE of Krakow; 49°29'/20°06'.

Ostrow Szlachecki, Pol.; pop. 8; 38 km E of Krakow; 50°02'/20°29'.

Ostrow Volhynia, LDL. This pre-World War I community was not found in BGN gazetteers.

Ostrow Wielkopolski, Pol. (Ostrowo); pop. 170; 88 km NNE of Wroclaw; 51°39'/17°49'; CAHJP, HSL, JGFF, LDS.

Ostrowy, Pol. (Ostrovy); pop. 138; 32 km NNW of Czestochowa; 50°59'/19°04'; HSL, SF.

Ostrowy Baranowskie, Pol.; pop. 21; 101 km WNW of Przemysl; 50°19'/21°39'.

Ostrowy Tuszowskie, Pol.; pop. 1; 101 km WNW of Przemysl; 50°18'/21°39'.

Ostrozec, *see* Ostrozhets.

Ostrozen, Pol.; pop. 19; 75 km ESE of Warszawa; 51°48'/21°45'.

Ostrozhets, Ukr. (Ostrozec); pop. 624; 50 km W of Rovno; 50°40'/25°33'; AMG, COH, EDRD, GUM4, LDL, SF.

Ostrozske Predmesti, Cz.; pop. 53; 62 km ESE of Brno; 48°59'/17°24'.

Ostrusza, Pol.; pop. 6; 88 km ESE of Krakow; 49°47'/21°01'.

Ostruv; See listings below. *See also* Ostrov; Ostrow.

Ostruv (near Bobrka), Ukr.; pop. 54; 50 km SE of Lvov; 49°28'/24°16'.

Ostruv (near Kalush), Ukr.; pop. 26; 88 km SE of Lvov; 49°10'/24°38'.

Ostruv (near Kamenka Strumilovska), Ukr.; pop. 10; 45 km ENE of Lvov; 49°56'/24°36'.

Ostruv (near Lutsk), Ukr.; pop. 3; 69 km WNW of Rovno; 50°59'/25°33'.

Ostruv (near Lvov), Ukr.; pop. 89; 26 km SSW of Lvov; 49°40'/23°52'.

Ostruv (near Tarnopol), Ukr.; 120 km ESE of Lvov; 49°29'/25°35'; GUM4, GUM5.

Ostrykol, Pol. (Ostrykol Wloscianski); pop. 24; 88 km NW of Bialystok; 53°44'/22°26'; AMG.

Ostrykol Wloscianski, *see* Ostrykol.

Ostryna, Byel. (Astrin, Istrin, Ostrin); pop. 1,067; 195 km WSW of Minsk; 53°44'/24°32'; COH, EJ, GA, GUM3, GUM5, HSL, JGFF, LDL, LYV, SF, YB.

Ostrz, *see* Oster.

Ostrzeszow, Pol. (Schildberg); pop. 122; 75 km NE of Wroclaw; 51°25'/17°57'; CAHJP, HSL, JGFF, LDS.

Osveya, Byel.; pop. 700; 157 km WNW of Vitebsk; 56°01'/28°06'; HSL.

Osviet, LDL. This pre-World War I community was not found in BGN gazetteers.

Osvracin, Cz.; pop. 3; 120 km SW of Praha; 49°31'/13°03'.

Oswiecim, Pol. (Auschwitz, Aushvits, Oshpetzin, Oshpitsin, Oshvitsin, Oshvitzin, Oshvyentsim, Ospinzi); pop. 4,950; 50 km WSW of Krakow; 50°02'/19°14'; AMG, CAHJP, COH, EGRS, EJ, FRG, GA, GUM3, GUM4, GUM5, GUM6, HSL, HSL2, JGFF, LDL, LYV, PHGBW, PHP1, PHP2, PHP3, PHP4, POCEM, SF, YB. As the location of the infamous Auschwitz concentration camp, most sources refer to the camp rather than the town.

Osyakow, *see* Osjakow.

Osyetsk, *see* Osiek.

Oszczerze, Pol.; pop. 27; 69 km ENE of Warszawa; 52°18'/22°00'.

Oszczow, Pol.; pop. 44; 126 km NE of Przemysl; 50°33'/24°04'; GUM4, GUM5.

Oszlar, Hung.; 32 km SE of Miskolc; 47°53'/21°02'; HSL, HSL2.

Oszmiana, *see* Oshmyany.

Oszro, Hung.; 94 km ESE of Nagykanizsa; 45°53'/17°55'; HSL. This town was located on a pre-World War I map, but does not appear in contemporary gazetteers.

Osztopan, Hung.; pop. 22; 50 km ENE of Nagykanizsa; 46°31'/17°40'.

Otach Tyrg, *see* Ataki.

Otaci Sat, *see* Ataki.

Otaci Targ, *see* Ataki.

Otalez, Pol.; pop. 31; 94 km NE of Krakow; 50°21'/21°14'.

Otchakov, *see* Ochakov.

Oteni, Rom.; pop. 3; 139 km ESE of Cluj; 46°15'/25°15'.

Otfinow, Pol.; pop. 30; 62 km ENE of Krakow; 50°11'/20°49'.

Otinya, *see* Otynya.

Otiski Vrh, Yug.; pop. 1; 114 km NW of Zagreb; 46°35'/15°03'.

Otmet, Pol. (Ottmuth); 88 km SW of Czestochowa;

50°29'/17°58'; GUM3, GUM4, PHP3.

Otocac, Yug.; 120 km SSW of Zagreb; 44°52'/15°14'; GUM4.

Otoczna, Pol.; 50 km E of Poznan; 52°20'/17°42'; EDRD, GA, GUM4, GUM5.

Otomani, Rom.; pop. 42; 126 km WNW of Cluj; 47°26'/22°14'; HSL.

Otrocz, Pol.; pop. 28; 50 km S of Lublin; 50°49'/22°35'.

Otschakow, *see* Ochakov.

Ottensheim, Aus.; pop. 4; 107 km NE of Salzburg; 48°20'/14°11'.

Ottensoos, Germ.; pop. 38; 19 km NE of Nurnberg; 49°31'/11°21'; CAHJP, GUM5, HSL, HSL2, JGFF, PHGB.

Ottenstein, Germ.; 56 km SSW of Hannover; 51°57'/09°24'; LDS.

Otterberg, Germ.; 88 km SSW of Frankfurt am Main; 49°30'/07°46'; HSL, JGFF.

Otterskirchen, Germ. (Holzing); 133 km NE of Munchen; 48°37'/13°17'; PHGB.

Ottersleben, Germ. (Gross Ottersleben); 107 km NW of Leipzig; 52°06'/11°35'; HSL.

Otterstadt, Germ.; 82 km NW of Stuttgart; 49°22'/08°27'; EJ, LDS.

Otteveny, Hung.; pop. 5; 120 km W of Budapest; 47°44'/17°29'.

Otting, Germ. BGN lists two possible localities with this name located at 47°56'/12°42' and 48°53'/10°48'. GUM5.

Ottingen, Germ. (Oettingen); pop. 88; 69 km SSW of Nurnberg; 48°57'/10°36'; GED, HSL, HSL2, JGFF, PHGB.

Otwock, Poland: Boys drawing water from the town pump.

Ottmuth, *see* Otmet.

Ottobeuren, Germ.; 101 km WSW of Munchen; 47°56'/10°18'; PHGB.

Ottrau, Germ.; pop. 17; 94 km NNE of Frankfurt am Main; 50°48'/09°23'; JGFF, LDS.

Ottweiler, Germ.; pop. 55; 133 km SW of Frankfurt am Main; 49°23'/07°10'; GED, GUM5.

Ottynia, *see* Otynya.

Ottyniowice, *see* Ottynovitse.

Ottynovitse, Ukr. (Ottyniowice); pop. 20; 50 km SE of Lvov; 49°26'/24°19'.

Otvock, *see* Otwock.

Otvosk, *see* Otwock.

Otvoskonyi, Hung.; pop. 12; 32 km ESE of Nagykanizsa; 46°17'/17°22'.

Otvotsk, *see* Otwock.

Otvovice, Cz.; pop. 2; 19 km WNW of Praha; 50°13'/14°16'.

Otwock, Pol. (Oshvotsk, Otvosk, Otvotsk, Ushvotsk); pop. 5,408; 26 km ESE of Warszawa; 52°08'/21°19'; AMG, COH, EDRD, EJ, FRG, GA, GUM3, GUM4, GUM5, GUM6, HSL, HSL2, ISH2, JGFF, LYV, PHP1, PHP4, SF, YB.

Otyn, Pol. (Deutsch Wartenberg); pop. 1; 107 km SW of Poznan; 51°51'/15°43'; AMG.

Otynya, Ukr. (Otinya, Ottynia); pop. 1,728; 88 km WNW of Chernovtsy; 48°44'/24°51'; COH, EDRD, EGRS, GUM4, GYLA, HSL, HSL2, JGFF, LDL, PHP2, SF.

Ovadno, Ukr. (Owadno); pop. 14; 120 km N of Lvov; 50°55'/24°24'.

Ovanta, *see* Alanta.

Ovenhausen, Germ.; pop. 10; 69 km SSW of Hannover; 51°47'/09°18'; GED.

Ovenstadt, Germ.; pop. 4; 50 km W of Hannover; 52°25'/08°58'.

Oventrop, *see* Oeventrop.

Ovidiopol, Ukr. (Ovidipol); 38 km SW of Odessa; 46°16'/30°26'; JGFF, LDL, SF.

Ovidipol, *see* Ovidiopol.

Ovlochin, Ukr. (Ovlochym, Owloczym); pop. 45; 139 km N of Lvov; 51°05'/24°15'.

Ovlochym, *see* Ovlochin.

Ovruch, Ukr. (Ovrutch, Owrucz); pop. 3,400; 150 km WNW of Kiyev; 51°19'/28°48'; EDRD, GUM3, GUM4, HSL, LDL, SF.

Ovrutch, *see* Ovruch.

Ovsemerov, Byel. (Owsiemirow); pop. 29; 32 km ESE of Pinsk; 52°00'/26°29'.

Owadno, *see* Ovadno.

Owadow, Pol.; pop. 2; 62 km ESE of Lodz; 51°23'/20°08'.

Owanta, *see* Alanta.

Owloczym, *see* Ovlochin.

Ownia, Pol.; pop. 15; 69 km NW of Lublin; 51°42'/21°55'.

Owrucz, *see* Ovruch.

Owsiemirow, *see* Ovsemerov.

Oxintea, *see* Oksentiya.

Oyber Visheve, *see* Viseu de Sus.

Oygstova, *see* Augustow.

Oyshitz, *see* Novaya Ushitsa.

Oytz, *see* Auce.

Ozalj, Yug.; pop. 7; 45 km SW of Zagreb; 45°37'/15°29'.

Ozanna, *see* Ozenna.

Ozarichi, Byel. (Ozaritch); pop. 1,238; 120 km W of Gomel; 52°28'/29°16'; SF.

Ozarichi (Polesie), Byel. (Ozarycze); 38 km NW of Pinsk; 52°24'/25°51'; GUM4.

Ozarinet, *see* Ozarintsy.

Ozarintsy, Ukr. (Ozarinet); 88 km SSW of Vinnitsa; 48°32'/27°48'; PHR1.

Ozaritch, *see* Ozarichi.

Ozarkov, *see* Ozorkow.

Ozarov, *see* Ozarow.

Ozarow, Pol. (Ozarov, Ozharov, Ozhorov); pop. 2,258; 75 km SW of Lublin; 50°53'/21°40'; AMG, COH, FRG, GA, GUM3, GUM5, GYLA, HSL, JGFF, LDS, PHP1, POCEM, SF, YB.

Ozarow (Warszawa), Pol.; pop. 54; 19 km WSW of Warszawa; 52°13'/20°49'.

Ozarow Przy Lugowie, Pol.; pop. 6; 26 km WNW of Lublin; 51°20'/22°19'.

Ozarycze, *see* Ozarichi (Polesie).

Ozd, Hung.; pop. 197; 38 km WNW of Miskolc; 48°13'/20°18'; AMG, GUM3, HSL, HSL2, LDL, LDS, PHH.

Ozdamicze, *see* Olgomel.

Ozdfalu, Hung.; pop. 3; 101 km ESE of Nagykanizsa;

45°56'/18°01'.

Ozdititch, *see* Ozyutichi.

Ozdiuticz, LDL. This pre-World War I community was not found in BGN gazetteers.

Ozdziutycze, *see* Ozyutichi.

Ozegow, Pol.; pop. 15; 50 km NNW of Czestochowa; 51°11'/18°53'.

Ozenna, Pol. (Ozanna); pop. 43; 56 km NNW of Przemysl; 50°17'/22°32'.

Ozerany, *see* Ozeryany (Wolyn II).

Ozerany (Nowogrodek), Byel.; pop. 4; 139 km SW of Minsk; 53°24'/25°39'.

Ozeri, *see* Ozery.

Ozernitsa, Byel. (Jeziernica); pop. 162; 62 km ENE of Pinsk; 52°17'/27°01'.

Ozernyani, *see* Ozernyany.

Ozernyany, Ukr. (Jezierna, Ozernyani, Uzirna, Uzyerni, Yezherne, Yezhyerna, Yezirna); pop. 835; 101 km E of Lvov; 49°38'/25°20'; AMG, COH, EGRS, GUM3, GUM4, GUM5, GYLA, HSL, JGFF, LDL, LYV, PHP2, SF, YB.

Ozero, (Jezioro);

Ozero (Polesie), Ukr.; pop. 82; 120 km NNE of Rovno; 51°34'/26°55'.

Ozero (Wolyn), Ukr.; pop. 21; 107 km N of Rovno; 51°30'/26°13'.

Ozersk, USSR (Darkehmen); pop. 12; 107 km ESE of Kaliningrad; 54°25'/22°01'; JGFF.

Ozery, Byel. (Jeziory, Ozeri, Ozhor, Ozor, Ozra, Ozyori, Yezhore, Yeziori, Yezyori); pop. 867; 221 km WSW of Minsk; 53°43'/24°11'; EJ, GA, GUM3, HSL, LDL, LYV, SF, WS.

Ozeryany, Ukr. (Jezierzany, Ozieran, Yezerzhany, Yezezhany, Yezherzani, Yezierne, Yezyerzany); pop. 1,302; 69 km N of Chernovtsy; 48°53'/25°57'; AMG, CAHJP, COH, EDRD, EGRS, GUM4, GUM5, HSL, HSL2, JGFF, LDL, LYV, PHP2, YB.

Ozeryany (Stanislawow), Ukr.; pop. 14; 82 km WNW of Chernovtsy; 48°48'/25°06'; GUM3.

Ozeryany (Wolyn), Ukr. (Jezierzany, Ozhiran, Ozyeran, Uziran, Yezerzani); pop. 340; 114 km WNW of Rovno; 51°01'/24°48'; SF.

Ozeryany (Wolyn II), Ukr. (Ozerany, Ozierany, Oziran); pop. 796; 19 km SSW of Rovno; 50°28'/26°02'; JGFF, SF.

Ozga, Pol.; pop. 34; 56 km NNE of Czestochowa; 51°14'/19°28'.

Ozharov, *see* Ozarow.

Ozhidiv, Ukr. (Ozydow); pop. 132; 62 km ENE of Lvov; 49°58'/24°49'; HSL.

Ozhiran, *see* Ozeryany (Wolyn).

Ozhor, *see* Ozery.

Ozhorov, *see* Ozarow.

Oziaty, *see* Ozyaty.

Ozieran, *see* Ozeryany.

Ozierany, *see* Ozeryany (Wolyn II).

Ozimina, Ukr.; pop. 12; 62 km SW of Lvov; 49°28'/23°24'. This town was located on an interwar map of Poland but does not appear in contemporary gazetteers. Map coordinates are approximate.

Oziran, *see* Ozeryany (Wolyn II).

Ozmanbuk, Hung.; pop. 4; 62 km NNW of Nagykanizsa; 46°55'/16°41'.

Ozmiana, *see* Oshmany.

Ozomla, Aus. AMG, PHP2. This town was not found in BGN gazetteers under the given spelling.

Ozor, *see* Ozery.

Ozora, Hung.; pop. 72; 94 km SSW of Budapest; 46°45'/18°24'; PHH.

Ozorkov, *see* Ozorkow.

Ozorkow, Pol. (Ozarkov, Ozorkov); pop. 4,949; 32 km NW of Lodz; 51°58'/19°17'; AMG, CAHJP, COH, EDRD, EJ, GA, GUM3, GUM4, GUM5, HSL, HSL2, JGFF, LDL, LDS, LYV, PHP1, PHP4, SF, YB.

Ozorow, Pol.; pop. 22; 75 km E of Warszawa; 52°07'/22°02'.

Ozra, *see* Ozery.

Oztza, *see* Ustse Zelene.

Ozun, Rom. (Uzon); pop. 44; 157 km N of Bucuresti; 45°48'/25°51'; HSL.

Ozyaty, Byel. (Oziaty); pop. 5; 133 km WSW of Pinsk; 52°06'/24°09'.

Ozydow, *see* Ozhidiv.

Ozyeran, *see* Ozeryany (Wolyn).

Ozynna, HSL. This pre-World War I community was not found in BGN gazetteers.

Ozyori, *see* Ozery.

Ozyutichi, Ukr. (Ozdititch, Ozdziutycze); pop. 739; 107 km W of Rovno; 50°51'/24°43'; GUM3, SF.

Paasdorf, Aus.; pop. 3; 45 km N of Wien; 48°32'/16°32'.

Pabaiskas, Lith.; pop. 22; 62 km NE of Kaunas; 55°10'/24°46'.

Pabazi, Lat.; pop. 2; 38 km NNE of Riga; 57°14'/24°24'.

Pabenits, *see* Pabianice.

Paberze, Lith. (Padbradje, Podberezha); 38 km NNW of Vilnius; 54°56'/25°14'; JGFF, LDL, SF.

Pabianice, Pol. (Pabenits, Pabjanice, Pabnitz, Pabyanets, Pabyanitse); pop. 7,336; 13 km SSW of Lodz; 51°40'/19°22'; AMG, CAHJP, COH, EDRD, EJ, FRG, GA, GUM3, GUM4, GUM5, HSL, HSL2, JGFF, LDL, LDS, PHP1, PHP4, POCEM, SF, YB.

Pabierowice, Pol.; pop. 6; 50 km S of Warszawa; 51°51'/20°55'.

Pabirze, Lith. (Pebirzih); pop. 1; 88 km ENE of Siauliai; 56°11'/24°39'; YL.

Pabjanice, *see* Pabianice.

Pabnitz, *see* Pabianice.

Pabrade, Lith. (Podbrodz, Podbrodze, Podbrodzie); 50 km NNE of Vilnius; 55°00'/25°47'; AMG, COH, GUM3, GUM4, GUM5, GUM6, HSL, JGFF, SF, YB.

Pabyanets, *see* Pabianice.

Pabyanitse, *see* Pabianice.

Pacanow, Pol. (Patsanov); pop. 1,689; 88 km NE of Krakow; 50°24'/21°03'; AMG, COH, GUM3, GUM4, GUM5, LDS, LYV.

Pachnowola, Pol.; pop. 7; 50 km WNW of Lublin; 51°25'/21°54'.

Pachow, Pol.; pop. 4; 94 km WNW of Lodz; 52°18'/18°28'.

Pachten, Germ.; pop. 3; 163 km SW of Frankfurt am Main; 49°21'/06°43'.

Pacierzow, Pol.; pop. 7; 26 km NE of Czestochowa; 50°54'/19°24'.

Pacin, Hung. (Paczin); pop. 98; 82 km NE of Miskolc; 48°20'/21°50'; AMG, HSL, JGFF, PHH.

Pacir, Yug.; pop. 23; 146 km NW of Beograd; 45°54'/19°27'.

Pacov, Cz.; pop. 124; 82 km SE of Praha; 49°29'/15°01'.

Pacsa, Hung.; pop. 96; 38 km N of Nagykanizsa; 46°43'/17°01'; HSL, LDS.

Pacureni, Rom.; pop. 2; 75 km E of Cluj; 46°39'/24°33'.

Paczin, *see* Pacin.

Paczyna, Pol.; pop. 6; 56 km SSW of Czestochowa; 50°25'/18°34'.

Padaflesa, *see* Podplesa.

Padaflesha, *see* Podplesa.

Padar, Hung.; 50 km N of Nagykanizsa; 46°51'/17°01'; HSL.

Padberg, Germ.; 126 km SSW of Hannover; 51°24'/08°46'; LDS.

Padbradje, *see* Paberze.

Padbuz, *see* Podbuzh.

Padej, Yug.; pop. 28; 120 km NNW of Beograd; 45°50'/20°10'.

Paderborn, Germ.; pop. 310; 101 km SSW of Hannover; 51°43'/08°46'; EJ, GED, GUM4, GUM5, GUM6, HSL, JGFF, LDS.

Paderewek, Pol.; pop. 5; 88 km SSW of Bialystok; 52°33'/22°20'.

Padew, Pol.; pop. 81; 114 km WNW of Przemysl; 50°26'/21°30'.

Padina, Yug.; pop. 33; 38 km NNE of Beograd; 45°07'/20°44'.

Padoc, *see* Podobovets.

Padubysys, Lith. (Bazilian, Bazilionai); 19 km SSW of Siauliai; 55°48'/23°08'; GUM5, YL.

Paezereliai, Lith.; pop. 155; 38 km WNW of Kaunas;

55°04'/23°22'.

Paezeriai, Lith.; pop. 24; 56 km NNE of Kaunas; 55°22'/24°17'.

Pagiriai, Lith. (Pagiris, Pegir, Pogir); pop. 83; 62 km NNE of Kaunas; 55°21'/24°24'; JGFF, LDL, SF, YL.

Pagiris, *see* Pagiriai.

Pagorzyna, Pol.; pop. 10; 107 km WSW of Przemysl; 49°42'/21°21'.

Pahi, Hung.; pop. 1; 75 km WNW of Szeged; 46°43'/19°24'.

Pahres, Germ.; 38 km WNW of Nurnberg; 49°37'/10°39'; GUM5, JGFF, PHGB.

Paide, Est. (Veisenshtein, Weissenstein); 75 km ESE of Tallinn; 58°54'/25°33'; PHLE.

Paingeni, Rom.; pop. 5; 75 km E of Cluj; 46°41'/24°34'.

Pajakow, Pol.; pop. 14; 56 km W of Lublin; 51°23'/21°48'.

Pajeczno, Pol. (Payentchno); pop. 618; 45 km NNW of Czestochowa; 51°09'/19°00'; CAHJP, COH, GA, GUM3, GUM4, LDS, PHP1, SF.

Pajuris, Lith. (Payora, Payuris, Piora, Poyuri?); 94 km WSW of Siauliai; 55°41'/21°56'; LDL, SF, YL.

Pakens, Germ.; pop. 2; 133 km W of Hamburg; 53°38'/08°00'.

Pakod, Hung.; pop. 19; 62 km N of Nagykanizsa; 46°58'/17°00'.

Pakon, *see* Pakuonis.

Pakosc, Pol. (Pakosch, Pakosz); pop. 35; 88 km NE of Poznan; 52°48'/18°06'; GUM3, LDS.

Pakosch, *see* Pakosc.

Pakosz, *see* Pakosc.

Pakoszowka, Pol.; pop. 13; 50 km SW of Przemysl; 49°38'/22°06'.

Pakrac, Yug. (Pakracz); pop. 209; 101 km ESE of Zagreb; 45°26'/17°12'; HSL, PHY.

Pakracz, *see* Pakrac.

Pakroujas, *see* Pakruojis.

Pakroujis, *see* Pakruojis.

Pakroy, *see* Pakruojis.

Pakruois, *see* Pakruojis.

Pakruojis, Lith. (Pakroujas, Pakroujis, Pakroy, Pakruois, Pakruojus, Pokroy); pop. 454; 38 km ENE of Siauliai; 55°58'/23°52'; GUM5, HSL, JGFF, LDL, SF, YL.

Pakruojus, *see* Pakruojis.

Paks, Hung.; pop. 767; 101 km S of Budapest; 46°38'/18°52'; AMG, COH, HSL, HSL2, JGFF, LDL, LDS, PHH, YB.

Pakuonis, Lith. (Pakon); pop. 51; 26 km SE of Kaunas; 54°43'/24°03'; YL.

Palad, Hung.; 157 km E of Miskolc; 48°02'/22°57'; COH, HSL, LDL. This town was located on a pre-World War I map, but does not appear in contemporary gazetteers.

Palade, Rom.; 69 km WNW of Bucuresti; 44°41'/25°18'; GUM4.

Paladia, *see* Paladiya.

Paladiya, Mold. (Paladia); pop. 30; 176 km NW of Kishinev; 48°15'/27°26'.

Palad Veliky, COH, HSL. This pre-World War I community was not found in BGN gazetteers.

Palanca, *see* Palanka.

Palanga, Lith. (Palonga, Polaga, Polangen, Polengen, Polonga); pop. 455; 139 km WSW of Siauliai; 55°55'/21°03'; AMG, EJ, GUM5, HSL, SF, YL.

Palanka, Mold. (Palanca); pop. 24; 62 km WNW of Kishinev; 47°20'/28°12'; GUM5.

Palany, Ukr. (Polapy); pop. 56; 163 km N of Lvov; 51°19'/23°57'.

Palarikovo, Cz. (Slovensky Meder); pop. 55; 69 km E of Bratislava; 48°03'/18°04'.

Palashevka, Ukr. (Pauszowka); pop. 61; 75 km NNW of Chernovtsy; 48°58'/25°34'.

Palatca, Rom.; pop. 8; 32 km NE of Cluj; 46°51'/23°59'; HSL.

Palchintsy, Ukr. (Palczynce, Paltchintz); 107 km S of Rovno; 49°41'/26°14'; HSL, SF.

Palczynce, *see* Palchintsy.

Paldiski, Est. (Baltiiskii Port, Baltisch Port); pop. 1; 38 km WSW of Tallinn; 59°20'/24°06'.

Paleniec, Pol.; pop. 2; 32 km NNE of Lodz; 51°58'/19°45'.

Palesnica, Pol.; pop. 14; 69 km ESE of Krakow; 49°48'/20°48'.

Paleu, Rom. (Hegykozpalyi); pop. 9; 133 km WNW of Cluj; 47°07'/21°58'.

Palfa, Hung.; pop. 15; 94 km S of Budapest; 46°43'/18°38'; HSL.

Palfalu, *see* Paylova.

Palfalva, *see* Pavlovce.

Palhaza, Hung.; pop. 29; 82 km W of Miskolc; 48°11'/19°45'.

Palikije, Pol.; pop. 10; 19 km WSW of Lublin; 51°14'/22°19'.

Palin, Hung.; 13 km NNW of Nagykanizsa; 46°30'/16°59'; HSL, HSL2.

Paller, HSL. This pre-World War I community was not found in BGN gazetteers.

Palmiry, Pol.; 19 km WNW of Warszawa; 52°22'/20°47'; PHP4.

Palmnicken, *see* Yantarnyy.

Palmiry, Pol.; 19 km WNW of Warszawa; 52°22'/20°47'; PHP4.

Palmonostora, Hung.; pop. 4; 50 km NNW of Szeged; 46°38'/19°57'.

Palocse, *see* Plavec.

Palocz, *see* Pavlovce nad Uhom.

Palonga, *see* Palanga.

Palosremete, *see* Remeti.

Palota, Rom.; 139 km W of Cluj; 47°04'/21°50'; HSL, HSL2.

Palotabozsok, Hung.; pop. 11; 120 km WSW of Szeged; 46°08'/18°39'.

Palotailva, *see* Lunca Bradului.

Palotas, Hung.; pop. 20; 50 km NE of Budapest; 47°48'/19°36'; HSL.

Palovna, *see* Plawno.

Palsmane, Lat.; pop. 1; 133 km NE of Riga; 57°23'/26°11'.

Paltchintz, *see* Palchintsy.

Palterndorf, Aus.; pop. 3; 56 km NNE of Wien; 48°35'/16°49'.

Palticeni, *see* Falticeni.

Paltinoasa, Rom.; pop. 14; 133 km WNW of Iasi; 47°33'/25°57'.

Paluszyce, Pol.; pop. 9; 62 km ENE of Krakow; 50°13'/20°45'.

Pama, Aus.; pop. 18; 50 km ESE of Wien; 48°03'/17°02'.

Pamhagen, Aus.; pop. 8; 69 km SE of Wien; 47°42'/16°55'.

Pamiatkowo, Pol.; pop. 8; 26 km WNW of Poznan; 52°33'/16°41'.

Pamleny, Hung.; pop. 10; 50 km N of Miskolc; 48°30'/20°56'.

Pamorzany, *see* Pomoryany.

Pampali, Lat.; pop. 13; 126 km SW of Riga; 56°32'/22°13'.

Pampenai, Lith. (Pompeyan, Pompian, Pumpenai, Pumpenei, Pumpian); pop. 372; 69 km E of Siauliai; 55°56'/24°21'; COH, EJ, HSL, JGFF, LDL, SF, YL.

Pamusis, Lith.; 32 km NE of Siauliai; 56°05'/23°40'; JGFF.

Pana, Cz. (Pann); 82 km ENE of Bratislava; 48°14'/18°14'; HSL.

Panaci, Rom.; pop. 14; 146 km NE of Cluj; 47°16'/25°23'.

Panasesti, *see* Panasheshty.

Panasheshty, Mold. (Panasesti); pop. 25; 32 km WNW of Kishinev; 47°09'/28°31'.

Panca, *see* Panka.

Pancelcseh, *see* Panticeu.

Pancesti, Rom. BGN lists two possible localities with this name located at 46°13'/27°04' and 46°20'/27°05'. HSL.

Pancevo, Yug. (Pancsova); pop. 507; 13 km NE of Beograd; 44°52'/20°39'; AMG, GUM4, PHY.

Panciu, Rom.; pop. 677; 146 km S of Iasi; 45°54'/27°05'; EJ, GUM4, GUM5, LDL, PHR1.

Pancoja, Rom.; 146 km WSW of Cluj; 46°36'/21°45'; PHR1. This town was located on a pre-World War I map, but does not appear in contemporary gazetteers.

Pancota, *see* Pincota.

Pancsova, *see* Pancevo.

Pand, Hung.; pop. 16; 45 km ESE of Budapest; 47°21'/19°38'; LDS.

Pandelis, *see* Pandelys.

Pandelys, Lith. (Pandelis, Ponedel, Ponedeli, Ponidel); pop. 611; 120 km ENE of Siauliai; 56°01'/25°13'; HSL, SF, YL.

Panemune, Lith. (Panemunek, Panemunelis, Panemunes, Panemunlis, Penimonik, Poneman, Ponemune, Ponemunek,

Ponemuneki); pop. 102; 126 km W of Kaunas; 55°06'/21°54'; GUM5, HSL, JGFF, LDL, SF, YL.

Panemunek, *see* Panemune.

Panemunelis, *see* Panemune.

Panemunes, *see* Panemune.

Panemunis, Lith.; pop. 387; 126 km ENE of Siauliai; 56°03'/25°17'; GUM4, GUM6.

Panemunlis, *see* Panemune.

Paneriai, Lith. (Ponary); 32 km WNW of Vilnius; 54°47'/24°55'; EDRD, EJ, GA, GUM5, GUM6, ISH2, PHP4.

Panet, Rom.; pop. 1; 75 km ESE of Cluj; 46°33'/24°28'.

Panevezhis, *see* Panevezys.

Panevezio Velzis, *see* Panevezys.

Panevezys, Lith. (Panevezhis, Panevezio Velzis, Ponavezh, Ponevetz, Ponevezh, Poniewiez, Ponivez, Ponowitcz, Ponyevez, Pounivez, Punaviz); pop. 6,845; 69 km ESE of Siauliai; 55°44'/24°21'; AMG, EJ, GUM3, GUM4, GUM5, GUM6, HSL, ISH1, JGFF, LDL, SF, YL.

Panevtsy, Ukr. (Paniowce, Panovtse); pop. 26; 45 km NNE of Chernovtsy; 48°35'/26°19'.

Panic, Rom. (Gyerofalva); pop. 3; 69 km NW of Cluj; 47°12'/23°00'.

Panicke Dravce, Cz. (Panyit?); 126 km SW of Kosice; 48°17'/19°40'; HSL.

Paninka, *see* Poninka.

Paniowce, *see* Panevtsy.

Paniszczow, Pol.; pop. 63; 56 km S of Przemysl; 49°21'/22°34'.

Panka, Ukr. (Panca); pop. 25; 32 km SW of Chernovtsy; 48°10'/25°39'.

Panki, Pol.; pop. 52; 32 km WNW of Czestochowa; 50°53'/18°45'.

Pankovtse, Ukr. (Pankowce); pop. 23; 94 km ENE of Lvov; 49°57'/25°16'.

Pankowce, *see* Pankovtse.

Panlelcseh, *see* Panticeu.

Pann, *see* Pana.

Panosiskes, *see* Panoskiu Zydkaimis.

Panoskiu Zydkaimis, Lith. (Panosiskes, Panshishok); 45 km SW of Vilnius; 54°31'/24°44'; YL.

Panoteriai, Lith.; pop. 15; 50 km NE of Kaunas; 55°11'/24°26'.

Panovce, Cz. (Pany); 19 km SW of Kosice; 48°38'/21°04'; HSL.

Panovtse, *see* Panevtsy.

Panshishok, *see* Panoskiu Zydkaimis.

Panska Dolina, *see* Spania Dolina.

Pantalowice, Pol.; pop. 58; 32 km WNW of Przemysl; 49°57'/22°27'.

Panticeu, Rom. (Pancelcseh, Panlelcseh, Ponticeu); pop. 91; 38 km N of Cluj; 47°02'/23°34'; HSL, PHR2.

Pany, *see* Panovce.

Panyit, *possibly* Panicke Dravce.

Panyok, Hung.; pop. 10; 69 km NNE of Miskolc; 48°32'/21°22'.

Panyola, Hung.; pop. 42; 120 km E of Miskolc; 48°03'/22°24'; HSL, JGFF.

Panzareni, *see* Pynzareny.

Pap, Hung.; pop. 40; 101 km ENE of Miskolc; 48°13'/22°09'; HSL, LDS.

Papa, Hung.; pop. 2,567; 107 km N of Nagykanizsa; 47°20'/17°28'; AMG, EDRD, GUM5, HSL, HSL2, JGFF, LDL, LDS, PHH.

Papateszer, Hung.; pop. 39; 107 km WSW of Budapest; 47°23'/17°42'.

Papauti, Rom.; pop. 5; 157 km N of Bucuresti; 45°47'/26°08'.

Papenburg, Germ.; pop. 71; 176 km WNW of Hannover; 53°04'/07°24'; AMG, GUM3, GUM5, LDS.

Papendorf, Germ.; 114 km E of Rostock; 53°57'/13°49'; GUM5.

Papfalva, *see* Farna.

Papile, Lith. (Popielany, Popilan, Popilyan); pop. 257; 45 km WNW of Siauliai; 56°09'/22°48'; YL.

Papilis, *see* Papilys.

Papilys, Lith. (Papilis); pop. 47; 107 km ENE of Siauliai; 56°07'/25°00'; HSL, JGFF, LDL, SF.

Papkeszi, Hung.; pop. 3; 88 km SW of Budapest; 47°05'/18°05'.

Paplaka, Lat.; 170 km SW of Riga; 56°26'/21°27'; PHLE.

Paplin, Pol.; 62 km NE of Warszawa; 52°29'/21°53'; HSL.

Papoc, Hung.; pop. 17; 114 km N of Nagykanizsa; 47°25'/17°08'.

Papos, Hung.; pop. 33; 107 km E of Miskolc; 47°59'/22°15'; HSL, LDS.

Pappenheim, Germ.; 62 km S of Nurnberg; 48°56'/10°58'; GUM3, PHGB.

Paproc Mala, Pol.; pop. 23; 75 km SW of Bialystok; 52°52'/22°06'.

Parabuc, *see* Ratkovo.

Paracin, Yug.; pop. 6; 133 km SE of Beograd; 43°52'/21°25'.

Paracov, Cz. BGN lists two possible localities with this name located at 49°12'/14°00' and 49°28'/13°51'. HSL.

Parad, Hung.; pop. 9; 62 km SW of Miskolc; 47°55'/20°02'.

Paradyz, Pol.; pop. 117; 69 km SE of Lodz; 51°18'/20°08'; EDRD, GUM5, PHP1, PHP4.

Parafianka, Pol. (Parafjanka); pop. 6; 50 km WNW of Lublin; 51°33'/22°02'.

Parafianova, *see* Parafyanovo.

Parafianowo, *see* Parafyanovo.

Parafjanka, *see* Parafianka.

Parafjanowo, *see* Parafyanovo.

Parafyanovo, Byel. (Parafianova, Parafianowo, Parafjanowo); pop. 84; 120 km N of Minsk; 54°53'/27°36'; GUM4, SF, YB.

Parajd, *see* Praid.

Parasznya, Hung.; pop. 3; 13 km WNW of Miskolc; 48°10'/20°39'.

Paraul Negru, *see* Piriu Negru.

Parcevo, *see* Parczew.

Parchacz, *see* Parkhach.

Parchev, *see* Parczew.

Parcheve, *see* Parczew.

Parchim, Germ.; pop. 45; 82 km S of Rostock; 53°26'/11°51'; EJ, JGFF, LDS.

Parcice, Pol. (Partshits); pop. 11; 75 km WNW of Czestochowa; 51°14'/18°19'; FRG.

Parcova, *see* Parkova.

Parczew, Pol. (Parcevo, Parchev, Parcheve, Partchev, Partsev, Partzeva); pop. 4,005; 50 km NNE of Lublin; 51°38'/22°54'; AMG, CAHJP, COH, EDRD, EJ, GA, GUM3, GUM4, GUM5, GUM6, HSL, HSL2, JGFF, LDS, LYV, PHP3, PHP4, SF.

Pardolow, Pol.; pop. 4; 107 km ESE of Lodz; 51°07'/20°37'.

Pardubice, Cz. (Pardubitz); pop. 554; 94 km E of Praha; 50°02'/15°47'; EJ, GUM3, GUM5.

Pardubitz, *see* Pardubice.

Parhida, Rom.; pop. 15; 139 km WNW of Cluj; 47°14'/21°52'.

Pari, Hung.; 101 km ENE of Nagykanizsa; 46°35'/18°16'; HSL.

Parichi, Byel. (Poritch); pop. 2,535; 114 km WNW of Gomel; 52°48'/29°25'; GUM4, HSL, LDL, SF, YB.

Parincea, *see* Parincea Tirg.

Parincea Targ, *see* Parincea Tirg.

Parincea Tirg, Rom. (Parincea, Parincea Targ); pop. 148; 88 km SSW of Iasi; 46°29'/27°06'; HSL, PHR1.

Parjolteni, *see* Pyrzholteny.

Parjota, *see* Pyrzhota.

Parkany, GUM4, HSL, HSL2. A number of towns share this name. It was not possible to determine from available information which one is being referenced.

Parkhach, Ukr. (Parchacz); pop. 56; 56 km N of Lvov; 50°20'/24°13'.

Parkosz, Pol.; pop. 15; 101 km E of Krakow; 50°00'/21°20'.

Parkova, Mold. (Parcova); pop. 47; 170 km NW of Kishinev; 48°09'/27°24'.

Parlita, *see* Pyrlitsa.

Parlita Targ, *see* Pyrlitsa.

Parliti, *see* Pyrlitsa.

Parndorf, Aus.; pop. 36; 45 km ESE of Wien; 47°59'/16°51'.

Parnik, Cz.; pop. 9; 88 km NNW of Brno; 49°55'/16°26'.

Parnivka, *see* Konetspol.

Parnu, Est. (Pernau, Pernov); pop. 252; 120 km S of Tallinn; 58°24'/24°32'; PHLE.

Parochonsk, *see* Parokhonsk.

Parokhonsk, Byel. (Parochonsk); pop. 5; 26 km NE of Pinsk; 52°14'/26°27'.

Parole, Pol.; pop. 1; 32 km SSW of Warszawa; 52°02'/20°49'.

Parshischa, *see* Przysucha.

Parsow, Pol.; 32 km SE of Szczecin; 53°13'/14°43'; AMG.

Partchev, *see* Parczew.

Partenheim, Germ.; pop. 16; 50 km SW of Frankfurt am Main; 49°53'/08°04'; GUM5.

Partestii de Jos, Rom.; pop. 46; 133 km WNW of Iasi; 47°38'/25°58'.

Partestii de Sus, Rom.; pop. 45; 139 km WNW of Iasi; 47°39'/25°55'.

Partizanska Dreznica, Yug. (Dresnitz, Dreznica); 101 km SSW of Zagreb; 45°09'/15°06'; HSL.

Partsev, *see* Parczew.

Partshits, *see* Parcice.

Partynia, Pol.; pop. 1; 94 km ENE of Krakow; 50°13'/21°17'.

Partzeva, *see* Parczew.

Paruchy, Pol.; pop. 5; 94 km ESE of Lodz; 51°14'/20°34'.

Parva, Rom.; pop. 22; 101 km NE of Cluj; 47°24'/24°33'.

Parypsy, Ukr.; pop. 8; 50 km WNW of Lvov; 50°08'/23°32'.

Paryshche, Ukr. (Paryszcze); pop. 35; 101 km WNW of Chernovtsy; 48°40'/24°42'.

Parysow, Pol. (Porisov); pop. 1,906; 56 km ESE of Warszawa; 51°58'/21°41'; AMG, COH, EDRD, GA, GUM3, GUM4, GUM5, HSL, HSL2, JGFF, PHP4, SF, YB.

Paryszcze, *see* Paryshche.

Parzeczew, Pol. (Parzentchev); pop. 174; 26 km NW of Lodz; 51°57'/19°13'; CAHJP, HSL, PHP1, SF, WS.

Parzentchev, *see* Parzeczew.

Parzniewice, Pol.; pop. 41; 56 km S of Lodz; 51°18'/19°31'; HSL.

Parzniewiczki, Pol.; pop. 31; Described in the *Black Book* as being in the Lodz region of Poland, this town was not found in BGN gazetteers.

Parzno, Pol.; pop. 11; 45 km S of Lodz; 51°23'/19°15'.

Parzymiechy, Pol.; pop. 42; 45 km WNW of Czestochowa; 51°03'/18°44'; GA, GUM3, GUM5.

Pasareni, Rom. (Bacskamadaras, Baczkamadaras); pop. 4; 88 km ESE of Cluj; 46°29'/24°42'; HSL.

Pasca, Hung. PHH. This town was not found in BGN gazetteers under the given spelling.

Pascani, Rom.; 69 km W of Iasi; 47°15'/26°44'; EJ, GUM3, GUM4, GUM5, HSL, LDL, PHR1.

Pascauti, *see* Paskautsy.

Pasching, Aus.; pop. 2; 101 km NE of Salzburg; 48°15'/14°12'.

Pasechna, Ukr. (Pasetchna, Pasieczna); pop. 135; 114 km W of Chernovtsy; 48°34'/24°26'; LDL, PHP2, SF.

Pasechna (near Ivano Frankovsk), Ukr.; pop. 30; 114 km WNW of Chernovtsy; 48°56'/24°41'.

Pasetchna, *see* Pasechna.

Pasewalk, Germ.; pop. 47; 120 km N of Berlin; 53°31'/13°59'; CAHJP, HSL, LDS.

Pashvitin, *see* Pasvitinys.

Pasieczna, *see* Pasechna.

Pasieka Otfinowska, Pol.; pop. 10; 62 km ENE of Krakow; 50°10'/20°49'.

Pasieki, Pol.; pop. 26; 75 km WSW of Lublin; 51°12'/21°27'; PHP4.

Pasiene, Lat. (Pasienes); pop. 458; 114 km NE of Daugavpils; 56°17'/28°10'.

Pasienes, *see* Pasiene.

Pasika, Ukr. (Paszika); 170 km SSW of Lvov; 48°32'/22°54'; HSL.

Pasing, Germ.; 13 km WSW of Munchen; 48°09'/11°27'; PHGB.

Paskautsy, Mold. (Pascauti); pop. 17; 150 km WNW of Kishinev; 47°50'/27°17'.

Paskrzyn, Pol.; pop. 5; 62 km SE of Lodz; 51°14'/19°53'.

Paskudy, Pol.; pop. 55; 75 km N of Lublin; 51°51'/22°33'; EDRD, GUM3.

Paslek, Pol. (Preussisch Holland); pop. 60; 75 km ESE of Gdansk; 54°04'/19°40'; LDS.

Pasrinca, GUM4. This town was not found in BGN gazetteers under the given spelling.

Passau, Germ.; 150 km NE of Munchen; 48°35'/13°29'; GED, GUM3, HSL, PHGB.

Pastende, Lat.; pop. 2; 101 km W of Riga; 57°13'/22°31'.

Pastuchov, Cz.; 62 km NE of Bratislava; 48°26'/17°53'; HSL.

Pasturka, Pol.; pop. 6; 62 km NE of Krakow; 50°30'/20°34'.

Pasusvis, *see* Pasusvys.

Pasusvys, Lith. (Pasusvis); pop. 100; 45 km SE of Siauliai; 55°35'/23°36'.

Pasvalis, *see* Pasvalys.

Pasvalys, Lith. (Pasvalis, Pasvul, Posvol, Posvul); pop. 748; 69 km ENE of Siauliai; 56°04'/24°24'; AMG, COH, GUM4, HSL, JGFF, LDL, SF, YL.

Pasviatin, *see* Pasvitinys.

Pasvitinys, Lith. (Pashvitin, Pasviatin, Poshvitin, Poswetin); pop. 274; 45 km NE of Siauliai; 56°09'/23°49'; HSL, JGFF, LDL, SF, YL.

Pasvul, *see* Pasvalys.

Paszab, Hung.; pop. 47; 69 km ENE of Miskolc; 48°09'/21°41'; HSL.

Paszczyna, Pol.; pop. 14; 101 km WNW of Przemysl; 50°05'/21°31'.

Paszenki, Pol.; pop. 7; 62 km NNE of Lublin; 51°43'/23°08'.

Paszika, *see* Pasika.

Paszki Duze, Pol.; pop. 33; 62 km N of Lublin; 51°44'/22°36'.

Paszki Male, Pol.; pop. 14; 62 km N of Lublin; 51°45'/22°35'.

Paszkowice, Pol.; pop. 6; 75 km SE of Lodz; 51°14'/20°12'.

Paszkowka, Pol.; pop. 25; 26 km SW of Krakow; 49°57'/19°41'.

Paszowa, Pol.; pop. 48; 45 km SSW of Przemysl; 49°32'/22°26'; HSL.

Paszto, Hung.; pop. 414; 62 km NNE of Budapest; 47°55'/19°42'; AMG, HSL, HSL2, LDL, LDS, PHH.

Pasztowa Wola, Pol.; pop. 4; 88 km WSW of Lublin; 51°10'/21°21'.

Paszyn, Pol.; pop. 9; 82 km ESE of Krakow; 49°38'/20°47'; HSL.

Patahaza, *see* Revfalu.

Patal, Rom.; pop. 33; 114 km WNW of Cluj; 47°23'/22°27'.

Patka, Hung.; pop. 9; 50 km SW of Budapest; 47°17'/18°30'.

Patkow, Pol.; pop. 4; 75 km WNW of Lublin; 51°27'/21°35'.

Patkowice, *see* Zakliczyn.

Patkule, Lat.; pop. 1; 120 km NNW of Daugavpils; 56°54'/26°18'.

Patokryje, Cz.; pop. 5; 69 km WNW of Praha; 50°30'/13°42'.

Patosfa, Hung.; pop. 3; 62 km ESE of Nagykanizsa; 46°08'/17°40'.

Patrai, Greece (Patras); pop. 170; 176 km W of Athens; 38°14'/21°44'.

Patras, *see* Patrai.

Patrauti, Rom. (Patrautii de Jos, Patrautii de Sus, Petrauti, Petrauti de Jos, Petrauti de Sus, Petrautz); pop. 249; 126 km WNW of Iasi; 47°43'/26°12'; GUM4, PHR2.

Patrautii de Jos, *see* Patrauti.

Patrautii de Sus, *see* Patrauti.

Patro, Hung. (Nemespatro); pop. 3; 19 km SSE of Nagykanizsa; 46°19'/17°01'.

Patroha, Hung.; pop. 141; 94 km ENE of Miskolc; 48°10'/22°00'; AMG, GUM3, HSL, LDS, PHH.

Patryki, Byel.; pop. 27; 126 km W of Pinsk; 52°11'/24°19'; EDRD. This town was located on an interwar map of Poland but does not appear in contemporary gazetteers. Map coordinates are approximate.

Patrykozy, Pol.; pop. 46; 94 km ENE of Warszawa; 52°19'/22°20'.

Patsanov, *see* Pacanow.

Pattensen, Germ.; pop. 43; 19 km SSE of Hannover; 52°16'/09°46'; GED, HSL.

Patvarc, Hung.; pop. 10; 69 km N of Budapest; 48°04'/19°21'.

Paty, Hung.; pop. 33; 19 km W of Budapest; 47°31'/18°50'.

Patyod, Hung.; pop. 3; 139 km E of Miskolc; 47°52'/22°37'.

Paulinow, Pol.; pop. 62; 45 km S of Lodz; 51°24'/19°25'.

Paulshafen, *see* Pavilosta.

Paupine, *see* Paupyne.

Paupis, Lith. (Antanava); pop. 192; 50 km NNW of Kaunas; 55°17'/23°45'.

Paupyne, Lith. (Paupine); pop. 7; 146 km NNE of Vilnius; 55°51'/26°12'.

Pausa, Rom.; pop. 40; A number of towns share this name. It was not possible to determine from available information which one is being referenced.

Pauszowka, *see* Palashevka.

Pava, Rom.; pop. 7; 170 km N of Bucuresti; 45°53'/26°11'; HSL.

Pavalitch, *see* Pavoloch.

Pavdocz, Ukr. EDRD. This town was not found in BGN gazetteers under the given spelling.

Paversk, *see* Povorsk.

Pavilosta, Lat. (Paulshafen, Saka); 176 km WSW of Riga; 56°53'/21°11'; PHLE.

Pavlograd, Ukr. (Pawlograd); pop. 3,921; 69 km ENE of Dnepropetrovsk; 48°31'/35°52'; EJ, GUM4, HSL, HSL2, JGFF, SF.

Pavlov, Cz. (Pawlowka); 38 km S of Brno; 48°52'/16°40'; JGFF.

Pavlov (Wolyn), COH, EDRD, GUM3, GUM6. This town was not found in BGN gazetteers under the given spelling.

Pavlova, *see* Konetspol.

Pavlovce, Cz. (Palfalva); 94 km SW of Kosice; 48°20'/20°05'; HSL.

Pavlovce nad Uhom, Cz. (Palocz); pop. 137; 62 km E of Kosice; 48°37'/22°04'; HSL.

Pavlovka, Ukr. (Pawlowka); pop. 2; 114 km SW of Odessa; 45°58'/29°30'; PHR1, WS.

Pavlovo, Byel. (Pawlowo); AMG. A number of towns share this name. It was not possible to determine from available information which one is being referenced. SF identifies a town of Pawlowo 2 km SE of Ruzhany that does not appear in contemporary gazetteers.

Pavlovsk, USSR (Pawlowsk); 32 km SE of Leningrad; 59°41'/30°27'; HSL, SF.

Pavoloch, Ukr. (Pavalitch, Pawolotsch, Povoloch); pop. 1,837; 101 km SW of Kiyev; 49°52'/29°27'; EDRD, EJ, GYLA, JGFF, LDL, SF.

Pavylova, HSL. This pre-World War I community was not found in BGN gazetteers.

Pawezow, Pol.; pop. 3; 75 km E of Krakow; 50°04'/20°59'.

Pawliczka, Pol.; pop. 11; 75 km WSW of Lublin; 51°10'/21°26'.

Pawlograd, *see* Pavlograd.

Pawlokoma, Pol.; pop. 8; 38 km W of Przemysl; 49°49'/22°17'.

Pawlosiow, Pol.; pop. 15; 26 km NNW of Przemysl; 49°59'/22°39'.

Pawlow, SF. A number of towns share this name. It was not possible to determine from available information which one is being referenced.

Pawlowice, Pol.; pop. 45; 75 km WNW of Lublin; 51°37'/21°40'.

Pawlowka, Pol.; pop. 40; 50 km E of Lublin; 51°09'/23°13'; GUM4, HSL, LDL. *See also* Pavlov; Pavlovka.

Pawlow Nowy, Pol.; pop. 22; 107 km S of Bialystok; 52°13'/23°10'.

Pawlowo, Byel.; pop. 292; 114 km WNW of Pinsk; 52°50'/24°55'; HSL, SF. *See also* Pavlovo.

Pawlowo (Leszno area), Pol.; 75 km N of Wroclaw; 51°40'/17°12'; GA.

Pawlowsk, *see* Pavlovsk.

Pawlowska Wola, *see* Wola Pawlowska.

Pawlow Stary, Pol.; pop. 24; 107 km S of Bialystok; 52°13'/23°12'.

Pawolotsch, *see* Pavoloch.

Payentchno, *see* Pajeczno.

Payerbach, Aus.; pop. 1; 69 km SSW of Wien; 47°41'/15°51'.

Paylova, Hung. (Palfalu); 62 km SE of Nagykanizsa; 45°58'/17°29'; HSL. This town was located on a pre-World War I map, but does not appear in contemporary gazetteers.

Payora, *see* Pajuris.

Payuris, *see* Pajuris.

Pazardzhik, Bulg. (Tatar Pazardzhik); pop. 2,961; 101 km ESE of Sofija; 42°12'/24°20'; EJ.

Pazhevla, *see* Zelva.

Pazmandfalu, Hung.; pop. 2; 94 km W of Budapest; 47°34'/17°47'.

Pazmandhegy, Hung.; pop. 2; 94 km W of Budapest; 47°34'/17°46'.

Pazony, Hung.; 75 km E of Miskolc; 47°59'/21°48'; HSL. This town was located on a pre-World War I map, but does not appear in contemporary gazetteers.

Pchany, Ukr. (Pczany); pop. 32; 62 km S of Lvov; 49°21'/24°02'.

Pcim, Pol.; pop. 15; 45 km S of Krakow; 49°45'/19°58'; PHP3.

Pczany, *see* Pchany.

Pebirzih, *see* Pabirze.

Peceiu, Rom.; pop. 8; 69 km WNW of Cluj; 47°07'/22°53'.

Pecel, Hung.; pop. 194; 19 km E of Budapest; 47°29'/19°21'; GUM5, LDS, PHH.

Pecerady, Cz.; pop. 12; 32 km SSE of Praha; 49°50'/14°37'.

Pecestea, *see* Pecheshtya.

Pechalovka, Ukr. (Pieczalowka); pop. 40; 45 km NNE of Rovno; 50°56'/26°33'.

Pecharna, Ukr. (Pieczarna); pop. 9; 101 km S of Rovno; 49°45'/26°01'.

Pechenezhin, Ukr. (Peczenizyn, Peczynizyn, Petchinizhin); pop. 1,413; 82 km WNW of Chernovtsy; 48°31'/24°54'; COH, EGRS, GUM4, HSL, LDL, PHP2, SF, WS.

Pechenki, Ukr. (Pieczonki); pop. 13; 101 km N of Rovno; 51°29'/26°05'.

Pechera, HSL. This pre-World War I community was not found in BGN gazetteers.

Pecheshtya, Mold. (Pecestea); pop. 102; 88 km N of Kishinev; 47°43'/28°44'.

Pechikhvosty, Ukr. (Pieczychwosty);

Pechikhvosty (Lwow), Ukr.; pop. 62; 26 km NE of Lvov; 50°00'/24°18'; PHP2.

Pechikhvosty (Wolyn), Ukr.; pop. 53; 82 km NNE of Lvov; 50°30'/24°37'.

Pechniew, *see* Peczniew.

Pechora, Ukr. (Peciora, Pecora, Petchora, Potchera); 50 km SSE of Vinnitsa; 48°50'/28°42'; EDRD, GUM4, LDL, PHR1, SF.

Pechow, Pol.; pop. 9; 101 km SW of Lublin; 50°40'/21°28'.

Peciora, *see* Pechora.

Peckelsheim, Germ.; pop. 11; 101 km SSW of Hannover; 51°36'/09°08'; EJ, JGFF.

Pecky, Cz.; pop. 32; 38 km ENE of Praha; 50°06'/15°01'.

Peclawice, Pol.; pop. 9; 114 km NE of Krakow; 50°37'/21°19'.

Pecora, *see* Pechora.

Pecs, Hung. (Funfkirchen); pop. 3,486; 101 km ESE of Nagykanizsa; 46°05'/18°14'; AMG, COH, EDRD, GUM3, GUM4, HSL, JGFF, LDS, PHH.

Pecsely, Hung. (Nemespecsely); pop. 2; 82 km NE of Nagykanizsa; 46°57'/17°47'; HSL.

Pecsudvard, Hung.; pop. 3; 107 km ESE of Nagykanizsa; 46°01'/18°17'.

Pecsvarad, Hung.; pop. 126; 114 km ESE of Nagykanizsa; 46°09'/18°25'; GUM5, LDS, PHH.

Peczelice, Pol.; pop. 6; 75 km NE of Krakow; 50°27'/20°47'.

Peczenizyn, *see* Pechenezhin.

Peczniew, Pol. (Pechniew); pop. 58; 50 km W of Lodz; 51°48'/18°44'; PHP1.

Peczurkes, GUM3. This town was not found in BGN gazetteers under the given spelling.

Peczynizyn, *see* Pechenezhin.

Peggau, Aus.; pop. 1; 26 km NW of Graz; 47°12'/15°21'.

Pegir, *see* Pagiriai.

Pegnitz, Germ.; 50 km NE of Nurnberg; 49°45'/11°33'; GUM3, PHGB.

Peine, Germ.; pop. 124; 38 km E of Hannover; 52°19'/10°14'; AMG, GED, HSL.

Peirin, LDL. This pre-World War I community was not found in BGN gazetteers.

Peisern, *see* Pyzdry.

Peiskretscham, *see* Pyszaca.

Peitz, Germ.; pop. 6; 101 km ESE of Berlin; 51°52'/14°25'.

Peizer, *see* Pyzdry.

Pekin, Pol.; pop. 5; 50 km WNW of Krakow; 50°17'/19°14'.

Peklany, *see* Uzovske Peklany.

Pekoslaw, Pol.; pop. 13; 50 km N of Krakow; 50°31'/20°05'.

Pelcza, *see* Povcha.

Pelczyce, Pol. (Bernstein); pop. 20; 75 km ESE of Szczecin; 53°02'/15°18'; LDS.

Pelczyn, Pol.; pop. 7; 32 km ESE of Lublin; 51°10'/22°59'.

Pelczyska, Pol.; pop. 29; 56 km NE of Krakow; 50°22'/20°34'.

Peleniya, Mold. (Pelinia); pop. 121; 120 km NW of Kishinev; 47°52'/27°50'.

Peles, Rom. (Pelesul); pop. 63; BGN lists two possible localities with this name located at 46°20'/22°59' and 47°53'/22°49'.

Pelesalja, *see* Podplesa.

Pelesul, *see* Peles.

Pelhrimov, Cz. (Pilgram); pop. 122; 88 km SE of Praha; 49°26'/15°14'; JGFF, PHGBW.

Pelinia, *see* Peleniya.

Pelkinie, Pol.; pop. 43; 38 km NNW of Przemysl; 50°04'/22°38'; GA, GUM4, PHP3.

Pelnatycze, Pol.; pop. 7; 26 km NW of Przemysl; 49°58'/22°34'.

Pelsucz, *see* Plesivec.

Peltev, Ukr. (Poltew); pop. 76; 38 km ENE of Lvov; 49°52'/24°30'.

Pelvac Pelyva, *see* Bronowo Plewnik.

Pely, Hung.; pop. 6; 75 km SSW of Miskolc; 47°29'/20°21'.

Penc, Hung. (Felsopenc); pop. 16; 38 km N of Budapest; 47°48'/19°15'; LDS.

Penchivca, *see* Penkovka.

Peneszlek, Hung.; pop. 55; 114 km ESE of Miskolc; 47°38'/22°09'; HSL, PHH.

Penimonik, *see* Panemune.

Penkovka, Ukr. (Penchivca); 45 km S of Vinnitsa; 48°52'/28°15'; PHR1.

Penkule, Lat.; pop. 1; 75 km SW of Riga; 56°29'/23°12'.

Penski, *see* Penskiy.

Penskie, Pol.; pop. 7; 32 km WNW of Bialystok; 53°19'/22°49'.

Penskiy, USSR (Penski); pop. 23; 82 km S of Kursk; 51°01'/35°51'.

Penyaki, Ukr. (Pieniaki); pop. 14; 82 km ENE of Lvov; 49°54'/25°11'.

Penyige, Hung.; pop. 12; 133 km E of Miskolc; 47°59'/22°34'.

Penza, *see* Peza.

Penzberg, Germ.; pop. 1; 50 km S of Munchen; 47°45'/11°23'.

Penzig, *see* Piensk.

Penzlin, Germ.; 88 km ESE of Rostock; 53°30'/13°05'; JGFF, LDS.

Pepeni, *see* Pepeny.

Pepeny, Mold. (Pepeni); pop. 180; 82 km NW of Kishinev; 47°38'/28°21'.

Per, Hung.; pop. 13; 94 km W of Budapest; 47°37'/17°48'; HSL.

Perast, Yug.; pop. 1; 234 km W of Skopje; 42°29'/18°43'.

Peratin, Ukr. (Peratyn); pop. 29; 75 km NNE of Lvov; 50°19'/24°43'.

Peratyn, *see* Peratin.

Perbal, Hung.; pop. 6; 26 km WNW of Budapest; 47°36'/18°46'.

Perbenik, *see* Pribenik.

Perbete, *see* Pribeta.

Percauti, *see* Perkovtsy.

Perchtoldsdorf, Aus.; pop. 67; 13 km SSW of Wien; 48°07'/16°16'.

Pere, Hung.; pop. 23; 32 km NE of Miskolc; 48°17'/21°08'; HSL.

Perebrodye, Ukr. (Przebrody, Przebrodzie, Pshebrody); pop. 43; 139 km N of Rovno; 51°44'/26°59'.

Perebrodye (Wilen), Byel.; pop. 19; 182 km W of Vitebsk; 55°37'/27°24'.

Perechin, Ukr. (Perecin, Perecseny); pop. 1,042; 170 km SSW of Lvov; 48°44'/22°28'; AMG, HSL, JGFF.

Perecin, *see* Perechin.

Perecse, Hung.; pop. 2; 50 km N of Miskolc; 48°30'/21°00'.

Perecseny, *see* Perechin.

Pered, *see* Tesedikovo.

Pereg, Hung. (Peregh); pop. 11; 45 km S of Budapest; 47°10'/19°00'; HSL.

Peregh, *see* Pereg.

Pereginsko, Ukr. (Perehinsko); pop. 612; 120 km S of Lvov; 48°49'/24°11'; HSL, JGFF, PHP2.

Perehinsko, *see* Pereginsko.

Pereiaslav Khmel Nitskii, *see* Pereyaslav Khmelnitskiy.

Pereiaslavl, *see* Pereyaslav Khmelnitskiy.

Perejaslaw, *see* Pereyaslav Khmelnitskiy.

Perejaslaw Chmielnicki, *see* Pereyaslav Khmelnitskiy.

Pereked, Hung.; pop. 3; 114 km ESE of Nagykanizsa; 46°06'/18°23'.

Perekop, Byel.; 176 km NW of Pinsk; 53°28'/24°49'; JGFF.

Perekop Armyansk, HSL. This pre-World War I community was not found in BGN gazetteers.

Perelkowce, Pol. PHP2. This town was not found in BGN gazetteers under the given spelling.

Peremarton, Hung.; pop. 3; 82 km SW of Budapest; 47°07'/18°07'.

Peremilow, *possibly* Peremyl.

Peremorovka, Ukr. (Peremorowka); pop. 20; 45 km S of Rovno; 50°15'/26°12'.

Peremorowka, *see* Peremorovka.

Peremozhnoye, Ukr. (Chlopy, Khlopy); pop. 25; 38 km SW of Lvov; 49°38'/23°40'.

Peremyl, Ukr. (Peremilow?); pop. 22; 82 km SW of Rovno; 50°24'/25°10'.

Peremyshl, *see* Przemysl.

Peremyshlyany, Ukr. (Premishlan, Premishlian, Premislani, Przemyslany, Pshemishlani); pop. 2,051; 45 km ESE of Lvov; 49°40'/24°33'; AMG, COH, EDRD, EGRS, EJ, GUM3, GUM4, GUM5, GUM6, HSL, HSL2, JGFF, LDL, PHP2, SF.

Perenye, Hung.; pop. 10; 101 km NNW of Nagykanizsa; 47°18'/16°35'.

Pererita, *see* Pereryta.

Pererosl, Ukr. (Psherosl); pop. 24; 107 km WNW of Chernovtsy; 48°42'/24°38'.

Pereryta, Mold. (Pererita); pop. 21; 195 km WNW of Kishinev; 48°12'/26°56'.

Peresechino, Mold. (Peresecina, Pereslchina); pop. 241; 38 km NNW of Kishinev; 47°16'/28°46'.

Peresecina, *see* Peresechino.

Pereseka, Byel. (Peresieka); 114 km WNW of Gomel; 53°06'/29°41'; EDRD.

Peresieka, *see* Pereseka.

Pereslchina, *see* Peresechino.

Pereszleny, *see* Preselany.

Pereszteg, Hung.; pop. 4; 139 km NNW of Nagykanizsa; 47°36'/16°44'.

Perevolochna, Ukr. (Perewoloczna, Przewloczna); pop. 8; 56 km NE of Lvov; 50°03'/24°48'.

Perevorsk, *see* Przeworsk.

Perewoloczna, *see* Perevolochna.

Pereyaslav, *see* Pereyaslav Khmelnitskiy.

Pereyaslav Khmelnitskiy, Ukr. (Pereiaslav Khmel Nitskii, Pereiaslavl, Perejaslaw, Perejaslaw Chmielnicki, Pereyaslav, Pereyaslavl, Periyoslov); pop. 3,590; 75 km ESE of Kiyev;

256

50°05'/31°28'; EDRD, EJ, GUM4, HSL, LDL, SF.

Pereyaslavl, *see* Pereyaslav Khmelnitskiy.

Perezhiri, Byel.; 45 km W of Minsk; 53°58'/26°59'; JGFF.

Periam, Rom. (Perjamos, Perjamosch); 221 km SW of Cluj; 46°03'/20°52'; HSL, JGFF.

Periceiu, Rom.; pop. 23; 75 km WNW of Cluj; 47°14'/22°53'.

Peridroysk, *see* Piedruja.

Perii Vadului, Rom.; pop. 8; 69 km N of Cluj; 47°21'/23°34'.

Perin, Cz. BGN lists two possible localities with this name located at 41°33'/23°34' and 48°33'/21°12'. HSL.

Periyoslov, *see* Pereyaslav Khmelnitskiy.

Perjamos, *see* Periam.

Perjamosch, *see* Periam.

Perkata, Hung.; pop. 42; 56 km S of Budapest; 47°03'/18°48'; HSL.

Perkhovichi, Byel. (Pierzchowice); pop. 3; 133 km NNW of Pinsk; 53°15'/25°39'.

Perkovtsy, Ukr. (Percauti); pop. 14; 56 km NE of Chernovtsy; 48°27'/26°39'.

Perkupa, Hung.; pop. 14; 50 km NNW of Miskolc; 48°28'/20°42'; HSL.

Perlach, Germ.; pop. 5; 6 km ESE of Munchen; 48°07'/11°38'.

Perlasz, *see* Perlez.

Perleberg, Germ.; pop. 6; 120 km WNW of Berlin; 53°04'/11°52'; JGFF, LDS.

Perlez, Yug. (Perlasz); pop. 18; 50 km NNW of Beograd; 45°12'/20°23'; HSL.

Perlitz, *see* Pyrlitsa.

Pernarava, Lith.; pop. 1; 45 km NW of Kaunas; 55°16'/23°39'.

Pernau, *see* Parnu.

Pernik, *see* Pernink.

Pernink, Cz. (Pernik); pop. 5; 126 km W of Praha; 50°22'/12°47'.

Pernov, *see* Parnu.

Perocseny, Hung.; pop. 9; 62 km NNW of Budapest; 48°00'/18°52'.

Persenbeug, Aus.; pop. 4; 94 km WSW of Wien; 48°11'/15°04'; EDRD, GUM4.

Pershay, Byel.; 62 km W of Minsk; 54°02'/26°41'; JGFF.

Pershotravnevoye, Ukr. (Mokwin); pop. 22; 56 km NE of Rovno; 50°57'/26°48'.

Pertoca, Yug.; pop. 5; 114 km N of Zagreb; 46°46'/16°02'.

Pertschup, Lat. EDRD. This town was not found in BGN gazetteers under the given spelling.

Peruc, Cz.; pop. 7; 45 km WNW of Praha; 50°20'/13°58'.

Perve Numer, *see* Novo Zlatopol.

Pervomaysk, Ukr. (Bogopol, Bohopolia, Olviopol, Olwiopol, Orzel, Pierwomajsk); pop. 9,896; 94 km SE of Uman; 48°03'/30°52'; EDRD, EJ, GUM4, GUM5, GYLA, HSL, JGFF, LDL, SF.

Pervomaysk (near Kommunarsk), Ukr.; pop. 1,347; 227 km ESE of Kharkov; 48°38'/38°36'.

Pervomayskaya, Byel. (Sobakince); pop. 65; 189 km WSW of Minsk; 53°54'/24°39'.

Pervoye Maya, Byel. (Przyszychwosty, Pshyshykhvosty); pop. 21; 88 km W of Pinsk; 52°12'/24°49'.

Peschanka, Ukr. (Pestchanka, Pestschanka, Pistchanka, Pyeschanka); pop. 2,925; 120 km SW of Uman; 48°12'/28°53'; COH, EDRD, LDL, SF.

Peschanoye, Ukr. (Pestschannoje); 150 km WSW of Kharkov; 49°45'/34°09'; EDRD, GUM4.

Pesevichi, Byel. (Piesiewicze); pop. 6; 101 km WSW of Minsk; 53°53'/26°04'.

Pesheysh, *see* Przedecz.

Peski, Lat.; 13 km S of Daugavpils; 55°50'/26°32'; HSL, PHLE.

Peskovka, Ukr.; 69 km WNW of Kiyev; 50°41'/29°39'; HSL.

Peskovtsy, Byel. (Piaskowce); pop. 3; 157 km WSW of Minsk; 53°34'/25°10'.

Pesochnya, USSR; pop. 145; JGFF. This town was not found in BGN gazetteers under the given spelling.

Pest, *see* Budapest.

Pestchanka, *see* Peschanka.

Pestere, Rom.; pop. 2; 94 km WNW of Cluj; 47°01'/22°23'.

Pesterzsebet, Hung. (Pestszenterzsebet); pop. 4,522; 13 km SSE of Budapest; 47°26'/19°07'; COH, EJ, GUM5, GUM6, PHH.

Pesthidegkut, Hung.; pop. 67; 13 km WNW of Budapest; 47°34'/18°58'.

Pestimre, Hung. (Pestszentimre); pop. 99; 19 km SE of Budapest; 47°24'/19°12'; GUM3, PHH.

Pestlin, *see* Postolin.

Pestlorinc, Hung. (Pestszentlorinc, Pestszentlorine); pop. 986; 13 km ESE of Budapest; 47°26'/19°12'; AMG, GUM5, PHH.

Pestschanka, *see* Peschanka.

Pestschannoje, *see* Peschanoye.

Pestszenterzsebet, *see* Pesterzsebet.

Pestszentimre, *see* Pestimre.

Pestszentlorinc, *see* Pestlorinc.

Pestszentlorine, *see* Pestlorinc.

Pestujhely, Hung.; pop. 668; 6 km NNE of Budapest; 47°32'/19°07'; PHH.

Petchinizhin, *see* Pechenezhin.

Petchora, *see* Pechora.

Petchuz, *see* Petseri.

Petelea, Rom.; pop. 12; 88 km E of Cluj; 46°44'/24°43'.

Peteranec, Yug.; pop. 8; 82 km NE of Zagreb; 46°11'/16°54'.

Peterburg, *see* Leningrad.

Peterd, Hung.; pop. 6; 120 km ESE of Nagykanizsa; 45°58'/18°22'.

Peterfala, *see* Petrovce nad Laborcom.

Petergof, *see* Petrodvorets.

Peterhida, Hung.; pop. 6; 56 km SE of Nagykanizsa; 46°01'/17°22'.

Peteri, Hung.; 26 km ESE of Budapest; 47°23'/19°25'; LDS.

Peteritea, Rom.; pop. 12; 75 km N of Cluj; 47°25'/23°44'.

Peternieki, Lat.; pop. 2; 26 km SSW of Riga; 56°46'/23°57'.

Petersdorf, HSL. A number of towns share this name. It was not possible to determine from available information which one is being referenced.

Peterseg, *see* Szentpeterszeg.

Petershagen, Germ.; pop. 35; 50 km W of Hannover; 52°23'/08°58'; HSL.

Peterswaldau, GUM4, GUM5, GUM6. This town was not found in BGN gazetteers under the given spelling.

Petervasara, Hung.; pop. 57; 50 km WSW of Miskolc; 48°01'/20°06'; HSL, LDL, LDS, PHH.

Peteryasar, Hung. HSL2. This pre-World War I community was not found in BGN gazetteers.

Peticeni, *see* Peticheni.

Peticheni, Mold. (Peticeni); pop. 9; 56 km WNW of Kishinev; 47°14'/28°12'.

Petikozly, Cz.; pop. 5; 50 km NNE of Praha; 50°25'/14°49'.

Petin, Rom.; pop. 24; 120 km NNW of Cluj; 47°46'/22°58'; HSL.

Petipsy, Cz.; pop. 5; 82 km WNW of Praha; 50°19'/13°21'.

Petkowice, Pol.; pop. 16; 69 km SW of Lublin; 51°02'/21°37'.

Petkowo Wielkie, Pol.; pop. 4; 75 km SW of Bialystok; 52°43'/22°11'.

Petkowo Wymiarowo, Pol.; pop. 3; 75 km SW of Bialystok; 52°44'/22°12'.

Petlikowce Stare, Ukr.; pop. 46; 62 km NW of Chernovtsy; 48°45'/25°25'; GUM3. This town was located on an interwar map of Poland but does not appear in contemporary gazetteers. Map coordinates are approximate.

Petna, Pol.; pop. 9; 114 km ESE of Krakow; 49°34'/21°16'.

Petnehaza, Hung.; pop. 85; 94 km E of Miskolc; 48°04'/22°05'; AMG, HSL, LDS, PHH.

Petnichany, Ukr. (Pietniczany); pop. 12; 62 km S of Lvov; 49°22'/23°57'.

Petohaza, Hung.; pop. 7; 139 km N of Nagykanizsa; 47°36'/16°54'.

Peto Szinnye, *see* Svinica.

Petra, Rom.; 240 km W of Bucuresti; 44°27'/23°06'; HSL.

Petrashani, Ukr. (Petriceni); pop. 75; 69 km SW of Chernovtsy; 48°08'/25°04'.

Petrauti, *see* Patrauti.

Petrauti de Jos, *see* Patrauti.

Petrauti de Sus, *see* Patrauti.

Petrautz, *see* Patrauti.

Petreni, *see* Petreny.

Petreny, Mold. (Petreni); pop. 66; 126 km NW of Kishinev; 47°57'/27°57'.

Petreu, Rom.; pop. 23; 120 km WNW of Cluj; 47°20'/22°18'.

Petreve, *see* Petrova.

Petriceni, *see* Petrashani.

Petrijanec, Yug.; pop. 1; 69 km N of Zagreb; 46°21'/16°13'.

Petrijevci, Yug.; pop. 28; 176 km WNW of Beograd; 45°37'/18°32'.

Petrikau, *see* Piotrkow Trybunalski.

Petrikov, USSR; pop. 1,710; A number of towns share this name. It was not possible to determine from available information which one is being referenced. *See also* Piotrkow Trybunalski.

Petrikov Koyavsk, *see* Piotrkow Kujawski.

Petrila, Rom. (Petrilla); 150 km S of Cluj; 45°27'/23°25'; HSL, HSL2, PHR1.

Petrilaca de Mures, Rom.; pop. 12; 88 km E of Cluj; 46°41'/24°45'.

Petrilla, *see* Petrila.

Petrilov, Ukr. (Petrylow); pop. 11; 101 km NW of Chernovtsy; 48°59'/25°00'.

Petrindu, Rom.; pop. 5; 38 km WNW of Cluj; 46°56'/23°12'.

Petrinzel, Rom.; pop. 13; 38 km WNW of Cluj; 46°55'/23°09'.

Petrocz, *see* Petrovce nad Laborcom.

Petrodvorets, USSR (Petergof); pop. 81; 19 km WSW of Leningrad; 59°53'/29°54'; HSL.

Petroham, HSL. This pre-World War I community was not found in BGN gazetteers.

Petrohrad, Cz.; pop. 17; 69 km W of Praha; 50°08'/13°27'.

Petrokow, *see* Piotrkow Trybunalski.

Petrokrepost, USSR (Shlisselburg); pop. 57; 45 km ENE of Leningrad; 59°57'/31°02'.

Petronell, Aus.; pop. 5; 38 km E of Wien; 48°07'/16°51'.

Petropavlovka, Ukr.; 107 km E of Dnepropetrovsk; 48°27'/36°26'; HSL, JGFF, LDL, SF.

Petrosani, *see* Petrushany.

Petroseni, Rom. (Petroseny); 157 km S of Cluj; 45°25'/23°22'; AMG, HSL2.

Petroseny, *see* Petroseni.

Petroupim, Cz.; pop. 2; 38 km SE of Praha; 49°49'/14°45'.

Petrov, Ukr. (Petruv, Piotrow?); pop. 42; 75 km NW of Chernovtsy; 48°51'/25°17'.

Petrova, Rom. (Petreve); pop. 658; 133 km N of Cluj; 47°50'/24°14'; AMG, COH, GUM4, HSL, HSL2, LDL, PHR2, SM.

Petrova Bisztra, GUM3. This town was not found in BGN gazetteers under the given spelling.

Petrovac, Yug.; pop. 104; 88 km ESE of Beograd; 44°22'/21°25'.

Petrova Gora, USSR; 221 km ENE of Leningrad; 60°02'/34°13'; GUM4.

Petrovaradin, Yug.; 69 km NW of Beograd; 45°15'/19°53'; GUM4.

Petrovce, *see* Petrovce nad Laborcom.

Petrovce nad Laborcom, Cz. (Peterfala, Petrocz, Petrovce); 50 km ENE of Kosice; 48°48'/21°53'; AMG, COH, HSL.

Petroverovka, USSR; pop. 1,600; This town was not found in BGN gazetteers under the given spelling.

Petrovgrad, *see* Zrenjanin.

Petrovice, Cz.; pop. 60; 56 km WSW of Praha; 50°04'/13°39'.

Petrovitch, *see* Petrowitschi.

Petrovka, Ukr. (Ceaga); pop. 421; 120 km W of Odessa; 46°31'/29°10'; JGFF, LDL, SF.

Petrovka (near Kharkov), Ukr. (Petrovskoye); 26 km NE of Kharkov; 50°07'/36°32'; GUM4.

Petrovo Selo, Yug. (Petrovoszello); 150 km E of Beograd; 44°38'/22°26'; COH, EDRD, HSL, HSL2.

Petrovoszello, *see* Petrovo Selo.

Petrovskoye, *see* Petrovka (near Kharkov).

Petrowitschi, (Petrovitch, Pitrovitz); JGFF, LDL, SF. This town was not found in BGN gazetteers under the given spelling.

Petrowitz, JGFF. A number of towns share this name. It was not possible to determine from available information which one is being referenced.

Petrozavodsk, USSR; pop. 391; 309 km NE of Leningrad; 61°49'/34°20'.

Petrushany, Mold. (Petrosani); pop. 21; 150 km WNW of Kishinev; 47°51'/27°19'; HSL, LDL, PHR1.

Petruv, *see* Petrov.

Petrvald, Cz.; pop. 50; 146 km NE of Brno; 49°50'/18°24'; GUM4.

Petryche, Ukr. (Pietrycze); pop. 52; 50 km ENE of Lvov; 49°55'/24°43'.

Petrylow, *see* Petrilov.

Petrzalka, Cz.; pop. 241; 6 km SSW of Bratislava; 48°08'/17°07'; GUM5.

Petschau, *see* Becov nad Teplou.

Petseri, Est. (Petchuz); 82 km ESE of Tartu; 57°49'/27°36'; PHLE.

Pettau, *see* Ptuj.

Pewel Mala, Pol.; pop. 8; 62 km SW of Krakow; 49°40'/19°17'.

Pewel Wielka, Pol.; pop. 2; 62 km SSW of Krakow; 49°40'/19°21'.

Peza, Pol. (Penza); 69 km W of Bialystok; 53°14'/22°04'; JGFF.

Pezinok, Cz. (Bazin, Boesing, Bosing); pop. 418; 19 km NNE of Bratislava; 48°17'/17°16'; AMG, EJ, GUM4, HSL, HSL2.

Pfaffen Beerfurth, Germ.; pop. 24; 50 km SSE of Frankfurt am Main; 49°43'/08°52'; LDS.

Pfaffenhausen, Germ.; 88 km E of Frankfurt am Main; 50°06'/09°54'; CAHJP, PHGB, PHGB.

Pfaffenhofen, *see* Pfaffenhofen an der Ilm.

Pfaffenhofen an der Ilm, Germ. (Pfaffenhofen); 50 km N of Munchen; 48°32'/11°31'; PHGB.

Pfalz, Germ. GED, JGFF, PHGBW. This town was not found in BGN gazetteers under the given spelling.

Pfarrkirchen, Germ.; 107 km NE of Munchen; 48°26'/12°56'; GUM3, PHGB.

Pfarrweisach, Germ.; 82 km NNW of Nurnberg; 50°09'/10°44'; PHGB.

Pfeddersheim, Germ.; pop. 32; 56 km SSW of Frankfurt am Main; 49°38'/08°18'; PHGBW.

Pfeffenhausen, Germ.; 62 km NNE of Munchen; 48°40'/11°58'; PHGB.

Pfeningen, HSL. This pre-World War I community was not found in BGN gazetteers.

Pfersdorf, Germ.; 101 km NW of Nurnberg; 50°08'/10°10'; PHGB.

Pfersee, Germ.; 56 km WNW of Munchen; 48°21'/10°54'; CAHJP, HSL, JGFF, PHGB.

Pflaumheim, Germ.; pop. 2; 32 km ESE of Frankfurt am Main; 49°55'/09°04'; PHGB.

Pflaumloch, Germ.; 88 km SSW of Nurnberg; 48°51'/10°26'; HSL, PHGBW.

Pforzheim, Germ.; pop. 886; 38 km WNW of Stuttgart; 48°53'/08°42'; AMG, EDRD, EJ, GED, GUM5, JGFF, LDS, PHGBW.

Pfreimd, Germ.; 82 km ENE of Nurnberg; 49°30'/12°11'; PHGB.

Pfungstadt, Germ.; pop. 76; 38 km S of Frankfurt am Main; 49°48'/08°36'; CAHJP, HSL, JGFF, LDS.

Phalsburg, HSL. This pre-World War I community was not found in BGN gazetteers.

Phanagoria, *see* Sennaya.

Philippopolis, *see* Plovdiv.

Philippsburg, Germ.; pop. 50; 75 km WNW of Stuttgart;

49°14'/08°27'; HSL, JGFF, PHGBW.

Pholegandros, Greece EDRD. This town was not found in BGN gazetteers under the given spelling.

Piadyki, *see* Pyadyki.

Pianow, Pol.; 82 km NE of Czestochowa; 51°02'/20°10'; PHP1.

Pianowice, *see* Pyanovichi.

Piantnica, *see* Piatnica.

Piaseczna, *see* Pyasechna.

Piaseczno, Pol. (Piasetchna); pop. 2,256; 26 km SSE of Warszawa; 52°05'/21°02'; AMG, CAHJP, COH, EDRD, EJ, GA, GUM5, HSL, HSL2, JGFF, LDL, LDS, PHP1, PHP4, SF. *See also* Pyasechno.

Piasek, HSL. A number of towns share this name. It was not possible to determine from available information which one is being referenced.

Piasek Maly, Pol.; pop. 10; 69 km NE of Krakow; 50°23'/20°50'.

Piasek Wielki, Pol.; pop. 4; 69 km NE of Krakow; 50°22'/20°47'.

Piasetchna, *see* Piaseczno.

Piask, *see* Piaski Luterskie.

Piaska Stare, *see* Staryye Peski.

Piaski, Byel. (Piesk); pop. 1,249; 170 km NW of Pinsk; 53°21'/24°38'; AMG, COH, EJ, FRG, HSL, HSL2, JGFF, LDL, LYV, PHP1, PHP2, PHP3, SF, WS, YB. *See also* Piaski Luterskie. There are no less than 55 towns in Eastern Europe named Piaski. Holocaust sources tend to refer to the large labor camp of Piaski Luterskie in the Lublin area of Poland. Piaski means "sandy area."

Piaski (near Wielun), Pol.; pop. 33; 69 km WNW of Czestochowa; 51°13'/18°26'.

Piaski Luterskie, Pol. (Piask, Piaski); pop. 2,674; 26 km ESE of Lublin; 51°08'/22°52'; EDRD, GA, GUM3, GUM4, GUM5, HSL, LDS, POCEM, SF.

Piaski Stare, *see* Staryye Peski.

Piaski Szlacheckie, Pol.; pop. 34; 50 km ESE of Lublin; 50°56'/23°04'.

Piaski Wielkie, Pol.; pop. 53; 13 km SE of Krakow; 50°01'/19°59'.

Piaskovce, *see* Peskovtsy.

Piaskowka, Pol.; pop. 42; Described in the *Black Book* as being in the Kielce region of Poland, this town was not found in BGN gazetteers.

Piastow, Pol.; 13 km SW of Warszawa; 52°12'/20°51'; HSL.

Piategorsk, *see* Pyatigorsk.

Piatek, Pol. (Piontka); pop. 1,291; 38 km N of Lodz; 52°04'/19°29'; AMG, EDRD, GA, GUM3, GUM4, GUM5, HSL, HSL2, LDL, PHP1, SF.

Piaterota, *see* Katerinopol.

Piatigory, *see* Pyatigory.

Piatka, *see* Pyatka.

Piatkow, Pol.; pop. 108; 62 km WNW of Lublin; 51°27'/21°44'.

Piatkowa, Pol.; pop. 44; 45 km W of Przemysl; 49°53'/22°10'; HSL, PHP2.

Piatkowa (Krakow), Pol.; pop. 29; 82 km ESE of Krakow; 49°38'/20°46'; PHP3.

Piatkowce, Pol.; pop. 23; Described in the *Black Book* as being in the Tarnopol region of Poland, this town was not found in BGN gazetteers.

Piatkowisko, Pol.; pop. 5; 13 km SW of Lodz; 51°41'/19°18'.

Piatlpwce, GUM4. This town was not found in BGN gazetteers under the given spelling.

Piatnica, Pol. (Piantnica, Piontnitza); pop. 520; 69 km W of Bialystok; 53°12'/22°06'; HSL, JGFF, LDL, PHP4, SF, YB.

Piatohor, *see* Pyatigory.

Piatra, HSL, HSL2, JGFF. A number of towns share this name. It was not possible to determine from available information which one is being referenced.

Piatra Neamt, Rom.; pop. 101 km SW of Iasi; 46°55'/26°20'; AMG, CAHJP, GUM3, GUM4, HSL, JGFF, PHR1.

Piatyhory, *see* Pyatigory.

Picleu, Rom.; pop. 19; 107 km WNW of Cluj; 47°08'/22°16'.

Pidayets, *see* Podgaytsy.

Pidbish, *see* Podbuzh.

Pidhayets, *see* Podgaytsy.

Piechoty, Pol.; pop. 5; 107 km WNW of Przemysl; 50°24'/21°34'.

Pieczalowka, *see* Pechalovka.

Pieczarna, *see* Pecharna.

Pieczonki, *see* Pechenki.

Pieczychwosty, *see* Pechikhvosty.

Pieczyski, Pol.; pop. 3; 75 km SSW of Bialystok; 52°34'/22°35'.

Piedecauti, Rom.; pop. 52; This town was not found in BGN gazetteers under the given spelling.

Piedruja, Lat. (Friedrusk, Peridroysk, Piedrujas, Pridroisk, Pridruiska); pop. 203; 56 km E of Daugavpils; 55°48'/27°27'; COH, PHLE.

Piedrujas, *see* Piedruja.

Piekielnik, Pol.; pop. 7; 75 km S of Krakow; 49°28'/19°46'.

Piekiely, EGRS. This town was not found in BGN gazetteers under the given spelling.

Piekoszow, Pol.; pop. 39; 94 km ENE of Czestochowa; 50°53'/20°28'.

Piekuty, Pol. (Piekuty Nowe); pop. 20; 45 km SW of Bialystok; 52°51'/22°43'.

Piekuty Nowe, *see* Piekuty.

Pielancz, Pol. EDRD. This town was not found in BGN gazetteers under the given spelling.

Pielnia, Pol.; pop. 10; 56 km SW of Przemysl; 49°33'/22°04'.

Pienczykowek, Pol.; pop. 3; 69 km NW of Bialystok; 53°39'/22°37'.

Pienczykowo, Pol.; 69 km NW of Bialystok; 53°38'/22°37'; JGFF.

Pieniaki, *see* Penyaki.

Pieniany, Pol.; pop. 11; 101 km NNE of Przemysl; 50°29'/23°41'.

Pieniazki, Pol.; pop. 108; 62 km WNW of Bialystok; 53°33'/22°31'.

Pieniezno, Pol. (Mehlsack); pop. 17; 94 km E of Gdansk; 54°14'/20°08'.

Pienki, Pol.; 114 km SSE of Gdansk; 53°21'/18°52'; HSL.

Piensk, Pol. (Penzig); pop. 7; 139 km W of Wroclaw; 51°15'/15°03'.

Pierczhnica, (Pierychnica); pop. 180; Described in the *Black Book* as being in the Kielce region of Poland, this town was not found in BGN gazetteers.

Piersk, Pol.; pop. 8; 88 km WNW of Lodz; 52°13'/18°26'.

Pierszyce, Pol.; pop. 16; 62 km ENE of Krakow; 50°11'/20°48'.

Pierwomajsk, *see* Pervomaysk.

Pierychnica, *see* Pierczhnica.

Pierzchnianka, Pol.; pop. 9; 94 km NNE of Krakow; 50°42'/20°47'.

Pierzchow, Pol.; pop. 13; 32 km ESE of Krakow; 49°57'/20°18'.

Pierzchowice, *see* Perkhovichi.

Pierzyny, Pol.; pop. 7; 62 km NNW of Czestochowa; 51°17'/18°57'.

Piesiewicze, *see* Pesevichi.

Piesk, *see* Piaski.

Piestany, Cz. (Pistyan, Pistyan Postyen, Postyen, Pyesk); pop. 2,141; 75 km NE of Bratislava; 48°36'/17°50'; AMG, COH, EJ, GUM3, GUM4, GUM5, HSL, LDL, YB.

Piestrzec, Pol.; pop. 12; 82 km NE of Krakow; 50°23'/20°57'.

Pieterkanie, HSL. This pre-World War I community was not found in BGN gazetteers.

Pietkovitz, *see* Piotrkowice.

Pietkowo, Pol.; pop. 42; 32 km SSW of Bialystok; 52°54'/22°53'; GUM3.

Pietnice, *see* Pyatnitsa.

Pietniczany, *see* Petnichany.

Pietrasze, Byel. GUM3. A number of towns share this name. It was not possible to determine from available information which one is being referenced.

Pietrusy, Pol.; pop. 29; 107 km N of Lublin; 52°10'/22°41'.

Pietrusza Wola, Pol.; pop. 10; 82 km W of Przemysl; 49°49'/21°41'.

Pietrycze, *see* Petryche.

Pietrzejowa, Pol.; pop. 14; 88 km WNW of Przemysl; 50°04'/21°38'.

Pietrzykowice, Pol.; pop. 5; 69 km SW of Krakow; 49°42'/19°10'.

Pikalin, see Pikeliai.

Pikelen, see Pikeliai.

Pikeli, see Pikeliai.

Pikeliai, Lith. (Pikalin, Pikelen, Pikeli); pop. 286; 82 km WNW of Kaunas; 55°19'/22°48'; COH, GUM3, HSL, HSL2, JGFF, LDL, SF, YL.

Pikeliat, LDL. This pre-World War I community was not found in BGN gazetteers.

Pikov, HSL. A number of towns share this name. It was not possible to determine from available information which one is being referenced.

Pikulice, Pol.; pop. 68; 13 km S of Przemysl; 49°45'/22°47'; PHP2.

Pikulovitse, Ukr. (Pikulowice); pop. 36; 13 km ENE of Lvov; 49°52'/24°13'.

Pikulowice, see Pikulovitse.

Pila, Pol. (Schneidemuhl, Schneidermuhl, Schneidmuhl); pop. 620; 82 km NNW of Poznan; 53°09'/16°45'; AMG, CAHJP, EDRD, GUM3, HSL, JGFF, PHP4.

Pilaszkowice, Pol.; 32 km SE of Lublin; 50°59'/22°51'; GA.

Pilaviez, Ukr. EDRD. This town was not found in BGN gazetteers under the given spelling.

Pilawa, Pol. (Pylyava); pop. 179; 56 km ESE of Warszawa; 51°57'/21°32'; GYLA, HSL.

Pilchow, Pol. (Pilichow); pop. 13; 82 km SSW of Lublin; 50°37'/22°03'.

Pilcza, Pol.; pop. 33; 69 km ENE of Krakow; 50°13'/20°52'.

Pilczyca, Pol.; pop. 28; 75 km NE of Czestochowa; 51°02'/20°06'.

Pilda, Lat.; pop. 7; 94 km NE of Daugavpils; 56°27'/27°44'; PHLE.

Pilev, see Pulawy.

Pilgersdorf, Aus.; pop. 3; 82 km NE of Graz; 47°26'/16°21'.

Pilgram, see Pelhrimov.

Pilica, Pol. (Pilitsa, Pilitz, Pilts, Piltz); pop. 1,877; 50 km ESE of Czestochowa; 50°28'/19°39'; AMG, CAHJP, EDRD, EJ, GUM3, GUM4, GUM5, GUM6, HSL, JGFF, LDL, LDS, LYV, PHP1, PHP3, POCEM, SF, WS.

Pilichow, see Pilchow.

Piliny, Hung.; pop. 9; 82 km NNE of Budapest; 48°09'/19°36'.

Pilipche, Ukr. (Filipkowce); pop. 37; 45 km N of Chernovtsy; 48°38'/26°05'.

Pilipec, see Pilipets.

Pilipets, Ukr. (Filipec, Filipetz, Fulopfalva, Pilipec); pop. 300; 146 km S of Lvov; 48°40'/23°21'; HSL, SM.

Pilis, Hung.; pop. 136; 45 km ESE of Budapest; 47°17'/19°33'; HSL, LDS, PHH.

Pilisborosjeno, Hung.; pop. 3; 19 km NW of Budapest; 47°37'/19°00'.

Piliscsaba, Hung.; pop. 73; 26 km WNW of Budapest; 47°37'/18°50'; HSL.

Pilismarot, Hung.; pop. 9; 38 km NW of Budapest; 47°47'/18°53'.

Pilisszanto, Hung.; pop. 4; 26 km NW of Budapest; 47°40'/18°54'.

Pilisszentivan, Hung.; pop. 5; 19 km WNW of Budapest; 47°37'/18°54'.

Pilisvorosvar, Hung. (Vorosvar); pop. 117; 19 km NW of Budapest; 47°37'/18°55'; HSL, LDS, PHH.

Pilitsa, see Pilica.

Pilitz, see Pilica.

Piliva, see Pilyava.

Piljawa, see Pilyava.

Pillau, see Baltiysk.

Pillichsdorf, Aus.; pop. 2; 26 km NNE of Wien; 48°21'/16°32'.

Pillkallen, see Dobrovolsk.

Pilnikov, Cz.; pop. 1; 107 km NE of Praha; 50°31'/15°49'.

Pilov, see Pulawy.

Pilsach, Germ.; 38 km ESE of Nurnberg; 49°19'/11°30'; GUM3.

Pilsen, see Plzen.

Pil Ten, see Piltene.

Pilten, see Piltene.

Piltene, Lat. (Pil Ten, Pilten); pop. 53; 150 km W of Riga; 57°13'/21°40'; COH, HSL, JGFF, LDL, PHLE, SF.

Pilts, see Pilica.

Piltz, see Pilica.

Pilvishki, see Pilviskiai.

Pilvishok, see Pilviskiai.

Pilviskai, see Pilviskiai.

Pilviski, see Pilviskiai.

Pilviskiai, Lith. (Pilvishki, Pilvishok, Pilviskai, Pilviski, Pilviskis); pop. 961; 50 km SW of Kaunas; 54°43'/23°13'; COH, GUM3, GUM4, HSL, HSL2, JGFF, LDL, SF, YL.

Pilviskis, see Pilviskiai.

Pily, Ukr.; pop. 28; 38 km NNW of Lvov; 50°08'/23°53'.

Pilyava, Ukr. (Piliva, Piljawa, Spilyava); 88 km WNW of Vinnitsa; 49°36'/27°27'; HSL, LDL, SF.

Pilzne, see Pilzno.

Pilzno, Pol. (Pilzne); pop. 752; 101 km E of Krakow; 49°58'/21°18'; AMG, CAHJP, EGRS, GA, GUM3, GUM5, HSL, JGFF, LDL, LYV, PHP3, SF.

Pincehely, Hung. (Gorbenpinczehely, Gorbopincehely); pop. 171; 101 km SSW of Budapest; 46°41'/18°27'; HSL, LDL, LDS, PHH.

Pinchev, see Pinczow.

Pinchov, see Pinczow.

Pinchuv, see Pinczow.

Pincota, Rom. (Pancota); pop. 113; 157 km SW of Cluj; 46°20'/21°42'.

Pinczow, Pol. (Pinchev, Pinchov, Pinchuv, Pintchov); pop. 4,324; 69 km NNE of Krakow; 50°32'/20°32'; AMG, CAHJP, COH, EDRD, EJ, GA, GUM3, GUM4, GUM5, HSL, HSL2, JGFF, LDL, LDS, LYV, PHP1, PHP2, PHP3, SF, YB.

Piniava, Lith.; pop. 58; 69 km E of Siauliai; 55°47'/24°22'; YL.

Pinkafeld, Aus.; pop. 34; 56 km NE of Graz; 47°22'/16°07'.

Pinne, see Pniewy.

Pinsk, Byel.; pop. 17,513; 221 km SSW of Minsk; 52°07'/26°07'; AMG, CAHJP, COH, EDRD, EJ, GA, GUM3, GUM4, GUM5, GUM6, GYLA, HSL, HSL2, JGFF, LDL, LYV, PHP4, YB.

Pintak, Rom.; 56 km N of Cluj; 47°13'/23°32'; HSL. This town was located on a pre-World War I map, but does not appear in contemporary gazetteers.

Pintchov, see Pinczow.

Pinticu, Rom.; pop. 10; 75 km NE of Cluj; 46°57'/24°32'.

Pinzberg, Germ.; 32 km N of Nurnberg; 49°42'/11°06'; PHGB.

Pionki, Pol.; 82 km WNW of Lublin; 51°29'/21°27'; AMG, GA, GUM3, GUM4, GUM5, GUM6, HSL, PHP1, SF.

Piontka, see Piatek.

Piontnitza, see Piatnica.

Piora, see Pajuris.

Piorkow, Pol.; pop. 9; 114 km NE of Krakow; 50°48'/21°10'; GUM4.

Piorunka, Pol.; pop. 12; 101 km ESE of Krakow; 49°29'/21°00'.

Piotrkovitz, see Piotrkowice.

Piotrkow, Pol.; pop. 75; A number of towns share this name. It was not possible to determine from available information which one is being referenced. See also Piotrkow Trybunalski. There are three towns in Poland alone with the name Piotrkow, but the name by itself usually refers to the town of Piotrkow Trybunalski. See also Piotrkow Trybunalski and other listings below that have Piotrkow in their names.

Piotrkowice, Pol. (Pietkovitz, Piotrkovitz); pop. 248; 82 km NNE of Krakow; 50°40'/20°41'; SF.

Piotrkowice (near Poznan), Pol.; 38 km SSW of Poznan; 52°09'/16°44'; GUM3.

Piotrkowice (near Tuchow), Pol.; pop. 12; 82 km E of Krakow;

49°56'/21°01'; SF.

Piotrkow Kujawski, Pol. (Kujawien, Petrikov Koyavsk); pop. 742; 101 km ENE of Poznan; 52°34'/18°30'; CAHJP, COH, HSL, LDL, PHP4, SF.

Piotrkow Trybunalski, Pol. (Petrikau, Petrikov, Petrokow, Piotrkow, Piotrkow Trybunaski, Piotrkuv, Pyetrkov, Trybunalski); pop. 11,630; 45 km SSE of Lodz; 51°24'/19°41'; AMG, CAHJP, COH, EDRD, EJ, FRG, GA, GUM3, GUM4, GUM5, GUM6, HSL, HSL2, ISH2, ISH3, JGFF, LDL, LDS, LYV, PHP1, PHP2, PHP3, PHP4, POCEM, SF, YB.

Piotrkuv, *see* Piotrkow Trybunalski.

Piotrow, *possibly* Petrov.

Piotrowice (near Bielsko Biala), Pol.; pop. 25; 45 km WSW of Krakow; 49°59'/19°22'.

Piotrowice (near Kielce), Pol.; pop. 30; 101 km NNE of Krakow; 50°50'/20°40'.

Piotrowice (near Lublin), Pol. (Piotrowice Wielkie); pop. 16; 88 km W of Lublin; 51°26'/21°19'; GUM5.

Piotrowice (near Radom), Pol.; pop. 33; 101 km W of Lublin; 51°25'/21°09'.

Piotrowice Wielkie, *see* Piotrowice (near Lublin).

Piotrowka, Pol.; pop. 53; 69 km S of Warszawa; 51°42'/20°50'. This town could not be found on any maps, but a Polish gazetteer places it close to Rykaly, whose location is given here.

Piotrowo, Pol.; 45 km WNW of Poznan; 52°43'/16°30'; GA.

Piplin, *see* Zelenyy.

Pir, Rom. (Szilagyper); pop. 147; 120 km WNW of Cluj; 47°28'/22°22'; HSL, PHR2.

Piraeus, Greece (Piree); pop. 167; 13 km SW of Athens; 37°57'/23°38'; GUM5.

Piran, Yug. (Pirano); 189 km WSW of Zagreb; 45°32'/13°34'; PHY.

Pirano, *see* Piran.

Pir Atin, *see* Piryatin.

Piree, *see* Piraeus.

Piriatyn, *see* Piryatin.

Piricse, Hung.; pop. 73; 107 km ESE of Miskolc; 47°46'/22°09'; HSL, LDS, PHH.

Piringsdorf, Aus.; pop. 4; 82 km NE of Graz; 47°26'/16°25'.

Piriu Negru, Rom. (Paraul Negru); pop. 27; 139 km WNW of Iasi; 47°57'/26°10'.

Pirlitz, *see* Pyrlitsa.

Pirmasens, Germ.; pop. 800; 126 km SSW of Frankfurt am Main; 49°12'/07°36'; GED, GUM3, GUM5, HSL, JGFF.

Pirna, Germ.; pop. 23; 114 km ESE of Leipzig; 50°58'/13°56'; GUM3, GUM4.

Pirog, Pol.; pop. 11; 75 km S of Warszawa; 51°38'/21°05'.

Pirot, Yug.; pop. 114; 157 km NNE of Skopje; 43°09'/22°36'; GUM6, PHY.

Piryatin, Ukr. (Pir Atin, Piriatyn); pop. 3,885; 120 km SSW of Konotop; 50°15'/32°31'; EJ, GUM4, GUM5, HSL, JGFF, SF.

Pisarovina, Yug.; pop. 15; 32 km S of Zagreb; 45°35'/15°52'.

Pisarzowa, Pol.; pop. 40; 62 km ESE of Krakow; 49°42'/20°30'.

Pisatchna, *see* Pyasechna.

Piscaresti, *see* Piskareshty.

Piscolt, Rom. (Piscott, Piskolt); pop. 121; 133 km WNW of Cluj; 47°35'/22°18'; HSL, PHR2.

Piscopia, *see* Episcopia Bihorului.

Piscott, *see* Piscolt.

Pisek, Cz.; pop. 217; 94 km S of Praha; 49°18'/14°09'; AMG, HSL, HSL2.

Pishcha, Ukr. (Pish Tch, Piszcza); pop. 37; 195 km N of Lvov; 51°36'/23°50'; SF.

Pishchen, *see* Pistany.

Pishelot, *see* Pusalotas.

Pish Tch, *see* Pishcha.

Pishtyan, *see* Pistany.

Pishtzatz, *see* Piszczac.

Piskareshty, Mold. (Piscaresti); pop. 3; 88 km N of Kishinev; 47°45'/28°49'.

Piski, Pol.; pop. 71; 88 km WSW of Bialystok; 52°59'/21°52'; HSL.

Pisko, Hung.; pop. 6; 101 km ESE of Nagykanizsa; 45°49'/17°57'; HSL.

Piskolt, *see* Piscolt.

Piskorovitza, *see* Piskorowice.

Piskorowice, Pol. (Piskorovitza); pop. 76; 50 km NNW of Przemysl; 50°14'/22°31'; HSL, SF.

Piskowitz, Germ.; 126 km E of Leipzig; 51°17'/14°12'; HSL, HSL2.

Pistany, Cz. (Pishchen, Pishtyan, Pyeshtani); pop. 6; 50 km NW of Praha; 50°31'/14°04'; LYV.

Pistchanka, *see* Peschanka.

Pistin, *see* Pistyn.

Pistyan, *see* Piestany.

Pistyan Postyen, *see* Piestany.

Pistyn, Ukr. (Pistin); pop. 525; 69 km W of Chernovtsy; 48°21'/25°02'; COH, EDRD, EGRS, GUM3, GUM4, HSL, JGFF, PHP2, SF.

Pisz, Pol. (Johannisburg); pop. 195; 107 km WNW of Bialystok; 53°38'/21°48'; POCEM.

Piszcza, *see* Pishcha.

Piszczac, Pol. (Pishtzatz); pop. 394; 101 km NNE of Lublin; 51°58'/23°23'; GUM3, GUM5, HSL, HSL2, JGFF, LDL, POCEM, SF.

Piszczanica, GUM3. This town was not found in BGN gazetteers under the given spelling.

Piszke, Hung.; pop. 37; 50 km WNW of Budapest; 47°45'/18°29'; HSL.

Pitalovo, *see* Abrini.

Pitcheyev, *see* Pochayev.

Pitesti, Rom.; 107 km WNW of Bucuresti; 44°51'/24°52'; GUM4, HSL, PHR1.

Pitkovice, Cz.; pop. 5; 13 km ESE of Praha; 50°01'/14°35'.

Pitomaca, Yug.; pop. 20; 94 km ENE of Zagreb; 45°57'/17°14'.

Pitrovitz, *see* Petrowitschi.

Pitschen, Germ.; pop. 31; 75 km SSE of Berlin; 51°52'/13°35'.

Pitshayev, *see* Pochayev.

Pitten, Aus.; pop. 4; 56 km S of Wien; 47°43'/16°11'.

Pitusca, *see* Pitushka.

Pitushka, Mold. (Pitusca); pop. 30; 45 km WNW of Kishinev; 47°14'/28°25'.

Pitvaros, Hung.; pop. 17; 45 km ENE of Szeged; 46°19'/20°44'.

Piuski, Yug.; 139 km WSW of Zagreb; 45°40'/14°13'; HSL. This town was located on a pre-World War I map, but does not appear in contemporary gazetteers.

Pivasiunai, Lith.; pop. 18; 62 km SE of Kaunas; 54°28'/24°22'.

Pivnica, Yug.; pop. 1; 114 km E of Zagreb; 45°43'/17°29'.

Pivnishna, *see* Piwniczna.

Piwaki, Pol.; pop. 33; 62 km SSE of Lodz; 51°13'/19°46'.

Piwniczna, Pol. (Pivnishna); pop. 226; 88 km SE of Krakow; 49°26'/20°43'; EGRS, GUM5, HSL, HSL2, LDL, PHP3, POCEM, SF.

Piwonice, Pol.; pop. 7; 94 km WSW of Lodz; 51°44'/18°06'.

Pjatigory, *see* Pyatigory.

Pjatino, Byel. EDRD. This town was not found in BGN gazetteers under the given spelling.

Pjatki, *see* Pyatka.

Placiszewo, Pol.; pop. 16; 69 km NW of Warszawa; 52°46'/20°23'.

Placzkow, Pol.; pop. 25; 114 km ESE of Lodz; 51°08'/20°43'.

Plaesii de Jos, Rom.; pop. 2; 157 km SW of Iasi; 46°13'/26°06'.

Plaesii de Sus, Rom.; pop. 2; 150 km SW of Iasi; 46°14'/26°06'.

Plahteevca, *see* Plakhteyevka.

Plainesti, GUM4. This town was not found in BGN gazetteers under the given spelling.

Plaiul Cosmin, *see* Molodiya.

Plaiul Cosminului, *see* Molodiya.

Plakhteyevka, Ukr. (Plahteevca); pop. 20; 88 km SW of Odessa;

46°06'/29°43'.

Plana, Cz.; pop. 80; 126 km WSW of Praha; 49°52'/12°45'.

Plana nad Luznici, Cz.; pop. 21; 88 km SSE of Praha; 49°21'/14°42'.

Planany, Cz.; pop. 5; 38 km E of Praha; 50°03'/15°02'.

Plandiste, Yug. (Mariolana); pop. 90; 69 km NE of Beograd; 45°14'/21°08'.

Planegg, Germ.; pop. 32; 82 km SSE of Stuttgart; 48°06'/09°25'; GUM3.

Planice, Cz.; pop. 21; 107 km SSW of Praha; 49°23'/13°28'.

Planig, Germ.; 62 km SW of Frankfurt am Main; 49°52'/07°55'; JGFF.

Plashuv, *see* Plaszow.

Plaska, Pol.; pop. 17; 88 km N of Bialystok; 53°54'/23°15'; AMG.

Plaskowice, Pol.; pop. 3; 75 km SE of Lodz; 51°10'/20°04'.

Plass, *see* Plasy.

Plasy, Cz. (Plass); pop. 10; 75 km WSW of Praha; 49°56'/13°24'; HSL.

Plaszow, Pol. (Plashuv); 13 km ESE of Krakow; 50°03'/19°59'; AMG, EJ, FRG, GA, GUM3, GUM4, GUM5, GUM6, PHP3.

Platel, *see* Plateliai.

Plateliai, Lith. (Platel, Plotel); pop. 150; 94 km W of Siauliai; 56°03'/21°49'; HSL, LDL, SF, YL.

Platere, Lat.; pop. 3; 69 km E of Riga; 56°50'/25°13'.

Plattling, Germ.; pop. 13; 120 km NE of Munchen; 48°47'/12°52'; GED, GUM3, GUM5, PHGB.

Platz, Germ.; 88 km ENE of Frankfurt am Main; 50°16'/09°55'; GUM5, JGFF, PHGB.

Plau, Germ.; pop. 4; 75 km SSE of Rostock; 53°27'/12°16'; LDS.

Plaucha Male, *see* Malaya Plavucha.

Plaucha Velka, Ukr. (Plaucza Wielka); pop. 65; 94 km ESE of Lvov; 49°35'/25°14'.

Plaucza Mala, *see* Malaya Plavucha.

Plaucza Wielka, *see* Plaucha Velka.

Plaue, Germ.; 120 km SW of Leipzig; 50°47'/10°54'; LDS.

Plauen, Germ.; pop. 623; 94 km S of Leipzig; 50°30'/12°08'; EJ.

Plavalar, Rom.; pop. 3; 101 km WNW of Iasi; 47°34'/26°21'.

Plavanitza, *see* Plawanice.

Plavec, Cz. (Palocse); 69 km NW of Kosice; 49°16'/20°51'; HSL.

Plavinas, Lat.; pop. 3; 101 km NW of Daugavpils; 56°37'/25°43'; JGFF, PHLE.

Plavinu, *see* Tirumbaltgalvji.

Plavnica, Cz.; pop. 53; 75 km NW of Kosice; 49°17'/20°47'; HSL.

Plawanice, Pol. (Plavanitza); pop. 30; 75 km E of Lublin; 51°07'/23°39'; SF.

Plawce, Pol.; 26 km ESE of Poznan; 52°18'/17°17'; PHP2.

Plawie, Ukr.; pop. 81; 150 km S of Lvov; 48°35'/23°15'; HSL. This town was located on an interwar map of Poland but does not appear in contemporary gazetteers. Map coordinates are approximate.

Plawna, Pol.; pop. 2; 88 km ESE of Krakow; 49°45'/20°58'.

Plawno, Pol. (Palovna); pop. 566; 38 km NE of Czestochowa; 50°59'/19°28'; CAHJP, GUM5, HSL, HSL2, JGFF, LDS, PHP1, SF, YB.

Plawo, Pol.; pop. 53; 88 km SSW of Lublin; 50°34'/22°04'.

Plawowice, Pol.; pop. 5; 38 km NE of Krakow; 50°11'/20°25'.

Plaza, Pol.; pop. 38; 32 km W of Krakow; 50°06'/19°28'.

Plazow, Pol.; pop. 88; 69 km NNE of Przemysl; 50°19'/23°15'; PHP1, PHP4.

Plazow Lubelski, Pol. PHP4. This town was not found in BGN gazetteers under the given spelling.

Plebanowka, Ukr.; pop. 38; 75 km NNW of Chernovtsy; 48°55'/25°45'; PHP2. This town was located on an interwar map of Poland but does not appear in contemporary gazetteers. Map coordinates are approximate.

Plec, Pol.; pop. 6; 101 km ESE of Lodz; 51°25'/20°48'.

Plenikow, Ukr.; pop. 30; 75 km ESE of Lvov; 49°25'/24°45'.

This town was located on an interwar map of Poland but does not appear in contemporary gazetteers. Map coordinates are approximate.

Plesca, Rom.; 69 km WNW of Cluj; 47°05'/22°54'; HSL.

Pleschen, *see* Pleszew.

Pleseni, *see* Plesheny.

Pleshchany, Byel. (Pleszczany); pop. 7; 50 km NNW of Minsk; 54°17'/27°23'.

Pleshchenitsy, Byel. (Pleshtchenitz); pop. 738; 62 km N of Minsk; 54°25'/27°50'; COH, GUM4, JGFF, SF.

Plesheny, Mold. (Pleseni); pop. 11; 82 km SSW of Kishinev; 46°21'/28°21'.

Pleshtchenitz, *see* Pleshchenitsy.

Plesivec, Cz. (Pelsucz); pop. 240; 62 km WSW of Kosice; 48°33'/20°24'; AMG, HSL.

Plesna, Pol.; pop. 45; 75 km E of Krakow; 49°56'/20°57'; GUM5.

Plesnice, Cz.; pop. 5; 101 km SW of Praha; 49°46'/13°11'.

Plesovec, Cz.; 56 km ENE of Brno; 49°20'/17°23'; COH, HSL.

Pless, *see* Pszczyna.

Pleszczany, *see* Pleshchany.

Pleszew, Pol. (Pleschen); pop. 116; 82 km ESE of Poznan; 51°54'/17°48'; AMG, CAHJP, GUM5, HSL, JGFF, LDS.

Pleszow, Pol.; pop. 13; 13 km E of Krakow; 50°05'/20°07'; AMG.

Pleternica, Yug.; pop. 8; 150 km ESE of Zagreb; 45°17'/17°48'.

Plettenberg, Germ.; pop. 43; 75 km NE of Koln; 51°13'/07°53'; CAHJP.

Pleven, Bulg. (Plevna); pop. 860; 133 km NE of Sofija; 43°25'/24°37'; EJ, GUM4, GUM6, HSL.

Plevna, *see* Pleven.

Plewnia Nowa, Pol.; pop. 21; 82 km W of Lodz; 51°53'/18°19'; PHP1.

Plewnik, *see* Bronowo Plewnik.

Plieningen, Germ.; 13 km SSE of Stuttgart; 48°42'/09°13'; PHGBW.

Pligavki, Byel. (Plihawki); pop. 4; 126 km W of Vitebsk; 55°25'/28°14'.

Plihawki, *see* Pligavki.

Plintsk, *see* Plonsk.

Plisa, *see* Plissa.

Pliski, Ukr.; 56 km WSW of Konotop; 51°07'/32°26'; HSL.

Pliskov, Ukr.; pop. 1,420; 56 km ENE of Vinnitsa; 49°22'/29°17'; GUM5, HSL, JGFF, LDL, SF.

Plissa, Byel. (Plisa); pop. 302; 139 km W of Vitebsk; 55°13'/27°57'; AMG, COH, EJ, HSL, LDL, SF.

Plitvicka Jezera, Yug.; pop. 1; 107 km S of Zagreb; 44°53'/15°37'.

Plociczno, Pol.; pop. 30; 133 km WNW of Warszawa; 53°07'/19°42'.

Plock, Pol. (Plotsk, Plotzk); pop. 7,352; 94 km N of Lodz; 52°33'/19°42'; AMG, CAHJP, COH, EDRD, EJ, GUM3, GUM4, GUM5, GUM6, GYLA, HSL, HSL2, JGFF, LDL, LDS, LYV, PHP1, PHP2, PHP4, POCEM, SF, YB.

Ploesti, Rom.; pop. 62 km N of Bucuresti; 44°57'/26°01'; AMG, EJ, GUM4, GUM5, HSL, JGFF, PHR1.

Ploki, Pol.; pop. 6; 32 km WNW of Krakow; 50°12'/19°31'.

Ploksciai, Lith.; pop. 39; 50 km WNW of Kaunas; 55°05'/23°11'; JGFF.

Plomiany, Pol.; pop. 2; 107 km N of Lodz; 52°40'/19°19'.

Plomieniec, Pol.; pop. 15; 69 km ESE of Warszawa; 52°04'/21°52'.

Plomnitz, Germ.; 62 km NW of Leipzig; 51°45'/11°49'; EDRD.

Plonczyn, Pol.; pop. 1; 114 km N of Lodz; 52°42'/19°19'.

Plonitsa, Pol. (Plotnice); EDRD. This town was not found in BGN gazetteers under the given spelling.

Plonka, Pol.; pop. 37; 56 km SE of Lublin; 50°50'/22°59'.

Plonna, Pol.; pop. 36; 62 km SW of Przemysl; 49°26'/22°07'.

Plonowo, Pol.; pop. 4; 56 km SSW of Bialystok; 52°41'/22°49'.

Plonsk, Pol. (Plintsk, Plunsk); pop. 4,460; 56 km WNW of Warszawa; 52°38'/20°23'; AMG, CAHJP, COH, EDRD, EJ,

GA, GUM3, GUM4, GUM5, HSL, HSL2, ISH3, JGFF, LDL, LDS, LYV, PHP4, POCEM, SF, YB.

Plonszowice, Pol.; pop. 54; 13 km W of Lublin; 51°16'/22°25'.

Plontch, *see* Polaniec.

Plopana, *see* Plopana Tirg.

Plopana Tirg, Rom. (Plopana); pop. 176; 56 km SSW of Iasi; 46°41'/27°13'; GUM3.

Plopani, *see* Plopeni.

Plopeni, Rom. (Plopani); 75 km N of Bucuresti; 45°04'/25°59'; PHR1.

Plopenii Mari, Rom.; pop. 18; 101 km NW of Iasi; 47°53'/26°47'.

Plopi, *see* Plopy.

Plopis, Rom.; pop. 30; 94 km N of Cluj; 47°35'/23°46'; AMG, HSL.

Plopy, Mold. (Plopi); pop. 73; 163 km NW of Kishinev; 48°16'/27°41'.

Plosca, *see* Ploska.

Ploshchevo, Byel. (Ploszczewo); pop. 9; 26 km E of Pinsk; 52°07'/26°25'.

Ploska, Ukr. (Plosca); pop. 99; 75 km SW of Chernovtsy; 47°54'/25°08'; HSL, PHR2.

Ploskie, Pol. (Ploskie Glowne); pop. 20; 69 km SE of Lublin; 50°44'/23°11'; GUM4.

Ploskie Glowne, *see* Ploskie.

Ploskin, Byel.; pop. 15; 45 km N of Pinsk; 52°28'/26°16'.

Ploskirow, *see* Khmelnitskiy.

Plosnica, Pol.; pop. 5; 133 km NW of Warszawa; 53°17'/20°01'.

Ploszczewo, *see* Ploshchevo.

Plotel, *see* Plateliai.

Plotnica, *see* Plotnitsa.

Plotnice, *see* Plonitsa.

Plotnitsa, Byel. (Plotnica, Plotnitse, Plotnitza, Plotniza); pop. 236; 38 km E of Pinsk; 52°03'/26°39'; COH, HSL, LDL, LYV, SF.

Plotnitse, *see* Plotnitsa.

Plotnitza, *see* Plotnitsa.

Plotniza, *see* Plotnitsa.

Plotsk, *see* Plock.

Plotych, Ukr. (Plotycz); pop. 16; 114 km E of Lvov; 49°37'/25°34'.

Plotycz, *see* Plotych.

Plotzk, *see* Plock.

Plovdiv, Bulg. (Filibe, Philippopolis); pop. 5,092; 133 km ESE of Sofija; 42°09'/24°45'; EJ, GUM4, HSL, JGFF, LDL, LJEE.

Pluchow, Pol. PHP2. This town was not found in BGN gazetteers under the given spelling.

Plugov, Ukr. (Pluguv, Pluhow); pop. 36; 75 km E of Lvov; 49°45'/25°02'; GUM3, GUM4, GUM5.

Pluguv, *see* Plugov.

Pluhow, *see* Plugov.

Plumenau, *see* Plumlov.

Plumlov, Cz. (Plumenau); pop. 3; 45 km NNE of Brno; 49°28'/17°01'.

Plunge, Lith. (Plungian, Plungyan, Plungyany, Plunjen); pop. 1,815; 88 km WSW of Siauliai; 55°55'/21°51'; EDRD, EJ, GUM3, GUM5, HSL, HSL2, JGFF, LDL, SF, YL.

Plungian, *see* Plunge.

Plungyan, *see* Plunge.

Plungyany, *see* Plunge.

Plunjen, *see* Plunge.

Plunsk, *see* Plonsk.

Plusy, *see* Plyussy.

Plyushchevka, Ukr. (Yefingar); pop. 1,639; 157 km NE of Odessa; 47°24'/32°19'; JGFF.

Plyussy, Byel. (Plusy); pop. 44; 208 km WNW of Vitebsk; 55°49'/27°02'; GUM3.

Plzen, Cz. (Pilsen); pop. 3,094; 88 km SW of Praha; 49°45'/13°22'; AMG, EDRD, EJ, GUM3, GUM4, GUM5, GUM6, HSL, JGFF.

Pnevno, Ukr. (Pniewno); pop. 143; 139 km NW of Rovno; 51°40'/25°16'; GUM3, GUM4.

Pniatyn, *see* Pnyatyn.

Pniewnik, Pol.; pop. 21; 56 km ENE of Warszawa; 52°23'/21°49'.

Pniewno, *see* Pnevno.

Pniewo, Pol.; pop. 35; 56 km N of Lodz; 52°13'/19°37'; JGFF, PHP4.

Pniewy, Pol. (Pinne); pop. 99; 50 km W of Poznan; 52°31'/16°16'; HSL, JGFF.

Pniow, *see* Pnyuv.

Pniowno, Pol.; pop. 46; 56 km E of Lublin; 51°15'/23°21'.

Pnov, Cz.; pop. 1; 50 km E of Praha; 50°05'/15°09'.

Pnyatyn, Ukr. (Pniatyn); pop. 37; 56 km ESE of Lvov; 49°39'/24°41'.

Pnyuv, Ukr. (Pniow); pop. 286; 107 km WNW of Chernovtsy; 48°37'/24°32'; GA, PHP2.

Pobeda, Mold. (Voinescu); pop. 14; 56 km SW of Kishinev; 46°39'/28°18'.

Poberezany, Pol.; pop. 129; Described in the *Black Book* as being in the Lublin region of Poland, this town was not found in BGN gazetteers.

Pobereze, *see* Poberezhye.

Poberezhe, *see* Poberezhye.

Poberezhye, Ukr. (Pobereze, Poberezhe); pop. 200; 114 km WNW of Chernovtsy; 49°01'/24°50'; PHP2.

Pobezovice, Cz. (Ronsperg, Ronsperk); pop. 63; 139 km SW of Praha; 49°31'/12°48'; EJ, HSL, HSL2.

Pobiedziska, Pol. (Pudewitz); pop. 24; 26 km ENE of Poznan; 52°28'/17°18'.

Pobikra, *possibly* Pobikry.

Pobikry, Pol. (Pobikra?); pop. 12; 69 km SSW of Bialystok; 52°38'/22°39'; PHP4.

Pobitno, Pol.; pop. 43; 62 km WNW of Przemysl; 50°02'/22°02'.

Poblow, *see* Pobolovo.

Pobolov, *see* Pobolovo.

Pobolovo, Byel. (Poblow, Pobolov, Pobolow); 107 km WNW of Gomel; 53°01'/29°47'; LDL, SF.

Pobolow, *see* Pobolovo.

Pobuk, Ukr.; pop. 22; 94 km S of Lvov; 49°05'/23°36'; HSL. This town was located on an interwar map of Poland but does not appear in contemporary gazetteers. Map coordinates are approximate.

Poburzany, *see* Pobuzhany.

Pobuzhany, Ukr. (Poburzany); pop. 37; 45 km NE of Lvov; 50°01'/24°33'.

Pocepice, Cz.; pop. 9; 62 km S of Praha; 49°36'/14°22'.

Pochaev, *see* Pochayev.

Pochapka, Ukr. (Milyatyn Pochapki); pop. 32; 32 km ESE of Rovno; 50°27'/26°39'.

Pochayev, Ukr. (Pitcheyev, Pitshayev, Pochaev, Poczajow, Potchayev); 82 km SSW of Rovno; 50°01'/25°29'; EDRD, GUM5, HSL, LDL, SF, YB.

Pochembautsy, Mold. (Pochumbauts, Pociumbauti); pop. 34; 163 km WNW of Kishinev; 48°00'/27°19'.

Pochep, *see* Pochepy.

Pochepy, USSR (Pochep); pop. 3,616; 69 km SW of Bryansk; 52°55'/33°29'; EJ, HSL, LDL, SF.

Pochinok, USSR; pop. 528; 120 km N of Leningrad; 60°58'/30°11'.

Pochrebishtche, *see* Pogrebishche.

Pochumbauts, *see* Pochembautsy.

Pochumbeny, Mold. (Pociumbeni); pop. 25; 157 km WNW of Kishinev; 47°58'/27°18'.

Pocioveliste, Rom. (Pocsafalva, Pokafalva); 88 km WSW of Cluj; 46°42'/22°26'; HSL.

Pociumbauti, *see* Pochembautsy.

Pociumbeni, *see* Pochumbeny.

Pociuneliai, Lith. (Potzunel); 50 km ESE of Siauliai; 55°34'/23°52'; LDL, SF.

Pocsa, Hung.; pop. 4; 126 km ESE of Nagykanizsa;

45°54'/18°28'.

Pocsafalva, *see* Pocioveliste.

Pocsaj, Hung.; pop. 74; 120 km SE of Miskolc; 47°17'/21°49'; HSL, LDS, PHH.

Pocskai, Cz. (Ferencztelep); 13 km ESE of Kosice; 48°39'/21°24'; HSL. This town was located on a pre-World War I map, but does not appear in contemporary gazetteers.

Pocs Megyer, *see* Mariapocs.

Pocsmegyer, Hung.; pop. 8; 32 km N of Budapest; 47°43'/19°06'.

Pocspetri, Hung.; pop. 65; 94 km E of Miskolc; 47°53'/22°00'; PHH.

Poczajow, *see* Pochayev.

Poczajow Nowy, *see* Novyy Pochayev.

Podabovec, *see* Podobovets.

Podberezce, *see* Podberezye.

Podberezha, *see* Paberze.

Podberezie, *see* Podberezye.

Podberezye, Ukr. (Podberezce, Podberezie, Podbrezitz); pop. 22; 88 km NNE of Lvov; 50°32'/24°39'; SF.

Podbielko, *see* Podbielsko.

Podbielsko, Pol. (Podbielko); pop. 5; 82 km WSW of Bialystok; 52°55'/21°59'.

Podbogoniki, (Podbohonniki); pop. 24; Described in the *Black Book* as being in the Bialystok region of Poland, this town was not found in BGN gazetteers.

Podbohonniki, *see* Podbogoniki.

Podboransky Rohozec, Cz. (Nemecky Rohozec); pop. 20; 82 km W of Praha; 50°13'/13°16'.

Podborany, Cz.; pop. 121; 75 km W of Praha; 50°14'/13°25'.

Podborce, *see* Podbortse.

Podbori, Cz.; pop. 2; 82 km S of Praha; 49°25'/14°28'.

Podbortse, Ukr. (Podborce); pop. 50; 13 km ENE of Lvov; 49°51'/24°09'.

Podbrezi, Cz.; pop. 6; 126 km NNW of Brno; 50°16'/16°13'.

Podbrezitz, *see* Podberezye.

Podbrodz, *see* Pabrade.

Podbrodze, *see* Pabrade.

Podbrodzie, *see* Pabrade.

Podbrzezie, COH, HSL. A number of towns share this name. It was not possible to determine from available information which one is being referenced.

Podbuz, *see* Podbuzh.

Podbuzh, Ukr. (Padbuz, Pidbish, Podbuz, Podubus?); pop. 204; 82 km SW of Lvov; 49°20'/23°15'; EGRS, LDL, PHP2, SF.

Poddebce, *see* Poddembtse.

Poddebice, Pol. (Podembice, Podembitza); pop. 1,333; 38 km WNW of Lodz; 51°53'/18°57'; AMG, GA, GUM3, HSL, HSL2, JGFF, LDS, PHP1, PHP2, POCEM, SF.

Poddebtse, *see* Poddubtsy.

Poddembtse, Ukr. (Poddebce, Poddubce); pop. 20; 62 km NNW of Lvov; 50°21'/23°43'.

Poddobryanka, Byel.; pop. 1,127; 45 km SSE of Gomel; 52°05'/31°11'.

Poddubce, *see* Poddembtse.

Poddubtsy, Ukr. (Poddebtse); pop. 15; 56 km WNW of Rovno; 50°46'/25°31'.

Podebrady, Cz.; pop. 65; 50 km ENE of Praha; 50°09'/15°08'; EJ, HSL, HSL2.

Podedworze, Pol.; pop. 50; 69 km NNE of Lublin; 51°41'/23°12'; GUM5.

Podegrodzie, Pol.; pop. 8; 75 km SE of Krakow; 49°35'/20°36'.

Podelusy, Cz.; 32 km SSE of Praha; 49°50'/14°35'; HSL.

Podembice, *see* Poddebice.

Podembitza, *see* Poddebice.

Podemszczyzna, Pol.; pop. 70; 62 km NNE of Przemysl; 50°13'/23°18'.

Podgaitsy, *see* Podgaytsy.

Podgajci Podravski, Yug. (Podravski Podgajci); pop. 6; 176 km E of Zagreb; 45°44'/18°17'.

Podgajek, Pol.; pop. 79; 94 km S of Warszawa; 51°29'/20°55'.

Podgaychiki, Ukr. (Podhajczyki); pop. 34; 45 km SW of Lvov; 49°39'/23°31'; AMG, GUM4, HSL.

Podgaychiki (Tarnopol), Ukr.; pop. 24; 62 km WNW of Chernovtsy; 48°34'/25°10'; GUM4.

Podgaytse, *see* Podgaytsy.

Podgaytsy, Ukr. (Pidayets, Pidhayets, Podgaitsy, Podgajcy, Podgaytse, Podhaitza, Podhajce, Podhaytse); pop. 2,872; 101 km ESE of Lvov; 49°16'/25°08'; AMG, CAHJP, COH, EGRS, EJ, GUM3, GUM5, GUM6, GYLA, HSL, HSL2, JGFF, PHP2, PHP3, SF, YB.

Podgornoye, Ukr. (Culmea); pop. 4; 133 km WSW of Odessa; 46°15'/29°03'.

Podgorodishche, Ukr. (Podhorodyszcze); pop. 186; 32 km ESE of Lvov; 49°42'/24°19'; GUM3, PHP2.

Podgorodno, Ukr. (Podhorodno); pop. 42; 157 km N of Lvov; 51°15'/24°12'.

Podgorodtsy, Ukr. (Podhorodce); pop. 91; 88 km SSW of Lvov; 49°09'/23°25'; HSL.

Podgortse, Ukr. (Podhorce, Podhortzi); pop. 72; 75 km ENE of Lvov; 49°57'/24°59'; HSL, PHP2, SF.

Podgorza, *see* Podgorze.

Podgorze, Pol. (Podgorza); 13 km SE of Krakow; 50°02'/19°58'; AMG, EGRS, HSL, HSL2, JGFF, LDL, SF.

Podgorze Gazdy, Pol.; pop. 19; 82 km SW of Bialystok; 52°42'/22°08'.

Podgrodze, Ukr. (Podgrodzie); pop. 42; 62 km ESE of Lvov; 49°26'/24°36'.

Podgrodzie, *see* Podgrodze.

Podhaitsy, *see* Postavy.

Podhaitza, *see* Podgaytsy.

Podhajce, *see* Podgaytsy.

Podhajczyki, *see* Podgaychiki.

Podhajczyki Justynowe, Pol.; pop. 37; Described in the *Black Book* as being in the Tarnopol region of Poland, this town was not found in BGN gazetteers.

Podhaytse, *see* Podgaytsy.

Podhorce, *see* Podgortse.

Podhorce (near Tomaszow Lubelski), Pol.; pop. 40; 94 km NNE of Przemysl; 50°29'/23°32'.

Podhorod, Cz.; pop. 61; 82 km ENE of Kosice; 48°49'/22°18'.

Podhorodce, *see* Podgorodtsy.

Podhorodno, *see* Podgorodno.

Podhorodyszcze, *see* Podgorodishche.

Podhortzi, *see* Podgortse.

Podhradie, Cz.; 163 km W of Kosice; 49°05'/19°03'; AMG.

Podivin, Cz. (Kostel); pop. 196; 45 km SSE of Brno; 48°50'/16°51'; HSL, HSL2, LDL.

Podjarkow, *see* Podyarkov.

Podkamen, Ukr. (Podkamien); pop. 822; 94 km ENE of Lvov; 49°56'/25°19'; AMG, COH, EDRD, EGRS, EJ, GA, GUM3, HSL, HSL2, JGFF, LDL, PHP2, SF.

Podkamien, *see* Podkamen.

Podkamien (Stanislawow), Ukr.; pop. 104; 56 km SE of Lvov; 49°27'/24°29'; GUM4.

Podkamionka, Pol.; pop. 5; 32 km NNE of Bialystok; 53°22'/23°24'.

Podklasztorze, Pol.; pop. 5; 56 km SE of Lodz; 51°22'/19°53'.

Podkosciele, Pol.; pop. 69; 82 km ENE of Krakow; 50°09'/21°07'; PHP3.

Podkost, Cz.; pop. 4; 62 km NE of Praha; 50°29'/15°08'.

Podkowa, Pol.; 62 km W of Lodz; 51°49'/18°30'; PHP4.

Podlazice, Cz.; pop. 1; 94 km NW of Brno; 49°54'/15°57'.

Podlazie, Pol.; pop. 9; 62 km E of Czestochowa; 50°44'/20°02'.

Podlazowek, HSL. This pre-World War I community was not found in BGN gazetteers.

Podlesie, *see* Podlesye.

Podlesko, Pol.; pop. 16; 69 km ENE of Czestochowa; 50°55'/20°08'.

Podlesnoye, Ukr. (Dryshchuv, Dryszczow); pop. 49; 101 km SE of Lvov; 49°10'/24°54'.

Podlesye, (Podlesie); pop. 41; A number of towns share this name. It was not possible to determine from available information which one is being referenced.

Podleszany, Pol.; pop. 34; 107 km ENE of Krakow; 50°16'/21°25'.

Podlez, Pol.; pop. 20; 69 km SE of Warszawa; 51°45'/21°29'.

Podlipce, *see* Podliptse.

Podliptse, Ukr. (Podlipce); pop. 29; 75 km E of Lvov; 49°46'/25°03'.

Podliski, Ukr.; pop. 60; 56 km WSW of Lvov; 49°43'/23°15'.

Podliski Male, *see* Podliski Malyye.

Podliski Malyye, Ukr. (Podliski Male); pop. 14; 13 km NE of Lvov; 49°55'/24°10'.

Podliski Wielkie, Ukr.; pop. 37; 38 km SSE of Lvov; 49°35'/24°05'. This town was located on an interwar map of Poland but does not appear in contemporary gazetteers. Map coordinates are approximate.

Podlodow, Pol.; pop. 9; 101 km NNE of Przemysl; 50°29'/23°41'.

Podlodowka, Pol.; pop. 4; 50 km NW of Lublin; 51°39'/22°11'.

Podloziany, Pol.; pop. 25; Described in the *Black Book* as being in the Nowogrodek region of Poland, this town was not found in BGN gazetteers.

Podlyashe, *see* Biala Podlaska.

Podmanasterek, *see* Podmonasterek.

Podmanastyrek, Ukr.; pop. 6; 75 km NE of Lvov; 50°12'/24°56'.

Podmichale, *see* Podmikhale.

Podmikhale, Ukr. (Podmichale); pop. 46; 101 km SSE of Lvov; 49°00'/24°24'.

Podmoklice, Cz.; pop. 3; 88 km NE of Praha; 50°36'/15°20'.

Podmokly, Cz.; pop. 270; 56 km WSW of Praha; 49°57'/13°42'; GUM5.

Podmonasterek, Ukr. (Podmanasterek); pop. 6; 82 km SW of Lvov; 49°22'/23°15'.

Podniebyle, Pol.; pop. 8; 88 km WSW of Przemysl; 49°41'/21°37'.

Podniesno, Pol.; pop. 7; 82 km ENE of Warszawa; 52°18'/22°14'.

Podobin, Pol.; pop. 6; 56 km SSE of Krakow; 49°38'/20°06'.

Podobovec, *see* Podobovets.

Podobovets, Ukr. (Padoc, Podabovec, Podobovec, Podobovice, Podobovitz); pop. 250; 146 km S of Lvov; 48°40'/23°18'; GUM3, SM.

Podobovice, *see* Podobovets.

Podobovitz, *see* Podobovets.

Podobriyevka, Ukr. (Podobryanka); pop. 1,127; 82 km E of Konotop; 51°14'/34°24'; HSL, JGFF.

Podobryanka, *see* Podobriyevka.

Podole Nowe, Pol.; pop. 32; 50 km SE of Warszawa; 51°52'/21°19'.

Podolia; Not a town, but a region in the southwestern Ukraine.

Podolik, *see* Podwilk.

Podolin, *see* Podolinec.

Podolinec, Cz. (Podolin, Pudlein); pop. 169; 82 km NW of Kosice; 49°16'/20°32'; HSL.

Podolszyca, Pol. PHP4. This town was not found in BGN gazetteers under the given spelling.

Podorozhnoye, Ukr. (Lachowice Podrozne, Lyakhovitse Podruzhne); pop. 31; 75 km SSE of Lvov; 49°14'/24°12'.

Podplesa, Ukr. (Padaflesa, Padaflesha, Pelesalja); 157 km WSW of Chernovtsy; 48°08'/23°49'; COH, LYV, SM.

Podravska Moslavina, *see* Moslavina Podravska.

Podravska Slatina, Yug. (Slatina); pop. 262; 133 km E of Zagreb; 45°42'/17°42'; PHY.

Podravski Podgajci, *see* Podgajci Podravski.

Podrezy, Byel.; pop. 4; 126 km NW of Minsk; 54°53'/26°47'.

Podros, Byel.; pop. 1; 170 km NW of Pinsk; 53°16'/24°26'.

Podsarnie, Pol.; pop. 5; 62 km S of Krakow; 49°34'/19°48'.

Podsedziszow, Pol.; pop. 62; 56 km N of Krakow; 50°34'/20°03'.

Podskale, Pol.; pop. 6; 56 km ENE of Krakow; 50°14'/20°43'.

Podsosnow, *see* Podsosnuv.

Podsosnuv, Ukr. (Podsosnow); pop. 55; 32 km ESE of Lvov; 49°45'/24°21'.

Podsumowo, Pol.; pop. 10; 133 km N of Bialystok; 54°16'/22°58'.

Podsusze, Pol.; pop. 7; 62 km ENE of Warszawa; 52°17'/21°57'.

Podsvilye, Byel. (Podswile); pop. 10; 139 km WSW of Vitebsk; 55°09'/27°58'.

Podswile, *see* Podsvilye.

Podubus, *possibly* Podbuzh.

Podu Iloaei, *see* Podu Iloaie.

Podu Iloaie, Rom. (Podu Iloaei, Podul Iloaei, Podul Iloaiei); pop. 1,454; 26 km W of Iasi; 47°13'/27°16'; GUM4, JGFF, PHR1.

Podul Iloaei, *see* Podu Iloaie.

Podul Iloaiei, *see* Podu Iloaie.

Podul Turcului, *see* Podu Turcului.

Podunajske Biskupice, Cz. (Puspoki); 6 km E of Bratislava; 48°08'/17°13'; HSL.

Podusilna, Ukr.; pop. 22; 62 km ESE of Lvov; 49°31'/24°42'.

Podusow, *see* Podusuv.

Podusuv, Ukr. (Podusow); pop. 34; 56 km ESE of Lvov; 49°35'/24°41'.

Podu Turcului, Rom. (Podul Turcului); pop. 454; 114 km S of Iasi; 46°12'/27°23'; GUM4, LDL, PHR1.

Podvolitchisk, *see* Podvolochisk.

Podvolochisk, Ukr. (Podvolitchisk, Podwlocztska, Podwoloczyska); pop. 2,275; 126 km S of Rovno; 49°32'/26°09'; AMG, COH, EGRS, EJ, FRG, GA, GUM3, GUM4, GUM5, HSL, HSL2, JGFF, LDL, LYV, PHP2, SF.

Podvornoye, Ukr. (Chisla Salieva, Kishla Saliyeva); pop. 23; 50 km E of Chernovtsy; 48°18'/26°37'.

Podvysoka, *see* Podvysokoye.

Podvysokoye, Ukr. (Podvysoka, Podwysoka); pop. 57; 45 km WNW of Chernovtsy; 48°33'/25°31'; HSL, PHP2.

Podwerbce, Pol. PHP2. This town was not found in BGN gazetteers under the given spelling.

Podwilk, Pol. (Podolik); pop. 49; 62 km S of Krakow; 49°33'/19°44'; FRG.

Podwlocztska, *see* Podvolochisk.

Podwoloczyska, *see* Podvolochisk.

Podwysoka, *see* Podvysokoye.

Podyarkov, Ukr. (Podjarkow); pop. 80; 32 km ESE of Lvov; 49°44'/24°22'.

Podzamche, Ukr. (Podzamcze, Podzameczek); pop. 93; 82 km SW of Rovno; 50°04'/25°24'.

Podzamcze, Pol.; pop. 28; 82 km NE of Wroclaw; 51°18'/18°08'. *See also* Podzamche.

Podzameczek, *see* Podzamche.

Podzelva, *see* Zelva.

Podzelve, *see* Zelva.

Poeni, Rom. (Alsopojeni, Poenii de Jos); pop. 51; 56 km WNW of Cluj; 46°55'/22°54'.

Poenii de Jos, *see* Poeni.

Poenile de Sub Munte, *see* Poienile de Sub Munte.

Poenile Glodului, *see* Poienile Glodului.

Pogaceaua, Rom.; 56 km E of Cluj; 46°41'/24°18'; JGFF.

Poganyszentpeter, Hung.; pop. 4; 13 km SE of Nagykanizsa; 46°23'/17°04'.

Pogar, USSR (Pohar); pop. 628; 107 km SW of Bryansk; 52°33'/33°16'; HSL, LDL, SF.

Pogir, *see* Pagiriai.

Pogoarna, *see* Pogorna.

Pogodino, *see* Bluden.

Pogonesti, Rom.; pop. 12; 120 km S of Iasi; 46°09'/27°32'.

Pogorelovka, Ukr. (Pohorlauti); pop. 32; 32 km N of Chernovtsy; 48°33'/25°58'.

Pogorelovka (Wolyn), Ukr. (Pohorelowka); pop. 19; 45 km NE of Rovno; 50°51'/26°49'.

Pogoreltsy, Ukr. (Pogoryltse, Pogorzeliski, Pohorylce); pop. 91; 38 km ESE of Lvov; 49°44'/24°29'; AMG.

Pogorna, Mold. (Pogoarna, Pohoarna); pop. 70; 101 km NNW of Kishinev; 47°50'/28°30'.

Pogorska Wola, Pol.; pop. 14; 88 km E of Krakow; 50°01'/21°10'.

Pogoryltse, see Pogoreltsy.

Pogorz, Pol.; pop. 5; 88 km E of Krakow; 50°01'/21°08'.

Pogorzela, Pol. (Pogorzelle); pop. 7; 75 km SSE of Poznan; 51°49'/17°13'.

Pogorzeliski, see Pogoreltsy.

Pogorzelle, see Pogorzela.

Pogost, Byel. (Novi Pohost, Nowy Pohost, Pohost, Pohost Novi, Pohost Zagorodski, Pohost Zagorodzki, Pohost Zahorodni, Pohost Zaretchna); pop. 20; 88 km N of Minsk; 54°37'/27°34'; AMG, COH, EDRD, GUM3, GUM4, HSL, JGFF, LDL, LYV, SF, SF, SF, YB.

Pogost Novy, see Novyy Pogost.

Pogost Zagorodskiy, Byel. (Pohost Zagrodski, Pohost Zahorodny); pop. 530; 32 km NNE of Pinsk; 52°19'/26°21'; YB.

Pogranicze, Pol.; pop. 24; 82 km E of Lublin; 51°06'/23°42'.

Pogrebeny, Mold. (Pogribeni); pop. 21; 69 km N of Kishinev; 47°33'/28°55'.

Pogrebisce, see Pogrebishche.

Pogrebishche, Ukr. (Pochrebishtche, Pogrebisce, Pohorbishch, Pohrebyszcze, Pohybryszcze, Probishta); pop. 2,881; 62 km NE of Vinnitsa; 49°29'/29°16'; COH, EDRD, EJ, GYLA, JGFF, LDL, SF, WS.

Pogribeni, see Pogrebeny.

Pogulianka, see Mezciems.

Pogulyanka, see Mezciems.

Pogwizdow, Pol.; pop. 43; 56 km WNW of Przemysl; 50°07'/22°09'; PHP3.

Pohar, see Pogar.

Pohle, Germ.; 32 km SW of Hannover; 52°16'/09°20'; GED.

Pohl Gons, Germ. (Kirch Gons); pop. 24; 50 km N of Frankfurt am Main; 50°28'/08°39'; HSL, LDS.

Pohoarna, see Pogorna.

Pohorbishch, see Pogrebishche.

Pohorce, possibly Pokhortsy.

Pohorelice, Cz. (Pohrlitz); pop. 272; 26 km S of Brno; 48°59'/16°31'; EJ, GUM4, HSL, HSL2.

Pohorelowka, see Pogorelovka (Wolyn).

Pohorlauti, see Pogorelovka.

Pohorylce, see Pogoreltsy.

Pohost, see Pogost.

Pohost Novi, see Pogost.

Pohost Nowy, see Novyy Pogost.

Pohost Zagorodski, see Pogost.

Pohost Zagorodzki, see Pogost.

Pohost Zagrodski, see Pogost Zagorodskiy.

Pohost Zahorodni, see Pogost.

Pohost Zahorodny, see Pogost Zagorodskiy.

Pohost Zaretchna, see Pogost.

Pohost Zarzeczny, see Zarechnoye.

Pohrebyszcze, see Pogrebishche.

Pohrlitz, see Pohorelice.

Pohybryszcze, see Pogrebishche.

Poian, Rom.; 163 km SSW of Iasi; 46°04'/26°09'; HSL.

Poiana, see Poiana Marului.

Poiana Blenchii, Rom. (Blenkemezo); pop. 26; 62 km N of Cluj; 47°18'/23°45'; HSL.

Poiana Ilvei, Rom.; pop. 11; 107 km NE of Cluj; 47°21'/24°44'.

Poiana Marului, Rom. (Poiana); pop. 49; 176 km SSW of Cluj; 45°24'/22°33'; HSL.

Poiana Micului, Rom.; pop. 11; 146 km WNW of Iasi; 47°39'/25°46'.

Poiana Porcului, Rom.; pop. 4; 75 km N of Cluj; 47°25'/23°50'.

Poiana Sarata, Rom.; pop. 4; 146 km SSW of Iasi; 46°09'/26°27'.

Poiana Soroca, see Poyana.

Poieni, Rom. (Kissebes); 88 km S of Cluj; 46°00'/23°29'; HSL.

Poienile de Sub Munte, Rom. (Havasmezo, Kopkas, Poenile de Sub Munte, Poenile de Sub Muntz, Polien Riskeve, Ruski Pole, Ruspolyana, Ruszpolyana, Urmezo, Vermezif); pop. 726; 133 km NNE of Cluj; 47°49'/24°26'; HSL, LDL, PHR2, SM.

Poienile de Sub Muntz, see Poienile de Sub Munte.

Poienile Glodului, Rom. (Poenile Glodului, Polien Glod, Sajomezo); pop. 159; 114 km N of Cluj; 47°42'/24°07'; SM.

Poigen, Aus.; pop. 5; 82 km WNW of Wien; 48°42'/15°34'.

Pojawie, Pol.; pop. 12; 56 km ENE of Krakow; 50°09'/20°43'.

Pojbuky, Cz.; pop. 1; 69 km SE of Praha; 49°30'/14°54'.

Pojlo, Pol. PHP2. This town was not found in BGN gazetteers under the given spelling.

Pojorata, see Pojorita.

Pojoreni, see Pozhareny.

Pojorita, Rom. (Pojorata); pop. 79; 163 km NE of Cluj; 47°31'/25°27'.

Pokafalva, see Pocioveliste.

Pokatilovka, see Pokotilovka.

Pokhortse, see Pokhortsy.

Pokhortsy, Ukr. (Pohorce?, Pokhortse); pop. 56; 45 km SW of Lvov; 49°36'/23°34'.

Pokitilov, see Pokotilovka.

Pokoj, Pol. (Carlsruhe); pop. 42; 62 km ESE of Wroclaw; 50°55'/17°50'; POCEM.

Pokotilovka, Ukr. (Pokatilovka, Pikitilov, Pokotilovo); pop. 220; 13 km SW of Kharkov; 49°56'/36°09'; LDL, SF.

Pokotilovo, see Pokotilovka.

Pokroy, see Pakruojis.

Pokrzywnica, Pol.; 56 km NNE of Krakow; 50°32'/20°14'; COH, EDRD.

Pokrzywno, HSL. A number of towns share this name. It was not possible to determine from available information which one is being referenced.

Pokshivnits, see Koprzywnica.

Pokshivnitsa, see Koprzywnica.

Pokshivnitza, see Koprzywnica.

Pokucie, GUM4. This town was not found in BGN gazetteers under the given spelling.

Pokupsko, Yug.; pop. 6; 38 km S of Zagreb; 45°29'/16°00'.

Pola, see Pula.

Polaga, see Palanga.

Polaky, Cz.; pop. 5; 82 km WNW of Praha; 50°20'/13°21'.

Polana, see Polyana.

Polana Kobilecka, see Kobyletskaya Polyana.

Polana Kobilelca, Cz. HSL2. This pre-World War I community was not found in BGN gazetteers.

Polana Kosovska, see Kosovskaya Polyana.

Polana Velka, see Velka Polana.

Polanczyk, Pol.; pop. 11; 56 km SSW of Przemysl; 49°22'/22°26'.

Polangen, see Palanga.

Polaniec, Pol. (Plontch, Polenitz); pop. 1,025; 101 km NE of Krakow; 50°26'/21°17'; AMG, CAHJP, GA, GUM3, GUM5, HSL, JGFF, LDS, PHP3, SF, WS, YB. The *Black Book* also shows a Polaniec Donacja (pop. 30).

Polanka, see Polyanka.

Polanka (Nowogrodek), Byel. EDRD. This town was not found in BGN gazetteers under the given spelling.

Polanka Haller, Pol.; pop. 13; 19 km SSW of Krakow; 49°57'/19°47'.

Polanka Wielka, Pol.; pop. 7; 45 km WSW of Krakow; 49°59'/19°19'.

Polanky, Cz.; 94 km SE of Praha; 49°27'/15°22'; HSL.

Polanok, HSL. This pre-World War I community was not found in BGN gazetteers.

Polanow, Pol. (Pollnow); pop. 36; 133 km WSW of Gdansk; 54°07'/16°41'.

Polanowka, Pol.; pop. 28; A number of towns share this name. It was not possible to determine from available information which one is being referenced.

Polany, see Polyany.

Polany Surowiczne, Pol.; pop. 14; 75 km SW of Przemysl; 49°28'/21°53'.

Polapy, *see* Palany.

Polatycze, Pol.; pop. 2; 114 km NNE of Lublin; 52°03'/23°36'.

Polatzk, *see* Polotsk.

Polazie, Pol. (Polazie Swietochowskie); pop. 22; 56 km NE of Warszawa; 52°24'/21°46'.

Polazie Swietochowskie, *see* Polazie.

Polch, Germ.; pop. 48; 75 km SSE of Koln; 50°18'/07°19'.

Polczyn Zdroj, Pol. (Bad Polzin, Polzin); pop. 120; 107 km NE of Szczecin; 53°45'/16°05'; LDS.

Polen, Cz.; pop. 3; 114 km SW of Praha; 49°26'/13°11'; JGFF.

Polengen, *see* Palanga.

Polenitz, *see* Polaniec.

Poleshchina, *see* Skaune.

Polesie Duze, Pol.; pop. 5; 56 km WNW of Lublin; 51°25'/21°48'.

Poleski, COH. This town was not found in BGN gazetteers under the given spelling.

Polessk, USSR (Labiau); pop. 23; 45 km NE of Kaliningrad; 54°52'/21°07'.

Polesskoye, Ukr. (Chabna, Chabnoje, Kaganovich, Khabne, Khabnoye); pop. 1,710; 120 km NW of Kiyev; 51°14'/29°23'; EDRD, GUM4, HSL, LDL, SF.

Polgar, Hung. (Tiszapolgar); pop. 490; 38 km SE of Miskolc; 47°52'/21°07'; AMG, HSL, JGFF, LDL, LDS, PHH.

Polgardi, Hung.; pop. 56; 75 km SW of Budapest; 47°03'/18°18'; PHH.

Polianka, Cz. BGN lists two possible localities with this name located at 48°42'/21°21' and 48°52'/19°14'. HSL.

Police, *see* Politsy.

Police nad Metuji, Cz.; 133 km NE of Praha; 50°32'/16°14'; EJ.

Policka, Cz.; pop. 59; 62 km NW of Brno; 49°43'/16°16'.

Policko, Pol.; pop. 5; 62 km ESE of Poznan; 52°12'/17°52'.

Policzyzna, Pol.; pop. 9; 26 km SE of Lublin; 51°03'/22°48'.

Polien Glod, *see* Poienile Glodului.

Polien Kabileczky, *see* Kobyletskaya Polyana.

Polien Kosoviczki, *see* Kosovskaya Polyana.

Polien Kosovkiczki, COH. This town was not found in BGN gazetteers under the given spelling.

Polien Lipsa, *see* Lipsha.

Polien Riskeve, *see* Poienile de Sub Munte.

Poligon, Lith. EDRD, YB. Although Poligon is listed in the yizkor book for Svencionys (Swieciany), it does not appear in contemporary gazetteers.

Poligonowo, Lith. GUM3. Although Poligonowo is listed in the yizkor book for Svencionys (Swieciany), it does not appear in contemporary gazetteers.

Polina, Cz.; 82 km SW of Kosice; 48°30'/20°13'; HSL.

Polin Koviletski, COH. This town was not found in BGN gazetteers under the given spelling.

Polinow, Pol.; pop. 4; 114 km S of Bialystok; 52°09'/23°10'.

Polipsy, Cz.; pop. 2; 56 km ESE of Praha; 49°47'/15°04'.

Politow, Pol.; pop. 13; 101 km ESE of Lodz; 51°20'/20°45'.

Politse, *see* Politsy.

Politsy, Ukr. (Police, Politse, Pullitz); pop. 45; 82 km NNW of Rovno; 51°16'/26°03'.

Politsy (near Kamen Kashirskiy), Ukr.; pop. 23; 133 km NW of Rovno; 51°34'/25°07'.

Polivanov Iar, *see* Polivanov Yar.

Polivanov Yar, Ukr. (Polivanov Iar); pop. 5; 88 km NE of Chernovtsy; 48°32'/27°02'.

Poljana, Cz. AMG. A number of towns share this name. It was not possible to determine from available information which one is being referenced.

Polkow Sagaly, Pol.; pop. 45; 62 km ENE of Warszawa; 52°17'/21°56'.

Pollnow, *see* Polanow.

Polna, *see* Polonnoye.

Polnicka, Cz.; pop. 13; 69 km WNW of Brno; 49°36'/15°55'.

Polny Kesov, Cz. (Kesov); 69 km ENE of Bratislava; 48°10'/18°04'; JGFF.

Polochany, Byel. (Poloczany); pop. 10; 69 km WNW of Minsk; 54°13'/26°43'; GUM3.

Polock, *see* Polotsk.

Poloczany, *see* Polochany.

Polomia, Pol. (Polomyja); pop. 16; 62 km W of Przemysl; 49°54'/21°53'.

Polomyja, *see* Polomia.

Polona, *see* Polonnoye.

Polonechka, Byel. (Poloneczka); pop. 12; 101 km SW of Minsk; 53°21'/26°15'.

Poloneczka, *see* Polonechka.

Polonga, *see* Palanga.

Polonice, *see* Polonichi.

Polonichi, Ukr. (Polonice, Polonitse); pop. 47; 26 km ENE of Lvov; 49°52'/24°22'.

Polonichna, Ukr. (Poloniczna); pop. 50; 56 km NE of Lvov; 50°09'/24°38'.

Poloniczna, *see* Polonichna.

Polonitse, *see* Polonichi.

Polonka, Byel.; pop. 206; 120 km NNW of Pinsk; 53°09'/25°43'; GUM3, HSL, JGFF, SF.

Polonnoye, Ukr. (Polna, Polona); pop. 5,337; 107 km ESE of Rovno; 50°07'/27°31'; COH, EDRD, EJ, GUM4, HSL, HSL2, JGFF, SF, YB.

Poloske, Hung.; pop. 6; 45 km N of Nagykanizsa; 46°45'/16°56'; HSL.

Poloskefo, Hung.; pop. 5; 26 km NNW of Nagykanizsa; 46°36'/16°57'.

Polotsk, Byel. (Polatzk, Polock); pop. 8,186; 94 km WNW of Vitebsk; 55°29'/28°47'; AMG, EDRD, EJ, GUM4, GYLA, HSL, JGFF, LDL, PHLE, PHP3, SF.

Polovtse, Ukr. (Polowce); pop. 12; 82 km NNW of Chernovtsy; 49°00'/25°34'.

Polowce, *see* Polovtse.

Polpiec, Pol.; pop. 29; Described in the *Black Book* as being in the Lwow region of Poland, this town was not found in BGN gazetteers.

Polrzeczki, Pol.; pop. 5; 50 km SE of Krakow; 49°40'/20°14'.

Polsingen, Germ.; 62 km SSW of Nurnberg; 48°56'/10°43'; PHGB.

Poltava, Ukr. (Poltawa); pop. 18,476; 126 km SW of Kharkov; 49°35'/34°34'; AMG, EJ, GUM3, GUM4, GUM5, GUM6, HSL, JGFF, LDL, PHP1, PHP4, SF.

Poltawa, *see* Poltava.

Polten, Germ.; 56 km S of Munchen; 47°42'/11°18'; GUM5.

Poltew, *see* Peltev.

Poltosk, *see* Pultusk.

Poltsamaa, Est.; pop. 2; 56 km WNW of Tartu; 58°41'/25°58'; PHLE.

Polubicze, *see* Polubicze Wiejskie.

Polubicze Wiejskie, Pol. (Polubicze); pop. 5; 75 km NNE of Lublin; 51°47'/23°05'.

Polubny, Cz.; pop. 2; 101 km NNE of Praha; 50°46'/15°20'.

Poluchow Maly, *see* Polukhuv Maly.

Polukhuv Maly, Ukr. (Poluchow Maly); pop. 27; 56 km ESE of Lvov; 49°37'/24°41'.

Polunce, Pol.; pop. 6; 133 km N of Bialystok; 54°15'/23°19'.

Polusciewicze, *see* Polustseviche.

Polustseviche, Byel. (Polusciewicze); pop. 4; 94 km ENE of Pinsk; 52°22'/27°26'.

Polusze, Pol.; pop. 30; A number of towns share this name. It was not possible to determine from available information which one is being referenced.

Polya, Hung.; 82 km S of Budapest; 46°48'/19°00'; HSL.

Polyana, Ukr. (Polana); pop. 99; 94 km SW of Lvov; 49°32'/22°46'; AMG, HSL.

Polyana (near Lvov), Ukr.; pop. 35; 38 km SSE of Lvov; 49°35'/24°04'.

Polyanka, (Polanka); pop. 34; HSL, HSL2. A number of towns share this name. It was not possible to determine from available information which one is being referenced.

Polyanovgrad, Bulg. (Karnobat); pop. 330; 101 km SW of

Varna; 42°39'/26°59'; EJ.

Polyany, Ukr. (Polany); 56 km NNE of Rovno; 51°03'/26°39'; GUM3, GUM4, HSL, JGFF.

Polzela, Yug.; pop. 5; 94 km WNW of Zagreb; 46°17'/15°04'.

Polzin, see Polczyn Zdroj.

Pomarin, see Pomoryany.

Pomaz, Hung.; pop. 142; 19 km NNW of Budapest; 47°39'/19°02'; GUM5, LDS, LJEE, PHH.

Pombsen, Germ.; pop. 21; 82 km SSW of Hannover; 51°47'/09°04'; GUM5, JGFF.

Pomezi, Cz. (Limberk); pop. 3; 62 km NNW of Brno; 49°43'/16°19'.

Pomi, Rom.; pop. 79; 107 km NNW of Cluj; 47°42'/23°19'.

Pomiechowek, Pol. (Pomyekhovek); pop. 202; 26 km NW of Warszawa; 52°28'/20°44'; FRG, GUM3, GUM4, GUM5, PHP4.

Pommerania; Not a town, but a region of pre-World War I Germany that is now northwestern Poland.

Pommern; See Pommerania.

Pomoneta, Ukr. (Pomonieta); pop. 26; 62 km SE of Lvov; 49°24'/24°26'.

Pomonieta, see Pomoneta.

Pomortsy, Ukr. (Jaslowiec, Jazlowiec, Yazlivitz, Yazlovets); pop. 474; 82 km NW of Chernovtsy; 48°58'/25°26'; AMG, EGRS, GUM3, HSL, JGFF, LDL, PHP1, PHP2, SF.

Pomoryany, Ukr. (Pamorzany, Pomarin, Pomorzany, Pomorzhany); pop. 799; 75 km ESE of Lvov; 49°38'/24°56'; AMG, COH, EGRS, GUM4, HSL, HSL2, JGFF, LDL, PHP2, SF.

Pomorzany, see Pomoryany.

Pomorzhany, see Pomoryany.

Pompa, Mold.; pop. 4; 94 km NW of Kishinev; 47°39'/27°57'.

Pompeyan, see Pampenai.

Pompian, see Pampenai.

Pomyekhovek, see Pomiechowek.

Pomzovye, possibly Ponizovye.

Pon, see Punia.

Ponary, see Paneriai.

Ponavezh, see Panevezys.

Ponedel, see Pandelys.

Ponedeli, see Pandelys.

Poneman, see Panemune.

Ponemon, see Aukstoji Panemune.

Ponemune, see Panemune.

Ponemunek, see Panemune.

Ponemuneki, see Panemune.

Ponetow Dolny, Pol.; pop. 6; 69 km WNW of Lodz; 52°12'/18°46'.

Ponetow Gorny, Pol.; pop. 8; 69 km NW of Lodz; 52°12'/18°49'.

Ponevetz, see Panevezys.

Ponevezh, see Panevezys.

Poniatow, Pol.; 45 km SE of Lodz; 51°24'/19°46'; GUM3, GUM5, PHP4.

Poniatowa, Pol.; 32 km WSW of Lublin; 51°11'/22°08'; EDRD, GA, GUM3, GUM4, GUM5, GUM6, PHP1.

Ponice, Pol.; pop. 7; 62 km S of Krakow; 49°36'/19°59'.

Ponidel, see Pandelys.

Poniec, Pol. (Punitz); pop. 4; 82 km S of Poznan; 51°46'/16°48'.

Poniewiez, see Panevezys.

Poniewirz, Pol. PHP4. This town was not found in BGN gazetteers under the given spelling.

Ponik, Pol.; pop. 48; A number of towns share this name. It was not possible to determine from available information which one is being referenced.

Ponikovitsa, Ukr. (Ponikowica); pop. 111; 75 km NE of Lvov; 50°03'/25°04'.

Ponikowica, see Ponikovitsa.

Ponikwa, Pol.; 69 km WNW of Lublin; 51°29'/21°36'; GUM4, PHP2.

Poninka, Ukr. (Paninka); pop. 730; 101 km ESE of Rovno; 50°11'/27°32'; HSL, JGFF, SF.

Ponivez, see Panevezys.

Ponizovye, Byel. (Pomzovye?); 56 km NNE of Vitebsk; 55°37'/30°40'; GUM4.

Ponoara, Rom.; pop. 6; 75 km W of Cluj; 46°53'/22°40'.

Ponowitcz, see Panevezys.

Ponticeu, see Panticeu.

Ponyevez, see Panevezys.

Poon, see Punia.

Popeasca, see Popovka.

Popele, Ukr. (Popiele); pop. 50; 75 km SSW of Lvov; 49°19'/23°23'; GUM3, GUM4, PHP2.

Popelken, see Vysokoye (Kaliningrad area).

Popelnya, Ukr.; 94 km SW of Kiyev; 49°58'/29°27'; HSL, JGFF.

Poperczyn, Pol.; pop. 17; 45 km SE of Lublin; 50°55'/22°54'.

Popeshti de Sus, see Verkhniye Popeshty.

Popeshti Nouy, see Novyye Popeshty.

Popesti de Jos, see Novyye Popeshty.

Popesti de Sus, see Verkhniye Popeshty.

Popestii Noui, see Novyye Popeshty.

Popielany, see Papile.

Popiele, see Popele.

Popielnik, see Popiyelniki.

Popielniki, see Popiyelniki.

Popilan, see Papile.

Popilyan, see Papile.

Popinska Wolka, Pol.; pop. 22; Described in the Black Book as being in the Polesie region of Poland, this town was not found in BGN gazetteers.

Popiszki, Lith.; 146 km N of Vilnius; 55°51'/26°03'; HSL. This town was located on a pre-World War I map, but does not appear in contemporary gazetteers.

Popiuti, see Popovtsy.

Popiyelniki, Ukr. (Popielnik, Popielniki); pop. 100; 45 km W of Chernovtsy; 48°23'/25°20'; PHP2.

Popkowice, Pol.; pop. 28; 38 km SSW of Lublin; 50°59'/22°14'.

Poplawce, Pol.; pop. 3; 50 km NNE of Bialystok; 53°28'/23°35'.

Poplawy, Pol.; pop. 82; 56 km N of Warszawa; 52°42'/21°06'; PHP4.

Popovaca, Yug.; pop. 7; 56 km ESE of Zagreb; 45°34'/16°37'.

Popovichi, Ukr. (Popovitse, Popowice); pop. 26; 82 km WSW of Lvov; 49°44'/22°54'.

Popoviti, HSL. This pre-World War I community was not found in BGN gazetteers.

Popovitse, see Popovichi.

Popovka, Mold. (Popeasca); pop. 15; 69 km ESE of Kishinev; 46°36'/29°32'.

Popovtse, Ukr. (Popovtzi, Popowce, Popowcy, Popvtse); pop. 21; 94 km SSW of Rovno; 49°57'/25°23'; SF.

Popovtsy, Ukr. (Popiuti); 62 km SW of Vinnitsa; 48°54'/27°49'; PHR1.

Popovtzi, see Popovtse.

Popowa, Pol. PHP4. This town was not found in BGN gazetteers under the given spelling.

Popowce, see Popovtse.

Popowcy, see Popovtse.

Popowice, see Popovichi.

Popowo, GUM3. A number of towns share this name. It was not possible to determine from available information which one is being referenced.

Popowo Koscielne, Pol.; pop. 109; 38 km NNE of Poznan; 52°43'/17°16'; HSL, PHP4.

Poppenlauer, Germ.; pop. 54; 101 km NW of Nurnberg; 50°13'/10°14'; GUM3, GUM5, HSL, PHGB.

Popper, see Poprad.

Poprad, Cz. (Popper); pop. 1,022; 82 km WNW of Kosice; 49°03'/20°18'; AMG, EDRD, EJ, GUM4, GUM5, GUM6, HSL, LDL.

Poproc, Cz.; 94 km WSW of Kosice; 48°35'/20°02'; HSL.

Popvtse, see Popovtse.

Porabka, Pol.; pop. 119; 32 km NNW of Krakow; 50°20'/19°49'.

Porabki, Pol.; pop. 15; 114 km NNE of Krakow; 50°52'/20°54'.

Poraj, Pol.; pop. 69; 19 km SE of Czestochowa; 50°40'/19°13'.

Porasow, *see* Porozovo.

Porazyn, Pol.; 45 km WSW of Poznan; 52°19'/16°21'; JGFF.

Porcesti, Rom. (Disznajo); pop. 24; 88 km ENE of Cluj; 46°54'/24°47'; HSL.

Porchulyanka, Mold. (Porciuleanca); pop. 24; 170 km NW of Kishinev; 48°04'/27°16'.

Porciuleanca, *see* Porchulyanka.

Porcsalma, Hung.; pop. 186; 139 km E of Miskolc; 47°53'/22°34'; COH, HSL, PHH, YB.

Poreba, Pol.; pop. 79; 88 km NE of Krakow; 50°37'/20°52'; EDRD, HSL, JGFF.

Poreba Koceby, Pol.; pop. 139; 69 km NE of Warszawa; 52°42'/21°41'; PHP4.

Poreba Mala, Pol.; pop. 15; 82 km ESE of Krakow; 49°35'/20°43'.

Poreba Spytkowska, Pol.; pop. 8; 50 km ESE of Krakow; 49°57'/20°34'.

Poreba Srednia, Pol.; pop. 112; PHP4. Described in the *Black Book* as being in the Bialystok region of Poland, this town was not found in BGN gazetteers.

Poreba Zegoty, Pol.; pop. 7; 26 km WSW of Krakow; 50°04'/19°34'.

Porebishce, LDL. This pre-World War I community was not found in BGN gazetteers.

Poreby Dymarskie, Pol.; pop. 6; 88 km WNW of Przemysl; 50°19'/21°50'.

Porechye, Byel. (Porzeczce); pop. 181; 221 km WSW of Minsk; 53°53'/24°08'; COH, GUM3, HSL.

Porechye (Polesie), Byel.; pop. 20; 32 km WNW of Pinsk; 52°17'/25°49'.

Porejov, Cz.; pop. 7; 139 km WSW of Praha; 49°44'/12°36'.

Poricany, Cz.; pop. 5; 38 km ENE of Praha; 50°06'/14°56'; HSL.

Porin, Cz.; pop. 2; 82 km SSE of Praha; 49°25'/14°53'.

Porisov, *see* Parysow.

Poritch, *see* Parichi.

Porkhov, USSR; pop. 264; 69 km E of Pskov; 57°46'/29°32'.

Porladany, Hung.; 114 km N of Nagykanizsa; 47°23'/16°53'; HSL. This town was located on a pre-World War I map, but does not appear in contemporary gazetteers.

Pornice, Cz.; 38 km ENE of Brno; 49°15'/17°11'; HSL.

Porogi, Ukr. (Porohy); pop. 150; 133 km WNW of Chernovtsy; 48°41'/24°16'; HSL, PHP2.

Porohy, *see* Porogi.

Poromow, *see* Poromuv.

Poromuv, Ukr. (Poromow); pop. 12; 107 km N of Lvov; 50°45'/24°05'.

Poronin, Pol.; pop. 5; 88 km S of Krakow; 49°20'/20°01'; GUM3.

Porosavo, *see* Porozovo.

Poroshkov, Ukr. (Poroskov); 163 km SSW of Lvov; 48°40'/22°45'; HSL.

Porosiuki, Pol.; pop. 15; 94 km N of Lublin; 52°01'/23°04'.

Poroskov, *see* Poroshkov.

Porostov, Cz.; 69 km E of Kosice; 48°42'/22°11'; AMG.

Poroszlo, Hung.; pop. 154; 56 km S of Miskolc; 47°39'/20°40'; HSL, HSL2, LDS, PHH.

Poroze Stare, Pol.; pop. 2; 75 km W of Lodz; 51°56'/18°23'.

Porozovo, Byel. (Porasow, Porosavo, Porozow, Porzwye); pop. 567; 150 km WNW of Pinsk; 52°56'/24°22'; GUM4, HSL, LDL, SF, YB.

Porozow, *see* Porozovo.

Porpac, Hung.; pop. 2; 94 km NNW of Nagykanizsa; 47°15'/16°48'.

Porplishche, Byel. (Porpliszcze); pop. 19; 126 km N of Minsk; 54°58'/27°39'.

Porpliszcze, *see* Porplishche.

Porrogszentkiraly, Hung.; pop. 5; 19 km SSE of Nagykanizsa; 46°17'/17°03'.

Porshna, Ukr. (Porszna); pop. 27; 26 km S of Lvov; 49°43'/23°57'.

Porszna, *see* Porshna.

Porszombat, Hung.; pop. 7; 45 km NW of Nagykanizsa; 46°44'/16°35'.

Port, Rom.; pop. 12; 94 km WNW of Cluj; 47°14'/22°33'.

Portita, Rom.; pop. 4; 126 km NW of Cluj; 47°34'/22°25'.

Poruba, Cz.; 133 km NE of Bratislava; 48°50'/18°36'; HSL.

Poruba pod Vihorlatom, Cz. (Nemecka Poruba); pop. 106; 69 km ENE of Kosice; 48°50'/22°09'.

Porudenko, Ukr.; pop. 9; 50 km W of Lvov; 49°55'/23°19'.

Porudno, *see* Kalynivka.

Porumbacu de Sus, Rom. (Porumbacul de Sus, Porumbak); 133 km SE of Cluj; 45°43'/24°28'; EJ.

Porumbacul de Sus, *see* Porumbacu de Sus.

Porumbak, *see* Porumbacu de Sus.

Porumbenii Mari, Rom.; pop. 13; 133 km ESE of Cluj; 46°16'/25°08'.

Porumbenii Mici, Rom. (Kisgalambfalva); pop. 6; 133 km ESE of Cluj; 46°16'/25°06'; HSL.

Porumbesti, Rom. (Kokenyesd); pop. 92; 146 km NNW of Cluj; 47°59'/22°59'; PHR2.

Porumbrey, Mold. (Mitropolit); pop. 2; 38 km S of Kishinev; 46°42'/28°48'.

Poryte, Pol. (Poryte Szlacheckie); pop. 23; 75 km WNW of Bialystok; 53°22'/22°05'; PHP4.

Poryte Szlacheckie, *see* Poryte.

Porz, Germ.; pop. 64; 13 km ESE of Koln; 50°53'/07°03'; GED.

Porzecze, *see* Porechye.

Porzwye, *see* Porozovo.

Posa, Cz.; 45 km NE of Kosice; 48°50'/21°46'; HSL.

Posada Dolna, Pol. (Posada Felsztynnska?); pop. 44; 69 km S of Przemysl; 49°15'/22°42'.

Posada Felsztynnska, *possibly* Posada Dolna.

Posada Gorna, Pol.; pop. 2; 69 km SW of Przemysl; 49°34'/21°52'.

Posada Jacmierska, *see* Jacmierz.

Posada Jasliska, *see* Jasliska.

Posada Leska, Pol. (Posada Liska); pop. 10; 50 km SW of Przemysl; 49°29'/22°20'.

Posada Liska, *see* Posada Leska.

Posada Nowomiejska, *see* Posada Rybotycka.

Posada Olchowska, Pol.; pop. 324; 50 km SW of Przemysl; 49°33'/22°13'.

Posada Rybotycka, Pol. (Posada Nowomiejska); pop. 48; 19 km SSW of Przemysl; 49°40'/22°37'.

Posadow, Pol.; pop. 42; 107 km NNE of Przemysl; 50°30'/23°49'.

Posadowa, Pol.; pop. 11; 82 km ESE of Krakow; 49°40'/20°51'; PHP3.

Pose, Hung.; pop. 4; 107 km NNW of Nagykanizsa; 47°19'/16°34'.

Posejny, Pol.; pop. 16; 114 km N of Bialystok; 54°06'/23°22'.

Posen, *see* Poznan.

Posfa, Hung. (Csallokozposfa); pop. 16; 107 km N of Nagykanizsa; 47°20'/16°51'.

Poshvitin, *see* Pasvitinys.

Poskle, Pol.; pop. 3; 88 km E of Krakow; 50°01'/21°09'.

Posmus, *see* Posnas.

Posnas, Rom. (Posmus); pop. 20; 82 km NE of Cluj; 46°59'/24°35'.

Possneck, Germ.; pop. 16; 82 km SSW of Leipzig; 50°42'/11°36'.

Postaszowice, Pol.; pop. 7; 32 km ESE of Czestochowa; 50°40'/19°29'.

Postav, *see* Postavy.

Postavi, *see* Postavy.

Postavy, Byel. (Podhaitsy, Postav, Postavi, Postawy, Postov, Postow); pop. 368; 150 km NNW of Minsk; 55°07'/26°50'; AMG, COH, GUM3, GUM4, GUM5, HSL, SF, YB.

Postawy, *see* Postavy.

Postelberg, Cz. CAHJP, HSL. This pre-World War I community was not found in BGN gazetteers.

Postojna, Yug.; 133 km WSW of Zagreb; 45°47'/14°14'; GUM5.

Postojno, *see* Postoyno.

Postolin, Pol. (Pestlin); pop. 3; 56 km SE of Gdansk; 53°52'/19°04'.

Postoliska, Pol.; pop. 11; 38 km NE of Warszawa; 52°27'/21°28'.

Postoloprty, Cz.; pop. 127; 62 km WNW of Praha; 50°22'/13°42'; CAHJP.

Postov, *see* Postavy.

Postovice, Cz.; pop. 1; 38 km NW of Praha; 50°19'/14°08'.

Postow, *see* Postavy.

Postoyno, Ukr. (Postojno); pop. 16; 38 km NNW of Rovno; 50°55'/26°07'; GUM4.

Postrizin, Cz.; pop. 3; 19 km NNW of Praha; 50°14'/14°23'.

Postronna, Pol.; pop. 4; 101 km SW of Lublin; 50°38'/21°32'.

Postupice, Cz.; pop. 11; 45 km SE of Praha; 49°44'/14°47'.

Postyen, *see* Piestany.

Posvol, *see* Pasvalys.

Posvul, *see* Pasvalys.

Poswetin, *see* Pasvitinys.

Poswietne, Pol.; pop. 100; 88 km WNW of Lublin; 51°29'/21°22'.

Poswietne (near Opoczno), Pol.; pop. 26; 69 km ESE of Lodz; 51°32'/20°23'.

Poswietne (near Skierniewice), Pol.; pop. 49; 56 km ESE of Lodz; 51°34'/20°13'.

Potarzyca, Pol.; 62 km SE of Poznan; 51°55'/17°25'; GA.

Potau, Rom.; pop. 22; 114 km NNW of Cluj; 47°45'/23°07'.

Potchayev, *see* Pochayev.

Potchera, *see* Pechora.

Potek Zolti, *see* Zolotoy Potok.

Potik, *see* Zolotoy Potok.

Potiski Sveti Nikola, *see* Ostojicevo.

Potochishche, Ukr. (Potoczyska); pop. 96; 56 km NW of Chernovtsy; 48°44'/25°35'; JGFF, PHP2.

Potocska, HSL. This pre-World War I community was not found in BGN gazetteers.

Potoczyska, *see* Potochishche.

Potok, Pol. PHP3. A number of towns share this name. It was not possible to determine from available information which one is being referenced.

Potok (Byelorussia), Byel.; 133 km WSW of Vitebsk; 55°04'/28°10'; JGFF.

Potok (Czechoslovakia), Cz. HSL, HSL2. There are four towns in Czechoslovakia listed in the BGN named Potok. It is not possible to tell which is referenced here.

Potok (near Buchach), Ukr.; 88 km ESE of Lvov; 49°31'/25°02'; PHP2.

Potok B, Pol.; pop. 6; 56 km ESE of Lodz; 51°25'/20°05'.

Potok Gorny, Pol.; pop. 58; 69 km NNW of Przemysl; 50°23'/22°34'.

Potok Maly, Pol.; pop. 8; 62 km N of Krakow; 50°36'/20°14'.

Potok Senderki, *see* Potok Senderski.

Potok Senderski, Pol. (Potok Senderki); pop. 10; 88 km SE of Lublin; 50°33'/23°05'; GUM3.

Potok Stany, Pol.; pop. 47; Described in the *Black Book* as being in the Lublin region of Poland, this town was not found in BGN gazetteers.

Potok Stany Wies, Pol.; pop. 36; Described in the *Black Book* as being in the Lublin region of Poland, this town was not found in BGN gazetteers.

Potok Wielki (Kielce area), Pol.; pop. 31; 62 km N of Krakow; 50°36'/20°14'.

Potok Wielki (Lublin area), Pol.; pop. 29; 56 km SSW of Lublin; 50°47'/22°13'; GUM3.

Potok Zloti, *see* Zolotoy Potok.

Potok Zloty, *see* Zolotoy Potok.

Potolitch, *see* Potylich.

Potranka, Pol.; pop. 83; Described in the *Black Book* as being in the Stanislawow region of Poland, this town was not found in BGN gazetteers.

Potrete, Hung.; pop. 4; 38 km N of Nagykanizsa; 46°41'/16°57'.

Potsdam, Germ.; pop. 365; 26 km SW of Berlin; 52°24'/13°04'; GUM3, HSL, HSL2, LDS.

Potstejn, Cz.; pop. 4; 107 km NNW of Brno; 50°05'/16°19'.

Pottenbrunn, Aus.; pop. 4; 50 km W of Wien; 48°14'/15°42'.

Pottenstein, Aus.; pop. 21; 32 km SSW of Wien; 47°57'/16°05'; GUM3, PHGB.

Pottmes, Germ.; pop. 62 km NW of Munchen; 48°35'/11°06'; GUM5, PHGB.

Pottsching, Aus.; pop. 6; 50 km S of Wien; 47°48'/16°23'.

Poturzyn, Pol.; pop. 106; 120 km NNE of Przemysl; 50°34'/23°57'.

Potvorov, Cz.; pop. 4; 75 km WSW of Praha; 50°01'/13°24'.

Potycz, Pol.; pop. 2; 45 km SE of Warszawa; 51°55'/21°14'.

Potylich, Ukr. (Potolitch, Potylicz); pop. 269; 50 km NW of Lvov; 50°14'/23°34'; EGRS, HSL, LDL, PHP2, SF.

Potylicz, *see* Potylich.

Potyond, Hung.; pop. 3; 133 km N of Nagykanizsa; 47°33'/17°11'.

Potzneusiedl, Aus.; pop. 7; 45 km ESE of Wien; 48°02'/16°56'.

Potzunel, *see* Pociuneliai.

Pouchov, Cz.; pop. 1; 101 km ENE of Praha; 50°14'/15°51'.

Poucnik, Cz.; pop. 5; 26 km SW of Praha; 49°56'/14°11'.

Pounivez, *see* Panevezys.

Povazska Bystrica, Cz. (Bystrica); pop. 350; 133 km E of Brno; 49°07'/18°27'; GUM5, HSL.

Povcha, Ukr. (Pelcza); pop. 6; 56 km SW of Rovno; 50°22'/25°31'.

Povitye, Byel. (Powicie); pop. 107; 94 km WSW of Pinsk; 51°59'/24°46'.

Povoloch, *see* Pavoloch.

Povorsk, Ukr. (Paversk, Povursk, Poworsk); pop. 37; 107 km WNW of Rovno; 51°16'/25°08'; COH, LYV, SF.

Povrly, Cz. (Male Brezno); pop. 4; 69 km NNW of Praha; 50°40'/14°10'; HSL.

Povursk, *see* Povorsk.

Povyatov, (Powiatow); FRG. This town was not found in BGN gazetteers under the given spelling.

Powiatow, *see* Povyatov.

Powicie, *see* Povitye.

Poworsk, *see* Povorsk.

Powroznik, Pol.; pop. 17; 114 km SE of Krakow; 49°22'/20°58'.

Powsinek, Pol.; pop. 6; 19 km SE of Warszawa; 52°09'/21°06'.

Poyana, Mold. (Poiana Soroca); pop. 91; 107 km NNW of Kishinev; 47°55'/28°39'.

Poysdorf, Aus.; pop. 38; 56 km N of Wien; 48°40'/16°38'; AMG.

Poyuri, *possibly* Pajuris.

Pozarevac, Yug.; pop. 65; 62 km ESE of Beograd; 44°37'/21°12'.

Pozba, Cz.; pop. 94 km E of Bratislava; 48°07'/18°23'; COH, HSL.

Pozden, Cz.; pop. 5; 45 km WNW of Praha; 50°14'/13°57'.

Pozdisovce, Cz.; pop. 55; 45 km ENE of Kosice; 48°44'/21°51'; HSL.

Pozdziacz, Pol.; pop. 20; 19 km NE of Przemysl; 49°51'/22°58'.

Pozdzienice, Pol.; pop. 35; 38 km SSW of Lodz; 51°27'/19°11'.

Pozdzimezh, Ukr. (Pozdzimierz); pop. 58; 62 km N of Lvov; 50°21'/24°19'.

Pozdzimierz, *see* Pozdzimezh.

Pozega, Yug.; pop. 248; 114 km S of Beograd; 43°51'/20°02'.

Pozelva, *see* Zelva.

Pozeski Brestovac, *see* Brestovac Pozeski.

Pozhareny, Mold. (Pojoreni); pop. 1; 19 km SSW of Kishinev; 46°53'/28°41'.

Poznachowice Dolne, Pol.; pop. 3; 38 km SE of Krakow; 49°49'/20°07'; HSL.

Poznan, Pol. (Posen, Pozno); pop. 2,088; 157 km N of Wroclaw; 52°25'/16°58'; AMG, CAHJP, EJ, GA, GUM3, GUM4, GUM5, GUM6, HSL, HSL2, ISH2, JGFF, LDL, PHP1, PHP2, PHP3, PHP4.

Pozno, *see* Poznan.

Pozsony, *see* Bratislava.

Prabuty, Pol. (Riesenburg); pop. 65; 75 km SE of Gdansk; 53°46'/19°13'; LDS.

Prace Duze, Pol.; pop. 3; 38 km S of Warszawa; 51°59'/20°56'.

Prace Male, Pol.; pop. 8; 38 km S of Warszawa; 51°59'/20°54'.

Prachatice, Cz.; pop. 36; 126 km S of Praha; 49°01'/14°00'.

Prachnik, *see* Bobrka.

Pradla, Pol.; pop. 87; 45 km ESE of Czestochowa; 50°34'/19°39'.

Pradnik, Pol. (Pradnik Bialy); pop. 50; 6 km NE of Krakow; 50°06'/19°57'; JGFF.

Pradnik Bialy, *see* Pradnik.

Pradnik Czerwony, Pol.; pop. 110; 6 km E of Krakow; 50°05'/19°57'.

Prady, Pol.; 26 km SSW of Czestochowa; 50°38'/18°53'; GA.

Praga, Pol.; pop. 21,705; 6 km NE of Warszawa; 52°16'/21°05'; AMG, COH, GUM4, GUM5, GYLA, HSL, JGFF, LDL, LYV, PHP4, YB.

Prague, *see* Praha.

Praha, Cz. (Prague); pop. 31,751; 182 km WNW of Brno; 50°05'/14°28'; AMG, CAHJP, EDRD, EJ, GUM3, GUM4, GUM5, GUM6, HSL, HSL2, ISH1, ISH2, ISH3, JGFF, LDL, LJEE, PHP1, PHP2, PHP3.

Prahovo, Yug.; 176 km ESE of Beograd; 44°18'/22°35'; GUM4.

Praid, Rom. (Parajd); pop. 123; 120 km E of Cluj; 46°33'/25°08'; HSL, PHR2.

Prajila, *see* Prazhilo.

Praha (Prague) Czechoslovakia:
The Altneuschul Synagogue.

Prakhnik, *see* Pruchnik.

Prameny, Cz. (Sangerberg); pop. 3; 126 km WSW of Praha; 50°04'/12°44'.

Praporiste, Cz.; 133 km SW of Praha; 49°23'/13°01'; JGFF.

Prashka, *see* Praszka.

Prashke, *see* Praszka.

Prashki, *see* Praszka.

Prashnitz, *see* Przasnysz.

Praska, *see* Praszka.

Praskolesy, Cz.; 50 km SW of Praha; 49°52'/13°56'; HSL.

Praszka, Pol. (Prashka, Prashke, Prashki, Praska); pop. 1,663; 56 km WNW of Czestochowa; 51°03'/18°28'; AMG, CAHJP, COH, EDRD, GA, GUM3, GUM4, HSL, HSL2, LDS, LYV, PHP1, POCEM, SF.

Pratulin, Pol.; pop. 2; 114 km SSE of Bialystok; 52°10'/23°26'.

Prauliena, Lat. (Praulienas); pop. 3; 114 km NNW of Daugavpils; 56°50'/26°18'.

Praulienas, *see* Prauliena.

Prausnitz, *see* Prusice.

Pravda, Ukr. (Chorobrow); pop. 20; 82 km N of Lvov; 50°32'/24°10'.

Pravdinsk, USSR (Friedland [East Prussia]); pop. 33; 50 km ESE of Kaliningrad; 54°27'/21°01'.

Pravieniskes, Lith. (Pravinishok); 19 km ENE of Kaunas; 54°55'/24°14'; YL.

Pravikov, Cz.; pop. 5; 94 km SE of Praha; 49°20'/15°06'.

Pravinishok, *see* Pravieniskes.

Pravonin, Cz.; pop. 29; 62 km SE of Praha; 49°38'/14°57'.

Prayl, *see* Preili.

Prazhilo, Mold. (Prajila); pop. 109; 107 km NW of Kishinev; 47°51'/28°12'.

Prazuchy, Pol.; pop. 2; 75 km W of Lodz; 51°53'/18°20'.

Prcice, Cz.; pop. 24; 62 km S of Praha; 49°35'/14°33'.

Prebuz, Cz. (Fruhbuss); pop. 1; 133 km W of Praha; 50°22'/12°38'.

Predboj, Cz.; pop. 9; 19 km N of Praha; 50°14'/14°29'.

Predeal, Rom.; 133 km NNW of Bucuresti; 45°30'/25°34'; GUM3, GUM4.

Predlice, Cz.; pop. 12; 75 km NW of Praha; 50°40'/13°59'.

Predmesti, Cz.; pop. 44; 56 km NNW of Brno; 49°37'/16°25'.

Predocin, Pol.; pop. 16; 88 km WSW of Lublin; 51°09'/21°20'.

Predslav, Cz.; pop. 3; 107 km SW of Praha; 49°27'/13°21'.

Preekulen, *see* Priekule.

Pregrada, Yug.; pop. 16; 50 km NW of Zagreb; 46°10'/15°45'.

Prehoryle, Pol.; pop. 27; 126 km ESE of Lublin; 50°41'/24°04'.

Prehysov, Cz.; pop. 7; 107 km SW of Praha; 49°42'/13°08'.

Preil, *see* Preili.

Preili, Lat. (Prayl, Preil, Preilu, Preli); pop. 892; 50 km N of Daugavpils; 56°18'/26°43'; AMG, COH, HSL, JGFF, PHLE, SF.

Preilu, *see* Preili.

Preiskreitscham, HSL. This pre-World War I community was not found in BGN gazetteers.

Preli, *see* Preili.

Prelic, Cz.; pop. 2; 32 km WNW of Praha; 50°12'/14°03'.

Prelog, Yug.; pop. 21; 75 km NNE of Zagreb; 46°20'/16°37'.

Prelouc, Cz.; pop. 32; 82 km E of Praha; 50°02'/15°34'.

Preluki, Pol.; pop. 11; 69 km SSW of Przemysl; 49°20'/22°07'.

Premishla, *see* Przemysl.

Premishlan, *see* Peremyshlyany.

Premishlian, *see* Peremyshlyany.

Premislani, *see* Peremyshlyany.

Premisle, *see* Przemysl.

Pren, *see* Prienai.

Preny, *see* Prienai.

Prenzlau, Germ.; pop. 200; 94 km N of Berlin; 53°19'/13°52'; HSL, HSL2, ISH1, JGFF, LDS.

Prepelita, *see* Prepelitsa.

Prepelitsa, Mold. (Prepelita); pop. 35; 75 km NW of Kishinev; 47°35'/28°20'.

Preraslia, *see* Lalovo.

Prerau, *see* Prerov.

Prerov, Cz. (Prerau); pop. 278; 69 km NE of Brno; 49°27'/17°27'; HSL, HSL2.

Presekareni, Ukr. (Prisacareni); pop. 29; 32 km S of Chernovtsy; 48°04'/25°51'.

Preselany, Cz. (Pereszleny); pop. 53; 82 km NE of Bratislava; 48°27'/18°06'.

Presevo, Yug.; pop. 4; 38 km N of Skopje; 42°19'/21°39'.

Preshedborz, *see* Przedborz.

Preshov, *see* Presov.

Presov, Cz. (Eperies, Eperjes, Eperyos, Ererjes, Preshov, Preszow); pop. 4,858; 38 km N of Kosice; 49°00'/21°15'; AMG, COH, EJ, GUM3, GUM4, GUM5, GUM6, HSL, HSL2, JGFF, LDL, LDS, LYV, PHP3.

Presovtse, Ukr. (Presowce); 82 km E of Lvov; 49°40'/25°06'; GUM5.

Presowce, *see* Presovtse.

Pressath, Germ.; 69 km NE of Nurnberg; 49°46'/11°56'; PHGB.

Pressbaum, Aus.; pop. 16; 19 km WSW of Wien; 48°11'/16°05'.

Pressburg, *see* Bratislava.

Pressisch Stargard, *see* Starogard.

Prestice, Cz.; pop. 78; 101 km SW of Praha; 49°34'/13°19'; GUM4.

Preszow, *see* Presov.

Pretzfeld, Germ.; 38 km N of Nurnberg; 49°45'/11°11'; GUM5, HSL, PHGB.

Preussische Stargard, *see* Starogard.

Preussisch Eylau, *see* Bagrationovsk.

Preussisch Friedland, *see* Debrzno.

Preussisch Holland, *see* Paslek.

Preussisch Oldendorf, Germ.; pop. 14; 82 km WSW of Hannover; 52°18'/08°30'.

Preveza, Greece; pop. 217; 82 km S of Ioannina; 38°58'/20°45'.

Prezerosl, Pol. PHP4. This town was not found in BGN gazetteers under the given spelling.

Prezhemisel, *see* Przemysl.

Pria, Rom.; pop. 15; 62 km WNW of Cluj; 47°03'/22°53'.

Pribenik, Cz. (Perbenik); 69 km ESE of Kosice; 48°23'/22°00'; HSL.

Pribeta, Cz. (Perbete); 88 km ESE of Bratislava; 47°54'/18°19'; COH, GUM5, HSL, HSL2.

Pribilesti, Rom.; pop. 13; 94 km NNW of Cluj; 47°34'/23°22'; HSL.

Pribor, Cz. (Freiberg); pop. 72; 120 km NE of Brno; 49°39'/18°09'; AMG, GUM3, GUM4, GUM6.

Pribram, Cz.; pop. 298; 56 km SSW of Praha; 49°42'/14°01'; AMG.

Prichsenstadt, Germ.; pop. 55; 62 km WNW of Nurnberg; 49°49'/10°21'; GUM5, PHGB.

Pricovy, Cz.; pop. 3; 50 km S of Praha; 49°40'/14°23'.

Pridroisk, *see* Piedruja.

Pridruiska, *see* Piedruja.

Priekopa, Cz.; pop. 82; 170 km NE of Bratislava; 49°06'/18°56'; AMG.

Priekule, Lat. (Preekulen, Priekules); pop. 24; 163 km SW of Riga; 56°26'/21°35'; PHLE.

Priekules, *see* Priekule.

Priement, *see* Przemet.

Priemhausen, *see* Stargard Szczecinski.

Prienai, Lith. (Pren, Preny); pop. 954; 38 km S of Kaunas; 54°38'/23°57'; COH, GUM3, GUM4, HSL, JGFF, LDL, SF, YL.

Prievidza, Cz. (Privigye); pop. 825; 133 km NE of Bratislava; 48°46'/18°38'; AMG, GUM5, HSL.

Prigrevica, Yug. (Prigrevica Sveti Ivan); pop. 13; 146 km WNW of Beograd; 45°41'/19°05'.

Prigrevica Sveti Ivan, *see* Prigrevica.

Prijedor, Yug.; pop. 45; 107 km SE of Zagreb; 44°59'/16°42'; PHY.

Prilbichi, Ukr. (Przylbic, Pshilbitse); pop. 23; 38 km W of Lvov; 49°53'/23°28'.

Prilepov, Cz.; pop. 5; 69 km S of Praha; 49°30'/14°15'.

Prilog, Rom.; pop. 21; 126 km NNW of Cluj; 47°51'/23°19'.

Priluki, Ukr. (Przyluka); pop. 9,001; 88 km SSW of Konotop; 50°36'/32°24'; EDRD, EJ, GUM4, GYLA, HSL, HSL2, JGFF, LDL, SF.

Priluki (near Berdichev), Ukr.; pop. 2,162; 19 km E of Vinnitsa; 49°13'/28°43'; SF.

Priluki (near Ovruch), Ukr. (Dedkovitchu, Dedukhi, Didkovitch, Didkovitz); 144 km NW of Kiyev; 51°28'/28°52'; SF.

Primda, Cz.; pop. 3; 139 km SW of Praha; 49°40'/12°41'.

Primkenau, *see* Przemkow.

Primorskoye, Ukr. (Nogaysk); pop. 186; 214 km SE of Dnepropetrovsk; 46°44'/36°21'; HSL.

Primorskoye (Bessarabia I), Ukr. (Budachi); pop. 12; 69 km SSW of Odessa; 45°58'/30°17'.

Primorskoye (Bessarabia II), Ukr. (Sagani); pop. 8; Described in the *Black Book* as being in the Bessarabia region of Romania, this town was not found in BGN gazetteers.

Principele Carol, *see* Krasnoarmeyskoye.

Pripyat, Ukr. (Butmer); pop. 8; 182 km WNW of Rovno; 51°30'/24°07'.

Prisacareni, *see* Presekareni.

Prisecnice, Cz.; pop. 1; 107 km WNW of Praha; 50°28'/13°08'.

Prislup, *see* Lukvitsa. The *Black Book* refers to a second Przyslup (pop. 44) in the county of Turka in Stanislawow province. The only other town named Przyslup on an interwar map of Poland appears northwest of the town of Turka in Lwow province. Neither Prislup nor Przyslup appears in contemporary gazetteers.

Pristina, Yug.; pop. 370; 75 km NNW of Skopje; 42°40'/21°10'; GUM4, PHY.

Pristoupim, Cz.; pop. 13; 32 km E of Praha; 50°03'/14°53'.

Pritkov, Cz.; pop. 1; 82 km NW of Praha; 50°41'/13°50'.

Prittlbach, Germ.; 19 km NW of Munchen; 48°17'/11°26'; PHGBW.

Pritzwalk, Germ.; 107 km WNW of Berlin; 53°09'/12°11'; EJ.

Privalki, Byel. (Przewalka); pop. 8; 240 km W of Minsk; 53°57'/23°55'.

Privigye, *see* Prievidza.

Priyutnaya, *see* Priyutnoye.

Priyutnoye, Ukr. (Priyutnaya); 146 km ESE of Dnepropetrovsk; 47°44'/36°40'; JGFF.

Prizren, Yug.; pop. 11; 62 km WNW of Skopje; 42°13'/20°45'; GUM4.

Probezhna, Ukr. (Probuzhne, Probuzna); pop. 1,226; 88 km N of Chernovtsy; 49°02'/25°59'; COH, EGRS, GUM5, GUM6, GYLA, HSL, HSL2, LDL, PHP2, SF.

Probishta, *see* Pogrebishche.

Probstdorf, Aus.; pop. 2; 19 km E of Wien; 48°10'/16°36'.

Probulov, Cz.; pop. 3; 69 km S of Praha; 49°30'/14°09'.

Probuzhne, *see* Probezhna.

Probuzna, *see* Probezhna.

Prochnik, Pol.; 50 km E of Gdansk; 54°14'/19°28'; AMG.

Procisne, Pol.; pop. 29; 75 km S of Przemysl; 49°12'/22°40'.

Prockau, *see* Prokowo.

Prode, *see* Brody.

Prokocice, Pol.; pop. 3; 50 km ENE of Krakow; 50°12'/20°34'.

Prokocim, Pol.; pop. 22; 13 km SE of Krakow; 50°01'/20°00'; GUM4, GUM5, PHP3.

Prokowo, Pol. (Prockau); 32 km W of Gdansk; 54°22'/18°10'; JGFF.

Prokurawa, HSL. This pre-World War I community was not found in BGN gazetteers.

Proletarskiy, Ukr.; 170 km ESE of Dnepropetrovsk; 47°31'/36°50'; JGFF.

Promna, Pol.; pop. 32; 69 km S of Warszawa; 51°41'/20°57'.

Proniewicze, Pol.; pop. 2; 45 km S of Bialystok; 52°48'/23°12'.

Propoisk, *see* Slavgorod.

Prosau, Cz. BGN lists two possible localities with this name located at 49°58'/12°50' and 50°09'/12°39'. HSL.

Proscureni, *see* Proskuryany.

Prosec, Cz.; 82 km NW of Brno; 49°48'/16°07'; HSL.

Proshnits, *see* Przasnysz.

Proshnitz, *see* Przasnysz.

Proshovitza, *see* Proszowice.

Prosienica, Pol.; pop. 58; 82 km SW of Bialystok; 52°53'/22°02'.

Proskau, *see* Proszkow.

Proskuren, *see* Proskuryany.

Proskurov, *see* Khmelnitskiy.

Proskuryany, Mold. (Proscureni, Proskuren); pop. 35; 150 km WNW of Kishinev; 47°52'/27°15'.

Prosmyky, Cz.; pop. 7; 50 km NW of Praha; 50°31'/14°06'.

Prossnitz, *see* Prostejov.

Prostejov, Cz. (Prossnitz); pop. 1,442; 50 km NE of Brno; 49°28'/17°07'; AMG, CAHJP, EJ, GUM3, GUM4, HSL, HSL2.

Prostibor, Cz.; pop. 6; 126 km SW of Praha; 49°39'/12°54'.

Prostken, see Prostki.

Prostki, Pol. (Prostken); pop. 56; 82 km NW of Bialystok; 53°42'/22°25'; GA.

Prostyn, Pol.; pop. 136; 82 km NE of Warszawa; 52°40'/21°59'; HSL.

Prosyanaya, Ukr.; 107 km ESE of Dnepropetrovsk; 48°07'/36°23'; HSL.

Proszew, Pol.; pop. 25; Described in the *Black Book* as being in the Lublin region of Poland, this town was not found in BGN gazetteers.

Proszkow, Pol. (Proskau); JGFF. This town was not found in BGN gazetteers under the given spelling.

Proszowice, Pol. (Proshovitza); pop. 1,307; 32 km NE of Krakow; 50°12'/20°18'; AMG, CAHJP, COH, GUM3, GUM4, GUM5, HSL, JGFF, POCEM, SF.

Proszowki, Pol.; pop. 23; 45 km ESE of Krakow; 49°59'/20°26'.

Protivin, Cz.; pop. 23; 107 km S of Praha; 49°12'/14°13'; HSL.

Provadiya, Bulg.; pop. 153; 38 km WSW of Varna; 43°11'/27°26'; EJ.

Proyanovska, Lith. EDRD. This town was not found in BGN gazetteers under the given spelling.

Prozorki, see Prozoroki.

Prozoroki, Byel. (Prozorki); pop. 134; 126 km W of Vitebsk; 55°18'/28°13'.

Pruchna, Pol.; pop. 16; 94 km WSW of Krakow; 49°52'/18°41'.

Pruchnik, Pol. (Prakhnik, Pruchnik Miasto, Prukhnik, Prukhnik Myasto); pop. 877; 26 km WNW of Przemysl; 49°55'/22°31'; COH, EDRD, EGRS, GUM3, GUM5, HSL, JGFF, LDL, LDS, LYV, PHP2, PHP3, SF.

Pruchnik Miasto, see Pruchnik.

Pruchnik Wies, Pol.; pop. 92; 26 km WNW of Przemysl; 49°54'/22°31'.

Prudnik, Pol. (Neustadt in Oberschlesien); pop. 100; 94 km SE of Wroclaw; 50°19'/17°35'; HSL, JGFF, LDS, POCEM.

Prugy, Hung.; pop. 31; 38 km E of Miskolc; 48°05'/21°15'.

Prukhnik, see Pruchnik.

Prukhnik Myasto, see Pruchnik.

Prundu Birgaului, Rom. (Borgoprund, Prundul Bargaului); pop. 325; 101 km NE of Cluj; 47°13'/24°44'; AMG, HSL, HSL2, LDL, PHR2.

Prundul Bargaului, see Prundu Birgaului.

Pruneni, Rom.; pop. 10; 38 km N of Cluj; 47°02'/23°43'.

Prunerov, Cz.; pop. 10; 94 km WNW of Praha; 50°25'/13°16'.

Prushkov, see Pruszkow.

Prusice, Pol. (Prausnitz); 38 km N of Wroclaw; 51°22'/16°58'; EJ.

Prusicko, Pol.; pop. 2; 32 km N of Czestochowa; 51°02'/19°12'.

Prusie, Pol.; pop. 7; 75 km NE of Przemysl; 50°15'/23°32'.

Prusiek, Pol.; pop. 9; 56 km SW of Przemysl; 49°32'/22°08'.

Prusinow, see Prusinuv.

Prusinuv, Ukr. (Prusinow); pop. 32; 62 km N of Lvov; 50°21'/24°02'.

Pruske, Cz.; pop. 59; 114 km E of Brno; 49°02'/18°13'.

Prussia; Not a town, but the largest state of the German Empire prior to World War I. Prior to 1871, Prussia was a separate nation.

Prusy, Ukr.; pop. 65; 62 km SW of Lvov; 49°28'/23°27'.

Prusy (near Lvov), Ukr.; pop. 22; 13 km ENE of Lvov; 49°52'/24°11'.

Pruszki Wielkie, Pol.; pop. 4; 56 km WSW of Bialystok; 53°06'/22°19'.

Pruszk Male, Pol. PHP4. This town was not found in BGN gazetteers under the given spelling.

Pruszkow, Pol. (Prushkov); pop. 971; 19 km SW of Warszawa; 52°10'/20°50'; AMG, COH, EDRD, GA, GUM4, GUM5, GUM6, HSL, HSL2, LYV, PHP4, POCEM, SF, YB.

Prutting, Germ.; pop. 5; 50 km ESE of Munchen; 47°54'/12°12'.

Pruzana, see Pruzhany.

Pruzany, see Pruzhany.

Pruzhana, see Pruzhany.

Pruzhany, Byel. (Pruzana, Pruzany, Pruzhana, Pruzhani, Pruzhene, Pruzin); pop. 4,152; 120 km WNW of Pinsk; 52°33'/24°28'; AMG, COH, EDRD, EJ, GA, GUM3, GUM4, GUM5, GUM6, HSL, JGFF, LDL, SF, YB.

Pruzhene, see Pruzhany.

Pruzin, see Pruzhany.

Pryamobalka, Ukr. (Denevitz); pop. 9; 126 km SW of Odessa; 45°53'/29°18'.

Pryben, HSL. This pre-World War I community was not found in BGN gazetteers.

Pryvetroye, see Svinyukhi.

Przadlo, GA. This town was not found in BGN gazetteers under the given spelling.

Przashysz, see Przasnysz.

Przasnysz, Pol. (Prashnitz, Proshnits, Proshnitz, Przashysz, Pshasnish); pop. 2,158; 88 km N of Warszawa; 53°02'/20°53'; AMG, CAHJP, COH, GA, GUM3, GUM4, GUM5, HSL, JGFF, LDL, LDS, LYV, PHP1, PHP4, SF, YB.

Przckopana, Pol.; pop. 83; Described in the *Black Book* as being in the Lwow region of Poland, this town was not found in BGN gazetteers.

Przebieczany, Pol.; pop. 11; 19 km ESE of Krakow; 49°59'/20°07'.

Przebrody, see Perebrodye.

Przebrodzie, see Perebrodye.

Przechowo, Pol.; pop. 5; 107 km S of Gdansk; 53°24'/18°25'.

Przeciszow, Pol.; pop. 27; 38 km WSW of Krakow; 50°01'/19°23'.

Przeclaw, Pol. (Pshetslav, Pshetzlov); pop. 158; 101 km WNW of Przemysl; 50°12'/21°28'; EGRS, GUM5, HSL, PHP3, SF, YB.

Przeczow, Pol.; pop. 13; 101 km NE of Krakow; 50°25'/21°12'.

Przeczyca, Pol.; pop. 2; 101 km W of Przemysl; 49°54'/21°22'.

Przedborz, Pol. (Preshedborz, Pshedbosh, Pshedbozh, Pshedburz); pop. 3,749; 62 km NE of Czestochowa; 51°05'/19°53'; AMG, CAHJP, COH, EDRD, EJ, GA, GUM3, GUM5, HSL, HSL2, JGFF, LDL, LDS, LYV, PHP1, POCEM, SF, WS, YB.

Przedecz, Pol. (Pesheysh, Pshaych, Pshayts, Pshaytsh, Pshech, Pshedech, Pshedesh, Pshedetz); pop. 840; 75 km NW of Lodz; 52°20'/18°54'; AMG, CAHJP, COH, FRG, HSL, HSL2, JGFF, LYV, PHP1, PHP4, SF, YB.

Przedmiescie, Pol.; pop. 111; 50 km WNW of Przemysl; 50°04'/22°13'.

Przedmiescie (near Zelechow), Pol.; pop. 78; 56 km WSW of Lublin; 51°09'/21°43'.

Przedmiescie Dubieckie, Pol.; pop. 25; 32 km W of Przemysl; 49°51'/22°22'.

Przedmiescie Kludzie, Pol.; pop. 38; 56 km WSW of Lublin; 51°10'/21°47'.

Przedmiescie Sedziszowskie, Pol.; pop. 35; 82 km WNW of Przemysl; 50°04'/21°43'.

Przedmoscie, Pol.; pop. 3; 62 km WNW of Czestochowa; 51°06'/18°26'; GA, PHP1.

Przedzel, Pol.; pop. 28; 88 km S of Lublin; 50°29'/22°14'; HSL.

Przegalina, Pol. (Przegaliny); 19 km E of Gdansk; 54°19'/18°55'; GA.

Przegaliny, see Przegalina.

Przegaliny Duze, Pol. (Przegaliny Wielkie); pop. 32; 69 km N of Lublin; 51°50'/22°53'.

Przegaliny Male, Pol.; pop. 36; 69 km N of Lublin; 51°49'/22°52'.

Przegaliny Wielkie, see Przegaliny Duze.

Przegorzaly, Pol.; pop. 3; 13 km SW of Krakow; 50°03'/19°52'.

Przemet, Pol. (Priement, Przemiat); 62 km SW of Poznan; 52°01'/16°18'; GA.

Przemiat, see Przemet.

Przemiwolki, see Pshemivulki.

Przemkow, Pol. (Primkenau); pop. 1; 94 km WNW of Wroclaw; 51°31'/15°48'.

Przemocze, Pol. LDS. This town was not found in BGN

gazetteers under the given spelling.

Przemysl, Pol. (Peremyshl, Premishla, Premisle, Prezhemisel, Pshemishel, Pshemyshl, Pshemysl); pop. 12,326; 163 km S of Lublin; 49°47'/22°47'; AMG, CAHJP, COH, EDRD, EGRS, EJ, FRG, GA, GUM3, GUM4, GUM5, GUM6, GYLA, HSL, HSL2, ISH1, ISH3, JGFF, LDL, LYV, PHP2, PHP3, PHP4, POCEM, SF, YB.

Przemyslany, *see* Peremyshlyany.

Przenosza, Pol.; pop. 15; 45 km SE of Krakow; 49°46'/20°10'; PHP3.

Przerab, Pol.; pop. 92; 56 km NE of Czestochowa; 51°09'/19°43'; AMG.

Przeradowo, Pol.; pop. 15; 62 km N of Warszawa; 52°47'/21°13'.

Przeradz Maly, Pol.; pop. 7; 114 km WNW of Warszawa; 53°02'/19°48'.

Przerosl, Pol.; pop. 185; 133 km NNW of Bialystok; 54°15'/22°39'; HSL, JGFF, LDS, POCEM, SF. *See also* Psherosl. There is a second town named Przerosl northeast of Kolno at 53°33'/21°39'.

Przeslaw, Pol.; pop. 41; Described in the *Black Book* as being in the Kielce region of Poland, this town was not found in BGN gazetteers.

Przesmyki, Pol.; pop. 28; 101 km S of Bialystok; 52°16'/22°35'.

Przestrzele, Pol.; pop. 23; Described in the *Black Book* as being in the Bialystok region of Poland, this town was not found in BGN gazetteers.

Przewale, *see* Pshovaly.

Przewalka, *see* Privalki.

Przewaly, *see* Pshovaly.

Przewloczna, *see* Perevolochna.

Przewloka, *see* Pshevloka.

Przewodow, Pol.; pop. 34; 114 km NE of Przemysl; 50°28'/23°56'.

Przewodziszowice, Pol.; pop. 4; 26 km ESE of Czestochowa; 50°38'/19°23'.

Przeworsk, Pol. (Perevorsk, Pshevarsk, Pshevorsk); pop. 1,457; 38 km NW of Przemysl; 50°04'/22°30'; AMG, COH, EGRS, EJ, GA, GUM3, GUM4, GUM5, HSL, HSL2, JGFF, LDL, LYV, PHP2, PHP3, POCEM, SF.

Przewrotne, Pol.; pop. 19; 75 km WNW of Przemysl; 50°13'/21°57'.

Przezdziecko, Pol.; pop. 54; 69 km SW of Bialystok; 52°52'/22°15'.

Przyborow, Pol.; pop. 28; 62 km SSW of Krakow; 49°37'/19°22'.

Przyborowice Gorne, Pol.; pop. 130; 45 km WNW of Warszawa; 52°33'/20°31'; PHP4.

Przybowka, Pol.; pop. 20; 82 km W of Przemysl; 49°48'/21°40'.

Przybradz, Pol.; pop. 7; 38 km SW of Krakow; 49°57'/19°25'.

Przybylow, Pol.; pop. 32; A number of towns share this name. It was not possible to determine from available information which one is being referenced.

Przybyslawice, Pol.; pop. 67; 45 km N of Krakow; 50°27'/20°04'.

Przybyszew, Pol.; pop. 104; 69 km S of Warszawa; 51°40'/20°51'; LDS, PHP4.

Przybyszowka, Pol.; pop. 69; 62 km WNW of Przemysl; 50°03'/21°57'.

Przybyszowy, Pol.; pop. 7; 88 km ESE of Lodz; 51°12'/20°18'.

Przybyszyn, Pol.; pop. 14; 69 km SSW of Bialystok; 52°38'/22°33'.

Przychojec, Pol.; pop. 9; 62 km NW of Przemysl; 50°18'/22°24'.

Przyglow, Pol. (Pshiglov); pop. 5; 50 km SE of Lodz; 51°23'/19°50'; GUM4, GUM5, PHP1, SF.

Przygody, Pol.; pop. 30; 88 km E of Warszawa; 52°15'/22°16'.

Przyjmy, Pol.; pop. 46; A number of towns share this name. It was not possible to determine from available information which one is being referenced.

Przykalety, Pol.; pop. 28; Described in the *Black Book* as being in the Bialystok region of Poland, this town was not found in BGN gazetteers.

Przylbic, *see* Prilbichi.

Przyleczek, Pol.; pop. 2; 56 km NNE of Krakow; 50°34'/20°15'.

Przylek, Pol.; pop. 46; 101 km WNW of Przemysl; 50°16'/21°37'; GA.

Przylogi, Pol.; pop. 5; 101 km NE of Czestochowa; 51°05'/20°27'.

Przylubie, Pol.; pop. 2; 114 km NE of Poznan; 53°04'/18°18'.

Przyluka, *see* Priluki.

Przypust, Pol.; 126 km NNW of Lodz; 52°49'/18°54'; PHP4.

Przyrab, Pol.; pop. 4; 50 km NNE of Krakow; 50°30'/20°19'.

Przyrow, Pol. (Psherov, Shperov); pop. 802; 26 km E of Czestochowa; 50°48'/19°31'; AMG, CAHJP, GA, GUM3, GUM4, GUM5, JGFF, LDS, PHP1, SF.

Przyrownica, Pol.; pop. 7; 26 km W of Lodz; 51°46'/19°04'; PHP1.

Przysieka, Pol. (Przysieki); pop. 131; 38 km E of Czestochowa; 50°45'/19°39'.

Przysieka (Krakow area), Pol.; pop. 8; 50 km N of Krakow; 50°29'/20°00'.

Przysieki, *see* Przysieka.

Przysiersk, Pol.; pop. 5; 107 km S of Gdansk; 53°26'/18°18'.

Przysietnica, Pol.; pop. 41; 50 km WSW of Przemysl; 49°44'/22°03'.

Przyslup, *see* Lukvitsa.

Przystajn, Pol.; pop. 78; 32 km WNW of Czestochowa; 50°53'/18°42'; AMG.

Przystajnia, Pol.; pop. 11; 88 km WSW of Lodz; 51°35'/18°11'.

Przystan, *see* Pshistan.

Przysucha, Pol. (Parshischa, Pshischa); pop. 2,153; 94 km ESE of Lodz; 51°22'/20°37'; AMG, COH, EDRD, EJ, GA, GUM3, GUM4, GUM5, HSL, HSL2, JGFF, LDL, LDS, PHP1, PHP4, POCEM, SF.

Przyszowa, Pol.; pop. 18; 69 km SE of Krakow; 49°39'/20°30'.

Przyszychwosty, *see* Pervoye Maya.

Przytkowice, Pol.; pop. 20; 26 km SSW of Krakow; 49°55'/19°41'; AMG.

Przytoczno, Pol.; pop. 20; 50 km NW of Lublin; 51°37'/22°16'.

Przytuly, Pol.; pop. 37; 94 km N of Warszawa; 53°04'/21°10'.

Przytyk, Pol. (Pshitik, Pshitikhl); pop. 1,852; 94 km S of Warszawa; 51°28'/20°54'; AMG, COH, EDRD, EJ, FRG, GUM3, GUM4, GUM5, HSL, LDS, LYV, PHP1, PHP3, PHP4, POCEM, SF, YB.

Przywitowo, Pol.; pop. 14; 133 km WNW of Warszawa; 53°03'/19°34'.

Przywoz, Pol.; pop. 7; 50 km NW of Czestochowa; 51°09'/18°43'.

Psare, Cz.; pop. 4; 50 km ESE of Praha; 49°45'/14°58'.

Psary (Kielce), Pol.; pop. 26; 120 km NNE of Krakow; 50°56'/20°53'.

Psary (Stanislawow), Ukr.; pop. 20; 62 km SE of Lvov; 49°25'/24°28'.

Pschelautsch, HSL. This pre-World War I community was not found in BGN gazetteers.

Pseves, Cz.; pop. 2; 69 km NE of Praha; 50°21'/15°18'.

Pshasnish, *see* Przasnysz.

Pshaych, *see* Przedecz.

Pshayts, *see* Przedecz.

Pshaytsh, *see* Przedecz.

Pshebrody, *see* Perebrodye.

Pshech, *see* Przedecz.

Pshedbosh, *see* Przedborz.

Pshedbozh, *see* Przedborz.

Pshedburz, *see* Przedborz.

Pshedech, *see* Przedecz.

Pshedesh, *see* Przedecz.

Pshedetz, *see* Przedecz.

Pshemishel, *see* Przemysl.

Pshemishl, *see* Przemysl.

Pshemishlani, *see* Peremyshlyany.

Pshemivulki, Ukr. (Przemiwolki, Smerekov, Smerekow, Smerekuv); pop. 22; 26 km N of Lvov; 50°01'/24°03'.

Pshemysl, *see* Przemysl.

Pshenichnoye, Ukr. (Oktyabrdorf); 88 km NNE of Simferopol; 45°34'/34°47'.

Psherosl, *see* Pererosl.

Psherosla, *see* Lalovo.

Psherov, *see* Przyrow.

Pshetslav, *see* Przeclaw.

Pshetzlov, *see* Przeclaw.

Pshevaly, *see* Pshovaly.

Pshevarsk, *see* Przeworsk.

Pshevloka, Ukr. (Przewloka); pop. 38; 101 km NW of Chernovtsy; 49°07'/25°22'.

Pshevorsk, *see* Przeworsk.

Pshiglov, *see* Przyglow.

Pshilbitse, *see* Prilbichi.

Pshischa, *see* Przysucha.

Pshistan, Ukr. (Przystan); pop. 45; 45 km N of Lvov; 50°14'/23°57'; EDRD.

Pshitik, *see* Przytyk.

Pshitikhl, *see* Przytyk.

Pshovaly, Ukr. (Przewale, Przewaly, Pshevaly); pop. 20; 146 km N of Lvov; 51°08'/24°20'.

Pshyshykhvosty, *see* Pervoye Maya.

Pskov, USSR; pop. 1,338; 214 km NW of Velikiye Luki; 57°50'/28°20'; GUM4, HSL, JGFF, PHLE.

Pstragowa, Pol.; pop. 61; 75 km W of Przemysl; 49°56'/21°46'; PHP3.

Pstragowka, Pol.; pop. 5; 82 km W of Przemysl; 49°53'/21°37'.

Pszczew, Pol. (Betsche); pop. 28; 82 km W of Poznan; 52°28'/15°46'; JGFF, LDS.

Pszczyna, Pol. (Pless); 69 km WSW of Krakow; 49°58'/18°57'; HSL, HSL2, JGFF, LDS, PHP3, POCEM.

Pszon, (Pszonka); pop. 51; GUM4. Described in the *Black Book* as being in the Lublin region of Poland, this town was not found in BGN gazetteers.

Pszonka, *see* Pszon.

Ptaszki, *see* Skolimow Ptaszki.

Ptaszkowa, Pol.; pop. 21; 88 km ESE of Krakow; 49°37'/20°53'.

Ptuj, Yug. (Pettau); pop. 24; 75 km NNW of Zagreb; 46°25'/15°52'; PHY.

Puchaczow, Pol.; pop. 94; 26 km ENE of Lublin; 51°19'/22°58'; GUM5.

Puchaly, Pol.; 56 km SSW of Bialystok; 52°40'/22°50'; GA.

Puchberg am Schneeberg, Aus.; pop. 3; 56 km SSW of Wien; 47°47'/15°54'.

Puchiny, Byel. (Puczyny); 45 km N of Pinsk; 52°26'/26°09'; GUM3.

Puchov, Cz.; pop. 542; 120 km E of Brno; 49°08'/18°20'; HSL.

Puchovitch, *see* Pukhovichi.

Puchowitschi, *see* Pukhovichi.

Puck, Pol. (Putzig); pop. 31; 45 km NW of Gdansk; 54°42'/18°25'; GUM3, HSL, JGFF, LDS.

Puclice, Cz.; pop. 4; 120 km SW of Praha; 49°33'/13°01'; JGFF.

Puconci, Yug.; pop. 1; 107 km N of Zagreb; 46°43'/16°10'.

Puczyce, Pol. (Pushtshe); pop. 6; 101 km S of Bialystok; 52°16'/22°48'; FRG.

Puczyny, *see* Puchiny.

Puderbach, Germ.; pop. 36; 62 km ESE of Koln; 50°36'/07°37'.

Pudewitz, *see* Pobiedziska.

Pudlein, *see* Podolinec.

Puesti, *see* Puesti Sat.

Puesti Sat, Rom. (Puesti); pop. 187; 88 km S of Iasi; 46°25'/27°29'; GUM4, PHR1.

Pugacheny, Mold. (Pugoceni); pop. 9; 45 km ENE of Kishinev; 47°05'/29°21'.

Pugoceni, *see* Pugacheny.

Pugoy, Mold. (Puhoi); pop. 31; 26 km SE of Kishinev; 46°50'/29°02'.

Puhoi, *see* Pugoy.

Puikule, Lat.; pop. 5; 94 km NNE of Riga; 57°41'/24°53'.

Puini, Rom.; pop. 2; 38 km NE of Cluj; 46°54'/24°01'.

Pukhovichi, Byel. (Puchovitch, Puchowitschi); pop. 929; 56 km ESE of Minsk; 53°32'/28°15'; HSL, JGFF, LDL, SF.

Puklice, Cz. (Puklitz); 69 km W of Brno; 49°22'/15°40'; EJ.

Puklitz, *see* Puklice.

Pukov, Ukr. (Pukow); pop. 32; 75 km ESE of Lvov; 49°23'/24°42'.

Pukow, *see* Pukov.

Pula, Yug. (Pola); 139 km W of Beograd; 44°52'/18°41'; AMG, PHY.

Pulaczow, Pol.; pop. 5; 114 km NE of Krakow; 50°42'/21°08'.

Pulamiec, *see* Pulemets.

Pulanki, Pol.; pop. 18; 82 km W of Przemysl; 49°51'/21°37'.

Pulankowice, Pol.; pop. 10; 38 km SSW of Lublin; 50°58'/22°19'.

Pulav, *see* Pulawy.

Pulavi, *see* Pulawy.

Pulavy, *see* Pulawy.

Pulawy, Pol. (Novaya Aleksandriya, Pilev, Pilov, Pulav, Pulavi, Pulavy); pop. 3,221; 45 km WNW of Lublin; 51°25'/21°58'; AMG, CAHJP, COH, EDRD, EJ, GA, GUM3, GUM4, GUM5, HSL, HSL2, JGFF, LDS, LYV, PHP3, PHP4, POCEM, SF, YB.

Pulazie Swierze, Pol.; pop. 9; 50 km SW of Bialystok; 52°51'/22°37'.

Pulemets, Ukr. (Pulamiec); pop. 30; 189 km N of Lvov; 51°32'/23°43'.

Pulgany, Ukr. (Pulhany); pop. 26; 88 km NE of Lvov; 50°23'/24°53'.

Pulhany, *see* Pulgany.

Pulice, Cz.; 120 km ENE of Praha; 50°18'/16°09'; EJ.

Pulin, *see* Chervonoarmeysk.

Pulkau, Aus.; pop. 1; 69 km NW of Wien; 48°42'/15°51'; EDRD, EJ.

Pullach, *see* Pullach im Isartal.

Pullach im Isartal, Germ. (Pullach); 19 km S of Munchen; 48°03'/11°32'; GUM3.

Pullitz, *see* Politsy.

Pulmo, Ukr.; pop. 64; 189 km N of Lvov; 51°31'/23°47'.

Pultosk, *see* Pultusk.

Pultusk, Pol. (Poltosk, Pultosk); pop. 5,919; 56 km N of Warszawa; 52°43'/21°06'; AMG, COH, EDRD, EJ, GUM3, GUM4, HSL, HSL2, JGFF, LDL, LYV, PHP1, PHP4, SF, YB.

Pumpenai, *see* Pampenai.

Pumpenei, *see* Pampenai.

Pumpian, *see* Pampenai.

Punaviz, *see* Panevezys.

Pungesti, Rom.; pop. 167; 56 km S of Iasi; 46°42'/27°20'; PHR1.

Punia, Lith. (Pon, Poon); 50 km SSE of Kaunas; 54°31'/24°06'; JGFF, SF, YL.

Punitz, Aus.; pop. 3; 69 km ENE of Graz; 47°07'/16°21'. *See also* Poniec.

Punsk, Pol.; pop. 228; 133 km N of Bialystok; 54°15'/23°11'; LDS, PHP4, POCEM, SF, YB.

Purcari, *see* Purkary.

Pure, Lat.; pop. 2; 69 km W of Riga; 57°02'/22°54'.

Purgstall, Aus.; pop. 23; 94 km WSW of Wien; 48°03'/15°08'; JGFF.

Purkary, Mold. (Purcari); pop. 25; 75 km ESE of Kishinev; 46°33'/29°32'.

Purkersdorf, Aus.; pop. 73; 19 km WSW of Wien; 48°12'/16°10'.

Purmsati, Lat.; pop. 4; 170 km SW of Riga; 56°24'/21°31'.

Pusalotas, Lith. (Pishelot, Pushelat, Pushlat); pop. 243; 56 km E of Siauliai; 55°55'/24°15'; JGFF, LDL, SF, YL.

Pushelat, *see* Pusalotas.

Pushkin, USSR (Detskoye Selo, Tsarskoye Selo); pop. 537; 26 km SE of Leningrad; 59°43'/30°25'; EDRD, GUM4, HSL.

Pushlat, *see* Pusalotas.

Pushtshe, *see* Puczyce.

Puspokhatvan, Hung.; pop. 7; 32 km NNE of Budapest; 47°46'/19°22'.

Puspoki, *see* Podunajske Biskupice.

Puspokladany, Hung.; pop. 631; 88 km SSE of Miskolc; 47°19'/21°07'; AMG, GUM3, GUM5, HSL, LDS, PHH.

Puspoklak, Hung.; pop. 17; 120 km ESE of Nagykanizsa;

46°06'/18°31'.

Puspoknadasd, *see* Mecseknadasd.

Puspokszilagy, Hung.; pop. 7; 32 km NNE of Budapest; 47°44'/19°19'.

Puspoktamasi, Hung.; pop. 4; 82 km NNW of Nagykanizsa; 47°06'/16°48'.

Pustelnik, Pol. (Pustelnik Struga); pop. 368; 32 km ENE of Warszawa; 52°17'/21°28'; GA, GUM4, GUM5.

Pustelnik Struga, *see* Pustelnik.

Puste Ulany, Cz. (Pusztafodemes); 38 km ENE of Bratislava; 48°14'/17°34'; HSL.

Pustina, Lat. (Pustinas); pop. 7; 69 km ENE of Daugavpils; 55°58'/27°36'.

Pustinas, *see* Pustina.

Pustkow, Pol.; pop. 40; 101 km WNW of Przemysl; 50°09'/21°30'; EDRD, GA, GUM3, GUM4, GUM5, GUM6, PHP3.

Pustokha, Ukr. BGN lists two possible localities with this name located at 49°41'/28°44' and 49°42'/29°10'. JGFF.

Pustoshka, USSR; pop. 931; 107 km SW of Leningrad; 59°13'/29°00'.

Pustynia, Pol.; pop. 8; 101 km WNW of Przemysl; 50°05'/21°27'.

Puszcza Marianska, Pol. (Puszcza Marjanska); pop. 1; 56 km SW of Warszawa; 51°59'/20°21'.

Puszcza Marjanska, *see* Puszcza Marianska.

Puszczew, Pol.; pop. 5; 26 km WNW of Czestochowa; 50°53'/18°52'.

Puszta, Hung. BGN lists two possible localities with this name located at 46°37'/20°02' and 46°48'/16°51'. HSL.

Pusztacsalad, Hung.; pop. 3; 120 km N of Nagykanizsa; 47°29'/16°54'.

Pusztadobos, Hung.; pop. 100; 107 km E of Miskolc; 48°04'/22°14'; PHH.

Pusztaederics, Hung.; pop. 2; 32 km NW of Nagykanizsa; 46°39'/16°48'.

Pusztaegres, Hung.; 88 km SSW of Budapest; 46°50'/18°31'; HSL.

Pusztafodemes, *see* Puste Ulany.

Pusztafoldvar, Hung.; pop. 2; 62 km NE of Szeged; 46°32'/20°48'.

Pusztahidegkut, Rom.; 101 km NNW of Cluj; 47°36'/23°26'; HSL. This town was located on a pre-World War I map, but does not appear in contemporary gazetteers.

Pusztakmaras, Rom.; 45 km ENE of Cluj; 46°47'/24°08'; HSL. This town was located on a pre-World War I map, but does not appear in contemporary gazetteers.

Pusztakovacsi, Hung.; pop. 20; 50 km ENE of Nagykanizsa; 46°32'/17°35'; LDS.

Pusztamagyarod, Hung.; pop. 5; 26 km NW of Nagykanizsa; 46°36'/16°50'.

Pusztamerges, Hung.; pop. 1; 38 km W of Szeged; 46°20'/19°41'.

Pusztamiske, Hung.; pop. 5; 82 km NNE of Nagykanizsa; 47°04'/17°27'.

Pusztamonostor, Hung.; pop. 9; 56 km ENE of Budapest; 47°33'/19°48'.

Pusztaradvany, Hung.; pop. 4; 56 km NNE of Miskolc; 48°28'/21°08'.

Pusztaras, HSL. This pre-World War I community was not found in BGN gazetteers.

Pusztasomorja, Hung.; pop. 5; 150 km W of Budapest; 47°47'/17°07'.

Pusztaszabolcs, Hung.; pop. 12; 50 km SSW of Budapest; 47°08'/18°46'.

Pusztatold, *see* Told.

Pusztavam, Hung.; pop. 10; 62 km WSW of Budapest; 47°26'/18°14'; EDRD.

Pusztazamor, Hung.; pop. 2; 26 km SW of Budapest; 47°24'/18°47'.

Putiatynce, *see* Putyatintsy.

Putila, Ukr.; pop. 382; 69 km SW of Chernovtsy; 48°00'/25°05';

GUM4, JGFF, PHR2.

Putineshty, Mold. (Putinesti); pop. 31; 114 km NW of Kishinev; 47°50'/28°08'.

Putinesti, *see* Putineshty.

Putivel, *see* Putivl.

Putivl, Ukr. (Putivel); pop. 341; 50 km ENE of Konotop; 51°20'/33°52'; GUM3.

Putkowice Nagorne, Pol.; pop. 3; 88 km SSW of Bialystok; 52°28'/22°36'.

Putna, Rom.; pop. 214; 234 km SSW of Cluj; 44°56'/22°11'; JGFF.

Putnok, Hung.; pop. 723; 38 km WNW of Miskolc; 48°18'/20°26'; AMG, COH, GUM4, HSL, HSL2, LDL, PHH.

Putnowice Dolne, Pol.; pop. 12; 82 km ESE of Lublin; 50°58'/23°41'.

Putnowice Gorne, Pol.; pop. 9; 82 km ESE of Lublin; 50°56'/23°42'.

Putsuntei, Mold. (Putuntei Mari); pop. 37; 50 km NNW of Kishinev; 47°23'/28°35'.

Puttelange, HSL. This pre-World War I community was not found in BGN gazetteers.

Putuntei Mari, *see* Putsuntei.

Putureni, Rom.; pop. 3; 126 km NW of Iasi; 48°07'/26°50'.

Putyatintsy, Ukr. (Putiatynce); pop. 65; 69 km SE of Lvov; 49°23'/24°39'.

Putzig, *see* Jedrzejewo; Puck.

Puze, Lat.; pop. 5; 133 km W of Riga; 57°20'/22°01'.

Puzichi, Byel. (Puzicze); pop. 16; 94 km NE of Pinsk; 52°32'/27°15'.

Puzicze, *see* Puzichi.

Puznowka, Pol.; pop. 22; 50 km ESE of Warszawa; 51°59'/21°35'.

Pyadyki, Ukr. (Piadyki); pop. 40; 69 km WNW of Chernovtsy; 48°34'/25°04'; GUM5.

Pyanovichi, Ukr. (Pianowice, Pyanovitse); pop. 23; 62 km SW of Lvov; 49°35'/23°12'.

Pyanovitse, *see* Pyanovichi.

Pyasechna, Ukr. (Piaseczna, Pisatchna, Sandberg); pop. 32; 50 km S of Lvov; 49°27'/23°58'; GUM4, JGFF, SF.

Pyasechno, Ukr. (Piaseczno); pop. 101; 88 km N of Lvov; 50°38'/24°06'.

Pyaski Stare, *see* Staryye Peski.

Pyatidorozhnoye, USSR (Bladiau); pop. 5; 38 km SW of Kaliningrad; 54°30'/20°06'.

Pyatigorsk, Byel. (Piategorsk); 56 km WSW of Vitebsk; 55°05'/29°20'; GUM5, GYLA, JGFF.

Pyatigory, Ukr. (Piatigory, Piatohor, Piatyhory, Pjatigory); pop. 244; 69 km NNW of Uman; 49°21'/29°56'; GYLA, JGFF, LDL, SF.

Pyatikhatka, *see* Pyatikhatki.

Pyatikhatki, Ukr. (Pyatikhatka); pop. 304; 94 km WSW of Dnepropetrovsk; 48°25'/33°42'.

Pyatka, Ukr. (Piatka, Pjatki, Pyatki); 94 km N of Vinnitsa; 50°01'/28°22'; SF.

Pyatki, *see* Pyatka.

Pyatnitsa, Ukr. (Pietnice); pop. 36; 88 km SW of Lvov; 49°34'/22°50'; HSL.

Pychowice, Pol.; pop. 9; 13 km S of Krakow; 50°02'/19°54'.

Pyeschanka, *see* Peschanka.

Pyeshtani, *see* Pistany.

Pyesk, *see* Piestany.

Pyetrkov, *see* Piotrkow Trybunalski.

Pylyava, *see* Pilawa.

Pynzareny, Mold. (Panzareni); pop. 15; 114 km WNW of Kishinev; 47°37'/27°41'.

Pyritz, *see* Pyrzyce.

Pyrlits, *see* Pyrlitsa.

Pyrlitsa, Mold. (Parlita, Parlita Targ, Parliti, Perlitz, Pirlitz, Pyrlits); pop. 1,064; 82 km WNW of Kishinev; 47°20'/27°53'; LDL, PHR2, SF.

Pyrzholteny, Mold. (Parjolteni); pop. 22; 50 km WNW of

Kishinev; 47°12'/28°14'.

Pyrzhota, Mold. (Parjota); pop. 21; 150 km NW of Kishinev; 47°58'/27°26'.

Pyrzyce, Pol. (Pyritz); pop. 100; 45 km SE of Szczecin; 53°08'/14°53'; CAHJP, HSL, LDS.

Pysely, Cz.; pop. 12; 32 km SE of Praha; 49°53'/14°41'.

Pyshno, Byel.; 114 km WSW of Vitebsk; 54°58'/28°29'; GUM4.

Pyskowice, *see* Pyszaca.

Pyszaca, Pol. (Peiskretscham, Pyskowice); pop. 94; 50 km SSE of Poznan; 52°04'/17°04'; GUM3, GUM4, HSL, JGFF, POCEM.

Pyszkowce, GUM3. This town was not found in BGN gazetteers under the given spelling.

Pysznica, Pol.; pop. 191; 82 km S of Lublin; 50°34'/22°08'; GUM5, PHP3.

Pytowice, Pol.; pop. 2; 50 km NNE of Czestochowa; 51°12'/19°27'.

Pyzdry, Pol. (Peisern, Peizer); pop. 406; 56 km ESE of Poznan; 52°10'/17°42'; CAHJP, EDRD, GUM4, HSL, HSL2, JGFF, LDL, LDS, PHP1, SF.

Quadrath Ichendorf, Germ.; 19 km WSW of Koln; 50°56'/06°42'; GED.

Quakenbruck, Germ.; pop. 54; 120 km W of Hannover; 52°41'/07°57'; GUM5.

Quedlinburg, Germ.; pop. 45; 101 km WNW of Leipzig; 51°47'/11°09'; HSL.

Quenstedt, Germ.; pop. 111; 75 km WNW of Leipzig; 51°42'/11°28'.

Quetzen, Germ.; pop. 12; 45 km WSW of Hannover; 52°21'/09°02'.

Raab, *see* Gyor.

Raabs an der Thaya, Aus.; pop. 3; 94 km NW of Wien; 48°51'/15°30'.

Raba, Germ.; 38 km SSW of Leipzig; 51°01'/12°05'; HSL.

Rabacsanak, Hung.; pop. 2; 126 km N of Nagykanizsa; 47°32'/17°18'.

Rabacsecseny, Hung.; pop. 5; 120 km W of Budapest; 47°35'/17°26'.

Rabafuzes, Hung.; pop. 5; 82 km NW of Nagykanizsa; 46°59'/16°17'.

Rabahidveg, Hung.; pop. 49; 75 km NNW of Nagykanizsa; 47°04'/16°45'.

Rabakecol, Hung.; pop. 13; 120 km N of Nagykanizsa; 47°26'/17°07'.

Rabakecsked, Hung.; pop. 5; 114 km N of Nagykanizsa; 47°23'/17°06'.

Rabakovacsi, Hung.; pop. 9; 88 km N of Nagykanizsa; 47°10'/16°52'.

Rabapatona, Hung.; pop. 5; 120 km W of Budapest; 47°38'/17°29'.

Rabapordany, Hung.; pop. 6; 133 km W of Budapest; 47°34'/17°20'.

Rabaszentandras, Hung.; pop. 4; 120 km W of Budapest; 47°27'/17°20'.

Rabatamasi, Hung.; pop. 2; 133 km N of Nagykanizsa; 47°35'/17°10'.

Rabatotfalu, Hung.; pop. 5; 82 km WNW of Nagykanizsa; 46°56'/16°15'.

Raba Wyzna, Pol.; pop. 23; 62 km S of Krakow; 49°34'/19°54'.

Rabber, Germ.; pop. 7; 88 km WSW of Hannover; 52°19'/08°24'.

Rabe, Pol.; pop. 53; 56 km S of Przemysl; 49°22'/22°41'.

Rabensburg, Aus.; pop. 5; 62 km NNE of Wien; 48°39'/16°54'.

Rabenstein, Germ.; 157 km NE of Munchen; 49°02'/13°12'; GUM5.

Rabiany, Pol.; pop. 19; 56 km NE of Warszawa; 52°25'/21°47'.

Rabiez, Pol.; pop. 11; 45 km WNW of Warszawa; 52°31'/20°26'.

Rabka, Pol. (Rabke); pop. 172; 56 km S of Krakow; 49°37'/19°57'; AMG, COH, EGRS, GA, GUM3, GUM4, GUM5, GUM6, LYV, PHP3, POCEM, YB.

Rabke, *see* Rabka.

Rabnita, *see* Rybnitsa.

Raca, Cz. (Racistorf, Recse); pop. 51; 13 km N of Bratislava; 48°13'/17°09'; HSL.

Racaciuni, Rom.; pop. 176; 107 km SSW of Iasi; 46°20'/26°59'.

Racadony, *see* Adony.

Racalmas, Hung.; pop. 67; 62 km S of Budapest; 47°01'/18°57'; LDS, PHH.

Racaria, *see* Rakariya.

Racas, Rom. (Almasrakos); pop. 9; 101 km W of Cluj; 46°51'/22°17'.

Race, Yug.; 75 km NNW of Zagreb; 46°27'/15°40'; HSL.

Racesti, *see* Recheshty.

Racfeherto, HSL. This pre-World War I community was not found in BGN gazetteers.

Rachanie, Pol.; pop. 78; 101 km NNE of Przemysl; 50°32'/23°33'.

Rachesti, *see* Recheshty.

Rachev, *see* Rakhov.

Rachin, *see* Rakhinya.

Rachki, *see* Raczki.

Rachlau, Germ. (Wiesdorf); 139 km ENE of Leipzig; 51°21'/14°17'; GED.

Rachmanov, *see* Rakhmanov.

Rachmanow, *see* Rakhmanov.

Rachmanowo, *see* Rakhmanov.

Rachmistrivka, *see* Rotmistrovka.

Rachodoszcze, Pol.; pop. 15; 88 km SE of Lublin; 50°38'/23°17'.

Rachov, *see* Rakhov. *See also* Rachow.

Rachow, Pol.; pop. 46; 62 km SW of Lublin; 50°54'/21°53'.

Rachtig, Germ.; pop. 31; 114 km S of Koln; 49°58'/07°00'; AMG, GED, YB.

Raciaz, Pol. (Racionz, Ratziondzh, Rotshonz); pop. 1,682; 82 km WNW of Warszawa; 52°47'/20°07'; AMG, COH, GA, GUM3, GUM4, GUM6, HSL, JGFF, LDS, PHP1, PHP4, SF, YB.

Raciazek, Pol.; 133 km NNW of Lodz; 52°52'/18°49'; HSL.

Raciborowice, Pol.; pop. 24; 88 km ESE of Lublin; 50°57'/23°46'.

Raciborz, Pol. (Ratibor); pop. 640; 101 km SSW of Czestochowa; 50°05'/18°12'; CAHJP, GA, HSL, HSL2, JGFF, LDS, PHP3.

Racin, Cz.; 146 km S of Praha; 48°51'/14°04'; HSL.

Racinovci, Yug.; pop. 2; 120 km W of Beograd; 44°52'/18°58'.

Racionz, *see* Raciaz.

Racistorf, *see* Raca.

Raciszyn, Pol.; pop. 9; 45 km NW of Czestochowa; 51°06'/18°52'.

Raciula, *see* Rechula.

Rackeresztur, Hung.; pop. 13; 32 km SSW of Budapest; 47°16'/18°50'.

Rackeve, Hung.; pop. 146; 45 km S of Budapest; 47°10'/18°57'; GUM5, LDS, PHH.

Rackova, Cz.; 75 km ENE of Brno; 49°17'/17°38'; AMG.

Raclawice (Lodz), Pol.; pop. 35; 94 km WSW of Lodz; 51°31'/18°10'; PHP4.

Raclawice (Lwow), Pol.; pop. 25; 88 km S of Lublin; 50°31'/22°10'.

Raclawowka, Pol.; pop. 10; 69 km WNW of Przemysl; 50°01'/21°55'.

Racosul de Jos, Rom. (Alsorakos); 170 km NNW of Bucuresti; 45°53'/25°34'; HSL.

Racovat, *see* Rakovets.

Racsa, Rom.; pop. 21; 120 km NNW of Cluj; 47°49'/23°21'.

Raczki, Pol. (Hornheim, Rachki, Raczkow, Ratschki, Rotchky, Rotzk); pop. 533; 101 km NNW of Bialystok; 53°59'/22°47'; AMG, COH, HSL, JGFF, LDL, PHGBW, PHP4, SF, YB.

Raczki (Lodz area), Pol.; 62 km NE of Czestochowa; 51°01'/19°54'; SF.

Raczkow, Pol. (Rashkov); 62 km WSW of Lodz; 51°41'/18°33'; SF. *See also* Raczki.

Raczkowa, Pol.; pop. 11; 50 km SW of Przemysl; 49°39'/22°11'.

Raczna, Pol.; pop. 25; 13 km SW of Krakow; 50°01'/19°45'.

Raczyna, Pol.; pop. 61; 26 km WNW of Przemysl; 49°55'/22°27'; PHP3.

Radajowice, Pol.; pop. 11; 62 km ESE of Krakow; 49°47'/20°43'.

Radau, HSL. A number of towns share this name. It was not possible to determine from available information which one is being referenced.

Radauti, Rom. (Radauts, Radautsi, Radautz, Radevitz, Radivits, Radovitch, Radovits, Radoyts); pop. 5,647; 146 km WNW of Iasi; 47°51'/25°55'; AMG, COH, EDRD, EJ, GUM3, GUM4, HSL, HSL2, JGFF, LDL, LYV, PHR2, SF.

Radauti Dorohoi, Rom.; pop. 780; 133 km NW of Iasi; 48°14'/26°48'.

Radauts, see Radauti.

Radautsi, see Radauti.

Radautz, see Radauti.

Radava, Cz. (Rendva); 88 km E of Bratislava; 48°06'/18°18'; HSL.

Radawa, Pol.; pop. 44; 45 km N of Przemysl; 50°08'/22°46'.

Radawiec Duzy, Pol. (Radawiec Wielki); pop. 10; 13 km SW of Lublin; 51°12'/22°24'.

Radawiec Wielki, see Radawiec Duzy.

Radcha, Ukr. (Radcza); pop. 21; 114 km WNW of Chernovtsy; 48°51'/24°39'.

Radchisk, Byel. (Radchysk, Radczysk); pop. 57; 38 km ESE of Pinsk; 51°57'/26°34'.

Radchysk, see Radchisk.

Radcza, see Radcha.

Radcze, Pol.; pop. 10; 62 km NNE of Lublin; 51°46'/22°59'.

Radczysk, see Radchisk.

Radeberg, Germ.; pop. 9; 114 km E of Leipzig; 51°07'/13°55'; GUM4, GUM5.

Radebeul, Germ.; pop. 12; 94 km E of Leipzig; 51°06'/13°39'.

Radeccyzna, Pol.; pop. 44; Described in the *Black Book* as being in the Lublin region of Poland, this town was not found in BGN gazetteers.

Radechov, see Radekhov.

Radecznica, Pol.; pop. 59; 56 km SSE of Lublin; 50°45'/22°50'.

Radeikai, see Radeikiai.

Radeikiai, Lith. (Radeikai, Redyk); 101 km N of Vilnius; 55°33'/25°45'; YL.

Radekhov, Ukr. (Radechov, Radikhiv, Radikhov, Radzekhuv, Radzhekhuv, Radzichov, Radziechow); pop. 1,977; 62 km NNE of Lvov; 50°17'/24°39'; CAHJP, COH, EDRD, EGRS, EJ, GUM3, GUM4, HSL, JGFF, PHP2, SF, YB.

Radenice, see Radenitse.

Radenii Vechi, see Staryye Redeny.

Radenin, Cz.; pop. 18; 88 km SSE of Praha; 49°22'/14°51'.

Radenitse, Ukr. (Radenice); pop. 45; 62 km WSW of Lvov; 49°44'/23°11'.

Radeni Vek, see Staryye Redeny.

Radenthein, Aus.; pop. 2; 120 km SE of Salzburg; 46°48'/13°43'.

Radevil, see Chervonoarmeisk.

Radevitz, see Radauti.

Radgoshtch, see Radgoszcz.

Radgoszcz, Pol. (Radgoshtch); pop. 188; 82 km ENE of Krakow; 50°12'/21°07'; HSL, PHP3, SF.

Radic, Cz.; 50 km S of Praha; 49°43'/14°25'; HSL.

Radikhiv, see Radekhov.

Radikhov, see Radekhov.

Radimin, see Radzymin.

Radimishil, see Radomysl Wielki.

Radimishle, see Radomysl Wielki.

Radimishli Gadol, see Radomysl Wielki.

Radimno, see Radymno.

Radimov, Cz.; pop. 34; 94 km SSE of Praha; 49°18'/14°40'; HSL.

Radiskis, GUM6. This town was not found in BGN gazetteers under the given spelling.

Radivil, see Chervonoarmeisk.

Radivits, see Radauti.

Radkersburg, Aus.; pop. 4; 56 km SE of Graz; 46°42'/15°59'.

Radkov, Cz. (Ratkau); 114 km NE of Brno; 49°50'/17°46'; HSL, HSL2.

Radkovice, HSL. A number of towns share this name. It was not possible to determine from available information which one is being referenced.

Radlin, Pol.; pop. 38; 107 km NNE of Krakow; 50°52'/20°46'.

Radlje Ob Dravi, Yug. (Marenberg); pop. 1; 107 km NW of Zagreb; 46°37'/15°13'.

Radlo, Cz.; pop. 1; 88 km NNE of Praha; 50°42'/15°07'.

Radlov, see Radlow.

Radlovichi, Ukr. (Radlowice); pop. 44; 69 km SW of Lvov; 49°31'/23°15'; PHP2.

Radlow, Pol. (Radlov); pop. 174; 69 km E of Krakow; 50°05'/20°51'; AMG, EGRS, GUM5, HSL, PHP3, SF.

Radlowice, see Radlovichi.

Radna, Rom.; 163 km SW of Cluj; 46°06'/21°41'; GUM3, HSL, HSL2, JGFF, PHR1.

Radnice, Cz.; pop. 39; 69 km SW of Praha; 49°51'/13°36'.

Radnot, see Radnovce.

Radnotfaja, see Iernuteni.

Radnovce, Cz. (Radnot); 88 km SW of Kosice; 48°21'/20°13'; HSL, HSL2.

Radoaia, see Radoya.

Radoboj, Yug.; pop. 4; 50 km NNW of Zagreb; 46°10'/15°55'.

Radochonce, see Radokhontsy.

Radocina, see Radocyna.

Radocyna, Pol. (Radocina); pop. 13; 107 km SW of Przemysl; 49°28'/21°23'.

Radogoszcz, Pol.; pop. 188; 13 km NNW of Lodz; 51°49'/19°27'; CAHJP, GA, GUM3, GUM4, GUM5, PHP1.

Radojewice, Pol.; pop. 101 km NE of Poznan; 52°45'/18°25'; GA.

Radokhontse, see Radokhontsy.

Radokhontsy, Ukr. (Radochonce, Radokhontse); pop. 37; 75 km WSW of Lvov; 49°41'/23°00'.

Radolfzell, Germ.; pop. 6; 120 km S of Stuttgart; 47°44'/08°58'; EDRD, PHGBW.

Radom, Pol. (Rodem); pop. 24,465; 101 km W of Lublin; 51°25'/21°09'; AMG, CAHJP, COH, EDRD, EJ, GA, GUM3, GUM4, GUM5, GUM6, GYLA, HSL, HSL2, ISH1, ISH3, JGFF, LDL, LDS, LYV, PHP1, PHP3, PHP4, POCEM, SF, YB.

Radomin, see Radzymin.

Radomishel, see Radomysl Wielki.

Radomishl, see Radomysl Wielki.

Radomishla, see Radomysl Wielki.

Radomishle, see Radomysl Wielki.

Radomishli Rabati, see Radomysl Wielki.

Radomishl Vyelki, see Radomysl Wielki.

Radomsk, see Radomsko.

Radomsko, Pol. (Naya Radomsk, Novo Radomsk, Nowo Radomsko, Radomsk); pop. 7,774; 38 km NNE of Czestochowa; 51°04'/19°27'; AMG, CAHJP, COH, EJ, GA, GUM3, GUM4, GUM5, GUM6, HSL, HSL2, ISH3, JGFF, LDL, LDS, LYV, PHP1, POCEM, SF, YB.

Radomyshl, Ukr.; pop. 4,637; 94 km W of Kiyev; 50°30'/29°14'; AMG, COH, EDRD, EJ, GYLA, HSL, JGFF, SF. *See also* Radomysl.

Radomysl, (Radomyshl); *See also* Radomyshl and the towns listed below.

Radomysl (Nad Sanem), Pol.; pop. 366; 75 km SSW of Lublin; 50°41'/21°57'; AMG, EGRS, GA, HSL, HSL2, JGFF, LDL, PHP3, SF.

Radomysl (Wolyn), Ukr.; pop. 21; 69 km WSW of Rovno; 50°33'/25°16'.

Radomysl Maly, Pol. AMG, PHP3. This town was not found in BGN gazetteers under the given spelling.

Radomysl Wielki, Pol. (Gross Radomysl, Radimishil, Radimishle, Radimishli Gadol, Radomishel, Radomishl, Radomishl Vyelki, Radomishla, Radomishle, Radomishli Rabati); pop. 1,422; 94 km ENE of Krakow; 50°12'/21°16'; AMG, EGRS, GA, GUM3, GUM4, GUM5, HSL, JGFF,

LDL, LYV, PHP3, SF, YB.

Radonice, Cz. (Radonitz); 88 km W of Praha; 50°18'/13°17'; JGFF.

Radonitz, *see* Radonice.

Radoshevka, Ukr.; 75 km S of Rovno; 49°59'/26°08'; JGFF.

Radoshin, Ukr. (Radoszyn); pop. 29; 107 km WNW of Rovno; 51°09'/24°59'; EDRD.

Radoshitz, *see* Radoszyce.

Radoshkovichi, Byel. (Radoshkovitz, Radoszkowice, Radoszkowicze); pop. 1,215; 38 km NW of Minsk; 54°09'/27°14'; COH, EDRD, EJ, GUM3, GUM4, GUM5, GUM6, HSL, HSL2, JGFF, LDL, SF, YB.

Radoshkovitz, *see* Radoshkovichi.

Radosice, Cz.; pop. 1; 82 km SSW of Praha; 49°32'/13°44'.

Radostkow, Pol.; pop. 9; 19 km N of Czestochowa; 50°55'/19°09'.

Radostyan, Hung.; pop. 6; 19 km NW of Miskolc; 48°11'/20°40'.

Radoszkowice, *see* Radoshkovichi.

Radoszkowicze, *see* Radoshkovichi.

Radoszyce, Pol. (Radoshitz); pop. 1,278; 82 km NE of Czestochowa; 51°05'/20°14'; COH, EDRD, GA, GUM3, GUM5, HSL, HSL2, LDL, LDS, PHP1, POCEM, SF.

Radoszyce (Lvov area), Pol.; pop. 41; 75 km SSW of Przemysl; 49°18'/22°04'.

Radoszyn, *see* Radoshin.

Radoszyna, Pol.; 50 km ENE of Warszawa; 52°23'/21°43'; HSL.

Radotin, Cz.; pop. 38; 19 km SSW of Praha; 49°59'/14°22'.

Radounka, Cz.; pop. 2; 114 km SSE of Praha; 49°10'/15°00'.

Radous, Cz.; pop. 2; 45 km SW of Praha; 49°51'/14°01'.

Radovis, Yug. (Radoviste); pop. 1; 94 km ESE of Skopje; 41°38'/22°28'.

Radoviste, *see* Radovis.

Radovitch, *see* Radauti.

Radovits, *see* Radauti.

Radovljica, Yug.; pop. 5; 150 km WNW of Zagreb; 46°21'/14°11'.

Radovtsy, Ukr. (Rodavetz); 56 km WSW of Vinnitsa; 49°11'/27°43'; SF.

Radowaz, Pol.; pop. 6; 101 km SSW of Lublin; 50°34'/21°40'.

Radoya, Mold. (Radoaia); pop. 93; 94 km NW of Kishinev; 47°44'/28°10'.

Radoyts, *see* Radauti.

Radruz, Pol.; pop. 83; 62 km NE of Przemysl; 50°10'/23°25'.

Raducaneni, Rom.; pop. 204; 38 km ESE of Iasi; 46°57'/27°56'; GUM4, PHR1.

Radul, Ukr.; pop. 35; 157 km N of Kiyev; 51°50'/30°42'; JGFF.

Radulenii Vechi, *see* Staryye Radulyany.

Radulesti, HSL. A number of towns share this name. It was not possible to determine from available information which one is being referenced.

Radun, Byel.; pop. 671; 88 km SW of Minsk; 53°27'/26°22'; COH, EDRD, EJ, GA, GUM3, GUM4, GUM5, GUM6, HSL, JGFF, LDL, LYV, SF.

Radutiskiai, GUM3. This town was not found in BGN gazetteers under the given spelling.

Radvan, Cz. (Radvan nad Hronom); pop. 77; 150 km W of Kosice; 48°43'/19°08'.

Radvanc, LDL. This pre-World War I community was not found in BGN gazetteers.

Radvanice, Cz.; pop. 58; 69 km NE of Brno; 49°31'/17°29'.

Radvanichi, Byel. (Radwanicze Koscielne); pop. 25; 146 km WSW of Pinsk; 52°02'/24°00'.

Radvanka, Ukr.; 189 km SSW of Lvov; 48°37'/22°19'; AMG, HSL. This town was located on a pre-World War I map, but does not appear in contemporary gazetteers.

Radvan nad Hronom, *see* Radvan.

Radvanov, Ukr. (Ruzdvyany, Ruzdwiany); pop. 45; 88 km SE of Lvov; 49°12'/24°36'.

Radvantse, Ukr. (Radwance); pop. 11; 62 km NNE of Lvov; 50°18'/24°26'.

Radvany, Cz.; 32 km S of Kosice; 48°29'/21°09'; HSL, HSL2.

This town was located on a pre-World War I map, but does not appear in contemporary gazetteers.

Radvil, *see* Chervonoarmeisk.

Radvili, *see* Radviliskis.

Radvilishok, *see* Radviliskis.

Radvilishok Nemunelis, *see* Nemunelio Radviliskis.

Radviliskis, Lith. (Radvili, Radvilishok, Radzivilishki, Radzivilishok, Radziwiliszki, Rodvilishuk); pop. 847; 19 km ESE of Siauliai; 55°49'/23°32'; AMG, GUM3, GUM5, HSL, JGFF, LDL, SF, YL.

Radwan, Pol.; pop. 28; 82 km ENE of Krakow; 50°15'/21°03'.

Radwance, *see* Radvantse.

Radwanicze Koscielne, *see* Radvanichi.

Radwanowice, Pol.; pop. 13; 19 km WNW of Krakow; 50°09'/19°44'.

Radwanowka, Pol.; pop. 36; 56 km SSW of Lublin; 50°48'/22°13'.

Radycz, HSL. This pre-World War I community was not found in BGN gazetteers.

Radymno, Pol. (Radimno, Redem, Redim); pop. 883; 26 km N of Przemysl; 49°57'/22°50'; COH, EGRS, EJ, GA, GUM3, GUM4, GUM5, GYLA, HSL, HSL2, ISH1, JGFF, LDL, LYV, PHP3, POCEM, SF.

Radyn, LDL. This pre-World War I community was not found in BGN gazetteers.

Radzanov, *see* Radzanow.

Radzanow, Pol. (Radzanov, Radznow); pop. 900; 82 km S of Warszawa; 51°34'/20°52'; AMG, COH, HSL, JGFF, LDS, PHP4, SF, YB. Shown in the *Black Book* as Radznow.

Radzekhuv, *see* Radekhov.

Radzhekhuv, *see* Radekhov.

Radzhilov, *see* Radzilow.

Radzhivilov, *see* Chervonoarmeisk.

Radzice, Pol.; 75 km ESE of Lodz; 51°28'/20°25'; GUM4.

Radzichov, *see* Radekhov.

Radzicz, Pol.; pop. 10; 88 km N of Poznan; 53°12'/17°24'.

Radziechow, *see* Radekhov; Radzikhuv.

Radziechowy, Pol.; pop. 11; 75 km SW of Krakow; 49°39'/19°08'.

Radziecin, Pol.; pop. 10; 62 km SSE of Lublin; 50°42'/22°41'.

Radziejow, Pol.; pop. 599; 107 km ENE of Poznan; 52°37'/18°32'; AMG, COH, HSL, JGFF, PHP4.

Radziejow (Lublin area), Pol.; pop. 25; 88 km E of Lublin; 51°02'/23°46'.

Radziejowa, Pol.; pop. 10; 69 km SSW of Przemysl; 49°18'/22°21'.

Radziejowice, Pol.; pop. 2; 45 km SW of Warszawa; 52°00'/20°33'; GUM4.

Radziev Kusawski, Pol. EDRD. This town was not found in BGN gazetteers under the given spelling.

Radzikhuv, Ukr. (Radziechow); pop. 37; 150 km N of Lvov; 51°10'/24°05'.

Radziki Duze, Pol.; pop. 10; 133 km SSE of Gdansk; 53°10'/19°17'.

Radzilove, *see* Radzilow.

Radzilovichi, Byel. (Radzilowicze); pop. 44; 107 km ESE of Pinsk; 51°40'/27°33'.

Radzilow, Pol. (Radzhilov, Radzilove, Rodzilova); pop. 671; 62 km WNW of Bialystok; 53°24'/22°24'; AMG, COH, GUM3, GUM4, HSL, LDS, LYV, PHP4, SF.

Radzilowicze, *see* Radzilovichi.

Radzimin, *see* Radzymin.

Radziszow, Pol.; pop. 16; 26 km S of Krakow; 49°56'/19°49'; GUM5.

Radzivilishki, *see* Radviliskis.

Radzivilishok, *see* Radviliskis.

Radzivilov, *see* Chervonoarmeisk.

Radziwie, Pol.; pop. 41; BGN lists two possible localities with this name located at 52°44'/20°35' and 52°32'/19°42'.

Radziwiliszki, *see* Radviliskis.

Radziwilka, Pol.; pop. 4; 56 km W of Warszawa; 52°19'/20°11'.

Radziwillow, *see* Chervonoarmeisk.

Radziwillowka, Pol.; pop. 16; 88 km S of Bialystok; 52°23'/23°02'; AMG.

Radzmin, *see* Radzymin.

Radznow, *see* Radzanow.

Radzymin, Pol. (Radimin, Radomin, Radzimin, Radzmin, Rodimin, Rodzamin); pop. 2,209; 26 km NNE of Warszawa; 52°25'/21°11'; AMG, EDRD, EJ, GA, GUM3, GUM4, GUM5, HSL, HSL2, LDL, LYV, PHP1, PHP4, POCEM, SF, YB.

Radzyminek, Pol.; pop. 4; 56 km WNW of Warszawa; 52°35'/20°21'.

Radzyn, *see* Radzyn Podlaski.

Radzynek, Pol.; pop. 15; 139 km WNW of Warszawa; 53°02'/19°17'.

Radzyn Podlaski, Pol. (Kozirynek, Radzyn, Rodzin); pop. 2,895; 69 km N of Lublin; 51°47'/22°37'; AMG, CAHJP, COH, EDRD, EJ, GA, GUM3, GUM4, GUM5, GUM6, GYLA, HSL, HSL2, LDL, LDS, PHP3, PHP4, POCEM, SF, YB.

Rae, *see* Raekula.

Raekula, Est. (Rae); 126 km S of Tallinn; 58°21'/24°34'; PHLE.

Raesfeld, Germ.; 94 km N of Koln; 51°46'/06°51'; GED.

Rafajlowa, Ukr.; pop. 32; 126 km WSW of Chernovtsy; 48°05'/24°15'. This town was located on an interwar map of Poland but does not appear in contemporary gazetteers. Map coordinates are approximate.

Rafalovka, Ukr. (Rafalowka); pop. 556; 88 km NNW of Rovno; 51°22'/25°52'; AMG, EDRD, GUM3, GUM4, JGFF, LYV, SF. There is a second town of Rafalovka nearby at 51°19'/25°59'. The population figure combines the two.

Rafalowka, *see* Rafalovka.

Ragaly, Hung.; pop. 16; 38 km NW of Miskolc; 48°24'/20°31'; HSL.

Ragendorf, *see* Rajka.

Raggendorf, Aus.; pop. 4; 32 km NE of Wien; 48°23'/16°40'.

Ragla, Rom.; pop. 20; 82 km NE of Cluj; 47°04'/24°37'.

Ragne, *see* Rodna.

Ragola, *see* Ariogala.

Ragole, *possibly* Ariogala.

Ragova, *see* Raguva.

Ragusa, *see* Dubrovnik.

Raguva, Lith. (Ragova, Rogov, Rogove, Roguva); pop. 593; 88 km NNE of Kaunas; 55°34'/24°36'; GUM3, GUM5, HSL, HSL2, LDL, SF, YL.

Rahden, Germ.; pop. 60; 75 km W of Hannover; 52°26'/08°37'.

Rahlstedt, Germ.; pop. 5; 13 km NE of Hamburg; 53°36'/10°10'.

Raho, *see* Rakhov.

Rahov, *see* Rakhov.

Rahovo, *see* Rakhov.

Raigorod, (Raigrod, Raygrod); EDRD, JGFF. This town was not found in BGN gazetteers under the given spelling.

Raigorodok, *see* Raygorodok.

Raigrod, *see* Raigorod.

Raileanca, *see* Roylyanka.

Raileni, *see* Yuryevka.

Rain, Germ.; 75 km NW of Munchen; 48°41'/10°54'; PHGB.

Rainiai, Lith.; 62 km W of Siauliai; 55°58'/22°18'; GUM3.

Rajbrot, Pol. (Robret); pop. 31; 50 km ESE of Krakow; 49°50'/20°29'; HSL, SF.

Rajcza, Pol. (Reitcha); pop. 132; 88 km SSW of Krakow; 49°30'/19°07'; HSL, PHP3, SF.

Rajec, Cz.; pop. 85; 146 km E of Brno; 49°05'/18°38'.

Rajevo Selo, Yug.; pop. 6; 133 km W of Beograd; 44°56'/18°47'.

Rajgrod, Pol.; pop. 745; 75 km NW of Bialystok; 53°44'/22°42'; GA, GUM3, HSL, JGFF, LDL, LDS, PHP4, SF.

Rajgrodek, *see* Raygorodok.

Rajhenburg, *see* Brestanica.

Rajka, Hung. (Ragendorf); pop. 136; 150 km WNW of Budapest; 48°00'/17°12'; AMG, EJ, HSL, HSL2, JGFF, LDL, LDS, PHH.

Rajlovac, Yug.; pop. 41; 208 km SW of Beograd; 43°52'/18°19'.

Rajsk, Pol.; pop. 4; 38 km S of Bialystok; 52°51'/23°09'; GUM4.

Rajskie, *see* Rajskie Sakowczyk.

Rajskie Sakowczyk, Pol. (Rajskie); pop. 58; 62 km S of Przemysl; 49°19'/22°29'.

Rajsko, Pol.; 19 km SSE of Krakow; 49°59'/19°59'; GUM4, GUM5.

Rajsko Duze, Pol.; pop. 7; 56 km SSE of Lodz; 51°17'/19°41'.

Rajszew, Pol.; pop. 1; 19 km NW of Warszawa; 52°23'/20°51'.

Rajtarowice, *see* Verkhovtsy.

Rakaca, Hung.; pop. 28; 50 km N of Miskolc; 48°28'/20°54'; HSL.

Rakacaszend, Hung.; pop. 38; 50 km N of Miskolc; 48°28'/20°51'.

Rakamaz, Hung.; pop. 170; 50 km ENE of Miskolc; 48°08'/21°28'; HSL, PHH.

Rakariya, Mold. (Racaria); pop. 23; 139 km NW of Kishinev; 47°55'/27°37'.

Rakasz, *see* Rokosov.

Rakhin, *see* Rakhinya.

Rakhinya, Ukr. (Rachin, Rakhin); pop. 41; 101 km S of Lvov; 49°00'/24°02'.

Rakhmanov, Ukr. (Rachmanov, Rachmanow, Rachmanowo); pop. 62; 56 km S of Rovno; 50°08'/26°06'; SF.

Rakhov, Ukr. (Akna Raho, Berlebas, Bocsko Raho, Rachev, Rachov, Raho, Rahov, Rahovo); pop. 9,455; 133 km WSW of Chernovtsy; 48°03'/24°12'; AMG, COH, GUM3, GUM4, GUM6, HSL, HSL2, JGFF, LDL, SF, SM, YB.

Rakishik, *see* Rokiskis.

Rakishki, *see* Rokiskis.

Rakishok, *see* Rokiskis.

Rakiski, *see* Rokiskis.

Rakiszki, *see* Rokiskis.

Rakita, Ukr. (Rokita); 170 km WNW of Rovno; 51°34'/24°22'; GUM5.

Rakitin, *see* Rakitina.

Rakitina, Ukr. (Rakitin); pop. 2,559; 251 km NE of Konotop; 52°20'/36°27'.

Rakobuty, Ukr.; pop. 6; 45 km NE of Lvov; 50°00'/24°33'.

Rakoczifalva, Hung.; pop. 1; 101 km ESE of Budapest; 47°05'/20°14'.

Rakolupy, Pol.; pop. 97; 69 km ESE of Lublin; 50°58'/23°27'; GUM5.

Rakoniewice, Pol. (Rakwitz); pop. 22; 56 km SW of Poznan; 52°08'/16°18'; CAHJP, HSL.

Rakonitz, *see* Rakovnik.

Rakos, Hung.; 32 km ENE of Szeged; 46°18'/20°36'; HSL, HSL2.

Rakoscsaba, Hung.; pop. 221; 19 km E of Budapest; 47°29'/19°17'; PHH.

Rakoshegy, Hung.; pop. 251; 13 km ESE of Budapest; 47°28'/19°14'.

Rakoshino, Ukr. (Rakosin); pop. 400; 182 km SSW of Lvov; 48°28'/22°36'; AMG, HSL.

Rakosin, *see* Rakoshino.

Rakoskeresztur, Hung.; pop. 229; 13 km E of Budapest; 47°29'/19°15'; GUM5, HSL, PHH.

Rakosliget, Hung.; pop. 268; 19 km E of Budapest; 47°29'/19°16'; PHH.

Rakospalota, Hung.; pop. 2,567; 13 km NNE of Budapest; 47°34'/19°08'; AMG, COH, GUM5, HSL, LDL, PHH, YB.

Rakosszentmihaly, Hung.; pop. 829; 6 km NE of Budapest; 47°32'/19°10'; GUM5, PHH.

Rakoszyn, Pol.; pop. 11; 69 km E of Czestochowa; 50°39'/20°06'.

Rakottyas, *see* Rokytnik.

Rakov, SF. A number of towns share this name. It was not possible to determine from available information which one is being referenced.

Rakovchyk, Ukr. (Rakowczyk); pop. 30; 82 km WNW of Chernovtsy; 48°36'/24°57'.

Rakovec, AMG. A number of towns share this name. It was not possible to determine from available information which one is being referenced.

Rakovets, Mold. (Racovat, Rakowiec); pop. 37; 126 km NNW of Kishinev; 48°06'/28°24'.

Rakovets (Lwow), Ukr.; 32 km S of Lvov; 49°39'/24°01'; BLBK.

Rakovets (near Bogorodchany), Ukr.; pop. 34; 126 km WNW of Chernovtsy; 48°43'/24°23'.

Rakovets (near Gorodenka), Ukr.; pop. 68; 69 km NW of Chernovtsy; 48°48'/25°18'; COH.

Rakovice, HSL. A number of towns share this name. It was not possible to determine from available information which one is being referenced.

Rakovnik, Cz. (Rakonitz); pop. 188; 50 km W of Praha; 50°06'/13°45'; HSL.

Rakovo, Cz. (Nagyrakocz); 157 km NE of Bratislava; 48°59'/18°53'; HSL.

Rakow, Pol.; pop. 1,112; 101 km NE of Krakow; 50°41'/21°03'; CAHJP, COH, FRG, GA, GUM3, GUM5, JGFF, PHP1, POCEM, SF, WS, YB. SF refers to a Rakov close to Minsk that does not appear in contemporary gazetteers.

Rakow (near Jedrzejow), Pol.; pop. 111; 75 km NNE of Krakow; 50°39'/20°23'; LYV.

Rakow (near Volozhin), Byel.; pop. 1,421; 38 km W of Minsk; 53°58'/27°03'; COH, EDRD, EJ, GUM3, GUM4, GUM6, HSL, LDL, LYV.

Rakowa, Pol.; pop. 60; 38 km SW of Przemysl; 49°34'/22°24'; JGFF.

Rakowczyk, *see* Rakovchyk.

Rakowice, Pol.; pop. 34; 6 km E of Krakow; 50°05'/19°59'; GUM4, GUM5, PHP3.

Rakowiec, *see* Rakovets.

Raksa, Cz.; 150 km NE of Bratislava; 48°53'/18°53'; HSL.

Raksi, Hung.; pop. 6; 75 km ENE of Nagykanizsa; 46°31'/17°55'.

Rakszawa, Pol.; pop. 90; 56 km NW of Przemysl; 50°09'/22°15'.

Rakvere, Est. (Vezenberg, Wesenberg); pop. 100; 88 km E of Tallinn; 59°22'/26°20'; PHLE.

Rakwitz, *see* Rakoniewice.

Ralevka, Ukr. (Ralow?); pop. 34; 69 km SW of Lvov; 49°31'/23°15'.

Ralow, *possibly* Ralevka.

Ramazan, *see* Ramazany.

Ramazany, Mold. (Ramazan); pop. 4; 146 km NW of Kishinev; 47°59'/27°37'.

Ramgola, *see* Ramygala.

Ramien (near Radom), GUM5. This town was not found in BGN gazetteers under the given spelling.

Ramnicu Valcea, HSL, PHR1. This town was not found in BGN gazetteers under the given spelling.

Ramocsahaza, Hung.; pop. 117; 94 km E of Miskolc; 48°03'/22°00'; HSL.

Ramsbeck, Germ.; 107 km NE of Koln; 51°19'/08°24'; GUM5.

Ramsberg, Germ.; 45 km S of Nurnberg; 49°07'/10°56'; GUM3.

Ramuli, Lat.; pop. 4; 82 km NE of Riga; 57°13'/25°22'.

Ramygala, Lith. (Ramgola, Ramygola, Remigola); pop. 480; 75 km N of Kaunas; 55°31'/24°18'; HSL, JGFF, SF, YL.

Ramygola, *see* Ramygala.

Randegg, Germ.; pop. 79; 120 km S of Stuttgart; 47°43'/08°45'; EDRD, HSL, HSL2, JGFF, LDS, PHGBW.

Randersacker, Germ.; 88 km WNW of Nurnberg; 49°46'/09°59'; PHGB.

Ranischau, *possibly* Ranizow.

Ranizov, *see* Wola Ranizowska.

Ranizow, Pol. (Ranischau?); pop. 218; 75 km WNW of Przemysl; 50°16'/21°59'; AMG, EGRS, GUM5, LDL, PHP3.

Ranka, Lat. (Rankas); pop. 16; 126 km ENE of Riga; 57°13'/26°11'.

Rankas, *see* Ranka.

Rankweil, Aus.; pop. 1; 133 km W of Innsbruck; 47°17'/09°39'.

Ranstadt, Germ.; 38 km NNE of Frankfurt am Main; 50°21'/08°59'; JGFF.

Raona, HSL. This pre-World War I community was not found

in BGN gazetteers.

Rapa de Jos, *see* Ripa de Jos.

Rapa de Sus, *see* Ripa de Sus.

Rapel, *see* Rapla.

Rapla, Est. (Odenwald, Rapel, Rappel); 50 km S of Tallinn; 59°01'/24°47'; PHLE.

Rapolt, Hung.; pop. 9; 133 km E of Miskolc; 47°55'/22°34'.

Rappel, *see* Rapla.

Rappenau, *see* Bad Rappenau.

Rapsach, Cz.; pop. 6; 126 km WSW of Brno; 48°53'/14°57'.

Rapujineti, *see* Repuzhintsy.

Rapy Dylanskie, Pol.; pop. 4; 75 km SSE of Lublin; 50°36'/22°45'.

Raro, *possibly* Raros.

Raros, Hung. (Raro?); pop. 28; 38 km NNE of Szeged; 46°31'/20°24'; HSL.

Ras, *see* Rasice.

Rascaeti, *see* Raskaytsy.

Rascani Targ, *see* Ryshkany.

Raschkow, *see* Raszkow.

Rascruci, Rom.; pop. 7; 26 km NNE of Cluj; 46°55'/23°46'.

Rasdelnaja, *see* Razdelnaya.

Rasdelnaya, *see* Razdelnaya.

Rasein, *see* Raseiniai.

Raseinai, *see* Raseiniai.

Raseiniai, Lith. (Rasein, Raseinai, Rasseyn, Resein, Rosienie, Rossein, Rossieny); pop. 2,035; 69 km WNW of Kaunas; 55°22'/23°07'; AMG, COH, EJ, GUM3, GUM5, HSL, HSL2, LDL, SF, YL.

Rasgrad, *see* Razgrad.

Rashin, *see* Raszyn.

Rashkev, *see* Vad Rashkov.

Rashkov, Mold.; pop. 2,020; 114 km N of Kishinev; 47°57'/28°50'; EJ, LDL, SF. *See also* Raczkow.

Rasiadz, LDL. This pre-World War I community was not found in BGN gazetteers.

Rasice, Cz. (Ras); 75 km SW of Kosice; 48°28'/20°15'; HSL.

Rasina, Est. (Razina); 38 km ESE of Tartu; 58°12'/27°15'; LDL.

Rasinja, Yug.; pop. 3; 69 km NE of Zagreb; 46°11'/16°43'.

Rasiska, *see* Rozsoska.

Raskaytsy, Mold. (Rascaeti); pop. 36; 88 km ESE of Kishinev; 46°36'/29°47'.

Rasna, *see* Ryasno.

Rasony, *see* Rasonysapberencs.

Rasonysapberencs, Hung. (Abaujsap, Rasony, Szarazberencs); pop. 4; 32 km NNE of Miskolc; 48°19'/21°00'.

Raspenava, Cz.; pop. 6; 101 km NNE of Praha; 50°54'/15°08'.

Raspopeni, *see* Raspopeny.

Raspopeny, Mold. (Raspopeni); pop. 158; 88 km NNW of Kishinev; 47°45'/28°36'.

Rasseyn, *see* Raseiniai.

Rastatt, Germ.; pop. 197; 75 km W of Stuttgart; 48°51'/08°12'; GUM5, PHGBW.

Rastede, Germ.; pop. 22; 126 km WSW of Hamburg; 53°15'/08°12'.

Rastenburg, *see* Ketrzyn.

Rastice, Cz. (Gross Magendorf, Haluboki, Hluboki, Nagymagyar); 26 km E of Bratislava; 48°07'/17°25'; AMG, COH, HSL, HSL2, YB.

Rastoace, Rom.; pop. 71; GUM4. This town was not found in BGN gazetteers under the given spelling.

Rastoci, Rom.; pop. 10; 69 km N of Cluj; 47°22'/23°32'.

Rastolita, Rom.; pop. 93; 114 km ENE of Cluj; 46°59'/25°02'.

Rastov, Ukr. (Rastow, Rastuv); pop. 16; 139 km WNW of Rovno; 51°07'/24°26'.

Rastow, *see* Rastov.

Rastuv, *see* Rastov.

Raszitocsno, *see* Raztocno.

Raszkow, Pol. (Raschkow); BGN lists two possible localities with this name located at 50°35'/19°56' and 51°43'/17°44'.

JGFF, PHP2.

Raszocska, *see* Rozsoska.

Raszyn, Pol. (Rashin); pop. 63; 19 km SSW of Warszawa; 52°09'/20°55'; HSL, HSL2, SF.

Rataje Slupskie, Pol.; pop. 15; 82 km NE of Krakow; 50°19'/21°03'.

Ratchev, *see* Rogachev.

Ratenice, Cz.; pop. 6; 45 km E of Praha; 50°05'/15°04'.

Rathenow, Germ.; pop. 100; 75 km W of Berlin; 52°36'/12°20'; GUM3, LDS.

Ratibor, *see* Raciborz.

Ratin, Rom.; pop. 10; 75 km WNW of Cluj; 47°11'/22°51'.

Ratingen, Germ.; pop. 18; 45 km NNW of Koln; 51°18'/06°51'.

Ratisbon, *see* Regensburg.

Ratka, Hung.; 38 km NE of Miskolc; 48°13'/21°14'; COH, HSL.

Ratkau, *see* Radkov.

Ratkobisztro, *see* Ratkovske Bystre.

Ratkogomor, *see* Ratkova.

Ratkoszirak, HSL. This pre-World War I community was not found in BGN gazetteers.

Ratkoszuha, *see* Ratkovska Sucha.

Ratkova, Cz. (Ratkogomor); 88 km WSW of Kosice; 48°35'/20°06'; HSL.

Ratkovo, Yug. (Parabuc); pop. 26; 114 km WNW of Beograd; 45°27'/19°21'; PHY.

Ratkovska Bystre, *see* Ratkovske Bystre.

Ratkovska Sucha, Cz. (Ratkoszuha); 88 km WSW of Kosice; 48°35'/20°04'; HSL.

Ratkovske Bystre, Cz. (Ratkobisztro, Ratkovska Bystre); 88 km WSW of Kosice; 48°39'/20°03'; HSL.

Ratndorf, Ukr.; 195 km SSW of Dnepropetrovsk; 47°02'/33°19'.

Ratne, *see* Ratno.

Ratniceni, Lat. (Brigi, Brigu); pop. 27; 88 km ESE of Riga; 56°41'/25°24'.

Ratno, Ukr. (Ratne, Rotno); pop. 1,554; 170 km WNW of Rovno; 51°40'/24°31'; COH, EDRD, FRG, GUM3, GUM4, GUM5, HSL, JGFF, LDL, SF, YB.

Ratnycia, Lith. (Rotnica, Rotnitza); pop. 24; 107 km S of Kaunas; 54°00'/24°01'; COH, HSL, SF.

Ratosnya, Rom.; 107 km ENE of Cluj; 46°50'/25°00'; HSL. This town was located on a pre-World War I map, but does not appear in contemporary gazetteers.

Ratowo Piotrowo, Pol.; pop. 5; 82 km WSW of Bialystok; 53°04'/22°00'.

Ratschki, *see* Raczki.

Rattersdorf, Aus.; pop. 1; 88 km NE of Graz; 47°24'/16°30'.

Ratulow, Pol.; pop. 15; 88 km S of Krakow; 49°22'/19°54'.

Ratzebuhr, *see* Okonek.

Ratzeburg, Germ.; 56 km NE of Hamburg; 53°42'/10°46'; GUM3.

Ratziondzh, *see* Raciaz.

Rauchenwarth, Aus.; pop. 1; 19 km SE of Wien; 48°05'/16°31'.

Rauchersdorf, Pol.; pop. 29; 82 km NNW of Przemysl; 50°30'/22°22'.

Rauchwart im Burgenland, Aus.; pop. 4; 56 km ENE of Graz; 47°08'/16°14'.

Raudenai, Lith.; pop. 38; 38 km W of Siauliai; 56°01'/22°43'.

Raudenes, *see* Raudone.

Raudenis, *see* Raudone.

Raudnitz, *see* Rudzienice.

Raudnitz an der Elbe, *see* Roudnice nad Labem.

Raudondvaris, Lith. (Royter Hoyf); pop. 55; 13 km WNW of Kaunas; 54°56'/23°48'; GUM3, JGFF, YL.

Raudone, Lith. (Raudenes, Raudenis); pop. 80; 56 km WNW of Kaunas; 55°06'/23°08'; YL.

Rauischholzhausen, Germ.; 82 km N of Frankfurt am Main; 50°45'/08°53'; LDS.

Raum Bremerhaven, YB. This town was not found in BGN gazetteers under the given spelling.

Rauna, Lat. (Ronneburg, Ronnenburg); pop. 12; 101 km NE of Riga; 57°20'/25°37'; AMG.

Rauschenberg, Germ.; pop. 40; 94 km N of Frankfurt am Main; 50°53'/08°55'; HSL, LDS.

Rausnitz, HSL, HSL2. This pre-World War I community was not found in BGN gazetteers.

Rautel, *see* Reutsel.

Rauza, Lat. (Rauzas); pop. 2; 133 km NE of Riga; 57°24'/26°06'.

Rauzas, *see* Rauza.

Rava, *see* Rawa Mazowiecka.

Rava Mazovietzk, *see* Rawa Mazowiecka.

Rava Ruska, *see* Rava Russkaya.

Rava Russkaya, Ukr. (Rava Ruska, Rave, Ravi, Rawa Ruska); pop. 5,048; 50 km NW of Lvov; 50°15'/23°37'; AMG, COH, EDRD, EGRS, GUM3, GUM4, GUM5, HSL, HSL2, JGFF, LDL, PHP2, SF, YB.

Ravazd, Hung.; pop. 9; 101 km W of Budapest; 47°31'/17°45'.

Rave, *see* Rava Russkaya.

Ravelsbach, Aus.; pop. 6; 56 km NW of Wien; 48°33'/15°51'.

Rave Mazovyetsk, *see* Rawa Mazowiecka.

Ravensbruck, Germ.; 82 km NNW of Berlin; 53°12'/13°09'; AMG, GUM3, GUM4, GUM5, GUM6, PHGBW, PHP1, PHP3. Most sources refer to the Ravensbruck concentration camp.

Ravensburg, Germ.; pop. 35; 114 km SSE of Stuttgart; 47°47'/09°37'; EDRD, EJ, GUM3, PHGBW.

Ravi, *see* Rava Russkaya.

Ravne na Koroskem, Yug. (Gustanj); pop. 1; 120 km NW of Zagreb; 46°33'/14°58'.

Ravnitsa, *see* Ribnitsa.

Rawa Mazowiecka, Pol. (Rava, Rava Mazovietzk, Rave Mazovyetsk, Rawa Mazowiecki); pop. 3,018; 56 km ENE of Lodz; 51°46'/20°15'; AMG, CAHJP, COH, EDRD, GA, GUM3, GUM4, GUM5, HSL, HSL2, JGFF, LDL, LDS, LYV, PHP1, PHP4, POCEM, SF.

Rawa Ruska, *see* Rava Russkaya.

Rawicz, Pol. (Rawitsch); pop. 139; 69 km NNW of Wroclaw; 51°37'/16°52'; AMG, CAHJP, EJ, GA, GUM3, GUM4, GUM6, HSL, HSL2, JGFF, LDL, YB.

Rawitsch, *see* Rawicz.

Rawy, Pol. (Kurzatki Rawy); pop. 20; 88 km N of Warszawa; 53°02'/21°16'.

Raygorodok, Ukr. (Krasny Gorodok, Raigorodok, Rajgrodek); 157 km SE of Kharkov; 48°54'/37°43'; GYLA, SF.

Raygrod, *see* Raigorod.

Rayov, *see* Rejow.

Raysha, *see* Rzeszow.

Rayshe, *see* Rzeszow.

Raytarovitse, *see* Verkhovtsy.

Rayvits, *see* Rejowiec.

Rayvitz, *see* Rejowiec.

Razalimas, *see* Rozalimas.

Razbuneni, Rom.; pop. 20; 50 km N of Cluj; 47°09'/23°42'.

Razdelnaja, *see* Razdelnaya.

Razdelnaya, Ukr. (Rasdelnaja, Rasdelnaya, Razdelnaja); pop. 200; 62 km WNW of Odessa; 46°51'/30°05'; EDRD, SF.

Razesi, *see* Sarata Rezeshty.

Razgrad, Bulg. (Rasgrad); pop. 656; 120 km WNW of Varna; 43°32'/26°31'; EJ.

Razhnyatov, *see* Rozhnyuv.

Razhnyuv, Ukr. (Razniow); pop. 26; 75 km NE of Lvov; 50°04'/24°57'.

Razina, *see* Rasina.

Razino, Rom.; pop. 5; HSL. A number of towns share this name. It was not possible to determine from available information which one is being referenced.

Razniow, *see* Razhnyuv.

Razoare, Rom.; pop. 23; 82 km N of Cluj; 47°27'/23°47'.

Raztocno, Cz. (Raszitocsno); 139 km NE of Bratislava; 48°46'/18°46'; HSL.

Rchichtchev, *see* Rzhishchev.

Rdzawka, Pol.; 62 km S of Krakow; 49°35'/19°59'; JGFF.

Rebielice Szlacheckie, Pol.; pop. 47; 32 km NW of Czestochowa; 51°01'/18°51'.

Rebkow, Pol.; pop. 7; 56 km ESE of Warszawa; 51°53'/21°34'; HSL.

Rebra, Rom.; pop. 26; 94 km NE of Cluj; 47°19'/24°30'.

Rebreanu, Rom. (Entradam, Jidovita); pop. 135; 88 km NE of Cluj; 47°17'/24°26'; EJ, HSL, PHR2.

Rebrin, Cz.; 50 km E of Kosice; 48°42'/21°59'; HSL.

Rebrisoara, Rom. (Kisrebra); pop. 75; 88 km NE of Cluj; 47°17'/24°27'; HSL.

Rebzevits, see Rubezhevichi.

Reca, Cz. (Rega, Rethe); 32 km NE of Bratislava; 48°14'/17°28'; COH, HSL.

Recea, see Recha.

Recea Cristur, Rom.; pop. 17; 38 km NNW of Cluj; 47°04'/23°32'.

Recha, Mold. (Recea); pop. 28; BGN lists two possible localities with this name located at 47°13'/28°35' and 47°54'/27°41'.

Recheshty, Mold. (Racesti, Rachesti); pop. 24; 94 km NNW of Kishinev; 47°47'/28°34'.

Rechitsa, Byel. (Rzeczyca); pop. 7,386; 45 km WSW of Gomel; 52°22'/30°23'; EDRD, EJ, HSL, JGFF, SF.

Rechitsa (near Luninets), Byel.; pop. 53; 50 km ESE of Pinsk; 51°51'/26°48'.

Rechitsa (near Sarny), Ukr.; pop. 38; 133 km N of Rovno; 51°46'/26°33'.

Rechki, Ukr. (Rzyczki); pop. 30; 50 km NW of Lvov; 50°17'/23°39'.

Rechnitz, Aus. (Rohonc); pop. 170; 82 km NE of Graz; 47°18'/16°27'; GUM4, GUM5, HSL, HSL2, LDS.

Rechta, Pol.; pop. 29; 26 km S of Lublin; 51°03'/22°26'.

Rechula, Mold. (Raciula); pop. 20; 50 km WNW of Kishinev; 47°18'/28°21'.

Reci, Rom.; pop. 6; 163 km N of Bucuresti; 45°51'/25°56'.

Reckendorf, Germ.; pop. 20; 69 km NNW of Nurnberg; 50°01'/10°50'; GUM5, HSL, JGFF, PHGB.

Recklinghausen, Germ.; pop. 280; 82 km N of Koln; 51°37'/07°12'; AMG, EJ, GED, GUM3, GUM5, YB.

Recse, see Raca.

Recseny, HSL. This pre-World War I community was not found in BGN gazetteers.

Recsk, Hung.; pop. 48; 50 km SW of Miskolc; 47°56'/20°07'; HSL.

Recske, see Riecka.

Reczajska Wola, see Wola Reczajska.

Reczno, Pol.; pop. 8; 69 km NE of Czestochowa; 51°11'/19°52'; GUM5.

Reczpol, Pol.; pop. 26; 26 km SSW of Przemysl; 49°37'/22°36'.

Rede, Hung.; pop. 22; 88 km WSW of Budapest; 47°26'/17°55'; HSL.

Redem, see Radymno.

Redeni, see Redeny.

Redeny, Mold. (Redeni); pop. 30; 62 km WNW of Kishinev; 47°24'/28°13'.

Redics, Hung.; pop. 1; 45 km WNW of Nagykanizsa; 46°37'/16°30'.

Redim, see Radymno.

Rediu Mare, see Redyu Mare.

Redwitz, see Redwitz an der Rodach.

Redwitz an der Rodach, Germ. (Redwitz); 82 km N of Nurnberg; 50°10'/11°12'; CAHJP, PHGB.

Redyk, see Radeikiai.

Redyu Mare, Mold. (Rediu Mare); pop. 38; 170 km NW of Kishinev; 48°14'/27°31'.

Redzen Nowy, Pol.; pop. 5; 26 km E of Lodz; 51°43'/19°52'.

Redziny, Pol.; pop. 76; A number of towns share this name. It was not possible to determine from available information which one is being referenced.

Redziny Zabigalskie, Pol. (Redziny Zbigalskie); pop. 7; 38 km NNE of Krakow; 50°23'/20°14'.

Redziny Zbigalskie, see Redziny Zabigalskie.

Rees, Germ.; pop. 41; 101 km NNW of Koln; 51°46'/06°24'.

Reformatuskovacshaza, Hung.; pop. 34; 56 km NE of Szeged; 46°25'/20°54'.

Rega, see Reca.

Regat; Not a town, but a section of southern Romania.

Regensburg, Germ. (Ratisbon); pop. 427; 88 km ESE of Nurnberg; 49°01'/12°06'; AMG, CAHJP, EJ, GUM3, GUM4, GUM5, HSL, HSL2, JGFF, PHGB.

Regensheim, HSL. This pre-World War I community was not found in BGN gazetteers.

Regenstauf, Germ.; pop. 4; 88 km ESE of Nurnberg; 49°08'/12°08'.

Regenwalde, see Resko.

Regenye, Hung.; pop. 4; 101 km ESE of Nagykanizsa; 45°58'/18°10'.

Reghin, Rom. (Sachsisch Reen, Saechsisch Regen, Szaszregen); pop. 1,587; 88 km E of Cluj; 46°46'/24°42'; AMG, COH, EJ, HSL, HSL2, LDL, PHR2.

Regina Maria, see Semenovka (Bessarabia).

Regingen, HSL. This pre-World War I community was not found in BGN gazetteers.

Regmec, see Alsoregmec.

Regmitz, see Alsoregmec.

Regnow, Pol.; pop. 21; 62 km E of Lodz; 51°45'/20°23'.

Regoce, see Ridica.

Regoly, Hung.; pop. 21; 114 km SSW of Budapest; 46°35'/18°25'.

Regulice, Pol.; pop. 6; 26 km W of Krakow; 50°06'/19°32'.

Rehau, Germ.; 114 km NNE of Nurnberg; 50°15'/12°02'; GUM3, PHGB.

Rehburg, Germ.; pop. 25; 32 km WNW of Hannover; 52°28'/09°14'.

Rehden, Germ.; pop. 2; 88 km WNW of Hannover; 52°37'/08°29'.

Rehlovice, Cz.; pop. 1; 69 km NW of Praha; 50°36'/13°57'.

Rehna, Germ.; 75 km NE of Hamburg; 53°47'/11°03'; LDS.

Rehweiler, Germ.; pop. 2; 56 km WNW of Nurnberg; 49°46'/10°26'; PHGB.

Reichelsheim, Germ.; pop. 115; 50 km SSE of Frankfurt am Main; 49°43'/08°51'; AMG, JGFF.

Reichenau, Aus.; pop. 24; 69 km SSW of Wien; 47°42'/15°50'. See also Rychnov nad Kneznou.

Reichenau (Czechoslovakia), GUM3, GUM4, GUM5, HSL, HSL2. This pre-World War I community was not found in BGN gazetteers.

Reichenbach, Germ.; pop. 36; A number of towns share this name. It was not possible to determine from available information which one is being referenced. See also Dzierzoniow.

Reichenbach (Im Saale), Germ.; pop. 19; 82 km S of Leipzig; 50°37'/12°18'.

Reichenberg, Germ.; pop. 47; 88 km WNW of Nurnberg; 49°44'/09°55'; AMG, GUM5, HSL, HSL2, PHGB.

Reichenborn, Germ.; pop. 8; 62 km NW of Frankfurt am Main; 50°32'/08°11'.

Reichenburg, see Brestanica.

Reichensachsen, Germ.; pop. 86; 146 km NNE of Frankfurt am Main; 51°09'/10°00'; CAHJP, HSL.

Reichertshofen, Germ.; pop. 1; 75 km W of Munchen; 48°12'/10°36'; PHGB.

Reichmannsdorf, Germ.; 50 km NW of Nurnberg; 49°47'/10°42'; PHGB.

Reichraming, Aus.; pop. 1; 107 km ENE of Salzburg; 47°53'/14°27'.

Reichshof, Pol.; pop. 21; 88 km WNW of Przemysl; 50°05'/21°35'. This town was located on an interwar map of Poland but does not appear in contemporary gazetteers. Map coordinates are approximate.

Reichshof, see Rzeszow.

Reifenberg, Germ.; 38 km N of Nurnberg; 49°45'/11°08'; PHGB.

Reilingen, Germ.; pop. 21; 75 km NW of Stuttgart; 49°18'/08°34'; HSL, LDS, PHGBW.

Reilsheim, Germ.; 69 km NW of Stuttgart; 49°21'/08°47'; JGFF.

Reimerswalde, *see* Lesnowo.

Reinheim, Germ.; pop. 70; 38 km SSE of Frankfurt am Main; 49°49'/08°50'; LDS.

Reinzov, *see* Wola Ranizowska.

Reisen, *see* Rydzyna.

Reisha, *see* Rzeszow.

Reiskirchen, Germ.; pop. 38; 62 km N of Frankfurt am Main; 50°36'/08°50'; LDS.

Reistenhausen, Germ.; 62 km ESE of Frankfurt am Main; 49°46'/09°19'; PHGB.

Reitberg, Germ.; 101 km SW of Hamburg; 53°15'/08°34'; LDS.

Reitcha, *see* Rajcza.

Reiu, Germ. PHLE. This town was not found in BGN gazetteers under the given spelling.

Rejckov, Cz.; pop. 5; 82 km ESE of Praha; 49°37'/15°19'.

Rejow, Pol. (Rayov); 120 km ESE of Lodz; 51°06'/20°50'; SF.

Rejowiec, Pol. (Rayvits, Rayvitz, Reyovyets, Reyvits); pop. 1,827; 56 km ESE of Lublin; 51°05'/23°17'; AMG, COH, GA, GUM3, GUM4, GUM5, GUM6, HSL, HSL2, JGFF, LDS, LYV, POCEM, SF.

Rejstejn, Cz.; pop. 1; 126 km SSW of Praha; 49°09'/13°31'.

Rekishok, *see* Rokiskis.

Reklinets, Ukr. (Rekliniec); pop. 87; 45 km N of Lvov; 50°13'/24°15'.

Rekliniec, *see* Reklinets.

Rekoraj, Pol.; 32 km SE of Lodz; 51°31'/19°39'; GUM5.

Rekshin, Ukr. (Rekszyn); pop. 51; 69 km ESE of Lvov; 49°34'/24°50'; HSL.

Rekszovice, Pol. EDRD. This town was not found in BGN gazetteers under the given spelling.

Rekszyn, *see* Rekshin.

Rem, Hung.; pop. 12; 75 km WSW of Szeged; 46°15'/19°09'.

Remagen, Germ.; pop. 25; 50 km SE of Koln; 50°34'/07°14'; GUM5.

Rembate, *see* Lielvarde.

Rembertov, *see* Rembertow.

Rembertow, Pol. (Rembertov); pop. 369; 13 km E of Warszawa; 52°15'/21°10'; COH, EDRD, FRG, GUM3, GUM4, GUM5, HSL, HSL2, LYV, PHP4, SF, YB.

Rembieszyce, Pol.; pop. 4; 82 km E of Czestochowa; 50°46'/20°18'.

Remchitsy, Ukr. (Remczyce); pop. 40; 94 km N of Rovno; 51°25'/26°29'.

Remczyce, *see* Remchitsy.

Remel, Byel.; pop. 16; 82 km E of Pinsk; 52°03'/27°20'; JGFF.

Remenow, *see* Remenuv.

Remenuv, Ukr. (Remenow); pop. 34; 19 km NE of Lvov; 49°57'/24°12'.

Remet, *see* Mnisek nad Hnilcom.

Remete, Hung. (Alsoremete); 94 km NNE of Nagykanizsa; 47°08'/17°42'; AMG, HSL.

Remetea Chioarului, Rom.; pop. 51; 88 km N of Cluj; 47°32'/23°33'.

Remeti, Rom. (Palosremete, Remit); pop. 399; 139 km N of Cluj; 47°59'/23°38'; PHR2, SM.

Remeti Bihor, Rom.; pop. 37; 69 km W of Cluj; 46°51'/22°40'.

Remicov, Cz.; pop. 3; 69 km SSE of Praha; 49°31'/14°46'.

Remigola, *see* Ramygala.

Remit, *see* Remeti.

Remizovtse, *see* Remizovtsy.

Remizovtsy, Ukr. (Remizovtse, Remizowce); pop. 48; 69 km E of Lvov; 49°43'/24°53'.

Remizowce, *see* Remizovtsy.

Remlingen, Germ.; pop. 3; 82 km ESE of Frankfurt am Main; 49°48'/09°42'; PHGB.

Remscheid, Germ.; pop. 246; 32 km NNE of Koln; 51°11'/07°12'.

Remte, Lat.; pop. 3; 88 km WSW of Riga; 56°45'/22°42'.

Remus, Rom.; 56 km S of Bucuresti; 43°56'/25°59'; HSL.

Renardowice, Pol.; pop. 10; 69 km WSW of Krakow; 49°55'/18°59'.

Renceni, Lat.; pop. 2; 114 km NE of Riga; 57°44'/25°26'.

Renchen, Germ.; pop. 3; 88 km WSW of Stuttgart; 48°35'/08°01'; EDRD, PHGBW.

Rendejov, Cz.; pop. 2; 56 km ESE of Praha; 49°46'/15°05'.

Rendsburg, Germ.; pop. 30; 88 km NNW of Hamburg; 54°18'/09°40'; CAHJP, EJ, HSL, HSL2.

Rendva, *see* Radava.

Rengshausen, Germ.; pop. 3; 120 km NNE of Frankfurt am Main; 51°01'/09°32'.

Reni, Ukr.; pop. 1,201; 221 km SW of Odessa; 45°27'/28°17'; LDL, SF.

Rennertehausen, Germ.; pop. 9; 107 km N of Frankfurt am Main; 51°01'/08°41'; LDS.

Rennertshofen, Germ.; pop. 3; 82 km NW of Munchen; 48°45'/11°04'; PHGB.

Rentweinsdorf, Germ.; pop. 3; 75 km NNW of Nurnberg; 50°04'/10°48'; PHGB.

Repany, Cz.; pop. 1; 82 km W of Praha; 50°08'/13°20'.

Repcelak, Hung.; pop. 14; 114 km N of Nagykanizsa; 47°25'/17°01'.

Repcevis, Hung.; pop. 3; 120 km NNW of Nagykanizsa; 47°27'/16°41'.

Repechow, *see* Repekhuv.

Repedea, Rom. (Krievei, Oroszko, Ruszkirva); pop. 237; 133 km NNE of Cluj; 47°50'/24°24'; AMG, SM.

Repekhuv, Ukr. (Repechow); pop. 27; 50 km SE of Lvov; 49°32'/24°21'.

Repenye, *see* Repinne.

Repinne, Ukr. (Repenye, Ripina); 146 km S of Lvov; 48°35'/23°27'; AMG, SM.

Reppen, *see* Rzepin.

Reppen Ad Eilang, HSL. This pre-World War I community was not found in BGN gazetteers.

Repperndorf, Germ.; 75 km WNW of Nurnberg; 49°45'/10°07'; PHGB.

Reppine, GUM3. This town was not found in BGN gazetteers under the given spelling.

Repuzhintsy, Ukr. (Rapujineti); pop. 37; 45 km NNW of Chernovtsy; 48°39'/25°48'.

Repuzhyntse, Ukr. (Repuzynce); pop. 16; 62 km NW of Chernovtsy; 48°48'/25°28'.

Repuzynce, *see* Repuzhyntse.

Reschohlau, HSL. This pre-World War I community was not found in BGN gazetteers.

Resein, *see* Raseiniai.

Resetari, Yug.; pop. 10; 126 km ESE of Zagreb; 45°15'/17°26'.

Reshetilovka, Ukr. (Reszetilowka); 146 km NW of Dnepropetrovsk; 49°34'/34°04'; GUM4, HSL.

Resica, Cz. (Resta); 26 km SSW of Kosice; 48°33'/21°03'; HSL.

Resighea, Rom. (Reszege); pop. 4; 139 km WNW of Cluj; 47°36'/22°19'; COH, HSL.

Resita, Rom.; pop. 302; 208 km SSW of Cluj; 45°18'/21°55'; PHR1.

Resko, Pol. (Regenwalde); pop. 53; 69 km NE of Szczecin; 53°46'/15°24'; JGFF.

Resta, *see* Resica.

Resterzewe, HSL. This pre-World War I community was not found in BGN gazetteers.

Restevitz, LDL. This pre-World War I community was not found in BGN gazetteers.

Reszege, *see* Resighea.

Reszel, Pol. (Roessel, Rossel); pop. 28; 163 km WNW of Bialystok; 54°03'/21°01'.

Reszetilowka, *see* Reshetilovka.

Resznek, Hung.; pop. 3; 45 km WNW of Nagykanizsa; 46°40'/16°29'.

Ret, HSL. A number of towns share this name. It was not possible to determine from available information which one is being referenced.

Reteag, Rom. (Retteg); pop. 473; 62 km NNE of Cluj; 47°12'/24°01'; AMG, COH, HSL, HSL2, LDL, PHR2, YB.

Retfala, Yug. (Rieddorf); pop. 29; 170 km WNW of Beograd; 45°34'/18°39'.

Rethe, *see* Reca.

Rethimnon, Greece; 296 km SSE of Athens; 35°23'/24°28'; EDRD.

Reti, Hung. BGN lists two possible localities with this name located at 46°09'/18°56' and 46°59'/20°15'. HSL.

Retkovci, Yug.; pop. 12; 150 km WNW of Beograd; 45°14'/18°39'.

Retkozberencs, Hung.; pop. 15; 94 km ENE of Miskolc; 48°12'/22°01'; LDS.

Retovo, *see* Rietavas.

Retsag, Hung.; pop. 15; 50 km N of Budapest; 47°56'/19°08'.

Retteg, *see* Reteag.

Retz, Aus.; pop. 32; 75 km NW of Wien; 48°45'/15°57'.

Reuterstadt Stavenhagen, Germ. (Stavenhagen); pop. 29; 69 km ESE of Rostock; 53°42'/12°54'; HSL, LDS.

Reutlingen, Germ.; pop. 54; 38 km S of Stuttgart; 48°29'/09°13'; EDRD, EJ, PHGBW.

Reutsel, Mold. (Rautel); pop. 4; 114 km NW of Kishinev; 47°43'/27°49'.

Reutte, Aus.; pop. 3; 56 km WNW of Innsbruck; 47°29'/10°43'.

Rev, *see* Vad Cluj.

Revacauti Cernauti, *see* Revakouts.

Revakouts, Ukr. (Revacauti Cernauti); pop. 37; 19 km WNW of Chernovtsy; 48°22'/25°40'; COH.

Reval, *see* Tallinn.

Revaranyos, Hung.; pop. 38; 107 km ENE of Miskolc; 48°12'/22°16'; HSL.

Revel, *see* Tallinn.

Revfalu, Hung. (Patahaza); 94 km SE of Nagykanizsa; 45°49'/17°47'; LDS.

Revfulop, Hung.; pop. 33; 69 km NE of Nagykanizsa; 46°50'/17°38'; GUM4.

Revlaborcz, HSL. This pre-World War I community was not found in BGN gazetteers.

Revleanyvar, Hung.; pop. 33; 101 km ENE of Miskolc; 48°19'/22°03'.

Revna, Ukr. (Revna pe Ceremus); pop. 49; 13 km WNW of Chernovtsy; 48°20'/25°48'.

Revna pe Ceremus, *see* Revna.

Revnice, Cz.; pop. 24; 26 km SSW of Praha; 49°55'/14°15'.

Revnicov, Cz.; pop. 17; 50 km W of Praha; 50°11'/13°48'.

Rexingen, Germ.; pop. 301; 56 km SW of Stuttgart; 48°26'/08°39'; EJ, GUM3, GUM5, HSL, HSL2, PHGBW.

Reyersbach, Germ.; pop. 2; 107 km NE of Frankfurt am Main; 50°24'/10°10'; PHGB.

Reyovyets, *see* Rejowiec.

Reysen, *see* Rydzyna.

Reyvits, *see* Rejowiec.

Rezavlia, *see* Rozavlea.

Rezehne, *see* Rezekne.

Rezekne, Lat. (Rezehne, Rezhitsa, Rezhitse, Rezhitza, Rjeshiza, Rjetschiza, Rositten, Rzezyca); pop. 3,555; 88 km NNE of Daugavpils; 56°30'/27°19'; COH, EDRD, EJ, GUM4, GUM5, GYLA, HSL, JGFF, LDL, PHLE, SF.

Rezeni, *see* Rezeny.

Rezeny, Mold. (Rezeni); pop. 50; 32 km SSE of Kishinev; 46°46'/28°54'.

Rezhitsa, *see* Rezekne.

Rezhitse, *see* Rezekne.

Rezhitza, *see* Rezekne.

Rezi, Hung.; pop. 5; 50 km N of Nagykanizsa; 46°51'/17°13'.

Reziai, Lith. (Rezy); pop. 6; 50 km S of Vilnius; 54°15'/25°08'.

Rezina, Mold. (Rezina Sat?, Rezina Targ); pop. 2,889; 88 km N of Kishinev; 47°45'/28°58'; GUM5, SF.

Rezina Sat, *possibly* Rezina.

Rezina Targ, *see* Rezina.

Rezitza, *see* Rezekne.

Rezna, *see* Rozenmuiza.

Rezy, *see* Reziai.

Rhaunen, Germ.; pop. 56; 101 km SW of Frankfurt am Main; 49°51'/07°21'; JGFF.

Rheda, Germ.; pop. 56; 114 km SW of Hannover; 51°51'/08°18'; AMG.

Rhede, Germ.; pop. 101 km NNW of Koln; 51°50'/06°42'; GED.

Rhein, Germ. PHGBW, YB. A number of towns share this name. It was not possible to determine from available information which one is being referenced.

Rheinbach, Germ.; pop. 66; 45 km S of Koln; 50°38'/06°57'; GED.

Rheinberg, Germ.; pop. 9; 69 km NNW of Koln; 51°33'/06°36'; GED.

Rheinbischofsheim, Germ.; pop. 69; 94 km WSW of Stuttgart; 48°39'/07°55'; GUM3, LDS, PHGBW.

Rheinbollen, Germ.; 69 km WSW of Frankfurt am Main; 50°01'/07°40'; JGFF.

Rheinbrohl, Germ.; pop. 56 km SE of Koln; 50°30'/07°20'; GUM5.

Rheindahlen, Germ.; pop. 20; 45 km WNW of Koln; 51°09'/06°22'.

Rheine, Germ.; pop. 110; 150 km WSW of Hannover; 52°17'/07°27'; GUM5.

Rheinhausen, Germ.; pop. 65; 56 km NNW of Koln; 51°25'/06°45'; GED.

Rheinland-Pfalz; Not a town but a region of western Germany.

Rheinsberg, Germ.; pop. 3; 82 km NW of Berlin; 53°06'/12°53'.

Rheurdt, Germ.; pop. 69 km NW of Koln; 51°28'/06°28'; GED.

Rheydt, Germ.; pop. 270; 45 km WNW of Koln; 51°10'/06°27'.

Rhina, Germ.; pop. 182; 107 km NE of Frankfurt am Main; 50°45'/09°41'; LDS.

Rhoden, Germ.; pop. 114 km SSW of Hannover; 51°27'/09°01'; LDS.

Rhodes, Greece (Rhodos); pop. 2,000; 429 km ESE of Athens; 36°25'/28°10'; AMG, EDRD, GUM4.

Rhodos, *see* Rhodes.

Riashov, *see* Rzeszow.

Ribene, Lat. (Ribinishok, Ribiniski, Ribinsk, Rybinischki); pop. 300; 56 km N of Daugavpils; 56°21'/26°48'; LDL, PHLE, SF.

Ribinishki, *see* Silajani.

Ribinishok, *see* Ribene.

Ribiniski, *see* Ribene.

Ribinsk, *see* Ribene.

Ribnik, *see* Rybnik.

Ribnitsa, Bulg. (Ravnitsa); pop. 3,568; 189 km SE of Sofija; 41°28'/24°52'.

Ribnitz, *see* Ribnitzdamgarten.

Ribnitza, *see* Rybnitsa.

Ribnitzdamgarten, Germ. (Damgarten, Ribnitz); pop. 1; 32 km NE of Rostock; 54°15'/12°30'; HSL, LDS.

Ribotitch, *see* Rybotycze.

Ricany, Cz.; pop. 41; 19 km ESE of Praha; 49°59'/14°39'.

Richelsdorf, Germ.; pop. 41; 139 km NE of Frankfurt am Main; 50°59'/10°01'; LDS.

Richen, Germ.; pop. 22; 50 km NNW of Stuttgart; 49°10'/08°57'; LDS, PHGBW.

Richka, Ukr. (Rzyczka); pop. 33; A number of towns share this name. It was not possible to determine from available information which one is being referenced.

Richrath, Germ.; pop. 67; 26 km N of Koln; 51°08'/06°56'.

Richvol, *see* Rychwal.

Ricka, *see* Ricky.

Ricky, Cz. (Kispatak, Ricka, Ricske); 120 km N of Brno; 50°13'/16°28'; AMG, HSL, SM.

Ricse, Hung.; pop. 171; 88 km NE of Miskolc; 48°20'/21°58'; AMG, HSL, HSL2, PHH.

Ricske, *see* Ricky.

Ridica, Yug. (Regoce, Rigyica); 170 km NW of Beograd; 45°59'/19°06'; LDS.

Ridik, *see* Rudki.

Ridnik, *see* Rudnik.

Riduk, *see* Rudki.

Riebeni, *see* Silajani.

Riebini, Lat.; 56 km N of Daugavpils; 56°20'/26°48'; PHLE.

Riecka, Cz. (Recske); 82 km SW of Kosice; 48°20'/20°20'; HSL.

Rieddorf, *see* Retfala.

Riedenburg, Germ.; 75 km SE of Nurnberg; 48°58'/11°41'; PHGB.

Ried im Innkreis, Aus.; pop. 1; 56 km NNE of Salzburg; 48°13'/13°30'.

Riedlingen, Germ.; 75 km SSE of Stuttgart; 48°09'/09°28'; PHGBW.

Riegel, Germ.; 126 km SW of Stuttgart; 48°09'/07°45'; PHGBW.

Rieneck, Germ.; pop. 12; 69 km E of Frankfurt am Main; 50°06'/09°39'; GUM5, PHGB.

Riesa, Germ.; pop. 12; 69 km E of Leipzig; 51°18'/13°18'.

Riese, Lith. (Rzesza); 19 km NNW of Vilnius; 54°49'/25°17'; GUM3.

Riesenburg, *see* Prabuty.

Rietavas, Lith. (Retovo, Rietevas, Riteva, Riteve, Ritova); pop. 868; 94 km WSW of Siauliai; 55°44'/21°56'; COH, EJ, GUM3, GUM4, GUM5, HSL, JGFF, LDL, SF, YB, YL.

Rietberg, Germ.; 107 km SW of Hannover; 51°48'/08°26'; JGFF, LDS.

Rietevas, *see* Rietavas.

Rietzneuendorf, Germ.; pop. 1; 56 km SSE of Berlin; 52°01'/13°40'.

Rifin, LDL. This pre-World War I community was not found in BGN gazetteers.

Riga, Lat. (Rige); pop. 43,558; 189 km WNW of Daugavpils; 56°57'/24°06'; AMG, CAHJP, COH, EDRD, EJ, GUM3, GUM4, GUM5, GUM6, HSL, HSL2, ISH1, ISH2, JGFF, LDL, PHGBW, PHLE, PHP4, YB.

Rigacs, Hung.; pop. 1; 75 km N of Nagykanizsa; 47°04'/17°13'.

Rige, *see* Riga.

Riglitz, *see* Ryglice.

Rigyac, Hung.; pop. 5; 13 km W of Nagykanizsa; 46°28'/16°52'.

Rigyica, *see* Ridica.

Rijeka, Yug. (Fiume); 133 km SW of Zagreb; 45°21'/14°24'; EJ, HSL, PHY.

Rika, *see* Ryki.

Rike, *see* Ryki.

Riki, *see* Ryki.

Rikov, *see* Rykow.

Rimalov, *see* Grimaylov.

Rimanov, *see* Rymanow.

Rimarska Sec, *see* Rimavska Sec.

Rimaszecs, *see* Rimavska Sec.

Rimaszombat, *see* Rimavska Sobota.

Rimavska Sec, Cz. (Rimarska Sec, Rimaszecs); pop. 143; 88 km SW of Kosice; 48°18'/20°15'; HSL.

Rimavska Sobota, Cz. (Rimaszombat, Sobota Rimavska); pop. 1,240; 101 km SW of Kosice; 48°23'/20°02'; AMG, COH, HSL, HSL2, JGFF.

Rimavske Janovce, Cz. (Janosi); 94 km SW of Kosice; 48°21'/20°04'; HSL.

Rimbach, Germ.; pop. 85; 56 km S of Frankfurt am Main; 49°37'/08°46'; JGFF, LDS.

Rimbeck, Germ.; pop. 54; 107 km SSW of Hannover; 51°32'/09°03'; GED.

Rimnicu Sarat, Rom.; 133 km NNE of Bucuresti; 45°23'/27°03'; GUM4, JGFF.

Rimoc, Hung.; pop. 4; 69 km NNE of Budapest; 48°02'/19°32'.

Rimpar, Germ.; pop. 47; 94 km ESE of Frankfurt am Main; 49°51'/09°57'; GUM5, HSL, PHGB.

Rimse, Lith. (Rimshan, Rymszany); pop. 151; 120 km NNE of Vilnius; 55°32'/26°26'; LDL, SF.

Rimshan, *see* Rimse.

Ringen, HSL. A number of towns share this name. It was not possible to determine from available information which one is being referenced.

Rinn, Aus.; 13 km E of Innsbruck; 47°15'/11°30'; EDRD.

Rinteln, Germ.; pop. 95; 50 km SW of Hannover; 52°11'/09°05'.

Rinyaszentkiraly, Hung.; pop. 8; 45 km SE of Nagykanizsa; 46°09'/17°24'.

Ripa de Jos, Rom. (Alsorepa, Rapa de Jos); 88 km ENE of Cluj; 46°56'/24°46'; HSL.

Ripa de Sus, Rom. (Felsorepa, Rapa de Sus); pop. 21; 88 km ENE of Cluj; 46°55'/24°46'.

Ripanj, Yug.; pop. 3; 26 km S of Beograd; 44°38'/20°32'.

Ripiceni, Rom.; pop. 225; 94 km NNW of Iasi; 47°57'/27°09'; GUM4, PHR1.

Ripin, *see* Rypin.

Ripina, *see* Repinne.

Rippenheim, HSL. This pre-World War I community was not found in BGN gazetteers.

Risca, HSL. A number of towns share this name. It was not possible to determine from available information which one is being referenced.

Risha, *see* Rzeszow.

Rishkan, *see* Ryshkany.

Rishkani, *see* Ryshkany.

Riskeva, *see* Ruscova.

Riskeve, *see* Ruscova.

Riskova, *see* Ruscova.

Riskovi, *see* Ruscova.

Risnita, Rom.; 62 km S of Iasi; 46°40'/27°34'; HSL.

Rite, Lat. (Rites); pop. 2; 75 km WNW of Daugavpils; 56°11'/25°27'.

Rites, *see* Rite.

Riteva, *see* Rietavas.

Riteve, *see* Rietavas.

Ritova, *see* Rietavas.

Ritschenhausen, Germ.; pop. 2; 126 km NNW of Nurnberg; 50°31'/10°27'.

Ritschenwalde, *see* Ryczywol (near Poznan).

Ritterhude, Germ.; pop. 10; 88 km SW of Hamburg; 53°11'/08°45'.

Ritvin, *see* Rytwiany.

Ritzov, *see* Gritsev.

Rizan, *see* Rozan.

Rizchov, *see* Rzochow.

Rizinivka, *see* Ryzhanovka.

Rjasna, *see* Ryasno.

Rjavinti, *possibly* Rzhavintsy.

Rjepki, USSR; EDRD. This town was not found in BGN gazetteers under the given spelling.

Rjeshiza, *see* Rezekne.

Rjetschiza, *see* Rezekne.

Robec, Cz.; pop. 4; 56 km N of Praha; 50°33'/14°25'.

Robel, Germ.; pop. 88 km SSE of Rostock; 53°23'/12°36'; LDS.

Robret, *see* Rajbrot.

Rochlov, Cz.; pop. 2; 101 km SW of Praha; 49°44'/13°09'.

Rochov, Cz. (Rocov); pop. 20; 50 km NW of Praha; 50°27'/14°07'.

Rockenhausen, Germ.; pop. 74; 82 km SW of Frankfurt am Main; 49°38'/07°50'; GED, JGFF.

Rocov, *see* Rochov.

Rodach, Germ.; pop. 6; 101 km NNW of Nurnberg; 50°20'/10°47'; PHGB.

Rodalben, Germ.; pop. 75; 120 km SSW of Frankfurt am Main; 49°14'/07°38'; JGFF.

Rodatyche, Ukr. (Rodatycze); pop. 35; 38 km WSW of Lvov; 49°48'/23°32'.

Rodatycze, *see* Rodatyche.

Rodaun, Aus.; pop. 31; 13 km SW of Wien; 48°08'/16°16'.

Rodavetz, *see* Radovtsy.

Roddenau, Germ.; pop. 7; 114 km N of Frankfurt am Main; 51°03'/08°45'; LDS.

Rodelheim, HSL, HSL2. This pre-World War I community was not found in BGN gazetteers.

Rodelmaier, Germ.; pop. 3; 114 km ENE of Frankfurt am Main; 50°19'/10°17'; PHGB.

Rodelsee, Germ.; pop. 69 km WNW of Nurnberg; 49°44'/10°14'; GUM5, HSL, PHGB.

Rodem, *see* Radom.

Rodenberg, Germ.; pop. 27; 26 km WSW of Hannover; 52°19'/09°21'; HSL.

Rodewisch, Germ.; pop. 10; 88 km S of Leipzig; 50°32'/12°25'.

Rodgen, Germ.; 62 km N of Frankfurt am Main; 50°36'/08°45'; LDS.

Rodheim, Germ.; pop. 44; 62 km N of Frankfurt am Main; 50°37'/08°36'; GUM5, JGFF.

Rodimin, *see* Radzymin.

Roding, Germ.; 114 km E of Nurnberg; 49°12'/12°31'; PHGB.

Rodingen, Germ.; 38 km W of Koln; 50°58'/06°27'; ISH1.

Rodna, Rom. (Oradna, Ragne); pop. 299; 120 km NE of Cluj; 47°25'/24°49'; HSL, PHR2.

Rodvil, *see* Chervonoarmeisk.

Rodvilishuk, *see* Radviliskis.

Rodzamin, *see* Radzymin.

Rodzilova, *see* Radzilow.

Rodzin, *see* Radzyn Podlaski.

Rodzislav, Pol. EDRD. This town was not found in BGN gazetteers under the given spelling.

Roessel, *see* Reszel.

Roettingen, *see* Rottingen.

Rogachev, Byel. (Ratchev, Rogaczew, Rogaczow, Rogatchev, Rohaczew, Rohatchov); pop. 5,372; 94 km NW of Gomel; 53°05'/30°03'; EJ, GUM4, GYLA, HSL, JGFF, SF.

Rogacze, Pol.; pop. 23; 75 km S of Bialystok; 52°31'/23°14'.

Rogaczew, *see* Rogachev.

Rogaczow, *see* Rogachev.

Rogasen, *see* Rogozno Wielkopolskie.

Rogasevci, *see* Rogasovci.

Rogasovci, Yug. (Rogasevci); pop. 13; 120 km N of Zagreb; 46°48'/16°02'.

Rogatchev, *see* Rogachev.

Rogatica, Yug.; pop. 47; 163 km SSW of Beograd; 43°48'/19°01'; PHY.

Rogatin, Ukr. (Rohatin, Rohatyn, Rotin); pop. 2,233; 69 km SE of Lvov; 49°25'/24°37'; AMG, COH, EDRD, EGRS, EJ, GUM3, GUM4, GUM5, GUM6, GYLA, HSL, HSL2, JGFF, LDL, LYV, PHP2, PHP3, SF, YB.

Rogau, *see* Rogowo.

Rogienice Wielkie, Pol.; pop. 13; 75 km W of Bialystok; 53°17'/22°05'.

Rogienice Wlascianskie, *see* Rogienice Wypychy.

Rogienice Wypychy, Pol. (Rogienice Wlascianskie); pop. 24; 75 km W of Bialystok; 53°17'/22°06'.

Rogna, Rom.; 69 km N of Cluj; 47°20'/23°36'; HSL.

Rogojesti, Rom.; pop. 9; 139 km WNW of Iasi; 47°56'/26°10'.

Rogolin, Pol.; pop. 2; 82 km S of Warszawa; 51°34'/20°54'.

Rogov, *see* Raguva.

Rogove, *see* Raguva.

Rogow, Pol.; pop. 161; 26 km ENE of Lodz; 51°49'/19°51'; PHP1, PHP4.

Rogow (near Miechow), Pol.; pop. 30; 45 km N of Krakow; 50°27'/20°04'.

Rogow (near Radom), Pol.; pop. 34; 107 km WSW of Lublin; 51°12'/21°01'.

Rogowice, Pol.; pop. 6; 107 km ENE of Czestochowa; 51°03'/20°35'.

Rogow Komorniki, Pol. (Komorniki); pop. 24; 107 km WSW of Lublin; 51°12'/20°59'.

Rogowo, Pol. (Rogau); 56 km NE of Poznan; 52°43'/17°40'; AMG, GUM3.

Rogowo Falecin, Pol.; pop. 23; 69 km WNW of Warszawa; 52°37'/20°05'.

Rogoznica, Pol. (Gross Rosen); 50 km WSW of Wroclaw; 51°01'/16°18'; EDRD, GA, GUM3, GUM4, GUM5, PHP3.

Rogozniczka, Pol.; pop. 33; 94 km N of Lublin; 52°02'/22°53'.

Rogozno, Pol. (Rohozna); pop. 264; 38 km N of Poznan; 52°45'/17°01'; CAHJP, EJ, JGFF, LDL, LDS.

Rogozno (Kielce area), Pol.; pop. 10; 50 km SW of Lodz; 51°26'/18°58'.

Rogozno (near Jaworow), Ukr.; pop. 47; 50 km W of Lvov; 49°52'/23°21'; HSL, SF.

Rogozno (near Lancut), Pol.; pop. 4; 45 km NW of Przemysl; 50°04'/22°23'.

Rogozno (near Lublin), Pol.; pop. 4; 38 km NE of Lublin; 51°23'/22°59'; GUM4.

Rogozno (near Sambor), Ukr.; pop. 40; 75 km SW of Lvov; 49°38'/23°04'.

Rogozno (near Sieradz), Pol.; pop. 20; 50 km SW of Lodz; 51°26'/18°58'.

Rogozno Wielkopolski, *see* Rogozno Wielkopolskie.

Rogozno Wielkopolskie, Germ. (Rogasen, Rogozno Wielkopolski); 69 km SW of Berlin; 52°19'/12°23'; EJ, HSL, LDS.

Roguszyn, Pol.; pop. 4; 56 km ENE of Warszawa; 52°23'/21°51'.

Roguva, *see* Raguva.

Rohaczew, *see* Rogachev.

Rohatchov, *see* Rogachev.

Rohatin, *see* Rogatin.

Rohatyn, *see* Rogatin.

Rohia, Rom.; pop. 10; 75 km N of Cluj; 47°24'/23°51'.

Rohod, Hung.; pop. 120; 101 km E of Miskolc; 48°02'/22°08'; AMG, HSL.

Rohonc, *see* Rechnitz.

Rohozna, *see* Rogozno.

Rohozne, Ukr.; pop. 21; 82 km SW of Rovno; 50°05'/25°25'. This town was located on an interwar map of Poland but does not appear in contemporary gazetteers. Map coordinates are approximate.

Rohrbach, Germ.; pop. 43; 50 km SSE of Frankfurt am Main; 49°41'/08°53'; AMG, HSL, JGFF, LDS, PHGBW.

Rohrbach an der Teich, Aus.; pop. 4; 62 km ENE of Graz; 47°12'/16°17'.

Rohrbruch, *see* Rynarzewo.

Rohrenfurth, Germ.; pop. 12; 133 km NNE of Frankfurt am Main; 51°09'/09°33'; LDS.

Roisdorf, Germ.; 26 km SSE of Koln; 50°45'/07°00'; GED.

Rojtokmuzsaj, Hung.; pop. 3; 133 km N of Nagykanizsa; 47°33'/16°50'.

Rokamezo, *see* Lisicovo.

Rokatschuw, GUM3. This town was not found in BGN gazetteers under the given spelling.

Rokiciny, Pol.; pop. 63; 26 km ESE of Lodz; 51°40'/19°49'; PHP1.

Rokietnica, Pol.; pop. 60; 19 km NW of Przemysl; 49°54'/22°39'; PHP3.

Rokishki, *see* Rokiskis.

Rokishkis, *see* Rokiskis.

Rokishok, *see* Rokiskis.

Rokishuk, *see* Rokiskis.

Rokiskis, Lith. (Rakishik, Rakishki, Rakishok, Rakiski, Rakiszki, Rekishok, Rokishki, Rokishkis, Rokishok, Rokishuk); pop. 2,013; 139 km ENE of Siauliai; 55°58'/25°35'; AMG, COH, EJ, GUM3, GUM4, GUM5, JGFF, LDL, LYV, SF, YB, YL.

Rokita, *see* Rakita.

Rokitnica, *see* Rokitnitsa.

Rokitnitsa, Byel. (Rokitnica); pop. 25; 146 km W of Pinsk; 52°08'/23°59'.

Rokitno, *see* Rokitnoye.

Rokitno (near Luninets), Byel.; pop. 97; 56 km ENE of Pinsk; 52°13'/26°56'.

Rokitno (near Lvov), Ukr.; pop. 33; 19 km NW of Lvov; 49°57'/23°54'.

Rokitno Szlacheckie, Pol.; pop. 3; 45 km SE of Czestochowa; 50°26'/19°27'.

Rokitnoye, Ukr. (Rokitno); pop. 566; 101 km NNE of Rovno;

51°17'/27°13'; AMG, COH, EDRD, GUM3, GUM4, GUM6, LDL, LYV, SF, YB.

Rokosov, Ukr. (Rakasz); 195 km S of Lvov; 48°13'/23°11'; AMG, HSL.

Rokosowo, Pol.; 75 km S of Poznan; 51°47'/16°53'; GA.

Rokow, Pol.; pop. 9; 32 km SW of Krakow; 49°55'/19°31'.

Rokycany, Cz.; pop. 66; 75 km SW of Praha; 49°44'/13°36'.

Rokytnik, Cz. (Rakottyas); 88 km SW of Kosice; 48°24'/20°11'; HSL.

Rokytov, Cz. BGN lists two possible localities with this name located at 49°06'/21°59' and 49°19'/21°11'. HSL.

Role, Pol.; pop. 17; 88 km NNW of Lublin; 51°59'/22°25'.

Rollbach, Germ.; pop. 13; 56 km ESE of Frankfurt am Main; 49°46'/09°15'; GUM5, PHGB.

Rollfeld, Germ.; 50 km SE of Frankfurt am Main; 49°46'/09°11'; PHGB.

Rollshausen, Germ.; 75 km N of Frankfurt am Main; 50°43'/08°36'; LDS.

Roman, Rom.; 56 km SW of Iasi; 46°55'/26°55'; GUM4, HSL, JGFF, LJEE, PHR1.

Romancauti, *see* Romankovtsy.

Romand, Hung.; pop. 1; 94 km WSW of Budapest; 47°27'/17°48'.

Romanesti, *see* Bessarabka.

Romankovtsy, Ukr. (Romancauti); pop. 180; 94 km ENE of Chernovtsy; 48°30'/27°13'.

Romanov, *see* Dzerzhinsk.

Romanovka, Ukr.; pop. 2,672; A number of towns share this name. It was not possible to determine from available information which one is being referenced.

Romanovo, (Romanowo); JGFF, LDL, SF, YB. The name Romanovo is a common town name in pre-World War I Russia, no doubt named for the Romanoff line of czars. SF notes two towns named Romanovo. One is located 21 km east of Slutsk (53°01'/27°33') and a second east of Orsha. About 50 km east of Orsha is a town named Lenino (54°25'/31°08'), which was previously called Romanovo. The sources cited here seem to refer to the town in the Slutsk area.

Romanow, *see* Romanuv.

Romanowce, Pol.; pop. 12; 120 km N of Bialystok; 54°10'/23°16'.

Romanowe Siolo, Ukr.; pop. 49; 107 km N of Chernovtsy; 49°15'/25°55'; PHP2. This town was located on an interwar map of Poland but does not appear in contemporary gazetteers. Map coordinates are approximate.

Romanowka, *possibly* Romanuv.

Romanowka Powtrembowla, *see* Romanuv.

Romanowo, *see* Romanovo.

Romanuv, Ukr. (Romanow, Romanowka?, Romanowka Powtrembowla); pop. 20; 32 km ESE of Lvov; 49°42'/24°21'; GUM3, HSL, HSL2, LDL, PHP1, SF.

Romaszki, Pol.; 75 km NNE of Lublin; 51°50'/23°03'; GA.

Romejki, *see* Romeyki.

Romejko, *see* Romeyki.

Romen, *see* Romny.

Romeyki, Ukr. (Romejki, Romejko); pop. 22; 82 km N of Rovno; 51°16'/26°13'.

Romhany, Hung.; pop. 21; 50 km N of Budapest; 47°56'/19°16'.

Rominesti, HSL. A number of towns share this name. It was not possible to determine from available information which one is being referenced.

Romita, Rom.; pop. 11; 50 km NW of Cluj; 47°08'/23°12'.

Rommelhausen, Germ.; 26 km NE of Frankfurt am Main; 50°16'/08°58'; LDS.

Rommershausen, Germ.; pop. 11; 101 km N of Frankfurt am Main; 50°56'/09°11'.

Romny, Ukr. (Romen); pop. 9,747; 56 km SSE of Konotop; 50°45'/33°28'; EDRD, EJ, HSL, HSL2, LDL, SF.

Romodan, Ukr.; pop. 61; 146 km S of Konotop; 50°00'/33°20'.

Romonya, Hung.; pop. 2; 107 km ESE of Nagykanizsa; 46°05'/18°21'.

Romrod, Germ.; pop. 13; 82 km NNE of Frankfurt am Main; 50°43'/09°13'; JGFF.

Romshishok, *see* Rumsiskes.

Romsthal, Germ. (Eckardroth); pop. 26; 56 km NE of Frankfurt am Main; 50°19'/09°22'; LDS.

Romuli, Rom.; pop. 333; 107 km NNE of Cluj; 47°32'/24°26'.

Rona de Jos, Rom. (Alsorona, Unter Rina, Unterine); pop. 477; 133 km N of Cluj; 47°55'/24°01'; COH, GUM5, HSL, PHR2, SM.

Rona de Sus, Rom. (Felsorona, Ober Rina, Oberrine); pop. 410; 133 km N of Cluj; 47°54'/24°03'; AMG, COH, HSL, PHR2, SM.

Rona Sek, *see* Costiui.

Ronaszek, *see* Costiui.

Rondorf, Germ.; pop. 44; 13 km SSE of Koln; 50°52'/06°58'.

Ronneburg, *see* Rauna.

Ronnenburg, *see* Rauna.

Ronsperg, *see* Pobezovice.

Ronsperk, *see* Pobezovice.

Rontau, Rom.; pop. 3; 120 km W of Cluj; 47°01'/22°01'.

Roop, *see* Lielstraupe.

Ropa, Pol.; pop. 84; 101 km ESE of Krakow; 49°36'/21°03'; HSL.

Ropcea, *see* Ropcha.

Ropcha, Ukr. (Ropcea); pop. 91; 32 km SSW of Chernovtsy; 48°06'/25°46'; COH.

Ropchitse, *see* Ropczyce.

Ropczyce, Pol. (Ropchitse, Ropshits, Ropshitz); pop. 840; 88 km WNW of Przemysl; 50°03'/21°37'; CAHJP, COH, EDRD, EGRS, EJ, GA, GUM3, GUM5, HSL, HSL2, JGFF, LDL, LYV, PHP3, SF.

Ropianka, Pol.; pop. 9; 94 km SW of Przemysl; 49°29'/21°38'.

Ropica, Yug.; 94 km NNW of Skopje; 42°48'/21°02'; HSL.

Ropica Polska, Pol.; pop. 5; 107 km ESE of Krakow; 49°39'/21°15'.

Ropica Ruska, Pol.; pop. 18; 114 km ESE of Krakow; 49°36'/21°15'.

Ropienka, Pol.; pop. 41; 38 km SSW of Przemysl; 49°32'/22°31'; HSL.

Ropki, Pol.; pop. 4; 114 km ESE of Krakow; 49°28'/21°08'.

Ropshits, *see* Ropczyce.

Ropshitz, *see* Ropczyce.

Rortieyes Szentmihaly, *see* Htusovo.

Ros, *see* Ross.

Rosalia, *see* Rozavlsa.

Rosash, *see* Rossosz.

Rosavo, *see* Rossawa.

Rosbach, Germ.; pop. 31; 50 km ESE of Koln; 50°48'/07°37'; GED.

Rosdorf, Germ.; 101 km SSE of Hannover; 51°30'/09°54'; GED.

Rosebeck, Germ.; pop. 7; 101 km S of Hannover; 51°31'/09°15'.

Rosenau, *see* Roznava.

Rosenberg, *see* Ruzomberok; Susz.

Rosenheim, Germ.; 50 km ESE of Munchen; 47°51'/12°08'; AMG, GUM3, PHGB.

Rosenowsk, *see* Zilupe.

Rosenowski, *see* Rozenmuiza.

Rosenthal, Germ.; pop. 27; 101 km N of Frankfurt am Main; 50°58'/08°53'; LDS.

Rosh, *see* Ross.

Roshev, LDL. This pre-World War I community was not found in BGN gazetteers.

Rosiejow, Pol.; pop. 12; 38 km NE of Krakow; 50°20'/20°19'.

Rosienie, *see* Raseiniai.

Rosilno, Ukr. (Rosulna); pop. 154; 126 km WNW of Chernovtsy; 48°46'/24°22'; GUM5, PHP2.

Rosinhof, *see* Zilupe.

Rosinovsk, *see* Zilupe.

Rosiori de Vede, Rom. (Rosiorii de Vede); 94 km SW of Bucuresti; 44°07'/24°59'; GUM4, JGFF.

Rosiorii de Vede, *see* Rosiori de Vede.

Rosiori Satu Mare, Rom.; pop. 40; 133 km WNW of Cluj; 47°15'/21°57'.

Rositsa, Byel. (Rositza, Rosiza); pop. 7,386; 176 km WNW of Vitebsk; 55°55'/27°45'; LDL, SF.

Rositten, *see* Rezekne.

Rositza, *see* Rositsa.

Rosiza, *see* Rositsa.

Roska, HSL. This pre-World War I community was not found in BGN gazetteers.

Roskoshnaya, *see* Roskoshnyy.

Roskoshnoye, Ukr.; 146 km ESE of Dnepropetrovsk; 47°45'/36°38'; JGFF.

Roskoshnyy, Ukr. (Roskoshnaya, Roskosnaya); 75 km N of Uman; 49°23'/30°11'; HSL.

Roskosnaya, *see* Roskoshnyy.

Roskoviany, *see* Rozkovany.

Roslavichi, Ukr. (Roslovichi, Roslowitz); 26 km S of Kiyev; 50°15'/30°26'; COH, HSL.

Roslavl, USSR (Roslawlj); pop. 3,254; 107 km SE of Smolensk; 53°57'/32°52'; EDRD, GUM4, GUM5.

Roslawlj, *see* Roslavl.

Roslovichi, *see* Roslavichi.

Roslowitz, *see* Roslavichi.

Rosni, *see* Ryasno.

Rosochacz, *see* Rosokhach.

Rosochate, Pol.; pop. 8; 62 km S of Przemysl; 49°17'/22°37'.

Rosochate Koscielne, Pol.; pop. 61; 62 km SW of Bialystok; 52°52'/22°21'.

Rosochatka, Pol.; pop. 7; 82 km SSW of Gdansk; 53°43'/18°08'.

Rosochowaciec, *see* Rosokhovatets.

Rosochy, *see* Rosokhi.

Rosokhach, Ukr. (Rosochacz); pop. 72; 62 km WNW of Chernovtsy; 48°38'/25°14'; HSL.

Rosokhach (Tarnopol), Ukr.; pop. 59; 75 km NNW of Chernovtsy; 48°57'/25°48'.

Rosokhi, Ukr. (Rosochy, Rosokhy); pop. 26; 101 km SW of Lvov; 49°26'/22°47'.

Rosokhovatets, Ukr. (Rosochowaciec, Rosokhovatsets); pop. 56; 120 km S of Rovno; 49°33'/26°03'; GUM4.

Rosokhovatsets, *see* Rosokhovatets.

Rosokhy, *see* Rosokhi.

Rosolin, Pol.; pop. 14; 56 km S of Przemysl; 49°20'/22°36'.

Rosovice, Cz.; pop. 3; 50 km SSW of Praha; 49°46'/14°07'.

Rospesha, *see* Rozprza.

Rospsza, *see* Rozprza.

Ross, Byel. (Ros, Rosh); pop. 389; 176 km NW of Pinsk; 53°17'/24°24'; GUM3, GUM4, HSL, SF.

Rossava, Ukr.; 88 km SSE of Kiyev; 49°42'/30°57'; JGFF.

Rossawa, (Rosavo); LDL, SF. This town was not found in BGN gazetteers under the given spelling.

Rossbach, Germ.; 50 km ESE of Frankfurt am Main; 49°53'/09°15'; PHGB.

Rossdorf, Germ.; pop. 53; 126 km NE of Frankfurt am Main; 50°42'/10°13'; LDS.

Rossein, *see* Raseiniai.

Rossel, *see* Reszel.

Rossieny, *see* Raseiniai.

Rossing, Germ.; 26 km SSE of Hannover; 52°11'/09°49'; GED.

Rosslau, Germ.; pop. 20; 69 km N of Leipzig; 51°53'/12°15'; GUM3.

Rossosh, USSR; pop. 20; 195 km SE of Voronezh; 50°12'/39°35'.

Rossosz, Pol. (Rosash); pop. 365; 82 km NNE of Lublin; 51°51'/23°08'; COH, GUM3, GUM5, HSL, POCEM, SF.

Rossoszyca, Pol.; 45 km WSW of Lodz; 51°42'/18°47'; EDRD.

Rossow, Germ.; 88 km WNW of Berlin; 53°03'/12°34'; LDS.

Rossviegev, *possibly* Rosvigovo.

Rostki Strozne, Pol.; pop. 7; 69 km N of Warszawa; 52°51'/21°14'.

Rostkov, Cz.; pop. 6; 69 km NNE of Praha; 50°35'/14°56'.

Rostock, Germ.; pop. 350; 157 km NE of Hamburg; 54°05'/12°08'; EJ, GUM4, HSL, JGFF, LDS.

Rostoka, Pol.; pop. 70; 82 km E of Lublin; 51°03'/23°45'; AMG.

Rostoki, Ukr.; pop. 25; 62 km WSW of Chernovtsy; 48°11'/25°06'; COH.

Rostoki Dolne, Pol.; pop. 24; Described in the *Black Book* as being in the Lwow region of Poland, this town was not found in BGN gazetteers.

Rostov, USSR (Rostov na Donu, Rostov On Don, Rostow); pop. 26,323; 504 km SSE of Voronezh; 47°15'/39°45'; EDRD, GUM3, GUM4, GUM5, HSL, JGFF, LDL.

Rostov na Donu, *see* Rostov.

Rostov On Don, *see* Rostov.

Rostow, *see* Rostov.

Rosulna, *see* Rosilno.

Rosvegovo, *see* Rosvigovo.

Rosvigo, *see* Rosvigovo.

Rosvigovo, Ukr. (Rossviegev?, Rosvegovo, Rosvigo, Roszveg, Rozvigo); 182 km SSW of Lvov; 48°27'/22°43'; HSL.

Rosy, Pol.; pop. 1; 82 km ESE of Warszawa; 52°00'/22°04'.

Roszczep, Pol.; pop. 5; 32 km NE of Warszawa; 52°27'/21°19'.

Rosztoka, *see* Roztoka.

Roszveg, *see* Rosvigovo.

Rotchky, *see* Raczki.

Rotenburg, Germ.; pop. 120; 126 km NNE of Frankfurt am Main; 50°59'/09°43'; GUM4, LDS.

Rotenfels, Germ.; pop. 4; 62 km W of Stuttgart; 48°49'/08°18'; PHGBW.

Roteni, Rom. (Harasztkerek); pop. 6; 88 km ESE of Cluj; 46°28'/24°41'.

Rotenturm an der Pinka, Aus.; pop. 9; 62 km NE of Graz; 47°15'/16°15'.

Roth, *see* Roth bei Nurnberg.

Roth bei Nurnberg, Germ. (Roth); pop. 20; 32 km S of Nurnberg; 49°15'/11°06'; GUM3, JGFF, LDS, PHGB.

Rothenbach, Germ.; 13 km NE of Nurnberg; 49°29'/11°14'; PHGB.

Rothenburg, *see* Rothenburg Ob der Tauber.

Rothenburg Ob der Tauber, Germ. (Rothenburg); pop. 45; 62 km WSW of Nurnberg; 49°23'/10°11'; EDRD, GUM3, ISH1, PHGB, PHGBW.

Rothenfels, Germ.; 69 km ESE of Frankfurt am Main; 49°53'/09°36'; PHGB.

Rothenkirchen, Germ.; 107 km N of Nurnberg; 50°21'/11°19'; LDS.

Rotin, *see* Rogatin.

Rotmistrivka, Ukr. (Rachmistrivka, Rotmistrowka); 114 km NE of Uman; 49°08'/31°42'; GUM4, SF.

Rotmistrowka, *see* Rotmistrivka.

Rotnica, *see* Ratnycia.

Rotnitza, *see* Ratnycia.

Rotno, *see* Ratno.

Rotshonz, *see* Raciaz.

Rott, Germ.; pop. 31; 32 km ESE of Koln; 50°45'/07°16'; GED.

Rottenbauer, Germ.; 82 km WNW of Nurnberg; 49°43'/09°58'; PHGB.

Rottenburg, Germ.; 38 km SSW of Stuttgart; 48°28'/08°56'; PHGBW.

Rottendorf, Germ.; 88 km WNW of Nurnberg; 49°48'/10°02'; PHGB.

Rotthalmunster, Germ.; 126 km ENE of Munchen; 48°21'/13°12'; GUM3.

Rottingen, Germ. (Roettingen); 82 km W of Nurnberg; 49°31'/09°58'; EDRD, EJ, PHGB.

Rottum, Germ.; 101 km SE of Stuttgart; 48°02'/09°5?; PHGBW.

Rottweil, Germ.; pop. 88; 82 km SSW of Stuttga?; 48°10'/08°37'; GUM4, PHGBW.

Rotzk, *see* Raczki.

Roudne, Cz.; pop. 5; 133 km S of Praha; 48°56'/14°29'.

Roudnice nad Labem, Cz. (Raudnitz an der Elbe); pop. ?

Rovno, Ukraine: A Sabbath evening on Sidewalk Street when "the public goes for a stroll."

45 km NNW of Praha; 50°25'/14°15'; EJ.

Roupov, Cz.; pop. 7; 107 km SW of Praha; 49°32'/13°15'.

Rovbitsk, *see* Rovbitskaya.

Rovbitskaya, Byel. (Rovbitsk, Rowbick); pop. 37; 150 km WNW of Pinsk; 52°40'/24°05'.

Rovenshiny, GUM3. This town was not found in BGN gazetteers under the given spelling.

Rovigno, *see* Rovinj.

Rovina, Cz.; pop. 50; BGN lists two possible localities with this name located at 49°36'/14°24' and 49°55'/14°14'. AMG.

Rovine, Rom. (Rovine Pecica); pop. 155; 202 km SW of Cluj; 46°10'/21°04'; PHR1.

Rovine Pecica, *see* Rovine.

Rovinj, Yug. (Rovigno); 202 km SW of Zagreb; 45°05'/13°38'; PHY.

...winy, Byel. (Rowiny); pop. 46; 62 km W of Pinsk; 52°14'/25°13'.

...na, *see* Rovne; Rovnoye.

..., *see* Rovno.

Ukr. (Rovne, Rowne, Ruvne); pop. 21,702; 182 km NE ...vov; 50°37'/26°15'; AMG, CAHJP, COH, EDRD, EJ, GUM4, GUM5, GUM6, HSL, HSL2, JGFF, LDL, ... PHP4, SF, YB.

..., Ukr. (Rowno); pop. 52; 157 km N of Lvov; ...3°48'.

... Rovnoye.

(Cuporani, Rovna, Rovnoje); pop. 4; 133 km SW 46°01'/29°10'; HSL, LDL, SF.

Rownia); pop. 38; 107 km SSE of Lvov;

...itskaya.

pop. 3; 82 km WSW of Przemysl;

50 km S of Przemysl; 49°25'/22°36'; ...a.

... km SSW of Lublin; 50°53'/22°03'.

Frankfurt am Main; 49°35'/08°22';

...9A;

...op. 27; 75 km SW of Odessa;

46°17'/29°47'.

Royter Hoyf, *see* Raudondvaris.

Roza, Pol.; pop. 72; 101 km ENE of Krakow; 50°07'/21°18'; HSL.

Rozahegy, *see* Ruzomberok.

Rozalia, *see* Rozavlea.

Rozalimas, Lith. (Razalimas, Rozalinas, Rozaumas); pop. 173; 38 km E of Siauliai; 55°53'/23°53'; YL.

Rozalin, Pol.; pop. 29; 32 km SSW of Warszawa; 52°03'/20°46'.

Rozalinas, *see* Rozalimas.

Rozan, Pol. (Rizan, Rozhan, Ruzan, Ruzhan); pop. 1,646; 75 km N of Warszawa; 52°53'/21°25'; CAHJP, COH, FRG, GA, GUM3, GUM4, GUM5, GYLA, HSL, JGFF, LDL, LYV, PHP4, SF, YB.

Rozana, *see* Ruzhany.

Rozaniec, Pol.; pop. 72; 62 km N of Przemysl; 50°20'/22°49'; AMG, HSL.

Rozanka, *see* Rozhanka.

Rozan Nowy, *see* Novyy Rozhan.

Rozanowka, Pol.; pop. 22; GUM4, GUM5, PHP2. Described in the *Black Book* as being in the Tarnopol region of Poland, this town was not found in BGN gazetteers.

Rozanstvo, Yug.; pop. 1; 133 km S of Beograd; 43°43'/19°50'.

Rozaumas, *see* Rozalimas.

Rozavla, *see* Rozavlea.

Rozavlea, Rom. (Rezavlia, Rozalia, Rozavla); pop. 723; 120 km N of Cluj; 47°44'/24°13'; AMG, GUM3, HSL, PHR2, SM.

Rozavlsa, (Rosalia); HSL. This pre-World War I community was not found in BGN gazetteers.

Rozbeki, Lat. (Rozula); pop. 2; 75 km NE of Riga; 57°24'/24°58'.

Rozberice, Cz.; pop. 1; 94 km ENE of Praha; 50°16'/15°45'.

Rozbity Kamien, Pol.; pop. 19; 82 km ENE of Warszawa; 52°20'/22°11'.

Rozborz, Pol.; pop. 26; 32 km NW of Przemysl; 50°03'/22°33'; JGFF.

Rozborz Dlugi, Pol.; pop. 27; 26 km WNW of Przemysl; 49°57'/22°31'.

Rozborz Okragly, Pol.; pop. 13; 26 km WNW of Przemysl; 49°56'/22°30'.

Rozce, Pol.; pop. 2; 50 km S of Warszawa; 51°51'/20°46'.

Rozdalovice, Cz.; pop. 16; 56 km NE of Praha; 50°18'/15°11'.

Rozdelov, Cz.; pop. 1; 26 km W of Praha; 50°08'/14°05'.

Rozdilovichi, Ukr. (Rozdzialowice, Rozdzyalovitse); pop. 25; 50 km SW of Lvov; 49°40'/23°24'.

Rozdol, Ukr. (Rozdul); pop. 1,738; 50 km S of Lvov; 49°28'/24°04'; AMG, COH, EDRD, EGRS, EJ, GUM3, HSL, HSL2, LDL, PHP2, SF, WS.

Rozdul, see Rozdol.

Rozdzalow, Pol.; pop. 29; 69 km ESE of Lublin; 51°04'/23°30'.

Rozdzialowice, see Rozdilovichi.

Rozdzialy, Pol.; pop. 9; 62 km N of Warszawa; 52°46'/21°17'.

Rozdzin, Pol.; 45 km S of Lodz; 51°24'/19°14'; PHP3.

Rozdzyalovitse, see Rozdilovichi.

Rozembark, Pol.; pop. 34; 94 km ESE of Krakow; 49°46'/21°10'.

Rozenberg, see Rozovka.

Rozeni, Lat.; pop. 9; 107 km N of Riga; 57°53'/24°38'.

Rozenmuiza, Lat. (Rezna, Rosenowski); pop. 16; 88 km NE of Daugavpils; 56°26'/27°30'.

Rozenovski, see Zilupe.

Rozen Wielki, see Rozhen Velikiy.

Rozev, HSL. This pre-World War I community was not found in BGN gazetteers.

Rozhan, see Rozan.

Rozhanka, Byel. (Rozanka); pop. 542; 182 km NW of Pinsk; 53°32'/24°44'; AMG, COH, EDRD, GUM4, HSL, PHP2, SF, YB.

Rozhanovce, Cz.; 13 km NE of Kosice; 48°45'/21°21'; EJ.

Rozhanoy, see Ruzhany.

Rozhantov, see Rozhnyatov.

Rozhenovskaya, LDL. This pre-World War I community was not found in BGN gazetteers.

Rozhen Velikiy, Ukr. (Rozen Wielki, Rozhen Velki); pop. 36; 69 km WSW of Chernovtsy; 48°13'/25°04'.

Rozhen Velki, see Rozhen Velikiy.

Rozhinoy, see Ruzhany.

Rozhishch, see Rozhishche.

Rozhishche, Ukr. (Rozhishch, Rozhishtch, Rozishtchov, Rozishts, Rozyszcze); pop. 3,500; 75 km WNW of Rovno; 50°55'/25°16'; AMG, COH, GUM3, GUM4, GUM5, GYLA, HSL, LDL, SF, YB.

Rozhishtch, see Rozhishche.

Rozhniatov, see Rozhnyuv.

Rozhnov, Ukr. (Rozhnuv, Roznov, Roznow); pop. 418; 56 km W of Chernovtsy; 48°22'/25°13'; EDRD, GA, GUM5, HSL, LYV, PHP2, PHP3, PHR1, SF.

Rozhnuv, see Rozhnov.

Rozhnyatov, Ukr. (Rozhantov, Rozhnyatuv, Rozintov, Roznatov, Rozniatow, Roznitev); pop. 1,349; 107 km S of Lvov; 48°56'/24°09'; AMG, COH, EGRS, GUM4, GUM5, HSL, HSL2, JGFF, LDL, PHP2, YB.

Rozhnyatuv, see Rozhnyatov.

Rozhnyuv, Ukr. (Razhnyatov, Rozhniatov); 107 km NW of Chernovtsy; 49°00'/24°54'; SF.

Roziecin, Pol.; pop. 5; 82 km ESE of Lublin; 50°54'/23°35'.

Rozinovsk, see Zilupe.

Rozintov, see Rozhnyatov.

Rozishtchov, see Rozhishche.

Rozishts, see Rozhishche.

Rozkochow, Pol.; pop. 7; 32 km WSW of Krakow; 50°03'/19°29'.

Rozkopaczow, Pol.; pop. 27; 32 km NE of Lublin; 51°25'/22°52'.

Rozkovany, Cz. (Roskoviany); 50 km NNW of Kosice; 49°08'/20°59'; AMG.

Rozlozna, Cz.; 69 km WSW of Kosice; 48°37'/20°21'; HSL.

Rozlucz, Ukr.; pop. 67; 126 km SSW of Lvov; 48°55'/22°55'; PHP2. This town was located on an interwar map of Poland but does not appear in contemporary gazetteers. Map coordinates are approximate.

Rozmberk, see Rozmberk nad Vltavou.

Rozmberk nad Vltavou, Cz. (Rozmberk); pop. 17; 163 km S of Praha; 48°39'/14°22'.

Roznatov, see Rozhnyatov.

Roznava, Cz. (Rosenau); pop. 1,084; 50 km WSW of Kosice; 48°40'/20°32'; AMG, COH, GUM5, HSL, HSL2, LDL.

Roznevice, Cz.; 101 km WSW of Praha; 49°52'/13°04'; HSL.

Rozniatow, see Rozhnyatov.

Roznica, Pol.; pop. 8; 62 km ESE of Czestochowa; 50°37'/20°02'.

Rozniszew, Pol.; pop. 17; 56 km SSE of Warszawa; 51°48'/21°18'.

Roznitev, see Rozhnyatov.

Roznov, see Rozhnov.

Roznovec, HSL. This pre-World War I community was not found in BGN gazetteers.

Roznow, see Rozhnov.

Roznowka, Pol.; pop. 24; 82 km SSE of Lublin; 50°32'/22°45'.

Rozovka, Ukr. (Rozenberg); 195 km ESE of Dnepropetrovsk; 47°23'/37°04'; HSL.

Rozplucie, Pol.; pop. 7; 38 km NE of Lublin; 51°25'/23°01'.

Rozprza, Pol. (Rospesha, Rospsza); pop. 546; 56 km SSE of Lodz; 51°18'/19°38'; CAHJP, EDRD, GUM5, HSL, HSL2, LDL, LDS, PHP1, POCEM, SF, YB.

Rozpucie, Pol.; pop. 41; 38 km SW of Przemysl; 49°36'/22°25'; HSL.

Rozsafa, Hung.; pop. 4; 82 km ESE of Nagykanizsa; 46°01'/17°53'.

Rozsaly, Hung.; pop. 23; 150 km E of Miskolc; 47°55'/22°48'.

Rozsaszentmarton, Hung.; pop. 35; 56 km NE of Budapest; 47°47'/19°45'.

Rozsoska, Ukr. (Rasiska, Raszocska); 139 km S of Lvov; 48°42'/23°18'; SM. This town was located on a pre-World War I map, but does not appear in contemporary gazetteers.

Roztoka, Pol. (Rosztoka, Rustuka); 26 km W of Warszawa; 52°19'/20°37'; GA, HSL.

Roztoka (Lwow), Pol.; pop. 18; 32 km SW of Przemysl; 49°37'/22°28'.

Roztoka (near Nowy Sacz), Pol.; pop. 7; 62 km SE of Krakow; 49°37'/20°27'.

Roztoka (Romania), Rom.; 107 km NNW of Cluj; 47°42'/23°18'; SM.

Rozubowice, Pol.; pop. 8; 13 km SE of Przemysl; 49°44'/22°51'.

Rozula, see Rozbeki.

Rozvadov, Ukr. (Rozwadow); pop. 23; 45 km S of Lvov; 49°30'/23°57'.

Rozvaduv, see Lalovo.

Rozvidev, see Lalovo.

Rozvigo, see Rosvigovo.

Rozwadow, Pol.; pop. 1,790; 82 km SSW of Lublin; 50°35'/22°03'; AMG, COH, EDRD, EGRS, EJ, FRG, GUM3, GUM4, GUM5, HSL, JGFF, LDL, LYV, PHP2, PHP3, SF, YB. See also Rozvadov.

Rozwadowka, Pol.; pop. 55; 75 km NNE of Lublin; 51°45'/23°18'.

Rozwady, Pol.; pop. 32; 82 km ESE of Lodz; 51°23'/20°27'.

Rozwienica, Pol.; pop. 28; 26 km NW of Przemysl; 49°57'/22°36'.

Rozwory, Pol.; pop. 20; 94 km WSW of Bialystok; 53°06'/21°45'.

Rozworzany, Ukr.; pop. 28; 62 km SE of Lvov; 49°25'/24°25'. This town was located on an interwar map of Poland but does not appear in contemporary gazetteers. Map coordinates are approximate.

Rozyca, Pol.; pop. 8; 26 km E of Lodz; 51°44'/19°47'; PHP1.

Rozyszcze, see Rozhishche.

Rubanovka, Ukr.; 170 km S of Dnepropetrovsk; 47°00'/34°10'; SF.

Rubas, Lat.; pop. 11; 114 km SW of Riga; 56°24'/22°33'.

Rubashov, see Hrubieszow.

Rubel, Byel. (Rubiel); pop. 349; 69 km E of Pinsk; 51°58'/27°04'; AMG, GUM4, JGFF.

Rubene, Lat.; pop. 45 km WNW of Daugavpils; 56°08'/26°00'; PHLE.

Rubeshov, see Hrubieszow.

Rubezh, Byel. (Rubiez); pop. 22; 107 km NNE of Pinsk; 52°56'/26°46'.

Rubezhevichi, Byel. (Rebzevits, Rubiezewicze, Rubizhevich, Rubizhevitch, Rubyezheviche, Rubzhevits); pop. 903; 50 km SW of Minsk; 53°41'/26°52'; COH, GUM3, GUM4, GUM6, HSL, HSL2, JGFF, LDL, SF, YB.

Rubiel, *see* Rubel.

Rubiez, *see* Rubezh.

Rubiezewicze, *see* Rubezhevichi.

Rubischoff, *see* Hrubieszow.

Rubishov, *see* Hrubieszow.

Rubishoyv, *see* Hrubieszow.

Rubizhevich, *see* Rubezhevichi.

Rubizhevitch, *see* Rubezhevichi.

Rublenita, *see* Rublenitsa.

Rublenitsa, Mold. (Rublenita); pop. 3; 139 km NNW of Kishinev; 48°10'/28°12'.

Rubnik, *see* Rybnik.

Rubyezheviche, *see* Rubezhevichi.

Rubzhevits, *see* Rubezhevichi.

Rucava, Lat. (Rucavas); pop. 12; 202 km SW of Riga; 56°10'/21°09'.

Rucavas, *see* Rucava.

Ruchheim, Germ.; pop. 12; 75 km S of Frankfurt am Main; 49°28'/08°20'; GED.

Ruchocice, Pol. (Ruchocki Mlyn); 50 km SW of Poznan; 52°11'/16°21'; GA.

Ruchocki Mlyn, *see* Ruchocice.

Ruckeroth, Germ.; pop. 3; 69 km ESE of Koln; 50°34'/07°45'.

Ruckersdorf, Germ.; 13 km NE of Nurnberg; 49°30'/11°15'; GUM3, PHGB.

Ruckershausen, Germ.; pop. 24; A number of towns share this name. It was not possible to determine from available information which one is being referenced.

Ruckingen, Germ.; 26 km ENE of Frankfurt am Main; 50°10'/09°00'; AMG, HSL, LDS.

Rucsin, *see* Rukshin.

Ruczynow, Pol.; pop. 7; 75 km NE of Krakow; 50°28'/20°50'.

Ruda, Pol.; pop. 236; GUM5, HSL, HSL2. There are more than 75 towns in Poland named Ruda, which means "ore," undoubtedly referring to mining operations in the area. The three towns shown here are all in the Polish interwar province of Lublin, described in the *Black Book* as Ruda A (pop. 49), Ruda B (pop. 236) and Ruda in Chelm area (pop. 66). It is unclear from contemporary maps what are the exact locations of these towns. See also listings below.

Ruda (near Bobrka), Ukr.; pop. 18; 50 km SSE of Lvov; 49°27'/24°14'.

Ruda (near Garwolin), Pol.; pop. 28; 62 km ESE of Warszawa; 51°52'/21°35'.

Ruda (near Grojec), Pol.; pop. 7; 26 km NNE of Warszawa; 52°28'/21°09'.

Ruda (near Ilza), Pol.; pop. 26; 101 km WSW of Lublin; 51°01'/21°11'.

Ruda (near Lancut), Pol.; pop. 22; 69 km NW of Przemysl; 50°19'/22°21'.

Ruda (near Mielec), Pol.; pop. 28; 107 km ENE of Krakow; 50°17'/21°25'.

Ruda (near Minsk Mazowiecki), Pol.; pop. 5; 32 km E of Warszawa; 52°11'/21°28'.

Ruda (near Rogatin), Ukr.; pop. 5; 62 km ESE of Lvov; 49°28'/24°35'.

Ruda (near Ropczyce), Pol.; pop. 4; 88 km WNW of Przemysl; 50°08'/21°42'.

Ruda (near Stopnica), Pol.; pop. 13; 88 km NE of Krakow; 50°33'/20°55'.

Ruda (near Zhidachov), Ukr.; pop. 51; 69 km S of Lvov; 49°18'/24°06'.

Ruda (Vilnius area), Byel.; pop. 7; 146 km N of Minsk; 55°09'/27°20'.

Rudabanya, Hung.; pop. 42; 38 km NNW of Miskolc; 48°23'/20°38'; HSL.

Rudabanyacska, Hung.; pop. 17; 75 km NE of Miskolc; 48°25'/21°37'.

Ruda Bialaczowska, Pol.; pop. 20; 82 km ESE of Lodz; 51°16'/20°23'.

Ruda Brodska, Ukr. (Ruda Brodzka); pop. 50; 75 km NE of Lvov; 50°05'/24°56'.

Ruda Brodzka, *see* Ruda Brodska.

Ruda Huta, Pol. (Ruda Opalin); pop. 92; 75 km E of Lublin; 51°15'/23°36'; GA, GUM3.

Ruda Instytutowa, Pol.; pop. 25; Described in the *Black Book* as being in the Lublin region of Poland, this town was not found in BGN gazetteers.

Ruda Jaworska, *see* Ruda Yavorskaya.

Ruda Kameralna, Pol.; pop. 14; 69 km ESE of Krakow; 49°49'/20°45'.

Ruda Koscielna, Pol.; pop. 17; 75 km SW of Lublin; 50°57'/21°33'.

Ruda Kotlowska, Pol. PHP2. This town was not found in BGN gazetteers under the given spelling.

Ruda Krakovetska, Ukr. (Ruda Krakowiecka); pop. 21; 62 km W of Lvov; 49°59'/23°11'.

Ruda Krakowiecka, *see* Ruda Krakovetska.

Ruda Krechowska, *see* Ruda Krekhuvska.

Ruda Krekhuvska, Ukr. (Ruda Krechowska); pop. 12; 32 km NW of Lvov; 50°04'/23°49'.

Ruda Maleniecka, Pol.; pop. 12; 88 km NE of Czestochowa; 51°09'/20°13'; PHP1.

Rudamin, *see* Rudamina.

Rudamina, Lith. (Rudamin); pop. 98; 19 km SE of Vilnius; 54°35'/25°24'; LDL, SF, YL.

Rudance, *see* Rudantse.

Rudantse, Ukr. (Rudance); pop. 53; 26 km NE of Lvov; 49°57'/24°16'; PHP2.

Ruda Opalin, *see* Ruda Huta.

Ruda Pabianicka, Pol. (Ruda Pabianitzka, Ruda Pabjanicka); pop. 237; 13 km S of Lodz; 51°42'/19°27'; AMG, GUM3, GUM5, PHP1, SF.

Ruda Pabianitzka, *see* Ruda Pabianicka.

Ruda Pabjanicka, *see* Ruda Pabianicka.

Ruda Rozaniecka, Pol.; pop. 80; 62 km NNE of Przemysl; 50°19'/23°11'.

Ruda Seletska, Ukr. (Ruda Sielecka); pop. 44; 45 km NNE of Lvov; 50°09'/24°24'.

Ruda Sielecka, *see* Ruda Seletska.

Ruda Slaska, Pol. PHP3. This town was not found in BGN gazetteers under the given spelling.

Ruda Solska, Pol.; pop. 13; 82 km N of Przemysl; 50°29'/22°39'.

Ruda Talubska, Pol.; pop. 8; 62 km ESE of Warszawa; 51°52'/21°35'.

Rudaw, Pol.; pop. 6; 146 km SSE of Gdansk; 53°03'/19°00'.

Ruda Wielka, Pol.; pop. 40; 107 km W of Lublin; 51°18'/21°04'.

Ruda Woloska, *see* Ruda Wolowska.

Ruda Wolowska, Pol. (Ruda Woloska); pop. 12; 88 km NNE of Przemysl; 50°26'/23°29'.

Ruda Yavorskaya, Byel. (Ruda Jaworska); pop. 63; 163 km NW of Pinsk; 53°24'/25°07'; GUM3.

Ruda Zazamcze, Pol.; pop. 34; PHP3. Described in the *Black Book* as being in the Krakow region of Poland, this town was not found in BGN gazetteers.

Ruda Zelazna, Pol.; pop. 10; 88 km NNE of Przemysl; 50°25'/23°29'.

Ruddingshausen, Germ.; pop. 22; 69 km N of Frankfurt am Main; 50°41'/08°55'.

Rudelstadt, *see* Ciechanowiec.

Rudendorf, Germ.; pop. 1; 62 km NNW of Nurnberg; 50°00'/10°45'.

Rudenka, Pol.; pop. 22; 45 km SSW of Przemysl; 49°30'/22°26'.

Rudenko Ruske, Ukr. (Rudenko Ruskie); pop. 7; 75 km NE of Lvov; 50°17'/24°49'.

Rudenko Ruskie, *see* Rudenko Ruske.

Rudersberg, Germ.; 32 km NE of Stuttgart; 48°53'/09°32'; GUM3.

Rudersdorf, Germ.; 26 km E of Berlin; 52°27'/13°47'; HSL.

Rudesheim, Germ.; pop. 30; 56 km WSW of Frankfurt am Main; 49°59'/07°55'; GUM5.

Rudig, *see* Vroutek.

Rudigershagen, Germ.; 126 km SE of Hannover; 51°21'/10°26'; LDS.

Rudik, *see* Rudki.

Rudka, Pol. (Rudke); pop. 436; 75 km SSE of Lublin; 50°37'/22°59'; HSL, PHP2, SF.

Rudka (near Bransk), Pol.; pop. 28; 56 km SSW of Bialystok; 52°44'/22°44'; LYV.

Rudka (near Jaroslaw), Pol.; pop. 22; 50 km NNW of Przemysl; 50°14'/22°38'.

Rudka (Tarnopol), Ukr. (Cygany, Tsygany); pop. 117; 69 km N of Chernovtsy; 48°52'/26°06'.

Rudka Kijanska, Pol.; pop. 4; 32 km NE of Lublin; 51°26'/22°52'.

Rudka Skroda, Pol.; pop. 36; 82 km W of Bialystok; 53°18'/21°54'.

Rudke, *see* Rudka.

Rudki, Ukr. (Ridik, Riduk, Rudik); pop. 1,824; 50 km SW of Lvov; 49°39'/23°29'; AMG, COH, EDRD, EGRS, EJ, GUM3, GUM5, GUM5, HSL, HSL2, JGFF, LDL, LYV, PHP2, SF, YB.

Rudmanns, Aus.; pop. 1; 101 km WNW of Wien; 48°36'/15°13'.

Rudna Wielka, Pol.; pop. 13; 69 km WNW of Przemysl; 50°05'/21°57'.

Rudni, *see* Staraya Rudnya.

Rudnia, *see* Rudnya.

Rudnia Bobrowska, *see* Rudnya Bobrovska.

Rudnia Staryki, *see* Stariki.

Rudnica, *see* Ruzhnitsa.

Rudniew, Pol. PHP3. This town was not found in BGN gazetteers under the given spelling.

Rudnik, Pol. (Ridnik); pop. 805; 82 km NW of Przemysl; 50°26'/22°15'; AMG, COH, EDRD, EGRS, GUM3, GUM5, HSL, JGFF, LDL, PHP2, PHP3, POCEM, SF.

Rudniki, Ukr.; pop. 73; 45 km WNW of Chernovtsy; 48°26'/25°20'; AMG, GUM4.

Rudniki (near Czestochowa), Pol. (Rudniki Redziny); pop. 28; 19 km NE of Czestochowa; 50°53'/19°15'; PHP1, PHP4.

Rudniki (near Mosciska), Ukr.; pop. 58; 62 km WSW of Lvov; 49°48'/23°09'.

Rudniki (near Vilnius), *see* Rudninkai.

Rudniki (near Wielun), Pol.; pop. 33; 45 km WNW of Czestochowa; 51°02'/18°36'.

Rudniki (near Zhidachov), Ukr.; pop. 25; 50 km S of Lvov; 49°27'/23°55'.

Rudniki Redziny, *see* Rudniki (near Czestochowa).

Rudninkai, Lith. (Rudniki [Near Vilnius]); 32 km S of Vilnius; 54°26'/25°10'; GUM3, GUM6.

Rudnitsa, Ukr.; pop. 64; 114 km SW of Uman; 48°16'/28°54'.

Rudnitz, Germ.; 32 km NNE of Berlin; 52°43'/13°37'; GUM3.

Rudnitza, *see* Ruzhnitsa.

Rudno, Ukr.; pop. 24; 6 km WSW of Lvov; 49°50'/23°54'; HSL, HSL2, JGFF.

Rudno Dolne, Pol.; pop. 3; 32 km ENE of Krakow; 50°08'/20°20'.

Rudnok, Hung.; 56 km NE of Miskolc; 48°16'/21°30'; HSL.

Rudnya, Byel. (Rudnia); pop. 2,235; 56 km SE of Vitebsk; 54°48'/30°41'; GUM4, GUM6, HSL.

Rudnya (near Lida), Lith.; pop. 22; 82 km SSW of Vilnius; 54°04'/24°41'.

Rudnya (near Sarny), Ukr.; pop. 20; 101 km N of Rovno; 51°27'/26°25'.

Rudnya Bobrovska, Ukr. (Rudnia Bobrowska); pop. 4; 75 km NE of Rovno; 51°03'/27°04'; GUM4.

Rudnya Staryki, *see* Stariki.

Rudolfin, Pol.; pop. 33; 75 km E of Lublin; 51°07'/23°37'.

Rudolowice, Pol.; pop. 6; 26 km NW of Przemysl; 49°57'/22°37'.

Rudolstadt, Germ.; pop. 13; 94 km SW of Leipzig; 50°43'/11°20'.

Rudowa, HSL. This pre-World War I community was not found in BGN gazetteers.

Rudy, Pol.; pop. 68; Described in the *Black Book* as being in the Lwow region of Poland, this town was not found in BGN gazetteers.

Rudy Rysie, Pol.; pop. 15; 50 km E of Krakow; 50°03'/20°39'.

Rudzana, Pol. PHP4. This town was not found in BGN gazetteers under the given spelling.

Rudzeti, Lat.; pop. 3; 62 km N of Daugavpils; 56°25'/26°28'.

Rudzienice, Pol. (Raudnitz); 101 km SE of Gdansk; 53°38'/19°40'; HSL, HSL2.

Ruen, *see* Rujiena.

Rugaji, Lat. (Rugaju); pop. 120; 133 km N of Daugavpils; 57°00'/27°08'; PHLE.

Rugaju, *see* Rugaji.

Rugasesti, Rom.; pop. 2; 56 km N of Cluj; 47°14'/23°53'; HSL.

Rugenwalde, *see* Darlowo.

Rughi, Mold.; pop. 93; 170 km NW of Kishinev; 48°21'/27°53'.

Ruhpolding, Germ.; pop. 1; 88 km ESE of Munchen; 47°46'/12°39'.

Ruhrort, Germ.; pop. 400; 56 km NNW of Koln; 51°26'/06°45'.

Rujene, *see* Rujiena.

Rujiena, Lat. (Ruen, Rujene); pop. 71; 126 km NNE of Riga; 57°54'/25°19'; PHLE.

Rujnita, *see* Ruzhnitsa.

Rukainiai, Lith. (Rukojnie); 19 km ESE of Vilnius; 54°37'/25°30'; GUM4.

Rukojnie, *see* Rukainiai.

Rukshin, Ukr. (Rucsin); pop. 2; 45 km NE of Chernovtsy; 48°30'/26°24'.

Rulzheim, Germ.; pop. 184; 82 km WNW of Stuttgart; 49°10'/08°18'; GED, GUM5, HSL.

Rum, Hung.; pop. 33; 82 km N of Nagykanizsa; 47°08'/16°51'.

Ruma, Yug.; pop. 215; 56 km WNW of Beograd; 45°01'/19°49'; PHY.

Rumanov, *see* Rymanow.

Rumburk, Cz.; pop. 112; 101 km N of Praha; 50°57'/14°34'; AMG, GUM4.

Rumiske, *see* Rumsiskes.

Rummelsberg, *see* Miastko.

Rummelsburg, *see* Miastko.

Rumno, *see* Grimnoye.

Rumshishok, *see* Rumsiskes.

Rumsiskes, Lith. (Romshishok, Rumiske, Rumshishok); pop. 288; 26 km E of Kaunas; 54°51'/24°12'; HSL, JGFF, SF, YL.

Rundeni, Lat.; pop. 8; 94 km NE of Daugavpils; 56°16'/27°50'; PHLE.

Rungury, Ukr.; pop. 33; 82 km W of Chernovtsy; 48°29'/24°51'.

Runia, *see* Runina.

Runina, Cz. (Runia); 94 km NE of Kosice; 49°04'/22°25'; HSL.

Runkel, Germ.; pop. 4; 50 km WNW of Frankfurt am Main; 50°24'/08°10'; GUM5.

Ruppach, Germ.; 69 km WNW of Frankfurt am Main; 50°27'/07°53'; PHGBW.

Ruppichteroth, Germ.; 45 km E of Koln; 50°51'/07°29'; GED.

Ruprechtice, Cz.; pop. 21; 139 km NE of Praha; 50°38'/16°16'.

Rus, HSL. A number of towns share this name. It was not possible to determine from available information which one is being referenced.

Rusa, *see* Ruse.

Rusakovichi, Byel.; 45 km SE of Minsk; 53°31'/27°50'; GUM4.

Rusca Mokra, *see* Russkaya Mokraya.

Ruschuk, *see* Ruse.

Ruscova, Rom. (Riskeva, Riskeve, Riskova, Riskovi, Ruskava, Ruskova, Visa Orom, Visha Orom, Visooroszi); pop. 1,034; 126 km N of Cluj; 47°48'/24°17'; AMG, COH, HSL, LYV, PHR2, SM, YB.

Ruse, Bulg. (Rusa, Ruschuk, Rustchuk, Rustschuk); pop. 3,220; 170 km WNW of Varna; 43°50'/25°57'; EJ, GUM4, HSL,

LDL.

Rusen, *see* Rusyany.

Ruseni, *see* Rusyany.

Rusestii Noui, *see* Novyye Ruseshty.

Rusii Munti, Rom.; pop. 31; 94 km ENE of Cluj; 46°55'/24°51'.

Ruska, Pol. AMG, HSL. A number of towns share this name. It was not possible to determine from available information which one is being referenced.

Ruska Mokra, *see* Russkaya Mokraya.

Ruskava, *see* Ruscova.

Ruska Wies, Pol.; 26 km W of Przemysl; 49°49'/22°24'; PHP3.

Ruske, Cz.; 94 km NE of Kosice; 49°07'/22°21'; COH, HSL.

Ruskie, Pol.; pop. 7; 69 km S of Przemysl; 49°13'/22°36'.

Ruskie Piaski, Pol.; pop. 7; 56 km SE of Lublin; 50°49'/23°07'.

Ruski Krstur, Yug.; pop. 38; 120 km NW of Beograd; 45°34'/19°25'.

Ruski Pole, *see* Poienile de Sub Munte.

Ruskov, Cz.; 19 km E of Kosice; 48°41'/21°26'; HSL.

Ruskova, *see* Ruscova.

Ruskow, Pol.; pop. 6; 94 km S of Bialystok; 52°19'/22°44'.

Ruslek, Pol.; pop. 63; Described in the *Black Book* as being in the Lodz region of Poland, this town was not found in BGN gazetteers.

Rusl Moldovita, *see* Moldovita.

Rusne, Lith. (Russ); 146 km SW of Siauliai; 55°18'/21°22'; HSL.

Rusociny, Pol.; pop. 5; 32 km S of Lodz; 51°30'/19°30'.

Rusor, Rom.; 150 km S of Cluj; 45°32'/23°01'; HSL.

Rusov, Ukr. (Rusow, Rusuv); pop. 22; 38 km WNW of Chernovtsy; 48°31'/25°32'.

Rusovce, Cz. (Karlburg, Oroszvar); 19 km SSE of Bratislava; 48°03'/17°09'; JGFF.

Rusow, *see* Rusov.

Ruspolyana, *see* Poienile de Sub Munte.

Russ, *see* Rusne.

Russelsheim, Germ.; pop. 62; 26 km SW of Frankfurt am Main; 50°00'/08°25'; GED.

Russenbach, Germ.; 38 km N of Nurnberg; 49°46'/11°10'; GUM5.

Russkaja Mokra, *see* Russkaya Mokraya.

Russkaya Mokraya, Ukr. (Mokra Russ, Oroszmokra, Rusca Mokra, Ruska Mokra, Russkaja Mokra); 150 km W of Chernovtsy; 48°21'/23°54'; SM.

Russko Ivanovka, Ukr. (Ivanestii Vechi); pop. 44; 75 km WSW of Odessa; 46°22'/29°46'.

Russocice, Pol. (Vladislavov Rusochitza, Wladyslawow); pop. 293; 82 km WNW of Lodz; 52°06'/18°29'; LDL, PHP1, POCEM, SF.

Russow, Germ. BGN lists two possible localities with this name located at 51°51'/18°05' and 54°04'/11°39'. JGFF.

Rust, Germ.; pop. 38; 120 km SW of Stuttgart; 48°16'/07°44'; HSL, HSL2, JGFF, PHGBW.

Rustchuk, *see* Ruse.

Rustingen, Germ.; pop. 100; 88 km WNW of Hannover; 52°45'/08°34'.

Rustorf, Aus.; pop. 2; 62 km NE of Salzburg; 48°03'/13°47'.

Rustschuk, *see* Ruse.

Rustuka, *see* Roztoka.

Rustvechko, Ukr. (Rustweczko); pop. 29; 62 km WSW of Lvov; 49°46'/23°05'.

Rustweczko, *see* Rustvechko.

Rusuv, *see* Rusov.

Rusyany, Mold. (Rusen, Ruseni); pop. 35; 170 km NW of Kishinev; 48°13'/27°26'.

Rusyvel, *see* Sennoye.

Rusywel, *see* Sennoye.

Ruszelczyce, Pol.; pop. 26; 19 km W of Przemysl; 49°49'/22°31'.

Ruszkirva, *see* Repedea.

Ruszow, Pol.; pop. 25; 82 km SE of Lublin; 50°40'/23°20'.

Ruszpolyana, *see* Poienile de Sub Munte.

Ruthen, Germ. BGN lists two possible localities with this name located at 51°29'/08°27' and 53°29'/12°02'. GUM5.

Ruthenia; Not a town, but a region of the western Ukraine south of the Carpathian Mountains.

Rutka, Pol.; pop. 141; HSL, PHP4. A number of towns share this name. It was not possible to determine from available information which one is being referenced.

Rutka (Czechoslovakia), Cz.; 82 km WSW of Praha; 50°01'/13°16'; GUM3.

Rutki, Pol.; pop. 713; 50 km WSW of Bialystok; 53°06'/22°26'; CAHJP, COH, GA, GUM3, JGFF, LDL, LDS, SF.

Rutki Kossaki, Pol. PHP4. This town was not found in BGN gazetteers under the given spelling.

Ruttershausen, Germ.; 69 km N of Frankfurt am Main; 50°40'/08°42'; LDS.

Ruvne, *see* Rovno.

Ruzan, *see* Rozan.

Ruzas, Lat. (Ruzinas); pop. 39; 50 km WSW of Riga; 56°56'/23°16'.

Ruzdvyany, *see* Radvanov.

Ruzdwiany, *see* Radvanov.

Ruzhan, *see* Rozan.

Ruzhana, *see* Ruzhany.

Ruzhany, Byel. (Rozana, Rozhanoy, Rozhinoy, Ruzany, Ruzhana, Ruzhyn); pop. 2,400; 120 km WNW of Pinsk; 52°52'/24°53'; AMG, COH, EDRD, EJ, FRG, HSL, HSL2, JGFF, SF, YB.

Ruzhin, Ukr.; pop. 2,567; 75 km NE of Vinnitsa; 49°43'/29°14'; GUM4, HSL, HSL2, JGFF, SF.

Ruzhnitsa, Mold. (Rudnica, Rudnitza, Rujnita); pop. 81; 176 km NW of Kishinev; 48°15'/27°26'; SF.

Ruzhyn, *see* Ruzhany.

Ruzinas, *see* Ruzas.

Ruzodol, Cz.; pop. 25; 88 km NNE of Praha; 50°46'/15°02'.

Ruzomberok, Cz. (Liptorosenberg, Rosenberg, Rozahegy); 146 km WNW of Kosice; 49°05'/19°19'; AMG, EJ, GUM4, GUM5, HSL.

Ryasna, Byel.; pop. 739; 146 km SE of Vitebsk; 54°01'/31°12'.

Ryasno, Byel. (Rasna, Rjasna, Rosni); pop. 739; 189 km W of Pinsk; 52°23'/23°25'; LDL, SF.

Rybaki, Pol. (Lansk); 146 km ESE of Gdansk; 53°35'/20°29'; AMG, PHP4.

Rybare, Cz.; pop. 283; 114 km W of Praha; 50°14'/12°52'.

Rybczewice, Pol.; pop. 20; 38 km SE of Lublin; 51°02'/22°52'; GUM5.

Rybie Nowe, Pol.; pop. 10; 45 km SE of Krakow; 49°47'/20°20'.

Rybie Stare, Pol.; pop. 4; 45 km ESE of Krakow; 49°49'/20°20'.

Rybinischki, *see* Ribene.

Rybinsk, Ukr.; 94 km NW of Konotop; 51°55'/32°27'; HSL.

Rybionek, Pol.; pop. 7; 62 km WSW of Warszawa; 52°15'/20°03'.

Rybne, *see* Rybnoye.

Rybnica, (Alsoribnyicze); AMG, HSL. A number of towns share this name. It was not possible to determine from available information which one is being referenced.

Rybnica Vysnia, *see* Vysna Rybnica.

Rybnice, Cz. BGN lists two possible localities with this name located at 50°37'/15°24' and 49°55'/13°22'. HSL.

Rybnicna, Cz.; pop. 3; 107 km W of Praha; 50°08'/12°57'.

Rybnik, (Certlov, Ribnik, Rubnik); JGFF. A number of towns share this name. It was not possible to determine from available information which one is being referenced.

Rybniste, Cz.; pop. 2; 94 km N of Praha; 50°52'/14°30'.

Rybnitsa, Mold. (Rabnita, Ribnitza); 88 km N of Kishinev; 47°45'/29°00'; GUM4, GUM6, JGFF, PHR1, SF.

Rybno, *see* Rybnoye.

Rybnoye, Ukr. (Rybne, Rybno); pop. 24; 114 km SE of Lvov; 48°57'/24°36'; COH, HSL.

Ryboly, Pol.; pop. 2; 26 km SSE of Bialystok; 52°56'/23°16'.

Rybotycze, Pol. (Ribotitch); pop. 314; 26 km SSW of Przemysl; 49°39'/22°39'; EGRS, HSL, JGFF, LDL, PHP2, PHP3, POCEM, SF.

Rycerka Dolna, Pol.; pop. 15; 94 km SSW of Krakow; 49°29'/19°06'.

Rychcice, *see* Rykhtsitse.

Rychlocice, Pol.; pop. 7; 62 km SW of Lodz; 51°23'/18°49'.

Rychnov nad Kneznou, Cz. (Reichenau); pop. 96; 114 km NNW of Brno; 50°10'/16°17'.

Rychtal, Pol.; pop. 5; 56 km ENE of Wroclaw; 51°09'/17°51'.

Rychwal, Pol. (Richvol); pop. 244; 94 km WNW of Lodz; 52°04'/18°10'; GUM3, JGFF, PHP1, SF.

Ryczow, Pol.; 32 km SW of Krakow; 49°59'/19°33'; 45 km NW of Krakow; 50°26'/19°36'; HSL.

Ryczyca, Pol.; pop. 10; 62 km E of Warszawa; 52°11'/21°55'.

Ryczyska, Pol.; pop. 43; 75 km ESE of Warszawa; 51°52'/21°51'.

Ryczywol, Pol. (Ritchvol); pop. 82; 69 km SE of Warszawa; 51°41'/21°26'; CAHJP, HSL, JGFF, LDS, PHP2, PHP4, SF.

Ryczywol (near Poznan), Pol. (Ritschenwalde); pop. 79; 50 km NNW of Poznan; 52°49'/16°50'; POCEM.

Rydoduby, Ukr.; pop. 45; 56 km NW of Chernovtsy; 48°45'/25°35'. This town was located on an interwar map of Poland but does not appear in contemporary gazetteers. Map coordinates are approximate.

Rydzewo, HSL. A number of towns share this name. It was not possible to determine from available information which one is being referenced.

Rydzewo Folw, Pol.; pop. 26; Described in the *Black Book* as being in the Bialystok region of Poland, this town was not found in BGN gazetteers.

Rydzewo Pieniazek, Pol.; pop. 5; 62 km WNW of Bialystok; 53°28'/22°23'.

Rydzow, Pol.; pop. 54; 107 km ENE of Krakow; 50°14'/21°23'.

Rydzyna, Pol. (Reisen, Reysen); 75 km S of Poznan; 51°47'/16°39'; CAHJP, EJ, GA, HSL.

Rygalowka, Pol.; pop. 5; 75 km N of Bialystok; 53°44'/23°33'.

Ryglice, Pol. (Riglitz); pop. 259; 94 km E of Krakow; 49°53'/21°08'; EGRS, GUM4, GUM5, HSL, JGFF, LDL, PHP3, SF.

Rykhtsitse, Ukr. (Rychcice); pop. 73; 62 km SSW of Lvov; 49°23'/23°33'; HSL.

Ryki, Pol. (Rika, Rike, Riki); pop. 2,419; 62 km WNW of Lublin; 51°38'/21°56'; AMG, COH, EDRD, GA, GUM3, GUM4, GUM5, HSL, HSL2, JGFF, LYV, SF, YB.

Rykoszyn, Pol.; pop. 9; 94 km ENE of Czestochowa; 50°52'/20°25'.

Rykov, *see* Rykow.

Rykoviche, Ukr. (Rykowicze); pop. 22; 94 km NNE of Lvov; 50°38'/24°33'.

Rykow, Pol. (Rikov, Rykov); 101 km ESE of Lodz; 51°20'/20°47'; HSL, SF, SF.

Rykowicze, *see* Rykoviche.

Rylow, Pol. PHP2. This town was not found in BGN gazetteers under the given spelling.

Rylowa, Pol.; pop. 11; 56 km ENE of Krakow; 50°06'/20°40'.

Rylsk, Ukr.; pop. 245; 107 km NE of Konotop; 51°34'/34°40'; GUM4.

Rymachi, Ukr. (Rymacze); pop. 70; 150 km N of Lvov; 51°11'/23°54'.

Rymacze, *see* Rymachi.

Rymanow, Pol. (Rimanov, Rumanov); pop. 1,412; 69 km SW of Przemysl; 49°35'/21°52'; AMG, COH, EDRD, EGRS, EJ, GA, GUM3, GUM4, GUM5, HSL, HSL2, JGFF, LDL, LYV, POCEM, SF, YB.

Rymki, Byel.; pop. 22; 163 km NNW of Minsk; 55°18'/27°16'.

Rymszany, *see* Rimse.

Rynarzewo, Pol. (Netzwalde, Rohrbruch); 88 km NNE of Poznan; 53°04'/17°49'; LDS.

Rynholec, Cz.; pop. 6; 38 km W of Praha; 50°08'/13°55'.

Rynoltice, Cz.; pop. 3; 82 km N of Praha; 50°48'/14°49'.

Rynovice, Cz.; pop. 1; 88 km NNE of Praha; 50°44'/15°09'.

Rypiany, Ukr.; pop. 48; 126 km SSW of Lvov; 48°55'/22°55'. This town was located on an interwar map of Poland but does not appear in contemporary gazetteers. Map coordinates are approximate.

Rypin, Pol. (Ripin); pop. 2,791; 139 km WNW of Warszawa; 53°04'/19°27'; AMG, CAHJP, COH, EDRD, GUM3, GUM4, GUM5, HSL, HSL2, JGFF, LDS, LYV, PHP4, POCEM, SF, YB.

Rypne, Ukr.; pop. 4; 120 km S of Lvov; 48°49'/24°08'; HSL.

Ryschkonowka, LDL. This pre-World War I community was not found in BGN gazetteers.

Ryshkany, Mold. (Rascani Targ, Rishkan, Rishkani, Ryskany); pop. 2,060; 146 km NW of Kishinev; 47°58'/27°33'; EJ, HSL, SF.

Ryskany, *see* Ryshkany.

Ryszkowa Wola, Pol.; pop. 16; 38 km N of Przemysl; 50°04'/22°52'.

Rytarowice, *see* Verkhovtsy.

Rytele, Pol. (Rytele Swieckie); pop. 46; 88 km SW of Bialystok; 52°41'/22°07'.

Rytele Swieckie, *see* Rytele.

Rytlow, Pol.; pop. 11; 75 km NE of Czestochowa; 51°02'/20°06'.

Rytro, Pol.; pop. 19; 88 km SE of Krakow; 49°29'/20°41'; GA, GUM3, GUM5, PHP3.

Rytwiany, Pol. (Ritvin); pop. 40; 107 km NE of Krakow; 50°32'/21°12'; SF, YB.

Ryzanowka, *see* Ryzhanovka.

Ryzhanovka, Ukr. (Rizinivka, Ryzanowka); 50 km NNE of Uman; 49°06'/30°43'; GYLA, LDL, SF.

Ryzhishchev, *see* Rzhishchev.

Rzabiec, Pol.; pop. 6; 69 km ENE of Czestochowa; 50°50'/20°04'.

Rzachowa, Pol.; pop. 6; 50 km ENE of Krakow; 50°08'/20°37'.

Rzaska, Pol.; pop. 5; 6 km WNW of Krakow; 50°06'/19°50'.

Rzasnia, Pol.; pop. 118; 56 km N of Czestochowa; 51°14'/19°03'; GUM3.

Rzasnik, Pol.; pop. 25; 82 km NNE of Warszawa; 52°50'/21°42'.

Rzazew, Pol.; pop. 24; 101 km E of Warszawa; 52°08'/22°29'.

Rzechow, Pol.; pop. 9; 82 km WSW of Lublin; 51°08'/21°23'.

Rzeczki, Byel.; pop. 83; There are two towns in the former Polish province of Wilen, located at 54°35'/25°06' and 55°26'/27°37'. *Also see* Rzyczki.

Rzeczyca, Pol.; pop. 186; 82 km S of Lublin; 50°32'/22°42'; CAHJP, GUM5, PHP2. *See also* Rechitsa.

Rzeczyca (near Lodz), Pol.; 45 km WSW of Lodz; 51°44'/18°51'; CAHJP.

Rzeczyca (near Tomaszow Mazowiecki), Pol.; pop. 91; 62 km E of Lodz; 51°36'/20°18'.

Rzeczyca Ziemianska, Pol.; pop. 3; 50 km SSW of Lublin; 50°51'/22°11'.

Rzedzianowice, Pol.; pop. 52; 107 km ENE of Krakow; 50°19'/21°24'.

Rzedzin, Pol.; pop. 79; 82 km E of Krakow; 50°01'/21°03'.

Rzegocina, *see* Zegocina.

Rzeki, Pol.; pop. 4; 50 km WSW of Przemysl; 49°45'/22°09'. *See also* Rzeki Male.

Rzeki Male, Pol. (Rzeki); pop. 85; 26 km NE of Czestochowa; 50°53'/19°25'; PHP1.

Rzeki Wielkie, Pol.; pop. 11; 26 km NE of Czestochowa; 50°53'/19°25'.

Rzekun, Pol.; pop. 49; 101 km WSW of Bialystok; 53°03'/21°38'.

Rzemien, Pol.; pop. 5; 101 km WNW of Przemysl; 50°13'/21°31'.

Rzepedz, Pol.; pop. 28; 69 km SW of Przemysl; 49°22'/22°06'.

Rzepiennik, *see* Rzepiennik Strzyzewski.

Rzepiennik Biskupi, Pol.; pop. 33; 88 km ESE of Krakow; 49°48'/21°05'; PHP3.

Rzepiennik Marciszowski, Pol. PHP3. This town was not found in BGN gazetteers under the given spelling.

Rzepiennik Strzyzews, *see* Rzepiennik Strzyzewski.

Rzepiennik Strzyzewski, Pol. (Rzepiennik, Rzepiennik Strzyzews); pop. 224; 88 km ESE of Krakow; 49°48'/21°03'; EGRS, GA, GUM3, GUM4, GUM5, HSL, PHP3.

Rzepin, Pol. (Reppen); pop. 33; 133 km SSE of Szczecin; 52°21'/14°49'; GUM3, GUM5.

Rzepki, Pol.; pop. 18; 26 km SE of Lodz; 51°36'/19°38'.

Rzeplin, Pol.; pop. 21; 107 km NE of Przemysl; 50°28'/23°52'; PHP3.

Rzepnik, Pol.; pop. 2; 75 km W of Przemysl; 49°48'/21°45'.

Rzepniow, *see* Zhepnyuv.

Rzerzeczyce, Pol.; pop. 13; 19 km NE of Czestochowa; 50°54'/19°20'.

Rzesna Polska, Pol.; pop. 63; Described in the *Black Book* as being in the Lwow region of Poland, this town was not found in BGN gazetteers.

Rzesza, *see* Riese.

Rzeszotary, Pol.; pop. 10; 19 km SSE of Krakow; 49°57'/19°58'.

Rzeszotary Chwaly, Pol.; pop. 3; 107 km WNW of Warszawa; 52°53'/19°50'.

Rzeszotary Gortaty, Pol.; pop. 9; 101 km WNW of Warszawa; 52°52'/19°49'.

Rzeszotkow, Pol.; pop. 17; 94 km ENE of Warszawa; 52°17'/22°23'.

Rzeszow, Pol. (Raysha, Rayshe, Reichshof, Reisha, Riashov, Risha, Zheshov, Zheshuv, Zhezhov); pop. 11,361; 62 km WNW of Przemysl; 50°03'/22°00'; AMG, COH, EDRD, EGRS, EJ, FRG, GA, GUM3, GUM4, GUM5, GUM6, HSL, HSL2, JGFF, LDL, LYV, PHGBW, PHP1, PHP2, PHP3, PHP4, POCEM, SF, YB.

Rzeszowek, Pol.; pop. 4; 69 km E of Czestochowa; 50°45'/20°04'.

Rzewnie, Pol.; pop. 2; 69 km N of Warszawa; 52°50'/21°21'.

Rzewuski Stare, Pol.; pop. 2; 101 km S of Bialystok; 52°16'/22°37'.

Rzezawa, Pol.; pop. 49; 45 km E of Krakow; 49°59'/20°31'.

Rzezyca, *see* Rezekne.

Rzgow, Pol. (Zhagov); pop. 93; 13 km SSE of Lodz; 51°40'/19°30'; CAHJP, GA, PHP1, SF.

Rzhavintsy, Ukr. (Rjavinti?); pop. 43; 32 km NNE of Chernovtsy; 48°31'/26°05'.

Rzhev, USSR; pop. 780; 120 km SW of Kalinin; 56°15'/34°20'; GUM4, GUM6, JGFF.

Rzhishcev, *see* Rzhishchev.

Rzhishchev, Ukr. (Orzistchov, Rchichtchev, Ryzhishchev, Rzhishcev, Ryszczow, Zhishchuv); pop. 1,608; 62 km SE of Kiyev; 49°58'/31°03'; AMG, EDRD, HSL, LDL, SF.

Rzhishchev (Wolyn), Ukr.; pop. 5; 82 km NE of Lvov; 50°21'/24°47'.

Rzochow, Pol. (Rizchov); pop. 53; 107 km WNW of Przemysl; 50°15'/21°29'; HSL, SF, WS.

Rzozow, Pol.; pop. 15; 19 km SSW of Krakow; 49°57'/19°49'.

Rzuchow, Pol.; pop. 21; A number of towns share this name. It was not possible to determine from available information which one is being referenced.

Rzuchowa, Pol.; pop. 7; 75 km E of Krakow; 49°57'/20°57'.

Rzucow, Pol.; pop. 10; 101 km ESE of Lodz; 51°17'/20°45'.

Rzyczka, *see* Richka.

Rzyczki, *see* Rechki.

Rzymki, Pol.; pop. 9; 75 km N of Lublin; 51°52'/22°29'.

Rzyszczow, *see* Rzhishchev.

Saabor, *see* Zabor.

Saalfeld, Germ.; pop. 33; a number of towns share this name. It was not possible to determine from available information which one is being referenced. *See also* Zalewo.

Saalstadt, Germ.; pop. 3; 120 km SSW of Frankfurt am Main; 49°19'/07°33'; GED.

Saarbrucken, Germ. (Saarbruecken, Saarland); pop. 2,650; 157 km SW of Frankfurt am Main; 49°14'/07°00'; AMG, EJ, GED, GUM3, GUM4, GUM5, HSL, JGFF, PHGBW, PHP1.

Saarbruecken, *see* Saarbrucken.

Saarburg, Germ.; 157 km S of Koln; 49°36'/06°33'; GUM5, HSL.

Saargemund, HSL. This pre-World War I community was not found in BGN gazetteers.

Saarland, *see* Saarbrucken.

Saarlouis, Germ.; pop. 274; 163 km SW of Frankfurt am Main; 49°19'/06°45'; HSL.

Saarwellingen, Germ.; pop. 151; 157 km SW of Frankfurt am Main; 49°21'/06°49'; GED, GUM5.

Saavar, *see* Zabor.

Saaz, *see* Zatec.

Saba, Ukr.; 50 km SSW of Odessa; 46°08'/30°23'; GUM4, HSL.

Sabac, Yug.; pop. 89; 62 km WSW of Beograd; 44°45'/19°43'; EDRD, GUM3, GUM4, ISH2, PHY.

Saba Targ, Ukr.; pop. 159; 50 km SSW of Odessa; 46°08'/30°23'.

Sabed, Rom.; pop. 3; 62 km E of Cluj; 46°40'/24°27'.

Sabila, *see* Sabile.

Sabile, Lat. (Sabila, Sabiles, Shabiln, Zabeln, Zobeln); pop. 305; 94 km W of Riga; 57°03'/22°35'; GUM4, GUM5, HSL, JGFF, PHLE, SF.

Sabiles, *see* Sabile.

Sabin, *see* Sawin.

Sabinka, Pol.; pop. 139; 82 km E of Warszawa; 52°11'/22°11'.

Sabinov, Cz. (Kisseben, Kisszeben, Zeben); pop. 1,480; 50 km NNW of Kosice; 49°06'/21°06'; AMG, COH, GUM4, GUM5, GUM6, HSL, HSL2, JGFF.

Sabinowka, *see* Sabinuvka.

Sabinuvka, Ukr. (Sabinowka); pop. 4; 75 km NNE of Lvov; 50°21'/24°39'.

Sabisa, Rom.; pop. 13; 114 km NNW of Cluj; 47°43'/23°20'.

Sabnie, Pol.; 88 km SSW of Bialystok; 52°31'/22°18'; HSL.

Sacalaia, Rom.; pop. 5; 32 km NE of Cluj; 46°58'/23°55'.

Sacalasau, Rom.; pop. 2; 107 km WNW of Cluj; 47°12'/22°18'.

Sacalaseni, Rom.; pop. 39; 94 km N of Cluj; 47°35'/23°34'.

Sacalul de Campi, Rom. (Mezoszakal); 50 km ESE of Cluj; 46°35'/24°11'; HSL. This town was located on a pre-World War I map, but does not appear in contemporary gazetteers.

Sacareni, *see* Sekareny.

Sacaseni, Rom.; pop. 47; 101 km NW of Cluj; 47°29'/22°41'.

Sacel, Rom. (Izaszacsal, Sicsel); pop. 651; 114 km NNE of Cluj; 47°38'/24°26'; AMG, GUM4, PHR2, SM.

Sachkhere, USSR; EDRD. This town was not found in BGN gazetteers under the given spelling.

Sachki, Ukr. (Sachtie); 202 km SE of Dnepropetrovsk; 47°10'/36°54'; HSL.

Sachsen, Germ.; 38 km SW of Nurnberg; 49°18'/10°39'; ISH2, PHGB.

Sachsenburg, Germ.; 82 km WSW of Leipzig; 51°17'/11°10'; AMG, GUM3, GUM5.

Sachsenflur, Germ.; 94 km W of Nurnberg; 49°31'/09°43'; LDS.

Sachsenhagen, Germ.; pop. 22; 32 km W of Hannover; 52°24'/09°16'.

Sachsenhausen, Germ.; 133 km N of Frankfurt am Main; 51°14'/09°01'; AMG, EDRD, GUM3, GUM4, GUM5, GUM6, ISH1, ISH2, PHGBW. Sachsenhausen was the site of a concentration camp. Sources more likely refer to the camp, not the town.

Sachsisch-Bereg, *see* Beregovo.

Sachsisch Reen, *see* Reghin.

Sachtie, *see* Sachki.

Sacueni, Rom. (Szekelyhid); pop. 547; 133 km WNW of Cluj; 47°21'/22°06'; HSL, HSL2, LDL, LDS, PHR2.

Sacurov, Cz. (Szacsur); 38 km NE of Kosice; 48°49'/21°42'; HSL.

Saczow, Pol.; pop. 4; 45 km S of Czestochowa; 50°26'/19°02'.

Sadaclia, *see* Sadakliya.

Sadacu, *see* Sadyk.

Sadagora, *see* Sadgura.

Sadagura, *see* Sadgura.

Sadakliya, Mold. (Sadaclia); pop. 4; 69 km S of Kishinev; 46°27'/28°53'.

Sadek, Cz.; 50 km SSW of Praha; 49°44'/13°59'; HSL.

Sadgora, *see* Sadgura.

Sadgura, Ukr. (Sadagora, Sadagura, Sdgora, Sadygera); pop. 1,488; 6 km N of Chernovtsy; 48°20'/25°57'; AMG, COH, EJ, GUM4, GUM5, GYLA, HSL, HSL2, JGFF, LDL,

PHR2, SF.

Sadki (near Ostrog), Ukr.; pop. 29; 32 km ESE of Rovno; 50°29'/26°41'.

Sadki (Tarnopol), Ukr.; pop. 23; 62 km NNW of Chernovtsy; 48°51'/25°34'; EDRD. It is likely that the Sadki described in EDRD is not indicated here, but is rather the Sadki in the eastern Ukraine.

Sadkowa, Pol.; pop. 33; 88 km WSW of Przemysl; 49°45'/21°34'.

Sadogora, Pol.; 62 km ENE of Wroclaw; 51°07'/17°54'; PHP2.

Sadoles, Pol.; pop. 10; 75 km NE of Warszawa; 52°39'/21°51'.

Sadov, Ukr. (Sadow); pop. 46; 94 km W of Rovno; 50°42'/24°56'; GUM3.

Sadova, Mold.; pop. 37; 45 km WNW of Kishinev; 47°11'/28°21'.

Sadova Vishnia, *see* Sudovaya Vishnya.

Sadow, *see* Sadov.

Sadowa, Pol.; 13 km WNW of Warszawa; 52°21'/20°50'; AMG.

Sadowa Wisnia, *see* Sudovaya Vishnya.

Sadowa Wiszna, *see* Sudovaya Vishnya.

Sadowa Wisznia, *see* Sudovaya Vishnya.

Sadowa Wisznia Miasto, *see* Sudovaya Vishnya.

Sadowie, Pol.; pop. 25; a number of towns share this name. It was not possible to determine from available information which one is being referenced.

Sadowna, *possibly* Sadowne.

Sadowne, Pol. (Sadowna?); pop. 245; 75 km NE of Warszawa; 52°39'/21°51'; GUM5, HSL.

Sadska, Cz.; pop. 13; 38 km ENE of Praha; 50°08'/14°59'.

Sadurki, Pol.; pop. 4; 19 km W of Lublin; 51°17'/22°17'; GUM4.

Sady, Pol.; pop. 27; 69 km ESE of Lublin; 50°57'/23°23'.

Sadygera, *see* Sadgura.

Sadyk, Mold. (Sadacu); pop. 17; 88 km S of Kishinev; 46°16'/28°31'.

Sadykierz Szlachecki, Pol.; pop. 33; Described in the *Black Book* as being in the Warszawa region of Poland, this town was not found in BGN gazetteers.

Sadzavka, Ukr. (Sadzawka); pop. 100; 88 km WNW of Chernovtsy; 48°34'/24°49'; PHP2.

Sadzavki, *see* Sadzhevka.

Sadzawka, *see* Sadzavka.

Sadzawki, *see* Sadzhevka.

Sadzhevka, Ukr. (Sadzavki, Sadzawki); pop. 22; 114 km N of Chernovtsy; 49°17'/26°09'.

Saechsisch Regen, *see* Reghin.

Safarikovo, Cz. (Tornala, Tornalja, Tornalya); pop. 887; 75 km SW of Kosice; 48°25'/20°20'; AMG, COH, EJ, GUM4, GUM5, GUM5, HSL, HSL2, LDL, LYV, YB.

Saffig, Germ.; 75 km SE of Koln; 50°23'/07°25'; GED.

Safov, Cz. (Schaffa); pop. 76; 75 km SW of Brno; 48°52'/15°44'; EJ, HSL, HSL2.

Sag, Rom. (Felsoszek); pop. 22; 221 km SW of Cluj; 45°39'/21°10'.

Sagan, *see* Zagan.

Sagani, *see* Primorskoye (Bessarabia II).

Sagaydak, Mold. (Sahaidac); pop. 14; 45 km S of Kishinev; 46°40'/28°51'.

Sagod, Hung.; pop. 1; 56 km NNW of Nagykanizsa; 46°52'/16°49'.

Sagujfalu, Hung.; pop. 10; 82 km NNE of Budapest; 48°06'/19°41'.

Sahaidac, *see* Sagaydak.

Saharna, *see* Sakharna.

Sahryn, Pol.; pop. 20; 107 km ESE of Lublin; 50°41'/23°48'.

Sahy, Cz. (Ipolysag); pop. 1,072; 139 km E of Bratislava; 48°04'/18°58'; AMG, COH, HSL, HSL2, LDL.

Saida, Germ.; 107 km ESE of Leipzig; 50°57'/13°47'; HSL.

Saikava, Lat. (Saikavas); pop. 33; 107 km N of Daugavpils; 56°46'/26°24'.

Saikavas, *see* Saikava.

Saint Nicolau Mare, GUM4. This town was not found in BGN gazetteers under the given spelling.

Saiti, *see* Saitsy.

Saitsy, Mold. (Saiti); pop. 23; 69 km SE of Kishinev; 46°30'/29°24'.

Sajan, Yug.; pop. 9; 120 km NNW of Beograd; 45°51'/20°16'.

Sajczyce, Pol.; pop. 17; 62 km E of Lublin; 51°15'/23°27'; GA.

Sajmiste, *see* Zemun.

Sajo, *see* Sieu.

Sajobabony, Hung.; pop. 5; 13 km NW of Miskolc; 48°10'/20°44'.

Sajoecseg, Hung.; pop. 22; 19 km N of Miskolc; 48°12'/20°47'; HSL.

Sajogomor, *see* Gemer.

Sajohidveg, Hung.; pop. 10; 13 km ESE of Miskolc; 48°00'/20°57'.

Sajoivanka, Hung.; pop. 16; 26 km NW of Miskolc; 48°16'/20°35'.

Sajokapolna, Hung.; pop. 4; 19 km NW of Miskolc; 48°12'/20°42'; HSL.

Sajokaza, Hung.; pop. 98; 26 km NW of Miskolc; 48°17'/20°35'; HSL, PHH.

Sajokazinc, *see* Kazincbarcika.

Sajokereszkur, Hung.; pop. 13; 13 km NNW of Miskolc; 48°10'/20°47'; HSL.

Sajolad, Hung.; pop. 21; 13 km ESE of Miskolc; 48°03'/20°54'; HSL.

Sajolaszlofalva, Hung.; pop. 2; 19 km NW of Miskolc; 48°11'/20°41'.

Sajomagyaros, *see* Sieu Magherus.

Sajomercse, Hung.; pop. 11; 32 km WNW of Miskolc; 48°15'/20°25'.

Sajomezo, *see* Poienile Glodului.

Sajonemeti, Hung.; pop. 4; 32 km WNW of Miskolc; 48°16'/20°23'; HSL.

Sajooros, Hung.; pop. 7; 26 km ESE of Miskolc; 47°57'/21°02'.

Sajopalfala, Hung.; pop. 6; 13 km NNE of Miskolc; 48°10'/20°51'.

Sajopetri, Hung.; pop. 21; 13 km ESE of Miskolc; 48°02'/20°54'.

Sajopuspoki, Hung.; pop. 2; 38 km WNW of Miskolc; 48°17'/20°21'; HSL.

Sajosenye, Hung.; pop. 13; 19 km N of Miskolc; 48°12'/20°50'.

Sajoszentandras, *see* Sieu Sfint.

Sajoszentpeter, Hung. (Baia Sprie, Felsobanya); pop. 597; 19 km NNW of Miskolc; 48°13'/20°43'; AMG, COH, GUM5, HSL, HSL2, JGFF, LDL, LDS, PHH, PHR2.

Sajoszoged, Hung.; pop. 20; 19 km SE of Miskolc; 47°57'/21°00'; HSL.

Sajovamos, Hung.; pop. 34; 19 km NNE of Miskolc; 48°11'/20°51'; HSL.

Sajovarkony, Hung.; pop. 102; 45 km WNW of Miskolc; 48°14'/20°19'; HSL.

Sajovelezd, Hung.; pop. 10; 32 km WNW of Miskolc; 48°16'/20°28'.

Saka, *see* Pavilosta.

Sakai, *see* Sakiai.

Sakarestie, Ukr. EDRD. This town was not found in BGN gazetteers under the given spelling.

Sakas, *see* Sakukrogs.

Sakee, *see* Sakiai.

Sakharna, Mold. (Saharna); pop. 36; 82 km N of Kishinev; 47°41'/28°58'.

Sakhnovshchina, Ukr.; pop. 150; 101 km NNE of Dnepropetrovsk; 49°08'/35°53'.

Saki, Ukr.; pop. 53; 45 km WNW of Simferopol; 45°08'/33°36'.

Sakiai, Lith. (Sakai, Sakee, Schaken, Schaki, Shakay, Shakee, Shaki, Shakyai, Suidine); pop. 1,267; 56 km W of Kaunas; 54°57'/23°03'; AMG, EJ, GUM3, GUM5, HSL, HSL2, JGFF, LDL, SF, YL.

Sakmir, *see* Satu Mare.

Sakod, Pol. EDRD. This town was not found in BGN gazetteers under the given spelling.

Sakovchizna, *see* Sharkovshchina.

Sakovichi, Byel. (Sakowicze); pop. 6; 94 km WNW of Minsk; 54°22'/26°23'.

Sakovshchina, Byel. (Sakowszczyzna); pop. 3; 82 km W of Minsk; 54°07'/26°22'.

Sakowicze, *see* Sakovichi.

Sakowszczyzna, *see* Sakovshchina.

Sakrau, GUM3, GUM4, PHP3. This town was not found in BGN gazetteers under the given spelling.

Saktmar, *see* Satu Mare.

Sakukrogs, Lat. (Sakas); pop. 73; 69 km SW of Riga; 56°33'/23°16'.

Sal, HSL. This pre-World War I community was not found in BGN gazetteers.

Sala, *see* Sellye.

Salacea, Rom.; pop. 45; 126 km WNW of Cluj; 47°28'/22°19'.

Salakas, Lith. (Salok, Saluk, Selok, Soloki); pop. 917; 114 km NNE of Vilnius; 55°35'/26°08'; AMG, GUM3, GUM4, HSL, JGFF, SF, YL.

Salamonowa, (Salamonowa Gora); pop. 39; Described in the *Black Book* as being in the Stanislawow region of Poland, this town was not found in BGN gazetteers.

Salamonowa Gora, *see* Salamonowa.

Salamony, *see* Salamony Grabowskie.

Salamony Grabowskie, Pol. (Salamony); pop. 10; 82 km SW of Lodz; 51°30'/18°22'.

Salank, *see* Shalanki.

Salanky, *see* Shalanki.

Salant, *see* Salantai.

Salanta, *see* Salonta.

Salantai, Lith. (Salant, Salanty, Selent); pop. 670; 107 km W of Siauliai; 56°04'/21°34'; COH, GUM4, HSL, HSL2, JGFF, LDL, LYV, SF, YL.

Salanty, *see* Salantai.

Salard, Rom. (Szalard); pop. 137; 133 km WNW of Cluj; 47°13'/22°03'; AMG, HSL, LDS, PHR2.

Salashe, Ukr. (Salasze); pop. 61; 50 km NNW of Lvov; 50°17'/23°51'.

Salaspils, Lat. (Kircholm); 19 km ESE of Riga; 56°51'/24°21'; EDRD, GUM3, GUM4, GUM5, PHLE.

Salasuri, Rom.; pop. 2; 101 km ESE of Cluj; 46°22'/24°46'.

Salasze, *see* Salashe.

Salat, *see* Salociai.

Salatig, Rom.; pop. 9; 75 km NW of Cluj; 47°22'/23°08'.

Salatiu, Rom.; pop. 6; 45 km NNE of Cluj; 47°06'/23°56'.

Salcininkai, Lith. (Soleczniki, Soleczniki Wielkie); 50 km S of Vilnius; 54°18'/25°23'; AMG, CAHJP.

Salcininkeliai, Lith. (Slutznik, Soletchnik); 38 km SSE of Vilnius; 54°23'/25°23'; LDL, SF.

Salcuta, *see* Salkutsa.

Salder, Germ.; pop. 5; 50 km ESE of Hannover; 52°08'/10°20'.

Saldobos, *see* Steblevka.

Saldobosh, *see* Steblevka.

Saldobus, *see* Steblevka.

Saldus, Lat. (Frauenburg, Freuenberg, Froienburg); pop. 375; 101 km WSW of Riga; 56°40'/22°30'; JGFF, LDL, LDS, PHLE, SF.

Salgotarjan, Hung.; pop. 1,135; 69 km W of Miskolc; 48°07'/19°49'; AMG, COH, GUM3, GUM5, HSL, LDL, LDS, PHH.

Salicea, Rom. (Szelicse); 13 km SSW of Cluj; 46°41'/23°32'; HSL.

Salisca, Rom.; pop. 15; 56 km N of Cluj; 47°13'/23°49'.

Salistea de Sus, Rom. (Felso Szelistye, Felsoszelistye, Selisht, Selist); pop. 377; 114 km NNE of Cluj; 47°39'/24°21'; COH, PHR2, SM.

Salka, *see* Szalka.

Salkaski Sveti Ivan, Yug.; pop. 20; This town was not found in BGN gazetteers under the given spelling.

Salkutsa, Mold. (Salcuta); pop. 36; 56 km SE of Kishinev; 46°34'/29°15'.

Sallel, *see* Silale.

Sallern, Germ.; 88 km ESE of Nurnberg; 49°01'/12°04'; PHGB.

Salmos, *see* Gondovo.

Salmunster, Germ.; pop. 52; 50 km NE of Frankfurt am Main; 50°17'/09°22'; LDS.

Salnita, Rom. (Erdoszallas); pop. 5; 75 km N of Cluj; 47°25'/23°40'.

Salnos, Lith. (Szolny); 75 km NE of Kaunas; 55°22'/24°43'; JGFF.

Salociai, Lith. (Salat, Selt); pop. 174; 75 km NE of Siauliai; 56°13'/24°24'; HSL, SF, YL.

Salok, *see* Salakas.

Salomvar, Hung.; pop. 10; 50 km NW of Nagykanizsa; 46°51'/16°40'.

Salonika, *see* Thessaloniki.

Saloniki, *see* Thessaloniki.

Salonta, Rom. (Salanta, Salonta Mare); pop. 740; 150 km W of Cluj; 46°48'/21°39'; PHR2.

Salonta Mare, *see* Salonta.

Salos, Lith. (Soly); 126 km E of Siauliai; 55°49'/25°22'; EDRD, GUM3, GUM4, GYLA.

Salsig, Rom.; pop. 49; 88 km NNW of Cluj; 47°32'/23°18'.

Saluk, *see* Salakas.

Salva, Rom. (Szalva); pop. 36; 82 km NNE of Cluj; 47°18'/24°21'; HSL.

Saly, Hung.; pop. 47; 19 km SSW of Miskolc; 47°57'/20°40'; HSL, PHH.

Salzberg, *see* Bochnia.

Salzburg, Aus.; pop. 198; 133 km NE of Innsbruck; 47°48'/13°02'; EDRD, EJ, GUM3, GUM5, HSL.

Salzhemmendorf, Germ.; pop. 7; 45 km S of Hannover; 52°04'/09°37'.

Salzkotten, Germ.; pop. 80; 107 km SW of Hannover; 51°40'/08°36'; JGFF.

Salzschlirf, *see* Bad Salzschlirf.

Salzuflen, *see* Bad Salzuflen.

Salzwedel, Germ.; pop. 64; 107 km ESE of Hamburg; 52°51'/11°09'; EJ, GUM3, GUM4, GUM5, GUM6, HSL.

Samac, *see* Samac Slavonski.

Samac Slavonski, Yug. (Samac); pop. 15; 163 km W of Beograd; 45°04'/18°29'.

Samakowce, Pol. PHP2. This town was not found in BGN gazetteers under the given spelling.

Samani, Lat.; 82 km ESE of Riga; 56°35'/25°15'; GUM3.

Samara, Rom.; 120 km WNW of Bucuresti; 44°50'/24°43'; JGFF, LDL.

Samaroviche, *see* Samarovichi.

Samarovichi, Byel. (Samaroviche, Samarowicze); pop. 20; 150 km NW of Pinsk; 53°12'/24°45'.

Samarowicze, *see* Samarovichi.

Samary, Ukr.; pop. 59; 182 km NW of Rovno; 51°52'/24°37'.

Samascani, *see* Samashkany.

Samashkany, Mold. (Samascani); pop. 143; 88 km N of Kishinev; 47°45'/28°42'.

Samber, *see* Sambor.

Sambor, Ukr. (Altshtot, Altstadt, Ir Yashan, Samber, Sambor Stary, Sambor Yashan); pop. 6,068; 69 km SW of Lvov; 49°31'/23°12'; AMG, CAHJP, COH, EDRD, EGRS, GA, GUM3, GUM4, GUM5, GUM6, GYLA, HSL, HSL2, JGFF, LDL, LYV, PHP2, PHP3, SF, YB.

Sambor Stary, *see* Sambor.

Sambor Yashan, *see* Sambor.

Samborz, Pol.; 56 km SW of Lodz; 51°28'/18°49'; POCEM.

Samborzec, Pol.; pop. 13; 88 km SW of Lublin; 50°39'/21°39'.

Samenheim, Germ. (Sammenheim); 56 km SSW of Nurnberg; 49°03'/10°43'; PHGB.

Samgorodok, Ukr. (Sangorodok, Shenderivka, Shinderivka, Szandorowka); pop. 1,244; 45 km NNE of Vinnitsa; 49°32'/28°51'; EDRD, JGFF, LDL, SF. BGN shows the spelling as Samgorodok; the correct name may be Sangorodok.

Sammenheim, *see* Samenheim.

Sammerein, *see* Samorin.

Samochvilocitch, *see* Samokhvalovichi.

Samocice, Pol.; pop. 23; 69 km ENE of Krakow; 50°16'/20°53'.

Samogitien, *see* Zmudz.

Samokhvalovichi, Byel. (Samochvilocitch); pop. 290; 19 km S of Minsk; 53°44'/27°30'; LDL, SF.

Samokleski Male, Pol.; 88 km NNE of Poznan; 53°04'/17°43'; GUM3.

Samokov, Bulg.; pop. 410; 45 km SSE of Sofija; 42°20'/23°33'; EJ.

Samoluskovtsy, Ukr. (Samoluskowce); pop. 24; 101 km N of Chernovtsy; 49°09'/26°07'.

Samoluskowce, *see* Samoluskovtsy.

Samorin, Cz. (Sammerein, Samorja, Somorja); pop. 945; 19 km ESE of Bratislava; 48°02'/17°19'; COH, HSL, JGFF, YB.

Samorja, *see* Samorin.

Samorzadki, Pol.; pop. 3; 75 km ESE of Warszawa; 51°50'/21°46'.

Samostrzalow, Pol.; pop. 6; 75 km NNE of Krakow; 50°35'/20°38'.

Samotevichi, Byel.; pop. 378; 107 km NNE of Gomel; 53°13'/31°50'; LDL, SF.

Samothrace, *see* Samothraki.

Samothraki, Greece (Samothrace); 1040 km NE of Athens; 40°27'/35°32'; EDRD.

Samotnia, Pol.; pop. 8; 107 km SW of Lublin; 50°38'/21°23'.

Samotschin, *see* Szamocin.

Samson, *see* Hajdusamson.

Samsonhaza, Hung.; pop. 3; 69 km NNE of Budapest; 47°59'/19°44'.

Samsonow, Pol.; pop. 50; 107 km ENE of Czestochowa; 50°59'/20°37'; GUM3, GUM5.

Samsud, Rom.; pop. 30; 82 km NW of Cluj; 47°21'/22°57'.

Samter, *see* Szamotuly.

Samuseni, Ukr.; pop. 5; 38 km N of Chernovtsy; 48°36'/26°04'.

Sanad, Yug.; pop. 21; 133 km NNW of Beograd; 45°58'/20°06'.

Sanapotek, *see* Valea Porcului.

Sanatauca, *see* Senatovka.

Sanc, *see* Kajdacs.

Sancauti, *see* Sankaitsy.

Sanda, HSL. This pre-World War I community was not found in BGN gazetteers.

Sandau, Germ.; 94 km WNW of Berlin; 52°47'/12°03'; HSL.

Sandberg, *see* Pyasechna.

Sandersleben, Germ.; pop. 9; 69 km WNW of Leipzig; 51°41'/11°34'; HSL, LDS.

Sandets, *see* Nowy Sacz.

Sandhausen, Germ.; pop. 24; 75 km NW of Stuttgart; 49°21'/08°39'; GED, LDS, PHGBW.

Sandhorst, Germ.; pop. 8; 163 km WSW of Hamburg; 53°29'/07°30'.

Sandomierz, Pol. (Sandomir, Sandomirzh, Sandomyerz, Sudomir, Tsoyzmir, Tsuyzmir, Tsuzmir, Tzoizmir, Zuzmir); pop. 2,641; 88 km SSW of Lublin; 50°41'/21°45'; AMG, CAHJP, COH, EDRD, EJ, GA, GUM3, GUM4, GUM5, GUM6, HSL, HSL2, JGFF, LDL, LDS, LYV, PHP1, PHP3, PHP4, POCEM, SF.

Sandominic, *see* Sindominic.

Sandomir, *see* Sandomierz.

Sandomirzh, *see* Sandomierz.

Sandomyerz, *see* Sandomierz.

Sandorfalu, HSL. This pre-World War I community was not found in BGN gazetteers.

Sandorfalva, Hung.; pop. 42; 19 km NNW of Szeged; 46°22'/20°06'.

Sandove Vishnie, *see* Sudovaya Vishnya.

Sandrif, *see* Sandrovo.

Sandrovo, Ukr. (Osandarfalva, Sandrif); 182 km WSW of Chernovtsy; 48°08'/23°31'; HSL, SM.

Sandurki, GA. This town was not found in BGN gazetteers

under the given spelling.

Sandz, *see* Nowy Sacz.

Sangeorgiul de Padure, *see* Singeorgiu de Padure.

Sangeorz Bai, *see* Singeorz Bai.

Sangerberg, *see* Prameny.

Sangerei, *see* Lazovsk.

Sangereii Noui, Mold.; pop. 23; 101 km NW of Kishinev; 47°43'/28°06'.

Sangerhausen, Germ.; pop. 19; 75 km W of Leipzig; 51°28'/11°18'.

Sangiorgiul de Padure, *see* Singeorgiu de Padure.

Sangorodok, *see* Samgorodok.

Saniob, *see* Sinioe.

Sanislau, Rom. (Szaniszlo); pop. 183; 139 km NW of Cluj; 47°38'/22°20'; COH, HSL, HSL2, JGFF, PHR2.

Sanka, Pol.; pop. 13; 19 km WSW of Krakow; 50°04'/19°39'.

Sankad, HSL. This pre-World War I community was not found in BGN gazetteers.

Sankaitsy, Mold. (Sancauti); pop. 46; 208 km NW of Kishinev; 48°23'/26°55'.

Sankt Andra, *see* Szentendre.

Sankt Blasien, Germ.; 139 km SSW of Stuttgart; 47°46'/08°08'; PHGBW.

Sankt Goar, Germ.; pop. 28; 69 km W of Frankfurt am Main; 50°09'/07°43'.

Sankt Goarshausen, Germ.; pop. 26; 69 km W of Frankfurt am Main; 50°09'/07°44'.

Sankt Ingbert, Germ.; pop. 76; 146 km SW of Frankfurt am Main; 49°17'/07°07'; GED, HSL.

Sankt Johann, *see* Mosonszentjanos.

Sankt Martin im Muhlkreise, Aus.; 101 km NE of Salzburg; 48°25'/14°02'; GUM5.

Sankt Nikolai, HSL. a number of towns share this name. It was not possible to determine from available information which one is being referenced.

Sankt Peter, *see* Mosonszentpeter.

Sankt Polten, Aus. (St Palten, St Poelten Stadt); pop. 1,603; 50 km WSW of Wien; 48°12'/15°38'; GUM4.

Sankt Tonis, Germ.; 50 km NW of Koln; 51°19'/06°30'; GED, GUM5.

Sankt Veit, *see* Sankt Veit im Pongau.

Sankt Veit im Pongau, Aus. (Sankt Veit, St Veit); 56 km SSE of Salzburg; 47°20'/13°09'; EJ.

Sankt Wendel, Germ. (St Wendel); pop. 130; 133 km SW of Frankfurt am Main; 49°28'/07°10'; EJ, GED.

Sanmartin, *see* Sinmartin.

Sanmartin Ciuc, *see* Sinmartin.

Sanmihaiul de Campie, *see* Sinmihaiu de Padure.

Sannicolal Mare, GUM4. This town was not found in BGN gazetteers under the given spelling.

Sannicolaul, Rom. PHR1. This town was not found in BGN gazetteers under the given spelling.

Sannicolaul Mare, *see* Sinnicolaw Mare.

Sannicolaul Roman, *see* Sinnicolau Romin.

Sanniki, Pol.; pop. 315; 69 km NNE of Lodz; 52°20'/19°52'; EDRD, GA, GUM3, PHP1, PHP4.

Sanoczek, Pol.; pop. 10; 56 km SW of Przemysl; 49°33'/22°09'.

Sanok, Pol. (Sanuk, Sonik); pop. 4,067; 50 km SW of Przemysl; 49°34'/22°12'; AMG, CAHJP, COH, EDRD, EGRS, EJ, GA, GUM3, GUM4, GUM5, GUM6, HSL, HSL2, ISH2, JGFF, LDL, LYV, PHP1, PHP2, PHP3, POCEM, SF, YB.

Sanpaul Cluj, *see* Sinpaul.

Sanski Most, Yug.; pop. 56; 126 km SSE of Zagreb; 44°46'/16°40'; PHY.

Sant, Rom.; pop. 30; 126 km NE of Cluj; 47°27'/24°54'.

Santa Maria, *see* Cojocna.

Santandrei Bihor, *see* Sintandrei.

Santau, Rom.; pop. 62; 114 km NW of Cluj; 47°31'/22°31'.

Santoczno, Pol.; pop. 88 km SE of Szczecin; 52°51'/15°21'; POCEM.

Santomischel, *see* Zaniemysl.

Santov, *see* Santovka.

Sarajevo, Yugoslavia: Jewish cemetery.

Santovka, Cz. (Santov); 120 km E of Bratislava; 48°09'/18°46'; HSL, JGFF.

Sants, *see* Nowy Sacz.

Sanuk, *see* Sanok.

Sanvasii, Rom. (Nyaradszentlaszlo); HSL. This pre-World War I community was not found in BGN gazetteers.

Sany, Cz.; pop. 6; 56 km ENE of Praha; 50°08'/15°15'; JGFF.

Sanz, *see* Nowy Sacz.

Sap, Hung.; 107 km SE of Miskolc; 47°15'/21°22'; HSL, LDS.

Sapaguv, Ukr. (Sapahow); pop. 24; 101 km SE of Lvov; 49°03'/24°36'.

Sapahow, *see* Sapaguv.

Sapanta, *see* Sapinta.

Sapci, Yug.; 182 km W of Beograd; 45°11'/18°13'; GUM4.

Sapezhanka, Ukr. (Sapiezanka); pop. 22; 38 km NNE of Lvov; 50°05'/24°20'.

Sapiezanka, *see* Sapezhanka.

Sapinta, Rom. (Sapanta, Sepinka, Spinka, Szaplonca); pop. 999; 139 km N of Cluj; 47°58'/23°42'; AMG, COH, GUM4, LDL, PHR2, SM.

Saponta, Rom. AMG, HSL. This pre-World War I community was not found in BGN gazetteers.

Sapte Bani, *possibly* Shishkany.

Sapte Sate, Mold.; pop. 34; 50 km WSW of Kishinev; 46°59'/28°12'.

Sar, *see* Sur.

Sarajevo, Yug. (Bosna Serai, Serajevo); pop. 8,190; 195 km SW of Beograd; 43°50'/18°25'; AMG, CAHJP, EDRD, EJ, GUM4, GUM6, HSL, ISH1, LJEE, PHY.

Saranchuki, Ukr. (Saranczuki); pop. 24; 94 km ESE of Lvov; 49°21'/24°59'.

Saranczuki, *see* Saranchuki.

Sarand, Hung.; 101 km SE of Miskolc; 47°24'/21°38'; AMG, LDS.

Sararia, *see* Zheltyy Yar.

Sarasau, Rom. (Szarvaszo); pop. 194; 139 km N of Cluj; 47°57'/23°49'.

Sarata, Ukr.; pop. 316; 94 km SW of Odessa; 46°01'/29°40'; YB.

Sarata Galbena, Mold.; pop. 55; 45 km SSW of Kishinev; 46°44'/28°31'.

Sarata Noua, *see* Novaya Sarata.

Sarata Rezeshty, Mold. (Razesi); pop. 2; 62 km SW of Kishinev; 46°37'/28°15'.

Sarata Veche, *see* Staraya Sarata.

Saratel, Rom. (Szeretfalva); pop. 44; 69 km NE of Cluj; 47°03'/24°25'; HSL.

Sarateni Orhei, *see* Staryye Sarateny.

Saratica Veche, *see* Saratsika Veke.

Saratov, USSR; 530 km E of Voronezh; 51°30'/45°55'; AMG, EDRD, EJ, GUM4, GUM5, HSL, JGFF, LDL.

Saratova, USSR; pop. 6,717; 530 km E of Voronezh; 51°30'/45°55'.

Saratsika Veke, Mold. (Saratica Veche); pop. 2; 50 km SSW of Kishinev; 46°36'/28°32'.

Sarauad, Rom.; pop. 17; 107 km NW of Cluj; 47°29'/22°37'.

Saravale, Rom.; 234 km SW of Cluj; 46°04'/20°44'; JGFF.

Saray, *see* Seirijai.

Sarazsadany, Hung. (Bodrogzsadany); pop. 4; 56 km NE of Miskolc; 48°16'/21°30'.

Sarbesti, *see* Sherbeshty.

Sarbi, *see* Sirbi.

Sarbi Maramures, *see* Sirbi.

Sarbinowo, Pol.; 13 km ENE of Poznan; 52°26'/17°10'; GA.

Sarbogard, Hung. (Alsokortvelyes); pop. 404; 75 km SSW of Budapest; 46°53'/18°38'; AMG, GUM5, HSL, LDL, LDS, PHH.

Sarbov, Cz.; 82 km N of Kosice; 49°25'/21°38'; HSL.

Sarcau, Rom.; pop. 3; 120 km WNW of Cluj; 47°12'/22°09'.

Sarcova, *see* Syrkovo.

Sard, Rom. (Magyarsard); 75 km S of Cluj; 46°08'/23°32'; AMG, HSL.

Sardu, Rom.; pop. 4; 19 km WNW of Cluj; 46°52'/23°23'.

Saregres, Hung.; pop. 5; 94 km SSW of Budapest; 46°47'/18°36'.

Sarengrad, Yug.; pop. 4; 107 km WNW of Beograd; 45°14'/19°17'; HSL.

Sarghieni, *see* Sergii.

Sargorog, *see* Shargorod.

Sarheya, *see* Seirijai.

Sari, Hung.; pop. 42; 38 km SE of Budapest; 47°13'/19°17'.

Sarisap, Hung.; pop. 11; 38 km WNW of Budapest; 47°41'/18°41'.

Sarisske Bohdanovce, Cz. (Sarosbogdany); 19 km N of Kosice; 48°51'/21°19'; HSL.

Sarisske Cierne, Cz. (Carna, Carno); pop. 110; 75 km N of Kosice; 49°21'/21°24'.

Sarisske Luky, Cz. (Sebeskellemes); pop. 315; 38 km N of Kosice; 49°01'/21°16'; HSL.

Sarkad, Hung.; pop. 245; 114 km NE of Szeged; 46°45'/21°23'; HSL, LDS, PHH.

Sarkadkeresztur, Hung.; pop. 10; 114 km NE of Szeged; 46°48'/21°23'; LDS.

Sarkan, Cz. (Sarkany); 114 km ESE of Bratislava; 47°52'/18°34'; HSL.

Sarkany, *see* Sarkan.

Sarkeresztes, Hung.; pop. 1; 62 km SW of Budapest; 47°15'/18°21'.

Sarkeresztur, Hung.; pop. 49; 69 km SSW of Budapest; 47°00'/18°33'.

Sarkeyschina, *see* Sharkovshchina.

Sarkeystsene, *see* Sharkovshchina.

Sarkoz, *see* Livada.

Sarkozujlac, *see* Livada Noua.

Sarmas, Rom.; pop. 23; 45 km E of Cluj; 46°45'/24°10'; EDRD, EJ, GUM3, GUM4, HSL, PHR1.

Sarmasag, Rom.; pop. 48; 88 km NW of Cluj; 47°21'/22°50'; HSL.

Sarmasel, Rom. (Kissarmas, Nagysarmas, Novi Dvor, Novi Dvur, Novradeker, Novy Dvor, Sarmaselu, Sarmasul, Sarmasul Mare); 45 km E of Cluj; 46°45'/24°11'; EJ, HSL, HSL2, PHR1.

Sarmaselu, *see* Sarmasel.

Sarmasul, *see* Sarmasel.

Sarmasul Mare, *see* Sarmasel.

Sarmellek, Hung.; pop. 3; 38 km NNE of Nagykanizsa; 46°43'/17°10'.

Sarnak, *see* Sarnaki.

Sarnaki, Pol. (Sarnak); pop. 1,198; 94 km S of Bialystok; 52°19'/22°53'; AMG, COH, EDRD, GA, GUM3, GUM4, GUM5, HSL, LDS, LYV, PHP1, POCEM, SF, YB.

Sarne, *see* Sarnowa.

Sarni, *see* Sarny.

Sarnki, *see* Sarnki Gurne.

Sarnki Dolne, Ukr.; pop. 36; 82 km SE of Lvov; 49°16'/24°44'.

Sarnki Gorne, *see* Sarnki Gurne.

Sarnki Gurne, Ukr. (Sarnki, Sarnki Gorne); pop. 78; 82 km SE of Lvov; 49°18'/24°44'.

Sarnow, Pol.; pop. 34; 26 km WNW of Lodz; 51°51'/19°09'.

Sarnow (Kielce), Pol.; pop. 5; 56 km SSW of Lodz; 51°22'/19°01'.

Sarnow (Lublin), Pol.; pop. 7; 62 km WNW of Lublin; 51°28'/21°46'.

Sarnowa, Pol. (Sarne); 69 km N of Wroclaw; 51°38'/16°54'; CAHJP, EDRD.

Sarnowek, Pol.; pop. 5; 82 km SW of Lublin; 51°01'/21°27'.

Sarny, Ukr. (Sarni); pop. 2,808; 88 km N of Rovno; 51°20'/26°36'; AMG, COH, EDRD, EJ, FRG, GA, GUM3, GUM4, GUM5, GUM6, ISH1, JGFF, LDL, LYV, SF, YB.

Sarny (Lvov area), Ukr.; pop. 29; 62 km W of Lvov; 49°55'/23°10'.

Sarok, Hung.; pop. 2; 126 km SW of Szeged; 45°51'/18°37'.

Saros, Hung.; 114 km WSW of Szeged; 45°59'/18°45'; HSL, HSL2.

Sarosbogdany, *see* Sarisske Bohdanovce.

Sarosd, Hung.; pop. 46; 62 km SSW of Budapest; 47°03'/18°39'.

Sarospatak, Hung.; pop. 1,096; 62 km NE of Miskolc; 48°19'/21°35'; AMG, COH, GUM4, GUM5, HSL, HSL2, JGFF, LDL, LDS, PHH.

Sarosreviscse, *see* Blatne Revistia.

Sarowo, Pol.; pop. 47; Described in the *Black Book* as being in the Polesie region of Poland, this town was not found in BGN gazetteers.

Sarpilis, Hung.; pop. 4; 107 km WSW of Szeged; 46°15'/18°45'.

Sarretudvari, Hung.; pop. 115; 101 km SSE of Miskolc; 47°14'/21°12'; HSL, LDS, PHH.

Sarsig, Rom.; pop. 4; 120 km WNW of Cluj; 47°15'/22°11'.

Sarstedt, Germ.; pop. 15; 26 km SE of Hannover; 52°14'/09°51'.

Sarszentagota, Hung.; pop. 11; 75 km SSW of Budapest; 46°58'/18°34'.

Sarszentmihaly, Hung.; pop. 6; 69 km SW of Budapest; 47°09'/18°20'.

Sarszentmiklos, Hung.; pop. 19; 75 km SSW of Budapest; 46°52'/18°38'.

Sarto, HSL, HSL2. This pre-World War I community was not found in BGN gazetteers.

Sarud, Hung.; pop. 15; 62 km S of Miskolc; 47°35'/20°36'; HSL.

Saru Mare, (Szatmar Nemeti, Szatmarnemeti); LDL. This pre-World War I community was not found in BGN gazetteers.

Sarvar, Hung.; pop. 790; 94 km N of Nagykanizsa; 47°15'/16°56'; AMG, COH, EDRD, GUM3, GUM5, GUM6, HSL, LDL, LDS, PHH.

Sarzyna, Pol.; pop. 68; 69 km NW of Przemysl; 50°21'/22°21'.

Sasar, Rom.; pop. 37; 101 km N of Cluj; 47°39'/23°30'.

Sasarm, Rom.; pop. 14; 69 km NNE of Cluj; 47°13'/24°13'.

Sasci, Rom. PHR1. This town was not found in BGN gazetteers under the given spelling.

Sascut, *see* Sascut Sat.

Sascut Sat, Rom. (Sascut); pop. 102; 120 km S of Iasi; 46°11'/27°04'; GUM4.

Sasd, Hung.; pop. 92; 88 km E of Nagykanizsa; 46°15'/18°07'; GUM4, HSL, PHH.

Saseni, Mold.; pop. 25; 45 km NW of Kishinev; 47°22'/28°30'.

Sashalom, Hung.; pop. 523; GUM5, PHH. a number of towns share this name. It was not possible to determine from available information which one is being referenced.

Sasiadka, Pol.; pop. 2; 56 km SSE of Lublin; 50°45'/22°53'.

Sasiadowice, Pol.; pop. 33; Described in the *Black Book* as being in the Lwow region of Poland, this town was not found in BGN gazetteers.

Sasmacken, *see* Valdemarpils.

Sasmaken, *see* Valdemarpils.

Sasnava, Lith.; pop. 16; 38 km SW of Kaunas; 54°39'/23°28'.

Sasov, Ukr. (Sasow, Sassov); pop. 1,096; 69 km ENE of Lvov; 49°52'/24°57'; AMG, COH, EDRD, EGRS, EJ, GUM3, GUM4, GUM5, HSL, HSL2, JGFF, LDL, PHP2, SF.

Sasovka, Ukr.; 163 km SSW of Lvov; 48°34'/23°04'; AMG, HSL.

Sasow, *see* Sasov.

Sassanfahrt, Germ.; 45 km NNW of Nurnberg; 49°48'/10°59'; PHGB.

Sassmacken, *see* Valdemarpils.

Sassov, *see* Sasov.

Sastin, Cz.; pop. 189; 62 km N of Bratislava; 48°38'/17°09'.

Sasuoliai, Lith. (Sesuoliai, Sheshvil, Soshly); pop. 129; 62 km NW of Vilnius; 55°11'/24°57'; HSL, JGFF, YL.

Sasvar, *see* Vinogradov.

Sasveres, Rom. (Szaszvaros); 120 km E of Cluj; 46°33'/25°07'; HSL.

Sata, Hung.; pop. 19; 32 km WNW of Miskolc; 48°11'/20°24'; HSL.

Satanov, Ukr. (Satanow); pop. 2,359; 107 km N of Chernovtsy; 49°15'/26°16'; COH, EJ, GYLA, HSL, HSL2, JGFF, LDL, PHP2, SF.

Satanow, *see* Satanov.

Sataviace, GUM4. This town was not found in BGN gazetteers under the given spelling.

Satinu, HSL. This pre-World War I community was not found in BGN gazetteers.

Satmar, *see* Satu Mare.

Satmarel, Rom.; pop. 20; 126 km NW of Cluj; 47°44'/22°48'.

Satoraljaujhely, Hung. (Ujhely); pop. 4,690; 75 km NE of Miskolc; 48°24'/21°40'; AMG, COH, EJ, GUM3, GUM4, GUM5, HSL, HSL2, JGFF, LDL, LDS, PHH, PHP3.

Sat Sugatag, *see* Satu Sugatag.

Sattel, *see* Sedlonov.

Satulung, Rom.; pop. 28; 94 km NNW of Cluj; 47°34'/23°26'; GUM4.

Satu Mare, Rom. (Sakmir, Saktmar, Satmar, Szatmar); pop. 11,533; 126 km NW of Cluj; 47°48'/22°53'; AMG, EJ, GUM3, GUM4, GUM5, GUM6, HSL, HSL2, JGFF, LYV, PHP3, PHR2.

Satu Mare (Bucovina), Rom.; pop. 53; BGN lists two possible localities with this name located at 47°21'/25°37' and 47°50'/26°01'.

Satu Nou de Jos, Rom. (Alsoujfalu, Statul Nou de Jos); 101 km N of Cluj; 47°37'/23°34'; HSL.

Satu Nou na Saud, Rom.; pop. 20; 146 km WSW of Cluj; 46°38'/21°42'.

Satu Sugatag, Rom. (Falusugatag, Sat Sugatag, Sugatag, Sugatag Sat); pop. 89; 120 km N of Cluj; 47°48'/23°54'; SM.

Sauca, Rom.; pop. 23; 114 km WNW of Cluj; 47°28'/22°29'.

Saucenita, Rom.; pop. 6; 120 km WNW of Iasi; 47°53'/26°23'.

Sauerbrunn, Aus.; pop. 39; 56 km S of Wien; 47°46'/16°20'.

Sauka, Lat. (Saukas); pop. 25; 82 km WNW of Daugavpils; 56°17'/25°29'.

Saukas, *see* Sauka.

Saukenai, Lith. (Shavkany, Shikian, Shokian, Shukian, Szawkiany); pop. 324; 32 km SW of Siauliai; 55°48'/22°53'; GUM5, HSL, JGFF, LDL, SF, WS, YL.

Saulgau, Germ.; 88 km SSE of Stuttgart; 48°01'/09°30'; EDRD, GUM3, PHGBW.

Saulia, Rom. (Mezosaly); 50 km ESE of Cluj; 46°38'/24°13'; HSL.

Sauran, *see* Savran.

Sausneja, Lat.; pop. 5; 101 km E of Riga; 56°48'/25°42'.

Savadisla, Rom. (Tordaszentlaszlo); 13 km SW of Cluj; 46°41'/23°27'; HSL.

Savchin, Ukr. (Sawczyn); pop. 10; 75 km N of Lvov; 50°28'/24°10'.

Saveni, Rom.; pop. 1,774; 107 km NW of Iasi; 47°57'/26°52'; GUM4, PHR1.

Saviena, Lat. (Savienas); pop. 6; 94 km NNW of Daugavpils; 56°40'/26°06'.

Savienas, *see* Saviena.

Savin, *see* Sawin.

Savoly, Hung.; 32 km NE of Nagykanizsa; 46°35'/17°16'; HSL.

Savran, Ukr. (Sauran); pop. 3,415; 75 km S of Uman; 48°08'/30°05'; EJ, JGFF, PHR1, SF.

Sawczyn, *see* Savchin.

Sawice, Pol.; pop. 46; 101 km SSW of Bialystok; 52°21'/22°30'.

Sawin, Pol. (Sabin, Savin); pop. 361; 62 km ENE of Lublin; 51°16'/23°26'; AMG, FRG, GA, GUM5, GUM6, HSL, HSL2, LDL, POCEM, SF.

Sawtschonki, Byel. EDRD. This town was not found in BGN gazetteers under the given spelling.

Saxony; Not a town, but a region of Germany that was once a duchy.

Saybusch, *see* Zywiec.

Sazava, Cz.; pop. 32; 69 km WNW of Brno; 49°34'/15°51'.

Sazgony, LDL. This pre-World War I community was not found in BGN gazetteers.

Sborny, *see* Sbornyy.

Sbornyy, Byel. (Sborny, Subari, Subory); 94 km N of Gomel; 53°15'/31°29'; SF.

Sburash, *see* Zburazh.

Scaziet, *see* Skazinets.

Scazinet, GUM4, GUM6. This town was not found in BGN gazetteers under the given spelling.

Schaafheim, Germ.; pop. 19; 32 km ESE of Frankfurt am Main; 49°55'/09°01'.

Schabokritsch, *see* Zhabokrich.

Schadeck, Germ.; pop. 5; 50 km WNW of Frankfurt am Main; 50°24'/08°10'.

Schaffa, *see* Safov.

Schafhausen, Germ.; 19 km WSW of Stuttgart; 48°43'/08°54'; PHGBW.

Schaftlach, Germ.; pop. 2; 45 km SSE of Munchen; 47°47'/11°41'.

Schaftlarn, *see* Unterschaftlarn.

Schaken, *see* Sakiai.

Schaki, *see* Sakiai.

Schamaiten, *see* Zmudz.

Schandorf, Germ.; 133 km W of Hannover; 52°41'/07°50'; GUM5.

Scharfenort, *see* Ostrorog.

Scharmbeck, Germ.; pop. 50; BGN lists two possible localities with this name located at 53°14'/08°48' and 53°21'/10°09'.

Scharowka, *see* Sharovechka.

Schassburg, *see* Sighisoara.

Schat, *see* Seda.

Schattendorf, Aus.; pop. 6; 56 km SSE of Wien; 47°43'/16°30'; GUM4, GUM5.

Schattmannsdorf, *see* Casta.

Schauboden, Aus.; pop. 1; 94 km WSW of Wien; 48°05'/15°08'.

Schauernheim, Germ.; pop. 2; 75 km S of Frankfurt am Main; 49°26'/08°18'.

Schaulen, *see* Siauliai.

Schavli, *see* Siauliai.

Schedniow, Pol. PHP4. This town was not found in BGN gazetteers under the given spelling.

Scheer, Germ.; 82 km S of Stuttgart; 48°04'/09°17'; JGFF.

Schegove, *see* Strzegowo.

Schegovo, *see* Strzegowo.

Scheibbs, Aus.; pop. 11; 88 km WSW of Wien; 48°00'/15°10'; EDRD.

Scheiblingkirchen, Aus.; pop. 8; 69 km S of Wien; 47°39'/16°08'.

Scheidegg, Germ.; pop. 1; 146 km SW of Munchen; 47°35'/09°51'.

Scheinfeld, Germ.; pop. 60; 50 km WNW of Nurnberg; 49°40'/10°28'; GUM5, HSL, JGFF, PHGB.

Schelldorf, Germ.; 69 km SSE of Nurnberg; 48°53'/11°25'; PHGB.

Schemeshits, *see* Strzemieszyce Wielkie.

Schemnitz, *see* Banska Stiavnica.

Schempin, *see* Czempin.

Schemyeshitse, *see* Strzemieszyce Wielkie.

Schenklengsfeld, Germ.; pop. 170; 120 km NE of Frankfurt am Main; 50°49'/09°51'; HSL, LDS.

Scheppach, Germ.; 88 km WNW of Munchen; 48°24'/10°26'; PHGB.

Scherfede, Germ.; 107 km SSW of Hannover; 51°32'/09°02'; GED.

Schermeisel, *see* Trzemeszno Lubuskie.

Scherps, *see* Sierpc.

Scherwind, *see* Kutuzovo.

Schesslitz, Germ.; pop. 31; 62 km N of Nurnberg; 49°59'/11°02'; PHGB.

Schieder, Germ.; 62 km SSW of Hannover; 51°55'/09°09'; LDS.

Schiefbahn, Germ.; 45 km NW of Koln; 51°14'/06°32'; GED.

Schienen, Germ.; 126 km S of Stuttgart; 47°41'/08°54'; PHGBW.

Schierstein, *see* Wiesbaden.

Schierstein (Now Wiesbaden), Germ.; pop. 62; 32 km WSW of Frankfurt am Main; 50°05'/08°15'.

Schiffelbach, Germ.; 101 km N of Frankfurt am Main; 50°57'/08°59'; LDS.

Schifferstadt, Germ.; pop. 39; 82 km S of Frankfurt am Main; 49°23'/08°22'; GED, GUM5.

Schildberg, *see* Ostrzeszow.

Schildesche, Germ. LDS. This town was not found in BGN

gazetteers under the given spelling.

Schima, *see* Zim.

Schippenbeil, *see* Sepopol.

Schirwindt, *see* Kutuzovo.

Schivelbein, *see* Swidwin.

Schizuv, *see* Strzyzow.

Schkeuditz, Germ.; pop. 43; 19 km NW of Leipzig; 51°24'/12°13'.

Schladming, Aus.; pop. 3; 69 km ESE of Salzburg; 47°23'/13°41'.

Schlaining, *see* Stadtschlaining.

Schlangen, Germ.; pop. 25; 88 km SW of Hannover; 51°49'/08°50'.

Schlawe, *see* Slawno.

Schleswig, Germ.; pop. 3; 114 km NNW of Hamburg; 54°31'/09°33'; HSL.

Schleusingen, Germ.; pop. 31; 120 km NNW of Nurnberg; 50°31'/10°45'.

Schlichtingsheim, *see* Szlinokiemie.

Schlipsheim, Germ.; 62 km WNW of Munchen; 48°23'/10°47'; PHGB.

Schlitz, Germ.; pop. 44; 88 km NE of Frankfurt am Main; 50°40'/09°34'; GED.

Schliwischewzi, *see* Sljivosevci.

Schlochau, *see* Czmon.

Schlock, *see* Sloka.

Schlok, *see* Sloka.

Schloppe, *see* Czlopa.

Schluchtern, Germ.; pop. 375; 69 km NE of Frankfurt am Main; 50°21'/09°31'; AMG, GUM5, HSL, HSL2, JGFF, LDS.

Schluchtern (Baden), Germ.; pop. 31; 50 km NNW of Stuttgart; 49°09'/09°06'; PHGBW.

Schlusselfeld, Germ.; 45 km NW of Nurnberg; 49°46'/10°38'; PHGB.

Schmalkalden, Germ.; pop. 77; 146 km SW of Leipzig; 50°43'/10°27'; HSL, HSL2, JGFF, LDS.

Schmallenberg, Germ.; pop. 44; 94 km ENE of Koln; 51°09'/08°18'.

Schmalnau, Germ.; pop. 53; 88 km NE of Frankfurt am Main; 50°27'/09°47'.

Schmerinka, *see* Zhmerinka.

Schmiedeberg, Germ.; 107 km ESE of Leipzig; 50°51'/13°41'; GUM3, GUM5.

Schmiegel, *see* Smigiel.

Schmieheim, Germ.; pop. 134; 114 km SW of Stuttgart; 48°17'/07°52'; PHGBW.

Schmollnitz, *see* Smolnik.

Schnaitsee, GUM3. This town was not found in BGN gazetteers under the given spelling.

Schnaittach, Germ.; pop. 46; 26 km NE of Nurnberg; 49°34'/11°21'; CAHJP, EJ, GUM3, GUM5, HSL, JGFF, PHGB.

Schneebergerhof, Germ.; 69 km SW of Frankfurt am Main; 49°41'/07°53'; GED.

Schneidemuhl, *see* Pila. GUM4 and GUM5 notes a camp named Schneidemuhle in the Rheinland-Pfalz region of Germany. It does not appear in contemporary gazetteers.

Schneidermuhl, *see* Pila.

Schneidmuhl, *see* Pila.

Schnodsenbach, Germ.; pop. 3; 56 km WNW of Nurnberg; 49°41'/10°26'; PHGB.

Schobdach, Germ.; 56 km SSW of Nurnberg; 49°02'/10°37'; PHGB.

Schochow, HSL. This pre-World War I community was not found in BGN gazetteers.

Schocken, *see* Skoki.

Schodnica, *see* Skhodnitsa.

S Chodnitza, *see* Skhodnitsa.

Schoenberg, *see* Sumperk. CAHJP has documents from a town in Germany. There are a number of German towns with that name.

Schoenlanke, *see* Trzcianka.

Scholanowo, GUM5. This town was not found in BGN gazetteers under the given spelling.

Schollkrippen, Germ.; pop. 57; 38 km E of Frankfurt am Main; 50°04'/09°14'; GUM5, PHGB.

Schomberg Dautmergen, *see* Dautmergen.

Schonberg, *see* Krasna Hora nad Vltavou; Skaistkalne.

Schonberg (Bavaria), Germ. AMG, GUM3. A number of towns in Bavaria share this name.

Schonbrunn, Pol. PHP3. a number of towns share this name. It was not possible to determine from available information which one is being referenced.

Schondra, Germ.; pop. 2; 88 km ENE of Frankfurt am Main; 50°16'/09°52'; GUM5, PHGB.

Schonebeck, Germ.; pop. 79; 94 km NW of Leipzig; 52°01'/11°45'; GUM3, GUM5, HSL.

Schonfeld, Germ.; 75 km SSW of Koln; 50°19'/06°31'; ISH1.

Schongau, Germ.; pop. 5; 62 km SW of Munchen; 47°49'/10°54'; PHGB.

Schongeising, Germ.; pop. 1; 32 km WSW of Munchen; 48°08'/11°12'.

Schonholthausen, Germ.; 75 km NE of Koln; 51°11'/08°01'; LDS.

Schoningen, Germ.; pop. 31; 88 km E of Hannover; 52°08'/10°57'; GED, LDS.

Schonlanke, *see* Trzcianka.

Schonstadt, Germ.; 94 km N of Frankfurt am Main; 50°53'/08°50'; LDS.

Schontal, Germ.; 69 km N of Stuttgart; 49°20'/09°30'; PHGBW.

Schonungen, Germ.; pop. 33; 88 km NW of Nurnberg; 50°03'/10°19'; GUM5, JGFF, PHGB.

Schopfheim, Germ.; pop. 26; 163 km SSW of Stuttgart; 47°39'/07°49'; PHGBW.

Schopfloch, Germ.; pop. 45; 69 km SW of Nurnberg; 49°07'/10°18'; CAHJP, GED, GUM5, HSL, JGFF, PHGB, PHGBW.

Schoppenstedt, Germ.; pop. 1; 75 km ESE of Hannover; 52°08'/10°47'.

Schorndorf, Germ.; 26 km ENE of Stuttgart; 48°48'/09°32'; GUM3, PHGBW.

Schornsheim, Germ.; pop. 45; 50 km SW of Frankfurt am Main; 49°51'/08°10'.

Schornweisach, Germ.; 45 km WNW of Nurnberg; 49°40'/10°39'; PHGB.

Schorov, Cz.; pop. 5; 69 km ESE of Praha; 49°52'/15°23'.

Schorrentin, Germ.; 50 km ESE of Rostock; 53°51'/12°46'; JGFF.

Schorzingen, Germ.; 75 km SSW of Stuttgart; 48°11'/08°45'; GUM3, GUM5, PHGBW.

Schossberg, HSL, HSL2. This pre-World War I community was not found in BGN gazetteers.

Schossenreuth, HSL. This pre-World War I community was not found in BGN gazetteers.

Schotmar, Germ.; pop. 44; 75 km SW of Hannover; 52°04'/08°46'; LDS.

Schotten, Germ.; pop. 75; 56 km NNE of Frankfurt am Main; 50°30'/09°08'; GUM5, JGFF.

Schozach, Germ.; 38 km N of Stuttgart; 49°04'/09°13'; PHGBW.

Schramberg, Germ.; pop. 4; 82 km SW of Stuttgart; 48°14'/08°23'; PHGBW.

Schrecksbach, Germ.; pop. 94 km NNE of Frankfurt am Main; 50°50'/09°17'; JGFF, LDS.

Schrick, Aus.; 38 km NNE of Wien; 48°30'/16°37'; AMG.

Schriesheim, Germ.; pop. 40; 75 km S of Frankfurt am Main; 49°29'/08°40'; LDS, PHGBW.

Schrimm, *see* Srem.

Schrobenhausen, Germ.; pop. 1; 50 km NW of Munchen; 48°33'/11°16'.

Schroda, *see* Sroda Wielkopolska.

Schubin, *see* Szubin.

Schulenburg, Germ.; 26 km SSE of Hannover; 52°12'/09°47'; HSL.

Schulitz, *see* Solec Kujawski.

Schumlau, *possibly* Shumlyany.

Schupbach, Germ.; pop. 10; 56 km WNW of Frankfurt am Main; 50°27'/08°10'; GUM5.

Schuttorf, Germ.; 157 km N of Koln; 52°19'/07°14'; GED.

Schutt Szerdahly, *see* Dunajska Streda.

Schutzen, Germ.; 38 km E of Munchen; 48°07'/12°03'; HSL, HSL2.

Schwaan, Germ.; pop. 6; 26 km S of Rostock; 53°57'/12°07'; LDS.

Schwabach, Germ.; 19 km S of Nurnberg; 49°20'/11°02'; CAHJP, GUM3, HSL, HSL2, JGFF, LDL, LDS, PHGB, PHGBW.

Schwabenheim, Germ. BGN lists two possible localities with this name located at 49°27'/08°38' and 49°56'/08°06'. GED, JGFF.

Schwabisch, GUM5. This town was not found in BGN gazetteers under the given spelling.

Schwabisch Gmund, Germ.; pop. 90; 45 km ENE of Stuttgart; 48°48'/09°47'; GED, GUM3, PHGBW.

Schwabisch Hall, Germ. (Hall); pop. 110; 56 km NE of Stuttgart; 49°06'/09°44'; GED, GUM3, GUM5, JGFF, PHGBW.

Schwabmunchen, Germ.; pop. 1; 62 km W of Munchen; 48°11'/10°45'; GUM3, PHGB.

Schwaighausen, Germ.; 101 km WSW of Munchen; 48°01'/10°15'; PHGB.

Schwalenberg, Germ.; 69 km SSW of Hannover; 51°52'/09°12'; LDS.

Schwanberg, Aus.; pop. 1; 38 km SSW of Graz; 46°45'/15°12'.

Schwandorf, *see* Schwandorf In Bayern.

Schwandorf In Bayern, Germ. (Schwandorf); pop. 26; 75 km E of Nurnberg; 49°20'/12°07'; AMG, GUM3, GUM4, GUM5, PHGB.

Schwaneburg, *see* Gulbene.

Schwanenbruckl, *see* Mostek.

Schwanenburg, *see* Gulbene.

Schwanfeld, Germ.; pop. 81; 88 km WNW of Nurnberg; 49°55'/10°08'; GUM5, HSL, HSL2, PHGB.

Schwarza, Germ.; 133 km NNW of Nurnberg; 50°38'/10°32'; CAHJP, JGFF, LDS.

Schwarzach, Germ.; 126 km NE of Munchen; 48°55'/12°49'; LDS.

Schwarzenau, *see* Czerniejewo.

Schwarzenberg, Germ.; 88 km SSE of Leipzig; 50°33'/12°47'; PHGBW.

Schwarzenborn, Germ.; 107 km NNE of Frankfurt am Main; 50°55'/09°27'; GUM3, LDS.

Schwarzenbruck, Germ.; pop. 5; 19 km ESE of Nurnberg; 49°21'/11°14'.

Schwarzenfeld, Germ.; 75 km E of Nurnberg; 49°23'/12°08'; GUM3.

Schwarzheide, Germ.; 107 km ENE of Leipzig; 51°29'/13°52'; GUM4, GUM5.

Schwarzwald, Germ.; 126 km SW of Leipzig; 50°46'/10°44'; PHGBW.

Schwebheim, Germ.; 82 km WNW of Nurnberg; 49°59'/10°15'; PHGB.

Schwechat, Aus.; pop. 57; 13 km ESE of Wien; 48°08'/16°28'.

Schwedt, Germ.; pop. 111; 88 km NE of Berlin; 53°04'/14°18'; HSL, LDS.

Schwegenheim, Germ.; pop. 25; 88 km WNW of Stuttgart; 49°16'/08°19'; GED.

Schweich, Germ.; pop. 84; 133 km S of Koln; 49°49'/06°45'.

Schweidnitz, *see* Swidnica.

Schweinberg, Germ. AMG. a number of towns share this name. It was not possible to determine from available information which one is being referenced.

Schweinfurt, Germ.; pop. 363; 88 km NW of Nurnberg; 50°03'/10°14'; AMG, CAHJP, EJ, GUM4, GUM5, HSL, HSL2, PHGB.

Schweinsberg, Germ.; pop. 30; 82 km N of Frankfurt am Main; 50°46'/08°58'; AMG, LDS.

Schweinshaupten, Germ.; pop. 25; 94 km NW of Nurnberg; 50°11'/10°34'; CAHJP, PHGB.

Schweinspoint, Germ.; pop. 1; 82 km S of Nurnberg; 48°45'/10°57'.

Schweissing, *see* Svojsin.

Schwelm, Germ.; pop. 54; 45 km NNE of Koln; 51°17'/07°17'; GED.

Schwenningen, *see* Schwenningen am Neckar.

Schwenningen am Neckar, Germ. (Schwenningen); 94 km SSW of Stuttgart; 48°04'/08°32'; GUM3, HSL, PHGBW.

Schweppenhausen, Germ.; pop. 18; 69 km SW of Frankfurt am Main; 49°55'/07°48'; JGFF.

Schwerin, *see* Skwierzyna.

Schwersenz, *see.* Swarzedz.

Schwertberg, Aus.; pop. 9; 126 km NE of Salzburg; 48°16'/14°35'; JGFF.

Schwerte, Germ.; pop. 63; 69 km NNE of Koln; 51°27'/07°34'; JGFF.

Schwetz bei Graudenz, HSL. This pre-World War I community was not found in BGN gazetteers.

Schwetzingen, Germ.; pop. 73; 82 km S of Frankfurt am Main; 49°23'/08°34'; GED, HSL, PHGBW.

Schwiebus, *see* Swiebodzin.

Schymanzy, *see* Simaniskiai.

Scianka, *see* Stinka.

Scinawa, Pol. (Steinau am Oder); pop. 24; 56 km WNW of Wroclaw; 51°25'/16°25'; JGFF, POCEM.

Sciony, Pol.; pop. 9; 38 km SSW of Bialystok; 52°50'/22°49'.

Scldwersenz, *see* Swarzedz.

Scorteni, *see* Skortseny.

Sculeni, *see* Skulyany.

Sculeni Moldova, *see* Skulyany.

Sculeni Targ, *see* Skulyany.

Scumpia, *see* Skumpiya.

Sdeh Lavan, *see* Bila Cirkev.

Sdeh Menocha, *see* Kalininskoye.

Sde Lavan, *see* Belaya Tserkov.

Sde Menucha, *see* Kalininskoye.

Sebastapol, *see* Sevastopol.

Sebes, Rom.; 94 km S of Cluj; 45°58'/23°34'; HSL, HSL2, JGFF.

Sebesh, *see* Sebeza.

Sebeskellemes, *see* Sarisske Luky.

Sebespatak, Cz.; 62 km WSW of Kosice; 48°40'/20°26'; HSL. This town was located on a pre-World War I map, but does not appear in contemporary gazetteers.

Sebez, *see* Sebeza.

Sebeza, Lat. (Sebesh, Sebez, Sebezh, Siebiez); 139 km N of Daugavpils; 57°06'/27°04'; HSL, LDL, SF.

Sebezh, *see* Sebeza.

Sebirov, Cz.; pop. 9; 62 km SE of Praha; 49°34'/14°49'.

Sebis, Rom. (Borossebes); 120 km SW of Cluj; 46°22'/22°07'; HSL, PHR1.

Sebnitz, Germ.; pop. 12; 146 km E of Leipzig; 50°58'/14°17'.

Sebuzin, Cz.; pop. 2; 62 km NW of Praha; 50°35'/14°04'.

Sebyezh, USSR; pop. 1,813; COH. This town was not found in BGN gazetteers under the given spelling.

Sec, Cz. (Frankova, Szecs); 126 km N of Brno; 50°13'/17°14'; AMG, HSL.

Secatura, Rom.; 114 km SSW of Iasi; 46°27'/26°35'; HSL.

Sece, Lat.; pop. 5; 88 km ESE of Riga; 56°33'/25°23'.

Secemin, Pol.; pop. 224; 50 km E of Czestochowa; 50°46'/19°50'; LDS.

Secereni, GUM3. This town was not found in BGN gazetteers under the given spelling.

Secheslav, *see* Dnepropetrovsk.

Sechov, Cz.; 69 km ESE of Praha; 49°42'/15°14'; SF.

Sechtem, Germ.; 26 km S of Koln; 50°47'/06°57'; GED.

Seciny, Pol. EDRD. This town was not found in BGN gazetteers under the given spelling.

Seckenburg, *see* Zapovednoye.

Seckenheim, Germ.; 69 km S of Frankfurt am Main; 49°30'/08°28'; PHGBW.

Seckmauern, Germ.; 45 km SE of Frankfurt am Main; 49°47'/09°07'; LDS.

Secovce, Cz.; pop. 1,055; 26 km E of Kosice; 48°42'/21°39'; AMG, COH, HSL, JGFF.

Secovska Polianka, *see* Secovska Polianka.

Secovska Polianka, Cz. (Secovska Polanka); pop. 51; 32 km ENE of Kosice; 48°47'/21°42'.

Secueni, Rom.; 69 km SW of Iasi; 46°51'/26°50'; EJ.

Secureni Sat, *see* Sekuren.

Secureni Targ, *see* Sokiryany.

Secyminek, *see* Secymin Polski.

Secymin Niemiecki, Pol.; pop. 21; 38 km WNW of Warszawa; 52°24'/20°26'.

Secymin Polski, Pol. (Secyminek); pop. 53; 38 km WNW of Warszawa; 52°23'/20°26'.

Seda, Lith. (Schat, Siad, Sod, Syad, Syady); pop. 815; 82 km WNW of Siauliai; 56°10'/22°06'; COH, HSL, HSL2, JGFF, SF, YL.

Sedlcanky, Cz.; pop. 7; 26 km NE of Praha; 50°10'/14°47'.

Sedlcany, Cz.; pop. 88; 50 km S of Praha; 49°40'/14°25'.

Sedlec, Cz.; pop. 43; 62 km S of Praha; 49°34'/14°32'.

Sedletin, Cz.; pop. 6; 94 km WNW of Brno; 49°43'/15°34'.

Sedlice, JGFF. a number of towns share this name. It was not possible to determine from available information which one is being referenced.

Sedlishche, Ukr. (Siedliszcze); 146 km WNW of Rovno; 51°25'/24°32'; GUM4. There are two towns in Volynia named Sedlishche, one at 51°25/24°32 and the other at 51°40/25°22.

Sedliska, Cz. (Siedliska, Szedliszka); 45 km NE of Kosice; 48°54'/21°44'; HSL. *See also* Selisko.

Sedlonov, Cz. (Sattel); 133 km NNW of Brno; 50°20'/16°19'; HSL.

Sedlov, Cz.; pop. 3; 50 km E of Praha; 49°58'/15°09'.

Sedmpany, Cz.; pop. 6; 62 km ESE of Praha; 49°42'/15°04'.

Sedowice, Pol.; pop. 26; BGN lists two possible localities with this name located at 50°30'/20°21' and 51°34'/21°59'.

Seduva, Lith. (Shadov, Shadova, Shadove, Shedeva, Szadow); pop. 916; 32 km ESE of Siauliai; 55°46'/23°46'; EJ, HSL, HSL2, JGFF, LDL, SF, YL.

Sedziejowice, Pol.; pop. 30; 38 km SW of Lodz; 51°31'/19°02'; PHP1.

Sedziszow, Pol. (Sedziszow Malopolski, Sendeshov, Sendishev, Sendziszov, Shendeshov); pop. 861; 82 km WNW of Przemysl; 50°04'/21°42'; AMG, COH, EDRD, GA, GUM3, GUM5, HSL, HSL2, JGFF, LDL, PHP3, POCEM, SF.

Sedziszow (near Jedrzejow), Pol.; pop. 448; 32 km N of Krakow; 50°35'/20°04'; CAHJP, EGRS, SF, YB.

Sedziszowa, Pol.; pop. 21; 88 km ESE of Krakow; 49°44'/20°58'.

Sedziszow Malopolski, *see* Sedziszow.

Seebach, Germ. LDS. a number of towns share this name. It was not possible to determine from available information which one is being referenced.

Seebad Heringsdorf, Germ.; pop. 12; 133 km E of Rostock; 53°58'/14°10'.

Seebenstein, Aus.; pop. 4; 62 km S of Wien; 47°41'/16°08'.

Seeburg, Germ.; 50 km WNW of Leipzig; 51°29'/11°42'; HSL.

Seeheim, Germ.; pop. 21; 45 km S of Frankfurt am Main; 49°46'/08°40'.

Seehof, Germ.; 56 km NNW of Nurnberg; 49°56'/10°57'; PHGB.

Seelow, Germ.; pop. 13; 69 km E of Berlin; 52°31'/14°23'; LDS.

Seelowitz, *see* Zidlochovice.

Seelze, Germ.; pop. 5; 13 km WNW of Hannover; 52°24'/09°36'.

Seesen, Germ.; pop. 50; 62 km SE of Hannover; 51°54'/10°11'; CAHJP, EJ, GED, GUM5, HSL.

Seeshaupt, Germ.; 38 km SSW of Munchen; 47°50'/11°18'; GUM5.

Sege, *see* Tiszacsege.

Segeberg, *see* Bad Segeberg.

Segesvar, *see* Sighisoara.

Segewald, *see* Sigulda.

Segewold, *see* Sigulda.

Segilong, HSL. This pre-World War I community was not found in BGN gazetteers.

Segnitz, Germ.; pop. 2; 75 km WNW of Nurnberg; 49°40'/10°08'; HSL, PHGB.

Sehl, Germ.; pop. 6; 94 km SSE of Koln; 50°08'/07°11'.

Sehnde, Germ.; pop. 15; 19 km ESE of Hannover; 52°19'/09°57'.

Seibersbach, Germ.; pop. 17; 69 km WSW of Frankfurt am Main; 49°58'/07°43'.

Seifriedsberg, Germ.; 82 km W of Munchen; 48°16'/10°33'; PHGB.

Seimeni, *see* Semenovka.

Seini, Rom. (Szinervaralja); pop. 673; 114 km NNW of Cluj; 47°45'/23°17'; EJ, HSL, LDL, PHR2.

Seiny, *see* Sejny.

Seirijai, Lith. (Saray, Sarheya, Serai, Seree, Serehai, Serey, Serheya, Serijai, Seyriay, Sierijai); pop. 880; 82 km S of Kaunas; 54°14'/23°49'; AMG, COH, GUM3, HSL, HSL2, JGFF, LDL, LDS, LYV, SF, YL.

Seitzersdorf Wolfpassing, Aus.; pop. 1; 26 km NW of Wien; 48°24'/16°05'.

Sejas, *see* Zilini.

Sejdorf, *see* Okrouhlicka.

Sejny, Pol. (Seiny, Senya, Synee); pop. 661; 114 km N of Bialystok; 54°06'/23°21'; AMG, COH, GUM3, GUM4, HSL, HSL2, JGFF, LDL, LDS, PHP4, POCEM, SF.

Sekareny, Mold. (Sacareni); pop. 4; 38 km W of Kishinev; 47°02'/28°20'.

Sekernica, *see* Sokirnitsa.

Sekernice, *see* Sokirnitsa.

Sekhuv, Ukr. (Siechow); pop. 32; 82 km S of Lvov; 49°12'/24°01'.

Sekiryani, *see* Sokiryany.

Seklence, *see* Szeklencze.

Sekow, Pol.; pop. 1; 50 km ENE of Lublin; 51°22'/23°15'.

Sekowa, Pol.; pop. 3; 107 km ESE of Krakow; 49°37'/21°12'.

Sekowa Wola, *see* Wola Sekowa.

Sekuren, Ukr. (Secureni Sat); pop. 39; 107 km ENE of Chernovtsy; 48°27'/27°23'.

Sekureni Targ, *see* Sokiryany.

Sekurian, *see* Sokiryany.

Sekursko, Pol.; pop. 7; 38 km ENE of Czestochowa; 50°53'/19°37'.

Sela, Lith.; 88 km NNE of Vilnius; 55°26'/25°53'; GUM4.

Selb, Germ.; 107 km NNE of Nurnberg; 50°10'/12°08'; GUM3, PHGB.

Selburg, *see* Selpils.

Selce, *see* Selets (Carpathia).

Seldin, *see* Svodin.

Selemet, Mold.; pop. 58; 50 km SSE of Kishinev; 46°35'/28°55'.

Selent, *see* Salantai.

Seleshche, Ukr. (Selistea, Selistea Veche); pop. 167; 45 km WSW of Chernovtsy; 48°12'/25°24'.

Selestovo, HSL. This pre-World War I community was not found in BGN gazetteers.

Seletice, Cz.; pop. 2; 56 km NE of Praha; 50°20'/15°06'.

Seletin, *see* Selyatin.

Selets, Byel. (Selitz, Seltz, Sielec); pop. 238; 101 km WNW of Pinsk; 52°35'/24°53'; YB.

Selets (Carpathia), (Selce); AMG, GUM3. This town was not found in BGN gazetteers under the given spelling.

Selets (near Pruzhany), Byel.; 114 km W of Pinsk; 52°14'/24°29'; HSL.

Selets (near Radekhov), Ukr. (Selets Benkuv, Sielec Bienkow);

pop. 81; 50 km NNE of Lvov; 50°11'/24°25'; JGFF, SF.

Selets (near Sambor), Ukr.; pop. 78; 69 km SW of Lvov; 49°27'/23°18'.

Selets (near Sokal), Ukr.; pop. 175; 56 km N of Lvov; 50°19'/24°12'; HSL, PHP2.

Selets (Nowogrodek), Byel.; pop. 34; 146 km WSW of Minsk; 53°40'/25°25'; GUM4.

Selets (Stanislawow), Ukr.; pop. 24; 107 km SE of Lvov; 49°02'/24°44'.

Selets (Wolyn), Ukr.; pop. 51; 107 km N of Lvov; 50°46'/24°23'.

Selets Benkuv, see Selets (near Radekhov).

Seletz, see Skulyany.

Seleus, Rom. (Csiger Szollos); pop. 27; 150 km SW of Cluj; 46°23'/21°43'.

Seliba, Byel. (Sheliba Dikshitz); 94 km ESE of Minsk; 53°37'/28°58'; GUM5, JGFF, LDL, SF.

Selibice, Cz.; 69 km WNW of Praha; 50°21'/13°37'; HSL.

Seligenstadt, Germ.; pop. 150; 26 km ESE of Frankfurt am Main; 50°03'/08°59'.

Selish, see Vinogradov.

Selishche, Ukr. (Selishchi, Sieliszcze Male, Slishtch Zuta, Slishtcha); pop. 2; 82 km NNE of Rovno; 51°12'/26°54'; JGFF, SF.

Selishchi, see Selishche.

Selisht, see Salistea de Sus.

Selishty, Mold. (Selishtya, Selistea Hotin, Selts); pop. 40; 56 km WNW of Kishinev; 47°10'/28°09'.

Selishtya, see Selishty.

Selisko, Ukr. (Sedliska); pop. 28; 26 km SE of Lvov; 49°40'/24°08'.

Selist, see Salistea de Sus.

Seliste, Rom. (Szelistye); 126 km SW of Cluj; 46°02'/22°23'; COH, HSL.

Selistea, see Seleshche.

Selistea Hotin, see Selishty.

Selistea Veche, see Seleshche.

Selitz, see Selets.

Sellye, Hung. (Sala); pop. 54; 94 km SE of Nagykanizsa; 45°52'/17°51'; HSL, LDS, PHH.

Selm, Germ.; pop. 8; 94 km NNE of Koln; 51°42'/07°28'.

Selmecbanya, see Banska Stiavnica.

Selo, Byel.; 50 km ESE of Vitebsk; 54°55'/30°48'; HSL.

Selok, see Salakas.

Selo Slatina, see Solotvina.

Selpils, Lat. (Selburg, Zel Burg); pop. 1; 94 km NW of Daugavpils; 56°35'/25°39'.

Selt, see Salociai.

Selters, Germ.; pop. 97; 75 km ESE of Koln; 50°32'/07°46'; JGFF.

Selts, see Selishty.

Seltz, see Selets.

Selyatin, Ukr. (Seletin); pop. 737; 75 km SW of Chernovtsy; 47°52'/25°13'; GUM4, PHR2.

Selyeb, Hung.; pop. 15; 32 km NNE of Miskolc; 48°20'/20°58'; HSL.

Selzen, Germ.; pop. 9; 45 km SW of Frankfurt am Main; 49°52'/08°15'.

Semakovtse, see Semakovtsy.

Semakovtsy, Ukr. (Semakovtse, Siemakowce); pop. 81; 56 km NW of Chernovtsy; 48°46'/25°32'.

Semakovtsy (near Kolomyya), Ukr.; pop. 57; 56 km WNW of Chernovtsy; 48°29'/25°12'.

Sembach, Germ.; 88 km SSW of Frankfurt am Main; 49°31'/07°51'; GED, JGFF.

Semcice, Cz.; pop. 1; 50 km NE of Praha; 50°22'/15°00'.

Semelishok, see Semeliskes.

Semeliskes, Lith. (Semelishok, Semeliskiai, Semilishok, Semilshouk); pop. 274; 45 km WSW of Vilnius; 54°40'/24°40'; GUM4, GUM5, SF, YL.

Semeliskiai, see Semeliskes.

Semeljci, Yug.; pop. 10; 170 km WNW of Beograd;

45°27'/18°32'.

Semendria, see Smederevo.

Semenki, Ukr. (Seminca); 69 km ESE of Vinnitsa; 48°50'/29°07'; GUM4, PHR1.

Semenovka, Ukr. (Seimeni, Semianovka, Semonovka); pop. 852; 182 km WNW of Dnepropetrovsk; 49°36'/33°10'; EDRD, HSL, JGFF, LDL, SF. *See also* Semenuvka. There are 50 towns named Semenovka in the USSR, mostly in the Ukraine. The two largest are in the northern Ukraine, northwest of Novgorod Severskiy at 49°36'/33°10', and in the southern Ukraine west of Poltava at 52°10'/32°35'. The population figure appears to refer to the northern town.

Semenovka (Bessarabia), Mold. (Regina Maria); pop. 5; 50 km SW of Kishinev; 46°42'/28°18'.

Semenuvka, Ukr. (Semenovka); pop. 39; 69 km NW of Chernovtsy; 48°47'/25°18'.

Semerovo, Cz. (Komaromszemere); 94 km E of Bratislava; 48°01'/18°21'; AMG, HSL.

Semgallen, see Zemgale.

Semianovka, see Semenovka.

Semiduby, Ukr.; pop. 11; 38 km SW of Rovno; 50°21'/25°49'.

Semigostichi, Byel. (Semikhostiche, Siemihoscicze); pop. 39; 88 km E of Pinsk; 52°06'/27°25'.

Semikhostiche, see Semigostichi.

Semilishok, see Semeliskes.

Semilshouk, see Semeliskes.

Semin, Cz.; 75 km E of Praha; 50°03'/15°32'; HSL.

Seminca, see Semenki.

Semjen, Hung.; pop. 27; 94 km NE of Miskolc; 48°21'/21°58'; HSL.

Semkowce, Pol. PHP2. This town was not found in BGN gazetteers under the given spelling.

Semlin, see Zemun.

Semmering, Aus.; pop. 26; 69 km N of Graz; 47°38'/15°49'.

Semnevice, Cz.; pop. 7; 126 km SW of Praha; 49°36'/12°55'.

Semonovka, see Semenovka.

Semsa, Cz. (Semse); 13 km WSW of Kosice; 48°41'/21°07'; HSL.

Semse, see Semsa.

Semyanovka, Ukr. (Siemianowka); pop. 31; 26 km S of Lvov; 49°40'/23°55'; HSL.

Semyatich, see Siemiatycze.

Semyatitcha, see Siemiatycze.

Sena, see Senno.

Senatovka, Mold. (Sanatauca); pop. 106; 120 km N of Kishinev; 48°01'/28°42'.

Senava, see Snezna.

Senca, see Svatusa.

Sendelbach, Germ.; 19 km ENE of Nurnberg; 49°29'/11°22'; PHGB.

Sendeshov, see Sedziszow.

Sendishev, see Sedziszow.

Sendziszov, see Sedziszow.

Senec, Cz. (Szempc, Szempcz, Szenc, Szencz); pop. 502; 19 km NE of Bratislava; 48°13'/17°24'; COH.

Senftenberg, Germ.; pop. 27; 120 km SSE of Berlin; 51°31'/14°01'; HSL, HSL2.

Senheim, Germ.; 101 km SSE of Koln; 50°05'/07°13'; LDL.

Senica, Cz.; pop. 867; 62 km N of Bratislava; 48°41'/17°22'; EJ, GUM4, HSL.

Seniver, see Sinevir Polyana.

Senkevicevka, see Senkevichevka.

Senkevichevka, Ukr. (Senkevicevka, Senkevitchovka, Sienkiewiczowka); 88 km WSW of Rovno; 50°32'/25°02'; AMG, SF.

Senkevitchovka, see Senkevichevka.

Senkovitse, Ukr. (Senkowice); pop. 21; 50 km NW of Lvov; 50°15'/23°43'.

Senkowice, see Senkovitse.

Senkuv, Ukr. (Sienkow); 75 km NE of Lvov; 50°18'/24°46'; YB.

Sennaya, Ukr. (Phanagoria); 227 km ENE of Simferopol;

306

45°17'/37°00'; EJ.

Sennfeld, Germ.; pop. 55; 75 km N of Stuttgart; 49°23'/09°23'; JGFF, LDS, PHGBW.

Senno, Byel. (Sena); pop. 1,847; 56 km SSW of Vitebsk; 54°49'/29°43'; HSL, JGFF, LDL, SF.

Sennoye, Ukr. (Rusyvel, Rusywel); pop. 27; 38 km E of Rovno; 50°33'/26°49'.

Seno, *see* Sienno.

Senohraby, Cz.; pop. 8; 26 km SE of Praha; 49°54'/14°43'.

Sensburg, *see* Mragowo.

Senta, Yug. (Zenta); pop. 1,457; 126 km NNW of Beograd; 45°56'/20°05'; AMG, CAHJP, GUM5, HSL, HSL2, LDL, PHY.

Sentes, *see* Svatus.

Sentus, *see* Svatus.

Senya, *see* Sejny.

Senyo, Hung.; pop. 39; 82 km E of Miskolc; 48°00'/21°53'; HSL.

Sepekov, *see* Lisnice.

Sepenberg, GUM3. This town was not found in BGN gazetteers under the given spelling.

Sepichow, Pol.; pop. 11; 62 km NE of Krakow; 50°19'/20°46'.

Sepinka, *see* Sapinta.

Sepizishok, *see* Zapyskis.

Sepnica, Pol.; pop. 6; 101 km WNW of Przemysl; 50°04'/21°31'.

Sepolno, Pol. (Zempelburg); pop. 183; 120 km SSW of Gdansk; 53°27'/17°32'; AMG, HSL, JGFF, POCEM.

Sepopol, Pol. (Schippenbeil); pop. 25; 150 km E of Gdansk; 54°16'/21°01'; AMG, GUM4.

Sepsiszentgyorgy, *see* Sfintu Gheorghe.

Ser, Rom.; pop. 16; 88 km NW of Cluj; 47°23'/22°58'.

Seradz, *see* Sieradz.

Serafince, *see* Serafintsy.

Serafintsy, Ukr. (Serafince); pop. 87; 50 km NW of Chernovtsy; 48°39'/25°33'.

Serai, *see* Seirijai.

Serajevo, *see* Sarajevo.

Serbauti, Rom.; pop. 14; 133 km WNW of Iasi; 47°49'/26°09'.

Serbeni, Rom.; pop. 4; 101 km E of Cluj; 46°43'/24°52'.

Serbia; Not a town, but an independent nation prior to World War I. Serbia is now a constituent republic of Yugoslavia.

Serbinow, Pol.; pop. 41; 107 km ENE of Czestochowa; 51°03'/20°33'.

Serczyn, HSL. This pre-World War I community was not found in BGN gazetteers.

Serechowicze, *see* Serekhovichi.

Sered, Cz. (Szered, Szereda); pop. 1,300; 45 km NE of Bratislava; 48°17'/17°44'; COH, EDRD, GUM3, GUM4, GUM5, GUM6, HSL, HSL2, JGFF.

Seredeiu, Rom.; pop. 3; 62 km WNW of Cluj; 47°06'/22°57'.

Seredina Buda, Ukr.; pop. 1,176; 126 km NNE of Konotop; 52°11'/34°03'.

Seredkevychi, Ukr. (Ulitsko Serendkevich); pop. 61; 45 km NW of Lvov; 50°09'/23°33'.

Seredne, Ukr.; pop. 27; 182 km SSW of Lvov; 48°32'/22°30'; HSL.

Seredneye, Ukr. (Serednie, Szerednye); pop. 1,300; 182 km SSW of Lvov; 48°32'/22°30'; AMG, COH, GUM6, LDL.

Serednica, Pol.; pop. 23; 38 km SSW of Przemysl; 49°30'/22°31'.

Serednie, *see* Seredneye.

Serednie Male, Pol.; pop. 7; 62 km S of Przemysl; 49°18'/22°34'.

Serednie Wielkie, Pol.; pop. 55; 62 km SSW of Przemysl; 49°24'/22°13'.

Serednik, *see* Seredzius.

Seredzice, Pol.; pop. 6; 101 km WSW of Lublin; 51°09'/21°11'.

Seredzius, Lith. (Serednik, Srednik, Srednius); pop. 449; 38 km WNW of Kaunas; 55°05'/23°25'; HSL, JGFF, LDL, SF, YL.

Seree, *see* Seirijai.

Seregelyes, Hung.; pop. 93; 56 km SSW of Budapest; 47°06'/18°35'; PHH.

Serehai, *see* Seirijai.

Serekhovichi, Ukr. (Serechowicze); pop. 59; 139 km WNW of

Rovno; 51°25'/24°40'.

Serene, *see* Serenes.

Serenes, Lat. (Serene); 82 km ESE of Riga; 56°34'/25°13'; PHLE.

Serenyfalva, Hung. (Serenyifalva); pop. 4; 38 km WNW of Miskolc; 48°19'/20°24'.

Serenyifalva, *see* Serenyfalva.

Serepets, *see* Sierpc.

Seres, Bulg.; pop. 500; This town was not found in BGN gazetteers under the given spelling.

Seret, *see* Siret.

Seretets, Ukr.; 101 km ENE of Lvov; 49°52'/25°23'; JGFF.

Sereth, *see* Siret.

Serey, *see* Seirijai.

Sergeyevka, Ukr. (Sergheevca); pop. 22; 82 km SW of Odessa; 46°00'/29°57'.

Sergheevca, *see* Sergeyevka.

Sergii, Ukr. (Sarghieni, Syrgiyeni); pop. 204; 75 km SW of Chernovtsy; 47°59'/25°06'; PHR2.

Serheya, *see* Seirijai.

Serijai, *see* Seirijai.

Serke, *see* Sirkovce.

Serniawy, Pol.; pop. 16; 56 km ENE of Lublin; 51°21'/23°22'.

Sernichki, Byel. (Serniczki); pop. 3; 13 km ESE of Pinsk; 52°04'/26°15'.

Serniczki, *see* Sernichki.

Sernik, *see* Serniki Pervyye.

Serniki, *see* Serniki Pervyye.

Serniki Pervyye, Ukr. (Sernik, Serniki); pop. 987; 139 km N of Rovno; 51°49'/26°14'; AMG, COH, EDRD, GUM3, GUM4, GUM6, HSL, HSL2, LDL, SF.

Serock, Pol. (Serotsk, Serotzk, Sierck, Sierock, Srotsk); pop. 2,295; 32 km N of Warszawa; 52°31'/21°04'; AMG, CAHJP, COH, EJ, GA, GUM3, GUM4, GUM5, HSL, HSL2, JGFF, LDL, LYV, PHP1, PHP4, SF, YB.

Seroczyn, Pol. (Serotchin); pop. 179; 69 km ESE of Warszawa; 52°01'/21°56'; LDS, SF.

Serokomla, Pol.; pop. 140; 56 km NNW of Lublin; 51°42'/22°20'; EDRD, GUM3, GUM4, GUM5, HSL, SF.

Serotchin, *see* Seroczyn.

Serotsk, *see* Serock.

Serotzk, *see* Serock.

Serpec, *see* Sierpc.

Serpelice, Pol.; pop. 5; 101 km S of Bialystok; 52°17'/23°03'.

Serpenita, Rom. (Serpiniec); pop. 2; 101 km NNW of Iasi; 48°02'/27°06'; PHP2.

Serpiniec, *see* Serpenita.

Serpnevoye, Ukr. (Leiptig); pop. 50; 133 km WSW of Odessa; 46°18'/29°01'.

Serrai, Greece; pop. 529; 69 km NNE of Thessaloniki; 41°03'/23°33'.

Sesik, *see* Siesikai.

Sesovce, HSL. This pre-World War I community was not found in BGN gazetteers.

Sessenbach, Germ.; 75 km ESE of Koln; 50°28'/07°39'; PHGBW.

Sesslach, Germ.; 88 km NNW of Nurnberg; 50°11'/10°51'; PHGB.

Sestaci, *see* Shestachi.

Sestokai, *see* Shostaki.

Sesuoliai, *see* Sasuoliai.

Seta, Lith. (Shaty, Shet, Shod, Shot); pop. 440; 50 km NNE of Kaunas; 55°17'/24°15'; GUM3, GUM4, HSL.

Seubelsdorf, Germ.; pop. 8; 82 km N of Nurnberg; 50°08'/11°03'; PHGB.

Seussen, Germ.; 101 km NE of Nurnberg; 50°02'/12°09'; PHGB.

Sevastapol, *see* Sevastopol.

Sevastopol, Ukr. (Sebastapol, Sevastapol, Sewastopol); pop. 5,204; 56 km SW of Simferopol; 44°36'/33°32'; EJ, GUM4, GUM5, HSL, HSL2, SF.

Severskaya, GUM4. This town was not found in BGN

Sevetin, Cz.; pop. 6; 114 km S of Praha; 49°06'/14°35'.

Sevirova, *see* Sevirovo.

Sevirovo, Mold. (Sevirova); pop. 32; 114 km NW of Kishinev; 47°56'/28°09'.

Sevliush, *see* Vinogradov.

Sevljus, *see* Vinogradov.

Sevlussky Ardov, GUM3. This town was not found in BGN gazetteers under the given spelling.

Sevsk, USSR (Siewsk); pop. 279; 126 km S of Bryansk; 52°09'/34°30'.

Sewastopol, *see* Sevastopol.

Sewerionowo, Pol. PHP4. This town was not found in BGN gazetteers under the given spelling.

Sewerynow, *see* Sewerynowka.

Sewerynowka, Pol. (Sewerynow); pop. 22; 38 km WSW of Lublin; 51°10'/22°05'.

Sewlusz, *see* Vinogradov.

Seyriay, *see* Seirijai.

Sfantu Gheorghe, *see* Sfintu Gheorghe.

Sfantul Gheorghe, *see* Sfintu Gheorghe.

Sfintu Gheorghe, Rom. (Sepsiszentgyorgy, Sfantu Gheorghe, Sfantul Gheorghe, St Gheorghe); pop. 378; 62 km ESE of Cluj; 46°27'/24°14'; HSL, PHR2.

Sfintu Ilie, Rom.; pop. 21; 120 km WNW of Iasi; 47°38'/26°13'.

Shaba, *see* Shabo.

Shabiln, *see* Sabile.

Shabo, Ukr. (Shaba, Szaba); 50 km SSW of Odessa; 46°08'/30°23'; YB.

Shadek, *see* Szadek.

Shadov, *see* Seduva.

Shadova, *see* Seduva.

Shadove, *see* Seduva.

Shakay, *see* Sakiai.

Shakee, *see* Sakiai.

Shakev, *see* Osjakow.

Shakhi, Ukr. (Shakhy, Szachy); pop. 17; 126 km N of Rovno; 51°37'/26°53'.

Shakhy, *see* Shakhi.

Shaki, *see* Sakiai.

Shakyai, *see* Sakiai.

Shalanki, Ukr. (Salank, Salanky); 202 km SSW of Lvov; 48°13'/22°53'; HSL, JGFF.

Shamloya, *see* Simleu Silvaniei.

Shamovo, Byel.; pop. 601; 133 km SE of Vitebsk; 54°12'/31°22'; EDRD.

Shandrovets, Ukr. (Szandrowiec); pop. 38; 114 km SW of Lvov; 49°10'/22°51'.

Shandrovka, *see* Camgorodok.

Shargorod, Ukr. (Sargorog, Sharigrad, Sharigrod, Szarogrod); pop. 2,697; 56 km SSW of Vinnitsa; 48°45'/28°05'; EDRD, EJ, GUM3, GUM4, GUM6, JGFF, PHR1, SF.

Sharigrad, *see* Shargorod.

Sharigrod, *see* Shargorod.

Sharkotsina, *see* Sharkovshchina.

Sharkovshchina, Byel. (Sakovchizna, Sarkeyschina, Sarkeystsene, Sharkotsina, Sharkoyshchina, Szarkowszczyzna); pop. 615; 170 km N of Minsk; 55°22'/27°28'; COH, EDRD, EJ, GUM3, GUM4, GUM6, HSL, LDL, LYV, SF, YB.

Sharkoyshchina, *see* Sharkovshchina.

Sharovechka, Ukr. (Scharowka, Sharovka, Sharovochka); 114 km W of Vinnitsa; 49°25'/26°55'; LDL, SF.

Sharovka, *see* Sharovechka.

Sharovochka, *see* Sharovechka.

Sharpantsa, Ukr. (Sharpantse, Szarpance); pop. 20; 88 km NNE of Lvov; 50°33'/24°32'.

Sharpantse, *see* Sharpantsa.

Shashkowka, GUM4. This town was not found in BGN gazetteers under the given spelling.

Shasmaken, *see* Valdemarpils.

Shatava, Ukr. (Shatova, Shatowa, Shitova); 75 km NE of Chernovtsy; 48°46'/26°43'; LDL, SF.

Shatova, *see* Shatava.

Shatowa, *see* Shatava.

Shatsk, Ukr. (Shatzk, Szack); pop. 238; 189 km N of Lvov; 51°30'/23°57'; AMG, GUM3, GUM4, SF.

Shatsk (Byelorussia), Byel.; pop. 684; 56 km SSE of Minsk; 53°25'/27°41'.

Shaty, *see* Seta.

Shatzk, *see* Shatsk.

Shaulyai, *see* Siauliai.

Shaumyan, *see* Shaumyana.

Shaumyana, USSR (Shaumyan); pop. 200; 611 km SSE of Voronezh; 46°22'/40°34'; GUM4.

Shavkany, *see* Saukenai.

Shavl, *see* Siauliai.

Shavlan, *see* Siaulenai.

Shavlian, *see* Siaulenai.

Shawli, *see* Siauliai.

Shchavnits, *see* Szczawnica Nizna.

Shchavnitsa Vizhna, *see* Szczawnica Nizna.

Shchebreshin, *see* Szczebrzeszyn.

Shchedrin, Byel.; pop. 1,759; 114 km WNW of Gomel; 52°53'/29°33'; COH, EJ, HSL, HSL2, SF, YB.

Shchedrogir, Ukr. (Shchodrokhoshche, Szczodrohoszcze); pop. 76; 170 km NW of Rovno; 51°48'/24°47'.

Shchekochin, *see* Szczekociny.

Sh Chekotckin, *see* Szczekociny.

Shchekotsini, *see* Szczekociny.

Shchenets, Byel. (Szczeniec); 208 km WSW of Minsk; 53°42'/24°25'; GYLA.

Shcheploty, Ukr. (Szczeploty); pop. 14; 56 km WNW of Lvov; 50°05'/23°21'.

Shcheptitsy, Ukr. (Sheptytse, Szeptyce); pop. 41; 50 km SW of Lvov; 49°39'/23°25'.

Shcherbakov, GUM4. This town was not found in BGN gazetteers under the given spelling.

Shcherbanka, Ukr.; 50 km WNW of Odessa; 46°42'/30°11'; JGFF.

Shcherbinovo, Byel. (Szczerbinowo); pop. 11; 94 km N of Pinsk; 52°55'/26°07'.

Shcherchevo, Byel. (Szczerczewo); pop. 8; 139 km W of Pinsk; 52°25'/24°09'.

Shcherets, Ukr. (Shtcherzetz, Szczerec, Szczerzec); pop. 712; 45 km WNW of Lvov; 50°07'/23°34'; COH, EDRD, EGRS, GUM5, HSL, JGFF, PHP2, SF.

Shchetinka, Byel.; 139 km N of Gomel; 53°40'/31°13'; GUM4.

Shchigry, USSR; pop. 58; This town was not found in BGN gazetteers under the given spelling.

Shchirets, Ukr.; 32 km SSW of Lvov; 49°39'/23°52'; JGFF.

Shchityn, Ukr. (Szczytyn); pop. 48; 163 km NW of Rovno; 51°47'/24°52'.

Shchodrokhoshche, *see* Shchedrogir.

Shchors, Ukr. (Snovsk, Snovsr, Snowsk); pop. 2,416; 107 km WNW of Konotop; 51°49'/31°56'; HSL, SF.

Sh Chuchin, *see* Shchuchin.

Shchuchin, Byel. (Sh Chuchin, Shtsutsin, Shtutsin, Stuchin, Stutchin); 189 km WSW of Minsk; 53°36'/24°45'; LYV, SF.

Shchurovichi, Ukr. (Shchurovitse, Shtervitz, Shtruvits, Szcrzorowice, Szczurowice); pop. 100; 88 km NE of Lvov; 50°16'/25°02'; EGRS, HSL, LDL, PHP2, SF, YB.

Shchurovitse, *see* Shchurovichi.

Shchutsin, *see* Szczucin.

Shebreshin, *see* Szczebrzeszyn.

Shedeva, *see* Seduva.

Shedlets, *see* Siedlce.

Shedlishtza, *see* Lalovo.

Shedlitz, *see* Siedlce.

Sheev, *see* Sieu.

Shegyni, Ukr. (Shekhyne, Szechynie); pop. 32; 75 km WSW of Lvov; 49°48'/22°58'.

Shekhyne, *see* Shegyni.

Shelib, *see* Vselyub.

Sheliba Dikshitz, *see* Seliba.

Shelvov, Ukr. (Szelwow); pop. 4; 101 km W of Rovno; 50°43'/24°47'.

Shemezova, *see* Siemiezowo.

Shemezovo, *see* Siemiezowo.

Shena, *see* Sienno.

Shenberg, *see* Skaistkalne.

Shenderivka, *see* Samgorodok.

Shendeshov, *see* Sedziszow.

Shepel, Ukr. (Czepel, Szepel); pop. 42; 82 km W of Rovno; 50°47'/25°07'; GUM6.

Shepetivke, *see* Shepetovka.

Shepetovka, Ukr. (Shepetivke, Szepetowka); pop. 3,916; 75 km ESE of Rovno; 50°11'/27°04'; AMG, COH, EJ, GUM4, GUM5, GYLA, HSL, JGFF, LYV, PHP2, SF.

Shepit, Ukr. (Shipotele Suchevey, Sipotele pe Siret, Sipotele Sucevei); pop. 89; 82 km SW of Chernovtsy; 47°48'/25°10'.

Sheps, *see* Sierpc.

Shepsk, *see* Sierpc.

Sheptytse, *see* Shcheptitsy.

Sheradz, *see* Sieradz.

Sherbeshty, Mold. (Sarbesti); pop. 136; 101 km NW of Kishinev; 47°47'/28°17'.

Sheredz, *see* Sieradz.

Sheresheva, *see* Shereshevo.

Shereshevo, Byel. (Sheresheva, Shereshov, Shereshuv, Shershev, Shershova, Shershovi, Szereszow); pop. 1,341; 139 km WNW of Pinsk; 52°33'/24°13'; AMG, COH, GUM3, GUM5, HSL, HSL2, JGFF, LDL, SF, YB.

Shereshov, *see* Shereshevo.

Shereshuv, *see* Shereshevo.

Sherpts, *see* Sierpc.

Sherptz, *see* Sierpc.

Shersheniovtse, Ukr. (Szereszniowce, Szerszeniowce); pop. 50; 62 km NNW of Chernovtsy; 48°49'/25°49'; PHP2.

Shershev, *see* Shereshevo.

Shershova, *see* Shereshevo.

Shershovi, *see* Shereshevo.

Shervinty, *see* Sirvintos.

Sheshvil, *see* Sasuoliai.

Shestachi, Mold. (Sestaci); pop. 47; 101 km N of Kishinev; 47°52'/28°45'.

Shet, *see* Seta.

Shevchenkovo, Ukr.; pop. 445; 69 km ESE of Kharkov; 49°41'/37°09'.

Shevchenkovo (Bessarabia), Ukr. (Caramahmet); pop. 6; 150 km SW of Odessa; 45°33'/29°20'.

Shevershin, *see* Szczebrzeszyn.

Shiaulai, *see* Siauliai.

Shidlov, *see* Szydlow.

Shidlova, *see* Siluva.

Shidlovets, *see* Szydlowiec.

Shidlovits, *see* Szydlowiec.

Shidlovitz, *see* Szydlowiec.

Shidlovtse, *see* Szydlowiec.

Shidlovtsy, Ukr. (Szydlowce); pop. 4; 82 km N of Chernovtsy; 49°00'/26°13'; GUM5.

Shidlovtza, *see* Szydlowiec.

Shidlovyets, *see* Szydlowiec.

Shidra, *see* Sidra.

Shikian, *see* Saukenai.

Shilauts, *see* Shilovtsy.

Shilel, *see* Silale.

Shileti, *see* Silale.

Shilin, Byel. (Szylin); pop. 10; 82 km WNW of Pinsk; 52°26'/25°02'.

Shilovtsy, Ukr. (Shilauts, Silauti); pop. 82; 26 km NE of Chernovtsy; 48°27'/26°11'.

Shimantza, *see* Simaniskiai.

Shimberg, *see* Skaistkalne.

Shimkaits, *see* Simkaiciai.

Shimkovtsy, Ukr. (Szymkowce); pop. 20; 62 km SSE of Rovno; 50°06'/26°24'.

Shimsk, *see* Shumskoye.

Shinderivka, *see* Samgorodok.

Shinova, *see* Sieniawa.

Shipentsi, *see* Shipintsy.

Shipintsy, Ukr. (Shipentsi, Sipeniti); pop. 79; 19 km WNW of Chernovtsy; 48°22'/25°45'.

Shipka, Mold. (Sipca); pop. 20; 101 km N of Kishinev; 47°50'/28°49'.

Shipotele Suchevey, *see* Shepit.

Shiraduv, *see* Zyrardow.

Shiradz, *see* Sieradz.

Shirautsi de Zhos, *see* Shirovtsy.

Shirokoye, Ukr. (Chebabcea); pop. 9; 75 km SSW of Odessa; 45°58'/30°05'; GUM4.

Shirovtsy, Ukr. (Shirautsi de Zhos, Sirautii de Sus); pop. 47; 32 km NE of Chernovtsy; 48°25'/26°20'.

Shirvent, *see* Sirvintos.

Shirvint, *see* Sirvintos.

Shishaki, Ukr.; 163 km WSW of Kharkov; 49°53'/34°00'; GUM4.

Shishkany, Mold. (Sapte Bani?); pop. 117; 50 km WSW of Kishinev; 46°59'/28°12'.

Shishkovtse, Ukr.; 88 km ENE of Lvov; 49°53'/25°15'; JGFF.

Shishkovtsy, *see* Shyshkovtse.

Shistka, *see* Shostka.

Shitomir, *see* Zhitomir.

Shitova, *see* Shatava.

Shklin, Ukr. (Szklin); pop. 28; 88 km WSW of Rovno; 50°34'/25°00'.

Shklo, Ukr. (Szklo); pop. 53; 38 km WNW of Lvov; 49°57'/23°32'; HSL, PHP2.

Shklov, Byel. (Szklow); pop. 3,119; 114 km S of Vitebsk; 54°13'/30°18'; CAHJP, EJ, GUM4, GYLA, HSL, HSL2, JGFF, LDL, PHP1, SF.

Shkod, *see* Skuodas.

Shkodvil, *see* Skaudvile.

Shkud, *see* Skuodas.

Shkudvil, *see* Skaudvile.

Shkudy, *see* Skuodas.

Shkuntiki, Byel. (Shkuntsiki, Szkunciki); pop. 51; 157 km W of Vitebsk; 55°22'/27°41'.

Shkuntsiki, *see* Shkuntiki.

Shlapan, Ukr. (Szlapan); pop. 22; 150 km NNW of Rovno; 51°52'/25°28'.

Shlaveshnia, *see* Slovechno.

Shlisselburg, *see* Petrokrepost.

Shlok, *see* Sloka.

Shmankovtse, Ukr. (Szmankowce); pop. 30; 82 km N of Chernovtsy; 49°00'/25°55'.

Shnadova, *see* Sniadowo.

Shnadovi, *see* Sniadowo.

Shnipishuk, *see* Snipiskes.

Shnodovo, *see* Sniadowo.

Shnyadovo, *see* Sniadowo.

Shnyatin, *see* Snyatyn.

Sho, Byel. (Szo); pop. 1; 126 km WSW of Vitebsk; 55°11'/28°14'.

Shod, *see* Seta.

Shodina, *see* Siaudine.

Shokian, *see* Saukenai.

Sholdaneshty, Mold. (Soldanesti); pop. 150; 94 km N of Kishinev; 47°49'/28°48'.

Sholomenitse, Ukr. (Szolomienice); pop. 26; 38 km SW of Lvov; 49°44'/23°32'.

Shomova, *see* Shumovka.

Shomsk, *see* Shumskoye.

Shonberg, *see* Skaistkalne.

Shosli, *see* Zasliai.

Shostaki, Ukr. (Sestokai, Szostakow); pop. 10; 32 km NW of Lvov; 50°07'/23°46'.

Shostka, Ukr. (Shistka); pop. 467; 75 km N of Konotop; 51°52'/33°29'.

Shot, *see* Seta.

Shovits, *see* Subata.

Shpanov, Ukr. (Szpanow); pop. 6; 13 km N of Rovno; 50°40'/26°16'.

Shperov, *see* Przyrow.

Shpikolosy, Ukr. (Szpikolosy); pop. 20; 75 km NNE of Lvov; 50°27'/24°31'; JGFF.

Shpikov, Ukr. (Spikov); pop. 1,361; 56 km S of Vinnitsa; 48°47'/28°34'; SF.

Shpola, Ukr.; pop. 5,379; 94 km NE of Uman; 49°02'/31°25'; HSL, JGFF, LDL, SF, YB.

Shransk, *see* Szrensk.

Shrensk, *see* Szrensk.

Shrentsk, *see* Szrensk.

Shtabin, *see* Sztabin.

Shtchertzov, *see* Szczercow.

Shtcherzetz, *see* Shcherets.

Shtefaneshty, Mold. (Stefanesti, Stefanesti Soroca); pop. 23; 88 km NNW of Kishinev; 47°44'/28°25'; EJ, GUM4, GUM5, HSL, JGFF, PHR1.

Shtehkeva, *see* Szczakowa.

Shtekechin, *see* Szczekociny.

Shtekishin, *see* Szczekociny.

Shtekotchin, *see* Szczekociny.

Shtervitz, *see* Shchurovichi.

Shtip, *see* Shtit.

Shtirotava, GUM5. This town was not found in BGN gazetteers under the given spelling.

Shtit, Bulg. (Shtip); pop. 480; 202 km SSW of Varna; 41°49'/26°22'.

Shtoklishok, *see* Stakliskes.

Shtoptsi, *see* Stolbtsy.

Shtruvits, *see* Shchurovichi.

Shtsitsin, *see* Szczucin.

Shtsutsin, *see* Shchuchin.

Shtubiyeny, Mold. (Stiubieni); pop. 79; 150 km NW of Kishinev; 48°02'/27°32'.

Shtutsin, *see* Shchuchin.

Shtzovnitz, *see* Szczawnica.

Shubbotz, *see* Siubaiciai.

Shubitz, *see* Subata.

Shubkov, Ukr. (Shuvkov, Szubkow); pop. 22; 26 km WNW of Rovno; 50°42'/26°01'; SF.

Shubotch, *see* Subata.

Shukian, *see* Saukenai.

Shulganuvka, Ukr. (Szulhanowka); pop. 23; 75 km NNW of Chernovtsy; 48°58'/25°43'.

Shumen, *see* Kolarovgrad.

Shumiachi, USSR (Shumiatch, Shumyachi); pop. 1,394; 120 km SSE of Smolensk; 53°47'/32°24'; HSL, LDL, SF. This town was located on a pre-World War I map, but does not appear in contemporary gazetteers.

Shumiatch, *see* Shumiachi.

Shumilino, Byel.; pop. 483; 38 km W of Vitebsk; 55°18'/29°37'.

Shumilovo, Ukr. (Sumilova); 50 km SW of Uman; 48°29'/29°41'; GUM4, PHR1.

Shumla, *see* Kolarovgrad.

Shumlyany, Ukr. (Schumlau?, Szumlany); pop. 62; 88 km ESE of Lvov; 49°17'/24°53'.

Shumovka, Byel. (Shomova); 139 km NNE of Gomel; 53°33'/32°01'; SF.

Shumsk, *see* Shumskoye.

Shumskoye, Ukr. (Shimsk, Shomsk, Shumsk, Szumsk); pop. 1,717; 62 km S of Rovno; 50°07'/26°07'; AMG, COH, EDRD, GUM3, GUM4, GUM6, GYLA, HSL, JGFF, LDL, SF, YB.

Shumyachi, *see* Shumiachi.

Shurvilishuk, *see* Surviliskis.

Shury, Mold. (Suri); pop. 113; 139 km NW of Kishinev; 48°06'/27°52'.

Shushki, Ukr. (Szuszki); pop. 9; 139 km WNW of Rovno; 51°21'/24°37'.

Shutz, *see* Suceava.

Shuvalovo Ozerki, USSR; pop. 125; 26 km N of Leningrad; 60°02'/30°18'.

Shuvinishok, *see* Suvainiskis.

Shuvkov, *see* Shubkov.

Shvaneburg, *see* Gulbene.

Shvekshni, *see* Sveksna.

Shveksna, *see* Sveksna.

Shverzna, *see* Stolbtsy.

Shvidostch, *see* Svedasai.

Shvintzion, *see* Svencionys.

Shvir, *see* Svir.

Shvyentshitse, *see* Swiecica.

Shvyentsiani, *see* Svencionys.

Shvyerzhen, *see* Stolbtsy.

Shvyetsiani, *see* Svencionys.

Shwartz Stimme, *see* Belaya Tserkov.

Shwartz Tomah, *see* Bila Cirkev.

Shyena, *see* Sienno.

Shypovtse, Ukr. (Szypowce); pop. 37; 62 km NNW of Chernovtsy; 48°50'/25°49'; PHP2.

Shyshkovtse, Ukr. (Shishkovtsy, Siscauti, Szyszkowce); pop. 26; 50 km N of Chernovtsy; 48°42'/26°02'; COH.

Siad, *see* Seda.

Sialenai, *see* Siaulenai.

Sianki, *see* Syanki.

Sianow, Pol. (Zanow); 139 km NE of Szczecin; 54°13'/16°17'; LDS.

Siarkowszczyna, *see* Sporkovshchizna.

Siary, Pol.; pop. 14; 107 km ESE of Krakow; 49°38'/21°11'.

Siaudine, Lith. (Shodina); YL. a number of towns share this name. It was not possible to determine from available information which one is being referenced.

Siaulenai, Lith. (Shavlan, Shavlian, Sialenai); pop. 237; 32 km SSE of Siauliai; 55°41'/23°24'; HSL, JGFF, SF, YL.

Siauliai, Lith. (Schaulen, Schavli, Shaulyai, Shavl, Shawli, Shiaulai, Silaliai, Szawle); pop. 5,338; 120 km NNW of Kaunas; 55°56'/23°19'; AMG, CAHJP, COH, EJ, GUM3, GUM4, GUM5, GUM6, HSL, HSL2, ISH3, JGFF, LDL, SF, YL.

Sibenik, Yug.; pop. 28; 234 km S of Zagreb; 43°44'/15°53'; PHY.

Sibiu, Rom. (Hermannstadt, Hermanstadt, Nagyszeben); 120 km SSE of Cluj; 45°48'/24°09'; EJ, HSL, HSL2, JGFF, PHR1.

Sibrina, Cz.; pop. 3; 13 km E of Praha; 50°04'/14°40'.

Sic, Rom.; pop. 50; BGN lists two possible localities with this name located at PHR2.

Sichow, *see* Sikhov.

Sickershausen, Germ.; 69 km WNW of Nurnberg; 49°43'/10°11'; PHGB.

Sickingen, Germ. BGN lists two possible localities with this name located at 49°06'/08°48' and 49°06'/08°48'. PHGBW.

Siclod, Rom.; pop. 21; 114 km E of Cluj; 46°31'/25°03'.

Sico Branko, *see* Bronka.

Sicsel, *see* Sacel.

Siculeni, Rom.; pop. 13; 163 km SW of Iasi; 46°25'/25°45'.

Siczeslaw, *see* Dnepropetrovsk.

Sid, Yug.; pop. 59; 107 km WNW of Beograd; 45°08'/19°14'; HSL, PHY.

Sidluva, *see* Siluva.

Sidorov, Ukr. (Sidorow); pop. 63; 82 km N of Chernovtsy; 49°01'/26°10'.

Sidorow, *see* Sidorov.

Sidra, Pol. (Shidra, Sidre); pop. 455; 56 km NNE of Bialystok; 53°34'/23°27'; COH, FRG, GUM3, HSL, LDL, POCEM,

SF, WS.

Sidre, *see* Sidra.

Sidzina, Pol.; pop. 23; 56 km S of Krakow; 49°37'/19°44'.

Siebenhirten, *see* Siebenhirten bei Wien.

Siebenhirten bei Wien, Aus. (Siebenhirten); pop. 25; 13 km SSW of Wien; 48°07'/16°18'.

Siebiez, *see* Sebeza.

Siechow, *see* Sekhuv.

Sieciechow, Pol.; pop. 118; 69 km WNW of Lublin; 51°33'/21°45'.

Sieciechowice, Pol.; pop. 17; 26 km N of Krakow; 50°15'/19°59'.

Sieczychy, Pol.; pop. 38; 62 km NNE of Warszawa; 52°44'/21°30'.

Siedlanka, Pol.; pop. 20; 56 km NW of Przemysl; 50°16'/22°26'; JGFF.

Siedlce, Pol. (Shedlets, Shedlitz); pop. 14,685; 88 km E of Warszawa; 52°10'/22°18'; AMG, CAHJP, COH, EDRD, EJ, GA, GUM3, GUM4, GUM5, GUM6, HSL, HSL2, ISH1, ISH3, JGFF, LDL, LDS, LYV, PHP1, PHP4, POCEM, SF, YB.

Siedlce (Nowy Sacz area), Pol.; pop. 21; 75 km ESE of Krakow; 49°41'/20°47'.

Siedleczka, Pol.; pop. 24; 38 km WNW of Przemysl; 49°58'/22°22'.

Siedliska, Pol.; pop. 92; 32 km NNW of Lublin; 51°28'/22°29'; AMG. *See also* Sedliska.

Siedliska (near Jaworow), Pol.; pop. 35; 75 km NE of Przemysl; 50°16'/23°34'; GUM3.

Siedliska (near Przemysl), Pol.; pop. 33; 13 km E of Przemysl; 49°46'/22°54'.

Siedliska (near Rzeszow), Pol.; pop. 26; 38 km WSW of Przemysl; 49°46'/22°15'; CAHJP.

Siedliska Bogusz, Pol.; pop. 11; 94 km W of Przemysl; 49°55'/21°25'.

Siedlisko, (Carolath); LDS. a number of towns share this name. It was not possible to determine from available information which one is being referenced.

Siedliszcze, Pol.; pop. 754; 45 km E of Lublin; 51°12'/23°10'; CAHJP, COH, EDRD, GA, GUM3, GUM5, LDS, POCEM, SF, YB. *See also* Sedlishche.

Siedliszcze (near Hrubieszow), Pol.; pop. 22; 88 km E of Lublin; 51°01'/23°49'.

Siedliszcze (near Wlodawa), Pol.; pop. 36; 75 km ENE of Lublin; 51°17'/23°39'.

Siedliszcze Male, *see* Male Sedlishche.

Siedliszcze Wielkie, Pol.; pop. 21; Described in the *Black Book* as being in the Wolyn region of Poland, this town was not found in BGN gazetteers.

Siedliszowice, Pol.; pop. 23; 62 km ENE of Krakow; 50°11'/20°46'.

Siefersheim, Germ.; 62 km SW of Frankfurt am Main; 49°48'/07°57'; GUM5.

Siegburg, Germ.; pop. 250; 26 km ESE of Koln; 50°48'/07°12'; GED, HSL, HSL2.

Siegelsbach, Germ.; pop. 20; 62 km NNW of Stuttgart; 49°16'/09°05'; PHGBW.

Siegen, Germ.; pop. 100; 75 km E of Koln; 50°52'/08°02'; GED, GUM5.

Siegertshofen, Germ.; 69 km W of Munchen; 48°15'/10°39'; PHGB.

Sieghartskirchen, Aus.; pop. 1; 32 km W of Wien; 48°15'/16°00'.

Sieglar, Germ.; pop. 20; 26 km SE of Koln; 50°48'/07°08'; GED.

Siegless, *see* Sigless.

Siegmar, *see* Siegmarschonau.

Siegmarschonau, Germ. (Siegmar); pop. 33; 62 km SE of Leipzig; 50°49'/12°51'.

Siegritz, Germ. BGN lists two possible localities with this name located at 49°51'/11°13' and 49°52'/12°05'. GUM5.

Siekierczyce, Ukr.; pop. 23; 82 km SSW of Lvov; 49°15'/23°25'.

This town was located on an interwar map of Poland but does not appear in contemporary gazetteers. Map coordinates are approximate.

Sieksate, Lat.; pop. 6; 139 km WSW of Riga; 56°43'/21°54'.

Sielce, HSL. a number of towns share this name. It was not possible to determine from available information which one is being referenced.

Sielec, Pol.; pop. 207; 69 km ESE of Lublin; 51°02'/23°31'; AMG, GUM5, HSL, HSL2, JGFF, SF. *See also* Selets.

Sielec (near Przemysl), Pol.; pop. 12; 13 km ESE of Przemysl; 49°46'/22°49'.

Sielec (near Tarnobrzeg), Pol.; pop. 3; 94 km SSW of Lublin; 50°38'/21°44'.

Sielec Bienkow, *see* Selets (near Radekhov).

Sielec Zawonie, Pol. PHP2. This town was not found in BGN gazetteers under the given spelling.

Sielen, Germ.; pop. 4; 101 km S of Hannover; 51°33'/09°23'; GED.

Sieliszcze, Byel.; 26 km NE of Pinsk; 52°12'/26°26'; COH, HSL, JGFF.

Sieliszcze Male, *see* Selishche.

Sielpia Duza, Pol. (Sielpia Wielka); pop. 22; 94 km NE of Czestochowa; 51°07'/20°21'.

Sielpia Wielka, *see* Sielpia Duza.

Siemakowce, *see* Semakovtsy.

Siemianowice, *see* Siemianowice Slaskie.

Siemianowice Slaskie, Pol. (Laurahutte, Siemianowice, Siemianowitz); 56 km S of Czestochowa; 50°18'/19°02'; AMG, GUM3, GUM4, GUM5, JGFF, LDS, PHP3.

Siemianowitz, *see* Siemianowice Slaskie.

Siemianowka, *see* Semyanovka.

Siemiatycze, Pol. (Semyatich, Semyatitcha); pop. 3,718; 82 km S of Bialystok; 52°27'/22°53'; AMG, COH, EDRD, EJ, GA, GUM3, GUM5, GUM6, HSL, JGFF, LDL, LYV, PHP4, POCEM, SF, YB.

Siemiechow, Pol.; pop. 25; 75 km ESE of Krakow; 49°51'/20°55'.

Siemien, Pol.; pop. 36; 50 km N of Lublin; 51°38'/22°46'; GUM5.

Siemieniczki, Pol.; pop. 9; 45 km N of Lodz; 52°07'/19°26'.

Siemierz, Pol.; pop. 32; 94 km SE of Lublin; 50°35'/23°31'.

Siemiezowo, (Shemezova, Shemezovo); LDL, SF. This town was not found in BGN gazetteers under the given spelling.

Siemiginow, Ukr.; pop. 25; 126 km S of Lvov; 48°45'/23°45'. This town was located on an interwar map of Poland but does not appear in contemporary gazetteers. Map coordinates are approximate.

Siemihoscicze, *see* Semigostichi.

Siemikowce, *see* Siemkowce.

Siemionowicze, Byel.; pop. 43; 139 km NNW of Minsk; 55°05'/27°05'. This town was located on an interwar map of Poland but does not appear in contemporary gazetteers. Map coordinates are approximate.

Siemionowka, Pol.; pop. 21; 50 km ESE of Bialystok; 52°54'/23°50'.

Siemiony, Pol.; pop. 4; 62 km SSW of Bialystok; 52°37'/22°47'.

Siemkowce, (Siemikowce); PHP2. This town was not found in BGN gazetteers under the given spelling.

Siemkowice, Pol.; pop. 21; 56 km NNW of Czestochowa; 51°13'/18°54'; PHP1.

Siemnice, Pol.; 101 km NNE of Przemysl; 50°33'/23°38'; JGFF.

Siemszyce, Pol.; pop. 14; 50 km NW of Lodz; 52°05'/19°06'.

Siemuszowa, Pol.; pop. 31; 45 km SW of Przemysl; 49°36'/22°19'.

Sieniawa, Pol. (Shinova); pop. 1,071; 50 km NNW of Przemysl; 50°12'/22°38'; COH, EGRS, GA, GUM3, GUM4, HSL, HSL2, JGFF, LDL, PHP2, PHP3, POCEM, SF. The *Black Book* notes a town named Sieniawa (pop. 60) in the interwar Polish province of Tarnopol that does not appear in interwar or contemporary gazetteers.

Sieniawa (near Sanok), Pol.; pop. 15; 62 km SW of Przemysl;

49°33'/21°56'.

Sieniawka, Pol.; pop. 34; 56 km NNE of Przemysl; 50°09'/23°18'.

Sieniec, Pol.; pop. 5; 62 km NW of Czestochowa; 51°15'/18°41'.

Sieniewice, Pol.; pop. 21; 82 km SSW of Bialystok; 52°26'/22°40'.

Sienkiewicze, *see* Sinkevichi.

Sienkiewiczowka, *see* Senkevichevka.

Sienkow, *see* Senkuv.

Sienna, Pol.; 69 km ESE of Krakow; 49°43'/20°42'; EDRD.

Siennica, Pol.; pop. 560; 45 km ESE of Warszawa; 52°06'/21°37'; COH, EDRD, GA, HSL, LDS, PHP4.

Siennica Krolewska, Pol.; pop. 6; 56 km ESE of Lublin; 50°59'/23°17'.

Siennica Nadolna, Pol.; pop. 3; 50 km ESE of Lublin; 51°01'/23°12'; GUM4.

Siennica Rozana, Pol. BGN lists two possible localities with this name located at 50°59'/23°20' and 51°00'/21°19'. GUM5.

Sienno, Pol. (Seno, Shena, Shyena, Syeno); pop. 735; 82 km WSW of Lublin; 51°05'/21°28'; COH, GA, GUM5, HSL, JGFF, LDS, LYV.

Siennow, Pol.; pop. 62; 26 km WNW of Przemysl; 49°58'/22°30'.

Siepietnica, Pol.; pop. 8; 107 km ESE of Krakow; 49°46'/21°18'.

Siepraw, Pol.; pop. 28; 26 km SSE of Krakow; 49°55'/19°59'.

Sieprawice, Pol.; pop. 6; 13 km WNW of Lublin; 51°18'/22°24'.

Sieradz, Pol. (Seradz, Sheradz, Sheredz, Shiradz); pop. 2,835; 56 km SW of Lodz; 51°36'/18°45'; AMG, CAHJP, COH, EDRD, EJ, FRG, GA, GUM3, GUM4, HSL, HSL2, JGFF, LYV, PHP1, PHP3, PHP4, POCEM, SF.

Sierakosce, Pol.; pop. 16; 19 km S of Przemysl; 49°40'/22°46'.

Sierakow, Pol. (Sierakow Wielkopolski, Zirke); pop. 24; 62 km WNW of Poznan; 52°39'/16°06'; CAHJP, HSL.

Sierakow Wielkopolski, *see* Sierakow.

Sierck, *see* Serock.

Siercza, Pol.; pop. 20; 19 km SE of Krakow; 49°59'/20°03'.

Sierijai, *see* Seirijai.

Siernicze Wielkie, Pol.; pop. 2; 69 km E of Poznan; 52°25'/18°01'.

Sierock, *see* Serock.

Sierpc, Pol. (Scherps, Serepets, Serpec, Sheps, Shepsk, Sherpts, Sherptz); pop. 2,861; 114 km WNW of Warszawa; 52°53'/19°40'; AMG, COH, EDRD, EJ, GA, GUM3, GUM4, GUM5, HSL, HSL2, JGFF, LDL, LDS, LYV, PHP1, PHP4, POCEM, SF, WS, YB.

Sierpow, Pol.; pop. 7; 38 km NW of Lodz; 52°01'/19°15'.

Siersburg, Germ.; 170 km SW of Frankfurt am Main; 49°22'/06°39'; GED.

Sierzawy, Pol.; pop. 30; 114 km SW of Lublin; 50°57'/21°02'.

Siesartis, Lith. (Sisarte); 75 km NE of Kaunas; 55°18'/24°54'; JGFF.

Siesiaki, *see* Siesikai.

Siesikai, Lith. (Sesik, Siesiaki); pop. 125; 62 km NE of Kaunas; 55°18'/24°30'; YL.

Sietesz, Pol.; pop. 39; 38 km WNW of Przemysl; 49°59'/22°22'.

Sietnica, Pol.; pop. 18; 94 km ESE of Krakow; 49°46'/21°08'.

Sieu, Rom. (Gross Schogen, Sajo, Sheev, Sif); pop. 324; 120 km N of Cluj; 47°43'/24°13'; AMG, HSL, PHR2, SM.

Sieul Mare, Rom. (Nagysajo); HSL. This pre-World War I community was not found in BGN gazetteers.

Sieu Magherus, Rom. (Sajomagyaros); pop. 63; 69 km NE of Cluj; 47°05'/24°23'; HSL, PHR2.

Sieu Nasaud, Rom.; pop. 98; 82 km NE of Cluj; 47°00'/24°37'.

Sieu Odorhei, Rom.; pop. 16; 69 km NE of Cluj; 47°09'/24°19'.

Sieu Sfaniu, *see* Sieu Sfint.

Sieu Sfint, Rom. (Sajoszentandras, Sieu Sfaniu); 69 km NE of Cluj; 47°09'/24°18'; HSL.

Sieut, Rom.; pop. 10; 82 km NE of Cluj; 46°59'/24°39'.

Siewierz, Pol.; pop. 266; 38 km SSE of Czestochowa; 50°28'/19°14'; AMG.

Siewsk, *see* Sevsk.

Sif, *see* Sieu.

Sigelki, Pol. (Sygielki); pop. 15; 69 km NNW of Przemysl; 50°22'/22°25'.

Sighet, Rom. (Maramaros Sighet, Maramarossziget, Sighetul Marmatiei, Sigut, Sihat, Syhot Marmaroski, Sziget); pop. 10,609; 133 km N of Cluj; 47°56'/23°53'; AMG, COH, EJ, GUM3, GUM4, GUM5, GUM6, HSL, HSL2, JGFF, LDL, LYV, PHP2, PHR2, SM, YB.

Sighet Suburbana Iapa, Rom.; pop. 466; Described in the *Black Book* as being in the Transylvania region of Romania, this town was not found in BGN gazetteers.

Sighetul Marmatiei, *see* Sighet.

Sighisoara, Rom. (Schassburg, Segesvar); 114 km ESE of Cluj; 46°13'/24°48'; HSL, HSL2, PHR1.

Sigless, Aus. (Siegless); pop. 4; 50 km S of Wien; 47°47'/16°23'.

Sigmaringen, Germ.; 82 km S of Stuttgart; 48°05'/09°13'; PHGBW.

Sigmundsherberg, Aus.; pop. 3; 69 km NW of Wien; 48°41'/15°45'.

Sigulda, Lat. (Segewald, Segewold, Zegevol D); pop. 7; 50 km NE of Riga; 57°09'/24°51'; PHLE.

Sigut, *see* Sighet.

Sihat, *see* Sighet.

Sihnea, GUM4. This town was not found in BGN gazetteers under the given spelling.

Sikabony, *see* Male Blahovo.

Sikarlo, Rom. (Csikarlo); 107 km NNW of Cluj; 47°42'/23°24'; HSL. This town was located on a pre-World War I map, but does not appear in contemporary gazetteers.

Sikator, Hung.; pop. 3; 94 km WSW of Budapest; 47°26'/17°51'.

Sikernica, *see* Sokirnitsa.

Sikhov, Ukr. (Sichow); pop. 55; 13 km SE of Lvov; 49°47'/24°04'.

Siklos, Hung.; pop. 404; 120 km ESE of Nagykanizsa; 45°51'/18°18'; HSL, LDS, PHH.

Siklosbodony, Hung.; pop. 1; 101 km ESE of Nagykanizsa; 45°55'/18°07'.

Siklosnagyfalu, Hung.; pop. 3; 126 km ESE of Nagykanizsa; 45°49'/18°22'.

Sikorzyce, Pol.; pop. 6; 62 km ENE of Krakow; 50°11'/20°47'.

Sikuran, *see* Sokiryany.

Silajani, Lat. (Ribinishki, Riebeni); pop. 348; 56 km NNE of Daugavpils; 56°21'/26°56'.

Silale, Lith. (Sallel, Shilel, Shileti); pop. 670; 88 km SW of Siauliai; 55°28'/22°12'; GUM5, HSL, LDL, SF, YL.

Silauti, *see* Shilovtsy.

Silava, *see* Siluva.

Silca, *see* Silica.

Silea Nirajului, Rom.; pop. 10; 101 km E of Cluj; 46°36'/24°55'.

Silenai, HSL. a number of towns share this name. It was not possible to determine from available information which one is being referenced.

Silene, Lat. (Silenes); pop. 213; 26 km ESE of Daugavpils; 55°45'/26°47'; PHLE.

Silenes, *see* Silene.

Silesia; A region now partially in Poland and Czechoslovakia.

Silev, *see* Vselyub.

Silica, Cz. (Silca, Szilicze); 56 km SW of Kosice; 48°33'/20°32'; AMG, HSL.

Silicka Jablonica, Cz. (Jabloncza); 50 km SW of Kosice; 48°34'/20°37'; HSL.

Silindru, Rom. (Erselend); pop. 26; 139 km WNW of Cluj; 47°26'/22°03'.

Silistra, Bulg.; pop. 205; 114 km NW of Varna; 44°07'/27°16'; EJ.

Silixen, Germ.; pop. 18; 50 km SW of Hannover; 52°08'/09°04'.

Siliyov, *see* Sulejow.

Sillein, *see* Zilina.

Sillian, Aus.; pop. 1; 94 km ESE of Innsbruck; 46°45'/12°25'.

Silmala, Lat. (Malta); pop. 356; 69 km NNE of Daugavpils; 56°24'/27°06'; COH, GA, HSL2, PHLE.

Silmerzitz, *see* Sulmierzyce.

Silnica Wielka, Pol.; pop. 10; 45 km NE of Czestochowa; 50°56'/19°42'.

Silniczka, Pol.; pop. 39; 50 km NE of Czestochowa; 50°56'/19°46'.

Silute, Lith. (Geidekrug, Heidekrug, Szylokarczma); 133 km SW of Siauliai; 55°21'/21°29'; GUM3, GUM5, JGFF.

Siluva, Lith. (Shidlova, Sidluva, Silava); pop. 365; 50 km S of Siauliai; 55°32'/23°14'; HSL, LDL, SF, YL.

Silvas, see Slivnik.

Sima, Hung.; pop. 3; 50 km NE of Miskolc; 48°18'/21°18'.

Simaniskiai, Lith. (Schymanzy, Shimantza); 32 km S of Siauliai; 55°41'/23°17'; LDL, SF.

Simasag, Hung.; pop. 5; 114 km N of Nagykanizsa; 47°25'/16°51'.

Simeiz, Ukr.; pop. 32; 62 km S of Simferopol; 44°25'/34°01'.

Simferopol, Ukr. (Symferopol); pop. 2,500; 309 km ESE of Odessa; 44°57'/34°06'; EDRD, GUM4, GUM5, HSL, HSL2, JGFF, LDL, SF.

Simian, Rom.; pop. 73; 139 km WNW of Cluj; 47°29'/22°06'.

Simisna, Rom.; pop. 65; 56 km N of Cluj; 47°13'/23°37'; HSL.

Simkaiciai, Lith. (Shimkaits); pop. 41; 62 km WNW of Kaunas; 55°13'/22°59'; GUM5, YL.

Simla, LDL. This pre-World War I community was not found in BGN gazetteers.

Simleul Silvaniei, see Simleu Silvaniei.

Simleu Silvaniei, Rom. (Shamloya, Simleul Silvaniei, Somlyo, Szilagysomlyo); pop. 1,568; 75 km WNW of Cluj; 47°14'/22°48'; AMG, CAHJP, EJ, GUM3, GUM6, HSL, LDL, PHR2.

Simmern, Germ.; pop. 56; 82 km WSW of Frankfurt am Main; 49°59'/07°31'; AMG, GED, JGFF.

Simmershausen, Germ. JGFF. a number of towns share this name. It was not possible to determine from available information which one is being referenced.

Simna, see Simnas.

Simnas, Lith. (Simna, Simno); pop. 662; 62 km S of Kaunas; 54°24'/23°39'; COH, HSL, JGFF, SF, YL.

Simno, see Simnas.

Simonfa, Hung.; pop. 2; 62 km ESE of Nagykanizsa; 46°17'/17°50'.

Simoniai, Lith.; pop. 79; 62 km ENE of Siauliai; 56°04'/24°19'.

Simonov, Ukr. (Symonow); pop. 2; 26 km E of Rovno; 50°35'/26°38'.

Simonovce, Cz. (Simonyi); 94 km SW of Kosice; 48°16'/20°07'; LDS.

Simonovichi, Byel. (Symonoviche, Symonowicze); pop. 83; 69 km W of Pinsk; 52°17'/25°07'.

Simontornya, Hung.; pop. 74; 94 km SSW of Budapest; 46°45'/18°33'; HSL, PHH.

Simonyi, see Simonovce.

Simpach, Cz.; pop. 5; 82 km SE of Praha; 49°26'/14°59'.

Sinaia, Rom.; 114 km NNW of Bucuresti; 45°21'/25°33'; HSL.

Sinautii de Jos, Rom.; pop. 1; 139 km WNW of Iasi; 47°59'/26°08'.

Sincai, Rom.; pop. 6; 62 km E of Cluj; 46°39'/24°23'.

Sincrai, Rom.; 56 km SSE of Cluj; 46°17'/23°45'; JGFF.

Sindelfingen, Germ.; 13 km SW of Stuttgart; 48°42'/09°01'; EDRD, PHGBW.

Sindolsheim, Germ.; 82 km N of Stuttgart; 49°29'/09°27'; LDS, PHGBW.

Sindominic, Rom. (Csikszentdomokos, Sandominic); pop. 40; 150 km SW of Iasi; 46°35'/25°47'.

Sindresti, Rom.; pop. 2; 101 km N of Cluj; 47°36'/23°42'.

Sineljnikov, see Sinelnikovo.

Sinelnikovo, Ukr. (Sineljnikov); pop. 1,309; 45 km ESE of Dneropetrovsk; 48°20'/35°31'; EDRD, GUM4, HSL.

Sineshty, Mold. (Sinesti); pop. 117; 75 km WNW of Kishinev; 47°24'/28°03'.

Sinesti, see Sineshty.

Sinevir, Ukr. (Felsoszinever, Sinovir); 157 km S of Lvov; 48°29'/23°38'; AMG, GUM4.

Sinevir Polyana, Ukr. (Alsoszinever, Seniver, Sinevirskaya Polyana, Siniyvir Polyana, Sinovirska Polana, Szinever); 146 km S of Lvov; 48°35'/23°41'; HSL, SM.

Sinevirskaya Polyana, see Sinevir Polyana.

Sinfalva, see Cornesti.

Singen, Germ.; 120 km S of Stuttgart; 47°46'/08°50'; AMG, PHGBW.

Singeorgiu de Padure, Rom. (Erdoszentgyorgy, Sangeorgiul de Padure, Sangiorgiul de Padure, Singiorgiu de Padure); pop. 227; 101 km ESE of Cluj; 46°26'/24°50'; HSL, HSL2, LDL, PHR2.

Singeorz Bai, Rom. (Olahszentgyorg, Sangeorz Bai); pop. 97; 101 km NE of Cluj; 47°22'/24°41'; HSL, PHR2.

Singhofen, Germ.; pop. 25; 62 km WNW of Frankfurt am Main; 50°17'/07°50'; JGFF.

Singiorgiu de Padure, see Singeorgiu de Padure.

Singureni, see Syngureny.

Siniavka, see Sinyavka.

Siniawka, see Sinyavka.

Siniec, see Budy Bielanskie.

Sinioe, Rom. (Saniob); pop. 41; 214 km ENE of Bucuresti; 44°38'/28°45'.

Siniyvir Polyana, see Sinevir Polyana.

Sinjava, see Staraya Sinyava.

Sinjawka, see Sinyavka.

Sinkevichi, Byel. (Sienkiewicze, Sinkiewicze); pop. 27; 75 km ENE of Pinsk; 52°13'/27°15'; GUM3.

Sinkiewicze, see Sinkevichi.

Sinkov, see Bogdanovka (Tarnopol).

Sinkow, see Bogdanovka (Tarnopol).

Sinmartin, Rom. (Mezoszentmarton, Sanmartin, Sanmartin Ciuc, Sinmartin Ciuc); pop. 77; 163 km SW of Iasi; 46°16'/25°56'; HSL.

Sinmartin Ciuc, see Sinmartin.

Sinmihaiu de Padure, Rom. (Sanmihaiul de Campie); 101 km E of Cluj; 46°44'/24°52'; PHR2.

Sinnicolaul Roman, see Sinnicolau Romin.

Sinnicolau Romin, Rom. (Sannicolaul Roman, Sinnicolaul Roman); pop. 21; 146 km W of Cluj; 46°57'/21°44'.

Sinnicolaw Mare, Rom. (Nagyszentmiklos, Sannicolaul Mare); HSL. This pre-World War I community was not found in BGN gazetteers.

Sinogora, Pol.; pop. 8; 126 km NW of Warszawa; 53°06'/19°47'.

Sinole, Lat. (Sinoles); pop. 8; 146 km ENE of Riga; 57°15'/26°30'.

Sinoles, see Sinole.

Sinolin, Pol. EDRD. This town was not found in BGN gazetteers under the given spelling.

Sinovir, see Sinevir.

Sinovirska Polana, see Sinevir Polyana.

Sinovka, see Sinyavka.

Sinpaul, Rom. (Sanpaul Cluj, Sinpaul Cluj); pop. 30; 150 km ESE of Cluj; 46°11'/25°23'.

Sinpaul Cluj, see Sinpaul.

Sinpetru, Rom. BGN lists two possible localities with this name located at 45°33'/22°55' and 45°43'/25°38'. JGFF.

Sinpetru de Cimpie, Rom. (Uzdiszentpeter); 50 km E of Cluj; 46°43'/24°16'; HSL.

Sinsheim, Germ.; pop. 79; 56 km NNW of Stuttgart; 49°15'/08°53'; AMG, GUM3, GUM5, JGFF, LDS, PHGBW.

Sintandrei, Rom. (Santandrei Bihor, Sintandrei Bihor); pop. 28; 139 km W of Cluj; 47°04'/21°52'.

Sintandrei Bihor, see Sintandrei.

Sintautai, Lith.; pop. 10; 56 km WSW of Kaunas; 54°53'/23°00'.

Sintchy, see Svatusa.

Sintereag, Rom. (Somkerek); pop. 131; 69 km NE of Cluj; 47°11'/24°18'; HSL, HSL2, PHR2.

Sinteu, Rom. (Huta Voivozi); pop. 6; 94 km WNW of Cluj; 47°09'/22°29'.

Sintimreu, Rom. (Hegykozszentimre); 133 km WNW of Cluj;

47°15'/22°03'; LDS.

Sinyavka, Byel. (Siniavka, Siniawka, Sinjawka, Sinovka); pop. 379; 101 km N of Pinsk; 52°58'/26°28'; COH, HSL, HSL2, LYV, SF, YB.

Sinzenich, Germ.; 38 km SSW of Koln; 50°40'/06°39'; AMG.

Sinzheim, Germ.; 75 km WSW of Stuttgart; 48°46'/08°10'; HSL.

Sinzig, Germ.; 50 km SE of Koln; 50°33'/07°15'; EDRD.

Sinzishok, *see* Snipiskes.

Sioagard, Hung.; pop. 9; 120 km W of Szeged; 46°24'/18°39'.

Siobutka, *see* Sloboda.

Siodlo, Pol.; pop. 2; 50 km ESE of Warszawa; 52°05'/21°42'.

Siofok, Hung.; pop. 287; 94 km NE of Nagykanizsa; 46°54'/18°03'; LDS, PHH.

Siojut, Hung. (Jut); pop. 5; 101 km SW of Budapest; 46°53'/18°08'.

Siolko, *see* Syulko.

Siolkowa, Pol.; pop. 15; 94 km ESE of Krakow; 49°39'/20°57'.

Siomaros, Hung.; pop. 8; 101 km SW of Budapest; 46°53'/18°09'.

Siostrzytow, Pol.; pop. 60; 32 km E of Lublin; 51°11'/22°59'.

Sipbachzell, Aus.; pop. 1; 88 km NE of Salzburg; 48°06'/14°07'.

Sipca, *see* Shipka.

Sipeniti, *see* Shipintsy.

Sipotele, Rom. BGN lists two possible localities with this name located at 44°03'/27°58' and 45°46'/26°47'. AMG.

Sipotele pe Siret, *see* Shepit.

Sipotele Sucevei, *see* Shepit.

Sipoteni, *see* Sipoteny.

Sipoteny, Mold. (Sipoteni); pop. 104; 56 km WNW of Kishinev; 47°16'/28°11'.

Sirautii de Sus, *see* Shirovtsy.

Sirbi, Rom. (Sarbi, Sarbi Maramures, Sirbi Maramures); pop. 95; 114 km N of Cluj; 47°46'/23°57'; PHR2, SM.

Sirbi Maramures, *see* Sirbi.

Sirem, Cz.; pop. 12; 69 km W of Praha; 50°14'/13°30'.

Siret, Rom. (Seret, Sereth); pop. 2,121; 146 km WNW of Iasi; 47°57'/26°04'; AMG, EJ, GUM4, HSL, HSL2, JGFF, LDL, PHP2, PHR2, SF.

Sireti, *see* Sirets.

Sirets, Mold. (Sireti); pop. 3; 19 km NW of Kishinev; 47°08'/28°43'.

Sirioara, Rom.; pop. 20; 62 km NE of Cluj; 47°06'/24°17'.

Sirk, Cz.; 88 km WSW of Kosice; 48°37'/20°06'; HSL.

Sirkovce, Cz. (Serke); 101 km SW of Kosice; 48°17'/20°05'; HSL.

Sirnek, *see* Sirnik.

Sirnik, Cz. (Sirnek); 45 km ESE of Kosice; 48°31'/21°49'; HSL.

Sirok, Hung.; pop. 24; 50 km SW of Miskolc; 47°56'/20°12'; HSL.

Siroke, Cz.; 45 km NW of Kosice; 49°00'/20°57'; AMG, HSL.

Siroke Trebcice, Cz. (Weiten Trebetitsch); 75 km W of Praha; 50°17'/13°23'; HSL.

Sirokyluh, *see* Leh.

Sirota, Mold.; pop. 3; 62 km N of Kishinev; 47°32'/28°47'.

Sirotino, Byel.; pop. 660; 38 km WNW of Vitebsk; 55°23'/29°37'.

Sirvint, *see* Sirvintos.

Sirvintai, *see* Sirvintos.

Sirvintos, Lith. (Shervinty, Shirvent, Shirvint, Sirvint, Sirvintai); pop. 1,053; 50 km NW of Vilnius; 55°03'/24°57'; GUM5, HSL, JGFF, LDL, SF.

Sisak, Yug.; pop. 230; 45 km SE of Zagreb; 45°29'/16°22'; PHY.

Sisarte, *see* Siesartis.

Siscauti, *see* Shyshkovtse.

Sisky, GUM3. This town was not found in BGN gazetteers under the given spelling.

Sislevitch, *see* Svisloch.

Sislevits, *see* Svisloch.

Sislevitsh, *see* Svisloch.

Sisterea, Rom.; pop. 3; 126 km WNW of Cluj; 47°09'/22°05'.

Sitaniec, Pol.; pop. 24; 69 km SE of Lublin; 50°46'/23°15'.

Sitce, *see* Bolshiye Sittsy.

Sitkowka, Pol.; 94 km NNE of Krakow; 50°49'/20°34'; GUM4.

Sitnitsa, Byel. (Sytnica); pop. 13; 88 km ENE of Pinsk; 52°12'/27°22'.

Sitno, Pol.; pop. 34; 75 km ESE of Lublin; 50°45'/23°23'; GA.

Siubaiciai, Lith. (Shubbotz); 13 km E of Siauliai; 55°55'/23°30'; JGFF.

Siucice, Pol.; pop. 30; 69 km SE of Lodz; 51°15'/20°02'.

Sivac, Yug.; pop. 133 km NW of Beograd; 45°42'/19°23'; PHY.

Sivka Voynilov, Ukr. (Siwka Wojnilowska); pop. 17; 88 km SE of Lvov; 49°11'/24°32'.

Siwka Wojnilowska, *see* Sivka Voynilov.

Sjenica, Yug.; pop. 19; 176 km S of Beograd; 43°16'/20°00'.

Sjeverin, Yug.; pop. 24; 163 km SSW of Beograd; 43°36'/19°23'.

Skadle, Pol.; pop. 36; 75 km ENE of Krakow; 50°15'/20°55'. This town was located on an interwar map of Poland but does not appear in contemporary gazetteers. Map coordinates are approximate.

Skadovsk, Ukr.; pop. 172; 163 km NW of Simferopol; 46°07'/32°55'.

Skadvile, *see* Skaudvile.

Skaigirren, HSL. This pre-World War I community was not found in BGN gazetteers.

Skaista, Lat. (Skaistas); pop. 16; 50 km ENE of Daugavpils; 55°57'/27°19'; PHLE.

Skaistas, *see* Skaista.

Skaistkalne, Lat. (Schonberg, Shenberg, Shimberg, Shonberg, Skaistkalnes, Skaitskalne); pop. 152; 75 km SE of Riga; 56°23'/24°39'; PHLE, SF.

Skaistkalnes, *see* Skaistkalne.

Skaitskalne, *see* Skaistkalne.

Skal, *see* Skala Podolskaya.

Skala, Pol.; pop. 604; 82 km SW of Lublin; 50°54'/21°33'; AMG, COH, GUM4, HSL, SF. See also Skala Podolskaya.

Skala Podolskaya, Ukr. (Skal, Skala); pop. 1,555; 62 km N of Chernovtsy; 48°51'/26°12'; AMG, CAHJP, COH, EDRD, EGRS, GUM3, GUM4, GUM5, GYLA, HSL, HSL2, JGFF, LDL, PHP2, PHP3, SF, YB.

Skalat, Ukr. (Skalat Stary); pop. 2,919; 133 km N of Chernovtsy; 49°26'/25°59'; AMG, COH, EDRD, EGRS, GUM3, GUM4, GUM5, HSL, HSL2, JGFF, PHP2, SF, YB.

Skalat Stary, *see* Skalat.

Skala Zbruch, Ukr.; 69 km NE of Chernovtsy; 48°42'/26°36'; JGFF.

Skalbmierz, Pol.; pop. 700; 45 km NE of Krakow; 50°20'/20°25'; AMG, COH, GUM3, GUM4, GUM6, HSL.

Skalica, Cz.; pop. 637; 56 km ESE of Brno; 48°51'/17°14'; HSL, HSL2.

Skalka, Cz. (Kebharec); pop. 1; 101 km WSW of Brno; 49°01'/15°13'.

Skalmierzyce, *see* Skalmierzyce Nowe.

Skalmierzyce Nowe, Pol. (Skalmierzyce); pop. 12; 101 km WSW of Lodz; 51°43'/17°59'; JGFF.

Skalna, Cz. (Vildstejn); pop. 9; 150 km W of Praha; 50°10'/12°22'.

Skaly, Pol.; pop. 20; 107 km SW of Lublin; 50°55'/21°10'.

Skape, Pol.; 126 km S of Gdansk; 53°13'/18°37'; POCEM.

Skapiskis, Lith. (Skopishok, Skopiskis); pop. 215; 114 km E of Siauliai; 55°53'/25°12'; JGFF, YL.

Skarby, Byel.; pop. 6; 189 km W of Minsk; 53°57'/24°40'.

Skarishov, *see* Skaryszew.

Skaros, Cz.; 19 km SE of Kosice; 48°35'/21°23'; HSL.

Skarszewy, Pol.; pop. 40; 38 km SSW of Gdansk; 54°04'/18°27'; LDS, POCEM.

Skaryszew, Pol. (Skarishov); pop. 820; 88 km W of Lublin; 51°19'/21°15'; GA, GUM3, GUM5, HSL, SF.

Skarzhisk, *see* Kamienna.

Skarzisko Kamyena, *see* Kamienna.

Skarzyn, Pol.; pop. 20; 56 km ENE of Warszawa; 52°21'/21°50'.

Skarzysko, *see* Kamienna.

Skarzysko Kamienna, Pol.; pop. 1,590; 120 km WSW of Lublin; 51°07'/20°54'; AMG, COH, EDRD, EJ, GA, GUM3, GUM4, GUM5, GUM6, HSL, LYV, PHP1, PHP2, PHP3, PHP4, SF, YB.

Skarzysko Koscielne, Pol.; pop. 14; 114 km WSW of Lublin; 51°09'/20°56'.

Skarzysko Ksiazece, Pol.; pop. 1; 120 km ESE of Lodz; 51°09'/20°51'.

Skasov, Cz.; pop. 4; 101 km SW of Praha; 49°31'/13°26'.

Skaudvile, Lith. (Bugai, Shkodvil, Shkudvil, Skadvile, Skodvil); pop. 1,017; 75 km SSW of Siauliai; 55°25'/22°37'; COH, GUM3, HSL, JGFF, LDL, SF, YL.

Skaune, Lat. (Poleshchina, Skaunes); pop. 94; 94 km ENE of Daugavpils; 56°08'/28°00'; PHLE.

Skaunes, see Skaune.

Skavin, see Skawina.

Skavshin, Byel.; 126 km NE of Pinsk; 52°32'/27°50'; JGFF.

Skawa, Pol.; pop. 4; 56 km S of Krakow; 49°37'/19°54'.

Skawce, Pol.; pop. 23; 38 km SSW of Krakow; 49°48'/19°35'.

Skawica, Pol.; pop. 10; 50 km SSW of Krakow; 49°41'/19°38'.

Skawina, Pol. (Skavin, Skovina); pop. 282; 19 km SSW of Krakow; 49°59'/19°50'; AMG, COH, EDRD, EGRS, GUM4, GUM5, HSL, PHP3, SF.

Skazinets, (Scaziet); PHR1. This town was not found in BGN gazetteers under the given spelling.

Skelivka, Ukr. (Felshtyn, Felsztein, Felsztin, Felsztyn); pop. 534; 88 km SW of Lvov; 49°32'/22°58'; COH, EGRS, JGFF, LDL, PHP2, SF, WS.

Skem, see Skiemonys.

Skemoniai, see Skiemonys.

Skemonis, see Skiemonys.

Skepe, Pol.; pop. 268; 126 km N of Lodz; 52°52'/19°21'; HSL, PHP4.

Skernyevits, see Skierniewice.

Skeshino, see Skrzynno.

Skhodnitsa, Ukr. (S Chodnitza, Schodnica); pop. 689; 88 km SSW of Lvov; 49°14'/23°21'; AMG, EDRD, EGRS, HSL, HSL2, LDL, PHP2, SF, YB.

Skibniew Podawce, Pol.; pop. 62; 82 km NE of Warszawa; 52°30'/22°11'.

Skiby, Ukr.; pop. 31; 157 km N of Lvov; 51°14'/24°07'; HSL.

Skidel, Byel.; pop. 2,231; 208 km NW of Pinsk; 53°35'/24°15'; AMG, CAHJP, COH, EDRD, EJ, GUM3, GUM5, GYLA, HSL, HSL2, LDL, SF.

Skiemanys, see Skiemonys.

Skiemonys, Lith. (Skem, Skemoniai, Skemonis, Skiemanys, Skimian, Skomian); pop. 128; 88 km N of Vilnius; 55°25'/25°16'; JGFF, LDL, SF, YL.

Skierbieszow, Pol.; pop. 106; 69 km ESE of Lublin; 50°51'/23°22'.

Skierniewice, Pol. (Skernyevits, Skiernivitz); pop. 4,333; 50 km NE of Lodz; 51°58'/20°09'; AMG, COH, EDRD, EJ, GA, GUM3, GUM4, GUM5, GYLA, HSL, HSL2, JGFF, LDL, LDS, LYV, PHP1, PHP3, POCEM, SF, YB.

Skiernivitz, see Skierniewice.

Skimian, see Skiemonys.

Skladow, Pol.; pop. 1; 50 km NW of Lublin; 51°35'/22°12'.

Sklad Solny, Pol.; pop. 15; 19 km NNE of Przemysl; 49°55'/22°54'.

Skloby, Pol.; pop. 14; 101 km ESE of Lodz; 51°15'/20°42'.

Sknifishuk, see Snipiskes.

Sknilov, Ukr. (Sknilow); pop. 38; 13 km SW of Lvov; 49°48'/23°57'; GUM4, HSL, YB.

Sknilow, see Sknilov; Skniluv.

Skniluv, Ukr. (Sknilow); pop. 29; BGN lists two possible localities with this name located at 49°48'/23°57' and 49°52'/24°38'.

Skobelka, Ukr.; pop. 83; 88 km NNE of Lvov; 50°30'/24°47'.

Skoczkowo, Pol.; pop. 8; 101 km WNW of Warszawa; 52°51'/19°50'.

Skoczow, Pol. (Skotschau); pop. 207; 88 km SW of Krakow; 49°48'/18°48'; AMG, PHP3.

Skoczow/Wilamowice, Pol. POCEM. This town was not found in BGN gazetteers under the given spelling.

Skodotzishok, see Skudutiskis.

Skoduciszki, see Skudutiskis.

Skodvil, see Skaudvile.

Skoki, Pol. (Schocken); pop. 66; 32 km NNE of Poznan; 52°40'/17°10'; HSL, POCEM.

Skoki (near Kock), Pol.; pop. 23; 56 km N of Lublin; 51°43'/22°40'.

Skoki Male, Pol.; pop. 4; 101 km N of Lodz; 52°36'/19°25'.

Skol, see Sokal.

Skola, see Skole.

Skole, Ukr. (Skola); pop. 2,410; 94 km S of Lvov; 49°02'/23°31'; AMG, COH, EDRD, EGRS, EJ, GUM3, GUM4, GUM5, HSL, HSL2, ISH1, JGFF, PHP2, SF, YB.

Skolimow, Pol.; pop. 5; 26 km SE of Warszawa; 52°05'/21°07'; HSL.

Skolimow Ptaszki, Pol. (Ptaszki); pop. 12; 107 km N of Lublin; 52°10'/22°34'.

Skolin, Pol.: pop. 17; 32 km NE of Przemysl; 50°00'/23°10'.

Skoloszow, Pol.; pop. 188; 19 km N of Przemysl; 49°56'/22°49'; PHP3.

Skolyszyn, Pol.; pop. 12; 107 km WSW of Przemysl; 49°45'/21°21'.

Skomian, see Skiemonys.

Skomielna Czarna, Pol.; pop. 3; 45 km S of Krakow; 49°44'/19°50'.

Skomlin, Pol.; pop. 21; 69 km WNW of Czestochowa; 51°11'/18°23'.

Skomorochy, see Skomorokhy.

Skomorochy Duze, Pol. (Skomorochy Wielkie); pop. 3; 82 km ESE of Lublin; 50°51'/23°31'.

Skomorochy Wielkie, see Skomorochy Duze.

Skomorokhy, Ukr. (Skomorochy); pop. 20; 82 km NW of Chernovtsy; 48°55'/25°22'; HSL.

Skopanie, Pol.; pop. 4; 107 km SSW of Lublin; 50°28'/21°34'.

Skopin, HSL. This pre-World War I community was not found in BGN gazetteers.

Skopishok, see Skapiskis.

Skopiskis, see Skapiskis.

Skopje, Yug. (Skoplje, Uskub, Uskup); pop. 3,000; 322 km SSE of Beograd; 42°00'/21°29'; CAHJP, EDRD, EJ, GUM4, GUM5, GUM6, PHY.

Skoplje, see Skopje.

Skopow, Pol.; pop. 14; 19 km W of Przemysl; 49°50'/22°30'.

Skorcz, Pol.; pop. 19; 62 km S of Gdansk; 53°48'/18°32'.

Skorczow, Pol.; pop. 3; 45 km NE of Krakow; 50°15'/20°27'.

Skorczyce, Pol.; pop. 11; 38 km SW of Lublin; 51°01'/22°12'.

Skordiow, Pol. (Skordjow); pop. 4; 82 km E of Lublin; 51°06'/23°44'.

Skordjow, see Skordiow.

Skoriki, Ukr. (Skoryki); pop. 32; 120 km S of Rovno; 49°36'/26°08'.

Skorkow, Pol.; pop. 16; 82 km ENE of Czestochowa; 50°52'/20°13'.

Skorkowice, Pol.; pop. 42; 69 km SE of Lodz; 51°14'/20°03'.

Skornica, see Skornice.

Skornice, Pol. (Skornica); pop. 17; 75 km NE of Czestochowa; 51°09'/20°05'.

Skorocice, Pol.; pop. 8; 62 km NE of Krakow; 50°24'/20°39'.

Skorodintsy, Ukr. (Skorodynce); pop. 45; 88 km NNW of Chernovtsy; 49°04'/25°45'.

Skorodne, Pol.; pop. 127; 62 km S of Przemysl; 49°17'/22°39'.

Skorodnica, Pol.; pop. 76; 56 km NE of Lublin; 51°32'/23°18'.

Skorodnoye, Byel.; 170 km SW of Gomel; 51°38'/28°50'; JGFF.

Skorodynce, see Skorodintsy.

Skortseny, Mold. (Scorteni); pop. 108; 75 km NNW of Kishinev; 47°38'/28°39'.

Skoryki, see Skoriki.

Skorynki, Byel.; pop. 10; 94 km NNW of Pinsk; 52°53'/25°52'.

Skorzeszyce, Pol.; pop. 2; 107 km NNE of Krakow; 50°50'/20°53'.

Skorzow, Pol.; pop. 6; 75 km NE of Krakow; 50°32'/20°45'.

Skotarsky, HSL. This pre-World War I community was not found in BGN gazetteers.

Skotniki, Pol.; pop. 55; 75 km NE of Czestochowa; 51°12'/19°56'; CAHJP. CAHJP refers to a town in the Lwow province. It does not appear in contemporary gazetteers.

Skotniki (near Sandomierz), Pol.; pop. 33; 94 km SSW of Lublin; 50°37'/21°39'.

Skotschau, *see* Skoczow.

Skovina, *see* Skawina.

Skovyatin, Ukr. (Skowiatyn); pop. 32; 50 km N of Chernovtsy; 48°44'/26°02'.

Skowiatyn, *see* Skovyatin.

Skowierzyn, Pol.; pop. 17; 82 km SSW of Lublin; 50°41'/21°55'.

Skrabske, Cz. (Strabicovo); 45 km NNE of Kosice; 49°01'/21°35'; AMG, HSL.

Skraglevka, Ukr. (Skralevka, Skrolifka); 88 km N of Vinnitsa; 49°57'/28°32'; SF.

Skralevka, *see* Skraglevka.

Skride, *see* Skruda.

Skrigalovo, *see* Skrygalovo.

Skrigalow, *see* Skrygalovo.

Skrihalov, *see* Skrygalovo.

Skrivare, *see* Skriveri.

Skriveri, Lat. (Skrivare); pop. 10; 75 km ESE of Riga; 56°39'/25°08'; PHLE.

Skrobaczow, Pol.; pop. 12; 82 km NE of Krakow; 50°27'/20°54'.

Skroda, *see* Skroda Wielka.

Skroda Wielka, Pol. (Skroda); pop. 8; 75 km WNW of Bialystok; 53°26'/22°06'.

Skrolifka, *see* Skraglevka.

Skronina, Pol.; pop. 3; 82 km ESE of Lodz; 51°17'/20°23'.

Skruda, (Skride); FRG. a number of towns share this name. It was not possible to determine from available information which one is being referenced.

Skrudaliena, Lat. (Skrudelino); 13 km ESE of Daugavpils; 55°49'/26°43'; PHLE.

Skrudelino, *see* Skrudaliena.

Skrudki, Pol.; pop. 4; 56 km WNW of Lublin; 51°34'/22°03'; GA.

Skrunda, Lat. (Skrundas); pop. 53; 133 km WSW of Riga; 56°41'/22°01'; PHLE.

Skrundas, *see* Skrunda.

Skrwilno, Pol.; pop. 69; 126 km WNW of Warszawa; 53°01'/19°36'.

Skrybicze, Pol.; 13 km SE of Bialystok; 53°04'/23°14'; HSL.

Skrygalovo, Byel. (Skrigalovo, Skrigalow, Skrihalov); pop. 866; 150 km WSW of Gomel; 52°06'/28°49'; LDL, SF.

Skryhiczyn, Pol.; pop. 215; 94 km ESE of Lublin; 50°59'/23°56'; HSL.

Skrzydlna, Pol.; pop. 42; 45 km SE of Krakow; 49°46'/20°11'; GUM4, PHP3.

Skrzynka, Pol.; pop. 47; 82 km ENE of Krakow; 50°16'/21°03'.

Skrzynno, Pol. (Skeshino); pop. 191; 94 km ESE of Lodz; 51°22'/20°43'; AMG, GA, PHP1, SF.

Skrzypaczowice, Pol.; pop. 8; 107 km SSW of Lublin; 50°34'/21°33'.

Skrzypny Ostrow, Pol.; pop. 14; 88 km NNE of Przemysl; 50°31'/23°25'.

Skrzyszew, Pol.; pop. 5; 75 km N of Lublin; 51°51'/22°29'.

Skrzyszow, Pol.; 94 km WNW of Przemysl; 50°04'/21°33'; GUM4.

Skuczynki, GUM4. This town was not found in BGN gazetteers under the given spelling.

Skudutishkis, *see* Skudutiskis.

Skudutiskis, Lith. (Skodotzishok, Skoduciszki, Skudutishkis); 82 km N of Vilnius; 55°23'/25°27'; SF.

Skulen, *see* Skulyany.

Skuleni, *see* Skulyany.

Skuliani, *see* Skulyany.

Skuljany, *see* Skulyany.

Skulsk, Pol.; pop. 228; 94 km ENE of Poznan; 52°29'/18°20'; AMG, CAHJP, COH, GUM3, GUM4, HSL2, PHP1, SF.

Skulyany, Mold. (Sculeni, Sculeni Moldova, Sculeni Targ, Seletz, Skulen, Skuleni, Skuliani, Skuljany); pop. 1,207; 101 km WNW of Kishinev; 47°20'/27°37'; GUM3, GUM4, PHR1, SF.

Skumpiya, Mold. (Scumpia); pop. 36; 101 km WNW of Kishinev; 47°28'/27°44'.

Skuodas, Lith. (Shkod, Shkud, Shkudy, Szkudy); pop. 1,310; 120 km W of Siauliai; 56°16'/21°32'; AMG, COH, EJ, GUM3, GUM5, GUM6, HSL, HSL2, JGFF, LYV, SF, YB, YL.

Skupec, Cz.; pop. 3; 101 km WSW of Praha; 49°52'/13°07'.

Skupowo, Pol.; pop. 5; 50 km ESE of Bialystok; 52°50'/23°42'.

Skurche, Ukr. (Skurcze); pop. 31; 88 km W of Rovno; 50°39'/24°59'.

Skurcze, *see* Skurche.

Skurowa, Pol.; pop. 9; 101 km W of Przemysl; 49°53'/21°23'.

Skuszew, Pol.; pop. 10; 50 km NNE of Warszawa; 52°35'/21°29'.

Skutec, Cz.; pop. 31; 88 km NW of Brno; 49°51'/16°00'.

Skvazhava Nova, Ukr. (Skwarzawa Nowa); pop. 46; 26 km NNW of Lvov; 50°03'/23°53'.

Skver, *see* Skvira.

Skvira, Ukr. (Skver, Skwira); pop. 4,681; 94 km SSW of Kiyev; 49°44'/29°40'; EDRD, EJ, GUM4, HSL, JGFF, SF.

Skvorec, Cz.; pop. 4; 19 km E of Praha; 50°03'/14°44'.

Skvrnov, Cz.; pop. 7; 45 km ESE of Praha; 49°54'/15°00'.

Skwarzawa Nowa, *see* Skvazhava Nova.

Skwierzyna, Pol. (Schwerin); pop. 200; 101 km W of Poznan; 52°36'/15°30'; AMG, EJ, GUM3, GUM4, GUM5, HSL, HSL2, ISH1, JGFF, LDS, POCEM.

Skwira, *see* Skvira.

Skwirtne, Pol.; pop. 1; 114 km ESE of Krakow; 49°30'/21°12'.

Skwirzowa, Pol.; pop. 6; 101 km SW of Lublin; 50°36'/21°30'.

Skycov, Cz. (Szkeco, Szkiczo); 107 km NE of Bratislava; 48°31'/18°25'; HSL.

Skytaly, Cz.; pop. 3; 82 km W of Praha; 50°10'/13°18'.

Slabce, Cz.; pop. 5; 56 km WSW of Praha; 50°00'/13°42'.

Slabkowice, Pol.; pop. 9; 75 km NE of Krakow; 50°31'/20°46'.

Slaboszewice, Pol.; pop. 32; 88 km SW of Lublin; 50°45'/21°32'.

Slaboszow, Pol.; pop. 2; 45 km NNE of Krakow; 50°23'/20°17'.

Slaboszowice, Pol.; pop. 12; 62 km N of Krakow; 50°35'/20°12'.

Sladeckovce, *see* Sladkovicovo.

Sladki Vrh, Yug.; pop. 4; 107 km NNW of Zagreb; 46°41'/15°45'.

Sladkovicovo, Cz. (Mocsonok, Sladeckovce, Velky Dioseg, Velky Diosek); pop. 135; 45 km ENE of Bratislava; 48°12'/17°39'; HSL.

Sladkovodnaya, *see* Sladkovodnoye.

Sladkovodnoye, Ukr. (Sladkovodnaya); 163 km ESE of Dnepropetrovsk; 47°34'/36°45'; JGFF.

Sladkow Maly, Pol.; pop. 29; 82 km NE of Krakow; 50°35'/20°45'.

Sladow, Pol.; 50 km W of Warszawa; 52°23'/20°18'; PHP4.

Slakovci, Yug.; pop. 8; 133 km WNW of Beograd; 45°13'/18°57'.

Slampe, Lat.; pop. 3; 50 km WSW of Riga; 56°51'/23°17'.

Slanec, Cz.; pop. 70; 19 km ESE of Kosice; 48°38'/21°29'; HSL.

Slanica, Cz. (Szlani); 150 km WNW of Kosice; 49°24'/19°31'; HSL.

Slanska Huta, Cz. (Szalanczi); 19 km ESE of Kosice; 48°35'/21°28'; HSL.

Slany, Cz.; pop. 111; 32 km WNW of Praha; 50°14'/14°06'.

Slapsko, Cz.; 62 km SSE of Praha; 49°35'/14°46'; HSL.

Slatina, *see* Podravska Slatina; Slatioara.

Slatina (Czechoslovakia), Cz.; pop. 47; AMG. Described in the *Black Book* as being in the Bohemia region of Czechoslovakia, this town was not found in BGN gazetteers.

Slatinany, Cz.; pop. 10; 101 km NW of Brno; 49°55'/15°49'.

Slatinita, Rom.; pop. 5; 88 km NE of Cluj; 47°13'/24°33'.

Slatinske Doly, *see* Solotvina.

Slatinski Drenovac, Yug.; pop. 13; 133 km E of Zagreb; 45°33'/17°43'.

Slatioara, Rom. (Izasopatak, Slatina); pop. 120; 120 km W of Iasi; 47°23'/26°06'; COH, GUM3, GUM5, HSL, HSL2, PHR1.

Slatioara (Marmaros), Rom.; 114 km N of Cluj; 47°45'/24°06'; SM.

Slavansk, *see* Slavyansk.

Slavantai, Lith.; 88 km S of Kaunas; 54°10'/23°40'; JGFF.

Slavatich, *see* Slawatycze.

Slavchynenta, (Slawczyn); pop. 29; 120 km NW of Minsk; 54°44'/26°29'. a number of towns share this name. It was not possible to determine from available information which one is being referenced.

Slavechino, *see* Slovechno.

Slaventyn, *see* Slavyatin.

Slaveshna, *see* Slovechno.

Slavgorod, Byel. (Propoisk, Slawgorod); pop. 1,513; 120 km N of Gomel; 53°27'/31°00'; HSL, SF.

Slavin, *see* Slavnya.

Slavjansk, *see* Slavyansk.

Slavkov, *see* Slawkow.

Slavkovce, Cz. (Slavkovcze); 50 km E of Kosice; 48°36'/21°55'; AMG, HSL.

Slavkovcze, *see* Slavkovce.

Slavkov u Brna, Cz. (Austerlitz, Neu Sedlitz, Nove Sedlice); pop. 106; 19 km ESE of Brno; 49°09'/16°52'; EJ, HSL, HSL2.

Slavna, Ukr. (Slawna); pop. 33; 75 km E of Lvov; 49°43'/25°02'.

Slavnya, Byel. (Slavin, Slawnja); 101 km NNW of Gomel; 53°18'/30°48'; LDL, SF.

Slavonice, Cz. (Zladings); pop. 75; 94 km WSW of Brno; 48°59'/15°21'.

Slavonska Pozega, Yug.; pop. 123; 139 km ESE of Zagreb; 45°20'/17°41'; AMG, GUM4, PHY.

Slavonski Brod, Yug. (Brod Slavonski); pop. 423; 170 km ESE of Zagreb; 45°09'/18°02'; HSL, PHY.

Slavskoye, Ukr. (Slawsko); 120 km S of Lvov; 48°51'/23°27'; HSL, PHP2.

Slavuta, Ukr. (Slawuta, Slovita, Slowita); pop. 4,701; 56 km ESE of Rovno; 50°18'/26°52'; EJ, GUM3, GUM4, GUM5, HSL, HSL2, JGFF, LDL, SF.

Slavyansk, Ukr. (Slavansk, Slavjansk); pop. 1,260; 157 km SE of Kharkov; 48°52'/37°37'; EDRD, GUM4, HSL, SF.

Slavyatin, Ukr. (Slaventyn, Slawentyn); pop. 21; 88 km ESE of Lvov; 49°18'/24°52'.

Slawa, Pol.; 88 km SW of Poznan; 51°53'/16°04'; GUM5, HSL.

Slawatycze, Pol. (Slavatich, Slovotitch); pop. 902; 88 km NE of Lublin; 51°45'/23°33'; COH, GA, GUM3, GUM5, HSL, JGFF, LDS, LYV, POCEM, SF.

Slawczyn, *see* Slavchynenta.

Slawek, *see* Wolomin.

Slawentyn, *see* Slavyatin.

Slawetschno, *see* Slovechno.

Slawgorod, *see* Slavgorod.

Slawkow, Pol. (Slavkov); pop. 610; 50 km WNW of Krakow; 50°18'/19°24'; AMG, COH, GUM3, GUM4, HSL, HSL2, SF.

Slawna, *see* Slavna.

Slawnja, *see* Slavnya.

Slawno, Pol. (Schlawe); pop. 80; 126 km WSW of Gdansk; 54°21'/16°41'.

Slawsko, *see* Slavskoye.

Slawuta, *see* Slavuta.

Slecin, Pol.; pop. 4; 69 km E of Czestochowa; 50°40'/20°05'.

Sledy, Ukr.; 82 km SSW of Vinnitsa; 48°36'/27°57'; GUM4.

Slemien, Pol.; pop. 8; 62 km SSW of Krakow; 49°43'/19°23'; HSL.

Slepcany, Cz. (Szelepcseny); 94 km ENE of Bratislava; 48°19'/18°20'; HSL.

Sleshin, *see* Zbrachlin.

Slesin, *see* Zbrachlin.

Slifia Chadash, *see* Slupia Nowa.

Slipcze, Pol.; pop. 31; 114 km ESE of Lublin; 50°46'/24°01'.

Slishch, *see* Sosnovoye.

Slishch Gadol, *see* Sosnovoye.

Slisht, *see* Sosnovoye.

Slishtcha, *see* Selishche.

Slishtch Gadol, *see* Sosnovoye.

Slishtch Zuta, *see* Selishche.

Slisht Gadol, *see* Sosnovoye.

Sliven, *see* Slivno.

Slivki, Ukr. (Sliwki); pop. 45; 126 km S of Lvov; 48°46'/24°12'; HSL.

Slivna, Rom.; 126 km SSE of Iasi; 46°05'/27°56'; PHR1.

Slivnik, Cz. (Silvas, Szilvasujfalu); 26 km ESE of Kosice; 48°36'/21°33'; AMG, HSL.

Slivno, Bulg. (Sliven); pop. 625; 146 km SW of Varna; 42°40'/26°19'; EJ, HSL.

Sliwice, Pol.; pop. 7; 75 km SSW of Gdansk; 53°43'/18°11'; JGFF.

Sliwki, *see* Slivki.

Sljivosevci, Yug. (Schliwischewzi); pop. 14; 170 km E of Zagreb; 45°39'/18°14'.

Slnck, Pol. PHP4. This town was not found in BGN gazetteers under the given spelling.

Slobkovitz, *see* Solobkovtsy.

Sloboda, Ukr. (Siobutka, Sloboda Rungurska); pop. 62; 82 km W of Chernovtsy; 48°27'/24°49'; HSL, JGFF, SF.

Sloboda Dolinska, *possibly* Sloboda Dubenska.

Sloboda Dubenska, Ukr. (Sloboda Dolinska?); pop. 28; 120 km S of Lvov; 48°51'/24°07'.

Sloboda Rungurska, *see* Sloboda.

Slobodka, Pol. PHP2, PHP4. a number of towns share this name. It was not possible to determine from available information which one is being referenced. *See also* Vilyampolskaya Sloboda.

Slobodka (Novogrudok); FRG refers to a village near Novogrudok called in Yiddish "Slobodke." There are numerous villages in the area called Slobodka or Sloboda. The *Black Book* shows no town in the Nowogrodek province with these names that had more than 10 Jews.

Slobodka (Stanislawow), Ukr.; pop. 23; 50 km WNW of Chernovtsy; 48°35'/25°22'.

Slobodka (Tarnopol), Ukr.; pop. 27; 82 km N of Chernovtsy; 48°59'/26°00'.

Slobodka (Wilen), Byel.; pop. 141; There are numerous towns named Slobodka in the area. It was not possible to determine which one is described here.

Slobodka Konkolnicka, *see* Slobudka Konkolnicka.

Slobodka Koszylowiecka, Pol.; pop. 31; Described in the *Black Book* as being in the Tarnopol region of Poland, this town was not found in BGN gazetteers.

Slobodka Lesna, *see* Lesnaya Slobodka.

Slobodka Mushkatovka, Ukr. (Mushkatovtse, Muszkatowce); pop. 26; 56 km N of Chernovtsy; 48°48'/26°06'.

Slobodka Nikolskaya, *see* Nikolskaya.

Slobodka Polna, Ukr.; pop. 18; 50 km WNW of Chernovtsy; 48°35'/25°22'.

Slobodka Strusowska, Pol.; pop. 26; Described in the *Black Book* as being in the Tarnopol region of Poland, this town was not found in BGN gazetteers.

Slobodke, *see* Vilyampolskaya Sloboda.

Slobodzeya Beltsy, Mold. (Slobodziya Belts, Slobozia Balti); pop. 190; 114 km NW of Kishinev; 47°47'/27°55'.

Slobodzeya Voronkovo, Mold. (Sloboda Vorancau); pop. 30; 126 km NNW of Kishinev; 48°04'/28°28'.

Slobodziya Belts, *see* Slobodzeya Beltsy.

Slobozia, Mold.; pop. 24; 88 km ESE of Kishinev; 46°30'/29°45'.

Slobozia Balti, *see* Slobodzeya Beltsy.

Slobozia Banilei, Rom.; pop. 162; This town was not found in

BGN gazetteers under the given spelling.

Slobozia Barancea, Rom.; pop. 21; This town was not found in BGN gazetteers under the given spelling.

Slobozia Comarestilor, Rom.; pop. 43; This town was not found in BGN gazetteers under the given spelling.

Slobozia Dobrusa, *see* Dobrusha.

Slobozia Hanesti, Rom.; pop. 13; 94 km NW of Iasi; 47°55'/27°00'.

Slobozia Hodjinesti, *see* Khodorozha.

Slobozia Horodistea, *see* Khodorozha.

Slobozia Pruncului, Rom.; pop. 8; 133 km WNW of Iasi; 47°45'/26°04'.

Slobozia Vorancau, *see* Slobodzeya Voronkovo.

Slobudka Konkolnitska, Ukr. (Slobodka Konkolnicka); pop. 39; 101 km SE of Lvov; 49°11'/24°49'.

Slobudka Lesna, *see* Lesnaya Slobodka.

Slocina, Pol.; pop. 18; 56 km WNW of Przemysl; 50°02'/22°03'; PHP3.

Sloczow, HSL. This pre-World War I community was not found in BGN gazetteers.

Slodkow, Pol. BGN lists two possible localities with this name located at 50°54'/22°17' and 52°01'/18°26'. JGFF.

Sloka, Lat. (Schlock, Schlok, Shlok); pop. 21; 32 km WSW of Riga; 56°57'/23°36'; AMG, EJ, GUM3, GUM4, PHLE, SF.

Slomka, Pol.; pop. 59; 50 km SSE of Krakow; 49°41'/20°07'.

Slomka (near Bochnia), Pol.; pop. 24; 38 km E of Krakow; 50°01'/20°28'.

Slomniczki Nowe, *see* Slomniki.

Slomnik, *see* Slomniki.

Slomniki, Pol. (Slomniczki Nowe, Slomnik, Solemnik); pop. 1,460; 26 km NNE of Krakow; 50°15'/20°06'; AMG, COH, GUM3, GUM4, GUM5, HSL, HSL2, LYV, SF.

Slona, Pol.; pop. 5; 75 km ESE of Krakow; 49°50'/20°51'.

Slonim, Byel.; pop. 6,917; 126 km NW of Pinsk; 53°06'/25°19'; AMG, CAHJP, COH, EDRD, EJ, GA, GUM3, GUM4, GUM5, GUM6, HSL, HSL2, JGFF, LDL, LYV, PHP1, PHP4, SF, YB.

Slopkovitz, *see* Solobkovtsy.

Slopnica, *see* Slopnice.

Slopnice, Pol. (Slopnica); pop. 40; 56 km SE of Krakow; 49°42'/20°21'; HSL.

Sloszewo, Pol.; 62 km ENE of Poznan; 52°27'/17°55'; HSL.

Slotfina, *see* Solotvina.

Slotopol, *see* Zlatopol.

Slotowa, Pol.; pop. 7; 94 km E of Krakow; 49°57'/21°17'.

Slotvina, *see* Solotwina.

Slotwina, Pol.; pop. 28; 75 km SW of Krakow; 49°43'/19°05'; GUM5.

Slotwiny, Pol.; pop. 98; 101 km ESE of Krakow; 49°26'/20°57'; AMG, JGFF.

Slovec, Cz.; pop. 1; 62 km ENE of Praha; 50°14'/15°20'.

Slovechno, Byel. (Shlaveshnia, Slavechino, Slaveshna, Slawetschno); 157 km SW of Gomel; 51°38'/29°04'; LDL, SF.

Slovenia; Not a town, but a constituent republic of Yugoslavia.

Slovenska Ves, Cz.; 82 km WNW of Kosice; 49°14'/20°26'; AMG.

Slovenske Darmoty, Cz.; pop. 56; 163 km E of Bratislava; 48°06'/19°18'.

Slovenske Raslavice, Cz. (Vysne Raslavice); 56 km N of Kosice; 49°09'/21°19'.

Slovensky Kajna, (Kajna); JGFF. This town was not found in BGN gazetteers under the given spelling.

Slovensky Meder, *see* Palarikovo.

Slovita, *see* Slavuta.

Slovotitch, *see* Slawatycze.

Slowikowa, Pol.; pop. 19; 75 km ESE of Krakow; 49°42'/20°44'.

Slowita, *see* Slavuta.

Sluchocin, Pol.; pop. 7; 62 km E of Warszawa; 52°14'/21°58'.

Sluck, *see* Slutsk.

Slucz, Pol.; pop. 22; 62 km WNW of Bialystok; 53°26'/22°20';

HSL.

Sluhy, Cz.; pop. 5; 19 km NNE of Praha; 50°11'/14°34'.

Sluknov, Cz.; pop. 3; 107 km N of Praha; 51°01'/14°28'.

Slupca, Pol. (Sluptza); pop. 1,426; 62 km E of Poznan; 52°17'/17°53'; COH, EDRD, GUM3, GUM4, HSL2, JGFF, PHP1, SF.

Slupcza, Pol.; pop. 3; 75 km SW of Lublin; 50°46'/21°49'.

Slupeczno, Pol.; pop. 19; 45 km SSE of Lublin; 50°55'/22°44'.

Slupia, *see* Slupia Nowa.

Slupia Nadbrzezna, Pol.; pop. 4; 62 km SW of Lublin; 50°57'/21°48'.

Slupia Nowa, Pol. (Nowa Slupia, Slifia Chadash, Slupia, Stara Slupia?); pop. 956; 107 km SW of Lublin; 50°52'/21°06'; AMG, CAHJP, COH, GUM5, JGFF, LDL, PHP4, SF, YB.

Slupica, Pol.; pop. 3; 82 km W of Lublin; 51°25'/21°24'.

Slupiec, Pol.; pop. 31; 94 km NE of Krakow; 50°20'/21°12'; CAHJP.

Slupna, *see* Myslowice.

Slupno, Pol.; pop. 20; 19 km NNE of Warszawa; 52°24'/21°09'.

Slupow, Pol.; pop. 11; 45 km NNE of Krakow; 50°22'/20°19'.

Slupsk, Pol. (Stolp); pop. 470; 107 km W of Gdansk; 54°27'/17°02'; GUM3, GUM4, JGFF, LDS.

Sluptza, *see* Slupca.

Slutsk, Byel. (Sluck, Slutzk); pop. 8,358; 101 km S of Minsk; 53°01'/27°33'; AMG, EDRD, EJ, GUM3, GUM4, GUM5, HSL, HSL2, JGFF, LDL, LYV, PHP2, SF, YB.

Slutsk (near Leningrad), USSR; pop. 281; 32 km SE of Leningrad; 59°41'/30°27'.

Slutzk, *see* Slutsk.

Slutznik, *see* Salcininkeliai.

Sluzewo, Pol. (Sluzheva); pop. 259; 120 km NE of Poznan; 52°51'/18°39'; EDRD, GA, HSL, JGFF, PHP4, SF, YB.

Sluzheva, *see* Sluzewo.

Smalininkai, Lith.; 82 km W of Kaunas; 55°05'/22°35'; GUM5, JGFF.

Smalvai, *see* Smalvos.

Smalvos, Lith. (Smalvai, Smolwy); pop. 13; 126 km NNE of Vilnius; 55°38'/26°22'.

Smardzewo, Pol.; 82 km WNW of Warszawa; 52°37'/19°55'; GA.

Smarkow, Pol.; pop. 8; 101 km ESE of Lodz; 51°12'/20°33'.

Smederevo, Yug. (Semendria, Smederovo); pop. 83; 38 km ESE of Beograd; 44°39'/20°56'; EJ, PHY.

Smederov, Cz.; pop. 5; 88 km SW of Praha; 49°34'/13°35'.

Smederovo, *see* Smederevo.

Smela, Ukr. (Smila); pop. 6,867; 133 km NE of Uman; 49°14'/31°53'; EDRD, GYLA, HSL, JGFF, LDL, SF.

Smeloa, SF. This town was not found in BGN gazetteers under the given spelling.

Smeloya, *see* Smeola.

Smeola, (Smeloya, Smiela); AMG. This town was not found in BGN gazetteers under the given spelling.

Smerdyna, Pol.; pop. 5; 114 km NE of Krakow; 50°36'/21°20'.

Smereczka, *see* Smereczyna.

Smereczyna, (Smereczka); pop. 22; Described in the *Black Book* as being in the Stanislawow region of Poland, this town was not found in BGN gazetteers.

Smerek, Pol.; pop. 43; 75 km S of Przemysl; 49°10'/22°29'.

Smerekov, *see* Pshemivulki.

Smerekow, *see* Pshemivulki.

Smerekowiec, Pol.; pop. 21; 114 km ESE of Krakow; 49°31'/21°14'.

Smerekuv, *see* Pshemivulki.

Smichov, HSL, HSL2, JGFF. This town was not found in BGN gazetteers under the given spelling.

Smidary, Cz.; pop. 4; 75 km NE of Praha; 50°18'/15°29'.

Smidovich, *see* Smidovicha.

Smidovicha, USSR (Smidovich); 637 km SSE of Voronezh; 46°14'/41°08'.

Smidyn, Ukr. (Smidyn Zablocie); pop. 22; 146 km WNW of Rovno; 51°18'/24°26'.

Smidyn Zablocie, *see* Smidyn.

Smiechen, Pol.; pop. 3; 75 km NW of Czestochowa; 51°19'/18°25'.

Smiechowice, Pol.; 94 km SW of Lublin; 50°40'/21°38'; AMG.

Smiedzyborz, *see* Medzhibozh.

Smiela, *see* Smeola.

Smielnik, Pol.; pop. 6; 82 km NW of Lodz; 52°22'/18°47'.

Smigiel, Pol. (Schmiegel); pop. 13; 56 km SSW of Poznan; 52°01'/16°32'; HSL, JGFF.

Smigno, Pol.; pop. 11; 75 km E of Krakow; 50°05'/21°00'.

Smila, *see* Smela.

Smilg, *see* Smilgiai.

Smilgiai, Lith. (Smilg); pop. 37; 50 km E of Siauliai; 55°48'/24°01'; SF.

Smilkov, Cz.; pop. 12; 62 km SSE of Praha; 49°36'/14°37'.

Smilno, Cz.; 82 km N of Kosice; 49°23'/21°21'; AMG, HSL.

Smilovichi, Byel. (Smilovitch); pop. 1,748; 32 km ESE of Minsk; 53°45'/28°01'; JGFF, LDL, SF.

Smilovitch, *see* Smilovichi.

Smilten, *see* Smiltene.

Smiltene, Lat. (Smilten); pop. 217; 120 km NE of Riga; 57°26'/25°54'; COH, PHLE, SF.

Smirice, Cz.; pop. 15; 101 km ENE of Praha; 50°18'/15°53'.

Smochowice, GA. This town was not found in BGN gazetteers under the given spelling.

Smodna, Ukr.; pop. 24; 56 km W of Chernovtsy; 48°19'/25°08'.

Smogorzow, Pol.; 88 km ESE of Lodz; 51°24'/20°38'; GUM5, PHP1.

Smolanica, *see* Smolyanitsa.

Smolany, Pol.; pop. 45; 120 km N of Bialystok; 54°11'/23°13'.

Smolavitch, *see* Smolevichi.

Smolechy, Pol.; pop. 6; 82 km SW of Bialystok; 52°48'/22°01'.

Smolensk, USSR; pop. 12,887; 195 km SE of Velikiye Luki; 54°49'/32°04'; AMG, EDRD, EJ, GUM4, GUM5, JGFF, LDL, PHP4.

Smolevichi, Byel. (Smolavitch, Smolewicze); pop. 1,566; 45 km NE of Minsk; 54°02'/28°05'; EDRD, GUM4, GUM5, GYLA, HSL, SF.

Smolewicze, *see* Smolevichi.

Smolewo, Pol.; pop. 5; 75 km SW of Bialystok; 52°44'/22°15'.

Smolian, *see* Smolyany.

Smolin, Ukr.; pop. 91; 50 km WNW of Lvov; 50°09'/23°28'.

Smoljany, *see* Smolyany.

Smolna, Ukr.; pop. 37; 88 km SSW of Lvov; 49°17'/23°11'.

Smolnica, *see* Smolnitsa.

Smolnick, *see* Smolnik.

Smolnicka Huta, Cz. (Szomolnokhutta); 38 km W of Kosice; 48°45'/20°47'; HSL.

Smolnik, Pol. (Schmollnitz, Smolnick); pop. 60; 69 km S of Przemysl; 49°13'/22°42'; AMG, HSL.

Smolnik (near Baligrod), Pol.; pop. 47; 75 km SSW of Przemysl; 49°16'/22°08'.

Smolnik (Slovakia), Cz. (Szmolnok); 38 km W of Kosice; 48°44'/20°45'; GUM5, HSL.

Smolniki, Pol.; 133 km NNW of Bialystok; 54°17'/22°53'; HSL.

Smolnitsa, Ukr. (Smolnica); pop. 20; 101 km SW of Lvov; 49°28'/22°43'.

Smolotely, Cz.; pop. 3; 56 km SSW of Praha; 49°37'/14°08'.

Smolugi, Pol.; pop. 5; 62 km S of Bialystok; 52°37'/22°55'.

Smolwy, *see* Smalvos.

Smolyanitsa, Byel. (Smolanica); pop. 12; 120 km WNW of Pinsk; 52°42'/24°38'.

Smolyany, Byel. (Smolian, Smoljany); pop. 950; 69 km S of Vitebsk; 54°36'/30°04'; GUM4, SF.

Smordva, Ukr. (Smordwa); pop. 14; 50 km WSW of Rovno; 50°29'/25°32'; GUM3.

Smordwa, *see* Smordva.

Smorgon, Byel. (Smorgonie, Smurgainiai); pop. 4,000; 107 km WNW of Minsk; 54°29'/26°24'; AMG, COH, EDRD, EJ, GUM3, GUM5, HSL, HSL2, JGFF, LDL, LYV, SF, YB.

Smorgonie, *see* Smorgon.

Smorodek, Ukr. (Smorodzk); pop. 48; 139 km N of Rovno; 51°47'/26°44'.

Smorodzk, *see* Smorodek.

Smoryn, Pol.; pop. 15; 69 km SSE of Lublin; 50°40'/22°47'.

Smorze Dolne, Pol.; pop. 60; Described in the *Black Book* as being in the Stanislawow region of Poland, this town was not found in BGN gazetteers.

Smorze Miasteczko, Pol.; pop. 129; HSL, PHP2. Described in the *Black Book* as being in the Stanislawow region of Poland, this town was not found in BGN gazetteers.

Smoszew, Pol.; 82 km NNE of Wroclaw; 51°40'/17°30'; LDS.

Smotrich, Ukr. (Smotritch); pop. 1,835; 82 km NNE of Chernovtsy; 48°57'/26°33'; AMG, COH, LDL, SF, YB.

Smotritch, *see* Smotrich.

Smrdov, Cz.; pop. 2; 75 km ESE of Praha; 49°44'/15°25'.

Smrock, Pol.; pop. 7; 69 km N of Warszawa; 52°50'/21°11'.

Smrzovka, Cz. (Morchenstern); pop. 13; 88 km NNE of Praha; 50°44'/15°14'; EJ.

Smurgainiai, *see* Smorgon.

Smykowce, Ukr.; pop. 29; 107 km N of Chernovtsy; 49°15'/25°45'. This town was located on an interwar map of Poland but does not appear in contemporary gazetteers. Map coordinates are approximate.

Snakov, Cz.; 69 km NNW of Kosice; 49°19'/21°03'; HSL.

Snamenka, *see* Znamenka.

Snegi, Byel. (Sniegi); pop. 3; 182 km N of Minsk; 55°27'/27°19'.

Snepele, Lat.; pop. 2; 133 km WSW of Riga; 56°50'/21°57'.

Snetin, *see* Snyatyn.

Snezna, Cz. (Senava); 146 km W of Praha; 50°18'/12°30'; HSL.

Sniadow, *see* Sniadowo.

Sniadowka, Pol.; pop. 11; 45 km NW of Lublin; 51°31'/22°11'.

Sniadowo, Pol. (Shnadova, Shnadovi, Shnodovo, Shnyadovo, Sniadow); pop. 386; 82 km WSW of Bialystok; 53°02'/22°00'; CAHJP, GA, GUM3, HSL, HSL2, LDL, LDS, LYV, PHP4, POCEM, SF, WS.

Sniatin, *see* Snyatyn.

Sniatycze, Pol.; pop. 32; 94 km ESE of Lublin; 50°39'/23°32'.

Sniatyn, *see* Snyatyn.

Sniatynka, *see* Snyatynka.

Sniedzanowo, Pol. (Sniedzianowo); pop. 7; 107 km WNW of Warszawa; 52°52'/19°45'.

Sniedzianowo, *see* Sniedzanowo.

Sniegi, *see* Snegi.

Snietnica, Pol.; pop. 52; 107 km ESE of Krakow; 49°31'/21°04'; AMG.

Snigirevka, Ukr.; 170 km NE of Odessa; 47°04'/32°49'; GUM4.

Snikere, Lat.; pop. 1; 88 km SW of Riga; 56°23'/23°06'.

Snina, Cz.; pop. 1,413; 75 km NE of Kosice; 48°59'/22°09'; HSL, JGFF.

Snipiskes, Lith. (Shnipishuk, Sinzishok, Sknifishuk); HSL2, SF. Snipiskes is a section of the city of Vilnius.

Snitin, *see* Snyatyn.

Snitkiv, *see* Snitkov.

Snitkov, Ukr. (Snitkiv, Snitkowo); 82 km SW of Vinnitsa; 48°48'/27°38'; SF, WS.

Snitkowo, *see* Snitkov.

Snitovo, Byel. (Snitowo); pop. 34; 45 km W of Pinsk; 52°08'/25°27'.

Snitowo, *see* Snitovo.

Snochowice, Pol.; pop. 11; 82 km ENE of Czestochowa; 50°57'/20°19'.

Snopkow, Pol.; pop. 7; 13 km NW of Lublin; 51°19'/22°29'.

Snopousovy, Cz.; pop. 4; 94 km SW of Praha; 49°37'/13°23'.

Snov, Byel. (Snow, Snuv); pop. 401; 107 km SW of Minsk; 53°13'/26°24'; EDRD, GUM3, HSL, SF.

Snovich, Ukr. (Snowicz); pop. 24; 69 km E of Lvov; 49°44'/24°56'.

Snovidov, Ukr. (Snowidow); pop. 51; 82 km NW of Chernovtsy; 48°52'/25°17'.

Snovidoviche, *see* Snovidovichi.

Snovidovichi, Ukr. (Snovidoviche, Snowidowicze); pop. 78; 114 km NE of Rovno; 51°17'/27°24'.

Snovsk, *see* Shchors.

Snovsr, *see* Shchors.

Snow, *see* Snov.

Snowicz, *see* Snovich.

Snowidow, *see* Snovidov.

Snowidowicze, *see* Snovidovichi.

Snowsk, *see* Shchors.

Snuv, *see* Snov.

Snyatin, *see* Snyatyn.

Snyatyn, Ukr. (Shnyatin, Snetin, Sniatin, Sniatyn, Snitin, Snyatin); pop. 3,248; 32 km WNW of Chernovtsy; 48°27'/25°34'; AMG, CAHJP, COH, EDRD, EGRS, EJ, GA, GUM3, GUM4, GUM5, GUM6, GYLA, HSL, HSL2, JGFF, LDL, LYV, PHP2, SF.

Snyatynka, Ukr. (Sniatynka); pop. 38; 62 km SSW of Lvov; 49°24'/23°30'.

Sob, GUM3. This town was not found in BGN gazetteers under the given spelling.

Sobakince, *see* Pervomayskaya.

Sobcice, Cz.; pop. 3; 82 km NE of Praha; 50°22'/15°31'.

Sobedruhy, Cz. (Soborten); pop. 64; 75 km NW of Praha; 50°40'/13°52'; EJ.

Sobehrdy, Cz.; pop. 3; 38 km SE of Praha; 49°49'/14°44'.

Sobernheim, Germ.; pop. 80; 82 km SW of Frankfurt am Main; 49°48'/07°39'; GED.

Sobesin, Cz.; pop. 2; 50 km ESE of Praha; 49°48'/14°57'.

Sobeslav, Cz.; pop. 80; 94 km SSE of Praha; 49°16'/14°43'.

Sobianowice, Pol.; pop. 11; 13 km NE of Lublin; 51°18'/22°41'.

Sobiatyn, Pol.; pop. 15; 69 km S of Bialystok; 52°34'/23°07'.

Sobibor, Pol.; pop. 31; 75 km NE of Lublin; 51°29'/23°39'; EDRD, EJ, GA, GUM3, GUM4, PHGBW, PHP2, PHP3, PHP4, SF, YB. This is the location of a large concentration camp during the Holocaust; sources may refer to the camp.

Sobiecin, Pol.; pop. 2; 32 km N of Przemysl; 50°01'/22°45'.

Sobienie Jeziory, Pol.; pop. 1,439; 45 km SE of Warszawa; 51°56'/21°19'; EDRD, GA, GUM5.

Sobienie Szlacheckie, Pol.; pop. 5; 45 km SE of Warszawa; 51°57'/21°20'.

Sobieseki, Pol.; pop. 7; 75 km WSW of Lodz; 51°37'/18°20'.

Sobieska Wola, Pol.; pop. 52; 38 km SE of Lublin; 50°58'/22°46'.

Sobieszyn, Pol.; pop. 16; 50 km NW of Lublin; 51°36'/22°10'.

Sobiska, Pol.; pop. 15; 56 km NW of Lublin; 51°43'/22°15'.

Sobkov, *see* Sobkow.

Sobkow, Pol. (Sobkov); pop. 400; 82 km NNE of Krakow; 50°42'/20°28'; EDRD, GUM3, GUM5, LDS, SF.

Sobolev, *see* Sobolew.

Soboleve, *see* Sobolew.

Sobolevka, Ukr. (Sobolewka, Sobolivka); pop. 1,201; 133 km S of Uman; 47°42'/29°33'; HSL, LDL, SF.

Sobolew, Pol. (Sobolev, Soboleve, Sobolewa, Sobolewo); pop. 561; 75 km SE of Warszawa; 51°44'/21°40'; COH, FRG, GA, HSL, LYV, PHP4, YB.

Sobolew (near Lublin), Pol.; pop. 69; 38 km NNW of Lublin; 51°31'/22°29'; GUM3, GUM5.

Sobolewa, *see* Sobolew.

Sobolewka, *see* Sobolevka.

Sobolewo, *see* Sobolew.

Sobolivka, *see* Sobolevka.

Sobolow, Pol.; pop. 6; 38 km ESE of Krakow; 49°55'/20°21'.

Soboniowice, Pol.; pop. 6; 19 km SSE of Krakow; 49°59'/19°59'.

Sobor, Hung.; pop. 2; 120 km N of Nagykanizsa; 47°29'/17°23'.

Soborten, *see* Sobedruhy.

Sobota, Pol.; pop. 356; 45 km N of Lodz; 52°07'/19°41'; COH, GA, JGFF, LDL, LDS, PHP1, POCEM, SF, YB.

Sobota Rimavska, *see* Rimavska Sobota.

Sobotiste, Cz. (Szombat); pop. 71; 69 km N of Bratislava; 48°43'/17°24'; HSL.

Sobotka, Pol. (Zobten); 26 km SSW of Wroclaw; 50°53'/16°45'; HSL, HSL2, SF.

Sobotsh, *see* Subacius.

Sobrance, Cz. (Szobrancz); pop. 1,933; 69 km ENE of Kosice; 48°45'/22°11'; AMG, COH, HSL, HSL2, JGFF.

Sobrinowo, GUM4. This town was not found in BGN gazetteers under the given spelling.

Socha, Pol. BGN lists two possible localities with this name located at 51°45'/18°35' and 51°07'/21°54'. PHP4.

Sochaczew, Pol. (Sochatchev, Sochoczew, Sokhachev); pop. 2,419; 56 km WSW of Warszawa; 52°14'/20°15'; AMG, CAHJP, EDRD, EJ, GA, GUM3, GUM5, HSL, HSL2, ISH2, JGFF, LDL, LYV, PHP1, PHP4, POCEM, SF, YB.

Sochatchev, *see* Sochaczew.

Sochatchin, *see* Sochocin.

Sochocin, Pol. (Sochatchin); pop. 406; 56 km NW of Warszawa; 52°41'/20°28'; AMG, HSL, JGFF, LDS, PHP4, SF.

Sochoczew, *see* Sochaczew.

Socond, Rom.; pop. 18; 101 km NW of Cluj; 47°34'/22°57'.

Soconzel, Rom.; pop. 10; 94 km NW of Cluj; 47°31'/23°00'.

Soczewka, Pol.; pop. 8; 94 km N of Lodz; 52°32'/19°34'.

Sod, *see* Seda.

Sodel, Germ.; pop. 38 km N of Frankfurt am Main; 50°24'/08°48'; LDS.

Soest, Germ.; pop. 192; 107 km NE of Koln; 51°35'/08°07'; CAHJP, GED.

Sofia, *see* Sofiya.

Sofievka, *see* Zofyuvka.

Sofiya, Bulg. (Sofia); pop. 27,289; 378 km WSW of Varna; 42°41'/23°19'; AMG, EJ, GUM4, GUM5, GUM6, HSL, HSL2, JGFF, LJEE.

Sofiya (Bessarabia), Mold.; pop. 108; 133 km NW of Kishinev; 47°57'/27°52'.

Sofiyevka, *see* Zofyuvka.

Sogel, Germ.; pop. 80; 157 km WNW of Hannover; 52°51'/07°31'; GUM5, LDS.

Soha Balca, *see* Sukha Balka.

Sohmerhausen, *see* Sommerhausen.

Sohrau, HSL, HSL2, LDS. This town was not found in BGN gazetteers under the given spelling.

Sohren, Germ.; pop. 26; 101 km WSW of Frankfurt am Main; 49°56'/07°19'.

Soimi, *see* Soyma.

Soimuseni, Rom.; pop. 4; 69 km NNW of Cluj; 47°20'/23°23'.

Sojkowa, Pol.; pop. 15; 82 km NW of Przemysl; 50°24'/22°03'.

Sojmy, *see* Soyma.

Sojtor, Hung.; pop. 51; 32 km NNW of Nagykanizsa; 46°40'/16°51'; PHH.

Sok, Cz. (Sook); 62 km E of Bratislava; 48°06'/17°58'; HSL, HSL2.

Sokal, Ukr. (Skol); pop. 4,360; 75 km N of Lvov; 50°29'/24°17'; AMG, CAHJP, COH, EDRD, EGRS, EJ, GA, GUM3, GUM4, GUM5, HSL, LDL, LYV, PHP2, SF, YB.

Sokhachev, *see* Sochaczew.

Sokirnitsa, Ukr. (Sekernica, Sekernice, Sikernica, Szcklencze); pop. 685; 189 km WSW of Chernovtsy; 48°07'/23°23'; AMG, COH, GUM3, HSL, SM.

Sokiryany, Ukr. (Secureni Targ, Sekiryani, Sekureni Targ, Sekurian, Sikuran, Sokorone); pop. 4,216; 107 km ENE of Chernovtsy; 48°27'/27°25'; COH, EDRD, EJ, GUM4, GYLA, HSL, HSL2, JGFF, LDL, LYV, PHR2, SF, YB.

Sokol, Ukr. (Sukul); pop. 167; 82 km WNW of Rovno; 51°03'/25°20'; HSL, JGFF.

Sokol (Krakow), Pol.; pop. 33; 107 km ESE of Krakow; 49°39'/21°11'.

Sokola, Ukr. (Sokole); 45 km NE of Lvov; 50°04'/24°30'; AMG, JGFF.

Sokole, *see* Sokola.

Sokoli, *see* Sokoly.

Sokoliki, Ukr.; pop. 340; 114 km SW of Lvov; 49°06'/22°52'; HSL, LDL.

Sokoliki Gorskie, Pol. PHP2. This town was not found in BGN gazetteers under the given spelling.

Sokolivka, *see* Sokolovka.

320

Sokolka, Pol. (Sokolke); pop. 2,821; 45 km NNE of Bialystok; 53°25'/23°30'; AMG, COH, EDRD, EJ, FRG, GA, GUM3, GUM5, HSL, HSL2, JGFF, LYV, POCEM, SF, YB.

Sokolke, see Sokolka.

Sokolniki, Pol.; pop. 22; 82 km WNW of Czestochowa; 51°19'/18°20'; GUM3, GUM4, GUM5, PHP1.

Sokolniki (Lwow), Ukr. (Sokolniky); pop. 25; 13 km S of Lvov; 49°47'/23°59'; GUM6.

Sokolniki Suche, Pol.; pop. 11; 94 km ESE of Lodz; 51°23'/20°47'.

Sokolniky, see Sokolniki (Lwow).

Sokolov, USSR; pop. 455; a number of towns share this name. It was not possible to determine from available information which one is being referenced. See also Sokolow. See also Sokoluv.

Sokolov (Czechoslovakia), Cz. (Falkenau, Falknov nad Ohri); pop. 170; 126 km W of Praha; 50°11'/12°38'; GUM3, HSL.

Sokolovac, Yug.; pop. 23; a number of towns share this name. It was not possible to determine from available information which one is being referenced.

Sokolovka, Ukr. (Justingrad, Sokolivka, Sokolowka, Sokoluvka, Stara Vies, Sukhovole, Yustigrod, Zahojpole, Zaluzie); 38 km NNW of Uman; 49°02'/30°09'; EDRD, JGFF, LDL, SF.

Sokolovka (Lwow), Ukr.; pop. 67; 38 km SE of Lvov; 49°34'/24°18'.

Sokolovka (Stanislawow), Ukr.; pop. 32; 69 km WSW of Chernovtsy; 48°17'/25°00'.

Sokolovka (Tarnopol), Ukr.; pop. 460; 62 km NE of Lvov; 50°02'/24°51'; EGRS, GUM3, HSL, HSL2, PHP2, PHP3, SF.

Sokolow, Pol. (Sokolov, Sokolow Malopolski); pop. 1,351; 62 km NW of Przemysl; 50°14'/22°07'; AMG, CAHJP, COH, EGRS, FRG, GA, GUM3, GUM5, HSL2, ISH2, JGFF, LDL, PHP2, PHP3, SF, YB. See also Sokoluv.

Sokolow (near Plock), Pol.; 75 km NNW of Lodz; 52°23'/19°20'; GUM5.

Sokolowa Wola, Pol.; pop. 30; 56 km S of Przemysl; 49°22'/22°37'.

Sokolow bei Stryj, SF. This town was not found in BGN gazetteers under the given spelling.

Sokolowice, Pol.; pop. 6; 50 km ENE of Krakow; 50°10'/20°35'.

Sokolowka, see Sokolovka.

Sokolow Malopolski, see Sokolow.

Sokolow Podlaski, Pol.; pop. 4,430; 82 km ENE of Warszawa; 52°24'/22°15'; AMG, COH, EDRD, EJ, GA, GUM3, GUM4, GUM5, GUM6, HSL, LDS, LYV, PHP1, PHP4, SF.

Sokoluv, Ukr.; pop. 237; 82 km NW of Chernovtsy; 48°56'/25°20'; HSL. See also Sokolow.

Sokoluv (near Podgaytsy), Ukr.; pop. 30; 82 km NW of Chernovtsy; 48°56'/25°20'.

Sokoluvka, see Sokolovka.

Sokoly, Pol. (Sokoli); pop. 1,558; 38 km SW of Bialystok; 52°59'/22°42'; AMG, CAHJP, COH, GUM3, GUM4, HSL, JGFF, LDS, LYV, PHP4, SF, YB.

Sokoly Nowosiolki, Pol. LDS. This town was not found in BGN gazetteers under the given spelling.

Sokorone, see Sokiryany.

Sokszelitz, LDL. This pre-World War I community was not found in BGN gazetteers.

Sokszelocz, HSL. This pre-World War I community was not found in BGN gazetteers.

Sokul, see Sokol.

Sol, Cz.; pop. 57; 38 km NE of Kosice; 48°56'/21°36'; HSL.

Sola, see Staraya Sol.

Solany, Cz.; pop. 7; 56 km WNW of Praha; 50°27'/13°55'; HSL.

Solca, Rom. (Solka); pop. 191; 146 km WNW of Iasi; 47°42'/25°51'; SF.

Soldanesti, see Sholdaneshty.

Soldin, see Mysliborz.

Solduba, Rom. (Szoldobagy); pop. 11; 107 km NNW of Cluj;

47°36'/23°03'; HSL.

Solec, Pol. (Soletz); pop. 898; 56 km WSW of Lublin; 51°08'/21°46'; AMG, COH, EDRD, GA, GUM3, HSL, HSL2, SF. The Black Book notes a town named Solec (pop. 45) in the interwar Polish province of Lwow that does not appear in contemporary gazetteers.

Solec Kujawski, Pol. (Schulitz); pop. 33; 114 km NE of Poznan; 53°05'/18°15'; LDS.

Solec nad Wisla, Pol. AMG, GUM5. This town was not found in BGN gazetteers under the given spelling.

Solec Zdroj, GUM5. This town was not found in BGN gazetteers under the given spelling.

Soleczniki, see Salcininkai.

Soleczniki Wielkie, see Salcininkai.

Solemnik, see Slomniki.

Soletchnik, see Salcininkeliai.

Soletz, see Solec.

Solikamsk, GUM4, GUM5. This town was not found in BGN gazetteers under the given spelling.

Solin, Yug.; 251 km SSE of Zagreb; 43°33'/16°30'; EJ.

Solina, Pol.; pop. 46; 50 km SSW of Przemysl; 49°23'/22°28'.

Solingen, Germ.; pop. 290; 32 km N of Koln; 51°11'/07°05'; GUM4, GUM5.

Solinka, Pol.; pop. 26; 82 km SSW of Przemysl; 49°10'/22°14'.

Solipse, GUM5. This town was not found in BGN gazetteers under the given spelling.

Solivar, Cz. (Sovar); pop. 52; 38 km N of Kosice; 48°59'/21°16'; HSL.

Soljani, Yug.; pop. 6; 120 km W of Beograd; 44°57'/18°59'.

Solka, see Solca.

Sollenau, Aus.; pop. 4; 45 km S of Wien; 47°53'/16°15'; GUM3.

Solln, Germ.; pop. 30; 13 km SSW of Munchen; 48°04'/11°31'.

Sollos, see Vinogradov.

Solnice, Cz.; pop. 12; 120 km NNW of Brno; 50°12'/16°15'.

Solnicka, Cz.; pop. 56 km ESE of Kosice; 48°29'/21°58'; JGFF.

Solobkovtsy, Ukr. (Slobkovitz, Slopkovitz); pop. 1,145; 114 km NNE of Chernovtsy; 49°05'/26°55'; COH, EDRD, JGFF, SF.

Solocma, Rom.; pop. 11; 114 km ESE of Cluj; 46°29'/24°59'.

Soloki, see Salakas.

Solona, Rom.; pop. 8; 62 km NNW of Cluj; 47°16'/23°24'.

Solonet, Rom.; pop. 32; 45 km NNW of Iasi; 47°30'/27°27'. See also Solonets.

Solonets, Mold. (Solonet); pop. 27; 120 km NNW of Kishinev; 48°00'/28°25'.

Solonka, Pol.; pop. 20; 62 km W of Przemysl; 49°55'/21°58'.

Solotvina, Ukr. (Akna Szlatina, Doly Slatinski, Falu Szlatina, Selo Slatina, Slatinske Doly, Slotfina, Solotvino, Solotvinske Kopalne, Szlatina); 157 km WSW of Chernovtsy; 47°57'/23°54'; AMG, COH, GUM3, GUM5, GUM6, JGFF, SM.

Solotvino, see Solotvina.

Solotvinske Kopalne, see Solotvina.

Solotwina, Ukr. (Slotvina); pop. 610; 120 km WNW of Chernovtsy; 48°42'/24°25'; EGRS, HSL, HSL2, LDL, PHP2, SF.

Solova, Ukr. (Solowa); pop. 21; 32 km ESE of Lvov; 49°45'/24°24'.

Solovastru, Rom. (Gorgenyoroszdalu); pop. 4; 88 km E of Cluj; 46°46'/24°46'; HSL.

Solowa, see Solova.

Solpa Mala, Ukr.; pop. 8; 50 km NE of Rovno; 50°45'/26°53'.

Solt, Hung.; pop. 53; 82 km S of Budapest; 46°48'/19°00'; PHH.

Soltaneshty, Mold. (Soltanesti); pop. 1; 56 km W of Kishinev; 47°03'/28°07'.

Soltanesti, see Soltaneshty.

Soltau, Germ.; pop. 6; 69 km S of Hamburg; 52°59'/09°50'.

Soltsy, USSR; pop. 150; 133 km ENE of Pskov; 58°12'/30°30'.

Soltvadkert, Hung.; pop. 384; 69 km WNW of Szeged; 46°35'/19°23'; HSL, LDL, PHH.

Soltykow, Pol.; pop. 33; BGN lists two possible localities with this name located at 51°21'/21°11' and 51°09'/20°42'.

Soltysy, Pol.; 56 km WNW of Czestochowa; 51°06'/18°32'; GA.

Solukow, Ukr.; pop. 22; 126 km S of Lvov; 48°45'/23°55'. This town was located on an interwar map of Poland but does not appear in contemporary gazetteers. Map coordinates are approximate.

Soly, *see* Salos.

Solymar, Hung.; pop. 4; 13 km WNW of Budapest; 47°35'/18°56'.

Som, Hung.; pop. 10; 101 km NE of Nagykanizsa; 46°48'/18°09'; HSL.

Somaly, *see* Sumal.

Somberek, Hung.; pop. 13; 120 km WSW of Szeged; 46°05'/18°40'; LDS.

Sombor, Yug. (Zombor); pop. 1,175; 150 km NW of Beograd; 45°46'/19°07'; COH, EDRD, EJ, GUM3, GUM4, HSL, HSL2, JGFF, LDS, PHY, YB.

Somborn, Germ.; pop. 42; 69 km NNE of Koln; 51°30'/07°21'.

Somcuta Mare, Rom. (Nagysomkut); pop. 799; 88 km N of Cluj; 47°31'/23°28'; HSL, JGFF, PHR2.

Somerpalu, Est.; 69 km S of Tartu; 57°51'/26°48'; PHLE.

Somerseta, Lat. (Aglona); 45 km NE of Daugavpils; 56°08'/27°01'; EDRD, PHLE.

Somes, *see* Someseni.

Someseni, Rom. (Somes); pop. 48; 114 km NNW of Cluj; 47°45'/23°12'.

Somes Odorhei, Rom. (Szamosudvarhely); 69 km NNW of Cluj; 47°19'/23°16'; HSL.

Somfalu, *see* Drienove.

Somianka, Pol.; pop. 4; 38 km NNE of Warszawa; 52°34'/21°18'.

Somin, Ukr.; pop. 3; 150 km N of Lvov; 51°12'/24°20'.

Somkad, Hung. (Sonkad); 146 km E of Miskolc; 48°03'/22°45'; HSL.

Somkerek, *see* Sintereag.

Somlojeno, Hung.; pop. 4; 82 km N of Nagykanizsa; 47°07'/17°22'.

Somloszollos, Hung.; pop. 15; 88 km N of Nagykanizsa; 47°10'/17°22'.

Somlovasarhely, Hung.; pop. 16; 82 km N of Nagykanizsa; 47°07'/17°23'.

Somlyo, *see* Simleu Silvaniei.

Somlyocsehi, GUM4. This town was not found in BGN gazetteers under the given spelling.

Sommerach, Germ.; 75 km WNW of Nurnberg; 49°50'/10°12'; PHGB.

Sommerau, Germ.; 50 km ESE of Frankfurt am Main; 49°50'/09°15'; GUM5, PHGB.

Sommerein, Aus.; pop. 3; 32 km SE of Wien; 47°59'/16°39'; HSL.

Sommerhausen, Germ. (Sohmerhausen); 82 km WNW of Nurnberg; 49°42'/10°02'; CAHJP, GUM5, HSL2, PHGB.

Somogy, Hung.; pop. 6; 107 km ESE of Nagykanizsa; 46°07'/18°19'.

Somogyacsa, Hung.; pop. 2; 75 km ENE of Nagykanizsa; 46°35'/17°57'.

Somogyapati, Hung.; pop. 9; 69 km ESE of Nagykanizsa; 46°05'/17°45'.

Somogyaszalo, Hung.; pop. 2; 62 km E of Nagykanizsa; 46°27'/17°49'.

Somogyfajsz, Hung.; pop. 2; 50 km ENE of Nagykanizsa; 46°31'/17°34'.

Somogyfeheregyhaz, Hung.; pop. 1; 32 km NE of Nagykanizsa; 46°34'/17°18'.

Somogyfok, Hung.; 94 km NE of Nagykanizsa; 46°53'/18°01'; HSL.

Somogyharsagy, Hung.; pop. 5; 62 km ESE of Nagykanizsa; 46°10'/17°47'.

Somogyhatvan, Hung.; pop. 1; 62 km ESE of Nagykanizsa; 46°07'/17°43'.

Somogyjad, Hung.; pop. 3; 56 km ENE of Nagykanizsa;

46°30'/17°42'.

Somogykiliti, HSL. This pre-World War I community was not found in BGN gazetteers.

Somogysamson, Hung.; pop. 13; 32 km NE of Nagykanizsa; 46°35'/17°18'.

Somogysard, Hung.; pop. 4; 45 km E of Nagykanizsa; 46°25'/17°36'.

Somogysimonyi, Hung.; pop. 2; 19 km ENE of Nagykanizsa; 46°29'/17°13'.

Somogyszentpal, Hung.; pop. 13; 45 km NE of Nagykanizsa; 46°39'/17°29'.

Somogyszil, Hung.; pop. 60; 75 km ENE of Nagykanizsa; 46°31'/18°00'; JGFF, LDS, PHH.

Somogyszob, Hung.; pop. 38; 26 km ESE of Nagykanizsa; 46°18'/17°18'.

Somogyudvarhely, Hung.; pop. 4; 32 km SE of Nagykanizsa; 46°10'/17°12'.

Somogyvamos, Hung.; pop. 12; 56 km ENE of Nagykanizsa; 46°34'/17°41'.

Somogyvar, Hung.; pop. 20; 56 km NE of Nagykanizsa; 46°35'/17°40'; GUM5.

Somorja, *see* Samorin.

Somoshuyvar, *see* Gherla.

Somosko, Hung.; pop. 3; 69 km W of Miskolc; 48°10'/19°52'.

Somoskoujfalu, Hung.; pop. 42; 69 km W of Miskolc; 48°10'/19°50'.

Somotor, Cz. (Szomotor); pop. 113; 56 km ESE of Kosice; 48°24'/21°49'; HSL.

Sompolna, *see* Sompolno.

Sompolno, Pol. (Sompolna); pop. 1,149; 94 km WNW of Lodz; 52°23'/18°31'; COH, GUM3, GUM5, HSL2, PHP1, SF.

Soms, HSL. This pre-World War I community was not found in BGN gazetteers.

Sonczyce, Pol.; pop. 29; Described in the *Black Book* as being in the Nowogrodek region of Poland, this town was not found in BGN gazetteers.

Sondernheim, Germ.; 75 km WNW of Stuttgart; 49°11'/08°22'; JGFF.

Sondershausen, Germ.; pop. 67; 101 km W of Leipzig; 51°22'/10°52'; HSL.

Sondova Vishniah, *see* Sudovaya Vishnya.

Sonik, *see* Sanok.

Sonina, Pol.; pop. 10; 50 km WNW of Przemysl; 50°04'/22°17'.

Sonkad, *see* Somkad.

Sonneberg, Germ.; pop. 25; 107 km N of Nurnberg; 50°21'/11°10'; AMG.

Sonnefeld, Germ.; 88 km N of Nurnberg; 50°13'/11°08'; JGFF.

Sonsbeck, Germ.; pop. 8; 88 km NW of Koln; 51°37'/06°22'.

Sonsk, Pol.; pop. 3; 62 km NNW of Warszawa; 52°47'/20°43'; GUM4.

Sonta, Yug.; pop. 47; 139 km WNW of Beograd; 45°36'/19°06'.

Sontheim, *see* Sontheim an der Brenz.

Sontheim an der Brenz, Germ. (Sontheim); pop. 60; 88 km ESE of Stuttgart; 48°33'/10°17'; GED, HSL, HSL2, PHGBW.

Sontra, Germ.; pop. 82; 139 km NNE of Frankfurt am Main; 51°04'/09°56'; GED, HSL, LDS.

Sook, *see* Sok.

Sopachiv, Ukr. (Sopachuv, Sopaczow); 94 km NNW of Rovno; 51°25'/25°53'; GUM4.

Sopachuv, *see* Sopachiv.

Sopaczow, *see* Sopachiv.

Sopje, Yug.; pop. 13; 133 km E of Zagreb; 45°48'/17°45'.

Sopochinie, *see* Sopotskin.

Sopochkinye, *see* Sopotskin.

Sopockine, *see* Sopotskin.

Sopockinie, *see* Sopotskin.

Soponya, Hung.; pop. 14; 75 km SSW of Budapest; 47°01'/18°27'.

Soporu de Cimpie, Rom. (Mezoszopor, Soporul de Campi); 32 km E of Cluj; 46°42'/24°00'; HSL.

Soporul de Campi, *see* Soporu de Cimpie.

Soporul de Jos, *see* Supuru de Jos.

Sopot, Pol. (Zoppot, Zoppot Freistaat); pop. 1,500; 19 km NW of Gdansk; 54°27'/18°34'; AMG, GUM3, GUM4, HSL, POCEM.

Sopotkin, *see* Sopotskin.

Sopotnia Mala, Pol.; pop. 20; 69 km SSW of Krakow; 49°37'/19°16'.

Sopotnice, Cz.; pop. 6; 107 km NNW of Brno; 50°04'/16°21'.

Sopotskin, Byel. (Sopochinie, Sopochkinye, Sopockin, Sopockine, Sopockinie, Sopotkin, Sopotzkin); pop. 888; 251 km NW of Pinsk; 53°50'/23°39'; AMG, COH, EDRD, GUM5, GYLA, HSL, JGFF, LDL, LYV, PHP4, SF, WS, YB.

Sopotzkin, *see* Sopotskin.

Sopov, Ukr. (Sopow); pop. 28; 75 km WNW of Chernovtsy; 48°31'/24°59'.

Sopow, *see* Sopov.

Soprashl, *see* Suprasl.

Soprec, Cz.; pop. 1; 75 km ENE of Praha; 50°06'/15°33'.

Sopron, Hung. (Odenburg); pop. 1,861; 146 km NNW of Nagykanizsa; 47°41'/16°36'; COH, EJ, GUM3, GUM4, GUM5, HSL, ISH2, LDL, LDS, PHH.

Sopronbanfalva, *see* Kertvaros.

Sopronhorpacs, Hung.; pop. 4; 120 km NNW of Nagykanizsa; 47°29'/16°44'.

Sopronkeresztur, *see* Deutschkreutz.

Sopronkovesd, Hung.; pop. 2; 133 km NNW of Nagykanizsa; 47°33'/16°45'.

Sopronszecseny, Hung.; pop. 3; 139 km NNW of Nagykanizsa; 47°36'/16°45'.

Sopte, Hung.; pop. 1; 101 km NNW of Nagykanizsa; 47°17'/16°39'.

Sopteriu, Rom.; pop. 13; 56 km ENE of Cluj; 46°48'/24°21'.

Sorau, *see* Zary.

Sorau Seifersdorf, *see* Zary.

Sorbin, Pol.; pop. 6; 114 km ESE of Lodz; 51°07'/20°42'.

Sorgenloch, Germ.; pop. 2; 45 km SW of Frankfurt am Main; 49°53'/08°12'.

Sorkifalud, Hung. (Sorkikisfalud); pop. 4; 82 km NNW of Nagykanizsa; 47°08'/16°44'.

Sorkikapolna, Hung.; pop. 3; 82 km NNW of Nagykanizsa; 47°08'/16°42'.

Sorkikisfalud, *see* Sorkifalud.

Soroca, *see* Soroki.

Sorocko, *see* Sorotsko.

Soroka, *see* Soroki.

Soroki, Mold. (Soroca, Soroka); pop. 5,452; 133 km NNW of Kishinev; 48°09'/28°18'; COH, EJ, GUM4, GUM6, GYLA, HSL, HSL2, JGFF, LDL, PHP2, PHR2, SF.

Soroki (Stanislawow), Ukr.; pop. 20; 50 km WNW of Chernovtsy; 48°37'/25°22'.

Soroksar, Hung.; pop. 245; 19 km SSE of Budapest; 47°24'/19°07'; GUM5, GUM6, HSL, LDS, PHH.

Sorok Tatary, *see* Keturiasdesimt Totoriu.

Sorotsko, Ukr. (Sorocko); pop. 53; 126 km N of Chernovtsy; 49°23'/25°52'.

Sosen, Cz.; pop. 3; 69 km WSW of Praha; 50°05'/13°32'.

Sosenka, Byel.; pop. 76; 75 km NNW of Minsk; 54°31'/27°14'; COH, JGFF.

Sosenki Jajki, Pol.; pop. 28; 107 km E of Warszawa; 52°11'/22°34'.

Soshichno, Ukr. (Soszyczno); pop. 47; 133 km WNW of Rovno; 51°28'/24°53'.

Soshly, *see* Sasuoliai.

Soshno, Byel. (Soszno); pop. 17; 26 km NE of Pinsk; 52°15'/26°21'.

Sosnica, *see* Sosnitsa.

Sosnicowice, Pol. (Kieferstadtel); 75 km SSW of Czestochowa; 50°17'/18°32'; LDS.

Sosniczany, Pol.; pop. 14; 94 km SW of Lublin; 50°37'/21°36'.

Sosnitsa, Ukr. (Sosnica, Sosnitza); pop. 1,141; 56 km WNW of Konotop; 51°32'/32°30'; EGRS, HSL, PHP3, SF, SF.

Sosnitza, *see* Sosnitsa.

Sosnki, GUM4. This town was not found in BGN gazetteers under the given spelling.

Sosnovets, *see* Sosnowiec.

Sosnovice, *see* Sosnowiec.

Sosnovits, *see* Sosnowiec.

Sosnovitz, *see* Sosnowiec.

Sosnovitza, *see* Sosnowica.

Sosnovoye, Ukr. (Ljudwipol, Ludvipol, Ludwipol, Lyudvipol, Slishch, Slishch Gadol, Slisht, Slisht Gadol, Slishtch Gadol); pop. 916; 62 km NE of Rovno; 50°50'/27°00'; COH, EDRD, GUM3, GUM4, GUM5, JGFF, LYV, SF, YB.

Sosnovyets, *see* Sosnowiec.

Sosnow, Ukr.; pop. 25; 133 km N of Chernovtsy; 49°28'/26°10'. This town was located on an interwar map of Poland but does not appear in contemporary gazetteers. Map coordinates are approximate.

Sosnowa Wola, Pol.; pop. 9; 45 km SW of Lublin; 50°59'/22°00'.

Sosnowe, Pol.; pop. 11; 69 km E of Warszawa; 52°09'/21°57'.

Sosnowica, Pol. (Sosnovitza); pop. 275; 50 km NE of Lublin; 51°31'/23°05'; GA, GUM3, GUM5, HSL, HSL2, SF.

Sosnowe, Pol.; pop. 75 km NE of Czestochowa; 51°12'/20°00'; AMG, GA, PHP1.

Sosnowiec, Pol. (Sosnovets, Sosnovice, Sosnovits, Sosnovitz, Sosnovyets); pop. 13,646; 56 km S of Czestochowa; 50°18'/19°10'; AMG, CAHJP, COH, EDRD, EJ, GA, GUM3, GUM4, GUM5, GUM6, GUM6, HSL, HSL2, JGFF, LDL, LYV, PHP3, POCEM, SF, YB.

Sosnowiec Niwka, Pol. POCEM. This town was not found in BGN gazetteers under the given spelling.

Sosnowiec Srodula, GUM5, GUM6. This town was not found in BGN gazetteers under the given spelling.

Sosnowka, Pol.; pop. 20; GUM4, PHP4. a number of towns share this name. It was not possible to determine from available information which one is being referenced.

Sosolowka, *see* Sosolyuvka.

Sosolyuvka, Ukr. (Sosolowka); pop. 23; 75 km N of Chernovtsy; 48°55'/25°50'.

Sostofalva, Hung.; pop. 13; 19 km NE of Miskolc; 48°09'/21°00'.

Sosvertike, Hung.; pop. 3; 94 km SE of Nagykanizsa; 45°50'/17°52'.

Soszno, *see* Soshno.

Soszyce, Pol.; pop. 8; 50 km ENE of Lodz; 51°46'/20°11'.

Soszyczno, *see* Soshichno.

Sotern, Germ.; pop. 95; 126 km SW of Frankfurt am Main; 49°36'/07°05'; JGFF.

Souflion, Greece; pop. 37; 283 km ENE of Thessaloniki; 41°12'/26°18'.

Soutice, Cz.; pop. 14; 56 km ESE of Praha; 49°44'/15°04'.

Souvrat, Cz.; pop. 2; 101 km NE of Praha; 50°29'/15°43'.

Sovar, *see* Solivar.

Sovarad, *see* Sovata.

Sovata, Rom. (Sovarad, Szovata); pop. 90; 114 km E of Cluj; 46°35'/25°04'; HSL, PHR2.

Sovenyhaza, Hung.; pop. 14; 32 km NNW of Szeged; 46°29'/20°05'.

Sovetsk, USSR (Tilsit); pop. 800; 101 km NE of Kaliningrad; 55°05'/21°53'; AMG, GUM5, HSL, LDL.

Sovits, *see* Subata.

Sowin, Pol.; 50 km NNE of Lublin; 51°37'/22°55'; GUM3.

Sowina, Pol.; 94 km W of Przemysl; 49°50'/21°30'; AMG.

Sowliny, Pol.; pop. 120; 50 km SE of Krakow; 49°44'/20°25'; PHP3.

Soyma, Ukr. (Soimi, Sojmy, Vizkoz); 150 km S of Lvov; 48°34'/23°29'; SM.

Spachbrucken, Germ.; pop. 6; 32 km SSE of Frankfurt am Main; 49°51'/08°50'; LDS.

Spaichingen, Germ.; 88 km SSW of Stuttgart; 48°05'/08°43'; GUM3, PHGBW.

Spala, Pol.; pop. 35; 50 km ESE of Lodz; 51°32'/20°08'; PHP1.

Spalene Porici, Cz.; pop. 37; 82 km SW of Praha; 49°37'/13°37'.

Spandau, Germ.; pop. 604; 19 km W of Berlin; 52°33'/13°12'.

Spandowerhagen, Germ.; 101 km ENE of Rostock; 54°09'/13°42'; GUM4.

Spangenberg, Germ.; pop. 94; 133 km NNE of Frankfurt am Main; 51°07'/09°40'; LDS.

Spania Dolina, Cz. (Panska Dolina); 150 km W of Kosice; 48°49'/19°08'; HSL.

Spannberg, Aus.; pop. 4; 38 km NNE of Wien; 48°27'/16°44'.

Sparach, *see* Zbarazh.

Spares, Lat.; pop. 10; 120 km WSW of Riga; 56°50'/22°11'.

Spartak, Ukr.; 296 km ESE of Kharkov; 48°12'/39°20'.

Spas, Ukr.; pop. 113; 114 km S of Lvov; 48°53'/24°04'; HSL, PHP2.

Spas (Lwow), Ukr.; pop. 50; 94 km SW of Lvov; 49°24'/22°58'.

Spas (Tarnopol), Ukr.; pop. 23; 38 km NE of Lvov; 50°03'/24°29'.

Spas Demensk, USSR (Spas Dement); pop. 161; 133 km ESE of Smolensk; 54°24'/34°01'.

Spas Dement, *see* Spas Demensk.

Spasow, Pol.; pop. 24; PHP2. Described in the *Black Book* as being in the Lwow region of Poland, this town was not found in BGN gazetteers.

Spassk, GUM4. This town was not found in BGN gazetteers under the given spelling.

Speckswinkel, Germ.; 94 km N of Frankfurt am Main; 50°52'/09°03'; LDS.

Spergau, Germ.; 26 km WSW of Leipzig; 51°18'/12°02'; GUM3.

Spermezeu, Rom. (Ispanmezo); pop. 154; 69 km NNE of Cluj; 47°18'/24°09'; AMG, HSL, PHR2.

Speyer, Germ. (Altspeyer, Spires); pop. 350; 82 km NW of Stuttgart; 49°19'/08°26'; CAHJP, EJ, GED, GUM3, GUM4, GUM5, HSL, JGFF, PHGBW.

Spiczyn, Pol.; pop. 28; 19 km NE of Lublin; 51°21'/22°46'.

Spiegelau, Germ.; 157 km NE of Munchen; 48°55'/13°22'; GUM3.

Spielberg, Germ.; 101 km NNE of Nurnberg; 50°10'/12°03'; PHGB.

Spieszyn, Pol.; pop. 4; 56 km SSW of Bialystok; 52°40'/22°49'.

Spikov, *see* Shpikov.

Spilyava, *see* Pilyava.

Spindleruv Mlyn, Cz.; pop. 63; 107 km NE of Praha; 50°44'/15°37'.

Spinka, *see* Sapinta.

Spinus, Rom. (Hagymadfalva); pop. 23; 120 km WNW of Cluj; 47°12'/22°12'.

Spires, *see* Speyer.

Spisicbukovica, Yug. (Neu Bukowitz, Nova Bukovica); pop. 34; 101 km ENE of Zagreb; 45°52'/17°18'.

Spisska Bela, Cz. (Szepesbela); pop. 157; 75 km WNW of Kosice; 49°11'/20°28'; HSL.

Spisska Nova Ves, Cz. (Iglo, Neudorf); pop. 733; 56 km WNW of Kosice; 48°57'/20°34'; GUM4, GUM5, HSL, JGFF.

Spisska Sobota, Cz. (Georgenberg); pop. 82; 75 km WNW of Kosice; 49°04'/20°20'.

Spisska Stara Ves, Cz.; pop. 295; 101 km NW of Kosice; 49°23'/20°22'.

Spisska Vlachy, *see* Spisske Vlachy.

Spisske Podhradie, Cz. (Kirchdrauf, Szepesvaralja); pop. 419; 50 km WNW of Kosice; 49°00'/20°45'; AMG, GUM4, GUM5, HSL.

Spisske Vlachy, Cz. (Spisska Vlachy, Szepesolaszi, Wallendorf); pop. 138; 45 km WNW of Kosice; 48°57'/20°48'; HSL, JGFF, LDL.

Spital am Pyhrn, Aus.; pop. 1; 101 km E of Salzburg; 47°39'/14°20'.

Spital am Semmering, Aus.; pop. 1; 69 km N of Graz; 47°36'/15°45'.

Spitkovitz, *see* Spytkowice.

Spittal, *see* Spittal an der Drau.

Spittal an der Drau, Aus. (Spittal); pop. 6; 114 km SSE of Salzburg; 46°48'/13°30'.

Split, Yug.; pop. 210; 258 km S of Zagreb; 43°31'/16°26'; EJ, GUM4, GUM6, JGFF, PHY.

Sporice, Cz.; pop. 6; 82 km WNW of Praha; 50°27'/13°23'.

Sporkovshchizna, Byel. (Siarkowszczyna); 146 km W of Minsk; 53°57'/25°20'; GUM5.

Sporovo, Byel. (Sporow, Sporuv); pop. 26; 62 km WNW of Pinsk; 52°25'/25°20'.

Sporow, *see* Sporovo.

Sporuv, *see* Sporovo.

Sporysz, Pol.; pop. 10; 62 km SW of Krakow; 49°41'/19°14'; PHP3.

Sprendling, *see* Sprendlingen.

Sprendlingen, Germ. (Sprendling); pop. 94; 13 km S of Frankfurt am Main; 50°01'/08°42'; GUM3, GUM5, JGFF, YB.

Sprottau, *see* Szprudowo.

Sprowa, Pol.; pop. 13; 56 km ESE of Czestochowa; 50°36'/19°54'.

Spurcani, Rom.; pop. 5; 101 km WNW of Cluj; 47°15'/22°25'.

Spytkowice, Pol. (Spitkovitz); pop. 21; 62 km S of Krakow; 49°35'/19°50'; HSL, SF.

Sramtura, *see* Strimtura.

Srbin, Cz.; pop. 6; 26 km ESE of Praha; 49°59'/14°45'.

Srbobran, Yug.; pop. 50; 101 km NW of Beograd; 45°33'/19°48'.

Srebrenica, Yug.; pop. 4; 126 km SW of Beograd; 44°06'/19°18'.

Srednia, Pol.; pop. 26; 19 km WNW of Przemysl; 49°50'/22°35'.

Srednia Mala, *see* Srednie Male.

Srednia Wies (Lublin), Pol.; pop. 22; 45 km SE of Lublin; 50°54'/22°50'.

Srednia Wies (Lwow), Pol.; pop. 38; 56 km SSW of Przemysl; 49°25'/22°22'.

Srednica, Pol.; 50 km SW of Bialystok; 52°53'/22°34'; HSL.

Srednica Pawlowieta, Pol.; pop. 21; Described in the *Black Book* as being in the Bialystok region of Poland, this town was not found in BGN gazetteers.

Srednie Duze, Pol. (Srednie Wieksze); pop. 4; 56 km SE of Lublin; 50°51'/23°01'.

Srednie Male, Pol. (Srednia Mala); pop. 26; 56 km SE of Lublin; 50°50'/23°02'.

Srednie Wieksze, *see* Srednie Duze.

Srednik, *see* Seredzius.

Srednius, *see* Seredzius.

Sredniye Zhory, Mold. (Jora de Mijloc, Zhora de Mizhlok); pop. 22; 56 km N of Kishinev; 47°28'/29°06'.

Srednjaja Poguljanka, Lat. EDRD. This town was not found in BGN gazetteers under the given spelling.

Srem, Pol. (Schrimm); pop. 103; 45 km S of Poznan; 52°05'/17°01'; CAHJP, EJ, HSL, JGFF, LDS.

Sremska Mitrovica, Yug.; pop. 115; 75 km W of Beograd; 44°58'/19°37'; GUM4, GUM5, PHY.

Sremski Karlovci, Yug.; pop. 2; 62 km WNW of Beograd; 45°12'/19°56'.

Srlin, Cz.; pop. 1; 88 km S of Praha; 49°22'/14°27'.

Srock, Pol. (Srock Czastkowy, Srock Prywatny, Srocko, Srocko Prywatne, Srotzko); pop. 119; 32 km SE of Lodz; 51°32'/19°38'; AMG, GUM5, PHP1, SF.

Srock Czastkowy, *see* Srock.

Srocko, *see* Srock.

Srocko Prywatne, *see* Srock.

Srock Prywatny, *see* Srock.

Sroda, *see* Sroda Wielkopolska.

Sroda Slaska, Pol. (Neumarkt); pop. 62; 32 km WNW of Wroclaw; 51°10'/16°36'; LDL, LDS, POCEM.

Sroda Wielkopolska, Pol. (Schroda, Sroda); pop. 80; 38 km ESE of Poznan; 52°14'/17°17'; CAHJP, GUM4, HSL, JGFF.

Srodborow, Pol.; 32 km ESE of Warszawa; 52°06'/21°19'; PHP4.

Srodula, GUM5, PHP3. This town was not found in BGN gazetteers under the given spelling.

Srokowo, Pol. (Drengfurth); pop. 4; 163 km WNW of Bialystok; 54°13'/21°31'.

Sromowce Wyzne, Pol.; pop. 3; 82 km SSE of Krakow; 49°25'/20°21'.

Srotsk, *see* Serock.

Srotzko, *see* Srock.

Srpske Moravice, Yug.; pop. 6; 82 km SW of Zagreb; 45°26'/15°02'.

Srpski Itebej, Yug.; pop. 5; 88 km N of Beograd; 45°34'/20°43'.

St.Petersburg, *see* Leningrad.

Stabichov, *see* Stobykhva.

Stablack, *see* Dolgorukovo.

Stabnits, *see* Stopnica.

Stacewicze, Pol.; pop. 8; 38 km S of Bialystok; 52°50'/23°04'.

Stachov, *see* Stakhovo.

Stachow, *see* Stakhovo.

Stackeln, *see* Strenci.

Stadecken, Germ.; pop. 7; 45 km SW of Frankfurt am Main; 49°55'/08°08'.

Stadeln, Germ.; 13 km WNW of Nurnberg; 49°31'/10°59'; PHGB.

Staden, Germ.; pop. 21; 32 km NNE of Frankfurt am Main; 50°20'/08°55'; LDS.

Stadice, Cz.; pop. 7; 69 km NW of Praha; 50°37'/13°58'.

Stadlec, Cz.; pop. 10; 82 km S of Praha; 49°23'/14°30'.

Stadtamhof, Germ.; 88 km ESE of Nurnberg; 49°02'/12°06'; PHGB.

Stadtbergen, Germ.; 56 km WNW of Munchen; 48°22'/10°51'; PHGB.

Stadthagen, Germ.; pop. 31; 38 km WSW of Hannover; 52°19'/09°12'; GED.

Stadtlauringen, Germ.; pop. 5; 101 km NW of Nurnberg; 50°11'/10°22'; PHGB.

Stadtlengsfeld, Germ. (Lengsfeld); pop. 32; 126 km NE of Frankfurt am Main; 50°47'/10°08'; HSL, HSL2, JGFF, LDS.

Stadtlohn, Germ.; 120 km N of Koln; 51°59'/06°56'; GED, GUM5.

Stadtoldendorf, Germ.; pop. 47; 56 km S of Hannover; 51°54'/09°39'; LDS.

Stadtschlaining, Aus. (Schlaining, Varosszalonak); pop. 19; 69 km NE of Graz; 47°19'/16°17'; LDS.

Stadtschwarzach, Germ.; 75 km WNW of Nurnberg; 49°48'/10°13'; PHGB.

Staedtel, *see* Miejsce.

Staffelstein, Germ.; 75 km N of Nurnberg; 50°06'/10°59'; PHGB.

Stahlavy, Cz.; pop. 7; 82 km SW of Praha; 49°40'/13°30'.

Stainach, Aus.; pop. 4; 88 km ESE of Salzburg; 47°32'/14°06'.

Staje, *see* Staye.

Stakcin, Cz.; pop. 386; 82 km NE of Kosice; 49°00'/22°14'.

Stakein, HSL. This pre-World War I community was not found in BGN gazetteers.

Stakhovo, Byel. (Stachov, Stachow); pop. 140; 45 km E of Pinsk; 52°05'/26°43'; LDL, SF.

Stakliskes, Lith. (Shtoklishok, Stakliskis, Stoklishok); pop. 391; 45 km SE of Kaunas; 54°36'/24°19'; COH, GUM3, HSL, SF, YL.

Stakliskis, *see* Stakliskes.

Stale, Pol.; pop. 20; 94 km SSW of Lublin; 50°34'/21°45'.

Stalin, Ukr.; pop. 749; 214 km E of Dnepropetrovsk; 48°00'/37°48'. *See also* Varna (Bulgaria).

Stalin Donezk, *see* Donetsk.

Stalindorf, *see* Izluchistoye.

Stalinesti, *see* Stalnovtsy.

Stalingrad, *see* Volgograd.

Stalino, *see* Donetsk.

Stalinogrod, *see* Katowice.

Stalinsk, GUM4. This town was not found in BGN gazetteers under the given spelling.

Stalluponen, *see* Nesterov (Rfsr).

Stalnia, Pol. (Stalownia); pop. 3; 45 km N of Lublin; 51°34'/22°32'.

Stalnovtsy, Ukr. (Stalinesti); pop. 39; 45 km E of Chernovtsy; 48°18'/26°33'.

Stalowa Wola, Pol.; 88 km SSW of Lublin; 50°34'/22°03'; GA, GUM3, GUM4, GUM5, GUM6, PHP2, PHP3.

Stalownia, *see* Stalnia.

Stammheim, Germ.; 32 km NNE of Frankfurt am Main; 50°19'/08°55'; LDS.

Stampfen, *see* Stupava.

Stana Salaj, *see* Stina.

Stanceni, *see* Stinceni.

Staneleviche, Byel.; 163 km NW of Pinsk; 53°13'/24°36'; GUM6.

Staneshti, *see* Stanesti.

Staneshti de Sus, Ukr. (Stanestii de Sus pe Ceremus); pop. 35; 32 km SSE of Chernovtsy; 48°05'/26°04'; GUM4.

Staneshti de Zhos, Ukr. (Stanestii de Jos pe Ceremus), Unter Stanestie); pop. 622; 32 km SSE of Chernovtsy; 48°04'/26°05'; COH, EDRD, JGFF, PHR2.

Stanesti, Rom. (Staneshti); 75 km NW of Iasi; 47°40'/27°01'; HSL.

Stanestii de Jos pe Ceremus, *see* Staneshti de Zhos.

Stanestii de Sus pe Ceremus, *see* Staneshti de Sus.

Stangau, Aus.; pop. 1; 26 km SW of Wien; 48°06'/16°07'.

Stangenhagen, Germ.; pop. 4; 38 km SSW of Berlin; 52°13'/13°06'.

Staniatki, Pol.; pop. 3; 19 km ESE of Krakow; 50°01'/20°12'; PHP3.

Stanimaka, *see* Asenovgrad.

Stanimirz, Ukr.; pop. 40; 62 km SE of Lvov; 49°25'/24°25'. This town was located on an interwar map of Poland but does not appear in contemporary gazetteers. Map coordinates are approximate.

Stanin, Pol.; pop. 131; 75 km NNW of Lublin; 51°53'/22°12'; AMG, GA, HSL, SF.

Stanisic, Yug.; pop. 80; 157 km NW of Beograd; 45°56'/19°10'; PHY.

Stanislau, *see* Ivano Frankovsk.

Stanislaucic, Rom. PHR1. This town was not found in BGN gazetteers under the given spelling.

Stanislav, *see* Ivano Frankovsk.

Stanislavchik, Ukr. (Stanislavcik, Stanislavtchik, Stanislawczyk); pop. 165; 69 km NE of Lvov; 50°10'/24°54'; COH, EGRS, GUM4, JGFF, LDL, PHP2, SF, YB.

Stanislavcik, *see* Stanislavchik.

Stanislavov, *see* Ivano Frankovsk.

Stanislavtchik, *see* Stanislavchik.

Stanislavuvka, Ukr. (Stanislawowka); pop. 4; 133 km N of Lvov; 50°59'/24°20'.

Stanislawczyk, *see* Stanislavchik.

Stanislawow, *see* Ivano Frankovsk. Sources generally refer to the town of Ivano Frankovsk. See also listings below.

Stanislawow (near Bilgoraj), Pol.; pop. 13; 88 km SE of Lublin; 50°33'/23°08'.

Stanislawow (near Chelm), Pol.; pop. 11; 75 km ENE of Lublin; 51°19'/23°36'.

Stanislawow (near Czestochowa), Pol.; pop. 31; 32 km NW of Czestochowa; 51°02'/18°51'.

Stanislawow (near Gora Pulawska), Pol.; pop. 12; 50 km WNW of Lublin; 51°24'/21°54'.

Stanislawow (near Konskie), Pol.; pop. 45; 107 km ESE of Lodz; 51°15'/20°48'.

Stanislawow (near Opatow), Pol.; pop. 4; 101 km SW of Lublin; 50°48'/21°16'.

Stanislawow (near Opoczno), Pol.; pop. 13; 69 km E of Lodz; 51°34'/20°29'.

Stanislawow (near Tczow), Pol.; pop. 20; 101 km W of Lublin; 51°18'/21°05'.

Stanislawow (Warszawa), Pol.; pop. 495; 38 km ENE of Warszawa; 52°18'/21°33'.

Stanislawow Duzy, Pol.; pop. 2; 32 km NW of Lublin; 51°28'/22°23'.

Stanislawowka, *see* Stanislavuvka.

Stanisle, *see* Ivano Frankovsk.

Stanislo, *see* Ivano Frankovsk.

Stanislowow, *see* Ivano Frankovsk.

Staniszewo, Pol.; pop. 3; 38 km W of Gdansk; 54°24'/18°05'.

Staniszewskie, Pol.; pop. 20; 75 km WNW of Przemysl; 50°15'/22°00'; GA, GUM5.

Stanke Dimitrov, Bulg. (Dupnitsa, Marek); pop. 960; 56 km S of Sofija; 42°16'/23°07'; EJ, GUM4.

Stankov, Cz. (Mestys Stankov); pop. 24; 114 km SW of Praha; 49°33'/13°04'; JGFF.

Stankova, Ukr. (Stankowa); pop. 32; 82 km SSE of Lvov; 49°09'/24°18'.

Stankovce, Cz. (Sztankocz); 32 km ENE of Kosice; 48°46'/21°40'; HSL.

Stankovice, HSL. a number of towns share this name. It was not possible to determine from available information which one is being referenced.

Stankowa, Pol.; pop. 37; 38 km SW of Przemysl; 49°34'/22°27'. *See also* Stankova.

Stany (Kielce), Pol.; pop. 23; 38 km W of Czestochowa; 50°52'/18°38'.

Stany (Lwow), Pol.; pop. 41; 88 km NW of Przemysl; 50°27'/21°59'.

Stany Male, Pol.; pop. 3; 88 km ENE of Warszawa; 52°18'/22°16'.

Staporkow, Pol. (Stomporkow); pop. 67; 101 km ESE of Lodz; 51°09'/20°33'; GUM5, PHP1, SF.

Stara, Pol.; pop. 23; 69 km SE of Lodz; 51°14'/19°58'.

Stara Bystrica, Cz.; pop. 64; 170 km ENE of Brno; 49°21'/18°57'.

Starachowice, *see* Wierzbnik.

Stara Dala, *see* Hurbanovo.

Stara Huta, Pol.; pop. 29; a number of towns share this name. It was not possible to determine from available information which one is being referenced.

Stara Kanjiza, *see* Kanjiza.

Starakhovits, *see* Wierzbnik.

Stara Kuznia, *see* Stara Kuznica.

Stara Kuznica, Pol. (Stara Kuznia); 69 km S of Czestochowa; 50°14'/18°52'; PHP3.

Stara Lubovna, Cz.; pop. 752; 75 km NW of Kosice; 49°18'/20°42'; AMG, GUM4, HSL.

Stara Moravica, Yug. (Kossuthfalva, Omoravicza); pop. 78; 139 km NW of Beograd; 45°52'/19°28'; PHY.

Stara Paka, Cz. (Altpaka); 88 km NE of Praha; 50°31'/15°30'; GUM3.

Stara Palanka, *see* Staro Poljance.

Stara Pazova, Yug.; pop. 68; 32 km WNW of Beograd; 44°59'/20°10'.

Stara Siol, *see* Staraya Sol.

Stara Slupia, *possibly* Slupia Nowa.

Stara Sol, *see* Staraya Sol.

Stara Tura, Cz.; pop. 50; 82 km NNE of Bratislava; 48°47'/17°42'.

Stara Vies, *see* Sokolovka.

Stara Wies, Ukr.; pop. 45; 62 km SSW of Lvov; 49°23'/23°31'; EDRD, HSL, PHP3, SF, SF.

Starawies, *see* Ulica Starowiejska.

Stara Wies (near Brzozow), Pol.; pop. 7; 56 km WSW of Przemysl; 49°43'/22°01'.

Stara Wies (near Cimarowa), Pol.; pop. 31; 62 km SE of Krakow; 49°41'/20°26'.

Stara Wies (near Grybow), Pol.; pop. 30; 56 km SE of Krakow; 49°40'/20°24'.

Stara Wies (near Krasne), Pol.; pop. 51; 32 km ENE of Lublin; 51°18'/22°59'.

Stara Wies (near Siedlce), Pol.; pop. 14; 107 km E of Warszawa; 52°14'/22°34'.

Stara Wies (near Tomaszow Lubelski), Pol.; pop. 16; 114 km ESE of Lublin; 50°36'/23°51'.

Stara Wies (near Zamosc), Pol.; pop. 9; 69 km ESE of Lublin; 50°55'/23°20'.

Stara Wies Rychwalska, Pol.; pop. 14; 94 km WNW of Lodz; 52°04'/18°11'.

Staraya Bogdanovka, Mold. (Bogdaneasca Veche); pop. 5; 62 km S of Kishinev; 46°28'/28°50'.

Staraya Chelakovka, Mold. (Ciolacu Vechi, Ciolacu Vechiu); pop. 21; 88 km WNW of Kishinev; 47°29'/27°52'.

Staraya Dashevka, *see* Dashev.

Staraya Kobuska, Mold. (Cobusca Veche); pop. 28; 32 km E of Kishinev; 46°58'/29°11'.

Staraya Kotelnya, Ukr. (Kotelnia, Kotelnja, Kotelnua, Kotelnya, Kotolina Hayashana); pop. 896; 101 km N of Vinnitsa; 50°06'/28°58'; LDL, SF.

Staraya Obrezha, Mold. (Obreja Veche); pop. 30; 120 km WNW of Kishinev; 47°41'/27°40'.

Staraya Rudnja, *see* Staraya Rudnya.

Staraya Rudnya, Byel. (Rudni, Staraya Rudnja); 69 km WNW of Gomel; 52°50'/30°17'; LDL, SF.

Staraya Russa, USSR; pop. 1,301; 182 km ENE of Pskov; 58°00'/31°23'; HSL.

Staraya Sarata, Mold. (Sarata Veche); pop. 3; 101 km WNW of Kishinev; 47°31'/27°44'.

Staraya Sinyava, Ukr. (Sinjava); 75 km WNW of Vinnitsa; 49°36'/27°37'; EDRD, JGFF.

Staraya Sol, Ukr. (Sola, Stara Siol, Stara Sol); pop. 211; 88 km SW of Lvov; 49°29'/22°58'; EGRS, HSL, LDL, PHP2, SF.

Staraya Tsarichanka, Ukr. (Tariceanca Veche); pop. 18; 69 km SW of Odessa; 46°17'/29°52'.

Staraya Ushitsa, Ukr. (Ushitse Podolye, Ushitza); pop. 1,003; 94 km NE of Chernovtsy; 48°35'/27°08'; GYLA, HSL, SF.

Staraya Ves Gorby, Ukr. (Staroye Selo); pop. 80; 45 km NW of Lvov; 50°11'/23°40'.

Staraya Yablona, Mold. (Iablona Veche, Yablona); pop. 37; 126 km WNW of Kishinev; 47°48'/27°37'.

Staraya Yelenovka, Ukr. (Gelenuvka Stara, Helenowka Stara); pop. 32; 82 km WNW of Rovno; 50°59'/25°17'.

Stara Zagora, Bulg. (Stara Zagura); pop. 490; 189 km E of Sofija; 42°25'/25°38'; EJ, GUM5.

Stara Zagura, *see* Stara Zagora.

Starciu, *see* Stirciu.

Starczewice, Pol.; pop. 5; 94 km SSW of Bialystok; 52°24'/22°37'.

Starczewo Duze, Pol. (Starczewo Wielkie); pop. 3; 75 km WNW of Warszawa; 52°40'/20°10'.

Starczewo Wielkie, *see* Starczewo Duze.

Starczynow, Pol.; pop. 2; 38 km WNW of Krakow; 50°16'/19°28'.

Stare, Cz. (Zemplensztara?); 50 km NE of Kosice; 48°52'/21°52'; HSL.

Stare Bielsko, Pol.; pop. 39; 69 km SW of Krakow; 49°50'/19°01'.

Stare Brody, Ukr.; pop. 186; 88 km NE of Lvov; 50°04'/25°10'.

Stare Bystre, Pol.; pop. 3; 75 km S of Krakow; 49°26'/19°55'.

Stare Miasto, Ukr.; pop. 84; 62 km SE of Lvov; 49°25'/24°33'; PHP2, PHP3.

Stare Miasto (Lodz), Pol.; pop. 38; 88 km E of Poznan; 52°11'/18°13'.

Stare Miasto (Lwow), Pol.; pop. 65; 56 km NW of Przemysl; 50°17'/22°26'.

Stare Selo, *see* Staroye Selo.

Stare Siolo (Lwow), Pol.; pop. 41; 45 km N of Przemysl; 50°09'/22°58'.

Stare Siolo (Polesie), Ukr.; pop. 49; 133 km NNE of Rovno; 51°37'/27°08'.

Stare Stawy, Pol.; pop. 3; 50 km WSW of Krakow; 50°01'/19°13'.

Stargard, *see* Stargard Szczecinski.

Stargard Szczecinski, Pol. (Priemhausen, Stargard); pop. 310; 38 km ESE of Szczecin; 53°20'/15°03'; CAHJP, GUM4, GUM6, HSL, LDS.

Stari Banovci, Yug.; pop. 1; 26 km NW of Beograd; 44°59'/20°17'.

Staridob, *see* Starodub.

Stariki, Ukr. (Rudnia Staryki, Rudnya Staryki); pop. 26; 94 km NNE of Rovno; 51°14'/27°06'.

Stari Mikanovci, Yug.; pop. 11; 163 km WNW of Beograd; 45°17'/18°33'.

Starinka, *see* Starinki.

Starinki, Byel. (Starinka); 50 km WSW of Minsk; 53°52'/26°46'; HSL.

Stari Sivac, Yug.; pop. 70; This town was not found in BGN gazetteers under the given spelling.

Stariy Yarov, Ukr. (Jazow Nowy?, Jazow Stary); pop. 50; 45 km WNW of Lvov; 49°59'/23°26'.

Starkenburg, GUM4. a number of towns share this name. It was not possible to determine from available information which one is being referenced.

Starkov, Cz.; pop. 5; 133 km NE of Praha; 50°32'/16°10'.

Starna, Cz. (Sztarnya); 75 km SW of Kosice; 48°26'/20°20'; HSL.

Starnberg, Germ.; pop. 18; 26 km SW of Munchen; 48°00'/11°21'; GUM3.

Starobel Sk, *see* Starobelsk.

Starobelsk, Ukr. (Starobel Sk, Starobielsk, Starobyelsk); pop. 210; 208 km ESE of Kharkov; 49°16'/38°56'.

Starobielsk, *see* Starobelsk.

Starobin, Byel.; pop. 1,427; 114 km NE of Pinsk; 52°44'/27°28'; JGFF, SF, YB.

Starobud, *see* Starodub.

Starobyelsk, *see* Starobelsk.

Starodub, USSR (Staridob, Starobud); pop. 3,317; 133 km SW of Bryansk; 52°35'/32°42'; EDRD, EJ, GUM4, GUM5, HSL, JGFF, LDL, SF.

Starogard, Pol. (Pressisch Stargard, Preussische Stargard, Starogard Gdanski); pop. 125; 45 km S of Gdansk; 53°58'/18°33'; AMG, CAHJP, GUM3, HSL, HSL2, LDS.

Starogard Gdanski, *see* Starogard.

Starokamienna, Pol.; pop. 7; 69 km N of Bialystok; 53°41'/23°19'.

Starokazachye, Ukr. (Cazaci, Eigenheim); pop. 136; 62 km WSW of Odessa; 46°20'/29°59'.

Starokonstantinov, Ukr. (Starokonstantynow); pop. 6,934; 107 km WNW of Vinnitsa; 49°45'/27°13'; COH, EJ, HSL, JGFF, LDL, SF.

Starokonstantynow, *see* Starokonstantinov.

Staromamayevtsy, *see* Altmamayeshti.

Staromieszczyzna, Pol. PHP2. This town was not found in BGN gazetteers under the given spelling.

Staroniwa, Pol.; pop. 15; 62 km WNW of Przemysl; 50°02'/21°58'.

Staro Poljance, Yug. (Stara Palanka); pop. 80; 101 km NW of Skopje; 42°44'/20°50'.

Staroscin, Pol.; pop. 15; 26 km NW of Lublin; 51°24'/22°25'.

Staroselia, *see* Staroselye.

Staroselja, *see* Staroselye.

Staroselye, Ukr. (Frumusica Veche, Staroselia, Staroselja); pop. 12; 101 km WSW of Odessa; 46°20'/29°28'; SF.

Starosielce, Pol.; pop. 66; 6 km WSW of Bialystok; 53°08'/23°05'; PHP4.

Starostwo Zwolen, Pol.; pop. 22; Described in the *Black Book* as being in the Kielce region of Poland, this town was not found in BGN gazetteers.

Staroye Selo, *see* Staraya Ves Gorby.

Starozreby, Pol.; pop. 49; 75 km WNW of Warszawa; 52°38'/19°59'.

Starunia, Ukr.; pop. 168; 114 km W of Chernovtsy; 48°25'/24°25'; HSL, PHP2. This town was located on an interwar map of Poland but does not appear in contemporary gazetteers. Map coordinates are approximate.

Starya Dorogi, *see* Staryye Dorogi.

Starya Russa, GUM4. This town was not found in BGN gazetteers under the given spelling.

Staryava, Ukr. (Starzawa); pop. 94; 94 km SW of Lvov; 49°30'/22°46'.

Staryava (near Mostiska), Ukr.; pop. 35; 69 km W of Lvov; 49°52'/23°03'.

Stary Dzikow, *see* Dzikow Stary.

Starye Dorogi, *see* Staryye Dorogi.

Stary Harcov, Cz.; pop. 23; 88 km NNE of Praha; 50°46'/15°06'.

Staryi Bykhov, *see* Bykhov.

Stary Kornin, Pol.; pop. 16; 50 km SE of Bialystok; 52°42'/23°27'.

Stary Krim, *see* Staryy Krym.

Stary Oleksiniec, *see* Staryy Oleksinets.

Stary Oskol, USSR; pop. 106; 45 km SSW of Voronezh; 51°20'/37°50'; GUM4, GUM5.

Stary Rynek, Pol.; pop. 32; Described in the *Black Book* as being in the Wilen region of Poland, this town was not found in BGN gazetteers.

Stary Sacz, Pol. (Alt Sandez, Alt Sanz, Tzantz Yashan); pop. 553; 75 km SE of Krakow; 49°34'/20°39'; AMG, COH, EDRD, EGRS, GA, GUM5, HSL, LDL, PHP3, SF.

Stary Sambor, *see* Staryy Sambor.

Stary Targ, Pol. (Altmark); pop. 6; 56 km SE of Gdansk; 53°56'/19°11'.

Staryy Badrazh, Mold. (Badragii Vechi); pop. 47; 170 km WNW of Kishinev; 48°03'/27°07'.

Staryy Chartoriysk, Ukr. (Chartorisk, Chartoriysk, Czartorysk, Tshartorisk); pop. 220; 75 km NNW of Rovno; 51°13'/25°53'; AMG, COH, EDRD, FRG, JGFF, SF.

Staryye Bilicheny, Mold. (Biliceni); pop. 28; 94 km NW of Kishinev; 47°39'/28°03'.

Staryye Brynzeny, Mold. (Branzenii Vechi); pop. 21; 75 km NNW of Kishinev; 47°39'/28°29'.

Staryye Choropkany, Mold. (Cioropcanii Vechi); pop. 5; 94 km WNW of Kishinev; 47°24'/27°43'.

Staryye Dorogi, Byel. (Starya Dorogi, Starye Dorogi); pop. 1,050; 107 km SE of Minsk; 53°02'/28°16'; GUM4, LDL, SF, YB.

Staryye Fundury, Mold. (Funduri); pop. 83; 120 km NW of Kishinev; 47°45'/27°43'.

Staryye Kitskany, Mold. (Chitcani Vechi, Kitskani Vek); pop. 27; 75 km NNW of Kishinev; 47°36'/28°30'.

Staryye Kukoneshty (Bessarabia), Mold. (Cuconestii Vechi); pop. 70; 163 km WNW of Kishinev; 47°58'/27°09'; HSL.

Staryye Limbeny, Mold. (Limbenii Vechi); pop. 26; 120 km WNW of Kishinev; 47°42'/27°37'.

Staryye Negureny, Mold. (Negureni Vek, Negurenii Vechi Orhei); pop. 65; 82 km WNW of Kishinev; 47°25'/27°53'.

Staryye Peski, Byel. (Piaska Stare, Piaski Stare, Pyaski Stare); pop. 28; 75 km WNW of Pinsk; 52°30'/25°13'.

Staryye Radulyany, Mold. (Raduleni Vechi); pop. 34; 120 km NNW of Kishinev; 47°59'/28°16'.

Staryye Redeny, Mold. (Radeni Vek, Radenii Vechi); pop. 62; 69 km WNW of Kishinev; 47°18'/28°00'.

Staryye Sarateny, Mold. (Sarateni Orhei); pop. 71; 62 km NNW of Kishinev; 47°32'/28°33'.

Staryye Tomashevtsy, Ukr. (Tomaszowce); pop. 53; 82 km SSE of Lvov; 49°09'/24°26'.

Staryy Krym, Ukr. (Stary Krim); pop. 150; 82 km ENE of Simferopol; 45°02'/35°06'.

Staryy Nizhborok, Ukr. (Nizborg Stary, Nizhborg Stary); pop. 52; 94 km N of Chernovtsy; 49°08'/26°03'; HSL.

Staryy Oleksinets, Ukr. (Stary Oleksiniec); pop. 23; 101 km SSW of Rovno; 49°50'/25°33'.

Staryy Oskol, USSR; pop. 106; 50 km SSW of Voronezh; 51°17'/37°51'.

Staryy Sambor, Ukr. (Altshtat, Stary Sambor); pop. 1,534; 88 km SW of Lvov; 49°26'/23°00'; AMG, COH, EDRD, EGRS, GUM3, HSL, HSL2, JGFF, LDL, PHP2, SF, YB.

Starzawa, *see* Staryava.

Starzechowice, Pol.; pop. 5; 75 km SE of Lodz; 51°11'/20°05'.

Starzenice, Pol.; pop. 8; 62 km NW of Czestochowa; 51°14'/18°38'.

Stashev, see Staszow.

Stashule, Byel. (Staszule); pop. 2; 170 km WNW of Vitebsk; 55°45'/27°38'.

Stashuv, see Staszow.

Stassfurt, Germ.; pop. 25; 82 km NW of Leipzig; 51°52'/11°35'; GUM3, LDS.

Staszkowka, Pol.; pop. 17; 88 km ESE of Krakow; 49°46'/21°02'.

Staszow, Pol. (Stashev, Stashuv); pop. 4,704; 101 km NE of Krakow; 50°33'/21°10'; AMG, CAHJP, COH, EDRD, EJ, GA, GUM3, GUM4, GUM5, GUM6, HSL, HSL2, JGFF, LDL, LDS, LYV, PHP3, PHP4, POCEM, SF, YB.

Staszule, see Stashule.

Stattersdorf, Aus.; pop. 2; 50 km WSW of Wien; 48°11'/15°38'.

Statul Nou de Jos, see Satu Nou de Jos.

Statzendorf, Aus.; pop. 1; 56 km W of Wien; 48°18'/15°38'.

Stauceni (Bessarabia), Rom.; pop. 27; Described in the *Black Book* as being in the Bessarabia region of Romania, this town was not found in BGN gazetteers.

Stauceni (Bucovina), Rom.; pop. 192; 88 km WNW of Iasi; 47°43'/26°45'.

Staudernheim, Germ.; pop. 24; 82 km SW of Frankfurt am Main; 49°47'/07°41'; JGFF.

Staufen, Germ.; 150 km SW of Stuttgart; 47°53'/07°44'; GED, PHGBW.

Staufenberg, Germ.; 69 km N of Frankfurt am Main; 50°40'/08°43'; LDS.

Stavchany, Ukr. (Stawczany); pop. 45; 19 km SW of Lvov; 49°46'/23°50'.

Stavechki, see Stavochki.

Stavenhagen, see Reuterstadt Stavenhagen.

Stavische, see Stavishche.

Stavishcha, see Stavishche.

Stavishchany, Ukr. (Uniow, Uniyev); pop. 79; 69 km S of Rovno; 50°03'/26°17'.

Stavishche, Ukr. (Stavische, Stavishcha, Stawiszcze); 75 km N of Uman; 49°23'/30°12'; GUM4, HSL, JGFF, LDL, SF, YB.

Stavishin, see Stawiszyn.

Stavisk, see Stawiski.

Staviska, Ukr.; 69 km W of Lvov; 49°51'/23°02'; JGFF.

Staviski, see Stawiski.

Stavki, Ukr. (Stawki); pop. 35; 139 km N of Lvov; 51°04'/24°11'; AMG, HSL, PHP4.

Stavki Krasnenske, Ukr. (Stawki Krasninskie); pop. 20; 114 km N of Chernovtsy; 49°19'/26°12'.

Stavna, see Stavnoye.

Stavnoye, Ukr. (Stavna, Sztawna); 133 km SW of Lvov; 49°00'/22°41'; HSL.

Stavochki, Ukr. (Stavechki, Staweczki); 139 km N of Lvov; 51°05'/24°10'; GUM3.

Stavok, Ukr. (Stawek); pop. 41; 38 km N of Rovno; 50°55'/26°12'.

Stavropol, USSR; pop. 1,381; 781 km SSE of Voronezh; 45°03'/41°49'.

Staw, Pol.; pop. 27; BGN lists two possible localities with this name located at 51°15'/18°37' and 51°42'/18°23'.

Stawce, Pol.; pop. 18; 45 km S of Lublin; 50°53'/22°32'.

Stawczany, see Stavchany.

Staweczki, see Stavochki.

Stawek, see Stavok.

Stawiski, Pol. (Stavisk, Staviski); pop. 1,920; 69 km WNW of Bialystok; 53°22'/22°09'; AMG, COH, GA, GUM3, GUM4, GUM5, GYLA, HSL, HSL2, JGFF, PHP4, POCEM, SF, YB.

Stawisza, Pol.; pop. 3; 107 km ESE of Krakow; 49°30'/21°05'.

Stawiszcze, see Stavishche.

Stawiszyn, Pol. (Stavishin); pop. 672; 88 km W of Lodz; 51°55'/18°09'; AMG, GUM3, HSL, HSL2, JGFF, LDL, LDS, PHP1, SF.

Stawki, see Stavki.

Stawki Krasninskie, see Stavki Krasnenske.

Staw Noakowski, Pol.; pop. 32; 56 km SE of Lublin; 50°49'/23°01'.

Stawowiczki, Pol.; pop. 4; 69 km ESE of Lodz; 51°19'/20°12'.

Staye, Ukr. (Staje); pop. 40; 62 km NNW of Lvov; 50°23'/23°53'; HSL.

St Chegova, see Strzegowo.

Stebbach, Germ.; pop. 8; 50 km NNW of Stuttgart; 49°09'/08°58'; JGFF, LDS, PHGBW.

Steblev, Ukr.; 94 km NNE of Uman; 49°24'/31°06'; JGFF.

Steblevka, Ukr. (Saldobos, Saldobosh, Saldobus, Szaldobos); 182 km WSW of Chernovtsy; 48°05'/23°25'; AMG, COH, HSL, SM.

Steblova, Cz.; pop. 1; 94 km ENE of Praha; 50°06'/15°45'.

Stebne, see Stebni.

Stebni, Ukr. (Stebne); pop. 9; 75 km SW of Chernovtsy; 48°06'/24°59'.

Stebnik, Ukr.; pop. 30; 69 km SSW of Lvov; 49°18'/23°34'; AMG, EGRS, HSL, HSL2, PHP2.

Stebnik (near Drogobych), Ukr.; pop. 134; 69 km SSW of Lvov; 49°18'/23°34'.

Stechovice, Cz.; pop. 27; BGN lists two possible localities with this name located at 49°15'/13°46' and 49°51'/14°24'. JGFF.

Steckelsdorf, Germ.; 75 km W of Berlin; 52°36'/12°17'; GUM3.

Stecowa, see Stetseva.

Stedra, Cz.; pop. 20; BGN lists two possible localities with this name located at 50°03'/13°07' and 50°06'/12°33'.

Stefan, see Stepan.

Stefanesti, see Shtefaneshty.

Stefanesti Soroca, see Shtefaneshty.

Stefankowice, Pol. (Stepankowice); pop. 52; 101 km ESE of Lublin; 50°55'/23°51'.

Steffenshagen, Germ.; 107 km S of Rostock; 53°12'/12°07'; HSL.

Stefkowa, see Stetkowa.

Stegersbach, Aus.; pop. 2; 56 km ENE of Graz; 47°10'/16°10'.

Stehelceves, Cz.; pop. 3; 19 km WNW of Praha; 50°10'/14°12'.

Steibtz, see Stolbtsy.

Steimel, Germ.; pop. 16; 62 km ESE of Koln; 50°37'/07°38'.

Stein, see Stein an der Donau.

Steinach, see Steinach an der Saale.

Steinach an der Saale, Germ. (Steinach); pop. 36; 101 km ENE of Frankfurt am Main; 50°17'/10°06'; EJ, GED, GUM3, GUM5, HSL, HSL2, LDS, PHGB.

Steinamanger, see Szombathely.

Stein am Kocher, Germ.; pop. 12; 62 km N of Stuttgart; 49°16'/09°18'; PHGBW.

Stein an der Donau, Aus. (Stein); pop. 80; 62 km WNW of Wien; 48°24'/15°35'; EDRD, JGFF.

Steinau am Oder, see Scinawa.

Steinbach, (Gyekes, Gyerkes); HSL, HSL2, JGFF. a number of towns share this name. It was not possible to determine from available information which one is being referenced.

Steinbach (Bavaria), Germ.; 62 km E of Frankfurt am Main; 50°01'/09°36'; PHGB.

Steinbach (Hessen), Germ.; 56 km N of Frankfurt am Main; 50°33'/08°47'; LDS.

Steinbach (Wurttemberg), Germ.; 56 km NE of Stuttgart; 49°06'/09°45'; PHGBW.

Steinbach am Donnersberg, Germ.; pop. 22; 75 km SSW of Frankfurt am Main; 49°36'/07°57'; GED.

Steinbach am Glan, Germ.; pop. 34; GED. Described in the *Black Book* as being in the Rheinland-Pfalz region of Germany, this town was not found in BGN gazetteers.

Steinbach bei Hall, Germ.; 56 km NE of Stuttgart; 49°06'/09°45'; HSL.

Stein bei Nurnberg, Germ.; 13 km SW of Nurnberg; 49°25'/11°01'; PHGB.

Steinberg, Germ.; 56 km N of Frankfurt am Main; 50°32'/08°42'; AMG, LDS.

Steinberg (Bavaria), Germ. PHGB. This town was not found in BGN gazetteers under the given spelling.

Steinbergen, Germ.; 45 km SW of Hannover; 52°13'/09°07';

GED.

Stein Bockenheim, Germ.; 62 km SW of Frankfurt am Main; 49°46'/07°58'; JGFF.

Steinbruch, GUM5. a number of towns share this name. It was not possible to determine from available information which one is being referenced.

Steinfurth, Germ.; 38 km N of Frankfurt am Main; 50°24'/08°45'; LDS.

Steinhart, Germ.; 69 km SSW of Nurnberg; 48°58'/10°40'; HSL, PHGB.

Steinhausen Bielsk Podlaski, SF. This town was not found in BGN gazetteers under the given spelling.

Steinheim, Germ.; pop. 69; 69 km SSW of Hannover; 51°51'/09°06'; GED, LDS.

Steinheim am Main, Germ.; pop. 49; 19 km E of Frankfurt am Main; 50°07'/08°55'.

Steinhude, Germ.; 26 km WNW of Hannover; 52°27'/09°21'; GED.

Steinitz, see Zdanice.

Steinsfurt, Germ.; pop. 36; 56 km NNW of Stuttgart; 49°14'/08°55'; LDS.

Stejera, Rom.; pop. 2; 82 km NNW of Cluj; 47°27'/23°26'.

Steken, Cz.; pop. 2; 94 km S of Praha; 49°16'/14°01'.

Steklinek, Pol.; pop. 6; 139 km NNW of Lodz; 52°58'/19°00'.

Stelbach, see Tichy Potok.

Stempina, see Stepina.

Stendal, Germ.; pop. 62; 107 km W of Berlin; 52°36'/11°51'; EJ, HSL, LDS.

Stende, Lat. (Stenden); 101 km W of Riga; 57°11'/22°33'; PHLE.

Stenden, see Stende.

Steniatyn, Pol.; pop. 24; 107 km NNE of Przemysl; 50°31'/23°47'. See also Stenyatin.

Stenovice, Cz.; pop. 13; 88 km SW of Praha; 49°40'/13°24'; HSL, HSL2.

Stenyatin, Ukr. (Steniatyn); pop. 99; 82 km N of Lvov; 50°32'/24°22'; EDRD, EJ.

Stepan, Ukr. (Stefan, Szczepan); pop. 1,325; 62 km N of Rovno; 51°08'/26°18'; AMG, COH, GUM3, GUM4, JGFF, LDL, SF, YB.

Stepanchi, see Stepanki.

Stepancy, see Stepantsy.

Stepangorod, Ukr. (Stepangrod); pop. 60; 120 km N of Rovno; 51°38'/26°11'.

Stepangrod, see Stepangorod.

Stepanki, Ukr. (Stepanchi); 69 km SSW of Vinnitsa; 48°47'/27°52'; GUM5, PHR1.

Stepankowice, see Stefankowice.

Stepantsy, Ukr. (Stepancy, Stepnitz); 101 km SE of Kiyev; 49°42'/31°18'; EDRD, LDL, SF.

Stepina, Pol. (Stempina); pop. 4; 88 km W of Przemysl; 49°53'/21°34'; PHP3.

Stepkow, Pol.; pop. 10; 50 km NNE of Lublin; 51°37'/22°57'.

Stepnitz, see Stepantsy.

Stepocice, Pol.; pop. 29; 50 km NNE of Krakow; 50°26'/20°20'.

Steppach, Germ.; 38 km NW of Nurnberg; 49°46'/10°48'; HSL, HSL2, PHGB, PHGB.

Sterbfritz, Germ.; pop. 95; 69 km NE of Frankfurt am Main; 50°19'/09°37'; LDS.

Sterdin, see Sterdyn.

Sterdyn, Pol. (Esterdin, Sterdin); pop. 710; 82 km SW of Bialystok; 52°35'/22°18'; COH, EDRD, GA, GUM4, GUM5, HSL, LYV, SF.

Sterkowitz, see Strkovice.

Sterkrade, Germ.; pop. 90; 62 km N of Koln; 51°28'/06°52'. Sterkrade is now part of Oberhausen, Germany.

Sternberg, Germ.; pop. 2; 50 km SSW of Rostock; 53°42'/11°49'. See also Sternberk.

Sternberg Barntrup, Germ.; 62 km SW of Hannover; 52°02'/08°56'; LDS.

Sternberk, Cz. (Sternberg); pop. 94; 82 km NNE of Brno;

49°44'/17°18'; HSL, LDS.

Stertzev, see Szczercow.

Sterzhausen, Germ.; pop. 6; 88 km N of Frankfurt am Main; 50°51'/08°42'; LDS.

Sterzyca, GA. This town was not found in BGN gazetteers under the given spelling.

Steti, Cz.; pop. 43; 45 km NNW of Praha; 50°27'/14°23'.

Stetkowa, Pol. (Stefkowa); pop. 41; 45 km SSW of Przemysl; 49°26'/22°30'; HSL.

Stetseva, Ukr. (Stecowa, Stetsova); pop. 118; 38 km WNW of Chernovtsy; 48°31'/25°34'; PHP2.

Stetsova, see Stetseva.

Stetteldorf, see Stetteldorf am Wagram.

Stetteldorf am Wagram, Aus. (Stetteldorf); pop. 6; 32 km WNW of Wien; 48°24'/16°01'.

Stettin, see Szczecin.

Steypts, see Stolbtsy.

Steyr, Aus.; pop. 78; 107 km ENE of Salzburg; 48°03'/14°25'; CAHJP, GUM3, GUM5.

Stezery, Cz.; pop. 3; 94 km ENE of Praha; 50°13'/15°45'.

Steznica, Pol.; pop. 34; 62 km SSW of Przemysl; 49°20'/22°20'.

Stezyca, Pol.; pop. 125; 69 km WNW of Lublin; 51°35'/21°47'; HSL.

St Gheorghe, see Sfintu Gheorghe.

Stiene, Lat.; pop. 1; 56 km NNE of Riga; 57°26'/24°32'.

Stilskoye, Ukr. (Stulsko); pop. 27; 45 km SSE of Lvov; 49°32'/24°05'.

Stina, Rom. (Felsonyarto, Stana Salaj); pop. 26; 94 km NW of Cluj; 47°31'/22°58'.

Stinceni, Rom. (Godemesterhaza, Stanceni); pop. 35; 126 km ENE of Cluj; 46°59'/25°14'.

Stinka, Ukr. (Scianka, Stsyanka); pop. 47; 88 km NW of Chernovtsy; 48°55'/25°15'.

Stinkenbrunn, Aus.; pop. 3; 45 km S of Wien; 47°50'/16°25'.

Stip, Yug.; pop. 626; 69 km ESE of Skopje; 41°44'/22°12'; PHY.

Stipshausen, Germ.; pop. 14; 101 km WSW of Frankfurt am Main; 49°51'/07°17'.

Stirciu, Rom. (Bogdanhaza, Starciu); pop. 62 km WNW of Cluj; 47°05'/22°55'; HSL.

Stirin, Cz.; pop. 6; 26 km SE of Praha; 49°55'/14°36'.

Stitchin, see Szczucin.

Stitnik, Cz. (Csetnik); pop. 71; 62 km WSW of Kosice; 48°40'/20°22'; HSL.

Stitsin, see Szczucin.

Stiubieni, see Shtubiyeny.

Stiyanev, see Stoyanov.

Stizhemeshitz, see Strzemieszyce Wielkie.

Stobiecko Miejskie, Pol.; pop. 15; 38 km NNE of Czestochowa; 51°05'/19°23'.

Stobierna, Pol.; pop. 67; 62 km WNW of Przemysl; 50°09'/22°05'.

Stoboru, Rom.; pop. 2; 32 km WNW of Cluj; 46°56'/23°17'.

Stobychwa, see Stobykhva.

Stobykhva, Ukr. (Stabichov, Stobychwa); 114 km NW of Rovno; 51°24'/25°11'; SF.

Stochek, see Stoczek.

Stochek Lukovski, see Stoczek Lukowski.

Stock, HSL. a number of towns share this name. It was not possible to determine from available information which one is being referenced.

Stocka, Pol. AMG. a number of towns share this name. It was not possible to determine from available information which one is being referenced.

Stockach, Germ.; 107 km S of Stuttgart; 47°51'/09°01'; GUM4, PHGBW.

Stockerau, Aus.; pop. 104; 26 km NW of Wien; 48°23'/16°13'; AMG.

Stockheim, Germ.; 38 km NE of Frankfurt am Main; 50°20'/09°01'; LDS.

Stoczek, Pol. (Stochek); pop. 1,962; 56 km SE of Warszawa; 51°53'/21°31'; AMG, COH, GUM3, GUM5, JGFF, LYV.

Stoczek (Bialystok), Pol.; pop. 112; 69 km ESE of Bialystok; 52°42'/23°52'.

Stoczek (near Lochow), Pol. (Stok); pop. 1,221; 69 km NE of Warszawa; 52°33'/21°54'; GA, GUM4, GUM5.

Stoczek Gajowka, Pol.; pop. 33; Described in the *Black Book* as being in the Lublin region of Poland, this town was not found in BGN gazetteers.

Stoczek Lukowski, Pol. (Stochek Lukovski); 75 km ESE of Warszawa; 51°57'/21°58'; LDL, LYV, POCEM, SF.

Stod, Cz.; pop. 49; 107 km SW of Praha; 49°38'/13°10'.

Stodolichi, USSR (Stodolishche); pop. 329; 82 km SE of Smolensk; 54°10'/32°38'.

Stodolishche, *see* Stodolichi.

Stodolna, Mold.; pop. 17; 69 km N of Kishinev; 47°33'/29°01'.

Stodoly, Pol.; pop. 22; 82 km SW of Lublin; 50°49'/21°35'.

Stoiana, Rom. (Eszteny); pop. 9; 32 km N of Cluj; 47°01'/23°41'.

Stoibtz, *see* Stolbtsy.

Stoicani, *see* Stoykany.

Stojaciszka, *see* Svencionys.

Stojaciszki, COH, GUM3, YB. This town was not found in BGN gazetteers under the given spelling.

Stojadla, Pol.; pop. 11; 38 km E of Warszawa; 52°11'/21°32'.

Stojance, *see* Stoyantsy.

Stojanow, *see* Stoyanov.

Stojeszyn, Pol.; pop. 22; 56 km S of Lublin; 50°46'/22°17'.

Stojice, Cz.; 82 km E of Praha; 49°58'/15°37'; HSL.

Stojowice, Pol.; pop. 6; 26 km SE of Krakow; 49°54'/20°03'.

Stok, Pol.; pop. 167; 69 km NE of Warszawa; 52°33'/21°54'; COH, GUM3, GUM4, HSL, PHP4, YB. *See also* Stoczek (near Lochow).

Stoki Male, Pol.; pop. 7; 75 km SW of Lublin; 50°58'/21°33'.

Stoki Stare, Pol.; pop. 6; 75 km SW of Lublin; 50°58'/21°33'.

Stok Lacki, Pol.; pop. 39; 94 km E of Warszawa; 52°10'/22°21'.

Stoklishok, *see* Stakliskes.

Stokov, Cz.; pop. 3; 133 km WSW of Praha; 49°51'/12°38'.

Stok Ruski, Pol.; pop. 3; 101 km E of Warszawa; 52°13'/22°27'; GA, GUM3, GUM5.

Stoky, Cz.; pop. 33; 88 km WNW of Brno; 49°30'/15°35'.

Stolany, Cz.; pop. 3; 94 km E of Praha; 49°56'/15°45'.

Stolbtsy, Byel. (Shtoptsi, Shverzna, Shvyerzhen, Steibtz, Steypts, Stoibtz, Stolbtzi, Stolpts, Stopts, Stoybts, Stoypts, Stoyvetz, Sverzhne, Swierzen); pop. 1,428; 69 km SW of Minsk; 53°29'/26°44'; AMG, COH, EDRD, EJ, GUM3, GUM4, GUM5, GUM6, HSL, JGFF, LDL, PHP1, SF, YB.

Stolbtzi, *see* Stolbtsy.

Stolevitch, *see* Stolovichi.

Stolin, Byel.; pop. 2,966; 56 km ESE of Pinsk; 51°53'/26°51'; AMG, COH, EDRD, EJ, GA, GUM4, GUM5, GYLA, HSL, HSL2, JGFF, LDL, LYV, PHP4, SF, YB.

Stollhofen, Germ.; 82 km WSW of Stuttgart; 48°46'/08°03'; LDS, PHGBW.

Stolniceni, *see* Stolnicheny.

Stolniceni (I), *see* Stolnichany.

Stolnichany, Mold. (Stolniceni [I]); pop. 20; 157 km NW of Kishinev; 48°03'/27°21'.

Stolnicheny, Mold. (Stolniceni); pop. 32; 94 km WNW of Kishinev; 47°25'/27°43'.

Stolniki, Pol.; pop. 4; 62 km E of Lodz; 51°40'/20°23'.

Stolno, Pol.; pop. 3; 120 km S of Gdansk; 53°19'/18°31'.

Stolovichi, Byel. (Stolevitch, Stolowicze, Stolowitschi); pop. 251; 120 km SW of Minsk; 53°13'/26°02'; GUM3, HSL, SF.

Stolowicze, *see* Stolovichi.

Stolowitschi, *see* Stolovichi.

Stolp, *see* Slupsk.

Stolpe, Germ.; 69 km NE of Berlin; 52°59'/14°07'; HSL.

Stolpno, *see* Miedzyrzec Podlaski.

Stolpts, *see* Stolbtsy.

Stolzenau, Germ.; pop. 35; 45 km WNW of Hannover; 52°31'/09°04'; JGFF.

Stomfa, *see* Stupava.

Stommeln, Germ.; 19 km WNW of Koln; 51°01'/06°46'; GED, YB.

Stomporkov, *see* Staporkow.

Stoob, Aus.; pop. 8; 82 km S of Wien; 47°31'/16°28'.

Stopchatuv, Ukr. (Stopczatow); pop. 32; 69 km W of Chernovtsy; 48°25'/24°59'.

Stopczatow, *see* Stopchatuv.

Stopini, Lat.; pop. 12; 19 km E of Riga; 56°56'/24°23'.

Stopnica, Pol. (Stabnits, Stopnits, Stopnitsa, Stovnitz, Stoybnits); pop. 3,328; 82 km NE of Krakow; 50°26'/20°57'; AMG, COH, EDRD, EJ, FRG, GA, GUM3, GUM4, GUM5, GYLA, HSL, JGFF, LDS, LYV, POCEM, SF.

Stopnits, *see* Stopnica.

Stopnitsa, *see* Stopnica.

Stoptchet, *see* Yablonov.

Stopts, *see* Stolbtsy.

Storchnest, *see* Osieczna.

Stordjinet, *see* Storozhinets.

Storkow, Germ.; 45 km ESE of Berlin; 52°15'/13°56'; CAHJP, JGFF, LDS.

Storndorf, Germ.; pop. 28; 75 km NNE of Frankfurt am Main; 50°39'/09°16'.

Storojinet, *see* Storozhinets.

Storojineti, *see* Storozhinets.

Storona, Ukr. (Stronna); pop. 34; 82 km SW of Lvov; 49°20'/23°12'.

Storozhinets, Ukr. (Stordjinet, Storojinet, Storojineti, Storozynetz, Strizinitz, Strozynetz); pop. 2,482; 26 km SW of Chernovtsy; 48°10'/25°43'; COH, EDRD, EJ, GUM4, GYLA, HSL, HSL2, JGFF, LDL, PHR2, SF.

Storozhov, Ukr. (Storozhuv, Storozow); pop. 36; 69 km ENE of Rovno; 50°44'/27°16'.

Storozhuv, *see* Storozhov.

Storozow, *see* Storozhov.

Storozynetz, *see* Storozhinets.

Stoshany, Byel. (Stoszany); pop. 28; 32 km N of Pinsk; 52°19'/26°08'.

Stoszany, *see* Stoshany.

Stottera, Aus.; pop. 2; 56 km SSE of Wien; 47°46'/16°28'.

Stovnitz, *see* Stopnica.

Stoyanov, Ukr. (Stiyanev, Stojanow, Stoyanuv); pop. 657; 75 km NNE of Lvov; 50°22'/24°39'; AMG, EGRS, HSL, JGFF, PHP2, SF, YB.

Stoyantse, *see* Stoyantsy.

Stoyantsy, Ukr. (Stojance, Stoyantse); pop. 47; 50 km WSW of Lvov; 49°46'/23°17'.

Stoyanuv, *see* Stoyanov.

Stoybnits, *see* Stopnica.

Stoybts, *see* Stolbtsy.

Stoykany, Mold. (Stoicani); pop. 26; 120 km NNW of Kishinev; 48°03'/28°22'.

Stoypts, *see* Stolbtsy.

Stoyvetz, *see* Stolbtsy.

St Palten, *see* Sankt Polten.

St Poelten Stadt, *see* Sankt Polten.

Strabicovo, *see* Skrabske.

Strabla, Pol.; pop. 1; 32 km S of Bialystok; 52°54'/23°07'.

Strachocina, Pol.; pop. 17; 50 km SW of Przemysl; 49°37'/22°06'; HSL.

Strachovitza, *see* Wierzbnik.

Strachowka, Pol.; pop. 27; 50 km NE of Warszawa; 52°26'/21°39'; PHP4.

Stradlice, Pol.; pop. 6; 50 km NE of Krakow; 50°15'/20°32'.

Stradom, Pol. EJ. Stradom does not appear in contemporary gazetteers, but is described in EJ as being near Krakow.

Stradomka, Pol.; pop. 6; 32 km ESE of Krakow; 49°56'/20°19'.

Straelen, Germ.; pop. 15; 75 km NW of Koln; 51°27'/06°16'.

Straja, Rom.; pop. 134; 170 km WNW of Iasi; 47°55'/25°33'.

Strakonice, Cz.; pop. 178; 101 km SSW of Praha; 49°16'/13°54'; HSL, JGFF.

Stralo, GUM3. This town was not found in BGN gazetteers

under the given spelling.

Stralsund, Germ.; pop. 140; 62 km NE of Rostock; 54°18'/13°06'; CAHJP, EDRD, HSL.

Stramba, see Strymba.

Strambu Baiutului, see Strimbu Baiut.

Stramtura, see Strimtura.

Strananny, Cz. (Sztrainyan); 50 km ENE of Kosice; 48°46'/21°56'; HSL.

Strancice, Cz.; pop. 3; 19 km ESE of Praha; 49°57'/14°41'.

Stranny, Cz.; pop. 5; 45 km S of Praha; 49°45'/14°30'.

Strascheny, see Strasheny.

Straschitz, see Strasice.

Straseni, see Strasheny.

Strasheny, Mold. (Strascheny, Straseni); pop. 73; 26 km WNW of Kishinev; 47°08'/28°36'; EDRD.

Strashevitse, Ukr. (Straszewice); pop. 95; 82 km SW of Lvov; 49°27'/23°04'.

Strasice, Cz. (Straschitz); 62 km SW of Praha; 49°44'/13°46'; HSL, HSL2.

Strasov, Cz.; pop. 4; 75 km E of Praha; 50°05'/15°31'.

Strassburg, see Aiud.

Strassgang, Aus.; pop. 31; 6 km SW of Graz; 47°02'/15°24'.

Strassnitz, see Straznice.

Strass Somerein, see Hegyeshalom.

Straszecin, Pol.; pop. 17; 107 km E of Krakow; 50°04'/21°22'.

Straszewice, see Strashevitse.

Straszydle, Pol.; pop. 15; 56 km W of Przemysl; 49°54'/21°59'.

Stratin, Ukr. (Stratyn, Stratyn Miasto, Stratyn Myasto, Stretin); pop. 155; 69 km ESE of Lvov; 49°28'/24°42'; EGRS, HSL, HSL2, LDL, PHP2, SF.

Stratyn, see Stratin.

Stratyn Miasto, see Stratin.

Stratyn Myasto, see Stratin.

Straubing, Germ.; pop. 110; 114 km NNE of Munchen; 48°53'/12°34'; EJ, GED, GUM3, HSL, PHGB.

Straupe, see Lielstraupe.

Strausberg, Germ.; pop. 36; 38 km ENE of Berlin; 52°35'/13°53'; AMG.

Strawczyn, Pol.; pop. 1; 94 km ENE of Czestochowa; 50°57'/20°25'.

Straz, Cz.; pop. 45; 126 km SW of Praha; 49°40'/12°47'; PHP4.

Strazde, Lat.; pop. 2; 82 km W of Riga; 57°08'/22°44'.

Strazdemuiza, see Strazdumuiza.

Strazdenhof, see Strazdumuiza.

Strazdumuiza, Lat. (Strazdemuiza, Strazdenhof, Strazdu Mujzha); 13 km NE of Riga; 56°59'/24°14'; EDRD, PHLE.

Strazdu Mujzha, see Strazdumuiza.

Straznice, Cz. (Strassnitz); pop. 282; 56 km ESE of Brno; 48°54'/17°19'; EJ, HSL, HSL2.

Strazow, Pol.; pop. 24; 56 km WNW of Przemysl; 50°04'/22°07'.

Strazske, Cz. (Ormezo); pop. 60; 50 km NE of Kosice; 48°52'/21°50'; HSL, JGFF.

Strba, Cz. (Csorba); 94 km WNW of Kosice; 49°04'/20°05'; HSL.

Strecno, Cz. (Sztrecsen); 157 km E of Brno; 49°11'/18°52'; AMG.

Streczyn, Pol. (Streczyn Nowy); pop. 29; 38 km E of Lublin; 51°15'/23°08'.

Streczyn Nowy, see Streczyn.

Streda nad Bodrog, see Streda nad Bodrogom.

Streda nad Bodrogom, Cz. (Bodrogszerdahely, Streda nad Bodrog, Streda nad Bodrok, Streda nad Bodrokom); pop. 127; 56 km ESE of Kosice; 48°22'/21°46'; HSL.

Streda nad Bodrok, see Streda nad Bodrogom.

Streda nad Bodrokom, see Streda nad Bodrogom.

Stredna Apsa, COH. This town was not found in BGN gazetteers under the given spelling.

Stredni Apsa, Rom. (Kozepapsa, Mitel Apsa); 139 km N of Cluj; 47°59'/23°54'; COH, GUM4, SM.

Stregoborzyce, Pol.; pop. 6; 26 km ENE of Krakow; 50°08'/20°18'.

Strehlen, see Strzelin.

Strekov, Cz. (Kert); pop. 66; 101 km ESE of Bratislava; 47°54'/18°25'; AMG.

Strekowa Gora, see Gora Strykowa.

Strelisk, see Novyye Strelishcha.

Streliske, Lith.; 101 km WNW of Siauliai; 56°24'/21°57'; AMG.

Strelitz, Germ.; 101 km NNW of Berlin; 53°20'/13°06'; CAHJP, HSL2, LDS.

Strelki, Ukr. (Strzylki); pop. 242; 94 km SW of Lvov; 49°20'/22°59'; PHP2, PHP3.

Strelna, USSR; pop. 41; 13 km SW of Leningrad; 59°51'/30°02'.

Strelno, see Strzelno.

Strelsk, Ukr. (Strzelsk); pop. 98; 94 km N of Rovno; 51°26'/26°39'.

Stremiltsh, see Strzemilcze.

Strenci, Lat. (Stackeln, Strencu); pop. 34; 120 km NE of Riga; 57°37'/25°41'; PHLE.

Strencu, see Strenci.

Strenice, Cz.; pop. 3; 45 km NNE of Praha; 50°24'/14°50'.

Streptov, Ukr. (Streptow); pop. 32; 38 km NE of Lvov; 50°02'/24°27'.

Streptow, see Streptov.

Streshin, Byel.; pop. 1,244; 69 km WNW of Gomel; 52°43'/30°07'; SF.

Stretin, see Stratin.

Strezimir, Cz.; pop. 19; 69 km SSE of Praha; 49°32'/14°37'.

Strezivojice, Cz.; pop. 3; 50 km N of Praha; 50°29'/14°33'.

Stri, see Stryy.

Stria, see Stryy.

Stribrniky, Cz.; pop. 3; 69 km NW of Praha; 50°40'/14°03'.

Stribro, Cz.; pop. 152; 114 km SW of Praha; 49°45'/13°00'.

Strichevka, USSR; EDRD. This town was not found in BGN gazetteers under the given spelling.

Striegau, see Strzegom.

Strigovo, Byel. (Strychowo, Stryhowo); pop. 15; 126 km W of Pinsk; 52°18'/24°17'.

Strikov, see Strykow.

Strilbichi, Ukr. (Strzelbic?, Stshelbitse); pop. 84; 88 km SW of Lvov; 49°27'/22°59'.

Strimba, HSL, HSL2. a number of towns share this name. It was not possible to determine from available information which one is being referenced.

Strimbu Baiut, Rom. (Strambu Baiutului); pop. 21; 101 km N of Cluj; 47°36'/23°59'.

Strimtere, see Strimtura.

Strimtura, Rom. (Sramtura, Stramtura, Strimtere, Szurdok); pop. 369; 120 km N of Cluj; 47°47'/24°08'; AMG, COH, GUM4, HSL, HSL2, PHR2, SM.

Strisev, see Strzyzow.

Strishuv, see Strzyzow.

Strisov, see Strusov.

Strizev, see Strzyzow.

Strizhavka, Ukr.; 13 km NNW of Vinnitsa; 49°19'/28°28'; GUM4.

Strizhuv, see Strzyzow.

Strizinitz, see Storozhinets.

Strizov, see Strzyzow.

Strkovice, Cz. (Sterkowitz); 62 km WNW of Praha; 50°20'/13°39'; JGFF.

Strmilov, Cz.; pop. 10; 107 km WSW of Brno; 49°10'/15°12'.

Strobin, Pol.; pop. 5; 62 km SW of Lodz; 51°20'/18°49'.

Strobow, Pol.; 50 km NE of Lodz; 51°55'/20°10'; PHP1.

Strojno, Lat.; 107 km W of Riga; 57°01'/22°19'; HSL. This town was located on a pre-World War I map, but does not appear in contemporary gazetteers.

Stromiec, Pol. (Stromiec Zagajnik); pop. 189; 75 km S of Warszawa; 51°39'/21°06'.

Stromiec Zagajnik, see Stromiec.

Stronibaby, Ukr.; 50 km ENE of Lvov; 49°56'/24°38'; HSL.

Stronie, Pol.; pop. 6; 32 km SSW of Krakow; 49°50'/19°40'.

Stronna, see Storona.

Stronsdorf, Aus.; pop. 1; 56 km N of Wien; 48°39'/16°17'.

Stropkov, Cz. (Sztropko); pop. 2,190; 56 km NNE of Kosice; 49°12'/21°39'; AMG, COH, GUM4, GUM6, HSL, JGFF, LDL, PHP2, PHP3, YB.

Stroza, Pol.; pop. 26; 45 km SSW of Lublin; 50°54'/22°16'.

Stroze, Pol. (Stroze Wyzne); pop. 49; 88 km ESE of Krakow; 49°40'/20°58'; HSL, PHP3.

Stroze Male, Pol.; pop. 4; 50 km SW of Przemysl; 49°33'/22°11'.

Stroze Wyzne, see Stroze.

Strozowka, Pol.; pop. 91; 101 km ESE of Krakow; 49°41'/21°08'.

Strozynetz, see Storozhinets.

Strubowiska, Pol.; pop. 22; 75 km S of Przemysl; 49°11'/22°25'.

Struchi Krasnye, USSR; pop. 77; This town was not found in BGN gazetteers under the given spelling.

Strugureni, Rom.; pop. 19; 50 km NE of Cluj; 46°59'/24°12'.

Strumbagalve, Lith. (Strumbaglow); 82 km SSW of Kaunas; 54°16'/23°20'; JGFF.

Strumbaglow, see Strumbagalve.

Strumica, Yug.; pop. 5; 114 km ESE of Skopje; 41°26'/22°39'.

Strumien, Pol.; pop. 56; 88 km WSW of Krakow; 49°55'/18°46'.

Strumilova, Pol. AMG, COH. This town was not found in BGN gazetteers under the given spelling.

Strumkovka, Ukr. (Surty, Szurte); pop. 149; 195 km SSW of Lvov; 48°30'/22°14'; HSL.

Strumok, Ukr. (Cismele); pop. 60; 133 km SW of Odessa; 45°43'/29°27'.

Strumpfelbrunn, Germ.; pop. 18; 75 km SSE of Frankfurt am Main; 49°28'/09°05'; GUM5, PHGBW.

Strupcice, Cz.; pop. 2; 82 km WNW of Praha; 50°28'/13°32'.

Strupice, Pol.; pop. 4; 101 km SW of Lublin; 50°54'/21°15'.

Strupiechow, Pol. BGN lists two possible localities with this name located at 51°42'/20°53' and 52°20'/21°55'. HSL.

Strupkow, see Strupkuv.

Strupkuv, Ukr. (Strupkow); pop. 24; 94 km WNW of Chernovtsy; 48°42'/24°49'.

Strusov, Ukr. (Strisov, Strusow); pop. 579; 120 km NNW of Chernovtsy; 49°20'/25°37'; AMG, EGRS, HSL, HSL2, JGFF, LDL, PHP2, SF, YB.

Strusow, see Strusov.

Strusy, Pol.; pop. 23; 94 km ENE of Warszawa; 52°16'/22°23'.

Strutin, Ukr. (Folvark, Folvarki, Folwarki Male); pop. 34; 62 km E of Lvov; 49°47'/24°55'.

Struza, Pol. BGN lists two possible localities with this name located at 50°54'/22°16' and 51°09'/22°55'. AMG.

Struzna, Cz. (Kysibl); pop. 6; 107 km W of Praha; 50°11'/13°00'.

Strwiazyk, Pol.; pop. 18; 45 km S of Przemysl; 49°27'/22°34'.

Stry, see Stryy.

Strychance, see Strygantse.

Strychowo, see Strigovo.

Strygantse, Ukr. (Strychance); pop. 35; BGN lists two possible localities with this name located at 49°01'/24°55' and 49°34'/24°51'.

Stryhowo, see Strigovo.

Stryj, see Stryy.

Stryje, see Stryy.

Stryjowka, Ukr.; pop. 22; 107 km S of Rovno; 49°45'/25°42'. This town was located on a pre-World War I map, but does not appear in contemporary gazetteers.

Strykow, Pol. (Strikov); pop. 1,998; 26 km NNE of Lodz; 51°54'/19°36'; AMG, CAHJP, GA, GUM5, HSL, HSL2, JGFF, LDL, LDS, LYV, PHP1, PHP4, SF.

Strymba, Mold. (Stramba); pop. 35; 120 km NW of Kishinev; 47°50'/27°50'.

Stryszawa, Pol.; pop. 29; 50 km SSW of Krakow; 49°43'/19°31'; PHP3.

Stryszow, Pol.; pop. 4; 38 km SSW of Krakow; 49°50'/19°37'; JGFF.

Stryy, Ukr. (Stri, Stria, Stry, Stryj, Stryje); pop. 10,988; 75 km S of Lvov; 49°15'/23°51'; AMG, CAHJP, COH, EDRD, EGRS, GA, GUM3, GUM4, GUM5, GUM6, GYLA, HSL, HSL2, JGFF, LDL, PHP2, SF, YB.

Strzalki, Pol.; pop. 29; a number of towns share this name. It was not possible to determine from available information which one is being referenced.

Strzalkow, Pol.; 45 km NNE of Czestochowa; 51°03'/19°29'; PHP1.

Strzalkowce, see Stshalkovtse.

Strzegom, Pol. (Striegau); pop. 74; 50 km WSW of Wroclaw; 50°58'/16°21'; GUM3, LDS, POCEM.

Strzegowo, Pol. (Schegove, Schegovo, St Chegova, Strzygov); pop. 591; 88 km NW of Warszawa; 52°54'/20°17'; AMG, COH, EDRD, GA, GUM3, GUM4, GUM5, HSL, LDL, LYV, PHP4, POCEM, SF, YB.

Strzelbic, possibly Strilbichi.

Strzelce, see Strzelce Opolskie.

Strzelce Krajenskie, Pol. (Friedeberg); pop. 55; 94 km ESE of Szczecin; 52°52'/15°32'; CAHJP, LDS.

Strzelce Opolskie, Pol. (Gross Strehlitz, Strzelce); pop. 145; 69 km SW of Czestochowa; 50°31'/18°18'; HSL, HSL2, LDS.

Strzelce Wielkie, Pol.; pop. 22; 50 km ENE of Krakow; 50°07'/20°35'.

Strzelcza, Ukr.; pop. 22; 62 km NNE of Lvov; 50°15'/24°35'. This town was located on an interwar map of Poland but does not appear in contemporary gazetteers. Map coordinates are approximate.

Strzelczyska, GUM4, PHP2. This town was not found in BGN gazetteers under the given spelling.

Strzelecin, Pol.; pop. 69; 69 km N of Poznan; 53°02'/16°57'; GUM3.

Strzelin, Pol. (Strehlen); pop. 36; 38 km SSE of Wroclaw; 50°47'/17°04'.

Strzeliska, see Novyye Strelishcha.

Strzeliska Nowe, see Novyye Strelishcha.

Strzeliska Stare, see Stsheliska Stare.

Strzelno, Pol. (Strelno); pop. 61; 88 km ENE of Poznan; 52°38'/18°12'; GUM5, HSL, JGFF.

Strzelsk, see Strelsk.

Strzemieszyce, see Strzemieszyce Wielkie.

Strzemieszyce Wielkie, Pol. (Schemeshits, Schemyeshitse, Stizhemeshitz, Strzemieszyce, Stumishts, Stushmishts); pop. 1,304; 56 km SSE of Czestochowa; 50°19'/19°17'; AMG, COH, EDRD, GUM3, GUM4, HSL, HSL2, PHP3, SF.

Strzemilcze, Ukr. (Stremiltsh); pop. 35; 75 km ENE of Lvov; 49°55'/25°05'; EGRS, PHP2, YB. This town was located on an interwar map of Poland but does not appear in contemporary gazetteers. Map coordinates are approximate.

Strzeszkowice Male, Pol.; pop. 5; 19 km SSW of Lublin; 51°09'/22°26'.

Strzeszyn, Pol.; pop. 25; 101 km ESE of Krakow; 49°44'/21°11'; GA, JGFF.

Strzewo, see Tczew.

Strzygov, see Strzegowo.

Strzylcze, possibly Novyye Strelishcha.

Strzylki, see Strelki.

Strzynew, GA. This town was not found in BGN gazetteers under the given spelling.

Strzyzow, Pol. (Schizuv, Strisev, Strishuv, Strizev, Strizhuv, Strizov); pop. 1,104; 75 km W of Przemysl; 49°52'/21°48'; AMG, COH, EGRS, FRG, GA, GUM3, GUM4, GUM5, HSL, HSL2, JGFF, LDL, LYV, PHP3, SF, YB.

Strzyzow (Lublin), Pol.; pop. 68; 114 km ESE of Lublin; 50°51'/24°02'.

Stshalkovtse, Ukr. (Strzalkowce); pop. 27; 56 km N of Chernovtsy; 48°46'/25°59'.

Stshelbitse, see Strilbichi.

Stsheliska Stare, Ukr. (Strzeliska Stare); pop. 24; 50 km SE of Lvov; 49°32'/24°25'.

Stsyanka, see Stinka.

Stubienko, Pol.; pop. 57; 19 km NNE of Przemysl; 49°55'/22°56'.

Stubig, Germ.; 62 km N of Nurnberg; 50°00'/11°05'; PHGB.

Stubnianske Teplice, see Turcianske Teplice.

Stubno, Pol.; pop. 25; 19 km NE of Przemysl; 49°54'/22°58'.

Stuchin, see Shchuchin.

Studena, see Nizhne Studenyy.

Studene, Cz.; 32 km S of Praha; 49°53'/14°29'; HSL.

Studene Vizhne, see Verkhne Studenyy.

Studenne, Pol.; pop. 11; 62 km S of Przemysl; 49°17'/22°27'.

Studiny, Ukr. (Studzinie); pop. 3; 101 km WNW of Rovno; 50°54'/24°51'.

Studna, see Verkhne Studenyy.

Studzianka, Pol.; 88 km NNE of Lublin; 51°56'/23°13'; GA.

Studzianki, Pol. (Studzianki Tartak); pop. 45; 45 km S of Lublin; 50°54'/22°25'.

Studzianki Tartak, see Studzianki.

Studzieniec, Pol.; pop. 24; 75 km NNE of Lodz; 52°23'/19°54'.

Studzinie, see Studiny.

Stuhlingen, Germ.; 126 km SSW of Stuttgart; 47°44'/08°26'; JGFF, PHGBW.

Stuhlweissenburg, see Szekesfehervar.

Stuhm, see Sztum.

Stulany, Cz.; 56 km N of Kosice; 49°09'/21°24'; HSL.

Stulln, Germ.; 75 km E of Nurnberg; 49°25'/12°08'; GUM5.

Stulno, Pol.; pop. 12; 75 km ENE of Lublin; 51°23'/23°37'.

Stulpicani, Rom.; pop. 151; 139 km W of Iasi; 47°28'/25°46'; PHR2.

Stulsko, see Stilskoye.

Stumishts, see Strzemieszyce Wielkie.

Stupava, Cz. (Stampfen, Stomfa); pop. 232; 19 km NNW of Bratislava; 48°17'/17°02'; HSL, LDL.

Stupki, Pol.; pop. 36; GUM3, GUM4, GUM5, PHP2. a number of towns share this name. It was not possible to determine from available information which one is being referenced.

Stuposiany, Pol.; pop. 77; 75 km S of Przemysl; 49°11'/22°42'.

Sturdzeny, Mold. (Sturzeni Balti); pop. 27; 146 km WNW of Kishinev; 47°55'/27°27'.

Sturzeni Balti, see Sturdzeny.

Sturzelberg, Germ.; 26 km NNW of Koln; 51°08'/06°49'; JGFF.

Sturzeni Tighina, Mold.; pop. 76; 75 km SE of Kishinev; 46°26'/29°17'.

Stushmishts, see Strzemieszyce Wielkie.

Stutchin, see Shchuchin.

Stutsin, see Szczucin.

Stuttgart, Germ. (Cannstatt); pop. 4,900; 150 km SSE of Frankfurt am Main; 48°46'/09°11'; AMG, EJ, GED, GUM3, GUM4, GUM5, GUM6, HSL, HSL2, ISH1, JGFF, LDL, PHGBW.

Stuttgart Cannstadt, Germ.; pop. 322; Described in the *Black Book* as being in the Baden-Wurttemberg region of Germany, this town was not found in BGN gazetteers.

Stutthof, see Sztutowo.

Stuzica, Byel.; 139 km NNW of Gomel; 53°40'/30°26'; HSL. This town was located on a pre-World War I map, but does not appear in contemporary gazetteers.

Stuzno, Pol.; pop. 3; 82 km ESE of Lodz; 51°21'/20°25'.

St Veit, see Sankt Veit im Pongau.

St Wendel, see Sankt Wendel.

Stydyn Maly, Ukr.; pop. 29; 50 km NNW of Rovno; 51°01'/26°10'.

Stydyn Velki, see Bolshoy Stydin.

Stydyn Wielki, see Bolshoy Stydin.

Stykow, Pol.; 101 km WSW of Lublin; 51°00'/21°09'; PHP3.

Stynawa, HSL. This pre-World War I community was not found in BGN gazetteers.

Stynawa Nizna, Ukr.; pop. 68; 126 km S of Lvov; 48°45'/23°35'. This town was located on an interwar map of Poland but does not appear in contemporary gazetteers. Map coordinates are approximate.

Suares, Rom. (Szovaros); 45 km N of Cluj; 47°08'/23°43'; HSL. This town was located on a pre-World War I map, but does not appear in contemporary gazetteers.

Subacius, Lith. (Sobotsh); pop. 352; 94 km E of Siauliai; 55°44'/24°47'; GUM3, HSL, LDL, SF, YL.

Subari, see Sbornyy.

Subata, Lat. (Shovits, Shubitz, Shubotch, Sovits, Subatas, Subate, Subbat); pop. 455; 45 km WNW of Daugavpils; 56°01'/25°54'; LDL, PHLE, SF.

Subatas, see Subata.

Subate, see Subata.

Subbat, see Subata.

Subbotniki, Byel. (Subotniki); pop. 55; 120 km W of Minsk; 54°06'/25°45'.

Subcarpathian Ruthenia; See Ruthenia.

Subina, Pol.; 38 km E of Lodz; 51°40'/19°57'; GUM5.

Subl, Germ.; pop. 120; This town was not found in BGN gazetteers under the given spelling.

Subory, see Sbornyy.

Subotica, Yug. (Maria Theresiopol, Szabadka); pop. 3,758; 157 km NNW of Beograd; 46°06'/19°40'; AMG, COH, EDRD, EJ, GUM4, HSL, HSL2, JGFF, PHY.

Subotniki, see Subbotniki.

Sucany, Cz. (Szuczan); pop. 120; 170 km E of Brno; 49°06'/19°00'; HSL.

Suceava, Rom. (Shutz, Suchava, Suczawa, Sutchava); pop. 3,533; 114 km WNW of Iasi; 47°38'/26°15'; AMG, EDRD, EJ, GUM4, GUM6, HSL, JGFF, LDL, PHP2, PHR2, SF.

Sucaveni, see Suchaveni.

Sucevita, Rom.; pop. 10; 157 km WNW of Iasi; 47°47'/25°43'.

Sucha, Pol. (Sukha, Sukhe); pop. 332; 45 km SSW of Krakow; 49°44'/19°36'; AMG, COH, EGRS, GUM3, GUM5, HSL, LYV, PHP3, SF, YB.

Sucha (near Radom), Pol.; pop. 204; 75 km W of Lublin; 51°26'/21°31'; HSL.

Sucha Beskidzka, GA. This town was not found in BGN gazetteers under the given spelling.

Sucha Bronka, see Bronka.

Suchadol, see Sukhodul.

Sucha Gorna, Pol.; pop. 11; 38 km WNW of Lodz; 51°59'/19°07'.

Suchaja Balta, possibly Sukhaya Balka Pervyy Uchastok.

Suchari, see Sukhari.

Suchary, see Sukhari.

Suchastov, see Sukhostav.

Suchava, see Suceava.

Suchaveni, Ukr. (Suceveni); pop. 33; 38 km S of Chernovtsy; 48°03'/25°50'; COH.

Suchawa, Pol.; pop. 31; 69 km NE of Lublin; 51°30'/23°26'; SF.

Sucha Wola, see Suchowola.

Sucha Wolka, Pol.; pop. 13; 62 km SW of Lublin; 50°55'/21°55'.

Suchcice, Pol.; pop. 22; 88 km NNE of Warszawa; 52°56'/21°39'.

Suchdol, Cz.; 107 km NE of Brno; 49°39'/17°56'; HSL.

Suchedniev, see Suchedniow.

Suchedniow, Pol. (Suchedniev, Sukhedniev); pop. 912; 120 km ENE of Czestochowa; 51°04'/20°50'; AMG, COH, EDRD, GA, GUM3, GUM4, GUM5, HSL, LDL, LYV, SF.

Suchelipie, Pol.; pop. 50; 50 km SE of Lublin; 50°54'/22°57'.

Suchestaw, Pol. PHP4. This town was not found in BGN gazetteers under the given spelling.

Suchocin, Pol.; 26 km NW of Warszawa; 52°25'/20°47'; YB.

Suchodol, see Sukhodul.

Suchodol Wypychy, Pol.; pop. 7; 107 km S of Bialystok; 52°11'/22°36'.

Suchodoly, Pol.; pop. 52; 32 km ESE of Lublin; 51°05'/22°58'; GUM4. See also Sukhodoly.

Suchomasty, Cz.; pop. 9; 32 km SW of Praha; 49°54'/14°04'.

Suchopol, see Sukhopol.

Suchorzow, Pol.; pop. 4; 107 km SSW of Lublin; 50°30'/21°35'.

Suchostan, see Sukhostav.

Suchostaw, see Sukhostav.

Suchowce, possibly Sukhnovtse.

Suchowola, Pol. (Sucha Wola); pop. 1,262; 56 km N of Bialystok; 53°35'/23°06'; AMG, EDRD, GA, HSL, HSL2, JGFF, POCEM, SF, WS, YB. See also Sukhovolya.

Suchowola (Lodz), Pol.; pop. 2; 50 km N of Czestochowa;

51°12'/19°04'.

Suchowola (Lwow), Pol.; pop. 40; 45 km N of Przemysl; 50°08'/23°01'.

Suchowola (near Parczew), Pol.; pop. 32; 56 km N of Lublin; 51°42'/22°44'; GUM5.

Suchozebry, Pol.; pop. 83; 82 km ENE of Warszawa; 52°16'/22°15'.

Suchteln, Germ.; pop. 27; 56 km WNW of Koln; 51°17'/06°23'.

Suchy Grunt, Pol.; pop. 13; 88 km ENE of Krakow; 50°16'/21°08'; AMG.

Suciu de Jos, Rom. (Suciul de Jos); 82 km N of Cluj; 47°27'/23°59'; HSL.

Suciu de Sus, Rom. (Felsoszocs, Felsoszucs, Suciul de Sus); pop. 75; 82 km N of Cluj; 47°26'/24°02'; HSL.

Suciul de Jos, *see* Suciu de Jos.

Suciul de Sus, *see* Suciu de Sus.

Sucutard, Rom.; pop. 14; 38 km NE of Cluj; 46°54'/24°04'.

Suczawa, *see* Suceava.

Sudak, Ukr.; pop. 26; 69 km E of Simferopol; 44°51'/34°58'; HSL.

Sudarca, *see* Sudarka.

Sudarg, *see* Sudargas.

Sudargai, *see* Sudargas.

Sudargas, Lith. (Sudarg, Sudargai, Sudargi); 82 km W of Kaunas; 55°03'/22°38'; HSL, LDL, YL.

Sudargi, *see* Sudargas.

Sudarka, Mold. (Sudarca); pop. 39; 170 km NW of Kishinev; 48°18'/27°47'.

Sudche, Ukr. (Sudcze); pop. 39; 139 km NNW of Rovno; 51°44'/25°35'.

Sudcze, *see* Sudche.

Sudejov, Cz.; pop. 5; 56 km ESE of Praha; 49°52'/15°06'.

Sudenburg, Germ.; 101 km NW of Leipzig; 52°06'/11°36'; EJ.

Sudheim, Germ.; pop. 5; 82 km SSE of Hannover; 51°40'/09°59'.

Sudilkov, Ukr.; pop. 1,842; 82 km ESE of Rovno; 50°10'/27°08'; HSL, JGFF, LDL, SF.

Sudkowice, *see* Sudokovitse.

Sudlohn, Germ.; 114 km N of Koln; 51°56'/06°52'; GED, GUM5, LDS.

Sudokovitse, USSR (Sudkowice); pop. 49; Described in the *Black Book* as being in the Lwow region of Poland, this town was not found in BGN gazetteers.

Sudomir, *see* Sandomierz.

Sudovaya Vishnya, Ukr. (Sadova Vishnia, Sadowa Wisnia, Sadowa Wiszna, Sadowa Wisznia, Sadowa Wisznia Miasto, Sandove Vishnie, Sondova Vishniah, Wisznia); pop. 1,039; 50 km WSW of Lvov; 49°47'/23°22'; COH, EGRS, GUM3, GUM4, GUM5, GYLA, HSL, HSL2, LDL, LYV, PHP2, SF.

Sudurau, Rom. (Ersszodoro); pop. 1; 120 km WNW of Cluj; 47°32'/22°27'.

Sudzha, USSR; pop. 53; 88 km SW of Kursk; 51°12'/35°15'.

Sudzuna, LDL. This pre-World War I community was not found in BGN gazetteers.

Suedasai, COH. This town was not found in BGN gazetteers under the given spelling.

Sufczyce, Pol.; pop. 13; 94 km NE of Krakow; 50°28'/21°05'.

Sufczyna, Pol.; pop. 30; 26 km WSW of Przemysl; 49°44'/22°29'.

Sugatag, *see* Satu Sugatag.

Sugatag Sat, *see* Satu Sugatag.

Sugenheim, Germ.; pop. 56; 50 km WNW of Nurnberg; 49°36'/10°26'; CAHJP, GUM5, PHGB.

Suharau, Rom.; pop. 48; 139 km NW of Iasi; 48°08'/26°25'.

Suhl, Germ.; pop. 120; 133 km NNW of Nurnberg; 50°36'/10°42'; JGFF, LDS.

Suhopolje, Yug.; pop. 28; 120 km E of Zagreb; 45°48'/17°30'.

Suhoverca, Rom.; pop. 47; This town was not found in BGN gazetteers under the given spelling.

Suidine, *see* Sakiai.

Suiug, Rom.; pop. 20; 107 km WNW of Cluj; 47°19'/22°26'.

Suiunduc, *see* Chistovodnoye.

Sukach, Ukr. (Sukacze); pop. 29; 170 km WNW of Rovno; 51°25'/24°10'. This town was located on an interwar map of Poland but does not appear in contemporary gazetteers. Map coordinates are approximate.

Sukach (Polesie), Byel.; pop. 15; 82 km N of Pinsk; 52°47'/26°23'.

Sukacze, *see* Sukach.

Sukha, *see* Sucha.

Sukha Balka, (Soha Balca); PHR1. This town was not found in BGN gazetteers under the given spelling.

Sukhari, Byel. (Suchari, Suchary); 94 km NW of Minsk; 54°36'/26°55'; AMG, LDL, SF.

Sukhaya Balka, *see* Sukhaya Balka Pervyy Uchastok.

Sukhayabalka, *see* Sukhaya Balka Pervyy Uchastok.

Sukhaya Balka Pervyy Uchastok, Ukr. (Suchaja Balta?, Sukhaya Balka, Sukhayabalka); 114 km N of Odessa; 47°26'/31°11'; GUM3.

Sukhe, *see* Sucha.

Sukhedniev, *see* Suchedniow.

Sukhinichi, USSR; pop. 66; 120 km NNE of Bryansk; 54°07'/35°21'.

Sukhnovtse, Ukr. (Suchowce?); pop. 39; 107 km S of Rovno; 49°40'/26°03'.

Sukhodol, *see* Sukhodul.

Sukhodoly, Ukr. (Suchodoly); pop. 33; 82 km ENE of Lvov; 50°00'/25°07'; PHP2.

Sukhodul, Ukr. (Suchadol, Suchodol, Sukhodol); pop. 39; 126 km S of Lvov; 48°48'/24°01'; SF.

Sukhodul (Lwow), Ukr.; pop. 36; 32 km SE of Lvov; 49°37'/24°10'.

Sukhopol, Byel. (Suchopol); pop. 46; 150 km WNW of Pinsk; 52°39'/24°10'.

Sukhostav, Ukr. (Suchastov, Suchostan, Suchostaw); pop. 378; 94 km N of Chernovtsy; 49°08'/25°52'; EGRS, HSL, JGFF, PHP2, SF.

Sukhovole, *see* Sokolovka.

Sukhovolya, (Suchowola).

Sukhovolya (Polesie), Ukr.; pop. 9; 88 km NNW of Rovno; 51°20'/25°58'.

Sukhovolya (Tarnopol), Ukr.; pop. 23; 88 km ENE of Lvov; 50°00'/25°15'.

Sukhovolya (Wolyn), Ukr.; pop. 8; 75 km ENE of Rovno; 50°41'/27°19'; LYV.

Sukoro, Hung.; pop. 4; 50 km SW of Budapest; 47°14'/18°37'.

Sukosd, Hung.; pop. 48; 88 km W of Szeged; 46°17'/19°00'.

Sukowate, Pol.; pop. 6; 69 km SSW of Przemysl; 49°21'/22°12'.

Sula, Pol.; pop. 20; a number of towns share this name. It was not possible to determine from available information which one is being referenced.

Sulatycze, *see* Sulyatichi.

Sulbiny, Pol. (Sulbiny Dolne); pop. 37; 62 km ESE of Warszawa; 51°52'/21°39'.

Sulbiny Dolne, *see* Sulbiny.

Sulborowice, Pol.; pop. 18; 75 km NE of Czestochowa; 51°12'/20°02'.

Sulechow, Pol. (Zullichau); pop. 38; 101 km SW of Poznan; 52°05'/15°37'; HSL, LDS.

Sulecin, Pol. (Zielenzig); pop. 82; 120 km SSE of Szczecin; 52°26'/15°06'; POCEM.

Suleje, Pol.; pop. 47; 88 km N of Lublin; 51°58'/22°26'.

Sulejovice, Cz.; pop. 5; 56 km NW of Praha; 50°30'/14°03'.

Sulejow, Pol. (Siliyov, Suliyov); pop. 2,133; 56 km SE of Lodz; 51°22'/19°53'; AMG, CAHJP, GA, GUM3, GUM4, GUM5, HSL, JGFF, LDS, PHP1, SF.

Sulejow (Warszawa area), Pol.; pop. 24; 45 km NE of Warszawa; 52°27'/21°34'; PHP4.

Sulejowek, Pol.; pop. 42; 19 km E of Warszawa; 52°15'/21°17'; GA.

Sulelmed, *see* Ulmeni.

Sulgostow, Pol.; pop. 12; 88 km ESE of Lodz; 51°31'/20°38'.

Sulichevo, Byel. (Suliczewo); pop. 13; 75 km WSW of Pinsk; 52°06'/25°02'.

Suliczewo, *see* Sulichevo.

Sulina, Rom.; 270 km SE of Iasi; 45°09'/29°40'; GUM4.

Sulinci, Yug.; pop. 5; 120 km N of Zagreb; 46°50'/16°12'.

Sulingen, Germ.; pop. 27; 69 km WNW of Hannover; 52°41'/08°48'.

Sulislav, Cz.; pop. 4; 107 km SW of Praha; 49°45'/13°05'.

Sulita, *see* Novyye Selishty.

Sulita Sat, *see* Sulitsa Noua.

Sulita Targ, *see* Novyye Selishty.

Sulita Tirg, *see* Novyye Selishty.

Sulitsa Noua, Ukr. (Sulita Sat); pop. 126; 32 km ESE of Chernovtsy; 48°13'/26°17'.

Suliyov, *see* Sulejow.

Sulkovice, *see* Sulkowice.

Sulkowice, Pol. (Sulkovice); pop. 74; 32 km S of Krakow; 49°51'/19°48'; HSL, PHP3.

Sulkowszczyzna, Pol.; pop. 59; Described in the *Black Book* as being in the Lwow region of Poland, this town was not found in BGN gazetteers.

Sulmeizhitza, *see* Sulmierzyce.

Sulmice, Pol.; pop. 6; 69 km ESE of Lublin; 50°53'/23°19'.

Sulmierzyce, Pol. (Silmerzitz, Sulmeizhitza); pop. 343; 50 km N of Czestochowa; 51°11'/19°12'; AMG, CAHJP, PHP1, SF.

Suloszyn, Pol.; pop. 4; 45 km N of Lublin; 51°36'/22°31'.

Sulow, Pol.; pop. 30; 56 km SE of Lublin; 50°46'/22°58'; GA.

Sulowiec, Pol.; pop. 8; 56 km SE of Lublin; 50°47'/22°54'.

Sulyatichi, Ukr. (Sulatycze, Sulyatyche); pop. 42; 82 km SSE of Lvov; 49°12'/24°08'.

Sulyatyche, *see* Sulyatichi.

Sulz, Germ.; 62 km SSW of Stuttgart; 48°22'/08°38'; HSL, LDS, PHGBW.

Sulzbach, *see* Sulzbach am Main.

Sulzbach am Main, Germ. (Sulzbach); 38 km ESE of Frankfurt am Main; 49°54'/09°09'; CAHJP, EJ, HSL, HSL2, JGFF, PHGB.

Sulzbach Rosenberg, Germ.; 50 km ENE of Nurnberg; 49°30'/11°45'; PHGB.

Sulzbung, Germ.; pop. 42; Described in the *Black Book* as being in the Oberpfalz region of Germany, this town was not found in BGN gazetteers.

Sulzburg, Germ.; pop. 120; 150 km SW of Stuttgart; 47°51'/07°43'; CAHJP, GED, JGFF, PHGB, PHGBW.

Sulzburg Baden, *see* Bad Sulzburg.

Sulzdorf, *see* Sulzdorf an der Lederhecke.

Sulzdorf an der Lederhecke, Germ. (Sulzdorf); 94 km NNW of Nurnberg; 50°14'/10°34'; HSL, HSL2, PHGB.

Sulze, Germ.; 50 km NNE of Hannover; 52°46'/10°02'; LDS.

Sumal, Rom. (Somaly); pop. 17; 101 km WNW of Cluj; 47°17'/22°34'; HSL.

Sumeg, Hung.; pop. 296; 69 km N of Nagykanizsa; 46°59'/17°17'; EDRD, GUM5, LDS, PHH.

Sumilova, *see* Shumilovo.

Sumony, Hung.; pop. 4; 88 km ESE of Nagykanizsa; 45°58'/17°55'.

Sumperk, Cz. (Mahrisch Schonberg, Schoenberg); pop. 204; 94 km N of Brno; 49°58'/16°58'; AMG.

Sumuleu, Rom.; pop. 3; 157 km SW of Iasi; 46°23'/25°50'.

Sumy, Ukr. (Sumy R); pop. 2,418; 114 km ESE of Konotop; 50°54'/34°48'; HSL, LDL.

Sumy R, *see* Sumy.

Suncuius, Rom.; pop. 11; 82 km W of Cluj; 46°56'/22°32'.

Suniperk, *see* Vysluni.

Sunja, Yug.; pop. 9; 69 km SE of Zagreb; 45°21'/16°33'.

Suntazi, Lat.; pop. 1; 50 km E of Riga; 56°55'/24°57'.

Suplacu de Barcau, Rom. (Berettyoszeplak, Suplacul de Barcau); pop. 125; 94 km WNW of Cluj; 47°15'/22°32'; PHR2.

Suplacul de Barcau, *see* Suplacu de Barcau.

Suplingen, Germ.; 114 km E of Hannover; 52°17'/11°20';

GUM3.

Supranowka, *see* Supranuvka.

Supranuvka, Ukr. (Supranowka); pop. 29; 120 km S of Rovno; 49°33'/26°05'.

Suprashl, *see* Suprasl.

Suprasl, Pol. (Soprashl, Suprashl, Suprasle); pop. 390; 19 km NE of Bialystok; 53°13'/23°21'; COH, GUM3, GUM4, HSL, JGFF, LYV, PHP1, SF.

Suprasle, *see* Suprasl.

Supuru de Jos, Rom. (Alsoszopor, Alsoszouor, Soporul de Jos, Supurul de Jos); pop. 118; 94 km NW of Cluj; 47°28'/22°48'; HSL, PHR2.

Supuru de Sus, Rom. (Felsoszopor, Supurul de Sus); pop. 73; 101 km NW of Cluj; 47°26'/22°46'.

Supurul de Jos, *see* Supuru de Jos.

Supurul de Sus, *see* Supuru de Sus.

Sur, Hung. (Sar); pop. 16; 82 km WSW of Budapest; 47°22'/18°02'; HSL.

Surany, Cz. (Gross Surany, Nagy Surany, Nagysurany); pop. 772; 82 km E of Bratislava; 48°05'/18°11'; COH, EJ, HSL, HSL2, JGFF, LDL.

Surasch, USSR; EDRD. This town was not found in BGN gazetteers under the given spelling.

Suraz, Pol.; pop. 120; 26 km SSW of Bialystok; 52°57'/22°57'; CAHJP, LDL, LDS, SF.

Surazh, USSR; pop. 2,190; HSL, JGFF, SF. a number of towns share this name. It was not possible to determine from available information which one is being referenced.

Surazh (near Vitebsk), Byel.; pop. 669; 45 km NE of Vitebsk; 55°25'/30°44'; SF.

Surcea, Rom.; pop. 4; 170 km N of Bucuresti; 45°53'/26°05'.

Surchow, Pol.; pop. 5; 62 km ESE of Lublin; 50°56'/23°16'.

Surduc, Rom. (Elesdszurdok, Szurduk); pop. 125; 56 km NNW of Cluj; 47°15'/23°21'; HSL, PHR2.

Suri, *see* Shury.

Surochow, Pol.; pop. 42; 32 km N of Przemysl; 50°02'/22°46'.

Surowica, Pol.; pop. 19; 75 km SW of Przemysl; 49°27'/21°55'.

Surty, *see* Strumkovka.

Suruceni, *see* Surucheny.

Surucheny, Mold. (Suruceni); pop. 9; 13 km WSW of Kishinev; 46°59'/28°40'.

Surviliskis, Lith. (Shurvilishuk); pop. 104; 69 km N of Kaunas; 55°27'/24°02'; HSL, LDL, SF.

Susa, Yug.; 32 km ESE of Zagreb; 45°38'/16°17'; HSL.

Susak, Yug.; pop. 95; 133 km SW of Zagreb; 45°20'/14°26'; GUM4.

Susek, Yug.; pop. 3; 88 km WNW of Beograd; 45°13'/19°32'; HSL.

Susenii Bargaului, *see* Susenii Birgaului.

Susenii Birgaului, Rom. (Susenii Bargaului); pop. 49; 101 km NE of Cluj; 47°13'/24°42'.

Susetice, Cz.; pop. 6; 62 km S of Praha; 49°34'/14°30'.

Sushitsa Velikaya, Ukr. (Sushitsa Velka, Suszyca Wielka); pop. 35; 94 km SW of Lvov; 49°30'/22°50'.

Sushitsa Velka, *see* Sushitsa Velikaya.

Sushno, Ukr. (Suszno); pop. 31; 62 km NNE of Lvov; 50°20'/24°33'.

Susice, Cz.; pop. 132; 120 km SSW of Praha; 49°14'/13°31'; AMG.

Susiec, Pol.; pop. 15; 75 km N of Przemysl; 50°25'/23°12'.

Susk, Ukr.; pop. 32; BGN lists two possible localities with this name located at 50°47'/26°07' and 50°57'/25°26'. HSL.

Suskowola, Pol.; pop. 6; 75 km WNW of Lublin; 51°28'/21°29'.

Suskrajowice, Pol.; pop. 12; 82 km NE of Krakow; 50°33'/20°48'.

Susleni, *see* Susleny.

Susleny, Mold. (Susleni); pop. 110; 50 km N of Kishinev; 47°25'/28°59'.

Sussen, Germ.; 45 km E of Stuttgart; 48°41'/09°46'; PHGBW.

Susz, Pol. (Rosenberg); pop. 102; 82 km SE of Gdansk; 53°43'/19°21'; HSL, HSL2, JGFF, LDS. There was a second town in interwar Poland (pop. 32) named Rosenberg in the province of Lwow near Rawa Ruska. Its current name is not known.

Suszczyn, Ukr.; pop. 29; 88 km NNW of Chernovtsy; 49°05'/25°45'. This town was located on an interwar map of Poland but does not appear in contemporary gazetteers. Map coordinates are approximate.

Suszno, see Sushno.

Suszow, Pol.; pop. 12; 120 km NE of Przemysl; 50°33'/23°57'.

Suszyca Wielka, see Sushitsa Velikaya.

Sutchava, see Suceava.

Sutoru, Rom.; pop. 6; 38 km WNW of Cluj; 46°59'/23°15'.

Sutto, Hung.; pop. 5; 56 km WNW of Budapest; 47°45'/18°27'.

Suvainiskis, Lith. (Shuvinishok, Suvenishki, Suyainishok); 126 km ENE of Siauliai; 56°10'/25°17'; LDL, SF, YL.

Suvalk, see Suwalki.

Suvalki, see Suwalki.

Suvenishki, see Suvainiskis.

Suwalki, Pol. (Suvalk, Suvalki); pop. 5,747; 114 km NNW of Bialystok; 54°06'/22°56'; AMG, CAHJP, COH, EDRD, FRG, GUM3, GUM4, GUM5, HSL, HSL2, JGFF, LDL, LDS, LYV, PHP4, POCEM, SF, YB.

Suwin, Pol.; pop. 19; 45 km NNE of Warszawa; 52°35'/21°15'.

Suyainishok, see Suvainiskis.

Suza, Yug.; pop. 12; 170 km WNW of Beograd; 45°47'/18°47'.

Suzun, GUM4. This town was not found in BGN gazetteers under the given spelling.

Svalava, see Svalyava.

Svalavska Nelipa, GUM3. This town was not found in BGN gazetteers under the given spelling.

Svalyava, Ukr. (Svalava); pop. 6,535; 163 km SSW of Lvov; 48°33'/22°59'; AMG, GUM6, HSL, HSL2.

Svarichov, Ukr. (Svarychuv, Swaryczow); pop. 41; 107 km SSE of Lvov; 48°57'/24°11'; YB.

Svaritsevichi, Ukr. (Svarytseviche, Swarycewicze); pop. 54; 126 km N of Rovno; 51°43'/26°16'; GUM3, GUM4, GUM6.

Svarychuv, see Svarichov.

Svaryn, Ukr. (Swaryn, Swarynie); pop. 23; 176 km NW of Rovno; 51°58'/25°02'.

Svarytseviche, see Svaritsevichi.

Svati Mikulov, see Svaty Mikulas.

Svati Mikulow, see Mikulov.

Svatki, Byel. (Swatki); pop. 6; 101 km NNW of Minsk; 54°45'/27°05'.

Svatus, Cz. (Sentes, Sentus); pop. 99; 62 km E of Kosice; 48°41'/22°08'; JGFF.

Svatusa, Cz. (Senca, Sintchy); 94 km E of Bratislava; 48°07'/18°20'; LDL, SF.

Svaty Benadik, Cz. (Svaty Benedik); pop. 50; 114 km ENE of Bratislava; 48°21'/18°34'.

Svaty Benedik, see Svaty Benadik.

Svaty Jakub, Cz. (Szentjakab); 150 km W of Kosice; 48°46'/19°08'; HSL.

Svaty Jur, Cz.; pop. 125; 19 km NNE of Bratislava; 48°15'/17°13'; GUM4.

Svaty Mikulas, Cz. (Svati Mikulov); 88 km E of Bratislava; 47°56'/18°19'; GUM3.

Svedasai, Lith. (Shvidostch, Sviadoshts); pop. 245; 120 km N of Vilnius; 55°41'/25°22'; HSL, JGFF, SF, YL.

Sveksna, Lith. (Shvekshni, Shveksna, Svieksniai); pop. 519; 114 km SW of Siauliai; 55°31'/21°37'; GUM3, GUM4, GUM5, HSL, LDL, SF, YL.

Svenchan, see Svencionys.

Svencioneliai, Lith. (Nowe Swieciany); 69 km NNE of Vilnius; 55°10'/26°00'; COH, GUM3, YB.

Svencionys, Lith. (Shvintzion, Shvyentsiani, Shvyetsiani, Stojaciszka, Svenchan, Sventsian, Sventsiany, Sventzion, Swenziany, Swieciany); 75 km NE of Vilnius; 55°09'/26°10'; AMG, COH, GUM3, GUM4, GUM5, GUM6, HSL, JGFF, LDL, SF, YB.

Sventezeris, Lith.; pop. 23; 82 km S of Kaunas; 54°14'/23°39'.

Sventsian, see Svencionys.

Sventsiany, see Svencionys.

Sventzion, see Svencionys.

Sverdlov, see Sverdlovsk.

Sverdlovsk, Ukr. (Sverdlov); 69 km NNW of Simferopol; 45°29'/33°56'.

Sverzhna, see Novyy Sverzhen.

Sverzhne, see Stolbtsy.

Svessa, Ukr.; pop. 12; 94 km NNE of Konotop; 51°57'/33°57'.

Sveta Jana, see Gorica Svetojanska.

Svete, Lat.; pop. 1; 50 km SSW of Riga; 56°35'/23°40'.

Sveti Ivan Zabno, see Zabno.

Sveti Ivan Zelina, see Zelina.

Sveti Petar Cvrstec, see Cvrstec.

Svetla nad Sazavou, Cz. (Svetla nad Sazvou); pop. 79; 82 km ESE of Praha; 49°40'/15°24'.

Svetla nad Sazvou, see Svetla nad Sazavou.

Svetlice, Cz. (Vilag); 75 km NE of Kosice; 49°10'/22°02'; HSL.

Svetlodolinskoye, Ukr. (Lichtental); pop. 14; 101 km SW of Odessa; 46°05'/29°35'.

Svetlovodsk, Ukr. (Novo Georgijevsk, Novogeorgievsk, Novogeorgiyevsk); pop. 1,427; 146 km WNW of Dnepropetrovsk; 49°05'/33°15'; LDL, SF.

Svetnov, Cz.; pop. 2; 69 km WNW of Brno; 49°37'/15°57'.

Svetozarevo, Yug. (Jagodina); pop. 24; 114 km SE of Beograd; 43°59'/21°15'.

Sviadoshts, see Svedasai.

Svidnicka, Cz.; 82 km N of Kosice; 49°23'/21°34'; COH, HSL.

Svidnik, Ukr. (Swidnik); pop. 21; 94 km SSW of Lvov; 49°15'/23°09'.

Svidova, Ukr. (Swidowa); pop. 51; 69 km NNW of Chernovtsy; 48°52'/25°44'; GUM4, PHP2.

Sviecany, see Swiecany.

Svieksniai, see Sveksna.

Sviench, see Svinyukhi.

Svihov, Cz.; pop. 26; 107 km SW of Praha; 49°29'/13°17'; EJ, HSL.

Svilaj, Yug.; pop. 3; 176 km W of Beograd; 45°07'/18°18'.

Svilajnac, Yug.; pop. 6; 82 km SE of Beograd; 44°14'/21°11'.

Svilengrad, Bulg.; 208 km SSW of Varna; 41°46'/26°12'; GUM5.

Svinare, Cz.; pop. 10; 26 km SW of Praha; 49°54'/14°11'.

Svinarin, Ukr. (Swinarzyn); pop. 6; 120 km WNW of Rovno; 50°57'/24°40'.

Svinica, Cz. (Peto Szinnye); 19 km ENE of Kosice; 48°44'/21°28'; HSL.

Sviniochi, see Svinyukhi.

Svinomazy, Cz.; pop. 4; 101 km WSW of Praha; 49°50'/13°03'.

Svinyukhi, Ukr. (Pryvetroye, Sviench, Sviniochi, Swiniuchy); pop. 173; 101 km NNE of Lvov; 50°38'/24°45'; EDRD, GUM3, JGFF, SF. According to legend, Svinyukhi was once called Romanov to honor the czar. When the residents killed the royal tax collector, the czar changed the name in anger to Svinyukhi, which means "pig town."

Svionik, Cz. HSL2. This pre-World War I community was not found in BGN gazetteers.

Svir, Byel. (Shvir, Svyriai, Swir); 133 km NW of Minsk; 54°51'/26°24'; AMG, COH, GUM3, GUM4, GUM5, HSL, HSL2, JGFF, LYV, SF, YB.

Svirzh, Ukr. (Swirz); pop. 184; 45 km ESE of Lvov; 49°39'/24°26'; EGRS, GUM3, GUM4, PHP2, SF.

Svisloch, Byel. (Sislevitch, Sislevits, Sislevitsh, Svislovitch, Svislovitz, Swislocz); pop. 1,959; 170 km WNW of Pinsk; 53°02'/24°06'; COH, FRG, GUM3, GUM5, GYLA, HSL, JGFF, LDL, SF, YB.

Svisloch (near Bobruysk), Byel. (Svislotch); pop. 742; 107 km ESE of Minsk; 53°26'/28°59'; EJ, SF.

Svislotch, see Svisloch (near Bobruysk).

Svislovitch, see Svisloch.

Svislovitz, see Svisloch.

Svistelniki, Ukr. (Swistelniki); pop. 28; 88 km ESE of Lvov; 49°18'/24°48'.

Svitavy, Cz. (Zwittau); pop. 197; 69 km NNW of Brno; 49°45'/16°28'; EJ, GUM4, HSL.

Svitkov, Cz.; pop. 7; 88 km E of Praha; 50°02'/15°43'.

Svityaz, Ukr. (Switaz); pop. 42; 182 km N of Lvov; 51°29'/23°51'.

Svodin, Cz. (Seldin); pop. 74; 107 km E of Bratislava; 47°55'/18°30'.

Svojetice, Cz.; pop. 7; 26 km ESE of Praha; 49°58'/14°44'.

Svojetin, Cz.; pop. 8; 62 km W of Praha; 50°11'/13°37'.

Svojsin, Cz. (Schweissing); pop. 13; 120 km SW of Praha; 49°46'/12°55'; HSL.

Svorotva, Byel. (Sworotwa Mala, Sworotwa Wielka); pop. 24; 133 km SW of Minsk; 53°22'/25°47'; GUM3.

Svoyatichi, Byel. (Swojatycze); pop. 17; 120 km SW of Minsk; 53°09'/26°21'.

Svoychuv, Ukr. (Swojczow, Swojczowka); pop. 29; 120 km N of Lvov; 50°53'/24°32'.

Svrabov, Cz.; pop. 3; 75 km SSE of Praha; 49°27'/14°38'.

Svratka, Cz.; pop. 8; 75 km NW of Brno; 49°43'/16°02'.

Svyataya Volya, Byel. (Swieta Wola); pop. 185; 62 km NW of Pinsk; 52°32'/25°41'.

Svyatsk, USSR; pop. 588; 202 km SW of Bryansk; 52°40'/31°33'.

Svyriai, see Svir.

Swarycewicze, see Svaritsevichi.

Swaryczow, see Svarichov.

Swaryn, see Svaryn.

Swarynie, see Svaryn.

Swarzedz, Pol. (Schwersenz, Scldwersenz); pop. 61; 13 km E of Poznan; 52°25'/17°05'; CAHJP, EJ, GA, HSL, JGFF, PHP1.

Swarzow, Pol.; pop. 8; 75 km ENE of Krakow; 50°12'/20°57'.

Swatki, see Svatki.

Swedow, Pol.; pop. 2; 26 km N of Lodz; 51°55'/19°33'.

Swenziany, see Svencionys.

Swiadoszcz, LDL. This pre-World War I community was not found in BGN gazetteers.

Swiatkowa Wielka, Pol.; pop. 6; 101 km WSW of Przemysl; 49°32'/21°26'.

Swiatniki, Pol.; 13 km SW of Lodz; 51°42'/19°19'; JGFF.

Swicciany, Pol. PHP1. This town was not found in BGN gazetteers under the given spelling.

Swider, Pol.; pop. 45; 26 km ESE of Warszawa; 52°07'/21°15'; GUM4.

Swidle, Pol.; pop. 7; 75 km W of Lodz; 51°54'/18°25'.

Swidnica, Pol. (Schweidnitz); pop. 146; 45 km SW of Wroclaw; 50°51'/16°30'; EJ, GUM3, GUM4, HSL, LDS, POCEM.

Swidnik, see Svidnik.

Swidowa, see Svidova.

Swidry Stare, Pol.; pop. 31; 13 km NNW of Warszawa; 52°19'/20°58'.

Swidwin, Pol. (Schivelbein); pop. 148; 88 km NE of Szczecin; 53°46'/15°47'; JGFF.

Swiebodna, Pol.; pop. 18; 26 km WNW of Przemysl; 49°55'/22°27'.

Swiebodzice, Pol.; 50 km SW of Wroclaw; 50°52'/16°20'; POCEM.

Swiebodzin, Pol. (Schwiebus); pop. 90; 101 km WSW of Poznan; 52°15'/15°32'; GUM3.

Swiecany, Pol. (Sviecany); pop. 48; 101 km ESE of Krakow; 49°46'/21°17'; EDRD.

Swieciany, see Svencionys.

Swiecica, Pol. (Shvyentshitse); pop. 23; 88 km SW of Lublin; 50°43'/21°35'; FRG, GUM3.

Swiecie, Pol.; pop. 171; 107 km S of Gdansk; 53°25'/18°27'; EDRD.

Swieciechow, Pol.; pop. 21; 62 km SW of Lublin; 50°57'/21°52'.

Swiedziebnia, Pol.; pop. 5; 139 km WNW of Warszawa; 53°09'/19°33'.

Swiercna, see Novyy Sverzhen.

Swierczkow, Pol.; pop. 13; 69 km E of Krakow; 50°01'/20°55'.

Swierszczow, Pol.; pop. 6; 45 km ENE of Lublin; 51°20'/23°11'.

Swierzan Novy, see Novyy Sverzhen.

Swierze, Pol.; pop. 294; 82 km E of Lublin; 51°13'/23°44'; AMG, CAHJP, COH, GUM4, GUM5, HSL, HSL2, LDS, POCEM.

Swierze Gorne, Pol.; pop. 7; 75 km SE of Warszawa; 51°40'/21°29'.

Swierzen, see Stolbtsy.

Swierzen Nowy, see Novyy Sverzhen.

Swierzen Stary, possibly Novyy Sverzhen.

Swierzowa Ruska, Pol.; pop. 1; 101 km WSW of Przemysl; 49°33'/21°26'.

Swiesielice, Pol.; pop. 5; 69 km WSW of Lublin; 51°14'/21°38'.

Swieta Wola, see Svyataya Volya.

Swiete, Pol.; pop. 30; 19 km N of Przemysl; 49°55'/22°51'.

Swietochlowice, Pol.; 62 km S of Czestochowa; 50°17'/18°55'; AMG, GUM3, GUM4, PHP3.

Swietochow, Pol.; pop. 6; 38 km SSW of Warszawa; 51°58'/20°48'.

Swietochow Stary, Pol.; pop. 19; 56 km ENE of Warszawa; 52°23'/21°45'.

Swietoniowa, Pol.; pop. 4; 45 km NW of Przemysl; 50°06'/22°26'.

Swietoslaw, Pol.; pop. 13; 146 km NNW of Lodz; 53°00'/18°59'.

Swiety Krzyz, Pol.; pop. 9; 114 km SW of Lublin; 50°52'/21°03'; GUM4.

Swilcza, Pol.; pop. 58; 69 km WNW of Przemysl; 50°04'/21°55'; GUM5.

Swinarzyn, see Svinarin.

Swinemunde, see Swinoujscie.

Swiniuchy, see Svinyukhi.

Swinna Poreba, Pol.; pop. 5; 38 km SW of Krakow; 49°50'/19°32'.

Swinoujscie, Pol. (Swinemunde); pop. 70; 56 km NNW of Szczecin; 53°55'/14°15'.

Swir, see Svir.

Swirydy, Pol.; pop. 29; 45 km SSW of Bialystok; 52°48'/22°52'; GUM4, PHP4.

Swirz, see Svirzh.

Swislocz, see Svisloch.

Swisloczany, Pol.; pop. 10; 50 km E of Bialystok; 53°05'/23°52'.

Swistelniki, see Svistelniki.

Switarzow, Pol.; pop. 21; Described in the Black Book as being in the Lwow region of Poland, this town was not found in BGN gazetteers.

Switaz, see Svityaz.

Swojatycze, see Svoyatichi.

Swojczow, see Svoychuv.

Swojczowka, see Svoychuv.

Sworotwa Mala, see Svorotva.

Sworotwa Wielka, see Svorotva.

Swory, Pol.; pop. 27; 101 km N of Lublin; 52°05'/22°56'; JGFF.

Swoszowa, Pol.; pop. 17; 94 km E of Krakow; 49°51'/21°14'; PHP3.

Swoszowice, Pol.; pop. 90; 19 km S of Krakow; 49°59'/19°56'.

Syad, see Seda.

Syady, see Seda.

Syalava, Hung. HSL2. This pre-World War I community was not found in BGN gazetteers.

Syanki, Ukr. (Sianki); pop. 119; 126 km SSW of Lvov; 49°01'/22°54'; GUM4, PHP2.

Sycewicze, see Sychevichi.

Syche, Byel. (Syczew, Tzihav); 114 km SW of Minsk; 53°11'/26°20'; SF.

Sychevichi, Byel. (Sycewicze); pop. 5; 45 km NW of Minsk; 54°13'/27°14'.

Sychevka, Ukr.; pop. 327; 26 km W of Uman; 48°48'/29°52'.

Sychi, Byel. (Sycze); pop. 4; 182 km W of Pinsk; 52°13'/23°28'.

Sycina, Cz.; pop. 2; 50 km NE of Praha; 50°22'/14°56'.

Sycow, Pol. (Gross Wartenberg, Grosz Wartenberg); pop. 52; 56 km NE of Wroclaw; 51°18'/17°43'; LDS.

Sycyna, Pol. BGN lists two possible localities with this name located at 51°19'/21°37' and 52°02'/22°57'. JGFF.

Sycze, *see* Sychi.

Syczew, *see* Syche.

Syczow, Pol.; pop. 24; 88 km ESE of Lublin; 51°01'/23°45'.

Syczyn, Pol.; pop. 47; 45 km ENE of Lublin; 51°17'/23°15'.

Syeno, *see* Sienno.

Sygielki, *see* Sigelki.

Sygniowka, *see* Sygnyuvka.

Sygnyuvka, Ukr. (Sygniowka); pop. 158; 13 km SW of Lvov; 49°49'/23°57'.

Syhot Marmaroski, *see* Sighet.

Syke, Germ.; pop. 40; 82 km WNW of Hannover; 52°54'/08°50'.

Sykorice, Cz.; pop. 6; 38 km WSW of Praha; 50°02'/13°56'.

Symferopol, *see* Simferopol.

Symonoviche, *see* Simonovichi.

Symonow, *see* Simonov.

Symonowicze, *see* Simonovichi.

Synee, *see* Sejny.

Syngureny, Mold. (Singureni); pop. 19; 120 km NW of Kishinev; 47°50'/27°51'.

Synowodzko Nizne, Pol. PHP2. This town was not found in BGN gazetteers under the given spelling.

Synowodzko Wyzne, *see* Verkhneye Sinevidnoye.

Syretsk, GUM4, GUM5. This town was not found in BGN gazetteers under the given spelling.

Syrgiyeni, *see* Sergii.

Syrkovo, Mold. (Sarcova); pop. 61; 88 km N of Kishinev; 47°44'/28°49'.

Syrokomia, Pol. EDRD. This town was not found in BGN gazetteers under the given spelling.

Syrovatka, Cz.; pop. 1; 82 km ENE of Praha; 50°09'/15°40'.

Sytnica, *see* Sitnitsa.

Syulko, Ukr. (Siolko); pop. 51; 88 km SE of Lvov; 49°08'/24°30'.

Szaba, *see* Shabo.

Szabadbattyan, Hung.; pop. 8; 69 km SW of Budapest; 47°07'/18°23'.

Szabadegyhaza, Hung. (Szolgaegyhaza); pop. 18; 56 km SSW of Budapest; 47°04'/18°41'.

Szabadhidveg, Hung.; pop. 34; 94 km SSW of Budapest; 46°49'/18°17'.

Szabadka, *see* Subotica.

Szabadszallas, Hung.; pop. 120; 75 km SSE of Budapest; 46°53'/19°13'; HSL, HSL2, LDS, PHH.

Szabatist, LDL. This pre-World War I community was not found in BGN gazetteers.

Szabelnia, Ukr.; pop. 32; 26 km SW of Lvov; 49°45'/23°45'. This town was located on an interwar map of Poland but does not appear in contemporary gazetteers. Map coordinates are approximate.

Szabolcs, Hung.; pop. 5; 56 km ENE of Miskolc; 48°11'/21°30'; AMG, GUM4, HSL.

Szabolcsbaka, Hung.; pop. 83; 101 km ENE of Miskolc; 48°09'/22°09'; HSL, LDS, PHH.

Szabolcsveresmart, Hung. (Veresmart, Vorosmart); pop. 25; 94 km ENE of Miskolc; 48°18'/22°01'; HSL, LDS.

Szachy, *see* Shakhi.

Szack, *see* Shatsk.

Szacsur, *see* Sacurov.

Szada, Hung.; pop. 9; 26 km NE of Budapest; 47°38'/19°19'; HSL.

Szadek, Pol. (Shadek); pop. 800; 38 km WSW of Lodz; 51°41'/18°59'; AMG, COH, EDRD, GA, HSL, JGFF, LDS, PHP1, SF.

Szadello, *see* Zadiel.

Szadkowice, Pol.; 38 km WSW of Lodz; 51°40'/18°59'; POCEM.

Szadow, *see* Seduva.

Szaflary, Pol.; pop. 18; 75 km S of Krakow; 49°26'/20°02'.

Szajk, Hung.; pop. 4; 133 km WSW of Szeged; 45°59'/18°32'.

Szajol, Hung.; pop. 25; 101 km ESE of Budapest; 47°11'/20°18'.

Szajowka, Pol.; pop. 6; 56 km ESE of Lublin; 50°52'/23°09'.

Szak, Hung.; pop. 7; 69 km W of Budapest; 47°32'/18°11'.

Szakacsi, Hung.; pop. 12; 38 km N of Miskolc; 48°23'/20°52'.

Szakal, *see* Korosszakal.

Szakald, Hung.; pop. 29; 19 km SE of Miskolc; 47°57'/20°55'; HSL.

Szakaly, Hung.; pop. 16; 107 km ENE of Nagykanizsa; 46°32'/18°23'.

Szakasz, Rom.; 107 km NW of Cluj; 47°35'/22°53'; HSL. This town was located on a pre-World War I map, but does not appear in contemporary gazetteers.

Szakcs, Hung.; pop. 37; 88 km ENE of Nagykanizsa; 46°33'/18°07'.

Szaki, *see* Sakiai.

Szakmar, Hung.; 94 km WNW of Szeged; 46°34'/19°04'; GUM4.

Szakolca, *see* Szakolcza.

Szakolcza, (Szakolca); LDS. This town was not found in BGN gazetteers under the given spelling.

Szakoly, Hung.; pop. 76; 94 km ESE of Miskolc; 47°46'/21°55'; PHH.

Szakony, Hung.; pop. 8; 120 km NNW of Nagykanizsa; 47°26'/16°43'.

Szala, Cz.; 126 km E of Kosice; 48°24'/22°53'; HSL. This town was located on a pre-World War I map, but does not appear in contemporary gazetteers.

Szalanczi, *see* Slanska Huta.

Szalanta, Hung.; pop. 5; 107 km ESE of Nagykanizsa; 45°57'/18°14'.

Szalapa, Hung.; pop. 5; 69 km N of Nagykanizsa; 46°59'/17°09'.

Szalard, *see* Salard.

Szaldobos, *see* Steblevka.

Szalka, Hung. (Salka); pop. 50; 114 km W of Szeged; 46°17'/18°38'; HSL, LDL.

Szalkeszentmarton, Hung.; pop. 26; 69 km S of Budapest; 46°58'/19°00'.

Szalonna, Hung.; pop. 41; 45 km N of Miskolc; 48°27'/20°45'; GUM5, HSL.

Szalowa, Pol.; pop. 5; 94 km ESE of Krakow; 49°41'/21°02'.

Szalva, *see* Salva.

Szambokret, HSL. This pre-World War I community was not found in BGN gazetteers.

Szamocin, Pol. (Samotschin); pop. 44; 69 km N of Poznan; 53°02'/17°08'; CAHJP.

Szamosangyalos, Hung.; pop. 14; 139 km E of Miskolc; 47°52'/22°40'.

Szamosbecs, Hung.; pop. 10; 146 km E of Miskolc; 47°52'/22°42'; AMG, HSL.

Szamosdob, *see* Doba.

Szamosfalva, Rom.; 6 km NE of Cluj; 46°47'/23°39'; HSL. This town was located on a pre-World War I map, but does not appear in contemporary gazetteers.

Szamosker, Hung.; pop. 37; 120 km E of Miskolc; 48°01'/22°25'.

Szamoskorod, *see* Corod.

Szamoskrasso, *see* Caraseu.

Szamosormezo, GUM3. This town was not found in BGN gazetteers under the given spelling.

Szamossalyi, Hung.; pop. 84; 133 km E of Miskolc; 47°54'/22°37'; PHH.

Szamosseplak, Rom.; 75 km NNW of Cluj; 47°23'/23°17'; HSL. This town was located on a pre-World War I map, but does not appear in contemporary gazetteers.

Szamosszeg, Hung.; pop. 94; 120 km E of Miskolc; 48°03'/22°22'; HSL, JGFF, PHH.

Szamostatarfalva, Hung.; pop. 3; 139 km E of Miskolc; 47°52'/22°40'.

Szamosudvarhely, *see* Somes Odorhei.

Szamosujlak, Hung.; 133 km E of Miskolc; 47°55'/22°36'; HSL.

Szamosujvar, *see* Gherla.

Szamosuovar, Rom.; 45 km NNE of Cluj; 47°02'/23°54'; HSL2. This town was located on a pre-World War I map, but does not appear in contemporary gazetteers.

Szamotuly, Pol. (Samter); pop. 264; 32 km WNW of Poznan; 52°37'/16°35'; CAHJP, HSL, JGFF.

Szanda, Hung.; pop. 4; 56 km NNE of Budapest; 47°56'/19°27'.

Szandorowka, *see* Samgorodok.

Szandrowiec, *see* Shandrovets.

Szaniawy, Pol. (Szaniawy Poniaty); pop. 41; 82 km N of Lublin; 51°57'/22°32'.

Szaniawy Matysy, Pol.; pop. 31; 45 km N of Lublin; 51°35'/22°35'. This town was located on an interwar map of Poland but does not appear in contemporary gazetteers. Map coordinates are approximate.

Szaniawy Poniaty, *see* Szaniawy.

Szaniec, Pol.; pop. 25; 69 km NE of Krakow; 50°31'/20°41'.

Szaniszlo, *see* Sanislau.

Szanto, *see* Abaujszanto.

Szany, Hung.; pop. 37; 120 km N of Nagykanizsa; 47°28'/17°18'; PHH.

Szapar, Hung.; pop. 4; 82 km WSW of Budapest; 47°19'/18°02'; HSL.

Szaplonca, *see* Sapinta.

Szar, Hung.; pop. 10; 45 km WSW of Budapest; 47°29'/18°31'.

Szarajowka, Pol.; pop. 5; 69 km N of Przemysl; 50°23'/22°52'.

Szara Wola, Pol.; pop. 5; 88 km NNE of Przemysl; 50°30'/23°22'.

Szarazberencs, *see* Rasonysapberencs.

Szarazd, Hung.; pop. 2; 114 km SSW of Budapest; 46°34'/18°26'.

Szarazkek, Hung.; pop. 9; 38 km NNE of Miskolc; 48°23'/21°02'.

Szarbkow, Pol.; pop. 2; 75 km NE of Krakow; 50°33'/20°39'.

Szarbsko, Pol.; pop. 7; 69 km SE of Lodz; 51°15'/19°56'.

Szare, Pol.; pop. 12; 88 km SW of Krakow; 49°34'/19°03'.

Szarfold, Hung.; pop. 4; 139 km N of Nagykanizsa; 47°36'/17°07'; HSL.

Szarkowszczyzna, *see* Sharkovshchina.

Szarogrod, *see* Shargorod.

Szarpance, *see* Sharpantsa.

Szaruty, Pol.; pop. 4; 75 km ENE of Warszawa; 52°21'/22°03'.

Szarvas, Hung.; pop. 787; 75 km N of Szeged; 46°52'/20°33'; AMG, GUM3, GUM5, HSL, HSL2, LDL, LDS, PHH.

Szarvasgede, Hung.; pop. 4; 50 km NE of Budapest; 47°49'/19°39'.

Szarvaszo, *see* Sarasau.

Szarwark, Pol.; pop. 5; 82 km ENE of Krakow; 50°08'/21°04'.

Szarygrod, Pol. PHP2. This town was not found in BGN gazetteers under the given spelling.

Szaszfa, Hung.; pop. 18; 50 km N of Miskolc; 48°28'/20°57'; HSL.

Szaszfellak, *see* Feleac.

Szaszlekence, *see* Lechinta.

Szaszlona, *see* Luna de Sus.

Szaszmegyes, HSL. This pre-World War I community was not found in BGN gazetteers.

Szasznadas, *see* Nadasu Sasesc.

Szasznyires, *see* Nires.

Szaszregen, *see* Reghin.

Szaszujfalu, *see* Noul Sasesc.

Szaszvar, Hung.; pop. 49; 107 km E of Nagykanizsa; 46°16'/18°23'.

Szaszvaros, *see* Sasveres.

Szatmar, *see* Satu Mare.

Szatmarcseke, Hung.; pop. 91; 139 km E of Miskolc; 48°05'/22°38'; GUM3, PHH.

Szatmarhegy, Rom.; 114 km NW of Cluj; 47°40'/22°53'; HSL. This town was located on a pre-World War I map, but does not appear in contemporary gazetteers.

Szatmar Nemeti, *see* Saru Mare.

Szatmarnemeti, *see* Saru Mare.

Szatmar Okorito, *see* Szatmarokorito.

Szatmarokorito, Hung. (Fulpos, Szatmar Okorito); pop. 126; 133 km E of Miskolc; 47°55'/22°31'; AMG, HSL, PHH.

Szatmar Udvari, *see* Odoreu.

Szatmarudvari, *see* Odoreu.

Szatok, Hung.; pop. 14; 56 km N of Budapest; 47°57'/19°14'.

Szava, Hung.; pop. 1; 107 km ESE of Nagykanizsa; 45°54'/18°11'; HSL.

Szawkiany, *see* Saukenai.

Szawle, *see* Siauliai.

Szawly, Pol.; pop. 9; 107 km N of Lublin; 52°10'/22°42'.

Szazhalombatta, Hung.; pop. 23; 26 km SSW of Budapest; 47°20'/18°56'.

Szcklencze, *see* Sokirnitsa.

Szcrzorowice, *see* Shchurovichi.

Szczakowa, Pol. (Shtehkeva); pop. 405; 50 km WNW of Krakow; 50°14'/19°17'; AMG, COH, EDRD, EGRS, GUM3, GUM4, HSL, PHP3, SF.

Szczawa, *see* Szczawo.

Szczawin, Pol.; pop. 22; a number of towns share this name. It was not possible to determine from available information which one is being referenced.

Szczawne, Pol.; pop. 38; 62 km SW of Przemysl; 49°24'/22°08'; JGFF.

Szczawnica, Pol. (Shtzovnitz, Szczawnica Wyzna); pop. 199; 82 km SE of Krakow; 49°26'/20°30'; COH, EGRS, GUM3, GUM5, HSL, PHP3, SF, YB.

Szczawnica Kroscienko, Pol. POCEM. This town was not found in BGN gazetteers under the given spelling.

Szczawnica Nizna, Pol. (Shchavnits, Shchavnitsa Vizhna); pop. 40; 82 km SE of Krakow; 49°26'/20°29'; LYV.

Szczawnica Wyzna, *see* Szczawnica.

Szczawnik, Pol.; pop. 7; 101 km SE of Krakow; 49°23'/20°52'.

Szczawo, Pol. (Szczawa); pop. 15; 62 km SE of Krakow; 49°36'/20°18'.

Szczeberka, Pol.; 94 km NNW of Bialystok; 53°56'/22°57'; PHP4.

Szczebrzeszyn, Pol. (Shchebreshin, Shebreshin, Shevershin, Szebrzeszyn); pop. 2,644; 62 km SE of Lublin; 50°42'/22°58'; AMG, CAHJP, COH, EDRD, EJ, GA, GUM3, GUM4, GUM5, HSL, HSL2, JGFF, LDL, LDS, PHP2, PHP4, POCEM, SF, YB.

Szczechowo, Pol.; pop. 6; 120 km WNW of Warszawa; 52°54'/19°37'.

Szczecin, Pol. (Stettin); pop. 2,701; 202 km WNW of Poznan; 53°27'/14°31'; AMG, EJ, GUM3, GUM4, GUM5, GUM6, HSL, HSL2, JGFF, LDS, PHGBW, POCEM, SF.

Szczecinek, Pol. (Neustettin); pop. 124; 146 km SW of Gdansk; 53°43'/16°42'; HSL, LDS.

Szczeglacin, Pol.; pop. 15; 94 km SSW of Bialystok; 52°22'/22°36'; GUM5.

Szczeglice, Pol.; pop. 2; 107 km SW of Lublin; 50°41'/21°19'.

Szczeglin, GA. a number of towns share this name. It was not possible to determine from available information which one is being referenced.

Szczekarzewo, Pol.; pop. 6; 126 km WNW of Warszawa; 52°54'/19°24'.

Szczekocin, *see* Szczekociny.

Szczekociny, Pol. (Sh Chekotckin, Shchekochin, Shchekotsini, Shtekechin, Shtekishin, Shtekotchin, Szczekocin); pop. 2,532; 56 km ESE of Czestochowa; 50°38'/19°50'; AMG, CAHJP, COH, EDRD, GA, GUM4, GUM5, HSL, HSL2, JGFF, LDL, LDS, LYV, SF, YB.

Szczelatyn, Pol.; pop. 11; 82 km ESE of Lublin; 50°49'/23°30'.

Szczeniec, *see* Shchenets.

Szczepan, *see* Stepan.

Szczepancowa, Pol.; pop. 13; 75 km WSW of Przemysl; 49°41'/21°42'.

Szczepanek, Pol.; pop. 5; 32 km NE of Warszawa; 52°23'/21°26'.

Szczepankowo, Pol.; 75 km WSW of Bialystok; 53°08'/21°57'; JGFF, LDS.

Szczepanow, Ukr.; pop. 23; 88 km E of Lvov; 49°38'/25°09'. This town was located on a pre-World War I map, but does not appear in contemporary gazetteers.

Szczepanowice, Pol.; pop. 21; 75 km E of Krakow; 49°57'/20°54'.

Szczepiatyn, Pol.; pop. 52; 101 km NE of Przemysl; 50°26'/23°50'.

Szczeploty, *see* Shcheploty.

Szczerbinowo, *see* Shcherbinovo.

Szczercow, Pol. (Shtchertzov, Stertzev); pop. 1,513; 50 km SSW of Lodz; 51°20'/19°07'; CAHJP, PHP1.

Szczerczewo, *see* Shcherchevo.

Szczerec, *see* Shcherets.

Szczerzec, *see* Shcherets.

Szczesliwice, Pol.; pop. 5; 13 km SSW of Warszawa; 52°12'/20°57'.

Szczodrohoszcze, *see* Shchedrogir.

Szczotkowice, Pol.; pop. 10; 45 km NE of Krakow; 50°21'/20°20'.

Szczucice, Pol.; pop. 2; 94 km SW of Lublin; 50°51'/21°24'.

Szczucin, Pol. (Shchutsin, Shtsitsin, Stitchin, Stitsin, Stutsin); pop. 491; 88 km ENE of Krakow; 50°18'/21°04'; CAHJP, EGRS, GUM5, HSL, HSL2, LDL, LYV, PHP3, POCEM, SF.

Szczuczki, Pol.; pop. 6; 26 km WSW of Lublin; 51°14'/22°11'.

Szczuczyn (Bialystok area), Pol.; pop. 2,506; 75 km WNW of Bialystok; 53°34'/22°18'; GA, GUM4, GUM5, HSL, HSL2, JGFF, LDL, LDS, PHP4, POCEM, SF, YB.

Szczuczyn (Novogrudok area), Byel.; pop. 1,036; 189 km WSW of Minsk; 53°36'/24°45'; COH, EDRD, GUM3, GUM4, HSL, JGFF, LYV, YB.

Szczukowice, Pol.; pop. 16; 101 km ENE of Czestochowa; 50°54'/20°31'.

Szczukowskie Gorki, *see* Gorki Szczukowskie.

Szczurowa, Pol.; pop. 132; 50 km ENE of Krakow; 50°07'/20°39'; GUM5, PHP3.

Szczurowice, *see* Shchurovichi.

Szczutkow, Pol.; pop. 40; 45 km NNE of Przemysl; 50°06'/23°08'.

Szczygly Gorne, Pol.; pop. 5; 75 km NNW of Lublin; 51°52'/22°20'.

Szczypiorno, Pol.; 101 km WSW of Lodz; 51°44'/18°02'; PHP1.

Szczyrk, Pol.; pop. 10; 75 km SW of Krakow; 49°43'/19°02'.

Szczyrzyc, Pol.; pop. 1; 38 km SE of Krakow; 49°47'/20°11'.

Szczytno, Pol. (Ortelsburg); pop. 120; 150 km WNW of Bialystok; 53°34'/21°00'; AMG, POCEM.

Szczytno (near Sochaczew), Pol.; pop. 21; 45 km WSW of Warszawa; 52°15'/20°21'.

Szczytyn, *see* Shchityn.

Szdek, Pol.; pop. 535; Described in the *Black Book* as being in the Lodz region of Poland, this town was not found in BGN gazetteers.

Szeben, HSL, HSL2. This pre-World War I community was not found in BGN gazetteers.

Szebeny, Hung.; pop. 3; 120 km WSW of Szeged; 46°08'/18°36'.

Szebnie, Pol.; 82 km WSW of Przemysl; 49°46'/21°36'; EDRD, GUM3, GUM4, GUM5, PHP2, PHP3.

Szebrzeszyn, *see* Szczebrzeszyn.

Szechynie, *see* Shegyni.

Szecs, *see* Sec.

Szecsegres, HSL, HSL2. This pre-World War I community was not found in BGN gazetteers.

Szecseny, Hung.; pop. 356; 75 km NNE of Budapest; 48°05'/19°31'; HSL, HSL2, LDL, LDS, PHH.

Szecsenyhalaszi, Hung.; pop. 6; 75 km NNE of Budapest; 48°08'/19°31'.

Szecsisziget, Hung.; pop. 3; 38 km WNW of Nagykanizsa; 46°34'/16°36'.

Szecskeresztur, *see* Kerestur.

Szederjes, HSL. This pre-World War I community was not found in BGN gazetteers.

Szederkeny, Hung.; pop. 6; 120 km ESE of Nagykanizsa; 46°00'/18°28'; HSL.

Szedliszka, *see* Sedliska.

Szedres, Hung.; pop. 57; 114 km W of Szeged; 46°29'/18°41'; HSL, PHH.

Szeg, HSL. This pre-World War I community was not found in BGN gazetteers.

Szeged, Hung. (Szegedin); pop. 4,161; 163 km SE of Budapest; 46°15'/20°10'; AMG, GUM3, GUM4, GUM5, GUM6, HSL, HSL2, JGFF, LDS, PHH.

Szegedin, *see* Szeged.

Szeghalom, Hung.; pop. 220; 120 km SSE of Miskolc; 47°02'/21°10'; LDL, LDS, PHH.

Szegi, Hung.; pop. 54; 45 km ENE of Miskolc; 48°12'/21°23'; AMG, HSL.

Szegilong, Hung.; pop. 18; 45 km ENE of Miskolc; 48°13'/21°24'; PHH.

Szegimalom, HSL. This pre-World War I community was not found in BGN gazetteers.

Szegszard, HSL. This pre-World War I community was not found in BGN gazetteers.

Szegvar, Hung.; pop. 63; 45 km N of Szeged; 46°35'/20°14'; PHH.

Szek, Hung.; 75 km ESE of Budapest; 47°12'/20°01'; HSL.

Szekely, Hung.; pop. 88 km E of Miskolc; 48°04'/21°57'; AMG, HSL.

Szekelyhid, *see* Sacueni.

Szekelykeresztur, *see* Cristur.

Szekelykocsard, *see* Cucerdea.

Szekelyudvarhely, *see* Odorhei.

Szekeres, *see* Kisszekeres.

Szekesfehervar, Hung. (Stuhlweissenburg); pop. 2,450; 56 km SW of Budapest; 47°12'/18°25'; AMG, COH, EJ, GUM3, GUM4, GUM5, HSL, ISH1, LDS, PHH.

Szeklencze, (Seklence); GUM6. This town was not found in BGN gazetteers under the given spelling.

Szekszard, Hung.; pop. 567; 114 km W of Szeged; 46°21'/18°43'; GUM5, PHH.

Szelepcseny, *see* Slepcany.

Szeleslonka, *see* Leh.

Szeleveny, Hung.; pop. 2; 69 km N of Szeged; 46°48'/20°12'.

Szelicse, *see* Salicea.

Szelistye, *see* Seliste.

Szelkow, *see* Szelkow Stary.

Szelkow Nowy, Pol.; pop. 141; PHP4. Described in the *Black Book* as being in the Warszawa region of Poland, this town was not found in BGN gazetteers.

Szelkow Stary, Pol. (Szelkow); pop. 10; 69 km N of Warszawa; 52°50'/21°13'; JGFF.

Szello, Hung.; pop. 4; 120 km ESE of Nagykanizsa; 46°04'/18°28'.

Szelwow, *see* Shelvov.

Szemenye, Hung.; pop. 2; 82 km N of Nagykanizsa; 47°06'/16°54'.

Szemere, Hung.; pop. 31; 50 km NNE of Miskolc; 48°28'/21°06'; HSL.

Szemlak, Rom.; 214 km SW of Cluj; 46°07'/20°55'; HSL. This town was located on a pre-World War I map, but does not appear in contemporary gazetteers.

Szempc, *see* Senec.

Szempcz, *see* Senec.

Szenc, *see* Senec.

Szencz, *see* Senec.

Szend, Hung.; pop. 12; 69 km W of Budapest; 47°33'/18°10'.

Szendehely, Hung.; pop. 8; 45 km N of Budapest; 47°51'/19°07'; HSL.

Szendro, Hung.; pop. 277; 38 km N of Miskolc; 48°24'/20°44'; HSL, HSL2, LDL, LDS, PHH.

Szendrolad, Hung.; pop. 6; 38 km N of Miskolc; 48°21'/20°45'.

Szenes Ofalu, LDL. This pre-World War I community was not found in BGN gazetteers.

Szenta, Hung.; pop. 6; 26 km SE of Nagykanizsa; 46°15'/17°11'; COH.

Szentadorjan, *see* Lispeszentadorjan.

Szentandras, Hung.; pop. 88 km S of Budapest; 46°45'/18°55'; HSL, HSL2, LDS.

Szentanna, *see* Liptovska Anna.

Szentantalfa, Hung.; pop. 11; 82 km NE of Nagykanizsa; 46°55'/17°41'.

Szentbekkalla, Hung.; pop. 1; 69 km NNE of Nagykanizsa; 46°53'/17°34'.

Szentbenedek, Hung. (Marosszentbenedeko?); 88 km NE of Szeged; 46°36'/21°14'; HSL.

Szentdemeter, *see* Dumitreni.

Szente, Hung.; pop. 13; 56 km N of Budapest; 47°58'/19°17'.

Szentendre, Hung. (Sankt Andra); pop. 229; 26 km N of Budapest; 47°40'/19°05'; GUM3, GUM4, HSL, LDS, PHH.

Szentes, Hung.; pop. 666; 50 km N of Szeged; 46°39'/20°16'; AMG, GUM4, GUM5, HSL, HSL2, JGFF, LDS, PHH.

Szentetornya, Hung.; pop. 8; 56 km NNE of Szeged; 46°35'/20°38'.

Szentgal, Hung.; pop. 88; 94 km NNE of Nagykanizsa; 47°07'/17°44'; PHH.

Szentgalosker, Hung.; pop. 1; 69 km ENE of Nagykanizsa; 46°30'/17°53'.

Szentgotthard, Hung.; pop. 178; 82 km NW of Nagykanizsa; 46°57'/16°17'; AMG, LDS, PHH.

Szentgrot, *see* Kisszentgrot.

Szentgyorgy, HSL, LDS. a number of towns share this name. It was not possible to determine from available information which one is being referenced.

Szentgyorgyabrany, *see* Nyirabrany.

Szentgyorgyvolgy, Hung.; pop. 13; 50 km WNW of Nagykanizsa; 46°44'/16°25'.

Szentimre, Hung.; 101 km ESE of Nagykanizsa; 46°10'/18°15'; HSL.

Szentistvan, Hung.; pop. 33; 45 km S of Miskolc; 47°46'/20°40'; COH, HSL.

Szentivan, *see* Kiskunlachaza.

Szentjakab, *see* Svaty Jakub.

Szentjobb, HSL. This pre-World War I community was not found in BGN gazetteers.

Szentkatalin, Hung.; pop. 2; 88 km ESE of Nagykanizsa; 46°10'/18°03'.

Szentkiraly, HSL. a number of towns share this name. It was not possible to determine from available information which one is being referenced.

Szentlaszlo, Hung.; 69 km ESE of Nagykanizsa; 46°09'/17°50'; HSL.

Szentlerant, Hung.; pop. 3; 82 km NNW of Nagykanizsa; 47°07'/16°45'.

Szentliszlo, Hung.; pop. 4; 26 km NW of Nagykanizsa; 46°35'/16°50'.

Szentlorinc, Hung.; pop. 56; 88 km ESE of Nagykanizsa; 46°03'/17°59'; HSL, LDS, PHH.

Szentlorinckata, Hung.; pop. 11; 50 km ENE of Budapest; 47°31'/19°45'; LDS.

Szentmarton, HSL, HSL2. This pre-World War I community was not found in BGN gazetteers.

Szentmartonkata, Hung.; pop. 38; 45 km E of Budapest; 47°27'/19°42'; HSL, LDS.

Szentmihaly, Hung.; 56 km S of Budapest; 47°04'/18°53'; LDS.

Szentmihalytelke, HSL. This pre-World War I community was not found in BGN gazetteers.

Szentnagyfalva, HSL. This pre-World War I community was not found in BGN gazetteers.

Szentpeter, HSL, HSL2, LDL. This pre-World War I community was not found in BGN gazetteers.

Szentpeterfa, Hung.; pop. 4; 88 km NW of Nagykanizsa; 47°06'/16°29'.

Szentpeterszeg, Hung. (Peterseg); pop. 13; 114 km SE of Miskolc; 47°14'/21°37'; HSL, LDS.

Szentpeterur, Hung.; pop. 1; 45 km N of Nagykanizsa; 46°46'/17°02'.

Szentsimon, Hung.; pop. 10; 45 km WNW of Miskolc; 48°14'/20°14'; HSL.

Szenttamas, Hung.; 45 km NE of Miskolc; 48°12'/21°18'; LDS.

Szeparowce, Ukr. (Szperowce); pop. 37; 75 km WSW of Chernovtsy; 48°15'/24°55'; JGFF, PHP2. This town was located on an interwar map of Poland but does not appear in contemporary gazetteers. Map coordinates are approximate.

Szepel, *see* Shepel.

Szepes, LDL. This pre-World War I community was not found in BGN gazetteers.

Szepesbela, *see* Spisska Bela.

Szepesolaszi, *see* Spisske Vlachy.

Szepesvaralja, *see* Spisske Podhradie.

Szepetk, *see* Szepetnek.

Szepetnek, Hung. (Szepetk); pop. 14; 6 km SW of Nagykanizsa; 46°26'/16°54'; HSL.

Szepetowka, *see* Shepetovka.

Szephalom, Hung.; pop. 32; 75 km NE of Miskolc; 48°26'/21°38'.

Szeplak, HSL. a number of towns share this name. It was not possible to determine from available information which one is being referenced.

Szeptyce, *see* Shcheptitsy.

Szerdahely, Hung.; 133 km N of Nagykanizsa; 47°35'/16°52'; COH, HSL, HSL2. This town was located on a pre-World War I map, but does not appear in contemporary gazetteers.

Szered, *see* Sered.

Szereda, *see* Sered.

Szeredmye, *see* Seredneye.

Szeremle, Hung. (Hajduhaz); pop. 3; 101 km WSW of Szeged; 46°09'/18°53'; GUM5.

Szerencs, Hung.; pop. 955; 32 km ENE of Miskolc; 48°10'/21°12'; AMG, HSL, HSL2, JGFF, LDL, LDS, PHH.

Szerep, Hung.; pop. 37; 101 km SSE of Miskolc; 47°14'/21°09'; HSL, LDS.

Szereszniowce, *see* Shersheniovtse.

Szereszow, *see* Shereshevo.

Szeretfalva, *see* Saratel.

Szergeny, Hung.; pop. 5; 107 km N of Nagykanizsa; 47°19'/17°16'.

Szerszeniowce, *see* Shersheniovtse.

Szerzyny, Pol.; pop. 65; 101 km ESE of Krakow; 49°49'/21°16'.

Szete, *see* Kubanovo.

Szewnia, Pol.; pop. 11; 82 km SE of Lublin; 50°38'/23°10'.

Sziget, *see* Sighet.

Szigetbecse, Hung.; pop. 3; 50 km S of Budapest; 47°08'/18°57'.

Szigetcsep, Hung.; pop. 8; 32 km S of Budapest; 47°16'/18°59'.

Szigetmonostor, Hung.; pop. 5; 26 km N of Budapest; 47°41'/19°07'.

Szigetszentmiklos, Hung.; pop. 51; 26 km S of Budapest; 47°21'/19°03'.

Szigetvar, Hung. (Szigevar); pop. 338; 75 km ESE of Nagykanizsa; 46°03'/17°48'; HSL, JGFF, LDS, PHH.

Szigevar, *see* Szigetvar.

Szigliget, Hung.; pop. 6; 56 km NNE of Nagykanizsa; 46°48'/17°26'; HSL.

Szihalom, Hung.; pop. 13; 45 km SSW of Miskolc; 47°46'/20°29'; HSL.

Szikso, *see* Szikszo.

Szikszo, Hung. (Szikso); pop. 785; 19 km NE of Miskolc; 48°12'/20°56'; AMG, COH, HSL, HSL2, JGFF, LDL, PHH, YB.

Szil, Hung. (Szill); pop. 46; 126 km N of Nagykanizsa; 47°30'/17°14'; EDRD, LDS, PHH.

Szilagycse, LDL. This pre-World War I community was not found in BGN gazetteers.

Szilagycseh, *see* Cehu Silvaniei.

Szilagykraszna, HSL, HSL2, LDL. This pre-World War I community was not found in BGN gazetteers.

Szilagynagyfalu, *see* Nusfalau.

Szilagyper, *see* Pir.

Szilagysomlyo, *see* Simleu Silvaniei.

Szilagyvalko, HSL. This pre-World War I community was not found in BGN gazetteers.

Szilas, HSL, HSL2. a number of towns share this name. It was not possible to determine from available information which one is being referenced.

Szilasarkany, *see* Szilsarkany.

Szilas Balhas, *see* Mezoszilas.

Szilasbalhas, *see* Mezoszilas.

Szilicze, *see* Silica.

Szill, *see* Szil.

Szilsarkany, Hung. (Szilasarkany); pop. 27; 133 km W of Budapest; 47°33'/17°16'; LDL, LDS.

Szilvasszentmarton, Hung.; pop. 5; 62 km ESE of Nagykanizsa; 46°17'/17°44'.

Szilvasujfalu, *see* Slivnik.

Szilvasvarad, Hung.; pop. 27; 32 km WSW of Miskolc; 48°06'/20°24'.

Szin, Hung.; pop. 32; 50 km NNW of Miskolc; 48°30'/20°40'; HSL.

Szind, Rom.; 26 km SSE of Cluj; 46°35'/23°43'; HSL. This town was located on a pre-World War I map, but does not appear in contemporary gazetteers.

Szinervaralja, *see* Seini.

Szinever, *see* Sinevir Polyana.

Szinpetri, Hung.; pop. 3; 50 km NNW of Miskolc; 48°29'/20°38'.

Szinye, HSL. This pre-World War I community was not found in BGN gazetteers.

Szirak, Hung.; pop. 36; 50 km NNE of Budapest; 47°50'/19°32'; HSL, LDS.

Szirma, Hung.; pop. 27; 6 km ESE of Miskolc; 48°04'/20°50'; HSL.

Szirmabesenyo, Hung.; 13 km N of Miskolc; 48°09'/20°48'; HSL.

Szkeco, *see* Skycov.

Szkiczo, *see* Skycov.

Szklarka Myslniewska, Pol.; pop. 5; 75 km NE of Wroclaw; 51°27'/17°49'.

Szklin, *see* Shklin.

Szklo, *see* Shklo.

Szklow, *see* Shklov.

Szkodna, Pol.; pop. 16; 82 km W of Przemysl; 49°59'/21°39'.

Szkolki, Pol.; pop. 1; 56 km NE of Poznan; 52°45'/17°37'.

Szkudy, *see* Skuodas.

Szkunciki, *see* Shkuntiki.

Szlachecki Las, Pol.; pop. 23; 56 km W of Lublin; 51°19'/21°46'.

Szlachtowa, Pol.; pop. 2; 88 km SE of Krakow; 49°25'/20°32'.

Szlani, *see* Slanica.

Szlapan, *see* Shlapan.

Szlasy Lozino, Pol.; pop. 11; 82 km N of Warszawa; 52°56'/21°01'.

Szlatina, *see* Solotvina.

Szlatyn, Pol.; pop. 34; 94 km NNE of Przemysl; 50°26'/23°41'.

Szlembark, Pol.; pop. 8; 75 km SSE of Krakow; 49°29'/20°13'.

Szlichtyngowa, *see* Szlinokiemie.

Szlininka, Pol.; pop. 35; Described in the *Black Book* as being in the Wilen region of Poland, this town was not found in BGN gazetteers.

Szlinokiemie, Pol. (Schlichtingsheim, Szlichtyngowa); pop. 3; 126 km N of Bialystok; 54°14'/23°09'; JGFF, LDS.

Szmankowce, *see* Shmankovtse.

Szmilowka, Pol. PHP3. This town was not found in BGN gazetteers under the given spelling.

Szmolnok, *see* Smolnik (Slovakia).

Szo, *see* Sho.

Szob, Hung.; pop. 100; 38 km NW of Budapest; 47°49'/18°52'; COH, GUM4, HSL, PHH.

Szoboticza, Yug.; 163 km SSE of Zagreb; 44°22'/16°31'; HSL. This town was located on a pre-World War I map, but does not appear in contemporary gazetteers.

Szobrancz, *see* Sobrance.

Szoc, Hung. (Szocs); 75 km NNE of Nagykanizsa; 47°01'/17°31'; HSL.

Szoce, Hung.; pop. 4; 62 km NW of Nagykanizsa; 46°53'/16°35'.

Szocs, *see* Szoc.

Szod, Hung.; pop. 67; 32 km N of Budapest; 47°43'/19°12'.

Szogliget, Hung.; pop. 7; 56 km NNW of Miskolc; 48°31'/20°41'.

Szojva, GUM3. This town was not found in BGN gazetteers under the given spelling.

Szokolya, Hung.; pop. 28; 45 km N of Budapest; 47°52'/19°01'.

Szolad, Hung.; pop. 5; 75 km NE of Nagykanizsa; 46°47'/17°51'.

Szoldobagy, *see* Solduba.

Szolgaegyhaza, *see* Szabadegyhaza.

Szollos, *see* Vinogradov.

Szollosardo, Hung.; pop. 3; 45 km NNW of Miskolc; 48°27'/20°38'; HSL.

Szollosgyorok, Hung.; pop. 28; 62 km NE of Nagykanizsa; 46°43'/17°41'.

Szolnok, Hung.; pop. 2,098; 94 km ESE of Budapest; 47°11'/20°12'; COH, EJ, GUM3, GUM4, GUM5, HSL, HSL2, JGFF, LDS, PHH.

Szolny, *see* Salnos.

Szolocsina, HSL. This pre-World War I community was not found in BGN gazetteers.

Szolomienice, *see* Sholomenitse.

Szolyva, LDL. This pre-World War I community was not found in BGN gazetteers.

Szomajom, *see* Kaposfo.

Szombat, *see* Sobotiste.

Szombathely, Hung. (Steinamanger); pop. 3,482; 94 km NNW of Nagykanizsa; 47°14'/16°37'; AMG, COH, EDRD, EJ, GUM3, GUM4, GUM5, HSL, HSL2, JGFF, LDL, LDS, PHH.

Szomod, Hung.; pop. 3; 56 km WNW of Budapest; 47°41'/18°21'.

Szomolnokhutta, *see* Smolnicka Huta.

Szomor, Hung.; pop. 3; 32 km WNW of Budapest; 47°35'/18°40'.

Szomotor, *see* Somotor.

Szony, Hung.; pop. 43; 69 km WNW of Budapest; 47°44'/18°10'.

Szopienice, Pol.; pop. 6; 56 km WNW of Krakow; 50°16'/19°07'; AMG, GUM3, GUM4, PHP3.

Szorce, Pol.; pop. 6; 38 km WNW of Bialystok; 53°18'/22°41'.

Szorcowka, Pol.; pop. 6; 75 km ESE of Lublin; 50°49'/23°26'.

Szoreg, Hung.; pop. 35; 13 km SE of Szeged; 46°13'/20°12'.

Szostakow, *see* Shostaki.

Szovaros, *see* Suares.

Szovat, *see* Hajduszovat.

Szovata, *see* Sovata.

Szowsko, Pol.; pop. 20; 32 km NNW of Przemysl; 50°03'/22°43'.

Szpanow, *see* Shpanov.

Szperowce, *see* Szeparowce.

Szpetal Dolny, Pol.; pop. 75; 107 km NNW of Lodz; 52°40'/19°05'.

Szpikolosy, Pol.; pop. 26; 101 km ESE of Lublin; 50°52'/23°56'. *See also* Shpikolosy.

Szprotawa, *see* Szprudowo.

Szprudowo, Pol. (Sprottau, Szprotawa); pop. 28; 56 km SSE of Gdansk; 53°54'/18°48'; LDS, POCEM.

Szransk, *see* Szrensk.

Szrensk, Pol. (Sherensk, Shransk, Shrensk, Shrentsk, Szransk); pop. 613; 101 km NW of Warszawa; 53°01'/20°07'; COH, EDRD, EJ, GUM3, HSL, JGFF, LDS, LYV, PHP1, PHP4, SF, YB.

Sztabin, Pol. (Shtabin); pop. 62; 69 km N of Bialystok; 53°41'/23°06'; GYLA, HSL, HSL2, JGFF, SF.

Sztalinvaros, Hung. (Dunapentele, Dunaujvaros); pop. 94; 62 km S of Budapest; 46°59'/18°56'; LDS, PHH.

Sztankocz, *see* Stankovce.

Sztarnya, *see* Starna.

Sztawna, *see* Stavnoye.

Sztrainyan, *see* Stranany.

Sztrecsen, *see* Strecno.

Sztrojna, GUM3. This town was not found in BGN gazetteers under the given spelling.

Sztropko, *see* Stropkov.

Sztum, Pol. (Stuhm); pop. 46; 50 km SE of Gdansk; 53°56'/19°02'; LDS, POCEM.

Sztutowo, Pol. (Stutthof); 38 km E of Gdansk; 54°20'/19°11';

EDRD, GA, GUM3, GUM4, GUM5, GUM6, JGFF, PHLE, PHP3.

Szubin, Pol. (Schubin); pop. 77; 82 km NNE of Poznan; 53°01'/17°45'; GUM3, HSL, PHP1, POCEM.

Szubkow, *see* Shubkov.

Szuczan, *see* Sucany.

Szufnarowa, Pol.; pop. 23; 88 km W of Przemysl; 49°55'/21°38'.

Szugy, Hung.; pop. 32; 62 km N of Budapest; 48°02'/19°20'; LDS.

Szuha, Hung.; pop. 6; 69 km WSW of Miskolc; 47°59'/19°55'; HSL.

Szuhabaranka, *see* Bronka.

Szuhafo, Hung. (Felso Szuha, Felsoszuha); pop. 5; 45 km NW of Miskolc; 48°25'/20°27'; HSL.

Szuhakallo, Hung.; pop. 12; 26 km NNW of Miskolc; 48°17'/20°40'; HSL.

Szuhogy, Hung.; pop. 10; 38 km NNW of Miskolc; 48°23'/20°41'.

Szulborze, Pol.; pop. 8; 75 km SW of Bialystok; 52°46'/22°13'; PHP4.

Szulhanowka, *see* Shulganuvka.

Szuliman, Hung.; pop. 1; 69 km ESE of Nagykanizsa; 46°08'/17°48'.

Szulok, Hung.; pop. 13; 62 km SE of Nagykanizsa; 46°03'/17°33'.

Szulz, HSL. This pre-World War I community was not found in BGN gazetteers.

Szumiacz, Ukr.; pop. 40; 126 km SSW of Lvov; 48°55'/22°55'. This town was located on an interwar map of Poland but does not appear in contemporary gazetteers. Map coordinates are approximate.

Szumlany, *see* Shumlyany.

Szumowa, Pol. PHP4. This town was not found in BGN gazetteers under the given spelling.

Szumowo, Pol. (Szumowo Nowe); pop. 125; 75 km WSW of Bialystok; 52°56'/22°05'; PHP4.

Szumowo Gora, Pol.; pop. 56; Described in the *Black Book* as being in the Bialystok region of Poland, this town was not found in BGN gazetteers.

Szumowo Nowe, *see* Szumowo.

Szumsk, *see* Shumskoye.

Szumsko, Pol.; pop. 8; 107 km NE of Krakow; 50°42'/21°06'.

Szurani, LDL. This pre-World War I community was not found in BGN gazetteers.

Szurdok, *see* Strimtura.

Szurdokpuspoki, Hung.; pop. 12; 62 km NE of Budapest; 47°51'/19°41'.

Szurduk, *see* Surduc.

Szurte, *see* Strumkovka.

Szury, Pol.; pop. 56; 126 km N of Bialystok; 54°13'/23°01'.

Szuszki, *see* Shushki.

Szwajkowce, Ukr.; pop. 23; 56 km N of Chernovtsy; 48°45'/25°55'. This town was located on an interwar map of Poland but does not appear in contemporary gazetteers. Map coordinates are approximate.

Szychowice, Pol.; pop. 11; 120 km ESE of Lublin; 50°41'/23°59'.

Szydlow, Pol. (Shidlov); pop. 660; 94 km NE of Krakow; 50°36'/21°00'; AMG, CAHJP, COH, FRG, GA, GUM3, GUM5, LDL, PHP3, PHP4, SF, YB.

Szydlowce, *see* Shidlovtsy.

Szydlowek, Pol.; pop. 23; 101 km NNE of Krakow; 50°53'/20°39'.

Szydlowiec, Pol. (Shidlovets, Shidlovits, Shidlovitz, Shidlovtse, Shidlovtza, Shidlovyets, Zhidlovetza); pop. 5,501; 114 km ESE of Lodz; 51°14'/20°51'; AMG, COH, EDRD, EJ, GA, GUM3, GUM4, GUM5, GUM6, GUM6, GYLA, HSL, HSL2, JGFF, LDL, LDS, LYV, PHP1, POCEM, SF, YB.

Szyk, Pol.; pop. 16; 45 km SE of Krakow; 49°48'/20°19'.

Szylin, *see* Shilin.

Szylokarczma, *see* Silute.

Szymanowa, Pol. PHP4. This town was not found in BGN gazetteers under the given spelling.

Szymbark, Pol.; pop. 50; 101 km ESE of Krakow; 49°38'/21°06'.

Szymkowce, *see* Shimkovtsy.

Szymonka, Pol.; 133 km WNW of Bialystok; 53°54'/21°39'; PHP2.

Szymony, Pol.; pop. 18; 56 km E of Warszawa; 52°11'/21°50'.

Szynkarzyzna, Pol.; pop. 23; 62 km NE of Warszawa; 52°37'/21°45'.

Szyperki, Pol.; pop. 5; 82 km S of Lublin; 50°34'/22°18'.

Szypliszki, Pol.; pop. 9; 133 km N of Bialystok; 54°15'/23°04'.

Szypowce, *see* Shypovtse.

Szyszkowce, *see* Shyshkovtse.

Tab, Hung.; pop. 482; 88 km NE of Nagykanizsa; 46°44'/18°02'; AMG, GUM5, HSL, HSL2, LDL, LDS, PHH.

Tabajd, Hung.; pop. 10; 38 km W of Budapest; 47°24'/18°38'.

Tabarz, Germ.; 133 km SW of Leipzig; 50°53'/10°31'; GUM3.

Tabaszowa, Pol.; pop. 4; 69 km ESE of Krakow; 49°45'/20°42'.

Tabkowice, Pol.; pop. 39; Described in the *Black Book* as being in the Kielce region of Poland, this town was not found in BGN gazetteers.

Tabor, Cz.; pop. 345; 82 km SSE of Praha; 49°25'/14°40'; EJ, HSL, HSL2, JGFF.

Tac, Hung.; pop. 26; 69 km SW of Budapest; 47°05'/18°24'.

Tachau, *see* Tachov.

Tachov, Cz. (Tachau); pop. 223; 133 km WSW of Praha; 49°48'/12°38'; AMG, EJ, HSL, HSL2, JGFF.

Tachovo, *see* Tyachev.

Tacovo, *see* Tyachev.

Taczow, Pol.; pop. 8; 94 km S of Warszawa; 51°28'/21°02'.

Tadaiki, Lat.; pop. 1; 170 km WSW of Riga; 56°31'/21°26'.

Tadanie, *see* Tadany.

Tadany, Ukr. (Tadanie); pop. 45; 45 km NE of Lvov; 50°05'/24°25'.

Tadten, Aus.; pop. 7; 69 km SE of Wien; 47°46'/16°59'.

Taffilalth, *see* Tafilelt.

Tafilelt, (Taffilalth); LDL. This pre-World War I community was not found in BGN gazetteers.

Taga, Rom. (Czege); 38 km NE of Cluj; 46°57'/24°03'; AMG.

Tagancha, Ukr. (Tagancza, Tahantcha); 114 km SE of Kiyev; 49°35'/31°17'; LDL, SF.

Tagancza, *see* Tagancha.

Taganrog, USSR; pop. 2,633; 498 km S of Voronezh; 47°12'/38°56'; EJ, GUM4, GUM5, HSL.

Tagara, *see* Tsygira.

Tagyon, Hung.; pop. 3; 75 km NE of Nagykanizsa; 46°54'/17°41'.

Tahantcha, *see* Tagancha.

Taharin, LDL. This pre-World War I community was not found in BGN gazetteers.

Tahert, HSL. This pre-World War I community was not found in BGN gazetteers.

Tahitotfalu, Hung.; pop. 23; 32 km N of Budapest; 47°45'/19°06'.

Tahnauti, *see* Tsekhnauts.

Tailfingen, Germ.; 62 km S of Stuttgart; 48°15'/09°01'; GUM3, PHGBW.

Takacsi, Hung.; pop. 6; 114 km N of Nagykanizsa; 47°24'/17°29'.

Takaros, *see* Takarostanya.

Takarostanya, Hung. (Takaros); 45 km E of Miskolc; 47°59'/21°24'; HSL.

Takonin, Cz.; pop. 2; 50 km SE of Praha; 49°46'/14°50'.

Takos, Hung.; pop. 21; 120 km ENE of Miskolc; 48°09'/22°26'.

Taksony, Hung.; pop. 33; 26 km S of Budapest; 47°20'/19°05'; GUM5.

Taktaharkany, Hung.; pop. 72; 32 km E of Miskolc; 48°05'/21°08'; GUM5, HSL, PHH.

Taktakenez, Hung.; pop. 13; 32 km E of Miskolc; 48°03'/21°13'.

Taktalachik, Pol. PHP3. This town was not found in BGN gazetteers under the given spelling.

Taktaszada, Hung.; pop. 19; 32 km ENE of Miskolc; 48°07'/21°11'; HSL.

Talaborfalu, *see* Tereblya.

Talalayevka, Ukr. (Talaljewka); 26 km W of Uman; 48°46'/29°55'; PHR1.

Talaljewka, *see* Talalayevka.

Talamas, HSL. This pre-World War I community was not found in BGN gazetteers.

Talheim, Germ.; pop. 90; 94 km SSW of Stuttgart; 48°01'/08°40'; EJ, GED, PHGBW.

Taliandorogd, Hung.; pop. 5; 82 km NNE of Nagykanizsa; 46°59'/17°34'.

Talka, Byel.; 75 km SE of Minsk; 53°22'/28°21'; GUM4.

Tallesbrunn, Aus.; pop. 4; 32 km NE of Wien; 48°21'/16°46'.

Tallin, *see* Tallinn.

Tallinn, Est. (Reval, Revel, Tallin); pop. 2,010; 163 km WNW of Tartu; 59°25'/24°45'; COH, GUM4, GUM5, GUM6, HSL, LDL, PHLE.

Tallos, *see* Tomasikovo.

Tallya, Hung. (Dorgo); pop. 196; 38 km NE of Miskolc; 48°14'/21°14'; COH, HSL, HSL2, LDL, LDS, PHH.

Talmach, *see* Tlumach.

Talmaciu, *see* Lazaret.

Talmatch, *see* Tlumach.

Talmaz, Mold.; pop. 308; 75 km ESE of Kishinev; 46°38'/29°40'.

Talminovichi, Byel. (Talminowicze); pop. 9; 101 km N of Pinsk; 52°57'/26°22'.

Talminowicze, *see* Talminovichi.

Talna, *see* Talnoye.

Talnoe, *see* Talnoye.

Talnoje, *see* Talnoye.

Talnoya, *see* Talnoye.

Talnoye, Ukr. (Talna, Talnoe, Talnoje, Talnoya); pop. 4,169; 38 km NE of Uman; 48°53'/30°42'; EDRD, EJ, GUM4, HSL, JGFF, LDL, SF.

Talsen, *see* Talsi.

Talsi, Lat. (Talsen, Talsn, Tilsen); pop. 605; 94 km WNW of Riga; 57°15'/22°36'; GUM4, HSL, JGFF, LDL, PHLE, SF.

Talsn, *see* Talsi.

Tamaia, Rom.; pop. 19; 101 km NNW of Cluj; 47°36'/23°22'.

Tamasa, Rom. (Almasszent Tamasi); pop. 5; 38 km WNW of Cluj; 46°57'/23°11'.

Tamasda, Rom.; 157 km WSW of Cluj; 46°38'/21°33'; HSL.

Tamaseni, Rom.; pop. 73; 146 km NNW of Cluj; 48°01'/23°09'.

Tamaseu, Rom.; pop. 15; 139 km WNW of Cluj; 47°13'/21°56'.

Tamasi, Hung.; pop. 211; 101 km ENE of Nagykanizsa; 46°38'/18°17'; PHH.

Tamaveni, Rom. PHR1. This town was not found in BGN gazetteers under the given spelling.

Tammiste, *see* Tammistu.

Tammistu, Est. (Tammiste); 120 km SSW of Tallinn; 58°27'/23°53'; PHLE.

Tamna, Est.; 94 km E of Tallinn; 59°16'/26°18'; HSL.

Tamsweg, Aus.; 94 km SE of Salzburg; 47°08'/13°48'; EJ.

Tanatari, *see* Tanatary.

Tanatary, Mold. (Tanatari); pop. 11; 56 km ESE of Kishinev; 46°43'/29°25'.

Tancs, *see* Tonciu.

Tangermunde, Germ.; pop. 24; 101 km W of Berlin; 52°33'/11°57'; LDS.

Tann, *see* Tann Bei Fulda.

Tann Bei Fulda, Germ. (Tann); pop. 72; 114 km NE of Frankfurt am Main; 50°39'/10°01'; GUM3, JGFF.

Tantareni Orehi, *see* Tsyntsareni.

Tantareni Tighina, *see* Tsyntsareny.

Tanvald, Cz.; pop. 9; 94 km NNE of Praha; 50°44'/15°18'.

Tap, Hung.; pop. 11; 94 km W of Budapest; 47°31'/17°50'; HSL, HSL2.

Tape, Hung.; pop. 9; 6 km NE of Szeged; 46°16'/20°13'.

Tapiau, *see* Gvardeysk.

Tapin, Pol.; pop. 28; 19 km NW of Przemysl; 49°55'/22°41'.

Tapiobicske, Hung.; pop. 61; 50 km ESE of Budapest; 47°22'/19°41'; LDS, PHH.

Tapiogyorgye, Hung.; pop. 74; 69 km ESE of Budapest; 47°20'/19°57'; HSL, PHH.

Tapiosag, Hung.; 45 km E of Budapest; 47°24'/19°37'; LDS.

Tapiosap, Hung.; pop. 17; 32 km E of Budapest; 47°27'/19°30'.

Tapiosuly, Hung.; pop. 76; 38 km E of Budapest; 47°27'/19°33'; GUM5, LDS, PHH.

Tapioszecso, Hung.; pop. 21; 45 km E of Budapest; 47°27'/19°36'; LDS.

Tapioszele, Hung.; pop. 88; 62 km ESE of Budapest; 47°20'/19°53'; HSL, LDS, PHH.

Tapioszentmarton, Hung.; pop. 21; 56 km ESE of Budapest; 47°20'/19°45'; LDS.

Tapioszollos, Hung. (Halesz); 62 km ESE of Budapest; 47°18'/19°51'; HSL.

Tapolca, Hung.; pop. 706; 62 km NNE of Nagykanizsa; 46°53'/17°26'; HSL, LDS, PHH.

Tapolcafo, Hung.; pop. 26; 107 km N of Nagykanizsa; 47°17'/17°31'.

Tapolcany, *see* Topolcany.

Tapsony, Hung.; pop. 5; 32 km ENE of Nagykanizsa; 46°28'/17°20'; HSL.

Tapszentmiklos, Hung.; pop. 19; 94 km WSW of Budapest; 47°30'/17°51'.

Tarachkos, *see* Tarasovka.

Tarackoz, *see* Tarasovka.

Taraclia Cahul, Mold.; pop. 46; 126 km S of Kishinev; 45°54'/28°40'.

Taraclia Tighina, *see* Tarakliya.

Taracs Kraszna, Ukr. (Krasnishore, Krasznisora); 146 km WSW of Chernovtsy; 48°14'/23°56'; COH, HSL, LYV.

Taracujfalu, *see* Neresnitsa.

Taraczkos, *see* Tarasovka.

Taracz Krazna, *see* Krasna.

Tarakliya, Mold. (Taraclia Tighina); pop. 151; 50 km SSE of Kishinev; 46°34'/29°07'.

Tarany, Hung.; pop. 12; 38 km SE of Nagykanizsa; 46°11'/17°18'.

Tarasca, *see* Tarashcha.

Taraseni Cernauti, *possibly* Tarashany.

Tarashany, Ukr. (Taraseni Cernauti?); pop. 52; 26 km SSE of Chernovtsy; 48°07'/26°01'.

Tarashcha, Ukr. (Tarasca, Tarashtcha, Taraszcza); pop. 3,222; 94 km N of Uman; 49°34'/30°30'; AMG, GUM4, JGFF, SF.

Tarashtcha, *see* Tarashcha.

Tarasits, *see* Tarasovka.

Tarasivka, *see* Khutor Tarasivka.

Taraskowo, Pol.; pop. 3; 62 km W of Bialystok; 53°13'/22°17'.

Tarasov, Cz. A number of towns share this name. It was not possible to determine from available information which one is being referenced.

Tarasovka, Ukr. (Tarachkos, Tarackoz, Taraczkos, Tarasits, Tarassiwka, Tereselpatak, Teresheł, Teresif, Teresova, Terisel); pop. 693; 157 km WSW of Chernovtsy; 48°12'/23°49'; AMG, HSL, LYV, PHR1, SM.

Tarassiwka, *see* Tarasovka.

Taraszcza, *see* Tarashcha.

Tarcal, Hung.; pop. 321; 45 km ENE of Miskolc; 48°08'/21°21'; AMG, COH, GUM3, HSL, HSL2, LDS, PHH.

Tarcea, Rom. (Erstarcsa); pop. 21; 133 km WNW of Cluj; 47°27'/22°11'.

Tarcesti, Rom.; pop. 3; 126 km ESE of Cluj; 46°22'/25°08'.

Tarcze, Pol.; 94 km E of Warszawa; 52°08'/22°25'; HSL.

Tarczyn, Pol. (Tartchin); pop. 1,427; 38 km S of Warszawa; 51°58'/20°50'; AMG, COH, GA, GUM3, GUM4, HSL, HSL2, LDS, PHP1, PHP4, SF.

Tard, Hung.; pop. 27; 32 km SSW of Miskolc; 47°53'/20°37'.

Tardona, Hung.; pop. 8; 19 km WNW of Miskolc; 48°10'/20°32'; HSL.

Tardos, *see* Tardosbanya.

Tardosbanya, Hung. (Tardos); 50 km WNW of Budapest; 47°40'/18°27'; HSL.

Tardosked, *see* Tvrdosovce.

Tareni, *see* Tsarevka.

Tarfalu, *see* Holatin.

Targin, *see* Tauragnai.

Targonie Wielkie, Pol.; pop. 4; 38 km W of Bialystok; 53°11'/22°37'.

Targonie Wity, Pol.; pop. 9; 32 km W of Bialystok; 53°10'/22°39'.

Targovica, *see* Torgovitsa.

Targovishche, *see* Turovichi.

Targoviste, *see* Torgovitsa.

Targovitsa, *see* Torgovitsa.

Targovitza, *see* Torgovitsa.

Targow, Pol. PHP4. This town was not found in BGN gazetteers under the given spelling.

Targowek, Pol.; pop. 8; 6 km NE of Warszawa; 52°16'/21°03'; HSL.

Targowica, *see* Torgovitsa.

Targowiska, Pol.; pop. 42; 69 km WSW of Przemysl; 49°38'/21°50'.

Targowisko, Pol.; pop. 25; 32 km ESE of Krakow; 49°59'/20°18'.

Targowiszcze, *see* Turovichi.

Targowitza, *see* Torgovitsa.

Targu Frumos, *see* Tirgu Frumos.

Targu Gloduri, *see* Tirgu Gloduli.

Targu Jiu, *see* Tirgu Jiu.

Targu Laposului, *see* Tirgu Lapus.

Targul Bujor, GUM4. This town was not found in BGN gazetteers under the given spelling.

Targul Frumos, *see* Tirgu Frumos.

Targul Jiu, *see* Tirgu Jiu.

Targul Lapush, *see* Tirgu Lapus.

Targul Lapusului, *see* Tirgu Lapus.

Targul Mures, *see* Tirgu Mures.

Targul Ocna, *see* Tirgu Ocna.

Targu Lopus, *see* Tirgu Lapus.

Targul Secuiesc, *see* Tirgu Secuesc.

Targu Miresh, *see* Tirgu Mures.

Targu Mores, *see* Tirgu Mures.

Targu Myres, *see* Tirgu Mures.

Targu Neamt, *see* Tirgu Neamt.

Targu Ocna, *see* Tirgu Ocna.

Targu Sacuiesc, *see* Tirgu Secuesc.

Targy Neanirom, *see* Tirgu Neamt.

Tarian, Rom.; pop. 17; 139 km W of Cluj; 47°04'/21°48'.

Tariceanca Veche, *see* Staraya Tsarichanka.

Tarigrad, *see* Glavan.

Tarjan, Hung.; pop. 6; 45 km WNW of Budapest; 47°37'/18°31'; HSL.

Tarkan, Bulg.; 101 km WNW of Varna; 43°49'/26°57'; HSL.

Tarkan Maly, HSL. This pre-World War I community was not found in BGN gazetteers.

Tarkan Velky, HSL. This pre-World War I community was not found in BGN gazetteers.

Tarkany, Hung.; 82 km W of Budapest; 47°35'/18°00'; HSL.

Tarkow, Pol.; 101 km ENE of Warszawa; 52°16'/22°31'; HSL2.

Tarle, *see* Tarlow.

Tarleh, *see* Tarlow.

Tarlisua, *see* Tirlisua.

Tarlo, Pol.; pop. 5; 38 km N of Lublin; 51°31'/22°42'.

Tarlow, Pol. (Tarle, Tarleh, Tarluv); pop. 1,052; 62 km SW of Lublin; 51°00'/21°43'; AMG, COH, GA, GUM3, GUM5, HSL, LDS, LYV, SF.

Tarluv, *see* Tarlow.

Tarna, *see* Tarnow.

Tarnalelesz, Hung.; pop. 18; 45 km WSW of Miskolc; 48°03'/20°11'.

Tarna Mare, Rom. (Nagytarna); pop. 349; 101 km WNW of Iasi; 47°29'/26°20'; AMG, HSL, PHR2.

Tarnamera, Hung.; pop. 33; 69 km SSW of Miskolc; 47°39'/20°10'; HSL.

Tarnaors, Hung.; pop. 5; 69 km ENE of Budapest; 47°36'/20°03'.

Tarnaszentmaria, Hung.; pop. 1; 50 km SW of Miskolc; 47°53'/20°12'.

Tarnaszentmiklos, Hung.; pop. 16; 69 km SSW of Miskolc; 47°32'/20°23'; HSL.

Tarnava, Ukr. (Tarnawa, Ternava); pop. 44; 88 km SW of Lvov; 49°33'/22°48'; AMG, GUM3, HSL.

Tarnavka, Ukr.; pop. 33; 69 km SW of Rovno; 50°15'/25°29'; CAHJP.

Tarnawa, *see* Tarnava.

Tarnawa Nizna, Pol.; pop. 115; PHP2. Described in the *Black Book* as being in the Stanislawow region of Poland, this town was not found in BGN gazetteers.

Tarnawatka, Pol.; pop. 12; 94 km SE of Lublin; 50°32'/23°23'; JGFF.

Tarnawa Wyzna, Pol.; pop. 55; Described in the *Black Book* as being in the Stanislawow region of Poland, this town was not found in BGN gazetteers.

Tarnawka, Pol.; pop. 92; 38 km WNW of Przemysl; 49°57'/22°17'; HSL. A list of Galician towns shows many towns named Tarnawka. The *Black Book* notes one (pop. 47), near Skole in the interwar Polish province of Tarnopol, that does not appear in contemporary gazetteers.

Tarnazsadany, Hung.; pop. 11; 62 km SSW of Miskolc; 47°40'/20°10'.

Tarno, Yug.; 32 km E of Zagreb; 45°44'/16°22'; AMG.

Tarnobrzeg, Pol. (Dikow, Dzhikev, Tarnobrzeg Dzikow); pop. 2,146; 94 km SSW of Lublin; 50°35'/21°41'; AMG, CAHJP, COH, EDRD, EGRS, EJ, GA, GUM3, GUM4, GUM5, HSL, HSL2, JGFF, LDL, PHP3, POCEM, SF, YB.

Tarnobrzeg Dzikow, *see* Tarnobrzeg.

Tarnogora, Pol.; pop. 107; 56 km ESE of Lublin; 50°53'/23°08'; HSL, SF.

Tarnogrod, Pol.; pop. 2,238; 69 km N of Przemysl; 50°22'/22°45'; AMG, CAHJP, COH, EDRD, GA, GUM3, GUM4, GUM5, GUM6, HSL, HSL2, JGFF, LYV, PHP1, PHP2, PHP3, SF, YB.

Tarnok, Hung.; pop. 40; 32 km SW of Budapest; 47°22'/18°51'.

Tarnopol, *see* Ternopol.

Tarnoruda, *see* Tarnorudka.

Tarnorudka, Ukr. (Tarnoruda); pop. 148; 126 km N of Chernovtsy; 49°25'/26°14'; EGRS, GUM3, HSL, LDL, PHP2, SF.

Tarnoszyn, Pol.; pop. 23; 101 km NE of Przemysl; 50°25'/23°48'.

Tarnov, *see* Tarnow.

Tarnova Hotin, Mold.; pop. 31; 157 km NW of Kishinev; 48°13'/27°40'.

Tarnova Soroca, *see* Tyrnovo.

Tarnovitsa Lesna, Ukr. (Tarnovitsa Lesnaya?, Tarnowica Lesna); pop. 55; 101 km WNW of Chernovtsy; 48°41'/24°38'.

Tarnovitsa Lesnaya, *possibly* Tarnovitsa Lesna.

Tarnovitsa Polna, *see* Ternovitsa.

Tarnovka, *see* Ternovka.

Tarnow, Pol. (Tarna, Tarnov, Tarnuv, Torne, Tornen); pop. 15,608; 75 km E of Krakow; 50°01'/20°59'; AMG, CAHJP, COH, EDRD, EGRS, EJ, FRG, GA, GUM3, GUM4, GUM5, GUM6, GYLA, HSL, HSL2, ISH1, ISH2, ISH3, JGFF, LDL, LDS, LYV, PHP1, PHP2, PHP3, PHP4, POCEM, SF, YB.

Tarnow (Siedlce area), Pol.; pop. 32; 62 km SE of Warszawa; 51°48'/21°27'.

Tarnowica Lesna, *see* Tarnovitsa Lesna.

Tarnowica Polna, *see* Ternovitsa.

Tarnowice, Pol.; pop. 45 km SSW of Czestochowa; 50°26'/18°50'; GUM3, GUM5, PHP3.

Tarnowiec, *see* Tarnowskie Gory.

Tarnowitz, *see* Tarnowskie Gory.

Tarnowka, Pol. JGFF. A number of towns share this name. It was not possible to determine from available information which one is being referenced.

Tarnowko, Pol.; pop. 1; 50 km NW of Poznan; 52°47'/16°36'.

Tarnowo, Pol. JGFF. A number of towns share this name. It

was not possible to determine from available information which one is being referenced.

Tarnowo Podgorne, Pol.; pop. 3; 26 km W of Poznan; 52°28'/16°40'.

Tarnowskie Gory, Pol. (Tarnowiec, Tarnowitz); 45 km SSW of Czestochowa; 50°27'/18°52'; AMG, HSL, LDS, PHP3, POCEM.

Tarnuv, *see* Tarnow.

Tarogen, *see* Taurage.

Tarovitz, *see* Torgovitsa.

Tarpa, Hung.; pop. 245; 133 km E of Miskolc; 48°06'/22°32'; AMG, COH, GUM5, HSL, HSL2, PHH.

Tarsolt, *see* Tirsolt.

Tartakov, Ukr. (Tartakow, Tartakow Miasto, Tartakuv, Tartakuv Miasto, Tartekev); pop. 1,039; 75 km N of Lvov; 50°28'/24°24'; AMG, COH, EDRD, EGRS, EJ, GUM4, HSL, HSL2, LDL, LYV, PHP2, SF, YB.

Tartakow, *see* Tartakov.

Tartakow Miasto, *see* Tartakov.

Tartakuv, *see* Tartakov.

Tartakuv Miasto, *see* Tartakov.

Tartaria, Rom. (Felsotatarlaka, Tatarlaua); 101 km S of Cluj; 45°56'/23°25'; HSL.

Tartarov, *see* Kremintsy.

Tartchin, *see* Tarczyn.

Tartekev, *see* Tartakov.

Tartkowice, Pol. PHP2. This town was not found in BGN gazetteers under the given spelling.

Tartolcz, *see* Tirsolt.

Tartu, Est. (Derpt, Dorpa, Dorpat, Juriew, Jurjew, Tur Ev, Yuriev, Yuryev); pop. 846; 163 km ESE of Tallinn; 58°23'/26°43'; COH, EJ, GUM4, HSL, HSL2, JGFF, LDL, PHLE.

Taruj Falu, *see* Neresnitsa.

Tarutino, Ukr. (Anciokrak, Antchikrok); pop. 1,546; 126 km WSW of Odessa; 46°12'/29°09'; EJ, GUM4, LDL, PHR2, SF, YB. *See also* Tauteny.

Tarutino Nou, Ukr.; pop. 4; 126 km WSW of Odessa; 46°28'/29°07'.

Tarvydai, Lith. (Dimitravas); 133 km W of Siauliai; 55°58'/21°14'; GUM5.

Tarzik, *see* Irza.

Tashnad, *see* Tasnad.

Taska, Hung.; pop. 3; 45 km NE of Nagykanizsa; 46°37'/17°32'.

Taslac, *see* Kamenskoye (Bessarabia).

Tasnad, Rom. (Tashnad, Tasnad Blaja, Trestenberg); pop. 823; 107 km NW of Cluj; 47°29'/22°35'; GUM3, HSL, HSL2, JGFF, LDL, PHR2, YB.

Tasnad Blaja, *see* Tasnad.

Tasnadszanto, *see* Tasnadu Nou.

Tasnadu Nou, Rom. (Tasnadszanto); 114 km NW of Cluj; 47°31'/22°34'; HSL.

Tass, Hung.; pop. 49; 62 km S of Budapest; 47°01'/19°02'; HSL, HSL2, LDS.

Taszar, Hung.; 75 km E of Nagykanizsa; 46°22'/17°55'; HSL.

Taszyce, Pol.; pop. 10; 19 km SE of Krakow; 49°57'/20°04'.

Tata, Hung. (Toti, Totis); pop. 315; 56 km WNW of Budapest; 47°39'/18°19'; GUM3, HSL, HSL2, LDS.

Tatabanya, Hung.; pop. 64; 50 km W of Budapest; 47°34'/18°25'; PHH.

Tatahaza, Hung.; pop. 12; 69 km WSW of Szeged; 46°11'/19°18'.

Tatar Bunar, *see* Tatarbunary.

Tatarbunary, Ukr. (Tatar Bunar); pop. 1,202; 114 km SW of Odessa; 45°51'/29°37'; HSL, HSL2, SF.

Tatar Copceac, *see* Kopchak.

Tataresti, Rom.; pop. 24; 114 km NNW of Cluj; 47°41'/23°00'.

Tatarka, Byel.; 114 km ESE of Minsk; 53°15'/28°50'; HSL.

Tatarlaua, *see* Tartaria.

Tatarovca, *see* Tatarovka.

Tatarovka, Ukr. (Tatarovca); 88 km SW of Uman; 48°23'/29°11'; PHR1.

Tatarow, *possibly* Kremintsy.

Tatar Pazardzhik, *see* Pazardzhik.

Tatarsk, USSR; pop. 864; 69 km SSW of Smolensk; 54°15'/31°34'; GUM4, LDL, SF.

Tatarszentgyorgy, Hung.; pop. 19; 56 km SE of Budapest; 47°04'/19°23'.

Tatary, Ukr.; pop. 41; 56 km SW of Lvov; 49°31'/23°27'; PHP1.

Tatatovaros, Hung. PHH. This town was not found in BGN gazetteers under the given spelling.

Tatce, Cz.; pop. 3; 38 km E of Praha; 50°05'/14°59'.

Tatzmannsdorf, Aus.; pop. 26; This town was not found in BGN gazetteers under the given spelling.

Tauberbischofsheim, Germ.; pop. 111; 88 km ESE of Frankfurt am Main; 49°37'/09°40'; EDRD, GUM5, JGFF, PHGBW.

Tauberrettersheim, Germ.; pop. 21; 88 km W of Nurnberg; 49°30'/09°56'; GUM5, PHGB.

Taujenai, Lith. (Taunus, Tavian, Tvian); pop. 91; 82 km NE of Kaunas; 55°24'/24°45'; AMG, HSL, JGFF, LDL, SF, YL.

Taul, *see* Tsaul.

Taunus, *see* Taujenai.

Taurage, Lith. (Tarogen, Taurik, Taurogen, Tauroggen, Taurogi, Tavrogi, Tevrig, Tovrik); pop. 1,777; 101 km SW of Siauliai; 55°15'/22°17'; AMG, COH, EJ, GUM3, GUM4, GUM5, HSL, HSL2, JGFF, LDL, SF, YL.

Tauragnai, Lith. (Targin); pop. 477; 94 km N of Vilnius; 55°27'/25°49'; HSL, YL.

Taureni, Rom. (Mezotohat); 45 km ESE of Cluj; 46°34'/24°05'; HSL.

Taurik, *see* Taurage.

Taurkalne, *see* Taurkalni.

Taurkalni, Lat. (Taurkalne); pop. 7; 133 km WSW of Riga; 56°57'/21°57'.

Taurogen, *see* Taurage.

Tauroggen, *see* Taurage.

Taurogi, *see* Taurage.

Taurov, Ukr. (Taurow); pop. 48; 101 km ESE of Lvov; 49°32'/25°17'.

Taurow, *see* Taurov.

Tausendblum, Aus.; pop. 27; 38 km WSW of Wien; 48°11'/15°52'.

Tauseni, Rom.; pop. 2; 26 km NE of Cluj; 46°52'/23°55'.

Taut, Rom. (Feketeto?); 133 km WSW of Cluj; 46°43'/21°51'; HSL.

Tautelec, Rom. (Hegykoztottelek, Tottelek); pop. 7; 126 km WNW of Cluj; 47°09'/22°02'; HSL.

Tauteni, *see* Tauteny.

Tauteny, Ukr. (Tarutino, Tauteni, Toiteres, Tuteres); pop. 80; 32 km NNW of Chernovtsy; 48°34'/25°52'; CAHJP, PHR2, SF.

Tauteu, Rom.; pop. 82; 114 km WNW of Cluj; 47°16'/22°20'.

Tautii de Sus, Rom.; pop. 32; 101 km N of Cluj; 47°39'/23°39'.

Tavarna, *see* Tovarne.

Tavian, *see* Taujenai.

Tavrogi, *see* Taurage.

Tchais, LDL. This pre-World War I community was not found in BGN gazetteers.

Tchorznica, Pol.; pop. 8; 88 km SSW of Bialystok; 52°30'/22°22'.

Tczew, Pol. (Dirchau, Dirschau, Dirschaw, Strzewo); pop. 93; 32 km SSE of Gdansk; 54°06'/18°48'; AMG, CAHJP, GUM5, HSL, LDS.

Teaca, Rom. (Teckendorf, Teke); pop. 115; 69 km ENE of Cluj; 46°55'/24°31'; HSL, HSL2, PHR2.

Teceu Mic, Rom.; pop. 41; 146 km N of Cluj; 48°00'/23°35'.

Tech, *see* Tyachev.

Techobuz, Cz.; pop. 2; 75 km SE of Praha; 49°31'/14°56'.

Techonice, Cz.; pop. 4; 107 km SSW of Praha; 49°22'/13°34'.

Teci, GUM4. This town was not found in BGN gazetteers under the given spelling.

Teckendorf, *see* Teaca.

Tecs, *see* Tyachev.

Tecso, *see* Tyachev.

Tecuci, Rom.; 150 km S of Iasi; 45°52'/27°25'; EJ, GUM4, GUM5, GUM6.

Teczki, Pol.; pop. 19; 94 km N of Lublin; 52°02'/22°37'.

Teesdorf, Aus.; pop. 9; 32 km S of Wien; 47°57'/16°17'.

Teghea, Rom.; pop. 11; 114 km NW of Cluj; 47°35'/22°44'.

Teglas, Hung.; pop. 174; 75 km ESE of Miskolc; 47°43'/21°41'; HSL, HSL2, LDS, PHH, YB.

Tegoborze, Pol.; pop. 12; 69 km ESE of Krakow; 49°43'/20°38'.

Tehinia, *see* Bendery.

Tehovec, Cz.; pop. 3; 26 km ESE of Praha; 49°59'/14°44'.

Teis, Rom. BGN lists two possible localities with this name located at 45°36'/27°04' and 44°58'/25°24'. HSL.

Teitz, GUM6. This town was not found in BGN gazetteers under the given spelling.

Teius, Rom.; pop. 181; 69 km S of Cluj; 46°12'/23°41'; GUM4, PHR1.

Teke, *see* Teaca.

Tekehaza, Hung.; 170 km ENE of Miskolc; 48°07'/23°06'; HSL. This town was located on a pre-World War I map, but does not appear in contemporary gazetteers.

Tekovske Luzany, Cz. (Gross Sallo, Tekovske Luzianicy, Tekovske Sarluzky); pop. 180; 107 km E of Bratislava; 48°06'/18°32'; COH, HSL, LDL.

Tekovske Luzianicy, *see* Tekovske Luzany.

Tekovske Sarluzky, *see* Tekovske Luzany.

Tekucha, Ukr. (Tekucza); pop. 83; 82 km W of Chernovtsy; 48°23'/24°48'.

Tekucza, *see* Tekucha.

Telaki, Pol. (Telek); pop. 51; 88 km NE of Warszawa; 52°34'/22°10'; HSL, SF, WS.

Telatyn, Pol.; pop. 52; 114 km NNE of Przemysl; 50°32'/23°51'; HSL.

Telc, Cz.; pop. 78; 88 km WSW of Brno; 49°11'/15°28'; GUM5.

Telchan, *see* Telekhany.

Telchea, *see* Telechia.

Telchia, *see* Telechia.

Telciu, Rom. (Telcs); pop. 204; 94 km NNE of Cluj; 47°26'/24°24'; PHR2.

Telcs, *see* Telciu.

Telechany, *see* Telekhany.

Telechia, Rom. (Telchea, Telchia); pop. 35; 163 km N of Bucuresti; 45°52'/26°02'.

Telechi Recea, Rom. (Telekirecse); 157 km SE of Cluj; 45°44'/24°56'; HSL.

Telechiu, Rom.; pop. 12; 107 km WNW of Cluj; 47°03'/22°16'.

Telechon, *see* Telekhany.

Telegd, *possibly* Tileagd.

Telek, *see* Telaki.

Telekani, *see* Telekhany.

Telekhan, *see* Telekhany.

Telekhany, Byel. (Lahiszyn, Logishin, Lohishin, Lohiszyn, Telchan, Telechany, Telechon, Telekani, Telekhan); pop. 463; 50 km NNW of Pinsk; 52°31'/25°51'; COH, GUM4, GYLA, HSL, JGFF, LDL, LYV, SF, YB.

Telekirecse, *see* Telechi Recea.

Telenesht, *see* Teleneshty.

Telenesht Targ, *see* Teleneshty.

Teleneshty, Mold. (Telenesht, Telenesht Targ, Telenesti, Telenesti Sat, Telenesti Targ); pop. 2,811; 69 km NW of Kishinev; 47°30'/28°22'; HSL, JGFF, SF.

Telenesti, *see* Teleneshty.

Telenesti Sat, *see* Teleneshty.

Telenesti Targ, *see* Teleneshty.

Teleseu, *see* Teleshovo.

Telesheu, *see* Teleshovo.

Teleshovo, Mold. (Teleseu, Telesheu); pop. 24; 38 km NNW of Kishinev; 47°16'/28°43'.

Telesnica Oszwarowa, Pol.; pop. 224; 50 km S of Przemysl; 49°23'/22°33'; PHP2.

Telesnica Sanna, Pol.; pop. 13; 56 km S of Przemysl; 49°22'/22°31'.

Telfs, Aus.; pop. 3; 26 km W of Innsbruck; 47°18'/11°04'.

Telgte, GUM5, YB. A number of towns share this name. It was not possible to determine from available information which one is being referenced.

Telince, Cz. (Tild); 94 km ENE of Bratislava; 48°14'/18°22'; HSL.

Telkibanya, Hung.; pop. 17; 62 km NE of Miskolc; 48°29'/21°22'.

Telschi, *see* Telsiai.

Telse, *see* Telsiai.

Telsen, COH. This town was not found in BGN gazetteers under the given spelling.

Telsh, *see* Telsiai.

Tel She, *see* Telsiai.

Telshie, *see* Telsiai.

Telsia, LDL. This pre-World War I community was not found in BGN gazetteers.

Telsiai, Lith. (Tel She, Telschi, Telse, Telsh, Telshie, Telsze, Teltsch, Telz, Telzh); pop. 1,545; 69 km W of Siauliai; 55°59'/22°15'; AMG, COH, FRG, GUM3, GUM4, GUM5, HSL, HSL2, JGFF, LDL, SF, YB, YL.

Telsze, *see* Telsiai.

Teltsch, *see* Telsiai.

Telz, *see* Telsiai.

Telzh, *see* Telsiai.

Temelenti Lapusna, *see* Temeleutsy.

Temeleuts, *see* Temeleutsy.

Temeleutsy, Mold. (Temelenti Lapusna, Temeleuts); pop. 20; 62 km WNW of Kishinev; 47°15'/28°05'.

Temelin, Cz.; pop. 7; 107 km S of Praha; 49°12'/14°21'.

Temerin, Yug.; pop. 92; 82 km NW of Beograd; 45°25'/19°53'; GUM4, PHY.

Temerovtse, Ukr. (Temerowce); pop. 25; 94 km SE of Lvov; 49°06'/24°36'.

Temerowce, *see* Temerovtse.

Temesrekas, HSL. This pre-World War I community was not found in BGN gazetteers.

Temesvar, *see* Timisoara.

Temesvar Gyarvaros, HSL. This pre-World War I community was not found in BGN gazetteers.

Temesvar Josefvaros, HSL. This pre-World War I community was not found in BGN gazetteers.

Temeszow, Pol.; pop. 3; 45 km WSW of Przemysl; 49°42'/22°14'; HSL.

Temir Chan Shura, LDL. This pre-World War I community was not found in BGN gazetteers.

Tempelburg, *see* Czaplinek.

Templin, Germ.; 75 km N of Berlin; 53°07'/13°30'; HSL.

Tempoczow, Pol.; pop. 18; 38 km NE of Krakow; 50°19'/20°21'.

Tenczynek, Pol.; pop. 22; 26 km W of Krakow; 50°07'/19°37'; PHP3.

Tenetniki, Ukr.; pop. 17; 82 km SE of Lvov; 49°14'/24°32'.

Tengod, Hung.; pop. 9; 88 km NE of Nagykanizsa; 46°42'/18°06'.

Teniatyska, Pol.; pop. 21; 82 km NNE of Przemysl; 50°20'/23°34'.

Tenje, GUM4, GUM5. This town was not found in BGN gazetteers under the given spelling.

Tenk, Hung.; pop. 3; 62 km SSW of Miskolc; 47°39'/20°21'; HSL.

Tenke, *see* Tinca.

Tentea, Rom. (Czente); pop. 4; 50 km NE of Cluj; 47°00'/24°08'.

Teodorsgof, Ukr. (Teodorshof, Theodorshof); pop. 17; 32 km NNE of Lvov; 50°05'/24°12'.

Teodorshof, *see* Teodorsgof.

Teodory, Pol.; pop. 3; 26 km SW of Lodz; 51°35'/19°12'; PHP1.

Teofipol, Ukr. (Chan, Tiofipol); pop. 1,483; 88 km SSE of Rovno; 49°50'/26°25'; JGFF, SF.

Teosin, Pol.; pop. 41; 82 km E of Lublin; 51°09'/23°45'.

Tepe, Hung.; pop. 3; 101 km SE of Miskolc; 47°19'/21°35'; LDS.

Tepla Mesto, Cz.; pop. 22; 114 km WSW of Praha; 49°49'/12°57'.

Teplice, Cz. (Teplice Sanov, Teplitz, Teplitz Schoenau, Teplitz Schonau); pop. 3,128; 75 km NW of Praha; 50°38'/13°50'; AMG, CAHJP, EJ, GUM3, GUM5, HSL, HSL2, JGFF.

Teplice Sanov, see Teplice.

Teplik, Ukr.; pop. 3,062; 38 km WSW of Uman; 48°40'/29°44'; EDRD, GUM4, JGFF, PHR1, SF, YB.

Teplitz, see Teplice.

Teplitz Schoenau, see Teplice.

Teplitz Schonau, see Teplice.

Teptin, Cz.; pop. 5; 32 km SSE of Praha; 49°53'/14°34'.

Terasiwka, see Khutor Tarasivka.

Teratyn, Pol.; pop. 55; 88 km ESE of Lublin; 50°54'/23°46'.

Tereben, Byel.; pop. 15; 45 km N of Pinsk; 52°27'/26°20'.

Terebes, see Trebisov.

Terebesfejer Patak, see Delovoye.

Terebesti, Rom.; pop. 7; 120 km NW of Cluj; 47°41'/22°43'.

Terebezhov, Byel. (Terebezhuv, Terebiezow); pop. 40; 50 km ESE of Pinsk; 51°49'/26°43'.

Terebezhuv, see Terebezhov.

Terebiezow, see Terebezhov.

Terebin, Pol.; pop. 25; 101 km ESE of Lublin; 50°44'/23°49'.

Terebla, see Tereblya.

Tereble, see Tereblya.

Tereblecea, see Terebleshti.

Tereblecea Noua, see Terebleshti.

Tereblecesa Noua, see Terebleshti.

Terebleshti, Ukr. (Tereblecea, Tereblecea Noua, Tereblecesa Noua); pop. 35; 38 km SSE of Chernovtsy; 48°02'/26°04'.

Tereblichi, Byel. (Tereblicze); pop. 21; 88 km E of Pinsk; 52°01'/27°26'.

Tereblicze, see Tereblichi.

Tereblya, Ukr. (Talaborfalu, Terebla, Tereble); 170 km WSW of Chernovtsy; 48°07'/23°36'; AMG, HSL, SM.

Terebna, Mold.; pop. 70; 163 km WNW of Kishinev; 48°03'/27°15'.

Terebovlya, Ukr. (Trebevle, Trembovla, Trembowla); pop. 1,486; 114 km NNW of Chernovtsy; 49°18'/25°43'; AMG, CAHJP, COH, EDRD, EGRS, GUM3, GUM4, GUM5, GYLA, HSL, HSL2, JGFF, LDL, PHP2, SF, YB.

Terehegy, Hung.; pop. 1; 114 km ESE of Nagykanizsa; 45°52'/18°13'.

Teremne, see Teremno.

Teremno, Ukr. (Teremne); pop. 6; 50 km S of Rovno; 50°13'/26°14'; GUM4.

Tereny, Hung.; pop. 6; 56 km NNE of Budapest; 47°57'/19°27'.

Terep, see Trip.

Teres, GA. This town was not found in BGN gazetteers under the given spelling.

Tereselpatak, see Tarasovka.

Tereshel, see Tarasovka.

Tereshkovtsy, Ukr. (Tereszkowce); pop. 8; 94 km WSW of Rovno; 50°32'/24°53'.

Tereshpol, see Tereszpol.

Teresif, see Tarasovka.

Teresin, see Tereszyn.

Tereske, Hung.; pop. 20; 56 km N of Budapest; 47°57'/19°12'.

Teresnev, see Trzezniow.

Teresov, Cz.; 56 km SW of Praha; 49°54'/13°42'; COH, HSL.

Teresova, see Tarasovka.

Teresow, Pol.; pop. 7; 45 km E of Czestochowa; 50°48'/19°43'.

Terespol, Pol. (Terespoli, Terespolia, Terespolya); pop. 1,024; 120 km SSE of Bialystok; 52°05'/23°37'; COH, HSL, HSL2, JGFF, LDL, LDS, LYV, PHP4, SF.

Terespoli, see Terespol.

Terespolia, see Terespol.

Terespolya, see Terespol.

Tereszkowce, see Tereshkovtsy.

Tereszpol, Pol. (Tereshpol); pop. 29; 82 km SSE of Lublin; 50°34'/22°56'; SF.

Teresztenye, Hung. (Trestena); pop. 3; 45 km NNW of Miskolc; 48°27'/20°37'; COH, HSL.

Tereszyn, Pol. (Teresin); 13 km SW of Lublin; 51°12'/22°25'; GUM3.

Terezin, Cz. (Theresienstadt); pop. 103; 50 km NW of Praha; 50°31'/14°09'; AMG, EJ, GUM3, GUM4, GUM5, GUM6, ISH3, PHGBW. Terezin was the location of Theresienstadt concentration camp. Some sources may refer to the camp rather than the town.

Terisel, see Tarasovka.

Terka, Pol.; pop. 12; 62 km SSW of Przemysl; 49°18'/22°26'.

Terlica, see Terlitsa.

Terliczka, Pol.; pop. 9; 62 km WNW of Przemysl; 50°06'/22°05'.

Terlitsa, Ukr. (Terlica, Terlitza); 45 km WNW of Uman; 48°56'/29°42'; COH, JGFF, LDL, SF.

Terlitza, see Terlitsa.

Terlo, Ukr. (Terlo Rustakalne, Terlo Rustikalne, Terlo Rustykalne, Terlo Szlacheckie); pop. 50; 101 km SW of Lvov; 49°28'/22°46'; EGRS.

Terlo Rustakalne, see Terlo.

Terlo Rustikalne, see Terlo.

Terlo Rustykalne, see Terlo.

Terlo Szlacheckie, see Terlo.

Termesivy, Cz.; pop. 3; 88 km WNW of Brno; 49°36'/15°37'.

Terna, Cz.; 50 km N of Kosice; 49°07'/21°14'; JGFF.

Ternava, see Tarnava.

Ternets, Ukr. (Ternits); pop. 1,051; 150 km WNW of Rovno; 51°36'/24°41'.

Terneve, see Ternovo.

Ternits, see Ternets.

Ternive, see Trnava.

Ternopol, Ukr. (Tarnopol); pop. 13,768; 120 km E of Lvov; 49°33'/25°35'; AMG, COH, EDRD, EGRS, EJ, GA, GUM3, GUM4, GUM5, GUM6, HSL, HSL2, JGFF, LDL, PHP1, PHP2, PHP3, SF, YB.

Ternopolye, Ukr. (Dornfeld); 32 km S of Lvov; 49°38'/23°57'; PHP1.

Ternova, Ukr.; 101 km NNE of Chernovtsy; 49°01'/26°47'; AMG, GUM3.

Ternovitsa, Ukr. (Tarnovitsa Polna, Tarnowica Polna); pop. 25; 88 km WNW of Chernovtsy; 48°47'/24°56'.

Ternovka, Ukr. (Tarnovka, Ternowka); pop. 3,081; 32 km SSW of Uman; 48°32'/29°58'; GUM4, HSL, HSL2, LDL, SF, YB.

Ternovo, Ukr. (Kokenyes, Terneve, Trnovo nad Teresvon); 163 km WSW of Chernovtsy; 48°05'/23°45'; AMG, GUM5, SM.

Ternowka, see Ternovka.

Terpilovka, Ukr. (Terpilowka); pop. 56; 114 km S of Rovno; 49°37'/26°03'.

Terpilowka, see Terpilovka.

Tershuvo, Ukr. (Terszow); pop. 61; 88 km SW of Lvov; 49°24'/22°59'.

Terszow, see Tershuvo.

Tervete, Lat. (Tervetes); pop. 8; 69 km SW of Riga; 56°29'/23°24'.

Tervetes, see Tervete.

Tes, HSL. A number of towns share this name. It was not possible to determine from available information which one is being referenced.

Tesa, Hung.; pop. 4; 62 km NNW of Budapest; 48°02'/18°51'.

Tesanj, Yug.; pop. 18; 195 km WSW of Beograd; 44°37'/18°00'.

Tesanovci, Yug.; pop. 7; 107 km N of Zagreb; 46°41'/16°15'.

Tesare nad Zitavou, Cz. (Barstaszar); 94 km ENE of Bratislava; 48°20'/18°22'; HSL.

Teschen, see Cieszyn.

Teschenmoschel, Germ.; pop. 21; 88 km SW of Frankfurt am Main; 49°38'/07°44'; GED, JGFF.

Tescureni, see Teshkureny.

Tesedikovo, Cz. (Pered); pop. 130; 56 km E of Bratislava; 48°06'/17°51'.

Tesenfa, Hung.; pop. 2; 114 km ESE of Nagykanizsa; 45°49'/18°07'.

Teshin, *see* Cieszyn.

Teshkureny, Mold. (Tescureni); pop. 13; 82 km WNW of Kishinev; 47°24'/27°57'.

Tesin, *see* Cesky Tesin. Tesin, Czechoslovakia and Cieszyn, Poland are twin cities.

Tesin Cesky, *see* Cesky Tesin.

Teskov, Cz.; pop. 1; 62 km SW of Praha; 49°48'/13°42'.

Teslic, Yug.; pop. 16; 195 km ESE of Zagreb; 44°37'/17°52'.

Tesmag, *see* Tesmak.

Tesmak, Cz. (Tesmag); 139 km E of Bratislava; 48°04'/18°59'; HSL.

Tesov, Ukr. (Tesow); pop. 26; 32 km ESE of Rovno; 50°30'/26°38'.

Tesow, *see* Tesov.

Tessin, Germ.; 26 km E of Rostock; 54°02'/12°28'; CAHJP, LDS.

Tet, Hung.; pop. 178; 120 km W of Budapest; 47°31'/17°31'; HSL, HSL2, LDS, PHH.

Tetcani, *see* Tetskany.

Tetche, Rom. (Czeczke, Tetchea); 101 km WNW of Cluj; 47°03'/22°19'; AMG, HSL.

Tetchea, *see* Tetche.

Teteny, HSL. This pre-World War I community was not found in BGN gazetteers.

Teterow, Germ.; pop. 38; 50 km SE of Rostock; 53°47'/12°34'; LDS.

Tetetlen, Hung.; pop. 61; 94 km SSE of Miskolc; 47°19'/21°18'; AMG, GUM3, HSL, LDS, PHH.

Tetevchitse, Ukr. (Tetewczyce); pop. 20; 75 km NNE of Lvov; 50°20'/24°42'.

Tetewczyce, *see* Tetevchitse.

Tetiev, *see* Tetiyev.

Tetin, Cz. BGN lists two possible localities with this name located at 49°57'/14°06' and 50°25'/15°38'. HSL.

Tetiyev, Ukr. (Tetiev); 82 km NW of Uman; 49°23'/29°40'; EDRD, EJ, HSL, JGFF, LDL, SF.

Tetov, Cz.; 69 km E of Praha; 50°05'/15°27'; HSL.

Tetsh, *see* Tyachev.

Tetskany, Ukr. (Tetcani); pop. 67; 82 km E of Chernovtsy; 48°10'/26°59'.

Tetszentkut, Hung.; 120 km WSW of Budapest; 47°29'/17°30'; LDS.

Tetyanov, USSR; pop. 1,563; This town was not found in BGN gazetteers under the given spelling.

Teunz, Germ.; pop. 5; 94 km ENE of Nurnberg; 49°29'/12°23'; PHGB.

Tevel, Hung.; pop. 22; 114 km E of Nagykanizsa; 46°25'/18°27'; HSL.

Tevli, Byel. (Tewle, Tewli); pop. 49; 126 km W of Pinsk; 52°20'/24°15'; HSL.

Tevrig, *see* Taurage.

Tewle, *see* Tevli.

Tewli, *see* Tevli.

Thale, Germ.; pop. 21; 101 km WNW of Leipzig; 51°45'/11°03'.

Thaleischweiler, Germ.; pop. 11; 120 km SSW of Frankfurt am Main; 49°16'/07°34'; GED, JGFF.

Thalfang, Germ.; pop. 45; 126 km SW of Frankfurt am Main; 49°45'/07°00'; JGFF.

Thalmassing, Germ. (Thalmessingen); pop. 42; 50 km SSE of Nurnberg; 49°05'/11°13'; CAHJP, GUM3, HSL, PHGB.

Thalmessingen, *see* Thalmassing.

Thann, Germ.; pop. 38; 38 km NE of Munchen; 48°16'/12°03'; HSL, HSL2, LDS.

Thannhausen, Germ.; pop. 82 km W of Munchen; 48°17'/10°28'; PHGB.

Thebes, Greece; 56 km NW of Athens; 38°19'/23°19'; GUM4.

Theilheim, Germ.; pop. 81; 82 km WNW of Nurnberg; 49°45'/10°02'; GUM5, JGFF, PHGB.

Themar, Germ.; pop. 64; 120 km NNW of Nurnberg; 50°30'/10°38'; LDS.

Theodorshof, *see* Teodorsgof.

Theodosia, *see* Feodosiya.

Theresienstadt, *see* Terezin.

Thessaloniki, Greece (Salonika, Saloniki); pop. 55,250; 208 km NE of Ioannina; 40°38'/22°58'; CAHJP, COH, GUM3, GUM4, GUM5, GUM6, HSL, ISH1, ISH3, JGFF, LDL, PHP2, YB.

Thessaly, Greece; 101 km E of Ioannina; 39°30'/22°00'; GUM4.

Thishky, *see* Tryskiai.

Tholey, Germ.; pop. 41; 139 km SW of Frankfurt am Main; 49°29'/07°04'; GED.

Thonischen, *see* Tyniste.

Thorenburg, *see* Turda.

Thorn, *see* Torun.

Thum, Germ. BGN lists two possible localities with this name located at 50°41'/12°58' and 50°42'/06°31'. AMG.

Thundorf, *see* Thundorf in Unterfranken.

Thundorf in Unterfranken, Germ. (Thundorf); 101 km NW of Nurnberg; 50°12'/10°19'; PHGB.

Thungen, Germ.; pop. 180; 82 km E of Frankfurt am Main; 49°57'/09°51'; GUM5, PHGB.

Thungfeld, Germ.; pop. 38 km NW of Nurnberg; 49°45'/10°47'; PHGB.

Thur, Germ.; pop. 19; 69 km SSE of Koln; 50°21'/07°17'.

Thuringia; Not a town, but a region of central Germany.

Thurnau, Germ.; 69 km N of Nurnberg; 50°01'/11°23'; PHGB.

Thurndorf, Germ.; 50 km NE of Nurnberg; 49°46'/11°39'; PHGB.

Tiacevo, *see* Tyachev.

Tiachev, *see* Tyachev.

Tiacheva, *see* Tyachev.

Tiaczowo, *see* Tyachev.

Tiapcze, *see* Tyapche.

Tiba, Cz. BGN lists two possible localities with this name located at 46°21'/25°48' and 48°31'/20°23'. HSL.

Tibana, Rom.; 32 km SSW of Iasi; 46°59'/27°20'; PHR1.

Tibava, Cz.; pop. 93; 75 km ENE of Kosice; 48°45'/22°14'; AMG.

Tibeni, Rom.; pop. 41; 139 km WNW of Iasi; 47°49'/26°02'.

Tibirica, *see* Tsibirika.

Tibolddaroc, Hung.; pop. 70; 26 km SSW of Miskolc; 47°55'/20°38'; HSL, JGFF, PHH.

Tibulovca, GUM4, PHR1. This town was not found in BGN gazetteers under the given spelling.

Ticau, Rom.; pop. 7; 82 km NNW of Cluj; 47°26'/23°18'.

Ticha, Cz.; 120 km NE of Brno; 49°34'/18°14'; HSL.

Ticheniz, *see* Tikhinichi.

Tichy Potok, Cz. (Stelbach); 62 km NW of Kosice; 49°09'/20°47'; HSL, HSL2.

Ticu, Rom. (Forgacskut); pop. 10; 38 km WNW of Cluj; 46°55'/23°15'.

Tiengen, Germ.; pop. 87; 146 km SSW of Stuttgart; 47°38'/08°16'; GED, GUM5, JGFF, PHGBW, YB.

Tiganasi, Rom.; pop. 100; 26 km NW of Iasi; 47°20'/27°28'; PHR1.

Tiganesti, *see* Tsyganeshty.

Tiganestii de Cris, Rom.; pop. 4; 107 km WNW of Cluj; 47°07'/22°17'.

Tigau, Rom.; pop. 6; 62 km NE of Cluj; 47°04'/24°20'.

Tigech, Mold. (Tigheci); pop. 5; 75 km SSW of Kishinev; 46°24'/28°23'.

Tigerfeld, Germ.; 62 km SSE of Stuttgart; 48°16'/09°23'; PHGBW.

Tigheci, *see* Tigech.

Tighina, *see* Bendery.

Tiginia, *see* Bendery.

Tiha, Cz.; 120 km ENE of Kosice; 48°56'/22°49'; HSL, HSL2. This town was located on a pre-World War I map, but does not appear in contemporary gazetteers.

Tiha Birgaului, Rom. (Borgotiha); 101 km NE of Cluj; 47°14'/24°46'; HSL.

Tihany, Hung.; pop. 5; 88 km NE of Nagykanizsa; 46°55'/17°54'.

Tihau, Rom.; pop. 2; 56 km NNW of Cluj; 47°13'/23°21'.

Tikhinichi, Byel. (Ticheniz, Titchinitz); pop. 420; 114 km WNW of Gomel; 53°10'/29°52'; SF.

Tikhvin, USSR; pop. 176; 182 km E of Leningrad; 59°39'/33°31'.

Tikotsin, *see* Tykocin.

Tiktin, *see* Tykocin.

Tilaj, Hung.; pop. 7; 50 km N of Nagykanizsa; 46°48'/17°03'.

Tild, *see* Telince.

Tileagd, Rom. (Mezo Telegd, Mezotelegd, Telegd?); pop. 296; 114 km WNW of Cluj; 47°04'/22°12'; HSL, LDL, PHR2.

Tilitch, *see* Tylicz.

Tilsen, *see* Talsi.

Tilsit, *see* Sovetsk.

Tilza, Lat. (Tilzas); pop. 46; 126 km NNE of Daugavpils; 56°54'/27°22'; GUM4, PHLE.

Tilzas, *see* Tilza.

Timborg, *see* Tymbark.

Timisoara, Rom. (Temesvar, Timiszora); pop. 9,368; 214 km SW of Cluj; 45°45'/21°13'; EJ, GUM4, GUM6, HSL, HSL2, JGFF, LDL, LDS, PHR1.

Timiszora, *see* Timisoara.

Timkovichi, Byel. (Timkovitz); pop. 1,093; 101 km SSW of Minsk; 53°04'/26°59'; GYLA, JGFF, LDL, SF, YB.

Timkovitz, *see* Timkovichi.

Tina Bargaului, *see* Tina Birgaului.

Tina Birgaului, Rom. (Tina Bargaului); pop. 37; Described in the *Black Book* as being in the Transylvania region of Romania, this town was not found in BGN gazetteers.

Tinaud, Rom.; pop. 11; 94 km WNW of Cluj; 47°03'/22°26'.

Tinca, Rom. (Tenke); 126 km WSW of Cluj; 46°46'/21°57'; HSL, PHR1.

Tinets, Ukr. (Tyniec); GUM3, GUM5, PHP3. This town was not found in BGN gazetteers under the given spelling.

Tinnye, Hung.; pop. 68; 26 km WNW of Budapest; 47°37'/18°47'; HSL, LDL, LDS, PHH.

Tiofipol, *see* Teofipol.

Tipilesti, Mold.; pop. 25; 107 km NW of Kishinev; 47°49'/28°08'.

Tipolovka Veche, GUM4. This town was not found in BGN gazetteers under the given spelling.

Tirashpol, Mold. (Tiraspol, Tyraspol); pop. 6,398; 114 km S of Kishinev; 46°03'/28°49'; EJ, GUM3, GUM4, GUM5, HSL, JGFF, PHR1, SF.

Tiraspol, *see* Tirashpol.

Tirava Vilaska, *see* Tyrawa Woloska.

Tirek, *see* Turek.

Tirgiu Lapus, *see* Tirgu Lapus.

Tirgu, *see* Tirgu Secuesc.

Tirgu Frumos, Rom. (Targu Frumos, Targul Frumos); pop. 1,608; 45 km W of Iasi; 47°12'/27°00'; CAHJP, EJ, GUM4, HSL, LDL, PHR1.

Tirgu Gloduli, (Targu Gloduri); PHR1. This town was not found in BGN gazetteers under the given spelling.

Tirgu Jiu, Rom. (Targu Jiu, Targul Jiu); 195 km S of Cluj; 45°03'/23°17'; GUM3, GUM4, GUM5, GUM6, PHR1.

Tirgu Lapus, Rom. (Magyarlapos, Targu Laposului, Targu Lopus, Targul Lapush, Targul Lapusului, Tirgiu Lapus); pop. 689; 82 km N of Cluj; 47°27'/23°52'; CAHJP, COH, HSL, JGFF, LDL, PHR2, YB.

Tirgu Mures, Rom. (Marosvasarhely, Naymarkt, Neumark am Mures, Neumarkt, Targu Miresh, Targu Mores, Targu Myres, Targul Mures, Torgu Muresh); pop. 5,193; 75 km ESE of Cluj; 46°33'/24°34'; AMG, COH, EJ, GUM3, GUM4, GUM5, GUM6, HSL, JGFF, LDL, LYV, PHR2, YB.

Tirgu Neamt, Rom. (Targu Neamt, Targy Neanirom); 94 km W of Iasi; 47°12'/26°22'; AMG, EJ, JGFF, PHR1.

Tirgu Ocna, Rom. (Targu Ocna, Targul Ocna); 120 km SSW of Iasi; 46°17'/26°37'; GUM3, GUM4, LDL.

Tirgu Secuesc, Rom. (Targu Sacuiesc, Targul Secuiesc, Tirgu, Tirgu Secuiesc); pop. 68; 170 km SSW of Iasi; 46°00'/26°08';

HSL, PHR2.

Tirgu Secuiesc, *see* Tirgu Secuesc.

Tirimia Mare, Ukr. (Nagyteremi); 107 km W of Chernovtsy; 48°27'/24°30'; HSL.

Tirimioara, Rom.; pop. 3; 82 km ESE of Cluj; 46°27'/24°33'.

Tirkosla, *see* Tirksliai.

Tirkshla, *see* Tirksliai.

Tirksliai, Lith. (Tirkosla, Tirkshla); pop. 119; 75 km WNW of Siauliai; 56°16'/22°19'; GUM3, HSL, LDL, SF, YL.

Tirlisua, Rom. (Felsoilosva, Tarlisua); pop. 26; 82 km NNE of Cluj; 47°23'/24°11'.

Tirnoy, *see* Trnava.

Tirnoya, *see* Trnava.

Tirol; Not a town, but a region of Austria.

Tirschenreuth, Germ.; pop. 25; 101 km NE of Nurnberg; 49°53'/12°21'; GUM3, PHGB.

Tirschtiegel, *see* Trzciel.

Tirsolt, Rom. (Tarsolt, Tartolcz); pop. 123; 139 km NNW of Cluj; 47°57'/23°21'; HSL, PHR2.

Tirumbaltgalvji, Lat. (Plavinu); pop. 636; 94 km NW of Daugavpils; 56°35'/25°50'.

Tirza, Lat.; pop. 4; 139 km ENE of Riga; 57°08'/26°26'; PHLE.

Tisachege, *see* Tiszacsege.

Tisauti, Rom.; pop. 9; 107 km WNW of Iasi; 47°37'/26°18'.

Tishevits, *see* Tyszowce.

Tishevitz, *see* Tyszowce.

Tishovits, *see* Tyszowce.

Tishovtse, *see* Tyszowce.

Tishvits, *see* Tyszowce.

Tishvitz, *see* Tyszowce.

Tisice, Cz.; pop. 5; 26 km N of Praha; 50°16'/14°33'.

Tisinec, Cz. (Tisinyecz); 62 km NNE of Kosice; 49°14'/21°38'; HSL.

Tisinyecz, *see* Tisinec.

Tiska, *see* Tuska.

Tismenitz, *see* Tysmenitsa.

Tismice, Cz.; pop. 5; 26 km E of Praha; 50°04'/14°49'.

Tisova, JGFF. A number of towns share this name. It was not possible to determine from available information which one is being referenced.

Tisovec, Cz.; pop. 64; 94 km WSW of Kosice; 48°41'/19°57'.

Tisralunka, *see* Luh.

Tist, *see* Tust.

Tiszaabadszalok, Hung.; 75 km S of Miskolc; 47°29'/20°39'; HSL. This town was located on a pre-World War I map, but does not appear in contemporary gazetteers.

Tiszaadony, Hung.; pop. 48; 114 km ENE of Miskolc; 48°14'/22°18'; HSL.

Tiszababolna, Hung.; pop. 4; 50 km S of Miskolc; 47°41'/20°49'; HSL.

Tiszabecs, Hung.; pop. 49; 150 km E of Miskolc; 48°06'/22°49'; HSL.

Tiszabercel, Hung.; pop. 175; 69 km ENE of Miskolc; 48°09'/21°39'; LDS, PHH.

Tiszabezded, Hung. (Bezded, Bezdedtelek); pop. 73; 107 km NE of Miskolc; 48°22'/22°09'; AMG, HSL, LDS, PHH.

Tiszabo, Hung.; pop. 32; 94 km S of Miskolc; 47°18'/20°29'; HSL, LDS, PHH.

Tiszabogdany, *see* Bogdan.

Tiszaborkut, *see* Kvasy.

Tiszabud, *see* Tiszavasvari.

Tiszabura, Hung.; pop. 17; 75 km S of Miskolc; 47°27'/20°28'.

Tiszacsecse, Hung.; pop. 5; 146 km E of Miskolc; 48°06'/22°45'.

Tiszacsege, Hung. (Chege, Csege, Sege, Tisachege); pop. 145; 50 km SSE of Miskolc; 47°42'/21°00'; HSL, LDS, LYV, PHH.

Tiszadada, Hung.; pop. 157; 38 km E of Miskolc; 48°02'/21°15'; AMG, HSL, LDL, LDS, PHH.

Tiszaderzs, Hung.; pop. 9; 69 km S of Miskolc; 47°31'/20°39'.

Tiszadob, Hung.; pop. 101; 32 km ESE of Miskolc; 48°01'/21°10'; HSL, PHH.

Tiszadorogma, Hung.; pop. 52; 50 km SSE of Miskolc; 47°41'/20°52'; HSL, PHH.

Tiszaeszlar, Hung.; pop. 61; 50 km E of Miskolc; 48°03'/21°28'; EJ, HSL, PHH.

Tiszafeyeenyhaz, *see* Bila Cirkev.

Tiszafoldvar, Hung.; pop. 115; 88 km N of Szeged; 46°59'/20°15'; LDS, PHH.

Tiszafured, Hung.; pop. 506; 56 km S of Miskolc; 47°37'/20°46'; COH, GUM5, HSL, HSL2, LDL, LDS, PHH.

Tiszaigar, Hung.; pop. 25; 69 km S of Miskolc; 47°32'/20°48'; HSL.

Tiszainoka, Hung.; pop. 3; 75 km N of Szeged; 46°54'/20°09'.

Tiszakanyar, Hung.; pop. 16; 88 km ENE of Miskolc; 48°15'/21°58'; LDS.

Tiszakaracsonfalva, *see* Craciunesti.

Tiszakarad, Hung.; pop. 46; 69 km ENE of Miskolc; 48°12'/21°43'.

Tiszakecske, Hung. (Ujkecke); 82 km N of Szeged; 46°56'/20°06'; LDS.

Tiszakerecseny, Hung.; pop. 49; 114 km ENE of Miskolc; 48°16'/22°18'; HSL.

Tiszakeszi, Hung.; pop. 47; 38 km SE of Miskolc; 47°47'/21°00'; HSL.

Tiszakorod, Hung.; pop. 21; 146 km E of Miskolc; 48°06'/22°43'; HSL.

Tiszakurt, Hung.; pop. 6; 75 km N of Szeged; 46°53'/20°07'.

Tiszaladany, Hung.; 50 km E of Miskolc; 48°04'/21°25'; HSL.

Tiszalok, Hung.; pop. 405; 45 km E of Miskolc; 48°01'/21°23'; AMG, COH, GUM4, HSL, LDS, PHH.

Tiszalonka, GUM5. This town was not found in BGN gazetteers under the given spelling.

Tiszaluc, Hung. (Tiszaluk); pop. 174; 26 km ESE of Miskolc; 48°02'/21°05'; HSL, PHH.

Tiszaluk, *see* Tiszaluc.

Tiszamogyoros, Hung.; pop. 17; 114 km ENE of Miskolc; 48°19'/22°14'.

Tiszanagyfalu, Hung.; pop. 15; 56 km E of Miskolc; 48°06'/21°29'.

Tiszanana, Hung.; pop. 43; 62 km S of Miskolc; 47°34'/20°32'; HSL.

Tiszaors, Hung.; pop. 5; 69 km S of Miskolc; 47°31'/20°50'; HSL.

Tiszapalkonya, Hung.; pop. 40; 32 km SE of Miskolc; 47°53'/21°04'; HSL.

Tiszapolgar, *see* Polgar.

Tiszapuspoki, Hung.; pop. 8; 101 km ESE of Budapest; 47°13'/20°19'.

Tiszarad, Hung.; pop. 5; 75 km ENE of Miskolc; 48°07'/21°48'.

Tiszaroff, Hung.; pop. 58; 82 km S of Miskolc; 47°24'/20°27'; HSL, PHH.

Tiszasas, Hung.; pop. 16; 69 km N of Szeged; 46°49'/20°05'.

Tiszasuly, Hung.; pop. 44; 82 km S of Miskolc; 47°23'/20°24'.

Tiszaszalka, Hung.; pop. 92; 114 km ENE of Miskolc; 48°11'/22°19'; GUM3, HSL, PHH.

Tiszaszederkeny, Hung.; pop. 24; 32 km ESE of Miskolc; 47°56'/21°05'; HSL.

Tiszaszentimre, Hung.; pop. 48; 75 km S of Miskolc; 47°29'/20°44'; HSL, LDS, PHH.

Tiszaszentmarton, Hung.; pop. 56; 114 km NE of Miskolc; 48°23'/22°14'; LDS, PHH.

Tisza Szipma, COH. This town was not found in BGN gazetteers under the given spelling.

Tiszaszollas, HSL. This pre-World War I community was not found in BGN gazetteers.

Tiszaszollos, Hung.; pop. 58; 62 km S of Miskolc; 47°34'/20°44'; HSL.

Tiszatardos, Hung.; pop. 11; 45 km E of Miskolc; 48°03'/21°23'.

Tiszatarjan, Hung.; pop. 20; 32 km SE of Miskolc; 47°50'/21°01'; HSL.

Tiszaug, Hung.; pop. 1; 69 km N of Szeged; 46°51'/20°04'.

Tiszaujfalu, Hung.; pop. 11; 69 km NNW of Szeged; 46°48'/20°01'.

Tisza Ujlak, *see* Vilok.

Tiszavalk, Hung.; 50 km S of Miskolc; 47°41'/20°45'; HSL.

Tiszavarkony, Hung.; pop. 17; 94 km N of Szeged; 47°04'/20°11'.

Tiszavasvari, Hung. (Tiszabud); pop. 99; 45 km ESE of Miskolc; 47°58'/21°21'; LDS, PHH.

Tiszavere, *see* Virismort.

Tiszaveresmart, *see* Virismort.

Tiszavid, Hung.; pop. 13; 114 km ENE of Miskolc; 48°12'/22°18'; HSL.

Tisztaberek, Hung.; pop. 15; 150 km E of Miskolc; 47°57'/22°48'.

Titchin, *see* Tyczyn.

Titchinitz, *see* Tikhinichi.

Titel, Yug.; pop. 67; 50 km NNW of Beograd; 45°13'/20°18'; GUM4, HSL, PHY.

Titovo Uzice, Yug. (Uzice); pop. 21; 120 km SSW of Beograd; 43°52'/19°51'.

Titov Veles, Yug. (Veles); pop. 6; 45 km SE of Skopje; 41°42'/21°48'.

Tittmoning, Germ.; 88 km E of Munchen; 48°04'/12°46'; GUM4, GUM5, GUM6.

Tiuriv, *see* Tyvrov.

Tivadar, Hung.; pop. 17; 133 km E of Miskolc; 48°04'/22°31'.

Tizmenitza, *see* Tysmenitsa.

Tlashch, *see* Tluszcz.

Tlashts, *see* Tluszcz.

Tlist, *see* Tust.

Tlomats, *see* Tlumach.

Tluchowo, Pol.; pop. 60; 114 km N of Lodz; 52°45'/19°28'.

Tlumach, Ukr. (Talmach, Talmatch, Tlomats, Tlumacz, Tlumatch); pop. 2,012; 94 km WNW of Chernovtsy; 48°52'/25°00'; AMG, COH, EDRD, EGRS, EJ, GUM3, GUM4, GUM5, GYLA, HSL, HSL2, LYV, PHP2, SF, YB.

Tlumachik, *see* Tolmachik.

Tlumacz, *see* Tlumach.

Tlumaczyk, *see* Tolmachik.

Tlumatch, *see* Tlumach.

Tlushch, *see* Tluszcz.

Tlust, *see* Tust.

Tlusta, *see* Tolstoye.

Tluste, *see* Tolstoye.

Tluste Miasto, *see* Tolstoye.

Tluste Myasto, *see* Tolstoye.

Tlustenke, *see* Tolstenkoye.

Tlustenkie, *see* Tolstenkoye.

Tluste Wies, *see* Tolstoye.

Tlustice, Cz.; pop. 12; 50 km SW of Praha; 49°51'/13°53'.

Tlustovousy, Cz.; pop. 1; 26 km E of Praha; 50°05'/14°46'.

Tlustowa, Pol.; pop. 30; Described in the *Black Book* as being in the Krakow region of Poland, this town was not found in BGN gazetteers.

Tluszcz, Pol. (Tlashch, Tlashts, Tlushch); pop. 437; 38 km NE of Warszawa; 52°25'/21°27'; COH, GA, GUM3, GUM5, HSL, LYV, PHP4, SF, YB.

Tluyst, *see* Tust.

Tman, Cz.; 32 km WNW of Praha; 50°17'/14°08'; AMG.

Toalmas, Hung.; pop. 20; 45 km ENE of Budapest; 47°31'/19°40'; LDS.

Tobitschau, *see* Tovacov.

Tochovice, Cz.; pop. 5; 69 km SSW of Praha; 49°36'/13°59'.

Tocuz, *see* Tokuz.

Toczek, Pol. (Tost, Toszek); 56 km SW of Czestochowa; 50°27'/18°31'; HSL, JGFF, LDS, POCEM.

Toczyska, Pol.; pop. 31; 82 km ESE of Warszawa; 51°59'/22°02'.

Tofej, Hung.; pop. 18; 32 km NW of Nagykanizsa; 46°40'/16°48'.

Toging, Germ.; 62 km SE of Nurnberg; 49°01'/11°34'; PHGB.

Tohat, HSL. A number of towns share this name. It was not possible to determine from available information which one is being referenced.

Tomaszow Lubelski, Poland: From left to right are a "shtibl" (small synagogue) of the Belzer Hassidim, a large synagogue, and a "bes hamidresh" (house of prayer and study).

Toiteres, *see* Tauteny.

Tokaj, Hung. (Tokay); pop. 959; 50 km ENE of Miskolc; 48°07'/21°25'; AMG, COH, GUM3, GUM4, HSL, HSL2, JGFF, LDL, LDS, PHH.

Tokary, Pol.; pop. 20; 94 km S of Bialystok; 52°20'/22°42'.

Tokay, *see* Tokaj.

Toke Terebes, *see* Trebisov.

Toketerebes, *see* Trebisov.

Toki, Ukr.; pop. 53; 114 km S of Rovno; 49°38'/26°13'.

Tokmak, Ukr. (Bolshoi Tokmak); pop. 1,898; 146 km SSE of Dnepropetrovsk; 47°14'/35°44'; GUM4, HSL, SF.

Tokod, Hung.; pop. 13; 45 km WNW of Budapest; 47°43'/18°40'.

Tokol, Hung.; pop. 74; 26 km S of Budapest; 47°19'/18°58'; GUM5, PHH.

Tokuz, Mold. (Tocuz); pop. 43; 62 km SE of Kishinev; 46°32'/29°18'.

Tolbukhin, Bulg. (Dobrich); pop. 312; 45 km NNW of Varna; 43°34'/27°50'; EJ, GUM4.

Tolcsva, Hung.; pop. 481; 50 km NE of Miskolc; 48°17'/21°27'; AMG, EJ, HSL, HSL2, LDL, LDS, PHH.

Told, Hung. (Pusztatold); pop. 10; 126 km SE of Miskolc; 47°07'/21°39'; LDS.

Toldal, Rom. (Toldalag); pop. 6; 75 km E of Cluj; 46°42'/24°35'; HSL.

Toldalag, *see* Toldal.

Tole, Ukr.; 32 km SSW of Simferopol; 44°43'/33°49'; GUM4.

Tolgyes, Hung.; 126 km E of Miskolc; 47°58'/22°28'; COH, HSL.

Tolmachevo, Byel. (Tolmaczewo); pop. 10; 94 km E of Pinsk; 52°02'/27°32'.

Tolmachik, Ukr. (Tlumachik, Tlumaczyk); pop. 127; 82 km WNW of Chernovtsy; 48°35'/24°54'; PHP2.

Tolnacs, Hung.; pop. 12; 50 km N of Budapest; 47°56'/19°07'.

Tolmaczewo, *see* Tolmachevo.

Tolna, Hung.; pop. 258; 107 km W of Szeged; 46°26'/18°47'; EDRD, HSL, LDS, PHH.

Tolnanemedi, Hung.; pop. 22; 101 km SSW of Budapest; 46°43'/18°29'.

Tolochin, Byel. (Toloschin, Tolotchin, Tolotschin); pop. 1,910; 94 km S of Vitebsk; 54°25'/29°42'; HSL, JGFF, LDL, SF.

Toloschin, *see* Tolochin.

Tolotchin, *see* Tolochin.

Tolotschin, *see* Tolochin.

Tolshchev, Ukr. (Tolshchuv, Tolszczow); pop. 22; 26 km SE of Lvov; 49°42'/24°07'; HSL.

Tolshchuv, *see* Tolshchev.

Tolstenkoye, Ukr. (Tlustenke, Tlustenkie); pop. 40; 82 km N of Chernovtsy; 49°01'/26°04'.

Tolstoye, Ukr. (Tlusta, Tluste, Tluste Miasto, Tluste Myasto, Tluste Wies, Touste, Toyst); pop. 1,196; 62 km NNW of Chernovtsy; 48°50'/25°44'; AMG, CAHJP, COH, EGRS, EJ, GUM3, GUM4, GUM5, GUM6, GYLA, HSL, HSL2, JGFF, LDL, PHP2, SF, YB.

Tolszczow, *see* Tolshchev.

Tolukow, Pol.; pop. 40; Described in the *Black Book* as being in the Stanislawow region of Poland, this town was not found in BGN gazetteers.

Tomai, *see* Novaya Sarata.

Tomashevka, Byel. (Tomashov); 182 km SW of Pinsk; 51°33'/23°36'; SF.

Tomashgorod, Ukr. (Tomaszgrod); pop. 190; 101 km NNE of Rovno; 51°22'/27°05'.

Tomashov, *see* Tomashevka.

Tomashov Khadash, *see* Tomaszow Mazowiecki.

Tomashov Lublinski, *see* Tomaszow Lubelski.

Tomashov Pyetirkov, *see* Tomaszow Mazowiecki.

Tomashov Ravski, *see* Tomaszow Mazowiecki.

Tomashpol, Ukr.; pop. 3,252; 82 km S of Vinnitsa; 48°32'/28°31'; EJ, HSL, HSL2, JGFF, LDL, SF.

Tomashuv Lubelski, *see* Tomaszow Lubelski.

Tomashuv Mazovyetsk, *see* Tomaszow Mazowiecki.

Tomashuv Mazovyetski, *see* Tomaszow Mazowiecki.

Tomashuv Pyetirkov, *see* Tomaszow Mazowiecki.

Tomasikovo, Cz. (Tallos); 45 km E of Bratislava; 48°05'/17°42'; HSL.

Tomaszgrod, *see* Tomashgorod.

Tomaszow, Pol.; pop. 21; 50 km NNE of Krakow; 50°27'/20°23'; AMG, COH, HSL2, JGFF, LDL.

Tomaszowce, *see* Staryye Tomashevtsy.

Tomaszowek, Pol.; pop. 6; 56 km ESE of Lodz; 51°27'/20°08'.

Tomaszowice, Pol.; pop. 21; 19 km W of Lublin; 51°17'/22°23'.

Tomaszowka, Pol.; pop. 27; 69 km ENE of Lublin; 51°21'/23°30'; GA, GUM3, HSL.

Tomaszow Lubelski, Pol. (Tomashov Lublinski, Tomashuv Lubelski); pop. 4,643; 88 km NNE of Przemysl; 50°27'/23°25'; AMG, CAHJP, EDRD, EJ, GA, GUM3, GUM4, GUM5, HSL, JGFF, LDL, LDS, LYV, PHP2, PHP4, POCEM, SF, YB.

Tomaszow Mazowiecki, Pol. (Tomashov Khadash, Tomashov Pyetirkov, Tomashov Ravski, Tomashuv Mazovyetsk, Tomashuv Mazovyetski, Tomashuv Pyetirkov, Tomaszow Piotrkov, Tomaszow Rawski); pop. 10,070; 45 km ESE of Lodz; 51°32'/20°01'; AMG, CAHJP, COH, EDRD, EJ, GA, GUM3, GUM4, GUM5, GUM6, HSL, JGFF, LDL, LDS, LYV, PHP1, PHP4, POCEM, SF, YB.

Tomaszow Piotrkov, *see* Tomaszow Mazowiecki.

Tomaszow Rawski, *see* Tomaszow Mazowiecki.

Tomawa, Pol.; pop. 9; 62 km SSE of Lodz; 51°15'/19°47'.

Tome, Lat.; pop. 3; 45 km ESE of Riga; 56°45'/24°38'.

Tomestii Vechi, *see* Tompeshti Vek.

Tomina, Yug.; pop. 1; 133 km SSE of Zagreb; 44°43'/16°42'.

Tomor, Hung.; pop. 17; 32 km N of Miskolc; 48°20'/20°53'; HSL.

Tomord, Hung.; pop. 1; 107 km NNW of Nagykanizsa; 47°22'/16°41'.

Tomorkeny, Hung.; pop. 6; 45 km NNW of Szeged; 46°37'/20°02'.

Tompeshti Vek, Mold. (Tomestii Vechi); pop. 13; 133 km WNW of Kishinev; 47°39'/27°20'.

Tonciu, Rom. (Tancs); 69 km ENE of Cluj; 46°47'/24°33'; HSL.

Tonie, Pol.; pop. 11; 6 km NNW of Krakow; 50°07'/19°55'.

Tonovo, Byel. (Tonowo); pop. 8; 56 km SW of Minsk; 53°43'/26°46'.

Tonowo, *see* Tonovo.

Toorof, *see* Turov.

Top, Rom. (Czoptelke); pop. 6; 45 km NNE of Cluj; 47°04'/24°00'.

Topa de Cris, Rom.; pop. 3; 82 km WNW of Cluj; 46°59'/22°34'.

Topa Mica, Rom.; pop. 6; 26 km NW of Cluj; 46°57'/23°23'.

Topanfalva, Rom.; 62 km SSW of Cluj; 46°22'/23°03'; HSL. This town was located on a pre-World War I map, but does not appear in contemporary gazetteers.

Topczykaly, Pol.; pop. 4; 50 km SSE of Bialystok; 52°42'/23°16'.

Topla, Yug.; 120 km WNW of Zagreb; 46°29'/14°46'; HSL.

Toplica, Yug. BGN lists two possible localities with this name located at 41°24'/21°45' and 41°52'/20°53'. AMG.

Toplistse, *see* Toplita.

Toplita, Rom. (Maroshevitz, Marosheviz, Moroshevis, Moroshhevis, Toplistse, Toplita Mures, Toplitsa Mures, Toplitse); pop. 746; 133 km ENE of Cluj; 46°55'/25°20'; AMG, COH, HSL, HSL2, LDL, LYV, PHR2.

Toplita Ciuc, Rom. (Csiktaplocza); pop. 31; 163 km SW of Iasi; 46°22'/25°48'.

Toplita Mures, *see* Toplita.

Toplitsa Mures, *see* Toplita.

Toplitse, *see* Toplita.

Topola, Yug.; 69 km SSE of Beograd; 44°16'/20°42'; COH, GUM5, GUM5, HSL.

Topola Krolewska, Pol.; pop. 14; 45 km NW of Lodz; 52°05'/19°12'.

Topolcany, Cz. (Nagytapolcsany, Tapolcany); pop. 2,991; 88 km NE of Bratislava; 48°34'/18°11'; AMG, COH, EJ, GUM3, GUM4, GUM5, GUM6, HSL, HSL2, JGFF, LDL, YB.

Topolcianky, Cz. (Kistapolcsany); 101 km NE of Bratislava; 48°25'/18°25'; HSL.

Topolnica Rustykalna, *see* Topolnitsa.

Topolnica Szlachecka, Ukr.; pop. 34; 120 km SSW of Lvov; 48°55'/23°05'. This town was located on an interwar map of Poland but does not appear in contemporary gazetteers. Map coordinates are approximate.

Topolnitsa, Ukr. (Topolnica Rustykalna); pop. 54; 94 km SW of Lvov; 49°19'/23°01'.

Topolno, *see* Topulno.

Topolsica, Yug.; pop. 4; 107 km WNW of Zagreb; 46°25'/15°00'.

Topolska, Ukr. (Topolsko); pop. 9; 107 km SSE of Lvov; 48°55'/24°14'.

Topolsko, *see* Topolska.

Toponar, Hung.; pop. 8; 62 km E of Nagykanizsa; 46°23'/17°50'; HSL.

Topor, Pol.; pop. 21; 69 km E of Warszawa; 52°08'/21°56'.

Toporauti, *see* Toporovtsy.

Toporov, Ukr. (Toporow); pop. 689; 56 km NE of Lvov; 50°07'/24°43'; AMG, EGRS, GUM3, HSL, HSL2, LDL, PHP2, SF, YB.

Toporovtse, *see* Toporovtsy.

Toporovtsy, Ukr. (Toporauti, Toporovtse, Toporowce); pop. 217; 19 km NE of Chernovtsy; 48°23'/26°07'.

Toporow, *see* Toporov.

Toporowce, *see* Toporovtsy.

Topulno, Ukr. (Topolno); pop. 36; 75 km WNW of Rovno; 50°56'/25°17'.

Topusko, Yug.; 62 km S of Zagreb; 45°18'/15°59'; GUM4.

Toraceni, *see* Torichi.

Torba, Rom. (Torboszlo); pop. 3; 101 km E of Cluj; 46°33'/24°53'; HSL.

Torbagy, Hung.; pop. 8; 19 km WSW of Budapest; 47°28'/18°49'.

Torbin, *see* Turobin.

Torboszlo, *see* Torba.

Torchin, Ukr. (Torczyn, Tortchin); pop. 1,480; 88 km W of Rovno; 50°46'/25°00'; AMG, EJ, GUM3, GUM5, HSL, JGFF, LDL, SF, YB.

Torczyn, *see* Torchin.

Torczynowice, *see* Torganovichi.

Torda, *see* Turda.

Tordas, Hung.; pop. 9; 32 km SW of Budapest; 47°21'/18°45'.

Tordaszentlaszlo, *see* Savadisla.

Torek, *see* Turek.

Toretz, *see* Turets.

Torez, Ukr.; 264 km E of Dnepropetrovsk; 48°02'/38°35'; JGFF.

Torganovichi, Ukr. (Torczynowice, Torganovitse, Torhanowice); pop. 59; 75 km SW of Lvov; 49°29'/23°05'.

Torganovitse, *see* Torganovichi.

Torgau, Germ.; pop. 10; 56 km NE of Leipzig; 51°34'/13°00'; EJ, GUM3, GUM4, GUM5.

Torgovitsa, Ukr. (Targovica, Targoviste, Targovitsa, Targovitza, Targowica, Targowitza, Tarovitz, Torgowica, Trovits, Truvitz); pop. 640; 56 km WSW of Rovno; 50°33'/25°24'; LYV, PHR1, WS, YB.

Torgovitsa (Stanislawow), Ukr.; pop. 26; 50 km WNW of Chernovtsy; 48°36'/25°26'.

Torgovitsa (Ukraine), Ukr.; 45 km E of Uman; 48°39'/30°47'; COH, EDRD, SF.

Torgowica, *see* Torgovitsa.

Torgu Muresh, *see* Tirgu Mures.

Torhanowice, *see* Torganovichi.

Torichi, Ukr. (Toraceni); pop. 58; 75 km SW of Chernovtsy; 48°01'/25°04'; PHR2.

Torki (near Przemysl), Pol.; pop. 20; 13 km NE of Przemysl; 49°50'/22°56'.

Torki (near Tartakow), Ukr.; pop. 26; 75 km NNE of Lvov; 50°25'/24°35'.

Torkn, Pol. PHP4. This town was not found in BGN gazetteers under the given spelling.

Torn, *see* Torun.

Torna, *see* Turna nad Bodvou.

Tornabarakony, Hung.; pop. 8; 50 km N of Miskolc; 48°30'/20°49'.

Tornakapolna, Hung.; pop. 4; 50 km NNW of Miskolc; 48°28'/20°37'.

Tornala, *see* Safarikovo.

Tornalja, *see* Safarikovo.

Tornalya, *see* Safarikovo.

Tornanadaska, Hung.; pop. 4; 56 km N of Miskolc; 48°34'/20°47'.

Tornaszentandras, Hung.; pop. 7; 56 km N of Miskolc; 48°31'/20°47'.

Torne, *see* Tarnow.

Tornen, *see* Tarnow.

Tornocz, *see* Trnovec nad Vahom.

Tornya, *see* Torun (Ukraine).

Tornyosnemeti, Hung.; pop. 4; 62 km NNE of Miskolc; 48°31'/21°16'; HSL.

Tornyospalca, Hung.; pop. 103; 107 km ENE of Miskolc; 48°16'/22°11'; HSL, JGFF, PHH.

Toroczko, Rom.; 45 km S of Cluj; 46°27'/23°34'; HSL. This town was located on a pre-World War I map, but does not appear in contemporary gazetteers.

Torokbalint, Hung.; pop. 93; 13 km SW of Budapest; 47°26'/18°55'; HSL, PHH.

Torok Becse, *see* Novi Becej.

Torokbecse, *see* Novi Becej.

Torok Kanyizsa, *see* Novi Knezevac.

Torokkoppany, Hung.; pop. 6; 82 km ENE of Nagykanizsa; 46°36'/18°03'.

Torokszentmiklos, Hung.; pop. 629; 107 km ESE of Budapest; 47°11'/20°25'; GUM5, HSL, LDL, LDS, PHH.

Toronya, *see* Torun (Ukraine).

Toropets, USSR; pop. 1,158; 69 km ENE of Velikiye Luki; 56°30'/31°39'; GUM5.

Toroszowka, *see* Turaszowka.

Torske, *see* Torskoye.

Torskie, *see* Torskoye.

Torskoye, Ukr. (Torske, Torskie); pop. 58; 56 km NNW of Chernovtsy; 48°46'/25°41'.

Tortchin, *see* Torchin.

Tortel, Hung.; pop. 19; 75 km ESE of Budapest; 47°07'/19°56'; LDS.

Torun, Pol. (Thorn, Torn); pop. 354; 126 km NE of Poznan; 53°02'/18°36'; AMG, CAHJP, COH, GUM3, GUM4, GUM5, JGFF, LDS, PHP1.

Torun (Ukraine), Ukr. (Tornya, Toronya); 139 km S of Lvov; 48°40'/23°34'; HSL, PHP3, SM.

Torysk, *see* Turiysk.

Toshvitse, *see* Tyszowce.

Tosie, Pol.; pop. 30; 88 km SW of Bialystok; 52°38'/22°09'.

Tosno, USSR; pop. 13; 56 km ESE of Leningrad; 59°33'/30°53'.

Tosok, *see* Tosokberend.

Tosokberend, Hung. (Tosok); pop. 1; 88 km NNE of Nagykanizsa; 47°06'/17°32'.

Tost, *see* Toczek.

Tostedt, Germ.; pop. 2; 32 km SSW of Hamburg; 53°17'/09°43'.

Toszeg, Hung.; pop. 47; 94 km ESE of Budapest; 47°06'/20°09'.

Toszek, *see* Toczek.

Totbanhegyes, Hung.; 56 km NE of Szeged; 46°27'/20°54'; HSL. This town was located on a pre-World War I map, but does not appear in contemporary gazetteers.

Totfalu, *see* Kerkatotfalu.

Totgyork, *see* Galgagyork.

Toti, *see* Tata.

Totis, *see* Tata.

Totkomlos, Hung.; pop. 192; 45 km NE of Szeged; 46°25'/20°44'; GUM4, HSL, LDS, PHH.

Totszentmarton, Hung.; pop. 5; 13 km SW of Nagykanizsa; 46°25'/16°49'.

Totszerdahely, Hung.; pop. 5; 19 km SW of Nagykanizsa; 46°24'/16°48'.

Tottelek, *see* Tautelec.

Totujfalu, Hung.; 75 km SE of Nagykanizsa; 45°54'/17°39'; JGFF.

Totvazsony, Hung.; pop. 11; 88 km NNE of Nagykanizsa; 47°01'/17°47'; HSL.

Touchovice, Cz.; pop. 6; 56 km WNW of Praha; 50°18'/13°44'.

Tousen, Cz.; pop. 3; 19 km NE of Praha; 50°10'/14°43'.

Touste, *see* Tolstoye.

Toustobaby, Ukr.; pop. 45; 133 km S of Lvov; 48°45'/23°25'. This town was located on an interwar map of Poland but does not appear in contemporary gazetteers. Map coordinates are approximate.

Touzim, Cz.; pop. 41; 107 km WSW of Praha; 50°04'/13°00'.

Tovacov, Cz. (Tobitschau); pop. 56; 56 km NE of Brno; 49°26'/17°17'; HSL, HSL2.

Tovarne, Cz. (Tavarna); 50 km NE of Kosice; 48°55'/21°46'; AMG, HSL.

Tovarnik, Yug. BGN lists two possible localities with this name located at 44°48'/19°58' and 45°10'/19°09'. GUM4.

Tovaros, Hung.; pop. 343; 56 km WNW of Budapest; 47°39'/18°20'.

Tovis, Cz.; pop. 5; 50 km NE of Brno; 49°21'/17°19'; HSL. This town was located on a pre-World War I map, but does not appear in contemporary gazetteers.

Tovrik, *see* Taurage.

Toyst, *see* Tolstoye.

Trabelsdorf, Germ.; pop. 16; 56 km NW of Nurnberg; 49°54'/10°44'; GUM5, JGFF, PHGB.

Traby, Byel.; pop. 511; 114 km W of Minsk; 54°09'/25°55'; COH, EDRD, HSL, SF.

Trachenberg, *see* Zmigrod.

Trachomin, Pol. PHP4. This town was not found in BGN gazetteers under the given spelling.

Trachtenberg, *possibly* Zmigrod.

Traiskirchen, Aus.; pop. 17; 26 km S of Wien; 48°01'/16°17'.

Traismauer, Aus.; pop. 1; 50 km WNW of Wien; 48°21'/15°44'.

Trajanow, *see* Troyanov.

Trakai, Lith. (Traken, Trok, Troki); pop. 300; 26 km WSW of Vilnius; 54°38'/24°56'; AMG, COH, EDRD, EJ, GUM3, GUM4, GUM6, HSL, JGFF, LDL, SF, YB.

Traken, *see* Trakai.

Tranis, Rom.; pop. 13; 69 km NNW of Cluj; 47°20'/23°18'.

Tranisu, Rom.; pop. 1; 56 km W of Cluj; 46°51'/22°50'.

Tranowo, Pol.; pop. 54; Described in the *Black Book* as being in the Bialystok region of Poland, this town was not found in BGN gazetteers.

Transbor, Pol.; pop. 5; 56 km ESE of Warszawa; 52°01'/21°42'.

Transnistra; Not a town, but a region of the Ukraine between the Dniester and Bug Rivers.

Transylvania; Not a town, but a region of Romania.

Trape, *see* Traupis.

Trapovka, Ukr. (Tropoclo); pop. 6; 114 km SW of Odessa; 45°48'/29°42'.

Trappstadt, Germ.; pop. 15; 101 km NNW of Nurnberg; 50°19'/10°35'; GUM5, PHGB.

Trashkin, *see* Troskunai.

Trashkon, *see* Troskunai.

Traskianai, *see* Troskunai.

Traszkuny, *see* Troskunai.

Tratnowice, Pol.; pop. 5; 19 km NE of Krakow; 50°12'/20°07'.

Traunkirchen, Aus.; pop. 4; 56 km ENE of Salzburg; 47°50'/13°47'.

Traunstein, Germ.; 88 km ESE of Munchen; 47°53'/12°39'; GUM3.

Traupis, Lith. (Trape, Truppa); pop. 62; 88 km NNE of Kaunas; 55°31'/24°45'; JGFF.

Traustadt, Germ.; pop. 2; 69 km NW of Nurnberg; 49°56'/10°26'; PHGB.

Trautenau, *see* Trutnov.

Trautskirchen, Germ.; 38 km WSW of Nurnberg; 49°27'/10°36'; PHGB.

Travnik, Yug.; pop. 364; 214 km SE of Zagreb; 44°14'/17°40'; EJ, GUM4, PHY.

Trawniki, Pol.; pop. 93; 32 km ESE of Lublin; 51°08'/23°00'; EDRD, GA, GUM3, GUM4, GUM5, GUM6, HSL, PHP4.

Trawy, Pol.; pop. 26; 50 km NE of Warszawa; 52°25'/21°44'; HSL.

Trbovlje, Yug.; pop. 3; 88 km WNW of Zagreb; 46°10'/15°03'.

Trciana, *see* Trzciana.

Trebbin, Germ.; pop. 11; 38 km S of Berlin; 52°13'/13°12'; LDS.

Trebechovice Pod Orebem, Cz.; pop. 47; 107 km ENE of Praha; 50°12'/16°00'.

Trebevle, *see* Terebovlya.

Trebic, Cz. (Trebitsch); pop. 335; 56 km W of Brno; 49°18'/15°53'; CAHJP, EJ, HSL, HSL2.

Trebice Dolne, Pol.; pop. 19; 101 km SSW of Bialystok; 52°19'/22°30'.

Trebice Gorne, Pol.; pop. 7; 101 km SSW of Bialystok; 52°19'/22°32'.

Trebichovice, Cz.; pop. 9; 32 km WNW of Praha; 50°11'/14°05'.

Trebisauti, *see* Trebiskauts.

Trebiskauts, Mold. (Trebisauti); pop. 21; 195 km NW of Kishinev; 48°21'/27°11'.

Trebisov, Cz. (Terebes, Toke Terebes, Toketerebes); pop. 2,791; 38 km E of Kosice; 48°38'/21°43'; COH, GUM3, GUM4, GUM6, HSL, JGFF.

Trebitsch, *see* Trebic.

Trebivlice, Cz.; pop. 15; 56 km WNW of Praha; 50°27'/13°54'.

Treblin, *see* Trzebielino.

Treblinka, Pol.; 88 km SW of Bialystok; 52°40'/22°02'; EJ, GA, GUM3, GUM4, GUM5, JGFF, PHGBW, PHP1, PHP3, PHP4, SF. Treblinka is the location of an extermination camp during the Holocaust. Most sources refer to the camp rather than the town.

Trebnitz, *see* Trzebnica.

Treboc, Cz.; pop. 6; 50 km W of Praha; 50°13'/13°45'.

Trebon, Cz.; pop. 55; 126 km SSE of Praha; 49°01'/14°47'.

Trebotov, Cz.; pop. 2; 19 km SSW of Praha; 49°58'/14°18'.

Trebovle, Cz.; pop. 2; 38 km E of Praha; 50°02'/14°58'.

Trebowiec, Pol.; pop. 6; 107 km WSW of Lublin; 51°10'/21°04'.

Trebujeni, *see* Trebuzheny.

Trebur, Germ.; pop. 23; 26 km SSW of Frankfurt am Main; 49°55'/08°24'.

Trebusa, *see* Delovoye.

Trebusan, *see* Delovoye.

Trebusany, *see* Delovoye.

Trebuzheny, Mold. (Trebujeni); pop. 6; 45 km N of Kishinev; 47°19'/28°59'.

Tregist, Aus.; pop. 1; 26 km W of Graz; 47°05'/15°09'.

Treis, Germ.; pop. 50; 88 km SSE of Koln; 50°11'/07°18'.

Treis an der Lumda, Germ.; pop. 30; 69 km N of Frankfurt am Main; 50°40'/08°47'.

Treitza, *see* Troitsa.

Trembovla, *see* Terebovlya.

Trembowla, *see* Terebovlya.

Tremessen, *see* Trzemeszno.

Trencianska Tepla, Cz.; pop. 133; 107 km E of Brno; 48°56'/18°07'.

Trencianska Turna, Cz. (Turna); 101 km NNE of Bratislava; 48°51'/18°01'; AMG.

Trencianske Teplice, Cz. (Trencsenteplicz); pop. 233; 114 km E of Brno; 48°55'/18°10'; GUM5, JGFF.

Trencin, Cz. (Trencsen, Trentschin); pop. 2,282; 107 km NNE of Bratislava; 48°54'/18°02'; AMG, EJ, GUM4, GUM5, HSL, JGFF.

Trencsen, *see* Trencin.

Trencsenteplicz, *see* Trencianske Teplice.

Trendel, Germ.; 62 km SSW of Nurnberg; 48°56'/10°42'; PHGB.

Trendelburg, Germ.; pop. 4; 94 km S of Hannover; 51°35'/09°25'.

Trennfurt, Germ.; 50 km ESE of Frankfurt am Main; 49°47'/09°11'; PHGB.

Trenscen, LDL, LDS. This town was not found in BGN gazetteers under the given spelling.

Trentschin, *see* Trencin.

Trepec, Cz. (Trepecz); 50 km NNE of Kosice; 49°03'/21°42'; HSL.

Trepecz, *see* Trepec.

Treptow, *see* Trzebiatow.

Treptow an der Riga, *see* Trzebiatow.

Treshebin, *see* Trzebinia.

Treskonice, Cz.; pop. 10; 62 km WNW of Praha; 50°16'/13°39'.

Trest, Cz. (Triesch); pop. 98; 88 km W of Brno; 49°18'/15°29'; EJ, HSL, HSL2.

Tresta, *possibly* Tresta Rzadowa.

Tresta Rzadowa, Pol. (Tresta?); 50 km ESE of Lodz; 51°28'/20°01'; POCEM.

Trestena, *see* Teresztenye.

Trestenberg, *see* Tasnad.

Trestiana, Rom.; pop. 23; 26 km SE of Iasi; 46°59'/27°47'.

Trestina, *see* Trzcianne.

Tretowo, GA. This town was not found in BGN gazetteers under the given spelling.

Treuburg, *see* Olecko.

Treuchtlingen, Germ.; pop. 119; 62 km S of Nurnberg; 48°57'/10°55'; CAHJP, GUM3, GUM5, ISH1, PHGB.

Treuenbrietzen, Germ.; pop. 12; 56 km SSW of Berlin; 52°06'/12°52'.

Treves, *see* Trier.

Treysa, Germ.; pop. 120; 101 km N of Frankfurt am Main; 50°55'/09°12'; GUM5, JGFF, LDS.

Treznea, Rom.; pop. 23; 56 km NW of Cluj; 47°06'/23°07'.

Trhonice, Cz.; pop. 3; 56 km NW of Brno; 49°38'/16°15'.

Tria, Rom.; pop. 30; 114 km WNW of Cluj; 47°14'/22°16'.

Triberg, Germ.; pop. 8; 101 km SW of Stuttgart; 48°08'/08°14'; PHGBW.

Tribsees, Germ.; pop. 3; 45 km ENE of Rostock; 54°06'/12°46'.

Tribuhovtsy, *see* Tribukhovtsy.

Tribukhovtsy, Ukr. (Tribuhovtsy, Trybuchowce); pop. 138; 101 km N of Chernovtsy; 49°09'/26°10'; PHP2. The *Black Book* notes two other communities named Trybuchowce in interwar Poland, one near Buchach and a second in Lwow province. Neither appear in BGN gazetteers.

Tribuswinkel, Aus.; pop. 8; 26 km S of Wien; 48°00'/16°16'.

Trichaty, GUM3. This town was not found in BGN gazetteers under the given spelling.

Tridubi, *see* Triduby.

Triduby, Ukr. (Tridubi); 82 km SSE of Uman; 48°04'/30°25'; PHR1.

Trier, Germ. (Treves); pop. 800; 139 km S of Koln; 49°45'/06°38'; AMG, EDRD, EJ, GED, GUM5, HSL, JGFF, LDS, YB.

Triesch, *see* Trest.

Triesdorf, Germ.; pop. 40; 45 km SW of Nurnberg; 49°12'/10°40'.

Trifaneshty, Mold. (Trifanesti); pop. 23; 120 km NW of Kishinev; 47°57'/28°08'.

Trifanesti, *see* Trifaneshty.

Trifeshti, *see* Trifeshty.

Trifeshty, Mold. (Trifeshti, Trifesti Orhei); pop. 27; 82 km N of Kishinev; 47°41'/28°49'.

Trifesti Orhei, *see* Trifeshty.

Trihati, GUM4, PHR1. This town was not found in BGN gazetteers under the given spelling.

Trikata, Lat.; pop. 3; 114 km NE of Riga; 57°33'/25°42'.

Trikkala, Greece; pop. 480; 75 km E of Ioannina; 39°33'/21°46'.

Trilesy, Ukr.; 69 km SW of Kiyev; 49°59'/29°50'; JGFF.

Trinca, *see* Trinka.

Trinec, Cz.; pop. 138; 157 km NE of Brno; 49°41'/18°39'; AMG, GUM4.

Trinka, Mold. (Trinca); pop. 64; 182 km NW of Kishinev; 48°13'/27°07'.

Trip, Rom. (Terep); pop. 195; 133 km N of Cluj; 47°56'/23°23';

PHR2.

Trishig, *see* Tryskiai.

Trishik, *see* Tryskiai.

Trishky, *see* Tryskiai.

Trishkyay, *see* Tryskiai.

Trisk, *see* Turiysk.

Triskinie, *see* Tryskine.

Triskovitz, *see* Truskavets.

Trittenheim, Germ.; pop. 31; 133 km WSW of Frankfurt am Main; 49°49'/06°54'; JGFF.

Trizs, Hung.; pop. 2; 45 km NW of Miskolc; 48°26'/20°30'.

Trmice, Cz.; pop. 36; 75 km NW of Praha; 50°39'/14°00'.

Trmova, Cz. (Durmaul); 94 km W of Praha; 50°16'/13°10'; HSL.

Trnava, Cz. (Kekenyes, Kukyenyes, Nagyszombat, Ternive, Tirnoy, Tirnoya, Tyrnau); pop. 3,170; 45 km NE of Bratislava; 48°22'/17°36'; AMG, COH, EJ, GUM4, GUM5, HSL, HSL2, LDL, LDS, LYV.

Trnovany, Cz.; pop. 400; BGN lists two possible localities with this name located at 50°19'/13°36' and 50°33'/14°11'.

Trnovec nad Vahom, Cz. (Tornocz); pop. 51; 62 km E of Bratislava; 48°09'/17°56'; HSL.

Trnovo nad Teresvon, *see* Ternovo.

Trobitz, Germ.; 82 km NE of Leipzig; 51°36'/13°26'; GUM5.

Trochenbrod, *see* Zofyuvka.

Trochinbrod, *see* Zofyuvka.

Trofaiach, Aus.; 50 km NW of Graz; 47°25'/15°00'; GUM5.

Troganov, *see* Troyanov.

Troisdorf, Germ.; 19 km ESE of Koln; 50°49'/07°10'; GED.

Troita, *see* Troitskoye.

Troitsa, Ukr. (Treitza, Trojca); pop. 96; 56 km WNW of Chernovtsy; 48°27'/25°14'; PHP2, SF.

Troitskoye, Mold. (Troita); pop. 41; 56 km SSE of Kishinev; 46°31'/29°02'.

Trojanovka, *see* Troyanovka.

Trojanowka, *see* Troyanovka.

Trojca, *see* Troitsa.

Trojczyce, Pol.; pop. 22; 13 km N of Przemysl; 49°53'/22°46'.

Trok, *see* Trakai.

Trokeli, Byel. (Trokiele); pop. 52; 139 km W of Minsk; 54°02'/25°25'.

Trokhinbrod, *see* Zofyuvka.

Trokhnibrod, *see* Zofyuvka.

Troki, *see* Trakai.

Trokiele, *see* Trokeli.

Tropie, Pol.; pop. 44; 62 km ESE of Krakow; 49°48'/20°40'.

Tropoclo, *see* Trapovka.

Tropova, *see* Tropovo.

Tropovci, Yug.; pop. 2; 101 km N of Zagreb; 46°39'/16°06'.

Tropovo, Ukr. (Tropova); 75 km SSW of Vinnitsa; 48°39'/27°56'; GUM4.

Troppau, *see* Opava.

Trosciance, *see* Trostsyantse.

Troscianiec, *see* Trostyanets.

Troscianiec Wielki, Ukr.; pop. 23; 101 km ESE of Lvov; 49°25'/25°15'. This town was located on an interwar map of Poland but does not appear in contemporary gazetteers. Map coordinates are approximate.

Troscianka, Pol.; 45 km N of Bialystok; 53°28'/23°22'; GUM3.

Troshkon, *see* Troskunai.

Troskav, *see* Truskava.

Troskunai, Lith. (Trashkin, Trashkon, Traskianai, Traszkuny, Troshkon); pop. 424; 101 km NNE of Kaunas; 55°36'/24°51'; AMG, HSL, JGFF, SF, YL.

Trostberg, Germ.; 69 km E of Munchen; 48°02'/12°33'; GUM3, GUM5.

Trostenets, Ukr. (Trosteniec); pop. 14; 50 km N of Rovno; 51°02'/26°16'.

Trosteniec, *see* Trostenets.

Trostinet, Rom. PHR1. This town was not found in BGN gazetteers under the given spelling.

Trostinets, GUM4, GUM5. A number of towns share this name. It was not possible to determine from available information which one is being referenced.

Trostsyantse, Ukr. (Trosciance); pop. 43; 114 km NW of Chernovtsy; 49°04'/24°56'.

Trostyanets, Ukr. (Troscianiec); pop. 1,335; 82 km SW of Uman; 48°31'/29°11'; EDRD, EJ, GUM4, HSL.

Trostyanets (near Dolina), Ukr.; pop. 29; 94 km S of Lvov; 49°04'/24°01'.

Trostyanets (near Snyatyn), Ukr.; pop. 33; 56 km W of Chernovtsy; 48°25'/25°14'.

Trostyanets (Wolyn), Ukr.; pop. 75; 45 km SSW of Rovno; 50°20'/25°53'.

Troszyn, Pol.; pop. 38; 94 km WSW of Bialystok; 53°02'/21°45'.

Troszyn Niemiecki, Pol.; pop. 15; 82 km N of Lodz; 52°27'/19°51'.

Trotsk, *see* Chapayevsk.

Trovits, *see* Torgovitsa.

Troyanivka, *see* Troyanovka.

Troyanov, Ukr. (Trajanow, Troganov); 101 km N of Vinnitsa; 50°07'/28°33'; HSL, LDL, SF.

Troyanovka, Ukr. (Trojanovka, Trojanowka, Troyanivka); pop. 212; 88 km SSE of Rovno; 49°50'/26°30'; AMG, GUM3, GUM4, GUM5, LDL, LYV, SF.

Trpinja, Yug.; pop. 2; 139 km WNW of Beograd; 45°25'/18°54'.

Trpisty, Cz.; pop. 2; 107 km WSW of Praha; 49°49'/13°04'.

Trstena, Cz.; pop. 322; 139 km WNW of Kosice; 49°22'/19°37'.

Trstena na Ostrove, Cz. (Nadasd); pop. 51; 38 km ESE of Bratislava; 47°55'/17°30'; HSL.

Trubchevsk, USSR; pop. 182; 82 km SSW of Bryansk; 52°36'/33°46'.

Trubki, Ukr.; pop. 13; 88 km N of Lvov; 50°35'/24°30'.

Truchanow, Ukr.; pop. 51; 126 km S of Lvov; 48°45'/23°35'; HSL, PHP2. This town was located on an interwar map of Poland but does not appear in contemporary gazetteers. Map coordinates are approximate.

Trudering, *see* Kirchtrudering.

Trudovoye, Ukr. (Draculea); pop. 5; 139 km SW of Odessa; 45°37'/29°24'.

Trudy, Byel.; pop. 123; 75 km WNW of Vitebsk; 55°38'/29°22'.

Trugenhofen, Germ.; 82 km NW of Munchen; 48°47'/11°00'; PHGB.

Trumau, Aus.; pop. 1; 32 km S of Wien; 47°59'/16°20'.

Trunstadt, Germ.; 56 km NW of Nurnberg; 49°56'/10°45'; PHGB.

Truppa, *see* Traupis.

Truseni, *see* Trusheny.

Trusheny, Mold. (Truseni); pop. 8; 13 km WNW of Kishinev; 47°04'/28°40'.

Trushkovitse, *see* Truskavets.

Trusk, *see* Turiysk.

Truskava, Lith. (Troskav); 62 km N of Kaunas; 55°26'/24°14'; SF.

Truskavets, Ukr. (Triskovitz, Trushkovitse, Truskawice, Truskawiec); pop. 149; 75 km SSW of Lvov; 49°17'/23°30'; EGRS, GUM4, PHP2, SF.

Truskawice, *see* Truskavets.

Truskawiec, *see* Truskavets.

Truskolasy, Pol.; pop. 266; 26 km WNW of Czestochowa; 50°52'/18°50'.

Trutnov, Cz. (Trautenau); pop. 397; 114 km NE of Praha; 50°34'/15°54'; HSL.

Truvitz, *see* Torgovitsa.

Trybuchowce, *see* Tribukhovtsy.

Trybunalski, *see* Piotrkow Trybunalski.

Tryliski, Byel.; pop. 19; 45 km WNW of Pinsk; 52°15'/25°32'.

Tryncza, Pol.; pop. 7; 45 km NNW of Przemysl; 50°10'/22°34'.

Trynosy, Pol.; pop. 10; 88 km NNE of Warszawa; 52°53'/21°46'.

Tryputna, Ukr. (Tryputnia); pop. 44; 107 km N of Rovno; 51°33'/26°19'; JGFF.

Tryputnia, *see* Tryputna.

Tryskiai, Lith. (Thishky, Trishig, Trishik, Trishky, Trishkyay); pop. 335; 45 km W of Siauliai; 56°04'/22°35'; HSL, JGFF, SF, YL.

Tryskine, Ukr. (Triskinie); pop. 43; 94 km N of Rovno; 51°23'/26°27'.

Trysolie, Ukr. EDRD. This town was not found in BGN gazetteers under the given spelling.

Trysten, Ukr.; pop. 5; 101 km WNW of Rovno; 50°56'/24°56'.

Trywieza, Pol.; pop. 7; 45 km SE of Bialystok; 52°49'/23°32'.

Trzas, Pol.; pop. 11; 56 km N of Czestochowa; 51°14'/19°17'.

Trzciana, USSR (Trciana); See listings below.

Trzciana (near Bochnia), Pol.; pop. 38; 45 km ESE of Krakow; 49°51'/20°22'.

Trzciana (near Mielec), Pol.; pop. 28; 107 km ENE of Krakow; 50°19'/21°21'.

Trzcianice, see Trzciniec.

Trzciniec, Pol. (Trzcianice); pop. 58; 32 km SSW of Przemysl; 49°35'/22°30'.

Trzcianka, Pol. (Schoenlanke, Schonlanke); pop. 380; 75 km NW of Poznan; 53°02'/16°27'; EJ, HSL, JGFF, LDS, PHP4.

Trzcianka (Bialystok), Pol.; pop. 127; 139 km N of Bialystok; 54°19'/23°01'.

Trzcianne, Pol. (Trestina); pop. 1,401; 45 km WNW of Bialystok; 53°20'/22°41'; AMG, GA, GUM3, GUM4, HSL, LDL, LDS, SF.

Trzciel, Pol. (Tirschtiegel); pop. 22; 75 km WSW of Poznan; 52°22'/15°52'; GA, HSL, LDS, POCEM.

Trzcieniec, Pol.; pop. 24; 62 km N of Krakow; 50°38'/20°06'; HSL.

Trzebce, Pol.; pop. 13; 62 km NE of Czestochowa; 51°03'/19°49'.

Trzebciny, Pol.; pop. 2; 82 km SSW of Gdansk; 53°38'/18°11'.

Trzebiatow, Pol. (Treptow, Treptow an der Riga); pop. 50; 82 km NNE of Szczecin; 54°04'/15°16'; HSL.

Trzebica, Pol.; pop. 18; 82 km NE of Krakow; 50°20'/20°59'.

Trzebielino, Pol. (Treblin); pop. 9; 101 km WSW of Gdansk; 54°12'/17°05'.

Trzebieszow, Pol.; pop. 83; 88 km N of Lublin; 52°00'/22°33'.

Trzebiez, Pol. (Ziegenort); pop. 6; 26 km N of Szczecin; 53°39'/14°31'.

Trzebina, Pol.; pop. 4; 75 km ESE of Lodz; 51°26'/20°22'; HSL2.

Trzebinia, Pol. (Chebin, Chebinya, Chubin, Treshebin, Trzebinia Miasteczko, Trzebinia Miasto, Tshebin); pop. 1,150; 32 km WNW of Krakow; 50°10'/19°29'; AMG, COH, EDRD, EGRS, GUM3, GUM4, GUM5, HSL, LDL, LYV, PHP3, POCEM, SF, YB.

Trzebinia Miasteczko, see Trzebinia.

Trzebinia Miasto, see Trzebinia.

Trzebinia Wies, Pol.; pop. 185; 75 km SW of Krakow; 49°39'/19°13'.

Trzebionka, Pol.; pop. 51; 38 km W of Krakow; 50°10'/19°27'.

Trzebnica, Germ. (Trebnitz); pop. 42; 283 km ESE of Berlin; 51°13'/17°00'; ISH1.

Trzebos, Pol.; pop. 33; 62 km WNW of Przemysl; 50°12'/22°09'; JGFF.

Trzebucza, Pol.; pop. 13; 62 km E of Warszawa; 52°14'/21°54'.

Trzebuska, Pol.; pop. 47; 69 km WNW of Przemysl; 50°13'/22°04'.

Trzemesnia, see Trzemeszno Lubuskie.

Trzemeszno, Pol. (Tremessen); pop. 37; 62 km ENE of Poznan; 52°34'/17°50'; LDS, PHP1.

Trzemeszno Lubuskie, Pol. (Schermeisel, Trzemesnia, Trzemiesnia); pop. 27; 114 km W of Poznan; 52°26'/15°15'.

Trzemiesnia, see Trzemeszno Lubuskie.

Trzepnica, Pol.; pop. 22; 62 km SSE of Lodz; 51°13'/19°44'.

Trzeskowice, see Trzeszkowice.

Trzesn, Pol.; pop. 24; 82 km SSW of Lublin; 50°40'/21°47'.

Trzesniow, see Trzezniow.

Trzesowka, Pol.; pop. 5; 94 km WNW of Przemysl; 50°17'/21°41'.

Trzeszczany, Pol.; pop. 80; 94 km ESE of Lublin; 50°50'/23°45'.

Trzeszkowice, Pol. (Trzeskowice); pop. 64; 19 km E of Lublin; 51°15'/22°48'.

Trzetrzewina, see Trzetrzewino.

Trzetrzewino, Pol. (Trzetrzewina); pop. 3; 75 km ESE of Krakow; 49°38'/20°38'.

Trzezniow, Pol. (Teresnev, Trzesniow); pop. 22; 62 km WSW of Przemysl; 49°39'/21°57'.

Trzydnik, Pol.; 50 km SSW of Lublin; 50°52'/22°08'; GUM5.

Tsants, see Nowy Sacz.

Tsapovka, Ukr. (Capowce); pop. 76; 69 km NNW of Chernovtsy; 48°52'/25°36'.

Tsarevka, Mold. (Tareni); pop. 18; 88 km N of Kishinev; 47°45'/28°53'.

Tsarichanka, Ukr. (Tzaritchanka, Zaritchanka, Zaritschanka); 69 km NW of Dnepropetrovsk; 48°57'/34°29'; LDL, SF.

Tsaritsyn, see Volgograd.

Tsarizin, see Volgograd.

Tsarnovitz, see Chernavchitsy.

Tsarskoye Selo, see Pushkin.

Tsaul, Mold. (Taul); pop. 84; 157 km NW of Kishinev; 48°13'/27°41'.

Tscenkowic, EGRS. This town was not found in BGN gazetteers under the given spelling.

Tschaschniki, see Chashniki.

Tschepin, see Cepin.

Tschereja, see Chereya.

Tschernewzi, see Chernevtsy.

Tschernigov, see Chernigov.

Tschertorija Novaya, (Chartariya Chadasha); LDL, SF. This town was not found in BGN gazetteers under the given spelling.

Tschetschelnik, see Chechelnik.

Tschigirin, USSR; EDRD. This town was not found in BGN gazetteers under the given spelling.

Tschippendorf, see Cepari.

Tschoplowitz bei Brieg, HSL. This pre-World War I community was not found in BGN gazetteers.

Tschudnowo, Ukr. EDRD. This town was not found in BGN gazetteers under the given spelling.

Tsebluv, Ukr. (Ceblow); pop. 16; 69 km N of Lvov; 50°25'/24°03'.

Tsechanovik, see Cekoniskes.

Tsegovo, see Tsekhuv.

Tsekhnauts, Mold. (Tahnauti); pop. 31; 88 km N of Kishinev; 47°45'/28°52'.

Tsekhuv, Ukr. (Cergowa?, Tsegovo); pop. 20; 88 km NNE of Lvov; 50°28'/24°47'.

Tselenzh, Ukr. (Cielaz); pop. 7; 75 km N of Lvov; 50°31'/24°16'.

Tselkoviche Velikoye, Ukr. (Ciolkowicze Wielkie, Tselkoviche Velke); pop. 24; 114 km NNW of Rovno; 51°35'/25°57'.

Tselkoviche Velke, see Tselkoviche Velikoye.

Tsemezhintse, see Chemerintsy.

Tsenyava, Ukr. (Ceniawa); pop. 6; 114 km S of Lvov; 48°53'/24°10'.

Tsenyuv, Ukr. (Ceniow); pop. 22; 88 km ESE of Lvov; 49°31'/25°06'.

Tseptseviche Male, see Tseptsevichi.

Tseptsevichi, Ukr. (Cepcewicze Male, Tseptseviche Male); pop. 49; 88 km N of Rovno; 51°22'/26°24'.

Tseshanov, see Cieszanow.

Tshartorisk, see Staryy Chartoriysk.

Tshastar, see Czastary.

Tshebin, see Trzebinia.

Tshekhanov, see Ciechanow.

Tshekhanovets, see Ciechanowiec.

Tshekhanovits, see Ciechanowiec.

Tshenstokhov, see Czestochowa.

Tshervinsk, see Czerwinsk nad Wisla.

Tsheshanov, see Cieszanow.

Tshizheva, see Czyzew.

Tshmelev, see Cmielow.

Tsibirika, Mold. (Tibirica); pop. 71; 56 km NW of Kishinev; 47°22'/28°22'.

Tsibulev, *see* Tsibulevo.

Tsibulevo, Ukr. (Tsibulev); pop. 1,000; 163 km ENE of Uman; 48°49'/32°30'; EDRD.

Tsiekishok, *see* Cekiske.

Tsirin, Byel. (Cyryn, Tzirin); pop. 11; 107 km SW of Minsk; 53°24'/26°09'; SF.

Tsisuv, *see* Tysov.

Tsituvian, *see* Tytuvenai.

Tsmen Pervsha, Byel. (Cmien?); pop. 21; 38 km ESE of Pinsk; 51°58'/26°37'.

Tsna, Byel. (Chiny, Cna); pop. 23; 62 km ENE of Pinsk; 52°15'/27°00'.

Tsoyzmir, *see* Sandomierz.

Tsuman, Ukr. (Cuman); 38 km WNW of Rovno; 50°50'/25°53'; GUM4.

Tsutsilov, *see* Tsutsyluv.

Tsutsnyuv, Ukr. (Cucniow); pop. 5; 107 km N of Lvov; 50°47'/24°04'.

Tsutsyluv, Ukr. (Cucylow, Tsutsilov); pop. 67; 107 km WNW of Chernovtsy; 48°44'/24°39'.

Tsuyzmir, *see* Sandomierz.

Tsuzmir, *see* Sandomierz.

Tsyganeshty, Mold. (Tiganesti); pop. 46; 38 km NW of Kishinev; 47°18'/28°33'.

Tsygany, *see* Rudka (Tarnopol).

Tsygira, Mold. (Tagara); pop. 17; 88 km WNW of Kishinev; 47°27'/27°54'.

Tsyntsareni, Mold. (Tantareni Orehi); pop. 51; 69 km NNW of Kishinev; 47°34'/28°34'.

Tsyntsareny, Mold. (Tantareni Tighina); pop. 29; 26 km ESE of Kishinev; 46°54'/29°09'.

Tsyr, Ukr. (Cyr); pop. 76; 150 km NW of Rovno; 51°49'/25°17'.

Tsyurupinsk, Ukr. (Aleshki, Oleszki); pop. 755; 150 km ENE of Odessa; 46°37'/32°43'; GUM4.

Tubingen, Germ.; pop. 137; 32 km S of Stuttgart; 48°32'/09°03'; GED, GUM3, GUM5, HSL, PHGBW.

Tuchan, Pol.; pop. 6; 56 km NNW of Czestochowa; 51°13'/18°57'.

Tuchanie, Pol.; pop. 34; 88 km E of Lublin; 51°02'/23°48'.

Tuchapy, Ukr. (Tuczapy); pop. 52; 45 km W of Chernovtsy; 48°24'/25°22'.

Tuchel, *see* Tuchola.

Tuchersfeld, Germ.; 45 km NNE of Nurnberg; 49°47'/11°22'; PHGB.

Tuchin, Ukr. (Tuczyn, Tuczyn Nowy, Tutchin, Tutchin Kripah, Tutsin); pop. 2,159; 26 km NE of Rovno; 50°42'/26°34'; AMG, COH, EDRD, EJ, GA, GUM3, GUM4, GUM5, GUM6, HSL, HSL2, JGFF, LDL, LYV, SF, YB.

Tuchla, *see* Tukhlya.

Tuchlin, Pol.; pop. 24; BGN lists two possible localities with this name located at 52°38'/21°41' and 53°49'/21°48'.

Tuchne, Ukr. (Tuczna); pop. 69; 50 km ESE of Lvov; 49°34'/24°28'.

Tuchola, Pol. (Tuchel); pop. 118; 101 km SSW of Gdansk; 53°35'/17°51'; GA, GUM5, HSL, JGFF, POCEM.

Tucholka, Ukr.; pop. 58; 150 km S of Lvov; 48°35'/23°15'; HSL. This town was located on an interwar map of Poland but does not appear in contemporary gazetteers. Map coordinates are approximate.

Tuchorice, Cz.; pop. 7; 56 km WNW of Praha; 50°16'/13°40'.

Tuchov, *see* Tuchow.

Tuchow, Pol. (Tuchov); pop. 328; 88 km E of Krakow; 49°54'/21°04'; AMG, EDRD, EGRS, GA, GUM3, GUM4, GUM5, GUM6, HSL, PHP3, SF.

Tuchowicz, Pol.; pop. 11; 82 km NNW of Lublin; 51°54'/22°14'.

Tuchowicze, *see* Tukhovichi.

Tuchume, *see* Tukums.

Tuckum, *see* Tukums.

Tuczapy, Pol.; pop. 33; 107 km ESE of Lublin; 50°37'/23°46'.

See also Tuchapy.

Tuczna, *see* Tuchne.

Tuczno, Pol. (Tutz); pop. 33; 101 km NW of Poznan; 53°11'/16°09'.

Tuczyn, *see* Tuchin.

Tuczyn Nowy, *see* Tuchin.

Tudorkovitse, Ukr. (Tudorkowice); pop. 41; 88 km N of Lvov; 50°35'/24°10'.

Tudorkowice, *see* Tudorkovitse.

Tuhnice, Cz.; pop. 48; 114 km W of Praha; 50°14'/12°55'.

Tukhlya, Ukr. (Tuchla); pop. 88; 114 km S of Lvov; 48°55'/23°28'; AMG, HSL.

Tukhovichi, Byel. (Tuchowicze); 88 km NNW of Pinsk; 52°49'/25°58'; GUM4.

Tukkum, *see* Tukums.

Tukkums, *see* Tukums.

Tuktin, *see* Tykocin.

Tukum, *see* Tukums.

Tukums, Lat. (Tuchume, Tuckum, Tukkum, Tukkums, Tukum); pop. 970; 56 km WSW of Riga; 56°57'/23°09'; COH, EJ, GUM3, HSL, JGFF, PHLE, SF.

Tula, *see* Tuula.

Tulbing, Aus.; pop. 3; 19 km WNW of Wien; 48°17'/16°07'.

Tulcea, Rom.; pop. 227 km NE of Bucuresti; 45°10'/28°48'; GUM4, JGFF, PHR1.

Tulchin, Ukr. (Tulcin, Tulczyn, Tultchin); pop. 7,708; 69 km SE of Vinnitsa; 48°41'/28°52'; EDRD, EJ, GUM3, GUM4, GUM6, GYLA, HSL, JGFF, PHP2, PHR1, SF.

Tulcin, *see* Tulchin.

Tulczyn, *see* Tulchin.

Tulghes, Rom. (Gyergyotol, Tulghes Ciuc); pop. 255; 139 km WSW of Iasi; 46°57'/25°46'; PHR2.

Tulghes Ciuc, *see* Tulghes.

Tulichev, Ukr. (Tuliczow); pop. 18; 120 km WNW of Rovno; 51°00'/24°39'.

Tuliczow, *see* Tulichev.

Tuliglowy, *see* Tuligolovy.

Tuligolovy, Ukr. (Tuliglowy); pop. 23; 45 km SW of Lvov; 49°36'/23°38'.

Tulishkov, *see* Tuliszkow.

Tuliszkow, Pol. (Tulishkov); pop. 260; 88 km WNW of Lodz; 52°05'/18°18'; CAHJP, PHP1, SF.

Tulkowice, Pol. BGN lists two possible localities with this name located at 49°54'/21°43' and 50°45'/21°38'. PHP3.

Tulln, Aus.; pop. 72; 26 km WNW of Wien; 48°20'/16°03'.

Tulovo, Byel. (Tulowo); pop. 5; 146 km NW of Pinsk; 53°05'/24°44'.

Tulovo (Vitebsk area), Byel.; 13 km ENE of Vitebsk; 55°13'/30°18'; GUM4.

Tulowo, *see* Tulovo.

Tultchin, *see* Tulchin.

Tuluga, GUM3. This town was not found in BGN gazetteers under the given spelling.

Tume, Lat.; pop. 1; 62 km W of Riga; 56°58'/23°03'.

Tumilovichi, Byel. (Tumilowicze); pop. 2; 126 km N of Minsk; 54°56'/27°57'.

Tumilowicze, *see* Tumilovichi.

Tumin, Ukr.; pop. 15; 120 km N of Lvov; 50°51'/24°36'.

Tumirz, *see* Tumizh.

Tumizh, Ukr. (Tumirz); pop. 29; 114 km NW of Chernovtsy; 49°05'/24°53'.

Tumlin, Pol.; pop. 35; 107 km ENE of Czestochowa; 50°58'/20°35'.

Tumringen, Germ. LDS, PHGBW. This town was not found in BGN gazetteers under the given spelling.

Tundern, Germ.; pop. 3; 50 km SSW of Hannover; 52°04'/09°22'.

Tunyog, Hung.; pop. 87; 126 km E of Miskolc; 47°58'/22°27'; AMG, HSL, LDS, PHH.

Tur, Ukr.; pop. 30; 182 km WNW of Rovno; 51°40'/24°17'; HSL, HSL2.

Tura, Hung.; pop. 96; 45 km NE of Budapest; 47°37'/19°36'; HSL, PHH.

Tura Luka, Cz. (Turoluka); 75 km NNE of Bratislava; 48°45'/17°32'; HSL.

Turaszowka, Pol. (Toroszowka, Turaszowka Vel Toroszowka); pop. 48; 75 km WSW of Przemysl; 49°44'/21°43'.

Turaszowka Vel Toroszowka, *see* Turaszowka.

Turawa Wolaska, *see* Tyrawa Woloska.

Turbe, Yug.; pop. 45; 214 km SE of Zagreb; 44°15'/17°35'; COH.

Turbia, Pol.; pop. 45; 82 km SSW of Lublin; 50°38'/21°59'.

Turbin, *see* Turobin.

Turbuta, Rom.; pop. 2; 56 km NNW of Cluj; 47°15'/23°19'.

Turc, Rom. AMG, GUM5. This town was not found in BGN gazetteers under the given spelling.

Turcianske Teplice, Cz. (Stubnianske Teplice); pop. 101; 150 km NE of Bratislava; 48°52'/18°52'.

Turciansky Svaty Martin, Cz.; pop. 1,373; 163 km NE of Bratislava; 49°04'/18°56'.

Turcz, *see* Turt.

Turda, Rom. (Aranyos Torda, Thorenburg, Torda); pop. 10; 26 km SE of Cluj; 46°34'/23°47'; EJ, GUM4, GUM6, HSL, JGFF, LDL, LDS, PHR1.

Turdeni, Rom.; pop. 4; 126 km ESE of Cluj; 46°23'/25°06'.

Tur Dolny, Pol.; pop. 9; 62 km NNE of Krakow; 50°32'/20°25'.

Turdosin, *see* Tvarozna.

Turdossin, *see* Tvarozna.

Turea, Rom.; pop. 2; 19 km WNW of Cluj; 46°51'/23°21'.

Turec, Cz.; pop. 6; 94 km W of Praha; 50°15'/13°12'.

Tureczki Nizne, Ukr.; pop. 58; 146 km SSW of Lvov; 48°45'/22°55'. This town was located on an interwar map of Poland but does not appear in contemporary gazetteers. Map coordinates are approximate.

Tureczki Wyzne, Ukr.; pop. 47; 146 km SSW of Lvov; 48°45'/22°55'. This town was located on an interwar map of Poland but does not appear in contemporary gazetteers. Map coordinates are approximate.

Turek, Pol. (Tirek, Torek); pop. 2,678; 75 km WNW of Lodz; 52°02'/18°30'; AMG, CAHJP, COH, EDRD, GA, GUM3, GUM4, HSL, JGFF, LYV, PHP1, POCEM, SF.

Tureni, Rom.; pop. 11; 26 km SSE of Cluj; 46°37'/23°42'.

Turets, Byel. (Toretz, Turetz, Turez, Turzec, Turzets); pop. 452; 88 km SW of Minsk; 53°31'/26°19'; COH, EDRD, GUM3, GUM4, GUM5, HSL, JGFF, LYV, SF, YB.

Turetz, *see* Turets.

Tur Ev, *see* Tartu.

Turev, *see* Turov.

Turez, *see* Turets.

Turgu Ocna, GUM3. This town was not found in BGN gazetteers under the given spelling.

Turia, Rom. BGN lists two possible localities with this name located at 44°27'/24°28' and 46°02'/26°03'. HSL.

Turilche, Ukr. (Turylcze); pop. 13; 56 km N of Chernovtsy; 48°46'/26°12'; PHP2.

Turinka, Ukr. (Turynka); pop. 64; 38 km N of Lvov; 50°08'/24°03'; HSL.

Turi Remety, *see* Turyanremety.

Turisk, *see* Turiysk.

Turistvandi, Hung.; pop. 36; 139 km E of Miskolc; 48°03'/22°39'.

Turiysk, Ukr. (Torysk, Trisk, Trusk, Turijsk, Turisk, Turzisk, Turzysk, Turzysk Przedmiescie); pop. 1,081; 133 km WNW of Rovno; 51°06'/24°32'; COH, EDRD, GUM3, GYLA, HSL, JGFF, LDL, LYV, PHP4, SF, YB.

Turja, Pol.; pop. 30; A number of towns share this name. It was not possible to determine from available information which one is being referenced.

Turjaremete, HSL. This pre-World War I community was not found in BGN gazetteers.

Turje, Hung.; pop. 59; 69 km N of Nagykanizsa; 46°59'/17°06'.

Turka, Ukr.; pop. 4,201; 62 km WNW of Chernovtsy; 48°35'/25°08'; AMG, EGRS, EJ, GUM3, GUM4, GUM5, GUM6, HSL, HSL2, JGFF, LDL, PHP2, PHP3, SF.

Turka (Lwow), Ukr.; pop. 4,117; 101 km SSW of Lvov; 49°09'/23°02'; EDRD, GUM5, SF, YB.

Turka (near Chelm), Pol.; pop. 56; 88 km E of Lublin; 51°08'/23°48'; GUM5.

Turkeve, Hung.; pop. 220; 107 km NNE of Szeged; 47°06'/20°45'; LDS, PHH.

Turkowice, Pol. (Turkowicze); pop. 26; 107 km ESE of Lublin; 50°40'/23°44'.

Turkowicze, *see* Turkowice.

Turkowo, Pol.; 38 km WSW of Poznan; 52°24'/16°26'; GA.

Turlava, Lat.; pop. 4; 146 km WSW of Riga; 56°48'/21°47'.

Turmantas, Lith. (Turmont); 139 km NNE of Vilnius; 55°42'/26°27'; YL.

Turmont, *see* Turmantas.

Turn, Cz.; pop. 6; 75 km NW of Praha; 50°38'/13°50'; HSL. This town was located on a pre-World War I map, but does not appear in contemporary gazetteers.

Turna, *see* Trencianska Turna.

Turna Mala, Pol.; pop. 7; 88 km S of Bialystok; 52°22'/22°53'.

Turna nad Bodvou, Cz. (Aalaiy Torna, Torna); pop. 262; 32 km SW of Kosice; 48°36'/20°53'; HSL, LDL.

Turnau, Aus.; 62 km NNW of Graz; 47°33'/15°20'; EJ, HSL, HSL2.

Turno, Pol.; pop. 22; 50 km NE of Lublin; 51°33'/23°10'.

Turnov, Cz.; pop. 93; 75 km NNE of Praha; 50°35'/15°10'; EJ.

Turnu Severin, Rom.; 246 km S of Cluj; 44°38'/22°40'; EDRD, GUM4, GUM6, PHR1.

Turobin, Pol. (Torbin, Turbin); pop. 965; 50 km SSE of Lublin; 50°50'/22°44'; AMG, CAHJP, COH, EDRD, GUM4, GUM5, GUM6, HSL, HSL2, JGFF, LDL, LDS, LYV, SF, YB.

Turobowice, Pol.; 69 km E of Lodz; 51°45'/20°29'; GUM4.

Turoluka, *see* Tura Luka.

Turosl, Pol.; 114 km WNW of Bialystok; 53°31'/21°36'; HSL.

Turov, Byel. (Toorof, Turev); pop. 2,171; 114 km E of Pinsk; 52°04'/27°44'; HSL, HSL2, JGFF, LDL, SF.

Turovichi, Ukr. (Targovishche, Targowiszcze); pop. 54; 146 km WNW of Rovno; 51°10'/24°24'.

Turovka, Ukr. (Turowka); 126 km N of Chernovtsy; 49°24'/26°10'; GUM3.

Turowka, *see* Turovka.

Tur Piaski, Pol.; pop. 6; 62 km NNE of Krakow; 50°32'/20°25'.

Turricse, Hung.; pop. 11; 146 km E of Miskolc; 47°58'/22°46'.

Turt, Rom. (Turcz); pop. 352; 139 km NNW of Cluj; 47°59'/23°13'; HSL, LDL, PHR2.

Turterebes, *see* Turulung.

Turulung, Rom. (Turterebes); pop. 207; 133 km NNW of Cluj; 47°56'/23°05'; PHR2.

Turvekonya, Rom.; 120 km NNW of Cluj; 47°48'/23°23'; HSL. This town was located on a pre-World War I map, but does not appear in contemporary gazetteers.

Tury, Pol.; pop. 34; A number of towns share this name. It was not possible to determine from available information which one is being referenced.

Turyanremety, Ukr. (Turi Remety); 163 km SSW of Lvov; 48°43'/22°36'; JGFF.

Turye, Ukr. (Tuzhe); pop. 77; 62 km NE of Lvov; 50°05'/24°50'.

Turylcze, *see* Turilche.

Turyn, USSR; 133 km E of Kaliningrad; 54°38'/22°34'; HSL. This town was located on a pre-World War I map, but does not appear in contemporary gazetteers.

Turynka, *see* Turinka.

Turza, Pol.; 38 km SE of Czestochowa; 50°28'/19°23'; GUM4. *See also* Tuzhe.

Turzansk, Pol.; pop. 32; 69 km SW of Przemysl; 49°22'/22°09'.

Turza Wielka, *see* Bolshaya Turya.

Turza Wilcza, Pol.; pop. 1; 114 km N of Lodz; 52°44'/19°25'.

Turza Wileka, Pol. PHP2. This town was not found in BGN gazetteers under the given spelling.

Turze, Pol.; pop. 199; 32 km SSW of Przemysl; 49°35'/22°34'; PHP2.

Turzec, see Turets.

Turzets, see Turets.

Turzisk, see Turiysk.

Turzovka, Cz.; pop. 75; 146 km ENE of Brno; 49°24'/18°38'.

Turzysk, see Turiysk.

Turzysk Przedmiescie, see Turiysk.

Tushin, see Tuszyn.

Tushkuv, Ukr. (Tuszkow); pop. 37; 62 km N of Lvov; 50°24'/23°59'.

Tusice, Cz. (Tussa); 38 km ENE of Kosice; 48°44'/21°45'; HSL.

Tuska, Ukr. (Csuszka, Tiska); 146 km S of Lvov; 48°35'/23°24'; SM. This town was located on a pre-World War I map, but does not appear in contemporary gazetteers.

Tuske, see Ujdombovar.

Tuskeszentpeter, Hung.; pop. 8; 62 km N of Nagykanizsa; 46°58'/17°04'.

Tusko, Hung.; 101 km ENE of Nagykanizsa; 46°38'/18°17'; HSL.

Tussa, see Tusice.

Tussenhausen, Germ. (Angelberg); 75 km WSW of Munchen; 48°06'/10°34'; PHGB.

Tust, Cz. (Tist, Tlist, Tlust, Tluyst, Tuyst); pop. 11; 133 km WSW of Brno; 48°53'/14°53'; LYV.

Tustanovitse, Ukr. (Tustanowice); pop. 2,803; 75 km SSW of Lvov; 49°17'/23°27'; EGRS.

Tustanowice, see Tustanovitse.

Tustoglowy, Pol.; pop. 22; GUM4. Described in the *Black Book* as being in the Tarnopol region of Poland, this town was not found in BGN gazetteers.

Tuszkow, see Tushkuv.

Tuszow, Pol.; pop. 3; 26 km S of Lublin; 51°05'/22°32'; GUM6.

Tuszow Narodowy, Pol.; pop. 12; 114 km ENE of Krakow; 50°22'/21°28'.

Tuszyma, Pol.; pop. 15; 101 km WNW of Przemysl; 50°12'/21°31'.

Tuszyn, Pol. (Tushin); pop. 1,271; 26 km SSE of Lodz; 51°36'/19°33'; AMG, CAHJP, COH, GUM4, HSL, HSL2, LDS, PHP1, SF.

Tutchin, see Tuchin.

Tutchin Kripah, see Tuchin.

Tuteres, see Tauteny.

Tutin, Yug.; pop. 6; 146 km NW of Skopje; 42°59'/20°20'.

Tutos, HSL. This pre-World War I community was not found in BGN gazetteers.

Tutovichi, Ukr. (Tutowicze); pop. 60; 88 km N of Rovno; 51°21'/26°22'.

Tutowicze, see Tutovichi.

Tutsin, see Tuchin.

Tuttlingen, Germ.; pop. 20; 94 km S of Stuttgart; 47°59'/08°49'; PHGBW.

Tutz, see Tuczno.

Tutzing, Germ.; pop. 5; 38 km SSW of Munchen; 47°55'/11°17'.

Tuula, Est. (Tula); 26 km SW of Tallinn; 59°16'/24°28'; JGFF, LDL.

Tuyst, see Tust.

Tuzha Velka, see Bolshaya Turya.

Tuzhe, see Turye.

Tuzhiluv, Ukr. (Tuzylow); pop. 21; 101 km SSE of Lvov; 48°59'/24°15'.

Tuzla, Yug.; pop. 314; 146 km WSW of Beograd; 44°33'/18°41'; PHY. See also Tuzly.

Tuzly, Ukr. (Tuzla); pop. 118; 88 km SSW of Odessa; 45°52'/30°05'.

Tuzora, see Kalarash.

Tuzser, Hung.; pop. 78; 107 km ENE of Miskolc; 48°21'/22°08'; HSL, PHH.

Tuzylow, see Tuzhiluv.

Tvardita, see Tvarditsa.

Tvarditsa, Mold. (Tvardita); pop. 6; 101 km S of Kishinev; 46°09'/28°58'.

Tvarozna, Cz. (Durand, Durelsdorf, Turdosin, Turdossin, Tvrdosin); pop. 97; 139 km WNW of Kosice; 49°07'/19°28'; AMG, GUM5.

Tver, see Kalinin.

Tverai, Lith.; pop. 102; 75 km WSW of Siauliai; 55°44'/22°09'; GUM5, HSL, LDL, SF, YL.

Tverdopillya, Ukr. (Hartfeld); pop. 19; 32 km WSW of Lvov; 49°50'/23°35'.

Tverdyn, Ukr. (Twerdyn); pop. 19; 114 km W of Rovno; 50°53'/24°45'.

Tverdza, Ukr. (Twierdza); pop. 29; 62 km WSW of Lvov; 49°48'/23°09'.

Tverecius, Lith. (Twerecz); 107 km NE of Vilnius; 55°19'/26°36'; GUM3.

Tvian, see Taujenai.

Tvrdosin, see Tvarozna.

Tvrdosovce, Cz. (Tardosked); 69 km E of Bratislava; 48°06'/18°04'; AMG.

Twardogora, Pol. (Festenberg); pop. 36; 50 km NE of Wroclaw; 51°22'/17°28'; HSL, LDS, PHP3.

Twarogi Mazury, Pol.; pop. 5; 69 km SSW of Bialystok; 52°35'/22°38'.

Twerdyn, see Tverdyn.

Twerecz, see Tverecius.

Twierdza, Pol.; pop. 148; 82 km W of Przemysl; 49°50'/21°38'; PHP3. See also Tverdza.

Twistringen, Germ.; pop. 30; 82 km WNW of Hannover; 52°48'/08°39'; GUM5, JGFF.

Tworki, Pol.; 19 km SW of Warszawa; 52°10'/20°50'; PHP4.

Tworkowa, Pol.; pop. 20; 62 km ESE of Krakow; 49°52'/20°40'.

Tworog, Pol.; pop. 5; 38 km SW of Czestochowa; 50°32'/18°42'.

Tworowice, Pol.; pop. 6; 56 km NE of Czestochowa; 51°06'/19°44'.

Tworyczow, Pol.; pop. 6; 56 km SE of Lublin; 50°47'/22°56'.

Tworylne, Pol.; pop. 30; 62 km S of Przemysl; 49°17'/22°29'.

Tyachev, Ukr. (Tachovo, Tacovo, Tech, Tecs, Tecso, Tetsh, Tiacevo, Tiachev, Tiacheva, Tiaczowo); pop. 12,661; 176 km WSW of Chernovtsy; 48°01'/23°35'; AMG, COH, GUM3, GUM6, HSL, HSL2, LDL, LYV, SM.

Tyapche, Ukr. (Tiapcze); pop. 3; 94 km S of Lvov; 49°02'/23°54'.

Tyble, Pol.; pop. 13; 82 km WNW of Czestochowa; 51°18'/18°18'.

Tyborow, Pol.; pop. 1; 50 km E of Warszawa; 52°10'/21°40'.

Tycha, Pol.; pop. 27; 62 km WNW of Przemysl; 50°03'/22°00'; HSL. This town was located on a pre-World War I map, but does not appear in contemporary gazetteers.

Tychy, Pol.; 69 km W of Krakow; 50°08'/18°59'; POCEM.

Tyczyn, Pol. (Titchin); pop. 957; 56 km WNW of Przemysl; 49°58'/22°02'; AMG, EGRS, GA, GUM5, PHP3, POCEM, SF.

Tykocin, Pol. (Tikotsin, Tiktin, Tuktin, Tykotsin); pop. 1,461; 26 km W of Bialystok; 53°12'/22°47'; CAHJP, COH, EJ, FRG, GUM3, GUM4, HSL, HSL2, JGFF, LDL, LDS, LYV, PHP2, PHP4, POCEM, SF, YB.

Tykotsin, see Tykocin.

Tylicz, Pol. (Tilitch); pop. 139; 114 km ESE of Krakow; 49°24'/21°02'; AMG, GUM5, HSL, PHP3, SF.

Tylmanowa, Pol.; pop. 32; 82 km SE of Krakow; 49°29'/20°25'; HSL.

Tylwica, Pol.; pop. 1; 26 km ESE of Bialystok; 53°02'/23°28'.

Tylza, Pol. PHP4. This town was not found in BGN gazetteers under the given spelling.

Tymbark, Pol. (Timborg); pop. 94; 50 km SE of Krakow; 49°44'/20°20'; EGRS, HSL, PHP3, SF.

Tymienica, see Tymienica Stara.

Tymienica Stara, Pol. (Tymienica); pop. 19; 62 km W of Lublin; 51°17'/21°41'.

Tymowa, Pol.; pop. 59; 56 km ESE of Krakow; 49°51'/20°38'; HSL.

Tynec, see Tynec nad Sazavou.

Tynec nad Sazavou, Cz. (Tynec); pop. 20; 32 km SSE of Praha; 49°50'/14°36'.

Tynice, Cz.; pop. 6; 75 km S of Praha; 49°29'/14°24'.

Tyniec, *see* Tinets.

Tyniewicze Male, Pol.; pop. 6; 38 km SE of Bialystok; 52°51'/23°28'.

Tyniewicze Wielkie, Pol.; pop. 5; 38 km SE of Bialystok; 52°52'/23°29'.

Tyniowice, Pol.; pop. 8; 19 km NW of Przemysl; 49°56'/22°34'; HSL.

Tyniste, Cz. (Thonischen); 94 km W of Praha; 50°09'/13°11'; AMG.

Tynistko, Cz.; pop. 3; 101 km NNW of Brno; 50°00'/16°06'.

Tyn nad Vltavou, Cz. (Moldautein); pop. 24; 101 km S of Praha; 49°14'/14°25'; EJ.

Tynne, *see* Tynnoye.

Tynnoye, Ukr. (Tynne); pop. 64; 75 km NNE of Rovno; 51°10'/26°47'.

Typin, Pol.; pop. 34; 94 km NNE of Przemysl; 50°29'/23°35'.

Tyraspol, *see* Tirashpol.

Tyrawa Solna, Pol.; pop. 32; 38 km SW of Przemysl; 49°37'/22°17'.

Tyrawa Woloska, Pol. (Tirava Vilaska, Turawa Wolaska); pop. 299; 45 km SW of Przemysl; 49°35'/22°22'; EGRS, GUM5, LDL, PHP2, PHP3, SF.

Tyria, LDL. This pre-World War I community was not found in BGN gazetteers.

Tyrnau, *see* Trnava.

Tyrnavos, GUM4. This town was not found in BGN gazetteers under the given spelling.

Tyrnovo, Mold. (Tarnova Soroca); pop. 201; 157 km NW of Kishinev; 48°10'/27°40'.

Tyshkovtse, *see* Tyshkovtsy.

Tyshkovtsy, Ukr. (Tyshkovtse, Tyszkowce); pop. 129; 62 km NW of Chernovtsy; 48°42'/25°22'; PHP2.

Tyskowa, Pol.; pop. 5; 69 km SSW of Przemysl; 49°18'/22°22'.

Tysmenichany, Ukr. (Tysmieniczany); pop. 64; 107 km WNW of Chernovtsy; 48°46'/24°40'.

Tysmenitsa, Ukr. (Tismenitz, Tizmenitza, Tysmienica); pop. 1,300; 101 km WNW of Chernovtsy; 48°54'/24°51'; AMG, COH, EGRS, EJ, HSL, HSL2, JGFF, LDL, PHP2, PHP3, SF, YB.

Tysmienica, *see* Tysmenitsa.

Tysmienica (near Lublin), Pol.; pop. 33; 45 km NNE of Lublin; 51°34'/22°51'.

Tysmieniczany, *see* Tysmenichany.

Tysov, Ukr. (Cisow, Cisow Las, Tsisuv); pop. 31; 94 km S of Lvov; 49°03'/23°47'.

Tyszki Gostery, Pol.; pop. 26; Described in the *Black Book* as being in the Bialystok region of Poland, this town was not found in BGN gazetteers.

Tyszkowce, *see* Tyshkovtsy.

Tyszowce, Pol. (Tishevits, Tishevitz, Tishovits, Tishovtse, Tishvits, Tishvitz, Toshvitse, Tyszviec); pop. 2,451; 107 km ESE of Lublin; 50°37'/23°42'; AMG, CAHJP, COH, EDRD, EJ, GA, GUM3, GUM4, GUM5, HSL, HSL2, JGFF, LDS, LYV, PHP1, PHP4, SF, YB.

Tyszviec, *see* Tyszowce.

Tytavenai, *see* Tytuvenai.

Tytuvenai, Lith. (Citavjan, Tsituvian, Tytavenai, Tzitavian); pop. 221; 45 km S of Siauliai; 55°36'/23°12'; GUM3, GUM5, HSL, JGFF, SF, YL.

Tyukod, Hung.; pop. 98; 133 km E of Miskolc; 47°51'/22°33'; HSL, PHH.

Tyvrov, Ukr. (Tiuriv); 32 km S of Vinnitsa; 49°01'/28°30'; PHR1.

Tywonia, Pol.; pop. 6; 32 km NNW of Przemysl; 50°02'/22°38'.

Tzantz Yashan, *see* Stary Sacz.

Tzanz, *see* Nowy Sacz.

Tzaritchanka, *see* Tsarichanka.

Tzarna Dunayetz, *see* Czarny Dunajec.

Tzeikishok, *see* Cekiske.

Tzezhkovitz, *see* Ciezkowice.

Tzieshinov, *see* Cieszanow.

Tzihav, *see* Syche.

Tzirin, *see* Tsirin.

Tzishova, *see* Cieszowa.

Tzitavian, *see* Tytuvenai.

Tzitzov, *see* Cycow.

Tzizhav, *see* Czyzew.

Tzoizmir, *see* Sandomierz.

Uberlingen, Germ.; 120 km S of Stuttgart; 47°46'/09°10'; EDRD, GUM3, PHGBW.

Ubieszyn, Pol.; pop. 10; 45 km NNW of Przemysl; 50°10'/22°35'.

Ubinie, Ukr.; pop. 20; 45 km ESE of Lvov; 49°35'/24°25'; YB. This town was located on an interwar map of Poland but does not appear in contemporary gazetteers. Map coordinates are approximate.

Ubla, Cz. (Ublya); pop. 136; 88 km ENE of Kosice; 48°54'/22°24'; AMG, HSL.

Ublya, *see* Ubla.

Uboc, Cz.; pop. 2; 120 km SW of Praha; 49°27'/13°05'.

Ubrez, Cz. (Ubrezs); pop. 50; 62 km ENE of Kosice; 48°47'/22°08'; HSL.

Ubrezs, *see* Ubrez.

Ubrodowice, Pol.; pop. 14; 101 km ESE of Lublin; 50°55'/23°52'.

Uchanie, Pol. (Uhanie); pop. 1,010; 82 km ESE of Lublin; 50°54'/23°38'; AMG, EDRD, GA, GUM3, GUM5, LDS, POCEM.

Uchanka, Pol.; pop. 7; 94 km E of Lublin; 51°05'/23°52'.

Uchomir, Ukr. EDRD. This town was not found in BGN gazetteers under the given spelling.

Uchte, Germ.; pop. 16; 56 km W of Hannover; 52°30'/08°55'.

Uchtenhagen, Germ.; pop. 1; 114 km W of Berlin; 52°47'/11°51'.

Uciana, *see* Utena.

Uciskow, Pol.; pop. 10; 69 km NE of Krakow; 50°20'/20°48'.

Uciszow, *see* Utsishkuv.

Uckingen, HSL. This pre-World War I community was not found in BGN gazetteers.

Udalec, Pol.; pop. 46; AMG. Described in the *Black Book* as being in the Lublin region of Poland, this town was not found in BGN gazetteers.

Udavske, Cz. (Udva); pop. 63; 62 km NE of Kosice; 48°59'/21°58'; HSL.

Udem, Germ.; pop. 22; 94 km NW of Koln; 51°40'/06°18'.

Uderwangen, *see* Chekhovo.

Udingen, Germ.; 45 km SW of Koln; 50°44'/06°29'; GUM5.

Udlice, Cz. (Eidlitz); pop. 17; 82 km WNW of Praha; 50°26'/13°28'; EJ, HSL, HSL2.

Udobnoye, Ukr. (Han Casla); pop. 6; 50 km WSW of Odessa; 46°23'/30°03'.

Udovo, Yug.; pop. 1; 107 km SE of Skopje; 41°21'/22°27'.

Udrc, Cz.; pop. 12; 101 km W of Praha; 50°08'/13°05'.

Udrycze, Pol.; pop. 30; 69 km ESE of Lublin; 50°48'/23°17'.

Udrzyn, Pol.; pop. 49; 69 km NE of Warszawa; 52°40'/21°44'.

Udva, *see* Udavske.

Udvard, *see* Dvory nad Zitavou.

Udvari, Hung.; pop. 17; 114 km S of Budapest; 46°36'/18°31'; HSL, LDS.

Udvarnok, *see* Dvorniky.

Uedainiai, *see* Utena.

Uehlfeld, *see* Uhlfeld.

Uelsen, Germ. (Ulsen); 176 km N of Koln; 52°30'/06°53'; GED, LDS.

Uelzen, Germ.; pop. 35; 75 km SE of Hamburg; 52°58'/10°34'.

Ufa, HSL, JGFF. This town was not found in BGN gazetteers under the given spelling.

Uffenheim, Germ.; pop. 77; 62 km W of Nurnberg; 49°32'/10°15'; GUM3, GUM5, JGFF, PHGB.

Ugale, Lat. (Ugalen, Ugales); pop. 24; 133 km W of Riga; 57°16'/22°02'; HSL, PHLE.

Ugalen, *see* Ugale.

Ugales, *see* Ugale.

Ugar, HSL. A number of towns share this name. It was not possible to determine from available information which one is being referenced.

Ugertse Nezabitovske, *see* Ugry.

Uglya, Ukr. (Igla, Igle, Uhla); 170 km WSW of Chernovtsy; 48°09'/23°37'; AMG, GUM5, LYV, SM.

Ugnev, Ukr. (Hivnev, Hivniv, Hovniv, Uhnow, Univ, Unov); pop. 1,832; 62 km NNW of Lvov; 50°22'/23°45'; COH, EGRS, GUM3, HSL, LDL, PHP2, SF, YB.

Ugod, Hung.; pop. 26; 114 km WSW of Budapest; 47°19'/17°36'; COH.

Ugolets, Byel. (Uholec); pop. 6; 62 km E of Pinsk; 52°01'/27°04'.

Ugorniki, Ukr. (Uhorniki); pop. 85; 114 km WNW of Chernovtsy; 48°55'/24°46'.

Ugorniki (near Tlumach), Ukr.; pop. 35; 94 km WNW of Chernovtsy; 48°52'/25°02'. This town was located on an interwar map of Poland but does not appear in contemporary gazetteers. Map coordinates are approximate.

Ugornya, *see* Gergelyiugornya.

Ugra, *see* Biharugra.

Ugrinkovtsy, Ukr. (Ugrynkovtse, Ugrynokovtse, Uhrynkowce); pop. 43; 50 km NNW of Chernovtsy; 48°44'/25°45'.

Ugrutiu, Rom.; pop. 7; 32 km NW of Cluj; 47°00'/23°22'.

Ugry, Ukr. (Ugertse Nezabitovske, Uherce Niezabitowskie, Uhry); pop. 51; 32 km SW of Lvov; 49°44'/23°37'; HSL.

Ugrynkovtse, *see* Ugrinkovtsy.

Ugrynokovtse, *see* Ugrinkovtsy.

Ugrynuv Sredni, Ukr. (Uhrynow Sredni); pop. 24; 107 km SSE of Lvov; 48°55'/24°22'.

Uhanie, *see* Uchanie.

Uherce, Pol. (Uherce Mineralne); pop. 51; 50 km SSW of Przemysl; 49°28'/22°25'.

Uherce Mineralne, *see* Uherce.

Uherce Niezabitowskie, *see* Ugry.

Uherske Hradiste, Cz. (Ungarisch Hradisch, Ungarsich Hradich); pop. 353; 62 km E of Brno; 49°04'/17°27'; EJ.

Uhersko, Ukr.; pop. 23; 69 km S of Lvov; 49°19'/23°54'.

Uhersky Brod, Cz. (Brod Uhersky, Broda, Ungarisch Brod); pop. 529; 75 km E of Brno; 49°02'/17°39'; EDRD, EJ, GUM3, GUM5, HSL, HSL2.

Uhersky Ostroh, Cz. (Ungarisch Ostrau, Ungarish Ostra); pop. 355; 62 km ESE of Brno; 48°59'/17°23'; HSL.

Uhla, *see* Uglya.

Uhlfeld, Germ. (Uehlfeld); pop. 66; 38 km WNW of Nurnberg; 49°40'/10°44'; CAHJP, GUM5, HSL, HSL2, JGFF, PHGB, PHGBW.

Uhlirske Janovice, Cz.; pop. 89; 50 km ESE of Praha; 49°53'/15°04'.

Uhnin, Pol. (Unin); pop. 86; 50 km NNE of Lublin; 51°35'/23°02'; HSL.

Uhnow, *see* Ugnev.

Uholec, *see* Ugolets.

Uhonice, Cz.; pop. 2; 19 km WSW of Praha; 50°03'/14°11'.

Uhorniki, *see* Ugorniki.

Uhrineves, Cz.; pop. 42; 13 km ESE of Praha; 50°02'/14°36'; AMG.

Uhrov, Cz.; pop. 4; 88 km ESE of Praha; 49°48'/15°34'.

Uhrusk, Pol.; pop. 27; 75 km ENE of Lublin; 51°18'/23°38'; GUM5.

Uhry, *see* Ugry.

Uhrynkowce, *see* Ugrinkovtsy.

Uhrynow, *see* Dubrovka (Lwow).

Uhrynow Sredni, *see* Ugrynuv Sredni.

Uhy, Cz.; pop. 5; 26 km NW of Praha; 50°17'/14°17'.

Uila, Rom.; pop. 6; 75 km ENE of Cluj; 46°56'/24°37'.

Uioara, *see* Uioara de Sus.

Uioara de Sus, Rom. (Felsomarosujvar, Marosujvar, Uioara); 50 km SE of Cluj; 46°23'/23°53'; HSL, HSL2, PHR1.

Uivar, Rom. (Ujvar); 240 km SW of Cluj; 45°39'/20°54'; COH, HSL.

Ujanowice, Pol.; pop. 16; 62 km ESE of Krakow; 49°45'/20°34'; GUM4.

Ujazd, Pol. (Ujest, Uyazd); pop. 792; 69 km SW of Czestochowa; 50°23'/18°21'; CAHJP, EDRD, EJ, GA, GUM3, GUM4, GUM6, HSL, JGFF, LDS, PHP1, POCEM, SF.

Ujazdow, Pol.; pop. 26; 62 km ENE of Lublin; 51°23'/23°23'; GA.

Ujazdowek, Pol.; 50 km NE of Czestochowa; 51°03'/19°39'; GA.

Ujcsanalos, Hung.; pop. 11; 19 km ENE of Miskolc; 48°08'/21°01'.

Ujdombovar, Hung. (Odombovar, Tuske); pop. 27; 88 km E of Nagykanizsa; 46°23'/18°09'; HSL, LDS.

Ujejsce, Pol.; pop. 15; 50 km SSE of Czestochowa; 50°24'/19°15'.

Ujest, *see* Ujazd.

Ujezd, HSL2. A number of towns share this name. It was not possible to determine from available information which one is being referenced.

Ujezna, Pol.; pop. 12; 38 km NW of Przemysl; 50°04'/22°35'.

Ujfala, Rom.; 240 km SW of Cluj; 46°04'/20°37'; HSL, HSL2. This town was located on a pre-World War I map, but does not appear in contemporary gazetteers.

Ujfeherto, Hung. (Micske); pop. 1,228; 75 km ESE of Miskolc; 47°48'/21°41'; AMG, GUM3, HSL, JGFF, LDL, LDS, PHH.

Ujgyor, HSL. This pre-World War I community was not found in BGN gazetteers.

Ujhartyan, Hung.; pop. 16; 45 km SE of Budapest; 47°13'/19°23'.

Ujhely, *see* Satoraljaujhely.

Ujkanizsa, HSL. This pre-World War I community was not found in BGN gazetteers.

Ujkecke, *see* Tiszakecske.

Ujkecske, Hung.; pop. 163; 82 km N of Szeged; 46°56'/20°05'; LDS, PHH.

Ujkenez, Hung.; pop. 12; 107 km ENE of Miskolc; 48°15'/22°14'.

Ujker, Hung.; pop. 18; 120 km N of Nagykanizsa; 47°28'/16°49'.

Ujkigyos, Hung.; pop. 15; 75 km NE of Szeged; 46°35'/21°02'.

Ujkowice, Pol.; pop. 43; 13 km NW of Przemysl; 49°51'/22°43'.

Ujlak, *see* Velke Zaluzie.

Ujleta, Hung.; pop. 8; 107 km ESE of Miskolc; 47°28'/21°53'.

Ujlorincfalva, Hung.; pop. 1; 56 km S of Miskolc; 47°38'/20°36'.

Ujmalomsok, Hung.; pop. 2; 120 km N of Nagykanizsa; 47°27'/17°24'.

Ujpazua, HSL. This pre-World War I community was not found in BGN gazetteers.

Ujpest, Hung.; pop. 11,396; 13 km NNW of Budapest; 47°34'/19°05'; AMG, COH, GUM3, GUM5, HSL, LDL, LDS, PHH, YB.

Ujradna, Rom.; 126 km NE of Cluj; 47°27'/24°54'; HSL. This town was located on a pre-World War I map, but does not appear in contemporary gazetteers.

Ujscie, Pol. (Uscz); pop. 21; 75 km NNW of Poznan; 53°03'/16°45'.

Ujscie Jezuickie, Pol.; pop. 37; 62 km NE of Krakow; 50°15'/20°45'.

Ujsoly, Pol.; pop. 41; 88 km SSW of Krakow; 49°29'/19°09'.

Ujszalok, HSL. This pre-World War I community was not found in BGN gazetteers.

Ujszalonta, Hung. (Nagyszalonta); 120 km NE of Szeged; 46°48'/21°30'; EJ, HSL, LDS.

Ujszasz, Hung.; pop. 35; 82 km ESE of Budapest; 47°18'/20°05'.

Ujvar, *see* Uivar.

Ujvarfalva, Hung.; pop. 5; 45 km E of Nagykanizsa; 46°26'/17°35'.

Ujvaros, *see* Komarom.

Ujvasar, Pol.; pop. 103; AMG, GUM3, GUM4, GUM5, HSL, HSL2, LYV, PHP2, PHP3. Described in the *Black Book* as being in the Lwow region of Poland, this town was not found in BGN gazetteers.

Ujvasar (Bohemia), Cz.; pop. 1; 163 km S of Praha; 48°39'/14°26'.

Ujvasar (Silesia), Pol.; 88 km SSW of Czestochowa; 50°07'/18°32'; CAHJP.

Uj Verbasz, *see* Vrbas.

Ujvidek, *see* Novi Sad.

Ukk, Hung. (Ilk); pop. 2; 75 km N of Nagykanizsa; 47°03'/17°13'; PHH.

Ukmerge, Lith. (Valkemir, Vil Komir, Vilkamir, Vilkmerge, Vilkomierz, Vilkomir, Wilkomierz, Wilkomir); pop. 3,885; 69 km NE of Kaunas; 55°15'/24°45'; AMG, COH, EJ, GUM3, GUM4, GUM5, GUM6, HSL, HSL2, JGFF, LDL, SF, YL.

Ulan, Pol.; pop. 9; 69 km N of Lublin; 51°49'/22°29'; GUM5.

Ulanica, Pol.; pop. 16; 45 km W of Przemysl; 49°51'/22°11'.

Ulaniki, *see* Ulyaniki.

Ulanov, Ukr. (Ulanow); pop. 2,151; 56 km NW of Vinnitsa; 49°42'/28°08'; FRG, SF.

Ulanovshchina, Byel. (Ulanowszczyzna); pop. 6; 50 km WNW of Minsk; 54°13'/27°00'.

Ulanow, Pol.; pop. 861; 88 km S of Lublin; 50°29'/22°16'; AMG, COH, EDRD, EGRS, GUM3, GUM5, HSL, JGFF, LDL, LYV, PHP2, PHP3, POCEM, SF. *See also* Ulanov. Some references refer to the town as being in the Lublin area. Others state it is in the Lvov area. All are undoubtedly referring to the same community as the map coordinates shown here are about halfway between Lublin and Lvov.

Ulanowice, Pol.; pop. 15; 107 km SW of Lublin; 50°40'/21°23'.

Ulanowszczyzna, *see* Ulanovshchina.

Ulanski Zarzyc, *see* Zarzyc Ulanski.

Ulashkovitz, *see* Ulashkovtsy.

Ulashkovtsy, Ukr. (Ulashkovitz, Ulaszkowce); pop. 138; 69 km N of Chernovtsy; 48°54'/25°49'; EGRS, GUM4, HSL, LDL, PHP2, SF.

Ulaszkowce, *see* Ulashkovtsy.

Ulatowo, Pol.; pop. 20; 107 km N of Warszawa; 53°11'/20°57'.

Ulazow, Pol.; pop. 180; 56 km N of Przemysl; 50°17'/23°00'; PHP2.

Ulcani, Rom.; pop. 3; 139 km ESE of Cluj; 46°21'/25°17'.

Ulciug, Rom.; pop. 4; 82 km NNW of Cluj; 47°26'/23°11'.

Ulhowek, Pol.; pop. 13; 101 km NE of Przemysl; 50°27'/23°48'.

Ulic, Cz.; pop. 74; 88 km NE of Kosice; 48°58'/22°26'; COH, HSL.

Ulica Starowiejska, Pol. (Starawies); pop. 4; 88 km E of Warszawa; 52°10'/22°18'.

Ulichno, Ukr. (Uliczno); pop. 50; 75 km S of Lvov; 49°14'/23°39'.

Ulicko, (Ulicko Zarebne); pop. 48; Described in the *Black Book* as being in the Lwow region of Poland, this town was not found in BGN gazetteers.

Ulicko Zarebne, *see* Ulicko.

Uliczno, *see* Ulichno.

Ulina Wielka, Pol.; pop. 10; 32 km N of Krakow; 50°19'/19°54'.

Ulitsko Serendkevich, *see* Seredkevychi.

Ulizerka, *see* Olizarka.

Uljanik, Yug.; pop. 23; 82 km ESE of Zagreb; 45°32'/17°01'.

Ulla, Byel.; pop. 1,119; 62 km W of Vitebsk; 55°14'/29°15'; GYLA, HSL, JGFF, LDL, SF.

Ullo, Hung.; pop. 102; 26 km ESE of Budapest; 47°23'/19°21'; LDS, PHH.

Ullstadt, Germ.; pop. 6; 50 km WNW of Nurnberg; 49°37'/10°29'; PHGB.

Ulm, Germ.; pop. 586; 88 km WSW of Stuttgart; 48°34'/08°03'; AMG, EDRD, EJ, GED, GUM3, GUM4, GUM5, HSL, PHGBW.

Ulma, Mold. (Ulmu); pop. 29; 19 km W of Kishinev; 47°01'/28°33'.

Ulmbach, Germ.; pop. 32; 62 km NE of Frankfurt am Main; 50°22'/09°25'; HSL.

Ulmeni, Rom. (Sulelmed); 82 km NNE of Bucuresti; 45°04'/26°39'; HSL, PHR2.

Ulmeni Salj, Rom.; pop. 116; 82 km NNW of Cluj; 47°28'/23°18'.

Ulmet, Germ.; pop. 15; 107 km SW of Frankfurt am Main; 49°35'/07°27'; GED.

Ulmu, *see* Ulma.

Ulrichskirchen, Aus.; pop. 3; 26 km N of Wien; 48°24'/16°29'.

Ulrichstein, Germ.; pop. 50; 69 km NNE of Frankfurt am Main; 50°35'/09°12'; LDS.

Ulsen, *see* Uelsen.

Ulucz, Pol.; pop. 210; 38 km SW of Przemysl; 49°41'/22°17'; EGRS, HSL, PHP3.

Ulvuvek, Ukr. (Ulwowek); pop. 18; 82 km N of Lvov; 50°33'/24°18'.

Ulwowek, *see* Ulvuvek.

Ulyaniki, Ukr. (Ulaniki); 82 km WNW of Rovno; 50°50'/25°07'; GUM3.

Uman, Ukr. (Human); pop. 22,179; 139 km ESE of Vinnitsa; 48°45'/30°13'; AMG, EDRD, GUM4, GUM5, HSL, JGFF, LDL, SF.

Umance, *see* Umantse.

Umantse, Ukr. (Umance); pop. 9; 94 km WSW of Rovno; 50°37'/24°53'.

Umer, Pol.; pop. 8; 107 km ENE of Czestochowa; 50°59'/20°34'.

Umianowice, Pol.; pop. 6; 69 km NNE of Krakow; 50°34'/20°31'.

Umieszcz, Pol.; pop. 3; 88 km WSW of Przemysl; 49°43'/21°33'.

Umka, Yug.; pop. 3; 19 km SSW of Beograd; 44°41'/20°19'.

Umurga, Lat.; pop. 1; 75 km NNE of Riga; 57°31'/24°48'.

Uncsest, *see* Oncesti.

Und, Hung.; pop. 5; 120 km NNW of Nagykanizsa; 47°29'/16°42'.

Unecha, USSR; pop. 1,409; 120 km SW of Bryansk; 52°52'/32°42'; JGFF.

Unesov, Cz.; pop. 2; 94 km WSW of Praha; 49°53'/13°09'.

Unewel, Pol.; pop. 11; 50 km ESE of Lodz; 51°27'/20°05'.

Ungarisch Brod, *see* Uhersky Brod.

Ungarisch Hradisch, *see* Uherske Hradiste.

Ungarisch Ostrau, *see* Uhersky Ostroh.

Ungarish Ostra, *see* Uhersky Ostroh.

Ungarsich Hradisch, *see* Uherske Hradiste.

Ungedanken, Germ.; 120 km N of Frankfurt am Main; 51°07'/09°13'; LDS.

Ungeni, *see* Ungeny.

Ungen Tyrg, *see* Ungeny.

Ungeny, Mold. (Ungen Tyrg, Ungeni, Ungheni, Ungheni Mures, Ungheni Targ); pop. 1,390; 82 km WNW of Kishinev; 47°12'/27°48'; GUM4, HSL, HSL2, LDL, SF.

Ungheni, *see* Ungeny.

Ungheni Mures, *see* Ungeny.

Ungheni Targ, *see* Ungeny.

Ungstein, Germ.; 82 km SSW of Frankfurt am Main; 49°29'/08°11'; JGFF.

Unguras, Rom. (Balvanyosvaralja, Unguras Salaj); pop. 34; 50 km NNE of Cluj; 47°07'/24°03'.

Unguras Salaj, *see* Unguras.

Ungureni, HSL. A number of towns share this name. It was not possible to determine from available information which one is being referenced.

Ungurmuiza, *see* Medni.

Ungvar, *see* Uzhgorod.

Ungwar, *see* Uzhgorod.

Unhost, Cz.; pop. 24; 26 km WSW of Praha; 50°05'/14°09'.

Uniatycze, *see* Unyatychi.

Uniayev, *see* Uniejow.

Unicov, Cz. (Maehrisch Neustadt); pop. 39; 75 km NNE of Brno; 49°46'/17°08'.

Unieck, Pol.; pop. 12; 82 km NW of Warszawa; 52°52'/20°12'.

Uniejow, Pol. (Uniayev); pop. 1,100; 50 km WNW of Lodz; 51°58'/18°48'; AMG, CAHJP, COH, GA, HSL, HSL2, JGFF, PHP1, SF.

Unierzyz, Pol.; pop. 4; 82 km NW of Warszawa; 52°51'/20°18'.

Unin, *see* Uhnin.

Uniow, *see* Stavishchany.

Uniszowa, Pol.; pop. 13; 88 km E of Krakow; 49°53'/21°07'.

Uniszowice, Pol.; pop. 8; 13 km WSW of Lublin; 51°15'/22°27'.

Univ, *see* Ugnev.

Uniyev, *see* Stavishchany.

Unkel, Germ.; 45 km SE of Koln; 50°36'/07°13'; GUM5.

Unna, Germ.; pop. 168; 82 km NNE of Koln; 51°32'/07°41'; GED.

Unov, *see* Ugnev.

Unruhstadt, *see* Kargowa.

Unrukstadt, *see* Kargowa.

Unsdorf, LDL. This pre-World War I community was not found in BGN gazetteers.

Unsleben, Germ.; pop. 114; 114 km ENE of Frankfurt am Main; 50°23'/10°16'; GUM5, HSL, PHGB.

Unteni, *see* Unteny.

Unteny, Rom. (Unteni); pop. 5; 32 km N of Iasi; 47°25'/27°35'.

Unteralba, Germ.; pop. 6; 126 km NE of Frankfurt am Main; 50°43'/10°07'.

Unteraltertheim, Germ.; pop. 38; 88 km ESE of Frankfurt am Main; 49°44'/09°44'; GUM5, PHGB.

Unter Apsa, *see* Nizhna Apsha.

Unterbalbach, Germ.; 94 km W of Nurnberg; 49°32'/09°45'; EJ, PHGBW.

Unterberg, Aus.; pop. 225; 32 km SE of Salzburg; 47°34'/13°19'.

Unterbissingen, Germ.; 94 km WNW of Munchen; 48°42'/10°37'; PHGB.

Unter Bistra, *see* Nizhnyaya Bystraya.

Unterdeufstetten, Germ.; 75 km SW of Nurnberg; 49°03'/10°14'; PHGBW.

Unterdorf, Germ.; 82 km SW of Stuttgart; 48°14'/08°22'; PHGBW.

Untereisenheim, Germ.; pop. 10; 82 km WNW of Nurnberg; 49°53'/10°09'; PHGB.

Untererthal, Germ.; pop. 19; 82 km ENE of Frankfurt am Main; 50°09'/09°53'; GUM5, PHGB.

Unterfarrnbach, Germ.; 13 km WNW of Nurnberg; 49°30'/10°57'; PHGB.

Unterfrauenhaid, Aus.; pop. 3; 75 km SSE of Wien; 47°34'/16°30'.

Untergrombach, Germ.; pop. 56; 56 km WNW of Stuttgart; 49°05'/08°33'; GUM5, JGFF, LDS, PHGBW.

Unterhaching, Germ.; pop. 5; 19 km SSE of Munchen; 48°03'/11°38'.

Unterine, *see* Rona de Jos.

Unterlaimbach, Germ.; 50 km WNW of Nurnberg; 49°38'/10°29'; PHGB.

Unterlanzendorf, Aus.; pop. 2; 19 km SE of Wien; 48°06'/16°27'.

Unterleichtersbach, Germ.; 82 km ENE of Frankfurt am Main; 50°16'/09°49'; PHGB.

Unterleinach, Germ.; 82 km ESE of Frankfurt am Main; 49°52'/09°49'; PHGB.

Unterlimpurg, Germ.; 56 km NE of Stuttgart; 49°07'/09°45'; PHGBW.

Untermaubach, Germ.; 45 km SW of Koln; 50°44'/06°27'; GED.

Untermaxfeld, Germ.; pop. 1; 69 km NNW of Munchen; 48°42'/11°13'.

Untermerzbach, Germ.; pop. 7; 82 km NNW of Nurnberg; 50°08'/10°51'; PHGB.

Unternzenn, Germ.; 45 km WSW of Nurnberg; 49°27'/10°29'; PHGB.

Unterolberndorf, Aus.; pop. 2; 32 km N of Wien; 48°26'/16°29'.

Unterpiesting, *see* Markt Piesting.

Unterpleichfeld, Germ.; 88 km WNW of Nurnberg; 49°52'/10°04'; PHGB.

Unterpullendorf, Aus.; pop. 2; 88 km SSE of Wien; 47°28'/16°32'.

Unterrabnitz, Aus.; pop. 5; 82 km NE of Graz; 47°27'/16°22'.

Unterretzbach, Aus.; pop. 2; 69 km NNW of Wien; 48°46'/16°00'.

Unterriedenberg, Germ.; pop. 34; 88 km ENE of Frankfurt am Main; 50°19'/09°52'; GUM3, GUM5, PHGB.

Unterriexingen, Germ.; 26 km NW of Stuttgart; 48°56'/09°04'; GUM3, GUM4, PHGBW.

Unter Rina, *see* Rona de Jos.

Unterschaftlarn, Germ. (Schaftlarn); pop. 3; 26 km SSW of Munchen; 47°59'/11°28'.

Unterschupf, Germ.; 94 km ESE of Frankfurt am Main; 49°31'/09°41'; JGFF, LDS.

Unterschwandorf, Germ. BGN lists two possible localities with this name located at 47°57'/09°00' and 48°32'/08°41'. PHGBW.

Untersiebenbrunn, Aus.; pop. 9; 32 km ENE of Wien; 48°15'/16°44'.

Unter Stanestie, *see* Staneshti de Zhos.

Unterwaldbehrungen, Germ.; 114 km NE of Frankfurt am Main; 50°25'/10°11'; PHGB.

Unterwalden; According to the *Black Book*, this town was located in the Polish interwar province of Tarnopol. It could not be located in interwar or contemporary gazetteers.

Unterwalden (Tarnopol area), Pol.; pop. 45; GUM3. Described in the *Black Book* as being in the Tarnopol region of Poland, this town was not found in BGN gazetteers.

Unter Wisho, *see* Viseu de Jos.

Unterwurmbach, Germ.; 50 km SSW of Nurnberg; 49°07'/10°44'; PHGB.

Uny, Hung.; pop. 2; 32 km WNW of Budapest; 47°38'/18°44'; LDS.

Unyatyche, *see* Unyatychi.

Unyatychi, Ukr. (Uniatycze, Unyatyche); pop. 33; 75 km SSW of Lvov; 49°22'/23°25'.

Upesgriva, Lat.; pop. 3; 82 km WNW of Riga; 57°23'/23°01'.

Upice, Cz.; pop. 83; 120 km NE of Praha; 50°31'/16°01'.

Upina, *see* Upyna.

Upor, Cz.; 38 km ESE of Kosice; 48°35'/21°40'; HSL.

Uppony, Hung.; 32 km WNW of Miskolc; 48°13'/20°26'; HSL.

Upyna, Lith. (Upina, Upynas); 75 km SW of Siauliai; 55°27'/22°27'; HSL, JGFF, LDL, SF, YL.

Upynas, *see* Upyna.

Ura, Hung.; pop. 48; 139 km E of Miskolc; 47°49'/22°37'; HSL.

Uraiujfalu, Hung.; pop. 32; 107 km N of Nagykanizsa; 47°22'/16°59'.

Uraj, Hung.; pop. 5; 45 km WNW of Miskolc; 48°15'/20°16'.

Urbach, Germ.; pop. 26; 13 km ESE of Koln; 50°53'/07°05'.

Urbau, *see* Vrbovec.

Urberach, Germ.; pop. 4; 19 km SE of Frankfurt am Main; 49°58'/08°48'; JGFF.

Urdenovac, Yug. (Durdenovac); pop. 47; 157 km E of Zagreb; 45°33'/18°03'.

Urdevac, Yug. (Djurdjevac, Durdevac); pop. 29; 88 km NE of Zagreb; 46°02'/17°04'.

Urechye, Byel. (Uretcha); pop. 148; 107 km SSE of Minsk; 52°57'/27°54'; HSL, SF, YB.

Uretcha, *see* Urechye.

Uri, Hung.; 38 km E of Budapest; 47°25'/19°32'; LDS.

Urisor, Rom. (Alor); pop. 146; 50 km NNE of Cluj; 47°10'/23°53'; PHR2.

Uritsk, USSR; pop. 43; This town was not found in BGN gazetteers under the given spelling.

Uriu, Rom.; pop. 42; 62 km NNE of Cluj; 47°12'/24°03'.

Urlich, Cz.; 120 km N of Brno; 50°13'/16°56'; HSL.

Urman, Ukr.; pop. 23; 75 km ESE of Lvov; 49°34'/24°57'.

Urmenis, Rom. (Bukkormenyes, Urmenisu); pop. 25; 56 km E of Cluj; 46°46'/24°22'.

Urmenisu, *see* Urmenis.

Urmeny, *see* Mojmirovce.

Urmezo, *see* Poienile de Sub Munte.

Urmini, Ukr. EDRD. This town was not found in BGN

Ustilug, Ukraine: Gathering at the Lug River for Tashlekh, a Rosh Hashanah ritual to wash away one's sins.

gazetteers under the given spelling.

Urmitz, Germ.; 69 km SE of Koln; 50°25'/07°31'; GED.

Urosevac, Yug.; pop. 3; 50 km NW of Skopje; 42°22'/21°10'.

Uroz, *see* Urozh.

Urozh, Ukr. (Uroz); pop. 42; 82 km SW of Lvov; 49°22'/23°15'.

Urshe, *see* Orsha.

Urspringen, Germ.; pop. 86; 75 km ESE of Frankfurt am Main; 49°54'/09°41'; GUM5, HSL, JGFF, PHGB.

Ursus, GUM5. This town was not found in BGN gazetteers under the given spelling.

Urszulin, Pol.; pop. 26; 50 km NE of Lublin; 51°24'/23°12'.

Urych, Ukr. (Urycz); pop. 151; 88 km SSW of Lvov; 49°11'/23°24'; PHP2.

Urycz, *see* Urych.

Urzedow, Pol. (Orzendov, Urzendov, Urzendow, Uzhendov); pop. 284; 38 km SW of Lublin; 50°59'/22°09'; AMG, CAHJP, COH, FRG, GUM5, JGFF, POCEM, SF.

Urzejowice, Pol.; pop. 31; 38 km NW of Przemysl; 50°01'/22°28'.

Urzendov, *see* Urzedow.

Urzendow, *see* Urzedow.

Urzicem, Rom. PHR1. This town was not found in BGN gazetteers under the given spelling.

Urziceni, Rom. (Csanalos); pop. 135; 139 km NW of Cluj; 47°44'/22°24'.

Uschiki Dolne, *see* Ustrzyki Dolne.

Uschomir, *see* Ushomir.

Uschpol, *see* Uzpaliai.

Uschurod, *see* Uzhgorod.

Uscie Biskupie, *see* Ustye.

Uscieczko, *see* Ustechko.

Uscie Ruskie, Pol.; pop. 15; 107 km ESE of Krakow; 49°31'/21°08'.

Uscie Solne, Pol. (Ishtcha Solna); pop. 28; 45 km ENE of Krakow; 50°07'/20°32'; HSL, HSL2, JGFF, SF.

Uscie Zielone, *see* Ustse Zelene.

Uscilug, *see* Ustilug.

Uscz, *see* Ujscie.

Usenborn, Germ.; 45 km NE of Frankfurt am Main; 50°22'/09°07'; JGFF, LDS.

Ushach, *see* Ushachi.

Ushachi, Byel. (Ushach, Ushatchi, Ushatz, Ushots); pop. 807; 101 km WSW of Vitebsk; 55°11'/28°37'; GUM4, HSL, JGFF, LDL, SF.

Ushatchi, *see* Ushachi.

Ushatz, *see* Ushachi.

Ushiokov, *see* Osjakow.

Ushitse Podolye, *see* Staraya Ushitsa.

Ushitza, *see* Staraya Ushitsa.

Ushkovitse, Ukr. (Uszkowice); pop. 54; 50 km ESE of Lvov; 49°38'/24°33'.

Ushnya, Ukr. (Usznia); pop. 120; 62 km ENE of Lvov; 49°53'/24°55'; PHP2.

Ushomir, Ukr. (Uschomir); 150 km WNW of Kiyev; 50°51'/28°28'; HSL, LDL, SF.

Ushots, *see* Ushachi.

Ushvotsk, *see* Otwock.

Usichi, Ukr. (Usicki, Usicze); pop. 24; 88 km W of Rovno; 50°46'/25°05'; GUM3.

Usicki, *see* Usichi.

Usicze, *see* Usichi.

Usingen, Germ.; pop. 74; 32 km NW of Frankfurt am Main; 50°20'/08°32'.

Uskub, *see* Skopje.

Uskup, *see* Skopje.

Uslar, Germ.; pop. 24; 82 km S of Hannover; 51°40'/09°39'.

Usma, Lat. (Usmas); pop. 4; 120 km W of Riga; 57°13'/22°09'.

Usmas, *see* Usma.

Usnik, Pol.; pop. 21; 82 km WSW of Bialystok; 53°05'/21°55'.

Usov, Cz. (Aussee); 75 km N of Brno; 49°48'/17°01'; EJ, HSL, HSL2.

Usovice, Cz.; pop. 2; 126 km WSW of Praha; 49°57'/12°43'.

Ustchorna, Ukr. (Kenigsfeld, Kiraly Mezo, Ustcorna); 146 km W of Chernovtsy; 48°19'/23°56'; GUM3, HSL, SM.

Ustcorna, *see* Ustchorna.

Ustechko, Ukr. (Uscieczko); pop. 244; 56 km NW of Chernovtsy; 48°46'/25°36'; HSL, HSL2, JGFF, PHP2.

Ustek, Cz. (Auscha); pop. 75; 62 km NNW of Praha; 50°35'/14°21'; EJ.

Ustenskoye Pervoye, Ukr. (Derman); pop. 32; 32 km S of Rovno; 50°22'/26°14'; SF.

Usti, AMG. A number of towns share this name. It was not possible to determine from available information which one is being referenced.

Ustia, *see* Ustye.

Ustianowa, Pol. (Ustjanowa); pop. 96; 45 km SSW of Przemysl; 49°26'/22°32'; HSL, PHP2.

Ustila, *see* Ustilug.

Ustilug, Ukr. (Austile, Ostila, Uscilug, Ustila); pop. 2,723; 120 km N of Lvov; 50°52'/24°09'; AMG, COH, EDRD, GYLA, HSL, HSL2, LDL, SF, YB.

Usti nad Labem, Cz. (Aussig); pop. 976; 69 km NW of Praha; 50°40'/14°02'; EJ, GUM4, GUM5, GUM6, HSL, JGFF.

Usti nad Orlici, Cz.; pop. 37; 94 km NNW of Brno; 49°59'/16°24'.

Ustjanowa, *see* Ustianowa.

Ustrasin, Cz.; pop. 5; 94 km SE of Praha; 49°23'/15°10'.

Ustrik, *see* Ustrzyki Dolne.

Ustrobna, Pol.; pop. 15; 75 km WSW of Przemysl; 49°45'/21°42'.

Ustron, Pol.; pop. 125; 94 km SW of Krakow; 49°43'/18°48'; PHP3.

Ustrzyk, Pol.; pop. 4; 69 km SSE of Krakow; 49°31'/20°12'.

Ustrzyki Dolne, Pol. (Astrik, Estrik, Istrik, Istryk, Uschiki Dolne, Ustrik); pop. 1,768; 45 km S of Przemysl; 49°26'/22°35'; AMG, COH, EGRS, GUM4, GUM5, HSL, HSL2, JGFF, LDL, LYV, PHP2, PHP3, POCEM, SF, YB.

Ustrzyki Gorne, Pol.; pop. 56; 82 km S of Przemysl; 49°06'/22°39'.

Ustse Zelene, Ukr. (Ishtcha Zilona, Oztza, Uscie Zielone); pop. 550; 107 km NW of Chernovtsy; 49°02'/24°58'; COH, EGRS, GUM3, GYLA, HSL, JGFF, LDL, PHP2, SF.

Ustye, Mold. (Uscie Biskupie, Ustia, Ustzi Beskopia); pop. 37; EGRS, JGFF, LDL, SF. A number of towns share this name. It was not possible to determine from available information which one is being referenced.

Ustye (Bessarabia), Mold.; 120 km WNW of Kishinev; 47°40'/27°36'; PHR1.

Ustzi Beskopia, *see* Ustye.

Uszczyn, Pol.; pop. 8; 45 km SE of Lodz; 51°24'/19°47'; PHP1.

Uszew, Pol.; pop. 48; 56 km ESE of Krakow; 49°55'/20°37'.

Uszka, Hung.; pop. 12; 157 km E of Miskolc; 48°04'/22°52'.

Uszkowice, *see* Ushkovitse.

Usznia, *see* Ushnya.

Uszod, Hung.; pop. 29; 101 km WNW of Szeged; 46°34'/18°55'; HSL.

Utena, Lith. (Uciana, Uedainiai, Utian, Utien, Utiyan, Utsiany, Utsjany, Utsyany, Utyan, Utyana); pop. 2,485; 94 km N of Vilnius; 55°30'/25°36'; COH, EDRD, EJ, GUM3, GUM4, GUM5, GUM6, HSL, HSL2, JGFF, LDL, LYV, SF, YB, YL.

Utery, Cz.; pop. 3; 107 km WSW of Praha; 49°56'/13°00'.

Utian, *see* Utena.

Utien, *see* Utena.

Utiyan, *see* Utena.

Utomir, USSR; pop. 1,749; This town was not found in BGN gazetteers under the given spelling.

Utoropy, Ukr.; pop. 16; 69 km W of Chernovtsy; 48°23'/24°59'.

Utphe, Germ.; pop. 5; 45 km N of Frankfurt am Main; 50°26'/08°53'.

Utsiany, *see* Utena.

Utsishkuv, Ukr. (Uciszow); pop. 24; 50 km ENE of Lvov; 49°55'/24°40'.

Utsjany, *see* Utena.

Utsyany, *see* Utena.

Uttenreuth, Germ.; 19 km N of Nurnberg; 49°36'/11°05'; PHGB.

Uttrichshausen, Germ.; 82 km NE of Frankfurt am Main; 50°25'/09°44'; LDS.

Utyan, *see* Utena.

Utyana, *see* Utena.

Utzwingen, Germ.; 75 km SSW of Nurnberg; 48°57'/10°30'; PHGB.

Uvarovichi, Byel. (Uvarovitchi); 26 km NW of Gomel; 52°36'/30°44'; GUM4, SF.

Uvarovitchi, *see* Uvarovichi.

Uwin, *possibly* Uzin.

Uyazd, *see* Ujazd.

Uzava, Lat. (Wizewo); pop. 7; 163 km W of Riga; 57°14'/21°27'.

Uzava (near Artemovsk), Ukr.; 202 km SE of Kharkov; 48°32'/38°00'; JGFF, SF. This town was located on a pre-World War I map, but does not appear in contemporary gazetteers.

Uzbloc, *see* Uzbolot.

Uzbolot, Byel. (Uzbloc); pop. 7; 75 km WNW of Minsk; 54°11'/26°32'.

Uzda, Byel.; pop. 1,564; 50 km SSW of Minsk; 53°27'/27°13'; COH, GUM4, GUM5, GUM6, HSL, JGFF, SF.

Uzdiszentpeter, *see* Sinpetru de Cimpie.

Uzhendov, *see* Urzedow.

Uzhgorod, Ukr. (Ungvar, Ungwar, Uschurod, Uzhhorod, Uzhorod); pop. 7,357; 189 km SSW of Lvov; 48°37'/22°18'; AMG, COH, EJ, GUM3, GUM4, GUM5, GUM6, HSL, HSL2, ISH3, JGFF, LDL, LYV, YB.

Uzhhorod, *see* Uzhgorod.

Uzhorod, *see* Uzhgorod.

Uzice, *see* Titovo Uzice.

Uzin, Ukr. (Uwin?); pop. 59; 114 km WNW of Chernovtsy; 48°59'/24°49'.

Uziran, *see* Ozeryany (Wolyn).

Uzirna, *see* Ozernyany.

Uzlany, *see* Uzlyany.

Uzlian, *see* Uzlyany.

Uzlion, *see* Uzlyany.

Uzlovoye, Ukr. (Batyu, Choliv, Cholojow, Holojow); pop. 793; 56 km NNE of Lvov; 50°14'/24°33'; AMG, EGRS, EJ, GUM3, HSL, LDL, PHP2, SF, YB.

Uzlyany, Byel. (Uzlany, Uzlian, Uzlion); 32 km SSE of Minsk; 53°37'/27°43'; JGFF, LDL, SF, WS.

Uznoga, Byel. (Uznoha); pop. 24; 101 km NNE of Pinsk; 52°54'/26°50'.

Uznoha, *see* Uznoga.

Uzon, *see* Ozun.

Uzovske Peklany, Cz. (Peklany); 45 km NNW of Kosice; 49°05'/21°02'; HSL.

Uzpaliai, Lith. (Oshpol, Uschpol, Uzpalis); pop. 551; 114 km N of Vilnius; 55°39'/25°35'; HSL, JGFF, YL.

Uzpalis, *see* Uzpaliai.

Uzvent, *see* Uzventis.

Uzventis, Lith. (Uzvent); pop. 173; 45 km SW of Siauliai; 55°47'/22°39'; AMG, GUM3, GUM5, HSL, JGFF, YL.

Uzyerni, *see* Ozernyany.

Vabalnik, *see* Vabalninkas.

Vabalninkas, Lith. (Vabalnik, Vobolnik, Wobolniki); pop. 441; 94 km ENE of Siauliai; 55°58'/24°45'; COH, GUM4, HSL, JGFF, LDL, SF, YL.

Vac, Hung. (Waitzen); pop. 1,934; 38 km N of Budapest; 47°47'/19°08'; AMG, EJ, GUM4, GUM5, GUM6, HSL,

HSL2, LDL, LDS, LJEE, PHH.

Vacaresti, Rom.; 69 km NW of Bucuresti; 44°51'/25°29'; GUM4.

Vacbottyan, Hung.; pop. 1; 26 km NNE of Budapest; 47°42'/19°18'.

Vacduka, Hung.; pop. 7; 32 km N of Budapest; 47°45'/19°13'.

Vach, Germ.; 13 km NW of Nurnberg; 49°32'/10°58'; PHGB.

Vacha, Germ.; pop. 90; 126 km NE of Frankfurt am Main; 50°50'/10°01'; HSL, LDS.

Vachartyan, Hung.; pop. 6; 32 km NNE of Budapest; 47°44'/19°16'.

Vachnovka, *see* Vakhnovka.

Vackisujfalu, Hung.; pop. 3; 32 km NNE of Budapest; 47°42'/19°21'.

Vacratot, Hung.; pop. 11; 32 km NNE of Budapest; 47°43'/19°14'.

Vacszentlaszlo, Hung.; pop. 6; 32 km ENE of Budapest; 47°35'/19°32'.

Vaculesti, Rom.; pop. 22; 120 km WNW of Iasi; 47°53'/26°25'.

Vadasz, Rom.; 146 km WSW of Cluj; 46°38'/21°40'; HSL. This town was located on a pre-World War I map, but does not appear in contemporary gazetteers.

Vad Bihor, *see* Vadu Crisului.

Vad Cluj, Rom. (Rev); 56 km N of Cluj; 47°12'/23°45'; HSL.

Vaden, *see* Vodyany.

Vadeni Soroca, *see* Vodyany.

Vadkert, Hung.; 101 km SSW of Budapest; 46°41'/18°32'; HSL, HSL2.

Vad Maramures, Rom. (Farkasrev); pop. 156; 126 km N of Cluj; 47°53'/23°57'; AMG, GUM3, HSL, PHR2, SM.

Vadna, Hung.; pop. 27; 26 km NW of Miskolc; 48°16'/20°34'; HSL.

Vadokliai, Lith.; pop. 79; 75 km NNE of Kaunas; 55°30'/24°30'.

Vadovits, *see* Wadowice.

Vadovitse, *see* Wadowice.

Vadovitz, *see* Wadowice.

Vad Rashkov, Mold. (Rashkev, Vadu Rascu, Vadu Rashky, Wad Raschkow); pop. 1,970; 107 km N of Kishinev; 47°56'/28°49'; EJ, PHR2, SF.

Vadu Crisului, Rom. (Vad Bihor); pop. 63; 82 km WNW of Cluj; 46°59'/22°31'.

Vadul Nistrului, *see* Brodok.

Vadu Mures, Rom.; pop. 50; 94 km E of Cluj; 46°36'/24°47'.

Vadu Rascu, *see* Vad Rashkov.

Vadu Rashky, *see* Vad Rashkov.

Vag, Hung.; pop. 5; 120 km N of Nagykanizsa; 47°27'/17°13'.

Vagas, Rom.; 150 km NNW of Cluj; 48°06'/23°12'; HSL.

Vagsellye, LDL. This pre-World War I community was not found in BGN gazetteers.

Vagszered, LDL. This pre-World War I community was not found in BGN gazetteers.

Vag Ujhely, *see* Nove Mesto nad Vahom.

Vag Vecse, *see* Veca.

Vaida Camaras, Rom. (Vajdakamaras); pop. 4; 32 km ENE of Cluj; 46°50'/23°57'; HSL.

Vaigeva, *see* Vaiguva.

Vaigova, *see* Vaiguva.

Vaiguva, Lith. (Vaigeva, Vaigova); pop. 118; 45 km SW of Siauliai; 55°42'/22°45'; GUM3, GUM5, HSL, LDL, SF, YL.

Vaihingen, *see* Vaihingen an der Enz.

Vaihingen an der Enz, Germ. (Vaihingen); 26 km NW of Stuttgart; 48°56'/08°58'; GUM3, GUM4, PHGBW.

Vaike Maarja, Est.; 88 km NNW of Tartu; 59°08'/26°15'; PHLE.

Vainode, Lat. (Vainoden, Vainodes); pop. 120; 146 km SW of Riga; 56°26'/21°52'; PHLE.

Vainoden, *see* Vainode.

Vainodes, *see* Vainode.

Vainutas, Lith. (Veinuta, Vonota, Vynota); pop. 348; 114 km SW of Siauliai; 55°22'/21°50'; GUM4, HSL, LDL, SF, YL.

Vaisal, *see* Vasilyevka (Bessarabia).

Vaja, Hung.; pop. 220; 107 km E of Miskolc; 48°00'/22°10'; COH, HSL, PHH.

Vajan, *see* Vojany.

Vajany, *see* Vojany.

Vajar, HSL. This pre-World War I community was not found in BGN gazetteers.

Vajatjulkan, *see* Vulcan.

Vajdacska, Hung.; pop. 62; 69 km NE of Miskolc; 48°19'/21°40'; AMG, PHH.

Vajdahunyad, HSL. This pre-World War I community was not found in BGN gazetteers.

Vajdakamaras, *see* Vaida Camaras.

Vajdaszeg, Rom.; 50 km SE of Cluj; 46°25'/23°57'; HSL. This town was located on a pre-World War I map, but does not appear in contemporary gazetteers.

Vajdaszentivany, HSL. This pre-World War I community was not found in BGN gazetteers.

Vajnag, *see* Vonigovo.

Vajszlo, Hung.; pop. 44; 101 km ESE of Nagykanizsa; 45°51'/17°59'; GUM5.

Vajta, Hung.; pop. 4; 94 km S of Budapest; 46°43'/18°40'.

Vakhnovka, Ukr. (Vachnovka, Vichnifka, Wachnowka); pop. 2,101; 32 km NE of Vinnitsa; 49°19'/28°51'; EDRD, JGFF, LDL, SF.

Val, Hung.; pop. 22; 38 km SW of Budapest; 47°22'/18°41'.

Valaksincz, *see* Aleksince.

Valana, GUM6. This town was not found in BGN gazetteers under the given spelling.

Valasske Klobouky, Cz. (Valesske Klobouky); pop. 49; 101 km E of Brno; 49°09'/18°00'.

Valasske Mezirici, Cz. (Mezirici Valesske, Wallachisch Meseritsch); pop. 142; 101 km NE of Brno; 49°28'/17°58'.

Valava, *see* Walawa.

Valcau de Jos, Rom. (Alsovalko, Valcaul de Jos); pop. 96; 75 km WNW of Cluj; 47°07'/22°44'; GUM5, PHR2.

Valcaul de Jos, *see* Valcau de Jos.

Valcaul Ungureasca, Rom. (Magyarvalko); 45 km W of Cluj; 46°47'/23°02'; HSL. This town was located on a pre-World War I map, but does not appear in contemporary gazetteers.

Valcov, *see* Vilkovo.

Valdai, Lat.; 38 km W of Riga; 57°00'/23°30'; PHLE.

Valdemarpils, Lat. (Sasmacken, Sasmaken, Sassmacken, Shasmaken); pop. 161; 101 km WNW of Riga; 57°22'/22°35'; JGFF, LDL, PHLE, SF.

Valea, *see* Valea Mica.

Valea Draganului, Rom.; pop. 3; 56 km WNW of Cluj; 46°55'/22°53'.

Valea Grosilor, Rom.; pop. 2; 56 km N of Cluj; 47°14'/23°45'.

Valea Hranei, Rom.; pop. 5; 56 km N of Cluj; 47°13'/23°33'.

Valea Loznei, Rom.; pop. 10; 62 km NNW of Cluj; 47°16'/23°30'.

Valea Lui Mihai, Rom. (Ermihalydalva); pop. 1,535; 139 km WNW of Cluj; 47°31'/22°09'; AMG, JGFF, PHR2.

Valea Lui Vlad, *see* Valya Rusuluy.

Valea Mica, Rom. (Kis Patak, Kispast, Valea); pop. 4,000; 157 km N of Bucuresti; 45°47'/25°59'.

Valea Neagra de Cris, Rom.; pop. 11; 75 km W of Cluj; 46°57'/22°38'.

Valea Perjei Noua, *see* Valya Perzhiy Noue.

Valea Porcului, Rom. (Disznopataka, Sanapotek); 126 km N of Cluj; 47°53'/23°59'; SM.

Valea Rea, Rom. (Diospatak); 101 km SSW of Iasi; 46°23'/26°56'; GUM4, PHR1.

Valea Rusului, *see* Valya Rusuluy.

Valea Scurta, Rom.; pop. 4; 163 km SSW of Iasi; 46°06'/26°12'.

Valea Seaca, Rom.; pop. 66; 150 km NNW of Cluj; 48°05'/23°10'.

Valea Ternei, Rom. (Harmaspatak); HSL. This pre-World War I community was not found in BGN gazetteers.

Valea Ungurasului, Rom.; pop. 10; 56 km NE of Cluj;

47°05'/24°07'.

Valea Ungurului, Rom. (Magyarpatak); HSL. A number of towns share this name. It was not possible to determine from available information which one is being referenced.

Valea Vinului, Rom.; pop. 57; 114 km NNW of Cluj; 47°43'/23°11'.

Valea Viseului, Rom. (Viso Volgy, Visovolgy); pop. 83; 133 km N of Cluj; 47°55'/24°10'; HSL, SM.

Valegotsulovo, *see* Dolinskoye.

Valehotzulovo, *see* Dolinskoye.

Valendorf, Ukr. (Dombo?); 150 km WSW of Chernovtsy; 48°11'/23°53'; HSL. This town was located on a pre-World War I map, but does not appear in contemporary gazetteers.

Valeni, Rom. (Danpataka, Mikolapatak, Valeny); 120 km N of Cluj; 47°47'/24°01'; SM.

Valeni Maramures, Rom.; pop. 62; Described in the *Black Book* as being in the Transylvania region of Romania, this town was not found in BGN gazetteers.

Valentova, Cz. (Balintfalva); 157 km NE of Bratislava; 48°58'/18°53'; HSL.

Valeny, *see* Valeni.

Valesske Klobouky, *see* Valasske Klobouky.

Valeva, Rom.; pop. 75; This town was not found in BGN gazetteers under the given spelling.

Valevka, Byel. (Walowka); pop. 10; 120 km SW of Minsk; 53°28'/25°54'.

Valga, Est. (Valka); pop. 262; 82 km SSW of Tartu; 57°47'/26°02'; PHLE. *See also* Valka.

Valiatin, *see* Velyatin.

Valjevo, Yug.; pop. 25; 82 km SSW of Beograd; 44°16'/19°53'.

Valk, *see* Valka.

Valka, Lat. (Valga, Valk, Walk); pop. 65; 146 km NE of Riga; 57°46'/26°00'; COH, HSL, JGFF, PHLE. *See also* Valga.

Valkaja, Ukr.; 182 km SSW of Lvov; 48°31'/22°28'; HSL. This town was located on a pre-World War I map, but does not appear in contemporary gazetteers.

Valkemir, *see* Ukmerge.

Valki, Ukr. (Walki); pop. 29; 50 km SW of Kharkov; 49°50'/35°37'; GUM4.

Valkininkas, Lith. (Olkenik, Olkeniki, Olkieniki, Olkienniki, Olkinik, Olknik, Volknik); 50 km SSW of Vilnius; 54°21'/24°50'; COH, EDRD, GUM4, HSL, JGFF, LDL, SF, WS, YB.

Valko, Hung.; pop. 21; 32 km ENE of Budapest; 47°34'/19°31'; HSL.

Vallaj, Hung.; pop. 21; 126 km ESE of Miskolc; 47°46'/22°23'.

Vallendar, Germ.; pop. 125; 82 km WNW of Frankfurt am Main; 50°24'/07°38'; GED.

Valley, Germ.; 32 km SE of Munchen; 47°54'/11°47'; PHGB.

Valmiera, Lat. (Velma, Velmar, Vol Mar, Wolmar); pop. 127; 101 km NE of Riga; 57°33'/25°24'; COH, PHLE, SF.

Valpovo, Yug.; pop. 30; 189 km WNW of Beograd; 45°39'/18°25'; PHY.

Valtaiki, Lat.; pop. 15; 146 km WSW of Riga; 56°42'/21°48'.

Valtcha, *see* Volchi.

Valuyki, USSR; pop. 84; 170 km S of Voronezh; 50°14'/38°08'.

Valy, Cz.; 82 km E of Praha; 50°02'/15°37'; HSL.

Valya Perzhiy Noue, Mold. (Valea Perjei Noua); pop. 10; 114 km S of Kishinev; 46°02'/28°56'.

Valya Rusuluy, Mold. (Valea Lui Vlad, Valea Rusului); pop. 1,281; 107 km WNW of Kishinev; 47°28'/27°35'.

Vama, Rom. (Vamfalu); 126 km N of Cluj; 47°50'/23°24'; HSL, JGFF.

Vama (Bucovina), Rom.; pop. 392; 150 km WNW of Iasi; 47°34'/25°41'.

Vama (Satu Mare), Rom.; pop. 213; 126 km N of Cluj; 47°50'/23°24'; PHR2.

Vama Turului, GUM4. This town was not found in BGN gazetteers under the given spelling.

Vamberk, Cz.; pop. 5; 107 km NNW of Brno; 50°07'/16°18'.

Vames Odriheiu, Rom. (Vamosudvarhely); 82 km ESE of Cluj; 46°24'/24°34'; HSL.

Vamfalu, *see* Vama.

Vamos, *see* Alsovamos.

Vamosatya, Hung.; pop. 35; 120 km ENE of Miskolc; 48°12'/22°25'.

Vamosgyork, Hung.; pop. 25; 62 km NE of Budapest; 47°41'/19°56'; HSL.

Vamoslaz, *see* Chislaz.

Vamosmikola, Hung.; pop. 133; 56 km NNW of Budapest; 47°59'/18°47'; COH, GUM4, HSL, PHH.

Vamosoroszi, Hung.; pop. 7; 146 km E of Miskolc; 47°59'/22°41'.

Vamospercs, Hung.; pop. 288; 107 km ESE of Miskolc; 47°32'/21°54'; HSL, LDS, PHH, YB.

Vamosudvarhely, *see* Vames Odriheiu.

Vamosujfalu, Hung.; pop. 25; 50 km NE of Miskolc; 48°16'/21°28'; GUM4.

Vanagishki, Byel. (Wanagiszki); pop. 6; 214 km NNW of Minsk; 55°47'/26°56'.

Vanatori, *see* Vyantory.

Vanchikauts Mar, *see* Vanchikovtsy.

Vanchikovtsy, Ukr. (Vanchikauts Mar, Vancicautii Mici); pop. 20; 45 km E of Chernovtsy; 48°13'/26°27'.

Vancicautii Mici, *see* Vanchikovtsy.

Vancsfalva, *see* Oncesti.

Vancsod, Hung.; pop. 51; 120 km SE of Miskolc; 47°12'/21°39'; LDS.

Vandsburg, *see* Wiecbork.

Vandzene, Lat.; pop. 1; 88 km WNW of Riga; 57°20'/22°48'.

Vandziogala, Lith. (Vendziogala); pop. 335; 32 km N of Kaunas; 55°07'/23°58'; GUM3, GUM5, YL.

Vankovichi, Ukr. (Vankovitse, Wankowice); pop. 22; 56 km SW of Lvov; 49°38'/23°18'.

Vankovitse, *see* Vankovichi.

Vanovichi, *see* Vanovitse.

Vanovitse, Ukr. (Vanovichi, Waniowice); pop. 172; 75 km SW of Lvov; 49°29'/23°07'; PHP2.

Vanvolnica, *see* Wawolnica.

Vanvolnitsa, *see* Wawolnica.

Vanyarc, Hung.; pop. 36; 50 km NNE of Budapest; 47°50'/19°27'.

Vanyola, Hung.; pop. 2; 114 km WSW of Budapest; 47°23'/17°35'.

Vanyuv, Ukr. (Waniow); pop. 37; 62 km N of Lvov; 50°22'/24°06'.

Vapniarca, *see* Vapnyarka.

Vapnyarka, Ukr. (Vapniarca); pop. 667; 82 km SSE of Vinnitsa; 48°32'/28°46'; EJ, GUM3, GUM4, GUM6, PHR1.

Vaprova, *see* Vyprovo.

Varadia, Rom.; pop. 246 km SSW of Cluj; 45°05'/21°32'; HSL.

Varaiu, Rom.; pop. 4; 75 km NNW of Cluj; 47°23'/23°27'.

Varaklani, Lat. (Varaklanu, Varaklyany, Varklian, Varkliani); pop. 24; 88 km N of Daugavpils; 56°37'/26°44'; AMG, HSL, JGFF, LDL, PHLE, SF.

Varaklanu, *see* Varaklani.

Varaklyany, *see* Varaklani.

Varalmas, HSL. This pre-World War I community was not found in BGN gazetteers.

Varanno, *see* Vranov nad Toplou.

Varaszo, Hung.; pop. 6; 50 km WSW of Miskolc; 48°02'/20°07'.

Varatchenka, *see* Verenchanka.

Varatic, *see* Varatik.

Varatik, Mold. (Varatic); pop. 68; 157 km WNW of Kishinev; 47°55'/27°16'.

Varatytsk, Byel. (Varotytsk, Waratyck); pop. 21; 50 km WNW of Pinsk; 52°17'/25°27'.

Varazdin, Yug.; pop. 486; 62 km N of Zagreb; 46°18'/16°20'; HSL, HSL2, PHY.

Varazdinske Toplice, Yug.; pop. 23; 56 km NNE of Zagreb; 46°13'/16°26'.

Varboc, Hung.; pop. 5; 50 km NNW of Miskolc; 48°28'/20°39'.

Varchofki, *see* Verkhovka.

Varda, Hung.; 56 km E of Nagykanizsa; 46°27'/17°44'; HSL.

Vardomichi, Byel. (Wardomicze Stare); pop. 11; 101 km N of Minsk; 54°43'/27°41'.

Vardz Dresht, *see* Varzareshty.

Varel, Germ.; pop. 58; 126 km WSW of Hamburg; 53°24'/08°08'.

Varena, Lith. (Oran, Orany, Warna); pop. 399; 75 km SW of Vilnius; 54°13'/24°34'; AMG, COH, GUM3, GUM4, HSL, JGFF, LDL, SF, YL.

Varenholz, Germ.; 56 km SW of Hannover; 52°10'/08°59'; LDS.

Varenz, *see* Novo Ukrainka (Lwow).

Varenzh, *see* Novoukrainka.

Varenz Miasto, *see* Novo Ukrainka (Lwow).

Varez, *see* Novo Ukrainka (Lwow).

Varez Miasto, *see* Novo Ukrainka (Lwow).

Vargata, Rom. (Csikfalva); pop. 9; 94 km E of Cluj; 46°34'/24°48'; HSL.

Vargede, HSL. This pre-World War I community was not found in BGN gazetteers.

Vari, *see* Vary.

Varin, Cz.; pop. 134; 163 km E of Brno; 49°12'/18°53'.

Varka, *see* Warka.

Varkava, Lat. (Varkavas); pop. 35; 45 km WNW of Daugavpils; 56°04'/25°57'.

Varkavas, *see* Varkava.

Varklian, *see* Varaklani.

Varkliani, *see* Varaklani.

Varkony, *see* Vrakun.

Varkoviche, *see* Varkovichi.

Varkovichi, Ukr. (Varkoviche, Varkovits, Warkowicze, Warkowicze); pop. 886; 26 km SW of Rovno; 50°28'/25°58'; AMG, COH, EDRD, GUM3, GUM4, LDL, SF.

Varkovits, *see* Varkovichi.

Varme, Lat.; pop. 4; 114 km WSW of Riga; 56°52'/22°14'.

Varmezo, *see* Buciumi.

Varna, *see* Varniai.

Varna (Bulgaria), Bulg. (Stalin); pop. 2,050; 378 km ENE of Sofija; 43°13'/27°55'; EJ, GUM4, GUM5, GUM6. *See also* Varniai, Lithuania.

Varnenai, *see* Baleliai Antrieji.

Varniai, Lith. (Medininkai, Miedniki, Varna, Vorna, Vorne, Vorni, Wornie); pop. 823; 62 km SW of Siauliai; 55°45'/22°22'; HSL, HSL2, JGFF, LDL, SF, YL.

Varnita, *see* Varnitsa.

Varnitsa, Mold. (Varnita); pop. 22; 50 km ESE of Kishinev; 46°52'/29°29'.

Varnov, COH. This town was not found in BGN gazetteers under the given spelling.

Varnsdorf, Cz. (Warensdorf); pop. 211; 94 km N of Praha; 50°55'/14°37'; HSL.

Varosa, YB. This town was not found in BGN gazetteers under the given spelling.

Varoslod, Hung.; pop. 8; 101 km NNE of Nagykanizsa; 47°09'/17°39'.

Varosmajor, Hung. EDRD. This town was not found in BGN gazetteers under the given spelling.

Varosszalonak, *see* Stadtschlaining.

Varosvar, HSL. This pre-World War I community was not found in BGN gazetteers.

Varotytsk, *see* Varatytsk.

Varpalanka, Ukr.; 182 km SSW of Lvov; 48°26'/22°41'; AMG, HSL. This town was located on a pre-World War I map, but does not appear in contemporary gazetteers.

Varpalota, Hung.; pop. 227; 75 km SW of Budapest; 47°12'/18°08'; HSL, LDL, PHH.

Varsad, Hung.; pop. 5; 114 km ENE of Nagykanizsa; 46°32'/18°31'.

Varsany, Hung. (Kalinciakovo); 94 km N of Szeged; 47°03'/20°16'; HSL, HSL2, LDS.

Varsava, *see* Warszawa.

Varshau, *see* Warszawa.

Varshe, *see* Warszawa.

Varshilovka, *see* Voroshilovka.

Varsolcz, HSL. This pre-World War I community was not found in BGN gazetteers.

Varsolt, *see* Virsoli.

Vartejeni Colonie, *possibly* Vertyuzhany.

Vartejenii Sat, *see* Vertyuzhany.

Varticauti, *see* Vaskautsy.

Vartuzhen, *see* Vertyuzhany.

Varvareni, *see* Varvarovka.

Varvarovka, Mold. (Varvareni, Vorvorovka, Warwarowka); pop. 22; 107 km NNW of Kishinev; 47°53'/28°19'; PHR1, SF.

Varviz, Rom.; pop. 12; 101 km WNW of Cluj; 47°13'/22°26'; HSL.

Vary, Ukr. (Vari); 214 km SSW of Lvov; 48°08'/22°43'; AMG, HSL.

Varzareshty, Mold. (Vardz Dresht, Varzaresti); pop. 205; 50 km W of Kishinev; 47°07'/28°12'; JGFF.

Varzaresti, *see* Varzareshty.

Varzari, Rom. (Fuves); pop. 6; 101 km WNW of Cluj; 47°12'/22°28'.

Varzhan, *see* Veivirzenai.

Vas, Yug.; 94 km SW of Zagreb; 45°29'/14°53'; YB.

Vasad, Rom. (Ersvasad); pop. 39; 133 km WNW of Cluj; 47°31'/22°16'; HSL.

Vasarhely, Cz.; 38 km E of Kosice; 48°42'/21°48'; GUM6, HSL, HSL2. This town was located on a pre-World War I map, but does not appear in contemporary gazetteers.

Vasarosbec, Hung.; pop. 4; 62 km ESE of Nagykanizsa; 46°11'/17°44'.

Vasarosdombo, Hung.; pop. 1; 88 km E of Nagykanizsa; 46°18'/18°09'.

Vasarosmiske, Hung.; pop. 4; 94 km N of Nagykanizsa; 47°12'/17°04'.

Vasarosnameny, Hung. (Vasarosnemeny); pop. 764; 114 km ENE of Miskolc; 48°08'/22°19'; AMG, GUM5, HSL, HSL2, JGFF, LDL, PHH.

Vasarosnemeny, *see* Vasarosnameny.

Vasboldogasszony, Hung.; pop. 6; 62 km NNW of Nagykanizsa; 46°57'/16°53'.

Vascau, Rom. (Vaskoh); 88 km SW of Cluj; 46°28'/22°28'; HSL.

Vascauti, *see* Vashkovtsy.

Vascauti Hotin, *see* Vashkovtsy Khotin.

Vascauti Orhei, *see* Vyshkautsy.

Vascauti pe Ceremus, *see* Vashkovtsy.

Vascauti Soroca, Mold.; pop. 34; 45 km N of Kishinev; 47°22'/28°49'.

Vasckauti, *see* Vashkovtsy.

Vashilkova, *see* Wasilkow.

Vashki, *see* Vaskai.

Vashkouts, *see* Vashkovtsy.

Vashkovtsy, Ukr. (Vascauti, Vascauti pe Ceremus, Vasckauti, Vashkouts, Voshkavitch, Washkoutz); pop. 856; 32 km WNW of Chernovtsy; 48°23'/25°31'; GUM3, GUM4, GUM5, GYLA, JGFF, SF.

Vashkovtsy Khotin, Ukr. (Vascauti Hotin); pop. 44; 88 km ENE of Chernovtsy; 48°25'/27°08'.

Vashniev, *see* Wasniow.

Vasica, Yug.; 107 km WNW of Beograd; 45°06'/19°11'; HSL.

Vasieni Orhei, *see* Vasiyeny.

Vasilau, *see* Vasilou.

Vasileutis, Rom.; pop. 41; 75 km NNW of Iasi; 47°49'/27°17'.

Vasilevichi, Byel. (Wasilewicze); pop. 10; 101 km WNW of Minsk; 54°26'/26°22'.

Vasilishak, *see* Vasilishki.

Vasilishki, Byel. (Vasilishak, Vasilishok, Wasiliszki); pop. 1,223; 176 km WSW of Minsk; 53°47'/24°51'; COH, EDRD, GUM3, GUM4, GUM5, HSL, HSL2, JGFF, LDL, SF, YB.

Vasilishok, *see* Vasilishki.

Vasilkov, Ukr. (Vassilkovo); pop. 3,061; 32 km SSW of Kiyev; 50°11'/30°19'; EDRD, JGFF.

Vasilkovtsy, Ukr. (Wasylkowce); pop. 157; 88 km N of Chernovtsy; 49°05'/26°04'; PHP2.

Vasilou, Ukr. (Vasilau); pop. 231; 38 km NNW of Chernovtsy; 48°36'/25°50'.

Vasilyevka, Ukr. HSL.

Vasilyevka (Bessarabia), Ukr. (Vaisal); pop. 12; 176 km SW of Odessa; 45°38'/28°50'.

Vasimony, LDL. This pre-World War I community was not found in BGN gazetteers.

Vasiyeny, Mold. (Vasieni Orhei); pop. 24; 56 km NW of Kishinev; 47°27'/28°26'.

Vaskai, Lith. (Vashki, Vaskiai, Voshki, Voski); pop. 267; 62 km NE of Siauliai; 56°10'/24°12'; COH, HSL, JGFF, LDL, SF, YL.

Vaskautsy, Mold. (Varticauti); pop. 51; 114 km NNW of Kishinev; 47°57'/28°31'.

Vaskiai, *see* Vaskai.

Vaskoh, *see* Vascau.

Vaskoutsi, *see* Vyshkautsy.

Vaskut, Hung.; pop. 17; 88 km WSW of Szeged; 46°07'/18°59'; LDS.

Vaslauti, *see* Vaslouts.

Vaslouts, Ukr. (Vaslauti); pop. 31; 19 km N of Chernovtsy; 48°27'/25°56'.

Vaslui, Rom.; 62 km SSE of Iasi; 46°38'/27°44'; EJ, GUM3, GUM4, HSL, JGFF, LDL, PHR1.

Vasmegyer, Hung.; pop. 45; 82 km ENE of Miskolc; 48°07'/21°49'; HSL.

Vassilivtchin, Ukr. EDRD. This town was not found in BGN gazetteers under the given spelling.

Vassilkovo, *see* Vasilkov.

Vasszecseny, Hung.; pop. 10; 88 km NNW of Nagykanizsa; 47°11'/16°46'.

Vasvar, Hung.; pop. 223; 75 km NNW of Nagykanizsa; 47°03'/16°48'; AMG, HSL, LDS, PHH.

Vasyuki, Byel. (Wasiuki); pop. 8; 107 km WNW of Minsk; 54°31'/26°15'.

Vaszar, Hung.; pop. 7; 120 km WSW of Budapest; 47°24'/17°31'.

Vaszoly, Hung.; pop. 3; 82 km NE of Nagykanizsa; 46°56'/17°46'.

Vat, Hung.; pop. 3; 101 km NNW of Nagykanizsa; 47°17'/16°47'; HSL.

Vatich, Mold. (Vatici); pop. 9; 45 km NNW of Kishinev; 47°21'/28°37'.

Vatici, *see* Vatich.

Vatra Dornei, Rom. (Dorna Vatra, Dorna Watra); pop. 1,750; 146 km NE of Cluj; 47°21'/25°22'; EDRD, GUM3, GUM4, GUM5, HSL, JGFF, PHR2, SF.

Vatra Moldovitei, Rom.; pop. 136; 157 km WNW of Iasi; 47°39'/25°34'; PHR2.

Vatta, Hung.; pop. 10; 26 km S of Miskolc; 47°55'/20°45'; HSL.

Vatyn, Ukr. (Watyn); pop. 10; 94 km W of Rovno; 50°40'/24°53'.

Vaverka, Byel. (Wawiorka); pop. 7; 170 km WSW of Minsk; 53°50'/24°58'.

Vavolnitsa, *see* Wawolnica.

Vayslits, *see* Wislica.

Vaytovka, *see* Voytovka.

Vcheraishe, *see* Vcherayshe.

Vcherayshe, Ukr. (Vcheraishe); pop. 1,072; 88 km NNE of Vinnitsa; 49°52'/29°09'.

Veca, Cz. (Vag Vecse); pop. 61; 56 km ENE of Bratislava; 48°10'/17°54'; HSL, LDL.

Vecamuiza, Lat. (Althaif, Althof); 75 km SSE of Riga; 56°21'/24°26'; JGFF.

Vecdoles, Lat. (Doles); pop. 8; 75 km ENE of Riga; 57°10'/25°17'.

Vecgulbene, *see* Gulbene.

Vechec, Cz. (Vehecz); pop. 9; 32 km NE of Kosice; 48°52'/21°38'; HSL.

Vechelde, Germ.; 50 km E of Hannover; 52°16'/10°23'; GUM3, GUM6.

Vechorki, Ukr. (Wieczorki); 50 km N of Lvov; 50°17'/24°04'; GUM3.

Vechta, Germ.; pop. 13; 107 km WNW of Hannover; 52°43'/08°17'; GED, JGFF.

Vecmemele, Lat. (Altmemelhof); 94 km SE of Riga; 56°16'/25°03'; JGFF.

Vecpiebalga, Lat.; pop. 2; 107 km ENE of Riga; 57°01'/25°50'.

Vecpils, Lat.; pop. 4; 163 km WSW of Riga; 56°38'/21°29'.

Vecsaule, Lat.; pop. 6; 62 km SSE of Riga; 56°26'/24°20'.

Vecses, Hung.; pop. 160; 19 km ESE of Budapest; 47°24'/19°17'; HSL, PHH.

Veczke, *see* Escu.

Veczvarde, Lat. (Zvarde); pop. 5; 101 km SW of Riga; 56°34'/22°38'.

Vegardo, Hung.; pop. 5; 69 km NE of Miskolc; 48°20'/21°36'.

Vegegyhaza, Hung.; pop. 28; 56 km ENE of Szeged; 46°23'/20°52'; HSL.

Veger, *see* Vegeriai.

Vegeriai, Lith. (Veger); pop. 102; 56 km NW of Siauliai; 56°24'/22°57'; GUM3, HSL, LDL, SF, YL.

Vegesack, Germ. (Aumund); pop. 110; 101 km SW of Hamburg; 53°10'/08°37'.

Vegrov, *see* Wegrow.

Vehecz, *see* Vechec.

Vehlen, Germ. BGN lists two possible localities with this name located at 52°16'/09°06' and 52°26'/12°19'. GED.

Veinuta, *see* Vainutas.

Veisee, *see* Veisiejai.

Veisejai, *see* Veisiejai.

Veisenshtein, *see* Paide.

Veisiejai, Lith. (Veisee, Veisejai, Vishay, Vishaya, Wiejsieje); pop. 516; 94 km S of Kaunas; 54°06'/23°42'; COH, GUM5, HSL, JGFF, LDL, LDS, SF, YL.

Veislitz, *see* Wislica.

Veitshochheim, Germ.; pop. 53; 88 km ESE of Frankfurt am Main; 49°50'/09°52'; GUM5, PHGB.

Veiveriai, Lith. (Vevia, Vyver); pop. 137; 19 km SSW of Kaunas; 54°46'/23°43'; JGFF, YL.

Veivirzenai, Lith. (Varzhan, Verzanai?, Verzian, Vevirzenai, Vevirzhon, Vievirzenai); pop. 259; 114 km SW of Siauliai; 55°36'/21°36'; GUM4, GUM5, HSL, SF, YL.

Vejava, Lat.; pop. 1; 107 km E of Riga; 56°55'/25°53'.

Vejprty, Cz.; pop. 36; 114 km WNW of Praha; 50°30'/13°02'.

Vejvanov, Cz.; pop. 2; 62 km SW of Praha; 49°52'/13°39'.

Veke, *see* Vojka.

Vekerd, Hung.; pop. 5; 120 km SSE of Miskolc; 47°06'/21°24'; LDS.

Vekshna, *see* Vieksniai.

Vekshne, *see* Vieksniai.

Vekshni, *see* Vieksniai.

Velatin, *see* Velete.

Velava, HSL. This pre-World War I community was not found in BGN gazetteers.

Velbert, Germ.; pop. 62; 50 km N of Koln; 51°20'/07°03'.

Velburg, Germ.; 50 km ESE of Nurnberg; 49°14'/11°41'; PHGB.

Velcherul de Campi, Rom. (Mezovelker); 45 km E of Cluj; 46°41'/24°12'; HSL. This town was located on a pre-World War I map, but does not appear in contemporary gazetteers.

Velcice, Cz. (Velsecz, Velsicz); 94 km NE of Bratislava; 48°25'/18°18'; HSL, HSL2.

Velden, Germ.; 38 km NE of Nurnberg; 49°37'/11°31'; PHGB.

Veldenz, Germ.; pop. 7; 126 km WSW of Frankfurt am Main; 49°53'/07°01'.

Veldes, GUM5. This town was not found in BGN gazetteers under the given spelling.

Veldhausen, Germ.; 176 km N of Koln; 52°31'/07°00'; LDS.

Veldzirsh, *see* Veldzizh.

Veldzizh, Ukr. (Veldzirsh, Weldzirz); pop. 220; 114 km S of Lvov; 48°54'/23°55'; AMG, HSL, LDL, PHP2, SF.

Velebudice, Cz.; pop. 3; 75 km WNW of Praha; 50°29'/13°38'.

Velemer, Hung.; pop. 2; 56 km WNW of Nagykanizsa; 46°44'/16°23'.

Velemichi, Byel. (Wielemicze); pop. 5; 75 km E of Pinsk; 52°01'/27°14'.

Velemin, Cz.; pop. 5; 62 km NW of Praha; 50°32'/13°59'.

Velen, Germ.; 114 km N of Koln; 51°54'/06°59'; GED.

Velena, *see* Vilani.

Velenovy, Cz.; pop. 3; 107 km SSW of Praha; 49°22'/13°33'.

Veles, *see* Titov Veles.

Velesin, Cz.; pop. 2; 146 km S of Praha; 48°50'/14°28'.

Velete, Hung. (Velatin); 69 km NNE of Nagykanizsa; 46°53'/17°34'; HSL.

Veletice, Cz.; pop. 5; 69 km WNW of Praha; 50°18'/13°35'.

Velezd, *possibly* Fulesd.

Velhartice, Cz.; pop. 21; 120 km SSW of Praha; 49°16'/13°24'; JGFF.

Velichka, *see* Wieliczka.

Velichovky, Cz.; pop. 2; 107 km NE of Praha; 50°21'/15°51'.

Velika Gorica, Yug.; pop. 19; 13 km SE of Zagreb; 45°44'/16°04'.

Velika Kikinda, *see* Kikinda.

Velika Kladusa, Yug.; pop. 1; 75 km S of Zagreb; 45°11'/15°49'.

Velika Kopanica, Yug.; pop. 8; 170 km W of Beograd; 45°10'/18°24'; COH.

Velikaya Berestovit, *see* Brzostowica.

Velikaya Berestovitsa, *see* Bolshaya Berestovitsa.

Velikaya Berezovitsa, Ukr. (Berezovitsa Velka, Berezowica Wielka); pop. 30; 126 km ESE of Lvov; 49°30'/25°37'.

Velikaya Glusha, Ukr. (Wielka Hlusza); pop. 224; 157 km NW of Rovno; 51°49'/25°03'.

Velikaya Gorozhanka, Ukr. (Gorozhanna Volka, Horozanna Wielka); pop. 49; 38 km S of Lvov; 49°35'/23°50'.

Velikaya Khodachka, Ukr. (Chodaczkow Maly, Chodaczkow Wielki, Khodachkuv Velki); pop. 40; 114 km ESE of Lvov; 49°29'/25°26'; GUM3, GUM5.

Velikaya Osnitsa, Ukr. (Osnica Wielka); pop. 7; 69 km NNW of Rovno; 51°11'/25°57'.

Velike Zaluzie, *see* Velke Zaluzie.

Veliki Beckerek, *see* Zrenjanin.

Veliki Berezny, *see* Velikiy Bereznyy.

Velikie Mosty, *see* Velikiye Mosty.

Veliki Grdevac, Yug.; pop. 25; 82 km E of Zagreb; 45°46'/17°04'.

Velikiy Bereznyy, Ukr. (Kisberenzna, Kisberezna, Veliki Berezny, Velke Berezne, Velky Berezny); pop. 2,404; 150 km SW of Lvov; 48°54'/22°28'; AMG, GUM3, JGFF.

Velikiy Bychkov, Ukr. (Bicskof, Bikivics, Bochkuv, Bukkospatak, Bukovec, Nagy Bocska, Veliky Bockov); pop. 1,708; 146 km WSW of Chernovtsy; 47°58'/24°01'; AMG, HSL, JGFF, SM.

Velikiye Berezhtsy, Ukr. (Berezce, Berezcy, Berezhtse, Brezitz); pop. 181; 75 km SSW of Rovno; 50°06'/25°37'; SF.

Velikiye Borki, Ukr. (Borki Wielkie); pop. 16; 126 km S of Rovno; 49°31'/25°45'; GUM3, GUM4, GUM5, GUM6, PHP2.

Velikiye Chornokontsy, Ukr. (Charnokontse, Charnokontse Velk, Czarnokonce Wielkie); pop. 79; 75 km N of Chernovtsy; 48°58'/26°02'.

Velikiye Glibovichi, Ukr. (Chlebowice Wielkie, Khlebovitse Velki); pop. 95; 32 km SE of Lvov; 49°37'/24°14'.

Velikiye Korchitsy, Byel. (Korczyce Wielkie); pop. 7; 120 km WSW of Pinsk; 52°07'/24°22'.

Velikiye Luki, *see* Bolshiye Luki.

Velikiye Mosty, Ukr. (Augustowa Ad Ratam, Gross Mosty, Mohast Rabati, Most Gadol, Most Rabati, Mosti Vielkie, Mosty, Mosty Wielkie, Velikie Mosty); pop. 1,142; 45 km N of Lvov; 50°14'/24°09'; COH, EDRD, EGRS, EJ, FRG, GUM3, GUM4, GUM5, HSL, HSL2, LDL, LYV, PHP2, SF, YB.

Velikiye Zagaytsy, Ukr. (Zahajce); pop. 8; 75 km S of Rovno; 50°00'/26°02'; GUM4, PHP2.

Velikiy Kochurov, Ukr. (Cuciurul Mare); pop. 224; 19 km S of Chernovtsy; 48°11'/25°53'.

Velikiy Lyuben, Ukr. (Lubien [Lwow], Lubien Wielki); pop. 204; 26 km SW of Lvov; 49°44'/23°44'; PHP2.

Velikiy Zhvanchik, Ukr. (Zhvanchik, Zvancik, Zvantchik, Zwanchik); 94 km NE of Chernovtsy; 48°46'/26°59'; GYLA, LDL, SF.

Veliko Gradiste, Yug.; pop. 9; 82 km E of Beograd; 44°46'/21°32'.

Velikoselka, Ukr. (Zelechow Wielki, Zelekhuv Velke, Zhelekhuv Velke); pop. 31; 32 km NE of Lvov; 50°00'/24°26'; EGRS.

Velikoye Selo, Byel. (Velke Selo, Wielkie Siolo); pop. 24; 133 km WNW of Pinsk; 52°38'/24°19'.

Veliky Bockov, *see* Velikiy Bychkov.

Velikye Luki, USSR (Weliki Luki); pop. 1,627; 6 km SSW of Velikiye Luki; 56°19'/30°31'; LDL.

Velim, Cz.; pop. 6; 50 km E of Praha; 50°04'/15°06'.

Veliona, *see* Veliuona.

Veliony, *see* Vilani.

Veliuona, Lith. (Veliona, Vilan, Vileny, Vilon, Wielona); pop. 355; 45 km WNW of Kaunas; 55°05'/23°17'; HSL, HSL2, JGFF, SF, YL.

Velizh, USSR (Vielizh, Wieliz); pop. 3,274; 94 km SE of Velikiye Luki; 55°36'/31°12'; HSL, HSL2, LDL, SF.

Velka, *see* Velka Pri Poprade.

Velka Bytca, Cz.; pop. 488; 139 km ENE of Brno; 49°13'/18°34'; GUM5.

Velka Ida, Cz. (Nagyida); pop. 111; 82 km WNW of Kosice; 49°04'/20°17'; AMG, HSL, HSL2.

Velka Lomnica, Cz. (Grosslomnitz); pop. 51; 82 km WNW of Kosice; 49°07'/20°22'.

Velka Luc, Cz. (Nagy Lucs, Nagylucs); 32 km ESE of Bratislava; 47°59'/17°31'; HSL.

Velka Polana, Cz. (Polana Velka); pop. 83; 88 km NE of Kosice; 49°05'/22°19'; AMG, GUM3.

Velka Pri Poprade, Cz. (Felk, Felka, Ida, Velka, Welka); pop. 85; 82 km WNW of Kosice; 49°04'/20°17'.

Velka Ves nad Iplom, Cz. (Nagyfalu); 146 km E of Bratislava; 48°05'/19°06'; HSL, HSL2.

Velke Berezne, *see* Velikiy Bereznyy.

Velke Kapusany, Cz. (Kapusany, Nagy Kapos, Nagykapos); pop. 1,327; 62 km E of Kosice; 48°33'/22°05'; AMG, HSL, HSL2, LDL.

Velke Kopany, GUM3. This town was not found in BGN gazetteers under the given spelling.

Velke Kostolany, Cz. (Nagykosztolany); pop. 58; 56 km NE of Bratislava; 48°30'/17°43'; HSL.

Velke Levare, Cz. (Grossschutzen, Nagylevard); pop. 60; 45 km NNW of Bratislava; 48°30'/17°00'.

Velke Ludince, Cz. (Nagy Olved); 107 km E of Bratislava; 47°58'/18°31'; HSL.

Velke Mezirici, Cz. (Gross Mesereitsch); pop. 89; 50 km WNW of Brno; 49°21'/16°01'.

Velkenye, *see* Vlkyna.

Velke Ripnany, Cz. (Velke Rypnany); pop. 64; 75 km NE of Bratislava; 48°30'/17°59'.

Velke Rypnany, *see* Velke Ripnany.

Velke Selo, *see* Velikoye Selo.

Velke Trakany, Cz. (Velky Tarkan); pop. 134; 75 km ESE of Kosice; 48°23'/22°06'.

Velke Ulany, Cz. (Nagy Fodemes, Velky Fedimes, Velky Fedymes); pop. 54; 38 km ENE of Bratislava; 48°10'/17°35'; HSL.

Velke Zaluzie, Cz. (Ujlak, Velike Zaluzie); pop. 124; 62 km ENE of Bratislava; 48°18'/17°57'; AMG, HSL, HSL2, JGFF.

Velki, Lat.; pop. 1; 107 km ENE of Riga; 57°04'/25°50'; AMG.

Velky Berezny, *see* Velikiy Bereznyy.

Velky Bysterec, Cz.; 157 km WNW of Kosice; 49°13'/19°17'; HSL.

Velky Dioseg, *see* Sladkovicovo.

Velky Diosek, *see* Sladkovicovo.

Velky Fedimes, *see* Velke Ulany.

Velky Fedymes, *see* Velke Ulany.

Velky Gyres, *see* Velky Hores.

Velky Hores, Cz. (Nagy Geres, Velky Gyres); pop. 71; 62 km ESE of Kosice; 48°23'/21°55'; HSL.

Velky Mader, *see* Calovo.

Velky Meder, *see* Calovo.

Velky Saris, Cz.; pop. 75; 45 km N of Kosice; 49°03'/21°12'; HSL.

Velky Tarkan, *see* Velke Trakany.

Velm, Aus.; pop. 3; 26 km SSE of Wien; 48°02'/16°26'.

Velma, *see* Valmiera.

Velmar, *see* Valmiera.

Velsecz, *see* Velcice.

Velsicz, *see* Velcice.

Veltruby, Cz. (Weltrub); 50 km E of Praha; 50°05'/15°11'; HSL.

Veltrusy, Cz.; pop. 9; 26 km NW of Praha; 50°16'/14°20'.

Velun, *see* Velyun.

Velvary, Cz.; pop. 57; 26 km NW of Praha; 50°17'/14°15'.

Velyatin, Ukr. (Valiatin); 195 km WSW of Chernovtsy; 48°06'/23°19'; SM.

Velyun, Ukr. (Velun, Vielun, Vyelun, Wielun); pop. 22; 120 km N of Rovno; 51°39'/26°40'.

Velzis, *see* Velzys.

Velzys, Lith. (Velzis); 75 km ESE of Siauliai; 55°42'/24°26'; HSL.

Vemend, Hung.; pop. 22; 120 km WSW of Szeged; 46°09'/18°37'.

Vencsello, Hung.; pop. 57; 56 km ENE of Miskolc; 48°10'/21°34'; HSL, HSL2, PHH.

Vendegi, *see* Hostovce nad Bodvou.

Venden, *see* Cesis.

Vendersheim, Germ.; pop. 6; 50 km SW of Frankfurt am Main; 49°52'/08°04'.

Vendichany, Ukr. (Vindiceni); pop. 600; 82 km SSW of Vinnitsa; 48°38'/27°48'; PHR1.

Vendziogala, *see* Vandziogala.

Venev, USSR; pop. 21; 157 km SSE of Moskva; 54°22'/38°15'.

Vengerov, *see* Wegrow.

Vengrov, *see* Wegrow.

Vengrova, *see* Wegrow.

Vengrove, *see* Wegrow.

Venningen, Germ.; pop. 29; 94 km WNW of Stuttgart; 49°17'/08°10'; CAHJP, GED.

Ventspils, Lat. (Vindava, Vindoi, Windall, Windau, Windawa); pop. 1,258; 163 km W of Riga; 57°24'/21°31'; COH, EJ, GUM3, GUM4, GUM5, HSL, JGFF, PHLE, SF.

Vepriai, Lith.; pop. 18; 50 km NE of Kaunas; 55°09'/24°34'.

Verba, *see* Verezheny.

Verbal, *see* Virbalis.

Verbasz, *possibly* Vrbas.

Verbauti, *see* Verbouts.

Verbche Male, Ukr. (Werbcze Male); pop. 35; 75 km N of Rovno; 51°13'/26°18'.

Verbche Velke, *see* Bolshaya Verbcha.

Verbionzh Vyzhny, Ukr. (Wierbiaz Nizny); pop. 82; 75 km WNW of Chernovtsy; 48°30'/24°59'.

Verbizh, Ukr. (Werbiz); 38 km S of Lvov; 49°33'/23°54'; EJ.

Verbo, *see* Vrbove.

Verbocz, *see* Vrbovce.

Verbouts, Ukr. (Verbauti); pop. 37; 26 km N of Chernovtsy; 48°29'/25°55'.

Verbovets, Ukr. (Verbovitz, Werbowez); 94 km SW of Vinnitsa; 48°44'/27°26'; LDL, SF.

Verbovets (Stanislawow), Pol.; pop. 131; PHP2. Described in the *Black Book* as being in the Stanislawow region of Poland, this town was not found in BGN gazetteers.

Verbovitz, *see* Verbovets.

Verbovtsy, Ukr. (Wierzbowce, Wierzbowiec); pop. 30; 50 km WNW of Chernovtsy; 48°37'/25°23'.

Verbovtsy (Tarnopol), Ukr.; pop. 31; 26 km N of Chernovtsy; 48°29'/25°55'.

Verbyany, Ukr. (Vezhbyany, Wierzbiany); pop. 59; 45 km WNW of Lvov; 50°03'/23°26'.

Verchany, Ukr. (Wierczany); pop. 21; 69 km S of Lvov; 49°16'/23°54'.

Verchnedneprovsk, *see* Verkhnedneprovsk.

Verchovka, *see* Verkhovka.

Verden, Germ.; pop. 80; 69 km NW of Hannover; 52°55'/09°14'.

Vereb, Hung.; pop. 2; 45 km SW of Budapest; 47°19'/18°37'.

Verecky Nizni, *see* Nizhniye Veretski.

Verecski, GUM3. This town was not found in BGN gazetteers under the given spelling.

Verecze, *possibly* Nizhniye Veretski.

Verejeni Orhei, *see* Verezheny.

Verejeni Soroca, *see* Verezhen.

Veremiyevka, Ukr. (Jeremjejewka, Yarmievka); 182 km NE of Uman; 49°22'/32°33'; LDL, SF.

Verenchanka, Ukr. (Varatchenka, Vranceni, Vrauceni); pop. 258; 32 km NW of Chernovtsy; 48°33'/25°44'; SF.

Verenkeu, *see* Voronkovo.

Veresegyhaz, Hung.; pop. 59; 19 km NNE of Budapest; 47°39'/19°17'; PHH.

Vereshitsa, Ukr. (Wereszyce); pop. 51; 32 km WNW of Lvov; 50°00'/23°38'.

Veresmart, *see* Szabolcsveresmart.

Vereyki, Byel. (Werejki); pop. 9; 182 km WNW of Pinsk; 53°15'/24°12'.

Verezhen, Mold. (Verejeni Soroca); pop. 37; 182 km NW of Kishinev; 48°26'/27°37'. *See also* Verezheny.

Verezheny, Mold. (Verba, Verejeni Orhei, Verezhen); pop. 26; 62 km NW of Kishinev; 47°32'/28°28'; EDRD, SF, SF.

Vergali, Lat.; pop. 5; 176 km WSW of Riga; 56°42'/21°12'.

Verhovca, GUM4, PHR1. This town was not found in BGN gazetteers under the given spelling.

Verhovka, *see* Verkhovka.

Verice, Cz.; 38 km SE of Praha; 49°47'/14°46'; GUM6.

Verkhi, Ukr. (Werchy); pop. 28; 126 km NW of Rovno; 51°27'/25°06'.

Verkhnedneprovsk, Ukr. (Verchnedneprovsk, Verkhne Dnyeprovsk, Wierchniednieprowsk); pop. 914; 56 km WNW of Dnepropetrovsk; 48°39'/34°20'; LDL, SF.

Verkhne Dnyeprovsk, *see* Verkhnedneprovsk.

Verkhnedvinsk, Byel. (Drissa, Dryssa); pop. 1,265; 157 km WNW of Vitebsk; 55°47'/27°56'; GUM5, HSL, LDL, SF.

Verkhne Studenyy, Ukr. (Felsohidegpatak, Studene Vizhne, Studna, Vysni Studeny); 139 km S of Lvov; 48°44'/23°21'; SM.

Verkhneye Krivche, Ukr. (Krzywcze Gorne); pop. 362; 50 km N of Chernovtsy; 48°42'/26°07'; EGRS, LDL.

Verkhneye Sinevidnoye, Ukr. (Synowodzko Wyzne); pop. 341; 88 km S of Lvov; 49°06'/23°35'; GUM3, HSL, PHP2.

Verkhneye Vodyanoye, Ukr. (Felso Apsa, Felsoapsa, Ober Apsa, Vizhna Apsha, Vysna Apsa, Vysni Apsa); pop. 1,175; 150 km WSW of Chernovtsy; 48°00'/23°58'; COH, GUM3, HSL, SM.

Verkhneye Vysotskoye, Ukr. (Visotzki Vizhna, Vysotsko Vyzhne, Wysocka Wyzne); 126 km SSW of Lvov; 48°57'/23°04'; SF.

Verkhniy Berezov, Ukr. (Berezow Wyzny, Berezuv Vyzhny); pop. 48; 82 km W of Chernovtsy; 48°25'/24°49'.

Verkhniye Popeshty, Mold. (Popeshti de Sus, Popesti de Sus); pop. 22; 139 km NW of Kishinev; 48°06'/28°01'.

Verkhniye Zhory, Mold. (Jora de Sus); pop. 11; 56 km N of Kishinev; 47°29'/29°04'.

Verkhniy Maydan, Ukr. (Majdan Gorny, Maydan Gurny); pop. 43; 101 km WNW of Chernovtsy; 48°37'/24°40'.

Verkhniy Yasenov, Ukr. (Jasieniow Gorny, Jasienow, Yasenuv Gorny, Yasenuv Gurny); pop. 34; 75 km WSW of Chernovtsy; 48°10'/24°57'.

Verkhnov, Ukr. (Verkhnuv, Wierzchniow?); pop. 20; 107 km N of Lvov; 50°46'/24°10'.

Verkhnuv, *see* Verkhnov.

Verkhnyaya Albota, Mold. (Albota); pop. 7; 120 km S of Kishinev; 45°58'/28°28'.

Verkhnyaya Bystra, Ukr. (Felsobisztra, Ober Bistra, Vysni Bystry); 139 km S of Lvov; 48°38'/23°31'; SM.

Verkhnyaya Maryanovka, Mold. (Marianca de Sus); pop. 12; 56 km SE of Kishinev; 46°39'/29°19'.

Verkholesye, Byel. (Wierzcholesie); pop. 38; 126 km WSW of Pinsk; 52°05'/24°18'.

Verkhova Bibikovo, Ukr. EDRD. This town was not found in BGN gazetteers under the given spelling.

Verkhovichi, Byel. (Wierzchowice); pop. 59; 182 km W of Pinsk; 52°29'/23°31'.

Verkhovina, Ukr. (Zabia, Zabie, Zhabeye, Zhabya, Zhabye); pop. 673; 88 km WSW of Chernovtsy; 48°09'/24°47'; COH, EDRD, EGRS, GUM3, LDL, PHP2, SF.

Verkhovka, Ukr. (Varchofki, Verchovka, Verhovka, Werchowka, Werkievka, Worchowka); 88 km SW of Uman; 48°26'/29°10'; EDRD, LDL, SF.

Verkhovtsy, Ukr. (Rajtarowice, Raytarovitse, Rytarowice); pop. 70; 69 km SW of Lvov; 49°38'/23°06'; PHP2.

Vermezif, *see* Poienile de Sub Munte.

Vermis, Rom.; pop. 11; 62 km NE of Cluj; 47°00'/24°19'.

Verne, Germ.; pop. 5; 114 km SW of Hannover; 51°41'/08°34'.

Veroia, Greece (Beroea); pop. 424; 69 km WSW of Thessaloniki; 40°32'/22°11'; EJ.

Verotze, *see* Virovitica.

Verovice, Cz.; 114 km NE of Brno; 49°33'/18°07'; GUM3.

Verpelet, Hung.; pop. 146; 50 km SW of Miskolc; 47°51'/20°14'; AMG, HSL, HSL2, LDL, LDS, LYV, PHH.

Verpole, Ukr. BGN lists two possible localities with this name located at 47°57'/26°06' and 48°32'/24°16'. HSL.

Verro, *see* Voru.

Verseg, Hung.; pop. 41; 45 km NE of Budapest; 47°43'/19°33'.

Versend, Hung.; pop. 1; 126 km ESE of Nagykanizsa; 45°59'/18°31'.

Versmold, Germ.; pop. 30; 114 km SW of Hannover; 52°03'/08°09'.

Vertes, Hung.; pop. 89; 114 km ESE of Miskolc; 47°23'/21°52'; HSL, LDS, PHH.

Vertesboglar, Hung.; pop. 2; 45 km WSW of Budapest; 47°26'/18°32'.

Vertessomlo, Hung.; pop. 5; 56 km W of Budapest; 47°31'/18°22'.

Vertesszollos, Hung.; pop. 14; 56 km W of Budapest; 47°37'/18°23'.

Vertujeni, *see* Vertyuzhany.

Vertuzhen, *see* Vertyuzhany.

Vertyuzhani, *see* Vertyuzhany.

Vertyuzhany, Mold. (Kolonie Wertizany, Vartejeni Colonie?, Vartejenii Sat, Vartuzhen, Vertujeni, Vertuzhen, Vertyuzhani); pop. 1,834; 114 km NNW of Kishinev; 47°59'/28°33'; EJ, PHR2, SF.

Verushev, *see* Wieruszow.

Verveghiu, Rom.; pop. 13; 75 km NW of Cluj; 47°19'/23°06'.

Verzanai, *possibly* Veivirzenai.

Verzhbelova, *see* Virbalis.

Verzhbnik, *see* Wierzbnik.

Verzhbnik Starakhov, *see* Wierzbnik.

Verzhboloro, *see* Virbalis.

Verzhbolov, *see* Virbalis.

Verzian, *see* Veivirzenai.

Vese, Hung.; pop. 7; 26 km E of Nagykanizsa; 46°25'/17°18'.

Veselaya Dolina, Ukr. (Cleastitz); pop. 56; 114 km WSW of Odessa; 46°14'/29°20'.

Veselaya Yevreyka, Ukr.; 146 km ESE of Dnepropetrovsk; 47°41'/36°37'; JGFF.

Veselicko, JGFF. A number of towns share this name. It was not possible to determine from available information which one is being referenced.

Veseli nad Moravou, Cz. (Wessely); pop. 64; 62 km ESE of Brno; 48°57'/17°24'; HSL, HSL2.

Veselinovo, Ukr.; 101 km N of Odessa; 47°21'/31°14'; PHR1.

Veselov, Cz.; pop. 6; 94 km W of Praha; 50°07'/13°08'.

Veselyy Kut, Ukr.; pop. 31; 126 km SW of Odessa; 46°03'/29°17'.

Vesenberg, Ukr. (Wiesenberg); pop. 23; 19 km N of Lvov; 50°00'/24°01'; GUM3, GUM5, HSL.

Veshinta, *see* Viesintos.

Veshkhnyakovtse, Ukr. (Wierzchniakowce); pop. 15; 62 km N of Chernovtsy; 48°49'/26°00'.

Vestenbergsgreuth, Germ.; 45 km WNW of Nurnberg; 49°41'/10°38'; PHGB.

Vestiena, Lat.; pop. 4; 114 km E of Riga; 56°52'/25°53'.

Veszkeny, Hung.; pop. 5; 139 km N of Nagykanizsa; 47°36'/17°05'.

Veszprem, Hung. (Weissbrunn); pop. 850; 101 km SW of Budapest; 47°06'/17°55'; EJ, GUM4, GUM5, HSL, HSL2, JGFF, LDS, PHH.

Veszprempinkoc, Hung.; pop. 3; 82 km N of Nagykanizsa; 47°06'/17°17'.

Veszpremvarsany, Hung.; pop. 35; 94 km WSW of Budapest; 47°26'/17°50'; JGFF.

Veszto, Hung.; pop. 159; 114 km NE of Szeged; 46°55'/21°16'; HSL, PHH.

Vetca, Rom.; pop. 2; 101 km ESE of Cluj; 46°21'/24°47'.

Vetes, *see* Vetis.

Vetis, Rom. (Vetes); pop. 53; 133 km NW of Cluj; 47°48'/22°46'; GUM4, HSL.

Vetka, Byel. (Viatka, Vyetka); pop. 2,094; 19 km NNE of Gomel; 52°33'/31°10'; GUM4, HSL, SF.

Vetly, Ukr. (Wietly); pop. 43; 163 km NW of Rovno; 51°53'/25°07'.

Vetrni, Cz.; pop. 56; 150 km S of Praha; 48°46'/14°17'.

Vettweib, *see* Vettweiss.

Vettweiss, Germ. (Vettweib); 38 km SW of Koln; 50°44'/06°36'; COH, GED, GUM5.

Vevia, *see* Veiveriai.

Vevinceni, GUM4. This town was not found in BGN gazetteers under the given spelling.

Vevirzenai, *see* Veivirzenai.

Vevirzhon, *see* Veivirzenai.

Veviya, *see* Vievis.

Vez, Cz.; pop. 2; 94 km WNW of Brno; 49°34'/15°28'.

Vezaiciai, Lith. (Vezhaychey, Visaytz, Wieshajzie); 114 km WSW of Siauliai; 55°43'/21°29'; SF.

Vezenberg, *see* Rakvere.

Vezendiu, Rom.; pop. 5; 126 km NW of Cluj; 47°35'/22°26'.

Vezhaychey, *see* Vezaiciai.

Vezhbenzh, Ukr. (Wierzbiaz); pop. 19; 69 km N of Lvov; 50°26'/24°04'.

Vezhbichno, Ukr. (Wierzbiczno); pop. 21; 126 km WNW of Rovno; 50°59'/24°37'.

Vezhbitsa, Ukr. (Wierzbica); pop. 20; 56 km SE of Lvov; 49°23'/24°24'.

Vezhblyany, Ukr. (Wierzblany); pop. 80; 26 km N of Lvov; 50°02'/24°03'.

Vezhbova, Ukr. (Wierzbow?); pop. 70; 56 km NNW of Chernovtsy; 48°47'/25°45'; PHP2.

Vezhbyany, *see* Verbyany.

Vezseny, Hung.; pop. 9; 94 km N of Szeged; 47°02'/20°13'.

Vgocsakomlos, *see* Comlausa.

Viatka, *see* Vetka.

Viazin, *see* Vyazyn.

Viazma, *see* Vyazma.

Vibranovka, *see* Vybranovka.

Vichin, Byel. (Wiczyn); pop. 26; 62 km ENE of Pinsk; 52°16'/26°57'.

Vichnifka, *see* Vakhnovka.

Vichyne, Ukr. (Wiczynie); pop. 15; 94 km WNW of Rovno; 50°55'/24°58'.

Vicolenii Mari, Rom.; pop. 2; 94 km NW of Iasi; 47°53'/26°51'.

Vicovu de Jos, Rom. (Vicovul de Jos); pop. 65; 163 km WNW

Vienna (Wien), Austria: Hassidim on the Gaussplatz.

of Iasi; 47°54'/25°44'.

Vicovu de Sus, Rom. (Vicovul de Sus); pop. 334; 163 km WNW of Iasi; 47°56'/25°41'; GUM4, PHR2.

Vicovul de Jos, *see* Vicovu de Jos.

Vicovul de Sus, *see* Vicovu de Sus.

Vicsap, HSL. This pre-World War I community was not found in BGN gazetteers.

Vicsapapati, *see* Vycapy Opatovce.

Vicski, *see* Vuchkovo.

Vidava, *see* Widawa.

Vidhostice, Cz.; pop. 6; 82 km W of Praha; 50°09'/13°22'.

Vidin, Bulg.; pop. 1,445; 146 km NNW of Sofija; 43°59'/22°52'; EJ, GUM4, GUM5, HSL, HSL2, JGFF.

Vidinov, Ukr. (Vidynuv, Widynow); pop. 51; 38 km WNW of Chernovtsy; 48°27'/25°26'.

Vidishok, *see* Vidiskiai.

Vidiskiai, Lith. (Vidishok); 75 km NE of Kaunas; 55°18'/24°52'; SF, YL.

Vidnava, Cz.; pop. 4; 139 km N of Brno; 50°22'/17°11'.

Vidochov, Cz.; pop. 5; 94 km NE of Praha; 50°31'/15°34'.

Vidomlya, Byel. (Widomla); pop. 5; 157 km W of Pinsk; 52°19'/23°47'.

Vidpuszta, Hung.; 69 km ESE of Miskolc; 47°45'/21°30'; HSL.

Vidrany, *see* Vydran.

Vidsmuiza, Lat.; pop. 13; 75 km N of Daugavpils; 56°29'/26°50'.

Vidukla, *see* Vidukle.

Vidukle, Lith. (Vidukla); pop. 221; 62 km SSW of Siauliai; 55°24'/22°54'; COH, GUM3, HSL, JGFF, LDL, SF, YL.

Vidynuv, *see* Vidinov.

Vidz, *see* Vidzy.

Vidzh, *see* Vidzy.

Vidziai, *see* Vidzy.

Vidzin, Cz.; pop. 3; 107 km WSW of Praha; 49°58'/12°59'.

Vidzy, Byel. (Vidz, Vidzh, Vidziai, Widze); pop. 316; 182 km NNW of Minsk; 55°24'/26°38'; COH, GUM3, GUM4, GUM6, HSL, JGFF, LDL, LYV, SF, YB.

Viechtach, Germ.; pop. 2; 139 km NNE of Munchen; 49°05'/12°53'; GUM3.

Vieksniai, Lith. (Vekshna, Vekshne, Vekshni, Wekschni); pop. 497; 56 km WNW of Siauliai; 56°14'/22°31'; GUM3, HSL, JGFF, LDL, SF, YL.

Vielbassen, (Kielbaszyn?); PHP4. This town was not found in BGN gazetteers under the given spelling.

Vielipoli, *see* Wielopole Skrzynskie.

Vielishev, *see* Waliszew.

Vielizh, *see* Velizh.

Vielun, *see* Velyun.

Vienna, *see* Wien.

Viereth, Germ.; 56 km NNW of Nurnberg; 49°56'/10°47'; PHGB.

Viernheim, Germ.; pop. 100; 69 km S of Frankfurt am Main; 49°32'/08°35'; JGFF, LDS.

Viersen, Germ.; pop. 140; 50 km WNW of Koln; 51°15'/06°23'; GED.

Vierzhbinik, *see* Wierzbnik.

Vieshmezhitz, *see* Wysmierzyce.

Viesintai, *see* Viesintos.

Viesintos, Lith. (Veshinta, Viesintai, Vishinta); pop. 188; 107 km E of Siauliai; 55°42'/24°59'; GUM5, LDL, SF, YL.

Viesite, Lat. (Eckengraf, Wessen); pop. 187; 82 km WNW of

Daugavpils; 56°21'/25°33'; PHLE.

Viesites, Lat.; pop. 187; 126 km ENE of Riga; 57°14'/26°03'.

Vietalva, Lat.; pop. 3; 107 km NW of Daugavpils; 56°44'/25°46'.

Vietz, *see* Witnica.

Vievirzenai, *see* Veivirzenai.

Vievis, Lith. (Veviya); pop. 304; 38 km W of Vilnius; 54°46'/24°48'; GUM4, GUM5, HSL, SF, YL.

Viforoasa, Rom. (Havadto); pop. 24; 94 km ESE of Cluj; 46°26'/24°48'.

Vigantpetend, Hung. (Zalapetend); pop. 3; 75 km NNE of Nagykanizsa; 46°58'/17°38'.

Vigoda, *see* Vygoda.

Viile Apei, Rom. (Apahegy); pop. 9; 114 km NNW of Cluj; 47°46'/23°18'.

Viishora, Mold. (Viisoara); pop. 24; 126 km WNW of Kishinev; 47°37'/27°27'; JGFF.

Viisoara, *see* Viishora.

Vijnicioara, *see* Vizhnichioara Mika.

Vijnita, *see* Vizhnitsa.

Viktoruv, Ukr. (Wiktorow); pop. 76; 101 km SE of Lvov; 49°03'/24°38'.

Vilag, *see* Svetlice.

Vilagos, HSL. A number of towns share this name. It was not possible to determine from available information which one is being referenced.

Vilaka, Lat. (Mariengauzen, Marienhausen, Marinhoiz, Mariyanovo, Vilakas, Vilaki, Viliaki, Vilyaka); pop. 510; 163 km NNE of Daugavpils; 57°11'/27°41'; COH, HSL, LDL, PHLE, SF.

Vilakas, *see* Vilaka.

Vilaki, *see* Vilaka.

Vilan, *see* Veliuona.

Vilanec, Cz. (Willenz); 82 km W of Brno; 49°20'/15°35'; HSL.

Vilani, Lat. (Velena, Veliony, Vileni, Vilenu, Vilion, Wellan); pop. 396; 82 km N of Daugavpils; 56°33'/26°57'; PHLE, SF.

Vilanov, *see* Wilanow.

Vilaucea, *possibly* Vilyavche.

Vilbel, *see* Bad Vilbel.

Vilce, Lat.; pop. 1; 75 km SSW of Riga; 56°25'/23°33'.

Vildstejn, *see* Skalna.

Vileika, *see* Naujoji Vilnia.

Vileni, *see* Vilani.

Vilenu, *see* Vilani.

Vileny, *see* Veliuona.

Vileyka, Byel. (Wilejka); pop. 710; 82 km NW of Minsk; 54°30'/26°55'; COH, EDRD, GUM3, GUM4, GUM5, GYLA, JGFF, SF, YB.

Vilhovitz, *see* Vilkovtsy.

Viliaki, *see* Vilaka.

Viliampol, *see* Vilijampole.

Vilice, Cz.; pop. 9; 62 km SE of Praha; 49°34'/14°52'.

Vilich Rheindorf, Germ.; 26 km SE of Koln; 50°45'/07°08'; GED.

Vilietchka, *see* Wieliczka.

Vilijampole, Lith. (Viliampol, Wiliampole); 6 km NW of Kaunas; 54°55'/23°53'; EDRD, FRG, JGFF, LDL.

Vilion, *see* Vilani.

Vilitsa, Ukr. (Wilica); pop. 10; 182 km N of Lvov; 51°29'/24°03'.

Viliya, Ukr. (Wilja); pop. 6; 50 km S of Rovno; 50°12'/26°17'.

Viliya (near Kremenets), Ukr.; pop. 20; 69 km S of Rovno; 50°03'/25°54'.

Viliya (near Ostrog), Ukr.; pop. 24; 50 km S of Rovno; 50°12'/26°17'.

Viljandi, Est. (Fellin); pop. 121; 62 km W of Tartu; 58°24'/25°36'; PHLE.

Viljevo, Yug.; pop. 6; 163 km E of Zagreb; 45°45'/18°04'.

Vilkamir, *see* Ukmerge.

Vilkatch, *see* Wielkie Oczy.

Vilkavisk, *see* Vilkaviskis.

Vilkaviskis, Lith. (Vilkavisk, Vilkovishk, Vilkovishki, Volkovisk,

Volkovyshki, Wilkowyszki, Wylkowyszki); pop. 3,206; 62 km SW of Kaunas; 54°39'/23°02'; CAHJP, COH, EDRD, EJ, GUM3, HSL, HSL2, JGFF, SF, WS, YL. *See also* Volkovysk.

Vilkene, Lat.; pop. 2; 75 km NNE of Riga; 57°37'/24°34'.

Vilkhovits, *see* Vilkovtsy.

Vilki, *see* Vilkija.

Vilkija, Lith. (Vilki); pop. 829; 32 km WNW of Kaunas; 55°03'/23°35'; GUM5, HSL, JGFF, SF, YL.

Vilkmerge, *see* Ukmerge.

Vilkomierz, *see* Ukmerge.

Vil Komir, *see* Ukmerge.

Vilkomir, *see* Ukmerge.

Vilkovishk, *see* Vilkaviskis.

Vilkovishki, *see* Vilkaviskis.

Vilkovisk, *see* Volkovysk.

Vilkovo, Ukr. (Valcov); pop. 176; 150 km SSW of Odessa; 45°24'/29°35'.

Vilkovtsy, Ukr. (Irhocz, Irholch, Irholcz, Irholo, Vilhovitz, Vilkhovits, Vulchovce, Vulkhovtse); 133 km WSW of Chernovtsy; 48°01'/24°10'; LYV, SM.

Villach, Aus.; pop. 26; 133 km SW of Graz; 46°36'/13°50'; GUM5.

Villany, Hung.; pop. 81; 126 km ESE of Nagykanizsa; 45°52'/18°27'; PHH.

Villanykovesd, Hung.; pop. 2; 126 km ESE of Nagykanizsa; 45°53'/18°26'.

Villigen, Germ. PHGBW. This town was not found in BGN gazetteers under the given spelling.

Villingen, Germ. (Wellingen?); pop. 56; 94 km SSW of Stuttgart; 48°04'/08°28'; EJ, HSL.

Villmar, Germ.; pop. 30; 50 km WNW of Frankfurt am Main; 50°23'/08°12'; GUM5, JGFF.

Vilmany, Hung.; 50 km NNE of Miskolc; 48°25'/21°14'; HSL.

Vilna, *see* Vilnius.

Vilnia, *see* Vilnius.

Vilnius, Lith. (Vilna, Vilnia, Vilno, Vilnyus, Wilna, Wilno); pop. 55,006; 94 km E of Kaunas; 54°41'/25°19'; AMG, CAHJP, COH, EJ, FRG, GA, GUM3, GUM4, GUM5, GUM6, HSL, HSL2, ISH1, ISH2, ISH3, JGFF, LDL, LYV, PHP1,

Vilna (Vilnius), Lithuania: Peddler in the Jewish ghetto.

375

PHP2, PHP3, PHP4, SF, YB, YL.

Vilno, *see* Vilnius.

Vilnyus, *see* Vilnius.

Vilok, Ukr. (Tisza Ujlak, Vylok); 214 km SSW of Lvov; 48°06'/22°50'; AMG, GUM3, HSL2, JGFF.

Vilon, *see* Veliuona.

Vilonya, Hung.; pop. 2; 88 km SW of Budapest; 47°07'/18°04'.

Vilova, *see* Vilovo.

Vilovo, Yug. (Vilova); 56 km NW of Beograd; 45°15'/20°10'; HSL.

Vilsbiburg, Germ.; 62 km NE of Munchen; 48°27'/12°21'; PHGB.

Vilseck, Germ.; pop. 6; 56 km NE of Nurnberg; 49°37'/11°48'; PHGB.

Vilshana, *see* Olshana.

Vilshofen, Germ.; pop. 21; 133 km NE of Munchen; 48°38'/13°11'; GUM3, PHGB.

Vilyaka, *see* Vilaka.

Vilyampolskaya Sloboda, Lith. (Slobodka, Slobodke); 6 km NNE of Kaunas; 54°55'/23°55'; COH, EDRD, FRG, HSL, LDL, SF.

Vilyavche, Ukr. (Vilaucea?); pop. 320; 38 km W of Chernovtsy; 48°20'/25°22'.

Vima Mare, Rom.; pop. 4; 75 km N of Cluj; 47°23'/23°43'.

Vima Mica, Rom. (Dragavilma); pop. 6; 75 km N of Cluj; 47°24'/23°43'.

Vimperk, Cz.; pop. 80; 126 km S of Praha; 49°03'/13°47'.

Vinac, Yug.; pop. 2; 202 km SE of Zagreb; 44°16'/17°17'.

Vinar, Hung.; pop. 4; 107 km N of Nagykanizsa; 47°19'/17°17'.

Vindava, *see* Ventspils.

Vindiceni, *see* Vendichany.

Vindoi, *see* Ventspils.

Vindornyafok, Hung.; pop. 2; 50 km N of Nagykanizsa; 46°51'/17°11'.

Vindornyalak, Hung.; pop. 1; 56 km N of Nagykanizsa; 46°53'/17°12'.

Vindornyaszollos, Hung.; pop. 4; 56 km N of Nagykanizsa; 46°54'/17°10'.

Vingard, Rom.; 88 km SSE of Cluj; 46°01'/23°45'; HSL.

Vinica, Yug. (Nyek); pop. 23; 82 km E of Skopje; 41°53'/22°30'; HSL.

Vinif, *see* Vonigovo.

Viniki, *see* Vinniki.

Vinitza, *see* Vinnitsa.

Vinkovci, Yug.; pop. 647; 139 km WNW of Beograd; 45°17'/18°49'; COH, HSL, PHY.

Vinkovitz, *see* Vinkovtsy.

Vinkovtsy, Ukr. (Vinkovitz, Vonkovtsy); pop. 1,854; 94 km WSW of Vinnitsa; 49°02'/27°14'; JGFF, LDL, SF.

Vinksniniai, Lith. (Winkshnin); 101 km ENE of Siauliai; 56°13'/24°54'; JGFF.

Vinniki, Ukr. (Viniki, Winniki); pop. 250; 13 km E of Lvov; 49°49'/24°08'; AMG, EGRS, GUM4, GUM5, GUM6, HSL, PHP2, SF.

Vinniki (near Drogobych), Ukr.; pop. 44; 75 km SW of Lvov; 49°24'/23°16'.

Vinnitsa, Ukr. (Vinitza, Winnica, Winnitsa, Winniza); pop. 21,812; 139 km WNW of Uman; 49°14'/28°29'; EDRD, EJ, GUM3, GUM4, GUM5, HSL, HSL2, JGFF, LDL, PHP2, SF, YB.

Vinograd, USSR; pop. 1,108; EDRD, JGFF. A number of towns share this name. It was not possible to determine from available information which one is being referenced.

Vinograd (near Tlumach), Ukr. (Winograd); pop. 70; 101 km WNW of Chernovtsy; 48°45'/24°46'.

Vinogradnoye, Ukr. (Hasan Batar); pop. 4; 150 km SW of Odessa; 45°48'/29°00'.

Vinogradov, Ukr. (Beregszollos, Bialostok, Nagyszollos, Sasvar, Selish, Sevliush, Sevljus, Sewlusz, Sollos, Szollos, Winogradow); pop. 8,424; 202 km S of Lvov; 48°09'/23°02'; AMG, COH, EDRD, EJ, GUM3, GUM4, GUM6, HSL,

HSL2, JGFF, LDL, YB.

Vinogradovka, Ukr. (Burgugi); pop. 15; 126 km SW of Odessa; 45°50'/29°23'.

Vinoj, *see* Vinozh.

Vinovi, *see* Czechowka Dolna.

Vinozh, Ukr. (Vinoj); 82 km SSW of Vinnitsa; 48°42'/27°42'; PHR1.

Vintileanca, *see* Vitelyuvka.

Vintu de Jos, Rom. (Alvinc, Vintul de Jos); 88 km S of Cluj; 46°00'/23°28'; HSL, PHR1.

Vintul de Jos, *see* Vintu de Jos.

Vintul de Sus, Rom. (Felvincz); HSL. This pre-World War I community was not found in BGN gazetteers.

Vionzova, Ukr. (Wiazowa); pop. 23; 32 km N of Lvov; 50°07'/23°59'.

Viragos, Hung.; pop. 6; 133 km SW of Szeged; 45°53'/18°29'.

Virbain, *see* Virbalis.

Virbalin, *see* Virbalis.

Virbalis, Lith. (Verbal, Verzhbelova, Verzhboloro, Verzhbolov, Virbain, Virbalin, Virbaln, Virbolin, Wierzbolow, Wirballen); pop. 1,233; 75 km SW of Kaunas; 54°38'/22°49'; EJ, GUM5, HSL, HSL2, JGFF, LDL, SF, YL.

Virbaln, *see* Virbalis.

Virbolin, *see* Virbalis.

Virchow, *see* Wierzchowo.

Virdayn Katan, *see* Kisvarda.

Virek, *see* Wyryki.

Virena, *see* Irena.

Virga, Lat.; pop. 8; 170 km WSW of Riga; 56°29'/21°25'.

Virismort, Rom. (Tiszavere, Tiszaveresmart, Wiresmort); pop. 98; 139 km N of Cluj; 47°57'/23°58'; GUM4, PHR2, SM.

Viroshov, *see* Wieruszow.

Virovitica, Yug. (Verotze); pop. 233; 107 km ENE of Zagreb; 45°50'/17°23'; PHY.

Virsoli, Rom. (Varsolt, Virsolt); pop. 23; 69 km WNW of Cluj; 47°12'/22°56'.

Virsolt, *see* Virsoli.

Visakio Ruda, Lith. (Visoki Ruda, Vysoka Ruda, Wysoka Ruda); pop. 80; 38 km SW of Kaunas; 54°48'/23°26'; LDL, SF.

Visa Orom, *see* Ruscova.

Visaytz, *see* Vezaiciai.

Visea, Rom.; pop. 4; 26 km NE of Cluj; 46°52'/23°52'.

Visegrad, Yug.; pop. 107; 150 km SSW of Beograd; 43°48'/19°17'; PHY.

Viseu de Jos, Rom. (Alsoviso, Unter Wisho, Viseul de Jos); pop. 604; 126 km NNE of Cluj; 47°44'/24°22'; EJ, GUM3, HSL, SM.

Viseu de Mijloc, Rom. (Kozepviso, Mitel Wisho, Viseul de Mijloc); pop. 530; 126 km NNE of Cluj; 47°43'/24°24'; EJ, SM.

Viseu de Sus, Rom. (Felshevisho, Ober Visho, Ober Wisho, Oyber Visheve, Vishya, Viso); pop. 3,734; 126 km NNE of Cluj; 47°43'/24°26'; AMG, EJ, GUM4, GUM6, HSL, LDL, PHR2, SM.

Viseul de Jos, *see* Viseu de Jos.

Viseul de Mijloc, *see* Viseu de Mijloc.

Visha Orom, *see* Ruscova.

Vishay, *see* Veisiejai.

Vishaya, *see* Veisiejai.

Vishegrod, *see* Wyszogrod.

Vishegrodek, *see* Vyshgorodok.

Vishenka, Ukr. (Wiszenka); pop. 36; 56 km WSW of Lvov; 49°42'/23°14'.

Vishenka Mala, Ukr.; pop. 84; 38 km WNW of Lvov; 50°04'/23°37'.

Vishenki, (Wiszenki);

Vishev, Byel. (Vishuv, Wiszow); pop. 20; 133 km NNW of Pinsk; 53°14'/25°32'.

Vishinki, *see* Wiszenki.

Vishinta, *see* Viesintos.

Vishkovo, Ukr. (Viskovo, Vyskovo, Vyskovo nad Tisou); 189 km WSW of Chernovtsy; 48°03'/23°25'; AMG, SM.

Vishky, *see* Viski.

Vishnava, *see* Vishnevo.

Vishnev, *see* Vishnevo.

Vishneva, *see* Vishnevo.

Vishnevets, Ukr. (Vishnevits, Vishniets, Vishnivitz, Vishnyovyets, Wisnievicze, Wisniowiec, Wisniowiec Nowy, Wisnowiec); pop. 2,825; 88 km SSW of Rovno; 49°54'/25°45'; EDRD, EGRS, EJ, FRG, GUM3, HSL, JGFF, LDL, LYV, SF, YB.

Vishnevits, *see* Vishnevets.

Vishnevka, Mold. (Visinesti); pop. 76; 82 km S of Kishinev; 46°20'/28°27'.

Vishnevo, Byel. (Vishnava, Vishnev, Vishneva, Vishniva, Viszniew, Wisznievo, Wiszniew, Wiszniewo); pop. 579; 94 km W of Minsk; 54°08'/26°14'; EDRD, GUM3, GUM4, HSL, LDL, SF, SF, YB.

Vishnevoye, Ukr. (Noul Caragaci); pop. 15; 107 km SSW of Odessa; 45°48'/29°47'.

Vishnich Novy, *see* Wisnicz Nowy.

Vishniets, *see* Vishnevets.

Vishnits, *see* Wisnicz Nowy.

Vishnitz, *see* Wisnicz Nowy.

Vishnitza, *see* Wisznice.

Vishniva, *see* Vishnevo.

Vishnivchik, Ukr. (Wisniowczyk); pop. 73; 114 km NNW of Chernovtsy; 49°14'/25°22'.

Vishnivchik (near Peremyshlyany), Ukr.; pop. 16; 56 km E of Lvov; 49°42'/24°45'.

Vishnivitz, *see* Vishnevets.

Vishnova, *see* Wisniowa.

Vishnyovyets, *see* Vishnevets.

Vishnyuv, Ukr. (Wiszniow); pop. 50; 150 km N of Lvov; 51°12'/24°02'.

Vishogrod, *see* Wyszogrod.

Vishogrud, *see* Wyszogrod.

Vishogrudek, *see* Vyshgorodok.

Vishtenitz, *see* Vistytis.

Vishtinetz, *see* Vistytis.

Vishtinits, *see* Vistytis.

Vishuv, *see* Vishev.

Vishya, *see* Viseu de Sus.

Visinesti, *see* Vishnevka.

Visk, *see* Vyskovce nad Iplom.

Viski, Lat. (Vishky, Visku); pop. 529; 26 km NE of Daugavpils; 56°03'/26°47'; JGFF, PHLE, SF.

Viskit, *see* Wiskitki.

Viskovo, *see* Vishkovo.

Visku, *see* Viski.

Vislava, Cz.; 75 km NNE of Kosice; 49°17'/21°40'; HSL.

Viso, *see* Viseu de Sus.

Visoca, *see* Vysoka.

Visoka D Lita, *see* Vysokoye.

Visoka Litovsk, *see* Vysokoye.

Visoka Mazovietzk, *see* Wysokie Mazowieckie.

Visoke Dlita, *see* Vysokoye.

Visoke Litovsk, *see* Vysokoye.

Visoke Mazovyetsk, *see* Wysokie Mazowieckie.

Visoki, *see* Wysokie Mazowieckie.

Visokidvar, *see* Aukstadvaris.

Visoki Dvor, *see* Aukstadvaris.

Visokidvor, *see* Aukstadvaris.

Visokie Litevskie, *see* Vysokoye.

Visokie Mazovyetsk, *see* Wysokie Mazowieckie.

Visoki Ruda, *see* Visakio Ruda.

Visoko, Yug.; pop. 113; 208 km SW of Beograd; 43°59'/18°11'; COH, PHY.

Visokoya, *see* Vysokoye.

Visonta, Hung.; pop. 15; 69 km SW of Miskolc; 47°47'/20°02'; HSL.

Visooroszi, *see* Ruscova.

Visotsk, *see* Vysotsk.

Visotzk, *see* Vysotsk.

Visotzki Vizhna, *see* Verkhneye Vysotskoye.

Viso Volgy, *see* Valea Viseului.

Visovolgy, *see* Valea Viseului.

Viss, Hung.; pop. 19; 56 km ENE of Miskolc; 48°13'/21°31'.

Vistytis, Lith. (Vishtenitz, Vishtinetz, Vishtinits, Wisztyniec); pop. 222; 94 km SW of Kaunas; 54°27'/22°43'; HSL, HSL2, JGFF, LDL, SF, YL.

Viszniew, *see* Vishnevo.

Vita, Rom.; pop. 16; 50 km NE of Cluj; 47°02'/24°09'.

Vitaz, Cz.; 38 km NW of Kosice; 48°58'/20°57'; JGFF.

Vitchevka, Ukr. (Wiczowka); pop. 66; 139 km N of Rovno; 51°50'/26°18'.

Vitebsk, Byel. (Witebsk); pop. 37,013; 221 km NE of Minsk; 55°12'/30°11'; AMG, EDRD, EJ, GUM3, GUM4, GUM5, GUM6, HSL, HSL2, JGFF, LDL, LYV, PHLE, PHP3, SF, YB.

Vitelevka, *see* Vitelyuvka.

Vitelyuvka, Ukr. (Vintileanca, Vitelevka); pop. 24; 13 km NW of Chernovtsy; 48°24'/25°48'.

Vititchna, *see* Wytyczno.

Vitka, Hung.; pop. 96; 114 km E of Miskolc; 48°06'/22°19'; HSL, JGFF, LDS, PHH.

Vitkov, *see* Novyy Vitkov.

Vitkovice, Cz. (Witkowitz); pop. 689; 139 km NE of Brno; 49°49'/18°16'; HSL.

Vitkuv Novy, *see* Novyy Vitkov.

Vitnyed, Hung.; pop. 5; 133 km N of Nagykanizsa; 47°35'/16°59'.

Vitrupes, Lat.; pop. 2; 56 km SSW of Riga; 56°33'/23°32'.

Vittencz, LDL. This pre-World War I community was not found in BGN gazetteers.

Vivikoni, GUM3, GUM4, GUM5. This town was not found in BGN gazetteers under the given spelling.

Vizakna, *see* Ocna Sibiului.

Vizhgorodok, *see* Vyshgorodok.

Vizhna, *see* Wizna.

Vizhna Apsha, *see* Verkhneye Vodyanoye.

Vizhnichioara Mika, Ukr. (Vijnicioara, Vizhnichiora Mika); pop. 227; 56 km WSW of Chernovtsy; 48°12'/25°12'; PHR2.

Vizhnichiora Mika, *see* Vizhnichioara Mika.

Vizhnitsa, Ukr. (Vijnita, Viznits, Wiznitz); pop. 2,666; 56 km WSW of Chernovtsy; 48°15'/25°11'; COH, EDRD, EJ, GUM4, GYLA, HSL, HSL2, JGFF, LDL, PHP2, PHP3, PHR2, SF.

Vizhnitz, *see* Wisnicz Nowy.

Vizhon, *see* Wizajny.

Vizhun, *see* Vyzuonos.

Vizina, Cz.; pop. 4; 38 km SSW of Praha; 49°50'/14°06'.

Vizion, *see* Vyzuonos.

Vizkoz, *see* Soyma.

Vizmberk, *see* Loucna nad Desnou.

Vizna, *see* Wisna.

Viznits, *see* Vizhnitsa.

Vizounous, *see* Vyzuonos.

Vizovice, Cz. (Wisowitz); pop. 50; 88 km ENE of Brno; 49°13'/17°51'.

Vizslas, Hung.; pop. 6; 69 km WSW of Miskolc; 48°03'/19°49'.

Vizsoly, Hung.; pop. 50; 45 km NE of Miskolc; 48°23'/21°13'; HSL, PHH.

Vizvar, Hung.; pop. 9; 45 km SE of Nagykanizsa; 46°05'/17°14'; HSL.

Vlachovo, Cz. (Olahpatak); 62 km W of Kosice; 48°47'/20°25'; HSL.

Vladicina, *see* Vladychen.

Vladicini, *see* Vladychen.

Vladikavkaz, *see* Ordzhonikidze.

Vladimir, COH. A number of towns share this name. It was not possible to determine from available information which one is being referenced.

Vladimirci, Yug.; pop. 3; 62 km SW of Beograd; 44°37'/19°47'.

Vladimirets, Ukr. (Vlodimiretz, Vlodzhimyerzets, Wladimirez, Wlodzimierzec); pop. 1,263; 94 km N of Rovno; 51°25'/26°08'; COH, FRG, GUM3, GUM4, GUM5, JGFF, LDL, LYV, SF, YB.

Vladimirovo, Bulg. (Liuta); 101 km N of Sofija; 43°32'/23°23'; HSL.

Vladimir Volinski, *see* Vladimir Volynskiy.

Vladimir Volynskiy, Ukr. (Ladmir, Lodmer, Lodomeria, Ludomir, Vladimir Volinski, Vlodzimyerz, Wlodzimierz Wolynski); pop. 5,917; 114 km N of Lvov; 50°51'/24°20'; AMG, CAHJP, COH, EJ, GUM3, GUM4, GUM5, GUM6, HSL, JGFF, LDL, PHP2, SF, YB.

Vladislauca, Rom. PHR1. This town was not found in BGN gazetteers under the given spelling.

Vladislavov, *see* Kudirkos Naumiestis.

Vladislavov Rusochitza, *see* Russocice.

Vladnik, *see* Novyye Veledniki.

Vladova, *see* Wlodawa.

Vladovka, Ukr. BGN lists two possible localities with this name located at 47°10'/35°59' and 50°55'/29°02'. JGFF.

Vladychen, Ukr. (Imputita, Vladicina, Vladicini); pop. 3; 195 km SW of Odessa; 45°34'/28°36'.

Vlaha, Rom. (Magyarfenes); 13 km SW of Cluj; 46°42'/23°27'; HSL.

Vlasenica, Yug.; pop. 60; 146 km SW of Beograd; 44°11'/18°57'; EDRD, PHY.

Vlasim, Cz.; pop. 87; 56 km SE of Praha; 49°42'/14°54'.

Vlasinesti, Rom.; pop. 26; 101 km NW of Iasi; 47°56'/26°53'.

Vlasovtse, Byel. (Wlasowce); pop. 33; 50 km SW of Pinsk; 51°59'/25°28'.

Vlatzlavek, *see* Wloclawek.

Vlcany, Cz. (Farkasd, Farkazd); pop. 171; 62 km E of Bratislava; 48°02'/17°57'; COH, HSL.

Vlceves, Cz.; pop. 3; 88 km SSE of Praha; 49°21'/14°54'.

Vlkancice, Cz.; pop. 1; 38 km ESE of Praha; 49°54'/14°54'.

Vlkonice, Cz.; pop. 56; A number of towns share this name. It was not possible to determine from available information which one is being referenced.

Vlkosovice, Cz.; pop. 43; 88 km SSE of Praha; 49°20'/14°58'.

Vlkyna, Cz. (Velkenye); 88 km SW of Kosice; 48°17'/20°18'; HSL.

Vlkys, Cz.; pop. 16; 107 km SW of Praha; 49°43'/13°05'.

Vlodava, *see* Wlodawa.

Vlodavi, *see* Wlodawa.

Vlodavka, Byel. (Vlodofka, Wlodawka); pop. 271; 182 km SW of Pinsk; 51°32'/23°34'; HSL, HSL2, JGFF, LDL, SF.

Vlodeve, *see* Wlodawa.

Vlodimiretz, *see* Vladimirets.

Vlodislovov, *see* Kudirkos Naumiestis.

Vlodofka, *see* Vlodavka.

Vlodova, *see* Wlodawa.

Vlodzhimyerzets, *see* Vladimirets.

Vlodzimyerz, *see* Vladimir Volynskiy.

Vloshtchovi, *see* Wloszczowa.

Vlotho, Germ.; pop. 70; 69 km SW of Hannover; 52°10'/08°51'.

Vlotslavek, *see* Wloclawek.

Vloyn, *see* Vranov nad Toplou.

Vobolnik, *see* Vabalninkas.

Vochov, Cz.; pop. 2; 94 km SW of Praha; 49°46'/13°17'.

Vocin, Yug.; pop. 2; 120 km E of Zagreb; 45°37'/17°32'; PHY.

Vodhany, *see* Vodnany.

Vodinci, Yug. (Vodjinci); pop. 9; 150 km WNW of Beograd; 45°17'/18°37'.

Vodislav, *see* Wodzislaw.

Vodislov, *see* Wodzislaw.

Vodjinci, *see* Vodinci.

Vodnany, Cz. (Vodhany); pop. 114; 107 km S of Praha; 49°09'/14°11'; JGFF.

Vodniki, Ukr. (Wodniki); pop. 48; 26 km ESE of Lvov; 49°42'/24°14'.

Vodslivy, Cz.; pop. 2; 38 km ESE of Praha; 49°51'/14°50'.

Vodyany, Mold. (Vaden, Vadeni Soroca); pop. 24; 126 km NNW of Kishinev; 48°01'/28°14'.

Vodzislav, *see* Wodzislaw.

Voelkermarkt, *see* Volkermarkt.

Voevodeasa, Rom.; pop. 66; 150 km WNW of Iasi; 47°48'/25°46'.

Vohburg, *see* Vohburg an der Donau.

Vohburg an der Donau, Germ. (Vohburg); 75 km N of Munchen; 48°46'/11°37'; PHGB.

Vohin, *see* Wohyn.

Vohl, Germ.; pop. 35; 126 km N of Frankfurt am Main; 51°12'/08°56'; JGFF.

Voinescu, *see* Pobeda.

Voiniceni, Rom. (Mezoszabad); 75 km E of Cluj; 46°37'/24°32'; HSL.

Voinilov, *see* Voynilov.

Voitinel, Rom.; pop. 1; 157 km WNW of Iasi; 47°53'/25°46'.

Voitovca, *see* Voytovka.

Voitzeshkov, *see* Wojcieszkow.

Voivozi, Rom. (Almaszeg); pop. 24; 101 km WNW of Cluj; 47°13'/22°24'; HSL.

Vojakovac, Yug.; pop. 4; 56 km NE of Zagreb; 46°05'/16°36'.

Vojany, Cz. (Vajan, Vajany); pop. 61; 56 km E of Kosice; 48°34'/21°59'; HSL.

Vojka, Cz. (Veke); 56 km ESE of Kosice; 48°28'/21°55'; GUM5, HSL.

Vojkov, Cz.; pop. 76; 56 km S of Praha; 49°39'/14°31'.

Vojnice, Cz. (Batorkeszi, Batorove Kesy); pop. 130; 101 km ESE of Bratislava; 47°50'/18°25'; HSL, LDL, LDS.

Vojnilow, *see* Voynilov.

Vokany, Hung.; pop. 8; 120 km ESE of Nagykanizsa; 45°54'/18°20'.

Voke, Lith. (Waka); 19 km SW of Vilnius; 54°38'/25°05'; AMG.

Vola, *see* Wola Zelechowska.

Vola Kshishtoporska, *see* Wola Krzysztoporska.

Volanka, Ukr. (Wolanka); 75 km SSW of Lvov; 49°18'/23°26'; JGFF.

Volborzh, *see* Wolborz.

Volbrom, *see* Wolbrom.

Volchansk, Ukr. (Wolczansk); pop. 223; 62 km NE of Kharkov; 50°18'/36°57'.

Volchatyche, Ukr. (Wolczatycze); pop. 31; 56 km SE of Lvov; 49°24'/24°20'.

Volche, Ukr. (Wolcza Dolna); pop. 21; 107 km SW of Lvov; 49°13'/22°53'.

Volchi, Ukr. (Valtcha, Wolcze); pop. 86; 126 km WSW of Chernovtsy; 48°03'/24°19'; HSL, SF.

Volchin, Byel. (Voltchin, Wolczyn); pop. 180; 189 km W of Pinsk; 52°17'/23°19'; AMG, COH, HSL, LDL, SF.

Volchinets (Hotin), Ukr. (Volcineti Hotin); pop. 20; 75 km ENE of Chernovtsy; 48°27'/26°55'.

Volchinets (Lapusna), Ukr. (Volcineyi Lapusna); pop. 162; 38 km S of Chernovtsy; 48°01'/25°57'.

Volchinets (Stanislowow), Ukr.; pop. 55; 114 km WNW of Chernovtsy; 48°57'/24°45'.

Volchishchovitsa, Ukr. (Wolczyszczowice); pop. 29; 50 km WSW of Lvov; 49°44'/23°18'.

Volchkov Perevoz, Ukr. (Wilczy Przewoz); pop. 18; 150 km N of Lvov; 51°11'/23°47'.

Volchkovtsy, Ukr. (Wolczkowce); pop. 62; 45 km WNW of Chernovtsy; 48°28'/25°24'.

Volchovec, GUM3. This town was not found in BGN gazetteers under the given spelling.

Volchowo, LDL. This pre-World War I community was not found in BGN gazetteers.

Volcineti Hotin, *see* Volchinets (Hotin).

Volcineyi Lapusna, *see* Volchinets (Lapusna).

Volcsej, Hung.; pop. 7; 120 km NNW of Nagykanizsa; 47°29'/16°46'.

Volduchy, Cz.; pop. 3; 69 km SW of Praha; 49°47'/13°38'.

Volec, Cz.; 82 km ENE of Praha; 50°07'/15°34'; HSL.

Volegotsulovo, *see* Dolinskoye.

Voletice, Cz.; pop. 1; 94 km NW of Brno; 49°55'/16°02'.

Voletiny, Cz.; pop. 5; 120 km NE of Praha; 50°35'/15°57'.

Volgograd, USSR (Stalingrad, Tsaritsyn, Tsarizin); pop. 1,985; 549 km ESE of Voronezh; 48°45'/44°30'; GUM3, GUM4, GUM6, HSL, LDL.

Volia, *see* Lunna.

Volintiri, *see* Volontirovka.

Volintza, *see* Volyntsy.

Volitsa, (Wolica);

Volitsa (near Dobromil), Ukr.; pop. 9; 62 km WSW of Lvov; 49°48'/23°05'.

Volitsa (near Nesterov), Ukr.; pop. 22; 45 km N of Lvov; 50°14'/24°06'.

Volitsa (near Podgaytsy), Ukr.; pop. 23; 75 km ESE of Lvov; 49°34'/24°56'.

Volitsa (near Skalat), Ukr.; pop. 2; 114 km N of Chernovtsy; 49°16'/26°13'.

Volitsa Derevlyanska, Ukr. (Derevlyany, Derewlany, Wolica Derewianska); pop. 22; 45 km NE of Lvov; 50°02'/24°31'.

Volitsa Gnizdchuvsk, Ukr. (Wolica Hnizdyczowska); pop. 23; A number of towns share this name. It was not possible to determine from available information which one is being referenced.

Volka, *see* Vulka Popinskaya.

Volkach, Germ.; 75 km WNW of Nurnberg; 49°52'/10°14'; PHGB.

Volkany, *see* Vulcan (near Brasov).

Volkavisk, *see* Volkovysk.

Volkermarkt, Aus. (Voelkermarkt); pop. 6; 75 km SW of Graz; 46°39'/14°38'.

Volkershausen, Germ.; 120 km NE of Frankfurt am Main; 50°29'/10°17'; JGFF, LDS.

Volkersleier, Germ.; pop. 36; 82 km ENE of Frankfurt am Main; 50°11'/09°47'; AMG, GUM5, PHGB.

Volkhov, USSR (Volkhovstroy); pop. 20; 120 km E of Leningrad; 59°55'/32°20'.

Volkhovstroy, *see* Volkhov.

Volkmarsen, Germ.; pop. 42; 120 km S of Hannover; 51°24'/09°07'; AMG, HSL, JGFF.

Volkmerz, Germ.; pop. 24; Described in the *Black Book* as being in the Hessen region of Germany, this town was not found in BGN gazetteers.

Volknik, *see* Valkininkas.

Volkolamsk, USSR; pop. 24; This town was not found in BGN gazetteers under the given spelling.

Volkolata, Byel. (Wolkolata); pop. 55; 126 km N of Minsk; 54°56'/27°22'; GUM3.

Volkov, Ukr. (Volkuv, Wolkow); pop. 46; 50 km ESE of Lvov; 49°37'/24°36'.

Volkovintsy, Ukr. (Wolkowinz, Wolkowinzy); 62 km WSW of Vinnitsa; 49°12'/27°40'; EDRD, SF.

Volkovisk, *see* Vilkaviskis.

Volkovonovke, *see* Wolka Wojnowska.

Volkovtse, *see* Volkovtsy.

Volkovtsy, Ukr. (Volkovtse, Wolkowce); pop. 38; 56 km N of Chernovtsy; 48°46'/26°05'; PHP2.

Volkovyshki, *see* Vilkaviskis.

Volkovysk, Byel. (Vilkovisk, Volkavisk, Wolkowysk); pop. 5,130; 163 km WNW of Pinsk; 53°10'/24°28'; AMG, COH, EDRD, EJ, GA, GUM3, GUM4, GUM5, GYLA, HSL, HSL2, JGFF, LDL, LYV, SF, YB. There is also a town in Lithuania called Vilkaviskis.

Volkovyye, Ukr. (Wolkowyje); pop. 112; 69 km SW of Rovno; 50°22'/25°23'.

Volkuv, *see* Volkov.

Volkuv (Lwow), Ukr.; pop. 26; 26 km SSE of Lvov; 49°43'/24°04'.

Vollmerz, Germ.; 69 km NE of Frankfurt am Main; 50°20'/09°35'; JGFF, LDS.

Volma, Byel. (Wolma); pop. 153; 38 km WSW of Minsk; 53°52'/26°57'; COH, SF, YB.

Vol Mar, *see* Valmiera.

Volna, Byel. (Wolna); pop. 21; 107 km SW of Minsk; 53°18'/26°14'.

Volnoye, Ukr. (Iserlia); pop. 8; 139 km SW of Odessa; 45°59'/29°03'.

Volo, *see* Volos.

Voloavele, *see* Volovy.

Voloca pe Derelui, *see* Voloka.

Volochisk, Ukr. (Volotchisk, Woloczysk); pop. 2,068; 126 km S of Rovno; 49°32'/26°10'; HSL, JGFF, PHP2, SF.

Volodarka, Ukr.; 88 km NNW of Uman; 49°31'/29°55'; EDRD, HSL, JGFF, SF.

Volodarsk, *see* Volodarsk Volynskiy.

Volodarsko Tolstovski, USSR; pop. 902; This town was not found in BGN gazetteers under the given spelling.

Volodarskoye, Ukr.; pop. 2,068; 221 km ESE of Dnepropetrovsk; 47°12'/37°20'.

Volodarsk Volynsk, *see* Volodarsk Volynskiy.

Volodarsk Volynskiy, Ukr. (Goroshki, Horoschki, Horoshki, Kotozovo, Kutuzov Volodarsk, Kutuzowe Volodarskoe, Volodarsk, Volodarsk Volynsk); pop. 2,068; 150 km W of Kiyev; 50°36'/28°27'; GUM4, SF.

Volodeni, Mold.; pop. 32; 182 km NW of Kishinev; 48°14'/27°12'.

Voloka, Ukr. (Voloca pe Derelui); pop. 35; 19 km S of Chernovtsy; 48°12'/25°56'; HSL, JGFF.

Volokhi, Ukr. (Wolochy); pop. 13; 62 km N of Chernovtsy; 48°51'/26°12'.

Volomin, *see* Wolomin.

Volonov, *see* Wolanow.

Volontirovka, Mold. (Volintiri, Voluntir, Wolontir); pop. 420; 88 km SE of Kishinev; 46°26'/29°37'; SF, YB.

Volos, Greece (Volo); pop. 948; 146 km S of Thessaloniki; 39°22'/22°57'; CAHJP, GUM4, HSL, JGFF.

Voloshcha, Ukr. (Woloszcza); pop. 36; 50 km SSW of Lvov; 49°30'/23°36'.

Voloshchizna, Ukr. (Woloszczyzna); pop. 27; 32 km SE of Lvov; 49°37'/24°14'.

Volosov, Ukr. (Volosuv, Wolosow); pop. 46; 107 km WNW of Chernovtsy; 48°44'/24°40'.

Volostkov, Ukr. (Volostkuv, Wolostow?); pop. 58; 50 km WSW of Lvov; 49°45'/23°19'.

Volostkuv, *see* Volostkov.

Volosuv, *see* Volosov.

Volosuvka, Ukr. (Wolosowka); pop. 31; 88 km E of Lvov; 49°40'/25°13'.

Volosyanka, Ukr. (Wolosianka); pop. 67; 126 km S of Lvov; 48°47'/23°26'; HSL, PHP2.

Volotchisk, *see* Volochisk.

Volovat, Rom.; pop. 9; 146 km WNW of Iasi; 47°49'/25°54'.

Volove, *see* Mezhgorye.

Volovec, *see* Volovets.

Volovel, Byel. (Wolowil); pop. 65; 82 km W of Pinsk; 52°08'/24°58'.

Volovets, Ukr. (Volovec); pop. 500; 139 km SSW of Lvov; 48°43'/23°11'; AMG.

Volovice, Cz.; 126 km S of Praha; 49°00'/13°58'; AMG.

Volovo, *see* Mezhgorye.

Volovy, Mold. (Voloavele); pop. 16; 126 km NNW of Kishinev; 48°06'/28°18'.

Volozhin, Byel. (Volozhyn, Woloskin, Wolozyn); pop. 1,434; 75 km W of Minsk; 54°05'/26°32'; CAHJP, COH, EJ, FRG, GA, GUM3, GUM4, GUM5, GUM6, GUM6, HSL, HSL2, JGFF, LDL, LYV, PHP4, SF, YB.

Volozhyn, *see* Volozhin.

Volp, *see* Volpa.

Volpa, Byel. (Volp, Wolpa); pop. 941; 182 km NW of Pinsk; 53°22'/24°22'; COH, EJ, GUM3, GUM4, GUM5, HSL, HSL2, JGFF, SF, WS, YB.

Volsvin, Ukr. (Wolswin); pop. 67; 56 km N of Lvov;

50°20'/24°18'.

Voltchin, *see* Volchin.

Voltchkii, Ukr. EDRD. This town was not found in BGN gazetteers under the given spelling.

Voluntir, *see* Volontirovka.

Voluta, Byel. (Woluta); pop. 19; 62 km NE of Pinsk; 52°28'/26°48'.

Volya Arlamovskaya, Ukr. (Arlamowska Wola); pop. 21; 56 km WSW of Lvov; 49°50'/23°14'.

Volya Blazhovska, Ukr. (Wola Blazowska); pop. 41; 82 km SW of Lvov; 49°24'/23°08'.

Volya Gnoynitska, Ukr. (Wola Gnojnicka); pop. 33; 62 km W of Lvov; 49°56'/23°07'.

Volya Vysotska, Ukr. (Wola Wysocka); pop. 45; 32 km NNW of Lvov; 50°05'/23°56'.

Volyne, Cz. (Wolin, Wollin); pop. 67; 114 km S of Praha; 49°10'/13°53'; HSL, HSL2.

Volynhia; Not a town, but a region of the northwestern Ukraine. During the interwar period, it comprised the Polish province of Wolyn.

Volynskiy, *see* Khutor Shevchenko.

Volyntsy, Byel. (Volintza); pop. 457; 88 km N of Gomel; 53°12'/31°00'; LDL, SF.

Volytsya, Ukr. (Wolica Komarowa); pop. 38; 62 km N of Lvov; 50°23'/24°21'.

Vonchotzk, *see* Wachock.

Vondsavek, YB. This town was not found in BGN gazetteers under the given spelling.

Vonigovo, Ukr. (Vajnag, Vinif, Vonihofo, Vonihovo); 176 km WSW of Chernovtsy; 48°04'/23°32'; AMG, JGFF, SM.

Vonihofo, *see* Vonigovo.

Vonihovo, *see* Vonigovo.

Vonkovtsy, *see* Vinkovtsy.

Vonock, Hung.; pop. 3; 107 km N of Nagykanizsa; 47°19'/17°10'.

Vonota, *see* Vainutas.

Vonseva, *see* Wasewo.

Vonsosh, *see* Wasosz.

Vonvolitz, *see* Wawolnica.

Vonvolnits, *see* Wawolnica.

Vonvolnitza, *see* Wawolnica.

Vorancau, *see* Voronkovo.

Vorchin, Ukr. (Worczyn); pop. 2; 120 km N of Lvov; 50°55'/24°13'.

Vorden, Germ.; pop. 221; 114 km W of Hannover; 52°29'/08°06'; LDS.

Vorderberg, Pol.; pop. 55; A number of towns share this name. It was not possible to determine from available information which one is being referenced.

Vorgulintsy, Ukr. (Vorvolintse, Worwolince); pop. 85; 56 km NNW of Chernovtsy; 48°48'/25°44'.

Vorke, *see* Warka.

Vorna, *see* Varniai.

Vorne, *see* Varniai.

Vorni, *see* Varniai.

Vorniceni, Rom. (Vorniceni Dorohoi); pop. 25; 120 km WNW of Iasi; 47°34'/26°08'.

Vorniceni Dorohoi, *see* Vorniceni.

Vorniceni Lapusna, *see* Vornicheny.

Vornicheni, *see* Vornicheny.

Vornicheny, Mold. (Vorniceni Lapusna, Vornicheni); pop. 58; 38 km WNW of Kishinev; 47°09'/28°26'.

Vorobin, Ukr. (Worobin); FRG. This town was not found in BGN gazetteers under the given spelling.

Voroblyachin, Ukr. (Wroblaczyn); pop. 43; 50 km WNW of Lvov; 50°08'/23°28'.

Vorokhta, Ukr. (Worochta); pop. 196; 101 km WSW of Chernovtsy; 48°17'/24°34'; GUM4, GUM5, PHP2.

Vorokomle, Ukr. (Worokomla); pop. 29; 146 km NW of Rovno; 51°42'/25°04'.

Voronchin, Ukr. (Woronczyn); pop. 5; 101 km WNW of Rovno; 50°55'/24°53'.

Voronezh, Ukr. (Woronesch, Woronez); 62 km N of Konotop; 51°46'/33°28'; EDRD, EJ, HSL, LDL, SF.

Voronino, Byel. (Woronino); pop. 8; 101 km NNE of Pinsk; 52°55'/26°40'.

Voronki, Ukr. (Woronki); pop. 21; 107 km N of Rovno; 51°33'/26°06'.

Voronkov, Ukr. (Woronkow); 38 km ESE of Kiyev; 50°13'/30°54'; SF.

Voronkovo, Mold. (Verenkeu, Vorancau); pop. 40; 126 km NNW of Kishinev; 48°05'/28°31'.

Voronok, USSR; pop. 93; 157 km SW of Bryansk; 52°21'/32°34'; LDL, SF.

Voronov, *see* Voronovo.

Voronova, *see* Voronovo.

Voronove, *see* Voronovo.

Voronovita, *see* Voronovitsa (Bessarabia).

Voronovitsa, Ukr.; pop. 1,572; 19 km ESE of Vinnitsa; 49°06'/28°41'.

Voronovitsa (Bessarabia), Ukr. (Voronovita); pop. 12; 62 km NE of Chernovtsy; 48°33'/26°41'.

Voronovo, Byel. (Voronov, Voronova, Voronove, Werenow, Woronowo); 150 km W of Minsk; 54°09'/25°19'; EDRD, GUM3, GUM5, GUM6, JGFF, LDL, LYV, SF, YB.

Vorontsovka, HSL. A number of towns share this name. It was not possible to determine from available information which one is being referenced.

Voronuv, Byel. (Woronow); pop. 980; 150 km W of Minsk; 54°09'/25°19'; COH, HSL.

Voronuv (Stanislawow), Ukr.; pop. 28; 69 km NW of Chernovtsy; 48°45'/25°18'.

Voronyaki, Ukr. (Woroniaki); pop. 26; 62 km E of Lvov; 49°47'/24°54'.

Voropayevo, Byel. (Woropajewo); pop. 31; 146 km NNW of Minsk; 55°09'/27°13'.

Vorosbereny, Hung.; pop. 17; 94 km SW of Budapest; 47°03'/18°01'.

Voroshilovgrad, Ukr. (Lugansk, Lugoj, Lugos, Lugosch, Luhansk, Woroszylowgrad); pop. 7,132; 270 km ESE of Kharkov; 48°34'/39°20'; EJ, GUM4, HSL, JGFF, LDL, PHR1, SF.

Voroshilovka, Ukr. (Varshilovka, Vorosilovca, Woroschilowka); pop. 1,079; 26 km SSW of Vinnitsa; 49°03'/28°20'; LDL, PHR1, SF.

Voroshilovo, Mold. (Dusmani); pop. 27; 133 km WNW of Kishinev; 47°43'/27°28'.

Voroshilovsk, *see* Kommunarsk.

Vorosilovca, *see* Voroshilovka.

Vorosmart, *see* Szabolcsveresmart.

Vorosvar, *see* Pilisvorosvar.

Vorotet, *see* Vorotets.

Vorotets, Mold. (Vorotet); pop. 25; 69 km N of Kishinev; 47°33'/28°52'.

Vorotsevichi, Byel. (Worocewicze); pop. 31; 50 km WSW of Pinsk; 52°06'/25°23'.

Vorru, Hung.; pop. 3; 45 km N of Nagykanizsa; 46°45'/17°02'.

Vors, Hung.; pop. 4; 32 km NNE of Nagykanizsa; 46°40'/17°16'.

Voru, Est. (Verro, Vyru, Werro); pop. 103; 69 km SSE of Tartu; 57°50'/27°03'; JGFF, PHLE.

Vorvolintse, *see* Vorgulintsy.

Vorvorovka, *see* Varvarovka.

Vor Wedenthal, HSL. This pre-World War I community was not found in BGN gazetteers.

Vorzel, Ukr.; pop. 14; 32 km WNW of Kiyev; 50°33'/30°09'.

Vosendorf, Aus.; pop. 20; 13 km S of Wien; 48°07'/16°20'.

Voshchantsy, Ukr. (Woszczance); pop. 29; 50 km SW of Lvov; 49°40'/23°25'.

Voshkavitch, *see* Vashkovtsy.

Voshki, *see* Vaskai.

Voski, *see* Vaskai.

Voslab, *see* Wojslaw.

Voslabeni, *see* Voslobeni.

Voslobeni, Rom. (Voslabeni); pop. 29; 157 km E of Cluj; 46°39'/25°38'.

Votice, Cz. (Wotitz); pop. 116; 56 km SSE of Praha; 49°39'/14°39'; EJ.

Votokom, Hung. LDS. This town was not found in BGN gazetteers under the given spelling.

Votslavsk, *see* Wloclawek.

Voul Romin, (Olahujfalu); HSL. This pre-World War I community was not found in BGN gazetteers.

Voydislav, *see* Wodzislaw.

Voykovitse, Ukr. (Wojkowice); pop. 11; 56 km WSW of Lvov; 49°47'/23°14'.

Voynilov, Ukr. (Voinilov, Vojnilow, Wojnilow); pop. 944; 88 km SE of Lvov; 49°08'/24°30'; EGRS, GYLA, HSL, JGFF, LDL, PHP2, SF.

Voynitch, *see* Wojnicz.

Voynitsa, Ukr. (Wojnica); pop. 6; 114 km NNE of Lvov; 50°47'/24°40'; GUM3.

Voyska, *see* Voyskaya.

Voyskaya, Byel. (Voyska, Wojska); pop. 19; 170 km W of Pinsk; 52°24'/23°38'.

Voyslavitse, Ukr. (Wojslawice); pop. 86; 82 km N of Lvov; 50°34'/24°12'.

Voytovka, Ukr. (Vaytovka, Voitovca); 62 km SW of Uman; 48°25'/29°32'; GUM4, PHR1.

Voyutin, Ukr. (Wojutyn); pop. 32; 88 km W of Rovno; 50°39'/25°00'; GUM3.

Voyutychi, Ukr. (Wojutycze); pop. 29; 69 km SW of Lvov; 49°33'/23°06'.

Voznesensk, Ukr. (Voznessenk, Wozniesiensk); pop. 5,116; 133 km N of Odessa; 47°33'/31°20'; EJ, HSL, JGFF, LDL, SF.

Voznessenk, *see* Voznesensk.

Voznovshchina, Byel. (Voznovshchyzna, Woznowszczyzna); pop. 49; 114 km N of Minsk; 54°50'/27°35'.

Voznovshchyzna, *see* Voznovshchina.

Vrabi, Cz.; pop. 4; 19 km NE of Praha; 50°11'/14°40'.

Vrable, Cz.; pop. 736; 88 km ENE of Bratislava; 48°15'/18°19'; AMG, GUM3, HSL.

Vradievka, *see* Vradiyevka.

Vradiyevka, Ukr. (Vradievka); 107 km SSE of Uman; 47°52'/30°36'; JGFF.

Vrakun, Cz. (Varkony); 45 km ESE of Bratislava; 47°57'/17°36'; HSL, HSL2.

Vrananany, Cz.; pop. 11; 32 km NNW of Praha; 50°19'/14°22'.

Vranceni, *see* Verenchanka.

Vrani, Yug. (Alsovarany); A number of towns share this name. It was not possible to determine from available information which one is being referenced.

Vranik, Yug.; 157 km S of Zagreb; 44°26'/15°42'; HSL.

Vranjevo, *see* Novi Becej.

Vranov, *see* Vranov nad Toplou.

Vranov nad Dyji, Cz.; pop. 98; 69 km SW of Brno; 48°54'/15°49'.

Vranov nad Toplou, Cz. (Frain, Varanno, Vloyn, Vranov); pop. 1,828; 38 km NE of Kosice; 48°54'/21°41'; 38 km NE of Kosice; 48°54'/21°41'; AMG, CAHJP, GUM4, HSL, HSL2, JGFF.

Vrany, Cz.; pop. 5; 38 km WNW of Praha; 50°20'/14°01'.

Vrapce, Yug.; pop. 129; A number of towns share this name. It was not possible to determine from available information which one is being referenced.

Vratsa, Bulg.; pop. 125; 62 km N of Sofija; 43°12'/23°33'; EJ, GUM4.

Vrauceni, *see* Verenchanka.

Vrbanja, Yug.; 126 km W of Beograd; 44°59'/18°56'; HSL.

Vrbas, Yug. (Uj Verbasz, Verbasz?); 107 km NW of Beograd; 45°34'/19°39'; COH, GUM3, HSL, PHY.

Vrbnica, Cz. (Fuzeser); 50 km E of Kosice; 48°41'/21°53'; AMG, HSL.

Vrbovce, Cz. (Verbocz); pop. 61; 75 km N of Bratislava; 48°48'/17°28'; AMG, HSL.

Vrbove, Cz. (Verbo); pop. 600; 75 km NNE of Bratislava; 48°38'/17°44'; CAHJP, COH, GUM4, HSL, HSL2, LDL, YB.

Vrbovec, Cz. (Urbau); 56 km SSW of Brno; 48°49'/16°06'; HSL.

Vrbovsko, Yug.; pop. 14; 82 km SW of Zagreb; 45°22'/15°05'.

Vrcen, Cz.; pop. 9; 88 km SW of Praha; 49°31'/13°37'.

Vrchlabi, Cz.; pop. 111; 101 km NE of Praha; 50°38'/15°36'.

Vrcholtovice, Cz.; pop. 17; 62 km SSE of Praha; 49°36'/14°45'.

Vrdnik, Yug.; pop. 1; 62 km WNW of Beograd; 45°08'/19°47'.

Vreden, Germ.; pop. 44; 126 km N of Koln; 52°02'/06°50'; GED, GUM5.

Vreskovice, Cz.; pop. 2; 107 km SW of Praha; 49°32'/13°16'.

Vrnjci, Yug.; pop. 1; 139 km SSE of Beograd; 43°37'/20°53'.

Vronik, *see* Wronki.

Vrotsuv, Ukr. (Wrocow); pop. 20; 13 km W of Lvov; 49°52'/23°49'.

Vroutek, Cz. (Rudig); pop. 40; 75 km W of Praha; 50°11'/13°23'; HSL.

Vrsac, Yug. (Werschetz); pop. 404; 69 km NE of Beograd; 45°07'/21°18'; CAHJP, PHY.

Vrsce, Cz.; pop. 2; 62 km NE of Praha; 50°19'/15°19'.

Vrskman, Cz.; pop. 1; 82 km WNW of Praha; 50°29'/13°30'.

Vrsta, Yug.; pop. 1; 107 km S of Zagreb; 44°54'/15°50'.

Vrublevshchina, Byel. (Wroblewszczyzna); pop. 11; 69 km N of Minsk; 54°28'/27°35'.

Vrudky, *see* Vrutky.

Vrutice, Cz.; pop. 3; 50 km NNW of Praha; 50°30'/14°17'.

Vrutky, Cz. (Vrudky); pop. 419; 163 km E of Brno; 49°07'/18°55'; GUM4, GUM5.

Vsechromy, Cz.; pop. 4; 19 km SE of Praha; 49°57'/14°39'.

Vsejany, Cz.; pop. 7; 38 km NE of Praha; 50°15'/14°57'.

Vselyub, Byel. (Shelib, Silev, Wsielub); pop. 297; 114 km WSW of Minsk; 53°43'/25°48'; AMG, GUM3, SF, YB.

Vsemyslice, Cz.; pop. 13; 101 km S of Praha; 49°13'/14°21'.

Vseradice, Cz.; pop. 10; 38 km SW of Praha; 49°53'/14°07'; HSL.

Vseruby, Cz.; pop. 44; 94 km SW of Praha; 49°50'/13°15'.

Vsetin, Cz. (Wsetin); pop. 101; 101 km ENE of Brno; 49°20'/18°00'; EJ, HSL.

Vtelno, Cz.; pop. 2; 69 km WNW of Praha; 50°29'/13°40'.

Vuchkovo, Ukr. (Vicski, Vuckovo, Vucskomezo); 163 km S of Lvov; 48°27'/23°32'; SM.

Vuckovo, *see* Vuchkovo.

Vucskomezo, *see* Vuchkovo.

Vukovar, Yug. (Wukowar); pop. 306; 133 km WNW of Beograd; 45°21'/19°00'; GUM4, GUM6, PHY.

Vulcan, Rom. (Vajatjulkan); pop. 341; 157 km S of Cluj; 45°23'/23°16'; GUM3, HSL, PHR1.

Vulcan (near Brasov), Rom. (Volkany); 146 km NNW of Bucuresti; 45°38'/25°25'; HSL, HSL2.

Vulcanesti, *see* Vulkaneshty.

Vulchovce, *see* Vilkovtsy.

Vulka, Ukr. (Wulka); pop. 20; 69 km ESE of Lvov; 49°27'/24°47'.

Vulka Mazovetska, *see* Vulka Mazovetskaya.

Vulka Mazovetskaya, Ukr. (Vulka Mazovetska, Wulka Mazowiecka); pop. 136; 50 km NNW of Lvov; 50°15'/23°52'; PHP2.

Vulkaneshty, Mold. (Vulcanesti); pop. 2; 150 km S of Kishinev; 45°41'/28°24'.

Vulka Popinskaya, Byel. (Volka, Wolka); pop. 49; 62 km WSW of Pinsk; 52°06'/25°09'.

Vulka Ugruska, Ukr. (Wolka Uhruska); pop. 3; 163 km NNW of Lvov; 51°18'/23°39'.

Vulkhovtse, *see* Vilkovtsy.

Vurka, *see* Warka.

Vurke, *see* Warka.

Vuyvichi, Byel. (Wujwicze); pop. 34; 26 km E of Pinsk; 52°03'/26°30'.

Vyantory, Mold. (Vanatori); pop. 27; 56 km WNW of Kishinev;

47°11'/28°06'.

Vyazma, USSR (Viazma); pop. 506; 146 km ENE of Smolensk; 55°12'/34°17'; GUM4, GUM5, HSL, JGFF, LDL.

Vyazovka, Ukr. (Wjasowka); 75 km NE of Dnepropetrovsk; 48°45'/35°49'; HSL, SF.

Vyazyn, Byel. (Viazin, Wiazyn); pop. 137; 62 km NW of Minsk; 54°25'/27°10'; COH, HSL, SF.

Vyborg, USSR; 126 km WNW of Leningrad; 60°42'/28°45'; HSL.

Vybranovka, Ukr. (Vibranovka, Wybranowka); pop. 101; 38 km SE of Lvov; 49°33'/24°13'; EGRS, HSL, PHP2, SF.

Vycapy Opatovce, Cz. (Vicsapapati); pop. 61; 75 km NE of Bratislava; 48°25'/18°05'; HSL.

Vyderta, Ukr. (Wyderta); pop. 25; 150 km NW of Rovno; 51°44'/25°01'.

Vydran, Cz. (Vidrany); 82 km NNE of Kosice; 49°17'/21°56'; HSL.

Vydranitsa, Ukr. (Wydranica); pop. 13; 163 km WNW of Rovno; 51°37'/24°33'.

Vyelun, *see* Velyun.

Vyershuv, *see* Wieruszow.

Vyerushov, *see* Wieruszow.

Vyerushuv, *see* Wieruszow.

Vyerzbnik, *see* Wierzbnik.

Vyerzhbanik, *see* Wierzbnik.

Vyetka, *see* Vetka.

Vygnanka, Ukr. (Wygnanka); pop. 631; 88 km N of Chernovtsy; 49°02'/25°49'.

Vygoda, Ukr. (Vigoda, Wygoda); pop. 89; 107 km S of Lvov; 48°56'/23°55'; HSL, PHP2, SF. *See also* Wolica Wygoda.

Vygoda (Transnistria), Ukr.; 26 km WNW of Odessa; 46°37'/30°25'; GUM4, PHR1.

Vygolovichi, Byel. (Wyholowicze); pop. 1; 94 km NNW of Minsk; 54°41'/27°07'.

Vykan, Cz.; pop. 1; 26 km ENE of Praha; 50°07'/14°49'.

Vyklice, Cz.; pop. 2; 75 km NW of Praha; 50°39'/13°57'.

Vylok, *see* Vilok.

Vynota, *see* Vainutas.

Vyprovo, Mold. (Vaprova); pop. 39; 50 km NW of Kishinev; 47°23'/28°34'.

Vypyski, Ukr. (Wypiski); pop. 29; 50 km ESE of Lvov; 49°40'/24°39'.

Vyritsa, USSR; pop. 49; 56 km SSE of Leningrad; 59°25'/30°21'.

Vyru, *see* Voru.

Vysehorovice, Cz.; pop. 8; 26 km ENE of Praha; 50°07'/14°47'.

Vyshgorodok, Ukr. (Vishegrodek, Vishogrudek, Vizhgorodok, Wyszogrodek, Wyzgrodek); pop. 944; 101 km S of Rovno; 49°46'/25°58'; COH, GUM5, HSL, LYV, SF, YB.

Vyshkautsy, Mold. (Vascauti Orhei, Vaskoutsi); pop. 30; 56 km N of Kishinev; 47°26'/29°05'.

Vyshkov, Ukr. (Vyshkuv, Wyszkow); pop. 61; 133 km S of Lvov; 48°44'/23°39'.

Vyshkovo, Byel. (Wyszkowo); 26 km NW of Minsk; 54°04'/27°24'; GUM3.

Vyshkuv, *see* Vyshkov.

Vyska, HSL. This pre-World War I community was not found in BGN gazetteers.

Vyskov, Cz. (Wischau); pop. 113; 32 km NE of Brno; 49°17'/17°00'; EJ, HSL, HSL2.

Vyskovce nad Iplom, Cz. (Visk); 133 km E of Bratislava; 48°03'/18°52'; AMG, HSL, HSL2.

Vyskovo, *see* Vishkovo.

Vyskovo nad Tisou, *see* Vishkovo.

Vysluni, Cz. (Suniperk); pop. 2; 101 km WNW of Praha; 50°28'/13°14'.

Vysna Apsa, *see* Verkhneye Vodyanoye.

Vysna Jablonka, Cz. (Vysnia Jablonka); 82 km NE of Kosice; 49°09'/22°07'; HSL.

Vysna Kamenica, Cz.; 19 km NE of Kosice; 48°47'/21°29'; AMG.

Vysna Mysla, Cz. (Felsomislye); 13 km ESE of Kosice;

48°38'/21°23'; HSL.

Vysna Orlik, *see* Vysny Orlik.

Vysna Radvan, Cz.; pop. 90; 69 km NE of Kosice; 49°08'/21°56'.

Vysna Rybnica, Cz. (Felsoribnycze, Rybnica Vysnia); pop. 102; 69 km ENE of Kosice; 48°49'/22°11'; HSL.

Vysna Slana, Cz. (Felsosajo); 69 km W of Kosice; 48°47'/20°19'; HSL.

Vysne Raslavice, *see* Slovenske Raslavice.

Vysne Remety, Cz. (Felsoremete, Vysni Remete, Vysni Remety); 69 km ENE of Kosice; 48°50'/22°10'; HSL.

Vysne Revistia, Cz. (Felsoreviscse); 62 km ENE of Kosice; 48°44'/22°06'. A number of towns share this name. It was not possible to determine from available information which one is being referenced.

Vysnia Jablonka, *see* Vysna Jablonka.

Vysni Apsa, *see* Verkhneye Vodyanoye.

Vysni Bystry, *see* Verkhnyaya Bystra.

Vysni Orlik, *see* Vysny Orlik.

Vysni Remete, *see* Vysne Remety.

Vysni Remety, *see* Vysne Remety.

Vysni Studeny, *see* Verkhne Studenyy.

Vysni Verecky, HSL. This pre-World War I community was not found in BGN gazetteers.

Vysnyj Svidnik, Cz. (Vysny Svidnik); pop. 727; 69 km N of Kosice; 49°18'/21°34'; AMG, COH, HSL.

Vysny Klatov, Cz. (Felsotokes); 13 km WNW of Kosice; 48°45'/21°08'; HSL.

Vysny Orlik, Cz. (Vysna Orlik, Vysni Orlik); pop. 67; 75 km N of Kosice; 49°21'/21°30'.

Vysny Svidnik, *see* Vysnyj Svidnik.

Vysochanskoye, Ukr. (Lac); pop. 5; 126 km W of Odessa; 46°29'/29°03'.

Vysoka, Mold. (Visoca); pop. 49; 157 km NW of Kishinev; 48°15'/27°55'.

Vysoka Ruda, *see* Visakio Ruda.

Vysokaya, Byel. (Vysoke, Vysoko); 75 km WNW of Pinsk; 52°24'/25°06'; EDRD, HSL.

Vysoke, *see* Vysokaya.

Vysoke Myto, Cz.; pop. 89; 94 km NNW of Brno; 49°57'/16°10'; GUM5.

Vysoko, *see* Vysokaya.

Vysokovskaya, USSR; pop. 25; 422 km NE of Moskva; 57°23'/43°54'.

Vysokoye, Byel. (Visoka D Lita, Visoka Litovsk, Visoke Dlita, Visoke Litovsk, Visoke Litevskie, Visokoya, Wysoki Litovsk, Wysokie Litewskie); pop. 1,902; 189 km W of Pinsk; 52°22'/23°22'; COH, EJ, HSL, JGFF, LDL, SF.

Vysokoye (Kaliningrad area), USSR (Popelken); pop. 10; 75 km ENE of Kaliningrad; 54°48'/21°36'.

Vysotsk, Ukr. (Visotsk, Visotzk, Wysock); pop. 893; 133 km N of Rovno; 51°44'/26°39'; COH, GUM3, GUM4, GUM5, HSL, SF, YB.

Vysotsko Vyzhne, *see* Verkhneye Vysotskoye.

Vyver, *see* Veiveriai.

Vyzhlovichi, Byel. (Vyzhlovidze, Wyzlowicze); pop. 20; 26 km WNW of Pinsk; 52°11'/25°51'.

Vyzhlovidze, *see* Vyzhlovichi.

Vyzhnyany, Ukr. (Wyzniany); pop. 30; 32 km E of Lvov; 49°48'/24°25'.

Vyzonous, *see* Vyzuonos.

Vyzuonai, *see* Vyzuonos.

Vyzuonis, *see* Vyzuonos.

Vyzuonos, Lith. (Vizhun, Vizion, Vizounous, Vyzonous, Vyzuonai, Vyzuonis, Wizuny); pop. 367; 107 km N of Vilnius; 55°36'/25°30'; HSL, JGFF, SF, WS, YL.

Waag, Germ.; 32 km NE of Koln; 51°09'/07°20'; PHGB.

Waal, Germ.; 56 km WSW of Munchen; 48°00'/10°47'; PHGB.

Wabrzezno, Pol.; pop. 92; 120 km SSE of Gdansk; 53°17'/18°57'.

Wachbach, Germ.; pop. 8; 88 km NNE of Stuttgart; 49°27'/09°47'; GED, PHGBW.

Wachenbuchen, Germ.; pop. 84; 19 km NE of Frankfurt am Main; 50°10'/08°52'; AMG, LDS.

Wachenheim, Germ.; pop. 24; 62 km SSW of Frankfurt am Main; 49°38'/08°10'; EDRD, GED, HSL.

Wachenheim an der Weinstrasse, Germ.; pop. 20; 82 km SSW of Frankfurt am Main; 49°26'/08°12'.

Wachenhofen, Germ.; 69 km ESE of Nurnberg; 49°04'/11°51'; GUM3.

Wachnowka, see Vakhnovka.

Wachock, Pol. (Vonchotzk); pop. 468; 114 km WSW of Lublin; 51°04'/21°01'; AMG, GUM3, GUM5, HSL, POCEM, SF.

Wachtersbach, Germ.; pop. 58; 50 km NE of Frankfurt am Main; 50°16'/09°18'.

Wadgassen, Germ.; pop. 6; 163 km SW of Frankfurt am Main; 49°16'/06°47'.

Wadlew, Pol.; pop. 9; 32 km S of Lodz; 51°31'/19°25'.

Wadowice, Pol. (Vadovits, Vadovitse, Vadovitz); pop. 1,437; 45 km SW of Krakow; 49°53'/19°29'; AMG, COH, EDRD, EGRS, GA, GUM3, GUM4, GUM5, HSL, JGFF, LYV, PHP3, POCEM, SF, YB.

Wadowice Dolne, Pol.; pop. 23; 101 km ENE of Krakow; 50°17'/21°15'.

Wadowice Gorne, Pol.; pop. 8; 101 km ENE of Krakow; 50°16'/21°17'.

Wad Raschkow, see Vad Rashkov.

Waganowice, Pol.; pop. 7; 19 km NNE of Krakow; 50°14'/20°08'.

Waghausel, Germ.; 69 km NW of Stuttgart; 49°15'/08°30'; PHGBW.

Waging, see Watzing.

Waging am See, Aus.; pop. 26 km NNW of Salzburg; 47°57'/12°56'; GUM4, GUM6, PHGB.

Waglczew, Pol.; pop. 7; 62 km WSW of Lodz; 51°36'/18°33'.

Wagrowiec, Pol. (Wangrowitz, Wongrowitz); pop. 206; 45 km N of Poznan; 52°48'/17°12'; CAHJP, HSL.

Wagstadt, see Bilovec.

Wahrentrup, Germ.; pop. 2; 82 km SW of Hannover; 51°58'/08°43'.

Waiblingen, Germ.; 13 km NE of Stuttgart; 48°50'/09°18'; GUM3, PHGBW.

Waibstadt, Germ.; pop. 25; 62 km NNW of Stuttgart; 49°18'/08°56'; PHGBW.

Waidhaus, Germ.; pop. 11; 101 km ENE of Nurnberg; 49°39'/12°30'; PHGB.

Waidhofen, see Waidhofen an der Ybbs.

Waidhofen an der Thaya, Aus.; pop. 317; 107 km WNW of Wien; 48°49'/15°17'.

Waidhofen an der Ybbs, Aus. (Waidhofen); pop. 20; 114 km NW of Graz; 47°58'/14°46'.

Waidmannsfeld, Aus.; pop. 5; 50 km SSW of Wien; 47°52'/15°58'.

Waiern, Aus.; pop. 1; 107 km SW of Graz; 46°44'/14°05'.

Waischenfeld, Germ.; 50 km N of Nurnberg; 49°51'/11°21'; PHGB.

Waitzen, see Vac.

Waka, see Voke.

Wakijow, Pol.; pop. 14; 101 km ESE of Lublin; 50°41'/23°42'.

Walawa, Pol. (Valava); 13 km NNE of Przemysl; 49°53'/22°54'; SF.

Walberberg, Germ.; pop. 26 km S of Koln; 50°48'/06°55'; GED.

Walbrzych, Pol. (Waldenburg); 62 km SW of Wroclaw; 50°46'/16°17'; AMG, GUM3, GUM4, GUM5, GUM6, LDS, LJEE, PHP3, POCEM.

Walcz, Pol.; pop. 250; 94 km NNW of Poznan; 53°16'/16°28'; CAHJP, HSL, JGFF, LDS.

Waldberg, Germ.; 94 km ENE of Frankfurt am Main; 50°20'/10°00'; PHGB.

Waldbreitbach, Germ.; pop. 39; 56 km SE of Koln; 50°33'/07°25'; GUM5, LDS.

Waldegg, Aus.; pop. 3; 45 km SSW of Wien; 47°52'/16°02'.

Waldenburg, see Walbrzych.

Waldfischbach, Germ.; 114 km SSW of Frankfurt am Main; 49°17'/07°40'; GED.

Waldgrehweiler, Germ.; pop. 3; 82 km SW of Frankfurt am Main; 49°40'/07°44'.

Waldhausen, Germ.; 82 km SE of Frankfurt am Main; 49°28'/09°16'; LDS.

Waldheim, Germ.; 50 km ESE of Leipzig; 51°04'/13°01'; GUM4, GUM5.

Waldkirch, Germ.; 146 km SSW of Stuttgart; 47°40'/08°10'; PHGBW.

Waldmohr, Germ.; pop. 21; 126 km SW of Frankfurt am Main; 49°23'/07°20'.

Waldmunchen, Germ.; pop. 2; 120 km E of Nurnberg; 49°23'/12°43'; GUM3, PHGB.

Waldniel, Germ.; 56 km WNW of Koln; 51°14'/06°16'; GED.

Waldorf, Germ.; 26 km S of Koln; 50°46'/06°57'; GED, GUM5.

Waldsassen, Germ.; pop. 23; 107 km NE of Nurnberg; 50°00'/12°18'; PHGB, PHGB.

Waldshut, Germ.; 146 km SSW of Stuttgart; 47°37'/08°13'; GED, PHGBW.

Waldvisse, HSL. This pre-World War I community was not found in BGN gazetteers.

Waldwinkel, see Borek.

Walegozulowo, see Dolinskoye.

Walentynow, Pol.; pop. 20; 45 km E of Lodz; 51°40'/20°04'.

Walewskie, Pol.; pop. 149; 101 km NNW of Lodz; 52°35'/19°05'; PHP4. This town was located on an interwar map of Poland but does not appear in contemporary gazetteers. Map coordinates are approximate.

Walichnowy, Pol.; pop. 13; 75 km NW of Czestochowa; 51°18'/18°23'.

Walina, see Walinna.

Walinna, Pol. (Walina); pop. 7; 69 km NNE of Lublin; 51°50'/22°59'.

Waliszew, Pol. (Vielishev); 50 km N of Lodz; 52°10'/19°32'; SF.

Walk, see Valka.

Walki, see Valki.

Wallachia; Not a town, but a region of Romania.

Wallachisch Meseritsch, see Valasske Mezirici.

Wallau, Germ.; pop. 21; 101 km NNW of Frankfurt am Main; 50°56'/08°28'; GUM5.

Walldorf, Germ.; pop. 67; 75 km NW of Stuttgart; 49°20'/08°39'; GED, HSL, HSL2, JGFF, PHGBW. See also Walldorf an der Werra.

Walldorf an der Werra, Germ.; pop. 32; 133 km NE of Frankfurt am Main; 50°37'/10°23'; CAHJP, LDS. See also Walldorf.

Walldurn, Germ.; pop. 21; 75 km SE of Frankfurt am Main; 49°35'/09°22'; AMG, LDS, PHGBW.

Wallendorf, Germ.; 114 km SSW of Leipzig; 50°32'/11°12'; HSL. See also Spisske Vlachy.

Wallensen, Germ.; pop. 2; 45 km S of Hannover; 52°01'/09°37'.

Wallerstein, Germ.; pop. 24; 75 km SSW of Nurnberg; 48°53'/10°28'; AMG, CAHJP, GED, GUM5, HSL, HSL2, JGFF, PHGB, PHGBW, PHGB.

Wallertheim, Germ.; pop. 38; 56 km SW of Frankfurt am Main; 49°50'/08°03'; GUM5.

Wallhalben, Germ.; 126 km SSW of Frankfurt am Main; 49°19'/07°32'; GED.

Walowka, see Valevka.

Walpersbach, Aus.; pop. 5; 56 km S of Wien; 47°43'/16°14'.

Wal Ruda, Pol.; pop. 7; 62 km ENE of Krakow; 50°07'/20°48'.

Walsdorf, Germ.; 50 km NW of Nurnberg; 49°52'/10°47'; PHGB.

Walsrode, Germ.; pop. 9; 56 km NNW of Hannover; 52°52'/09°35'.

Walsum, Germ.; pop. 16; 69 km NNW of Koln; 51°32'/06°42'.

Waltersbruck, Germ.; pop. 8; 107 km N of Frankfurt am Main; 50°59'/09°12'; AMG.

Waltershausen, Germ.; 114 km NW of Nurnberg; 50°21'/10°24'; AMG, GUM3, PHGB.

Waltrop, Germ.; pop. 18; 82 km N of Koln; 51°38'/07°24'; GED.

Waly, GA. A number of towns share this name. It was not possible to determine from available information which one is being referenced.

Wampierzow, Pol.; pop. 101; 101 km ENE of Krakow; 50°18'/21°16'; PHP3.

Wanagiszki, *see* Vanagishki.

Wandsbek, Germ.; pop. 200; 13 km NNE of Hamburg; 53°34'/10°01'; CAHJP, GED, HSL, HSL2, LDL, PHGBW.

Wanfried, Germ.; pop. 33; 139 km SSE of Hannover; 51°11'/10°10'; CAHJP, LDS.

Wangen, Germ.; pop. 23; 133 km SSE of Stuttgart; 47°41'/09°50'; GUM3, HSL, JGFF, PHGBW.

Wangerin, *see* Wegorzyno.

Wangerooge, Germ.; pop. 6; 139 km W of Hamburg; 53°48'/07°54'.

Wangrowitz, *see* Wagrowiec.

Waniewo, Pol.; pop. 25; BGN lists two possible localities with this name located at 52°57'/23°33' and 53°04'/22°48'.

Waniow, *see* Vanyuv.

Waniowice, *see* Vanovitse.

Wankenheim, *see* Wankheim.

Wankheim, Germ. (Wankenheim); 38 km S of Stuttgart; 48°30'/09°06'; EJ, LDS, PHGBW.

Wankowa, Pol.; pop. 24; 38 km SSW of Przemysl; 49°31'/22°29'; HSL.

Wankowice, *see* Vankovichi.

Wannbach, Germ.; 62 km NE of Nurnberg; 49°45'/11°51'; GUM5, JGFF, PHGB.

Wanne Eickel, Germ.; pop. 270; 69 km N of Koln; 51°32'/07°10'.

Wanrispertz, GUM3. This town was not found in BGN gazetteers under the given spelling.

Wansdorf, Germ.; pop. 11; 26 km WNW of Berlin; 52°38'/13°05'.

Wansen, *see* Wiazow.

Wapienica, Pol.; pop. 11; 75 km SW of Krakow; 49°49'/18°59'.

Wapienne, Pol.; pop. 2; 107 km ESE of Krakow; 49°38'/21°17'.

Wapienno, Pol. (Wopienno); pop. 2; 82 km NE of Poznan; 52°50'/17°58'.

Wapowce, Pol.; pop. 8; 13 km WNW of Przemysl; 49°49'/22°40'.

Wara, Pol.; pop. 15; 38 km WSW of Przemysl; 49°46'/22°13'.

Waratyck, *see* Varatytsk.

Warburg, Germ.; pop. 150; 101 km S of Hannover; 51°30'/09°10'; CAHJP, GED, GUM3, GUM4, GUM5, JGFF, LDS.

Warchalow, *see* Warchalow Nowy.

Warchalow Nowy, Pol. (Warchalow); pop. 1; 32 km NNE of Lodz; 51°58'/19°43'.

Wardenburg, Germ.; pop. 8; 126 km WNW of Hannover; 53°04'/08°12'.

Wardomicze Stare, *see* Vardomichi.

Warele Stare, Pol.; pop. 5; 56 km SW of Bialystok; 52°47'/22°36'.

Waren, Germ.; pop. 24; 75 km SE of Rostock; 53°31'/12°41'; JGFF, LDS.

Warendorf, Germ.; pop. 41; 133 km SW of Hannover; 51°57'/07°59'; EJ, HSL, LDS.

Warensdorf, *see* Varnsdorf.

Warez, *see* Novoukrainka.

Warez Miasto, *see* Novo Ukrainka (Lwow).

Warfleth, Germ.; 107 km SW of Hamburg; 53°11'/08°32'; JGFF.

Warin, Germ.; 45 km SW of Rostock; 53°48'/11°42'; LDS.

Warka, Pol. (Varka, Vorke, Vurka, Vurke); pop. 2,176; 56 km SSE of Warszawa; 51°47'/21°12'; AMG, COH, EDRD, EJ, FRG, GA, GUM3, HSL, HSL2, JGFF, LDL, LDS, LYV, PHP4, SF, WS, YB.

Warkocz, Pol.; pop. 43; 88 km NNW of Lublin; 51°59'/22°10'.

Warkovicze, *see* Varkovichi.

Warkowicze, *see* Varkovichi.

Warlubie, Pol.; pop. 11; 88 km S of Gdansk; 53°35'/18°38'.

Warmsen, Germ.; pop. 13; 62 km W of Hannover; 52°28'/08°51'.

Warna, *see* Varena.

Warnemunde, Germ.; pop. 8; 13 km NNW of Rostock; 54°10'/12°05'.

Warnsdorf, Germ. BGN lists two possible localities with this name located at 53°15'/12°16' and 53°58'/10°49'. EDRD.

Warpechy Stare, Pol.; pop. 3; 38 km S of Bialystok; 52°52'/23°01'.

Warsaw, *see* Warszawa.

Warsawa, *see* Warszawa.

Warschau, *see* Warszawa.

Warstein, Germ.; pop. 15; 114 km NE of Koln; 51°27'/08°22'; GUM5, LDS.

Warszawa, Pol. (Varsava, Varshau, Varshe, Warsaw, Warsawa, Warschau); pop. 310,322; 120 km NE of Lodz; 52°15'/21°00'; AMG, CAHJP, EDRD, EJ, FRG, GA, GUM3, GUM4, GUM4, GUM5, GUM6, GYLA, HSL, HSL2, ISH1, ISH2, ISH3, JGFF, LDL, LDS, LJEE, LYV, PHP1, PHP2, PHP3, PHP4, POCEM, SF, YB.

Warta, Pol. (Dvart, Dvurt); pop. 2,025; 56 km WSW of Lodz; 51°42'/18°38'; AMG, CAHJP, COH, EDRD, GA, GUM3, GUM4, HSL, HSL2, JGFF, LDL, LDS, LYV, PHP1, POCEM, SF, YB.

Wartberg, Aus.; 56 km N of Graz; 47°31'/15°30'; HSL.

Wartenberg, Germ.; pop. 38 km NE of Munchen; 48°24'/11°59'; AMG, HSL, HSL2.

Wartenburg, Germ.; pop. 54; 62 km NNE of Leipzig; 51°49'/12°47'.

Warth, Aus. (Oberwarth); pop. 432; 94 km WSW of Innsbruck; 47°15'/10°11'.

Wartoslaw, Pol. (Neubruck); pop. 6; 56 km WNW of Poznan; 52°43'/16°18'.

Warwarowka, *see* Varvarovka.

Warwarynce, Ukr.; pop. 56; 88 km NNW of Chernovtsy; 49°05'/25°35'. This town was located on an interwar map of Poland but does not appear in contemporary gazetteers.

Warka, Poland: Exterior of wooden synagogue.

Map coordinates are approximate.

Warzyce, Pol.; pop. 14; 88 km WSW of Przemysl; 49°46'/21°33'; PHP3.

Warzyn, Pol.; pop. 8; 62 km N of Krakow; 50°38'/20°11'.

Wasewo, Pol. (Vonseva); pop. 261; 82 km NNE of Warszawa; 52°53'/21°40'; PHP4, SF.

Washkoutz, see Vashkovtsy.

Wasilewicze, see Vasilevichi.

Wasiliszki, see Vasilishki.

Wasilkow, Pol. (Vashilkova); pop. 950; 13 km NNE of Bialystok; 53°12'/23°13'; CAHJP, COH, EJ, GA, GUM3, GUM5, HSL, LDL, LDS, POCEM, SF, SF. See also Vasilkov, Ukraine.

Wasiuki, see Vasyuki.

Wasniow, Pol. (Vashniev); pop. 191; 101 km SW of Lublin; 50°54'/21°13'; GUM5, HSL, JGFF, SF, YB.

Wasosz, Pol. (Vonsosh); pop. 334; 69 km WNW of Bialystok; 53°31'/22°19'; CAHJP, GUM3, HSL, JGFF, LDS, PHP4, SF.

Wasosz Poduchowny, Pol.; pop. 11; 38 km NNW of Czestochowa; 51°04'/19°01'.

Wasowo, Pol.; 50 km WSW of Poznan; 52°22'/16°15'; GA.

Wassenberg, Germ.; pop. 10; 56 km WNW of Koln; 51°06'/06°09'; GUM5.

Wasseralfingen, Germ.; 69 km ENE of Stuttgart; 48°52'/10°06'; GUM3, GUM4.

Wasserburg, see Wasserburg am Inn.

Wasserburg am Inn, Germ. (Wasserburg); 50 km E of Munchen; 48°04'/12°14'; PHGB.

Wasserlos, Germ.; pop. 10; 26 km E of Frankfurt am Main; 50°04'/09°05'; GUM5, JGFF, LDS, PHGB.

Wasserndorf, Germ.; 69 km WNW of Nurnberg; 49°38'/10°12'; PHGB.

Wassertrudingen, Germ.; pop. 28; 56 km SSW of Nurnberg; 49°03'/10°36'; GUM5, PHGB.

Wasy, Pol.; pop. 12; 56 km E of Warszawa; 52°15'/21°50'.

Wasylkowce, see Vasilkovtsy.

Wasylow, Pol.; pop. 23; 114 km NNE of Przemysl; 50°33'/23°54'.

Waszkowica, GUM3, PHP2. This town was not found in BGN gazetteers under the given spelling.

Waszkowskie, Pol.; pop. 5; 62 km SW of Lodz; 51°25'/18°47'.

Watraszew, Pol.; pop. 4; 50 km SSE of Warszawa; 51°52'/21°09'.

Wattenheim, Germ. BGN lists two possible localities with this name located at 49°31'/08°04' and 49°41'/08°25'. JGFF.

Wattens, Aus.; pop. 5; 19 km ENE of Innsbruck; 47°17'/11°36'.

Wattenscheid, Germ.; pop. 160; 62 km N of Koln; 51°29'/07°08'.

Wattersdorf, Germ.; pop. 2; 38 km SE of Munchen; 47°52'/11°49'.

Watyn, see Vatyn.

Watzenborn, Germ.; 56 km N of Frankfurt am Main; 50°32'/08°43'; LDS.

Watzing, Germ. (Waging); 101 km E of Munchen; 47°56'/12°51'; GUM3.

Wawer, Pol.; pop. 89; 13 km E of Warszawa; 52°14'/21°09'; GUM3, GUM4, GUM5.

Wawern, Germ.; pop. 45; BGN lists two possible localities with this name located at 49°39'/06°33' and 50°07'/06°29'.

Wawiorka, see Vaverka.

Wawolnica, Pol. (Vanvolnica, Vanvolnitsa, Vavolnitsa, Vonvolitz, Vonvolnits, Vonvolnitza); pop. 1,500; 26 km W of Lublin; 51°17'/22°10'; COH, GA, GUM4, GUM5, HSL, LDS, LYV, SF.

Wawrzynow, Pol.; pop. 15; 94 km ESE of Lodz; 51°18'/20°35'.

Wawrzyszow, Pol.; pop. 6; 101 km S of Warszawa; 51°23'/20°55'.

Wechadlow, Pol.; pop. 16; 56 km NNE of Krakow; 50°28'/20°21'; AMG.

Wechterswinkel, Germ.; pop. 3; 114 km ENE of Frankfurt am Main; 50°23'/10°13'.

Weckesheim, Germ.; pop. 38 km N of Frankfurt am Main; 50°22'/08°51'; LDS.

Wedzina, see Wezina.

Weener, Germ.; pop. 142; 182 km WSW of Hamburg; 53°10'/07°21'; LDS.

Weeze, Germ.; pop. 12; 94 km NW of Koln; 51°38'/06°14'.

Wegeleben, Germ.; 101 km WNW of Leipzig; 51°53'/11°10'; LDS.

Wegleszyn, Pol.; pop. 62; 75 km E of Czestochowa; 50°46'/20°11'.

Weglin, Pol.; pop. 22; 56 km SSW of Lublin; 50°49'/22°07'.

Wegliska, Pol.; pop. 8; 56 km WNW of Przemysl; 50°10'/22°12'.

Weglowice, Pol. BGN lists two possible localities with this name located at 51°24'/18°13' and 50°49'/18°51'. JGFF.

Wegorzewo, Pol. (Angerburg); pop. 42; 150 km NW of Bialystok; 54°13'/21°44'; LDS.

Wegorzyno, Pol. (Wangerin); pop. 14; 69 km ENE of Szczecin; 53°32'/15°33'.

Wegrce, Pol. (Wegrce Panienskie); pop. 38; 88 km SW of Lublin; 50°42'/21°36'.

Wegrce Panienskie, see Wegrce.

Wegrow, Pol. (Vegrov, Vengerov, Vengrov, Vengrova, Vengrove, Wegrow Podlaski); pop. 5,148; 69 km ENE of Warszawa; 52°24'/22°01'; AMG, CAHJP, COH, EDRD, EJ, FRG, GA, GUM3, GUM4, GUM5, HSL, HSL2, JGFF, LDL, LDS, LYV, PHP1, PHP3, PHP4, SF, YB.

Wegrowka, HSL. This pre-World War I community was not found in BGN gazetteers.

Wegrow Podlaski, see Wegrow.

Wegrzce Wielkie, Pol.; pop. 3; 19 km ESE of Krakow; 50°01'/20°07'.

Wegrzyn, Pol.; pop. 2; 88 km NE of Czestochowa; 51°02'/20°19'.

Wegrzynow, Pol.; pop. 25; BGN lists two possible localities with this name located at 50°34'/19°55' and 51°01'/20°28'.

Wehen, Germ.; pop. 22; 38 km W of Frankfurt am Main; 50°09'/08°11'; GUM5.

Wehlau, see Znamensk.

Wehr, Germ.; 170 km SSW of Stuttgart; 47°38'/07°44'; PHGBW.

Wehrda, Germ.; pop. 28; 88 km N of Frankfurt am Main; 50°50'/08°45'; JGFF, LDS.

Wehrheim, Germ.; pop. 15; 32 km NNW of Frankfurt am Main; 50°18'/08°34'.

Weickersgruben, Germ.; 82 km E of Frankfurt am Main; 50°06'/09°48'; PHGB.

Weidach Durach, GUM3. This town was not found in BGN gazetteers under the given spelling.

Weiden, Germ.; pop. 168; 82 km NE of Nurnberg; 49°41'/12°10'; AMG, CAHJP, GED, GUM5, PHGB.

Weidenau, Germ. GED. A number of towns share this name. It was not possible to determine from available information which one is being referenced.

Weidenberg, Germ.; 75 km NNE of Nurnberg; 49°57'/11°43'; GUM5, PHGB.

Weidlingbach, Aus.; pop. 1; 13 km WNW of Wien; 48°16'/16°15'.

Weidnitz, Germ.; pop. 2; 82 km N of Nurnberg; 50°09'/11°14'; PHGB.

Weigenheim, Germ.; pop. 1; 62 km W of Nurnberg; 49°34'/10°16'; GUM3, GUM5, PHGB.

Weikersheim, Germ.; pop. 15; 82 km W of Nurnberg; 49°29'/09°55'; GED, HSL, HSL2, LDL, PHGBW.

Weil, see Weil am Rhein.

Weil am Rhein, Germ. (Weil); 176 km SSW of Stuttgart; 47°35'/07°38'; HSL, PHGBW.

Weilbach, Germ.; 62 km SE of Frankfurt am Main; 49°40'/09°13'; PHGB.

Weilburg, Germ.; pop. 90; 56 km NW of Frankfurt am Main; 50°29'/08°15'; CAHJP, HSL.

Weildorf, Germ.; 56 km SSW of Stuttgart; 48°22'/08°47'; PHGBW.

Weiler, see Weiler in Allgau.

Weiler in Allgau, Germ. (Weiler); 139 km SW of Munchen; 47°35'/09°55'; JGFF, LDS.

Weilerswist, Germ.; pop. 24; 26 km SSW of Koln; 50°46'/06°50'; GED.

Weilheim, Germ.; pop. 31; 139 km SSW of Stuttgart; 47°40'/08°14'; GUM3, PHGB.

Weil im Dorf, Germ.; 6 km NNE of Stuttgart; 48°47'/09°12'; PHGBW.

Weimar, Germ.; pop. 45; 75 km SW of Leipzig; 50°59'/11°19'; AMG, GUM3, HSL, HSL2, LDS.

Weimarschmieden, Germ.; 120 km NE of Frankfurt am Main; 50°33'/10°12'; PHGB.

Weimersheim, Germ.; 50 km S of Nurnberg; 49°03'/10°55'; PHGB.

Weinern, HSL, HSL2. A number of towns share this name. It was not possible to determine from available information which one is being referenced.

Weingarten, Germ.; pop. 76; 56 km WNW of Stuttgart; 49°03'/08°32'; AMG, JGFF, LDS, PHGBW.

Weingraben, Aus.; pop. 5; 82 km NE of Graz; 47°31'/16°22'.

Weinheim, Germ.; pop. 157; 62 km S of Frankfurt am Main; 49°33'/08°40'; GED, GUM5, JGFF, LDS, PHGBW.

Weinsberg, Germ.; pop. 50 km N of Stuttgart; 49°09'/09°17'; PHGBW.

Weisbach, Germ.; 107 km NE of Frankfurt am Main; 50°25'/10°05'; PHGB.

Weisendorf, Germ.; pop. 2; 26 km WNW of Nurnberg; 49°37'/10°50'; JGFF, PHGB.

Weisenheim am Sand, Germ.; 69 km SSW of Frankfurt am Main; 49°31'/08°15'; GED.

Weiskirchen, Germ.; pop. 32; 146 km SW of Frankfurt am Main; 49°33'/06°49'.

Weismain, Germ.; 75 km N of Nurnberg; 50°05'/11°14'; PHGB.

Weissbrunn, see Veszprem.

Weissenau, Germ.; 120 km SSE of Stuttgart; 47°46'/09°36'; CAHJP.

Weissenbach, GUM5. A number of towns share this name. It was not possible to determine from available information which one is being referenced.

Weissenberg, Germ.; 50 km NE of Nurnberg; 49°35'/11°44'; GUM5.

Weissenburg, see Weissenburg in Bayern.

Weissenburg in Bayern, Germ. (Weissenburg); 50 km S of Nurnberg; 49°02'/10°59'; EDRD, EJ, GUM3, HSL, HSL2, PHGB, PHP2.

Weissenfels, Germ.; pop. 165; 32 km SW of Leipzig; 51°12'/11°58'; EJ, GUM3, LDS.

Weissenhorn, Germ.; 88 km ESE of Stuttgart; 48°18'/10°10'; PHGB.

Weissenstein, Germ.; 50 km E of Stuttgart; 48°42'/09°54'; PHGBW. See also Paide.

Weisskirchen, see Weisskirchen in Steiermark.

Weisskirchen in Steiermark, Aus. (Weisskirchen); 56 km W of Graz; 47°09'/14°44'; HSL, HSL2.

Weisstein, Pol.; pop. 16; 62 km SW of Wroclaw; 50°47'/16°15'.

Weisweiler, Germ.; 50 km WSW of Koln; 50°49'/06°19'; GUM5.

Weitenegg, Aus.; pop. 1; 75 km W of Wien; 48°13'/15°17'.

Weiten Trebetitsch, see Siroke Trebcice.

Weiterstadt, Germ.; pop. 10; 26 km S of Frankfurt am Main; 49°54'/08°35'; LDS.

Weitra, Aus.; pop. 5; 120 km WNW of Wien; 48°42'/14°53'.

Weiz, Aus.; 26 km NNE of Graz; 47°13'/15°37'; HSL.

Wejherowo, Pol.; pop. 62; 45 km WNW of Gdansk; 54°36'/18°14'; GUM3, LDS.

Wekschni, see Vieksniai.

Welbhausen, Germ.; 62 km W of Nurnberg; 49°32'/10°13'; GUM5, HSL, JGFF, PHGB.

Weldzirz, see Veldzizh.

Weldziz, EGRS. This town was not found in BGN gazetteers under the given spelling.

Welecz, Pol.; pop. 8; 69 km NE of Krakow; 50°27'/20°40'.

Weledniki, see Novyye Veledniki.

Weliki Luki, see Velikye Luki.

Welka, see Velka Pri Poprade.

Wellan, see Vilani.

Wellingen, possibly Villingen.

Wellmich, Germ.; pop. 4; 69 km W of Frankfurt am Main; 50°10'/07°42'.

Wels, Aus.; pop. 20; 82 km NE of Salzburg; 48°10'/14°02'; GUM6.

Weltrub, see Veltruby.

Welzheim, Germ.; 38 km NE of Stuttgart; 48°53'/09°39'; GUM3, GUM5, PHGBW.

Wemding, Germ.; 69 km S of Nurnberg; 48°52'/10°43'; PHGB.

Wendelsheim, Germ.; 62 km SW of Frankfurt am Main; 49°46'/08°00'; JGFF.

Wenden, see Cesis.

Weniger Maertersdorf, see Eisenstadt.

Wenings, Germ.; pop. 51; 50 km NE of Frankfurt am Main; 50°23'/09°12'; GUM5, LDS.

Wenkheim, Germ.; pop. 62; 82 km ESE of Frankfurt am Main; 49°42'/09°42'; AMG, PHGBW.

Wenzen, Germ.; 62 km SSE of Hannover; 51°52'/09°49'; LDS.

Werachanie, Pol.; pop. 21; 101 km SE of Lublin; 50°32'/23°31'.

Werba, Ukr.; pop. 228; BGN lists two possible localities with this name located at 50°17'/25°37' and 50°56'/24°20'. AMG, COH, GUM3, HSL.

Werbcze, see Bolshaya Verbcha.

Werbcze Male, see Verbche Male.

Werbiz, see Verbizh.

Werbcze Wielkie, see Bolshaya Verbcha.

Werbkowice, Pol.; pop. 72; 94 km ESE of Lublin; 50°45'/23°46'; GA.

Werbowez, see Verbovets.

Werchowka, see Verkhovka.

Werchrata, Pol.; pop. 196; 75 km NE of Przemysl; 50°15'/23°29'; PHP2.

Werchy, see Verkhi.

Werden, Germ.; pop. 47; A number of towns share this name. It was not possible to determine from available information which one is being referenced.

Werdohl, Germ.; pop. 1; 69 km NE of Koln; 51°16'/07°46'.

Werejki, see Vereyki.

Weremien, Pol.; pop. 10; 50 km SSW of Przemysl; 49°28'/22°20'.

Werenow, see Voronovo.

Wereszczyn, Pol.; pop. 52; 50 km ENE of Lublin; 51°22'/23°13'; GUM4, GUM5.

Wereszyce, see Vereshitsa.

Wereszyn, Pol.; pop. 39; 120 km ESE of Lublin; 50°36'/23°56'; GUM3, GUM5.

Werkievka, see Verkhovka.

Werl, Germ.; pop. 90; 94 km NE of Koln; 51°33'/07°55'; GED.

Werlte, Germ.; pop. 40; 146 km WNW of Hannover; 52°51'/07°41'; GUM5.

Wermelskirchen, Germ.; pop. 1; 26 km NNE of Koln; 51°09'/07°13'.

Wernarz, Germ.; pop. 15; 75 km ENE of Frankfurt am Main; 50°17'/09°45'; PHGB.

Werne, see Werne an der Lippe.

Werne an der Lippe, Germ. (Werne); pop. 334; 94 km NNE of Koln; 51°40'/07°38'; AMG, LDS.

Werneck, Germ.; pop. 18; 94 km WNW of Nurnberg; 49°59'/10°06'; HSL, PHGB.

Wernigerode, Germ.; pop. 13; 94 km ESE of Hannover; 51°50'/10°47'; GUM3.

Werro, see Voru.

Werschau, Germ.; 50 km WNW of Frankfurt am Main; 50°21'/08°10'; HSL.

Werschetz, see Vrsac.

Werth, Germ.; 101 km NNW of Koln; 51°49'/06°30'; GED.

Wertheim, Germ.; pop. 110; 69 km ESE of Frankfurt am Main; 49°45'/09°31'; GUM5, JGFF, PHGBW.

Werther, Germ.; pop. 20; 94 km SW of Hannover; 52°04'/08°25'; HSL.

Wertingen, Germ.; 82 km WNW of Munchen; 48°33'/10°41'; GED, PHGB.

Werynia, Pol.; pop. 14; 88 km WNW of Przemysl; 50°15'/21°50'.

Weseke, Germ.; pop. 8; 114 km N of Koln; 51°55'/06°51'; GED.

Wesel, Germ.; pop. 170; 88 km NNW of Koln; 51°40'/06°37'; AMG, GED, HSL, HSL2.

Wesenberg, *see* Rakvere.

Wesermunde, *see* Bremerhaven.

Wesola, Pol.; pop. 65; 50 km W of Przemysl; 49°48'/22°06'; PHP1.

Wesolka, Pol.; pop. 20; 101 km N of Lublin; 52°05'/22°39'.

Wesolow, Pol.; pop. 37; 69 km ESE of Krakow; 49°52'/20°47'.

Wesseling, Germ.; pop. 61; 19 km SSE of Koln; 50°50'/06°59'; GED.

Wessely, *see* Veseli nad Moravou.

Wessen, *see* Viesite.

Westerburg, Germ.; pop. 102; 75 km WNW of Frankfurt am Main; 50°34'/07°59'; GUM5.

Westeregeln, Germ.; pop. 4; 101 km NW of Leipzig; 51°58'/11°24'; GUM5.

Westerholt, Germ. GED. A number of towns share this name. It was not possible to determine from available information which one is being referenced.

Westernkotten, Germ.; pop. 5; 126 km SW of Hannover; 51°38'/08°22'.

Westerstede, Germ.; pop. 29; 146 km WSW of Hamburg; 53°15'/07°56'.

Westhausen, HSL. A number of towns share this name. It was not possible to determine from available information which one is being referenced.

Westheim, Germ.; 62 km WNW of Munchen; 48°23'/10°49'; CAHJP, GUM3, HSL, LDS.

Westheim bei Hammelburg, Germ.; pop. 51; 88 km E of Frankfurt am Main; 50°07'/09°56'; GUM5, PHGB.

Westheim bei Hassfurt, Germ.; pop. 60; 75 km NW of Nurnberg; 49°59'/10°30'; GUM5, PHGB.

Westhofen, Germ. (Westhoffen); 56 km SSW of Frankfurt am Main; 49°42'/08°15'; EJ, HSL.

Westhoffen, *see* Westhofen.

Westphalia; Not a town but a region of northwestern Germany.

Westwahl, Germ. PHGBW. This town was not found in BGN gazetteers under the given spelling.

Wetlina, Pol.; pop. 8; 75 km S of Przemysl; 49°09'/22°29'.

Wetter, Germ.; pop. 80; 94 km N of Frankfurt am Main; 50°54'/08°43'.

Wettesingen, Germ.; pop. 1; 107 km S of Hannover; 51°27'/09°11'; JGFF.

Wetzlar, Germ.; pop. 147; 56 km NNW of Frankfurt am Main; 50°33'/08°30'; CAHJP, EDRD, EJ, GUM3, GUM4, HSL, HSL2, JGFF.

Wevelinghoven, Germ.; 32 km WNW of Koln; 51°06'/06°37'; EJ, GED.

Weyer, Germ.; pop. 40; 69 km W of Frankfurt am Main; 50°11'/07°43'; GUM5.

Weze, Pol.; pop. 10; 82 km ENE of Warszawa; 52°21'/22°09'.

Wezina, Pol. (Wedzina, Windeck); 38 km W of Czestochowa; 50°51'/18°39'; JGFF.

Wezyczyn, Pol.; pop. 9; 62 km ESE of Warszawa; 52°04'/21°49'.

White Field, *see* Belaya Tserkov.

White Russia; *See* Byelorussia.

Wiaczein Polski, Pol.; pop. 22; Described in the *Black Book* as being in the Warszawa region of Poland, this town was not found in BGN gazetteers.

Wiatowice, Pol.; pop. 6; 26 km ESE of Krakow; 49°57'/20°13'; HSL.

Wiazow, Pol. (Wansen); pop. 9; 32 km SE of Wroclaw; 50°49'/17°12'.

Wiazowa, *see* Vionzova.

Wiazowka, Pol.; pop. 7; 26 km ESE of Warszawa; 52°10'/21°18'; LDL.

Wiazowna, Pol.; pop. 272; 26 km ESE of Warszawa; 52°10'/21°18'; PHP4.

Wiazownica, Pol.; pop. 22; 38 km NNW of Przemysl; 50°05'/22°42'.

Wiazyn, *see* Vyazyn.

Wiciow, HSL. This pre-World War I community was not found in BGN gazetteers.

Wickede, Germ.; pop. 20; 88 km NE of Koln; 51°29'/07°52'.

Wickrath, Germ.; pop. 110; 45 km WNW of Koln; 51°08'/06°25'; GED.

Wiczowka, *see* Vitchevka.

Wiczyn, *see* Vichin.

Wiczynie, *see* Vichyne.

Widaczow, Pol.; pop. 24; 38 km WNW of Przemysl; 49°55'/22°19'.

Widawa, Pol. (Vidava); pop. 773; 56 km SW of Lodz; 51°26'/18°57'; CAHJP, COH, FRG, HSL, HSL2, JGFF, LDL, LDS, PHP1, POCEM, SF.

Widawka, Pol.; pop. 10; 50 km NE of Czestochowa; 51°07'/19°36'.

Widdern, Germ.; 62 km N of Stuttgart; 49°19'/09°25'; EDRD.

Widdig, Germ.; pop. 9; 26 km SSE of Koln; 50°47'/07°01'; GED.

Widelka, Pol.; pop. 38; 75 km WNW of Przemysl; 50°12'/21°53'.

Widelki, Pol.; pop. 16; 107 km NNE of Krakow; 50°46'/20°56'.

Widoki, Pol.; pop. 25; Described in the *Black Book* as being in the Kielce region of Poland, this town was not found in BGN gazetteers.

Widoma, Pol.; 19 km NNE of Krakow; 50°12'/20°01'; HSL.

Widomla, *see* Vidomlya.

Widuchowa, Pol. (Fiddichow); pop. 9; 45 km S of Szczecin; 53°07'/14°23'.

Widynow, *see* Vidinov.

Widze, *see* Vidzy.

Wiebelskirchen, Germ.; 139 km SW of Frankfurt am Main; 49°22'/07°11'; GED.

Wiecbork, Pol. (Vandsburg); pop. 64; 107 km N of Poznan; 53°21'/17°30'; LDS, POCEM.

Wiecierza, Pol.; pop. 5; 45 km S of Krakow; 49°45'/19°52'.

Wieckowice, Pol.; pop. 21; A number of towns share this name. It was not possible to determine from available information which one is being referenced.

Wieczorki, *see* Vechorki.

Wieden, Germ. AMG. A number of towns share this name. It was not possible to determine from available information which one is being referenced.

Wiedenbruck, Germ.; pop. 79; 114 km SW of Hannover; 51°50'/08°19'; AMG.

Wiedersbach, Germ.; 50 km SW of Nurnberg; 49°18'/10°27'; PHGB.

Wiejsieje, *see* Veisiejai.

Wieladki, Pol.; pop. 4; 56 km ENE of Warszawa; 52°24'/21°50'.

Wielatki Rosochate, Pol.; pop. 3; 45 km NNE of Warszawa; 52°38'/21°19'.

Wielemicze, *see* Velemichi.

Wielen, Pol. (Filehne, Wielen nad Notecia); pop. 54; 75 km WNW of Poznan; 52°54'/16°11'; CAHJP, HSL, HSL2, JGFF.

Wielen nad Notecia, *see* Wielen.

Wielgie, Pol.; pop. 24; 69 km NW of Czestochowa; 51°20'/18°43'.

Wielgie Grabowce, Pol.; pop. 25; Described in the *Black Book* as being in the Lublin region of Poland, this town was not found in BGN gazetteers.

Wielgolaskie Budki, *see* Budy Wielgoleskie.

Wielgomlyny Poduchowne, Pol.; pop. 10; 50 km NE of Czestochowa; 51°01'/19°47'.

Wielgorz, Pol.; pop. 10; 101 km E of Warszawa; 52°10'/22°29'.

Wielichow, *see* Wielichowo.

Wielichowo, Pol. (Wielichow); pop. 2; 56 km SW of Poznan; 52°07'/16°22'.

Wieliczka, Pol. (Velichka, Vilietchka); pop. 1,135; 19 km ESE of Krakow; 49°59'/20°04'; AMG, CAHJP, COH, EDRD, EGRS, EJ, GA, GUM3, GUM4, GUM5, GUM6, HSL, HSL2, JGFF, LDL, LYV, PHP3, POCEM, SF, YB.

Wieliczna, Pol.; pop. 22; 62 km NE of Warszawa; 52°33'/21°49'.

Wieliszew, Pol.; pop. 35; 26 km N of Warszawa; 52°27'/20°58'; LDS.

Wieliz, see Velizh.

Wielka Hlusza, see Velikaya Glusha.

Wielka Wies, Pol.; pop. 32; 62 km E of Krakow; 49°57'/20°49'; PHP3.

Wielka Wola, Pol.; 50 km E of Lodz; 51°38'/20°11'; EJ, PHP1.

Wielkie Drogi, Pol.; pop. 11; 19 km SW of Krakow; 49°58'/19°43'.

Wielkie Lunawy, Pol.; pop. 23; 114 km S of Gdansk; 53°23'/18°37'.

Wielkie Oczy, Pol. (Vilkatch); pop. 547; 38 km NE of Przemysl; 50°01'/23°09'; COH, EGRS, GUM4, HSL, JGFF, LDL, PHP1, PHP2, SF.

Wielkie Siolo, see Velikoye Selo.

Wielodroz, Pol.; pop. 3; 82 km N of Warszawa; 52°57'/21°00'.

Wielona, see Veliuona.

Wielopole, see Wielopole Skrzynskie.

Wielopole (Lwow), Pol.; pop. 26; 38 km W of Przemysl; 49°49'/22°17'.

Wielopole Skrzynskie, Pol. (Vielipoli, Wielopole); pop. 550; 88 km W of Przemysl; 49°57'/21°37'; AMG, COH, EDRD, EGRS, GUM3, GUM5, HSL, PHP3, SF.

Wielowies, Pol.; pop. 38; 94 km SSW of Lublin; 50°38'/21°45'.

Wielowies (near Katowice), Pol.; pop. 50 km SW of Czestochowa; 50°31'/18°38'; LDS, POCEM.

Wielun, Pol.; pop. 4,818; 62 km NW of Czestochowa; 51°13'/18°33'; AMG, CAHJP, COH, EDRD, EJ, GA, GUM3, GUM4, GUM5, GUM6, HSL, HSL2, JGFF, LDL, LDS, LYV, PHP1, PHP3, POCEM, SF, YB. See also Velyun.

Wien, Aus. (Vienna); pop. 176,034; 146 km NNE of Graz; 48°12'/16°22'; AMG, CAHJP, EDRD, GUM3, GUM4, GUM5, GUM6, HSL, HSL2, ISH1, ISH3, JGFF, LDL, PHP1, PHP2, PHP3, PHP4.

Wiener Neustadt, Aus.; pop. 685; 50 km S of Wien; 47°48'/16°15'; AMG, EDRD, GUM5.

Wieniawa, Pol.; pop. 101 km ESE of Lodz; 51°22'/20°48'; LDS.

Wieprz, Pol.; 50 km SW of Krakow; 49°53'/19°23'; PHP3.

Wieprzki, Pol.; pop. 17; 88 km SW of Lublin; 50°43'/21°40'.

Wierbiaz Nizny, see Verbionzh Vyzhny.

Wiercany, Pol.; pop. 2; 82 km WNW of Przemysl; 50°01'/21°45'.

Wierchniednieprowsk, see Verkhnedneprovsk.

Wierchomla, see Wierchomla Wielka.

Wierchomla Wielka, Pol. (Wierchomla); 101 km SE of Krakow; 49°25'/20°48'; PHP3.

Wierczany, see Verchany.

Wiersze, Pol.; pop. 6; 26 km WNW of Warszawa; 52°20'/20°40'.

Wieruszow, Pol. (Verushev, Viroshov, Vyershuv, Vyerushov, Vyerushuv); pop. 1,903; 88 km WNW of Czestochowa; 51°17'/18°10'; AMG, COH, EDRD, FRG, GA, GUM3, GUM4, GUM5, HSL, JGFF, LDL, LYV, PHP1, POCEM, SF, YB.

Wierzawice, Pol.; pop. 58; 56 km NW of Przemysl; 50°15'/22°28'.

Wierzbanowa, Pol.; pop. 9; 45 km SE of Krakow; 49°46'/20°08'.

Wierzbiany, see Verbyany.

Wierzbiaz, see Vezhbenzh.

Wierzbica, Pol.; pop. 81; 101 km WSW of Lublin; 51°15'/21°05'; POCEM, SF. See also Vezhbitsa.

Wierzbica (near Janow Lubelski), Pol.; pop. 9; 50 km SE of Lublin; 50°52'/22°56'.

Wierzbica (near Krasnystaw), Pol.; pop. 36; 56 km ENE of Lublin; 51°16'/23°20'.

Wierzbica (near Miechow), Pol.; pop. 31; 26 km NE of Krakow; 50°15'/20°10'.

Wierzbica (near Pinczow), Pol.; pop. 8; 75 km NNE of Krakow; 50°38'/20°35'; GUM5.

Wierzbica (near Rava Ruskayya), Pol.; pop. 45; 88 km NE of Przemysl; 50°21'/23°41'.

Wierzbica (near Stopnica), Pol.; pop. 4; 94 km NE of Krakow; 50°32'/21°02'.

Wierzbiczno, see Vezhbichno.

Wierzbinek, Pol.; pop. 1; 101 km NW of Lodz; 52°26'/18°31'.

Wierzblany, see Vezhblyany.

Wierzbna, Pol.; pop. 8; 32 km NW of Przemysl; 50°02'/22°36'.

Wierzbnik, Pol. (Starachowice, Starakhovits, Strachovitza, Verzhbnik, Verzhbnik Starakhov, Vierzhbinik, Vyerzbnik, Vyerzhbanik, Wierzbnik Starachow); pop. 2,159; 101 km WSW of Lublin; 51°03'/21°05'; AMG, COH, FRG, GA, GUM3, GUM4, GUM5, GUM6, HSL, HSL2, JGFF, LYV, PHP1, PHP4, POCEM, SF, YB.

Wierzbnik Starachow, see Wierzbnik.

Wierzbno, Pol.; 26 km NE of Krakow; 50°09'/20°15'; PHP3.

Wierzbolow, see Virbalis.

Wierzbow, possibly Vezhbova.

Wierzbowce, see Verbovtsy.

Wierzbowiec, see Verbovtsy.

Wierzchlas, Pol.; pop. 51; 62 km NW of Czestochowa; 51°13'/18°41'.

Wierzchlesie, Pol.; pop. 3; 32 km NE of Bialystok; 53°19'/23°33'.

Wierzchniakowce, see Veshkhnyakovtse.

Wierzchniow, possibly Verkhnov.

Wierzcholesie, see Verkholesye.

Wierzchow, Ukr.; pop. 20; 62 km S of Rovno; 50°05'/26°15'. This town was located on an interwar map of Poland but does not appear in contemporary gazetteers. Map coordinates are approximate.

Wierzchowice, see Verkhovichi.

Wierzchowina, Pol.; pop. 39; 50 km SE of Lublin; 50°51'/22°51'.

Wierzchowiska, Pol.; 56 km S of Lublin; 50°48'/22°25'; GA.

Wierzchownia, Pol. GUM4. A number of towns share this name. It was not possible to determine from available information which one is being referenced.

Wierzchowo, Pol. (Virchow); pop. 8; 107 km E of Szczecin; 53°27'/16°06'.

Wierzejki, Pol.; pop. 11; 94 km N of Lublin; 52°02'/22°34'.

Wiesbaden, Germ. (Schierstein); pop. 3,200; 32 km WSW of Frankfurt am Main; 50°05'/08°15'; AMG, EJ, GED, GUM4, GUM5, HSL, HSL2, JGFF, LDL.

Wieschowa, see Wieszowa.

Wiesdorf, see Rachlau.

Wieseck, Germ.; pop. 36; 62 km N of Frankfurt am Main; 50°36'/08°42'.

Wieselburg, Aus.; pop. 13; 94 km WSW of Wien; 48°08'/15°08'; HSL.

Wiesen, HSL. A number of towns share this name. It was not possible to determine from available information which one is being referenced.

Wiesenbach, Germ.; 82 km WSW of Nurnberg; 49°18'/10°02'; PHGBW.

Wiesenberg, see Vesenberg.

Wiesenbronn, Germ.; pop. 27; 62 km WNW of Nurnberg; 49°45'/10°18'; GUM5, PHGB.

Wiesenburg, Germ.; 82 km SW of Berlin; 52°07'/12°27'; HSL.

Wiesenfeld, Germ.; pop. 63; 75 km E of Frankfurt am Main; 49°59'/09°41'; GED, GUM5, PHGB.

Wiesent, Germ.; pop. 16; 107 km ESE of Nurnberg; 49°01'/12°23'.

Wiesenthau, Germ.; 32 km N of Nurnberg; 49°43'/11°08'; PHGB.

Wieshajzie, see Vezaiciai.

Wieska, Pol.; pop. 10; 82 km SSW of Bialystok; 52°33'/22°29'.

Wiesloch, Germ.; pop. 103; 69 km NW of Stuttgart; 49°18'/08°42'; GED, GUM5, LDS, PHGBW.

Wiesmath, Aus.; pop. 17; 69 km S of Wien; 47°37'/16°17'.

Wies Zolynia, see Zolynia.

Wieszowa, Pol. (Wieschowa); LDS. This town was not found in BGN gazetteers under the given spelling.

Wietlin, Pol.; pop. 81; 32 km N of Przemysl; 50°01'/22°49'.

Wietly, see Vetly.

Wietrzychowice, Pol.; pop. 71; 62 km ENE of Krakow; 50°12'/20°45'.

Wiewiec, Pol.; pop. 25; 45 km N of Czestochowa; 51°08'/19°14'.

Wiewiorka, Pol.; pop. 57; 107 km ENE of Krakow; 50°07'/21°21'.

Wiewiorow, Pol.; 88 km WSW of Lublin; 51°09'/21°21'; AMG.

Wiezyca, Pol.; 38 km SW of Gdansk; 54°14'/18°08'; GA.

Wiklow, Pol.; pop. 17; 32 km NNE of Czestochowa; 51°00'/19°18'.

Wiktorow, see Viktoruv.

Wilamowice, Pol.; pop. 31; 56 km SW of Krakow; 49°55'/19°10'; HSL.

Wilanow, Pol. (Vilanov); 19 km SE of Warszawa; 52°10'/21°06'; GUM3, GUM5, GUM6, HSL, PHP4, SF.

Wilanowo, Pol. GUM3, HSL. GUM3 states it is in the Vilnius area. It does not appear in interwar or contemporary gazetteers.

Wilatowen, see Wylatowo.

Wilcza, Pol.; pop. 24; 6 km NE of Przemysl; 49°48'/22°49'.

Wilczanka, Pol.; pop. 1; 50 km WNW of Lublin; 51°34'/22°04'.

Wilcza Wola, Pol.; pop. 45; 88 km WNW of Przemysl; 50°21'/21°56'.

Wilcze Nory, GUM4. This town was not found in BGN gazetteers under the given spelling.

Wilczki, Pol.; pop. 6; 126 km NNW of Warszawa; 53°23'/20°35'.

Wilczkowice, HSL. A number of towns share this name. It was not possible to determine from available information which one is being referenced.

Wilczopole, Pol.; pop. 17; 13 km SE of Lublin; 51°10'/22°39'.

Wilczyca, Pol.; pop. 7; 32 km WNW of Lodz; 51°51'/19°04'.

Wilczyn, Pol.; pop. 174; 82 km ENE of Poznan; 52°29'/18°10'; AMG, COH, GUM3, HSL, LDL, LDS.

Wilczy Przewoz, see Volchkov Perevoz.

Wilczyska, Pol.; 75 km ESE of Krakow; 49°42'/20°46'; HSL.

Wildbad, see Wildbad im Schwarzwald.

Wildbad im Schwarzwald, Germ. (Wildbad); 50 km WSW of Stuttgart; 48°45'/08°33'; PHGBW.

Wildeshausen, Germ.; pop. 17; 107 km WNW of Hannover; 52°54'/08°26'.

Wilejka, see Vileyka.

Wilga, Pol.; 50 km SE of Warszawa; 51°52'/21°23'; GA, GUM3, GUM4, GUM5, HSL.

Wilhelmow, Pol.; pop. 7; 69 km ESE of Lublin; 50°57'/23°29'.

Wilhelmpieckstadt Guben, Germ. (Guben); pop. 200; 107 km ESE of Berlin; 51°57'/14°43'; AMG, GUM5, GUM6, HSL, HSL2.

Wilhelmsburg, Aus.; pop. 27; 56 km WSW of Wien; 48°06'/15°36'; GUM3.

Wilhelmshaven, Germ.; pop. 170; 126 km WSW of Hamburg; 53°31'/08°08'; GUM3, GUM5.

Wilhermsdorf, Germ.; pop. 47; 26 km W of Nurnberg; 49°29'/10°43'; GUM5, JGFF, PHGB.

Wiliampole, see Vilijampole.

Wilica, see Vilitsa.

Wilja, see Viliya.

Wilkolaz, Pol. (Wilkolaz Poduchowny); pop. 17; 32 km SSW of Lublin; 51°01'/22°20'; HSL.

Wilkolaz Poduchowny, see Wilkolaz.

Wilkomierz, see Ukmerge.

Wilkomir, see Ukmerge.

Wilkoszewice, Pol.; pop. 5; 62 km NNE of Czestochowa; 51°15'/19°39'.

Wilkowa, Pol.; pop. 6; 94 km NE of Krakow; 50°27'/21°10'.

Wilkowice, Pol.; pop. 29; 69 km SW of Krakow; 49°46'/19°07'.

Wilkowiecko, Pol.; pop. 12; 26 km WNW of Czestochowa; 50°57'/18°52'.

Wilkowisko, Pol.; pop. 17; 50 km SE of Krakow; 49°46'/20°16'.

Wilkowyszki, see Vilkaviskis.

Willanzheim, Germ.; 62 km WNW of Nurnberg; 49°41'/10°14'; PHGB.

Willenz, see Vilanec.

Willingshausen, Germ.; 94 km NNE of Frankfurt am Main; 50°51'/09°12'; LDS.

Willmars, Germ.; pop. 36; 120 km NE of Frankfurt am Main; 50°30'/10°15'; GUM5, JGFF, PHGB.

Willmenrod, Germ.; pop. 4; 75 km WNW of Frankfurt am Main; 50°33'/07°58'.

Willstatt, Germ.; 101 km WSW of Stuttgart; 48°32'/07°53'; PHGBW.

Wilmersdorf, Germ.; 82 km NNE of Berlin; 53°07'/13°55'; HSL, HSL2.

Wilna, see Vilnius.

Wilno, see Vilnius.

Wiloczan, Lith. EDRD. This town was not found in BGN gazetteers under the given spelling.

Wimpassing, HSL. A number of towns share this name. It was not possible to determine from available information which one is being referenced.

Wimpfen, see Bad Wimpfen.

Wincentow, Pol.; pop. 21; 19 km SW of Lodz; 51°40'/19°16'.

Wincentowo, Pol.; pop. 31; 56 km NNE of Warszawa; 52°44'/21°23'.

Windall, see Ventspils.

Windau, see Ventspils.

Windawa, see Ventspils.

Windeck, see Wezina.

Windecken, Germ.; pop. 41; 19 km NE of Frankfurt am Main; 50°14'/08°53'; LDS.

Windesheim, Germ.; 69 km SW of Frankfurt am Main; 49°54'/07°49'; JGFF.

Windischgarsten, Aus.; pop. 3; 94 km E of Salzburg; 47°43'/14°20'.

Windsbach, Germ.; pop. 47; 32 km SSW of Nurnberg; 49°15'/10°49'; CAHJP, GUM5, PHGB.

Windsheim, Germ.; pop. 70; 50 km W of Nurnberg; 49°30'/10°25'; CAHJP, EDRD, EJ, GUM3, GUM5, PHGB.

Wingrany, Pol.; pop. 13; 139 km N of Bialystok; 54°21'/22°59'.

Winkshnin, see Vinksniniai.

Winna Chroly, Pol.; pop. 5; 62 km SSW of Bialystok; 52°41'/22°36'.

Winnica, see Vinnitsa.

Winniczki, Pol.; pop. 33; Described in the Black Book as being in the Lwow region of Poland, this town was not found in BGN gazetteers.

Winniki, see Vinniki.

Winnitsa, see Vinnitsa.

Winniza, see Vinnitsa.

Winnweiler, Germ.; pop. 30; 82 km SW of Frankfurt am Main; 49°34'/07°51'; GED, HSL, JGFF.

Winograd, see Vinograd (near Tlumach).

Winogradow, see Vinogradov.

Winsko, Pol. (Winzig); pop. 23; 50 km NW of Wroclaw; 51°28'/16°38'; POCEM.

Winterhausen, Germ.; 82 km WNW of Nurnberg; 49°42'/10°01'; GUM5, PHGB.

Wintrich, Germ.; pop. 6; 126 km WSW of Frankfurt am Main; 49°53'/06°57'.

Wintzenheim, see Winzenheim.

Winzenheim, Germ. (Wintzenheim); 62 km SW of Frankfurt am Main; 49°52'/07°52'; HSL, LDS.

Winzig, see Winsko.

Wiory, Pol.; pop. 8; 94 km ESE of Poznan; 51°59'/18°04'.

Wioska Radzyminska, Pol.; pop. 68; 19 km E of Warszawa; 52°15'/21°15'. This town was located on an interwar map of Poland but does not appear in contemporary gazetteers. Map coordinates are approximate.

Wiowka, Pol. PHP4. This town was not found in BGN gazetteers under the given spelling.

Wirballen, *see* Virbalis.

Wirdum, Germ.; pop. 2; 182 km WSW of Hamburg; 53°29'/07°12'.

Wirek, *see* Nowa Wies (near Katowice).

Wiresmort, *see* Virismort.

Wirges, Germ.; pop. 3; 75 km WNW of Frankfurt am Main; 50°28'/07°48'.

Wirkowice, Pol.; pop. 3; 56 km SE of Lublin; 50°52'/23°06'.

Wirow, Pol.; pop. 4; 88 km SSW of Bialystok; 52°26'/22°31'.

Wirsberg, Germ.; 82 km NNE of Nurnberg; 50°07'/11°36'; PHGB.

Wirsitz, *see* Wyrzysk.

Wiry, Pol. (Gross Wierau); 19 km SSW of Poznan; 52°19'/16°51'; LDS.

Wischau, *see* Vyskov.

Wiskienice, Pol.; pop. 10; 56 km N of Lodz; 52°12'/19°44'.

Wiskitki, Pol. (Viskit); pop. 951; 45 km SW of Warszawa; 52°05'/20°24'; AMG, COH, FRG, GA, GUM3, HSL, HSL2, LDS, PHP1, PHP4, POCEM, SF, YB.

Wisla, Pol. (Wisla Wielki); pop. 5; 88 km SW of Krakow; 49°40'/18°52'; EDRD, PHP3.

Wisla Wielki, *see* Wisla.

Wislica, Pol. (Vayslits, Veislitz, Wyslica); pop. 1,341; 62 km NE of Krakow; 50°21'/20°41'; AMG, COH, EDRD, GA, GUM4, GUM5, HSL, JGFF, LDL, LDS, PHP4, POCEM, SF, YB.

Wislitz, HSL. This pre-World War I community was not found in BGN gazetteers.

Wisloczek, Pol.; pop. 5; 69 km SW of Przemysl; 49°31'/21°53'.

Wislok Wielki, Pol.; pop. 40; 69 km SW of Przemysl; 49°24'/21°59'.

Wislowice, *see* Wislowiec.

Wislowiec, Pol. (Wislowice); pop. 2; 69 km ESE of Lublin; 50°49'/23°16'; COH, GUM5.

Wismar, Germ.; pop. 23; 50 km SW of Rostock; 53°54'/11°28'; EJ.

Wisna, (Vizna); LDL, SF, YB. This town was not found in BGN gazetteers under the given spelling.

Wisnicz, *see* Wisnicz Nowy.

Wisnicz Nowy, Pol. (Nowy Wisnicz, Vishnich Novy, Vishnits, Vishnitz, Vizhnitz, Wisnicz); pop. 1,273; 45 km ESE of Krakow; 49°55'/20°28'; AMG, CAHJP, COH, EGRS, GA, GUM3, GUM4, GUM5, HSL, JGFF, LDL, LDS, LYV, PHP3, POCEM, SF.

Wisnicz Stary, Pol.; pop. 19; 45 km ESE of Krakow; 49°55'/20°29'.

Wisnievicze, *see* Vishnevets.

Wisniewo, Pol. AMG. A number of towns share this name. It was not possible to determine from available information which one is being referenced.

Wisniowa, Pol. (Vishnova); pop. 55; 38 km SSE of Krakow; 49°47'/20°07'; COH, HSL, LDL, PHP3.

Wisniowa Gora, Pol. (Gora Wisniowa); pop. 56; 13 km ESE of Lodz; 51°43'/19°38'; GUM3, GUM5, PHP1.

Wisniowczyk, *see* Vishnivchik.

Wisniowiec, *see* Vishnevets.

Wisniowiec Nowy, *see* Vishnevets.

Wisnowiec, *see* Vishnevets.

Wisowitz, *see* Vizovice.

Wissek, *see* Wysoka.

Wissen, Germ.; pop. 11; 56 km E of Koln; 50°47'/07°45'; GED.

Wiszenka, *see* Vishenka.

Wiszenki, Ukr. (Vishinki); pop. 85; 75 km WNW of Rovno; 50°59'/25°21'; SF. *See also* Vishenki.

Wisznia, *see* Sudovaya Vishnya.

Wisznice, Pol. (Vishnitza); pop. 811; 82 km NNE of Lublin; 51°48'/23°13'; COH, EDRD, GA, GUM5, HSL, HSL2, LDS, SF.

Wiszniewo, *see* Vishnevo.

Wiszniew, *see* Vishnevo.

Wiszniewice, *see* Cycow.

Wiszniewo, *see* Vishnevo.

Wiszniow, Pol.; pop. 27; 120 km ESE of Lublin; 50°35'/23°54'. *See also* Vishnyuv.

Wiszow, *see* Vishev.

Wisztyniec, *see* Vistytis.

Witanowice, Pol.; pop. 10; 32 km SW of Krakow; 49°56'/19°33'.

Witaszyn, Pol.; pop. 6; 75 km S of Warszawa; 51°38'/20°53'.

Witebsk, *see* Vitebsk.

Witkow, Pol.; pop. 29; 120 km ESE of Lublin; 50°35'/23°59'; AMG, CAHJP, COH, EDRD, EJ, GA, GUM3, HSL.

Witkowitz, *see* Vitkovice.

Witkow Nowy, *see* Novyy Vitkov.

Witkowo, Pol. (Wittkowo); pop. 46; 56 km ENE of Poznan; 52°27'/17°48'; HSL.

Witkow Stary, *see* Novyy Vitkov.

Witnica, Pol. (Vietz); pop. 11; 94 km SSE of Szczecin; 52°40'/14°54'; POCEM.

Witoldow, Pol.; pop. 5; 107 km S of Bialystok; 52°13'/23°07'.

Witomino, Pol.; pop. 1; 26 km NW of Gdansk; 54°30'/18°30'.

Witoszynce, Pol.; pop. 6; 13 km SSW of Przemysl; 49°44'/22°44'.

Witow, Pol.; 88 km S of Krakow; 49°20'/19°49'; PHP1.

Witowice, Pol.; pop. 71; 38 km N of Krakow; 50°23'/19°56'.

Witowice Gorne, Pol.; pop. 25; 38 km N of Krakow; 50°23'/19°56'.

Witrynow, Pol.; pop. 27; 62 km SSW of Przemysl; 49°25'/22°15'. This town was located on an interwar map of Poland but does not appear in contemporary gazetteers. Map coordinates are approximate.

Wittelsberg, Germ.; pop. 8; 82 km N of Frankfurt am Main; 50°45'/08°51'; LDS.

Wittelshofen, Germ.; pop. 31; 62 km SW of Nurnberg; 49°04'/10°29'; GUM5, JGFF, PHGB.

Witten, Germ.; pop. 300; 56 km NNE of Koln; 51°26'/07°20'; AMG, GUM3.

Wittenberg, *see* Lutherstadt Wittenberg.

Wittenberge, Germ.; pop. 35; 126 km WNW of Berlin; 53°00'/11°45'; GUM3, GUM4.

Wittenburg, Germ.; 69 km E of Hamburg; 53°31'/11°04'; LDS.

Wittenheim, Germ. LDS. This town was not found in BGN gazetteers under the given spelling.

Wittkowo, *see* Witkowo.

Wittlich, Germ.; pop. 250; 114 km S of Koln; 49°59'/06°53'; GUM5.

Wittmund, Germ.; pop. 40; 146 km W of Hamburg; 53°34'/07°47'; AMG, LDS.

Wittstock, Germ.; 94 km NW of Berlin; 53°09'/12°30'; JGFF, LDS.

Witwica, Ukr.; pop. 34; 146 km S of Lvov; 48°35'/23°55'. This town was located on an interwar map of Poland but does not appear in contemporary gazetteers. Map coordinates are approximate.

Witzenhausen, Germ.; pop. 135; 120 km S of Hannover; 51°20'/09°52'; AMG, HSL, JGFF.

Wixhausen, Germ.; pop. 9; 26 km S of Frankfurt am Main; 49°56'/08°39'; LDS.

Wizajny, Pol. (Vizhon); pop. 332; 146 km NNW of Bialystok; 54°22'/22°51'; HSL, JGFF, LDS, PHP4, POCEM, SF.

Wizewo, *see* Uzava.

Wizna, Pol. (Vizhna); pop. 714; 50 km W of Bialystok; 53°12'/22°23'; CAHJP, GUM3, GUM4, GUM5, GUM6, JGFF, LDS, PHP4, SF.

Wiznitz, *see* Vizhnitsa.

Wizuny, *see* Vyzuonos.

Wizyn, Pol. PHP4. This town was not found in BGN gazetteers under the given spelling.

Wjasowka, *see* Vyazovka.

Wjasowok, SF. This town was not found in BGN gazetteers under the given spelling.

Wladimirez, *see* Vladimirets.

Wladyslawow, *see* Russocice.

Wladyslawowo, Pol.; 56 km NNW of Gdansk; 54°48'/18°25';

JGFF.

Wlasowce, *see* Vlasovtse.

Wlobczynce, Pol. PHP4. This town was not found in BGN gazetteers under the given spelling.

Wlochy, Pol.; pop. 13 km SW of Warszawa; 52°12'/20°55'; GUM4, GUM5, PHP2, PHP4.

Wloclawek, Pol. (Alt Lesle, Leslau, Leslo, Lesluya, Vlatzlavek, Vlotslavek, Votslavsk); pop. 9,595; 107 km NNW of Lodz; 52°39'/19°05'; AMG, COH, EDRD, EJ, GA, GUM3, GUM4, GUM5, GUM6, GYLA, HSL, HSL2, ISH3, JGFF, LDL, LDS, LYV, PHP1, PHP4, POCEM, SF, YB.

Wlodawa, Pol. (Vladova, Vlodava, Vlodavi, Vlodeve, Vlodova, Wlodowa); pop. 4,196; 82 km NE of Lublin; 51°34'/23°33'; AMG, CAHJP, COH, EDRD, EJ, GA, GUM3, GUM4, GUM5, GUM6, HSL, HSL2, JGFF, LDS, LYV, PHP3, POCEM, SF, YB.

Wlodawka, *see* Vlodavka.

Wlodowa, *see* Wlodawa.

Wlodowice, Pol.; pop. 71; 38 km SE of Czestochowa; 50°33'/19°27'.

Wlodzierzow, GUM5. This town was not found in BGN gazetteers under the given spelling.

Wlodzimierzec, *see* Vladimirets.

Wlodzimierzow, Pol.; 50 km SE of Lodz; 51°22'/19°50'; GUM4, PHP1.

Wlodzimierz Wolynski, *see* Vladimir Volynskiy.

Wloki, Pol. (Wloki Male, Wloki Piaski); pop. 255; 69 km WNW of Warszawa; 52°36'/20°09'; PHP4. BGN lists a town in Warszawa province, about 50 km east of Plock, that could not be found in contemporary gazetteers. The *Black Book* shows two towns in Warszawa province, Wloki Male (pop. 144) and Wloki Piaski (pop. 111).

Wloki Male, *see* Wloki.

Wloki Piaski, *see* Wloki.

Wlosan, Pol.; pop. 11; 26 km S of Krakow; 49°55'/19°55'.

Wloslawitz, *see* Wojslawice.

Wloszczowa, Pol. (Vloshtchovi); pop. 2,910; 62 km ENE of Czestochowa; 50°52'/19°58'; AMG, COH, EDRD, GA, GUM4, GUM5, HSL, HSL2, LDS, PHP4, POCEM, SF.

Wloszczowice, Pol.; pop. 11; 75 km NNE of Krakow; 50°38'/20°37'.

Wnetrzne, Pol.; pop. 29; 82 km NW of Lublin; 51°54'/22°05'.

Wobolniki, *see* Vabalninkas.

Woczerjasche, LDL. This pre-World War I community was not found in BGN gazetteers.

Wodna, Pol.; pop. 20; 38 km W of Krakow; 50°10'/19°26'.

Wodniki, *see* Vodniki.

Wodokaczka, Pol.; pop. 23; 26 km NNE of Bialystok; 53°18'/23°17'.

Wodynie, Pol.; pop. 34; 69 km ESE of Warszawa; 52°03'/21°58'; LDS.

Wodzierady, Pol.; 26 km WSW of Lodz; 51°43'/19°09'; PHP1.

Wodzinek, Pol.; pop. 23; A number of towns share this name. It was not possible to determine from available information which one is being referenced.

Wodzislaw, Pol. (Vodislav, Vodislov, Vodzislav, Voydislav); pop. 2,839; 56 km N of Krakow; 50°32'/20°12'; AMG, COH, EJ, GA, GUM3, GUM5, HSL, JGFF, LDS, LYV, PHP1, PHP3, PHP4, SF, YB.

Wohin, HSL. This pre-World War I community was not found in BGN gazetteers.

Wohlau, *see* Wolow.

Wohnbach, Germ.; 45 km N of Frankfurt am Main; 50°26'/08°50'; LDS.

Wohra, Germ.; pop. 36; 101 km N of Frankfurt am Main; 50°56'/08°57'; GUM5.

Wohrd, *see* Nurnberg.

Wohyn, Pol. (Vohin, Wohyn Lubelski); pop. 1,025; 62 km N of Lublin; 51°45'/22°47'; AMG, COH, GUM4, GUM5, LDS, POCEM, SF.

Wohyn Lubelski, *see* Wohyn.

Wojakowa, Pol.; pop. 16; 56 km ESE of Krakow; 49°49'/20°34'.

Wojaszowka, Pol.; pop. 8; 82 km WSW of Przemysl; 49°47'/21°41'.

Wojciechow, Pol.; pop. 24; 38 km E of Lublin; 51°11'/23°04'; LDL.

Wojciechow (near Przedborz), Pol.; pop. 20; 69 km NE of Czestochowa; 51°04'/19°59'.

Wojciechowka, Pol.; pop. 3; 69 km NW of Lublin; 51°44'/22°05'.

Wojcieszkow, Pol. (Voitzeshkov); pop. 86; 62 km NNW of Lublin; 51°46'/22°19'; GUM5, SF.

Wojcieszyce, Pol.; pop. 3; 107 km SW of Lublin; 50°35'/21°27'.

Wojcina, Pol.; pop. 9; 82 km NE of Krakow; 50°18'/20°59'.

Wojcza, Pol.; pop. 8; 82 km NE of Krakow; 50°24'/20°59'; GUM5.

Wojewodki Dolne, Pol.; pop. 12; 82 km ENE of Warszawa; 52°22'/22°14'.

Wojewodki Gorne, Pol.; pop. 3; 82 km ENE of Warszawa; 52°22'/22°15'.

Wojkow, Pol.; pop. 29; 114 km WNW of Przemysl; 50°27'/21°30'.

Wojkowa, Pol.; pop. 5; 114 km SE of Krakow; 49°21'/21°00'.

Wojkowice, *see* Voykovitse; Wojkowice Komorne.

Wojkowice Komorne, Pol. (Wojkowice); pop. 21; 50 km S of Czestochowa; 50°22'/19°04'.

Wojkowka, Pol.; pop. 6; 75 km WSW of Przemysl; 49°47'/21°42'.

Wojnarowa, Pol.; pop. 44; 82 km ESE of Krakow; 49°40'/20°56'.

Wojnica, *see* Voynitsa.

Wojnicz, Pol. (Voynitch); pop. 164; 62 km E of Krakow; 49°58'/20°50'; EGRS, GUM3, GUM5, HSL, PHP3, SF.

Wojnilow, *see* Voynilov.

Wojnow, Pol.; pop. 22; 107 km S of Bialystok; 52°13'/22°35'.

Wojska, *see* Voyskaya.

Wojslaw, Pol. (Voslab); pop. 24; 107 km ENE of Krakow; 50°16'/21°27'; HSL.

Wojslawice, Pol. (Wloslawitz); pop. 835; 82 km ESE of Lublin; 50°55'/23°33'; AMG, COH, EJ, GUM3, GUM4, GUM5, HSL, JGFF, LDL, LDS, LYV, POCEM, SF, YB. See also Voyslavitse.

Wojszki, Pol.; pop. 8; 26 km SSE of Bialystok; 52°56'/23°13'.

Wojszyce, Pol.; pop. 5; 56 km N of Lodz; 52°13'/19°32'.

Wojszyn, Pol.; pop. 9; 45 km W of Lublin; 51°21'/21°57'.

Wojtkowa, Pol.; pop. 113; 32 km SSW of Przemysl; 49°34'/22°34'; PHP2.

Wojtkowka, Pol.; pop. 58; 32 km SSW of Przemysl; 49°34'/22°35'.

Wojtostwo, Pol. (Wojtowstwo); pop. 32; 50 km SE of Lodz; 51°20'/19°51'.

Wojtowa, Pol.; pop. 50; 107 km ESE of Krakow; 49°42'/21°19'.

Wojtowstwo, *see* Wojtostwo.

Wojtyniow, Pol.; pop. 13; 114 km ESE of Lodz; 51°06'/20°44'.

Wojty Zamoscie, Pol.; pop. 21; Described in the *Black Book* as being in the Warszawa region of Poland, this town was not found in BGN gazetteers.

Wojutycze, *see* Voyutychi.

Wojutyn, *see* Voyutin.

Wokowice, Pol.; pop. 13; 56 km E of Krakow; 50°01'/20°42'.

Wola, AMG, HSL, HSL2, LDL. A number of towns share this name. It was not possible to determine from available information which one is being referenced.

Wola Baraniecka, Ukr.; pop. 45; 94 km SW of Lvov; 49°15'/23°05'. This town was located on an interwar map of Poland but does not appear in contemporary gazetteers. Map coordinates are approximate.

Wola Batorska, Pol.; pop. 28; 26 km E of Krakow; 50°04'/20°16'.

Wola Blakowa, Pol.; pop. 36; 45 km N of Czestochowa; 51°08'/19°18'.

Wola Blazowska, *see* Volya Blazhovska.

Wola Bledowa, Pol.; pop. 6; 26 km NNE of Lodz; 51°56'/19°38'.

Wola Blizocka, Pol.; pop. 4; 50 km NW of Lublin; 51°37'/22°15'.

Wola Bokrzycka, Pol. (Wola Boksycka); pop. 6; 94 km NE of

Krakow; 50°36'/20°54'.

Wola Boksycka, *see* Wola Bokrzycka.

Wola Branicka, Pol.; pop. 6; 26 km N of Lodz; 51°56'/19°28'.

Wola Brzeznicka, Pol.; pop. 13; 101 km WNW of Przemysl; 50°06'/21°30'.

Wola Brzostecka, Pol.; pop. 13; 94 km W of Przemysl; 49°54'/21°28'.

Wola Buchowska, Pol.; pop. 29; 38 km NNW of Przemysl; 50°06'/22°36'.

Wola Bystrzycka, Pol.; pop. 8; 62 km NNW of Lublin; 51°46'/22°20'.

Wola Chomejowa, Pol.; pop. 7; 69 km N of Lublin; 51°47'/22°28'.

Wola Cicha, Pol.; pop. 7; 69 km WNW of Przemysl; 50°08'/21°58'.

Wola Cieklinska, Pol.; pop. 6; 101 km WSW of Przemysl; 49°39'/21°23'.

Wola Czolnowska, Pol.; pop. 6; 45 km NW of Lublin; 51°33'/22°11'.

Wola Dereznianska, Pol. (Dereznianska Wola); pop. 5; 82 km N of Przemysl; 50°29'/22°40'.

Wola Dolholucka, Pol.; pop. 34; Described in the *Black Book* as being in the Stanislawow region of Poland, this town was not found in BGN gazetteers.

Wola Domatkowska, Pol.; pop. 3; 88 km WNW of Przemysl; 50°12'/21°43'.

Wola Duchacka, Pol.; pop. 12; 13 km SE of Krakow; 50°02'/19°59'; GUM4, GUM5, PHP3.

Wola Filipowska, Pol.; pop. 24; 26 km W of Krakow; 50°08'/19°35'.

Wola Gnojnicka, *see* Volya Gnoynitska.

Wola Gorzanska, Pol.; pop. 10; 62 km SSW of Przemysl; 49°19'/22°23'.

Wola Greboszowska, Pol.; pop. 16; 69 km ENE of Krakow; 50°15'/20°48'.

Wola Gulowska, Pol.; pop. 14; 56 km NW of Lublin; 51°43'/22°14'.

Wola Idzikowska, Pol.; pop. 20; 32 km ESE of Lublin; 51°06'/22°59'.

Wola Jachowa, Pol. (Wola Jackowa); pop. 23; 107 km NNE of Krakow; 50°51'/20°52'.

Wola Jackowa, *see* Wola Jachowa.

Wola Jajkowska, Pol.; pop. 26; 45 km N of Czestochowa; 51°06'/19°07'.

Wola Jakubowa, Ukr.; pop. 26; 69 km SSW of Lvov; 49°20'/23°35'. This town was located on an interwar map of Poland but does not appear in contemporary gazetteers. Map coordinates are approximate.

Wola Jasienicka, Pol.; 101 km WSW of Przemysl; 49°46'/21°24'; PHP3.

Wola Justowska, Pol.; pop. 6; 6 km SW of Krakow; 50°04'/19°53'.

Wola Kaluska, Pol. (Kaluska Wola); pop. 229; 56 km E of Warszawa; 52°10'/21°47'; PHP4.

Wola Kanigowska, Pol.; pop. 6; 82 km NW of Warszawa; 52°53'/20°23'.

Wola Karczewska, Pol.; pop. 6; 32 km ESE of Warszawa; 52°08'/21°23'.

Wola Korybutowa, Pol.; pop. 9; 38 km E of Lublin; 51°14'/23°05'.

Wola Korycka, Pol.; pop. 27; 82 km WNW of Lublin; 51°44'/21°45'.

Wola Korytnicka, Pol.; pop. 27; 62 km NE of Warszawa; 52°25'/21°49'.

Wola Korzeniecka, Pol.; pop. 5; 26 km SW of Przemysl; 49°42'/22°30'.

Wola Kotkowska, Pol. (Kotkowska Wola); pop. 5; 56 km NNE of Czestochowa; 51°10'/19°37'.

Wola Krzysztoporska, Pol. (Vola Kshishtoporska); pop. 79; 50 km SSE of Lodz; 51°21'/19°35'; PHP1, SF.

Wola Krzywiecka, Pol. (Krzywiecka Wola); pop. 27; 13 km W

of Przemysl; 49°49'/22°35'.

Wola Laska, Pol. (Laska Wola); pop. 33; A number of towns share this name. It was not possible to determine from available information which one is being referenced.

Wola Magnuszewska, Pol.; pop. 6; 62 km SE of Warszawa; 51°46'/21°22'.

Wola Malowana, Pol.; pop. 27; 50 km NE of Czestochowa; 51°04'/19°38'.

Wola Mazowiecka, Pol. PHP2. This town was not found in BGN gazetteers under the given spelling.

Wola Michowa, Pol.; pop. 148; 82 km SSW of Przemysl; 49°14'/22°09'; JGFF, PHP2, PHP3.

Wola Miedniewska, Pol.; 50 km SW of Warszawa; 52°06'/20°18'; GA.

Wola Mielecka, Pol.; pop. 17; 107 km ENE of Krakow; 50°17'/21°22'.

Wola Mlocka, Pol.; pop. 4; 69 km NW of Warszawa; 52°47'/20°25'.

Wola Morawicka, Pol.; pop. 4; 88 km NNE of Krakow; 50°44'/20°38'.

Wola Mystkowska, Pol. (Mystkowska Wola); pop. 20; 45 km NNE of Warszawa; 52°38'/21°20'.

Wola Niechcicka Nowa, Pol. (Niechcicka Wola Nowa); pop. 45; 56 km SSE of Lodz; 51°16'/19°35'.

Wola Nieszkowska, Pol.; pop. 3; 38 km ESE of Krakow; 49°54'/20°23'.

Wola Nizna, Pol.; pop. 5; 75 km SW of Przemysl; 49°27'/21°51'.

Wolanka, *see* Volanka.

Wolanow, Pol. (Volonov); pop. 318; 101 km S of Warszawa; 51°23'/20°58'; AMG, GA, GUM3, GUM4, GUM5, LDS, SF.

Wola Obszanska, Pol. (Obszanska Wola); pop. 77; 62 km N of Przemysl; 50°19'/22°55'.

Wola Okrzejska, Pol.; 62 km NW of Lublin; 51°46'/22°09'; GUM3.

Wola Pawlowska, Pol. (Pawlowska Wola); pop. 29; 56 km SW of Lublin; 51°04'/21°47'; AMG, PHP1.

Wola Pelkinska, *see* Wolka Pelkinska.

Wola Pieczyska, Pol.; pop. 3; 45 km S of Warszawa; 51°56'/21°03'.

Wola Plawska, Pol.; pop. 6; 107 km ENE of Krakow; 50°21'/21°24'.

Wola Przemykowska, Pol.; pop. 62; 50 km ENE of Krakow; 50°10'/20°39'.

Wola Przybyslawska, Pol.; pop. 12; 26 km WNW of Lublin; 51°24'/22°20'; GUM4.

Wola Radlowska, Pol.; pop. 4; 62 km E of Krakow; 50°05'/20°50'.

Wola Radziszowska, Pol.; pop. 28; 26 km SSW of Krakow; 49°55'/19°47'.

Wola Ranizowska, Pol. (Ranizov, Reinzov); pop. 90; 82 km WNW of Przemysl; 50°18'/21°58'; GUM5, PHP3, SF.

Wola Rasztowska, Pol.; pop. 29; 32 km NE of Warszawa; 52°27'/21°18'.

Wola Reczajska, Pol. (Reczajska Wola); pop. 20; 26 km ENE of Warszawa; 52°19'/21°24'.

Wola Rozwieniecka, Pol.; pop. 16; 26 km NW of Przemysl; 49°58'/22°34'.

Wola Rusinowska, Pol.; pop. 13; 94 km WNW of Przemysl; 50°22'/21°50'.

Wola Sekowa, Pol. (Sekowa Wola); pop. 5; 62 km SW of Przemysl; 49°30'/22°01'; HSL.

Wola Siennicka, Pol.; pop. 5; 62 km ESE of Lublin; 51°00'/23°20'.

Wola Sniatycka, Pol.; pop. 52; Described in the *Black Book* as being in the Lublin region of Poland, this town was not found in BGN gazetteers.

Wola Solecka, Pol.; pop. 13; 56 km WSW of Lublin; 51°12'/21°43'.

Wola Suchozebrska, Pol.; pop. 9; 82 km E of Warszawa; 52°15'/22°14'.

Wola Szczygielkowa, Pol.; pop. 16; 114 km SW of Lublin;

50°54'/20°58'.

Wola Szkucka, Pol.; pop. 4; 82 km NE of Czestochowa; 51°07'/20°07'.

Wola Trebska, Pol.; pop. 2; 69 km N of Lodz; 52°20'/19°31'.

Wola Trzydnicka, Pol.; pop. 6; 69 km NW of Lublin; 51°50'/22°08'.

Wola Uhruska, Pol.; pop. 58; 75 km ENE of Lublin; 51°19'/23°38'.

Wola Wadowska, Pol.; pop. 61; 94 km ENE of Krakow; 50°16'/21°11'.

Wolawce, Pol.; pop. 5; 75 km E of Lublin; 51°04'/23°35'.

Wola Wegierska, Pol.; pop. 13; 19 km WNW of Przemysl; 49°51'/22°35'.

Wola Wereszczynska, Pol.; pop. 27; 45 km NE of Lublin; 51°26'/23°08'.

Wola Wezykowa, Pol.; pop. 8; 45 km SW of Lodz; 51°28'/19°01'.

Wola Wielka, Pol.; pop. 22; 75 km NNE of Przemysl; 50°18'/23°24'.

Wola Wisniowa, Pol.; pop. 5; 62 km ENE of Czestochowa; 50°50'/20°00'.

Wola Wodynska, Pol.; pop. 7; 75 km ESE of Warszawa; 52°02'/22°01'.

Wola Wydrzyna, Pol.; pop. 8; 50 km N of Czestochowa; 51°12'/19°09'.

Wola Wysocka, *see* Volya Vysotska.

Wola Zabierzowska, Pol.; pop. 5; 32 km E of Krakow; 50°04'/20°21'.

Wola Zaleska, Pol. (Zaleska Wola); pop. 26; 26 km NNE of Przemysl; 49°59'/22°59'.

Wola Zambrowska, Pol.; pop. 7; 62 km WSW of Bialystok; 52°58'/22°16'.

Wola Zamkowa, Pol. (Zamkowa Wola); pop. 23; 114 km SW of Lublin; 50°49'/21°05'; PHP1.

Wola Zarczycka, Pol. (Wola Zarczyska); pop. 101; 69 km NW of Przemysl; 50°18'/22°15'; PHP3.

Wola Zarczyska, *see* Wola Zarczycka.

Wola Zdakowska, Pol.; pop. 8; 114 km NE of Krakow; 50°25'/21°25'.

Wola Zelechowska, Pol. (Vola, Wola Zelichowska); 82 km NW of Lublin; 51°49'/21°52'; HSL, SF.

Wola Zelichowska, *see* Wola Zelechowska.

Wola Zglobienska, Pol.; 69 km WNW of Przemysl; 50°00'/21°49'; PHP3.

Wola Zycinska, Pol.; pop. 9; 56 km NE of Czestochowa; 50°57'/19°49'.

Wola Zycka, Pol.; pop. 4; 75 km WNW of Lublin; 51°41'/21°44'.

Wola Zydowska, Pol.; pop. 1; 75 km NNE of Krakow; 50°36'/20°39'.

Wola Zyrakowska, Pol.; pop. 4; 101 km WNW of Przemysl; 50°06'/21°25'.

Wolbattendorf, Germ.; 114 km S of Leipzig; 50°19'/11°51'; PHGB.

Wolbeck, Germ.; pop. 34; 120 km NNE of Koln; 51°55'/07°44'; LDS.

Wolborz, Pol. (Volborzh); pop. 443; 38 km SE of Lodz; 51°30'/19°50'; AMG, CAHJP, EJ, GUM4, GUM5, HSL, HSL2, LDL, LDS, PHP1, SF, YB.

Wolbrom, Pol. (Volbrom); pop. 4,276; 38 km NNW of Krakow; 50°24'/19°46'; AMG, CAHJP, COH, EDRD, GA, GUM3, GUM4, GUM5, HSL, HSL2, ISH1, ISH3, LDL, LDS, LYV, PHP1, PHP3, POCEM, SF, YB.

Wolchowo, LDL. This pre-World War I community was not found in BGN gazetteers.

Wolcza Dolna, *see* Volche.

Wolczansk, *see* Volchansk.

Wolczatycze, *see* Volchatyche.

Wolcze, *see* Volchi.

Wolczkowce, *see* Volchkovtsy.

Wolczyn, Pol. (Konstadt); pop. 80; 75 km E of Wroclaw; 51°01'/18°03'; LDS, POCEM. *See also* Volchin.

Wolczyny, Pol.; pop. 47; 75 km ENE of Lublin; 51°26'/23°39'.

Wolczyszczowice, *see* Volchishchovitsa.

Woldenberg, *see* Dobiegniew.

Woldenburg, *see* Dobiegniew.

Wolfenbuttel, Germ.; pop. 125; 62 km ESE of Hannover; 52°10'/10°33'; AMG, CAHJP, GUM4, HSL, LDS.

Wolferode, Germ.; 94 km N of Frankfurt am Main; 50°53'/08°59'; LDS.

Wolfhagen, Germ.; pop. 78; 126 km S of Hannover; 51°19'/09°10'; GED, LDS.

Wolframs Eschenbach, Germ.; 38 km SW of Nurnberg; 49°14'/10°44'; PHGB.

Wolfratshausen, Germ.; pop. 20; 32 km SSW of Munchen; 47°55'/11°25'; GUM3, GUM5.

Wolfsberg, Aus.; 50 km SW of Graz; 46°50'/14°50'; EDRD, GUM4, GUM5, GUM5, GUM6.

Wolfsegg, Germ.; 75 km ESE of Nurnberg; 49°06'/11°59'; GUM5, PHGB.

Wolfsheim, Germ.; 56 km SW of Frankfurt am Main; 49°52'/08°02'; HSL.

Wolfskehlen, Germ.; pop. 3; 32 km SSW of Frankfurt am Main; 49°51'/08°30'; GUM5.

Wolfsmunster, Germ.; 75 km E of Frankfurt am Main; 50°05'/09°44'; PHGB.

Wolgast, Germ.; pop. 28; 107 km E of Rostock; 54°03'/13°46'.

Wolica, Pol.; pop. 57; 88 km NNE of Krakow; 50°46'/20°29'; PHP1, PHP3. *See also* Volitsa.

Wolica (near Jaslo), Pol.; pop. 5; 94 km WSW of Przemysl; 49°44'/21°31'.

Wolica (near Sanok), Pol.; pop. 7; 56 km SW of Przemysl; 49°31'/22°06'.

Wolica (near Stopnica), Pol.; pop. 64; 88 km NE of Krakow; 50°34'/20°58'.

Wolica Derewianska, *see* Volitsa Derevlyanska.

Wolica Hnizdyczowska, *see* Volitsa Gnizdychuvsk.

Wolica Komarowa, *see* Volytsya.

Wolica Lugowa, Pol.; pop. 4; 82 km WNW of Przemysl; 50°05'/21°43'.

Wolica Wygoda, Ukr. YB. Wolica Wygoda could not be found in contemporary gazetteers. It is listed in the yizkor book for Radekhov (Radziechow). There is a town of Vygoda at 50°19'/24°51', 20 km east of Radekhov.

Wolin, Pol.; 45 km N of Szczecin; 53°50'/14°36'; LDS. *See also* Volyne.

Wolina, Pol.; pop. 5; 88 km S of Lublin; 50°30'/22°12'.

Wolka, Byel.; pop. 24; 69 km NE of Pinsk; 52°21'/26°59'. *See also* Vulka Popinskaya.

Wolka Baltowska, Pol.; pop. 3; 75 km SW of Lublin; 51°02'/21°32'.

Wolka Batorska, Pol.; pop. 7; 45 km S of Lublin; 50°52'/22°31'.

Wolka Bielinska, Pol.; pop. 5; 88 km S of Lublin; 50°28'/22°17'.

Wolka Biska, Pol. (Biska Wolka); pop. 4; 75 km NNW of Przemysl; 50°26'/22°35'.

Wolka Bodzechowska, Pol.; pop. 7; 82 km SW of Lublin; 50°56'/21°27'.

Wolka Cycowska, Pol.; pop. 20; 38 km ENE of Lublin; 51°19'/23°07'.

Wolka Domaszewska, Pol.; 69 km NNW of Lublin; 51°50'/22°21'; GA.

Wolka Dulecka, Pol.; pop. 16; 94 km ENE of Krakow; 50°12'/21°16'.

Wolka Goscieradowska, Pol.; pop. 9; 56 km SSW of Lublin; 50°52'/22°02'.

Wolka Gruszczynska, Pol.; pop. 11; 50 km SE of Warszawa; 51°51'/21°21'.

Wolka Horyniecka, Pol.; pop. 55; 62 km NNE of Przemysl; 50°11'/23°19'.

Wolka Horyszowska, Pol.; pop. 3; 82 km ESE of Lublin; 50°44'/23°25'.

Wolka Jedlanska, Pol.; pop. 20; Described in the *Black Book* as being in the Kielce region of Poland, this town was not found in BGN gazetteers.

Wolka Kanska, Pol.; pop. 21; 38 km ESE of Lublin; 51°08'/23°05'; GUM4.

Wolka Karwicka, Pol.; pop. 8; 75 km ESE of Lodz; 51°25'/20°25'.

Wolka Katna, Pol.; pop. 4; 26 km WNW of Lublin; 51°26'/22°17'.

Wolka Klucka, Pol.; pop. 15; 88 km ENE of Czestochowa; 50°59'/20°22'.

Wolka Konopna, Pol.; pop. 7; 94 km N of Lublin; 52°02'/22°28'.

Wolka Krzykowska, Pol.; pop. 7; 38 km ESE of Lodz; 51°34'/19°53'.

Wolka Labunska, Pol.; pop. 5; 94 km SE of Lublin; 50°38'/23°23'.

Wolka Lancuchowska, Pol.; pop. 14; 26 km ENE of Lublin; 51°16'/22°54'.

Wolka Leszczanska, Pol.; 75 km ESE of Lublin; 51°01'/23°38'; GUM5.

Wolka Letowska, Pol.; pop. 19; 75 km NW of Przemysl; 50°18'/22°12'.

Wolka Lubielska, Pol.; pop. 53; 62 km NNE of Warszawa; 52°46'/21°24'.

Wolka Lukowska, Pol.; pop. 3; 69 km N of Warszawa; 52°52'/20°56'.

Wolka Malkowa, Pol.; pop. 7; 45 km NW of Przemysl; 50°08'/22°31'.

Wolka Medrzechowska, Pol.; pop. 7; 82 km ENE of Krakow; 50°16'/21°02'.

Wolka Nieliska, Pol.; pop. 21; 56 km SE of Lublin; 50°49'/23°06'.

Wolka Ogryzkowa, Pol.; pop. 5; 45 km NNW of Przemysl; 50°08'/22°34'.

Wolka Okopska, Pol.; pop. 23; Described in the *Black Book* as being in the Lublin region of Poland, this town was not found in BGN gazetteers.

Wolka Panienska, Pol.; pop. 6; 82 km SE of Lublin; 50°42'/23°19'.

Wolka Pelkinska, Pol. (Wola Pelkinska); pop. 24; 38 km NNW of Przemysl; 50°05'/22°37'.

Wolka Petkowska, Pol.; pop. 5; 69 km SW of Lublin; 51°01'/21°38'.

Wolka Petrylowska, Pol.; pop. 6; 56 km ENE of Lublin; 51°21'/23°25'.

Wolka Proszewska, Pol.; pop. 6; 75 km ENE of Warszawa; 52°17'/22°04'.

Wolka Przekory, Pol.; pop. 14; 50 km NNE of Warszawa; 52°40'/21°19'.

Wolka Putnowicka, *see* Wolka Putnowiecka.

Wolka Putnowiecka, Pol. (Wolka Putnowicka); pop. 19; 82 km ESE of Lublin; 50°57'/23°40'.

Wolka Radzyminska, Pol.; pop. 3; 26 km N of Warszawa; 52°25'/21°06'.

Wolka Skotnicka, Pol.; pop. 2; 69 km SE of Lodz; 51°13'/19°57'.

Wolka Sokolowska, Pol.; pop. 42; 69 km NW of Przemysl; 50°15'/22°12'.

Wolka Szczytynska, Pol.; pop. 52; Described in the *Black Book* as being in the Polesie region of Poland, this town was not found in BGN gazetteers.

Wolka Tanewska, Pol.; pop. 44; 88 km S of Lublin; 50°30'/22°16'.

Wolka Uhruska, *see* Vulka Ugruska.

Wolka Wojcieszkowska, Pol.; pop. 27; 62 km WNW of Lublin; 51°32'/21°49'.

Wolka Wojnowska, Pol. (Volkovonovke); 82 km SW of Lublin; 50°53'/21°34'; FRG.

Wolka Zaleska, Pol.; pop. 5; 38 km SSW of Bialystok; 52°50'/22°52'.

Wolki, Pol.; 88 km E of Gdansk; 54°11'/19°59'; PHP4.

Wolkolata, *see* Volkolata.

Wolkow, *see* Volkov.

Wolkowce, *see* Volkovtsy.

Wolkowiany, Pol.; pop. 39; 82 km ESE of Lublin; 51°02'/23°40'.

Wolkowinz, *see* Volkovintsy.

Wolkowinzy, *see* Volkovintsy.

Wolkowyja, Pol.; pop. 14; 56 km SSW of Przemysl; 49°20'/22°25'.

Wolkowyje, *see* Volkovyye.

Wolkowysk, *see* Volkovysk.

Wolkowysko, Pol. PHP4. This town was not found in BGN gazetteers under the given spelling.

Wollenberg, Germ.; 62 km NNW of Stuttgart; 49°18'/09°02'; LDS, PHGBW.

Wollin, *see* Volyne.

Wollmarshausen, Germ.; 107 km SSE of Hannover; 51°29'/10°05'; JGFF.

Wollstein, *see* Wolsztyn.

Wolma, *see* Volma.

Wolmar, *see* Valmiera.

Wolna, *see* Volna.

Wolnianka Mala, Ukr.; pop. 77; 69 km WSW of Rovno; 50°35'/25°15'. This town was located on an interwar map of Poland but does not appear in contemporary gazetteers. Map coordinates are approximate.

Wolnianka Wielka, Pol.; pop. 189; Described in the *Black Book* as being in the Wolyn region of Poland, this town was not found in BGN gazetteers.

Wolnica Niechmirowska, Pol.; pop. 6; 69 km NNW of Czestochowa; 51°22'/18°45'.

Wolochy, *see* Volokhi.

Woloczysk, *see* Volochisk.

Wolodz, Pol.; pop. 11; 38 km WSW of Przemysl; 49°44'/22°13'; AMG.

Wolomin, Pol. (Slawek, Volomin); pop. 3,079; 19 km NE of Warszawa; 52°21'/21°15'; AMG, COH, EDRD, EJ, GA, GUM3, GUM4, GUM5, HSL, LDL, LYV, PHP4, SF, YB.

Wolontir, *see* Volontirovka.

Wolosate, Pol.; pop. 24; 88 km S of Przemysl; 49°04'/22°42'.

Wolosianka, *see* Volosyanka.

Wolosianka Wielka, Ukr.; pop. 28; 120 km SSW of Lvov; 48°55'/23°05'. This town was located on an interwar map of Poland but does not appear in contemporary gazetteers. Map coordinates are approximate.

Woloska, Pol. (Woloska Wies); pop. 216; 69 km SSW of Przemysl; 49°15'/22°25'; JGFF, PHP2. This town was located on an interwar map of Poland but does not appear in contemporary gazetteers. Map coordinates are approximate.

Woloska Wies, *see* Woloska.

Woloskin, *see* Volozhin.

Wolosow, *see* Volosov.

Wolosowka, *see* Volosuvka.

Wolostow, *possibly* Volostkov.

Wolosza, Ukr.; pop. 22; 26 km NNE of Rovno; 50°45'/26°25'. This town was located on an interwar map of Poland but does not appear in contemporary gazetteers. Map coordinates are approximate.

Woloszcza, *see* Voloshcha.

Woloszczyzna, *see* Voloshchizna.

Wolow, Pol. (Wohlau); pop. 29; 107 km NE of Czestochowa; 51°08'/20°36'; GUM4.

Wolowa, *see* Mezhgorye.

Wolowe, *see* Mezhgorye.

Wolowice, Pol.; pop. 3; 19 km SW of Krakow; 49°59'/19°44'.

Wolowiec, Pol.; pop. 4; 107 km WSW of Przemysl; 49°32'/21°22'.

Wolowil, *see* Volovel.

Wolowitz, HSL. This pre-World War I community was not found in BGN gazetteers.

Wolozyce, GUM4. This town was not found in BGN gazetteers under the given spelling.

Wolozyn, *see* Volozhin.

Wolpa, *see* Volpa.

Wolsau, Germ.; pop. 2; 94 km NE of Nurnberg; 50°00'/12°07'.

Wolswin, *see* Volsvin.

Wolsztyn, Pol. (Wollstein); pop. 64; 69 km SW of Poznan; 52°07'/16°08'; CAHJP, GUM5, HSL, JGFF.

Woluszewo, Pol.; pop. 4; 133 km NE of Poznan; 52°54'/18°45'.

Woluta, *see* Voluta.

Wonfurt, Germ.; 75 km NW of Nurnberg; 50°01'/10°28'; PHGB.

Wongrowitz, *see* Wagrowiec.

Woniacze Dobrowola, Pol.; pop. 60; Described in the *Black Book* as being in the Polesie region of Poland, this town was not found in BGN gazetteers.

Wonsees, Germ.; 62 km N of Nurnberg; 49°59'/11°18'; PHGB.

Wopienno, *see* Wapienno.

Woquard, Germ.; pop. 2; 189 km WSW of Hamburg; 53°26'/07°06'.

Worblingen, Germ.; 120 km S of Stuttgart; 47°44'/08°52'; JGFF, PHGBW.

Worchowka, *see* Verkhovka.

Worczyn, *see* Vorchin.

Worl, HSL. This pre-World War I community was not found in BGN gazetteers.

Worlitz, Germ.; 62 km N of Leipzig; 51°50'/12°25'; HSL, LDS.

Wormditt, *see* Orneta.

Worms, Germ.; pop. 1,194; 56 km SSW of Frankfurt am Main; 49°38'/08°21'; AMG, CAHJP, EDRD, EJ, GED, GUM3, GUM4, GUM5, HSL, JGFF, LDS, PHGBW, PHP3, PHP4, YB.

Wornie, *see* Varniai.

Worobin, *see* Vorobin.

Worocewicze, *see* Vorotsevichi.

Worochta, *see* Vorokhta.

Worokomla, *see* Vorokomle.

Woronczyn, *see* Voronchin.

Woronesch, *see* Voronezh.

Woronez, *see* Voronezh.

Woroniaki, *see* Voronyaki.

Woroniec, Pol.; 75 km NNE of Lublin; 51°49'/23°02'; GA.

Woronino, *see* Voronino.

Woronki, *see* Voronki.

Woronkow, *see* Voronkov.

Woronovitsy, Ukr. EDRD. This town was not found in BGN gazetteers under the given spelling.

Woronow, *see* Voronuv.

Woronowo, *see* Voronovo.

Woropajewo, *see* Voropayevo.

Woroschilowka, *see* Voroshilovka.

Woroszylowgrad, *see* Voroshilovgrad.

Worpswede, Germ.; pop. 1; 75 km SW of Hamburg; 53°13'/08°56'.

Worrstadt, Germ.; pop. 50; 50 km SW of Frankfurt am Main; 49°50'/08°06'; GED, GUM5.

Worth am Main, Germ.; pop. 23; 50 km ESE of Frankfurt am Main; 49°48'/09°10'; PHGB.

Worth an der Donau, Germ.; pop. 107 km ESE of Nurnberg; 49°01'/12°24'; GUM3, GUM5.

Worwolince, *see* Vorgulintsy.

Woskorzenice Duze, Pol. (Woskrzenice Wielkie); 101 km NNE of Lublin; 52°03'/23°16'; GA.

Woskrzenice Wielkie, *see* Woskorzenice Duze.

Wossnesenk, GUM5. This town was not found in BGN gazetteers under the given spelling.

Woszczance, *see* Voshchantsy.

Woszczkowo, Pol.; 75 km N of Wroclaw; 51°41'/17°00'; GA.

Wotitz, *see* Votice.

Wozniczna, Pol.; pop. 8; 75 km E of Krakow; 49°57'/20°58'.

Wozniesiensk, *see* Voznesensk.

Woznowszczyzna, *see* Voznovshchina.

Wozuczyn, Pol.; pop. 11; 101 km NNE of Przemysl; 50°34'/23°34'.

Wreby, Pol.; pop. 36; 120 km ESE of Lublin; 50°35'/23°55'. This town was located on an interwar map of Poland but does not appear in contemporary gazetteers. Map coordinates are approximate.

Wreczyca Wielka, Pol.; pop. 8; 19 km WNW of Czestochowa; 50°51'/18°56'.

Wreschen, *see* Wrzesnia.

Wrexen, Germ.; 107 km SSW of Hannover; 51°31'/09°00'; GUM3.

Wriezen, Germ.; pop. 127; 56 km NE of Berlin; 52°43'/14°08'; HSL, LDS.

Wroblaczyn, *see* Voroblyachin.

Wroblewszczyzna, *see* Vrublevshchina.

Wroblik Krolewski, Pol.; pop. 26; 69 km WSW of Przemysl; 49°37'/21°52'.

Wroblik Szlachecki, Pol.; pop. 52; 69 km WSW of Przemysl; 49°37'/21°53'; JGFF.

Wroblowice, Pol.; pop. 25; 75 km ESE of Krakow; 49°53'/20°52'.

Wroblowka, Pol.; pop. 6; 75 km S of Krakow; 49°28'/19°53'.

Wrocien, Pol.; pop. 3; 50 km NW of Bialystok; 53°32'/22°51'.

Wrocieryz, Pol.; pop. 14; 56 km NNE of Krakow; 50°30'/20°23'.

Wroclaw, Pol. (Breslau, Bresslau); pop. 24,433; 150 km W of Czestochowa; 51°05'/17°00'; AMG, CAHJP, EDRD, EJ, GUM3, GUM4, GUM5, GUM6, HSL, HSL2, ISH1, ISH3, JGFF, LDL, LDS, LJEE, PHGBW, PHP1, PHP2, PHP3, PHP4, POCEM.

Wrocow, *see* Vrotsuv.

Wroczyny, Pol.; pop. 5; 56 km NNW of Lodz; 52°13'/19°16'.

Wronin, Pol.; pop. 18; 19 km NE of Krakow; 50°09'/20°12'.

Wronka, Germ. JGFF. A number of towns share this name. It was not possible to determine from available information which one is being referenced.

Wronke, *see* Wronki.

Wronki, Pol. (Vronik, Wronke); pop. 187; 50 km WNW of Poznan; 52°43'/16°24'; CAHJP, EJ, GUM3, HSL, LDS, PHP2.

Wronow, Pol.; pop. 39; 45 km WNW of Lublin; 51°28'/22°03'.

Wronowice, Pol.; pop. 30; 107 km ESE of Lublin; 50°41'/23°45'.

Wrzaca, Pol. (Wrzaca Wielka); 82 km WNW of Lodz; 52°01'/18°25'; POCEM.

Wrzaca Wielka, *see* Wrzaca.

Wrzawy, Pol.; pop. 13; 75 km SSW of Lublin; 50°43'/21°51'.

Wrzepia, Pol.; pop. 17; 50 km E of Krakow; 50°05'/20°33'.

Wrzesnia, Pol. (Wreschen); pop. 151; 45 km E of Poznan; 52°19'/17°35'; AMG, GUM4, HSL, HSL2, JGFF, LDS, PHP1.

Wrzeszczewo, Pol. (Wrzeszewo); pop. 1; 139 km SSE of Gdansk; 53°10'/19°21'.

Wrzeszewo, *see* Wrzeszczewo.

Wschowa, Pol. (Fraustadt); pop. 125; 82 km SSW of Poznan; 51°48'/16°19'; AMG, HSL, JGFF, LDS, POCEM.

Wsetin, *see* Vsetin.

Wsielub, *see* Vselyub.

Wszerzecz, Pol.; pop. 6; 82 km WSW of Bialystok; 53°07'/21°56'.

Wujowka, Pol.; pop. 33; 45 km NE of Warszawa; 52°27'/21°35'.

Wujskie, Pol.; pop. 6; 45 km SW of Przemysl; 49°33'/22°18'.

Wujwicze, *see* Vuyvichi.

Wukowar, *see* Vukovar.

Wulfrath, Germ.; pop. 3; 45 km N of Koln; 51°17'/07°03'.

Wulka, *see* Vulka.

Wulka Mazowiecka, *see* Vulka Mazovetskaya.

Wulzeshofen, Aus.; pop. 9; 62 km N of Wien; 48°43'/16°18'.

Wunsiedel, Germ.; pop. 4; 94 km NE of Nurnberg; 50°02'/12°01'; PHGB.

Wunstorf, Germ.; pop. 53; 26 km WNW of Hannover; 52°26'/09°25'; AMG, GED.

Wuppertal, Germ. (Elberfeld, Wuppertal Elberfeld); pop. 2,500; 45 km NNE of Koln; 51°16'/07°11'; AMG, EJ, GED, GUM3, GUM5, HSL, HSL2, PHGBW.

Wuppertal Barmen, Germ.; pop. 730; 45 km NNE of Koln; 51°16'/07°11'.

Wuppertal Elberfeld, *see* Wuppertal.

Wurselen, Germ.; pop. 20; 62 km WSW of Koln; 50°49'/06°08'.

Wurzburg, Germ. (Wuerzburg); pop. 2,145; 94 km ESE of

Frankfurt am Main; 49°48'/09°56'; AMG, CAHJP, EDRD, EJ, GED, GUM3, GUM4, GUM5, GUM6, HSL, HSL2, JGFF, LDL, PHGB, PHGBW.

Wustensachsen, Germ.; pop. 90; 107 km NE of Frankfurt am Main; 50°30'/10°01'; GUM5, JGFF.

Wusterhausen, Germ.; 75 km WNW of Berlin; 52°53'/12°28'; LDS.

Wusterwitz, Germ.; pop. 1; 69 km WSW of Berlin; 52°23'/12°24'.

Wybranowka, *see* Vybranovka.

Wychodz, *see* Wychodzc.

Wychodzc, Pol. (Wychodz); pop. 67; 45 km WNW of Warszawa; 52°24'/20°25'.

Wyciaze, Pol.; pop. 36; 19 km E of Krakow; 50°04'/20°10'.

Wyczerpy Dolne, Pol. (Wyczerpy Gorne); pop. 69; 13 km NNE of Czestochowa; 50°51'/19°11'.

Wyczerpy Gorne, *see* Wyczerpy Dolne.

Wyczolki, Pol. PHP2. A number of towns share this name. It was not possible to determine from available information which one is being referenced.

Wyderta, *see* Vyderta.

Wydminy, Pol.; 120 km NW of Bialystok; 53°59'/22°02'; POCEM.

Wydranica, *see* Vydranitsa.

Wydreja, Byel. EDRD. This town was not found in BGN gazetteers under the given spelling.

Wydzna, *see* Wydzno.

Wydzno, (Wydzna); pop. 24; Described in the *Black Book* as being in the Lwow region of Poland, this town was not found in BGN gazetteers.

Wygajny, Pol. PHP4. This town was not found in BGN gazetteers under the given spelling.

Wygnanka, *see* Vygnanka.

Wygoda, *see* Vygoda.

Wygwizdow, Pol. BGN lists two possible localities with this name located at 51°06'/19°57' and 51°29'/21°38'. HSL.

Wyhalew, Pol. (Wyhalow); pop. 61; 62 km NE of Lublin; 51°37'/23°10'.

Wyhalow, *see* Wyhalew.

Wyholowicze, *see* Vygolovichi.

Wylatowo, Pol. (Wilatowen); 69 km NE of Poznan; 52°37'/17°56'; LDS.

Wylewa, Pol.; pop. 38; 50 km NNW of Przemysl; 50°12'/22°38'.

Wylezin, Pol.; pop. 3; 69 km NW of Lublin; 51°43'/21°55'.

Wylkowyszki, *see* Vilkaviskis.

Wylow, Pol.; pop. 7; 107 km ENE of Krakow; 50°13'/21°24'.

Wyludzin, Pol.; pop. 22; 62 km W of Bialystok; 53°14'/22°16'.

Wymysle Niemieckie, Pol.; pop. 10; 82 km N of Lodz; 52°26'/19°51'.

Wymyslin, Pol.; pop. 22; 126 km N of Lodz; 52°52'/19°20'.

Wymyslow, Pol.; pop. 41; A number of towns share this name. It was not possible to determine from available information which one is being referenced.

Wypalenisko, Pol.; pop. 88; Described in the *Black Book* as being in the Lodz region of Poland, this town was not found in BGN gazetteers.

Wypiski, *see* Vypyski.

Wypychy, Pol.; pop. 2; 38 km SSW of Bialystok; 52°52'/22°57'.

Wyrebow, Pol.; pop. 15; 94 km NE of Czestochowa; 51°03'/20°21'.

Wyrozeby Podawce, Pol.; pop. 67; Described in the *Black Book* as being in the Lublin region of Poland, this town was not found in BGN gazetteers.

Wyryki, Pol. (Virek, Wyryki Polod, Wyryki Wola); pop. 61; 69 km NE of Lublin; 51°34'/23°23'; SF.

Wyryki Polod, *see* Wyryki.

Wyryki Wola, *see* Wyryki.

Wyrzysk, Pol. (Wirsitz); pop. 18; 82 km N of Poznan; 53°08'/17°16'; AMG.

Wyslica, *see* Wislica.

Wysmierzyce, Pol. (Vieshmezhitz); pop. 109; 75 km S of

Warszawa; 51°37'/20°50'; GA, SF.

Wysocin, Pol.; pop. 9; 62 km W of Lublin; 51°19'/21°41'.

Wysock, *see* Vysotsk.

Wysocka Wyzne, *see* Verkhneye Vysotskoye.

Wysocko, Pol.; pop. 28; 26 km N of Przemysl; 49°59'/22°49'.

Wysocko Nizne, Ukr.; pop. 141; 139 km SSW of Lvov; 48°45'/23°05'; PHP2. This town was located on an interwar map of Poland but does not appear in contemporary gazetteers. Map coordinates are approximate.

Wysocko Wyzne, Ukr.; pop. 220; 157 km SSW of Lvov; 48°35'/23°05'; PHP2. This town was located on an interwar map of Poland but does not appear in contemporary gazetteers. Map coordinates are approximate.

Wysoczany, Pol.; pop. 4; 56 km SW of Przemysl; 49°27'/22°10'.

Wysocze, Pol.; pop. 14; 88 km NNE of Warszawa; 52°53'/21°42'.

Wysoka, Pol. (Wissek); pop. 60; 45 km SE of Czestochowa; 50°26'/19°22'; JGFF, POCEM.

Wysoka (near Lancut), Pol.; pop. 52; 50 km WNW of Przemysl; 50°03'/22°16'; PHP3.

Wysoka Lelowska, Pol.; pop. 6; 26 km SE of Czestochowa; 50°38'/19°20'.

Wysoka Powrzeszow, Pol.; pop. 20; Described in the *Black Book* as being in the Lwow region of Poland, this town was not found in BGN gazetteers.

Wysoka Ruda, *see* Visakio Ruda.

Wysokidwor, *see* Aukstadvaris.

Wysokie, Pol.; pop. 285; 45 km SSE of Lublin; 50°55'/22°40'; AMG, EDRD, GUM4, GUM5, HSL, HSL2, JGFF, LDS, POCEM.

Wysokie (near Zamosc), Pol.; pop. 67; 69 km SE of Lublin; 50°45'/23°12'; HSL.

Wysokie Litewskie, *see* Vysokoye.

Wysokie Mazowieckie, Pol. (Visoka Mazovietzk, Visoke Mazovyetsk, Visoki, Visokie Mazovyetsk); pop. 1,898; 50 km SW of Bialystok; 52°55'/22°31'; AMG, CAHJP, GA, GUM3, GUM4, GUM5, HSL, JGFF, LDL, LDS, LYV, PHP4, POCEM, SF, WS, YB.

Wysoki Litovsk, *see* Vysokoye.

Wysowa, Pol.; pop. 49; 114 km ESE of Krakow; 49°26'/21°11'.

Wyspa, Ukr.; pop. 33; 94 km SSE of Lvov; 49°05'/24°25'. This town was located on an interwar map of Poland but does not appear in contemporary gazetteers. Map coordinates are approximate.

Wystepy, Pol.; pop. 5; 75 km ENE of Czestochowa; 50°52'/20°12'.

Wyszatyce, Pol.; pop. 12; 13 km NE of Przemysl; 49°51'/22°53'.

Wyszkow, Pol.; pop. 4,412; 50 km NNE of Warszawa; 52°36'/21°28'; AMG, COH, EDRD, EJ, FRG, GUM3, GUM5, GUM6, HSL, HSL2, JGFF, LDL, LYV, PHP1, PHP2, PHP4, POCEM, SF, YB. *See also* Vyshkov.

Wyszkow (Lublin), Pol.; pop. 40; 69 km ENE of Warszawa; 52°19'/22°01'.

Wyszkowo, *see* Vyshkovo.

Wyszmontow, Pol.; pop. 7; 75 km SW of Lublin; 50°52'/21°39'.

Wysznica, Pol. PHP4. This town was not found in BGN gazetteers under the given spelling.

Wyszogrod, Pol. (Vishegrod, Vishogrod, Vishogrud); pop. 2,465; 56 km W of Warszawa; 52°23'/20°12'; AMG, CAHJP, COH, EDRD, EJ, GA, HSL, HSL2, LDS, LYV, PHP1, PHP4, POCEM, SF, YB.

Wyszogrodek, *see* Vyshgorodok.

Wyszomierz, Pol.; pop. 30; 75 km SW of Bialystok; 52°53'/22°04'.

Wyszonki, Pol. (Wyszonki Koscielne); pop. 177; 56 km SSW of Bialystok; 52°45'/22°37'; PHP4.

Wyszonki Koscielne, *see* Wyszonki.

Wytrzyszczka, Pol.; pop. 5; 62 km ESE of Krakow; 49°49'/20°38'.

Wytyczno, Pol. (Vititchna, Wytyczno Lowiszow); pop. 74; 56 km NE of Lublin; 51°26'/23°16'; SF.

Wytyczno Lowiszow, *see* Wytyczno.

Wywoz, Pol.; pop. 5; 82 km ESE of Lodz; 51°24'/20°30'.

Wyzgrodek, *see* Vyshgorodok.

Wyzlow, Ukr.; pop. 8; 32 km N of Lvov; 50°05'/24°05'. This town was located on an interwar map of Poland but does not appear in contemporary gazetteers. Map coordinates are approximate. The *Black Book* notes a second town named Wyzlow (pop. 33) in the Polish interwar province of Stanislawow. It could not be found in interwar or contemporary gazetteers.

Wyzlowicze, *see* Vyzhlovichi.

Wyzna Jablonka, (Jablonka Wyzna); pop. 86; This town was not found in BGN gazetteers under the given spelling.

Wyzne, Pol.; pop. 10; 62 km W of Przemysl; 49°56'/21°53'; HSL.

Wyznianka, Pol.; pop. 3; 45 km SSW of Lublin; 50°56'/22°09'.

Wyzniany, *see* Vyzhnyany.

Wyznica, Pol.; pop. 4; 45 km SSW of Lublin; 50°56'/22°09'.

Wyzwa Nowa, *see* Novaya Vyzhva.

Wyzwa Stara, *possibly* Novaya Vyzhva.

Wyzyce, Pol.; pop. 3; 38 km E of Krakow; 50°05'/20°29'.

Wzdol, Pol.; pop. 46; 120 km NNE of Krakow; 50°58'/20°53'.

Wzdow, Pol.; pop. 28; 56 km WSW of Przemysl; 49°39'/21°59'; GUM4.

Xanten, Germ.; pop. 19; 88 km NW of Koln; 51°40'/06°27'; EDRD, HSL.

Xanthi, Greece; pop. 718; 170 km NE of Thessaloniki; 41°07'/24°56'; CAHJP, EDRD.

Xiaz, *see* Ksiaz Wielki.

Xions, *see* Ksiaz Wielki.

Yablanna, *see* Jablonna.

Yablanov, *see* Yablonov.

Yablona, *see* Staraya Yablona.

Yablonevo, Ukr. (Jablonewo); 150 km ESE of Kiyev; 49°57'/32°32'; SF.

Yablonitsa, Ukr. (Jablonica, Jablonice, Jablonitza); AMG, PHP2.

Yablonitsa (near Kuty), Ukr.; pop. 98; 107 km W of Chernovtsy; 48°19'/24°29'; GUM4, GUM5, HSL, JGFF.

Yablonitsa (near Yasinya), Ukr.; pop. 51; 107 km W of Chernovtsy; 48°19'/24°29'.

Yablonka, Ukr. (Jablonka); pop. 246; 126 km WNW of Chernovtsy; 48°42'/24°18'; LDL, PHP2.

Yablonka (Wolyn), Ukr.; 56 km N of Rovno; 51°03'/26°28'; GUM3.

Yablonov, Ukr. (Jablanow, Jablonow, Stoptchet, Yablanov, Yablonuv); pop. 834; 75 km W of Chernovtsy; 48°24'/24°57'; EDRD, EGRS, GUM4, HSL, LDL, PHP2, SF, WS.

Yablonov (near Turka), Ukr.; pop. 103; 101 km SE of Lvov; 49°12'/24°51'.

Yablonov (Tarnopol), Ukr.; pop. 20; 101 km N of Chernovtsy; 49°09'/25°52'.

Yablonovka, Ukr. (Jablonowka); pop. 23; 50 km NE of Lvov; 50°01'/24°36'.

Yablonuv, *see* Yablonov.

Yadimov, *see* Adamow.

Yadov, *see* Jadow.

Yadove, *see* Jadow.

Yadvinuvka, Ukr. (Jadwinowka); pop. 6; 94 km WSW of Rovno; 50°33'/24°55'.

Yagelnitsa, Ukr. (Jagielnica, Yagelnitza); pop. 988; 75 km NNW of Chernovtsy; 48°57'/25°44'; COH, EGRS, GUM3, GUM6, HSL, JGFF, LYV, PHP2, SF.

Yagelnitsa Stara, Ukr. (Jagielnica Stara); pop. 33; 82 km NNW of Chernovtsy; 48°59'/25°42'.

Yagelnitza, *see* Yagelnitsa.

Yagestov, *see* Augustow.

Yagistov, *see* Augustow.

Yaglevichi, Byel. (Jaglewicze); pop. 19; 88 km NW of Pinsk; 52°42'/25°23'.

Yagodin, Ukr. (Jagodzin, Yagodzin); pop. 30; 150 km N of Lvov; 51°12'/23°55'.

Yagodzin, *see* Yagodin.

Yagotin, Ukr. (Jagotin, Yagotina); pop. 1,431; 88 km E of Kiyev; 50°17'/31°46'; GUM4, GUM5, JGFF, SF.

Yagotina, *see* Yagotin.

Yagustova, *see* Augustow.

Yakimchitse, *see* Yakimchitsy.

Yakimchitsy, Ukr. (Jakimczyce, Yakimchitse); pop. 23; 32 km SSW of Lvov; 49°38'/23°44'.

Yakimovtsy, USSR (Akimovici); JGFF. A number of towns share this name. It was not possible to determine from available information which one is being referenced.

Yakoviche, Ukr. (Jakowicze); pop. 8; 107 km N of Lvov; 50°47'/24°34'.

Yakovlevo, *see* Jakowlewo.

Yakovshtat, *see* Jekabpils.

Yaktoruv, Ukr. (Jaktorow); pop. 31; 45 km E of Lvov; 49°44'/24°34'; GUM3, GUM4, GUM5, GUM6, PHP2.

Yakubovka, Ukr. (Jakobowka, Jakubowka, Yakubuvka); pop. 34; 56 km NNW of Chernovtsy; 48°47'/25°40'; PHP2.

Yakubuvka, *see* Yakubovka.

Yaloch, Byel. (Jalocz); pop. 10; 62 km WSW of Pinsk; 52°07'/25°13'.

Yaloveny, Mold. (Ialoveni); pop. 11; 13 km SSW of Kishinev; 46°56'/28°47'.

Yalpuzheny, Mold. (Ialpugeni); pop. 8; 50 km S of Kishinev; 46°35'/28°37'.

Yalta, Ukr. (Ialta, Jalta); pop. 2,353; 56 km S of Simferopol; 44°30'/34°10'; EDRD, GUM4, GUM5, HSL, JGFF, LDL, SF.

Yaltuchkov, Ukr. (Jaltichkov); EDRD. This town was not found in BGN gazetteers under the given spelling.

Yaltushkov, Ukr. (Jaltuskow); pop. 1,397; 75 km SW of Vinnitsa; 48°59'/27°30'; SF.

Yaluvka, *see* Jalowka.

Yambol, Bulg. (Iambol); pop. 925; 139 km SW of Varna; 42°29'/26°30'; EJ, GUM5.

Yamelnitsa, Ukr. (Jamielnica); pop. 33; 88 km SSW of Lvov; 49°10'/23°29'.

Yamne, Ukr. (Jamne); pop. 21; 38 km NE of Lvov; 50°03'/24°26'; HSL.

Yampol, Ukr. (Iampol, Jampol); HSL, JGFF, LDL, PHR1.

Yampol (Podolia), Ukr.; pop. 1,184; 114 km S of Vinnitsa; 48°15'/28°17'; GUM4, GUM6, SF.

Yampol (Wolyn), Ukr.; pop. 1,823; 75 km S of Rovno; 49°58'/26°15'; EJ, PHP2, SF, YB.

Yanchin, *see* Ivanovka (Tarnopol).

Yaneskel, *see* Joniskelis.

Yanev, *see* Janow Lubelski.

Yanevichi, Ukr. (Janiewicze); pop. 30; 26 km WSW of Rovno; 50°35'/25°56'.

Yanev Podlaski, *see* Janow Podlaski.

Yanev Shedletzki, *see* Janow Podlaski.

Yanina, *see* Ioannina.

Yanishke, *see* Joniskis.

Yanishki, *see* Joniskis.

Yanishok, *see* Joniskis.

Yanishov, *possibly* Januszew.

Yanishpol, LDL. This pre-World War I community was not found in BGN gazetteers.

Yaniv, *see* Janow Lubelski.

Yanofka, *see* Ivanovka.

Yanov, *see* Janow Podlaski.

Yanova, *see* Jonava.

Yanove, *see* Jonava.

Yanoviche, Byel. (Janowicze); pop. 2; 107 km N of Pinsk; 53°00'/26°39'.

Yanovichi, Byel. (Janovichi, Janowiczi); pop. 1,345; 38 km ENE of Vitebsk; 55°17'/30°42'; GUM4, LDL, SF, YB.

Yanovitch, *see* Janowiec. See also Yanovichi.

Yanovka, *see* Ivanovka.

Yanov Podlaski, *see* Janow Podlaski.

Yanov Polski, *see* Janow Lubelski.

Yanov Sokolski, *see* Janow Sokolski.

Yantarnyy, USSR (Palmnicken); 38 km WNW of Kaliningrad; 54°52'/19°57'; GUM3, GUM4, GUM5.

Yantsevichi, Byel. (Jancewicze); pop. 11; 157 km W of Minsk; 53°55'/25°08'.

Yanushevichi, *see* Ivanovka (near Zhitomir).

Yanuv, *see* Janow Lubelski.

Yanuv Podolsk, *see* Janow Podlaski.

Yapolots, Ukr. (Japoloc); pop. 14; 50 km N of Rovno; 50°59'/26°16'.

Yarchev, *see* Jarczew.

Yaremcha, Ukr. (Jaremcze); pop. 56; 107 km W of Chernovtsy; 48°27'/24°33'; GUM4.

Yargara, *see* Yargora.

Yargora, Mold. (Iargara, Yargara); pop. 56; 69 km SSW of Kishinev; 46°26'/28°27'.

Yarichuv, *see* Jarczew.

Yarichuv Novi, *see* Jarczew.

Yarichuv Novy, *see* Jarczew.

Yarishev, *see* Yaryshev.

Yarishevo, *see* Yaryshev.

Yarishov, *see* Yaryshev.

Yarmievka, *see* Veremiyevka.

Yarmolinits, *see* Yarmolintsy.

Yarmolintsy, Ukr. (Jarmolince, Yarmolinits, Yarmolintza); 69 km WSW of Uman; 48°45'/29°17'; COH, JGFF, LDL, SF, WS.

Yarmolintza, *see* Yarmolintsy.

Yaroslav, *see* Jaroslaw.

Yaroslavka, Ukr. (Iaroslava); pop. 2; 75 km SW of Odessa; 46°05'/29°53'.

Yarovoye, Ukr. (Diulmeni); pop. 5; 133 km SW of Odessa; 46°03'/29°06'.

Yartchev, *see* Novyy Yarychev.

Yartchovka, *see* Jarczow.

Yartsevo, USSR; pop. 515; 214 km E of Leningrad; 59°19'/33°57'.

Yaruga, Ukr. (Jaruga); 107 km S of Vinnitsa; 48°20'/28°03'; LDL, PHR1, SF.

Yaryshev, Ukr. (Iarisav, Jaryschew, Yarishev, Yarishevo, Yarishov); 101 km SSW of Vinnitsa; 48°32'/27°38'; HSL, LDL, SF.

Yasen, Byel.; pop. 295; 114 km ESE of Minsk; 53°13'/28°56'.

Yasen Polnyy, Ukr. (Jasieniow Polny, Yasenuv Polny); pop. 109; 45 km NW of Chernovtsy; 48°37'/25°32'.

Yasenitsa, Ukr. (Jasienice, Jasionka Masiowa); pop. 46; 101 km SSW of Lvov; 49°12'/23°10'; PHP2.

Yasenitsa Solna, Ukr. (Jasienica Solna, Jasienica Zamkowa?); pop. 31; 75 km SSW of Lvov; 49°20'/23°22'.

Yasenov, Ukr. (Jasienow); 75 km ENE of Lvov; 49°58'/25°03'; GUM4, HSL, PHP2.

Yasenuv Gorny, *see* Verkhniy Yasenov.

Yasenuv Gurny, *see* Verkhniy Yasenov.

Yasenuv Polny, *see* Yasenev Polnyy.

Yasevichi, Byel. (Jasiewicze); pop. 14; 139 km N of Minsk; 55°05'/27°52'.

Yashinovka, *see* Jasionowka.

Yashinovke, *see* Jasionowka.

Yashinowka, *see* Jasionowka.

Yashnitza, *see* Jasienica Rosielna.

Yasigola, LDL. This pre-World War I community was not found in BGN gazetteers.

Yasinitza, *see* Jasienica Rosielna.

Yasinuvka, Ukr. (Jasinowka); 101 km WNW of Rovno; 50°59'/24°57'; GUM3, JGFF.

Yasinya, Ukr. (Iasin, Iasinia, Jasina, Korosmezo); pop. 1,403; 114 km WSW of Chernovtsy; 48°16'/24°21'; AMG, COH, GUM3, GUM4, HSL, JGFF, LDL, SM.

Yaskovichi, Byel. (Jaskowicze); pop. 32; 107 km NE of Pinsk; 52°34'/27°31'; HSL.

Yaskovichi (near Luninets), Byel.; pop. 16; 82 km NNE of Pinsk; 52°42'/26°40'.

Yasla, *see* Jaslo.

Yaslany, *see* Jaslany.

Yaslo, *see* Jaslo.

Yasnogorka, Ukr. (Jasnogorka, Yasnogurka); pop. 21; 82 km NNE of Rovno; 51°12'/26°57'.

Yasnogurka, *see* Yasnogorka.

Yasnoye, USSR (Kaukehmen); pop. 100; 88 km NE of Kaliningrad; 55°11'/21°33'.

Yastshembitsa, Ukr. (Jastrzebica); pop. 64; 56 km NNE of Lvov; 50°19'/24°21'.

Yasvainiai, *see* Josvainiai.

Yasven, *see* Josvainiai.

Yatra, Byel. (Jatra); pop. 37; 126 km SW of Minsk; 53°25'/25°48'.

Yavarzna, *see* Jaworzno.

Yavche, Ukr. (Jawcze); pop. 38; 69 km SE of Lvov; 49°21'/24°31'.

Yavora, Ukr. (Jawora); pop. 77; 101 km SW of Lvov; 49°12'/23°03'.

Yavoriv, *see* Yavorov.

Yavornik, *see* Jawornik Polski.

Yavorov, Ukr. (Javorov, Jaworow, Yavoriv); pop. 2,405; 45 km W of Lvov; 49°56'/23°23'; AMG, COH, EDRD, EGRS, EJ, GUM3, GUM4, GUM5, GYLA, HSL, HSL2, JGFF, LDL, LYV, PHP2, PHP3, SF, YB. *See also* Yavoruv.

Yavorov (near Kossuv), Ukr.; pop. 73; 69 km WSW of Chernovtsy; 48°15'/24°59'.

Yavoruv, Ukr. (Yavorov); pop. 89; 107 km WNW of Chernovtsy; 48°39'/24°31'.

Yavoruvka, Ukr. (Jaworowka); pop. 42; 107 km SSE of Lvov; 48°58'/24°26'.

Yavorzhne, *see* Jaworzno.

Yavorzno, *see* Jaworzno.

Yavozhne, *see* Jaworzno.

Yayechkovichi, Byel. (Jajeczkowicze); pop. 8; 32 km WSW of Pinsk; 52°05'/25°40'.

Yaykovtse, Ukr. (Jajkowce); pop. 22; 69 km SSE of Lvov; 49°16'/24°11'.

Yazlivitz, *see* Pomortsy.

Yazlovets, *see* Pomortsy.

Yazvinki, Byel. (Jazwinki); pop. 9; 56 km ENE of Pinsk; 52°15'/26°55'.

Yazyl, Byel.; 107 km SSE of Minsk; 52°59'/27°58'; JGFF.

Ybbs, *see* Ybbs an der Donau.

Ybbs an der Donau, Aus. (Ybbs); pop. 130; 94 km WSW of Wien; 48°10'/15°05'.

Yedinets, *see* Yedintsy.

Yedintsy, Mold. (Edineti, Edineti Sat?, Edineti Targ, Edinita, Edinita Targ, Jedincy, Yedinets); pop. 5,349; 170 km NW of Kishinev; 48°10'/27°19'; EDRD, EJ, GUM3, GUM4, GUM4, HSL, HSL2, JGFF, LYV, PHR2, SF, YB. The *Black Book* also notes the town of Edineti Sat (pop. 401).

Yedlinsk, *see* Jedlinsk.

Yedlitch, *see* Jedlicze.

Yedvabna, *see* Jedwabne.

Yedwabne, *see* Jedwabne.

Yedzheyov, *see* Jedrzejow.

Yefingar, *see* Plyushchevka.

Yefremov, USSR; pop. 126; 163 km N of Voronezh; 53°09'/38°07'; GUM5.

Yekabpils, *see* Jekabpils.

Yekaterinodar, *see* Krasnodar.

Yekaterinopol, *see* Katerinopol.

Yekaterinoslav, *see* Dnepropetrovsk.

Yekaterinovka, Mold. (Ecaterineanca); pop. 9; 50 km S of Kishinev; 46°35'/28°45'.

Yekimoutsy, Mold. (Echimauti); pop. 13; 82 km N of Kishinev; 47°42'/28°54'.

Yelekhovichi, Ukr. (Jelechowice); 62 km E of Lvov; 49°50'/24°55'; GUM4.

Mitau — Große Straße

Yelgava (Jelgava) Latvia: Broad Street.

Yelenovka, Mold. (Ilineuca, Ilineuka); pop. 21; 107 km WNW of Kishinev; 47°38'/27°43'.

Yelets, USSR; pop. 1,017; 107 km N of Voronezh; 52°37'/38°30'.

Yelgava, *see* Jelgava.

Yelin, *see* Jelen.

Yelisavetgrod, *see* Kirovograd.

Yelizarov, Ukr. (Elizarow); pop. 11; 94 km NNE of Lvov; 50°29'/24°54'.

Yelizavelgrad, *see* Kirovograd.

Yelizavetgradka, Ukr.; 163 km ENE of Uman; 48°49'/32°24'; JGFF.

Yelizavetovka, Ukr. (Gura Vailor); pop. 4; 114 km WSW of Odessa; 46°24'/29°17'.

Yelmicheno, *see* Yemilchino.

Yelmiheno, *see* Yemilchino.

Yelno, Byel. (Jelno); pop. 42; 94 km ENE of Pinsk; 52°18'/27°25'.

Yelnya, USSR; pop. 567; 75 km E of Smolensk; 54°36'/33°13'.

Yelok, *see* Ylakiai.

Yelsk, Byel.; 146 km SW of Gomel; 51°48'/29°09'; LDL.

Yemilchino, Ukr. (Emiltchina, Jemilcino, Yelmicheno, Yelmiheno); pop. 1,383; 114 km ENE of Rovno; 50°52'/27°48'; GUM4, SF.

Yenakievo, *see* Yenakiyevo.

Yenakiyevo, Ukr. (Yenakievo); pop. 2,396; 240 km E of Dnepropetrovsk; 48°14'/38°13'; LDL.

Yendrikhov, *see* Andrychow.

Yendzheva, *see* Jedrzejow.

Yendzheyev, *see* Jedrzejow.

Yendzhiov, *see* Jedrzejow.

Yendziv, *see* Jedrzejow.

Yenishok, *see* Joniskis.

Yeremichi, Byel. (Jeremicze, Yeremitcha); pop. 113; 88 km SW of Minsk; 53°34'/26°20'; COH, HSL, LDL, LYV, SF, YB.

Yeremitcha, *see* Yeremichi.

Yereslev, *see* Jaroslaw.

Yerkhi, Byel. (Jerchy); pop. 3; 82 km NNW of Minsk; 54°34'/27°13'.

Yermokliya, Mold. (Ermoclia); pop. 14; 69 km ESE of Kishinev; 46°35'/29°31'.

Yernyes, *see* Kopasnovo.

Yevgenyevka, Ukr. (Evghenita); pop. 4; 120 km WSW of Odessa; 46°23'/29°13'.

Yevpatoria, *see* Yevpatoriya.

Yevpatoriya, Ukr. (Eupatoria, Evpatoriia, Gezlev, Goslow, Jevpatorija, Koslov, Koslow, Kozlov, Yevpatoria); pop. 2,409; 62 km WNW of Simferopol; 45°12'/33°22'; EDRD, EJ, GUM4, GUM5, HSL, HSL2, JGFF, LDL, SF.

Yeysi, *see* Jejse.

Yezapol, *see* Zhovten.

Yezerzani, *see* Ozeryany (Wolyn).

Yezerzhany, *see* Ozeryany. According to the *Black Book*, there were two towns in Poland called Jezierzany, one in Wolyn province and one in Tarnopol province. The latter was the larger community.

Yezezhanka, Ukr. (Jezierzanka); pop. 160; 82 km E of Lvov; 49°39'/25°05'; PHP2.

Yezezhany, *see* Ozeryany.

Yezherne, *see* Ozernyany.

Yezherzani, *see* Ozeryany.

Yezhore, *see* Ozery.

Yezhov, *see* Jezow.

Yezhyerna, *see* Ozernyany.

Yezierne, *see* Ozeryany.

Yeziori, *see* Ozery.

Yeziorna, *see* Jeziorna Krolewska.

Yezirna, *see* Ozernyany.

Yezna, *see* Jieznas.

Yeznas, *see* Jieznas.

Yezyerzany, *see* Ozeryany.

Yezyori, *see* Ozery.

Ylakai, *see* Ylakiai.

Ylakiai, Lith. (Illok, Illoki, Yelok, Ylakai, Ylok); pop. 409; 101 km WNW of Siauliai; 56°17'/21°51'; HSL, JGFF, LDL, SF, YL.

Ylok, *see* Ylakiai.

Yoblonka, *see* Jablonka.

Yod, *see* Iody.

Yodi, *see* Iody.

Zabludow, Poland: A street scene.

Yodlava, *see* Jodlowa.
Yoed, *see* Ieud.
Yohonishkel, *see* Joniskelis.
Yoid, *see* Ieud.
Yonava, *see* Jonava.
Yonev, *see* Janow Lubelski.
Yonishkel, *see* Joniskelis.
Yonishkis, *see* Joniskis.
Yonishok, *see* Joniskis.
Yonushkel, *see* Joniskelis.
Yorburg, *see* Jurbarkas.
Yordanev, *see* Jordanow.
Yordanov, *see* Jordanow.
Yorvorig, *see* Jurbarkas.
Yoshlisk, *see* Jasliska.
Yostkovitz, *see* Jastkowice.
Yosvain, *see* Josvainiai.
Yosven, *see* Josvainiai.
Yozefov, *see* Jozefow.
Yozifif Veisil, *see* Jozefow (Nad Wisla).
Yozint, *see* Juzintai.
Yuchavitz, *see* Yukhovichi.
Yukhnov, USSR; pop. 34; 176 km N of Bryansk; 54°45'/35°14'.
Yukhnovichi, Byel. (Juchnowicze); pop. 47; 26 km WSW of Pinsk; 52°07'/25°43'.
Yukhovichi, Byel. (Juchowitschi, Yuchavitz); pop. 349; 133 km WNW of Vitebsk; 56°02'/28°39'; SF.
Yuratishki, Byel. (Juraciszki); pop. 25; 107 km W of Minsk; 54°02'/25°56'.

Yuravitch, *see* Yurevichi.
Yurbarkas, *see* Jurbarkas.
Yurburg, *see* Jurbarkas.
Yurcheny, Mold. (Iurceni); pop. 56; 45 km W of Kishinev; 47°05'/28°16'.
Yurevichi, Byel. (Jurovice, Yuravitch); pop. 1,139; 114 km SW of Gomel; 51°57'/29°32'; HSL, LDL, SF.
Yuriev, *see* Tartu.
Yurkovtsy, Ukr. (Iurcauti); pop. 47; 26 km N of Chernovtsy; 48°30'/25°56'.
Yurovshchina, Ukr. (Labun); 101 km ESE of Rovno; 50°01'/27°22'; COH, LDL, SF.
Yuryev, *see* Tartu.
Yuryevka, Ukr. (Raileni); pop. 6; 114 km WSW of Odessa; 46°22'/29°18'.
Yushkevichi, Byel. (Juszkiewicze); pop. 2; 126 km NNW of Minsk; 54°56'/26°57'.
Yustigrod, *see* Sokolovka.
Yuzefin, Ukr. (Jozefin); pop. 322; 126 km NNE of Rovno; 51°33'/27°23'.
Yuzefov, *see* Jozefow.
Yuzefov Ardinatzki, *see* Jozefow.
Yuzefovka, *see* Yuzefuvka.
Yuzefpol, *see* Iosipovka.
Yuzefuv, *see* Jozefow.
Yuzefuvka, Ukr. (Jozefowka, Yuzefovka); pop. 44; 56 km NNW of Lvov; 50°20'/23°44'.
Yuzhenistsy, *see* Yuzhenitse.
Yuzhenitse, Ukr. (Iujineti, Yuzhenistsy, Yuzhenitsy); pop. 51; 32

km NW of Chernovtsy; 48°32'/25°40'.

Yuzhenitsy, *see* Yuzhenitse.

Yuzny Poselok, USSR; pop. 28; This town was not found in BGN gazetteers under the given spelling.

Yuzovka, *see* Donetsk.

Zab, Pol.; pop. 6; 88 km S of Krakow; 49°21'/19°57'.

Zabajka, Pol.; pop. 10; 69 km WNW of Przemysl; 50°09'/21°57'.

Zabala, Rom.; pop. 4; 170 km N of Bucuresti; 45°54'/26°11'; HSL.

Zabalj, Yug.; pop. 41; 75 km NW of Beograd; 45°23'/20°04'; PHY.

Zabar, HSL. A number of towns share this name. It was not possible to determine from available information which one is being referenced.

Zabava, Ukr. (Zabawa); pop. 26; 69 km NNE of Lvov; 50°23'/24°33'; GUM5, PHP3.

Zabawa, *see* Zabava.

Zabce, Pol.; pop. 20; 94 km N of Lublin; 52°01'/22°44'.

Zabcze, Pol.; pop. 23; 120 km NE of Przemysl; 50°33'/24°00'.

Zabcze Murowane, *see* Zhabche Murovane.

Zabelin, *see* Izabelin.

Zabeln, *see* Sabile.

Zaberfeld, Germ.; 38 km NW of Stuttgart; 49°04'/08°56'; PHGBW.

Zabia, *see* Verkhovina.

Zabianka, Pol.; pop. 30; 69 km WNW of Lublin; 51°42'/21°51'.

Zabia Wola, Pol.; pop. 85; 19 km S of Lublin; 51°07'/22°31'.

Zabie, *see* Verkhovina.

Zabiec, Pol.; pop. 55; 88 km NE of Krakow; 50°21'/21°05'.

Zabiele Wielkie, Pol.; pop. 47; 94 km N of Warszawa; 53°05'/21°22'.

Zabierzow, Pol. (Zbiershav); pop. 49; 32 km E of Krakow; 50°04'/20°20'; SF.

Zabin, COH. A number of towns share this name. It was not possible to determine from available information which one is being referenced.

Zabinka, *see* Zhabinka.

Zabki, Pol.; pop. ?; 13 km NE of Warszawa; 52°17'/21°07'; GUM4.

Zabkow, Pol.; pop. 5; 82 km ENE of Warszawa; 52°26'/22°10'.

Zabkowice, Pol.; pop. 230; 50 km SSE of Czestochowa; 50°23'/19°17'; AMG, COH, HSL, JGFF, LDS, PHP3.

Zablatov, *see* Zabolotov.

Zabledza, Pol.; pop. 16; 88 km E of Krakow; 49°56'/21°04'.

Zablocie, Pol.; pop. 624; 26 km ESE of Krakow; 49°58'/20°11'; EGRS, GUM5.

Zablodov, *see* Zabludow.

Zablodova, *see* Zabludow.

Zablotce, *see* Zabolottsy.

Zablotov, *see* Zabolotov.

Zablotow, *see* Zabolotov.

Zablotse, *see* Zabolotye.

Zablotse (Wolyn), Ukr.; pop. 40; 133 km N of Lvov; 50°59'/24°11'.

Zablotuv, *see* Zabolotov.

Zabludove, *see* Zabludow.

Zabludow, Pol. (Zablodov, Zablodova, Zabludove, Zabluduv); pop. 1,817; 19 km ESE of Bialystok; 53°01'/23°21'; COH, EDRD, EJ, FRG, GA, GUM3, GYLA, HSL, HSL2, JGFF, LDL, LYV, PHP4, SF, WS, YB.

Zabluduv, *see* Zabludow.

Zablutov, *see* Zabolotov.

Zabnica, Pol.; pop. ?; 82 km SW of Krakow; 49°35'/19°09'; COH, HSL.

Zabnik, Pol. BGN lists two possible localities with this name located at 46°18'/16°27' and 51°31'/17°32'. HSL.

Zabno, Pol. (Sveti Ivan Zabno, Zhabno, Zobni); pop. 361; 69 km ENE of Krakow; 50°08'/20°54'; AMG, COH, EGRS, GA, GUM5, HSL, JGFF, LDL, PHP3, POCEM, SF.

Zabno (Lublin), Pol.; pop. 36; 50 km SSE of Lublin; 50°51'/22°47'.

Zabno (Yugoslavia), Yug.; pop. 20; 50 km NE of Zagreb; 45°57'/16°36'.

Zabocrici, *see* Zhanokrich.

Zabok, Yug.; pop. 6; 32 km NNW of Zagreb; 46°02'/15°55'.

Zabokliky, Cz.; pop. 4; 75 km WNW of Praha; 50°19'/13°28'.

Zabokreky nad Nitrou, Cz.; pop. 170; 107 km NE of Bratislava; 48°38'/18°18'; HSL.

Zabokritz, *see* Zhabokrich.

Zabolotce, *see* Zabolottsi.

Zabolotov, Ukr. (Zablatov, Zablotov, Zablotow, Zablotuv, Zablutov); pop. 1,454; 50 km WNW of Chernovtsy; 48°28'/25°18'; AMG, COH, EDRD, EGRS, EJ, GUM5, HSL, HSL2, LDL, LYV, PHP2, SF, YB.

Zabolottsi, Ukr. (Zabolotce); pop. 7; 88 km N of Lvov; 50°38'/24°16'.

Zabolottsy, Ukr. (Zablotce); pop. 32; 69 km NE of Lvov; 50°02'/24°58'.

Zabolotye, (Zablotse);

Zabolotye (Nowogrodek), Byel.; pop. 49; 126 km NNW of Pinsk; 53°11'/25°50'.

Zabolotye (Polesie), Byel.; pop. 21; 150 km WSW of Pinsk; 52°03'/23°51'.

Zabor, Pol. (Saabor, Saavar); pop. 1; 101 km SW of Poznan; 51°57'/15°43'; HSL2.

Zabori, Cz.; pop. 22; A number of towns share this name. It was not possible to determine from available information which one is being referenced.

Zaborovtsy, Byel. (Zaborowce); pop. 31; 38 km N of Pinsk; 52°24'/26°07'.

Zaborowce, *see* Zaborovtsy.

Zaborowice, Pol.; pop. 25; 101 km ENE of Czestochowa; 51°03'/20°29'.

Zaborye, Ukr. (Zaborze); pop. 42; 50 km NNW of Lvov; 50°17'/23°45'.

Zaborze, *see* Zaborye.

Zabotec, Cz.; pop. 907; Described in the *Black Book* as being in the Bohemia region of Czechoslovakia, this town was not found in BGN gazetteers.

Zabovresky, Cz.; pop. 195; A number of towns share this name. It was not possible to determine from available information which one is being referenced.

Zaboze, Pol. PHP2. This town was not found in BGN gazetteers under the given spelling.

Zabratowka, Pol.; pop. 16; 50 km WNW of Przemysl; 49°58'/22°12'.

Zabreh, Cz. (Hohenstadt); pop. 35; 82 km N of Brno; 49°53'/16°52'; HSL, HSL2, JGFF.

Zabrezhye, Byel. (Zabrzez); pop. 97; 82 km WNW of Minsk; 54°11'/26°28'.

Zabriceni, *see* Zabrichen.

Zabrichen, Mold. (Zabriceni); pop. 84; 170 km NW of Kishinev; 48°05'/27°15'.

Zabrodi, Cz.; pop. 120 km NE of Praha; 50°27'/16°07'; HSL.

Zabrody, Pol.; 107 km NW of Warszawa; 53°07'/20°24'; EJ. EJ describes Zabrody as a suburb of Mlawa. *See also* Mlawa.

Zabrodzie, Pol.; pop. 56; A number of towns share this name. It was not possible to determine from available information which one is being referenced.

Zabrze, Pol. (Hindenburg); pop. 1,200; 56 km SSW of Czestochowa; 50°19'/18°47'; EJ, GUM4, GUM5, LDS, POCEM.

Zabrzez, *see* Zabrezhye.

Zabud, Pol. PHP4. This town was not found in BGN gazetteers under the given spelling.

Zabuze, Pol.; pop. 23; 94 km S of Bialystok; 52°19'/23°03'; EDRD, GUM4.

Zabuzhye, Ukr. JGFF. A number of towns share this name. It was not possible to determine from available information which one is being referenced.

Zacharin, LDL. This pre-World War I community was not found in BGN gazetteers.

Zacheta, Pol.; pop. 270; Described in the *Black Book* as being in the Kielce region of Poland, this town was not found in

BGN gazetteers.

Zachorzow, Pol.; pop. 3; 69 km ESE of Lodz; 51°21'/20°11'.

Zacler, Cz.; pop. 3; 120 km NE of Praha; 50°39'/15°54'.

Zacretje, Yug.; pop. 6; 38 km NNW of Zagreb; 46°05'/15°55'.

Zaczernie, Pol.; pop. 3; 62 km WNW of Przemysl; 50°06'/22°01'.

Zaczopki, Pol.; pop. 26; 114 km SSE of Bialystok; 52°10'/23°25'.

Zadar, Yug. (Zara); 195 km S of Zagreb; 44°07'/15°15'; CAHJP, PHY.

Zaden, *see* Zhaden.

Zadibi, Ukr. (Zadyby); pop. 3; 126 km WNW of Rovno; 51°08'/24°38'.

Zadiel, Cz. (Szadello); 38 km SW of Kosice; 48°37'/20°50'; HSL.

Zadna, *see* Zadneye.

Zadne, *see* Zadneye.

Zadnevo, USSR (Zadnya); 126 km E of Leningrad; 59°36'/32°24'; COH, HSL.

Zadneye, Ukr. (Zadna, Zadne, Zadnya, Zaenya); 176 km S of Lvov; 48°21'/23°14'; HSL, SM.

Zadnishevka, Ukr. (Zadniszowka); pop. 93; 126 km S of Rovno; 49°31'/26°08'.

Zadniszowka, *see* Zadnishevka.

Zadnya, *see* Zadnevo; Zadneye.

Zadorfala, *see* Zadorfalva.

Zadorfalva, Hung. (Zadorfala); pop. 11; 45 km NW of Miskolc; 48°23'/20°29'; HSL.

Zadova, *see* Zhadova.

Zadowa, *see* Zhadova.

Zadubce, Pol.; pop. 4; 94 km ESE of Lublin; 50°51'/23°46'.

Zadubie, *see* Zadubye.

Zadubrovtse, *see* Zadubrovtsy.

Zadubrovtsy, Ukr. (Zadubrovtse); 45 km WNW of Chernovtsy; 48°32'/25°27'; JGFF.

Zadubye, Byel. (Zadubie); pop. 8; 56 km NNE of Pinsk; 52°32'/26°27'.

Zadunayevka, Ukr. (Dunareanca); pop. 4; 146 km SW of Odessa; 45°50'/29°06'.

Zadvyzhe, Ukr. (Zadworze); pop. 78; GUM4, GUM4. Described in the *Black Book* as being in the Tarnopol region of Poland, this town was not found in BGN gazetteers.

Zadworze, *see* Zadvyzhe.

Zadyby, *see* Zadibi.

Zadziele, Pol.; pop. 11; 62 km SW of Krakow; 49°44'/19°12'.

Zadzielsko, Ukr.; pop. 70; 157 km SSW of Lvov; 48°35'/23°05'; HSL. This town was located on an interwar map of Poland but does not appear in contemporary gazetteers. Map coordinates are approximate.

Zaenya, *see* Zadneye.

Zagacie, Pol.; 69 km NE of Czestochowa; 51°01'/20°02'; GA.

Zagajew, Pol.; pop. 1; 62 km WSW of Lodz; 51°42'/18°35'.

Zagan, Pol. (Sagan); pop. 100; 133 km WNW of Wroclaw; 51°37'/15°19'; GUM3, GUM4, GUM6, LDS.

Zagarancea, *see* Zagorancha.

Zagare, Lith. (Nei Zhagar, Novo Zhagory, Zager, Zager Chadash, Zagere, Zagory, Zhagar, Zhagare, Zhager, Zhagory); pop. 1,928; 50 km N of Siauliai; 56°21'/23°15'; COH, EJ, GUM3, GUM4, GUM5, HSL, HSL2, JGFF, LDL, SF, YL.

Zagaykany, Mold. (Zahaicana); pop. 14; 26 km NNE of Kishinev; 47°10'/28°57'.

Zagaypol, Ukr. (Zahajpol); pop. 48; 56 km WNW of Chernovtsy; 48°32'/25°13'; HSL, PHP2.

Zager, *see* Zagare.

Zager Chadash, *see* Zagare.

Zagere, *see* Zagare.

Zaglebie Dabrowskie, GUM4, GUM5, GUM6. This town was not found in BGN gazetteers under the given spelling.

Zaglinki, *see* Glinyanka.

Zagnansk, Pol.; 114 km ENE of Czestochowa; 50°59'/20°41'; GUM3.

Zagorancha, Mold. (Zagarancea); pop. 2; 82 km WNW of Kishinev; 47°14'/27°46'.

Zagoreczko, Pol.; pop. 25; Described in the *Black Book* as being in the Lwow region of Poland, this town was not found in BGN gazetteers.

Zagorna, Mold. (Zahorna, Zakharna); pop. 4; 94 km NNW of Kishinev; 47°48'/28°33'.

Zagorow, Pol. (Zagrova); pop. 807; 69 km ESE of Poznan; 52°10'/17°54'; AMG, COH, GUM3, GUM4, HSL2, PHP1, SF.

Zagorsko, *see* Zgorsko.

Zagory, *see* Zagare.

Zagorye, Ukr. (Zagurzhe); pop. 194; 56 km SW of Lvov; 49°37'/23°22'.

Zagorz, Pol. (Zagorzh); pop. 392; 50 km SW of Przemysl; 49°31'/22°16'; EGRS, HSL, HSL2, LDL, PHP3, SF.

Zagorzany, Pol.; pop. 54; 101 km ESE of Krakow; 49°42'/21°11'.

Zagorze, Pol.; pop. 282; 56 km NE of Czestochowa; 51°03'/19°45'; AMG, PHP1, PHP2. *See also* Zagurzhe.

Zagorze (near Krakow), Pol.; pop. 19; 19 km WSW of Krakow; 50°02'/19°39'; GUM3, GUM4.

Zagorze (near Rudki), Pol.; pop. 40; 38 km WNW of Przemysl; 49°57'/22°22'.

Zagorze (Warszawa area), Pol.; 62 km ENE of Lodz; 51°48'/20°20'; GUM4.

Zagorze Knihynickie, *see* Zaguzhe Konkolnitske.

Zagorzh, *see* Zagorz.

Zagorzyce, Pol.; pop. 28; 82 km WNW of Przemysl; 50°02'/21°41'.

Zagorzynek, Pol.; pop. 12; 94 km WSW of Lodz; 51°45'/18°06'.

Zagozdzie, Pol. (Zagozdzon); pop. 37; 82 km NNW of Lublin; 51°56'/22°07'.

Zagozdzon, *see* Zagozdzie.

Zagra, Rom.; pop. 17; 82 km NNE of Cluj; 47°20'/24°17'.

Zagrab, *see* Zagreb.

Zagreb, Yug. (Agram, Zagrab); pop. 8,702; 365 km WNW of Beograd; 45°48'/16°00'; AMG, EJ, GUM3, GUM4, GUM5, GUM6, HSL, HSL2, ISH1, JGFF, LJEE, PHP1, PHY.

Zagreblya, *see* Zagreblye.

Zagreblye, Ukr. (Zagreblya, Zagrobela); pop. 36; 50 km S of Rovno; 50°11'/26°17'.

Zagrobela, *see* Zagreblye.

Zagroda, Pol.; pop. 56; 62 km ESE of Lublin; 51°01'/23°22'.

Zagrodki, Pol.; pop. 13; 69 km NNW of Przemysl; 50°21'/22°33'.

Zagrody Skalbmierskie, Pol.; pop. 24; 75 km ENE of Krakow; 50°12'/21°00'.

Zagrova, *see* Zagorow.

Zagurzhe, *see* Zagorye.

Zaguzhe Konkolnitske, Ukr. (Zagorze Knihynickie); pop. 27; 94 km SE of Lvov; 49°13'/24°49'.

Zagvozdye, *see* Zagvuzdzh.

Zagvuzdzh, Ukr. (Zagvozdye, Zagwozdz); pop. 28; 114 km SE of Lvov; 48°55'/24°40'.

Zagwozdz, *see* Zagvuzdzh.

Zagyvapalfalva, Hung.; pop. 26; 75 km WSW of Miskolc; 48°04'/19°47'.

Zagyvarekas, Hung.; pop. 10; 82 km ESE of Budapest; 47°16'/20°08'; HSL.

Zagyvaszanto, Hung.; pop. 15; 56 km NE of Budapest; 47°47'/19°41'; HSL.

Zahaicana, *see* Zagaykany.

Zahajce, *see* Velikiye Zagaytsy.

Zahajki, Pol.; pop. 25; 82 km N of Lublin; 51°57'/22°50'.

Zahajpol, *see* Zagaypol.

Zaharesti, Rom.; 120 km WNW of Iasi; 47°35'/26°09'; GUM4.

Zahariceni, *see* Zakharicheni.

Zahati, HSL. This pre-World War I community was not found in BGN gazetteers.

Zahoczewie, Pol.; pop. 43; 62 km SSW of Przemysl; 49°23'/22°16'.

Zahojpole, *see* Sokolovka.

Zahony, Hung.; pop. 53; 114 km NE of Miskolc; 48°25'/22°11'; PHH.

Zahorany, Cz.; pop. 24; A number of towns share this name. It was not possible to determine from available information which one is being referenced.

Zahorb, HSL. This pre-World War I community was not found in BGN gazetteers.

Zahorna, see Zagorna.

Zahutyn, Pol.; pop. 12; 50 km SW of Przemysl; 49°32'/22°15'.

Zaibis, EGRS, LDL. This pre-World War I community was not found in BGN gazetteers.

Zaicani, see Zaykany.

Zaim, Mold.; pop. 30; 62 km SE of Kishinev; 46°37'/29°21'.

Zajecar, Yug.; pop. 23; 176 km ESE of Beograd; 43°54'/22°17'.

Zajecov, Cz.; pop. 6; 56 km SW of Praha; 49°46'/13°51'.

Zajeczyce, see Zayenchitse.

Zajezdec, Cz.; pop. 9; 101 km NW of Brno; 49°56'/15°56'.

Zajta, Hung.; pop. 12; 150 km E of Miskolc; 47°54'/22°48'.

Zakanale, Pol.; pop. 8; 107 km S of Bialystok; 52°12'/23°06'.

Zakany, Hung.; pop. 55; 19 km S of Nagykanizsa; 46°17'/16°57'; PHH.

Zakharevka, see Zakharicheni.

Zakharicheni, Ukr. (Zahariceni, Zakharevka); pop. 38; 56 km WSW of Chernovtsy; 48°12'/25°08'; COH.

Zakharna, see Zagorna.

Zakhlin, see Zychlin.

Zakilkov, see Zaklikow.

Zakinthos, Greece; pop. 138; 214 km S of Ioannina; 37°47'/20°54'.

Zakliczewo, Pol. (Zakliczowo); pop. 7; 69 km N of Warszawa; 52°51'/21°07'.

Zakliczowo, see Zakliczewo.

Zakliczyn, Pol. (Opatkowice, Patkowice, Zoklitchin); pop. 295; 69 km ESE of Krakow; 49°52'/20°49'; EGRS, GA, GUM3, GUM5, HSL, PHP3, SF.

Zaklikov, see Zaklikow.

Zaklikow, Pol. (Zakilkov, Zaklikov, Zaklikow Tartak, Zoklikov); pop. 1,403; 62 km SSW of Lublin; 50°46'/22°07'; AMG, COH, EDRD, GA, GUM3, GUM5, HSL, HSL2, LDS, LYV, PHP3, POCEM, SF.

Zaklikow Tartak, see Zaklikow.

Zaklodzie, Pol.; pop. 34; 56 km SSE of Lublin; 50°46'/22°51'.

Zakmur, Yug.; pop. 1; 208 km SSW of Beograd; 43°27'/18°42'.

Zakopane, Pol. (Koscielisko, Zakopona); pop. 533; 94 km S of Krakow; 49°18'/19°58'; AMG, EGRS, GA, GUM3, GUM4, GUM5, GUM6, HSL, LDL, LYV, PHP3, POCEM, SF, YB.

Zakopona, see Zakopane.

Zakow, Pol.; pop. 15; 50 km ESE of Warszawa; 52°04'/21°40'.

Zakowa, Pol.; 26 km SE of Krakow; 49°56'/20°07'; HSL.

Zakowice, Pol.; pop. 37; 101 km W of Lublin; 51°23'/21°08'.

Zakowice Nowe, Pol.; pop. 28; Described in the *Black Book* as being in the Lodz region of Poland, this town was not found in BGN gazetteers.

Zakowola, Pol.; pop. 8; 75 km N of Lublin; 51°52'/22°42'.

Zakowska Huta, see Huta Zakowska.

Zakrakowka, Pol. CAHJP. Although, this town does not appear in contemporary gazetteers, it was located in the vicinity of Miechow, Poland.

Zakret, Pol.; pop. 8; 19 km E of Warszawa; 52°13'/21°16'.

Zakrochim, see Zakroczym.

Zakrochin, see Zakroczym.

Zakrocz, Pol.; pop. 19; 133 km WNW of Warszawa; 53°02'/19°28'.

Zakroczym, Pol. (Zakrochim, Zakrochin, Zakrotchim, Zakrotchin); pop. 1,865; 32 km WNW of Warszawa; 52°26'/20°38'; AMG, CAHJP, COH, GUM4, GUM5, GUM6, HSL, HSL2, JGFF, LDL, LDS, LYV, PHP4, POCEM, SF.

Zakrotchim, see Zakroczym.

Zakrotchin, see Zakroczym.

Zakrzew, Pol.; pop. 31; 75 km N of Lublin; 51°52'/22°33'; GUM5, HSL, HSL2.

Zakrzowek, Pol. (Zakrzowek Majoracki); pop. 408; 38 km S of Lublin; 50°57'/22°24'; AMG, COH, GA, GUM3, GUM4, GUM5, HSL.

Zakrzowek Majoracki, see Zakrzowek.

Zakrzowek Szlachecki, Pol.; pop. 3; 38 km N of Czestochowa; 51°03'/19°13'.

Zakrzyze, Pol.; pop. 6; 38 km SE of Lublin; 50°58'/22°47'.

Zakszuwek, Pol. EDRD. This town was not found in BGN gazetteers under the given spelling.

Zakupy, Cz.; pop. 2; 69 km N of Praha; 50°41'/14°39'.

Zaky, Cz.; pop. 5; 69 km ESE of Praha; 49°53'/15°22'.

Zala, Hung. BGN lists two possible localities with this name located at 45°52'/14°28' and 46°44'/18°00'. COH.

Zalaapati, Hung.; pop. 35; 38 km N of Nagykanizsa; 46°44'/17°07'.

Zalabaksa, Hung.; pop. 10; 45 km WNW of Nagykanizsa; 46°42'/16°33'.

Zalaber, Hung.; pop. 37; 62 km N of Nagykanizsa; 46°58'/17°02'.

Zalabesenyo, see Botfa.

Zalaboldogfa, Hung.; pop. 2; 56 km NNW of Nagykanizsa; 46°54'/16°46'.

Zalacsany, Hung.; pop. 15; 50 km N of Nagykanizsa; 46°48'/17°07'.

Zalaegerszeg, Hung.; pop. 1,041; 50 km NNW of Nagykanizsa; 46°50'/16°51'; GUM5, GUM6, HSL, LDS, PHH.

Zalaerdod, Hung.; pop. 2; 75 km N of Nagykanizsa; 47°03'/17°08'.

Zalagalsa, Hung.; pop. 3; 82 km N of Nagykanizsa; 47°06'/17°16'.

Zalagyomoro, Hung.; pop. 8; 69 km N of Nagykanizsa; 47°01'/17°14'.

Zalahalap, Hung.; pop. 10; 69 km NNE of Nagykanizsa; 46°55'/17°28'.

Zalaigrice, Hung.; pop. 5; 45 km N of Nagykanizsa; 46°45'/17°01'.

Zalaistvand, Hung.; pop. 4; 62 km N of Nagykanizsa; 46°55'/16°59'.

Zalakoppany, Hung.; pop. 13; 56 km N of Nagykanizsa; 46°53'/17°05'.

Zalalovo, Hung. (Zalaovo); pop. 115; 56 km NW of Nagykanizsa; 46°51'/16°36'; LDS, PHH.

Zalamerenye, Hung.; pop. 5; 26 km NNE of Nagykanizsa; 46°34'/17°06'.

Zalamihalyfa, HSL. This pre-World War I community was not found in BGN gazetteers.

Zalan, Rom.; pop. 3; 176 km N of Bucuresti; 45°57'/25°49'.

Zalanow, see Zalanuv.

Zalanuv, Ukr. (Zalanow); pop. 61; 62 km SE of Lvov; 49°28'/24°32'.

Zalaovo, see Zalalovo.

Zalapetend, see Vigantpetend.

Zalas, Pol.; pop. 20; 107 km W of Bialystok; 53°26'/21°34'.

Zalasowa, Pol.; pop. 18; 88 km E of Krakow; 49°56'/21°08'.

Zalaszabar, Hung.; pop. 4; 32 km N of Nagykanizsa; 46°39'/17°07'.

Zalaszanto, Hung.; pop. 20; 56 km N of Nagykanizsa; 46°53'/17°14'.

Zalaszentbalazs, Hung.; pop. 10; 26 km NNW of Nagykanizsa; 46°35'/16°55'.

Zalaszentgrot, Hung.; pop. 171; 62 km N of Nagykanizsa; 46°57'/17°05'; LDS, PHH.

Zalaszentivan, Hung.; pop. 23; 56 km N of Nagykanizsa; 46°53'/16°54'.

Zalaszentjakab, Hung.; pop. 2; 13 km NE of Nagykanizsa; 46°29'/17°08'.

Zalaszentlaszlo, Hung.; pop. 7; 56 km N of Nagykanizsa; 46°53'/17°07'.

Zalaszentlorinc, Hung.; pop. 5; 62 km NNW of Nagykanizsa; 46°55'/16°53'.

Zalaszentmihaly, Hung.; pop. 41; 38 km N of Nagykanizsa; 46°43'/16°57'.

Zalata, Hung.; pop. 6; 101 km SE of Nagykanizsa; 45°49'/17°53'.

Zalatarnok, Hung.; pop. 13; 38 km NW of Nagykanizsa; 46°42'/16°46'.

Zalau, Rom. (Zilah); pop. 429; 69 km NW of Cluj; 47°12'/23°03'; AMG, HSL, PHR2.

Zalaudvarnok, Hung.; pop. 4; 62 km N of Nagykanizsa; 46°55'/17°07'.

Zalaujlak, Hung.; pop. 3; 19 km NNE of Nagykanizsa; 46°33'/17°05'.

Zalavar, Hung.; pop. 7; 32 km NNE of Nagykanizsa; 46°40'/17°10'.

Zalaveg, Hung.; pop. 7; 69 km N of Nagykanizsa; 47°00'/17°02'.

Zalavye, Ukr. (Zalawie); pop. 23; 114 km NNE of Rovno; 51°23'/27°20'.

Zalawie, see Zalavye.

Zalazhtsy, see Dzialoszyce.

Zalazie, see Zalazye.

Zalazy, Pol.; pop. 17; 62 km W of Lublin; 51°23'/21°44'.

Zalazye, Byel. (Zalazie); pop. 8; 107 km NE of Pinsk; 52°45'/27°17'.

Zale, Pol.; pop. 24; 139 km WNW of Warszawa; 53°02'/19°19'.

Zalecze Male, Pol.; pop. 4; 45 km NW of Czestochowa; 51°05'/18°43'.

Zalecze Wielkie, Pol.; pop. 13; 45 km WNW of Czestochowa; 51°05'/18°41'.

Zalene, see Zelene.

Zalenieki, Lat.; pop. 1; 62 km SSW of Riga; 56°32'/23°31'.

Zalesany, Cz.; pop. 8; 38 km E of Praha; 50°02'/15°01'; HSL.

Zalese, (Zalesie);

Zalese (near Chortkov), Ukr.; pop. 38; 75 km N of Chernovtsy; 48°56'/25°54'.

Zalese (near Gorodok), Ukr.; pop. 18; 19 km WNW of Lvov; 49°54'/23°44'.

Zalese (near Kamen Kashirskiy), Ukr.; pop. 4; 139 km NW of Rovno; 51°33'/24°57'.

Zalese (near Kobrin), Byel.; pop. 4; 114 km W of Pinsk; 52°13'/24°29'.

Zalese (near Zolochev), Ukr.; pop. 6; 62 km E of Lvov; 49°47'/24°49'.

Zaleshchiki, Ukr. (Zaleshchyki, Zaleszcyki, Zaleszczyki, Zaleszczyki Stare, Zaleszczyski, Zalishchik, Zolishtchik); pop. 2,485; 45 km NNW of Chernovtsy; 48°38'/25°44'; AMG, COH, EDRD, EGRS, GA, GUM3, GUM4, GUM5, GUM6, GYLA, HSL, HSL2, JGFF, LDL, LYV, PHP2, PHP4, SF.

Zaleshchyki, see Zaleshchiki.

Zaleshits, see Dzialoszyce.

Zalesiany, Pol.; pop. 5; 13 km SSW of Bialystok; 53°04'/23°04'.

Zalesie, see Zalese. There are no less than 78 towns in Poland named Zalesie, which means "place beyond the woods." See listings below.

Zalesie (near Brest), Pol.; pop. 18; 107 km NNE of Lublin; 52°02'/23°22'.

Zalesie (near Jedrzejow), Pol.; pop. 4; 69 km E of Czestochowa; 50°47'/20°08'.

Zalesie (near Lancut), Pol.; pop. 11; 62 km WNW of Przemysl; 50°01'/22°02'.

Zalesie (near Lublin), Pol.; pop. 7; 19 km N of Lublin; 51°22'/22°38'.

Zalesie (near Lukow), Pol.; pop. 36; 82 km NNW of Lublin; 51°57'/22°19'.

Zalesie (near Nisko), Pol.; pop. 21; 82 km NW of Przemysl; 50°24'/22°04'.

Zalesie (near Nowy Sacz), Pol.; pop. 62 km SE of Krakow; 49°37'/20°21'; CAHJP.

Zalesie (near Radom), Pol.; pop. 4; 88 km WSW of Lublin; 51°15'/21°17'.

Zalesie (near Rzeszow), Pol.; pop. 10; 62 km WNW of Przemysl; 50°01'/22°02'.

Zalesie (near Wegrow), Pol.; pop. 29; 62 km ENE of Warszawa; 52°25'/21°53'.

Zalesie (near Wloszczowa), Pol.; pop. 7; 62 km NE of Czestochowa; 50°59'/19°58'.

Zalesie Krasienskie, see Zalesie Kraszenskie.

Zalesie Kraszenskie, Pol. (Zalesie Krasienskie); pop. 6; 45 km ESE of Lublin; 51°07'/23°11'.

Zaleska Wola, see Wola Zaleska.

Zalesye, USSR (Mehlauken); pop. 11; 69 km ENE of Kaliningrad; 54°51'/21°32'.

Zalesye (near Borshchev), Ukr.; pop. 21; 45 km NNE of Chernovtsy; 48°40'/26°14'.

Zaleszcyki, see Zaleshchiki.

Zaleszczyki, see Zaleshchiki.

Zaleszczyki Stare, see Zaleshchiki.

Zaleszczyski, see Zaleshchiki.

Zalewo, Pol. (Saalfeld); pop. 44; 88 km ESE of Gdansk; 53°50'/19°36'.

Zalha, Rom.; pop. 14; 50 km N of Cluj; 47°11'/23°32'; HSL.

Zalhostice, Cz.; pop. 2; 50 km NW of Praha; 50°31'/14°05'.

Zalin, Pol. BGN lists two possible localities with this name located at 44°51'/16°15' and 51°13'/23°38'. GUM3.

Zaliosia, Lith.; pop. 24; This town was not found in BGN gazetteers under the given spelling.

Zalipie, Pol.; 69 km ENE of Krakow; 50°14'/20°51'; PHP2.

Zalishchik, see Zaleshchiki.

Zalisocze, Pol.; pop. 28; 88 km E of Lublin; 51°09'/23°47'.

Zaliszcze, Pol.; pop. 51; 62 km NNE of Lublin; 51°39'/23°09'; HSL.

Zalite, Lat.; pop. 2; 45 km S of Riga; 56°39'/24°05'.

Zalkod, Hung.; pop. 5; 50 km ENE of Miskolc; 48°11'/21°28'.

Zalkove, see Nesterov.

Zalkva, see Nesterov.

Zalnoc, Rom.; pop. 21; 94 km WNW of Cluj; 47°22'/22°41'.

Zalokets, Ukr. (Zalokiec); pop. 67; 88 km SSW of Lvov; 49°18'/23°15'.

Zalokiec, see Zalokets.

Zalosce, see Zalozhtsy.

Zaloscie, see Zalozhtsy.

Zaloshits, see Dzialoszyce.

Zaloshitz, see Dzialoszyce.

Zaloshts, see Zalozhtsy.

Zalozce, see Zalozhtsy.

Zalozhtsy, Ukr. (Zalosce, Zaloscie, Zaloshts, Zalozce, Zalozhtza, Zalozitz, Zilozitz); pop. 524; 94 km E of Lvov; 49°47'/25°22'; AMG, EGRS, GUM3, GUM4, GUM6, HSL, HSL2, JGFF, PHP2, SF.

Zalozhtza, see Zalozhtsy.

Zalozitz, see Zalozhtsy.

Zalshits, see Dzialoszyce.

Zalszyn, Pol.; 107 km WNW of Warszawa; 52°45'/19°36'; HSL.

Zaluche, Ukr. (Zalucze); pop. 72; 32 km WNW of Chernovtsy; 48°24'/25°31'. The Black Book notes two towns in Stanislawow province, Zalucze nad Prutem and Zalucze nad Czeremoszen. Only one town in the area named Zaluche appears in contemporary gazetteers.

Zaluchow, see Zalukhuv.

Zalucze, Pol.; pop. 40; 45 km NE of Lublin; 51°24'/23°07'. See also Zaluche.

Zaluczne, Pol.; pop. 2; 69 km S of Krakow; 49°30'/19°50'.

Zaluhe, Pol.; pop. 51; Described in the Black Book as being in the Stanislawow region of Poland, this town was not found in BGN gazetteers.

Zalukh, Ukr. (Zaluzhye); pop. 80; 50 km WNW of Lvov; 50°04'/23°24'.

Zalukhuv, Ukr. (Zaluchow); pop. 43; 163 km NW of Rovno; 51°50'/24°52'.

Zalukiew, Ukr.; pop. 120; 101 km WNW of Chernovtsy; 48°45'/24°45'; PHP2. This town was located on an interwar map of Poland but does not appear in contemporary gazetteers. Map coordinates are approximate.

Zaluski, Pol.; pop. 30; 19 km SSW of Warszawa; 52°10'/20°56'.

Zalutycze, see Zalyutichi.

Zaluz, Pol.; pop. 31; 50 km SW of Przemysl; 49°32'/22°18'.

Zaluze, Byel.; pop. 33; 88 km N of Pinsk; 52°49'/26°03'; PHP2. *See also* Zaluzhe; Zaluzhye.

Zaluzhe, Ukr. (Zaluze); pop. 26; 69 km SE of Lvov; 49°24'/24°36'.

Zaluzhe (Lwow), Ukr.; pop. 26; 45 km WNW of Lvov; 49°58'/23°25'.

Zaluzhye, *see* Zalukh.

Zaluzi, Cz.; pop. 82 km SSE of Praha; 49°25'/14°43'; HSL.

Zaluzie, *see* Sokolovka.

Zalyutichi, Byel. (Zalutycze); pop. 24; 101 km NE of Pinsk; 52°24'/27°32'.

Zam, Rom.; pop. 20; 120 km SW of Cluj; 46°00'/22°27'.

Zamardi, Hung. (Balatonzamardi); pop. 14; 88 km NE of Nagykanizsa; 46°53'/17°57'.

Zamarski, Pol.; pop. 3; 94 km SW of Krakow; 49°48'/18°41'.

Zamarstynow, Pol.; pop. 2,914; EGRS. Described in the *Black Book* as being in the Lwow region of Poland, this town was not found in BGN gazetteers.

Zamberk, Cz.; pop. 38; 107 km N of Brno; 50°06'/16°28'.

Zambrov, *see* Zambrow.

Zambrow, Pol. (Zambrov, Zambruv, Zembrov, Zembrova, Zembrove, Zombrov); pop. 3,216; 62 km WSW of Bialystok; 52°59'/22°15'; AMG, CAHJP, COH, EJ, FRG, GA, GUM3, HSL, HSL2, JGFF, LDL, LDS, LYV, PHP4, POCEM, SF, YB.

Zambruv, *see* Zambrow.

Zambrzeniec Nowy, Pol. (Zambrzyniec Nowy); pop. 6; 62 km NE of Warszawa; 52°31'/21°50'.

Zambrzyniec Nowy, *see* Zambrzeniec Nowy.

Zambski Koscielne, Pol.; pop. 33; 62 km N of Warszawa; 52°46'/21°14'.

Zambski Stare, Pol.; pop. 2; 56 km N of Warszawa; 52°45'/21°14'.

Zamch, Pol. (Zamek); pop. 150; 62 km N of Przemysl; 50°19'/23°02'; JGFF.

Zamchozhi, Mold. (Zamosi); pop. 5; 32 km NNW of Kishinev; 47°12'/28°44'.

Zamechow, *see* Zamekhov.

Zameczek, *see* Zamochek.

Zamek, *see* Zamch.

Zamek (Lwow), Ukr.; pop. 72; 45 km NW of Lvov; 50°10'/23°39'.

Zamekhov, Ukr. (Zamechow, Zamichov); 88 km SW of Vinnitsa; 48°52'/27°22'; COH, EDRD, JGFF, LDL, SF, YB.

Zamety, Pol.; pop. 7; 94 km W of Lodz; 51°59'/18°11'.

Zamichov, *see* Zamekhov.

Zamiechow, Pol.; pop. 11; 19 km NNW of Przemysl; 49°56'/22°45'.

Zamienie, Pol.; pop. 8; 38 km ESE of Warszawa; 52°09'/21°30'.

Zamiescie, Pol.; pop. 34; 50 km SE of Krakow; 49°44'/20°21'.

Zamkowa Wola, *see* Wola Zamkowa.

Zamliche, Ukr. (Zamlicze); pop. 16; 107 km N of Lvov; 50°44'/24°33'.

Zamlicze, *see* Zamliche.

Zamlynie, *see* Zamlynye.

Zamlynye, Ukr. (Zamlynie); pop. 22; 146 km N of Lvov; 51°08'/23°58'.

Zamochek, Ukr. (Zameczek); pop. 41; 38 km N of Lvov; 50°08'/23°57'.

Zamoczyn, HSL. This pre-World War I community was not found in BGN gazetteers.

Zamojsce, Pol.; pop. 15; 19 km N of Przemysl; 49°56'/22°49'.

Zamolodycze, Pol.; pop. 68; 62 km NE of Lublin; 51°34'/23°13'.

Zamoly, Hung.; pop. 42; 56 km SW of Budapest; 47°19'/18°25'.

Zamorocze, HSL. This pre-World War I community was not found in BGN gazetteers.

Zamosc, Pol. (Zamoshch, Zamoshtch, Zamoshtsh, Zamostie, Zamotch); pop. 9,328; 75 km SE of Lublin; 50°43'/23°15'; AMG, CAHJP, COH, EDRD, EJ, FRG, GA, GUM3, GUM4, GUM5, GUM6, HSL, HSL2, JGFF, LDL, LDS, LYV, PHP2, PHP3, PHP4, POCEM, SF, YB.

Zamosc (near Piotrkow Trybunalski), Pol.; pop. 67; 26 km ESE of Lodz; 51°37'/19°43'; PHP1.

Zamoscie, Pol.; pop. 31; A number of towns share this name. It was not possible to determine from available information which one is being referenced.

Zamosc Mierzejewo, Pol.; pop. 48; 82 km N of Warszawa; 52°59'/21°15'.

Zamoshch, *see* Zamosc.

Zamoshtch, *see* Zamosc.

Zamoshtsh, *see* Zamosc.

Zamoshye (Polesie), Byel. (Zamosze [Polesie]); pop. 26; 50 km NE of Pinsk; 52°23'/26°43'.

Zamoshye (Wilen), Byel. (Zamosze [Wilen]); pop. 28; 69 km N of Minsk; 54°28'/27°55'.

Zamosi, *see* Zamchozhi.

Zamostea, Rom. (Zamostre); 133 km WNW of Iasi; 47°52'/26°12'; PHR2.

Zamostea Storojinet, *see* Zamostye.

Zamostie, *see* Zamosc.

Zamostre, *see* Zamostea.

Zamosty, Byel.; pop. 305; 157 km W of Pinsk; 52°24'/23°48'.

Zamostye, Ukr. (Zamostea Storojinet); pop. 129; 45 km W of Chernovtsy; 48°21'/25°25'.

Zamosze (Polesie), *see* Zamoshye (Polesie).

Zamosze (Wilen), *see* Zamoshye (Wilen).

Zamotch, *see* Zamosc.

Zamshany, Ukr. (Zamszany); pop. 62; 157 km WNW of Rovno; 51°34'/24°34'.

Zamszany, *see* Zamshany.

Zamuescie, Pol. PHP3. This town was not found in BGN gazetteers under the given spelling.

Zamulince, *see* Zamulintse.

Zamulintse, Ukr. (Zamulince); pop. 48; 62 km WNW of Chernovtsy; 48°29'/25°11'.

Zaniemysl, Pol. (Santomischel); pop. 12; 38 km SE of Poznan; 52°10'/17°12'; CAHJP, HSL, HSL2, JGFF, LDS.

Zaniow, Pol. PHP2. This town was not found in BGN gazetteers under the given spelling.

Zanivye, Byel. (Zaniwie); pop. 12; 88 km W of Pinsk; 52°14'/24°51'.

Zaniwie, *see* Zanivye.

Zanka, Hung.; pop. 8; 75 km NE of Nagykanizsa; 46°53'/17°41'.

Zanow, *see* Sianow.

Zaolzie, Pol. EDRD. This town was not found in BGN gazetteers under the given spelling.

Zaorle, Pol.; 62 km N of Wroclaw; 51°34'/17°04'; GA.

Zapadnaya Dvina, USSR; pop. 439; 94 km E of Velikiye Luki; 56°16'/32°04'.

Zapalow, Pol.; pop. 64; 38 km N of Przemysl; 50°05'/22°53'; HSL.

Zapiskis, *see* Zapyskis.

Zapoeoze, *see* Zaporozhye.

Zaporizhia, *see* Zaporozhye.

Zaporoze, *see* Zaporozhye.

Zaporozhe, *see* Zaporozhye.

Zaporozhia, *see* Zaporozhye.

Zaporozhye, Ukr. (Aleksandrovsk, Aleksandrowsk, Alexandrovsk, Zapoeoze, Zaporizhia, Zaporoze, Zaporozhe, Zaporozhia); pop. 11,319; 75 km SSE of Dnepropetrovsk; 47°49'/35°11'; EDRD, EJ, GUM4, GUM5, GYLA, HSL, JGFF, LDL, SF.

Zaporze, Pol.; pop. 14; 56 km SSE of Lublin; 50°46'/22°49'.

Zapovednoye, USSR (Seckenburg); pop. 57; 69 km NE of Kaliningrad; 55°04'/21°24'.

Zaprudy, Byel.; pop. 12; 114 km W of Pinsk; 52°20'/24°34'; HSL, SF.

Zaprudze, Byel. (Zaprudzie); pop. 4; 157 km N of Minsk; 55°14'/27°40'.

Zaprudzie, *see* Zaprudze.

Zapyskis, Lith. (Sepizishok, Zapiskis); pop. 293; 19 km W of Kaunas; 54°55'/23°40'; GUM5, HSL, YL.

Zapytov, Ukr. (Zapytow); pop. 26; 19 km NE of Lvov; 49°55'/24°12'.

Zapytow, *see* Zapytov.

Zara, *see* Zadar.

Zaradawa, Pol.; pop. 17; 45 km N of Przemysl; 50°09'/22°48'.

Zarajec, Pol.; pop. 11; 56 km S of Lublin; 50°48'/22°18'.

Zaran, *see* Zarenai.

Zarasai, Lith. (Ezerenai, Ezherena, Ezherene, Ezreni, Jeziorosy, Novo Aleksandrovsk, Novoaleksandrovsk); pop. 1,329; 133 km NNE of Vilnius; 55°44'/26°15'; AMG, EDRD, EJ, GUM3, GUM4, GUM5, HSL, JGFF, LDL, SF, YL.

Zaravice, Cz.; pop. 8; 82 km ENE of Praha; 50°06'/15°34'.

Zarczyn, Pol.; 69 km NNE of Poznan; 52°57'/17°32'; AMG.

Zarebe Koscielne, *see* Zareby Koscielne.

Zarebi Koschelne, *see* Zareby Koscielne.

Zareby, Pol.; 120 km N of Warszawa; 53°18'/21°02'; HSL2.

Zareby Koscielne, Pol. (Zarebe Koscielne, Zarebi Koschelne, Zarembi Koshchelne, Zaremby, Zaremby Koscielne, Zaromb); pop. 1,254; 82 km SW of Bialystok; 52°45'/22°08'; AMG, CAHJP, COH, EDRD, GUM3, GYLA, HSL, JGFF, LDS, LYV, PHP4, SF, YB.

Zarechanka, Ukr. (Lanchkorun, Lantskorun, Lantzekronia, Laskorun); pop. 1,638; 75 km NNE of Chernovtsy; 48°54'/26°23'; SF.

Zarechka, Byel. (Zarzeczka); pop. 11; 69 km WSW of Pinsk; 52°03'/25°07'. The *Black Book* notes a second town named Zarechka (pop. 24) in Polesie province in the vicinity of Osowce (Osovtse) that does not appear in contemporary gazetteers.

Zarechnoye, Ukr. (Pohost Zarzeczny); pop. 264; 139 km N of Rovno; 51°49'/26°08'.

Zarechye, Ukr. (Zarzecze); pop. 67; 101 km W of Chernovtsy; 48°31'/24°39'. *See also* Zazheche. The *Black Book* also notes two towns in Wolyn province named Zarzecze. One is near Vladimir Volynskiy (pop. 6); the second is near Lutsk (pop. 5). Neither appears in contemporary gazetteers.

Zarechye (near Slonim), Byel.; pop. 12; 94 km NW of Pinsk; 52°52'/25°30'.

Zarechye (near Stolbtsy), Byel.; pop. 23; 56 km SW of Minsk; 53°35'/26°51'.

Zarechye (Tarnopol), Ukr.; pop. 26; 101 km W of Chernovtsy; 48°31'/24°39'.

Zarembi Koshchelne, *see* Zareby Koscielne.

Zaremby, *see* Zareby Koscielne.

Zaremby Koscielne, *see* Zareby Koscielne.

Zarenai, Lith. (Zaran); pop. 174; 69 km WSW of Siauliai; 55°50'/22°13'; YL.

Zarica, Cz. AMG, COH. A number of towns share this name. It was not possible to determine from available information which one is being referenced.

Zaricany, Cz.; pop. 9; 75 km E of Praha; 49°58'/15°28'.

Zaritchanka, *see* Tsarichanka.

Zaritschanka, *see* Tsarichanka.

Zaritz, HSL. This pre-World War I community was not found in BGN gazetteers.

Zarki, Pol. (Zharik, Zharki, Zhurik); pop. 2,536; 26 km ESE of Czestochowa; 50°38'/19°23'; AMG, CAHJP, COH, EDRD, GA, GUM3, GUM4, GUM5, GUM6, HSL, JGFF, LDS, LYV, PHP1, PHP4, POCEM, SF, YB.

Zarnov, *see* Zarnow.

Zarnovica, Cz.; pop. 84; 126 km NE of Bratislava; 48°29'/18°44'.

Zarnovitza, *see* Zarnowiec.

Zarnow, Pol. (Zarnov, Zharnov, Zsarno); pop. 919; 75 km SE of Lodz; 51°15'/20°11'; GUM5, HSL, JGFF, LDL, LDS, PHP1, PHP3, PHP4, SF. The *Black Book* also shows a town of Zarnow Kantoria (pop. 40).

Zarnowce, *see* Zhornishche.

Zarnowiec, Pol. (Zarnovitza); pop. 946; 50 km N of Krakow; 50°29'/19°52'; AMG, CAHJP, COH, GUM3, GUM4, GUM5, GUM5, HSL, HSL2, LDL, LDS, PHP1, SF.

Zarnowiec (near Krosno), Pol.; pop. 22; 82 km WSW of Przemysl; 49°42'/21°39'; HSL.

Zarnowka, Pol.; pop. 26; 62 km ENE of Warszawa; 52°16'/21°53'.

Zarnowo, Pol.; 82 km NNW of Bialystok; 53°50'/22°53'; HSL.

Zarojani, *see* Zarozhan.

Zaromb, *see* Zareby Koscielne.

Zaronovo, Byel. (Novo); 26 km WNW of Vitebsk; 55°18'/29°52'. This town was not found in BGN gazetteers under the given spelling.

Zarowie, Byel.; pop. 38; 114 km N of Pinsk; 53°05'/26°15'. This town was located on an interwar map of Poland but does not appear in contemporary gazetteers. Map coordinates are approximate.

Zarowka, Pol.; pop. 54; 94 km ENE of Krakow; 50°10'/21°14'; AMG.

Zarownie, Pol.; pop. 10; 114 km WNW of Przemysl; 50°25'/21°32'.

Zarozhan, Ukr. (Zarojani); pop. 90; 32 km NE of Chernovtsy; 48°25'/26°19'.

Zarshin, *see* Zarszyn.

Zarszyn, Pol. (Zarshin); pop. 181; 62 km SW of Przemysl; 49°35'/22°01'; EGRS, HSL, PHP3, SF, YB.

Zarubince, Ukr.; pop. 26; 126 km N of Chernovtsy; 49°25'/25°45'; HSL. This town was located on an interwar map of Poland but does not appear in contemporary gazetteers. Map coordinates are approximate.

Zarudnia, Pol.; pop. 16; 69 km E of Lublin; 51°14'/23°35'.

Zarudnyce, Ukr.; 56 km W of Uman; 48°50'/29°25'; PHR1. This town was located on a pre-World War I map, but does not appear in contemporary gazetteers.

Zaruzie, Pol.; pop. 13; 88 km W of Bialystok; 53°09'/21°49'.

Zary, Pol. (Sorau, Sorau Seifersdorf); pop. 90; 146 km WNW of Wroclaw; 51°38'/15°09'; AMG, JGFF.

Zarya, Ukr. (Camcic); pop. 18; 101 km SW of Odessa; 45°59'/29°42'.

Zaryszyn, Pol.; pop. 20; 45 km NNE of Krakow; 50°27'/20°15'.

Zarzecze, Pol. PHP2. A number of towns share this name. It was not possible to determine from available information which one is being referenced. *See also* Zarechye.

Zarzecze (Kielce), Pol.; pop. 9; 56 km S of Lodz; 51°18'/19°16'.

Zarzecze (near Jaroslaw), Pol.; pop. 7; 26 km NW of Przemysl; 49°59'/22°33'.

Zarzecze (near Jaslo), Pol.; pop. 23; 94 km WSW of Przemysl; 49°41'/21°29'.

Zarzecze (near Nisko), Pol.; pop. 29; 82 km S of Lublin; 50°32'/22°12'.

Zarzecze (near Nowy Sacz), Pol.; pop. 12; 69 km SE of Krakow; 49°33'/20°25'.

Zarzecze (near Radom), Pol.; pop. 19; 56 km WNW of Lublin; 51°25'/21°51'.

Zarzecze (near Zamosc), Pol.; pop. 15; 75 km SE of Lublin; 50°39'/23°10'.

Zarzecze (Slaskie), Pol.; pop. 7; 69 km S of Czestochowa; 50°11'/18°58'.

Zarzeczka, *see* Zarechka.

Zarzezce (near Nowy Sacz), Pol.; pop. 12; Described in the *Black Book* as being in the Krakow region of Poland, this town was not found in BGN gazetteers.

Zarzyc Ulanski, Pol. (Ulanski Zarzyc); pop. 27; 69 km N of Lublin; 51°48'/22°28'.

Zasadne, Pol.; pop. 4; 69 km SE of Krakow; 49°36'/20°20'.

Zasanie, Pol.; 6 km NW of Przemysl; 49°48'/22°46'; EJ.

Zasavica, Yug.; 163 km W of Beograd; 45°02'/18°25'; EJ, GUM4, GUM5.

Zashkov, Ukr. (Zashkuv, Zaszkow); pop. 70; 19 km N of Lvov; 49°57'/23°59'; HSL.

Zashkuv, *see* Zashkov.

Zasiecie, GUM3. This town was not found in BGN gazetteers under the given spelling.

Zasimy, Byel. (Zosimy); pop. 2; 120 km W of Pinsk; 52°21'/24°27'.

Zaskevichi, Byel. (Zaskrevitz); 82 km WNW of Minsk; 54°24'/26°37'; SF.

Zaskevitchi, LDL. This pre-World War I community was not found in BGN gazetteers.

Zaskov, Cz. (Zaskow); 157 km WNW of Kosice; 49°10'/19°13'; GYLA, LDL, SF.

Zaskow, *see* Zaskov.

Zaskrevitz, *see* Zaskevichi.

Zaskrodzie, Pol.; pop. 6; 82 km WNW of Bialystok; 53°24'/22°01'.

Zasla, *see* Zasliai.

Zaslav, *see* Izyaslav.

Zaslavl, Byel. (Izaslav, Iziaslav, Zaslaw); pop. 368; 26 km WNW of Minsk; 54°00'/27°17'; GUM4, GUM5, HSL, HSL2, JGFF, LDL, PHP3, SF.

Zaslaw, *see* Izyaslav; Zaslavl.

Zaslawie, GUM5, HSL, PHP2, PHP3. This town was not found in BGN gazetteers under the given spelling.

Zasle, *see* Zasliai.

Zasliai, Lith. (Shosli, Zasla, Zasle, Zhosla, Zosli); pop. 1,067; 45 km E of Kaunas; 54°52'/24°36'; GUM5, HSL, JGFF, LDL, SF, YL.

Zaslov, *see* Izyaslav.

Zasmuky, Cz.; pop. 7; 45 km ESE of Praha; 49°57'/15°02'.

Zasov, *see* Zassow.

Zassow, Pol. (Zasov); pop. 61; 101 km ENE of Krakow; 50°08'/21°20'; SF, YB.

Zastave, Ukr. (Zastawie); pop. 64; 62 km NNW of Lvov; 50°23'/23°45'; HSL. *See also* Zastavye.

Zastavna, Ukr.; pop. 635; 32 km NNW of Chernovtsy; 48°31'/25°51'; COH, EJ, GUM4, HSL, JGFF, LYV, PHR2, SF.

Zastavne, Ukr. (Zdzary Wielkie); pop. 7; 88 km N of Lvov; 50°35'/24°16'.

Zastavye, Byel. (Zastave); pop. 20; 56 km WNW of Pinsk; 52°18'/25°19'; COH, YB.

Zastawa, Pol.; pop. 15; 62 km ESE of Bialystok; 52°42'/23°50'.

Zastawie, Pol.; pop. 39; 82 km NNW of Lublin; 51°57'/22°10'. *See also* Zastave.

Zasule, *see* Zasulye.

Zasulye, Byel. (Zasule); pop. 4; 56 km SW of Minsk; 53°34'/26°50'.

Zaszkow, *see* Zashkov.

Zaszkowice, Ukr.; pop. 28; 56 km S of Lvov; 49°25'/23°45'. This town was located on an interwar map of Poland but does not appear in contemporary gazetteers. Map coordinates are approximate.

Zatec, Cz. (Saaz); 69 km WNW of Praha; 50°20'/13°33'; EJ.

Zatiscea, *see* Zatishye.

Zatishye, Ukr. (Zatiscea); 120 km NW of Odessa; 47°20'/29°51'; PHR1.

Zaton, Byel.; 69 km WNW of Gomel; 52°46'/30°05'; HSL, HSL2.

Zator, Pol.; pop. 436; 38 km SW of Krakow; 49°59'/19°27'; CAHJP, COH, EGRS, HSL, LDL, PHP3, SF.

Zatory, Pol.; pop. 58; 45 km N of Warszawa; 52°36'/21°11'; AMG, POCEM.

Zatrzebin, GUM4, GUM5. This town was not found in BGN gazetteers under the given spelling.

Zatwarnica, Pol.; pop. 82; 69 km S of Przemysl; 49°13'/22°34'.

Zau, *see* Zau de Cimpie.

Zauan, Rom. (Zavan); pop. 22; 88 km WNW of Cluj; 47°14'/22°40'.

Zaube, Lat.; pop. 9; 69 km ENE of Riga; 57°00'/25°16'.

Zau de Cimpie, Rom. (Bzau, Mezozah, Zau); 45 km ESE of Cluj; 46°36'/24°08'; HSL.

Zavadka, Ukr. (Zawadka); pop. 90; 88 km SSE of Lvov; 49°06'/24°15'.

Zavadov, Ukr. (Zavaduv, Zavidov, Zawadow); pop. 70; 50 km WNW of Lvov; 50°04'/23°23'; GUM3, HSL, PHP2, SF.

Zavaduv, *see* Zavadov.

Zavale, Ukr. (Zawale); pop. 73; 26 km WNW of Chernovtsy; 48°23'/25°36'; JGFF. The *Black Book* notes a second town of Zawale (pop. 120) in the interwar Polish province of Wolyn.

Zavalov, Ukr. (Zavaluv, Zawalow); pop. 137; 107 km ESE of Lvov; 49°12'/25°02'; EGRS, GUM4, HSL, HSL2, JGFF, LDL, PHP2, SF.

Zavaluv, *see* Zavalov.

Zavan, *see* Zauan.

Zavertse, *see* Zawiercie.

Zavichost, *see* Zawichost.

Zavichvost, *see* Zawichost.

Zavidche, Ukr. (Zawidcze); pop. 82; 88 km NE of Lvov; 50°18'/24°56'; YB.

Zavidchitsy, Byel. (Zawidczyce); pop. 10; 13 km SSW of Pinsk; 52°03'/26°03'.

Zavidov, *see* Zavadov.

Zavidova, *see* Zavidovo.

Zavidovici, Yug.; pop. 147; 189 km WSW of Beograd; 44°27'/18°09'; PHY.

Zavidovitse, Ukr. (Zawidowice); pop. 15; 32 km SW of Lvov; 49°42'/23°39'.

Zavidovo, Cz. (Zavidova); 56 km WSW of Praha; 50°04'/13°37'; AMG.

Zavirtcha, *see* Zawiercie.

Zavlekov, Cz.; pop. 6; 114 km SSW of Praha; 49°20'/13°29'.

Zavod, (Zawod); GUM3. A number of towns share this name. It was not possible to determine from available information which one is being referenced.

Zavody, Ukr.; pop. 251; 107 km SE of Kharkov; 49°09'/37°05'.

Zavoy, Ukr. (Zawoj); pop. 126; 107 km SSE of Lvov; 48°56'/24°25'.

Zavyerche, *see* Zawiercie.

Zawada (Nowy Sacz area), Pol.; pop. 103; 82 km ESE of Krakow; 49°35'/20°44'; GUM5.

Zawada (Piotrkowskie), Pol.; pop. 22; 50 km N of Lublin; 51°38'/22°35'; GA, PHP1.

Zawadka, *see* Zavadka.

Zawadka Morochowska, Pol.; pop. 9; 62 km SW of Przemysl; 49°28'/22°09'.

Zawadka Osiecka, Pol. PHP3. This town was not found in BGN gazetteers under the given spelling.

Zawadow, *see* Zavadov.

Zawady, Pol.; pop. 93; 94 km ENE of Warszawa; 52°22'/22°22'; GA.

Zawale, *see* Zavale.

Zawalow, Pol.; pop. 20; 88 km ESE of Lublin; 50°45'/23°33'. *See also* Zavalov.

Zawan, *possibly* Zvon.

Zawarza, Pol.; pop. 7; 56 km NE of Krakow; 50°24'/20°30'.

Zawerow, LDL, SF. This town was not found in BGN gazetteers under the given spelling.

Zawichost, Pol. (Zavichost, Zavichvost); pop. 2,000; 69 km SW of Lublin; 50°48'/21°51'; AMG, CAHJP, COH, EDRD, EJ, GA, GUM3, GUM5, GYLA, HSL, HSL2, LDL, LDS, PHP3, SF.

Zawidcze, *see* Zavidche.

Zawidczyce, *see* Zavidchitsy.

Zawidowice, *see* Zavidovitse.

Zawidza, Pol.; pop. 5; 107 km SSW of Lublin; 50°32'/21°30'.

Zawiercie, Pol. (Zavertse, Zavirtcha, Zavyerche); pop. 6,095; 38 km SE of Czestochowa; 50°30'/19°26'; AMG, CAHJP, COH, EDRD, EJ, GA, GUM3, GUM4, GUM5, GUM6, HSL, HSL2, ISH2, JGFF, LDL, LYV, PHP3, POCEM, SF, YB.

Zawiselcze, Pol.; pop. 7; 88 km SSW of Lublin; 50°40'/21°44'.

Zawisty Dzikie, Pol.; pop. 181; 88 km SW of Bialystok; 52°41'/22°04'; PHP4.

Zawiszyn, Pol. BGN lists two possible localities with this name located at 52°30'/21°41' and 52°58'/18°17'. PHP4.

Zawitala, Pol.; pop. 51; 62 km NW of Lublin; 51°41'/22°08'; GUM3.

Zawod, *see* Zavod.

Zawoda, Pol.; pop. 45; 56 km E of Warszawa; 52°13'/21°48'.

Zawoj, Pol.; pop. 21; 62 km S of Przemysl; 49°16'/22°27'; PHP2. *See also* Zavoy.

Zawoja, Pol.; pop. 58; 50 km SSW of Krakow; 49°40'/19°34'.

Zawoz, Pol.; pop. 18; 56 km SSW of Przemysl; 49°21'/22°27'.

Zaybash, *see* Zywiec.

Zaybush, *see* Zywiec.

Zayenchitse, Ukr. (Zajeczyce); pop. 14; 107 km NNE of Lvov; 50°42'/24°43'.

Zaykany, Mold. (Zaicani); pop. 71; 150 km NW of Kishinev; 47°59'/27°22'.

Zazamcze, Pol.; 107 km NNW of Lodz; 52°40'/19°02'; PHP3.

Zazheche, Ukr. (Zarechye); pop. 106; 120 km WNW of Chernovtsy; 48°43'/24°25'.

Zazolkiew, Pol.; pop. 6; 50 km ESE of Lublin; 50°58'/23°08'.

Zazule, Ukr.; pop. 68; 82 km ESE of Lvov; 49°25'/24°55'. This town was located on an interwar map of Poland but does not appear in contemporary gazetteers. Map coordinates are approximate.

Zazulince, *see* Zazulintsy.

Zazulintse, *see* Zazulintsy.

Zazulintsy, Ukr. (Zazulince, Zazulintse); pop. 33; 38 km N of Chernovtsy; 48°35'/25°55'.

Zbarav, *see* Zborov.

Zbaraz, *see* Zbarazh.

Zbarazh, Ukr. (Sparach, Zbaraz, Zbarezh); pop. 2,982; 107 km S of Rovno; 49°40'/25°47'; AMG, COH, EDRD, EGRS, EJ, GA, GUM3, GUM4, GUM6, GYLA, HSL, HSL2, JGFF, LDL, LYV, PHP2, SF, YB.

Zbarezh, *see* Zbarazh.

Zbaszyn, Pol. (Bentschen); pop. 54; 75 km WSW of Poznan; 52°15'/15°56'; GUM3, GUM4, GUM5, GUM6, GUM6, HSL, ISH3, PHP1, PHP3, PHP4.

Zbelutka, Pol. (Zbielutka); pop. 14; 107 km NE of Krakow; 50°44'/21°07'.

Zbenice, Cz. (Zbenitz); pop. 3; 62 km SSW of Praha; 49°35'/14°06'; HSL.

Zbenitz, *see* Zbenice.

Zbereze, Pol.; pop. 29; 82 km ENE of Lublin; 51°24'/23°42'.

Zberezh, *see* Zburazh.

Zbielutka, *see* Zbelutka.

Zbiershav, *see* Zabierzow.

Zbigniewice, Pol.; pop. 16; 101 km SW of Lublin; 50°37'/21°30'.

Zbijow, Pol.; pop. 8; 107 km WSW of Lublin; 51°11'/20°59'.

Zbik, Pol.; pop. 5; 19 km WNW of Krakow; 50°09'/19°40'.

Zbikow, Pol. PHP4. This town was not found in BGN gazetteers under the given spelling.

Zbikowice, Pol.; pop. 12; 62 km ESE of Krakow; 49°45'/20°36'; GUM4.

Zbiroh, Cz.; pop. 7; 56 km SW of Praha; 49°51'/13°46'.

Zbizuby, Cz.; pop. 1; 50 km ESE of Praha; 49°49'/15°01'.

Zbludowice, Pol.; pop. 17; 69 km NE of Krakow; 50°26'/20°45'.

Zbludza, Pol.; pop. 7; 69 km SE of Krakow; 49°36'/20°21'.

Zboiska, Pol.; pop. 72; 82 km WSW of Przemysl; 49°35'/21°42'; HSL.

Zbojna, Pol.; pop. 109; 88 km W of Bialystok; 53°15'/21°48'; HSL, JGFF.

Zbojno, Pol.; pop. 24; 101 km WNW of Warszawa; 52°45'/19°45'.

Zbora, Ukr.; pop. 45; 88 km SSE of Lvov; 49°07'/24°15'; HSL.

Zborov, Ukr. (Zbarav, Zborow); pop. 1,184; 88 km E of Lvov; 49°40'/25°09'; AMG, COH, EDRD, EGRS, EJ, GA, GUM3, GUM4, GUM5, GUM6, GYLA, HSL, HSL2, JGFF, LDL, PHP2, PHP4, SF, YB.

Zborow, Pol.; pop. 32; 75 km NE of Krakow; 50°23'/20°54'. *See also* Zborov.

Zborowice, Pol.; pop. 15; 88 km ESE of Krakow; 49°46'/20°59'.

Zbozenna, Pol.; pop. 6; 94 km ESE of Lodz; 51°23'/20°42'.

Zbrachlin, Pol. (Sleshin, Slesin); pop. 304; 126 km NNW of Lodz; 52°47'/18°52'; AMG, COH, GUM3, LDS, PHP1, SF.

Zbraslav, Cz.; pop. 40; 19 km S of Praha; 49°58'/14°24'.

Zbraslavice, Cz.; pop. 22; 62 km ESE of Praha; 49°49'/15°11'.

Zbrodzice, Pol.; pop. 10; 75 km NE of Krakow; 50°29'/20°46'.

Zbuch, Cz.; pop. 3; 101 km SW of Praha; 49°41'/13°13'.

Zbuczyn, Pol.; pop. 103; 101 km N of Lublin; 52°05'/22°26'.

Zbudza, Cz. (Izbugya); 50 km ENE of Kosice; 48°49'/21°54'; HSL.

Zburaz, *see* Zburazh.

Zburazh, Byel. (Sburash, Zberezh, Zburaz); 150 km WSW of Pinsk; 51°46'/23°59'; SF.

Zbuzany, Cz.; pop. 2; 19 km SW of Praha; 50°01'/14°17'.

Zbydniow, Pol.; pop. 32; 82 km SSW of Lublin; 50°38'/21°57'; HSL.

Zbydniowice, Pol.; pop. 15; 19 km SSE of Krakow; 49°58'/19°57'.

Zbylitowska Gora, Pol. (Zglobice); pop. 12; 75 km E of Krakow; 49°59'/20°55'.

Zbyszewo, Pol.; pop. 6; 107 km NNW of Lodz; 52°40'/19°17'.

Zbyszyce, Pol.; pop. 36; 69 km ESE of Krakow; 49°43'/20°40'.

Zbytkow, Pol.; pop. 4; 88 km WSW of Krakow; 49°56'/18°45'.

Zdala, Yug.; pop. 11; 101 km NE of Zagreb; 46°10'/17°09'.

Zdana, Cz. (Hernadzsadany); pop. 59; 19 km SE of Kosice; 48°36'/21°21'; LDL.

Zdanice, Cz. (Steinitz); pop. 98; 32 km ESE of Brno; 49°04'/17°02'; HSL, HSL2.

Zdanow, *see* Zhdanov.

Zdanowice, Pol.; pop. 7; 69 km N of Krakow; 50°40'/20°09'.

Zdar, *see* Mesto Zdar.

Zdebuzeves, Cz.; pop. 8; 50 km ESE of Praha; 49°47'/14°58'.

Zdechovice, Cz. (Zdechowitz); 69 km E of Praha; 50°01'/15°28'; HSL.

Zdechovitz, *see* Zdziechowice.

Zdechowitz, *see* Zdechovice.

Zdiar, Cz. BGN lists two possible localities with this name located at 49°08'/20°44' and 49°16'/20°16'. GUM4.

Zdice, Cz.; pop. 9; 38 km SW of Praha; 49°54'/13°59'.

Zdikov, Cz.; pop. 8; 126 km SSW of Praha; 49°05'/13°42'.

Zditovo, Byel. (Zdzitow); pop. 2; 69 km WNW of Pinsk; 52°25'/25°15'.

Zdolbica, *see* Zdolbitsa.

Zdolbitsa, Ukr. (Zdolbica); pop. 2; 19 km S of Rovno; 50°30'/26°15'.

Zdolbunov, Ukr. (Zdolbunow); pop. 1,262; 19 km S of Rovno; 50°31'/26°15'; AMG, COH, EDRD, GUM3, GUM4, GUM5, HSL, JGFF, LDL, LYV, SF.

Zdolbunow, *see* Zdolbunov.

Zdonia, Pol.; pop. 5; 69 km ESE of Krakow; 49°51'/20°48'.

Zdounek, *see* Zdounky.

Zdounky, Cz. (Zdounek); pop. 28; 50 km ENE of Brno; 49°14'/17°19'.

Zdow, Pol.; pop. 22; 38 km ESE of Czestochowa; 50°36'/19°32'.

Zdrochec, Pol.; pop. 2; 62 km ENE of Krakow; 50°08'/20°50'.

Zdrody, Pol. (Zdrody Stare); pop. 22; 32 km SW of Bialystok; 52°57'/22°47'.

Zdrody Stare, *see* Zdrody.

Zdroje, GA. A number of towns share this name. It was not possible to determine from available information which one is being referenced.

Zdrzychow, Pol.; pop. 13; 32 km WNW of Lodz; 51°51'/19°06'.

Zdunska Vola, *see* Zdunska Wola.

Zdunska Volye, *see* Zdunska Wola.

Zdunska Wola, Pol. (Dinskivola, Zdunska Vola, Zdunska Volye, Zdunske Volye); pop. 7,885; 45 km SW of Lodz; 51°36'/18°56'; AMG, CAHJP, COH, EDRD, EJ, GA, GUM3, GUM4, GUM5, GUM6, GYLA, HSL, HSL2, JGFF, LDS, LYV, PHP1, POCEM, SF, YB.

Zdunske Volye, *see* Zdunska Wola.

Zduny, Pol.; 69 km NNE of Wroclaw; 51°39'/17°23'; CAHJP, LDS.

Zdynia, Pol.; pop. 52; 114 km SW of Przemysl; 49°29'/21°17'; HSL.

408

Zdzanne, Pol.; pop. 22; 62 km ESE of Lublin; 51°01'/23°23'.

Zdzar, Pol.; pop. 8; 62 km E of Warszawa; 52°12'/21°57'.

Zdzary Wielkie, see Zastavne.

Zdzhentsiol, see Dyatlovo.

Zdziar Wielki, Pol.; pop. 8; 75 km WNW of Warszawa; 52°38'/20°03'.

Zdziarzec, Pol.; pop. 23; 94 km ENE of Krakow; 50°10'/21°16'.

Zdziechowice, Pol. (Zdechovitz); pop. 22; 62 km SSW of Lublin; 50°47'/22°07'; SF.

Zdzieci, Pol.; pop. 5; 101 km NE of Krakow; 50°25'/21°13'; GUM4.

Zdzilowice, Pol.; pop. 33; 50 km S of Lublin; 50°49'/22°32'.

Zdzitow, see Zditovo.

Zebegeny, Hung.; pop. 6; 38 km NNW of Budapest; 47°48'/18°55'.

Zeben, see Sabinov.

Zebrak, Pol.; pop. 24; 75 km E of Warszawa; 52°04'/22°05'.

Zebry Falbogi, Pol.; pop. 8; 56 km NNW of Warszawa; 52°44'/20°53'.

Zebry Laskowiec, Pol.; pop. 24; 69 km SW of Bialystok; 52°42'/22°21'.

Zebry Wierzchlas, Pol.; pop. 6; 94 km N of Warszawa; 53°03'/21°23'.

Zebrzydowice, Pol.; 94 km WSW of Krakow; 49°53'/18°37'; GA.

Zeckendorf, Germ.; 62 km N of Nurnberg; 49°57'/11°04'; GUM5, JGFF, PHGB.

Zedechoyv, see Zhidachov.

Zegartowice, Pol.; pop. 23; 62 km NNE of Krakow; 50°33'/20°24'.

Zegevol D, see Sigulda.

Zegiestow, Pol.; pop. 12; 101 km SE of Krakow; 49°23'/20°48'; GUM5, PHP3.

Zeglce, Pol.; pop. 22; 82 km WSW of Przemysl; 49°40'/21°40'.

Zegocina, Pol. (Rzegocina); pop. 16; 50 km ESE of Krakow; 49°48'/20°26'.

Zehdenick, Germ.; pop. 32; 56 km N of Berlin; 52°59'/13°20'.

Zehun, Cz.; pop. 3; 62 km ENE of Praha; 50°08'/15°17'.

Zehusice, Cz.; pop. 8; 69 km E of Praha; 49°58'/15°25'.

Zeibush, see Zywiec.

Zeil, Germ.; 75 km NW of Nurnberg; 50°01'/10°36'; PHGB, PHGBW.

Zeilitzheim, Germ.; pop. 39; 82 km WNW of Nurnberg; 49°54'/10°16'; GUM5, HSL, PHGB.

Zeilsheim, Germ.; 13 km WSW of Frankfurt am Main; 50°06'/08°30'; GUM3.

Zeimelis, Lith. see Zeimys.

Zeimiai, Lith. (Zheim, Zheime, Ziem); pop. 110; 13 km NE of Siauliai; 55°58'/23°25'; GUM3, JGFF, LDL, SF, YL.

Zeimys, Lith. (Zeimelis, Zemel, Zheimel, Ziemel); pop. 378; 56 km NE of Siauliai; 56°17'/24°00'; COH, HSL, JGFF, SF, YL.

Zeiselmauer, Aus.; pop. 1; 19 km WNW of Wien; 48°20'/16°10'.

Zeitlofs, Germ.; pop. 34; 75 km ENE of Frankfurt am Main; 50°16'/09°40'; GUM5, HSL, JGFF, LDS, PHGB.

Zeitz, Germ.; pop. 5; 32 km SSW of Leipzig; 51°03'/12°09'; GUM3, GUM5.

Zejbis, Cz.; pop. 6; 126 km SSW of Praha; 49°13'/13°18'.

Zekhlin, see Zychlin.

Zelanka, Pol.; pop. 32; Described in the *Black Book* as being in the Wolyn region of Poland, this town was not found in BGN gazetteers.

Zelav, see Zelow.

Zelazowka, Pol.; pop. 27; 75 km ENE of Krakow; 50°08'/21°00'.

Zel Burg, see Selpils.

Zelczyna, Pol.; pop. 3; 19 km SSW of Krakow; 49°58'/19°45'.

Zeldec, see Zheldets.

Zelea, see Zetea.

Zelechow, Pol. (Zhelekhov, Zhelichov); pop. 4,806; 82 km NW of Lublin; 51°49'/21°54'; AMG, COH, EDRD, EJ, FRG, GA, GUM3, GUM4, GUM5, GYLA, HSL, HSL2, JGFF, LDL, PHP3, POCEM, SF, YB.

Zelechow Wielki, see Velikoselka.

Zelekhuv Velke, see Velikoselka.

Zelena, Rom.; pop. 66; COH. A number of towns share this name. It was not possible to determine from available information which one is being referenced. *See also* Zulnya.

Zelena (Bucovina), Ukr. (Zeleneu); pop. 39; 26 km W of Chernovtsy; 48°21'/25°38'.

Zelenaya, Ukr. (Zielona); pop. 112; 120 km W of Chernovtsy; 48°32'/24°20'; GUM3, GUM4, PHP2.

Zelene, Cz. (Zalene); 114 km WSW of Kosice; 48°26'/19°47'; JGFF.

Zeleneu, see Zelena (Bucovina).

Zelenitsa, Ukr. (Zielenica); pop. 25; 69 km N of Chernovtsy; 48°53'/26°00'; GUM4, HSL.

Zeleno, Ukr. (Andruha, Andrukha); pop. 49; 107 km N of Rovno; 51°30'/26°06'.

Zelenoe Pole, see Zelenopolye.

Zelenopol Ye, (Myodla);

Zelenopolye, Ukr. (Zelenoe Pole); pop. 1,559; 170 km ESE of Dnepropetrovsk; 47°33'/36°51'; JGFF.

Zelenovka, GUM4. A number of towns share this name. It was not possible to determine from available information which one is being referenced.

Zeleny Gay, see Zelenyy Gay.

Zelenyy, USSR (Piplin); pop. 4; 62 km ENE of Kaliningrad; 54°52'/21°27'.

Zelenyy Gay, Ukr. (Zeleny Gay); pop. 25; 120 km SSE of Dnepropetrovsk; 47°24'/35°22'.

Zelezna Ruda, Cz.; pop. 28; 139 km SSW of Praha; 49°08'/13°14'.

Zelezniki, Pol.; pop. 25; 75 km NE of Warszawa; 52°28'/22°04'; HSL.

Zelezny Brod, Cz.; pop. 34; 82 km NNE of Praha; 50°38'/15°15'; JGFF.

Zelichow, Pol. (Zelikhov); pop. 36; 62 km ENE of Krakow; 50°14'/20°50'; LYV, PHP4.

Zeliezovce, Cz. (Zseliz); pop. 752; 120 km E of Bratislava; 48°03'/18°40'; COH, GUM4, HSL.

Zelikhov, see Zelichow.

Zelina, Yug. (Sveti Ivan Zelina); pop. 6; 32 km NE of Zagreb; 45°58'/16°16'.

Zelinow, COH, HSL. This pre-World War I community was not found in BGN gazetteers.

Zeliszew, Pol.; pop. 30; 69 km E of Warszawa; 52°08'/21°59'.

Zeliv, Cz.; pop. 3; 88 km SE of Praha; 49°32'/15°14'.

Zelizna, Pol.; pop. 5; 75 km N of Lublin; 51°52'/22°57'.

Zelizy, Cz.; pop. 5; 45 km N of Praha; 50°25'/14°28'.

Zell, Germ.; pop. 34; 107 km WSW of Frankfurt am Main; 50°02'/07°11'; EJ, JGFF, PHGB.

Zellerndorf, Aus.; pop. 7; 62 km NW of Wien; 48°41'/15°57'; HSL.

Zellin, see Celldomolk.

Zellingen, Germ.; 82 km ESE of Frankfurt am Main; 49°54'/09°49'; PHGB.

Zelovo, Byel. (Ziolovo, Ziolowo); pop. 32; 88 km W of Pinsk; 52°15'/24°49'.

Zelow, Pol. (Zelav); pop. 1,816; 38 km SSW of Lodz; 51°28'/19°14'; AMG, COH, EDRD, GA, GUM3, GUM4, GUM5, HSL, HSL2, PHP1, SF, YB.

Zelowek, Pol.; pop. 8; 38 km SSW of Lodz; 51°29'/19°15'.

Zeltingen, Germ.; pop. 17; 114 km S of Koln; 49°57'/07°01'; GED, YB.

Zeltweg, Aus.; pop. 3; 56 km W of Graz; 47°11'/14°45'.

Zelva, Lith. (Pazhevla, Podzelva, Podzelve, Pozelva, Zelve, Zelwa); pop. 364; 62 km NNW of Vilnius; 55°13'/25°06'; JGFF, LDL, SF, SF, YB, YL. EJ refers to the Byelorussian town of Zelwa. *See also* Zelwa.

Zelve, see Zelva.

Zelvyany, Byel. (Zelwiany); pop. 43; 182 km NW of Pinsk; 53°24'/24°32'.

Zelwa, Byel.; pop. 1,319; 146 km NW of Pinsk; 53°09'/24°49'; AMG, EJ, GUM3, GUM4, HSL, LYV, PHP4. *See also*

409

Zelva.

Zelwiany, *see* Zelvyany.

Zelzin, Pol.; pop. 31; Described in the *Black Book* as being in the Bialystok region of Poland, this town was not found in BGN gazetteers.

Zemaiciu Kalvarija, Lith. (Kalwarya); pop. 25; 82 km W of Siauliai; 56°07'/22°01'.

Zemaiciu Naumiestis, Lith. (Ir Chadash Sugind, Neishtat Sugind, Neustadt Sugind, Nishtot Tavrig); 120 km SW of Siauliai; 55°22'/21°42'; HSL, JGFF, SF, YL.

Zemaitija, *see* Zmudz.

Zemaitkiemis, Lith.; pop. 207; 75 km NNW of Vilnius; 55°18'/24°58'.

Zembin, Byel.; pop. 838; 75 km NNE of Minsk; 54°22'/28°13'; SF.

Zembreni, *see* Zembreny.

Zembreny, Mold. (Zembreni); pop. 4; 26 km S of Kishinev; 46°50'/28°50'.

Zembrov, *see* Zambrow.

Zembrova, *see* Zambrow.

Zembrove, *see* Zambrow.

Zembrzus Mokry Grunt, Pol.; pop. 8; 120 km NNW of Warszawa; 53°17'/20°40'.

Zembrzyce, Pol.; pop. 64; 38 km SSW of Krakow; 49°47'/19°36'; AMG, HSL.

Zemel, *see* Zeimys.

Zemgale, Lat. (Semgallen, Zemgola, Zemigalliia); 26 km S of Daugavpils; 55°43'/26°28'; PHLE.

Zemgola, *see* Zemgale.

Zemianska Olca, Cz. (Nemesocsa); pop. 82; 69 km ESE of Bratislava; 47°48'/17°52'; AMG, HSL.

Zemigalliia, *see* Zemgale.

Zemite, Lat.; pop. 3; 82 km WSW of Riga; 56°56'/22°48'.

Zemne, Cz.; 69 km E of Bratislava; 47°59'/18°00'; HSL.

Zempelburg, *see* Sepolno.

Zempeln, *see* Zemplin.

Zemplen, *see* Zemplin.

Zemplenagard, Hung.; pop. 137; 101 km NE of Miskolc; 48°21'/22°05'; AMG, HSL, PHH.

Zemplensztara, *possibly* Stare.

Zemplin, Cz. (Zempeln, Zemplen); 50 km ESE of Kosice; 48°26'/21°49'; HSL, JGFF.

Zemun, Yug. (Sajmiste, Semlin); pop. 523; 6 km WSW of Beograd; 44°50'/20°24'; CAHJP, EJ, GUM4, GUM5, HSL, PHY.

Zemunik, *see* Donji Zemunik.

Zendek, Pol.; pop. 2; 38 km S of Czestochowa; 50°30'/19°06'.

Zenica, Yug.; pop. 234; 214 km SW of Beograd; 44°13'/17°55'; COH, EJ, PHY.

Zenkov, Ukr. (Zienkow, Zinkow); pop. 608; 133 km W of Kharkov; 50°12'/34°22'.

Zenonow, Pol.; pop. 9; 101 km W of Lublin; 51°21'/21°11'.

Zenta, *see* Senta.

Zentene, Lat.; pop. 1; 69 km W of Riga; 57°08'/22°59'.

Zepce, Yug.; pop. 71; 195 km WSW of Beograd; 44°26'/18°03'; PHY.

Zeran, Pol.; pop. 28; 13 km NNW of Warszawa; 52°18'/20°59'; GUM4.

Zeran Duzy, Pol.; pop. 9; 88 km N of Warszawa; 53°02'/21°30'.

Zeravice, Cz. AMG. A number of towns share this name. It was not possible to determine from available information which one is being referenced.

Zerbst, Germ.; pop. 120; 82 km NNW of Leipzig; 51°58'/12°05'; COH, EJ, HSL, JGFF, LDS.

Zerczyce, Pol.; pop. 4; 75 km S of Bialystok; 52°29'/23°05'.

Zerechowa, Pol.; pop. 9; 62 km SSE of Lodz; 51°14'/19°45'.

Zerf, Germ.; pop. 15; 150 km SW of Frankfurt am Main; 49°36'/06°41'; GED.

Zerind, Rom. (Nagyzerind); 157 km WSW of Cluj; 46°37'/21°31'; HSL, PHR1.

Zerkovice, (Zerkowitz); HSL. This pre-World War I community

was not found in BGN gazetteers.

Zerkow, Pol.; 62 km ESE of Poznan; 52°04'/17°34'; CAHJP, JGFF.

Zerkowitz, *see* Zerkovice.

Zernica Nizna, Pol.; pop. 27; 56 km SSW of Przemysl; 49°24'/22°19'.

Zernica Wyzna, Pol.; pop. 23; 56 km SSW of Przemysl; 49°23'/22°20'.

Zerniki, Pol.; pop. 20; 101 km NNE of Przemysl; 50°29'/23°45'.

Zernsdorf, Germ.; 32 km SE of Berlin; 52°18'/13°42'; HSL.

Zerocin, Pol.; pop. 7; 82 km N of Lublin; 51°57'/22°55'.

Zeroslawice, Pol.; pop. 5; 38 km SE of Krakow; 49°50'/20°15'.

Zerwana, Pol.; pop. 33; 19 km N of Krakow; 50°11'/19°59'.

Zery Czubiki, Pol.; pop. 11; 69 km SSW of Bialystok; 52°36'/22°40'.

Zerzen, Pol.; pop. 14; 13 km ESE of Warszawa; 52°11'/21°08'.

Zetea, Rom. (Zelea); pop. 22; 139 km ESE of Cluj; 46°23'/25°22'.

Zetl, *see* Dyatlovo.

Zeulenroda, Germ.; pop. 4; 75 km S of Leipzig; 50°39'/11°59'.

Zeven, Germ.; pop. 22; 56 km SW of Hamburg; 53°18'/09°17'.

Zezmar, *see* Ziezmariai.

Zezmer, *see* Ziezmariai.

Zezulin, Pol.; pop. 81; 26 km NE of Lublin; 51°21'/22°51'; JGFF.

Zgardesti, *see* Zgordeshty.

Zgaritza, *see* Zguritsa.

Zgerzh, *see* Zgierz.

Zgierz, Pol. (Zgerzh, Zgyerz); pop. 3,828; 19 km NNW of Lodz; 51°51'/19°25'; AMG, CAHJP, COH, EDRD, EJ, GA, GUM3, GUM4, GUM5, GUM6, GYLA, HSL, HSL2, JGFF, LDS, LYV, PHP1, PHP4, SF, YB.

Zglechow, Pol.; pop. 6; 50 km ESE of Warszawa; 52°06'/21°40'.

Zglobice, *see* Zbylitowska Gora.

Zglobien, Pol.; pop. 56; 75 km WNW of Przemysl; 50°01'/21°51'; PHP3.

Zgorany, Ukr. (Zhorany); pop. 51; 170 km N of Lvov; 51°21'/23°59'.

Zgordeshty, Mold. (Zgardesti); pop. 25; 75 km NW of Kishinev; 47°32'/28°12'.

Zgorsko, Pol. (Zagorsko); pop. 22; 94 km ENE of Krakow; 50°14'/21°17'.

Zgorzelec, *see* Gorlitz.

Zgosca, Yug.; pop. 16; 202 km SW of Beograd; 44°08'/18°08'.

Zgurit, *see* Zguritsa.

Zgurita, *see* Zguritsa.

Zguritsa, Mold. (Kolonie Zgurica, Zgaritza, Zgurit, Zgurita); pop. 2,541; 146 km NW of Kishinev; 48°08'/28°01'; EDRD, EJ, GYLA, LDL, SF.

Zgurovka, Ukr.; 94 km ENE of Kiyev; 50°30'/31°47'; SF.

Zgyerz, *see* Zgierz.

Zhabche Murovane, Ukr. (Zabcze Murowane); pop. 19; 69 km N of Lvov; 50°25'/24°06'.

Zhabeye, *see* Verkhovina.

Zhabinka, Byel. (Zabinka); pop. 445; 146 km W of Pinsk; 52°12'/24°01'; COH, HSL, LDL, SF.

Zhabka, Mold. (Japca, Zhapka); pop. 32; 114 km N of Kishinev; 47°59'/28°42'.

Zhabno, *see* Zabno.

Zhabokrich, Ukr. (Schabokritsch, Zabokritz, Zhabokritch); pop. 500; 101 km SW of Uman; 48°23'/28°59'; LDL, SF.

Zhabokritch, *see* Zhabokrich.

Zhabya, *see* Verkhovina.

Zhabye, *see* Verkhovina.

Zhaden, Ukr. (Zaden); pop. 35; 133 km N of Rovno; 51°43'/26°50'.

Zhadova, Ukr. (Jadova, Jadova Noua, Zadova, Zadowa); pop. 468; 38 km SW of Chernovtsy; 48°12'/25°31'; HSL, PHR2.

Zhagar, *see* Zagare.

Zhagare, *see* Zagare.

Zhager, *see* Zagare.

Zhagory, *see* Zagare.

Zhagov, *see* Rzgow.

Zhanokrich, (Zabocrici); PHR1. This town was not found in BGN gazetteers under the given spelling.

Zhapka, *see* Zhabka.

Zharik, *see* Zarki.

Zharki, *see* Zarki.

Zharnov, *see* Zarnow.

Zhavgur, Mold. (Javgur); pop. 18; 56 km S of Kishinev; 46°33'/28°37'.

Zhdanov, Ukr. (Mariupol, Zdanow); pop. 7,332; 240 km ESE of Dnepropetrovsk; 47°06'/37°33'; EDRD, EJ, GUM4, GUM5, HSL, LDL, PHP2, SF.

Zheim, *see* Zeimiai.

Zheime, *see* Zeimiai.

Zheimel, *see* Zeimys.

Zheldets, Ukr. (Zeldec); pop. 66; 32 km N of Lvov; 50°06'/24°10'.

Zhelekhov, *see* Zelechow.

Zhelekhuv Velke, *see* Velikoselka.

Zheleznodorozhnyy, USSR (Gerdauen); pop. 15; 69 km ESE of Kaliningrad; 54°22'/21°19'.

Zhelichov, *see* Zelechow.

Zheltyy Yar, Ukr. (Sararia); pop. 14; 94 km SSW of Odessa; 45°52'/29°56'.

Zheludok, Byel. (Zoludek); pop. 1,053; 176 km WSW of Minsk; 53°36'/24°59'; COH, EDRD, GUM4, GUM5, GUM6, HSL, HSL2, SF, YB.

Zhepnyuv, Ukr. (Rzepniow); pop. 31; 38 km NE of Lvov; 49°59'/24°30'.

Zheravne, *see* Zhuravno.

Zheredov, *see* Zyrardow.

Zheshov, *see* Rzeszow.

Zheshuv, *see* Rzeszow.

Zhetl, *see* Dyatlovo.

Zhevitza, *see* Drzewica.

Zhevreny, Mold. (Jevreni); pop. 32; 38 km NNE of Kishinev; 47°16'/29°04'.

Zhezhmariai, *see* Ziezmariai.

Zhezhov, *see* Rzeszow.

Zhichlin, *see* Zychlin.

Zhidachov, Ukr. (Zedechoyv, Zhidatchov, Zidatchov, Zidichev, Zidichuv, Zydaczov, Zydaczow); pop. 823; 56 km SSE of Lvov; 49°23'/24°08'; CAHJP, COH, EGRS, EJ, GUM3, HSL, HSL2, LDL, LYV, PHP2, SF, WS.

Zhidatchov, *see* Zhidachov.

Zhidik, *see* Zidikai.

Zhidiki, *see* Zidikai.

Zhidlovetza, *see* Szydlowiec.

Zhidovska Grebla, Ukr. EDRD. This town was not found in BGN gazetteers under the given spelling.

Zhikhlin, *see* Zychlin.

Zhilkovke, *see* Zolkiewka.

Zhirardov, *see* Zyrardow.

Zhiravno, *see* Zhuravno.

Zhirmuny, Byel. (Zyrmuny); pop. 100; 157 km W of Minsk; 54°01'/25°13'; GUM3, JGFF.

Zhirovichi, *see* Zhirovitsy.

Zhirovitsy, Byel. (Zhirovichi, Zyrowice); pop. 48; 114 km NW of Pinsk; 53°01'/25°21'.

Zhishchuv, *see* Rzhishchev.

Zhitkovichi, Byel.; pop. 925; 120 km ENE of Pinsk; 52°14'/27°52'; HSL, LDL, SF.

Zhitnovichi, Byel. (Zytnowicze); pop. 3; 13 km SW of Pinsk; 52°04'/25°59'.

Zhitomir, Ukr. (Jitomir, Shitomir, Zytomierz); pop. 30,001; 120 km N of Vinnitsa; 50°15'/28°40'; COH, EJ, GUM4, GUM5, GUM6, HSL, JGFF, LDL, PHP2, SF.

Zhivacher, (Jivatov); EDRD. This town was not found in BGN gazetteers under the given spelling.

Zhivachev, Ukr. (Zhyvachuv, Zywaczow); pop. 51; 75 km WNW of Chernovtsy; 48°48'/25°10'.

Zhivatov, *see* Zhivotovka.

Zhivits, *see* Zywiec.

Zhivitz, *see* Zywiec.

Zhivotov, *see* Zhivotovka.

Zhivotovka, Ukr. (Zhivatov, Zhivotov, Zivotov, Zywatow); 69 km NW of Uman; 49°14'/29°32'; HSL, JGFF, SF.

Zhivyets, *see* Zywiec.

Zhizdra, USSR (Zhuzdra); pop. 554; 56 km NNE of Bryansk; 53°41'/34°40'.

Zhizhmore E, *see* Ziezmariai.

Zhizhmory, *see* Ziezmariai.

Zhlobin, Byel.; pop. 3,531; 82 km WNW of Gomel; 52°54'/30°03'; GUM4, HSL, LDL, SF.

Zhmerinka, Ukr. (Schmerinka, Zmerinka); pop. 4,380; 32 km SW of Vinnitsa; 49°02'/28°06'; EDRD, EJ, GUM3, GUM4, GUM5, HSL, JGFF, SF.

Zhmigrod, *see* Zmigrod.

Zhmud, *see* Zmudz.

Zhnibrody, Ukr. (Znibrody); pop. 26; 75 km NW of Chernovtsy; 48°54'/25°26'.

Zholchuv, Ukr. (Zolczow); pop. 21; 75 km SE of Lvov; 49°21'/24°43'.

Zholinia, *see* Zolynia.

Zholkev, *see* Nesterov.

Zholkeva, *see* Nesterov.

Zholkevka, *see* Zolkiewka.

Zholkevke, *see* Zolkiewka.

Zholkin, Byel. (Zhulkin, Zolkin, Zolkinie); pop. 57; BGN lists two possible localities with this name located at 51°21'/26°08' and 51°54'/26°20'. FRG.

Zholkva, *see* Nesterov.

Zholkve, *see* Nesterov.

Zholobki, Ukr. (Zolobki); pop. 8; 56 km S of Rovno; 50°08'/25°59'.

Zholudek, *see* Bolshoy Zhelutsk.

Zholudsk, *see* Kolonie Zoludzk.

Zhora de Mizhlok, *see* Sredniye Zhory.

Zhora de Zhos, *see* Nizhniye Zhory.

Zhorany, *see* Zgorany.

Zhoremin, *see* Zuromin.

Zhornishche, Ukr. (Zarnowce); 50 km ESE of Vinnitsa; 49°04'/29°05'; JGFF, PHP4.

Zhornuv, Ukr. (Zornow); pop. 28; 26 km SW of Rovno; 50°31'/25°57'.

Zhosla, *see* Zasliai.

Zhovtantsy, Ukr. (Zoltance); pop. 293; 26 km NE of Lvov; 49°59'/24°14'; PHP2.

Zhovten, Ukr. (Azipolia, Chesybesy, Czesybiesy, Ezupol, Jezupol, Yezapol, Zowten); pop. 188; 107 km SE of Lvov; 49°02'/24°47'; EGRS, HSL, HSL2, LDL, PHP2, SF.

Zhuchovitch, *see* Bolshiye Zhukhovichi.

Zhukov (Stanislawow), Ukr.; pop. 35; 75 km WNW of Chernovtsy; 48°42'/25°06'.

Zhukov (Tarnopol), Ukr.; pop. 46; 56 km E of Lvov; 49°43'/24°48'.

Zhukovitchi, *see* Bolshiye Zhukhovichi.

Zhukovka, USSR; pop. 674; 50 km WNW of Bryansk; 53°32'/33°45'.

Zhulitse, Ukr. (Zulice); pop. 21; 62 km ENE of Lvov; 49°52'/24°52'.

Zhulkev, *see* Nesterov.

Zhulkiewka, *see* Zolkiewka.

Zhulkin, *see* Zholkin.

Zhulkyev, *see* Nesterov.

Zhuprany, Byel. (Zuprany); 114 km WNW of Minsk; 54°28'/26°05'; AMG, HSL.

Zhuravichi, Byel. (Zuravitch, Zuravitz Yashan); pop. 1,140; 94 km NNW of Gomel; 53°15'/30°33'; COH, HSL, HSL2, JGFF, LDL, SF.

Zhuravno, Ukr. (Zheravne, Zhiravno, Zuravna, Zurawno); pop.

411

865; 75 km SSE of Lvov; 49°15'/24°17'; COH, EDRD, EGRS, EJ, GUM3, GUM4, GUM5, HSL, HSL2, LDL, PHP2, PHP3, SF.

Zhurevichi, Byel. (Zurewicze); pop. 4; 75 km WNW of Minsk; 54°14'/26°37'.

Zhurik, *see* Zarki.

Zhuromin, *see* Zuromin.

Zhurov, *see* Dzhuruv.

Zhuzdra, *see* Zhizdra.

Zhuzhel, Ukr. (Zuzel); pop. 31; 62 km N of Lvov; 50°24'/24°03'.

Zhvanchik, *see* Velikiy Zhvanchik.

Zhvanets, Ukr. (Zvanitz, Zvantz, Zwaniec, Zwanitse); pop. 1,383; 50 km NE of Chernovtsy; 48°33'/26°30'; EGRS, GYLA, HSL, HSL2, JGFF, LDL, SF.

Zhychin, Byel. (Zyczyn); pop. 4; 101 km WNW of Pinsk; 52°28'/24°46'.

Zhyvachuv, *see* Zhivachev.

Ziabki, *see* Zyabki.

Ziarkowice, GUM3. This town was not found in BGN gazetteers under the given spelling.

Zichovice, Cz.; pop. 17; 107 km SSW of Praha; 49°16'/13°38'.

Zics, Hung.; pop. 11; 82 km NE of Nagykanizsa; 46°41'/17°59'.

Zidatchov, *see* Zhidachov.

Zidichev, *see* Zhidachov.

Zidichuv, *see* Zhidachov.

Zidik, *see* Zidikai.

Zidikai, Lith. (Zhidik, Zhidiki, Zidik, Zidikiai, Zydikiai); pop. 799; 94 km WNW of Siauliai; 56°19'/22°01'; GUM3, HSL, HSL2, JGFF, SF, YL.

Zidikiai, *see* Zidikai.

Zidlochovice, Cz. (Seelowitz); pop. 48; 19 km S of Brno; 49°02'/16°37'.

Zidneves, Cz.; pop. 1; 56 km NE of Praha; 50°25'/15°00'.

Ziebice, *see* Zrebice.

Ziechenau, *see* Ciechanow.

Ziegelhausen, Germ.; 75 km NNW of Stuttgart; 49°25'/08°46'; PHGBW.

Ziegelhutte, HSL. A number of towns share this name. It was not possible to determine from available information which one is being referenced.

Ziegenhain, Germ.; pop. 63; 101 km NNE of Frankfurt am Main; 50°55'/09°15'; GUM3, GUM5, HSL, LDS.

Ziegenort, *see* Trzebiez.

Zielence, Pol. PHP2. This town was not found in BGN gazetteers under the given spelling.

Zielenica, *see* Zelenitsa.

Zieleniec, Pol. PHP2. A number of towns share this name. It was not possible to determine from available information which one is being referenced.

Zielenzig, *see* Sulecin.

Zielin, HSL. This pre-World War I community was not found in BGN gazetteers.

Zielona, *see* Zelenaya.

Zielona Gora, Pol. (Gruenberg, Grunberg); pop. 50; 114 km SW of Poznan; 51°56'/15°30'; GUM3, GUM4, GUM5, GUM6, HSL.

Zielonka, Pol.; pop. 60; 75 km WNW of Przemysl; 50°16'/22°03'; GUM3, GUM4, PHP3.

Zielonki, Pol.; pop. 28; 6 km N of Krakow; 50°07'/19°56'; GUM5, PHP4.

Zielow, Germ. CAHJP. CAHJP states it is in the Lodz province of Poland. It does not appear in interwar or contemporary gazetteers.

Zielun, Pol. (Zilin); pop. 366; 133 km NW of Warszawa; 53°10'/19°51'; PHP4, SF.

Ziem, *see* Zeimiai.

Ziemblice, Pol.; pop. 7; 101 km NE of Krakow; 50°33'/21°07'.

Ziemel, *see* Zeimys.

Ziemetshausen, Germ.; pop. 1; 82 km W of Munchen; 48°18'/10°32'.

Ziempniow, Pol.; pop. 14; 94 km ENE of Krakow; 50°20'/21°14'.

Zienkow, *see* Zenkov.

Zierenberg, Germ.; pop. 57; 120 km S of Hannover; 51°22'/09°19'.

Ziersdorf, Aus.; pop. 4; 50 km NW of Wien; 48°31'/15°55'.

Zietil, *see* Dyatlovo.

Zieverich, Germ.; 26 km W of Koln; 50°57'/06°37'; GED.

Ziezmariai, Lith. (Zezmar, Zezmer, Zhezhmariai, Zhizhmore E, Zhizhmory, Zyzmory); pop. 1,205; 38 km E of Kaunas; 54°48'/24°27'; COH, GUM3, GUM4, GUM5, HSL, JGFF, LDL, SF, YL.

Zihle, Cz.; pop. 27; 75 km WSW of Praha; 50°03'/13°23'.

Zihobce, Cz.; pop. 3; 114 km SSW of Praha; 49°13'/13°38'.

Zilah, *see* Zalau.

Zilin, *see* Zielun.

Zilina, Cz. (Sillein, Zsolna); pop. 2,888; 150 km ENE of Brno; 49°13'/18°44'; AMG, EJ, GUM3, GUM4, GUM5, GUM6, HSL, JGFF.

Zilini, Lat. (Sejas); pop. 4; 88 km NNW of Daugavpils; 56°39'/26°05'.

Zilistea, HSL. This pre-World War I community was not found in BGN gazetteers.

Ziliz, Hung.; pop. 8; 26 km N of Miskolc; 48°15'/20°48'.

Zilkevke, *see* Zolkiewka.

Zilozitz, *see* Zalozhtsy.

Zilupe, Lat. (Rosenowsk, Rosinhof, Rosinovsk, Rozenovski, Rozinovsk); pop. 600; 114 km NE of Daugavpils; 56°23'/28°07'; PHLE, SF.

Zim, Cz. (Schima); 69 km NW of Praha; 50°35'/13°58'; HSL.

Zimany, Hung.; pop. 8; 75 km E of Nagykanizsa; 46°25'/17°55'.

Zimbor, Rom. (Kolozs Zsombor, Magyarnagyszombor, Zimboru, Zsombor); pop. 87; 38 km NW of Cluj; 47°00'/23°16'; HSL, PHR2.

Zimboru, *see* Zimbor.

Zimmersrode, Germ.; pop. 44; 107 km N of Frankfurt am Main; 51°00'/09°14'; LDS.

Zimna Voda, Ukr. (Kaltwasser, Zimna Woda); pop. 22; 13 km WSW of Lvov; 49°49'/23°54'; GUM4, GUM5, GUM6, HSL.

Zimna Woda, *see* Zimna Voda.

Zimno, Pol.; pop. 35; 101 km NNE of Przemysl; 50°31'/23°44'.

Zimnochy Swiechy, Pol.; pop. 5; 26 km S of Bialystok; 52°57'/23°05'.

Zimnowoda, Pol. BGN lists two possible localities with this name located at 50°38'/21°15' and 52°17'/21°47'. HSL.

Zimor, Cz.; pop. 3; 62 km NNW of Praha; 50°35'/14°19'.

Zinkov, Ukr.; pop. 2,999; 101 km WSW of Vinnitsa; 49°05'/27°04'; COH, GYLA, HSL, JGFF, LDL, SF.

Zinkovtsy, Ukr. (Zinkowitz); 69 km NE of Chernovtsy; 48°42'/26°36'; GYLA.

Zinkow, *see* Zenkov.

Zinkowitz, *see* Zinkovtsy.

Zinovyevsk, *see* Kirovograd.

Zinowjewsk, *see* Kirovograd.

Zinten, *see* Kornevo.

Ziolkow, Pol.; pop. 27; 26 km NE of Lublin; 51°20'/22°48'.

Ziolovo, *see* Zelovo.

Ziolowo, *see* Zelovo.

Zipov, Cz. (Izsep); 32 km NNW of Kosice; 48°58'/21°06'; HSL.

Ziras, Lat.; pop. 6; 157 km W of Riga; 57°11'/21°34'.

Zirc, Hung.; pop. 65; 94 km SW of Budapest; 47°16'/17°52'; PHH.

Zirke, *see* Sierakow.

Zirndorf, Germ.; pop. 63; 13 km WSW of Nurnberg; 49°27'/10°57'; GUM5, PHGB.

Zirovnice, Cz.; pop. 7; 107 km W of Brno; 49°15'/15°12'.

Zishkov, LDL. This pre-World War I community was not found in BGN gazetteers.

Zissersdorf, Aus. BGN lists two possible localities with this name located at 48°24'/16°08' and 48°49'/15°37'. HSL.

Zistersdorf, Aus.; pop. 37; 50 km NNE of Wien; 48°32'/16°45'.

Zitenice, Cz.; pop. 6; 56 km NNW of Praha; 50°33'/14°10'.

Zitiste, Yug.; pop. 150; 82 km N of Beograd; 45°29'/20°33'.

Zitl, *see* Dyatlovo.

Zittau, Germ.; pop. 104; 176 km E of Leipzig; 50°54'/14°50'; AMG, GUM3, GUM5.

Zivanice, Cz.; pop. 1; 82 km E of Praha; 50°04'/15°39'.

Zivotov, *see* Zhivotovka.

Zladings, *see* Slavonice.

Zlata Idka, Cz. (Aranyidka); 19 km WNW of Kosice; 48°45'/21°01'; HSL.

Zlatarif, *see* Zlatary.

Zlatary, Ukr. (Zlatarif); 182 km WSW of Chernovtsy; 48°12'/23°30'; SM. This town was located on a pre-World War I map, but does not appear in contemporary gazetteers.

Zlate Hory (Bohemia), Cz. (Kamberk); pop. 17; 62 km SE of Praha; 49°36'/14°50'.

Zlate Hory (Moravia), Cz. (Cukmantl); pop. 34; 133 km NNE of Brno; 50°16'/17°24'.

Zlate Moravce, Cz. (Aranyosmarot); pop. 725; 101 km ENE of Bratislava; 48°23'/18°24'; AMG, GUM4, GUM5, HSL, LDL.

Zlatna, Rom. AMG. A number of towns share this name. It was not possible to determine from available information which one is being referenced.

Zlatopol, Ukr. (Slotopol, Zlotopol); pop. 3,863; 120 km S of Dnepropetrovsk; 47°24'/35°01'; EDRD, EJ, HSL, HSL2, JGFF, LDL, SF.

Zlazno, Ukr.; pop. 64; 45 km N of Rovno; 50°56'/26°13'.

Zlin, *see* Gottwaldov.

Zlobnica, Pol.; pop. 12; 56 km N of Czestochowa; 51°14'/19°15'.

Zlochev, *see* Zolochev.

Zlochuv, *see* Zolochev.

Zlocieniec, Pol. (Falkenburg); pop. 51; 94 km ENE of Szczecin; 53°32'/16°00'.

Zlockie, Pol.; pop. 6; 107 km SE of Krakow; 49°23'/20°54'.

Zloczew, Pol. (Zlotshev); pop. 1,959; 69 km SW of Lodz; 51°25'/18°37'; AMG, EDRD, FRG, HSL, HSL2, JGFF, LDS, LYV, PHP1, POCEM, SF, YB.

Zloczow, *see* Zolochev.

Zlonice, Cz.; pop. 15; 32 km WNW of Praha; 50°17'/14°06'.

Zlonin, Cz.; pop. 3; 19 km N of Praha; 50°13'/14°31'.

Zlosyn, Cz.; pop. 9; 26 km NNW of Praha; 50°17'/14°22'.

Zlota, Pol.; pop. 33; 56 km NE of Krakow; 50°23'/20°36'.

Zlotchev, *see* Zolochev.

Zlote, *see* Zolotoye.

Zloti Potok, *see* Zolotoy Potok.

Zlotki, Pol.; pop. 72; BGN lists two possible localities with this name located at 52°39'/21°59' and 52°45'/22°26'.

Zlotkovitse, *see* Zolotkovichi.

Zlotkowice, *see* Zolotkovichi.

Zlotkowo, Pol.; 13 km NW of Poznan; 52°31'/16°50'; GA.

Zlotniki, Ukr.; pop. 114; 114 km NNW of Chernovtsy; 49°17'/25°23'; AMG, EGRS, HSL, LDL, PHP2, SF.

Zlotniki (near Mielec), Pol.; pop. 54; 114 km ENE of Krakow; 50°19'/21°25'.

Zlotolin, *see* Zolotolin.

Zlotopol, *see* Zlatopol.

Zlotoryja, Germ. (Goldberg); 227 km ESE of Berlin; 51°07'/15°54'; HSL, LDS.

Zlotow, Pol. (Flatau, Flatow); pop. 186; 107 km N of Poznan; 53°21'/17°03'; AMG, HSL, JGFF, LDS.

Zlotowa, EGRS, JGFF. This town was not found in BGN gazetteers under the given spelling.

Zlotshev, *see* Zloczew.

Zloty Potok, Pol. (Zolotoi Potok); pop. 7; 26 km ESE of Czestochowa; 50°43'/19°27'; AMG, JGFF, PHP1.

Zlozeniec, Pol.; pop. 2; 45 km NW of Krakow; 50°26'/19°39'.

Zlutice, Cz.; pop. 49; 94 km W of Praha; 50°06'/13°11'.

Zlynka, USSR; pop. 586; 202 km SW of Bryansk; 52°24'/31°45'; HSL, JGFF.

Zmajevac, Yug.; pop. 23; 170 km WNW of Beograd; 45°48'/18°48'.

Zmerinka, *see* Zhmerinka.

Zmiarki, Pol.; pop. 4; 50 km NNE of Lublin; 51°36'/23°01'.

Zmiennica, Pol.; pop. 25; 62 km WSW of Przemysl; 49°42'/21°58'.

Zmiev, *see* Zmiyev.

Zmigrod, Pol. (Trachenberg, Trachtenberg?, Zhmigrod); pop. 27; 50 km NNW of Wroclaw; 51°28'/16°55'; AMG, GUM3, GUM4, GUM5, HSL, HSL2, JGFF, LDL, LDS.

Zmigrod Nowy, Pol. (Nowy Zmigrod, Zmygrod Nowy); pop. 940; 88 km WSW of Przemysl; 49°37'/21°32'; COH, EGRS, EJ, GA, JGFF, PHP3, POCEM, SF.

Zmigrod Stary, Pol.; pop. 6; 94 km WSW of Przemysl; 49°36'/21°34'.

Zmijow, *see* Zmiyev.

Zmijowiska, Pol.; pop. 24; 45 km NE of Przemysl; 50°02'/23°12'.

Zminne, Pol.; pop. 7; 56 km N of Lublin; 51°40'/22°47'.

Zmiyev, Ukr. (Zmiev, Zmijow); pop. 40; 38 km SSE of Kharkov; 49°41'/36°21'.

Zmorzna Wola, *see* Zmozna Wola.

Zmozna Wola, Pol. (Zmorzna Wola); pop. 5; 56 km SSE of Lodz; 51°18'/19°44'.

Zmudz, Pol. (Samogitien, Schamaiten, Zemaitija, Zhmud); pop. 40; 82 km ESE of Lublin; 51°01'/23°40'; GUM4, GUM5.

Zmygrod Nowy, *see* Zmigrod Nowy.

Zmyslowka, Pol.; pop. 39; 50 km NW of Przemysl; 50°10'/22°22'.

Znacevo, *see* Znyatsevo.

Znaim, *see* Znojmo.

Znamenka, Ukr. (Bolshoya Znamenka, Snamenka); pop. 774; 176 km W of Dnepropetrovsk; 48°43'/32°38'; GUM4, HSL, LDL, SF.

Znamensk, USSR (Wehlau); pop. 26; 50 km E of Kaliningrad; 54°37'/21°13'.

Zniatyn, Pol.; pop. 68; 114 km NE of Przemysl; 50°29'/23°59'.

Znibrody, *see* Zhnibrody.

Zniesienie, Ukr.; pop. 1,972; 69 km SSW of Rovno; 50°05'/25°45'; EGRS. This town was located on an interwar map of Poland but does not appear in contemporary gazetteers. Map coordinates are approximate.

Znin, Pol.; pop. 134; 69 km NE of Poznan; 52°51'/17°44'; AMG, GUM5.

Znojmo, Cz. (Znaim); pop. 743; 56 km SW of Brno; 48°51'/16°03'; EJ.

Znosichi, Ukr. (Znosicze); pop. 20; 75 km NNE of Rovno; 51°13'/26°42'.

Znosicze, *see* Znosichi.

Znyatsevo, Ukr. (Znacevo); 189 km SSW of Lvov; 48°29'/22°31'; AMG.

Zobeln, *see* Sabile.

Zoblas, YB. This town was not found in BGN gazetteers under the given spelling.

Zobni, *see* Zabno.

Zobten, *see* Sobotka.

Zochow, HSL. This pre-World War I community was not found in BGN gazetteers.

Zofiowka, *see* Zofyuvka.

Zofiuvka, *see* Zofyuvka.

Zofjowka, *see* Zofyuvka.

Zofyuvka, Ukr. (Sofievka, Sofiovka, Sofiyevka, Trochenbrod, Trochinbrod, Trokhinbrod, Trokhnibrod, Zofiowka, Zofiuvka, Zofjowka); pop. 1,531; 50 km WNW of Rovno; 50°55'/25°42'; AMG, COH, GUM3, GUM4, GUM5, HSL, JGFF, LYV, SF.

Zohatyn, Pol.; pop. 35; 32 km WSW of Przemysl; 49°44'/22°21'.

Zohor, Cz.; 26 km NW of Bratislava; 48°19'/16°59'; GUM6, HSL.

Zoklikov, *see* Zaklikow.

Zoklitchin, *see* Zakliczyn.

Zolczow, *see* Zholchuv.

Zolin, *see* Zolynia.

Zolinia, *see* Zolynia.

413

Zolishtchik, *see* Zaleshchiki.

Zolkevka, *see* Zolkiewka.

Zolkiew, Pol.; pop. 23; 45 km SE of Lublin; 50°54'/22°51'; AMG. *See also* Nesterov.

Zolkiewka, Pol. (Zhilkovka, Zholkevka, Zholkevke, Zhulkiewka, Zilkevke, Zolkevka); pop. 1,308; 45 km SE of Lublin; 50°54'/22°50'; AMG, COH, EDRD, GA, GUM3, GUM4, GUM5, HSL, HSL2, JGFF, LDL, LDS, LYV, PHP1, POCEM, SF.

Zolkin, *see* Zholkin.

Zolkinie, *see* Zholkin.

Zolkow, Pol. (Zylkow); pop. 25; 94 km WSW of Przemysl; 49°43'/21°29'; PHP3.

Zolobki, *see* Zholobki.

Zolobow, Pol.; pop. 20; Described in the *Black Book* as being in the Wolyn region of Poland, this town was not found in BGN gazetteers.

Zolocari, *see* Liman.

Zolochev, Ukr. (Zlochev, Zlochuv, Zloczow, Zlotchev); pop. 5,744; 62 km E of Lvov; 49°48'/24°54'; COH, EGRS, EJ, GA, GUM3, GUM4, GUM5, GUM6, JGFF, PHP2, SF, YB.

Zoloteanca, *see* Zolotiyevka.

Zolotiyevka, Mold. (Zoloteanca); pop. 3; 45 km SE of Kishinev; 46°44'/29°12'.

Zolotkovichi, Ukr. (Zlotkovitse, Zlotkowice); pop. 37; 69 km WSW of Lvov; 49°43'/23°03'.

Zolotoi Potok, *see* Zloty Potok.

Zolotolin, Ukr. (Zlotolin); pop. 28; 56 km N of Rovno; 51°03'/26°18'.

Zolotonosha, Ukr. (Zolotonosza); pop. 5,180; 139 km ESE of Kiyev; 49°40'/32°02'; GUM4, HSL, JGFF, LDL, SF.

Zolotonosza, *see* Zolotonosha.

Zolotoye, Ukr. (Zlote); pop. 21; 126 km N of Rovno; 51°40'/26°29'.

Zolotoy Potok, Ukr. (Potek Zolti, Potik, Potok Zloti, Potok Zloty, Zloti Potok); pop. 895; 75 km NW of Chernovtsy; 48°54'/25°20'; AMG, EGRS, GUM3, GUM5, HSL, HSL2, JGFF, LDL, LYV, PHP2, PHP4, SF.

Zoltance, *see* Zhovtantsy.

Zoludek, *see* Zheludok.

Zoludzik, *possibly* Bolshoy Zhelutsk.

Zoludzk, *see* Kolonie Zoludzk.

Zoludzk Maly, Pol.; pop. 72; Described in the *Black Book* as being in the Polesie region of Poland, this town was not found in BGN gazetteers.

Zoludzk Wielki, Pol.; pop. 30; Described in the *Black Book* as being in the Polesie region of Poland, this town was not found in BGN gazetteers.

Zolynia, Pol. (Wies Zolynia, Zholinia, Zolin, Zolinia, Zolynia Miasteczko); pop. 569; 50 km NW of Przemysl; 50°10'/22°19'; AMG, COH, EGRS, GUM5, HSL, HSL2, JGFF, LDL, PHP3, SF.

Zolynia Miasteczko, *see* Zolynia.

Zomba, Hung.; pop. 33; 120 km W of Szeged; 46°24'/18°34'; GUM5, HSL.

Zombor, *see* Sombor.

Zombrov, *see* Zambrow.

Zons, Germ.; 26 km NNW of Koln; 51°07'/06°51'; GED, JGFF.

Zoppot, *see* Sopot.

Zoppot Freistaat, *see* Sopot.

Zornow, *see* Zhornuv.

Zory, Pol.; 88 km S of Czestochowa; 50°03'/18°42'; CAHJP, HSL, LDS, PHP3, POCEM.

Zoschingen, Germ.; 82 km E of Stuttgart; 48°40'/10°19'; PHGB.

Zosimy, *see* Zasimy.

Zosinek, Pol.; pop. 10; 32 km SW of Lublin; 51°05'/22°14'.

Zosli, *see* Zasliai.

Zossen, Germ.; 38 km S of Berlin; 52°13'/13°27'; CAHJP, GUM3.

Zowten, *see* Zhovten.

Zozhetsiol, *see* Dyatlovo.

Zozow, LDL, SF. This town was not found in BGN gazetteers under the given spelling.

Zrebice, Pol. (Ziebice); 19 km ESE of Czestochowa; 50°44'/19°20'; GUM6, POCEM.

Zrecin, Pol.; pop. 11; 75 km WSW of Przemysl; 49°40'/21°42'.

Zrenjanin, Yug. (Gross Becskerek, Nagybecskerek, Petrovgrad, Veliki Beckerek); pop. 1,352; 69 km NNW of Beograd; 45°23'/20°23'; AMG, EJ, GUM4, PHY.

Zrotowice, HSL. This pre-World War I community was not found in BGN gazetteers.

Zruc, *see* Zruc nad Sazavou.

Zruc nad Sazavou, Cz. (Zruc); pop. 22; 62 km ESE of Praha; 49°44'/15°06'.

Zsabar, *see* Jabar.

Zsadany, Hung.; pop. 19; 126 km NE of Szeged; 46°55'/21°30'; HSL, LDS.

Zsaka, Hung.; pop. 50; 120 km SE of Miskolc; 47°08'/21°26'; HSL, LDS, PHH.

Zsambek, Hung.; pop. 80; 32 km W of Budapest; 47°33'/18°43'; GUM4, HSL, LDS, PHH.

Zsambok, Hung.; pop. 29; 45 km ENE of Budapest; 47°33'/19°37'; HSL.

Zsarno, *see* Zarnow.

Zsarolyan, Hung.; pop. 9; 133 km E of Miskolc; 47°57'/22°36'.

Zschachwitz, Germ.; 114 km ESE of Leipzig; 51°00'/13°51'; GUM3, GUM6.

Zselickisfalud, Hung.; pop. 6; 62 km ESE of Nagykanizsa; 46°16'/17°44'.

Zseliz, *see* Zeliezovce.

Zsennye, Hung.; pop. 1; 82 km NNW of Nagykanizsa; 47°07'/16°49'.

Zsetl, *see* Dyatlovo.

Zsibo, *see* Jibou.

Zsira, Hung.; pop. 2; 120 km NNW of Nagykanizsa; 47°27'/16°41'.

Zsok, HSL. This pre-World War I community was not found in BGN gazetteers.

Zsolcza, HSL. This pre-World War I community was not found in BGN gazetteers.

Zsolna, *see* Zilina.

Zsombor, *see* Zimbor.

Zsujta, Hung.; pop. 16; 56 km NNE of Miskolc; 48°30'/21°17'.

Zsulest, *see* Giulesti.

Zsurk, Hung.; pop. 62; 114 km NE of Miskolc; 48°25'/22°13'; HSL.

Zuara, HSL. This pre-World War I community was not found in BGN gazetteers.

Zubensko, Pol.; pop. 7; 82 km SSW of Przemysl; 49°14'/22°07'; JGFF.

Zubki Duze, Pol.; pop. 13; 50 km E of Lodz; 51°42'/20°12'.

Zubkow, *see* Zubkuv.

Zubkuv, Ukr. (Zubkow); pop. 17; 62 km NNE of Lvov; 50°24'/24°24'.

Zubogy, Hung.; pop. 5; 38 km NW of Miskolc; 48°23'/20°35'.

Zubole, Pol.; pop. 21; 45 km WNW of Bialystok; 53°21'/22°40'.

Zubov Most, Ukr. (Zubowmosty); pop. 18; 38 km NNE of Lvov; 50°09'/24°19'.

Zubowice, Pol.; pop. 14; 101 km ESE of Lublin; 50°37'/23°34'.

Zubowmosty, *see* Zubov Most.

Zubracze, Pol.; pop. 14; 75 km SSW of Przemysl; 49°13'/22°16'.

Zubreshty, Mold. (Zubresti); pop. 45; 38 km NW of Kishinev; 47°14'/28°31'.

Zubresti, *see* Zubreshty.

Zubrzyca Dolna, Pol.; pop. 1; 69 km S of Krakow; 49°32'/19°41'.

Zubrzyca Gorna, Pol.; pop. 17; 62 km S of Krakow; 49°34'/19°39'.

Zubrzyca Wielka, Pol.; pop. 7; 50 km NE of Bialystok; 53°23'/23°44'.

Zubrzyce, Pol. PHP3. This town was not found in BGN gazetteers under the given spelling.

Zubrzyk, Pol.; pop. 4; 101 km SE of Krakow; 49°24'/20°46'; AMG.

Zuchorzyce, Ukr.; pop. 22; 26 km ESE of Lvov; 49°45'/24°15'. This town was located on an interwar map of Poland but does not appear in contemporary gazetteers. Map coordinates are approximate.

Zuchow, Pol. PHP3. This town was not found in BGN gazetteers under the given spelling.

Zuchowicze, see Bolshiye Zhukhovichi.

Zuelz, see Bielsko Biala.

Zuffenhausen, Germ.; 13 km NNW of Stuttgart; 48°50'/09°11'; PHGBW.

Zukov, see Zukow.

Zukow, Pol. (Zukov); pop. 35; 56 km NNE of Przemysl; 50°17'/23°10'; HSL, SF.

Zukow Dwor, Pol.; pop. 24; Described in the *Black Book* as being in the Lublin region of Poland, this town was not found in BGN gazetteers.

Zukowice Nowe, Pol.; pop. 30; 88 km E of Krakow; 50°05'/21°08'.

Zukowice Stare, Pol.; pop. 18; 82 km E of Krakow; 50°05'/21°07'.

Zulice, see Zhulitse.

Zulinya, see Zulnya.

Zullichau, see Sulechow.

Zulnya, Ukr. (Zelena, Zulinya); pop. 3; 62 km N of Rovno; 51°09'/26°23'; JGFF, SF.

Zulpich, Germ.; pop. 100; 38 km SSW of Koln; 50°42'/06°39'; GED.

Zundorf, Germ.; 13 km ESE of Koln; 50°52'/07°03'; GED.

Zuntersbach, Germ.; 82 km ENE of Frankfurt am Main; 50°19'/09°44'; LDS.

Zupanie, Pol.; pop. 20; Described in the *Black Book* as being in the Stanislawow region of Poland, this town was not found in BGN gazetteers.

Zupanja, Yug.; pop. 25; 146 km W of Beograd; 45°04'/18°42'.

Zupawa, Pol.; pop. 10; 88 km SSW of Lublin; 50°35'/21°47'.

Zuprany, see Zhuprany.

Zuraki, Ukr.; pop. 64; 114 km W of Chernovtsy; 48°25'/24°25'. This town was located on an interwar map of Poland but does not appear in contemporary gazetteers. Map coordinates are approximate.

Zuravitch, see Zhuravichi.

Zuravitz Yashan, see Zhuravichi.

Zuravna, see Zhuravno.

Zurawce, Pol.; pop. 104; 88 km NNE of Przemysl; 50°23'/23°34'.

Zurawica, Pol.; pop. 80; 6 km N of Przemysl; 49°49'/22°48'.

Zurawiczki, Pol.; pop. 22; 32 km NW of Przemysl; 50°01'/22°31'.

Zurawieniec, Pol.; pop. 30; 45 km N of Lublin; 51°36'/22°33'.

Zurawin, Pol.; pop. 55; 69 km S of Przemysl; 49°14'/22°44'.

Zurawnica, Pol.; pop. 6; 69 km SE of Lublin; 50°39'/22°59'.

Zurawno, see Zhuravno.

Zurewicze, see Zhurevichi.

Zurndorf, Aus.; pop. 17; 56 km ESE of Wien; 47°58'/17°00'.

Zurobice, Pol.; pop. 27; 69 km S of Bialystok; 52°32'/22°56'.

Zuromin, Pol. (Zhoremin, Zhuromin); pop. 1,902; 114 km NW of Warszawa; 53°04'/19°55'; AMG, COH, GUM4, HSL, JGFF, LDL, LDS, LYV, PHP4, SF.

Zurow, see Dzhuruv.

Zurowisty, EGRS. This town was not found in BGN gazetteers under the given spelling.

Zuzel, see Zhuzhel.

Zuzmir, see Sandomierz.

Zvala, Cz.; 88 km NE of Kosice; 49°08'/22°14'; AMG.

Zvancik, see Velikiy Zhvanchik.

Zvanitz, see Zhvanets.

Zvantchik, see Velikiy Zhvanchik.

Zvantz, see Zhvanets.

Zvarde, see Veczvarde.

Zvenigorodka, Ukr. (Zwenigorodka, Zwinogrodka); pop. 6,584; 62 km NE of Uman; 49°05'/30°58'; GUM4, GUM5, HSL, JGFF, LDL, SF.

Zver, see Zvur.

Zverovichi, Byel.; 107 km ESE of Vitebsk; 54°31'/31°17'; EJ.

Zvestov, Cz.; pop. 8; 56 km SE of Praha; 49°38'/14°48'.

Zvestovice, Cz.; pop. 3; 82 km ESE of Praha; 49°51'/15°31'.

Zviagel, see Novograd Volynskiy.

Zvierznitz, see Zwierzyniec.

Zvihil, see Novograd Volynskiy.

Zvikovec, Cz.; pop. 4; 56 km WSW of Praha; 49°57'/13°41'.

Zvil, see Novograd Volynskiy.

Zviniace, *possibly* Zvinyachka.

Zviniatch, see Dzvinyach.

Zvinyach, Ukr. (Zwiniacz); pop. 34; 50 km NNW of Chernovtsy; 48°42'/25°44'; HSL.

Zvinyacheye, Ukr. (Zwiniacze); pop. 9; 94 km NNE of Lvov; 50°30'/24°54'.

Zvinyachka, Ukr. (Dzwiniaczka, Zviniace?); pop. 139; 38 km NNE of Chernovtsy; 48°35'/26°15'; GUM4.

Zvirgzdene, Lat.; pop. 8; 101 km NE of Daugavpils; 56°34'/27°40'.

Zvizhdzhe, Ukr. (Zwizdze); pop. 6; 38 km NNW of Rovno; 50°54'/26°11'.

Zvolen, Cz.; pop. 662; 150 km WSW of Kosice; 48°35'/19°08'.

Zvolin, see Zwolen.

Zvon, Byel. (Zawan?); pop. 26; 107 km WSW of Vitebsk; 55°04'/28°33'.

Zvonickov, Cz. (Mannelsdorf); pop. 1; 94 km WNW of Praha; 50°20'/13°15'.

Zvorastea, see Zvoristea.

Zvoristea, Rom. (Zvorastea); pop. 28; 126 km WNW of Iasi; 47°50'/26°17'.

Zvornik, Yug.; pop. 75; 120 km SW of Beograd; 44°23'/19°07'; PHY.

Zvur, Ukr. (Zver, Zwor); 82 km SW of Lvov; 49°23'/23°06'; HSL.

Zvyezhinets, see Zwierzyniec.

Zwanchik, see Velikiy Zhvanchik.

Zwaniec, see Zhvanets.

Zwanitse, see Zhvanets.

Zwardon, Pol.; pop. 5; 94 km SW of Krakow; 49°31'/18°59'.

Zweibrucken, Germ.; pop. 155; 133 km SW of Frankfurt am Main; 49°15'/07°22'; AMG, GED, GUM5, HSL, JGFF, LDS, PHP1.

Zwenigorodka, see Zvenigorodka.

Zwesten, Germ.; pop. 80; 114 km N of Frankfurt am Main; 51°03'/09°11'.

Zwiahl, see Novograd Volynskiy.

Zwiartow, Pol.; pop. 4; 101 km SE of Lublin; 50°34'/23°30'.

Zwickau, Germ.; pop. 473; 69 km SSE of Leipzig; 50°44'/12°30'; EJ, GUM3, GUM4, GUM5, JGFF.

Zwiefalten, Germ.; 62 km SSE of Stuttgart; 48°14'/09°28'; PHGBW.

Zwieniacz, Pol. PHP2. This town was not found in BGN gazetteers under the given spelling.

Zwiernik, Pol.; pop. 14; 94 km E of Krakow; 49°57'/21°13'.

Zwierzchow, Pol.; 50 km S of Lodz; 51°22'/19°27'; GA.

Zwierzyn, Pol.; pop. 3; 50 km SSW of Przemysl; 49°27'/22°23'.

Zwierzyniec, Pol. (Zvierznitz, Zvyezhinets); 75 km SSE of Lublin; 50°36'/22°58'; FRG, GUM5, HSL, HSL2, PHP1, POCEM, SF.

Zwiesel, Germ.; 150 km NE of Munchen; 49°01'/13°14'; GED, GUM3.

Zwingenberg, Germ.; pop. 41; 50 km S of Frankfurt am Main; 49°43'/08°37'; GED, LDS.

Zwiniacz, see Zvinyach.

Zwiniacze, see Zvinyacheye.

Zwinogrodka, see Zvenigorodka.

Zwir, Pol.; pop. 13; 19 km E of Warszawa; 52°13'/21°15'.

Zwittau, see Svitavy.

Zwizdze, see Zvizhdzhe.

Zwoelfaxing, *see* Zwolfaxing.

Zwola, Pol.; pop. 21; 75 km ESE of Warszawa; 51°53'/21°53'; HSL, HSL2.

Zwolen, Pol. (Zvolin, Zwolin); pop. 3,787; 69 km W of Lublin; 51°21'/21°36'; AMG, CAHJP, COH, EDRD, EJ, FRG, GA, GUM3, GUM4, GUM5, HSL, HSL2, LDL, LDS, LYV, PHP4, SF, YB. The *Black Book* also shows a town of Zwolen Wojtowstwo (pop. 96).

Zwolfaxing, Aus. (Zwoelfaxing); 19 km SE of Wien; 48°06'/16°28'; EJ.

Zwolin, *see* Zwolen.

Zwor, *see* Zvur.

Zyabki, Byel. (Ziabki); pop. 65; 126 km W of Vitebsk; 55°16'/28°10'.

Zychlin, Pol. (Zakhlin, Zekhlin, Zhichlin, Zhikhlin); pop. 2,701; 62 km N of Lodz; 52°15'/19°37'; AMG, COH, EDRD, EJ, GA, GUM3, GUM4, GUM5, HSL, JGFF, LDL, LDS, LYV, PHP1, PHP4, POCEM, SF, YB.

Zychorzyn, Pol.; pop. 6; 82 km ESE of Lodz; 51°27'/20°32'.

Zyck Niemiecki, Pol.; pop. 7; 75 km W of Warszawa; 52°25'/19°55'.

Zyck Polski, Pol.; pop. 7; 75 km W of Warszawa; 52°25'/19°56'.

Zyczyn, *see* Zhychin.

Zydaczov, *see* Zhidachov.

Zydaczow, *see* Zhidachov.

Zydikiai, *see* Zidikai.

Zydowskie, Pol.; pop. 12; 101 km SW of Przemysl; 49°28'/21°29'.

Zylin, GUM5. This town was not found in BGN gazetteers under the given spelling.

Zylkow, *see* Zolkow.

Zyrakow, Pol.; pop. 10; 107 km E of Krakow; 50°05'/21°24'.

Zyrardow, Pol. (Shiraduv, Zheredov, Zhirardov); pop. 2,547; 45 km SW of Warszawa; 52°04'/20°26'; AMG, COH, EDRD, EJ, FRG, GA, GUM3, GUM4, GUM5, GYLA, HSL, HSL2, LYV, PHP1, PHP4, POCEM, SF, YB.

Zyrmuny, *see* Zhirmuny.

Zyrowice, *see* Zhirovitsy.

Zyrzyn, Pol.; pop. 22; 50 km WNW of Lublin; 51°30'/22°06'.

Zytniow Rzedowy, Pol.; pop. 47; 45 km WNW of Czestochowa; 51°01'/18°34'.

Zytnowicze, *see* Zhitnovichi.

Zytomierz, *see* Zhitomir.

Zywaczow, *see* Zhivachev.

Zywatow, *see* Zhivotovka.

Zywiec, Pol. (Saybusch, Zaybash, Zaybush, Zeibush, Zhivits, Zhivitz, Zhivyets); pop. 624; 69 km SW of Krakow; 49°41'/19°13'; COH, GUM3, GUM4, HSL, JGFF, LYV, PHP3, POCEM, SF.

Zyzmory, *see* Ziezmariai.

Listing of Town Names
by the
Daitch-Mokotoff Soundex System

Listing of Town Names
by the Daitch-Mokotoff Soundex System

      The Daitch-Mokotoff Soundex System is to be used when the exact spelling of a town name is unknown or uncertain. Town names on this list are grouped by the way they sound, rather than in alphabetical order. The special considerations of Slavic and other Eastern European names are addressed in this soundex system.

      The first step is to encode the name using the coding chart (directions below). Then match the code with the numbers on the soundex list. Adjacent to the numbers are the names of towns. Select a town name and look for it in the Listing of Towns section.

      The rules for converting names into Daitch-Mokotoff code numbers are listed here. First turn briefly to the coding chart on the next page to familiarize yourself with the concept, and then return to the specific coding instructions on this page.

1. Town names are translated into codes of six digits. Each sound in the name is assigned a number, as listed in the coding chart on the next page.

2. The letters A, E, I, O, U, J and Y are always coded at the beginning of a name, as in Augsburg (074797). In any other situation, they are ignored, except when two of these particular letters form a pair and the pair comes before a vowel, as in Breuer (791900), but not Freud.

   The letter H is coded at the beginning of a name, as in Halberstadt (587943) or preceding a vowel, as in Mannheim (665600). Otherwise it is not coded.

3. When adjacent sounds combine to form a larger sound, they are given the code number of that larger sound, as in Chernowitz, which is coded Chernowi-tz (496740), rather than Chernowi-t-z (496734).

4. When adjacent letters have the same code number, they are coded as one sound, as in Cherkassy, which is coded Cherkassy (495400), rather than Cherka-s-sy (495440). When two identical letters or sounds are separated by a vowel, they are coded separately. Thus, Zalisocze is coded Zalisocze (484400), not Zalisocze (484000).

   Exceptions to this rule are the letter combinations "MN" and "NM" whose letters are coded separately, as in Kleinman, which is coded 586660, not 586600.

5. When a name consists of more than one word, it is coded as if it were one word, such as Nowy Targ, which is treated as Nowytarg (673950).

6. Several letters and letter combinations may produce more than one sound. The letter and letter combinations CH, CK, C, J and RZ are assigned two possible code numbers. Be sure to try both possibilities.

7. When a name lacks enough coded sounds to fill the six digits, the remaining digits are coded as zeroes, as in Berlin (798600), which has only four sounds to be coded (B-R-L-N).

Examples:

Town Name	Alternate Spelling
C e n io w (467000)	Ts e n yu v (467000)
H o l u b i c a (587400)	G o l u b i ts a (587400)
P rz e m y s l (646470)	P sh e m e sh i l (646470)
R o s o ch o w a c ie c (944744) or (945744)	R o s o k ho v a ts e ts (945744)

Daitch-Mokotoff Soundex Coding Chart

Letter	Alternate Spelling	Start of a Name	Before a Vowel	Any Other Situation
AI	AJ, AY	0	1	N/C
AU		0	7	N/C
A		0	N/C	N/C
B		7	7	7
CHS		5	54	54
CH	Try KH (5) and TCH (4)			
CK	Try K (5) and TSK (45)			
CZ	CS, CSZ, CZS	4	4	4
C	Try K (5) and TZ (4)			
DRZ	DRS	4	4	4
DS	DSH, DSZ	4	4	4
DZ	DZH, DZS	4	4	4
D	DT	3	3	3
EI	EJ, EY	0	1	N/C
EU		1	1	N/C
E		0	N/C	N/C
FB		7	7	7
F		7	7	7
G		5	5	5
H		5	5	N/C
IA	IE, IO, IU	1	N/C	N/C
I		0	N/C	N/C
J	Try Y (1) and DZH (4)			
KS		5	54	54
KH		5	5	5
K		5	5	5
L		8	8	8
MN			66	66
M		6	6	6
NM			66	66
N		6	6	6
OI	OJ, OY	0	1	N/C
O		0	N/C	N/C
P	PF, PH	7	7	7
Q		5	5	5

N/C = not coded

Daitch-Mokotoff Soundex Coding Chart
(continued)

Letter	Alternate Spelling	Start of a Name	Before a Vowel	Any Other Situation
RZ, RS	Try RTZ (94) and ZH (4)			
R		9	9	9
SCHTSCH	SCHTSH, SCHTCH	2	4	4
SCH		4	4	4
SHTCH	SHCH, SHTSH	2	4	4
SHT	SCHT, SCHD	2	43	43
SH		4	4	4
STCH	STSCH, SC	2	4	4
STRZ	STRS, STSH	2	4	4
ST		2	43	43
SZCZ	SZCS	2	4	4
SZT	SHD, SZD, SD	2	43	43
SZ		4	4	4
S		4	4	4
TCH	TTCH, TTSCH	4	4	4
TH		3	3	3
TRZ	TRS	4	4	4
TSCH	TSH	4	4	4
S	TTS, TTSZ, TC	4	4	4
TZ	TTZ, TZS, TSZ	4	4	4
T		3	3	3
UI	UJ, UY	0	1	N/C
U	UE	0	N/C	N/C
V		7	7	7
W		7	7	7
X		5	54	54
Y		1	N/C	N/C
ZDZ	ZDZH, ZHDZH	2	4	4
ZD	ZHD	2	43	43
ZH	ZS, ZSCH, ZSH	4	4	4
Z		4	4	4

N/C = not coded

421

000000	Ai, Aue, Ay, Uhy	036783	Odenwald
010000	Oaia	036784	Odenwaldstettin
014000	Ujejsce	036795	Odenberg, Odenburg
014300	Ujazd, Ujest, Ujezd, Uyazd	036900	Jitomir, Utomir
014370	Ujazdow	036930	Uttenreuth
014375	Ujazdowek	037000	Udovo, Udva, Utphe
014600	Ujezna	037300	Jidovita
015000	Ajak	037430	Odobesti
016000	Aiyina	037450	Otvosk, Otvotsk, Udavske
016300	Iujineti	037456	Otvoskonyi
016740	Ujanowice	037500	Otvock, Otwock
017000	Iojib	037600	Otteveny
017390	Ayibator	037610	Udobnoye
017974	Uj Verbasz	037670	Otfinow
030000	Ada, Ade, Aiud, Atea, Atia, Atya, Ete, Iad, Ida, Ieud, Ioda, Iody, Iuda	037740	Otvovice
		037800	Odjivol
031600	Utiyan	037860	Edwahlen
033000	Adjud, Atid, Eted	037890	Ottweiler
033454	Adutiskis	037900	Udvari
033750	Adjudu Vechi	037930	Udvard
034000	Adacs, Etes, Idos, Odess, Odessa	037960	Ottobeuren
034300	Odesti	037965	Udvarnok
034314	Ideciu de Jos	038000	Attala, Edole, Itel, Ojdula
034378	Adasztevel	038400	Eidlitz, Otalez, Udalec, Udlice
034395	Otaci Targ	038438	Edelstal
034430	Otaci Sat	038439	Adelsdorf
034579	Otiski Vrh	038450	Odelsk
034600	Adaseni, Aidhausen, Atasiene, Edesheim, Odyzyn, Otoczna	038460	Adelsheim
		038479	Adelsberg
034831	Ideciul de Jos	038500	Eddelak
035000	Atachi, Ataki, Etyek	038600	Adelnau, Edeleny, Idalin
035395	Otach Tyrg	038656	Ettlingen, Ittlingen
035400	Otocac	038670	Odolanow
035460	Aidhausen	038746	Adelebsen
035560	Eydtkuhen	038765	Edelfingen
035600	Itcani, Odheim, Oedheim	038770	Adolfow
035659	Itcani Gara	039000	Iadara, Odorau, Odoreu, Odorhei, Ottrau, Utery
035660	Eydtkuhnen, Itcani Noui		
035740	Odechowiec	039300	Oderady
035900	Atkar, Ediger	039360	Eterdam
036000	Adoni, Adony, Atany, Eutin, Odheim, Oedheim, Oteni, Otinya, Ottynia, Otyn, Otynya, Udem, Uedainiai, Utena, Utian, Utien, Utyan, Utyana	039365	Ederding
		039400	Adorjas, Otrocz, Udrc, Udrycze
		039433	Otterstadt
		039446	Oettershausen
		039459	Otterskirchen
		039460	Atratzheim, Eddersheim, Odrizhin, Odryzyn
036300	Adand, Edineti, Edinita, Otmet, Ottmuth		
		039487	Ottersleben
036339	Edineti Targ, Edinita Targ	039500	Odorhei
036343	Edineti Sat	039544	Uttrichshausen
036396	Attendorn	039560	Ederheim, Odrzykon
036400	Adamos, Adams, Adamus, Athens	039570	Odrekhova, Odrzechowa
036436	Ottenstein	039600	Ederheim, Idrany, Udrzyn
036440	Ottensoos	039656	Odernheim
036460	Ottensheim	039660	Odernheim
036500	Otting	039669	Adrianu Mare
036530	Adancata	039678	Adrianopol
036534	Adancata Storojinet, Adancata Strojinet	039700	Eitorf, Utoropy
		039740	Odrowaz
036560	Edingen, Etingen, Ettenheim, Odenheim, Oettingen, Ottingen, Udingen	039745	Odrowazek
		039765	Uderwangen
		039780	Odrzywol
036576	Edenkoben	039783	Eiterfeld
036595	Odenkirchen	039794	Idar Oberstein
036600	Ettenheim, Idunum, Odenheim, Otomani	039795	Oderberg, Otterberg
		040000	Aciua, Acs, Acsa, As, Asch, Auce, Auscha, Auseu, Aussee, Autz, Eschau, Iasi, Iaz, Iza, Ocs, Ocsa, Oitz, Oos, Osie, Osoj, Ossa, Ostrz, Oytz, Oztza, Ujscie, Uscz
036630	Admont		
036650	Attnang		
036700	Adamov, Adamow, Odonow		
036740	Autunowatz, Ottyniowice, Ottynovitse		
		041000	Isaje
036750	Odenbach	041450	Ujscie Jezuickie
036779	Odombovar, Ujdombovar		

041500	Osijek
041536	Osijekdonji Grad
041700	Isayev
043000	Acsad, Adjud, Adzud, Asite, Aszod, Ecsed, Egyed, Ociete, Ocsod, Osht, Ozd, Oziaty, Ozyaty, Usti, Ustia, Ustye, Uszod, Uzda
043100	Ostoje
043147	Ostojicevo
043170	Ostojow
043300	Egyeduta, Ehrstadt
043340	Ozdititch, Ozdiuticz
043400	Ozdziutycze
043450	Ustechko
043457	Izdeshkovo
043460	Ostashin, Ostaszyn
043463	Uzdiszentpeter
043490	Acsteszer
043500	Ozyutichi, Ustek
043570	Eustachow
043596	Ustcorna
043600	Ehrsten, Eszteny, Idstein, Ostheim, Ostin
043630	Ostende
043638	Usti nad Labem
043639	Usti nad Orlici
043640	Ozdamicze
043641	Istenmezeje
043645	Ustenskoye Pervoye
043654	Oestinghausen, Ostinghausen
043670	Ustianowa, Ustjanowa
043678	Estenfeld
043679	Ostheim vor der Rhon
043690	Isztimer
043700	Izdby, Ostape, Ostapie, Ozhidiv, Ozydow
043740	Ostobuz, Ostobuzh
043746	Ostffyasszonyfa
043750	Adjudu Vechi, Izdebki
043755	Izdebki Kosmy
043757	Izdebki Blazeje, Izdebki Wasy, Ostapkowce
043760	Istebna, Osthafen, Osthofen, Osztopan
043763	Istvandi
043764	Jistebnice
043765	Istabnik, Izdebnik
043770	Ostapovo
043780	Ozdfalu
043800	Astileu, Austile, Ostila, Ustila
043850	Ustilug
043874	Osada Lubicz, Ostalovitse, Ostalowice
043900	Esztar, Istra, Oster, Ostor, Ostra, Ostre, Ostrz, Ustrzyk
043930	Osterode, Ostroda
043935	Ostredek
043936	Esterdin, Ostereiden, Osterode am Harz, Ostretin
043938	Ustrzyki Dolne
043939	Osterdorf
043940	Istras, Ostoros, Ostrusza
043944	Ostroshitskiy Gorodok, Ostrozec, Ostrozhets
043945	Ostrozske Predmesti
043946	Ostreznica, Ostrozen, Ustrasin
043950	Astrik, Estrik, Istrik, Istryk, Oestrich, Ostraha, Ostrich, Ostrog, Ustrik
043954	Ostrogozhsk, Ostrogozsk
043956	Eszteregnye, Esztergom
043957	Ostercappeln, Osterkappeln

043958 Osterholz Scharmbeck, Ostrykol, Ostrykol Wloscianski
043959 Ostrogorsk, Ustrzyki Gorne
043960 Astrin, Istrin, Ostrin, Ostryna, Ustron
043964 Ostromecz Krolewski, Ostromeczyn
043965 Ostra Mogila, Ostringen, Ostromech Krulevski, Ostromichi, Ostronek
043967 Oster Novoselitz
043969 Ostromer
043970 Jisterpy, Ostrava, Ostrov, Ostrova, Ostrovy, Ostrow, Ostrowo, Ostrowy, Ostruv, Ostrzeszow
043973 Ostrowy Tuszowskie
043974 Ostrava Slezska, Ostrovets, Ostrovitz, Ostrovitza, Ostrovtse, Ostrow Szlachecki, Ostrowczyk Polny, Ostrowiec, Ostrowsko
043975 Esterwegen, Ostrovchik Polny, Ostrow Kaliski, Ostrow Krolewski, Ostrowek, Ostrowiec Kielecki, Ostrowiec Swietokrzyski, Ostrowik
043976 Ostrov Mazovyetska, Ostrovna, Ostrovno, Ostrow Mazowiecka, Ostrow Mazowiecki, Ustrobna
043977 Ostorw Polnochy, Ostrow Polnocny, Ostrow Poludniowy, Ostrow Volhynia, Ostrow Wielkopolski, Ostrowy Baranowskie
043978 Osterfeld, Ostropol, Ostropolia, Ostrov Lubelski, Ostrow Lubelski
043979 Osterberg, Osterburken
043980 Osterholz Scharmbeck
043984 Austerlitz
043985 Ostroleka
043986 Ostrolenka
043995 Ostrorog
044000 Acis, Ociesc, Oschatz, Osiecza, Oyshitz, Ujszasz, Ushatchi, Ushatz, Ushitza, Ushots, Usicze, Uzice
044300 Idzesti
044340 Ozdiuticz
044480 Izaszacsal
044486 Ishtcha Solna, Ishtcha Zilona
044500 Aisheshuk, Aishishak, Aishishuk, Eishishki, Eishishuk, Eishyshok, Ejszyszki, Eshishuk, Eyshishok, Isaszeg, Ocieseki, Oshetsk, Oshetzk, Osyetsk, Uscieczko, Usicki
044540 Eisiskes, Eyshishkes
044570 Uciskow, Utsishkuv
044600 Osecna, Osieciny, Osieczna, Uszczyn
044650 Osoczniki
044700 Ostrzeszow, Oszczow, Uciszow
044735 Izasopatak
044738 Ushitse Podolye
044860 Iszczolna, Uscie Solne, Uscie Zielone, Ustse Zelene
044870 Izaslaw, Iziaslav, Izyaslav, Oscislowo
044878 Izyaslavl
044940 Oszczerze
045000 Aschach, Aussig, Ecka, Ecseg, Egyek, Escu, Esseg, Eszek,

Iska, Iski, Isky, Iszka, Izky, Izsak, Ocieka, Osek, Oshik, Osieck, Osiek, Ozga, Ushach, Ushachi, Usichi, Ustrzyk, Uszka
045386 Uschiki Dolne, Ustrzyki Dolne
045400 Isaccea, Iszkaz
045446 Iskrzyczyn, Oskrzesince, Oskzhesintse
045460 Iskrzynia
045593 Osiek Grodowski
045596 Ustrzyki Gorne
045600 Iskan, Izakonyha, Odrzykon
045650 Izakonyka, Osochniki
045700 Isakov, Isakovo, Isakow, Isakuv, Izsakfa, Oczakowbia, Oczkow, Odrzechowa, Oshiokov, Osiakow, Osjakov, Osjakow, Osyakow, Otchakov, Otschakow, Ozegow, Ushiokov, Uskub, Uskup
045740 Askovitz, Idzikowice, Ushkovitse, Uszkowice
045787 Agyagfalva
045800 Eskullo
045830 Ishkold
045840 Iszkoldz
045860 Aizkalni
045866 Ishcholnyany
045870 Oshekhlib, Oshekhliby
045930 Asakert, Assakurt, Osagard, Uzhgorod
045943 Atzgersdorf, Iskorost
045946 Iskrzyczyn, Oskrzesince
045956 Euskirchen
045958 Aizkraukle
045960 Iskrzynia
045970 Osekruv, Osiekrow
046000 Ajszyn, Asen, Assen, Asune, Aysyn, Ecseny, Eschenau, Esen, Essen, Iasin, Iasinia, Icna, Isjum, Issum, Itchnia, Izyum, Jicin, Ocna, Ocseny, Osann, Osno, Ossan, Ozanna, Ozenna, Ozon, Ozun, Ozynna, Uciana, Udrzyn, Ushnya, Usma, Usznia, Utsiany, Utsjany, Utsyany, Uzin, Uzon
046300 Ocnita
046314 Ocna de Jos
046318 Ocna Dejului
046344 Ocna de Sus
046359 Ocnita Gara
046360 Eisenhuttenstadt
046370 Uzhendov
046397 Aschendorf, Ashendorf, Osandarfalva, Ossendorf
046400 Asenz, Asunes, Esens, Jieznas, Usmas
046433 Eisenstadt
046438 Essen Steele
046450 Osnitsk
046453 Ocna Sugatag
046460 Aschenhausen, Eschenhausen, Osencin
046478 Ocna Sibiului
046500 Eisenach, Osinki, Osnick, Usnik, Uznoga, Uznoha
046536 Eisenhuttenstadt
046546 Aschenhausen, Assinghausen, Eschenhausen, Essen Heisingen
046560 Assenheim, Essenheim,

Essingen, Usingen
046578 Eisenkappel, Isnuchpol, Osnica Wielka
046590 Essen Kray
046600 Asmena, Assenheim, Essenheim, Oshmana, Oshmene, Oshmiana, Oshmina, Oshmyany, Osmiana, Osmiany, Oszmiana, Ozimina, Ozmiana
046630 Asminta
046665 Ismaning
046675 Ozmanbuk
046700 Asszonyfa, Aszanfo
046730 Isnovat
046740 Ishnovets
046750 Eisenbach
046759 Asenovgrad
046795 Atzenbrugg, Eisenberg, Eisenburg, Osnabruck
046796 Usenborn
046800 Ismail, Izmail, Osmola, Ozomla
046840 Osmolice, Ujcsanalos
046860 Osmolin
046900 Uschomir, Ushomir
046940 Eisenerz
046943 Eisenarzt
046953 Etzenricht
047000 Isep, Izby, Izow, Izsep, Izuv, Ojcow, Osova, Osowa, Ossovo, Ossowa, Usov, Uszew, Uzava
047100 Osveya
047300 Aispute, Aizpute, Osviet
047400 Auschwitz, Aushvits, Auspitz, Ispas, Izbica, Izbitsa, Izbitz, Izbitza, Izbugya, Izhevtsy, Osovtse, Osovtsy, Osowce, Usovice
047430 Izbeshty, Izbestea, Izbishtya
047439 Aszubeszterce
047450 Oshvotsk, Ushvotsk
047457 Uscie Biskupie, Ustzi Beskopia, Uzovske Peklany
047460 Oshpetzin, Oshpitsin, Oshvitsin, Oshvitzin, Oswiecim
047479 Osovtsy Pervyye
047500 Aschbach, Ausbach, Esbach, Eschwege, Iuzovka, Osowek, Osowa
047551 Izbica Kujawska
047567 Izbica Nowa, Ossowka Nowa
047587 Izbica Lubelska, Izbica Lubelski
047600 Asvany, Ispina
047630 Uzvent
047634 Uzventis
047640 Ispanmezo, Osobnica, Ospinzi
047646 Oshvyentsim
047650 Osipenko, Osipienko
047656 Aspang Markt, Utzwingen
047679 Aschaffenburg
047745 Osowa Wyskasa, Osowa Wyszka
047750 Iosipovka, Osipovichi
047800 Azipolia, Ezupol, Odjivol, Odrzywol, Oshpol, Uschpol, Uzpaliai
047830 Eisfeld, Izvalta, Uzbolot
047840 Uzbloc, Uzpalis
047850 Osoblaha
047860 Izabelin
047890 Eschweiler, Essweiler
047900 Asvar, Isper, Izvoare, Izvory
047946 Osvracin

424

047950	Asperg	
047956	Eisbergen	
047957	Asperhofen	
047960	Aspern	
047966	Aspern an der Donau	
047970	Asperhofen	
047980	Izvoarele	
048000	Aszalo, Isola, Issel, Izola, Osli, Ossala, Ozalj, Ujsoly	
048360	Eysolden	
048400	Oselce, Osielec	
048450	Iasliska	
048500	Ujszalok, Uscilug	
048543	Izluchistoye	
048600	Oselin, Oslany, Uzlany, Uzlian, Uzlion, Uzlyany	
048630	Ujszalonta	
048656	Aislingen, Esslingen, Esslingen am Neckar	
048690	Aschileu Mare	
048700	Osehlib, Oslip	
048710	Uzlovoye	
048730	Iaslovat	
048740	Oslawica	
048750	Eschelbach, Isselbach	
048754	Oslaw Gzarny	
048756	Eschelbach an der Ilm	
048759	Oslavy Charne	
048760	Eisleben	
048778	Oslav Byaly, Oslaw Bialy	
048795	Eschollbrucken, Isselburg	
048796	Eschelbronn	
048900	Asslar, Oszlar, Uslar	
048960	Eslarn	
049000	Asare, Aseri, Aszar, Ecser, Oszro, Ozeri, Ozero, Ozery, Ozhor, Ozor, Ozora, Ozra, Ozyori, Ujgyor	
049100	Osorheiu	
049300	Uschurod, Uzhhorod, Uzhorod	
049350	Oseredek	
049370	Oserdow	
049400	Azarce, Azartsy, Ozaritch, Ozarycze	
049446	Eschershausen	
049450	Ozersk, Uscie Ruskie	
049487	Aschersleben, Oschersleben	
049500	Ozarichi	
049510	Osorheiu	
049570	Ozarkov, Ozorkov, Ozorkow	
049600	Assern, Ezerenai, Ezherena, Ezherene, Ezreni, Ozerany, Ozeryany, Ozhiran, Ozieran, Ozierany, Oziran, Ozyeran, Ustchorna, Uziran, Uzirna, Uzyerni	
049630	Ozarinet	
049640	Ozarintsy, Ozernitsa	
049660	Ozernyani, Ozernyany	
049700	Ozarov, Ozarow, Ozharov, Ozhorov, Ozorow	
049774	Ozarow Przy Lugowie	
049779	Ozarow Przy Lugowie	
049783	Eiserfeld	
049800	Iserlia	
049860	Iserlia Noua, Iserlohn	
049874	Israelovca	
049875	Israilovka, Izrailovka	
050000	Ajka, Aka, Eckau, Eich, Ighiu, Iik, Oggau, Ukk	
053000	Ochota, Uchte, Ugod	
053540	Ohatkocs	
053636	Ochtendung	
053640	Ochotnica	
053643	Aktenstadt	
053650	Uchtenhagen	
053653	Ochotnica Dolna	
053655	Uchtenhagen	
053679	Aegidienberg, Agidienberg	
053745	Oktyabrskiy, Oktyabrskoi Revolyutsii	
053790	Oktyabr	
053793	Oktyabrdorf	
053795	Oktyabrskiy, Oktyabrskoi Revolyutsii	
053850	Aggtelek, Agtelek	
053900	Acatari	
053936	Echterdingen	
053946	Eichtersheim	
053950	Achtyrka, Akhtyrka	
053964	Ekaterinoslav	
053966	Ecaterineanca	
053970	Ochtrup	
054000	Acas, Ahaus, Akos, Eges, Ochoza, Oksa	
054100	Okrzeja	
054300	Akaszto, Igesti	
054317	Aukstoji Panemune	
054330	Eichstatt, Igstadt	
054336	Eichstetten	
054337	Aukshtadvaris, Aukstadvaris	
054340	Oksiutycze	
054370	Agustov, Augustov, Augustow, Oygstova	
054373	Augustowa Ad Ratam	
054400	Ujkigyos	
054430	Egyhazashetye	
054436	Egyhazasdengeleg	
054500	Okecske, Ujkecke, Ujkecske	
054580	Ikskile	
054600	Ahausen, Eggesin, Exin, Ikazan, Ikazn, Ochedzyn, Okocim	
054630	Oxintea	
054631	Oksentiya	
054640	Ochsenhausen	
054654	Ochsenhausen	
054678	Ochsenfeld	
054679	Aegidienberg, Agidienberg, Ochsenfurt	
054780	Augspil	
054784	Augspils	
054787	Agasfalva, Akosfalva	
054795	Augsburg	
054800	Echzell	
054857	Aix la Chapelle	
055000	Aichach	
055700	Ochakov	
056000	Aachen, Achim, Aegina, Aigen, Aken, Egen, Ichnya, Igene, Ogony, Okany, Okna, Okne, Okno, Okny, Uchanie, Uhanie	
056160	Okmiyan	
056300	Echimauti, Ignatei	
056350	Ignatki	
056370	Ignatow	
056375	Eigentovka, Ignatovka, Ignatowka	
056400	Achneish, Ignatsey, Ignecz, Oknitsa, Uhonice, Ujkanizsa, Ujkenez	
056430	Aknist, Akniste	
056434	Aknistes	
056453	Aknasugatag, Okna Sugatag	
056460	Egenhausen, Eichenhausen, Ichenhausen	
056470	Ignacow	
056483	Akna Szlatina	
056500	Okonek, Uchanka	
056546	Egenhausen, Eichenhausen, Ichenhausen	
056560	Ehingen, Eigenheim, Ockenheim, Uckingen	
056570	Agenhof	
056574	Ignacow Szlachecki	
056597	Eckengraf	
056600	Akemene, Akmene, Akmian, Eigenheim, Eihumen, Igumen, Ihumen, Ockenheim, Okmian, Okmjan	
056640	Okmianica, Okmyanitsa	
056650	Okuninka	
056670	Ochmanow	
056700	Agenhof, Okuniev, Okuniew, Okunyev, Ugnev	
056740	Akimovici, Ogonowice	
056750	Akimovka, Okuniuwek	
056780	Eichenbuhl	
056783	Eggenfelden	
056795	Eggenburg	
056860	Ignalina	
056865	Ignalinko	
056900	Iachmir, Uchomir	
056950	Akna Raho, Ukmerge	
057000	Akovo, Iecava, Okip, Okopy, Okup, Okupy	
057400	Ickowice, Ujkowice	
057430	Iacobesti	
057433	Iakobshtadt	
057600	Iacobeni	
057800	Egbeli	
057870	Agfalva	
057890	Eichweiler	
058000	Akali, Ekel, Igal, Igla, Iglau, Igle, Iglo, Ugale, Uglya	
058300	Iclod, Iglita, Iklad	
058370	Oglyadov	
058379	Iklodbordoce	
058386	Iclodul Mare	
058400	Okolica, Okolitsa, Ugales, Ugolets, Uholec	
058446	Acholshausen	
058460	Eggolsheim, Oklesna	
058466	Okolicna na Ostrove	
058475	Egelsbach, Igelsbach	
058480	Iclozel	
058560	Ickelheim, Iggelheim	
058600	Aglona, Aklin, Egeln, Eglaine, Ickelheim, Iggelheim, Igolomia, Ogulin, Ugalen	
058650	Igling	
058700	Okalewo, Okyu Alb	
058743	Egloffstein	
058770	Ochlopow, Okhlopov	
058870	Ochiul Alb	
059000	Agrij, Eger, Oger, Ogra, Ogre, Ohare, Ugar, Ugra, Ugry, Ujker	
059100	Okrzeja	
059300	Agard, Akarattya, Egerhat, Ogrody, Okorito, Ugrutiu	
059361	Ogorodnoye	
059364	Ogrodniczki, Ogrodzieniec	
059365	Ogorodnya Gomelskaya	
059393	Eckardroth	
059400	Aghiresu, Agries, Agris, Egeres, Egersee, Igrici, Igricze, Ogres, Oharice, Uherce	
059430	Iegheriste	
059446	Ockershausen	

059450	Egercsehi, Egerszeg, Egerszog, Okorsk, Uhersko	063900	Amdor, Amdur, Indra, Indura	064500	Insko, Ionyaska, Onusky, Onyszki
059454	Uhersky Ostroh	063914	Andrijasevci	064540	Oniskis, Onuskis
059457	Okorsk Wielki, Uhersky Brod	063917	Andreyev, Andriejava, Andrzejewo, Andrzejow, Ondrejovce	064560	Oniscani, Onishkany, Onitskany
059458	Aghiresu Cluj			064595	Anciokrak, Antchikrok, Enskirchen
059459	Uherske Hradiste	063930	Andrid, Endred, Endrod	064600	Amsana, Amshana, Emmetzheim
059460	Igersheim	063936	Entradam, Unterriedenberg		
059464	Ogrodzieniec, Ugertse Nezabitovske, Uherce Niezabitowskie	063937	Unterdeufstetten	064635	Enyedszentkiraz
		063939	Unterdorf	064640	Encsencs
		063943	Andrashida, Unter Stanestie	064650	Omniszonka
059466	Uherce Mineralne	063944	Andrasocz	064656	Aynzingen, Einsingen, Eynzingen
059470	Ogershof	063945	Andruszkowice		
059479	Iharosbereny	063946	Untereisenheim	064670	Amshinov
059480	Egreshely	063947	Andrespol, Andrushovka, Andruszowka, Unterretzbach, Unterschaftlarn, Unterschupf, Unterschwandorf, Untersiebenbrunn	064693	Enzenreith
059486	Ogorzeliny			064700	Unesov, Unicov, Uniszowa
059497	Eckarts Rupboden			064740	Uniszowice
059500	Egerag, Egregy, Ogarka, Okorag			064750	Ansbach, Imsbach
059530	Egerhat			064795	Innsbruck
059576	Equarhofen	063950	Andruha, Andrukha, Anturke, Intorok, Inturik, Inturk, Inturke, Unterhaching	064840	Angyalos
059593	Egerhart			064876	Unsleben
059600	Achern, Agram, Eggern, Igren, Ugornya			064879	Amschelberg
		063954	Unterriexingen	064943	Inzersdorf, Inzersdorf bei Wien
059635	Ajkarendek	063955	Unterhaching	065000	Enichioi, Inke, Inucu, Onga, Umka, Unecha, Unieck
059640	Okormezo	063957	Andrichov, Andrikhov, Andrychow, Jindrichuv Hradec		
059650	Okrajnik, Ugorniki, Uhorniki			065360	Inheiden
059657	Ugrinkovtsy, Ugrynkovtse, Ugrynokovtse	063959	Untergrombach	065365	Ungedanken
		063960	Unterine	065393	Engetried
059660	Agrinion, Akerman, Akkerman	063964	Andranishok, Andrionishkis, Andrioniskis, Andronischki, Unternzenn	065430	Aniksht, Anikst, Anykst, Onikshty, Unhost
059674	Achremowce, Akhremovtsy, Ugrynuv Sredni			065436	Ungstein
				065440	Anyksciai
059675	Okhrimovka	063965	Andernach, Andornak, Andryjanki, Untermaxfeld	065450	Anikshchyai
059740	Egerbocs, Igrovitsa			065600	Ungeni, Ungeny, Ungheni
059750	Egerbegy	063967	Untermaubach	065639	Ungen Tyrg, Ungheni Targ
059760	Equarhofen	063969	Untermerzbach	065656	Ingenheim
059785	Egervolgy	063970	Andreev	065660	Ingenheim
059790	Egervar, Ikervar	063974	Unter Apsa, Unter Bistra, Unter Wisho, Unterbissingen, Unterpiesting	065669	Ungheni Mures
059800	Okrouhla, Okruhla			065693	Angenrod
059845	Okrouhlicka			065740	Inacovce
059870	Egerlovo	063976	Andrupene, Indarapnici, Indarepnish, Unterrabnitz	065760	Encovany
059930	Egerhart			065790	Ungvar, Ungwar
060000	Ineu, Oni, Unna, Uny	063978	Andreapol, Endrefalva, Unterbalbach, Unterpleichfeld, Unterpullendorf, Unterwaldbehrungen, Unterwalden	065800	Unkel
061700	Uniayev, Uniejow, Uniyev			065830	Anhalt, Anholt
063000	Amati, Andau, Antau, Emod, Enyed, Ianauti, India, Inota, Ond, Onod, Onut, Und			065839	Angelturn
				065840	Anghelus, Engels, Ingulec, Ingulets
063100	Indija	063979	Unterberg, Unterfarrnbach, Unterfrauenhaid, Unterwurmbach	065843	Angelsdorf, Ingolstadt
063300	Ondod			065856	Ingelheim
063400	Andocs, Antas, Uniatycze			065859	Engelhartstetten
063460	Antosin, Antosino	063983	Unteraltertheim	065860	Anklam, Ingelheim
063500	Unyatyche, Unyatychi	063985	Unterleichtersbach	065879	Angelberg
063560	Onitcani	063986	Unterlaimbach, Unterlanzendorf, Unterleinach, Unterlimpurg	065890	Engelhartstetten
063580	Antokol			065900	Engure, Enniger
063586	Antakalnis	063987	Unteralba, Unterolberndorf	065916	Angereii Noui
063600	Antin, Emden, Inheiden, Unteni, Unteny	063993	Untererthal	065940	Unguras
		063996	Unter Rina	065944	Ungarisch Ostrau, Ungarish Ostra, Unguras Salaj
063656	Endingen	064000	Ainazi, Amacz, Ance, Emes, Emmes, Ems, Enciu, Encs, Endsee, Enese, Enns, India, Ioneasca, Jince, Onuca		
063660	Antonin, Antoniny			065945	Ungarsich Hradisch
063664	Antonin Stary			065946	Ingershem
063665	Antoninek			065947	Ungarisch Brod
063666	Antonin Nowy	064170	Andrzejewo, Andrzejow	065949	Ungarisch Hradisch
063670	Antanava, Antoniow, Antonov, Antonovo, Antonow, Antonowo, Antonuv	064300	Imsady, Ineshty, Inesti, Oneshty, Onesti, Unhost	065960	Angern, Ungureni
				065964	Ungurmuiza
		064336	Amstetten	065966	Angermunde
063674	Antonovtsy, Antonowce, Antonowiecka, Antunovac	064340	Ahmecetca	065979	Angerburg
		064370	Omstov	066000	Anin, Imeni, Ioannina, Uhnin, Uman, Unin
063675	Antonivka, Antonovka, Antonowka, Antonuvka	064377	Omstibova		
		064380	Einsiedel	066300	Aumund
063678	Antonopol	064390	Aumeisteri	066365	Amendingen, Emmendingen
063700	Ondava	064397	Insterburg, Unsdorf	066397	Ammendorf, Immendorf
063780	Antapoli, Antepolye, Antipolye, Antopol, Antopole	064400	Ances, Umieszcz	066400	Inancs, Umance, Umantse
		064430	Oncesti, Uncsest	066454	Anenska Studanka
063850	Antolka	064487	Amtchislav, Amtzislov, Omtchislav		
063873	Antalept, Antaliepte				

066460	Immenhausen
066500	Enmianki, Enying
066546	Immenhausen
066700	Ananiev, Ananyev
066740	Umianowice
066795	Amoneburg
066930	Immenroda, Immenrode
067000	Uhnow, Uniow, Univ, Unov
067300	Ambud, Ombod
067330	Imputita
067446	Imbshausen
067500	Einbeck
067560	Embken
067570	Ambukow, Ambukuv
067644	Invancice
067650	Ampfing
067656	Impfingen
067800	Anapol, Annapol, Annapoli, Annopol, Iambol, Iampol, Unewel
067830	Inwald
067840	Inowlodz
067876	Ampfelwang
067890	Annweiler
067934	Imbradas
067947	Ambrozfalva
067948	Inowroclaw
067950	Amberg, Annaberg
067957	Annaberg Buchholz, Anufrehifka
067975	Onufriewka
068000	Emilia, Emilja, Imola, Omuli
068300	Anhalt, Anholt
068365	Eimeldingen
068460	Emiltchina, Emiltchine
068560	Emlichheim
068600	Emilin, Jimlin
068640	Imielnica
068645	Ujmalomsok
068650	Imling, Immling
068930	Eimelrod
069000	Amur, Umer
069365	Emmerdingen
069400	Ammersee, Anarcs
069433	Emmerstedt, Unruhstadt
069440	Unierzyz
069446	Einartshausen
069459	Emersacker
069500	Emmerich, Umurga
069530	Anrochte
069543	Unrukstadt
069646	Amur Nishni Dnjeprowsk
069650	Imerinka
069740	Omoravicza
069750	Amorbach
070000	Aba, Apa, Ape, Aub, Epe, Iba, Ievve, Ip, Ipp, Ivia, Ivye, Iwia, Iwie, Iwje, Jibou, Oaffa, Ufa
071600	Oboyan
073000	Abda, Abod, Abud, Apateu, Apati, Apatiu, Apt, Apta, Ivot, Obuda
073100	Abadaja, Opatija
073400	Obytce
073437	Apatistvanfalva
073460	Ipthausen
073500	Obdach, Ujvidek
073574	Opatkowice, Opatkowice Drewniane, Opatkowice Pojalowskie
073594	Apatkeresztur
073600	Apatin, Ovadno, Owadno
073640	Obdenice
073675	Auf dem Bock

073700	Jivatov, Opatov, Opatow, Owadow
073740	Ejwidowicze, Opatowice, Opatowiec
073749	Abaujdevecser
073750	Eyvidovichi, Obodovka, Obodowka, Opatowek
073780	Apatfalu, Ovidiopol, Ovidipol
073787	Apatfalva
073860	Apetlon
073900	Eupatoria, Obodr
073910	Evpatoriia
073930	Abterode
073960	Avdarma
074000	Abbazia, Abus, Apc, Apes, Avas, Epfishe, Obecse, Obesce, Obice, Obsza, Obycz, Opaci, Opacie, Opsa, Opshe, Uboc, Ujpazua, Upice
074300	Ivesti, Ujpest
074330	Aubstadt
074350	Apostag
074360	Eppstein
074387	Apostolovo
074397	Ebsdorf
074400	Apsicsa, Aufsess
074436	Oboz Zjednoczenia Narodowego
074450	Obrzycko
074500	Ebeczk, Opochka, Opoczka
074568	Opoczka Mala
074574	Ivashkovtsy, Ivaskovice, Iwaszkowce
074577	Episcopia Bihoruliu, Episcopia Bihorului
074597	Upesgriva
074600	Aufhausen, Ipsheim, Opoczno, Oposhno, Oposhnya, Oposna, Opotchna, Ubieszyn
074630	Abaujszanto
074640	Obecnice, Opocnice
074645	Obszanska Wola
074650	Opacionka
074697	Ovsemerov, Owsiemirow
074700	Abaujsap, Opozdzew
074740	Ivatzvitch, Iwacewicze
074750	Ivatsevichi
074780	Avasujfalu, Ovidiopol
074787	Abosfalva
074794	Avasujvaros
074840	Apsilsa
074850	Abadszalok
074865	Abaujszolnok
074870	Oficjalow
074900	Ujvasar
075000	Apagy, Aubach, Obbach, Obych, Opachi, Opaka, Opaki
075300	Apahida
075396	Apacatorna
075460	Aufhausen
075500	Apahegy
075600	Eubigheim, Iobageni, Opochno
075630	Evghenita
075700	Iwkowa, Obiechow, Obukhov, Opechowo
075900	Abaujker
075930	Ofeherto, Ujfeherto
075956	Aufkirchen
076000	Abony, Apheim, Ivan, Ivanyi, Iwanie, Obanya, Ofen, Offenau, Oppein, Ownia, Ubinie, Upina, Uppony, Upyna, Uwin
076300	Avanta, Ebneth, Ovanta, Owanta

076393	Ivandarda
076397	Oeventrop, Oventrop
076400	Ebensee, Ivanc, Ivancea, Ivancsa, Ivanec, Ivanice, Ivanici, Ivanitz, Ivanusca, Ivenets, Ivienic, Ivnica, Ivnitza, Iwanicze, Iwieniec, Iwonicz, Obnize, Upynas
076430	Ibanesti, Ivaneshti, Ivanesti
076431	Ivanestii Noui, Ivanestii Vechi
076433	Ovenstadt
076440	Eibenschitz, Ivancice
076443	Iwonicz Zdroj
076450	Ivaniska, Ivansk, Ivanska, Ivantchik, Ivanushka, Iwaniska, Iwanisko
076460	Obenhausen, Ovenhausen
076474	Iwancewicze
076475	Ivantseviche
076478	Ebensfeld
076479	Abensberg
076483	Ivano Zolot
076500	Ivancha, Ivanichi, Ivaniki, Ivanka, Iwaniki
076530	Ivancauti
076546	Obenhausen, Ovenhausen
076560	Abenheim, Ebingen, Eppingen, Offingen, Oppenheim, Uffenheim
076570	Appenhof, Ivankov, Iwankow
076574	Ivanhkovitz, Ivankovtsy, Iwankowicze
076575	Ivankoviche, Ivankovichi
076578	Apanagyfalu, Apanagyfalva
076579	Ivanka Pri Dunaji
076593	Ivangorod, Iwanogorod
076600	Abenheim, Oppenheim, Uffenheim
076700	Appenhof, Ivanovo
076719	Appenweier
076736	Ivanbattyan
076740	Eiwanowitz, Ivanhkovitz, Ivanovice, Ivanovtse, Ivanovtsy, Iwanowice
076743	Ivane Puste, Iwanie Puste
076746	Ivanovice na Hane
076748	Ivanovo Selo
076750	Epfenbach, Ivanovka, Iwanowka, Offenbach
076756	Offenbach am Glan, Offenbach am Main, Offenbach in der Pfalz
076780	Ivanopol
076793	Ebenfurth
076795	Offenburg, Ofienburg
076796	Ibbenburen, Ivana Franka, Ivano Frankovo, Ivano Frankovsk, Iwano Frankowsk
077000	Iwowe, Obava, Opava
077400	Abovce
077600	Iphofen
077847	Avafelsofalu
077870	Abafalva
077900	Abaujvar
078000	Abeil, Abel, Abeli, Abeliai, Ipel, Ipoly, Iwla, Jiblea, Obel, Obeliai, Opalya, Opalyi, Opola, Opole, Ubla, Ublya, Ujfala
078174	Oblajovice
078300	Apolda, Aufeld, Auffeld, Oploty
078360	Opladen
078364	Ipolydamasd

078395	Affaltrach	079560	Oberhaching, Obrigheim	079986	Obererlenbach
078396	Ipolytarnoc	079564	Obergunzburg	080000	Ilia, Ilja, Ilya, Ohlau, Uhla,
078400	Obilic, Oboltsy, Oboltzi, Obolzy	079567	Obergimpern		Uila, Ujhely, Ulla, Ullo
078433	Eibelstadt	079576	Oberkaufungen	081000	Aloja, Auleja, Eleja
078450	Ipolysag, Ipolyszog, Oplucko,	079585	Oberglogau	081396	Aalaiy Torna
	Oplutsko	079586	Ober Gleen, Ober Klingen,	081700	Olejow, Oleyev
078457	Ipelske Predmostie		Obergleen	081759	Olejowa Korniow, Olejowa
078458	Ipelske Ulany	079587	Oberhollabrunn		Korolowka, Oleyeva Kornyuv,
078460	Eppelsheim, Owloczym	079596	Obergrombach		Oleyeva Korolevka, Oleyeva
078470	Obilicevo	079600	Abram, Abrany, Abrene, Abrini,		Korolyuvka, Oleyevo
078475	Ebelsbach		Ebern, Ibrany, Ibrony,		Korolevka
078500	Abaujlak		Obernau, Oberrine, Obran,	083000	Aldea, Alita, Alite, Ialta, Oelde,
078560	Oblekon, Ovlochin, Ovlochym		Obryn, Oparany		Olad, Olita, Ujleta
078600	Apalina, Ewelin, Opalin, Oplany,	079630	Abramut	083400	Alitus, Alt Oytch, Alt Oytz,
	Oppeln	079639	Oberndorf, Oberndorf an der		Altaussee, Alytus
078630	Iablonita		Melk	083463	Alt Sandez
078640	Opalenica, Opalenitza	079643	Oberramstadt	083464	Alt Sanz
078645	Opaleniska, Opalenisko	079646	Obermassing, Obernzenn	083536	Altkettenhof
078650	Ipolnyak, Obelniki	079648	Obermoschel, Obernzell	083546	Eldagsen
078660	Iablona Noua	079650	Obornik, Oborniki	083584	Alt Kolziglow
078675	Iablona Veche	079654	Ober Mockstadt	083593	Altkrautheim
078736	Ipoly Fodemes	079656	Efringen	083595	Aldekerk
078795	Apfelberg	079657	Obbornhofen	083600	Ahlden, Alattyan, Altdamm,
078878	Opole Lubelski, Opole Lubelskie	079658	Ober Ingelheim, Oberingelbach		Altena, Altona
078960	Oblarn, Oeblarn	079659	Obernkirchen	083630	Oltenita
079000	Eberau, Obora, Obra, Opary,	079660	Abrehnen	083639	Altendorf, Eltendorf
	Opory, Uivar, Ujvar, Upor	079664	Ebermannstadt	083640	Altenhasslau
079175	Obreja Veche	079670	Abramowo, Obbornhofen	083643	Altenstadt, Altenstein
079190	Obereuerheim	079674	Abramovce	083646	Altenschonbach
079195	Obereuerheim	079675	Abramowka	083654	Altenhasslau
079300	Abrud, Obryte	079679	Abrany Borsod, Ebernburg,	083656	Aldingen, Altenkunstadt
079343	Abrud Sat		Obernbreit	083659	Altengronau, Altenkirchen
079360	Abertamy, Obertin, Obertyn,	079687	Obernalb	083660	Eltmann
	Obratan	079695	Oberammergau	083661	Altmamayeshti
079367	Oberreidenbach, Oberriedenberg	079700	Oberwia, Obierwia, Obrow	083663	Altenundem
079374	Obradovci, Ubrodowice	079739	Oberpetersdorf	083668	Altmemelhof
079376	Abrudbanya	079740	Ober Apsa, Ober Visho, Ober	083674	Alten Buseck
079386	Oberdollendorf		Wisho, Obrowiec, Uvarovitchi	083675	Altenbogge
079387	Oberthulba	079743	Ober Bistra	083676	Altenbamberg
079396	Obertraun	079746	Oberowisheim	083679	Altenburg, Oldenburg
079397	Oberdorf, Oberdorf in	079747	Oyber Visheve	083683	Altenlotheim, Altmuhldorf
	Wurtemberg	079748	Oberwesel	083690	Altenahr, Altenmuhr
079400	Eperies, Eperjes, Eperyos, Obritz,	079750	Eberbach, Uvarovichi	083695	Altmark
	Obrocz, Oporets, Ovrutch,	079756	Oberwikon	083700	Althaif, Althof, Ohladow,
	Owrucz, Ubrez, Ubrezs,	079764	Oberrabnitz		Ulatowo
	Ujvaros	079776	Oberpfaffenhofen	083730	Altwied
079433	Eberstadt	079779	Oberbieber	083739	Altwiedermus
079434	Oberstotzingen	079783	Oberbildein,	083750	Altpaka
079435	Oberstockstall		Oberwaldbehrungen,	083760	Alt Ofen
079436	Oberstein, Obersteinabrunn		Oberwaltersdorf	083780	Aldoboly, Eltville
079437	Obristvi	079784	Oberwollstadt	083790	Aldebro
079439	Oberstdorf, Oberstreu	079785	Oberpleichfeld	083794	Alt Breisach
079440	Eberschutz, Iwierzyce, Oporzec	079786	Oberpullendorf	083796	Altberun
079444	Oparszczyzna	079787	Ujvarfalva	083848	Alt Lesle
079445	Obersitzko	079789	Oberweiler, Oberweilersbach	083853	Altlichtenwarth
079446	Eppertshausen, Obertshausen,	079793	Oberwart, Oberwarth	083864	Alt Landsberg
	Oberzissen, Oepfershausen	079794	Obervorschutz	083865	Altlengbach
079450	Eperjeske, Obrzycko	079795	Oberberg, Oberbrechen	083866	Altleiningen
079460	Ebersheim, Obarzym, Oberhausen	079800	Ibraila, Oberaula	083946	Oldersum
079464	Eversmuiza	079839	Oberaltertheim	083947	Oldrisov, Oltarzew
079466	Ober Seemen, Oberseemen	079843	Oberlistingen, Oberloisdorf,	083957	Oldrichov
079470	Ober Asphe, Oberasphe,		Oberlustadt	083970	Altdorf
	Obrazow	079847	Oberelsbach	084000	Aleus, Algyo, Alzey, Elyus, Ilza,
079475	Ebersbach	079860	Ober Olm		Ilzha, Oels, Olesha, Olesza,
079476	Obersiebenbrunn, Oppertshofen	079864	Oberlahnstein, Oberlanzendorf		Ols, Ulic, Ulucz
079478	Eberswalde, Oberessfeld	079865	Oberlangenstadt, Uberlingen	084300	Alcsut, Alesd, Alsedziai,
079479	Oberschwarzach, Obritzberg	079866	Oberlenningen		Alshad, Alsiad, Alushta,
079480	Oberzell	079870	Oberhollabrunn		Elesd
079500	Aporka, Ebrach, Iburg, Ovruch	079896	Oberlauringen	084330	Altshtat, Altshtot, Altstadt,
079540	Oberkotzau	079948	Oberursel		Ullstadt
079543	Ebereichsdorf	079960	Ober Rina	084340	Alsoidecs
079546	Ebergassing, Oberhausen	079964	Ober Ramstadt	084360	Olsztyn
079556	Oberhaching	079967	Oberehrenbach	084365	Olsztynek

084374	Alsodabas, Alsodobsza
084380	Alistal
084385	Alsotelekes, Elesdlok
084390	Alcedar
084396	Alsoderna
084397	Alsdorf, Elsdorf
084400	Alsedziai, Oleszyce, Olszyc, Olszyce
084410	Alsosajo
084430	Ilisesti
084440	Alsocece
084443	Oleszyce Stare
084450	Alsosack, Alsosag, Alsoszuha, Alsozsuk
084454	Alsosegesd
084463	Alsoszenterzsebet
084467	Alsoszinever
084478	Algyogyafalu, Alsosofalva
084479	Alsoszopor, Alszopor
084484	Alsoszeleste, Alsoszelistye, Alsozsolca, Alsozsolcza
084485	Alsoszalok
084487	Algyogyalfalu
084490	Alsocsora, Alsoszouor
084493	Alsogyertany, Alsosarad
084500	Alacska, Aleshki, Allesk, Alsok, Elecske, Elzach, Illocska, Olaszka, Olecko, Oledzkie, Oleshiche, Oleshki, Olesk, Oleski, Olesko, Oleszki, Olosig, Ulciug, Ulicko
084530	Alsogod
084535	Alsohidegpatak
084548	Alsokosaly, Olszyc Szlachecki
084549	Ulitsko Serendkevich
084550	Alsogagy
084553	Alsohahot
084556	Alsohagymas
084560	Oliscani, Olishkany
084565	Alsohangony
084569	Alsohomorod
084570	Oleshkuv, Oleszkowo
084574	Ulashkovitz, Ulashkovtsy, Ulaszkowce
084576	Also Kubin, Alsokubin
084580	Alsogalla
084584	Alsokalocsa
084586	Alsokalinfalva
084593	Alsokortvelyes
084594	Alsogorzsony
084600	Alesheim, Alsenai, Alsheim, Alzenau, Elasson, Olesno, Oleszno, Olsana, Olshan, Olshana, Olshani, Olshany, Olszana, Olszany, Olszyn, Olszyny, Uelsen, Uelzen, Uliczno, Ulsen
084634	Olahszentgyorg
084640	Alsenz, Olesnica, Olesznica, Olshanitsa, Olszanica
084648	Alsomislye
084650	Alsonyek, Oleshonki, Olesniki, Olshanik, Olszanik, Olszynka
084656	Also Mochnya, Olszanka Mala
084663	Alsonemedi
084664	Alsonemesapati
084666	Alzenau in Unterfranken
084670	Alsonovaj
084690	Alsomera
084694	Alsoneresznice
084698	Alsonyarlo
084700	Ilosva, Olaszfa, Olcsva, Olshevo, Olsov, Olszewo, Ulazow
084716	Alsobajom, Alsopojeni
084719	Altspeyer
084730	Alsopaty
084734	Alsovadasz, Elisabethstadt
084735	Alsobudak, Elizabetgrod
084736	Alsopeteny
084738	Olszow Dolny
084740	Alsoapsa, Alsoviso, Olszowiec
084743	Alsobisztra
084750	Alsbach, Alsvika, Alsviki, Olszowka
084755	Alsopahok
084764	Alsovamos, Olszewnica, Olszownica
084765	Olszewnica Mala, Olszewnica Wielka
084773	Olcsvaapati
084780	Alsoujfalu
084783	Alsfeld
084785	Alsobolkeny, Alsovalko
084793	Alsovaradja, Alsowartberg
084794	Alsoberecki, Alsovaradja, Alsovereczke
084795	Olsberg
084796	Alsoabrany, Alsofernezely, Alsovarany
084845	Alsolieszko, Olaszliszka
084847	Alsoolcsva
084850	Alsoujlak
084863	Also Lendva
084874	Alsolapos
084935	Elesdszurdok
084940	Alsoors
084950	Alsorajk, Olizarka, Ulizerka
084954	Alsorakos
084956	Alsoregmec
084960	Alsorona
084963	Alsoremete
084965	Alsoronok
084970	Alsoorbo, Alsorepa, Elizarow
084976	Alsoribnyicze
085000	Alag, Elek, Elk, Ilk, Illok, Illoki, Ilok, Olik, Olika, Oliki, Olyka, Ujlak
085390	Alchedary
085400	Elkush, Olkush, Olkusz
085417	Alekseyevka
085430	Aleksat, Alukst, Illukst, Illuxt, Ilokst, Ilukst, Ilukste
085434	Aleksotas, Ilukstes
085439	Ulica Starowiejska
085440	Olekshitsa
085444	Olekszyce
085460	Aleksin, Aluksna, Aluksne, Elksni, Elksnu, Olekshin
085463	Aleksander, Aleksandreni, Aleksandreny, Aleksandreshty, Aleksandria, Aleksandriia, Aleksandrija, Aleksandriya, Aleksandrov, Aleksandrovka, Aleksandrovki, Aleksandrovo, Aleksandrovsk, Aleksandrovski, Aleksandrow, Aleksandrow Kujawski, Aleksandrow Lodzki, Aleksandrowice, Aleksandrowka, Aleksandrowki, Aleksandrowo, Aleksandrowsk, Aleksandrya, Alexandreni, Alexandreni Targ, Alexandresti, Alexandria, Alexandroupolis, Alexandrovka, Alexandrovsk
085464	Aleksinac, Aleksince, Aleksnitz, Oleksince, Oleksinets Novy, Oleksintse
085465	Oleksianka
085493	Olahkocsard
085497	Ulicko Zarebne
085600	Ulcani, Ulichno
085639	Alikendorf
085650	Olching, Olkenik, Olkeniki, Olkienniki, Olkienniki, Olkinik, Olknik
085670	Olganow
085680	Olgomel
085730	Olahapati
085740	Olchowce, Olchowiec, Olkhovets, Olkhovtsy
085745	Olchowczyk
085750	Olchowka, Olkoviche, Olkovichi, Ulhowek
085780	Ol Gopol, Olahujfalu, Olgapol, Olgopol, Olhopol
085900	Alker
085944	Elgershausen
085947	Elgersburg
086000	Aalen, Ahlem, Ahlen, Ahlon, Ilina, Ilino, Iljino, Olaine, Ulan, Ulm, Ulma, Ulmu
086300	Alanta, Alland, Alunta, Ellend, Ileanda, Oleanita, Ulmet
086369	Ileanda Mare
086397	Allendorf, Allendorf an der Lumda, Allendorf an der Werra, Eilendorf
086400	Aljmas, Almas, Almasu, Alunis, Alunish, Alunisu, Ilanets, Ilince, Ilinets, Ilineuca, Iliniec, Ilintse, Ilintsy, Iljincy, Illmitz, Ilnica, Jilemnice, Olmuetz, Olmutz, Olomouc, Olyanitsa, Ulanica
086430	Almosd, Olanesti, Oloneshty
086436	Allenstein
086450	Almaszeg
086454	Ulanski Zarzyc
086456	Elmshagen
086458	Almas Galgo
086460	Elnhausen, Olnhausen
086463	Almasszent Tamasi
086464	Almasmezo
086468	Almasmalom
086469	Almasu Mare, Alunisu Mures
086480	Almasel
086495	Almasrakos
086496	Elmshorn
086500	Ilineuka, Ilnik, Ilniki, Ulaniki, Uljanik, Ulyaniki
086546	Elnhausen, Olnhausen
086560	Ellingen, Illingen
086574	Olnkhovtsy
086600	Ilmenau, Olmany, Ulmeni
086647	Allmannshofen, Allmendshofen, Elmendshofen
086648	Ulmeni Salj
086700	Ulanov, Ulanow
086740	Ulanowice
086744	Ulanowszczyzna
086745	Ulanovshchina
086750	Olenowka, Ulmbach
086785	Ulina Wielka
086794	Almaujvaros
086975	Eleonorowka
087000	Alap, Alave, Alba, Alove, Elva, Ilava, Ilawa, Ilba, Illoba, Ilow,

	Ilowa, Jihlava, Jilava, Olawa, Olbo, Olovi, Olovo, Olpe
087180	Alba Iulia, Alba Julia, Albaiulia
087300	Albota
087340	Alvitas
087350	Olahpatak
087390	Alfter
087400	Albishe, Ilawcze
087430	Albesti
087431	Albestii Bistritei
087450	Olevsk, Olewsk, Olivsk
087460	Albisheim, Ilvesheim, Olbiecin
087500	Ulhowek
087560	Ialpugeni
087570	Albigowa
087600	Alpen, Elben, Ialoveni, Olpin, Olpini, Olpiny
087640	Alvinc, Ilva Mica
087650	Elbing
087656	Ellwangen
087670	Alibanfa
087690	Alibunar, Ilva Mare
087693	Alpenrod
087700	Ilvov
087750	Ulvuvek, Ulwowek
087780	Olviopol, Olwiopol
087800	Olapolia, Olhopol
087830	Uehlfeld, Uhlfeld
087850	Elblag
087860	Alflen
087900	Alpar
087930	Alberti, Alparet, Olpret
087937	Albertfalva
087939	Albertirsa
087943	Olbersdorf
087947	Albersweiler
087960	Alwernia, Olbernhau
087965	Olbernhau
087967	Olbramovice
087978	Elberfeld
088740	Olahlapos
089000	Alor, Ellar, Ilioara
089433	Ellerstadt
089451	Uhlirske Janovice
089460	Allersheim, Ellersheim
089500	Ellrich, Illerich
089543	Ulrichstein
089545	Ulrichskirchen
089560	Alerheim, Illereichen
089600	Alerheim
089647	Ujlorincfalva
089656	Ailringen
089750	Ellerbach
090000	Oar, Or, Orhei, Uhry, Uioara, Ura, Uraj, Uri, Uriu
091460	Ir Yashan
091780	Uraiujfalu
093000	Arad, Ardo, Arta, Erd, Irota, Ohrid, Oradea, Orda
093170	Ordejov
093300	Arded, Ardud, Ehrstadt, Erdod
093314	Oarta de Jos
093344	Oarta de Sus
093350	Erdudka, Ortiteag
093385	Erdotelek
093394	Erdotarcsa
093400	Aradac, Ordasei, Ordashey
093430	Ardusat, Erdoszada
093440	Uioara de Sus
093447	Artyszczow
093456	Erdocsokonya
093457	Artyshchuv
093463	Erdoszentgyorgy
093470	Artasow, Artasuv
093480	Arduzel
093484	Erdoszallas
093530	Ordogkut
093574	Erdokovesd
093578	Ordogfala
093593	Erdokurt
093595	Erdokerek
093597	Erdohorvati
093600	Ardan, Ardany, Ehrsten, Eraadony, Erteny, Oradna, Ujhartyan, Ujradna
093630	Artand
093640	Ardanhaza
093643	Iordaneshte, Iordanesti
093650	Erding
093654	Ardanhaza
093658	Eradengeleg
093660	Iordaneni
093664	Erdmannsdorf
093669	Erdmannrode
093670	Ardanovo
093674	Ardanovce, Artemovsk, Artemowsk, Urdenovac
093675	Iordanovka
093679	Ortenberg, Ortenburg
093694	Iara de Mures
093700	Ardovo, Ordow, Orduv
093740	Urdevac
093750	Erdevik, Oradovka, Orodowka
093760	Erdobenye
093795	Erdberg
093840	Ortelec, Ortilos
093847	Ortelsburg
093854	Ortel Ksiazecy
093859	Ortel Krolewski
093865	Ortlingerhausen
093970	Ohrdruf
094000	Arys, Ercsi, Irhocz, Irsa, Irshe, Irsi, Irsya, Irza, Oras, Orasa, Orci, Oros, Orsha, Orsoy, Orsza, Uretcha, Uroz, Urozh, Urshe, Urycz
094174	Urzejowice
094300	Ihriste, Orastie
094340	Orestias
094360	Orosztony
094370	Urzedow
094390	Ersszodoro
094394	Erstarcsa
094400	Arciz, Artsiz, Artziz, Irzadze, Oroshaza, Oryszcze, Orzysz, Ursus
094457	Orzeszkowka
094460	Erzhausen, Urzicem, Urziceni
094470	Orzistchov
094475	Orzeszowka
094500	Oreske, Orishche, Oroszko, Uhrusk, Uritsk
094546	Ersekcsanad
094570	Orzechow
094573	Ersekvadkert
094574	Orishkovtsy, Oryshkovtse, Oryszkowce, Orzechowce, Orzechowiec
094576	Orzechow Nowy, Orzechowno
094579	Ersekujvar
094600	Aerzen, Ariseni, Arzen, Arzheim, Iurceni, Oraseni, Orasu Nou
094636	Orszentmiklos
094637	Orzendov, Urzendov, Urzendow
094640	Oroszmezo
094654	Ordshonikidze, Ordzhonikidze
094659	Oroszmokra
094700	Iarisav, Iarisev, Irsava, Irshava, Oracov, Orsava, Orsova, Oryszew
094710	Orosfaia
094719	Orschweier
094737	Erzsebetbanya
094740	Arosheviz, Orishovtsy, Urosevac
094743	Ersvasad
094750	Oroszveg
094767	Oryszew Nowy
094780	Orosfala, Oroszfala
094785	Erzhvilek, Erzhvilkas, Erzvilkas, Erzvilki
094790	Oroszvar
094796	Urspringen
094800	Oroszlo, Orzel
094843	Orasul Stalin
094860	Orasul Nou, Oroszlany, Urszulin
094863	Erselend
094864	Orasul Nou Satu Mare
094870	Iaroslava, Oroslavje, Orszulewo
094900	Urisor
095000	Arak, Arka, Aurach, Aurich, Erk, Irig, Oracu, Orak, Orhei, Urechye, Urych
095100	Arokaja
095170	Orgeyev
095300	Arahida, Archid, Arokto, Iurcauti
095340	Ir Chadash, Ir Khadash
095344	Ir Chadash Sugind
095400	Arcus, Argos, Arkos, Arokhaza, Irhocz
095439	Erksdorf
095448	Arokszallas
095464	Iregszemcse
095476	Archshofen
095490	Erkeseru
095493	Oregcserto
095600	Argenau, Iorcani, Orkeny
095647	Argenschwang
095690	Erkner
095700	Ihrhove, Jirikov, Jirkov, Orhaiv, Oriachov, Oriekhov, Orikhov, Orjechow
095740	Ergkavas, Erkavas, Orahovica, Orekhovets
095750	Orchowek
095760	Orekhovno, Oriechowno, Oriekhovno
095785	Erkobolkut
095800	Airiogala, Arcalia, Argel, Ariogala, Ergli, Iragola, Irholo
095840	Irholcz
095847	Ergoldsbach
095849	Argelsried
095850	Irholch, Oreglak
095856	Arheilgen
095860	Erkeln, Orhalom
095864	Erkelenz
095900	Iargara
095930	Erkrath
095937	Erkortvelyes
096000	Arnau, Ernei, Irena, Irina, Oran, Orany
096300	Aranyod, Arnot, Iermut, Orneta
096350	Aranyidka
096360	Iernuteni
096365	Iermata Neagra

096379	Erndtebruck	097800	Orfalu	139460	Jutroschin, Jutrosin
096387	Arandelovac	097836	Erfelden	139750	Jueterbog, Juterbog
096393	Erendred	097890	Ahrweiler	140000	Jac, Jajce, Jasi, Jassy, Jaszo,
096400	Aranyos, Arinis, Ormezo,	097900	Arbore, Arborea		Jejse, Jozsa, Yeysi
	Urmezo, Urmitz	097930	Erfurt	141700	Jedrzejewo, Jedrzejow,
096430	Arioneshty, Arionesti	097950	Urberach		Yedzheyov
096433	Arnstadt	098000	Arlo, Erlaa, Erlau, Erlui, Irholo,	143000	Jasd
096434	Ernsthausen		Irrel, Orel, Orla, Orle, Orlya,	143400	Jaszdozsa
096436	Arnstein, Ernestinehof,		Oryol	143570	Jastkow
	Ernestinovo	098360	Orladany	143574	Jastkowice, Yostkovitz
096437	Arnostovice	098400	Erolaszi, Irholcz, Orelec	143593	Yustigrod
096439	Ahrensdorf, Aranyos Torda	098450	Orlicky, Orliczko	143640	Jasa Tomic
096440	Oranczyce	098460	Arolsen	143659	Justingrad
096460	Armsheim	098500	Irholch, Urlich	143850	Jasztelek
096461	Aranzenii Vechi	098560	Arheilgen	143900	Jastary, Jastrzab, Jastrzebia,
096464	Aranyosmegyes	098600	Aurelin, Orhalom		Jastrzebie
096469	Aranyosmarot	098654	Oerlinghausen	143940	Jastrzebica, Jastrzebice,
096475	Ernsbach	098656	Erlangen		Jastrzebiec
096476	Ermetzhofen	098659	Orlingerhausen	143945	Jastrzebska Wola, Jastrzebsko
096478	Arnsfelde, Arnswalde	098674	Arlamowska Wola		Stare
096479	Ahrensburg, Arnsberg	098675	Erlenbach, Erlenbach bei Dahn	143946	Jastrzebie Smiary
096494	Aranyosgyeres	098680	Orly Male	143950	Jastrzebik
096540	Oranchitsy	098700	Arlava, Arloff, Aurelow, Erlauf,	143954	Jastrzabka Stara
096560	Ihringen, Ohringen		Orlova, Orlove, Orlovo,	143956	Jastrzabka Nowa
096574	Uhrynkowce		Orlowa	143970	Jastrow, Jastrowie, Jastrowo
096580	Ermoclia	098717	Erlaa bei Wien	143979	Jastrebarsko
096583	Ermihalydalva	098739	Orlow Drewniany	144400	Jedziszcze
096587	Ermihalyfalva	098740	Orlowicze	144500	Jaciazek, Jaszsag
096600	Eremieni, Orinin, Urman,	098745	Orlovskaya	144600	Yezezhany
	Urmeny, Urmini	098750	Erlbach, Orlovichi, Orlowka,	144636	Jaszszentandras
096637	Ornontowice		Orlowko, Orluvka	144638	Jaszszentlaszlo
096640	Armenis, Ormenyes, Urmenis,	098760	Ir Lavan	144650	Yezezhanka
	Urmenisu	098785	Orly Wielkie	144700	Jaszczew
096645	Armensk, Armiansk Bazar,	098796	Erlabrunn	144830	Jaszczulty
	Armyansk	099400	Ererjes	145000	Jajczaki
096646	Arannyosmeggyes	114574	Jajeczkowicze	145490	Jaszkiser
096654	Aranymegges, Aranyomeggyes	114575	Yayechkovichi	145586	Jaszjakohalma
096679	Oranienburg	116400	Jajinci	145700	Jashkov
096700	Ornbau, Ornowo, Uhrynow	130000	Jata, Jod, Jody, Jut, Yod, Yodi,	145740	Jaskowice, Jaskowicze,
096740	Uhrineves		Yoed, Yoid		Juszkiewicze
096749	Uhrynow Sredni	134000	Jutas	145750	Jucica Veche, Yaskovichi,
096783	Ehrenfeld	136000	Judenau		Yushkevichi
096794	Ehrenbreitstein	136397	Jeutendorf, Judendorf	145800	Yasigola
096795	Arenberg, Arneburg	136400	Jedincy, Yedinets, Yedintsy	145916	Jaszkarajeno
096837	Arnoldowo	136475	Jedenspeigen	145955	Jaszkerekegyhaza
096843	Arnoldstein	136700	Yadimov	146000	Jacnia, Jasien, Jasina, Jasine,
096847	Arnoldsweiler	136750	Judenbach		Jasiunai, Jaszuny, Jesin,
096860	Aranylona	136795	Judenburg		Jesiona, Jezena, Yasen,
096930	Ermreuth	137000	Jadova, Jadovo, Jadow, Yadov,		Yasinya, Yezna
096944	Ermershausen		Yadove	146100	Yasnoye
097000	Arva, Erp, Ihrhove, Orawa, Orb,	137400	Juodupis	146179	Josenii Bargaului, Josenii
	Orhaiv, Orow, Oryava, Uhrov,	137500	Judovka		Birgaului
	Urbau	137600	Jadova Noua	146300	Juzintai, Yozint
097300	Erwitte, Oravita	137650	Jadowniki	146350	Jesentuki
097350	Erpatak	137656	Jadowniki Mokre	146400	Jasienica, Jasienice, Jasmuiza,
097363	Oroftiana de Sus	137670	Jadwinow		Jesenice, Jessnitz, Jeznas,
097400	Ihrowica, Orawitza	137675	Jadwinowka, Yadvinuvka		Yasenitsa, Yashnitza,
097430	Arpasteu, Arpasti, Arpasto	137760	Jedwabne, Yedvabna, Yedwabne		Yasinitza, Yeznas,
097433	Erbstadt	138000	Jedle		Yuzhenitsy, Yuzhenitse,
097440	Erpuzice	138400	Jedlice, Jedlicze, Yedlitch		Yuzhenitsy
097450	Orawczyk	138600	Jedelina, Jedlany, Jedlina,	146448	Yasenitsa Solna
097458	Oravska Lesna		Jedlnia, Jedlno	146450	Jesenske
097473	Erbes Budesheim	138645	Jedlinsk, Yedlinsk	146500	Jasionka, Jesenik
097475	Arbesbach	138650	Jedlinki	146543	Jasiennik Stary
097500	Auerbach, Erbach, Euerbach,	138683	Jedlnia Letnisko	146546	Jasienica Zamkowa
	Orawka, Urbach	138700	Jadlowa, Jodlowa, Yodlava	146547	Jasienica Sufczynska
097563	Auerbach an der Bergstrasse	138740	Jadlowice	146548	Jasienica Solna
097600	Irpen	138750	Jodlowka	146564	Jasionka Masiowa
097639	Erbendorf	138753	Jodlowka Tuchowska	146567	Jasieniec Nowy
097640	Ervenice, Orvanitsa, Orwianica	138765	Jodlownik	146594	Jasienica Rosielna, Jazienica
097656	Erbenheim	139000	Jatra, Yatra		Ruska
097657	Arvanagyfalu	139170	Jedrzejewo, Jedrzejow	146595	Jasnogorka, Yasnogorka,
097660	Erbenheim	139417	Jedrezejow		Yasnogurka

431

Code	Names
146600	Juzmin
146700	Jasienow, Yasenov
146738	Jasna Podlopien
146740	Jasenovac, Yastshembitsa
146748	Yuzny Poselok
146750	Jasienowka, Jasinowka, Jasionowk, Jasionowka, Yashinovka, Yashinovke, Yashinowka, Yasinuvka
146759	Jasieniow Gorny, Yasenuv Gorny, Yasenuv Gurny
146778	Jasieniow Polny, Jasienow Polny, Yasenev Polnyy, Yasenuv Polny
146940	Jacmierz
147000	Jaczew, Jadziwia, Jasiow, Jasov, Jasova, Jastrzab, Jastrzebia, Jastrzebie, Jazovo, Jazwie, Jezow, Jezowe, Yezhov
147300	Jaszapati
147400	Jasiewicze, Jastrzebica, Jastrzebice, Jastrzebiec
147439	Jazow Stary
147450	Jazowsko
147454	Jastrzebsko Stare
147457	Jastrzebska Wola
147469	Jastrzebie Smiary
147500	Jastrzebik, Jaswojki, Josbach, Jozefka, Juzowka, Yasevichi, Yuzovka
147543	Jastrzabka Stara
147567	Jastrzabka Nowa
147600	Jasvainiai, Jazwiny, Josvainiai, Jozefin, Yasvainiai, Yasven, Yosvain, Yosven, Yuzefin
147649	Jaszfenyszaru
147650	Jazwinki, Yazvinki
147670	Jazow Nowy
147700	Josefov, Josefow, Josvafo, Jozefow, Yozefov, Yuzefov, Yuzefuv
147743	Jozefow Stary
147750	Jozefowka, Yuzefovka, Yuzefuvka
147774	Yozifif Veisil
147793	Yuzefov Ardinatzki
147800	Jaswily, Jaszfalu, Jezupol, Juzefpol, Yezapol, Yuzefpol
147844	Jaszfelsoszentgyorgy
147950	Jesberg
147960	Jaszbereny
148000	Jasiel, Jaslo, Yasla, Yaslo, Yazyl
148360	Jaszladany
148439	Jetzelsdorf
148446	Jaszalsoszentgyorgy
148450	Jasliska, Yoshlisk
148570	Jaslikow
148600	Jaslany, Yaslany
148740	Jaslowiec, Jazlovice, Jazlowiec, Joslowitz, Yazlivitz, Yazlovets
149000	Jezioro, Jeziory, Jezor, Yezhore, Yeziori, Yezyori
149400	Jeziorosy
149460	Jezierzany, Yezerzani, Yezerzhany, Yezherzani, Yezyerzany
149465	Jezierzanka
149500	Jeziorko
149544	Jaszarokszallas
149600	Jezerne, Jezierna, Jeziorany, Jeziorna, Yezherne, Yezhyerna, Yezierne, Yeziorna, Yezirna
149640	Jezerance, Jeziernica
149659	Jeziorna Krolewska
149679	Jeziorna Oborska
149750	Jasiorowka
150000	Jak, Jeke
153140	Jucu de Jos
153600	Jagodina, Jagodne, Jagotin, Yagodin, Yagotin, Yagotina
153963	Yekaterinodar
153964	Jekaterynoslaw, Yekaterinoslav
153967	Yekaterinopol, Yekaterinovka
153970	Jaktorow, Yaktoruv
154370	Yagestov, Yagistov, Yagustova
154400	Jaksice
154600	Jagodzin, Jugesheim, Yagodzin
154640	Jagodziniec
154664	Jaksmanice
154700	Jugoszow
154795	Jochsberg
155439	Jakac Stara
156000	Juchen
156400	Yekimoutsy
156440	Jakimczyce
156458	Yohonishkel
156479	Johannisburg
156500	Jagonak
156540	Yakimchitse, Yakimchitsy
156560	Jugenheim
156600	Jugenheim
156700	Jachymov, Yukhnov
156740	Juchnowicze, Yakimovtsy
156750	Jachimowka, Yukhnovichi
157000	Jakfa, Jakuby, Jogeva
157400	Jacovce, Jajkowce, Jakowicze, Juchowitschi, Jugovici, Jugowice, Yaykovtse, Yuchavitz
157433	Jakobstadt, Yakovshtat
157456	Jacobshagen
157500	Jakowki, Yakoviche, Yukhovichi
157596	Jackowo Gorne
157600	Jacobeni, Jakubben, Jakubin
157700	Jakubow
157750	Jakobowka, Jakubowka, Yakubovka, Yakubuvka
157840	Jekabpils, Jekobpils, Yekabpils
157870	Jakfalva, Jakowlewo, Yakovlevo
158000	Jagiela, Jagiella
158314	Jucul de Jos
158640	Jagielnica, Yagelnitsa, Yagelnitza
158644	Yagelnitsa Stara
158654	Jagielnica Stara
158740	Jaglewicze, Jaklovce
158750	Yaglevichi
159639	Jaegerndorf, Jagerndorf
160000	Jamne, Jena, Jeno, Yamne
161850	Jaunijelgaua
161857	Jaunijelgava
163000	Jand
163860	Jamna Dolna
163917	Jendrzejov
163957	Yendrikhov
163960	Yantarnyy
164000	Jamnitz, Janisze, Janosi, Jaunauce, Jemnice, Joniec
164170	Jendrzejov, Yendzheyev
164300	Janoshida
164360	Jenstejn
164400	Janoshaza
164500	Janischki, Yanishke, Yanishki, Yanishok, Yenishok, Yonishok
164540	Joniskis, Yonishkis
164574	Januszkowice
164580	Yaneskel, Yonishkel, Yonushkel
164584	Joniskelis
164600	Janczyn, Januszno
164700	Janczowa, Januszew, Yanishov, Yendzheva, Yendzhiov, Yendziv
164740	Jancewicze
164750	Yantsevichi, Yanushevichi
164780	Yanishpol
164798	Jaunsvirlauka
164860	Janoshalma
165000	Jamniki, Jank, Jankai, Janochy, Jenikau, Jenke, Jenki, Jonik, Jonnik
165170	Yenakiyevo
165600	Jemgum, Yanchin
165683	Janki Mlode
165700	Janikowo, Jankowa, Janukow, Junikowo, Yenakievo
165740	Janikowice, Jankowce, Jankowice, Jenkovce
165750	Jankowka
165764	Jungbunzlau
165796	Jungfernhof
165876	Jaungulbene, Jaungulbenes
165960	Jamna Gorna
166000	Janina, Joanin, Joanina, Joniny, Yanina
166400	Jammince
166700	Janinow
167000	Janov, Janova, Janovo, Janow, Janowa, Janowo, Jonava, Yanev, Yaniv, Yanov, Yanova, Yanove, Yanuv, Yonava, Yonev
167396	Janow Trembowelski
167400	Janiewicze, Janovice, Janowice, Janowicze, Janowiczi, Janowiec, Janowitz, Yanovitch
167438	Yanev Shedletzki
167458	Janow Sokolski, Yanov Sokolski
167463	Janovice nad Uhlavou
167500	Janovichi, Janowka, Yanevichi, Yanofka, Yanoviche, Yanovichi, Yanovka
167563	Janowiec nad Wisla
167578	Janowiec Wielkopolski
167670	Janow Nowy
167738	Janow Podlaski, Yanev Podlaski, Yanov Podlaski, Yanuv Podolsk
167784	Janow Polski, Yanov Polski
167785	Jaunpiebalga, Jaunpiebalgas
167800	Jampol, Yambol, Yampol
167878	Janow Lubelski
167970	Jumprava
167974	Jumpravas
167976	Jumpravmuiza
168358	Jaunlatgale
168460	Jaunlaicene, Jemilcino
168560	Yemilchino
168570	Jaunjelgava
168574	Jaunjelgavas
168640	Jamielnica, Yamelnitsa
169300	Jumurda
169439	Jennersdorf
170000	Jaba, Jewe, Johvi
173900	Yevpatoria
173910	Jevpatorija, Yevpatoriya
174000	Japca, Jawcze, Jobbagyi, Jovsa
174500	Jevicko
174600	Yavozhne
174740	Jawiszowice
175000	Jabuka, Yavche
175400	Jobahaza
175675	Yevgenyevka

175900	Javgur	
175940	Jabocritch	
176300	Jabenita	
176460	Jebenhausen	
176546	Jebenhausen	
176590	Yefingar	
176740	Jevineves	
178400	Japoloc, Yapolots	
178600	Jablon, Jablonna, Yablanna, Yablona	
178637	Jablon Dabrowa	
178640	Jabloncza, Jablonec, Jablonica, Jablonice, Jablonitsa, Jablonitza, Yablonitsa	
178650	Jablonka, Yablonka, Yoblonka	
178654	Jablon Koscielna, Jablonka Swierszczewo	
178655	Jablonka Koscielna	
178656	Jablonec nad Nisou, Jablonka Nizna	
178657	Jablonica Polska, Jablonka Wyzna, Jablunkov	
178659	Jablonica Ruska	
178670	Jablanow, Jablonewo, Jablonow, Yablanov, Yablonevo, Yablonov, Yablonuv	
178675	Jablonowka, Yablonovka	
178677	Jablonne V Podjestedi	
178684	Jablonna Lacka	
178685	Jablonna Legionowo	
178694	Jablonna Ruska	
179000	Jabar, Javor, Jawor, Jawora, Jever, Yavora	
179400	Jaworze	
179438	Jaworze Dolne	
179440	Jaworzec	
179450	Jaworsko	
179459	Jaworze Gorne	
179460	Jaworzno, Yavarzna, Yavorzhne, Yavorzno	
179464	Jaworzyna Slaska	
179465	Jaworznik	
179484	Jawor Solecki	
179500	Jaworki	
179600	Jevreni	
179650	Jawornik, Yavornik	
179657	Jawornik Polski, Jawornik Przedmiescie	
179659	Jawornik Ruski	
179670	Yefremov	
179700	Javorov, Jaworow, Yavoriv, Yavorov, Yavoruv	
179740	Javaravas	
179750	Jaworowka, Yavoruvka	
180000	Jolo	
183000	Jalta, Yalta	
183457	Jaltichkov, Jaltuskow, Yaltuchkov, Yaltushkov	
184000	Jalocz, Jelcza, Jelec, Yelets	
184500	Yelsk	
184600	Jelesnia	
184700	Jelsava, Jolsva, Juliszew	
184730	Jalzabet	
184735	Jelissawetgrad, Yelisavetgrod, Yelizavetgradka	
184737	Yelizavetovka	
184785	Yelizavelgrad	
184970	Yelizarov	
185000	Jelka, Juelich, Julich, Yaloch, Yelok	
185700	Jelgava, Yelgava	
185740	Jelechowice, Jelgavas, Jelochowice	
185750	Yelekhovichi	
186000	Jelen, Jelenje, Jelna, Jelnia, Jelno, Yelin, Yelno, Yelnya	
186400	Jeleniec	
186500	Jelonki	
186560	Johlingen, Yelmicheno, Yelmiheno	
186568	Jelonka Mala	
186573	Jelenkowate	
186590	Jelenia Gora	
186700	Jeleniewo	
186750	Yelenovka	
187000	Jahlow, Jalow, Jalowe, Jelewo	
187460	Yalpuzheny	
187500	Jalovka, Jalowka, Yaluvka	
187600	Yaloveny	
187800	Juljopol	
190000	Jauer, Jure	
193140	Jora de Jos	
193440	Jora de Sus	
193450	Yuratishki	
193500	Jurydyka	
193640	Jardanhaza	
193654	Jardanhaza	
193670	Jordanow, Jordanowo, Yordanev, Yordanov	
193684	Jora de Mijloc	
193745	Jaretowskie Pole	
193790	Jartypory	
194000	Jerice, Jeryze, Jurca	
194300	Jarzt	
194400	Jerzyce	
194450	Juraciszki	
194750	Jureczkowa	
194600	Jarocin, Jaroszyn, Jarotschin	
194700	Jaraczew, Jaraczewo, Jaratschewo, Jarczew, Jarczow, Jaryczow, Jaryschew, Yarchev, Yarishev, Yarishevo, Yarishov, Yartchev, Yartsevo, Yaryshev	
194743	Jaryczow Stary	
194750	Yartchovka	
194767	Jaryczow Nowy	
194800	Jarzyly, Jeruzal	
194860	Jeruzalema	
194870	Jaroslav, Jaroslaw, Yaroslav, Yereslev	
194874	Jaroslavice, Jaroslawiec	
194875	Yaroslavka	
195000	Jaruga, Jerchy, Jurki, Yaruga, Yerkhi	
195300	Jurcauti	
195600	Yurcheny	
195639	Jarkendorf	
195700	Jurkow, Yarichuv	
195740	Jarkovac, Yurkovtsy	
195767	Yarichuv Novi, Yarichuv Novy	
195860	Jurkalne	
195864	Jurkalnes	
195900	Yargara, Yargora	
196000	Jarmi	
196175	Jeremjejewka	
196300	Jarnuty	
196374	Jarentowskie Pole	
196400	Jaremcze, Jarnice, Jeremicze, Yeremitcha, Yernyes	
196500	Yaremcha, Yeremichi	
196581	Yermokliya	
196643	Jormannsdorf	
196740	Jaronowice	
196750	Jareniowka, Yarmievka	
196800	Jurmala	
196864	Jarmolince, Yarmolinits, Yarmolintsy, Yarmolintza	
196900	Jaromer	
197000	Juriew, Jurjew, Yuriev, Yuryev	
197100	Yarovoye	
197400	Jarowica, Jarpice, Jurovice, Yuravitch	
197440	Jarewiszcze	
197456	Yurovshchina	
197500	Yurevichi, Yuryevka	
197640	Jarovnice	
197950	Jurborg, Jurburg, Yorburg, Yorvorig, Yurburg	
197954	Jurbarkas, Yurbarkas	
210000	Staje, Staye	
213800	Stojadla	
214000	Stojice	
214450	Stojaciszka, Stojaciszki	
214600	Stojeszyn	
216000	Stoiana	
216400	Stojance, Stoyantse, Stoyantsy	
216700	Stiyanev, Stojanow, Stoyanov, Stoyanuv	
217400	Stojowice	
219000	Stejera	
230000	Shtit, Steti, Stod	
234000	Stadice	
234794	Stadtschwarzach	
234866	Stadtschlaining	
235600	Stadecken, Stadthagen	
235700	Stetkowa, Szczutkow	
235740	Szczotkowice	
235930	Stuttgart	
235935	Stuttgart Cannstadt	
236000	Shchityn, Staden, Stettin, Studena, Studene, Studenne, Studiny, Studna, Szczytno, Szczytyn	
236400	Studzieniec	
236500	Shchetinka, Stitnik, Studzianka, Studzianki	
236539	Studzianki Tartak	
236570	Stadtamhof	
236680	Stydyn Maly	
236700	Stadtamhof	
236746	Studene Vizhne	
236785	Stydyn Velki, Stydyn Wielki	
237000	Stutthof, Sztutowo, Zditovo, Zdzitow	
237956	Stadtbergen	
238000	Staedtel, Stodoly	
238363	Stadtoldendorf	
238397	Stetteldorf, Stetteldorf am Wagram	
238400	Stadlec	
238450	Stodolishche	
238500	Stodolichi	
238600	Stadeln, Stadtlohn, Stodolna	
238631	Statul Nou de Jos	
238654	Stadtlengsfeld	
238965	Stadtlauringen	
239000	Stedra, Stottera	
239439	Stattersdorf	
239544	Szczodrohoszcze	
239545	Shchodrokhoshche	
239590	Shchedrogir	
239600	Shchedrin	
239656	Staudernheim	
239660	Staudernheim	
240000	Zdice, Zdzieci	
244000	Stezyca, Stuzica, Szczucice, Szczyrzyc	
244600	Shtsitsin, Shtsutsin	
245000	Stochek, Stocka, Stoczek, Szczuczki	

245517	Stoczek Gajowka
245700	Zdrzychow
245746	Strzeszkowice Male
245750	Staszkowka
245857	Stoczek Lukowski
246000	Shchutsin, Shtutsin, Stauceni, Stitchin, Stitsin, Stoshany, Stoszany, Strzeszyn, Studzinie, Stutchin, Stutsin, Stuzno, Szczecin, Szczucin, Szczuczyn
246397	Statzendorf
246400	Steznica, Studzieniec
246440	Stizhemeshitz, Stushmishts
246500	Studzianka, Studzianki, Szczecinek
246539	Studzianki Tartak
247000	Stashev, Stashuv, Staszow, Stecowa, Stetseva, Stetsova, Strzyzow
247400	Stacewicze
247640	Shtzovnitz
247930	Stassfurt
248000	Stashule, Staszule
248740	Szczesliwice
249000	Stezery
250000	Stock, Stok, Stoky
254390	Stoki Stare
254600	Shchekotsini, Shtekishin, Shtekotchin, Stakcin, Szczekocin, Szczekociny
255000	Stockach
255600	Shchekochin, Shtekechin
255700	St Chegova
255857	Stochek Lukovski
256000	Shchuchin, Stakein, Steken, Stockheim, Stoicani, Stoykany, Strzegom, Stuchin
256800	Stoki Male
257000	Shtehkeva, Stachov, Stachow, Stakhovo, Stokov, Strzegowo, Strzygov, Stykow, Szczakowa, Szczechowo, Zdikov
257400	Stechovice, Szczukowice, Zdechovice, Zdechovitz, Zdechowitz, Zdziechowice
257455	Szczukowskie Gorki
258400	Szczeglice
258439	Steckelsdorf
258450	Shtoklishok, Stok Lacki, Stoklishok
258454	Stakliskes, Stakliskis
258460	Szczeglacin
258474	Stehelceves
258596	Szczygly Gorne
258600	Stackeln, Szczeglin
258650	Steklinek
259000	Shchigry, Stockerau
259450	Stok Ruski
259470	Szczekarzewo
259475	Stegersbach
259500	St Gheorghe
260000	Stany, Stein, Stiene, Stina, Stuhm, Sztum, Zdana, Zdonia, Zduny, Zdynia, Zdzanne
263000	Steinhude, Stende
263500	Staniatki
263600	Stenden, Steniatyn, Stenyatin
263800	Stendal
264000	Shchenets, Steinitz, Szczeniec, Zdanice
264300	Staneshti, Stanesti
264313	Stanestii de Jos pe Ceremus, Stanestii de Sus pe Ceremus, Stanestii de Zhos

264334	Staneshti de Sus, Staneshti de Zhos
264400	Stanisic, Strzemieszyce, Stumishts
264478	Strzemieszyce Wielkie
264578	Zdunska Vola, Zdunska Volye, Zdunska Wola, Zdunske Volye
264600	Stanceni, Stinceni
264670	Steinhausen Bielsk Podlaski
264700	Staniszewo
264745	Staniszewskie
264793	Steinsfurt
264800	Stana Salaj, Stanislau, Stanisle, Stanislo, Zdzhentsiol
264844	Stanislaucic
264870	Stanislav
264874	Stanislavchik, Stanislavcik, Stanislavtchik, Stanislawczyk
264877	Stanislavov, Stanislavuvka, Stanislawow, Stanislawow Duzy, Stanislawowka, Stanislowow
265000	Stainach, Stangau, Steinach, Stinka, Stsyanka, Zdounek, Zdounky
265300	Steinhude
265363	Stanke Dimitrov
265400	Sztankocz
265467	Steinhausen Bielsk Podlaski
265600	Stammheim, Steinheim
265639	Steinach an der Saale
265650	Stangenhagen
265655	Stangenhagen
265666	Steinheim am Main
265679	Stinkenbrunn
265700	Stankov, Stankova, Stankowa
265740	Stankovce, Stankovice
265930	Steinhart
266000	Stammheim, Stanin, Steinheim
266390	Steinau am Oder
266393	Stein an der Donau
266500	Stanimaka
266559	Stein am Kocher
266659	Steinamanger
266660	Steinheim am Main
266800	Stany Male
266940	Stanimirz
267000	Stomfa, Strzynew, Stynawa, Zdanow, Zhdanov
267169	Stein bei Nurnberg
267400	Stenovice, Zdanowice
267500	Steinbach
267560	Stein Bockenheim
267563	Steinbach am Donnersberg
267565	Stein Bockenheim, Steinbach am Glan
267571	Steinbach bei Hall
267600	Stampfen, Stempina
267646	Stynawa Nizna
267930	Steinfurth
267950	Steinberg, Steinbruch
267956	Steinbergen
267957	Stomporkov
268000	Steimel
268400	Strzemilcze
268600	Stommeln
268750	Staneleviche
269300	Steinhart
270000	Shtip, Staw, Stip, Stoob, Strzewo, Szczawa, Szczawo, Zdow
271600	Shtubiyeny

273000	St Veit
273400	Shcheptitsy
273600	Szczepiatyn
273947	St.Petersburg
274000	Shtoptsi, Stavische, Stawce, Stawisza, Steibtz, Steypts, Stoibtz, Stopts, Stoybts, Stoypts, Stoyvetz
274300	Stoptchet
274370	Stopczatow
274400	Stawiszcze, Stepocice
274460	Stipshausen, Szczebrzeszyn
274500	Stavechki, Stavishcha, Stavishche, Stavisk, Staviska, Staviski, Stavochki, Staweczki, Stawiski
274560	Stavishchany
274600	Stavishin, Stawczany, Stawiszyn, Stuposiany
274740	Zdebuzeves
275000	Stavki, Stavok, Stawek, Stawki, Stebbach, Steppach, Stubig, Stupki
275370	Stopchatuv
275594	Stavki Krasnenske, Stawki Krasninskie
275600	Stavchany
275645	Stobiecko Miejskie
275700	Stabichov, Stefkowa, Stepkow, Stobychwa, Stobykhva
276000	Shtabin, Staufen, Stavna, Stebne, Stebni, Stefan, Stepan, Stepina, Stiubieni, Stopini, Stubno, Szczawin, Szczawne, Szczepan, Sztabin, Sztawna
276100	Stavnoye
276380	St Wendel
276400	Shchavnits, Stabnits, Stepancy, Stepantsy, Stepnitz, Stopnica, Stopnits, Stopnitsa, Stovnitz, Stoybnits, Szczawnica
276430	Shtefaneshty, Stefanesti
276434	Stefanesti Soroca
276456	Steffenshagen
276470	Szczepancowa
276474	Shchavnitsa Vizhna
276500	Stebnik, Stepanchi, Stepanki, Stubienko, Szczawnik, Szczepanek
276556	Stavenhagen
276559	Szczawnica Kroscienko
276560	Stavenhagen
276564	Szczawnica Nizna
276570	Szczepankowo
276574	Staw Noakowski, Stefankowice, Stepankowice, Szczawnica Wyzna
276593	Stepangorod, Stepangrod
276645	Stubnianske Teplice
276700	Szczepanow
276740	Szczepanowice
276795	Staufenberg
277000	Stupava
277450	Stawowiczki
278300	Shcheploty, Szczeploty
278360	St Palten
278364	St Poelten Stadt
278436	Staffelstein
278500	Stablack
278700	Steblev, Steblova
278750	Steblevka
279000	Stoboru

279460	Shchebreshin, Szczebrzeszyn	
279500	Szczeberka	
279570	Staporkow	
279600	Stobierna, Szczypiorno	
279780	Stavropol	
280000	Stale, Zdala	
283600	Szczelatyn	
284000	Strzelce, Strzelcza, Strzylcze	
284450	Strzelczyska	
284500	Strzeliska, Strzelsk, Stulsko	
284510	Stilskoye	
284543	Strzeliska Stare, Stsheliska Stare	
284567	Strzeliska Nowe	
284591	Strzelce Krajenskie	
284600	Stolzenau, Strzelecin	
284784	Strzelce Opolskie	
284785	Strzelce Wielkie	
285000	Strzalki, Strzylki	
285700	Strzalkow	
285740	Strzalkowce, Stshalkovtse	
285760	Stollhofen	
286000	Stalin, Stalino, Stalnia, Stolany, Stolin, Stolno, Strzelin, Strzelno, Stulany, Stulln, Stulno	
286364	Stalin Donezk	
286397	Stalindorf	
286430	Stalinesti	
286450	Stalinsk	
286460	Stolniceni	
286500	Stolniki	
286560	Stolnichany, Stolnicheny, Stuhlingen	
286593	Stalingrad, Stalinogrod	
286740	Stalnovtsy	
286794	Sztalinvaros	
287000	Stahlavy, Stolp, Stolpe	
287400	Stolbtsy, Stolbtzi, Stolevitch, Stolowicze, Stolowitschi, Stolpts, Strzelbic, Stshelbitse, Zdolbica, Zdolbitsa, Zdzilowice	
287467	Stuhlweissenburg	
287500	Stelbach, Stolovichi	
287560	Stulpicani	
287600	Stalownia, Stollhofen, Stolpno	
287660	Stalluponen	
287670	Zdolbunov, Zdolbunow	
287780	Stalowa Wola	
290000	Stara, Stare, Steyr, Stri, Stria, Stry, Stryj, Stryje, Stryy, Zdar, Zdiar, Zdzar	
291000	Straja, Zdroje	
291178	Staraya Yablona	
291186	Staraya Yelenovka	
291197	Stariy Yarov	
291347	Staraya Dashevka	
291440	Staraya Ushitsa	
291467	Staraya Sinyava	
291480	Staraya Sol, Staroye Selo	
291493	Staraya Sarata	
291495	Staraya Tsarichanka	
291538	Staraya Kotelnya	
291574	Staraya Kobuska	
291585	Staraya Chelakovka	
291630	Storojinet, Storojineti	
291745	Staraya Ves Gorby	
291753	Staraya Bogdanovka	
291794	Staraya Obrezha	
291936	Staraya Rudnja, Staraya Rudnya	
291940	Staraya Russa	
293000	Zdrody	
293439	Zdrody Stare	
293600	Sterdin, Sterdyn, Stradom, Stratin, Stratyn, Stretin, Strutin	
293630	Stordjinet	
293637	Streda nad Bodrog, Streda nad Bodrogom, Streda nad Bodrok, Streda nad Bodrokom	
293647	Staryye Tomashevtsy	
293650	Stradomka	
293664	Stratyn Miasto, Stratyn Myasto	
293674	Stredna Apsa, Stredni Apsa	
293700	Shtirotava, Staridob, Starodub	
293800	Stara Dala	
293840	Stradlice	
293900	Stara Tura	
293950	Stary Targ, Starya Dorogi, Starye Dorogi, Staryye Dorogi	
294000	Shcherets, Shchirets, Shchors, Starciu, Stirciu, Straz, Stroza, Stroze, Strusy, Struza, Szczerec, Szczyrzyc	
294300	Strazde	
294360	Strazdenhof	
294364	Strazdemuiza, Strazdu Mujzha, Strazdumuiza	
294365	Strazdenhof	
294370	Stare Stawy	
294374	Starostwo Zwolen	
294380	Straszydle	
294400	Shtcherzetz, Stary Sacz, Sterzyca, Straschitz, Strasice, Szczerzec, Zdziarzec	
294439	Zdrody Stare	
294460	Sterzhausen, Straszecin	
294469	Strass Somerein	
294500	Strazske	
294565	Strassgang	
294570	Stary Dzikow	
294574	Starzechowice, Strzeszkowice Male	
294580	Stary Oskol, Staryy Oskol	
294590	Stara Zagora, Stara Zagura	
294600	Staroscin, Strascheny, Straseni, Strasheny, Strecno, Streczyn, Streshin, Struzna, Strzeszyn, Sturdzeny, Sztrecsen	
294630	Stordjinet	
294635	Sturzeni Tighina	
294640	Starzenice, Storozhinets, Storozynetz, Strassnitz, Straznice, Strizinitz, Strozynetz	
294667	Streczyn Nowy	
294670	Starczynow	
294678	Sturzeni Balti	
294679	Stary Sambor, Staryy Sambor	
294680	Stroze Male	
294690	Strezimir	
294700	Shtchertzov, Starzawa, Stertzev, Storozhov, Storozhuv, Storozow, Strasov, Strazow, Strisev, Strishuv, Strisov, Strizev, Strizhuv, Strizov, Strusov, Strusow, Stryszawa, Stryszow, Strzyzow, Szczercow, Szczerczewo	
294714	Strezivojice	
294734	Starczewo Duze	
294740	Starczewice, Stari Sivac, Strashevitse, Straszewice	
294746	Stroze Wyzne	
294750	Strizhavka, Strozowka	
294778	Starczewo Wielkie	
294795	Strassburg, Strausberg	
294800	Stara Siol, Stara Sol, Stare Selo, Stare Siolo, Staroselia, Staroselja, Staroselye	
294840	Starosielce	
294870	Stara Slupia	
294879	Sturzelberg	
294936	Staryye Sarateny	
294970	Starozreby	
295000	Stariki, Striegau, Szczyrk	
295300	Stara Huta	
295400	Zdrochec	
295450	Starokazachye	
295456	Staryye Kitskany	
295460	Stara Kuznia, Strachocina	
295464	Stara Kuznica	
295564	Staryye Kukoneshty	
295594	Struchi Krasnye	
295600	Strzegom	
295640	Stara Kanjiza, Strakonice, Strychance, Strygantse	
295643	Starokonstantinov, Starokonstantynow, Storchnest	
295660	Starokamienna	
295679	Starkenburg	
295700	Shcherchevo, Starkov, Storkow, Strekov, Strigovo, Strikov, Strychowo, Strykow, Strzegowo, Strzygov, Zdrzychow	
295740	Starachowice, Starakhovits, Sterkowitz, Strachovitza, Strkovice	
295750	Strachowka, Strichevka	
295759	Strekowa Gora	
295794	Stregoborzyce	
295930	Stargard, Starogard, Sterkrade	
295934	Stargard Szczecinski	
295935	Starogard Gdanski	
295939	Staryy Chartoriysk	
295947	Stary Harcov	
295960	Stary Krim, Staryy Krym, Strugureni	
295966	Stary Kornin	
295975	Staryye Choropkany	
296000	Starna, Starunia, Stirin, Storona, Stranny, Strojno, Stronie, Stronna, Sztarnya, Sztrojna	
296390	Stramtura, Strimtere, Strimtura	
296397	Storndorf	
296400	Strenci, Strenice, Stromiec, Strumica	
296430	Stare Miasto	
296439	Stronsdorf	
296440	Strancice, Strzemieszyce	
296444	Staromieszczyzna	
296447	Strzemieszyce Wielkie	
296479	Staryy Nizhborok	
296500	Starinka, Starinki, Strencu, Strumok	
296545	Stromiec Zagajnik	
296567	Stari Mikanovci	
296575	Strumkovka	
296596	Staryye Negureny	
296600	Stranany, Strumien, Sztrainyan	
296617	Staromamayevtsy	
296700	Staroniwa, Stramba, Strimba, Strymba, Strzynew	
296758	Strumbagalve, Strumbaglow	
296770	Stronibaby	
296771	Strambu Baiutului, Strimbu Baiut	
296787	Strumpfelbrunn	
296795	Starnberg, Sternberg, Sternberg Barntrup, Sternberk	

296840	Stremiltsh, Strzemilcze	311786	Daujoji Vilnia	338749	Dittlofsroda
296870	Strmilov, Strumilova	314000	Teius	338750	Dettelbach, Dyatlovichi
296974	Stara Moravica	314370	Dojazdow	338763	Doudleby nad Orlici
297000	Staryava, Straupe, Strba, Stryhowo, Strzewo, Szczurowa	316000	Daujenai, Dauyen, Taujenai	339000	Dejtar, Deter, Detter, Ditrau, Ditro, Dudar, Tatary,
297300	Starobud	319000	Dijir		Teodory
297370	Streptov, Streptow	330000	Dad, Deda, Deta, Detta, Doda, Tata, Taut, Tauteu, Tet, Toti	339300	Datterode
297394	Staryy Badrazh	331344	Tautii de Sus	339400	Toiteres, Tuteres
297400	Shchurovitse, Shtervitz, Shtruvits, Stara Vies, Stara Wies, Starawies, Strupice, Szczurowice	331700	Tetiyev	339430	Tataresti
		333600	Dytiatyn	339433	Duderstadt
		333794	Tatatovaros	339450	Tatarsk
297439	Stara Bystrica, Stare Bystre	333860	Tetetlen	339457	Teodorsgof
297440	Strupcice	334000	Dedes, Tatce, Theodosia, Totis, Tutos	339463	Tatarszentgyorgy
297450	Staryye Peski, Strwiazyk			339470	Teodorshof, Theodorshof
297460	Strawczyn	334397	Dedesdorf	339476	Ditterswind
297470	Stara Pazova	334468	Dzieduszyce Male	339500	Tatarka
297495	Stara Wies Rychwalska	334478	Dzieduszyce Wielkie	339534	Ditrohodas
297500	Shchurovichi, Stara Paka, Stryjowka, Sztropko	334600	Deidesheim	339574	Tatar Copceac, Tudorkovitse, Tudorkowice
		334950	Totgyork		
297570	Shcherbakov, Staryi Bykhov, Strabicovo, Stropkov, Strupiechow, Strupkow, Strupkuv	335000	Dedga, Dedukhi, Detek, Detk, Tadaiki	339586	Dederkaly Male
		335400	Tatahaza	339700	Tatarow, Teterow
		335600	Tetcani	339740	Tatarovca
		335684	Totkomlos	339749	Tatar Pazardzhik
297600	Starobin, Strobin	335700	Dyatkovo	339750	Tatarovka
297639	Staryye Fundury	335740	Dedkovitchu, Diatkowice, Didkovitch, Didkovitz, Dyatkovtse, Dyatkovtsy, Dziatkowicze	339769	Tatar Bunar, Tatarbunary
297650	Shcherbanka, Straubing			339800	Tatarlaua
297670	Shcherbinovo, Szczerbinowo			340000	Decs, Des, Dessau, Desze, Deutz, Dicio, Dicso, Diez, Dosha, Tac, Tass, Teaca, Teci, Tecs, Tecso, Teis, Teitz, Tes, Tesa, Tetche, Tetchea, Tetsh, Tosie, Tussa, Tutz, Tuzhe
297674	Stari Banovci				
297700	Strobow				
297745	Strubowiska	335750	Dyadkovichi		
297800	Strabla	336000	Datyn, Tadanie, Tadany, Tadten, Tauteni, Tauteny, Teteny, Tetin, Tutin		
297845	Stare Bielsko, Starobel Sk, Starobelsk, Starobielsk, Starobyelsk				
		336300	Dihtinet, Dihtineti	341963	Deutsch Jahrndorf
		336350	Didymoteikhou, Didymotihou	343000	Diosod, Dusetai, Dusetoi, Dusiat, Dusjaty, Dusyat, Tisauti, Tist, Tost, Touste, Toyst, Tust, Tuyst
297850	Zdzary Wielkie, Zdziar Wielki	336400	Dettensee		
297856	Staryye Bilicheny	336460	Dettenhausen		
297864	Staro Poljance	336546	Dettenhausen		
297865	Stara Palanka	336560	Dettingen, Deutenheim, Dietenheim, Dittenheim, Dottenheim	343300	Tiszadada, Tostedt
297900	Stribro			343400	Dusetos
297930	Stare Brody			343570	Tesedikovo
297940	Sterbfritz	336576	Dietenhofen, Dudenhofen	343587	Tustoglowy
297964	Staryye Brynzeny	336600	Deutenheim, Dittenheim, Dottenheim	343600	Destna, Tiszaadony
297965	Stribrniky			343640	Destnice
298000	Stralo	336665	Tittmoning	343674	Tustanovitse, Tustanowice
298400	Strelitz, Strzelce, Strzelcza, Strzylcze	336700	Datnuva, Dotnava, Dotneva, Dotnuva, Tetyanov	343700	Tiszadob
				343770	Toustobaby
298445	Strzelczyska	336760	Dudenhofen	343795	Tisztaberek
298450	Strelisk, Streliske, Strelsk, Strzeliska, Strzelsk	336783	Dattenfeld	343800	Duzy Dol
		336795	Diedenbergen	343934	Tiszatardos
298454	Strzeliska Stare	336830	Detmold	343940	Tiszaderzs
298456	Strzeliska Nowe	336956	Dautmergen	343956	Tiszadorogma
298459	Strzelce Krajenskie	337000	Dautova, Dedova, Detva, Dydiowa, Tetiev, Tetov	343960	Tiszatarjan
298460	Strzelecin			343970	Teesdorf
298463	Stralsund	337400	Tutowicze	344000	Dacice, Dasice, Datschitz, Daudzese, Deshaza, Dozice, Dziedzice, Taszyce, Tisice, Tusice
298478	Strzelce Opolskie, Strzelce Wielkie	337439	Deda Bisztra		
		337440	Tetewczyce, Titovo Uzice		
298500	Strelki, Strzalki, Strzylki	337460	Totvazsony		
298546	Stary Oleksiniec, Staryy Oleksinets	337500	Tutovichi	344300	Desest, Desesti
		337540	Tetevchitse	344369	Dicio St Martin
298570	Strzalkow	337600	Tatabanya, Tytavenai, Tytuvenai	344395	Tiszaszederkeny
298574	Strzalkowce	337640	Totbanhegyes	344400	Tiszacsecse, Tiszasas
298600	Straelen, Strehlen, Strelna, Strelno, Strzelin, Strzelno	337654	Totbanhegyes	344500	Tiszacsege, Toczyska
		337784	Titov Veles	344635	Tetszentkut
298676	Staryye Limbeny	337800	Totfalu, Totujfalu	344636	Dicsoszentmarton, Tiszaszentimre, Tiszaszentmarton, Totszentmarton
298740	Strzelbic	338000	Titel		
298750	Strilbichi	338400	Tautelec		
298776	Stara Lubovna	338460	Diedelsheim, Dudelsheim		
299360	Staryye Redeny	338500	Tottelek	344646	Deutsch Tschantschendorf
299386	Staryye Radulyany	338600	Datteln	344760	Tisza Szipma
299400	Starya Russa	338656	Tuttlingen	344800	Tiszasuly
299650	Stary Rynek	338700	Dedilov, Doudleby, Dyatlovo	344840	Tiszazollas, Tiszazollos
300000	Dej, Doh	338740	Dziatlowicze	344850	Tiszaszalka
310000	Daia, Deja				

344890	Tiszaeszlar	346670	Tuczyn Nowy
344935	Totszerdahely	346700	Dusanov, Dusanow, Tesenfa
345000	Deszk, Diosig, Dioszeg, Taska,	346735	Disznopataka
	Teczki, Thishky, Tiska, Tiszaug,	346740	Dezanovac, Tesanovci
	Toczek, Tosok, Toszeg, Toszek,	346750	Dietzenbach
	Tuska, Tuske, Tusko	346900	Dezmer, Dezmir
345148	Detskoye Selo	347000	Dachev, Dascova, Dasev,
345400	Tiszakeszi		Dashava, Dashev, Dashiev,
345450	Tiszakecske		Daszawa, Dezhov, Dydiowa,
345463	Tuskeszentpeter		Taczow, Tczew, Tesov, Tesow,
345500	Tisachege		Tiacevo, Tiachev, Tiaczowo,
345543	Tyszki Gostery		Tisova, Tiszabo, Tuczapy,
345600	Desakna, Tetskany		Tuszow, Tyachev, Tysov
345640	Dezginzhe	347164	Tiszafeyeenyhaz
345650	Dezghinge	347300	Tiszabud, Tiszavid
345690	Tiszakanyar	347350	Diospatak
345700	Dyczkow, Dyshkovo, Teskov,	347400	Dusowce, Tishevits, Tishevitz,
	Tushkuv, Tuszkow, Tyskowa		Tishovits, Tishovtse, Tishvits,
345740	Daszkiewicze, Deszkowice,		Tishvitz, Tisovec, Tiszabecs,
	Dzietrzkowice, Tyshkovtse,		Toshvitse, Tyszowce, Tyszviec
	Tyshkovtsy, Tyszkowce	347433	Tiszabezded
345750	Daschkowka, Dashkavka,	347475	Tiszapuspoki
	Dashkeviche, Dashkevichi,	347479	Tiszavasvari
	Dashkovka	347480	Diosviszlo
345796	Tosokberend	347485	Tiszaabadszalok
345800	Dioskal	347500	Daszowka, Diespeck
345836	Deutsch Kaltenbrunn	347536	Tiszabogdany
345900	Tiszaigar	347596	Deutsch Wagram
345930	Tiszakarad, Tiszakorod, Tiszakurt	347693	Tuszow Narodowy
345940	Deutschkreitz, Deutschkreutz	347700	Dyszobaba
345946	Tiszakaracsonfalva,	347786	Tiszababolna
	Tiszakerecseny	347800	Tiszaujfalu
345960	Tescureni, Teshkureny	347837	Tiszafoldvar
345964	Diz Gramzda	347850	Tiszavalk, Tuzha Velka
346000	Dausenau, Decin, Desna, Deszno,	347856	Tiszapalkonya
	Diessen, Diosjeno, Disna,	347859	Tiszapolgar
	Disne, Dysina, Dzieczyna,	347900	Tiszabura, Tiszavere
	Tagyon, Tauseni, Teosin,	347930	Tiszafured
	Tesanj, Teschen, Teshin, Tesin,	347936	Deutsch Wartenberg
	Tessin, Titchin, Tosno, Tousen,	347946	Tiszaveresmart
	Touzim, Tuczna, Tuczno,	347948	Tiszabercel
	Tuczyn, Tushin, Tuszyma,	347950	Daseburg, Duisburg
	Tuszyn, Tutchin, Tutsin, Tyczyn	347953	Tiszaborkut
346100	Disznajo	347956	Tiszavarkony
346300	Tashnad, Tasnad	347959	Duisburg Ruhrort
346360	Tasnadu Nou	348000	Dassel, Deisel, Deutsch Eylau,
346361	Desantnoye		Diszel, Dzieciol, Thessaly,
346378	Tasnad Blaja, Tausendblum		Tuzla, Tuzly
346400	Desenice, Desznica, Teceu Mic,	348360	Tiszaladany
	Tisinec, Tisinyecz, Tismice,	348397	Dusseldorf
	Titchinitz	348400	Taslac, Teslic, Tiszaluc
346430	Disznosd	348440	Dziasloszyce
346445	Tesin Cesky	348500	Tisza Ujlak, Tiszalok, Tiszaluk
346460	Deisenhausen, Tussenhausen	348650	Thessaloniki, Tiszalonka
346463	Tasnadszanto	348700	Dziedzilow, Tuzhiluv, Tuzylow
346480	Teschenmoschel	349000	Diosgyor, Dizser, Taszar,
346494	Tiszamogyoros		Tuzora, Tuzser
346497	Disznoshorvat	349300	Tiszarad
346500	Disneg, Duschnik, Dusniky,	349400	Tiszaors
	Dusnok, Dzietrzniki, Tesmag,	349634	Tesare nad Zitavou
	Tesmak, Tiszainoka, Tutzing	349700	Tiszaroff
346546	Deisenhausen, Tussenhausen	349865	Tisralunka
346560	Dossenheim	350000	Dachau, Daka, Daug, Daugai,
346574	Tscenkowic		Daugi, Deg, Doaga, Doge,
346578	Tiszanagyfalu		Doig, Doyg, Duka, Tachau,
346597	Tutchin Kripah		Taga, Tech, Teghea, Teke,
346600	Dossenheim, Dusmani, Dziecinin,		Ticau, Ticha, Ticu, Tigau,
	Tiszanana		Tiha, Tihau, Tokaj, Tokay,
346640	Tismenitz, Tizmenitza,		Toki, Tycha, Tychy
	Tysmenitsa, Tysmienica	353000	Dagda, Dagde, Tohat, Tokod,
346643	Tatzmannsdorf		Tyukod
346646	Tysmieniczany	353378	Tahitotfalu
346656	Tysmenichany	353400	Dagdas

353430	Taktaszada
353563	Dhidhimotikon
353564	Taktakenez
353595	Taktaharkany
353600	Tiktin, Tuktin
353630	Dhidhimotikon
353640	Dikhtenets
353700	Dokudow
353845	Taktalachik
353974	Toke Terebes, Toketerebes
354000	Takacsi, Takos, Tecuci,
	Tekucza, Tigheci, Tocuz,
	Tokuz
354300	Duksht
354340	Dukstas, Dukstos
354400	Dokshits, Dokshitse, Dokshitsy,
	Dokshitsya, Dokshitz,
	Dugscitz
354430	Dukszty
354440	Dokszyce
354460	Deksznie
354600	Diuksyn, Doksany, Dyuksin,
	Taksony, Tikotsin, Tykocin,
	Tykotsin
354700	Duchcov
354750	Dachsbach
354800	Dugo Selo
355000	Tekucha, Tigech
355400	Tekehaza
356000	Tehinia, Tighina, Tiginia,
	Tihany, Tuchan, Tuchanie,
	Tuchin, Tuchne, Tuchume,
	Tuckum, Tukkum, Tukum
356100	Dignaja
356397	Deggendorf, Teckendorf
356400	Duchnice, Tagancza, Tahantcha,
	Techonice, Ticheniz, Tiganasi,
	Tukkums, Tukums
356430	Tiganesti
356431	Tiganestii de Cris
356500	Doging, Dziekanka, Tagancha,
	Tikhinichi, Toging, Tokmak
356560	Deggingen, Dockingen
356600	Takonin
356700	Dachnow, Duchnow, Dziekanow
356750	Dakhnovichi
356766	Dziekanow Niemiecki
356778	Dziekanow Polski
356950	Taganrog
357000	Dakovo, Daugava, Dikow,
	Djakovo, Tachov, Tachovo,
	Tacovo, Tiacheva, Tuchapy,
	Tuchov, Tuchow
357350	Tichy Potok
357400	Diakovce, Techobuz, Tehovec,
	Tochovice, Touchovice,
	Tuchowicz, Tuchowicze
357437	Dogwizdow
357454	Tekovske Sarluzky
357456	Dukhovshchina
357458	Tekovske Luzany, Tekovske
	Luzianicy
357500	Tukhovichi
357600	Tikhvin
357800	Ducka Wola
357840	Daugapils, Daugavpils
357940	Tegoborze
357958	Tiha Birgaului
358000	Daugailiai, Dikla, Dukla, Tokol,
	Tuchel, Tuchla, Tuchola,
	Tukhlya
358400	Teglas
358450	Daugeliszki

358500	Tucholka	364400	Dancshaza, Dencshaza, Dnesice, Domousice	365656	Dungenheim	
358600	Tuchlin			365660	Dungenheim	
359000	Dukor, Dukora, Tagara, Tokary	364460	Dondyushany	365700	Danichuv, Dankow, Denkow, Domacheva, Domacheve, Domachevo, Domachuv, Dunkov, Dziunkow	
359300	Tahert	364500	Danzig, Donetsk, Dunaszeg, Dyniska			
359400	Duga Resa, Takaros, Tuchorice	364540	Dunaszekcso			
359436	Takarostanya	364543	Dunajska Streda			
359478	Tuchersfeld	364558	Dniestrzyk Holowiecki	365740	Dankovtsy, Dunkowice, Timkovitz	
359600	Taharin	364559	Donji Skugric			
359700	Ducherow, Dukrowo	364570	Tomasikovo	365745	Dunkowiczki	
359736	Diguri Putna	364574	Deniskowicze	365750	Denkowek, Timkovichi	
359783	Tigerfeld	364575	Deniskovichi	365783	Thungfeld	
360000	Dahn, Dainiai, Dany, Demnia, Demnya, Dno, Domnau, Tamna, Tann, Tenje, Thann, Thum, Tinnye, Tomai, Tome, Tonie, Tume, Tynne	364578	Dinskivola	365830	Dunakiliti	
		364593	Tomashgorod, Tomaszgrod	365847	Dinkelsbuhl	
		364600	Danceni, Domacyny, Domaszno, Tamaseni, Thannhausen, Thonischen	365865	Dinglingen	
				365876	Dingolfing	
				365900	Dankera, Dankere, Dymokury	
361000	Tamaia, Tynnoye	364634	Dunaszentgyorgy	365930	Donji Grad	
361400	Dunayets	364636	Danszentmiklos	365936	Damgarten	
361700	Dunajow, Dunayev, Duneiav	364637	Dunaszentbenedek	365943	Dunaharaszti	
361740	Dunajevcy, Dunayevitz, Dunayevtsy	364639	Deinzendorf	365966	Tangermunde	
		364650	Tenczynek	366000	Dainjenai, Damieni, Demene, Demmin, Domnin, Domony, Dziemiany, Dziemionna, Tman, Tomina, Tumin	
363000	Demete, Demjata, Dinauti, Tahnauti, Tentea, Tinaud	364656	Donaueschingen			
		364665	Donji Zemunik			
363430	Dindesti	364700	Daniczow, Denysow, Domaczewo, Domaczow, Domashov, Domashuv, Domaszow, Domatcheva, Domatchov, Temeszow, Tomashav, Tomaszow	366360	Dominteni, Dominteny	
363450	Teniatyska			366378	Tyn nad Vltavou	
363460	Dondusani, Dondyushany			366400	Damenice, Damienice, Demenyhaza, Dunamocs, Tymienica	
363465	Dondosani Gara					
363500	Demotika, Dundaga					
363540	Dundagas			366430	Damienesti, Domanesti	
363570	Domatkow			366436	Diemantstein	
363650	Tenetniki	364740	Daniszewice, Tomaszowce, Tomaszowice	366450	Demyansk	
363700	Dantova, Demidov, Demidow, Demiduv			366474	Domanjsevci, Domanjsovci	
		364745	Domaszewska Wolka	366479	Demantsfurth	
363740	Dimidovca	364746	Domaszowce Nowe	366480	Domamysl	
363744	Demidowszyzna	364750	Dunsbach, Tamsweg, Tomashevka, Tomaszowek, Tomaszowka	366500	Demenka	
363745	Demidovshchina, Demidovshchyzna			366543	Tymienica Stara	
				366584	Donji Miholjac	
363750	Dandowka, Demidovka, Demidowka, Demiduvka	364753	Tomashov Khadash	366600	Dmenin, Dminin	
		364764	Domaszewnica, Tomashuv Mazovyetsk, Tomashuv Mazovyetski, Tomaszow Mazowiecki	366700	Damianow, Domanowo, Duninow	
363797	Donja Dubrava					
363860	Dentlein			366734	Duninow Duzy	
363866	Dentlein am Forst			366740	Domanovca, Domonovca	
363900	Domotori, Tanatari, Tanatary	364773	Tomashov Pyetirkov, Tomashuv Pyetirkov, Tomaszow Piotrkov	366743	Domanowo Stare	
363917	Dmitriyevka			366750	Domanevka, Dumanovka	
363930	Dumitrita	364780	Danczypol, Tomashpol	366767	Duninow Nowy	
363960	Dumitreni, Tundern	364787	Tomashov Lublinski, Tomashuv Lubelski, Tomaszow Lubelski	366850	Dennenlohe	
363963	Tantareni Tighina			366867	Donji Milanovac	
363969	Tantareni Orehi	364790	Temesvar	367000	Dabie, Dambia, Dambye, Damnov, Deba, Debie, Dinov, Dombe, Dombie, Dombo, Dombye, Domnovo, Dunaiv, Dynow, Tomawa, Tonovo, Tonowo, Tymowa	
363970	Dmitriev, Dmitrov, Dmytrow, Thundorf	364791	Temesvar Josefvaras			
		364794	Temesvar Gyarvaros			
363973	Dymitrow Duzy	364797	Tomashov Ravski, Tomaszow Rawski			
363974	Dimitravas, Dmitrovsk, Dmitrovsk Orlovskiy, Dmytrowice					
		364800	Domoszlo			
		364840	Domazlice			
363975	Dmitrovka, Dmitrowka	364850	Deneslak	367178	Tann bei Fulda	
363976	Dymitrow Maly, Thundorf in Unterfranken	364856	Dinslaken	367300	Dunapataj	
		364900	Demecser, Domazhir, Domazyr, Timisoara, Timiszora	367350	Danpataka	
363978	Demeterfalva			367374	Donji Vidovec	
364000	Damice, Damis, Damoc, Demycze, Domashe, Domasze, Domitz, Domos, Domosu, Dzianisz, Tamasa, Tamaseu, Tamasi, Tancs, Taunus, Teunz, Tinca, Tinets, Tonciu, Tuhnice, Tumizh, Tynec, Tynice, Tyniec			367400	Dabaca, Dabas, Dahnovici, Danowice, Debica, Debicze, Debitsa, Dembica, Dembits, Dembitsa, Dembitz, Dembiza, Denevitz, Dinewitz, Dinovits, Dinovitz, Dinovtsy, Dunavecse, Dunovits, Tyniowice	
		364935	Duna Szerdahely, Dunaszerdahely			
		364954	Temesrekas			
		365000	Damak, Dancu, Danku, Donieck, Dunika, Tenk, Tenke, Tunyog			
364300	Domsod, Tamasda, Tammiste, Tammistu, Tyniste	365300	Dancauti, Domahida, Tengod			
364315	Danestii Chioarului	365400	Domokos, Dunaegyhaza, Dunakeszi	367437	Tompeshti Vek	
364317	Tomestii Vechi			367457	Debska Wola	
364330	Dannstadt	365460	Damacuseni, Thannhausen	367460	Debrzno	
364350	Tynistko	365584	Donji Caglic	367468	Tyniewicze Male	
364370	Domostawa	365586	Dmochy Glinki	367470	Tempoczow	
364374	Donja Stubica	365600	Dancheny, Dienheim, Dimacheni, Thungen, Tiengen	367478	Tyniewicze Wielkie	
364395	Dniestrzyk Holowiecki	365634	Tynec nad Sazavou	367487	Debeslavtse, Debeslawce	

438

367500	Dabki, Dambach, Debeikiai, Demievka, Donbki
367540	Dombegyhaz
367570	Donji Vakuf
367600	Dabjon, Debina, Debna, Debno, Dembina, Dembno, Tamaveni
367638	Dunapentele
367640	Debienica
367643	Dabie Miasto
367650	Debnik, Debniki, Dembinka
367700	Debow, Debowa, Dziembowo
367740	Debowce, Debowica, Debowiec
367784	Deby Wolskie
367785	Dab Wielki, Debe Wielkie
367790	Dombovar
367800	Dompole
367830	Domefolde, Tanvald
367837	Dunafoldvar
367840	Debeljaca
367860	Deblin, Demblin, Templin
367879	Tempelburg
367900	Daber, Debur
367930	Debrad, Debrod, Dombrad, Donauworth
367934	Dombiratos
367939	Dnieprodzierzynsk
367940	Damborice, Damboritz, Debrisch, Dunaujvaros
367946	Debercseny, Deborzyn, Debrecen, Debretsin
367949	Dneprodzerzhinsk, Dnieprodzierzynsk, Dnyeprodzerzinsk
367950	Dinaburg, Dinnyeberki, Duenaburg, Dunaberg, Dunaburg, Timborg, Tymbark
367958	Tina Bargaului, Tina Birgaului
367960	Debren
367964	Dabronc
367970	Dabrowa, Dombrova, Dombrove, Dziembrow
367973	Dabrowa Tarnowska, Dabrowa Tworki, Dnepropetrovsk, Dniepropetrovsk
367974	Dabrovica, Dabrowa Dzieciel, Dabrowa Szlachecka, Dabrowica, Dabrowice, Dabrowiece, Dambrovitsa, Dombrovits, Dombrovitsa, Dombrovitza
367975	Dabrova Gornicha, Dabrowa Gornicza, Dabrowa K Pabianic, Dabrowa Kozlowska, Dabrowka Dolna, Dabrowka Koscielna, Dabrowka Lug, Dabrowka Morska, Dabrowka Niemiecka, Dabrowka Ruska, Dabrowka Stany, Dabrowka Starzenska, Dabrowka Szczepanowska, Dabrowka Szlachecka, Dabrowka Tuchowska, Dabrowka Wylazy, Dabrowki Brenskie, Dambrova Gurnicha, Dombrava Gornitsha, Dombrove Gur, Dombrowa Gornicza
367976	Dabrowno, Dambraveni, Dombroven, Dombroveni, Dumbraveni, Dumbraveny
367977	Dabrowa Bialostocka, Dabrowa Wielka
367978	Dabrowa Lazy
367979	Dabrowa Rusiecka,

	Dumbravioara
368000	Danila, Danul
368400	Danilcze, Temeleuts, Temeleutsy
368439	Demmelsdorf
368460	Domuluzhany
368500	Dunalka
368560	Domulugeni
368600	Temelin, Tumlin
368638	Temelenti Lapusna
368640	Dunaalmas
368700	Danielow, Danilov, Danilovo
368740	Danilevitch, Danilovtse, Danilowce, Danilowicze, Dunalovitch, Dunilovicze, Dunilowicze, Tumilowicze
368750	Danilowka, Danul Vechi, Danul Vechiu, Dunilovichi, Tumilovichi
369000	Dimer, Dunarea, Dymer, Themar, Tomor
369300	Diemerode, Tomord
369400	Domaradz, Tumirz
369560	Tomorkeny
369564	Temir Chan Shura
369600	Temerin
369640	Dunareanca
369656	Tumringen
369740	Temerovtse, Temerowce
370000	Dabie, Dambia, Dambye, Deba, Debie, Deva, Dob, Doba, Doboj, Dombe, Dombie, Dombo, Dombye, Dovhe, Duba, Dubi, Duboj, Duboy, Tab, Tap, Tape, Tapiau, Tepe, Tiba, Tofej, Top
371740	Dubejovice
373000	Davod, Tabajd
373400	Davidhaza
373430	Davideshte, Davidesti
373500	Davidka
373540	Davidhaza
373570	Davidkovo, Davitkov
373574	Davidkovtse, Dawidkowce
373593	David Gorodok, David Horodok, Davidgrodek, Davidgrudek, Dawidgrodek
373594	Topa de Cris
373600	Davideni, Teptin
373650	Devyatniki, Dziewietniki
373700	Davidov, Dawidow
373750	Davidovka, Davydovka
373900	Tivadar
374000	Dabaca, Dabas, Debica, Debicze, Debitsa, Dembica, Dembits, Dembitsa, Dembitz, Dembiza, Dipsa, Dipse, Divizia, Dobcza, Dobocza, Doboz, Dobrz, Dobschau, Dobsza, Dubas, Dubiciai, Dubicze, Thebes, Tiapcze, Tobitschau, Tovis
374100	Diviziya
374396	Twistringen
374400	Dobczyce, Dobrzyca, Dobrzyce, Dobshitz, Dopshitz, Dziewieczyce, Tapioszecso
374450	Dvozhyshche
374470	Dobrzeszow
374500	Dibetsk, Dobuzek, Dovsk, Dowsk, Dubetsk, Dubetsko, Dubiecko, Dubietzko, Dubyetsko, Tapiosag, Topusko
374570	Debska Wola, Dobrzechow,

	Dobrzykow
374580	Topczykaly
374600	Debrzno, Dobiecin, Dobieszyn, Doboseni, Dobrzany, Dobsina, Dobzhany, Dobzhin, Dubeczno, Dubetchna, Dubicsany, Tapsony
374636	Tapioszentmarton, Tapszentmiklos
374650	Dobrzanka
374657	Dobrzankowo
374658	Dobrzyn Golub, Dobzhin Golub
374663	Dobrzyn nad Drewca, Dobrzyn nad Drweca, Dobrzyn nad Wisla, Dobzhin nad Drvents
374700	Divisov, Tabaszowa, Tapiosap, Tovacov
374730	Dobspuda
374740	Divisovice, Dobieszowice, Dubosevica
374800	Dziewiecioly, Tapiosuly, Tapioszele
374840	Tapioszollos
374870	Debeslavtse, Debeslawce, Dobrzelow
374874	Dobieslawice
374900	Devecser, Deveczer, Dobyasser, Dubasari, Dubosar, Dubossary
374916	Diviciorii Mari, Diviciorii Mici
374940	Dziewiecierz, Tapiogyorgye
375000	Dabki, Dambach, Debeikiai, Dobeik, Dovge, Dovhe, Dubka, Dvyk, Dybki, Tyapche
375400	Dombegyhaz, Dwikozy
375670	Dobiegniew
375700	Dobkov, Dybkow
375740	Dobkowice, Tabkowice
375845	Dovgaliszek, Dowgieliszki
376000	Dabjon, Debina, Debna, Debno, Dembina, Dembno, Dewin, Diepenau, Divin, Diwin, Dobeni, Doveny, Dubene, Dubin, Dubina, Dubiny, Dubna, Dubno, Dupin, Dyvin, Dywin, Dziewin, Tapin, Tavian, Tibana, Tibeni, Tvian, Typin, Tywonia
376300	Dubanti
376400	Debienica, Doba Mica, Dubines, Dupnitsa, Topa Mica
376430	Dabie Miasto
376450	Devenishki, Dewenishki, Divenishok, Dvinsk, Dwinsk, Dziewieniszki
376454	Dieveniskes
376500	Debnik, Debniki, Dembinka, Dibenka, Dubenka, Dubienka, Dubingai, Dubingiai, Dubinik, Dubnik, Dubyenka
376560	Tubingen
376563	Dubnica nad Vahom
376700	Dubinovo, Dubinowo
376740	Dobanovci, Dubanevitse, Dubaniowice
376787	Topanfalva
376900	Doba Mare, Toponar
377000	Debow, Debowa, Doupov, Dubova, Dubove, Dubovo, Dubowa, Dubowe, Dubowo,

	Tibava		Tverecius		Dabrowiece, Dambrovitsa,
377100	Dubovoje, Dubovoye	379444	Dworzyszcze		Dobrovice, Dombrovits,
377400	Debowce, Debowica, Debowiec,	379445	Dworzysk, Dworzyska		Dombrovitsa, Dombrovitza,
	Dubovec, Dubovtsy, Dubowce	379450	Dobruska, Dubrojsk		Dubrovits, Dubrovitsa,
377450	Tapiobicske	379460	Deberceny, Deborzyn,		Dubrowica, Toporovtse,
377600	Devavanya		Debrecen, Debretsin,		Toporovtsy, Toporowce,
377785	Dubova Balka		Doborcseny, Dobraczyn,		Tworowice
377800	Teofipol, Tiofipol		Dobrassen, Dobrocina,	379744	Doubravcice
377840	Deby Wolskie		Dobrodzien, Dobrosin,	379745	Dubrovsk
377850	Dab Wielki, Debe Wielkie		Tvarozna	379747	Tauberbischofsheim
377900	Dombovar	379464	Dobricionesti	379750	Dabrova Gornicha, Dabrowa
378000	Davle, Depoyla, Dobele,	379470	Dobrosov, Dobrzeszow,		Gornicza, Dabrowa K
	Dziewule, Tevel, Tevli, Tewle,		Tworyczow		Pabianic, Dabrowa
	Tewli, Topla, Topola, Tyble	379474	Dworszowice Koscielne,		Kozlowska, Dabrowka Dolna,
378100	Dupljaja		Dworszowice Pakoszowe		Dabrowka Koscielna,
378134	Dobolii de Sus	379480	Dobricel		Dabrowka Lug, Dabrowka
378300	Dobolt, Toplita	379485	Dobra Szlachecka		Morska, Dabrowka
378344	Toplita Ciuc	379500	Dieburg, Doborhegy, Dobrich,		Niemiecka, Dabrowka Ruska,
378345	Depultycze Krolewskie		Dubroka, Dworaki, Tavrogi,		Dabrowka Stany, Dabrowka
378369	Toplita Mures		Tevrig, Tovrik, Tworki,		Starzenska, Dabrowka
378394	Tibolddaroc		Tworog		Szczepanowska, Dabrowka
378400	Debeljaca, Diepholz, Dziepulc,	379540	Dobrokoz		Szlachecka, Dabrowka
	Tapolca, Teplice, Teplitz,	379543	Dobrohostow, Dworaki Staski		Tuchowska, Dabrowka
	Toplica, Toplistse, Toplitse	379550	Doborhegy		Wylazy, Dabrowki Brenskie,
378430	Tipilesti	379560	Dobricany, Dobrochin		Dambrova Gurnicha,
378440	Topolsica	379564	Twarogi Mazury		Dombrava Gornitsha,
378446	Teplice Sanov, Teplitz Schoenau,	379570	Dobrkow, Dobruchow,		Dombrove Gur, Dombrowa
	Teplitz Schonau		Dobrzechow, Dobrzykow,		Gornicza, Dubravka,
378450	Dupliska, Topolska, Topolsko		Tworkowa		Dubrovka
378465	Topolcianky	379574	Dobrichovice, Dobrocovice	379756	Doubravcany
378469	Toplitsa Mures	379598	Dvur Kralove, Dvur Kralove nad	379760	Dabrowno, Dambraveni,
378500	Teplik		Lab, Dvur Kralove nad Labem		Dombroven, Dombroveni,
378560	Tapolcany, Topolcany	379600	Dauborn, Debren, Dobrany,		Dubrovno, Dumbraveni,
378570	Tapolcafo		Dobreni, Dobrin, Dobron,		Dumbraveny
378598	Topola Krolewska		Dobrzany, Tavarna, Tovarne	379765	Dobrovnik, Dubrovnik
378600	Deblin, Demblin, Diefflen,	379630	Dobronauti	379770	Dabrowa Bialostocka, Dabrowa
	Dobeln, Doblen, Dubbelin,	379634	Dvory nad Zitavou		Wielka
	Dublany, Dublyany, Dvilne,	379636	Dobra nad Ondavou	379780	Dabrowa Lazy, Dobrowola
	Dziewuliny, Topolno, Topulno	379640	Dabronc, Dobronouts, Dubranec	379784	Dobrovelichkovka, Dobrovolsk
378640	Topolnitsa	379643	Dobre Miasto	379785	Dobra Velka
378643	Tepla Mesto	379648	Dobra Misla, Dobromysl	379786	Dobropole Mateuszowka,
378654	Topolnica Szlachecka	379650	Dobranka, Dobrinka, Dobrjanka,		Dobrovlyany, Dobrowlany
378659	Topolnica Rustykalna		Dobryanka, Dobrynka,	379790	Dabrowa Rusiecka,
378740	Dapalovce, Dublovice, Tibulovca		Dobrzanka, Dvorniky,		Dumbravioara
378757	Tipolovka Veche		Dwernik, Tovarnik	379860	Tworylne
378830	Taffilalth, Tafilelt	379656	Daubringen	379870	Dobrylow, Dobrzelow
379000	Daber, Davor, Debur, Dobra,	379657	Dobrzankowo	379943	Dobra Rustykalna
	Dobre, Dobry, Dobrz, Tabor,	379658	Dobrzyn Golub	380000	Dale, Dalj, Dlha, Dlhe, Dolha,
	Topor, Tver, Tverai	379660	Dobrynin		Dolhe, Dolia, Doly, Duoly,
379100	Dobriya	379663	Dobrzyn nad Drewca, Dobrzyn		Dyle, Tallya, Taul, Thale,
379300	Debrad, Debrod, Dombrad,		nad Drweca, Dobrzyn nad		Tholey, Tilaj, Tole, Tula,
	Dvart, Dvurt, Toporauti		Wisla		Tuula
379330	Tvardita	379670	Dubryniow	381700	Delejow, Deleyuv
379340	Dombiratos, Tvarditsa	379671	Dobrin Bay Dervents	383000	Dailydai, Djoltai, Dojlidy,
379346	Tvrdosin	379674	Dobronovtsy		Doylidy, Tild, Told
379347	Tvrdosovce	379675	Dobranowka	383400	Delatycze
379359	Twardogora	379678	Dobron Velika	383500	Delyatichi, Delyatyche
379360	Differten, Dobrodzien, Tverdyn,	379680	Dobra Mala, Dobromil,	383600	Delatyn, Deliatin, Delyatin,
	Twerdyn		Dobromyl		Telatyn
379370	Dobrotow, Dobrotuv	379695	Dobromirka	383700	Dlutow, Dzialdowo
379378	Tverdopillya	379700	Dabrowa, Dobrava, Dobriv,	383800	Toldal
379379	Dobrotvor, Dobrotwor		Dombrowa, Dombrove,	383850	Toldalag
379394	Tauberrettersheim		Doubrava, Dubrava, Dubrave,	384000	Doles, Tallos, Talsi, Tel She,
379400	Damborice, Damboritz, Debrisch,		Dubrova, Dubrovo, Dubrowa,		Telc, Telciu, Telcs, Teleseu,
	Dobrcz, Dobris, Dobrose,		Dubrowo, Toporov, Toporow,		Telesheu, Telschi, Telse,
	Dobrush, Dobrusha, Dobrzyca,		Tyborow, Tyvrov		Telsh, Telshie, Telsia, Telsiai,
	Dobrzyce, Dubarsi, Dvorce,	379730	Dabrowa Tarnowska, Dabrowa		Telsze, Teltsch, Telz, Telzh,
	Dvorets, Dvoretz, Tabarz,		Tworki, Dobrovody,		Tilitch, Tilza, Tulcea, Tylicz,
	Tibirica, Tovaros, Tverdza,		Dobrowoda, Dobrowody		Tylza
	Twerecz, Twierdza	379737	Dobrovitov	384300	Tilsit, Tlist, Tlust, Tlusta,
379436	Dobrostany	379740	Dabrovica, Dabrowa Dzieciel,		Tluste, Tluyst
379440	Doberschutz, Dobrociesz,		Dabrowa Szlachecka,	384310	Tolstoye
	Dobroszyce, Dworzec,		Dabrowica, Dabrowice,	384340	Tlustice

384364	Tluste Miasto, Tluste Myasto
384365	Tlustenke, Tlustenkie, Tolstenkoye
384370	Tlustowa
384374	Tluste Wies, Tlustovousy
384400	Daleszyce, Dalishitza, Delitzsch, Dolzyca, Dzialoshitz, Dzialoszyce, Dzyaloshitse, Tilzas, Tlashts, Tluszcz, Tolgyes
384470	Tolshchev, Tolszczow
384500	Dolsk, Dolzhka, Dolzhki, Dolzhok, Dolzig, Dolzka, Dolzki, Dylazki, Tlashch, Tlushch
384570	Tolshchuv, Tulishkov, Tuliszkow
384574	Dlazkovice
384600	Dolesheim, Dzialoszyn, Dzyaloshin, Talsen, Talsn, Telsen, Tilsen, Toloschin, Tolotchin, Tolotschin, Tulcin, Tulczyn, Tultchin
384654	Telesnica Oszwarowa, Telesnica Sanna
384670	Dolishnev
384674	Dluzniewice
384680	Dulcza Mala
384700	Daleshova, Daleszowa, Delcevo, Dlazov, Teleshovo, Tolcsva, Tulichev, Tuliczow
384740	Daleszewice
384785	Dulcza Wielka
384789	Thaleischweiler
384795	Dilsberg
384796	Tallesbrunn
384836	Doly Slatinski
385000	Delacheu, Delakeu, Dillich, Dlha, Dlhe, Dlouha, Dlugie, Dolge, Dolha, Dolhe, Talka, Telaki, Telchea, Telchia, Telechia, Telechiu, Telek, Tuluga
385100	Dolgoye
385300	Telegd, Telgte, Tileagd
385400	Tulghes
385438	Dlugosiodlo
385444	Tulghes Ciuc
385460	Dolgesheim
385485	Dluga Szlachecka
385566	Dlugie Kamienskie
385600	Dulken, Talheim, Telchan, Telechany, Telechon, Telekani, Telekhan, Telekhany, Theilheim, Tolochin, Tulchin
385656	Delkenheim
385660	Delkenheim
385670	Dolginov, Dolginovo, Dolhinov, Dolhinow, Dolhinuv
385674	Dlouhonovice
385694	Dzialki Morozowalskie
385700	Dalachow, Dalechowy, Dolgov, Tluchowo, Tolukow
385737	Dolhe Podbuskie
385740	Dalechowice, Dalekowice, Dlouha Ves, Dluga Wies, Tulkowice
385747	Dolhobyczow
385750	Dylagowka
385760	Telkibanya
385780	Dlugovolya, Dlugowola, Dolgovolya
385793	Dolhobrody, Dolhobrot
385794	Dlugoborz
385830	Dlouha Lhota
385853	Dlouha Lhota
385870	Tuliglowy, Tuligolovy

385940	Telechi Recea, Telekirecse
385956	Dielkirchen
385957	Dolgorukovo
386000	Dohlen, Dolin, Dolina, Dolna, Dolne, Dzialyn, Talheim, Tallin, Tallinn, Talna, Talnoe, Theilheim, Tolna, Tulln
386100	Talnoje, Talnoya, Talnoye
386348	Dolna Tuzla
386374	Dolmatovshchina, Dolmatowszczyzna
386395	Taliandorogd
386400	Dalnicz, Talamas, Talmaciu, Talmatch, Talmaz, Telince, Tlomats, Tlumacz, Tlumatch, Toalmas, Tolmacs
386430	Telenesht, Teleneshty, Telenesti
386433	Telenesht Targ, Telenesti Targ
386434	Telenesti Sat
386450	Tlumachik, Tlumaczyk, Tolmachik
386451	Dolinskoye
386459	Dolne Zahorany
386460	Dielmissen
386463	Dolni Zandov
386465	Thalmassing, Thalmessingen
386470	Tolmaczewo
386500	Dalnich, Dalnik, Talmach, Tlumach
386560	Dillingen
386564	Dolni Kounice
386566	Dillingen an der Donau
386570	Tolmachevo
386576	Dolni Kubin, Dolny Kubin
386598	Dolni Kralovice
386600	Diulmeni, Dolinen, Dolineni, Doliniany, Dolinyany, Dulmen
386646	Dellmensingen
386659	Delmenhorst
386663	Tolnanemedi
386670	Tylmanowa
386674	Talminowicze
386675	Talminovichi
386690	Delmenhorst
386700	Dalnow, Dolhinov, Dolhinow, Dolhinuv
386747	Dolni Bousov
386750	Dalanowka
386837	Dolna Ludova
386845	Dolny Lieskov
386857	Dolni Lukavice
386863	Dolnja Lendava
386900	Dealu Mare, Dealumare
386940	Dalimerice
387000	Daliowa, Daljowa, Dilif, Dolovo, Duliby, Dulovo, Dulowa, Tulovo, Tulowo
387100	Delovoye
387370	Dolhe Podbuskie
387400	Djulaves, Dulaves, Telfs, Tylwica
387457	Doly Biskupie
387470	Dolhobyczow
387500	Dulabka
387560	Tolbukhin
387650	Thalfang, Tulbing
387656	Tailfingen
387870	Dulfalva, Dulofalva
387930	Dolhobrody, Dolhobrot
387978	Talaborfalu
388175	Talalayevka
388750	Talaljewka
388900	Deljiler
390000	Dara, Dor, Dora, Thur, Tria,

	Tur, Tura, Turea, Turia, Turja, Turje, Tury, Turye, Tyria
391000	Druja, Druya
391670	Trajanow, Troyanov
391675	Trojanovka, Trojanowka, Troyanivka, Troyanovka
391679	Treuenbrietzen
391780	Taruj Falu
393000	Darda, Darot, Dert, Dridu, Druta, Durdy, Tard, Tartu, Torda, Troita, Trudy, Turda, Turt
393400	Tardos, Tordas
393453	Tardosked
393460	Turdosin, Turdossin
393463	Tordaszentlaszlo
393476	Tardosbanya
393570	Tartakov, Tartakow, Tartakuv, Tartekev
393574	Tartkowice
393576	Tartakow Miasto, Tartakuv Miasto
393600	Driten, Tardona, Tarutino, Teratyn, Trautenau, Trstena, Turdeni
393650	Trzydnik
393656	Dertingen, Trittenheim
393660	Tarutino Nou, Trittenheim
393663	Dortmund
393664	Trstena na Ostrove
393670	Trutnov
393674	Durdenovac, Tratnowice
393678	Dridu Movila
393700	Dratow, Tretowo, Tridubi, Triduby
393710	Trudovoye
393740	Djurdjevac, Durdevac
393800	Tortel
393840	Tartolcz
393860	Tur Dolny
393900	Druitory, Tartaria
393960	Drutarnia
393965	Trudering
393970	Dierdorf, Tartarov
393974	Turterebes
393975	Duritoarya Veke, Duruitoarea Veche
394000	Derc, Derzs, Dirschau, Drissa, Drisy, Drutsa, Dryssa, Durusa, Tarasca, Tarcea, Tarcze, Teres, Tirza, Toretz, Torez, Treis, Treitza, Treysa, Triesch, Trizs, Troitsa, Trojca, Trzas, Turc, Turcz, Turec, Turets, Turetz, Turez, Turricse, Turza, Turze
394300	Dersida, Dorosauti, Drozdy, Drusti, Trest, Tresta
394330	Traustadt
394358	Tirschtiegel
394360	Dorsten, Dresden, Drezden, Drozdin, Drozdni, Drozdnie, Drozdyn, Dursztyn, Teresztenye, Trestena, Trestiana, Trestina, Trysten
394363	Trostinet
394364	Trostenets, Trosteniec, Trostinets, Trostyanets
394365	Drezdenko
394367	Trestenberg
394370	Drozdov
394376	Turistvandi

394378	Dorstfeld	
394379	Trostberg	
394394	Tresta Rzadowa	
394397	Triesdorf, Troisdorf	
394400	Derezyce, Doroshitse, Dracic, Druzec, Tarashtcha, Tarasits, Taraszcza, Trojczyce, Turzec, Turzets	
394430	Tarcesti	
394450	Turzisk, Turzysk	
394457	Turzysk Przedmiescie	
394460	Trzeszczany	
394470	Dryszczow	
394500	Derecske, Deresk, Drujsk, Druysk, Tarashcha, Tarzik, Tereske, Toroczko, Torske, Torskie, Torysk, Trishig, Trishik, Trishky, Trishkyay, Trisk, Trotsk, Trusk, Tryskiai, Turijsk, Turisk, Turiysk	
394510	Torskoye, Troitskoye	
394540	Tarachkos, Taraczkos	
394559	Dreissigacker	
394560	Dzierzgon, Trashkin, Trashkon, Traskianai, Traszkuny, Triskinie, Troshkon, Troskunai, Tryskine	
394564	Treskonice, Tureczki Nizne	
394565	Drozgenik, Druskieniki	
394566	Druskininkai	
394570	Drazgow, Druzykowa, Dryshchuv, Dzierzgow, Dzierzgowo, Taraskowo, Troskav, Truskava	
394574	Dzierzkowice, Tereshkovtsy, Tereszkowce, Triskovitz, Trushkovitse, Truskavets, Truskawice, Truskawiec, Trzeskowice, Trzeszkowice, Tureczki Wyzne	
394577	Druzkow Pusty	
394578	Droshkopol, Drushkopla, Drushkopol, Druszkopol, Druzhkopol, Druzkopol	
394584	Truskolasy	
394594	Taracs Kraszna, Taracz Krazna	
394595	Traiskirchen, Trautskirchen	
394600	Derazhna, Derazhnia, Derazhno, Derazhnya, Derazne, Dercen, Dereczyn, Dereshnja, Deretchin, Dorosinie, Dorszyn, Draceni, Drasne, Dreisen, Dretchin, Driceni, Driesen, Drodzyn, Drossen, Drozen, Drozyn, Drzazna, Tarashany, Tarczyn, Tartchin, Teresin, Tereszyn, Terezin, Toraceni, Torczyn, Tortchin, Trciana, Treznea, Troszyn, Truseni, Trusheny, Trzciana, Trzcianne, Trzesn	
394615	Druzhnaya Gorka	
394630	Dracinet, Dracineti	
394639	Treis an der Lumda	
394640	Dresnitz, Dreznica, Trosciance, Troscianiec, Trostsyantse, Trzcianice, Trzcianiec, Trzcieniec	
394643	Theresienstadt	
394645	Darshonishok, Darshunishok, Darsuniskis, Turcianske Teplice, Turciansky Svaty Martin, Turzansk	
394648	Dereznia Solska	

394649	Taraseni Cernauti
394650	Dereczanka, Droesing, Drosing, Troscianka, Trzcianka
394657	Drasenhofen, Tariceanca Veche, Troscianiec Wielki
394660	Dzierzaniny
394664	Dereznianska Wola
394666	Troszyn Niemiecki
394669	Targy Neanirom
394670	Drasenhofen, Drazniew, Dzierzoniow, Teresnev, Trzesniow, Trzezniow
394674	Torczynowice
394679	Traismauer
394693	Tirschenreuth
394695	Drassmarkt
394700	Derzow, Dirschaw, Dorozhev, Dorozow, Drazdzewo, Dreszew, Duraczow, Dzierzby, Tarasov, Teresif, Teresov, Teresova, Teresow, Tershuvo, Terszow
394730	Drisviat, Drisvyaty, Dryswiaty
394735	Dzierzbotki
394740	Djurdjevac
394748	Dzierzby Szlacheckie
394750	Doerzbach, Dorzbach, Tarasivka, Tarasovka, Tarassiwka, Terasiwka, Toroszowka, Trzesowka, Turaszowka, Turzovka
394757	Turaszowka Vel Toroszowka
394760	Druzbin, Dzierzbin, Treshebin
394780	Tereshpol, Terespol, Terespoli, Terespolia, Terespolya, Tereszpol, Tirashpol, Tiraspol, Tyraspol
394784	Turza Wilcza
394785	Turza Wielka, Turza Wileka
394795	Diersburg, Drassburg
394800	Tereshel, Terisel, Trysolie, Trzciel, Turosl
394830	Tarsolt, Tirsolt
394846	Drasliceni
394856	Draslicheny
394870	Doroslovo
394873	Tereselpatak
394874	Druzylowicze
394875	Druzhilovichi
395000	Darag, Dirchau, Dorgo, Dorog, Dorohoi, Dorok, Draga, Dragu, Drighiu, Drochia, Taurage, Taurik, Taurogi, Terka, Tirek, Tirgu, Torek, Torgau, Torichi, Torki, Trakai, Trok, Troki, Turek, Turka
395100	Drokiya I, Targu Jiu, Tirgu Jiu
395110	Drokiya Ii
395170	Drohojow
395300	Darcauti, Trichaty, Trihati, Trikata
395367	Dragutinovo, Trachtenberg
395386	Treuchtlingen
395400	Darkauts, Derkautsy, Doroghaza, Dorohucza, Tarackoz
395430	Dragoesti, Tregist
395446	Torokszentmiklos
395450	Dorohusk
395451	Targu Sacuiesc, Tirgu Secuiesc
395454	Tirgu Secuesc
395460	Dragosen, Dragoseni, Dragusheny, Drohiczyn, Drohitchin, Targu Ocna, Tirgu

	Ocna, Turgu Ocna
395461	Dragusenii Noui, Dragusenii Vechi
395466	Dragusheni Nouy, Drohiczyn nad Bugiem
395467	Dragasymuv, Drahasymow
395470	Drahisevo, Drogoszewo
395475	Drohiczowka
395480	Tirkosla, Tirkshla, Tirksliai
395500	Terehegy
395540	Derekegyhaz
395560	Derhichin, Drogichin, Drohichin
395564	Torok Kanyizsa
395575	Drogichevka, Drogichuvka
395583	Targu Gloduri, Tirgu Gloduli
395590	Drochia Gara
395600	Dargun, Derechin, Derhichin, Dorogma, Dragany, Dragunia, Droginia, Drugnia, Durkheim, Targin, Tarkan, Tarkany, Tarogen, Tauragnai, Taurogen, Tauroggen, Torchin, Torkn, Traken
395640	Drachinets, Trhonice
395643	Draganeshti, Draganesti, Dragoneshty
395648	Drahomysl, Drogomyshl, Drohomysl
395650	Druckenik
395657	Trugenhofen
395660	Darkehmen, Trachomin
395663	Targu Neamt, Tirgu Neamt
395668	Tarkan Maly
395670	Doraganova, Troganov, Truchanow, Trugenhofen
395673	Targonie Wity
395674	Torganovitse, Torhanowice
395675	Torganovichi
395678	Dragonyfalva, Targonie Wielkie, Tarkan Velky
395679	Trachenberg, Trochenbrod, Trochinbrod, Trokhinbrod, Trokhnibrod
395694	Dragimiresht, Dragomirest, Dragomiresti, Drohomirczany, Targu Miresh, Targu Mores, Targu Myres, Tirgu Mures, Torgu Muresh
395695	Drogomirchany
395697	Dragomerfalva
395700	Darachow, Darakhov, Dorogov, Doroguv, Dorohow, Dragovo, Drahiv, Drahov, Drahova, Drahovo, Drhovy, Druchowa, Drukhov, Drukhova, Durkov, Dziergova, Targow, Tarkow, Turkeve, Turkowo
395734	Drahobudice
395738	Drochow Dolny
395740	Dorogobuzh, Drahobuz, Drahovce, Drahovec, Drogobycz, Drohobitch, Drohobycz, Drohowyze, Drzkovce, Targovica, Targovitsa, Targovitza, Targowica, Targowitza, Torgovitsa, Torgowica, Torok Becse, Torokbecse, Turkowice, Turkowicze
395743	Targoviste
395744	Targowiszcze
395745	Drohobyczka, Targovishche,

442

	Targowiska, Targowisko
395750	Drogobich, Drogobych, Drohobich, Targowek
395760	Torokkoppany
395780	Drogowle, Taracujfalu
395786	Dragavilma, Torokbalint
395793	Dorogobratovo
395796	Targu Frumos, Tirgu Frumos
395800	Draculea, Tarcal, Trikkala, Trokeli, Trokiele
395810	Tarakliya, Targul Jiu
395835	Taraclia Tighina
395840	Dragalic
395845	Targul Secuiesc
395846	Targul Ocna
395855	Taraclia Cahul
395860	Drochlin, Taurkalne, Taurkalni
395869	Targul Mures
395871	Targul Bujor
395874	Targu Laposului, Targu Lopus, Tirgiu Lapus, Tirgu Lapus
395878	Dregelypalank
395879	Targul Frumos
395887	Targul Lapush, Targul Lapusului
395930	Tarigrad
396000	Darany, Dehrn, Dereneu, Derenie, Derna, Dernau, Dirna, Djurin, Dorna, Drama, Drinja, Drnje, Duhren, Duren, Durnau, Tarany, Tareni, Tarian, Tarjan, Tarna, Tarno, Taureni, Teremne, Teremno, Tereny, Terna, Thorn, Thurnau, Tirnoy, Torn, Torna, Torne, Tornya, Toronya, Torun, Trumau, Tureni, Turn, Turna, Turnau, Turno, Turyn, Tyrnau
396100	Tirnoya
396300	Durand, Dyormot
396380	Trendel
396387	Trendelburg
396397	Dorndorf, Thurndorf
396400	Darnica, Darnitsa, Dormitz, Drinjaca, Drnis, Ternets, Ternits, Tornocz, Tranis, Tranisu, Trhonice, Trinca, Trinec, Trmice, Tryncza, Trynosy
396430	Dornesti
396433	Darmstadt, Trunstadt
396436	Dirmstein, Drensteinfurt, Tarnazsadany, Traunstein
396440	Dremcice
396460	Dranceni, Drinceni, Tarnoszyn, Tremessen, Trencin, Trencsen, Trenscen, Trentschin, Trzemesnia, Trzemeszno, Trzemiesnia
396461	Drancenii de Sus
396463	Dorna Cindrenilor, Tarnaszentmaria, Tarnaszentmiklos, Tornaszentandras, Trencsenteplicz
396464	Trencianska Tepla, Trencianska Turna, Trencianske Teplice
396466	Tornyosnemeti
396468	Trzemeszno Lubuskie
396470	Dransheva, Termesivy
396478	Dransfeld, Tornyospalca
396479	Transbor, Turnu Severin
396480	Darmysl, Dorrmoschel
396490	Dernisoara

396500	Dornach, Tarnok, Trinka, Turinka, Turynka
396560	Dormagen, Dornheim, Dornigheim
396563	Dorna Candrenilor
396578	Tornakapolna
396579	Drengfurth
396590	Tarnogora
396593	Durnkrut, Tarnogrod
396595	Traunkirchen
396600	Derman, Dornheim, Dornum, Dramin, Dramino, Tornen
396630	Dormand, Turmont
396634	Tornanadaska, Turmantas
396637	Turna nad Bodvou
396643	Darmanesti
396650	Dermanka
396680	Turna Mala
396690	Tarna Mare, Tarnamera, Tirimia Mare
396700	Derenev, Dernow, Drahnov, Drienove, Tarnava, Tarnawa, Tarnov, Tarnow, Tarnowo, Tarnuv, Ternava, Terneve, Ternive, Ternova, Ternovo, Tranowo, Trmova, Trnava, Turnov, Tyrnovo
396735	Tarnawatka
396739	Dorna Vatra, Dorna Watra
396740	Drahnovice, Tarnowice, Tarnowiec, Tarnowitz, Ternovitsa, Torhanowice, Tyrnavos
396745	Tarnobrzeg, Tarnobrzeg Dzikow, Tarnowskie Gory
396747	Tarnovitsa Polna
396748	Tarnovitsa Lesna, Tarnovitsa Lesnaya
396749	Tarnova Soroca
396750	Dereniowka, Dernuvka, Dornbach, Tarnavka, Tarnawka, Tarnovka, Tarnowka, Tarnowko, Ternovka, Ternowka
396753	Tarnova Hotin
396756	Trnovec nad Vahom
396757	Tarnowica Polna
396758	Tarnowica Lesna
396760	Trnovany
396763	Trnovo nad Teresvon
396764	Tarnawa Nizna
396773	Tarnowo Podgorne
396774	Tarnawa Wyzna
396778	Trembovla, Trembowla
396780	Tarnopol, Ternopol, Ternopolye
396783	Dornfeld, Tirumbaltgalvji
396793	Dyhernfurth, Trennfurt
396795	Derenburg, Dornberg, Dramburg, Tarnobrzeg, Tarnobrzeg Dzikow, Thorenburg, Tornabarakony
396796	Dornbirn
396800	Drmoul, Duerrmaul, Durmaul, Tornala, Tornalja, Tornalya
396884	Tarnalelesz
396900	Tirimioara
396930	Tarnoruda
396935	Tarnorudka
396940	Tarnaors
396946	Dromersheim
396963	Turyanremety
397000	Darevo, Darewo, Darow, Darva, Dorpa, Drhovy, Drove,

	Drupia, Durbe, Durova, Tarpa, Taurov, Taurow, Terep, Tiuriv, Toorof, Torba, Traby, Trape, Trawy, Trip, Tropie, Troppau, Truppa, Tur Ev, Turbe, Turbia, Turev, Turov
397150	Trofaiach
397160	Trebujeni
397300	Derpt, Dorpat, Tarvydai, Tervete, Turbuta
397340	Tervetes
397360	Tryputna, Tryputnia
397370	Trebotov, Treptow, Trzebiatow
397376	Treptow an der Riga
397400	Darvas, Dorbozy, Drabesi, Drzewica, Tarovitz, Terebes, Toropets, Traupis, Trebic, Trebitsch, Treboc, Trebusa, Trepec, Trepecz, Treves, Trobitz, Trovits, Truvitz, Trywieza, Trzebce, Trzebica, Trzebiez, Trzebos, Trzebucza
397430	Terebesti, Trebisauti, Trifeshti, Trifeshty, Trpisty
397433	Trappstadt
397438	Trebice Dolne
397439	Dravasztara, Trifesti Orhei
397440	Tribsees
397450	Dravacsehi, Drawsko, Drebsk, Trzebuska, Tur Piaski
397454	Trebiskauts
397457	Drawsko Pomorskie
397459	Trebice Gorne
397460	Derebcin, Trebusan, Trebusany, Trebuzheny, Trzebciny
397470	Terebezhov, Terebezhuv, Terebiezow, Trebisov, Trzebieszow
397471	Terebesfejer Patak
397476	Tribuswinkel
397478	Dravaszabolcs
397480	Torboszlo
397486	Tyrawa Solna
397489	Durboslar
397500	Derevok, Derewek, Drobich, Durbach, Torbagy, Trubki, Turovichi, Turovka, Turowka
397530	Drepcauti
397560	Derebchin, Turvekonya
397574	Drepkovtsy, Trebechovice pod Orebem, Trebichovice, Tribuhovtsy, Tribukhovtsy, Trubchevsk, Trybuchowce
397580	Tropoclo
397593	Dravograd
397594	Dravakeresztur
397596	Dorfe Haaren
397600	Darabani, Darbenai, Darbian, Darbyenay, Derevna, Derevno, Derewina, Derewna, Derewno, Dorbenai, Dorbian, Dorbyan, Dorbyany, Dorfen, Dorpen, Drawno, Dribin, Dribino, Drobian, Drobin, Drobyan, Drwinia, Drybin, Durben, Tereben, Terebin, Terebna, Torbin, Trebbin, Trebon, Trpinja, Trzebina, Trzebinia, Turbin, Turobin
397610	Darevnaya, Derevnaya
397630	Derbent, Derventa
397640	Drewnica, Trebnitz, Trzebnica,

	Trzepnica	415900	Zajecar		Sadgura, Sadogora, Sadygera
397643	Trifaneshty, Trifanesti	415943	Sajokeresztur	435944	Sadykierz Szlachecki
397650	Drewnik, Travnik, Trawniki, Trzebionka	416000	Sajan	436000	Cetinje, Ciudin, Cseteny, Czudyn, Satinu, Schotten, Shodina, Siaudine, Sitno, Sudheim, Suidine, Trstena, Zaden, Zadna, Zadne, Zadnya, Zaton, Zhaden, Zsadany
397656	Durrwangen	416340	Suiunduc		
397660	Drobnin	416400	Sajomezo		
397664	Trzebinia Miasteczko, Trzebinia Miasto	416450	Suyainishok		
397665	Drabinianka	416494	Sajomagyaros		
397674	Trzebinia Wies	416540	Zayenchitse		
397684	Trybunalski	416630	Sajonemeti	436100	Zadneye
397700	Drabov, Tropova, Tropovo	416940	Sajomercse	436175	Zadunayevka
397740	Drobovice, Trebowiec, Tropovci, Turobowice	417000	Cejov	436314	Satu Nou de Jos
397744	Drabowszczyzna	417390	Sajopetri	436397	Schattendorf
397745	Drabovshchyzna, Dravapiski	417475	Sajopuspoki	436400	Schodnica, Sietnica, Sitaniec, Sitnitsa, Sytnica, Zitenice
397750	Dravafok, Trapovka	417500	Szajowka		
397780	Terebovlya, Trbovlje, Trebevle, Trebovle	417640	Sajovamos	436475	Zadnishevka, Zadniszowka
		417650	Sajoivanka	436500	Csetnik, Trzydnik, Zehdenick
397784	Tirava Vilaska, Trebivlice, Turawa Wolaska, Tyrawa Woloska	417760	Sajobabony	436560	Dietenheim
		417843	Sajovelezd	436576	Dietenhofen
397800	Dorfel, Tarfalu, Terebla, Tereble, Tereblya	417850	Czaje Wolka	436643	Satu Nou na Saud, Schattmannsdorf, Trstena na Ostrove
		417878	Sajopalfala		
397840	Tereblecea, Tereblicze	417956	Sajovarkony		
397843	Terebleshti, Trabelsdorf	418000	Szajol	436650	Sde Menucha
397844	Tereblecesa Noua	418300	Sajolad	436700	Satanov, Satanow, Schedniow, Tschudnowo, Zadnevo
397846	Tereblecea Noua	418487	Sajolaszlofalva		
397850	Tereblichi	419400	Sajooros	436740	Rzedzianowice, Zidneves, Zytnowicze
397860	Derevlyany, Derewlany, Treblin, Trzebielino	430000	Chet, Csot, Csota, Gyod, Sady, Saida, Saiti, Sata, Schat, Seda, Seta, Shaty, Shet, Shod, Shot, Siad, Sid, Sieut, Sod, Sutto, Syad, Syady, Szada, Szete, Szod, Zajta, Zetea, Zittau, Zsujta	436750	Zhitnovichi
397865	Treblinka			436760	Sedmpany
397875	Terpilovka, Terpilowka			436794	Zytniow Rzedowy
397900	Daruvar, Trebur			436795	Diedenbergen, Sudenburg
397937	Dorobertovo, Dorobratovo			436900	Satmar, Satu Mare, Schotmar, Shitomir, Sudomir, Szatmar, Zhitomir
397950	Treuburg, Triberg				
398000	Derlo, Dorolea, Tarle, Tarleh, Tarlo, Terlo	431000	Ciudeiu	436937	Szatmar Udvari, Szatmarudvari
		431700	Sudejov	436940	Zytomierz
398300	Dorolt	431740	Sedziejowice	436945	Szatmarcseke
398400	Drildzh, Driltch, Tarlisua, Terlica, Terlitsa, Terlitza, Tirlisua, Trilesy, Turylcze	433800	Cetatele	436950	Szatmarhegy
		433870	Cetatea Alba	436955	Szatmarhegy
		434000	Ciotusza, Czudec, Czudez, Sietesz, Sitce, Soutice, Sudcze, Suedasai, Zatec, Zatiscea, Zatishye	436959	Szatmar Okorito, Szatmarokorito
398439	Durelsdorf			436966	Szatmar Nemeti, Szatmarnemeti
398450	Terliczka, Tryliski			436969	Syhot Marmaroski
398485	Terlo Szlacheckie	434300	Zitiste	436980	Satmarel
398500	Derylaki, Drilch, Durlach, Tura Luka, Turilche, Turoluka	434468	Dzedushitse Male, Dzieduszyce Male	437000	Sadov, Sadova, Sadow, Sadowa, Sadowie, Seduva, Shadov, Shadova, Shadove, Shatava, Shatova, Shatowa, Shedeva, Shitova, Szadow, Zadibi, Zadova, Zadowa, Zadubie, Zadubye, Zadyby, Zhadova
		434478	Dzieduszyce Wielkie		
398600	Drahlin	434535	Sat Sugatag, Satu Sugatag		
398650	Turulung	434670	Zau de Cimpie		
398700	Darlowo, Drelow, Tarlow, Tarluv, Turlava	434700	Zhidatchov, Zidatchov, Zidichev, Zydaczov, Zydaczow		
398943	Terlo Rustakalne, Terlo Rustikalne, Terlo Rustykalne	434938	Schutt Szerdahly	437174	Sudovaya Vishnya
		435000	Citcau, Csatka, Dzaudhikau, Sadacu, Sadek, Sadki, Sadyk, Schadeck, Scheidegg, Shadek, Sudak, Sudche, Szadek, Szatok, Szdek, Zhidik, Zhidiki, Zidik, Zidikai, Zidikiai, Zydikiai	437400	Sataviace, Sedowice, Zadubce, Zadvyzhe
399000	Trier				
399630	Turi Remety, Turjaremete			437450	Zydowskie
400000	Sahy, Sho, Sieu, Szo, Zau			437455	Zhidovska Grebla
410000	Sajo			437600	Citavjan, Sadowna, Sadowne, Tsituvian, Tzitavian
413000	Siojut	435500	Dzaudhikau		
414000	Sejas	435600	Chitcani, Sudheim	437746	Sadova Vishnia, Sadowa Wisnia, Sadowa Wiszna, Sadowa Wisznia, Sadowa Wisznia Miasto
414340	Zajezdec	435665	Sdeh Menocha		
414400	Zajeczyce	435674	Chitcani Vechi		
414500	Sajoecseg	435700	Dyatkovo, Sadkowa, Zedechoyv, Zhidachov, Zidichuv		
414530	Sajoszoged			437936	Cetvertinovca, Chetvertinovka, Chetvertnya, Czetwiertnia
414600	Sajosenye	435740	Diatkowice, Dyatkovtse, Dyatkovtsy, Dziatkowicze, Sudkowice, Sudokovitse, Szadkowice		
414636	Sajoszentandras			437940	Zadworze
414637	Sajoszentpeter			437964	Zatwarnica
414700	Zajecov	435750	Dyadkovichi, Sitkowka, Zhitkovichi	437974	Zadubrovtse, Zadubrovtsy
415000	Csajag, Suiug			438000	Csatalja, Czudel, Sattel, Siodlo, Sodel, Szadello, Zadiel, Zadziele, Zetl, Zhetl, Zietil, Zitl, Zsetl
415375	Sajohidveg	435800	Sadaclia		
415400	Sajokaza	435810	Sadakliya		
415464	Sajokazinc	435876	Sdeh Lavan	438360	Sedletin
415690	Sajogomor	435900	Sadagora, Sadagura, Sadgora,	438400	Ciutelec, Sadoles, Sedlec,
415786	Sajokapolna				

	Sedlice, Shedlets, Shedlitz, Siedlce	443670	Czestoniew	445917	Suskrajowice
438430	Ciutulesti	443700	Csesztve, Siostrzytow, Zastave, Zastavye, Zastawa, Zastawie	445930	Zaskrodzie
438440	Shedlishtza, Siedliszcze	443736	Chistovodnoye	445940	Szecsegres, Zaskrodzie
438446	Siedliszcze Male	443740	Sasiadowice	445943	Szecskeresztur
438447	Siedliszcze Wielkie	443760	Zastavna, Zastavne	445954	Ciceu Giurgesti
438450	Sedlishche, Sedliska, Siedleczka, Siedliska, Siedlisko, Szedliszka, Zadzielsko	443787	Sostofalva	445960	Chiscareni
		443797	Czestoborowice	445970	Ciceu Corabia
		443863	Chistelnita	445974	Zaskrevitz
438457	Siedliska Bogusz	443870	Czystylow	446000	Cedzyna, Cheshin, Chisinau, Ciazen, Ciecina, Cieszyn, Cieszyna, Cieszyny, Cisna, Czudzin, Czyzyny, Diessen, Diosjeno, Drzazna, Dzieczyna, Dzisna, Rzasnia, Rzedzin, Saseni, Schutzen, Seciny, Seesen, Seussen, Sidzina, Sosen, Soshno, Soszno, Sudzuna, Sushno, Sussen, Suszno, Suzun, Sycina, Sycyna, Syczyn, Szecseny, Szuczan, Trzciana, Trzcianne, Trzesn, Zasanie, Zasimy, Zosimy, Zossen, Zyczyn, Zyrzyn
438460	Diedelsheim	443900	Czastary, Rzeszotary, Sisterea, Tshastar, Zhizdra, Zhuzdra		
438474	Siedliszowice				
438560	Sedlcany	443943	Zistersdorf		
438565	Sedlcanky	443950	Csesztreg		
438570	Sudilkov	443957	Rzeszotary Chwaly		
438574	Zidlochovice	443959	Rzeszotary Gortaty		
438600	Sudlohn	443970	Siostrzytow		
438650	Satulung, Siedlanka	444000	Cesis, Cisiec, Dziedzice, Rzeczyca, Rzezyca, Sajczyce, Siucice, Soszyce, Susice, Susiec, Zasiecie		
438670	Sedlonov				
438700	Citoliby, Dyatlovo, Sedlov, Shidlov, Shidlova, Sidluva, Szydlow				
		444530	Szecsisziget		
438740	Dziatlowicze, Shidlovets, Shidlovits, Shidlovitz, Shidlovtse, Shidlovtsy, Shidlovtza, Shidlovyets, Szydlowce, Szydlowiec, Zeitlofs, Zhidlovetza	444600	Soszyczno, Suszczyn, Trzeszczany	446100	Sausneja
		444657	Csicsogyongyfalva	446179	Susenii Bargaului, Susenii Birgaului
		444700	Cieciszew, Rzhishcev, Rzhishchev, Rzyszczow, Sedziszow, Sedziszowa	446300	Chisindia, Saucenita
				446340	Szasznadas
438750	Dyatlovichi, Szydlowek	444768	Sedziszow Malopolski	446400	Chisindia, Cicenice, Sosnica, Sosnitsa, Sosnitza, Trzcianice, Trzcianiec, Trzcieniec, Zazamcze
438760	Sde Lavan	444785	Sushitsa Velikaya, Sushitsa Velka		
439000	Ceadar, Cetariu, Csatar, Csitar, Schieder, Shidra, Sidra, Sidre, Sieu Odorhei, Sojtor, Sudurau, Sutoru, Zadar, Zator, Zatory				
		444800	Zozhetsiol	446440	Szaszmegyes
		444870	Siczeslaw	446460	Sosniczany
		445000	Chishki, Chizhki, Csuszka, Czeczke, Czyszki, Czyzyki, Diosig, Dioszeg, Dziczki, Rzaska, Rzeczki, Rzyczka, Rzyczki, Sachki, Sadska, Schozach, Sesik, Shatsk, Shatzk, Shishaki, Shushki, Sieczychy, Siesiaki, Siesikai, Sisak, Sisky, Susak, Susek, Susk, Szuszki, Zazheche	446500	Chesniki, Csesznek, Czesniki, Dzietrzniki, Rzasnik, Sosenka, Sosnki, Trzcianka, Tschaschniki, Zasmuky, Zosinek
439400	Chetrosu, Sudarca, Szederjes, Szedres				
439500	Cidreag, Sadurki, Sieu Odorhei, Sudarg, Sudargai, Sudargi, Sudarka				
				446515	Sosenki Jajki
439540	Sudargas			446560	Sasmacken, Sasmaken, Sassmacken, Shasmaken, Zoschingen
439560	Szederkeny				
439600	Cetireni, Chetyreny, Sotern				
439700	Schuttorf, Sejdorf, Sidorov, Sidorow	445300	Sascut, Siscauti	446574	Sosnicowice
		445343	Sascut Sat	446594	Chisineu Cris
439760	Trzetrzewina, Trzetrzewino, Zatrzebin	445346	Cesky Tesin	446600	Ciocmani, Dziecinin, Secemin
		445397	Ceska Trebova	446650	Secyminek
439780	Zadorfala	445439	Cesky Sternberk	446666	Secymin Niemiecki
439787	Zadorfalva	445458	Ceska Skalice	446678	Secymin Polski
439865	Ceadar Lunga	445466	Rzeczyca Ziemianska	446700	Cheshanov, Cieszanow, Czosnow, Sasnava, Sosnow, Sosnowe, Trzesniow, Trzezniow, Tseshanov, Tsheshanov, Tsutsnyuv, Tzieshinov
439880	Satoraljaujhely	445596	Cesky Krumlov		
440000	Ceaca, Cece, Ceica, Chesa, Chitch, Ciceu, Ciisia, Ciucea, Ciz, Csecs, Csecse, Csiz, Csosz, Csucsa, Csuz, Czausy, Czyze, Diez, Gyugye, Rzesza, Saaz, Saitsy, Sasci, Sauca, Sec, Sece, Shutz, Sic, Sudzha, Susa, Susz, Suza, Sycze, Szecs, Szoc, Szoce, Szocs, Tchais, Trzas, Zeitz, Zics	445598	Cesky Heralec		
		445600	Sazgony, Shishkany, Soshichno		
		445674	Csicsogombas		
		445700	Cecehov, Cieszkowy, Czyzykow, Sieciechow, Zashkov, Zashkuv, Zaskov, Zaskow, Zaszkow, Zhishchuv, Zishkov		
				446710	Sosnovoye
				446740	Cheznovice, Rzedzianowice, Sosnovets, Sosnovice, Sosnovits, Sosnovitz, Sosnovitza, Sosnovyets, Sosnowica, Sosnowice, Sosnowiec
		445731	Ceske Budejovice		
441740	Cecejovce, Sedziejowice	445740	Ciezkowice, Cizkovice, Dzietrzkowice, Shishkovtse, Shishkovtsy, Shyshkovtse, Sieciechowice, Szyszkowce, Trzeskowice, Trzeszkowice, Tzezhkovitz, Zaskevitchi, Zaszkowice		
443000	Cista, Czyste, Diosod, Sasd, Soest				
443140	Suciu de Jos				
443376	Czystadebina			446750	Dietzenbach, Sessenbach, Sosnowka
443400	Sestaci, Susetice				
443440	Czestocice, Suciu de Sus	445750	Shashkowka, Zaskevichi	446754	Sosnowiec Srodula
443500	Chistag, Sasiadka, Sestokai, Shestachi, Shistka, Shostaki, Shostka	445780	Suskowola	446756	Sosnowiec Niwka
		445785	Suszyca Wielka	446778	Sosnowa Wola
		445786	Ceske Velenice	446784	Rzesna Polska
443570	Chestokhova, Czestochowa, Rzeszotkow, Szostakow	445793	Cesky Brod	446793	Sassanfahrt
		445800	Dioskal	446800	Cismele
443574	Czastkowice	445870	Ceska Lipa	446840	Szecsenyhalaszi
443597	Czystohorb	445900	Sachkhere	446900	Tsoyzmir, Tsuyzmir, Tsuzmir,
443600	Sastin, Zasadne				

	Tzoizmir, Zezmar, Zezmer, Zhezhmariai, Zhizhmore E, Zhizhmory, Ziezmariai, Zuzmir, Zyzmory
446930	Schossenreuth
446940	Szasznyires
447000	Chizeve, Chizheva, Chizhevo, Ciacova, Cieszowa, Cisow, Cycow, Czieschowa, Czyzew, Czyzewo, Czyzow, Rzazew, Rzeszow, Rzezawa, Rzozow, Rzucow, Saczow, Sasov, Sasow, Sassov, Sazava, Schizuv, Suceava, Suczawa, Suszow, Sutchava, Sycow, Syczew, Syczow, Szaszfa, Tshizheva, Tsisuv, Tzishova, Tzitzov, Tzizhav, Zasov, Zassow, Zheshov, Zheshuv, Zhezhov, Zozow
447300	Seeshaupt, Sucevita
447350	Diospatak
447400	Chesybesy, Ciceuvic, Cieszybiesy, Cisovice, Czesybiesy, Czyzowice, Sesovce, Sycewicze, Zasavica
447468	Czuczewicze Male
447478	Czuczewicze Wielkie
447480	Diosviszlo
447500	Czyzowka, Diespeck, Rzeszowek, Sadzavka, Sadzavki, Sadzawka, Sadzawki, Sadzhevka, Sasovka, Soczewka, Trzesowka, Zaczopki
447548	Czyzewo Koscielne Wies
447600	Cesvaine, Czezwin, Sieu Sfaniu, Suceveni, Trzetrzewina, Trzetrzewino, Zatrzebin
447630	Sieu Sfint
447800	Sheshvil, Szaszujfalu
447840	Cisow Las
447850	Szaszfellak
447900	Sasvar, Szaszvar
447935	Sosvertike
447940	Sasveres, Szaszvaros
447950	Schassburg, Schossberg
448000	Chisalau, Ciesle, Ciuciulea, Csaszlo, Dzieciol, Sacel, Sasuoliai, Sesuoliai, Shosli, Sicsel, Soshly, Trzciel, Zadiel, Zadziele, Zasla, Zasle, Zasliai, Zasule, Zasulye, Zazule, Zhosla, Zhuzhel, Zosli, Zuzel
448314	Suciul de Jos
448344	Suciul de Sus
448400	Cecelice, Chislaz, Ciuslice, Schesslitz
448440	Dziasloszyce
448450	Zadzielsko
448487	Chisla Salieva
448500	Sesslach
448564	Szaszlekence
448570	Zazolkiew
448600	Ciuciuleni, Sashalom, Susleni, Susleny, Szaszlona, Zezulin
448640	Cicelnic, Zazulince, Zazulintse, Zazulintsy
448650	Chetschelnik, Chitchilnik, Czeczelnik, Tschetschelnik
448673	Szazhalombatta
448679	Zeiselmauer
448700	Cieciulow, Czaslaw, Dzedziluv, Dziedzilow, Tsutsilov, Tsutsyluv, Zaslav, Zaslaw, Zaslawie, Zaslov

448740	Chislavici, Sislevitch, Sislevits, Sislevitsh
448750	Cecylowka, Sosolowka, Sosolyuvka
448780	Zaslavl
448900	Zacler
449000	Chesereu, Cizer, Csaszar, Csizer, Diosgyor, Sasar, Szacsur
449300	Sisarte
449340	Siesartis
449383	Csaszartoltes
449439	Seitzersdorf Wolfpassing, Zissersdorf
449450	Czeczersk
449500	Cesarka, Cieciorki
449560	Szaszregen
449600	Sasarm, Secereni, Zaczernie
449800	Cicirlau
450000	Ceaga, Chege, Chegea, Cig, Csege, Cseke, Csog, Czege, Gyugy, Rzeki, Sag, Saka, Sakai, Sakee, Saki, Sakiai, Sauka, Schaki, Sege, Shakay, Shakee, Shakhi, Shakhy, Shaki, Shakyai, Socha, Sok, Sook, Sucha, Sukha, Sukhe, Syche, Sychi, Syke, Szachy, Szack, Szajk, Szak, Szaki, Szeg, Szegi, Szek, Szugy, Szuha, Szyk, Zaky, Zsaka, Zsok
451000	Ceheiu, Ciheiu, Ciocaia, Czekaje
451700	Czugujew, Zagajew
451783	Suchaja Balta
451785	Sukhaya Balka, Sukhaya Balka Pervyy Uchastok, Sukhayabalka
453000	Csekut, Sachtie, Sagod, Sakod, Shkod, Shkud, Shkudy, Sighet, Sigut, Sihat, Szeged, Sziget, Szkudy, Zacheta, Zahati
453345	Skudutishkis, Skudutiskis
453400	Cechtice, Ciocotis, Sahaidac, Schkeuditz, Skuodas, Skutec
453445	Skodotzishok, Skoduciszki
453470	Szigetcsep
453479	Sighet Suburbana Iapa
453500	Sagaydak, Sugatag
453543	Sugatag Sat
453600	Sechtem, Szegedin, Szkodna, Zahutyn, Zohatyn
453640	S Chodnitza, Skhodnitsa
453650	Skotniki
453664	Szigetmonostor
453670	Suchedniev, Suchedniow, Sukhedniev
453690	Saktmar
453740	Szigetbecse
453745	Skadovsk
453780	Shkodvil, Shkudvil, Skadvile, Skaudvile, Skodvil
453784	Csiktaplocza
453787	Csehetfalva
453790	Szigetvar
453800	Cehetel, Skadle, Skidel, Skytaly, Suchadol, Suchdol, Suchodol, Suchodoly, Sukhodol, Sukhodoly, Sukhodul
453860	Suchteln
453869	Sighetul Marmatiei
453877	Suchodol Wypychy
453900	Secatura, Sikator
453930	Sucutard
453945	Skotarsky

453960	Csakathurn, Csaktornya
454000	Csokas, Gyekes, Sakas, Saukas, Skotschau, Sukacze, Szakacsi, Szakasz, Szakcs, Szikso, Szkeco, Szkiczo, Zagacie, Zagozdzie, Zahajce, Zgosca
454300	Cechesti, Cihost, Dzukste, Scaziet, Sieksate, Skaista, Sukosd, Zagozdzie
454340	Skaistas
454358	Skaistkalne, Skaistkalnes
454360	Suchostan
454370	Cichostow, Suchastov, Suchestaw, Suchostaw, Sukhostav, Zegiestow
454374	Ciechostowice
454386	Skrzydlna
454400	Suchcice, Szikszo, Zakrzyze, Zehusice
454463	Csikszentdomokos, Csikszentmihaly, Szigetszentmiklos
454470	Skrzyszew, Skrzyszow
454475	Zakszuwek
454479	Sachsisch-Bereg
454484	Sokszelitz, Sokszelocz
454493	Csikszereda, Szekszard
454495	Saechsisch Regen
454496	Sachsisch Reen
454500	Cekiske, Tsiekishok, Tzeikishok
454565	Zaguzhe Konkolnitske
454570	Skoczkowo
454586	Skaitskalne
454600	Diuksyn, Dyuksin, Rzegocina, Sacaseni, Sachsen, Skeshino, Skrzynno, Sochatchin, Sochocin, Suchocin, Zagozdzon, Zegocina
454630	Scazinet
454640	Sachsenhausen, Skazinets
454650	Ciechocinek, Sachsenhagen, Skrzynka, Skuczynki
454654	Sachsenhausen
454655	Sachsenhagen
454678	Sachsenflur
454679	Sachsenburg
454680	Csiksomlyo
454700	Skasov, Skoczow, Skuszew, Skycov, Sochaczew, Sochatchev, Sochoczew, Sokhachev, Zahoczewie, Zakrzew
454747	Skrzypaczowice
454750	Zakrzowek
454754	Zakrzowek Szlachecki
454756	Zakrzowek Majoracki
454759	Szekesfehervar
454760	Cehu Sivaniei
454764	Skrzypny Ostrow
454778	Skoczow/Wilamowice
454790	Segesvar, Suchozebry
454870	Secheslav
454876	Cehu Silvaniei, Cehu Silvaniei
454900	Sighisoara
454930	Szegszard
454974	Szcrzorowice
455000	Csokako, Skoki, Sukach, Szuhogy, Zahajki
455345	Sh Chekotckin
455600	Sh Chuchin, Zagaykany, Zahaicana
455680	Skoki Male
455740	Zschachwitz

455800	Szuhakallo
455954	Sakukrogs
455960	Skaigirren, Sucha Gorna
455963	Suchy Grunt
456000	Csakany, Csokmo, Cygany, Czajkin, Rzekun, Sacueni, Sagan, Sagani, Saukenai, Schaken, Schocken, Secueni, Seeheim, Shegyni, Shekhyne, Shikian, Shokian, Shukian, Siegen, Skaune, Skem, Sucany, Szakony, Szechynie, Tsygany, Zagan, Zahony, Zaicani, Zakany, Zaykany, Zehun, Zhychin, Ziechenau
456300	Cigand, Socond
456340	Zakinthos
456350	Shkuntiki
456360	Chok Maydan, Cioc Maidan
456363	Cegenydanyad
456397	Zeckendorf
456400	Cekanice, Ciechomice, Segnitz, Skaunes, Tsekhnauts
456430	Suchomasty, Tsyganeshty
456450	Shkuntsiki, Szkunciki
456454	Cekoniskes
456480	Soconzel
456500	Dziekanka, Sukhinichi
456554	Ciechanki Krzesimowskie
456559	Ciechanki Krzesimowskie
456560	Seckenheim, Sickingen, Sugenheim, Ziegenhain
456600	Ciechomin, Csokmany, Seckenheim, Skemoniai, Skimian, Skomian, Sugenheim, Ziegenhain
456638	Cukmantl
456640	Skemonis, Skiemanys, Skiemonys
456645	Zagnansk, Zyck Niemiecki
456649	Sigmundsherberg
456700	Chekhanov, Chekhanove, Ciechanow, Dziekanow, Scumpia, Tshekhanov
456710	Skumpiya
456740	Chekhanovits, Chekhanovtse, Ciechanowiec, Sukhnovtse, Tshekhanovets, Tshekhanovits
456745	Sakhnovshchina, Sknifishuk
456746	Csokonyavisonta
456750	Sygniowka, Sygnyuvka, Tsechanovik
456766	Dziekanow Niemiecki
456778	Dziekanow Polski
456795	Seckenburg
456796	Seckmauern
456800	Rzeki Male, Zakanale
456860	Skomlin, Szegimalom
456864	Skomielna Czarna
456870	Sknilov, Sknilow, Skniluv
456900	Sakmir, Siegmar, Szakmar, Zakmur
456930	Ziegenort
456946	Siegmarschonau
456950	Skomorochy, Skomorokhy
456953	Skomorochy Duze
456957	Skomorochy Wielkie
456965	Sigmaringen
457000	Cejkov, Cekow, Chekhovo, Chukhovo, Cichawa, Csokva, Czajkow, Czajkowa, Czchow, Czechow, Czuchowo, Czukow, Djakovo, Dzhikev, Dzikov, Dzikow, Rzachowa, Rzechow, Rzgow, Rzochow, Rzuchow, Rzuchowa, Saikava, Schegove, Schegovo, Schochow, Sechov, Seehof, Sekhuv, Sekow, Sekowa, Shakev, Sichow, Siechow, Sikhov, Skape, Skawa, Skepe, Skiby, Skopje, Sojkowa, Suchava, Suchawa, Szuhafo, Tsegovo, Tsekhuv, Tzihav, Zakow, Zakowa, Zakupy, Zhagov, Zhukov, Zochow, Zuchow, Zukov, Zukow
457300	Sukowate
457360	Skovyatin, Skowiatyn
457379	Zukow Dwor
457400	Chaykovichi, Chaykovitse, Czajkowice, Czechowice, Diakovce, Drzkovce, Dzikowiec, Saikavas, Sakowicze, Secovce, Skawce, Skawica, Skupec, Suchowce, Szychowice, Zagvuzdzh, Zagwozdz, Zakowice, Zhuchovitch, Zhukovitchi, Zichovice, Zihobce, Zuchowicze
457430	Zagvozdye
457439	Dzikow Stary
457440	Zagvozdye
457443	Zukowice Stare
457444	Sakowszczyzna
457450	Skopishok
457454	Skapiskis, Skopiskis, Sucha Beskidzka
457455	Zakowska Huta
457456	Sakovshchina
457457	Secovska Polanka, Secovska Polianka
457460	Skavshin
457463	Zagyvaszanto
457467	Zakowice Nowe, Zukowice Nowe
457476	Skvazhava Nova
457500	Cechowka, Dzygovka, Sakovichi, Sychevichi, Sychevka, Zhukovka
457538	Czechowka Dolna
457546	Sakovchizna
457600	Sikabony, Skavin, Skawina, Skopanie, Skopin, Skovina, Suchaveni, Zakopane, Zakopona
457630	Csikvand
457670	Dzikow Nowy
457677	Skibniew Podawce
457700	Skopow, Skupowo
457765	Czuchow Pienki
457780	Sekowa Wola
457787	Zagyvapalfalva
457800	Sagujfalu, Skoplje, Sucha Wola, Suchopol, Suchowola, Suhopolje, Sukhopol, Sukhovole, Sukhovolya, Zagaypol, Zahajpol, Zahojpole, Zakowola
457830	Segewald, Segewold, Zegevol D
457840	Soha Balca
457845	Zyck Polski
457850	Rzeki Wielkie, Skobelka, Sucha Wolka, Sukha Balka
457870	Csikfalva
457900	Csakvar, Skver, Skvira, Skwira,
	Szegvar, Szigevar
457936	Skwirtne
457940	Cichoborz, Cichoburz, Skvorec, Suhoverca
457946	Skowierzyn, Skwierzyna
457947	Skwarzawa Nowa, Skwirzowa
457950	Segeberg, Siegburg
457954	Zagyvarekas
457960	Csakbereny
457965	Sico Branko, Sucha Bronka, Szuhabaranka
457967	Skvrnov
458000	Cehal, Cigla, Csogle, Csokaly, Csokoly, Shklo, Skal, Skala, Skaly, Skol, Skola, Skole, Sogel, Sokal, Sokol, Sokola, Sokole, Sokoli, Sokoly, Sokul, Szakal, Szakaly, Szakoly, Szekely, Szklo, Szokolya
458100	Sacalaia
458300	Cegled, Cehalut, Csegold, Siclod, Sigulda, Skalat, Szakald, Szekelyhid, Zaklodzie, Ziegelhutte
458343	Skalat Stary
458348	Sklad Solny
458360	Chekolteny, Ciocalteni
458370	Skladow
458379	Cegledbercel, Scldwersenz, Szekelyudvarhely
458400	Csaholc, Czachulec, Sacalasau, Siegless, Sigless, Siklos, Skalica, Szakolca, Szakolcza, Zaklodzie, Zeglce
458450	Skulsk
458453	Cikolasziget
458460	Sacalaseni, Skolyszyn, Zakliczyn, Ziegelhausen, Zoklitchin
458465	Siklosnagyfalu
458470	Skoloszow, Zakliczewo, Zakliczowo
458473	Siklosbodony
458475	Siegelsbach
458476	Cehul Sivaniei
458479	Skala Zbruch
458487	Cehul Silvaniei
458500	Sigelki, Skalka, Sokoliki, Sokolka, Sokolke, Sygielki, Szkolki
458530	Szigliget, Szogliget, Ziegelhutte
458546	Ziegelhausen
458549	Szekelykocsard
458559	Sokoliki Gorskie
458570	Zakilkov, Zaklikov, Zaklikow, Zglechow, Zoklikov
458573	Zaklikow Tartak
458594	Szekelykeresztur
458600	Cegielnia, Ciechlin, Cieklin, Sculeni, Shklin, Siculeni, Skalna, Skolin, Skulen, Skuleni, Skuliani, Skuljany, Skulyany, Szeghalom, Szihalom, Szklin, Zakhlin, Zekhlin, Zhichlin, Zhikhlin, Zychlin
458639	Sculeni Targ
458640	Seklence, Szcklencze, Szeklencze
458650	Segilong, Sokolniki, Sokolniky, Szegilong, Zaglinki
458654	Sokolniki Suche
458668	Sculeni Moldova
458670	Skolimow

458674	Sokoly Nowosiolki
458677	Skolimow Ptaszki
458694	Skalmierzyce, Skalmierzyce Nowe
458700	Ceglow, Shklov, Skloby, Sokolov, Sokolow, Sokoluv, Suchelipie, Szklow
458737	Zaglebie Dabrowskie
458738	Skala Podolskaya
458740	Sokolovac, Sokolowice, Zglobice
458750	Chukalovka, Chukaluvka, Czukalowka, Skelivka, Sokolivka, Sokolovka, Sokolowka, Sokoluvka
458760	Zglobien
458768	Sokolow Malopolski
458769	Skalbmierz
458771	Sokolow bei Stryj
458773	Sokolow Podlaski
458778	Sokolowa Wola
458835	Sacalul de Campi
458900	Sieglar
458956	Szklarka Myslniewska
459000	Cychry, Sakrau, Suchari, Suchary, Suharau, Sukhari, Sukoro, Tsygira, Zagare, Zager, Zagere, Zagory, Zagorye, Zagra, Zhagar, Zhagare, Zhager, Zhagory, Zohor
459300	Sioagard, Skride, Skroda, Skruda, Zacretje, Zagroda, Zakret, Zgurit, Zgurita
459343	Zgardesti, Zgordeshty
459345	Zagrody Skalbmierskie
459350	Skrudki, Zagrodki
459360	Scorteni, Skorodne
459361	Skorodnoye
459364	Skorodintsy, Skorodnica, Skorodynce
459370	Skordiow, Skordjow
459374	Zegartowice
459378	Skroda Wielka
459386	Skrudaliena, Skrudelino, Skrzydlna
459400	Siegritz, Skaros, Skorcz, Skurcze, Sykorice, Szekeres, Zagorz, Zagorze, Zagorzh, Zagurzhe, Zakrocz, Zakrzyze, Zgaritza, Zgerzh, Zgierz, Zguritsa
459430	Ciucuresti, Sakarestie, Zaharesti
459440	Siekierczyce, Sikorzyce, Skorczyce, Skorocice, Zagorzyce, Zuchorzyce
459444	Skorzeszyce
459445	Skarzhisk, Skarzisko Kamyena, Skarzysko, Skarzysko Kamienna, Skarzysko Koscielne, Skarzysko Ksiazece, Zagrody Skalbmierskie
459446	Sickershausen
459450	Sekursko, Zagoreczko, Zagorsko, Zgorsko
459456	Zagorze Knihynickie
459459	Sieghartskirchen
459460	Skarzyn, Skortseny, Skryhiczyn, Zagorzany, Zahariceni, Zakroczym, Zakrotchim, Zakrotchin, Zychorzyn
459465	Zagorzynek
459470	Dzigorzew, Skarishov, Skarszewy, Skaryszew, Skorczow, Skordiow, Skordjow, Skorzow, Skrzyszew, Skrzyszow, Suchorzow, Zachorzow

459474	Czekarzewice
459476	Siegertshofen
459484	Csiger Szollos, Zgorzelec
459500	Skoriki, Skoryki, Skurche
459534	Zager Chadash
459560	Zakharicheni, Zakrochim, Zakrochin
459570	Skorkow
459574	Skorkowice
459575	Zakrakowka
459587	Skraglevka, Skrigalovo, Skrigalow, Skrihalov, Skrygalovo
459600	Cegoreni, Chegoreny, Chigirin, Sacareni, Saharna, Sakharna, Sekareny, Sekiryani, Sekuren, Sekurian, Sikuran, Skrzynno, Sokiryany, Sokorone, Tschigirin, Zacharin, Zagorna, Zahorany, Zahorna, Zakharna, Zgorany
459630	Skrunda
459634	Skrundas
459639	Secureni Targ, Sekureni Targ
459640	Sekernica, Sekernice, Sikernica, Skornica, Skornice, Sokirnitsa, Zagarancea
459643	Secureni Sat
459650	Skorynki, Skrzynka, Zagorancha
459660	Skronina
459664	Chekur Menzhir
459669	Cecur Menjir
459674	Skernyevits, Skierniewice, Skiernivitz
459700	Sacurov, Skarby, Skurowa, Zagorow, Zagrab, Zagreb, Zagrova, Zahorb, Zakrzew
459740	Cicarovce, Skrybicze
459745	Skrabske
459747	Skierbieszow, Skrobaczow, Skrzypaczowice
459750	Zakharevka, Zakrzowek, Zgurovka
459754	Zakrzowek Szlachecki
459756	Zakrzowek Majoracki
459764	Skrzypny Ostrow
459780	Zagreblya, Zagreblye, Zagrobela
459786	Skrwilno
459790	Skrivare, Skriveri
459800	Cicarlau, Csikarlo, Sikarlo
459860	Chigirleni, Chigirleny
459875	Skralevka, Skrolifka
459974	Szcrzorowice
460000	Cean, Chiny, Cna, Csany, Csoma, Gyoma, Gyon, Sany, Schima, Sciony, Seini, Seiny, Sejny, Sena, Senno, Seno, Senya, Senyo, Shena, Shyena, Sienna, Sienno, Sihnea, Sima, Simna, Simno, Sinioe, Soimi, Sojmy, Som, Soyma, Sumy, Sunja, Syeno, Synee, Szany, Szin, Szinye, Szony, Tsna, Zaenya, Zaim, Zam, Zauan, Zeimiai, Zemne, Zheim, Zheime, Ziem, Zim, Zimno, Zsennye
461000	Sennaya, Sennoye, Sinaia
461600	Szomajom
461700	Zmijov, Zmiyev
461740	Zmajevac
461745	Zmijowiska
463000	Centa, Csenyete, Czente, Sanad,

	Sanda, Sandau, Sant, Santau, Sehnde, Senta, Sinteu, Sonta, Szanda, Szanto, Szend, Szenta, Szente, Szind, Szomod, Zamety, Zemite, Zenta, Zhmud
463100	Zemaitija
463131	Sinautii de Jos
463300	Sintautai
463396	Szentadorjan, Szentetornya
463400	Sanatauca, Sandets, Semyatitcha, Sentes, Sentus, Siemiatycze, Sniatycze, Suntazi, Szentes
463437	Szentistvan
463440	Chentatzitza
463460	Sandhausen, Santoczno
463470	Sendeshov, Sendishev, Shendeshov
463494	Szentgyorgyabrany
463495	Szentgyorgy, Szentgyorgyvolgy
463500	Schnaittach, Semyatich, Zendek
463538	Szentkatalin
463539	Szentgotthard
463546	Sandhausen
463564	Zemaitkiemis
463570	Snitkiv, Snitkov, Snitkowo, Szentjakab
463580	Szendehely, Szentgal
463584	Szentgalosker
463593	Szentgrot
463594	Sandhorst
463598	Szentkiraly
463600	Samotnia, Schamaiten, Shnyatin, Smidyn, Smodna, Snetin, Sniatin, Sniatyn, Snitin, Snyatin, Snyatyn, Sontheim, Szentanna, Zentene, Zinten, Zniatyn
463638	Szentantalfa
463639	Santandrei Bihor, Sintandrei, Sintandrei Bihor, Szentandras, Szentdemeter, Szentendre
463640	Chendu Mic, Snietnica, Szenttamas
463647	Smidyn Zablocie
463648	Santomischel
463650	Ciemietniki, Sniatynka, Snyatynka
463657	Szentnagyfalva
463658	Saint Nicolau Mare, Szentmihaly, Szentmihalytelke
463663	Sontheim an der Brenz
463664	Sandominic, Sindominic
463670	Sniedzianowo
463680	Schneidemuhl, Schneidmuhl
463690	Chendu Mare, Sandomir, Santa Maria, Sintimreu, Szentimre
463693	Szentmarton, Szentmartonkata
463694	Sandomierz, Sandomirzh, Sandomyerz
463700	Chinyadevo, Cinadovo, Santov, Semiduby, Shnadova, Shnadovi, Shnodovo, Shnyadovo, Sniadow, Sniadowo, Snitovo, Snitowo, Szentjobb
463739	Szentpeter, Szentpeterfa, Szentpeterszeg, Szentpeterur
463740	Csanadapaca, Smidovich
463750	Samotevichi, Santovka, Senatovka, Smidovicha, Sniadowka

448

463758	Szentbekkalla
463760	Szentivan
463763	Szentbenedek
463774	Sandove Vishnie, Sondova Vishniah
463783	Csanadpalota
463790	Csantaver
463795	Sandberg, Schmiedeberg
463800	Schontal, Szamotuly
463846	Sindolsheim
463848	Szentlaszlo, Szentliszlo
463850	Csanytelek
463864	Chendul Mic, Chintelnic
463869	Chendul Mare
463875	Sendelbach
463876	Sindelfingen
463896	Szentlerant, Szentlorinc, Szentlorinckata
463900	Center, Csomoder, Samter, Schondra, Smidary, Somotor, Sontra, Szendro, Szomotor
463940	Samothrace, Sandhorst, Smotritch
463943	Sindresti
463944	Sondershausen
463947	Zuntersbach
463948	Sandersleben
463950	Samothraki, Sandurki, Sintereag, Smotrich
463960	Sondernheim
463965	Sondernheim
463968	Schneidermuhl
463970	Sandrif, Sandrovo, Schandorf, Smederevo, Smederov, Smederovo, Zundorf
463974	Shandrovets, Szandrowiec
463975	Shandrovka, Shenderivka, Shinderivka, Szandorowka
463978	Sandorfalu, Sandorfalva
463983	Szendrolad
464000	Cenac, Chemnitz, Chinocz, Czaniec, Czanyz, Dzianisz, Gyimes, Samac, Sanc, Sandz, Sants, Sanz, Schemnitz, Schnaitsee, Semsa, Semse, Senca, Senec, Senica, Shumiatch, Siemnice, Sieniec, Siennica, Simeiz, Simnas, Siniec, Sintchy, Sjenica, Somes, Soms, Szaniec, Szenc, Szencz, Szumiacz, Tsants, Tzanz, Zamiescie, Zamojsce, Zamosc, Zamoscie, Zamoshye, Zamosi, Zamosze, Zamotch, Zamuescie, Zeimys, Zenica, Zmudz, Zons
464146	Tzantz Yashan
464300	Ciniseuti, Ciumesti, Sajmiste, Samsud, Sieu Nasaud, Sineshty, Sinesti, Zamostea, Zamostie, Zamosty, Zamostye
464330	Schonstadt
464339	Szamostatarfalva
464340	Gyenesdias
464343	Zamostea Storojinet
464347	Chenstochov
464357	Chenstokhov, Tshenstokhov
464370	Szamosdob
464379	Somogyudvarhely, Szamosudvarhely
464390	Somes Odorhei, Zamostre
464395	Somes Odorhei
464397	Samostrzalow
464400	Chinisheutsy, Gyongyos, Samocice, Schemeshits,

	Schemyeshitse, Semcice, Siemszyce, Somogyacsa, Sonczyce, Zamoshtch, Zamoshtsh, Znosicze
464439	Gyongyostarjan
464440	Gyenesdias
464450	Sinzishok
464460	Ziemetshausen
464468	Gyongyosmellek
464470	Sendziszov
464473	Gyongyospata
464480	Somogyaszalo
464484	Gyongyoshalasz
464486	Gyongyoshalmaj
464494	Gyongyosoroszi
464496	Gyongyosherman
464500	Sanoczek, Shimsk, Shomsk, Shumsk, Simasag, Sinzig, Somosko, Sonsk, Szamosszeg, Szumsk, Szumsko, Zameczek, Zamochek, Zamoshch, Znosichi
464510	Shumskoye
464534	Czumsk Duzy
464547	Gyimeskozeplak, Gyimeskozeplock
464560	Samascani, Samashkany
464564	Sanski Most
464569	Zamosc Mierzejewo
464578	Somoskoujfalu
464587	Zemaiciu Kalvarija
464590	Szamosker
464593	Szamoskorod
464594	Szamoskrasso
464600	Chimisheny, Cimiseni, Samotschin, Samson, Samuseni, Simisna, Sinsheim, Sinzheim, Snezna, Soimuseni, Someseni, Szamocin, Trzemesnia, Trzemeszno, Trzemiesnia, Zamoczyn, Zamshany, Zamszany, Zniesienie
464640	Samsonhaza, Tsemezhintse
464648	Szamosangyalos
464650	Sinzenich
464654	Samsonhaza
464660	Szentsimon
464664	Zemaiciu Naumiestis
464670	Samsonow, Sniedzanowo, Sniedzianowo
464675	Schnodsenbach
464678	Zmozna Wola
464687	Trzemeszno Lubuskie
464700	Chenstchov, Shemezova, Shemezovo, Siemiezowo, Siemuszowa, Smoszew, Znacevo, Znyatsevo
464730	Somogyapati
464740	Ciemiezowice, Szamosbecs
464750	Gyimesbukk, Smrzovka, Sonsbeck
464780	Szenes Ofalu
464785	Szamosseplak
464787	Szamosfalva
464790	Somoshuyvar, Szamosujvar, Szamosuovar
464794	Smiedzyborz
464795	Sensburg
464800	Chimiashla, Chimishli, Cimislia, Czimisli, Sanislau, Szamossalyi, Szaniszlo
464810	Chimishliya, Cimislija

464850	Szamosujlak
464870	Samostrzalow
464875	Zmyslowka
464960	Tsyntsareni, Tsyntsareny
464964	Szamosormezo
465000	Chenak, Chenga, Chinkeu, Cimochy, Cincau, Csonge, Dshankoi, Dzhankoi, Dzhankoy, Gyongy, Gyonk, Rzymki, Sanka, Sanniki, Sanok, Sanuk, Schongau, Scianka, Shumiachi, Shumyachi, Sianki, Sincai, Snegi, Sniegi, Somogy, Sonik, Sumeg, Syanki, Zamch, Zamek, Zanka
465137	Sinmihaiu de Padure
465140	Suncuius
465183	Sanmihaiul de Campie
465300	Cinkota, Csengod, Sancauti, Sankad, Somkad, Somogyjad, Sonkad
465315	Sankt Johann
465336	Sankt Tonis
465359	Sankt Goar, Sankt Goarshausen
465360	Samogitien
465363	Sankt Andra
465365	Sankt Ingbert, Sankt Nikolai
465369	Sankt Martin im Muhlkreise, Somcuta Mare
465373	Sankt Peter, Sankt Veit, Sankt Veit im Pongau
465376	Sankt Wendel, Somogyhatvan
465378	Sankt Blasien, Sankt Polten
465400	Csomakoz, Sankaitsy, Shimkaits, Simkaiciai, Zamchozhi
465435	Semigostichi, Semikhostiche
465440	Siemihoscicze
465463	Somogyszentpal
465464	Somogysamson
465465	Schongeising
465466	Somogysimonyi
465470	Somogyszob
465475	Zimnochy Swiechy
465480	Somogyszil
465487	Samac Slavonski
465493	Somogysard
465553	Csonkahegyhat
465583	Somogykiliti
465598	Siennica Krolewska
465600	Dienheim, Schmieheim, Senheim, Singen, Smiechen, Smigno
465638	Siennica Nadolna
465670	Siemiginow
465700	Chinkov, Dziunkow, Samokov, Senkuv, Siemiechow, Sienkow, Sinkov, Sinkow, Smichov, Snakov, Zamechow, Zamekhov, Zamichov, Zamiechow, Zenkov, Zienkow, Zinkov, Zinkow
465740	Samakowce, Semakovtse, Semakovtsy, Semkowce, Senkovitse, Senkowice, Shimkovtsy, Siemakowce, Siemikowce, Siemkowce, Siemkowice, Sienkiewicze, Sinkiewicze, Smiechowice, Smochowice, Smykowce, Snochowice, Somogyfajsz, Szymkowce, Zinkovtsy, Zinkowitz

465747 Senkevicevka, Senkevitchovka, Sienkiewiczowka
465750 Sinkevichi, Somogyfok
465757 Senkevichevka
465759 Somogyfeheregyhaz
465760 Singhofen
465764 Somogyvamos
465778 Zamkowa Wola
465784 Samochvilocitch
465787 Samokhvalovichi
465790 Somogyvar
465800 Schmiegel, Smigiel, Zemgale, Zemgola
465810 Zemigalliia
465834 Schonholthausen
465845 Samokleski Male
465860 Semgallen
465865 Schenklengsfeld
465876 Sinnicolaw Mare
465880 Sannicolaul
465886 Sannicolal Mare, Sannicolaul Mare
465889 Sannicolaul Roman, Sinnicolaul Roman
465896 Sinnicolau Romin
465900 Chenger, Csenger, Sangerei, Sincrai, Sinogora, Snikere
465916 Sangereii Noui
465930 Csongrad, Zhmigrod, Zmigrod
465934 Zmigrod Stary
465935 Samgorodok, Sangorodok
465936 Zmigrod Nowy, Zmygrod Nowy
465940 Sangerhausen, Sieu Magherus
465944 Szynkarzyzna
465945 Somogyharsagy
465946 Csengersima, Siennica Rozana
465947 Sangeorz Bai, Singeorz Bai, Smogorzow
465950 Somkerek, Zhanokrich
465953 Singeorgiu de Padure, Singiorgiu de Padure
465954 Sangerhausen
465958 Sangeorgiul de Padure, Sangiorgiul de Padure
465960 Singureni, Syngureny
465975 Snigirevka
465978 Csengerujfalu
465979 Sangerberg
466000 Ciumeni, Cmien, Csomeny, Csomonya, Czmon, Dzhamany, Dziemiany, Dziemionna, Rzemien, Samani, Schienen, Seimeni, Semin, Semjen, Senheim, Shaumyan, Shaumyana, Shumen, Siemien, Siemiony, Simian, Simoniai, Simonyi, Snina, Somin, Sonina, Sumony, Szemenye, Szymony, Tsuman, Zamienie, Zemun, Zimany, Zminne, Znaim, Znin, Znojmo
466300 Csomend
466390 Semendria
466396 Simontornya
466400 Schymanzy, Seminca, Shimantza, Zmiennica
466436 Diemantstein
466450 Siemieniczki, Simaniskiai
466458 Zemianska Olca
466480 Zaniemysl
466500 Chemenik, Semenki, Somianka, Szymonka, Zemunik
466560 Samenheim, Sammenheim,

Schoningen, Schonungen
466574 Shmankovtse, Szmankowce
466600 Samenheim, Sammenheim
466645 Znamensk
466650 Snamenka, Znamenka
466700 Simonfa, Simonov, Symonow, Szymanowa, Zenonow
466740 Siemianowice, Siemianowitz, Siemionowicze, Simonovce, Symonowicze
466744 Siemianowice Slaskie
466750 Semenovka, Semenuvka, Semianovka, Semonovka, Semyanovka, Siemianowka, Siemionowka, Simonovichi, Symonoviche
466797 Tsmen Pervsha
466900 Ceanu Mare
467000 Ceniawa, Ceniow, Cieniawa, Csimpo, Saniob, Scinawa, Senava, Shamovo, Shinova, Shomova, Sianow, Sieniawa, Siennow, Siniava, Sinjava, Snov, Snow, Snuv, Szaniawy, Szumowa, Szumowo, Tsenyava, Tsenyuv, Zaniow, Zanivye, Zaniwie, Zanow, Zmiev, Zomba
467300 Szombat, Zimna Voda, Zimna Woda, Zimnowoda
467350 Sanapotek
467367 Senftenberg
467370 Snovidov, Snowidow
467374 Snowidowicze
467375 Snovidoviche, Snovidovichi
467380 Szombathely
467390 Sinpetru, Szinpetri
467393 Sinpetru de Cimpie
467394 Cimpia Truzii
467400 Cineves, Csonopyca, Czempisz, Sanvasii, Semnevice, Sieniewice, Snovich, Snowicz, Szempc, Szempcz
467440 Zembrzyce
467446 Zembrzus Mokry Grunt
467450 Shnipishuk, Snovsk, Snowsk
467454 Snipiskes, Zambski Stare
467455 Zambski Koscielne
467456 Synowodzko Nizne
467457 Synowodzko Wyzne
467465 Zambrzeniec Nowy, Zambrzyniec Nowy
467470 Snopousovy
467490 Snovsr
467500 Schonebeck, Sembach, Shumovka, Sieniawka, Simpach, Siniavka, Siniawka, Sinjawka, Sinovka, Sinyavka, Zsambek, Zsambok
467570 Snopkow
467590 Szumowo Gora
467593 Szambokret
467600 Czempin, Schempin, Zembin
467630 Cimpinita
467634 Szaniawy Matysy
467670 Szumowo Nowe, Ziempniow
467700 Dziembowo
467745 Zinovyevsk, Zinowjewsk
467763 Szaniawy Poniaty
467800 Sinpaul, Snepele, Somfalu
467830 Scheinfeld, Schonfeld, Sennfeld, Sonnefeld
467840 Ziemblice

467858 Sanpaul Cluj, Sinpaul Cluj
467860 Sompolna, Sompolno, Zempeln, Zemplen, Zemplin
467864 Templensztara
467865 Cimpulung la Tisa, Cimpulung Moldovenesc, Zemplenagard
467870 Csomafalva, Sinfalva
467879 Zempl...
467900 Sam..., ..bor, Seniver, Sinevir, Sinovir, Sombor, Szinever, Zimbor, Zimboru, Zombor, Zsombor
467914 Sambor Yashan
467930 Zhnibrody, Znibrody
467940 Samborz, Zembrzyce
467943 Sambor Stary
467944 Samborzec
467945 Sinevirskaya Polyana, Sinovirska Polana
467946 Zembrzus Mokry Grunt
467950 Schoenberg, Schonberg, Shenberg, Shimberg, Shonberg, Somberek, Sonneberg, Sumperk, Suniperk, Szymbark, Zamberk
467953 Schomberg Dautmergen
467959 Schneebergerhof
467960 Schonbrunn, Somborn, Zembreni, Zembreny
467965 Zambrzeniec Nowy, Zambrzyniec Nowy
467970 Dziembrow, Zambrov, Zambrow, Zambruv, Zembrov, Zembrova, Zembrove, Zombrov
467978 Simferopol, Sinevir Polyana, Siniyvir Polyana, Symferopol
468000 Schumlau, Shumla, Simla, Sinole, Smela, Smeloa, Smeola, Smiela, Smila, Somaly, Somlyo, Sumal, Sumuleu, Zamoly, Zemel, Zheimel, Ziemel
468100 Shamloya, Smeloya
468160 Somlojeno
468340 Schonholthausen, Zamolodycze
468360 Smilten, Smiltene
468380 Smolotely
468400 Cenalos, Cimelice, Cmolas, Csanalos, Semeljci, Sinoles, Zamlicze, Zeimelis
468450 Semelishok, Semeliskiai, Semilishok, Semilshouk, Somlyocsehi
468454 Semeliskes
468457 Samoluskovtsy, Samoluskowce
468484 Somloszollos
468487 Simleu Silvaniei
468500 Smilg, Smilgiai, Smolechy, Smolugi, Szemlak, Zamliche
468570 Smilkov
468583 Schmalkalden
468600 Schmalnau, Semlin, Shumilino, Shumlyany, Sinolin, Smilno, Smolany, Smolian, Smolin, Smoljany, Smolna, Smolyany, Szumlany, Zamlynie, Zamlynye
468640 Schmollnitz, Smolanica, Smolnica, Smolnitsa, Smolyanitsa, Zamulince, Zamulintse
468645 Smolensk

468650	Schoenlanke, Schonlanke, Smielnik, Smolnick, Smolnik, Smolniki, Szmolnok
468653	Szomolnokhutta
468655	Smolnicka Huta
468657	Sineljnikov, Sinelnikovo
468665	Smalininkai
468679	Schmallenberg
468700	Chem..., Csmolif, Czmielov, ʒh ... ʌ, Smalvai, Smolewo, Smolwy, Sumilova, Tshmelev
468740	Smalvos, Smilovitch, Smolavitch, Smolewicze
468749	Somlovasarhely
468750	Schnellbach, Smilovichi, Smolevichi, Szmilowka
468848	Simleul Silvaniei
469000	Chinari, Ciumara, Csomor, Czemery, Gyomore, Gyomro, Samara, Samary, Samorja, Sommerau, Somorja, Sumy R, Szemere, Szomor, Zimor
469300	Diemerode, Zamardi
469350	Smorodek
469360	Sanmartin, Sinmartin, Smerdyna
469364	Sanmartin Ciuc, Sinmartin Ciuc
469370	Smordva, Smordwa, Smrdov
469400	Siemierz, Siomaros, Smirice, Zamorocze
469430	Somerseta
469435	Samorzadki
469436	Zamarstynow
469438	Smorze Dolne
469446	Simmershausen
469450	Smereczka, Smorodzk, Zamarski
469460	Smereczyna, Sohmerhausen, Sommerhausen
469464	Ciemierzynce, Ciemierzyniec, Smorze Miasteczko
469467	Zmorzna Wola
469470	Smardzewo
469474	Ciemierzowice
469493	Zimmersrode
469500	Smerek, Smrock, Sommerach, Zmiarki
469546	Sohmerhausen, Sommerhausen
469560	Smorgon, Smorgonie, Smurgainiai
469570	Smarkow, Smerekov, Smerekow, Smerekuv
469574	Smerekowiec
469600	Cemerne, Ciomirna, Ciumarna, Sammerein, Samorin, Simmern, Smoryn, Sommerein
469640	Chemerintsy
469650	Chemernik, Chemyerniki, Czemierniki, Schmerinka, Semmering, Zhmerinka, Zmerinka
469700	Semerovo, Senohraby
469740	Chemerovitz, Chemerovtsy, Czemerowce, Samarowicze
469750	Samaroviche, Samarovichi, Smrzovka
469780	Somerpalu
469798	Szinervaralja
469800	Csomorlo
470000	Ceaba, Cefa, Cheb, Cibu, Csaba, Csap, Csapi, Cseb, Cseffa, Csep, Csepa, Csob, Csobaj, Csop, Rzhev, Saba, Sap, Schaffa, Shaba, Shabo, Sheev, Sibiu, Sif, Sob, Sofia, Sopje,

	Szaba, Szava, Szob, Szojva, Zab, Zabia, Zabie, Zaube, Zavoy, Zawoj, Zhabya, Zhabye, Zsibo
471000	Sofiya, Zawoja, Zhabeye
471340	Svojetice, Swojatycze
471350	Svoyatichi
471360	Svojetin
471700	Zbijow
471745	Chapayevsk
471750	Sofiyevka
471900	Speyer
473000	Csabdi, Csapod, Csobad, Sabed, Schwedt, Shepit, Sobota, Sopot, Sopte, Sovata, Subata, Subate, Subbat, Svete, Swiete, Szovat, Szovata, Zabud, Zavod, Zavody, Zawada, Zawady, Zawod, Zawoda, Zoppot, Zwittau
473157	Svaty Jakub
473160	Sveta Jana
473178	Svyataya Volya
473190	Svaty Jur
473370	Szabadhidveg
473400	Sheptytse, Shvidostch, Subatas, Subotica, Svatus, Svatusa, Svedasai, Svityaz, Switaz, Szeptyce, Szoboticza, Zabotec, Zawidcze
473430	Sapte Sate, Sobotiste, Szabatist
473440	Sviadoshts, Swiadoszcz, Zawidczyce
473480	Savadisla
473487	Swietoslaw
473497	Svetozarevo
473500	Schobdach, Siobotka, Sobotka, Svatki, Swatki, Szabadka, Szepetk, Zavadka, Zavidche, Zawadka
473537	Szabadhidveg
473540	Szabadegyhaza, Zavidchitsy
473544	Swiety Krzyz, Zawadka Osiecka
473560	Sopotkin
473569	Zawadka Morochowska
473570	Svitkov, Swietochow, Zbytkow
473574	Spitkovitz, Spytkowice, Swietochow Stary
473577	Swiatkowa Wielka
473587	Swietochlowice
473594	Swiety Krzyz
473596	Seebad Heringsdorf
473600	Schauboden, Sevetin, Sipoteni, Sipoteny, Sobiatyn, Svodin, Zhovten, Zobten, Zowten
473613	Zapadnaya Dvina
473640	Schweidnitz, Siepietnica, Sopotnice, Swidnica, Zhovtantsy
473645	Svidnicka
473650	Dziewietniki, Subbotniki, Subotniki, Svidnik, Swiatniki, Swidnik, Szepetnek
473658	Svati Mikulov, Svati Mikulow, Svaty Mikulas
473668	Sopotnia Mala
473670	Svetnov, Swietoniowa, Zbydniow
473674	Zbydniowice
473700	Svidova, Svitavy, Swedow, Swidowa, Trzebiatow, Zapytov, Zapytow, Zavadov, Zavaduv, Zavidov, Zavidova, Zavidovo, Zawadow, Zhivatov, Zhivotov,

	Zivotov, Zywatow
473736	Szabadbattyan
473739	Sveti Petar Cvrstec
473740	Zavidovici, Zavidovitse, Zawidowice
473750	Shepetivke, Shepetovka, Szepetowka, Zhivotovka
473760	Sapte Bani, Swidwin, Swiedziebnia
473763	Svaty Benadik, Svaty Benedik
473764	Sveti Ivan Zabno, Sveti Ivan Zelina
473780	Swieta Wola
473794	Zoppot Freistaat
473800	Sipotele, Spittal, Swidle, Zawitala
473838	Svetlodolinskoye, Szpetal Dolny
473840	Svetlice
473844	Sipotele Sucevei
473845	Shipotele Suchevey
473850	Czoptelke, Schaftlach
473863	Spittal an der Drau, Svetla nad Sazavou, Svetla nad Sazvou
473864	Spital am Semmering
473867	Spital am Pyhrn
473874	Sipotele pe Siret, Svetlovodsk
473896	Schaftlarn
473900	Sobedruhy, Sopteriu, Swider
473943	Swidry Stare
473947	Switarzow
473950	Saba Targ
473967	Sobota Rimavska
474000	Cepice, Drzewica, Dzevice, Dzhevitza, Dzibice, Rzabiec, Rzepedz, Sabac, Sabisa, Sapci, Sawice, Saybusch, Scheibbs, Sebes, Sebesh, Sebez, Sebeza, Sebezh, Sebis, Sebyezh, Sheps, Shovits, Shubbotz, Shubitz, Shubotch, Siebiez, Sipca, Siubaiciai, Sivac, Sobotsh, Sovits, Spas, Svessa, Swiecie, Szepes, Trzebce, Trzebica, Trzebiez, Trzebos, Trzebucza, Zabce, Zabcze, Zabiec, Zaboze, Zabrze, Zabuze, Zabuzhye, Zaibis, Zapoeoze, Zawidza, Zawoz, Zaybash, Zaybush, Zbudza, Zeibush, Zejbis, Zepce, Zhevitza, Zhivits, Zhivitz, Zhivyets, Ziebice, Zwizdze, Zywiec
474300	Csabacsud
474340	Cvrstec
474345	Zawisty Dzikie
474360	Zwesten
474366	Spas Demensk, Spas Dement
474370	Zvestov
474374	Zebrzydowice, Zvestovice
474378	Sebastapol, Sevastapol, Sevastopol, Sewastopol
474386	Svistelniki, Swistelniki
474400	Dziewieczyce, Sobcice, Subacius, Sufczyce, Swiecica, Zabrzez, Zbyszyce, Zubrzyce, Zvizhdzhe
474450	Sepizishok
474460	Szebrzeszyn
474463	Sepsiszentgyorgy
474475	Spisicbukovica
474500	Sevsk, Shepsk, Siewsk, Sobieseki, Sobiska, Sovetsk,

	Spassk, Svyatsk, Szowsko, Trzebuska, Zboiska, Zubrzyk
474538	Zubrzyca Dolna
474540	Zapiskis, Zapyskis
474543	Rzewuski Stare, Spisska Stara Ves
474547	Spisska Sobota
474559	Zubrzyca Gorna
474560	Sopochkinye, Sopockin, Sopotskin, Sopotzkin
474567	Spisska Nova Ves
474570	Swieciechow
474573	Spisske Podhradie
474578	Sobieska Wola, Spisska Bela, Spisska Vlachy, Spisske Vlachy, Zubrzyca Wielka
474586	Sebeskellemes
474600	Sawczyn, Schafhausen, Sebuzin, Shvyetsiani, Sobesin, Sobiecin, Sobieszyn, Spiczyn, Spieszyn, Sufczyna, Svojsin, Swieciany, Trzebciny, Zawiszyn, Zbaszyn, Zbozenna, Zbuczyn, Zbuzany
474640	Zvyezhinets
474650	Sapezhanka, Sapiezanka, Sawtschonki, Schweissing
474656	Schwetzingen
474697	Zabcze Murowane
474700	Sopaczow, Spasow, Swojczow, Swoszowa, Trzebieszow, Zbizuby, Zbyszewo, Zhivachev, Zywaczow
474715	Schwetz bei Graudenz
474735	Sebespatak
474740	Swoszowice
474746	Cepcewicze Male
474747	Cepcewicze Wielkie Obolonie, Cepcewicze Wielkie Smolki
474750	Swojczowka, Tseptsevichi
474756	Tseptseviche Male
474760	Swiedziebnia
474780	Szepesbela
474798	Szepesvaralja
474800	Dziewiecioly, Zwiesel
474840	Svislotch, Swiesielice, Swislocz, Szabadszallas, Szepesolaszi, Zawiselcze
474846	Swisloczany
474850	Svisloch
474870	Sobeslav
474874	Svislovitch, Svislovitz
474940	Dziewiecierz
475000	Rzepki, Saffig, Scheppach, Schupbach, Schweich, Seebach, Shipka, Siofok, Zabajka, Zabki, Zabok, Zbik, Zbuch, Zhabka, Zhapka, Ziabki, Zubogy, Zwickau, Zyabki
475300	Schwechat
475340	Zubki Duze
475400	Cibakhaza
475430	Zavichost, Zawichost
475460	Schafhausen, Schwaighausen, Shvekshni, Shveksna, Sveksna, Svieksniai, Swicciany
475476	Speckswinkel
475480	Sipbachzell
475600	Savchin, Schaafheim, Schopfheim, Shavkany, Sopochinie, Sopockine, Sopockinie, Sviecany, Swiecany, Szawkiany, Zebegeny
475640	Sobakince

475656	Schwegenheim, Spaichingen
475657	Shevchenkovo
475660	Schwegenheim
475674	Zbigniewice
475697	Zhabche Murovane
475700	Cewkow, Cvikov, Sapaguv, Sapahow, Sepekov, Sepichow, Shpikov, Shubkov, Shuvkov, Sobkov, Sobkow, Sopachiv, Sopachuv, Spikov, Svihov, Svoychuv, Szubkov, Zabkow, Zbikow, Zhyvachuv, Zubkow, Zubkuv
475740	Szwajkowce, Zabkowice, Zbikowice, Zvikovec
475743	Zavichvost
475768	Sivka Voynilov, Siwka Wojnilowska
475795	Spachbrucken
475800	Spiegelau, Zviagel, Zvihil
475840	Shpikolosy, Szpikolosy
475850	Zabokliky
475900	Zhavgur, Zhivacher
475940	Schabokritsch, Zabocrici, Zabokritz, Zhabokritch
475950	Csipkerek, Zhabokrich
475956	Zabokreky nad Nitrou
476000	Cepin, Chebin, Chebinya, Csebeny, Csehbanya, Czubin, Diepenau, Dziewin, Rzepin, Rzewnie, Sabin, Sabnie, Saveni, Saviena, Savin, Sawin, Schaafheim, Schiefbahn, Schopfheim, Schubin, Schwaan, Soponya, Sowin, Sowina, Subina, Suwin, Szeben, Szebeny, Szebnie, Szewnia, Szubin, Trzebina, Trzebinia, Tschepin, Tshebin, Zabin, Zabno, Zavan, Zawan, Zbojna, Zbojno, Zeben, Zeven, Zhabno, Zobni, Zupanie, Zupanja, Zvon
476149	Sobienie Jeziory
476300	Sapanta, Sapinta, Saponta, Sipeniti, Spandau
476349	Sventezeris
476359	Sfantu Gheorghe, Sfintu Gheorghe
476365	Dzeventniki
476379	Spandowerhagen
476380	Sfintu Ilie
476385	Sfantul Gheorghe
476386	Spania Dolina
476389	Spindleruv Mlyn
476397	Schwandorf, Schwandorf in Bayern, Tschippendorf
476400	Ciubanca, Dzwiniacz, Rzhavintsy, Savienas, Sebnitz, Sepnica, Shipentsi, Shipintsy, Sovenyhaza, Spinus, Svinica, Swinoujscie, Szopienice, Trzebnica, Trzepnica, Zabnica, Zbenice, Zbenitz, Zhvanets, Zivanice, Zvanitz, Zvantz, Zviniace, Zviniatch, Zwaniec, Zwanitse, Zwieniacz, Zwiniacz, Zwiniacze
476433	Schoppenstedt
476436	Seebenstein
476438	Dzwiniacz Dolny
476440	Shvyentshitse
476450	Dziewieniszki, Dzvinsk,

	Dzwiniaczka, Shuvinishok, Suvenishki, Zhvanchik, Zubensko, Zvancik, Zvantchik, Zvinyachka, Zwanchik
476454	Dieveniskes, Suvainiskis
476459	Dzwiniacz Gorny
476460	Shvintzion, Shvyentsiani, Sventsian, Sventsiany, Sventzion, Swenziany, Zuffenhausen
476464	Svencionys
476468	Svencioneliai
476473	Schweinshaupten
476476	Schweinspoint
476479	Schweinsberg
476485	Sobienie Szlacheckie
476500	Csobanka, Dzvinyach, Dzwonek, Rzepiennik, Rzepnik, Sabinka, Sepinka, Sibenik, Spinka, Sviench, Sviniochi, Svinyukhi, Svionik, Swiniuchy, Trzebionka, Zabianka, Zabinka, Zabnik, Zhabinka, Zvinyach
476510	Zvinyacheye
476543	Rzepiennik Strzyzews, Rzepiennik Strzyzewski
476544	Rzepiennik Strzyzews, Rzepiennik Strzyzewski
476546	Zuffenhausen
476560	Svenchan
476567	Spangenberg, Zwingenberg
476569	Rzepiennik Marciszowski
476570	Zvonickov
476574	Rzepiennik Biskupi
476593	Dzvinogorod, Dzvinogrud, Dzwinogrod, Siebenhirten, Siebenhirten bei Wien, Zvenigorodka, Zwenigorodka, Zwinogrodka
476640	Svinomazy
476643	Trzebinia Miasteczko, Trzebinia Miasto
476656	Schwenningen, Schwenningen am Neckar
476663	Swinemunde
476679	Schwanenbruckl, Schwanenburg
476700	Dziwnow, Dzwonowa, Rzepniow, Sabinov, Shpanov, Szpanow, Zhepnyuv
476740	Sobianowice, Soboniowice, Trzebinia Wies
476750	Dziwnowek, Sabinowka, Sabinuvka
476780	Schippenbeil
476783	Schwanfeld
476793	Schweinfurt
476795	Schwanberg, Schwaneburg, Schweinberg, Sepenberg, Shvaneburg, Spannberg
476797	Swinna Poreba
476900	Svinare
476930	Siebenhirten, Siebenhirten bei Wien
476946	Swinarzyn
476960	Svinarin
476970	Szufnarowa
477000	Dzbow, Safov, Sopov, Sopow, Zabava, Zabawa, Zipov, Zupawa
477360	Swiebodna
477361	Zapovednoye

477386	Czepow Dolny	478700	Ceblow, Chepelov, Ciepelow, Ciepielewo, Ciepielow, Czepielow, Sobolev, Soboleve, Sobolew, Sobolewa, Sobolewo, Sobolow, Spilyava, Svalava, Svalyava, Tsebluv, Tsibulev, Tsibulevo, Zapalow, Zavalov, Zavaluv, Zawalow	479460	Chiperceni, Schwarzenau, Shebreshin, Shevershin, Shverzna, Shvyerzhen, Siefersheim, Sverzhna, Sverzhne, Swiercna, Swierzen, Szebrzeszyn, Zabriceni, Zwierzyn
477400	Chebabcea, Czepowiczi, Schwabisch, Schwiebus, Shypovtse, Szypowce, Zubowice			479464	Schwersenz, Swierzen Stary, Zvierznitz, Zwierzyniec
477440	Swiebodzice			479466	Swierzan Novy, Swierzen Nowy
477456	Schwabisch Gmund			479467	Schwarzenberg, Schwarzenborn, Schwarzenbruck, Schwarzenfeld
477458	Schwabisch Hall	478737	Cieplewo Dworskie		
477460	Swiebodzin	478745	Svalavska Nelipa		
477500	Schwabach, Sofievka, Sofiovka, Tsapovka, Zofiowka, Zofiuvka, Zofjowka, Zofyuvka	478747	Tschoplowitz bei Brieg	479470	Swaryczow, Swarzow, Zabierzow, Zbiershav
		478749	Shuvalovo Ozerki		
		478750	Schiffelbach, Sobolevka, Sobolewka, Sobolivka	479474	Swarycewicze
477560	Schwebheim			479475	Seibersbach, Svaritsevichi, Svarytseviche
477600	Schwebheim	478754	Zwoelfaxing, Zwolfaxing		
477640	Schweppenhausen	478760	Schivelbein	479478	Schwarzwald
477643	Zubov Most, Zubowmosty	478785	Czaple Wielkie, Zabiele Wielkie	479479	Seifriedsberg, Swierzowa Ruska
477654	Schweppenhausen	478795	Spielberg	479480	Soprashl, Suprashl, Suprasl, Suprasle
477656	Schwabenheim	478900	Szaflary		
477660	Schwabenheim	478945	Czaple Ruskie	479487	Zbraslav, Zbraslavice
477665	Schwabmunchen	479000	Cepari, Ceparia, Cifer, Csovar, Saabor, Saavar, Shvir, Sobor, Sovar, Subari, Subory, Svir, Svyriai, Swir, Swory, Szapar, Zabar, Zabor, Zabori, Zaborye, Zabreh, Zabrze, Zbiroh, Zbora, Zsabar, Zver, Zvur, Zwir, Zwor	479500	Csepreg, Csibrak, Cyprki, Dieburg, Seeburg, Sparach, Spergau, Szyperki, Tsibirika, Zavyerche, Zebrak, Zieverich, Zubrzyk
477800	Sepopol, Zabia Wola				
477836	Zwiefalten				
477900	Sobibor				
477945	Zabovresky				
477956	Zweibrucken				
478000	Chapli, Cibla, Csavoly, Csepel, Czaple, Czepel, Czepiele, Dziewule, Sabila, Sabile, Savoly, Schavli, Shavl, Shawli, Shepel, Shpola, Spala, Subl, Svilaj, Szawle, Szawly, Szepel, Zabala, Zabalj, Zavale, Zawale, Zubole, Zvala, Zvil, Zwiahl, Zwola			479538	Zubrzyca Dolna
		479100	Chepariya	479543	Zvirgzdene
		479300	Schwerte, Sobehrdy, Souvrat, Sovarad, Sprottau, Swirydy, Zabrodi, Zabrody, Zabrodzie, Zaprudy, Zaprudzie, Zvarde	479559	Zubrzyca Gorna
				479560	Spurcani, Zabrichen
				479570	Safarikovo, Svarichov, Svarychuv
478300	Cepeleuti, Split, Zabolotye	479314	Supuru de Jos	479574	Sporkovshchizna
478340	Zablotce, Zabolotce, Zabolottsi, Zabolottsy	479340	Cvrstec	479578	Zubrzyca Wielka
		479344	Supuru de Sus	479586	Zbrachlin
478350	Zbelutka, Zbielutka	479346	Soporu de Cimpie	479600	Savran, Sborny, Sbornyy, Schwerin, Sibrina, Sjeverin, Sopron, Svaryn, Swaryn, Swarynie, Zhevreny, Zhuprany, Zuprany
478370	Zablatov, Zablodov, Zablodova, Zablotov, Zablotow, Zablotuv, Zabludove, Zabludow, Zabluduv, Zablutov, Zabolotov	479350	Spartak, Svratka		
		479360	Soborten, Zwardon		
		479370	Svorotva, Szprotawa, Szprudowo, Zwiartow		
		479374	Zebrzydowice		
478374	Zbludowice, Zbylitowska Gora	479375	Zabratowka	479635	Csabrendek
478400	Chepeleuts, Chepeleutsy, Cieplice, Cybulice, Czaplice, Diepholz, Dziepulc, Sabiles, Sevliush, Sevljus, Sewlusz, Swilcza, Szabolcs, Zabledza, Zablocie, Zablotse, Zbludza, Zoblas	479376	Sworotwa Mala	479638	Sprendling, Sprendlingen
		479377	Sworotwa Wielka	479640	Sobrance, Spermezeu, Szobrancz
		479379	Schwertberg		
		479387	Sverdlov, Sverdlovsk	479644	Sopronszecseny
		479400	Cioburciu, Sburash, Schwarza, Siewierz, Soprec, Spares, Spires, Sporice, Sporysz, Svirzh, Swierze, Swirz, Szovaros, Zaborze, Zabrezhye, Zabrodzie, Zabrzez, Zaporizhia, Zaporoze, Zaporozhe, Zaporozhia, Zaporozhye, Zaporze, Zaprudze, Zaprudzie, Zavertse, Zavirtcha, Zawarza, Zawiercie, Zbaraz, Zbarazh, Zbarezh, Zbereze, Zberezh, Zburaz, Zburazh, Zubracze, Zubrzyce	479650	Zvornik, Zwiernik
478430	Ciuflesti			479656	Sobernheim
478439	Seubelsdorf			479657	Sopronkovesd
478450	Szypliszki			479659	Sopronhorpacs, Sopronkereszturr
478459	Sevlussky Ardov			479660	Sobernheim
478475	Szabolcsbaka			479670	Sewerionowo, Sewerynow, Sobrinowo
478479	Szabolcsveresmart				
478500	Czaplaki, Dzibulki, Schopfloch, Suvalk, Suvalki, Suwalki, Szeplak			479675	Sewerynowka, Supranowka, Supranuvka
				479676	Sopronbanfalva
478537	Suplacu de Barcau			479690	Sopronhorpacs
478570	Zavlekov			479700	Sebirov, Sevirova, Sevirovo, Shperov, Siepraw, Sporovo, Sporow, Sporuv, Sprowa, Zawerow, Zbarav, Zborov, Zborow
478583	Suplacul de Barcau				
478600	Chaplino, Ciepliny, Diefflen, Dziewuliny, Rzeplin, Schwelm, Sepolno, Shabiln, Shavlan, Shavlian, Souflion, Sowliny, Szabelnia, Szephalom, Trzebielino, Zabelin, Zabeln, Zobeln, Zvolen, Zvolin, Zwolen, Zwolin	479430	Schwarzheide, Zubreshty, Zubresti, Zvorastea, Zvoristea		
		479433	Schifferstadt	479740	Czubrowice, Sieprawice, Szeparowce, Szperowce, Zaborovtsy, Zaborowce, Zaborowice, Zborowice
		479436	Shwartz Tomah		
		479440	Swarzedz, Zbrodzice		
		479443	Shwartz Stimme		
		479447	Swierszczow	479750	Zverovichi
478640	Svilajnac, Szaplonca	479450	Schwarzach	479770	Svrabov
478650	Czaplinek	479451	Severskaya	479783	Zaberfeld
478656	Suplingen	479457	Swierczkow, Zwierzchow	479787	Zebry Falbogi
478659	Scheiblingkirchen, Svilengrad	479459	Swierze Gorne	479794	Zebry Wierzchlas
478679	Schwalenberg, Spalene Porici			479831	Soporul de Jos, Supurul de Jos
478680	Czaple Male				

479834	Supurul de Sus
479835	Soporul de Campi
479845	Zebry Laskowiec
480000	Cel, Celje, Celle, Ciula, Gyala, Gyalu, Gyula, Gyulaj, Sal, Sala, Saly, Saulia, Sehl, Sela, Sellye, Selo, Shaulyai, Shiaulai, Siaulai, Sluhy, Sol, Sola, Soly, Suhl, Sula, Szala, Szello, Szil, Szill, Tsaul, Zala, Zalau, Zale, Zalha, Zeil, Zelea, Zell, Zihle, Zilah
481000	Suleje
481600	Silajani
481700	Siliyov, Sulejow, Suliyov
481740	Sulejovice
481750	Sulejowek
483000	Ciolt, Csolt, Csolto, Djoltai, Dzholtay, Salat, Salatiu, Selt, Shileti, Silauti, Silute, Sledy, Solt, Soltau, Sulita, Szolad, Zalata, Zalite, Zlota, Zlote
483100	Zolotoye
483173	Zolotoi Potok, Zolotoy Potok
483175	Zolotiyevka
483190	Zheltyy Yar
483350	Zlata Idka
483395	Sulita Targ, Sulita Tirg
483400	Czelatyce, Saldus, Schildesche, Seletice, Soltysy, Sulatycze, Zalutycze, Zeldec, Zheldets, Zlutice
483430	Sulita Sat
483500	Salatig, Sulyatichi, Sulyatyche, Zalyutichi, Zheludok, Zholudek, Zlotki, Zoludek
483570	Slodkow, Soltykow, Zlotkowo
483573	Sladkovodnaya, Sladkovodnoye
483574	Sladeckovce, Zlotkovitse, Zlotkowice
483575	Sladkovicovo, Zolotkovichi
483576	Sladkow Maly
483579	Sladki Vrh
483590	Zlate Hory
483600	Seldin, Seletin, Selyatin, Slatina, Soldin, Szlatina, Szlatyn, Zlatna
483630	Slatinita
483640	Zoloteanca, Zolotonosha, Zolotonosza, Zoltance
483643	Sholdaneshty, Soldanesti, Soltaneshty, Soltanesti
483645	Slatinske Doly, Slatinski Drenovac
483650	Cieletniki, Zlotniki
483654	Zladings
483656	Zeltingen
483660	Slatinany
483665	Schladming
483685	Celldomolk, Czelldomolk
483697	Zlate Moravce
483700	Dzialdowo, Sladow, Slotowa, Solduba, Zlotow, Zlotowa
483735	Soltvadkert, Zloti Potok, Zloty Potok
483740	Saldobos, Saldobosh, Saldobus, Szaldobos
483750	Szoldobagy, Zeltweg
483760	Slotfina, Slotvina, Slotwina, Slotwiny, Solotvina, Solotvino, Solotwina
483764	Solotvinske Kopalne
483780	Slotopol, Zlatopol, Zlotopol
483795	Schildberg
483796	Zalaudvarnok
483860	Zlotolin, Zolotolin
483900	Salder, Slatioara, Zlatary, Zlotoryja
483940	Selters
483965	Zalatarnok
483970	Schelldorf, Zlatarif
484000	Chelitch, Chelodz, Cielaz, Cielcza, Czeladz, Salacea, Salashe, Salasze, Salicea, Salisca, Salociai, Salos, Schlitz, Schulitz, Seelze, Selce, Selets, Seletz, Seleus, Selish, Selitz, Selts, Seltz, Shilauts, Sielce, Sielec, Silca, Silica, Slucz, Solca, Solec, Soletz, Sollos, Soltsy, Sulz, Sulze, Szelicse, Szilas, Szilicze, Szollos, Szulz, Zalas, Zalazie, Zalazy, Zalazye, Zalese, Zalesie, Zalesye, Zaliosia, Zalosce, Zaloscie, Zalozce, Zalucze, Zaluz, Zaluze, Zaluzhe, Zaluzhye, Zaluzi, Zaluzie, Zaolzie, Zelizy, Zhulitse, Ziliz, Zseliz, Zsolcza, Zuelz, Zulice
484300	Ciulesti, Selisht, Selishty, Selishtya, Selist, Seliste, Selistea, Slisht, Szelistye, Zilistea, Zsulest
484330	Saalstadt
484334	Salistea de Sus
484340	Zalhostice
484353	Selistea Hotin, Slisht Gadol
484367	Celestynow
484370	Selestovo
484375	Selistea Veche
484376	Zalaistvand
484390	Silistra
484397	Sulzdorf, Sulzdorf an der Lederhecke
484400	Czulczyce, Dzialoshitz, Dzialoszyce, Dzyaloshitse, Sieliszcze, Slishtcha, Zalazhtsy, Zaleshits, Zalisocze, Zaliszcze, Zaloshits, Zaloshitz, Zaloshts, Zalozhtsy, Zalozhtza, Zalozitz, Zalshits, Zilozitz
484443	Slishtch Zuta
484445	Zaleszczyski
484450	Zaleszcyki, Zaleszczyki, Zalishchik, Zolishtchik
484453	Slishtch Gadol
484454	Zaleszczyki Stare
484468	Sieliszcze Male
484500	Cieloszka, Salsig, Seleshche, Selishche, Selishchi, Selisko, Slishch, Slutsk, Slutzk, Zaluski, Zholudsk, Zoludzik, Zoludzk
484536	Salzkotten
484550	Zaleshchiki, Zaleshchyki
484553	Slishch Gadol
484568	Zoludzk Maly
484578	Zaleska Wola, Zoludzk Wielki
484589	Salzschlirf
484594	Zalesie Krasienskie, Zalesie Kraszenskie
484600	Czolczyn, Dzialoszyn, Dzyaloshin, Selzen, Slecin, Sleshin, Slesin, Slocina, Solocma, Sulecin, Sulitsa Noua, Suloszyn, Szolocsina, Zalacsany, Zalesany, Zalesiany, Zalszyn, Zaluczne,
	Zeilitzheim, Zeilsheim, Zelczyna, Zelizna, Zelzin, Zlazno, Zlosyn
484630	Zalaszanto
484635	Zalaszentgrot, Zalaszentjakab
484636	Zalaszentmihaly
484637	Zalaszentbalazs, Zalaszentivan
484638	Zalaszentlaszlo, Zalaszentlorinc
484639	Zheleznodorozhnyy
484640	Zlocieniec, Zlozeniec
484650	Slutznik, Soleczniki, Soletchnik, Zelezniki
484656	Schleusingen
484657	Soleczniki Wielkie
484663	Salzhemmendorf
484665	Salcininkai, Salcininkeliai
484679	Zelezny Brod
484680	Zalecze Male
484690	Zalagyomoro
484693	Zelezna Ruda
484700	Dzelzava, Sloczow, Sloszewo, Sluzewo, Sluzheva, Suliczewo, Zalasowa, Zeliszew, Zlochev, Zloczew, Zloczow, Zlotchev, Zlotshev, Zolczow, Zolochev
484738	Salzwedel
484740	Zeliezovce
484750	Schleswig, Sulzbach, Zelazowka
484756	Sulzbach am Main
484759	Sulzbach Rosenberg
484765	Selets Benkuv, Sulzbung
484780	Szilas Balhas, Szilasbalhas
484784	Salaspils
484785	Szilas Balhas, Szilasbalhas, Zalecze Wielkie
484786	Salzuflen
484790	Zalaszabar
484795	Salzberg, Salzburg, Sulzburg, Sulzburg Baden
484836	Selo Slatina
484846	Szlasy Lozino
484865	Szeleslonka
484870	Sulislav
484878	Schlusselfeld
484879	Shlisselburg
484900	Salasuri
484930	Szollosardo
484950	Szollosgyorok
484956	Szilasarkany, Szilsarkany
485000	Czilka, Salka, Salok, Saluk, Saulgau, Schlochau, Schlock, Schlok, Selok, Shlok, Siolko, Sloka, Sluck, Solka, Soloki, Syulko, Szalka, Szulok, Zalha, Zaluche, Zaluhe, Zalukh, Zlockie, Zullichau
485178	Silicka Jablonica
485300	Gyalakuta, Salcuta, Zalkod
485365	Schlichtingsheim, Szlichtyngowa
485370	Szlachtowa
485396	Salgotarjan, Schluchtern
485400	Gyulahaza, Gyulakeszi, Salakas, Salkutsa, Szilagycse, Szilagycseh, Zalokets, Zalokiec
485434	Zalhostice
485437	Sulgostow
485439	Solec Zdroj
485454	Salkaski Sveti Ivan
485460	Silixen, Sluchocin
485463	Szalkeszentmarton
485468	Szilagysomlyo
485474	Csallokozposfa

485476	Sielec Zawonie
485478	Zselickisfalud
485500	Csillaghegy
485517	Solec Kujawski
485540	Szolgaegyhaza
485584	Szlachecki Las
485594	Szilagykraszna
485600	Ciolacu Nou, Czolhany, Zholkin, Zhulkin, Zolkin, Zolkinie
485637	Solec nad Wisla
485643	Seligenstadt
485645	Solikamsk
485657	Szilagynagyfalu
485670	Sluknov
485675	Shulganuvka, Szulhanowka
485694	Dzialki Morozowalskie
485700	Siolkowa, Solukow, Sulechow, Sulichevo, Szelkow, Zalkove, Zalkva, Zaluchow, Zalukhuv, Zalukiew, Zelechow, Zelichow, Zelikhov, Zhelekhov, Zhelichov, Zholchuv, Zholkev, Zholkeva, Zholkva, Zholkve, Zhulkev, Zhulkyev, Ziolkow, Zlochuv, Zolkiew, Zolkow, Zylkow
485740	Celakovice, Celkovice, Slakovci, Sulkovice, Sulkowice
485743	Szelkow Stary
485744	Sulkowszczyzna
485747	Ciolkowicze Wielkie
485750	Ciolacu Vechi, Ciolacu Vechiu, Zhilkovke, Zholkevka, Zholkevke, Zhulkiewka, Zilkevke, Zolkevka, Zolkiewka
485757	Tselkoviche Velikoye, Tselkoviche Velke
485760	Zalakoppany
485765	Sielec Bienkow
485767	Szelkow Nowy
485778	Zelechow Wielki, Zelekhuv Velke, Zhelekhuv Velke
485785	Szilagyvalko
485790	Szilagyper
485840	Zalagalsa
485870	Zalahalap
485900	Zolocari
485940	Zalaigrice
485945	Zalaegerszeg
485946	Szylokarczma
485956	Dielkirchen
485976	Schollkrippen
486000	Celiny, Chelem, Chelm, Chelmno, Chelmo, Ciuleni, Czolhany, Dzialyn, Schaulen, Selm, Shilin, Sialenai, Siaulenai, Sielen, Silenai, Silene, Sillein, Sillian, Slany, Slona, Solany, Solin, Solina, Soljani, Sollenau, Solln, Solona, Sulina, Szalonna, Szlani, Szolny, Szylin, Zalan, Zalene, Zalin, Zelena, Zelene, Zeleneu, Zeleno, Zelenyy, Zelina, Zellin, Zholinia, Zielin, Zielona, Zielun, Zilin, Zilina, Zilini, Zlin, Zolin, Zolinia, Zolynia, Zsolna, Zulinya, Zulnya, Zylin
486100	Zelenaya
486300	Chelinta, Salant, Salanta, Salantai, Salanty, Salnita, Salonta, Selemet, Selent, Solonet, Szalanta
486369	Salonta Mare
486390	Silindru

486400	Chelmce, Chelmiec, Chelmza, Salmos, Salnos, Silenes, Slanec, Slanica, Solnice, Solonets, Sulinci, Sulmice, Szalanczi, Tselenzh, Zalnoc, Zelenitsa, Zielence, Zielenica, Zieleniec, Zlonice
486440	Sulmeizhitza
486450	Silniczka, Solnicka, Zielenzig
486455	Slanska Huta
486456	Slomniczki Nowe
486460	Dielmissen
486476	Selmecbanya
486500	Chelmek, Csolnok, Salank, Salanky, Salonika, Saloniki, Shalanki, Slnck, Slomka, Slomnik, Slomniki, Solemnik, Solinka, Solonka, Szolnok, Zalenieki, Zelanka, Zeleny Gay, Zelenyy Gay, Zielonka, Zielonki, Zlynka
486560	Schlangen, Solingen, Sulingen, Szlinokiemie, Zellingen
486578	Chelmiec Polski, Silnica Wielka
486587	Zalamihalyfa
486590	Zielona Gora
486600	Diulmeni, Salamony, Slemien, Slonim, Szuliman, Zlonin
486630	Chelmeniti, Chelmenti
486640	Sholomenitse, Szolomienice
486643	Salmunster, Zolynia Miasteczko
486650	Schlaining, Szlininka
486659	Salamony Grabowskie
486670	Salamonowa
486675	Salamonowa Gora
486700	Scholanowo, Slampe, Zalanow, Zalanuv, Zelinow
486750	Szulhanowka, Zelenovka
486780	Zelenoe Pole, Zelenopolye
486781	Zelenopol Ye
486790	Salomvar
486795	Schulenburg, Szlembark
486800	Silmala
486900	Gyalumare, Sieul Mare, Solymar
486918	Silea Nirajului
486930	Zeulenroda
486944	Silmerzitz, Sulmierzyce
486960	Zalamerenye
487000	Celiv, Celivo, Chelb, Czlopa, Salva, Schlawe, Schloppe, Seelow, Selb, Seliba, Selyeb, Shelib, Silava, Silev, Siluva, Slawa, Slupia, Solova, Solowa, Sulow, Syalava, Szalapa, Szalowa, Szalva, Szolyva, Zalaovo, Zalavye, Zalawie, Zalewo, Zalipie, Zelav, Zeliv, Zelovo, Zelow, Zelva, Zelve, Zelwa, Zielow, Zilupe, Ziolovo, Ziolowo
487300	Slavuta, Slawuta, Sloboda, Slovita, Slowita, Zalaapati
487337	Sloboda Dubenska
487338	Sloboda Dolinska
487340	Sielpia Duza, Slawatycze, Slovotitch
487350	Slavatich, Slobodka, Slobodke
487354	Sheliba Dikshitz, Slobodka Strusowska
487355	Slobodka Konkolnicka, Slobodka Koszylowiecka, Slobudka Konkolnitska
487356	Slobodka Mushkatovka,

	Slobodka Nikolskaya
487357	Slobodka Polna
487358	Slobodka Lesna, Slobudka Lesna
487360	Slavyatin
487363	Zalapetend
487396	Sloboda Rungurska
487400	Czolowiec, Czulowice, Djulaves, Gyulevesz, Seelowitz, Selibice, Shilovtsy, Silvas, Slabce, Slipcze, Sliwice, Slobozia, Slovec, Slupca, Slupcza, Slupica, Slupiec, Sluptza, Solipse, Sulowiec
487417	Slobodzeya Beltsy, Slobodzeya Voronkovo, Slobodziya Belts
487437	Slobozia Dobrusa
487439	Solovastru
487450	Slapsko, Slawsko, Slupsk
487451	Slavskoye
487453	Slobozia Hodjinesti
487454	Slobozia Hodjinesti
487456	Slobozia Comarestilor, Slobozia Hanesti
487459	Slobozia Horodistea
487460	Schlipsheim, Shlaveshnia, Slaveshna, Slawczyn, Slawetschno, Slupeczno, Szelepcseny, Zalabesenyo
487463	Szilvasszentmarton
487470	Slaboszow
487474	Schliwischewzi, Slaboszewice, Slaboszowice, Sljivosevci
487476	Slobozia Banilei
487478	Slobozia Balti, Szilvasujfalu
487479	Slobozia Barancea, Slobozia Pruncului, Slobozia Vorancau, Szilvasvarad
487500	Slawek, Slivki, Sliwki, Zalaveg, Zelowek, Zholobki, Zolobki, Zulpich
487534	Slifia Chadash
487540	Zalabaksa
487560	Slavechino, Slepcany, Slovechno
487566	Slavchynenta
487570	Slavkov, Slawkow, Slowikowa
487574	Slabkowice, Slavkovce, Slavkovcze, Slobkovitz, Slopkovitz, Solobkovtsy
487577	Slavkov u Brna
487593	Slavgorod, Slawgorod
487597	Gyulafehervar
487600	Shlapan, Slavin, Slavna, Slavnya, Slawna, Slawnja, Slawno, Sliven, Slivna, Slivno, Slupna, Slupno, Sulbiny, Szeleveny, Szlapan, Zelvyany, Zelwiany, Zhlobin
487630	Slavantai
487636	Slaventyn, Slawentyn
487637	Slupia Nadbrzezna
487638	Sulbiny Dolne
487640	Slavonice, Slopnica, Slopnice, Zlobnica
487645	Slavansk, Slavjansk, Slavonska Pozega, Slavonski Brod, Slavyansk, Slovenska Ves, Slovenske Darmoty, Slovenske Raslavice, Slovensky Kajna, Slovensky Meder
487650	Slivnik
487670	Slupia Nowa

487680	Solpa Mala
487700	Shelvov, Slupow, Szelwow, Zolobow
487740	Dzilbowiec
487785	Sielpia Wielka
487830	Saalfeld
487835	Zalaboldogfa
487840	Selpils
487900	Gyulavari, Solivar, Zalaber, Zalavar
487933	Gyulafiratot
487940	Szulborze
487950	Selburg, Zel Burg
487974	Sulborowice
488000	Sallel, Shilel, Silale, Silaliai
488500	Zalaujlak
488630	Sulelmed
488700	Zalalovo
489300	Gyalaret, Salard, Szalard
489330	Zalaerdod
489600	Sallern
489639	Zellerndorf
490000	Cere, Cheriu, Csor, Cyr, Gyar, Gyor, Gyore, Gyoro, Gyure, Gyuro, Sar, Saray, Sari, Scheer, Ser, Serai, Seree, Serey, Serrai, Seyriay, Shury, Siary, Sohrau, Sorau, Sur, Suri, Szar, Szare, Szury, Tsyr, Zara, Zary, Zarya, Zory, Zsira, Zuara
491000	Chereya, Sarheya, Seirijai, Serheya, Serijai, Sierijai, Tschereja
491400	Zarajec
491600	Zarojani
491700	Sarajevo, Serajevo
491750	Szarajowka
493000	Cered, Csarda, Csaroda, Czered, Sarata, Sarauad, Sard, Sardu, Sarto, Sarud, Schroda, Sered, Seret, Sereth, Siret, Sireti, Sirota, Sroda, Surty, Szaruty, Szered, Szereda, Szurte
493100	Seredeiu
493134	Sirautii de Sus
493379	Sarretudvari
493400	Ceradice, Certeze, Cheretezh, Chertezh, Csertesz, Czertez, Seredzius, Seretets, Surduc
493440	Zhora de Zhos
493460	Certizne, Czertyzne
493484	Sroda Slaska
493500	Certege, Szurdok, Szurduk
493570	Czortkow
493574	Czortkow Stary, Szurdokpuspoki
493575	Saratica Veche, Seredkevychi
493580	Szerdahely
493587	Sarata Galbena
493600	Chirutnea, Sarata Noua, Seredne, Seredne, Sirotino, Srednia, Szerednye, Zarudnia
493610	Seredneye
493614	Sredniye Zhory
493617	Srednjaja Poguljanka
493634	Srednie Duze
493640	Serednica, Srednica, Srednius, Zarudnyce
493648	Zhora de Mizhlok
493650	Serednik, Srednik
493657	Srednica Pawlowieta
493668	Seredne Male, Srednia Mala, Srednie Male
493673	Seredina Buda

493674	Srednia Wies
493675	Srednie Wieksze
493678	Seredne Wielkie
493685	Gyertyanliget
493690	Sarateni Orhei
493695	Sarateni Orhei
493700	Saratov, Saratova, Shiraduv, Zaradawa, Zheredov
493740	Czortowiec, Zrotowice
493745	Czartowczyk
493750	Sarata Veche
493785	Sroda Wielkopolska
493787	Szeretfalva
493797	Srodborow
493800	Saratel, Srodula
493850	Gyortelek
493865	Chiriet Lunga
493870	Certlov, Cserhathalap
493916	Tschertorija Novaya
493944	Sarata Rezeshty
493945	Czartorysk, Tshartorisk
493970	Dierdorf
494000	Cherche, Cherechiu, Cheres, Cheresh, Chereusa, Circ, Cires, Ciresi, Cserjes, Czaryz, Czercze, Czeress, Gyeres, Sarasau, Saros, Seradz, Seres, Sheradz, Sheredz, Shiradz, Sieradz, Siercza, Sirets, Soroca, Suares, Surasch, Suraz, Surazh, Surcea, Szorce, Zarasai, Zarica, Zaritz, Zaruzie, Zgyerz, Ziras, Zirc, Zruc
494100	Ciresoaia
494146	Ciresoaia Somes
494300	Ciorasti, Sarosd, Szarazd
494330	Sarstedt
494344	Shirautsi de Zhos
494360	Czorsztyn, Sarazsadany, Schierstein
494380	Gyergyotol
494397	Ziersdorf
494400	Seredzice, Seredzius, Zarzecze, Zarzecze, Zerczyce
494440	Rzerzeczyce
494450	Zarzeczka
494460	Cserhatszentivan
494463	Gyergyoszentmiklos
494500	Chersk, Czersk, Czyrczyk, Gyorocske, Gyorsag, Sarsig, Serotsk, Serotzk, Sorocko, Sorotsko, Srocko, Srotsk, Srotzko, Syretsk, Zarechka
494514	Tsarskoye Selo
494530	Gyorsziget
494549	Sarisske Cierne
494550	Szarazkek
494560	Dzierzgon
494570	Dzierzgow, Dzierzgowo
494573	Sarisske Bohdanovce
494574	Dzierzkowice
494575	Saratsika Veke
494576	Czersk Pomorski
494580	Gyergyohollo
494585	Sarisske Luky
494586	Zarzyc Ulanski
494600	Cherson, Sarzyna, Schriesheim, Serczyn, Seroczyn, Serotchin, Suruceni, Szerzyny, Tsaritsyn, Tsarizin, Zarczyn, Zarozhan, Zarshin, Zarszyn, Zaryszyn, Zerocin, Zerzen, Zrecin

494635	Gyeresszentkiraly, Sarszentagota
494636	Gyorszentmarton, Sarszentmihaly, Sarszentmiklos
494637	Gyorszentivan
494640	Tchorznica
494645	Dzerzhinsk
494650	Tzaritchanka, Zaritchanka, Zaritschanka
494656	Schorzingen
494660	Dzierzaniny
494670	Dzierzoniow, Gyorasszonyfa
494674	Shersheniovtse, Szereszniowce, Szerszeniowce
494680	Gyorzamoly
494690	Gyorszemere
494700	Chirsova, Czerchawa, Dzierzby, Sarcova, Sarisap, Sheresheva, Shereshevo, Shereshov, Shereshuv, Shershev, Shershova, Shershovi, Sierzawy, Szereszow
494730	Gyorszabadi
494735	Dzierzbotki, Sarospatak
494748	Dzierzby Szlacheckie
494750	Zery Czubiki
494753	Sarosbogdany
494760	Dzierzbin
494764	Gyorsovenyhaz
494794	Sorau Seifersdorf
494795	Diersburg, Siersburg
494796	Szarazberencs
494800	Czersl
494874	Zeroslawice
494878	Gyergyoalfalu
494974	Sarosreviscse
494980	Circirlau
495000	Cirak, Cseoreg, Csurgo, Csurog, Sarcau, Sarok, Schrick, Serehai, Sergii, Serke, Serock, Sierck, Sierock, Sirk, Sirok, Siroke, Soroka, Soroki, Srock, Szirak, Szoreg, Zarechye, Zarki, Zharik, Zharki, Zhurik, Zirke, Zsurk, Zuraki
495100	Sarheya, Serheya, Shirokoye
495160	Syrgiyeni
495175	Sergeyevka
495300	Sarkad
495339	Sorok Tatary
495359	Sarkadkeresztur
495387	Cserhathalap
495397	Siroke Trebcice
495400	Cherkassy, Cherkoss, Czerkasy, Gyerkes, Sarkoz, Sierakosce
495430	Chircaesti
495443	Srock Czastkowy
495446	Cserhatszentivan
495456	Sharkoyshchina
495460	Sarkeyschina, Sarkeystsene, Sharkotsina
495475	Schrecksbach
495484	Sarkozujlac
495490	Soroksar
495547	Sorkikisfalud
495578	Sorkikapolna
495600	Cercany, Gyorkony, Sarghieni, Sarkan, Sarkany, Surucheny, Syrokomia, Szergeny, Zaricany
495610	Zarechnoye
495634	Zruc nad Sazavou
495640	Cerhenice

495650 Tsarichanka, Zarechanka
495656 Csurgonagymarton
495663 Saargemund
495680 Serokomla
495685 Sorgenloch
495700 Cergowa, Cherikov, Cherkhava, Czarkow, Czarukow, Czerykow, Dziergova, Dzurkiv, Dzurkow, Dzurkuv, Sierakow, Srokowo, Surchow, Surochow, Syrkovo, Zerechowa, Zerkow, Zyrakow
495735 Gyurkapataka
495740 Serechowicze, Sergheevca, Sirkovce, Zerkovice, Zerkowitz, Ziarkowice
495744 Siarkowszczyna, Szarkowszczyzna
495745 Sharkovshchina
495750 Serekhovichi, Szorcowka
495765 Cerkiewnik
495778 Sierakow Wielkopolski
495783 Sorkifalud
495787 Gyorkefalva
495797 Srock Prywatny, Srocko Prywatne
495800 Cirgali, Sirokyluh
495840 Seregelyes
495930 Shargorod, Sharigrad, Sharigrod, Szarogrod, Szarygrod
495940 Saregres
495943 Sarkeresztes, Sarkeresztur
495950 Sargorog
496000 Charna, Cherin, Cherna, Cierna, Cihrin, Ciorna, Csorna, Cyryn, Czarna, Czarne, Czarnia, Czarny, Czehryn, Czermna, Czermno, Czerna, Czernia, Czyrna, Djurin, Dzhurin, Dzuryn, Sahryn, Sarne, Sarni, Sarny, Sauran, Schrimm, Serene, Sirem, Sohren, Srem, Surany, Szirma, Szurani, Tsirin, Tzirin, Zaran, Zarenai, Zeran, Zhorany, Zsarno, Zyrzyn
496170 Cherneyev, Cherneyuv, Cherniyuv, Czerniejewo, Czerniejow, Czernijow
496300 Cernauti, Ciornita, Dyormot, Dzhormot, Gyarmat, Gyirmot, Sarand, Zerind
496340 Zeran Duzy
496360 Chernyatin, Czerniatyn, Schorrentin
496361 Charni Dunayets, Czarny Dunajec, Tzarna Dunayetz
496390 Sramtura
496397 Schorndorf, Zirndorf, Zurndorf
496400 Cerhenice, Cernauca, Cernici, Chernche, Chernich, Chernitsa, Chirianca, Czarnca, Czeremcha, Czerncze, Czernica, Czernice, Czerniec, Sarmas, Serenes, Szerencs
496430 Cernesti
496439 Cherny Ostrov, Chernyy Ostrov, Czarna Ostrov, Czarna Struga, Zernsdorf
496450 Saranczuki, Sarmasag, Sernichki, Serniczki, Sherensk, Shransk, Shrensk, Shrentsk, Szransk, Szrensk, Zhornishche
496455 Sremski Karlovci
496456 Sremska Mitrovica
496460 Cernosin, Cheremoshno, Czeremoszno, Czerniczyn,

Czerniecin, Schornsheim
496470 Chernichov, Czerniachow, Czernichow
496474 Charnushovitse, Chernyshevskoye, Czarnuszowice, Czernichowce
496475 Czernichowek
496478 Siernicze Wielkie
496480 Sarmasel, Sarmaselu, Sarmasul, Schermeisel
496486 Sarmasul Mare
496487 Chernyye Oslavy
496493 Czarna Srednia
496500 Cernuchi, Cherinka, Chernukhi, Cyranka, Czarnikau, Czernik, Sarnak, Sarnaki, Sarnki, Sernik, Serniki, Sirnek, Sirnik, Zerniki
496538 Sarnki Dolne
496540 Ciornohuzi, Csarnohaza
496550 Saranchuki
496559 Czarniecka Gora, Sarnki Gorne, Sarnki Gurne
496560 Schauernheim
496564 Charnokontse, Charnokontse Velk, Chernokinits, Czarnokonce Wielkie, Zernica Nizna
496565 Czarnokoniecka Wola
496570 Chernigov, Chernikhov, Chernyakhov, Czarnkow, Czernihow, Czernikowo, Tschernigov
496574 Chernikhovtsy, Chernyakhovsk, Zernica Wyzna
496575 Chernigovka
496579 Serniki Pervyye
496587 Czarnoglow
496593 Sarengrad
496600 Cerniny, Chernyany, Czermin, Czerniany, Schauernheim, Zhirmuny, Zhoremin, Zhuromin, Zuromin, Zyrmuny
496660 Zrenjanin
496700 Ceranow, Cernov, Chernev, Czerniewo, Czerniow, Sarnow, Sarnowa, Serniawy, Zaremby, Zarnov, Zarnow, Zarnowo, Zaromb, Zaronovo, Zharnov, Zhornuv, Zornow
496730 Cernevti
496735 Cerni Potok, Czarny Potok
496740 Cernawicy, Cernevcy, Cernovcy, Cernovice, Chernevtsi, Chernevtsy, Chernivitz, Chernovitsy, Chernovitz, Chernovtsy, Czarniewice, Czarnowaz, Czarnowiec, Czerniewicze, Czerniowce, Czernovitz, Czernowitz, Tsarnovitz, Tschernewzi, Zarnovica, Zarnovitza, Zarnowce, Zarnowiec
496744 Chernavchitse, Chernavchitsy, Czernawczyce
496745 Chernovtsky, Schornweisach
496746 Szirmabesenyo
496747 Cernowitze Bukovina, Sromowce Wyzne
496750 Chernavka, Chernevka, Czernewka, Sarnowek, Scharmbeck, Zarnowka
496754 Zarembi Koshchelne, Zaremby

Koscielne
496780 Chernobil, Chernobyl
496783 Csornyefold
496785 Czarna Wielka, Czarna Wielkie
496787 Serenyfalva, Serenyifalva
496795 Schramberg, Zierenberg
496800 Csernely, Szeremle
496840 Cernoleuca, Chernelitsa, Czarnolas, Czarnolozy, Czernelica
496850 Sarmellek
496870 Chernilyava, Czernilawa
496875 Chernolevka
496900 Saru Mare
496940 Cioara Murza, Cioara Murzei
497000 Chirov, Cirava, Cserep, Csorba, Czahrow, Dzhuruv, Dzurow, Sarbi, Sarowo, Schorov, Sirbi, Szerep, Zareby, Zarowie, Zerf, Zhurov, Zurow
497300 Scherfede, Serbauti
497350 Syrovatka
497400 Cerevic, Chiribis, Csorvas, Dzerves, Scherps, Serepets, Serpec, Sherpts, Sherptz, Shirovtsy, Sierpc, Surowica, Szarvas, Szarvaszo, Zaravice, Zeravice, Zhirovitsy, Zrebice, Zuravitch, Zurawce, Zurawica, Zurewicze, Zurobice, Zyrowice
497414 Zuravitz Yashan
497430 Sarbesti, Sherbeshty, Zerbst, Zurowisty
497440 Chereposhetz
497450 Sharovechka, Sharovochka, Szarbsko, Zurawiczki
497453 Srpski Itebej, Szarvasgede
497456 Srpske Moravice
497500 Chiripkeu, Ciripcau, Scharowka, Sharovka, Tsarevka, Zarowka, Zhirovichi, Zhuravichi, Zhurevichi
497530 Cerepcauti
497548 Zarebe Koscielne, Zarebi Koschelne, Zareby Koscielne
497561 Cioropcanii Noui, Cioropcanii Vechi
497570 Cherepkovo, Szarbkow
497574 Cherepkovtsy
497593 Sarbogard
497600 Cherven, Chervin, Chervona, Chirpan, Czerbin, Czerwien, Czerwin, Czerwona, Dzerbene, Serbeni, Sorbin, Srbin, Zarownie, Zerwana, Zheravne, Zhiravno, Zhuravno, Zuravna, Zurawin, Zurawno
497630 Scherwind, Schirwindt, Serpenita, Shervinty, Shirvent, Shirvint, Sirvint, Sirvintai
497634 Sirvintos
497640 Schrobenhausen, Serafince. Serafintsy, Serpiniec, Sharpantsa, Sharpantse, Szarpance, Zarubince, Zirovnice, Zurawieniec, Zurawnica
497645 Czerwinsk, Czerwinsk nad Wisla, Tshervinsk, Tsyurupinsk
497650 Cservenka, Czerwonka

497654	Cerveny Kostelec, Schrobenhausen	531430	Codaiesti	535616	Cotiugenii Mari
497658	Chervono Glinskoye	531477	Huta Jozefow	535669	Cotiugeni Mari
497659	Chervonograd, Czerwona Gora	531593	Kitai Gorod, Kitay Gorod	535697	Huta Komarowska, Huta Komorowska
497670	Sarbinowo, Serbinow	533000	Hadad, Hodod	535700	Chodkow, Chodkowo, Gatkow, Hutkow
497671	Serpnevoye	533400	Chotutice		
497678	Czerwona Wola	533440	Hajdeu de Sus	535740	Katy Kupce
497679	Chervony Prapor, Chervonyy Prapor, Czerwony Bor	533558	Kotyatiche Golyn	535745	Kotkowska Wola
		533584	Hajduteglas	535767	Chodkow Nowy
497693	Czerwonohrad, Scharfenort	533600	Coadjuthen	535787	Hadikfalva
497696	Chervonoarmeisk, Chervonoarmeysk, Chervonoarmeyskoye, Sarbi Maramures, Sirbi Maramures	533700	Katadfa	535846	Huta Golcieynow
		533797	Huta Dabrowa	535930	Kitaigorod
		533950	Hajdudorog	535950	Geidekrug, Heidekrug
		533957	Huta Deregowska	535987	Huta Krolewska
497700	Sarbov, Sierpow	534000	Cadca, Chodecz, Chodetch, Chodziez, Chotycze, Chotys, Cotusca, Gadac, Hadziacz, Hatuica, Hetes, Hidas, Hodac, Hodasz, Hodgya, Hodiatch, Hodisa, Hodisu, Hodosa, Kadcza, Kadysz, Kajdacs, Katyciai, Kittsee, Kotcse, Koteschau, Kutaso	536000	Catina, Chodoun, Chotin, Chotyn, Chudin, Cothen, Gadany, Gadna, Gdynia, Gudzion, Gudziunai, Hajdieni, Hatten, Hoteni, Hotin, Huedin, Huten, Kadan, Kadino, Kaidan, Katona, Kdyne, Kedainai, Kedainiai, Keidan, Keidany, Keydan, Khotin, Kiejdany, Koden, Kodima, Kodni, Kodnia, Kodnja, Kodnya, Kodyma, Kothen, Kotun, Kuidany, Kutina, Kutno, Kutyn, Kytin
497796	Srbobran				
497800	Cserepfalu, Gyorujfalu, Saravale, Szara Wola				
497830	Szarfold				
497840	Sarpilis, Serpelice				
497845	Shurvilishuk, Surviliskis				
497865	Saarwellingen				
497870	Gyerofalva	534300	Codaesti, Goteshty, Gotesti		
497900	Gyorvar, Sarvar	534330	Guttstadt, Hettstadt		
497950	Saarburg, Szarwark	534344	Hodosa de Ciuc		
497956	Saarbrucken, Saarbruecken	534386	Chotcza Dolna		
497960	Sauerbrunn	534390	Kuty Stare, Kuty Stary		
497964	Srebrenica	534400	Chotesice, Gdeshitse, Gdeszyce, Hodousice	536350	Guttentag
498000	Chiraleu, Chirileu, Zaorle			536397	Gattendorf, Huttendorf, Kottendorf
498400	Chirales, Saarlouis	534450	Goduzischki, Haydutsishok, Heidotzishok, Hidotzishok, Hoduciszki		
498600	Cerlina, Cherlina, Srlin, Zsarolyan			536400	Chodenice, Chotynicze, Chotyniec, Chudenice, Kiydantsy, Kodeniec, Kujdance, Kuydantse
498630	Saarland	534500	Gdeshichi, Hajduczok, Kutyska, Kutyski		
498770	Cirlibaba				
498776	Cirlibaba Noua	534538	Guta Sukhodolska, Huta Suchodolska, Khuta Sukhodolska	536430	Hodjinesti
499000	Sararia, Sirioara			536435	Gut am Steg
499370	Zhirardov, Zyrardow	534543	Kutaski Stare	536439	Godemesterhaza
500000	Gey	534559	Kutaski Grady	536450	Chotimsk, Gdansk, Khotimsk
510000	Gaje, Gaya, Haieu, Hajo, Hoya, Kije	534574	Huta Zakowska	536474	Hodmezovasarhely
		534576	Chodaczkow Maly	536479	Gudensberg
513000	Caiuti, Chajety	534577	Chodaczkow Wielki, Khodachkuv Velki	536500	Gauting, Goding, Goeding, Gudenieki, Hotinka, Hutting, Khotynichi
513395	Caiuti Tirg				
513600	Kojetein, Kojetin	534586	Huta Szklana		
513650	Kajetanka	534596	Chotcza Gorna	536540	Hetenyegyhaza, Khotenchitsy
514000	Gajec, Hajos, Kajaszo	534600	Chotysany, Gdeszyn, Heidesheim, Kotegyan, Kotyudzhen, Kotyuzhany	536544	Huttengesass
514400	Gajecice			536547	Heidingsfeld
514463	Kajaszoszentpeter			536560	Goettingen, Gottingen, Hattingen, Heidenheim, Huttenheim
514600	Cojocna, Hojesin	534646	Hajdusamson		
514686	Gaje Smolenskie	534663	Hidasnemeti		
514700	Hejocsaba	534670	Chotcza Nowa	536566	Huttenheim in Bayern
514863	Hejoszalonta	534700	Chodaczew, Hodyszewo, Htusovo, Hudcov, Khoteshov, Kotozovo, Kutuzovo	536570	Kitanchevo
515943	Hejokereszhtur			536574	Hadynkowce
516000	Caian, Gaujiena			536579	Kottingbrunn
516460	Gaje Nizne, Gaye Nizhne	534730	Hajduszovat	536586	Cotu Miculinti, Guta Mikhalin, Huta Michalinska
516461	Gay Nizhniye	534748	Hajduszoboszlo		
516640	Caianu Mic	534778	Kutuzov Volodarsk, Kutuzowe Volodarskoe	536590	Kutna Hora
516784	Kijany Blizsze			536600	Chotynin, Cotman, Heidenheim, Hodonin, Hudonin, Huttenheim
516864	Caianul Mic	534785	Godziesze Wielkie		
517000	Chojewo, Kijew, Kijow, Kiyev	534795	Godesberg		
517400	Gejovce	534840	Hidashollos	536640	Hajdananasz, Hajdunanas
517460	Gaje Wyzne	534860	Guta Zelena, Huta Zielona	536643	Hettmannsdorf
517600	Kujawien	535000	Catcau, Gadiach, Gadyach, Gudigai, Hadich, Heideck, Hideaga, Kitki	536660	Huttenheim in Bayern
517650	Hajowniki			536700	Chotomow, Chudnov, Chudnow, Cudnov, Cudnow, Hadynow, Kaidanovo, Katy Nowe, Kaydanovo, Keidanov, Koidanovo, Koydanovo, Kujdanow, Kuydanuv
517700	Hejobaba, Hejopapi				
517850	Gaje Wielkie	535300	Ghitcauti		
519000	Gajar, Gajary, Kajar	535340	Hajduhadhaz		
519479	Hoyerswerda	535354	Hajduhadhaz, Hajduhodkaz		
530000	Cadea, Cheud, Chidea, Cut, Cuta, Gad, Gata, Getye, Ghida, Gotha, Gut, Guta, Hat, Het, Hete, Hida, Hodi, Hody, Huta, Katy, Kety, Kide, Kotaj, Kuta, Kuty	535400	Ghidighici, Gutahaza, Hajduhaz, Ketegyhaza		
		535500	Gidigich	536750	Hottenbach, Huttenbach, Kettenbach
		535587	Huta Gogolowska		
		535600	Cotiugeni, Kotyugany	536786	Kuttenplan

536795	Huttenberg
536796	Gutenbrunn
536800	Heidemuhle
536900	Chotymyr, Hadamar, Khotimir
536940	Chotimierz
536948	Hadmersleben
536954	Heidenreichstein
537000	Cadow, Chodov, Chudovo, Cotova, G Dov, Gdov, Gdow, Godowa, Goduv, Hodow, Kitev, Kitov, Kitow, Kotov, Kotova, Kotowy, Kotuv, Kutev, Kutjevo, Kutow
537360	Ketbodony
537364	Huta Obedynska
537400	Chotowitz, Cottbus, Gadebusch, Gudovac, Hodowica, Katovice, Katowice, Kattowitz, Kottbus
537430	Cadobesti, Kadobeste
537444	Hatowszczyzna
537445	Huta Brzuska
537450	Kotovsk, Kotowsk
537451	Kotovskoye
537496	Hajdabesernin, Hajduboszormeny, Hajdubozormeny
537500	Hetbukk, Hidveg, Kettwig, Kotowka
537539	Kettwig A D Ruhr
537540	Hajdubagos, Hajdubogosz
537593	Hidvegardo
537600	Chotoviny, Guty Bujno, Hatvan, Kadobna
537640	Chodywance
537657	Huta Bankowa
537740	Huta Voivozi, Kadobovtsy
537780	Kotowa Wola
537786	Chodova Plana
537837	Gottwaldov
537864	Guta Polonetska, Huta Polonicka, Huta Poloniecka
537870	Kutyfalva
537876	Huta Plebanska
537900	Chotebor
537945	Huta Brzuska
537958	Katy Wroclawskie
538000	Catalu, Cataly, Chodel, Chodla, Chudel, Gidla, Gidle, Goddelau, Godeliai, Godollo, Katoly, Kethely, Kiduliai, Kotel
538400	Catalusa, Kotlice
538430	Chutuleshty
538458	Hadle Szklarskie
538460	Heidelsheim
538479	Cadolzburg, Kettlasbrunn
538497	Chotel Czerwony
538500	Kadziolki, Kotelek
538564	Hadle Kanczuckie
538586	Katlakalna, Katlakalns
538600	Cataleni, Gadalin, Ghiduleni, Giduleny, Kadzielnia, Kotelnia, Kotelnja, Kotelnua, Kotelnya
538640	Hidalmas, Kotelnice
538650	Cotu Lung
538651	Kotolina Hayashana
538679	Quedlinburg
538700	Chotylow, Chotylub, Chudlovo, Getlovo, Ghetlova, Godilieva, Godlawo, Godlewo
538745	Kadlubiska
538750	Kadlubek
538760	Kotlovina
538769	Godlewo Mierniki
538774	Godlewo Backi
538778	Godlewo Wielkie
538779	Kutylowo Perysie
538795	Heidelberg, Kadlburg
538800	Catalul
538865	Cotul Lung
538970	Giedlarowa
539000	Chadyr, Chidry, Codor, Godre, Hutar, Kadar, Khidry, Kidry, Kietrz, Kotra
539300	Gatarta, Hodarauti, Kadarta
539356	Quadrath Ichendorf
539394	Khutor Tarasivka
539400	Gadoros, Giedraiciai, Hethars, Kedzierz, Ketrosy, Khodoreuts, Khodoroutsy, Khodorozha
539434	Keturiasdesimt Totoriu
539439	Hadersdorf
539465	Kedzierzyn Kozle
539467	Katarzynow, Katarzynow Nowy
539475	Khutor Shevchenko
539476	Haidershofen
539478	Hadersfeld
539480	Gutersloh
539500	Giedraicai
539530	Kadarkut
539546	Kudirkos Naumiestis
539570	Chodorkov, Chodorkow, Hodorkov, Khodorkov
539574	Choderkowce, Khoderkovtse
539580	Hedrehely
539600	Gedern, Katerina, Katerini, Katherine, Ketrzyn
539640	Kudrintsy, Kudrintz, Kudrynce
539648	Keterinoslav
539656	Gau Odernheim, Heddernheim, Hedernheim
539660	Gau Odernheim, Heddernheim, Hedernheim, Kotormany
539675	Katerinovka
539676	Khutor Novinki
539678	Katerinopol
539679	Katrynburg
539700	Choderev, Chodorov, Chodorow, Hitdorf, Khodorov, Khodorow, Kodrab, Kotoriba
539740	Gedrevitz, Gedrovitz
539750	Chadorowka
539783	Gutorfolde
539785	Keturvalakiai
539790	Hedervar
539795	Katerburg
539850	Gederlak
539865	Chadyr Lunga
540000	Cauas, Chaussy, Chausy, Chios, Chiuza, Chocz, Choss, Chotch, Chyse, Coas, Cuceu, Cuci, Cuhca, Gac, Gacs, Gecse, Geisa, Gicze, Gocs, Gocz, Gosca, Gozha, Heci, Hejce, Hoza, Hugyaj, Hujcze, Husi, Husia, Hyza, Kac, Kacs, Kaschau, Kasha, Kashau, Kashoy, Kassa, Keci, Kecso, Ketsch, Khios, Kietrz, Kis, Kitsee, Kocs, Kos, Krsy, Kusze, Kuziai, Kuzie
541000	Caseiu, Coseiu, Cucioaia
541700	Kosciejow
541740	Kasejovice
541743	Huziejow Stary
543000	Casta, Chiced, Chiesd, Chiuesti, Chust, Chyste, Cosauti, Costiui, Gaesti, Geszt, Grzeda,
	Hosht, Hostau, Hust, Huste, Huszt, Jgesti, Kecsed, Khust, Kishuta, Kisida, Kiszte, Kosd, Kusti, Kysta
543160	Gizhdiyany
543300	Kostedt
543344	Khazhdeu de Sus
543360	Kostatin
543378	Kistotfalu
543400	Gesztes
543430	Costesti, Kostesht, Kosteshti, Kosteshty
543437	Costesti Balti
543438	Costesti Lapusna, Kosteshty Lapusna
543439	Gozd Stary
543460	Costiceni
543474	Hostisovce
543500	Hostka, Keszteg, Kistokaj, Krzatka
543540	Husztkoz
543570	Gostkow
543574	Kostiukovitch
543575	Kostyukovichi
543600	Coadjuthen, Costini, Gostini, Gostomia, Gostyn, Gostynie, Gozdzielin, Gusiatyn, Gustanj, Gusten, Gusyatin, Gusztyn, Hostinne, Hostoun, Hostynne, Husiatin, Husiatyn, Husten, Kazatin, Kostany, Kosten, Kustany
543630	Kuestendje
543636	Kostantin Yashan, Kostentin, Kostiantinograd
543638	Kustendil, Kyustendil
543640	Hostomice, Hostomitz, Kostajnica, Kostenice, Kostintsy, Kuestendje
543645	Kustanszeg
543650	Choustnik, Kotzting
543656	Geistingen
543660	Gostinin, Gostynin
543663	Gesstemunde und Lehe
543670	Kasdanov
543675	Haustenbeck, Kostenevichi
543680	Gostomel, Hostomlia
543683	Kostomloty
543700	Gostov, Hostow, Kastav, Kosztowa, Krzetow
543740	Chystovice, Gostwica, Hostivice, Hustopece
543745	Gozdowska Wola
543746	Hostovce nad Bodvou
543750	Kostevichi
543780	Kostopol
543784	Kistapolca, Kistapolcsany
543787	Kossuthfalva
543800	Gesztely, Gostila, Kaczy Dol, Kadzhidla, Kadzidlo, Keszthely, Kostel, Kostely
543840	Kesztolc, Kostelec, Kosteletz
543843	Kastelyosdombo
543847	Gotse Delchev
543850	Kistelek
543856	Kostelec nad Cernymi Lesy, Kostelec nad Labem, Kostelec nad Orlici
543860	Castellaum, Kastellaun, Kostelan, Kostolany, Kostolna, Kostuleny, Kosztelany
543864	Kishtelnitsa

543865	Kostelniki
543867	Kostelni Briza, Kostolna Pri Dunaji
543876	Gozd Lipinski
543900	Castoria, Kashedar, Kastoria, Keszter, Koisedary, Koschedary, Koshedar, Koshedary, Koshidar, Kostera, Kostry, Kostrza Ryje, Kostrzyna, Koszedary, Kozodrza, Krstur
543916	Costrijeni
543930	Cuzdrioada, Gesztered
543940	Kaishiadorys, Kaisiadoris, Kaisiadorys, Kistarcsa
543947	Kostrizhevka
543950	Kestrich
543960	Kisterenye, Kistoronya, Kostrina, Kostroma, Kostrzeszyn, Kustrin
543964	Hesse Darmstadt, Kistormas
543970	Castrov, Gestorf, Gustorf, Gustrow, Hessdorf, Kustrawa
543974	Kostarowce
543979	Castrop Rauxel
543990	Cusdrioara, Cuzdrioara
544000	Cacica, Cazaci, Chincis, Chodziez, Choziez, Godzisz, Hadziacz, Hiezyce, Hodiatch, Hogyesz, Hoshtch, Hosszuaszo, Hoszcza, Husasau, Huszcza, Kacice, Kadzice, Kaszyce, Kigyos, Kisac, Kishaza, Kosauts, Koshitse, Koshitz, Kosice, Kosoutsy, Koszyce, Kozodrza, Krzyz, Kshaz, Ksiaz, Ksice, Xiaz
544300	Kisecsed, Kisecset
544357	Krzystkowice
544360	Kiszsidany
544386	Kozice Dolne
544400	Kishegyes
544436	Ksiezostany
544440	Krzciecice
544460	Kozaczyzna
544500	Gizycko, Gosciszka, Grzeska, Gutsisko, Gzhatsk, Huciska, Hucisko, Krzesk
544510	Kazatskoye
544517	Hucisko Jawornickie
544559	Krzesk Krolowa Niwa
544575	Hucisko Pikulskie
544576	Gutsisko Penyatske, Krzeczkowo Mianowskie
544579	Gutsisko Brodzke, Hucisko Brodzke
544596	Kozice Gorne
544600	Choszczno, Chrzczony, Gasocin, Goszczyn, Kostrzeszyn, Krzcin, Krzecin, Krzesiny
544630	Kisasszond
544646	Ksiaznice Male
544650	Chrzczanka, Krzesinki
544670	Chszczonow, Krzczonow, Krzeczanowo
544674	Krzyzanowice
544679	Kotzschenbroda
544694	Ksiezomierz
544700	Chaszczow, Chocieszow, Choszczow, Hoszczewo, Koce Schaby, Krzeczow, Krzeszow, Krzyzowa
544740	Cazaciovca, Kesheshovitz, Krzeszowice, Krzeszowiec
544745	Krszywcze Gorne
544750	Kozaczowka, Krzeszowka,

	Krzyzowka, Kshesivka
544759	Krzeszow Gorny
544763	Krzyzewo Nadrzeczne
544764	Krzyzewo Nadrzeczne
544765	Krzyzowniki
544780	Ksiezpol
544784	Ksiezopole Smolaki
544785	Godziesze Wielkie, Kosicze Wielkie, Kshaz Vyelki, Ksiaz Wielki
544836	Hessisch Oldendorf
544840	Kisujszallas
544853	Hessisch Lichtenau
544860	Hegyeshalom, Krzeslin
545000	Cacak, Gadiach, Gadyach, Gaski, Geisig, Geseke, Gieski, Goshcha, Gotsk, Gozdzik, Guchok, Gusak, Gushcha, Hacki, Hoshch, Hoshcha, Huczko, Hugyag, Hujsko, Husaki, Kaczka, Kaczko, Kazsok, Kecsege, Keszeg, Kiczki, Kisag, Kossaki, Koszeg, Kotsk, Kotzk, Kozaki, Krzak, Kysak
545160	Kiskajan
545353	Keszohidegkut
545360	Hosszuheteny
545390	Kissikator
545394	Koszegdoroszlo
545400	Kaszahaza
545460	Kozachizna
545493	Koszegszerdahely
545584	Kosicky Klecenov
545600	Gissigheim, Kitskan, Kitskany
545630	Kecskemet, Kiskend
545636	Koziki Majdan
545639	Kiskundorozsma
545640	Kiskinizs, Kiskunmajsa
545658	Kiskunhalas
545663	Kisigmand
545675	Kitskani Vek
545676	Kysucke Nove Mesto
545678	Kiskunfelegyhaza
545680	Kiskunhalas
545685	Kiskunlachaza
545696	Kiskomarom
545700	Goshchevo, Gusakov, Haskovo, Husakov, Hussakow, Hyskov, Khashchuv, Khaskovo, Kisskowo, Kiszkowo, Kozuchow
545710	Khashchevoye
545731	Khashchevatoye, Kochkovatoye
545740	Kosciukowicze
545750	Kozachovka, Kozachuvka, Kozuchowek, Krzykawka
545778	Kozuchow Wielki
545785	Kosiche Velke
545800	Cascalia, Cazaclia, Kiskallo
545810	Kashkaliya, Kazakliya
545867	Kisgalambfalva
545870	Kozieglowy
545900	Kiskore, Kozia Gora
545940	Kisgercze, Kiskoros, Kisszekeres
545947	Grzegorzew, Grzegorzewice
545950	Kosogorka
545956	Hochkirchen
545970	Kisgorbo, Kiskirva
545973	Kiskorpad
546000	Causani, Cazin, Cazma, Checiny, Chenciny, Chentchin, Chocen, Chocim, Chocznia, Chotzen,

	Chyrzyna, Chyzyny, Coseni, Couasna, Cusma, Gaischin, Gaisin, Gaissin, Gajsin, Gatchina, Gauzeni, Gauzeny, Gayshin, Gaysin, Giessen, Gosan, Goscino, Gudzion, Gudziunai, Gusino, Haissin, Haisyn, Hajdieni, Hajsyn, Hausen, Hazin, Heciu Nou, Heessen, Heishin, Heisin, Hessen, Hessheim, Husen, Husynne, Hyzne, Kaczyn, Kasin, Kasina, Kaszony, Kausany, Kaushany, Kautzen, Kazan, Kcynia, Ketrzyn, Khisinau, Kicin, Kocin, Kosani, Koscian, Koshany, Kosheny, Kosin, Kosina, Kosino, Kosiny, Kosna, Kossyn, Kostrzyna, Kosyno, Kozian, Koziany, Kozin, Koziny, Kozma, Kozyan, Kozyany, Kuciunai, Kucmeh, Kuczany, Kusin, Kusma, Kuznia, Quetzen
546160	Causanii Noui
546170	Kaznejov
546300	Cusmed, Geiss Nidda, Gzhenda, Kishind, Kiszindia, Ksanti, Xanthi
546359	Kisszentgrot
546360	Kasentin, Kesznyeten, Kosintin, Kosnitin, Xanten
546367	Kozmadombja
546380	Hessental
546386	Kasna Dolna
546397	Gassendorf, Hautzendorf, Kasendorf
546400	Cacinci, Casunca, Grzmiaca, Hasmas, Hasznos, Hosszumezo, Keshionzh, Khotsimezh, Kiszindia, Kosienice, Kosmacz, Kozhenits, Kozhenitz, Kozhnitz, Kozienice, Kozieniec, Kozmice, Koznitz, Krzymosze, Kshanzh, Kshoynzh, Kushnitsa, Kusnice, Kuzhnitsa, Kuzmice, Kuzmicze, Kuznica, Kuznitse, Kuznitza, Xions
546430	Cazanesti, Godzhineshty, Hodjinesti, Kazaneshty
546436	Heusenstamm
546439	Kocin Stary
546440	Chocienczyce, Goscienczyce
546450	Chocimsk, Kazanzhik
546459	Krzyncze Gorne
546461	Hasnasenii Mari
546468	Kozmice Male
546470	Kocmyrzow
546478	Kisenzhopol, Kshanzh Vyelki
546479	Kazincbarcika
546500	Chashnik, Chashniki, Gussing, Husinka, Kashunka, Kasinka, Kazanka, Kazanki, Koshnik, Kosmach, Kozhanka, Kuzmichi, Kuzniaki
546540	Cazangic, Hasenhecke Siedlung
546543	Kuznica Stara
546554	Hasenhecke Siedlung
546559	Kuznica Grabowska
546560	Geisenheim, Geisingen,

	Hussingen, Kissenheim, Kissingen, Kitzingen
546578	Kuznica Blonska
546579	Kisungvar
546593	Chyrzyna Korytniki, Kozangrodek, Kozhan Gorodok, Kozhangrudek, Kozhanhorodok
546595	Giesenkirchen
546596	Kasna Gorna
546600	Causani Noui, Cozmeni, Geisenheim, Kisnana, Kissenheim, Kisunyom, Kitsman, Koschmin, Kosemin, Kosman, Kotzman, Kozmeny, Kozmin, Kozomin, Krzemienna, Kuzmin, Kuzmina, Kuzmino
546630	Cuzminti, Kisnemedi
546640	Kosmonosy, Krzemienica, Krzemieniec, Kshemyenyets, Kuzmintsy
546643	Gossmannsdorf, Gossmannsdorf am Main, Hausmannstatten
546645	Krzemienczuk
546650	Kozminek, Kozminka
546660	Kisnameny
546665	Hausmenning
546670	Causani Novi, Kocin Nowy
546700	Chocianow, Chocimow, Chrzanow, Cucniow, K Shonev, Kaczonowy, Kazanov, Kazanow, Kaznow, Keshanov, Keshenev, Keshinov, Khshanov, Khshanuv, Kishinev, Kiszyniow, Koczanow, Koszanowo, Krzymow, Kshanev, Kshanov, Kusnive
546730	Gazenpot, Hasenpot, Hasenpoth, Hazenpot, Hoznpot
546739	Hasan Batar
546740	Chocianowice, Cudzynowice, Koczanowicze, Koscieniewicze
546745	Krzymowskie
546746	Husne Wyzne
546750	Kaczanowka
546767	Kozinowo Nowe
546783	Geisenfeld
546784	Hotzenplotz
546785	Kasina Wielka, Kosina Wielka, Krzynowloga Mala, Krzynowloga Wielka
546790	Kiszombor
546793	Hatzenport
546795	Hauzenberg
546800	Grzymala
546850	Kazanlik, Kazanluk
546857	Grzymalkow
546870	Grzymalow, Gzhimalov
546875	Grzymalowka
546900	Geismar, Kazmir, Kismarja, Kuzmir
546930	Kisnarda, Kozhanhorodok
546935	Kazhaneradok
546936	Kismarton
546940	Chocimierz, Cusmirca, Kazimierz, Kazimierza, Kazimyerz, Kazmierz
546943	Kazimierz Dolny, Kazimyerz Dolni
546946	Kazimierz nad Wisla, Kazimierza Mala
546947	Kazimierz Biskupi, Kazimierza Wielka, Kazimierzowka
546950	Kasmark, Kazimirka, Kesmark, Kezmarok, Kushmirka

546970	Kasimirov, Kazimirov, Kazimirovo, Kocmyrzow
546974	Hecznarowice
546975	Kazimierowka
547000	Cacova, Casva, Cuzap, Gasawa, Gasewo, Goshevo, Goshov, Gusev, Haczow, Hoczew, Hoszewo, Hoszow, Husow, Hussow, Kashov, Kaszew, Kazhba, Kesov, Koczow, Kosciow, Kosev, Koseva, Kosevo, Kosewo, Kosov, Kosow, Kosowy, Kossewo, Kossov, Kossovo, Kossow, Kossuv, Koszow, Kozeve, Koziowa, Kozova, Kozovo, Kozowa, Krzywe, Kucow, Kuzova
547160	Kisbajom
547300	Geisweid, Kisapati, Kosobudy, Kozubata, Krzywda
547350	Kis Patak, Kisbodak, Kispatak
547364	Gospodinci
547369	Kisbudmer
547400	Chcebuz, Cosbuc, Cuizovca, Giesebitz, Gospic, Huczwice, Husovice, Kasubassa, Keshepitz, Kisapsa, Kisovce, Kispec, Kissebes, Kosciewicze, Kossowitz, Kozepviso, Kozia Wies, Krzepice, Krzewica, Krzywcza, Krzywce, Krzywica, Krzywice, Krzywicze, Kshepits, Kshepitse, Kucewicze
547430	Kispast, Kispest
547437	Gosprzydowa
547438	Krzywcze Dolne
547439	Kosow Stary, Kossow Stary
547440	Krzywczyce
547450	Hoszowczyk, Krzywiczki
547451	Kosovskaya Polyana
547456	Kosovska Mitrovica
547457	Kosovska Polana, Kosovska Polyana
547459	Krzywcze Gorne
547460	Kisbagyon, Krzywoszyn
547490	Kisvasarhely, Kisvaszar
547495	Kisvasarhely
547500	Catzbach, Coswig, Grzywka, Hatzbach, Hosbach, Kaschowka, Kashivka, Kashofka, Kaszowka, Kisvejke, Kosovka, Kozovka, Ksebki, Kshivcha, Kshivche, Kutsevichi, Kuyzovka
547538	Kshyvche Dolne
547545	Gasowka Skwarki
547548	Kosuv Hutsulski
547558	Kosow Huculski
547559	Kshivche Gurne
547574	Grzywkowicze
547575	Gzhivkoviche
547578	Krzywiecka Wola
547585	Gasowka Oleksin
547590	Kosova Hora
547600	Grzebienie, Kacwin, Kisbanya, Kisseben, Kisszeben, Krzepin, Krzywin
547640	Kisfenes, Kociubince
547645	Kociubinczyki
547650	Krzewianki
547655	Kotsyubinchiki, Kotsyubinchyki
547700	Grzybow, Grzybowo

547740	Grzybowice, Kozepapsa, Kozowowice
547784	Kosewo Wloscianskie, Kosov Polski
547785	Krzywowolka
547800	Hossufalu, Hosszufalu, Hosszupalyi, Kisfalu, Kuczewola, Kysibl
547830	Coesfeld, Kispalad
547836	Gossfelden
547840	Cuzaplac
547845	Kosov Lacki, Kosov Latski, Kosow Lacki, Kossow Lacki
547850	Cuzaplacu, Gesia Wolka, Kospallag, Kozeplak, Krzywoluka, Kshyvoluka
547865	Kosciflniki, Krzywulanka
547900	Kisber
547930	Hassfurt, Kishvarda, Kispirit, Kisvarda
547935	Kisbarathegy
547937	Gosprzydowa
547943	Hosszupereszteg
547945	Kasperske Hory, Kossow Ruski
547946	Kisberezna, Kisberzseny, Kisvarsany
547950	Hausberge, Kisberki, Kodzborg, Kozepborgo, Krzywy Rog, Kuczbork, Kutzberg, Kysperk
547956	Hausberge an der Porta
547964	Kisberezna
547970	Kocborowo
547973	Kisbarapati
547974	Ksawerow Stary
547975	Kashperovka
547976	Krzyworownia
548000	Casel, Cassel, Chioselia, Cociulia, Cosel, Gacsaly, Gidzel, Hegyalja, Hotzila, Huzele, Kasely, Kasheli, Kassel, Kecel, Khozhel, Kiscell, Kisczell, Kislau, Kocsola, Kosel, Koszoly, Koziol, Kozle, Kusel
548100	Kisseliya
548300	Cuciulat, Kisleta, Kislod
548336	Caslita Dunare
548360	Kisladany
548400	Kejzlice, Kisielice, Kislitsa, Kisszallas, Kozelec, Kozelets, Kozeletz, Kozhelitse, Kozielec
548439	Katzelsdorf
548450	Koscieliska, Koscielisko, Kozelsk
548474	Heci Lespezi
548481	Kishla Saliyeva
548500	Haslach, Hassloch, Hazlach, Hessloch, Kadziolki, Koshlyaki, Kozlaki
548570	Kosciolkow
548596	Geiselhoring
548600	Cosuleni, Goslin, Gozdzielin, Hazslin, Kadzielnia, Kasilan, Katsaleny, Kiselin, Kisgyalan, Kisielin, Kislonya, Koeslin, Koslin, Koszalin, Kozlin
548630	Hogyoliomad
548640	Kesellymeszo, Kisalmas, Kozlinicze
548650	Kislang, Koscielniki, Kostselniki, Kozielniki, Kozliniche, Kozlinichi
548654	Kaslomkzo

548656	Geislingen A Steige	
548700	Caslav, Cucylow, Gezlev, Goslow, Hazlov, Huszlew, Kiselev, Kisielew, Kisielow, Kisilva, Kiszolow, Koselovo, Koshelevo, Koshelovo, Koslov, Koslow, Koszelewy, Kozlov, Kozlow, Kozlowa, Kozluv, Kozolupy	
548740	Caslovce, Choslovitz, Hoslovitz, Kasselowitz, Koszylowce	
548744	Kislowszczyzna, Koslowszczyzna, Kozlowszczyzna	
548745	Caslavsko, Kislovodsk, Kislovshchizna, Kozlovshchina, Kozlovshchyzna	
548746	Kozlowstchine	
548748	Kozlow Szlachecki	
548750	Haselbach, Kesselbach, Khislavichi, Khoslavichi, Kisielowka, Kozlowek	
548756	Kislovchina	
548763	Geiselwind	
548793	Kozlova Ruda, Kozlowa Ruda	
548900	Geislar, Goslar, Koslar	
548930	Kazlu Ruda, Kizil Orda	
548960	Geiselhoring	
549000	Gescher, Guzar, Kaiserau, Katscher, Kisar, Kisgyor, Kocser, Kostrza Ryje, Koszary, Kozara, Kozari, Kuzary	
549300	Chocerady, Cucerdea, Kocsord	
549360	Kishartyan	
549370	Goscieradow	
549400	Hagyaros, Kedzierz, Kisorycze, Kisrecse, Koserz, Kosorice	
549439	Kaisersdorf	
549440	Kaisersesch	
549450	Kisraska	
549460	Koscierzyna	
549465	Kedzierzyn Kozle	
549475	Kisrozvagy	
549479	Hagyarosborond	
549483	Kaiserslautern	
549500	Kisorichi	
549567	Koczargi Nowe	
549600	Koziarnia	
549630	Cosarnita, Kusgyarmat	
549640	Kissarmas, Koshernitsa	
549648	Kozarmisleny	
549650	Kozirynek	
549700	Gasiorowo, Kaczorowy, Koszarawa, Koszarowa	
549740	Kosarovce	
549783	Kaiserwald	
549790	Kisrebra, Kozarvar	
549839	Kaiserlautern	
549864	Cuciurul Mic	
549869	Cuciurul Mare	
549900	Cuzorioara	
550000	Cako, Coka, Cucu, Cuhea, Gaiki, Geoagiu, Geyche, Gheghie, Gige, Goagiu, Goch, Guyche, Haag, Hage, Hegy, Hock, Hoghia, Hohe, Kak, Kek, Kock, Koka, Kuchoyya	
551000	Kuchoya	
551700	Chuguyev	
553000	Hahot, Kakad, Kehida, Kokad, Kokot	
553175	Cocuetii Vechi	
553450	Koktishka, Kuktiskiai	
553454	Kuktiskes	
554000	Cacuciu, Chechis, Cheuchis, Chichisa, Chiochis, Gehaus, Gichitse, Gichitsy, Kakics, Kakucs, Kakush, Kekcse, Kekes, Kocudza, Kukec, Kuketse, Kuketze, Kukuci, Kukucze	
554300	Hochst, Kakasd, Keccsed	
554330	Hochstadt, Kochstadt	
554336	Hochstadt am Main, Hochstadt an der Aisch, Hochstadt an der Donau, Hochstatten	
554363	Hochst im Odenwald	
554386	Kocudza Dolna	
554390	Hoxter	
554400	Kokasice	
554463	Hegyhatszentjakab, Hegyhatszentpeter	
554480	Chechis Salaj	
554500	Kokoszki, Kokuszka	
554517	Kukhotskaya Volya	
554560	Guxhagen	
554580	Gac Sokola	
554600	Gochsheim, Hechtsheim, Hochhausen, Kohiszyn	
554700	Kukizov, Kukizow	
554719	Hochspeyer	
554730	Hachtchevaty	
554760	Cuxhaven	
555400	Hegykoz	
555433	Hegykoztottelek	
555439	Hegykozcsatar	
555446	Hegykozszentimre	
555478	Hegykozpalyi	
555650	Chechochinek	
555700	Gogikev	
555780	Kuchecka Wola	
555930	Hagi Curda	
556000	Cochem, Cohani, Gaggenau, Gegeny, Gigen, Hagen, Hagenau, Heegheim, Hochheim, Hohenau, Kachin, Kechnie, Kochon, Koconia, Kuchany	
556300	Hoheinod, Kikinda	
556378	Hagymadfalva	
556393	Hohentrudingen	
556397	Kochendorf	
556400	Gaiganz, Hagymas, Kekenyes, Kokenyes, Koknese, Kukyenyes	
556430	Kokenyesd, Kukhneshty	
556431	Cuconestii Vechi	
556433	Hohenstadt	
556436	Hohenstein	
556440	Kokneses	
556460	Hohenhausen, Kokenhausen, Kokenhusen	
556484	Hohen Sulzen, Hohensalza	
556486	Hohensolms	
556487	Hagymaslapos	
556500	Hegymeg, Hoheneich	
556546	Hohenhausen, Kokengauzen, Kokenhausen, Kokenhusen	
556547	Gaukonigshofen	
556560	Goggingen, Hechingen, Hockenheim, Kuchenheim	
556568	Hohenhameln	
556595	Hochneukirch	
556600	Hockenheim, Kaukehmen, Kuchenheim	
556640	Hohenems	
556666	Hochheim am Main	
556680	Hohenhameln	
556700	Chechinov, Hagenow, Kochanov, Kochanova, Kokhanovo	
556740	Chechanovitz, Kaganovich, Kochanovce, Kochanovitch, Kukunjevac	
556750	Hagenbach, Kachanovka, Kochanovichi, Kochanowka, Kokhanavka, Kokhanovichi, Kokhanovka	
556783	Hohenfeld	
556793	Hagnaufurt	
556795	Hachenburg, Hagenburg, Hohenberg, Quakenbruck	
556867	Hohenlimburg	
556960	Hohenraunau	
556979	Hohenruppersdorf	
557000	Cakova, Chechiav, Chechov, Gochevo, Hacava, Hokov, Kakawa, Kakova, Kecovo	
557390	Gagybator	
557400	Cakovci, Cakovec, Cucavca, Gajkowice	
557500	Hohebach, Kachovka, Kakhovka, Kukavka	
557635	Gagyvendegi	
557639	Kokava nad Rimavicou	
557696	Kokava na Rimavica	
557800	Hegyfalu	
557850	Hac Wielka	
557859	Hochwolkersdorf	
557950	Hochberg	
558000	Cahul, Chechly, Chuchel, Chuchulya, Gugel, Kagul, Kahul, Kikol, Kochel, Kukaly	
558100	Kochuliya	
558400	Caglic, Kuklicze	
558478	Kukulloszeplak	
558500	Kuklichi	
558560	Heuchelheim, Hochelheim	
558570	Koglhof	
558576	Huckelhoven	
558600	Chuchuleny, Gogolin, Hehalom, Heuchelheim, Hochelheim, Kogilno, Kohilno	
558650	Chechelnik, Chichelnik	
558656	Hechlingen	
558700	Chechlowo, Chocholow, Gogolevo, Gogolow, Guklivyy, Hohalov, Hukliva, Kaclowa, Kochlew, Koglhof	
558740	Kochlowice	
558750	Chechelevka, Goclawek, Kakolowka, Kokalofka	
558760	Huckelhoven	
558764	Kakolewnica, Kakolownica	
558795	Kockelburg	
558970	Koclerov	
559000	Haiger, Kichary, Kuchary	
559431	Cuhurestii de Jos	
559437	Kuchary Zydowskie	
559450	Chechersk	
559460	Cucuruzeni, Kokorozeny	
559600	Gagarin, Kokorin	
559700	Cachrov, Chagrov, Chagruv, Kagerava, Kocurow	
559789	Gaugrehweiler	
559795	Hocherberg	
559850	Haigerloch, Kacorlak, Kagarlyk	
560000	Canea, Cania, Cham, Chan, Chania, Chne, Chojna, Chojny, Ckyne, Cun, Ganya, Gayna, Gumna, Gunja, Haan, Hahn, Hajna, Hamm, Hanau, Hanna, Hayna, Haynau,	

464

	Hamor, Hemer, Kanyar, Kaynary, Kemer, Kemeri, Kenyeri, Komoro, Komory, Konar, Konary, Konyar	
569175	Cainarii Vechi, Kaynariy Vek	
569300	Comrat, Homorod, Homorud, Homrod, Kainreith, Komeirid, Komrat, Kunreuth	
569331	Homorodu de Jos	
569356	Homorodkemenyfalva	
569358	Homorodokland	
569360	Hemmerden	
569365	Heimertingen	
569370	Konradow	
569383	Homorodul de Jos	
569386	Homorodalmas	
569400	Camarasu, Kamoroc, Kimirz, Konrac	
569430	Comaresti, Komara Osada, Komareshti	
569436	Hammerstein	
569453	Gemerske Dechtare	
569460	Camarzana, Giumiurdzhina, Gommersheim, Heimerzheim, Komorzan	
569463	Homorodszentmarton	
569470	Konarzewo	
569475	Gummersbach	
569484	Gomorszollos	
569500	Gemmerich, Kammerich, Komarichi	
569530	Homrogd	
569540	Heinrichs	
569547	Heinrichs B Weitra	
569570	Henrykow	
569593	Komar Gorod, Komargorod	
569600	Komarin, Komarne, Komarno, Komarom, Kommern, Komorn	
569644	Komarom Csicso	
569646	Komaromszemere	
569650	Komarnik, Komarniki, Komorniki	
569656	Gomaringen	
569700	Comarova, Knurow, Komarov, Komarove, Komarovo, Komarow, Komarowo, Komorowo, Komrov	
569740	Komarovec, Komarovtsi	
569743	Komarow Osada	
569750	Komarovka, Komarowka	
569757	Komarowka Podlaska	
569794	Komarvaros	
569873	General Poetas	
570000	Caffa, Cajba, Chop, Chybie, Cop, Copou, Cubei, Gava, Gebe, Gepiu, Giby, Hapai, Hof, Hoff, Hoof, Hubo, Kaba, Kaffa, Kapi, Kepa, Kiev, Kjew, Kobaj, Koovi, Kovi, Kupa, Kyjov	
571000	Cufoaia	
571593	Kopai Gorod	
571640	Chvojenec	
571750	Kubajowka, Kubayuvka	
573000	Caputh, Chibed, Havad, Havadto, Kaputh	
573400	Kohfidisch	
573430	Cobatesti	
573450	Kvietiski	
573500	Kvatki, Kvetkai	
573570	Kopetkowa	
573574	Chwedkowicze, Kopatkevitch	
573575	Khvedkovichi, Kopatkevichi	
573600	Khvaydan	
573670	Kvetinov	
573700	Hebdow, Kopytow, Kopytowa	
573750	Hobodovka	
573860	Kopidlno	
573863	Kaptalantoti	
573867	Kaptalanfa	
573950	Copou Targ, Copu Targ	
573956	Kepa Tarchominska	
573960	Kvedarna	
573970	Chvateruby	
574000	Chobedza, Chybice, Cupca, Gaubitsch, Gavieze, Gebice, Gewitsch, Ghipes, Habic, Havas, Heves, Heviz, Hubice, Hubicze, Kavas, Kawec, Kobiztcha, Kobuzie, Kopacze, Kopiec, Kopis, Kopys, Kovac, Kovaszo, Kupce, Kups, Kvasi, Kvasy	
574300	Cabesti, Gvozd, Gwozdziec, Hwozd, Kabeshti, Kapust, Kopisty, Kopust, Kovesd	
574330	Hovestadt	
574336	Hofstetten, Hoppstadten	
574340	Gvozdets, Gvozdetz, Gvozdits, Gvozduts	
574346	Capusu de Cimpie	
574360	Capustani, Capustiani, Kapustyany	
574364	Gwozdziec Miasto	
574368	Gwozdziec Maly	
574370	Gvozdova, Gvozdovo	
574375	Gvozdovka, Gvozdovka Vtoraya, Gvozdovke, Gvozdowka	
574380	Gwizdaly	
574385	Gwizdalki	
574400	Gaviezes, Givozits, Gvodzhits, Gwozdziec, Kawczyce, Kobyzszcza, Kovacica, Kovacshaza, Kovecses, Kvacice	
574414	Gvozhdziyets Malyy	
574440	Gvozhdzhyets	
574446	Gvodzhzhyets Miasta, Gvozhdzhyets Miasto	
574463	Heviz Szent Andras, Hevizszentandras	
574470	Kwieciszewo	
574500	Kavsko, Kawsko, Kobyzhcha, Kopchak, Kopeisk, Kopishche, Kubeczki, Kupishki, Kupishok	
574540	Kaposszekcso, Kapsukas, Kupiskis	
574560	Cobusca Noua	
574564	Gwozdziec Miasto	
574568	Gwozdziec Maly	
574570	Gabcikovo	
574575	Cobusca Veche	
574580	Koveskal	
574590	Hevesugra	
574594	Kaposkereszur	
574600	Copaceni, Covasna, Cupcina, Cupseni, Gebiczyna, Habitzheim, Kapashne, Kapusany, Kaweczyn, Kopczany, Kupusina, Kvasiny, Kwidzyn	
574637	Kaposszentbenedek, Kaweczyn Debicki	
574640	Havasmezo, Kopaczynce, Kopczynce, Kopitshinets, Koptchintz, Kopyczynce, Kupczynce	
574643	Kapciamiestis	
574644	Kaweczyn Sedziszowski	
574653	Gwoznica Dolna, Havasnagydalu, Kopcseny Kittse	
574654	Kobrzyniec Stary	
574655	Gwoznica Gorna	
574656	Kobrzyniec Nowy	
574660	Kwaszenina	
574670	Kopasnovo	
574674	Kvasnovice	
574678	Capu Cimpului	
574690	Kaposmero	
574700	Gibaszew, Gibaszewo, Hefziba, Kapisova, Kaposfo, Kiwaczow, Koptchevo, Koptsiva, Kupiczow, Kvasuv, Kwasow	
574730	Kopocsapati	
574750	Kopaczowka, Koptsevichi	
574754	Kovacsvagas	
574764	Koprzywnica, Kopshevnitza, Kopshivnitsa	
574780	Kapospula, Kupiczwola	
574790	Kaposvar	
574793	Kaposfured	
574800	Gapsal, Haapsalu, Hapsal, Hapsil, Kvatchali, Kwaczala	
574817	Kepa Celejowska	
574835	Capasul de Campi	
574850	Kaposujlak	
574853	Kovesliget	
574860	Gwizdzilny	
574870	Gawrzylowa	
574930	Kovacsret	
574935	Kaposszerdahely	
574950	Hevizgyork	
575000	Copcui, Gaibach, Gubiche, Heubach, Hobbach, Hopkie, Kepki, Kobaki, Kopache, Kopachi, Kopki, Kupka, Kupkuy	
575345	Kepa Chotecka	
575398	Capu Codrului	
575400	Kopkas, Kovchitsy, Kubekhaza	
575469	Hofgeismar	
575473	Kovchitsy Vtoryye	
575600	Hofheim, Kopacheny, Kupchina, Kupchino, Kvacany	
575640	Kopachintsy, Kopachynitse, Kopychintsy, Kupchintsy	
575663	Hofheim am Taunus	
575678	Capu Campului	
575700	Kupichov, Kwikow	
575740	Kvakovce	
575750	Kopachovka	
575780	Kupichvolya	
575930	Copaigorod, Kopaigorod, Kopaygorod	
575940	Kebharec, Kovagoors	
576000	Cabin, Cabuna, Cajvana, Chabna, Chibene, Chubin, Cubani, Gabin, Gabon, Gevonai, Gieben, Guben, Gubin, Heepen, Hofheim, Hubin, Kapani, Kapini, Kapinu, Keipene, Kepno, Khabne, Kobanya, Kopin, Kopojno, Kovin, Kovno, Kowno, Kuban, Kubyn, Kupen, Kupin, Kupna	
576100	Chabnoje, Khabnoye	
576300	Kobnat, Kovend, Kovnat, Kownaty	
576360	Kovnyatin, Kowniatyn	
576379	Hofamt Priel	

576400	Capnic, Cavnic, Copanca, Gavanoasa, Gavanosy, Gevonis, Hubienice
576445	Hubin Czeski, Kownaciska
576446	Hebenshausen
576450	Kupiansk, Kupjansk, Kupyansk
576463	Koppanyszanto
576500	Gappenach, Huwniki, Kopanka
576560	Goppingen, Heppenheim, Hoffenheim, Kaubenheim, Kippenheim, Kuppenheim
576566	Heppenheim an der Bergstrasse, Heppenheim an der Wiese
576576	Kapnikbanya
576593	Huffenhardt
576600	Heppenheim, Hoffenheim, Kaubenheim, Kippenheim, Kuppenheim
576630	Hofheim am Taunus
576654	Hofnungstal
576660	Heppenheim an der Bergstrasse, Heppenheim an der Wiese
576700	Chopniow, Hivnev, Hivniv, Hovniv, Kubanovo
576744	Kupnovitse Stare, Kupnowice Stare
576754	Kupnovichi Staryye
576795	Coppenbrugge, Kapfenberg, Koppenbrugge
576930	Huffenhardt
577000	Cabov, Hubova, Hubovo, Kviv
577400	Capowce, Chobowicze, Chopovitch
577476	Chabowo Swiniary
577500	Chabowka, Chopovichi, Khabovichi
577864	Kepa Falenicka
577900	Kapuvar
578000	Cavala, Cavalla, Cuple, Gbely, Hobol, Kabeliai, Kapiel, Kapoli, Kapolia, Kapoly, Kappel, Kapulye, Kavala, Kavalla, Kobiel, Kobiele, Koblo, Kobyla, Kobyle, Kobylea, Kopil, Kopyl, Kopyly, Koval, Kovel, Kovla, Kovle, Kowal, Kowel, Kupel, Kupil, Kval
578300	Copeleuti, Cubolta, Kabold, Kowald, Kubolta, Kvilda
578370	Chobultow, Gabultow, Gebeltov, Giebultow, Khobultova
578400	Chabielice, Chvalec, Cobalca, Gablitz, Kaplica, Kaplice, Kapolcs, Kobylice, Koviljaca, Kublitch, Kublitschi
578430	Chufleshty
578433	Giebelstadt
578439	Koblo Stare
578446	Cubles Somesani
578450	Kovalishki, Kowaliszki
578451	Kobyletskaya Polyana
578460	Cobalceni, Kobylczyna
578474	Gawluszowice
578478	Kobiletsa Polyana
578479	Gevelsberg, Gobelsburg
578486	Cublesul Ungureasca
578500	Kobelaki, Kobeliaki, Kobelyaki, Kobielaki, Kobiliack, Kobiliak, Kobiljak, Kobylaki, Kobylka, Koflach, Kublich, Kublichi
578530	Cubulcut
578560	Kobalchin
578567	Kobialki Nowe

578570	Kowalkow
578577	Havlickuv Brod
578578	Kobylecka Polana
578600	Caplani, Cobalea Noua, Coplean, Kapellen, Kapelln, Kaplany, Kapolna, Kobilnye, Kobleny, Kobylany, Kobylin, Kobylino, Kobylnya, Kopaliny, Kwilina
578640	Chvalenice, Coblenz, Copalnic, Gaflenz, Kaplonosy, Koblenz, Kobylnica, Koplancy, Koplanus
578646	Kapolnasnyek
578650	Kobilnik, Kobilniki, Kobylnik, Kobylniki
578656	Copalnic Manastur, Kapolnokhonostor, Kapolnokmonostor
578657	Kobylnica Woloska
578659	Kobylany Gorne, Kobylnica Ruska
578674	Kaplanowicze
578675	Kaplanoviche
578680	Kobiele Male
578700	Chwalowo, Gawlow, Kaplava, Keblov, Kopalow, Kopylow, Kowalowy, Kuflew
578740	Chwalowice, Hawlowice, Kaplavas
578750	Cobalea Veche, Kapulovka, Kopylovka
578764	Kowale Panskie
578774	Kepa Lubawska
578779	Khvalovo Pervoye
578780	Kobyla Wola, Kobyle Pole, Kobylepole
578785	Kobiele Wielkie, Kobylowloki
578795	Havelberg
579000	Copru, Haber, Habry, Hvar, Koper
579300	Gibart, Kibart, Kibarti, Kibarty, Koprod, Kubarty, Kybartai
579345	Gvardeiskoye, Gvardeysk, Gvardeyskoye
579370	Habartov
579400	Kebharec, Kivercy, Kivertsy, Kivertzi, Kiwerce, Koprusa
579430	Capresti, Kapreschty, Kapresht, Kapreshti, Kapreshty
579433	Kieferstadtel
579435	Capresti Colonie
579437	Chworostow, Khvorostov
579439	Kobersdorf
579444	Kepa Rzeczycka
579450	Kavarsk, Kovarsk
579454	Kavarskas, Kovarskas, Koverskas
579460	Gaworzyna, Kobierzyn
579470	Govartchov, Gowarczow
579479	Habersbirk
579500	Chobruchi, Coburg, Heuberg, Kyburg
579560	Kipercheny
579600	Cuporani, Gaborjan, Gawrony, Geberjen, Habern, Habrina, Havarna, Havirna, Kaufbeuren, Kobern, Kobrin, Kobryn
579630	Kovarremete
579640	Kaproncza, Kevermes
579650	Kaufering
579654	Kobrzyniec Stary
579656	Kobrzyniec Nowy
579660	Kaberneeme
579700	Gabrovo, Govorova, Govorove,

	Goworowo
579740	Chabarovice, Kaperowce
579750	Kvrievka
579764	Koprivnica, Koprzywnica
579779	Goworowo Probostwo
579796	Kovarberence
579800	Covurlui, Kovyrluy
579840	Hybralec
579843	Gavrileshte, Gavrilesti
579844	Hawrylczyce
579854	Gavrilchitsy
579870	Gawrzylowa
579875	Gavrilovka, Gavryluvka, Hawrylowka
580000	Calle, Cholui, Cluj, Gelej, Ghioli, Gilau, Golle, Hall, Halle, Haly, Hel, Hola, Kaal, Kal, Kall, Kallo, Kaly, Kehl, Kiel, Klaj, Kohlo, Koil, Kojly, Kol, Kolo, Koyl, Kuhl, Kul, Kula, Kuliai, Kuyl
581000	Kilija, Kiliya, Kolaje, Kuleje
581674	Cluj Napoca
581700	Cholojow, Golejow, Holojow
581780	Gulay Pole, Guljai Polje, Gulyay Pole, Kulhaje Wielkie
581794	Golaia Pristan, Golaya Pristan
583000	Calata, Coldau, Coltau, Galati, Glott, Golet, Golta, Halta, Hiliuti, Hollad, Jklad, Kaladei, Kald, Keled, Klattau, Kloda, Klodau, Klode, Kolleda, Kolodja, Kolodya, Kolta, Kolut
583100	Kolodeje
583163	Kolodeje nad Luznici
583170	Kolodziejow
583174	Galatii Bistritei
583175	Kolodeyevka, Kolodziejowka
583336	Gualdo Tadino
583400	Galautas
583446	Golotczyzna
583450	Kolodishchi
583460	Hildesheim
583464	Glod Somes
583470	Gladyszow, Koldyczewo
583500	Golotki, Holotki, Kuldiga
583540	Gildehaus
583570	Koldychevo
583574	Goldkops
583600	Gledeny, Gledin, Glodeni, Glodyany, Hilden, Hludno, Holatin, Holotin, Holten, Huliatin, Kladam, Kladanj, Kladno, Kletna, Kletnya, Klodne, Klodno, Koldin, Koledziany, Kolodna, Kolodne
583610	Kletnaya
583640	Klodnica, Kolodentse, Kolodnica, Kolodnitsa
583643	Goldenstadt
583646	Kaltensundheim
583648	Haldensleben
583650	Kaletnik, Klodzienko
583656	Gleidingen, Gol Dingen, Goldingen
583657	Goldenhof
583659	Kaldenkirchen
583660	Kaltanenai, Kaltinenai, Keltinan, Koltinenai, Koltiniani, Koltininai, Koltyniany
583664	Hildmannsfeld

583670 Goldenhof, Kladnev, Kladniow
583671 Kaletten bei Libau
583675 Gladenbach
583676 Hiltenfingen
583678 Klodno Velikoye, Klodno Velke, Klodno Wielkie
583679 Heldenbergen
583683 Kaltenleutgeben
583693 Kaltennordheim
583696 Glod Maramures
583700 Coltovo, Glodowo, Goldap, Kladovo, Kladova, Klatovy, Klodava, Klodawa, Klodeve, Klodove, Klodowa, Koltov, Koltow
583749 Kaltwasser
583750 Gladbeck, Goldbach
583795 Goldberg, Hildburghausen
583800 Calatele
583900 Coltirea
583946 Geldersheim
583960 Caldern, Geldern, Haldern, Haltern, Kaldern
583970 Kalladorf, Kladruby, Kolodruby
583975 Kolodrobka
584000 Chaltch, Chaltz, Cholotschje, Clus, Culcea, Galacs, Galatz, Galoc, Geleziai, Gelse, Gilsa, Glatz, Glesch, Glusha, Gluzy, Golcza, Gols, Gulacs, Guls, Halaszi, Halesz, Halic, Halicz, Hals, Halze, Helitch, Holic, Holice, Holleschau, Holudza, Hulcze, Hulice, Huls, Kalios, Kalis, Kalisch, Kalish, Kalisz, Kalius, Kallies, Kallos, Kalocsa, Kaloz, Kalusa, Kalush, Kalusz, Kaluza, Kaluze, Kalyus, Kelc, Kelts, Keltz, Khiliutsy, Kielce, Kilts, Kiltz, Klecz, Kletchei, Kluzh, Klyz, Kolacze, Kolcse, Kolets, Kolis, Kolish, Kolodja, Kolodya, Kolozs, Kulaschi, Kulesz, Kulus
584165 Goltsch Jenikau
584170 Kolodzeyuv, Kolodziejow
584175 Kolodziejowka
584300 Galeshty, Galesti, Giulesti, Hulsede, Kaliste, Kohlscheid, Kolesd
584330 Hallstadt, Hallstatt, Hollstadt
584340 Cleastitz
584350 Golystok
584358 Kielsztyglov
584360 Goldstein, Hellstein
584384 Clausthal Zellerfeld
584386 Klecza Dolna
584390 Klaster
584396 Klosterneuburg
584397 Gelsdorf, Gleusdorf, Halsdorf, Kelsterbach, Klostar Ivanic
584398 Klosterlechfeld
584400 Chalcis, Galszecs, Glushitsa, Gluszyca, Holashitz, Holsice, Kalaszyce, Kalyszyce, Kleszcze, Klodzice, Kluczyce, Kludzice, Kolaczyce, Kolashitz, Kolatchitz
584448 Kulczyce Szlacheckie
584460 Geilshausen, Holzhausen
584464 Haluszczynce
584467 Kolozs Zsombor
584470 Hleszczawa, Kleshtchov, Kleszczow

584476 Kleszczowna
584480 Kleshtchel, Kleszczele
584494 Kulczyce Rustykalne
584500 Chyliczki, Glisk, Glusk, Glussk, Halusk, Hlusk, Hulskie, Kalisk, Kalisko, Kalushki, Klecko, Kleshchi, Kletsk, Kletzk, Kletzko, Klezk, Klodzko, Klucek, Klucko, Klusk, Klyusk, Kolacsko, Kolishki, Kolushki, Koluszki, Kolyshki
584530 Cliscauti
584534 Glusko Duze
584540 Klishkutz
584548 Kulesze Koscielne
584568 Kloski Mlynowieta
584570 Glushkov, Glushkovo, Gluszkow, Goloskov, Goloskovo, Goloskowo, Goloskuv, Hluzkowo, Holoskov, Holoskow, Holuczkow, Kleczkowo, Kletchkovo, Kulichkov, Kuliczkow
584574 Glushkovskoye, Klaszkovce, Kleshkovtsy, Klischkowcy, Klishkovtsy, Kluczkowice, Klushkevitz, Kluszkowce, Kolaczkowice, Kulachkovtsy, Kulaczkowce
584576 Kleshchuvna, Klishchevna
584577 Kliczkow Wielki
584578 Kaluska Wola
584580 Kleshchel, Kleshchele
584587 Keiltchiglov, Kielczyglow, Kielczyglowek
584600 Galaseni, Galashany, Galczyn, Gielczyn, Glodyany, Gluszyn, Golecin, Goleczyna, Golizna, Golshany, Hillesheim, Hlucin, Holshan, Holshani, Holszany, Holzheim, Kalacsin, Kalushin, Kaluszyn, Kelecin, Kelecseny, Klasna, Klasni, Klasno, Kleczany, Klicin, Klosno, Kolcino, Koledziany, Koltchin, Kulaszne, Kulczyn, Kulsheim, Kultschiny
584610 Kolesnoye
584630 Holosnita
584640 Goloshnitsa, Holoszynce
584650 Holzing, Klodzienko, Kolesniki
584656 Gelsungen, Hilzingen
584657 Klucznikowice
584659 Gelsenkirchen
584660 Kallosemjen
584663 Holzminden
584665 Glasmanka, Glazmanka, Glazmanke, Glazminka
584670 Glaznow, Halcnow, Kalsnava, Kalusz Nowy, Klecenov
584674 Kalsnavas
584679 Klausenberg, Klausenburg, Kluyzenburg
584690 Culciu Mare
584700 Calceva, Galosfa, Gielzow, Golcowa, Goleshuv, Goleszow, Gulzow, Helesfa, Hlasivo, Hlizov, Holesov, Holeszow, Holishev, Kalicsava, Kalocfa, Kielczawa, Kielczew, Kleczew, Kleczewo, Kleczow, Klesov, Klesow, Kleszewo, Kletcheva, Klichev, Klisov, Kliszow,

Kloczew, Klosova, Klusow, Klyuchev, Klyzow, Koliszowy, Kolozuby
584730 Kulsovat
584739 Galos Petrei, Galos Petreu, Galospetreu, Galospetri
584740 Kielczewice, Kolesovice, Kulsobocs
584743 Kleszewo Stare
584750 Hilsbach, Kielczewek
584768 Kluczow Maly
584769 Kalisz Pomorski
584778 Kluczow Wielki
584780 Holzappel
584784 Hulcza Wloscianska
584785 Kalusa Vulchovce
584790 Kolozhvar, Kolozsvar, Kolozvar
584794 Kolozsborsa
584795 Heilsberg, Kluczbork
584796 Heilsbronn
584837 Kulesze Litewka
584840 Kalocsalaz
584869 Culciul Mare
584900 Kolczer
584930 Klusserath
584979 Gilserberg
585000 Galgau, Galgo, Galich, Gilgau, Glauchau, Glogau, Glogo, Golgau, Hluk, Kaluga, Kleck, Klichy, Klooga, Kolaki, Kolek, Kolk, Kolke, Kolki, Kulgai
585178 Kulhaje Wielkie
585300 Colcauti, Gialacuta, Kolked
585360 Klokotnia, Klokotyna
585400 Chalkis, Galgoc, Galgocz, Hollohaza, Khalkis, Klekacz, Klekacze, Kolikoutsy, Kulchitsy
585433 Gluckstadt, Glueckstadt
585448 Kulchitse Shlyakhetske
585450 Galgauska
585456 Kolaki Zagnatowo
585460 Gau Algesheim
585474 Klokocevci
585479 Kalksburg
585495 Galgagyork
585530 Galgaguta
585548 Kolaki Koscielne
585574 Galgaheviz
585600 Cologne, Gollheim, Kelechin, Kelheim, Klacany, Klecany, Klicany, Kolchino, Kulchin, Kulchiny
585640 Galgamacsa, Gloggnitz
585643 Heiligenstadt
585675 Hilchenbach
585679 Gilgenburg, Gleichenberg, Gleichenberg Dorf, Klagenfurt
585700 Glogov, Glogow, Gluchov, Gluchow, Glukhov, Golkow, Hluchov, Kielkow, Klikov, Klukowo, Kolocava, Kolochava, Kulichow, Kuligow, Kulikov, Kulikow
585710 Kalchevaya
585716 Golcuv Jenikov
585740 Glogowice, Gluchowice, Glukhovitse, Golkovice, Golkowice, Haligovce, Hlohovec, Kolechowice, Kulakovtse, Kulakowce
585743 Gluchow Stawki

467

585745 Galkovshchina, Hlohovicky
585747 Kolechowice Folwark
585750 Galkowek, Glogowek, Kulikovka
585765 Golcuvjenikov
585768 Glogow Malopolski
585778 Klyuchuv Velki, Kulikovo Pole
585797 Gulcha Pervaya
585800 Kalikal, Klikol, Klikole, Klykoliai
585860 Kolokolin
585900 Calkar, Golgora, Golgory, Goligor, Gologory, Kalkar, Klakar, Kologury, Kolohury
585930 Hulchrath
585940 Gologorica
585950 Gologorki, Gologurki
585974 Gleicherwiesen
585975 Kalagarovka, Kalaharowka
586000 Calma, Calna, Chilia Noua, Chlina, Chylin, Chylonia, Chylonja, Coln, Culmea, Galeny, Galina, Galiniai, Glehn, Gleina, Glina, Glinah, Gline, Glini, Glinna, Glinne, Golin, Golina, Gollheim, Gollin, Golne, Golnie, Golyn, Haleny, Hallein, Halmaj, Halmeu, Halmi, Halom, Hehlen, Hlina, Holmi, Holonie, Holyn, Kalami, Kalin, Kalina, Kaliny, Kalme, Kalna, Kalne, Kalni, Kelheim, Kelin, Kelm, Kelme, Kelmy, Keln, Khelem, Khelm, Kholm, Kholmy, Kielno, Klin, Kliny, Klunya, Koeln, Kolano, Kolimia, Kolin, Koln, Kolna, Kolne, Kolno, Kolomai, Kolomea, Kolomey, Kolomyia, Kolomyja, Kolomyya, Kolonia, Kolumna, Kulm, Kulno
586100 Calomija, Glinnoye, Glinoya, Kolimeya
586150 Glinojeck
586300 Calmatui, Climauti, Colonita, Galanta, Ghelinta, Hlinita, Kalamata
586340 Koln Deutz
586354 Kleindexen
586360 Kolendzyany
586370 Klimetow
586380 Hellenthal
586390 Holendry
586394 Halle an der Saale
586400 Chlumec, Cholmetch, Gelencze, Gelenes, Gellenhaza, Gelnica, Glinice, Glinitsa, Golancz, Gollantsch, Gollnitz, Hlomcza, Kalmatsuy, Kalnica, Kelemes, Kelencze, Klamos, Klanjec, Klenec, Klenocz, Klimautsy, Klimiec, Klinec, Klintsy, Klintzi, Klinzy, Klomnice, Klonice, Klonitse, Kolinec, Kolnica, Kolonice, Koloniec, Kolonitsa, Kulimaz
586430 Calinesti, Calinesti I, Galanesti, Halmasd, Halmosd, Hlemyzdi, Kalineshty, Kalinest
586431 Calinesti II
586433 Helmstadt, Helmstedt
586435 Calinesti Cuparencu
586436 Calinesti Enache, Kleinostheim, Kleinsteinach
586438 Kleinneusiedl

586439 Chylin Stary, Glina Stara
586449 Kolonia Szczerbacka
586450 Glinsko, Hlinsko, Kalnicki, Kolonja Izaaka, Kolonsk
586451 Glinskoye
586457 Kalinciakovo
586459 Kolonie Zgurica
586460 Gelnhausen, Glinzheny, Kolendzyany
586464 Kolonia Synajska, Kolonia Synyska, Kolonie Synaska, Kolonja Synajska
586470 Gelmyazov, Glemjasow, Glemyazovo, Helmiazov
586479 Kolano Swierczyno
586484 Kolonie Zoludzk
586485 Kleinschlag
586498 Kolonja Izraelska
586500 Glinik, Glinka, Glinki, Glomcha, Golinka, Golonki, Golonog, Golynka, Halamky, Holinka, Holynka, Kalinka, Kalnik, Kholmech, Klejniki, Kleyniki, Kolanki, Kolyanki
586530 Colencauti
586540 Gellenhaza
586546 Gelnhausen
586549 Glinik Sredni, Kolonie Kaiserau
586559 Glinik Charzewski, Glinik Gorny
586560 Gailingen
586563 Chlumec nad Cidlinou, Klingenthal, Kolonie Ignitowka
586566 Kilingi Nomme, Klingenmunster
586567 Glingeni Balti, Klingenberg am Main
586569 Glingeni Orhei
586570 Kalnikow
586574 Kalinkovitch, Klimkovice, Klimkovtse, Klimkowce, Kolinkovtsy
586575 Kalinkovichi, Kleinheubach, Klimkovka, Klimkowka
586583 Kalaniec Litewski
586584 Kleineicholzheim
586594 Klein Krotzenburg, Kleinkrotzenburg
586595 Geilenkirchen
586598 Kleinkarlbach
586600 Gliniany, Glinyany, Kalinin, Kiliman, Koloman, Kulmain
586630 Klimonty
586637 Klementov, Klementowice, Klimentov, Klimentow, Klimontow
586638 Kelementelke
586639 Kalinindorf
586640 Kelmentsy
586643 Calimanesti, Golymin Stary, Klein Umstadt
586645 Kalininskoye
586647 Klemensow
586650 Glinianka, Glinianki, Glinyanka
586659 Kaliningrad
586665 Glan Munchweiler
586678 Golymin Polnoc
586680 Gliny Male, Koln Mulheim
586685 Koln Mulheim
586690 Glina Mare
586693 Klein Nordlingen
586700 Chilia Nova, Chlaniow, Choloniow, Gielniow, Gielniow, Goleniow, Gollnow, Halimba, Helenow, Kalinovo, Kalinow,

Kholonev, Klenova, Klimov, Klimovo, Klimow, Klonowa, Kolanow
586740 Kalinowice, Kalinowiec, Klanovice, Klenovec, Klenowitz, Klimovitch, Klimovitz, Klimowice, Klimowicze
586743 Kleineibstadt
586744 Kalinowszczyzna
586745 Glenbochek, Glinovietzk, Kalinovshchizna
586750 Galambok, Glemboka, Glemboke, Glembokie, Hollenbach, Kalinovka, Kalinowka, Kalinuvka, Kalynivka, Kleinheubach, Klimovichi, Klimovka, Kolenivka, Kulmbach
586754 Gelenuvka Stara, Helenowka Stara
586756 Kleinbockenheim
586759 Kleinweikersdorf
586770 Klembow
586775 Klembovka, Klembow Koscielny
586780 Galinovolya, Halinowola
586783 Kalniboloto
586784 Kleinwallstadt
586785 Glinno Wielkie, Gliny Wielkie, Golina Wielka, Kalina Wielka
586793 Klaynvardayn, Kleinbardorf, Kleinwardein, Kolonia Bardo Dolne, Kolonie Wertizany
586794 Kleinwarasdorf
586795 Colmberg, Hallenberg, Hollenberg
586800 Kalnel
586840 Kalnalis
586848 Kleinalsleben
586865 Kleinlangheim
586877 Kolonie Lvovo
586900 Kelemer, Kolmar
586938 Kleinerdlingen
586943 Kleinrust
586944 Helmarshausen
586956 Klein Reken
586960 Helmern
586970 Kielnarowa
587000 Calbe, Calovo, Calw, Chlopy, Choliv, Cholvi, Cleve, Culpiu, Golab, Gollub, Golobi, Goloby, Golop, Golub, Golubie, Holobi, Holoby, Holubie, Kalevi, Kalov, Kaluv, Kelebia, Khlopy, Kilb, Klapy, Kleve, Klew, Kolby, Kulawa, Kulyava
587300 Calafat, Golobudy, Holobudy, Hylvaty, Klaipeda, Klajpeda, Klejpeda
587317 Klavdiyevo Tarasovo
587340 Hlavatce
587350 Klwatka
587357 Klwatecka Wolka
587360 Chlopiatyn, Clivodin, Klivodin
587370 Holobutow, Kolpytov
587373 Klavdyevo Tarasovka
587374 Golub Dobrzyn, Golub Dobzhin
587379 Golub Dobrzyn
587400 Calabasi, Chlewice, Chlopice, Cholowice, Chulovitse, Cleves, Culevcea, Galewice,

468

	Galibicy, Galvacs, Ghilvaci, Giulvaz, Glayvits, Gleiwitz, Gliwice, Golbice, Golubitsa, Holubica, Holubicze, Hulboca, Hulewicze, Hulievcza, Keleviz, Kielbasa, Kielbasy, Kolbas
587430	Clivesti, Khliveshte
587440	Chlopczyce, Glubczyce
587443	Gola Przystan
587450	Chlevieska, Chlewiska, Gleboczek, Glubochek, Golovetsko, Holowiecko, Klobucko, Klobutsk, Klobutzk, Kolobrzeg
587451	Golovetskoye
587457	Chlewska Wola, Hluboczek Wielki
587460	Chlewczany, Golovatchino, Golowtschin, Holovtchin, Kelbassen, Kielbasin, Kielbaszyn
587464	Holowczynce
587467	Chlebiczyn Polny
587468	Chlebiczyn Lesny
587470	Glavtchev, Glowaczow, Glowaczowa, Kolbasov, Kolbasuv, Kolbishov, Kolbushov, Kolbushova, Kolbuszowa
587473	Klavdyevo Tarasovka, Kolbuszowa Dolna
587475	Kolbuszowa Gorna
587500	Chulovichi, Gleboka, Glebokie, Glubokie, Golubichi, Gulboka, Gulevichi, Haluboki, Hluboka, Hluboki, Holovke, Khlebwka, Klobouk, Klobouky, Klobuck, Klobuky
587510	Glebokoye, Glubokoye, Glybokaya
587538	Gilowka Dolna
587560	Golovkino, Khlevchany
587563	Hluboka nad Vltavou
587564	Golovchyntse
587570	Chlopkow, Globikowa, Holoubkov
587574	Klobukowice
587596	Klepie Gorne
587600	Chlebna, Galben, Geleven, Gelvan, Gelvonai, Gelvoniai, Gielwany, Gilvan, Glavan, Globino, Glovna, Glovno, Glowno, Golovno, Gulbene, Gulbiny, Holowno, Holubin, Holubina, Holubine, Kalvene, Kalvini, Klevan, Klewan, Klovainiai, Klovian, Kolpino
587634	Calafindesti
587639	Calbe an der Saale
587640	Chlopeniczi, Cholopenitch, Cholopenitschi, Gelvonis, Gelvonys, Golubinci, Hlavenec, Hlubieniec, Kielpiniec, Kluwince
587650	Glowienka, Holowienki, Kallwang, Kalwang, Kholopenichi
587656	Kloppenheim
587659	Cholewiana Gora
587660	Kloppenheim
587670	Klewinowo
587674	Golovanevsk, Holavenevsk
587675	Klebanovka, Klebanowka, Klebanuvka
587679	Cloppenburg
587700	Halbow, Hlibow, Kielbow, Klevov, Klwow

587740	Glebowice, Glebowicze, Glubowce, Kolbowicze
587744	Chlebowice Swirskie, Khlebovitse Svizhske
587747	Chlebowice Wielkie, Khlebovitse Velki
587750	Chlebowka, Chlopowka, Glebuvka, Klapowka, Klubovka, Kolbovichi
587774	Kolibabovce
587800	Chliple, Holiapol, Holubla, Khliple, Kolbiel, Kolobeel
587830	Hollfeld
587843	Hilpoltstein
587870	Kalevi Liiva
587900	Calvaria, Kalawaria, Kalvaria, Kalwaria, Kalwarja, Kalwarya
587910	Kalvarija, Kalvariya, Kalwariya
587930	Calvorde, Koloverta, Koloverti, Kolowerta
587943	Gola Pristan, Gola Przystan, Halberstadt, Holia Pristan
587945	Golowierzchy
587947	Kalwaria Zebrzydowska, Kalwarja Zebrzydowska
587950	Glauberg, Holberg, Kolberg, Kolobrzeg, Kyllburg
587957	Kulparkow, Kulparkuv
587960	Heilbronn, Hollabrunn
587965	Hilbringen
587970	Kleparov, Kleparow
587975	Kalwaria Paclawska, Kalwarja Paclawska
588430	Galilesti
588450	Kauleliskiai
589000	Chilioara, Kulro
589400	Calarasi, Kalaras, Kalarash
589439	Calarasi Targ
589443	Calarasi Sat
589470	Klarysew
589500	Hollrich
589560	Golerkany, Holercani
589639	Hallerndorf
589700	Kolarovo
589745	Hole Rawskie
589759	Kolarovgrad
590000	Carei, Chari, Gara, Gaure, Gauri, Ger, Gera, Gier, Gor, Gora, Gorai, Goraj, Goray, Gory, Guhrau, Gur, Haar, Harhaj, Hoor, Horia, Ker, Kray, Krsy
591000	Coruia
591386	Kiriyet Lunga
591400	Grojec, Gruyets
591543	Gorajec Stara
591545	Gorajec Zagroble
591650	Kiriyanka, Krajenka, Krojanke
591655	Krajenka Chelmno
591690	Carei Mare
591700	Craiova, Grajewo, Grayavah
591740	Karajewicze, Krajowice
591767	Krajow Nowy
591780	Crijopol
591878	Goraj Lubelski
593000	Cordau, Corjauti, Corjeuti, Corod, Gerde, Geroda, Gerthe, Gorod, Gorodye, Grady, Gruta, Grzeda, Hartau, Hered, Herta, Hird, Horde, Horhat, Horodia, Horodziej, Hort, Hrud, Hurth, Karad, Karait, Kert, Kerta, Krata,

	Kratie, Krutyje, Krutyye, Kurd
593100	Gardeja, Gorodeia, Gorodeya, Krutiye, Krutuje
593146	Curtuiuseni, Curtuiusieni
593400	Chorodetz, Chortitz, Chortotza, Curtici, Gorodets, Gorodisce, Greiditz, Grodziec, Grudziadz, Horodca, Horodec, Horodets, Horodziec, Karditsa, Kartuzy, Khortitsa, Korotycze
593430	Gradistea, Horodistea
593436	Hradiste Mnichovo, Krautostheim
593437	Horodystawice
593438	Horodistea Lapusna
593439	Grady Stare
593440	Chorodishtch, Gorodischtsche, Horodyszcze
593445	Horodyszcze Krolewskie
593450	Gorodishche, Gradysk, Herdecke, Kratecko
593451	Kartusskaya Bereza
593455	Gorodyshche Krulevske, Gorodyshche Krulevski
593460	Curtusieni, Harthausen, Hradesin, Krotoschin, Krotoszyn
593466	Kroatisch Minihof
593479	Kardasova Recice, Kartoz Brezah, Kartuz Bereze
593487	Gorodyslavichi, Gorodyslavitse, Grodyslawice, Kreta Sloboda
593500	Gorodka, Gorodok, Gradki, Graydik, Grodek, Grodig, Grottkau, Grudek, Horodek, Horodok, Hradek, Hradki, Hrudek, Korotichi, Korytki, Krzatka
593514	Grudek Yagyelonski
593515	Grodek Jagiellonski
593534	Kretki Duze
593540	Gradacac, Kurta Keszi
593554	Kratka Kesy, Kratke Kesy
593559	Hradec Kralove
593560	Hardheim
593563	Grodek Nadbuzny
593570	Chortkev, Chortkov, Grodkow
593574	Grodkowice, Hrtkovci
593575	Gorodkovka
593578	Kretki Wielkie
593580	Girtagola, Girtakol
593584	Korytki Lesne
593596	Gratkorn
593600	Chrudim, Garadna, Gardani, Gardony, Gehrden, Gerdauen, Girdani, Gordinya, Gordynya, Gorodna, Gorodno, Gorodnya, Gradin, Gradina, Grodne, Grodno, Hardheim, Herrieden, Herten, Horden, Horodna, Horodne, Horodno, Hriteni, Hurodno, Kartena, Kiryutnya, Kratonohy, Krautheim, Kurityan
593610	Krutnoye
593640	Gardzienice, Gherta Mica, Gorodnitsa, Graudenz, Horodnica, Horodnitza, Korytnica, Korytnitsa
593643	Gordineshty, Gordinesti Hotin,

	Gorodnista
593644	Gardzienice Stare
593648	Hordynia Szlachecka
593650	Gorodenka, Grayding, Graydung, Graydunk, Greding, Greiding, Hertnik, Horodenka, Korytniki, Kretinga, Kretinge
593653	Grotniki Duze
593656	Kretingen, Krettingen, Krottingen
593657	Grudna Kepska
593658	Kretingale
593659	Grudna Gorna
593660	Hradenin
593664	Hartmanice
593667	Hartmanov
593670	Grady Nowe
593678	Gardanfalva
593679	Hardenberg, Hirtenberg
593694	Hordynia Rustykalna
593700	Gertop, Hartop, Krotovo, Krotowo, Krzetow
593740	Chortovets, Grodowice, Grotowice, Hrotovice, Hrottowitz, Kretowce
593749	Hartop Soroca
593750	Kordowka, Kretowka
593760	Kortovian, Kurdyban, Kurtavenai, Kurtuvenai, Kurtuvian, Kurtvvenai
593767	Kurdwanow, Kurdwanowka
593769	Gertop Mare, Hartop Mare
593783	Hartfeld, Karatfold
593784	Kortvelyes
593786	Cartofleanca, Hartopul Mare, Kartoflyanka
593787	Grady Polewne
593794	Kertvaros
593800	Gorodlo, Griedel, Horodle, Horodlo
593840	Kortelisy, Kortilisy
593856	Gardelegen
593870	Gorodilovo
593874	Gorodlovitse, Horodlowice
593900	Curatura, Krstur, Kuratura
593915	Chartariya Chadasha
593930	Craidorott, Harderode
593945	Chartorisk, Chartoriysk
593970	Kirtorf, Kordorf
593980	Craidorol
593983	Craidorlt, Craidorolt
594000	Caraseu, Charz, Creaca, Cris, Gartz, Garz, Geras, Gerausa, Gerce, Geres, Gerse, Gertsa, Ghiris, Ghirisa, Gorizia, Gorizy, Gorodye, Gracze, Graetz, Gratz, Graz, Greiz, Gritsa, Gritza, Gritze, Gross, Grossau, Grutse, Gruz, Gruzdziai, Harc, Harczo, Harz, Hirics, Horice, Horodia, Horodz, Horodzei, Horodzhyey, Horodziej, Hurez, Karasz, Karcsa, Karez, Karos, Karsy, Kercz, Kertsh, Korec, Korets, Koretz, Koric, Koritz, Koros, Kracie, Kratzau, Kraziai, Krc, Krec, Kreuzau, Krise, Kroz, Kroze, Krozhe, Kruce, Kruz, Krzyz, Kurash, Kurasz, Kyritz
594143	Gross Jestin
594170	Gorzejowa
594300	Carcedea, Choreshty, Chrast, Garzdai, Gorzad, Gorzd,

	Gorzed, Gorzh D, Gorzhdy, Gruzd, Gruzdziai, Hirschaid, Horosauti, Kercsed, Keresd, Korost, Koryst
594330	Corestauti, Horostyta, Keresztete, Keresztut
594336	Gerstetten
594338	Cristottul Mare
594340	Crisceatec, Grushatytse, Harastas, Harasztos, Hristici, Hrusiatycze, Hruszatyce, Keresztes, Korestautsy
594343	Cristesti
594347	Keresztespuspoki, Korostishov, Korostyshev, Korostyszow
594350	Grushatichi, Grusyatychi, Khristichi
594354	Grosstaxen
594357	Chorostkov, Chorostkow, Chrostkowo, Khorostkov, Krystkowice, Krzystkowice
594359	Harasztkerek, Kurzatki Rawy
594360	Chrastany, Chrustne, Garsden, Horstein, Hrastin, Kereszteny, Korosten, Krastine, Krastini, Kristiania
594364	Christianstadt, Cristinesti, Horst Emscher
594367	Chrusty Nowe, Khristinovka, Krestyanovka, Kristinopol, Krystynopol
594369	Horstmar
594370	Chorostow, Chrastava, Gorzedow, Karzdaba, Khorostov, Korostov, Korostuv
594374	Chroustovice, Horazdovice, Karzdabas, Korostowice
594375	Grodztwo Kowal
594378	Krustpils
594379	Christburg
594380	Herstelle, Horesedly, Horosedl
594383	Cristolt, Cristoltel
594384	Carastelec, Cristelec
594390	Crestur, Cristur, Kerestur, Kereszter, Keresztur
594394	Gross Ottersleben, Korostarcsa
594395	Gora Strykowa
594397	Geresdorf, Gorsdorf, Kraisdorf
594398	Cristorel
594400	Chorosciec, Choroshtch, Choroszcz, Chroscice, Gorzyce, Grodziec, Grudziadz, Horodziec, Horschitz, Horsice, Khoroshoutsi, Khorostsets, Korzec, Korzets, Korzhets, Korzysc, Krasic
594430	Corcesti, Cracesti, Grozeshti, Grozeshty, Grozesti, Kracest
594436	Grosi Satu Mare, Grossostheim
594439	Grady Stare, Gross Strehlitz
594440	Horoszczyce, Krzciecice
594443	Kroczyce Stare
594446	Grossschutzen
594450	Grodzhisk, Grodzisk, Grodzisko, Grozitsk, Korczyska
594453	Grodzisko Dolne
594454	Grosssachsen
594455	Grodzisko Gorne
594456	Grodzhisk Mazovyets, Grodzisk Mazowiecki, Grodzisko Miasteczko, Grodzisko Miasto, Gross Schogen
594457	Grodzisk Wielkopolski

594459	Grosssiegharts
594460	Gorzyczany, Gruszczyn, Krasiczyn, Krasocin
594464	Grosi Somes
594465	Kroshtzinka
594469	Gross Zimmern
594470	Carsicov, Chruszczow
594478	Korczyce Wielkie
594479	Chruszczobrod
594480	Gross Sallo
594483	Gross Schlatten
594490	Crucisor
594496	Gross Surany
594500	Gorecko, Goroshki, Gorsk, Gorutsko, Gresk, Gressk, Grushka, Grzeska, Horoschki, Horoshki, Horsk, Horucko, Hureczko, Kerecke, Kerecki, Kerecky, Keretski, Keretzky, Koroshegy, Krichka, Krusk, Krychka, Kryczka, Krysk, Krzesk, Kursk
594510	Gorskoye
594530	Criscauti, Hercegcut, Hercegkut, Horoscauti
594535	Kreshchatik
594538	Grosskadolz
594540	Krishkautsy
594545	Karsakiskis
594546	Hercegszanto
594554	Gross Kackschen
594559	Krzesk Krolowa Niwa
594560	Giershagen, Krasichin, Krusicany
594565	Kroshchenke
594567	Grodzkie Nowe, Herzogenburg
594568	Horoszki Male
594569	Herzogenaurach, Herzogenrath
594570	Gireshkov, Gorshkov, Gorzakiew, Gorzkow, Hriskov, Karyshkov, Khoroskiv, Khroskev, Korzkiew, Kraczkowa, Kraskow, Kuraszkow
594573	Grishkabod, Grishkabud, Griskabodis, Griskabudis, Korosszegapati
594574	Gorszkowice, Gorzkowice, Hercegovac, Kraszkowice
594575	Charishkifka, Gorischkowka, Goryshkovka, Horyschkowka
594576	Krzeczkowo Mianowskie
594578	Hercegfalva
594580	Korosszakal
594584	Grosseicholzheim
594590	Ghirasa Ghira, Gross Gerau, Grossgerau, Hara Sghira
594593	Grossgartach, Grosskrut, Harzgerode
594594	Grezegerzova, Gross Krotzenburg, Grosskrotzenburg
594597	Gross Karben, Grosskarben
594598	Grosskarlbach
594600	Charzyno, Chorzen, Chorzyna, Chrzczony, Crasna, Creussen, Crossen, Garcin, Garsene, Gauersheim, Ghiriseni, Girisheni, Girisheny, Gorcsony, Gorczyn, Gorzno, Griesheim, Grischino, Grishino, Grozny, Groznyy, Gruczno, Gruesen, Grusen,

Harsany, Heresznye,
Horitschon, Karasin, Karitchin,
Karsin, Kartchin, Kerecseny,
Kherson, Korczyn, Korczyna,
Koricin, Koristchan, Koritschan,
Korsun, Korycin, Koryciny,
Koryczany, Korzenna,
Korzenno, Krasna, Krasne,
Krasnei, Krasno, Krasny,
Kraszna, Krcin, Kroczyn,
Krosin, Krosna, Krosno,
Kruszyna, Krzcin, Krzecin,
Krzesiny, Kurczyno, Kursenai,
Kurseniai, Kurshan, Kurshany,
Kurshjan, Kurzany, Kurzeme,
Kurzyna
594610 Krasnaye, Krasnoya, Krasnoye
594614 Krasnaya Sloboda
594617 Krasnaya Volya
594630 Grozinti, Karacsond, Kerecsend
594636 Hroznetin
594638 Gorzen Dolny
594639 Grosseneder, Krasnodar,
Kritzendorf, Krosno Odrzanskie
594640 Charsnitza, Charsznica,
Chorosnica, Corcmaz,
Gardzienice, Garesnica,
Gorczenica, Grozintsi,
Kharshnitse, Khorosnitsa,
Korosmezo, Korzenica,
Korzeniec, Krasnica, Krasnitsa,
Krasnocz, Krasznoc, Krosnica,
Krosnice, Kureshnitsa,
Kurzeniec
594643 Craciunesti, Gross Mosty, Gross
Umstadt, Korzeniste,
Krasinstav, Krasnistav,
Krasnistov, Krasnostav,
Krasnostavtse, Krasnostavtsy,
Krasnostawce, Krasny Ostrov,
Krasnystav, Krasnystaw
594644 Gardzienice Stare
594645 Karczmiska
594646 Crasnaseni, Krasniczyn,
Krasnosheny, Krosno
Odrzanskie
594647 Gorishnyy Dzvinyach, Korsun
Shevchenkovskiy
594648 Krasnoe Selo, Krasnoselka,
Krasnoselye, Krasnoshelets,
Krasnoshelts, Krasnosielc,
Krosnoshiltz
594649 Gross Mesereitsch,
Grossenzersdorf, Krasnishore,
Krasnisora, Krasznisora
594650 Chrzczanka, Gorozhanka,
Gorzanka, Gressenich,
Gurzenich, Horozanka,
Karczemka, Krashnik, Krasnik,
Kreutznach, Kreuznach,
Krocienko, Kroschenke,
Kroscienko, Krosenko,
Kroshinka, Kroshnik,
Krosienko, Krosinek, Krushnik,
Krusznik, Krzesinki
594651 Kreznica Jara
594653 Krasny Oktyabr, Krasnyy Oktyabr
594654 Krasnokutsk
594655 Krasnokuck
594656 Greussenheim, Gross Magendorf,
Grossenkneten, Grotzingen,
Kerzenheim, Krasna Kamienka,
Krasnyye Okny, Kreuzingen,

Kroscienko Nizne
594657 Karasznokvajda, Kroscienko
Wyzne
594659 Gorzen Gorny,
Korosnagyharsany, Krasna
Hora nad Vltavoa, Krasna
Hora nad Vltavou,
Krasnograd, Krasnogrod,
Krasny Gorodok,
Kurzanhradek
594660 Greussenheim, Kersemjen,
Kerzenheim, Krasienin,
Kruszyniany
594664 Grasmannsdorf
594665 Grossenenglis, Krasnyanka,
Krasznamihalyfalva
594668 Kurzyna Mala
594670 Garasymuv, Grady Nowe,
Harasymow, Harszymow,
Karaczynow, Korzeniew,
Korzeniow, Krashanov,
Kreshanov, Kretsnif,
Krosnowa, Krzczonow,
Krzeczanowo
594673 Crasna Putnei, Krasna Putna,
Krasne Potockie, Krasnoputna
594674 Grossen Buseck, Hryczynowicze,
Kracinovce, Krasna Wies,
Krasnovce, Kroshnivitz,
Krosniewice, Krzyzanowice
594678 Gorozhanna Volka, Horozanna
Wielka, Karacson Falva,
Karacsonfalva, Krasna Wola,
Krasnapole, Krasnapoli,
Krasnopol, Krasnopole,
Krasnopole Malastowki,
Krasnopolye, Krassnapolje,
Krasznafalu, Krisnipolye,
Krosnopolia
594679 Korschenbroich, Krasnobrod,
Krasny Brod, Krotzenburg
594680 Craciunel
594684 Crasna Iliesti, Crasna Ilschi,
Crasnaleuca, Krasna Ilski,
Krasnoilsk
594685 Krasnaluk, Krasnoluka,
Krasnoluki
594686 Grossen Linden, Grossenlinden,
Grossmuhlingen
594687 Krasna Lipa
594690 Garsa Mare, Kurzanhradek
594693 Kreuzenort
594694 Korczyn Rustykalny
594696 Krasnoarmeyskoye
594700 Chorzewa, Chorzow, Cracow,
Gorodzuv, Gorosheve,
Gorzow, Graziowa, Grezow,
Gricev, Gritsev, Grizew,
Grosow, Grozov, Grozovo,
Gruseva, Grushev, Grushevo,
Gruszow, Gurzuf, Harisof,
Haritzev, Horodzow,
Horoszowa, Hrozovo, Hrozow,
Hrushov, Hrusov, Hruszew,
Hruszow, Karachev, Karcsava,
Karczew, Karsava, Kartchev,
Kartshev, Kirsova, Korczew,
Korczow, Korshev, Korshuv,
Korsov, Korsove, Korsow,
Korszow, Korzhevo, Kraczew,
Kraczow, Krasew, Krauszow,
Krauzow, Krecow, Kreshiv,
Kreshov, Krichev, Kricov,

Kricsif, Kritchev, Krostchov,
Krzeczow, Krzeszow,
Krzyzowa
594730 Grossbeti
594739 Grosspetersdorf
594740 Charzewice, Choroszewicze,
Gieraszowice, Groszowice,
Grushevtsy, Hruszowice,
Hruszwica, Karczowice,
Karsavas, Khoroshovtsy,
Korzhevtsy, Kraczewice,
Kraszewice, Krizevci,
Kruschwitz, Kruswica,
Kruszwica, Krysovitse,
Krysowice, Krzeszowice,
Krzeszowiec
594744 Choroszewsszczyce, Krasowo
Czestki
594745 Gross Becskerek, Horesovicky,
Horsovsky Tyn, Krszywcze
Gorne
594747 Grushvitsy Pervyye, Kraszewo
Czubaki
594748 Gorzow Slaski
594749 Karassu Basar, Karasu Bazar,
Karasubazar, Kraso Bazar
594750 Graisbach, Grezowka,
Grossheubach, Grushevka,
Grushuvka, Hroszowka,
Hruszowka, Karsavka,
Korshovka, Korsovka,
Korsovke, Korsowka,
Kreisbach, Krzeszowka,
Krzyzowka, Kurozweki
594754 Khoroshovchitsy
594756 Gross Bockenheim
594759 Grossweikersdorf, Krzeszow
Gorny
594760 Giershofen, Krocben,
Kurozvany, Kurozwany
594765 Harsewinkel, Krzyzowniki
594767 Kryspinow
594776 Grosspoppen
594778 Gorzow Wielkopolski, Gruszow
Wielki, Horyszow Polski,
Krasowo Wielkie
594779 Gross Bieberau
594780 Krizhopol, Kryzhopol, Kryzopol
594783 Charciabalda, Gersfeld,
Herschfeld, Hersfeld,
Herzfeld, Karsfeld Allach
594787 Grady Polewne, Harsfalva,
Kracsfalva, Kricsfalva,
Kriesfalva
594789 Garzweiler
594790 Gross Wierau, Har Shafer
594793 Gross Wartenberg,
Grosswardein, Grosz
Wartenberg
594794 Gora Siewierska, Gross
Breesen, Grosswarasdorf,
Horyszow Ruski
594795 Hersbruck, Herschberg,
Hirschberg, Kirschberg,
Kraitzburg, Kreitsburg,
Kreitzburg, Kreutzburg,
Kreuzberg, Kreuzburg, Kruczy
Borek
594800 Chortzel, Chorzele, Chrosla,
Greetsiel, Guruslau, Hersel,
Kerdzhali, Khorzel, Khorzele,
Khorzhel, Kirdzhali, Korezule,
Kraslau, Kurdzhali

471

594830	Kurzelaty
594836	Korosladany
594840	Chruslice, Korzelice, Kraslice
594845	Kryczylsk
594848	Grossalsleben
594850	Korozluky
594853	Kercseliget
594860	Chruslina, Gorzelnia, Gross Leine, Krzeslin
594864	Grosslomnitz, Krushelnitsa, Kruszelnica
594865	Chruslanki Jozefowskie, Chruslanki Mazanowskie, Grosslangheim, Kruszelnica Rustykalna, Kruszelnica Szlachecka
594870	Chorzelow, Grosolovo, Horodzilow, Korszylow, Krasilov, Krasilova, Krasilow, Kraslava, Kraslave, Kresilov, Kreslawa, Krocehlavy, Kruzlowa, Kurzelow
594874	Goryslawice
594875	Khorshyluvka, Korshyluvka, Kraslavka, Kraslavke, Kreslavaka, Kreslavka
594876	Grosselfingen
594878	Kreslaval
594900	Gruisor, Kuresare, Kuressaare
594930	Gross Rhuden
594936	Gross Radomysl
594946	Gross Rosen
594947	Grossrussbach
594953	Gross Rhuden
594960	Hirschhorn
594979	Grossropperhausen
594990	Gross Rohrheim
594995	Gross Rohrheim
595000	Caracui, Chorki, Curug, Garki, Gergo, Giurgiu, Gor'kiy, Gorki, Gorkiy, Gurghiu, Harhaj, Harka, Hereg, Hurka, Hurko, Karakuy, Karge, Kerch, Keregky, Krakau, Krakiai, Krako, Krakoy, Kregi, Kriukai, Krok, Kroke, Krucha, Kruk, Kruki, Kryg, Krzak, Kurki
595143	Kirkayeshty
595174	Kragujevac
595300	Giorocuta, Girokuta, Horhat, Hrochot
595337	Kerkatotfalu
595350	Gorgeteg
595360	Hora Kutna
595385	Kerekteleki
595393	Kirchtrudering
595397	Kirchdorf, Kirchdrauf
595400	Gractz, Harkacs, Horgos, Hrkac, Krakes
595417	Caragacii Vechi
595430	Corocaesti, Gargzdai, Gargzhday
595439	Gorecko Stare, Grochy Stare, Kreigsdorf
595445	Gorki Szczukowskie, Karkaziskes
595450	Gorchtchik
595460	Cara Hasan, Caracuseni, Herxheim, Karagasany, Karakushany, Karakushen, Kirchohsen
595467	Kirchschonbach
595473	Gorica Svetojanska
595478	Georgswalde
595479	Kriegshaber

595485	Kirchschlag, Kirchschlag bei Linz
595493	Gorki Srednie
595500	Karcag, Kerekheg, Kerekhegy
595534	Kerkakutas
595540	Kerekegyhaza
595541	Gorka Koscejowska
595564	Kirch Gons
595578	Krokocka Wola
595583	Kerkaiklod
595597	Gorki Grabienskie
595600	Gheorgheni, Gorican, Harheim, Harkany, Herkheim, Horkheim, Kereknye, Kirchen, Kirchhain, Kirchheim, Korchyn, Korchynie, Korycany, Kurchino
595630	Gurahont
595635	Gorgenyhodak
595639	Kirchendorf
595640	Georgenhausen, Gracanica, Krhanice, Krokmazy, Kruchenicze, Krukenitsa, Krukienice
595645	Georgensgmund
595646	Gorgenyszentimre
595650	Crehange, Krukhinichi
595654	Georgenhausen
595655	Gorgenykakucs
595663	Kirchheim an der Weinstrasse
595664	Gura Camenca, Kirchheim im Schwaben
595665	Gura Kamenka
595670	Karachinuv, Krakanova, Krakenovo, Krakinava, Krakinova, Krakinovo, Krekenava, Krekenova
595675	Grichinovichi
595678	Kircheimbolanden, Kirchheimbolanden
595679	Georgenberg, Kirchenbirk
595680	Karack Maly
595690	Gura Cainari, Gura Humora, Gura Kaynary, Gurahumora
595694	Gorgenyoroszdalu, Gorgenyorsova
595698	Gura Humorului
595700	Charkow, Charukuv, Gorokhov, Grochov, Grochow, Horchov, Horkhov, Horkhuv, Horochow, Hrhov, Kargowa, Kharkov, Korouhev, Krakow, Krakuv, Krcava, Krechow, Krekhov, Krichevo, Krichovo, Kricovo, Kriukav, Krjukow, Krugov, Kruguv, Kruhow, Krukow, Krychow, Kryukov
595740	Choragwica, Harkabuz, Hrejkovice, Krakovets, Krakovitz, Krakowice, Krakowiec, Krechowce, Krechowice, Krekhovitse, Krekhovtse
595744	Krukowszczyzna
595748	Kargowa Zielona
595750	Chorkowka, Grochowka, Koryukovka, Krekhovichi, Krukowka, Krzykawka
595764	Crikvenica
595778	Grochow Wloscianski
595780	Hrycowola
595785	Gorki Wielkie
595790	Hara Kbira

595794	Gorki Borze
595795	Kirchberg
595800	Caracal, Cracalia, Gergely, Gergelyi, Kirkilai, Kirklyay, Korcula, Krugel, Krugla, Krugle, Krugloe, Kruhel, Kurkil, Kurkla, Kurkli, Kurkliai
595810	Krugloye
595840	Grocholice, Grocholitza
595845	Krichilsk
595850	Kruglik, Kruglyak
595855	Cruglic Hotin
595859	Cruglic Orhei, Gergelyiugornya
595860	Gorokholina, Horocholina, Kircholm
595864	Girkalnis
595865	Creglingen
595876	Gura Galbena
595878	Kruhel Wielki
595879	Gora Kalwaria, Gora Kalwarja, Gorka Lubartowska, Gura Kalvaria, Gura Kalwariska
595900	Kerkira, Krickerhau, Kriegerhay
595930	Kirchardt
595936	Kirchherten
595944	Hergershausen
595947	Grzegorzew, Grzegorzewice
595950	Krickerhau, Kriegerhay
595955	Grigore Gika Vode, Grigori Ghica Voda
595960	Chorherrn, Chorochoryn, Khorokhorin
595964	Hohr Grenzhausen
595970	Gregorov, Gregoruv, Hrehorow
595974	Grgurevci, Grygorowicze
595978	Grigoriopol
596000	Carna, Carno, Chorna, Chyrzyna, Corni, Garany, Garrin, Gaureny, Gaurini, Gerjen, Ghireni, Gorane, Gorno, Goruna, Grain, Gran, Granne, Greene, Grimma, Gronau, Grun, Haaren, Haren, Harheim, Harina, Herina, Herne, Horanie, Horn, Horna, Hornya, Horrem, Hoyren, Hranie, Hurnie, Kirn, Koren, Korma, Kornie, Kornye, Korom, Kourim, Krain, Krajno, Kranj, Kremna, Kremno, Kriaunai, Kromau, Kromy, Kron, Krouna, Krymno, Kurima, Kuryany
596100	Carmeiu, Grimnoye
596300	Corinth, Gerend, Gorond, Goronda, Gorund, Granaut, Granauti, Grind, Haromhuta, Herend, Korond
596340	Kurantice
596344	Gaureni de Sus
596345	Harmuthsachsen
596346	Gora Motyczna, Hernadcsany
596355	Hernadkak
596357	Hory Matky Bozi
596359	Gerendkeresztur, Grind Cristur, Hernadkercs
596360	Carnateni, Grindeni
596364	Gramatneusiedl
596366	Hernadnemeti
596373	Hernadpetri
596374	Hernadvecse

596380 Cornitel
596391 Grinauti Raia
596394 Kramatorsk
596400 Chramec, Crimmitschau, Garnsee, Gerenyes, Girincs, Granica, Granice, Grenci, Grinauts, Grinautsi, Grinautsy, Gromiec, Gronitza, Grzmiaca, Harmacz, Harmas, Hernecs, Horyniec, Hranice, Karanac, Karmacs, Karnozia, Kernitsa, Kiernica, Kiernozia, Korenetz, Korenice, Kornica, Kornice, Kornitsa, Kornitz, Kornitza, Korniza, Koronco, Kremnica, Kremnitz, Krems, Kremyz, Krenice, Krenitz, Krhanice, Kriaunos, Krimice, Krinec, Krinitza, Kruonis, Krynica, Krzymosze, Kurenets
596430 Carnesti, Cornest, Cornesti, Gornesti, Kornesht, Korneshty, Kornesty, Kyrneshty
596431 Gornostayevka, Hornostaje
596433 Cornesti Targ, Crumstadt, Gruenstadt, Grunstadt, Kornesht Targ, Kornesht Tyrg, Kronstadt, Kronstetten
596434 Gramzdas, Hrimezdice, Korneshty Sabany
596435 Cornesti Gara
596437 Gornja Stubica, Gornostaypol, Hornistopol
596439 Chorny Ostrov, Cornyj Ostrov
596443 Granicesti, Harnicesti, Hernadzsadany, Hornicest
596445 Karancssag
596446 Grenzhausen
596450 Carynskie, Choromsk, Grenzach, Khoromsk, Korrenzig, Kramsk, Krinichki, Krnsko
596454 Karancskeszi
596455 Kranjska Gora
596457 Gorynska Wola
596458 Hermeskeil
596459 Krzyncze Gorne
596460 Gernsheim, Grundsheim, Kirnatseny
596461 Gorna Dzhumaya
596463 Hernadszentandras, Krems an der Donau
596464 Krincinas
596470 Gronzeva, Horincevo
596473 Harmaspatak
596474 Caram Sebes, Caransebes, Crensovci, Karniszewice, Kernasovca, Kromszewice
596475 Gernsbach, Kramaszowka
596476 Horni Cepen, Horny Cepen, Kormocbanya
596478 Gruensfeld, Grunsfeld
596479 Garmisch Partenkirchen, Karancsbereny, Kransberg, Krantsberg, Kranzberg
596480 Karancsalja
596484 Grundzales
596487 Horne Saliby, Hornie Saliby, Karancslapujto
596490 Kremsier
596495 Horni Cerekev
596500 Gairing, Garnek, Gorniki, Gremyach, Grinki, Gromnik, Herink, Hornigi, Karnich,

Kornichi, Kornik, Kreinik, Krienek, Krinek, Krinki, Krinok, Krnjak, Kronach, Krynka, Krynki, Kurnik
596530 Harangod, Haromhuta
596537 Korniaktow
596543 Krynica Zdroj
596545 Grenkeshek, Grinkishok, Grinkiskis
596546 Horinghausen
596547 Krynki Sobole
596560 Cronheim, Gremheim, Hornheim, Hurnheim
596564 Horni Hincina
596570 Gorinchovo, Horincovo, Krajnikov
596574 Chrancovice, Hrynkowce, Krynica Wies
596575 Germakovka, Germakowka, Korynkovka, Kramkowka Duza, Kramkowka Wielka
596576 Kurniki Iwanczanskie
596587 Krenglbach
596590 Crna Gora, Hermagor
596593 Chyrzyna Korytniki, Goringrod, Goryngrad, Horyngrad Krupa, Horyngrod
596600 Cormani, Corneni, Cremenia, Cronheim, Geranony, Gieranony, Goranin, Gremheim, Grimmen, Hornheim, Hurnheim, Keremjen, Korman, Kornin, Kremmen, Krnany, Krzemienna, Kurmeni
596630 Caramahmet, Crainimat, Kormend
596639 Krone an der Brahe
596640 Kormanice, Kremenets, Kremenits, Kremenitz, Kremintsy, Kremyanitsa, Krimianitza, Krzemienica, Krzemieniec
596643 Hermannstadt, Hermanstadt
596644 Cremenciuc
596645 Hermanszeg, Kremenchuk, Krementchug, Kremienczuk, Krzemienczuk
596646 Horni Hyncina
596653 Grimancauti
596654 Grimankautsy
596655 Kremenchug
596656 Groningen, Gruningen
596658 Gornji Miholjac
596664 Hermann Mestetz
596670 Germanuv, Hermanow, Hermanowa
596674 Hermanovce, Hermanovice, Hermanowice, Hermanowicze, Karmanowice
596675 Germanovichi, Germanovka, Germanowka, Gronenbach, Guermanovka, Hermanovka
596676 Hermanuv Mestec
596680 Crnomelj
596686 Gornji Milanovac
596694 Kromau Mahrisch
596700 Choronow, Chreniow, Chrzanow, Cornova, Granov, Granow, Granuv, Gromovo, Gronov, Gronow, Grynyava, Haromfa, Hornowo, Hronov, Hryniawa, Hryniow, Karniewo, Karniow,

Kornevo, Korniow, Kornova, Kornovo, Kornyuv, Korompa, Koronowo, Krnov, Krzymow
596730 Karnobat
596739 Gornji Petrovci
596740 Gorna Wies, Granowiec, Hrinovca
596743 Kornwestheim
596745 Krzymowskie
596747 Grunow Spiegelberg
596750 Chromowka, Grombach, Horrenbach, Khrenovka, Krempachy, Krombach, Krompach, Krompachy, Krumbach, Krumpach
596756 Krumbach Markt
596760 Krempna
596764 Horni Benesov
596765 Herrnbaumgarten
596780 Goromboly
596783 Crainfeld, Grunwald
596785 Krzynowloga Mala, Krzynowloga Wielka
596795 Gruenberg, Grunberg, Hornburg, Kirnberg, Kornburg, Korneuburg, Kronberg
596800 Grzymala
596830 Krimulda
596837 Horni Litvinov
596857 Grzymalkow
596866 Kornelimunster
596870 Grimaylov, Grzymalow, Herrenalb, Krimilev, Krimilov, Kromolow, Krumlov
596874 Kornalowice
596875 Grzymalowka, Kornelowka
596876 Krumlov Moravsky
596900 Gheria Mare
596930 Gernrode
596940 Kromeriz
596945 Gory Morskie
596946 Germersheim
597000 Chorewo, Chorow, Chrapy, Chyrow, Corabia, Corbu, Corfu, Corjeva, Criva, Garba, Garbou, Ghirova, Girbou, Girovo, Goruv, Grabie, Gribo, Griby, Griva, Grivo, Griwa, Grybai, Gurba, Horb, Hrhov, Hrip, Hrob, Hrywa, Hurby, Karb, Kariv, Karow, Karuv, Khirov, Khorevo, Khorov, Khyrov, Kirf, Kirov, Kirowo, Korb, Koriv, Korop, Korpoi, Koruv, Korva, Krape, Kreva, Krevo, Krewo, Krievei, Kripa, Kriva, Krive, Krivoi, Krobia, Krpy, Krupa, Krupe, Krywa, Krzywe, Kurov, Kurow, Kuruv
597100 Crepaja
597149 Crivoje Ozero, Krivoie Oziero, Krivoje Ozero, Krivoye Ozero
597195 Krivay Rog, Krivoi Rog, Krivoj Rog, Krivoy Rog
597300 Chrewt, Grabiuti, Herbede, Karpathy, Karpety, Krzywda, Kurivody
597337 Krywe a/d Tworylne
597350 Garbatka, Gryvyatki, Hrywiatki, Krovatka, Krowatka
597353 Horvatkut

597356	Horvatkimle
597360	Carabeteni, Grivita Noua, Gura Putein, Gura Putnei
597365	Kuropatniki
597374	Harbutowice, Horobatowice
597375	Garbatowka, Karabetovka
597380	Gura Putilei, Kriftel
597386	Krepa Dolna
597387	Horvatlovo
597390	Karwodrza
597400	Corpaci, Crivitz, Garbocz, Grabiec, Gryfice, Horovce, Horovice, Horpacs, Hrobce, Hrobec, Karwodrza, Kerepec, Kerepes, Koropets, Koropiec, Koropitz, Koropuz, Koropuzh, Krappitz, Krepice, Krevz, Kriftch, Krivich, Krivitch, Krivitsa, Krivitsh, Kropitz, Krowice, Krzepice, Krzewica, Krzywcza, Krzywcze, Krzywica, Krzywice, Krzywicze, Kurovitse, Kurovtsy, Kurowce, Kurowice
597430	Carpesti, Corbesti, Hervest, Karpeshty
597433	Gerbstedt, Harpstedt, Kropstadt
597436	Herbstein
597437	Krivsoudov
597438	Krzywcze Dolne
597439	Grabie Stare
597440	Graboszyce, Hrivcice, Krzywczyce, Kurovischtscha
597443	Horvatzsidany
597450	Charpaczka, Chribska, Grobzig, Horbacka, Kharpachka, Korbecke, Krupsko, Krzywiczki
597459	Krzywcze Gorne
597460	Coropceni, Grabocin, Hrabesin, Krivoshin, Krzywoszyn
597467	Gora Wisniowa, Grubisno Polje
597470	Greboszow, Hrubieszow, Hrubishov, Hrubyeshuv
597474	Carapciu pe Ceremus, Carapciu pe Siret
597478	Greifswald
597479	Grabce Wreckie
597480	Carevo Selo
597490	Krivazer, Krivoe Ozero
597500	Churovichi, Corbach, Gerbach, Gorbakha, Grabki, Grzywka, Karapchu, Karbach, Karpach, Korbach, Koropki, Krifch, Krivch, Krivichi, Krivka, Krufch, Krupka, Krupki, Krywka, Kurovichi
597534	Grabki Duze
597546	Krowica Sama
597548	Krepa Koscielna
597558	Krowica Holodowska Wies
597560	Korobcheny
597570	Gorbakov, Gorbkuv, Grabkow, Grebkow, Horbakow, Horbkow, Hrabkov, Karapchiv, Karavukovo
597574	Grzywkowicze, Kharapchiu pe Siret, Kharapchou pe Ceremus, Krapkowice
597578	Krzywiecka Wola
597580	Gura Bacului, Gura Bykuluy
597583	Krivoklat
597584	Krowica Lasowa
597593	Kirovograd, Kirowograd
597600	Carbuna, Chrapon, Chrapun,

	Gorpin, Graben, Grabiny, Grebenau, Grebien, Grobin, Grobina, Grovin, Grubna, Gryfin, Gryfino, Grzebienie, Horpin, Hrivno, Hurben, Karbuna, Karpfen, Karvina, Karvinna, Karwina, Kerpen, Khrapun, Korabina, Korpona, Krapina, Kravany, Kriewen, Kroben, Kroeben, Kropine, Kruopine, Krupina, Krzepin, Krzywin
597635	Garbenteich
597637	Korfantow
597640	Garabonc, Grafenhausen, Grobinas, Krobonosz, Krobonosza
597643	Corvinesti, Grebenstein, Kroppenstedt
597650	Crvenka, Grabianka, Grabniki, Grebenka, Grebenki, Greifenhagen, Horepniky, Krowinka, Krowniki, Krzewianki
597654	Grafenhausen
597655	Greifenhagen
597656	Grebenhain
597660	Carpineni, Chrbonin, Grebenhain, Karpineny
597670	Grabianow, Grebenov, Hrebenow, Hrobonovo, Hurbanovo, Krobanow
597674	Charbinowice, Gravenwiesbach
597676	Gorbenpinczehely
597677	Kaerpen B Bergheim
597679	Grafenberg, Grafenwoerth, Grafenwohr, Grafenworth, Greifenberg, Grevenbroich
597700	Garbov, Garbova, Garbow, Gorbovo, Grabov, Grabova, Grabow, Grabowa, Grabowie, Grebow, Gribev, Gribiv, Gribov, Gribuv, Grubov, Grybow, Grzybow, Grzybowo, Horbow, Krjupow, Krupove, Krupowie
597730	Garbovat, Harbovat
597731	Garbova de Jos
597740	Gerbovets, Grabovets, Grabovits, Grabovitz, Grabovtsy, Grabovyets, Grabowce, Grabowiec, Grybovitsa, Grzybowice, Gyrbovets, Hrabovec, Hroubovice, Karpowicze
597743	Grabowce Dolne
597750	Grabovka, Grabowka, Karpovichi
597754	Karwowo Krzywanice
597759	Karwowo Krzywanice
597760	Kropivna, Kropiwna
597764	Gorbopincehely
597765	Grabownica Starzenska, Kropevnik, Kropivnik, Kropiwnik, Kropiwnik Nowy, Kropiwnik Stary
597784	Gorbo Belecska
597785	Krzywowolka
597786	Kriva Palanka
597794	Grabow Rycki
597800	Chraboly, Gorval, Gorwal, Grobla, Horval, Hrebla, Kereplye, Kripuli, Krypule,

	Kuropole, Kuropolye
597830	Grywald, Krefeld
597840	Chrypalicze, Garbolc
597850	Khrypaliche, Krzywoluka
597860	Chryplin, Garvilin, Garvolin, Garwolin, Khryplin, Kropelin
597865	Krzywulanka
597870	Korablew
597874	Gora Pulawska, Korablew Zagrodniki
597875	Gorowo Ilaweckie, Karpilovka, Karpilowka
597876	Grafelfing
597890	Gura Vailor
597900	Krawara
597930	Herford
597940	Chroberz
597945	Kravarsko
597950	Harburg, Horburg, Kraiburg, Krzywy Rog
597956	Kraiburg am Inn
597957	Harburg Wilhelmsburg
597960	Gerabronn, Herbern, Herborn
597970	Chorobrow
597976	Krivorovnya, Krzyworownia
598000	Choral, Chorol, Gerla, Gherla, Giruliai, Harlau, Hirlau, Kerelo, Khorli, Khorly, Khorol, Kiraly, Krali, Kruhle, Krula
598170	Charlejow
598300	Carolath, Kirald, Korlat
598340	Krole Duze
598360	Corlateni
598367	Charlottenburg
598374	Gieraltowiczki, Giraltovce
598379	Grala Dabrowizna
598394	Kiralydarocz, Kyralydarocz
598400	Goerlitz, Goorlitz, Gorlice, Gorlits, Gorlitse, Gorlitz, Gorlitza, Horelice, Horlacea, Karelic, Karelits, Kiralyhaza, Korelicze, Korelitz, Kyrieleis
598433	Karlstadt
598436	Gerolstein, Karlstein
598439	Karlsdorf, Krole Stare
598446	Geroldshausen, Herleshausen
598460	Crailsheim, Gorliczyna, Herrlisheim, Kriltsin
598473	Carlsbad, Karlsbad, Karlzbad
598474	Gory Luszowskie
598476	Gerolzhofen, Karlshafen
598479	Carlosburg, Carlsberg, Karlsburg
598493	Karlsrode
598495	Carlsruhe, Karlsruhe
598500	Karlich, Karlik, Koreliche, Korelichi, Kraliky
598570	Karlikow, Krolikow
598577	Gierlachow Blizszy
598578	Krolik Polski, Krolik Woloski
598586	Kiraly Helmec
598600	Criuleni, Karlin, Karlino, Karolin, Korlin, Kriulyany, Kruhlany
598630	Kurlandia
598635	Kairlindach
598640	Kiraly Mezo, Kurlandia
598643	Karalnnstadt
598650	Karolinka, Kierling, Krailling
598654	Herlinghausen
598656	Herrlingen
598657	Gerlenhofen

474

598670	Gerlenhofen
598674	Karolinow Stary
598676	Karlin Pinsk
598695	Karl Marx Stadt, Karla Marksa, Karlmarxstadt
598700	Garliava, Gerleve, Gorliava, Gralewo, Karlow, Karluv, Korolevo, Kralupy, Krilev, Krilov, Krylovo, Krylow
598740	Carlovca, Chrolowice, Karlovac, Karlowice, Kraljevica, Krolevets, Krolewice, Krolewiec
598744	Krolewszczyzna
598745	Kralovske Porici, Kralovsky Chlmec, Kralovsky Chlumec, Krolewska Huta, Krolewskie Bagno, Krulevshchina, Krulovsky
598750	Gorlovka, Karlovka, Karolowka, Karolyuvka, Kirilovka, Korilifka, Korolovka, Korolowka, Korolyuvka, Kurylowka
598756	Kraljevcani
598763	Kralovo nad Tisou, Kralupy nad Vltavou
598765	Gerolfingen
598770	Carlibaba, Kirlibaba
598776	Carlibaba Noua
598778	Charlupia Wielka
598779	Karlovy Vary
598780	Kiralyfala
598794	Krolowa Ruska
598795	Karlburg
598859	Garlele Garariei
598864	Kiralyhelmec
598930	Kiralyret
599000	Kryry
599373	Carierde Piatra
599400	Gura Rosie
599600	Chorherrn
599744	Gora Ropczycka
600000	Neaua
610000	Maia
611640	Noyaya Mysh
611786	Naujoji Vilnia
613000	Maiad
614400	Majoshaza, Nei Ushitz
614435	Naujasis Daugeliskis, Naujasis Daugiliskis
614590	Nei Zhagar
614634	Naya Sandets
614640	Nay Sants
614700	Mijaczow
614740	Majaczewice
616000	Mayen
616338	Neuendettelsau
616397	Neuendorf Uber Furstenwald
616400	Mayence, Meienci, Neuenhaus, Nijemci
616434	Naujamiestis
616540	Neuenhaus
616560	Neuengamme
616595	Neuenkirchen
616796	Neuenbrunslar
616930	Neuenried
616953	Neuenmarkt
617500	Majowka
617600	Nejepin
617850	Nei Vileika
619000	Maieru
619364	Naya Radomsk
619430	Maioresti
619600	Meiranu

619610	Meirani
630000	Mad, Mada, Madei, Matei, Meudt, Miody, Mitau, Mitoi, Myta, Nidda, Nietiahy
631700	Matiejow
631740	Mutejovice
633000	Mateuti, Mititei, Neded
633450	Mediedischki
633790	Nadudvar
633850	Matetelke
634000	Madocsa, Majtis, Matcze, Mateutsy, Matuizai, Matujzy, Matyus, Medias, Mediasch, Medisa, Mitoc, Mittsau, Mnetes, Motis, Motycz, Nadas, Nadasu, Nadis, Nedecz, Nededza, Nudysze, Nudyzhe
634300	Nadasd, Nadushita, Nadusita
634370	Mietustwo
634375	Nadezhdovka
634400	Medgyes
634440	Medgyeshaza
634444	Nadasu Sasesc
634454	Medgyesegyhaza
634600	Mauthausen, Nadazhin, Neutitschein, Neutitschin
634610	Nadezhnaya
634700	Nedezow
634735	Motycze Poduchowne
634745	Nudyzhi Peski
634750	Matysowka
634850	Mateszalka
634893	Mediasul Aurit, Mediesul Aurit
634930	Mediesu Aurit
635000	Matuk, Matukai, Meducha, Medukha, Medyka, Mitcau, Nejdek, Neuteich, Nidek, Notig
635600	Nideggen
635639	Madchendorf
635700	Matkiv, Matkow, Metkow, Nadejkov, Nietkow
635750	Mitkovka
635786	Mitocu Balan
635794	Neuteich Freistaat
635800	Matkule
635840	Matkules
636000	Madohn, Madon, Madona, Maidan, Majdan, Maydan, Medin, Medina, Medna, Medni, Medynia, Medynya, Miedna, Modena, Modohn, Nadma, Neteni, Neudamm, Neudenau
636339	Majdan Tatarski, Maydan Tatarski
636400	Medenica, Medenice, Medenitsa, Mednitz, Nedomice
636436	Neidenstein, Niedenstein
636439	Majdan Ostrowski, Majdan Starowiejski, Majdan Stary, Maydan Stary
636459	Majdan Skierbieszowski, Majdan Skordiow, Majdan Skordjow
636467	Majdan Sieniawski
636474	Majdan Sopocki
636480	Neutomischel
636493	Majdan Sredni, Maydan Sredni
636500	Majdanek, Miedniki, Miedzianka, Nedinge, Neuotting
636545	Majdan Kozic Dolnych
636547	Majdan Krzywski
636557	Majdan Kukawiecki, Majdan

	Kukawski
636560	Medingenai
636580	Nadimihali
636585	Medynia Glogowska
636594	Majdan Krasieninski
636596	Majdan Gorny, Maydan Gurny
636597	Majdan Krzywski
636598	Majdan Krolewski
636600	Mettmann, Mutenin
636650	Medininkai
636680	Majdan Maly
636740	Nedanovce
636783	Mittenwald
636794	Majdan Wierzchowinski, Majdan Wierzchowski
636795	Neidenburg
636846	Majdan Lesniowski
636865	Medynia Lancucka
636877	Majdan Lipiwiecki
636938	Majdan Radlinski
637000	Mateev, Mitava, Mitawa
637174	Matwijowce, Nedoboyevtsy
637300	Medvedzie, Mittweida, Nedabauti
637340	Medveditch
637345	Medwiedischki
637350	Medvedichi, Medvedka
637374	Medvedovce
637375	Medvedevka, Medvedovka, Medwjedowka
637400	Matwica, Matyjowce, Medvedzie, Mitwitz, Motwica, Mutvitsa, Mutwica
637415	Medvezhaya Gora
637440	Nadbrzezie
637500	Medebach
637600	Netphen
637674	Medvinovtsy, Miedwinowicze
637800	Nadujfalu, Niedabyl
637830	Madfeld
637870	Natafalva
637940	Nadbrzezie, Netvorice
637959	Mitburger
637960	Nadvorna, Nadworna, Nodvorna
637961	Nadvornaya
637974	Motvarjavci, Motvarjevci
638000	Meteliai, Miadziol, Model, Motel, Motele, Motila, Motol, Motyle, Motyli, Myadel, Myadl, Myodla, Nadalj, Neutal, Niedziela
638400	Matolcs, Nadlac
638439	Miadziol Stary, Mittelstreu
638440	Medlesice
638460	Mittelsinn
638474	Modliszewice
638500	Mehtelek
638600	Madalin, Madliena, Mitulin, Modlany, Modlin, Nadolany, Nottuln
638640	Modlnica
638645	Modlniczka
638650	Meidling, Modling, Mydlniki
638656	Neidlingen
638667	Modlin Nowy
638670	Miadziol Nowy
638700	Mydlow
638740	Mitel Apsa, Mitel Wisho, Mydlowiec
638744	Modliboshitz, Modlibozhits
638754	Mittelbexbach
638779	Mittel Biberach

638794	Modliborzitse, Modliborzyce	
638900	Nuttlar	
638967	Mittelehrenbach	
639000	Modor, Modra, Netra, Neutra, Niedary, Nitaure, Nitra, Nyitra	
639170	Modrzejow	
639350	Mitterteich	
639367	Niederrodenbach	
639375	Niedertaufkirchen	
639394	Matraderecske	
639396	Niederrodern	
639400	Madaras, Miedzierza, Modrice, Modrycz, Modrzyc, Mytarz	
639433	Mutterstadt, Niederstetten	
639436	Niederstein	
639439	Mattersdorf	
639440	Nedrazice	
639443	Madaras Satu Mare	
639446	Niederzissen	
639454	Madarsky Seldin	
639460	Muddersheim, Nadarzyn, Neitersen, Neuterhausen	
639475	Niedarczow Gorny, Nieder Eschbach	
639479	Mattersburg	
639480	Nieder Saulheim	
639483	Nieder Selters	
639484	Matraszollos, Mitterscholtz, Niedersulz	
639485	Nieder Saulheim	
639486	Niederschleinz	
639500	Modrych, Modrychi	
639540	Niederhochstadt	
639546	Neuterhausen	
639554	Niederhochstadt	
639556	Niederhagenthal	
639560	Niederhagenthal	
639561	Nadrechnoye	
639566	Modry Kamen	
639570	Medrzechow	
639574	Nedrahovice	
639586	Niederholm, Niederklein	
639594	Niederkreuzstetten	
639595	Niederkirchen, Niederkruchten	
639600	Metriena, Modryn, Nautreni, Nautrenu	
639633	Niederntudorf	
639638	Niedermittlau	
639639	Mitterndorf an der Fischa	
639640	Nieder Moos	
639648	Niedermoschel	
639649	Niedermeiser	
639654	Nieder Mockstadt	
639660	Nieder Ohmen	
639663	Niedermendig	
639664	Matramindszent	
639668	Niedermemmel	
639675	Matranovak, Nyitra Novak	
639679	Niedernberg	
639680	Niederemmel	
639694	Niedermarsberg	
639700	Nadrybie, Naydorf, Netreba, Neu Dorf, Neudorf	
639737	Nadrybie Dwor, Niederweidbach	
639740	Mitrovica, Niedrzwice	
639743	Niederabsdorf	
639746	Nieder Wiesen	
639748	Nieder Weisel	
639750	Moderowka	
639753	Niedrzwica Duza	
639755	Niedrzwica Koscielna	
639757	Niedrzwica Wielka	
639760	Nyitrabanya	
639771	Neudorf bei Parndorf	
639779	Niederbieber	
639780	Matraballa, Neudorfl, Niederbuhl	
639783	Mitropolit	
639784	Niederwollstadt	
639789	Niederflorstadt	
639795	Neu Oderberg	
639796	Niederbronn, Niederwerrn	
639797	Matraverebely	
639800	Niederaula	
639840	Niederleis	
639843	Niederlustadt	
639846	Niederelsungen	
639860	Nieder Olm, Niederholm	
639864	Niederlahnstein	
639964	Nieder Ramstadt	
640000	Macs, Majs, Maschau, Maza, Medze, Miase, Mica, Miejsce, Misca, Moca, Mociu, Mocs, Mocsa, Moisei, Moiseu, Mush, Nacza, Nassau, Neisse, Neuss, Nezsa, Nica, Nis, Nysa	
641000	Moiseiu	
641700	Maciejow, Maciejowa, Matseyev, Matsyeyuv, Modrzejow, Muzijovo	
641740	Maciejowice	
641743	Maciejow Stary	
643000	Maishad, Mast, Maytshet, Meisad, Meschede, Meytshet, Misiad, Mitshat, Most, Mosty, Motsit, Nagyida, Nasaud, Negyed	
643300	Musteata, Nagyatad, Nayshtut, Neishtat, Neustadt	
643337	Nishtat Tavrig	
643340	Nestedice	
643345	Mesto Touskov, Nayshtot Shaki, Neishtat Sugind, Neustadt Sugind, Neyshtadt Shaki	
643349	Neishtat Shervint	
643353	Neishtat Kudirko, Neustadtgodens	
643360	Nagyteteny, Nastatten, Neustettin	
643363	Neustadt an der Aisch, Neustadt an der Dibau, Neustadt an der Haardt, Neustadt an der Saale, Neustadt an der Waldnaab, Neustadt an der Weinstrasse, Neustadt in der Pfalz	
643365	Neustadt am Kulm, Neustadt in Hessen	
643367	Neustadt in Oberschlesien	
643368	Neustadt in Oldenwald	
643369	Neustadt am Rubenberge	
643371	Neustadt bei Coburg, Neustadt bei Pinne	
643373	Neishtat Oif der Piltza	
643376	Nayshtot Ponivez	
643379	Neustadt A Warthe	
643380	Neishtetel, Neustadtel	
643384	Neustadtles	
643400	Mesetice, Mestec, Mosedis, Mozdzierz, Mustyatsa, Nagyhodos, Nizatycze	
643439	Mesto Stare, Mesto Zdar	
643443	Mestys Stankov	
643446	Nastaszczyn	
643450	Mediedischki, Mostishche, Mostiska	
643456	Nastashchin	
643460	Mesteceni, Nastashino	
643470	Mstishaw, Mstisov, Mstyczow	
643487	Mstislavl	
643500	Miastko, Mostek, Mostki	
643530	Mezotohat	
643538	Most Gadol	
643559	Mestec Kralove	
643560	Mesztegnyo	
643570	Mystkow	
643574	Miastkow Stary, Mystkowska Wola	
643575	Mestkovka, Miastkovka, Myastkovka, Mystkowiec Stary	
643600	Nagydem, Niesten	
643640	Nestanitse, Nestemice, Niestanice	
643645	Nestanishki, Niestaniszki	
643680	Mosty Male	
643700	Mastov, Mistow, Mostovoi, Mostow, Mstow, Mustvee	
643710	Mostovoye	
643736	Neustift an der Rosalia	
643740	Nagydobos	
643760	Nadstawem	
643770	Mstibovo, Neustupov	
643784	Nagytapolcsany	
643785	Mosti Vielkie, Mosty Wielkie	
643786	Mostowlany	
643800	Moczydly, Neusiedl	
643840	Mocidlec, Neu Sedlitz, Neuzedlisch	
643843	Mszadla Stara	
643853	Mezo Telegd, Mezotelegd	
643867	Moczydla Nowe, Mszadla Nowa	
643875	Mistelbach, Mistelbach an der Zaya	
643877	Mesto Libava	
643878	Mistelfeld	
643900	Mezotur, Misdroy, Mostar, Niezdara, Nozdrzec, Nustar	
643940	Mesterhaza	
643947	Nestrasovice	
643950	Nagydorog	
643954	Mesterhaza	
643956	Mezotarkany	
643960	Nagyadorjan, Nagytarna, Nagyteremi	
643965	Maustrenk	
643970	Nesterov, Nesterow	
643973	Most Rabati	
643974	Nesterovtsy, Nesterowce	
643976	Nussdorf an der Traisen	
643979	Nestervarca, Nestervarka	
643984	Neustrelitz	
644000	Medias, Mediasch, Megyaszo, Megyes, Meszes, Mezica, Mezozah, Mizocz, Mizotch, Modrzyc, Modzhits, Modzhitz, Modzits, Moscice, Mozyrz, Nasice, Negyes, Neusatz, Nidzica, Nieciecz, Nieciecza, Niedzica, Noszyce, Nozdrzec	
644100	Nagysajo	
644300	Mezocsat, Nagyacsad, Nagyecsed	
644313	Micestii de Campie, Micestii de Cimpie	
644391	Miedzyzdroje	
644395	Nagyesztergar	
644400	Mezosas, Miedzyrzec, Miedzyrzecz, Nagycsecs,	

	Niszczyce
644450	Moshtchisk, Moshtsiska
644459	Miedzyrzecze Gorne
644470	Mieczyszczow
644478	Miedzyrzecz Volhyn, Miedzyrzecz Wielkopolski
644500	Mezoseg, Miescisko, Mosciska, Moshatzik
644540	Nagyszakacsi
644559	Miedzyrzec Korzecki
644560	Mezocsokonya
644563	Nagyczigand
644573	Miedzyrzec Podlaski
644578	Miedzyrzec Wolyn, Miedzyrzec Wolynski
644580	Mezoszakal, Nagyszokoly
644594	Nagyszekeres
644600	Mezocsan, Mezogyan, Miedzeszyn, Nasiczne
644630	Nagycsomote
644634	Mezoszentgyorgy
644636	Mezoszentmarton, Nagyszentmiklos
644640	Moszczanica, Moszczaniec, Moszczenica, Nagyszenas
644648	Mazzesinsel
644650	Miedzeszynek, Nagycenk
644653	Nagysomkut
644656	Moszczenica Nizna
644660	Nagysimonyi
644670	Mszczonow
644673	Nagyszombat
644676	Moszczona Panska
644679	Mezozombor
644690	Mezoszemere
644700	Meciszow, Mojzeszow, Nagysap
644730	Mezoszabad
644740	Miedzyswiec, Nosaczewicze
644760	Nagyszeben
644780	Nagycsepely
644787	Megyesfalva
644790	Mezoszopor
644800	Mezosaly
644840	Mezoszilas, Nagyszollos
644863	Nagyszalonta
644870	Mscislaw
644874	Niecieslawice
644893	Mediasul Aurit, Mediesul Aurit
644930	Mediesu Aurit
644960	Nagy Surany, Nagysurany
644963	Nagyzerind
644964	Nagysarmas
645000	Maszki, Mazeikai, Mazeiki, Mazeikiai, Mazheik, Mazheiki, Mazheyk, Mazheyki, Mazik, Meskai, Mezheyki, Mezyk, Micske, Miske, Mizach, Mizoch, Mniszek, Mniszki, Mozejki, Nisk, Niska, Nisko, Noski, Nyrsko
645100	Mayskoye
645140	Nesukhoyezhe, Niesuchojeze
645300	Mascauti, Miedzychod, Nagykata
645360	Nieszkodna
645374	Mushkatovtse, Muszkatowce
645375	Muszkatowka
645400	Mashkautsy, Meshkots, Meskuiciai, Nagygec, Nezkizh, Niesuchash
645438	Nagykosztolany
645440	Mezohegyes
645447	Mecsekszabolcs
645450	Moshchisk

645460	Mezokaszony
645463	Noski Snietne
645476	Nsagyszeben
645563	Nagy Kikinda
645564	Nagykokenyes
645600	Miskiniai, Miszkinie, Nagykonyi, Niscani, Nishkany
645630	Nagykend
645634	Mecseknadasd
645636	Mnisek nad Hnilcom
645640	Maszkienice, Moscanci, Nagykanizsa, Nagykinizs, Nesuchonzhi, Niskienicze
645650	Niskenichi
645663	Mezokemenytelke, Nagyigmand, Nagykamond
645670	Mshchonov
645680	Mydzk Maly
645696	Mezokomarom
645700	Medrzechow, Meshkov, Miaskowo, Miedzechow, Mieschkow, Mieszkow, Misjakow, Mizikov, Mizyakov, Mniszkow, Moshkov, Moskva, Moszkow, Mozgawa, Mushkev, Myczkow, Myszkow, Nieszkow, Nizkov, Noskov
645740	Mezokapus, Mezokovacs, Mieskowicze, Mishkovitz, Mishkovtsy, Myczkowce, Myshkovtse, Myszkowce, Myszkowice, Nagy Kapos, Nagykapos, Nagykovacsi, Niskiewicze, Noskovtsy, Noskowcy
645743	Mezokovesd, Nagykovesd
645744	Mezokovacshaza
645745	Meshchovsk
645746	Nieszkowice Male
645750	Meskoviche, Miaskivka, Mjaskowka, Myshakuvka, Myszakowka
645767	Myszkow Nowy
645796	Nagykapornak
645800	Maishagola, Maisiagala, Maisiogala, Mecsekalja, Mejszagola, Nagykallo
645830	Mrzyglod, Mrzyglody, Nagyiklod, Nagyikold
645840	Meziklasi, Miskolc, Miskolcz
645853	Nagykolked
645875	Moskalowka, Moskaluvka, Moskalyuvka
645900	Meschigorie, Mezgorje, Mezhgorye, Nagykoru
645940	Miedzygorz, Nagy Geres, Nagykoros
645943	Mezokeresztes, Nagygeresd
645947	Moskarzew, Moskorzew, Nieskurzow Stary
645950	Messkirch, Nagykereki
645970	Nagykirva
645973	Nagykorpad
645980	Nagykaroly
646000	Macin, Mecin, Mecina, Meissen, Meseni, Mesno, Miaczyn, Mieczyn, Miedzna, Miedzno, Misheny, Mizun, Moiseni, Moschin, Mosciany, Mosina, Moson, Mostsyany, Mosuni, Mseno, Mszana, Mszanna, Mucsony, Mushina, Muszne, Muszyna, Myshin, Myszyn,

	Nadzin, Necin, Nezhin, Nezin, Nieczajna, Niezyn, Nizyn, Nuseni
646100	Nizhneye
646148	Nizhneye Selishche
646149	Nizhniye Zhory
646155	Nizhniye Kugureshty
646159	Nizhneye Krivche
646174	Nizhniy Bistri, Nizhniye Bistri, Nizhnyaya Bystraya, Nizhnyaya Viznitse
646178	Nizhnyaya Belka, Nizna Jablonka
646179	Nizhniye Veretski
646300	Mosaneti, Nagyenyed, Nagynad
646340	Neu Sandez
646386	Meshana Dolna, Mszana Dolna
646400	Maszaniec, Mezciems, Mishenits, Mishenitz, Mishinyets, Mishnits, Mizhinets, Mizyniec, Moscenica, Moshanets, Mshanets, Mszaniec, Mysenec, Myszyniec, Necemice, Neisantz, Nusmice
646430	Mezimesti, Mezimosti
646433	Nizhne Studenyy, Nizni Studeny
646436	Mezimosti nad Nezarkou
646439	Mizun Stary
646450	Mtsensk
646463	Mosonszentjanos, Mosonszentmiklos, Mosonszentpeter
646470	Neznasov, Neznazov
646474	Nizna Sebastova, Nizni Sebes
646480	Nagymuzsaly
646484	Nizni Seliste
646485	Meszna Szlachecka
646486	Mosonszolnok, Nizna Slana
646487	Nizni Slavkov, Nizny Slavkov
646490	Mezomegyer, Nagy Megyer, Nagymagyar, Nagymegyer
646497	Mosonmagyarovar
646500	Massing, Mezonyek, Miedzianka, Mocsonok, Moszenki, Musnik, Muszynka, Nedzinge
646540	Mezomehes, Nagymagocs
646546	Messinghausen
646560	Matzenheim, Meisenheim, Metzingen, Miesenheim, Muschenheim
646565	Mezonagymihaly
646567	Messenkamp
646570	Misiankov
646574	Nizankowice, Nizhankovitz, Nozankovitz
646575	Nizhankovichi
646576	Nizne Cabiny
646579	Messingwerk
646580	Nadzhmihali, Nagymihaly
646584	Majsamiklosvar
646596	Mszana Gorna
646600	Matzenheim, Meisenheim, Miesenheim, Muschenheim, Musninuai
646648	Nizna Mysla
646650	Musninkai, Nagymanyok
646670	Neznanuv, Nieznanow
646674	Nieznanowice
646697	Miedzna Murowana
646700	Mazanow, Nizhnev, Nizhnov, Nizniow

477

646740	Nacina Ves, Nacyna Ves, Nazina Ves, Nizhna Apsha, Nizni Apsa
646743	Nizhne Bystraya, Nizni Bystry
646745	Meszna Opacka
646750	Massenbach
646754	Massenbachhausen
646785	Mecina Wielka
646794	Nihzni Vierecki, Nizhni Verecki, Nizhni Veretski, Nizni Verecki, Nizni Verecky
646795	Neu Isenburg, Nizhni Vereki
646800	Neszmely
646930	Mezonyarad
646936	Nagymarton
646940	Nagymaros, Nagyniyres
646977	Nizny Hrabovec
646985	Nizni Orlik, Nizny Orlik
647000	Machev, Maczev, Mashev, Mashuv, Masiewo, Massow, Maszew, Maszewo, Maszow, Matsiov, Mdzewo, Miasowa, Mishev, Mishov, Miszewo, Mniszew, Mniszow, Moscow, Motchiov, Msciow, Mycow, Myczow, Myshev, Myszow, Nadzow, Nesfoyya, Nieszawa, Nishava, Noiszew, Nojszew, Nosov, Nosow, Noszvaj
647100	Msciwoje, Nesfoaia
647160	Nagyabajom, Nagybajom
647300	Niedzwiada
647340	Maszewo Duze
647350	Nezbodka, Niedzwiadka
647360	Mezobodon, Nagybatony
647364	Nagy Fodemes
647369	Nagybudmer
647370	Niezabitow
647393	Mezopeterd
647400	Maczevice, Masiewicze, Medzhibozh, Medzibezh, Medziboz, Medzibozh, Mezhibezh, Mezhibozh, Mezhvitsa, Miedzyboz, Misiewicze, Motchevitz, Nagybajcs, Neshviz, Nesvizh, Niedrzwice, Niedzwiedz, Niesviez, Nieswicz, Nieswiez, Nishviz, Nyeshvyezh
647434	Nezvestice
647440	Niedzwiedzica
647450	Mazowiecki, Nagy Bocska, Nagybocsko, Nezviska, Niezwiska
647459	Nagybecskerek
647460	Nagyvazsony, Nagyvisnyo
647470	Nazavizuv, Nazawizow, Nezavizov
647493	Nagybicserd
647500	Maseviche, Masevichi, Massbach, Mazoviechi, Mosbach, Mossbach, Musbach, Mussbach, Nosovka
647530	Nagyfuged
647534	Niedrzwica Duza
647554	Niedrzwica Koscielna
647565	Nagybakonak
647578	Niedrzwica Wielka
647600	Nagy Banya, Nagybanya, Nagybuny, Nagyivan, Nieswin
647640	Nagybanhegyes
647654	Nagybanhegyes
647680	Maszewo Male
647700	Mscibow, Mszibowo
647734	Nezbavetice

647760	Nagybabony
647800	Micfalau, Musfalau, Nagyfalu, Nagypali, Nagypall, Nusfalau
647830	Netzwalde
647845	Nacpolsk
647850	Nagyveleg
647859	Mezovelker
647870	Mezofalva
647900	Mezovari, Nezvir, Niezwir
647930	Nagy Varad, Nagybarod, Nagypirit, Nagyvarad
647940	Miedzyborz, Nagybarca
647945	Nagybaracska
647946	Nagyborzsony, Nagyvarsany
647947	Nagyborzsova
647950	Mezapark, Misburg, Moosburg, Mosberg, Nagy Bereg, Nagybereg, Nagyberki, Nizhborg
647954	Mezaparks, Nizborg Stary, Nizborg Szlachecki, Nizhborg Stary
647956	Nizborg Nowy, Nizhborg Novy, Nizhborg Novyy
647960	Mezobereny, Nagybereny, Nisporeni, Nisporeny
648000	Macsola, Mcely, Medzula, Messel, Miadziol, Miszla, Moczula, Muszaly, Nasal, Naszaly, Neusohl, Niedziela
648300	Nagyleta, Noua Sulita
648340	Myslatycze
648350	Myshlyatichi, Myslyatyche
648360	Mezoladany
648379	Nagyletavertes
648400	Miedzyles, Misslitz, Moczalec, Nagy Lucs, Nagyhalasz, Nagylaz, Nagyloc, Nagylucs, Neusalz
648439	Miadziol Stary
648440	Moczuliszcze
648450	Mosalsk, Naselsk, Nashelsk, Nasielsk, Nasyelsk
648457	Nasielska Wola
648460	Messelhausen, Nagyalasony, Nagylozna
648500	Masluchy, Mezolak, Moczulki, Nagylak, Nagylok, Nussloch
648546	Messelhausen
648570	Myslakow, Niesulkow
648574	Myslachowice, Myslakowice, Myslkovice
648600	Myslina, Mysliny, Nagylonya
648630	Nagyilonda
648640	Maslomiaca, Mishlenitse, Mishlenitz, Mishlinits, Myslenice
648648	Nagylengyel
648650	Metzling, Moczulniki, Moisling, Nagylang
648670	Miadziol Nowy
648700	Maslow, Muzylow, Myslow, Myslowa, Nagyilva, Niesulowo, Noszlop
648710	Mysloboje, Mysloboye
648730	Nagy Olved
648740	Maslovice, Maslowice, Meuselwitz, Mojslawice, Myslowice, Myslowitz, Naslavcea, Naslawice, Nosalewice
648750	Nashlavcha
648753	Modzele Wygoda

648767	Moslavina Podravska
648790	Mezolabore
648793	Nagylevard
648794	Medzilaborce, Mezolaborc, Mysliborz
648936	Nesselroden
649000	Magyaro, Mazury, Megyer, Miszory, Mocira, Mocsar, Moczary, Mozir, Mozyr, Mozyrz, Myszory, Nagyar
649300	Mogyorod, Nagyrada, Nagyrede, Nagyret
649330	Magyaratad
649340	Magyartes, Naceradec
649367	Magyardombegyhaz
649400	Meseritz, Mezoors, Mezritsh, Mezyryczy, Miedzierza, Miedzyrzec, Miedzyrzecz, Mogyoros, Mozdzierz, Nagyoroszi, Nagyrocze
649438	Mezeritz D'lita
649440	Myedzirzets
649446	Magyarszogyen
649447	Myedzirzets Podlask
649450	Magyarcseke, Magyarszek
649453	Mezeritch Katan, Mezeritz Gadol
649459	Mezyrycz Korecki, Miedzyrzecze Gorne
649460	Nagyharsany
649463	Magyarcsanad
649467	Magyarszombatfa
649470	Nosarzewo
649475	Nagyrozvagy
649478	Mezirici Valesske, Miedzyrzecz Volhyn, Miedzyrzecz Wielkopolski
649493	Magyarsard, Magyarszerdahely
649500	Mezerich, Mezherichi, Mezhirech, Mezhirechye, Mezhirichi, Mezhrechye, Mezrich
649540	Magyarkeszi, Nagyrakocz, Nagyrakos
649553	Mezerich Gadol
649559	Mezerich Korets, Miedzyrzec Korzecki
649560	Magyarigen
649564	Magyargencs
649568	Magyarkimle
649569	Magyarhomorog
649573	Miedzyrzec Podlaski
649578	Magyarkoblos, Miedzyrzec Wolyn, Miedzyrzec Wolynski
649594	Magyarkeresztur
649595	Magyaregregy
649600	Messern, Mosoreni, Mosorin
649645	Magyarmecske
649654	Magyarnagyszombor
649663	Magyarnandor
649664	Magyarnemegye, Mezoermenyas
649677	Maziarnia Wawrzkowa, Mazyarnya Vavrshkova
649690	Magyarhomorog
649700	Mesherov, Mezhirov, Mezirov, Mzurow, Nagyrabe
649735	Magyarpatak
649740	Metzerwisse
649750	Mazurowka, Mazuruvka
649760	Magyarbanhegyes
649764	Magyarfenes
649765	Magyarbanhegyes
649780	Magyarboly, Magyarujfalu

649783	Magyarfold	
649785	Magyarbolkeny, Magyarvalko	
649786	Magyarpolany	
649787	Magyarfalva	
649790	Magyarovar	
649793	Magyarfrata	
649864	Magyaralmas	
649874	Magyarlapos	
650000	Macau, Maga, Magy, Mako, Mochy, Much, Muchea, Muhi, Nacha, Nak, Nyek	
651000	Nehoiu	
651700	Macheyuv	
651740	Nahujowice	
651750	Makeyevka, Makiyevka, Naguyevichi	
653000	Makad, Makod, Micauti, Mocod, Nachod	
653300	Ngytad	
653400	Nikitycze	
653500	Nikityche	
653600	Nectiny, Nichiteni	
653640	Myketyntse, Mykietynce	
653645	Mechetinskaya	
653700	Mokotow	
653795	Magdeburg	
653875	Magdalowka	
654000	Magocs, Micus, Mikautsy, Mikes, Mogos, Mohacs, Mokca, Neuhaus, Nikitsch	
654300	Mihoesti	
654330	Mikstat	
654337	Ncustadt bei Pinne	
654350	Makkoshotyka	
654360	Negostina	
654397	Maxdorf, Mohast Rabati, Niksdorf	
654400	Makocice, Micasasa, Mikeszasza, Mokrzec, Mokrzesz, Mokshets, Niechcice, Niksic	
654430	Mogosesti	
654433	Mixstadt	
654439	Miekisz Stary	
654450	Mokrzyska	
654460	Maxsain	
654470	Mechishchev, Mokrzyszow	
654478	Meggyesfalva	
654500	Makoszka, Mokrsko, Nogaysk	
654570	Mechishchuv	
654578	Niechcicka Wola Nowa	
654594	Mokrsko Rzadowe	
654600	Makasan, Makaseni, Makoszyn, Meckesheim, Megesheim, Miechocin, Mokrzany, Mokzhany, Nagoszyn, Naukseni, Nekezseny, Neuhausen, Niechodzin	
654640	Maksimets	
654650	Naguzhanka	
654670	Miekisz Nowy	
654674	Maksymovitse, Maksymowice	
654675	Maksimovichi, Maksymowka, Maksymuvka	
654700	Mukacevo, Mukaczewo, Nagachev, Nahaczow, Niechaczewo	
654740	Mikaszewicze, Mikuszowice	
654746	Niksowizna	
654750	Mikashevichi	
654835	Miheseul de Campi	
654853	Magosliget, Nikisialka Duza	
654856	Nikisialka Mala	
654860	Maxglan	
654874	Negoslavci	
655400	Mikohaza	
655700	Mukachevo, Nekhachevo	
656000	Magne, Miekina, Miekinia, Mugeni, Mukane, Mukanie, Nauheim, Neheim, Nieheim	
656170	Nagnajow	
656300	Mochnata, Mochnate	
656397	Magendorf, Michendorf, Mogendorf	
656400	Magnesia, Nikinci	
656430	Mogneszty	
656439	Muggensturm	
656457	Mochnaczka Wyzna	
656460	Meckenhausen	
656470	Magnashev, Magnuszew	
656475	Neuhemsbach	
656480	Mackenzell	
656500	Maconka	
656543	Neheim Husten	
656546	Meckenhausen	
656560	Maihingen, Meckenheim, Nackenheim	
656600	Machnin, Meckenheim, Nackenheim	
656700	Machnow, Mechnov	
656740	Michniowice, Negniavitch	
656750	Machnowek, Machnowka, Makhnovka, Mochnovka, Negnevichi	
656900	Maikammer, Neuhammer	
656930	Mechenried	
656970	Niechmirow	
657000	Machowa, Machyov, Maikop, Majkow, Makov, Makova, Makovi, Makow, Maykov, Maykuv, Mchawa, Mekhev, Michov, Michow, Miechov, Miechow, Mihova, Mikhov, Mikhova, Mikif, Mikova, Mikow, Mnichow, Mochowo, Mychow, Myekhov, Nackowo, Nagov, Nagovo, Neuhof, Niagova, Nockowa, Nyagova	
657100	Migovoye	
657300	Mokobody	
657400	Mackowice, Michowice, Miechowice, Miechowiec, Miechowitz, Mocovice, Nakvasha, Nakwasza, Niechobrz, Niegowic, Nihowice	
657460	Nagawczyna	
657468	Miechowice Male	
657470	Miokovicevo, Nekvasovy	
657478	Miechowice Wielkie	
657500	Muchawka, Mukhavka, Nigovichi, Nikhovichi	
657534	Makowiec Duzy	
657594	Miechow Charsznica	
657600	Mihoveni, Mokwin, Neuhofen	
657645	Niegowoniczki	
657647	Makov Mazovyetsk, Makow Mazowiecki	
657663	Neuhofen an der Krems	
657730	Makow Podhalanski	
657735	Makow Podhalanski	
657800	Mihaifalau, Nikopol	
657840	Nikopolis	
657870	Mikofalva	
657879	Michow Lubartowski	
657900	Niechobrz	
657934	Mnichovo Hradiste	
657940	Mikepercs	
657943	Makowa Rustykalna	
657945	Nekhvoroshcha	
658000	Mahal, Michle, Micola, Micula, Mikola, Mikoly, Mikula, Mochula, Mogila, Mohol, Nakel, Nakiel, Naklo, Nikla, Nikolai	
658170	Mikolajow, Mikolayev, Nikolajev, Nikolajew, Nikolayev	
658174	Mikolajowice	
658175	Nikolayevka, Nikolayevka Novorossiyskaya	
658177	Mikolajow Wielkie	
658300	Maglod, Mihald, Nagold	
658340	Nyekladhaza	
658354	Nyekladhaza	
658364	Neuhaldensleben	
658385	Mihalytelke	
658400	Michalcze, Mihalcea, Mikleus, Miklos, Miklusy, Mikulec, Mueglitz, Muglitz	
658430	Miclesti, Mikleshty	
658433	Michelstadt	
658439	Michaelsdorf	
658440	Mikulczyce, Mikultschutz	
658450	Makolusky, Michaliszki, Mikhalishki, Mykaliskiai	
658451	Nikolskaya, Nikolskaya Sloboda, Nikolskaya Slobodka	
658454	Mikaliskis, Nikolski Slobodka	
658460	Michelhausen, Mihalaseni, Mikuliczyn	
658470	Michalczowa, Mikolasov	
658474	Mikluszowice, Mikulasovice	
658479	Nagelsberg, Nagelsberg bei Runzelsau, Nichelsburg, Nickelsburg, Nikolsburg	
658500	Michalok, Mihalka, Mihalko, Mikhalche, Mikolajki, Mochulki, Naklik	
658546	Michelhausen	
658560	Mikulichin, Nikolaiken	
658574	Michalkovice, Michalkowice	
658600	Mglin, Michalany, Michalin, Mihaileni, Mikhalin, Mikhayleny, Mikulino, Mogilna, Mogilno, Mogilyany, Mohilno, Neukalen, Neukollin	
658636	Naklo nad Notecia	
658640	Mihaileanca, Mikolintza, Mikulince, Mikulincie, Mikulintsy, Mogelnitsa, Mogelnitse, Mogelnitza, Mogielnica, Mohelnice, Nakel Netze, Nakielnica, Nicolaenca	
658650	Mikhaylyanka	
658670	Muglinov	
658678	Nieklan Wielki	
658679	Mecklenburg	
658700	Mecholupy, Meclov, Michalova, Michalowo, Michelob, Mihalyfa, Mikolow, Mikulov, Mogilev, Mohilev, Nikolaev, Nocoleav	
658735	Mikolapatak	
658740	Michalovce, Michalowice, Michalowitz, Mihalevich, Mikhalovich, Mikhalowitz, Naglowice, Nicolaevca, Nieglowice, Niklovitse, Niklowice, Noglovitz	
658750	Michailowka, Michajlowka,	

	Michalowek, Michalowka, Michaylovka, Michelbach, Mikhailovka, Mikhalevichi, Mikhalovka, Mikhaylovichi, Mikhaylovka, Mochalivka, Niklovichi
658756	Michelbach an der Lucke, Michelbach Markt
658759	Mikhailovgrad, Mikhaylovgrad
658773	Mogilev Podolski, Mogilev Podolskiy, Mohilev Podolsk
658780	Michalpol, Michelpolia, Mikhalpol
658783	Michelfeld
658900	Maklar
659000	Machory, Magare, Magarei, Maghera, Magura, Mohora, Mokra, Mokre, Nagor, Nakory, Nakri, Neckarau, Nyoger
659100	Negreia
659300	Moigrad, Naugard, Nograd
659347	Nogradadsap
659357	Nogradkovesd
659360	Mokrotyn
659364	Nogradmegyer
659369	Nogradmarcal
659373	Nogradpatak
659379	Nogradberczel, Nogradbertsel, Nogradveroce
659400	Mokrets, Mokroc, Mokrzec, Mokrzesz, Negressi, Niekurza, Nikrace
659430	Negresti, Nicoresti
659434	Negresti Satu Mare
659436	Neckar Steinach, Neckarsteinach
659439	Mokra Strona
659450	Makarska, Mokrosek, Mokrzyska
659458	Nogradszakal
659460	Nagorzany
659465	Nagorzanka
659468	Nagortse Male, Nahorce Male
659469	Neckarzimmern
659470	Mokrzyszow, Niekrasow, Nogradsap
659475	Necrasovca Noua
659486	Neckarsulm
659498	Neagra Sarului
659500	Makarki, Mokrsko, Nagorki
659560	Neukirchen
659566	Neckargemund
659594	Mokrsko Rzadowe
659596	Mokra Germ
659600	Mokrany, Mokrin, Mokryany, Mokrzany, Nagorna, Negreni, Nicoreni, Nikoreny, Nochern
659610	Nagornoye
659617	Negurenii Vechi Orhei
659640	Makrancz, Mokrance
659650	Mechernich
659667	Mokrany Nove
659675	Mokre Niwki, Negureni Vek
659700	Magerov, Magierow, Magriv, Makarov, Mokrovo, Mokrowo, Nahoruby, Negrovo
659740	Mokra Wies, Negreviz, Negrivits, Negriviz, Negrovec, Negrovets
659747	Neckarbischofsheim
659750	Makarowka
659787	Negerfalva
659840	Negrileasa
659843	Negril Esti, Negrilesti
659870	Magura Ilvei, Mokrelipie
659940	Mokra Russ
660000	Manau, Mema, Mena, Mien,

	Mienia, Minaj, Minau, Mineu, Mnin, Mohnya, Monaj, Myena, Nana, Nauen, Nima, Nomme, Nujno, Nuyno, Nyim, Nyomja
661600	Nemajunai, Nimayin
663000	Mand, Maneuti, Mantua, Mende, Mintia, Mintiu, Monyhad, Nemeti, Nemti
663400	Mandac, Moniatycze
663500	Mandok, Myndyk
663530	Mendicauti
663540	Mendikauts
663600	Manetin, Menden, Minden, Munden, Muntenia, Nemteni
663659	Nemetmokra
663700	Mantov, Mantova, Nienadowa
663750	Nienadowka
663780	Nemetboly, Nemetfalu
663790	Montabaur, Montebaur, Nemetujvar
663796	Nemetbarnag
663800	Neumetely
663830	Nemetlad
663856	Mindelheim
663860	Mindelheim
663878	Neumittelwalde
663940	Nandras, Nandraz
663943	Mandresti, Myndreshty
663944	Nentershausen
663970	Mondorf
663975	Nandorfehervar
664000	Mainz, Majnicz, Manasi, Meinz, Menes, Monaco, Monashi, Muntz, Munus, Nanas, Nancy, Neamtz, Nemes, Nemiz, Niemce, Niemcza, Niemnietz, Nimizshe
664300	Menschede, Moinesti, Monast, Namest, Nanest, Nanesti
664317	Mamaestii Vechi
664330	Nemesded
664336	Neunstetten
664340	Naumestis
664344	Manastezhets
664345	Monastyrshchina, Naumiestis Kudirkos
664356	Mainstockheim
664363	Namest nad Oslavou
664368	Nemesdomolk
664370	Namestovo, Niemstow
664390	Minster, Monastir, Monostor, Muenster, Munster, Munsterhausen
664393	Nemestordemic
664394	Manasterczany, Manasterz, Manasterzec, Manasterzh, Monasterishtche, Monasteriska, Monasteryska, Monasterzec, Monasterzyska, Monastiristch, Monastirshtchina, Monastrishch, Monastrishtch, Monastyrets, Monastyrisce, Monastyrishche, Monastyriska, Monostorszeg
664395	Manasterek, Monasterek, Monastyrshchina, Munsterhausen
664396	Munstermaifeld
664397	Monostorapati, Monostorpalyi, Munsterberg, Munstereifel
664398	Manasturel
664400	Nemesocsa, Nemosice

664436	Nemetzsidany
664460	Munzesheim
664500	Minsk, Nemeske
664516	Nemetskaya Mokra
664540	Nemeskocs
664553	Minsk Khadash
664564	Minsk Mazovyets, Minsk Mazovyetsk, Minsk Mazowiecki
664583	Nemeskolta
664584	Nemesgulacs
664590	Nemesker
664594	Nemesgorzsony
664600	Meinsen, Nemeshany, Nemtseny
664630	Mindszent
664633	Nemesnadudvar
664636	Nemesszentandras
664639	Nemessandorhaza
664654	Mensengesass
664656	Menzingen, Munsingen, Nenzenheim, Neunzenheim
664660	Nenzenheim, Neunzenheim
664679	Munzenberg
664700	Nemsova
664730	Nemesapati, Nemesvid
664739	Nemespatro
664746	Mainz Weisenau
664748	Nemespecsely
664750	Mansbach, Nemesbikk, Nemesbuk
664764	Nemesvamos
664780	Monosbel
664794	Nemesborzova
664795	Mansburg
664800	Monzel, Namslau
664836	Nemesladony
664850	Menslage, Nemesszalok
664856	Nanczulka Mala
664867	Nemesleanyfalu
664870	Namyslow
664890	Mainzlar
664900	Manzar, Minzhir
664940	Menzyryczy
664944	Myendzirzets, Myendzirzets Podlas
664950	Menzhirichi
664960	Monzernheim
664965	Monzernheim
665000	Maineck, Mank, Maynich, Minoga, Moniaki, Monok, Munich, Niemojki, Noniucha
665178	Nemecke Jablonne
665314	Nimigea de Jos
665344	Nimigea de Sus
665400	Munkacs, Munkacz, Munkatsch
665430	Nemaksht, Nemoksht, Nemokshty, Nemuksht
665435	Monchsdeggingen
665440	Nemaksciai
665450	Nemakscai
665493	Monchsroth
665600	Mannheim, Mengen, Monheim, Munchen, Neumagen
665658	Monchen Gladbach, Monchengladbach, Munchen Gladbach
665659	Nemecka Mokra
665700	Nankif, Nankovo
665730	Monkavid, Monkobody
665740	Manicovca, Mankowicze, Minkovitz, Minkovtsy, Minkowce
665750	Mankoviche, Mankovka

665789	Munchweiler, Munchweiler an der Alsenz	
665793	Nemecky Brod	
665795	Monchberg, Munchberg, Muncheberg	
665797	Nemecka Poruba	
665800	Mangali, Mangalu, Mengele	
665846	Mingolsheim	
665850	Nanchulka	
665870	Moncalvo	
665900	Mingir	
665936	Munchreith an der Thaya	
665954	Nemecky Rohozec	
665956	Neunkirchen	
665965	Mengeringhausen	
666000	Mahnaym, Mamino, Mannheim, Mieniany, Mimon, Monheim, Munina, Niemen	
666340	Nemunaitis	
666400	Nemenitz, Nemunayts, Niemenietz, Niemienice	
666439	Neumuenster, Neumunster	
666460	Nemencine, Nementchin, Nemenzin, Niemenczyn	
666560	Meiningen, Memmingen, Mommenheim	
666600	Mommenheim, Nemonien, Niemonany, Niemoniany	
666719	Nonnenweier	
666740	Niemianowice	
666849	Nemunelis Radviliskis	
666893	Nemunelis Radviliskis	
667000	Maniowy, Nanova, Nanowa, Nemnovo, Niemnowo	
667400	Maniewicze, Manivits, Manyevich, Mianowice, Monavitz, Monevitch, Monowice, Niehniewicze, Niemowicze, Nienowice, Nimptsch	
667500	Manevichi, Manyevichi, Mianowek, Nemovichi	
667870	Nanfalva	
667946	Meimbressen	
667950	Momberg, Naumburg, Nienborg, Nienburg, Nymburk	
667953	Numbrecht	
667957	Neunburg Vorm Wald	
667960	Mainbernheim	
667965	Mainbernheim	
668000	Memel	
668439	Mannelsdorf, Memmelsdorf	
668500	Mamaliga, Mamalyga	
668655	Mumling Grumbach	
668656	Momlingen	
668700	Nemiluv, Niemilow	
669000	Monariu, Monor, Mumor, Nemir, Niemir, Nyomar	
669300	Mainroth	
669400	Men Yryczy, Nemerci, Neumerice, Nimerice	
669433	Munnerstadt	
669439	Mannersdorf am Leithagebirge, Mannersdorf an der March	
669456	Meinerzhagen	
669460	Neumorschen	
669470	Niemiryczow	
669500	Naymark, Nemerchi, Nemerichi, Neumark, Niemirki, Noymark	
669530	Naymarkt, Neumarkt, Noymarkt	
669534	Neumarkt Sankt Veit	
669536	Neumarkt an der Raab, Neumarkt an der Ybbs, Neumarkt im Schlesien, Neumarkt in der Oberpfalz	
669566	Neumark am Mures	
669600	Nimoreni, Nimoreny	
669700	Nemirov, Nemirova, Niemirow, Nyemiruv	
669740	Mojmirovce	
670000	Miava, Mniow, Myjava, Nivy, Niwy, Nova, Novaj, Novo, Nowe	
671178	Novaya Yablona	
671340	Novaya Odessa	
671380	Napajedla	
671396	Novajidrany	
671397	Novaya Derevnya	
671439	Novaya Strelishcha	
671440	Novaja Usica, Novaya Ushitsa	
671460	Novy Jicin	
671493	Novaya Sarata	
671498	Novaya Iserliya	
671574	Novaya Kobuska	
671585	Novaya Chelakovka	
671597	Novaia Greblia	
671640	Novaya Mysh	
671659	Novaya Nekrasovka	
671700	Nawojowa	
671746	Novaya Basan	
671747	Novaya Vyzhva	
671759	Nowojowa Gora	
671767	Novaya Ivanovka	
671795	Novaya Praga	
671854	Novaya Aleksandriya	
671860	Novoyelnya, Nowojelnia	
671947	Novi Yarichev, Novyy Yarychev	
671960	Neubeuern	
673000	Nefta, Neuwied, Niuved	
673400	Novi Odessa	
673600	Napadeni, Napadeny, Niewodna	
673640	Novitanitz, Nowotaniec	
673648	Nowy Tomysl	
673664	Moftinu Mic	
673686	Moftinul Mic	
673700	Napadova, Napadovo	
673757	Nowd Bychow	
673790	Novi Dvor, Novi Dvur, Novy Dvor, Novyy Dvor, Nowy Dwor	
673796	Nowy Dwor Maziowecki, Nowy Dwor Mazowiecki	
673800	Neuwedell	
673860	Nevetlen	
673878	Nevetlefalu	
673935	New Tredegar	
673946	Novyye Dorosini	
673950	Novi Targ, Novy Targ, Nowy Targ, Nowyja Dorogi	
673954	Novyye Dragusheny	
673974	Niewiatrowice	
674000	Nepos, Nivitse, Niwice, Novitsa, Nowica	
674300	Nehvizdy, Nove Sady, Novi Sad, Novi Sadi, Novo Sadi, Novosad, Novosady, Nowa Schita	
674350	Niewistka	
674370	Nowy Staw	
674380	Nove Sedlo, Nowosiadlo	
674384	Nove Sedlice, Nove Sedliste, Novosedlice	
674394	Nove Straseci	
674395	Nove Strakonice	
674398	Novye Strelishche, Novyye Strelishcha	
674400	Nawodzice, Nova Oshitza, Novo Cice, Novoshitse, Novy Sacz, Nowoszyce, Nowy Sacz	
674460	Niebieszczany, Nieprzesnia	
674500	Niebocko, Nivetsk, Niwiska, Novi Sach, Novska, Novyye Sochi	
674570	Neu Bidschow, Nowy Dzikow	
674580	Novy Oskol	
674584	Nawsie Kolaczyckie	
674585	Nowosiclka Jazlowiecka	
674586	Novosokolniki	
674590	Nova Zagora, Novo Zhagory	
674594	Nowy Zagorz	
674600	Nevesinje, Niewiescin	
674640	Novi Sansh	
674649	Novi Senzhari, Novyye Sanzhary	
674650	Nove Zamky	
674659	Nowy Zmigrod	
674670	Nowo Sinjawa	
674700	Neubitschow	
674730	Nowy Swiat	
674744	Nawsie Brzosteckie	
674746	Nowe Swieciany	
674757	Novozibkov, Novozybkov, Novozybkow, Nowosybkow	
674794	Nawsie Brzosteckie, Novyy Sverzhen, Nowy Swershen, Nowy Swierzen	
674800	Nowa Sol, Nowe Siolo	
674837	Novo Zlatopol, Novo Zlatopolskaya, Novyy Zlatopol	
674840	Navaselicza, Novo Selitsa, Novoselica, Novoselice, Novoselitsa, Novoseliza, Novoseltsy, Nowosielce, Nowosielec, Nowosielica	
674843	Novyye Selishty	
674845	Nowosielce Gniewosz, Nowosielce Kozickie	
674850	Novoselki, Novosyulka, Novosyulki, Nowosiolka, Nowosiolki	
674851	Novosyulka Yazlovets, Novosyulki Yazlovets, Novsyulka Yazlovetska, Nowosiolka Jazlowiecka	
674853	Nowosiolki Dydynskie	
674855	Novoselka Kostyukova, Novoselki Gostsinne, Nowociolka Kosciukowa, Nowosiolki Goscinne, Nowosiolki Kadynalskie	
674856	Nowosiolki Nowoczeskie	
674857	Nowosiolki Przednie	
674858	Nowosiolki Liskie	
674859	Novosyulki Ruske	
674870	Nowa Slupia	
674874	Novoselovskoye	
674875	Novoselovka	
674957	Nova Cerekev	
675000	Nivki, Niweck, Niwka, Niwki, Novak, Novaky, Nupaky	
675400	Neviges	
675500	Novyye Gechi	
675640	Nova Kanjiza	
675643	Novo Konstantinov, Novokonstantinov, Novyy Konstantinov, Nowo Konstantinow	
675647	Novi Knezevac, Novi Knezvac	
675700	Napekow, Neubukow	
675740	Neu Bukowitz	

481

675780	Nova Kapela	
675790	Nefcover	
675840	Nieweglosz	
675870	Neveklov, Nevekolov	
675900	Napkor, Nowa Gora	
675930	Novgorod, Novogorod, Novogrod, Nowgorod, Nowogard, Nowogrod	
675934	Nova Gradiska, Novaharod Siversk, Novgorod Seversk, Novgorod Severski, Novgorod Severskiy	
675935	Novogrudek, Novogrudok, Novohorodek, Novohorodok, Nowogrodek, Nowogrudok	
675937	Novograd Volynsk, Novograd Volynskij, Novograd Volynskiy	
675940	Nova Gorica	
675944	Nowy Korzec	
675946	Novi Kortchin, Nowy Korczyn	
675951	Novo Georgijevsk, Novogeorgiyevsk	
675956	Novi Korchin	
675957	Novogeorgievsk	
675960	Nova Crnja	
675965	Nova Ukrainka, Nova Ukreinka, Novo Ukrainka, Novoukrainka	
675975	Novyye Choropkany	
675978	Nowa Grobla	
676000	Meppen, Nowiny	
676360	Nowomodna	
676386	Nowy Modlin	
676400	Nova Muzh, Nowa Mysz	
676430	Nove Mesto, Nove Miasto, Nove Miesto, Novi Miasto, Novo Mesto, Novoe Mesto, Nowe Miasto	
676436	Nove Mesto na Morave, Nove Mesto nad Metuji, Nove Mesto nad Vahom, Nowe Miasto nad Pilica, Nowe Miasto nad Warta	
676438	Nowe Miasto Lubawskie	
676457	Novomoskovsk, Nowomoskowsk	
676480	Nepomysl	
676500	Nepomuk, Novinki	
676593	Novomigrod	
676596	Nowiny Horynieckie	
676645	Novo Minsk, Novominsk	
676759	Nowiny Pokarczmiska	
676793	Nowiny Brdowskie	
676847	Novo Milosevo, Nowa Maliszewa	
676860	Novo Malin, Nowe Mlyny, Nowomalin	
676946	Nowe Marcinkowo	
676957	Novo Markovka	
676959	Novo Mirgorod, Novomirgorod, Novomirogorod, Nowomirgorod	
676970	Novi Marof	
677357	Novyy Vitkov	
677360	Nowy Bytom	
677374	Novi Vitebsk, Novo Vitebsk, Novyy Vitebsk	
677400	Nova Ves, Novi Becej, Nowa Wies, Nowawes	
677436	Novi Bezdan	
677437	Novo Fastov	
677439	Nova Bystrice	
677443	Nowa Wies Czudecka	
677445	Novobrzesk, Nowe Brzesko	
677446	Nowa Brzeznica	
677457	Novo Pashkovo	
677460	Nova Bason, Novo Basan	
677464	Nowy Wisnicz	
677470	Nova Pazova, Novy Bydzov	
677490	Novi Pazar	
677500	Novi Bug, Novy Bug, Novyy Bug, Nowyi Bug	
677517	Novyy Pochayev	
677543	Novi Pohost, Novyy Pogost, Nowy Pohost	
677566	Novy Bohumin	
677570	Novi Pikov, Novyy Pikov, Novyy Pykiv	
677574	Nova Bukovica	
677600	Nova Bana	
677635	Nove Benatky	
677743	Novyye Popeshty	
677800	Nowa Biala, Nowe Pole, Nowopole	
677836	Novyye Veledniki	
677837	Novo Poltavka, Novopoltavka	
677845	Novo Vileisk, Nowe Polaszki	
677850	Nova Vilejka, Nowa Wilejka	
677935	Nowy Bartkow	
677945	Novobrzesk, Nowe Brzesko	
677946	Nowa Brzeznica	
677950	Nova Praga, Novi Praga	
677964	Novo Vorontsovka	
677974	Novi Vrbas	
677976	Nowe Warpno	
677985	Novo Priluki	
678000	Nabla, Nebel, Nevel	
678300	Mayfeld, Neufeld	
678360	Nohfelden	
678363	Neufeld an der Leitha	
678400	Nebiliec, Nebilitz, Niebylec	
678530	Nepolcauti	
678540	Nepolkouts, Nepolokouts	
678546	Novo Aleksandrovsk, Novoaleksandrovsk, Novy Oleksiniec, Novyy Aleksinets, Novyy Oleksinets, Nowy Aleksiniec	
678574	Nepolokovtsy	
678640	Nepolomits, Nieplomitza, Niepolomice, Nyepolomitse	
678700	Nebilovy, Nebylov, Nebyluv, Niebylow	
678757	Nowy Lupkow	
678760	Novo Labun	
679000	Navaria, Navarja, Navria, Nawaria, Nawarja, Nawarya, Nevir, Nivra, Niwra	
679100	Navariya	
679300	Nabrad, Naprad, Napradea, Nieporet, Nove Hrady	
679344	Noworodczyce	
679350	Navahredek, Navaredok, Novaredok, Novradok	
679354	Novorodchitsy	
679359	Novradeker	
679364	Novo Radomsk, Nowo Radomsko	
679370	Neporotova, Neporotovo	
679400	Mavruciai, Mevrotsh, Nabroz, Neporadza, Nieporaz, Niewierz, Nova Raca	
679433	Neu Freistett	
679439	Nebersdorf	
679440	Nawarzyce	
679443	Novyye Ruseshty	
679445	Novorossiysk	
679460	Nieprzesnia, Novyy Rozhan	
679461	Naberezhnoye	
679465	Novy Hrozenkov	
679470	Movorzhev	
679500	Nabburg, Neubruck	
679563	Neuburg an der Donau, Neuburg an der Kammel	
679570	Nevrokop, Niewirkow	
679600	Neubrunn, Nevaran, Nevarenai, Nievern	
679630	Navarnet	
679636	Neubrandenburg	
679640	Navyrnets	
679700	Naprawa, Neuwarp, Niebrow	
679760	Nifribony	
680000	Mala, Male, Malyi, Melle, Milej, Milie, Mol, Naila	
681000	Miliye	
681430	Malayeshty	
681566	Malaya Kamenka	
681584	Malaya Glusha	
681700	Malejowa, Milejow	
681749	Malaya Vishera	
681787	Malaya Plavucha	
681850	Malaya Luka	
681876	Malaya Lopenitsa	
681948	Maloyaroslavets, Maloyaroslavets Pervyy, Maloyaroslavets Vtordy	
683000	Mala Ida, Malat, Maletai, Maljaty, Malta, Malut, Malyat, Meliat, Meliata, Mellete, Milota, Moletai, Moliat	
683100	Molodiya	
683340	Molodziatycze	
683360	Mlodiatyn, Mlodyatyn, Moldautein	
683400	Maletos, Mali Idjos, Mali Idos, Milatycze, Moliatitch, Molodycz	
683450	Molotychki, Molyatichki, Molytichki	
683460	Molodeczno, Molodetchno	
683476	Moldauischbanid	
683500	Milyatyche, Molyatichi	
683560	Molodechno	
683570	Mlodochow, Molodkov, Molotkow, Molotkuv	
683586	Neu Lettgallen	
683600	Milatyn, Milyatin, Milyatyn	
683640	Mlodnice	
683670	Mladenovo, Mladonov, Mlodzianowo	
683675	Milyatyn Pochapki	
683679	Miltenberg, Milyatyn Buryny	
683700	Mlodow, Moldava, Moldova, Molodova, Molodovo, Molodow, Molotow, Nelidovo, Nieledwia	
683730	Moldovita	
683744	Mlada Vozice	
683745	Moldawsko	
683748	Moldova Sulita	
683763	Moldava nad Bodvou	
683780	Melitopol	
683784	Mlada Boleslav	
683870	Molodylow, Molodyluv	
683940	Malodruzy, Milodroz	
683943	Maly Trostenets, Maly Trostinec, Maly Trostyanets, Malyy Trostenets	
683960	Mala Torona, Mala Trna	
683970	Muhldorf	
683976	Male Tarpno	
684000	Malec, Malecz, Malesze, Malic, Malsch, Melits, Melitz,	

	Meltsy, Mielce, Mielec, Milacze, Milas, Milcza, Milica, Milicz, Militsch, Moletch, Myelets, Nielisz
684300	Milesauti, Mileshty, Milisauti, Moleshty, Molesti, Moltchad
684316	Milestii Mari, Milestii Mici
684336	Muhlstetten
684340	Molodziatycze
684360	Milostin, Mlodiatyn, Mlodyatyn
684370	Malastow
684378	Malaesti Balti
684384	Male Sedlishche
684400	Malczyce, Malesice, Mali Idjos, Malocice, Malsice, Milaytchitz, Milejczyce, Molczadz, Mulczyce
684440	Noul Sasesc
684443	Molczadz Stacja Kolejowa
684450	Mielciesko
684460	Mlodziszyn
684500	Malacka, Malacky, Malatzka, Mehlsack, Meiliski, Meiliskiai, Mieleszki, Mileszki, Nalchik
684548	Malice Koscielne
684570	Malociechowo
684574	Mlcechvosty
684586	Milzkalne
684600	Malcin, Malczyn, Maluszyn, Maluzyn, Meleseni, Meleshen, Melesheny, Milicin, Milosna, Molocneea, Molsheim, Muhlhausen
684617	Mijlocenii Bargaului, Mijlocenii Birgaului
684656	Melsungen
684670	Mlodzianowo
684675	Molczanowka
684700	Malczew, Malczow, Malesov, Maleszowa, Maliszow, Milaczew, Mlodzowy, Molozew, Molozow, Naleczow
684715	Malsch bei Heidelberg
684717	Malsch bei Wiesloch
684734	Mlodzawy Duze, Mlodzowy Duze
684740	Malaszewicze, Nalzovice
684743	Malaszewicze Duze
684745	Milaczewskie Mlyny
684768	Maleszewo Male
684783	Malsfeld
684785	Malusy Wielkie
684800	Milasel
684870	Miloslaw
684874	Miloslavitch, Miloslawicze
684875	Miloslavichi
684940	Maly Saris
684957	Mala Cerkwica
685000	Malachy, Malech, Malechy, Malki, Milcha, Milik, Mologhia
685300	Melykut, Molchad
685400	Malchitse, Molchadz, Mulchitsy
685440	Maligoshtch, Malogoszcz
685460	Muhlhausen
685474	Nelahozeves
685497	Mlekosrby
685500	Meleghegy, Mielcuchy
685597	Malyy Kochurov
685600	Malchin, Malken, Malkinia, Mehlauken, Mulheim, Mullheim
685634	Male Chyndice
685638	Malkinia Dolna
685659	Malkinia Gorna
685663	Muhlheim an der Ruhr, Mulheim an der Ruhr

685666	Muhlheim am Main, Mulheim am Mosel
685674	Milochniewice
685675	Molchanovka
685700	Malchow, Malechow, Malekhuv, Malkow, Melgiew, Milakowo, Milkow, Nalechov, Nalechuv
685740	Malachowice, Malkiewicze, Malkowice
685743	Malyy Gvozdets
685750	Malakhovka, Malkevichi
685840	Mala Glusza, Mala Khlusha
685940	Maly Gyres, Maly Hores
685954	Noul Caragaci
685970	Mala Kriva
686000	Malin, Malina, Maljuny, Malmo, Malom, Malyn, Miehlen, Miliana, Milin, Milno, Mlynne, Mlyny, Mohylany, Muhlen, Mulheim, Mullheim, Neu Ulm
686300	Malinti, Malonty, Mlenauti
686400	Maleniec, Malenitz, Malinec, Malintsy, Malnas, Malu Mic, Melnitsa, Melnitse, Melnitza, Mielnica, Mielnice, Mileanca, Mlyniec, Myelnitsa
686443	Molnaszecsod
686450	Malinsk, Malynsk, Malynska
686460	Mielniczne
686470	Nalenczow, Nalentchov
686473	Melnitsa Podolskaya
686476	Mlyn Spindleruv
686500	Malinka, Malyinka, Meilnik, Melnich, Melnik, Melonek, Mielnik
686560	Nellingen, Neulingen
686570	Nalenchov, Nalenchuv, Naleynchiv
686575	Neulengbach
686630	Muhlheim an der Ruhr, Mulheim an der Ruhr
686656	Neu Leininen, Neuleininen
686660	Muhlheim am Main, Mulheim am Mosel
686700	Malinuv, Malnow, Mielnow, Milanow, Milnowo, Mlinov, Mlinuv, Mlynow
686734	Mlyn Wojtostwo
686740	Milanowicze, Mlynovtse, Mlynowce
686743	Malanowo Stare
686750	Malinovka, Malinowka, Malinuvka, Milanowek, Milyanovichi
686843	Malyye Mileshty
686847	Malyy Malyshev
686900	Malu Mare, Mlynary, Molnari
686940	Mlynarze
686944	Malomierzyce
687000	Malawa, Malova, Malpa, Milawa, Milewo, Mlava, Mlawa, Mohylew, Mohylow, Molev
687300	Malovata, Molovata
687400	Mala Wies, Milewicze, Mulawicze
687440	Milawczyce
687450	Milevsko
687456	Mallwischken
687500	Melbach, Melbeck, Milevichi, Milovka, Milowka, Muehlbach, Muhlbach, Nalbach, Nalibok, Naliboki
687574	Mali Bukovec, Nielepkowice

687590	Malowa Gora
687600	Nelepino, Nelipeno
687656	Mulfingen
687745	Milewo Brzegedy
687795	Milewo Brzegedy
687800	Malopole
687830	Muhlfeld
687850	Maly Plock
687857	Male Blahovo
687940	Melperts
687943	Mala Berestovitsa
687946	Male Brezno
687950	Mahlberg, Mailberg, Malborg, Malbork
688400	Mala Hlusza
688670	Male Lunawy
688765	Maly Lipnik
689300	Malorita, Maloryta
689400	Mullrose
689457	Male Raskovce
689543	Mellrichstadt
689565	Maloarkhangelsk
689700	Millerovo
689800	Malyye Orly
690000	Mehr, Mior, Miory, Mir, Mor, Murau, Naira, Narai, Nera, Nur, Nyiri
691670	Mariyanovo
691678	Marijampol, Marijampole
691700	Narajow, Narayev, Narayuv
691750	Narajewka, Narayevka
691764	Narajow Miasto
693000	Maritei, Mord, Mordy, Narty, Nereta, Nord, Norta, Nyarad, Nyaradto, Nyirad
693164	Martijanec
693300	Nyirtet
693400	Mradice, Narodici, Naroditch, Neretas, Nyirtass
693439	Nart Stary
693460	Nordhausen
693500	Maradik, Narodichi, Nordeck
693546	Nordhausen
693560	Nordheim
693567	Nordheim vor der Rhon
693587	Nyaradgalfalva
693596	Nordhorn
693600	Martonyi, Mirotyn, Mortini, Mratin, Norden, Nordheim, Northeim, Nyiradony
693640	Martinis, Martinus, Martonos
693643	Martinesti, Nordenstadt
693656	Nordenham, Nurtingen
693659	Norten Hardenberg
693660	Martineni, Nordenham
693670	Martinova, Martynow, Nart Nowy, Nordheim vor der Rhon
693674	Martinovca, Martonvasar, Martynow Stary, Martynuv Stary
693675	Martynovka
693676	Martynow Nowy, Martynuv Novy
693678	Martonfalva
693679	Nordenburg
693739	Moara de Piatra, Moara de Pyatre
693740	Neratovice
693850	Mertloch
693865	Nordlingen
693900	Nyirtura
693940	Nyirderzs

693947	Maria Theresiopol	694778	Mrozowa Wola	695778	Markowo Wolka
693950	Mordarka, Nordrach	694780	Morzywol	695780	Markobel, Markopol
693960	Nordhorn	694783	Marisfeld	695789	Merchweiler
693970	Mardorf	694790	Marosujvar	695800	Marcali
694000	Maraza, Marca, Marius,	694795	Marosborgo, Meersburg,	695830	Marcalto, Mrigolod, Mrzyglod,
	Mauruciai, Meretch, Meritz,		Merseburg		Mrzyglody
	Merts, Mertsh, Mircze, Moers,	694800	Marazli, Mariselu, Nyirgyulaj	695836	Markoldendorf
	Mors, Mrocza, Mrozy, Narocz,	694817	Marazleyevka	695840	Meerholz, Nyirgelse
	Nerusai, Nerushay, Nires,	694834	Marosludas	695843	Marculesti, Marculesti Colonie,
	Nirza, Nyires, Nyirjes	694840	Nyirszollos		Markuleshti, Markuleshty,
694170	Mordzejow	694860	Marcelina, Martselin		Markulesty, Markulisti
694300	Maeriste, Meresti, Mirsid,	694869	Miresul Mare	695846	Markelsheim
	Nyiracsad	694870	Miroslav	695859	Marcalgergelyi
694336	Murstetten, Nordstetten	694874	Miroslavas, Miroslawiec	695865	Mariakalnok
694340	Nea Orestias	694876	Marazlaveni	695875	Merkulovichi
694366	Nordstemmen	694878	Maragyulafalva	695879	Markkleeberg
694397	Maehrisch Truebau	694900	Marosjara	695930	Mirgorod
694400	Marzysz, Mierzyce, Mirashasa,	694930	Nyaradszereda	695931	Mirhorod Yashan
	Mirocice, Mirzec, Nerezice,	695000	Marek, Marki, Marok, Merch,	695936	Margareten, Margaretten
	Nirzas, Nurzec, Nyereshaza		Merech, Merk, Miereckie,	695940	Nyirkarasz, Nyirkercs
694430	Marasesti		Morag, Moragy, Nyirjako,	695943	Murakeresztur
694439	Maehrisch Ostrau, Mahrisch		Nyrsko	695944	Mercurea Ciuc, Miercurea Ciuc
	Ostrau, Mahrish Ostrau	695300	Marcauti, Marghita, Marghuta,	695969	Mercurea Nirajului, Miercurea
694460	Marzecin, Merzhausen,		Margita, Markt, Morichida,		Nirajului
	Morzyczyn		Nyirkata	695976	Markgrafneusiedl
694467	Mahrisch Schonberg	695336	Marktheidenfeld	695987	Mur Kirilovtsy
694470	Marciszow	695353	Marcauti Hotin	696000	Marhan, Meerane, Mernye,
694485	Murzzuschlag	695374	Markt Piesting		Miron, Miryn, Mohrin,
694490	Nyircsaszari	695378	Margitfalu, Margitfalva,		Moreni, Moryn, Muran,
694500	Meretske, Merzig, Mierzejki,		Margitfaul		Murany, Murnau, Noara
	Moroski	695379	Markt Berolzheim, Marktbreit		Noua, Nyrany
694547	Murska Sobota	695393	Markt Rettenbach, Marktredwitz	696300	Nyirmada
694559	Murski Crnci	695398	Markt Erlbach	696360	Marandeni, Marandeny
694570	Morszkow, Mroczkow	695400	Markeutsy, Nyaregyhaza,	696380	Marienthal
694574	Mroczkowice		Nyiregyhaza	696397	Mahrendorf, Nierendorf
694580	Nyircsaholy	695433	Markstadt	696400	Marinhoiz, Marjanci, Merunice,
694590	Marosugra	695437	Markostav, Markostaw,		Naramice, Nurmuiza
694596	Maehrisch Kromau		Marktsteft	696439	Marianosztra
694600	Marciena, Maruszyna, Mercin,	695439	Marksdorf	696450	Narinsk, Norinsk
	Merdzene, Mierzen, Mirocin,	695440	Markusica	696458	Marianske Lazne
	Moroczyn, Morozeni,	695445	Markauciskes	696460	Mareniceni, Marienhausen,
	Morozeny, Morshin, Morszyn,	695460	Marxheim, Merxheim		Merinitseni, Mornsheim
	Mricna, Mrotschen, Murczyn,	695470	Markushev, Markushov,	696475	Maria Anzbach
	Mureseni, Nierodzim, Nurzyna		Markuszow, Markuszowa	696534	Marianca de Sus
694617	Muresenii Bargaului, Muresenii	695474	Markusovce	696540	Marinhoiz
	Birgaului	695478	Markusfalu, Nyergesujfalu	696544	Nyirmeggyes
694630	Marsinita	695479	Maerkisch Friedland, Markisch	696546	Mariengauzen, Marienhausen
694637	Marosszentbenedeko		Friedland	696560	Marenicheni, Marnheim,
694638	Nyaradszentlaszlo	695500	Marchegg		Mehringen, Mohringen,
694640	Marshintsy, Mrazhnitsa, Mraznica,	695560	Margecany		Mohrungen, Moringen,
	Neresnica, Neresnice,	695591	Marki Grojeckie		Muhringen
	Neresnitsa, Neresniza,	695600	Margine, Marginea, Margonya,	696567	Marjanka Nowa
	Neuraussnitz		Marhan, Merken, Merkine,	696570	Marienhafe
694643	Maehrisch Neustadt, Morszyn		Miorcani, Morochno	696583	Nyirmihalydi
	Zdroj	695636	Mergentheim	696595	Marina Gorka
694656	Marcinkance, Marcinkonys	695639	Markendorf	696600	Marna Noua, Marnheim,
694657	Marcinkowice	695643	Morchenstern		Mironim
694660	Marsneni	695656	Merchingen	696700	Marianowo, Marienhafe,
694673	Muraszombat	695659	Markneukirchen, Merkengersch		Marjanowo, Miernow
694674	Marcinowice	695660	Margonin	696730	Marienbad
694678	Moroczna Wielka	695663	Mariakemend	696740	Marinovca, Moranwica
694690	Miresu Mare	695670	Markuniow	696750	Marinovka, Marjanowka,
694700	Mieroszow	695678	Morochna Velka		Maryanovka, Maryanuvka
694730	Mersevat	695700	Markowa, Mirkow, Morochow,	696780	Mariampol, Mariampole,
694737	Maehrisch Budwitz		Mragowo, Nyrkov, Nyrkow		Marinopol, Maryampol,
694740	Maroshevitz, Marosheviz,	695740	Markowice, Markowicze		Mirnopolye
	Marosvecs, Mierzwica,	695743	Marki Pustelnik	696786	Marjampol Miasto
	Moroshevis, Moroshhevis	695744	Markowszczyzna	696793	Marienwerder
694745	Maehrisch Weisskirchen,	695745	Markovshchizna	696795	Marenberg, Marianow
	Morozovsk	695750	Markivka, Markoviche,		Rogowski, Marienberg,
694749	Marosvasarhely		Markovka, Markowka		Marienburg, Marjanow
694750	Merzbach	695765	Morgownik		Rogowski, Merenberg,
694753	Marosbogat, Marosbogata	695770	Marokpapi		Norenberg, Nuremberg,

484

	Nurnberg
696900	Mura Mare
696936	Nyirmartonfalva
696944	Maramaros Sighet
696945	Maramarossziget
697000	Merefa, Murafa, Murava, Murawa, Muryjovo, Narev, Narew, Nariav, Narva, Narve, Narwa, Norap
697100	Nyirvaja
697140	Narva Joesu, Narva Joesuu
697164	Mauer bei Amstetten
697176	Mauer bei Wein
697390	Nyirbator
697400	Mariapocs, Marvits, Marvitz, Merovce, Moravec, Moravica, Moravitza, Morawica, Morawiec, Morovic, Muravica, Muravitsa, Murawica
697439	Mirow Stary
697453	Moravska Trebova
697454	Moravska Ostrava, Morawska Ostrawa
697455	Moravsky Krumlov
697456	Murawskie Nadbuzne
697457	Moravske Budejovice
697458	Moravske Lieskove
697460	Morawczyna, Nyirpazony
697479	Nyirvasvari
697500	Marbach, Mauerbach, Meerbeck, Narevka, Narevke, Narewka, Nehrybka
697530	Nyirbogat
697536	Nyirbogdany
697563	Marbach an der Donau
697567	Marbach am Walde
697568	Narevka Mala, Narewka Mala
697600	Marwino, Moravany, Morawiany, Murowin, Neuruppin
697650	Maravianka, Marwianka, Morawianki, Norvenich
697654	Murowana Goslin, Murowana Goslina
697659	Maravna Krilovitz, Murovano Kurilovtsy, Murovanyye Kurilovtsy
697700	Murav Evo, Muravievo, Murawjewo
697740	Moraveves
697800	Mariupol, Marvile, Marwile, Miropol, Mrowla, Narovl, Narovla, Narovlya, Narowla
697835	Nyirbeltek
697836	Morfelden
697840	Nyirpilis
697900	Maribor
697946	Nyirparasznya
697950	Marburg
697956	Marburg an der Lahn
697960	Nyirabrany, Nyiribrony
698000	Marl, Merlau, Mierlau, Narol, Nyarlo
698400	Meerholz, Morlaca
698474	Maroldsweisach
698540	Nyirlugos
698600	Mariolana
698643	Narol Miasto, Narol Myasto
698700	Marlow, Nyirlovo
698740	Narol Wies
698743	Marloffstein
699300	Mirarid
699310	Mirhorod Yashan
699350	Muraratka

700000	Baj, Bia, Buj, Foi
710000	Baja, Beje, Buia, Vaja
713000	Baiut, Bajot
713400	Wojutycze
713500	Voyutychi
713600	Voyutin, Wojutyn
713856	Vajatjulkan
714000	Baius, Bayush, Beius
714300	Biyesht, Biyeshty
714430	Baiasesti
714600	Pajeczno
714750	Wojaszowka
714790	Baia Sprie
715700	Bujakow, Pajakow, Wojakowa
715740	Vojakovac
716000	Boian, Bojan, Bojonye, Boyan, Boyany, Poian, Poiana, Poieni, Poyana, Vajan, Vajany, Vojany
716400	Bojaniec, Boyanets, Boyanitz, Bujanhaza
716460	Boianceni, Payentchno
716493	Poiana Sarata
716494	Poiana Soroca
716540	Bujanhaza
716560	Beienheim
716600	Beienheim
716658	Poiana Micului
716698	Poiana Marului
716700	Bojanow, Bojanowo
716750	Bojanowka
716786	Poiana Blenchii
716795	Poiana Porcului
716834	Poienile de Sub Munte, Poienile de Sub Muntz
716858	Poienile Glodului
716870	Poiana Ilvei
716900	Baia Mare, Boiu Mare
717000	Bujawa, Pojawie, Vejava
717353	Wojewodki Dolne
717355	Wojewodki Gorne
717400	Bojowice, Boyevitse
717500	Boyovichi, Wujowka
718000	Beuel
718567	Bujaly Gniewosze
718600	Bijeljina
718654	Bujaly Mikosze
719000	Bujor, Bujoru, Payora, Poyuri, Vajar, Weyer
719300	Feiurd, Fejerd, Pojorata, Pojorita
719360	Feiurdeni
719380	Baiertal, Baierthal, Bayertal
719400	Fejercse, Pajuris, Payuris
719439	Baiersdorf
719500	Boyarka
719573	Boyarka Budayevka
719600	Beuern, Pojoreni, Waiern
719750	Feuerbach, Payerbach
719787	Fejerfalva
730000	Baita, Bajdy, Batya, Batyu, Bedo, Bejdy, Beudiu, Bod, Bodia, Boid, Bojt, Bota, Buda, Bude, Budey, Budi, Budy, Fadd, Fot, Padej, Paide, Paty, Pettau, Potau, Ptuj, Vajta, Vat, Vatta, Vidziai, Vita
731400	Pidayets, Pidhayets
731740	Bodziejowice, Budejovice
733000	Patyod
733360	Budateteny
733400	Batiatycze, Bitetice
733483	Bad Deutsch Altenburg
733500	Batyatychi

733640	Putiatynce, Putyatintsy
733643	Bad Tennstedt
733794	Podedworze
733840	Bad Tolz, Budatelec
733850	Budatelke
733946	Pyatidorozhnoye
733956	Bad Durkheim, Bad Durrheim
733958	Podu Turcului
733960	Bad Durrheim
734000	Batiz, Batiza, Bodhaza, Bodos, Bothaza, Botiz, Botiza, Budcza, Budes, Budis, Budus, Butiza, Buttos, Fatezh, Feodosia, Feodosja, Feodosya, Padoc, Pitusca, Podhaitsy, Podhaitza, Podhajce, Podhaytse, Potycz, Vadasz, Vatici, Vetca, Vetes, Vetis, Vitaz, Votice, Waidhaus, Wotitz
734100	Feodosiia, Feodosiya
734300	Bodesti, Budesti, Feteshty, Fetesti, Pitesti
734340	Vidhostice
734350	Wittstock
734360	Bad Soden
734366	Bad Soden am Taunus
734369	Budesti Maramures
734370	Wojtostwo
734436	Botiz Satu Mare
734450	Potoczyska
734500	Bataszek, Biedaszki, Pitushka, Podhajczyki, Potocska, Ptaszki, Vajdacska, Vajdaszeg, Vidishok, Vidiskiai
734510	Podhajczyki Justynowe
734547	Potiski Sveti Nikola
734570	Ptaszkowa
734579	Bad Segeberg
734584	Budy Zaklasztorne
734600	Badacin, Badiceni, Botosana, Botosani, Botoshani, Budesheim, Peticeni, Peto Szinnye, Vititchna, Witaszyn, Wytyczno
734636	Badacsonytomaj
734637	Vajdaszentivany
734639	Badacsonytordemic
734640	Witoszynce, Wojty Zamoscie
734650	Budy Usniackie, Pottsching
734656	Wettesingen
734687	Wytyczno Lowiszow
734696	Botiza Maramures
734700	Boduszow, Bodziaczow, Bottschow, Budisava, Patosfa, Podusow, Podusuv, Widaczow
734787	Bad Schwalbach
734800	Bad Ischl, Baita Salaj, Buduslau
734845	Bad Salzschlirf
734846	Bad Salzungen
734847	Bad Salzuflen, Bad Sulzburg
734860	Podusilna
734870	Budislav, Vodislav, Vodislov, Voydislav
735000	Badicu, Batak, Batakai, Batakiai, Batka, Batok, Betok, Bodajk, Bodak, Bodiky, Bodki, Botak, Botik, Botoka, Botoki, Budachi, Budcha, Butka, Patka, Piadyki, Piatek, Piatka, Pjatki, Potik, Potok, Pyadyki, Pyatka, Pyatki, Vatich, Vetka, Viatka,

	Vitka, Vyetka, Widdig, Widoki
735140	Pidhayets
735150	Podgajek
735300	Piedecauti
735347	Bad Godesberg
735350	Pyatikhatka, Pyatikhatki
735395	Weidach Durach
735400	Bedahaza, Bedohaza, Bodhaza, Budahaz, Budakeszi, Patahaza, Petohaza, Podgaitsy, Podgajcy, Podgaytse, Podgaytsy, Podhaitsy, Podhaitza, Podhajce, Podhaytse, Waidhaus
735430	Podkost
735434	Vidhostice
735436	Badgastein, Potok Stany, Potok Stany Wies
735437	Budy Augustowskie
735440	Bydgoszcz
735450	Bidgoshch, Podhajczyki, Potochishche, Wodokaczka
735451	Podhajczyki Justynowe
735460	Wadgassen
735463	Potok Senderki, Potok Senderski
735465	Bad Kissingen
735473	Podgajci Podravski
735480	Petikozly, Podkosciele
735483	Potek Zolti, Potok Zloti, Potok Zloty
735487	Buda Koshelevo
735550	Podgaychiki
735596	Potok Gorny
735600	Badichany, Bietigheim, Bodigheim, Botoken, Peticheni, Vodhany, Votokom
735630	Vajdahunyad
735639	Bad Gandersheim
735646	Budki Neznanovske, Budki Nieznanowskie
735650	Bad Konig
735654	Bad Koenigswart
735660	Podkamen, Podkamien
735665	Podkamionka
735670	Bad Honnef
735679	Bad Homburg, Bad Homburg vor der Hohe
735680	Potok Maly
735683	Badyku Moldavskoye
735694	Vaida Camaras, Vajdakamaras
735700	Bedkow, Bedziechow, Bitkov, Bitkow, Bodzyachuv, Budkov, Budkow, Budkuv, Bytkov, Fiddichow, Fitkow, Fitkuv, Patkow, Piatkow, Piatkowa, Pietkowo, Podkowa, Potok B, Vidochov, Vitkov, Widuchowa, Witkow, Witkowo, Wittkowo, Wojtkowa
735740	Bedkowice, Budkovce, Patkowice, Petkowice, Piatkowce, Pietkovitz, Pitkovice, Vitkovice, Witkowitz
735743	Witkow Stary
735745	Piatkowisko
735746	Putkowice Nagorne
735750	Wojtkowka
735760	Waidhofen
735766	Waidhofen an der Thaya, Waidhofen an der Ybbs
735767	Vitkuv Novy, Witkow Nowy
735776	Petkowo Wymiarowo
735778	Petkowo Wielkie
735785	Potok Wielki

735800	Betigola, Betygala, Betygola, Patkule, Vad Cluj, Vadokliai, Vidukla, Vidukle
735840	Budakalasz
735843	Podklasztorze
735900	Patokryje, Piatigory, Piatohor, Pjatigory, Pyatigory
735930	Podegrodzie, Podgrodzie, Podhorod, Podhradie, Vadkert
735934	Podgorodishche, Podgorodtsy, Podhorodce, Podhorodyszcze
735936	Podgorodno, Podhorodno
735940	Podegrodzie, Podgortse, Podgorza, Podgorze, Podgrodze, Podgrodzie, Podhorce, Podhortzi, Podhradie
735945	Piategorsk, Podgorze Gazdy, Pyatigorsk
735946	Bad Kreuznach
735947	Bad Harzburg, Bad Hersfeld
735948	Vadu Crisului
735961	Podgornoye
735967	Bad Hornburg
735974	Budy Krepskie
736000	Badan, Baden, Badin, Batin, Batony, Battonya, Batyn, Beuthen, Biten, Boden, Bodony, Bohdan, Botany, Budin, Budina, Budon, Butani, Buten, Buteni, Butyny, Byten, Bytom, Byton, Futoma, Padina, Petin, Petna, Pitten, Pjatino, Putna, Vaden, Vadna, Vatyn, Vidin, Vodhany, Vodyany, Watyn, Weiden, Weidenau, Widoma, Wieden, Witten, Wodna, Wodynie
736169	Bad Neuenahr, Batanii Mari
736300	Potyond, Vitnyed
736316	Putuntei Mari
736360	Bodjentin
736396	Bytom Odrzanski
736397	Bodendorf, Weiten Trebetitsch
736400	Bad Ems, Bodenmais, Bodonci, Budimci, Budince, Fedemes, Piatnica, Pietnice, Pitomaca, Pottmes, Pyatnitsa, Vittencz, Vodinci, Vodjinci, Wattens, Weidnitz, Witnica
736430	Putineshty, Putinesti, Wattenscheid
736433	Bad Neustadt an der Saale
736436	Pottenstein
736444	Podemszczyzna
736450	Bytomsko
736457	Podunajske Biskupice
736460	Bad Oeynhausen, Bettenhausen, Budinscina, Buttenhausen, Pattensen, Pietniczany, Podniesno
736464	Bytom Odrzanski
736480	Bedziemysl
736494	Vadeni Soroca
736500	Buding, Budniki, Putnok, Vodniki, Weitenegg, Wodniki
736540	Petnehaza
736546	Bad Oeynhausen, Bettenhausen, Buttenhausen
736560	Bad Nauheim, Bettingen, Bodenheim, Bottingheim, Budingen, Buttenheim, Feudenheim, Petnichany,

	Wattenheim, Wittenheim
736570	Butenkovo
736580	Podmichale, Podmikhale, Podmokly
736584	Podmoklice
736600	Bodenheim, Budynin, Buttenheim, Feudenheim, Vodnany, Wattenheim, Witomino, Wittenheim, Wydminy
736630	Wittmund
736639	Budyne nad Ohri
736643	Batmonostor, Podmanasterek, Podmanastyrek, Podmonasterek
736647	Waidmannsfeld
736658	Bad Mingolsheim
736700	Budanov, Vidinov, Vidnava, Vidynuv, Widynow, Wojtyniow
736736	Baden Baden
736740	Bdeneves, Poddembtse, Podembice, Podembitza, Witanowice
736743	Putnowice Dolne
736745	Putnowice Gorne
736746	Buttenwiesen
736750	Bohdanowka
736780	Podniebyle
736783	Battenfeld, Bodenfelde
736789	Badenweiler
736795	Battenberg, Weidenberg, Wiedenbruck, Wittenberg, Wittenberge, Wittenburg
736796	Pottenbrunn
736800	Budymle, Budymlya, Vidomlya, Voitinel, Widomla
736900	Bodmer, Butmer
736940	Budomierz, Vadu Mures
736950	Bednarka
736956	Bad Mergentheim
736969	Vad Maramures
736970	Bednarov, Bednarow, Bednaruv
737000	Batovo, Batyjow, Batyyuv, Betfia, Botfa, Budva, Buetow, Butow, Bytow, Padew, Vidava, Widawa, Witow, Wojtowa
737300	Bataapati
737340	Budvietis
737400	Batowice, Budevitz, Budvieciai, Budvitch, Budweis, Budwiecie, Padbuz, Petipsy, Pidbish, Podbuz, Podbuzh, Poddebce, Poddebice, Poddebtse, Poddubce, Poddubtsy, Podubus, Pudewitz, Pytowice, Vadovits, Vadovitse, Vadovitz, Vettweiss, Voitovca, Wadowice, Wiatowice, Witowice, Witwica
737430	Budapest, Vidpuszta
737437	Wojtowstwo
737438	Wadowice Dolne
737440	Padubysys, Podbrzezie
737450	Podvysoka, Podwysoka, Vitebsk, Witebsk
737451	Podvysokoye
737459	Wadowice Gorne, Witowice Gorne
737480	Bad Voslau
737484	Bodvaszilas

737500	Bad Buchau, Budafok, Vaytovka, Voytovka, Widawka	
737565	Podbogoniki, Podbohonniki	
737590	Vad Bihor	
737600	Podivin, Podobin, Waidhofen	
737660	Waidhofen an der Thaya, Waidhofen an der Ybbs	
737676	Bad Wimpfen	
737700	Vettweiß	
737740	Podabovec, Podobovec, Podobovets, Podobovice, Podobovitz	
737800	Bedeval, Bedevla, Bedevle, Bedevlia, Bedevlya, Bidevle, Putivel, Putivl	
737830	Botpalad, White Field	
737836	Bad Wildungen	
737840	Padaflesa, Padaflesha, Podplesa	
737844	Podvolitchisk, Podwlocztska, Podwoloczyska	
737845	Podbielsko	
737846	Bad Polzin	
737850	Podbielko, Podwilk	
737854	Podvolochisk	
737858	Budy Wielgoleskie	
737864	Budy Bielanskie	
737865	Bad Aibling, Bodvalenke	
737870	Badfalva, Budfalva, Fiatfalva	
737878	Bad Vilbel	
737900	Podbori	
737916	Bad Freienwalde	
737917	Podobriyevka	
737930	Padbradje, Podbrodzie, Podebrady	
737935	Bedburdyck	
737939	Bad Friedrichshall	
737940	Padbradje, Patvarc, Pitvaros, Podberezce, Podberezha, Podberezie, Podberezye, Podborce, Podbortse, Podbrezi, Podbrodz, Podbrodze, Podbrodzie, Podbrzezie	
737944	Podbrezitz	
737945	Budy Barczackie	
737947	Bad Worishofen	
737950	Bedburg, Bitburg, Bodvarako, Padberg	
737956	Badbergen	
737960	Budaabrany, Podborany	
737961	Podvornoye	
737964	Podboransky Rohozec	
737965	Bad Berneck, Bad Berneck im Fichtelgebirge, Fedvernik, Poddobryanka, Podobryanka	
737966	Bad Pyrmont	
737970	Potvorov	
737974	Podwerbce	
738000	Badalo, Battelau, Bitla, Bitola, Bitolj, Bitolja, Botla, Butla, Patal, Petelea, Podu Iloaei, Putila, Vetly, Wietly	
738100	Podu Iloaie	
738356	Budiul de Campie	
738370	Podlodow, Witoldow	
738375	Podlodowka	
738395	Podul Turcului	
738400	Bodolz, Podelusy, Podlazie, Podlesie, Podlesye, Podlez, Podlyashe, Potolitch, Potylicz	
738440	Podlazice, Podolszyca	
738450	Podlesko, Podliski	
738456	Podliski Male, Podliski Malyye	
738457	Podliski Wielkie	

738460	Beddelhausen, Podleszany, Podloziany	
738461	Podlesnoye	
738475	Podlazowek	
738476	Wittelshofen	
738479	Wittelsberg	
738500	Podolik, Potylich, Widelka, Widelki, Wittlich	
738543	Bad Lauchstadt	
738546	Beddelhausen	
738564	Butelka Nizna	
738574	Butelka Wyzna, Petlikowce Stare	
738600	Bedlne, Bedlno, Bethlen, Betlen, Podolin, Pudlein, Vtelno, Wetlina, Wietlin	
738640	Podolinec	
738643	Vadul Nistrului	
738650	Bedlenko, Puttelange	
738655	Budy Lancuckie	
738657	Weidlingbach	
738670	Podole Nowe	
738693	Biadoliny Radlowskie	
738700	Batelov, Budylov, Budylow, Pitalovo, Vietalva, Wadlew	
738740	Piatlpwce, Podlipce, Podliptse	
738747	Bad Lippspringe	
738750	Vitelevka, Vitelyuvka	
738760	Badljevina	
738796	Buttelborn	
738800	Podul Iloaei	
738810	Podul Iloaiei	
739000	Batar, Bator, Batyr, Beodra, Buduri, Padar, Patrai, Patro, Peteri, Petra, Petreu, Piatra, Piatyhory, Weitra, Wetter	
739100	Piedruja, Wydreja	
739140	Piedrujas	
739164	Petrijanec	
739170	Pietrzejowa	
739174	Petrijevci	
739300	Butthard, Butthart, Patrauti, Peterd, Peterhida, Peteritea, Petrauti, Piaterota, Podhorod, Potrete, Vyderta, Wodzierady, Wyderta	
739313	Patrautii de Jos, Patrautii de Sus	
739331	Petrauti de Jos	
739334	Petrauti de Sus	
739340	Podhorodce, Podhorodyszcze	
739360	Podhorodno	
739379	Petrodvorets	
739396	Vatra Dornei	
739400	Batarci, Batarciu, Batarcs, Batorz, Bedrc, Budaors, Buderaz, Buderazh, Fodorhaz, Fodorhaza, Patras, Petrautz, Petrocz, Pietrasze, Pietrusy, Pietrycze, Podhorce, Podhortzi, Podrezy, Podros	
739433	Weiterstadt	
739439	Petersdorf, Wattersdorf	
739440	Potarzyca	
739445	Wytrzyszczka	
739450	Biedrusko, Peterseg, Vadu Rascu, Vadu Rashky	
739456	Petershagen	
739457	Vad Rashkov, Wad Raschkow	
739460	Petrashani, Petriceni, Petrosani, Petroseni, Petroseny, Petrushany, Pfeddersheim, Poturzyn	
739461	Podorozhnoye	
739470	Watraszew	

739471	Bodersweier	
739474	Petrozavodsk	
739475	Wiedersbach	
739478	Peterswaldau, Pietrusza Wola	
739490	Peteryasar	
739500	Botragy, Buderich, Patroha, Patryki, Petrikau, Petryche	
739516	Badragii Noui	
739517	Badragaii Vechi, Badragii Vechi	
739530	Peterhida	
739540	Batorkeszi, Fodorhaz, Fodorhaza, Patrykozy	
739543	Bodrogzsadany	
739547	Bodrogkisfalud	
739549	Bodrogszerdahely	
739560	Bad Reichenhall, Petroham, Pieterkanie	
739565	Bad Reichenhall	
739570	Petergof, Petrikov, Petrokow, Piotrkow, Piotrkuv, Podjarkow, Podyarkow, Pyetrkov	
739573	Piotrkow Trybunalski, Piotrkow Trybunaski	
739574	Badrzychowice, Bedrykowce, Biedrzykowice, Bodrog Vecs, Pietrzykowice, Piotrkovitz, Piotrkowice, Wietrzychowice	
739575	Petrikov Koyavsk, Piotrkow Kujawski	
739584	Bodrogolaszi	
739586	Bodroghalom	
739594	Bodrogkeresztur	
739597	Petrokrepost	
739600	Baturin, Baturyn, Petreni, Petreny, Putureni, Vetrni, Vidrany, Vydran, Widdern	
739630	Petrindu	
739640	Peteranec, Vydranitsa, Wydranica	
739648	Petrinzel	
739650	Peternieki, Potranka	
739660	Baturnin, Butrimoniai	
739663	Piatra Neamt	
739664	Biedermannsdorf, Butrimants, Butrimontz, Butrimonys, Butyrmantsy	
739665	Butrimonicai	
739670	Witrynow	
739680	Petronell	
739683	Vatra Moldovitei	
739700	Bad Orb, Bottrop, Petreve, Petrov, Petrova, Petruv, Piotrow, Piotrowo	
739740	Petrovac, Petrovce, Petrovice, Petrovitch, Petrowitschi, Petrowitz, Piotrowice, Pitrovitz, Vitrupes	
739745	Petrovskoye, Podravska Moslavina, Podravska Slatina, Podravski Podgajci	
739746	Petrovce nad Laborcom	
739747	Piotrowice Wielkie	
739748	Petrovo Selo, Petrovoszello	
739749	Petervasara	
739750	Paderewek, Petrovka, Piotrowka, Puderbach	
739754	Batorove Kesy	
739759	Petrova Gora, Petrovgrad	
739760	Bad Rappenau, Petroupim	
739774	Petrova Bisztra	
739778	Petropavlovka	
739780	Peterfala	

739783	Bitterfeld, Petrvald
739793	Petrovaradin
739795	Peterburg
739796	Paderborn
739797	Petroverovka
739800	Petrila, Petrilla
739850	Petrzalka
739853	Petrilaca de Mures
739870	Petrilov, Petrylow
739930	Petrohrad
740000	Bac, Bacia, Bacs, Bacsa, Bacsi, Bacza, Baseu, Baytsh, Baza, Bazsi, Becej, Beitch, Bejsce, Bes, Betsche, Beudiu, Beytch, Bezi, Biecz, Biusa, Boc, Bocs, Bodia, Bous, Boze, Buc, Bucea, Bugyi, Buss, Bussu, Buza, Buzau, Bzau, Fajsz, Fugyi, Pacsa, Pasca, Passau, Pausa, Pecs, Peitz, Petschau, Peza, Pisz, Pocsa, Pocsaj, Posa, Pose, Puze, Vac, Vas, Veca, Veisee, Vese, Vez, Vidz, Vidzh, Vidziai, Vidzy, Vietz, Visea, Vishay, Vishya, Viso, Viss, Wasy, Weeze, Weiz, Weze, Widze, Wischau, Wojcza, Ybbs
741000	Bacioiu, Bucsoaia, Peceiu, Veisejai, Veisiejai, Vishaya, Wiejsieje
741600	Vasiyeny, Vsejany
741700	Bezejow, Pietrzejowa, Pitcheyev, Pitshayev, Poczajow, Potchayev
741740	Bodziejowice, Bozejovice, Bystrzejowice
741767	Poczajow Nowy
743000	Basaid, Bezid, Bicsad, Biesti, Biezdziedza, Bosta, Buzita, Byst, Bzite, Facsad, Paszto, Pest, Pozdziacz, Puesti, Puszta, Pyrzhota, Vasad, Veszto, Viesite, Vrsta
743140	Viseu de Jos
743146	Posada Jacmierska
743148	Posada Jasliska
743300	Bezded
743340	Vistytis
743353	Pesthidegkut
743374	Pusztadobos
743383	Pusztatold
743385	Bezdedtelek
743386	Posada Dolna
743394	Pusztaederics
743400	Besztece, Brzotice, Pozdzienice, Przedecz, Pshedesh, Pshedetz, Viesites, Wyszatyce
743430	Puesti Sat
743440	Viseu de Sus
743450	Pustoshka
743460	Przytoczno, Westhausen
743469	Pusztasomorja, Pusztazamor
743470	Bistuszowa
743474	Postaszowice, Pozdisovce
743478	Pusztaszabolcs
743483	Pusztacsalad
743500	Biesiadka, Przytyk, Pshedech, Pshitik, Pustokha
743535	Pusztahidegkut
743540	Bustyahaza
743569	Pusztakmaras
743570	Pastuchov, Pustkow
743574	Przytkowice, Pusztakovacsi
743580	Pshitikhl

743594	Pusztaegres
743596	Posada Gorna
743600	Bastheim, Bastunai, Bastuny, Bezdan, Bezidu Nou, Bistina, Bostyn, Brzotin, Bushtina, Bushtyna, Bustina, Bustino, Piestany, Pishtyan, Pistany, Pistin, Pistyan, Pistyn, Postojna, Postojno, Postoyno, Postyen, Potsdam, Potstejn, Pozden, Pustina, Pustynia, Pyeshtani, Vestiena, Vsetin, Weisstein, Westheim, Wsetin
743630	Pastende
743640	Bestemac, Bezdonys, Przedmiescie, Przedmoscie, Pustinas, Vishtenitz, Vishtinetz, Vishtinits, Wisztyniec
743643	Przedmiescie Dubieckie
743644	Przedmiescie Sedziszowskie
743645	Przedmiescie Kludzie, Pusztamiske, Wustensachsen
743649	Pusztamagyarod
743650	Beshtemak
743664	Pusztamonostor
743670	Bezidu Nov
743671	Westheim bei Hammelburg, Westheim bei Hassfurt
743674	Pistyan Postyen
743676	Posada Nowomiejska
743679	Festenberg, Vestenbergsgreuth
743684	Viseu de Mijloc
743690	Pestimre
743695	Pusztamerges
743700	Fastov, Piastow, Posadow, Posadowa, Postav, Postavi, Postavy, Postawy, Postov, Postow, Wystepy, Wzdow
743736	Pusztafodemes
743740	Bestovice, Postovice, Postupice, Pshedbosh, Pshedbozh
743760	Bestvina, Bestwina, Pusztavam, Westhofen, Westhoffen
743778	Pasztowa Wola
743780	Bacstopolya, Bozodujfalu, Westwahl
743783	Pusztafoldvar
743784	Posada Felsztynnska
743793	Pecsudvard
743794	Przedborz, Pshedburz
743800	Pestujhely, Przadlo, Przytuly, Wzdol
743830	Festelita
743840	Feshtelitsa
743845	Posada Leska, Posada Liska, Postoliska
743857	Posada Olchowska
743860	Bezidul Nou, Pestlin, Postolin, Puste Ulany
743865	Pustelnik, Pustelnik Struga
743879	Postelberg, Postoloprty
743896	Pestlorinc
743900	Bistra, Bisztra, Bucsitura, Bystra, Bystre, Bystry, Bystrzece, Bystrzyca, Pestere, Piestrzec, Pyzdry
743930	Bistrita, Bustehrad
743937	Bistrita Bargaului, Bistrita Birgaului, Pusztaradvany
743939	Bisztraterebes
743940	Beszterec, Bistritch, Bystrica, Bystrice, Bystritschi, Pusztaras,

	Wusterhausen
743943	Westerstede
743944	Bezdruzice
743946	Beszterce Naszod, Bystrice Mala, Bystrice Nove, Postrizin
743947	Besztercebanya, Bystrice pod Hostynem, Pesterzsebet
743950	Bystraki, Bystrichi, Pasturka
743954	Wusterhausen
743957	Pstragowa, Pstragowka
743958	Westeregeln, Westerholt
743960	Postronna
743965	Westernkotten
743970	Betzdorf, Paasdorf, Poysdorf, Wiesdorf
743973	Posada Rybotycka
743974	Bystrowice, Bystrzejowice, Wusterwitz
743977	Biestrzykow Wielki
743979	Westerburg
743980	Westerholt
744000	Bazos, Beszyce, Bezhitsa, Biczyce, Biezdziedza, Bischitz, Bisses, Biszca, Biszcza, Bitshutsh, Bocecea, Bosaca, Boshaza, Bosiacz, Brzesc, Brzescie, Brzezce, Brzezie, Bucecea, Bucici, Buczacz, Buszcze, Butchatch, Buzias, Buzica, Buzice, Bysice, Bystrzece, Bystrzyca, Byszyce, Fuzes, Pesheysh, Petchuz, Piestrzec, Pish Tch, Piszcza, Podsusze, Pozdziacz, Pshayts, Pshaytsh, Pshischa, Puczyce, Pushtshe, Puzicze, Pyrzyce, Pyszaca, Vasica, Vecses, Vezaiciai, Visaytz, Visoca, Vrsac, Vrsce, Wasosz, Wieshajzie, Wiezyca, Wojszyce, Wrzaca, Wyciaze, Wysocze, Wyzyce
744300	Bacesti, Baisesti, Basesti, Bazesti, Bazosd, Pecestea
744350	Brzhostik, Brzostek, Przezdziecko
744360	Przystajn, Przystajnia, Przystan, Pshistan
744364	Przysietnica
744370	Brzostowa
744374	Brzostowica, Brzozdowce, Brzozdowce Miasto, Bzhostovitsa, Bzhostovitsa Mala, Bzhostovitsa Vielka, Bzhostovitsa Vyelka
744375	Brzostowa Gora, Brzostowica Mala, Brzostowica Wielka
744397	Betziesdorf
744400	Brzeszcze, Pishtzatz, Piszczac, Przashysz, Przeczyca, Wojcieszyce
744433	Brzoza Stadnicka
744450	Przezdziecko, Wytrzyszczka
744470	Podsedziszow, Przeciszow, Wrzeszczewo
744500	Bacieczki, Brzesko, Brzuska, Brzyska, Brzyski, Budziska, Pieczyski, Przysieka, Przysieki, Przysucha, Visotsk, Visotzk, Vysotsk, Wyrzysk, Wysocko
744533	Brzoski Tatary
744551	Brzesc Kujawski

744563 Brzesc nad Bugiem, Bzhesbch nad Bugyem
744567 Brzesko Nowe, Bzesko Nowe
744570 Voitzeshkov, Wojcieszkow, Woszczkowo
744574 Brzozki Brzezinskie, Przyszychwosty, Pshyshykhvosty, Visotzki Vizhna, Vysotsko Vyzhne
744578 Brzyska Wola
744579 Brzozki Brzezinskie, Pozeski Brestovac
744583 Brzesc Litewski
744584 Budy Zaklasztorne
744598 Brzoza Krolewska, Fizesu Gherlii
744600 Bezhezhin, Bischhausen, Brzesciany, Brzezany, Brzezhany, Brzezin, Brzezina, Brzeziny, Brzezna, Brzyzna, Budziszyn, Bzezan, Bzhezhani, Bzhezina, Bzhezini, Bzheziny, Pasetchna, Pasieczna, Paszczyna, Piaseczna, Piaseczno, Piasetchna, Pisatchna, Pszczyna, Vasszecseny, Wezyczyn, Wozuczyn, Wrzesnia, Wysocin, Wysoczany
744636 Pestszentimre
744638 Bucsuszentlaszlo, Pestszentlorinc, Pestszentlorine, Vacszentlaszlo
744639 Pestszenterzsebet
744640 Brzeznica, Bzhezhnitsa, Piszczanica, Przasnysz, Pshasnish, Woszczance
744650 Brzezinka, Brzezinki, Budy Usniackie, Budziszynek, Przesmyki
744654 Brzeznica Stara
744655 Brzeznica Ksiazeca
744657 Brzeznica Bychawska
744667 Brzydzyn Nowy
744670 B Zhesha Nova, Podsosnow, Podsosnuv
744696 Puszcza Marianska, Puszcza Marjanska
744700 Bodziaczow, Brzezawa, Brzozow, Fasciszowa, Przeczow, Przyszowa, Pszczew, Puszczew, Wrzeszewo
744735 Wasosz Poduchowny
744740 Brzaczowice, Brzezowiec, Brzozowiec, Pasusvis, Pasusvys
744743 Brzozow Stary
744750 Brzezowka, Faszczowka
744753 Brzozowica Duza
744756 Brzozowica Mala
744757 Brzozowica Wielka
744760 Fuzesabony
744793 Buziasfurdo
744800 Bogyiszlo, Bogyoszlo, Przedzel, Przestrzele
744845 Brzezie Laskowa
744850 Bodzasujlak
744859 Fizesul Gherlei
744860 Wies Zolynia
744870 Przeclaw, Przeslaw, Przyslup, Pshetslav, Pshetzlov, Vodzislav, Wodzislaw
744900 Fuzeser
744945 Przysiersk
744963 Fuzesgyarmat
745000 Baczki, Baisk, Bashuki, Baszuki, Bausk, Bauska, Bauske, Becske,

Beska, Bicske, Biisk, Bisk, Biysk, Bocicau, Bocki, Bocska, Boisk, Bosyach, Boysk, Brzeg, Brzegi, Bucki, Bucsko, Bucyki, Busag, Bushche, Bushyki, Busk, Busko, Buszyki, Butsyki, Buzaki, Buzsak, Bzheg, Fischach, Pasieki, Pasika, Paszika, Pecky, Peski, Piasek, Piask, Piaski, Piesk, Pisek, Pishcha, Piski, Pisko, Piszke, Piuski, Pocskai, Pozega, Pshaych, Pshech, Putzig, Puzichi, Pyesk, Vascau, Vashki, Vaskai, Vaskiai, Vaskoh, Vasyuki, Veczke, Vezhaychey, Vicski, Vishky, Visk, Viski, Visku, Visoki, Visoko, Voshki, Voski, Voyska, Vyska, Vysoka, Vysoke, Vysoko, Wachock, Wasiuki, Weseke, Wieseck, Wieska, Wissek, Wojska, Wojszki, Wujskie, Wysock, Wysoka, Wysokie
745100 Visokoya, Voyskaya, Vysokaya, Vysokoye
745140 Przychojec
745169 Bocicoiu Mare
745180 Bocicoiel
745186 Bocicoiul Mare
745300 Pascauti, Paskudy, Piscott, Przygody, Vascauti, Vasckauti, Vaskut, Viskit
745340 Paszki Duze
745349 Vascauti Soroca
745350 Wiskitki
745353 Vascauti Hotin
745374 Vascauti pe Ceremus
745376 Pasieka Otfinowska
745379 Visoki Dvor, Visokidvar, Visokidvor, Wysokidwor
745383 Visoka D Lita, Visoke Dlita
745386 Brzeg Dolny
745390 Vascauti Orhei
745395 Vascauti Orhei
745400 Bes Ghioz, Besh Gioz, Buzahaza, Paskautsy, Vashkouts, Vaskautsy, Vaskoutsi, Vizkoz, Vyshkautsy, Washkoutz
745437 Budy Augustowskie
745439 Boiska Stare, Busk Zadroi, Busko Zdroj, Piaska Stare, Piaski Stare, Pyaski Stare
745460 Paskrzyn
745464 Woskrzenice Wielkie
745473 Boczki Swidrowo
745485 Piaski Szlacheckie
745600 Bashkany, Boscana, Bozicany, Pascani, Pasechna, Pesochnya, Pishchen, Pushkin, Pyasechna, Pyasechno, Veitshochheim, Veszkeny, Vizakna
745630 Vysoke Myto
745639 Bacskamadaras, Baczkamadaras
745640 Voshchantsy, Vucskomezo, Wiskienice
745645 Vysochanskoye
745646 Wysocko Nizne
745647 Visoka Mazovietzk, Visoke Mazovyetsk, Visoki Mazovyetsk, Wysokie Mazovyetsk, Wysokie

Mazowieckie
745656 Fussgonheim
745657 Veshkhnyakovtse
745660 Fussgonheim, Vrskman
745680 Paszki Male, Piasek Maly
745700 Beczkow, Bedziechow, Beeskow, Bicskof, Bishkiv, Bishkuv, Biszkow, Bochkuv, Bodzechow, Bodzyachuv, Botcheikev, Botcheikovo, Bozykow, Brzechow, Buczkow, Buszkow, Piscopia, Przechowo, Pskov, Vishkovo, Viskovo, Vuchkovo, Vyshkov, Vyshkovo, Vyshkuv, Vyskov, Vyskovo, Wojciechow, Wyszkow, Wyszkowo
745740 Badrzychowice, Biedrzykowice, Biskopitza, Biskovitse, Biskowice, Biskupice, Biskupiec, Biskupitz, Boskovice, Boskowitz, Bozkovice, Brzuchowice, Buczkowice, Buskovice, Buszkowice, Paszkowice, Peskovtsy, Piaskowce, Pietrzykowice, Piskowitz, Pyskowice, Pyszkowce, Vashkovtsy, Voshkavitch, Waszkowica, Wietrzychowice
745743 Pieczychwosty
745745 Buczkowska Wola, Buszkowiczki, Vashkovtsy Khotin, Vysokovskaya, Waszkowskie
745746 Biskupice Melsztynskie, Vyskovce nad Iplom, Wysocka Wyzne, Wysocko Wyzne
745748 Biskupice Lubelskie
745749 Biskupice Radlowskie
745750 Biskovichi, Fashchevka, Paszkowka, Peskovka, Piaskowka, Wojciechowka
745760 Przckopana
745763 Vyskovo nad Tisou
745774 Wysoka Powrzeszow
745778 Biestrzykow Wielki
745779 Wysoka Powrzeszow
745780 Boska Wola
745785 Biska Wolka, Piasek Wielki, Piaski Wielkie, Wrzaca Wielka
745800 Baisa Gala, Baisagole, Baisogala, Baisogola, Bascalia, Beisogala, Podskale, Poskle
745810 Bashkaliya
745830 Piscolt, Piskolt, Przykalety
745837 Visoka Litovsk, Visoke Litovsk, Visokie Litevskie, Wysoki Litovsk, Wysokie Litewskie
745839 Piaski Luterskie
745860 Przegalina, Przegaliny
745863 Przegaliny Duze
745866 Przegaliny Male
745867 Przegaliny Wielkie
745870 Przyglow, Pshiglov
745876 Vecgulbene
745887 Wysoka Lelowska
745900 Besiekiery
745930 Bazakeretlye, Visakio Ruda, Visegrad, Vishegrod,

745935 Vishogrod, Vishogrud, Visoki Ruda, Vysoka Ruda, Wysoka Ruda, Wyszogrod

745935 Vishegrodek, Vishogrudek, Vizhgorodok, Vyshgorodok, Wyszogrodek, Wyzgrodek

745943 Piscaresti, Piskareshty

745946 Peiskretscham, Wioska Radzyminska, Woskorzenice Duze

745948 Przegorzaly

745950 Bocsko Raho

745956 Weiskirchen, Weisskirchen, Weisskirchen in Steiermark

745960 Paskrzyn, Vsechromy

745964 Woskrzenice Wielkie

745974 Budy Krepskie, Piskorovitza, Piskorowice, Vysehorovice

746000 Bacseni, Bassum, Bautzen, Bazin, Bazna, Bedzin, Beocin, Besenyo, Besiny, Besno, Bezeny, Bezenye, Bezin, Beznea, Bezoyn, Biezun, Bizun, Bocian, Bocsum, Bogyan, Bosen, Bosyne, Bozieni, Brzana, Brzyna, Bucium, Buciumi, Bucsum, Bucyn, Budzhin, Budzin, Budzyn, Busno, Butsin, Butsyn, Buzany, Buzhany, Byczyna, Byezhun, Bysen, Bzin, Focsani, Pacin, Paczin, Paczyna, Pasiene, Paszyn, Pazony, Pcim, Pczany, Pitschen, Posejny, Posen, Pozno, Pozsony, Przyjmy, Pszon, Puczyny, Pyshno, Vezseny, Viazin, Viazma, Vidzin, Vizhna, Vizhon, Vizhun, Vizina, Vizion, Vizna, Vocin, Vodyany, Vyazma, Vyazyn, Vyzuonai, Waitzen, Wedzina, Weissenau, Wessen, Wezina, Wiazyn, Wiczyn, Wiczynie, Wiesen, Wisna, Wissen, Wisznia, Wizajny, Wizna, Wizuny, Wizyn, Wojcina, Wojszyn, Wydzna, Wydzno, Wyzne

746100 Peschanoye, Pestschannoje

746134 Bozienii de Sus

746178 Vysna Jablonka, Vysnia Jablonka, Wyzna Jablonka

746300 Besenyod, Przemet, Przemiat, Putsuntei, Veshinta, Vezendiu, Viesintai, Vishinta, Visonta, Wiesent, Wiesenthau, Wiesmath

746340 Viesintos

746360 Bodjentin, Bodzentin, Bodzentyn

746365 Budszentmihaly

746369 Bozinta Mare

746370 Bazantov

746385 Besenyotelek

746386 Basnia Dolna

746393 Ybbs an der Donau

746397 Bausendorf, Busendorf, Vosendorf, Weisendorf

746400 Basnice, Bisenz, Bzenec, Pasienes, Podzamcze, Posmus, Posnas, Pozdzienice, Pozdzimezh, Przemocze, Przenosza, Pysznica, Vezendiu, Vidsmuiza, Vishniets, Vishnits, Vishnitz, Vishnitza, Vizhnitsa, Vizhnitz, Viznits, Vizounous, Vodjinci, Vyzonous,

746430 Visinesti

746433 Vysni Studeny

746436 Buciumi Satu Mare, Veisenshtein, Weissenstein

746438 Potzneusiedl

746440 Vieshmezhitz

746443 Wisnicz Stary

746450 Besenyszog, Podzameczek

746454 Bosanski Samac

746455 Bosanska Gradiska, Bosanska Krupa

746456 Bosanski Novi

746457 Bosanski Brod, Bosanski Petrovac

746460 Busenhausen, Peczenizyn, Peczynizyn, Petchinizhin, Witzenhausen, Wozniczna

746464 Voznesensk, Wozniesiensk

746465 Voznessenk, Wossnesenk

746467 Wisnicz Nowy

746473 Vysny Svidnik, Vysnyj Svidnik

746480 Bedziemysl, Buciumi Salaj, Przemysl, Pshemishel, Pshemishl, Pshemysl

746484 Vsemyslice

746486 Przemyslany, Pshemishlani, Vysna Slana

746490 Bosna Serai, Pocs Megyer, Pocsmegyer, Vasmegyer

746500 Boesing, Bosing, Bzinek, Facimiech, Pasching, Pasing, Paszenki, Peschanka, Pestchanka, Pestschanka, Pezinok, Pieczonki, Pistchanka, Podzamche, Possneck, Poucnik, Pszonka, Pyeschanka, Vishenka, Vishenki, Vishinki, Watzing, Wiszenka, Wiszenki, Wodzinek, Wyszonki

746534 Bason Chadash

746546 Busenhausen, Witzenhausen

746554 Wyszonki Koscielne

746560 Baisingen, Bassenheim, Bessingen, Bissingen, Fischingen

746561 Pshenichnoye

746566 Vysna Kamenica, Weisenheim am Sand

746567 Vishnich Novy

746568 Vishenka Mala

746570 Przemkow

746573 Bezmichowa Dolna

746574 Beshenkowitschi, Bishenkovitz, Bjeschenkowitschi, Poznachowice Dolne

746575 Beshenkovichi, Bezmichowa Gorna

746578 Bosingfeld

746583 Vysny Klatov

746596 Basnia Gorna, Vizhnichioara Mika, Vizhnichiora Mika, Weissenhorn

746600 Bassenheim, Budzynin, Poznan, Vasimony, Vyzhnyany, Weismain, Wyzniany

746630 Pazmandhegy

746635 Pazmandhegy

746636 Fischamend Markt

746637 Pazmandfalu, Wyszmontow

746648 Vysna Mysla

746650 Wyznianka

746660 Weisenheim am Sand

746680 Vecmemele

746700 Besenov, Biezanow, Bizinev, Bizinov, Biznov, Bodzanov, Bodzanow, Bucniow, Budzanov, Budzanow, Budzanuv, Butsnev, Patsanov, Peczniew, Podsumowo, Vashniev, Vishnava, Vishnev, Vishneva, Vishnevo, Vishniva, Vishnova, Vishnyuv, Viszniew, Wasniow, Wisniewo, Wisniowa, Wisznievo, Wiszniew, Wiszniewo, Wiszniow

746710 Vishnevoye

746730 Pociumbauti

746740 Bazanowice, Vishnevets, Vishnevits, Vishnivitz, Vishnyovyets, Vizhna Apsha, Vysna Apsa, Vysni Apsa, Wisnievicze, Wisniowiec, Wisnowiec, Wiszniewice

746743 Vysni Bystry

746744 Woznowszczyzna

746745 Vishnivchik, Voznovshchina, Voznovshchyzna, Wisniowczyk

746750 Puznowka, Vishnevka, Weissenbach, Wiesenbach

746756 Wisniowiec Nowy

746759 Wisniowa Gora

746760 Pociumbeni

746783 Waischenfeld, Wiesenfeld

746784 Bozieni Bals, Weissenfels, Wiaczein Polski

746785 Przemiwolki, Pshemivulki

746794 Vysni Verecky

746795 Beutzenburg, Bisamberg, Boizenburg, Busenberg, Vesenberg, Vezenberg, Vizmberk, Wassenberg, Weissenberg, Weissenburg, Weissenburg in Bayern, Wesenberg, Wiesenberg, Wiesenburg

746796 Watzenborn, Wiesenbronn

746800 Pociuneliai, Potzunel

746900 Bezmir, Vasieni Orhei, Wismar

746937 Vysna Radvan

746940 Pozdzimierz, Wyszomierz

746944 Wysmierzyce

746948 Vysne Raslavice

746950 Vasieni Orhei

746955 Bismarch Hutte

746960 Weissenhorn

746963 Vysne Remety, Vysni Remete, Vysni Remety

746974 Vysne Revistia

746976 Vysna Rybnica

746985 Vysna Orlik, Vysni Orlik, Vysny Orlik

747000 Baczow, Bashova, Baszowa, Bazow, Becov, Beszowa, Boczow, Bozhev, Bozhuv, Bucow, Butzow, Byczow, Pacov, Paszab, Paszowa, Posfa, Pozba, Vicsap, Vishev, Vishuv, Wasewo, Wasowo, Wiazow, Wiazowa, Wiciow, Wieschowa, Wieszowa, Wiszow, Wizewo, Wrzawy, Wrzepia, Wschowa, Wysowa,

	Wyspa
747300	Buzovita
747360	Pashvitin, Pasviatin, Poshvitin, Poswetin, Poswietne, Vacbottyan, Wiesbaden
747364	Pasvitinys
747370	Przewodow, Przywitowo
747390	Pocspetri
747400	Bezivce, Bezovce, Bizovac, Boshevitch, Bozovice, Bozovici, Bozoviciu, Bozovics, Busovca, Butschowitz, Buzovitsa, Bzowiec, Piesiewicze, Pocepice, Przywoz, Pseves, Vezhbitsa, Vizovice, Wisowitz
747430	Przypust
747433	Bischofstetten
747439	Wyzwa Stara
747447	Przewodziszowice
747450	Busovisko, Busowisko
747460	Bischofsheim, Przebieczany, Przybyszyn
747470	Przybyszew, Przybyszowy
747475	Przybyszowka
747479	Bischofsberg, Bischofsburg, Bischofswerder
747480	Bacs Peczello
747487	Przybyslawice
747490	Fugyivasarhely
747495	Fugyivasarhely
747500	Bushovka, Butzbach, Fischbach, Fischbachau, Fuzovka, Pauszowka, Pesevichi, Puspoki, Vitchevka, Vyazovka, Weisbach, Wiazowka, Wiczowka, Wjasowka, Wjasowok
747530	Bacsbokod
747536	Puspoktamasi
747537	Puspokhatvan
747544	Puspokszilagy
747559	Bzowiec Gorny
747560	Vezhbichno
747563	Puspoknadasd
747583	Puspokladany
747585	Puspoklak
747600	Busowno, Bussowno, Vezhbyany, Wiazowna
747630	Bischwind
747640	Vezhbenzh, Wiazownica
747670	Wyzwa Nowa
747700	Vezhbova
747730	Vicsapapati
747750	Przybowka
747785	Vecpiebalga
747800	Bezwola, Pasvul, Pazhevla, Podsvilye, Podswile, Posvol, Posvul, Przewale, Przewaly, Pshevaly, Pshovaly
747830	Bocfolde
747835	Vasboldogasszony
747840	Pasvalis, Pasvalys, Vecpils
747843	Pocioveliste
747845	Bazavluchok
747846	Przewloczna
747850	Fuzvolgy, Pasewalk, Przewalka, Przewloka, Pshevloka, Viso Volgy, Visovolgy
747858	Budy Wielgoleskie
747860	Vezhblyany
747864	Budy Bielanskie
747870	Buzafalva, Pocsafalva, Przybylow
747879	Bacs Folovar
747890	Butzweiler, Weisweiler

747900	Becvary, Vasvar, Vizvar
747930	Beiseforth, Bezbrudy, Pecsvarad, Przebrody, Przebrodzie, Pshebrody, Veczvarde
747936	Przewrotne
747940	Przebrodzie, Przybradz
747945	Budy Barczackie, Przeworsk, Pshevarsk, Pshevorsk
747950	Bischberg, Wiecbork
747960	Bischbrunn, Fischborn, Veszprem, Weissbrunn
747967	Veszprempinkoc, Veszpremvarsany
747970	Przyborow
747974	Przyborowice Gorne
748000	Bazalia, Bazilia, Bazylia, Bozsaly, Bushila, Busila, Pecel, Pecsely, Pysely, Vaisal, Vajszlo, Vasilau, Vasilou, Vaslui, Vaszoly, Vecsaule, Vizsoly, Wesel, Wesola, Wessely, Wisla
748100	Bazaliia, Bazalija, Bazaliya
748117	Veselaya Yevreyka
748138	Veselaya Dolina
748300	Pishelot, Pushelat, Pushlat, Vaslauti
748314	Viseul de Jos
748340	Pusalotas, Vasileutis
748356	Budiul de Campie
748360	Pyrzholteny
748368	Viseul de Mijloc
748400	Bosilec, Peczelice, Pschelautsch, Vaslouts, Vayslits, Veislitz, Vizslas, Wislica, Wislitz, Wyslica
748450	Bizeljsko, Przyleczek, Vasilishak, Vasilishki, Vasilishok, Veselicko, Wasiliszki, Wisloczek
748470	Fassoldshof
748500	Buzuluk, Paslek, Petrzalka, Przylek, Przylogi, Przyluka, Wesolka, Wiesloch, Wyczolki
748530	Veselyy Kut
748570	Vashilkova, Vasilkov, Vassilkovo, Wasilkow
748574	Vasilkovtsy, Wasylkowce
748578	Wislok Wielki
748596	Baczal Gorny
748600	Bazilian, Bazilionai, Besalma, Beshalma, Vysluni
748636	Veseli nad Moravou
748640	Bacsalmas
748650	Wesseling
748655	Budy Lancuckie
748670	Veselinovo
748700	Bohslov, Boslev, Budslav, Budslaw, Butslav, Butzlav, Podzelva, Podzelve, Pozelva, Przylubie, Veselov, Vislava, Vodslivy, Voslab, Vselyub, Wasylow, Wesolow, Wojslaw, Wsielub, Wyzlow
748740	Fajslawice, Przylbic, Pshilbitse, Voyslavitse, Vyzhlovidze, Wasilewicze, Wislowice, Wislowiec, Wojslawice, Wyzlowicze
748745	Votslavsk
748746	Vassilivtchin
748750	Pieczalowka, Vasilevichi, Vasilyevka, Vyzhlovichi
748760	Voslabeni, Voslobeni

748785	Wisla Wielki
748795	Wieselburg
748900	Boslar, Wetzlar
749000	Bazar, Bosyry, Bozsor, Buzhory, Pacir, Paezeriai, Peciora, Peizer, Petchora, Petseri, Potchera, Psare, Psary, Vaszar, Viishora, Viisoara
749300	Bezered, Pecerady, Wodzierady
749340	Vseradice
749364	Bejcgyertyanos
749370	Przeradowo
749376	Fuzerradvany
749393	Wassertrudingen
749400	Visooroszi, Wiecierza, Woczerjasche
749436	Vasarosdombo
749440	Wszerzecz
749446	Brzerzusnia
749450	Pazardzhik
749464	Vasarosmiske
749466	Vasarosnameny, Vasarosnemeny
749468	Przeradz Maly
749470	Pacierzow, Pisarzowa
749474	Vasarosbec
749480	Przerosl, Psherosl, Psherosla
749500	Wieczorki
749540	Peczurkes
749560	Bosarkany
749568	Fuzerkomlos
749570	Podjarkow, Podyarkov
749580	Vasarhely
749587	Biserica Alba
749600	Pasareni, Peisern, Pieczarna, Podsarnie, Pozhareny, Visa Orom, Visha Orom
749639	Wasserndorf
749640	Pasrinca
749660	Boszormeny
749663	Wesermunde
749700	Przerab, Przyrab, Przyrow, Psherov, Vseruby
749738	Wyczerpy Dolne
749740	Bizerewicze, Pozarevac
749750	Bessarabka, Bizherevichi
749759	Wyczerpy Gorne
749760	Pisarovina
749764	Przyrownica
749795	Wasserburg, Wasserburg am Inn
749800	Paezereliai, Vasarhely
749840	Wasserlos
749873	Bocsarlapujto
749876	Wasseralfingen
750000	Bacau, Bachoy, Backau, Bak, Baka, Baki, Baych, Bicai, Bigge, Bock, Boka, Bucha, Buchau, Buck, Bugai, Bugaj, Buk, Buki, Byk, Byki, Fiuk, Fuge, Fughiu, Pahi, Peggau, Pokoj, Puck, Pugoy, Puhoi, Vach, Vacha, Vag, Veke, Vojka, Voke, Waag, Waka
751000	Bachoyu, Bogeiu
751600	Bogojina
751700	Bogojevo, Pochayev, Wakijow
753000	Bagota, Bakta, Bikity, Bogad, Bogata, Bogate, Bogdaj, Bohata, Faget, Fokto, Fugod, Pakod, Piechoty, Piekuty, Vechta, Vigoda, Vygoda, Wickede, Wygoda
753140	Beica de Jos

753300	Bagdad, Feketeto
753314	Bogata de Jos
753344	Bogata de Sus
753400	Bektez, Bekteze, Bogdasa, Bohatice, Bohutycze, Feketic
753440	Beica de Sus
753450	Feketeszek
753496	Feketegyarmat
753500	Vacduka, Viechtach
753540	Bogat Koze
753543	Bogatkozetanya
753570	Bogoduchow, Bogodukhov
753574	Bohatkowce
753600	Bechtheim, Bogdan, Bogdany, Bogutyn, Bohutyn, Pachten, Pogodino
753630	Bogdand
753640	Bochotnica, Bogdanhaza
753645	Bagdoniske, Bogdaneasca Veche
753654	Bogdanhaza
753655	Bochotnica Koscielna
753664	Bogdanantz
753670	Piekuty Nowe
753674	Bogdanovca
753675	Bogdanovka, Bogdanowka, Bogdanuvka
753694	Bogata Muras
753735	Feketepatak
753765	Feuchtwangen
753780	Backa Topola
753800	Bagatele
753840	Vecdoles
753846	Bechtolsheim
753870	Pokitilov, Pokotilovo, Wechadlow
753875	Pokatilovka, Pokotilovka
753896	Baktaloranthaza
753930	Fekete Ardo, Feketeerdo
753947	Wachtersbach, Wechterswinkel
753970	Viktoruv, Wiktorow
753984	Bohatery Lesne
754000	Bakoca, Baksa, Bekecs, Bekes, Bekiesza, Bihac, Bogacs, Bogosza, Bogoz, Bogushe, Bogushi, Bohusze, Buhusi, Bykos, Pakosc, Pakosch, Pakosz, Paks, Pogaceaua, Pokucie, Vagas, Vechec, Vehecz, Wychodz
754300	Baksht, Bakshty, Biksad, Biksti, Bixad, Bukkosd, Pecheshtya, Pogost, Pohost
754330	Fuchsstadt, Wagstadt
754345	Pogost Zagorodskiy, Pohost Zagorodski, Pohost Zagorodzki, Pohost Zagrodski, Pohost Zahorodni, Pohost Zahorodny
754349	Pohost Zaretchna, Pohost Zarzeczny
754353	Buxtehude
754367	Pogost Novy, Pohost Novi, Pohost Nowy
754379	Baksht Borishoka
754400	Bogucice, Bogutschuetz, Wychodzc
754430	Bakszty, Bikszad, Bogzeshty, Bogzesti
754438	Buksztel
754460	Wixhausen
754478	Wegrzce Wielkie
754480	Bicaz Salaj
754490	Bachtchisarai, Bachtshisarai
754500	Vegesack
754560	Wekschni
754568	Vgocsakomlos
754600	Baksheny, Boghiceni, Bogoszyn, Pugoceni, Vekshna, Vekshne, Vekshni, Vieksniai, Weckesheim, Wegrzyn
754636	Bekesszentandras
754646	Bekessamson
754649	Bekasmegyer, Bekesmegyer
754670	Wegrzynow
754700	Bekescsaba, Bohusov, Piekoszow, Puchaczow
754735	Bukkospatak
754740	Boguschewitschi, Bohoshevitch, Bukaczowce, Bukotchovitz, Bukshevitz
754745	Bogushevsk, Bogushevskoye
754750	Bogushevichi, Boguszowka, Pakoszowka
754760	Pokrzywno
754764	Pokrzywnica, Pokshivnits, Pokshivnitsa, Pokshivnitza
754780	Vackisujfalu
754795	Boxberg
754800	Vagsellye, Waghausel
754870	Boguslav, Boguslaw, Bohuslaw, Pekoslaw
754874	Bagaslavishkis, Bagaslaviskis, Bogoslavishok
754877	Boguslawowka
754930	Vagszered
754940	Bukkzserc
755000	Buchach, Bukkhegy
755400	Vegegyhaza
755463	Bukkszenterzsebet, Bukkszentmarton
755490	Bachchysaray, Bakhchisarai, Bakhchisaray
755600	Bogicheny, Pugacheny
755700	Bocheykovo, Bugakov, Bugakow
755740	Bukachevtsy
755743	Pechikhvosty
755780	Boguchwala
755934	Backo Gradiste
756000	Bagna, Bechyne, Beckum, Begno, Bekeny, Bochnia, Bochum, Bockum, Bogen, Bokhnia, Bokiny, Bokony, Boohom, Buchen, Buchenau, Bugojno, Bukin, Fechheim, Pakon, Pchany, Pekin, Poigen, Puchiny, Vichin, Vichyne, Vohin, Vokany, Vykan, Wehen, Wohin, Wygajny
756300	Bachmut, Bakhmut, Boconad
756364	Bakonytamasi
756373	Vigantpetend
756400	Bachmac, Bachmatch, Bagienica, Biegonice, Bokinicze, Bukmuiza, Pakens, Pakuonis, Pegnitz, Puconci, Vecamuiza
756430	Pogonesti
756450	Bakonszeg, Fokinsk
756460	Pechenezhin
756463	Bakonyszentivan, Bakonyszentkiraly, Bakonyszentlaszlo, Poganyszentpeter
756467	Bakonyszombathely
756487	Bakonyoszlop
756493	Bakonygyirot
756496	Bakonycsernye
756500	Bakhmach, Bakonyjako, Behanky, Bokinichi, Pechenki,
	Pochinok, Waging
756530	Bakonykuti
756559	Bokinka Krolewska
756560	Bochingen, Bockenheim, Fechenheim, Vaihingen, Wachenheim, Weigenheim
756564	Waging am See
756566	Vaihingen an der Enz, Wachenheim an der Weinstrasse
756576	Bakonykoppany, Wachenhofen
756600	Bockenheim, Bohumin, Fechenheim, Wachenheim, Weigenheim
756643	Backi Monostor
756650	Backnang, Vygnanka, Wygnanka
756660	Bakonynana, Wachenheim an der Weinstrasse
756700	Bochanow, Bohunovo, Pacanow, Pechniew
756730	Bachnowate, Bagnovate, Bakhnovate, Bochnovata
756740	Bogoniowice, Pochembautsy, Pochumbauts, Waganowice
756743	Bekenypuszta
756750	Bickenbach, Buchenbach, Fechenbach, Vachnovka, Vakhnovka, Vichnifka, Wachnowka
756756	Wachenbuchen
756760	Pochumbeny, Wachenhofen
756765	Bakonybank
756780	Bakonybel, Pachnowola
756796	Buchenbeuren
756800	Begoml
756900	Bagamer, Vaike Maarja
757000	Bachow, Bachuv, Backov, Bakow, Beckov, Bekheve, Bichava, Bicheva, Bichov, Biechow, Biejkow, Bikhava, Bochov, Bockow, Bokov, Bokow, Bokuv, Buchowo, Bukhovo, Bukov, Bukova, Bukowa, Bychawa, Bychow, Byckov, Bykev, Bykhov, Bykjov, Bykov, Bykow, Bykuv, Pachow, Pechow, Pikov, Pochaev, Pochep, Pochepy, Pouchov, Puchov, Pukov, Pukow, Vaigeva, Vaigova, Vaiguva, Vochov, Vojkov, Vuckovo, Wojkow, Wojkowa
757100	Bichevaya
757300	Bucovat
757314	Vicovu de Jos
757344	Vicovu de Sus
757397	Backi Petrovac, Backo Petrovo Selo
757400	Backowice, Bajkowce, Bajkowitz, Bakowce, Bakowice, Bechovice, Bikivics, Bochavitz, Bojkovice, Buchowice, Bucovice, Bukavitz, Bukovec, Bukovecz, Bukowice, Bukowiec, Bykovets, Bykovice, Bykovtse, Bykovtsy, Bykowcy, Fokovci, Puchovitch, Puchowitschi, Pychowice, Vag Vecse, Voykovitse, Wieckowice, Wojkowice, Wokowice
757437	Pogwizdow, Wygwizdow

757444	Buchowszczyzna Nowa
757450	Bakavsk, Bikovsk, Bukovska, Bukowsko, Pokupsko
757456	Bakowski Mlyn, Wojkowice Komorne
757458	Bukowski Las
757470	Bogwidzowy
757500	Bikowek, Bykovka, Fachbach, Pochapka, Pukhovichi, Wachbach, Wojkowka
757590	Bakowa Gora
757596	Bakowa Gorna
757600	Bechhofen, Beckhofen, Bukovina, Bukowina
757633	Becov nad Teplou
757640	Bukovnica
757650	Bukovinka, Bukowinka
757680	Bukowa Mala, Byckov Malyj
757737	Vycapy Opatovce
757800	Bogopol, Bohopolia
757831	Vicovul de Jos
757834	Vicovul de Sus
757860	Backa Polana
757865	Backa Palanka
757870	Bukkfalva, Pokafalva
757900	Vukovar, Wukowar
757950	Buchberg, Buckeburg
757956	Puchberg am Schneeberg
757965	Fegyvernek
758000	Bihale, Bogel, Buchel, Buchloe, Picleu, Piekiely, Pikeli, Pikeliai, Puchaly, Puikule, Vag Ujhely
758300	Bocholt, Pikeliat, Vechelde
758400	Bekolce, Buchholz, Buchlicze, Pikulice, Puclice, Puklice, Puklitz, Vyklice
758430	Vaculesti
758450	Wegliska
758460	Peckelsheim, Wegleszyn
758464	Bagolasanc
758470	Waglczew
758480	Baglyasalja
758500	Bagolyuk
758600	Beclean, Peklany, Pikalin, Pikelen, Weglin
758616	Vicolenii Mari
758650	Piekielnik, Pogulianka, Pogulyanka
758700	Bachlowa, Buglov, Bugluv, Wiklow
758740	Boglewice, Peclawice, Pikulovitse, Pikulowice, Weglowice
758745	Bagailaviskis
758750	Bichlbach, Pechalovka, Vygolovichi
758753	Boglewicki Tartak
758760	Wegeleben
758780	Bagolyfalu
758900	Boglar
758947	Bakalarzewo
758970	Baklerava, Baklerove, Baklrovo
759000	Bachory, Bakar, Bihar, Biharea, Bogarja, Bogoria, Bogorja, Bogoryja, Bokor, Bychory, Pagiriai, Pakroy, Pechera, Pechora, Pecora, Pegir, Pogar, Pogir, Pohar, Pokroy, Veger, Vegeriai
759140	Pakroujas, Pakroujis, Pakruojis, Pakruojus
759300	Beograd, Vegardo, Vekerd, Wickrath, Woquard
759330	Vacratot

759345	Bihardioszeg, Bogoroditsk
759346	Bogoroditsyn, Bohorodczany, Bohorodczany Stare, Bohorodyczyn
759356	Bogorodchany, Bogorodychyn
759360	Vachartyan
759364	Bihardancshaza
759367	Bagrationovsk
759379	Biharudvary, Biharudvori
759393	Bihartorda
759400	Bachorz, Fagaras, Fagarasi, Fogaras, Pagiris, Pakrac, Pakracz, Pakruois, Pogorz, Pohorce, Pokhortse, Pokhortsy, Vcheraishe, Vcherayshe, Wegrce
759430	Bucharest, Bucuresti, Vacaresti
759445	Bihardioszeg
759457	Pogorska Wola
759459	Weickersgruben
759460	Pagorzyna, Wegorzyno, Weikersheim
759470	Wegorzewo
759476	Wegrce Panienskie
759478	Wegrzce Wielkie
759480	Pogorzela, Pogorzelle
759484	Pogorzeliski
759496	Fehergyarmat
759500	Bacharach, Vechorki
759590	Biharugra
759594	Biharkeresztes
759600	Bugryn, Bukharino, Pacureni, Pecharna, Pogoarna, Pogorna, Pohoarna, Wegrzyn
759640	Bukkaranyos, Fegernic, Pogranicze
759643	Bagrineshti, Bagrineshty, Bagrinesti
759657	Biharnagybajom
759664	Bukkormenyes
759670	Wegrzynow
759675	Bagrinovka
759700	Becherov, Beharov, Vegrov, Wegrow
759740	Bogrovice, Pogrebisce, Wagrowiec
759744	Pochrebishtche
759745	Pogrebishche, Pohorbishch
759747	Biharpuspoki
759750	Bogrowka, Wegrowka
759760	Pogrebeny, Pogribeni, Pokrzywno
759764	Pokrzywnica
759773	Wegrow Podlaski
759794	Fehervarcsurgo
759830	Pohorlauti
759840	Pogoreltsy, Pogoryltse, Pohorelice, Pohorylce
759850	Feherlak
759875	Pogorelovka, Pohorelowka
759963	Feheryarmat
760000	Bahn, Bahnea, Bain, Bajna, Ban, Bana, Banie, Banja, Banya, Bauni, Bena, Bene, Beny, Benye, Bina, Binau, Boimie, Bojmie, Bonn, Bonnya, Bun, Fiume, Fony, Fujna, Fuyna, Pama, Pana, Pann, Pany, Peine, Pinne, Poeni, Pomi, Pon, Poon, Puini, Punia, Vama, Vienna, Vinoj, Wien, Wohyn
761314	Poenii de Jos

763000	Bahmutea, Bainet, Baineti, Band, Banhida, Bonyhad, Bunde, Fonyed, Fonyod, Pand, Panet, Panyit, Vainode, Veinuta, Vijnita, Vindoi, Vonota, Vynota, Windau
763160	Bontaieni
763300	Bontida
763314	Vintu de Jos
763400	Bondyrz, Panticeu, Ponticeu, Vainodes, Vainutas
763459	Windischgarsten
763460	Vindiceni, Windesheim
763500	Benediki, Pintak, Pinticu, Piontka, Vendegi, Windeck
763560	Vendichany, Windecken
763563	Benatky nad Jizerou
763570	Bendkov, Pamiatkowo
763574	Benadikovce, Benedikovce
763580	Vandziogala, Vendziogala
763581	Fundukleyevka
763587	Fundu Galbena, Fundukleewka
763600	Bendin, Bentheim, Finthen, Pniatyn, Pnyatyn, Vainoden, Venden, Wenden
763640	Piantnica, Piontnitza
763650	Wemding
763683	Fundu Moldovei
763686	Fantanele Nasaud
763687	Fantana Alba
763700	Poniatow, Poniatowa, Vindava, Windawa
763738	Ponetow Dolny
763759	Ponetow Gorny
763784	Bantapolcsany
763800	Ponedel, Ponedeli, Ponidel, Windall
763831	Vintul de Jos
763834	Vintul de Sus
763840	Pandelis, Pandelys
763846	Wendelsheim
763864	Vintileanca
763868	Fandul Moldovei, Fundul Moldovei
763874	Pantalowice
763900	Bender, Benderi, Bendery, Bondyrz, Funduri, Panoteriai, Vanatori, Vyantory
763940	Winterhausen
763946	Vendersheim
763950	Wintrich
763954	Winterhausen
763960	Wnetrzne
763964	Vindornyaszollos
763965	Bindermichl
763967	Vindornyafok
763968	Vindornyalak
763970	Bendorf, Bondorf, Bundorf
763974	Bendorf Sayn, Bondarovca
763976	Bandrow Narodowy
763980	Vama Turului
764000	Behynce, Bieniasze, Bieniec, Boncza, Fajnica, Panaci, Panca, Panciu, Panic, Penc, Penza, Pomaz, Pomezi, Ponice, Poniec, Punitz, Vamos, Vinac, Vinica, Vinitza, Vinnitsa, Vinozh, Vojnice, Voynitch, Voynitsa, Winnica, Winnitsa, Winniza, Wojnica, Wojnicz
764300	Baneshty, Banesti, Benesat, Boinesti, Bomst, Bonczida,

	Vamosatya, Vancsod	765100	Pancoja		Piniava, Pniewo, Pniewy,
764330	Bonstadt	765300	Banhida, Pancota, Pincota		Pniow, Pnov, Pnyuv, Pompa,
764379	Vamosudvarhely, Woniacze	765374	Bania Kotowska		Vanyuv, Venev, Vinif, Vinovi,
	Dobrowola	765378	Boncodfolde		Waniewo, Waniow, Wieniawa,
764380	Wunsiedel	765397	Panicke Dravce		Wojnow
764395	Vames Odriheiu	765400	Bunkas	767160	Pompeyan
764397	Fohnsdorf, Wansdorf, Wunstorf	765430	Pungesti	767195	Banova Jaruga
764400	Banhegyes, Pamusis, Vonsosh,	765433	Pfungstadt	767340	Ponowitcz
	Wonsees	765440	Banhegyes	767360	Bonbaden
764430	Panasesti, Panasheshty, Pancesti	765446	Banokszentgyorgy	767400	Banovce, Boniowice, Fonovice,
764450	Panshishok	765450	Vanagishki, Vonchotzk,		Panevtsy, Paniowce, Panovce,
764454	Panosiskes		Wanagiszki		Panovtse, Pianowice,
764470	Paniszczow	765460	Benhausen, Bennigsen		Ponavezh, Ponevetz,
764500	Bujniczki, Fancsika, Penski,	765466	Vinksniniai, Winkshnin		Ponevezh, Poniewiez, Ponivez,
	Penskie, Penskiy, Penzig,	765546	Vanchikauts Mar		Ponyevez, Pounivez, Punaviz,
	Pieniazki, Piensk, Pinsk, Punsk,	765560	Pamhagen		Pyanovitse, Vanovitse,
	Voinescu, Winniczki, Winsko,	765574	Vanchikovtsy		Waniowice
	Winzig	765600	Benakani, Beniakon, Benyakoni,	767440	Panevezhis, Panevezys
764531	Vancicautii Mici		Bieniakonie, Bingen, Paingeni,	767460	Pombsen
764538	Panska Dolina		Pamhagen, Wangen,	767463	Banovce nad Bebravou,
764543	Banska Stiavnica, Panoskiu		Wankheim, Weinheim,		Banovce nad Ondavou
	Zydkaimis		Wenkheim	767465	Wimpassing
764559	Banatski Karlovac	765656	Wankenheim	767478	Panevezio Velzis
764570	Pienczykowo	765660	Wankenheim	767500	Banovichi, Baumbach,
764574	Banska Bystrica	765700	Pinchov, Pinchuv, Ponikwa,		Bonevichi, Pyanovichi,
764575	Pienczykowek		Vonigovo, Vonihofo,		Vanovichi, Wannbach,
764580	Pincehely, Vandziogala,		Vonihovo, Wankowa		Wohnbach
	Vendziogala	765740	Bankwitz, Benkovce, Benkovtse,	767595	Funfkirchen
764596	Banatsko Arandelovo		Bienkowce, Pankovtse,	767600	Pampenai, Pnevno, Pniewno,
764600	Bendzin, Benhausen, Bensheim,		Pankowce, Penchivca,		Pniowno, Pompian,
	Bentschen, Pieniezno,		Ponikovitsa, Ponikowica,		Pumpenai, Pumpenei,
	Vandzene, Voiniceni, Wansen,		Vankovitse, Vinkovci,		Pumpian, Wimpfen
	Wenzen, Windsheim, Wnetrzne		Vinkovitz, Vinkovtsy,	767630	Banffyhunyad
764637	Wincentow, Wincentowo		Vonkovtsy, Wankowice	767650	Pniewnik
764656	Wintzenheim, Winzenheim	765750	Penkovka, Pomiechowek,	767800	Banfalu, Pampali, Vamfalu
764658	Vamosmikola		Pomyekhovek, Vankovichi	767830	Benfeld, Bonfeld
764660	Wintzenheim, Winzenheim	765773	Bonkowo Podlesne	767840	Vonvolitz
764700	Benesov, Pancevo, Pancsova,	765783	Pinkafeld	767864	Vanvolnica, Vanvolnitsa,
	Pinchev, Pinczow, Pintchov,	765784	Banja Koviljaca		Vonvolnits, Vonvolnitza
	Pomzovye, Ponizovye, Vionzova,	765800	Baimaclia, Bengel, Penkule,	767870	Banfalva, Fenyofalva
	Vonseva		Wanne Eickel	767890	Winnweiler
764740	Bieniaszowice	765810	Baymakliya	767930	Wanfried, Wonfurt
764750	Vondsavek, Wandsbek,	765900	Phanagoria	767940	Poniewirz
	Windsbach	765930	Vingard, Vinograd, Winograd	767947	Bania Berezow, Banya Berezov,
764763	Benesov nad Ploucnici	765936	Vinogradnoye, Weingarten		Banya Berezuv, Wampierzow
764765	Binswangen	765937	Vinogradov, Vinogradovka,	767950	Bamberg, Bomberg, Vamberk,
764780	Vamosujfalu		Winogradow		Vimperk
764784	Ventspils	765950	Wangerooge	767956	Bahnbrucken
764787	Vancsfalva	765960	Wangerin, Wingrany	768000	Banila, Panyola, Vanyola
764793	Binsforth, Bohmisch Brod	765969	Weniger Maertersdorf	768347	Poenile de Sub Munte
764794	Vamospercs	765970	Vengerov, Vengrov, Vengrova,	768500	Banja Luka, Banya Luka,
764795	Bensberg, Penzberg, Pinzberg,		Vengrove		Bonya Luka
	Vandsburg, Weinsberg	765973	Banhorvat	768538	Banlaktolmecs
764800	Bumsla, Fenesel, Fensel, Finisel,	765974	Wangrowitz, Wongrowitz	768583	Poenile Glodului
	Vencsello	765976	Weingraben	768600	Pamleny
764835	Fenyeslitke	765980	Winna Chroly	768630	Bonnland
764840	Pancelcseh, Vamoslaz	766000	Banin, Bonin, Pieniany,	768700	Banilov, Voinilov, Vojnilow,
764850	Peneszlek		Weinheim		Voynilov, Wojnilow
764860	Penzlin, Wymyslin	766300	Pomoneta, Pomonieta, Vemend	768749	Banila pe Ceremus, Banila pe
764866	Wymysle Niemieckie	766400	Vima Mica		Siret
764870	Boehmisch Leipa, Bohmisch	766500	Paninka, Poninka	768784	Wohyn Lubelski
	Leipa, Wymyslow	766540	Wenings	768840	Panlelcseh
764900	Vijnicioara	766560	Pfeningen, Venningen	769000	Binarea, Paneriai, Ponary,
764940	Vamosoroszi	766600	Banunin, Panemune, Poneman,		Ponoara, Vinar, Weener,
764950	Vamosgyork		Ponemon, Ponemune		Weimar
764960	Panzareni, Pynzareny	766640	Panemunes, Panemunis	769300	Benroth
764970	Binczarowa	766650	Panemunek, Penimonik,	769358	Benrath Hilden
765000	Bajmok, Banachi, Bank, Banka,		Ponemunek, Ponemuneki	769387	Bonyretalap
	Bankau, Baunach, Finke,	766684	Panemunelis, Panemunlis	769400	Pomortsy, Vanyarc
	Panka, Panki, Panyok, Penyaki,	766795	Bonenburg	769460	Pamorzany, Pomorzany,
	Penyige, Pieniaki, Pienki,	766900	Vima Mare		Pomorzhany, Weimersheim
	Pionki, Ponik, Vajnag, Viniki,	767000	Banfe, Beniowa, Bonow, Bonuv,	769463	Weimarschmieden
	Vinniki, Vonock, Winniki		Bunov, Fenyofo, Pianow,	769479	Wanrispertz

769600	Pomarin, Pomoryany, Weinern
769643	Wiener Neustadt
769700	Banreve, Binarowa, Wojnarowa
769730	Banhorvat
769750	Bonarowka
770000	Baba, Pap, Papa, Pava, Vevia
771000	Veviya
771865	Popiyelniki
771900	Babi Yar
773000	Babdiu, Babot, Babta, Babtai, Bobota, Bobt, Bobty, Papauti, Pobeda, Popiuti, Povitye
773400	Pavdocz, Voevodeasa
773490	Papateszer
773500	Babadag
773600	Bobiatyn, Bobyatyn, Pobitno
773700	Povyatov, Powiatow
774000	Babcza, Babcze, Babdiu, Babice, Babocsa, Bibice, Fuves, Pabazi, Papoc, Papos, Paupis, Popeasca, Popvtse, Powicie, Vievis, Voivozi, Wieprz, Wiewiec, Wujwicze, Wywoz
774300	Babesti, Bobeshti, Bobesti
774316	Popestii Noui
774330	Babstadt, Waibstadt
774331	Popesti de Jos
774334	Popeshti de Sus, Popesti de Sus
774360	Popeshti Nouy
774430	Babasesti
774450	Pobiedziska
774460	Wabrzezno
774470	Wawrzyszow
774500	Popiszki, Vypyski, Wieprzki, Wypiski
774540	Pabaiskas
774574	Povazska Bystrica
774600	Biebesheim, Boffzen, Pivasiunai, Pobuzhany
774640	Bobrzyniec
774650	Powsinek
774670	Wawrzynow
774700	Pawezow
774740	Pobezovice
775000	Babche, Babiak, Babiche, Babichy, Piwaki, Pobuk, Pojbuky, Povcha, Vuyvichi, Wiowka, Wypychy
775400	Papkeszi
775496	Befegsurany
775600	Vivikoni
775700	Babicheva, Babichova, Babuchow
775740	Popkowice
775860	Babahalma, Bobohalma
775900	Pobikra, Pobikry
776000	Babeni, Babin, Babony, Bobbin, Paupine, Paupyne, Pepeni, Pepeny, Wapienne, Wapienno, Wopienno
776360	Bovenden
776397	Papendorf
776400	Babince, Babintse, Babintsy, Fabianhaza, Pabenits, Pabianice, Pabjanice, Pabnitz, Pabyanets, Pabyanitse, Pivnica, Piwonice, Wapienica
776430	Babimost
776457	Popinska Wolka
776460	Babenhausen, Bobenhausen, Bobenhausen Zwei, Pfaffenhausen, Pfeffenhausen, Pivnishna, Piwniczna, Vevinceni
776474	Fabiansebestyen

776500	Babanka, Babynka, Bobinka, Fabianki, Fabjanki
776540	Fabianhaza
776546	Babenhausen, Bobenhausen, Bobenhausen Zwei, Pfaffenhausen, Pfeffenhausen
776560	Bobenheim, Bopfingen, Pappenheim
776566	Bobenheim am Berg
776576	Pfaffenhofen, Pfaffenhofen an der Ilm
776593	Babina Greda
776600	Bobenheim, Pappenheim
776649	Babonymegyer
776660	Bobenheim am Berg
776700	Vejvanov
776740	Babinowicze
776750	Babinovichi
776760	Pfaffenhofen, Pfaffenhofen an der Ilm
776785	Bobino Wielkie
776795	Papenburg
776797	Pfaffen Beerfurth
776879	Poppenlauer
776940	Vapniarca
776950	Vapnyarka
777000	Bobov, Bobova, Bobowa, Bobowo, Popowa, Popowo
777300	Popoviti
777400	Bobovtsy, Popovaca, Popovitse, Popovtse, Popovtsy, Popovtzi, Popowce, Popowcy, Popowice, Wapowce
777500	Popovichi, Popovka
777548	Popowo Koscielne
777600	Bobovna, Bobovnya
778000	Babule, Bobly, Byblo, Papile, Popele, Popiele
778340	Bobletici
778350	Bobletichi
778400	Biblis, Papilis, Papilys, Pavalitch, Pawolotsch
778430	Bobuleshty, Bobulesti, Pavilosta
778439	Bubel Stary
778450	Pawliczka
778459	Wiebelskirchen
778470	Pawlosiow
778479	Babelsberg
778500	Paplaka, Pavoloch, Povoloch
778560	Pawlokoma, Popelken
778593	Pavlograd, Pawlograd
778600	Babolna, Bobalna, Paplin, Piplin, Popelnya, Popilan, Popilyan
778640	Bivolu Mic, Bobulince, Vavolnitsa, Wawolnica
778645	Wypalenisko
778650	Popielnik, Popielniki, Vabalnik, Vobolnik, Wobolniki
778656	Waiblingen
778657	Wevelinghoven
778665	Vabalninkas
778680	Pewel Mala
778690	Bivolu Mare
778700	Papfalva, Pavlov, Pavlova, Pavlovo, Pavylova, Pawlow, Pawlowo, Poblow, Pobolov, Pobolovo, Pobolow, Poplawy
778740	Pavlovce, Pawlowice, Poplawce
778743	Pawlow Stary
778745	Pavlovsk, Pawlowsk, Pawlowska Wola
778746	Pavlovce nad Uhom
778750	Pavlovka, Pawlowka

778767	Pawlow Nowy
778785	Pewel Wielka
778800	Bublelai, Bubleliai
778857	Bubel Lukowisko
778900	Bivolari
779000	Bebra, Bibra, Bober, Bobr, Bobri, Bobry, Popper, Veiveriai, Vepriai, Vyver, Wawer, Wieprz
779300	Bobroidy, Bobroydy, Boppard, Pabrade, Poprad, Vejprty
779380	Wuppertal
779387	Wuppertal Barmen
779388	Wuppertal Elberfeld
779400	Babarc, Paberze, Pabirze, Pebirzih, Pobereze, Poberezhe, Poberezhye, Poproc, Viforoasa
779440	Bobryszce, Pohybryszcze
779450	Bobroisk, Bobruisk, Bobrujsk, Bobruysk, Paversk, Povorsk, Povursk, Poworsk
779460	Poberezany, Poburzany, Poperczyn, Veivirzenai, Vevirzenai, Vevirzhon, Vievirzenai, Wabrzezno
779465	Powroznik
779470	Wawrzyszow
779500	Biberach, Bibergau, Biebrich, Boberka, Bobrek, Bobrik, Bobrka, Boiberik, Boyberik, Vaverka, Vohburg, Vyborg, Wawiorka, Wieprzki, Wiewiorka
779530	Bobrokut
779559	Bobrek Karf
779563	Biberach an der Riss, Vohburg an der Donau
779568	Paproc Mala
779569	Biebrich am Rhein
779579	Bobrik Pervyy
779600	Bebrene, Wawern
779640	Bobrinets, Bobrinitz, Bobrynetz, Bobrzyniec
779645	Bobrinskaia
779656	Beverungen
779670	Wawrzynow
779675	Vibranovka, Vybranovka, Wybranowka
779700	Bavorov, Baworow, Bobrowe, Vaprova, Vyprovo, Wiewiorow
779713	Bobrovy Jut
779740	Bavorovice, Bobrovica, Bobrovitsa, Bobrovitsy, Bobrovitza, Bobrowicze, Pabierowice
779750	Bobrovichi, Bobrowka
779753	Bobrovy Kut, Bobrovyy Kut
779765	Bobrovnik, Bobrowniki, Bobrowniki Wielkie
779800	Povrly
780000	Bala, Bel, Bela, Beliu, Beluj, Bely, Biala, Biel, Bila, Blaj, Boehl, Bohl, Bol, Bolho, Boly, Bolya, Buhl, Byala, Filea, Filia, Fule, Paleu, Pely, Pila, Pillau, Pily, Plau, Plaue, Pohle, Pojlo, Pola, Polya, Pula, Val, Valea, Vallaj, Valley, Valy, Vohl, Vola, Volia, Volo, Waal, Wallau, Waly, Wehlau, Weil, Wilja,

	Wohlau, Wola
781000	Belaya, Viliya
781430	Bulayeshty
781437	Wola Justowska
781464	Wola Jasienicka
781495	Belaia Tserkov, Belaya Tserkov
781570	Wola Jachowa, Wola Jackowa
781574	Wola Jajkowska
781577	Wola Jakubowa
781596	Belaya Krinitsa
781613	Blajenii de Jos, Blajenii de Sus
781678	Vilijampole
781700	Belejow, Beleyev
781750	Belaya Vaka, Falejowka
781800	Blajel
781854	Plaiul Cosmin, Plaiul Cosminului
783000	Balajt, Balta, Balti, Balut, Baluti, Baluty, Belauti, Belda, Beled, Belut, Bladiau, Bled, Bolda, Feled, Flatau, Fulda, Palad, Palade, Paladia, Palota, Pilda, Valdai, Velete, Vlotho, Voluta, Woluta
783100	Paladiya
783175	Baltoja Voke, Baltoji Voke
783400	Bielatycze, Boletice, Falatycze, Feldesz, Foldes, Palatca, Palotas, Plotycz, Polatycze, Veldes, Veletice, Voletice
783430	Foltesti
783437	Bledostowo
783446	Wildeshausen
783450	Baltiysk, Paldiski, Poltosk, Pultosk, Pultusk
783451	Baltiiskii Port
783460	Falticeni, Palticeni, Veldhausen, Vladicina, Vladicini, Waldhausen
783479	Baltisch Port
783484	Vladislauca
783487	Vladislavov, Vladislavov Rusochitza, Vlodislovov, Wladyslawow, Wladyslawowo
783500	Beltiug, Bildugi, Bildyugi, Bildziugi, Bildziuki, Boldog, Foldeak, Plotych, Valtaiki, Volduchy, Waldegg, Wieladki
783534	Beltekhodos
783545	Wola Duchacka
783546	Boldogasszony, Veldhausen, Waldhausen
783560	Vladychen, Waldheim
783575	Vladikavkaz
783578	Boldogkoujfalu
783579	Boldogkovaralja
783594	Wielatki Rosochate
783595	Feldkirch, Waldkirch
783597	Waldgrehweiler
783600	Balatina, Balaton, Baldone, Beldno, Blatna, Blodno, Blotnia, Blotnya, Bluden, Bludna, Bolotino, Bolotnya, Flieden, Pil Ten, Pilten, Piltene, Polten, Valiatin, Velatin, Velden, Velyatin, Voletiny, Volodeni, Waldheim
783614	Bialy Dunajec
783635	Wola Domatkowska
783637	Balatonudvari
783640	Beltinci, Bludenz, Feledince, Paltinoasa, Plotnica, Plotnice, Plotnitsa, Plotnitse, Plotnitza, Plotniza, Veldenz

783644	Balatoncsicso
783646	Balatonszemes, Balatonszentgyorgy, Balatonzamardi
783647	Balatonszabadi
783649	Balatonmagyarod, Balatonszarszo
783650	Bludniki, Vladnik, Weledniki
783656	Balatonkenese, Baldingen, Feldmoching, Fladungen
783658	Balatonakali, Balatonkiliti
783659	Balatonkeresztur
783660	Blutenam
783663	Balatonendred
783665	Waldmunchen
783670	Baltinava, Baltinova, Baltinove
783674	Balatonbozsok, Baltinavas
783675	Balatonboglar, Balatonfokajar
783679	Balatonbereny, Balatonfured, Baldenburg, Plettenberg, Waldenburg, Woldenberg, Woldenburg
783680	Balatonujhely, Waldniel
783685	Balatonujlak
783686	Balatonalmadi
783688	Balatonlelle
783690	Vladimir, Waldmohr
783694	Balatonaracs, Vladimirci, Vladimirets, Vlodimiretz, Wladimirez
783697	Blatne Revistia, Valdemarpils, Vladimir Volinski, Vladimir Volynskiy, Vladimirovo
783700	Baltow, Beldow, Bledov, Bledow, Bledowa, Bludov, Bludow, Boldva, Flatow, Peltev, Politow, Poltava, Poltawa, Poltew, Vladava, Vlodava, Vlodavi, Vlodeve, Vlodova, Wlodawa, Wlodowa, Wylatowo
783730	Wildbad
783736	Wildbad im Schwarzwald
783740	Plahteevca, Waldvisse, Wlodowice
783745	Palotabozsok
783747	Waldfischbach
783750	Baltowka, Feldbach, Vladovka, Vlodavka, Vlodofka, Wlodawka
783751	Plitvicka Jezera
783760	Wilatowen
783765	Feldafing, Waldwinkel
783780	Feldoboly
783785	Palad Veliky
783790	Feldebro, Foldvar
783793	Waldbreitbach
783795	Waldberg
783800	Platel, Plateliai, Plotel
783830	Biala Dlita
783858	Wola Dolholucka
783865	Plattling
783870	Palotailva
783880	Wola Dolholucka
783900	Feldru, Foldra, Platere
783936	Wola Trzydnicka
783940	Veltrusy, Wielodroz
783943	Bliedersdorf, Boldureshti, Boldureshty, Bolduresti
783944	Waltershausen
783945	Volodarsk, Volodarsk Volynsk, Volodarsk Volynskiy, Volodarsko Tolstovski, Volodarskoye
783946	Wola Dereznianska

783947	Waltersbruck, Wlodzierzow
783950	Volodarka
783956	Valea Draganului
783960	Valea Ternei, Walldurn
783963	Palterndorf
783964	Pleternica
783966	Baltrimontz, Bultrimantz
783970	Veltruby, Waldorf, Walldorf, Waltrop, Weildorf, Weltrub
783974	Wola Trebska
783976	Walldorf an der Werra
784000	Balc, Balice, Balsa, Beelitz, Belauts, Belice, Belisce, Belitsa, Belitza, Beltsy, Beltz, Belus, Belusa, Belz, Belza, Belzy, Bielce, Bielcza, Bielica, Bielice, Bielitz, Bilca, Bilcze, Bileca, Bilicz, Bilitz, Bilitza, Bladiau, Bulz, Bylice, Bylitse, Falcio, Falciu, Feleac, Fels, Floss, Folusz, Folyas, Paladia, Palhaza, Palocse, Palocz, Pelcza, Peles, Pfalz, Pilcza, Pilica, Pilis, Pilitsa, Pilitz, Pilts, Piltz, Plass, Plasy, Platz, Plaza, Plec, Plesca, Pless, Plisa, Plissa, Plosca, Plusy, Plyussy, Polazie, Police, Politse, Politsy, Polusze, Pulice, Pullitz, Valtcha, Veles, Velizh, Vielizh, Vilaucea, Vilce, Vilice, Vilitsa, Volcsej, Volec, Volitsa, Volos, Volytsya, Walcz, Welecz, Wels, Wieliz, Wilcza, Wilica, Wolcze, Wolica, Wolodz, Wolosza, Wolsau
784131	Plaesii de Jos
784134	Plaesii de Sus
784135	Bolshoi Tokmak
784139	Bolshaya Turya
784140	Felsojozsa
784143	Bolshaya Seidemenukha, Bolshiye Sittsy, Bolshoy Stydin
784145	Bolshiye Zhukhovichi
784146	Bolshiye Asnashany, Bolshoya Znamenka
784147	Bolshoye Osovo
784148	Bolshoy Zhelutsk
784164	Felsojanosfa
784170	Blizejov
784178	Bolshaya Belina
784179	Bolshaya Berestovit, Bolshaya Berestovitsa, Bolshaya Verbcha
784185	Bolschaja Aleksandrovka, Bolshiye Luki, Bolshoya Aleksandrovka
784186	Bolshaya Lenina
784187	Bolshoi Lepeticha
784196	Bolshaya Romanowka
784198	Bolshiye Orly
784300	Bulaesti, Faleshti, Faleshty, Falesti, Felcsut, Filesti, Fulesd, Ploesti, Velezd, Waldshut, Wolosate
784330	Billstedt, Bollstadt, Willstatt
784336	Fliesteden
784339	Felsotatarlaka
784340	Polesie Duze, Wolczatycze
784350	Belostok, Bialistok, Bialostok, Bialystok

784354	Felsotokes
784357	Volostkov, Volostkuv, Wola Zdakowska
784360	Blesteni, Felshtin, Felshtyn, Felsztein, Felsztin, Felsztyn, Vildstejn, Wollstein, Wolsztyn
784364	Bleshtenautsy, Wola Trzydnicka
784370	Wolostow
784374	Felsodabas, Felsodobos, Felsodobsza, Wola Zydowska
784383	Felsotold
784385	Balazstelke
784386	Wolcza Dolna
784394	Bolestraszyce
784395	Felsodorgicse, Felsotarkany
784396	Boloshodyormot, Felsoderna
784397	Floisdorf, Volitsa Derevlyanska, Walsdorf
784400	Belzec, Belzhets, Belzhetz, Belzhits, Belzhitse, Belzhitza, Belzyce, Bildzhuis, Blazice, Falecice, Paluszyce, Pelczyce, Pelsucz, Pilczyca, Valea Seaca, Velcice, Veldzizh, Velsecz, Velsicz, Velzis, Velzys, Weldziz, Wilczyca, Woloszcza, Wolozyce
784410	Felsosajo
784440	Felsocece, Felsoszocs, Felsoszucs
784446	Woloszczyzna
784447	Wolczyszczowice
784450	Felso Szuha, Felsoszek, Felsoszuha, Pelczyska, Polrzeczki, Volotchisk, Wilczyska, Wola Zycka, Woloczysk
784454	Felsoiszkaz, Felsosegesd
784458	Wola Szczygielkowa
784460	Blizocin, Pleszczany, Plociczno, Policzyzna, Waldsassen
784463	Felsoszentmarton
784464	Pleshtchenitz, Wola Zycinska
784466	Felsoszemenye
784467	Felsoszinever
784470	Placiszewo, Ploszczewo, Vloshtchovi, Wloszczowa
784473	Blyszczywody, Felsoszovat, Polazie Swietochowskie
784474	Wloszczowice
784476	Wulzeshofen
784478	Felsosofalu
784479	Felsoszopor, Pulazie Swierze
784480	Felso Szeli, Felsoszeli
784483	Bilcze Zlote, Felsoszelt
784484	Felso Szelistye, Felsoszelistye, Felsozsolca
784496	Balashadzharmat, Balassagyarmat, Boloshodyormot
784500	Belecke, Belecko, Belecska, Belsk, Belzig, Bielsk, Bielsko, Bildyugi, Bildzhugi, Bildziugi, Bildziuki, Bilsk, Bilsko, Blashka, Blaszki, Blazek, Blazki, Bolcske, Byelsk, Byelsko, Felgyogy, Pilsach, Plaska, Pliski, Ploska, Ploskie, Plotsk, Plotzk, Polatzk, Poleski, Polessk, Policka, Policko, Poloske, Polotsk, Velichka, Vilietchka, Vilseck, Voloshcha, Voltchkii, Wieliczka, Wilczki, Wola Cicha, Woloska
784510	Polesskoye
784517	Belskaya Volya
784530	Felsogod
784535	Falusugatag, Felsohidegpatak
784540	Bildzhugis
784543	Blieskastel
784545	Wola Szkucka
784546	Voloshchizna
784547	Wola Suchozebrska
784550	Felsogagy
784553	Felsohahot
784558	Ploskie Glowne, Valasske Klobouky, Valesske Klobouky
784560	Pleshchany, Ploskin, Poleshchina, Woloskin
784564	Pleshchenitsy, Valasske Mezirici, Volitsa Gnizdychuvsk
784567	Bleshchanovka
784570	Blaszkowa, Blazkowa, Bolshakovo, Placzkow, Pliskov, Ploshchevo, Poloskefo, Wola Sekowa
784573	Bielsk Podlaski, Bielsko Podlaskie, Blyshchyvody, Byelsk Podlaski
784574	Bliskowice, Pilaszkowice, Plaskowice, Volchkovtsy, Wilczkowice, Wola Idzikowska, Wolczkowce, Woloska Wies
784575	Plyushchevka
784577	Volchkov Perevoz
784578	Bielska Wola, Bielsko Biala, Byelsko Biala
784580	Felsogalla
784584	Felsokalocsa, Felsokelecseny
784586	Felsokalinfalva, Wola Cieklinska
784587	Wola Zglobienska
784593	Valea Scurta
784595	Felsoegregy
784597	Ploskirow
784600	Balaceana, Balceana, Baluczyn, Belezna, Bieliczna, Bilczyn, Biliceni, Blatzheim, Blesen, Blizhin, Blizin, Blizna, Blizne, Blizyn, Blotzheim, Blsany, Bolesiny, Felczyn, Flotzheim, Pelczyn, Pilsen, Pilzne, Pilzno, Pleschen, Pleseni, Plesheny, Plesna, Plzen, Poloczany, Poltsamaa, Polzin, Velesin, Vilshana, Vlasim, Volozhin, Volozhyn, Voltchin, Walsum, Welzheim, Wieliczna, Wilczyn, Wiloczan, Wlosan, Wolczyn, Wolczyny, Wolozyn, Wylezin, Wyludzin
784618	Volcineyi Lapusna
784630	Pilisszanto
784634	Wola Sniatycka
784635	Volcineti Hotin
784636	Police nad Metuji
784637	Pilisszentivan
784638	Felizienthal
784639	Blasendorf
784640	Palczynce, Palesnica, Paltchintz, Plesnice, Plosnica, Vlasenica
784643	Balasineshty, Balasinesti, Polczyn Zdroj, Vlasinesti
784644	Felsomezos
784645	Wola Siennicka, Wolczansk
784648	Felsomislye, Felsomocsolad
784650	Blizianka, Bloshniki, Bloszniki, Felsonyek, Volosyanka, Wilczanka, Wolosianka
784654	Balozsameggyes
784656	Polsingen
784657	Wola Zamkowa, Wolosianka Wielka
784660	Felsonana, Palsmane
784664	Felsomindszent, Felsomonoster
784670	Bolozhinov, Bolozynow, Felicjanow
784675	Fels am Wagram
784676	Felicjanow Nowy
784679	Flossenburg, Wola Zambrowska
784680	Plaucza Mala
784690	Felsomera, Wilcze Nory
784693	Felsonyarad, Felsonyarto, Pilismarot
784694	Felsomarosujvar, Vlodzhimyerzets, Vlodzimyerz, Wlodzimierz Wolynski, Wlodzimierzec, Wlodzimierzow
784700	Bialaczow, Bialatchov, Bialoczev, Bialyszewo, Bilczow, Blazev, Blazhova, Blazov, Blazow, Blazowa, Bledzew, Blezhovo, Blezowo, Blizow, Bolizuby, Bolszow, Faliszew, Faliszow, Piliscsaba, Plashuv, Plaszow, Plazow, Pleszew, Pleszow, Pulaczow, Valcov, Vielishev, Volosov, Volosuv, Waliszew, Wieliszew, Wolosow, Woluszewo
784730	Felsopaty
784734	Felsovadasz
784735	Balicze Podgorne, Felso Batka
784736	Felsopeteny
784739	Balicze Podrozne
784740	Belasovice, Belsbocs, Belsobocs, Bielszowice, Bolsewits, Bolsewitz, Bolshevetz, Bolshovtse, Bolshovtsy, Bolshovtzi, Bolszowce, Felshevisho, Felso Apsa, Felsoapsa, Plesivec, Plesovec, Polusciewicze, Vlasovtse, Vlceves, Wlasowce
784743	Felsobisztra, Felsobisztre
784746	Felsovizniecze, Felsoviznieczee
784747	Wilczy Przewoz
784750	Faliszowka, Palashevka, Polustseviche, Volosuvka, Wolosowka
784755	Felsopahok
784759	Blozew Gorna
784760	Felsoban, Felsobanya, Paulshafen, Vilshofen, Volsvin, Wolswin
784764	Felsopenc
784779	Vilsbiburg
784780	Bielitz Biala, Byelits Biala, Wilcza Wola, Wilczopole
784785	Plaucza Wielka
784787	Balazsfalva, Plazow Lubelski
784790	Felszopor
784793	Felsovaradja
784794	Felsoberecki, Felsovaradja, Pilisborosjeno, Pilisvorosvar, Wola Zabierzowska
784795	Felsberg, Felsoberekszo, Phalsburg
784796	Felsoabrany
784797	Wilczy Przewoz
784800	Pelesalja, Pelesul, Polzela
784836	Falu Szlatina
784840	Faluzsolcza

784843	Bolshały Seidemenukha
784845	Wola Solecka, Wola Zaleska
784847	Felsoilosva
784857	Wola Zelechowska, Wola Zelichowska
784867	Wola Czolnowska
784870	Belyye Oslavy, Boleslav, Boleslaw, Boleslev
784874	Boleslawiec, Felsolapos, Wloslawitz
784875	Vlatzlavek, Vlotslavek
784900	Balauseri, Belozera, Belozerye, Bilazor
784930	Walsrode
784940	Felsoors, Veldzirsh, Weldzirz
784944	Wola Zarczycka, Wola Zarczyska
784947	Wlodzierzow
784950	Belozerka, Bialozorka, Bieloserka, Bielozierka, Bielozorka, Felsoireg, Felsorajk
784954	Felsoregec
784955	Bielozerka Hagdolah
784957	Bela Cerkva, Biala Cerkiew, Biala Tserkov, Bieloserka Bolshoi, Bila Cirkev, Wola Zyrakowska
784960	Felsorona
784963	Felsoremete, Palosremete
784965	Felsoronok
784970	Felsorepa
784974	Felsorevisce, Felsoreviscse
784976	Felsohrabonicza, Felsoribnycze
785000	Balchi, Balichi, Balki, Balog, Beloky, Bialka, Bilak, Bilche, Bileag, Bilichi, Bilka, Bilke, Bilki, Bilky, Bleich, Blochy, Bolho, Bolyk, Bolyok, Felk, Felka, Fulek, Plock, Ploki, Polaga, Polaky, Polch, Polock, Pulkau, Pullach, Valga, Valk, Valka, Valki, Valko, Valuyki, Velka, Velki, Vilag, Vilaka, Vilaki, Vileika, Vileyka, Viliaki, Vilki, Villach, Vilok, Vilyaka, Vlaha, Volche, Volchi, Volka, Voloka, Volokhi, Vulka, Vylok, Walk, Walki, Welka, Wielgie, Wilejka, Wilga, Wlochy, Wloki, Wolka, Wolki, Wolochy, Wulka
785100	Palikije, Vaikaja, Vilkija
785138	Wolka Jedlanska
785145	Velikiye Zagaytsy
785146	Velikaya Osnitsa
785147	Velikiy Zhvanchik
785148	Velikoye Selo
785153	Velikaya Khodachka
785155	Velikiy Kochurov
785158	Velikaya Glusha, Velikiye Glibovichi
785159	Velikaya Gorozhanka, Velikiye Chornokontsy, Velikiye Korchitsy
785164	Velikiye Mosty
785174	Velikiy Bychkov
785179	Velikaya Berestovit, Velikaya Berestovitsa, Velikaya Berezovitsa, Velikiy Bereznyy, Velikiye Berezhtsy, Velikiye Borki
785185	Velikiye Luki
785187	Velikiy Lyuben
785300	Balcauti, Bologd, Flacht, Velka Ida
785313	Balcautii de Jos

785314	Valcau de Jos
785317	Plakhteyevka
785345	Velky Dioseg, Velky Diosek
785350	Volchatyche
785357	Wola Kotkowska
785360	Biala Katan
785364	Wolka Domaszewska
785367	Wolka Tanewska
785370	Belchatov, Belchatow, Belkhatov
785375	Belchatowek
785380	Biala Gadol
785384	Wolka Dulecka
785386	Bialki Dolne
785395	Velke Trakany, Velky Tarkan, Wielkie Drogi
785397	Wolica Derewianska
785400	Balkautsy, Belcus, Belochitz, Belogusha, Bialohusza, Bilghez, Blihusz, Fulehaz, Palhaza, Vilagos, Vilakas, Vilkatch, Vlkys, Wielkie Oczy
785430	Wolgast
785434	Balkauts de Zhos
785439	Felixdorf, Pillichsdorf
785440	Ploksciai
785443	Vola Kshishtoporska, Wola Krzysztoporska, Wolka Szczytynska
785445	Baliche Zazhechne, Velky Dioseg, Velky Diosek, Wola Okrzejska
785450	Volochisk
785453	Wolka Skotnicka
785457	Volchishchovitsa, Wolka Cycowska
785458	Wolka Sokolowska
785460	Blexen
785464	Valaksincz, Wallachisch Meseritsch
785474	Falkusovce, Vlkosovice, Wilkoszewice, Wola Krzywiecka
785480	Velke Selo, Wielkie Siolo
785483	Bilche Zolotoye
785484	Velike Zaluzie, Velke Zaluzie, Wolka Zaleska
785485	Bilka Shlyakhetska, Bilka Szlachecka, Velikoselka
785487	Valegotsulovo, Valehotzulovo, Volegotsulovo, Walegozulowo
785494	Velky Saris
785500	Volkach
785536	Wolka Katna
785543	Velke Kostolany
785545	Wolka Krzykowska
785549	Wolka Goscieradowska
785556	Velika Kikinda
785564	Wolka Kanska
785567	Wolka Konopna
785569	Wolica Komarowa
785574	Velke Kapusany, Wolka Okopska
785576	Velika Kopanica, Velke Kopany
785583	Velika Kladusa
785584	Wolka Klucka
785593	Veliki Grdevac, Veliko Gradiste, Volgograd
785594	Velika Gorica, Velky Gyres, Velky Hores, Vulka Ugruska, Wolka Gruszczynska, Wolka Horyszowska, Wolka Ogryzkowa
785595	Wolka Krzykowska

785596	Bialki Gorne, Wolka Horyniecka
785597	Wielgie Grabowce, Wolka Karwicka
785598	Bilka Krolewska, Bilka Krulevska
785600	Balkany, Balkunai, Balkuny, Baluchin, Bialogon, Billigheim, Bolchany, Falkenau, Fellheim, Pelkinie, Poligon, Polochany, Pulgany, Pulhany, Velkenye, Vilkene, Villigen, Vlcany, Vlkyna, Volchin, Volkany, Vulcan, Weilheim
785617	Wola Chomejowa
785637	Blh nad Iplom
785639	Pholegandros, Velky Mader, Velky Meder, Wolka Medrzechowska
785640	Falkensee, Palchintsy, Pohl Gons, Vlkonice, Volchinets
785643	Falkenstein, Velikie Mosty, Vulcanesti, Vulkaneshty, Wolica Hnizdyczowska
785644	Vlkancice
785645	Volchansk, Wolka Medrzechowska
785647	Vulka Mazovetska, Vulka Mazovetskaya, Wulka Mazowiecka
785649	Pullach im Isartal, Velke Mezirici
785650	Volknik
785656	Bolkenhain, Flehingen
785657	Wola Kanigowska
785660	Belyy Kamen, Bialikomin, Bialy Kamien, Bialykamien, Bilkamin, Bolkenhain
785661	Bolganymajor
785664	Volya Gnoynitska, Wola Gnojnicka
785665	Valkininkas
785670	Poligonowo, Walichnowy
785676	Falknov nad Ohri
785679	Falkenberg, Falkenburg
785680	Plaucha Male, Wloki Male
785684	Wolka Nieliska
785685	Wolka Malkowa
785686	Wielgomlyny Poduchowne
785690	Valkemir, Vil Komir, Vilkamir, Vilkomir, Wilkomir
785694	Vilkomierz, Volkmarsen, Volkmerz, Wilkomierz
785695	Vilkmerge
785700	Bilichov, Bolechov, Bolechow, Bolekhov, Bolkhov, Bolkow, Bolochow, Bolokhuv, Bulkovo, Bulkowo, Filakovo, Pilchow, Pilichow, Pluchow, Plugov, Pluguv, Pluhow, Vilkovo, Vlachovo, Volchowo, Volkhov, Volkov, Volkovyye, Volkuv, Wielichow, Wielichowo, Wilkowa, Wolchowo, Wolkow, Wolkowyja, Wolkowyje
785734	Velka Bytca
785735	Wolka Petkowska
785736	Velky Fedimes, Velky Fedymes, Wolka Putnowicka, Wolka Putnowiecka
785739	Baliche Podruzhne, Voloca pe

	Derelui, Wolka Batorska, Wolka Petrylowska
785740	Bolkovce, Vilhovitz, Vilkhovits, Vilkovtsy, Volchovec, Volkovtse, Volkovtsy, Vulchovce, Vulkhovtse, Wielka Wies, Wilkowice, Wolkowce
785743	Velky Bysterec, Volkhovstroy
785744	Wolka Wojcieszkowska
785745	Blagovshchina, Polkow Sagaly, Vilkaviskis, Vilkaviskis, Vilkovishk, Vilkovishki, Vilkovisk, Volkavisk, Volkovisk, Volkovyshki, Volkovysk, Wilkowiecko, Wilkowisko, Wilkowyszki, Wloki Piaski, Wolka Biska, Wolka Bodzechowska, Wolka Przekory, Wolkowysk, Wolkowysko, Wylkowyszki
785746	Velka Ves nad Iplom
785750	Belchowka, Pligavki, Plihawki, Velichovky
785753	Wolica Wygoda
785757	Veliky Bockov
785759	Blagoevgrad, Veliki Beckerek
785760	Wolkowiany
785764	Blachownia Slaska, Volkovintsy, Wolkowinz, Wolkowinzy
785766	Wolka Panienska
785767	Volkovonovke, Wolka Wojnowska
785768	Poluchow Maly, Polukhuv Maly
785776	Vulka Popinskaya
785780	Wielka Wola
785783	Wolka Baltowska
785785	Plaucha Velka, Wolka Pelkinska
785786	Velka Polana, Wolka Bielinska
785794	Bolechow Ruski, Veliki Berezny, Velke Berezne, Velky Berezny, Wolka Proszewska
785795	Wolka Przekory
785797	Velka Pri Poprade
785810	Balakleya, Balakliya
785830	Volkolata, Wolkolata
785831	Valcaul de Jos
785836	Velke Ludince
785837	Wolka Letowska
785840	Velka Luc, Wielka Hlusza, Wilkolaz
785844	Wolka Leszczanska
785845	Wielgolaskie Budki, Wola Kaluska
785847	Wilkolaz Poduchowny
785850	Velikye Luki, Weliki Luki
785857	Wolica Lugowa, Wolka Lukowska
785860	Pillkallen, Velke Ulany
785864	Velka Lomnica, Volkolamsk, Wilhelmsburg, Wilhelmshaven
785865	Valcaul Ungureasca, Wolka Lancuchowska
785867	Wielkie Lunawy, Wilhelmow, Wilhelmpieckstadt Guben
785870	Balaklava
785874	Wola Gulowska
785875	Wloclawek
785876	Wallhalben, Wolka Labunska
785878	Wolka Lubielska
785879	Velke Levare
785900	Belogorye, Biala Gora, Bilgoraj, Bilgoray, Polgar
785930	Baligrod, Belgard, Belgorod, Belgrad, Belgrade, Beligrod, Bialogard, Bleicherode,

	Bolgrad, Polgardi
785933	Belgorod Dnestrovski, Belgorod Dnestrovskii, Belgorod Dnestrovskiy
785934	Velhartice
785935	Belgorodka, Belogorodka, Bielogorodka, Bilhorodki, Byelogorodka
785936	Wola Korytnicka
785940	Belokorets, Fulokercs, Wielgorz
785943	Pilgersdorf, Wola Krzysztoporska
785944	Bialokorzec, Bilohorszcze, Volkershausen
785945	Balkerishki, Belogorsk, Bilogorshche, Wola Korycka, Wola Okrzejska, Wolka Uhruska
785946	Wola Gorzanska, Wola Korzeniecka, Wolka Radzyminska
785947	Wola Karczewska
785948	Valea Grosilor, Volkersleier
785950	Belegregy
785956	Vilich Rheindorf
785957	Bela Crkva, Biala Krakowska, Byala Cherkova
785960	Bialogorne, Pilgram, Vilich Rheindorf
785964	Belokrinitsa, Bialokrynica, Wilhermsdorf
785967	Pelhrimov
785969	Voelkermarkt, Volkermarkt
785973	Wola Korybutowa
785974	Bilokorovitch, Wola Greboszowska, Wola Krzywiecka
785975	Belokorovichi
785976	Velke Ripnany, Velke Rypnany
785983	Velcherul de Campi
785986	Belkiralymezo
786000	Balin, Balon, Beelen, Beleni, Belin, Belina, Bielin, Bieliny, Bilan, Bilin, Bilina, Bjelina, Blonie, Bloyna, Byelin, Bylany, Fellheim, Fellin, Filehne, Palany, Palin, Pelinia, Pielnia, Piliny, Plana, Plauen, Plonna, Polana, Polany, Polen, Polina, Poljana, Polna, Polomia, Polomyja, Polona, Polyana, Polyany, Pulhany, Pulin, Pulmo, Valana, Valeni, Valeny, Vehlen, Velen, Velena, Velim, Veliona, Veliony, Veliuona, Velm, Velma, Velun, Velyun, Vielun, Vilan, Vilani, Vileni, Vilenu, Vileny, Vilion, Villany, Vilna, Vilnia, Vilno, Vilon, Vilonya, Vloyn, Volma, Volna, Volyne, Vyelun, Walina, Walinna, Weilheim, Wellan, Wielen, Wielona, Wielun, Wilna, Wilno, Wolin, Wolina, Wollin, Wolma, Wolna
786100	Peleniya, Polonnoye, Volnoye
786300	Falenty, Viljandi
786340	Pelnatycze
786343	Plandiste
786367	Walentynow, Wola Miedniewska
786370	Blendov, Blh nad Iplom, Valentova
786378	Balintfalva

786390	Flondora, Vallendar, Volintiri, Voluntir, Wolontir
786397	Bollendorf, Valendorf, Volontirovka, Wallendorf, Weil im Dorf
786400	Balnaca, Belenyes, Belinitch, Bieliniec, Bilence, Bilenec, Biliniec, Falenica, Falenits, Falenitsa, Falenitz, Palanca, Paleniec, Pielancz, Planice, Plomnitz, Plonitsa, Plontch, Polaniec, Polenitz, Polonice, Polonitse, Polunce, Pulamiec, Pulemets, Valea Mica, Vilanec, Vilnius, Vilnyus, Volintza, Volyntsy, Wielemicze, Willenz
786430	Balaneshty, Balanesti, Balinesti, Plainesti
786433	Ballenstedt
786435	Wola Mystkowska
786439	Byliny Stare
786450	Bieluniszki, Blansko, Plintsk, Plonsk, Plunsk, Polanczyk, Polnicka, Polonechka, Poloneczka, Volynskiy
786457	Wola Nieszkowska
786460	Plonczyn, Plungyan, Plungyany, Poloniczna, Wallensen, Willanzheim, Wola Nizna
786464	Falencia Miedzeszyn
786474	Plonszowice, Wola Mazowiecka
786479	Balmazujvaros, Flensburg
786497	Polany Surowiczne
786500	Belinek, Belynichi, Bielinek, Bielniki, Bolnik, Felling, Fulnek, Palanga, Palanka, Palonga, Planegg, Planig, Plonka, Plunge, Polanka, Polanky, Polanok, Polianka, Polonga, Polonichi, Polonka, Polyanka, Pulanki, Velemichi, Volanka, Wellmich, Wolanka
786544	Willingshausen
786545	Wola Niechcicka Nowa
786547	Polana Kosovska, Polien Kosoviczki, Polien Kosovkiczki, Polny Kesov
786558	Polanka Haller
786559	Balanca Grosi
786560	Balingen, Bullenheim, Flonheim, Palmnicken, Pflaumheim, Plungian, Polangen, Polengen, Polonichna, Villingen, Wellingen
786564	Blenkemezo, Wola Magnuszewska
786565	Wolnica Niechmirowska
786568	Bilinka Mala
786570	Pilnikov, Plenikow, Wola Michowa
786573	Bieliny Kapitulne
786574	Belinkovitch, Pulankowice, Villanykovesd
786575	Belynkovichi
786578	Polana Kobilecka, Polana Kobilelca, Polanka Wielka, Polien Kabileczky, Polin Koviletski
786583	Polien Glod
786593	Valea Neagra de Cris
786594	Beilngries, Valea Ungurasului

786598	Valea Ungurului
786600	Bullenheim, Flonheim, Pflaumheim, Planany, Plomiany, Plumenau, Plunjen, Velemin, Vilmany, Volomin, Wolomin
786630	Felnemet
786636	Wielen nad Notecia
786638	Blumenthal, Blumenthal bei Hellenthall, Plana nad Luznici
786640	Plomieniec
786643	Beli Manastir, Palmonostora
786646	Flamanzeni, Flamynzeny
786650	Balninkai
786656	Plieningen, Wolnianka Mala
786657	Wolnianka Wielka
786693	Willmenrod
786696	Valeni Maramures
786700	Blinow, Bolimov, Bolimow, Folmava, Paulinow, Plonowo, Polanow, Polinow, Pollnow, Velenovy, Vilanov, Volonov, Wilanow, Wilanowo, Wolanow
786730	Bielany Budy
786740	Balanovca, Blanowice, Bolanowice, Bolyanovitse, Wilamowice
786750	Bolyanovichi, Polanowka
786759	Polyanovgrad
786780	Viliampol, Wiliampole
786784	Vilyampolskaya Sloboda
786785	Bilina Velikaya, Bilina Velka, Bilina Wielka, Polana Velka
786795	Ballenberg, Blomberg, Wollenberg
786845	Wola Mielecka, Wola Mlocka
786850	Pflaumloch
786870	Plumlov
786874	Polien Lipsa
786876	Wola Malowana
786900	Palmiry, Valmiera, Velemer, Velmar, Villmar, Vol Mar, Wolmar
786940	Vollmerz, Willmars
786943	Wilmersdorf
786944	Wollmarshausen
786945	Polien Riskeve
786946	Flamersheim
786947	Flammersfeld
786956	Weil am Rhein
786960	Weil am Rhein
786974	Wola Morawicka
787000	Balf, Balvi, Balvu, Balwa, Belev, Bielavi, Bielawa, Bielawy, Bielowy, Bolve, Bolvi, Buhlow, Byelov, Filibe, Palfa, Paylova, Pilawa, Pilev, Piliva, Piljawa, Pilov, Pilyava, Plawie, Plawo, Plopi, Plopy, Polapy, Pulav, Pulavi, Pulavy, Pulawy, Pylyava, Valava, Valeva, Valjevo, Velava, Viile Apei, Viljevo, Vilova, Vilovo, Volove, Volovo, Volovy, Volp, Volpa, Walawa, Wolow, Wolowa, Wolowe, Wolpa, Wyhalew, Wyhalow, Wylewa, Wylow
787300	Bilavati, Volovat
787340	Velebudice
787363	Wolbattendorf
787364	Wola Wodynska
787370	Plovdiv
787374	Bela pod Bezdezem, Wola Wadowska
787378	Belapatfalva
787384	Biala Podlaska
787386	Bielawa Dolna
787394	Wola Batorska
787396	Wola Wydrzyna
787400	Belovizh, Belovtse, Belovtsy, Bialowieza, Bialowiz, Bielowce, Bielowice, Bilovec, Blovice, Bolboaca, Bolevec, Bolewice, Boljevci, Bulboaca, Felpec, Filipec, Filipetz, Fulpos, Pilaviez, Pilipec, Pilipets, Plavec, Plawce, Plopis, Polipsy, Polovtse, Polowce, Polpiec, Polubicze, Vilhovitz, Volovec, Volovets, Volovice, Wielowies, Wolawce, Wolowice, Wolowiec, Wolowitz, Wyholowicze
787417	Bolbocii Vechi
787430	Biala Poshet
787439	Fulposdaroc, Wola Bystrzycka
787443	Wola Brzostecka
787445	Volya Vysotska, Wola Bystrzycka, Wola Pieczyska, Wola Wysocka
787446	Belowschtschina, Wola Brzeznicka
787450	Bialabzheg, Bialobrzeg, Bialobrzegi, Bolovsk, Bolowsk, Pilvishki, Pilvishok, Pilviskai, Pilviski, Pilviskiai, Walbrzych, Walewskie, Wolfsegg
787454	Pilviskis
787457	Wola Wezykowa
787458	Wolfskehlen
787460	Biala Wyzna, Bielowizna, Vielbassen, Welbhausen, Wola Wydrzyna, Wolfsheim
787464	Belobozhnitsa, Bialoboznica, Wlobczynce, Wola Obszanska
787465	Wola Przemykowska
787466	Wolfsmunster
787467	Wola Wisniowa
787474	Polubicze Wiejskie, Wola Przybyslawska
787479	Philippsburg, Wolfsberg
787480	Valea Viseului
787484	Fulopszallas
787490	Balavasar
787500	Biala Waka, Bielawki, Bilaevka, Bolbochi, Bul'boka, Fellbach, Pilipche, Valevka, Vilyavche, Walowka, Weilbach, Wolbeck
787544	Wola Bokrzycka, Wola Boksycka
787546	Welbhausen
787556	Wolfhagen
787560	Wolfhagen
787574	Filipkowce, Wola Buchowska
787578	Pelvac Pelyva
787594	Wola Bokrzycka, Wola Wegierska
787600	Palovna, Plavinu, Plawna, Plawno, Pleven, Plevna, Plopana, Plopani, Plopeni, Polubny
787616	Plopenii Mari
787639	Plopana Tirg
787640	Balabanca, Felvincz, Plavanitza, Plavinas, Plavnica, Plawanice
787643	Balabaneshty, Balabanesti
787647	Balvanyosvaralja
787650	Balabanka, Plewnik
787667	Plewnia Nowa
787671	Polivanov Iar, Polivanov Yar
787673	Wolfenbuttel
787675	Bala Banovka, Balabanovka, Balabanowka, Plebanowka
787680	Valea Vinului
787700	Filipova, Filipow, Valpovo
787740	Filipowice, Plawowice
787750	Filipowka
787784	Philippopolis
787787	Wola Pawlowska
787800	Belopolye, Bialopole, Byelopolye, Felfalu, Fulopfalu, Palfalu, Vielipoli, Vilbel, Voloavele, Volovel, Wielopole, Wolowil
787830	Biale Blota, Bielefeld, Bielfeld
787837	Wola Bledowa
787840	Biala Bilits
787844	Wola Blizocka
787845	Biala Bielsko, Biala Opolskie, Wielopole Skrzynskie
787847	Volya Blazhovska, Wola Blazowska
787850	Biala Wielka, Wola Wielka
787856	Wola Pelkinska
787857	Wola Blakowa
787870	Folyfalva, Fulopfalva, Palfalva
787874	Wola Plawska
787877	Wola Filipowska
787890	Bollweiler, Plavalar
787900	Belavar, Belber, Bialy Bor, Bilbor, Bjelovar, Velvary
787916	Valea Perjei Noua
787930	Belfort, Bialobrodzie, Velbert, Wolferode, Wulfrath
787934	Belvardgyula
787940	Belovarec, Bialobrodzie, Bialoworce, Bilovarets, Bilvaritz, Volborzh, Wolborz
787941	Valya Perzhiy Noue
787943	Wola Brzostecka
787944	Wola Wereszczynska, Wolfratshausen
787945	Balberiskis, Balbieriskis, Balbirishok, Balbirishuk, Balbirshuk
787946	Wola Brzeznicka
787947	Walpersbach
787950	Bialobrzeg, Bialobrzegi, Folvark, Folvarki, Velburg, Walbrzych, Weilburg
787955	Folvark Karasin
787956	Folwarki Male
787958	Valea Porcului
787959	Folwark Raducki
787960	Volbrom, Wolbrom
787964	Wola Baraniecka, Wola Branicka, Wolframs Eschenbach
787965	Wola Przemykowska
787974	Wola Przybyslawska
787979	Walberberg
788163	Baleliai Antrieji
788165	Valea Lui Mihai
788178	Valea Lui Vlad
788450	Wola Laska
788460	Valea Loznei
788500	Bialoleka
788640	Wilhelmsburg, Wilhelmshaven
788670	Wilhelmow, Wilhelmpieckstadt Guben
788750	Belilovka

788760	Wallhalben
789000	Paller, Valea Rea, Weiler
789300	Wal Ruda
789340	Velhartice
789350	Bilhorodki
789360	Wallertheim
789387	Wola Radlowska
789430	Balaureshty, Balauresti, Floreshty, Floresti
789434	Floresti Sat
789435	Floresti Cluj
789436	Floresti Noui, Wallerstein
789437	Wola Rasztowska
789439	Floridsdorf, Florisdorf
789445	Wola Reczajska
789447	Wola Radziszowska
789450	Polrzeczki, Wola Uhruska
789460	Bellersheim, Florsheim
789467	Wola Rusinowska
789474	Weilerswist
789476	Wola Rozwieniecka
789480	Valea Rusului, Valya Rusuluy
789570	Palarikovo
789600	Florina, Valea Hranei
789636	Florentynowo
789640	Wilhermsdorf
789647	Wola Ranizowska
789650	Florynka
789660	Voul Romin
789670	Floryjanowa, Pelhrimov
789685	Weiler in Allgau
789745	Biala Ravska, Biala Rawska
789750	Billerbeck
789867	Volya Arlamovskaya
790000	Bar, Bara, Ber, Bere, Berea, Bereh, Beroea, Biery, Bira, Biri, Bor, Boria, Borja, Brehy, Buer, Forro, Pari, Per, Pere, Piora, Pir, Piree, Poraj, Porohy, Pria, Pure, Vari, Vary, Verro, Vorru, Voru, Vyru, Wara, Wehr, Werro, Wiory, Wiry, Wohra
791000	Varaiu, Veroia
791361	Priyutnaya, Priyutnoye
791390	Prijedor
791487	Pereiaslav Khmel Nitskii, Pereiaslavl, Perejaslaw, Perejaslaw Chmielnicki, Pereyaslav, Pereyaslav Khmelnitskiy, Pereyaslavl, Periyoslov
791548	Boruja Koscielna
791600	Brejeni
791649	Verejeni Soroca
791650	Freyung
791674	Proyanovska
791678	Freienwalde
791679	Freuenberg, Froienburg
791680	Freienohl
791690	Verejeni Orhei
791695	Verejeni Orhei
791700	Berejow, Porejov
791738	Perii Vadului
791800	Prajila
791879	Frei Laubersheim
793000	Barot, Barth, Baruth, Bayreuth, Beret, Berhida, Berta, Borauti, Borhid, Borod, Borota, Brad, Brod, Broda, Brody, Burty, Farad, Forth, Frata, Fuerth, Furta, Furth, Parad, Parajd, Parhida, Parjota, Pered, Pirot,

	Port, Poryte, Prady, Praid, Prode, Pyrzhota, Varadia, Varda, Viereth, Vrsta, Warta, Warth, Wehrda, Werth, Wohrd
793160	Burdujeni, Vertujeni
793161	Vartejenii Sat
793165	Vartejeni Colonie
793170	Bardejov
793175	Vradiyevka
793300	Portita, Vorotet
793310	Bartodzieje
793316	Fratautii Noi, Fratautii Noui, Fratuatii Noui
793317	Bartodzieje Podlesne, Fratautii pe Suceava, Fratautii Vechi
793330	Berettyodeda
793360	Bortiatyn, Bortyatin
793374	Bertotovce
793379	Bardudvarnok
793386	Bardo Dolne
793400	Baratos, Bardos, Bordosiu, Bortaycze, Bratca, Brates, Brtec, Brzotice, Firtusu, Paradyz, Pertoca, Przedecz, Varatic, Vertes, Vorotets, Vrutice
793410	Bartodzieje
793417	Bartodzieje Podlesne
793430	Bardesti
793431	Partestii de Jos, Partestii de Sus
793440	Bartoszyce
793450	Varatytsk, Varotytsk
793460	Bratuseni, Bratushany, Predocin, Przytoczno, Vartuzhen, Vertuzhen, Vertyuzhani, Vertyuzhany
793463	Berettyoszentmarton, Fertoszentmiklos
793464	Partizanska Dreznica
793468	Vertessomlo
793470	Bardichev, Bartishaw, Bartoszewo, Berdichev, Berditchev, Berditchov, Berdyczow
793474	Bartosovce
793475	Vertesboglar
793478	Berettyoszeplak, Fertoszeplak
793484	Vertesszollos
793485	Poryte Szlacheckie
793487	Bratislava, Bratyslawa, Brod Slavonski, Wartoslaw
793500	Beretke, Bratka, Bretcu, Bretka, Brodok, Bruttig, Friedek, Frydek, Fryedek, Przytyk, Varatik, Vroutek, Vrudky, Vrutky, Waratyck
793530	Varticauti
793556	Berettykohany
793564	Frydek Mistek
793570	Berdechow, Bortkov, Bortkow, Bortkuv, Pritkov
793574	Bartkowice, Berdykovtse, Bratkovtse, Bratkowce, Bratkowice, Burdiakowce, Burdyakovtse, Burdyakovtsy, Burdykovshchina, Przytkowice
793575	Bratkow Gorny, Bratkowka
793577	Bartkowa Posadowa
793594	Brod Uhersky
793600	Barten, Bartne, Boratyn, Borodina, Borodino, Bratian, Bratjan, Bredtheim, Breitenau,

	Bretten, Brodina, Brzotin, Fordon, Forteni, Partynia, Peratin, Peratyn, Pir Atin, Piriatyn, Piryatin, Porudno, Verden, Vorden, Vreden, Werden, Wertheim, Wirdum
793638	Freudental, Freudenthal
793639	Fertoendred, Worth an der Donau
793640	Bartnitz, Brodanci, Brodnica, Brodnitsa, Brudnica, Brudnice, Przedmiescie, Przedmoscie
793643	Bartenstein, Freudenstadt, Predmesti, Przedmiescie Dubieckie
793644	Przedmiescie Sedziszowskie, Wardomicze Stare
793645	Berd Ansk, Berdiansk, Berdjansk, Berdyansk, Bierdjansk, Przedmiescie Kludzie
793647	Friedensfeld
793650	Barodeinka, Boradianka, Borodyanka, Bortniki, Bratnik, Porudenko, Pradnik, Prudnik, Prutting, Vardomichi, Vrdnik
793653	Virdayn Katan
793654	Pradnik Czerwony
793656	Partenheim, Wertingen
793657	Pradnik Bialy
793658	Boratyniec Lacki
793660	Fridman, Frydman, Partenheim
793663	Ferdinand, Ferdinandovac
793665	Bartininkai
793666	Worth am Main
793670	Bortnow, Bortnuv
793673	Breitenwaida
793675	Breidenbach, Breitenbach, Breitenbach am Herzberg, Brodenbach
793676	Breitenwang
793678	Furth im Wald
793679	Bardenberg, Breitenberg, Freudenberg, Freudenburg, Wardenburg, Wartenberg, Wartenburg
793680	Breitenlee
793700	Bardiow, Bartfa, Bierutow, Brdov, Brdow, Predboj
793740	Brdovec, Britavca, Pardubice, Pardubitz
793744	Berdowszczyzna
793746	Barodbeznye
793750	Britavka, Britovka, Vradievka
793760	Protivin
793765	Furtwangen
793780	Berettyoujfalu
793783	Bartfeld, Bartfeldt
793787	Bardfalva
793794	Przedborz
793795	Friedberg, Friedberg an der Ach, Friedburg, Friedeberg, Wartberg
793798	Berettyovaralja
793800	Bartele, Barteliai, Bortele, Brodla, Freital, Pradla, Predeal, Przadlo, Przytuly, Werdohl
793830	Bartoldy
793840	Predlice
793850	Bordulaki, Bordulyaki

793860	Berehy Dolne, Bratuleni, Bratuleny, Pratulin
793863	Friedland, Frydlant
793869	Borodul Mare
793870	Pardolow
793874	Bartolovec
793875	Prittlbach
793876	Fridolfing
793877	Bratolyubovka
793890	Bredelar
793900	Bardar, Werther
793945	Friedrusk, Peridroysk, Pridroisk, Pridruiska
793954	Fridrikhshtadt, Friedrichsburg, Friedrichsgmund, Friedrichshafen, Friedrichshof, Friedrichstadt
793957	Frydrychowice
793964	Bratronice
793970	Brotdorf, Fraydorf
793978	Fredropol
793979	Vorderberg
794000	Barashi, Barasj, Barca, Barciai, Barcs, Barycz, Barysh, Barysz, Baurcei, Berescie, Bereza, Berezce, Berezcy, Berezo, Berzai, Birca, Bircza, Birtch, Birzai, Birze, Birzh, Birzhi, Birzi, Bors, Borsa, Borsha, Brasso, Bratz, Breaza, Breza, Brezah, Briaza, Brojce, Broos, Bruesau, Brus, Bruss, Brusy, Brzesc, Brzescie, Brzezce, Brzezie, Bursz, Fericea, Firiza, Foroeucs, Frics, Pahres, Perecse, Pershay, Peruc, Pfersee, Piraeus, Piricse, Poritch, Porz, Prosau, Prusie, Prusy, Pyritz, Pyrzyce, Varadia, Varaszo, Varez, Varosa, Varshau, Varshe, Verecze, Verice, Verotze, Vors, Vratsa, Vrsac, Vrsce, Vyritsa, Warez, Warschau, Werschau, Wiersze, Wrzaca
794100	Brezoaia, Brezoya, Periceiu
794300	Barsad, Berest, Berestye, Bersad, Bershad, Bershty, Berszad, Berszada, Berszty, Berzete, Borsod, Braesti, Brest, Fauresti, Ferest, Feresti, Forst, Friesoythe, Perast, Pressath, Varsad
794317	Prostejov
794330	Berstadt, Bierstadt, Borrstadt, Burstadt, Fraustadt, Freistadt, Freistett, Freystadt, Frystat, Worrstadt
794339	Braesti Dorohoi
794340	Barstyciai, Breshtitz, Prace Duze, Prestice
794344	Birsau de Sus
794345	Berestechko, Beresteczko, Berestetchka, Brestitski
794347	Borsodcsaba
794349	Barstaszar
794350	Brzhostik, Brzostek, Frastak, Fristik, Frysztak, Pereszteg, Prostki
794351	Brest Kujavsk
794354	Borsodgeszt
794356	Prostken
794359	Borsodharsany

794360	Birschton, Birshtan, Birshton, Birstein, Britsiteni, Burshtin, Burshtyn, Bursztyn, Forostna, Furstenau, Pristina, Prostyn, Przystajn, Przystajnia, Przystan, Varazdin, Warstein
794363	Borsodnadasd, Brist nad Bugie
794364	Birstonas, Brestanica, Furstenzell, Przysietnica, Varazdinske Toplice
794367	Fuerstenberg, Furstenberg, Furstenfeld, Furstenfeldbruck, Furstenfelde, Furstenforst, Furstenwalde
794370	Beresdowo, Berezdiv, Berezdov, Bristev, Brzostowa, Porostov
794373	Borsodbota
794374	Berestovets, Berestovitsa, Berestovitz, Berestovitza, Berestowiec, Brestovits, Brizdowitz, Bruzdovitz, Brzostowica, Brzozdowce, Brzozdowce Miasto
794375	Brestovac Pozeski, Brzostowa Gora, Brzostowica Mala, Brzostowica Wielka
794376	Borsodivanka, Pristoupim
794379	Preshedborz, Prostibor
794383	Brest Litovsk, Brest Litowsk
794385	Beresztelke
794390	Borsodharsany, Brister, Brustura, Brustury, Brusztura
794394	Brusturesti, Brusturoasa, Vardz Dresht
794397	Pershotravnevoye, Pfersdorf
794400	Barcice, Barczaca, Berezhtse, Berzasca, Boroczyce, Borsec, Brezice, Brezitz, Brudzice, Bruzyca, Bryshce, Bryszcze, Brzeszcze, Burzec, Burzuc, Parcice, Parshischa, Partshits, Paryszcze, Pierszyce, Porzecze, Prcice, Prosec, Prusice, Przashysz, Przeczyca, Vereshitsa, Warzyce, Wereszyce, Werschetz, Wirsitz
794430	Porcesti
794433	Brzoza Stadnicka
794439	Bircza Stara, Poroze Stare
794443	Burczyce Stare, Pressisch Stargard, Preussische Stargard
794446	Borsuczyzna, Bryszcze Samojlowka
794450	Berzaska, Burzysk, Prusicko
794457	Borschtschagowka
794458	Preussisch Holland
794460	Borzecin, Broszecin, Peresecina, Procisne, Wereszczyn
794463	Borsodszentmarton
794464	Breaza Somes, Prisecnice
794465	Borzecinek
794469	Borsodszemere
794470	Borshchev, Borshtchev, Borszczow, Bruszczowa, Parzeczew, Przeciszow, Wrzeszczewo
794474	Barszczowice, Brezezowicz
794475	Borszczowka
794479	Borsosbereny, Preussisch Friedland
794480	Bayrischzell, Preussisch Eylau
794483	Preussisch Oldendorf
794490	Borsosgyor

794495	Borsodszirak
794500	Baracska, Barcika, Berecyk, Beresk, Bereska, Beresko, Berezhki, Berezki, Berzek, Borceag, Borszeg, Borszek, Borzychy, Brcko, Breisach, Brisk, Brzesko, Brzuska, Brzyska, Brzyski, Fersig, Paryshche, Pereseka, Peresieka, Piersk, Porosiuki, Prashka, Prashke, Prashki, Praska, Praszka, Prazuchy, Proskau, Prusiek, Pruske, Przysieka, Przysieki, Przysucha, Verecski, Verseg, Wierzejki, Wyrzysk
794530	Broscauti
794531	Broscautii Noui, Broscautii Vechi
794533	Broscauti Dorohoi, Brzoski Tatary
794535	Brisk D Koya
794538	Brisk D Lita, Brisk Dlita
794540	Veresegyhaz
794543	Brusko Stare
794546	Borsuchizna
794551	Brisk Kuyavsk, Brzesc Kujawski
794557	Borshchagovka
794560	Peresechino
794563	Brzesc nad Bugiem
794565	Wierzchniakowce
794566	Pierzchnianka
794567	Brusko Nowe, Brzesko Nowe, Wierzchniow
794568	Pruszk Male
794570	Barczkow, Borshchov, Borshchuv, Borzechow, Braskov, Pierzchow, Poroshkov, Poroskov, Proszkow, Prushkov, Pruszkow, Wierzchow, Wierzchowo
794574	Barshchovitse, Bruskovtsy, Burdiakowce, Burdyakovtse, Burdyakovtsy, Pierzchowice, Przyszychwosty, Vreskovice, Wierzchowice, Wierzchowiska
794575	Borshagovka, Borshchevka, Borshchovichi
794576	Pereshchepino, Wierzchowina, Wierzchownia
794578	Brzyska Wola, Pruszki Wielkie, Wreczyca Wielka
794579	Brodski Varos
794580	Berzgale, Birzgale, Borsa Cluj
794583	Brzesc Litewski
794584	Praskolesy, Wierzchlas, Wierzchlesie, Wierzcholesie
794593	Bereza Kartuska, Bereza Kartuskaya
794594	Preiskretscham
794596	Presekareni, Prisacareni, Proscureni, Proskuren, Proskuryany
794597	Proskurov
794598	Brzoza Krolewska
794600	Barciany, Barcin, Barsana, Bartschin, Barzan, Barzna, Beresino, Berezan, Berezany, Berezene, Berezhany, Berezin, Berezina, Berezino, Berezna, Berezne, Berezno, Berson, Berzaune, Berzhan, Berzin,

Birsana, Borszyn, Borzna,
Brezan, Brezhen, Brezheny,
Brezhin, Brezhna, Brezin,
Brezina, Breziny, Brezne,
Brezno, Briceni, Briesen,
Britshan, Britshani, Broceni,
Brodshin, Brotchin, Brzesciany,
Brzezany, Brzezhany, Brzezin,
Brzezina, Brzeziny, Brzezna,
Brzyzna, Frasan, Frasin,
Friesen, Friesheim, Furceni,
Paracin, Parasznya, Parzno,
Perecin, Perecseny, Perocseny,
Pforzheim, Pierzyny, Porazyn,
Porshna, Porszna, Pruzana,
Pruzany, Pruzhana, Pruzhani,
Pruzhany, Pruzhene, Pruzin,
Varsany, Varzhan, Verezhen,
Verezheny, Verzanai, Verzian,
Viersen, Vrauceni, Vrcen,
Warzyn, Wereszyn, Wierczany,
Worczyn, Wreschen, Wriezen,
Wrocien, Wroczyny, Wrzesnia

794610	Prosyanaya
794619	Varosmajor
794630	Versend
794634	Brudzen Duzy
794639	Briceni Targ
794640	Barodsomos, Berezhnits, Bereznica, Bereznitsa, Berzence, Berzhnitse, Berznits, Birzu Muiza, Breznice, Breznitz, Brusnica, Brzeznica, Friesenhausen, Pierczhnica, Prashnitz, Prausnitz, Proshnits, Proshnitz, Prosienica, Prossnitz, Przasnysz
794643	Briceni Sat, Brusno Stare, Varez Miasto, Warez Miasto
794645	Berdiansk, Berdjansk, Berdyansk, Bierdjansk
794647	Parzentchev
794648	Prezhemisel
794650	Bereznek, Berezniak, Berezniaki, Bereznyaki, Berzniki, Bierznik, Boradianka, Borodyanka, Borosznok, Brezinka, Brusnik, Brzezinka, Brzezinki, Freising, Parzymiechy, Prosmyky, Przesmyki, Varatchenka
794654	Barsinghausen, Brzeznica Stara, Friesenhausen
794655	Breznicki Hum, Brzeznica Ksiazeca
794656	Bereznica Nizna, Bretzenheim, Friesenheim
794657	Beresnegowatoje, Bereznegovatoye, Bereznica Wyzna, Brzeznica Bychawska
794659	Bereznica Rustykalna
794660	Bretzenheim, Burzenin, Friesenheim
794663	Brezno nad Hronom
794667	Brusno Nowe, Brzydzyn Nowy
794669	Borosneu Mare
794670	Bierzanow, Broshnyuv, Broszniow, Prusinow, Prusinuv
794673	Brezhnovata, Porszombat
794674	Broshnev Osada, Parzniewice, Parzniewiczki
794675	Persenbeug
794678	Barczanfalva, Brezny Velky

794680	Prace Male
794683	Versmold
794693	Veresmart, Virismort, Vorosmart, Wiresmort
794696	Borsa Maramures, Borsha Maramuresh, Borsha Marmorosh
794700	Barczewo, Bardiow, Bereziv, Berezov, Berezovo, Berezow, Berezuv, Borisov, Borshov, Borszow, Borusowa, Borysowo, Borzava, Brasov, Brezov, Brezova, Briceva, Britcheva, Brudzew, Brzezawa, Brzozow, Paracov, Parcevo, Parchev, Parcova, Parczew, Parsow, Partchev, Partsev, Partzeva, Parysow, Pertschup, Porasow, Porisov, Porosavo, Porozovo, Porozow, Porzwye, Prehysov, Presevo, Preshov, Presov, Preszow, Proszew, Przeczow, Przyszowa, Varsava, Verushev, Viroshov, Vrotsuv, Vyershuv, Vyerushov, Vyerushuv, Warsaw, Warsawa, Warszawa, Wieruszow, Wrocow, Wrzeszewo
794740	Berezovca, Berezovitsa, Berzevicze, Borossebes, Boryczewicze, Braszewice, Brezowice, Brzaczowice, Brzezowiec, Brzozowiec, Presovtse, Presowce, Proshovitza, Proszowice, Wierzawice, Wierzbiaz, Wierzbica, Worocewicze
794743	Brzozow Stary
794744	Borysowszczyzna
794746	Berezovitsa Mala, Wierzbiczno
794747	Berezovitsa Velka
794749	Berezow Sredni
794750	Barishevka, Baryschewka, Beresovka, Berezovka, Berozovka, Borishovka, Borisovka, Borshivka, Borysowka, Borysuvka, Brzezowka, Proszowki, Vorotsevichi, Vradievka
794753	Brzozowica Duza
794756	Brezovica nad Torysou, Brzozowica Mala
794757	Berezovica Wielka, Brzozowica Wielka
794760	Pressbaum, Wierzbiany, Wierzbna, Wierzbno
794764	Berezow Nizny, Berezuv Nizhny
794765	Verzhbnik, Verzhbnik Starakhov, Vierzhbinik, Vyerzbnik, Vyerzhbanik, Wierzbinek, Wierzbnik, Wierzbnik Starachow
794767	Wierzbanowa
794770	Wierzbow
794773	Brezova pod Bradlom, Wyrozeby Podawce
794774	Berezow Wyzny, Berezuv Vyzhny, Wierzbowce, Wierzbowiec
794780	Borispol
794783	Pretzfeld
794784	Berzpils, Bor Zapilski
794785	Pritzwalk

794786	Wierzblany
794787	Verzhbelova, Verzhbolov, Wierzbolow
794789	Verzhboloro
794790	Borzavar, Varosvar, Vorosvar
794794	Barsbaracska
794795	Pressburg, Wirsberg, Wuerzburg, Wurzburg
794796	Vorosbereny
794800	Barzila, Bercel, Birsula, Birzula, Breslau, Bresslau, Poroszlo, Prazhilo, Przedzel, Przestrzele, Virsoli, Vorzel
794830	Varoslod, Varsolt, Virsolt
794834	Barsaul de Sus
794840	Berezlozhi, Varsolcz
794845	Brzezie Laskowa
794850	Berezlogi
794856	Pereslchina
794860	Pereszleny, Porcsalma, Preselany, Wurselen
794864	Porciuleanca
794865	Varosszalonak
794870	Berislav, Beryslav, Borislav, Boryslaw, Braclav, Braclaw, Braslav, Braslaw, Bratslav, Bratslow, Bratzlav, Breclav, Breslav, Breslev, Brusilov, Predslav, Prislup, Przeclaw, Przeslaw, Przyslup, Voroshilovo, Wroclaw
794874	Boryslawice, Voroshilovsk, Vorosilovca
794875	Boryslawka, Varshilovka, Voroshilovgrad, Voroshilovka, Woroschilowka, Woroszylowgrad
794890	Fritzlar
794900	Perezhiri, Varzari
794940	Wrocieryz
794943	Varzareshty, Varzaresti
794945	Borszorcsok, Przysiersk
794948	Prezerosl
794950	Fryszerka, Prozorki, Prozoroki
794960	Prizren
795000	Baraki, Bargau, Barki, Baurchi, Bercu, Bereg, Beregi, Berge, Berghia, Beurig, Borak, Borek, Bork, Borka, Borki, Braga, Brak, Brake, Brieg, Brigi, Brigu, Brok, Bruck, Brzeg, Brzegi, Burg, Burgau, Faragau, Farago, Parichi, Paruchy, Pereg, Peregh, Pirog, Porechye, Porogi, Praga, Prague, Praha, Prockau, Prugy, Varka, Vereyki, Verkhi, Virek, Virga, Vorke, Vurka, Vurke, Warka, Werchy, Werejki, Wirek, Wyryki
795140	Przychojec
795300	Berhida, Borcut, Borhid, Furged, Parhida, Percauti, Pereked, Perkata, Przygody, Vargata, Vargede, Vorokhta, Worochta
795340	Prachatice
795343	Brykuta Stara
795345	Berchtesgaden
795350	Borgotiha
795384	Perchtoldsdorf
795386	Brzeg Dolny

503

795394	Beregdaroc	
795397	Burgdorf	
795400	Barkaszo, Berchez, Berkesz, Bruex, Burgas, Farcasa, Parchacz, Parkosz, Viragos, Warkocz, Wirges	
795410	Berchezoaia	
795430	Berkesd, Burgezd, Farkasd, Farkazd	
795436	Burgsteinfurt	
795438	Purgstall	
795439	Birkesdorf, Borek Stary	
795440	Beregszasz, Prokocice	
795443	Berchisesti	
795453	Forgacskut	
795457	Borchtchagovka	
795458	Bergisch Gladbach	
795460	Berghausen, Bruchhausen, Burghausen, Burgsinn, Prokocim, Wrexen	
795463	Beregszentmiklos, Porrogszentkiraly	
795464	Prichsenstadt	
795470	Barchaczow, Barkasovo, Farkasgyepu	
795473	Berkeszpataka	
795479	Bergzabern	
795480	Bruchsal	
795484	Beregszollos	
795485	Borek Szlachecki, Burghaslach, Farkaslaka	
795496	Beregsurany	
795497	Farkasrev	
795500	Berkach, Borochiche, Burgugi, Parkhach	
795530	Borek Kuty	
795547	Bereg Hasva	
795597	Burg Grafenrode	
795600	Berchan, Bergen, Bergheim, Berkheim, Birkenau, Borken, Borogani, Borogany, Bragin, Brahin, Brichany, Bricheni, Brohin, Brucken, Bruckenau, Brykon, Burghaun, Burgheim, Forchheim, Frechen, Furcheny, Parchim, Parkany, Perechin, Poricany, Pruchna, Varkony, Verchany, Vorchin, Vrakun, Wehrheim, Werachanie, Wiercany	
795611	Verkhniy Yasenov	
795614	Verkhneye Sinevidnoye, Verkhniye Zhory	
795615	Verkhneye Krivche	
795616	Verkhniy Maydan, Verkhnyaya Maryanovka	
795617	Verkhneye Vodyanoye, Verkhneye Vysotskoye, Verkhniy Berezov, Verkhniye Popeshty, Verkhnyaya Bystra	
795618	Verkhnyaya Albota	
795630	Beregomet, Bergomet, Berhomet, Berkhomet	
795636	Verchnedneprovsk, Verkhne Dnyeprovsk, Verkhnedneprovsk, Wierchniednieprowsk	
795637	Berhomet pe Prut, Berhomete pe Siret, Verkhnedvinsk	
795639	Borgentreich, Bricheni Targ, Bruck an der Grossglocknerstrasse, Bruckneudorf	
795640	Bregenz, Fericanci, Pierychnica	
795643	Bricheni Sat, Burgkundstadt, Burgkunstadt, Verkhne Studenyy	
795645	Parochonsk, Parokhonsk, Pereginsko, Perehinsko	
795646	Borki Nizinskie, Verecky Nizni	
795650	Berching, Berg im Gau, Borkenhagen, Prachnik, Prakhnik, Prochnik, Pruchnik, Prukhnik	
795655	Borkenhagen	
795656	Breckenheim, Pruchnik Miasto, Prukhnik Myasto	
795657	Pruchnik Wies	
795659	Freckenhorst	
795660	Bergkamen, Breckenheim, Vrskman	
795665	Bergen Enkheim	
795670	Borek Nowy, Burkanow, Burkanuv, Verkhnov, Verkhnuv	
795675	Burgambach	
795678	Barcanfalva, Birkenfeld	
795679	Birkenwerder	
795680	Vorokomle, Wierchomla, Worokomla	
795684	Borgo Mijloceni	
795687	Wierchomla Wielka	
795690	Freckenhorst	
795694	Borgo Muraseni	
795700	Barchow, Barkava, Beregovo, Berehovo, Berehowo, Borchow, Bricheva, Brichevo, Briukhovo, Brykov, Brykow, Brzechow, Burhave, Parcheve, Parkova, Perekop, Perkupa, Piorkow, Porkhov, Prahovo, Pricovy, Priekopa, Prokowo, Przechowo, Varkava, Virchow	
795730	Brackwede	
795740	Barchovice, Barkavas, Berkovitsa, Brzuchowice, Fricovce, Perkovtsy, Varkavas, Varkovits, Verhovca, Verkhovtsy, Warkovicze, Warkowicze, Wirkowice	
795746	Borkowizna	
795749	Beregboszormeny, Berekboszormeny	
795750	Bryukhovichi, Burakowka, Buryakovka, Perkhovichi, Varchofki, Varkoviche, Varkovichi, Verchovka, Verhovka, Verkhovichi, Verkhovka, Werchowka, Werkievka, Worchowka	
795760	Beregbene, Frickhofen, Przckopana, Verkhovina	
795777	Verkhova Bibikovo	
795780	Beregujfalu, Wyryki Wola	
795783	Barchfeld, Wyryki Polod	
795784	Borek Falecki	
795785	Borek Wielkopolski, Borki Wielkie, Wrzaca Wielka	
795795	Borki Wyrki, Burgebrach	
795796	Berg vor Nideggen, Borgoprund, Burgbernheim, Perekop Armyansk	
795797	Burgpreppach	
795798	Burgbrohl	
795800	Brackel, Brakel, Briegel, Brigel, Burgel, Fragel, Priekule, Vergali	
795830	Przykalety	
795837	Vrcholtovice	
795840	Barchholz, Borgholz, Burglesau, Priekules, Verkholesye	
795844	Borgholzhausen, Burgholzhausen	
795860	Brokeln, Burgeln, Forgolany, Preekulen, Przegalina, Przegaliny, Varaklani, Varaklanu, Varaklyany, Varklian, Varkliani	
795863	Przegaliny Duze	
795864	Vorgulintsy	
795865	Porchulyanka	
795866	Przegaliny Male	
795867	Przegaliny Wielkie	
795870	Przyglow, Vrchlabi, Warchalow	
795873	Barglow Dworny	
795876	Warchalow Nowy	
795890	Birklar	
795896	Berglern, Burgellern	
795900	Purcari, Purkary	
795930	Pregrada, Werchrata	
795936	Bergrothenfels	
795943	Berekeresztur, Bor u Chroustovic, Borghorst, Purkersdorf	
795947	Burkhardsfelden	
795948	Przegorzaly	
795954	Beregrakos	
795956	Bergkirchen, Pfarrkirchen	
795960	Berehy Gorne	
795970	Prokurawa	
795974	Prigrevica	
795975	Prigrevica Sveti Ivan	
795976	Burggrafenrode	
795980	Prehoryle	
796000	Baran, Barna, Bereni, Bernau, Beroun, Birini, Borinya, Borynia, Braunau, Brieni, Brin, Brno, Bruenn, Brunau, Brunn, Brunnau, Bryn, Brzana, Brzyna, Buhryn, Buren, Burin, Buryn, Farna, Frain, Parnu, Peirin, Perenye, Periam, Perin, Pernau, Piran, Pirano, Pirna, Porin, Pren, Preny, Prienai, Promna, Przyjmy, Varanno, Varena, Varin, Varme, Varna, Varniai, Verne, Virena, Vorna, Vorne, Vorni, Vrani, Vrany, Waren, Warin, Warna, Wehrheim, Werne, Werynia, Wornie	
796175	Veremiyevka	
796300	Barand, Berend, Berent, Berente, Berhomet, Berindu, Berinta, Fornad, Pfreimd, Primda, Przemet, Przemiat, Varnita	
796330	Wormditt	
796340	Brandeis	
796343	Biernaty Stare	
796345	Brandysek, Frantiskov, Frantiskov Lazne	
796346	Bermuthshain, Brandys nad Labem, Brandys nad Orlici	
796360	Berindan	
796365	Fremdingen	
796367	Brandenburg, Frondenberg	
796370	Berhomet pe Prut, Berhomete pe Siret	

796374	Bernatovice, Brandwica
796378	Bernatfalva
796379	Prundu Birgaului
796380	Bruntal
796387	Prundul Bargaului
796397	Barntrup, Berndorf, Berrendorf, Brenndorf, Ferndorf, Frauendorf, Parndorf, Wahrentrup, Warendorf
796400	Bairamcea, Bajramtscha, Baranca, Barancea, Baroncea, Beiramtch, Berencs, Biruintsa, Bornitz, Borynicze, Branc, Bronica, Bronitsa, Burenice, Burnosy, Farmos, Ferneziu, Firnitz, Forroencs, Frumosu, Frunza, Parincea, Perjamos, Perjamosch, Pornice, Przemocze, Przenosza, Varenz, Varenzh, Varmezo, Varnitsa, Vermis, Voronezh, Vrnjci, Worms, Woronesch, Woronez, Woroniec
796430	Bahrinesti, Braneshty, Branistea, Purmsati
796433	Bernstadt, Bernstadt in Schlesien, Frenstat, Frenstat pod Radhostem
796436	Bernstein
796438	Ferencztelep
796439	Brunsdorf, Frensdorf, Parincea Targ, Parincea Tirg, Varnsdorf, Warensdorf, Warnsdorf
796440	Baranczyce, Bronczyce, Bronocice, Frumosica, Frumusica
796445	Branszczyk
796450	Beryansk, Bransk, Branska, Braynsk, Breinsk, Bryansk, Burniszki, Frumushika
796455	Brianska Gora, Brunska Gora
796456	Bernadzki Most, Frumusica Noua
796457	Bren Osuchowski, Frumusica Veche
796459	Bromskirchen
796460	Bernhausen, Branzeni, Brynzeny, Franusin, Frohnhausen, Priemhausen, Vorniceni, Vranceni, Warmsen, Woronczyn
796461	Branzenii Vechi, Peremozhnoye
796463	Baranyaszentgyorgy, Vorniceni Dorohoi
796464	Pirmasens, Varenz Miasto
796468	Vorniceni Lapusna
796470	Vermezif
796475	Braunsbach, Braunschweig, Brunswick, Vorontsovka
796478	Principele Carol
796479	Bernecebarati, Braunsberg, Franzburg
796480	Frumosul, Peremyshl, Premishla, Premisle, Prenzlau, Przemysl
796486	Peremyshlyany, Premishlan, Premishlian, Premislani, Przemyslany
796487	Bronislawowka
796500	Barancha, Barnag, Beiramich, Bornich, Boronka, Boryniche, Bremke, Brnik, Bronka, Farynki, Fehring, Parnik, Pernik, Piorunka, Verenkeu, Vorancau, Voronki, Voronok,
	Voronyaki, Vranik, Vronik, Werneck, Woroniaki, Woronki, Wronka, Wronke, Wronki
796543	Bernkastel Cues, Bernkastel Kues, Frankstadt, Piringsdorf
796545	Frankisch Crumbach
796546	Bernhausen, Frohnhausen, Priemhausen
796560	Bieringen, Bornheim, Brenken, Frankenau, Primkenau, Viernheim, Vornicheni, Vornicheny, Voronchin
796563	Frankenthal
796565	Verenchanka
796567	Frankenberg, Frankenwinheim
796570	Brankow, Frankova, Przemkow, Voronkov, Voronkovo, Woronkow
796576	Brancovenesti, Briancovenesti, Brincovenesti
796579	Frankfort On The Main, Frankfurt am Hochst, Frankfurt am Main, Frankfurt am Rodelheim, Frankfurt an der Oder
796584	Varenholz
796590	Piriu Negru
796593	Wernigerode
796594	Behringersdorf, Frankershausen
796595	Frauenkirchen
796600	Barmen, Beremiany, Beremyany, Bornheim, Bremen, Brunen, Furmany, Poronin, Prameny, Pruneni, Varenai, Viernheim, Voronino, Vranany, Weremien, Woronino, Wronin
796630	Beremend, Priement
796639	Werne an der Lippe
796640	Brnenec, Firminis, Furmenyes
796650	Pernink
796654	Baranyamagocs
796657	Brunn am Gebirge
796663	Warnemunde
796670	Bierun Nowy, Furmanow
796679	Branjin Vrh
796700	Baranov, Baranow, Baranowo, Barniv, Bernow, Bornov, Boronow, Braniewa, Braniewo, Breanova, Broniewo, Broniow, Broumov, Brunava, Bryanovo, Byrnovo, Pernov, Poromow, Poromuv, Varnov, Voronov, Voronova, Voronove, Voronovo, Voronuv, Vranjevo, Vranov, Werenow, Woronow, Woronowo, Wronow
796730	Voronovita
796740	Baranovich, Baranovitch, Baranovitsh, Baranowice, Baranowicze, Baranowitz, Barnabas, Bronowice, Proniewicze, Voronovitsa, Woronovitsy, Wronowice
796743	Berenbostel, Porumbesti
796745	Brunaviski, Brunavitzik, Brunovishok, Brunovitshok, Brunovitzik
796746	Baranow Sandomierski
796749	Barnova Soroca
796750	Baranivka, Baranovichi, Baranovka, Baranowka, Baronovka, Branewka,
	Bronnbach, Parnivka, Porumbak
796753	Porumbacu de Sus
796758	Porumbacul de Sus
796760	Birnbaum
796761	Porumbenii Mari, Porumbenii Mici
796763	Baranow nad Wieprzem, Vranov nad Dyji, Vranov nad Toplou
796765	Brno Venkov
796778	Bronowo Plewnik
796780	Frampol, Franpol
796783	Fahrenwalde
796784	Braunfels
796785	Pryamobalka, Przemiwolki
796787	Barnafalva
796789	Bronnweiler
796790	Porumbrey
796794	Brenn Poritschen
796795	Bernburg, Brauneberg, Brennberg, Bromberg, Frauenberg, Frauenburg, Frombork
796800	Baremel, Beremel, Beremelia, Boremel, Boromel, Peremyl
796836	Frohnleiten
796840	Borumlaca, Brunnlitz, Varenholz
796845	Wermelskirchen
796850	Baromlak, Braunlage
796870	Peremilow
796934	Bernartice
796936	Peremarton
796940	Wernarz
796943	Frimmersdorf
796945	Primorskoye
796946	Framersheim
796957	Bremerhaven
796970	Bremerhaven, Pernarava, Prunerov
796975	Peremorovka, Peremorowka
796979	Bremervorde
797000	Baraboi, Baraboy, Barby, Berfa, Berovo, Borov, Borove, Borow, Borowa, Borowe, Breb, Burhave, Parva, Poreba, Poruba, Verba, Verbo, Vereb, Vrabi, Wejherowo, Werba, Wirow, Wreby, Wrzawy, Wrzepia
797100	Borovaja, Borovaya, Borovoye
797161	Pervoye Maya
797170	Voropayevo, Woropajewo
797300	Perbete, Prabuty, Pravda, Pribeta, Pripyat, Verbauti
797310	Provadiya
797340	Virovitica
797363	Vor Wedenthal
797364	Pravdinsk
797369	Poreby Dymarskie
797370	Przewodow, Przywitowo
797391	Pryvetroye
797400	Barabas, Barwica, Barwice, Bauerwitz, Beravci, Bierwce, Borovtse, Borowica, Borowiec, Bravica, Bravicea, Bravitcha, Brawicza, Fruhbuss, Parabuc, Parypsy, Porpac, Prebuz, Preveza, Prievidza, Privigye, Przywoz, Varboc, Varviz, Verbasz, Verbizh, Verbocz, Verbouts,

	Verhovca, Verovice, Vrapce, Vrbas, Werbcze, Werbiz
797430	Barbesti, Berbesht, Berbesti, Borbest, Probishta, Przypust
797439	Probstdorf
797440	Pohrebyszcze, Porebishce
797447	Przewodziszowice
797450	Borovsk, Pfarrweisach, Propoisk
797453	Poreba Zegoty
797460	Braviceni, Probezhna, Probuzhne, Probuzna, Przebieczany, Przybyszyn
797464	Wierbiaz Nizny
797468	Werbcze Male
797470	Przybyszew, Przybyszowy
797473	Poreba Spytkowska, Worpswede
797475	Przybyszowka
797478	Werbcze Wielkie
797487	Przybyslawice
797493	Poreba Srednia
797500	Bauerbach, Borivka, Borofka, Borovichi, Borovka, Braubach, Bravicha, Fauerbach, Forbach, Porabka, Porabki, Verhovka, Verveghiu
797543	Warpechy Stare
797547	Poreba Koceby
797560	Bravicheny
797568	Verbche Male
797570	Pravikov
797571	Fauerbach bei Nidda
797574	Werbkowice
797578	Verbche Velke
797590	Borowa Gora
797600	Berveni, Brvany, Burwin, Pryben, Verbyany, Virbain, Vorobin, Vrbanja, Worobin
797640	Borownica, Vrbnica
797645	Pervomaysk, Pervomayskaya, Pierwomajsk, Pravieniskes, Pravinishok
797647	Verbionzh Vyzhny
797650	Barwinek, Parafianka, Parafjanka, Perbenik, Pribenik
797656	Berwangen
797660	Pravonin
797669	Perve Numer
797670	Brwinow, Parafianova, Parafianowo, Parafjanowo, Parafyanovo
797680	Poreba Mala
797696	Breb Maramures
797700	Vrbove, Wyrebow
797737	Poruba pod Vihorlatom
797740	Verbovets, Verbovitz, Verbovtsy, Vrbovce, Vrbovec, Werbowez
797745	Vrbovsko
797750	Przybowka
797800	Barbele, Borfalu, Borvely, Perbal, Przewale, Przewaly, Verbal, Verpole, Vrable
797830	Barwalde, Freiwaldau, Furfeld, Prepelita, Varpalota, Verpelet, Warfleth
797833	Barwald Dolny
797836	Beerfelden
797837	Fryvaldov
797840	Prepelitsa, Virbalis
797843	Borvalaszut, Pribilesti
797844	Porpliszcze
797845	Porplishche
797846	Perewoloczna, Przewloczna, Wroblaczyn

797850	Privalki, Przewalka, Przewloka
797854	Wroblik Szlachecki
797855	Wroblik Krolewski
797856	Perevolochna, Voroblyachin
797860	Fehrbellin, Virbalin, Virbaln, Virbolin, Wirballen
797864	Vorvolintse, Worwolince
797865	Varpalanka, Worblingen
797870	Barafalva, Probulov, Przybylow
797874	Vrublevshchina, Wroblewszczyzna, Wroblowice
797875	Wroblowka
797900	Brovari, Brovary, Browary, Pribor
797930	Perebrodye, Przebrody
797936	Przewrotne
797940	Perebrodye, Przybradz
797943	Praporiste
797945	Perevorsk, Przeworsk
797947	Barbircheff
797950	Freiberg, Freiburg, Warburg
797956	Freiburg im Breisgau
797957	Forwarki Wielkie
797960	Pribram, Varvareni
797964	Warwarynce
797970	Przyborow
797974	Borowirowszczyzna, Przyborowice Gorne
797975	Varvarovka, Vorvorovka, Warwarowka
798000	Berlohy, Borla, Borolea, Braila, Breila, Bril, Bruel, Bruhl, Firlej, Frille, Parole, Prayl, Preil, Preili, Preilu, Preli, Varel, Werl, Worl
798170	Firlejow
798175	Firlejowka, Firleyuvka
798300	Baraolt, Barlad, Berlad, Birlad, Parlita, Parliti, Werlte
798339	Parlita Targ
798360	Barladeni, Barlyadyany, Farladeny, Farladyany, Parjolteni, Porladany, Pyrzholteny
798363	Farladani Tighina
798394	Proletarskiy
798396	Fraulautern
798400	Brilice, Perlasz, Perlez, Perlitz, Pirlitz, Pohrlitz, Prelic, Prelouc, Pyrlits, Pyrlitsa, Worlitz
798430	Borlesti
798439	Warele Stare
798450	Przyleczek
798460	Barlyadyany, Berolzheim, Farladyany
798465	Freilassing
798500	Berlochy, Berlogy, Brylki, Perlach, Prelog, Preluki, Prilog, Priluki, Przylek, Przylogi, Przyluka
798565	Berlichingen
798570	Brelikow, Frelichow
798574	Perelkowce
798600	Berlin, Bralin, Brilon, Prauliena
798630	Berlinti
798639	Frielendorf
798640	Berlintsy, Brylince, Praulienas, Varalmas
798643	Burlaneshty, Burlanesti
798650	Barlinek, Brolniki
798656	Berlinchen
798659	Paraul Negru

798700	Barylow, Baryluv, Brailov, Brailow, Bralov, Firleev, Przylubie, Warlubie
798740	Barlibas, Berlebas, Przylbic
798750	Birlovka, Prilbichi
798770	Prilepov
798780	Barlafalu
798795	Berleburg, Perleberg
799000	Prerau
799300	Pererita, Pereryta
799330	Borrstadt, Worrstadt
799350	Borohradek
799370	Przeradowo
799446	Brzerzusnia
799468	Przeradz Maly
799480	Pererosl, Preraslia, Przerosl
799600	Freren
799700	Prerov, Przerab, Przyrab, Przyrow
799764	Przyrownica
800000	Laa, Le, Leh, Luh, Luhy
814569	Lajoskomarom
814640	Lajosmizse, Lejasciems
816000	Lujeni
817000	Lojowa, Loyev
819300	Lujerdiu
819400	Lujerdiu
830000	Lad, Lada, Lauda, Let, Lettau, Lhota, Lhuta, Liady, Lida, Lite, Littau, Liuta, Lode, Lueta, Luta, Lyadi, Lyady
831000	Litija
833000	Ludad, Lutita
833600	Litetiny, Litiatyn, Lityatin
833650	Lotatniki
833700	Lititov, Lututov, Lututow
834000	Ladce, Ladhaza, Latacz, Ledec, Letca, Lidice, Lodes, Lodus, Ludus, Lutcza
834500	Latoszek, Ledyczek
834600	Ladosno, Ladyczyn, Ladyshin, Ladyzhin, Latczyn, Latyczyn
834650	Ladyzhinka, Ladyzinka, Lodishenka
834665	Ladizhnenka
834700	Latyczow, Letichev, Letitchev
834836	Ludosul de Muras
835000	Ladek, Latach, Letky, Litka, Litke, Lutki, Luttich
835300	Lajtakata
835400	Ladhaza
835439	Ladek Zdroj
835634	Ledec nad Sazavou
835700	Letichuv
835740	Lodygowice
835750	Lutkowka
835950	Leutkirch
835964	Ludcrinetz
835970	Lodherov
836000	Ladany, Ladejn, Laden, Lathen, Laudona, Letenye, Letiny, Letnia, Letnya, Liten, Litene, Liteni, Litin, Lityn, Litynia, Litynya, Lodyna, Ludany, Ludin, Ludynia, Ludynie, Lyudyn, Lyudyne
836300	Letmathe
836379	Lad nad Warta
836397	Ladendorf, Ludendorf
836400	Ladance, Ladantse, Ladantsy, Ladmoc, Laudonas, Lednica, Lodenice
836430	Ludenscheid

836450	Lutynsk, Lyutynsk
836480	Litomysl
836500	Latanka, Ludinka, Luttange
836546	Ludinghausen
836576	Leidenhofen
836670	Lodyna Nova, Lodyna Nowa
836700	Ludinovo
836740	Ladmovce, Ludeniewicze
836750	Laudenbach, Lyudenevichi
836760	Ladanybene, Leidenhofen
836795	Ladenburg, Lautenburg
836875	Ludmilowka
836900	Ladmir, Ladomer, Ljutomer, Lodmer, Lodomeria, Ludomir
836940	Leitmeritz, Litomerice
836945	Lutamiersk, Lutomiersk
836970	Ladomirova
836974	Ladimirevci, Ladimirewzi
837000	Letov, Lietuva, Litva, Litwa, Lotow, Lutowo
837400	Ladowicze, Latowicz, Latowicze, Ledvice, Letowice, Litovice, Litovizh, Litowiz, Lotovitch
837450	Litevisk, Litovisk, Lutoviska, Lutowiska
837460	Ladbesenyo, Ludvisin, Ludwisin, Ludwiszyn
837500	Lyadovichi
837547	Ludwigsburg, Ludwigshafen
837548	Ludwigslust
837549	Ludwigshorst
837570	Ludwikow, Ludwikowo
837600	Letownia, Liduvian, Ludwin, Lyduvenai
837650	Lidvinka, Litvinki, Litwinki
837670	Lidvinov, Litvonovo, Ludwinow
837674	Liudvinavas
837680	Lotwa Mala
837780	Ljudwipol, Ludvipol, Ludwipol, Lyudvipol
837800	Litovel
837830	Littfeld
837945	Liutavariskes
837950	Ludberg, Ludbreg
838000	Litol
838460	Liedolsheim
838700	Litohlavy
839300	Letohrad, Lothard
839400	Lutoryz
839430	Luthorst
839433	Lutherstadt Wittenberg
839446	Leutershausen
839476	Leitershofen
839500	Ledurga
839560	Lauterecken
839600	Latrany, Lutrini
839700	Lodherov
839750	Lauterbach
839796	Lauterbrunn
840000	Lac, Laca, Laisa, Lajsce, Laschia, Lash, Lasha, Lasi, Lasse, Lassee, Lasu, Lazi, Lazo, Lazy, Les, Lesu, Leutschau, Lezce, Lissa, Litschau, Locs, Lodz, Lodzh, Losch, Losha, Losie, Loza, Lozdzee, Luc, Luca, Ludza, Lusca, Luze, Lysa, Lyse
841000	Lozdzieje
841569	Liuzii Homoru Lui
841590	Lysaja Gora
843000	Lazdei, Lazdey, Lazhdai, Lezdi, Lozdzieje
843100	Lazdijai
843300	Lustadt
843400	Lisiatycze, Lostice
843487	Las Toczylowo
843500	Lasotki, Lisyatychi
843600	Lazdona, Lazduny, Lestina, Listany, Lustenau
843640	Lustenice
843690	Lastomir
843700	Lastovo
843740	Lastovce
843750	Lastivka, Lastowki, Lastuvki, Lostowka
843760	Listvin, Listwin
843770	Las Debowy
843970	Lisdorf, Loosdorf
844000	Laczhaz, Laidzes, Lecycza, Leczyca, Lisets, Lisitse, Lisitz, Loschitz, Loshits, Loshitz, Losiacz, Losice, Lositse, Luczyce, Lysets, Lysica, Lysiec
844300	Lozisht
844350	Leszczatka
844370	Leszczatow
844390	Liza Stara
844500	Lasitsk, Laszczki, Laziska, Lezajsk, Lezhaysk
844570	Leshchkuv, Leszczkow
844600	Lasocin, Lasoczyn, Laszczyn, Leszczyn, Lososna, Lososno
844638	Lososina Dolna
844640	Laidzesciems, Leszczance
844650	Leszczanka
844659	Lososina Gorna
844700	Laszczow, Loshtchov
844730	Leszczowate
844738	Leszczawa Dolna
844750	Laszczowka, Leszczawka
844759	Leszczawa Gorna
844760	Legyesbenye
845000	Lacko, Laczka, Lasick, Lask, Laski, Lasko, Laszki, Lecka, Lesko, Lisek, Lishki, Lisk, Liska, Liski, Lisko, Liszki, Liszko, Litzki, Losk, Losyach, Lucka, Lushki, Lusk, Luszki, Lutsk, Lutzk, Luytsk, Luzhki, Luzk, Luzki, Luzkye
845100	Lascaia
845300	Laskod
845370	Leshchatuv
845386	Laszki Dolne, Luzek Dolny, Luzhek Dolny, Lyashki Dolne
845439	Lysiec Stary
845470	Laskaczev, Laskazhev
845485	Ladzkie Szlacheckie, Lyadske Shlyakhetske
845546	Laszki Goscincowe
845596	Laszki Gorne, Lyashki Gurne
845598	Laszki Krolewskie
845600	Leshchin
845640	Leshchantse
845645	Lisichansk
845650	Lesechniki
845700	Lashchov, Lashkuv, Laskow, Laskuv, Lasochow, Laszkow, Latzkawa, Latzkeva, Latzkova, Letzkova, Lezachow, Lieskova, Lisicovo, Liskava, Liskeva, Liskiava, Liskova, Liskovo, Lysakow, Lyskovo, Lyskow, Lyskuv
845730	Liskowate
845740	Laskovtsy, Laskowce, Laskowice, Laskowicze, Laskowiec, Leskovac, Leszkowice, Lichkovtse, Liczkowce, Liskovitz, Luchkovtsy, Lyszkowice, Lyszkowicze
845743	Liszkopuszta
845744	Laczki Brzeskie
845747	Laskowicze Wielkie
845748	Laskowice Olawskie
845750	Laskowka, Leskovichi, Lyaskovichi, Lysakowek
845757	Lyaskoviche Velke
845780	Laska Wola
845785	Luytsk Vilka
845794	Laczki Brzeskie
845860	Laisgol M
845900	Lisia Gora, Lysa Gora
845947	Laskarzev, Laskarzew
845960	Laskorun, Lyskornia
845970	Laskarov, Laskerov, Laskirov
846000	Laasan, Laczna, Lasin, Lazany, Leczna, Leczyn, Leshnya, Lesna, Lessen, Leszna, Leszno, Letschin, Leuseni, Leusheni, Leusheny, Lezany, Lezyny, Liezen, Liozna, Liozno, Lisen, Lishnya, Lisna, Liszna, Lisznia, Liszno, Liutchin, Liutsyn, Ljuzyn, Loetzen, Losno, Lotzen, Loucen, Loucim, Lozin, Lozina, Lozna, Lozno, Lscin, Luczany, Ludzen, Ludzin, Luschan, Lusino, Lutsen, Luzan, Luzany, Luzhany, Luzna, Lyusino, Lyutsin, Lzin
846100	Lesnoye
846148	Lesnaya Slobodka
846158	Lesnoy Khlebichin
846300	Lucinet
846400	Laschinca, Leschnitz, Lesenice, Lesienice, Lesnica, Lisienica, Lisnice, Litshenitz, Losiniec, Losonc, Losoncz, Lucenec, Lutschinez
846436	Lesencetomaj
846440	Lucincic
846443	Lesenceistvand
846450	Lezansk, Lizansk, Lizhensk, Lozansky, Lzhansk
846500	Lesnyaki, Liesing, Lisianka, Lisinka, Lisnyaki, Luzhanka, Lysanka, Lysyanka
846534	Lisnik Duzy
846559	Lodzinka Gorna
846564	Lazne Kynzvart
846578	Lesnica Opolska
846600	Lozniany
846630	Lecninta
846633	Loucna nad Desnou
846643	Litzmannstadt, Litzmanstadt
846690	Lozna Mare
846700	Leshnev, Leshnov, Lesniow, Lesnowo, Leszinow, Leszniow, Lisnowo, Loshnev, Loszniow, Luszniewo, Lyushnevo
846738	Lesna Podlaska
846740	Lesniovitse, Lesniowice, Luczanowice
846745	Laznowska Wola
846750	Lesnevichi, Lezanowka, Lezhanovka, Lezhanuvka,

	Lishnevka, Lishniovka, Lishnivka, Lisnovka, Liszniowka
846780	Lecznowola
846793	Lesno Brdo
846854	Lozno Aleksandrovka
846900	Lecsmer, Lesmir, Leuseni Orhei
846940	Lucmierz, Ludzimierz
846950	Leuseni Orhei
847000	Laasphe, Laizuva, Laszow, Latzuva, Layzheve, Lazow, Leizeva, Lisow, Lisowa, Lisowo, Lozova, Lozovia, Lozovo, Luszawa, Lysow
847100	Lozovaja, Lozovaya
847300	Lisaveta
847365	Lazy pod Makytou
847400	Lasowice, Lespezi, Lisovitse, Lisowce, Lisowice, Luszowice, Lysowiec
847450	Lazovsk
847459	Luszowice Gorne
847463	Lispeszentadorjan
847500	Laszowka, Lisobiki, Lisoviki, Lysobyki
847594	Luszawa Karczma
847865	Lusci Palanka
847870	Lucfalva
847950	Lidzbark, Lisberg
847957	Lidzbark Warminski
848000	Leslau, Leslo, Loslau
848100	Lesluya
848454	Lutzelsachsen
848600	Laisholm
848700	Laslovo
848740	Luslawice
849000	Lazarea, Lazuri, Lieser, Liezere
849300	Lazaret
849400	Liezeres
849470	Latchorzew
849600	Lozorno
850000	Jlok, Laage, Lage, Lak, Laka, Leghea, Leiha, Leki, Lich, Liege, Liegi, Liga, Lika, Loka, Lucha, Luck, Luga, Lugi, Lugoj, Luhe, Luka, Lukoy, Luky, Luoka, Luoke, Lyck, Ylakai, Ylakiai, Ylok
853000	Lagedi, Lakta, Lhota, Lhuta, Lichty, Loket, Lugde
853386	Lakta Dolna
853400	Loktyshi, Loktysze
853500	Lokietka
853596	Lakta Gorna
853600	Legden, Lichtenau, Ligatne, Lochotin
853638	Lichtental
853643	Lichtenstadt
853670	Lochtynowo
853678	Lichtenfels
853679	Lichtenberg
853700	Lahodow
853860	Leki Dolne
853978	Lichterfelde
854000	Lagisza, Lakocsa, Lehocz, Lekeciai, Lokacze, Lokatchi, Luchcze, Lugazi, Lugos, Lugosch, Lukshi, Luksiai
854330	Lokstedt
854396	Leihgestern
854446	Leka Szczucinska
854466	Lagisza Cmentarna
854500	Lahoisk, Logoisk, Logosk, Logoysk, Lukiszki

854594	Lukatz Kreuz
854600	Lahiszyn, Liksna, Lochocin, Logishin, Lohishin, Lohiszyn, Lucaceni, Lukaczin, Lukoszyn, Luxheim, Lykoszyn
854639	Leksandrowa
854679	Laxenburg
854700	Laguszow
854750	Lukashevka, Lukaszewka
854854	Laka Szlachecka
854855	Lackie Szlacheckie, Leki Szlacheckie
855000	Lechicha, Logig, Lokach, Lokachi, Lukach, Lyukhcha, Lyukhche
855600	Lukacheny
855750	Lukachevka
855840	Lugi Golasze
855960	Leki Gorne
855987	Leki Krolewskie
856000	Lachen, Lauchheim, Lechna, Leeheim, Legina, Lekenye, Ligem, Ligum, Ligumai, Luchin, Luchine, Luchini, Luginy, Luhin, Lygumai
856300	Lechinta, Legend
856400	Legnica, Legonice, Liegnitz, Lockenhaus, Locknitz, Loknica, Loknitsa, Luchinets
856430	Loganeshty, Loganesti
856450	Lekinsko, Lochynsko, Luchinchik, Lugansk, Luhansk
856470	Legniszewo
856500	Lechenich, Lekenik, Loknik, Luknik
856540	Lockenhaus
856600	Lauknen, Ligmian, Ligmiany
856680	Legenyemihly
856700	Legionowo, Luknif
856740	Lukanowice, Lukjanowicze
856750	Lackenbach, Lakompak, Lukyanovichi
856783	Luckenwalde
856800	Luka Mala
856846	Legenyealsomihal
856930	Lichenroth
857000	Lachawa, Lachva, Lachwa, Lagow, Lakhva, Lakhwa, Laukuba, Laukuva, Lecava, Lechow, Leckava, Leckawa, Lekawa, Lgov, Lickov, Likeva, Likeve, Likova, Lochov, Lochow, Logiv, Loykeva, Loykova, Luhova, Lukov, Lukova, Lukovo, Lukow, Lukowa, Lukowe, Lukowo, Luykeve
857300	Lucavita
857340	Likavitos
857383	Lucavatul de Jos, Lucavatul de Sus
857386	Luchow Dolny
857400	Lachovici, Lachovitch, Lachowce, Lachowcy, Lachowice, Lachowicze, Lahovec, Lahoviz, Lakhovtsy, Lecavas, Lechovice, Lechovich, Lechovicz, Lechowitz, Lekawica, Lekhevich, Lekhovich, Liachovitch, Liachovitz, Ljachowzy, Lochovice, Lochvitza, Lochwica, Lokhvitsa,

	Lokhvitza, Lukavec, Lukavets, Lukavitsa, Lukavytsa, Lukawica, Lukawiec, Lukovitsa, Lukowica, Lukvitsa, Lyakhovitse, Lyakhovtsy
857444	Lyakhovitse Zazhechke
857449	Lachowice Zarzeczne
857463	Lukavets Maydan
857473	Lachowice Podrozne, Lyakhovitse Podruzhne
857500	Lakhoviche, Lechowek, Lukowek, Lyakhovitse, Lyakhovichi
857567	Lagowica Nowa
857596	Luchow Gorny
857600	Lichwin
857633	Lukov nad Toplou
857650	Lagiewniki
857675	Logvinoviche
857800	Luga Wola
857830	Lechfeld
857850	Lackie Wielkie, Leki Wielkie, Lugi Wielkie, Luka Wielka, Luki Wielkie
858650	Leh Lunka
859300	Legrad, Lekart
859435	Laka Rustykalna
859500	Lacarak
859740	Lekarovce
859857	Lager Lechfeld
860000	Laehn, Lahn, Lan, Lania, Lany, Lauenau, Laun, Lemniu, Line, Lohne, Lom, Lomna, Lone, Lonie, Lonya, Louny, Luhyna, Luna, Lunna, Lunno
863000	Jleanda, Landau, Lanieta, Lenti, Lindau
863140	Luna de Jos
863430	Landeshut
863431	Lentestii de Jos
863439	Landestreu
863440	Luna de Sus
863500	Landeck, Lindach
863560	Lindheim
863564	Landek im Schlesien
863567	Landek im Westpreussen
863578	Lentikapolna
863594	Lindhorst
863600	Leontina, Linden, Lindheim
863639	Landau an der Isar, Landau in der Pfalz
863643	Lindenschied
863671	Linden bei Hannover
863679	Lundenburg
863700	Lendava, Leontyevo, Lyntupy
863740	Lentupis
863797	Landvarov, Landvorova, Landwarow
863931	Laa an der Thaya
863940	Lindhorst
863943	Lendersdorf
863944	Lendershausen
863970	Londorf
864000	Lemes, Lenci, Lencze, Lienz, Linitz, Linz, Lomaz, Lomazy, Lomnica, Lomnice, Lomnitz, Lomza, Lomzha, Lunca
864300	Landshut, Lantsut, Lantzut
864380	Landstuhl
864397	Landstrew
864400	Lenesice, Lentshits, Lintchitz, Lomzyca, Luntzitz

864474	Lomzycza Wyzna
864500	Lansk, Linsk
864596	Lanchkorun, Lanskroun, Lantskorun, Lantzekronia, Lencze Gorne
864600	Lamsheim, Lanczyn, Lanshin, Lantchin, Lemesany, Lencin, Lenczna, Lentchna, Leoncin
864640	Lemniu Somes
864656	Lenzingen
864659	Lanzenkirchen
864690	Linz am Rhein
864695	Linz am Rhein
864740	Lemieszewicze
864750	Lemeshevichi
864783	Lohnsfeld
864795	Landsberg, Landsberg am Lech, Landsberg an der Prosna, Landsberg an der Warthe, Landsberg Ost Preussen
864796	Lamspringe
864800	Lemsal, Lemzal
864833	Lengyeltoti
864848	Lengyelszallas
864900	Luncsoara
865000	Lanek, Lanka, Lemgo, Lenke, Linkah, Linnich, Lynki
865300	Lancut, Lankti, Lencauti
865314	Lunca de Jos
865340	Langadas
865353	Lencauti Hotin
865400	Lenchitsa, Linchits, Linkitz
865430	Langside
865439	Langsdorf, Lomnica Zdroj
865450	Linkiskiai
865478	Lengsfeld
865496	Lunga Cernei de Jos
865500	Lenchicha, Lunchich
865564	Lang Gons
865600	Lanchin, Langen, Lauingen, Lenchna, Lingen, Linkani, Lymgumai
865637	Langendiebach
865639	Langendorf
865643	Langenscheid
865646	Langenzenn
865647	Langendiebach, Langenschwalbach, Langenschwarz
865648	Langensalza, Langenselbold
865649	Langenzersdorf
865660	Linkmenai, Lyngmiany
865664	Linkmenys
865678	Langenbielau, Langenfeld, Lingenfeld
865679	Langen Bergheim, Langenberg, Langenbrucken
865680	Lanki Male
865683	Langenaltheim
865684	Langenlois
865686	Langenlonsheim
865699	Langenrohr
865700	Leonhoff, Linkeve, Linkova, Linkovo, Linkowo, Linkuva
865740	Lenkovtsy
865783	Lengfeld
865789	Langweiler
865793	Lunca Bradului
865946	Lenkersheim
865950	Lengerich
865960	Lanckorona
865975	Langerwehe
866000	Leimen, Lenin, Lenino, Leonin,

	Liman, Lniano, Lounin, Lunen, Lunin
866397	Lenindorf
866400	Luninets, Luniniec, Luninits, Luninitz, Luninyets
866430	Lom u Mostu
866451	Leninskaya Kopalnya, Leninskoye
866500	Lomianek, Lomianki
866559	Lomianki Gorne
866560	Loningen
866593	Leningrad
866680	Lenina Mala
866681	Lenina Malaya
866700	Limanowa, Limonov
866785	Lenina Velka, Lenina Wielka
867000	Leonhoff, Linevo, Linow, Linowo, Lyniew, Lyniow
867400	Lanovits, Lanovitz, Lanovtse, Lanovtsy, Lanowce, Lanowice, Lanowicze, Lanowiec, Limbazhi, Limbazi, Lounovice
867460	Lambsheim
867500	Laimbach, Lembeck, Limbach
867600	Lempino
867617	Limbenii Vechi
867785	Luniewo Wielkie
867800	Leonpol, Lunavolia, Lunna Wola
867845	Lany Polskie, Lany Polskie
867850	Lany Wielkie
867930	Lemforde, Lompirt
867934	Lampertice
867936	Lampertheim
867950	Lauenberg, Lauenburg, Lemberg, Limberk, Limburg, Lohnberg, Lueneburg, Luneburg
867954	Lamprechtshausen
867956	Limburg an der Lahn
867959	Luneburger Heide
869000	Limmer, Lnare
869378	Lenardfalu
869394	Lenarddaroc
869433	Lonnerstadt
869439	Loimersdorf
869440	Lenarczyce
869460	Leimersheim, Lommersum
870000	Labiau, Lapi, Lapiai, Lapy, Lauf, Leba, Leova, Leovo, Leva, Levo, Libau, Liboi, Liebau, Lipa, Lipau, Lipie, Lippo, Liw, Lobau, Lof, Lovo, Lubau
871000	Liboya, Liepaja
871740	Libejovice
873000	Labod, Lipot, Livada, Lopaty, Lyebed
873300	Liptod
873378	Liptotepla, Liptoteplicska
873400	Libedice, Lipetitcha, Lopatycze, Lubotice
873436	Livada Satu Mare, Lyptosztmiklo
873463	Liptoszentmiklos
873500	Leiptig, Lopatki, Lopatyche
873555	Lepeticha Hagdola
873600	Lebedin, Lebiedyn, Livada Noua, Lobodno, Lopatin, Lopatna, Lopatno, Lopatyn, Lopayton, Lubotin, Lubotyn, Lubtheen, Lyubotin
873640	Lopatnic
873643	Lubotyn Stary

873650	Lopatnik
873700	Lebedevo, Lebedov, Lebedowa, Lebiedziew, Lubatowa, Lubitow, Lyubitov
873745	Liptovska Anna, Liptovska Tepla, Liptovska Teplicka, Liptovsky Hradok, Liptovsky Mikulas, Liptovsky Svaty Mikulas, Lubitowska Wolka
873750	Lyubitovka
873774	Lapy Debowizna
873860	Labatlan
873940	Libodrice
873946	Liptorosenberg
874000	Labacz, Labedz, Labes, Labetz, Lapitch, Lapos, Lapus, Leibitz, Levice, Levoca, Libez, Libiaz, Libidza, Libusza, Liepas, Lipca, Lipcse, Lipec, Lipica, Lipsa, Lipsha, Liubitch, Livezi, Liwcze, Lovich, Lowce, Lowcza, Lowicz, Loyvitch, Lubasch, Lubasz, Lubca, Lubce, Lubcz, Lubcza, Lubec, Lubiaz, Lubica, Lubicz, Lubocz, Lubrza, Lubsza, Lubtch, Lubtse, Lubz, Luyvich, Lyubsha, Lyubyaz
874330	Liebstadt, Lippstadt
874386	Lipitsa Dolna
874396	Lubostron
874397	Leubsdorf
874400	Lapczyca, Leobschuetz, Leobschutz, Libesice, Liebesice, Ljubescica, Lobositz, Lovosice, Lowczyce
874500	Layptsig, Layptsik, Leipzig, Lipsk, Lipsko, Lowczyk, Lowisko, Lubbecke, Lubiczko, Lupisuki
874560	Lubycza Kam
874563	Lipsk nad Biebrza, Lipsko nad Wisla
874564	Lubycza Kniazie
874568	Lopuszka Mala
874573	Lipskie Budy
874578	Lopuszka Wielka
874596	Lipitsa Gurna
874598	Lubycza Krolewska
874600	Labischin, Labiszyn, Lapshin, Lapszyn, Lapushna, Lapusna, Lawoczne, Lepseny, Libusin, Lipceni, Lipiczany, Lopatchna, Loposhna, Lopuszna, Lopuszno, Lubaczyn, Lubiczyn, Lubzina
874640	Lipcsemezo, Lobsens, Lobsenz, Lobzenica, Lopushnitsa, Lopusznica
874646	Lapsze Nizne
874656	Lopsingen
874658	Lopuszanka Lechniowa
874700	Lapiszow, Lapszow, Lebiedziew, Libatchov, Libiszow, Liubachev, Lobozew, Lowczow, Lubaczow, Lubashov, Lubaszewo, Lubaszowa, Lubatchov, Lubeczow, Lubieszow, Lubishov, Lyubashev, Lyubeshov, Lyubichev
874736	Lovaszpatona

874740	Libceves, Libesovice
874746	Lapsze Wyzne
874750	Lobaczowka, Lowczowek, Lubashovka, Lyubashevka
874785	Libiaz Wielki
874796	Lippspringe, Lovasbereny
874800	Lapusel
874900	Lubezere
875000	Labach, Laibach, Lapichi, Laubach, Lipik, Lipki, Lubch, Lubeck, Luebeck, Lyubch, Lyubcha, Lyubech
875386	Lipica Dolna
875400	Lapiguz, Libouchec
875460	Libickozma
875485	Liwki Szlacheckie
875596	Lipica Gorna
875600	Lavochne, Libocany, Lipcani, Lipcany, Lipcheny, Lipkan, Lipkany, Lubochiny, Lyubachin, Lyubokhiny
875639	Lipcani Targ
875643	Lipcani Sat
875700	Lavkov, Lavkovo, Levkiev, Levkov, Lewkow, Libechov, Libechuyv, Lipkow, Lopuchowa, Lopukhov, Lubachov, Lubachowy, Lubichuv, Lupkow
875740	Libochovice, Liebochowitz, Lubikowicze
875750	Lobachevka, Lyubikovichi
875760	Libochovany
875786	Lipecka Palana
875860	Liepkalne
875864	Liepkalns
875900	Libochora, Libohora, Libokhora, Libuchora, Libukhora, Liebochora
875950	Luby Kurki
875970	Lipa Krepa
876000	Labun, Labunie, Lauban, Laupheim, Lavini, Lebeny, Leipheim, Leiwen, Leoben, Lepna, Liban, Liben, Libien, Libna, Liboun, Libyne, Lieben, Liebenau, Liepna, Lipen, Lipiny, Lipna, Lipne, Lipno, Lipon, Lippehne, Liuban, Livani, Livno, Livny, Livonia, Ljuban, Lopon, Lovyn, Lowen, Lowinia, Luban, Lubana, Lubben, Luben, Lubenia, Lubiana, Lubiane, Lubien, Lubienia, Lubin, Lubnie, Lubno, Lubny, Lupeni, Lyuban
876175	Livenii Vechi
876386	Lipiny Dolne
876400	Lapinoz, Leibnitz, Liepnas, Lipence, Lipnic, Lipnica, Lipnitza, Liubonitch, Ljubonitschi, Lubanas, Lubenec, Lubenets, Lubenitchi, Lubience
876433	Loewenstadt
876450	Lipnicka, Lipniczka, Lipniscek, Lipnishki, Lipnishky, Lipnishok, Lipnishuk, Lipniszki, Lipniszok
876468	Lopenitsa Mala
876480	Libomysl
876483	Laufenselden
876500	Labunki, Leipnik, Libinky, Liebing, Lipinki, Lipniaki, Lipnik, Lipniki, Lopianka,

	Lopienka, Lopiennik, Lubenichi, Lubienka, Lubienko, Lubinka, Lubonik, Lyubonichi
876517	Lubien Kujawski
876538	Lipnica Dolna
876543	Lupianka Stara
876559	Lopiennik Gorny
876560	Lebenhan
876563	Lipnik nad Becou
876564	Lubianki Nizsze
876568	Lipnica Mala, Lipnik Maly, Lopienica Mala
876569	Lipnica Murowana
876570	Lievenhof, Livenhof, Liwenhof
876578	Lipnica Wielka
876584	Lipa Miklas, Lopiennik Lacki
876596	Lipiny Gorne
876600	Lebenhan
876670	Lipina Nowa, Lipiny Nowe
876700	Lapanow, Lapnov, Lewniowa, Lievenhof, Livenhof, Liwenhof, Lubanow
876740	Lohwinowicze, Lubno Opace
876744	Lewin Brzeski
876780	Levinpol
876783	Liebenwalde
876785	Lubien Wielki
876787	Libanfalva
876794	Lewin Brzeski
876795	Lowenberg
876800	Liubomil, Luboml, Lyuboml
876874	Luboml Wies, Lyuboml Wies
876940	Lubomierz
876950	Lubomirka
877000	Labowa, Lapovo, Libava, Libawa, Libov, Libova, Lipova, Lipowa, Liubova, Lubawa, Lubova, Lubow, Lviv, Lvov, Lvovo, Lwow, Lwowo
877300	Lipovat
877390	Lovopetri
877400	Lipovec, Lipovets, Lipovetz, Lipovtse, Lipovtsy, Lipowce, Lipowice, Lipowiec, Liubavas, Lubavich, Lubavitch, Lyubavitch
877440	Lipowczyce
877453	Libavske Udoli
877478	Lubowicz Wielki
877500	Lipovka, Lipowka, Lubavichi, Lwowek, Lyubavichi
877548	Lwowek Slaski
877600	Libevne, Libovne
878000	Leopol, Lepel, Level, Lubela, Lubella, Lubla, Lubola, Lyubelya
878370	Leopoldow, Leopoldowo
878400	Lieblos, Liplas, Lublica
878439	Leopoldsdorf, Leopoldsdorf im Marchfelde
878450	Lubelski
878480	Leopoldshall
878500	Levelek
878596	Lublo Krempach
878600	Lipljan, Ljubljana, Lublin
878630	Liflandia
878640	Liflandia, Lubliniec, Lublinitz
878654	Leipalingis, Leipolingis, Lubliniec Stary
878656	Lubliniec Nowy
878658	Liublin Colonie
878700	Lupolovo

878750	Leplevka, Leplowka
878900	Liblar
879000	Laubere, Liubar, Luber, Lubrza, Lyubar
879300	Laferte, Lipperode
879370	Levertev, Levertov, Libertow, Lieber Tov, Lubartov, Lubartow, Lyubartov
879400	Liberec, Liborice, Lieberose, Livberze
879439	Leobersdorf
879440	Luborzitza, Luborzyca
879458	Liebarska Lucka
879478	Laufersweiler
879500	Lauberg, Lebork
879546	Leverkusen
879570	Lawrykow
879637	Librantowa
879640	Lubraniec, Lubranitz, Lyubranets
879700	Lavrov, Lavruv, Lawrow
879764	Librava Mesto
881000	Leleiu
884000	Leles, Lelesz, Lielauce
884397	Lielstraupe
884400	Leltchitz, Leltzitz
884783	Lulsfeld
885400	Lelchitsy
885560	Lielkokini
885700	Lelikov, Lelikow, Lelikuv
885750	Lelechowka, Lelekhovka
886000	Lalin, Leliunai
886783	Lilienfeld
887000	Lalova, Lalovo, Lelev, Lelewo, Leliwa, Lelow
887400	Lahlapos, Lelowice
887800	Liliopol, Liljopol
887930	Lielvarde
889000	Lollar
890000	Lahr, Leer, Lohr, Lohra, Lorau
893000	Lehrte, Loretto
893600	Leordina, Lerdene, Lerdine
894000	Larissa, Leros, Lorsch
895000	Larga, Lerche, Lorrach
895300	Laurahutte
895736	Lohrhaupten
896000	Lern
896397	Larindorf
896400	Lorinci
896436	Lehrensteinsfeld
896660	Lohr am Main
897000	Lorev
897360	Lohrhaupten
897950	Lehrberg
900000	Rae
910000	Reiu
914000	Rajec
915000	Rijeka
916000	Rujene, Rujiena
917000	Rayov, Rejow
917400	Rejowiec, Reyovyets
917480	Rajevo Selo
919475	Reyersbach
930000	Radau, Rede, Ret, Rethe, Reti, Reutte, Rheda, Rhede, Rheydt, Rite, Roth, Rott, Ruda
931000	Radoaia, Radoya
931487	Rataje Slupskie
931700	Radziejow, Radziejowa
931740	Radajowice, Radojewice, Radziejowice
931794	Ruda Jaworska, Ruda

	Yavorskaya
933000	Radauti
933395	Radauti Dorohoi
933400	Rodatycze
933450	Radutiskiai
933500	Rodatyche
933600	Radotin
933700	Rydoduby
933874	Ruda Talubska
934000	Radauts, Radautsi, Radautz, Radcza, Radcze, Radic, Radous, Radoyts, Radycz, Redics, Rhodes, Rhodos, Ridica, Rites
934357	Radostkow
934360	Radostyan
934400	Radoshitz, Radosice, Radoszyce
934450	Radczysk
934464	Ruda Zazamcze
934540	Radiskis
934574	Radoshkovitz, Radoszkowice, Radoszkowicze
934575	Radoshkovichi
934600	Radocina, Radocyna, Radoshin, Radoszyn, Radoszyna, Radziecin, Ratosnya, Rudesheim
934640	Radecznica
934750	Radoshevka
934760	Ratisbon
934845	Ruda Seletska, Ruda Sielecka, Ruda Slaska, Ruda Solska
934846	Ruda Zelazna
935000	Radcha, Radeikai, Radeikiai, Ratka, Ratkau, Redyk, Reteag, Retteg, Ridik, Riduk, Rodach, Rudig, Rudik, Rudka, Rudke, Rudki, Rutka, Rutki
935300	Ruda Huta
935387	Ruda Kotlowska
935440	Radgoshtch, Radgoszcz, Radogoszcz
935446	Radecczyzna
935450	Radchisk, Radchysk, Ratkoszuha
935459	Rudka Skroda
935479	Retkozberencs
935486	Ruda Koscielna
935495	Ratkoszirak
935516	Rudka Kijanska
935545	Rutki Kossaki
935569	Ratkogomor
935600	Rodgen, Rodheim
935640	Radochonce, Radokhontse, Radokhontsy, Rojtokmuzsaj
935660	Raducaneni
935698	Ruda Kameralna
935700	Radechov, Radekhov, Radikhiv, Radikhov, Radkov, Radziechow, Radziechowy, Ratkova, Ratkovo
935740	Radkovice, Retkovci
935743	Ratkobisztro
935745	Ratkovska Bystre, Ratkovska Sucha, Ratkovske Bystre
935945	Rudigershagen
935947	Radkersburg
935957	Ruda Krakovetska, Ruda Krakowiecka, Ruda Krechowska, Ruda Krekhuvska
936000	Radimno, Radna, Radom, Radun, Radymno, Radyn, Rahden, Ratin, Ratne, Ratno, Raudenai, Raudone, Redem, Redeni, Redeny, Redim, Rehden,

	Rhoden, Rodaun, Roddenau, Rodem, Rodheim, Rodna, Roteni, Rotin, Rotno, Rottum, Roudne, Rudni, Rudnia, Rudno, Rudnya, Ruthen
936175	Radenii Vechi
936300	Radnot
936360	Radenthein
936371	Radnotfaja
936379	Raudondvaris
936386	Rudno Dolne
936396	Rotenturm an der Pinka
936397	Ratndorf, Rottendorf, Rudendorf
936400	Radenice, Radenitse, Radnice, Radonice, Radonitz, Ratenice, Ratnycia, Raudenes, Raudenis, Raudnitz, Rotnica, Rotnitza, Rudance, Rudantse, Rudnica, Rudnitsa, Rudnitz, Rudnitza, Rudzienice
936433	Ruda Instytutowa
936439	Rotmistrovka, Rotmistrowka, Rudnia Staryki, Rudnya Staryki
936450	Radomsk, Radomsko
936460	Ratniceni
936463	Raudnitz an der Elbe, Roudnice nad Labem
936480	Radimishil, Radimishle, Radomishel, Radomishl, Radomishla, Radomishle, Radomyshl, Radomysl
936485	Radimishli Gadol
936486	Radomysl Maly
936487	Radomishl Vyelki, Radomysl Wielki
936489	Radomishli Rabati
936500	Radounka, Ridnik, Roding, Rudenka, Rudnik, Rudniki, Rudnok
936544	Ruddingshausen
936560	Ratingen, Rodingen, Roettingen, Rottingen
936594	Rudenko Ruske, Rudenko Ruskie, Rudniki Redziny
936595	Rothenkirchen
936600	Radenin, Radimin, Radomin, Rethimnon, Rodimin, Rudamin, Rudamina
936640	Rudmanns
936650	Rudninkai
936659	Ried im Innkreis
936700	Radimov, Rathenow, Rudniew
936740	Radnovce
936750	Radeni Vek, Rothenbach
936779	Rottenbauer, Rudnia Bobrowska, Rudnya Bobrovska
936784	Rotenfels, Rothenfels
936785	Rudna Wielka
936795	Riedenburg, Rodenberg, Rotenburg, Rothenburg, Rothenburg Ob der Tauber, Rottenburg
936864	Ruda Maleniecka
936900	Rediu Mare, Redyu Mare
937000	Radava, Radawa, Radoboj, Retovo, Riteva, Riteve, Ritova, Rudaw, Rudowa
937169	Roth bei Nurnberg
937400	Radevitz, Radivits, Radovis, Radovitch, Radovits,

	Radovtsy, Radowaz, Redwitz, Rietavas, Rietevas, Rodavetz, Rodewisch
937430	Radoviste
937463	Redwitz an der Rodach
937479	Rudy Przeworskie
937534	Radawiec Duzy
937547	Radziev Kusawski
937578	Radawiec Wielki
937600	Radvan, Radvany, Radwan, Ritvin, Rudabanya, Rytwiany
937640	Radvanc, Radvanice, Radvantse, Radwance
937645	Radwanicze Koscielne, Rudabanyacska
937650	Radvanichi, Radvanka
937663	Radvan nad Hronom
937670	Radvanov
937674	Radwanowice
937675	Radwanowka
937739	Ratowo Piotrowo
937764	Ruda Pabianicka, Ruda Pabianitzka, Ruda Pabjanicka
937800	Radebeul, Radevil, Radivil, Radvil, Radvili, Retfala, Rodvil, Rottweil
937840	Radovljica
937845	Radvilishok, Radvilishok Nemunelis, Radviliskis, Rodvilishuk, Ruda Woloska
937847	Ruda Bialaczowska
937850	Ruda Wielka
937860	Ruda Opalin
937874	Ruda Wolowska
937900	Ratibor
937945	Ruda Brodska, Ruda Brodzka
937950	Radeberg, Reitberg, Rietberg
938000	Radlo, Radul, Rautel, Rytele
938400	Rodelsee
938430	Radulesti
938433	Rudelstadt, Rudolstadt
938475	Rytele Swieckie
938560	Rodelheim
938600	Radlin, Rodelheim
938617	Radulenii Vechi
938619	Rodelmaier
938656	Reutlingen, Riedlingen
938664	Rotthalmunster
938700	Radlov, Radlow, Ratulow, Rytlow
938739	Radlje Ob Dravi
938740	Radlowice, Rudolowice
938748	Radolfzell
938750	Radlovichı
938760	Rodalben, Rudolfin
939000	Rytro
939300	Ritterhude
939400	Radruz, Rudy Rysie
939433	Reuterstadt Stavenhagen
939439	Rattersdorf, Rudersdorf
939446	Ruttershausen
939464	Ruda Rozaniecka
939479	Rudersberg
939530	Ritterhude
939570	Royter Hoyf
939700	Rieddorf
939740	Rajtarowice, Raytarovitse, Rytarowice
940000	Raca, Race, Racsa, Rajcza, Ras, Rauza, Raysha, Rayshe, Reca, Recea, Reci, Recse, Rees, Reisha, Reitcha, Retz, Rezi, Reziai, Rezy, Ricse,

511

Code	Name
	Riesa, Riese, Risca, Risha, Ros, Rosh, Ross, Rosy, Roza, Rozce, Rus, Rusa, Ruse, Russ
941663	Rusii Munti
941700	Radziejow, Radziejowa, Rosiejow
941740	Radziejowice
943000	Resita, Resta, Rozdzialy, Rudzeti, Rust
943300	Rastatt, Rastede
943400	Rastice, Rastoace, Rastoci
943460	Raszitocsno, Raztocno
943500	Rostock, Rostoka, Rostoki, Rosztoka, Roztoka, Rustuka
943538	Rostoki Dolne
943543	Rostki Strozne
943570	Rostkov
943600	Rejstejn, Rositten
943640	Reistenhausen
943654	Reistenhausen
943656	Rustingen
943679	Rastenburg
943700	Rastov, Rastow, Rastuv, Rostov, Rostow
943740	Restevitz, Rozdzialowice, Rozdzyalovitse
943745	Rustvechko, Rustweczko
943760	Ruzdvyany, Ruzdwiany
943763	Rostov na Donu, Rostov On Don
943800	Rozdol, Rozdul, Ruzodol
943830	Rastolita
943861	Rasdelnaja, Rasdelnaya, Razdelnaja, Razdelnaya
943870	Rozdelov
943874	Rozdalovice
943875	Reshetilovka, Reszetilowka, Rozdilovichi
943900	Resetari
943947	Resterzewe
943970	Roisdorf, Rosdorf, Rossdorf, Rustorf
944000	Raciaz, Radzice, Radzicz, Rasiadz, Rasice, Rauzas, Razesi, Resica, Rezhitsa, Rezhitse, Rezhitza, Rezitza, Rigyac, Rigyica, Rjeshiza, Rjetschiza, Rosash, Rositsa, Rositza, Rosiza, Rossosh, Rossosz, Rozyca, Ruzas, Ryczyca
944300	Racesti
944316	Rusestii Noui
944397	Racistorf
944400	Rossoszyca, Rozhishtch, Rozishts, Rozyszcze, Russocice
944470	Rozishtchov, Ryzhishchev
944500	Raciazek, Rasiska, Raszocska, Rozhishch, Rozhishche, Rozsoska, Ryczyska
944578	Reczajska Wola
944600	Raciszyn, Radziecin, Roziecin, Rusociny
944636	Rozsaszentmarton
944700	Radziszow, Roszczep
944870	Rodzislav
945000	Rachki, Raczki, Rajsk, Rajskie, Rajsko, Ratschki, Rechki, Recsk, Recske, Resighea, Resko, Reszege, Retsag, Richka, Ricka, Ricky, Ricske, Riecka, Roska, Rosochy, Rosokhi, Rosokhy, Rotchky, Rotzk, Ruschuk, Ruska, Ruske, Ruskie, Rustchuk, Rustschuk
945165	Russkaja Mokra, Russkaya Mokraya
945300	Rascaeti, Rosochate
945340	Radziki Duze, Rajsko Duze
945350	Rosochatka
945354	Rosochate Koscielne
945400	Raskaytsy, Rosochacz
945457	Rajskie Sakowczyk
945460	Roskoshnyy
945461	Roskoshnaya, Roskoshnoye, Roskosnaya
945500	Rosokhach, Rozahegy
945543	Ruski Krstur
945570	Rozkochow
945593	Ruski Krstur
945600	Rezekne, Rishkan, Rishkani, Ryshkany, Ryskany
945639	Rascani Targ
945659	Rusca Mokra, Ruska Mokra
945675	Ryschkonowka
945700	Raczkow, Raczkowa, Radzekhuv, Radzhekhuv, Radzichov, Radziechow, Radziechowy, Radzikhuv, Raschkow, Rashkev, Rashkov, Raszkow, Riskeva, Riskeve, Riskova, Riskovi, Rizchov, Ruskava, Ruskov, Ruskova, Ruskow
945734	Rosokhovatets
945740	Ruska Wies
945744	Rosochowaciec, Rosokhovatsets
945745	Ruskie Piaski
945747	Rozkopaczow
945750	Rusakovichi
945760	Roskoviany, Rozkovany
945767	Russko Ivanovka
945778	Ryszkowa Wola
945780	Ruski Pole
945930	Rasgrad, Razgrad
945940	Rascruci
945943	Recea Cristur
945956	Reiskirchen
945970	Ruszkirva
946000	Racin, Raczna, Raczyna, Radzyn, Rasein, Raseinai, Raseiniai, Rashin, Rasina, Rasinja, Rasna, Rasony, Rasseyn, Raszyn, Razina, Razino, Recseny, Reczno, Redziny, Reisen, Resein, Reysen, Rezehne, Rezeni, Rezeny, Rezina, Rezna, Rizan, Rjasna, Rodzin, Rosenau, Rosienie, Rosni, Rossein, Rossieny, Rozan, Rozana, Rozdzin, Rozeni, Rozhan, Rozhanoy, Rozhinoy, Rucsin, Rudzana, Rusen, Ruseni, Rusne, Rusyany, Ruzan, Ruzany, Ruzhan, Ruzhana, Ruzhany, Ruzhin, Ruzhyn, Ryasna, Ryasno, Rydzyna
946163	Rietzneuendorf
946300	Risnita
946370	Razhnyatov, Rozhantov, Rozhniatov, Rozhnyatov, Rozhnyatuv, Rozintov, Roznatov, Rozniatow, Roznitev
946380	Rosenthal
946395	Rezina Targ
946400	Racionz, Ratziondzh, Rausnitz, Rotshonz, Rozaniec, Rozaumas, Rozenmuiza, Roznica, Rudzienice, Ruzhnitsa, Ruzinas
946430	Rezina Sat
946437	Rozanstvo
946460	Ritschenhausen
946470	Rozniszew
946475	Redziny Zabigalskie, Redziny Zbigalskie
946479	Rasonysapberencs
946500	Radzynek, Resznek, Rossing, Rozanka, Rozhanka
946546	Ritschenhausen
946560	Rosenheim
946570	Rosinhof
946600	Radzimin, Radzmin, Radzymin, Rodzamin, Rosenheim
946650	Radzyminek
946670	Redzen Nowy, Rozan Nowy
946700	Radzanov, Radzanow, Radznow, Razhnyuv, Razniow, Rosinhof, Rozhnov, Rozhnuv, Rozhnyuv, Roznava, Roznov, Roznow, Ruczynow
946738	Radzyn Podlaski
946740	Racinovci, Rozhanovce, Roznevice, Roznovec
946745	Rosenowsk, Rosenowski, Rosinovsk, Rozenovski, Rozhenovskaya, Rozinovsk
946750	Rizinivka, Rozanowka, Roznowka, Russenbach, Ryzanowka, Ryzhanovka
946783	Ritschenwalde
946785	Rozen Wielki, Rozhen Velikiy, Rozhen Velki
946795	Rauschenberg, Riesenburg, Rosenberg, Rozembark, Rozenberg, Rozmberk, Rozmberk nad Vltavou, Ruzomberok
946900	Rediu Mare, Redyu Mare
947000	Rachev, Radziwie, Rajszew, Ratchev, Riashov, Ritzov, Rocov, Rosavo, Roshev, Rossava, Rossawa, Rossow, Rozev, Rozsafa, Ruscova, Rusov, Rusow, Russow, Rusuv, Ruszow, Ryczow, Rydzewo, Rydzow
947300	Rozwady
947356	Rozbity Kamien
947370	Rozvadov, Rozvaduv, Rozvidev, Rozwadow
947375	Rozwadowka
947400	Rosovice, Rospesha, Rospsza, Rozprza, Rozpucie, Rusovce
947479	Rudy Przeworskie
947500	Rdzawka, Rosbach, Rosebeck, Rossbach, Rosvigo, Roszveg, Rozbeki, Rozvica, Rozvigo
947547	Radziev Kusawski
947570	Rossviegev, Rosvegovo, Rosvigovo
947593	Racfeherto
947640	Rozwienica
947660	Razbuneni
947670	Raspenava
947740	Rozubowice
947760	Raspopeni, Raspopeny
947764	Rydzewo Pieniazek
947787	Rydzewo Folw

947800	Reczpol, Rezavlia, Ritchvol, Rozavla, Rozavlea, Rusyvel, Rusywel, Ryczywol	954474	Rekszovice	957000	Rachov, Rachow, Rackeve, Rackova, Ragova, Raguva, Rahov, Rahovo, Rakhov, Rakov, Rakovo, Rakow, Rakowa, Rejckov, Rikov, Rochov, Rogov, Rogove, Rogow, Rogowo, Roguva, Rokow, Rucava, Rykov, Rykow
947830	Raesfeld	954500	Rakishik, Rakishki, Rakishok, Rakiski, Rakiszki, Rakoshegy, Rekishok, Rokishki, Rokishok, Rokishuk		
947840	Rozavlsa, Rozplucie				
947845	Radzivilishki, Radzivilishok, Radziwiliszki	954540	Rokishkis, Rokiskis		
		954594	Rakoskeresztur		
947850	Radziwilka	954600	Racaciuni, Rakoshino, Rakosin, Rakoszyn, Reichsheim, Rekshin, Rogasen, Rogozno, Roguszyn, Rohozna, Rohozne, Rokiciny, Roxheim, Rukshin, Rykoszyn		
947860	Ruspolyana, Ruszpolyana			957300	Racovat, Rakobuty
947870	Radzhivilov, Radzivilov, Radziwillow			957400	Rakovec, Rakovets, Rakovice, Rakowice, Rakowiec, Rakwitz, Rogowice, Rucavas, Rykowicze
947875	Radziwillowka				
947900	Ratzebuhr, Rozprza, Rozwory				
947940	Raciborz, Rozberice, Rozborz	954636	Rakosszentmihaly		
947943	Rozborz Dlugi	954640	Rogoznica	957450	Rakovchyk, Rakowczyk
947945	Rozborz Okragly	954645	Rogozniczka	957500	Rykoviche
947946	Rozworzany	954656	Rexingen	957569	Rogow Komorniki
947950	Ratzeburg	954678	Rogozno Wielkopolski, Rogozno Wielkopolskie	957650	Rakovnik
947974	Raciborowice			957784	Rogowo Falecin
948000	Raciula, Reschohlau, Reszel, Reutsel, Roessel, Rosalia, Rossel, Rosslau, Rozalia, Rozdzialy, Rozsaly, Rozula	954700	Rakoscsaba, Reichshof, Rogachev, Rogaczew, Rogaczow, Rogatchev, Rohaczew, Rohatchov, Rokatschuw, Rokosov, Rokosowo	957800	Richvol, Rychwal
				957900	Rakvere
				957936	Rauchwart im Burgenland
				958000	Rachlau, Raekula, Ragaly, Ragla, Ragola, Ragole, Rechula, Regoly, Riegel
948400	Rozlucz				
948440	Ruszelczyce				
948446	Rauischholzhausen	954740	Rogasevci, Rogasovci		
948460	Rozlozna, Russelsheim	954783	Rakospalota	958400	Regulice, Riglitz, Ryglice
948500	Ruslek	954787	Rakoczifalva	958439	Richelsdorf
948600	Rosilno, Rosolin, Rosulna, Rozalin	954831	Racosul de Jos	958440	Rychlocice
		954853	Rakosliget	958460	Reichelsheim
948640	Razalimas, Rozalimas, Rozalinas	955463	Rakacaszend	958600	Rogolin
948683	Rusl Moldovita	955470	Rchichtchev	958640	Racalmas, Reklinets, Rekliniec
948700	Radzhilov, Radzilove, Radzilow, Rodzilova, Rozdzalow	955600	Rokycany	958654	Recklinghausen
		955686	Ruchocki Mlyn	958700	Rakolupy, Rochlov
948740	Radzilowicze, Roslowitz, Rozdzialowice, Rozdzyalovitse	956000	Rachanie, Rachin, Ragne, Rakhin, Rakhinya, Regenye, Reghin, Reichenau, Rhein, Rheine, Rhina, Ricany, Richen, Rogna, Ruchheim, Rukainiai, Rukojnie	958740	Raclawice
				958750	Rygalowka
948750	Radzilovichi, Roslavichi, Roslovichi			958775	Raclawowka
				959000	Racaria, Rekoraj
948780	Roslavl, Roslawlj			959100	Rakariya
949000	Razoare, Rusor	956386	Rheindahlen	959300	Raigorod, Raigrod, Rajgrod, Raygrod, Rheurdt, Richrath, Ruckeroth
949137	Rosiorii de Vede	956397	Ragendorf, Raggendorf, Reckendorf		
949373	Rosiori de Vede				
949400	Rudy Rysie	956400	Rakamaz, Rakonitz, Rechnitz, Regmec, Regmitz, Rohonc, Rokamezo	959350	Raigorodok, Rajgrodek, Raygorodok
949436	Rosiori Satu Mare				
949538	Rycerka Dolna			959439	Rackeresztur, Rauchersdorf, Ruckersdorf
950000	Raho, Rajka, Recha, Rega, Rehau, Riga, Rige, Rika, Rike, Riki, Rogau, Rohia, Rughi, Ryki	956437	Regenstauf		
		956439	Rachmistrivka	959446	Ruckershausen
		956454	Reichensachsen	959476	Reichertshofen
		956460	Regensheim, Rheinhausen, Rockenhausen	959665	Reichraming
951000	Rugaji, Rugaju			960000	Rain, Rainiai, Raona, Rauna, Rehna, Rem, Reni, Rhein, Rheine, Rhina, Rinn, Romny, Ruen, Rum, Ruma, Rumno, Runia
951430	Rogojesti				
953000	Rakita, Rechta, Rheda, Rhede, Rheydt, Rohod, Rokita	956477	Rogienice Wypychy		
		956478	Rogienice Wielkie, Rogienice Wlascianskie		
953400	Rakottyas, Rhodes, Rhodos, Rogatica				
		956479	Regensburg, Rheinsberg	963000	Remet, Remete, Remeti, Remit, Remte, Romita, Rontau, Rujnita
953440	Rachodoszcze	956546	Rheinhausen, Rockenhausen		
953500	Rachtig	956560	Regingen, Ruckingen		
953600	Racadony, Rakitin, Rakitina, Rhoden, Rogatin, Rohatin, Rohatyn, Rokitno	956600	Rhaunen	963140	Rona de Jos
		956643	Reichmannsdorf	963170	Rendejov
		956670	Rachmanov, Rachmanow, Rachmanowo, Rakhmanov	963440	Rona de Sus
				963500	Randegg
953610	Rokitnoye			963598	Remetea Chioarului
953640	Rokietnica, Rokitnica, Rokitnitsa	956690	Regina Maria	963600	Romodan, Rundeni
		956700	Regnow	963700	Rendva
953648	Rokitno Szlacheckie	956740	Rakoniewice	963759	Remeti Bihor
953650	Rokytnik	956747	Rheinbischofsheim	963764	Rentweinsdorf
953700	Rokytov	956750	Reichenbach, Rheinbach	963860	Rheindahlen, Rinteln
953800	Rychtal	956763	Rychnov nad Kneznou	963945	Randersacker
954000	Racas, Ragusa, Rakaca, Rakasz, Rakos, Raksa, Raksi, Rechitsa, Regoce, Rigacs, Rogacze	956783	Regenwalde, Rugenwalde	963970	Rondorf
		956786	Rheinbollen	964000	Ranischau, Remus, Rimoc, Rimse, Rymacze
		956793	Rauchenwarth		
954300	Rachesti, Recheshty	956795	Reichenberg, Reichenburg, Rheinberg	964300	Remscheid
954400	Ruchocice, Rychcice, Rykhtsitse			964330	Ranstadt
954430	Rugasesti	956796	Reichenborn	964380	Romsthal
954460	Rekszyn	956798	Rheinbrohl	964400	Remczyce, Rimaszecs
954470	Rakszawa				

964450	Romshishok, Rumshishok	969470	Rynarzewo	976470	Revnicov
964454	Rumsiskes	969476	Rennertshofen	976474	Rava Mazovietzk, Rave
964500	Romaszki, Rona Sek, Ronaszek,	969478	Reimerswalde		Mazovyetsk, Rawa
	Rumiske	970000	Raab, Raba, Rabe, Rava, Rave,		Mazowiecka, Rawa
964540	Ramocsahaza		Ravi, Rawy, Rev, Roop, Ropa		Mazowiecki
964600	Ramazan, Ramazany, Renceni,	971630	Rapujineti	976479	Rabensburg, Ravensbruck,
	Rimshan, Rymszany	973000	Repedea		Ravensburg
964635	Rinyaszentkiraly	973140	Rapa de Jos, Ripa de Jos	976500	Ribnik, Ropianka, Ropienka,
964673	Rimaszombat	973378	Rabatotfalu		Rubnik, Rybionek, Rybnik
964700	Ranizov, Ranizow, Reinzov,	973400	Ribotitch, Rybotycze	976560	Rippenheim
	Remicov	973440	Rapa de Sus, Ripa de Sus	976574	Rybnica Vysnia
964740	Remizovtse, Remizovtsy,	973640	Rabatamasi	976600	Rippenheim
	Remizowce	973864	Rapy Dylanskie	976650	Rownianki
964750	Ramsbeck	974000	Rabiez, Rawicz, Rawitsch,	976659	Ravne na Koroskem
964790	Rheinsberg		Rayvits, Rayvitz, Reyvits,	976700	Rybie Nowe
964795	Ramsberg, Rendsburg, Ronsperg,		Robec, Ropcea, Ropica,	976744	Rovine Pecica
	Ronsperk		Rubas, Rubezh, Rubiez	976749	Revna pe Ceremus
965000	Ranka, Rieneck, Romejki,	974300	Ravazd	976750	Rubanovka
	Romejko, Romeyki, Rymachi,	974390	Rybie Stare	976795	Reifenberg
	Rymki	974400	Ropczyce, Ropshits, Ropshitz	977000	Roupov
965400	Rankas, Remchitsy	974460	Rabacsecseny	977360	Rabapatona
965446	Rengshausen	974500	Rapsach, Rovbitsk	977440	Rabafuzes
965493	Rimnicu Sarat	974510	Rovbitskaya	977460	Raba Wyzna
965600	Reinheim, Remagen, Renchen,	974600	Ripiceni	977936	Rabapordany
	Ringen, Romhany	974636	Rabaszentandras	978000	Rapel, Rapla, Rappel, Reval,
965780	Rankweil	974639	Raabs an der Thaya		Revel, Revfalu, Robel, Rubel,
965784	Ramnicu Valcea	974640	Repuzhintsy, Repuzhyntse,		Rubiel, Ryboly
965800	Ramgola, Ramygala, Ramygola,		Repuzynce	978300	Rapolt
	Remigola, Runkel	974650	Rabacsanak	978365	Ruhpolding
965840	Rynholec	974700	Rubashov, Rubeshov,	978448	Rebielice Szlacheckie
965900	Rungury		Rubischoff, Rubishov,	978475	Ravelsbach
966000	Ramien, Reinheim, Rhaunen,		Rubishoyv	978630	Rublenita
	Roman, Romen, Romhany,	974740	Rebzevits, Repcevis,	978640	Rublenitsa
	Romonya, Runina		Rubiezewicze, Rubizhevich,	978679	Revleanyvar
966300	Romand		Rubizhevitch, Rubzhevits,	978700	Rafajlowa, Revfulop
966430	Romanesti, Rominesti		Rybczewice	978750	Rafalovka, Rafalowka
966530	Romancauti	974750	Rubezhevichi, Rubyezheviche	978794	Revlaborcz
966574	Romankovtsy	974850	Repcelak	978900	Rehweiler
966700	Remenow, Remenuv, Rimanov,	975000	Rabka, Rabke, Rjepki, Ropcha,	979000	Rabber, Rebra, Rybare
	Romanov, Romanovo,		Ropki, Rowbick, Ruppach,	979300	Rajbrot, Robret
	Romanow, Romanowo,		Rybaki	979450	Rava Ruska, Rawa Ruska
	Romanuv, Rumanov, Rymanow	975349	Revacauti Cernauti	979451	Rava Russkaya
966740	Romanowce	975375	Rabahidveg	979490	Rebrisoara
966748	Romanowe Siolo	975393	Ruppichteroth	979500	Rehburg
966750	Romanovka, Romanowka	975400	Revakouts, Ropchitse	979534	Ruprechtice
966757	Romanowka Powtrembowla	975453	Rabakecsked	979600	Rebreanu, Rebrin
966795	Ronnenburg	975580	Rabakecol	979634	Reformatuskovacshaza
967300	Rembate	975600	Rovigno	979639	Repperndorf
967400	Rynovice	975700	Rebkow, Repechow, Repekhuv	979640	Revaranyos
967440	Rembieszyce	975740	Rabakovacsi	980000	Role
967451	Rimavske Janovce	975784	Ropica Polska	984330	Rahlstedt
967454	Rimavska Sec, Rimavska Sobota	975945	Ropica Ruska	984460	Rollshausen
967470	Rheinbischofsheim	976000	Rabiany, Rappenau, Repany,	984500	Rylsk
967500	Rheinbach, Rimbach, Rimbeck		Repenye, Repinne, Reppen,	984600	Reilsheim, Rulzheim
967860	Rheinbollen		Reppine, Revna, Ribene,	986000	Raileni
967900	Rimpar		Riebeni, Riebini, Rifin,	986400	Raileanca
967937	Rembertov, Rembertow		Ripanj, Ripin, Ripina, Rovina,	986500	Roylyanka
967950	Rajhenburg, Rheinberg,		Rovine, Rovinj, Roviny,	986560	Reilingen
	Ronneburg, Rumburk		Rovna, Rovne, Rovno,	987000	Ralow, Rylow, Rylowa
967969	Raum Bremerhaven		Rovnya, Rowiny, Rowne,	987400	Rajlovac, Rehlovice
967980	Rheinbrohl		Rownia, Rowno, Rubene,	987500	Ralevka, Rollbach
968000	Ramuli, Remel, Romuli		Ruvne, Rybne, Rybno,	987830	Rollfeld
968340	Rynoltice		Rypiany, Rypin, Rypne	990000	Raro
968400	Rynholec	976100	Rovnoje, Rovnoye, Rybnoye	993000	Rheurdt
968460	Rommelhausen	976300	Rabnita, Rjavinti	993144	Rortieyes Szentmihaly
968479	Rummelsberg, Rummelsburg	976386	Reppen Ad Eilang	994000	Raros
968546	Rommelhausen	976400	Ravnitsa, Revnice, Ribnitsa,	996793	Rohrenfurth
968656	Remlingen		Ribnitz, Ribnitza, Rybnica,	997500	Rohrbach
968700	Rimalov		Rybnice, Rybnitsa	997563	Rohrbach an der Teich
969300	Romrod	976430	Rybniste	997950	Rohrbruch
969354	Rennertehausen	976436	Rabenstein, Ribnitzdamgarten	999300	Ruhrort
969374	Renardowice	976450	Ribinishki, Ribinishok, Ribiniski,		
969446	Rommershausen		Ribinsk, Rybinischki, Rybinsk		
969454	Rimarska Sec	976460	Rovenshiny, Rybnicna		